CORPORATIONS AND OTHER BUSINESS ASSOCIATIONS

STATUTES, RULES, AND FORMS

2020 Edition

Edited by

DOUGLAS K. MOLL

Beirne, Maynard & Parsons, L.L.P.
Professor of Law
University of Houston Law Center

WEST
ACADEMIC
PUBLISHING

COPYRIGHT © 1985, 1987, 1989, 1991–1994, 1996 WEST PUBLISHING CO.
© West, a Thomson business, 1997–2008
© 2009–2012 Thomson Reuters
© 2013 LEG, Inc. d/b/a West Academic Publishing
© 2014–2019 LEG, Inc. d/b/a West Academic
© 2020 LEG, Inc. d/b/a West Academic
    444 Cedar Street, Suite 700
    St. Paul, MN 55101
    1-877-888-1330

Printed in the United States of America

ISBN: 978-1-68467-961-4

PREFACE

_____

First, a hearty thanks to Professor Jeffrey Bauman for all of his hard work on prior editions. This edition largely follows the template that he left behind.

Second, I received invaluable help from Ashley Arrington of the O'Quinn Law Library at the University of Houston Law Center. Ashley was of great assistance in updating and editing many of these materials.

Finally, I welcome any comments or suggestions for additions (or deletions) to these materials. I can be reached via email at dmoll@central.uh.edu.

DOUGLAS K. MOLL

June 2020

PREFACE

TABLE OF CONTENTS

CORPORATIONS AND OTHER BUSINESS ASSOCIATIONS

STATUTES, RULES, AND FORMS

2020 Edition

I. AGENCY

A. RESTATEMENT (SECOND) OF AGENCY (1958)

(Selected Sections and Comments)

Table of Sections

1

RESTATEMENT (SECOND) OF AGENCY (1958)

TOPIC 2. INTERPRETATION OF AUTHORITY AND APPARENT AUTHORITY

TITLE A. AUTHORITY

TITLE B. INTERPRETATION OF APPARENT AUTHORITY

CHAPTER 4. RATIFICATION

TOPIC 1. DEFINITIONS

TOPIC 2. WHEN AFFIRMANCE RESULTS IN RATIFICATION

TOPIC 3. WHAT CONSTITUTES AFFIRMANCE

TOPIC 4. LIABILITIES

CHAPTER 5. TERMINATION OF AGENCY POWERS

TOPIC 1. TERMINATION OF AUTHORITY

TITLE A. INFERRED FROM ORIGINAL MANIFESTATION IN LIGHT OF SUBSEQUENT EVENTS

RESTATEMENT (SECOND) OF AGENCY (1958)

3

RESTATEMENT (SECOND) OF AGENCY (1958)

TITLE D.   DEFENSES AND LIABILITY AFFECTED BY SUBSEQUENT EVENTS

TOPIC 3.   UNDISCLOSED PRINCIPAL

TITLE A.   CREATION OF LIABILITY BY AUTHORIZED ACTS

TITLE B.   CREATION OF LIABILITY BY UNAUTHORIZED ACTS

TITLE C.   DEFENSES AND LIABILITY AFFECTED BY SUBSEQUENT EVENTS

CHAPTER 7.   LIABILITY OF PRINCIPAL TO THIRD PERSON; TORTS

TOPIC 1.   LIABILITY FOR PERSONAL VIOLATION OF DUTY

TOPIC 2.   LIABILITY FOR AUTHORIZED CONDUCT OR CONDUCT INCIDENTAL THERETO

TITLE A.   IN GENERAL

TITLE B.   TORTS OF SERVANTS

WHO IS A SERVANT

SCOPE OF EMPLOYMENT

RESTATEMENT (SECOND) OF AGENCY (1958)

TITLE C. AGENTS' TORTS; LIABILITY NOT DEPENDENT UPON RELATION OF MASTER AND SERVANT

IN GENERAL

MISREPRESENTATIONS

TITLE D. CONDUCT WITHIN APPARENT AUTHORITY OR EMPLOYMENT

CHAPTER 10. LIABILITY OF THIRD PERSON TO PRINCIPAL

TOPIC 1. CONTRACTS; DISCLOSED AGENCY

TOPIC 2. CONTRACTS; UNDISCLOSED AGENCY

TOPIC 5. EFFECT OF RATIFICATION

RESTATEMENT (SECOND) OF AGENCY (1958)

CHAPTER 11. LIABILITY OF AGENT TO THIRD PERSONS

TOPIC 1. CONTRACTS AND CONVEYANCES

TITLE A. AGENT A PARTY TO A TRANSACTION CONDUCTED BY HIMSELF

TITLE B. AGENT NOT PARTY TO TRANSACTION CONDUCTED BY HIMSELF

TITLE C. DEFENSES AND EFFECTS OF SUBSEQUENT EVENTS

TOPIC 3. TORTS

CHAPTER 13. DUTIES AND LIABILITIES OF AGENT TO PRINCIPAL

TOPIC 1. DUTIES

TITLE B. DUTIES OF SERVICE AND OBEDIENCE

TITLE C. DUTIES OF LOYALTY

TOPIC 2. LIABILITIES

TOPIC 4. DUTIES AND LIABILITIES OF PARTICULAR KINDS OF AGENTS

CHAPTER 14. DUTIES AND LIABILITIES OF PRINCIPAL TO AGENT

TOPIC 1. CONTRACTUAL AND RESTITUTIONAL DUTIES AND LIABILITIES

TITLE A. INTERPRETATION OF CONTRACTS AND LIABILITIES THEREUNDER

CHAPTER 1. INTRODUCTORY MATTERS

TOPIC 1. DEFINITIONS

§ 1. Agency; Principal; Agent

(1) Agency is the fiduciary relation which results from the manifestation of consent by one person to another that the other shall act on his behalf and subject to his control, and consent by the other so to act.

(2) The one for whom action is to be taken is the principal.

(3) The one who is to act is the agent.

Comment b. Agency a legal concept. Agency is a legal concept which depends upon the existence of required factual elements: the manifestation by the principal that the agent shall act for him, the agent's acceptance of the undertaking and the understanding of the parties that the principal is to be in control of the undertaking. The relation which the law calls agency does not depend upon the intent of the parties to create it, nor their belief that they have done so. To constitute the relation, there must be an agreement, but not necessarily a contract, between the parties; if the agreement results in the factual relation between them to which are attached the legal consequences of agency, an agency exists although the parties did not call it agency and did not intend the legal consequences of the relation to

7

follow. Thus, when one who asks a friend to do a slight service for him, such as to return for credit goods recently purchased from a store, neither one may have any realization that they are creating an agency relation or be aware of the legal obligations which would result from performance of the service. On the other hand, one may believe that he has created an agency when in fact the relation is that of seller and buyer. *See* § 14J. The distinction between agency and other relations, such as those of trust, buyer and seller, and others are stated in Sections 14A to 14O. The distinction between the kind of agent called a servant and a non-servant agent is stated in Section 2.

When it is doubtful whether a representative is the agent of one or the other of two contracting parties, the function of the court is to ascertain the factual relation of the parties to each other and in so doing can properly disregard a statement in the agreement that the agent is to be the agent of one rather than of the other, or a statement by the parties as to the legal relations which are thereby created. *See* § 14L. The agency relation results if, but only if, there is an understanding between the parties which, as interpreted by the court, creates a fiduciary relation in which the fiduciary is subject to the directions of the one on whose account he acts. It is the element of continuous subjection to the will of the principal which distinguishes the agent from other fiduciaries and the agency agreement from other agreements. The characteristics which tend to indicate an agency or a non-agency relation are stated in Sections 12 to 14O.

§ 2.   Master; Servant; Independent Contractor

(1)   A master is a principal who employs an agent to perform service in his affairs and who controls or has the right to control the physical conduct of the other in the performance of the service.

(2)   A servant is an agent employed by a master to perform service in his affairs whose physical conduct in the performance of the service is controlled or is subject to the right to control by the master.

(3)   An independent contractor is a person who contracts with another to do something for him but who is not controlled by the other nor subject to the other's right to control with respect to his physical conduct in the performance of the undertaking. He may or may not be an agent.

Comment a. Servants and non-servant agents. A master is a species of principal, and a servant is a species of agent. The words "master" and "servant" are herein used to indicate the relation from which arises both the liability of an employer for the physical harm caused to third persons by the tort of an employee (*see* §§ 219–249) and the special duties and immunities of an employer to the employee. *See* §§ 473–528. Although for brevity the definitions in this Section refer only to the control or right to control the physical conduct of the servant, there are many factors which are considered by the courts in defining the relation. These factors which distinguish a servant from an independent contractor are stated in Section 220. The distinction between servants and agents who are not servants is of importance for the purposes of the Sections referred to. Statements made in the Restatement of this Subject as applicable to principals or agents are, unless otherwise stated, applicable to masters and servants. The rules as to liability of a principal for the torts of agents who are not servants are stated in Sections 250–267, and those with respect to his liability in tort to such agents in Sections 470–472. The duties of servants to masters and their liabilities to third persons are in general the same as those of agents who are not servants. However, servants may have only custody, as distinguished from possession of goods entrusted to them by the master (*see* § 339, Comment *g* and § 349), and a servant, because of his position, may not be responsible for mistakes made by him as to facts upon which his authority depends, whereas an agent who is not a servant would be responsible. *See* Comment *c* on § 383.

§ 3.   General Agent; Special Agent

(1)   A general agent is an agent authorized to conduct a series of transactions involving a continuity of service.

(2)   A special agent is an agent authorized to conduct a single transaction or a series of transactions not involving continuity of service.

§ 4. Disclosed Principal; Partially Disclosed Principal; Undisclosed Principal

(1) If, at the time of a transaction conducted by an agent, the other party thereto has notice that the agent is acting for a principal and of the principal's identity, the principal is a disclosed principal.

(2) If the other party has notice that the agent is or may be acting for a principal but has no notice of the principal's identity, the principal for whom the agent is acting is a partially disclosed principal.

(3) If the other party has no notice that the agent is acting for a principal, the one for whom he acts is an undisclosed principal.

§ 7. Authority

Authority is the power of the agent to affect the legal relations of the principal by acts done in accordance with the principal's manifestations of consent to him.

§ 8. Apparent Authority

Apparent authority is the power to affect the legal relations of another person by transactions with third persons, professedly as agent for the other, arising from and in accordance with the other's manifestations to such third persons.

§ 8A. Inherent Agency Power

Inherent agency power is a term used in the restatement of this subject to indicate the power of an agent which is derived not from authority, apparent authority or estoppel, but solely from the agency relation and exists for the protection of persons harmed by or dealing with a servant or other agent.

§ 8B. Estoppel; Change of Position

(1) A person who is not otherwise liable as a party to a transaction purported to be done on his account, is nevertheless subject to liability to persons who have changed their positions because of their belief that the transaction was entered into by or for him, if

(a) he intentionally or carelessly caused such belief, or

(b) knowing of such belief and that others might change their positions because of it, he did not take reasonable steps to notify them of the facts.

(2) An owner of property who represents to third persons that another is the owner of the property or who permits the other so to represent, or who realizes that third persons believe that another is the owner of the property, and that he could easily inform the third persons of the facts, is subject to the loss of the property if the other disposes of it to third persons who, in ignorance of the facts, purchase the property or otherwise change their position with reference to it.

(3) Change of position, as the phrase is used in the restatement of this subject, indicates payment of money, expenditure of labor, suffering a loss or subjection to legal liability.

TOPIC 2. KNOWLEDGE AND NOTICE

§ 9. Notice

(1) A person has notice of a fact if he knows the fact, has reason to know it, should know it, or has been given notification of it.

(2) A person is given notification of a fact by another if the latter

(a) informs him of the fact by adequate or specified means or of other facts from which he has reason to know or should know the facts: or

(b) does an act which, under the rules applicable to the transaction, has the same effect on the legal relations of the parties as the acquisition of knowledge or reason to know.

(3) A person has notice of a fact if his agent has knowledge of the fact, reason to know it or should know it, or has been given a notification of it, under circumstances coming within the rules applying to the liability of a principal because of notice to his agent.

Comment d. Reason to know. A person has reason to know of a fact if he has information from which a person of ordinary intelligence, or of the superior intelligence which such person may have, would infer that the fact in question exists or that there is such a substantial chance of its existence that, if exercising reasonable care with reference to the matter in question, his action would be predicated upon the assumption of its possible existence. The inference drawn need not be that the fact exists; it is sufficient that the likelihood of its existence is so great that a person of ordinary intelligence, or of the superior intelligence which the person in question has, would, if exercising ordinary prudence under the circumstances, govern his conduct as if the fact existed, until he could ascertain its existence or non-existence. The words "reason to know" do not necessarily import the existence of a duty to others to ascertain facts; the words are used both where the actor has a duty to another and where he would not be acting adequately in the protection of his own interests were he not to act with reference to the facts which he has reason to know. One may have reason to know a fact although he does not make the inference of its existence which would be made by a reasonable person in his position and with his knowledge, whether his failure to make such inference is due to inferior intelligence or to a failure properly to exercise such intelligence as he has. A person of superior intelligence or training has reason to know a fact if a person with his mental capacity and attainments would draw such an inference from the facts known to him. On the other hand, "reason to know" imports no duty to ascertain facts not to be deduced as inferences from facts already known; one has reason to know a fact only if a reasonable person in his position would infer such fact from other facts already known to him.

Further, a person has reason to know facts only if the circumstances are such that any unconscious knowledge would be made conscious if such person were to meet the required standards with reference to memory, consideration for the interests of others, or, in some instances, consideration for one's own interests. Thus, one who had no reason to remember facts once known would not at a later time have reason to know the facts. *See* Sections 276 and 277, which deal with situations in which this distinction may be crucial in determining the liability of the principal because of what an agent has reason to know.

TOPIC 3. ESSENTIAL CHARACTERISTICS OF RELATION

§ 13. Agent as a Fiduciary

An agent is a fiduciary with respect to matters within the scope of his agency.

§ 14. Control by Principal

A principal has the right to control the conduct of the agent with respect to matters entrusted to him.

Comment a. The right of control by the principal may be exercised by prescribing what the agent shall or shall not do before the agent acts, or at the time when he acts, or at both times. The principal's right to control is continuous and continues as long as the agency relation exists, even though the principal agreed that he would not exercise it. Thus, the agent is subject to a duty not to act contrary to the principal's directions, although the principal has agreed not to give such directions. *See* § 33. Further, the principal has power to revoke the agent's authority, although this would constitute a breach of his contract with him. *See* § 118. The agent cannot obtain specific performance of the principal's agreement. If the agent has notice of facts from which he should infer that the principal does not wish him to act as originally specified, the agent's authority is terminated, suspended, or modified accordingly. *See* § 108. The control of the principal does not, however, include control at every moment; its exercise may be very attenuated and, as where the principal is physically absent, may be ineffective.

The extent of the right to control the physical acts of the agent is an important factor in determining whether or not a master-servant relation between them exists. *See* § 220.

Comment b. If it is otherwise clear that there is an agency relation, as in the case of recognized agents such as attorneys at law, factors, or auctioneers, the principal, although he has contracted with the agent not to exercise control and to permit the agent the free exercise of his discretion, nevertheless has power to give lawful directions which the agent is under a duty to obey if he continues to act as such. *See* § 385. If the existence of an agency relation is not otherwise clearly shown, as where the issue is whether a trust or an agency has been created, the fact that it is understood that the person acting is not to be subject to the control of the other as to the manner of performance determines that the relation is not that of agency. *See* § 14B.

TOPIC 4. AGENCY DISTINGUISHED FROM OTHER RELATIONS

§ 14H. Agents or Holders of a Power Given for Their Benefit

One who holds a power created in the form of an agency authority, but given for the benefit of the power holder or of a third person, is not an agent of the one creating the power.

§ 14O. Security Holder Becoming a Principal

A creditor who assumes control of his debtor's business for the mutual benefit of himself and his debtor, may become a principal, with liability for the acts and transactions of the debtor in connection with the business.

Comment a. A security holder who merely exercises a veto power over the business acts of his debtor by preventing purchases or sales above specified amounts does not thereby become a principal. However, if he takes over the management of the debtor's business either in person or through an agent, and directs what contracts may or may not be made, he becomes a principal, liable as any principal for the obligations incurred thereafter in the normal course of business by the debtor who has now become his general agent. The point at which the creditor becomes a principal is that at which he assumes de facto control over the conduct of his debtor, whatever the terms of the formal contract with his debtor may be.

Where there is an assignment for the benefit of creditors, the latter may become the principals of the assignee if they exercise control over transactions entered into by him on their behalf.

CHAPTER 2. CREATION OF RELATION

TOPIC 1. MUTUAL CONSENT AND CONSIDERATION

§ 15. Manifestations of Consent

An agency relation exists only if there has been a manifestation by the principal to the agent that the agent may act on his account, and consent by the agent so to act.

TOPIC 3. CAPACITY OF PARTIES TO RELATION

§ 23. Agent Having Interests Adverse to Principal

One whose interests are adverse to those of another can be authorized to act on behalf of the other; it is a breach of duty for him so to act without revealing the existence and extent of such adverse interests.

CHAPTER 3. CREATION AND INTERPRETATION
OF AUTHORITY AND APPARENT AUTHORITY

TOPIC 1.   METHODS OF MANIFESTING CONSENT

§ 26.   Creation of Authority; General Rule

Except for the execution of instruments under seal or for the performance of transactions required by statute to be authorized in a particular way, authority to do an act can be created by written or spoken words or other conduct of the principal which, reasonably interpreted, causes the agent to believe that the principal desires him so to act on the principal's account.

§ 27.   Creation of Apparent Authority: General Rule

Except for the execution of instruments under seal or for the conduct of transactions required by statute to be authorized in a particular way, apparent authority to do an act is created as to a third person by written or spoken words or any other conduct of the principal which, reasonably interpreted, causes the third person to believe that the principal consents to have the act done on his behalf by the person purporting to act for him.

TOPIC 2.   INTERPRETATION OF AUTHORITY
AND APPARENT AUTHORITY

TITLE A.   AUTHORITY

§ 32.   Applicability of Rules for Interpretation of Agreements

Except to the extent that the fiduciary relation between principal and agent requires special rules, the rules for the interpretation of contracts apply to the interpretation of authority.

§ 33.   General Principle of Interpretation

An agent is authorized to do, and to do only, what it is reasonable for him to infer that the principal desires him to do in the light of the principal's manifestations and the facts as he knows or should know them at the time he acts.

§ 34.   Circumstances Considered in Interpreting Authority

An authorization is interpreted in light of all accompanying circumstances, including among other matters:

(a)   the situation of the parties, their relations to one another, and the business in which they are engaged;

(b)   the general usages of business, the usages of trades or employments of the kind to which the authorization relates, and the business methods of the principal;

(c)   facts of which the agent has notice respecting the objects which the principal desires to accomplish;

(d)   the nature of the subject matter, the circumstances under which the act is to be performed and the legality or illegality of the act; and

(e)   the formality or informality, and the care, or lack of it, with which an instrument evidencing the authority is drawn.

§ 35. When Incidental Authority is Inferred

Unless otherwise agreed, authority to conduct a transaction includes authority to do acts which are incidental to it, usually accompany it, or are reasonably necessary to accomplish it.

§ 39. Inference That Agent is to Act Only for Principal's Benefit

Unless otherwise agreed, authority to act as agent includes only authority to act for the benefit of the principal.

§ 43. Acquiescence by Principal in Agent's Conduct

(1) Acquiescence by the principal in conduct of an agent whose previously conferred authorization reasonably might include it, indicates that the conduct was authorized; if clearly not included in the authorization, acquiescence in it indicates affirmance.

(2) Acquiescence by the principal in a series of acts by the agent indicates authorization to perform similar acts in the future.

TITLE B. INTERPRETATION OF APPARENT AUTHORITY

§ 49. Interpretation of Apparent Authority Compared with Interpretation of Authority

The rules applicable to the interpretation of authority are applicable to the interpretation of apparent authority except that:

(a) manifestations of the principal to the other party to the transaction are interpreted in light of what the other party knows or should know instead of what the agent knows or should know, and

(b) if there is a latent ambiguity in the manifestations of the principal for which he is not at fault, the interpretation of apparent authority is based on the facts known to the principal.

CHAPTER 4. RATIFICATION

TOPIC 1. DEFINITIONS

§ 82. Ratification

Ratification is the affirmance by a person of a prior act which did not bind him but which was done or professedly done on his account, whereby the act, as to some or all persons, is given effect as if originally authorized by him.

Comment c. A unique concept. The concept of ratification is not a legal fiction, but denotes the legal consequences which result from a series of events beginning with a transaction inoperative as to the principal, and ending in an act of validation. The statement that there is a relation back to the time of the original act is fictitious in form, but in effect, it is a statement of liabilities. The concept is unique. It does not conform to the rules of contracts, since it can be accomplished without consideration to or manifestation by the purported principal and without fresh consent by the other party. Further, it operates as if the transaction were complete at the time and place of the first event, rather than the last, as in the normal case of offer and acceptance. It does not conform to the rules of torts, since the ratifier may become responsible for a harm which was not caused by him, his property or his agent. It can not be justified on a theory of restitution, since the ratifier may not have received a benefit, nor the third person a deprivation. Nor is ratification dependent upon a doctrine of estoppel, since there may be ratification although neither the agent nor the other party suffer a loss resulting from a statement of affirmance or a failure to disavow. However, in some cases in which ratification is claimed, the principal's liability can be based upon unjust enrichment or estoppel, either in addition to or as alternative to his liability based on ratification. *See* §§ 103, 104.

§ 83.   Affirmance

Affirmance is either

    (a)   a manifestation of an election by one on whose account an unauthorized act has been done to treat the act as authorized, or

    (b)   conduct by him justifiable only if there were such an election.

TOPIC 2.   WHEN AFFIRMANCE RESULTS IN RATIFICATION

§ 84.   What Acts Can be Ratified

    (1)   An act which, when done, could have been authorized by a purported principal, or if an act of service by an intended principal, can be ratified if, at the time of affirmance, he could authorize such an act.

    (2)   An act which, when done, the purported or intended principal could not have authorized, he cannot ratify, except an act affirmed by a legal representative whose appointment relates back to or before the time of such act.

§ 85.   Purporting to Act as Agent as a Requisite for Ratification

    (1)   Ratification does not result from the affirmance of a transaction with a third person unless the one acting purported to be acting for the ratifier.

    (2)   An act of service not involving a transaction with a third person is subject to ratification if, but only if, the one doing the act intends or purports to perform it as the servant of another.

§ 87.   Who Can Affirm

To become effective as ratification, the affirmance must be by the person identified as the principal at the time of the original act or, if no person was then identified, by the one for whom the agent intended to act.

§ 88.   Affirmance After Withdrawal of Other Party or Other Termination of Original Transaction

To constitute ratification, the affirmance of a transaction must occur before the other party has manifested his withdrawal from it either to the purported principal or to the agent, and before the offer or agreement has otherwise terminated or been discharged.

§ 89.   Affirmance After Change of Circumstances

If the affirmance of a transaction occurs at a time when the situation has so materially changed that it would be inequitable to subject the other party to liability thereon, the other party has an election to avoid liability.

§ 90.   Affirmance After Rights Have Crystallized

If an act to be effective in creating a right against another or to deprive him of a right must be performed before a specific time, an affirmance is not effective against the other unless made before such time.

§ 91.   Knowledge of Principal at Time of Affirmance

    (1)   If, at the time of affirmance, the purported principal is ignorant of material facts involved in the original transaction, and is unaware of his ignorance, he can thereafter avoid the effect of the affirmance.

(2) Material facts are those which substantially affect the existence or extent of the obligations involved in the transaction, as distinguished from those which affect the values or inducements involved in the transaction.

TOPIC 3. WHAT CONSTITUTES AFFIRMANCE

§ 93. Methods and Formalities of Affirmance

(1) Except as stated in Subsection (2), affirmance can be established by any conduct of the purported principal manifesting that he consents to be a party to the transaction, or by conduct justifiable only if there is ratification.

(2) Where formalities are requisite for the authorization of an act, its affirmance must be by the same formalities in order to constitute a ratification.

(3) The affirmance can be made by an agent authorized so to do.

§ 94. Failure to Act as Affirmance

An affirmance of an unauthorized transaction can be inferred from a failure to repudiate it.

§ 95. Necessity of Communicating Manifestation of Affirmance

The manifestation of a definitive election by the principal constitutes affirmance without communication to the agent, to the other party, or to other persons.

§ 97. Bringing Suit or Basing Defense as Affirmance

There is affirmance if the purported principal, with knowledge of the facts, in an action in which the third person or the purported agent is an adverse party:

(a) brings suit to enforce promises which were part of the unauthorized transaction or to secure interests which were the fruit of such transaction and to which he would be entitled only if the act had been authorized; or

(b) bases a defense upon the unauthorized transaction as though it were authorized; or

(c) continues to maintain such suit or base such defense.

§ 98. Receipt of Benefits as Affirmance

The receipt by a purported principal, with knowledge of the facts, of something to which he would not be entitled unless an act purported to be done for him were affirmed, and to which he makes no claim except through such act, constitutes an affirmance unless at the time of such receipt he repudiates the act. If he repudiates the act, his receipt of benefits constitutes an affirmance at the election of the other party to the transaction.

§ 99. Retention of Benefits as Affirmance

The retention by a purported principal, with knowledge of the facts and before he has changed his position, of something which he is not entitled to retain unless an act purported to be done on his account is affirmed, and to which he makes no claim except through such act, constitutes an affirmance unless at the time of such retention he repudiates the act. Even if he repudiates the act, his retention constitutes an affirmance at the election of the other party to the transaction.

TOPIC 4.   LIABILITIES

§ 100.   Effect of Ratification; In General

Except as stated in Section 101, the liabilities resulting from ratification are the same as those resulting from authorization if, between the time when the original act was performed and when it was affirmed, there has been no change in the capacity of the principal or third person or in the legality of authorizing or performing the original act.

§ 100A.   Relation Back in Time and Place

The liabilities of the parties to a ratified act or contract are determined in accordance with the law governing the act or contract at the time and place it was done or made. Whether the conduct of the purported principal is an affirmance depends upon the law at the time and place when and where the principal consents or acts.

§ 101.   Exceptions to Normal Effect of Ratification

Ratification is not effective:

(a)   in favor of a person who, by misrepresentation or duress, has caused the affirmance;

(b)   in favor of the agent against the principal if the principal is obliged to affirm in order to protect his own interests; or

(c)   in diminution of the rights or other interests of persons not parties to the transaction which were acquired in the subject matter before affirmance.

CHAPTER 5. TERMINATION OF AGENCY POWERS

TOPIC 1.   TERMINATION OF AUTHORITY

TITLE A.   INFERRED FROM ORIGINAL MANIFESTATION IN LIGHT OF SUBSEQUENT EVENTS

§ 105.   Lapse of Time

Authority conferred for a specified time terminates at the expiration of that period; if no time is specified, authority terminates at the end of a reasonable period.

§ 106.   Accomplishment of Authorized Act

The authority of an agent to perform a specified act or to accomplish a specified result terminates when the act is done or the result is accomplished by the agent or by another, except that if the act is done or the result is accomplished by a person other than the agent, the manifestations of the principal to the agent determine whether the authority terminates at once or when the agent has notice of it.

§ 107.   Happening of Specified Events

If the terms of the authorization specifically provide that an authority is to continue until a specified event happens or during the continuance of specified conditions, whether the authority terminates at once upon the happening of the event or the cessation of the condition or only when the agent has notice of such happening or cessation depends upon the interpretation of the principal's manifestation in light of all circumstances.

§ 108. Happening of Unspecified Events or Changes; In General

(1) The authority of an agent terminates or is suspended when the agent has notice of the happening of an event or of a change in circumstances from which he should reasonably infer that the principal does not consent to the further exercise of authority or would not consent if he knew the facts.

(2) The agent's authority revives upon the restoration of the original situation within a reasonable time if the agent has no notice that the principal's position has been changed.

§ 109. Change in Value or Business Conditions

The authority of an agent terminates or is suspended when he has notice of a change in value of the subject matter or a change in business conditions from which he should infer that the principal, if he knew of it, would not consent to the further exercise of the authority.

§ 110. Loss or Destruction of Subject Matter

Unless otherwise agreed, the loss or destruction of the subject matter of the authority or the termination of the principal's interest therein terminates the agent's authority to deal with reference to it, either at once or when the agent has notice of it, dependent upon the manifestation of the principal to the agent.

§ 111. Loss of Qualification of Principal or Agent

The loss of or failure to acquire a qualification by the agent without which it is illegal to do an authorized act, or a similar loss or failure by the principal, of which the agent has notice, terminates the agent's authority to act if thereafter he should infer that the principal, if he knew the facts, would not consent to the further exercise of the authority.

§ 112. Disloyalty of Agent

Unless otherwise agreed, the authority of an agent terminates if, without knowledge of the principal, he acquires adverse interests or if he is otherwise guilty of a serious breach of loyalty to the principal.

§ 113. Bankruptcy of Agent

The bankruptcy or insolvency of an agent terminates his authority to conduct transactions in which the state of his credit would so affect the interests of the principal that the agent should infer that the principal, if he knew the facts, would not consent to the further exercise of the authority.

§ 114. Bankruptcy of Principal

The bankruptcy or the substantial impairment of the assets of the principal, of which the agent has notice, terminates his authority as to transactions which he should infer the principal no longer consents to have conducted for him.

§ 115. War

The outbreak of a war of which the agent has notice terminates his authority if the conditions are thereby so changed that he should infer that the principal, if he knew the facts, would not consent to the further exercise of the authority.

§ 116. Change of Law

A change of law of which the agent has notice and which causes the execution of his authority to be illegal, or which otherwise materially changes the effect of its execution, terminates his authority, if he should infer that the principal, if he knew the circumstances, would not consent to the further exercise of the authority.

TITLE B.   TERMINATION BY MUTUAL CONSENT, REVOCATION, OR RENUNCIATION

§ 117.   Mutual Consent

The authority of an agent terminates in accordance with the terms of an agreement between the principal and agent so to terminate it.

§ 118.   Revocation or Renunciation

Authority terminates if the principal or the agent manifests to the other dissent to its continuance.

§ 119.   Manner of Revocation or Renunciation

Authority created in any manner terminates when either party in any manner manifests to the other dissent to its continuance or, unless otherwise agreed, when the other has notice of dissent.

TITLE C.   LOSS OF CAPACITY AND IMPOSSIBILITY

§ 120.   Death of Principal

(1)   The death of the principal terminates the authority of the agent without notice to him, except as stated in subsections (2) and (3) and in the caveat.

(2)   Until notice of a depositor's death, a bank has authority to pay checks drawn by him or by agents authorized by him before death.

(3)   Until notice of the death of the holder of a check deposited for collection, the bank in which it is deposited and those to which the check is sent for collection have authority to go forward with the process of collection.

Caveat:

No inference is to be drawn from the rule stated in this Section that an agent does not have power to bind the estate of a deceased principal in transactions dependent upon a special relation between the agent and the principal, such as trustee and beneficiary, or in transactions in which special rules are applicable, as in dealings with negotiable instruments.

§ 121.   Death of Agent

The death of the agent terminates the authority.

§ 122.   Loss of Capacity of Principal or Agent

(1)   Except as stated in the caveat, the loss of capacity by the principal has the same effect upon the authority of the agent during the period of incapacity as has the principal's death.

(2)   The agent's loss of capacity to do an act for the principal terminates or suspends his authority.

Caveat:

The Institute expresses no opinion as to the effect of the principal's temporary incapacity due to a mental disease.

§ 123. Death or Loss of Capacity of Joint Principals or Agents

The death or loss of capacity of one of two or more joint principals terminates the authority of an agent to act on their joint account to the same extent as the loss of capacity of a single principal. The death or loss of capacity of one of two or more agents authorized to act only jointly terminates the authority of the survivor.

§ 124. Impossibility

There is a termination of the agent's authority:

(a) to create interests in or otherwise deal with a particular subject matter, when it is destroyed;

(b) to affect the interests of the principal in a particular subject matter, when the principal has lost his interests in it;

(c) to enter into transactions with particular persons when they die or lose capacity to become parties to such transactions; or

(d) to effectuate results when, by a change of law or other circumstances, the transactions which the agent is authorized to conduct do not effectuate such results.

TITLE D. EFFECT OF TERMINATION OF AUTHORITY

§ 124A. Effect of Termination of Authority Upon Apparent Authority and Other Powers

The termination of authority does not thereby terminate apparent authority. All other powers of the agent resulting from the relation terminate except powers necessary for the protection of his interests or of those of the principal.

TOPIC 2. TERMINATION OF APPARENT AUTHORITY

§ 125. By Notice of Termination of Authority, or of Principal's Consent, or of a Basic Error

Apparent authority, not otherwise terminated, terminates when the third person has notice of:

(a) the termination of the agent's authority;

(b) a manifestation by the principal that he no longer consents; or

(c) facts, the failure to reveal which, were the transaction with the principal in person, would be ground for rescission by the principal.

Comment b. Apparent authority can exist only as long as the third person, to whom the principal has made a manifestation of authority, continues reasonably to believe that the agent is authorized. He does not have this reasonable belief if he has reason to know that the principal has revoked, or that the agent has renounced the authority, or that such time has elapsed or such events have happened after the authorization as to require the reasonable inference that the agent's authority has terminated. If the authority terminated only because the agent has notice of the happening of an event, the apparent authority may not terminate although the third person has notice of the event (*see* Comment *d*); it is terminated, however, if he knows that the agent has notice of it. In such case, it would be a breach of duty to the principal for the agent to act, and a third person having notice of this can acquire no rights against the principal by thereafter dealing with the agent. The third person has notice of the termination of authority, although he does not know the facts, if he has reason to know them or if, knowing the facts, he would, if reasonable, draw the inference that the authority is terminated, although in fact he unreasonably infers that it is not. He is also bound by a notification given him by the principal in accordance with the rules stated in Section 136.

TOPIC 5.   TERMINATION OF POWERS GIVEN AS SECURITY

§ 138.   Definition

A power given as security is a power to affect the legal relations of another, created in the form of an agency authority, but held for the benefit of the power holder or a third person and given to secure the performance of a duty or to protect a title, either legal or equitable, such power being given when the duty or title is created or given for consideration.

§ 139.   Termination of Powers Given as Security

(1)   Unless otherwise agreed, a power given as security is not terminated by:

(a)   revocation by the creator of the power;

(b)   surrender by the holder of the power, if he holds for the benefit of another;

(c)   the loss of capacity during the lifetime of either the creator of the power or the holder of the power; or

(d)   the death of the holder of the power, or, if the power is given as security for a duty which does not terminate at the death of the creator of the power, by his death.

(2)   A power given as security is terminated by its surrender by the beneficiary, if of full capacity; or by the happening of events which, by its terms, discharges the obligations secured by it, or which makes its execution illegal or impossible.

CHAPTER 6. LIABILITY OF PRINCIPAL TO THIRD PERSONS; CONTRACTS AND CONVEYANCES

TOPIC 1.   GENERAL PRINCIPLES

§ 140.   Liability Based Upon Agency Principles

The liability of the principal to a third person upon a transaction conducted by an agent, or the transfer of his interests by an agent, may be based upon the fact that:

(a)   the agent was authorized;

(b)   the agent was apparently authorized; or

(c)   the agent had a power arising from the agency relation and not dependent upon authority or apparent authority.

§ 143.   Effect of Ratification

Upon ratification with knowledge of the material facts, the principal becomes responsible for contracts and conveyances made for him by one purporting to act on his account as if the transaction had been authorized, if there has been no supervening loss of capacity by the principal or change in the law which would render illegal the authorization or performance of such a transaction.

TOPIC 2.   DISCLOSED OR PARTIALLY DISCLOSED PRINCIPAL

TITLE A.   CREATION OF LIABILITY BY AUTHORIZED ACTS

§ 144.   General Rule

A disclosed or partially disclosed principal is subject to liability upon contracts made by an agent acting within his authority if made in proper form and with the understanding that the principal is a party.

TITLE C. CREATION OF LIABILITY BY UNAUTHORIZED ACTS

§ 159. Apparent Authority

A disclosed or partially disclosed principal is subject to liability upon contracts made by an agent acting within his apparent authority if made in proper form and with the understanding that the apparent principal is a party. The rules as to the liability of a principal for authorized acts, are applicable to unauthorized acts which are apparently authorized.

§ 160. Violation of Secret Instructions

A disclosed or partially disclosed principal authorizing an agent to make a contract, but imposing upon him limitations as to incidental terms intended not to be revealed, is subject to liability upon a contract made in violation of such limitations with a third person who has no notice of them.

§ 161. Unauthorized Acts of General Agent

A general agent for a disclosed or partially disclosed principal subjects his principal to liability for acts done on his account which usually accompany or are incidental to transactions which the agent is authorized to conduct if, although they are forbidden by the principal, the other party reasonably believes that the agent is authorized to do them and has no notice that he is not so authorized.

§ 161A. Unauthorized Acts of Special Agents

A special agent for a disclosed or partly disclosed principal has no power to bind his principal by contracts or conveyances which he is not authorized or apparently authorized to make, unless the principal is estopped, or unless:

    (a) the agent's only departure from his authority or apparent authority is

        (i) in naming or disclosing the principal, or

        (ii) in having an improper motive, or

        (iii) in being negligent in determining the facts upon which his authority is based, or

        (iv) in making misrepresentations; or

    (b) the agent is given possession of goods or commercial documents with authority to deal with them.

TITLE D. DEFENSES AND LIABILITY AFFECTED BY SUBSEQUENT EVENTS

§ 179. Rights Between Third Person and Agent

Unless otherwise agreed, the liability of a disclosed or partially disclosed principal is not affected by any rights or liabilities existing between the other party and the agent at the time the contract is made.

§ 180. Defenses of Principal; In General

A disclosed or partially disclosed principal is entitled to all defenses arising out of a transaction between his agent and a third person. He is not entitled to defenses which are personal to the agent.

TOPIC 3.   UNDISCLOSED PRINCIPAL

TITLE A.   CREATION OF LIABILITY BY AUTHORIZED ACTS

§ 186.   General Rule

An undisclosed principal is bound by contracts and conveyances made on his account by an agent acting within his authority, except that the principal is not bound by a contract which is under seal or which is negotiable, or upon a contract which excludes him.

TITLE B.   CREATION OF LIABILITY BY UNAUTHORIZED ACTS

§ 194.   Acts of General Agents

A general agent for an undisclosed principal authorized to conduct transactions subjects his principal to liability for acts done on his account, if usual or necessary in such transactions, although forbidden by the principal to do them.

§ 195.   Acts of Manager Appearing to be Owner

An undisclosed principal who entrusts an agent with the management of his business is subject to liability to third persons with whom the agent enters into transactions usual in such businesses and on the principal's account, although contrary to the directions of the principal.

§ 195A.   Unauthorized Acts of Special Agents

A special agent for an undisclosed principal has no power to bind his principal by contracts or conveyances which he is not authorized to make unless:

    (a)   the agent's only departure from his authority is

        (i)   in not disclosing his principal, or

        (ii)   in having an improper motive, or

        (iii) in being negligent in determining the facts upon which his authority is based, or

        (iv)   in making misrepresentations; or

    (b)   the agent is given possession of goods or commercial documents with authority to deal with them.

TITLE C.   DEFENSES AND LIABILITY AFFECTED BY SUBSEQUENT EVENTS

§ 203.   Defenses of Undisclosed Principal; In General

An undisclosed principal is entitled to all defenses arising out of a transaction with an agent, but not defenses which are personal to the agent.

§ 205.   Power of Agent to Modify Contract Before Disclosure of Principal

Until the existence of the principal is disclosed, an agent who has made a contract for an undisclosed principal has power to cancel the contract and to modify it with binding effect upon the principal if the contract or conveyance, as modified, is authorized or is within the inherent power of the agent to make.

CHAPTER 7. LIABILITY OF PRINCIPAL TO THIRD PERSON; TORTS

TOPIC 1. LIABILITY FOR PERSONAL VIOLATION OF DUTY

§ 212. Principal Intends Conduct or Consequences

A person is subject to liability for the consequences of another's conduct which results from his directions as he would be for his own personal conduct if, with knowledge of the conditions, he intends the conduct, or if he intends its consequences, unless the one directing or the one acting has a privilege or immunity not available to the other.

§ 213. Principal Negligent or Reckless

A person conducting an activity through servants or other agents is subject to liability for harm resulting from his conduct if he is negligent or reckless:

(a) in giving improper or ambiguous orders of in failing to make proper regulations; or

(b) in the employment of improper persons or instrumentalities in work involving risk of harm to others:

(c) in the supervision of the activity; or

(d) in permitting, or failing to prevent, negligent or other tortious conduct by persons, whether or not his servants or agents, upon premises or with instrumentalities under his control.

§ 214. Failure of Principal to Perform Non-Delegable Duty

A master or other principal who is under a duty to provide protection for or to have care used to protect others or their property and who confides the performance of such duty to a servant or other person is subject to liability to such others for harm caused to them by the failure of such agent to perform the duty.

TOPIC 2. LIABILITY FOR AUTHORIZED CONDUCT OR CONDUCT INCIDENTAL THERETO

TITLE A. IN GENERAL

§ 215. Conduct Authorized but Unintended by Principal

A master or other principal who unintentionally authorizes conduct of a servant or other agent which constitutes a tort to a third person is subject to liability to such person.

§ 216. Unauthorized Tortious Conduct

A master or other principal may be liable to another whose interests have been invaded by the tortious conduct of a servant or other agent, although the principal does not personally violate a duty to such other or authorize the conduct of the agent causing the invasion.

TITLE B. TORTS OF SERVANTS

§ 219. When Master is Liable for Torts of His Servants

(1) A master is subject to liability for the torts of his servants committed while acting in the scope of their employment.

(2) A master is not subject to liability for the torts of his servants acting outside the scope of their employment, unless:

    (a)   the master intended the conduct or the consequences, or

    (b)   the master was negligent or reckless, or

    (c)   the conduct violated a non-delegable duty of the master, or

    (d)   the servant purported to act or to speak on behalf of the principal and there was reliance upon apparent authority, or he was aided in accomplishing the tort by the existence of the agency relation.

WHO IS A SERVANT

§ 220.   Definition of Servant

(1)   A servant is a person employed to perform services in the affairs of another and who with respect to the physical conduct in the performance of the services is subject to the other's control or right to control.

(2)   In determining whether one acting for another is a servant or an independent contractor, the following matters of fact, among others, are considered:

    (a)   the extent of control which, by the agreement, the master may exercise over the details of the work;

    (b)   whether or not the one employed is engaged in a distinct occupation or business;

    (c)   the kind of occupation, with reference to whether, in the locality, the work is usually done under the direction of the employer or by a specialist without supervision;

    (d)   the skill required in the particular occupation;

    (e)   whether the employer or the workman supplies the instrumentalities, tools, and the place of work for the person doing the work;

    (f)   the length of time for which the person is employed;

    (g)   the method of payment, whether by the time or by the job;

    (h)   whether or not the work is a part of the regular business of the employer;

    (i)   whether or not the parties believe they are creating the relation of master and servant; and

    (j)   whether the principal is or is not in business.

SCOPE OF EMPLOYMENT

§ 228.   General Statement

(1)   Conduct of a servant is within the scope of employment if, but only if:

    (a)   it is of the kind he is employed to perform;

    (b)   it occurs substantially within the authorized time and space limits;

    (c)   it is actuated, at least in part, by a purpose to serve the master; and

    (d)   if force is intentionally used by the servant against another, the use of force is not unexpectable by the master.

(2)   Conduct of a servant is not within the scope of employment if it is different in kind from that authorized, far beyond the authorized time or space limits, or too little actuated by a purpose to serve the master.

§ 229.   Kind of Conduct Within Scope of Employment

(1)   To be within the scope of the employment, conduct must be of the same general nature as that authorized, or incidental to the conduct authorized.

(2)   In determining whether or not the conduct, although not authorized, is nevertheless so similar to or incidental to the conduct authorized as to be within the scope of employment, the following matters of fact are to be considered:

(a)   whether or not the act is one commonly done by such servants;

(b)   the time, place and purpose of the act;

(c)   the previous relations between the master and the servant;

(d)   the extent to which the business of the master is apportioned between different servants;

(e)   whether or not the act is outside the enterprise of the master or, if within the enterprise, has not been entrusted to any servant;

(f)   whether or not the master has reason to expect that such an act will be done;

(g)   the similarity in quality of the act done to the act authorized;

(h)   whether or not the instrumentality by which the harm is done has been furnished by the master to the servant;

(i)   the extent of departure from the normal method of accomplishing an authorized result; and

(j)   whether or not the act is seriously criminal.

Comment a. As stated in Section 212, a master is responsible for an act or result which he intends the servant to perform or achieve if the servant acts because of his directions. Also, as stated in Section 215, a master is responsible for authorized but unintended conduct. Thus, a servant is authorized to do anything which is reasonably regarded as incidental to the work specifically directed or which is usually done in connection with such work. The scope of employment includes not only such acts but also other acts which, as between the master and servant, the servant is not privileged to do. The limits of the scope of employment are dependent upon the facts of the particular case, and no more definite statement can profitably be made concerning them than that made in Subsection (2). Since the phrase "scope of the employment," is used for the purpose of determining the liability of the master for the conduct of servants, the ultimate question is whether or not it is just that the loss resulting from the servant's acts should be considered as one of the normal risks to be borne by the business in which the servant is employed.

The factors here stated have primary reference to the physical activities of servants. The special rules which deal with situations in which the master may be liable for deceit, false arrest or attachment and similar matters are stated in Sections 246–264.

§ 230.   Forbidden Acts

An act, although forbidden, or done in a forbidden manner, may be within the scope of employment.

§ 231.   Criminal or Tortious Acts

An act may be within the scope of employment although consciously criminal or tortious.

§ 232.   Failure to Act

The failure of a servant to act may be conduct within the scope of employment.

§ 233.   Time of Service

Conduct of a servant is within the scope of employment only during a period which has a reasonable connection with the authorized period.

§ 234.   Area of Service

Conduct is within the scope of employment only in the authorized area or in a locality not unreasonably distant from it.

§ 235.   Conduct not for Purpose of Serving Master

An act of a servant is not within the scope of employment if it is done with no intention to perform it as a part of or incident to a service on account of which he is employed.

§ 236.   Conduct Actuated by Dual Purpose

Conduct may be within the scope of employment, although done in part to serve the purposes of the servant or of a third person.

§ 237.   Re-entry into Employment

A servant who has temporarily departed in space or time from the scope of employment does not re-enter it until he is again reasonably near the authorized space and time limits and is acting with the intention of serving his master's business.

TITLE C.   AGENTS' TORTS; LIABILITY NOT DEPENDENT UPON RELATION OF MASTER AND SERVANT

IN GENERAL

§ 250.   Non-Liability for Physical Harm by Non-Servant Agents

A principal is not liable for physical harm caused by the negligent physical conduct of a non-servant agent during the performance of the principal's business, if he neither intended nor authorized the result nor the manner of performance, unless he was under a duty to have the act performed with due care.

§ 251.   Liability for Physical Harm Caused by a Servant or a Non-Servant Agent

A principal is subject to liability for physical harm to the person or the tangible things of another caused by the negligence of a servant or a non-servant agent:

(a)   in the performance of an act which the principal is under a duty to have performed with care; and

(b)   in the making of a representation which the agent is authorized or apparently authorized to make or which is within the power of the agent to make for the principal.

§ 252.   Mistaken Action by Agents

If a servant or other agent, authorized to do an act provided certain conditions exist, and to determine whether or not such conditions exist, does the act in the erroneous belief that such conditions do exist and thereby commits a tort, the principal is subject to liability for the act.

§ 253.   Tortious Institution or Conduct of Legal Proceedings

A principal who authorizes a servant or other agent to institute or conduct such legal proceedings as in his judgment are lawful and desirable for the protection of the principal's interests is subject to liability to a person against whom proceedings reasonably adapted to accomplish the principal's purposes are tortiously brought by the agent.

§ 254. Defamation

A principal is subject to liability for a defamatory statement by a servant or other agent if the agent was authorized, or if, as to the person to whom he made the statement, he was apparently authorized to make it.

§ 255. Acts of Subservants and Other Subagents

The rules applicable to the liability of a principal for the acts of agents, are applicable to his liability for subservants and other subagents insofar as their conduct has relation to the principal's affairs.

MISREPRESENTATIONS

§ 256. Knowledge of Principal When Agent Innocently Makes a Misrepresentation

If a principal knows facts unknown to a servant or other agent and which are relevant to a transaction which the agent is authorized to conduct, and, because of his justifiable ignorance, the agent makes a material misstatement of facts, the principal:

(a) is subject to liability for an intentional misrepresentation, if he believed the agent would make the statement, or for a negligent misrepresentation, if he had reason to know the agent would make the statement.

(b) is not subject to liability in tort if he had no reason to know that the agent would enter into such a transaction, or if, after acquiring the information, he had no way of communicating with the agent.

§ 257. Misrepresentations; In General

A principal is subject to liability for loss caused to another by the other's reliance upon a tortious representation of a servant or other agent, if the representation is:

(a) authorized;

(b) apparently authorized; or

(c) within the power of the agent to make for the principal.

Comment g. Physical harm. The rule stated in this Section applies to physical harm resulting from the misrepresentation, as well as to economic loss. Thus, an agent authorized to direct travelers causes his employer to be liable if he negligently directs them to a dangerous place in which they are harmed.

§ 258. Incidental Misrepresentations

In the absence of an exculpatory agreement, a principal authorizing a servant or other agent to enter into negotiations to which representations concerning the subject matter thereof are usually incident is subject to liability for loss caused to the other party to the transaction by tortious misrepresentations of the agent upon matters which the principal might reasonably expect would be the subject of representations, provided the other party has no notice that the representations are unauthorized.

§ 259.   Rescission of Transaction for Misrepresentations of Agent

(1)   A transaction into which one is induced to enter by reliance upon untrue and material representations as to the subject matter, made by a servant or other agent entrusted with its preliminary or final negotiations, is subject to rescission at the election of the person deceived.

(2)   Change of position by the principal:

    (a)   is a defense if the agent has no power to bind the principal by the misrepresentations;

    (b)   is not a defense if the principal was liable for the misrepresentations.

Caveat:

No statement is made as to the defense of change of position if the misrepresentation, although within the power of the agent to make for the principal, was not tortious.

§ 260.   Contracts Limiting Liability for Agent's Misrepresentations

(1)   An innocent principal can, by contract with another, relieve himself of liability for deceit because of unauthorized fraud by a servant or other agent upon the other party.

(2)   A contract with, or a conveyance to, the principal obtained by his agent through misrepresentations can be rescinded by the other party to the contract or conveyance prior to a change of position by the principal, even though the contract provides that "it shall not be affected by misrepresentations not contained therein" and includes a statement that the agent has made no representations.

Caveat:

The rule stated in Subsection (2) is not intended to deny the possibility that the principal and the other party can make a binding agreement that the other party shall not be able to avoid the transaction because of his reliance upon misrepresentations made by the agent.

§ 261.   Agent's Position Enables Him to Deceive

A principal who puts a servant or other agent in a position which enables the agent, while apparently acting within his authority, to commit a fraud upon third persons is subject to liability to such third persons for the fraud.

Comment a. The principal is subject to liability under the rule stated in this Section although he is entirely innocent, has received no benefit from the transaction, and, as stated in Section 262, although the agent acted solely for his own purposes. Liability is based upon the fact that the agent's position facilitates the consummation of the fraud, in that from the point of view of the third person the transaction seems regular on its face and the agent appears to be acting in the ordinary course of the business confided to him.

§ 262.   Agent Acts for His Own Purposes

A person who otherwise would be liable to another for the misrepresentations of one apparently acting for him is not relieved from liability by the fact that the servant or other agent acts entirely for his own purposes, unless the other has notice of this.

§ 263.   Property Acquired for Principal by Fraud of Agent

Unless he has changed his position, a principal whose servant or other agent has fraudulently acquired property for him, holds it subject to the interests of the defrauded person. If the principal is liable in tort for the fraud of the agent, his change of position after acquiring the property is not a defense.

§ 264. Misrepresentations by Subservants and Other Subagents

The rules applicable to representations by servants and other agents are applicable to representations by subservants and other subagents made in connection with transactions conducted for the principal.

TITLE D.   CONDUCT WITHIN APPARENT AUTHORITY OR EMPLOYMENT

§ 265. General Rule

(1)   A master or other principal is subject to liability for torts which result from reliance upon, or belief in, statements or other conduct within an agent's apparent authority.

(2)   Unless there has been reliance, the principal is not liable in tort for conduct of a servant or other agent merely because it is within his apparent authority or apparent scope of employment.

§ 266. Physical Harm Caused by Reliance Upon Representations

A purported master or other principal is subject to liability for physical harm caused to others or to their belongings by their reasonable reliance upon the tortious representations of one acting within his apparent authority or apparent scope of employment.

§ 267. Reliance Upon Care or Skill of Apparent Servant or Other Agent

One who represents that another is his servant or other agent and thereby causes a third person justifiably to rely upon the care or skill of such apparent agent is subject to liability to the third person for harm caused by the lack of care or skill of the one appearing to be a servant or other agent as if he were such.

CHAPTER 10.   LIABILITY OF THIRD PERSON TO PRINCIPAL

TOPIC 1.   CONTRACTS; DISCLOSED AGENCY

§ 292. General Rule

The other party to a contract made by an agent for a disclosed or partially disclosed principal, acting within his authority, apparent authority or other agency power, is liable to the principal as if he had contracted directly with the principal, unless the principal is excluded as a party by the form or terms of the contract.

§ 293. Principal Excluded From Transaction

The other party to a contract made by an agent on behalf of a disclosed or partially disclosed principal does not become liable to such principal upon it in an action at law if the principal is excluded as a party by the form or terms of the contract.

§ 298. Defenses of Other Party

The other party to a contract made by an agent on behalf of a disclosed or partially disclosed principal has all the defenses which he would have had against the principal if the principal had made the contract under the same circumstances.

§ 299. Rights Between Other Party and Agent

Unless otherwise agreed, the liability of the other party to a disclosed or partially disclosed principal upon a contract made by an agent is not affected by any rights or liabilities then existing between the other party and the agent.

TOPIC 2.   CONTRACTS; UNDISCLOSED AGENCY

§ 302.   General Rule

A person who makes a contract with an agent of an undisclosed principal, intended by the agent to be on account of his principal and within the power of such agent to bind his principal, is liable to the principal as if the principal himself had made the contract with him, unless he is excluded by the form or terms of the contract, unless his existence is fraudulently concealed or unless there is set-off or a similar defense against the agent.

§ 303.   Principal Excluded From Transaction

A person with whom an agent makes a contract on account of an undisclosed principal is not liable in an action at law brought upon the contract by such principal:

    (a)   if the contract is in the form of a sealed or negotiable instrument; or

    (b)   if the terms of the contract exclude liability to any undisclosed principal or to the particular principal.

§ 304.   Agent Misrepresents Existence of Principal

A person with whom an agent contracts on account of an undisclosed principal can rescind the contract if he was induced to enter into it by a representation that the agent was not acting for a principal and if, as the agent or principal had notice, he would not have dealt with the principal.

§ 306.   Rights Between Other Party and Agent

(1)   If the agent has been authorized to conceal the existence of the principal, the liability to an undisclosed principal of a person dealing with the agent within his power to bind the principal is diminished by any claim which such person may have against the agent at the time of making the contract and until the existence of the principal becomes known to him, if he could set off such claim in an action against the agent.

(2)   If the agent is authorized only to contract in the principal's name, the other party does not have set-off for a claim due him from the agent unless the agent has been entrusted with the possession of chattels which he disposes of as directed or unless the principal has otherwise misled the third person into extending credit to the agent.

§ 308.   Defenses of Other Party

In an action by an undisclosed principal against the other party to a contract, the other party has all the defenses, except those of a purely procedural nature:

    (a)   which he would have had against the principal if the principal had made the contract under the same circumstances,

    (b)   which he had against the agent until the discovery of the principal, unless the agent was authorized to contract only in the principal's name.

§ 309.   Principal Cannot or Does not Give Required Performance

Acts done or offered to be done by an undisclosed principal which, if performed by a person other than the agent, are not substantially those which the contract contemplates, are not effective as a performance or as a tender of performance of the contract.

§ 310. When Performance Must be Rendered to Principal

An undisclosed principal upon whose account an agent has acted within his power to bind the principal in making a contract, unless he is excluded by its terms, can require the other party to render performance to him instead of to the agent, except in the case of personal services or where performance to the principal would subject the other to a substantially different liability from that contemplated.

TOPIC 5. EFFECT OF RATIFICATION

§ 319. General Rule

Where a purported servant or other agent has entered into a transaction with a third person, its ratification by the purported master or other principal has the same effect upon the liabilities of the third person to the principal as an original authorization.

CHAPTER 11. LIABILITY OF AGENT TO THIRD PERSONS

TOPIC 1. CONTRACTS AND CONVEYANCES

TITLE A. AGENT A PARTY TO A TRANSACTION CONDUCTED BY HIMSELF

§ 320. Principal Disclosed

Unless otherwise agreed, a person making or purporting to make a contract with another as agent for a disclosed principal does not become a party to the contract.

§ 321. Principal Partially Disclosed

Unless otherwise agreed, a person purporting to make a contract with another for a partially disclosed principal is a party to the contract.

§ 322. Principal Undisclosed

An agent purporting to act upon his own account, but in fact making a contract on account of an undisclosed principal, is a party to the contract.

§ 326. Principal Known to be Nonexistent or Incompetent

Unless otherwise agreed, a person who, in dealing with another, purports to act as agent for a principal whom both know to be nonexistent or wholly incompetent, becomes a party to such a contract.

TITLE B. AGENT NOT PARTY TO TRANSACTION CONDUCTED BY HIMSELF

§ 328. Liability of Authorized Agent for Performance of Contract

An agent, by making a contract only on behalf of a competent disclosed or partially disclosed principal whom he has power so to bind, does not thereby become liable for its nonperformance.

§ 329. Agent Who Warrants Authority

A person who purports to make a contract, conveyance or representation on behalf of another who has full capacity but whom he has no power to bind, thereby becomes subject to liability to the other party thereto upon an implied warranty of authority, unless he has manifested that he does not make such warranty or the other party knows that the agent is not so authorized.

§ 330. Liability for Misrepresentation of Authority

A person who tortiously misrepresents to another that he has authority to make a contract, conveyance, or representation on behalf of a principal whom he has no power to bind, is subject to liability to the other in an action of tort for loss caused by reliance upon such misrepresentation.

TITLE C. DEFENSES AND EFFECTS OF SUBSEQUENT EVENTS

§ 333. Rights Between Other Party and Principal

Unless otherwise agreed, the liability of an agent upon a contract between a third person and the principal to which the agent is a party is not affected by any rights or liabilities existing between the third person and the principal not arising from the transaction, except that, with the consent of the principal, the agent can set off a claim which the principal would have in an action brought against him.

§ 334. Defenses of Agent; In General

In an action against an agent upon a contract between a third person and the principal to which the agent is a party, the agent has all the defenses which arise out of the transaction itself and also those which he has personally against the third person; defenses which are personal to the principal are not available to the agent.

§ 335. Agent Surety for Principal

In an action brought against an agent upon a contract to which the agent is a party but under which the primary duty of performance rests upon the principal, the agent has the defenses available to a surety.

§ 336. Election by Other Party to Hold Principal; Agency Disclosed

Unless otherwise agreed, the agent of a disclosed or partially disclosed principal who is a party to a contract made by another with such principal is not relieved from liability upon the contract by the determination of the other party to look to the principal alone, nor, unless the agent and the principal are joint contractors, by the fact that the other gets a judgment against the principal. He is relieved from liability to the extent that he is prejudiced thereby if he changes his position in justifiable reliance upon a manifestation of the other that he will look solely to the principal for performance.

§ 337. Election by Other Party to Hold Principal; Agency Undisclosed

An agent who has made a contract on behalf of an undisclosed principal is not relieved from liability by the determination of the other party thereto to look to the principal alone for the performance of the contract. He is discharged from liability if the other obtains a judgment against the principal, or, to the extent that he is prejudiced thereby, if he changes his position in justifiable reliance upon the other's manifestation that he will look solely to the principal for payment.

TOPIC 3. TORTS

§ 343. General Rule

An agent who does an act otherwise a tort is not relieved from liability by the fact that he acted at the command of the principal or on account of the principal, except where he is exercising a privilege of the principal, or a privilege held by him for the protection of the principal's interests, or where the principal owes no duty or less than the normal duty of care to the person harmed.

CHAPTER 13. DUTIES AND LIABILITIES OF AGENT TO PRINCIPAL

TOPIC 1. DUTIES

TITLE B. DUTIES OF SERVICE AND OBEDIENCE

§ 377. Contractual Duties

A person who makes a contract with another to perform services as an agent for him is subject to a duty to act in accordance with his promise.

§ 379. Duty of Care and Skill

(1) Unless otherwise agreed, a paid agent is subject to a duty to the principal to act with standard care and with the skill which is standard in the locality for the kind of work which he is employed to perform and, in addition, to exercise any special skill that he has.

(2) Unless otherwise agreed, a gratuitous agent is under a duty to the principal to act with the care and skill which is required of persons not agents performing similar gratuitous undertakings for others.

§ 381. Duty to Give Information

Unless otherwise agreed, an agent is subject to a duty to use reasonable efforts to give his principal information which is relevant to affairs entrusted to him and which, as the agent has notice, the principal would desire to have and which can be communicated without violating a superior duty to a third person.

§ 383. Duty to Act Only as Authorized

Except when he is privileged to protect his own or another's interests, an agent is subject to a duty to the principal not to act in the principal's affairs except in accordance with the principal's manifestation of consent.

§ 385. Duty to Obey

(1) Unless otherwise agreed, an agent is subject to a duty to obey all reasonable directions in regard to the manner of performing a service that he has contracted to perform.

(2) Unless he is privileged to protect his own or another's interests, an agent is subject to a duty not to act in matters entrusted to him on account of the principal contrary to the directions of the principal, even though the terms of the employment prescribe that such directions shall not be given.

TITLE C. DUTIES OF LOYALTY

§ 387. General Principle

Unless otherwise agreed, an agent is subject to a duty to his principal to act solely for the benefit of the principal in all matters connected with his agency.

§ 388. Duty to Account for Profits Arising Out of Employment

Unless otherwise agreed, an agent who makes a profit in connection with transactions conducted by him on behalf of the principal is under a duty to give such profit to the principal.

§ 389.   Acting as Adverse Party Without Principal's Consent

Unless otherwise agreed, an agent is subject to a duty not to deal with his principal as an adverse party in a transaction connected with his agency without the principal's knowledge.

§ 390.   Acting as Adverse Party with Principal's Consent

An agent who, to the knowledge of the principal, acts on his own account in a transaction in which he is employed has a duty to deal fairly with the principal and to disclose to him all facts which the agent knows or should know would reasonably affect the principal's judgment, unless the principal has manifested that he knows such facts or that he does not care to know them.

§ 391.   Acting for Adverse Party Without Principal's Consent

Unless otherwise agreed, an agent is subject to a duty to his principal not to act on behalf of an adverse party in a transaction connected with his agency without the principal's knowledge.

Comment b. Where act not inconsistent with agent's duty. An agent can properly deal with the other party to a transaction if such dealing is not inconsistent with his duties to the principal. Thus, an agent employed to sell can properly lend money to the buyer to complete the purchase or he may "split" his commission with the buyer, unless because of business policy or otherwise it is understood that he is not to do so.

§ 392.   Acting for Adverse Party with Principal's Consent

An agent who, to the knowledge of two principals, acts for both of them in a transaction between them, has a duty to act with fairness to each and to disclose to each all facts which he knows or should know would reasonably affect the judgment of each in permitting such dual agency, except as to a principal who has manifested that he knows such facts or does not care to know them.

§ 393.   Competition as to Subject Matter of Agency

Unless otherwise agreed, an agent is subject to a duty not to compete with the principal concerning the subject matter of his agency.

§ 394.   Acting for One with Conflicting Interests

Unless otherwise agreed, an agent is subject to a duty not to act or to agree to act during the period of his agency for persons whose interests conflict with those of the principal in matters in which the agent is employed.

§ 395.   Using or Disclosing Confidential Information

Unless otherwise agreed, an agent is subject to a duty to the principal not to use or to communicate information confidentially given him by the principal or acquired by him during the course of or on account of his agency or in violation of his duties as agent, in competition with or to the injury of the principal, on his own account or on behalf of another, although such information does not relate to the transaction in which he is then employed, unless the information is a matter of general knowledge.

§ 396.   Using Confidential Information After Termination of Agency

Unless otherwise agreed, after the termination of the agency, the agent:

(a)   has no duty not to compete with the principal;

(b)   has a duty to the principal not to use or to disclose to third persons, on his own account or on account of others, in competition with the principal or to his injury, trade secrets, written lists of names, or other similar confidential matters given to him only for the principal's use or acquired by the agent in violation of duty. The agent is entitled to use general information concerning the method of business of the principal and the names of the customers retained in his memory, if not acquired in violation of his duty as agent;

(c)   has a duty to account for profits made by the sale or use of trade secrets and other confidential information, whether or not in competition with the principal;

(d)   has a duty to the principal not to take advantage of a still subsisting confidential relation created during the prior agency relation.

§ 398.   Confusing or Appearing to Own Principal's Things

Unless otherwise agreed, an agent receiving or holding things on behalf of the principal is subject to a duty to the principal not to receive or deal with them so that they will appear to be his own, and not so to mingle them with his own things as to destroy their identity.

TOPIC 2.   LIABILITIES

§ 399.   Remedies of Principal

A principal whose agent has violated or threatens to violate his duties has an appropriate remedy for such violation. Such remedy may be:

(a)   an action on the contract of service;

(b)   an action for losses and for the misuse of property;

(c)   an action in equity to enforce the provisions of an express trust undertaken by the agent;

(d)   an action for restitution, either at law or in equity;

(e)   an action for an accounting;

(f)   an action for an injunction;

(g)   set-off or counterclaim;

(h)   causing the agent to be made party to an action brought by a third person against the principal;

(i)   self-help;

(j)   discharge; or

(k)   refusal to pay compensation or rescission of the contract of employment.

§ 401.   Liability for Loss Caused

An agent is subject to liability for loss caused to the principal by any breach of duty.

§ 402.   Liability for Misuse of Principal's Property

(1)   An agent is subject to liability to the principal for the value of a chattel, a chose in action, or money which he holds for the principal and to the immediate possession of which the principal is entitled, together with interest thereon if the amount is liquidated, or damages, if the agent:

(a)   intentionally or negligently destroys it or causes its loss;

(b)   uses it for his own purposes under an adverse claim;

(c)   unreasonably refuses to surrender it on demand;

(d)   manifests that he will not surrender it except on conditions which he is not privileged to exact;

(e)   makes delivery of it to a person to whom he is not authorized to deliver it;

(f)   improperly causes the title or indicia of title to be placed in his own name, if either this is done in bad faith or the thing substantially depreciates in value while the title is so held because of his wrongful conduct;

(g)   deviates substantially from his authority in its transfer to a third person in a sale or purchase; or

(h)   intentionally and substantially deviates from his authority in dealing with the possession of the thing, and the chattel suffers substantial harm during the course of such wrongful dealing or because of it.

(2)   An agent who deviates substantially from his authority in the transfer of land belonging to the principal or who, in bad faith, causes the title of such land to be placed in his own name, is subject to liability to the principal for the value of the land.

§ 403. Liability for Things Received in Violation of Duty of Loyalty

If an agent receives anything as a result of his violation of a duty of loyalty to the principal, he is subject to a liability to deliver it, its value, or its proceeds, to the principal.

§ 404. Liability for Use of Principal's Assets

An agent who, in violation of duty to his principal, uses for his own purposes or those of a third person assets of the principal's business is subject to liability to the principal for the value of the use. If the use predominates in producing a profit he is subject to liability, at the principal's election, for such profit; he is not, however, liable for profits made by him merely by the use of time which he has contracted to devote to the principal unless he violates his duty not to act adversely or in competition with the principal.

§ 407. Principal's Choice of Remedies

(1)   If an agent has received a benefit as a result of violating his duty of loyalty, the principal is entitled to recover from him what he has so received, its value, or its proceeds, and also the amount of damage thereby caused; except that, if the violation consists of the wrongful disposal of the principal's property, the principal cannot recover its value and also what the agent received in exchange therefor.

(2)   A principal who has recovered damages from a third person because of an agent's violation of his duty of loyalty is entitled nevertheless to obtain from the agent any profit which the agent improperly received as a result of the transaction.

TOPIC 4. DUTIES AND LIABILITIES OF PARTICULAR KINDS OF AGENTS

§ 422. Agents in Charge of Land or Chattels

Unless otherwise agreed, an agent who has charge of land or chattels for his principal is subject to a duty to the principal to use reasonable care in their protection, to use them only in accordance with the directions of the principal and for his benefit, and to surrender them upon demand or upon the termination of the agency.

§ 423. Agents Holding a Title

Unless otherwise agreed, an agent who holds the title to something for the principal is subject to a duty to the principal to use reasonable care in the protection of the title which he so holds, to act in accordance with the directions of the principal, to use it only for the principal's benefit, and to transfer it upon demand or upon the termination of the agency.

CHAPTER 14.   DUTIES AND LIABILITIES OF PRINCIPAL TO AGENT

TOPIC 1.   CONTRACTUAL AND RESTITUTIONAL DUTIES AND LIABILITIES

TITLE A.   INTERPRETATION OF CONTRACTS AND LIABILITIES THEREUNDER

§ 432.   Duty to Perform Contract

A principal is subject to a duty to an agent to perform the contract which he has made with the agent.

§ 433.   Duty to Furnish Opportunity for Work

A principal does not, by contracting to employ an agent, thereby promise to provide him with an opportunity for work, but the circumstances under which the agreement for employment is made or the nature of the employment may warrant an inference of such a promise.

§ 434.   Duty not to Interfere with Agent's Work

A principal who has contracted to afford an agent an opportunity to work has a duty to refrain from unreasonably interfering with his work.

§ 435.   Duty to Give Agent Information

Unless otherwise agreed, it is inferred that a principal contracts to use care to inform the agent of risks of physical harm or pecuniary loss which, as the principal has reason to know, exist in the performance of authorized acts and which he has reason to know are unknown to the agent. His duty to give other information depends upon the agreement between them.

§ 436.   Duty to Keep and Render Accounts

Unless otherwise agreed, a master has a duty to keep and render accounts of the amount due from him to a servant; whether principals of other agents have such a duty depends upon the method of compensation, the fact that the agent operates or does not operate an independent enterprise, the customs of business and other similar factors.

§ 437.   Duty of Good Conduct

Unless otherwise agreed, a principal who has contracted to employ an agent has a duty to conduct himself so as not to harm the agent's reputation nor to make it impossible for the agent, consistently with his reasonable self-respect or personal safety, to continue in the employment.

§ 438.   Duty of Indemnity; The Principle

(1)   A principal is under a duty to indemnify the agent in accordance with the terms of the agreement with him.

(2)   In the absence of terms to the contrary in the agreement of employment, the principal has a duty to indemnify the agent where the agent

    (a)   makes a payment authorized or made necessary in executing the principal's affairs or, unless he is officious, one beneficial to the principal, or

    (b)   suffers a loss which, because of their relation, it is fair that the principal should bear.

§ 439.   When Duty of Indemnity Exists

Unless otherwise agreed, a principal is subject to a duty to exonerate an agent who is not barred by the illegality of his conduct to indemnify him for:

     (a)   authorized payments made by the agent on behalf of the principal;

     (b)   payments upon contracts upon which the agent is authorized to make himself liable, and upon obligations arising from the possession or ownership of things which he is authorized to hold on account of the principal;

     (c)   payments of damages to third persons which he is required to make on account of the authorized performance of an act which constitutes a tort or a breach of contract;

     (d)   expenses of defending actions by third persons brought because of the agent's authorized conduct, such actions being unfounded but not brought in bad faith; and

     (e)   payments resulting in benefit to the principal, made by the agent under such circumstances that it would be inequitable for indemnity not to be made.

§ 440.   When No Duty of Indemnity

Unless otherwise agreed, the principal is not subject to a duty to indemnify an agent:

     (a)   for pecuniary loss or other harm, not of benefit to the principal, arising from the performance of unauthorized acts or resulting solely from the agent's negligence or other fault; or

     (b)   if the principal has otherwise performed his duties to the agent, for physical harm caused by the performance of authorized acts, for harm suffered as a result of torts, other than the tortious institution of suits, committed upon the agent by third persons because of his employment, or for harm suffered by the refusal of third persons to deal with him; or

     (c)   if the agent's loss resulted from an enterprise which he knew to be illegal.

§ 441.   Duty to Pay Compensation

Unless the relation of the parties, the triviality of the services, or other circumstances, indicate that the parties have agreed otherwise, it is inferred that a person promises to pay for services which he requests or permits another to perform for him as his agent.

§ 442.   Period of Employment

Unless otherwise agreed, mutual promises by principal and agent to employ and to serve create obligations to employ and to serve which are terminable upon notice by either party; if neither party terminates the employment, it may terminate by lapse of time or by supervening events.

B. RESTATEMENT (THIRD) OF AGENCY (2006)

(with Selected Comments)

Table of Sections

CHAPTER 1.   INTRODUCTORY MATTERS

TOPIC 1.   DEFINITIONS AND TERMINOLOGY

CHAPTER 2.   PRINCIPLES OF ATTRIBUTION

TOPIC 1.   ACTUAL AUTHORITY

TOPIC 2.   APPARENT AUTHORITY

TOPIC 3.   RESPONDEAT SUPERIOR

TOPIC 4.   RELATED DOCTRINES

CHAPTER 3.   CREATION AND TERMINATION OF AUTHORITY AND AGENCY RELATIONSHIPS

TOPIC 1.   CREATING AND EVIDENCING ACTUAL AUTHORITY

TOPIC 2.   CREATING APPARENT AUTHORITY

TOPIC 3.   CAPACITY TO ACT AS PRINCIPAL OR AGENT

RESTATEMENT (THIRD) OF AGENCY (2006)

TOPIC 4.   TERMINATION OF AGENT'S POWER

TITLE A.   TERMINATION OF ACTUAL AUTHORITY

TITLE B.   TERMINATION OF APPARENT AUTHORITY

TITLE C.   IRREVOCABLE POWERS

TOPIC 5.   AGENTS WITH MULTIPLE PRINCIPALS

CHAPTER 4.   RATIFICATION

CHAPTER 5.   NOTIFICATIONS AND NOTICE

CHAPTER 6.   CONTRACTS AND OTHER TRANSACTIONS WITH THIRD PARTIES

TOPIC 1.   PARTIES TO CONTRACTS

TOPIC 2.   RIGHTS, LIABILITIES, AND DEFENSES

TITLE A.   GENERAL

RESTATEMENT (THIRD) OF AGENCY (2006)

CHAPTER 1. INTRODUCTORY MATTERS

TOPIC 1.   DEFINITIONS AND TERMINOLOGY

§ 1.01   Agency Defined

Agency is the fiduciary relationship that arises when one person (a "principal") manifests assent to another person (an "agent") that the agent shall act on the principal's behalf and subject to the principal's control, and the agent manifests assent or otherwise consents so to act.

Comment f. Principal's power and right of interim control.

(1).   Principal's power and right of interim control—in general. An essential element of agency is the principal's right to control the agent's actions. Control is a concept that embraces a wide spectrum of meanings, but within any relationship of agency the principal initially states what the agent shall and shall not do, in specific or general terms. Additionally, a principal has the right to give interim instructions or directions to the agent once their relationship is established. Within an organization the right to control its agents is essential to the organization's ability to function, regardless of its size, structure, or degree of hierarchy or complexity. In an organization, it is often another agent, one holding a supervisory position, who gives the directions. For definitions of the terms "superior" and "subordinate" coagents, *see* § 1.04(9). A principal may exercise influence over an agent's actions in other ways as well. Incentive structures that reward the agent for achieving results affect the agent's actions. In an organization, assigning a specified function with a functionally descriptive title to a person tends to control activity because it manifests what types of activity are approved by the principal to all who know of the function and title, including their holder.

A relationship of agency is not present unless the person on whose behalf action is taken has the right to control the actor. Thus, if a person is appointed by a court to act as a receiver, the receiver is not the agent of the person whose affairs the receiver manages because the appointing court retains the power to control the receiver.

A principal's control over an agent will as a practical matter be incomplete because no agent is an automaton who mindlessly but perfectly executes commands. A principal's power to give instructions, created by the agency relationship, does not mean that all instructions the principal gives are proper. An agent's duty of obedience does not require the agent to obey instructions to commit a crime or a tort or to violate established professional standards. *See* § 8.09(2). Moreover, an agent's duty of obedience does not supersede the agent's power to resign and terminate the agency relationship. *See* § 3.10.

The power to give interim instructions distinguishes principals in agency relationships from those who contract to receive services provided by persons who are not agents. In many agreements to provide services, the agreement between the service provider and the recipient specifies terms and conditions creating contractual obligations that, if enforceable, prescribe or delimit the choices that the service provider has the right to make. In particular, if the service provider breaches a contractual obligation, the service recipient has a claim for breach of contract. The service provider may be constrained by both the existence of such an obligation and the prospect of remedies for breach of contract. The fact that such an agreement imposes constraints on the service provider does not mean that the service recipient has an interim right to give instructions to the provider. Thus, setting standards in an agreement for acceptable service quality does not of itself create a right of control. Additionally, if a service provider is retained to give an independent assessment, the expectation of independence is in tension with a right of control in the service recipient.

To the extent the parties have created a relationship of agency, however, the principal has a power of control even if the principal has previously agreed with the agent that the principal will not give interim instructions to the agent or will not otherwise interfere in the agent's exercise of discretion. However, a principal who has made such an agreement but then subsequently exercises its power of control may breach contractual duties owed to the agent, and the agent may have remedies available for the breach.

If an agent disregards or contravenes an instruction, the doctrine of actual authority, defined in § 2.01, governs the consequences as between the principal and the agent. Section 8.09 states an agent's duties to act only within the scope of actual authority and to comply with lawful instructions. The rights and obligations of the third party with whom the agent interacts are governed by the doctrines of actual authority and apparent authority. Doctrines of estoppel, restitution, and ratification are also relevant under some circumstances. *See* §§ 2.03, 2.05–2.07, and 4.01–4.08.

The principal's right of control in an agency relationship is a narrower and more sharply defined concept than domination or influence more generally. Many positions and relationships give one person the ability to dominate or influence other persons but not the right to control their actions. Family ties, friendship, perceived expertise, and religious beliefs are often the source of influence or dominance, as are the variety of circumstances that create a strong position in bargaining. A position of dominance or influence does not in itself mean that a person is a principal in a relationship of agency with the person over whom dominance or influence may be exercised. A relationship is one of agency only if the person susceptible to dominance or influence has consented to act on behalf of the other and the other has a right of control, not simply an ability to bring influence to bear.

The right to veto another's decisions does not by itself create the right to give affirmative directives that action be taken, which is integral to the right of control within common-law agency. Thus, a debtor does not become a creditor's agent when a loan agreement gives the creditor veto rights over decisions the debtor may make. Moreover, typically a debtor does not consent to act on behalf of the creditor as opposed to acting in its own interests.

The principal's right of control presupposes that the principal retains the capacity throughout the relationship to assess the agent's performance, provide instructions to the agent, and terminate the agency relationship by revoking the agent's authority. *See* § 3.10 on the principal's power to revoke authority. Under the common law of agency, as stated in Restatement Second, Agency § 122(1), a durable agency power, one that survives the principal's loss of mental competence, was not feasible because of the loss of control by the principal. Section 3.08(2), like statutes in all states, recognizes the efficacy of durable powers, which enable an agent to act on behalf of a principal incapable of exercising control. Legitimating the power does not eliminate the risks for the principal that are inherent when the agent is not subject to direction or termination by the principal.

(2). Principal's power and right of interim control—corporate context. Many questions testing the nature of the right of control arise as a result of the legal consequences of incorporating or creating a juridical or legal person distinct from its shareholders, its governing body, and its agents. A corporation's agents are its own because it is a distinct legal person; they are not the agents of other affiliated corporations unless, separately, an agency relation has been created between the agents and the affiliated corporation. Similarly, the hierarchical link between a local union and its international affiliate does not by itself create a relationship of agency between the local and the international.

Although a corporation's shareholders elect its directors and may have the right to remove directors once elected, the directors are neither the shareholders' nor the corporation's agents as defined in this section, given the treatment of directors within contemporary corporation law in the United States. Directors' powers originate as the legal consequence of their election and are not conferred or delegated by shareholders. Although corporation statutes require shareholder approval for specific fundamental transactions, corporation law generally invests managerial authority over corporate affairs in a board of directors, not in shareholders, providing that management shall occur by or under the board of directors. Thus, shareholders ordinarily do not have a right to control directors by giving binding instructions to them. If the statute under which a corporation has been incorporated so permits, shareholders may be allocated power to give binding instructions to directors through a provision in the corporation's articles or through a validly adopted shareholder agreement. The fact that a corporation statute may refer to directors as the corporation's "agents" for a particular purpose does not place directors in an agency relationship with shareholders for purposes of the common law of agency. In any event, directors' ability to bind the corporation is invested in the directors as a board, not in individual directors acting unilaterally. A director may, of course, also be an employee or officer (who may or may not be an employee) of the corporation, giving the director an additional and separate conventional position or role as an agent. Fellow directors may, with that director's consent, appoint a director as an agent to act on behalf of the corporation in some respect or matter.

Comment g. Acting on behalf of. The common-law definition of agency requires as an essential element that the agent consent to act on the principal's behalf, as well as subject to the principal's control. From the standpoint of the principal, this is the purpose for creating the relationship. The common law of agency encompasses employment as well as nonemployment relations. Employee and nonemployee agents who represent their principal in transactions with third parties act on the principal's account and behalf. Employee-agents whose work does not involve transactional interactions with third parties also act "on behalf of" their employer-principal. By consenting to act on behalf of the principal, an agent who is an employee consents to do the work that the employer directs and to do it subject to the employer's instructions. In either case, actions "on behalf of" a principal do not necessarily entail that the principal will benefit as a result.

In any relationship created by contract, the parties contemplate a benefit to be realized through the other party's performance. Performing a duty created by contract may well benefit the other party but the performance is that of an agent only if the elements of agency are present. A purchaser is not "acting on behalf of" a supplier in a distribution relationship in which goods are purchased from the supplier for resale. A purchaser who resells goods supplied by another is acting as a principal, not an agent. However, courts may treat a trademark licensee as the agent of the licensor in certain situations, with the result that the licensor is liable to third parties for defective goods produced by licensees.

An actor who acts under the immediate control of another person is not that person's agent unless the actor has agreed to act on the person's behalf. For example, a foreman or supervisor in charge of a crew of laborers exercises full and detailed control over the laborers' work activities. The relationship between the foreman and the laborers is not an agency relationship despite the foreman's full control, nor is their relationship one of subagency. Section 1.04(8) defines subagency. The foreman and the laborers are coagents of a common employer who occupy different strata within an organizational hierarchy. *See* § 1.04(9), which defines "superior" and "subordinate" coagents. The foreman's role of direction, defined by the organization, does not make the laborers the foreman's own agents. The laborers act on behalf of their common employer, not the foreman. Likewise, the captain of a ship and its crew are coagents, hierarchically stratified, who have consented to act on behalf of their common principal, the ship's owner.

It is possible to create a power to affect a person's legal relations to be exercised for the benefit of the holder of the power. Such powers typically are created as security for the interests of the holder or otherwise to benefit a person other than the person who creates the power. Consequently, the holder of such a power is not an agent as defined in this section, even though the power has the form of agency and, if exercised, will result in some of agency's legal consequences. The creator does not have a right to control the power holder's use of the power, and the power holder is not under a duty to use it in the interests of the creator. Sections 3.12–3.13 specifically treat powers given as security.

Relationships of agency are among the larger family of relationships in which one person acts to further the interests of another and is subject to fiduciary obligations. Agency is not antithetical to these other relationships, and whether a fiduciary is, additionally, an agent of another depends on the circumstances of the particular relationship. For example, as defined in Restatement Third, Trusts § 2, a trust is a fiduciary relationship with respect to property that arises from a manifestation of intention to create that relationship; a trustee is not an agent of the settlor or beneficiaries unless the terms of the trust subject the trustee to the control of either the settlor or the beneficiaries. Principals in agency relationships have power to terminate authority and thus remove the agent; trust beneficiaries, in contrast, do not have power to remove the trustee.

As agents, all employees owe duties of loyalty to their employers. The specific implications vary with the position the employee occupies, the nature of the employer's assets to which the employee has access, and the degree of discretion that the employee's work requires. However ministerial or routinized a work assignment may be, no agent, whether or not an employee, is simply a pair of hands, legs, or eyes. All are sentient and, capable of disloyal action, all have the duty to act loyally. For further discussion of the scope of fiduciary duty, *see* § 8.01, Comment *c*.

§ 1.02   Parties' Labeling and Popular Usage not Controlling

An agency relationship arises only when the elements stated in § 1.01 are present. Whether a relationship is characterized as agency in an agreement between parties or in the context of industry or popular usage is not controlling.

§ 1.03   Manifestation

A person manifests assent or intention through written or spoken words or other conduct.

§ 1.04   Terminology

(1)   *Coagents.* Coagents have agency relationships with the same principal. A coagent may be appointed by the principal or by another agent actually or apparently authorized by the principal to do so.

(2)   *Disclosed, undisclosed, and unidentified principals.*

(a)   *Disclosed principal.* A principal is disclosed if, when an agent and a third party interact, the third party has notice that the agent is acting for a principal and has notice of the principal's identity.

(b)   *Undisclosed principal.* A principal is undisclosed if, when an agent and a third party interact, the third party has no notice that the agent is acting for a principal.

(c)   *Unidentified principal.* A principal is unidentified if, when an agent and a third party interact, the third party has notice that the agent is acting for a principal but does not have notice of the principal's identity.

(3)   *Gratuitous agent.* A gratuitous agent acts without a right to compensation.

(4)   *Notice.* A person has notice of a fact if the person knows the fact, has reason to know the fact, has received an effective notification of the fact, or should know the fact to fulfill a duty owed to another person. Notice of a fact that an agent knows or has reason to know is imputed to the principal as stated in §§ 5.03 and 5.04. A notification given to or by an agent is effective as notice to or by the principal as stated in § 5.02.

(5)   *Person.* A person is (a) an individual; (b) an organization or association that has legal capacity to possess rights and incur obligations; (c) a government, political subdivision, or instrumentality or entity created by government; or (d) any other entity that has legal capacity to possess rights and incur obligations.

(6)   *Power given as security.* A power given as security is a power to affect the legal relations of its creator that is created in the form of a manifestation of actual authority and held for the benefit of the holder or a third person. It is given to protect a legal or equitable title or to secure the performance of a duty apart from any duties owed the holder of the power by its creator that are incident to a relationship of agency under § 1.01.

(7)   *Power of attorney.* A power of attorney is an instrument that states an agent's authority.

(8) *Subagent.* A subagent is a person appointed by an agent to perform functions that the agent has consented to perform on behalf of the agent's principal and for whose conduct the appointing agent is responsible to the principal. The relationship between an appointing agent and a subagent is one of agency, created as stated in § 1.01.

(9) *Superior and subordinate coagents.* A superior coagent has the right, conferred by the principal, to direct a subordinate coagent.

(10) *Trustee and agent-trustee.* A trustee is a holder of property who is subject to fiduciary duties to deal with the property for the benefit of charity or for one or more persons, at least one of whom is not the sole trustee. An agent-trustee is a trustee subject to the control of the settlor or of one or more beneficiaries.

CHAPTER 2. PRINCIPLES OF ATTRIBUTION

TOPIC 1. ACTUAL AUTHORITY

§ 2.01 Actual Authority

An agent acts with actual authority when, at the time of taking action that has legal consequences for the principal, the agent reasonably believes, in accordance with the principal's manifestations to the agent, that the principal wishes the agent so to act.

Comment b. Terminology. As defined in this section, "actual authority" is a synonym for "true authority," a term used in some opinions. The definition in this section does not attempt to classify different types of actual authority on the basis of the degree of detail in the principal's manifestation, which may consist of written or spoken words or other conduct. *See* § 1.03. As commonly used, the term "express authority" often means actual authority that a principal has stated in very specific or detailed language.

The term "implied authority" has more than one meaning. "Implied authority" is often used to mean actual authority either (1) to do what is necessary, usual, and proper to accomplish or perform an agent's express responsibilities or (2) to act in a manner in which an agent believes the principal wishes the agent to act based on the agent's reasonable interpretation of the principal's manifestation in light of the principal's objectives and other facts known to the agent. These meanings are not mutually exclusive. Both fall within the definition of actual authority. Section 2.02, which delineates the scope of actual authority, subsumes the practical consequences of implied authority.

The term "inherent agency power," used in Restatement Second, Agency, and defined therein by § 8A, is not used in this Restatement. Inherent agency power is defined as "a term used . . . to indicate the power of an agent which is derived not from authority, apparent authority or estoppel, but solely from the agency relation and exists for the protection of persons harmed by or dealing with a servant or other agent." Other doctrines stated in this Restatement encompass the justifications underpinning § 8A, including the importance of interpretation by the agent in the agent's relationship with the principal, as well as the doctrines of apparent authority, estoppel, and restitution.

§ 2.02 Scope of Actual Authority

(1) An agent has actual authority to take action designated or implied in the principal's manifestations to the agent and acts necessary or incidental to achieving the principal's objectives, as the agent reasonably understands the principal's manifestations and objectives when the agent determines how to act.

(2) An agent's interpretation of the principal's manifestations is reasonable if it reflects any meaning known by the agent to be ascribed by the principal and, in the absence of any meaning known to the agent, as a reasonable person in the agent's position would interpret the manifestations in light of the context, including circumstances of which the agent has notice and the agent's fiduciary duty to the principal.

(3)   An agent's understanding of the principal's objectives is reasonable if it accords with the principal's manifestations and the inferences that a reasonable person in the agent's position would draw from the circumstances creating the agency.

TOPIC 2.   APPARENT AUTHORITY

§ 2.03   Apparent Authority

Apparent authority is the power held by an agent or other actor to affect a principal's legal relations with third parties when a third party reasonably believes the actor has authority to act on behalf of the principal and that belief is traceable to the principal's manifestations.

TOPIC 3.   RESPONDEAT SUPERIOR

§ 2.04   Respondeat Superior

An employer is subject to liability for torts committed by employees while acting within the scope of their employment.

TOPIC 4.   RELATED DOCTRINES

§ 2.05   Estoppel to Deny Existence of Agency Relationship

A person who has not made a manifestation that an actor has authority as an agent and who is not otherwise liable as a party to a transaction purportedly done by the actor on that person's account is subject to liability to a third party who justifiably is induced to make a detrimental change in position because the transaction is believed to be on the person's account, if

(1)   the person intentionally or carelessly caused such belief, or

(2)   having notice of such belief and that it might induce others to change their positions, the person did not take reasonable steps to notify them of the facts.

§ 2.06   Liability of Undisclosed Principal

(1)   An undisclosed principal is subject to liability to a third party who is justifiably induced to make a detrimental change in position by an agent acting on the principal's behalf and without actual authority if the principal, having notice of the agent's conduct and that it might induce others to change their positions, did not take reasonable steps to notify them of the facts.

(2)   An undisclosed principal may not rely on instructions given an agent that qualify or reduce the agent's authority to less than the authority a third party would reasonably believe the agent to have under the same circumstances if the principal had been disclosed.

Comment c. Rationale. The principle stated in this section will result in liability in a relatively small number of cases in which a third party deals with an agent but has no notice that the agent represents the interests of another. Under subsection (1), a principal is subject to liability to a third party who is justifiably induced to make a detrimental change in position by the conduct of an agent acting without actual authority when the principal has notice of the agent's conduct and its likely impact on third parties and fails to take reasonable steps to inform them of the facts. The underlying principle is consistent with the estoppel doctrine stated in § 2.05. Under subsection (2), a principal is subject to liability to a third party when the third party would have no reason to inquire into the scope of the agent's authority if the third party knew the agent acted on behalf of a principal. The principal may not rely on qualifications or reductions to the agent's authority when the doctrine of apparent authority would make the qualification or restriction ineffective as to an agent acting on behalf of a disclosed or an unidentified principal. In such cases, the principal has chosen to place the agent in a position in which it is reasonable for third parties to believe that the agent has authority consistent with the position.

The rule stated in this section, like the doctrine of apparent authority, protects third parties by backstopping actual authority when circumstances might otherwise permit the principal opportunistically to speculate at the expense of third parties. *See* § 2.03, Comment *c*. Apparent authority does not arise when a principal is undisclosed because no manifestation has been made that the actor with whom the third party interacts has authority to act as an agent.

A further rationale for the doctrine stated in this section is protection of the reasonable expectations of third parties who deal with an ongoing enterprise following an undisclosed sale to a new owner, whether or not affiliated in some manner with the former owner, when the former owner continues to operate the enterprise as agent on behalf of the new owner. The enterprise's new owner, as undisclosed principal, would or reasonably should expect that third parties will continue to deal with the now-agent as if no change had occurred. If the agent operates a business under the agent's name, the appearance to the third party may be that the agent owns the business and that its assets will be available to satisfy business-related obligations incurred by the agent. The opportunity for speculation provided the principal would emerge when the principal has limited the agent's authority and the agent enters into a contract that exceeds the agent's actual authority. Then, if the contract is advantageous to the principal, neither the principal nor the agent will raise the agent's lack of authority and the third party will not know of it. On the other hand, if the contract then is disadvantageous to the principal, the principal may assert lack of authority as a defense.

The doctrine allocates to the principal the risk that the agent will deviate from the principal's instructions while doing acts that are consistent with the apparent position the agent occupies, which are acts that third parties would anticipate an agent in such a position would have authority to do and may well be acts that are foreseeable to the principal. Such acts are especially likely to be foreseeable when they are consistent with the agent's position although they contravene the principal's instructions.

A third party who deals with an actor, lacking notice that the actor is someone's agent, does not expect the liability of any person in addition to the immediate actor with whom the third party deals. Estoppel's perspective is broader but less well defined. The question is whether it is unjust, in particular circumstances, to permit a principal who has chosen to deal through an agent but to remain undisclosed to have the benefit of restrictions on the agent's authority. In the instance in which the rule is applicable, it is unlikely that the third party will inquire into the status of the immediate actor or seek to identify the existence of restrictions on that actor's right to interact with legal consequences for the third party. The need to make such inquiries, in the circumstances to which this doctrine applies, is unlikely to occur to a reasonable third party, and making the inquiry may be difficult or its cost may seem excessive relative to the magnitude of the particular transaction. When a third party previously dealt with the agent as the owner of the business now managed by the agent, the third party may assume that inquiry is unnecessary for transactions similar to prior transactions. Separately, if an undisclosed principal has notice of an agent's unauthorized actions and notice that a third party will as a consequence be induced to make a detrimental change in position, the undisclosed principal may be estopped to deny the agent's authority. The undisclosed principal may avoid estoppel by disclosing the agent's status and the extent of the agent's authority.

The doctrine encompasses deviations from actual authority of a sort that would not lead a reasonable third party to inquire separately into the scope of the agent's authority. Such deviations are foreseeable to the principal and are likely not to be contested by any principal, whether or not undisclosed, when they appear likely to benefit the principal.

§ 2.07 Restitution of Benefit

If a principal is unjustly enriched at the expense of another person by the action of an agent or a person who appears to be an agent, the principal is subject to a claim for restitution by that person.

CHAPTER 3. CREATION AND TERMINATION OF AUTHORITY AND AGENCY RELATIONSHIPS

TOPIC 1.   CREATING AND EVIDENCING ACTUAL AUTHORITY

§ 3.01   Creation of Actual Authority

Actual authority, as defined in § 2.01, is created by a principal's manifestation to an agent that, as reasonably understood by the agent, expresses the principal's assent that the agent take action on the principal's behalf.

§ 3.02   Formal Requirements

If the law requires a writing or record signed by the principal to evidence an agent's authority to bind a principal to a contract or other transaction, the principal is not bound in the absence of such a writing or record. A principal may be estopped to assert the lack of such a writing or record when a third party has been induced to make a detrimental change in position by the reasonable belief that an agent has authority to bind the principal that is traceable to a manifestation made by the principal.

Comment b. Equal-dignity requirements. Creating actual authority under § 3.01 does not require a writing or other formality. However, legislation in many states imposes what is often termed an "equal dignity" requirement for the creation of authority or agency applicable to specific types of agreements. As with the Statute of Frauds more generally, the purpose is to prevent fraud and perjury by safeguarding the principal against agreements made by an agent who lacks authority. Under an equal-dignity rule, if a transaction is unenforceable unless the party to be charged has agreed in writing to be bound, an agent's authority to enter into such a transaction on behalf of a principal must likewise be in writing. Such rules also apply to ratification. *See* § 4.02, Comment *e.* If an agent acted with apparent authority as defined in § 2.03 but no writing or record evidences the agent's authority, the principal is not bound to contracts or other transactions to which an equal-dignity rule applies.

A writing includes "any intentional reduction to tangible form," *see* Restatement Second, Contracts § 131, Comment *d.* A record includes an electronic record that is given the legal effect of a writing. Electronic records are given the legal effect of paper-and-ink writings by legislation, including the Uniform Electronic Transactions Act § 7 (1999) and the federal Electronic Signatures in Global and National Commerce Act § 101(a) (2000). A writing is signed by the principal by affixing a symbol that evidences intention to authenticate the writing. *See* Restatement Second, Contracts § 134. Similarly, an electronic record is signed by attaching to it an electronic sound, symbol, or process that is adopted with the intention of signing the record. *See* Uniform Electronic Transactions Act § 2(8).

Equal-dignity rules are either elements in a statute of frauds or are stated in separate statutes. Equal-dignity rules apply when a statute of frauds requires the underlying agreement to be evidenced by a writing signed by the party to be charged, including agreements for the sale or lease of land and suretyship agreements. On the scope of contracts to which statutes of frauds apply, *see* Restatement Second, Contracts § 110. Equal-dignity rules are inapplicable when a writing is required by agreement but not by law. However, a contract may not be binding when a contractual provision itself requires that the principal sign personally.

Equal-dignity rules have been applied with some stringency. For example, when one spouse acts as the agent of the other who owns property, or as an agent when both spouses own property jointly, the equal-dignity rule requires the agent-spouse's authorization to be in writing. If a principal executes a contract but leaves blanks that are completed by the agent, the contract may not be enforceable against the principal if the third party has notice that the agent may fill in the blanks only when the agent is authorized in writing to do so.

Nevertheless, the application of equal-dignity rules should not outrun their purpose. Equal-dignity rules do not apply when an action on a contract is brought by the principal against a third party. An equal-dignity rule may be satisfied by a writing or record executed by a principal following the agent's execution of the contract or transaction. Moreover, if an agent has acted without actual authority, as well as without prior written authorization, the principal would be able to ratify the transaction by a signed writing, see § 4.01, Comment *e*, so long as the principal ratifies prior to a manifestation from the third party that the third party has withdrawn from the transaction, *see* § 4.05(1). Additionally, an equal-dignity rule does not create a defense that an agent may assert against the third party, such as when the agent misrepresents authority. On an agent's warranties of authority, *see* § 6.10. On an agent's representations, *see* § 6.11.

TOPIC 2. CREATING APPARENT AUTHORITY

§ 3.03 Creation of Apparent Authority

Apparent authority, as defined in § 2.03, is created by a person's manifestation that another has authority to act with legal consequences for the person who makes the manifestation, when a third party reasonably believes the actor to be authorized and the belief is traceable to the manifestation.

TOPIC 3. CAPACITY TO ACT AS PRINCIPAL OR AGENT

§ 3.04 Capacity to Act as Principal

(1) An individual has capacity to act as principal in a relationship of agency as defined in § 1.01 if, at the time the agent takes action, the individual would have capacity if acting in person.

(2) The law applicable to a person that is not an individual governs whether the person has capacity to be a principal in a relationship of agency as defined in § 1.01, as well as the effect of the person's lack or loss of capacity on those who interact with it.

(3) If performance of an act is not delegable, its performance by an agent does not constitute performance by the principal.

§ 3.05 Capacity to Act as Agent

Any person may ordinarily be empowered to act so as to affect the legal relations of another. The actor's capacity governs the extent to which, by so acting, the actor becomes subject to duties and liabilities to the person whose legal relations are affected or to third parties.

TOPIC 4. TERMINATION OF AGENT'S POWER

TITLE A. TERMINATION OF ACTUAL AUTHORITY

§ 3.06 Termination of Actual Authority—In General

An agent's actual authority may be terminated by:

(1) the agent's death, cessation of existence, or suspension of powers as stated in § 3.07(1) and (3); or

(2) the principal's death, cessation of existence, or suspension of powers as stated in § 3.07(2) and (4); or

(3) the principal's loss of capacity, as stated in § 3.08(1) and (3); or

(4) an agreement between the agent and the principal or the occurrence of circumstances on the basis of which the agent should reasonably conclude that the principal no longer would assent to the agent's taking action on the principal's behalf, as stated in § 3.09; or

(5) a manifestation of revocation by the principal to the agent, or of renunciation by the agent to the principal, as stated in § 3.10(1); or

(6) the occurrence of circumstances specified by statute.

Comment b. Agreement between principal and agent and changes in circumstances. The basis for actual authority is a manifestation of assent made by a principal to an agent. *See* § 3.01. When the manifestation is embodied in an agreement that specifies circumstances under which the agent's actual authority shall terminate, occurrence of a specified circumstance effects termination of the principal's expressed assent. Regardless of whether the initial agreement contains a termination provision, mutual agreement to terminate the agency relationship is always effective to terminate the agent's actual authority. *See* § 3.09.

Following the principal's manifestation of assent to an agent, circumstances may change such that, at the time the agent takes action, it is not reasonable for the agent to believe that the principal at that time consents to the action being taken on the principal's behalf even though the principal has not manifested dissent to the action by that time. For example, the agent may become insolvent and have notice that it is important to the principal to be represented by a solvent agent. The agent may lose capacity to bind itself by a contract or to become subject to other obligations and have notice that it is important to the principal that the agent retain such capacity. Events that are totally outside the control of the agent or the principal may also make it unreasonable for the agent to believe that the principal consents to the agent's action. For example, if the principal retains the agent to sell goods in a particular geographically defined market, the occurrence of war or widespread civil unrest may so impair the value of the agent's efforts to the principal that the agent would not be reasonable in believing the principal wishes the agent to sell into the territory. The agent then lacks actual authority so to act but would have acted with actual authority had the agent acted prior to the change in circumstances. The focal point for determining whether an agent acted with actual authority is the time of action, not the time of the principal's manifestation, which may be earlier. *See* §§ 2.01 and 2.02.

An alternate analysis of the impact of changed circumstances, as set forth in Restatement Second, Agency, requires the use of at least two distinct focal points. First, it is posited that an agent has actual authority up until the agent receives notice of the changed circumstances. Notice that circumstances have changed, beyond those operative when the principal manifested consent to the agent, then implicitly modifies either the principal's manifestation of consent or the actual authority it engenders on the basis of the agent's reasonable belief in the principal's consent. *See* Restatement Second, Agency, Introductory Note to Chapter 5. Moreover, if circumstances thereafter revert to those present originally, the agent's actual authority, having once existed but thereafter having been terminated, is again revived. *See* Restatement Second, Agency § 108(2). This Restatement does not follow this alternate pattern of analysis because it is unnecessary in light of the nature of actual authority and the rules that determine whether an agent acted with actual authority. *See* §§ 2.01–2.02.

§ 3.07 Death, Cessation of Existence, and Suspension of Powers

(1) The death of an individual agent terminates the agent's actual authority.

(2) The death of an individual principal terminates the agent's actual authority. The termination is effective only when the agent has notice of the principal's death. The termination is also effective as against a third party with whom the agent deals when the third party has notice of the principal's death.

(3) When an agent that is not an individual ceases to exist or commences a process that will lead to cessation of existence or when its powers are suspended, the agent's actual authority terminates except as provided by law.

(4) When a principal that is not an individual ceases to exist or commences a process that will lead to cessation of its existence or when its powers are suspended, the agent's actual authority terminates except as provided by law.

§ 3.08 Loss of Capacity

(1) An individual principal's loss of capacity to do an act terminates the agent's actual authority to do the act. The termination is effective only when the agent has notice that the principal's loss of

capacity is permanent or that the principal has been adjudicated to lack capacity. The termination is also effective as against a third party with whom the agent deals when the third party has notice that the principal's loss of capacity is permanent or that the principal has been adjudicated to lack capacity.

(2)   A written instrument may make an agent's actual authority effective upon a principal's loss of capacity, or confer it irrevocably regardless of such loss.

(3)   If a principal that is not an individual loses capacity to do an act, its agent's actual authority to do the act is terminated.

§ 3.09   Termination by Agreement or by Occurrence of Changed Circumstances

An agent's actual authority terminates (1) as agreed by the agent and the principal, subject to the provisions of § 3.10; or (2) upon the occurrence of circumstances on the basis of which the agent should reasonably conclude that the principal no longer would assent to the agent's taking action on the principal's behalf.

§ 3.10   Manifestation Terminating Actual Authority

(1)   Notwithstanding any agreement between principal and agent, an agent's actual authority terminates if the agent renounces it by a manifestation to the principal or if the principal revokes the agent's actual authority by a manifestation to the agent. A revocation or a renunciation is effective when the other party has notice of it.

(2)   A principal's manifestation of revocation is, unless otherwise agreed, ineffective to terminate a power given as security or to terminate a proxy to vote securities or other membership or ownership interests that is made irrevocable in compliance with applicable legislation. *See* §§ 3.12–3.13.

TITLE B.   TERMINATION OF APPARENT AUTHORITY

§ 3.11   Termination of Apparent Authority

(1)   The termination of actual authority does not by itself end any apparent authority held by an agent.

(2)   Apparent authority ends when it is no longer reasonable for the third party with whom an agent deals to believe that the agent continues to act with actual authority.

TITLE C.   IRREVOCABLE POWERS

§ 3.12   Power Given as Security; Irrevocable Proxy

(1)   A power given as security is a power to affect the legal relations of its creator that is created in the form of a manifestation of actual authority and held for the benefit of the holder or a third person. This power is given to protect a legal or equitable title or to secure the performance of a duty apart from any duties owed the holder of the power by its creator that are incident to a relationship of agency under § 1.01. It is given upon the creation of the duty or title or for consideration. It is distinct from actual authority that the holder may exercise if the holder is an agent of the creator of the power.

(2)   A power to exercise voting rights associated with securities or a membership interest may be conferred on a proxy through a manifestation of actual authority. The power may be given as security under (1) and may be made irrevocable in compliance with applicable legislation.

§ 3.13   Termination of Power Given as Security or Irrevocable Proxy

(1)   A power given as security or an irrevocable proxy is terminated by an event that

(a)   discharges the obligation secured by the power or terminates the interest secured or supported by the proxy, or

(b)   makes its execution illegal or impossible, or

(c)   constitutes an effective surrender of the power or proxy by the person for whose benefit it was created or conferred.

(2)   Unless otherwise agreed, neither a power given as security nor a proxy made irrevocable as provided in § 3.12(2) is terminated by:

(a)   a manifestation revoking the power or proxy made by the person who created it; or

(b)   surrender of the power or proxy by its holder if it is held for the benefit of another person, unless that person consents; or

(c)   loss of capacity by the creator or the holder of the power or proxy; or

(d)   death of the holder of the power or proxy, unless the holder's death terminates the interest secured or supported by the power or proxy; or

(e)   death of the creator of the power or proxy, if the power or proxy is given as security for the performance of a duty that does not terminate with the death of its creator.

TOPIC 5.   AGENTS WITH MULTIPLE PRINCIPALS

§ 3.14   Agents with Multiple Principals

An agent acting in the same transaction or matter on behalf of more than one principal may be one or both of the following:

(a)   a subagent, as stated in § 3.15; or

(b)   an agent for coprincipals, as stated in § 3.16.

§ 3.15   Subagency

(1)   A subagent is a person appointed by an agent to perform functions that the agent has consented to perform on behalf of the agent's principal and for whose conduct the appointing agent is responsible to the principal. The relationships between a subagent and the appointing agent and between the subagent and the appointing agent's principal are relationships of agency as stated in § 1.01.

(2)   An agent may appoint a subagent only if the agent has actual or apparent authority to do so.

Comment b. Subagency contrasted with coagency. Agency creates a personal relationship between principal and agent; an agent's delegation of power to another person to act on behalf of the principal is inconsistent with the undertaking made when a person consents to act as agent on behalf of a principal. However, a principal may empower an agent to appoint another agent to act on the principal's behalf. The second agent may be a subagent or a coagent. *See* Comment *d* for discussion of the consequences that follow if the second agent is characterized as a subagent.

An agent who appoints a subagent delegates to the subagent power to act on behalf of the principal that the principal has conferred on the agent. A subagent acts subject to the control of the appointing agent, and the principal's legal position is affected by action taken by the subagent as if the action had been taken by the appointing agent. Thus, a subagent has two principals, the appointing agent and that agent's principal. Although an appointing agent has the right and duty to control a subagent, the interests and instructions of the appointing agent's principal are paramount. *See* Comment *d*.

In contrast, an agent who appoints a coagent does not delegate power held by the agent to the coagent. By empowering an agent to appoint a coagent, the principal creates a mechanism through which to generate additional relationships of agency between the principal and persons chosen by the agent. Coagents, although they may occupy dominant and subordinate positions within an organizational hierarchy, share a common principal.

A person appointed by an agent to act on behalf of the agent's principal is a subagent if the appointing agent has agreed with the principal that the appointing agent shall be responsible to the principal for the agent's conduct. Such agreement may be express or implied. For example, employees of an appointing agent whom the agent designates to act on behalf of the appointing agent's principal are presumed to be subagents, not coagents of the appointing agent. When an agent is itself a corporation or other legal person, its officers, employees, partners, or members who are designated to work on the principal's account are subagents. In contrast, when a manager within an organization hires persons as employees of the organization, those hired are presumed to be the hiring manager's coagents and not subagents. Employees of a single organization are presumed to be coagents of that organization, not subagents.

Comment c. Creation of subagency. An agent has actual authority to create a relationship of subagency when the agent reasonably believes, based on a manifestation from the principal, that the principal consents to the appointment of a subagent. For the definition of actual authority, *see* § 2.01. For the means by which a principal creates it, *see* § 3.01.

A principal's consent to the appointment of a subagent may be express or implied. For example, a principal's consent to the appointment of subagents may be implied when the principal retains an individual as agent to carry out a number of transactions and has notice that the amount of work involved exceeds the agent's individual capability or requires action that the agent may not legally perform, such as action for which the law requires a license. Implied consent to appoint subagents is also present when an agent is itself a person that is not an individual, such as a corporation.

Subagents may be appointed in series. This would occur when a subagent has actual or apparent authority to appoint another for whose conduct the appointing subagent is responsible.

An agent may have apparent authority to appoint a subagent if the principal has made a manifestation to third parties that the agent has such authority. Section 1.03 defines manifestation. Section 2.03 defines apparent authority; § 3.03 states how it is created. A principal may make a manifestation that an agent has actual authority to appoint subagents by placing the agent in a position in which agents customarily have such authority without notice to third parties that the agent's authority does not include the appointment of subagents. A subagent appointed by an agent acting with only apparent authority may act on behalf of the principal with actual authority. *See* Comment *d*.

If an agent acts without actual or apparent authority in purporting to appoint a subagent, the person so appointed is the agent solely of the appointing agent and is not the principal's subagent unless the principal ratifies the appointment. On the requisites for ratification, *see* Chapter 4.

In emergencies and other unforeseen circumstances, when communication between agent and principal is not feasible, an agent's actual authority to take action to protect the principal's interests may permit the agent to appoint a subagent although the principal has not previously manifested consent to the agent to make such an appointment. *See* § 2.02, Comment *d*.

A person may be appointed as a subagent even though the person does not expect to be compensated for actions taken.

Comment d. Consequences of subagency. As between a principal and third parties, it is immaterial that an action was taken by a subagent as opposed to an agent directly appointed by the principal. In this respect, subagency is governed by a principle of transparency that looks from the subagent to the principal and through the appointing agent. As to third parties, an action taken by a subagent carries the legal consequences for the principal that would follow were the action instead taken by the appointing agent. . . .

When a subagent works on a principal's account, notifications received by the subagent are effective as notifications to the principal to the same extent as if the principal had appointed the subagent directly. Likewise, notice of facts the subagent knows or has reason to know is imputed to the principal to the same extent as if the principal had appointed the subagent directly. . . .

As among a principal, an appointing agent, and a subagent, the fact that action is taken by a subagent may carry different or additional legal consequences than if the action were taken directly by the appointing agent or by a coagent of the appointing agent. The legal consequences of subagency reflect the distinct significance of (1) the relationship between an appointing agent and a subagent; (2) the relationship between a principal and an appointing agent; and (3) the relationship between a principal and a subagent. An appointing agent is responsible to the principal for the subagent's conduct. This may subject an appointing agent to liability for loss incurred by the principal as a consequence of misconduct by a subagent. A contract between the principal and the appointing agent that requires or permits the appointment of subagents will often delineate the extent of the appointing agent's liability and will require indemnification by the principal of the appointing agent. In contrast, an agent is subject to liability stemming from a coagent's conduct only when the agent's own conduct subjects the agent to liability. *See* § 7.01, Comments *b* and *d*.

Statutes may change the results that would otherwise follow when a subagent takes action. For example, under Article 4 of the Uniform Commercial Code, when the owner of an item deposits it with a bank for collection, the depositary bank is treated as the agent of the item's owner. If the depositary bank sends the item for collection to another bank, the collecting bank is treated as the owner's subagent. *See* U.C.C. § 4–201(a). However, under U.C.C. § 4–202, although a depositary bank has a duty to use ordinary care in selecting intermediaries and in giving proper instructions to them, it is not liable for another bank's "insolvency, neglect, misconduct, mistake, or default. . . ."

Although an appointing agent is responsible for a subagent's action and has the right and duty to control the subagent, the principal's interests and instructions are nonetheless paramount. Several specific doctrines reflect this general point. If a subagent acts without actual or apparent authority, only the principal may ratify the subagent's action; ratification by an appointing agent is effective only when the principal has authorized the appointing agent to ratify on its behalf. Moreover, a subagent is a fiduciary, as is any agent. *See* § 1.01. A subagent owes duties of loyalty to the principal as well as to the appointing agent. *See* §§ 8.01–8.06, which state the specifics of these duties. A subagent owes a duty of obedience to the principal as well as to the appointing agent. *See* § 8.09(2). However, the principal's rights as to the subagent are superior to rights of the appointing agent, even in the event of conflict or disagreement between principal and appointing agent.

If a subagent is appointed by an agent who acts with only apparent authority, the subagent is privileged to act on behalf of the principal because the subagent, on the basis of the principal's manifestation, reasonably believes that the appointing agent acted with the principal's consent in appointing the subagent. As a consequence, the principal is subject to liability to the subagent to indemnify the subagent as stated in § 8.14. The appointing agent, having acted without actual authority in appointing the subagent, is subject to liability to the principal as stated in § 8.09(1). The subagent is not subject to liability to third parties on the basis that the subagent breached warranties of authority. *See* § 6.10.

A principal's duties to a subagent are those owed to any agent, but the principal is not subject to duties created by agreement between the appointing agent and the subagent, including the appointing agent's agreement to compensate the subagent. *See* § 8.13, Comment *d*. A subagent may have set-off rights against the principal. *See* § 6.06.

Comment e. Termination of subagent's actual and apparent authority. Whether a subagent acts with actual authority depends on three separate consensual relationships: (1) between principal and appointing agent; (2) between appointing agent and subagent; and (3) between principal and subagent. A subagent's actual authority terminates upon notice to the subagent that any of these relationships is severed.

Additionally, circumstances that terminate an agent's actual authority by operation of law likewise terminate a subagent's authority. Thus, notice of the death of a principal or of an appointing agent terminates a subagent's actual authority, as does notice that the principal has revoked an appointing agent's actual authority. *See* §§ 3.07(2) and 3.10(1). If the relationship between an appointing agent and a subagent is severed, for example by notice of the appointing agent's death or loss of capacity, the subagent no longer acts under the control of the appointing agent who had responsibility for the subagent's acts. If a subagent is a lawyer who represents a client having diminished capacity, the lawyer's duties are as stated in Restatement Third, The Law Governing Lawyers § 24.

Additionally, a principal may terminate a subagent's actual authority by making a manifestation of revocation directly to the subagent or to the appointing agent. A manifestation revoking a subagent's actual authority made by the principal to the appointing agent should not be effective, in most circumstances, as to the subagent until the subagent has notice of it. A principal has rights and responsibilities of ultimate control, including ultimate control over chains of command and channels of communication. A principal may choose how best to communicate with a subagent, including how best to convey notice that the subagent's actual authority has been revoked. If the principal chooses to rely exclusively on the appointing agent as the channel of communication with the subagent, the principal at least ordinarily should bear the risk that the appointing agent will not duly deliver notice of revocation to the subagent.

In contrast, under the rule stated in Restatement Second, Agency § 137, Comment *b*, when a principal terminates a subagent's authority by giving notice of termination to the appointing agent, "the subagent's authority terminates only when the agent has had an opportunity to communicate with him." If the appointing agent, having had the opportunity to communicate with the subagent, does not do so, or does not do so effectively, the rule as stated in Restatement Second allocates to the subagent the risk of acting without actual authority, although the subagent lacks notice that the principal wishes to terminate the subagent's authority. The notice requirement stated in this Restatement instead allocates to the principal the risk that notice of revocation communicated only to the appointing agent may not reach the subagent. So allocating the risk is supported by a well-reasoned case in the real-estate context. The principal should bear this risk because the principal has consented to the appointment of subagents and because a subagent should be under no greater risk than is an agent of unwittingly taking an unauthorized action following the termination of actual authority.

A subagent may continue to act with apparent authority following termination of the subagent's actual authority when third parties reasonably believe that the subagent continues to act with actual authority on the basis of manifestations traceable to the appointing agent or the principal. *See* § 3.11.

Comment f. Transactions in real estate. Under the common-law rule in most states, a real-estate broker or salesperson associated with a broker who successfully markets property to a prospective buyer (hereinafter the "showing broker") is treated as the subagent of the broker with whom a prospective seller has listed the property (hereinafter the "listing broker"), even if the showing broker is not the listing broker's employee or associate. Conventional terminology applies the term "broker" or "real-estate broker" to a person holding a license to provide brokerage services. A broker may use the services of salespeople, who may be employees of the broker or the broker's nonemployee associates. Except where the context otherwise requires, the remainder of this Comment refers to all as "brokers."

The better rule, followed in a minority of states, characterizes a showing broker as the agent of the prospective buyer, and not the seller's subagent, when the terms of the relationship between the showing broker and the prospective buyer reasonably reflect the buyer's expectation that the showing broker represents the buyer. The minority rule is consistent with the policy reflected in legislation in a majority of states that explicitly permits a prospective buyer to appoint a real-estate broker to act as the buyer's agent.

A showing broker may be characterized as: (1) the seller's subagent, regardless of whether the broker has a relationship with the buyer that constitutes a relationship of agency as defined by § 1.01; (2) the buyer's agent when the relationship between buyer and broker constitutes a relationship of agency as defined by § 1.01; or (3) neither the agent nor the subagent of buyer or seller. If a showing broker is characterized as acting as agent for both buyer and seller, or as agent for buyer and subagent for seller, the agent is in a position of dual agency because the showing broker represents adverse parties to the same transaction. *See* § 8.03.

As the seller's subagent, a showing broker is presumed not to have a relationship of agency with the buyer and does not owe an agent's fiduciary duties to the buyer. It is well-settled, as a matter of industry practice and regulation as well as common-law agency, that a broker in a single real-estate transaction may not represent both buyer and seller unless both know of and consent to the dual representation. Unless such consent is given, a broker who represents both buyer and seller may forfeit any commission otherwise payable to the broker. *See* § 8.03, Comment *d.* In a transaction involving the same property, buyer and seller have interests that are adverse. The benefit that a seller will receive through a higher sales price will be paid by the buyer. Moreover, a broker who represents a prospective seller or buyer of property may have material information that, if disclosed to the other party, will disadvantage the broker's client. For example, information about the seller's reservation price—the lowest price at which the seller may be willing to sell—is material to price negotiations between the seller and prospective buyers. For further treatment of dual agency, *see* § 8.03.

The mechanism through which a relationship of subagency arises is an offer of a unilateral contract of subagency, made by the listing broker to showing brokers, that is accepted by the showing broker who produces a buyer able and willing to purchase the property at the listing price and terms or at other terms acceptable to the seller. Such an offer is often made when a listing broker lists property with a multiple listing service ("MLS"). A multiple listing service is an agreement among brokers in a particular geographic market to pool information about their listings. A showing broker may also become a subagent in the absence of MLS participation through a relationship of cooperation with the listing broker. When a showing broker produces an offer from a buyer to purchase at the seller's stated listing price and on terms otherwise consistent with the listing agreement, conventional MLS terms require that the listing broker split the commission to be paid by the seller with the successful showing broker.

The legal consequences of how a showing broker is characterized carry corresponding advantages as well as disadvantages from the standpoint of buyers and sellers of real estate. Characterizing a showing broker as the seller's subagent orients the showing broker's duties exclusively to the seller, with the implication that the broker must disclose to the seller all material information the broker learns about the buyer. This disadvantages a buyer if the showing broker discloses information the buyer has provided to the seller or the listing broker, such as the maximum price the buyer is willing to pay to acquire property. However, this characterization may be advantageous to the buyer if the showing broker induces the buyer to purchase a property through fraud because the buyer may rescind the transaction. For the circumstances under which a misrepresentation makes a contract voidable, *see* Restatement Second, Contracts § 164(1). To be sure, a seller may not perceive this consequence to be fair when the seller has had no contact with a showing broker who induces a purchase through fraud. In contrast, if a showing broker acts as a buyer's agent, the buyer will be limited to remedies against the broker if the seller is innocent of the fraud and has in good faith given value or changed position in reliance on the transaction. *See* Restatement Second, Contracts § 164(2). Neither buyer nor seller benefits if a showing broker is not characterized as either the seller's subagent or the buyer's agent because the duties of a nonagent showing broker are indeterminate. However, principals in real-estate transactions may benefit if nonagent showing brokers charge lower commissions than brokers who act as agents and subagents.

The common-law rule applicable to agency relationships in this context should reflect the reasonable expectations of prospective buyers and sellers of property and the real-estate professionals who act on their behalf. If a broker has agreed to assist a prospective buyer, it is reasonable for the prospective buyer to expect that the broker does not owe duties of loyalty to the seller of property that the buyer purchases. Treating a showing broker as the seller's subagent is likely to conflict with the expectations of a buyer to whom the showing broker has given guidance and, in many instances, advice. Moreover, a seller may reasonably expect that, as the seller's subagent, the showing broker will be loyal to the seller's interests and will not compromise them through advice or information that the showing broker may share with buyers. If a showing broker is treated as a buyer's agent, although the buyer loses the availability of rescission as a remedy in some situations, the buyer gains the advantages of representation by a professional whom the buyer is free to choose. Real-estate professionals are best served by rules that clarify the identity of parties to whom particular duties are owed and that do not create the risk of inadvertently acting as a dual agent for buyer and seller.

Empirical results confirm the significance to buyers of retaining the services of an agent who has clearly defined duties to represent the buyer, even when the agent is compensated by splitting a commission that will be payable from the proceeds of a sale and that will be augmented the greater the sale price. In Georgia, following the enactment of a statute that encourages buyers to retain their own agents, the average time required to sell a house fell, as did reported sale prices of expensive houses. Additionally, a large majority of buyers chose to be represented by their own agent.

Statutes in many states expressly permit prospective buyers to retain licensed real-estate brokers as agents. Since 1993, the Realtors' Association has permitted listing brokers to offer showing brokers, as an alternative to a relationship of subagency, a relationship of "cooperation and compensation" that is compatible both with a showing broker who acts as a buyer's agent as well as with a showing broker who acts as the seller's subagent.

Unless a statute so requires, a writing should not be necessary to establish that a prospective buyer and a real-estate broker have consented to create a relationship of agency. *See* § 3.02, Comment *e*, for discussion of statutes that impose a writing requirement on agreements to pay commissions to brokers. Statutes in some states require a written agreement to create a relationship of agency with either a listing broker or a buyer's agent.

If a prospective buyer does not create a relationship of agency as defined in § 1.01 with a showing broker, the showing broker should be treated as the seller's subagent if the seller has expressly or impliedly consented to the appointment of subagents by the listing broker. The showing broker should not be treated as the buyer's agent when no relationship of agency as defined in § 1.01 has been created between the buyer and the showing broker, nor should the showing broker be treated as an intermediary who acts as no one's agent, unless a statute so requires.

If a prospective buyer consents to a relationship of agency as defined in § 1.01 with a particular real-estate broker, it is incompatible with the duties thereby created for that broker additionally to act as subagent for the seller of property that the buyer purchases unless the buyer knows of the subagency and consents to it and unless the seller knows of and consents to the broker's relationship with the buyer. On consent by a principal to conduct by an agent that would otherwise breach the agent's duties of loyalty to the principal, *see* § 8.06. A broker retained by a prospective buyer would become a dual agent if the broker also acts as subagent on behalf of the seller of the property purchased by the buyer who is represented by the broker. This would occur if the property's owner lists it with the buyer's broker or if the buyer's broker is also characterized as the subagent of the property's owner. If the property in which a buyer is interested is listed in a MLS under terms that designate a successful showing broker as the seller's subagent, that designation should not be operative without the consent of a buyer who has previously retained the showing broker as the buyer's agent.

However, an agent is not a dual agent if there is no substantial risk that the agent's action on behalf of one principal will materially and adversely affect the agent's action on behalf of another principal. *See* § 8.03. An agent retained by a buyer does not become a dual agent by taking ministerial actions on behalf of a seller. Dual agency, as noted above, results when the broker whom a buyer has retained to act as the buyer's agent also serves as listing agent for the property purchased by the buyer, whether at the outset of the buyer's relationship with the broker or thereafter if the owner of the property lists it for sale with that broker. Under the common-law rule in most states, a broker has a relationship of agency with each of the broker's clients although the clients have agreed to be represented by individuals among the broker's cohort of employees and associates. Thus, a broker would be characterized as a dual agent when one employee or associate serves as the designated agent of a buyer and another serves as the seller's designated agent. Statutes in some states explicitly permit the practice of designated dual agency and impose specific writing and disclosure requirements. In contrast, a few statutes categorically prohibit dual agency in transactions but permit the use of nonagent intermediaries, as described below.

Relationships among brokers, sellers, and buyers have been recharacterized by statutes enacted by many states since the late 1980s. Statutes in many states expressly permit prospective buyers to retain licensed real-estate brokers to act as their agents. However, these statutes are disparate in specifying the default rule that characterizes a showing broker when a buyer has not appointed that broker as agent. Several statutes provide that subagency shall not be deemed to be created automatically or through participation in a MLS. Some statutes provide that, if no written agreement establishes a relationship of agency or subagency, a broker is treated as a "transaction broker," "transaction coordinator," or "facilitator" who does not act as either party's agent or subagent. Some statutes that permit the use of such nonagent intermediaries specify the duties owed by the intermediary. Many statutes make subagency the default characterization, either explicitly or implicitly by not specifying an alternative. Other statutes require specific types of disclosure, such as disclosure to a prospective buyer that a seller's agent represents the seller. Several statutes permit the parties to create a relationship of "designated dual agency" not subject to the usual consequences of dual agency, in which one sales associate in a real-estate brokerage represents the seller of a property and the other its buyer. Some statutes characterize such brokers as "limited agents," specifying their duties. Some statutes explicitly prohibit "designated dual agency." Statutes in a few states explicitly abrogate the common law of agency.

§ 3.16   Agent for Coprincipals

Two or more persons may as coprincipals appoint an agent to act for them in the same transaction or matter.

CHAPTER 4.   RATIFICATION

§ 4.01   Ratification Defined

(1)   Ratification is the affirmance of a prior act done by another, whereby the act is given effect as if done by an agent acting with actual authority.

(2)   A person ratifies an act by

(a)   manifesting assent that the act shall affect the person's legal relations, or

(b)   conduct that justifies a reasonable assumption that the person so consents.

(3)   Ratification does not occur unless

(a)   the act is ratifiable as stated in § 4.03,

(b)   the person ratifying has capacity as stated in § 4.04,

(c)   the ratification is timely as stated in § 4.05, and

(d)   the ratification encompasses the act in its entirety as stated in § 4.07.

Comment b. The nature and effect of ratification. As the term is used in agency law, ratification is both an act and a set of effects. The act of ratification consists of an externally observable manifestation of assent to be bound by the prior act of another person. When the prior act did not otherwise affect the legal relations of the ratifier, ratification provides the basis on which the ratifier's legal relations are affected by the act. The set of effects that ratification creates are the consequences of actual authority. That is, when a person ratifies another's act, the legal consequence is that the person's legal relations are affected as they would have been had the actor been an agent acting with actual authority at the time of the act.

In most jurisdictions, ratification may create a relationship of agency when none existed between the actor and the ratifier at the time of the act. It is necessary that the actor have acted or purported to act on behalf of the ratifier. *See* § 4.03. This limits the range of ratifiable acts to those done by an actor who is an agent or who is not an agent but pretends to be.

Ratification often serves the function of clarifying situations of ambiguous or uncertain authority. A principal's ratification confirms or validates an agent's right to have acted as the agent did. That is, an agent's action may have been effective to bind the principal to the third party, and the third party to the principal, because the agent acted with apparent authority. *See* § 2.03. If the principal ratifies the agent's act, it is thereafter not necessary to establish that the agent acted with apparent authority. Moreover, by replicating the effects of actual authority, the principal's ratification eliminates claims the principal would otherwise have against the agent for acting without actual authority. *See* § 8.09, Comment *b*. The principal's ratification may also eliminate claims that third parties could assert against the agent when the agent has purported to be authorized to bind the principal but the principal is not bound. *See* § 6.10. Ratification is effective even when the third party knew that the agent lacked authority to bind the principal but nonetheless dealt with the agent.

Much of the doctrine applicable to ratification either determines the validity and significance of the principal's assent or makes ratification unavailable or limits its effects when unfair consequences otherwise would follow. Although ratification creates the legal effects of actual authority, it reverses in time the sequence between an agent's conduct and the principal's manifestation of assent. If the principal ratifies, the relevant time for determining legal consequences is the time of the agent's act. *See* § 4.02, Comment *b*. Thus, if the agent purported to commit the principal to a transaction, the principal and third party become bound as of the time of the agent's commitment when the principal ratifies. If the agent's act constituted a tort, the time of the act is the time as of which the principal becomes vicariously liable, if the principal ratifies the agent's act. If the agent receives a notification, or learns information relevant to the action the agent takes, the notification is effective as to the principal, and knowledge of the information is imputed to the principal, as of the time of the agent's act if the principal ratifies it. *See* § 5.02, which covers notifications.

The sole requirement for ratification is a manifestation of assent or other conduct indicative of consent by the principal. To be effective as a ratification, the principal's assent need not be communicated to the agent or to third parties whose legal relations will be affected by the ratification. *See* Comment *d*. The principal is not bound by a ratification made without knowledge of material facts about the agent's act unless the principal chose to ratify with awareness that such knowledge was lacking. *See* § 4.06. When there are two or more coprincipals, each must ratify to be bound. In most cases in which the outcome turns on whether a principal has ratified, the claim of ratification is asserted by a third party who seeks to bind the principal in the absence of other bases to attribute the legal consequences of an agent's act to the principal. It is fair to hold the principal to such consequences when the principal has, after the fact, assented to the agent's act. The principal's ability to ratify also enables the principal to create a clear basis on which to hold the third party to transactions that are desirable from the principal's perspective. The doctrines stated in §§ 4.05, 4.07, and 4.08 deny the principal the power to ratify when the result of ratification would be unfair. Absent such circumstances, it is not unfair to bind the third party when the principal elects to ratify a transaction because the result binds the third party only as originally anticipated or hoped, which is to the terms of a transaction with the principal.

The effects of the principal's ratification are also fair to the agent because by assenting to the agent's act the principal usually eliminates claims that the principal or the third party might otherwise assert against the agent. Ratification is an all-or-nothing proposition in two basic respects. First, in most cases, by ratifying the principal eliminates claims the principal might otherwise have against the agent for acting without actual authority. *See* § 4.02(2) for exceptions to this general principle. Were the doctrine otherwise, the principal could speculate at the agent's expense by ratifying a transaction as against the third party, but holding the agent accountable if, after the time of ratification, the transaction turned out to be a losing proposition for the principal. Second, a principal must ratify a single transaction in its entirety, thereby becoming subject to its burdens as well as enjoying its benefits. *See* § 4.07.

§ 4.02   Effect of Ratification

(1)   Subject to the exceptions stated in subsection (2), ratification retroactively creates the effects of actual authority.

(2)   Ratification is not effective:

(a)   in favor of a person who causes it by misrepresentation or other conduct that would make a contract voidable;

(b)   in favor of an agent against a principal when the principal ratifies to avoid a loss; or

(c)   to diminish the rights or other interests of persons, not parties to the transaction, that were acquired in the subject matter prior to the ratification.

§ 4.03   Acts That May be Ratified

A person may ratify an act if the actor acted or purported to act as an agent on the person's behalf.

§ 4.04   Capacity to Ratify

(1)   A person may ratify an act if

(a)   the person existed at the time of the act, and

(b)   the person had capacity as defined in § 3.04 at the time of ratifying the act.

(2)   At a later time, a principal may avoid a ratification made earlier when the principal lacked capacity as defined in § 3.04.

§ 4.05   Timing of Ratification

A ratification of a transaction is not effective unless it precedes the occurrence of circumstances that would cause the ratification to have adverse and inequitable effects on the rights of third parties. These circumstances include:

(1)   any manifestation of intention to withdraw from the transaction made by the third party;

(2)   any material change in circumstances that would make it inequitable to bind the third party, unless the third party chooses to be bound; and

(3)   a specific time that determines whether a third party is deprived of a right or subjected to a liability.

§ 4.06   Knowledge Requisite to Ratification

A person is not bound by a ratification made without knowledge of material facts involved in the original act when the person was unaware of such lack of knowledge.

§ 4.07   No Partial Ratification

A ratification is not effective unless it encompasses the entirety of an act, contract, or other single transaction.

§ 4.08   Estoppel to Deny Ratification

If a person makes a manifestation that the person has ratified another's act and the manifestation, as reasonably understood by a third party, induces the third party to make a detrimental change in position, the person may be estopped to deny the ratification.

CHAPTER 5. NOTIFICATIONS AND NOTICE

§ 5.01   Notifications and Notice—In General

(1) A notification is a manifestation that is made in the form required by agreement among parties or by applicable law, or in a reasonable manner in the absence of an agreement or an applicable law, with the intention of affecting the legal rights and duties of the notifier in relation to rights and duties of persons to whom the notification is given.

(2) A notification given to or by an agent is effective as notification to or by the principal as stated in § 5.02.

(3) A person has notice of a fact if the person knows the fact, has reason to know the fact, has received an effective notification of the fact, or should know the fact to fulfill a duty owed to another person.

(4) Notice of a fact that an agent knows or has reason to know is imputed to the principal as stated in §§ 5.03 and 5.04.

§ 5.02   Notification Given by or to an Agent

(1) A notification given to an agent is effective as notice to the principal if the agent has actual or apparent authority to receive the notification, unless the person who gives the notification knows or has reason to know that the agent is acting adversely to the principal as stated in § 5.04.

(2) A notification given by an agent is effective as notification given by the principal if the agent has actual or apparent authority to give the notification, unless the person who receives the notification knows or has reason to know that the agent is acting adversely to the principal as stated in § 5.04.

§ 5.03   Imputation of Notice of Fact to Principal

For purposes of determining a principal's legal relations with a third party, notice of a fact that an agent knows or has reason to know is imputed to the principal if knowledge of the fact is material to the agent's duties to the principal, unless the agent

     (a)   acts adversely to the principal as stated in § 5.04, or

     (b)   is subject to a duty to another not to disclose the fact to the principal.

Comment c. Imputation within organizational principals. Imputation doctrines, like common-law agency in general, treat a juridical person that is an organization as one legal person. Organizations generally function by subdividing work or activities into specific functions that are assigned to different people. *See* § 1.03, Comment *c.* Within an organization, the work done by some agents consists of obtaining information on the basis of which coagents take action. Imputation recognizes that an organization constitutes one legal person and that its link to the external world is through its agents, including those whose assigned function is to receive, collect, report, or record information for organizational purposes. . . .

The nature and scope of the duties assigned to an agent are key to imputation within an organization. . . .

An organization's large size does not in itself defeat imputation, nor does the fact that an organization has structured itself internally into separate departments or divisions. Organizations are treated as possessing the collective knowledge of their employees and other agents, when that knowledge is material to the agents' duties, however the organization may have configured itself or its internal practices for transmission of information.

If an agent has learned a fact under circumstances that impose a duty on the agent not to reveal it to a principal, notice of that fact is not imputed to that principal. Thus, notice of a fact that an agent learns in confidence from one principal is not imputed to another principal. For further discussion, *see* Comment *e.*

An organization may put in place internal restrictions on how information is handled and transmitted to assist in fulfilling duties of confidentiality owed to its clients. Such restrictions are common in multifunction financial-services firms.

If information is communicated within an organization contrary to a prohibition imposed by an internal barrier on communication, the firm is charged with notice of the information. . . . Prior communications that contravene an organization's internal barrier call the barrier's general effectiveness into question. A barrier is not likely to be effective or to appear credible when personnel who possess nonpublic information work on shared projects with personnel whose job functions involve trading or other activity that would be aided by access to nonpublic information. Indicia of commitment to the barrier at an organization's highest levels enhance its credibility, as does consistent imposition of sanctions when violations are known to have occurred. A barrier's credibility will also be enhanced by regular review of its efficacy by a suitable organ of internal governance, such as an internal audit or regulatory department or an independent audit or other committee of a board of directors.

Barriers on intra-organization transmission of nonpublic information may also be strongly encouraged or required by law or regulation, which evolves as circumstances require. For example, the SEC's Rule 14e–3(b), promulgated under § 14(e) of the Securities Exchange Act, provides that a person (other than a natural person) will not be subject to liability for trading on the basis of nonpublic information about an impending tender offer if the person has established reasonable policies to ensure that individuals who make decisions to trade in securities of the target corporation do not receive information about the bid possessed by other individuals within the same firm. Such barriers may also be required by law. For example, the Insider Trading and Securities Fraud Enforcement Act of 1988 requires broker-dealers and investment advisers to establish and maintain written procedures to prevent misuse of inside information. *See* 15 U.S.C. § 78*o*(f). National banks are required by the Office of the Comptroller of the Currency to use internal barriers to prevent bank trust departments from unlawfully obtaining nonpublic information from other bank departments. *See* 12 C.F.R. § 9.5.

An internal barrier on communication of nonpublic information does not provide a defense to the legal consequences of a failure to take action in light of information that is otherwise freely available. . . .

§ 5.04 An Agent Who Acts Adversely to a Principal

For purposes of determining a principal's legal relations with a third party, notice of a fact that an agent knows or has reason to know is not imputed to the principal if the agent acts adversely to the principal in a transaction or matter, intending to act solely for the agent's own purposes or those of another person. Nevertheless, notice is imputed

(a) when necessary to protect the rights of a third party who dealt with the principal in good faith; or

(b) when the principal has ratified or knowingly retained a benefit from the agent's action.

A third party who deals with a principal through an agent, knowing or having reason to know that the agent acts adversely to the principal, does not deal in good faith for this purpose.

Comment b. Exception to imputation—in general. The doctrine stated in this section is an exception to the general rule, stated in § 5.03, that notice is imputed to a principal of a fact that an agent knows or has reason to know if knowledge of the fact is material to the agent's duties to the principal and to the principal's legal relations with third parties. The exception stated in this section is often termed the "adverse interest" exception. There is no imputation if an agent acts adversely to the principal. The adverse-interest exception is subject to two exclusions or exceptions. First, as stated in subsection (a), notice is imputed to the principal of facts that an agent who acts adversely knows or has reason to know when necessary to protect the rights of a third party who has dealt with the principal in good faith. Second, as stated in subsection (b), notice is imputed to a principal when the principal ratifies the agent's action or knowingly retains a benefit from the agent's action, although the agent acted adversely to the principal.

A third party who knows or has reason to know that an agent acts adversely to the principal, and who deals with the principal through the agent, has not dealt in good faith and may not rely on the adverse-interest exception. Thus, imputation protects innocent third parties but not those who know or have reason to know that an agent is not likely to transmit material information to the principal.

The rule stated in this section, like the rule stated in § 5.03, is applicable only for purposes of determining a principal's legal relations with a third party. Thus, notice is not imputed for purposes of determining rights and liabilities as between principal and agent. As a consequence, imputation does not furnish a basis on which an agent may defend against a claim by the principal.

If a principal ratifies action taken by an agent, the principal is bound by the legal consequences of that action as if the principal had knowledge of all the facts known by the agent. Section 4.01(2) states how a principal may ratify an agent's action, including by retaining a benefit produced by the agent's action. *See* Comment *d* for further discussion.

This section states a well-established doctrine. Partnership legislation has long incorporated the principle that a partnership is not charged with the knowledge of a partner who acts adversely to it. Under § 12 of the Uniform Partnership Act (1914) and § 102(f) of the Uniform Partnership Act (1997), a partnership is charged with a partner's knowledge, "except in the case of a fraud on the partnership committed by or with the consent of that partner."

However, as stated above, in order to protect third parties who deal with the principal in good faith, common-law agency doctrine encompasses exclusions to the exception to imputation when an agent acts adversely. As stated in subsection (a), the adverse-interest exception to imputation does not defeat the rights of a third party who dealt in good faith with the principal through an agent. Common-law agency also recognizes that a principal may elect to ratify the actions of an adversely acting agent. Taken as a whole, the common-law doctrine reflects a balance among factors that, if pressed in isolation to their respective extremes, would lead to divergent outcomes.

Ordinarily, an agent's failure to disclose a material fact to a principal does not defeat imputation, nor does the fact that the agent's action otherwise constitutes a breach of a duty owed the principal. *See* § 5.03, Comment *b*. For an agent's duty to provide information to the principal, *see* § 8.11. A principal's opportunity to monitor an agent and create incentives for the proper handling of information warrant imputing an agent's knowledge to the principal even when the agent has breached duties of disclosure to the principal. Moreover, imputation does not rest on an identification between principal and agent but rather on the fact that a principal's agents link it to the external world for purposes of obtaining and conveying information as well as taking action.

When an agent acts for the agent's own purposes or those of another person, the principal may be subject to liability to third parties because the agent may reasonably appear to be acting as the principal's representative with actual authority. *See* § 2.03. Likewise, notice of material facts known to an agent is imputed to the principal when the agent deals with a third party who reasonably believes the agent to be authorized so to act for the principal. However, this section does not protect a third party who knows or has reason to know that an agent acts adversely to the principal. If the third party colludes with the agent against the principal or otherwise knows or has reason to know that the agent is acting adversely to the principal, the third party should not expect that the agent will fulfill duties of disclosure owed to the principal.

CHAPTER 6. CONTRACTS AND OTHER TRANSACTIONS WITH THIRD PARTIES

TOPIC 1. PARTIES TO CONTRACTS

§ 6.01 Agent for Disclosed Principal

When an agent acting with actual or apparent authority makes a contract on behalf of a disclosed principal,

(1) the principal and the third party are parties to the contract; and

(2) the agent is not a party to the contract unless the agent and third party agree otherwise.

§ 6.02 Agent for Unidentified Principal

When an agent acting with actual or apparent authority makes a contract on behalf of an unidentified principal,

(1) the principal and the third party are parties to the contract; and

(2) the agent is a party to the contract unless the agent and the third party agree otherwise.

§ 6.03 Agent for Undisclosed Principal

When an agent acting with actual authority makes a contract on behalf of an undisclosed principal,

(1) unless excluded by the contract, the principal is a party to the contract;

(2) the agent and the third party are parties to the contract; and

(3) the principal, if a party to the contract, and the third party have the same rights, liabilities, and defenses against each other as if the principal made the contract personally, subject to §§ 6.05–6.09.

Comment d. Circumstances that affect rights or liabilities of undisclosed principal; contract excluding undisclosed principal as party. An undisclosed principal does not become a party to a contract if the contract excludes the principal. An explicit exclusion limits the third party's manifestation of assent to be bound. Such an explicit exclusion provides a simple device through which a third party may exclude the interests of persons other than those identified as parties to the contract. An undisclosed principal is not excluded from a contract by language stating that the contract is not assignable.

In contrast, an undisclosed principal and an agent may agree that the agent alone shall be liable on a contract. An agreement between an undisclosed principal and an agent cannot effectively exclude the principal as a party to the contract because the third party has not assented to such exclusion.

By dealing on behalf of an undisclosed principal, an agent does not implicitly represent that the agent is not acting for a principal. This is because it is usually not material to a third party whether the person with whom the third party deals, and who becomes subject to liability on contracts made with the third party, acts as an agent for an undisclosed principal. *See* § 6.11, Comment *d.* If an agent falsely represents that the agent does not act on behalf of a principal, the third party may avoid a contract made with the agent under the circumstances stated in § 6.11(4). A third party may avoid a contract made by an agent acting for an undisclosed principal if the agent or the principal knows or has reason to know that the third party would not have dealt with the principal as a party to the contract. *See id. See also* § 6.02, Comment *c.*

The nature of the performance that a contract requires determines whether performance by an undisclosed principal will be effective as performance under the contract and whether an undisclosed principal can require that the third party render performance to the principal. Performance by an undisclosed principal is not effective as performance under a contract if the third party has a substantial interest in receiving performance from the agent who made the contract. This limit corresponds to the limit on delegability of performance of a duty as stated in Restatement Second, Contracts § 318(2).

The nature of the performance that a contract requires from a third party determines whether an undisclosed principal is entitled to receive that performance. An undisclosed principal may not require that a third party render performance to the principal if rendering performance to the principal would materially change the nature of the third party's duty, materially increase the burden or risk imposed on the third party, or materially impair the third party's chance of receiving return performance. These limits correspond to the limits imposed on assignment of a contractual right. *See* Restatement Second, Contracts § 317(2).

§ 6.04   Principal Does not Exist or Lacks Capacity

Unless the third party agrees otherwise, a person who makes a contract with a third party purportedly as an agent on behalf of a principal becomes a party to the contract if the purported agent knows or has reason to know that the purported principal does not exist or lacks capacity to be a party to a contract.

TOPIC 2.   RIGHTS, LIABILITIES, AND DEFENSES

TITLE A.   GENERAL

§ 6.05   Contract That is Unauthorized in Part or That Combines Orders of Several Principals

(1) If an agent makes a contract with a third party that differs from the contract that the agent had actual or apparent authority to make only in an amount or by the inclusion or exclusion of a separable part, the principal is subject to liability to the third party to the extent of the contract that the agent had actual or apparent authority to make if

(a) the third party seasonably makes a manifestation to the principal of willingness to be bound; and

(b) the principal has not changed position in reasonable reliance on the belief that no contract bound the principal and the third party.

(2) Two or more principals may authorize the same agent to make separate contracts for them. If the agent makes a single contract with a third party on the principals' behalves that combines the principals' separate orders or interests and calls for a single performance by the third party,

(a) if the agent purports to make the combined contract on behalf of disclosed principals, the agent is subject to liability to the third party for breach of the agent's warranty of authority as stated in § 6.10, unless the separate principals are bound by the combined contract;

(b) if the principals are unidentified or undisclosed, the third party and the agent are the only parties to the combined contract; and

(c) unless the agent acted with actual or apparent authority to bind each of the principals to the combined contract,

(i) subject to (1), none of the separate principals is subject to liability on the combined contract; and

(ii) the third party is not subject to liability on the combined contract to any of the separate principals.

§ 6.06   Setoff

(1)   When an agent makes a contract on behalf of a disclosed or unidentified principal, unless the principal and the third party agree otherwise,

(a)   the third party may not set off any amount that the agent independently owes the third party against an amount the third party owes the principal under the contract; and

(b)   the principal may not set off any amount that the third party independently owes the agent against an amount the principal owes the third party under the contract.

(2)   When an agent makes a contract on behalf of an undisclosed principal,

(a)   the third party may set off

(i)   any amount that the agent independently owed the third party at the time the agent made the contract and

(ii)   any amount that the agent thereafter independently comes to owe the third party until the third party has notice that the agent acts on behalf of a principal against an amount the third party owes the principal under the contract;

(b)   after the third party has notice that the agent acts on behalf of a principal, the third party may not set off any amount that the agent thereafter independently comes to owe the third party against an amount the third party owes the principal under the contract unless the principal consents; and

(c)   the principal may not set off any amount that the third party independently owes the agent against an amount that the principal owes the third party under the contract, unless the principal and the third party agree otherwise.

(3)   Unless otherwise agreed, an agent who is a party to a contract may not set off any amount that the principal independently owes the agent against an amount that the agent owes the third party under the contract. However, with the principal's consent, the agent may set off any amount that the principal could set off against an amount that the principal owes the third party under the contract.

TITLE B.   SUBSEQUENT DEALINGS BETWEEN THIRD PARTY AND PRINCIPAL OR AGENT

§ 6.07   Settlement with Agent by Principal or Third Party

(1)   A principal's payment to or settlement of accounts with an agent discharges the principal's liability to a third party with whom the agent has made a contract on the principal's behalf only when the principal acts in reasonable reliance on a manifestation by the third party, not induced by misrepresentation by the agent, that the agent has settled the account with the third party.

(2)   A third party's payment to or settlement of accounts with an agent discharges the third party's liability to the principal if the agent acts with actual or apparent authority in accepting the payment or settlement.

(3)   When an agent has made a contract on behalf of an undisclosed principal,

(a)   until the third party has notice of the principal's existence, the third party's payment to or settlement of accounts with the agent discharges the third party's liability to the principal;

(b)   after the third party has notice of the principal's existence, the third party's payment to or settlement of accounts with the agent discharges the third party's liability to the principal if the agent acts with actual or apparent authority in accepting the payment or settlement; and

(c)   after receiving notice of the principal's existence, the third party may demand reasonable proof of the principal's identity and relationship to the agent. Until such proof is received, the third party's payment to or settlement of accounts in good faith with the agent discharges the third party's liability to the principal.

§ 6.08   Other Subsequent Dealings Between Third Party and Agent

(1)   When an agent has made a contract with a third party on behalf of a disclosed or unidentified principal, subsequent dealings between the agent and the third party may increase or diminish the principal's rights or liabilities to the third party if the agent acts with actual or apparent authority or the principal ratifies the agent's action.

(2)   When an agent has made a contract with a third party on behalf of an undisclosed principal,

(a)   until the third party has notice of the principal's existence, subsequent dealings between the third party and the agent may increase or diminish the rights or liabilities of the principal to the third party if the agent acts with actual authority, or the principal ratifies the agent's action; and

(b)   after the third party has notice of the principal's existence, subsequent dealings between the third party and the agent may increase or diminish the principal's rights or liabilities to the third party if the agent acts with actual or apparent authority or the principal ratifies the agent's action.

§ 6.09   Effect of Judgment Against Agent or Principal

When an agent has made a contract with a third party on behalf of a principal, unless the contract provides otherwise,

(1)   the liability, if any, of the principal or the agent to the third party is not discharged if the third party obtains a judgment against the other; and

(2)   the liability, if any, of the principal or the agent to the third party is discharged to the extent a judgment against the other is satisfied.

TITLE C.   AGENT'S WARRANTIES AND REPRESENTATIONS

§ 6.10   Agent's Implied Warranty of Authority

A person who purports to make a contract, representation, or conveyance to or with a third party on behalf of another person, lacking power to bind that person, gives an implied warranty of authority to the third party and is subject to liability to the third party for damages for loss caused by breach of that warranty, including loss of the benefit expected from performance by the principal, unless

(1)   the principal or purported principal ratifies the act as stated in § 4.01; or

(2)   the person who purports to make the contract, representation, or conveyance gives notice to the third party that no warranty of authority is given; or

(3)   the third party knows that the person who purports to make the contract, representation, or conveyance acts without actual authority.

§ 6.11   Agent's Representations

(1)   When an agent for a disclosed or unidentified principal makes a false representation about the agent's authority to a third party, the principal is not subject to liability unless the agent acted with actual or apparent authority in making the representation and the third party does not have notice that the agent's representation is false.

(2)   A representation by an agent made incident to a contract or conveyance is attributed to a disclosed or unidentified principal as if the principal made the representation directly when the agent had actual or apparent authority to make the contract or conveyance unless the third party knew or

had reason to know that the representation was untrue or that the agent acted without actual authority in making it.

(3)   A representation by an agent made incident to a contract or conveyance is attributed to an undisclosed principal as if the principal made the representation directly when

    (a)   the agent acted with actual authority in making the representation, or

    (b)   the agent acted without actual authority in making the representation but had actual authority to make true representations about the same matter.

The agent's representation is not attributed to the principal when the third party knew or had reason to know it was untrue.

(4)   When an agent who makes a contract or conveyance on behalf of an undisclosed principal falsely represents to the third party that the agent does not act on behalf of a principal, the third party may avoid the contract or conveyance if the principal or agent had notice that the third party would not have dealt with the principal.

CHAPTER 7. TORTS—LIABILITY OF AGENT AND PRINCIPAL

TOPIC 1.   AGENT'S LIABILITY

§ 7.01   Agent's Liability to Third Party

An agent is subject to liability to a third party harmed by the agent's tortious conduct. Unless an applicable statute provides otherwise, an actor remains subject to liability although the actor acts as an agent or an employee, with actual or apparent authority, or within the scope of employment.

§ 7.02   Duty to Principal; Duty to Third Party

An agent's breach of a duty owed to the principal is not an independent basis for the agent's tort liability to a third party. An agent is subject to tort liability to a third party harmed by the agent's conduct only when the agent's conduct breaches a duty that the agent owes to the third party.

TOPIC 2.   PRINCIPAL'S LIABILITY

§ 7.03   Principal's Liability—In General

(1)   A principal is subject to direct liability to a third party harmed by an agent's conduct when

    (a)   as stated in § 7.04, the agent acts with actual authority or the principal ratifies the agent's conduct and

        (i)   the agent's conduct is tortious, or

        (ii)   the agent's conduct, if that of the principal, would subject the principal to tort liability; or

    (b)   as stated in § 7.05, the principal is negligent in selecting, supervising, or otherwise controlling the agent; or

    (c)   as stated in § 7.06, the principal delegates performance of a duty to use care to protect other persons or their property to an agent who fails to perform the duty.

(2)   A principal is subject to vicarious liability to a third party harmed by an agent's conduct when

    (a)   as stated in § 7.07, the agent is an employee who commits a tort while acting within the scope of employment; or

(b)   as stated in § 7.08, the agent commits a tort when acting with apparent authority in dealing with a third party on or purportedly on behalf of the principal.

Comment d. Agents with multiple principals. An agent who commits a tort may have more than one principal for at least some purposes. On agents with multiple principals in general, *see* Chapter 3, Topic 5. In the context of a principal's liability on the basis of an agent's tort, it is helpful to distinguish among three different types of relationships: (1) subagency; (2) employees who are "borrowed" by one employer from another employer; and (3) officers of interrelated entities.

(1) Subagency. A subagent is a person appointed by an agent to perform functions that the agent has consented to perform on behalf of the principal. *See* § 3.15(1). For general discussion of the consequences of subagency, *see* § 3.15, Comment *d.* A subagent may be an employee of the appointing agent. When a subagent is an employee, as defined in § 7.07(3), of the appointing agent, the appointing agent is subject to vicarious liability for torts committed by the subagent within the scope of employment. *See* § 7.07. Both the appointing agent and the principal are subject to vicarious liability when a subagent acts with apparent authority in committing a tort, as stated in § 7.08. An appointing agent may be subject to liability for torts of a subagent who is not an employee. For example, when a law firm assigns work on behalf of a client to a "temporary" lawyer who is neither a member of the firm nor its employee, the firm creates a relationship of subagency with the "temporary" lawyer that subjects it to liability to its client for acts and omissions of the "temporary" lawyer. *See* Restatement Third, The Law Governing Lawyers § 58, Comment *e.*

A relationship of subagency does not result when an agent appoints a coagent. Coagents share a common principal, although they may occupy dominant and subordinate positions in an organizational hierarchy. *See* § 3.15, Comment *b.* An agent who has authority to hire a coagent is not subject to vicarious liability for the coagent's tortious conduct.

(2) "Lent employees," or "borrowed servants." When work requires specialized skills or equipment or requires that an actor perform a task on less than a full-time basis, it is not unusual that the actor who performs the work is employed by a firm that contracts to provide the actor's services to another firm. The types of actors who work through such arrangements vary greatly, as does the nature of the work they do. These arrangements span the range of highly skilled professionals, including nurses, lawyers, and other members of licensed professions; office workers; skilled construction workers; and unskilled manual laborers. The risks of injury to third parties posed by such work vary, as do the settings in which work is performed. Moreover, the specifics of such arrangements vary in several respects. These include the duration of an actor's placement in a particular workplace and the provision of supervision, training, and tools needed to perform work. An actor's employer may provide requisite training, furnish the actor with specialized equipment needed for work, and reassign the actor with frequency. Alternatively, the actor may work on a long-term basis within a particular firm using tools and receiving training provided by that firm.

When an actor negligently injures a third party while performing work for the firm that has contracted for the actor's services, the question is whether that firm (often termed the "special employer") or the initial employer (often termed the "general employer"), or both, should be subject to liability to the third party. Liability should be allocated to the employer in the better position to take measures to prevent the injury suffered by the third party. An employer is in that position if the employer has the right to control an employee's conduct. When both a general and special employer have the right to control an employee's conduct, the practical history of direction may establish that one employer in fact ceded its right of control to the other, whether through its failure to exercise the right or otherwise.

It is a question of fact whether a general or a special employer, or both, have the right to control an employee's conduct. Factors that a court may consider in making this determination include the extent of control that an employer may exercise over the details of an employee's work and the timing of the work; the relationship between the employee's work and the nature of the special employer's business; the nature of the employee's work, the skills required to perform it, and the degree of supervision customarily associated with the work; the duration of the employee's work in the special employer's firm; the identity of the employer who furnishes equipment or other instrumentalities requisite to performing the work; and the method of payment for the work.

Many cases allocate liability in this context on the basis that a general employer has an exclusive right of control over employees assigned to work for clients of the general employer. This presupposes that ties between a general employer and an assigned employee will remain strong despite the employee's emplacement in the special employer's workplace where the employee's performance will often be subject to some degree of direction and monitoring by members of the special employer's management. It may also reflect assumptions about links between the general employer and the risk that third parties will be injured when work is done in a special employer's workplace. A general employer is in a position to screen prospective employees to determine their general aptitude and fitness; a general employer may also provide training to those it selects for employment. If a general employer assigns an employee and furnishes the employee with equipment to use in performing assigned work, the general employer is also in a position to impose requirements for the proper usage and maintenance of the equipment. A general employer may also be in a better position to provide insurance coverage for an employee's actions. Any presumption that a general employer has the right to control an employee may be rebutted by proving factual indicia that the right has been assumed by a special employer. Even within the same jurisdiction, it may be difficult to predict whether a given set of indicia will demonstrate that a special employer has assumed the right of control.

However, a significant number of cases allocate liability to a special employer on the basis of its right and ability to direct a borrowed employee's specific actions in its workplace. A justification for this approach is that a borrowed employee may retain only formal ties to a general employer, depending on the duration and nature of the borrowed employee's relationship with the special employer, which weakens the likelihood that the general employer retains any practical capacity to control the borrowed employee's conduct. This approach also reflects the possibility that a special employer may in fact be in the better position to exercise control in a manner that reduces the risk of injury to third parties. This possibility may be especially likely when the nature of a borrowed employee's work requires coordinated effort as part of a skilled team and close direction or supervision by the team's leader. Some cases allocate liability to both general and special employer on the basis that both exercised control over the employee and both benefited to some degree from the employee's work.

A related question, arising when the third party injured by an actor's negligence is an employee of the special employer, is the applicability of workers'-compensation insurance law to the employee's claims. Although these questions may often be related as a practical matter, workers'-compensation questions are beyond the scope of this Restatement.

(3) Officers of interrelated entities. The fact that a corporation or other entity owns a majority of the voting equity in another entity does not create a relationship of agency between them or between each entity and the other's agents. Likewise, common ownership of multiple entities does not create relationships of agency among them. *See* § 1.01, Comment *f(2)*. An entity becomes the agent of another entity, and an individual becomes an entity's agent, only when they are linked by the elements of an agency relationship as stated in § 1.01.

Within a related group of corporations or other entities the same individuals may serve as officers or directors of more than one entity. An overlapping cast in multiple organizational roles does not in itself create relationships of agency that are not otherwise present.

When the same individuals serve multiple entities as their officers, directors, or employees, it may become necessary to determine the entity to which an individual's conduct should be attributed. There is a general presumption that contracts and other transactions entered into by a shared officer are attributed to the entity for which the officer purports to be acting. A rationale for this presumption is that the identity of the party who will be bound by a contract or transaction is often material to the other party to the contract or transaction. *See* § 6.01, Comment *b*. This rationale does not support applying the same presumption when a shared officer's conduct is tortious, especially when the party injured by the conduct has not chosen to engage in a transaction conducted by the shared officer.

Moreover, that an officer purports to act on behalf of a particular entity does not create a basis for attribution that corresponds to policies and objectives that underlie contemporary tort law. When harm is caused negligently, these objectives include remedying an injustice that has been inflicted on a plaintiff by a defendant and providing a defendant with appropriate safety incentives. *See* Restatement Third, Torts: Liability for Physical Harm § 6, Comment *d* (Proposed Final Draft No. 1, 2005). On harm that is caused intentionally, *see id.* § 5, Comment *a*. Likewise, the contract-based presumption is inapt when a shared officer's conduct violates a statute that proscribes or regulates conduct, particularly conduct outside a transactional context.

§ 7.04   Agent Acts with Actual Authority

A principal is subject to liability to a third party harmed by an agent's conduct when the agent's conduct is within the scope of the agent's actual authority or ratified by the principal; and

(1)   the agent's conduct is tortious, or

(2)   the agent's conduct, if that of the principal, would subject the principal to tort liability.

§ 7.05   Principal's Negligence in Conducting Activity Through Agent; Principal's Special Relationship with Another Person

(1)   A principal who conducts an activity through an agent is subject to liability for harm to a third party caused by the agent's conduct if the harm was caused by the principal's negligence in selecting, training, retaining, supervising, or otherwise controlling the agent.

(2)   When a principal has a special relationship with another person, the principal owes that person a duty of reasonable care with regard to risks arising out of the relationship, including the risk that agents of the principal will harm the person with whom the principal has such a special relationship.

§ 7.06   Failure in Performance of Principal's Duty of Protection

A principal required by contract or otherwise by law to protect another cannot avoid liability by delegating performance of the duty, whether or not the delegate is an agent.

§ 7.07   Employee Acting Within Scope of Employment

(1)   An employer is subject to vicarious liability for a tort committed by its employee acting within the scope of employment.

(2)   An employee acts within the scope of employment when performing work assigned by the employer or engaging in a course of conduct subject to the employer's control. An employee's act is not within the scope of employment when it occurs within an independent course of conduct not intended by the employee to serve any purpose of the employer.

(3)   For purposes of this section,

(a)   an employee is an agent whose principal controls or has the right to control the manner and means of the agent's performance of work, and

(b)   the fact that work is performed gratuitously does not relieve a principal of liability.

Comment c. Conduct in the performance of work and scope of employment. An employee's conduct is within the scope of employment when it constitutes performance of work assigned to the employee by the employer. The fact that the employee performs the work carelessly does not take the employee's conduct outside the scope of employment, nor does the fact that the employee otherwise makes a mistake in performing the work. Likewise, conduct is not outside the scope of employment merely because an employee disregards the employer's instructions.

. . . [T]he fact that an employee's action violates a generally applicable law, such as a speeding limit, does not by itself place the employee's conduct outside the scope of employment. These results are not surprising. An employee may believe that the employer wishes the employee to disregard an inconvenient constraint when the employee fears that compliance would jeopardize completing the employee's assigned mission at all or completing it on or ahead of schedule. Although the employee's belief may be mistaken, it is compatible with acting in an assigned role to do an assigned task. However, the character, extreme nature, or other circumstances accompanying an employee's actions may demonstrate that the employee's course of conduct is independent of performing work assigned by the employer and intended solely to further the employee's own purposes. . . .

An employee's failure to take action may also be conduct within the scope of employment. For example, an employee's failure to do work assigned by the employer, when harm to a third party results, under some circumstances may constitute negligence. A negligent action "frequently involves a failure to take a reasonable precaution. . . . [which] can be described as an omission, and it hence can be said that the omission is itself negligent." Restatement Third, Torts: Liability for Physical Harm § 3, Comment c (Proposed Final Draft No. 1, 2005).

An employee's assigned work may include tasks that contemplate the necessity of using physical force to complete the assigned work. . . . An employee's assigned duties may also place the employee in situations in which physical consequences may follow in an uninterrupted sequence from verbal exchanges with third parties. An escalation in the pitch of an employee's conduct does not by itself transform the conduct into an independent course of conduct that represents a departure not within the scope of employment. It is a question of fact what motivated an employee's conduct as verbal exchanges escalate or when an employee's use of physical force becomes more pronounced.

In determining whether an employee's tortious conduct is within the scope of employment, the nature of the tort is relevant, as is whether the conduct also constitutes a criminal act. An employee's intentionally criminal conduct may indicate a departure from conduct within the scope of employment, not a simple escalation. The nature and magnitude of the conduct are relevant to determining the employee's intention at the time. . . .

The determinative question is whether the course of conduct in which the tort occurred is within the scope of employment. Intentional torts and other intentional wrongdoing may be within the scope of employment. For example, if an employee's job duties include determining the prices at which the employer's output will be sold to customers, the employee's agreement with a competitor to fix prices is within the scope of employment unless circumstances establish a departure from the scope of employment. Likewise, when an employee's job duties include making statements to prospective customers to induce them to buy from the employer, intentional misrepresentations made by the employee are within the scope of employment unless circumstances establish that the employee has departed from it.

An employee may engage in conduct, part of which is within the scope of employment and part of which is not. . . .

When an employee's tortious conduct is outside the scope of employment, alternate theories of liability may be available against the employer. . . .

§ 7.08 Agent Acts with Apparent Authority

A principal is subject to vicarious liability for a tort committed by an agent in dealing or communicating with a third party on or purportedly on behalf of the principal when actions taken by the agent with apparent authority constitute the tort or enable the agent to conceal its commission.

CHAPTER 8. DUTIES OF AGENT AND PRINCIPAL TO EACH OTHER

TOPIC 1.   AGENT'S DUTIES TO PRINCIPAL

TITLE A.   GENERAL FIDUCIARY PRINCIPLE

§ 8.01   General Fiduciary Principle

An agent has a fiduciary duty to act loyally for the principal's benefit in all matters connected with the agency relationship.

TITLE B.   DUTIES OF LOYALTY

§ 8.02   Material Benefit Arising Out of Position

An agent has a duty not to acquire a material benefit from a third party in connection with transactions conducted or other actions taken on behalf of the principal or otherwise through the agent's use of the agent's position.

Comment e. Remedies. When an agent breaches the duty stated in this section, the principal may recover monetary relief from the agent and, in appropriate circumstances, from any third party who participated in the agent's breach. A principal may avoid a contract entered into by the agent with a third party who participated in the agent's breach of duty. The principal may recover any material benefit received by the agent through the agent's breach, the value of the benefit, or proceeds of the benefit retained by the agent. The principal may also recover damages for any harm caused by the agent's breach. If an agent's breach of duty involves a wrongful disposal of assets of the principal, the principal cannot recover both the value of the asset and what the agent received in exchange. If a principal recovers damages from a third party as a consequence of an agent's breach of fiduciary duty, the principal remains entitled to recover from the agent any benefit that the agent improperly received from the transaction.

If a principal seeks to recover a material benefit received by an agent, the value of the benefit, or its proceeds, the principal's recovery is not subject to a deduction for expenses incurred by the agent to induce a third party to confer the benefit on the agent.

However, if an agent breaches the agent's fiduciary duty by taking personal advantage of a business opportunity as discussed in Comment *d*, the principal may recover property that the agent acquired through the breach only if the principal reimburses the agent. The amount of reimbursement is either the amount paid by the agent for the property or the amount for which the principal could have obtained the property, whichever is less. *See* Restatement of Restitution §§ 194, 195; Principles of Corporate Governance: Analysis and Recommendations, Comment to § 5.05(e) and Illustration 13.

§ 8.03   Acting as or on Behalf of an Adverse Party

An agent has a duty not to deal with the principal as or on behalf of an adverse party in a transaction connected with the agency relationship.

Comment b. Rationale. As a fiduciary, an agent has a duty to the principal to act loyally in the principal's interest in all matters in connection with the agency relationship. *See* § 8.01. The rule stated in this section is a specific application of this general principle. When an agent deals with the principal on the agent's own account, the agent's own interests are irreconcilably in tension with the principal's interests because the interest of each is furthered by action—negotiating a higher or a lower price, for example—that is incompatible with the interests of the other. If an agent acts on behalf of the principal in a transaction with the agent, the agent's duty to act loyally in the principal's interest conflicts with the agent's self-interest. Even if the agent's divided loyalty does not result in demonstrable harm to the principal, the agent has breached the agent's duty of undivided loyalty.

Likewise, an agent who acts on behalf of more than one principal in a transaction between or among the principals has breached the agent's duty of loyalty to each principal through undertaking service to multiple principals that divides the agent's loyalty.

A principal may consent to conduct by an agent that would otherwise constitute a breach of the agent's duty. See § 8.06. On consent by multiple principals when an agent conducts a transaction between or among the principals, see § 8.06(2).

The duty stated in this section is formulated broadly. So long as the transaction in which an agent acts as or on behalf of an adverse party is connected with the agency relationship, the agent is subject to the duty although the agent does not have direct or indirect responsibility for conducting the transaction on behalf of the principal. The breadth of this formulation requires that an agent disclose adverse interests to the principal so that the principal may evaluate, as only the principal is situated to do, how best to protect its interests in light of the agent's interest. See § 8.06. The breadth of the formulation also makes it unnecessary for a principal to prescribe its agents' duties and prohibit outside interests that its agents may have or acquire with great specificity in formulating the initial terms of its relationship with its agents.

A principal's knowledge that an agent deals as or on behalf of an adverse party does not relieve the agent of duties to the principal in connection with that transaction. Under the rule stated in § 8.06, the agent has a duty to deal fairly with the principal and to disclose to the principal all facts of which the agent has notice that are reasonably relevant to the principal's exercise of judgment, unless the principal has manifested that the principal already knows them or does not wish to know them. Thus, a principal's knowledge that its agent acts as or on behalf of an adverse party does not convert the relationship between principal and agent into an arm's-length relationship. Moreover, as stated in § 8.11, an agent has a duty to use reasonable effort to furnish information to the principal although the agent does not deal as or on behalf of an adverse party.

It is, of course, possible that an agent may assume an adverse position in which the agent may not legally discharge the duties of disclosure that the agent owes to the principal because the agent owes a duty to another person not to disclose a fact that §§ 8.06 and 8.11 require be disclosed to the principal. In Illustration 3, for example, A's duties to T Corporation may prohibit A's disclosure of new product developments to T Corporation's customer, P Corporation. Unless it is possible for T Corporation to shield A from access to facts that A will have a duty to disclose to P Corporation, A's position is not tenable, and consequently A must withdraw as P Corporation's agent.

However, an agent whose acts on behalf of a party consist solely of ministerial acts that require no exercise of discretion, judgment, or skill does not act on behalf of that party for purposes of determining whether the agent acts adversely to another principal. Thus, one principal's agent who performs only ministerial acts for another does not become a dual agent.

A custom in an industry that permits self-dealing by agents, if unknown to the principal, does not relieve the agent of the duty to refrain from self-dealing. If an agreement between principal and agent grants the agent discretion to take such adverse action, the agent is subject to a contract-law duty of good faith and fair dealing in exercising the discretion. See § 8.01, Comment b.

Many business-organization statutes contain provisions that address self-dealing conduct on the part of specified organizational actors. Under contemporary partnership legislation, a partner has a duty to "refrain from dealing with the partnership in the conduct or winding up of the partnership business as or on behalf of a party having an interest adverse to the partnership. . . ." Rev. Unif. Partnership Act § 404(b)(2). Similarly, a manager of a limited-liability company (LLC) has a comparable duty, as does a member of a member-managed LLC. See Unif. Limited Liability Company Act § 409(b)(2). Many corporation statutes have provisions applicable to transactions between a corporation and a director, or between a corporation and an officer, in which mechanisms are specified through which the director or officer may fulfill duties owed to the corporation in connection with the transaction. See Principles of Corporate Governance: Analysis and Recommendations § 5.02.

§ 8.04   Competition

Throughout the duration of an agency relationship, an agent has a duty to refrain from competing with the principal and from taking action on behalf of or otherwise assisting the principal's competitors. During that time, an agent may take action, not otherwise wrongful, to prepare for competition following termination of the agency relationship.

§ 8.05   Use of Principal's Property; Use of Confidential Information

An agent has a duty

(1)   not to use property of the principal for the agent's own purposes or those of a third party; and

(2)   not to use or communicate confidential information of the principal for the agent's own purposes or those of a third party.

§ 8.06   Principal's Consent

(1)   Conduct by an agent that would otherwise constitute a breach of duty as stated in §§ 8.01, 8.02, 8.03, 8.04, and 8.05 does not constitute a breach of duty if the principal consents to the conduct, provided that

(a)   in obtaining the principal's consent, the agent

(i)   acts in good faith,

(ii)   discloses all material facts that the agent knows, has reason to know, or should know would reasonably affect the principal's judgment unless the principal has manifested that such facts are already known by the principal or that the principal does not wish to know them, and

(iii)   otherwise deals fairly with the principal; and

(b)   the principal's consent concerns either a specific act or transaction, or acts or transactions of a specified type that could reasonably be expected to occur in the ordinary course of the agency relationship.

(2)   An agent who acts for more than one principal in a transaction between or among them has a duty

(a)   to deal in good faith with each principal,

(b)   to disclose to each principal

(i)   the fact that the agent acts for the other principal or principals, and

(ii)   all other facts that the agent knows, has reason to know, or should know would reasonably affect the principal's judgment unless the principal has manifested that such facts are already known by the principal or that the principal does not wish to know them, and

(c)   otherwise to deal fairly with each principal.

TITLE C.   DUTIES OF PERFORMANCE

§ 8.07   Duty Created by Contract

An agent has a duty to act in accordance with the express and implied terms of any contract between the agent and the principal.

§ 8.08 Duties of Care, Competence, and Diligence

Subject to any agreement with the principal, an agent has a duty to the principal to act with the care, competence, and diligence normally exercised by agents in similar circumstances. Special skills or knowledge possessed by an agent are circumstances to be taken into account in determining whether the agent acted with due care and diligence. If an agent claims to possess special skills or knowledge, the agent has a duty to the principal to act with the care, competence, and diligence normally exercised by agents with such skills or knowledge.

Comment b. Common-law and statutory duties of care; regulatory duties. A principal and an agent may establish benchmarks or other measures for the effort and skill to be expected from the agent. For example, a contract between principal and agent may specify measures for the effort that the agent has a duty to expend in pursuing the principal's objectives. An agent may also guarantee by contract that the agent's work will be successful in achieving an objective or that the agent's work will be satisfactory to the principal. On conditions that an obligor be satisfied with an obligee's performance, *see* Restatement Second, Contracts § 228. A contract may also, in appropriate circumstances, raise or lower the standard of performance to be expected of an agent or specify the remedies or mechanisms of dispute resolution available to the principal. Regardless of their content, contractually shaped or contractually created duties are grounded in the mutual assent of agent and principal.

In contrast to § 8.06, the rule stated in this section articulates a broader role for general agreements that a principal and an agent may make in advance. If an agreement between principal and agent is otherwise enforceable, it may define the standard of performance applicable to the agent across the board in general terms and without the specificity required under § 8.06(1)(b) for consent by a principal to conduct by an agent that would otherwise breach a duty of loyalty owed to the principal under §§ 8.01, 8.02, 8.03, 8.04, or 8.05. Moreover, a principal's consent under § 8.06 is ineffective unless in obtaining the consent the agent acted consistently with the requirements stated in § 8.06(1)(a) or (2).

The duties stated in this section will often overlap with an agent's duties of performance that are express or implied terms of a contract between principal and agent. However, the duties stated in this section are tort-law duties because they "denote the fact that the actor is required to conduct himself in a particular manner at the risk that if he does not do so he becomes subject to liability to another to whom the duty is owed for any injury sustained by such other, of which that actor's conduct is a legal cause." Restatement Second, Torts § 4. Tort law imposes duties of care on an agent because the agent undertakes to act on behalf of the principal, because the principal's reliance on that undertaking is foreseeable by the agent, and because it is often socially useful that an agent fulfill the agent's undertaking to the principal. *See* Restatement Second, Torts § 323; Restatement Third, Torts: Liability for Physical Harm § 42 (Proposed Final Draft No. 1, 2005).

The overlap between duties derived from tort law and from an agent's contract with the principal will often provide the principal with alternative remedies when a breach of duty subjects the agent to liability. In particular, an agent is subject to liability to the principal for all harm, whether past, present, or prospective, caused the principal by the agent's breach of the duties stated in this section. *See* Restatement Second, Torts § 910. The agent's liability includes an obligation to indemnify the principal when a wrongful act by the agent subjects the principal to vicarious liability to a third person. *See* §§ 7.07 and 7.08. One agent's breach of the duties stated in this section does not bar an innocent principal from recovery against another agent who is also subject to liability.

Statutory provisions may also be relevant in determining the duties of care owed by an agent. For example, some organizational statutes establish standards of conduct for officers and others who act on behalf of an organization. Under § 8.42(a)(2) of the Model Business Corporation Act, an officer must act, in performing the officer's duties, "with the care that a person in like position would reasonably exercise under similar circumstances. . . ." The Revised Uniform Partnership Act states that a partner owes a duty of care to the partnership and to other partners "in the conduct and winding up of the partnership business" that is limited to "refraining from engaging in grossly negligent or reckless conduct, intentional misconduct, or a knowing violation of law." Rev. Unif. Partnership Act

§ 404(c). The Uniform Limited Liability Company Act imposes a comparable standard on an LLC's managers and members who are also managers. Unif. Limited Liability Co. Act § 409(c) and (h)(2).

An agent's conduct may be subject to regulation by statutes, administrative rules, or rules of a particular profession. An agent's violation of such a statute or rule does not in itself establish that the agent breached the agent's duty to the principal stated in this section. If the statute or rule is designed to protect persons in the principal's position, the trier of fact may consider the agent's violation of the statute in defining and applying the standard stated in this section.

§ 8.09 Duty to Act Only Within Scope of Actual Authority and to Comply with Principal's Lawful Instructions

(1) An agent has a duty to take action only within the scope of the agent's actual authority.

(2) An agent has a duty to comply with all lawful instructions received from the principal and persons designated by the principal concerning the agent's actions on behalf of the principal.

§ 8.10 Duty of Good Conduct

An agent has a duty, within the scope of the agency relationship, to act reasonably and to refrain from conduct that is likely to damage the principal's enterprise.

§ 8.11 Duty to Provide Information

An agent has a duty to use reasonable effort to provide the principal with facts that the agent knows, has reason to know, or should know when

(1) subject to any manifestation by the principal, the agent knows or has reason to know that the principal would wish to have the facts or the facts are material to the agent's duties to the principal; and

(2) the facts can be provided to the principal without violating a superior duty owed by the agent to another person.

§ 8.12 Duties Regarding Principal's Property—Segregation, Record-Keeping, and Accounting

An agent has a duty, subject to any agreement with the principal,

(1) not to deal with the principal's property so that it appears to be the agent's property;

(2) not to mingle the principal's property with anyone else's; and

(3) to keep and render accounts to the principal of money or other property received or paid out on the principal's account.

TOPIC 2. PRINCIPAL'S DUTIES TO AGENT

§ 8.13 Duty Created by Contract

A principal has a duty to act in accordance with the express and implied terms of any contract between the principal and the agent.

Comment d. Compensation—other issues. Unless an agreement between a principal and an agent indicates otherwise, a principal has a duty to pay compensation to an agent for services that the agent provides. An agreement that an agent will not have a right to compensation for services provided may be implied from the agent's relationship to the principal or from the trivial nature of the services requested. The amount of compensation due may be determined by the terms of agreement between principal and agent and may be fixed in amount or made contingent on whether the agent achieves stated outcomes or on other criteria. An agreement between a principal and an agent may also set the agent's right to compensation at an amount or rate that is standard or customary in a particular industry. If an agent has a right to be paid compensation by a principal but the amount due cannot be determined on the basis of the terms of the parties' agreement, the agent is entitled to the value of the services provided by the agent.

A principal's duty to pay compensation to an agent does not extend to fulfilling an agent's duties to pay compensation to subagents engaged by the agent, unless the principal so agrees. *See* § 3.15, Comment *d*, for an extended discussion of the consequences of subagency relationships. Thus, unless a principal agrees otherwise, the principal is not a guarantor of obligations undertaken by its agent to pay subagents appointed by the agent. Were the rule otherwise, a principal would bear the risk that an appointing agent would make generous arrangements with a subagent in exchange for payments by the subagent or would be tempted for other reasons to disregard the principal's interests in making arrangements with a subagent.

In contrast, a principal's duties of indemnity extend to subagents appointed by agents of the principal. *See* § 8.14, Comment *b*.

§ 8.14 Duty to Indemnify

A principal has a duty to indemnify an agent

(1) in accordance with the terms of any contract between them; and

(2) unless otherwise agreed,

   (a) when the agent makes a payment

      (i) within the scope of the agent's actual authority, or

      (ii) that is beneficial to the principal, unless the agent acts officiously in making the payment; or

   (b) when the agent suffers a loss that fairly should be borne by the principal in light of their relationship.

§ 8.15 Principal's Duty to Deal Fairly and in Good Faith

A principal has a duty to deal with the agent fairly and in good faith, including a duty to provide the agent with information about risks of physical harm or pecuniary loss that the principal knows, has reason to know, or should know are present in the agent's work but unknown to the agent.

Comment d. Duty to refrain from conduct likely to injure agent's business reputation or reasonable self-respect. This duty is the reciprocal of an agent's duty of good conduct as stated in § 8.10. Although a principal is not subject to a duty of loyalty to an agent, the principal's duty to deal with an agent fairly and in good faith requires that the principal refrain from conduct that is likely to injure the agent's business reputation through the agent's association with the principal. Likewise, a principal has a duty to refrain from conduct that will injure the agent's reasonable self-respect if the association continues.

The nature of the agent's work and other circumstances of the relationship between principal and agent are relevant to whether a principal's conduct breaches this duty.

II. PARTNERSHIPS

A. UNIFORM PARTNERSHIP ACT (1914)

Table of Sections

PART I.   PRELIMINARY PROVISIONS

PART II.   NATURE OF A PARTNERSHIP

PART III.   RELATIONS OF PARTNERS TO PERSONS DEALING WITH THE PARTNERSHIP

PART IV.   RELATIONS OF PARTNERS TO ONE ANOTHER

PART V.   PROPERTY RIGHTS OF A PARTNER

PART I.   PRELIMINARY PROVISIONS

§ 1.   Name of Act

This act may be cited as Uniform Partnership Act.

§ 2.   Definition of Terms

In this act, "Court" includes every court and judge having jurisdiction in the case.

"Business" includes every trade, occupation, or profession.

"Person" includes individuals, partnerships, corporations, and other associations.

"Bankrupt" includes bankrupt under the Federal Bankruptcy Act or insolvent under any state insolvent act.

"Conveyance" includes every assignment, lease, mortgage, or encumbrance.

"Real property" includes land and any interest or estate in land.

§ 3.   Interpretation of Knowledge and Notice

(1)   A person has "knowledge" of a fact within the meaning of this act not only when he has actual knowledge thereof, but also when he has knowledge of such other facts as in the circumstances shows bad faith.

(2)   A person has "notice" of a fact within the meaning of this act when the person who claims the benefit of the notice:

(a)   States the fact to such person, or

(b)   Delivers through the mail, or by other means of communication, a written statement of the fact to such person or to a proper person at his place of business or residence.

§ 4.   **Rules of Construction**

(1)   The rule that statutes in derogation of the common law are to be strictly construed shall have no application to this act.

(2)   The law of estoppel shall apply under this act.

(3)   The law of agency shall apply under this act.

(4)   This act shall be so interpreted and construed as to effect its general purpose to make uniform the law of those states which enact it.

(5)   This act shall not be construed so as to impair the obligations of any contract existing when the act goes into effect, nor to affect any action or proceedings begun or right accrued before this act takes effect.

§ 5.   **Rules for Cases not Provided for in this Act**

In any case not provided for in this act the rules of law and equity, including the law merchant, shall govern.

PART II.   NATURE OF A PARTNERSHIP

§ 6.   **Partnership Defined**

(1)   A partnership is an association of two or more persons to carry on as co-owners a business for profit.

(2)   But any association formed under any other statute of this state, or any statute adopted by authority, other than the authority of this state, is not a partnership under this act, unless such association would have been a partnership in this state prior to the adoption of this act; but this act shall apply to limited partnerships except in so far as the statutes relating to such partnerships are inconsistent herewith.

COMMENT

Subdivision (1). Explanation of the Reason for the Words Employed in the Definition. The first inquiry is, Why say a partnership is "an association of two or more persons"? In view of the fact that the word "association" itself implies the acting together of two or more persons, why not merely say that a partnership is an association to carry on business in which the members are co-owners of the business? The word person includes, as stated in section 2, supra, "individuals, partnerships, corporations, and other associations." The definition as worded thus asserts, what would be doubtful if the words "of two or more persons" were omitted, namely, that any one of these associations may become members of a partnership. It is true that if two or more corporations attempt to form a partnership the contract may be ultra vires as to both (*Boyd v. American Carbon Black Co.* (1897) 37 Atl. 937, 182 Pa.St. 206); but the capacity of corporations to contract is a question of corporation law. Under the present law it appears that a partnership can, as such, be a member of another partnership, if that was the intent of the parties. [*Raymond v. Putnam* (1862) 44 N.H. 160; *Cheap v. Cramond* (1821), 4 Barn. & Ald. 663, 6 E.C.L. 645; *In re Hamilton* (1880) 1 Fed. 800; *Riddle v. Whitehill* (1890) 10 S.Ct. 924, 135 U.S. 621, 34 U.S. (L.Ed.) 282.]

The words "to carry on as co-owners a business" remove any doubt in the following case: A and B sign partnership articles and make their agreed contributions to the common fund. A refuses to carry on business as agreed. Is there a partnership to be wound up in accordance with the provisions of Part VI "Dissolution and Winding-up"? The words quoted require an affirmative answer to this question. If the words "carrying on business" had been used, in the case given, no partnership would exist, and Part VI would not apply.

The definition asserts that the associates are "co-owners" of the business. This distinguishes a partnership from an agency—an association of principal and agent. A business is a series of acts directed toward an end. Ownership involves the power of ultimate control. To state that partners are co-owners of a business is to state that they each have the power of ultimate control.

Lastly, the definition asserts that the business is for profit. Partnership is a branch of our commercial law; it has developed in connection with a particular business association, and it is, therefore, essential that the operation of the act should be confined to associations organized for profit.

In view of the many definitions of a partnership which have been proposed, it is desirable to note the reasons for the omission of certain ideas expressed in some of the definitions cited by Lindley in his work on Partnership, pp. 11, 12.

It is not indicated that the association must be a voluntary one. In the domain of private law the term association necessarily involves the idea that the association is voluntary.

To say that the association must be created by contract, is not only unnecessary, but in view of the varied use of the word "contract" in our law, if the word is used an explanation would have to be made as to whether the contract could be implied, and if so, whether it could be implied in law or only implied as a fact. By merely saying that it is an association these difficulties are avoided.

Again, it is not said that the business must be lawful business. The effect of the unlawfulness of the business is dealt with under Part VI "Dissolution and Winding-up." Section 31(3), *infra*, provides that dissolution is produced "By any event which makes it unlawful for the business of the partnership to be carried on or for the members to carry it on in partnership." If the business is wholly unlawful, then the partnership is dissolved the moment it is created. The omission of the word "lawful" in the definition does not prevent this result. Very often, however, a business may be in part lawful and in part unlawful. Hotel-keepers may run a "dive." Placing the word "lawful" before the word business in the definition would tend to throw a doubt on the propriety of the orderly winding up of such a business as a partnership.

§ 7.   Rules for Determining the Existence of a Partnership

In determining whether a partnership exists, these rules shall apply:

(1)   Except as provided by section 16 persons who are not partners as to each other are not partners as to third persons.

(2)   Joint tenancy, tenancy in common, tenancy by the entireties, joint property, common property, or part ownership does not of itself establish a partnership, whether such co-owners do or do not share any profits made by the use of the property.

(3)   The sharing of gross returns does not of itself establish a partnership, whether or not the persons sharing them have a joint or common right or interest in any property from which the returns are derived.

(4)   The receipt by a person of a share of the profits of a business is prima facie evidence that he is a partner in the business, but no such inference shall be drawn if such profits were received in payment:

(a)   As a debt by installments or otherwise,

(b)   As wages of an employee or rent to a landlord,

(c)   As an annuity to a widow or representative of a deceased partner,

(d)   As interest on a loan, though the amount of payment vary with the profits of the business,

(e)   As the consideration for the sale of the good-will of a business or other property by installments or otherwise.

§ 8.   Partnership Property

(1)   All property originally brought into the partnership stock or subsequently acquired by purchase or otherwise, on account of the partnership, is partnership property.

(2)   Unless the contrary intention appears, property acquired with partnership funds is partnership property.

(3)   Any estate in real property may be acquired in the partnership name. Title so acquired can be conveyed only in the partnership name.

(4)   A conveyance to a partnership in the partnership name, though without words of inheritance, passes the entire estate of the grantor unless a contrary intent appears.

PART III.   RELATIONS OF PARTNERS TO PERSONS DEALING WITH THE PARTNERSHIP

§ 9.   Partner Agent of Partnership as to Partnership Business

(1)   Every partner is an agent of the partnership for the purpose of its business, and the act of every partner, including the execution in the partnership name of any instrument, for apparently carrying on in the usual way the business of the partnership of which he is a member binds the partnership, unless the partner so acting has in fact no authority to act for the partnership in the particular matter, and the person with whom he is dealing has knowledge of the fact that he has no such authority.

(2)   An act of a partner which is not apparently for the carrying on of the business of the partnership in the usual way does not bind the partnership unless authorized by the other partners.

(3)   Unless authorized by the other partners or unless they have abandoned the business, one or more but less than all the partners have no authority to:

(a)   Assign the partnership property in trust for creditors or on the assignee's promise to pay the debts of the partnership,

(b)   Dispose of the good-will of the business,

(c)   Do any other act which would make it impossible to carry on the ordinary business of a partnership,

(d)   Confess a judgment,

(e)   Submit a partnership claim or liability to arbitration or reference.

(4)   No act of a partner in contravention of a restriction on authority shall bind the partnership to persons having knowledge of the restriction.

§ 10.   Conveyance of Real Property of the Partnership

(1)   Where title to real property is in the partnership name, any partner may convey title to such property by a conveyance executed in the partnership name; but the partnership may recover such property unless the partner's act binds the partnership under the provisions of paragraph (1) of section 9, or unless such property has been conveyed by the grantee or a person claiming through such grantee to a holder for value without knowledge that the partner, in making the conveyance, has exceeded his authority.

(2)   Where title to real property is in the name of the partnership, a conveyance executed by a partner, in his own name, passes the equitable interest of the partnership, provided the act is one within the authority of the partner under the provisions of paragraph (1) of section 9.

(3)   Where title to real property is in the name of one or more but not all the partners, and the record does not disclose the right of the partnership, the partners in whose name the title stands may convey title to such property, but the partnership may recover such property if the partners' act does not bind the partnership under the provisions of paragraph (1) of section 9, unless the purchaser or his assignee, is a holder for value, without knowledge.

(4)   Where the title to real property is in the name of one or more or all the partners, or in a third person in trust for the partnership, a conveyance executed by a partner in the partnership name, or

in his own name, passes the equitable interest of the partnership, provided the act is one within the authority of the partner under the provisions of paragraph (1) of section 9.

(5)   Where the title to real property is in the names of all the partners a conveyance executed by all the partners passes all their rights in such property.

§ 11.   Partnership Bound by Admission of Partner

An admission or representation made by any partner concerning partnership affairs within the scope of his authority as conferred by this act is evidence against the partnership.

§ 12.   Partnership Charged with Knowledge of or Notice to Partner

Notice to any partner of any matter relating to partnership affairs, and the knowledge of the partner acting in the particular matter, acquired while a partner or then present to his mind, and the knowledge of any other partner who reasonably could and should have communicated it to the acting partner, operate as notice to or knowledge of the partnership, except in the case of a fraud on the partnership committed by or with the consent of that partner.

§ 13.   Partnership Bound by Partner's Wrongful Act

Where, by any wrongful act or omission of any partner acting in the ordinary course of the business of the partnership or with the authority of his co-partners, loss or injury is caused to any person, not being a partner in the partnership, or any penalty is incurred, the partnership is liable therefor to the same extent as the partner so acting or omitting to act.

§ 14.   Partnership Bound by Partner's Breach of Trust

The partnership is bound to make good the loss:

(a)   Where one partner acting within the scope of his apparent authority receives money or property of a third person and misapplies it; and

(b)   Where the partnership in the course of its business receives money or property of a third person and the money or property so received is misapplied by any partner while it is in the custody of the partnership.

§ 15.   Nature of Partner's Liability

All partners are liable

(a)   Jointly and severally for everything chargeable to the partnership under sections 13 and 14.

(b)   Jointly for all other debts and obligations of the partnership; but any partner may enter into a separate obligation to perform a partnership contract.

§ 16.   Partner by Estoppel

(1)   When a person, by words spoken or written or by conduct, represents himself, or consents to another representing him to any one, as a partner in an existing partnership or with one or more persons not actual partners, he is liable to any such person to whom such representation has been made, who has, on the faith of such representation, given credit to the actual or apparent partnership, and if he has made such representation or consented to its being made in a public manner he is liable to such person, whether the representation has or has not been made or communicated to such person so giving credit by or with the knowledge of the apparent partner making the representation or consenting to its being made.

(a) When a partnership liability results, he is liable as though he were an actual member of the partnership.

(b) When no partnership liability results, he is liable jointly with the other persons, if any, so consenting to the contract or representation as to incur liability, otherwise separately.

(2) When a person has been thus represented to be a partner in an existing partnership, or with one or more persons not actual partners, he is an agent of the persons consenting to such representation to bind them to the same extent and in the same manner as though he were a partner in fact, with respect to persons who rely upon the representation. Where all the members of the existing partnership consent to the representation, a partnership act or obligation results; but in all other cases it is the joint act or obligation of the person acting and the persons consenting to the representation.

§ 17.   Liability of Incoming Partner

A person admitted as a partner into an existing partnership is liable for all the obligations of the partnership arising before his admission as though he had been a partner when such obligations were incurred, except that this liability shall be satisfied only out of partnership property.

PART IV.   RELATIONS OF PARTNERS TO ONE ANOTHER

§ 18.   Rules Determining Rights and Duties of Partners

The rights and duties of the partners in relation to the partnership shall be determined, subject to any agreement between them, by the following rules:

(a) Each partner shall be repaid his contributions, whether by way of capital or advances to the partnership property and share equally in the profits and surplus remaining after all liabilities, including those to partners, are satisfied; and must contribute towards the losses, whether of capital or otherwise, sustained by the partnership according to his share in the profits.

(b) The partnership must indemnify every partner in respect of payments made and personal liabilities reasonably incurred by him in the ordinary and proper conduct of its business, or for the preservation of its business or property.

(c) A partner, who in aid of the partnership makes any payment or advance beyond the amount of capital which he agreed to contribute, shall be paid interest from the date of the payment or advance.

(d) A partner shall receive interest on the capital contributed by him only from the date when repayment should be made.

(e) All partners have equal rights in the management and conduct of the partnership business.

(f) No partner is entitled to remuneration for acting in the partnership business, except that a surviving partner is entitled to reasonable compensation for his services in winding up the partnership affairs.

(g) No person can become a member of a partnership without the consent of all the partners.

(h) Any difference arising as to ordinary matters connected with the partnership business may be decided by a majority of the partners; but no act in contravention of any agreement between the partners may be done rightfully without the consent of all the partners.

§ 19.   Partnership Books

The partnership books shall be kept, subject to any agreement between the partners, at the principal place of business of the partnership, and every partner shall at all times have access to and may inspect and copy any of them.

§ 20.   Duty of Partners to Render Information

Partners shall render on demand true and full information of all things affecting the partnership to any partner or the legal representative of any deceased partner or partner under legal disability.

§ 21.   Partner Accountable as a Fiduciary

(1)   Every partner must account to the partnership for any benefit, and hold as trustee for it any profits derived by him without the consent of the other partners from any transaction connected with the formation, conduct, or liquidation of the partnership or from any use by him of its property.

(2)   This section applies also to the representatives of a deceased partner engaged in the liquidation of the affairs of the partnership as the personal representatives of the last surviving partner.

§ 22.   Right to an Account

Any partner shall have the right to a formal account as to partnership affairs:

    (a)   If he is wrongfully excluded from the partnership business or possession of its property by his co-partners,

    (b)   If the right exists under the terms of any agreement,

    (c)   As provided by section 21,

    (d)   Whenever other circumstances render it just and reasonable.

§ 23.   Continuation of Partnership Beyond Fixed Term

(1)   When a partnership for a fixed term or particular undertaking is continued after the termination of such term or particular undertaking without any express agreement, the rights and duties of the partners remain the same as they were at such termination, so far as is consistent with a partnership at will.

(2)   A continuation of the business by the partners or such of them as habitually acted therein during the term, without any settlement or liquidation of the partnership affairs, is prima facie evidence of a continuation of the partnership.

PART V.   PROPERTY RIGHTS OF A PARTNER

§ 24.   Extent of Property Rights of a Partner

The property rights of a partner are (1) his rights in specific partnership property, (2) his interest in the partnership, and (3) his right to participate in the management.

§ 25.   Nature of a Partner's Right in Specific Partnership Property

(1)   A partner is co-owner with his partners of specific partnership property holding as a tenant in partnership.

(2)   The incidents of this tenancy are such that:

    (a)   A partner, subject to the provisions of this act and to any agreement between the partners, has an equal right with his partners to possess specific partnership property for partnership purposes; but he has no right to possess such property for any other purpose without the consent of his partners.

(b)   A partner's right in specific partnership property is not assignable except in connection with the assignment of rights of all the partners in the same property.

(c)   A partner's right in specific partnership property is not subject to attachment or execution, except on a claim against the partnership. When partnership property is attached for a partnership debt the partners, or any of them, or the representatives of a deceased partner, cannot claim any right under the homestead or exemption laws.

(d)   On the death of a partner his right in specific partnership property vests in the surviving partner or partners, except where the deceased was the last surviving partner, when his right in such property vests in his legal representative. Such surviving partner or partners, or the legal representative of the last surviving partner, has no right to possess the partnership property for any but a partnership purpose.

(e)   A partner's right in specific partnership property is not subject to dower, curtesy, or allowances to widows, heirs, or next of kin.

§ 26.   Nature of Partner's Interest in the Partnership

A partner's interest in the partnership is his share of the profits and surplus, and the same is personal property.

§ 27.   Assignment of Partner's Interest

(1)   A conveyance by a partner of his interest in the partnership does not of itself dissolve the partnership, nor, as against the other partners in the absence of agreement, entitle the assignee, during the continuance of the partnership, to interfere in the management or administration of the partnership business or affairs, or to require any information or account of partnership transactions, or to inspect the partnership books; but it merely entitles the assignee to receive in accordance with his contract the profits to which the assigning partner would otherwise be entitled.

(2)   In case of a dissolution of the partnership, the assignee is entitled to receive his assignor's interest and may require an account from the date only of the last account agreed to by all the partners.

§ 28.   Partner's Interest Subject to Charging Order

(1)   On due application to a competent court by any judgment creditor of a partner, the court which entered the judgment, order, or decree, or any other court, may charge the interest of the debtor partner with payment of the unsatisfied amount of such judgment debt with interest thereon; and may then or later appoint a receiver of his share of the profits, and of any other money due or to fall due to him in respect of the partnership, and make all other orders, directions, accounts and inquiries which the debtor partner might have made, or which the circumstances of the case may require.

(2)   The interest charged may be redeemed at any time before foreclosure, or in case of a sale being directed by the court may be purchased without thereby causing a dissolution:

(a)   With separate property, by any one or more of the partners, or

(b)   With partnership property, by any one or more of the partners with the consent of all the partners whose interests are not so charged or sold.

(3)   Nothing in this act shall be held to deprive a partner of his right, if any, under the exemption laws, as regards his interest in the partnership.

PART VI. DISSOLUTION AND WINDING UP

§ 29. Dissolution Defined

The dissolution of a partnership is the change in the relation of the partners caused by any partner ceasing to be associated in the carrying on as distinguished from the winding up of the business.

§ 30. Partnership not Terminated by Dissolution

On dissolution the partnership is not terminated, but continues until the winding up of partnership affairs is completed.

§ 31. Causes of Dissolution

Dissolution is caused:

(1) Without violation of the agreement between the partners,

(a) By the termination of the definite term or particular undertaking specified in the agreement,

(b) By the express will of any partner when no definite term or particular undertaking is specified,

(c) By the express will of all the partners who have not assigned their interests or suffered them to be charged for their separate debts, either before or after the termination of any specified term or particular undertaking,

(d) By the expulsion of any partner from the business bona fide in accordance with such a power conferred by the agreement between the partners;

(2) In contravention of the agreement between the partners, where the circumstances do not permit a dissolution under any other provision of this section, by the express will of any partner at any time;

(3) By any event which makes it unlawful for the business of the partnership to be carried on or for the members to carry it on in partnership;

(4) By the death of any partner;

(5) By the bankruptcy of any partner or the partnership;

(6) By decree of court under section 32.

§ 32. Dissolution by Decree of Court

(1) On application by or for a partner the court shall decree a dissolution whenever:

(a) A partner has been declared a lunatic in any judicial proceeding or is shown to be of unsound mind,

(b) A partner becomes in any other way incapable of performing his part of the partnership contract,

(c) A partner has been guilty of such conduct as tends to affect prejudicially the carrying on of the business,

(d) A partner wilfully or persistently commits a breach of the partnership agreement, or otherwise so conducts himself in matters relating to the partnership business that it is not reasonably practicable to carry on the business in partnership with him,

(e) The business of the partnership can only be carried on at a loss,

(f)   Other circumstances render a dissolution equitable.

(2)   On the application of the purchaser of a partner's interest under sections 27 or 28:

(a)   After the termination of the specified term or particular undertaking,

(b)   At any time if the partnership was a partnership at will when the interest was assigned or when the charging order was issued.

§ 33.   General Effect of Dissolution on Authority of Partner

Except so far as may be necessary to wind up partnership affairs or to complete transactions begun but not then finished, dissolution terminates all authority of any partner to act for the partnership,

(1)   With respect to the partners,

(a)   When the dissolution is not by the act, bankruptcy or death of a partner; or

(b)   When the dissolution is by such act, bankruptcy or death of a partner, in cases where section 34 so requires.

(2)   With respect to persons not partners, as declared in section 35.

§ 34.   Right of Partner to Contribution From Co-partners After Dissolution

Where the dissolution is caused by the act, death or bankruptcy of a partner, each partner is liable to his co-partners for his share of any liability created by any partner acting for the partnership as if the partnership had not been dissolved unless

(a)   The dissolution being by act of any partner, the partner acting for the partnership had knowledge of the dissolution, or

(b)   The dissolution being by the death or bankruptcy of a partner, the partner acting for the partnership had knowledge or notice of the death or bankruptcy.

§ 35.   Power of Partner to Bind Partnership to Third Persons After Dissolution

(1)   After dissolution a partner can bind the partnership except as provided in Paragraph (3).

(a)   By any act appropriate for winding up partnership affairs or completing transactions unfinished at dissolution;

(b)   By any transaction which would bind the partnership if dissolution had not taken place, provided the other party to the transaction

(i)   Had extended credit to the partnership prior to dissolution and had no knowledge or notice of the dissolution; or

(ii)   Though he had not so extended credit, had nevertheless known of the partnership prior to dissolution, and, having no knowledge or notice of dissolution, the fact of dissolution had not been advertised in a newspaper of general circulation in the place (or in each place if more than one) at which the partnership business was regularly carried on.

(2)   The liability of a partner under Paragraph (1b) shall be satisfied out of partnership assets alone when such partner had been prior to dissolution

(a)   Unknown as a partner to the person with whom the contract is made; and

(b)   So far unknown and inactive in partnership affairs that the business reputation of the partnership could not be said to have been in any degree due to his connection with it.

(3)   The partnership is in no case bound by any act of a partner after dissolution

(a) Where the partnership is dissolved because it is unlawful to carry on the business, unless the act is appropriate for winding up partnership affairs; or

(b) Where the partner has become bankrupt; or

(c) Where the partner has no authority to wind up partnership affairs; except by a transaction with one who

(i) Had extended credit to the partnership prior to dissolution and had no knowledge or notice of his want of authority; or

(ii) Had not extended credit to the partnership prior to dissolution, and; having no knowledge or notice of his want of authority, the fact of his want of authority has not been advertised in the manner provided for advertising the fact of dissolution in Paragraph (1b II).

(4) Nothing in this section shall affect the liability under Section 16 of any person who after dissolution represents himself or consents to another representing him as a partner in a partnership engaged in carrying on business.

§ 36.　　Effect of Dissolution on Partner's Existing Liability

(1) The dissolution of the partnership does not of itself discharge the existing liability of any partner.

(2) A partner is discharged from any existing liability upon dissolution of the partnership by an agreement to that effect between himself, the partnership creditor and the person or partnership continuing the business; and such agreement may be inferred from the course of dealing between the creditor having knowledge of the dissolution and the person or partnership continuing the business.

(3) Where a person agrees to assume the existing obligations of a dissolved partnership, the partners whose obligations have been assumed shall be discharged from any liability to any creditor of the partnership who, knowing of the agreement, consents to a material alteration in the nature or time of payment of such obligations.

(4) The individual property of a deceased partner shall be liable for all obligations of the partnership incurred while he was a partner but subject to the prior payment of his separate debts.

§ 37.　　Right to Wind Up

Unless otherwise agreed the partners who have nor wrongfully dissolved the partnership or the legal representative of the last surviving partner, not bankrupt, has the right to wind up the partnership affairs; provided, however, that any partner, his legal representative or his assignee, upon cause shown, may obtain winding up by the court.

§ 38.　　Rights of Partners to Application of Partnership Property

(1) When dissolution is caused in any way, except in contravention of the partnership agreement, each partner, as against his co-partners and all persons claiming through them in respect of their interests in the partnership, unless otherwise agreed, may have the partnership property applied to discharge its liabilities, and the surplus applied to pay in cash the net amount owing to the respective partners. But if dissolution is caused by expulsion of a partner, bona fide under the partnership agreement and if the expelled partner is discharged from all partnership liabilities, either by payment or agreement under section 36(2), he shall receive in cash only the net amount due him from the partnership.

(2) When dissolution is caused in contravention of the partnership agreement the rights of the partners shall be as follows:

(a) Each partner who has not caused dissolution wrongfully shall have,

(i)   All the rights specified in paragraph (1) of this section, and

(ii)   The right, as against each partner who has caused the dissolution wrongfully, to damages for breach of the agreement.

(b)   The partners who have not caused the dissolution wrongfully, if they all desire to continue the business in the same name, either by themselves or jointly with others, may do so, during the agreed term for the partnership and for that purpose may possess the partnership property, provided they secure the payment by bond approved by the court, or pay to any partner who has caused the dissolution wrongfully, the value of his interest in the partnership at the dissolution, less any damages recoverable under clause (2a II) of this section, and in like manner indemnify him against all present or future partnership liabilities.

(c)   A partner who has caused the dissolution wrongfully shall have:

(i)   If the business is not continued under the provisions of paragraph (2b) all the rights of a partner under paragraph (1), subject to clause (2a II), of this section,

(ii)   If the business is continued under paragraph (2b) of this section the right as against his co-partners and all claiming through them in respect of their interests in the partnership, to have the value of his interest in the partnership, less any damages caused to his co-partners by the dissolution, ascertained and paid to him in cash, or the payment secured by bond approved by the court, and to be released from all existing liabilities of the partnership; but in ascertaining the value of the partner's interest the value of the good-will of the business shall not be considered.

§ 39.   Rights Where Partnership is Dissolved for Fraud or Misrepresentation

Where a partnership contract is rescinded on the ground of the fraud or misrepresentation of one of the parties thereto, the party entitled to rescind is, without prejudice to any other right, entitled,

(a)   To a lien on, or a right of retention of, the surplus of the partnership property after satisfying the partnership liabilities to third persons for any sum of money paid by him for the purchase of an interest in the partnership and for any capital or advances contributed by him; and

(b)   To stand, after all liabilities to third persons have been satisfied, in the place of the creditors of the partnership for any payments made by him in respect of the partnership liabilities; and

(c)   To be indemnified by the person guilty of the fraud or making the representation against all debts and liabilities of the partnership.

§ 40.   Rules for Distribution

In settling accounts between the partners after dissolution, the following rules shall be observed, subject to any agreement to the contrary:

(a)   The assets of the partnership are:

(i)   The partnership property,

(ii)   The contributions of the partners necessary for the payment of all the liabilities specified in clause (b) of this paragraph.

(b)   The liabilities of the partnership shall rank in order of payment, as follows:

(i)   Those owing to creditors other than partners,

(ii)   Those owing to partners other than for capital and profits,

(iii)   Those owing to partners in respect of capital,

(iv) Those owing to partners in respect of profits.

(c) The assets shall be applied in the order of their declaration in clause (a) of this paragraph to the satisfaction of the liabilities.

(d) The partners shall contribute, as provided by section 18(a) the amount necessary to satisfy the liabilities; but if any, but not all, of the partners are insolvent, or, not being subject to process, refuse to contribute, the other partners shall contribute their share of the liabilities, and, in the relative proportions in which they share the profits, the additional amount necessary to pay the liabilities.

(e) An assignee for the benefit of creditors or any person appointed by the court shall have the right to enforce the contributions specified in clause (d) of this paragraph.

(f) Any partner or his legal representative shall have the right to enforce the contributions specified in clause (d) of this paragraph, to the extent of the amount which he has paid in excess of his share of the liability.

(g) The individual property of a deceased partner shall be liable for the contributions specified in clause (d) of this paragraph.

(h) When partnership property and the individual properties of the partners are in possession of a court for distribution, partnership creditors shall have priority on partnership property and separate creditors on individual property, saving the rights of lien or secured creditors as heretofore.

(i) Where a partner has become bankrupt or his estate insolvent the claims against his separate property shall rank in the following order:

(i) Those owing to separate creditors,

(ii) Those owing to partnership creditors,

(iii) Those owing to partners by way of contribution.

§ 41.   Liability of Persons Continuing the Business in Certain Cases

(1) When any new partner is admitted into an existing partnership, or when any partner retires and assigns (or the representative of the deceased partner assigns) his rights in partnership property to two or more of the partners, or to one or more of the partners and one or more third persons, if the business is continued without liquidation of the partnership affairs, creditors of the first or dissolved partnership are also creditors of the partnership so continuing the business.

(2) When all but one partner retire and assign (or the representative of a deceased partner assigns) their rights in partnership property to the remaining partner, who continues the business without liquidation of partnership affairs, either alone or with others, creditors of the dissolved partnership are also creditors of the person or partnership so continuing the business.

(3) When any partner retires or dies and the business of the dissolved partnership is continued as set forth in paragraphs (1) and (2) of this section, with the consent of the retired partners or the representative of the deceased partner, but without any assignment of his right in partnership property, rights of creditors of the dissolved partnership and of the creditors of the person or partnership continuing the business shall be as if such assignment had been made.

(4) When all the partners or their representatives assign their rights in partnership property to one or more third persons who promise to pay the debts and who continue the business of the dissolved partnership, creditors of the dissolved partnership are also creditors of the person or partnership continuing the business.

(5) When any partner wrongfully causes a dissolution and the remaining partners continue the business under the provisions of section 38(2b), either alone or with others, and without liquidation of

the partnership affairs, creditors of the dissolved partnership are also creditors of the person or partnership continuing the business.

(6) When a partner is expelled and the remaining partners continue the business either alone or with others, without liquidation of the partnership affairs, creditors of the dissolved partnership are also creditors of the person or partnership continuing the business.

(7) The liability of a third person becoming a partner in the partnership continuing the business, under this section, to the creditors of the dissolved partnership shall be satisfied out of partnership property only.

(8) When the business of a partnership after dissolution is continued under any conditions set forth in this section the creditors of the dissolved partnership, as against the separate creditors of the retiring or deceased partner or the representative of the deceased partner, have a prior right to any claim of the retired partner or the representative of the deceased partner against the person or partnership continuing the business, on account of the retired or deceased partner's interest in the dissolved partnership or on account of any consideration promised for such interest or for his right in partnership property.

(9) Nothing in this section shall be held to modify any right of creditors to set aside any assignment on the ground of fraud.

(10) The use by the person or partnership continuing the business of the partnership name, or the name of a deceased partner as part thereof, shall not of itself make the individual property of the deceased partner liable for any debts contracted by such person or partnership.

§ 42. Rights of Retiring or Estate of Deceased Partner When the Business is Continued

When any partner retires or dies, and the business is continued under any of the conditions set forth in section 41 (1, 2, 3, 5, 6), or section 38(2b) without any settlement of accounts as between him or his estate and the person or partnership continuing the business, unless otherwise agreed, he or his legal representative as against such persons or partnership may have the value of his interest at the date of dissolution ascertained, and shall receive as an ordinary creditor an amount equal to the value of his interest in the dissolved partnership with interest, or, at his option or at the option of his legal representative, in lieu of interest, the profits attributable to the use of his right in the property of the dissolved partnership; provided that the creditors of the dissolved partnership as against the separate creditors, or the representative of the retired or deceased partner, shall have priority on any claim arising under this section, as provided by section 41(8) of this act.

§ 43. Accrual of Actions

The right to an account of his interest shall accrue to any partner, or his legal representative, as against the winding up partners or the surviving partners or the person or partnership continuing the business, at the date of dissolution, in the absence of any agreement to the contrary.

PART VII. MISCELLANEOUS PROVISIONS

§ 44. When Act Takes Effect

This act shall take effect on the _____ day of _____ one thousand nine hundred and _____.

§ 45. Legislation Repealed

All acts or parts of acts inconsistent with this act are hereby repealed.

B. REVISED UNIFORM PARTNERSHIP ACT (1997)

Table of Sections

ARTICLE 1. GENERAL PROVISIONS

ARTICLE 2. NATURE OF PARTNERSHIP

ARTICLE 3. RELATIONS OF PARTNERS TO PERSONS DEALING WITH PARTNERSHIP

ARTICLE 4. RELATIONS OF PARTNERS TO EACH OTHER AND TO PARTNERSHIP

ARTICLE 5. TRANSFEREES AND CREDITORS OF PARTNER

REVISED UNIFORM PARTNERSHIP ACT (1997)

ARTICLE 6. PARTNER'S DISSOCIATION

ARTICLE 7. PARTNER'S DISSOCIATION
WHEN BUSINESS NOT WOUND UP

ARTICLE 8. WINDING UP PARTNERSHIP BUSINESS

ARTICLE 9. CONVERSIONS AND MERGERS

ARTICLE 10. LIMITED LIABILITY PARTNERSHIP

ARTICLE 11. FOREIGN LIMITED LIABILITY PARTNERSHIP

ARTICLE 12. MISCELLANEOUS PROVISIONS

ARTICLE 1.   GENERAL PROVISIONS

§ 101.   Definitions

In this [Act]:

(1)   "Business" includes every trade, occupation, and profession.

(2)   "Debtor in bankruptcy" means a person who is the subject of:

    (i)   an order for relief under Title 11 of the United States Code or a comparable order under a successor statute of general application; or

    (ii)   a comparable order under federal, state, or foreign law governing insolvency.

(3)   "Distribution" means a transfer of money or other property from a partnership to a partner in the partner's capacity as a partner or to the partner's transferee.

(4)   "Foreign limited liability partnership" means a partnership that:

    (i)   is formed under laws other than the laws of this State; and

    (ii)   has the status of a limited liability partnership under those laws.

(5)   "Limited liability partnership" means a partnership that has filed a statement of qualification under Section 1001 and does not have a similar statement in effect in any other jurisdiction.

(6)   "Partnership" means an association of two or more persons to carry on as co-owners a business for profit formed under Section 202, predecessor law, or comparable law of another jurisdiction.

(7)   "Partnership agreement" means the agreement, whether written, oral, or implied, among the partners concerning the partnership, including amendments to the partnership agreement.

(8)   "Partnership at will" means a partnership in which the partners have not agreed to remain partners until the expiration of a definite term or the completion of a particular undertaking.

(9)   "Partnership interest" or "partner's interest in the partnership" means all of a partner's interests in the partnership, including the partner's transferable interest and all management and other rights.

(10)   "Person" means an individual, corporation, business trust, estate, trust, partnership, association, joint venture, government, governmental subdivision, agency, or instrumentality, or any other legal or commercial entity.

(11)   "Property" means all property, real, personal, or mixed, tangible or intangible, or any interest therein.

(12)   "State" means a State of the United States, the District of Columbia, the Commonwealth of Puerto Rico, or any territory or insular possession subject to the jurisdiction of the United States.

(13)   "Statement" means a statement of partnership authority under Section 303, a statement of denial under Section 304, a statement of dissociation under Section 704, a statement of dissolution under Section 805, a statement of merger under Section 907, a statement of qualification under Section

1001, a statement of foreign qualification under Section 1102, or an amendment or cancellation of any of the foregoing.

    (14) "Transfer" includes an assignment, conveyance, lease, mortgage, deed, and encumbrance.

COMMENT

    These Comments include the original Comments to the Revised Uniform Partnership Act (RUPA or the Act) and the new Comments to the Limited Liability Partnership Act Amendments to the Uniform Partnership Act (1994). The new Comments regarding limited liability partnerships are integrated into the RUPA Comments.

    The RUPA continues the definition of "business" from Section 2 of the Uniform Partnership Act (UPA).

    RUPA uses the more contemporary term "debtor in bankruptcy" instead of "bankrupt." The definition is adapted from the new Georgia Partnership Act, Ga. Code Ann. § 14–8–2(1). The definition does not distinguish between a debtor whose estate is being liquidated under Chapter 7 of the Bankruptcy Code and a debtor who is being rehabilitated under Chapter 11, 12, or 13 and includes both. The filing of a voluntary petition under Section 301 of the Bankruptcy Code constitutes an order for relief, but the debtor is entitled to notice and an opportunity to be heard before the entry of an order for relief in an involuntary case under Section 303 of the Code. The term also includes a debtor who is the subject of a comparable order under state or foreign law.

    The definition of "distribution" is new and adds precision to the accounting rules established in Sections 401 and 807 and related sections. Transfers to a partner in the partner's capacity as a creditor, lessor, or employee of the partnership, for example, are not "distributions."

    The definition of a "foreign limited liability partnership" includes a partnership formed under the laws of another State, foreign country, or other jurisdiction provided it has the status of a limited liability partnership in the other jurisdiction. Since the scope and nature of foreign limited liability partnership liability shields may vary in different jurisdictions, the definition avoids reference to similar or comparable laws. Rather, the definition incorporates the concept of a limited liability partnership in the foreign jurisdiction, however defined in that jurisdiction. The reference to formation "under laws other than the laws of this State" makes clear that the definition includes partnerships formed in foreign countries as well as in another State.

    The definition of a "limited liability partnership" makes clear that a partnership may adopt the special liability shield characteristics of a limited liability partnership simply by filing a statement of qualification under Section 1001. A partnership may file the statement in this State regardless of where formed. When coupled with the governing law provisions of Section 106(b), this definition simplifies the choice of law issues applicable to partnerships with multi-state activities and contacts. Once a statement of qualification is filed, a partnership's internal affairs and the liability of its partners are determined by the law of the State where the statement is filed. *See* Section 106(b). The partnership may not vary this particular requirement. *See* Section 103(b)(9).

    The reference to a "partnership" in the definition of a limited liability partnership makes clear that the RUPA definition of the term rather than the UPA concept controls for purposes of a limited liability partnership. Section 101(6) defines a "partnership" as "an association of two or more persons to carry on as co-owners a business for profit formed under Section 202, predecessor law, or comparable law of another jurisdiction." Section 202(b) further provides that "an association formed under a statute other than this [Act], a predecessor statute, or a comparable statute of another jurisdiction is not a partnership under this [Act]." This language was intended to clarify that a limited partnership is not a RUPA general partnership. It was not intended to preclude the application of any RUPA general partnership rules to limited partnerships where limited partnership law otherwise adopts the RUPA rules. *See* Comments to Section 202(b) and Prefatory Note.

    The effect of these definitions leaves the scope and applicability of RUPA to limited partnerships to limited partnership law, not to sever the linkage between the two Acts in all cases. Certain provisions of RUPA will continue to govern limited partnerships by virtue of Revised Uniform Limited Partnership Act (RULPA) Section 1105 which provides that "in any case not provided for in this [Act] the provisions of the Uniform Partnership Act govern." The RUPA partnership definition includes partnerships formed under the UPA. Therefore, the limited liability partnership rules will govern limited partnerships "in any case not provided for" in RULPA. Since RULPA does not provide for any rules applicable to a limited partnership becoming a limited liability partnership, the limited liability partnership rules should apply to limited partnerships that file a statement of qualification.

Partner liability deserves special mention. RULPA Section 403(b) provides that a general partner of a limited partnership "has the liabilities of a partner in a partnership without limited partners." Thus limited partnership law expressly references general partnership law for general partner liability and does not separately consider the liability of such partners. The liability of a general partner of a limited partnership that becomes a LLLP would therefore be the liability of a general partner in an LLP and would be governed by Section 306. The liability of a limited partner in a LLLP is a more complicated matter. RULPA Section 303(a) separately considers the liability of a limited partner. Unless also a general partner, a limited partner is not liable for the obligations of a limited partnership unless the partner participates in the control of the business and then only to persons reasonably believing the limited partner is a general partner. Therefore, arguably limited partners in a LLLP will have the specific RULPA Section 303(c) liability shield while general partners will have a superior Section 306(c) liability shield. In order to clarify limited partner liability and other linkage issues, States that have adopted RUPA, these limited liability partnership rules, and RULPA may wish to consider an amendment to RULPA. A suggested form of such an amendment is:

SECTION 1107.   LIMITED LIABILITY LIMITED PARTNERSHIP.

(a)   A limited partnership may become a limited liability partnership by:

(1)   obtaining approval of the terms and conditions of the limited partnership becoming a limited liability limited partnership by the vote necessary to amend the limited partnership agreement except, in the case of a limited partnership agreement that expressly considers contribution obligations, the vote necessary to amend those provisions;

(2)   filing a statement of qualification under Section 1001(c) of the Uniform Partnership Act (1994); and

(3)   complying with the name requirements of Section 1002 of the Uniform Partnership Act (1994).

(b)   A limited liability limited partnership continues to be the same entity that existed before the filing of a statement of qualification under Section 1001(c) of the Uniform Partnership Act (1994).

(c)   Sections 306(c) and 307(b) of the Uniform Partnership Act (1994) apply to both general and limited partners of a limited liability limited partnership.

"Partnership" is defined to mean an association of two or more persons to carry on as co-owners a business for profit formed under Section 202 (or predecessor law or comparable law of another jurisdiction), that is, a general partnership. Thus, as used in RUPA, the term "partnership" does not encompass limited partnerships, contrary to the use of the term in the UPA. Section 901(3) defines "limited partnership" for the purpose of Article 9, which deals with conversions and mergers of general and limited partnerships.

The definition of "partnership agreement" is adapted from Section 101(9) of RULPA. The RUPA definition is intended to include the agreement among the partners, including amendments, concerning either the affairs of the partnership or the conduct of its business. It does not include other agreements between some or all of the partners, such as a lease or loan agreement. The partnership agreement need not be written; it may be oral or inferred from the conduct of the parties.

Any partnership in which the partners have not agreed to remain partners until the expiration of a definite term or the completion of a particular undertaking is a "partnership at will." The distinction between an "at-will" partnership and a partnership for "a definite term or the completion of a particular undertaking" is important in determining the rights of dissociating and continuing partners following the dissociation of a partner. *See* Sections 601, 602, 701(b), 801(a), 802(b), and 803.

It is sometimes difficult to determine whether a partnership is at will or is for a definite term or the completion of a particular undertaking. Presumptively, every partnership is an at-will partnership. *See, e.g., Stone v. Stone*, 292 So. 2d 686 (La. 1974); *Frey v. Hauke*, 171 Neb. 852, 108 N.W.2d 228 (1961). To constitute a partnership for a term or a particular undertaking, the partners must agree (i) that the partnership will continue for a definite term or until a particular undertaking is completed and (ii) that they will remain partners until the expiration of the term or the completion of the undertaking. Both are necessary for a term partnership; if the partners have the unrestricted right, as distinguished from the power, to withdraw from a partnership formed for a term or particular undertaking, the partnership is one at will, rather than a term partnership.

To find that the partnership is formed for a definite term or a particular undertaking, there must be clear evidence of an agreement among the partners that the partnership (i) has a minimum or maximum duration or (ii) terminates at the conclusion of a particular venture whose time is indefinite but certain to occur. *See, e.g., Stainton v. Tarantino*, 637 F. Supp. 1051 (E.D. Pa. 1986) (partnership to dissolve no later than December 30, 2020); *Abel v. American Art Analog, Inc.*, 838 F.2d 691 (3d Cir. 1988) (partnership purpose to market an art book); *68th Street Apts., Inc. v. Lauricella*, 362 A.2d 78 (N.J. Super. Ct. 1976) (partnership purpose to construct an apartment building). A partnership to conduct a business which may last indefinitely, however, is an at-will partnership, even though there may be an obligation of the partnership, such as a mortgage, which must be repaid by a certain date, absent a specific agreement that no partner can rightfully withdraw until the obligation is repaid. *See, e.g., Page v. Page*, 55 Cal. 2d. 192, 359 P.2d 41 (1961) (partnership purpose to operate a linen supply business); *Frey v. Hauke, supra* (partnership purpose to contract and operate a bowling alley); *Girard Bank v. Haley*, 460 Pa. 237, 332 A.2d 443 (1975) (partnership purpose to maintain and lease buildings).

"Partnership interest" or "partner's interest in the partnership" is defined to mean all of a partner's interests in the partnership, including the partner's transferable interest and all management and other rights. A partner's "transferable interest" is a more limited concept and means only his share of the profits and losses and right to receive distributions, that is, the partner's economic interests. *See* Section 502 and Comment. *Compare* RULPA § 101(10) ("partnership interest" includes partner's economic interests only).

The definition of "person" is the usual definition used by the National Conference of Commissioners on Uniform State Laws (NCCUSL or the Conference). The definition includes other legal or commercial entities such as limited liability companies.

"Property" is defined broadly to include all types of property, as well as any interest in property.

The definition of "State" is the Conference's usual definition.

The definition of "statement" is new and refers to one of the various statements authorized by RUPA to enhance or limit the agency authority of a partner, to deny the authority or status of a partner, or to give notice of certain events, such as the dissociation of a partner or the dissolution of the partnership. *See* Sections 303, 304, 704, 805, and 907. Generally, Section 105 governs the execution, filing, and recording of all statements. The definition also makes clear that a statement of qualification under Section 1001 and a statement of foreign qualification under Section 1102 are considered statements. Both qualification statements are therefore subject to the execution, filing, and recordation rules of Section 105.

"Transfer" is defined broadly to include all manner of conveyances, including leases and encumbrances.

§ 102.   Knowledge and Notice

(a)   A person knows a fact if the person has actual knowledge of it.

(b)   A person has notice of a fact if the person:

    (1)   knows of it;

    (2)   has received a notification of it; or

    (3)   has reason to know it exists from all of the facts known to the person at the time in question.

(c)   A person notifies or gives a notification to another by taking steps reasonably required to inform the other person in ordinary course, whether or not the other person learns of it.

(d)   A person receives a notification when the notification:

    (1)   comes to the person's attention; or

(2)   is duly delivered at the person's place of business or at any other place held out by the person as a place for receiving communications.

(e)   Except as otherwise provided in subsection (f), a person other than an individual knows, has notice, or receives a notification of a fact for purposes of a particular transaction when the individual conducting the transaction knows, has notice, or receives a notification of the fact, or in any event when the fact would have been brought to the individual's attention if the person had exercised reasonable diligence. The person exercises reasonable diligence if it maintains reasonable routines for communicating significant information to the individual conducting the transaction and there is reasonable compliance with the routines. Reasonable diligence does not require an individual acting for the person to communicate information unless the communication is part of the individual's regular duties or the individual has reason to know of the transaction and that the transaction would be materially affected by the information.

(f)   A partner's knowledge, notice, or receipt of a notification of a fact relating to the partnership is effective immediately as knowledge by, notice to, or receipt of a notification by the partnership, except in the case of a fraud on the partnership committed by or with the consent of that partner.

COMMENT

The concepts and definitions of "knowledge," "notice," and "notification" draw heavily on Section 1–201(25) to (27) of the Uniform Commercial Code (UCC). The UCC text has been altered somewhat to improve clarity and style, but in general no substantive changes are intended from the UCC concepts. "A notification" replaces the UCC's redundant phrase, "a notice or notification," throughout the Act.

A person "knows" a fact only if that person has actual knowledge of it. Knowledge is cognitive awareness. That is solely an issue of fact. This is a change from the UPA Section 3(1) definition of "knowledge" which included the concept of "bad faith" knowledge arising from other known facts.

"Notice" is a lesser degree of awareness than "knows" and is based on a person's: (i) actual knowledge; (ii) receipt of a notification; or (iii) reason to know based on actual knowledge of other facts and the circumstances at the time. The latter is the traditional concept of inquiry notice.

Generally, under RUPA, statements filed pursuant to Section 105 do not constitute constructive knowledge or notice, except as expressly provided in the Act. See Section 301(1) (generally requiring knowledge of limitations on partner's apparent authority). Properly recorded statements of limitation on a partner's authority, on the other hand, generally constitute constructive knowledge with respect to the transfer of real property held in the partnership name. See Sections 303(d)(1), 303(e), 704(b), and 805(b). The other exceptions are Sections 704(c) (statement of dissociation effective 90 days after filing) and 805(c) (statement of dissolution effective 90 days after filing).

A person "receives" a notification when (i) the notification is delivered to the person's place of business (or other place for receiving communications) or (ii) the recipient otherwise actually learns of its existence.

The sender "notifies" or gives a notification by making an effort to inform the recipient, which is reasonably calculated to do so in ordinary course, even if the recipient does not actually learn of it.

The Official Comment to UCC Section 1–201(26), on which this subsection is based, explains that "notifies" is the word used when the essential fact is the proper dispatch of the notice, not its receipt. When the essential fact is the other party's receipt of the notice, that is stated.

A notification is not required to be in writing. That is a change from UPA Section 3(2)(b). As under the UCC, the time and circumstances under which a notification may cease to be effective are not determined by RUPA.

Subsection (e) determines when an agent's knowledge or notice is imputed to an organization, such as a corporation. In general, only the knowledge or notice of the agent conducting the particular transaction is imputed to the organization. Organizations are expected to maintain reasonable internal routines to insure that important information reaches the individual agent handling a transaction. If, in the exercise of reasonable diligence on the part of the organization, the agent should have known or had notice of a fact, or received a notification of it, the organization is bound. The Official Comment to UCC Section 1–201(27) explains:

> This makes clear that reason to know, knowledge, or a notification, although "received" for instance by a clerk in Department A of an organization, is effective for a transaction conducted in Department B only from the time when it was or should have been communicated to the individual conducting that transaction.

Subsection (e) uses the phrase "person other than an individual" in lieu of the UCC term "organization."

Subsection (f) continues the rule in UPA Section 12 that a partner's knowledge or notice of a fact relating to the partnership is imputed to the partnership, except in the case of fraud on the partnership. Limited partners, however, are not "partners" within the meaning of RUPA. *See* Comment 4 to Section 202. It is anticipated that RULPA will address the issue of whether notice to a limited partner is imputed to a limited partnership.

§ 103.   Effect of Partnership Agreement; Nonwaivable Provisions

(a)   Except as otherwise provided in subsection (b), relations among the partners and between the partners and the partnership are governed by the partnership agreement. To the extent the partnership agreement does not otherwise provide, this [Act] governs relations among the partners and between the partners and the partnership.

(b)   The partnership agreement may not:

(1)   vary the rights and duties under Section 105 except to eliminate the duty to provide copies of statements to all of the partners;

(2)   unreasonably restrict the right of access to books and records under Section 403(b);

(3)   eliminate the duty of loyalty under Section 404(b) or 603(b)(3), but:

(i)   the partnership agreement may identify specific types or categories of activities that do not violate the duty of loyalty, if not manifestly unreasonable; or

(ii)   all of the partners or a number or percentage specified in the partnership agreement may authorize or ratify, after full disclosure of all material facts, a specific act or transaction that otherwise would violate the duty of loyalty;

(4)   unreasonably reduce the duty of care under Section 404(c) or 603(b)(3);

(5)   eliminate the obligation of good faith and fair dealing under Section 404(d), but the partnership agreement may prescribe the standards by which the performance of the obligation is to be measured, if the standards are not manifestly unreasonable;

(6)   vary the power to dissociate as a partner under Section 602(a), except to require the notice under Section 601(1) to be in writing;

(7)   vary the right of a court to expel a partner in the events specified in Section 601(5);

(8)   vary the requirement to wind up the partnership business in cases specified in Section 801(4), (5), or (6);

(9)   vary the law applicable to a limited liability partnership under Section 106(b); or

(10)   restrict rights of third parties under this [Act].

COMMENT

1.   The general rule under Section 103(a) is that relations among the partners and between the partners and the partnership are governed by the partnership agreement. *See* Section 101(5). To the extent that the partners fail to agree upon a contrary rule, RUPA provides the default rule. Only the rights and duties listed in Section 103(b), and implicitly the corresponding liabilities and remedies under Section 405, are mandatory and cannot be waived or varied by agreement beyond what is authorized. Those are the only exceptions to the general principle that the provisions of RUPA with respect to the rights of the partners

inter se are merely default rules, subject to modification by the partners. All modifications must also, of course, satisfy the general standards of contract validity. *See* Section 104.

2. Under subsection (b)(1), the partnership agreement may not vary the requirements for executing, filing, and recording statements under Section 105, except the duty to provide copies to all the partners. A statement that is not executed, filed, and recorded in accordance with the statutory requirements will not be accorded the effect prescribed in the Act, except as provided in Section 303(d).

3. Subsection (b)(2) provides that the partnership agreement may not unreasonably restrict a partner or former partner's access rights to books and records under Section 403(b). It is left to the courts to determine what restrictions are reasonable. *See* Comment 2 to Section 403. Other information rights in Section 403 can be varied or even eliminated by agreement.

4. Subsection (b)(3) through (5) are intended to ensure a fundamental core of fiduciary responsibility. Neither the fiduciary duties of loyalty or care, nor the obligation of good faith and fair dealing, may be eliminated entirely. However, the statutory requirements of each can be modified by agreement, subject to the limitation stated in subsection (b)(3) through (5).

There has always been a tension regarding the extent to which a partner's fiduciary duty of loyalty can be varied by agreement, as contrasted with the other partners' consent to a particular and known breach of duty. On the one hand, courts have been loathe to enforce agreements broadly "waiving" in advance a partner's fiduciary duty of loyalty, especially where there is unequal bargaining power, information, or sophistication. For this reason, a very broad provision in a partnership agreement in effect negating any duty of loyalty, such as a provision giving a managing partner complete discretion to manage the business with no liability except for acts and omissions that constitute willful misconduct, will not likely be enforced. *See, e.g., Labovitz v. Dolan*, 189 Ill. App. 3d 403, 136 Ill. Dec. 780, 545 N.E.2d 304 (1989). On the other hand, it is clear that the remaining partners can "consent" to a particular conflicting interest transaction or other breach of duty, after the fact, provided there is full disclosure.

RUPA attempts to provide a standard that partners can rely upon in drafting exculpatory agreements. It is not necessary that the agreement be restricted to a particular transaction. That would require bargaining over every transaction or opportunity, which would be excessively burdensome. The agreement may be drafted in terms of types or categories of activities or transactions, but it should be reasonably specific.

A provision in a real estate partnership agreement authorizing a partner who is a real estate agent to retain commissions on partnership property bought and sold by that partner would be an example of a "type or category" of activity that is not manifestly unreasonable and thus should be enforceable under the Act. Likewise, a provision authorizing that partner to buy or sell real property for his own account without prior disclosure to the other partners or without first offering it to the partnership would be enforceable as a valid category of partnership activity.

Ultimately, the courts must decide the outer limits of validity of such agreements, and context may be significant. It is intended that the risk of judicial refusal to enforce manifestly unreasonable exculpatory clauses will discourage sharp practices while accommodating the legitimate needs of the parties in structuring their relationship.

5. Subsection (b)(3)(i) permits the partners, in their partnership agreement, to identify specific types or categories of partnership activities that do not violate the duty of loyalty. A modification of the statutory standard must not, however, be manifestly unreasonable. This is intended to discourage overreaching by a partner with superior bargaining power since the courts may refuse to enforce an overly broad exculpatory clause. *See, e.g., Vlases v. Montgomery Ward & Co.*, 377 F.2d 846, 850 (3d Cir. 1967) (limitation prohibits unconscionable agreements); *PPG Industries, Inc. v. Shell Oil Co.*, 919 F.2d 17, 19 (5th Cir. 1990) (apply limitation deferentially to agreements of sophisticated parties).

Subsection (b)(3)(ii) is intended to clarify the right of partners, recognized under general law, to consent to a known past or anticipated violation of duty and to waive their legal remedies for redress of that violation. This is intended to cover situations where the conduct in question is not specifically authorized by the partnership agreement. It can also be used to validate conduct that might otherwise not satisfy the "manifestly unreasonable" standard. Clause (ii) provides that, after full disclosure of all material facts regarding a specific act or transaction that otherwise would violate the duty of loyalty, it may be authorized or ratified by the partners. That authorization or ratification must be unanimous unless a lesser number or percentage is specified for this purpose in the partnership agreement.

6.   Under subsection (b)(4), the partners' duty of care may not be unreasonably reduced below the statutory standard set forth in Section 404(d), that is, to refrain from engaging in grossly negligent or reckless conduct, intentional misconduct, or a knowing violation of law.

For example, partnership agreements frequently contain provisions releasing a partner from liability for actions taken in good faith and in the honest belief that the actions are in the best interests of the partnership and indemnifying the partner against any liability incurred in connection with the business of the partnership if the partner acts in a good faith belief that he has authority to act. Many partnership agreements reach this same result by listing various activities and stating that the performance of these activities is deemed not to constitute gross negligence or willful misconduct. These types of provisions are intended to come within the modifications authorized by subsection (b)(4). On the other hand, absolving partners of intentional misconduct is probably unreasonable. As with contractual standards of loyalty, determining the outer limit in reducing the standard of care is left to the courts.

The standard may, of course, be increased by agreement to one of ordinary care or an even higher standard of care.

7.   Subsection (b)(5) authorizes the partners to determine the standards by which the performance of the obligation of good faith and fair dealing is to be measured. The language of subsection (b)(5) is based on UCC Section 1–102(3). The partners can negotiate and draft specific contract provisions tailored to their particular needs (*e.g.*, five days notice of a partners' meeting is adequate notice), but blanket waivers of the obligation are unenforceable. *See, e.g., PPG Indus., Inc. v. Shell Oil Co.*, 919 F.2d 17 (5th Cir. 1990); *First Security Bank v. Mountain View Equip. Co.*, 112 Idaho 158, 730 P.2d 1078 (Ct. App. 1986), *aff'd*, 112 Idaho 1078, 739 P.2d 377 (1987); *American Bank of Commerce v. Covolo*, 88 N.M. 405, 540 P.2d 1294 (1975).

8.   Section 602(a) continues the traditional UPA Section 31(2) rule that every partner has the power to withdraw from the partnership at any time, which power can not be bargained away. Section 103(b)(6) provides that the partnership agreement may not vary the power to dissociate as a partner under Section 602(a), except to require that the notice of withdrawal under Section 601(1) be in writing. The UPA was silent with respect to requiring a written notice of withdrawal.

9.   Under subsection (b)(7), the right of a partner to seek court expulsion of another partner under Section 601(5) can not be waived or varied (*e.g.*, requiring a 90-day notice) by agreement. Section 601(5) refers to judicial expulsion on such grounds as misconduct, breach of duty, or impracticability.

10.   Under subsection (b)(8), the partnership agreement may not vary the right of partners to have the partnership dissolved and its business wound up under Section 801(4), (5), or (6). Section 801(4) provides that the partnership must be wound up if its business is unlawful. Section 801(5) provides for judicial winding up in such circumstances as frustration of the firm's economic purpose, partner misconduct, or impracticability. Section 801(6) accords standing to transferees of an interest in the partnership to seek judicial dissolution of the partnership in specified circumstances.

11.   Subsection (b)(9) makes clear that a limited liability partnership may not designate the law of a State other than the State where it filed its statement of qualification to govern its internal affairs and the liability of its partners. *See* Sections 101(5), 106(b), and 202(a). Therefore, the selection of a State within which to file a statement of qualification has important choice of law ramifications, particularly where the partnership was formed in another State. *See* Comments to Section 106(b).

12.   Although stating the obvious, subsection(b)(10) provides expressly that the rights of a third party under the Act may not be restricted by an agreement among the partners to which the third party has not agreed. A non-partner who is a party to an agreement among the partners is, of course, bound. *Cf.* Section 703(c) (creditor joins release).

13.   The Article 9 rules regarding conversions and mergers are not listed in Section 103(b) as mandatory. Indeed, Section 907 states expressly that partnerships may be converted and merged in any other manner provided by law. The effect of compliance with Article 9 is to provide a "safe harbor" assuring the legal validity of such conversions and mergers. Although not immune from variation in the partnership agreement, noncompliance with the requirements of Article 9 in effecting a conversion or merger is to deny

that "safe harbor" validity to the transaction. In this regard, Sections 903(b) and 905(c)(2) require that the conversion or merger of a limited partnership be approved by all of the partners, notwithstanding a contrary provision in the limited partnership agreement. Thus, in effect, the agreement can not vary the voting requirement without sacrificing the benefits of the "safe harbor."

§ 104.　Supplemental Principles of Law

(a)　Unless displaced by particular provisions of this [Act], the principles of law and equity supplement this [Act].

(b)　If an obligation to pay interest arises under this [Act] and the rate is not specified, the rate is that specified in [applicable statute].

COMMENT

The principles of law and equity supplement RUPA unless displaced by a particular provision of the Act. This broad statement combines the separate rules contained in UPA Sections 4(2), 4(3), and 5. These supplementary principles encompass not only the law of agency and estoppel and the law merchant mentioned in the UPA, but all of the other principles listed in UCC Section 1–103: the law relative to capacity to contract, fraud, misrepresentation, duress, coercion, mistake, bankruptcy, and other common law validating or invalidating causes, such as unconscionability. No substantive change from either the UPA or the UCC is intended.

It was thought unnecessary to repeat the UPA Section 4(1) admonition that statutes in derogation of the common law are not to be strictly construed. This principle is now so well established that it is not necessary to so state in the Act. No change in the law is intended. *See* the Comment to RUPA Section 1101.

Subsection (b) is new. It is based on the definition of "interest" in Section 14–8–2(5) of the Georgia act and establishes the applicable rate of interest in the absence of an agreement among the partners. Adopting States can select the State's legal rate of interest or other statutory interest rate, such as the rate for judgments.

§ 105.　Execution, Filing, and Recording of Statements

(a)　A statement may be filed in the office of [the Secretary of State]. A certified copy of a statement that is filed in an office in another State may be filed in the office of [the Secretary of State]. Either filing has the effect provided in this [Act] with respect to partnership property located in or transactions that occur in this State.

(b)　A certified copy of a statement that has been filed in the office of the [Secretary of State] and recorded in the office for recording transfers of real property has the effect provided for recorded statements in this [Act]. A recorded statement that is not a certified copy of a statement filed in the office of the [Secretary of State] does not have the effect provided for recorded statements in this [Act].

(c)　A statement filed by a partnership must be executed by at least two partners. Other statements must be executed by a partner or other person authorized by this [Act]. An individual who executes a statement as, or on behalf of, a partner or other person named as a partner in a statement shall personally declare under penalty of perjury that the contents of the statement are accurate.

(d)　A person authorized by this [Act] to file a statement may amend or cancel the statement by filing an amendment or cancellation that names the partnership, identifies the statement, and states the substance of the amendment or cancellation.

(e)　A person who files a statement pursuant to this section shall promptly send a copy of the statement to every nonfiling partner and to any other person named as a partner in the statement. Failure to send a copy of a statement to a partner or other person does not limit the effectiveness of the statement as to a person not a partner.

(f)   The [Secretary of State] may collect a fee for filing or providing a certified copy of a statement. The [officer responsible for recording transfers of real property] may collect a fee for recording a statement.

COMMENT

1.   Section 105 is new. It mandates the procedural rules for the execution, filing, and recording of the various "statements" (see Section 101(11)) authorized by RUPA. Section 101(13) makes clear that a statement of qualification filed by a partnership to become a limited liability partnership is included in the definition of a statement. Therefore, the execution, filing, and recording rules of this section must be followed except that the decision to file the statement of qualification must be approved by the vote of the partners necessary to amend the partnership agreement as to contribution requirements. See Section 1001(b) and Comments.

No filings are mandatory under RUPA. In all cases, the filing of a statement is optional and voluntary. A system of mandatory filing and disclosure for partnerships, similar to that required for corporations and limited partnerships, was rejected for several reasons. First, RUPA is designed to accommodate the needs of small partnerships, which often have unwritten or sketchy agreements and limited resources. Furthermore, inadvertent partnerships are also governed by the Act, as the default form of business organization, in which case filing would be unlikely.

The RUPA filing provisions are, however, likely to encourage the voluntary use of partnership statements. There are a number of strong incentives for the partnership or the partners to file statements or for third parties, such as lenders or transferees of partnership property, to compel them to do so.

Only statements that are executed, filed, and, if appropriate (such as the authority to transfer real property), recorded in conformity with Section 105 have the legal consequences accorded statements by RUPA. The requirements of Section 105 cannot be varied in the partnership agreement, except the duty to provide copies of statements to all the partners. See Section 103(b)(1).

In most States today, the filing and recording of statements requires written documents. As technology advances, alternatives suitable for filing and recording may be developed. RUPA itself does not impose any requirement that statements be in writing. It is intended that the form or medium for filing and recording be left to the general law of adopting States.

2.   Section 105(a) provides for a single, central filing of all statements, as is the case with corporations, limited partnerships, and limited liability companies. The expectation is that most States will assign to the Secretary of State the responsibility of maintaining the filing system for partnership statements. Since a partnership is an entity under RUPA, all statements should be indexed by partnership name, not by the names of the individual partners.

Partnerships transacting business in more than one State will want to file copies of statements in each State because subsection (a) limits the legal effect of filed statements to property located or transactions occurring within the State. The filing of a certified copy of a statement originally filed in another State is permitted, and indeed encouraged, in order to avoid inconsistencies between statements filed in different States.

3.   Subsection (b), in effect, mandates the use of certified copies of filed statements for local recording in the real estate records by limiting the legal effect of recorded statements under the Act to those copies. The reason for recording only certified copies of filed statements is to eliminate the possibility of inconsistencies affecting the title to real property.

Subsection (c) requires that statements filed on behalf of a partnership, that is, the entity, be executed by at least two partners. Individual partners and other persons authorized by the Act to file a statement may execute it on their own behalf. To protect the partners and the partnership from unauthorized or improper filings, an individual who executes a statement as a partner must personally declare under penalty of perjury that the statement is accurate.

The amendment or cancellation of statements is authorized by subsection (d).

As a further safeguard against inaccurate or unauthorized filings, subsection (e) requires that a copy of every statement filed be sent to each partner, although the failure to do so does not limit the effectiveness of the statement. This requirement may, however, be eliminated in the partnership agreement. *See* Section 103(b)(1). Partners may also file a statement of denial under Section 304.

4.   A filed statement may be amended or canceled by any person authorized by the Act to file an original statement. The amendment or cancellation must state the name of the partnership so that it can be properly indexed and found, identify the statement being amended or canceled, and the substance of the amendment or cancellation. An amendment generally has the same operative effect as an original statement. A cancellation of extraordinary authority terminates that authority. A cancellation of a limitation on authority revives a previous grant of authority. *See* Section 303(d). The subsequent filing of a statement similar in kind to a statement already of record is treated as an amendment, even if not so denominated. Any substantive conflict between filed statements operates as a cancellation of authority under Section 303.

§ 106.   Governing Law

(a)   Except as otherwise provided in subsection (b), the law of the jurisdiction in which a partnership has its chief executive office governs relations among the partners and between the partners and the partnership.

(b)   The law of this State governs relations among the partners and between the partners and the partnership and the liability of partners for an obligation of a limited liability partnership.

COMMENT

The subsection (a) internal relations rule is new. *Cf.* RULPA § 901 (internal affairs governed by law of State in which limited partnership organized).

RUPA looks to the jurisdiction in which a partnership's chief executive office is located to provide the law governing the internal relations among the partners and between the partners and the partnership. The concept of the partnership's "chief executive office" is drawn from UCC Section 9–103(3)(d). It was chosen in lieu of the State of organization because no filing is necessary to form a general partnership, and thus the situs of its organization is not always clear, unlike a limited partnership, which is organized in the State where its certificate is filed.

The term "chief executive office" is not defined in the Act, nor is it defined in the UCC. Paragraph 5 of the Official Comment to UCC Section 9–103(3)(d) explains:

"Chief executive office" . . . means the place from which in fact the debtor manages the main part of his business operations. . . . Doubt may arise as to which is the "chief executive office" of a multi-state enterprise, but it would be rare that there could be more than two possibilities. . . . [The rule] will be simple to apply in most cases. . . .

In the absence of any other clear rule for determining a partnership's legal situs, it seems convenient to use that rule for choice of law purposes as well.

The choice-of-law rule provided by subsection (a) is only a default rule, and the partners may by agreement select the law of another State to govern their internal affairs, subject to generally applicable conflict of laws requirements. For example, where the partners may not resolve a particular issue by an explicit provision of the partnership agreement, such as the rights and duties set forth in Section 103(b), the law chosen will not be applied if the partners or the partnership have no substantial relationship to the chosen State or other reasonable basis for their choice or if application of the law of the chosen State would be contrary to a fundamental policy of a State that has a materially greater interest than the chosen State. *See* Restatement (Second) of Conflict of Laws § 187(2) (1971). The partners must, however, select only one State to govern their internal relations. They cannot select one State for some aspects of their internal relations and another State for others.

Contrasted with the variable choice-of-law rule provided by subsection (a), the law of the State where a limited liability partnership files its statement of qualification applies to such a partnership and may not be varied by the agreement of the partners. *See* Section 103(b)(9). Also, a partnership that files a statement of qualification in another State is not defined as a limited liability partnership in this State. *See* Section 101(5). Unlike a general partnership which may be formed without any filing, a partnership may only

109

become a limited liability partnership by filing a statement of qualification. Therefore, the situs of its organization is clear. Because it is often unclear where a general partnership is actually formed, the decision to file a statement of qualification in a particular State constitutes a choice-of-law for the partnership which cannot be altered by the partnership agreement. *See* Comments to Section 103(b)(9). If the partnership agreement of an existing partnership specifies the law of a particular State as its governing law, and the partnership thereafter files a statement of qualification in another State, the partnership agreement choice is no longer controlling. In such cases, the filing of a statement of qualification "amends" the partnership agreement on this limited matter. Accordingly, if a statement of qualification is revoked or canceled for a limited liability partnership, the law of the State of filing would continue to apply unless the partnership agreement thereafter altered the applicable law rule.

§ 107.   Partnership Subject to Amendment or Repeal of [Act]

A partnership governed by this [Act] is subject to any amendment to or repeal of this [Act].

COMMENT

The reservation of power provision is new. It is adapted from Section 1.02 of the Revised Model Business Corporation Act (RMBCA) and Section 1106 of RULPA.

As explained in the Official Comment to the RMBCA, the genesis of those provisions is *Trustees of Dartmouth College v. Woodward*, 17 U.S. (4 Wheat) 518 (1819), which held that the United States Constitution prohibits the application of newly enacted statutes to existing corporations, while suggesting the efficacy of a reservation of power provision. Its purpose is to avoid any possible argument that a legal entity created pursuant to statute or its members have a contractual or vested right in any specific statutory provision and to ensure that the State may in the future modify its enabling statute as it deems appropriate and require existing entities to comply with the statutes as modified.

ARTICLE 2.   NATURE OF PARTNERSHIP

§ 201.   Partnership as Entity

(a)   A partnership is an entity distinct from its partners.

(b)   A limited liability partnership continues to be the same entity that existed before the filing of a statement of qualification under Section 1001.

COMMENT

RUPA embraces the entity theory of the partnership. In light of the UPA's ambivalence on the nature of partnerships, the explicit statement provided by subsection (a) is deemed appropriate as an expression of the increased emphasis on the entity theory as the dominant model. *But see* Section 306 (partners' liability joint and several unless the partnership has filed a statement of qualification to become a limited liability partnership).

Giving clear expression to the entity nature of a partnership is intended to allay previous concerns stemming from the aggregate theory, such as the necessity of a deed to convey title from the "old" partnership to the "new" partnership every time there is a change of cast among the partners. Under RUPA, there is no "new" partnership just because of membership changes. That will avoid the result in cases such as *Fairway Development Co. v. Title Insurance Co.*, 621 F. Supp. 120 (N.D. Ohio 1985), which held that the "new" partnership resulting from a partner's death did not have standing to enforce a title insurance policy issued to the "old" partnership.

Subsection (b) makes clear that the explicit entity theory provided by subsection (a) applies to a partnership both before and after it files a statement of qualification to become a limited liability partnership. Thus, just as there is no "new" partnership resulting from membership changes, the filing of a statement of qualification does not create a "new" partnership. The filing partnership continues to be the same partnership entity that existed before the filing. Similarly, the amendment or cancellation of a statement of qualification under Section 105(d) or the revocation of a statement of qualification under Section 1003(c) does not terminate the partnership and create a "new" partnership. *See* Section 1003(d).

Accordingly, a partnership remains the same entity regardless of a filing, cancellation, or revocation of a statement of qualification.

§ 202. Formation of Partnership

(a) Except as otherwise provided in subsection (b), the association of two or more persons to carry on as co-owners a business for profit forms a partnership, whether or not the persons intend to form a partnership.

(b) An association formed under a statute other than this [Act], a predecessor statute, or a comparable statute of another jurisdiction is not a partnership under this [Act].

(c) In determining whether a partnership is formed, the following rules apply:

(1) Joint tenancy, tenancy in common, tenancy by the entireties, joint property, common property, or part ownership does not by itself establish a partnership, even if the co-owners share profits made by the use of the property.

(2) The sharing of gross returns does not by itself establish a partnership, even if the persons sharing them have a joint or common right or interest in property from which the returns are derived.

(3) A person who receives a share of the profits of a business is presumed to be a partner in the business, unless the profits were received in payment:

(i) of a debt by installments or otherwise;

(ii) for services as an independent contractor or of wages or other compensation to an employee;

(iii) of rent;

(iv) of an annuity or other retirement or health benefit to a beneficiary, representative, or designee of a deceased or retired partner;

(v) of interest or other charge on a loan, even if the amount of payment varies with the profits of the business, including a direct or indirect present or future ownership of the collateral, or rights to income, proceeds, or increase in value derived from the collateral; or

(vi) for the sale of the goodwill of a business or other property by installments or otherwise.

COMMENT

1. Section 202 combines UPA Sections 6 and 7. The traditional UPA Section 6(1) "definition" of a partnership is recast as an operative rule of law. No substantive change in the law is intended. The UPA "definition" has always been understood as an operative rule, as well as a definition. The addition of the phrase, "whether or not the persons intend to form a partnership," merely codifies the universal judicial construction of UPA Section 6(1) that a partnership is created by the association of persons whose intent is to carry on as co-owners a business for profit, regardless of their subjective intention to be "partners." Indeed, they may inadvertently create a partnership despite their expressed subjective intention not to do so. The new language alerts readers to this possibility.

As under the UPA, the attribute of co-ownership distinguishes a partnership from a mere agency relationship. A business is a series of acts directed toward an end. Ownership involves the power of ultimate control. To state that partners are co-owners of a business is to state that they each have the power of ultimate control. See Official Comment to UPA § 6(1). On the other hand, as subsection (c)(1) makes clear, passive co-ownership of property by itself, as distinguished from the carrying on of a business, does not establish a partnership.

2. Subsection (b) provides that business associations organized under other statutes are not partnerships. Those statutory associations include corporations, limited partnerships, and limited liability

companies. That continues the UPA concept that general partnership is the residual form of for profit business association, existing only if another form does not.

A limited partnership is not a partnership under this definition. Nevertheless, certain provisions of RUPA will continue to govern limited partnerships because RULPA itself, in Section 1105, so requires "in any case not provided for" in RULPA. For example, the rules applicable to a limited liability partnership will generally apply to limited partnerships. *See* Comment to Section 101(5) (definition of a limited liability partnership). In light of that RULPA Section 1105, UPA Section 6(2), which provides that limited partnerships are governed by the UPA, is redundant and has not been carried over to RUPA. It is also more appropriate that the applicability of RUPA to limited partnerships be governed exclusively by RULPA. For example, a RULPA amendment may clarify certain linkage questions regarding the application of the limited liability partnership rules to limited partnerships. *See* Comment to Section 101(5) for a suggested form of such an amendment.

It is not intended that RUPA change any common law rules concerning special types of associations, such as mining partnerships, which in some jurisdictions are not governed by the UPA.

Relationships that are called "joint ventures" are partnerships if they otherwise fit the definition of a partnership. An association is not classified as a partnership, however, simply because it is called a "joint venture."

An unincorporated nonprofit organization is not a partnership under RUPA, even if it qualifies as a business, because it is not a "for profit" organization.

3.　　Subsection (c) provides three rules of construction that apply in determining whether a partnership has been formed under subsection (a). They are largely derived from UPA Section 7, and to that extent no substantive change is intended. The sharing of profits is recast as a rebuttable presumption of a partnership, a more contemporary construction, rather than as prima facie evidence thereof. The protected categories, in which receipt of a share of the profits is not presumed to create a partnership, apply whether the profit share is a single flat percentage or a ratio which varies, for example, after reaching a dollar floor or different levels of profits.

Like its predecessor, RUPA makes no attempt to answer in every case whether a partnership is formed. Whether a relationship is more properly characterized as that of borrower and lender, employer and employee, or landlord and tenant is left to the trier of fact. As under the UPA, a person may function in both partner and nonpartner capacities.

Paragraph (3)(v) adds a new protected category to the list. It shields from the presumption a share of the profits received in payment of interest or other charges on a loan, "including a direct or indirect present or future ownership in the collateral, or rights to income, proceeds, or increase in value derived from the collateral." The quoted language is taken from Section 211 of the Uniform Land Security Interest Act. The purpose of the new language is to protect shared-appreciation mortgages, contingent or other variable or performance-related mortgages, and other equity participation arrangements by clarifying that contingent payments do not presumptively convert lending arrangements into partnerships.

4.　　Section 202(e) of the 1993 Act stated that partnerships formed under RUPA are general partnerships and that the partners are general partners. That section has been deleted as unnecessary. Limited partners are not "partners" within the meaning of RUPA, however.

§ 203.　Partnership Property

Property acquired by a partnership is property of the partnership and not of the partners individually.

COMMENT

All property acquired by a partnership, by transfer or otherwise, becomes partnership property and belongs to the partnership as an entity, rather than to the individual partners. This expresses the substantive result of UPA Sections 8(1) and 25.

Neither UPA Section 8(1) nor RUPA Section 203 provides any guidance concerning when property is "acquired by" the partnership. That problem is dealt with in Section 204.

UPA Sections 25(2)(c) and (e) also provide that partnership property is not subject to exemptions, allowances, or rights of a partner's spouse, heirs, or next of kin. Those provisions have been omitted as unnecessary. No substantive change is intended. Those exemptions and rights inure to the property of the partners, and not to partnership property.

§ 204. When Property is Partnership Property

(a) Property is partnership property if acquired in the name of:

    (1) the partnership; or

    (2) one or more partners with an indication in the instrument transferring title to the property of the person's capacity as a partner or of the existence of a partnership but without an indication of the name of the partnership.

(b) Property is acquired in the name of the partnership by a transfer to:

    (1) the partnership in its name; or

    (2) one or more partners in their capacity as partners in the partnership, if the name of the partnership is indicated in the instrument transferring title to the property.

(c) Property is presumed to be partnership property if purchased with partnership assets, even if not acquired in the name of the partnership or of one or more partners with an indication in the instrument transferring title to the property of the person's capacity as a partner or of the existence of a partnership.

(d) Property acquired in the name of one or more of the partners, without an indication in the instrument transferring title to the property of the person's capacity as a partner or of the existence of a partnership and without use of partnership assets, is presumed to be separate property, even if used for partnership purposes.

COMMENT

1. Section 204 sets forth the rules for determining when property is acquired by the partnership and, hence, becomes partnership property. It is based on UPA Section 8(3), as influenced by the recent Alabama and Georgia modifications. The rules govern the acquisition of personal property, as well as real property, that is held in the partnership name. *See* Section 101(9).

2. Subsection (a) governs the circumstances under which property becomes "partnership property," and subsection (b) clarifies the circumstances under which property is acquired "in the name of the partnership." The concept of record title is emphasized, although the term itself is not used. Titled personal property, as well as all transferable interests in real property acquired in the name of the partnership, are covered by this section.

Property becomes partnership property if acquired (1) in the name of the partnership or (2) in the name of one or more of the partners with an indication in the instrument transferring title of either (i) their capacity as partners or (ii) of the existence of a partnership, even if the name of the partnership is not indicated. Property acquired "in the name of the partnership" includes property acquired in the name of one or more partners in their capacity as partners, but only if the name of the partnership is indicated in the instrument transferring title.

Property transferred to a partner is partnership property, even though the name of the partnership is not indicated, if the instrument transferring title indicates either (i) the partner's capacity as a partner or (ii) the existence of a partnership. This is consonant with the entity theory of partnership and resolves the troublesome issue of a conveyance to fewer than all the partners but which nevertheless indicates their partner status.

3.   Ultimately, it is the intention of the partners that controls whether property belongs to the partnership or to one or more of the partners in their individual capacities, at least as among the partners themselves. RUPA sets forth two rebuttable presumptions that apply when the partners have failed to express their intent.

First, under subsection (c), property purchased with partnership funds is presumed to be partnership property, notwithstanding the name in which title is held. The presumption is intended to apply if partnership credit is used to obtain financing, as well as the use of partnership cash or property for payment. Unlike the rule in subsection (b), under which property is deemed to be partnership property if the partnership's name or the partner's capacity as a partner is disclosed in the instrument of conveyance, subsection (c) raises only a presumption that the property is partnership property if it is purchased with partnership assets.

That presumption is also subject to an important caveat. Under Section 302(b), partnership property held in the name of individual partners, without an indication of their capacity as partners or of the existence of a partnership, that is transferred by the partners in whose name title is held to a purchaser without knowledge that it is partnership property is free of any claims of the partnership.

Second, under subsection (d), property acquired in the name of one or more of the partners, without an indication of their capacity as partners and without use of partnership funds or credit, is presumed to be the partners' separate property, even if used for partnership purposes. In effect, it is presumed in that case that only the use of the property is contributed to the partnership.

4.   Generally, under RUPA, partners and third parties dealing with partnerships will be able to rely on the record to determine whether property is owned by the partnership. The exception is property purchased with partnership funds without any reference to the partnership in the title documents. The inference concerning the partners' intent from the use of partnership funds outweighs any inference from the State of the title, subject to the overriding reliance interest in the case of a purchaser without notice of the partnership's interest. This allocation of risk should encourage the partnership to eliminate doubt about ownership by putting title in the partnership.

5.   UPA Section 8(4) provides, "A transfer to a partnership in the partnership name, even without words of inheritance, passes the entire estate or interest of the grantor unless a contrary intent appears." It has been omitted from RUPA as unnecessary because modern conveyancing law deems all transfers to pass the entire estate or interest of the grantor unless a contrary intent appears.

ARTICLE 3.   RELATIONS OF PARTNERS TO PERSONS DEALING WITH PARTNERSHIP

§ 301.   Partner Agent of Partnership

Subject to the effect of a statement of partnership authority under Section 303:

(1)   Each partner is an agent of the partnership for the purpose of its business. An act of a partner, including the execution of an instrument in the partnership name, for apparently carrying on in the ordinary course the partnership business or business of the kind carried on by the partnership binds the partnership, unless the partner had no authority to act for the partnership in the particular matter and the person with whom the partner was dealing knew or had received a notification that the partner lacked authority.

(2)   An act of a partner which is not apparently for carrying on in the ordinary course the partnership business or business of the kind carried on by the partnership binds the partnership only if the act was authorized by the other partners.

COMMENT

1.   Section 301 sets forth a partner's power, as an agent of the firm, to bind the partnership entity to third parties. The rights of the partners among themselves, including the right to restrict a partner's authority, are governed by the partnership agreement and by Section 401.

The agency rules set forth in Section 301 are subject to an important qualification. They may be affected by the filing or recording of a statement of partnership authority. The legal effect of filing or recording a statement of partnership authority is set forth in Section 303.

2.   Section 301(1) retains the basic principles reflected in UPA Section 9(1). It declares that each partner is an agent of the partnership and that, by virtue of partnership status, each partner has apparent authority to bind the partnership in ordinary course transactions. The effect of Section 301(1) is to characterize a partner as a general managerial agent having both actual and apparent authority co-extensive in scope with the firm's ordinary business, at least in the absence of a contrary partnership agreement.

Section 301(1) effects two changes from UPA Section 9(1). First, it clarifies that a partner's apparent authority includes acts for carrying on in the ordinary course "business of the kind carried on by the partnership," not just the business of the particular partnership in question. The UPA is ambiguous on this point, but there is some authority for an expanded construction in accordance with the so-called English rule. *See, e.g., Burns v. Gonzalez*, 439 S.W.2d 128, 131 (Tex. Civ. App. 1969) (dictum); *Commercial Hotel Co. v. Weeks*, 254 S.W. 521 (Tex. Civ. App. 1923). No substantive change is intended by use of the more customary phrase "carrying on in the ordinary course" in lieu of the UPA phrase "in the usual way." The UPA and the case law use both terms without apparent distinction.

The other change from the UPA concerns the allocation of risk of a partner's lack of authority. RUPA draws the line somewhat differently from the UPA.

Under UPA Section 9(1) and (4), only a person with knowledge of a restriction on a partner's authority is bound by it. Section 301(1) provides that a person who has received a notification of a partner's lack of authority is also bound. The meaning of "receives a notification" is explained in Section 102(d). Thus, the partnership may protect itself from unauthorized acts by giving a notification of a restriction on a partner's authority to a person dealing with that partner. A notification may be effective upon delivery, whether or not it actually comes to the other person's attention. To that extent, the risk of lack of authority is shifted to those dealing with partners.

On the other hand, as used in the UPA, the term "knowledge" embodies the concept of "bad faith" knowledge arising from other known facts. As used in RUPA, however, "knowledge" is limited to actual knowledge. *See* Section 102(a). Thus, RUPA does not expose persons dealing with a partner to the greater risk of being bound by a restriction based on their purported reason to know of the partner's lack of authority from all the facts they did know. *Compare* Section 102(b)(3) (notice).

With one exception, this result is not affected even if the partnership files a statement of partnership authority containing a limitation on a partner's authority. Section 303(f) makes clear that a person dealing with a partner is not deemed to know of such a limitation merely because it is contained in a filed statement of authority. Under Section 303(e), however, all persons are deemed to know of a limitation on the authority of a partner to transfer real property contained in a recorded statement. Thus, a recorded limitation on authority concerning real property constitutes constructive knowledge of the limitation to the whole world.

3.   Section 301(2) is drawn directly from UPA Section 9(2), with conforming changes to mirror the new language of subsection (1). Subsection (2) makes it clear that the partnership is bound by a partner's actual authority, even if the partner has no apparent authority. Section 401(j) requires the unanimous consent of the partners for a grant of authority outside the ordinary course of business, unless the partnership agreement provides otherwise. Under general agency principles, the partners can subsequently ratify a partner's unauthorized act. *See* Section 104(a).

4.   UPA Section 9(3) contains a list of five extraordinary acts that require unanimous consent of the partners before the partnership is bound. RUPA omits that section. That leaves it to the courts to decide the outer limits of the agency power of a partner. Most of the acts listed in UPA Section 9(3) probably remain outside the apparent authority of a partner under RUPA, such as disposing of the goodwill of the business, but elimination of a statutory rule will afford more flexibility in some situations specified in UPA Section 9(3). In particular, it seems archaic that the submission of a partnership claim to arbitration always requires unanimous consent. *See* UPA § 9(3)(e).

5.   Section 301(1) fully reflects the principle embodied in UPA Section 9(4) that the partnership is not bound by an act of a partner in contravention of a restriction on his authority known to the other party.

§ 302.   Transfer of Partnership Property

(a)   Partnership property may be transferred as follows:

(1)   Subject to the effect of a statement of partnership authority under Section 303, partnership property held in the name of the partnership may be transferred by an instrument of transfer executed by a partner in the partnership name.

(2)   Partnership property held in the name of one or more partners with an indication in the instrument transferring the property to them of their capacity as partners or of the existence of a partnership, but without an indication of the name of the partnership, may be transferred by an instrument of transfer executed by the persons in whose name the property is held.

(3)   Partnership property held in the name of one or more persons other than the partnership, without an indication in the instrument transferring the property to them of their capacity as partners or of the existence of a partnership, may be transferred by an instrument of transfer executed by the persons in whose name the property is held.

(b)   A partnership may recover partnership property from a transferee only if it proves that execution of the instrument of initial transfer did not bind the partnership under Section 301 and:

(1)   as to a subsequent transferee who gave value for property transferred under subsection (a)(1) and (2), proves that the subsequent transferee knew or had received a notification that the person who executed the instrument of initial transfer lacked authority to bind the partnership; or

(2)   as to a transferee who gave value for property transferred under subsection (a)(3), proves that the transferee knew or had received a notification that the property was partnership property and that the person who executed the instrument of initial transfer lacked authority to bind the partnership.

(c)   A partnership may not recover partnership property from a subsequent transferee if the partnership would not have been entitled to recover the property, under subsection (b), from any earlier transferee of the property.

(d)   If a person holds all of the partners' interests in the partnership, all of the partnership property vests in that person. The person may execute a document in the name of the partnership to evidence vesting of the property in that person and may file or record the document.

COMMENT

1.   Section 302 replaces UPA Section 10 and provides rules for the transfer and recovery of partnership property. The language is adapted in part from Section 14–8–10 of the Georgia partnership statute.

2.   Subsection (a)(1) deals with the transfer of partnership property held in the name of the partnership and subsection (a)(2) with property held in the name of one or more of the partners with an indication either of their capacity as partners or of the existence of a partnership. Subsection (a)(3) deals with partnership property held in the name of one or more of the partners without an indication of their capacity as partners or of the existence of a partnership. Like the general agency rules in Section 301, the power of a partner to transfer partnership property under subsection (a)(1) is subject to the effect under Section 303 of the filing or recording of a statement of partnership authority. These rules are intended to foster reliance on record title.

UPA Section 10 covers only real property. Section 302, however, also governs the transfer of partnership personal property acquired by instrument and held in the name of the partnership or one or more of the partners.

3.   Subsection (b) deals with the right of the partnership to recover partnership property transferred by a partner without authority. Subsection (b)(1) deals with the recovery of property held in either the name of the partnership or the name of one or more of the partners with an indication of their capacity as partners

or of the existence of a partnership, while subsection (b)(2) deals with the recovery of property held in the name of one or more persons without an indication of their capacity as partners or of the existence of a partnership.

In either case, a transfer of partnership property may be avoided only if the partnership proves that it was not bound under Section 301 by the execution of the instrument of initial transfer. Under Section 301, the partnership is bound by a transfer in the ordinary course of business, unless the transferee actually knew or had received a notification of the partner's lack of authority. *See* Section 102(a) and (d). The reference to Section 301, rather than Section 301(1), is intended to clarify that a partner's actual authority is not revoked by Section 302. *Compare* UPA § 10(1) (refers to partner's authority under Section 9(1)).

The burden of proof is on the partnership to prove the partner's lack of authority and, in the case of a subsequent transferee, the transferee's knowledge or notification thereof. Thus, even if the transfer to the initial transferee could be avoided, the partnership may not recover the property from a subsequent purchaser or other transferee for value unless it also proves that the subsequent transferee knew or had received a notification of the partner's lack of authority with respect to the initial transfer. Since knowledge is required, rather than notice, a remote purchaser has no duty to inquire as to the authority for the initial transfer, even if he knows it was partnership property.

The burden of proof is on the transferee to show that value was given. Value, as used in this context, is synonymous with valuable consideration and means any consideration sufficient to support a simple contract.

The burden of proof on all other issues is allocated to the partnership because it is generally in a better position than the transferee to produce the evidence. Moreover, the partnership may protect itself against unauthorized transfers by ensuring that partnership real property is held in the name of the partnership and that a statement of partnership authority is recorded specifying any limitations on the partners' authority to convey real property. Under Section 303(e), transferees of real property held in the partnership name are conclusively bound by those limitations. On the other hand, transferees can protect themselves by insisting that the partnership record a statement specifying who is authorized to transfer partnership property. Under Section 303(d), transferees for value, without actual knowledge to the contrary, may rely on that grant of authority.

4. Subsection (b)(2) replaces UPA Section 10(3) and provides that partners who hold partnership property in their own names, without an indication in the record of their capacity as partners or of the existence of a partnership, may transfer good title to a transferee for value without knowledge or a notification that it was partnership property. To recover the property under this subsection, the partnership has the burden of proving that the transferee knew or had received a notification of the partnership's interest in the property, as well as of the partner's lack of authority for the initial transfer.

5. Subsection (c) is new and provides that property may not be recovered by the partnership from a remote transferee if any intermediate transferee of the property would have prevailed against the partnership. *Cf.* Uniform Fraudulent Transfer Act, §§ 8(a) (subsequent transferee from bona fide purchaser protected), 8(b)(2) (same).

6. Subsection (d) is new. The UPA does not have a provision dealing with the situation in which all of the partners' interests in the partnership are held by one person, such as a surviving partner or a purchaser of all the other partners' interests. Subsection (d) allows for clear record title, even though the partnership no longer exists as a technical matter. When a partnership becomes a sole proprietorship by reason of the dissociation of all but one of the partners, title vests in the remaining "partner," although there is no "transfer" of the property. The remaining "partner" may execute a deed or other transfer of record in the name of the non-existent partnership to evidence vesting of the property in that person's individual capacity.

7. UPA Section 10(2) provides that, where title to real property is in the partnership name, a conveyance by a partner in his own name transfers the partnership's equitable interest in the property. It has been omitted as was done in Georgia and Florida. In this situation, the conveyance is clearly outside the chain of title and so should not pass title or any interest in the property. UPA Section 10(2) dilutes, albeit slightly, the effect of record title and is, therefore, inconsistent with RUPA's broad policy of fostering reliance on the record.

UPA Section 10(4) and (5) have also been omitted. Those situations are now adequately covered by Section 302(a).

§ 303.   Statement of Partnership Authority

(a)   A partnership may file a statement of partnership authority, which:

    (1)   must include:

        (i)   the name of the partnership;

        (ii)   the street address of its chief executive office and of one office in this State, if there is one;

        (iii)   the names and mailing addresses of all of the partners or of an agent appointed and maintained by the partnership for the purpose of subsection (b); and

        (iv)   the names of the partners authorized to execute an instrument transferring real property held in the name of the partnership; and

    (2)   may state the authority, or limitations on the authority, of some or all of the partners to enter into other transactions on behalf of the partnership and any other matter.

(b)   If a statement of partnership authority names an agent, the agent shall maintain a list of the names and mailing addresses of all of the partners and make it available to any person on request for good cause shown.

(c)   If a filed statement of partnership authority is executed pursuant to Section 105(c) and states the name of the partnership but does not contain all of the other information required by subsection (a), the statement nevertheless operates with respect to a person not a partner as provided in subsections (d) and (e).

(d)   Except as otherwise provided in subsection (g), a filed statement of partnership authority supplements the authority of a partner to enter into transactions on behalf of the partnership as follows:

    (1)   Except for transfers of real property, a grant of authority contained in a filed statement of partnership authority is conclusive in favor of a person who gives value without knowledge to the contrary, so long as and to the extent that a limitation on that authority is not then contained in another filed statement. A filed cancellation of a limitation on authority revives the previous grant of authority.

    (2)   A grant of authority to transfer real property held in the name of the partnership contained in a certified copy of a filed statement of partnership authority recorded in the office for recording transfers of that real property is conclusive in favor of a person who gives value without knowledge to the contrary, so long as and to the extent that a certified copy of a filed statement containing a limitation on that authority is not then of record in the office for recording transfers of that real property. The recording in the office for recording transfers of that real property of a certified copy of a filed cancellation of a limitation on authority revives the previous grant of authority.

(e)   A person not a partner is deemed to know of a limitation on the authority of a partner to transfer real property held in the name of the partnership if a certified copy of the filed statement containing the limitation on authority is of record in the office for recording transfers of that real property.

(f)   Except as otherwise provided in subsections (d) and (e) and Sections 704 and 805, a person not a partner is not deemed to know of a limitation on the authority of a partner merely because the limitation is contained in a filed statement.

(g)   Unless earlier canceled, a filed statement of partnership authority is canceled by operation of law five years after the date on which the statement, or the most recent amendment, was filed with the [Secretary of State].

COMMENT

1.   Section 303 is new. It provides for an optional statement of partnership authority specifying the names of the partners authorized to execute instruments transferring real property held in the name of the partnership. It may also grant supplementary authority to partners, or limit their authority, to enter into other transactions on behalf of the partnership. The execution, filing, and recording of statements is governed by Section 105.

RUPA follows the lead of California and Georgia in authorizing the optional filing of statements of authority. Filing a statement of partnership authority may be deemed to satisfy the disclosure required by a State's fictitious name statute, if the State so chooses.

Section 105 provides for the central filing of statements, rather than local filing. However, to be effective in connection with the transfer of real property, a statement of partnership authority must also be recorded locally with the land records.

2.   The most important goal of the statement of authority is to facilitate the transfer of real property held in the name of the partnership. A statement must specify the names of the partners authorized to execute an instrument transferring that property.

Under subsection (d)(2), a recorded grant of authority to transfer real property held in the name of the partnership is conclusive in favor of a transferee for value without actual knowledge to the contrary. A partner's authority to transfer partnership real property is affected by a recorded statement only if the property is held in the name of the partnership. A recorded statement has no effect on the partners' authority to transfer partnership real property that is held other than in the name of the partnership. In that case, by definition, the record will not indicate the name of the partnership, and thus the partnership's interest would not be disclosed by a title search. See Section 204. To be effective, the statement recorded with the land records must be a certified copy of the original statement filed with the Secretary of State. See Section 105(b).

The presumption of authority created by subsection (d)(2) operates only so long as and to the extent that a limitation on the partner's authority is not contained in another recorded statement. This is intended to condition reliance on the record to situations where there is no conflict among recorded statements, amendments, or denials of authority. See Section 304. If the record is in conflict regarding a partner's authority, transferees must go outside the record to determine the partners' actual authority. This rule is modified slightly in the case of a cancellation of a limitation on a partner's authority, which revives the previous grant of authority.

Under subsection (e), third parties are deemed to know of a recorded limitation on the authority of a partner to transfer real property held in the partnership name. Since transferees are bound under Section 301 by knowledge of a limitation on a partner's authority, they are bound by such a recorded limitation. Of course, a transferee with actual knowledge of a limitation on a partner's authority is bound under Section 301, whether or not there is a recorded statement of limitation.

3.   A statement of partnership authority may have effect beyond the transfer of real property held in the name of the partnership. Under subsection (a)(2), a statement of authority may contain any other matter the partnership chooses, including a grant of authority, or a limitation on the authority, of some or all of the partners to enter into other transactions on behalf of the partnership. Since Section 301 confers authority on all partners to act for the partnership in ordinary matters, the real import of such a provision is to grant extraordinary authority, or to limit the ordinary authority, of some or all of the partners.

The effect given to such a provision is different from that accorded a provision regarding the transfer of real property. Under subsection (d)(1), a filed grant of authority is binding on the partnership, in favor of a person who gives value without actual knowledge to the contrary, unless limited by another filed statement. That is the same rule as for statements involving real property under subsection 301(d)(2). There is, however, no counterpart to subsection (e) regarding a filed limitation of authority. To the contrary, subsection (f) makes clear that filing a limitation of authority does not operate as constructive knowledge of a partner's lack of authority with respect to non-real property transactions.

Under Section 301, only a third party who knows or has received a notification of a partner's lack of authority in an ordinary course transaction is bound. Thus, a limitation on a partner's authority to transfer personal property or to enter into other non-real property transactions on behalf of the partnership, contained in a filed statement of partnership authority, is effective only against a third party who knows or has received a notification of it. The fact of the statement being filed has no legal significance in those transactions, although the filed statement is a potential source of actual knowledge to third parties.

4.   It should be emphasized that Section 303 concerns the authority of partners to bind the partnership to third persons. As among the partners, the authority of a partner to take any action is governed by the partnership agreement, or by the provisions of RUPA governing the relations among partners, and is not affected by the filing or recording of a statement of partnership authority.

5.   The exercise of the option to file a statement of partnership authority imposes a further disclosure obligation on the partnership. Under subsection (a)(1), a filed statement must include the street address of its chief executive office and of an office in the State (if any), as well as the names and mailing addresses of all of the partners or, alternatively, of an agent appointed and maintained by the partnership for the purpose of maintaining such a list. If an agent is appointed, subsection (b) provides that the agent shall maintain a list of all of the partners and make it available to any person on request for good cause shown. Under subsection (c), the failure to make all of the required disclosures does not affect the statement's operative effect, however.

6.   Under subsection (g), a statement of authority is canceled by operation of law five years after the date on which the statement, or the most recent amendment, was filed.

7.   Section 308(c) makes clear that a person does not become a partner solely because he is named as a partner in a statement of partnership authority filed by another person. *See also* Section 304 ("person named as a partner" may file statement of denial).

§ 304.   Statement of Denial

A partner or other person named as a partner in a filed statement of partnership authority or in a list maintained by an agent pursuant to Section 303(b) may file a statement of denial stating the name of the partnership and the fact that is being denied, which may include denial of a person's authority or status as a partner. A statement of denial is a limitation on authority as provided in Section 303(d) and (e).

COMMENT

Section 304 is new and complements Section 303. It provides partners (and persons named as partners) an opportunity to deny any fact asserted in a statement of partnership authority, including denial of a person's status as a partner or of another person's authority as a partner. A statement of denial must be executed, filed, and recorded pursuant to the requirements of Section 105.

Section 304 does not address the consequences of a denial of partnership. No adverse inference should be drawn from the failure of a person named as a partner to deny such status, however. *See* Section 308(c) (person not liable as a partner merely because named in statement as a partner).

A statement of denial operates as a limitation on a partner's authority to the extent provided in Section 303. Section 303(d) provides that a filed or recorded statement of partnership authority is conclusive, in favor of purchasers without knowledge to the contrary, so long as and to the extent that a limitation on that authority is not contained in another filed or recorded statement. A filed or recorded statement of denial operates as such a limitation on authority, thereby precluding reliance on an inconsistent grant of authority. Under Section 303(d), a filed or recorded cancellation of a statement of denial that operates as a limitation on authority revives the previous grant of authority.

Under Section 303(e), a recorded statement of denial of a partner's authority to transfer partnership real property held in the partnership name constitutes constructive knowledge of that limitation.

§ 305.   Partnership Liable for Partner's Actionable Conduct

(a)   A partnership is liable for loss or injury caused to a person, or for a penalty incurred, as a result of a wrongful act or omission, or other actionable conduct, of a partner acting in the ordinary course of business of the partnership or with authority of the partnership.

(b)   If, in the course of the partnership's business or while acting with authority of the partnership, a partner receives or causes the partnership to receive money or property of a person not a partner, and the money or property is misapplied by a partner, the partnership is liable for the loss.

COMMENT

Section 305(a), which is derived from UPA Section 13, imposes liability on the partnership for the wrongful acts of a partner acting in the ordinary course of the partnership's business or otherwise within the partner's authority. The scope of the section has been expanded by deleting from UPA Section 13, "not being a partner in the partnership." This is intended to permit a partner to sue the partnership on a tort or other theory during the term of the partnership, rather than being limited to the remedies of dissolution and an accounting. *See also* Comment 2 to Section 405.

The section has also been broadened to cover no-fault torts by the addition of the phrase, "or other actionable conduct."

The partnership is liable for the actionable conduct or omission of a partner acting in the ordinary course of its business or "with the authority of the partnership." This is intended to include a partner's apparent, as well as actual, authority, thereby bringing within Section 305(a) the situation covered in UPA Section 14(a).

The phrase in UPA Section 13, "to the same extent as the partner so acting or omitting to act," has been deleted to prevent a partnership from asserting a partner's immunity from liability. This is consistent with the general agency rule that a principal is not entitled to its agent's immunities. *See* Restatement (Second) of Agency § 217(b) (1957). The deletion is not intended to limit a partnership's contractual rights.

Section 305(b) is drawn from UPA Section 14(b), but has been edited to improve clarity. It imposes strict liability on the partnership for the misapplication of money or property received by a partner in the course of the partnership's business or otherwise within the scope of the partner's actual authority.

§ 306.   Partner's Liability

(a)   Except as otherwise provided in subsections (b) and (c), all partners are liable jointly and severally for all obligations of the partnership unless otherwise agreed by the claimant or provided by law.

(b)   A person admitted as a partner into an existing partnership is not personally liable for any partnership obligation incurred before the person's admission as a partner.

(c)   An obligation of a partnership incurred while the partnership is a limited liability partnership, whether arising in contract, tort, or otherwise, is solely the obligation of the partnership. A partner is not personally liable, directly or indirectly, by way of contribution or otherwise, for such an obligation solely by reason of being or so acting as a partner. This subsection applies notwithstanding anything inconsistent in the partnership agreement that existed immediately before the vote required to become a limited liability partnership under Section 1001(b).

COMMENT

1.   Section 306(a) changes the UPA rule by imposing joint and several liability on the partners for all partnership obligations where the partnership is not a limited liability partnership. Under UPA Section 15, partners' liability for torts is joint and several, while their liability for contracts is joint but not several. About ten States that have adopted the UPA already provide for joint and several liability. The UPA reference to "debts and obligations" is redundant, and no change is intended by RUPA's reference solely to "obligations."

121

Joint and several liability under RUPA differs, however, from the classic model, which permits a judgment creditor to proceed immediately against any of the joint and several judgment debtors. Generally, Section 307(d) requires the judgment creditor to exhaust the partnership's assets before enforcing a judgment against the separate assets of a partner.

2.   RUPA continues the UPA scheme of liability with respect to an incoming partner, but states the rule more clearly and simply. Under Section 306(a), an incoming partner becomes jointly and severally liable, as a partner, for all partnership obligations, except as otherwise provided in subsection (b). That subsection eliminates an incoming partner's personal liability for partnership obligations incurred before his admission as a partner. In effect, a new partner has no personal liability to existing creditors of the partnership, and only his investment in the firm is at risk for the satisfaction of existing partnership debts. That is presently the rule under UPA Sections 17 and 41(7), and no substantive change is intended. As under the UPA, a new partner's personal assets are at risk with respect to partnership liabilities incurred after his admission as a partner.

3.   Subsection (c) alters classic joint and several liability of general partners for obligations of a partnership that is a limited liability partnership. Like shareholders of a corporation and members of a limited liability company, partners of a limited liability partnership are not personally liable for partnership obligations incurred while the partnership liability shield is in place solely because they are partners. As with shareholders of a corporation and members of a limited liability company, partners remain personally liable for their personal misconduct.

In cases of partner misconduct, Section 401(c) sets forth a partnership's obligation to indemnify the culpable partner where the partner's liability was incurred in the ordinary course of the partnership's business. When indemnification occurs, the assets of both the partnership and the culpable partner are available to a creditor. However, Sections 306(c), 401(b), and 807(b) make clear that a partner who is not otherwise liable under Section 306(c) is not obligated to contribute assets to the partnership in excess of agreed contributions to share the loss with the culpable partner. (*See* Comments to Sections 401(b) and 807(b). regarding a slight variation in the context of priority of payment of partnership obligations.) Accordingly, Section 306(c) makes clear that an innocent partner is not personally liable for specified partnership obligations, directly or indirectly, by way of contribution or otherwise.

Although the liability shield protections of Section 306(c) may be modified in part or in full in a partnership agreement (and by way of private contractual guarantees), the modifications must constitute an intentional waiver of the liability protections. *See* Sections 103(b), 104(a), and 902(b). Since the mere act of filing a statement of qualification reflects the assumption that the partners intend to modify the otherwise applicable partner liability rules, the final sentence of subsection (c) makes clear that the filing negates inconsistent aspects of the partnership agreement that existed immediately before the vote to approve becoming a limited liability partnership. The negation only applies to a partner's personal liability for future partnership obligations. The filing however has no effect as to previously created partner obligations to the partnership in the form of specific capital contribution requirements.

Inter se contribution agreements may erode part or all of the effects of the liability shield. For example, Section 807(f) provides that an assignee for the benefit of creditors of a partnership or a partner may enforce a partner's obligation to contribute to the partnership. The ultimate effect of such contribution obligations may make each partner jointly and severally liable for all partnership obligations—even those incurred while the partnership is a limited liability partnership. Although the final sentence of subsection (c) negates such provisions existing before a statement of qualification is filed, it will have no effect on any amendments to the partnership agreement after the statement is filed.

The connection between partner status and personal liability for partnership obligations is severed only with respect to obligations incurred while the partnership is a limited liability partnership. Partnership obligations incurred before a partnership becomes a limited liability partnership or incurred after limited liability partnership status is revoked or canceled are treated as obligations of an ordinary partnership. *See* Sections 1001 (filing), 1003 (revocation), and 1006 (cancellation). Obligations incurred by a partnership during the period when its statement of qualification is administratively revoked will be considered as incurred by a limited liability partnership provided the partnership's status as such is reinstated within two years under Section 1003(e). *See* Section 1003(f).

When an obligation is incurred is determined by other law. *See* Section 104(a). Under that law, and for the limited purpose of determining when partnership contract obligations are incurred, the reasonable expectations of creditors and the partners are paramount. Therefore, partnership obligations under or relating to a note, contract, or other agreement generally are incurred when the note, contract, or other agreement is made. Also, an amendment, modification, extension, or renewal of a note, contract, or other agreement should not affect or otherwise reset the time at which a partnership obligation under or relating to that note, contract, or other agreement is incurred, even as to a claim that relates to the subject matter of the amendment, modification, extension, or renewal. A note, contract, or other agreement may expressly modify these rules and fix the time a partnership obligation is incurred thereunder.

For the limited purpose of determining when partnership tort obligations are incurred, a distinction is intended between injury and the conduct causing that injury. The purpose of the distinction is to prevent unjust results. Partnership obligations under or relating to a tort generally are incurred when the tort conduct occurs rather than at the time of the actual injury or harm. This interpretation prevents a culpable partnership from engaging in wrongful conduct and then filing a statement of qualification to sever the vicarious responsibility of its partners for future injury or harm caused by conduct that occurred prior to the filing.

§ 307.   Actions by and Against Partnership and Partners

(a)   A partnership may sue and be sued in the name of the partnership.

(b)   An action may be brought against the partnership and, to the extent not inconsistent with Section 306, any or all of the partners in the same action or in separate actions.

(c)   A judgment against a partnership is not by itself a judgment against a partner. A judgment against a partnership may not be satisfied from a partner's assets unless there is also a judgment against the partner.

(d)   A judgment creditor of a partner may not levy execution against the assets of the partner to satisfy a judgment based on a claim against the partnership unless the partner is personally liable for the claim under Section 306 and:

(1)   a judgment based on the same claim has been obtained against the partnership and a writ of execution on the judgment has been returned unsatisfied in whole or in part;

(2)   the partnership is a debtor in bankruptcy;

(3)   the partner has agreed that the creditor need not exhaust partnership assets;

(4)   a court grants permission to the judgment creditor to levy execution against the assets of a partner based on a finding that partnership assets subject to execution are clearly insufficient to satisfy the judgment, that exhaustion of partnership assets is excessively burdensome, or that the grant of permission is an appropriate exercise of the court's equitable powers; or

(5)   liability is imposed on the partner by law or contract independent of the existence of the partnership.

(e)   This section applies to any partnership liability or obligation resulting from a representation by a partner or purported partner under Section 308.

COMMENT

1.   Section 307 is new. Subsection (a) provides that a partnership may sue and be sued in the partnership name. That entity approach is designed to simplify suits by and against a partnership.

At common law, a partnership, not being a legal entity, could not sue or be sued in the firm name. The UPA itself is silent on this point, so in the absence of another enabling statute, it is generally necessary to join all the partners in an action against the partnership.

Most States have statutes or rules authorizing partnerships to sue or be sued in the partnership name. Many of those statutes, however, are found in the state provisions dealing with civil procedure rather than in the partnership act.

2.   Subsection (b) provides that suit generally may be brought against the partnership and any or all of the partners in the same action or in separate actions. It is intended to clarify that the partners need not be named in an action against the partnership. In particular, in an action against a partnership, it is not necessary to name a partner individually in addition to the partnership. This will simplify and reduce the cost of litigation, especially in cases of small claims where there are known to be significant partnership assets and thus no necessity to collect the judgment out of the partners' assets.

Where the partnership is a limited liability partnership, the limited liability partnership rules clarify that a partner not liable for the alleged partnership obligation may not be named in the action against the partnership unless the action also seeks to establish personal liability of the partner for the obligation. *See* subsections (b) and (d).

3.   Subsection (c) provides that a judgment against the partnership is not, standing alone, a judgment against the partners, and it cannot be satisfied from a partner's personal assets unless there is a judgment against the partner. Thus, a partner must be individually named and served, either in the action against the partnership or in a later suit, before his personal assets may be subject to levy for a claim against the partnership.

RUPA leaves it to the law of judgments, as did the UPA, to determine the collateral effects to be accorded a prior judgment for or against the partnership in a subsequent action against a partner individually. *See* Section 60 of the Second Restatement of Judgments (1982) and the Comments thereto.

4.   Subsection (d) requires partnership creditors to exhaust the partnership's assets before levying on a judgment debtor partner's individual property where the partner is personally liable for the partnership obligation under Section 306. That rule respects the concept of the partnership as an entity and makes partners more in the nature of guarantors than principal debtors on every partnership debt. It is already the law in some States.

As a general rule, a final judgment against a partner cannot be enforced by a creditor against the partner's separate assets unless a writ of execution against the partnership has been returned unsatisfied. Under subsection (d), however, a creditor may proceed directly against the partner's assets if (i) the partnership is a debtor in bankruptcy (*see* Section 101(2)); (ii) the partner has consented; or (iii) the liability is imposed on the partner independently of the partnership. For example, a judgment creditor may proceed directly against the assets of a partner who is liable independently as the primary tortfeasor, but must exhaust the partnership's assets before proceeding against the separate assets of the other partners who are liable only as partners.

There is also a judicial override provision in subsection (d)(4). A court may authorize execution against the partner's assets on the grounds that (i) the partnership's assets are clearly insufficient; (ii) exhaustion of the partnership's assets would be excessively burdensome; or (iii) it is otherwise equitable to do so. For example, if the partners who are parties to the action have assets located in the forum State, but the partnership does not, a court might find that exhaustion of the partnership's assets would be excessively burdensome.

5.   Although subsection (d) is silent with respect to pre-judgment remedies, the law of pre-judgment remedies already adequately embodies the principle that partnership assets should be exhausted before partners' assets are attached or garnished. Attachment, for example, typically requires a showing that the partnership's assets are being secreted or fraudulently transferred or are otherwise inadequate to satisfy the plaintiff's claim. A showing of some exigent circumstance may also be required to satisfy due process. *See Connecticut v. Doehr*, 501 U.S. 1, 16 (1991).

6.   Subsection (e) clarifies that actions against the partnership under Section 308, involving representations by partners or purported partners, are subject to Section 307.

§ 308.   Liability of Purported Partner

(a)   If a person, by words or conduct, purports to be a partner, or consents to being represented by another as a partner, in a partnership or with one or more persons not partners, the purported partner is liable to a person to whom the representation is made, if that person, relying on the representation, enters into a transaction with the actual or purported partnership. If the representation, either by the purported partner or by a person with the purported partner's consent, is made in a public manner, the purported partner is liable to a person who relies upon the purported partnership even if the purported partner is not aware of being held out as a partner to the claimant. If partnership liability results, the purported partner is liable with respect to that liability as if the purported partner were a partner. If no partnership liability results, the purported partner is liable with respect to that liability jointly and severally with any other person consenting to the representation.

(b)   If a person is thus represented to be a partner in an existing partnership, or with one or more persons not partners, the purported partner is an agent of persons consenting to the representation to bind them to the same extent and in the same manner as if the purported partner were a partner, with respect to persons who enter into transactions in reliance upon the representation. If all of the partners of the existing partnership consent to the representation, a partnership act or obligation results. If fewer than all of the partners of the existing partnership consent to the representation, the person acting and the partners consenting to the representation are jointly and severally liable.

(c)   A person is not liable as a partner merely because the person is named by another in a statement of partnership authority.

(d)   A person does not continue to be liable as a partner merely because of a failure to file a statement of dissociation or to amend a statement of partnership authority to indicate the partner's dissociation from the partnership.

(e)   Except as otherwise provided in subsections (a) and (b), persons who are not partners as to each other are not liable as partners to other persons.

COMMENT

Section 308 continues the basic principles of partnership by estoppel from UPA Section 16, now more accurately entitled "Liability of Purported Partner." Subsection (a) continues the distinction between representations made to specific persons and those made in a public manner. It is the exclusive basis for imposing liability as a partner on persons who are not partners in fact. As under the UPA, there is no duty of denial, and thus a person held out by another as a partner is not liable unless he actually consents to the representation. *See* the Official Comment to UPA Section 16. *Also see* Section 308(c) (no duty to file statement of denial) and Section 308(d) (no duty to file statement of dissociation or to amend statement of partnership authority).

Subsection (b) emphasizes that the persons being protected by Section 308 are those who enter into transactions in reliance upon a representation. If all of the partners of an existing partnership consent to the representation, a partnership obligation results. Apart from Section 308, the firm may be bound in other situations under general principles of apparent authority or ratification.

If a partnership liability results under Section 308, the creditor must exhaust the partnership's assets before seeking to satisfy the claim from the partners. *See* Section 307.

Subsections (c) and (d) are new and deal with potential negative inferences to be drawn from a failure to correct inaccurate or outdated filed statements. Subsection (c) makes clear that an otherwise innocent person is not liable as a partner for failing to deny his partnership status as asserted by a third person in a statement of partnership authority. Under subsection (d), a partner's liability as a partner does not continue after dissociation solely because of a failure to file a statement of dissociation.

Subsection (e) is derived from UPA Section 7(1). It means that only those persons who are partners as among themselves are liable as partners to third parties for the obligations of the partnership, except for liabilities incurred by purported partners under Section 308(a) and (b).

ARTICLE 4.   RELATIONS OF PARTNERS TO EACH OTHER AND TO PARTNERSHIP

§ 401.   Partner's Rights and Duties

(a)   Each partner is deemed to have an account that is:

(1)   credited with an amount equal to the money plus the value of any other property, net of the amount of any liabilities, the partner contributes to the partnership and the partner's share of the partnership profits; and

(2)   charged with an amount equal to the money plus the value of any other property, net of the amount of any liabilities, distributed by the partnership to the partner and the partner's share of the partnership losses.

(b)   Each partner is entitled to an equal share of the partnership profits and is chargeable with a share of the partnership losses in proportion to the partner's share of the profits.

(c)   A partnership shall reimburse a partner for payments made and indemnify a partner for liabilities incurred by the partner in the ordinary course of the business of the partnership or for the preservation of its business or property.

(d)   A partnership shall reimburse a partner for an advance to the partnership beyond the amount of capital the partner agreed to contribute.

(e)   A payment or advance made by a partner which gives rise to a partnership obligation under subsection (c) or (d) constitutes a loan to the partnership which accrues interest from the date of the payment or advance.

(f)   Each partner has equal rights in the management and conduct of the partnership business.

(g)   A partner may use or possess partnership property only on behalf of the partnership.

(h)   A partner is not entitled to remuneration for services performed for the partnership, except for reasonable compensation for services rendered in winding up the business of the partnership.

(i)   A person may become a partner only with the consent of all of the partners.

(j)   A difference arising as to a matter in the ordinary course of business of a partnership may be decided by a majority of the partners. An act outside the ordinary course of business of a partnership and an amendment to the partnership agreement may be undertaken only with the consent of all of the partners.

(k)   This section does not affect the obligations of a partnership to other persons under Section 301.

COMMENT

1.   Section 401 is drawn substantially from UPA Section 18. It establishes many of the default rules that govern the relations among partners. All of these rules are, however, subject to contrary agreement of the partners as provided in Section 103.

2.   Subsection (a) provides that each partner is deemed to have an account that is credited with the partner's contributions and share of the partnership profits and charged with distributions to the partner and the partner's share of partnership losses. In the absence of another system of partnership accounts, these rules establish a rudimentary system of accounts for the partnership. The rules regarding the settlement of the partners' accounts upon the dissolution and winding up of the partnership business are found in Section 807.

3.   Subsection (b) establishes the default rules for the sharing of partnership profits and losses. The UPA Section 18(a) rules that profits are shared equally and that losses, whether capital or operating, are shared in proportion to each partner's share of the profits are continued. Thus, under the default rule, partners share profits per capita and not in proportion to capital contribution as do corporate shareholders or partners in limited partnerships. *Compare* RULPA Section 504. With respect to losses, the qualifying phrase, "whether capital or operating," has been deleted as inconsistent with contemporary partnership accounting practice and terminology; no substantive change is intended.

If partners agree to share profits other than equally, losses will be shared similarly to profits, absent agreement to do otherwise. That rule, carried over from the UPA, is predicated on the assumption that partners would likely agree to share losses on the same basis as profits, but may fail to say so. Of course, by agreement, they may share losses on a different basis from profits.

The default rules apply, as does UPA Section 18(a), where one or more of the partners contribute no capital, although there is case law to the contrary. *See, e.g., Kovacik v. Reed*, 49 Cal. 2d 166, 315 P.2d 314 (1957); *Becker v. Killarney*, 177 Ill. App. 3d 793, 523 N.E.2d 467 (1988). It may seem unfair that the contributor of services, who contributes little or no capital, should be obligated to contribute toward the capital loss of the large contributor who contributed no services. In entering a partnership with such a capital structure, the partners should foresee that application of the default rule may bring about unusual results and take advantage of their power to vary by agreement the allocation of capital losses.

Subsection (b) provides that each partner "is chargeable" with a share of the losses, rather than the UPA formulation that each partner shall "contribute" to losses. Losses are charged to each partner's account as provided in subsection (a)(2). It is intended to make clear that a partner is not obligated to contribute to partnership losses before his withdrawal or the liquidation of the partnership, unless the partners agree otherwise. In effect, unless related to an obligation for which the partner is not personally liable under Section 306(c), a partner's negative account represents a debt to the partnership unless the partners agree to the contrary. Similarly, each partner's share of the profits is credited to his account under subsection (a)(1). Absent an agreement to the contrary, however, a partner does not have a right to receive a current distribution of the profits credited to his account, the interim distribution of profits being a matter arising in the ordinary course of business to be decided by majority vote of the partners.

However, where a liability to contribute at dissolution and winding up relates to a partnership obligation governed by the limited liability rule of Section 306(c), a partner is not obligated to contribute additional assets even at dissolution and winding up. *See* Section 807(b). In such a case, although a partner is not personally liable for the partnership obligation, that partner's interest in the partnership remains at risk. *See also* Comment to Section 401(c) relating to indemnification.

In the case of an operating limited liability partnership, the Section 306 liability shield may be partially eroded where the limited liability partnership incurs both shielded and unshielded liabilities. Where the limited liability partnership uses its assets to pay shielded liabilities before paying unshielded liabilities, each partner's obligation to contribute to the limited liability partnership for that partner's share of the unpaid and unshielded obligations at dissolution and winding up remains intact. The same issue is less likely to occur in the context of the termination of a limited liability partnership since a partner's contribution obligation is based only on that partner's share of unshielded obligations and the partnership will ordinarily use the contributed assets to pay unshielded claims first as they were the basis of the contribution obligations. *See* Comments to Section 807(b).

4.   Subsection (c) is derived from UPA Section 18(b) and provides that the partnership shall reimburse partners for payments made and indemnify them for liabilities incurred in the ordinary course of the partnership's business or for the preservation of its business or property. Reimbursement and indemnification is an obligation of the partnership. Indemnification may create a loss toward which the partners must contribute. Although the right to indemnification is usually enforced in the settlement of accounts among partners upon dissolution and winding up of the partnership business, the right accrues when the liability is incurred and thus may be enforced during the term of the partnership in an appropriate case. *See* Section 405 and Comment. A partner's right to indemnification under this Act is not affected by the partnership becoming a limited liability partnership. Accordingly, partners continue to share partnership losses to the extent of partnership assets.

5.   Subsection (d) is based on UPA Section 18(c). It makes explicit that the partnership must reimburse a partner for an advance of funds beyond the amount of the partner's agreed capital contribution, thereby treating the advance as a loan.

6.   Subsection (e), which is also drawn from UPA Section 18(c), characterizes the partnership's obligation under subsection (c) or (d) as a loan to the partnership which accrues interest from the date of the payment or advance. *See* Section 104(b) (default rate of interest).

7.   Under subsection (f), each partner has equal rights in the management and conduct of the business. It is based on UPA Section 18(e), which has been interpreted broadly to mean that, absent contrary agreement, each partner has a continuing right to participate in the management of the partnership and to be informed about the partnership business, even if his assent to partnership business decisions is not required. There are special rules regarding the partner vote necessary to approve a partnership becoming (or canceling its status as) a limited liability partnership. *See* Section 1001(b).

8.   Subsection (g) provides that partners may use or possess partnership property only for partnership purposes. That is the edited remains of UPA Section 25(2)(a), which deals in detail with the incidents of tenancy in partnership. That tenancy is abolished as a consequence of the entity theory of partnerships. *See* Section 501 and Comments.

9.   Subsection (h) continues the UPA Section 18(f) rule that a partner is not entitled to remuneration for services performed, except in winding up the partnership. Subsection (h) deletes the UPA reference to a "surviving" partner. That means any partner winding up the business is entitled to compensation, not just a surviving partner winding up after the death of another partner. The exception is not intended to apply in the hypothetical winding up that takes place if there is a buyout under Article 7.

10.   Subsection (i) continues the substance of UPA Section 18(g) that no person can become a partner without the consent of all the partners.

11.   Subsection (j) continues with one important clarification the UPA Section 18(h) scheme of allocating management authority among the partners. In the absence of an agreement to the contrary, matters arising in the ordinary course of the business may be decided by a majority of the partners. Amendments to the partnership agreement and matters outside the ordinary course of the partnership business require unanimous consent of the partners. Although the text of the UPA is silent regarding extraordinary matters, courts have generally required the consent of all partners for those matters. *See, e.g., Paciaroni v. Crane,* 408 A.2d 946 (Del. Ch. 1989); *Thomas v. Marvin E. Jewell & Co.,* 232 Neb. 261, 440 N.W.2d 437 (1989); *Duell v. Hancock,* 83 A.D.2d 762, 443 N.Y.S.2d 490 (1981).

It is not intended that subsection (j) embrace a claim for an objection to a partnership decision that is not discovered until after the fact. There is no cause of action based on that after-the-fact second-guessing.

12.   Subsection (k) is new and was added to make it clear that Section 301 governs partners' agency power to bind the partnership to third persons, while Section 401 governs partners' rights among themselves.

§ 402.   Distributions in Kind

A partner has no right to receive, and may not be required to accept, a distribution in kind.

COMMENT

Section 402 provides that a partner has no right to demand and receive a distribution in kind and may not be required to take a distribution in kind. That continues the "in kind" rule of UPA Section 38(*l*). The new language is suggested by RULPA Section 605.

This section is complemented by Section 807(a) which provides that, in winding up the partnership business on dissolution, any surplus after the payment of partnership obligations must be applied to pay in cash the net amount distributable to each partner.

§ 403.   Partner's Rights and Duties with Respect to Information

(a)   A partnership shall keep its books and records, if any, at its chief executive office.

(b)   A partnership shall provide partners and their agents and attorneys access to its books and records. It shall provide former partners and their agents and attorneys access to books and records pertaining to the period during which they were partners. The right of access provides the opportunity to inspect and copy books and records during ordinary business hours. A partnership may impose a reasonable charge, covering the costs of labor and material, for copies of documents furnished.

(c)   Each partner and the partnership shall furnish to a partner, and to the legal representative of a deceased partner or partner under legal disability:

(1)   without demand, any information concerning the partnership's business and affairs reasonably required for the proper exercise of the partner's rights and duties under the partnership agreement or this [Act]; and

(2)   on demand, any other information concerning the partnership's business and affairs, except to the extent the demand or the information demanded is unreasonable or otherwise improper under the circumstances.

COMMENT

1.   Subsection (a) provides that the partnership's books and records, if any, shall be kept at its chief executive office. It continues the UPA Section 19 rule, modified to include partnership records other than its "books," i.e., financial records. The concept of "chief executive office" comes from UCC Section 9–103(3)(d). *See* the Comment to Section 106.

Since general partnerships are often informal or even inadvertent, no books and records are enumerated as mandatory, such as that found in RULPA Section 105. Any requirement in UPA Section 19 that the partnership keep books is oblique at best, since it states merely where the books shall be kept, not that they shall be kept. Under RUPA, there is no liability to either partners or third parties for the failure to keep partnership books. A partner who undertakes to keep books, however, must do so accurately and adequately.

In general, a partnership should, at a minimum, keep those books and records necessary to enable the partners to determine their share of the profits and losses, as well as their rights on withdrawal. An action for an accounting provides an adequate remedy in the event adequate records are not kept. The partnership must also maintain any books and records required by state or federal taxing or other governmental authorities.

2.   Under subsection (b), partners are entitled to access to the partnership books and records. Former partners are expressly given a similar right, although limited to the books and records pertaining to the period during which they were partners. The line between partners and former partners is not a bright one for this purpose, however, and should be drawn in light of the legitimate interests of a dissociated partner in the partnership. For example, a withdrawing partner's liability is ongoing for pre-withdrawal liabilities and will normally be extended to new liabilities for at least 90 days. It is intended that a former partner be accorded access to partnership books and records as reasonably necessary to protect that partner's legitimate interests during the period his rights and liabilities are being wound down.

The right of access is limited to ordinary business hours, and the right to inspect and copy by agent or attorney is made explicit. The partnership may impose a reasonable charge for furnishing copies of documents. *Accord*, RULPA § 105(b).

A partner's right to inspect and copy the partnership's books and records is not conditioned on the partner's purpose or motive. *Compare* RMBCA Section 16.02(c)(*l*) (shareholder must have proper purpose to inspect certain corporate records). A partner's unlimited personal liability justifies an unqualified right of access to the partnership books and records. An abuse of the right to inspect and copy might constitute a violation of the obligation of good faith and fair dealing for which the other partners would have a remedy. *See* Sections 404(d) and 405.

Under Section 103(b)(2), a partner's right of access to partnership books and records may not be unreasonably restricted by the partnership agreement. Thus, to preserve a partner's core information rights despite unequal bargaining power, an agreement limiting a partner's right to inspect and copy partnership books and records is subject to judicial review. Nevertheless, reasonable restrictions on access to partnership books and records by agreement are authorized. For example, a provision in a partnership agreement denying partners access to the compensation of other partners should be upheld, absent any abuse such as fraud or duress.

3.   Subsection (c) is a significant revision of UPA Section 20 and provides a more comprehensive, although not exclusive, statement of partners' rights and duties with respect to partnership information other than books and records. Both the partnership and the other partners are obligated to furnish partnership information.

Paragraph (1) is new and imposes an affirmative disclosure obligation on the partnership and partners. There is no express UPA provision imposing an affirmative obligation to disclose any information other than the partnership books. Under some circumstances, however, an affirmative disclosure duty has been inferred from other sections of the Act, as well as from the common law, such as the fiduciary duty of good faith. Under UPA Section 18(e), for example, all partners enjoy an equal right in the management and conduct of the partnership business, absent contrary agreement. That right has been construed to require that every partner be provided with ongoing information concerning the partnership business. *See* Comment 7 to Section 401. Paragraph (1) provides expressly that partners must be furnished, without demand, partnership information reasonably needed for them to exercise their rights and duties as partners. In addition, a disclosure duty may, under some circumstances, also spring from the Section 404(d) obligation of good faith and fair dealing. *See* Comment 4 to Section 404.

Paragraph (2) continues the UPA rule that partners are entitled, on demand, to any other information concerning the partnership's business and affairs. The demand may be refused if either the demand or the information demanded is unreasonable or otherwise improper. That qualification is new to the statutory formulation. The burden is on the partnership or partner from whom the information is requested to show that the demand is unreasonable or improper. The UPA admonition that the information furnished be "true and full" has been deleted as unnecessary, and no substantive change is intended.

The Section 403(c) information rights can be waived or varied by agreement of the partners, since there is no Section 103(b) limitation on the variation of those rights as there is with respect to the Section 403(b) access rights to books and records. *See* Section 103(b)(2).

§ 404.   General Standards of Partner's Conduct

(a)   The only fiduciary duties a partner owes to the partnership and the other partners are the duty of loyalty and the duty of care set forth in subsections (b) and (c).

(b)   A partner's duty of loyalty to the partnership and the other partners is limited to the following:

(1)   to account to the partnership and hold as trustee for it any property, profit, or benefit derived by the partner in the conduct and winding up of the partnership business or derived from a use by the partner of partnership property, including the appropriation of a partnership opportunity;

(2)   to refrain from dealing with the partnership in the conduct or winding up of the partnership business as or on behalf of a party having an interest adverse to the partnership; and

(3)   to refrain from competing with the partnership in the conduct of the partnership business before the dissolution of the partnership.

(c)   A partner's duty of care to the partnership and the other partners in the conduct and winding up of the partnership business is limited to refraining from engaging in grossly negligent or reckless conduct, intentional misconduct, or a knowing violation of law.

(d)   A partner shall discharge the duties to the partnership and the other partners under this [Act] or under the partnership agreement and exercise any rights consistently with the obligation of good faith and fair dealing.

(e)   A partner does not violate a duty or obligation under this [Act] or under the partnership agreement merely because the partner's conduct furthers the partner's own interest.

(f)   A partner may lend money to and transact other business with the partnership, and as to each loan or transaction the rights and obligations of the partner are the same as those of a person who is not a partner, subject to other applicable law.

(g)   This section applies to a person winding up the partnership business as the personal or legal representative of the last surviving partner as if the person were a partner.

COMMENT

1.   Section 404 is new. The title, "General Standards of Partner's Conduct," is drawn from RMBCA Section 8.30. Section 404 is both comprehensive and exclusive. In that regard, it is structurally different from the UPA which touches only sparingly on a partner's duty of loyalty and leaves any further development of the fiduciary duties of partners to the common law of agency. *Compare* UPA Sections 4(3) and 21.

Section 404 begins by stating that the only fiduciary duties a partner owes to the partnership and the other partners are the duties of loyalty and care set forth in subsections (b) and (c) of the Act. Those duties may not be waived or eliminated in the partnership agreement, but the agreement may identify activities and determine standards for measuring performance of the duties, if not manifestly unreasonable. *See* Sections 103(b)(3)–(5).

Section 404 continues the term "fiduciary" from UPA Section 21, which is entitled "Partner Accountable as a Fiduciary." Arguably, the term "fiduciary" is inappropriate when used to describe the duties of a partner because a partner may legitimately pursue self-interest (*see* Section 404(e)) and not solely the interest of the partnership and the other partners, as must a true trustee. Nevertheless, partners have long been characterized as fiduciaries. *See, e.g., Meinhard v. Salmon,* 249 N.Y. 458, 463, 164 N.E. 545, 546 (1928) (Cardozo, J.). Indeed, the law of partnership reflects the broader law of principal and agent, under which every agent is a fiduciary. *See* Restatement (Second) of Agency § 13 (1957).

2.   Section 404(b) provides three specific rules that comprise a partner's duty of loyalty. Those rules are exclusive and encompass the entire duty of loyalty.

Subsection (b)(*l*) is based on UPA Section 21(1) and continues the rule that partnership property usurped by a partner, including the misappropriation of a partnership opportunity, is held in trust for the partnership. The express reference to the appropriation of a partnership opportunity is new, but merely codifies case law on the point. *See, e.g., Meinhard v. Salmon, supra; Fouchek v. Janicek,* 190 Ore. 251, 225 P.2d 783 (1950). Under a constructive trust theory, the partnership can recover any money or property in the partner's hands that can be traced to the partnership. *See, e.g., Yoder v. Hooper,* 695 P.2d 1182 (Colo. App. 1984), *aff'd,* 737 P.2d 852 (Colo. 1987); *Fortugno v. Hudson Manure Co.,* 51 N.J. Super. 482, 144 A.2d 207 (1958); *Harestad v. Weitzel,* 242 Or. 199, 536 P.2d 522 (1975). As a result, the partnership's claim is greater than that of an ordinary creditor. *See* Official Comment to UPA Section 21.

UPA Section 21(1) imposes the duty on partners to account for profits and benefits in all transactions connected with "the formation, conduct, or liquidation of the partnership." Reference to the "formation" of the partnership has been eliminated by RUPA because of concern that the duty of loyalty could be inappropriately extended to the pre-formation period when the parties are really negotiating at arm's length. *Compare Herring v. Offutt,* 295 A.2d 876 (Ct. App. Md. 1972), *with Phoenix Mutual Life Ins. Co. v. Shady Grove Plaza Limited Partnership,* 734 F. Supp. 1181 (D. Md. 1990), *aff'd,* 937 F.2d 603 (4th Cir. 1991). Once a partnership is agreed to, each partner becomes a fiduciary in the "conduct" of the business. Preformation negotiations are, of course, subject to the general contract obligation to deal honestly and without fraud.

Upon a partner's dissociation, Section 603(b)(3) limits the application of the duty to account for personal profits to those derived from matters arising or events occurring before the dissociation, unless the partner participates in winding up the partnership's business. Thus, after withdrawal, a partner is free to appropriate to his own benefit any new business opportunity thereafter coming to his attention, even if the partnership continues.

Subsection (b)(2) provides that a partner must refrain from dealing with the partnership as or on behalf of a party having an interest adverse to the partnership. This rule is derived from Sections 389 and 391 of the Restatement (Second) of Agency. Comment c to Section 389 explains that the rule is not based upon the harm caused to the principal, but upon avoiding a conflict of opposing interests in the mind of an agent whose duty is to act for the benefit of his principal.

Upon a partner's dissociation, Section 603(b)(3) limits the application of the duty to refrain from representing interests adverse to the partnership to the same extent as the duty to account. Thus, after withdrawal, a partner may deal with the partnership as an adversary with respect to new matters or events.

Section 404(b)(3) provides that a partner must refrain from competing with the partnership in the conduct of its business. This rule is derived from Section 393 of the Restatement (Second) of Agency and is an application of the general duty of an agent to act solely on his principal's behalf.

The duty not to compete applies only to the "conduct" of the partnership business; it does not extend to winding up the business, as do the other loyalty rules. Thus, a partner is free to compete immediately upon an event of dissolution under Section 801, unless the partnership agreement otherwise provides. A partner who dissociates without a winding up of the business resulting is also free to compete, because Section 603(b)(2) provides that the duty not to compete terminates upon dissociation. A dissociated partner is not, however, free to use confidential partnership information after dissociation. *See* Restatement (Second) of Agency § 393 cmt. e (1957). Trade secret law also may apply. *See* the Uniform Trade Secrets Act.

Under Section 103(b)(3), the partnership agreement may not "eliminate" the duty of loyalty. Section 103(b)(3)(i) expressly empowers the partners, however, to identify specific types or categories of activities that do not violate the duty of loyalty, if not manifestly unreasonable. As under UPA Section 21, the other partners may also consent to a specific act or transaction that otherwise violates one of the rules. For the consent to be effective under Section 103(b)(3)(ii), there must be full disclosure of all material facts regarding the act or transaction and the partner's conflict of interest. *See* Comment 5 to Section 103.

3.   Subsection (c) is new and establishes the duty of care that partners owe to the partnership and to the other partners. There is no statutory duty of care under the UPA, although a common law duty of care is recognized by some courts. *See, e.g., Rosenthal v. Rosenthal*, 543 A.2d 348, 352 (Me. 1988) (duty of care limited to acting in a manner that does not constitute gross negligence or willful misconduct).

The standard of care imposed by RUPA is that of gross negligence, which is the standard generally recognized by the courts. *See, e.g., Rosenthal v. Rosenthal, supra*. Section 103(b)(4) provides that the duty of care may not be eliminated entirely by agreement, but the standard may be reasonably reduced. *See* Comment 6 to Section 103.

4.   Subsection (d) is also new. It provides that partners have an obligation of good faith and fair dealing in the discharge of all their duties, including those arising under the Act, such as their fiduciary duties of loyalty and care, and those arising under the partnership agreement. The exercise of any rights by a partner is also subject to the obligation of good faith and fair dealing. The obligation runs to the partnership and to the other partners in all matters related to the conduct and winding up of the partnership business.

The obligation of good faith and fair dealing is a contract concept, imposed on the partners because of the consensual nature of a partnership. *See* Restatement (Second) of Contracts § 205 (1981). It is not characterized, in RUPA, as a fiduciary duty arising out of the partners' special relationship. Nor is it a separate and independent obligation. It is an ancillary obligation that applies whenever a partner discharges a duty or exercises a right under the partnership agreement or the Act.

The meaning of "good faith and fair dealing" is not firmly fixed under present law. "Good faith" clearly suggests a subjective element, while "fair dealing" implies an objective component. It was decided to leave the terms undefined in the Act and allow the courts to develop their meaning based on the experience of real cases. Some commentators, moreover, believe that good faith is more properly understood by what it excludes than by what it includes. *See* Robert S. Summers, *"Good Faith" in General Contract Law and the Sales Provisions of the Uniform Commercial Code*, 54 Va. L. Rev. 195, 262 (1968):

Good faith, as judges generally use the term in matters contractual, is best understood as an "excluder"—a phrase with no general meaning or meanings of its own. Instead, it functions to rule out many different forms of bad faith. It is hard to get this point across to persons used to thinking that every word must have one or more general meanings of its own—must be either univocal or ambiguous.

The UCC definition of "good faith" is honesty in fact and, in the case of a merchant, the observance of reasonable commercial standards of fair dealing in the trade. *See* UCC §§ 1–201(19), 2–103(b). Those definitions were rejected as too narrow or not applicable.

In some situations the obligation of good faith includes a disclosure component. Depending on the circumstances, a partner may have an affirmative disclosure obligation that supplements the Section 403 duty to render information.

Under Section 103(b)(5), the obligation of good faith and fair dealing may not be eliminated by agreement, but the partners by agreement may determine the standards by which the performance of the obligation is to be measured, if the standards are not manifestly unreasonable. *See* Comment 7 to Section 103.

5. Subsection (e) is new and deals expressly with a very basic issue on which the UPA is silent. A partner as such is not a trustee and is not held to the same standards as a trustee. Subsection (e) makes clear that a partner's conduct is not deemed to be improper merely because it serves the partner's own individual interest.

That admonition has particular application to the duty of loyalty and the obligation of good faith and fair dealing. It underscores the partner's rights as an owner and principal in the enterprise, which must always be balanced against his duties and obligations as an agent and fiduciary. For example, a partner who, with consent, owns a shopping center may, under subsection (e), legitimately vote against a proposal by the partnership to open a competing shopping center.

6. Subsection (f) authorizes partners to lend money to and transact other business with the partnership and, in so doing, to enjoy the same rights and obligations as a nonpartner. That language is drawn from RULPA Section 107. The rights and obligations of a partner doing business with the partnership as an outsider are expressly made subject to the usual laws governing those transactions. They include, for example, rules limiting or qualifying the rights and remedies of inside creditors, such as fraudulent transfer law, equitable subordination, and the law of avoidable preferences, as well as general debtor-creditor law. The reference to "other applicable law" makes clear that subsection (f) is not intended to displace those laws, and thus they are preserved under Section 104(a).

It is unclear under the UPA whether a partner may, for the partner's own account, purchase the assets of the partnership at a foreclosure sale or upon the liquidation of the partnership. Those purchases are clearly within subsection (f)'s broad approval. It is also clear under that subsection that a partner may purchase partnership assets at a foreclosure sale, whether the partner is the mortgagee or the mortgagee is an unrelated third party. Similarly, a partner may purchase partnership property at a tax sale. The obligation of good faith requires disclosure of the partner's interest in the transaction, however.

7. Subsection (g) provides that the prescribed standards of conduct apply equally to a person engaged in winding up the partnership business as the personal or legal representative of the last surviving partner, as if the person were a partner. This is derived from UPA Section 21(2), but now embraces the duty of care and the obligation of good faith and fair dealing, as well as the duty of loyalty.

§ 405.   Actions by Partnership and Partners

(a) A partnership may maintain an action against a partner for a breach of the partnership agreement, or for the violation of a duty to the partnership, causing harm to the partnership.

(b) A partner may maintain an action against the partnership or another partner for legal or equitable relief, with or without an accounting as to partnership business, to:

(1) enforce the partner's rights under the partnership agreement;

(2) enforce the partner's rights under this [Act], including:

(i) the partner's rights under Sections 401, 403, or 404;

(ii) the partner's right on dissociation to have the partner's interest in the partnership purchased pursuant to Section 701 or enforce any other right under Article 6 or 7; or

(iii) the partner's right to compel a dissolution and winding up of the partnership business under Section 801 or enforce any other right under Article 8; or

(3)   enforce the rights and otherwise protect the interests of the partner, including rights and interests arising independently of the partnership relationship.

(c)   The accrual of, and any time limitation on, a right of action for a remedy under this section is governed by other law. A right to an accounting upon a dissolution and winding up does not revive a claim barred by law.

COMMENT

1.   Section 405(a) is new and reflects the entity theory of partnership. It provides that the partnership itself may maintain an action against a partner for any breach of the partnership agreement or for the violation of any duty owed to the partnership, such as a breach of fiduciary duty.

2.   Section 405(b) is the successor to UPA Section 22, but with significant changes. At common law, an accounting was generally not available before dissolution. That was modified by UPA Section 22 which specifies certain circumstances in which an accounting action is available without requiring a partner to dissolve the partnership. Section 405(b) goes far beyond the UPA rule. It provides that, during the term of the partnership, partners may maintain a variety of legal or equitable actions, including an action for an accounting, as well as a final action for an accounting upon dissolution and winding up. It reflects a new policy choice that partners should have access to the courts during the term of the partnership to resolve claims against the partnership and the other partners, leaving broad judicial discretion to fashion appropriate remedies.

Under RUPA, an accounting is not a prerequisite to the availability of the other remedies a partner may have against the partnership or the other partners. That change reflects the increased willingness courts have shown to grant relief without the requirement of an accounting, in derogation of the so-called "exclusivity rule." *See, e.g., Farney v. Hauser*, 109 Kan. 75, 79, 198 Pac. 178, 180 (1921) ("[For] all practical purposes a partnership may be considered as a business entity"); *Auld v. Estridge*, 86 Misc. 2d 895, 901, 382 N.Y.S.2d 897, 901 (1976) ("No purpose of justice is served by delaying the resolution here on empty procedural grounds").

Under subsection (b), a partner may bring a direct suit against the partnership or another partner for almost any cause of action arising out of the conduct of the partnership business. That eliminates the present procedural barriers to suits between partners filed independently of an accounting action. In addition to a formal account, the court may grant any other appropriate legal or equitable remedy. Since general partners are not passive investors like limited partners, RUPA does not authorize derivative actions, as does RULPA Section 1001.

Subsection (b)(3) makes it clear that a partner may recover against the partnership and the other partners for personal injuries or damage to the property of the partner caused by another partner. *See, e.g., Duffy v. Piazza Construction Co.*, 815 P.2d 267 (Wash. App. 1991); *Smith v. Hensley*, 354 S.W.2d 744 (Ky. App.). One partner's negligence is not imputed to bar another partner's action. *See, e.g., Reeves v. Harmon*, 475 P.2d 400 (Okla. 1970); *Eagle Star Ins. Co. v. Bean*, 134 F.2d 755 (9th Cir. 1943) (fire insurance company not subrogated to claim against partners who negligently caused fire that damaged partnership property).

3.   Generally, partners may limit or contract away their Section 405 remedies. They may not, however, eliminate entirely the remedies for breach of those duties that are mandatory under Section 103(b). *See* Comment 1 to Section 103.

4.   Section 405(c) replaces UPA Section 43 and provides that other (i.e., non-partnership) law governs the accrual of a cause of action for which subsection (b) provides a remedy. The statute of limitations on such claims is also governed by other law, and claims barred by a statute of limitations are not revived by reason of the partner's right to an accounting upon dissolution, as they were under the UPA. The effect of those rules is to compel partners to litigate their claims during the life of the partnership or risk losing them. Because an accounting is an equitable proceeding, it may also be barred by laches where there is an undue delay in bringing the action. Under general law, the limitations periods may be tolled by a partner's fraud.

5. UPA Section 39 grants ancillary remedies to a person who rescinds his participation in a partnership because it was fraudulently induced, including the right to a lien on surplus partnership property for the amount of that person's interest in the partnership. RUPA has no counterpart provision to UPA Section 39, and leaves it to the general law of rescission to determine the rights of a person fraudulently induced to invest in a partnership. *See* Section 104(a).

§ 406. Continuation of Partnership Beyond Definite Term or Particular Undertaking

(a) If a partnership for a definite term or particular undertaking is continued, without an express agreement, after the expiration of the term or completion of the undertaking, the rights and duties of the partners remain the same as they were at the expiration or completion, so far as is consistent with a partnership at will.

(b) If the partners, or those of them who habitually acted in the business during the term or undertaking, continue the business without any settlement or liquidation of the partnership, they are presumed to have agreed that the partnership will continue.

COMMENT

Section 406 continues UPA Section 23, with no substantive change. Subsection (a) provides that, if a term partnership is continued without an express agreement beyond the expiration of its term or the completion of the undertaking, the partners' rights and duties remain the same as they were, so far as is consistent with a partnership at will.

Subsection (b) provides that if the partnership is continued by the partners without any settlement or liquidation of the business, it is presumed that the partners have agreed not to wind up the business. The presumption is rebuttable. If the partnership is continued under this subsection, there is no dissolution under (2)(iii). As a partnership at will, however, the partnership may be dissolved under (1) at any time.

ARTICLE 5. TRANSFEREES AND CREDITORS OF PARTNER

§ 501. Partner not Co-owner of Partnership Property

A partner is not a co-owner of partnership property and has no interest in partnership property which can be transferred, either voluntarily or involuntarily.

COMMENT

Section 501 provides that a partner is not a co-owner of partnership property and has no interest in partnership property that can be transferred, either voluntarily or involuntarily. Thus, the section abolishes the UPA Section 25(1) concept of tenants in partnership and reflects the adoption of the entity theory. Partnership property is owned by the entity and not by the individual partners. *See also* Section 203, which provides that property transferred to or otherwise acquired by the partnership is property of the partnership and not of the partners individually.

RUPA also deletes the references in UPA Sections 24 and 25 to a partner's "right in specific partnership property," although those rights are largely defined away by the detailed rules of UPA Section 25 itself. Thus, it is clear that a partner who misappropriates partnership property is guilty of embezzlement the same as a shareholder who misappropriates corporate property.

Adoption of the entity theory also has the effect of protecting partnership property from execution or other process by a partner's personal creditors. That continues the result under UPA Section 25(2)(c). Those creditors may seek a charging order under Section 504 to reach the partner's transferable interest in the partnership.

RUPA does not interfere with a partner's exemption claim in nonpartnership property. As under the UPA, disputes over whether specific property belongs to the partner or to the firm will likely arise in the context of an exemption claim by a partner.

A partner's spouse, heirs, or next of kin are not entitled to allowances or other rights in partnership property. That continues the result under UPA Section 25(2)(e).

§ 502.   Partner's Transferable Interest in Partnership

The only transferable interest of a partner in the partnership is the partner's share of the profits and losses of the partnership and the partner's right to receive distributions. The interest is personal property.

COMMENT

Section 502 continues the UPA Section 26 concept that a partner's only transferable interest in the partnership is the partner's share of profits and losses and right to receive distributions, that is, the partner's financial rights. The term "distribution" is defined in Section 101(3). *Compare* RULPA Section 101(10) ("partnership interest").

The partner's transferable interest is deemed to be personal property, regardless of the nature of the underlying partnership assets.

Under Section 503(b)(3), a transferee of a partner's transferable interest has standing to seek judicial dissolution of the partnership business.

A partner has other interests in the partnership that may not be transferred, such as the right to participate in the management of the business. Those rights are included in the broader concept of a "partner's interest in the partnership." *See* Section 101(9).

§ 503.   Transfer of Partner's Transferable Interest

(a) A transfer, in whole or in part, of a partner's transferable interest in the partnership:

(1) is permissible;

(2) does not by itself cause the partner's dissociation or a dissolution and winding up of the partnership business; and

(3) does not, as against the other partners or the partnership, entitle the transferee, during the continuance of the partnership, to participate in the management or conduct of the partnership business, to require access to information concerning partnership transactions, or to inspect or copy the partnership books or records.

(b) A transferee of a partner's transferable interest in the partnership has a right:

(1) to receive, in accordance with the transfer, distributions to which the transferor would otherwise be entitled;

(2) to receive upon the dissolution and winding up of the partnership business, in accordance with the transfer, the net amount otherwise distributable to the transferor; and

(3) to seek under Section 801(6) a judicial determination that it is equitable to wind up the partnership business.

(c) In a dissolution and winding up, a transferee is entitled to an account of partnership transactions only from the date of the latest account agreed to by all of the partners.

(d) Upon transfer, the transferor retains the rights and duties of a partner other than the interest in distributions transferred.

(e) A partnership need not give effect to a transferee's rights under this section until it has notice of the transfer.

(f) A transfer of a partner's transferable interest in the partnership in violation of a restriction on transfer contained in the partnership agreement is ineffective as to a person having notice of the restriction at the time of transfer.

COMMENT

1.   Section 503 is derived from UPA Section 27. Subsection (a)(1) states explicitly that a partner has the right to transfer his transferable interest in the partnership. The term "transfer" is used throughout RUPA in lieu of the term "assignment." *See* Section 101(10).

Subsection (a)(2) continues the UPA Section 27(1) rule that an assignment of a partner's interest in the partnership does not of itself cause a winding up of the partnership business. Under Section 601(4)(ii), however, a partner who has transferred substantially all of his partnership interest may be expelled by the other partners.

Subsection (a)(3), which is also derived from UPA Section 27(*l*), provides that a transferee is not, as against the other partners, entitled (i) to participate in the management or conduct of the partnership business; (ii) to inspect the partnership books or records; or (iii) to require any information concerning or an account of partnership transactions.

2.   The rights of a transferee are set forth in subsection (b). Under subsection (b)(1), which is derived from UPA Section 27(*l*), a transferee is entitled to receive, in accordance with the terms of the assignment, any distributions to which the transferor would otherwise have been entitled under the partnership agreement before dissolution. After dissolution, the transferee is also entitled to receive, under subsection (b)(2), the net amount that would otherwise have been distributed to the transferor upon the winding up of the business.

Subsection (b)(3) confers standing on a transferee to seek a judicial dissolution and winding up of the partnership business as provided in Section 801(6), thus continuing the rule of UPA Section 32(2).

Section 504(b) accords the rights of a transferee to the purchaser at a sale foreclosing a charging order. The same rule should apply to creditors or other purchasers who acquire partnership interests by pursuing UCC remedies or statutory liens under federal or state law.

3.   Subsection (c) is based on UPA Section 27(2). It grants to transferees the right to an account of partnership transactions, limited to the period since the date of the last account agreed to by all of the partners.

4.   Subsection (d) is new. It makes clear that unless otherwise agreed the partner whose interest is transferred retains all of the rights and duties of a partner, other than the right to receive distributions. That means the transferor is entitled to participate in the management of the partnership and remains personally liable for all partnership obligations, unless and until he withdraws as a partner, is expelled under Section 601(4)(ii), or is otherwise dissociated under Section 601.

A divorced spouse of a partner who is awarded rights in the partner's partnership interest as part of a property settlement is entitled only to the rights of a transferee. The spouse may instead be granted a money judgment in the amount of the property award, enforceable by a charging order in the same manner as any other money judgment against a partner. In neither case, however, would the spouse become a partner by virtue of the property settlement or succeed to any of the partner's management rights. *See, e.g., Warren v. Warren*, 12 Ark. App. 260, 675 S.W.2d 371 (1984).

5.   Subsection (e) is new and provides that the partnership has no duty to give effect to the transferee's rights until the partnership receives notice of the transfer. This is consistent with UCC Section 9–318(3), which provides that an "account debtor" is authorized to pay the assignor until the account debtor receives notification that the amount due or to become due has been assigned and that payment is to be made to the assignee. It further provides that the assignee, on request, must furnish reasonable proof of the assignment.

6.   Subsection (f) is new and provides that a transfer of a partner's transferable interest in the partnership in violation of a restriction on transfer contained in a partnership agreement is ineffective as to a person with timely notice of the restriction. Under Section 103(a), the partners may agree among themselves to restrict the right to transfer their partnership interests. Subsection (f) makes explicit that a transfer in violation of such a restriction is ineffective as to a transferee with notice of the restriction. *See* Section 102(b) for the meaning of "notice." RUPA leaves to general law and the UCC the issue of whether a transfer in violation of a valid restriction is effective as to a transferee without notice of the restriction.

Whether a particular restriction will be enforceable, however, must be considered in light of other law. *See* 11 U.S.C. § 541(c)(1) (property owned by bankrupt passes to trustee regardless of restrictions on transfer); UCC § 9–318(4) (agreement between account debtor and assignor prohibiting creation of security interest in a general intangible or requiring account debtor's consent is ineffective); *Battista v. Carlo*, 57 Misc. 2d 495, 293 N.Y.S.2d 227 (1968) (restriction on transfer of partnership interest subject to rules against unreasonable restraints on alienation of property) (dictum); *Tupper v. Kroc*, 88 Nev. 146, 494 P.2d 1275 (1972) (partnership interest subject to charging order even if partnership agreement prohibits assignments). *Cf. Tu-Vu Drive-In Corp. v. Ashkins*, 61 Cal. 2d 283, 38 Cal. Rptr. 348, 391 P.2d 828 (1964) (restraints on transfer of corporate stock must be reasonable). Even if a restriction on the transfer of a partner's transferable interest in a partnership were held to be unenforceable, the transfer might be grounds for expelling the partner-transferor from the partnership under Section 601(5)(ii).

7.　　Other rules that apply in the case of transfers include Section 601(4)(ii) (expulsion of partner who transfers substantially all of partnership interest); Section 601(6) (dissociation of partner who makes an assignment for benefit of creditors); and Section 801(6) (transferee has standing to seek judicial winding up).

§ 504.　　Partner's Transferable Interest Subject to Charging Order

(a)　On application by a judgment creditor of a partner or of a partner's transferee, a court having jurisdiction may charge the transferable interest of the judgment debtor to satisfy the judgment. The court may appoint a receiver of the share of the distributions due or to become due to the judgment debtor in respect of the partnership and make all other orders, directions, accounts, and inquiries the judgment debtor might have made or which the circumstances of the case may require.

(b)　A charging order constitutes a lien on the judgment debtor's transferable interest in the partnership. The court may order a foreclosure of the interest subject to the charging order at any time. The purchaser at the foreclosure sale has the rights of a transferee.

(c)　At any time before foreclosure, an interest charged may be redeemed:

(1)　by the judgment debtor;

(2)　with property other than partnership property, by one or more of the other partners; or

(3)　with partnership property, by one or more of the other partners with the consent of all of the partners whose interests are not so charged.

(d)　This [Act] does not deprive a partner of a right under exemption laws with respect to the partner's interest in the partnership.

(e)　This section provides the exclusive remedy by which a judgment creditor of a partner or partner's transferee may satisfy a judgment out of the judgment debtor's transferable interest in the partnership.

COMMENT

1.　　Section 504 continues the UPA Section 28 charging order as the proper remedy by which a judgment creditor of a partner may reach the debtor's transferable interest in a partnership to satisfy the judgment. Subsection (a) makes the charging order available to the judgment creditor of a transferee of a partnership interest. Under Section 503(b), the transferable interest of a partner or transferee is limited to the partner's right to receive distributions from the partnership and to seek judicial liquidation of the partnership. The court may appoint a receiver of the debtor's share of the distributions due or to become due and make all other orders that may be required.

2.　　Subsection (b) is new and codifies the case law under the UPA holding that a charging order constitutes a lien on the debtor's transferable interest. The lien may be foreclosed by the court at any time, and the purchaser at the foreclosure sale has the Section 503(b) rights of a transferee. For a general discussion of the charging order remedy, *see* 1 *Alan R. Bromberg & Larry E. Ribstein, Partnership* (1988), at 3:69.

3.   Subsection (c) continues the UPA Section 28(2) right of the debtor or other partners to redeem the partnership interest before the foreclosure sale. Redemption by the partnership (i.e., with partnership property) requires the consent of all the remaining partners. Neither the UPA nor RUPA provide a statutory procedural framework for the redemption.

4.   Subsection (d) provides that nothing in RUPA deprives a partner of his rights under the State's exemption laws. That is essentially the same as UPA Section 28(3).

5.   Subsection (e) provides that the charging order is the judgment creditor's exclusive remedy. Although the UPA nowhere states that a charging order is the exclusive process for a partner's individual judgment creditor, the courts have generally so interpreted it. *See, e.g., Matter of Pischke*, 11 B.R. 913 (E.D. Va. 1981); *Baum v. Baum*, 51 Cal. 2d 610, 335 P.2d 481 (1959); *Atlantic Mobile Homes, Inc. v. LeFever*, 481 So. 2d 1002 (Fla. App. 1986).

Notwithstanding subsection (e), there may be an exception for the enforcement of family support orders. Some States have unique statutory procedures for the enforcement of support orders. In Florida, for example, a court may issue an "income deduction order" requiring any person or entity providing "income" to the obligor of a support order to remit to the obligee or a depository, as directed by the court, a specified portion of the income. Fla. Stat. § 61.1301 (1993). "Income" is broadly defined to include any form of payment to the obligor, including wages, salary, compensation as an independent contractor, dividends, interest, or other payment, regardless of source. Fla. Stat. § 61.046(4) (1993). That definition includes distributions payable to an obligor partner. A charging order under RUPA would still be necessary to reach the obligor's entire partnership interest, however.

ARTICLE 6.   PARTNER'S DISSOCIATION

§ 601.   Events Causing Partner's Dissociation

A partner is dissociated from a partnership upon the occurrence of any of the following events:

(1)   the partnership's having notice of the partner's express will to withdraw as a partner or on a later date specified by the partner;

(2)   an event agreed to in the partnership agreement as causing the partner's dissociation;

(3)   the partner's expulsion pursuant to the partnership agreement;

(4)   the partner's expulsion by the unanimous vote of the other partners if:

(i)   it is unlawful to carry on the partnership business with that partner;

(ii)   there has been a transfer of all or substantially all of that partner's transferable interest in the partnership, other than a transfer for security purposes, or a court order charging the partner's interest, which has not been foreclosed;

(iii)   within 90 days after the partnership notifies a corporate partner that it will be expelled because it has filed a certificate of dissolution or the equivalent, its charter has been revoked, or its right to conduct business has been suspended by the jurisdiction of its incorporation, there is no revocation of the certificate of dissolution or no reinstatement of its charter or its right to conduct business; or

(iv)   a partnership that is a partner has been dissolved and its business is being wound up;

(5)   on application by the partnership or another partner, the partner's expulsion by judicial determination because:

(i)   the partner engaged in wrongful conduct that adversely and materially affected the partnership business;

(ii)   the partner willfully or persistently committed a material breach of the partnership agreement or of a duty owed to the partnership or the other partners under Section 404; or

(iii) the partner engaged in conduct relating to the partnership business which makes it not reasonably practicable to carry on the business in partnership with the partner;

(6) the partner's:

(i) becoming a debtor in bankruptcy;

(ii) executing an assignment for the benefit of creditors;

(iii) seeking, consenting to, or acquiescing in the appointment of a trustee, receiver, or liquidator of that partner or of all or substantially all of that partner's property; or

(iv) failing, within 90 days after the appointment, to have vacated or stayed the appointment of a trustee, receiver, or liquidator of the partner or of all or substantially all of the partner's property obtained without the partner's consent or acquiescence, or failing within 90 days after the expiration of a stay to have the appointment vacated;

(7) in the case of a partner who is an individual:

(i) the partner's death;

(ii) the appointment of a guardian or general conservator for the partner; or

(iii) a judicial determination that the partner has otherwise become incapable of performing the partner's duties under the partnership agreement;

(8) in the case of a partner that is a trust or is acting as a partner by virtue of being a trustee of a trust, distribution of the trust's entire transferable interest in the partnership, but not merely by reason of the substitution of a successor trustee;

(9) in the case of a partner that is an estate or is acting as a partner by virtue of being a personal representative of an estate, distribution of the estate's entire transferable interest in the partnership, but not merely by reason of the substitution of a successor personal representative; or

(10) termination of a partner who is not an individual, partnership, corporation, trust, or estate.

COMMENT

1. RUPA dramatically changes the law governing partnership breakups and dissolution. An entirely new concept, "dissociation," is used in lieu of the UPA term "dissolution" to denote the change in the relationship caused by a partner's ceasing to be associated in the carrying on of the business. "Dissolution" is retained but with a different meaning. *See* Section 802. The entity theory of partnership provides a conceptual basis for continuing the firm itself despite a partner's withdrawal from the firm.

Under RUPA, unlike the UPA, the dissociation of a partner does not necessarily cause a dissolution and winding up of the business of the partnership. Section 801 identifies the situations in which the dissociation of a partner causes a winding up of the business. Section 701 provides that in all other situations there is a buyout of the partner's interest in the partnership, rather than a windup of the partnership business. In those other situations, the partnership entity continues, unaffected by the partner's dissociation.

A dissociated partner remains a partner for some purposes and still has some residual rights, duties, powers, and liabilities. Although Section 601 determines when a partner is dissociated from the partnership, the consequences of the partner's dissociation do not all occur at the same time. Thus, it is more useful to think of a dissociated partner as a partner for some purposes, but as a former partner for others. For example, *see* Section 403(b) (former partner's access to partnership books and records). The consequences of a partner's dissociation depend on whether the partnership continues or is wound up, as provided in Articles 6, 7, and 8.

Section 601 enumerates all of the events that cause a partner's dissociation. Section 601 is similar in approach to RULPA Section 402, which lists the events resulting in a general partner's withdrawal from a limited partnership.

2.   Section 601(1) provides that a partner is dissociated when the partnership has notice of the partner's express will to withdraw as a partner, unless a later date is specified by the partner. If a future date is specified by the partner, other partners may dissociate before that date; specifying a future date does not bind the others to remain as partners until that date. See also Section 801(2)(i).

Section 602(a) provides that a partner has the power to withdraw at any time. The power to withdraw is immutable under Section 103(b)(6), with the exception that the partners may agree the notice must be in writing. This continues the present rule that a partner has the power to withdraw at will, even if not the right. See UPA Section 31(2). Since no writing is required to create a partner relationship, it was felt unnecessarily formalistic, and a trap for the unwary, to require a writing to end one. If a written notification is given, Section 102(d) clarifies when it is deemed received.

RUPA continues the UPA "express will" concept, thus preserving existing case law. Section 601(1) clarifies existing law by providing that the partnership must have notice of the partner's expression of will before the dissociation is effective. See Section 102(b) for the meaning of "notice."

3.   Section 601(2) provides expressly that a partner is dissociated upon an event agreed to in the partnership agreement as causing dissociation. There is no such provision in the UPA, but that result has been assumed.

4.   Section 601(3) provides that a partner may be expelled by the other partners pursuant to a power of expulsion contained in the partnership agreement. That continues the basic rule of UPA Section 31(1)(d). The expulsion can be with or without cause. As under existing law, the obligation of good faith under Section 404(d) does not require prior notice, specification of cause, or an opportunity to be heard. See Holman v. Coie, 11 Wash. App. 195, 522 P.2d 515, cert. denied, 420 U.S. 984 (1974).

5.   Section 601(4) empowers the partners, by unanimous vote, to expel a partner for specified causes, even if not authorized in the partnership agreement. This changes the UPA Section 31(1)(d) rule that authorizes expulsion only if provided in the partnership agreement. A partner may be expelled from a term partnership, as well as from a partnership at will. Under Section 103(a), the partnership agreement may change or abolish the partners' power of expulsion.

Subsection (4)(i) is derived from UPA Section 31(3). A partner may be expelled if it is unlawful to carry on the business with that partner. Section 801(4), on the other hand, provides that the partnership itself is dissolved and must be wound up if substantially all of the business is unlawful.

Subsection (4)(ii) provides that a partner may be expelled for transferring substantially all of his transferable interest in the partnership, other than as security for a loan. (He may, however, be expelled upon foreclosure.) This rule is derived from UPA Section 31(1)(c). To avoid the presence of an unwelcome transferee, the remaining partners may dissolve the partnership under Section 801(2)(ii), after first expelling the transferor partner. A transfer of a partner's entire interest may, in some circumstances, evidence the transferor's intention to withdraw under Section 601(1).

Subsection (4)(iii) provides for the expulsion of a corporate partner if it has filed a certificate of dissolution, its charter has been revoked, or its right to conduct business has been suspended, unless cured within 90 days after notice. This provision is derived from RULPA Section 402(9). The cure proviso is important because charter revocation is very common in some States and partner status should not end merely because of a technical noncompliance with corporate law that can easily be cured. Withdrawal of a voluntarily filed notice of dissolution constitutes a cure.

Subsection (4)(iv) is the partnership analogue of paragraph (iii) and is suggested by RULPA Section 402(8). It provides that a partnership that is a partner may be expelled if it has been dissolved and its business is being wound up. It is intended that the right of expulsion not be triggered solely by the dissolution event, but only upon commencement of the liquidation process.

6.   Section 601(5) empowers a court to expel a partner if it determines that the partner has engaged in specified misconduct. The enumerated grounds for judicial expulsion are based on the UPA Section 32(1) grounds for judicial dissolution. The application for expulsion may be brought by the partnership or any

partner. The phrase "judicial determination" is intended to include an arbitration award, as well as any final court order or decree.

Subsection (5)(i) provides for the partner's expulsion if the court finds that the partner has engaged in wrongful conduct that adversely and materially affected the partnership business. That language is derived from UPA Section 32(1)(c).

Subsection (5)(ii) provides for expulsion if the court determines that the partner willfully or persistently committed a material breach of the partnership agreement or of a duty owed to the partnership or to the other partners under Section 404. That would include a partner's breach of fiduciary duty. Paragraph (ii), together with paragraph (iii), carry forward the substance of UPA Section 32(1)(d).

Subsection (5)(iii) provides for judicial expulsion of a partner who engaged in conduct relating to the partnership business that makes it not reasonably practicable to carry on the business in partnership with that partner. Expulsion for such misconduct makes the partner's dissociation wrongful under Section 602(a)(ii) and may also support a judicial decree of dissolution under Section 801(5)(ii).

7.   Section 601(6) provides that a partner is dissociated upon becoming a debtor in bankruptcy or upon taking or suffering other action evidencing the partner's insolvency or lack of financial responsibility.

Subsection (6)(i) is derived from UPA Section 31(5), which provides for dissolution upon a partner's bankruptcy. *Accord* RULPA § 402(4)(ii). There is some doubt as to whether UPA Section 31(1) is limited to so-called "straight bankruptcy" under Chapter 7 or includes other bankruptcy relief, such as Chapter 11. Under RUPA Section 101(2), however, "debtor in bankruptcy" includes a person who files a voluntary petition, or against whom relief is ordered in an involuntary case, under any chapter of the Bankruptcy Code.

Initially, upon the filing of the bankruptcy petition, the debtor partner's transferable interest in the partnership will pass to the bankruptcy trustee as property of the estate under Section 541(a)(1) of the Bankruptcy Code, notwithstanding any restrictions on transfer provided in the partnership agreement. In most Chapter 7 cases, that will result in the eventual buyout of the partner's interest.

The application of various provisions of the federal Bankruptcy Code to Section 601(6)(i) is unclear. In particular, there is uncertainty as to the validity of UPA Section 31(5), and thus its RUPA counterpart, under Sections 365(e) and 541(c)(1) of the Bankruptcy Code. Those sections generally invalidate so-called *ipso facto* laws that cause a termination or modification of the debtor's contract or property rights because of the bankruptcy filing. As a consequence, RUPA Section 601(6)(i), which provides for a partner's dissociation by operation of law upon becoming a debtor in bankruptcy, may be invalid under the Supremacy Clause. *See, e.g., In the Matter of Phillips*, 966 F.2d 926 (5th Cir. 1992); *In re Cardinal Industries, Inc.*, 105 B.R. 385 (Bankr. S.D. Ohio 1989), 116 B.R. 964 (Bankr. S.D. Ohio 1990); *In re Corky Foods Corp.*, 85 B.R. 903 (Bankr. S.D. Fla. 1988). *But see, In re Catron*, 158 B.R. 629 (E.D. Va. 1993) (partnership agreement could not be assumed by debtor under Bankruptcy Code § 365(c)(1) because other partners excused by UPA from accepting performance by or rendering performance to party other than debtor and buyout option not invalid *ipso facto* clause under Code § 365 (e)), *aff'd per curiam*, 25 F.3d 1038 (4th Cir. 1994). RUPA reflects the policy choice, as a matter of state partnership law, that a partner be dissociated upon becoming a debtor in bankruptcy.

Subsection (6)(ii) is new and provides for dissociation upon a general assignment for the benefit of a partner's creditors. The UPA says nothing about an assignment for the benefit of creditors or the appointment of a trustee, receiver, or liquidator. Subsection (6)(iii) and (iv) cover the latter and are based substantially on RULPA Section 402(4) and (5).

8.   UPA Section 31(4) provides for the dissolution of a partnership upon the death of any partner, although by agreement the remaining partners may continue the partnership business. RUPA Section 601(7)(i), on the other hand, provides for dissociation upon the death of a partner who is an individual, rather than dissolution of the partnership. That changes existing law, except in those States previously adopting a similar non-uniform provision, such as California, Georgia, and Texas. Normally, under RUPA, the deceased partner's transferable interest in the partnership will pass to his estate and be bought out under Article 7.

Section 601(7)(ii) replaces UPA Section 32(1)(a) and provides for dissociation upon the appointment of a guardian or general conservator for partner who is an individual. The appointment itself operates as the event of dissociation, and no further order of the court is necessary.

Section 601(7)(iii) is based on UPA Section 32(1)(b) and provides for dissociation upon a judicial determination that an individual partner has in any other way become incapable of performing his duties under the partnership agreement. The intent is to include physical incapacity.

9.   Section 601(8) is new and provides for the dissociation of a partner that is a trust, or is acting as a partner by virtue of being a trustee of a trust, upon the distribution by the trust of its entire transferable interest in the partnership, but not merely upon the substitution of a successor trustee. The provision is inspired by RULPA Section 402(7).

10.   Section 601(9) is new and provides for the dissociation of a partner that is an estate, or is acting as a partner by virtue of being a personal representative of an estate, upon the distribution of the estate's entire transferable interest in the partnership, but not merely the substitution of a successor personal representative. It is based on RULPA Section 402(10). Under Section 601(7), a partner is dissociated upon death, however, and the estate normally becomes a transferee, not a partner.

11.   Section 601(10) is new and provides that a partner that is not an individual, partnership, corporation, trust, or estate is dissociated upon its termination. It is the comparable "death" analogue for other types of entity partners, such as a limited liability company.

§ 602.   Partner's Power to Dissociate; Wrongful Dissociation

(a)   A partner has the power to dissociate at any time, rightfully or wrongfully, by express will pursuant to Section 601(1).

(b)   A partner's dissociation is wrongful only if:

(1)   it is in breach of an express provision of the partnership agreement; or

(2)   in the case of a partnership for a definite term or particular undertaking, before the expiration of the term or the completion of the undertaking:

(i)   the partner withdraws by express will, unless the withdrawal follows within 90 days after another partner's dissociation by death or otherwise under Section 601(6) through (10) or wrongful dissociation under this subsection;

(ii)   the partner is expelled by judicial determination under Section 601(5);

(iii)   the partner is dissociated by becoming a debtor in bankruptcy; or

(iv)   in the case of a partner who is not an individual, trust other than a business trust, or estate, the partner is expelled or otherwise dissociated because it willfully dissolved or terminated.

(c)   A partner who wrongfully dissociates is liable to the partnership and to the other partners for damages caused by the dissociation. The liability is in addition to any other obligation of the partner to the partnership or to the other partners.

COMMENT

1.   Subsection (a) states explicitly what is implicit in UPA Section 31(2) and RUPA Section 601(1)—that a partner has the power to dissociate at any time by expressing a will to withdraw, even in contravention of the partnership agreement. The phrase "rightfully or wrongfully" reflects the distinction between a partner's power to withdraw in contravention of the partnership agreement and a partner's right to do so. In this context, although a partner can not be enjoined from exercising the power to dissociate, the dissociation may be wrongful under subsection (b).

2.   Subsection (b) provides that a partner's dissociation is wrongful only if it results from one of the enumerated events. The significance of a wrongful dissociation is that it may give rise to damages under

subsection (c) and, if it results in the dissolution of the partnership, the wrongfully dissociating partner is not entitled to participate in winding up the business under Section 804.

Under subsection (b), a partner's dissociation is wrongful if (1) it breaches an express provision of the partnership agreement or (2), in a term partnership, before the expiration of the term or the completion of the undertaking (i) the partner voluntarily withdraws by express will, except a withdrawal following another partner's wrongful dissociation or dissociation by death or otherwise under Section 601(6) through (10); (ii) the partner is expelled for misconduct under Section 601(5); (iii) the partner becomes a debtor in bankruptcy (see Section 101(2)); or (iv) a partner that is an entity (other than a trust or estate) is expelled or otherwise dissociated because its dissolution or termination was willful. Since subsection (b) is merely a default rule, the partnership agreement may eliminate or expand the dissociations that are wrongful or modify the effects of wrongful dissociation.

The exception in subsection (b)(2)(i) is intended to protect a partner's reactive withdrawal from a term partnership after the premature departure of another partner, such as the partnership's rainmaker or main supplier of capital, under the same circumstances that may result in the dissolution of the partnership under Section 801(2)(i). Under that section, a term partnership is dissolved 90 days after the bankruptcy, incapacity, death (or similar dissociation of a partner that is an entity), or wrongful dissociation of any partner, unless a majority in interest (see Comment 5(i) to Section 801 for a discussion of the term "majority in interest") of the remaining partners agree to continue the partnership. Under Section 602(b)(2)(i), a partner's exercise of the right of withdrawal by express will under those circumstances is rendered "rightful," even if the partnership is continued by others, and does not expose the withdrawing partner to damages for wrongful dissociation under Section 602(c).

A partner wishing to withdraw prematurely from a term partnership for any other reason, such as another partner's misconduct, can avoid being treated as a wrongfully dissociating partner by applying to a court under Section 601(5)(iii) to have the offending partner expelled. Then, the partnership could be dissolved under Section 801(2)(i) or the remaining partners could, by unanimous vote, dissolve the partnership under Section 801(2)(ii).

3.   Subsection (c) provides that a wrongfully dissociating partner is liable to the partnership and to the other partners for any damages caused by the wrongful nature of the dissociation. That liability is in addition to any other obligation of the partner to the partnership or to the other partners. For example, the partner would be liable for any damage caused by breach of the partnership agreement or other misconduct. The partnership might also incur substantial expenses resulting from a partner's premature withdrawal from a term partnership, such as replacing the partner's expertise or obtaining new financing. The wrongfully dissociating partner would be liable to the partnership for those and all other expenses and damages that are causally related to the wrongful dissociation.

Section 701(c) provides that any damages for wrongful dissociation may be offset against the amount of the buyout price due to the partner under Section 701(a), and Section 701(h) provides that a partner who wrongfully dissociates from a term partnership is not entitled to payment of the buyout price until the term expires.

Under UPA Section 38(2)(c)(II), in addition to an offset for damages, the goodwill value of the partnership is excluded in determining the value of a wrongfully dissociating partner's partnership interest. Under RUPA, however, unless the partnership's goodwill is damaged by the wrongful dissociation, the value of the wrongfully dissociating partner's interest will include any goodwill value of the partnership. If the firm's goodwill is damaged, the amount of the damages suffered by the partnership and the remaining partners will be offset against the buyout price. See Section 701 and Comments.

§ 603.   Effect of Partner's Dissociation

(a)   If a partner's dissociation results in a dissolution and winding up of the partnership business, Article 8 applies; otherwise, Article 7 applies.

(b)   Upon a partner's dissociation:

(1)   the partner's right to participate in the management and conduct of the partnership business terminates, except as otherwise provided in Section 803;

(2)   the partner's duty of loyalty under Section 404(b)(3) terminates; and

(3)   the partner's duty of loyalty under Section 404(b)(1) and (2) and duty of care under Section 404(c) continue only with regard to matters arising and events occurring before the partner's dissociation, unless the partner participates in winding up the partnership's business pursuant to Section 803.

COMMENT

1.   Section 603(a) is a "switching" provision. It provides that, after a partner's dissociation, the partner's interest in the partnership must be purchased pursuant to the buyout rules in Article 7 unless there is a dissolution and winding up of the partnership business under Article 8. Thus, a partner's dissociation will always result in either a buyout of the dissociated partner's interest or a dissolution and winding up of the business.

By contrast, under the UPA, every partner dissociation results in the dissolution of the partnership, most of which trigger a right to have the business wound up unless the partnership agreement provides otherwise. *See* UPA § 38. The only exception in which the remaining partners have a statutory right to continue the business is when a partner wrongfully dissolves the partnership in breach of the partnership agreement. *See* UPA § 38(2)(b).

2.   Section 603(b) is new and deals with some of the internal effects of a partner's dissociation. Subsection (b)(1) makes it clear that one of the consequences of a partner's dissociation is the immediate loss of the right to participate in the management of the business, unless it results in a dissolution and winding up of the business. In that case, Section 804(a) provides that all of the partners who have not wrongfully dissociated may participate in winding up the business.

Subsection (b)(2) and (3) clarify a partner's fiduciary duties upon dissociation. No change from current law is intended. With respect to the duty of loyalty, the Section 404(b)(3) duty not to compete terminates upon dissociation, and the dissociated partner is free immediately to engage in a competitive business, without any further consent. With respect to the partner's remaining loyalty duties under Section 404(b) and duty of care under Section 404(c), a withdrawing partner has a continuing duty after dissociation, but it is limited to matters that arose or events that occurred before the partner dissociated. For example, a partner who leaves a brokerage firm may immediately compete with the firm for new clients, but must exercise care in completing on-going client transactions and must account to the firm for any fees received from the old clients on account of those transactions. As the last clause makes clear, there is no contraction of a dissociated partner's duties under subsection (b)(3) if the partner thereafter participates in the dissolution and winding up the partnership's business.

ARTICLE 7.   PARTNER'S DISSOCIATION WHEN BUSINESS NOT WOUND UP

§ 701.   Purchase of Dissociated Partner's Interest

(a)   If a partner is dissociated from a partnership without resulting in a dissolution and winding up of the partnership business under Section 801, the partnership shall cause the dissociated partner's interest in the partnership to be purchased for a buyout price determined pursuant to subsection (b).

(b)   The buyout price of a dissociated partner's interest is the amount that would have been distributable to the dissociating partner under Section 807(b) if, on the date of dissociation, the assets of the partnership were sold at a price equal to the greater of the liquidation value or the value based on a sale of the entire business as a going concern without the dissociated partner and the partnership were wound up as of that date. Interest must be paid from the date of dissociation to the date of payment.

(c)   Damages for wrongful dissociation under Section 602(b), and all other amounts owing, whether or not presently due, from the dissociated partner to the partnership, must be offset against the buyout price. Interest must be paid from the date the amount owed becomes due to the date of payment.

(d)   A partnership shall indemnify a dissociated partner whose interest is being purchased against all partnership liabilities, whether incurred before or after the dissociation, except liabilities incurred by an act of the dissociated partner under Section 702.

(e)   If no agreement for the purchase of a dissociated partner's interest is reached within 120 days after a written demand for payment, the partnership shall pay, or cause to be paid, in cash to the dissociated partner the amount the partnership estimates to be the buyout price and accrued interest, reduced by any offsets and accrued interest under subsection (c).

(f)   If a deferred payment is authorized under subsection (h), the partnership may tender a written offer to pay the amount it estimates to be the buyout price and accrued interest, reduced by any offsets under subsection (c), stating the time of payment, the amount and type of security for payment, and the other terms and conditions of the obligation.

(g)   The payment or tender required by subsection (e) or (f) must be accompanied by the following:

(1)   a statement of partnership assets and liabilities as of the date of dissociation;

(2)   the latest available partnership balance sheet and income statement, if any;

(3)   an explanation of how the estimated amount of the payment was calculated; and

(4)   written notice that the payment is in full satisfaction of the obligation to purchase unless, within 120 days after the written notice, the dissociated partner commences an action to determine the buyout price, any offsets under subsection (c), or other terms of the obligation to purchase.

(h)   A partner who wrongfully dissociates before the expiration of a definite term or the completion of a particular undertaking is not entitled to payment of any portion of the buyout price until the expiration of the term or completion of the undertaking, unless the partner establishes to the satisfaction of the court that earlier payment will not cause undue hardship to the business of the partnership. A deferred payment must be adequately secured and bear interest.

(i)   A dissociated partner may maintain an action against the partnership, pursuant to Section 405(b)(2)(ii), to determine the buyout price of that partner's interest, any offsets under subsection (c), or other terms of the obligation to purchase. The action must be commenced within 120 days after the partnership has tendered payment or an offer to pay or within one year after written demand for payment if no payment or offer to pay is tendered. The court shall determine the buyout price of the dissociated partner's interest, any offset due under subsection (c), and accrued interest, and enter judgment for any additional payment or refund. If deferred payment is authorized under subsection (h), the court shall also determine the security for payment and other terms of the obligation to purchase. The court may assess reasonable attorney's fees and the fees and expenses of appraisers or other experts for a party to the action, in amounts the court finds equitable, against a party that the court finds acted arbitrarily, vexatiously, or not in good faith. The finding may be based on the partnership's failure to tender payment or an offer to pay or to comply with subsection (g).

COMMENT

1.   Article 7 is new and provides for the buyout of a dissociated partner's interest in the partnership when the partner's dissociation does not result in a dissolution and winding up of its business under Article 8. See Section 603(a). If there is no dissolution, the remaining partners have a right to continue the business and the dissociated partner has a right to be paid the value of his partnership interest. These rights can, of course, be varied in the partnership agreement. See Section 103. A dissociated partner has a continuing relationship with the partnership and third parties as provided in Sections 603(b), 702, and 703. See also Section 403(b) (former partner's access to partnership books and records).

2.   Subsection (a) provides that, if a partner's dissociation does not result in a windup of the business, the partnership shall cause the interest of the dissociating partner to be purchased for a buyout price determined pursuant to subsection (b). The buyout is mandatory. The "cause to be purchased" language is

REVISED UNIFORM PARTNERSHIP ACT (1997)

intended to accommodate a purchase by the partnership, one or more of the remaining partners, or a third party.

For federal income tax purposes, a payment to a partner for his interest can be characterized as a purchase of the partner's interest or as a liquidating distribution. The two have different tax consequences. RUPA permits either option by providing that the payment may come from either the partnership, as all of the continuing partners, or a third party purchaser.

3.   Subsection (b) provides how the "buyout price" is to be determined. The terms "fair market value" or "fair value" were not used because they are often considered terms of art having a special meaning depending on the context, such as in tax or corporate law. "Buyout price" is a new term. It is intended that the term be developed as an independent concept appropriate to the partnership buyout situation, while drawing on valuation principles developed elsewhere.

Under subsection (b), the buyout price is the amount that would have been distributable to the dissociating partner under Section 807(b) if, on the date of dissociation, the assets of the partnership were sold at a price equal to the greater of liquidation value or going concern value without the departing partner. Liquidation value is not intended to mean distress sale value. Under general principles of valuation, the hypothetical selling price in either case should be the price that a willing and informed buyer would pay a willing and informed seller, with neither being under any compulsion to deal. The notion of a minority discount in determining the buyout price is negated by valuing the business as a going concern. Other discounts, such as for a lack of marketability or the loss of a key partner, may be appropriate, however.

Since the buyout price is based on the value of the business at the time of dissociation, the partnership must pay interest on the amount due from the date of dissociation until payment to compensate the dissociating partner for the use of his interest in the firm. Section 104(b) provides that interest shall be at the legal rate unless otherwise provided in the partnership agreement. The UPA Section 42 option of electing a share of the profits in lieu of interest has been eliminated.

UPA Section 38(2)(c)(II) provides that the good will of the business not be considered in valuing a wrongfully dissociating partner's interest. The forfeiture of good will rule is implicitly rejected by RUPA. *See* Section 602(c) and Comment 3.

The Section 701 rules are merely default rules. The partners may, in the partnership agreement, fix the method or formula for determining the buyout price and all of the other terms and conditions of the buyout right. Indeed, the very right to a buyout itself may be modified, although a provision providing for a complete forfeiture would probably not be enforceable. *See* Section 104(a).

4.   Subsection (c) provides that the partnership may offset against the buyout price all amounts owing by the dissociated partner to the partnership, whether or not presently due, including any damages for wrongful dissociation under Section 602(c). This has the effect of accelerating payment of amounts not yet due from the departing partner to the partnership, including a long-term loan by the partnership to the dissociated partner. Where appropriate, the amounts not yet due should be discounted to present value. A dissociating partner, on the other hand, is not entitled to an add-on for amounts owing to him by the partnership. Thus, a departing partner who has made a long-term loan to the partnership must wait for repayment, unless the terms of the loan agreement provide for acceleration upon dissociation.

It is not intended that the partnership's right of setoff be construed to limit the amount of the damages for the partner's wrongful dissociation and any other amounts owing to the partnership to the value of the dissociated partner's interest. Those amounts may result in a net sum due to the partnership from the dissociated partner.

5.   Subsection (d) follows the UPA Section 38 rule and provides that the partnership must indemnify a dissociated partner against all partnership liabilities, whether incurred before or after the dissociation, except those incurred by the dissociated partner under Section 702.

6.   Subsection (e) provides that, if no agreement for the purchase of the dissociated partner's interest is reached within 120 days after the dissociated partner's written demand for payment, the partnership must pay, or cause to be paid, in cash the amount it estimates to be the buyout price, adjusted for any offsets allowed and accrued interest. Thus, the dissociating partner will receive in cash within 120 days of dissociation the undisputed minimum value of the partner's partnership interest. If the dissociated partner

§ 701

...ut price should be higher, suit may thereafter be brought as provided in subsection (i) claims that t... ...t of the buyout price determined by the court. This is similar to the procedure for to have th... value of dissenting shareholders' shares under RMBCA Sections 13.20–13.28. determin... ...e to be paid" language of subsection (a) is repeated here to permit either the partnership, one ...e continuing partners, or a third-party purchaser to tender payment of the estimated amount

or... Subsection (f) provides that, when deferred payment is authorized in the case of a wrongfully ...ting partner, a written offer stating the amount the partnership estimates to be the purchase price ...d be tendered within the 120-day period, even though actual payment of the amount may be deferred, ...ibly for many years. *See* Comment 8. The dissociated partner is entitled to know at the time of ...ssociation what amount the remaining partners think is due, including the estimated amount of any ...amages allegedly caused by the partner's wrongful dissociation that may be offset against the buyout price.

8. Subsection (g) provides that the payment of the estimated price (or tender of a written offer under subsection (f)) by the partnership must be accompanied by (1) a statement of the partnership's assets and liabilities as of the date of the partner's dissociation; (2) the latest available balance sheet and income statement, if the partnership maintains such financial statements; (3) an explanation of how the estimated amount of the payment was calculated; and (4) a written notice that the payment will be in full satisfaction of the partnership's buyout obligation unless the dissociated partner commences an action to determine the price within 120 days of the notice. Subsection (g) is based in part on the dissenters' rights provisions of RMBCA Section 13.25(b).

Those disclosures should serve to identify and narrow substantially the items of dispute between the dissociated partner and the partnership over the valuation of the partnership interest. They will also serve to pin down the parties as to their claims of partnership assets and values and as to the existence and amount of all known liabilities. *See* Comment 4. Lastly, it will force the remaining partners to consider thoughtfully the difficult and important questions as to the appropriate method of valuation under the circumstances, and in particular, whether they should use going concern or liquidation value. Simply getting that information on the record in a timely fashion should increase the likelihood of a negotiated resolution of the parties' differences during the 120-day period within which the dissociated partner must bring suit.

9. Subsection (h) replaces UPA Section 38(2)(c) and provides a somewhat different rule for payment to a partner whose dissociation before the expiration of a definite term or the completion of a particular undertaking is wrongful under Section 602(b). Under subsection (h), a wrongfully dissociating partner is not entitled to receive any portion of the buyout price before the expiration of the term or completion of the undertaking, unless the dissociated partner establishes to the satisfaction of the court that earlier payment will not cause undue hardship to the business of the partnership. In all other cases, there must be an immediate payment in cash.

10. Subsection (i) provides that a dissociated partner may maintain an action against the partnership to determine the buyout price, any offsets, or other terms of the purchase obligation. The action must be commenced within 120 days after the partnership tenders payment of the amount it estimates to be due or, if deferred payment is authorized, its written offer. This provision creates a 120-day "cooling off" period. It also allows the parties an opportunity to negotiate their differences after disclosure by the partnership of its financial statements and other required information.

If the partnership fails to tender payment of the estimated amount due (or a written offer, if deferred payment is authorized), the dissociated partner has one year after written demand for payment in which to commence suit.

If the parties fail to reach agreement, the court must determine the buyout price of the partner's interest, any offsets, including damages for wrongful dissociation, and the amount of interest accrued. If payment to a wrongfully dissociated partner is deferred, the court may also require security for payment and determine the other terms of the obligation.

Under subsection (i), attorney's fees and other costs may be assessed against any party found to have acted arbitrarily, vexatiously, or not in good faith in connection with the valuation dispute, including the partnership's failure to tender payment of the estimated price or to make the required disclosures. This provision is based in part on RMBCA Section 13.31(b).

§ 702.   Dissociated Partner's Power to Bind and Liability to Partnership

(a)   For two years after a partner dissociates without resulting in a dissolution and winding up of the partnership business, the partnership, including a surviving partnership under Article 9, is bound by an act of the dissociated partner which would have bound the partnership under Section 301 before dissociation only if at the time of entering into the transaction the other party:

(1)   reasonably believed that the dissociated partner was then a partner;

(2)   did not have notice of the partner's dissociation; and

(3)   is not deemed to have had knowledge under Section 303(e) or notice under Section 704(c).

(b)   A dissociated partner is liable to the partnership for any damage caused to the partnership arising from an obligation incurred by the dissociated partner after dissociation for which the partnership is liable under subsection (a).

COMMENT

1.   Section 702 deals with a dissociated partner's lingering apparent authority to bind the partnership in ordinary course partnership transactions and the partner's liability to the partnership for any loss caused thereby. It also applies to partners who withdraw incident to a merger under Article 9. *See* Section 906(e).

A dissociated partner has no actual authority to act for the partnership. *See* Section 603(b)(1). Nevertheless, in order to protect innocent third parties, Section 702(a) provides that the partnership remains bound, for two years after a partner's dissociation, by that partner's acts that would, before his dissociation, have bound the partnership under Section 301 if, and only if, the other party to the transaction reasonably believed that he was still a partner, did not have notice of the partner's dissociation, and is not deemed to have had knowledge of the dissociation under Section 303(e) or notice thereof under Section 704(c).

Under Section 301, every partner has apparent authority to bind the partnership by any act for carrying on the partnership business in the ordinary course, unless the other party knows that the partner has no actual authority to act for the partnership or has received a notification of the partner's lack of authority. Section 702(a) continues that general rule for two years after a partner's dissociation, subject to three modifications.

After a partner's dissociation, the general rule is modified, first, by requiring the other party to show reasonable reliance on the partner's status as a partner. Section 301 has no explicit reliance requirement, although the partnership is bound only if the partner purports to act on its behalf. Thus, the other party will normally be aware of the partnership and presumably the partner's status as such.

The second modification is that, under Section 702(a), the partnership is not bound if the third party has notice of the partner's dissociation, while under the general rule of Section 301 the partnership is bound unless the third party knows of the partner's lack of authority. Under Section 102(b), a person has "notice" of a fact if he knows or has reason to know it exists from all the facts that are known to him or he has received a notification of it. Thus, the partnership may protect itself by sending a notification of the dissociation to a third party, and a third party may, in any event, have a duty to inquire further based on what is known. That provides the partnership with greater protection from the unauthorized acts of a dissociated partner than from those of partners generally.

The third modification of the general apparent authority rule under Section 702(a) involves the effect of a statement of dissociation. Section 704(c) provides that, for the purposes of Sections 702(a)(3) and 703(b)(3), third parties are deemed to have notice of a partner's dissociation 90 days after the filing of a statement of dissociation. Thus, the filing of a statement operates as constructive notice of the dissociated partner's lack of authority after 90 days, conclusively terminating the dissociated partner's Section 702 apparent authority.

With respect to a dissociated partner's authority to transfer partnership real property, Section 303(e) provides that third parties are deemed to have knowledge of a limitation on a partner's authority to transfer real property held in the partnership name upon the proper recording of a statement containing such a limitation. Section 704(b) provides that a statement of dissociation operates as a limitation on the dissociated partner's authority for the purposes of Section 303(e). Thus, a properly recorded statement of dissociation operates as constructive knowledge of a dissociated partner's lack of authority to transfer real property held in the partnership name, effective immediately upon recording.

Under RUPA, therefore, a partnership should notify all known creditors of a partner's dissociation and may, by filing a statement of dissociation, conclusively limit to 90 days a dissociated partner's lingering agency power. Moreover, under Section 703(b), a dissociated partner's lingering liability for post-dissociation partnership liabilities may be limited to 90 days by filing a statement of dissociation. These incentives should encourage both partnerships and dissociating partners to file statements routinely. Those transacting substantial business with partnerships can protect themselves from the risk of dealing with dissociated partners, or relying on their credit, by checking the partnership records at least every 90 days.

2.   Section 702(b) is a corollary to subsection (a) and provides that a dissociated partner is liable to the partnership for any loss resulting from an obligation improperly incurred by the partner under subsection (a). In effect, the dissociated partner must indemnify the partnership for any loss, meaning a loss net of any gain from the transaction. The dissociated partner is also personally liable to the third party for the unauthorized obligation.

§ 703.   Dissociated Partner's Liability to Other Persons

(a)   A partner's dissociation does not of itself discharge the partner's liability for a partnership obligation incurred before dissociation. A dissociated partner is not liable for a partnership obligation incurred after dissociation, except as otherwise provided in subsection (b).

(b)   A partner who dissociates without resulting in a dissolution and winding up of the partnership business is liable as a partner to the other party in a transaction entered into by the partnership, or a surviving partnership under Article 9, within two years after the partner's dissociation, only if the partner is liable for the obligation under Section 306 and at the time of entering into the transaction the other party:

(1)   reasonably believed that the dissociated partner was then a partner;

(2)   did not have notice of the partner's dissociation; and

(3)   is not deemed to have had knowledge under Section 303(e) or notice under Section 704(c).

(c)   By agreement with the partnership creditor and the partners continuing the business, a dissociated partner may be released from liability for a partnership obligation.

(d)   A dissociated partner is released from liability for a partnership obligation if a partnership creditor, with notice of the partner's dissociation but without the partner's consent, agrees to a material alteration in the nature or time of payment of a partnership obligation.

COMMENT

Section 703(a) is based on UPA Section 36(1) and continues the basic rule that the departure of a partner does not of itself discharge the partner's liability to third parties for any partnership obligation incurred before dissociation. The word "obligation" is used instead of "liability" and is intended to include broadly both tort and contract liability incurred before dissociation. The second sentence states affirmatively that a dissociating partner is not liable for any partnership obligation incurred after dissociation except as expressly provided in subsection (b).

Section 703(b) is new and deals with the problem of protecting third parties who extend credit to the partnership after a partner's dissociation, believing that he is still a partner. It provides that the dissociated partner remains liable as a partner for transactions entered into by the partnership within two years after departure, if the other party does not have notice of the partner's dissociation and reasonably believes when entering the transaction that the dissociated partner is still a partner. The dissociated partner is not personally liable, however, if the other party is deemed to know of the dissociation under Section 303(e) or to have notice thereof under Section 704(c). Also, a dissociated partner is not personally liable for limited liability partnership obligations for which the partner is not personally liable under Section 306.

Section 703(b) operates similarly to Section 702(a) in that it requires reliance on the departed partner's continued partnership status, as well as lack of notice. Under Section 704(c), a statement of dissociation operates conclusively as constructive notice 90 days after filing for the purposes of Section 703(b)(3) and, under Section 704(b), as constructive knowledge when recorded for the purposes of Section 303(d) and (e).

Section 703(c) continues the rule of UPA Section 36(2) that a departing partner can bargain for a contractual release from personal liability for a partnership obligation, but it requires the consent of both the creditor and the remaining partners.

Section 703(d) continues the rule of UPA Section 36(3) that a dissociated partner is released from liability for a partnership obligation if the creditor, with notice of the partner's departure, agrees to a material alteration in the nature or time of payment, without that partner's consent. This rule covers all partner dissociations and is not limited, as is the UPA rule, to situations in which a third party "agrees to assume the existing obligations of a dissolved partnership."

In general under RUPA, as a result of the adoption of the entity theory, relationships between a partnership and its creditors are not affected by the dissociation of a partner or by the addition of a new partner, unless otherwise agreed. Therefore, there is no need under RUPA, as there is under the UPA, for an elaborate provision deeming the new partnership to assume the liabilities of the old partnership. *See* UPA Section 41.

The "dual priority" rule in UPA Section 36(4) is eliminated to reflect the abolition of the "jingle rule," providing that separate debts have first claim on separate property, in order to conform to the Bankruptcy Code. *See* Comment 2 to Section 807. A deceased partner's estate, and thus all of his individual property, remains liable for partnership obligations incurred while he was a partner, however.

§ 704. Statement of Dissociation

(a) A dissociated partner or the partnership may file a statement of dissociation stating the name of the partnership and that the partner is dissociated from the partnership.

(b) A statement of dissociation is a limitation on the authority of a dissociated partner for the purposes of Section 303(d) and (e).

(c) For the purposes of Sections 702(a)(3) and 703(b)(3), a person not a partner is deemed to have notice of the dissociation 90 days after the statement of dissociation is filed.

COMMENT

Section 704 is new and provides for a statement of dissociation and its effects. Subsection (a) authorizes either a dissociated partner or the partnership to file a statement of dissociation. Like other RUPA filings, the statement of dissociation is voluntary. Both the partnership and the departing partner have an incentive to file, however, and it is anticipated that those filings will become routine upon a partner's dissociation. The execution, filing, and recording of the statement is governed by Section 105.

Filing or recording a statement of dissociation has threefold significance:

(1) It is a statement of limitation on the dissociated partner's authority to the extent provided in Section 303(d) and (e). Under Section 303(d), a filed or recorded limitation on the authority of a partner destroys the conclusive effect of a prior grant of authority to the extent it contradicts the prior grant. Under Section 303(e), nonpartners are conclusively bound by a limitation on the authority of a partner to transfer real property held in the partnership name, if the statement is properly recorded in the real property records.

(2) Ninety days after the statement is filed, nonpartners are deemed to have notice of the dissociation and thus conclusively bound for purposes of cutting off the partner's apparent authority under Sections 301 and 702(a)(3).

(3)   Ninety days after the statement is filed, third parties are conclusively bound for purposes of cutting off the dissociated partner's continuing liability under Section 703(b)(3) for transactions entered into by the partnership after dissociation.

§ 705.   Continued Use of Partnership Name

Continued use of a partnership name, or a dissociated partner's name as part thereof, by partners continuing the business does not of itself make the dissociated partner liable for an obligation of the partners or the partnership continuing the business.

COMMENT

Section 705 is an edited version of UPA Section 41(10) and provides that a dissociated partner is not liable for the debts of the continuing business simply because of continued use of the partnership name or the dissociated partner's name as a part thereof. That prevents forcing the business to forego the good will associated with its name.

ARTICLE 8.   WINDING UP PARTNERSHIP BUSINESS

§ 801.   Events Causing Dissolution and Winding up of Partnership Business

A partnership is dissolved, and its business must be wound up, only upon the occurrence of any of the following events:

(1)   in a partnership at will, the partnership's having notice from a partner, other than a partner who is dissociated under Section 601(2) through (10), of that partner's express will to withdraw as a partner, or on a later date specified by the partner;

(2)   in a partnership for a definite term or particular undertaking:

(i)   within 90 days after a partner's dissociation by death or otherwise under Section 601(6) through (10) or wrongful dissociation under Section 602(b), the express will of at least half of the remaining partners to wind up the partnership business, for which purpose a partner's rightful dissociation pursuant to Section 602(b)(2)(i) constitutes the expression of that partner's will to wind up the partnership business;

(ii)   the express will of all of the partners to wind up the partnership business; or

(iii)   the expiration of the term or the completion of the undertaking;

(3)   an event agreed to in the partnership agreement resulting in the winding up of the partnership business;

(4)   an event that makes it unlawful for all or substantially all of the business of the partnership to be continued, but a cure of illegality within 90 days after notice to the partnership of the event is effective retroactively to the date of the event for purposes of this section;

(5)   on application by a partner, a judicial determination that:

(i)   the economic purpose of the partnership is likely to be unreasonably frustrated;

(ii)   another partner has engaged in conduct relating to the partnership business which makes it not reasonably practicable to carry on the business in partnership with that partner; or

(iii)   it is not otherwise reasonably practicable to carry on the partnership business in conformity with the partnership agreement; or

(6)   on application by a transferee of a partner's transferable interest, a judicial determination that it is equitable to wind up the partnership business:

     (i)   after the expiration of the term or completion of the undertaking, if the partnership was for a definite term or particular undertaking at the time of the transfer or entry of the charging order that gave rise to the transfer; or

     (ii)   at any time, if the partnership was a partnership at will at the time of the transfer or entry of the charging order that gave rise to the transfer.

COMMENT

1.   Under UPA Section 29, a partnership is dissolved every time a partner leaves. That reflects the aggregate nature of the partnership under the UPA. Even if the business of the partnership is continued by some of the partners, it is technically a new partnership. The dissolution of the old partnership and creation of a new partnership causes many unnecessary problems.

Under RULPA, limited partnerships dissolve far less readily than do general partnerships under the UPA. A limited partnership does not dissolve on the withdrawal of a limited partner, nor does it necessarily dissolve on the withdrawal of a general partner. *See* RULPA § 801(4).

RUPA's move to the entity theory is driven in part by the need to prevent a technical dissolution or its consequences. Under RUPA, not every partner dissociation causes a dissolution of the partnership. Only certain departures trigger a dissolution. The basic rule is that a partnership is dissolved, and its business must be wound up, only upon the occurrence of one of the events listed in Section 801. All other dissociations result in a buyout of the partner's interest under Article 7 and a continuation of the partnership entity and business by the remaining partners. *See* Section 603(a).

With only three exceptions, the provisions of Section 801 are merely default rules and may by agreement be varied or eliminated as grounds for dissolution. The first exception is dissolution under Section 801(4) resulting from carrying on an illegal business. The other two exceptions cover the power of a court to dissolve a partnership under Section 801(5) on application of a partner and under Section 801(6) on application of a transferee. *See* Comments 6–8 for further explanation of these provisions.

2.   Under RUPA, "dissolution" is merely the commencement of the winding up process. The partnership continues for the limited purpose of winding up the business. In effect, that means the scope of the partnership business contracts to completing work in process and taking such other actions as may be necessary to wind up the business. Winding up the partnership business entails selling its assets, paying its debts, and distributing the net balance, if any, to the partners in cash according to their interests. The partnership entity continues, and the partners are associated in the winding up of the business until winding up is completed. When the winding up is completed, the partnership entity terminates.

3.   Section 801 continues two basic rules from the UPA. First, it continues the rule that any member of an at-will partnership has the right to force a liquidation. Second, by negative implication, it continues the rule that the partners who wish to continue the business of a term partnership can not be forced to liquidate the business by a partner who withdraws prematurely in violation of the partnership agreement.

Those rules are gleaned from the separate UPA provisions governing dissolution and its consequences. Under UPA Section 31(1)(b), dissolution is caused by the express will of any partner when no definite term or particular undertaking is specified. UPA Section 38(1) provides that upon dissolution any partner has the right to have the business wound up. That is a default rule and applies only in the absence of an agreement affording the other partners a right to continue the business.

UPA Section 31(2) provides that a term partnership may be dissolved at any time, in contravention of the partnership agreement, by the express will of any partner. In that case, however, UPA Section 38(2)(b) provides that the nonbreaching partners may by unanimous consent continue the business. If the business is continued, they must buy out the breaching partner.

4.   Section 801(1) provides that a partnership at will is dissolved and its business must be wound up upon the partnership's having notice of a partner's express will to withdraw as a partner, unless a later effective date is specified by the partner. A partner at will who has already been dissociated in some other manner, such as a partner who has been expelled, does not thereafter have a right to cause the partnership to be dissolved and its business wound up.

If, after dissolution, none of the partners wants the partnership wound up, Section 802(b) provides that, with the consent of all the partners, including the withdrawing partner, the remaining partners may continue the business. In that event, although there is a technical dissolution of the partnership and, at least in theory, a temporary contraction of the scope of the business, the partnership entity continues and the scope of its business is restored. *See* Section 802(b) and Comment 2.

5.   Section 801(2) provides three ways in which a term partnership may be dissolved before the expiration of the term:

(i)   Subsection (2)(i) provides for dissolution after a partner's dissociation by death or otherwise under Section 601(6) to (10) or wrongful dissociation under Section 602(b), if within 90 days after the dissociation at least half of the remaining partners express their will to dissolve the partnership. Thus if a term partnership had six partners and one of the partners dies or wrongfully dissociates before the end of the term, the partnership will, as a result of the dissociation, be dissolved only if three of the remaining five partners affirmatively vote in favor of dissolution within 90 days after the dissociation.* This reactive dissolution of a term partnership protects the remaining partners where the dissociating partner is crucial to the successful continuation of the business. The corresponding UPA Section 38(2)(b) rule requires unanimous consent of the remaining partners to continue the business, thus giving each partner an absolute right to a reactive liquidation. Under UPA 1994, if the partnership is continued by the majority, any dissenting partner who wants to withdraw may do so rightfully under the exception to Section 602(b)(2)(i), in which case his interest in the partnership will be bought out under Article 7. By itself, however, a partner's vote not to continue the business is not necessarily an expression of the partner's will to withdraw, and a dissenting partner may still elect to remain a partner and continue in the business.

The Section 601 dissociations giving rise to a reactive dissolution are: (6) a partner's bankruptcy or similar financial impairment; (7) a partner's death or incapacity; (8) the distribution by a trust-partner of its entire partnership interest; (9) the distribution by an estate-partner of its entire partnership interest; and (10) the termination of an entity-partner. Any dissociation during the term of the partnership that is wrongful under Section 602(b), including a partner's voluntary withdrawal, expulsion or bankruptcy, also gives rise to a reactive dissolution. Those statutory grounds may be varied by agreement or the reactive dissolution may be abolished entirely.

Under Section 601(6)(i), a partner is dissociated upon becoming a debtor in bankruptcy. The bankruptcy of a partner or of the partnership is not, however, an event of dissolution under Section 801. That is a change from UPA Section 31(5). A partner's bankruptcy does, however, cause dissolution of a term partnership under Section 801(2)(i), unless a majority in interest of the remaining partners thereafter agree to continue the partnership. Affording the other partners the option of buying out the bankrupt partner's interest avoids the necessity of winding up a term partnership every time a partner becomes a debtor in bankruptcy.

Similarly, under Section 801(2)(i), the death of any partner will result in the dissolution of a term partnership, only if at least half of the remaining partners express their will to wind up the partnership's business. If dissolution does occur, the deceased partner's transferable interest in the partnership passes to his estate and must be bought out under Article 7. *See* Comment 8 to Section 601.

(ii)   Section 801(2)(ii) provides that a term partnership may be dissolved and wound up at any time by the express will of all the partners. That is merely an expression of the general rule that the partnership agreement may override the statutory default rules and that the partnership agreement, like any contract, can be amended at any time by unanimous consent.

UPA Section 31(1)(c) provides that a term partnership may be wound up by the express will of all the partners whose transferable interests have not been assigned or charged for a partner's separate debts. That

---

*   Prior to August 1997, Section 801(2)(i) provided that upon the dissociation of a partner in a term partnership by death or otherwise under Section 601(6) through (10) or wrongful dissociation under 602(b) the partnership would dissolve unless "a majority in interest of the remaining partners (including partners who have rightfully dissociated pursuant to Section 602(b)(2)(i)) agree to continue the partnership." This language was thought to be necessary for a term partnership to lack continuity of life under the Internal Revenue Act tax classification regulations. These regulations were repealed effective January 1, 1997. The current language, approved at the 1997 annual meeting of the National Conference of Commissioners on Uniform State Laws, allows greater continuity in a term partnership than the prior version of this subsection and UPA Section 38(2)(b).

rule reflects the belief that the remaining partners may find transferees very intrusive. This provision has been deleted, however, because the liquidation is easily accomplished under Section 801(2)(ii) by first expelling the transferor partner under Section 601(4)(ii).

(iii) Section 801(2)(iii) is based on UPA Section 31(1)(a) and provides for winding up a term partnership upon the expiration of the term or the completion of the undertaking.

Subsection (2)(iii) must be read in conjunction with Section 406. Under Section 406(a), if the partners continue the business after the expiration of the term or the completion of the undertaking, the partnership will be treated as a partnership at will. Moreover, if the partners continue the business without any settlement or liquidation of the partnership, under Section 406(b) they are presumed to have agreed that the partnership will continue, despite the lack of a formal agreement. The partners may also agree to ratify all acts taken since the end of the partnership's term.

6.   Section 801(3) provides for dissolution upon the occurrence of an event specified in the partnership agreement as resulting in the winding up of the partnership business. The partners may, however, agree to continue the business and to ratify all acts taken since dissolution.

7.   Section 801(4) continues the basic rule in UPA Section 31(3) and provides for dissolution if it is unlawful to continue the business of the partnership, unless cured. The "all or substantially all" proviso is intended to avoid dissolution for insubstantial or innocent regulatory violations. If the illegality is cured within 90 days after notice to the partnership, it is effective retroactively for purposes of this section. The requirement that an uncured illegal business be wound up cannot be varied in the partnership agreement. *See* Section 103(b)(8).

8.   Section 801(5) provides for judicial dissolution on application by a partner. It is based in part on UPA Section 32(1), and the language comes in part from RULPA Section 802. A court may order a partnership dissolved upon a judicial determination that: (i) the economic purpose of the partnership is likely to be unreasonably frustrated; (ii) another partner has engaged in conduct relating to the partnership business which makes it not reasonably practicable to carry on the business in partnership with that partner; or (iii) it is not otherwise reasonably practicable to carry on the partnership business in conformity with the partnership agreement. The court's power to wind up the partnership under Section 801(5) cannot be varied in the partnership agreement. *See* Section 103(b)(8).

RUPA deletes UPA Section 32(1)(e) which provides for dissolution when the business can only be carried on at a loss. That provision might result in a dissolution contrary to the partners' expectations in a start-up or tax shelter situation, in which case "book" or "tax" losses do not signify business failure. Truly poor financial performance may justify dissolution under subsection (5)(i) as a frustration of the partnership's economic purpose.

RUPA also deletes UPA Section 32(1)(f) which authorizes a court to order dissolution of a partnership when "other circumstances render a dissolution equitable." That provision was regarded as too open-ended and, given RUPA's expanded remedies for partners, unnecessary. No significant change in result is intended, however, since the interpretation of UPA Section 32(1)(f) is comparable to the specific grounds expressed in subsection (5). *See, e.g., Karber v. Karber*, 145 Ariz. 293, 701 P.2d 1 (Ct. App. 1985) (partnership dissolved on basis of suspicion and ill will, citing UPA §§ 32(1)(d) and (f)); *Fuller v. Brough*, 159 Colo. 147, 411 P.2d 18 (1966) (not equitable to dissolve partnership for trifling causes or temporary grievances that do not render it impracticable to carry on partnership business); *Lau v. Wong*, 1 Haw. App. 217, 616 P.2d 1031 (1980) (partnership dissolved where business operated solely for benefit of managing partner).

9.   Section 801(6) provides for judicial dissolution on application by a transferee of a partner's transferable interest in the partnership, including the purchaser of a partner's interest upon foreclosure of a charging order. It is based on UPA Section 32(2) and authorizes dissolution upon a judicial determination that it is equitable to wind up the partnership business (i) after the expiration of the partnership term or completion of the undertaking or (ii) at any time, if the partnership were a partnership at will at the time of the transfer or when the charging order was issued. The requirement that the court determine that it is equitable to wind up the business is new. The rights of a transferee under this section cannot be varied in the partnership agreement. *See* Section 103(b)(8).

§ 802.   Partnership Continues After Dissolution

(a)   Subject to subsection (b), a partnership continues after dissolution only for the purpose of winding up its business. The partnership is terminated when the winding up of its business is completed.

(b)   At any time after the dissolution of a partnership and before the winding up of its business is completed, all of the partners, including any dissociating partner other than a wrongfully dissociating partner, may waive the right to have the partnership's business wound up and the partnership terminated. In that event:

(1)   the partnership resumes carrying on its business as if dissolution had never occurred, and any liability incurred by the partnership or a partner after the dissolution and before the waiver is determined as if dissolution had never occurred; and

(2)   the rights of a third party accruing under Section 804(1) or arising out of conduct in reliance on the dissolution before the third party knew or received a notification of the waiver may not be adversely affected.

COMMENT

1.   Section 802(a) is derived from UPA Section 30 and provides that a partnership continues after dissolution only for the purpose of winding up its business, after which it is terminated. RUPA continues the concept of "termination" to mark the completion of the winding up process. Since no filing or other formality is required, the date will often be determined only by hindsight. No legal rights turn on the partnership's termination or the date thereof. Even after termination, if a previously unknown liability is asserted, all of the partners are still liable.

2.   Section 802(b) makes explicit the right of the remaining partners to continue the business after an event of dissolution if all of the partners, including the dissociating partner or partners, waive the right to have the business wound up and the partnership terminated. Only those "dissociating" partners whose dissociation was the immediate cause of the dissolution must waive the right to have the business wound up. The consent of wrongfully dissociating partners is not required.

3.   Upon waiver of the right to have the business wound up, Paragraph (1) of the subsection provides that the partnership entity may resume carrying on its business as if dissolution had never occurred, thereby restoring the scope of its business to normal. "Resumes" is intended to mean that acts appropriate to winding up, authorized when taken, are in effect ratified, and the partnership remains liable for those acts, as provided explicitly in paragraph (2).

If the business is continued following a waiver of the right to dissolution, any liability incurred by the partnership or a partner after the dissolution and before the waiver is to be determined as if dissolution had never occurred. That has the effect of validating transactions entered into after dissolution that might not have been appropriate for winding up the business, because, upon waiver, any liability incurred by either the partnership or a partner in those transactions will be determined under Sections 702 and 703, rather than Sections 804 and 806.

As to the liability for those transactions among the partners themselves, the partners by agreement may provide otherwise. Thus, a partner who, after dissolution, incurred an obligation appropriate for winding up, but not appropriate for continuing the business, may protect himself by conditioning his consent to the continuation of the business on the ratification of the transaction by the continuing partners.

Paragraph (2) of the subsection provides that the rights of third parties accruing under Section 804(1) before they knew (or were notified) of the waiver may not be adversely affected by the waiver. That is intended to mean the partnership is bound, notwithstanding a subsequent waiver of dissolution and resumption of its business, by a transaction entered into after dissolution that was appropriate for winding up the partnership business, even if not appropriate for continuing the business. Similarly, any rights of a third party arising out of conduct in reliance on the dissolution are protected, absent knowledge (or notification) of the waiver. Thus, for example, a partnership loan, callable upon dissolution, that has been called is not reinstated by a subsequent waiver. If the loan has not been called before the lender learns (or is notified) of the waiver, however, it may not thereafter be called because of the dissolution. On the other hand, a waiver does not reinstate a lease that is terminated by the dissolution itself.

§ 803. Right to Wind up Partnership Business

(a)　After dissolution, a partner who has not wrongfully dissociated may participate in winding up the partnership's business, but on application of any partner, partner's legal representative, or transferee, the [designate the appropriate court], for good cause shown, may order judicial supervision of the winding up.

(b)　The legal representative of the last surviving partner may wind up a partnership's business.

(c)　A person winding up a partnership's business may preserve the partnership business or property as a going concern for a reasonable time, prosecute and defend actions and proceedings, whether civil, criminal, or administrative, settle and close the partnership's business, dispose of and transfer the partnership's property, discharge the partnership's liabilities, distribute the assets of the partnership pursuant to Section 807, settle disputes by mediation or arbitration, and perform other necessary acts.

COMMENT

Section 803(a) is drawn from UPA Section 37. It provides that the partners who have not wrongfully dissociated may participate in winding up the partnership business. Wrongful dissociation is defined in Section 602. On application of any partner, a court may for good cause judicially supervise the winding up.

Section 803(b) continues the rule of UPA Section 25(2)(d) that the legal representative of the last surviving partner may wind up the business. It makes clear that the representative of the last surviving partner will not be forced to go to court for authority to wind up the business. On the other hand, the legal representative of a deceased partner, other than the last surviving partner, has only the rights of a transferee of the deceased partner's transferable interest. *See* Comment 8 to Section 601.

Section 803(c) is new and provides further guidance on the powers of a person who is winding up the business. It is based on Delaware Laws, Title 6, Section 17–803. The powers enumerated are not intended to be exclusive.

Subsection (c) expressly authorizes the preservation of the partnership's business or property as a going concern for a reasonable time. Some courts have reached that result without benefit of statutory authority. *See, e.g., Paciaroni v. Crane*, 408 A.2d 946 (Del. Ch. 1979). An agreement to continue the partnership business in order to preserve its going-concern value until sale is not a waiver of a partner's right to have the business liquidated.

The authorization of mediation and arbitration implements Conference policy to encourage alternative dispute resolution.

A partner's fiduciary duties of care and loyalty under Section 404 extend to winding up the business, except as modified by Section 603(b).

§ 804. Partner's Power to Bind Partnership After Dissolution

Subject to Section 805, a partnership is bound by a partner's act after dissolution that:

(1)　is appropriate for winding up the partnership business; or

(2)　would have bound the partnership under Section 301 before dissolution, if the other party to the transaction did not have notice of the dissolution.

COMMENT

Section 804 is the successor to UPA Sections 33(2) and 35, which wind down the authority of partners to bind the partnership to third persons.

Section 804(1) provides that partners have the authority to bind the partnership after dissolution in transactions that are appropriate for winding-up the partnership business. Section 804(2) provides that partners also have the power after dissolution to bind the partnership in transactions that are inconsistent with winding up. The partnership is bound in a transaction not appropriate for winding up, however, only if the partner's act would have bound the partnership under Section 301 before dissolution and the other party to the transaction did not have notice of the dissolution. *See* Section 102(b) (notice). *Compare* Section 301(1) (partner has apparent authority unless other party knows or has received a notification of lack of authority).

Section 804(2) attempts to balance the interests of the partners to terminate their mutual agency authority against the interests of outside creditors who have no notice of the partnership's dissolution. Even if the partnership is not bound under Section 804, the faithless partner who purports to act for the partnership after dissolution may be liable individually to an innocent third party under the law of agency. *See* Section 330 of the Restatement (Second) of Agency (agent liable for misrepresentation of authority), applicable under RUPA as provided in Section 104(a).

RUPA eliminates the special and confusing UPA rules limiting the authority of partners after dissolution. The special protection afforded by UPA Section 35(1)(b)(I) to former creditors and the lesser special protection afforded by UPA Section 35(1)(b)(II) to other parties who knew of the partnership before dissolution are both abolished. RUPA eschews these cumbersome notice provisions in favor of the general apparent authority rules of Section 301, subject to the effect of a filed or recorded statement of dissolution under Section 805. This enhances the protection of innocent third parties and imposes liability on the partnership and the partners who choose their fellow partner-agents and are in the best position to protect others by providing notice of the dissolution.

Also deleted are the special rules for unknown partners in UPA Section 35(2) and for certain causes of dissolution in UPA Section 35(3). Those, too, are inconsistent with RUPA's policy of adhering more closely to the general agency rules of Section 301.

Section 804 should be contrasted with Section 702, which winds down the power of a partner being bought out. The power of a dissociating partner is limited to transactions entered into within two years after the partner's dissociation. Section 804 has no time limitation. However, the apparent authority of partners in both situations is now subject to the filing of a statement of dissociation or dissolution, as the case may be, which operates to cut off such authority after 90 days.

§ 805.   Statement of Dissolution

(a)   After dissolution, a partner who has not wrongfully dissociated may file a statement of dissolution stating the name of the partnership and that the partnership has dissolved and is winding up its business.

(b)   A statement of dissolution cancels a filed statement of partnership authority for the purposes of Section 303(d) and is a limitation on authority for the purposes of Section 303(e).

(c)   For the purposes of Sections 301 and 804, a person not a partner is deemed to have notice of the dissolution and the limitation on the partners' authority as a result of the statement of dissolution 90 days after it is filed.

(d)   After filing and, if appropriate, recording a statement of dissolution, a dissolved partnership may file and, if appropriate, record a statement of partnership authority which will operate with respect to a person not a partner as provided in Section 303(d) and (e) in any transaction, whether or not the transaction is appropriate for winding up the partnership business.

COMMENT

1.   Section 805 is new. Subsection (a) provides that, after an event of dissolution, any partner who has not wrongfully dissociated may file a statement of dissolution on behalf of the partnership. The filing and recording of a statement of dissolution is optional. The execution, filing, and recording of the statement is governed by Section 105. The legal consequences of filing a statement of dissolution are similar to those of a statement of dissociation under Section 704.

2.   Subsection (b) provides that a statement of dissolution cancels a filed statement of partnership authority for the purposes of Section 303(d), thereby terminating any extraordinary grant of authority contained in that statement.

A statement of dissolution also operates as a limitation on authority for the purposes of Section 303(e). That section provides that third parties are deemed to know of a limitation on the authority of a partner to transfer real property held in the name of the partnership if a certified copy of the statement containing the limitation is recorded with the real estate records. In effect, a properly recorded statement of dissolution restricts the authority of all partners to real property transfers that are appropriate for winding up the business. Thus, third parties must inquire of the partnership whether a contemplated real property transfer is appropriate for winding up. After dissolution, the partnership may, however, file and record a new statement of authority that will bind the partnership under Section 303(d).

3.   Subsection (c) operates in conjunction with Sections 301 and 804 to wind down partners' apparent authority after dissolution. It provides that, for purposes of those sections, 90 days after the filing of a statement of dissolution nonpartners are deemed to have notice of the dissolution and the corresponding limitation on the authority of all partners. Sections 301 and 804 provide that a partner's lack of authority is binding on persons with notice thereof. Thus, after 90 days the statement of dissolution operates as constructive notice conclusively limiting the apparent authority of partners to transactions that are appropriate for winding up the business.

4.   Subsection (d) provides that, after filing and, if appropriate, recording a statement of dissolution, the partnership may file and record a new statement of partnership authority that will operate as provided in Section 303(d). A grant of authority contained in that statement is conclusive and may be relied upon by a person who gives value without knowledge to the contrary, whether or not the transaction is appropriate for winding up the partnership business. That makes the partners' record authority conclusive after dissolution, and precludes going behind the record to inquire into whether or not the transaction was appropriate for winding up.

§ 806.   Partner's Liability to Other Partners After Dissolution

(a)   Except as otherwise provided in subsection (b) and Section 306, after dissolution a partner is liable to the other partners for the partner's share of any partnership liability incurred under Section 804.

(b)   A partner who, with knowledge of the dissolution, incurs a partnership liability under Section 804(2) by an act that is not appropriate for winding up the partnership business is liable to the partnership for any damage caused to the partnership arising from the liability.

COMMENT

Section 806 is the successor to UPA Sections 33(1) and 34, which govern the rights of partners among themselves with respect to post-dissolution liability.

Subsection (a) provides that, except as provided in Section 306(a) and subsection (b), after dissolution each partner is liable to the other partners by way of contribution for his share of any partnership liability incurred under Section 804. That includes not only obligations that are appropriate for winding up the business, but also obligations that are inappropriate if within the partner's apparent authority. Consistent with other provisions of this Act, Section 806(a) makes clear that a partner does not have a contribution obligation with regard to limited liability partnership obligations for which the partner is not liable under Section 306. See Comments to Section 401(b).

Subsection (a) draws no distinction as to the cause of dissolution. Thus, as among the partners, their liability is treated alike in all events of dissolution. That is a change from UPA Section 33(l).

Subsection (b) creates an exception to the general rule in subsection (a). It provides that a partner, who with knowledge of the winding up nevertheless incurs a liability binding on the partnership by an act that is inappropriate for winding up the business, is liable to the partnership for any loss caused thereby.

Section 806 is merely a default rule and may be varied in the partnership agreement. See Section 103(a).

§ 807.   Settlement of Accounts and Contributions Among Partners

(a) In winding up a partnership's business, the assets of the partnership, including the contributions of the partners required by this section, must be applied to discharge its obligations to creditors, including, to the extent permitted by law, partners who are creditors. Any surplus must be applied to pay in cash the net amount distributable to partners in accordance with their right to distributions under subsection (b).

(b) Each partner is entitled to a settlement of all partnership accounts upon winding up the partnership business. In settling accounts among the partners, profits and losses that result from the liquidation of the partnership assets must be credited and charged to the partners' accounts. The partnership shall make a distribution to a partner in an amount equal to any excess of the credits over the charges in the partner's account. A partner shall contribute to the partnership an amount equal to any excess of the charges over the credits in the partner's account but excluding from the calculation charges attributable to an obligation for which the partner is not personally liable under Section 306.

(c) If a partner fails to contribute the full amount required under subsection (b), all of the other partners shall contribute, in the proportions in which those partners share partnership losses, the additional amount necessary to satisfy the partnership obligations for which they are personally liable under Section 306. A partner or partner's legal representative may recover from the other partners any contributions the partner makes to the extent the amount contributed exceeds that partner's share of the partnership obligations for which the partner is personally liable under Section 306.

(d) After the settlement of accounts, each partner shall contribute, in the proportion in which the partner shares partnership losses, the amount necessary to satisfy partnership obligations that were not known at the time of the settlement and for which the partner is personally liable under Section 306.

(e) The estate of a deceased partner is liable for the partner's obligation to contribute to the partnership.

(f) An assignee for the benefit of creditors of a partnership or a partner, or a person appointed by a court to represent creditors of a partnership or a partner, may enforce a partner's obligation to contribute to the partnership.

COMMENT

1. Section 807 provides the default rules for the settlement of accounts and contributions among the partners in winding up the business. It is derived in part from UPA Sections 38(1) and 40.

2. Subsection (a) continues the rule in UPA Section 38(l) that, in winding up the business, the partnership assets must first be applied to discharge partnership liabilities to creditors. For this purpose, any required contribution by the partners is treated as an asset of the partnership. After the payment of all partnership liabilities, any surplus must be applied to pay in cash the net amount due the partners under subsection (b) by way of a liquidating distribution.

RUPA continues the "in-cash" rule of UPA Section 38(1) and is consistent with Section 402, which provides that a partner has no right to receive, and may not be required to accept, a distribution in kind, unless otherwise agreed. The in-cash rule avoids the valuation problems that afflict unwanted in-kind distributions.

The partnership must apply its assets to discharge the obligations of partners who are creditors on a parity with other creditors. *See* Section 404(f) and Comment 6. In effect, that abolishes the priority rules in UPA Section 40(b) and (c) which subordinate the payment of inside debt to outside debt. Both RULPA and the RMBCA do likewise. *See* RULPA § 804; RMBCA §§ 6.40(f), 14.05(a). Ultimately, however, a partner whose "debt" has been repaid by the partnership is personally liable, as a partner, for any outside debt remaining unsatisfied, unlike a limited partner or corporate shareholder. Accordingly, the obligation to contribute sufficient funds to satisfy the claims of outside creditors may result in the equitable subordination of inside debt when partnership assets are insufficient to satisfy all obligations to non-partners.

. RUPA in effect abolishes the "dual priority" or "jingle" rule of UPA Section 40(h) and (i). Those sections gave partnership creditors priority as to partnership property and separate creditors priority as to separate property. The jingle rule has already been preempted by the Bankruptcy Code, at least as to Chapter 7 partnership liquidation proceedings. Under Section 723(c) of the Bankruptcy Code, and under RUPA, partnership creditors share pro rata with the partners' individual creditors in the assets of the partners' estates.

3. Subsection (b) provides that each partner is entitled to a settlement of all partnership accounts upon winding up. It also establishes the default rules for closing out the partners' accounts. First, the profits and losses resulting from the liquidation of the partnership assets must be credited or charged to the partners' accounts, according to their respective shares of profits and losses. Then, the partnership must make a final liquidating distribution to those partners with a positive account balance. That distribution should be in the amount of the excess of credits over the charges in the account. Any partner with a negative account balance must contribute to the partnership an amount equal to the excess of charges over the credits in the account provided the excess relates to an obligation for which the partner is personally liable under Section 306. The partners may, however, agree that a negative account does not reflect a debt to the partnership and need not be repaid in settling the partners' accounts.

Section 807(b) makes clear that a partner's contribution obligation to a partnership in dissolution only considers the partner's share of obligations for which the partner was personally liable under Section 306 ("unshielded obligations"). See Comments to Section 401(b) (partner contribution obligation to an operating partnership). Properly determined under this Section, the total required partner contributions will be sufficient to satisfy the partnership's total unshielded obligations. In special circumstances where a partnership has both shielded and unshielded obligations and the partner required contributions are used to first pay shielded partnership obligations, the partners may be required to make further contributions to satisfy the partnership unpaid unshielded obligations. The proper resolution of this matter is left to debtor-creditor law as well as the law governing the fiduciary obligations of the partners. See Section 104(a).

RUPA eliminates the distinction in UPA Section 40(b) between the liability owing to a partner in respect of capital and the liability owing in respect of profits. Section 807(b) speaks simply of the right of a partner to a liquidating distribution. That implements the logic of RUPA Sections 401(a) and 502 under which contributions to capital and shares in profits and losses combine to determine the right to distributions. The partners may, however, agree to share "operating" losses differently from "capital" losses, thereby continuing the UPA distinction.

4. Subsection (c) continues the UPA Section 40(d) rule that solvent partners share proportionately in the shortfall caused by insolvent partners who fail to contribute their proportionate share. The partnership may enforce a partner's obligation to contribute. See Section 405(a). A partner is entitled to recover from the other partners any contributions in excess of that partner's share of the partnership's liabilities. See Section 405(b)(iii).

5. Subsection (d) provides that, after settling the partners' accounts, each partner must contribute, in the proportion in which he shares losses, the amount necessary to satisfy partnership obligations that were not known at the time of the settlement. That continues the basic rule of UPA Section 40(d) and underscores that the obligation to contribute exists independently of the partnership's books of account. It specifically covers the situation of a partnership liability that was unknown when the partnership books were closed.

6. Under subsection (e), the estate of a deceased partner is liable for the partner's obligation to contribute to partnership losses. That continues the rule of UPA Section 40(g).

7. Subsection (f) provides that an assignee for the benefit of creditors of the partnership or of a partner (or other court appointed creditor representative) may enforce any partner's obligation to contribute to the partnership. That continues the rules of UPA Sections 36(4) and 40(e).

ARTICLE 9.   CONVERSIONS AND MERGERS

§ 901.   Definitions

In this article:

    (1)   "General partner" means a partner in a partnership and a general partner in a limited partnership.

    (2)   "Limited partner" means a limited partner in a limited partnership.

    (3)   "Limited partnership" means a limited partnership created under the [State Limited Partnership Act], predecessor law, or comparable law of another jurisdiction.

    (4)   "Partner" includes both a general partner and a limited partner.

COMMENT

1.   Article 9 is new. The UPA is silent with respect to the conversion or merger of partnerships, and thus it is necessary under the UPA to structure those types of transactions as asset transfers. RUPA provides specific statutory authority for conversions and mergers. It provides for continuation of the partnership entity, thereby simplifying those transactions and adding certainty to the legal consequences.

A number of States currently authorize the merger of limited partnerships, and some authorize them to merge with other business entities such as corporations and limited liability companies. A few States currently authorize the merger of a general and a limited partnership or the conversion of a general to a limited partnership.

2.   As Section 908 makes clear, the requirements of Article 9 are not mandatory, and a partnership may convert or merge in any other manner provided by law. Article 9 is merely a "safe harbor." If the requirements of the article are followed, the conversion or merger is legally valid. Since most States have no other established procedure for the conversion or merger of partnerships, it is likely that the Article 9 procedures will be used in virtually all cases.

3.   Article 9 does not restrict the provisions authorizing conversions and mergers to domestic partnerships. Since no filing is required for the creation of a partnership under RUPA, it is often unclear where a partnership is domiciled. Moreover, a partnership doing business in the State satisfies the definition of a partnership created under this Act since it is an association of two or more co-owners carrying on a business for profit. Even a partnership clearly domiciled in another State could easily amend its partnership agreement to provide that its internal affairs are to be governed by the laws of a jurisdiction that has enacted Article 9 of RUPA. No harm is likely to result from extending to foreign partnerships the right to convert or merge under local law.

4.   Because Article 9 deals with the conversion and merger of both general and limited partnerships, Section 901 sets forth four definitions distinguishing between the two types of partnerships solely for the purposes of Article 9. "Partner" includes both general and limited partners, and "general partner" includes general partners in both general and limited partnerships.

§ 902.   Conversion of Partnership to Limited Partnership

    (a)   A partnership may be converted to a limited partnership pursuant to this section.

    (b)   The terms and conditions of a conversion of a partnership to a limited partnership must be approved by all of the partners or by a number or percentage specified for conversion in the partnership agreement.

    (c)   After the conversion is approved by the partners, the partnership shall file a certificate of limited partnership in the jurisdiction in which the limited partnership is to be formed. The certificate must include:

    (1)   a statement that the partnership was converted to a limited partnership from a partnership;

(2)   its former name; and

(3)   a statement of the number of votes cast by the partners for and against the conversion and, if the vote is less than unanimous, the number or percentage required to approve the conversion under the partnership agreement.

(d)   The conversion takes effect when the certificate of limited partnership is filed or at any later date specified in the certificate.

(e)   A general partner who becomes a limited partner as a result of the conversion remains liable as a general partner for an obligation incurred by the partnership before the conversion takes effect. If the other party to a transaction with the limited partnership reasonably believes when entering the transaction that the limited partner is a general partner, the limited partner is liable for an obligation incurred by the limited partnership within 90 days after the conversion takes effect. The limited partner's liability for all other obligations of the limited partnership incurred after the conversion takes effect is that of a limited partner as provided in the [State Limited Partnership Act].

COMMENT

Section 902(a) authorizes the conversion of a "partnership" to a "limited partnership." Section 202(b) limits the usual RUPA definition of "partnership" to general partnerships. That definition is applicable to Article 9. If a limited partnership is contemplated, Article 9 uses the term "limited partnership." *See* Section 901(3).

Subsection (b) provides that the terms and conditions of the conversion must be approved by all the partners, unless the partnership agreement specifies otherwise for a conversion.

Subsection (c) provides that, after approval, the partnership must file a certificate of limited partnership which includes the requisite information concerning the conversion.

Subsection (d) provides that the conversion takes effect when the certificate is filed, unless a later effective date is specified.

Subsection (e) establishes the partners' liabilities following a conversion. A partner who becomes a limited partner as a result of the conversion remains fully liable as a general partner for any obligation arising before the effective date of the conversion, both to third parties and to other partners for contribution. Third parties who transact business with the converted partnership unaware of a partner's new status as a limited partner are protected for 90 days after the conversion. Since RULPA Section 201(a)(3) requires the certificate of limited partnership to name all of the general partners, and under RUPA Section 902(c) the certificate must also include a statement of the conversion, parties transacting business with the converted partnership can protect themselves by checking the record of the State where the limited partnership is formed (the State where the conversion takes place). A former general partner who becomes a limited partner as a result of the conversion can avoid the lingering 90-day exposure to liability as a general partner by notifying those transacting business with the partnership of his limited partner status.

Although Section 902 does not expressly provide that a partner's withdrawal upon a term partnership's conversion to a limited partnership is rightful, it was assumed that the unanimity requirement for the approval of a conversion would afford a withdrawing partner adequate opportunity to protect his interest as a condition of approval. This question is left to the partnership agreement if it provides for conversion without the approval of all the partners.

§ 903.   Conversion of Limited Partnership to Partnership

(a)   A limited partnership may be converted to a partnership pursuant to this section.

(b)   Notwithstanding a provision to the contrary in a limited partnership agreement, the terms and conditions of a conversion of a limited partnership to a partnership must be approved by all of the partners.

(c)   After the conversion is approved by the partners, the limited partnership shall cancel its certificate of limited partnership.

163

(d)   The conversion takes effect when the certificate of limited partnership is canceled.

(e)   A limited partner who becomes a general partner as a result of the conversion remains liable only as a limited partner for an obligation incurred by the limited partnership before the conversion takes effect. Except as otherwise provided in Section 306, the partner is liable as a general partner for an obligation of the partnership incurred after the conversion takes effect.

COMMENT

Section 903(a) authorizes the conversion of a limited partnership to a general partnership.

Subsection (b) provides that the conversion must be approved by all of the partners, even if the partnership agreement provides to the contrary. That includes all of the general and limited partners. *See* Section 901(4). The purpose of the unanimity requirement is to protect a limited partner from exposure to personal liability as a general partner without clear and knowing consent at the time of conversion. Despite a general voting provision to the contrary in the partnership agreement, conversion to a general partnership may never have been contemplated by the limited partner when the partnership investment was made.

Subsection (c) provides that, after approval of the conversion, the converted partnership must cancel its certificate of limited partnership. *See* RULPA § 203.

Subsection (d) provides that the conversion takes effect when the certificate of limited partnership is canceled.

Subsection (e) provides that a limited partner who becomes a general partner is liable as a general partner for all partnership obligations for which a general partner would otherwise be personally liable for if incurred after the effective date of the conversion, but still has only limited liability for obligations incurred before the conversion.

§ 904.   Effect of Conversion; Entity Unchanged

(a)   A partnership or limited partnership that has been converted pursuant to this article is for all purposes the same entity that existed before the conversion.

(b)   When a conversion takes effect:

(1)   all property owned by the converting partnership or limited partnership remains vested in the converted entity;

(2)   all obligations of the converting partnership or limited partnership continue as obligations of the converted entity; and

(3)   an action or proceeding pending against the converting partnership or limited partnership may be continued as if the conversion had not occurred.

COMMENT

Section 904 sets forth the effect of a conversion on the partnership. Subsection (a) provides that the converted partnership is for all purposes the same entity as before the conversion.

Subsection (b) provides that upon conversion: (1) all partnership property remains vested in the converted entity; (2) all obligations remain the obligations of the converted entity; and (3) all pending legal actions may be continued as if the conversion had not occurred. The term "entity" as used in Article 9 refers to either or both general and limited partnerships as the context requires.

Under subsection (b)(1), title to partnership property remains vested in the converted partnership. As a matter of general property law, title remains vested without further act or deed and without reversion or impairment.

§ 905.   Merger of Partnerships

(a)   Pursuant to a plan of merger approved as provided in subsection (c), a partnership may be merged with one or more partnerships or limited partnerships.

(b)   The plan of merger must set forth:

(1)   the name of each partnership or limited partnership that is a party to the merger;

(2)   the name of the surviving entity into which the other partnerships or limited partnerships will merge;

(3)   whether the surviving entity is a partnership or a limited partnership and the status of each partner;

(4)   the terms and conditions of the merger;

(5)   the manner and basis of converting the interests of each party to the merger into interests or obligations of the surviving entity, or into money or other property in whole or part; and

(6)   the street address of the surviving entity's chief executive office.

(c)   The plan of merger must be approved:

(1)   in the case of a partnership that is a party to the merger, by all of the partners, or a number or percentage specified for merger in the partnership agreement; and

(2)   in the case of a limited partnership that is a party to the merger, by the vote required for approval of a merger by the law of the State or foreign jurisdiction in which the limited partnership is organized and, in the absence of such a specifically applicable law, by all of the partners, notwithstanding a provision to the contrary in the partnership agreement.

(d)   After a plan of merger is approved and before the merger takes effect, the plan may be amended or abandoned as provided in the plan.

(e)   The merger takes effect on the later of:

(1)   the approval of the plan of merger by all parties to the merger, as provided in subsection (c);

(2)   the filing of all documents required by law to be filed as a condition to the effectiveness of the merger; or

(3)   any effective date specified in the plan of merger.

COMMENT

Section 905 provides a "safe harbor" for the merger of a general partnership and one or more general or limited partnerships. The surviving entity may be either a general or a limited partnership.

The plan of merger must set forth the information required by subsection (b), including the status of each partner and the manner and basis of converting the interests of each party to the merger into interests or obligations of the surviving entity.

Subsection (c) provides that the plan of merger must be approved: (1) by all the partners of each general partnership that is a party to the merger, unless its partnership agreement specifically provides otherwise for mergers; and (2) by all the partners, including both general and limited partners, of each limited partnership that is a party to the merger, notwithstanding a contrary provision in its partnership agreement, unless specifically authorized by the law of the jurisdiction in which that limited partnership is organized. Like Section 902(b), the purpose of the unanimity requirement is to protect limited partners from exposure to liability as general partners without their clear and knowing consent.

Subsection (d) provides that the plan of merger may be amended or abandoned at any time before the merger takes effect, if the plan so provides.

Subsection (e) provides that the merger takes effect on the later of: (1) approval by all parties to the merger; (2) filing of all required documents; or (3) the effective date specified in the plan. The surviving entity must file all notices and documents relating to the merger required by other applicable statutes governing the entities that are parties to the merger, such as articles of merger or a certificate of limited partnership. It may also amend or cancel a statement of partnership authority previously filed by any party to the merger.

§ 906.   Effect of Merger

(a)   When a merger takes effect:

(1)   the separate existence of every partnership or limited partnership that is a party to the merger, other than the surviving entity, ceases;

(2)   all property owned by each of the merged partnerships or limited partnerships vests in the surviving entity;

(3)   all obligations of every partnership or limited partnership that is a party to the merger become the obligations of the surviving entity; and

(4)   an action or proceeding pending against a partnership or limited partnership that is a party to the merger may be continued as if the merger had not occurred, or the surviving entity may be substituted as a party to the action or proceeding.

(b)   The [Secretary of State] of this State is the agent for service of process in an action or proceeding against a surviving foreign partnership or limited partnership to enforce an obligation of a domestic partnership or limited partnership that is a party to a merger. The surviving entity shall promptly notify the [Secretary of State] of the mailing address of its chief executive office and of any change of address. Upon receipt of process, the [Secretary of State] shall mail a copy of the process to the surviving foreign partnership or limited partnership.

(c)   A partner of the surviving partnership or limited partnership is liable for:

(1)   all obligations of a party to the merger for which the partner was personally liable before the merger;

(2)   all other obligations of the surviving entity incurred before the merger by a party to the merger, but those obligations may be satisfied only out of property of the entity; and

(3)   except as otherwise provided in Section 306, all obligations of the surviving entity incurred after the merger takes effect, but those obligations may be satisfied only out of property of the entity if the partner is a limited partner.

(d)   If the obligations incurred before the merger by a party to the merger are not satisfied out of the property of the surviving partnership or limited partnership, the general partners of that party immediately before the effective date of the merger shall contribute the amount necessary to satisfy that party's obligations to the surviving entity, in the manner provided in Section 807 or in the [Limited Partnership Act] of the jurisdiction in which the party was formed, as the case may be, as if the merged party were dissolved.

(e)   A partner of a party to a merger who does not become a partner of the surviving partnership or limited partnership is dissociated from the entity, of which that partner was a partner, as of the date the merger takes effect. The surviving entity shall cause the partner's interest in the entity to be purchased under Section 701 or another statute specifically applicable to that partner's interest with respect to a merger. The surviving entity is bound under Section 702 by an act of a general partner dissociated under this subsection, and the partner is liable under Section 703 for transactions entered into by the surviving entity after the merger takes effect.

COMMENT

Section 906 states the effect of a merger on the partnerships that are parties to the merger and on the individual partners.

Subsection (a) provides that when the merger takes effect: (1) the separate existence of every partnership that is a party to the merger (other than the surviving entity) ceases; (2) all property owned by the parties to the merger vests in the surviving entity; (3) all obligations of every party to the merger become the obligations of the surviving entity; and (4) all legal actions pending against a party to the merger may be continued as if the merger had not occurred or the surviving entity may be substituted as a party. Title to partnership property vests in the surviving entity without further act or deed and without reversion or impairment.

Subsection (b) makes the Secretary of State the agent for service of process in any action against the surviving entity, if it is a foreign entity, to enforce an obligation of a domestic partnership that is a party to the merger. The purpose of this rule is to make it more convenient for local creditors to sue a foreign surviving entity when the credit was extended to a domestic partnership that has disappeared as a result of the merger.

Subsection (c) provides that a general partner of the surviving entity is liable for (1) all obligations for which the partner was personally liable before the merger; (2) all other obligations of the surviving entity incurred before the merger by a party to the merger, which obligations may be satisfied only out of the surviving entity's partnership property; and (3) all obligations incurred by the surviving entity after the merger, limited to the surviving entity's property in the case of limited partners and also limited to obligations of the partnership for which the partner was personally liable under Section 306.

This scheme of liability is similar to that of an incoming partner under Section 306(b). Only the surviving partnership itself is liable for all obligations, including obligations incurred by every constituent party before the merger. A general partner of the surviving entity is personally liable for obligations of the surviving entity incurred before the merger by the partnership of which he was a partner and those incurred by the surviving entity after the merger. Thus, a general partner of the surviving entity is liable only to the extent of his partnership interest for obligations incurred before the merger by a constituent party of which he was not a general partner.

Subsection (d) requires general partners to contribute the amount necessary to satisfy all obligations for which they were personally liable before the merger, if such obligations are not satisfied out of the partnership property of the surviving entity, in the same manner as provided in Section 807 or the limited partnership act of the applicable jurisdiction, as if the merged party were then dissolved. *See* RULPA §§ 502, 608.

Subsection (e) provides for the dissociation of a partner of a party to the merger who does not become a partner in the surviving entity. The surviving entity must buy out that partner's interest in the partnership under Section 701 or other specifically applicable statute. If the state limited partnership act has a dissenter's rights provision providing a different method of determining the amount due a dissociating limited partner, it would apply, rather than Section 701, since the two statutes should be read *in pari materia*.

Although subsection (e) does not expressly provide that a partner's withdrawal upon the merger of a term partnership is rightful, it was assumed that the unanimity requirement for the approval of a merger would afford a withdrawing partner adequate opportunity to protect his interest as a condition of approval. This question is left to the partnership agreement if it provides for merger without the approval of all the partners.

Under subsection (e), a dissociating general partner's lingering agency power is wound down, pursuant to Section 702, the same as in any other dissociation. Moreover, a dissociating general partner may be liable, under Section 703, for obligations incurred by the surviving entity for up to two years after the merger. A dissociating general partner can, however, limit to 90 days his exposure to liability by filing a statement of dissociation under Section 704.

§ 907. Statement of Merger

(a) After a merger, the surviving partnership or limited partnership may file a statement that one or more partnerships or limited partnerships have merged into the surviving entity.

(b) A statement of merger must contain:

(1) the name of each partnership or limited partnership that is a party to the merger;

(2)   the name of the surviving entity into which the other partnerships or limited partnership were merged;

(3)   the street address of the surviving entity's chief executive office and of an office in this State, if any; and

(4)   whether the surviving entity is a partnership or a limited partnership.

(c)   Except as otherwise provided in subsection (d), for the purposes of Section 302, property of the surviving partnership or limited partnership which before the merger was held in the name of another party to the merger is property held in the name of the surviving entity upon filing a statement of merger.

(d)   For the purposes of Section 302, real property of the surviving partnership or limited partnership which before the merger was held in the name of another party to the merger is property held in the name of the surviving entity upon recording a certified copy of the statement of merger in the office for recording transfers of that real property.

(e)   A filed and, if appropriate, recorded statement of merger, executed and declared to be accurate pursuant to Section 105(c), stating the name of a partnership or limited partnership that is a party to the merger in whose name property was held before the merger and the name of the surviving entity, but not containing all of the other information required by subsection (b), operates with respect to the partnerships or limited partnerships named to the extent provided in subsections (c) and (d).

COMMENT

Section 907(a) provides that the surviving entity may file a statement of merger. The execution, filing, and recording of the statement are governed by Section 105.

Subsection (b) requires the statement to contain the name of each party to the merger, the name and address of the surviving entity, and whether it is a general or limited partnership.

Subsection (c) provides that, for the purpose of the Section 302 rules regarding the transfer of partnership property, all personal and intangible property which before the merger was held in the name of a party to the merger becomes, upon the filing of the statement of merger with the Secretary of State, property held in the name of the surviving entity.

Subsection (d) provides a similar rule for real property, except that real property does not become property held in the name of the surviving entity until a certified copy of the statement of merger is recorded in the office for recording transfers of that real property under local law.

Subsection (e) is a savings provision in the event a statement of merger fails to contain all of the information required by subsection (b). The statement will have the operative effect provided in subsections (c) and (d) if it is executed and declared to be accurate pursuant to Section 105(e) and correctly states the name of the party to the merger in whose name the property was held before the merger, so that it would be found by someone searching the record. *Compare* Section 303(c) (statement of partnership authority).

§ 908.   Nonexclusive

This article is not exclusive. Partnerships or limited partnerships may be converted or merged in any other manner provided by law.

COMMENT

Section 908 provides that Article 9 is not exclusive. It is merely a "safe harbor." Partnerships may be converted or merged in any other manner provided by statute or common law. Existing statutes in a few States already authorize the conversion or merger of general partnerships and limited partnerships. *See* Comment 1 to Section 901. Those procedures may be followed in lieu of Article 9.

ARTICLE 10. LIMITED LIABILITY PARTNERSHIP

§ 1001. Statement of Qualification

(a) A partnership may become a limited liability partnership pursuant to this section.

(b) The terms and conditions on which a partnership becomes a limited liability partnership must be approved by the vote necessary to amend the partnership agreement except, in the case of a partnership agreement that expressly considers obligations to contribute to the partnership, the vote necessary to amend those provisions.

(c) After the approval required by subsection (b), a partnership may become a limited liability partnership by filing a statement of qualification. The statement must contain:

(1) the name of the partnership;

(2) the street address of the partnership's chief executive office and, if different, the street address of an office in this State, if any;

(3) if the partnership does not have an office in this State, the name and street address of the partnership's agent for service of process;

(4) a statement that the partnership elects to be a limited liability partnership; and

(5) a deferred effective date, if any.

(d) The agent of a limited liability partnership for service of process must be an individual who is a resident of this State or other person authorized to do business in this State.

(e) The status of a partnership as a limited liability partnership is effective on the later of the filing of the statement or a date specified in the statement. The status remains effective, regardless of changes in the partnership, until it is canceled pursuant to Section 105(d) or revoked pursuant to Section 1003.

(f) The status of a partnership as a limited liability partnership and the liability of its partners is not affected by errors or later changes in the information required to be contained in the statement of qualification under subsection (c).

(g) The filing of a statement of qualification establishes that a partnership has satisfied all conditions precedent to the qualification of the partnership as a limited liability partnership.

(h) An amendment or cancellation of a statement of qualification is effective when it is filed or on a deferred effective date specified in the amendment or cancellation.

COMMENT

Any partnership may become a limited liability partnership by filing a statement of qualification. See Comments to Sections 101(6) and 202(b) regarding a limited partnership filing a statement of qualification to become a limited liability limited partnership. Section 1001 sets forth the required contents of a statement of qualification. The section also sets forth requirements for the approval of a statement of qualification, establishes the effective date of the filing (and any amendments) which remains effective until canceled or revoked, and provides that the liability of the partners of a limited liability partnership is not affected by errors or later changes in the statement information.

Subsection (b) provides that the terms and conditions on which a partnership becomes a limited liability partnership must be generally be approved by the vote necessary to amend the partnership agreement. This means that the act of becoming a limited liability partnership is equivalent to an amendment of the partnership agreement. Where the partnership agreement is silent as to how it may be amended, the subsection (b) vote requires the approval of every partner. Since the limited liability partnership rules are not intended to increase the vote necessary to amend the partnership agreement, where the partnership agreement specifically sets forth an amendment process, that process may be used. Where a partnership agreement sets forth several amendment procedures depending upon the nature of the amendment, the required vote will be that necessary to amend the contribution obligations of the partners. The specific "contribution" vote is preferred because the filing of the statement directly affects partner contribution obligations. Therefore, the language "considers contribution" should be broadly interpreted to include any amendment vote that indirectly affects any partner's contribution obligation such as a partner's obligation to "indemnify" other partners.

The unanimous vote default rule reflects the significance of a partnership becoming a limited liability partnership. In general, upon such a filing each partner is released from the personal contribution obligation imposed under this Act in exchange for relinquishing the right to enforce the contribution obligations of other partners under this Act. *See* Comments to Sections 306(c) and 401(b). The wisdom of this bargain will depend on many factors including the relative risks of the partners' duties and the assets of the partnership.

Subsection (c) sets forth the information required in a statement of qualification. The must include the name of the partnership which must comply with Section 1002 to identify the partnership as a limited liability partnership. The statement must also include the address of the partnership's chief executive office and, if different, the street address of any other office in this State. A statement must include the name and street address of an agent for service of process only if it does not have any office in this State.

As with other statements, a statement of qualification must be filed in the office of the Secretary of State. *See* Sections 101(13) and 105(a). Accordingly, a statement of qualification is executed, filed, and otherwise regarded as a statement under this Act. For example, a copy of a filed statement must be sent to every nonfiling partner unless otherwise provided in the partnership agreement. *See* Sections 105(e) and 103(b)(1). A statement of qualification must be executed by at least two partners under penalties of perjury that the contents of the statement are accurate. *See* Section 105(c). A person who files the statement must promptly send a copy of the statement to every nonfiling partner but failure to send the copy does not limit the effectiveness of the filed statement to a nonpartner. Section 105(e). The filing must be accompanied by the fee required by the Secretary of State. Section 105(f).

Subsection (d) makes clear that once a statement is filed and effective, the status of the partnership as a limited liability partnership remains effective until the partnership status is either canceled or revoked "regardless of changes in the partnership." Accordingly, a partnership that dissolves but whose business is continued under a business continuation agreement retains its status as a limited liability partnership without the need to refile a new statement. Also, limited liability partnership status remains even though a partnership may be dissolved, wound up, and terminated. Even after the termination of the partnership, the former partners of a terminated partnership would not be personally liable for partnership obligations incurred while the partnership was a limited liability partnership.

Subsection (d) also makes clear that limited liability partnership status remains effective until actual cancellation under Section 1003 or revocation under Section 105(d). Ordinarily the terms and conditions of becoming a limited liability partnership must be approved by the vote necessary to amend the partnership agreement. *See* Sections 1001(b), 306(c), and 401(j). Since the statement of cancellation may be filed by a person authorized to file the original statement of qualification, the same vote necessary to approve the filing of the statement of qualification must be obtained to file the statement of cancellation. *See* Section 105(d).

Subsection (f) provides that once a statement of qualification is executed and filed under subsection (c) and Section 105, the partnership assumes the status of a limited liability partnership. This status is intended to be conclusive with regard to third parties dealing with the partnership. It is not intended to affect the rights of partners. For example, a properly executed and filed statement of qualification conclusively establishes the limited liability shield described in Section 306(c). If the partners executing and filing the statement exceed their authority, the internal abuse of authority has no effect on the liability shield with regard to third parties. Partners may challenge the abuse of authority for purposes of establishing the liability of the culpable partners but may not effect the liability shield as to third parties. Likewise, third parties may not challenge the existence of the liability shield because the decision to file the statement lacked the proper vote. As a result, the filing of the statement creates the liability shield even when the required subsection (b) vote is not obtained.

§ 1002. Name

The name of a limited liability partnership must end with "Registered Limited Liability Partnership", "Limited Liability Partnership", "R.L.L.P.", "L.L.P.", "RLLP," or "LLP".

COMMENT

The name provisions are intended to alert persons dealing with a limited liability partnership of the presence of the liability shield. Because many jurisdictions have adopted the naming concept of a "registered" limited liability partnership, this aspect has been retained. These name requirements also distinguish limited partnerships and general partnerships that become limited liability partnerships because the new name must be at the end of and in addition to the general or limited partnership's regular name. *See* Comments to Section 101(6). Since the name identification rules of this section do not alter the regular name of the partnership, they do not disturb historic notions of apparent authority of partners in both general and limited partnerships.

§ 1003. Annual Report

(a) A limited liability partnership, and a foreign limited liability partnership authorized to transact business in this State, shall file an annual report in the office of the [Secretary of State] which contains:

(1) the name of the limited liability partnership and the State or other jurisdiction under whose laws the foreign limited liability partnership is formed;

(2) the street address of the partnership's chief executive office and, if different, the street address of an office of the partnership in this State, if any; and

(3) if the partnership does not have an office in this State, the name and street address of the partnership's current agent for service of process.

(b) An annual report must be filed between [January 1 and April 1] of each year following the calendar year in which a partnership files a statement of qualification or a foreign partnership becomes authorized to transact business in this State.

(c) The [Secretary of State] may revoke the statement of qualification of a partnership that fails to file an annual report when due or pay the required filing fee. To do so, the [Secretary of State] shall provide the partnership at least 60 days' written notice of intent to revoke the statement. The notice must be mailed to the partnership at its chief executive office set forth in the last filed statement of qualification or annual report. The notice must specify the annual report that has not been filed, the fee that has not been paid, and the effective date of the revocation. The revocation is not effective if the annual report is filed and the fee is paid before the effective date of the revocation.

(d) A revocation under subsection (c) only affects a partnership's status as a limited liability partnership and is not an event of dissolution of the partnership.

(e) A partnership whose statement of qualification has been revoked may apply to the [Secretary of State] for reinstatement within two years after the effective date of the revocation.

The application must state:

(1) the name of the partnership and the effective date of the revocation; and

(2) that the ground for revocation either did not exist or has been corrected.

(f) A reinstatement under subsection (e) relates back to and takes effect as of the effective date of the revocation, and the partnership's status as a limited liability partnership continues as if the revocation had never occurred.

COMMENT

Section 1003 sets forth the requirements of an annual report that must be filed by all limited liability partnerships and any foreign limited liability partnership authorized to transact business in this State. *See* Sections 101(5)(definition of a limited liability partnership) and 101(4)(definition of a foreign limited liability partnership). The failure of a limited liability partnership to file an annual report is a basis for the Secretary of State to administratively revoke its statement of qualification. *See* Section 1003(c). A foreign limited liability partnership that fails to file an annual report may not maintain an action or proceeding in this State. *See* Section 1103(a).

Subsection (a) generally requires that an annual report contain the same information required in a statement of qualification. *Compare* Sections 1001(a) and 1003(a). The differences are that the annual report requires disclosure of the State of formation of a foreign limited liability partnership but deletes the delayed effective date and limited liability partnership election statement provisions of a statement of qualification. As such, the annual report serves to update the information required in a statement of qualification. Under subsection (b), the annual report must be filed between January 1 and April 1 of each calendar year following the year in which a statement of qualification was filed or a foreign limited liability partnership becomes authorized to transact business. This timing requirement means that a limited liability partnership must make an annual filing and may not prefile multiple annual reports in a single year.

Subsection (c) sets forth the procedure for the Secretary of State to administratively revoke a partnership's statement of qualification for the failure to file an annual report when due or pay the required filing fee. The Secretary of State must provide a partnership at least 60 days' written notice of the intent to revoke the statement. The notice must be mailed to the partnership at the address of its chief executive office set forth in the last filed statement or annual report and must state the grounds for revocation as well as the effective date of revocation. The revocation is not effective if the stated problem is cured before the stated effective date.

Under subsection (d), a revocation only terminates the partnership's status as a limited liability partnership but is not an event of dissolution of the partnership itself. Where revocation occurs, a partnership may apply for reinstatement under subsection (e) within two years after the effective date of the revocation. The application must state that the grounds for revocation either did not exist or have been corrected. The Secretary of State may grant the application on the basis of the statements alone or require proof of correction. Under subsection (f), when the application is granted, the reinstatement relates back to and takes effect as of the effective date of the revocation. The relation back doctrine prevents gaps in a reinstated partnership's liability shield. *See* Comments to Section 306(c).

ARTICLE 11.   FOREIGN LIMITED LIABILITY PARTNERSHIP

§ 1101.   Law Governing Foreign Limited Liability Partnership

(a)   The law under which a foreign limited liability partnership is formed governs relations among the partners and between the partners and the partnership and the liability of partners for obligations of the partnership.

(b)   A foreign limited liability partnership may not be denied a statement of foreign qualification by reason of any difference between the law under which the partnership was formed and the law of this State.

(c)   A statement of foreign qualification does not authorize a foreign limited liability partnership to engage in any business or exercise any power that a partnership may not engage in or exercise in this State as a limited liability partnership.

COMMENT

Section 1101 provides that the laws where a foreign limited liability partnership is formed rather than the laws of this State govern both the internal relations of the partnership and liability of its partners for the obligations of the partnership. *See* Section 101(4)(definition of a foreign limited liability partnership). Section 106(b) provides that the laws of this State govern the internal relations of a domestic limited liability and the liability of its partners for the obligations of the partnership. *See* Sections 101(5)(definition of a domestic limited liability partnership). A partnership may therefore chose the laws of a particular jurisdiction by filing a statement of qualification in that jurisdiction. But there are limitations on this choice.

Subsections (b) and (c) together make clear that although a foreign limited liability partnership may not be denied a statement of foreign qualification simply because of a difference between the laws of its foreign jurisdiction and the laws of this State, it may not engage in any business or exercise any power in this State that a domestic limited liability partnership may not engage in or exercise. Under subsection (c), a foreign limited liability partnership that engages in a business or exercises a power in this State that a domestic may not engage in or exercise, does so only as [an] ordinary partnership without the benefit of the limited liability partnership liability shield set forth in Section 306(c). In this sense, a foreign limited liability partnership is treated the same as a domestic limited liability partnership. Also, the Attorney General may maintain an action to restrain a foreign limited liability partnership from transacting an unauthorized business in this State. *See* Section 1105.

§ 1102. Statement of Foreign Qualification

(a)   Before transacting business in this State, a foreign limited liability partnership must file a statement of foreign qualification. The statement must contain:

(1)   the name of the foreign limited liability partnership which satisfies the requirements of the State or other jurisdiction under whose law it is formed and ends with "Registered Limited Liability Partnership", "Limited Liability Partnership", "R.L.L.P.", "L.L.P.", "RLLP," or "LLP";

(2)   the street address of the partnership's chief executive office and, if different, the street address of an office of the partnership in this State, if any;

(3)   if there is no office of the partnership in this State, the name and street address of the partnership's agent for service of process; and

(4)   a deferred effective date, if any.

(b)   The agent of a foreign limited liability company for service of process must be an individual who is a resident of this State or other person authorized to do business in this State.

(c)   The status of a partnership as a foreign limited liability partnership is effective on the later of the filing of the statement of foreign qualification or a date specified in the statement. The status remains effective, regardless of changes in the partnership, until it is canceled pursuant to Section 105(d) or revoked pursuant to Section 1003.

(d)   An amendment or cancellation of a statement of foreign qualification is effective when it is filed or on a deferred effective date specified in the amendment or cancellation.

COMMENT

Section 1102 provides that a foreign limited liability partnership must file a statement of foreign qualification before transacting business in this State. The section also sets forth the information required in the statement. As with other statements, a statement of foreign qualification must be filed in the office of the Secretary of State. *See* Sections 101(13), 105(a), and 1001(c). Accordingly, a statement of foreign qualification is executed, filed, and otherwise regarded as a statement under this Act. *See* Section 101(13)(definition of a statement includes a statement of foreign qualification).

Subsection (a) generally requires the same information in a statement of foreign qualification as is required in a statement of qualification. *Compare* Section 1001(c). The statement of foreign qualification must include a name that complies with the requirements for domestic limited liability partnership under Section 1002 and must include the address of the partnership's chief executive office and, if different, the street address of any other office in this State. If a foreign limited liability partnership does not have any office in this State, the statement of foreign qualification must include the name and street address of an agent for service of process.

As with a statement of qualification, a statement of foreign qualification (and amendments) is effective when filed or at a later specified filing date. *Compare* Sections 1102(b) and (c) with Sections 1001(e) and (h). Likewise, a statement of foreign qualification remains effective until canceled by the partnership or revoked by the Secretary of State, regardless of changes in the partnership. *See* Sections 105(d) (statement cancellation) and Section 1003 (revocation for failure to file annual report or pay annual filing fee) and *Compare* Sections 1102(b) and 1001(e). Statement of qualification provisions regarding the relationship of the status of a foreign partnership relative to its initial filing of a statement are governed by foreign law and are therefore omitted from this section. *See* Sections 1001(f) (effect of errors and omissions) and (g)(filing establishes all conditions precedent to qualification).

§ 1103.   Effect of Failure to Qualify

(a)   A foreign limited liability partnership transacting business in this State may not maintain an action or proceeding in this State unless it has in effect a statement of foreign qualification.

(b)   The failure of a foreign limited liability partnership to have in effect a statement of foreign qualification does not impair the validity of a contract or act of the foreign limited liability partnership or preclude it from defending an action or proceeding in this State.

(c)   A limitation on personal liability of a partner is not waived solely by transacting business in this State without a statement of foreign qualification.

(d)   If a foreign limited liability partnership transacts business in this State without a statement of foreign qualification, the [Secretary of State] is its agent for service of process with respect to a right of action arising out of the transaction of business in this State.

COMMENT

Section 1103 makes clear that the only consequence of a failure to file a statement of foreign qualification is that the foreign limited liability partnership will not be able to maintain an action or proceeding in this State. The partnership's contracts remain valid, it may defend an action or proceeding, personal liability of the partners is not waived, and the Secretary of State is the agent for service of process with respect to claims arising out of transacting business in this State. Sections 1103(b)–(d). Once a statement of foreign qualification is filed, the Secretary of State may revoke the statement for failure to file an annual report but the partnership has the right to cure the failure for two years. *See* Section 1003(c) and (e). Since the failure to file a statement of foreign qualification has no impact on the liability shield of the partners, a revocation of a statement of foreign qualification also has no impact on the liability shield created under foreign laws. *Compare* Sections 1103(c) and 1003(f) (revocation of the statement of qualification of a domestic limited liability partnership removes partner liability shield unless filing problems cured within two years).

§ 1104.   Activities not Constituting Transacting Business

(a)   Activities of a foreign limited liability partnership which do not constitute transacting business for the purpose of this article include:

(1)   maintaining, defending, or settling an action or proceeding;

(2)   holding meetings of its partners or carrying on any other activity concerning its internal affairs;

(3)   maintaining bank accounts;

(4)   maintaining offices or agencies for the transfer, exchange, and registration of the partnership's own securities or maintaining trustees or depositories with respect to those securities;

(5)   selling through independent contractors;

(6)   soliciting or obtaining orders, whether by mail or through employees or agents or otherwise, if the orders require acceptance outside this State before they become contracts;

(7) creating or acquiring indebtedness, with or without a mortgage, or other security interest in property;

(8) collecting debts or foreclosing mortgages or other security interests in property securing the debts, and holding, protecting, and maintaining property so acquired;

(9) conducting an isolated transaction that is completed within 30 days and is not one in the course of similar transactions; and

(10) transacting business in interstate commerce.

(b) For purposes of this article, the ownership in this State of income-producing real property or tangible personal property, other than property excluded under subsection (a), constitutes transacting business in this State.

(c) This section does not apply in determining the contacts or activities that may subject a foreign limited liability partnership to service of process, taxation, or regulation under any other law of this State.

COMMENT

Because the Attorney General may restrain a foreign limited liability partnership from transacting an unauthorized business in this State and a foreign partnership may not maintain an action or proceeding in this State, the concept of "transacting business" in this State is important. To provide more certainty, subsection (a) sets forth ten separate categories of activities that do not constitute transacting business. Subsection (c) makes clear that the section only considers the definition of "transacting business" and as no impact on whether a foreign limited liability partnership's activities in this State subject it to service of process, taxation, or regulation under any other law of this State.

§ 1105. Action by [Attorney General]

The [Attorney General] may maintain an action to restrain a foreign limited liability partnership from transacting business in this State in violation of this article.

COMMENT

Section 1105 makes clear that the Attorney General may restrain a foreign limited liability from transacting an unauthorized business in this State. As a threshold matter, a foreign limited liability partnership must be "transacting business" in this State within the meaning of Section 1104. Secondly, the business transacted in this State must be that which could not be engaged in by a domestic limited liability partnership. *See* Section 1101(c). The fact that a foreign limited liability partnership has a statement of foreign qualification does not permit it to engage in any unauthorized business in this State or impair the power of the Attorney General to restrain the foreign partnership from engaging in the unauthorized business. *See* Section 1101(c).

ARTICLE 12. MISCELLANEOUS PROVISIONS

§ 1201. Uniformity of Application and Construction

This [Act] shall be applied and construed to effectuate its general purpose to make uniform the law with respect to the subject of this [Act] among States enacting it.

§ 1202. Short Title

This [Act] may be cited as the Uniform Partnership Act (1997).

§ 1203. Severability Clause

If any provision of this [Act] or its application to any person or circumstance is held invalid, the invalidity does not affect other provisions or applications of this [Act] which can be given effect without the invalid provision or application, and to this end the provisions of this [Act] are severable.

§ 1204. Effective Date

This [Act] takes effect . . . .

COMMENT

The effective date of the Act established by an adopting State has operative effects under Section 1206, which defers mandatory application of the Act to existing partnerships.

§ 1205. Repeals

Effective January 1, 199___, the following acts and parts of acts are repealed: [the State Partnership Act as amended and in effect immediately before the effective date of this [Act]].

COMMENT

This section repeals the adopting State's present general partnership act. The effective date of the repealer should not be any earlier than the date selected by that State in Section 1206(b) for the application of the Act to all partnerships.

§ 1206. Applicability

(a)   Before January 1, 199___, this [Act] governs only a partnership formed:

   (1)   after the effective date of this [Act], except a partnership that is continuing the business of a dissolved partnership under [Section 41 of the superseded Uniform Partnership Act]; and

   (2)   before the effective date of this [Act], that elects, as provided by subsection (c), to be governed by this [Act].

(b)   On and after January 1, 199___, this [Act] governs all partnerships.

(c)   Before January 1, 199___, a partnership voluntarily may elect, in the manner provided in its partnership agreement or by law for amending the partnership agreement, to be governed by this [Act]. The provisions of this [Act] relating to the liability of the partnership's partners to third parties apply to limit those partners' liability to a third party who had done business with the partnership within one year before the partnership's election to be governed by this [Act] only if the third party knows or has received a notification of the partnership's election to be governed by this [Act].

COMMENT

This section provides for a transition period in the applicability of the Act to existing partnerships, similar to that provided in the revised Texas partnership act. *See* Tex. Rev. Civ. Stat. Ann. art. 6132b–10.03 (Vernon Supp. 1994). Subsection (a) makes application of the Act mandatory for all partnerships formed after the effective date of the Act and permissive, by election, for existing partnerships. That affords existing partnerships and partners an opportunity to consider the changes effected by RUPA and to amend their partnership agreements, if appropriate.

Under subsection (b), application of the Act becomes mandatory for all partnerships, including existing partnerships that did not previously elect to be governed by it, upon a future date to be established by the adopting State. Texas, for example, deferred for five years mandatory compliance by existing partnerships.

Subsection (c) provides that an existing partnership may voluntarily elect to be governed by RUPA in the manner provided for amending its partnership agreement. Under UPA Section 18(h), that requires the consent of all the partners, unless otherwise agreed. Third parties doing business with the partnership must know or be notified of the election before RUPA's rules limiting a partner's liability become effective as to them. Those rules would include, for example, the provisions of Section 704 limiting the liability of a partner 90 days after the filing of a statement of dissociation. Without knowledge of the partnership's election, third parties would not be aware that they must check the record to ascertain the extent of a dissociated partner's personal liability.

§ 1207. Savings Clause

This [Act] does not affect an action or proceeding commenced or right accrued before this [Act] takes effect.

COMMENT

This section continues the prior law after the effective date of the Act with respect to a pending action or proceeding or a right accrued at the time of the effective date. Since courts generally apply the law that exists at the time an action is commenced, in many circumstances the new law of this Act would displace the old law, but for this section.

Almost all States have general savings statutes, usually as part of their statutory construction acts. These are often very broad. *Compare* Uniform Statute and Rule Construction Act § 16(a) (narrow savings clause). As RUPA is remedial, the more limited savings provisions in Section 1207 are more appropriate than the broad savings provisions of the usual general savings clause. *See generally*, Comment to Uniform Statute and Rule Construction Act § 16.

Pending "action" refers to a judicial proceeding, while "proceeding" is broader and includes administrative proceedings. Although it is not always clear whether a right has "accrued," the term generally means that a cause of action has matured and is ripe for legal redress. *See, e.g., Estate of Hoover v. Iowa Dept. of Social Services*, 299 Iowa 702, 251 N.W.2d 529 (1977); *Nielsen v. State of Wisconsin*, 258 Wis. 1110, 141 N.W.2d 194 (1966). An inchoate right is not enough, and thus, for example, there is no accrued right under a contract until it is breached.

[Sections 1208 through 1211 are necessary only for jurisdictions adopting Uniform Limited Liability Partnership Act Amendments after previously adopting Uniform Partnership Act (1994)]

§ 1208. Effective Date

These [Amendments] take effect . . . .

§ 1209. Repeals

Effective January 1, 199__, the following acts and parts of acts are repealed: [the Limited Liability Partnership amendments to the State Partnership Act as amended and in effect immediately before the effective date of these [Amendments]].

§ 1210. Applicability

(a) Before January 1, 199__, these [Amendments] govern only a limited liability partnership formed:

(1) on or after the effective date of these [Amendments], unless that partnership is continuing the business of a dissolved limited liability partnership; and

(2) before the effective date of these [Amendments], that elects, as provided by subsection (c), to be governed by these [Amendments].

(b) On and after January 1, 199__, these [Amendments] govern all partnerships.

(c) Before January 1, 199__, a partnership voluntarily may elect, in the manner provided in its partnership agreement or by law for amending the partnership agreement, to be governed by these [Amendments]. The provisions of these [Amendments] relating to the liability of the partnership's partners to third parties apply to limit those partners' liability to a third party who had done business with the partnership within one year before the partnership's election to be governed by these [Amendments], only if the third party knows or has received a notification of the partnership's election to be governed by these [Amendments].

(d)   The existing provisions for execution and filing a statement of qualification of a limited liability partnership continue until either the limited liability partnership elects to have this [Act] apply or January 1, 199__.

§ 1211.   Savings Clause

These [Amendments] do not affect an action or proceeding commenced or right accrued before these [Amendments] take effect.

C. REVISED UNIFORM PARTNERSHIP ACT (2013)

(with Selected Comments)

Table of Sections

[ARTICLE] 1.   GENERAL PROVISIONS

[ARTICLE] 2.   NATURE OF PARTNERSHIP

[ARTICLE] 3.   RELATIONS OF PARTNERS TO PERSONS DEALING WITH PARTNERSHIP

REVISED UNIFORM PARTNERSHIP ACT (2013)

[ARTICLE] 4. RELATIONS OF PARTNERS TO EACH OTHER AND TO PARTNERSHIP

[ARTICLE] 5. TRANSFERABLE INTERESTS AND RIGHTS OF TRANSFEREES AND CREDITORS

[ARTICLE] 6. DISSOCIATION

[ARTICLE] 7. PERSON'S DISSOCIATION AS A PARTNER WHEN BUSINESS NOT WOUND UP

[ARTICLE] 8. DISSOLUTION AND WINDING UP

[ARTICLE] 9. LIMITED LIABILITY PARTNERSHIP

[ARTICLE] 10.   FOREIGN LIMITED LIABILITY PARTNERSHIP

[ARTICLE] 11.   MERGER, INTEREST EXCHANGE, CONVERSION, AND DOMESTICATION

[PART] 1.   GENERAL PROVISIONS

[PART] 2.   MERGER

[PART] 3.   INTEREST EXCHANGE

[ARTICLE] 1.   GENERAL PROVISIONS

§ 101.   Short Title

This [act] may be cited as the Uniform Partnership Act.

§ 102.   Definitions

In this [act]:

(1)   "Business" includes every trade, occupation, and profession.

(2)   "Contribution", except in the phrase "right of contribution", means property or a benefit described in Section 403 which is provided by a person to a partnership to become a partner or in the person's capacity as a partner.

(3)   "Debtor in bankruptcy" means a person that is the subject of:

(A)   an order for relief under Title 11 of the United States Code or a comparable order under a successor statute of general application; or

(B)   a comparable order under federal, state, or foreign law governing insolvency.

(4)   "Distribution" means a transfer of money or other property from a partnership to a person on account of a transferable interest or in a person's capacity as a partner. The term:

(A) includes:

(i) a redemption or other purchase by a partnership of a transferable interest; and

(ii) a transfer to a partner in return for the partner's relinquishment of any right to participate as a partner in the management or conduct of the partnership's business or have access to records or other information concerning the partnership's business; and

(B) does not include amounts constituting reasonable compensation for present or past service or payments made in the ordinary course of business under a bona fide retirement plan or other bona fide benefits program.

(5) "Foreign limited liability partnership" means a foreign partnership whose partners have limited liability for the debts, obligations, or other liabilities of the foreign partnership under a provision similar to Section 306(c).

(6) "Foreign partnership" means an unincorporated entity formed under the law of a jurisdiction other than this state which would be a partnership if formed under the law of this state. The term includes a foreign limited liability partnership.

(7) "Jurisdiction", used to refer to a political entity, means the United States, a state, a foreign country, or a political subdivision of a foreign country.

(8) "Jurisdiction of formation" means the jurisdiction whose law governs the internal affairs of an entity.

(9) "Limited liability partnership", except in the phrase "foreign limited liability partnership" and in [Article] 11, means a partnership that has filed a statement of qualification under Section 901 and does not have a similar statement in effect in any other jurisdiction.

(10) "Partner" means a person that:

(A) has become a partner in a partnership under Section 402 or was a partner in a partnership when the partnership became subject to this [act] under Section 110; and

(B) has not dissociated as a partner under Section 601.

(11) "Partnership", except in [Article] 11, means an association of two or more persons to carry on as co-owners a business for profit formed under this [act] or that becomes subject to this [act] under [Article] 11 or Section 110. The term includes a limited liability partnership.

(12) "Partnership agreement" means the agreement, whether or not referred to as a partnership agreement and whether oral, implied, in a record, or in any combination thereof, of all the partners of a partnership concerning the matters described in Section 105(a). The term includes the agreement as amended or restated.

(13) "Partnership at will" means a partnership in which the partners have not agreed to remain partners until the expiration of a definite term or the completion of a particular undertaking.

(14) "Person" means an individual, business corporation, nonprofit corporation, partnership, limited partnership, limited liability company, [general cooperative association,] limited cooperative association, unincorporated nonprofit association, statutory trust, business trust, common-law business trust, estate, trust, association, joint venture, public corporation, government or governmental subdivision, agency, or instrumentality, or any other legal or commercial entity.

(15) "Principal office" means the principal executive office of a partnership or a foreign limited liability partnership, whether or not the office is located in this state.

(16) "Property" means all property, whether real, personal, or mixed or tangible or intangible, or any right or interest therein.

(17) "Record", used as a noun, means information that is inscribed on a tangible medium or that is stored in an electronic or other medium and is retrievable in perceivable form.

(18) "Registered agent" means an agent of a limited liability partnership or foreign limited liability partnership which is authorized to receive service of any process, notice, or demand required or permitted by law to be served on the partnership.

(19) "Registered foreign limited liability partnership" means a foreign limited liability partnership that is registered to do business in this state pursuant to a statement of registration filed by the [Secretary of State].

(20) "Sign" means, with present intent to authenticate or adopt a record:

    (A)   to execute or adopt a tangible symbol; or

    (B)   to attach to or logically associate with the record an electronic symbol, sound, or process.

(21) "State" means a state of the United States, the District of Columbia, Puerto Rico, the United States Virgin Islands, or any territory or insular possession subject to the jurisdiction of the United States.

(22) "Transfer" includes:

    (A)   an assignment;

    (B)   a conveyance;

    (C)   a sale;

    (D)   a lease;

    (E)   an encumbrance, including a mortgage or security interest;

    (F)   a gift; and

    (G)   a transfer by operation of law.

(23) "Transferable interest" means the right, as initially owned by a person in the person's capacity as a partner, to receive distributions from a partnership, whether or not the person remains a partner or continues to own any part of the right. The term applies to any fraction of the interest, by whomever owned.

(24) "Transferee" means a person to which all or part of a transferable interest has been transferred, whether or not the transferor is a partner.

§ 103.   Knowledge; Notice

    (a)   A person knows a fact if the person:

        (1)   has actual knowledge of it; or

        (2)   is deemed to know it under subsection (d)(1) or law other than this [act].

    (b)   A person has notice of a fact if the person:

        (1)   has reason to know the fact from all the facts known to the person at the time in question; or

        (2)   is deemed to have notice of the fact under subsection (d)(2).

    (c)   Subject to Section 117(f), a person notifies another person of a fact by taking steps reasonably required to inform the other person in ordinary course, whether or not those steps cause the other person to know the fact.

    (d)   A person not a partner is deemed:

        (1)   to know of a limitation on authority to transfer real property as provided in Section 303(g); and

        (2)   to have notice of:

(A) a person's dissociation as a partner 90 days after a statement of dissociation under Section 704 becomes effective; and

(B) a partnership's:

(i)   dissolution 90 days after a statement of dissolution under Section 802 becomes effective;

(ii) termination 90 days after a statement of termination under Section 802 becomes effective; and

(iii) participation in a merger, interest exchange, conversion, or domestication, 90 days after articles of merger, interest exchange, conversion, or domestication under [Article] 11 become effective.

(e) A partner's knowledge or notice of a fact relating to the partnership is effective immediately as knowledge of or notice to the partnership, except in the case of a fraud on the partnership committed by or with the consent of that partner.

§ 104. Governing Law

The internal affairs of a partnership and the liability of a partner as a partner for a debt, obligation, or other liability of the partnership are governed by:

(1) in the case of a limited liability partnership, the law of this state; and

(2) in the case of a partnership that is not a limited liability partnership, the law of the jurisdiction in which the partnership has its principal office.

§ 105. Partnership Agreement; Scope, Function, and Limitations

(a) Except as otherwise provided in subsections (c) and (d), the partnership agreement governs:

(1) relations among the partners as partners and between the partners and the partnership;

(2) the business of the partnership and the conduct of that business; and

(3) the means and conditions for amending the partnership agreement.

(b) To the extent the partnership agreement does not provide for a matter described in subsection (a), this [act] governs the matter.

(c) A partnership agreement may not:

(1) vary the law applicable under Section 104(1);

(2) vary the provisions of Section 110;

(3) vary the provisions of Section 307;

(4) unreasonably restrict the duties and rights under Section 408, but the partnership agreement may impose reasonable restrictions on the availability and use of information obtained under that section and may define appropriate remedies, including liquidated damages, for a breach of any reasonable restriction on use;

(5) alter or eliminate the duty of loyalty or the duty of care, except as otherwise provided in subsection (d);

(6) eliminate the contractual obligation of good faith and fair dealing under Section 409(d), but the partnership agreement may prescribe the standards, if not manifestly unreasonable, by which the performance of the obligation is to be measured;

(7) unreasonably restrict the right of a person to maintain an action under Section 410(b);

185

(8) relieve or exonerate a person from liability for conduct involving bad faith, willful or intentional misconduct, or knowing violation of law;

(9) vary the power of a person to dissociate as a partner under Section 602(a), except to require that the notice under Section 601(1) to be in a record;

(10) vary the grounds for expulsion specified in Section 601(5);

(11) vary the causes of dissolution specified in Section 801(4) or (5);

(12) vary the requirement to wind up the partnership's business as specified in Section 802(a), (b)(1), and (d);

(13) vary the right of a partner under Section 901(f) to vote on or consent to a cancellation of a statement of qualification;

(14) vary the right of a partner to approve a merger, interest exchange, conversion, or domestication under Section 1123(a)(2), 1133(a)(2), 1143(a)(2), or 1153(a)(2);

(15) vary the required contents of a plan of merger under Section 1122(a), plan of interest exchange under Section 1132(a), plan of conversion under Section 1142(a), or plan of domestication under Section 1152(a);

(16) vary any requirement, procedure, or other provision of this [act] pertaining to:

(A) registered agents; or

(B) the [Secretary of State], including provisions pertaining to records authorized or required to be delivered to the [Secretary of State] for filing under this [act]; or

(17) except as otherwise provided in Sections 106 and 107(b), restrict the rights under this [act] of a person other than a partner.

(d) Subject to subsection (c)(8), without limiting other terms that may be included in a partnership agreement, the following rules apply:

(1) The partnership agreement may:

(A) specify the method by which a specific act or transaction that would otherwise violate the duty of loyalty may be authorized or ratified by one or more disinterested and independent persons after full disclosure of all material facts; and

(B) alter the prohibition in Section 406(a)(2) so that the prohibition requires only that the partnership's total assets not be less than the sum of its total liabilities.

(2) To the extent the partnership agreement expressly relieves a partner of a responsibility that the partner would otherwise have under this [act] and imposes the responsibility on one or more other partners, the agreement also may eliminate or limit any fiduciary duty of the partner relieved of the responsibility which would have pertained to the responsibility.

(3) If not manifestly unreasonable, the partnership agreement may:

(A) alter or eliminate the aspects of the duty of loyalty stated in Section 409(b);

(B) identify specific types or categories of activities that do not violate the duty of loyalty;

(C) alter the duty of care, but may not authorize conduct involving bad faith, willful or intentional misconduct, or knowing violation of law; and

(D) alter or eliminate any other fiduciary duty.

(e) The court shall decide as a matter of law whether a term of a partnership agreement is manifestly unreasonable under subsection (c)(6) or (d)(3). The court:

(1)   shall make its determination as of the time the challenged term became part of the partnership agreement and by considering only circumstances existing at that time; and

(2)   may invalidate the term only if, in light of the purposes and business of the partnership, it is readily apparent that:

(A)   the objective of the term is unreasonable; or

(B)   the term is an unreasonable means to achieve the term's objective.

COMMENT

The Harmonization Project re-wrote this section, for the most part conforming this section to the corresponding section of ULLCA (2006).

Principal Provisions of the Act Concerning the Partnership Agreement

The partnership agreement is pivotal to a partnership, and Sections 105 through 107 are pivotal to this act. They must be read together, along with Section 102(12) (defining the partnership agreement).

This section performs five essential functions. Subsection (a) establishes the primacy of the partnership agreement in establishing *inter se* relations among the partners and partnership. Subsection (b) recognizes this act as comprising mostly default rules (i.e., gap fillers for issues as to which the partnership agreement provides no rule). Subsection (c) lists the few mandatory provisions of the act. Subsection (d) lists some provisions frequently found in partnership agreements, authorizing some unconditionally and others so long as "not manifestly unreasonable." Subsection (e) delineates in detail both the meaning of "not manifestly unreasonable" and the information relevant to determining a claim that a provision of a partnership agreement is manifestly unreasonable.

Section 106 details the effect of a partnership agreement on the partnership and on persons becoming partners. Section 107 concerns the effect of a partnership agreement on third parties.

Role and Inevitability of Partnership Agreement

Section 102(12) delineates a very broad scope for "partnership agreement." As a result, once a partnership comes into existence, a partnership agreement necessarily exists. *See* the comment to Section 102(12). Accordingly, this act refers to "the partnership agreement" rather than "a partnership agreement." This phrasing should not, however, be read to require a partnership or its partners to take any formal action to adopt a partnership agreement.

The partnership agreement is the exclusive consensual process for modifying this act's various default rules pertaining to relationships *inter se* the partners and between the partners and the partnership. Section 105(a). The partnership agreement also has power over "the obligations of a partnership and its partners to a person in the person's capacity as a transferee or person dissociated as a partner." Section 107(b). For the relationship between the partnership agreement and public records in the filing office, see Section 107(d).

The Partnership Agreement and the Fiduciary and Other Duties of Those Who Manage

One of the most complex questions in the law of unincorporated business organizations is the extent to which an agreement among the organization's owners can affect the fiduciary and other duties of those who have ultimate power to manage the organization—in a general partnership, the partners themselves. As explained in detail in the comment to Subsection (d)(3), this act rejects the notion that a contract can completely transform an inherently fiduciary relationship into a merely arm's length association. Within that limitation, however, this section provides substantial power to the partnership agreement to reshape, limit, and eliminate fiduciary and other managerial duties.

Subsection (a) recognizes that the partnership agreement is the map to the parties' deal and that any claim by a partner of managerial misconduct must be assessed first under the relevant terms of the partnership agreement. Subsection (d) specifically validates arrangements commonly used to reshape managerial duties and limit the consequences of breaching those duties. Subsection (c) contains relevant limitations, but those limitations: (i) must be read together with Subsection (d); and (ii) do not preclude the partnership agreement fundamentally redesigning the duties applicable to the partners. For the act's design of those duties, see Sections 408 and 409.

Subsection (a)—This section describes the very broad scope of a partnership's partnership agreement, which includes all matters constituting "internal affairs." *Compare* Section 105(a), with Section 104 (using the phrase "internal affairs" in stating a choice of law rule). This broad grant of authority is subject to the restrictions stated in Subsection (c), including the broad restriction stated in Subsection (c)(17) (concerning the rights of third parties under this act).

Subsection (a)(1)—This paragraph encompasses all the rights and duties of each partner, including rights and duties pertaining to transactions under Article 11.

Subsection (a)(3)—Under this provision, the partnership agreement can control both the quantum of consent required (*e.g.*, majority of partners) and the means by which the consent is manifested (*e.g.*, prohibiting modifications except when consented to in writing). *See* the comment to Section 107(a).

If the partnership agreement does not address the issue, Section 401(k) applies and requires the affirmative vote or consent of all the partners. Under Section 119 (supplemental principles of law), the parol evidence rule will apply to a written partnership agreement when appropriate under contract law.

Subsection (b)—To the extent the partnership agreement does not determine an *inter se* matter, this act determines the matter. The partnership agreement may vary any provision of this act pertaining to inter se matters, except as provided in Subsections (c) and (d).

Sometimes—but not always—the comments to this act refer to a variable provision as a "default rule" and a non-waivable provision as "mandatory." These references are merely to draw attention to the default/mandatory distinction in particular contexts and have neither the intent nor the power to affect the default/mandatory status of provisions of this act whose comments lack a comparable reference.

Subsection (c)—This subsection lists provisions of this act whose respective effects cannot be varied or may be varied subject to a stated limitation. For historical reasons, this subsection uses the words "vary" and "alter" interchangeably. No difference in meaning is intended.

If a person claims that a term of the partnership agreement violates this subsection, as a matter of ordinary procedural law the burden of proof is on the person making the claim.

Subsection (c)(1)—"[T]he law applicable under Section 104(1)" establishes the governing law for the internal affairs of a partnership. The organizers of a partnership make this choice of law by choosing to form a partnership under this act. Domestication to another jurisdiction will re-set the choice of law, see Sections 1151–56, but the partnership agreement cannot. *See* the comment to Section 104(1).

Subsection (c) contains no parallel prohibition on varying Section 901 (stating the governing law for foreign limited liability partnerships), because a prohibition is unnecessary. As a matter of fundamental contract law, an agreement among partners of one partnership is powerless to govern the affairs of another partnership.

Subsection (c)(3)—Under this act, a partnership is emphatically an entity, and the partners lack the power to alter that characteristic.

The cited section pertains to "actions by and against partnership and partners," arguably comes within Subsection (c)(17) (prohibiting the partnership agreement from "restrict[ing] the rights under this [act] of a person other than a partner"), but is specifically noted for the avoidance of doubt.

Subsection (c)(4)—Although phrased as a restriction, this provision grants substantial power to the partnership agreement.

Example: A law firm operates as a partnership, and the partnership agreement provides that a "Compensation Committee" periodically decides each partner's compensation. The agreement also states that only partners who are on the Compensation Committee may have access to the Committee's compensation decisions pertaining to other partners. This restriction is reasonable.

The act also empowers the partnership "as a matter within the ordinary course of its business [to] impose reasonable restrictions and conditions on access to and use of information" obtained under Section 408. *See* Section 408(j).

In determining whether a restriction is reasonable, a court might consider: (i) the danger or other problem the restriction seeks to avoid; (ii) the purpose for which the information is sought; and (iii) whether, in light of both the problem and the purpose, the restriction is reasonably tailored.

Subsection (c)(5)—This limitation is less powerful than might first appear, because Subsection (d) specifically authorizes substantial alterations to the duties of loyalty and care, including restricting and substantially eliminating those duties.

Subsection (c)(6)—Section 409(d) refers to the "contractual obligation of good faith and fair dealing," which contract law implies in every contract. The partnership agreement cannot eliminate this obligation, neither in whole (*i.e.*, generally) nor in part (*i.e.*, as applicable to specified situations).

However, a partnership agreement may "prescribe the standards . . . by which the performance of [that] obligation is to be measured."

Example: A partnership agreement designates a managing partner, provides that partner almost total control of the partnership's operations, and grants the partner the discretion to cause the partnership to enter into contracts with affiliates of the partner (so-called "Conflict Transactions"). The agreement further provides: "When causing the Company to enter into a Conflict Transaction, the Managing Partner complies with Section 409(d) of [this act] if a disinterested person, knowledgeable in the subject matter, states in writing that the terms and conditions of the Conflict Transaction are equivalent to the terms and conditions that would be agreed to by persons at arm's length in comparable circumstances." This provision "prescribes[s] the standards by which the performance of the [Section 409(d)] obligation is to be measured."

Example: Same facts as the previous example, except that, during the performance of a Conflict Transaction, the managing partner causes the partnership to waive material protections under the applicable contract. The standard stated in the previous example is inapposite to this conduct. Section 409(d) therefore applies to the conduct without any direct contractual delineation. (However, other terms of the agreement may be relevant to determining whether the conduct violates Section 409(d). *See* the comment to Section 409(d).)

Example: A partnership agreement designates a managing partner and gives that partner "sole discretion" to make various decisions. The agreement further provides: "Whenever this agreement requires or permits the Managing Partner to make a decision that has the potential to benefit one class of partners to the detriment of another class, the Managing Partner complies with Section 409(d) of [this act] if the Managing Partner makes the decision with:

    a.   the honest belief that the decision:

        i.   serves the best interests of the Partnership; or

        ii.   at least does not injure or otherwise disserve those interests; and

    b.   the reasonable belief that the decision breaches no partner's rights under this agreement."

This provision "prescribe[s] the standards by which the performance of the [Section 409(d)] obligation is to be measured." *Compare* Section 105(c)(6), with *Nemec v. Shrader*, 991 A.2d 1120 (Del. 2010) (considering such a situation in the context of the right to call preferred stock and deciding by a three-two vote that exercising the call did not breach the implied covenant of good faith and fair dealing).

A partnership agreement that seeks to prescribe standards for measuring the contractual obligation of good faith and fair dealing under Section 409(d) should expressly refer to the obligation. *See Gerber v. Enter. Prods. Hldgs., L.L.C.*, 67 A.3d 400, 418 (Del. 2013) (distinguishing between the implied contractual covenant and an express contractual obligation of "good faith" as stated in a limited partnership agreement).

For an explanation of the function and role of the covenant of good faith and fair dealing, see the comment to Section 409(d). For the rules delimiting the "not manifestly unreasonable" requirement, see Subsection (e).

Subsection (c)(7)—Section 410(b) delineates a partner's rights to "maintain an action against the partnership or another partner." It would be unreasonable to frustrate these rights but not unreasonable to channel their exercise. For example, the partnership agreement might select a forum, require pre-suit mediation, provide for arbitration, or require a pre-suit demand on a management committee before a partner files suit against the partnership. Similarly, it is not unreasonable to provide for liquidated damages consonant with the law of contracts. In contrast, it would be unreasonable for a partnership agreement to both: (i) require a partner intending to sue the partnership to make demand on a management committee before filing suit against the partnership regardless of futility; and (ii) bar taking the claim to court no matter how long the management committee ponders the demand.

Subsection (c)(8)—These restrictions are ubiquitous in the law of business entities and, in conjunction with other provisions of this section, control the otherwise very broad power of a partnership agreement to affect fiduciary and other duties. The restrictions are central to the raft of exculpatory provisions that sprung up in corporate statutes in response to *Smith v. Van Gorkum*, 488 A.2d 858 (Del. 1985), *overruled on other grounds by Gantler v. Stephens*, 965 A.2d 695 (Del. 2009). Delaware led the response with Delaware Code Annotated title 8, section 102(b)(7), and a number of LLC statutes have similar provisions. E.g., GA. CODE ANN. § 14–11–305(4)(A) (2011). For an extreme example, see Virginia Code Annotated section 13.1–1025 (B) (2012). In this context, "conduct" includes both acts and omissions. BLACK'S LAW DICTIONARY (9th ed. 2009) (defining conduct as "[p]ersonal behavior, whether by action or inaction").

The term "bad faith" has multiple meanings, and the context determines which meaning applies. In the context of the duty of loyalty, "bad faith" includes conduct motivated by ill will or other intent purposely to harm another person. The concept also includes conduct from which a person derives an improper personal benefit. See, e.g., *Mroz v. Hoaloha Na Eha, Inc.*, 410 F. Supp. 2d 919, 936–37 (D. Haw. 2005) (denying a motion to dismiss a claim that "the Majority Partners" were personally liable for the partnership's wrongful termination of the plaintiff; quoting the complaint as alleging that "the Majority Partners, individually and as a group, acted with malice and/or ill will, and/or with an intent to serve their own personal interests and/or without an intent to serve company interests, and/or outside of the scope of their authority and/or without justification"); *BOGNC, LLC v. Cornelius NC Self-Storage L.L.C.*, 10 CVS 19072, 2013 WL 1867065, at *9 (N.C. Super. [Business Court] May 1, 2013) (noting that "no . . . [exculpatory] provision may limit a manager's liability for acts known to be in conflict with the interests of the limited liability company, or for acts from which the manager derived an improper personal benefit") (citing N.C. Gen. Stat. § 57C–3–32(b)); *Lasica v. Savers Grp. of Minn., L.L.C.*, A12-0092, 2012 WL 3553246, at *2 (Minn. Ct. App. Aug. 20, 2012) (noting that an "individual seeking indemnification [under statute providing for indemnification)] must have acted in good faith and must not have received an improper personal benefit") (citing MINN. STAT. § 322B.699, subdivs. 2(a)(2), (3) (2010)).

In the context of the duty of care, the concept of bad faith comes primarily from corporate law and means an extreme breach of the duty (i.e., "the failure to exercise "honest judgment in the lawful and legitimate furtherance of corporate purposes"). *Deblinger v. Sani-Pine Products Co., Inc.*, 107 A.D.3d 659, 661 (N.Y. 2013) (quoting *Auerbach v. Bennett*, 393 N.E.2d 994 (N.Y. 1979)) (emphasis added) (internal quotation marks omitted).

Thus, when a plaintiff alleges bad faith as pertaining to the duty of care, "[t]he burden . . . is to show irrationality: a plaintiff must demonstrate that no reasonable business person could possibly authorize the action in good faith. Put positively, the decision must go so far beyond the bounds of reasonable business judgment that its only explanation is bad faith." *In re Tower Air, Inc.*, 416 F.3d 229, 238 (3d Cir. 2005) (discussing then prevailing Delaware law) (citation omitted); *see also KDW Restructuring & Liquidation Servs. L.L.C. v. Greenfield*, 874 F. Supp. 2d 213, 226 (S.D.N.Y. 2012) (referring to a lack of "a rationale corporate purpose" and "a disregard for the duty to examine all available information—*information that was readily at hand*") (emphasis added).

With regard to both the duty of loyalty and the duty of care, "bad faith" is entirely distinct from the meaning of "good faith" in the contractual covenant of good faith and fair dealing. *See* the comment to Section 409(d).

Subsection (c)(8) pertains to indirect as well as direct efforts to "relieve or exonerate" and thus limits how far a partnership agreement can go in providing for indemnification. *See* Section 401(c) (stating a default rule for indemnification).

Although this paragraph does not expressly address contracts between a partnership and a partner, the stated constraints must also apply to such contracts. If not, those constraints are effectively meaningless.

Example: A general partnership enters into a management contract with its sole managing partner, and the contract provides the partner exoneration for liability to the partnership even for willful and intentional misconduct. Most likely, contract law will treat the provision as against public policy and therefore unenforceable. RESTATEMENT (SECOND) OF CONTRACTS § 195(1) (1981) ("A term exempting a party from tort liability for harm caused intentionally or recklessly is unenforceable on grounds of public policy."). If not, a court should hold the provision unenforceable to avoid evisceration of Subsection (c)(8). (Or, the court could invoke the policy expressed in Subsection (c)(8) as grounds for holding the provision unenforceable under contract law.)

Subsection (c)(9)—As a result of this restriction, a partner always has the power to dissociate; the partnership agreement can only negate the right. This approach is consistent with the notions that: (i) a partnership is a voluntary association, see, e.g., *Gangl v. Gangl*, 281 N.W.2d 574, 580 (N.D. 1979) (stating that "[t]he term [association] connotes not only a group of two or more persons but also voluntariness"); (ii) the partnership relationship is essentially contractual, *see, e.g., Wallner v. Schmitz*, 239 Minn. 93, 95, 57 N.W.2d 821, 823 (1953) (stating that "[a] partnership is a contractual relationship as between the parties"); and (iii) only in exceptional circumstances does a party to a contract lack the power to breach, and courts will not enjoin a person to remain in an ongoing contractual relationship that involves trust and confidence. E. ALLAN FARNSWORTH, CONTRACTS § 12.7, at 781 (3d ed.1999) ("A court will not grant specific performance of a contract to provide a service that is personal in nature. This refusal . . . is based [in part] of the undesirability of compelling the continuance of personal relations after disputes have arisen and confidence and loyalty have been shaken and the undesirability, in some instances, of imposing what might seem like involuntary servitude.") (footnote omitted).

Subsection (c)(10)—The partnership agreement may not change the stated grounds for expulsion but may determine the forum in which a claim for expulsion under Section 601(5) is determined.

Subsection (c)(11)—The partnership agreement may not change the stated grounds for dissolution but may determine the forum in which a claim for dissolution under Section 801(4) or (5) is determined. For example, arbitration and forum selection clauses are commonplace in business relationships in general and in partnership agreements in particular.

The approach of this paragraph differs from the law of Delaware. *See Huatuco v. Satellite Healthcare*, CV 8465-VCG, 2013 WL 6460898, at *1, n.2 (Del. Ch. Dec. 9, 2013) (stating that "the right to judicial dissolution is a default right which the parties may eschew by contract" but reserving the question of "[w]hether the parties may, by contract, divest this Court of its authority to order a dissolution in all circumstances, even where it appears manifest that equity so requires—leaving, for instance, irreconcilable members locked away together forever like some alternative entity version of Sartre's *Huis Clos*").

Subsection (c)(12)—The cited provisions comprise the non-waivable aspects of winding up a dissolved partnership. The other provisions of Section 802 are default rules and therefore waivable.

Subsection (c)(13)—Section 901(f) requires the "the affirmative vote or consent of all the partners." The requirement is non-waivable, because canceling a statement of qualification eliminates the LLP liability shield and makes each partner automatically liable for partnership's obligations subsequently incurred.

Subsection (c)(14)—Sections 1123(a)(1), 1133(a)(1), 1143(a)(1), and 1153(a)(1) each requires the consent or the affirmative vote of all partners. The partnership agreement may modify these requirements. In contrast, under the sections stated in this subsection:

- each partner is protected from being merged, exchanged, converted, or domesticated "into" the status of a partner in a general partnership that is not a limited liability partnership (or a comparable "unshielded" position in some other organization) without the partner having *directly* consented to either:
  - the merger, interest exchange, conversion, or domestication; or
  - a partnership agreement provision that permits such transactions to occur with less than unanimous consent of the partners; and

- merely consenting to a partnership agreement provision that permits amendment of the partnership agreement with less than unanimous consent of the partners does not qualify as the requisite direct consent.

Subsection (c)(15)—Because these plans are the basic "deal documents" for each of the organic transactions contemplated in Article 11, the partnership agreement may not vary the contents of these plans.

Subsection (c)(16)—This prohibition is arguably implicit in Subsection (c)(17) (affecting rights under this act of third parties) but is stated expressly to avoid any doubt.

Subsection (c)(17)—This limitation pertains only to "the rights under this [act] of" third parties" other than partners. Moreover, the limitation is subject to two major exceptions: Section 106 (pertaining to the partnership agreement's relationship to the partnership itself and to persons becoming partners) and Section 107(b) (pertaining to the partnership agreement's power over the rights of transferees).

Subsection (d)—The partnership agreement has plenipotentiary power over the matters described in Subsection (a), except as specifically limited by Subsections (c) and (d)(3). However, for the convenience of practitioners and the courts, Paragraphs 1 and 2 list various terms often found in partnership agreements. No negative inference should be drawn about terms not listed; the listing is provided "without limiting other terms that may be included in a partnership agreement."

Paragraph 3 lists arrangements subject to the "not manifestly unreasonable" standard. Subsection (e) delineates that standard. The same standard applies to terms of a partnership agreement which seek to "prescribe the standards . . . by which the performance of the [contractual] obligation [of good faith and fair dealing under Section 409(d)] is to be measured." Subsection (c)(6).

Subsection (d)(1)(A)—An arrangement *not* involving "one or more disinterested and independent persons" acting "after full disclosure of all material facts" would "alter . . . the aspects of the duty of loyalty stated in Section 409(b)" and would therefore be subject to the "not manifestly unreasonable standard" of Subsection (d)(3)(A).

For the meaning of "material" as applied to information, see the comment to Section 409(f).

Subsection (d)(1)(B)—Section 405(a)(2) prohibits distributions by a limited liability partnership:

- *not merely* when, after the distribution, "the partnership's total assets would be less than the sum of its total liabilities";

- *but also* when, after the distribution, the assets would less than the total liabilities "plus the amount that would be needed, if the partnership were to be dissolved and wound up at the time of the distribution, to satisfy the preferential rights upon dissolution and winding up of partners and transferees whose preferential rights are superior to the rights of persons receiving the distribution."

The second part of the solvency test pertains to preferential rights to distributions, is thus a matter *inter se* the partners and any transferees, and is therefore subject to change in the partnership agreement.

In contrast, the first part of the solvency test protects third parties—creditors of the partnership—and therefore cannot be changed by the partnership agreement. Section 105(c)(17). Likewise, the partnership agreement cannot change the solvency test stated in Section 406(a)(1) (that "the partnership would not be able to pay its debts as they become due in the ordinary course of the partnership's business").

Subsection (d)(2)—The "not manifestly unreasonable" standard does not apply to partnership agreement provisions within this paragraph.

Example: ABC Company ("ABC") has three partners. ABC has two entirely separate lines of business, the Alpha business and the Beta business. Under ABC's partnership agreement:

- Partner 1's responsibilities pertain exclusively to the Alpha business, while responsibility for:

  o the Beta business is allocated exclusively to Partner 2; and

  o ABC's overall operation is allocated exclusively to Partner 3.

- Partner 2's responsibilities pertain exclusively to the Beta business, while responsibility for:

  o the Alpha business is allocated exclusively to Partner 1; and

  o ABC's overall operation is allocated exclusively to Partner 3.

- Partner 1 has no fiduciary duties pertaining to the Beta business.

- Partner 2 has no fiduciary duties pertaining to the Alpha business.

The elimination of Partner 1's fiduciary duties with regard to the Beta business and Partner 2's fiduciary duties with regard to the Alpha business are enforceable, without regard to the "manifestly unreasonable" standard of Subsection (d)(3).

Section (d)(3)—This act rejects the ultra-contractarian notion that fiduciary duty within a business organization is merely a set of default rules and seeks instead to balance the virtues of "freedom of contract" against the dangers that inescapably exist when some persons have power over the interests of others.

Nonetheless, a properly drafted partnership agreement may substantially alter and even eliminate fiduciary duties. Two important limitations exist. First, arrangements subject to this subsection may not be "manifestly unreasonable." *See* Subsection (e) (delineating this standard).

Second, the partnership agreement may not transform the relationship inter se partners and the partnership into an entirely arm's length arrangement. For example, displacement of fiduciary duties is effective only to the extent that the displacement is stated clearly and with particularity. This rule is fundamental in the jurisprudence of fiduciary duty. *See, e.g., Paige Capital Mgmt., L.L.C. v. Lerner Master Fund, L.L.C.*, Civ. A. No. 5502-CS, 2011 WL 3505355, at *31 (Del. Ch. Aug. 8, 2011) (stating that, even under a statute that "permits the waiver of fiduciary duties . . . such waivers must be set forth clearly"); *Kelly v. Blum*, Civ. A. No. 4516-VCP, 2010 WL 629850, at *10 n.70 (Del. Ch. Feb. 24, 2010) ("Having been granted great contractual freedom by the LLC Act, drafters of or parties to an LLC agreement should be expected to provide . . . clear and unambiguous provisions when they desire to expand, restrict or eliminate the operation of traditional fiduciary duties"). It would therefore be manifestly unreasonable for a partnership agreement to negate this rule.

Although Subsection (d)(3) does not expressly address contracts between a partnership and a partner, the stated constraints must also apply to such contracts. If not, those constraints are effectively meaningless.

Example: A general partnership enters into a management contract with its sole managing partner, and the contract provides that the duties of loyalty stated in Section 409(b) are entirely eliminated. If the partnership agreement were to so provide, the provision would be subject to the "manifestly unreasonable standard." Section 105(d)(3)(A). Absent the authorization provided by Section 105(d)(3)(A), the management contract's attempt to waive fiduciary duties may be unenforceable as a matter of public policy and contract law. *See Neubauer v. Goldfarb*, 108 Cal. App. 4th 47, 57, 133 Cal. Rptr. 2d 218 (2003) (stating that "waiver of corporate directors' and majority shareholders' fiduciary duties to minority shareholders in private close corporations is against public policy and a contract provision in a buy-sell agreement purporting to effect such a waiver is void"). If not, a court should hold the provision unenforceable nonetheless so as to avoid eviscerating Subsection (d)(3).

Subsection (d)(3)(A)—Subject to the "not manifestly unreasonable" standard, this paragraph empowers the partnership agreement to eliminate all aspects of the duty of loyalty listed in Section 409(b). The obligation of good faith and fair dealing, Section 409(d), would remain. *See* Subsection (c)(6). As to any other, uncodified aspects of the duty of loyalty, see Subsection (d)(3)(D) (empowering the partnership agreement to "alter or eliminate any other fiduciary duty").

Example: Joint Venture Partnership ("JV") is a general partnership, with two partners, Kappa, Inc. ("Kappa") and Lambda, LLC ("Lambda"). The partnership agreement provides that:

- JV is managed by a "board" consisting of one person appointed by Kappa and one person appointed by Lambda;

- each appointee:

    o   owes fiduciary and any other duties exclusively to the partner that made the appointment; and

    o   owes no duties to the other partner and the partnership.

The "not manifestly unreasonable" standard applies to these provisions under Subsection (d)(3)(A) and (D), and the provisions are not manifestly unreasonable. Note that the provisions do not affect the duties of Kappa and Lambda to each other.

Subsection (d)(3)(B)—Under this paragraph, a partnership agreement might provide that an affiliate of a partner will provide compensated services to the partnership at a price not exceeding market price, or that the partner may pursue opportunities that otherwise would be partnership opportunities. Such arrangements are commonplace and permissible.

Subsection (d)(3)(C)—In this context, "conduct" includes both acts and omissions. BLACK'S LAW DICTIONARY (9th ed. 2009) (defining conduct as "[p]ersonal behavior, whether by action or inaction"). Subject to the "not manifestly unreasonable" standard and the bedrock requirements stated here and in Subsection (c)(8), the partnership agreement can reduce the duty of care substantially. In particular, the partnership agreement can eliminate the aspects of the duty of care pertaining to gross negligence and recklessness.

This provision replicates in a particular context the general rule stated in Subsection (c)(8). For the meaning of "bad faith" in the context of the duty of care, see Subsection (c)(8), comment.

Subsection (e)—The "not manifestly unreasonable" concept became part of uniform business entity statutes when UPA (1997) imported the concept from the Uniform Commercial Code. (In the current version of the Uniform Commercial Code, the concept appears in Section 1–302(b).)

This subsection provides rules for applying the concept, specifying:

- who decides the issue of "manifestly unreasonable"
  - "the court . . . as a matter of law," Subsection (e);
- the framework for determining the issue
  - determination to be made "in light of the purposes, activities, and affairs of the partnership," Subsection (e)(2);
- the temporal setting for determining the issue
  - "[d]etermination [to be made] as of the time the challenged term became part of the partnership agreement," Subsection (e)(1); and
- what information is admissible for determining the issue
  - "[o]nly circumstances existing" when "the challenged term became part of the partnership agreement," Subsection (e)(1).

The subsection also provides a very demanding standard for persons claiming that a term of a partnership agreement is "manifestly unreasonable." "The court . . . may invalidate the term only if, in light of the purposes, and business of the partnership, it is *readily apparent* that: (A) the objective of the term is unreasonable; or (B) the term is an unreasonable means to achieve the term's objective." Subsection (e)(2) (emphasis added).

Subsection (e) is fundamental to this act, because: (i) this act generally defers to the agreement among the partners; and (ii) Subsection (e) safeguards the partnership agreement in at least four ways:

- Determining manifest unreasonableness *inter se* owners of an organization is a different task than doing so in a commercial context, where concepts like "usages of trade" are available to inform the analysis. Each business organization must be understood in its own terms and context.

- If loosely applied, the concept of "manifestly unreasonable" would permit a court to rewrite the partners' agreement, which would destroy the balance this act seeks to establish between freedom of contract and fiduciary duty.

- Case law has not adequately delineated the concept. *See, e.g., In re Brobeck, Phleger & Harrison L.L.P.*, 408 B.R. 318, 335 (Bankr. N.D. Cal. 2009) ("RUPA [UPA (1997)] does not define what is 'manifestly unreasonable' and the parties have not cited, nor can the court locate, a decision that defines the term. Absent case law or even a dictionary definition, the court must rely on its common sense to recognize something as manifestly unreasonable.").

- In the context of statutes permitting stock transfer restrictions unless "manifestly unreasonable," courts have often ignored the word "manifestly." *See, e.g., Brandt v. Somerville*, 692 N.W.2d 144, 152 (N.D. 2005) (stating that "in close corporations, a majority of courts have sustained restrictions that are determined to be reasonable in light of the relevant circumstances"); *Roof Depot, Inc. v. Ohman*, 638 N.W.2d 782, 786 (Minn. Ct. App. 2002) (stating that "the restrictions [on share transfer] are not 'manifestly unreasonable' because they are reasonable means to ensure that the management and control of the business remains in the group of investors or with people well known to them"); *Castriota v. Castriota*, 633 A.2d 1024, 1027–28 (N.J. App. Div. 1993) ("We are obliged to apply the statute in a manner consonant with its essential purpose to permit reasonable restrictions upon alienation.").

Subsection (e)(1)—The significance of the phrase "as of the time the term as challenged became part of the partnership agreement" is best shown by example.

Example: When a particular partnership comes into existence, its business plan is quite unusual and its success depends on the willingness of a particular individual to serve as the partnership's sole managing partner. This individual has a rare combination of skills, experiences, and contacts, which are particularly appropriate for the partnership's start-up. In order to induce the individual to accept the position of sole managing partner, the other partners are willing to have the partnership agreement significantly limit the managing partner's fiduciary duties. Several years later, when the partnership's operations have turned prosaic and the managing partner's talents and background are not nearly so crucial, a partner challenges the fiduciary duty limitations as manifestly unreasonable. The relevant time under Subsection (e)(1) is when the partnership began. Subsequent developments are not relevant, except as they might inferentially bear on the circumstances in existence at the relevant time.

Example: As initially adopted, a partnership agreement identifies a category of decisions ordinarily subject to the duty of loyalty and provides that "the managing partner's sole, reasonable discretion" satisfies the duty. A year later, the agreement is amended to delete the word "reasonable." Later, a partner claims that, without the word "reasonable," the provision is manifestly unreasonable. The relevant time under Subsection (e)(1) is when the agreement was amended, not when the agreement was initially adopted.

Subsection (e)(2)—If a person claims that a term of the partnership agreement is manifestly unreasonable under Subsections (c)(6) or (d)(3), as a matter of ordinary procedural law the person making the claim has the burden of proof.

§ 106. Partnership Agreement; Effect on Partnership and Person Becoming Partner; Preformation Agreement

(a) A partnership is bound by and may enforce the partnership agreement, whether or not the partnership has itself manifested assent to the agreement.

(b) A person that becomes a partner is deemed to assent to the partnership agreement.

(c) Two or more persons intending to become the initial partners of a partnership may make an agreement providing that upon the formation of the partnership the agreement will become the partnership agreement.

§ 107. Partnership Agreement; Effect on Third Parties and Relationship to Records Effective on Behalf of Partnership

(a) A partnership agreement may specify that its amendment requires the approval of a person that is not a party to the agreement or the satisfaction of a condition. An amendment is ineffective if its adoption does not include the required approval or satisfy the specified condition.

(b)   The obligations of a partnership and its partners to a person in the person's capacity as a transferee or person dissociated as a partner are governed by the partnership agreement. Subject only to a court order issued under Section 504(b)(2) to effectuate a charging order, an amendment to the partnership agreement made after a person becomes a transferee or is dissociated as a partner:

(1)   is effective with regard to any debt, obligation, or other liability of the partnership or its partners to the person in the person's capacity as a transferee or person dissociated as a partner; and

(2)   is not effective to the extent the amendment:

(A)   imposes a new debt, obligation, or other liability on the transferee or person dissociated as a partner; or

(B)   prejudices the rights under Section 701 of a person that dissociated as a partner before the amendment was made.

(c)   If a record delivered by a partnership to the [Secretary of State] for filing becomes effective and contains a provision that would be ineffective under Section 105(c) or (d)(3) if contained in the partnership agreement, the provision is ineffective in the record.

(d)   Subject to subsection (c), if a record delivered by a partnership to the [Secretary of State] for filing becomes effective and conflicts with a provision of the partnership agreement:

(1)   the agreement prevails as to partners, persons dissociated as partners, and transferees; and

(2)   the record prevails as to other persons to the extent they reasonably rely on the record.

§ 108.   Signing of Records to Be Delivered for Filing to [Secretary of State]

(a)   A record delivered to the [Secretary of State] for filing pursuant to this [act] must be signed as follows:

(1)   Except as otherwise provided in paragraphs (2) and (3), a record signed by a partnership must be signed by a person authorized by the partnership.

(2)   A record filed on behalf of a dissolved partnership that has no partner must be signed by the person winding up the partnership's business under Section 802(c) or a person appointed under Section 802(d) to wind up the business.

(3)   A statement of denial by a person under Section 304 must be signed by that person.

(4)   Any other record delivered on behalf of a person to the [Secretary of State] for filing must be signed by that person.

(b)   A record filed under this [act] may be signed by an agent. Whenever this [act] requires a particular individual to sign a record and the individual is deceased or incompetent, the record may be signed by a legal representative of the individual.

(c)   A person that signs a record as an agent or legal representative affirms as a fact that the person is authorized to sign the record.

§ 109.   Liability for Inaccurate Information in Filed Record

(a)   If a record delivered to the [Secretary of State] for filing under this [act] and filed by the [Secretary of State] contains inaccurate information, a person that suffers loss by reliance on the information may recover damages for the loss from:

(1)   a person that signed the record, or caused another to sign it on the person's behalf, and knew the information to be inaccurate at the time the record was signed; and

(2)   subject to subsection (b), a partner if:

(A) the record was delivered for filing on behalf of the partnership; and

(B) the partner knew or had notice of the inaccuracy for a reasonably sufficient time before the information was relied upon so that, before the reliance, the partner reasonably could have:

(i) effected an amendment under Section 901(f);

(ii) filed a petition under Section 112; or

(iii) delivered to the [Secretary of State] for filing a statement of change under Section 909 or a statement of correction under Section 116.

(b) To the extent the partnership agreement expressly relieves a partner of responsibility for maintaining the accuracy of information contained in records delivered on behalf of the partnership to the [Secretary of State] for filing under this [act] and imposes that responsibility on one or more other partners, the liability stated in subsection (a)(2) applies to those other partners and not to the partner that the partnership agreement relieves of the responsibility.

(c) An individual who signs a record authorized or required to be filed under this [act] affirms under penalty of perjury that the information stated in the record is accurate.

§ 110. Application to Existing Relationships

(a) Before [all-inclusive date], this [act] governs only:

(1) a partnership formed on or after [the effective date of this [act]]; and

(2) except as otherwise provided in subsection (c), a partnership formed before [the effective date of this [act]] which elects, in the manner provided in its partnership agreement or by law for amending the partnership agreement, to be subject to this [act].

(b) Except as otherwise provided in subsection (c), on and after [all-inclusive date] this [act] governs all partnerships.

(c) With respect to a partnership that elects pursuant to subsection (a)(2) to be subject to this [act], after the election takes effect the provisions of this [act] relating to the liability of the partnership's partners to third parties apply:

(1) before [all-inclusive date], to:

(A) a third party that had not done business with the partnership in the year before the election took effect; and

(B) a third party that had done business with the partnership in the year before the election took effect only if the third party knows or has been notified of the election; and

(2) on and after [all-inclusive date], to all third parties, but those provisions remain inapplicable to any obligation incurred while those provisions were inapplicable under paragraph (1)(B).

Legislative Note:

For states that have previously enacted UPA (1997): For these states this section is unnecessary. There is no need for a delayed effective date, even with regard to pre-existing partnerships. (Presumably, the "linkage" issue [discussed below] was addressed when UPA (1997) was enacted.)

For states that have not previously enacted UPA (1997): Each enacting jurisdiction should consider whether: (i) this act makes material changes to the "default" (or "gap filler") rules of the predecessor statute; and (ii) if so, whether Subsection (c) should carry forward any of those rules for pre-existing partnerships. In this assessment, the focus is on pre-existing partnerships that have left default rules in place, whether advisedly or not. The central question is whether, for such partnerships, expanding Subsection (c) is necessary to prevent material changes to the partners' "deal."

The "all-inclusive" date should be at least one year after the effective date of this act, Section 1206, but no more than two years.

The "linkage" issue—for states that still have ULPA (1976) or ULPA (1976/1985) in effect: These states should enact ULPA (2001) (Last Amended 2013) to take effect in conjunction with this act. If not, a state's current limited partnership act must be amended to link to this act.

§ 111.   Delivery of Record

(a)   Except as otherwise provided in this [act], permissible means of delivery of a record include delivery by hand, mail, conventional commercial practice, and electronic transmission.

(b)   Delivery to the [Secretary of State] is effective only when a record is received by the [Secretary of State].

§ 112.   Signing and Filing Pursuant to Judicial Order

(a)   If a person required by this [act] to sign a record or deliver a record to the [Secretary of State] for filing under this [act] does not do so, any other person that is aggrieved may petition [the appropriate court] to order:

(1)   the person to sign the record;

(2)   the person to deliver the record to the [Secretary of State] for filing; or

(3)   the [Secretary of State] to file the record unsigned.

(b)   If a petitioner under subsection (a) is not the partnership or foreign limited liability partnership to which the record pertains, the petitioner shall make the partnership or foreign partnership a party to the action.

(c)   A record filed under subsection (a)(3) is effective without being signed.

§ 113.   Filing Requirements

(a)   To be filed by the [Secretary of State] pursuant to this [act], a record must be received by the [Secretary of State], comply with this [act], and satisfy the following:

(1)   The filing of the record must be required or permitted by this [act].

(2)   The record must be physically delivered in written form unless and to the extent the [Secretary of State] permits electronic delivery of records.

(3)   The words in the record must be in English, and numbers must be in Arabic or Roman numerals, but the name of an entity need not be in English if written in English letters or Arabic or Roman numerals.

(4)   The record must be signed by a person authorized or required under this [act] to sign the record.

(5)   The record must state the name and capacity, if any, of each individual who signed it, either on behalf of the individual or the person authorized or required to sign the record, but need not contain a seal, attestation, acknowledgment, or verification.

(b)   If law other than this [act] prohibits the disclosure by the [Secretary of State] of information contained in a record delivered to the [Secretary of State] for filing, the [Secretary of State] shall file the record if the record otherwise complies with this [act] but may redact the information.

(c)   When a record is delivered to the [Secretary of State] for filing, any fee required under this [act] and any fee, tax, interest, or penalty required to be paid under this [act] or law other than this [act] must be paid in a manner permitted by the [Secretary of State] or by that law.

(d)   The [Secretary of State] may require that a record delivered in written form be accompanied by an identical or conformed copy.

(e)   The [Secretary of State] may provide forms for filings required or permitted to be made by this [act], but, except as otherwise provided in subsection (f), their use is not required.

(f)   The [Secretary of State] may require that a cover sheet for a filing be on a form prescribed by the [Secretary of State].

§ 114.   Effective Date and Time

Except as otherwise provided in Section 115 and subject to Section 116(c), a record filed under this [act] is effective:

(1)   on the date and at the time of its filing by the [Secretary of State], as provided in Section 117(b);

(2)   on the date of filing and at the time specified in the record as its effective time, if later than the time under paragraph (1);

(3)   at a specified delayed effective date and time, which may not be more than 90 days after the date of filing; or

(4)   if a delayed effective date is specified, but no time is specified, at 12:01 a.m. on the date specified, which may not be more than 90 days after the date of filing.

§ 115.   Withdrawal of Filed Record Before Effectiveness

(a)   Except as otherwise provided in Sections 1124, 1134, 1144, and 1154, a record delivered to the [Secretary of State] for filing may be withdrawn before it takes effect by delivering to the [Secretary of State] for filing a statement of withdrawal.

(b)   A statement of withdrawal must:

(1)   be signed by each person that signed the record being withdrawn, except as otherwise agreed by those persons;

(2)   identify the record to be withdrawn; and

(3)   if signed by fewer than all the persons that signed the record being withdrawn, state that the record is withdrawn in accordance with the agreement of all the persons that signed the record.

(c)   On filing by the [Secretary of State] of a statement of withdrawal, the action or transaction evidenced by the original record does not take effect.

§ 116.   Correcting Filed Record

(a)   A person on whose behalf a filed record was delivered to the [Secretary of State] for filing may correct the record if:

(1)   the record at the time of filing was inaccurate;

(2)   the record was defectively signed; or

(3)   the electronic transmission of the record to the [Secretary of State] was defective.

(b)   To correct a filed record, a person on whose behalf the record was delivered to the [Secretary of State] must deliver to the [Secretary of State] for filing a statement of correction.

(c)   A statement of correction:

(1)   may not state a delayed effective date;

(2)   must be signed by the person correcting the filed record;

(3)   must identify the filed record to be corrected;

(4)   must specify the inaccuracy or defect to be corrected; and

(5)   must correct the inaccuracy or defect.

(d)   A statement of correction is effective as of the effective date of the filed record that it corrects except for purposes of Section 103(d) and as to persons relying on the uncorrected filed record and adversely affected by the correction. For those purposes and as to those persons, the statement of correction is effective when filed.

§ 117.   Duty of [Secretary of State] to File; Review of Refusal to File; Delivery of Record by [Secretary of State]

(a)   The [Secretary of State] shall file a record delivered to the [Secretary of State] for filing which satisfies this [act]. The duty of the [Secretary of State] under this section is ministerial.

(b)   When the [Secretary of State] files a record, the [Secretary of State] shall record it as filed on the date and at the time of its delivery. After filing a record, the [Secretary of State] shall deliver to the person that submitted the record a copy of the record with an acknowledgment of the date and time of filing and, in the case of a statement of denial, also to the partnership to which the statement pertains.

(c)   If the [Secretary of State] refuses to file a record, the [Secretary of State] shall, not later than [15] business days after the record is delivered:

(1)   return the record or notify the person that submitted the record of the refusal; and

(2)   provide a brief explanation in a record of the reason for the refusal.

(d)   If the [Secretary of State] refuses to file a record, the person that submitted the record may petition [the appropriate court] to compel filing of the record. The record and the explanation of the [Secretary of State] of the refusal to file must be attached to the petition. The court may decide the matter in a summary proceeding.

(e)   The filing of or refusal to file a record does not:

(1)   affect the validity or invalidity of the record in whole or in part; or

(2)   create a presumption that the information contained in the record is correct or incorrect.

(f)   Except as otherwise provided by Section 909 or by law other than this [act], the [Secretary of State] may deliver any record to a person by delivering it:

(1)   in person to the person that submitted it;

(2)   to the address of the person's registered agent;

(3)   to the principal office of the person; or

(4)   to another address the person provides to the [Secretary of State] for delivery.

§ 118.   Reservation of Power to Amend or Repeal

The [legislature of this state] has power to amend or repeal all or part of this [act] at any time, and all limited liability partnerships and foreign limited liability partnerships subject to this [act] are governed by the amendment or repeal.

§ 119.   Supplemental Principles of Law

Unless displaced by particular provisions of this [act], the principles of law and equity supplement this [act].

[ARTICLE] 2.   NATURE OF PARTNERSHIP

§ 201.   Partnership as Entity

(a)   A partnership is an entity distinct from its partners.

(b)   A partnership is the same entity regardless of whether the partnership has a statement of qualification in effect under Section 901.

§ 202.   Formation of Partnership

(a)   Except as otherwise provided in subsection (b), the association of two or more persons to carry on as co-owners a business for profit forms a partnership, whether or not the persons intend to form a partnership.

(b)   An association formed under a statute other than this [act], a predecessor statute, or a comparable statute of another jurisdiction is not a partnership under this [act].

(c)   In determining whether a partnership is formed, the following rules apply:

(1)   Joint tenancy, tenancy in common, tenancy by the entireties, joint property, common property, or part ownership does not by itself establish a partnership, even if the co-owners share profits made by the use of the property.

(2)   The sharing of gross returns does not by itself establish a partnership, even if the persons sharing them have a joint or common right or interest in property from which the returns are derived.

(3)   A person who receives a share of the profits of a business is presumed to be a partner in the business, unless the profits were received in payment:

(A)   of a debt by installments or otherwise;

(B)   for services as an independent contractor or of wages or other compensation to an employee;

(C)   of rent;

(D)   of an annuity or other retirement or health benefit to a deceased or retired partner or a beneficiary, representative, or designee of a deceased or retired partner;

(E)   of interest or other charge on a loan, even if the amount of payment varies with the profits of the business, including a direct or indirect present or future ownership of the collateral, or rights to income, proceeds, or increase in value derived from the collateral; or

(F)   for the sale of the goodwill of a business or other property by installments or otherwise.

§ 203.   Partnership Property

Property acquired by a partnership is property of the partnership and not of the partners individually.

§ 204.   When Property Is Partnership Property

(a)   Property is partnership property if acquired in the name of:

(1)   the partnership; or

(2)   one or more partners with an indication in the instrument transferring title to the property of the person's capacity as a partner or of the existence of a partnership but without an indication of the name of the partnership.

(b)　Property is acquired in the name of the partnership by a transfer to:

(1)　the partnership in its name; or

(2)　one or more partners in their capacity as partners in the partnership, if the name of the partnership is indicated in the instrument transferring title to the property.

(c)　Property is presumed to be partnership property if purchased with partnership assets, even if not acquired in the name of the partnership or of one or more partners with an indication in the instrument transferring title to the property of the person's capacity as a partner or of the existence of a partnership.

(d)　Property acquired in the name of one or more of the partners, without an indication in the instrument transferring title to the property of the person's capacity as a partner or of the existence of a partnership and without use of partnership assets, is presumed to be separate property, even if used for partnership purposes.

[ARTICLE] 3.　RELATIONS OF PARTNERS TO PERSONS DEALING WITH PARTNERSHIP

§ 301.　Partner Agent of Partnership

Subject to the effect of a statement of partnership authority under Section 303, the following rules apply:

(1)　Each partner is an agent of the partnership for the purpose of its business. An act of a partner, including the signing of an instrument in the partnership name, for apparently carrying on in the ordinary course the partnership business or business of the kind carried on by the partnership binds the partnership, unless the partner did not have authority to act for the partnership in the particular matter and the person with which the partner was dealing knew or had notice that the partner lacked authority.

(2)　An act of a partner which is not apparently for carrying on in the ordinary course the partnership's business or business of the kind carried on by the partnership binds the partnership only if the act was actually authorized by all the other partners.

§ 302.　Transfer of Partnership Property

(a)　Partnership property may be transferred as follows:

(1)　Subject to the effect of a statement of partnership authority under Section 303, partnership property held in the name of the partnership may be transferred by an instrument of transfer signed by a partner in the partnership name.

(2)　Partnership property held in the name of one or more partners with an indication in the instrument transferring the property to them of their capacity as partners or of the existence of a partnership, but without an indication of the name of the partnership, may be transferred by an instrument of transfer signed by the persons in whose name the property is held.

(3)　Partnership property held in the name of one or more persons other than the partnership, without an indication in the instrument transferring the property to them of their capacity as partners or of the existence of a partnership, may be transferred by an instrument of transfer signed by the persons in whose name the property is held.

(b)　A partnership may recover partnership property from a transferee only if it proves that signing of the instrument of initial transfer did not bind the partnership under Section 301 and:

(1)　as to a subsequent transferee who gave value for property transferred under subsection (a)(1) and (2), proves that the subsequent transferee knew or had been notified that the person who signed the instrument of initial transfer lacked authority to bind the partnership; or

(2) as to a transferee who gave value for property transferred under subsection (a)(3), proves that the transferee knew or had been notified that the property was partnership property and that the person who signed the instrument of initial transfer lacked authority to bind the partnership.

(c) A partnership may not recover partnership property from a subsequent transferee if the partnership would not have been entitled to recover the property, under subsection (b), from any earlier transferee of the property.

(d) If a person holds all the partners' interests in the partnership, all the partnership property vests in that person. The person may sign a record in the name of the partnership to evidence vesting of the property in that person and may file or record the record.

§ 303.   Statement of Partnership Authority

(a) A partnership may deliver to the [Secretary of State] for filing a statement of partnership authority. The statement:

(1) must include the name of the partnership and:

(A) if the partnership is not a limited liability partnership, the street and mailing addresses of its principal office; or

(B) if the partnership is a limited liability partnership, the name and street and mailing addresses of its registered agent;

(2) with respect to any position that exists in or with respect to the partnership, may state the authority, or limitations on the authority, of all persons holding the position to:

(A) sign an instrument transferring real property held in the name of the partnership; or

(B) enter into other transactions on behalf of, or otherwise act for or bind, the partnership; and

(3) may state the authority, or limitations on the authority, of a specific person to:

(A) sign an instrument transferring real property held in the name of the partnership; or

(B) enter into other transactions on behalf of, or otherwise act for or bind, the partnership.

(b) To amend or cancel a statement of authority filed by the [Secretary of State], a partnership must deliver to the [Secretary of State] for filing an amendment or cancellation stating:

(1) the name of the partnership;

(2) if the partnership is not a limited liability partnership, the street and mailing addresses of the partnership's principal office;

(3) if the partnership is a limited liability partnership, the name and street and mailing addresses of its registered agent;

(4) the date the statement being affected became effective; and

(5) the contents of the amendment or a declaration that the statement is canceled.

(c) A statement of authority affects only the power of a person to bind a partnership to persons that are not partners.

(d) Subject to subsection (c) and Section 103(d)(1), and except as otherwise provided in subsections (f), (g), and (h), a limitation on the authority of a person or a position contained in an effective statement of authority is not by itself evidence of any person's knowledge or notice of the limitation.

(e)   Subject to subsection (c), a grant of authority not pertaining to transfers of real property and contained in an effective statement of authority is conclusive in favor of a person that gives value in reliance on the grant, except to the extent that if the person gives value:

(1)   the person has knowledge to the contrary;

(2)   the statement has been canceled or restrictively amended under subsection (b); or

(3)   a limitation on the grant is contained in another statement of authority that became effective after the statement containing the grant became effective.

(f)   Subject to subsection (c), an effective statement of authority that grants authority to transfer real property held in the name of the partnership, a certified copy of which statement is recorded in the office for recording transfers of the real property, is conclusive in favor of a person that gives value in reliance on the grant without knowledge to the contrary, except to the extent that when the person gives value:

(1)   the statement has been canceled or restrictively amended under subsection (b), and a certified copy of the cancellation or restrictive amendment has been recorded in the office for recording transfers of the real property; or

(2)   a limitation on the grant is contained in another statement of authority that became effective after the statement containing the grant became effective, and a certified copy of the later-effective statement is recorded in the office for recording transfers of the real property.

(g)   Subject to subsection (c), if a certified copy of an effective statement containing a limitation on the authority to transfer real property held in the name of a partnership is recorded in the office for recording transfers of that real property, all persons are deemed to know of the limitation.

(h)   Subject to subsection (i), an effective statement of dissolution is a cancellation of any filed statement of authority for the purposes of subsection (f) and is a limitation on authority for purposes of subsection (g).

(i)   After a statement of dissolution becomes effective, a partnership may deliver to the [Secretary of State] for filing and, if appropriate, may record a statement of authority that is designated as a post-dissolution statement of authority. The statement operates as provided in subsections (f) and (g).

(j)   Unless canceled earlier, an effective statement of authority is canceled by operation of law five years after the date on which the statement, or its most recent amendment, becomes effective. The cancellation is effective without recording under subsection (f) or (g).

(k)   An effective statement of denial operates as a restrictive amendment under this section and may be recorded by certified copy for purposes of subsection (f)(1).

§ 304.   Statement of Denial

A person named in a filed statement of authority granting that person authority may deliver to the [Secretary of State] for filing a statement of denial that:

(1)   provides the name of the partnership and the caption of the statement of authority to which the statement of denial pertains; and

(2)   denies the grant of authority.

§ 305. Partnership Liable for Partner's Actionable Conduct

(a) A partnership is liable for loss or injury caused to a person, or for a penalty incurred, as a result of a wrongful act or omission, or other actionable conduct, of a partner acting in the ordinary course of business of the partnership or with the actual or apparent authority of the partnership.

(b) If, in the course of the partnership's business or while acting with actual or apparent authority of the partnership, a partner receives or causes the partnership to receive money or property of a person not a partner, and the money or property is misapplied by a partner, the partnership is liable for the loss.

§ 306. Partner's Liability

(a) Except as otherwise provided in subsections (b) and (c), all partners are liable jointly and severally for all debts, obligations, and other liabilities of the partnership unless otherwise agreed by the claimant or provided by law.

(b) A person that becomes a partner is not personally liable for a debt, obligation, or other liability of the partnership incurred before the person became a partner.

(c) A debt, obligation, or other liability of a partnership incurred while the partnership is a limited liability partnership is solely the debt, obligation, or other liability of the limited liability partnership. A partner is not personally liable, directly or indirectly, by way of contribution or otherwise, for a debt, obligation, or other liability of the limited liability partnership solely by reason of being or acting as a partner. This subsection applies:

(1) despite anything inconsistent in the partnership agreement that existed immediately before the vote or consent required to become a limited liability partnership under Section 901(b); and

(2) regardless of the dissolution of the limited liability partnership.

(d) The failure of a limited liability partnership to observe formalities relating to the exercise of its powers or management of its business is not a ground for imposing liability on a partner for a debt, obligation, or other liability of the partnership.

(e) The cancellation or administrative revocation of a limited liability partnership's statement of qualification does not affect the limitation in this section on the liability of a partner for a debt, obligation, or other liability of the partnership incurred while the statement was in effect.

§ 307. Actions By and Against Partnership and Partners

(a) A partnership may sue and be sued in the name of the partnership.

(b) To the extent not inconsistent with Section 306, a partner may be joined in an action against the partnership or named in a separate action.

(c) A judgment against a partnership is not by itself a judgment against a partner. A judgment against a partnership may not be satisfied from a partner's assets unless there is also a judgment against the partner.

(d) A judgment creditor of a partner may not levy execution against the assets of the partner to satisfy a judgment based on a claim against the partnership unless the partner is personally liable for the claim under Section 306 and:

(1) a judgment based on the same claim has been obtained against the partnership and a writ of execution on the judgment has been returned unsatisfied in whole or in part;

(2) the partnership is a debtor in bankruptcy;

(3) the partner has agreed that the creditor need not exhaust partnership assets;

(4)   a court grants permission to the judgment creditor to levy execution against the assets of a partner based on a finding that partnership assets subject to execution are clearly insufficient to satisfy the judgment, that exhaustion of partnership assets is excessively burdensome, or that the grant of permission is an appropriate exercise of the court's equitable powers; or

(5)   liability is imposed on the partner by law or contract independent of the existence of the partnership.

(e)   This section applies to any debt, liability, or other obligation of a partnership which results from a representation by a partner or purported partner under Section 308.

§ 308.   Liability of Purported Partner

(a)   If a person, by words or conduct, purports to be a partner, or consents to being represented by another as a partner, in a partnership or with one or more persons not partners, the purported partner is liable to a person to whom the representation is made, if that person, relying on the representation, enters into a transaction with the actual or purported partnership. If the representation, either by the purported partner or by a person with the purported partner's consent, is made in a public manner, the purported partner is liable to a person who relies upon the purported partnership even if the purported partner is not aware of being held out as a partner to the claimant. If partnership liability results, the purported partner is liable with respect to that liability as if the purported partner were a partner. If no partnership liability results, the purported partner is liable with respect to that liability jointly and severally with any other person consenting to the representation.

(b)   If a person is thus represented to be a partner in an existing partnership, or with one or more persons not partners, the purported partner is an agent of persons consenting to the representation to bind them to the same extent and in the same manner as if the purported partner were a partner with respect to persons who enter into transactions in reliance upon the representation. If all the partners of the existing partnership consent to the representation, a partnership act or obligation results. If fewer than all the partners of the existing partnership consent to the representation, the person acting and the partners consenting to the representation are jointly and severally liable.

(c)   A person is not liable as a partner merely because the person is named by another as a partner in a statement of partnership authority.

(d)   A person does not continue to be liable as a partner merely because of a failure to file a statement of dissociation or to amend a statement of partnership authority to indicate the person's dissociation as a partner.

(e)   Except as otherwise provided in subsections (a) and (b), persons who are not partners as to each other are not liable as partners to other persons.

[ARTICLE] 4.   RELATIONS OF PARTNERS TO EACH OTHER AND TO PARTNERSHIP

§ 401.   Partner's Rights and Duties

(a)   Each partner is entitled to an equal share of the partnership distributions and, except in the case of a limited liability partnership, is chargeable with a share of the partnership losses in proportion to the partner's share of the distributions.

(b)   A partnership shall reimburse a partner for any payment made by the partner in the course of the partner's activities on behalf of the partnership, if the partner complied with this section and Section 409 in making the payment.

(c)   A partnership shall indemnify and hold harmless a person with respect to any claim or demand against the person and any debt, obligation, or other liability incurred by the person by reason of the person's former or present capacity as a partner, if the claim, demand, debt, obligation, or other liability does not arise from the person's breach of this section or Section 407 or 409.

(d) In the ordinary course of its business, a partnership may advance reasonable expenses, including attorney's fees and costs, incurred by a person in connection with a claim or demand against the person by reason of the person's former or present capacity as a partner, if the person promises to repay the partnership if the person ultimately is determined not to be entitled to be indemnified under subsection (c).

(e) A partnership may purchase and maintain insurance on behalf of a partner against liability asserted against or incurred by the partner in that capacity or arising from that status even if, under Section 105(c)(7), the partnership agreement could not eliminate or limit the person's liability to the partnership for the conduct giving rise to the liability.

(f) A partnership shall reimburse a partner for an advance to the partnership beyond the amount of capital the partner agreed to contribute.

(g) A payment or advance made by a partner which gives rise to a partnership obligation under subsection (b) or (f) constitutes a loan to the partnership which accrues interest from the date of the payment or advance.

(h) Each partner has equal rights in the management and conduct of the partnership's business.

(i) A partner may use or possess partnership property only on behalf of the partnership.

(j) A partner is not entitled to remuneration for services performed for the partnership, except for reasonable compensation for services rendered in winding up the business of the partnership.

(k) A difference arising as to a matter in the ordinary course of business of a partnership may be decided by a majority of the partners. An act outside the ordinary course of business of a partnership and an amendment to the partnership agreement may be undertaken only with the affirmative vote or consent of all the partners.

§ 402. Becoming Partner

(a) Upon formation of a partnership, a person becomes a partner under Section 202(a).

(b) After formation of a partnership, a person becomes a partner:

(1) as provided in the partnership agreement;

(2) as a result of a transaction effective under [Article] 11; or

(3) with the affirmative vote or consent of all the partners.

(c) A person may become a partner without:

(1) acquiring a transferable interest; or

(2) making or being obligated to make a contribution to the partnership.

§ 403. Form of Contribution

A contribution may consist of property transferred to, services performed for, or another benefit provided to the partnership or an agreement to transfer property to, perform services for, or provide another benefit to the partnership.

§ 404. Liability for Contribution

(a) A person's obligation to make a contribution to a partnership is not excused by the person's death, disability, termination, or other inability to perform personally.

(b)   If a person does not fulfill an obligation to make a contribution other than money, the person is obligated at the option of the partnership to contribute money equal to the value of the part of the contribution which has not been made.

(c)   The obligation of a person to make a contribution may be compromised only by the affirmative vote or consent of all the partners. If a creditor of a limited liability partnership extends credit or otherwise acts in reliance on an obligation described in subsection (a) without knowledge or notice of a compromise under this subsection, the creditor may enforce the obligation.

§ 405.   Sharing of and Right to Distributions Before Dissolution

(a)   Any distribution made by a partnership before its dissolution and winding up must be in equal shares among partners, except to the extent necessary to comply with a transfer effective under Section 503 or charging order in effect under Section 504.

(b)   Subject to Section 701, a person has a right to a distribution before the dissolution and winding up of a partnership only if the partnership decides to make an interim distribution.

(c)   A person does not have a right to demand or receive a distribution from a partnership in any form other than money. Except as otherwise provided in Section 806, a partnership may distribute an asset in kind only if each part of the asset is fungible with each other part and each person receives a percentage of the asset equal in value to the person's share of distributions.

(d)   If a partner or transferee becomes entitled to receive a distribution, the partner or transferee has the status of, and is entitled to all remedies available to, a creditor of the partnership with respect to the distribution. However, the partnership's obligation to make a distribution is subject to offset for any amount owed to the partnership by the partner or a person dissociated as partner on whose account the distribution is made.

§ 406.   Limitations on Distributions by Limited Liability Partnership

(a)   A limited liability partnership may not make a distribution, including a distribution under Section 806, if after the distribution:

(1)   the partnership would not be able to pay its debts as they become due in the ordinary course of the partnership's business; or

(2)   the partnership's total assets would be less than the sum of its total liabilities plus the amount that would be needed, if the partnership were to be dissolved and wound up at the time of the distribution, to satisfy the preferential rights upon dissolution and winding up of partners and transferees whose preferential rights are superior to the rights of persons receiving the distribution.

(b)   A limited liability partnership may base a determination that a distribution is not prohibited under subsection (a) on:

(1)   financial statements prepared on the basis of accounting practices and principles that are reasonable in the circumstances; or

(2)   a fair valuation or other method that is reasonable under the circumstances.

(c)   Except as otherwise provided in subsection (e), the effect of a distribution under subsection (a) is measured:

(1)   in the case of a distribution as defined in Section 102(4)(A), as of the earlier of:

(A)   the date money or other property is transferred or debt is incurred by the limited liability partnership; or

(B)   the date the person entitled to the distribution ceases to own the interest or rights being acquired by the partnership in return for the distribution;

(2)   in the case of any other distribution of indebtedness, as of the date the indebtedness is distributed; and

(3)   in all other cases, as of the date:

(A)   the distribution is authorized, if the payment occurs not later than 120 days after that date; or

(B)   the payment is made, if the payment occurs more than 120 days after the distribution is authorized.

(d)   A limited liability partnership's indebtedness to a partner or transferee incurred by reason of a distribution made in accordance with this section is at parity with the partnership's indebtedness to its general, unsecured creditors, except to the extent subordinated by agreement.

(e)   A limited liability partnership's indebtedness, including indebtedness issued as a distribution, is not a liability for purposes of subsection (a) if the terms of the indebtedness provide that payment of principal and interest is made only if and to the extent that a payment of a distribution could then be made under this section. If the indebtedness is issued as a distribution, each payment of principal or interest is treated as a distribution, the effect of which is measured on the date the payment is made.

(f)   In measuring the effect of a distribution under Section 806, the liabilities of a dissolved limited liability partnership do not include any claim that has been disposed of under Section 807, 808, or 809.

§ 407.   Liability for Improper Distributions by Limited Liability Partnership

(a)   Except as otherwise provided in subsection (b), if a partner of a limited liability partnership consents to a distribution made in violation of Section 406 and in consenting to the distribution fails to comply with Section 409, the partner is personally liable to the partnership for the amount of the distribution which exceeds the amount that could have been distributed without the violation of Section 406.

(b)   To the extent the partnership agreement of a limited liability partnership expressly relieves a partner of the authority and responsibility to consent to distributions and imposes that authority and responsibility on one or more other partners, the liability stated in subsection (a) applies to the other partners and not to the partner that the partnership agreement relieves of the authority and responsibility.

(c)   A person that receives a distribution knowing that the distribution violated Section 406 is personally liable to the limited liability partnership but only to the extent that the distribution received by the person exceeded the amount that could have been properly paid under Section 406.

(d)   A person against which an action is commenced because the person is liable under subsection (a) may:

(1)   implead any other person that is liable under subsection (a) and seek to enforce a right of contribution from the person; and

(2)   implead any person that received a distribution in violation of subsection (c) and seek to enforce a right of contribution from the person in the amount the person received in violation of subsection (c).

(e)   An action under this section is barred unless commenced not later than two years after the distribution.

§ 408.   Rights to Information of Partners and Persons Dissociated as Partner

(a)   A partnership shall keep its books and records, if any, at its principal office.

(b)   On reasonable notice, a partner may inspect and copy during regular business hours, at a reasonable location specified by the partnership, any record maintained by the partnership regarding the partnership's business, financial condition, and other circumstances, to the extent the information is material to the partner's rights and duties under the partnership agreement or this [act].

(c)   The partnership shall furnish to each partner:

(1)   without demand, any information concerning the partnership's business, financial condition, and other circumstances which the partnership knows and is material to the proper exercise of the partner's rights and duties under the partnership agreement or this [act], except to the extent the partnership can establish that it reasonably believes the partner already knows the information; and

(2)   on demand, any other information concerning the partnership's business, financial condition, and other circumstances, except to the extent the demand or the information demanded is unreasonable or otherwise improper under the circumstances.

(d)   The duty to furnish information under subsection (c) also applies to each partner to the extent the partner knows any of the information described in subsection (c).

(e)   Subject to subsection (j), on 10 days' demand made in a record received by a partnership, a person dissociated as a partner may have access to information to which the person was entitled while a partner if:

(1)   the information pertains to the period during which the person was a partner;

(2)   the person seeks the information in good faith; and

(3)   the person satisfies the requirements imposed on a partner by subsection (b).

(f)   Not later than 10 days after receiving a demand under subsection (e), the partnership in a record shall inform the person that made the demand of:

(1)   the information that the partnership will provide in response to the demand and when and where the partnership will provide the information; and

(2)   the partnership's reasons for declining, if the partnership declines to provide any demanded information.

(g)   A partnership may charge a person that makes a demand under this section the reasonable costs of copying, limited to the costs of labor and material.

(h)   A partner or person dissociated as a partner may exercise the rights under this section through an agent or, in the case of an individual under legal disability, a legal representative. Any restriction or condition imposed by the partnership agreement or under subsection (j) applies both to the agent or legal representative and to the partner or person dissociated as a partner.

(i)   Subject to Section 505, the rights under this section do not extend to a person as transferee.

(j)   In addition to any restriction or condition stated in its partnership agreement, a partnership, as a matter within the ordinary course of its business, may impose reasonable restrictions and conditions on access to and use of information to be furnished under this section, including designating information confidential and imposing nondisclosure and safeguarding obligations on the recipient. In a dispute concerning the reasonableness of a restriction under this subsection, the partnership has the burden of proving reasonableness.

§ 409.   Standards of Conduct for Partners

(a)   A partner owes to the partnership and the other partners the duties of loyalty and care stated in subsections (b) and (c).

(b)   The fiduciary duty of loyalty of a partner includes the duties:

(1) to account to the partnership and hold as trustee for it any property, profit, or benefit derived by the partner:

   (A) in the conduct or winding up of the partnership's business;

   (B) from a use by the partner of the partnership's property; or

   (C) from the appropriation of a partnership opportunity;

(2) to refrain from dealing with the partnership in the conduct or winding up of the partnership business as or on behalf of a person having an interest adverse to the partnership; and

(3) to refrain from competing with the partnership in the conduct of the partnership's business before the dissolution of the partnership.

(c) The duty of care of a partner in the conduct or winding up of the partnership business is to refrain from engaging in grossly negligent or reckless conduct, willful or intentional misconduct, or a knowing violation of law.

(d) A partner shall discharge the duties and obligations under this [act] or under the partnership agreement and exercise any rights consistently with the contractual obligation of good faith and fair dealing.

(e) A partner does not violate a duty or obligation under this [act] or under the partnership agreement solely because the partner's conduct furthers the partner's own interest.

(f) All the partners may authorize or ratify, after full disclosure of all material facts, a specific act or transaction by a partner that otherwise would violate the duty of loyalty.

(g) It is a defense to a claim under subsection (b)(2) and any comparable claim in equity or at common law that the transaction was fair to the partnership.

(h) If, as permitted by subsection (f) or the partnership agreement, a partner enters into a transaction with the partnership which otherwise would be prohibited by subsection (b)(2), the partner's rights and obligations arising from the transaction are the same as those of a person that is not a partner.

COMMENT

This section originated as UPA (1997) § 404. The 2011 and 2013 Harmonization amendments made one major substantive change; they "un-cabined" fiduciary duty. UPA (1997) § 404 had deviated substantially from UPA (1914) by purporting to codify all fiduciary duties owed by partners. This approach had a number of problems. Most notably, the exhaustive list of fiduciary duties left no room for the fiduciary duty owed by partners to each other—i.e., "the punctilio of an honor the most sensitive"). *Meinhard v. Salmon*, 164 N.E. 545, 546 (N.Y. 1928). Although UPA (1997) § 404(b) purported to state "[a] partner's duty of loyalty to the partnership *and the other partners*" (emphasis added), the three listed duties each protected the partnership and not the partners.

"Un-cabining" harmonized this act to ULLCA (2006), and this section states some of the core aspects of the fiduciary duty of loyalty, provides a duty of care, and incorporates the contractual obligation of good faith and fair dealing. The duties stated in this section are subject to the partnership agreement, but Sections 105(c) and (d) contain important limitations on the power of the partnership agreement to affect fiduciary and other duties and the obligation of good faith and fair dealing.

For the effect of dissociation on a person's duties under this section, see Section 603(b)(2).

Subsection (a)—This subsection recognizes two core managerial duties but, unlike UPA (1997), does not purport to be exhaustive. For example, many cases characterize a manager's duty to disclose as a fiduciary duty. *E.g., Lonergan v. EPE Holdings, L.L.C.*, 5 A.3d 1008, 1023 (Del. Ch. 2010) (stating that "in the limited partnership context, absent contractual modification, a general partner owes fiduciary duties that include a duty of full disclosure") (quotation marks omitted) (citation omitted); *Exxon Corp. v. Burglin*, 4 F.3d 1294, 1298 (5th Cir. 1993) ("Under Alaska law, a general partner stands in a fiduciary relationship with the limited partnership and thereby owes 'a fiduciary duty . . . to disclose information concerning partnership affairs.' ") (quoting *Parker v. N. Mixing Co.*, 756 P.2d 881, 894 (Alaska 1988)).

Subsection (b)—This subsection states three core aspects of the fiduciary duty of loyalty: (i) not "usurping" partnership opportunities or otherwise wrongly benefiting from the partnership's operations or property; (ii) avoiding conflict of interests in dealing with the partnership (whether directly or on behalf of another); and (iii) refraining from competing with the partnership. Essentially the same duties exist in agency law and under the law of all types of business organizations.

This subsection applies beginning with "the partnership's business," which by definition cannot exist before the partnership does; thus the stated duties do not apply to pre-formation activities.

The stated duties comprise a default rule. Under Section 105(d)(3)(A): "If not manifestly unreasonable, the partnership agreement may . . . alter or eliminate the aspects of the duty of loyalty stated in Section 409(b)."

Subsection (b)(1)—The phrase "hold as trustee" dates back to UPA (1914) § 21 and reflects the availability of disgorgement remedies, such as a constructive trust. In contrast to an actual trustee, a person subject to this duty does not: (i) face the special obstacles to consent characteristic of trust law; or (ii) enjoy protection for decisions taken in reliance on the governing instrument and other sources of information. *Cf.* Uniform Statutory Trust Entity Act (2009) (Last Amended 2013) § 506 ("A trustee [of a statutory trust] . . . is not liable to the trust or to a beneficial owner for breach of any duty, *including a fiduciary duty*, to the extent the breach results from reasonable reliance on: (i) a term of the governing instrument; (ii) a record of the statutory trust; or (iii) an opinion, report, or statement of another person that the person to which the opinion, report, or statement is made or delivered reasonably believes is within the other person's professional or expert competence and is made or delivered to the trustee . . . .") (emphasis added).

Subsection (b)(1)(A)—This provision is consistent with a basic principle of agency law—namely, that an agent may not benefit at all from the performance of the agency unless the principal consents. RESTATEMENT (THIRD) OF AGENCY § 8.06, cmt. c. (2006). Typically, however, the partnership agreement will legitimize particular benefits—*e.g.*, a management fee paid to a managing partner in addition to that partner's share of distributions. Also, an agreed allocation of distributions takes those benefits outside the reach of this provision.

Subsection (b)(1)(B)—For the expansive meaning of "property," see Section 102(16). The term includes confidential information.

Subsection (b)(1)(C)—This act does not specify what constitutes "a partnership opportunity," but ample case law exists. See, e.g., *Triple Five of Minn., Inc. v. Simon*, 404 F.3d 1088, 1096 (8th Cir. 2005) ("An opportunity that is closely related to the entity's existing or prospective line of business, would competitively advantage the partnership, and is one that the partnership has the financial ability, knowledge and experience to pursue is a partnership opportunity."); *Knudson v. Kyllo*, 831 N.W.2d 763, 767 (N.D. 2013) (explaining why conducting farming operations on land owned by others was a partnership opportunity while purchasing farmland was not).

The duty stated here continues through winding up, although in that context the scope of partnership opportunities inevitably narrows.

In most, if not all, situations, usurping a partnership opportunity also breaches the duty not to compete, Paragraph (b)(3), but not vice versa.

Subsection (b)(2)—In this context, the phrase "adverse interest" is a term of art, meaning "to be on the other side of the table" in some dealing with the partnership. Absent informed consent by the partnership, this duty is breached by the mere existence of the conflict of interest and the partnership need not prove that the outcome of the dealing was adverse to the partnership. *But see* Subsection (g) (permitting the defense of fairness).This duty continues through winding up.

Subsection (b)(3)—Although competition is often thought of in terms of potential customers, this duty applies equally to competition for resources, including employees. This duty ends when the partnership dissolves.

Subsection (c)—This act no longer refers to the duty of care as a fiduciary duty, because: the duty of care applies in many non-fiduciary situations; and (ii) breach of the duty of care is remediable in damages while breach of a fiduciary duty gives rise also to equitable remedies, including disgorgement, constructive trust, and rescission.

The change in label is consistent with the Restatement (Third) of Agency section 8.02 (2006), which refers to the agent's "fiduciary duty" to act loyally, but eschews the word "fiduciary" when stating the agent's duties of "care, competence, and diligence." *Id.* § 8.08. However, the label change is merely semantics; no change in the law is intended.

The partnership agreement can raise the standard of care, or subject to Sections 105(c)(8) and (d)(3)(C), lower it. A person's practical exposure for breaching the duty of care involves not only the standard of care but also any partnership agreement provision that: (i) exonerates the person from liability for breach of the duty of care, Section 105(c)(8); or (ii) entitles the person to indemnification despite such breach, Section 408(b), cmt.

Subsection (d)—This subsection refers to the "*contractual* obligation of good faith and fair dealing" (emphasis added) and thereby invokes the implied obligation that exists in every contract. *See* RESTATEMENT (SECOND) CONTRACTS § 205 (1981) ("Every contract imposes upon each party a duty of good faith and fair dealing in its performance and its enforcement."). The adjective ("contractual") should help avoid decisions like *Phelps v. Frampton*, 170 P.3d 474, 483 (Mont. 2007) (holding that Montana's version of UPA (1997) creates a statutory obligation of good faith and fair dealing separate from the implied contractual covenant).

At first glance, it may seem strange to apply a contractual obligation to statutory duties and rights— *i.e.*, duties and rights "under this [act]." However, for the most part those duties and rights apply to relationships *inter se* the partners and the partnership and function only to the extent not displaced by the partnership agreement. Those statutory default rules are thus intended to function like a contract; applying the contractual notion of good faith and fair dealing therefore makes sense.

The contractual obligation of "good faith" has nothing to do with the corporate concept of good faith that for years bedeviled courts and attorneys trying to understand: (i) Delaware's famous corporate law exoneration provision; and (ii) that provision's exception "for acts or omissions not in good faith." DEL. CODE ANN. tit. 8, § 102(b)(7) (2012). In that context, good faith is an aspect of the duty of loyalty. *See Stone ex rel. AmSouth Bancorporation v. Ritter*, 911 A.2d 362, 369–70 (Del. 2006).

Likewise, the contractual obligation of good faith and fair dealing has nothing to do with the "utmost good faith" sometimes used to describe the fiduciary duties that owners of closely held businesses owe each other. *See, e.g., Meinhard v. Salmon*, 477, 164 N.E. 545, 551 (NY 1928) ("[W]here parties engage in a joint enterprise each owes to the other the duty of the utmost good faith in all that relates to their common venture. Within its scope they stand in a fiduciary relationship."); *Donahue v. Rodd Electrotype Co. of New England, Inc.*, 328 N.E.2d 505, 515 (Mass. 1975) ("[S]tockholders in the close corporation owe one another substantially the same fiduciary duty in the operation of the enterprise that partners owe to one another. In our previous decisions, we have defined the standard of duty owed by partners to one another as the utmost good faith and loyalty.") (footnotes omitted) (citations omitted) (internal quotations omitted).

To the contrary, the contractual obligation of good faith and fair dealing is not a fiduciary duty, does not command altruism or self-abnegation, and does not prevent a partner from acting in the partner's own self-interest:

> "Fair dealing" is not akin to the fair process component of entire fairness, *i.e.*, whether the fiduciary acted fairly when engaging in the challenged transaction as measured by duties of loyalty and care .... It is rather a commitment to deal "fairly" in the sense of consistently with the terms of the parties' agreement and its purpose. Likewise "good faith" does not envision loyalty to the contractual counterparty, but rather faithfulness to the scope, purpose, and terms of the parties' contract. Both necessarily turn on the contract itself and what the parties would have agreed upon had the issue arisen when they were bargaining originally.

Gerber v. Enter. Prods. Holdings, L.L.C., 67 A.3d 400, 418–19 (Del. 2013) (quoting *ASB Allegiance Real Estate Fund v. Scion Breckenridge Managing Member, L.L.C.*, 50 A.3d 434, 440–42 (Del. Ch. 2012), *aff'd in part, rev'd in part on other grounds*, 68 A.3d 665 (Del. 2013); *see also* Subsection (e).

Courts should not use the contractual obligation to change *ex post facto* the parties' or this act's allocation of risk and power. To the contrary, the obligation should be used only to protect agreed-upon arrangements from conduct that is manifestly beyond what a reasonable person could have contemplated when the arrangements were made.

The partnership agreement or this act may grant discretion to a partner, and the contractual obligation of good faith and fair dealing is especially salient when discretion is at issue. However, a partner may properly exercise discretion even though another partner suffers as a consequence. Conduct does not violate the obligation of good faith and fair dealing merely because that conduct substantially prejudices a party. Indeed, parties allocate risk precisely because prejudice may occur.

The exercise of discretion constitutes a breach of the obligation of good faith and fair dealing only when the party claiming breach shows that the conduct has no honestly held purpose that legitimately comports with the parties' agreed-upon arrangements:

> An implied covenant claim . . . looks to the past. It is not a free-floating duty unattached to the underlying legal documents. It does not ask what duty the law should impose on the parties given their relationship at the time of the wrong, but *rather what the parties would have agreed to themselves had they considered the issue in their original bargaining positions at the time of contracting.*

Gerber v. Enter. Prods. Holdings, L.L.C., 67 A.3d 400, 418 (Del. 2013) (quoting *ASB Allegiance Real Estate Fund v. Scion Breckenridge Managing Member, L.L.C.*, 50 A.3d 434, 440–42 (Del. Ch. 2012), *aff'd in part, rev'd in part on other grounds*, 68 A.3d 665 (Del. 2013)).

In sum, the purpose of the contractual obligation of good faith and fair dealing is to protect the arrangement the partners have chosen for themselves, not to restructure that arrangement under the guise of safeguarding it.

As to the power of the partnership agreement to affect the contractual obligation of good faith and fair dealing, see Section 105(c)(6) (prohibiting elimination but allowing the agreement to "prescribe standards, if not manifestly unreasonable, by which the performance of the obligation is to be measured"). For examples, see Section 105(c)(6), comment. As to whether the obligation stated in this subsection applies to the benefit of transferees, see Section 107(b), comment.

Subsection (e)—A partner in a general partnership has at least two different roles: (i) as a party to the partnership agreement, with rights and obligations under that agreement; and (ii) as co-manager of the enterprise. This provision pertains to the first role. A partner's exercise of rights under the partnership agreement is subject to the obligation of good faith and fair dealing, Subsection (d), but a partner does not breach that contractual obligation "solely because the partner's conduct furthers the partner's own interest." In contrast, this provision is ineffective with regard to a partner's duties as co-manager. For example, a partner's liability under Section 409(b)(3) (prohibiting competition) is not "solely because the partner's conduct furthers the partner's own interest." Rather, the liability results from the breach of a specific obligation—*i.e.*, the codified aspect of the duty of loyalty that prohibits competition.

Subsection (f)—Here and elsewhere in this act, information "is material if there is a substantial likelihood that a reasonable [decision maker] would consider it important in deciding how to vote" or take other action under this act or the partnership agreements. See *Basic Inc. v. Levinson*, 485 U.S. 224, 231–32 (1988) (quoting *TSC Indus., Inc. v. Northway, Inc.*, 426 U.S. 438, 449 (1976)).

The partnership agreement can provide additional or different methods of authorization or ratification, subject to the strictures of Section 105(c)(5), (d)(1), and (d)(3)(A)(B) and (D).

Subsection (g)—This subsection codifies judge-made law applicable to all business entities. See, e.g., *Kahn v. Lynch Commc'n Sys., Inc.*, 638 A.2d 1110, 1116 (Del. 1994) (discussing "entire fairness" in the context of a corporation's merger with an affiliate); *Lonergan EPE Holdings, L.L.C.*, 5 A.3d 1008, 1019 (Del. Ch. 2010) (discussing "entire fairness" in the context of a limited partnership"); *Gottsacker v. Monnier*, 697 N.W.2d 436, 444 (Wis. 2005) (referring to "a willful failure to deal fairly with the LLC or its other members").

Subsection (h)—This subsection is the modern, reformulated version of a language that sought to overturn the now-defunct notion that debts to partners were categorically inferior to debts to non-partner creditors. *See, e.g.*, ULPA (2001) § 112 ("A partner may lend money to and transact other business with the limited partnership and has the same rights and obligations with respect to the loan or other transaction as a person that is not a partner."). The reformulation makes clear that this provision has nothing to do with the fiduciary duty pertaining to conflict of interests. *See BT-I v. Equitable Life Assurance Soc'y of the U.S.*, 75 Cal. App. 4th 1406, 1415 (Cal. Ct. App. 1999) (examining the prior formulation, explaining its history and stating "[w]e cannot discern anything in the purpose of [the prior formulation] that suggests an intent to affect a general partner's fiduciary duty to limited partners").

This subsection states a default rule. The partnership agreement may provide that debt to a partner (or partners generally) is subordinate to other partnership obligations. The agreement that creates the debt may do likewise.

§ 410. Actions by Partnership and Partners

(a) A partnership may maintain an action against a partner for a breach of the partnership agreement, or for the violation of a duty to the partnership, causing harm to the partnership.

(b) A partner may maintain an action against the partnership or another partner, with or without an accounting as to partnership business, to enforce the partner's rights and protect the partner's interests, including rights and interests under the partnership agreement or this [act] or arising independently of the partnership relationship.

(c) A right to an accounting on dissolution and winding up does not revive a claim barred by law.

§ 411. Continuation of Partnership Beyond Definite Term or Particular Undertaking

(a) If a partnership for a definite term or particular undertaking is continued, without an express agreement, after the expiration of the term or completion of the undertaking, the rights and duties of the partners remain the same as they were at the expiration or completion, so far as is consistent with a partnership at will.

(b) If the partners, or those of them who habitually acted in the business during the term or undertaking, continue the business without any settlement or liquidation of the partnership, they are presumed to have agreed that the partnership will continue.

[ARTICLE] 5. TRANSFERABLE INTERESTS AND RIGHTS OF TRANSFEREES AND CREDITORS

§ 501. Partner Not Co-Owner of Partnership Property

A partner is not a co-owner of partnership property and has no interest in partnership property which can be transferred, either voluntarily or involuntarily.

§ 502. Nature of Transferable Interest

A transferable interest is personal property.

§ 503. Transfer of Transferable Interest

(a) A transfer, in whole or in part, of a transferable interest:

(1) is permissible;

(2) does not by itself cause a person's dissociation as a partner or a dissolution and winding up of the partnership business; and

(3) subject to Section 505, does not entitle the transferee to:

(A) participate in the management or conduct of the partnership's business; or

(B) except as otherwise provided in subsection (c), have access to records or other information concerning the partnership's business.

(b)   A transferee has the right to:

(1)   receive, in accordance with the transfer, distributions to which the transferor would otherwise be entitled; and

(2)   seek under Section 801(5) a judicial determination that it is equitable to wind up the partnership business.

(c)   In a dissolution and winding up of a partnership, a transferee is entitled to an account of the partnership's transactions only from the date of dissolution.

(d)   A partnership need not give effect to a transferee's rights under this section until the partnership knows or has notice of the transfer.

(e)   A transfer of a transferable interest in violation of a restriction on transfer contained in the partnership agreement is ineffective if the intended transferee has knowledge or notice of the restriction at the time of transfer.

(f)   Except as otherwise provided in Section 601(4)(B), if a partner transfers a transferable interest, the transferor retains the rights of a partner other than the transferable interest transferred and retains all the duties and obligations of a partner.

(g)   If a partner transfers a transferable interest to a person that becomes a partner with respect to the transferred interest, the transferee is liable for the partner's obligations under Sections 404 and 407 known to the transferee when the transferee becomes a partner.

§ 504.   Charging Order

(a)   On application by a judgment creditor of a partner or transferee, a court may enter a charging order against the transferable interest of the judgment debtor for the unsatisfied amount of the judgment. A charging order constitutes a lien on a judgment debtor's transferable interest and requires the partnership to pay over to the person to which the charging order was issued any distribution that otherwise would be paid to the judgment debtor.

(b)   To the extent necessary to effectuate the collection of distributions pursuant to a charging order in effect under subsection (a), the court may:

(1)   appoint a receiver of the distributions subject to the charging order, with the power to make all inquiries the judgment debtor might have made; and

(2)   make all other orders necessary to give effect to the charging order.

(c)   Upon a showing that distributions under a charging order will not pay the judgment debt within a reasonable time, the court may foreclose the lien and order the sale of the transferable interest. The purchaser at the foreclosure sale obtains only the transferable interest, does not thereby become a partner, and is subject to Section 503.

(d)   At any time before foreclosure under subsection (c), the partner or transferee whose transferable interest is subject to a charging order under subsection (a) may extinguish the charging order by satisfying the judgment and filing a certified copy of the satisfaction with the court that issued the charging order.

(e)   At any time before foreclosure under subsection (c), a partnership or one or more partners whose transferable interests are not subject to the charging order may pay to the judgment creditor the full amount due under the judgment and thereby succeed to the rights of the judgment creditor, including the charging order.

(f)   This [act] does not deprive any partner or transferee of the benefit of any exemption law applicable to the transferable interest of the partner or transferee.

(g)   This section provides the exclusive remedy by which a person seeking in the capacity of a judgment creditor to enforce a judgment against a partner or transferee may satisfy the judgment from the judgment debtor's transferable interest.

§ 505.   Power of Legal Representative of Deceased

If a partner dies, the deceased partner's legal representative may exercise:

(1)   the rights of a transferee provided in Section 503(c); and

(2)   for purposes of settling the estate, the rights the deceased partner had under Section 408.

[ARTICLE] 6.   DISSOCIATION

§ 601.   Events Causing Dissociation

A person is dissociated as a partner when:

(1)   the partnership knows or has notice of the person's express will to withdraw as a partner, but, if the person has specified a withdrawal date later than the date the partnership knew or had notice, on that later date;

(2)   an event stated in the partnership agreement as causing the person's dissociation occurs;

(3)   the person is expelled as a partner pursuant to the partnership agreement;

(4)   the person is expelled as a partner by the affirmative vote or consent of all the other partners if:

(A)   it is unlawful to carry on the partnership business with the person as a partner;

(B)   there has been a transfer of all of the person's transferable interest in the partnership, other than:

(i)   a transfer for security purposes; or

(ii)   a charging order in effect under Section 504 which has not been foreclosed;

(C)   the person is an entity and:

(i)   the partnership notifies the person that it will be expelled as a partner because the person has filed a statement of dissolution or the equivalent, the person has been administratively dissolved, the person's charter or the equivalent has been revoked, or the person's right to conduct business has been suspended by the person's jurisdiction of formation; and

(ii)   not later than 90 days after the notification, the statement of dissolution or the equivalent has not been withdrawn, rescinded, or revoked, or the person's charter or the equivalent or right to conduct business has not been reinstated; or

(D)   the person is an unincorporated entity that has been dissolved and whose activities and affairs are being wound up;

(5)   on application by the partnership or another partner, the person is expelled as a partner by judicial order because the person:

(A)   has engaged or is engaging in wrongful conduct that has affected adversely and materially, or will affect adversely and materially, the partnership's business;

(B)   has committed willfully or persistently, or is committing willfully or persistently, a material breach of the partnership agreement or a duty or obligation under Section 409; or

(C)   has engaged or is engaging in conduct relating to the partnership's business which makes it not reasonably practicable to carry on the business with the person as a partner;

(6)   the person:

(A)   becomes a debtor in bankruptcy;

(B)   signs an assignment for the benefit of creditors; or

(C)   seeks, consents to, or acquiesces in the appointment of a trustee, receiver, or liquidator of the person or of all or substantially all the person's property;

(7)   in the case of an individual:

(A)   the individual dies;

(B)   a guardian or general conservator for the individual is appointed; or

(C)   a court orders that the individual has otherwise become incapable of performing the individual's duties as a partner under this [act] or the partnership agreement;

(8)   in the case of a person that is a testamentary or inter vivos trust or is acting as a partner by virtue of being a trustee of such a trust, the trust's entire transferable interest in the partnership is distributed;

(9)   in the case of a person that is an estate or is acting as a partner by virtue of being a personal representative of an estate, the estate's entire transferable interest in the partnership is distributed;

(10) in the case of a person that is not an individual, the existence of the person terminates;

(11) the partnership participates in a merger under [Article] 11 and:

(A)   the partnership is not the surviving entity; or

(B)   otherwise as a result of the merger, the person ceases to be a partner;

(12) the partnership participates in an interest exchange under [Article] 11 and, as a result of the interest exchange, the person ceases to be a partner;

(13) the partnership participates in a conversion under [Article] 11;

(14) the partnership participates in a domestication under [Article] 11 and, as a result of the domestication, the person ceases to be a partner; or

(15) the partnership dissolves and completes winding up.

§ 602.   Power to Dissociate as Partner; Wrongful Dissociation

(a)   A person has the power to dissociate as a partner at any time, rightfully or wrongfully, by withdrawing as a partner by express will under Section 601(1).

(b)   A person's dissociation as a partner is wrongful only if the dissociation:

(1)   is in breach of an express provision of the partnership agreement; or

(2)   in the case of a partnership for a definite term or particular undertaking, occurs before the expiration of the term or the completion of the undertaking and:

(A)   the person withdraws as a partner by express will, unless the withdrawal follows not later than 90 days after another person's dissociation by death or otherwise under Section 601(6) through (10) or wrongful dissociation under this subsection;

(B)   the person is expelled as a partner by judicial order under Section 601(5);

(C)   the person is dissociated under Section 601(6); or

(D)   in the case of a person that is not a trust other than a business trust, an estate, or an individual, the person is expelled or otherwise dissociated because it willfully dissolved or terminated.

(c)   A person that wrongfully dissociates as a partner is liable to the partnership and to the other partners for damages caused by the dissociation. The liability is in addition to any debt, obligation, or other liability of the partner to the partnership or the other partners.

§ 603.   Effect of Dissociation

(a)   If a person's dissociation results in a dissolution and winding up of the partnership business, [Article] 8 applies; otherwise, [Article] 7 applies.

(b)   If a person is dissociated as a partner:

(1)   the person's right to participate in the management and conduct of the partnership's business terminates, except as otherwise provided in Section 802(c); and

(2)   the person's duties and obligations under Section 409 end with regard to matters arising and events occurring after the person's dissociation, except to the extent the partner participates in winding up the partnership's business pursuant to Section 802.

(c)   A person's dissociation does not of itself discharge the person from any debt, obligation, or other liability to the partnership or the other partners which the person incurred while a partner.

[ARTICLE] 7.   PERSON'S DISSOCIATION AS A PARTNER WHEN BUSINESS NOT WOUND UP

§ 701.   Purchase of Interest of Person Dissociated as Partner

(a)   If a person is dissociated as a partner without the dissociation resulting in a dissolution and winding up of the partnership business under Section 801, the partnership shall cause the person's interest in the partnership to be purchased for a buyout price determined pursuant to subsection (b).

(b)   The buyout price of the interest of a person dissociated as a partner is the amount that would have been distributable to the person under Section 806(b) if, on the date of dissociation, the assets of the partnership were sold and the partnership were wound up, with the sale price equal to the greater of:

(1)   the liquidation value; or

(2)   the value based on a sale of the entire business as a going concern without the person.

(c)   Interest accrues on the buyout price from the date of dissociation to the date of payment, but damages for wrongful dissociation under Section 602(b), and all other amounts owing, whether or not presently due, from the person dissociated as a partner to the partnership, must be offset against the buyout price.

(d)   A partnership shall defend, indemnify, and hold harmless a person dissociated as a partner whose interest is being purchased against all partnership liabilities, whether incurred before or after the dissociation, except liabilities incurred by an act of the person under Section 702.

(e)   If no agreement for the purchase of the interest of a person dissociated as a partner is reached not later than 120 days after a written demand for payment, the partnership shall pay, or cause to be paid, in money to the person the amount the partnership estimates to be the buyout price and accrued interest, reduced by any offsets and accrued interest under subsection (c).

(f)   If a deferred payment is authorized under subsection (h), the partnership may tender a written offer to pay the amount it estimates to be the buyout price and accrued interest, reduced by any offsets under subsection (c), stating the time of payment, the amount and type of security for payment, and the other terms and conditions of the obligation.

(g)   The payment or tender required by subsection (e) or (f) must be accompanied by the following:

(1)   a statement of partnership assets and liabilities as of the date of dissociation;

(2)   the latest available partnership balance sheet and income statement, if any;

(3)   an explanation of how the estimated amount of the payment was calculated; and

(4)   written notice that the payment is in full satisfaction of the obligation to purchase unless, not later than 120 days after the written notice, the person dissociated as a partner commences an action to determine the buyout price, any offsets under subsection (c), or other terms of the obligation to purchase.

(h)   A person that wrongfully dissociates as a partner before the expiration of a definite term or the completion of a particular undertaking is not entitled to payment of any part of the buyout price until the expiration of the term or completion of the undertaking, unless the person establishes to the satisfaction of the court that earlier payment will not cause undue hardship to the business of the partnership. A deferred payment must be adequately secured and bear interest.

(i)   A person dissociated as a partner may maintain an action against the partnership, pursuant to Section 410(b)(2), to determine the buyout price of that person's interest, any offsets under subsection (c), or other terms of the obligation to purchase. The action must be commenced not later than 120 days after the partnership has tendered payment or an offer to pay or within one year after written demand for payment if no payment or offer to pay is tendered. The court shall determine the buyout price of the person's interest, any offset due under subsection (c), and accrued interest, and enter judgment for any additional payment or refund. If deferred payment is authorized under subsection (h), the court shall also determine the security for payment and other terms of the obligation to purchase. The court may assess reasonable attorney's fees and the fees and expenses of appraisers or other experts for a party to the action, in amounts the court finds equitable, against a party that the court finds acted arbitrarily, vexatiously, or not in good faith. The finding may be based on the partnership's failure to tender payment or an offer to pay or to comply with subsection (g).

§ 702.   Power to Bind and Liability of Person Dissociated as Partner

(a)   After a person is dissociated as a partner without the dissociation resulting in a dissolution and winding up of the partnership business and before the partnership is merged out of existence, converted, or domesticated under [Article] 11, or dissolved, the partnership is bound by an act of the person only if:

(1)   the act would have bound the partnership under Section 301 before dissociation; and

(2)   at the time the other party enters into the transaction:

(A)   less than two years has passed since the dissociation; and

(B)   the other party does not know or have notice of the dissociation and reasonably believes that the person is a partner.

(b)   If a partnership is bound under subsection (a), the person dissociated as a partner which caused the partnership to be bound is liable:

(1)   to the partnership for any damage caused to the partnership arising from the obligation incurred under subsection (a); and

(2)   if a partner or another person dissociated as a partner is liable for the obligation, to the partner or other person for any damage caused to the partner or other person arising from the liability.

§ 703.   Liability of Person Dissociated as Partner to Other Persons

(a)   Except as otherwise provided in subsection (b), a person dissociated as a partner is not liable for a partnership obligation incurred after dissociation.

(b)   A person that is dissociated as a partner is liable on a transaction entered into by the partnership after the dissociation only if:

(1)   a partner would be liable on the transaction; and

(2)   at the time the other party enters into the transaction:

(A)   less than two years has passed since the dissociation; and

(B)   the other party does not have knowledge or notice of the dissociation and reasonably believes that the person is a partner.

(c)   By agreement with a creditor of a partnership and the partnership, a person dissociated as a partner may be released from liability for a debt, obligation, or other liability of the partnership.

(d)   A person dissociated as a partner is released from liability for a debt, obligation, or other liability of the partnership if the partnership's creditor, with knowledge or notice of the person's dissociation but without the person's consent, agrees to a material alteration in the nature or time of payment of the debt, obligation, or other liability.

§ 704.   Statement of Dissociation

(a)   A person dissociated as a partner or the partnership may deliver to the [Secretary of State] for filing a statement of dissociation stating the name of the partnership and that the person has dissociated from the partnership.

(b)   A statement of dissociation is a limitation on the authority of a person dissociated as a partner for the purposes of Section 303.

§ 705.   Continued Use of Partnership Name

Continued use of a partnership name, or the name of a person dissociated as a partner as part of the partnership name, by partners continuing the business does not of itself make the person dissociated as a partner liable for an obligation of the partners or the partnership continuing the business.

[ARTICLE] 8.   DISSOLUTION AND WINDING UP

§ 801.   Events Causing Dissolution

A partnership is dissolved, and its business must be wound up, upon the occurrence of any of the following:

(1)   in a partnership at will, the partnership knows or has notice of a person's express will to withdraw as a partner, other than a partner that has dissociated under Section 601(2) through (10), but, if the person has specified a withdrawal date later than the date the partnership knew or had notice, on the later date;

(2)   in a partnership for a definite term or particular undertaking:

(A)   within 90 days after a person's dissociation by death or otherwise under Section 601(6) through (10) or wrongful dissociation under Section 602(b), the affirmative vote or consent of at least half of the remaining partners to wind up the partnership business, for which purpose a person's rightful dissociation pursuant to Section 602(b)(2)(A) constitutes that partner's consent to wind up the partnership business;

(B)   the affirmative vote or consent of all the partners to wind up the partnership business; or

(C)   the expiration of the term or the completion of the undertaking;

(3)   an event or circumstance that the partnership agreement states causes dissolution;

(4)   on application by a partner, the entry by [the appropriate court] of an order dissolving the partnership on the grounds that:

(A)   the conduct of all or substantially all the partnership's business is unlawful;

(B)   the economic purpose of the partnership is likely to be unreasonably frustrated;

(C)   another partner has engaged in conduct relating to the partnership business which makes it not reasonably practicable to carry on the business in partnership with that partner; or

(D)   it is otherwise not reasonably practicable to carry on the partnership business in conformity with the partnership agreement;

(5)   on application by a transferee, the entry by [the appropriate court] of an order dissolving the partnership on the ground that it is equitable to wind up the partnership business:

(A)   after the expiration of the term or completion of the undertaking, if the partnership was for a definite term or particular undertaking at the time of the transfer or entry of the charging order that gave rise to the transfer; or

(B)   at any time, if the partnership was a partnership at will at the time of the transfer or entry of the charging order that gave rise to the transfer; or

(6)   the passage of 90 consecutive days during which the partnership does not have at least two partners.

§ 802.   Winding Up

(a)   A dissolved partnership shall wind up its business and, except as otherwise provided in Section 803, the partnership continues after dissolution only for the purpose of winding up.

(b)   In winding up its business, the partnership:

(1)   shall discharge the partnership's debts, obligations, and other liabilities, settle and close the partnership's business, and marshal and distribute the assets of the partnership; and

(2)   may:

(A)   deliver to the [Secretary of State] for filing a statement of dissolution stating the name of the partnership and that the partnership is dissolved;

(B)   preserve the partnership business and property as a going concern for a reasonable time;

(C)   prosecute and defend actions and proceedings, whether civil, criminal, or administrative;

(D)   transfer the partnership's property;

(E)   settle disputes by mediation or arbitration;

(F)   deliver to the [Secretary of State] for filing a statement of termination stating the name of the partnership and that the partnership is terminated; and

(G)   perform other acts necessary or appropriate to the winding up.

(c)   A person whose dissociation as a partner resulted in dissolution may participate in winding up as if still a partner, unless the dissociation was wrongful.

(d)   If a dissolved partnership does not have a partner and no person has the right to participate in winding up under subsection (c), the personal or legal representative of the last person to have been a partner may wind up the partnership's business. If the representative does not exercise that right, a person to wind up the partnership's business may be appointed by the affirmative vote or consent of transferees owning a majority of the rights to receive distributions at the time the consent is to be effective. A person appointed under this subsection has the powers of a partner under Section 804 but is not liable for the debts, obligations, and other liabilities of the partnership solely by reason of having or exercising those powers or otherwise acting to wind up the partnership's business.

(e)   On the application of any partner or person entitled under subsection (c) to participate in winding up, the [appropriate court] may order judicial supervision of the winding up of a dissolved partnership, including the appointment of a person to wind up the partnership's business, if:

(1)   the partnership does not have a partner and within a reasonable time following the dissolution no person has been appointed under subsection (d); or

(2)   the applicant establishes other good cause.

§ 803.   Rescinding Dissolution

(a)   A partnership may rescind its dissolution, unless a statement of termination applicable to the partnership has become effective or [the appropriate court] has entered an order under Section 801(4) or (5)   dissolving the partnership.

(b)   Rescinding dissolution under this section requires:

(1)   the affirmative vote or consent of each partner; and

(2)   if the partnership has delivered to the [Secretary of State] for filing a statement of dissolution and:

(A)   the statement has not become effective, delivery to the [Secretary of State] for filing of a statement of withdrawal under Section 115 applicable to the statement of dissolution; or

(B)   the statement of dissolution has become effective, delivery to the [Secretary of State] for filing of a statement of rescission stating the name of the partnership and that dissolution has been rescinded under this section.

(c)   If a partnership rescinds its dissolution:

(1)   the partnership resumes carrying on its business as if dissolution had never occurred;

(2)   subject to paragraph (3), any liability incurred by the partnership after the dissolution and before the rescission has become effective is determined as if dissolution had never occurred; and

(3)   the rights of a third party arising out of conduct in reliance on the dissolution before the third party knew or had notice of the rescission may not be adversely affected.

§ 804.   Power to Bind Partnership After Dissolution

(a)   A partnership is bound by a partner's act after dissolution which:

(1)   is appropriate for winding up the partnership business; or

(2)   would have bound the partnership under Section 301 before dissolution if, at the time the other party enters into the transaction, the other party does not know or have notice of the dissolution.

(b)   A person dissociated as a partner binds a partnership through an act occurring after dissolution if:

(1)   at the time the other party enters into the transaction:

(A)   less than two years has passed since the dissociation; and

(B)   the other party does not know or have notice of the dissociation and reasonably believes that the person is a partner; and

(2)   the act:

(A)   is appropriate for winding up the partnership's business; or

(B)   would have bound the partnership under Section 301 before dissolution and at the time the other party enters into the transaction the other party does not know or have notice of the dissolution.

§ 805.   Liability After Dissolution of Partner and Person Dissociated as Partner

(a)   If a partner having knowledge of the dissolution causes a partnership to incur an obligation under Section 804(a) by an act that is not appropriate for winding up the partnership business, the partner is liable:

(1)   to the partnership for any damage caused to the partnership arising from the obligation; and

(2)   if another partner or person dissociated as a partner is liable for the obligation, to that other partner or person for any damage caused to that other partner or person arising from the liability.

(b)   Except as otherwise provided in subsection (c), if a person dissociated as a partner causes a partnership to incur an obligation under Section 804(b), the person is liable:

(1)   to the partnership for any damage caused to the partnership arising from the obligation; and

(2)   if a partner or another person dissociated as a partner is liable for the obligation, to the partner or other person for any damage caused to the partner or other person arising from the obligation.

(c)   A person dissociated as a partner is not liable under subsection (b) if:

(1)   Section 802(c) permits the person to participate in winding up; and

(2)   the act that causes the partnership to be bound under Section 804(b) is appropriate for winding up the partnership's business.

§ 806.   Disposition of Assets in Winding Up; When Contributions Required

(a)   In winding up its business, a partnership shall apply its assets, including the contributions required by this section, to discharge the partnership's obligations to creditors, including partners that are creditors.

(b)   After a partnership complies with subsection (a), any surplus must be distributed in the following order, subject to any charging order in effect under Section 504:

(1)   to each person owning a transferable interest that reflects contributions made and not previously returned, an amount equal to the value of the unreturned contributions; and

(2)   among persons owning transferable interests in proportion to their respective rights to share in distributions immediately before the dissolution of the partnership.

(c)   If a partnership's assets are insufficient to satisfy all its obligations under subsection (a), with respect to each unsatisfied obligation incurred when the partnership was not a limited liability partnership, the following rules apply:

(1)   Each person that was a partner when the obligation was incurred and that has not been released from the obligation under Section 703(c) and (d) shall contribute to the partnership for the purpose of enabling the partnership to satisfy the obligation. The contribution due from each of those persons is in proportion to the right to receive distributions in the capacity of a partner in effect for each of those persons when the obligation was incurred.

(2)   If a person does not contribute the full amount required under paragraph (1) with respect to an unsatisfied obligation of the partnership, the other persons required to contribute by paragraph (1) on account of the obligation shall contribute the additional amount necessary to

discharge the obligation. The additional contribution due from each of those other persons is in proportion to the right to receive distributions in the capacity of a partner in effect for each of those other persons when the obligation was incurred.

(3)   If a person does not make the additional contribution required by paragraph (2), further additional contributions are determined and due in the same manner as provided in that paragraph.

(d)   A person that makes an additional contribution under subsection (c)(2) or (3) may recover from any person whose failure to contribute under subsection (c)(1) or (2) necessitated the additional contribution. A person may not recover under this subsection more than the amount additionally contributed. A person's liability under this subsection may not exceed the amount the person failed to contribute.

(e)   If a partnership does not have sufficient surplus to comply with subsection (b)(1), any surplus must be distributed among the owners of transferable interests in proportion to the value of the respective unreturned contributions.

(f)   All distributions made under subsections (b) and (c) must be paid in money.

§ 807.   Known Claims Against Dissolved Limited Liability Partnership

(a)   Except as otherwise provided in subsection (d), a dissolved limited liability partnership may give notice of a known claim under subsection (b), which has the effect provided in subsection (c).

(b)   A dissolved limited liability partnership may in a record notify its known claimants of the dissolution. The notice must:

(1)   specify the information required to be included in a claim;

(2)   state that a claim must be in writing and provide a mailing address to which the claim is to be sent;

(3)   state the deadline for receipt of a claim, which may not be less than 120 days after the date the notice is received by the claimant;

(4)   state that the claim will be barred if not received by the deadline; and

(5)   unless the partnership has been throughout its existence a limited liability partnership, state that the barring of a claim against the partnership will also bar any corresponding claim against any partner or person dissociated as a partner which is based on Section 306.

(c)   A claim against a dissolved limited liability partnership is barred if the requirements of subsection (b) are met and:

(1)   the claim is not received by the specified deadline; or

(2)   if the claim is timely received but rejected by the limited liability partnership:

(A)   the partnership causes the claimant to receive a notice in a record stating that the claim is rejected and will be barred unless the claimant commences an action against the partnership to enforce the claim not later than 90 days after the claimant receives the notice; and

(B)   the claimant does not commence the required action not later than 90 days after the claimant receives the notice.

(d)   This section does not apply to a claim based on an event occurring after the date of dissolution or a liability that on that date is contingent.

§ 808. Other Claims Against Dissolved Limited Liability Partnership

(a) A dissolved limited liability partnership may publish notice of its dissolution and request persons having claims against the partnership to present them in accordance with the notice.

(b) A notice under subsection (a) must:

(1) be published at least once in a newspaper of general circulation in the [county] in this state in which the dissolved limited liability partnership's principal office is located or, if the principal office is not located in this state, in the [county] in which the office of the partnership's registered agent is or was last located;

(2) describe the information required to be contained in a claim, state that the claim must be in writing, and provide a mailing address to which the claim is to be sent;

(3) state that a claim against the partnership is barred unless an action to enforce the claim is commenced not later than three years after publication of the notice; and

(4) unless the partnership has been throughout its existence a limited liability partnership, state that the barring of a claim against the partnership will also bar any corresponding claim against any partner or person dissociated as a partner which is based on Section 306.

(c) If a dissolved limited liability partnership publishes a notice in accordance with subsection (b), the claim of each of the following claimants is barred unless the claimant commences an action to enforce the claim against the partnership not later than three years after the publication date of the notice:

(1) a claimant that did not receive notice in a record under Section 807;

(2) a claimant whose claim was timely sent to the partnership but not acted on; and

(3) a claimant whose claim is contingent at, or based on an event occurring after, the date of dissolution.

(d) A claim not barred under this section or Section 807 may be enforced:

(1) against a dissolved limited liability partnership, to the extent of its undistributed assets;

(2) except as otherwise provided in Section 809, if assets of the partnership have been distributed after dissolution, against a partner or transferee to the extent of that person's proportionate share of the claim or of the partnership's assets distributed to the partner or transferee after dissolution, whichever is less, but a person's total liability for all claims under this paragraph may not exceed the total amount of assets distributed to the person after dissolution; and

(3) against any person liable on the claim under Sections 306, 703, and 805.

§ 809. Court Proceedings

(a) A dissolved limited liability partnership that has published a notice under Section 808 may file an application with [the appropriate court] in the [county] where the partnership's principal office is located or, if the principal office is not located in this state, where the office of its registered agent is or was last located, for a determination of the amount and form of security to be provided for payment of claims that are reasonably expected to arise after the date of dissolution based on facts known to the partnership and:

(1) at the time of the application:

(A) are contingent; or

(B) have not been made known to the partnership; or

(2) are based on an event occurring after the date of dissolution.

(b)   Security is not required for any claim that is or is reasonably anticipated to be barred under Section 807.

(c)   Not later than 10 days after the filing of an application under subsection (a), the dissolved limited liability partnership shall give notice of the proceeding to each claimant holding a contingent claim known to the partnership.

(d)   In any proceeding under this section, the court may appoint a guardian ad litem to represent all claimants whose identities are unknown. The reasonable fees and expenses of the guardian, including all reasonable expert witness fees, must be paid by the dissolved limited liability partnership.

(e)   A dissolved limited liability partnership that provides security in the amount and form ordered by the court under subsection (a) satisfies the partnership's obligations with respect to claims that are contingent, have not been made known to the partnership, or are based on an event occurring after the date of dissolution, and such claims may not be enforced against a partner or transferee on account of assets received in liquidation.

§ 810.   Liability of Partner and Person Dissociated as Partner When Claim Against Partnership Barred

If a claim against a dissolved partnership is barred under Section 807, 808, or 809, any corresponding claim under Section 306, 703, or 805 is also barred.

[ARTICLE] 9.   LIMITED LIABILITY PARTNERSHIP

§ 901.   Statement of Qualification

(a)   A partnership may become a limited liability partnership pursuant to this section.

(b)   The terms and conditions on which a partnership becomes a limited liability partnership must be approved by the affirmative vote or consent necessary to amend the partnership agreement except, in the case of a partnership agreement that expressly addresses obligations to contribute to the partnership, the affirmative vote or consent necessary to amend those provisions.

(c)   After the approval required by subsection (b), a partnership may become a limited liability partnership by delivering to the [Secretary of State] for filing a statement of qualification. The statement must contain:

(1)   the name of the partnership;

(2)   the street and mailing addresses of the partnership's principal office and, if different, the street address of an office in this state, if any;

(3)   the name and street and mailing addresses in this state of the partnership's registered agent; and

(4)   a statement that the partnership elects to become a limited liability partnership.

(d)   A partnership's status as a limited liability partnership remains effective, regardless of changes in the partnership, until it is canceled pursuant to subsection (f) or administratively revoked pursuant to Section 903.

(e)   The status of a partnership as a limited liability partnership and the protection against liability of its partners for the debts, obligations, or other liabilities of the partnership while it is a limited liability partnership is not affected by errors or later changes in the information required to be contained in the statement of qualification.

(f)   A limited liability partnership may amend or cancel its statement of qualification by delivering to the [Secretary of State] for filing a statement of amendment or cancellation. The statement must be approved by the affirmative vote or consent of all the partners and state the name of the limited liability partnership and in the case of:

(1) an amendment, state the text of the amendment; and

(2) a cancellation, state that the statement of qualification is canceled.

§ 902. Permitted Names

(a) The name of a partnership that is not a limited liability partnership may not contain the phrase "Registered Limited Liability Partnership" or "Limited Liability Partnership" or the abbreviation "R.L.L.P.", "L.L.P.", "RLLP", or "LLP".

(b) The name of a limited liability partnership must contain the phrase "Registered Limited Liability Partnership" or "Limited Liability Partnership" or the abbreviation "R.L.L.P.", "L.L.P.", "RLLP", or "LLP".

(c) Except as otherwise provided in subsection (f), the name of a limited liability partnership, and the name under which a foreign limited liability partnership may register to do business in this state, must be distinguishable on the records of the [Secretary of State] from any:

(1) name of an existing person whose formation required the filing of a record by the [Secretary of State] and which is not at the time administratively dissolved;

(2) name of a limited liability partnership whose statement of qualification is in effect;

(3) name under which a person that is registered to do business in this state by the filing of a record by the [Secretary of State];

(4) name that is reserved under Section 903 or other law of this state providing for the reservation of a name by a filing of a record by the [Secretary of State];

(5) name that is registered under Section 904 or other law of this state providing for the registration of a name by a filing of a record by the [Secretary of State]; and

(6) a name registered under [this state's assumed or fictitious name statute].

(d) If a person consents in a record to the use of its name and submits an undertaking in a form satisfactory to the [Secretary of State] to change its name to a name that is distinguishable on the records of the [Secretary of State] from any name in any category of names in subsection (c), the name of the consenting person may be used by the person to which the consent was given.

(e) Except as otherwise provided in subsection (f), in determining whether a name is the same as or not distinguishable on the records of the [Secretary of State] from the name of another person, words, phrases, or abbreviations indicating a type of entity, such as "corporation", "corp.", "incorporated", "Inc.", "professional corporation", "PC", "P.C.", "professional association", "PA", "P.A.", "Limited", "Ltd.", "limited partnership", "LP", "L.P.", "limited liability partnership", "LLP", "L.L.P.", "registered limited liability partnership", "RLLP", "R.L.L.P.", "limited liability limited partnership", "LLLP", "L.L.L.P.", "registered limited liability limited partnership", "RLLLP", "R.L.L.L.P.", "limited liability company", "LLC", or "L.L.C.", "limited cooperative association", "limited cooperative", "LCA", or "L.C.A." may not be taken into account.

(f) A person may consent in a record to the use of a name that is not distinguishable on the records of the [Secretary of State] from its name except for the addition of a word, phrase, or abbreviation indicating the type of person as provided in subsection (e). In such a case, the person need not change its name pursuant to subsection (d).

(g) The name of a limited liability partnership or foreign limited liability partnership may not contain the words [insert prohibited words or words that may be used only with approval by an appropriate state agency].

(h)   A limited liability partnership or foreign limited liability partnership may use a name that is not distinguishable from a name described in subsection (c)(1) through (6) if the partnership delivers to the [Secretary of State] a certified copy of a final judgment of a court of competent jurisdiction establishing the right of the partnership to use the name in this state.

§ 903.   Administrative Revocation of Statement of Qualification

(a)   The [Secretary of State] may commence a proceeding under subsection (b) to revoke the statement of qualification of a limited liability partnership administratively if the partnership does not:

(1)   pay any fee, tax, interest, or penalty required to be paid to the [Secretary of State] not later than [six months] after it is due;

(2)   deliver [an annual] [a biennial] report to the [Secretary of State] not later than [six months] after it is due; or

(3)   have a registered agent in this state for [60] consecutive days.

(b)   If the [Secretary of State] determines that one or more grounds exist for administratively revoking a statement of qualification, the [Secretary of State] shall serve the partnership with notice in a record of the [Secretary of State's] determination.

(c)   If a limited liability partnership, not later than [60] days after service of the notice under subsection (b), does not cure or demonstrate to the satisfaction of the [Secretary of State] the nonexistence of each ground determined by the [Secretary of State], the [Secretary of State] shall administratively revoke the statement of qualification by signing a statement of administrative revocation that recites the grounds for revocation and the effective date of the revocation. The [Secretary of State] shall file the statement and serve a copy on the partnership pursuant to Section 116.

(d)   An administrative revocation under subsection (c) affects only a partnership's status as a limited liability partnership and is not an event causing dissolution of the partnership.

(e)   The administrative revocation of a statement of qualification of a limited liability partnership does not terminate the authority of its registered agent.

§ 904.   Reinstatement

(a)   A partnership whose statement of qualification has been revoked administratively under Section 903 may apply to the [Secretary of State] for reinstatement of the statement of qualification [not later than [two] years after the effective date of the revocation]. The application must state:

(1)   the name of the partnership at the time of the administrative revocation of its statement of qualification and, if needed, a different name that satisfies Section 902;

(2)   the address of the principal office of the partnership and the name and street and mailing addresses of its registered agent;

(3)   the effective date of administrative revocation of the partnership's statement of qualification; and

(4)   that the grounds for revocation did not exist or have been cured.

(b)   To have its statement of qualification reinstated, a partnership must pay all fees, taxes, interest, and penalties that were due to the [Secretary of State] at the time of the administrative revocation and all fees, taxes, interest, and penalties that would have been due to the [Secretary of State] while the partnership's statement of qualification was revoked administratively.

(c)   If the [Secretary of State] determines that an application under subsection (a) contains the required information, is satisfied that the information is correct, and determines that all payments required to be made to the [Secretary of State] by subsection (b) have been made, the [Secretary of State] shall:

(1)   cancel the statement of revocation and prepare a statement of reinstatement that states the [Secretary of State's] determination and the effective date of reinstatement; and

(2)   file the statement of reinstatement and serve a copy on the partnership.

(d)   When reinstatement under this section has become effective, the following rules apply:

(1)   The reinstatement relates back to and takes effect as of the effective date of the administrative revocation.

(2)   The partnership's status as a limited liability partnership continues as if the revocation had not occurred.

(3)   The rights of a person arising out of an act or omission in reliance on the revocation before the person knew or had notice of the reinstatement are not affected.

§ 905.   Judicial Review of Denial of Reinstatement

(a)   If the [Secretary of State] denies a partnership's application for reinstatement following administrative revocation of the partnership's statement of qualification, the [Secretary of State] shall serve the partnership with a notice in a record that explains the reasons for the denial.

(b)   A partnership may seek judicial review of denial of reinstatement in [the appropriate court] not later than [30] days after service of the notice of denial.

§ 906.   Reservation of Name

(a)   A person may reserve the exclusive use of a name that complies with Section 902 by delivering an application to the [Secretary of State] for filing. The application must state the name and address of the applicant and the name to be reserved. If the [Secretary of State] finds that the name is available, the [Secretary of State] shall reserve the name for the applicant's exclusive use for [120] days.

(b)   The owner of a reserved name may transfer the reservation to another person by delivering to the [Secretary of State] a signed notice in a record of the transfer which states the name and address of the person to which the reservation is being transferred.

§ 907.   Registration of Name

(a)   A foreign limited liability partnership not registered to do business in this state under [Article] 10 may register its name, or an alternate name adopted pursuant to Section 902, if the name is distinguishable on the records of the [Secretary of State] from the names that are not available under Section 902.

(b)   To register its name or an alternate name adopted pursuant to Section 902, a foreign limited liability partnership must deliver to the [Secretary of State] for filing an application stating the partnership's name, the jurisdiction and date of its formation, and any alternate name adopted pursuant to Section 902. If the [Secretary of State] finds that the name applied for is available, the [Secretary of State] shall register the name for the applicant's exclusive use.

(c)   The registration of a name under this section is effective for [one year] after the date of registration.

(d)   A foreign limited liability partnership whose name registration is effective may renew the registration for successive [one-year] periods by delivering, not earlier than [three months] before the expiration of the registration, to the [Secretary of State] for filing a renewal application that complies with this section. When filed, the renewal application renews the registration for a succeeding [one-year] period.

(e)   A foreign limited liability partnership whose name registration is effective may register as a foreign limited liability partnership under the registered name or consent in a signed record to the use of that name by another person that is not an individual.

§ 908.   Registered Agent

(a)   Each limited liability partnership and each registered foreign limited liability partnership shall designate and maintain a registered agent in this state. The designation of a registered agent is an affirmation of fact by the partnership or foreign partnership that the agent has consented to serve.

(b)   A registered agent for a limited liability partnership or registered foreign limited liability partnership must have a place of business in this state.

(c)   The only duties under this [act] of a registered agent that has complied with this [act] are:

(1)   to forward to the limited liability partnership or registered foreign limited liability partnership at the address most recently supplied to the agent by the partnership or foreign partnership any process, notice, or demand pertaining to the partnership or foreign partnership which is served on or received by the agent;

(2)   if the registered agent resigns, to provide the notice required by Section 907(c) to the partnership or foreign partnership at the address most recently supplied to the agent by the partnership or foreign partnership; and

(3)   to keep current the information with respect to the agent in the statement of qualification or foreign registration statement.

§ 909.   Change of Registered Agent or Address for Registered Agent by Limited Liability Partnership

(a)   A limited liability partnership or registered foreign limited liability partnership may change its registered agent or the address of its registered agent by delivering to the [Secretary of State] for filing a statement of change that states:

(1)   the name of the partnership or foreign partnership; and

(2)   the information that is to be in effect as a result of the filing of the statement of change.

(b)   The partners of a limited liability partnership need not approve the delivery to the [Secretary of State] for filing of:

(1)   a statement of change under this section; or

(2)   a similar filing changing the registered agent or registered office, if any, of the partnership in any other jurisdiction.

(c)   A statement of change under this section designating a new registered agent is an affirmation of fact by the limited liability partnership or registered foreign limited liability partnership that the agent has consented to serve.

(d)   As an alternative to using the procedure in this section, a limited liability partnership may amend its statement of qualification.

§ 910.   Resignation of Registered Agent

(a)   A registered agent may resign as an agent for a limited liability partnership or registered foreign limited liability partnership by delivering to the [Secretary of State] for filing a statement of resignation that states:

(1)   the name of the partnership or foreign partnership;

(2)   the name of the agent;

(3)   that the agent resigns from serving as registered agent for the partnership or foreign partnership; and

(4)   the address of the partnership or foreign partnership to which the agent will send the notice required by subsection (c).

(b)   A statement of resignation takes effect on the earlier of:

(1)   the 31st day after the day on which it is filed by the [Secretary of State]; or

(2)   the designation of a new registered agent for the limited liability partnership or registered foreign limited liability partnership.

(c)   A registered agent promptly shall furnish to the limited liability partnership or registered foreign limited liability partnership notice in a record of the date on which a statement of resignation was filed.

(d)   When a statement of resignation takes effect, the registered agent ceases to have responsibility under this [act] for any matter thereafter tendered to it as agent for the limited liability partnership or registered foreign limited liability partnership. The resignation does not affect any contractual rights the partnership or foreign partnership has against the agent or that the agent has against the partnership or foreign partnership.

(e)   A registered agent may resign with respect to a limited liability partnership or registered foreign limited liability partnership whether or not the partnership or foreign partnership is in good standing.

§ 911.   Change of Name or Address by Registered Agent

(a)   If a registered agent changes its name or address, the agent may deliver to the [Secretary of State] for filing a statement of change that states:

(1)   the name of the limited liability partnership or registered foreign limited liability partnership represented by the registered agent;

(2)   the name of the agent as currently shown in the records of the [Secretary of State] for the partnership or foreign partnership;

(3)   if the name of the agent has changed, its new name; and

(4)   if the address of the agent has changed, its new address.

(b)   A registered agent promptly shall furnish notice to the represented limited liability partnership or registered foreign limited liability partnership of the filing by the [Secretary of State] of the statement of change and the changes made by the statement.

Legislative Note: Many registered agents act in that capacity for many entities, and the Model Registered Agents Act (2006) (Last Amended 2013) provides a streamlined method through which a commercial registered agent can make a single filing to change its information for all represented entities. The single filing does not prevent an enacting state from assessing filing fees on the basis of the number of entity records affected. Alternatively the fees can be set on an incremental sliding fee or capitated amount based upon potential economies of costs for a bulk filing.

§ 912.   Service of Process, Notice, or Demand

(a)   A limited liability partnership or registered foreign limited liability partnership may be served with any process, notice, or demand required or permitted by law by serving its registered agent.

(b)   If a limited liability partnership or registered foreign limited liability partnership ceases to have a registered agent, or if its registered agent cannot with reasonable diligence be served, the partnership or foreign partnership may be served by registered or certified mail, return receipt requested, or by similar commercial delivery service, addressed to the partnership or foreign partnership at its principal office. The address of the principal office must be as shown in the partnership's or foreign partnership's most recent [annual] [biennial] report filed by the [Secretary of State]. Service is effected under this subsection on the earliest of:

(1)   the date the partnership or foreign partnership receives the mail or delivery by the commercial delivery service;

(2)   the date shown on the return receipt, if signed by the partnership or foreign partnership; or

(3)   five days after its deposit with the United States Postal Service, or with the commercial delivery service, if correctly addressed and with sufficient postage or payment.

(c)   If process, notice, or demand cannot be served on a limited liability partnership or registered foreign limited liability partnership pursuant to subsection (a) or (b), service may be made by handing a copy to the individual in charge of any regular place of business of the partnership or foreign partnership if the individual served is not a plaintiff in the action.

(d)   Service of process, notice, or demand on a registered agent must be in a written record.

(e)   Service of process, notice, or demand may be made by other means under law other than this [act].

§ 913.   [Annual] [Biennial] Report for [Secretary of State]

(a)   A limited liability partnership or registered foreign limited liability partnership shall deliver to the [Secretary of State] for filing [an annual] [a biennial] report that states:

(1)   the name of the partnership or registered foreign partnership;

(2)   the name and street and mailing addresses of its registered agent in this state;

(3)   the street and mailing addresses of its principal office;

(4)   the name of at least one partner; and

(5)   in the case of a foreign partnership, its jurisdiction of formation and any alternate name adopted under Section 1006.

(b)   Information in the [annual] [biennial] report must be current as of the date the report is signed by the limited liability partnership or registered foreign limited liability partnership.

(c)   The first [annual] [biennial] report must be delivered to the [Secretary of State] for filing after [January 1] and before [April 1] of the year following the calendar year in which the limited liability partnership's statement of qualification became effective or the registered foreign limited liability partnership registered to do business in this state. Subsequent [annual] [biennial] reports must be delivered to the [Secretary of State] for filing after [January 1] and before [April 1] of each [second] calendar year thereafter.

(d)   If [an annual] [a biennial] report does not contain the information required by this section, the [Secretary of State] promptly shall notify the reporting limited liability partnership or registered foreign limited liability partnership in a record and return the report for correction.

(e)   If [an annual] [a biennial] report contains the name or address of a registered agent which differs from the information shown in the records of the [Secretary of State] immediately before the report becomes effective, the differing information is considered a statement of change under Section 909.

[ARTICLE] 10.   FOREIGN LIMITED LIABILITY PARTNERSHIP

§ 1001.   Governing Law

(a)   The law of the jurisdiction of formation of a foreign limited liability partnership governs:

   (1)   the internal affairs of the partnership; and

   (2)   the liability of a partner as partner for a debt, obligation, or other liability of the foreign partnership.

(b)   A foreign limited liability partnership is not precluded from registering to do business in this state because of any difference between the law of its jurisdiction of formation and the law of this state.

(c)   Registration of a foreign limited liability partnership to do business in this state does not authorize the foreign partnership to engage in any business or exercise any power that a limited liability partnership may not engage in or exercise in this state.

§ 1002.   Registration to Do Business in This State

(a)   A foreign limited liability partnership may not do business in this state until it registers with the [Secretary of State] under this [article].

(b)   A foreign limited liability partnership doing business in this state may not maintain an action or proceeding in this state unless it has registered to do business in this state.

(c)   The failure of a foreign limited liability partnership to register to do business in this state does not impair the validity of a contract or act of the foreign partnership or preclude it from defending an action or proceeding in this state.

(d)   A limitation on the liability of a partner of a foreign limited liability partnership is not waived solely because the foreign partnership does business in this state without registering to do business in this state.

(e)   Section 1001(a) and (b) applies even if a foreign limited liability partnership fails to register under this [article].

§ 1003.   Foreign Registration Statement

To register to do business in this state, a foreign limited liability partnership must deliver a foreign registration statement to the [Secretary of State] for filing. The statement must state:

   (1)   the name of the partnership and, if the name does not comply with Section 902, an alternate name adopted pursuant to Section 1006(a);

   (2)   that the partnership is a foreign limited liability partnership;

   (3)   the partnership's jurisdiction of formation;

   (4)   the street and mailing addresses of the partnership's principal office and, if the law of the partnership's jurisdiction of formation requires the partnership to maintain an office in that jurisdiction, the street and mailing addresses of the required office; and

   (5)   the name and street and mailing addresses of the partnership's registered agent in this state.

§ 1004.   Amendment of Foreign Registration Statement

A registered foreign limited liability partnership shall deliver to the [Secretary of State] for filing an amendment to its foreign registration statement if there is a change in:

   (1)   the name of the partnership;

   (2)   the partnership's jurisdiction of formation;

(3)   an address required by Section 1003(4); or

(4)   the information required by Section 1003(5).

§ 1005.   Activities Not Constituting Doing Business

(a)   Activities of a foreign limited liability partnership which do not constitute doing business in this state under this [article] include:

(1)   maintaining, defending, mediating, arbitrating, or settling an action or proceeding;

(2)   carrying on any activity concerning its internal affairs, including holding meetings of its partners;

(3)   maintaining accounts in financial institutions;

(4)   maintaining offices or agencies for the transfer, exchange, and registration of securities of the partnership or maintaining trustees or depositories with respect to those securities;

(5)   selling through independent contractors;

(6)   soliciting or obtaining orders by any means if the orders require acceptance outside this state before they become contracts;

(7)   creating or acquiring indebtedness, mortgages, or security interests in property;

(8)   securing or collecting debts or enforcing mortgages or security interests in property securing the debts and holding, protecting, or maintaining property;

(9)   conducting an isolated transaction that is not in the course of similar transactions;

(10)   owning, without more, property; and

(11)   doing business in interstate commerce.

(b)   A person does not do business in this state solely by being a partner of a foreign limited liability partnership that does business in this state.

(c)   This section does not apply in determining the contacts or activities that may subject a foreign limited liability partnership to service of process, taxation, or regulation under law of this state other than this [act].

§ 1006.   Noncomplying Name of Foreign Limited Liability Partnership

(a)   A foreign limited liability partnership whose name does not comply with Section 902 may not register to do business in this state until it adopts, for the purpose of doing business in this state, an alternate name that complies with Section 902. A partnership that registers under an alternate name under this subsection need not comply with [this state's assumed or fictitious name statute]. After registering to do business in this state with an alternate name, a partnership shall do business in this state under:

(1)   the alternate name;

(2)   the partnership's name, with the addition of its jurisdiction of formation; or

(3)   a name the partnership is authorized to use under [this state's assumed or fictitious name statute].

(b)   If a registered foreign limited liability partnership changes its name to one that does not comply with Section 902, it may not do business in this state until it complies with subsection (a) by amending its registration to adopt an alternate name that complies with Section 902.

§ 1007. Withdrawal Deemed on Conversion to Domestic Filing Entity or Domestic Limited Liability Partnership

A registered foreign limited liability partnership that converts to a domestic limited liability partnership or to a domestic entity whose formation requires the delivery of a record to the [Secretary of State] for filing is deemed to have withdrawn its registration on the effective date of the conversion.

§ 1008. Withdrawal on Dissolution or Conversion to Nonfiling Entity Other than Limited Liability Partnership

(a) A registered foreign limited liability partnership that has dissolved and completed winding up or has converted to a domestic or foreign entity whose formation does not require the public filing of a record, other than a limited liability partnership, shall deliver a statement of withdrawal to the [Secretary of State] for filing. The statement must state:

(1) in the case of a partnership that has completed winding up:

(A) its name and jurisdiction of formation;

(B) that the partnership surrenders its registration to do business in this state; and

(2) in the case of a partnership that has converted:

(A) the name of the converting partnership and its jurisdiction of formation;

(B) the type of entity to which the partnership has converted and its jurisdiction of formation;

(C) that the converted entity surrenders the converting partnership's registration to do business in this state and revokes the authority of the converting partnership's registered agent to act as registered agent in this state on behalf of the partnership or the converted entity; and

(D) a mailing address to which service of process may be made under subsection (b).

(b) After a withdrawal under this section becomes effective, service of process in any action or proceeding based on a cause of action arising during the time the foreign limited liability partnership was registered to do business in this state may be made pursuant to Section 909.

§ 1009. Transfer of Registration

(a) When a registered foreign limited liability partnership has merged into a foreign entity that is not registered to do business in this state or has converted to a foreign entity required to register with the [Secretary of State] to do business in this state, the foreign entity shall deliver to the [Secretary of State] for filing an application for transfer of registration. The application must state:

(1) the name of the registered foreign limited partnership before the merger or conversion;

(2) that before the merger or conversion the registration pertained to a foreign limited liability partnership;

(3) the name of the applicant foreign entity into which the foreign limited liability partnership has merged or to which it has been converted and, if the name does not comply with Section 902, an alternate name adopted pursuant to Section 1006(a);

(4) the type of entity of the applicant foreign entity and its jurisdiction of formation;

(5) the street and mailing addresses of the principal office of the applicant foreign entity and, if the law of that entity's jurisdiction of formation requires the entity to maintain an office in that jurisdiction, the street and mailing addresses of that office; and

(6) the name and street and mailing addresses of the applicant foreign entity's registered agent in this state.

(b)   When an application for transfer of registration takes effect, the registration of the foreign limited liability limited partnership to do business in this state is transferred without interruption to the foreign entity into which the partnership has merged or to which it has been converted.

§ 1010.   Termination of Registration

(a)   The [Secretary of State] may terminate the registration of a registered foreign limited liability partnership in the manner provided in subsections (b) and (c) if the partnership does not:

(1)   pay, not later than [60] days after the due date, any fee, tax, interest, or penalty required to be paid to the [Secretary of State] under this [act] or law other than this [act];

(2)   deliver to the [Secretary of State] for filing, not later than [60] days after the due date, [an annual] [a biennial] report required under Section 913;

(3)   have a registered agent as required by Section 908; or

(4)   deliver to the [Secretary of State] for filing a statement of a change under Section 909 not later than [30] days after a change has occurred in the name or address of the registered agent.

(b)   The [Secretary of State] may terminate the registration of a registered foreign limited liability partnership by:

(1)   filing a notice of termination or noting the termination in the records of the [Secretary of State]; and

(2)   delivering a copy of the notice or the information in the notation to the partnership's registered agent or, if the partnership does not have a registered agent, to the partnership's principal office.

(c)   A notice or information in a notation under subsection (b) must include:

(1)   the effective date of the termination, which must be at least [60] days after the date the [Secretary of State] delivers the copy; and

(2)   the grounds for termination under subsection (a).

(d)   The authority of a registered foreign limited liability partnership to do business in this state ceases on the effective date of the notice of termination or notation under subsection (b), unless before that date the partnership cures each ground for termination stated in the notice or notation. If the partnership cures each ground, the [Secretary of State] shall file a record so stating.

§ 1011.   Withdrawal of Registration of Registered Foreign Limited Liability Partnership

(a)   A registered foreign limited liability partnership may withdraw its registration by delivering a statement of withdrawal to the [Secretary of State] for filing. The statement of withdrawal must state:

(1)   the name of the partnership and its jurisdiction of formation;

(2)   that the partnership is not doing business in this state and that it withdraws its registration to do business in this state;

(3)   that the partnership revokes the authority of its registered agent to accept service on its behalf in this state; and

(4)   an address to which service of process may be made under subsection (b).

(b)   After the withdrawal of the registration of a foreign limited liability partnership, service of process in any action or proceeding based on a cause of action arising during the time the partnership was registered to do business in this state may be made pursuant to Section 909.

§ 1012. **Action by [Attorney General]**

The [Attorney General] may maintain an action to enjoin a foreign limited liability partnership from doing business in this state in violation of this [article].

[ARTICLE] 11.   MERGER, INTEREST EXCHANGE, CONVERSION, AND DOMESTICATION

[PART] 1.   GENERAL PROVISIONS

§ 1101. **Definitions**

(1) "Acquired entity" means the entity, all of one or more classes or series of interests of which are acquired in an interest exchange.

(2) "Acquiring entity" means the entity that acquires all of one or more classes or series of interests of the acquired entity in an interest exchange.

(3) "Conversion" means a transaction authorized by [Part] 4.

(4) "Converted entity" means the converting entity as it continues in existence after a conversion.

(5) "Converting entity" means the domestic entity that approves a plan of conversion pursuant to Section 1143 or the foreign entity that approves a conversion pursuant to the law of its jurisdiction of formation.

(6) "Distributional interest" means the right under an unincorporated entity's organic law and organic rules to receive distributions from the entity.

(7) "Domestic", with respect to an entity, means governed as to its internal affairs by the law of this state.

(8) "Domesticated limited liability partnership" means a domesticating limited liability partnership as it continues in existence after a domestication.

(9) "Domesticating limited liability partnership" means the domestic limited liability partnership that approves a plan of domestication pursuant to Section 1153 or the foreign limited liability partnership that approves a domestication pursuant to the law of its jurisdiction of formation.

(10) "Domestication" means a transaction authorized by [Part] 5.

(11) "Entity":

(A) means:

    (i)   a business corporation;

    (ii)   a nonprofit corporation;

    (iii)   a general partnership, including a limited liability partnership;

    (iv)   a limited partnership, including a limited liability limited partnership;

    (v)   a limited liability company;

    [(vi) a general cooperative association;]

    (vii) a limited cooperative association;

    (viii) an unincorporated nonprofit association;

    (ix)   a statutory trust, business trust, or common-law business trust; or

    (x)   any other person that has:

        (I)   a legal existence separate from any interest holder of that person; or

(II) the power to acquire an interest in real property in its own name; and

(B) does not include:

(i) an individual;

(ii) a trust with a predominantly donative purpose or a charitable trust;

(iii) an association or relationship that is not an entity listed in subparagraph (A) and is not a partnership under the rules stated in [Section 202(c) of the Uniform Partnership Act (1997) (Last Amended 2013)] [Section 7 of the Uniform Partnership Act (1914)] or a similar provision of the law of another jurisdiction;

(iv) a decedent's estate; or

(v) a government or a governmental subdivision, agency, or instrumentality.

(12) "Filing entity" means an entity whose formation requires the filing of a public organic record. The term does not include a limited liability partnership.

(13) "Foreign", with respect to an entity, means an entity governed as to its internal affairs by the law of a jurisdiction other than this state.

(14) "Governance interest" means a right under the organic law or organic rules of an unincorporated entity, other than as a governor, agent, assignee, or proxy, to:

(A) receive or demand access to information concerning, or the books and records of, the entity;

(B) vote for or consent to the election of the governors of the entity; or

(C) receive notice of or vote on or consent to an issue involving the internal affairs of the entity.

(15) "Governor" means:

(A) a director of a business corporation;

(B) a director or trustee of a nonprofit corporation;

(C) a general partner of a general partnership;

(D) a general partner of a limited partnership;

(E) a manager of a manager-managed limited liability company;

(F) a member of a member-managed limited liability company;

[(G) a director of a general cooperative association;]

(H) a director of a limited cooperative association;

(I) a manager of an unincorporated nonprofit association;

(J) a trustee of a statutory trust, business trust, or common-law business trust; or

(K) any other person under whose authority the powers of an entity are exercised and under whose direction the activities and affairs of the entity are managed pursuant to the organic law and organic rules of the entity.

(16) "Interest" means:

(A) a share in a business corporation;

(B) a membership in a nonprofit corporation;

(C) a partnership interest in a general partnership;

(D) a partnership interest in a limited partnership;

(E)   a membership interest in a limited liability company;

[(F)   a share in a general cooperative association;]

(G)   a member's interest in a limited cooperative association;

(H)   a membership in an unincorporated nonprofit association;

(I)   a beneficial interest in a statutory trust, business trust, or common-law business trust; or

(J)   a governance interest or distributional interest in any other type of unincorporated entity.

(17) "Interest Exchange" means a transaction authorized by [Part] 3.

(18) "Interest holder" means:

(A)   a shareholder of a business corporation;

(B)   a member of a nonprofit corporation;

(C)   a general partner of a general partnership;

(D)   a general partner of a limited partnership;

(E)   a limited partner of a limited partnership;

(F)   a member of a limited liability company;

[(G)   a shareholder of a general cooperative association;]

(H)   a member of a limited cooperative association;

(I)   a member of an unincorporated nonprofit association;

(J)   a beneficiary or beneficial owner of a statutory trust, business trust, or common-law business trust; or

(K)   any other direct holder of an interest.

(19) "Interest holder liability" means:

(A)   personal liability for a liability of an entity which is imposed on a person:

(i)   solely by reason of the status of the person as an interest holder; or

(ii)   by the organic rules of the entity which make one or more specified interest holders or categories of interest holders liable in their capacity as interest holders for all or specified liabilities of the entity; or

(B)   an obligation of an interest holder under the organic rules of an entity to contribute to the entity.

(20) "Merger" means a transaction authorized by [Part] 2.

(21) "Merging entity" means an entity that is a party to a merger and exists immediately before the merger becomes effective.

(22) "Organic law" means the law of an entity's jurisdiction of formation governing the internal affairs of the entity.

(23) "Organic rules" means the public organic record and private organic rules of an entity.

(24) "Plan" means a plan of merger, plan of interest exchange, plan of conversion, or plan of domestication.

(25) "Plan of conversion" means a plan under Section 1142.

(26) "Plan of domestication" means a plan under Section 1152.

(27) "Plan of interest exchange" means a plan under Section 1132.

(28) "Plan of merger" means a plan under Section 1122.

(29) "Private organic rules" means the rules, whether or not in a record, that govern the internal affairs of an entity, are binding on all its interest holders, and are not part of its public organic record, if any. The term includes:

    (A) the bylaws of a business corporation;

    (B) the bylaws of a nonprofit corporation;

    (C) the partnership agreement of a general partnership;

    (D) the partnership agreement of a limited partnership;

    (E) the operating agreement of a limited liability company;

    [(F) the bylaws of a general cooperative association;]

    (G) the bylaws of a limited cooperative association;

    (H) the governing principles of an unincorporated nonprofit association; and

    (I) the trust instrument of a statutory trust or similar rules of a business trust or common-law business trust.

(30) "Protected agreement" means:

    (A) a record evidencing indebtedness and any related agreement in effect on [the effective date of this [act]];

    (B) an agreement that is binding on an entity on [the effective date of this [act]];

    (C) the organic rules of an entity in effect on [the effective date of this [act]]; or

    (D) an agreement that is binding on any of the governors or interest holders of an entity on [the effective date of this [act]].

(31) "Public organic record" means the record the filing of which by the [Secretary of State] is required to form an entity and any amendment to or restatement of that record. The term includes:

    (A) the articles of incorporation of a business corporation;

    (B) the articles of incorporation of a nonprofit corporation;

    (C) the certificate of limited partnership of a limited partnership;

    (D) the certificate of organization of a limited liability company;

    [(E) the articles of incorporation of a general cooperative association;]

    (F) the articles of organization of a limited cooperative association; and

    (G) the certificate of trust of a statutory trust or similar record of a business trust.

(32) "Registered foreign entity" means a foreign entity that is registered to do business in this state pursuant to a record filed by the [Secretary of State].

(33) "Statement of conversion" means a statement under Section 1145.

(34) "Statement of domestication" means a statement under Section 1155.

(35) "Statement of interest exchange" means a statement under Section 1135.

(36) "Statement of merger" means a statement under Section 1125.

(37) "Surviving entity" means the entity that continues in existence after or is created by a merger.

(38) "Type of entity" means a generic form of entity:

    (A) recognized at common law; or

    (B) formed under an organic law, whether or not some entities formed under that organic law are subject to provisions of that law that create different categories of the form of entity.

§ 1102. Relationship of [Article] to Other Laws

(a) This [article] does not authorize an act prohibited by, and does not affect the application or requirements of, law other than this [article].

(b) A transaction effected under this [act] may not create or impair a right, duty, or obligation of a person under the statutory law of this state relating to a change in control, takeover, business combination, control-share acquisition, or similar transaction involving a domestic merging, acquired, converting, or domesticating business corporation unless:

    (1) if the corporation does not survive the transaction, the transaction satisfies any requirements of the law; or

    (2) if the corporation survives the transaction, the approval of the plan is by a vote of the shareholders or directors which would be sufficient to create or impair the right, duty, or obligation directly under the law.

§ 1103. Required Notice or Approval

(a) A domestic or foreign entity that is required to give notice to, or obtain the approval of, a governmental agency or officer of this state to be a party to a merger must give the notice or obtain the approval to be a party to an interest exchange, conversion, or domestication.

(b) Property held for a charitable purpose under the law of this state by a domestic or foreign entity immediately before a transaction under this [article] becomes effective may not, as a result of the transaction, be diverted from the objects for which it was donated, granted, devised, or otherwise transferred unless, to the extent required by or pursuant to the law of this state concerning cy pres or other law dealing with nondiversion of charitable assets, the entity obtains an appropriate order of [the appropriate court] [the Attorney General] specifying the disposition of the property.

(c) A bequest, devise, gift, grant, or promise contained in a will or other instrument of donation, subscription, or conveyance which is made to a merging entity that is not the surviving entity and which takes effect or remains payable after the merger inures to the surviving entity.

(d) A trust obligation that would govern property if transferred to a nonsurviving entity applies to property that is transferred to the surviving entity under this section.

Legislative Note: As an alternative to enacting Subsection (a), a state may identify each of its regulatory laws that requires prior approval for a merger of a regulated entity, decide whether regulatory approval should be required for an interest exchange, conversion, or domestication, and make amendments as appropriate to those laws.

As with Subsection (a), an adopting state may choose to amend its various laws with respect to the nondiversion of charitable property to cover the various transactions authorized by this act as an alternative to enacting Subsection (b).

§ 1104. Nonexclusivity

The fact that a transaction under this [article] produces a certain result does not preclude the same result from being accomplished in any other manner permitted by law other than this [article].

§ 1105. Reference to External Facts

A plan may refer to facts ascertainable outside the plan if the manner in which the facts will operate upon the plan is specified in the plan. The facts may include the occurrence of an event or a determination or action by a person, whether or not the event, determination, or action is within the control of a party to the transaction.

§ 1106. Appraisal Rights

An interest holder of a domestic merging, acquired, converting, or domesticating partnership is entitled to contractual appraisal rights in connection with a transaction under this [article] to the extent provided in:

(1) the partnership's organic rules; or

(2) the plan.

[§ 1107. Excluded Entities and Transactions

(a) The following entities may not participate in a transaction under this [article]:

(1)

(2).

(b) This [article] may not be used to effect a transaction that:

(1)

(2).]

Legislative Note: Subsection (a) may be used by states that have special statutes restricted to the organization of certain types of entities. A common example is banking statutes that prohibit banks from engaging in transactions other than pursuant to those statutes.

Nonprofit entities may participate in transactions under this act with for-profit entities, subject to compliance with Section 1103. If a state desires, however, to exclude entities with a charitable purpose or to exclude other types of entities from the scope of this article, that may be done by referring to those entities in Subsection (a).

Subsection (b) may be used to exclude certain types of transactions governed by more specific statutes. A common example is the conversion of an insurance company from mutual to stock form. There may be other types of transactions that vary greatly among the states.

[PART] 2. MERGER

§ 1121. Merger Authorized

(a) By complying with this [part]:

(1) one or more domestic partnerships may merge with one or more domestic or foreign entities into a domestic or foreign surviving entity; and

(2) two or more foreign entities may merge into a domestic partnership.

(b) By complying with the provisions of this [part] applicable to foreign entities, a foreign entity may be a party to a merger under this [part] or may be the surviving entity in such a merger if the merger is authorized by the law of the foreign entity's jurisdiction of formation.

§ 1122. Plan of Merger

(a) A domestic partnership may become a party to a merger under this [part] by approving a plan of merger. The plan must be in a record and contain:

(1)   as to each merging entity, its name, jurisdiction of formation, and type of entity;

(2)   if the surviving entity is to be created in the merger, a statement to that effect and the entity's name, jurisdiction of formation, and type of entity;

(3)   the manner of converting the interests in each party to the merger into interests, securities, obligations, money, other property, rights to acquire interests or securities, or any combination of the foregoing;

(4)   if the surviving entity exists before the merger, any proposed amendments to:

    (A)   its public organic record, if any; or

    (B)   its private organic rules that are, or are proposed to be, in a record;

(5)   if the surviving entity is to be created in the merger:

    (A)   its proposed public organic record, if any; and

    (B)   the full text of its private organic rules that are proposed to be in a record;

(6)   the other terms and conditions of the merger; and

(7)   any other provision required by the law of a merging entity's jurisdiction of formation or the organic rules of a merging entity.

(b)   In addition to the requirements of subsection (a), a plan of merger may contain any other provision not prohibited by law.

§ 1123.   Approval of Merger

(a)   A plan of merger is not effective unless it has been approved:

(1)   by a domestic merging partnership, by all the partners of the partnership entitled to vote on or consent to any matter; and

(2)   in a record, by each partner of a domestic merging partnership which will have interest holder liability for debts, obligations, and other liabilities that are incurred after the merger becomes effective, unless:

    (A)   the partnership agreement of the partnership provides in a record for the approval of a merger in which some or all of its partners become subject to interest holder liability by the affirmative vote or consent of fewer than all the partners; and

    (B)   the partner consented in a record to or voted for that provision of the partnership agreement or became a partner after the adoption of that provision.

(b)   A merger involving a domestic merging entity that is not a partnership is not effective unless the merger is approved by that entity in accordance with its organic law.

(c)   A merger involving a foreign merging entity is not effective unless the merger is approved by the foreign entity in accordance with the law of the foreign entity's jurisdiction of formation.

§ 1124.   Amendment or Abandonment of Plan of Merger

(a)   A plan of merger may be amended only with the consent of each party to the plan, except as otherwise provided in the plan.

(b)   A domestic merging partnership may approve an amendment of a plan of merger:

(1)   in the same manner as the plan was approved, if the plan does not provide for the manner in which it may be amended; or

(2)   by its partners in the manner provided in the plan, but a partner that was entitled to vote on or consent to approval of the merger is entitled to vote on or consent to any amendment of the plan that will change:

(A)   the amount or kind of interests, securities, obligations, money, other property, rights to acquire interests or securities, or any combination of the foregoing, to be received by the interest holders of any party to the plan;

(B)   the public organic record, if any, or private organic rules of the surviving entity that will be in effect immediately after the merger be effective, except for changes that do not require approval of the interest holders of the surviving entity under its organic law or organic rules; or

(C)   any other terms or conditions of the plan, if the change would adversely affect the partner in any material respect.

(c)   After a plan of merger has been approved and before a statement of merger becomes effective, the plan may be abandoned as provided in the plan. Unless prohibited by the plan, a domestic merging partnership may abandon the plan in the same manner as the plan was approved.

(d)   If a plan of merger is abandoned after a statement of merger has been delivered to the [Secretary of State] for filing and before the statement becomes effective, a statement of abandonment, signed by a party to the plan, must be delivered to the [Secretary of State] for filing before the statement of merger becomes effective. The statement of abandonment takes effect on filing, and the merger is abandoned and does not become effective. The statement of abandonment must contain:

(1)   the name of each party to the plan of merger;

(2)   the date on which the statement of merger was filed by the [Secretary of State]; and

(3)   a statement that the merger has been abandoned in accordance with this section.

§ 1125.   Statement of Merger; Effective Date of Merger

(a)   A statement of merger must be signed by each merging entity and delivered to the [Secretary of State] for filing.

(b)   A statement of merger must contain:

(1)   the name, jurisdiction of formation, and type of entity of each merging entity that is not the surviving entity;

(2)   the name, jurisdiction of formation, and type of entity of the surviving entity;

(3)   a statement that the merger was approved by each domestic merging entity, if any, in accordance with this [part] and by each foreign merging entity, if any, in accordance with the law of its jurisdiction of formation;

(4)   if the surviving entity exists before the merger and is a domestic filing entity, any amendment to its public organic record approved as part of the plan of merger;

(5)   if the surviving entity is created by the merger and is a domestic filing entity, its public organic record, as an attachment; and

(6)   if the surviving entity is created by the merger and is a domestic limited liability partnership, its statement of qualification, as an attachment.

(c)   In addition to the requirements of subsection (b), a statement of merger may contain any other provision not prohibited by law.

(d)   If the surviving entity is a domestic entity, its public organic record, if any, must satisfy the requirements of the law of this state, except that the public organic record does not need to be signed.

(e)   A plan of merger that is signed by all the merging entities and meets all the requirements of subsection (b) may be delivered to the [Secretary of State] for filing instead of a statement of merger and on filing has the same effect. If a plan of merger is filed as provided in this subsection, references in this [article] to a statement of merger refer to the plan of merger filed under this subsection.

(f)   If the surviving entity is a domestic partnership, the merger becomes effective when the statement of merger is effective. In all other cases, the merger becomes effective on the later of:

     (1)   the date and time provided by the organic law of the surviving entity; and

     (2)   when the statement is effective.

§ 1126.   Effect of Merger

(a)   When a merger becomes effective:

     (1)   the surviving entity continues or comes into existence;

     (2)   each merging entity that is not the surviving entity ceases to exist;

     (3)   all property of each merging entity vests in the surviving entity without transfer, reversion, or impairment;

     (4)   all debts, obligations, and other liabilities of each merging entity are debts, obligations, and other liabilities of the surviving entity;

     (5)   except as otherwise provided by law or the plan of merger, all the rights, privileges, immunities, powers, and purposes of each merging entity vest in the surviving entity;

     (6)   if the surviving entity exists before the merger:

         (A)   all its property continues to be vested in it without transfer, reversion, or impairment;

         (B)   it remains subject to all its debts, obligations, and other liabilities; and

         (C)   all its rights, privileges, immunities, powers, and purposes continue to be vested in it;

     (7)   the name of the surviving entity may be substituted for the name of any merging entity that is a party to any pending action or proceeding;

     (8)   if the surviving entity exists before the merger:

         (A)   its public organic record, if any, is amended as provided in the statement of merger; and

         (B)   its private organic rules that are to be in a record, if any, are amended to the extent provided in the plan of merger;

     (9)   if the surviving entity is created by the merger, its private organic rules become effective and:

         (A)   if it is a filing entity, its public organic record becomes effective; and

         (B)   if it is a limited liability partnership, its statement of qualification becomes effective; and

     (10) the interests in each merging entity which are to be converted in the merger are converted, and the interest holders of those interests are entitled only to the rights provided to them under the plan of merger and to any appraisal rights they have under Section 1106 and the merging entity's organic law.

(b)   Except as otherwise provided in the organic law or organic rules of a merging entity, the merger does not give rise to any rights that an interest holder, governor, or third party would have upon a dissolution, liquidation, or winding up of the merging entity.

(c)   When a merger becomes effective, a person that did not have interest holder liability with respect to any of the merging entities and becomes subject to interest holder liability with respect to a domestic entity as a result of the merger has interest holder liability only to the extent provided by the organic law of that entity and only for those debts, obligations, and other liabilities that are incurred after the merger becomes effective.

(d)   When a merger becomes effective, the interest holder liability of a person that ceases to hold an interest in a domestic merging partnership with respect to which the person had interest holder liability is subject to the following rules:

(1)   The merger does not discharge any interest holder liability under this [act] to the extent the interest holder liability was incurred before the merger became effective.

(2)   The person does not have interest holder liability under this [act] for any debt, obligation, or other liability that is incurred after the merger becomes effective.

(3)   This [act] continues to apply to the release, collection, or discharge of any interest holder liability preserved under paragraph (1) as if the merger had not occurred and the surviving entity were the domestic merging entity.

(4)   The person has whatever rights of contribution from any other person as are provided by this [act], law other than this [act], or the partnership agreement of the domestic merging partnership with respect to any interest holder liability preserved under paragraph (1) as if the merger had not occurred.

(e)   When a merger has become effective, a foreign entity that is the surviving entity may be served with process in this state for the collection and enforcement of any debts, obligations, or other liabilities of a domestic merging partnership as provided in Section 119.

(f)   When a merger has become effective, the registration to do business in this state of any foreign merging entity that is not the surviving entity is canceled.

[PART] 3.   INTEREST EXCHANGE

§ 1131.   Interest Exchange Authorized

(a)   By complying with this [part]:

(1)   a domestic partnership may acquire all of one or more classes or series of interests of another domestic entity or a foreign entity in exchange for interests, securities, obligations, money, other property, rights to acquire interests or securities, or any combination of the foregoing; or

(2)   all of one or more classes or series of interests of a domestic partnership may be acquired by another domestic entity or a foreign entity in exchange for interests, securities, obligations, money, other property, rights to acquire interests or securities, or any combination of the foregoing.

(b)   By complying with the provisions of this [part] applicable to foreign entities, a foreign entity may be the acquiring or acquired entity in an interest exchange under this [part] if the interest exchange is authorized by the law of the foreign entity's jurisdiction of formation.

(c)   If a protected agreement contains a provision that applies to a merger of a domestic partnership but does not refer to an interest exchange, the provision applies to an interest exchange in which the domestic partnership is the acquired entity as if the interest exchange were a merger until the provision is amended after [the effective date of this [act]].

§ 1132. Plan of Interest Exchange

(a) A domestic partnership may be the acquired entity in an interest exchange under this [part] by approving a plan of interest exchange. The plan must be in a record and contain:

(1)   the name of the acquired entity;

(2)   the name, jurisdiction of formation, and type of entity of the acquiring entity;

(3)   the manner of converting the interests in the acquired entity into interests, securities, obligations, money, other property, rights to acquire interests or securities, or any combination of the foregoing;

(4)   any proposed amendments to the partnership agreement that are, or are proposed to be, in a record of the acquired entity;

(5)   the other terms and conditions of the interest exchange; and

(6)   any other provision required by the law of this state or the partnership agreement of the acquired entity.

(b)   In addition to the requirements of subsection (a), a plan of interest exchange may contain any other provision not prohibited by law.

§ 1133. Approval of Interest Exchange

(a)   A plan of interest exchange is not effective unless it has been approved:

(1)   by all the partners of a domestic acquired partnership entitled to vote on or consent to any matter; and

(2)   in a record, by each partner of the domestic acquired partnership that will have interest holder liability for debts, obligations, and other liabilities that are incurred after the interest exchange becomes effective, unless:

(A)   the partnership agreement of the partnership provides in a record for the approval of an interest exchange or a merger in which some or all its partners become subject to interest holder liability by the affirmative vote or consent of fewer than all the partners; and

(B)   the partner consented in a record to or voted for that provision of the partnership agreement or became a partner after the adoption of that provision.

(b)   An interest exchange involving a domestic acquired entity that is not a partnership is not effective unless it is approved by the domestic entity in accordance with its organic law.

(c)   An interest exchange involving a foreign acquired entity is not effective unless it is approved by the foreign entity in accordance with the law of the foreign entity's jurisdiction of formation.

(d)   Except as otherwise provided in its organic law or organic rules, the interest holders of the acquiring entity are not required to approve the interest exchange.

§ 1134. Amendment or Abandonment of Plan of Interest Exchange

(a)   A plan of interest exchange may be amended only with the consent of each party to the plan, except as otherwise provided in the plan.

(b)   A domestic acquired partnership may approve an amendment of a plan of interest exchange:

(1)   in the same manner as the plan was approved, if the plan does not provide for the manner in which it may be amended; or

(2)   by its partners in the manner provided in the plan, but a partner that was entitled to vote on or consent to approval of the interest exchange is entitled to vote on or consent to any amendment of the plan that will change:

(A)   the amount or kind of interests, securities, obligations, money, other property, rights to acquire interests or securities, or any combination of the foregoing, to be received by any of the partners of the acquired partnership under the plan;

(B)   the partnership agreement of the acquired partnership that will be in effect immediately after the interest exchange becomes effective, except for changes that do not require approval of the partners of the acquired partnership under this [act] or the partnership agreement; or

(C)   any other terms or conditions of the plan, if the change would adversely affect the partner in any material respect.

(c)   After a plan of interest exchange has been approved and before a statement of interest exchange becomes effective, the plan may be abandoned as provided in the plan. Unless prohibited by the plan, a domestic acquired partnership may abandon the plan in the same manner as the plan was approved.

(d)   If a plan of interest exchange is abandoned after a statement of interest exchange has been delivered to the [Secretary of State] for filing and before the statement becomes effective, a statement of abandonment, signed by the acquired partnership, must be delivered to the [Secretary of State] for filing before the statement of interest exchange becomes effective. The statement of abandonment takes effect on filing, and the interest exchange is abandoned and does not become effective. The statement of abandonment must contain:

(1)   the name of the acquired partnership;

(2)   the date on which the statement of interest exchange was filed by the [Secretary of State]; and

(3)   a statement that the interest exchange has been abandoned in accordance with this section.

§ 1135.   Statement of Interest Exchange; Effective Date of Interest Exchange

(a)   A statement of interest exchange must be signed by a domestic acquired partnership and delivered to the [Secretary of State] for filing.

(b)   A statement of interest exchange must contain:

(1)   the name of the acquired partnership;

(2)   the name, jurisdiction of formation, and type of entity of the acquiring entity; and

(3)   a statement that the plan of interest exchange was approved by the acquired partnership in accordance with this [part].

(c)   In addition to the requirements of subsection (b), a statement of interest exchange may contain any other provision not prohibited by law.

(d)   A plan of interest exchange that is signed by a domestic acquired partnership and meets all the requirements of subsection (b) may be delivered to the [Secretary of State] for filing instead of a statement of interest exchange and on filing has the same effect. If a plan of interest exchange is filed as provided in this subsection, references in this [article] to a statement of interest exchange refer to the plan of interest exchange filed under this subsection.

(e)   An interest exchange becomes effective when the statement of interest exchange is effective.

§ 1136.   Effect of Interest Exchange

(a)   When an interest exchange in which the acquired entity is a domestic partnership becomes effective:

(1)   the interests in the acquired partnership which are the subject of the interest exchange are converted, and the partners holding those interests are entitled only to the rights provided to them under the plan of interest exchange and to any appraisal rights they have under Section 1106;

(2)   the acquiring entity becomes the interest holder of the interests in the acquired partnership stated in the plan of interest exchange to be acquired by the acquiring entity; and

(3)   the provisions of the partnership agreement of the acquired partnership that are to be in a record, if any, are amended to the extent provided in the plan of interest exchange.

(b)   Except as otherwise provided in the partnership agreement of a domestic acquired partnership, the interest exchange does not give rise to any rights that a partner or third party would have upon a dissolution, liquidation, or winding up of the acquired partnership.

(c)   When an interest exchange becomes effective, a person that did not have interest holder liability with respect to a domestic acquired partnership and becomes subject to interest holder liability with respect to a domestic entity as a result of the interest exchange has interest holder liability only to the extent provided by the organic law of the entity and only for those debts, obligations, and other liabilities that are incurred after the interest exchange becomes effective.

(d)   When an interest exchange becomes effective, the interest holder liability of a person that ceases to hold an interest in a domestic acquired partnership with respect to which the person had interest holder liability is subject to the following rules:

(1)   The interest exchange does not discharge any interest holder liability under this [act] to the extent the interest holder liability was incurred before the interest exchange became effective.

(2)   The person does not have interest holder liability under this [act] for any debt, obligation, or other liability that is incurred after the interest exchange becomes effective.

(3)   This [act] continues to apply to the release, collection, or discharge of any interest holder liability preserved under paragraph (1) as if the interest exchange had not occurred.

(4)   The person has whatever rights of contribution from any other person as are provided by this [act], law other than this [act], or the partnership agreement of the domestic acquired partnership with respect to any interest holder liability preserved under paragraph (1) as if the interest exchange had not occurred.

[PART] 4.   CONVERSION

§ 1141.   Conversion Authorized

(a)   By complying with this [part], a domestic partnership may become:

(1)   a domestic entity that is a different type of entity; or

(2)   a foreign entity that is a different type of entity, if the conversion is authorized by the law of the foreign entity's jurisdiction of formation.

(b)   By complying with the provisions of this [part] applicable to foreign entities, a foreign entity that is not a foreign partnership may become a domestic partnership if the conversion is authorized by the law of the foreign entity's jurisdiction of formation.

(c)   If a protected agreement contains a provision that applies to a merger of a domestic partnership but does not refer to a conversion, the provision applies to a conversion of the partnership as if the conversion were a merger until the provision is amended after [the effective date of this [act]].

§ 1142. Plan of Conversion

(a) A domestic partnership may convert to a different type of entity under this [part] by approving a plan of conversion. The plan must be in a record and contain:

(1) the name of the converting partnership;

(2) the name, jurisdiction of formation, and type of entity of the converted entity;

(3) the manner of converting the interests in the converting partnership into interests, securities, obligations, money, other property, rights to acquire interests or securities, or any combination of the foregoing;

(4) the proposed public organic record of the converted entity if it will be a filing entity;

(5) the full text of the private organic rules of the converted entity which are proposed to be in a record;

(6) the other terms and conditions of the conversion; and

(7) any other provision required by the law of this state or the partnership agreement of the converting partnership.

(b) In addition to the requirements of subsection (a), a plan of conversion may contain any other provision not prohibited by law.

§ 1143. Approval of Conversion

(a) A plan of conversion is not effective unless it has been approved:

(1) by a domestic converting partnership, by all the partners of the partnership entitled to vote on or consent to any matter; and

(2) in a record, by each partner of a domestic converting partnership which will have interest holder liability for debts, obligations, and other liabilities that are incurred after the conversion becomes effective, unless:

(A) the partnership agreement of the partnership provides in a record for the approval of a conversion or a merger in which some or all of its partners become subject to interest holder liability by the affirmative vote or consent of fewer than all the partners; and

(B) the partner voted for or consented in a record to that provision of the partnership agreement or became a partner after the adoption of that provision.

(b) A conversion involving a domestic converting entity that is not a partnership is not effective unless it is approved by the domestic converting entity in accordance with its organic law.

(c) A conversion of a foreign converting entity is not effective unless it is approved by the foreign entity in accordance with the law of the foreign entity's jurisdiction of formation.

§ 1144. Amendment or Abandonment of Plan of Conversion

(a) A plan of conversion of a domestic converting partnership may be amended:

(1) in the same manner as the plan was approved, if the plan does not provide for the manner in which it may be amended; or

(2) by its partners in the manner provided in the plan, but a partner that was entitled to vote on or consent to approval of the conversion is entitled to vote on or consent to any amendment of the plan that will change:

(A) the amount or kind of interests, securities, obligations, money, other property, rights to acquire interests or securities, or any combination of the foregoing, to be received by any of the partners of the converting partnership under the plan;

　　　　(B)　the public organic record, if any, or private organic rules of the converted entity which will be in effect immediately after the conversion becomes effective, except for changes that do not require approval of the interest holders of the converted entity under its organic law or organic rules; or

　　　　(C)　any other terms or conditions of the plan, if the change would adversely affect the partner in any material respect.

　　(b)　After a plan of conversion has been approved by a domestic converting partnership and before a statement of conversion becomes effective, the plan may be abandoned as provided in the plan. Unless prohibited by the plan, a domestic converting partnership may abandon the plan in the same manner as the plan was approved.

　　(c)　If a plan of conversion is abandoned after a statement of conversion has been delivered to the [Secretary of State] for filing and before the statement becomes effective, a statement of abandonment, signed by the converting entity, must be delivered to the [Secretary of State] for filing before the statement of conversion becomes effective. The statement of abandonment takes effect on filing, and the conversion is abandoned and does not become effective. The statement of abandonment must contain:

　　　　(1)　the name of the converting partnership;

　　　　(2)　the date on which the statement of conversion was filed by the [Secretary of State]; and

　　　　(3)　a statement that the conversion has been abandoned in accordance with this section.

§ 1145.　Statement of Conversion; Effective Date of Conversion

　　(a)　A statement of conversion must be signed by the converting entity and delivered to the [Secretary of State] for filing.

　　(b)　A statement of conversion must contain:

　　　　(1)　the name, jurisdiction of formation, and type of entity of the converting entity;

　　　　(2)　the name, jurisdiction of formation, and type of entity of the converted entity;

　　　　(3)　if the converting entity is a domestic partnership, a statement that the plan of conversion was approved in accordance with this [part] or, if the converting entity is a foreign entity, a statement that the conversion was approved by the foreign entity in accordance with the law of its jurisdiction of formation;

　　　　(4)　if the converted entity is a domestic filing entity, its public organic record, as an attachment; and

　　　　(5)　if the converted entity is a domestic limited liability partnership, its statement of qualification, as an attachment.

　　(c)　In addition to the requirements of subsection (b), a statement of conversion may contain any other provision not prohibited by law.

　　(d)　If the converted entity is a domestic entity, its public organic record, if any, must satisfy the requirements of the law of this state, except that the public organic record does not need to be signed.

　　(e)　A plan of conversion that is signed by a domestic converting partnership and meets all the requirements of subsection (b) may be delivered to the [Secretary of State] for filing instead of a statement of conversion and on filing has the same effect. If a plan of conversion is filed as provided in this subsection, references in this [article] to a statement of conversion refer to the plan of conversion filed under this subsection.

　　(f)　If the converted entity is a domestic partnership, the conversion becomes effective when the statement of conversion is effective. In all other cases, the conversion becomes effective on the later of:

(1)   the date and time provided by the organic law of the converted entity; and

(2)   when the statement is effective.

§ 1146.   Effect of Conversion

(a)   When a conversion becomes effective:

(1)   the converted entity is:

(A)   organized under and subject to the organic law of the converted entity; and

(B)   the same entity without interruption as the converting entity;

(2)   all property of the converting entity continues to be vested in the converted entity without transfer, reversion, or impairment;

(3)   all debts, obligations, and other liabilities of the converting entity continue as debts, obligations, and other liabilities of the converted entity;

(4)   except as otherwise provided by law or the plan of conversion, all the rights, privileges, immunities, powers, and purposes of the converting entity remain in the converted entity;

(5)   the name of the converted entity may be substituted for the name of the converting entity in any pending action or proceeding;

(6)   if the converted entity is a limited liability partnership, its statement of qualification becomes effective;

(7)   the provisions of the partnership agreement of the converted entity which are to be in a record, if any, approved as part of the plan of conversion become effective; and

(8)   the interests in the converting entity are converted, and the interest holders of the converting entity are entitled only to the rights provided to them under the plan of conversion and to any appraisal rights they have under Section 1106.

(b)   Except as otherwise provided in the partnership agreement of a domestic converting partnership, the conversion does not give rise to any rights that a partner or third party would have upon a dissolution, liquidation, or winding up of the converting entity.

(c)   When a conversion becomes effective, a person that did not have interest holder liability with respect to the converting entity and becomes subject to interest holder liability with respect to a domestic entity as a result of the conversion has interest holder liability only to the extent provided by the organic law of the entity and only for those debts, obligations, and other liabilities that are incurred after the conversion becomes effective.

(d)   When a conversion becomes effective, the interest holder liability of a person that ceases to hold an interest in a domestic converting partnership with respect to which the person had interest holder liability is subject to the following rules:

(1)   The conversion does not discharge any interest holder liability under this [act] to the extent the interest holder liability was incurred before the conversion became effective.

(2)   The person does not have interest holder liability under this [act] for any debt, obligation, or other liability that is incurred after the conversion becomes effective.

(3)   This [act] continues to apply to the release, collection, or discharge of any interest holder liability preserved under paragraph (1) as if the conversion had not occurred.

(4)   The person has whatever rights of contribution from any other person as are provided by this [act], law other than this [act], or the organic rules of the converting entity with respect to any interest holder liability preserved under paragraph (1) as if the conversion had not occurred.

(e)   When a conversion has become effective, a foreign entity that is the converted entity may be served with process in this state for the collection and enforcement of any of its debts, obligations, and other liabilities as provided in Section 119.

(f)   If the converting entity is a registered foreign entity, its registration to do business in this state is canceled when the conversion becomes effective.

(g)   A conversion does not require the entity to wind up its affairs and does not constitute or cause the dissolution of the entity.

[PART] 5.   DOMESTICATION

§ 1151.   Domestication Authorized

(a)   By complying with this [part], a domestic limited liability partnership may become a foreign limited liability partnership if the domestication is authorized by the law of the foreign jurisdiction.

(b)   By complying with the provisions of this [part] applicable to foreign limited liability partnerships, a foreign limited liability partnership may become a domestic limited liability partnership if the domestication is authorized by the law of the foreign limited liability partnership's jurisdiction of formation.

(c)   If a protected agreement contains a provision that applies to a merger of a domestic limited liability partnership but does not refer to a domestication, the provision applies to a domestication of the limited liability partnership as if the domestication were a merger until the provision is amended after [the effective date of this [act]].

§ 1152.   Plan of Domestication

(a)   A domestic limited liability partnership may become a foreign limited liability partnership in a domestication by approving a plan of domestication. The plan must be in a record and contain:

(1)   the name of the domesticating limited liability partnership;

(2)   the name and jurisdiction of formation of the domesticated limited liability partnership;

(3)   the manner of converting the interests in the domesticating limited liability partnership into interests, securities, obligations, money, other property, rights to acquire interests or securities, or any combination of the foregoing;

(4)   the proposed statement of qualification of the domesticated limited liability partnership;

(5)   the full text of the provisions of the partnership agreement of the domesticated limited liability partnership that are proposed to be in a record;

(6)   the other terms and conditions of the domestication; and

(7)   any other provision required by the law of this state or the partnership agreement of the domesticating limited liability partnership.

(b)   In addition to the requirements of subsection (a), a plan of domestication may contain any other provision not prohibited by law.

§ 1153.   Approval of Domestication

(a)   A plan of domestication of a domestic domesticating limited liability partnership is not effective unless it has been approved:

(1)   by all the partners entitled to vote on or consent to any matter; and

(2)   in a record, by each partner that will have interest holder liability for debts, obligations, and other liabilities that are incurred after the domestication becomes effective, unless:

    (A) the partnership agreement of the domesticating partnership in a record provides for the approval of a domestication or merger in which some or all of its partners become subject to interest holder liability by the affirmative vote or consent of fewer than all the partners; and

    (B) the partner voted for or consented in a record to that provision of the partnership agreement or became a partner after the adoption of that provision.

(b) A domestication of a foreign domesticating limited liability partnership is not effective unless it is approved in accordance with the law of the foreign limited liability partnership's jurisdiction of formation.

§ 1154. Amendment or Abandonment of Plan of Domestication

(a) A plan of domestication of a domestic domesticating limited liability partnership may be amended:

    (1) in the same manner as the plan was approved, if the plan does not provide for the manner in which it may be amended; or

    (2) by its partners in the manner provided in the plan, but a partner that was entitled to vote on or consent to approval of the domestication is entitled to vote on or consent to any amendment of the plan that will change:

        (A) the amount or kind of interests, securities, obligations, money, other property, rights to acquire interests or securities, or any combination of the foregoing, to be received by any of the partners of the domesticating limited liability partnership under the plan;

        (B) the partnership agreement of the domesticated limited liability partnership that will be in effect immediately after the domestication becomes effective, except for changes that do not require approval of the partners of the domesticated limited liability partnership under its organic law or partnership agreement; or

        (C) any other terms or conditions of the plan, if the change would adversely affect the partner in any material respect.

(b) After a plan of domestication has been approved by a domestic domesticating limited liability partnership and before a statement of domestication becomes effective, the plan may be abandoned as provided in the plan. Unless prohibited by the plan, a domestic domesticating limited liability partnership may abandon the plan in the same manner as the plan was approved.

(c) If a plan of domestication is abandoned after a statement of domestication has been delivered to the [Secretary of State] for filing and before the statement becomes effective, a statement of abandonment, signed by the domesticating limited liability partnership, must be delivered to the [Secretary of State] for filing before the statement of domestication becomes effective. The statement of abandonment takes effect on filing, and the domestication is abandoned and does not become effective. The statement of abandonment must contain:

    (1) the name of the domesticating limited liability partnership;

    (2) the date on which the statement of domestication was filed by the [Secretary of State]; and

    (3) a statement that the domestication has been abandoned in accordance with this section.

§ 1155. Statement of Domestication; Effective Date of Domestication

(a) A statement of domestication must be signed by the domesticating limited liability partnership and delivered to the [Secretary of State] for filing.

(b) A statement of domestication must contain:

(1) the name and jurisdiction of formation of the domesticating limited liability partnership;

(2) the name and jurisdiction of formation of the domesticated limited liability partnership;

(3) if the domesticating limited liability partnership is a domestic limited liability partnership, a statement that the plan of domestication was approved in accordance with this [part] or, if the domesticating limited liability partnership is a foreign limited liability partnership, a statement that the domestication was approved in accordance with the law of its jurisdiction of formation; and

(4) the statement of qualification of the domesticated limited liability partnership, as an attachment.

(c) In addition to the requirements of subsection (b), a statement of domestication may contain any other provision not prohibited by law.

(d) The statement of qualification of a domesticated domestic limited liability partnership must satisfy the requirements of this [act], but the statement does not need to be signed.

(e) A plan of domestication that is signed by a domesticating domestic limited liability partnership and meets all the requirements of subsection (b) may be delivered to the [Secretary of State] for filing instead of a statement of domestication and on filing has the same effect. If a plan of domestication is filed as provided in this subsection, references in this [article] to a statement of domestication refer to the plan of domestication filed under this subsection.

(f) If the domesticated entity is a domestic partnership, the domestication becomes effective when the statement of domestication is effective. If the domesticated entity is a foreign partnership, the domestication becomes effective on the later of:

(1) the date and time provided in the organic law of the domesticated entity; and

(2) when the statement is effective.

§ 1156. Effect of Domestication

(a) When a domestication becomes effective:

(1) the domesticated entity is:

(A) organized under and subject to the organic law of the domesticated entity; and

(B) the same entity without interruption as the domesticating entity;

(2) all property of the domesticating entity continues to be vested in the domesticated entity without transfer, reversion, or impairment;

(3) all debts, obligations, and other liabilities of the domesticating entity continue as debts, obligations, and other liabilities of the domesticated entity;

(4) except as otherwise provided by law or the plan of domestication, all the rights, privileges, immunities, powers, and purposes of the domesticating entity remain in the domesticated entity;

(5) the name of the domesticated entity may be substituted for the name of the domesticating entity in any pending action or proceeding;

(6) the statement of qualification of the domesticated entity becomes effective;

(7) the provisions of the partnership agreement of the domesticated entity that are to be in a record, if any, approved as part of the plan of domestication become effective; and

(8) the interests in the domesticating entity are converted to the extent and as approved in connection with the domestication, and the partners of the domesticating entity are entitled

only to the rights provided to them under the plan of domestication and to any appraisal rights they have under Section 1106.

(b)   Except as otherwise provided in the organic law or partnership agreement of the domesticating limited liability partnership, the domestication does not give rise to any rights that a partner or third party would otherwise have upon a dissolution, liquidation, or winding up of the domesticating partnership.

(c)   When a domestication becomes effective, a person that did not have interest holder liability with respect to the domesticating limited liability partnership and becomes subject to interest holder liability with respect to a domestic limited liability partnership as a result of the domestication has interest holder liability only to the extent provided by this [act] and only for those debts, obligations, and other liabilities that are incurred after the domestication becomes effective.

(d)   When a domestication becomes effective, the interest holder liability of a person that ceases to hold an interest in a domestic domesticating limited liability partnership with respect to which the person had interest holder liability is subject to the following rules:

(1)   The domestication does not discharge any interest holder liability under this [act] to the extent the interest holder liability was incurred before the domestication became effective.

(2)   A person does not have interest holder liability under this [act] for any debt, obligation, or other liability that is incurred after the domestication becomes effective.

(3)   This [act] continues to apply to the release, collection, or discharge of any interest holder liability preserved under paragraph (1) as if the domestication had not occurred.

(4)   A person has whatever rights of contribution from any other person as are provided by this [act], law other than this [act], or the partnership agreement of the domestic domesticating limited liability partnership with respect to any interest holder liability preserved under paragraph (1) as if the domestication had not occurred.

(e)   When a domestication becomes effective, a foreign limited liability partnership that is the domesticated partnership may be served with process in this state for the collection and enforcement of any of its debts, obligations, and other liabilities as provided in Section 119.

(f)   If the domesticating limited liability partnership is a registered foreign entity, the registration of the partnership is canceled when the domestication becomes effective.

(g)   A domestication does not require a domestic domesticating limited liability partnership to wind up its business and does not constitute or cause the dissolution of the partnership.

[ARTICLE] 12.   MISCELLANEOUS PROVISIONS

§ 1201.   Uniformity of Application and Construction

In applying and construing this uniform act, consideration must be given to the need to promote uniformity of the law with respect to its subject matter among states that enact it.

§ 1202.   Relation to Electronic Signatures in Global and National Commerce Act

This [act] modifies, limits, and supersedes the Electronic Signatures in Global and National Commerce Act, 15 U.S.C. Section 7001 et seq., but does not modify, limit, or supersede Section 101(c) of that act, 15 U.S.C. Section 7001(c), or authorize electronic delivery of any of the notices described in Section 103(b) of that act, 15 U.S.C. Section 7003(b).

§ 1203.   Savings Clause

This [act] does not affect an action commenced, proceeding brought, or right accrued before [the effective date of this [act]].

§ 1204.   Severability Clause

If any provision of this [act] or its application to any person or circumstance is held invalid, the invalidity does not affect other provisions or applications of this [act] which can be given effect without the invalid provision or application, and to this end the provisions of this [act] are severable.]

Legislative Note: Include this section only if this state lacks a general severability statute or decision by the highest court of this state stating a general rule of severability.

§ 1205.   Repeals

The following are repealed:

(1)   [the state partnership act as [amended, and as] in effect immediately before [the effective date of this [act]]].

(2)   . . . .

(3)   . . . .

§ 1206.   Effective Date

This [act] takes effect. . . .

D. REVISED UNIFORM LIMITED PARTNERSHIP ACT (1976) WITH 1985 AMENDMENTS

(The 1985 Amendments are Indicated by Underscore and Strikeout)*

Table of Sections

---

* For a "clean" version of the 1985 RULPA, see the following statute at II(E).

ARTICLE 1
GENERAL PROVISIONS

§ 101.   Definitions

As used in this [Act], unless the context otherwise requires:

(1) "Certificate of limited partnership" means the certificate referred to in Section 201, and the certificate as amended or restated.

(2) "Contribution" means any cash, property, services rendered, or a promissory note or other binding obligation to contribute cash or property or to perform services, which a partner contributes to a limited partnership in his capacity as a partner.

(3) "Event of withdrawal of a general partner" means an event that causes a person to cease to be a general partner as provided in Section 402.

(4) "Foreign limited partnership" means a partnership formed under the laws of any ~~State~~ state other than this State and having as partners one or more general partners and one or more limited partners.

(5) "General partner" means a person who has been admitted to a limited partnership as a general partner in accordance with the partnership agreement and named in the certificate of limited partnership as a general partner.

(6) "Limited partner" means a person who has been admitted to a limited partnership as a limited partner in accordance with the partnership agreement ~~and named in the certificate of limited partnership as a limited partner~~.

(7) "Limited partnership" and "domestic limited partnership" mean a partnership formed by two or more persons under the laws of this State and having one or more general partners and one or more limited partners.

(8) "Partner" means a limited or general partner.

(9) "Partnership agreement" means any valid agreement, written or oral, of the partners as to the affairs of a limited partnership and the conduct of its business.

(10) "Partnership interest" means a partner's share of the profits and losses of a limited partnership and the right to receive distributions of partnership assets.

(11) "Person" means a natural person, partnership, limited partnership (domestic or foreign), trust, estate, association, or corporation.

(12) "State" means a state, territory, or possession of the United States, the District of Columbia, or the Commonwealth of Puerto Rico.

COMMENT

The definitions in this section clarify a number of uncertainties in the law existing ~~law~~ prior to the 1976 Act, and also make certain changes in such prior law. The 1985 Act makes very few additional changes in Section 101.

Contribution: this definition makes it clear that a present contribution of services and a promise to make a future payment of cash, contribution of property or performance of services are permissible forms for a contribution. ~~Accordingly, the present~~ Section 502 of the 1985 Act provides that a limited partner's promise to make a contribution is enforceable only when set out in a writing signed by the limited partner. (This result is not dissimilar from that under the 1976 Act, which required all promises of future contributions to be described in the certificate of limited partnership, which was to be signed by, among others, the partners making such promises.) The property or services contributed presently or ~~promise~~ promised to be contributed in the future must be accorded a value in the ~~certificate of limited partnership (Section 201(5))~~ partnership agreement or the partnership records required to be kept pursuant to Section

105, and, in the case of a promise, that value may determine the liability of a partner who fails to honor his agreement (Section 502). Section 3 of the ~~prior uniform law~~ 1916 Act did not permit a limited partner's contribution to be in the form of services, although that inhibition did not apply to general partners.

Foreign limited partnership: the Act only deals with foreign limited partnerships formed under the laws of another ~~"State"~~ "state" of the United States (*see* subdivision 12 of Section 101), and any adopting ~~State~~ state that desires to deal by statute with the status of entities formed under the laws of foreign countries must make appropriate changes throughout the Act. The exclusion of such entities from the Act was not intended to suggest that their "limited partners" should not be accorded limited liability by the courts of a ~~State~~ state adopting the Act. That question would be resolved by the choice-of-law rules of the forum ~~State~~ state.

General partner: this definition recognizes the separate functions of the partnership agreement and the certificate of limited partnership. The partnership agreement establishes the basic grant of management power to the persons named as general partners; but because of the passive role played by the limited partners, the separate, formal step of ~~embodying~~ memorializing that grant of power in the certificate of limited partnership has been preserved to emphasize its importance and to provide notice of the identity of the partnership's general partners to persons dealing with the partnership.

Limited partner: ~~as in~~ unlike the ~~case of~~ definition of general partners, this definition provides for admission of limited partners through the partnership agreement ~~and solemnization in the certificate of limited partnership. In addition, the definition makes it clear that being named in the certificate of limited partnership is a prerequisite to limited partner status. Failure to file does not, however, mean that the participant is a general partner or that he has general liability. See Sections 202(c) and 303~~ alone and does not require identification of any limited partner in the certificate of limited partnership (Section 201). Under the 1916 and the 1976 Acts, being named as a limited partner in the certificate of limited partnership was a statutory requirement and, in most if not all cases, probably also a prerequisite to limited partner status. By eliminating the requirement that the certificate of limited partnership contain the name, address, and capital contribution of each limited partner, the 1985 Act all but eliminates any risk that a person intended to be a limited partner may be exposed to liability as a general partner as a result of the inadvertent omission of any of that information from the certificate of limited partnership, and also dispenses with the need to amend the certificate of limited partnership upon the admission or withdrawal of, transfer of an interest by, or change in the address or capital contribution of, any limited partner.

Partnership agreement: the ~~prior uniform law~~ 1916 Act did not refer to the partnership agreement, assuming that all important matters affecting limited partners would be set forth in the certificate of limited partnership. Under modern practice, however, it has been common for the partners to enter into a comprehensive partnership agreement, only part of which was required to be included or summarized in the certificate of limited partnership. As reflected in Section 201 of the 1985 Act, the certificate of limited partnership is confined principally to matters respecting the partnership itself and the ~~addition and withdrawal~~ identity of general partners ~~and of capital~~, and other important issues are left to the partnership agreement. Most of the information formerly provided by, but no longer required to be included in, the certificate of limited partnership is now required to be kept in the partnership records (Section 105).

Partnership interest: this definition ~~is new~~ first appeared in the 1976 Act and is intended to define what it is that is transferred when a partnership interest is assigned.

§ 102.   Name

The name of each limited partnership as set forth in its certificate of limited partnership:

(1)   shall contain without abbreviation the words "limited partnership";

(2)   may not contain the name of a limited partner unless (i) it is also the name of a general partner or the corporate name of a corporate general partner, or (ii) the business of the limited partnership had been carried on under that name before the admission of that limited partner;

~~(3) may not contain any word or phrase indicating or implying that it is organized other than for a purpose stated in its certificate of limited partnership;~~

(4) (3)   may not be the same as, or deceptively similar to, the name of any corporation or limited partnership organized under the laws of this State or licensed or registered as a foreign corporation or limited partnership in this State; and

(5) (4)   may not contain the following words [here insert prohibited words].

COMMENT

Subdivision (2) of Section 102 has been carried over from Section 5 of the prior uniform law 1916 Act with certain editorial changes. The remainder of Section 102 is new first appeared in the 1976 Act and primarily reflects the intention to integrate the registration of limited partnership names with that of corporate names. Accordingly, Section 201 provides for central, State-wide state-wide filing of certificates of limited partnership, and subdivisions (3), and (4) and (5) of Section 102 contain standards to be applied by the filing officer in determining whether the certificate should be filed. Subdivision (1) requires that the proper name of a limited partnership contain the words "limited partnership" in full. Subdivision (3) of the 1976 Act has been deleted, to reflect the deletion from Section 201 of any requirement that the certificate of limited partnership describe the partnership's purposes or the character of its business.

§ 103.   Reservation of Name

(a)   The exclusive right to the use of a name may be reserved by:

(1)   any person intending to organize a limited partnership under this [Act] and to adopt that name;

(2)   any domestic limited partnership or any foreign limited partnership registered in this State which, in either case, intends to adopt that name;

(3)   any foreign limited partnership intending to register in this State and adopt that name; and

(4)   any person intending to organize a foreign limited partnership and intending to have it register in this State and adopt that name.

(b)   The reservation shall be made by filing with the Secretary of State an application, executed by the applicant, to reserve a specified name. If the Secretary of State finds that the name is available for use by a domestic or foreign limited partnership, he [or she] shall reserve the name for the exclusive use of the applicant for a period of 120 days. Once having so reserved a name, the same applicant may not again reserve the same name until more than 60 days after the expiration of the last 120-day period for which that applicant reserved that name. The right to the exclusive use of a reserved name may be transferred to any other person by filing in the office of the Secretary of State a notice of the transfer, executed by the applicant for whom the name was reserved and specifying the name and address of the transferee.

COMMENT

Section 103 is new first appeared in the 1976 Act. The prior uniform law 1916 Act did not provide for registration of names.

§ 104.   Specified Office and Agent

Each limited partnership shall continuously maintain in this State:

(1)   an office, which may but need not be a place of its business in this State, at which shall be kept the records required by Section 105 to be maintained; and

(2)   an agent for service of process on the limited partnership, which agent must be an individual resident of this State, a domestic corporation, or a foreign corporation authorized to do business in this State.

COMMENT

Section 104 ~~is new~~ first appeared in the 1976 Act. It requires that a limited partnership have certain minimum contacts with its State of organization, i.e., an office at which the constitutive documents and basic financial information is kept and an agent for service of process.

§ 105.   Records to be Kept

(a)   Each limited partnership shall keep at the office referred to in Section 104(1) the following:

(1)   a current list of the full name and last known business address of each partner ~~set forth,~~ separately identifying the general partners (in alphabetical order) and the limited partners (in alphabetical order~~,~~);

(2)   a copy of the certificate of limited partnership and all certificates of amendment thereto, together with executed copies of any powers of attorney pursuant to which any certificate has been executed~~,~~;

(3)   copies of the limited partnership's federal, state and local income tax returns and reports, if any, for the three most recent years~~, and~~;

(4)   copies of any then effective written partnership agreements and of any financial statements of the limited partnership for the three most recent years; and

(5)   unless contained in a written partnership agreement, a writing setting out:

(i)   the amount of cash and a description and statement of the agreed value of the other property or services contributed by each partner and which each partner has agreed to contribute;

(ii)   the times at which or events on the happening of which any additional contributions agreed to be made by each partner are to be made;

(iii)   any right of a partner to receive, or of a general partner to make, distributions to a partner which include a return of all or any part of the partner's contribution; and

(iv)   any events upon the happening of which the limited partnership is to be dissolved and its affairs wound up.

(b)   ~~Those records~~ Records kept under this section are subject to inspection and copying at the reasonable request and at the expense of any partner during ordinary business hours.

COMMENT

Section 105 ~~is new~~ first appeared in the 1976 Act. In view of the passive nature of the limited partner's position, it has been widely felt that limited partners are entitled to access to certain basic documents and information, including the certificate of limited partnership ~~and,~~ any partnership agreement, and a writing setting out certain important matters which, under the 1916 and 1976 Acts, were required to be set out in the certificate of limited partnership. In view of the great diversity among limited partnerships, it was thought inappropriate to require a standard form of financial report, and Section 105 does no more than require retention of tax returns and any other financial statements that are prepared. The names and addresses of the general partners are made available to the general public in the certificate of limited partnership.

§ 106.   Nature of Business

A limited partnership may carry on any business that a partnership without limited partners may carry on except [here designate prohibited activities].

COMMENT

Section 106 is identical to Section 3 of the ~~prior uniform law~~ 1916 Act. Many states require that certain regulated industries, such as banking, may be carried on only by entities organized pursuant to special statutes, and it is contemplated that the prohibited activities would be confined to the matters covered by those statutes.

§ 107.   Business Transactions of Partner with Partnership

Except as provided in the partnership agreement, a partner may lend money to and transact other business with the limited partnership and, subject to other applicable law, has the same rights and obligations with respect thereto as a person who is not a partner.

COMMENT

Section 107 makes a number of important changes in Section 13 of the ~~prior uniform law~~ 1916 Act. Section 13, in effect, created a special fraudulent conveyance provision applicable to the making of secured loans by limited partners and the repayment by limited partnerships of loans from limited partners. Section 107 leaves that question to a ~~State's~~ state's general fraudulent conveyance statute. In addition, Section 107 eliminates the prohibition in ~~former~~ Section 13 against a general ~~partner (as opposed to a limited partner)~~ partner's sharing pro rata with general creditors in the case of an unsecured loan. Of course, other doctrines developed under bankruptcy and insolvency laws may require the subordination of loans by partners under appropriate circumstances.

ARTICLE 2
FORMATION; CERTIFICATE OF LIMITED PARTNERSHIP

§ 201.   Certificate of Limited Partnership

(a)   In order to form a limited partnership, ~~two or more persons must execute~~ a certificate of limited partnership. ~~The certificate shall be~~ must be executed and filed in the office of the Secretary of State. ~~and~~ The certificate shall set forth:

(1)   the name of the limited partnership;

~~(2)   the general character of its business;~~

~~(3)~~ (2)   the address of the office and the name and address of the agent for service of process required to be maintained by Section 104;

~~(4)~~ (3)   the name and the business address of each general partner ~~(specifying separately the general partners and limited partners)~~;

~~(5)   the amount of cash and a description and statement of the agreed value of the other property or services contributed by each partner and which each partner has agreed to contribute in the future;~~

~~(6)   the times at which or events on the happening of which any additional contributions agreed to be made by each partner are to be made;~~

~~(7)   any power of a limited partner to grant the right to become a limited partner to an assignee of any part of his partnership interest, and the terms and conditions of the power;~~

~~(8)   if agreed upon, the time at which or the events on the happening of which a partner may terminate his membership in the limited partnership and the amount of, or the method of determining, the distribution to which he may be entitled respecting his partnership interest, and the terms and conditions of the termination and distribution;~~

~~(9)   any right of a partner to receive distributions of property, including cash from the limited partnership;~~

~~(10) any right of a partner to receive, or of a general partner to make, distributions to a partner which include a return of all or any part of the partner's contribution;~~

~~(11) any time at which or events upon the happening of which the limited partnership is to be dissolved and its affairs wound up;~~

~~(12) any right of the remaining general partners to continue the business on the happening of an event of withdrawal of a general partner; and~~

(4)   the latest date upon which the limited partnership is to dissolve; and

~~(13)~~ (5)   any other matters the general partners determine to include therein.

(b)   A limited partnership is formed at the time of the filing of the certificate of limited partnership in the office of the Secretary of State or at any later time specified in the certificate of limited partnership if, in either case, there has been substantial compliance with the requirements of this section.

COMMENT

The 1985 Act requires far fewer matters ~~required~~ to be set forth in the certificate of limited partnership ~~are not different in kind from those required by~~ than did Section 2 of the ~~prior uniform law, although certain additions and deletions have been made and the description has been revised to conform with the rest of the Act. In general, the certificate is intended to serve two functions: first, to place creditors on notice of the~~ 1916 Act and Section 201 of the 1976 Act. This is in recognition of the fact that the partnership agreement, not the certificate of limited partnership, has become the authoritative and comprehensive document for most limited partnerships, and that creditors and potential creditors of the partnership do and should refer to the partnership agreement and to other information furnished to them directly by the partnership and by others, not to the certificate of limited partnership, to obtain facts concerning the capital and finances of the partnership and ~~the rules regarding additional contributions to and withdrawals from the partnership; second, to clearly delineate the time at which persons become general partners and limited partners~~ other matters of concern. Subparagraph (b), which is based upon the ~~prior uniform law~~ 1916 Act, has been retained to make it clear that the existence of the limited partnership depends only upon compliance with this section. Its continued existence is not dependent upon compliance with other provisions of this Act.

§ 202.   Amendment to Certificate

(a)   A certificate of limited partnership is amended by filing a certificate of amendment thereto in the office of the Secretary of State. The certificate shall set forth:

(1)   the name of the limited partnership;

(2)   the date of filing the certificate; and

(3)   the amendment to the certificate.

(b)   Within 30 days after the happening of any of the following events, an amendment to a certificate of limited partnership reflecting the occurrence of the event or events shall be filed:

~~(1) a change in the amount or character of the contribution of any partner, or in any partner's obligation to make a contribution;~~

~~(2)~~ (1)   the admission of a new general partner;

~~(3)~~ (2)   the withdrawal of a general partner; or

~~(4)~~ (3)   the continuation of the business under Section 801 after an event of withdrawal of a general partner.

(c)   A general partner who becomes aware that any statement in a certificate of limited partnership was false when made or that any arrangements or other facts described have changed, making the certificate inaccurate in any respect, shall promptly amend the certificate, ~~but an amendment to show a change of address of a limited partner need be filed only once every 12 months.~~

266

(d)   A certificate of limited partnership may be amended at any time for any other proper purpose the general partners determine.

(e)   No person has any liability because an amendment to a certificate of limited partnership has not been filed to reflect the occurrence of any event referred to in subsection (b) of this ~~Section~~ section if the amendment is filed within the 30-day period specified in subsection (b).

(f)   A restated certificate of limited partnership may be executed and filed in the same manner as a certificate of amendment.

COMMENT

Section 202 ~~makes~~ of the 1976 Act made substantial changes in Section 24 of the ~~prior uniform law~~ 1916 Act. Further changes in this section are made by the 1985 Act. Paragraph (b) lists the basic events—the addition or withdrawal of ~~partners or capital or capital obligations~~ a general partner—that are so central to the function of the certificate of limited partnership that they require prompt amendment. With the elimination of the requirement that the certificate of limited partnership include the names of all limited partners and the amount and character of all capital contributions, the requirement of the 1916 and 1976 Acts that the certificate be amended upon the admission or withdrawal of limited partners or on any change in the partnership capital must also be eliminated. This change should greatly reduce the frequency and complexity of amendments to the certificate of limited partnership. Paragraph (c) makes it clear, as it was not clear under ~~subdivision (2)(g) of former~~ Section ~~24~~ 24(2)(g) of the 1916 Act, that the certificate of limited partnership is intended to be an accurate description of the facts to which it relates at all times and does not speak merely as of the date it is executed.

Paragraph (e) provides a "safe harbor" against claims of creditors or others who assert that they have been misled by the failure to amend the certificate of limited partnership to reflect changes in any of the important facts referred to in paragraph (b); if the certificate of limited partnership is amended within 30 days of the occurrence of the event, no creditor or other person can recover for damages sustained during the interim. Additional protection is afforded by the provisions of Section 304. The elimination of the requirement that the certificate of limited partnership identify all limited partners and their respective capital contributions may have rendered paragraph (e) an obsolete and unnecessary vestige. The principal, if not the sole, purpose of paragraph (e) in the 1976 Act was to protect limited partners newly admitted to a partnership from being held liable as general partners when an amendment to the certificate identifying them as limited partners and describing their contributions was not filed contemporaneously with their admission to the partnership. Such liability cannot arise under the 1985 Act because such information is not required to be stated in the certificate. Nevertheless, the 1985 Act retains paragraph (e) because it is protective of partners, shielding them from liability to the extent its provisions apply, and does not create or impose any liability.

Paragraph (f) is added in the 1985 Act to provide explicit statutory recognition of the common practice of restating an amended certificate of limited partnership. While a limited partnership seeking to amend its certificate of limited partnership may do so by recording a restated certificate which incorporates the amendment, that is by no means the only purpose or function of a restated certificate, which may be filed for the sole purpose of restating in a single integrated instrument all the provisions of a limited partnership's certificate of limited partnership which are then in effect.

§ 203.   Cancellation of Certificate

A certificate of limited partnership shall be cancelled upon the dissolution and the commencement of winding up of the partnership or at any other time there are no limited partners. A certificate of cancellation shall be filed in the office of the Secretary of State and set forth:

(1)   the name of the limited partnership;

(2)   the date of filing of its certificate of limited partnership;

(3)   the reason for filing the certificate of cancellation;

(4)   the effective date (which shall be a date certain) of cancellation if it is not to be effective upon the filing of the certificate; and

(5)   any other information the general partners filing the certificate determine.

COMMENT

Section 203 changes Section 24 of the ~~prior uniform law~~ 1916 Act by making it clear that the certificate of cancellation should be filed upon the commencement of winding up of the limited partnership. Section 24 provided for cancellation "when the partnership is dissolved."

§ 204.   Execution of Certificates

(a)   Each certificate required by this Article to be filed in the office of the Secretary of State shall be executed in the following manner:

(1)   an original certificate of limited partnership must be signed by all <u>general</u> partners ~~named therein~~;

(2)   a certificate of amendment must be signed by at least one general partner and by each other <u>general</u> partner designated in the certificate as a new <u>general</u> partner ~~or whose contribution is described as having been increased~~; and

(3)   a certificate of cancellation must be signed by all general partners~~;~~.

(b)   Any person may sign a certificate by an attorney-in-fact, but a power of attorney to sign a certificate relating to the admission, ~~or increased contribution,~~ of a <u>general</u> partner must specifically describe the admission ~~or increase~~.

(c)   The execution of a certificate by a general partner constitutes an affirmation under the penalties of perjury that the facts stated therein are true.

COMMENT

Section 204 collects in one place the formal requirements for the execution of certificates which were set forth in Sections 2 and 25 of the ~~prior uniform law~~ 1916 Act. Those sections required that each certificate be signed by all partners, and there developed an unnecessarily cumbersome practice of having each limited partner sign powers of attorney to authorize the general partners to execute certificates of amendment on their behalf. ~~Section 204 insures that each partner must sign a certificate when he becomes a partner or when the certificates reflect any increase in his obligation to make contributions.~~ <u>The 1976 Act, while simplifying the execution requirements, nevertheless required that an original certificate of limited partnership be signed by all partners and a certificate of amendment by all new partners being admitted to the limited partnership. However, the certificate of limited partnership is no longer required to include the name or capital contribution of any limited partner. Therefore, while the 1985 Act still requires all general partners to sign the original certificate of limited partnership, no limited partner is required to sign any certificate.</u> Certificates of amendment are required to be signed by only one general partner and all general partners must sign certificates of cancellation. ~~Section 204 prohibits blanket powers of attorney for the execution of certificates in many cases, since those conditions under which a partner is required to sign have been narrowed to circumstances of special importance to that partner.~~ The ~~former~~ requirement <u>in the 1916 Act</u> that all certificates be sworn ~~has been confined to statements by the general partners, recognizing that the limited partner's role is a limited one~~ <u>was deleted in the 1976 and 1985 Acts</u> as potentially an unfair trap for the unwary (*see, e.g.,* Wisniewski v. Johnson, 223 Va. 141, 286 S.E.2d 223 (1982)); <u>in its place, paragraph (c) now provides, as a matter of law, that the execution of a certificate by a general partner subjects him to the penalties of perjury for inaccuracies in the certificate.</u>

§ 205.   ~~Amendment or Cancellation~~ <u>Execution</u> by Judicial Act

If a person required by Section 204 to execute ~~a~~ <u>any</u> certificate ~~of amendment or cancellation~~ fails or refuses to do so, any other ~~partner, and any assignee of a partnership interest,~~ <u>person</u> who is adversely affected by the failure or refusal~~,~~ may petition the [designate the appropriate court] to direct the ~~amendment or cancellation~~ <u>execution of the certificate</u>. If the court finds that ~~the amendment or cancellation is proper~~ <u>it is proper for the certificate to be executed</u> and that any person so designated has failed or refused to execute the certificate, it shall order the Secretary of State to record an appropriate certificate ~~of amendment or cancellation~~.

COMMENT

Section 205 ~~changes~~ <u>of the 1976 Act changed</u> subdivisions (3) and (4) of Section 25 of the ~~prior uniform law~~ <u>1916 Act</u> by confining the persons who have standing to seek judicial intervention to partners and to those assignees who ~~are~~ <u>were</u> adversely affected by the failure or refusal of the appropriate persons to file a certificate of amendment or cancellation. <u>Section 205 of the 1985 Act reverses that restriction, and provides that any person adversely affected by a failure or refusal to file any certificate (not only a certificate of cancellation or amendment) has standing to seek judicial intervention.</u>

§ 206. Filing in Office of Secretary of State

(a) Two signed copies of the certificate of limited partnership and of any certificates of amendment or cancellation (or of any judicial decree of amendment or cancellation) shall be delivered to the Secretary of State. A person who executes a certificate as an agent or fiduciary need not exhibit evidence of his [or her] authority as a prerequisite to filing. Unless the Secretary of State finds that any certificate does not conform to law, upon receipt of all filing fees required by law he [or she] shall:

(1) endorse on each duplicate original the word "Filed" and the day, month and year of the filing thereof;

(2) file one duplicate original in his [or her] office; and

(3) return the other duplicate original to the person who filed it or his [or her] representative.

(b) Upon the filing of a certificate of amendment (or judicial decree of amendment) in the office of the Secretary of State, the certificate of limited partnership shall be amended as set forth therein, and upon the effective date of a certificate of cancellation (or a judicial decree thereof), the certificate of limited partnership is cancelled.

COMMENT

Section 206 ~~is new~~ <u>first appeared in the 1976 Act</u>. In addition to providing mechanics for the central filing system, the second sentence of this section does away with the requirement, formerly imposed by some local filing officers, that persons who have executed certificates under a power of attorney exhibit executed copies of the power of attorney itself. Paragraph (b) changes subdivision (5) of Section 25 of the ~~prior uniform law~~ <u>1916 Act</u> by providing that certificates of cancellation are effective upon their effective date under Section 203.

§ 207. Liability for False Statement in Certificate

If any certificate of limited partnership or certificate of amendment or cancellation contains a false statement, one who suffers loss by reliance on the statement may recover damages for the loss from:

(1) any person who executes the certificate, or causes another to execute it on his behalf, and knew, and any general partner who knew or should have known, the statement to be false at the time the certificate was executed; and

(2) any general partner who thereafter knows or should have known that any arrangement or other fact described in the certificate has changed, making the statement inaccurate in any respect within a sufficient time before the statement was relied upon reasonably to have enabled that general partner to cancel or amend the certificate, or to file a petition for its cancellation or amendment under Section 205.

COMMENT

Section 207 changes Section 6 of the ~~prior uniform law~~ 1916 Act by providing explicitly for the liability of persons who sign a certificate as agent under a power of attorney and by confining the obligation to amend a certificate of limited partnership in light of future events to general partners.

§ 208.   Scope of Notice

The fact that a certificate of limited partnership is on file in the office of the Secretary of State is notice that the partnership is a limited partnership and the persons designated therein as ~~limited~~ general partners are ~~limited~~ general partners, but it is not notice of any other fact.

COMMENT

Section 208 ~~is new~~ first appeared in the 1976 Act, and referred to the certificate's providing constructive notice of the status as limited partners of those so identified therein. The 1985 Act's deletion of any requirement that the certificate name limited partners required that Section 208 be modified accordingly.

By stating that the filing of a certificate of limited partnership only results in notice of the ~~limited~~ general liability of the ~~limited~~ general partners, ~~it~~ Section 208 obviates the concern that third parties may be held to have notice of special provisions set forth in the certificate. While this section is designed to preserve by implication the limited liability of limited partners, the ~~notice~~ implicit protection provided is not intended to change any liability of a limited partner which may be created by his action or inaction under the law of estoppel, agency, fraud, or the like.

§ 209.   Delivery of Certificates to Limited Partners

Upon the return by the Secretary of State pursuant to Section 206 of a certificate marked "Filed", the general partners shall promptly deliver or mail a copy of the certificate of limited partnership and each certificate of amendment or cancellation to each limited partner unless the partnership agreement provides otherwise.

COMMENT

This section ~~is new~~ first appeared in the 1976 Act.

ARTICLE 3
LIMITED PARTNERS

§ 301.   Admission of ~~Additional~~ Limited Partners

(a)   A person becomes a limited partner:

(1)   at the time the limited partnership is formed; or

(2)   at any later time specified in the records of the limited partnership for becoming a limited partner.

~~(a)~~ (b)   After the filing of a limited partnership's original certificate of limited partnership, a person may be admitted as an additional limited partner:

(1)   in the case of a person acquiring a partnership interest directly from the limited partnership, upon compliance with the partnership agreement or, if the partnership agreement does not so provide, upon the written consent of all partners; and

(2)   in the case of an assignee of a partnership interest of a partner who has the power, as provided in Section 704, to grant the assignee the right to become a limited partner, upon the exercise of that power and compliance with any conditions limiting the grant or exercise of the power.

(b) In each case under subsection (a), the person acquiring the partnership interest becomes a limited partner only upon amendment of the certificate of limited partnership reflecting that fact.

COMMENT

Section 301(a) is new; no counterpart was found in the 1916 or 1976 Acts. This section imposes on the partnership an obligation to maintain in its records the date each limited partner becomes a limited partner. Under the 1976 Act, one could not become a limited partner until an appropriate certificate reflecting his status as such was filed with the Secretary of State. Because the 1985 Act eliminates the need to name limited partners in the certificate of limited partnership, an alternative mechanism had to be established to evidence the fact and date of a limited partner's admission. The partnership records required to be maintained under Section 105 now serve that function, subject to the limitation that no person may become a limited partner before the partnership is formed (Section 201(b)).

Subdivision (1) of Section 301(a) 301(b) adds to Section 8 of the prior uniform law 1916 Act an explicit recognition of the fact that unanimous consent of all partners is required for admission of new limited partners unless the partnership agreement provides otherwise. Subdivision (2) is derived from Section 19 of the prior uniform law 1916 Act but abandons the former terminology of "substituted limited partner."

§ 302. Voting

Subject to Section 303, the partnership agreement may grant to all or a specified group of the limited partners the right to vote (on a per capita or other basis) upon any matter.

COMMENT

Section 302 is new first appeared in the 1976 Act, and must be read together with subdivision (b)(5) (b)(6) of Section 303. Although the prior uniform law 1916 Act did not speak specifically of the voting powers of limited partners, it is was not uncommon for partnership agreements to grant such power powers to limited partners. Section 302 is designed only to make it clear that the partnership agreement may grant such power to limited partners. If such powers are granted to limited partners beyond the "safe harbor" of subdivision (6) or (8) of Section 303(b)(5) 303(b), a court may (but of course need not) hold that, under the circumstances, the limited partners have participated in "control of the business" within the meaning of Section 303(a). Section 303(c) simply means makes clear that the exercise of powers beyond the ambit of Section 303(b) is not ipso facto to be taken as taking part in the control of the business.

§ 303. Liability to Third Parties

(a) Except as provided in subsection (d), a limited partner is not liable for the obligations of a limited partnership unless he [or she] is also a general partner or, in addition to the exercise of his [or her] rights and powers as a limited partner, he [or she] takes part participates in the control of the business. However, if the limited partner's participation partner participates in the control of the business is not substantially the same as the exercise of the powers of a general partner, he [or she] is liable only to persons who transact business with the limited partnership with actual knowledge of his participation in control reasonably believing, based upon the limited partner's conduct, that the limited partner is a general partner.

(b) A limited partner does not participate in the control of the business within the meaning of subsection (a) solely by doing one or more of the following:

(1) being a contractor for or an agent or employee of the limited partnership or of a general partner or being an officer, director, or shareholder of a general partner that is a corporation;

(2) consulting with and advising a general partner with respect to the business of the limited partnership;

(3) acting as surety for the limited partnership or guaranteeing or assuming one or more specific obligations of the limited partnership;

(4) ~~approving or disapproving an amendment to the partnership agreement~~ taking any action required or permitted by law to bring or pursue a derivative action in the right of the limited partnership; ~~or~~

~~(5) voting on one or more of the following matters:~~

(5) requesting or attending a meeting of partners;

(6) proposing, approving, or disapproving, by voting or otherwise, one or more of the following matters:

(i) the dissolution and winding up of the limited partnership;

(ii) the sale, exchange, lease, mortgage, pledge, or other transfer of all or substantially all of the assets of the limited partnership ~~other than in the ordinary course of its business~~;

(iii) the incurrence of indebtedness by the limited partnership other than in the ordinary course of its business;

(iv) a change in the nature of the business; ~~or~~

(v) the admission or removal of a general partner~~.~~;

(vi) the admission or removal of a limited partner;

(vii) a transaction involving an actual or potential conflict of interest between a general partner and the limited partnership or the limited partners;

(viii) an amendment to the partnership agreement or certificate of limited partnership; or

(ix) matters related to the business of the limited partnership not otherwise enumerated in this subsection (b), which the partnership agreement states in writing may be subject to the approval or disapproval of limited partners;

(7) winding up the limited partnership pursuant to Section 803; or

(8) exercising any right or power permitted to limited partners under this [Act] and not specifically enumerated in this subsection (b).

(c) The enumeration in subsection (b) does not mean that the possession or exercise of any other powers by a limited partner constitutes participation by him [or her] in the business of the limited partnership.

(d) A limited partner who knowingly permits his [or her] name to be used in the name of the limited partnership, except under circumstances permitted by Section 102(2), is liable to creditors who extend credit to the limited partnership without actual knowledge that the limited partner is not a general partner.

COMMENT

Section 303 makes several important changes in Section 7 of the ~~prior uniform law~~ 1916 Act. The first sentence of Section 303(a) ~~carries over the basic test from former Section 7—whether the limited partner "takes part in the control of the business"—in order to insure that judicial decisions under the prior uniform law remain applicable to the extent not expressly changed~~ differs from the text of Section 7 of the 1916 Act in that it speaks of participating (rather than taking part) in the control of the business; this was done for the sake of consistency with the second sentence of Section 303(a), not to change the meaning of the text. It is intended that judicial decisions interpreting the phrase "takes part in the control of the business" under the prior uniform law will remain applicable to the extent that a different result is not called for by other provisions of Section 303 and other provisions of the Act. The second sentence of Section 303(a) reflects a wholly new concept. ~~Because~~ in the 1976 Act that has been further modified in the 1985 Act. It was adopted partly because of the difficulty of determining when the "control" line has been overstepped, ~~it was thought it unfair to impose general partner's liability on a limited partner except to the extent that a third party~~

had knowledge of his participation in control of the business. On the other hand, in order to avoid permitting a limited partner to exercise all of the powers of a general partner while avoiding any direct dealings with third parties, the "is not substantially the same as" test was introduced but also (and more importantly) because of a determination that it is not sound public policy to hold a limited partner who is not also a general partner liable for the obligations of the partnership except to persons who have done business with the limited partnership reasonably believing, based on the limited partner's conduct, that he is a general partner. Paragraph (b) is intended to provide a "safe harbor" by enumerating certain activities which a limited partner may carry on for the partnership without being deemed to have taken part in control of the business. This "safe harbor" list has been expanded beyond that set out in the 1976 Act to reflect case law and statutory developments and more clearly to assure that limited partners are not subjected to general liability where such liability is inappropriate. Paragraph (d) is derived from Section 5 of the prior uniform law 1916 Act, but adds as a condition to the limited partner's liability the fact requirement that a limited partner must have knowingly permitted his name to be used in the name of the limited partnership.

§ 304. Person Erroneously Believing Himself [or Herself] Limited Partner

(a) Except as provided in subsection (b), a person who makes a contribution to a business enterprise and erroneously but in good faith believes that he [or she] has become a limited partner in the enterprise is not a general partner in the enterprise and is not bound by its obligations by reason of making the contribution, receiving distributions from the enterprise, or exercising any rights of a limited partner, if, on ascertaining the mistake, he [or she]:

(1) causes an appropriate certificate of limited partnership or a certificate of amendment to be executed and filed; or

(2) withdraws from future equity participation in the enterprise by executing and filing in the office of the Secretary of State a certificate declaring withdrawal under this section.

(b) A person who makes a contribution of the kind described in subsection (a) is liable as a general partner to any third party who transacts business with the enterprise (i) before the person withdraws and an appropriate certificate is filed to show withdrawal, or (ii) before an appropriate certificate is filed to show his status as a limited partner and, in the case of an amendment, after expiration of the 30-day period for filing an amendment relating to the person as a limited partner under Section 202 that he [or she] is not a general partner, but in either case only if the third party actually believed in good faith that the person was a general partner at the time of the transaction.

COMMENT

Section 304 is derived from Section 11 of the prior uniform law 1916 Act. The "good faith" requirement has been added in the first sentence of Section 304(a). The provisions of subdivision (2) of Section 304(a) are intended to clarify an ambiguity in the prior law by providing that a person who chooses to withdraw from the enterprise in order to protect himself from liability is not required to renounce any of his then current interest in the enterprise so long as he has no further participation as an equity participant. Paragraph (b) preserves the liability of the equity participant prior to withdrawal (and after the time for appropriate amendment in the case of a limited partnership) by such person from the limited partnership or amendment to the certificate demonstrating that such person is not a general partner to any third party who has transacted business with the person believing in good faith that he was a general partner.

Evidence strongly suggests that Section 11 of the 1916 Act and Section 304 of the 1976 Act were rarely used, and one might expect that Section 304 of the 1985 Act may never have to be used. Section 11 of the 1916 Act and Section 304 of the 1976 Act could have been used by a person who invested in a limited partnership believing he would be a limited partner but who was not identified as a limited partner in the certificate of limited partnership. However, because the 1985 Act does not require limited partners to be named in the certificate, the only situation to which Section 304 would now appear to be applicable is one in which a person intending to be a limited partner was erroneously identified as a general partner in the certificate.

§ 305.   Information

Each limited partner has the right to:

(1)   inspect and copy any of the partnership records required to be maintained by Section 105; and

(2)   obtain from the general partners from time to time upon reasonable demand (i) true and full information regarding the state of the business and financial condition of the limited partnership, (ii) promptly after becoming available, a copy of the limited partnership's federal, state and local income tax returns for each year, and (iii) other information regarding the affairs of the limited partnership as is just and reasonable.

COMMENT

Section 305 changes and restates the rights of limited partners to information about the partnership formerly provided by Section 10 of the ~~prior uniform law~~ 1916 Act. Its importance has increased as a result of the 1985 Act's substituting the records of the partnership for the certificate of limited partnership as the place where certain categories of information are to be kept.

Section 305, which should be read together with Section 105(b), provides a mechanism for limited partners to obtain information about the partnership useful to them in making decisions concerning the partnership and their investments in it. Its purpose is not to provide a mechanism for competitors of the partnership or others having interests or agendas adverse to the partnership's to subvert the partnership's business. It is assumed that courts will protect limited partnerships from abuses and attempts to misuse Section 305 for improper purposes.

ARTICLE 4
GENERAL PARTNERS

§ 401.   Admission of Additional General Partners

After the filing of a limited partnership's original certificate of limited partnership, additional general partners may be admitted ~~only~~ as provided in writing in the partnership agreement or, if the partnership agreement does not provide in writing for the admission of additional general partners, with the ~~specific~~ written consent of ~~each partner~~ all partners.

COMMENT

Section 401 is derived from, but represents a significant departure from, Section 9(1)(e) of the ~~prior law and carries over the unwaivable requirement that all limited partners must consent~~ 1916 Act and Section 401 of the 1976 Act, which required, as a condition to the admission of an additional general partner, that all limited partners consent and that such consent ~~must~~ specifically identify the general partner involved. Section 401 of the 1985 Act provides that the written partnership agreement determines the procedure for authorizing the admission of additional general partners, and that the written consent of all partners is required only when the partnership agreement fails to address the question.

§ 402.   Events of Withdrawal

Except as approved by the specific written consent of all partners at the time, a person ceases to be a general partner of a limited partnership upon the happening of any of the following events:

(1)   the general partner withdraws from the limited partnership as provided in Section 602;

(2)   the general partner ceases to be a member of the limited partnership as provided in Section 702;

(3)   the general partner is removed as a general partner in accordance with the partnership agreement;

(4) unless otherwise provided <u>in writing</u> in the ~~certificate of limited~~ partnership <u>agreement</u>, the general partner: (i) makes an assignment for the benefit of creditors; (ii) files a voluntary petition in bankruptcy; (iii) is adjudicated a bankrupt or insolvent; (iv) files a petition or answer seeking for himself [or herself] any reorganization, arrangement, composition, readjustment, liquidation, dissolution or similar relief under any statute, law, or regulation; (v) files an answer or other pleading admitting or failing to contest the material allegations of a petition filed against him [or her] in any proceeding of this nature; or (vi) seeks, consents to, or acquiesces in the appointment of a trustee, receiver, or liquidator of the general partner or of all or any substantial part of his [or her] properties;

(5) unless otherwise provided <u>in writing</u> in the ~~certificate of limited~~ partnership <u>agreement</u>, [120] days after the commencement of any proceeding against the general partner seeking reorganization, arrangement, composition, readjustment, liquidation, dissolution or similar relief under any statute, law, or regulation, the proceeding has not been dismissed, or if within [90] days after the appointment without his [or her] consent or acquiescence of a trustee, receiver, or liquidator of the general partner or of all or any substantial part of his [or her] properties, the appointment is not vacated or stayed or within [90] days after the expiration of any such stay, the appointment is not vacated;

(6) in the case of a general partner who is a natural person,

   (i)   his [or her] death; or

   (ii) the entry of an order by a court of competent jurisdiction adjudicating him [or her] incompetent to manage his [or her] person or his [or her] estate;

(7) in the case of a general partner who is acting as a general partner by virtue of being a trustee of a trust, the termination of the trust (but not merely the substitution of a new trustee);

(8) in the case of a general partner that is a separate partnership, the dissolution and commencement of winding up of the separate partnership;

(9) in the case of a general partner that is a corporation, the filing of a certificate of dissolution, or its equivalent, for the corporation or the revocation of its charter; or

(10) in the case of an estate, the distribution by the fiduciary of the estate's entire interest in the partnership.

COMMENT

Section 402 expands considerably the provisions of Section 20 of the ~~prior uniform law~~ <u>1916 Act</u> which provided for dissolution in the event of the retirement, death or insanity of a general partner. Subdivisions (1), (2) and (3) recognize that the general partner's agency relationship is terminable at will, although it may result in a breach of the partnership agreement giving rise to an action for damages. Subdivisions (4) and (5) reflect a judgment that, unless the limited partners agree otherwise, they ought to have the power to rid themselves of a general partner who is in such dire financial straits that he is the subject of proceedings under the National Bankruptcy ~~Act~~ <u>Code</u> or a similar provision of law. Subdivisions (6) through (10) simply elaborate on the notion of death in the case of a general partner who is not a natural person. ~~Of course, the addition of the words "and in the partnership statement" was not intended to suggest that liabilities to third parties could be affected by provisions in the partnership agreement.~~ <u>Subdivisions (4) and (5) differ from their counterparts in the 1976 Act, reflecting the policy underlying the 1985 revision of Section 201, that the partnership agreement, not the certificate of limited partnership, is the appropriate document for setting out most provisions relating to the respective powers, rights, and obligations of the partners inter se. Although the partnership agreement need not be written, the 1985 Act provides that, to protect the partners from fraud, these and certain other particularly significant provisions must be set out in a written partnership agreement to be effective for the purposes described in the Act.</u>

§ 403.   General Powers and Liabilities

(a)   Except as provided in this [Act] or in the partnership agreement, a general partner of a limited partnership has the rights and powers and is subject to the restrictions of a partner in a partnership without limited partners.

(b)   Except as provided in this [Act], a general partner of a limited partnership has the liabilities of a partner in a partnership without limited partners to persons other than the partnership and the other partners. Except as provided in this [Act] or in the partnership agreement, a general partner of a limited partnership has the liabilities of a partner in a partnership without limited partners to the partnership and to the other partners.

COMMENT

Section 403 is derived from Section 9(1) of the ~~prior uniform law~~ 1916 Act.

§ 404.   Contributions by General Partner

A general partner of a limited partnership may make contributions to the partnership and share in the profits and losses of, and in distributions from, the limited partnership as a general partner. A general partner also may make contributions to and share in profits, losses, and distributions as a limited partner. A person who is both a general partner and a limited partner has the rights and powers, and is subject to the restrictions and liabilities, of a general partner and, except as provided in the partnership agreement, also has the powers, and is subject to the restrictions, of a limited partner to the extent of his [or her] participation in the partnership as a limited partner.

COMMENT

Section 404 is derived from Section 12 of the ~~prior uniform law~~ 1916 Act and makes clear that the partnership agreement may provide that a general partner who is also a limited partner may exercise all of the powers of a limited partner.

§ 405.   Voting

The partnership agreement may grant to all or certain identified general partners the right to vote (on a per capita or any other basis), separately or with all or any class of the limited partners, on any matter.

COMMENT

Section 405 ~~is new~~ first appeared in the 1976 Act and is intended to make it clear that the Act does not require that the limited partners have any right to vote on matters as a separate class.

ARTICLE 5
FINANCE

§ 501.   Form of Contribution

The contribution of a partner may be in cash, property, or services rendered, or a promissory note or other obligation to contribute cash or property or to perform services.

COMMENT

As noted in the comment to Section 101, the explicit permission to make contributions of services expands Section 4 of the ~~prior uniform law~~ 1916 Act.

§ 502. Liability for Contribution

(a) A promise by a limited partner to contribute to the limited partnership is not enforceable unless set out in a writing signed by the limited partner.

(a) (b) Except as provided in the certificate of limited partnership agreement, a partner is obligated to the limited partnership to perform any enforceable promise to contribute cash or property or to perform services, even if he [or she] is unable to perform because of death, disability, or any other reason. If a partner does not make the required contribution of property or services, he [or she] is obligated at the option of the limited partnership to contribute cash equal to that portion of the value, as stated in the certificate of limited partnership records required to be kept pursuant to Section 105, of the stated contribution which has not been made.

(b) (c) Unless otherwise provided in the partnership agreement, the obligation of a partner to make a contribution or return money or other property paid or distributed in violation of this [Act] may be compromised only by consent of all partners. Notwithstanding the compromise, a creditor of a limited partnership who extends credit, or whose claim arises, otherwise acts in reliance on that obligation after the filing of the certificate of limited partnership or an amendment thereto partner signs a writing which, in either case, reflects the obligation, and before the amendment or cancellation thereof to reflect the compromise, may enforce the original obligation.

COMMENT

Section 502(a) is new; it has no counterpart in the 1916 or 1976 Act. Because, unlike the prior uniform acts, the 1985 Act does not require that promises to contribute cash, property, or services be described in the limited partnership certificate, to protect against fraud it requires instead that such important promises be in a signed writing.

Although Section 17(1) of the prior uniform law 1916 Act required a partner to fulfill his promise to make contributions, the addition of contributions in the form of a promise to render services means that a partner who is unable to perform those services because of death or disability as well as because of an intentional default is required to pay the cash value of the services unless the certificate of limited partnership partnership agreement provides otherwise.

Subdivision (b) (c) is derived from, but expands upon, Section 17(3) of the prior uniform law 1916 Act.

§ 503. Sharing of Profits and Losses

The profits and losses of a limited partnership shall be allocated among the partners, and among classes of partners, in the manner provided in writing in the partnership agreement. If the partnership agreement does not so provide in writing, profits and losses shall be allocated on the basis of the value, as stated in the certificate of limited partnership records required to be kept pursuant to Section 105, of the contributions made by each partner to the extent they have been received by the partnership and have not been returned.

COMMENT

Section 503 is new first appeared in the 1976 Act. The prior uniform law 1916 Act did not provide for the basis on which partners would share profits and losses in the absence of agreement. The 1985 Act differs from its counterpart in the 1976 Act by requiring that, to be effective, the partnership agreement provisions concerning allocation of profits and losses be in writing, and by its reference to records required to be kept pursuant to Section 105, the latter reflecting the 1985 changes in Section 201.

§ 504. Sharing of Distributions

Distributions of cash or other assets of a limited partnership shall be allocated among the partners and among classes of partners in the manner provided in writing in the partnership agreement. If the partnership agreement does not so provide in writing, distributions shall be made on the basis of the value, as stated in the certificate of limited partnership records required to be kept pursuant to Section 105, of the contributions made by each partner to the extent they have been received by the partnership and have not been returned.

COMMENT

Section 504 ~~is new~~ first appeared in the 1976 Act. The ~~prior uniform law~~ 1916 Act did not provide ~~for~~ the basis on which partners would share distributions in the absence of agreement. Section 504 also differs from its counterpart in the 1976 Act by requiring that, to be effective, the partnership agreement provisions concerning allocation of distributions be in writing, and in its reference to records required to be kept pursuant to Section 105, the latter reflecting the 1985 changes in Section 201. This section also recognizes that partners may choose to share in ~~distribution~~ distributions on a ~~different~~ basis ~~than~~ different from that on which they share in profits and losses.

ARTICLE 6
DISTRIBUTIONS AND WITHDRAWAL

§ 601.   Interim Distributions

Except as provided in this Article, a partner is entitled to receive distributions from a limited partnership before his [or her] withdrawal from the limited partnership and before the dissolution and winding up thereof~~:~~

~~(1)~~ to the extent and at the times or upon the happening of the events specified in the partnership agreement~~; and~~

~~(2) if any distribution constitutes a return of any part of his contribution under Section 608(c), to the extent and at the times or upon the happening of the events specified in the certificate of limited partnership.~~

COMMENT

Section 601 ~~is new~~ first appeared in the 1976 Act. The 1976 Act provisions have been modified to reflect the 1985 changes made in Section 201.

§ 602.   Withdrawal of General Partner

A general partner may withdraw from a limited partnership at any time by giving written notice to the other partners, but if the withdrawal violates the partnership agreement, the limited partnership may recover from the withdrawing general partner damages for breach of the partnership agreement and offset the damages against the amount otherwise distributable to him [or her].

COMMENT

Section 602 ~~is new~~ first appeared in the 1976 Act, but is generally derived from Section 38 of the Uniform Partnership Act.

§ 603.   Withdrawal of Limited Partner

A limited partner may withdraw from a limited partnership at the time or upon the happening of events specified ~~in the certificate of limited partnership and in accordance with~~ in writing in the partnership agreement. If the ~~certificate~~ agreement does not specify in writing the time or the events upon the happening of which a limited partner may withdraw or a definite time for the dissolution and winding up of the limited partnership, a limited partner may withdraw upon not less than six months' prior written notice to each general partner at his [or her] address on the books of the limited partnership at its office in this State.

COMMENT

Section 603 is derived from Section ~~16(e)~~ 16 of the ~~prior uniform law~~ 1916 Act. The 1976 Act provision has been modified to reflect the 1985 changes made in Section 201. This section additionally reflects the policy determination, also embodied in certain other sections of the 1985 Act, that to avoid fraud, agreements concerning certain matters of substantial importance to the partners will be enforceable only if in writing. If the partnership agreement does provide, in writing, whether a limited partner may withdraw and, if he may, when and on what terms and conditions, those provisions will control.

§ 604. Distribution Upon Withdrawal

Except as provided in this Article, upon withdrawal any withdrawing partner is entitled to receive any distribution to which he [or she] is entitled under the partnership agreement and, if not otherwise provided in the agreement, he [or she] is entitled to receive, within a reasonable time after withdrawal, the fair value of his [or her] interest in the limited partnership as of the date of withdrawal based upon his [or her] right to share in distributions from the limited partnership.

COMMENT

Section 604 ~~is new~~ first appeared in the 1976 Act. It fixes the distributive share of a withdrawing partner in the absence of an agreement among the partners.

§ 605. Distribution in Kind

Except as provided in writing in the ~~certificate of limited~~ partnership agreement, a partner, regardless of the nature of his [or her] contribution, has no right to demand and receive any distribution from a limited partnership in any form other than cash. Except as provided in writing in the partnership agreement, a partner may not be compelled to accept a distribution of any asset in kind from a limited partnership to the extent that the percentage of the asset distributed to him [or her] exceeds a percentage of that asset which is equal to the percentage in which he [or she] shares in distributions from the limited partnership.

COMMENT

The first sentence of Section 605 is derived from Section 16(3) of the ~~prior uniform law~~ 1916 Act; it also differs from its counterpart in the 1976 Act, reflecting the 1985 changes made in Section 201. The second sentence ~~is new~~ first appeared in the 1976 Act, and is intended to protect a limited partner (and the remaining partners) against a distribution in kind of more than his share of particular assets.

§ 606. Right to Distribution

At the time a partner becomes entitled to receive a distribution, he [or she] has the status of, and is entitled to all remedies available to, a creditor of the limited partnership with respect to the distribution.

COMMENT

Section 606 ~~is new~~ first appeared in the 1976 Act and is intended to make it clear that the right of a partner to receive a distribution, as between the partners, is not subject to the equity risks of the enterprise. On the other hand, since partners entitled to distributions have creditor status, there did not seem to be a need for the extraordinary remedy of Section 16(4)(a) of the ~~prior uniform law~~ 1916 Act, which granted a limited partner the right to seek dissolution of the partnership if he was unsuccessful in demanding the return of his contribution. It is more appropriate for the partner to simply sue as an ordinary creditor and obtain a judgment.

§ 607.   Limitations on Distribution

A partner may not receive a distribution from a limited partnership to the extent that, after giving effect to the distribution, all liabilities of the limited partnership, other than liabilities to partners on account of their partnership interests, exceed the fair value of the partnership assets.

COMMENT

Section 607 is derived from Section 16(1)(a) of the ~~prior uniform law~~ 1916 Act.

§ 608.   Liability Upon Return of Contribution

(a)   If a partner has received the return of any part of his [or her] contribution without violation of the partnership agreement or this [Act], he [or she] is liable to the limited partnership for a period of one year thereafter for the amount of the returned contribution, but only to the extent necessary to discharge the limited partnership's liabilities to creditors who extended credit to the limited partnership during the period the contribution was held by the partnership.

(b)   If a partner has received the return of any part of his [or her] contribution in violation of the partnership agreement or this [Act], he [or she] is liable to the limited partnership for a period of six years thereafter for the amount of the contribution wrongfully returned.

(c)   A partner receives a return of his [or her] contribution to the extent that a distribution to him [or her] reduces his [or her] share of the fair value of the net assets of the limited partnership below the value, as set forth in the ~~certificate of limited~~ partnership records required to be kept pursuant to Section 105, of his contribution which has not been distributed to him [or her].

COMMENT

Paragraph (a) is derived from Section 17(4) of the ~~prior uniform law~~ 1916 Act, but the one year statute of limitations has been added. Paragraph (b) is derived from Section 17(2)(b) of the ~~prior uniform law~~ 1916 Act but, again, a statute of limitations has been added.

Paragraph (c) ~~is new~~ first appeared in the 1976 Act. The provisions of former Section 17(2) that referred to the partner holding as "trustee" any money or specific property wrongfully returned to him have been eliminated. Paragraph (c) in the 1985 Act also differs from its counterpart in the 1976 Act to reflect the 1985 changes made in Sections 105 and 201.

ARTICLE 7
ASSIGNMENT OF PARTNERSHIP INTERESTS

§ 701.   Nature of Partnership Interest

A partnership interest is personal property.

COMMENT

This section is derived from Section 18 of the ~~prior uniform law~~ 1916 Act.

§ 702.   Assignment of Partnership Interest

Except as provided in the partnership agreement, a partnership interest is assignable in whole or in part. An assignment of a partnership interest does not dissolve a limited partnership or entitle the assignee to become or to exercise any rights of a partner. An assignment entitles the assignee to receive, to the extent assigned, only the distribution to which the assignor would be entitled. Except as provided in the partnership agreement, a partner ceases to be a partner upon assignment of all his [or her] partnership interest.

COMMENT

Section 19(1) of the ~~prior uniform law~~ 1916 Act provided simply that "a limited partner's interest is assignable," raising a question whether any limitations on the right of assignment were permitted. While the first sentence of Section 702 recognizes that the power to assign may be restricted in the partnership agreement, there was no intention to affect in any way the usual rules regarding restraints on alienation of personal property. The second and third sentences of Section 702 are derived from Section 19(3) of the ~~prior uniform law~~ 1916 Act. The last sentence ~~is new~~ first appeared in the 1976 Act.

§ 703.   Rights of Creditor

On application to a court of competent jurisdiction by any judgment creditor of a partner, the court may charge the partnership interest of the partner with payment of the unsatisfied amount of the judgment with interest. To the extent so charged, the judgment creditor has only the rights of an assignee of the partnership interest. This [Act] does not deprive any partner of the benefit of any exemption laws applicable to his [or her] partnership interest.

COMMENT

Section 703 is derived from Section 22 of the ~~prior uniform law~~ 1916 Act but has not carried over some provisions that were thought to be superfluous. For example, references in Section 22(1) to specific remedies have been omitted, as has a prohibition in Section 22(2) against discharge of the lien with partnership property. Ordinary rules governing the remedies available to a creditor and the fiduciary obligations of general partners will determine those matters.

§ 704.   Right of Assignee to Become Limited Partner

(a)   An assignee of a partnership interest, including an assignee of a general partner, may become a limited partner if and to the extent that ~~(1)~~ (i) the assignor gives the assignee that right in accordance with authority described in the ~~certificate of limited~~ partnership agreement, or ~~(2)~~ (ii) all other partners consent.

(b)   An assignee who has become a limited partner has, to the extent assigned, the rights and powers, and is subject to the restrictions and liabilities, of a limited partner under the partnership agreement and this [Act]. An assignee who becomes a limited partner also is liable for the obligations of his [or her] assignor to make and return contributions as provided in ~~Article~~ Articles 5 and 6. However, the assignee is not obligated for liabilities unknown to the assignee at the time he [or she] became a limited partner ~~and which could not be ascertained from the certificate of limited partnership~~.

(c)   If an assignee of a partnership interest becomes a limited partner, the assignor is not released from his [or her] liability to the limited partnership under Sections 207 and 502.

COMMENT

Section 704 is derived from Section 19 of the ~~prior uniform law~~ 1916 Act, but paragraph (b) defines more narrowly than Section 19 the obligations of the assignor that are automatically assumed by the assignee. Section 704 of the 1985 Act also differs from the 1976 Act to reflect the 1985 changes made in Section 201.

§ 705.   Power of Estate of Deceased or Incompetent Partner

If a partner who is an individual dies or a court of competent jurisdiction adjudges him [or her] to be incompetent to manage his [or her] person or his [or her] property, the partner's executor, administrator, guardian, conservator, or other legal representative may exercise all the partner's rights for the purpose of settling his [or her] estate or administering his [or her] property, including any power the partner had to give an assignee the right to become a limited partner. If a partner is a corporation, trust, or other entity and is dissolved or terminated, the powers of that partner may be exercised by its legal representative or successor.

COMMENT

Section 705 is derived from Section 21(1) of the ~~prior uniform law~~ 1916 Act. Former Section 21(2), making a deceased limited partner's estate liable for his liabilities as a limited partner was deleted as superfluous, with no intention of changing the liability of the estate.

ARTICLE 8
DISSOLUTION

§ 801. Nonjudicial Dissolution

A limited partnership is dissolved and its affairs shall be wound up upon the happening of the first to occur of the following:

(1)   at the time <u>specified in the certificate of limited partnership;</u>

(2)   ~~or~~ upon the happening of events specified <u>in writing</u> in the ~~certificate of limited~~ partnership <u>agreement;</u>

~~(2)~~ <u>(3)</u>   written consent of all partners;

~~(3)~~ <u>(4)</u>   an event of withdrawal of a general partner unless at the time there is at least one other general partner and the ~~certificate of limited~~ <u>written provisions of the</u> partnership <u>agreement</u> ~~permits~~ <u>permit</u> the business of the limited partnership to be carried on by the remaining general partner and that partner does so, but the limited partnership is not dissolved and is not required to be wound up by reason of any event of withdrawal, if, within 90 days after the withdrawal, all partners agree in writing to continue the business of the limited partnership and to the appointment of one or more additional general partners if necessary or desired; or

~~(4)~~ <u>(5)</u>   entry of a decree of judicial dissolution under Section 802.

COMMENT

Section 801 merely collects in one place all of the events causing dissolution. Paragraph (3) is derived from Sections 9(1)(g) and 20 of the ~~prior uniform law~~ 1916 Act, but adds the 90-day grace period. <u>Section 801 also differs from its counterpart in the 1976 Act to reflect the 1985 changes made in Section 201.</u>

§ 802. Judicial Dissolution

On application by or for a partner the [designate the appropriate court] court may decree dissolution of a limited partnership whenever it is not reasonably practicable to carry on the business in conformity with the partnership agreement.

COMMENT

Section 802 ~~is new~~ <u>first appeared in the 1976 Act.</u>

§ 803. Winding Up

Except as provided in the partnership agreement, the general partners who have not wrongfully dissolved a limited partnership or, if none, the limited partners, may wind up the limited partnership's affairs; but the [designate the appropriate court] court may wind up the limited partnership's affairs upon application of any partner, his [or her] legal representative, or assignee.

COMMENT

Section 803 ~~is new~~ first appeared in the 1976 Act and is derived in part from Section 37 of the Uniform ~~General~~ Partnership Act.

§ 804.   Distribution of Assets

Upon the winding up of a limited partnership, the assets shall be distributed as follows:

(1)   to creditors, including partners who are creditors, to the extent permitted by law, in satisfaction of liabilities of the limited partnership other than liabilities for distributions to partners under Section 601 or 604;

(2)   except as provided in the partnership agreement, to partners and former partners in satisfaction of liabilities for distributions under Section 601 or 604; and

(3)   except as provided in the partnership agreement, to partners first for the return of their contributions and secondly respecting their partnership interests, in the proportions in which the partners share in distributions.

COMMENT

Section 804 revises Section 23 of the ~~prior uniform law~~ 1916 Act by providing that (1) to the extent partners are also creditors, other than in respect of their interests in the partnership, they share with other creditors, (2) once the partnership's obligation to make a distribution accrues, it must be paid before any other distributions of an "equity" nature are made, and (3) general and limited partners rank on the same level except as otherwise provided in the partnership agreement.

ARTICLE 9
FOREIGN LIMITED PARTNERSHIPS

§ 901.   Law Governing

Subject to the Constitution of this State, (i) the laws of the state under which a foreign limited partnership is organized govern its organization and internal affairs and the liability of its limited partners, and (ii) a foreign limited partnership may not be denied registration by reason of any difference between those laws and the laws of this State.

COMMENT

Section 901 ~~is new~~ first appeared in the 1976 Act.

§ 902.   Registration

Before transacting business in this State, a foreign limited partnership shall register with the Secretary of State. In order to register, a foreign limited partnership shall submit to the Secretary of State, in duplicate, an application for registration as a foreign limited partnership, signed and sworn to by a general partner and setting forth:

(1)   the name of the foreign limited partnership and, if different, the name under which it proposes to register and transact business in this State;

(2)   the ~~state~~ State and date of its formation;

~~(3)   the general character of the business it proposes to transact in this State;~~

~~(4)~~ (3)   the name and address of any agent for service of process on the foreign limited partnership whom the foreign limited partnership elects to appoint; the agent must be an individual resident of this ~~state~~ State, a domestic corporation, or a foreign corporation having a place of business in, and authorized to do business in, this State;

~~(5)~~ (4) a statement that the Secretary of State is appointed the agent of the foreign limited partnership for service of process if no agent has been appointed under paragraph ~~(4)~~ (3) or, if appointed, the agent's authority has been revoked or if the agent cannot be found or served with the exercise of reasonable diligence;

~~(6)~~ (5) the address of the office required to be maintained in the ~~State~~ state of its organization by the laws of that ~~State~~ state or, if not so required, of the principal office of the foreign limited partnership; ~~and~~

~~(7) if the certificate of limited partnership filed in the foreign limited partnership's state of organization is not required to include the names and business addresses of the partners, a list of the names and addresses.~~

(6) the name and business address of each general partner; and

(7) the address of the office at which is kept a list of the names and addresses of the limited partners and their capital contributions, together with an undertaking by the foreign limited partnership to keep those records until the foreign limited partnership's registration in this State is cancelled or withdrawn.

COMMENT

Section 902 ~~is new~~ first appeared in the 1976 Act. It was thought that requiring a full copy of the certificate of limited partnership and all amendments thereto to be filed in each state in which the partnership does business would impose an unreasonable burden on interstate limited partnerships and that the information ~~on file was~~ Section 902 required to be filed would be sufficient to tell interested persons where they could write to obtain copies of those basic documents. Subdivision (3) of the 1976 Act has been omitted, and subdivisions (6) and (7) differ from their counterparts in the 1976 Act, to conform these provisions relating to the registration of foreign limited partnerships to the corresponding changes made by the Act in the provisions relating to domestic limited partnerships. The requirement that an application for registration be sworn to by a general partner is simply intended to produce the same result as is provided for in Section 204(c) with respect to certificates of domestic limited partnerships; the acceptance and endorsement by the Secretary of State (or equivalent authority) of an application which was not sworn by a general partner should be deemed a mere technical and insubstantial shortcoming, and should not result in the limited partners' being subjected to general liability for the obligations of the foreign limited partnership (*see* Section 907(c)).

§ 903. Issuance of Registration

(a) If the Secretary of State finds that an application for registration conforms to law and all requisite fees have been paid, he [or she] shall:

(1) endorse on the application the word "Filed," and the month, day and year of the filing thereof;

(2) file in his [or her] office a duplicate original of the application; and

(3) issue a certificate of registration to transact business in this State.

(b) The certificate of registration, together with a duplicate original of the application, shall be returned to the person who filed the application or his [or her] representative.

COMMENT

Section 903 first appeared in the 1976 Act.

§ 904. Name

A foreign limited partnership may register with the Secretary of State under any name, whether or not it is the name under which it is registered in its state of organization, that includes without abbreviation the words "limited partnership" and that could be registered by a domestic limited partnership.

COMMENT

Section 904 is new first appeared in the 1976 Act.

§ 905.   Changes and Amendments

If any statement in the application for registration of a foreign limited partnership was false when made or any arrangements or other facts described have changed, making the application inaccurate in any respect, the foreign limited partnership shall promptly file in the office of the Secretary of State a certificate, signed and sworn to by a general partner, correcting such statement.

COMMENT

Section 905 is new first appeared in the 1976 Act. It corresponds to the provisions of Section 202(c) relating to domestic limited partnerships.

§ 906.   Cancellation of Registration

A foreign limited partnership may cancel its registration by filing with the Secretary of State a certificate of cancellation signed and sworn to by a general partner. A cancellation does not terminate the authority of the Secretary of State to accept service of process on the foreign limited partnership with respect to [claims for relief] [causes of action] arising out of the transactions of business in this State.

COMMENT

Section 906 is new first appeared in the 1976 Act.

§ 907.   Transaction of Business Without Registration

(a)   A foreign limited partnership transacting business in this State may not maintain any action, suit, or proceeding in any court of this State until it has registered in this State.

(b)   The failure of a foreign limited partnership to register in this State does not impair the validity of any contract or act of the foreign limited partnership or prevent the foreign limited partnership from defending any action, suit, or proceeding in any court of this State.

(c)   A limited partner of a foreign limited partnership is not liable as a general partner of the foreign limited partnership solely by reason of having transacted business in this State without registration.

(d)   A foreign limited partnership, by transacting business in this State without registration, appoints the Secretary of State as its agent for service of process with respect to [claims for relief] [causes of action] arising out of the transaction of business in this State.

COMMENT

Section 907 is new first appeared in the 1976 Act.

§ 908.   Action by [Appropriate Official]

The [designate the appropriate official] may bring an action to restrain a foreign limited partnership from transacting business in this State in violation of this Article.

COMMENT

Section 908 is new first appeared in the 1976 Act.

ARTICLE 10
DERIVATIVE ACTIONS

§ 1001. Right of Action

A limited partner may bring an action in the right of a limited partnership to recover a judgment in its favor if general partners with authority to do so have refused to bring the action or if an effort to cause those general partners to bring the action is not likely to succeed.

COMMENT

Section 1001 ~~is new~~ first appeared in the 1976 Act.

§ 1002. Proper Plaintiff

In a derivative action, the plaintiff must be a partner at the time of bringing the action and (i) must have been a partner at the time of the transaction of which he [or she] complains or (ii) his [or her] status as a partner ~~had~~ must have devolved upon him [or her] by operation of law or pursuant to the terms of the partnership agreement from a person who was a partner at the time of the transaction.

COMMENT

Section 1002 ~~is new~~ first appeared in the 1976 Act.

§ 1003. Pleading

In a derivative action, the complaint shall set forth with particularity the effort of the plaintiff to secure initiation of the action by a general partner or the reasons for not making the effort.

COMMENT

Section 1003 ~~is new~~ first appeared in the 1976 Act.

§ 1004. Expenses

If a derivative action is successful, in whole or in part, or if anything is received by the plaintiff as a result of a judgment, compromise or settlement of an action or claim, the court may award the plaintiff reasonable expenses, including reasonable attorney's fees, and shall direct him [or her] to remit to the limited partnership the remainder of those proceeds received by him [or her].

COMMENT

Section 1004 ~~is new~~ first appeared in the 1976 Act.

ARTICLE 11
MISCELLANEOUS

§ 1101. Construction and Application

This [Act] shall be so applied and construed to effectuate its general purpose to make uniform the law with respect to the subject of this [Act] among states enacting it.

COMMENT

Because the principles set out in Sections 28(1) and 29 of the 1916 Act have become so universally established, it was felt that the 1976 and 1985 Acts need not contain express provisions to the same effect. However, it is intended that the principles enunciated in those provisions of the 1916 Act also apply to this Act.

§ 1102.   Short Title

This [Act] may be cited as the Uniform Limited Partnership Act.

§ 1103.   Severability

If any provision of this [Act] or its application to any person or circumstance is held invalid, the invalidity does not affect other provisions or applications of the [Act] which can be given effect without the invalid provision or application, and to this end the provisions of this [Act] are severable.

§ 1104.   Effective Date, Extended Effective Date and Repeal

Except as set forth below, the effective date of this [Act] is _____ and the following acts [list prior existing limited partnership acts] are hereby repealed:

(1)   The existing provisions for execution and filing of certificates of limited partnerships and amendments thereunder and cancellations thereof continue in effect until [specify time required to create central filing system], the extended effective date, and Sections 102, 103, 104, 105, 201, 202, 203, 204 and 206 are not effective until the extended effective date.

(2)   Section 402, specifying the conditions under which a general partner ceases to be a member of a limited partnership, is not effective until the extended effective date, and the applicable provisions of existing law continue to govern until the extended effective date.

(3)   Sections 501, 502 and 608 apply only to contributions and distributions made after the effective date of this [Act].

(4)   Section 704 applies only to assignments made after the effective date of this [Act].

(5)   Article 9, dealing with registration of foreign limited partnerships, is not effective until the extended effective date.

(6)   Unless otherwise agreed by the partners, the applicable provisions of existing law governing allocation of profits and losses (rather than the provisions of Section 503), distributions to a withdrawing partner (rather than the provisions of Section 604), and distribution of assets upon the winding up of a limited partnership (rather than the provisions of Section 804) govern limited partnerships formed before the effective date of this [Act].

COMMENT

Subdivisions (6) and (7) did not appear in Section 1104 of the 1976 Act. They are included in the 1985 Act to ensure that the application of the Act to limited partnerships formed and existing before the Act becomes effective would not violate constitutional prohibitions against the impairment of contracts.

§ 1105.   Rules for Cases not Provided for in this [Act]

In any case not provided for in this [Act] the provisions of the Uniform Partnership Act govern.

COMMENT

The result provided for in Section 1105 would obtain even in its absence in a jurisdiction which had adopted the Uniform Partnership Act, by operation of Section 6 of that act.

§ 1106.   Savings Clause

The repeal of any statutory provision by this [Act] does not impair, or otherwise affect, the organization or the continued existence of a limited partnership existing at the effective date of this [Act], nor does the repeal of any existing statutory provision by this [Act] impair any contract or affect any right accrued before the effective date of this [Act].

COMMENT

Section 1106 did not appear in the 1976 Act. It was included in the 1985 Act to ensure that the application of the Act to limited partnerships formed and existing before the Act becomes effective would not violate constitutional prohibitions against the impairment of contracts.

E. REVISED UNIFORM LIMITED PARTNERSHIP ACT (1985)

Table of Sections

ARTICLE 1.   GENERAL PROVISIONS.

ARTICLE 2.   FORMATION: CERTIFICATE OF LIMITED PARTNERSHIP.

ARTICLE 3.   LIMITED PARTNERS.

ARTICLE 4.   GENERAL PARTNERS.

ARTICLE 5.   FINANCE.

REVISED UNIFORM LIMITED PARTNERSHIP ACT (1985)

ARTICLE 6. DISTRIBUTIONS AND WITHDRAWAL.

ARTICLE 7. ASSIGNMENT OF PARTNERSHIP INTERESTS.

ARTICLE 8. DISSOLUTION.

ARTICLE 9. FOREIGN LIMITED PARTNERSHIPS.

ARTICLE 10. DERIVATIVE ACTIONS.

ARTICLE 11. MISCELLANEOUS.

ARTICLE 1
GENERAL PROVISIONS

§ 101. Definitions

As used in this [Act], unless the context otherwise requires:

(1) "Certificate of limited partnership" means the certificate referred to in Section 201, and the certificate as amended or restated.

(2) "Contribution" means any cash, property, services rendered, or a promissory note or other binding obligation to contribute cash or property or to perform services, which a partner contributes to a limited partnership in his capacity as a partner.

(3) "Event of withdrawal of a general partner" means an event that causes a person to cease to be a general partner as provided in Section 402.

(4) "Foreign limited partnership" means a partnership formed under the laws of any state other than this State and having as partners one or more general partners and one or more limited partners.

(5) "General partner" means a person who has been admitted to a limited partnership as a general partner in accordance with the partnership agreement and named in the certificate of limited partnership as a general partner.

(6) "Limited partner" means a person who has been admitted to a limited partnership as a limited partner in accordance with the partnership agreement.

(7) "Limited partnership" and "domestic limited partnership" mean a partnership formed by two or more persons under the laws of this State and having one or more general partners and one or more limited partners.

(8) "Partner" means a limited or general partner.

(9) "Partnership agreement" means any valid agreement, written or oral, of the partners as to the affairs of a limited partnership and the conduct of its business.

(10) "Partnership interest" means a partner's share of the profits and losses of a limited partnership and the right to receive distributions of partnership assets.

(11) "Person" means a natural person, partnership, limited partnership (domestic or foreign), trust, estate, association, or corporation.

(12) "State" means a state, territory, or possession of the United States, the District of Columbia, or the Commonwealth of Puerto Rico.

COMMENT

The definitions in this section clarify a number of uncertainties in the law existing prior to the 1976 Act, and also make certain changes in such prior law. The 1985 Act makes very few additional changes in Section 101.

Contribution: this definition makes it clear that a present contribution of services and a promise to make a future payment of cash, contribution of property or performance of services are permissible forms for a contribution. Section 502 of the 1985 Act provides that a limited partner's promise to make a contribution is enforceable only when set out in a writing signed by the limited partner. (This result is not dissimilar from that under the 1976 Act, which required all promises of future contributions to be described in the certificate of limited partnership, which was to be signed by, among others, the partners making such promises.) The property or services contributed presently or promised to be contributed in the future must be accorded a value in the partnership agreement or the partnership records required to be kept pursuant to Section 105, and, in the case of a promise, that value may determine the liability of a partner who fails to honor his agreement (Section 502). Section 3 of the 1916 Act did not permit a limited partner's contribution to be in the form of services, although that inhibition did not apply to general partners.

Foreign limited partnership: the Act only deals with foreign limited partnerships formed under the laws of another "state" of the United States (see subdivision 12 of Section 101), and any adopting state that desires to deal by statute with the status of entities formed under the laws of foreign countries must make appropriate changes throughout the Act. The exclusion of such entities from the Act was not intended to suggest that their "limited partners" should not be accorded limited liability by the courts of a state adopting the Act. That question would be resolved by the choice-of-law rules of the forum state.

General partner: this definition recognizes the separate functions of the partnership agreement and the certificate of limited partnership. The partnership agreement establishes the basic grant of management power to the persons named as general partners; but because of the passive role played by the limited partners, the separate, formal step of memorializing that grant of power in the certificate of limited partnership has been preserved to emphasize its importance and to provide notice of the identity of the partnership's general partners to persons dealing with the partnership.

Limited partner: unlike the definition of general partners, this definition provides for admission of limited partners through the partnership agreement alone and does not require identification of any limited partner in the certificate of limited partnership (Section 201). Under the 1916 and the 1976 Acts, being named as a limited partner in the certificate of limited partnership was a statutory requirement and, in most if not all cases, probably also a prerequisite to limited partner status. By eliminating the requirement that the certificate of limited partnership contain the name, address, and capital contribution of each limited partner, the 1985 Act all but eliminates any risk that a person intended to be a limited partner may be exposed to liability as a general partner as a result of the inadvertent omission of any of that information from the certificate of limited partnership, and also dispenses with the need to amend the certificate of limited partnership upon the admission or withdrawal of, transfer of an interest by, or change in the address or capital contribution of, any limited partner.

Partnership agreement: the 1916 Act did not refer to the partnership agreement, assuming that all important matters affecting limited partners would be set forth in the certificate of limited partnership. Under modern practice, however, it has been common for the partners to enter into a comprehensive partnership agreement, only part of which was required to be included or summarized in the certificate of limited partnership. As reflected in Section 201 of the 1985 Act, the certificate of limited partnership is confined principally to matters respecting the partnership itself and the identity of general partners, and other important issues are left to the partnership agreement. Most of the information formerly provided by, but no longer required to be included in, the certificate of limited partnership is now required to be kept in the partnership records (Section 105).

Partnership interest: this definition first appeared in the 1976 Act and is intended to define what it is that is transferred when a partnership interest is assigned.

§ 102.   Name

The name of each limited partnership as set forth in its certificate of limited partnership:

(1)   shall contain without abbreviation the words "limited partnership";

(2)   may not contain the name of a limited partner unless (i) it is also the name of a general partner or the corporate name of a corporate general partner, or (ii) the business of the limited partnership had been carried on under that name before the admission of that limited partner;

(3)   may not be the same as, or deceptively similar to, the name of any corporation or limited partnership organized under the laws of this State or licensed or registered as a foreign corporation or limited partnership in this State; and

(4)   may not contain the following words [here insert prohibited words].

COMMENT

Subdivision (2) of Section 102 has been carried over from Section 5 of the 1916 Act with certain editorial changes. The remainder of Section 102 first appeared in the 1976 Act and primarily reflects the intention to integrate the registration of limited partnership names with that of corporate names. Accordingly, Section 201 provides for central, state-wide filing of certificates of limited partnership, and subdivisions (3) and (4) of Section 102 contain standards to be applied by the filing officer in determining whether the certificate should be filed. Subdivision (1) requires that the proper name of a limited partnership contain the words "limited partnership" in full. Subdivision (3) of the 1976 Act has been deleted, to reflect the deletion from Section 201 of any requirement that the certificate of limited partnership describe the partnership's purposes or the character of its business.

§ 103.   Reservation of Name

(a)   The exclusive right to the use of a name may be reserved by:

(1)   any person intending to organize a limited partnership under this [Act] and to adopt that name;

(2)   any domestic limited partnership or any foreign limited partnership registered in this State which, in either case, intends to adopt that name;

(3)   any foreign limited partnership intending to register in this State and adopt that name; and

(4)   any person intending to organize a foreign limited partnership and intending to have it register in this State and adopt that name.

(b)   The reservation shall be made by filing with the Secretary of State an application, executed by the applicant, to reserve a specified name. If the Secretary of State finds that the name is available for use by a domestic or foreign limited partnership, he [or she] shall reserve the name for the exclusive use of the applicant for a period of 120 days. Once having so reserved a name, the same applicant may not again reserve the same name until more than 60 days after the expiration of the last 120-day period for which that applicant reserved that name. The right to the exclusive use of a reserved name may be transferred to any other person by filing in the office of the Secretary of State a notice of the transfer, executed by the applicant for whom the name was reserved and specifying the name and address of the transferee.

COMMENT

Section 103 first appeared in the 1976 Act. The 1916 Act did not provide for registration of names.

§ 104.   Specified Office and Agent

Each limited partnership shall continuously maintain in this State:

(1)   an office, which may but need not be a place of its business in this State, at which shall be kept the records required by Section 105 to be maintained; and

(2)   an agent for service of process on the limited partnership, which agent must be an individual resident of this State, a domestic corporation, or a foreign corporation authorized to do business in this State.

COMMENT

Section 104 first appeared in the 1976 Act. It requires that a limited partnership have certain minimum contacts with its State of organization, i.e., an office at which the constitutive documents and basic financial information is kept and an agent for service of process.

§ 105.   Records to be Kept

(a)   Each limited partnership shall keep at the office referred to in Section 104(1) the following:

(1)   a current list of the full name and last known business address of each partner, separately identifying the general partners (in alphabetical order) and the limited partners (in alphabetical order);

    (2)   a copy of the certificate of limited partnership and all certificates of amendment thereto, together with executed copies of any powers of attorney pursuant to which any certificate has been executed;

    (3)   copies of the limited partnership's federal, state and local income tax returns and reports, if any, for the three most recent years;

    (4)   copies of any then effective written partnership agreements and of any financial statements of the limited partnership for the three most recent years; and

    (5)   unless contained in a written partnership agreement, a writing setting out:

       (i)   the amount of cash and a description and statement of the agreed value of the other property or services contributed by each partner and which each partner has agreed to contribute;

       (ii)   the times at which or events on the happening of which any additional contributions agreed to be made by each partner are to be made;

       (iii) any right of a partner to receive, or of a general partner to make, distributions to a partner which include a return of all or any part of the partner's contribution; and

       (iv) any events upon the happening of which the limited partnership is to be dissolved and its affairs wound up.

    (b)   Records kept under this section are subject to inspection and copying at the reasonable request and at the expense of any partner during ordinary business hours.

COMMENT

Section 105 first appeared in the 1976 Act. In view of the passive nature of the limited partner's position, it has been widely felt that limited partners are entitled to access to certain basic documents and information, including the certificate of limited partnership, any partnership agreement, and a writing setting out certain important matters which, under the 1916 and 1976 Acts, were required to be set out in the certificate of limited partnership. In view of the great diversity among limited partnerships, it was thought inappropriate to require a standard form of financial report, and Section 105 does no more than require retention of tax returns and any other financial statements that are prepared. The names and addresses of the general partners are made available to the general public in the certificate of limited partnership.

§ 106.   Nature of Business

A limited partnership may carry on any business that a partnership without limited partners may carry on except [here designate prohibited activities].

COMMENT

Section 106 is identical to Section 3 of the 1916 Act.

Many states require that certain regulated industries, such as banking, may be carried on only by entities organized pursuant to special statutes, and it is contemplated that the prohibited activities would be confined to the matters covered by those statutes.

§ 107.   Business Transactions of Partner with Partnership

Except as provided in the partnership agreement, a partner may lend money to and transact other business with the limited partnership and, subject to other applicable law, has the same rights and obligations with respect thereto as a person who is not a partner.

COMMENT

Section 107 makes a number of important changes in Section 13 of the 1916 Act. Section 13, in effect, created a special fraudulent conveyance provision applicable to the making of secured loans by limited partners and the repayment by limited partnerships of loans from limited partners. Section 107 leaves that question to a state's general fraudulent conveyance statute. In addition, Section 107 eliminates the prohibition in Section 13 against a general partner's sharing pro rata with general creditors in the case of an unsecured loan. Of course, other doctrines developed under bankruptcy and insolvency laws may require the subordination of loans by partners under appropriate circumstances.

ARTICLE 2
FORMATION: CERTIFICATE OF LIMITED PARTNERSHIP

§ 201.   Certificate of Limited Partnership

(a)   In order to form a limited partnership, a certificate of limited partnership must be executed and filed in the office of the Secretary of State. The certificate shall set forth:

(1)   the name of the limited partnership;

(2)   the address of the office and the name and address of the agent for service of process required to be maintained by Section 104;

(3)   the name and the business address of each general partner;

(4)   the latest date upon which the limited partnership is to dissolve; and

(5)   any other matters the general partners determine to include therein.

(b)   A limited partnership is formed at the time of the filing of the certificate of limited partnership in the office of the Secretary of State or at any later time specified in the certificate of limited partnership if, in either case, there has been substantial compliance with the requirements of this section.

COMMENT

The 1985 Act requires far fewer matters to be set forth in the certificate of limited partnership than did Section 2 of the 1916 Act and Section 201 of the 1976 Act. This is in recognition of the fact that the partnership agreement, not the certificate of limited partnership, has become the authoritative and comprehensive document for most limited partnerships, and that creditors and potential creditors of the partnership do and should refer to the partnership agreement and to other information furnished to them directly by the partnership and by others, not to the certificate of limited partnership, to obtain facts concerning the capital and finances of the partnership and other matters of concern. Subparagraph (b), which is based upon the 1916 Act, has been retained to make it clear that the existence of the limited partnership depends only upon compliance with this section. Its continued existence is not dependent upon compliance with other provisions of this Act.

§ 202.   Amendment to Certificate

(a)   A certificate of limited partnership is amended by filing a certificate of amendment thereto in the office of the Secretary of State. The certificate shall set forth:

(1)   the name of the limited partnership;

(2)   the date of filing the certificate; and

(3)   the amendment to the certificate.

(b)   Within 30 days after the happening of any of the following events, an amendment to a certificate of limited partnership reflecting the occurrence of the event or events shall be filed:

(1)   the admission of a new general partner;

(2)   the withdrawal of a general partner; or

(3)   the continuation of the business under Section 801 after an event of withdrawal of a general partner.

(c)   A general partner who becomes aware that any statement in a certificate of limited partnership was false when made or that any arrangements or other facts described have changed, making the certificate inaccurate in any respect, shall promptly amend the certificate.

(d)   A certificate of limited partnership may be amended at any time for any other proper purpose the general partners determine.

(e)   No person has any liability because an amendment to a certificate of limited partnership has not been filed to reflect the occurrence of any event referred to in subsection (b) of this section if the amendment is filed within the 30-day period specified in subsection (b).

(f)   A restated certificate of limited partnership may be executed and filed in the same manner as a certificate of amendment.

COMMENT

Section 202 of the 1976 Act made substantial changes in Section 24 of the 1916 Act. Further changes in this section are made by the 1985 Act. Paragraph (b) lists the basic events—the addition or withdrawal of a general partner—that are so central to the function of the certificate of limited partnership that they require prompt amendment. With the elimination of the requirement that the certificate of limited partnership include the names of all limited partners and the amount and character of all capital contributions, the requirement of the 1916 and 1976 Acts that the certificate be amended upon the admission or withdrawal of limited partners or on any change in the partnership capital must also be eliminated. This change should greatly reduce the frequency and complexity of amendments to the certificate of limited partnership. Paragraph (c) makes it clear, as it was not clear under Section 24(2)(g) of the 1916 Act, that the certificate of limited partnership is intended to be an accurate description of the facts to which it relates at all times and does not speak merely as of the date it is executed.

Paragraph (e) provides a "safe harbor" against claims of creditors or others who assert that they have been misled by the failure to amend the certificate of limited partnership to reflect changes in any of the important facts referred to in paragraph (b); if the certificate of limited partnership is amended within 30 days of the occurrence of the event, no creditor or other person can recover for damages sustained during the interim. Additional protection is afforded by the provisions of Section 304. The elimination of the requirement that the certificate of limited partnership identify all limited partners and their respective capital contributions may have rendered paragraph (e) an obsolete and unnecessary vestige. The principal, if not the sole, purpose of paragraph (e) in the 1976 Act was to protect limited partners newly admitted to a partnership from being held liable as general partners when an amendment to the certificate identifying them as limited partners and describing their contributions was not filed contemporaneously with their admission to the partnership. Such liability cannot arise under the 1985 Act because such information is not required to be stated in the certificate. Nevertheless, the 1985 Act retains paragraph (e) because it is protective of partners, shielding them from liability to the extent its provisions apply, and does not create or impose any liability.

Paragraph (f) is added in the 1985 Act to provide explicit statutory recognition of the common practice of restating an amended certificate of limited partnership. While a limited partnership seeking to amend its certificate of limited partnership may do so by recording a restated certificate which incorporates the amendment, that is by no means the only purpose or function of a restated certificate, which may be filed for the sole purpose of restating in a single integrated instrument all the provisions of a limited partnership's certificate of limited partnership which are then in effect.

§ 203.   Cancellation of Certificate

A certificate of limited partnership shall be cancelled upon the dissolution and the commencement of winding up of the partnership or at any other time there are no limited partners. A certificate of cancellation shall be filed in the office of the Secretary of State and set forth:

(1)   the name of the limited partnership;

(2)   the date of filing of its certificate of limited partnership;

(3)   the reason for filing the certificate of cancellation;

(4)   the effective date (which shall be a date certain) of cancellation if it is not to be effective upon the filing of the certificate; and

(5)   any other information the general partners filing the certificate determine.

COMMENT

Section 203 changes Section 24 of the 1916 Act by making it clear that the certificate of cancellation should be filed upon the commencement of winding up of the limited partnership. Section 24 provided for cancellation "when the partnership is dissolved."

§ 204.   Execution of Certificates

(a)   Each certificate required by this Article to be filed in the office of the Secretary of State shall be executed in the following manner:

(1)   an original certificate of limited partnership must be signed by all general partners;

(2)   a certificate of amendment must be signed by at least one general partner and by each other general partner designated in the certificate as a new general partner; and

(3)   a certificate of cancellation must be signed by all general partners.

(b)   Any person may sign a certificate by an attorney-in-fact, but a power of attorney to sign a certificate relating to the admission of a general partner must specifically describe the admission.

(c)   The execution of a certificate by a general partner constitutes an affirmation under the penalties of perjury that the facts stated therein are true.

COMMENT

Section 204 collects in one place the formal requirements for the execution of certificates which were set forth in Sections 2 and 25 of the 1916 Act. Those sections required that each certificate be signed by all partners, and there developed an unnecessarily cumbersome practice of having each limited partner sign powers of attorney to authorize the general partners to execute certificates of amendment on their behalf. The 1976 Act, while simplifying the execution requirements, nevertheless required that an original certificate of limited partnership be signed by all partners and a certificate of amendment by all new partners being admitted to the limited partnership. However, the certificate of limited partnership is no longer required to include the name or capital contribution of any limited partner. Therefore, while the 1985 Act still requires all general partners to sign the original certificate of limited partnership, no limited partner is required to sign any certificate. Certificates of amendment are required to be signed by only one general partner and all general partners must sign certificates of cancellation. The requirement in the 1916 Act that all certificates be sworn was deleted in the 1976 and 1985 Acts as potentially an unfair trap for the unwary (see, e.g., Wisniewski v. Johnson, 223 Va. 141, 286 S.E.2d 223 (1982)); in its place, paragraph (c) now provides, as a matter of law, that the execution of a certificate by a general partner subjects him to the penalties of perjury for inaccuracies in the certificate.

§ 205.   Execution by Judicial Act

If a person required by Section 204 to execute any certificate fails or refuses to do so, any other person who is adversely affected by the failure or refusal may petition the [designate the appropriate court] to direct the execution of the certificate. If the court finds that it is proper for the certificate to be executed and that any person so designated has failed or refused to execute the certificate, it shall order the Secretary of State to record an appropriate certificate.

COMMENT

Section 205 of the 1976 Act changed subdivisions (3) and (4) of Section 25 of the 1916 Act by confining the persons who have standing to seek judicial intervention to partners and to those assignees who were adversely affected by the failure or refusal of the appropriate persons to file a certificate of amendment or cancellation. Section 205 of the 1985 Act reverses that restriction, and provides that any person adversely affected by a failure or refusal to file any certificate (not only a certificate of cancellation or amendment) has standing to seek judicial intervention.

§ 206.   Filing in Office of Secretary of State

(a)   Two signed copies of the certificate of limited partnership and of any certificates of amendment or cancellation (or of any judicial decree of amendment or cancellation) shall be delivered to the Secretary of State. A person who executes a certificate as an agent or fiduciary need not exhibit evidence of his [or her] authority as a prerequisite to filing. Unless the Secretary of State finds that any certificate does not conform to law, upon receipt of all filing fees required by law he [or she] shall:

(1)   endorse on each duplicate original the word "Filed" and the day, month and year of the filing thereof;

(2)   file one duplicate original in his [or her] office; and

(3)   return the other duplicate original to the person who filed it or his [or her] representative.

(b)   Upon the filing of a certificate of amendment (or judicial decree of amendment) in the office of the Secretary of State, the certificate of limited partnership shall be amended as set forth therein, and upon the effective date of a certificate of cancellation (or a judicial decree thereof), the certificate of limited partnership is cancelled.

COMMENT

Section 206 first appeared in the 1976 Act. In addition to providing mechanics for the central filing system, the second sentence of this section does away with the requirement, formerly imposed by some local filing officers, that persons who have executed certificates under a power of attorney exhibit executed copies of the power of attorney itself. Paragraph (b) changes subdivision (5) of Section 25 of the 1916 Act by providing that certificates of cancellation are effective upon their effective date under Section 203.

§ 207.   Liability for False Statement in Certificate

If any certificate of limited partnership or certificate of amendment or cancellation contains a false statement, one who suffers loss by reliance on the statement may recover damages for the loss from:

(1)   any person who executes the certificate, or causes another to execute it on his behalf, and knew, and any general partner who knew or should have known, the statement to be false at the time the certificate was executed; and

(2)   any general partner who thereafter knows or should have known that any arrangement or other fact described in the certificate has changed, making the statement inaccurate in any respect within a sufficient time before the statement was relied upon reasonably to have enabled that general partner to cancel or amend the certificate, or to file a petition for its cancellation or amendment under Section 205.

COMMENT

Section 207 changes Section 6 of the 1916 Act by providing explicitly for the liability of persons who sign a certificate as agent under a power of attorney and by confining the obligation to amend a certificate of limited partnership in light of future events to general partners.

§ 208.   Scope of Notice

The fact that a certificate of limited partnership is on file in the office of the Secretary of State is notice that the partnership is a limited partnership and the persons designated therein as general partners are general partners, but it is not notice of any other fact.

COMMENT

Section 208 first appeared in the 1976 Act, and referred to the certificate's providing constructive notice of the status as limited partners of those so identified therein. The 1985 Act's deletion of any requirement that the certificate name limited partners required that Section 208 be modified accordingly.

By stating that the filing of a certificate of limited partnership only results in notice of the general liability of the general partners, Section 208 obviates the concern that third parties may be held to have notice of special provisions set forth in the certificate. While this section is designed to preserve by implication the limited liability of limited partners, the implicit protection provided is not intended to change any liability of a limited partner which may be created by his action or inaction under the law of estoppel, agency, fraud, or the like.

§ 209.   Delivery of Certificates to Limited Partners

Upon the return by the Secretary of State pursuant to Section 206 of a certificate marked "Filed", the general partners shall promptly deliver or mail a copy of the certificate of limited partnership and each certificate of amendment or cancellation to each limited partner unless the partnership agreement provides otherwise.

COMMENT

This section first appeared in the 1976 Act.

ARTICLE 3
LIMITED PARTNERS

§ 301.   Admission of Limited Partners

(a)   A person becomes a limited partner:

    (1)   at the time the limited partnership is formed; or

    (2)   at any later time specified in the records of the limited partnership for becoming a limited partner.

(b)   After the filing of a limited partnership's original certificate of limited partnership, a person may be admitted as an additional limited partner:

    (1)   in the case of a person acquiring a partnership interest directly from the limited partnership, upon compliance with the partnership agreement or, if the partnership agreement does not so provide, upon the written consent of all partners; and

    (2)   in the case of an assignee of a partnership interest of a partner who has the power, as provided in Section 704, to grant the assignee the right to become a limited partner, upon the exercise of that power and compliance with any conditions limiting the grant or exercise of the power.

COMMENT

Section 301(a) is new; no counterpart was found in the 1916 or 1976 Acts. This section imposes on the partnership an obligation to maintain in its records the date each limited partner becomes a limited partner. Under the 1976 Act, one could not become a limited partner until an appropriate certificate reflecting his status as such was filed with the Secretary of State. Because the 1985 Act eliminates the need to name limited partners in the certificate of limited partnership, an alternative mechanism had to be established to evidence the fact and date of a limited partner's admission. The partnership records required to be maintained under Section 105 now serve that function, subject to the limitation that no person may become a limited partner before the partnership is formed (Section 201(b)).

Subdivision (1) of Section 301(b) adds to Section 8 of the 1916 Act an explicit recognition of the fact that unanimous consent of all partners is required for admission of new limited partners unless the partnership agreement provides otherwise. Subdivision (2) is derived from Section 19 of the 1916 Act but abandons the former terminology of "substituted limited partner."

§ 302.   Voting

Subject to Section 303, the partnership agreement may grant to all or a specified group of the limited partners the right to vote (on a per capita or other basis) upon any matter.

COMMENT

Section 302 first appeared in the 1976 Act, and must be read together with subdivision (b)(6) of Section 303. Although the 1916 Act did not speak specifically of the voting powers of limited partners, it was not uncommon for partnership agreements to grant such powers to limited partners. Section 302 is designed only to make it clear that the partnership agreement may grant such power to limited partners. If such powers are granted to limited partners beyond the "safe harbor" of subdivision (6) or (8) of Section 303(b), a court may (but of course need not) hold that, under the circumstances, the limited partners have participated in "control of the business" within the meaning of Section 303(a). Section 303(c) makes clear that the exercise of powers beyond the ambit of Section 303(b) is not ipso facto to be taken as taking part in the control of the business.

§ 303.   Liability to Third Parties

(a)   Except as provided in subsection (d), a limited partner is not liable for the obligations of a limited partnership unless he [or she] is also a general partner or, in addition to the exercise of his [or her] rights and powers as a limited partner, he [or she] participates in the control of the business. However, if the limited partner participates in the control of the business, he [or she] is liable only to persons who transact business with the limited partnership reasonably believing, based upon the limited partner's conduct, that the limited partner is a general partner.

(b)   A limited partner does not participate in the control of the business within the meaning of subsection (a) solely by doing one or more of the following:

(1)   being a contractor for or an agent or employee of the limited partnership or of a general partner or being an officer, director, or shareholder of a general partner that is a corporation;

(2)   consulting with and advising a general partner with respect to the business of the limited partnership;

(3)   acting as surety for the limited partnership or guaranteeing or assuming one or more specific obligations of the limited partnership;

(4)   taking any action required or permitted by law to bring or pursue a derivative action in the right of the limited partnership;

(5)   requesting or attending a meeting of partners;

(6)   proposing, approving, or disapproving, by voting or otherwise, one or more of the following matters:

(i)   the dissolution and winding up of the limited partnership;

(ii)   the sale, exchange, lease, mortgage, pledge, or other transfer of all or substantially all of the assets of the limited partnership;

(iii)   the incurrence of indebtedness by the limited partnership other than in the ordinary course of its business;

(iv) a change in the nature of the business;

(v) the admission or removal of a general partner;

(vi) the admission or removal of a limited partner;

(vii) a transaction involving an actual or potential conflict of interest between a general partner and the limited partnership or the limited partners;

(viii) an amendment to the partnership agreement or certificate of limited partnership; or

(ix) matters related to the business of the limited partnership not otherwise enumerated in this subsection (b), which the partnership agreement states in writing may be subject to the approval or disapproval of limited partners;

(7) winding up the limited partnership pursuant to Section 803; or

(8) exercising any right or power permitted to limited partners under this [Act] and not specifically enumerated in this subsection (b).

(c) The enumeration in subsection (b) does not mean that the possession or exercise of any other powers by a limited partner constitutes participation by him [or her] in the business of the limited partnership.

(d) A limited partner who knowingly permits his [or her] name to be used in the name of the limited partnership, except under circumstances permitted by Section 102(2), is liable to creditors who extend credit to the limited partnership without actual knowledge that the limited partner is not a general partner.

COMMENT

Section 303 makes several important changes in Section 7 of the 1916 Act. The first sentence of Section 303(a) differs from the text of Section 7 of the 1916 Act in that it speaks of participating (rather than taking part) in the control of the business; this was done for the sake of consistency with the second sentence of Section 303(a), not to change the meaning of the text. It is intended that judicial decisions interpreting the phrase "takes part in the control of the business" under the prior uniform law will remain applicable to the extent that a different result is not called for by other provisions of Section 303 and other provisions of the Act. The second sentence of Section 303(a) reflects a wholly new concept in the 1976 Act that has been further modified in the 1985 Act. It was adopted partly because of the difficulty of determining when the "control" line has been overstepped, but also (and more importantly) because of a determination that it is not sound public policy to hold a limited partner who is not also a general partner liable for the obligations of the partnership except to persons who have done business with the limited partnership reasonably believing, based on the limited partner's conduct, that he is a general partner. Paragraph (b) is intended to provide a "safe harbor" by enumerating certain activities which a limited partner may carry on for the partnership without being deemed to have taken part in control of the business. This "safe harbor" list has been expanded beyond that set out in the 1976 Act to reflect case law and statutory developments and more clearly to assure that limited partners are not subjected to general liability where such liability is inappropriate. Paragraph (d) is derived from Section 5 of the 1916 Act, but adds as a condition to the limited partner's liability the requirement that a limited partner must have knowingly permitted his name to be used in the name of the limited partnership.

§ 304. Person Erroneously Believing Himself [or Herself] Limited Partner

(a) Except as provided in subsection (b), a person who makes a contribution to a business enterprise and erroneously but in good faith believes that he [or she] has become a limited partner in the enterprise is not a general partner in the enterprise and is not bound by its obligations by reason of making the contribution, receiving distributions from the enterprise, or exercising any rights of a limited partner, if, on ascertaining the mistake, he [or she]:

    (1)   causes an appropriate certificate of limited partnership or a certificate of amendment to be executed and filed; or

    (2)   withdraws from future equity participation in the enterprise by executing and filing in the office of the Secretary of State a certificate declaring withdrawal under this section.

    (b)   A person who makes a contribution of the kind described in subsection (a) is liable as a general partner to any third party who transacts business with the enterprise (i) before the person withdraws and an appropriate certificate is filed to show withdrawal, or (ii) before an appropriate certificate is filed to show that he [or she] is not a general partner, but in either case only if the third party actually believed in good faith that the person was a general partner at the time of the transaction.

COMMENT

    Section 304 is derived from Section 11 of the 1916 Act. The "good faith" requirement has been added in the first sentence of Section 304(a). The provisions of subdivision (2) of Section 304(a) are intended to clarify an ambiguity in the prior law by providing that a person who chooses to withdraw from the enterprise in order to protect himself from liability is not required to renounce any of his then current interest in the enterprise so long as he has no further participation as an equity participant. Paragraph (b) preserves the liability of the equity participant prior to withdrawal by such person from the limited partnership or amendment to the certificate demonstrating that such person is not a general partner to any third party who has transacted business with the person believing in good faith that he was a general partner.

    Evidence strongly suggests that Section 11 of the 1916 Act and Section 304 of the 1976 Act were rarely used, and one might expect that Section 304 of the 1985 Act may never have to be used. Section 11 of the 1916 Act and Section 304 of the 1976 Act could have been used by a person who invested in a limited partnership believing he would be a limited partner but who was not identified as a limited partner in the certificate of limited partnership. However, because the 1985 Act does not require limited partners to be named in the certificate, the only situation to which Section 304 would now appear to be applicable is one in which a person intending to be a limited partner was erroneously identified as a general partner in the certificate.

§ 305.   Information

Each limited partner has the right to:

    (1)   inspect and copy any of the partnership records required to be maintained by Section 105; and

    (2)   obtain from the general partners from time to time upon reasonable demand (i) true and full information regarding the state of the business and financial condition of the limited partnership, (ii) promptly after becoming available, a copy of the limited partnership's federal, state and local income tax returns for each year, and (iii) other information regarding the affairs of the limited partnership as is just and reasonable.

COMMENT

    Section 305 changes and restates the rights of limited partners to information about the partnership formerly provided by Section 10 of the 1916 Act. Its importance has increased as a result of the 1985 Act's substituting the records of the partnership for the certificate of limited partnership as the place where certain categories of information are to be kept.

    Section 305, which should be read together with Section 105(b), provides a mechanism for limited partners to obtain information about the partnership useful to them in making decisions concerning the partnership and their investments in it. Its purpose is not to provide a mechanism for competitors of the partnership or others having interests or agendas adverse to the partnership's to subvert the partnership's business. It is assumed that courts will protect limited partnerships from abuses and attempts to misuse Section 305 for improper purposes.

ARTICLE 4
GENERAL PARTNERS

§ 401.   Admission of Additional General Partners

After the filing of a limited partnership's original certificate of limited partnership, additional general partners may be admitted as provided in writing in the partnership agreement or, if the partnership agreement does not provide in writing for the admission of additional general partners, with the written consent of all partners.

COMMENT

Section 401 is derived from, but represents a significant departure from, Section 9(1)(e) of the 1916 Act and Section 401 of the 1976 Act, which required, as a condition to the admission of an additional general partner, that all limited partners consent and that such consent specifically identify the general partner involved. Section 401 of the 1985 Act provides that the written partnership agreement determines the procedure for authorizing the admission of additional general partners, and that the written consent of all partners is required only when the partnership agreement fails to address the question.

§ 402.   Events of Withdrawal

Except as approved by the specific written consent of all partners at the time, a person ceases to be a general partner of a limited partnership upon the happening of any of the following events:

(1)   the general partner withdraws from the limited partnership as provided in Section 602;

(2)   the general partner ceases to be a member of the limited partnership as provided in Section 702;

(3)   the general partner is removed as a general partner in accordance with the partnership agreement;

(4)   unless otherwise provided in writing in the partnership agreement, the general partner: (i) makes an assignment for the benefit of creditors; (ii) files a voluntary petition in bankruptcy; (iii) is adjudicated a bankrupt or insolvent; (iv) files a petition or answer seeking for himself [or herself] any reorganization, arrangement, composition, readjustment, liquidation, dissolution or similar relief under any statute, law, or regulation; (v) files an answer or other pleading admitting or failing to contest the material allegations of a petition filed against him [or her] in any proceeding of this nature; or (vi) seeks, consents to, or acquiesces in the appointment of a trustee, receiver, or liquidator of the general partner or of all or any substantial part of his [or her] properties;

(5)   unless otherwise provided in writing in the partnership agreement, [120] days after the commencement of any proceeding against the general partner seeking reorganization, arrangement, composition, readjustment, liquidation, dissolution or similar relief under any statute, law, or regulation, the proceeding has not been dismissed, or if within [90] days after the appointment without his [or her] consent or acquiescence of a trustee, receiver, or liquidator of the general partner or of all or any substantial part of his [or her] properties, the appointment is not vacated or stayed or within [90] days after the expiration of any such stay, the appointment is not vacated;

(6)   in the case of a general partner who is a natural person,

(i)   his [or her] death; or

(ii)   the entry of an order by a court of competent jurisdiction adjudicating him [or her] incompetent to manage his [or her] person or his [or her] estate;

(7)   in the case of a general partner who is acting as a general partner by virtue of being a trustee of a trust, the termination of the trust (but not merely the substitution of a new trustee);

(8) in the case of a general partner that is a separate partnership, the dissolution and commencement of winding up of the separate partnership;

(9) in the case of a general partner that is a corporation, the filing of a certificate of dissolution, or its equivalent, for the corporation or the revocation of its charter; or

(10) in the case of an estate, the distribution by the fiduciary of the estate's entire interest in the partnership.

COMMENT

Section 402 expands considerably the provisions of Section 20 of the 1916 Act which provided for dissolution in the event of the retirement, death or insanity of a general partner. Subdivisions (1), (2) and (3) recognize that the general partner's agency relationship is terminable at will, although it may result in a breach of the partnership agreement giving rise to an action for damages. Subdivisions (4) and (5) reflect a judgment that, unless the limited partners agree otherwise, they ought to have the power to rid themselves of a general partner who is in such dire financial straits that he is the subject of proceedings under the National Bankruptcy Code or a similar provision of law. Subdivisions (6) through (10) simply elaborate on the notion of death in the case of a general partner who is not a natural person. Subdivisions (4) and (5) differ from their counterparts in the 1976 Act, reflecting the policy underlying the 1985 revision of Section 201, that the partnership agreement, not the certificate of limited partnership, is the appropriate document for setting out most provisions relating to the respective powers, rights, and obligations of the partners inter se. Although the partnership agreement need not be written, the 1985 Act provides that, to protect the partners from fraud, these and certain other particularly significant provisions must be set out in a written partnership agreement to be effective for the purposes described in the Act.

§ 403. General Powers and Liabilities

(a) Except as provided in this [Act] or in the partnership agreement, a general partner of a limited partnership has the rights and powers and is subject to the restrictions of a partner in a partnership without limited partners.

(b) Except as provided in this [Act], a general partner of a limited partnership has the liabilities of a partner in a partnership without limited partners to persons other than the partnership and the other partners. Except as provided in this [Act] or in the partnership agreement, a general partner of a limited partnership has the liabilities of a partner in a partnership without limited partners to the partnership and to the other partners.

COMMENT

Section 403 is derived from Section 9(1) of the 1916 Act.

§ 404. Contributions by General Partner

A general partner of a limited partnership may make contributions to the partnership and share in the profits and losses of, and in distributions from, the limited partnership as a general partner. A general partner also may make contributions to and share in profits, losses, and distributions as a limited partner. A person who is both a general partner and a limited partner has the rights and powers, and is subject to the restrictions and liabilities, of a general partner and, except as provided in the partnership agreement, also has the powers, and is subject to the restrictions, of a limited partner to the extent of his [or her] participation in the partnership as a limited partner.

COMMENT

Section 404 is derived from Section 12 of the 1916 Act and makes clear that the partnership agreement may provide that a general partner who is also a limited partner may exercise all of the powers of a limited partner.

§ 405.   Voting

The partnership agreement may grant to all or certain identified general partners the right to vote (on a per capita or any other basis), separately or with all or any class of the limited partners, on any matter.

COMMENT

Section 405 first appeared in the 1976 Act and is intended to make it clear that the Act does not require that the limited partners have any right to vote on matters as a separate class.

ARTICLE 5
FINANCE

§ 501.   Form of Contribution

The contribution of a partner may be in cash, property, or services rendered, or a promissory note or other obligation to contribute cash or property or to perform services.

COMMENT

As noted in the comment to Section 101, the explicit permission to make contributions of services expands Section 4 of the 1916 Act.

§ 502.   Liability for Contribution

(a)   A promise by a limited partner to contribute to the limited partnership is not enforceable unless set out in a writing signed by the limited partner.

(b)   Except as provided in the partnership agreement, a partner is obligated to the limited partnership to perform any enforceable promise to contribute cash or property or to perform services, even if he [or she] is unable to perform because of death, disability, or any other reason. If a partner does not make the required contribution of property or services, he [or she] is obligated at the option of the limited partnership to contribute cash equal to that portion of the value, as stated in the partnership records required to be kept pursuant to Section 105, of the stated contribution which has not been made.

(c)   Unless otherwise provided in the partnership agreement, the obligation of a partner to make a contribution or return money or other property paid or distributed in violation of this [Act] may be compromised only by consent of all partners. Notwithstanding the compromise, a creditor of a limited partnership who extends credit or otherwise acts in reliance on that obligation after the partner signs a writing which reflects the obligation and before the amendment or cancellation thereof to reflect the compromise may enforce the original obligation.

COMMENT

Section 502(a) is new; it has no counterpart in the 1916 or 1976 Act. Because, unlike the prior uniform acts, the 1985 Act does not require that promises to contribute cash, property, or services be described in the limited partnership certificate, to protect against fraud it requires instead that such important promises be in a signed writing.

Although Section 17(1) of the 1916 Act required a partner to fulfill his promise to make contributions, the addition of contributions in the form of a promise to render services means that a partner who is unable to perform those services because of death or disability as well as because of an intentional default is required to pay the cash value of the services unless the partnership agreement provides otherwise.

Subdivision (c) is derived from, but expands upon, Section 17(3) of the 1916 Act.

§ 503.   Sharing of Profits and Losses

The profits and losses of a limited partnership shall be allocated among the partners, and among classes of partners, in the manner provided in writing in the partnership agreement. If the partnership agreement does not so provide in writing, profits and losses shall be allocated on the basis of the value, as stated in the partnership records required to be kept pursuant to Section 105, of the contributions made by each partner to the extent they have been received by the partnership and have not been returned.

COMMENT

Section 503 first appeared in the 1976 Act. The 1916 Act did not provide the basis on which partners would share profits and losses in the absence of agreement. The 1985 Act differs from its counterpart in the 1976 Act by requiring that, to be effective, the partnership agreement provisions concerning allocation of profits and losses be in writing, and by its reference to records required to be kept pursuant to Section 105, the latter reflecting the 1985 changes in Section 201.

§ 504.   Sharing of Distributions

Distributions of cash or other assets of a limited partnership shall be allocated among the partners and among classes of partners in the manner provided in writing in the partnership agreement. If the partnership agreement does not so provide in writing, distributions shall be made on the basis of the value, as stated in the partnership records required to be kept pursuant to Section 105, of the contributions made by each partner to the extent they have been received by the partnership and have not been returned.

COMMENT

Section 504 first appeared in the 1976 Act. The 1916 Act did not provide the basis on which partners would share distributions in the absence of agreement. Section 504 also differs from its counterpart in the 1976 Act by requiring that, to be effective, the partnership agreement provisions concerning allocation of distributions be in writing, and in its reference to records required to be kept pursuant to Section 105, the latter reflecting the 1985 changes in Section 201. This section also recognizes that partners may choose to share in distributions on a basis different from that on which they share in profits and losses.

ARTICLE 6
DISTRIBUTIONS AND WITHDRAWAL

§ 601.   Interim Distributions

Except as provided in this Article, a partner is entitled to receive distributions from a limited partnership before his [or her] withdrawal from the limited partnership and before the dissolution and winding up thereof to the extent and at the times or upon the happening of the events specified in the partnership agreement.

COMMENT

Section 601 first appeared in the 1976 Act. The 1976 Act provisions have been modified to reflect the 1985 changes made in Section 201.

§ 602.   Withdrawal of General Partner

A general partner may withdraw from a limited partnership at any time by giving written notice to the other partners, but if the withdrawal violates the partnership agreement, the limited partnership may recover from the withdrawing general partner damages for breach of the partnership agreement and offset the damages against the amount otherwise distributable to him [or her].

COMMENT

Section 602 first appeared in the 1976 Act, but is generally derived from Section 38 of the Uniform Partnership Act.

§ 603.   Withdrawal of Limited Partner

A limited partner may withdraw from a limited partnership at the time or upon the happening of events specified in writing in the partnership agreement. If the agreement does not specify in writing the time or the events upon the happening of which a limited partner may withdraw or a definite time for the dissolution and winding up of the limited partnership, a limited partner may withdraw upon not less than six months' prior written notice to each general partner at his [or her] address on the books of the limited partnership at its office in this State.

COMMENT

Section 603 is derived from Section 16 of the 1916 Act. The 1976 Act provision has been modified to reflect the 1985 changes made in Section 201. This section additionally reflects the policy determination, also embodied in certain other sections of the 1985 Act, that to avoid fraud, agreements concerning certain matters of substantial importance to the partners will be enforceable only if in writing. If the partnership agreement does provide, in writing, whether a limited partner may withdraw and, if he may, when and on what terms and conditions, those provisions will control.

§ 604.   Distribution Upon Withdrawal

Except as provided in this Article, upon withdrawal any withdrawing partner is entitled to receive any distribution to which he [or she] is entitled under the partnership agreement and, if not otherwise provided in the agreement, he [or she] is entitled to receive, within a reasonable time after withdrawal, the fair value of his [or her] interest in the limited partnership as of the date of withdrawal based upon his [or her] right to share in distributions from the limited partnership.

COMMENT

Section 604 first appeared in the 1976 Act. It fixes the distributive share of a withdrawing partner in the absence of an agreement among the partners.

§ 605.   Distribution in Kind

Except as provided in writing in the partnership agreement, a partner, regardless of the nature of his [or her] contribution, has no right to demand and receive any distribution from a limited partnership in any form other than cash. Except as provided in writing in the partnership agreement, a partner may not be compelled to accept a distribution of any asset in kind from a limited partnership to the extent that the percentage of the asset distributed to him [or her] exceeds a percentage of that asset which is equal to the percentage in which he [or she] shares in distributions from the limited partnership.

COMMENT

The first sentence of Section 605 is derived from Section 16(3) of the 1916 Act; it also differs from its counterpart in the 1976 Act, reflecting the 1985 changes made in Section 201. The second sentence first appeared in the 1976 Act, and is intended to protect a limited partner (and the remaining partners) against a distribution in kind of more than his share of particular assets.

§ 606.   Right to Distribution

At the time a partner becomes entitled to receive a distribution, he [or she] has the status of, and is entitled to all remedies available to, a creditor of the limited partnership with respect to the distribution.

COMMENT

Section 606 first appeared in the 1976 Act and is intended to make it clear that the right of a partner to receive a distribution, as between the partners, is not subject to the equity risks of the enterprise. On the other hand, since partners entitled to distributions have creditor status, there did not seem to be a need for the extraordinary remedy of Section 16(4)(a) of the 1916 Act, which granted a limited partner the right to seek dissolution of the partnership if he was unsuccessful in demanding the return of his contribution. It is more appropriate for the partner to simply sue as an ordinary creditor and obtain a judgment.

§ 607.   Limitations on Distribution

A partner may not receive a distribution from a limited partnership to the extent that, after giving effect to the distribution, all liabilities of the limited partnership, other than liabilities to partners on account of their partnership interests, exceed the fair value of the partnership assets.

COMMENT

Section 607 is derived from Section 16(1)(a) of the 1916 Act.

§ 608.   Liability Upon Return of Contribution

(a)   If a partner has received the return of any part of his [or her] contribution without violation of the partnership agreement or this [Act], he [or she] is liable to the limited partnership for a period of one year thereafter for the amount of the returned contribution, but only to the extent necessary to discharge the limited partnership's liabilities to creditors who extended credit to the limited partnership during the period the contribution was held by the partnership.

(b)   If a partner has received the return of any part of his [or her] contribution in violation of the partnership agreement or this [Act], he [or she] is liable to the limited partnership for a period of six years thereafter for the amount of the contribution wrongfully returned.

(c)   A partner receives a return of his [or her] contribution to the extent that a distribution to him [or her] reduces his [or her] share of the fair value of the net assets of the limited partnership below the value, as set forth in the partnership records required to be kept pursuant to Section 105, of his contribution which has not been distributed to him [or her].

COMMENT

Paragraph (a) is derived from Section 17(4) of the 1916 Act, but the one year statute of limitations has been added. Paragraph (b) is derived from Section 17(2)(b) of the 1916 Act but, again, a statute of limitations has been added.

Paragraph (c) first appeared in the 1976 Act. The provisions of former Section 17(2) that referred to the partner holding as "trustee" any money or specific property wrongfully returned to him have been eliminated. Paragraph (c) in the 1985 Act also differs from its counterpart in the 1976 Act to reflect the 1985 changes made in Sections 105 and 201.

ARTICLE 7
ASSIGNMENT OF PARTNERSHIP INTERESTS

§ 701.   Nature of Partnership Interest

A partnership interest is personal property.

COMMENT

This section is derived from Section 18 of the 1916 Act.

§ 702.   Assignment of Partnership Interest

Except as provided in the partnership agreement, a partnership interest is assignable in whole or in part. An assignment of a partnership interest does not dissolve a limited partnership or entitle the assignee to become or to exercise any rights of a partner. An assignment entitles the assignee to receive, to the extent assigned, only the distribution to which the assignor would be entitled. Except as provided in the partnership agreement, a partner ceases to be a partner upon assignment of all his [or her] partnership interest.

COMMENT

Section 19(1) of the 1916 Act provided simply that "a limited partner's interest is assignable," raising a question whether any limitations on the right of assignment were permitted. While the first sentence of Section 702 recognizes that the power to assign may be restricted in the partnership agreement, there was no intention to affect in any way the usual rules regarding restraints on alienation of personal property. The second and third sentences of Section 702 are derived from Section 19(3) of the 1916 Act. The last sentence first appeared in the 1976 Act.

§ 703.   Rights of Creditor

On application to a court of competent jurisdiction by any judgment creditor of a partner, the court may charge the partnership interest of the partner with payment of the unsatisfied amount of the judgment with interest. To the extent so charged, the judgment creditor has only the rights of an assignee of the partnership interest. This [Act] does not deprive any partner of the benefit of any exemption laws applicable to his [or her] partnership interest.

COMMENT

Section 703 is derived from Section 22 of the 1916 Act but has not carried over some provisions that were thought to be superfluous. For example, references in Section 22(1) to specific remedies have been omitted, as has a prohibition in Section 22(2) against discharge of the lien with partnership property. Ordinary rules governing the remedies available to a creditor and the fiduciary obligations of general partners will determine those matters.

§ 704.   Right of Assignee to Become Limited Partner

(a)   An assignee of a partnership interest, including an assignee of a general partner, may become a limited partner if and to the extent that (i) the assignor gives the assignee that right in accordance with authority described in the partnership agreement, or (ii) all other partners consent.

(b)   An assignee who has become a limited partner has, to the extent assigned, the rights and powers, and is subject to the restrictions and liabilities, of a limited partner under the partnership agreement and this [Act]. An assignee who becomes a limited partner also is liable for the obligations of his [or her] assignor to make and return contributions as provided in Articles 5 and 6. However, the assignee is not obligated for liabilities unknown to the assignee at the time he [or she] became a limited partner.

(c)   If an assignee of a partnership interest becomes a limited partner, the assignor is not released from his [or her] liability to the limited partnership under Sections 207 and 502.

COMMENT

Section 704 is derived from Section 19 of the 1916 Act, but paragraph (b) defines more narrowly than Section 19 the obligations of the assignor that are automatically assumed by the assignee. Section 704 of the 1985 Act also differs from the 1976 Act to reflect the 1985 changes made in Section 201.

§ 705.   Power of Estate of Deceased or Incompetent Partner

If a partner who is an individual dies or a court of competent jurisdiction adjudges him [or her] to be incompetent to manage his [or her] person or his [or her] property, the partner's executor, administrator, guardian, conservator, or other legal representative may exercise all the partner's rights for the purpose of settling his [or her] estate or administering his [or her] property, including any power the partner had to give an assignee the right to become a limited partner. If a partner is a corporation, trust, or other entity and is dissolved or terminated, the powers of that partner may be exercised by its legal representative or successor.

COMMENT

Section 705 is derived from Section 21(1) of the 1916 Act. Former Section 21(2), making a deceased limited partner's estate liable for his liabilities as a limited partner was deleted as superfluous, with no intention of changing the liability of the estate.

ARTICLE 8
DISSOLUTION

§ 801.   Nonjudicial Dissolution

A limited partnership is dissolved and its affairs shall be wound up upon the happening of the first to occur of the following:

(1)   at the time specified in the certificate of limited partnership;

(2)   upon the happening of events specified in writing in the partnership agreement;

(3)   written consent of all partners;

(4)   an event of withdrawal of a general partner unless at the time there is at least one other general partner and the written provisions of the partnership agreement permit the business of the limited partnership to be carried on by the remaining general partner and that partner does so, but the limited partnership is not dissolved and is not required to be wound up by reason of any event of withdrawal if, within 90 days after the withdrawal, all partners agree in writing to continue the business of the limited partnership and to the appointment of one or more additional general partners if necessary or desired; or

(5)   entry of a decree of judicial dissolution under Section 802.

COMMENT

Section 801 merely collects in one place all of the events causing dissolution. Paragraph (3) is derived from Sections 9(1)(g) and 20 of the 1916 Act, but adds the 90-day grace period. Section 801 also differs from its counterpart in the 1976 Act to reflect the 1985 changes made in Section 201.

§ 802.   Judicial Dissolution

On application by or for a partner the [designate the appropriate court] court may decree dissolution of a limited partnership whenever it is not reasonably practicable to carry on the business in conformity with the partnership agreement.

COMMENT

Section 802 first appeared in the 1976 Act.

§ 803.   Winding Up

Except as provided in the partnership agreement, the general partners who have not wrongfully dissolved a limited partnership or, if none, the limited partners, may wind up the limited partnership's affairs; but the [designate the appropriate court] court may wind up the limited partnership's affairs upon application of any partner, his [or her] legal representative, or assignee.

COMMENT

Section 803 first appeared in the 1976 Act and is derived in part from Section 37 of the Uniform Partnership Act.

§ 804.   Distribution of Assets

Upon the winding up of a limited partnership, the assets shall be distributed as follows:

(1)   to creditors, including partners who are creditors, to the extent permitted by law, in satisfaction of liabilities of the limited partnership other than liabilities for distributions to partners under Section 601 or 604;

(2)   except as provided in the partnership agreement, to partners and former partners in satisfaction of liabilities for distributions under Section 601 or 604; and

(3)   except as provided in the partnership agreement, to partners first for the return of their contributions and secondly respecting their partnership interests, in the proportions in which the partners share in distributions.

COMMENT

Section 804 revises Section 23 of the 1916 Act by providing that (1) to the extent partners are also creditors, other than in respect of their interests in the partnership, they share with other creditors, (2) once the partnership's obligation to make a distribution accrues, it must be paid before any other distributions of an "equity" nature are made, and (3) general and limited partners rank on the same level except as otherwise provided in the partnership agreement.

ARTICLE 9
FOREIGN LIMITED PARTNERSHIPS

§ 901.   Law Governing

Subject to the Constitution of this State, (i) the laws of the state under which a foreign limited partnership is organized govern its organization and internal affairs and the liability of its limited partners, and (ii) a foreign limited partnership may not be denied registration by reason of any difference between those laws and the laws of this State.

COMMENT

Section 901 first appeared in the 1976 Act.

§ 902.   Registration

Before transacting business in this State, a foreign limited partnership shall register with the Secretary of State. In order to register, a foreign limited partnership shall submit to the Secretary of State, in duplicate, an application for registration as a foreign limited partnership, signed and sworn to by a general partner and setting forth:

(1)   the name of the foreign limited partnership and, if different, the name under which it proposes to register and transact business in this State;

(2)   the State and date of its formation;

(3)   the name and address of any agent for service of process on the foreign limited partnership whom the foreign limited partnership elects to appoint; the agent must be an

individual resident of this State, a domestic corporation, or a foreign corporation having a place of business in, and authorized to do business in, this State;

(4) a statement that the Secretary of State is appointed the agent of the foreign limited partnership for service of process if no agent has been appointed under paragraph (3) or, if appointed, the agent's authority has been revoked or if the agent cannot be found or served with the exercise of reasonable diligence;

(5) the address of the office required to be maintained in the state of its organization by the laws of that state or, if not so required, of the principal office of the foreign limited partnership;

(6) the name and business address of each general partner; and

(7) the address of the office at which is kept a list of the names and addresses of the limited partners and their capital contributions, together with an undertaking by the foreign limited partnership to keep those records until the foreign limited partnership's registration in this State is cancelled or withdrawn.

COMMENT

Section 902 first appeared in the 1976 Act. It was thought that requiring a full copy of the certificate of limited partnership and all amendments thereto to be filed in each state in which the partnership does business would impose an unreasonable burden on interstate limited partnerships and that the information Section 902 required to be filed would be sufficient to tell interested persons where they could write to obtain copies of those basic documents. Subdivision (3) of the 1976 Act has been omitted, and subdivisions (6) and (7) differ from their counterparts in the 1976 Act, to conform these provisions relating to the registration of foreign limited partnerships to the corresponding changes made by the Act in the provisions relating to domestic limited partnerships. The requirement that an application for registration be sworn to by a general partner is simply intended to produce the same result as is provided for in Section 204(c) with respect to certificates of domestic limited partnerships; the acceptance and endorsement by the Secretary of State (or equivalent authority) of an application which was not sworn by a general partner should be deemed a mere technical and insubstantial shortcoming, and should not result in the limited partners' being subjected to general liability for the obligations of the foreign limited partnership (see Section 907(c)).

§ 903. Issuance of Registration

(a) If the Secretary of State finds that an application for registration conforms to law and all requisite fees have been paid, he [or she] shall:

(1) endorse on the application the word "Filed," and the month, day and year of the filing thereof;

(2) file in his [or her] office a duplicate original of the application; and

(3) issue a certificate of registration to transact business in this State.

(b) The certificate of registration, together with a duplicate original of the application, shall be returned to the person who filed the application or his [or her] representative.

COMMENT

Section 903 first appeared in the 1976 Act.

§ 904. Name

A foreign limited partnership may register with the Secretary of State under any name, whether or not it is the name under which it is registered in its state of organization, that includes without abbreviation the words "limited partnership" and that could be registered by a domestic limited partnership.

COMMENT

Section 904 first appeared in the 1976 Act.

§ 905. Changes and Amendments

If any statement in the application for registration of a foreign limited partnership was false when made or any arrangements or other facts described have changed, making the application inaccurate in any respect, the foreign limited partnership shall promptly file in the office of the Secretary of State a certificate, signed and sworn to by a general partner, correcting such statement.

COMMENT

Section 905 first appeared in the 1976 Act. It corresponds to the provisions of Section 202(c) relating to domestic limited partnerships.

§ 906. Cancellation of Registration

A foreign limited partnership may cancel its registration by filing with the Secretary of State a certificate of cancellation signed and sworn to by a general partner. A cancellation does not terminate the authority of the Secretary of State to accept service of process on the foreign limited partnership with respect to [claims for relief] [causes of action] arising out of the transactions of business in this State.

COMMENT

Section 906 first appeared in the 1976 Act.

§ 907. Transaction of Business Without Registration

(a) A foreign limited partnership transacting business in this State may not maintain any action, suit, or proceeding in any court of this State until it has registered in this State.

(b) The failure of a foreign limited partnership to register in this State does not impair the validity of any contract or act of the foreign limited partnership or prevent the foreign limited partnership from defending any action, suit, or proceeding in any court of this State.

(c) A limited partner of a foreign limited partnership is not liable as a general partner of the foreign limited partnership solely by reason of having transacted business in this State without registration.

(d) A foreign limited partnership, by transacting business in this State without registration, appoints the Secretary of State as its agent for service of process with respect to [claims for relief] [causes of action] arising out of the transaction of business in this State.

COMMENT

Section 907 first appeared in the 1976 Act.

§ 908. Action by [Appropriate Official]

The [designate the appropriate official] may bring an action to restrain a foreign limited partnership from transacting business in this State in violation of this Article.

COMMENT

Section 908 first appeared in the 1976 Act.

ARTICLE 10
DERIVATIVE ACTIONS

§ 1001. Right of Action

A limited partner may bring an action in the right of a limited partnership to recover a judgment in its favor if general partners with authority to do so have refused to bring the action or if an effort to cause those general partners to bring the action is not likely to succeed.

COMMENT

Section 1001 first appeared in the 1976 Act.

§ 1002. Proper Plaintiff

In a derivative action, the plaintiff must be a partner at the time of bringing the action and (i) must have been a partner at the time of the transaction of which he [or she] complains or (ii) his [or her] status as a partner must have devolved upon him [or her] by operation of law or pursuant to the terms of the partnership agreement from a person who was a partner at the time of the transaction.

COMMENT

Section 1002 first appeared in the 1976 Act.

§ 1003. Pleading

In a derivative action, the complaint shall set forth with particularity the effort of the plaintiff to secure initiation of the action by a general partner or the reasons for not making the effort.

COMMENT

Section 1003 first appeared in the 1976 Act.

§ 1004. Expenses

If a derivative action is successful, in whole or in part, or if anything is received by the plaintiff as a result of a judgment, compromise or settlement of an action or claim, the court may award the plaintiff reasonable expenses, including reasonable attorney's fees, and shall direct him [or her] to remit to the limited partnership the remainder of those proceeds received by him [or her].

COMMENT

Section 1004 first appeared in the 1976 Act.

ARTICLE 11
MISCELLANEOUS

§ 1101. Construction and Application

This [Act] shall be so applied and construed to effectuate its general purpose to make uniform the law with respect to the subject of this [Act] among states enacting it.

COMMENT

Because the principles set out in Sections 28(1) and 29 of the 1916 Act have become so universally established, it was felt that the 1976 and 1985 Acts need not contain express provisions to the same effect. However, it is intended that the principles enunciated in those provisions of the 1916 Act also apply to this Act.

§ 1102. Short Title

This [Act] may be cited as the Uniform Limited Partnership Act.

§ 1103. Severability

If any provision of this [Act] or its application to any person or circumstance is held invalid, the invalidity does not affect other provisions or applications of the [Act] which can be given effect without the invalid provision or application, and to this end the provisions of this [Act] are severable.

§ 1104. Effective Date, Extended Effective Date and Repeal

Except as set forth below, the effective date of this [Act] is _____ and the following acts [list existing limited partnership acts] are hereby repealed:

(1) The existing provisions for execution and filing of certificates of limited partnerships and amendments thereunder and cancellations thereof continue in effect until [specify time required to create central filing system], the extended effective date, and Sections 102, 103, 104, 105, 201, 202, 203, 204 and 206 are not effective until the extended effective date.

(2) Section 402, specifying the conditions under which a general partner ceases to be a member of a limited partnership, is not effective until the extended effective date, and the applicable provisions of existing law continue to govern until the extended effective date.

(3) Sections 501, 502 and 608 apply only to contributions and distributions made after the effective date of this [Act].

(4) Section 704 applies only to assignments made after the effective date of this [Act].

(5) Article 9, dealing with registration of foreign limited partnerships, is not effective until the extended effective date.

(6) Unless otherwise agreed by the partners, the applicable provisions of existing law governing allocation of profits and losses (rather than the provisions of Section 503), distributions to a withdrawing partner (rather than the provisions of Section 604), and distribution of assets upon the winding up of a limited partnership (rather than the provisions of Section 804) govern limited partnerships formed before the effective date of this [Act].

COMMENT

Subdivisions (6) and (7) did not appear in Section 1104 of the 1976 Act. They are included in the 1985 Act to ensure that the application of the Act to limited partnerships formed and existing before the Act becomes effective would not violate constitutional prohibitions against the impairment of contracts.

§ 1105. Rules for Cases not Provided for in this [Act]

In any case not provided for in this [Act] the provisions of the Uniform Partnership Act govern.

COMMENT

The result provided for in Section 1105 would obtain even in its absence in a jurisdiction which had adopted the Uniform Partnership Act, by operation of Section 6 of that act.

§ 1106. Savings Clause

The repeal of any statutory provision by this [Act] does not impair, or otherwise affect, the organization or the continued existence of a limited partnership existing at the effective date of this [Act], nor does the repeal of any existing statutory provision by this [Act] impair any contract or affect any right accrued before the effective date of this [Act].

COMMENT

Section 1106 did not appear in the 1976 Act. It was included in the 1985 Act to ensure that the application of the Act to limited partnerships formed and existing before the Act becomes effective would not violate constitutional prohibitions against the impairment of contracts.

F. UNIFORM LIMITED PARTNERSHIP ACT (2001)

Table of Sections

[ARTICLE] 1. GENERAL PROVISIONS

[ARTICLE] 2. FORMATION; CERTIFICATE OF LIMITED PARTNERSHIP AND OTHER FILINGS

[ARTICLE] 3. LIMITED PARTNERS

UNIFORM LIMITED PARTNERSHIP ACT (2001)

[ARTICLE] 4.   GENERAL PARTNERS

[ARTICLE] 5.   CONTRIBUTIONS AND DISTRIBUTIONS

[ARTICLE] 6.   DISSOCIATION

[ARTICLE] 7.   TRANSFERABLE INTERESTS AND RIGHTS OF TRANSFEREES AND CREDITORS

[ARTICLE] 8.   DISSOLUTION

UNIFORM LIMITED PARTNERSHIP ACT (2001)

UNIFORM LIMITED PARTNERSHIP ACT (2001)

PREFATORY NOTE

The Act's Overall Approach

The new Limited Partnership Act is a "stand alone" act, "de-linked" from both the original general partnership act ("UPA") and the Revised Uniform Partnership Act ("RUPA"). To be able to stand alone, the Limited Partnership incorporates many provisions from RUPA and some from the Uniform Limited Liability Company Act ("ULLCA"). As a result, the new Act is far longer and more complex than its immediate predecessor, the Revised Uniform Limited Partnership Act ("RULPA").

The new Act has been drafted for a world in which limited liability partnerships and limited liability companies can meet many of the needs formerly met by limited partnerships. This Act therefore targets two types of enterprises that seem largely beyond the scope of LLPs and LLCs: (i) sophisticated, manager-entrenched commercial deals whose participants commit for the long term, and (ii) estate planning arrangements (family limited partnerships). This Act accordingly assumes that, more often than not, people utilizing it will want:

- strong centralized management, strongly entrenched, and
- passive investors with little control over or right to exit the entity

The Act's rules, and particularly its default rules, have been designed to reflect these assumptions.

The Decision to "De-Link" and Create a Stand Alone Act

Unlike this Act, RULPA is not a stand alone statute. RULPA was drafted to rest on and link to the UPA. RULPA Section 1105 states that "In any case not provided for in this [Act] the provisions of the Uniform Partnership Act govern." UPA Section 6(2) in turn provides that "this Act shall apply to limited partnerships except in so far as the statutes relating to such partnerships are inconsistent herewith." More particularly, RULPA Section 403 defines the rights, powers, restrictions and liabilities of a "general partner of a limited partnership" by equating them to the rights, powers, restrictions and liabilities of "a partner in a partnership without limited partners."

This arrangement has not been completely satisfactory, because the consequences of linkage are not always clear. *See, e.g., Frye v. Manacare Ltd.*, 431 So.2d 181, 183–84 (Fla. Dist. Ct. App. 1983) (applying UPA Section 42 in favor of a limited partner), *Porter v. Barnhouse*, 354 N.W.2d 227, 232–33 (Iowa 1984) (declining to apply UPA Section 42 in favor of a limited partner) and *Baltzell-Wolfe Agencies, Inc. v. Car Wash Investments No. 1, Ltd.*, 389 N.E.2d 517, 518–20 (Ohio App. 1978) (holding that neither the specific provisions of the general partnership statute nor those of the limited partnership statute determined the liability of a person who had withdrawn as general partner of a limited partnership). Moreover, in some instances the "not inconsistent" rules of the UPA can be inappropriate for the fundamentally different relations involved in a limited partnership.

In any event, the promulgation of RUPA unsettled matters. RUPA differs substantially from the UPA, and the drafters of RUPA expressly declined to decide whether RUPA provides a suitable base and link for the limited partnership statute. According to RUPA's Prefatory Note:

Partnership law no longer governs limited partnerships pursuant to the provisions of RUPA itself. First, limited partnerships are not "partnerships" within the RUPA definition. Second, UPA Section 6(2), which provides that the UPA governs limited partnerships in cases not provided for in the Uniform Limited Partnership Act (1976) (1985) ("RULPA") has been deleted. No substantive change in result is intended, however. Section 1105 of RULPA already provides that the UPA governs in any case not provided for in RULPA, and thus the express linkage in RUPA is unnecessary. Structurally, it is more appropriately left to RULPA to determine the applicability of RUPA to limited partnerships. It is contemplated that the Conference will review the linkage question carefully, although no changes in RULPA may be necessary despite the many changes in RUPA.

The linkage question was the first major issue considered and decided by this Act's Drafting Committee. Since the Conference has recommended the repeal of the UPA, it made no sense to recommend retaining the UPA as the base and link for a revised or new limited partnership act. The Drafting Committee therefore had to choose between recommending linkage to the new general partnership act (i.e., RUPA) or recommending de-linking and a stand alone act.

The Committee saw several substantial advantages to de-linking. A stand alone statute would:

- be more convenient, providing a single, self-contained source of statutory authority for issues pertaining to limited partnerships;

- eliminate confusion as to which issues were solely subject to the limited partnership act and which required reference (i.e., linkage) to the general partnership act; and

- rationalize future case law, by ending the automatic link between the cases concerning partners in a general partnership and issues pertaining to general partners in a limited partnership.

Thus, a stand alone act seemed likely to promote efficiency, clarity, and coherence in the law of limited partnerships.

In contrast, recommending linkage would have required the Drafting Committee to (1) consider each provision of RUPA and determine whether the provision addressed a matter provided for in RULPA; (2) for each RUPA provision which addressed a matter not provided for in RULPA, determine whether the provision stated an appropriate rule for limited partnerships; and (3) for each matter addressed both by RUPA and RULPA, determine whether RUPA or RULPA stated the better rule for limited partnerships.

That approach was unsatisfactory for at least two reasons. No matter how exhaustive the Drafting Committee's analysis might be, the Committee could not guarantee that courts and practitioners would reach the same conclusions. Therefore, in at least some situations linkage would have produced ambiguity. In addition, the Drafting Committee could not guarantee that all currently appropriate links would remain appropriate as courts begin to apply and interpret RUPA. Even if the Committee recommended linkage, RUPA was destined to be interpreted primarily in the context of general partnerships. Those interpretations might not make sense for limited partnership law, because the modern limited partnership involves fundamentally different relations than those involved in "the small, often informal, partnership" that is "[t]he primary focus of RUPA." RUPA, Prefatory Note.

The Drafting Committee therefore decided to draft and recommend a stand alone act.

Availability of LLLP Status

Following the example of a growing number of States, this Act provides for limited liability limited partnerships. In a limited liability limited partnership ("LLLP"), no partner—whether general or limited—is liable on account of partner status for the limited partnership's obligations. Both general and limited partners benefit from a full, status-based liability shield that is equivalent to the shield enjoyed by corporate shareholders, LLC members, and partners in an LLP.

This Act is designed to serve preexisting limited partnerships as well as limited partnerships formed after the Act's enactment. Most of those preexisting limited partnership will not be LLLPs, and accordingly the Act does not prefer or presume LLLP status. Instead, the Act makes LLLP status available through a simple statement in the certificate of limited partnership. *See* Sections 102(9), 201(a)(4) and 404(c).

UNIFORM LIMITED PARTNERSHIP ACT (2001)

Liability Shield for Limited Partners

RULPA provides only a restricted liability shield for limited partners. The shield is at risk for any limited partner who "participates in the control of the business." RULPA Section 303(a). Although this "control rule" is subject to a lengthy list of safe harbors, RULPA Section 303(b), in a world with LLPs, LLCs and, most importantly, LLLPs, the rule is an anachronism. This Act therefore eliminates the control rule and provides a full, status-based shield against limited partner liability for entity obligations. The shield applies whether or not the limited partnership is an LLLP. *See* Section 303.

Transition Issues

Following RUPA's example, this Act provides (i) an effective date, after which all newly formed limited partnerships are subject to this Act; (ii) an optional period, during which limited partnerships formed under a predecessor statute may elect to become subject to this Act; and (iii) a mandatory date, on which all preexisting limited partnerships become subject to this Act by operation of law.

A few provisions of this Act differ so substantially from prior law that they should not apply automatically to a preexisting limited partnership. Section 1206(c) lists these provisions and states that each remains inapplicable to a preexisting limited partnership, unless the limited partnership elects for the provision to apply.

Comparison of RULPA and this Act

The following table compares some of the major characteristics of RULPA and this Act. In most instances, the rules involved are "default" rules—i.e., subject to change by the partnership agreement.

Characteristic	RULPA	this Act
relationship to general partnership act	linked, Sections 1105, 403; UPA Section 6(2)	de-linked (but many RUPA provisions incorporated)
permitted purposes	subject to any specified exceptions, "any business that a partnership without limited partners may carry on, "Section 106	any lawful purpose, Section 104(b)
constructive notice via publicly filed documents	only that limited partnership exists and that designated general partners are general partners, Section 208	RULPA constructive notice provisions carried forward, Section 103(c), plus constructive notice, 90 days after appropriate filing, of: general partner dissociation and of limited partnership dissolution, termination, merger and conversion, Section 103(d)
duration	specified in certificate of limited partnership, Section 201(a)(4)	perpetual, Section 104(c); subject to change in partnership agreement
use of limited partner name in entity name	prohibited, except in unusual circumstances, Section 102(2)	permitted, Section108(a)
annual report	none	required, Section 210
limited partner liability for entity debts	none unless limited partner "participates in the control of the business" and person "transact[s] business with the limited partnership reasonably believing . . . that the limited partner is a general partner," Section 303(a); safe harbor	none, regardless of whether the limited partnership is an LLLP, "even if the limited partner participates in the management and control of the limited partnership," Section 303

UNIFORM LIMITED PARTNERSHIP ACT (2001)

Characteristic	RULPA	this Act
	lists many activities that do not constitute participating in the control of the business, Section 303(b)	
limited partner duties	none specified	no fiduciary duties "solely by reason of being a limited partner," Section 305(a); each limited partner is obliged to "discharge duties . . . and exercise rights consistently with the obligation of good faith and fair dealing," Section 305(b)
partner access to information—required records/information	all partners have right of access; no requirement of good cause; Act does not state whether partnership agreement may limit access; Sections 105(b) and 305(1)	list of required information expanded slightly; Act expressly states that partner does not have to show good cause; Sections 304(a), 407(a); however, the partnership agreement may set reasonable restrictions on access to and use of required information, Section 110(b)(4), and limited partnership may impose reasonable restrictions on the use of information, Sections 304(g) and 407(f)
partner access to information—other information	limited partners have the right to obtain other relevant information "upon reasonable demand," Section 305(2); general partner rights linked to general partnership act, Section 403	for limited partners, RULPA approach essentially carried forward, with procedures and standards for making a reasonable demand stated in greater detail, plus requirement that limited partnership supply known material information when limited partner consent sought, Section 304; general partner access rights made explicit, following ULLCA and RUPA, including obligation of limited partnership and general partners to volunteer certain information, Section 407; access rights provided for former partners, Sections 304 and 407
general partner liability for entity debts	complete, automatic and formally inescapable, Section 403(b) (n.b.—in practice, most modern limited partnerships have used a general partner that has its own liability shield; *e.g.,* a corporation or limited liability company)	LLLP status available via a simple statement in the certificate of limited partnership, Sections 102(9), 201(a)(4); LLLP status provides a full liability shield to all general partners, Section 404(c); if the limited partnership is not an LLLP, general partners are liable just as under RULPA, Section 404(a)
general partner duties	linked to duties of partners in a general partnership, Section 403	RUPA general partner duties imported, Section 408; general partner's non-compete duty continues during winding up, Section 408(b)(3)

UNIFORM LIMITED PARTNERSHIP ACT (2001)

Characteristic	RULPA	this Act
allocation of profits, losses and distributions	provides separately for sharing of profits and losses, Section 503, and for sharing of distributions, Section 504; allocates each according to contributions made and not returned	eliminates as unnecessary the allocation rule for profits and losses; allocates distributions according to contributions made, Section 503 (n.b.—in the default mode, the Act's formulation produces the same result as RULPA formulation)
partner liability for distributions	recapture liability if distribution involved "the return of . . . contribution"; one year recapture liability if distribution rightful, Section 608(a); six year recapture liability if wrongful, Section 608(b)	following ULLCA Sections 406 and 407, the Act adopts the RMBCA approach to improper distributions, Sections 508 and 509
limited partner voluntary dissociation	theoretically, limited partner may withdraw on six months notice unless partnership agreement specifies a term for the limited partnership or withdrawal events for limited partner, Section 603; practically, virtually every partnership agreement specifies a term, thereby eliminating the right to withdraw (n.b.—due to estate planning concerns, several States have amended RULPA to prohibit limited partner withdrawal unless otherwise provided in the partnership agreement)	no "right to dissociate as a limited partner before the termination of the limited partnership," Section 601(a); power to dissociate expressly recognized, Section 601(b)(1), but can be eliminated by the partnership agreement
limited partner involuntary dissociation	not addressed	lengthy list of causes, Section 601(b), taken with some modification from RUPA
limited partner dissociation—payout	"fair value . . . based upon [the partner's] right to share in distributions," Section 604	no payout; person becomes transferee of its own transferable interest, Section 602(3)
general partner voluntary dissociation	right exists unless otherwise provided in partnership agreement, Section 602; power exists regardless of partnership agreement, Section 602	RULPA rule carried forward, although phrased differently, Section 604(a); dissociation before termination of the limited partnership is defined as wrongful, Section 604(b)(2)
general partner involuntary dissociation	Section 402 lists causes	following RUPA, Section 603 expands the list of causes, including expulsion by court order, Section 603(5)
general partner dissociation—payout	"fair value . . . based upon [the partner's] right to share in distributions," Section 604, subject to offset for damages caused by wrongful withdrawal, Section 602	no payout; person becomes transferee of its own transferable interest, Section 605(5)
transfer of partner interest—nomenclature	"Assignment of Partnership Interest," Section 702	"Transfer of Partner's Transferable Interest," Section 702

UNIFORM LIMITED PARTNERSHIP ACT (2001)

Characteristic	RULPA	this Act
transfer of partner interest—substance	economic rights fully transferable, but management rights and partner status are not transferable, Section 702	same rule, but Sections 701 and 702 follow RUPA's more detailed and less oblique formulation
rights of creditor of partner	limited to charging order, Section 703	essentially the same rule, but, following RUPA and ULLCA, the Act has a more elaborate provision that expressly extends to creditors of transferees, Section 703
dissolution by partner consent	requires unanimous written consent, Section 801(3)	requires consent of "all general partners and of limited partners owning a majority of the rights to receive distributions as limited partners at the time the consent is to be effective," Section 801(2)
dissolution following dissociation of a general partner	occurs automatically unless all partners agree to continue the business and, if there is no remaining general partner, to appoint a replacement general partner, Section 801(4)	if at least one general partner remains, no dissolution unless "within 90 days after the dissociation . . . partners owning a majority of the rights to receive distributions as partners" consent to dissolve the limited partnership; Section 801(3)(A); if no general partner remains, dissolution occurs upon the passage of 90 days after the dissociation, unless before that deadline limited partners owning a majority of the rights to receive distributions owned by limited partners consent to continue the business and admit at least one new general partner and a new general partner is admitted, Section 801(3)(B)
filings related to entity termination	certificate of limited partnership to be cancelled when limited partnership dissolves and begins winding up, Section 203	limited partnership may amend certificate to indicate dissolution, Section 803(b)(1), and may file statement of termination indicating that winding up has been completed and the limited partnership is terminated, Section 203
procedures for barring claims against dissolved limited partnership	none	following ULLCA Sections 807 and 808, the Act adopts the RMBCA approach providing for giving notice and barring claims, Sections 806 and 807
conversions and mergers	no provision	Article 11 permits conversions to and from and mergers with any "organization," defined as "a general partnership, including a limited liability partnership; limited partnership, including a limited liability limited partnership; limited liability company; business trust;

Characteristic	RULPA	this Act
		corporation; or any other entity having a governing statute . . . [including] domestic and foreign entities regardless of whether organized for profit." Section 1101(8)
writing requirements	some provisions pertain only to written understandings; *see, e.g.,* Sections 401 (partnership agreement may "provide in writing for the admission of additional general partners"; such admission also permitted "with the written consent of all partners"), 502(a) (limited partner's promise to contribute "is not enforceable unless set out in a writing signed by the limited partner"), 801(2) and (3) (dissolution occurs "upon the happening of events specified in writing in the partnership agreement" and upon "written consent of all partners"), 801(4) (dissolution avoided following withdrawal of a general partner if "all partners agree in writing")	removes virtually all writing requirements; but does require that certain information be maintained in record form, Section 111

[ARTICLE] 1.   GENERAL PROVISIONS

§ 101.   Short Title

This [Act] may be cited as the Uniform Limited Partnership Act [year of enactment].

§ 102.   Definitions

In this [Act]:

(1)   "Certificate of limited partnership" means the certificate required by Section 201. The term includes the certificate as amended or restated.

(2)   "Contribution", except in the phrase "right of contribution," means any benefit provided by a person to a limited partnership in order to become a partner or in the person's capacity as a partner.

(3)   "Debtor in bankruptcy" means a person that is the subject of:

(A)   an order for relief under Title 11 of the United States Code or a comparable order under a successor statute of general application; or

(B)   a comparable order under federal, state, or foreign law governing insolvency.

(4)   "Designated office" means:

(A)   with respect to a limited partnership, the office that the limited partnership is required to designate and maintain under Section 114; and

(B)   with respect to a foreign limited partnership, its principal office.

(5)   "Distribution" means a transfer of money or other property from a limited partnership to a partner in the partner's capacity as a partner or to a transferee on account of a transferable interest owned by the transferee.

(6) "Foreign limited liability limited partnership" means a foreign limited partnership whose general partners have limited liability for the obligations of the foreign limited partnership under a provision similar to Section 404(c).

(7) "Foreign limited partnership" means a partnership formed under the laws of a jurisdiction other than this State and required by those laws to have one or more general partners and one or more limited partners. The term includes a foreign limited liability limited partnership.

(8) "General partner" means:

(A) with respect to a limited partnership, a person that:

(i) becomes a general partner under Section 401; or

(ii) was a general partner in a limited partnership when the limited partnership became subject to this [Act] under Section 1206(a) or (b); and

(B) with respect to a foreign limited partnership, a person that has rights, powers, and obligations similar to those of a general partner in a limited partnership.

(9) "Limited liability limited partnership", except in the phrase "foreign limited liability limited partnership", means a limited partnership whose certificate of limited partnership states that the limited partnership is a limited liability limited partnership.

(10) "Limited partner" means:

(A) with respect to a limited partnership, a person that:

(i) becomes a limited partner under Section 301; or

(ii) was a limited partner in a limited partnership when the limited partnership became subject to this [Act] under Section 1206(a) or (b); and

(B) with respect to a foreign limited partnership, a person that has rights, powers, and obligations similar to those of a limited partner in a limited partnership.

(11) "Limited partnership", except in the phrases "foreign limited partnership" and "foreign limited liability limited partnership", means an entity, having one or more general partners and one or more limited partners, which is formed under this [Act] by two or more persons or becomes subject to this [Act] under [Article] 11 or Section 1206(a) or (b). The term includes a limited liability limited partnership.

(12) "Partner" means a limited partner or general partner.

(13) "Partnership agreement" means the partners' agreement, whether oral, implied, in a record, or in any combination, concerning the limited partnership. The term includes the agreement as amended.

(14) "Person" means an individual, corporation, business trust, estate, trust, partnership, limited liability company, association, joint venture, government; governmental subdivision, agency, or instrumentality; public corporation, or any other legal or commercial entity.

(15) "Person dissociated as a general partner" means a person dissociated as a general partner of a limited partnership.

(16) "Principal office" means the office where the principal executive office of a limited partnership or foreign limited partnership is located, whether or not the office is located in this State.

(17) "Record" means information that is inscribed on a tangible medium or that is stored in an electronic or other medium and is retrievable in perceivable form.

(18) "Required information" means the information that a limited partnership is required to maintain under Section 111.

(19) "Sign" means:

(A) to execute or adopt a tangible symbol with the present intent to authenticate a record; or

(B) to attach or logically associate an electronic symbol, sound, or process to or with a record with the present intent to authenticate the record.

(20) "State" means a State of the United States, the District of Columbia, Puerto Rico, the United States Virgin Islands, or any territory or insular possession subject to the jurisdiction of the United States.

(21) "Transfer" includes an assignment, conveyance, deed, bill of sale, lease, mortgage, security interest, encumbrance, gift, and transfer by operation of law.

(22) "Transferable interest" means a partner's right to receive distributions.

(23) "Transferee" means a person to which all or part of a transferable interest has been transferred, whether or not the transferor is a partner.

COMMENT

This section contains definitions applicable throughout the Act. Section 1101 provides additional definitions applicable within Article 11.

Paragraph 8(A)(i) [General partner]—A partnership agreement may vary Section 401 and provide a process or mechanism for becoming a general partner which is different from or additional to the rules stated in that section. For the purposes of this definition, a person who becomes a general partner pursuant to a provision of the partnership agreement "becomes a general partner under Section 401."

Paragraph 10(A)(i) [Limited partner]—The Comment to Paragraph 8(A)(i) applies here as well. For the purposes of this definition, a person who becomes a limited partner pursuant to a provision of the partnership agreement "becomes a limited partner under Section 301."

Paragraph (11) [Limited partnership]—This definition pertains to what is commonly termed a "domestic" limited partnership. The definition encompasses: (i) limited partnerships originally formed under this Act, including limited partnerships formed under Section 1101(11) to be the surviving organization in a merger; (ii) any entity that becomes subject to this Act by converting into a limited partnership under Article 11; (iii) any preexisting domestic limited partnership that elects pursuant to Section 1206(a) to become subject to this Act; and (iv) all other preexisting domestic limited partnerships when they become subject to this Act under Section 1206(b).

Following the approach of predecessor law, RULPA Section 101(7), this definition contains two substantive requirements. First, it is of the essence of a limited partnership to have two classes of partners. Accordingly, under Section 101(11) a limited partnership must have at least one general and one limited partner. Section 801(3)(B) and (4) provide that a limited partnership dissolves if its sole general partner or sole limited partner dissociates and the limited partnership fails to admit a replacement within 90 days of the dissociation. The 90 day limitation is a default rule, but, in light of Section 101(11), a limited partnership may not indefinitely delay "having one or more general partners and one or more limited partners."

It is also of the essence of a limited partnership to have at least two partners. Section 101(11) codifies this requirement by referring to a limited partnership as "an entity . . . which is formed under this [Act] by two or more persons." Thus, while the same person may be both a general and limited partner, Section 113 (Dual Capacity), one person alone cannot be the "two persons" contemplated by this definition. However, nothing in this definition prevents two closely affiliated persons from satisfying the two person requirement.

Paragraph (13) [Partnership agreement]—Section 110 is essential to understanding the significance of the partnership agreement. *See also* Section 201(d) (resolving inconsistencies between the certificate of limited partnership and the partnership agreement).

Paragraph (21) [Transfer]—Following RUPA, this Act uses the words "transfer" and "transferee" rather than the words "assignment" and "assignee." *See* RUPA Section 503.

The reference to "transfer by operation of law" is significant in connection with Section 702 (Transfer of Partner's Transferable Interest). That section severely restricts a transferee's rights (absent the consent of the partners), and this definition makes those restrictions applicable, for example, to transfers ordered by a family court as part of a divorce proceeding and transfers resulting from the death of a partner.

Paragraph (23) [Transferee]—*See* comment to Paragraph 21 for an explanation of why this Act refers to "transferee" rather than "assignee."

§ 103. Knowledge and Notice

(a) A person knows a fact if the person has actual knowledge of it.

(b) A person has notice of a fact if the person:

(1) knows of it;

(2) has received a notification of it;

(3) has reason to know it exists from all of the facts known to the person at the time in question; or

(4) has notice of it under subsection (c) or (d).

(c) A certificate of limited partnership on file in the [office of the Secretary of State] is notice that the partnership is a limited partnership and the persons designated in the certificate as general partners are general partners. Except as otherwise provided in subsection (d), the certificate is not notice of any other fact.

(d) A person has notice of:

(1) another person's dissociation as a general partner, 90 days after the effective date of an amendment to the certificate of limited partnership which states that the other person has dissociated or 90 days after the effective date of a statement of dissociation pertaining to the other person, whichever occurs first;

(2) a limited partnership's dissolution, 90 days after the effective date of an amendment to the certificate of limited partnership stating that the limited partnership is dissolved;

(3) a limited partnership's termination, 90 days after the effective date of a statement of termination;

(4) a limited partnership's conversion under [Article] 11, 90 days after the effective date of the articles of conversion; or

(5) a merger under [Article] 11, 90 days after the effective date of the articles of merger.

(e) A person notifies or gives a notification to another person by taking steps reasonably required to inform the other person in ordinary course, whether or not the other person learns of it.

(f) A person receives a notification when the notification:

(1) comes to the person's attention; or

(2) is delivered at the person's place of business or at any other place held out by the person as a place for receiving communications.

(g) Except as otherwise provided in subsection (h), a person other than an individual knows, has notice, or receives a notification of a fact for purposes of a particular transaction when the individual conducting the transaction for the person knows, has notice, or receives a notification of the fact, or in any event when the fact would have been brought to the individual's attention if the person had exercised reasonable diligence. A person other than an individual exercises reasonable diligence if it maintains reasonable routines for communicating significant information to the individual conducting the transaction for the person and there is reasonable compliance with the routines. Reasonable diligence does not require an individual acting for the person to communicate information unless the communication is part of the individual's regular duties or the individual has reason to know of the transaction and that the transaction would be materially affected by the information.

(h)   A general partner's knowledge, notice, or receipt of a notification of a fact relating to the limited partnership is effective immediately as knowledge of, notice to, or receipt of a notification by the limited partnership, except in the case of a fraud on the limited partnership committed by or with the consent of the general partner. A limited partner's knowledge, notice, or receipt of a notification of a fact relating to the limited partnership is not effective as knowledge of, notice to, or receipt of a notification by the limited partnership.

COMMENT

Source—RUPA Section 102; RULPA Section 208.

Notice and the relationship among subsections (b), (c) and (d)—These subsections provide separate and independent avenues through which a person can have notice of a fact. A person has notice of a fact as soon as any of the avenues applies.

Example: A limited partnership dissolves and amends its certificate of limited partnership to indicate dissolution. The amendment is effective on March 1. On March 15, Person #1 has reason to know of the dissolution and therefore has "notice" of the dissolution under Section 103(b)(3) even though Section 103(d)(2) does not yet apply. Person #2 does not have actual knowledge of the dissolution until June 15. Nonetheless, under Section 103(d)(2) Person #2 has "notice" of the dissolution on May 30.

Subsection (c)—This subsection provides what is commonly called constructive notice and comes essentially verbatim from RULPA Section 208. As for the significance of constructive notice "that the partnership is a limited partnership," *see Water, Waste & Land, Inc. v. Lanham*, 955 P.2d 997, 1001–1003 (Colo. 1998) (interpreting a comparable provision of the Colorado LLC statute and holding the provision ineffective to change common law agency principles, including the rules relating to the liability of an agent that transacts business for an undisclosed principal).

As for constructive notice that "the persons designated in the certificate as general partners are general partners," Section 201(a)(3) requires the initial certificate of limited partnership to name each general partner, and Section 202(b) requires a limited partnership to promptly amend its certificate of limited partnership to reflect any change in the identity of its general partners. Nonetheless, it will be possible, albeit improper, for a person to be designated in the certificate of limited partnership as a general partner without having become a general partner as contemplated by Section 401. Likewise, it will be possible for a person to have become a general partner under Section 401 without being designated as a general partner in the certificate of limited partnership. According to the last clause of this subsection, the fact that a person is **not** listed . . . in the certificate as a general partner is **not** notice that the person is **not** a general partner. For further discussion of this point, *see* the Comment to Section 401.

If the partnership agreement and the public record are inconsistent, Section 201(d) applies (partnership agreement controls *inter se*; public record controls as to third parties who have relied). *See also* Section 202(b) (requiring the limited partnership to amend its certificate of limited partnership to keep accurate the listing of general partners), 202(c) (requiring a general partner to take corrective action when the general partner knows that the certificate of limited partnership contains false information), and 208 (imposing liability for false information in *inter alia* the certificate of limited partnership).

Subsection (d)—This subsection also provides what is commonly called constructive notice and works in conjunction with other sections of this Act to curtail the power to bind and personal liability of general partners and persons dissociated as general partners. *See* Sections 402, 606, 607, 804, 805, 1111, and 1112. Following RUPA (in substance, although not in form), the constructive notice begins 90 days after the effective date of the filed record. For the Act's rules on delayed effective dates, *see* Section 206(c).

The 90-day delay applies only to the constructive notice and not to the event described in the filed record.

Example: On March 15, X dissociates as a general partner from XYZ Limited Partnership by giving notice to XYZ. *See* Section 603(1). On March 20, XYZ amends its certificate of limited partnership to remove X's name from the list of general partners. *See* Section 202(b)(2).

X's **dissociation** is effective March 15. If on March 16 X purports to be a general partner of XYZ and under Section 606(a) binds XYZ to some obligation, X will be liable under Section 606(b) as a "person dissociated as a general partner."

On June 13 (90 days after March 15), the world has constructive notice of X's dissociation as a general partner. Beginning on that date, X will lack the power to bind XYZ. *See* Section 606(a)(2)(B) (person dissociated as a general partner can bind the limited partnership only if, *inter alia*, "at the time the other party enters into the transaction ... the other party does not have notice of the dissociation").

Constructive notice under this subsection applies to partners and transferees as well as other persons.

Subsection (e)—The phrase "person learns of it" in this subsection is equivalent to the phrase "knows of it" in subsection (b)(1).

Subsection (h)—Under this subsection and Section 302, information possessed by a person that is only a limited partner is not attributable to the limited partnership. However, information possessed by a person that is both a general partner and a limited partner is attributable to the limited partnership. *See* Section 113 (Dual Capacity).

§ 104. Nature, Purpose, and Duration of Entity

(a) A limited partnership is an entity distinct from its partners. A limited partnership is the same entity regardless of whether its certificate states that the limited partnership is a limited liability limited partnership.

(b) A limited partnership may be organized under this [Act] for any lawful purpose.

(c) A limited partnership has a perpetual duration.

COMMENT

Subsection (a)—Acquiring or relinquishing an LLLP shield changes only the rules governing a general partner's liability for subsequently incurred obligations of the limited partnership. The underlying entity is unaffected.

Subsection (b)—In contrast with RULPA Section 106, this Act does not require a limited partnership to have a business purpose. However, many of the Act's default rules presuppose at least a profit-making purpose. *See, e.g.,* Section 503 (providing for the sharing of distributions in proportion to the value of contributions), 701 (defining a transferable interest in terms of the right to receive distributions), 801 (allocating the right to consent to cause or avoid dissolution in proportion to partners' rights to receive distributions), and 812 (providing that, after a dissolved limited partnership has paid its creditors, "[a]ny surplus remaining ... must be paid in cash as a distribution" to partners and transferees). If a limited partnership is organized for an essentially non-pecuniary purpose, the organizers should carefully review the Act's default rules and override them as necessary via the partnership agreement.

Subsection (c)—The partnership agreement has the power to vary this subsection, either by stating a definite term or by specifying an event or events which cause dissolution. Sections 110(a) and 801(1). Section 801 also recognizes several other occurrences that cause dissolution. Thus, the public record pertaining to a limited partnership will not necessarily reveal whether the limited partnership actually has a perpetual duration.

The public record might also fail to reveal whether the limited partnership has in fact dissolved. A dissolved limited partnership may amend its certificate of limited partnership to indicate dissolution but is not required to do so. Section 803(b)(1).

Predecessor law took a somewhat different approach. RULPA Section 201(4) required the certificate of limited partnership to state "the latest date upon which the limited partnership is to dissolve." Although RULPA Section 801(2) provided for a limited partnership to dissolve "upon the happening of events specified in writing in the partnership agreement," RULPA Section 203 required the limited partnership to file a certificate of cancellation to indicate that dissolution had occurred.

§ 105.   Powers

A limited partnership has the powers to do all things necessary or convenient to carry on its activities, including the power to sue, be sued, and defend in its own name and to maintain an action against a partner for harm caused to the limited partnership by a breach of the partnership agreement or violation of a duty to the partnership.

COMMENT

This Act omits as unnecessary any detailed list of specific powers. The power to sue and be sued is mentioned specifically so that Section 110(b)(1) can prohibit the partnership agreement from varying that power. The power to maintain an action against a partner is mentioned specifically to establish that the limited partnership itself has standing to enforce the partnership agreement.

§ 106.   Governing Law

The law of this State governs relations among the partners of a limited partnership and between the partners and the limited partnership and the liability of partners as partners for an obligation of the limited partnership.

COMMENT

To partially define its scope, this section uses the phrase "relations among the partners of a limited partnership and between the partners and the limited partnership." Section 110(a) uses essentially identical language in defining the proper realm of the partnership agreement: "relations among the partners and between the partners and the partnership."

Despite the similarity of language, this section has no bearing on the power of a partnership agreement to vary other provisions of this Act. It is quite possible for a provision of this Act to involve "relations among the partners of a limited partnership and between the partners and the limited partnership" and thus come within this section, and yet not be subject to variation by the partnership agreement. Although Section 110(a) grants plenary authority to the partnership agreement to regulate "relations among the partners and between the partners and the partnership," that authority is subject to Section 110(b).

For example, Section 408 (General Standards of General Partner's Conduct) certainly involves "relations among the partners of a limited partnership and between the partners and the limited partnership." Therefore, according to this section, Section 408 applies to a limited partnership formed or otherwise subject to this Act. Just as certainly, Section 408 pertains to "relations among the partners and between the partners and the partnership" for the purposes of Section 110(a), and therefore the partnership agreement may properly address matters covered by Section 408. However, Section 110(b)(5), (6), and (7) limit the power of the partnership agreement to vary the rules stated in Section 408. *See also, e.g.*, Section 502(c) (stating creditor's rights, which are protected under Section 110(b)(13) from being restricted by the partnership agreement) and Comment to Section 509.

This section also applies to "the liability of partners as partners for an obligation of a limited partnership." The phrase "as partners" contemplates the liability shield for limited partners under Section 303 and the rules for general partner liability stated in Section 404. Other grounds for liability can be supplied by other law, including the law of some other jurisdiction. For example, a partner's contractual guaranty of a limited partnership obligation might well be governed by the law of some other jurisdiction.

Transferees derive their rights and status under this Act from partners and accordingly this section applies to the relations of a transferee to the limited partnership.

The partnership agreement may not vary the rule stated in this section. *See* Section 110(b)(2).

§ 107.   Supplemental Principles of Law; Rate of Interest

(a) Unless displaced by particular provisions of this [Act], the principles of law and equity supplement this [Act].

(b)   If an obligation to pay interest arises under this [Act] and the rate is not specified, the rate is that specified in [applicable statute].

COMMENT

Subsection (a)—This language comes from RUPA Section 104 and does not address an important question raised by the de-linking of this Act from the UPA and RUPA—namely, to what extent is the case law of general partnerships relevant to limited partnerships governed by this Act?

Predecessor law, RULPA Section 403, expressly equated the rights, powers, restrictions, and liabilities of a general partner in a limited partnership with the rights, powers, restrictions, and liabilities of a partner in a general partnership. This Act has no comparable provision. *See* Prefatory Note. Therefore, a court should not assume that a case concerning a general partnership is automatically relevant to a limited partnership governed by this Act. A general partnership case may be relevant by analogy, especially if (1) the issue in dispute involves a provision of this Act for which a comparable provision exists under the law of general partnerships; and (2) the fundamental differences between a general partnership and limited partnership are immaterial to the disputed issue.

§ 108.   Name

(a)   The name of a limited partnership may contain the name of any partner.

(b)   The name of a limited partnership that is not a limited liability limited partnership must contain the phrase "limited partnership" or the abbreviation "L.P." or "LP" and may not contain the phrase "limited liability limited partnership" or the abbreviation "LLLP" or "L.L.L.P."

(c)   The name of a limited liability limited partnership must contain the phrase "limited liability limited partnership" or the abbreviation "LLLP" or "L.L.L.P." and must not contain the abbreviation "L.P." or "LP."

(d)   Unless authorized by subsection (e), the name of a limited partnership must be distinguishable in the records of the [Secretary of State] from:

(1)   the name of each person other than an individual incorporated, organized, or authorized to transact business in this State; and

(2)   each name reserved under Section 109 [or other state laws allowing the reservation or registration of business names, including fictitious name statutes].

(e)   A limited partnership may apply to the [Secretary of State] for authorization to use a name that does not comply with subsection (d). The [Secretary of State] shall authorize use of the name applied for if, as to each conflicting name:

(1)   the present user, registrant, or owner of the conflicting name consents in a signed record to the use and submits an undertaking in a form satisfactory to the [Secretary of State] to change the conflicting name to a name that complies with subsection (d) and is distinguishable in the records of the [Secretary of State] from the name applied for;

(2)   the applicant delivers to the [Secretary of State] a certified copy of the final judgment of a court of competent jurisdiction establishing the applicant's right to use in this State the name applied for; or

(3)   the applicant delivers to the [Secretary of State] proof satisfactory to the [Secretary of State] that the present user, registrant, or owner of the conflicting name:

(A)   has merged into the applicant;

(B)   has been converted into the applicant; or

(C)   has transferred substantially all of its assets, including the conflicting name, to the applicant.

(f)   Subject to Section 905, this section applies to any foreign limited partnership transacting business in this State, having a certificate of authority to transact business in this State, or applying for a certificate of authority.

COMMENT

Subsection (a)—Predecessor law, RULPA Section 102, prohibited the use of a limited partner's name in the name of a limited partnership except in unusual circumstances. That approach derived from the 1916 Uniform Limited Partnership Act and has become antiquated. In 1916, most business organizations were either unshielded (*e.g.*, general partnerships) or partially shielded (*e.g.*, limited partnerships), and it was reasonable for third parties to believe that an individual whose own name appeared in the name of a business would "stand behind" the business. Today most businesses have a full shield (*e.g.*, corporations, limited liability companies, most limited liability partnerships), and corporate, LLC and LLP statutes generally pose no barrier to the use of an owner's name in the name of the entity. This Act eliminates RULPA's restriction and puts limited partnerships on equal footing with these other "shielded" entities.

Subsection (d)(1)—If a sole proprietor registers or reserves a business name under a fictitious name statute, that name comes within this provision. For the purposes of this provision, a sole proprietor doing business under a registered or reserved name is a "person other than an individual."

Subsection (f)—Section 905 permits a foreign limited partnership to obtain a certificate of authority under an alternate name if the foreign limited partnership's actual name does not comply with this section.

§ 109.   Reservation of Name

(a)   The exclusive right to the use of a name that complies with Section 108 may be reserved by:

(1)   a person intending to organize a limited partnership under this [Act] and to adopt the name;

(2)   a limited partnership or a foreign limited partnership authorized to transact business in this State intending to adopt the name;

(3)   a foreign limited partnership intending to obtain a certificate of authority to transact business in this State and adopt the name;

(4)   a person intending to organize a foreign limited partnership and intending to have it obtain a certificate of authority to transact business in this State and adopt the name;

(5)   a foreign limited partnership formed under the name; or

(6)   a foreign limited partnership formed under a name that does not comply with Section 108(b) or (c), but the name reserved under this paragraph may differ from the foreign limited partnership's name only to the extent necessary to comply with Section 108(b) and (c).

(b)   A person may apply to reserve a name under subsection (a) by delivering to the [Secretary of State] for filing an application that states the name to be reserved and the paragraph of subsection (a) which applies. If the [Secretary of State] finds that the name is available for use by the applicant, the [Secretary of State] shall file a statement of name reservation and thereby reserve the name for the exclusive use of the applicant for a 120 days.

(c)   An applicant that has reserved a name pursuant to subsection (b) may reserve the same name for additional 120-day periods. A person having a current reservation for a name may not apply for another 120-day period for the same name until 90 days have elapsed in the current reservation.

(d)   A person that has reserved a name under this section may deliver to the [Secretary of State] for filing a notice of transfer that states the reserved name, the name and street and mailing address of some other person to which the reservation is to be transferred, and the paragraph of subsection (a) which applies to the other person. Subject to Section 206(c), the transfer is effective when the [Secretary of State] files the notice of transfer.

§ 110. Effect of Partnership Agreement; Nonwaivable Provisions

(a) Except as otherwise provided in subsection (b), the partnership agreement governs relations among the partners and between the partners and the partnership. To the extent the partnership agreement does not otherwise provide, this [Act] governs relations among the partners and between the partners and the partnership.

(b) A partnership agreement may not:

(1) vary a limited partnership's power under Section 105 to sue, be sued, and defend in its own name;

(2) vary the law applicable to a limited partnership under Section 106;

(3) vary the requirements of Section 204;

(4) vary the information required under Section 111 or unreasonably restrict the right to information under Sections 304 or 407, but the partnership agreement may impose reasonable restrictions on the availability and use of information obtained under those sections and may define appropriate remedies, including liquidated damages, for a breach of any reasonable restriction on use;

(5) eliminate the duty of loyalty under Section 408, but the partnership agreement may:

(A) identify specific types or categories of activities that do not violate the duty of loyalty, if not manifestly unreasonable; and

(B) specify the number or percentage of partners which may authorize or ratify, after full disclosure to all partners of all material facts, a specific act or transaction that otherwise would violate the duty of loyalty;

(6) unreasonably reduce the duty of care under Section 408(c);

(7) eliminate the obligation of good faith and fair dealing under Sections 305(b) and 408(d), but the partnership agreement may prescribe the standards by which the performance of the obligation is to be measured, if the standards are not manifestly unreasonable;

(8) vary the power of a person to dissociate as a general partner under Section 604(a) except to require that the notice under Section 603(1) be in a record;

(9) vary the power of a court to decree dissolution in the circumstances specified in Section 802;

(10) vary the requirement to wind up the partnership's business as specified in Section 803;

(11) unreasonably restrict the right to maintain an action under [Article] 10;

(12) restrict the right of a partner under Section 1110(a) to approve a conversion or merger or the right of a general partner under Section 1110(b) to consent to an amendment to the certificate of limited partnership which deletes a statement that the limited partnership is a limited liability limited partnership; or

(13) restrict rights under this [Act] of a person other than a partner or a transferee.

COMMENT

Source—RUPA Section 103.

Subject only to subsection (b), the partnership agreement has plenary power to structure and regulate the relations of the partners *inter se*. Although the certificate of limited partnership is a limited partnership's foundational document, among the partners the partnership agreement controls. *See* Section 201(d).

The partnership agreement has the power to control the manner of its own amendment. In particular, a provision of the agreement prohibiting oral modifications is enforceable, despite any common law antagonism to "no oral modification" provisions. Likewise, a partnership agreement can impose "made in a record" requirements on other aspects of the partners' relationship, such as requiring consents to be made in a record and signed, or rendering unenforceable oral promises to make contributions or oral understandings as to "events upon the happening of which the limited partnership is to be dissolved," Section 111(9)(D). *See also* Section 801(1).

Subsection (b)(3)—The referenced section states who must sign various documents.

Subsection (b)(4)—In determining whether a restriction is reasonable, a court might consider: (i) the danger or other problem the restriction seeks to avoid; (ii) the purpose for which the information is sought; and (iii) whether, in light of both the problem and the purpose, the restriction is reasonably tailored. Restricting access to or use of the names and addresses of limited partners is not per se unreasonable.

Under this Act, general and limited partners have sharply different roles. A restriction that is reasonable as to a limited partner is not necessarily reasonable as to a general partner.

Sections 304(g) and 407(f) authorize the limited partnership (as distinguished from the partnership agreement) to impose restrictions on the use of information. For a comparison of restrictions contained in the partnership agreement and restrictions imposed unilaterally by the limited partnership, *see* the Comment to Section 304(g).

Subsection (b)(5)(A)—It is not per se manifestly unreasonable for the partnership agreement to permit a general partner to compete with the limited partnership.

Subsection (b)(5)(B)—The Act does not require that the authorization or ratification be by **disinterested** partners, although the partnership agreement may so provide. The Act does require that the disclosure be made to all partners, even if the partnership agreement excludes some partners from the authorization or ratification process. An interested partner that participates in the authorization or ratification process is subject to the obligation of good faith and fair dealing. Sections 305(b) and 408(d).

Subsection (b)(8)—This restriction applies only to the power of a person to dissociate as a general partner. The partnership agreement may eliminate the power of a person to dissociate as a limited partner.

Subsection (b)(9)—This provision should not be read to limit a partnership agreement's power to provide for arbitration. For example, an agreement to arbitrate all disputes—including dissolution disputes—is enforceable. Any other interpretation would put this Act at odds with federal law. *See Southland Corp. v. Keating*, 465 U.S. 1 (1984) (holding that the Federal Arbitration Act preempts state statutes that seek to invalidate agreements to arbitrate) and *Allied-Bruce Terminix Cos., Inc. v. Dobson*, 513 U.S. 265 (1995) (same). This provision does prohibit any narrowing of the substantive grounds for judicial dissolution as stated in Section 802.

> **Example:** A provision of a partnership agreement states that no partner may obtain judicial dissolution without showing that a general partner is in material breach of the partnership agreement. The provision is ineffective to prevent a court from ordering dissolution under Section 802.

Subsection (b)(11)—Section 1001 codifies a partner's right to bring a direct action, and the rest of Article 10 provides for derivative actions. The partnership agreement may not restrict a partner's right to bring either type of action if the effect is to undercut or frustrate the duties and rights protected by Section 110(b).

The reasonableness of a restriction on derivative actions should be judged in light of the history and purpose of derivative actions. They originated as an equitable remedy, intended to protect passive owners against management abuses. A partnership agreement may not provide that all derivative claims will be subject to final determination by a special litigation committee appointed by the limited partnership, because that provision would eliminate, not merely restrict, a partner's right to bring a derivative *action*.

Subsection (b)(12)—Section 1110 imposes special consent requirements with regard to transactions that might make a partner personally liable for entity debts.

Subsection (b)(13)—The partnership agreement is a contract, and this provision reflects a basic notion of contract law—namely, that a contract can **directly** restrict rights only of parties to the contract and of persons who derive their rights from the contract. A provision of a partnership agreement can be determined to be unenforceable against third parties under paragraph (b)(13) without therefore and automatically being unenforceable *inter se* the partners and any transferees. How the former determination affects the latter question is a matter of other law.

§ 111.   Required Information

A limited partnership shall maintain at its designated office the following information:

(1)   a current list showing the full name and last known street and mailing address of each partner, separately identifying the general partners, in alphabetical order, and the limited partners, in alphabetical order;

(2)   a copy of the initial certificate of limited partnership and all amendments to and restatements of the certificate, together with signed copies of any powers of attorney under which any certificate, amendment, or restatement has been signed;

(3)   a copy of any filed articles of conversion or merger;

(4)   a copy of the limited partnership's federal, state, and local income tax returns and reports, if any, for the three most recent years;

(5)   a copy of any partnership agreement made in a record and any amendment made in a record to any partnership agreement;

(6)   a copy of any financial statement of the limited partnership for the three most recent years;

(7)   a copy of the three most recent annual reports delivered by the limited partnership to the [Secretary of State] pursuant to Section 210;

(8)   a copy of any record made by the limited partnership during the past three years of any consent given by or vote taken of any partner pursuant to this [Act] or the partnership agreement; and

(9)   unless contained in a partnership agreement made in a record, a record stating:

(A)   the amount of cash, and a description and statement of the agreed value of the other benefits, contributed and agreed to be contributed by each partner;

(B)   the times at which, or events on the happening of which, any additional contributions agreed to be made by each partner are to be made;

(C)   for any person that is both a general partner and a limited partner, a specification of what transferable interest the person owns in each capacity; and

(D)   any events upon the happening of which the limited partnership is to be dissolved and its activities wound up.

COMMENT

Source—RULPA Section 105.

Sections 304 and 407 govern access to the information required by this section, as well as to other information pertaining to a limited partnership.

Paragraph (5)—This requirement applies to superseded as well as current agreements and amendments. An agreement or amendment is "made in a record "to the extent the agreement is "integrated" into a record and consented to in that memorialized form. It is possible for a partnership agreement to be made in part in a record and in part otherwise. *See* Comment to Section 110. An oral agreement that is subsequently inscribed in a record (but not consented to as such) was not "made in a record" and is not covered by paragraph (5). However, if the limited partnership happens to have such a record, Section 304(b) might and Section 407(a)(2) will provide a right of access.

Paragraph (8)—This paragraph does not require a limited partnership to make a record of consents given and votes taken. However, if the limited partnership has made such a record, this paragraph requires that the limited partnership maintain the record for three years. The requirement applies to any record made by the limited partnership, not just to records made contemporaneously with the giving of consent or voting. The three year period runs from when the record was made and not from when the consent was given or vote taken.

Paragraph (9)—Information is "contained in a partnership agreement made in a record" only to the extent that the information is "integrated" into a record and, in that memorialized form, has been consented to as part of the partnership agreement.

This paragraph is not a statute of frauds provision. For example, failure to comply with paragraph (9)(A) or (B) does not render unenforceable an oral promise to make a contribution. Likewise, failure to comply with paragraph (9)(D) does not invalidate an oral term of the partnership specifying "events upon the happening of which the limited partnership is to be dissolved and its activities wound up." *See also* Section 801(1).

Obversely, the mere fact that a limited partnership maintains a record in purported compliance with paragraph (9)(A) or (B) does not prove that a person has actually promised to make a contribution. Likewise, the mere fact that a limited partnership maintains a record in purported compliance with paragraph (9)(D) does not prove that the partnership agreement actually includes the specified events as causes of dissolution.

Consistent with the partnership agreement's plenary power to structure and regulate the relations of the partners *inter se*, a partnership agreement can impose "made in a record" requirements which render unenforceable oral promises to make contributions or oral understandings as to "events upon the happening of which the limited partnership is to be dissolved." *See* Comment to Section 110.

Paragraph (9)(A) and (B)—Often the partnership agreement will state in record form the value of contributions made and promised to be made. If not, these provisions require that the value be stated in a record maintained as part of the limited partnership's required information. The Act does not authorize the limited partnership or the general partners to set the value of a contribution without the concurrence of the person who has made or promised the contribution, although the partnership agreement itself can grant that authority.

Paragraph (9)(C)—The information required by this provision is essential for determining what happens to the transferable interests of a person that is both a general partner and a limited partner and that dissociates in one of those capacities but not the other. *See* Sections 602(3) and 605(5).

§ 112.   Business Transactions of Partner with Partnership

A partner may lend money to and transact other business with the limited partnership and has the same rights and obligations with respect to the loan or other transaction as a person that is not a partner.

COMMENT

Source—RULPA Section 107. *See also* RUPA Section 404(f) and ULLCA Section 409(f).

This section has no impact on a general partner's duty under Section 408(b)(2) (duty of loyalty includes refraining from acting as or for an adverse party) and means rather that this Act does not discriminate against a creditor of a limited partnership that happens also to be a partner. *See, e.g., BT-I v. Equitable Life Assurance Society of the United States,* 75 Cal.App.4th 1406, 1415, 89 Cal.Rptr.2d 811, 814 (Cal.App. 4 Dist.1999). and *SEC v. DuPont, Homsey & Co.,* 204 F. Supp. 944, 946 (D. Mass. 1962), vacated and remanded on other grounds, 334 F.2d 704 (1st Cir. 1964). This section does not, however, override other law, such as fraudulent transfer or conveyance acts.

§ 113.   Dual Capacity

A person may be both a general partner and a limited partner. A person that is both a general and limited partner has the rights, powers, duties, and obligations provided by this [Act] and the partnership agreement in each of those capacities. When the person acts as a general partner, the person is subject to the obligations, duties and restrictions under this [Act] and the partnership agreement for general partners. When the person acts as a limited partner, the person is subject to the obligations, duties and restrictions under this [Act] and the partnership agreement for limited partners.

COMMENT

Source—RULPA Section 404, redrafted for reasons of style.

§ 114. Office and Agent for Service of Process

(a) A limited partnership shall designate and continuously maintain in this State:

(1) an office, which need not be a place of its activity in this State; and

(2) an agent for service of process.

(b) A foreign limited partnership shall designate and continuously maintain in this State an agent for service of process.

(c) An agent for service of process of a limited partnership or foreign limited partnership must be an individual who is a resident of this State or other person authorized to do business in this State.

COMMENT

Subsection (a)—The initial designation occurs in the original certificate of limited partnership. Section 201(a)(2). A limited partnership may change the designation in any of three ways: a statement of change, Section 115, an amendment to the certificate, Section 202, and the annual report, Section 210(e). If a limited partnership fails to maintain an agent for service of process, substituted service may be made on the Secretary of State. Section 117(b). Although a limited partnership's failure to maintain an agent for service of process is not immediate grounds for administrative dissolution, Section 809(a), the failure will prevent the limited partnership from delivering to the Secretary of State for filing an annual report that complies with Section 210(a)(2). Failure to deliver a proper annual report is grounds for administrative dissolution. Section 809(a)(2).

Subsection (b)—The initial designation occurs in the application for a certificate of authority. *See* Section 902(a)(4). A foreign limited partnership may change the designation in either of two ways: a statement of change, Section 115, and the annual report, Section 210(e). If a foreign limited partnership fails to maintain an agent for service of process, substituted service may be made on the Secretary of State. Section 117(b). A foreign limited partnership's failure to maintain an agent for service of process is grounds for administrative revocation of the certificate of authority. Section 906(a)(3).

A foreign limited partnership need not maintain an office in this State.

§ 115. Change of Designated Office or Agent for Service of Process

(a) In order to change its designated office, agent for service of process, or the address of its agent for service of process, a limited partnership or a foreign limited partnership may deliver to the [Secretary of State] for filing a statement of change containing:

(1) the name of the limited partnership or foreign limited partnership;

(2) the street and mailing address of its current designated office;

(3) if the current designated office is to be changed, the street and mailing address of the new designated office;

(4) the name and street and mailing address of its current agent for service of process; and

(5) if the current agent for service of process or an address of the agent is to be changed, the new information.

(b) Subject to Section 206(c), a statement of change is effective when filed by the [Secretary of State].

339

COMMENT

Source—ULLCA Section 109.

Subsection (a)—The Act uses "may" rather than "shall" here because other avenues exist. A limited partnership may also change the information by an amendment to its certificate of limited partnership, Section 202, or through its annual report. Section 210(e). A foreign limited partnership may use its annual report. Section 210(e). However, neither a limited partnership nor a foreign limited partnership may wait for the annual report if the information described in the public record becomes inaccurate. *See* Sections 208 (imposing liability for false information in record) and 117(b) (providing for substitute service).

§ 116. Resignation of Agent for Service of Process

(a) In order to resign as an agent for service of process of a limited partnership or foreign limited partnership, the agent must deliver to the [Secretary of State] for filing a statement of resignation containing the name of the limited partnership or foreign limited partnership.

(b) After receiving a statement of resignation, the [Secretary of State] shall file it and mail a copy to the designated office of the limited partnership or foreign limited partnership and another copy to the principal office if the address of the office appears in the records of the [Secretary of State] and is different from the address of the designated office.

(c) An agency for service of process is terminated on the 31st day after the [Secretary of State] files the statement of resignation.

COMMENT

Source—ULLCA Section 110.

This section provides the only way an agent can resign without cooperation from the limited partnership or foreign limited partnership and the only way the agent, rather than the limited partnership or foreign limited partnership, can effect a change in the public record. *See* Sections 115(a) (Statement of Change), 202 (Amendment or Restatement of Certificate), and 210(e) (Annual Report), all of which involve the limited partnership or foreign limited partnership designating a replacement agent for service of process.

Subsection (c)—In contrast to most records authorized or required to be delivered to the filing officer for filing under this Act, a statement of resignation may not provide for a delayed effective date. This subsection mandates the effective date, and an effective date included in a statement of resignation is disregarded. *See also* Section 206(c).

§ 117. Service of Process

(a) An agent for service of process appointed by a limited partnership or foreign limited partnership is an agent of the limited partnership or foreign limited partnership for service of any process, notice, or demand required or permitted by law to be served upon the limited partnership or foreign limited partnership.

(b) If a limited partnership or foreign limited partnership does not appoint or maintain an agent for service of process in this State or the agent for service of process cannot with reasonable diligence be found at the agent's address, the [Secretary of State] is an agent of the limited partnership or foreign limited partnership upon whom process, notice, or demand may be served.

(c) Service of any process, notice, or demand on the [Secretary of State] may be made by delivering to and leaving with the [Secretary of State] duplicate copies of the process, notice, or demand. If a process, notice, or demand is served on the [Secretary of State], the [Secretary of State] shall forward one of the copies by registered or certified mail, return receipt requested, to the limited partnership or foreign limited partnership at its designated office.

(d) Service is effected under subsection (c) at the earliest of:

(1)   the date the limited partnership or foreign limited partnership receives the process, notice, or demand;

(2)   the date shown on the return receipt, if signed on behalf of the limited partnership or foreign limited partnership; or

(3)   five days after the process, notice, or demand is deposited in the mail, if mailed postpaid and correctly addressed.

(e)   The [Secretary of State] shall keep a record of each process, notice, and demand served pursuant to this section and record the time of, and the action taken regarding, the service.

(f)   This section does not affect the right to serve process, notice, or demand in any other manner provided by law.

COMMENT

Source—ULLCA Section 111.

Requiring a foreign limited partnership to name an agent for service of process is a change from RULPA. *See* RULPA Section 902(3).

§ 118.   Consent and Proxies of Partners

Action requiring the consent of partners under this [Act] may be taken without a meeting, and a partner may appoint a proxy to consent or otherwise act for the partner by signing an appointment record, either personally or by the partner's attorney in fact.

COMMENT

Source—ULLCA Section 404(d) and (e).

This Act imposes no meeting requirement and does not distinguish among oral, record, express and tacit consent. The partnership agreement may establish such requirements and make such distinctions.

[ARTICLE] 2.   FORMATION; CERTIFICATE OF LIMITED PARTNERSHIP AND OTHER FILINGS

§ 201.   Formation of Limited Partnership; Certificate of Limited Partnership

(a)   In order for a limited partnership to be formed, a certificate of limited partnership must be delivered to the [Secretary of State] for filing. The certificate must state:

(1)   the name of the limited partnership, which must comply with Section 108;

(2)   the street and mailing address of the initial designated office and the name and street and mailing address of the initial agent for service of process;

(3)   the name and the street and mailing address of each general partner;

(4)   whether the limited partnership is a limited liability limited partnership; and

(5)   any additional information required by [Article] 11.

(b)   A certificate of limited partnership may also contain any other matters but may not vary or otherwise affect the provisions specified in Section 110(b) in a manner inconsistent with that section.

(c)   If there has been substantial compliance with subsection (a), subject to Section 206(c) a limited partnership is formed when the [Secretary of State] files the certificate of limited partnership.

(d)   Subject to subsection (b), if any provision of a partnership agreement is inconsistent with the filed certificate of limited partnership or with a filed statement of dissociation, termination, or change or filed articles of conversion or merger:

(1)   the partnership agreement prevails as to partners and transferees; and

(2)   the filed certificate of limited partnership, statement of dissociation, termination, or change or articles of conversion or merger prevail as to persons, other than partners and transferees, that reasonably rely on the filed record to their detriment.

COMMENT

Source—RULPA Section 201.

A limited partnership is a creature of statute, and this section governs how a limited partnership comes into existence. A limited partnership is formed only if (i) a certificate of limited partnership is prepared and delivered to the specified public official for filing, (ii) the public official files the certificate, and (iii) the certificate, delivery and filing are in "substantial compliance" with the requirements of subsection (a). Section 206(c) governs when a limited partnership comes into existence.

Despite its foundational importance, a certificate of limited partnership is far less powerful than a corporation's articles of incorporation. Among partners and transferees, for example, the partnership agreement is paramount. *See* Section 201(d).

Subsection (a)(1)—Section 108 contains name requirements. To be acceptable for filing, a certificate of limited partnership must state a name for the limited partnership which complies with Section 108.

Subsection (a)(3)—This provision should be read in conjunction with Section 103(c) and Section 401. *See* the Comment to those sections.

Subsection (a)(4)—This Act permits a limited partnership to be a limited liability limited partnership ("LLLP"), and this provision requires the certificate of limited partnership to state whether the limited partnership is an LLLP. The requirement is intended to force the organizers of a limited partnership to decide whether the limited partnership is to be an LLLP.

Subject to Sections 406(b)(2) and 1110, a limited partnership may amend its certificate of limited partnership to add or delete a statement that the limited partnership is a limited liability limited partnership. An amendment deleting such a statement must be accompanied by an amendment stating that the limited partnership is **not** a limited liability limited partnership. Section 201(a)(4) does not permit a certificate of limited partnership to be silent on this point, except for pre-existing partnerships that become subject to this Act under Section 1206. *See* Section 1206(c)(2).

Subsection (d)—Source: ULLCA Section 203(c).

A limited partnership is a creature of contract as well as a creature of statute. It will be possible, albeit improper, for the partnership agreement to be inconsistent with the certificate of limited partnership or other specified public filings relating to the limited partnership. For those circumstances, this subsection provides the rule for determining which source of information prevails.

For partners and transferees, the partnership agreement is paramount. For third parties seeking to invoke the public record, actual knowledge of that record is necessary and notice under Section 103(c) or (d) is irrelevant. A third party wishing to enforce the public record over the partnership agreement must show reasonable reliance on the public record, and reliance presupposes knowledge.

This subsection does not expressly cover a situation in which (i) one of the specified filed records contains information in addition to, but not inconsistent with, the partnership agreement, and (ii) a person, other than a partner or transferee, detrimentally relies on the additional information. However, the policy reflected in this subsection seems equally applicable to that situation.

Responsibility for maintaining a limited partnership's public record rests with the general partner or partners. Section 202(c). A general partner's failure to meet that responsibility can expose the general partner to liability to third parties under Section 208(a)(2) and might constitute a breach of the general partner's duties under Section 408. In addition, an aggrieved person may seek a remedy under Section 205 (Signing and Filing Pursuant to Judicial Order).

§ 202. Amendment or Restatement of Certificate

(a) In order to amend its certificate of limited partnership, a limited partnership must deliver to the [Secretary of State] for filing an amendment or, pursuant to [Article] 11, articles of merger stating:

(1) the name of the limited partnership;

(2) the date of filing of its initial certificate; and

(3) the changes the amendment makes to the certificate as most recently amended or restated.

(b) A limited partnership shall promptly deliver to the [Secretary of State] for filing an amendment to a certificate of limited partnership to reflect:

(1) the admission of a new general partner;

(2) the dissociation of a person as a general partner; or

(3) the appointment of a person to wind up the limited partnership's activities under Section 803(c) or (d).

(c) A general partner that knows that any information in a filed certificate of limited partnership was false when the certificate was filed or has become false due to changed circumstances shall promptly:

(1) cause the certificate to be amended; or

(2) if appropriate, deliver to the [Secretary of State] for filing a statement of change pursuant to Section 115 or a statement of correction pursuant to Section 207.

(d) A certificate of limited partnership may be amended at any time for any other proper purpose as determined by the limited partnership.

(e) A restated certificate of limited partnership may be delivered to the [Secretary of State] for filing in the same manner as an amendment.

(f) Subject to Section 206(c), an amendment or restated certificate is effective when filed by the [Secretary of State].

COMMENT

Source—RULPA Section 202.

Subsection (b)—This subsection lists changes in circumstances which require an amendment to the certificate. Neither a statement of change, Section 115, nor the annual report, Section 210(e), suffice to report the addition or deletion of a general partner or the appointment of a person to wind up a limited partnership that has no general partner.

This subsection states an obligation of the limited partnership. However, so long as the limited partnership has at least one general partner, the general partner or partners are responsible for managing the limited partnership's activities. Section 406(a). That management responsibility includes maintaining accuracy in the limited partnership's public record. Moreover, subsection (c) imposes direct responsibility on any general partner that knows that the filed certificate of limited partnership contains false information.

Acquiring or relinquishing LLLP status also requires an amendment to the certificate. *See* Sections 201(a)(4), 406(b)(2), and 1110(b)(2).

Subsection (c)—This provision imposes an obligation directly on the general partners rather than on the limited partnership. A general partner's failure to meet that responsibility can expose the general partner to liability to third parties under Section 208(a)(2) and might constitute a breach of the general partner's duties under Section 408. In addition, an aggrieved person may seek a remedy under Section 205 (Signing and Filing Pursuant to Judicial Order).

Subsection (d)—A limited partnership that desires to change its name will have to amend its certificate of limited partnership. The new name will have to comply with Section 108. *See* Section 201(a)(1).

§ 203.   Statement of Termination

A dissolved limited partnership that has completed winding up may deliver to the [Secretary of State] for filing a statement of termination that states:

(1)   the name of the limited partnership;

(2)   the date of filing of its initial certificate of limited partnership; and

(3)   any other information as determined by the general partners filing the statement or by a person appointed pursuant to Section 803(c) or (d).

COMMENT

Under Section 103(d)(3), a filed statement of termination provides constructive notice, 90 days after the statement's effective date, that the limited partnership is terminated. That notice effectively terminates any apparent authority to bind the limited partnership.

However, this section is permissive. Therefore, it is not possible to use Section 205 (Signing and Filing Pursuant to Judicial Order) to cause a statement of termination to be filed.

This section differs from predecessor law, RULPA Section 203, which required the filing of a certificate of cancellation when a limited partnership dissolved.

§ 204.   Signing of Records

(a)   Each record delivered to the [Secretary of State] for filing pursuant to this [Act] must be signed in the following manner:

(1)   An initial certificate of limited partnership must be signed by all general partners listed in the certificate.

(2)   An amendment adding or deleting a statement that the limited partnership is a limited liability limited partnership must be signed by all general partners listed in the certificate.

(3)   An amendment designating as general partner a person admitted under Section 801(3)(B) following the dissociation of a limited partnership's last general partner must be signed by that person.

(4)   An amendment required by Section 803(c) following the appointment of a person to wind up the dissolved limited partnership's activities must be signed by that person.

(5)   Any other amendment must be signed by:

(A)   at least one general partner listed in the certificate;

(B)   each other person designated in the amendment as a new general partner; and

(C)   each person that the amendment indicates has dissociated as a general partner, unless:

(i)   the person is deceased or a guardian or general conservator has been appointed for the person and the amendment so states; or

(ii)   the person has previously delivered to the [Secretary of State] for filing a statement of dissociation.

(6)   A restated certificate of limited partnership must be signed by at least one general partner listed in the certificate, and, to the extent the restated certificate effects a change under any other paragraph of this subsection, the certificate must be signed in a manner that satisfies that paragraph.

(7)   A statement of termination must be signed by all general partners listed in the certificate or, if the certificate of a dissolved limited partnership lists no general partners, by the person appointed pursuant to Section 803(c) or (d) to wind up the dissolved limited partnership's activities.

(8)   Articles of conversion must be signed by each general partner listed in the certificate of limited partnership.

(9)   Articles of merger must be signed as provided in Section 1108(a).

(10) Any other record delivered on behalf of a limited partnership to the [Secretary of State] for filing must be signed by at least one general partner listed in the certificate.

(11) A statement by a person pursuant to Section 605(a)(4) stating that the person has dissociated as a general partner must be signed by that person.

(12) A statement of withdrawal by a person pursuant to Section 306 must be signed by that person.

(13) A record delivered on behalf of a foreign limited partnership to the [Secretary of State] for filing must be signed by at least one general partner of the foreign limited partnership.

(14) Any other record delivered on behalf of any person to the [Secretary of State] for filing must be signed by that person.

(b)   Any person may sign by an attorney in fact any record to be filed pursuant to this [Act].

COMMENT

Source—ULLCA Section 205.

This section pertains only to signing requirements and implies nothing about approval requirements. For example, Section 204(a)(2) requires that an amendment changing a limited partnership's LLLP status be signed by all **general** partners listed in the certificate, but under Section 406(b)(2) **all** partners must consent to that change unless otherwise provided in the partnership agreement.

A person who signs a record without ascertaining that the record has been properly authorized risks liability under Section 208.

Subsection (a)—The recurring reference to general partners "listed in the certificate" recognizes that a person might be admitted as a general partner under Section 401 without immediately being listed in the certificate of limited partnership. Such persons may have rights, powers and obligations despite their unlisted status, but they cannot act as general partners for the purpose of affecting the limited partnership's public record. *See* the Comment to Section 103(c) and the Comment to Section 401.

§ 205.   Signing and Filing Pursuant to Judicial Order

(a)   If a person required by this [Act] to sign a record or deliver a record to the [Secretary of State] for filing does not do so, any other person that is aggrieved may petition the [appropriate court] to order:

(1)   the person to sign the record;

(2)   deliver the record to the [Secretary of State] for filing; or

(3)   the [Secretary of State] to file the record unsigned.

(b)   If the person aggrieved under subsection (a) is not the limited partnership or foreign limited partnership to which the record pertains, the aggrieved person shall make the limited partnership or foreign limited partnership a party to the action. A person aggrieved under subsection (a) may seek the remedies provided in subsection (a) in the same action in combination or in the alternative.

(c)   A record filed unsigned pursuant to this section is effective without being signed.

COMMENT

Source—RULPA Section 205.

§ 206.   Delivery to and Filing of Records by [Secretary of State]; Effective Time and Date

(a)   A record authorized or required to be delivered to the [Secretary of State] for filing under this [Act] must be captioned to describe the record's purpose, be in a medium permitted by the [Secretary of State], and be delivered to the [Secretary of State]. Unless the [Secretary of State] determines that a record does not comply with the filing requirements of this [Act], and if all filing fees have been paid, the [Secretary of State] shall file the record and:

(1)   for a statement of dissociation, send:

(A)   a copy of the filed statement and a receipt for the fees to the person which the statement indicates has dissociated as a general partner; and

(B)   a copy of the filed statement and receipt to the limited partnership;

(2)   for a statement of withdrawal, send:

(A)   a copy of the filed statement and a receipt for the fees to the person on whose behalf the record was filed; and

(B)   if the statement refers to an existing limited partnership, a copy of the filed statement and receipt to the limited partnership; and

(3)   for all other records, send a copy of the filed record and a receipt for the fees to the person on whose behalf the record was filed.

(b)   Upon request and payment of a fee, the [Secretary of State] shall send to the requester a certified copy of the requested record.

(c)   Except as otherwise provided in Sections 116 and 207, a record delivered to the [Secretary of State] for filing under this [Act] may specify an effective time and a delayed effective date. Except as otherwise provided in this [Act], a record filed by the [Secretary of State] is effective:

(1)   if the record does not specify an effective time and does not specify a delayed effective date, on the date and at the time the record is filed as evidenced by the [Secretary of State's] endorsement of the date and time on the record;

(2)   if the record specifies an effective time but not a delayed effective date, on the date the record is filed at the time specified in the record;

(3)   if the record specifies a delayed effective date but not an effective time, at 12:01 a.m. on the earlier of:

(A)   the specified date; or

(B)   the 90th day after the record is filed; or

(4)   if the record specifies an effective time and a delayed effective date, at the specified time on the earlier of:

(A)   the specified date; or

(B)   the 90th day after the record is filed.

COMMENT

Source—ULLCA Section 206.

In order for a record prepared by a private person to become part of the public record under this Act, (i) someone must put a properly prepared version of the record into the possession of the public official specified in the Act as the appropriate filing officer, and (ii) that filing officer must determine that the record complies with the filing requirements of this Act and then officially make the record part of the public record. This Act refers to the first step as *delivery to the [Secretary of State] for filing* and refers to the second step as *filing*. Thus, under this Act "filing" is an official act.

Subsection (a)—The caption need only indicate the title of the record; *e.g.*, Certificate of Limited Partnership, Statement of Change for Limited Partnership.

Filing officers typically note on a filed record the fact, date and time of filing. The copies provided by the filing officer under this subsection should contain that notation.

This Act does not provide a remedy if the filing officer wrongfully fails or refuses to file a record.

Subsection (c)—This subsection allows most records to have a delayed effective date, up to 90 days after the date the record is filed by the filing officer. A record specifying a longer delay will **not** be rejected. Instead, under paragraph (c)(3) and (4), the delayed effective date is adjusted by operation of law to the "90th day after the record is filed." The Act does not require the filing officer to notify anyone of the adjustment.

§ 207. Correcting Filed Record

(a) A limited partnership or foreign limited partnership may deliver to the [Secretary of State] for filing a statement of correction to correct a record previously delivered by the limited partnership or foreign limited partnership to the [Secretary of State] and filed by the [Secretary of State], if at the time of filing the record contained false or erroneous information or was defectively signed.

(b) A statement of correction may not state a delayed effective date and must:

(1) describe the record to be corrected, including its filing date, or attach a copy of the record as filed;

(2) specify the incorrect information and the reason it is incorrect or the manner in which the signing was defective; and

(3) correct the incorrect information or defective signature.

(c) When filed by the [Secretary of State], a statement of correction is effective retroactively as of the effective date of the record the statement corrects, but the statement is effective when filed:

(1) for the purposes of Section 103(c) and (d); and

(2) as to persons relying on the uncorrected record and adversely affected by the correction.

COMMENT

Source—ULLCA Section 207.

A statement of correction is appropriate only to correct inaccuracies that existed or signatures that were defective "at the time of filing." A statement of correction may not be used to correct a record that was accurate when filed but has become inaccurate due to subsequent events.

Subsection (c)—Generally, a statement of correction "relates back." However, there is no retroactive effect: (1) for the purposes of constructive notice under Section 103(c) and (d); and (2) against persons who have relied on the uncorrected record and would be adversely affected if the correction related back.

§ 208. Liability for False Information in Filed Record

(a) If a record delivered to the [Secretary of State] for filing under this [Act] and filed by the [Secretary of State] contains false information, a person that suffers loss by reliance on the information may recover damages for the loss from:

(1) a person that signed the record, or caused another to sign it on the person's behalf, and knew the information to be false at the time the record was signed; and

(2)   a general partner that has notice that the information was false when the record was filed or has become false because of changed circumstances, if the general partner has notice for a reasonably sufficient time before the information is relied upon to enable the general partner to effect an amendment under Section 202, file a petition pursuant to Section 205, or deliver to the [Secretary of State] for filing a statement of change pursuant to Section 115 or a statement of correction pursuant to Section 207.

(b)   Signing a record authorized or required to be filed under this [Act] constitutes an affirmation under the penalties of perjury that the facts stated in the record are true.

COMMENT

This section pertains to both limited partnerships and foreign limited partnerships.

LLLP status is irrelevant to this section. The LLLP shield protects only to the extent that (i) the obligation involved is an obligation of the limited partnership or foreign limited partnership, and (ii) a partner is claimed to be liable for that obligation by reason of being a partner. This section does not address the obligations of a limited partnership or foreign limited partnership and instead imposes direct liability on signers and general partners.

Subsection (a)—This subsection's liability rules apply only to records (i) created by private persons ("delivered to the [Secretary of State] for filing"), (ii) which actually become part of the public record ("filed by the [Secretary of State]"). This subsection does not preempt other law, which might provide remedies for misleading information contained, for example, in a record that is delivered to the filing officer for filing but withdrawn before the filing officer takes the official action of filing the record.

Records filed under this Act are signed subject to the penalties for perjury. *See* subsection (b). This subsection therefore does not require a party who relies on a record to demonstrate that the reliance was reasonable. Contrast Section 201(d)(2), which provides that, if the partnership agreement is inconsistent with the public record, the public record prevails in favor of a person that is neither a partner nor a transferee and that reasonably relied on the record.

§ 209.   Certificate of Existence or Authorization

(a)   The [Secretary of State], upon request and payment of the requisite fee, shall furnish a certificate of existence for a limited partnership if the records filed in the [office of the Secretary of State] show that the [Secretary of State] has filed a certificate of limited partnership and has not filed a statement of termination. A certificate of existence must state:

(1)   the limited partnership's name;

(2)   that it was duly formed under the laws of this State and the date of formation;

(3)   whether all fees, taxes, and penalties due to the [Secretary of State] under this [Act] or other law have been paid;

(4)   whether the limited partnership's most recent annual report required by Section 210 has been filed by the [Secretary of State];

(5)   whether the [Secretary of State] has administratively dissolved the limited partnership;

(6)   whether the limited partnership's certificate of limited partnership has been amended to state that the limited partnership is dissolved;

(7)   that a statement of termination has not been filed by the [Secretary of State]; and

(8)   other facts of record in the [office of the Secretary of State] which may be requested by the applicant.

(b)   The [Secretary of State], upon request and payment of the requisite fee, shall furnish a certificate of authorization for a foreign limited partnership if the records filed in the [office of the

Secretary of State] show that the [Secretary of State] has filed a certificate of authority, has not revoked the certificate of authority, and has not filed a notice of cancellation. A certificate of authorization must state:

(1)   the foreign limited partnership's name and any alternate name adopted under Section 905(a) for use in this State;

(2)   that it is authorized to transact business in this State;

(3)   whether all fees, taxes, and penalties due to the [Secretary of State] under this [Act] or other law have been paid;

(4)   whether the foreign limited partnership's most recent annual report required by Section 210 has been filed by the [Secretary of State];

(5)   that the [Secretary of State] has not revoked its certificate of authority and has not filed a notice of cancellation; and

(6)   other facts of record in the [office of the Secretary of State] which may be requested by the applicant.

(c)   Subject to any qualification stated in the certificate, a certificate of existence or authorization issued by the [Secretary of State] may be relied upon as conclusive evidence that the limited partnership or foreign limited partnership is in existence or is authorized to transact business in this State.

COMMENT

Source—ULLCA Section 208.

A certificate of existence can reveal only information present in the public record, and under this Act significant information bearing on the status of a limited partnership may be outside the public record. For example, while this Act provides for a limited partnership to have a perpetual duration, Section 104(c), the partnership agreement may set a definite term or designate particular events whose occurrence will cause dissolution. Section 801(1). Dissolution is also possible by consent, Section 801(2), and, absent a contrary provision in the partnership agreement, will at least be at issue whenever a general partner dissociates. Section 801(3). Nothing in this Act requires a limited partnership to deliver to the filing officer for filing a record indicating that the limited partnership has dissolved.

A certificate of authorization furnished under this section is different than a certificate of authority filed under Section 904.

§ 210.   Annual Report for [Secretary of State]

(a)   A limited partnership or a foreign limited partnership authorized to transact business in this State shall deliver to the [Secretary of State] for filing an annual report that states:

(1)   the name of the limited partnership or foreign limited partnership;

(2)   the street and mailing address of its designated office and the name and street and mailing address of its agent for service of process in this State;

(3)   in the case of a limited partnership, the street and mailing address of its principal office; and

(4)   in the case of a foreign limited partnership, the State or other jurisdiction under whose law the foreign limited partnership is formed and any alternate name adopted under Section 905(a).

(b)   Information in an annual report must be current as of the date the annual report is delivered to the [Secretary of State] for filing.

(c)   The first annual report must be delivered to the [Secretary of State] between [January 1 and April 1] of the year following the calendar year in which a limited partnership was formed or a foreign limited partnership was authorized to transact business. An annual report must be delivered to the [Secretary of State] between [January 1 and April 1] of each subsequent calendar year.

(d)   If an annual report does not contain the information required in subsection (a), the [Secretary of State] shall promptly notify the reporting limited partnership or foreign limited partnership and return the report to it for correction. If the report is corrected to contain the information required in subsection (a) and delivered to the [Secretary of State] within 30 days after the effective date of the notice, it is timely delivered.

(e)   If a filed annual report contains an address of a designated office or the name or address of an agent for service of process which differs from the information shown in the records of the [Secretary of State] immediately before the filing, the differing information in the annual report is considered a statement of change under Section 115.

COMMENT

Source—ULLCA Section 211.

Subsection (d)—This subsection's rule affects only Section 809(a)(2) (late filing of annual report grounds for administrative dissolution) and any late fees that the filing officer might have the right to impose. For the purposes of subsection (e), the annual report functions as a statement of change only when "filed" by the filing officer. Likewise, a person cannot rely on subsection (d) to escape liability arising under Section 208.

[ARTICLE] 3.   LIMITED PARTNERS

§ 301.   Becoming Limited Partner

A person becomes a limited partner:

  (1)   as provided in the partnership agreement;

  (2)   as the result of a conversion or merger under [Article] 11; or

  (3)   with the consent of all the partners.

COMMENT

Source—RULPA Section 301.

Although Section 801(4) contemplates the admission of a limited partner to avoid dissolution, that provision does not itself authorize the admission. Instead, this section controls. Contrast Section 801(3)(B), which itself authorizes the admission of a general partner in order to avoid dissolution.

§ 302.   No Right or Power as Limited Partner to Bind Limited Partnership

A limited partner does not have the right or the power as a limited partner to act for or bind the limited partnership.

COMMENT

In this respect a limited partner is analogous to a shareholder in a corporation; status as owner provides neither the right to manage nor a reasonable appearance of that right.

The phrase "as a limited partner" is intended to recognize that: (i) this section does not disable a general partner that also owns a limited partner interest; (ii) the partnership agreement may as a matter of contract allocate managerial rights to one or more limited partners; and (iii) a separate agreement can empower and entitle a person that is a limited partner to act for the limited partnership in another capacity; *e.g.*, as an agent. *See* Comment to Section 305.

The fact that a limited partner *qua* limited partner has no power to bind the limited partnership means that, subject to Section 113 (Dual Capacity), information possessed by a limited partner is not attributed to the limited partnership. *See* Section 103(h).

This Act specifies various circumstances in which limited partners have consent rights, including:

- admission of a limited partner, Section 301(3)

- admission of a general partner, Section 401(4)

- amendment of the partnership agreement, Section 406(b)(1)

- the decision to amend the certificate of limited partnership so as to obtain or relinquish LLLP status, Section 406(b)(2)

- the disposition of all or substantially all of the limited partnership's property, outside the ordinary course, Section 406(b)(3)

- the compromise of a partner's obligation to make a contribution or return an improper distribution, Section 502(c)

- expulsion of a limited partner by consent of the other partners, Section 601(b)(4)

- expulsion of a general partner by consent of the other partners, Section 603(4)

- redemption of a transferable interest subject to charging order, using limited partnership property, Section 703(c)(3)

- causing dissolution by consent, Section 801(2)

- causing dissolution by consent following the dissociation of a general partner, when at least one general partner remains, Section 801(3)(A)

- avoiding dissolution and appointing a successor general partner, following the dissociation of the sole general partner, Section 801(3)(B)

- appointing a person to wind up the limited partnership when there is no general partner, Section 803(C)

- approving, amending or abandoning a plan of conversion, Section 1103(a) and (b)(2)

- approving, amending or abandoning a plan of merger, Section 1107(a) and (b)(2).

§ 303. No Liability as Limited Partner for Limited Partnership Obligations

An obligation of a limited partnership, whether arising in contract, tort, or otherwise, is not the obligation of a limited partner. A limited partner is not personally liable, directly or indirectly, by way of contribution or otherwise, for an obligation of the limited partnership solely by reason of being a limited partner, even if the limited partner participates in the management and control of the limited partnership.

COMMENT

This section provides a full, status-based liability shield for each limited partner, "even if the limited partner participates in the management and control of the limited partnership." The section thus eliminates the so-called "control rule" with respect to personal liability for entity obligations and brings limited partners into parity with LLC members, LLP partners and corporate shareholders.

The "control rule" first appeared in an uniform act in 1916, although the concept is much older. Section 7 of the original Uniform Limited Partnership Act provided that "A limited partner shall not become liable as a general partner [i.e., for the obligations of the limited partnership] unless . . . he takes part in the control of the business." The 1976 Uniform Limited Partnership Act (ULPA-1976) "carrie[d] over the basic test from former Section 7," but recognized "the difficulty of determining when the 'control' line has been overstepped." Comment to ULPA-1976, Section 303. Accordingly, ULPA-1976 tried to buttress the limited partner's shield by (i) providing a safe harbor for a lengthy list of activities deemed not to constitute participating in control, ULPA-1976, Section 303(b), and (ii) limiting a limited partner's "control rule" liability "only to persons who transact business with the limited partnership with actual knowledge of [the limited partner's] participation in control." ULPA-1976, Section 303(a). However, these protections were complicated by a countervailing rule which made a limited partner generally liable for the limited partnership's obligations "if the limited partner's participation in the control of the business is ... substantially the same as the exercise of the powers of a general partner." ULPA-1976, Section 303(a).

The 1985 amendments to ULPA-1976 (i.e., RULPA) further buttressed the limited partner's shield, removing the "substantially the same" rule, expanding the list of safe harbor activities and limiting "control rule" liability "only to persons who transact business with the limited partnership reasonably believing, based upon the limited partner's conduct, that the limited partner is a general partner."

In a world with LLPs, LLCs and, most importantly, LLLPs, the control rule has become an anachronism. This Act therefore takes the next logical step in the evolution of the limited partner's liability shield and renders the control rule extinct.

The shield established by this section protects only against liability for the limited partnership's obligations and only to the extent that the limited partner is claimed to be liable on account of being a limited partner. Thus, a person that is both a general and limited partner will be liable as a general partner for the limited partnership's obligations. Moreover, this section does not prevent a limited partner from being liable as a result of the limited partner's own conduct and is therefore inapplicable when a third party asserts that a limited partner's own wrongful conduct has injured the third party. This section is likewise inapplicable to claims by the limited partnership or another partner that a limited partner has breached a duty under this Act or the partnership agreement.

This section does not eliminate a limited partner's liability for promised contributions, Section 502 or improper distributions. Section 509. That liability pertains to a person's status as a limited partner but is **not** liability for an obligation of the limited partnership.

The shield provided by this section applies whether or not a limited partnership is a limited liability limited partnership.

§ 304.   Right of Limited Partner and Former Limited Partner to Information

(a)   On 10 days' demand, made in a record received by the limited partnership, a limited partner may inspect and copy required information during regular business hours in the limited partnership's designated office. The limited partner need not have any particular purpose for seeking the information.

(b)   During regular business hours and at a reasonable location specified by the limited partnership, a limited partner may obtain from the limited partnership and inspect and copy true and full information regarding the state of the activities and financial condition of the limited partnership and other information regarding the activities of the limited partnership as is just and reasonable if:

(1)   the limited partner seeks the information for a purpose reasonably related to the partner's interest as a limited partner;

(2)   the limited partner makes a demand in a record received by the limited partnership, describing with reasonable particularity the information sought and the purpose for seeking the information; and

(3)   the information sought is directly connected to the limited partner's purpose.

(c)   Within 10 days after receiving a demand pursuant to subsection (b), the limited partnership in a record shall inform the limited partner that made the demand:

(1)   what information the limited partnership will provide in response to the demand;

(2)   when and where the limited partnership will provide the information; and

(3)   if the limited partnership declines to provide any demanded information, the limited partnership's reasons for declining.

(d) Subject to subsection (f), a person dissociated as a limited partner may inspect and copy required information during regular business hours in the limited partnership's designated office if:

(1) the information pertains to the period during which the person was a limited partner;

(2) the person seeks the information in good faith; and

(3) the person meets the requirements of subsection (b).

(e) The limited partnership shall respond to a demand made pursuant to subsection (d) in the same manner as provided in subsection (c).

(f) If a limited partner dies, Section 704 applies.

(g) The limited partnership may impose reasonable restrictions on the use of information obtained under this section. In a dispute concerning the reasonableness of a restriction under this subsection, the limited partnership has the burden of proving reasonableness.

(h) A limited partnership may charge a person that makes a demand under this section reasonable costs of copying, limited to the costs of labor and material.

(i) Whenever this [Act] or a partnership agreement provides for a limited partner to give or withhold consent to a matter, before the consent is given or withheld, the limited partnership shall, without demand, provide the limited partner with all information material to the limited partner's decision that the limited partnership knows.

(j) A limited partner or person dissociated as a limited partner may exercise the rights under this section through an attorney or other agent. Any restriction imposed under subsection (g) or by the partnership agreement applies both to the attorney or other agent and to the limited partner or person dissociated as a limited partner.

(k) The rights stated in this section do not extend to a person as transferee, but may be exercised by the legal representative of an individual under legal disability who is a limited partner or person dissociated as a limited partner.

COMMENT

This section balances two countervailing concerns relating to information: the need of limited partners and former limited partners for access versus the limited partnership's need to protect confidential business data and other intellectual property. The balance must be understood in the context of fiduciary duties. The general partners are obliged through their duties of care and loyalty to protect information whose confidentiality is important to the limited partnership or otherwise inappropriate for dissemination. *See* Section 408 (general standards of general partner conduct). A limited partner, in contrast, "does not have any fiduciary duty to the limited partnership or to any other partner solely by reason of being a limited partner." Section 305(a). (Both general partners and limited partners are subject to a duty of good faith and fair dealing. Section 305(b) and 408(d)).

Like predecessor law, this Act divides limited partner access rights into two categories—required information and other information. However, this Act builds on predecessor law by:

- expanding slightly the category of required information and stating explicitly that a limited partner may have access to that information without having to show cause

- specifying a procedure for limited partners to follow when demanding access to other information

- specifying how a limited partnership must respond to such a demand and setting a time limit for the response

- retaining predecessor law's "just and reasonable" standard for determining a limited partner's right to other information, while recognizing that, to be "just and reasonable," a limited partner's demand for other information must meet at minimum standards of relatedness and particularity

- expressly requiring the limited partnership to volunteer known, material information when seeking or obtaining consent from limited partners

- codifying (while limiting) the power of the partnership agreement to vary limited partner access rights

- permitting the limited partnership to establish other reasonable limits on access

- providing access rights for former limited partners.

The access rights stated in this section are personal to each limited partner and are enforceable through a direct action under Section 1001(a). These access rights are in addition to whatever discovery rights a party has in a civil suit.

Subsection (a)—The phrase "required information" is a defined term. *See* Sections 102(18) and 111. This subsection's broad right of access is subject not only to reasonable limitations in the partnership agreement, Section 110(b)(4), but also to the power of the limited partnership to impose reasonable limitations on use. Unless the partnership agreement provides otherwise, it will be the general partner or partners that have the authority to use that power. *See* Section 406(a).

Subsection (b)—The language describing the information to be provided comes essentially verbatim from RULPA Section 305(a)(2)(i) and (iii). The procedural requirements derive from RMBCA Section 16.02(c). This subsection does not impose a requirement of good faith, because Section 305(b) contains a generally applicable obligation of good faith and fair dealing for limited partners.

Subsection (d)—The notion that former owners should have information rights comes from RUPA Section 403(b) and ULLCA Section 408(a). The access is limited to the required information and is subject to certain conditions.

Example: A person dissociated as a limited partner seeks data which the limited partnership has compiled, which relates to the period when the person was a limited partner, but which is beyond the scope of the information required by Section 111. No matter how reasonable the person's purpose and how well drafted the person's demand, the limited partnership is not obliged to provide the data.

Example: A person dissociated as a limited partner seeks access to required information pertaining to the period during which the person was a limited partner. The person makes a bald demand, merely stating a desire to review the required information at the limited partnership's designated office. In particular, the demand does not describe "with reasonable particularity the information sought and the purpose for seeking the information." *See* subsection (b)(2). The limited partnership is not obliged to allow access. The person must first comply with subsection (d), which incorporates by reference the requirements of subsection (b).

Subsection (f) and Section 704 provide greater access rights for the estate of a deceased limited partner.

Subsection (d)(2)—A duty of good faith is needed here, because a person claiming access under this subsection is no longer a limited partner and is no longer subject to Section 305(b). *See* Section 602(a)(2) (dissociation as a limited partner terminates duty of good faith as to subsequent events).

Subsection (g)—This subsection permits the limited partnership—as distinguished from the partnership agreement—to impose use limitations. Contrast Section 110(b)(4). Under Section 406(a), it will be the general partner or partners that decide whether the limited partnership will impose use restrictions.

The limited partnership bears the burden of proving the reasonableness of any restriction imposed under this subsection. In determining whether a restriction is reasonable, a court might consider: (i) the danger or other problem the restriction seeks to avoid; (ii) the purpose for which the information is sought; and (iii) whether, in light of both the problem and the purpose, the restriction is reasonably tailored. Restricting use of the names and addresses of limited partners is not per se unreasonable.

The following table compares the limitations available through the partnership agreement with those available under this subsection.

	partnership agreement	Section 304(g)
how restrictions adopted	by the consent of partners when they adopt or amend the partnership agreement, unless the partnership agreement provides another method of amendment	by the general partners, acting under Section 406(a)
what restrictions may be imposed	"reasonable restrictions on the availability and use of information obtained," Section 110(b)(4)	"reasonable restrictions on the use of information obtained"
burden of proof	the person challenging the restriction must prove that the restriction will "unreasonably restrict the right of information," Section 110(b)(4)	"the limited partnership has the burden of proving reasonableness"

Subsection (h)—Source: RUPA Section 403(b) and ULLCA Section 408(a).

Subsection (i)—Source: ULLCA Section 408(b).

The duty stated in this subsection is at the core of the duties owed the limited partners by a limited partnership and its general partners. This subsection imposes an affirmative duty to volunteer information, but that obligation is limited to information which is both material and known by the limited partnership. The duty applies to known, material information, even if the limited partnership does not know that the information is material.

A limited partnership will "know" what its general partners know. Section 103(h). A limited partnership may also know information known by the "individual conducting the transaction for the [limited partnership]." Section 103(g).

A limited partner's right to information under this subsection is enforceable through the full panoply of "legal or equitable relief" provided by Section 1001(a), including in appropriate circumstances the withdrawal or invalidation of improperly obtained consent and the invalidation or recision of action taken pursuant to that consent.

Subsection (k)—Section 304 provides no information rights to a transferee as transferee. Transferee status brings only the very limited information rights stated in Section 702(c).

It is nonetheless possible for a person that happens to be a transferee to have rights under this section. For example, under Section 602(a)(3) a person dissociated as a limited partner becomes a "mere transferee" of its own transferable interest. While that status provides the person no rights under this section, the status of person dissociated as a limited partner triggers rights under subsection (d).

§ 305. Limited Duties of Limited Partners

(a) A limited partner does not have any fiduciary duty to the limited partnership or to any other partner solely by reason of being a limited partner.

(b) A limited partner shall discharge the duties to the partnership and the other partners under this [Act] or under the partnership agreement and exercise any rights consistently with the obligation of good faith and fair dealing.

(c) A limited partner does not violate a duty or obligation under this [Act] or under the partnership agreement merely because the limited partner's conduct furthers the limited partner's own interest.

COMMENT

Subsection (a)—Fiduciary duty typically attaches to a person whose status or role creates significant power for that person over the interests of another person. Under this Act, limited partners have very limited power of any sort in the regular activities of the limited partnership and no power whatsoever justifying the imposition of fiduciary duties either to the limited partnership or fellow partners. It is possible for a partnership agreement to allocate significant managerial authority and power to a limited partner, but in that case the power exists not as a matter of status or role but rather as a matter of contract. The proper limit on such contract-based power is the obligation of good faith and fair dealing, not fiduciary duty, unless the partnership agreement itself expressly imposes a fiduciary duty or creates a role for a limited partner which, as a matter of other law, gives rise to a fiduciary duty. For example, if the partnership agreement makes a limited partner an agent for the limited partnership as to particular matters, the law of agency will impose fiduciary duties on the limited partner with respect to the limited partner's role as agent.

Subsection (b)—Source: RUPA Section 404(d). The same language appears in Section 408(d), pertaining to general partners.

The obligation of good faith and fair dealing is *not* a fiduciary duty, does not command altruism or self-abnegation, and does not prevent a partner from acting in the partner's own self-interest. Courts should not use the obligation to change *ex post facto* the parties' or this Act's allocation of risk and power. To the contrary, in light of the nature of a limited partnership, the obligation should be used only to protect agreed-upon arrangements from conduct that is manifestly beyond what a reasonable person could have contemplated when the arrangements were made.

The partnership agreement or this Act may grant discretion to a partner, and that partner may properly exercise that discretion even though another partner suffers as a consequence. Conduct does not violate the obligation of good faith and fair dealing merely because that conduct substantially prejudices a party. Indeed, parties allocate risk precisely because prejudice may occur. The exercise of discretion constitutes a breach of the obligation of good faith and fair dealing only when the party claiming breach shows that the conduct has no honestly-held purpose that legitimately comports with the parties' agreed-upon arrangements. Once such a purpose appears, courts should not second guess a party's choice of method in serving that purpose, unless the party invoking the obligation of good faith and fair dealing shows that the choice of method itself lacks any honestly-held purpose that legitimately comports with the parties' agreed-upon arrangements.

In sum, the purpose of the obligation of good faith and fair dealing is to protect the arrangement the partners have chosen for themselves, not to restructure that arrangement under the guise of safeguarding it.

§ 306. Person Erroneously Believing Self to be Limited Partner

(a) Except as otherwise provided in subsection (b), a person that makes an investment in a business enterprise and erroneously but in good faith believes that the person has become a limited partner in the enterprise is not liable for the enterprise's obligations by reason of making the investment, receiving distributions from the enterprise, or exercising any rights of or appropriate to a limited partner, if, on ascertaining the mistake, the person:

　　(1) causes an appropriate certificate of limited partnership, amendment, or statement of correction to be signed and delivered to the [Secretary of State] for filing; or

　　(2) withdraws from future participation as an owner in the enterprise by signing and delivering to the [Secretary of State] for filing a statement of withdrawal under this section.

(b) A person that makes an investment described in subsection (a) is liable to the same extent as a general partner to any third party that enters into a transaction with the enterprise, believing in good faith that the person is a general partner, before the [Secretary of State] files a statement of withdrawal, certificate of limited partnership, amendment, or statement of correction to show that the person is not a general partner.

(c)   If a person makes a diligent effort in good faith to comply with subsection (a)(1) and is unable to cause the appropriate certificate of limited partnership, amendment, or statement of correction to be signed and delivered to the [Secretary of State] for filing, the person has the right to withdraw from the enterprise pursuant to subsection (a)(2) even if the withdrawal would otherwise breach an agreement with others that are or have agreed to become co-owners of the enterprise.

COMMENT

Source—RULPA Section 304, substantially redrafted for reasons of style.

Subsection (a)(2)—The requirement that a person "withdraw[ ] from future participation as an owner in the enterprise" means, in part, that the person refrain from taking any further profit from the enterprise. The requirement does not mean, however, that the person is required to return previously obtained profits or forfeit any investment.

[ARTICLE] 4.   GENERAL PARTNERS

§ 401.   Becoming General Partner

A person becomes a general partner:

(1)   as provided in the partnership agreement;

(2)   under Section 801(3)(B) following the dissociation of a limited partnership's last general partner;

(3)   as the result of a conversion or merger under [Article] 11; or

(4)   with the consent of all the partners.

COMMENT

This section does not make a person's status as a general partner dependent on the person being so designated in the certificate of limited partnership. If a person does become a general partner under this section without being so designated:

* the limited partnership is obligated to promptly and appropriately amend the certificate of limited partnership, Section 202(b)(1);

* each general partner that knows of the anomaly is personally obligated to cause the certificate to be promptly and appropriately amended, Section 202(c)(1), and is subject to liability for failing to do so, Section 208(a)(2);

* the "non-designated" general partner has:

— all the rights and duties of a general partner to the limited partnership and the other partners, and

— the powers of a general partner to bind the limited partnership under Sections 402 and 403, but

— no power to sign records which are to be filed on behalf of the limited partnership under this Act

Example: By consent of the partners of XYZ Limited Partnership, G is admitted as a general partner. However, XYZ's certificate of limited partnership is not amended accordingly. Later, G—acting without actual authority—purports to bind XYZ to a transaction with Third Party. Third Party does not review the filed certificate of limited partnership before entering into the transaction. XYZ might be bound under Section 402.

Section 402 attributes to a limited partnership "[a]n act of a general partner . . . for apparently carrying on in the ordinary course the limited partnership's activities or activities of the kind carried on by the limited partnership." The limited partnership's liability under Section 402 does not depend on the "act of a general partner" being the act of a general partner designated in the certificate of limited partnership. Moreover, the notice provided by Section 103(c) does not undercut G's appearance of authority. Section 402 refers only to notice under Section 103(d) and, in any event, according to the second sentence of Section 103(c), the fact that a person is **not** listed as in the certificate as a general partner is **not** notice that the person is **not** a general partner. *See* Comment to Section 103(c).

Example: Same facts, except that Third Party does review the certificate of limited partnership before entering into the transaction. The result might still be the same.

The omission of a person's name from the certificate's list of general partners is **not** notice that the person is **not** a general partner. Therefore, Third Party's review of the certificate does not mean that Third Party knew, had received a notification or had notice that G lacked authority. At most, XYZ could argue that, because Third Party knew that G was not listed in the certificate, a transaction entered into by G could not appear to Third Party to be for apparently carrying on the limited partnership's activities in the ordinary course.

§ 402.   General Partner Agent of Limited Partnership

(a)   Each general partner is an agent of the limited partnership for the purposes of its activities. An act of a general partner, including the signing of a record in the partnership's name, for apparently carrying on in the ordinary course the limited partnership's activities or activities of the kind carried on by the limited partnership binds the limited partnership, unless the general partner did not have authority to act for the limited partnership in the particular matter and the person with which the general partner was dealing knew, had received a notification, or had notice under Section 103(d) that the general partner lacked authority.

(b)   An act of a general partner which is not apparently for carrying on in the ordinary course the limited partnership's activities or activities of the kind carried on by the limited partnership binds the limited partnership only if the act was actually authorized by all the other partners.

COMMENT

Source—RUPA Section 301. For the meaning of "authority" in subsection (a) and "authorized" in subsection (b), *see* RUPA Section 301, Comment 3 (stating that "Subsection (2) [of RUPA Section 301] makes it clear that the partnership is bound by a partner's *actual* authority, even if the partner has no apparent authority"; emphasis added).

The fact that a person is not listed in the certificate of limited partnership as a general partner is **not** notice that the person is **not** a partner and is **not** notice that the person lacks authority to act for the limited partnership. *See* Comment to Section 103(c) and Comment to Section 401.

Section 103(f) defines receipt of notification. Section 103(d) lists various public filings, each of which provides notice 90 days after its effective date.

Example: For the past ten years, X has been a general partner of XYZ Limited Partnership and has regularly conducted the limited partnership's business with Third Party. However, 100 days ago the limited partnership expelled X as a general partner and the next day delivered for filing an amendment to XYZ's certificate of limited partnership which stated that X was no longer a general partner. On that same day, the filing officer filed the amendment.

Today X approaches Third Party, purports [to still be] a general partner of XYZ and purports to enter into a transaction with Third Party on XYZ's behalf. Third Party is unaware that X has been expelled and has no reason to doubt . . . X's bona fides. Nonetheless, XYZ is not liable on the transaction. Under Section 103(d), Third Party has notice that X is dissociated and perforce has notice that X is not a general partner authorized to bind XYZ.

§ 403.   Limited Partnership Liable for General Partner's Actionable Conduct

(a)   A limited partnership is liable for loss or injury caused to a person, or for a penalty incurred, as a result of a wrongful act or omission, or other actionable conduct, of a general partner acting in the ordinary course of activities of the limited partnership or with authority of the limited partnership.

(b) If, in the course of the limited partnership's activities or while acting with authority of the limited partnership, a general partner receives or causes the limited partnership to receive money or property of a person not a partner, and the money or property is misapplied by a general partner, the limited partnership is liable for the loss.

COMMENT

Source—RUPA Section 305. For the meaning of "authority" in subsections (a) and (b), *see* RUPA Section 305, Comment. The third-to-last paragraph of that Comment states:

> The partnership is liable for the actionable conduct or omission of a partner acting in the ordinary course of its business or "with the authority of the partnership." This is intended to include a partner's apparent, as well as actual, authority, thereby bringing within Section 305(a) the situation covered in UPA Section 14(a).

The last paragraph of that Comment states:

> Section 305(b) is drawn from UPA Section 14(b), but has been edited to improve clarity. It imposes strict liability on the partnership for the misapplication of money or property received by a partner in the course of the partnership's business or otherwise within the scope of the partner's actual authority.

Section 403(a) of this Act is taken essentially verbatim from RUPA Section 305(a), and Section 403(b) of this Act is taken essentially verbatim from RUPA Section 305(b).

This section makes the limited partnership vicariously liable for a partner's misconduct. That vicarious[ ] liability in no way discharges or diminishes the partner's direct liability for the partner's own misconduct.

A general partner can cause a limited partnership to be liable under this section, even if the general partner is not designated as a general partner in the certificate of limited partnership. *See* Comment to Section 401.

§ 404. General Partner's Liability

(a) Except as otherwise provided in subsections (b) and (c), all general partners are liable jointly and severally for all obligations of the limited partnership unless otherwise agreed by the claimant or provided by law.

(b) A person that becomes a general partner of an existing limited partnership is not personally liable for an obligation of a limited partnership incurred before the person became a general partner.

(c) An obligation of a limited partnership incurred while the limited partnership is a limited liability limited partnership, whether arising in contract, tort, or otherwise, is solely the obligation of the limited partnership. A general partner is not personally liable, directly or indirectly, by way of contribution or otherwise, for such an obligation solely by reason of being or acting as a general partner. This subsection applies despite anything inconsistent in the partnership agreement that existed immediately before the consent required to become a limited liability limited partnership under Section 406(b)(2).

COMMENT

Source—RUPA Section 306.

Following RUPA and the UPA, this Act leaves to other law the question of when a limited partnership obligation is incurred.

Subsection (c)—For an explanation of the decision to provide for limited liability limited partnerships, *see* the Prefatory Note.

§ 405.   Actions by and Against Partnership and Partners

(a) To the extent not inconsistent with Section 404, a general partner may be joined in an action against the limited partnership or named in a separate action.

(b) A judgment against a limited partnership is not by itself a judgment against a general partner. A judgment against a limited partnership may not be satisfied from a general partner's assets unless there is also a judgment against the general partner.

(c) A judgment creditor of a general partner may not levy execution against the assets of the general partner to satisfy a judgment based on a claim against the limited partnership, unless the partner is personally liable for the claim under Section 404 and:

(1) a judgment based on the same claim has been obtained against the limited partnership and a writ of execution on the judgment has been returned unsatisfied in whole or in part;

(2) the limited partnership is a debtor in bankruptcy;

(3) the general partner has agreed that the creditor need not exhaust limited partnership assets;

(4) a court grants permission to the judgment creditor to levy execution against the assets of a general partner based on a finding that limited partnership assets subject to execution are clearly insufficient to satisfy the judgment, that exhaustion of limited partnership assets is excessively burdensome, or that the grant of permission is an appropriate exercise of the court's equitable powers; or

(5) liability is imposed on the general partner by law or contract independent of the existence of the limited partnership.

COMMENT

Source—RUPA Section 307.

If a limited partnership is a limited liability limited partnership throughout its existence, this section will bar a creditor of a limited partnership from impleading, suing or reaching the assets of a general partner unless the creditor can satisfy subsection (c)(5).

§ 406.   Management Rights of General Partner

(a) Each general partner has equal rights in the management and conduct of the limited partnership's activities. Except as expressly provided in this [Act], any matter relating to the activities of the limited partnership may be exclusively decided by the general partner or, if there is more than one general partner, by a majority of the general partners.

(b) The consent of each partner is necessary to:

(1) amend the partnership agreement;

(2) amend the certificate of limited partnership to add or, subject to Section 1110, delete a statement that the limited partnership is a limited liability limited partnership; and

(3) sell, lease, exchange, or otherwise dispose of all, or substantially all, of the limited partnership's property, with or without the good will, other than in the usual and regular course of the limited partnership's activities.

(c) A limited partnership shall reimburse a general partner for payments made and indemnify a general partner for liabilities incurred by the general partner in the ordinary course of the activities of the partnership or for the preservation of its activities or property.

(d) A limited partnership shall reimburse a general partner for an advance to the limited partnership beyond the amount of capital the general partner agreed to contribute.

(e) A payment or advance made by a general partner which gives rise to an obligation of the limited partnership under subsection (c) or (d) constitutes a loan to the limited partnership which accrues interest from the date of the payment or advance.

(f) A general partner is not entitled to remuneration for services performed for the partnership.

COMMENT

Source—RUPA Section 401 and ULLCA Section 404.

Subsection (a)—As explained in the Prefatory Note, this Act assumes that, more often than not, people utilizing the Act will want (i) strong centralized management, strongly entrenched, and (ii) passive investors with little control over the entity. Section 302 essentially excludes limited partners from the ordinary management of a limited partnership's activities. This subsection states affirmatively the general partners' commanding role. Only the partnership agreement and the express provisions of this Act can limit that role.

The authority granted by this subsection includes the authority to delegate. Delegation does not relieve the delegating general partner or partners of their duties under Section 408. However, the fact of delegation is a fact relevant to any breach of duty analysis.

Example: A sole general partner personally handles all "important paperwork" for a limited partnership. The general partner neglects to renew the fire insurance coverage on the a building owned by the limited partnership, despite having received and read a warning notice from the insurance company. The building subsequently burns to the ground and is a total loss. The general partner might be liable for breach of the duty of care under Section 408(c) (gross negligence).

Example: A sole general partner delegates responsibility for insurance renewals to the limited partnership's office manager, and that manager neglects to renew the fire insurance coverage on the building. Even assuming that the office manager has been grossly negligent, the general partner is not necessarily liable under Section 408(c). The office manager's gross negligence is not automatically attributed to the general partner. Under Section 408(c), the question is whether the general partner was grossly negligent (or worse) in selecting the general manager, delegating insurance renewal matters to the general manager and supervising the general manager after the delegation.

For the consequences of delegating authority to a person that is a limited partner, *see* the Comment to Section 305.

The partnership agreement may also provide for delegation and, subject to Section 110(b)(5)–(7), may modify a general partner's Section 408 duties.

Subsection (b)—This subsection limits the managerial rights of the general partners, requiring the consent of each general and limited partner for the specified actions. The subsection is subject to change by the partnership agreement, except as provided in Section 110(b)(12) (pertaining to consent rights established by Section 1110).

Subsection (c)—This Act does not include any parallel provision for limited partners, because they are assumed to be passive. To the extent that by contract or other arrangement a limited partner has authority to act on behalf of the limited partnership, agency law principles will create an indemnity obligation. In other situations, principles of restitution might apply.

Subsection (f)—Unlike RUPA Section 401(h), this subsection provides no compensation for winding up efforts. In a limited partnership, winding up is one of the tasks for which the limited partners depend on the general partner. There is no reason for the Act to single out this particular task as giving rise to compensation.

§ 407.　Right of General Partner and Former General Partner to Information

(a) A general partner, without having any particular purpose for seeking the information, may inspect and copy during regular business hours:

(1) in the limited partnership's designated office, required information; and

(2) at a reasonable location specified by the limited partnership, any other records maintained by the limited partnership regarding the limited partnership's activities and financial condition.

(b) Each general partner and the limited partnership shall furnish to a general partner:

(1) without demand, any information concerning the limited partnership's activities and activities reasonably required for the proper exercise of the general partner's rights and duties under the partnership agreement or this [Act]; and

(2) on demand, any other information concerning the limited partnership's activities, except to the extent the demand or the information demanded is unreasonable or otherwise improper under the circumstances.

(c) Subject to subsection (e), on 10 days' demand made in a record received by the limited partnership, a person dissociated as a general partner may have access to the information and records described in subsection (a) at the location specified in subsection (a) if:

(1) the information or record pertains to the period during which the person was a general partner;

(2) the person seeks the information or record in good faith; and

(3) the person satisfies the requirements imposed on a limited partner by Section 304(b).

(d) The limited partnership shall respond to a demand made pursuant to subsection (c) in the same manner as provided in Section 304(c).

(e) If a general partner dies, Section 704 applies.

(f) The limited partnership may impose reasonable restrictions on the use of information under this section. In any dispute concerning the reasonableness of a restriction under this subsection, the limited partnership has the burden of proving reasonableness.

(g) A limited partnership may charge a person dissociated as a general partner that makes a demand under this section reasonable costs of copying, limited to the costs of labor and material.

(h) A general partner or person dissociated as a general partner may exercise the rights under this section through an attorney or other agent. Any restriction imposed under subsection (f) or by the partnership agreement applies both to the attorney or other agent and to the general partner or person dissociated as a general partner.

(i) The rights under this section do not extend to a person as transferee, but the rights under subsection (c) of a person dissociated as a general may be exercised by the legal representative of an individual who dissociated as a general partner under Section 603(7)(B) or (C).

COMMENT

This section's structure parallels the structure of Section 304 and the Comment to that section may be helpful in understanding this section.

Subsection (b)—Source: RUPA Section 403(c).

Subsection (b)(1)—If a particular item of material information is apparent in the limited partnership's records, whether a general partner is obliged to disseminate that information to fellow general partners depends on the circumstances.

Example: A limited partnership has two general partners: each of which is regularly engaged in conducting the limited partnership's activities; both of which are aware of and have regular access to all significant limited partnership records; and neither of which has special responsibility for or knowledge about any particular aspect of those activities or the partnership records pertaining to any particular aspect of those activities. Most likely, neither general partner is obliged to draw the other general partner's attention to information apparent in the limited partnership's records.

Example: Although a limited partnership has three general partners, one is the managing partner with day-to-day responsibility for running the limited partnership's activities. The other two meet periodically with the managing general partner, and together with that partner function in a manner analogous to a corporate board of directors. Most likely, the managing general partner has a duty to draw the attention of the other general partners to important information, even if that information would be apparent from a review of the limited partnership's records.

In all events under subsection (b)(1), the question is whether the disclosure by one general partner is "reasonably required for the proper exercise" of the other general partner's rights and duties.

Subsection (f)—This provision is identical to Section 304(g) and the Comment to Section 304(g) is applicable here. Under this Act, general and limited partners have sharply different roles. A restriction that is reasonable as to a limited partner is not necessarily reasonable as to a general partner.

Subsection (g)—No charge is allowed for current general partners, because in almost all cases they would be entitled to reimbursement under Section 406(c). Contrast Section 304(h), which authorizes charges to current limited partners.

Subsection (i)—The Comment to Section 304(k) is applicable here.

§ 408.   General Standards of General Partner's Conduct

(a)   The only fiduciary duties that a general partner has to the limited partnership and the other partners are the duties of loyalty and care under subsections (b) and (c).

(b)   A general partner's duty of loyalty to the limited partnership and the other partners is limited to the following:

(1)   to account to the limited partnership and hold as trustee for it any property, profit, or benefit derived by the general partner in the conduct and winding up of the limited partnership's activities or derived from a use by the general partner of limited partnership property, including the appropriation of a limited partnership opportunity;

(2)   to refrain from dealing with the limited partnership in the conduct or winding up of the limited partnership's activities as or on behalf of a party having an interest adverse to the limited partnership; and

(3)   to refrain from competing with the limited partnership in the conduct or winding up of the limited partnership's activities.

(c)   A general partner's duty of care to the limited partnership and the other partners in the conduct and winding up of the limited partnership's activities is limited to refraining from engaging in grossly negligent or reckless conduct, intentional misconduct, or a knowing violation of law.

(d)   A general partner shall discharge the duties to the partnership and the other partners under this [Act] or under the partnership agreement and exercise any rights consistently with the obligation of good faith and fair dealing.

(e)   A general partner does not violate a duty or obligation under this [Act] or under the partnership agreement merely because the general partner's conduct furthers the general partner's own interest.

COMMENT

Source—RUPA Section 404.

This section does not prevent a general partner from delegating one or more duties, but delegation does not discharge the duty. For further discussion, *see* the Comment to Section 406(a).

If the partnership agreement removes a particular responsibility from a general partner, that general partner's fiduciary duty must be judged according to the rights and powers the general partner retains. For example, if the partnership agreement denies a general partner the right to act in a particular matter, the general partner's compliance with the partnership agreement cannot be a breach of fiduciary duty. However,

363

the general partner may still have a duty to provide advice with regard to the matter. That duty could arise from the fiduciary duty of care under Section 408(c) and the duty to provide information under Sections 304(i) and 407(b).

For the partnership agreement's power directly to circumscribe a general partner's fiduciary duty, *see* Section 110(b)(5) and (6).

Subsection (a)—The reference to "the other partners" does not affect the distinction between direct and derivative claims. *See* Section 1001(b) (prerequisites for a partner bringing a direct claim).

Subsection (b)—A general partner's duty under this subsection continues through winding up, since the limited partners' dependence on the general partner does not end at dissolution. *See* Comment to Section 406(f) (explaining why this Act provides no remuneration for a general partner's winding up efforts).

Subsection (d)—This provision is identical to Section 305(b) and the Comment to Section 305(b) is applicable here.

[ARTICLE] 5.   CONTRIBUTIONS AND DISTRIBUTIONS

§ 501.   Form of Contribution

A contribution of a partner may consist of tangible or intangible property or other benefit to the limited partnership, including money, services performed, promissory notes, other agreements to contribute cash or property, and contracts for services to be performed.

COMMENT

Source—ULLCA Section 401.

§ 502.   Liability for Contribution

(a)   A partner's obligation to contribute money or other property or other benefit to, or to perform services for, a limited partnership is not excused by the partner's death, disability, or other inability to perform personally.

(b)   If a partner does not make a promised non-monetary contribution, the partner is obligated at the option of the limited partnership to contribute money equal to that portion of the value, as stated in the required information, of the stated contribution which has not been made.

(c)   The obligation of a partner to make a contribution or return money or other property paid or distributed in violation of this [Act] may be compromised only by consent of all partners. A creditor of a limited partnership which extends credit or otherwise acts in reliance on an obligation described in subsection (a), without notice of any compromise under this subsection, may enforce the original obligation.

COMMENT

In contrast with predecessor law, RULPA Section 502(a), this Act does not include a statute of frauds provision covering promised contributions. Section 111(9)(A) does require that the value of a promised contribution be memorialized, but that requirement does not affect enforceability. *See* Comment to Section 111(9).

Subsection (a)—Source: RULPA Section 502(b).

Under common law principles of impracticability, an individual's death or incapacity will sometimes discharge a duty to render performance. Restatement (Second) of Contracts, Sections 261 and 262. This subsection overrides those principles.

Subsection (b)—RULPA Section 502(b).

This subsection is a statutory liquidated damage provision, exercisable at the option of the limited partnership, with the damage amount set according to the value of the promised, non-monetary contribution as stated in the required information.

Example: In order to become a limited partner, a person promises to contribute to the limited partnership various assets which the partnership agreement values at $150,000. In return for the person's promise, and in light of the agreed value, the limited partnership admits the person as a limited partner with a right to receive 25% of the limited partnership's distributions.

The promised assets are subject to a security agreement, but the limited partner promises to contribute them "free and clear." Before the limited partner can contribute the assets, the secured party forecloses on the security interest and sells the assets at a public sale for $75,000. Even if the $75,000 reflects the actual fair market value of the assets, under this subsection the limited partnership has a claim against the limited partner for "the value, as stated in the required information, of the stated contribution which has not been made"—[i.e.], $150,000.

This section applies "at the option of the limited partnership" and does not affect other remedies which the limited partnership may have under other law.

Example: Same facts as the previous example, except that the public sale brings $225,000. The limited partnership is not obliged to invoke this subsection and may instead sue for breach of the promise to make the contribution, asserting the $225,000 figure as evidence of the actual loss suffered as a result of the breach.

Subsection (c)—Source: ULLCA Section 402(b); RULPA Section 502(c). The first sentence of this subsection applies not only to promised contributions but also to improper distributions. *See* Sections 508 and 509. The second sentence, pertaining to creditor's rights, applies only to promised contributions.

§ 503. Sharing of Distributions

A distribution by a limited partnership must be shared among the partners on the basis of the value, as stated in the required records when the limited partnership decides to make the distribution, of the contributions the limited partnership has received from each partner.

COMMENT

This Act has no provision allocating profits and losses among the partners. Instead, the Act directly apportions the right to receive distributions.

Nearly all limited partnerships will choose to allocate profits and losses in order to comply with applicable tax, accounting and other regulatory requirements. Those requirements, rather than this Act, are the proper source of guidance for that profit and loss allocation.

Unlike predecessor law, this section apportions distributions in relation to the value of contributions received from each partner without regard to whether the limited partnership has returned any of those contributions. *Compare* RULPA Sections 503 and 504. This Act's approach produces the same result as predecessor law, so long as the limited partnership does not vary this section's approach to apportioning distributions.

This section's rule for sharing distributions is subject to change under Section 110. A limited partnership that does vary the rule should be careful to consider not only the tax and accounting consequences but also the "ripple" effect on other provisions of this Act. *See, e.g.*, Sections 801 and 803(c) (apportioning consent power in relation to the right to receive distributions).

§ 504. Interim Distributions

A partner does not have a right to any distribution before the dissolution and winding up of the limited partnership unless the limited partnership decides to make an interim distribution.

COMMENT

Under Section 406(a), the general partner or partners make this decision for the limited partnership.

§ 505.   No Distribution on Account of Dissociation

A person does not have a right to receive a distribution on account of dissociation.

COMMENT

This section varies substantially from predecessor law. RULPA Sections 603 and 604 permitted a limited partner to withdraw on six months notice and receive the fair value of the limited partnership interest, unless the partnership agreement provided the limited partner with some exit right or stated a definite duration for the limited partnership.

Under this Act, a partner that dissociates becomes a transferee of its own transferable interest. *See* Sections 602(a)(3) (person dissociated as a limited partner) and 605(a)(5) (person dissociated as a general partner).

§ 506.   Distribution in Kind

A partner does not have a right to demand or receive any distribution from a limited partnership in any form other than cash. subject to Section 812(b), a limited partnership may distribute an asset in kind to the extent each partner receives a percentage of the asset equal to the partner's share of distributions.

COMMENT

Source—RULPA Section 605.

§ 507.   Right to Distribution

When a partner or transferee becomes entitled to receive a distribution, the partner or transferee has the status of, and is entitled to all remedies available to, a creditor of the limited partnership with respect to the distribution. However, the limited partnership's obligation to make a distribution is subject to offset for any amount owed to the limited partnership by the partner or dissociated partner on whose account the distribution is made.

COMMENT

Source—RULPA Section 606.

This section's first sentence refers to distributions generally. Contrast Section 508(e), which refers to indebtedness issued as a distribution.

The reference in the second sentence to "dissociated partner" encompasses circumstances in which the partner is gone and the dissociated partner's transferable interest is all that remains.

§ 508.   Limitations on Distribution

(a) A limited partnership may not make a distribution in violation of the partnership agreement.

(b) A limited partnership may not make a distribution if after the distribution:

(1)   the limited partnership would not be able to pay its debts as they become due in the ordinary course of the limited partnership's activities; or

(2)   the limited partnership's total assets would be less than the sum of its total liabilities plus the amount that would be needed, if the limited partnership were to be dissolved, wound up, and terminated at the time of the distribution, to satisfy the preferential rights upon dissolution, winding up, and termination of partners whose preferential rights are superior to those of persons receiving the distribution.

(c)   A limited partnership may base a determination that a distribution is not prohibited under subsection (b) on financial statements prepared on the basis of accounting practices and principles that are reasonable in the circumstances or on a fair valuation or other method that is reasonable in the circumstances.

(d)   Except as otherwise provided in subsection (g), the effect of a distribution under subsection (b) is measured:

(1)   in the case of distribution by purchase, redemption, or other acquisition of a transferable interest in the limited partnership, as of the date money or other property is transferred or debt incurred by the limited partnership; and

(2)   in all other cases, as of the date:

(A)   the distribution is authorized, if the payment occurs within120 days after that date; or

(B)   the payment is made, if payment occurs more than120 days after the distribution is authorized.

(e)   A limited partnership's indebtedness to a partner incurred by reason of a distribution made in accordance with this section is at parity with the limited partnership's indebtedness to its general, unsecured creditors.

(f)   A limited partnership's indebtedness, including indebtedness issued in connection with or as part of a distribution, is not considered a liability for purposes of subsection (b) if the terms of the indebtedness provide that payment of principal and interest are made only to the extent that a distribution could then be made to partners under this section.

(g)   If indebtedness is issued as a distribution, each payment of principal or interest on the indebtedness is treated as a distribution, the effect of which is measured on the date the payment is made.

COMMENT

Source—ULLCA Section 406. *See also* RMBCA Section 6.40.

Subsection (c)—This subsection appears to impose a standard of ordinary care, in contrast with the general duty of care stated in Section 408(c). For a reconciliation of these two provisions, *see* Comment to Section 509(a).

§ 509.   Liability for Improper Distributions

(a)   A general partner that consents to a distribution made in violation of Section 508 is personally liable to the limited partnership for the amount of the distribution which exceeds the amount that could have been distributed without the violation if it is established that in consenting to the distribution the general partner failed to comply with Section 408.

(b)   A partner or transferee that received a distribution knowing that the distribution to that partner or transferee was made in violation of Section 508 is personally liable to the limited partnership but only to the extent that the distribution received by the partner or transferee exceeded the amount that could have been properly paid under Section 508.

(c)   A general partner against which an action is commenced under subsection (a) may:

(1)   implead in the action any other person that is liable under subsection (a) and compel contribution from the person; and

(2)   implead in the action any person that received a distribution in violation of subsection (b) and compel contribution from the person in the amount the person received in violation of subsection (b).

(d)   An action under this section is barred if it is not commenced within two years after the distribution.

COMMENT

Source—ULLCA Section 407. *See also* RMBCA Section 8.33.

In substance and effect this section protects the interests of creditors of the limited partnership. Therefore, according to Section 110(b)(13), the partnership agreement may not change this section in a way that restricts the rights of those creditors. As for a limited partnership's power to compromise a claim under this section, *see* Section 502(c).

Subsection (a)—This subsection refers both to Section 508, which includes in its subsection (c) a standard of ordinary care ("reasonable in the circumstances"), and to Section 408, which includes in its subsection (c) a general duty of care that is limited to "refraining from engaging in grossly negligent or reckless conduct, intentional misconduct, or a knowing violation of law."

A limited partnership's failure to meet the standard of Section 508(c) cannot by itself cause a general partner to be liable under Section 509(a). *Both* of the following would have to occur before a failure to satisfy Section 508(c) could occasion personal liability for a general partner under Section 509(a):

- the limited partnership "base[s] a determination that a distribution is not prohibited . . . on financial statements prepared on the basis of accounting practices and principles that are [not] reasonable in the circumstances or on a [not] fair valuation or other method that is [not] reasonable in the circumstances" [Section 508(c)]

AND

- the general partner's decision to rely on the improper methodology in consenting to the distribution constitutes "grossly negligent or reckless conduct, intentional misconduct, or a knowing violation of law" [Section 408(c)] or breaches some other duty under Section 408.

To serve the protective purpose of Sections 508 and 509, in this subsection "consent" must be understood as encompassing any form of approval, assent or acquiescence, whether formal or informal, express or tacit.

Subsection (d)—The subsection's limitation applies to the commencement of an action under subsection (a) or (b) and not to subsection (c), under which a general partner may implead other persons.

[ARTICLE] 6.   DISSOCIATION

§ 601.   Dissociation as Limited Partner

(a)   A person does not have a right to dissociate as a limited partner before the termination of the limited partnership.

(b)   A person is dissociated from a limited partnership as a limited partner upon the occurrence of any of the following events:

(1)   the limited partnership's having notice of the person's express will to withdraw as a limited partner or on a later date specified by the person;

(2)   an event agreed to in the partnership agreement as causing the person's dissociation as a limited partner;

(3)   the person's expulsion as a limited partner pursuant to the partnership agreement;

(4)   the person's expulsion as a limited partner by the unanimous consent of the other partners if:

(A)   it is unlawful to carry on the limited partnership's activities with the person as a limited partner;

368

(B)   there has been a transfer of all of the person's transferable interest in the limited partnership, other than a transfer for security purposes, or a court order charging the person's interest, which has not been foreclosed;

(C)   the person is a corporation and, within 90 days after the limited partnership notifies the person that it will be expelled as a limited partner because it has filed a certificate of dissolution or the equivalent, its charter has been revoked, or its right to conduct business has been suspended by the jurisdiction of its incorporation, there is no revocation of the certificate of dissolution or no reinstatement of its charter or its right to conduct business; or

(D)   the person is a limited liability company or partnership that has been dissolved and whose business is being wound up;

(5)   on application by the limited partnership, the person's expulsion as a limited partner by judicial order because:

(A)   the person engaged in wrongful conduct that adversely and materially affected the limited partnership's activities;

(B)   the person willfully or persistently committed a material breach of the partnership agreement or of the obligation of good faith and fair dealing under Section 305(b); or

(C)   the person engaged in conduct relating to the limited partnership's activities which makes it not reasonably practicable to carry on the activities with the person as limited partner;

(6)   in the case of a person who is an individual, the person's death;

(7)   in the case of a person that is a trust or is acting as a limited partner by virtue of being a trustee of a trust, distribution of the trust's entire transferable interest in the limited partnership, but not merely by reason of the substitution of a successor trustee;

(8)   in the case of a person that is an estate or is acting as a limited partner by virtue of being a personal representative of an estate, distribution of the estate's entire transferable interest in the limited partnership, but not merely by reason of the substitution of a successor personal representative;

(9)   termination of a limited partner that is not an individual, partnership, limited liability company, corporation, trust, or estate;

(10)   the limited partnership's participation in a conversion or merger under [Article] 11, if the limited partnership:

(A)   is not the converted or surviving entity; or

(B)   is the converted or surviving entity but, as a result of the conversion or merger, the person ceases to be a limited partner.

COMMENT

Source—RUPA Section 601.

This section adopts RUPA's dissociation provision essentially verbatim, except for provisions inappropriate to limited partners. For example, this section does not provide for the dissociation of a person as a limited partner on account of bankruptcy, insolvency or incompetency.

This Act refers to *a person's dissociation as a limited partner* rather than to the *dissociation of a limited partner*, because the same person may be both a general and a limited partner. *See* Section 113 (Dual Capacity). It is possible for a dual capacity partner to dissociate in one capacity and not in the other.

Subsection (a)—This section varies substantially from predecessor law. *See* Comment to Section 505.

Subsection (b)(1)—This provision gives a person the power to dissociate as a limited partner even though the dissociation is wrongful under subsection (a). See, however, Section 110(b)(8) (prohibiting the partnership agreement from eliminating the power of a person to dissociate as a *general* partner but imposing no comparable restriction with regard to a person's dissociation as a *limited* partner).

Subsection (b)(5)—In contrast to RUPA, this provision may be varied or even eliminated by the partnership agreement.

§ 602.   Effect of Dissociation as Limited Partner

(a)   Upon a person's dissociation as a limited partner:

(1)   subject to Section 704, the person does not have further rights as a limited partner;

(2)   the person's obligation of good faith and fair dealing as a limited partner under Section 305(b) continues only as to matters arising and events occurring before the dissociation; and

(3)   subject to Section 704 and [Article] 11, any transferable interest owned by the person in the person's capacity as a limited partner immediately before dissociation is owned by the person as a mere transferee.

(b)   A person's dissociation as a limited partner does not of itself discharge the person from any obligation to the limited partnership or the other partners which the person incurred while a limited partner.

COMMENT

Source—RUPA Section 603(b).

Subsection (a)(1)—In general, when a person dissociates as a limited partner, the person's rights as a limited partner disappear and, subject to Section 113 (Dual Status), the person's status degrades to that of a mere transferee. However, Section 704 provides some special rights when dissociation is caused by an individual's death.

Subsection (a)(3)—For any person that is both a general partner and a limited partner, the required records must state which transferable interest is owned in which capacity. Section 111(9)(C).

Article 11 provides for conversions and mergers. A plan of conversion or merger may provide for the dissociation of a person as a limited partner and may override the rule stated in this paragraph.

§ 603.   Dissociation as General Partner

A person is dissociated from a limited partnership as a general partner upon the occurrence of any of the following events:

(1)   the limited partnership's having notice of the person's express will to withdraw as a general partner or on a later date specified by the person;

(2)   an event agreed to in the partnership agreement as causing the person's dissociation as a general partner;

(3)   the person's expulsion as a general partner pursuant to the partnership agreement;

(4)   the person's expulsion as a general partner by the unanimous consent of the other partners if:

(A)   it is unlawful to carry on the limited partnership's activities with the person as a general partner;

(B)   there has been a transfer of all or substantially all of the person's transferable interest in the limited partnership, other than a transfer for security purposes, or a court order charging the person's interest, which has not been foreclosed;

(C) the person is a corporation and, within 90 days after the limited partnership notifies the person that it will be expelled as a general partner because it has filed a certificate of dissolution or the equivalent, its charter has been revoked, or its right to conduct business has been suspended by the jurisdiction of its incorporation, there is no revocation of the certificate of dissolution or no reinstatement of its charter or its right to conduct business; or

(D) the person is a limited liability company or partnership that has been dissolved and whose business is being wound up;

(5) on application by the limited partnership, the person's expulsion as a general partner by judicial determination because:

(A) the person engaged in wrongful conduct that adversely and materially affected the limited partnership activities;

(B) the person willfully or persistently committed a material breach of the partnership agreement or of a duty owed to the partnership or the other partners under Section 408; or

(C) the person engaged in conduct relating to the limited partnership's activities which makes it not reasonably practicable to carry on the activities of the limited partnership with the person as a general partner;

(6) the person's:

(A) becoming a debtor in bankruptcy;

(B) execution of an assignment for the benefit of creditors;

(C) seeking, consenting to, or acquiescing in the appointment of a trustee, receiver, or liquidator of the person or of all or substantially all of the person's property; or

(D) failure, within 90 days after the appointment, to have vacated or stayed the appointment of a trustee, receiver, or liquidator of the general partner or of all or substantially all of the person's property obtained without the person's consent or acquiescence, or failing within 90 days after the expiration of a stay to have the appointment vacated;

(7) in the case of a person who is an individual:

(A) the person's death;

(B) the appointment of a guardian or general conservator for the person; or

(C) a judicial determination that the person has otherwise become incapable of performing the person's duties as a general partner under the partnership agreement;

(8) in the case of a person that is a trust or is acting as a general partner by virtue of being a trustee of a trust, distribution of the trust's entire transferable interest in the limited partnership, but not merely by reason of the substitution of a successor trustee;

(9) in the case of a person that is an estate or is acting as a general partner by virtue of being a personal representative of an estate, distribution of the estate's entire transferable interest in the limited partnership, but not merely by reason of the substitution of a successor personal representative;

(10) termination of a general partner that is not an individual, partnership, limited liability company, corporation, trust, or estate; or

(11) the limited partnership's participation in a conversion or merger under [Article] 11, if the limited partnership:

(A) is not the converted or surviving entity; or

(B) is the converted or surviving entity but, as a result of the conversion or merger, the person ceases to be a general partner.

COMMENT

Source—RUPA Section 601.

This section adopts RUPA's dissociation provision essentially verbatim. This Act refers to *a person's dissociation as a general partner* rather than to the *dissociation of a general partner*, because the same person may be both a general and a limited partner. *See* Section 113 (Dual Capacity). It is possible for a dual capacity partner to dissociate in one capacity and not in the other.

Paragraph (1)—The partnership agreement may not eliminate this power to dissociate. *See* Section 110(b)(8).

Paragraph (5)—In contrast to RUPA, this provision may be varied or even eliminated by the partnership agreement.

§ 604.   Person's Power to Dissociate as General Partner; Wrongful Dissociation

(a)   A person has the power to dissociate as a general partner at any time, rightfully or wrongfully, by express will pursuant to Section 603(1).

(b)   A person's dissociation as a general partner is wrongful only if:

　(1)   it is in breach of an express provision of the partnership agreement; or

　(2)   it occurs before the termination of the limited partnership, and:

　　(A)   the person withdraws as a general partner by express will;

　　(B)   the person is expelled as a general partner by judicial determination under Section 603(5);

　　(C)   the person is dissociated as a general partner by becoming a debtor in bankruptcy; or

　　(D)   in the case of a person that is not an individual, trust other than a business trust, or estate, the person is expelled or otherwise dissociated as a general partner because it willfully dissolved or terminated.

(c)   A person that wrongfully dissociates as a general partner is liable to the limited partnership and, subject to Section 1001, to the other partners for damages caused by the dissociation. The liability is in addition to any other obligation of the general partner to the limited partnership or to the other partners.

COMMENT

Source—RUPA Section 602.

Subsection (a)—The partnership agreement may not eliminate this power. *See* Section 110(b)(8).

Subsection (b)(1)—The reference to "an express provision of the partnership agreement" means that a person's dissociation as a general partner in breach of the obligation of good faith and fair dealing is not wrongful dissociation for the purposes of this section. The breach might be actionable on other grounds.

Subsection (b)(2)—The reference to "before the termination of the limited partnership" reflects the expectation that each general partner will shepherd the limited partnership through winding up. *See* Comment to Section 406(f). A person's obligation to remain as general partner through winding up continues even if another general partner dissociates and even if that dissociation leads to the limited partnership's premature dissolution under Section 801(3)(A).

Subsection (c)—The language "subject to Section 1001" is intended to preserve the distinction between direct and derivative claims.

§ 605.   Effect of Dissociation as General Partner

(a)   Upon a person's dissociation as a general partner:

(1)   the person's right to participate as a general partner in the management and conduct of the partnership's activities terminates;

(2)   the person's duty of loyalty as a general partner under Section 408(b)(3) terminates;

(3)   the person's duty of loyalty as a general partner under Section 408(b)(1) and (2) and duty of care under Section 408(c) continue only with regard to matters arising and events occurring before the person's dissociation as a general partner;

(4)   the person may sign and deliver to the [Secretary of State] for filing a statement of dissociation pertaining to the person and, at the request of the limited partnership, shall sign an amendment to the certificate of limited partnership which states that the person has dissociated; and

(5)   subject to Section 704 and [Article] 11, any transferable interest owned by the person immediately before dissociation in the person's capacity as a general partner is owned by the person as a mere transferee.

(b)   A person's dissociation as a general partner does not of itself discharge the person from any obligation to the limited partnership or the other partners which the person incurred while a general partner.

COMMENT

Source—RUPA Section 603(b).

Subsection (a)(1)—Once a person dissociates as a general partner, the person loses all management rights as a general partner regardless of what happens to the limited partnership. This rule contrasts with RUPA Section 603(b)(1), which permits a dissociated general partner to participate in winding up in some circumstances.

Subsection (a)(4)—Both records covered by this paragraph have the same effect under Section 103(d)—namely, to give constructive notice that the person has dissociated as a general partner. The notice benefits the person by curtailing any further personal liability under Sections 607, 805, and 1111. The notice benefits the limited partnership by curtailing any lingering power to bind under Sections 606, 804, and 1112.

The limited partnership is in any event obligated to amend its certificate of limited partnership to reflect the dissociation of a person as general partner. *See* Section 202(b)(2). In most circumstances, the amendment requires the signature of the person that has dissociated. Section 204(a)(5)(C). If that signature is required and the person refuses or fails to sign, the limited partnership may invoke Section 205 (Signing and Filing Pursuant to Judicial Order).

Subsection (a)(5)—In general, when a person dissociates as a general partner, the person's rights as a general partner disappear and, subject to Section 113 (Dual Status), the person's status degrades to that of a mere transferee. For any person that is both a general partner and a limited partner, the required records must state which transferable interest is owned in which capacity. Section 111(9)(C).

Section 704 provides some special rights when an individual dissociates by dying. Article 11 provides for conversions and mergers. A plan of conversion or merger may provide for the dissociation of a person as a general partner and may override the rule stated in this paragraph.

§ 606.   Power to Bind and Liability to Limited Partnership Before Dissolution of Partnership of Person Dissociated as General Partner

(a)   After a person is dissociated as a general partner and before the limited partnership is dissolved, converted under [Article] 11, or merged out of existence under [Article 11], the limited partnership is bound by an act of the person only if:

(1)   the act would have bound the limited partnership under Section 402 before the dissociation; and

(2)   at the time the other party enters into the transaction:

(A)   less than two years has passed since the dissociation; and

(B)   the other party does not have notice of the dissociation and reasonably believes that the person is a general partner.

(b)   If a limited partnership is bound under subsection (a), the person dissociated as a general partner which caused the limited partnership to be bound is liable:

(1)   to the limited partnership for any damage caused to the limited partnership arising from the obligation incurred under subsection (a); and

(2)   if a general partner or another person dissociated as a general partner is liable for the obligation, to the general partner or other person for any damage caused to the general partner or other person arising from the liability.

COMMENT

Source—RUPA Section 702.

This Act contains three sections pertaining to the lingering power to bind of a person dissociated as a general partner:

- this section, which applies until the limited partnership dissolves, converts to another form of organization under Article 11, or is merged out of existence under Article 11;

- Section 804(b), which applies after a limited partnership dissolves; and

- Section 1112(b), which applies after a conversion or merger.

Subsection (a)(2)(B)—A person might have notice under Section 103(d)(1) as well as under Section 103(b).

Subsection (b)—The liability provided by this subsection is not exhaustive. For example, if a person dissociated as a general partner causes a limited partnership to be bound under subsection (a) and, due to a guaranty, some other person is liable on the resulting obligation, that other person may have a claim under other law against the person dissociated as a general partner.

§ 607.   Liability to Other Persons of Person Dissociated as General Partner

(a)   A person's dissociation as a general partner does not of itself discharge the person's liability as a general partner for an obligation of the limited partnership incurred before dissociation. Except as otherwise provided in subsections (b) and (c), the person is not liable for a limited partnership's obligation incurred after dissociation.

(b)   A person whose dissociation as a general partner resulted in a dissolution and winding up of the limited partnership's activities is liable to the same extent as a general partner under Section 404 on an obligation incurred by the limited partnership under Section 804.

(c)   A person that has dissociated as a general partner but whose dissociation did not result in a dissolution and winding up of the limited partnership's activities is liable on a transaction entered into by the limited partnership after the dissociation only if:

(1)   a general partner would be liable on the transaction; and

(2)   at the time the other party enters into the transaction:

(A)   less than two years has passed since the dissociation; and

(B)   the other party does not have notice of the dissociation and reasonably believes that the person is a general partner.

(d) By agreement with a creditor of a limited partnership and the limited partnership, a person dissociated as a general partner may be released from liability for an obligation of the limited partnership.

(e) A person dissociated as a general partner is released from liability for an obligation of the limited partnership if the limited partnership's creditor, with notice of the person's dissociation as a general partner but without the person's consent, agrees to a material alteration in the nature or time of payment of the obligation.

COMMENT

Source—RUPA Section 703.

A person's dissociation as a general partner does not categorically prevent the person from being liable as a general partner for subsequently incurred obligations of the limited partnership. If the dissociation results in dissolution, subsection (b) applies and the person will be liable as a general partner on any partnership obligation incurred under Section 804. In these circumstances, neither filing a statement of dissociation nor amending the certificate of limited partnership to state that the person has dissociated as a general partner will curtail the person's lingering exposure to liability.

If the dissociation does not result in dissolution, subsection (c) applies. In this context, filing a statement of dissociation or amending the certificate of limited partnership to state that the person has dissociated as a general partner will curtail the person's lingering liability. *See* subsection (c)(2)(B).

If the limited partnership subsequently dissolves as the result of some other occurrence (i.e., not a result of the person's dissociation as a general partner), subsection (c) continues to apply. In that situation, Section 804 will determine whether, for the purposes of subsection (c), the limited partnership has entered into a transaction after dissolution.

If the limited partnership is a limited liability limited partnership, these liability rules are moot.

Subsection (a)—The phrase "liability as a general partner for an obligation of the limited partnership" refers to liability under Section 404. Following RUPA and the UPA, this Act leaves to other law the question of when a limited partnership obligation is incurred.

Subsection (c)(2)(B)—A person might have notice under Section 103(d)(1) as well as under Section 103(b).

[ARTICLE] 7. TRANSFERABLE INTERESTS AND RIGHTS OF TRANSFEREES AND CREDITORS

§ 701. Partner's Transferable Interest

The only interest of a partner which is transferable is the partner's transferable interest. A transferable interest is personal property.

COMMENT

Source—RUPA Section 502.

Like all other partnership statutes, this Act dichotomizes each partner's rights into economic rights and other rights. The former are freely transferable, as provided in Section 702. The latter are not transferable at all, unless the partnership agreement so provides.

Although a partner or transferee owns a transferable interest as a present right, that right only entitles the owner to distributions if and when made. *See* Sections 504 (subject to any contrary provision in the partnership agreement, no right to interim distribution unless the limited partnership decides to make an interim distribution) and the Comment to Section 812 (subject to any contrary provision in the partnership agreement, no partner obligated to contribute for the purpose of equalizing or otherwise allocating capital losses).

§ 702.   Transfer of Partner's Transferable Interest

(a)   A transfer, in whole or in part, of a partner's transferable interest:

    (1)   is permissible;

    (2)   does not by itself cause the partner's dissociation or a dissolution and winding up of the limited partnership's activities; and

    (3)   does not, as against the other partners or the limited partnership, entitle the transferee to participate in the management or conduct of the limited partnership's activities, to require access to information concerning the limited partnership's transactions except as otherwise provided in subsection (c), or to inspect or copy the required information or the limited partnership's other records.

(b)   A transferee has a right to receive, in accordance with the transfer:

    (1)   distributions to which the transferor would otherwise be entitled; and

    (2)   upon the dissolution and winding up of the limited partnership's activities the net amount otherwise distributable to the transferor.

(c)   In a dissolution and winding up, a transferee is entitled to an account of the limited partnership's transactions only from the date of dissolution.

(d)   Upon transfer, the transferor retains the rights of a partner other than the interest in distributions transferred and retains all duties and obligations of a partner.

(e)   A limited partnership need not give effect to a transferee's rights under this section until the limited partnership has notice of the transfer.

(f)   A transfer of a partner's transferable interest in the limited partnership in violation of a restriction on transfer contained in the partnership agreement is ineffective as to a person having notice of the restriction at the time of transfer.

(g)   A transferee that becomes a partner with respect to a transferable interest is liable for the transferor's obligations under Sections 502 and 509. However, the transferee is not obligated for liabilities unknown to the transferee at the time the transferee became a partner.

COMMENT

Source—RUPA Section 503, except for subsection (g), which derives from RULPA Section 704(b). Following RUPA, this Act uses the words "transfer" and "transferee" rather than the words "assignment" and "assignee." *See* RUPA Section 503.

Subsection (a)(2)—The phrase "by itself" is significant. A transfer of all of a person's transferable interest could lead to dissociation via expulsion, Sections 601(b)(4)(B) and 603(4)(B).

Subsection (a)(3)—Mere transferees have no right to intrude as the partners carry on their activities as partners. Moreover, a partner's obligation of good faith and fair dealing under Sections 305(b) and 408(d) is framed in reference to "the limited partnership and the other partners." *See also* Comment to Section 1102(b)(3) and Comment to Section 1106(b)(3).

§ 703.   Rights of Creditor of Partner or Transferee

(a)   On application to a court of competent jurisdiction by any judgment creditor of a partner or transferee, the court may charge the transferable interest of the judgment debtor with payment of the unsatisfied amount of the judgment with interest. To the extent so charged, the judgment creditor has only the rights of a transferee. The court may appoint a receiver of the share of the distributions due or to become due to the judgment debtor in respect of the partnership and make all other orders, directions, accounts, and inquiries the judgment debtor might have made or which the circumstances of the case may require to give effect to the charging order.

(b)   A charging order constitutes a lien on the judgment debtor's transferable interest. The court may order a foreclosure upon the interest subject to the charging order at any time. The purchaser at the foreclosure sale has the rights of a transferee.

(c)   At any time before foreclosure, an interest charged may be redeemed:

(1)   by the judgment debtor;

(2)   with property other than limited partnership property, by one or more of the other partners; or

(3)   with limited partnership property, by the limited partnership with the consent of all partners whose interests are not so charged.

(d)   This [Act] does not deprive any partner or transferee of the benefit of any exemption laws applicable to the partner's or transferee's transferable interest.

(e)   This section provides the exclusive remedy by which a judgment creditor of a partner or transferee may satisfy a judgment out of the judgment debtor's transferable interest.

COMMENT

Source—RUPA Section 504 and ULLCA Section 504.

This section balances the needs of a judgment creditor of a partner or transferee with the needs of the limited partnership and non-debtor partners and transferees. The section achieves that balance by allowing the judgment creditor to collect on the judgment through the transferable interest of the judgment debtor while prohibiting interference in the management and activities of the limited partnership.

Under this section, the judgment creditor of a partner or transferee is entitled to a charging order against the relevant transferable interest. While in effect, that order entitles the judgment creditor to whatever distributions would otherwise be due to the partner or transferee whose interest is subject to the order. The creditor has no say in the timing or amount of those distributions. The charging order does not entitle the creditor to accelerate any distributions or to otherwise interfere with the management and activities of the limited partnership.

Foreclosure of a charging order effects a permanent transfer of the charged transferable interest to the purchaser. The foreclosure does not, however, create any rights to participate in the management and conduct of the limited partnership's activities. The purchaser obtains nothing more than the status of a transferee.

Subsection (a)—The court's power to appoint a receiver and "make all other orders, directions, accounts, and inquiries the judgment debtor might have made or which the circumstances of the case may require" must be understood in the context of the balance described above. In particular, the court's power to make orders "which the circumstances may require" is limited to "giv[ing] effect to the charging order."

Example: A judgment creditor with a charging order believes that the limited partnership should invest less of its surplus in operations, leaving more funds for distributions. The creditor moves the court for an order directing the general partners to restrict re-investment. This section does not authorize the court to grant the motion.

Example: A judgment creditor with a judgment for $10,000 against a partner obtains a charging order against the partner's transferable interest. The limited partnership is duly served with the order. However, the limited partnership subsequently fails to comply with the order and makes a $3000 distribution to the partner. The court has the power to order the limited partnership to turn over $3000 to the judgment creditor to "give effect to the charging order."

The court also has the power to decide whether a particular payment is a distribution, because this decision determines whether the payment is part of a transferable interest subject to a charging order. (To the extent a payment is not a distribution, it is not part of the transferable interest and is not subject to subsection (e). The payment is therefore subject to whatever other creditor remedies may apply.)

Subsection (c)(3)—This provision requires the consent of all the limited as well as general partners.

§ 704.   Power of Estate of Deceased Partner

If a partner dies, the deceased partner's personal representative or other legal representative may exercise the rights of a transferee as provided in section 702 and, for the purposes of settling the estate, may exercise the rights of a current limited partner under section 304.

COMMENT

Section 702 strictly limits the rights of transferees. In particular, a transferee has no right to participate in management in any way, no voting rights and, except following dissolution, no information rights. Even after dissolution, a transferee's information rights are limited. *See* Section 702(c).

This section provides special informational rights for a deceased partner's legal representative for the purposes of settling the estate. For those purposes, the legal representative may exercise the informational rights of a current limited partner under Section 304. Those rights are of course subject to the limitations and obligations stated in that section—*e.g.*, Section 304 (g) (restrictions on use) and (h) (charges for copies)— as well as any generally applicable limitations stated in the partnership agreement.

[ARTICLE] 8.   DISSOLUTION

§ 801.   Nonjudicial Dissolution

Except as otherwise provided in Section 802, a limited partnership is dissolved, and its activities must be wound up, only upon the occurrence of any of the following:

(1)   the happening of an event specified in the partnership agreement;

(2)   the consent of all general partners and of limited partners owning a majority of the rights to receive distributions as limited partners at the time the consent is to be effective;

(3)   after the dissociation of a person as a general partner:

(A)   if the limited partnership has at least one remaining general partner, the consent to dissolve the limited partnership given within 90 days after the dissociation by partners owning a majority of the rights to receive distributions as partners at the time the consent is to be effective; or

(B)   if the limited partnership does not have a remaining general partner, the passage of 90 days after the dissociation, unless before the end of the period:

(i)   consent to continue the activities of the limited partnership and admit at least one general partner is given by limited partners owning a majority of the rights to receive distributions as limited partners at the time the consent is to be effective; and

(ii)   at least one person is admitted as a general partner in accordance with the consent;

(4)   the passage of 90 days after the dissociation of the limited partnership's last limited partner, unless before the end of the period the limited partnership admits at least one limited partner; or

(5)   the signing and filing of a declaration of dissolution by the [Secretary of State] under Section 809(c).

COMMENT

This Act does not require that any of the consents referred to in this section be given in the form of a signed record. The partnership agreement has the power to impose that requirement. *See* Comment to Section 110.

In several provisions, this section provides for consent in terms of rights to receive distributions. Distribution rights of non-partner transferees are not relevant. Mere transferees have no consent rights, and their distribution rights are not counted in determining whether majority consent has been obtained.

Paragraph (1)—There is no requirement that the relevant provision of the partnership agreement be made in a record, unless the partnership agreement creates that requirement. However, if the relevant provision is not "contained in a partnership agreement made in a record," Section 111(9)(D) includes among the limited partnership's required information "a record stating . . . any events upon the happening of which the limited partnership is to be dissolved and its activities wound up."

Paragraph (2)—Rights to receive distributions owned by a person that is both a general and a limited partner figure into the limited partner determination only to the extent those rights are owned in the person's capacity as a limited partner. *See* Section 111(9)(C).

Example: XYZ is a limited partnership with three general partners, each of whom is also a limited partner, and 5 other limited partners. Rights to receive distributions are allocated as follows:

Partner #1 as general partner—3%
Partner #2 as general partner—2%
Partner #3 as general partner—1%
Partner #1 as limited partner—7%
Partner #2 as limited partner—3%
Partner #3 as limited partner—4%
Partner #4 as limited partner—5%
Partner #5 as limited partner—5%
Partner #6 as limited partner—5%
Partner #7 as limited partner—5%
Partner #8 as limited partner—5%
Several non-partner transferees, in the aggregate—55%

Distribution rights owned by persons as limited partners amount to 39% of total distribution rights. A majority is therefore anything greater than 19.5%. If only Partners 1, 2, 3 and 4 consent to dissolve, the limited partnership is not dissolved. Together these partners own as limited partners 19% of the distribution rights owned by persons as limited partners—just short of the necessary majority. For purposes of this calculation, distribution rights owned by non-partner transferees are irrelevant. So, too, are distribution rights owned by persons as general partners. (However, dissolution under this provision requires "the consent of all general partners.")

Paragraph (3)(A)—Unlike paragraph (2), this paragraph makes no distinction between distribution rights owned by persons as general partners and distribution rights owned by persons as limited partners. Distribution rights owned by non-partner transferees are irrelevant.

§ 802. Judicial Dissolution

On application by a partner the [appropriate court] may order dissolution of a limited partnership if it is not reasonably practicable to carry on the activities of the limited partnership in conformity with the partnership agreement.

COMMENT

Source—RULPA Section 802.

Section 110(b)(9) limits the power of the partnership agreement with regard to this section.

§ 803. Winding Up

(a) A limited partnership continues after dissolution only for the purpose of winding up its activities.

(b) In winding up its activities, the limited partnership:

(1) may amend its certificate of limited partnership to state that the limited partnership is dissolved, preserve the limited partnership business or property as a going concern for a reasonable time, prosecute and defend actions and proceedings, whether civil, criminal, or administrative, transfer the limited partnership's property, settle disputes by mediation or

arbitration, file a statement of termination as provided in Section 203, and perform other necessary acts; and

    (2)   shall discharge the limited partnership's liabilities, settle and close the limited partnership's activities, and marshal and distribute the assets of the partnership.

    (c)   If a dissolved limited partnership does not have a general partner, a person to wind up the dissolved limited partnership's activities may be appointed by the consent of limited partners owning a majority of the rights to receive distributions as limited partners at the time the consent is to be effective. A person appointed under this subsection:

    (1)   has the powers of a general partner under Section 804; and

    (2)   shall promptly amend the certificate of limited partnership to state:

    (A)   that the limited partnership does not have a general partner;

    (B)   the name of the person that has been appointed to wind up the limited partnership; and

    (C)   the street and mailing address of the person.

    (d)   On the application of any partner, the [appropriate court] may order judicial supervision of the winding up, including the appointment of a person to wind up the dissolved limited partnership's activities, if:

    (1)   a limited partnership does not have a general partner and within a reasonable time following the dissolution no person has been appointed pursuant to subsection (c); or

    (2)   the applicant establishes other good cause.

COMMENT

Source—RUPA Sections 802 and 803.

Subsection (b)(2)—A limited partnership may satisfy its duty to "discharge" a liability either by paying or by making an alternative arrangement satisfactory to the creditor.

Subsection (c)—The method for determining majority consent is analogous to the method applicable under Section 801(2). *See* the Comment to that paragraph.

A person appointed under this subsection is **not** a general partner and therefore is not subject to Section 408.

§ 804.   Power of General Partner and Person Dissociated as General Partner to Bind Partnership After Dissolution

    (a)   A limited partnership is bound by a general partner's act after dissolution which:

    (1)   is appropriate for winding up the limited partnership's activities; or

    (2)   would have bound the limited partnership under Section 402 before dissolution, if, at the time the other party enters into the transaction, the other party does not have notice of the dissolution.

    (b)   A person dissociated as a general partner binds a limited partnership through an act occurring after dissolution if:

    (1)   at the time the other party enters into the transaction:

    (A)   less than two years has passed since the dissociation; and

    (B)   the other party does not have notice of the dissociation and reasonably believes that the person is a general partner; and

    (2)   the act:

(A) is appropriate for winding up the limited partnership's activities; or

(B) would have bound the limited partnership under Section 402 before dissolution and at the time the other party enters into the transaction the other party does not have notice of the dissolution.

COMMENT

Subsection (a)—Source: RUPA Section 804.

Subsection (a)(2)—A person might have notice under Section 103(d)(2) (amendment of certificate of limited partnership to indicate dissolution) as well as under Section 103(b).

Subsection (b)—This subsection deals with the post-dissolution power to bind of a person dissociated as a general partner. Paragraph (1) replicates the provisions of Section 606, pertaining to the pre-dissolution power to bind of a person dissociated as a general partner. Paragraph (2) replicates the provisions of subsection (a), which state the post-dissolution power to bind of a general partner. For a person dissociated as a general partner to bind a dissolved limited partnership, the person's act will have to satisfy both paragraph (1) and paragraph (2).

Subsection (b)(1)(B)—A person might have notice under Section 103(d)(1) as well as under Section 103(b).

Subsection (b)(2)(B)—A person might have notice under Section 103(d)(2) (amendment of certificate of limited partnership to indicate dissolution) as well as under Section 103(b).

§ 805. Liability After Dissolution of General Partner and Person Dissociated as General Partner to Limited Partnership, Other General Partners, and Persons Dissociated as General Partner

(a) If a general partner having knowledge of the dissolution causes a limited partnership to incur an obligation under Section 804(a) by an act that is not appropriate for winding up the partnership's activities, the general partner is liable:

(1) to the limited partnership for any damage caused to the limited partnership arising from the obligation; and

(2) if another general partner or a person dissociated as a general partner is liable for the obligation, to that other general partner or person for any damage caused to that other general partner or person arising from the liability.

(b) If a person dissociated as a general partner causes a limited partnership to incur an obligation under Section 804(b), the person is liable:

(1) to the limited partnership for any damage caused to the limited partnership arising from the obligation; and

(2) if a general partner or another person dissociated as a general partner is liable for the obligation, to the general partner or other person for any damage caused to the general partner or other person arising from the liability.

COMMENT

Source—RUPA Section 806.

It is possible for more than one person to be liable under this section on account of the same limited partnership obligation. This Act does not provide any rule for apportioning liability in that circumstance.

Subsection (a)(2)—If the limited partnership is not a limited liability limited partnership, the liability created by this paragraph includes liability under Sections 404(a), 607(b), and 607(c). The paragraph also applies when a partner or person dissociated as a general partner suffers damage due to a contract of guaranty.

§ 806.   Known Claims Against Dissolved Limited Partnership

(a)   A dissolved limited partnership may dispose of the known claims against it by following the procedure described in subsection (b).

(b)   A dissolved limited partnership may notify its known claimants of the dissolution in a record. The notice must:

(1)   specify the information required to be included in a claim;

(2)   provide a mailing address to which the claim is to be sent;

(3)   state the deadline for receipt of the claim, which may not be less than 120 days after the date the notice is received by the claimant;

(4)   state that the claim will be barred if not received by the deadline; and

(5)   unless the limited partnership has been throughout its existence a limited liability limited partnership, state that the barring of a claim against the limited partnership will also bar any corresponding claim against any general partner or person dissociated as a general partner which is based on Section 404.

(c)   A claim against a dissolved limited partnership is barred if the requirements of subsection (b) are met and:

(1)   the claim is not received by the specified deadline; or

(2)   in the case of a claim that is timely received but rejected by the dissolved limited partnership, the claimant does not commence an action to enforce the claim against the limited partnership within 90 days after the receipt of the notice of the rejection.

(d)   This section does not apply to a claim based on an event occurring after the effective date of dissolution or a liability that is contingent on that date.

COMMENT

Source—ULLCA Section 807. *See also* RMBCA Section 14.06.

Paragraph (b)(5)—If the limited partnership has always been a limited liability limited partnership, there can be no liability under Section 404 for any general partner or person dissociated as a general partner.

§ 807.   Other Claims Against Dissolved Limited Partnership

(a)   A dissolved limited partnership may publish notice of its dissolution and request persons having claims against the limited partnership to present them in accordance with the notice.

(b)   The notice must:

(1)   be published at least once in a newspaper of general circulation in the [county] in which the dissolved limited partnership's principal office is located or, if it has none in this State, in the [county] in which the limited partnership's designated office is or was last located;

(2)   describe the information required to be contained in a claim and provide a mailing address to which the claim is to be sent;

(3)   state that a claim against the limited partnership is barred unless an action to enforce the claim is commenced within five years after publication of the notice; and

(4)   unless the limited partnership has been throughout its existence a limited liability limited partnership, state that the barring of a claim against the limited partnership will also bar any corresponding claim against any general partner or person dissociated as a general partner which is based on Section 404.

(c)   If a dissolved limited partnership publishes a notice in accordance with subsection (b), the claim of each of the following claimants is barred unless the claimant commences an action to enforce the claim against the dissolved limited partnership within five years after the publication date of the notice:

(1)   a claimant that did not receive notice in a record under Section 806;

(2)   a claimant whose claim was timely sent to the dissolved limited partnership but not acted on; and

(3)   a claimant whose claim is contingent or based on an event occurring after the effective date of dissolution.

(d)   A claim not barred under this section may be enforced:

(1)   against the dissolved limited partnership, to the extent of its undistributed assets;

(2)   if the assets have been distributed in liquidation, against a partner or transferee to the extent of that person's proportionate share of the claim or the limited partnership's assets distributed to the partner or transferee in liquidation, whichever is less, but a person's total liability for all claims under this paragraph does not exceed the total amount of assets distributed to the person as part of the winding up of the dissolved limited partnership; or

(3)   against any person liable on the claim under Section 404.

COMMENT

Source—ULLCA Section 808. *See also* RMBCA Section 14.07.

Paragraph (b)(4)—If the limited partnership has always been a limited liability limited partnership, there can be no liability under Section 404 for any general partner or person dissociated as a general partner.

§ 808.   Liability of General Partner and Person Dissociated as General Partner When Claim Against Limited Partnership Barred

If a claim against a dissolved limited partnership is barred under Section 806 or 807, any corresponding claim under Section 404 is also barred.

COMMENT

The liability under Section 404 of a general partner or person dissociated as a general partner is merely liability for the obligations of the limited partnership.

§ 809.   Administrative Dissolution

(a)   The [Secretary of State] may dissolve a limited partnership administratively if the limited partnership does not, within 60 days after the due date:

(1)   pay any fee, tax, or penalty due to the [Secretary of State] under this [Act] or other law; or

(2)   deliver its annual report to the [Secretary of State].

(b)   If the [Secretary of State] determines that a ground exists for administratively dissolving a limited partnership, the [Secretary of State] shall file a record of the determination and serve the limited partnership with a copy of the filed record.

(c)   If within 60 days after service of the copy the limited partnership does not correct each ground for dissolution or demonstrate to the reasonable satisfaction of the [Secretary of State] that each ground determined by the [Secretary of State] does not exist, the [Secretary of State] shall administratively dissolve the limited partnership by preparing, signing and filing a declaration of dissolution that states the grounds for dissolution. The [Secretary of State] shall serve the limited partnership with a copy of the filed declaration.

(d)   A limited partnership administratively dissolved continues its existence but may carry on only activities necessary to wind up its activities and liquidate its assets under Sections 803 and 812 and to notify claimants under Sections 806 and 807.

(e)   The administrative dissolution of a limited partnership does not terminate the authority of its agent for service of process.

COMMENT

Source—ULLCA Sections 809 and 810. *See also* RMBCA Sections 14.20 and 14.21.

Subsection (a)(1)—This provision refers solely to money due the specified filing officer and does not apply to other money due to the State.

Subsection (c)—The filing of a declaration of dissolution does not provide notice under Section 103(d).

§ 810.   Reinstatement Following Administrative Dissolution

(a)   A limited partnership that has been administratively dissolved may apply to the [Secretary of State] for reinstatement within two years after the effective date of dissolution. The application must be delivered to the [Secretary of State] for filing and state:

(1)   the name of the limited partnership and the effective date of its administrative dissolution;

(2)   that the grounds for dissolution either did not exist or have been eliminated; and

(3)   that the limited partnership's name satisfies the requirements of Section 108.

(b)   If the [Secretary of State] determines that an application contains the information required by subsection (a) and that the information is correct, the [Secretary of State] shall prepare a declaration of reinstatement that states this determination, sign, and file the original of the declaration of reinstatement, and serve the limited partnership with a copy.

(c)   When reinstatement becomes effective, it relates back to and takes effect as of the effective date of the administrative dissolution and the limited partnership may resume its activities as if the administrative dissolution had never occurred.

COMMENT

Source—ULLCA Section 811. *See also* RMBCA Section 14.22.

§ 811.   Appeal From Denial of Reinstatement

(a)   If the [Secretary of State] denies a limited partnership's application for reinstatement following administrative dissolution, the [Secretary of State] shall prepare, sign and file a notice that explains the reason or reasons for denial and serve the limited partnership with a copy of the notice.

(b)   Within 30 days after service of the notice of denial, the limited partnership may appeal from the denial of reinstatement by petitioning the [appropriate court] to set aside the dissolution. The petition must be served on the [Secretary of State] and contain a copy of the [Secretary of State's] declaration of dissolution, the limited partnership's application for reinstatement, and the [Secretary of State's] notice of denial.

(c)   The court may summarily order the [Secretary of State] to reinstate the dissolved limited partnership or may take other action the court considers appropriate.

Source—ULLCA Section 812.

§ 812.   Disposition of Assets; When Contributions Required

(a) In winding up a limited partnership's activities, the assets of the limited partnership, including the contributions required by this section, must be applied to satisfy the limited partnership's obligations to creditors, including, to the extent permitted by law, partners that are creditors.

(b) Any surplus remaining after the limited partnership complies with subsection (a) must be paid in cash as a distribution.

(c) If a limited partnership's assets are insufficient to satisfy all of its obligations under subsection (a), with respect to each unsatisfied obligation incurred when the limited partnership was not a limited liability limited partnership, the following rules apply:

(1) Each person that was a general partner when the obligation was incurred and that has not been released from the obligation under Section 607 shall contribute to the limited partnership for the purpose of enabling the limited partnership to satisfy the obligation. The contribution due from each of those persons is in proportion to the right to receive distributions in the capacity of general partner in effect for each of those persons when the obligation was incurred.

(2) If a person does not contribute the full amount required under paragraph (1) with respect to an unsatisfied obligation of the limited partnership, the other persons required to contribute by paragraph (1) on account of the obligation shall contribute the additional amount necessary to discharge the obligation. The additional contribution due from each of those other persons is in proportion to the right to receive distributions in the capacity of general partner in effect for each of those other persons when the obligation was incurred.

(3) If a person does not make the additional contribution required by paragraph (2), further additional contributions are determined and due in the same manner as provided in that paragraph.

(d) A person that makes an additional contribution under subsection (c)(2) or (3) may recover from any person whose failure to contribute under subsection (c)(1) or (2) necessitated the additional contribution. A person may not recover under this subsection more than the amount additionally contributed. A person's liability under this subsection may not exceed the amount the person failed to contribute.

(e) The estate of a deceased individual is liable for the person's obligations under this section.

(f) An assignee for the benefit of creditors of a limited partnership or a partner, or a person appointed by a court to represent creditors of a limited partnership or a partner, may enforce a person's obligation to contribute under subsection (c).

COMMENT

In some circumstances, this Act requires a partner to make payments to the limited partnership. *See, e.g.*, Sections 502(b), 509(a), 509(b), and 812(c). In other circumstances, this Act requires a partner to make payments to other partners. *See, e.g.*, Sections 509(c) and 812(d). In no circumstances does this Act require a partner to make a payment for the purpose of equalizing or otherwise reallocating capital losses incurred by partners.

Example: XYZ Limited Partnership ("XYZ") has one general partner and four limited partners. According to XYZ's required information, the value of each partner's contributions to XYZ are:

General partner—$5,000
Limited partner #1—$10,000

Limited partner #2—$15,000
Limited partner #3—$20,000
Limited partner #4—$25,000

XYZ is unsuccessful and eventually dissolves without ever having made a distribution to its partners. XYZ lacks any assets with which to return to the partners the value of their respective contributions. No partner is obliged to make any payment either to the limited partnership or to fellow partners to adjust these capital losses. These losses are not part of "the limited partnership's obligations to creditors." Section 812(a).

Example: Same facts, except that Limited Partner #4 loaned $25,000 to XYZ when XYZ was not a limited liability limited partnership, and XYZ lacks the assets to repay the loan. The general partner must contribute to the limited partnership whatever funds are necessary to enable XYZ to satisfy the obligation owned to Limited Partner #4 on account of the loan. Section 812(a) and (c).

Subsection (c)—Following RUPA and the UPA, this Act leaves to other law the question of when a limited partnership obligation is incurred.

[ARTICLE] 9.   FOREIGN LIMITED PARTNERSHIPS

§ 901.   Governing Law

(a)   The laws of the State or other jurisdiction under which a foreign limited partnership is organized govern relations among the partners of the foreign limited partnership and between the partners and the foreign limited partnership and the liability of partners as partners for an obligation of the foreign limited partnership.

(b)   A foreign limited partnership may not be denied a certificate of authority by reason of any difference between the laws of the jurisdiction under which the foreign limited partnership is organized and the laws of this State.

(c)   A certificate of authority does not authorize a foreign limited partnership to engage in any business or exercise any power that a limited partnership may not engage in or exercise in this State.

COMMENT

Source—ULLCA Section 1001 for subsections (b) and (c).

Subsection (a)—This subsection parallels and is analogous in scope and effect to Section 106 (choice of law for domestic limited partnerships).

§ 902.   Application for Certificate of Authority

(a)   A foreign limited partnership may apply for a certificate of authority to transact business in this State by delivering an application to the [Secretary of State] for filing. The application must state:

(1)   the name of the foreign limited partnership and, if the name does not comply with Section 108, an alternate name adopted pursuant to Section 905(a).

(2)   the name of the State or other jurisdiction under whose law the foreign limited partnership is organized;

(3) · the street and mailing address of the foreign limited partnership's principal office and, if the laws of the jurisdiction under which the foreign limited partnership is organized require the foreign limited partnership to maintain an office in that jurisdiction, the street and mailing address of the required office;

(4)   the name and street and mailing address of the foreign limited partnership's initial agent for service of process in this State;

(5)   the name and street and mailing address of each of the foreign limited partnership's general partners; and

(6) whether the foreign limited partnership is a foreign limited liability limited partnership.

(b) A foreign limited partnership shall deliver with the completed application a certificate of existence or a record of similar import signed by the [Secretary of State] or other official having custody of the foreign limited partnership's publicly filed records in the State or other jurisdiction under whose law the foreign limited partnership is organized.

COMMENT

Source—ULLCA Section 1002.

A certificate of authority applied for under this section is different than a certificate of authorization furnished under Section 209.

§ 903. Activities not Constituting Transacting Business

(a) Activities of a foreign limited partnership which do not constitute transacting business in this State within the meaning of this [article] include:

(1) maintaining, defending, and settling an action or proceeding;

(2) holding meetings of its partners or carrying on any other activity concerning its internal affairs;

(3) maintaining accounts in financial institutions;

(4) maintaining offices or agencies for the transfer, exchange, and registration of the foreign limited partnership's own securities or maintaining trustees or depositories with respect to those securities;

(5) selling through independent contractors;

(6) soliciting or obtaining orders, whether by mail or electronic means or through employees or agents or otherwise, if the orders require acceptance outside this State before they become contracts;

(7) creating or acquiring indebtedness, mortgages, or security interests in real or personal property;

(8) securing or collecting debts or enforcing mortgages or other security interests in property securing the debts, and holding, protecting, and maintaining property so acquired;

(9) conducting an isolated transaction that is completed within 30 days and is not one in the course of similar transactions of a like manner; and

(10) transacting business in interstate commerce.

(b) For purposes of this [article], the ownership in this State of income-producing real property or tangible personal property, other than property excluded under subsection (a), constitutes transacting business in this State.

(c) This section does not apply in determining the contacts or activities that may subject a foreign limited partnership to service of process, taxation, or regulation under any other law of this State.

COMMENT

Source—ULLCA Section 1003.

§ 904. Filing of Certificate of Authority

Unless the [Secretary of State] determines that an application for a certificate of authority does not comply with the filing requirements of this [Act], the [Secretary of State], upon payment of all filing fees, shall file the application, prepare, sign and file a certificate of authority to transact business in this state, and send a copy of the filed certificate, together with a receipt for the fees, to the foreign limited partnership or its representative.

COMMENT

Source—ULLCA Section 1004 and RULPA Section 903.

A certificate of authority filed under this section is different than a certificate of authorization furnished under Section 209.

§ 905. Noncomplying Name of Foreign Limited Partnership

(a) A foreign limited partnership whose name does not comply with Section 108 may not obtain a certificate of authority until it adopts, for the purpose of transacting business in this State, an alternate name that complies with Section 108. A foreign limited partnership that adopts an alternate name under this subsection and then obtains a certificate of authority with the name need not comply with [fictitious name statute]. After obtaining a certificate of authority with an alternate name, a foreign limited partnership shall transact business in this State under the name unless the foreign limited partnership is authorized under [fictitious name statute] to transact business in this State under another name.

(b) If a foreign limited partnership authorized to transact business in this State changes its name to one that does not comply with Section 108, it may not thereafter transact business in this State until it complies with subsection (a) and obtains an amended certificate of authority.

COMMENT

Source—ULLCA Section 1005.

§ 906. Revocation of Certificate of Authority

(a) A certificate of authority of a foreign limited partnership to transact business in this State may be revoked by the [Secretary of State] in the manner provided in subsections (b) and (c) if the foreign limited partnership does not:

(1) pay, within 60 days after the due date, any fee, tax or penalty due to the [Secretary of State] under this [Act] or other law;

(2) deliver, within 60 days after the due date, its annual report required under Section 210;

(3) appoint and maintain an agent for service of process as required by Section 114(b); or

(4) deliver for filing a statement of a change under Section 115 within 30 days after a change has occurred in the name or address of the agent.

(b) In order to revoke a certificate of authority, the [Secretary of State] must prepare, sign, and file a notice of revocation and send a copy to the foreign limited partnership's agent for service of process in this State, or if the foreign limited partnership does not appoint and maintain a proper agent in this State, to the foreign limited partnership's designated office. The notice must state:

(1) the revocation's effective date, which must be at least 60 days after the date the [Secretary of State] sends the copy; and

(2) the foreign limited partnership's failures to comply with subsection (a) which are the reason for the revocation.

(c)   The authority of the foreign limited partnership to transact business in this State ceases on the effective date of the notice of revocation unless before that date the foreign limited partnership cures each failure to comply with subsection (a) stated in the notice. If the foreign limited partnership cures the failures, the [Secretary of State] shall so indicate on the filed notice.

COMMENT

Source—ULLCA Section 1006.

§ 907.   Cancellation of Certificate of Authority; Effect of Failure to Have Certificate

(a)   In order to cancel its certificate of authority to transact business in this State, a foreign limited partnership must deliver to the [Secretary of State] for filing a notice of cancellation. The certificate is canceled when the notice becomes effective under Section 206.

(b)   A foreign limited partnership transacting business in this State may not maintain an action or proceeding in this State unless it has a certificate of authority to transact business in this State.

(c)   The failure of a foreign limited partnership to have a certificate of authority to transact business in this State does not impair the validity of a contract or act of the foreign limited partnership or prevent the foreign limited partnership from defending an action or proceeding in this State.

(d)   A partner of a foreign limited partnership is not liable for the obligations of the foreign limited partnership solely by reason of the foreign limited partnership's having transacted business in this State without a certificate of authority.

(e)   If a foreign limited partnership transacts business in this State without a certificate of authority or cancels its certificate of authority, it appoints the [Secretary of State] as its agent for service of process for rights of action arising out of the transaction of business in this State.

COMMENT

Source—RULPA Section 907(d); ULLCA Section 1008.

§ 908.   Action by [Attorney General]

The [Attorney General] may maintain an action to restrain a foreign limited partnership from transacting business in this state in violation of this [article].

COMMENT

Source—RULPA Section 908; ULLCA Section 1009.

[ARTICLE] 10.   ACTIONS BY PARTNERS

§ 1001.   Direct Action by Partner

(a)   Subject to subsection (b), a partner may maintain a direct action against the limited partnership or another partner for legal or equitable relief, with or without an accounting as to the partnership's activities, to enforce the rights and otherwise protect the interests of the partner, including rights and interests under the partnership agreement or this [Act] or arising independently of the partnership relationship.

(b)   A partner commencing a direct action under this section is required to plead and prove an actual or threatened injury that is not solely the result of an injury suffered or threatened to be suffered by the limited partnership.

(c)   The accrual of, and any time limitation on, a right of action for a remedy under this section is governed by other law. A right to an accounting upon a dissolution and winding up does not revive a claim barred by law.

COMMENT

Subsection (a)—Source: RUPA Section 405(b).

Subsection (b)—In ordinary contractual situations it is axiomatic that each party to a contract has standing to sue for breach of that contract. Within a limited partnership, however, different circumstances may exist. A partner does not have a direct claim against another partner merely because the other partner has breached the partnership agreement. Likewise a partner's violation of this Act does not automatically create a direct claim for every other partner. To have standing in his, her, or its own right, a partner plaintiff must be able to show a harm that occurs independently of the harm caused or threatened to be caused to the limited partnership.

The reference to "threatened" harm is intended to encompass claims for injunctive relief and does not relax standards for proving injury.

§ 1002. Derivative Action

A partner may maintain a derivative action to enforce a right of a limited partnership if:

(1) the partner first makes a demand on the general partners, requesting that they cause the limited partnership to bring an action to enforce the right, and the general partners do not bring the action within a reasonable time; or

(2) a demand would be futile.

COMMENT

Source—RULPA Section 1001.

§ 1003. Proper Plaintiff

A derivative action may be maintained only by a person that is a partner at the time the action is commenced and:

(1) that was a partner when the conduct giving rise to the action occurred; or

(2) whose status as a partner devolved upon the person by operation of law or pursuant to the terms of the partnership agreement from a person that was a partner at the time of the conduct.

COMMENT

Source—RULPA Section 1002.

§ 1004. Pleading

In a derivative action, the complaint must state with particularity:

(1) the date and content of plaintiff's demand and the general partners' response to the demand; or

(2) why demand should be excused as futile.

COMMENT

Source—RULPA Section 1003.

§ 1005. Proceeds and Expenses

(a) Except as otherwise provided in subsection (b):

(1) any proceeds or other benefits of a derivative action, whether by judgment, compromise, or settlement, belong to the limited partnership and not to the derivative plaintiff;

(2) if the derivative plaintiff receives any proceeds, the derivative plaintiff shall immediately remit them to the limited partnership.

(b)   If a derivative action is successful in whole or in part, the court may award the plaintiff reasonable expenses, including reasonable attorney's fees, from the recovery of the limited partnership.

COMMENT

Source—RULPA Section 1004.

[ARTICLE] 11.   CONVERSION AND MERGER

§ 1101.   Definitions

In this [article]:

(1) "Constituent limited partnership" means a constituent organization that is a limited partnership.

(2) "Constituent organization" means an organization that is party to a merger.

(3) "Converted organization" means the organization into which a converting organization converts pursuant to Sections 1102 through 1105.

(4) "Converting limited partnership" means a converting organization that is a limited partnership.

(5) "Converting organization" means an organization that converts into another organization pursuant to Section 1102.

(6) "General partner" means a general partner of a limited partnership.

(7) "Governing statute" of an organization means the statute that governs the organization's internal affairs.

(8) "Organization" means a general partnership, including a limited liability partnership; limited partnership, including a limited liability limited partnership; limited liability company; business trust; corporation; or any other person having a governing statute. The term includes domestic and foreign organizations whether or not organized for profit.

(9) "Organizational documents" means:

(A) for a domestic or foreign general partnership, its partnership agreement;

(B) for a limited partnership or foreign limited partnership, its certificate of limited partnership and partnership agreement;

(C) for a domestic or foreign limited liability company, its articles of organization and operating agreement, or comparable records as provided in its governing statute;

(D) for a business trust, its agreement of trust and declaration of trust;

(E) for a domestic or foreign corporation for profit, its articles of incorporation, bylaws, and other agreements among its shareholders which are authorized by its governing statute, or comparable records as provided in its governing statute; and

(F) for any other organization, the basic records that create the organization and determine its internal governance and the relations among the persons that own it, have an interest in it, or are members of it.

(10) "Personal liability" means personal liability for a debt, liability, or other obligation of an organization which is imposed on a person that co-owns, has an interest in, or is a member of the organization:

(A) by the organization's governing statute solely by reason of the person co-owning, having an interest in, or being a member of the organization; or

(B) by the organization's organizational documents under a provision of the organization's governing statute authorizing those documents to make one or more specified persons liable for all or specified debts, liabilities, and other obligations of the organization solely by reason of the person or persons co-owning, having an interest in, or being a member of the organization.

(11) "Surviving organization" means an organization into which one or more other organizations are merged. A surviving organization may preexist the merger or be created by the merger.

COMMENT

This section contains definitions specific to this Article.

§ 1102. Conversion

(a) An organization other than a limited partnership may convert to a limited partnership, and a limited partnership may convert to another organization pursuant to this section and Sections 1103 through 1105 and a plan of conversion, if:

(1) the other organization's governing statute authorizes the conversion;

(2) the conversion is not prohibited by the law of the jurisdiction that enacted the governing statute; and

(3) the other organization complies with its governing statute in effecting the conversion.

(b) A plan of conversion must be in a record and must include:

(1) the name and form of the organization before conversion;

(2) the name and form of the organization after conversion; and

(3) the terms and conditions of the conversion, including the manner and basis for converting interests in the converting organization into any combination of money, interests in the converted organization, and other consideration; and

(4) the organizational documents of the converted organization.

COMMENT

In a statutory conversion an existing entity changes its form, the jurisdiction of its governing statute or both. For example, a limited partnership organized under the laws of one jurisdiction might convert to:

- a limited liability company (or other form of entity) organized under the laws of the same jurisdiction,

- a limited liability company (or other form of entity) organized under the laws of another jurisdiction, or

- a limited partnership organized under the laws of another jurisdiction (referred to in some statutes as "domestication").

In contrast to a merger, which involves at least two entities, a conversion involves only one. The converting and converted organization are the same entity. *See* Section 1105(a). For this Act to apply to a conversion, either the converting or converted organization must be a limited partnership subject to this Act. If the converting organization is a limited partnership subject to this Act, the partners of the converting organization are subject to the duties and obligations stated in this Act, including Sections 304 (informational rights of limited partners), 305(b) (limited partner's obligation of good faith and fair dealing), 407 (informational rights of general partners), and 408 (general partner duties).

Subsection (a)(2)—Given the very broad definition of "organization," Section 1101(8), this Act authorizes conversions involving non-profit organizations. This provision is intended as an additional safeguard for that context.

Subsection (b)(3)—A plan of conversion may provide that some persons with interests in the converting organization will receive interests in the converted organization while other persons with interests in the converting organization will receive some other form of consideration. Thus, a "squeeze out" conversion is possible. As noted above, if the converting organization is a limited partnership subject to this Act, the partners of the converting organization are subject to the duties and obligations stated in this Act. Those duties would apply to the process and terms under which a squeeze out conversion occurs.

If the converting organization is a limited partnership, the plan of conversion will determine the fate of any interests held by mere transferees. This Act does not state any duty or obligation owed by a converting limited partnership or its partners to mere transferees. That issue is a matter for other law.

§ 1103. Action on Plan of Conversion by Converting Limited Partnership

(a) Subject to Section 1110, a plan of conversion must be consented to by all the partners of a converting limited partnership.

(b) Subject to Section 1110 and any contractual rights, after a conversion is approved, and at any time before a filing is made under Section 1104, a converting limited partnership may amend the plan or abandon the planned conversion:

(1) as provided in the plan; and

(2) except as prohibited by the plan, by the same consent as was required to approve the plan.

COMMENT

Section 1110 imposes special consent requirements for transactions which might cause a partner to have "personal liability," as defined in Section 1101(10) for entity debts. The partnership agreement may not restrict the rights provided by Section 1110. *See* Section 110(b)(12).

Subsection (a)—Like many of the rules stated in this Act, this subsection's requirement of unanimous consent is a default rule. Subject only to Section 1110, the partnership agreement may state a different quantum of consent or provide a completely different approval mechanism. Varying this subsection's rule means that a partner might be subject to a conversion (including a "squeeze out" conversion) without consent and with no appraisal remedy. If the converting organization is a limited partnership subject to this Act, the partners of the converting organization are subject to the duties and obligations stated in this Act. Those duties would apply to the process and terms under which the conversion occurs. However, if the partnership agreement allows for a conversion with less than unanimous consent, the mere fact a partner objects to a conversion does not mean that the partners favoring, arranging, consenting to or effecting the conversation have breached a duty under this Act.

§ 1104. Filings Required for Conversion; Effective Date

(a) After a plan of conversion is approved:

(1) a converting limited partnership shall deliver to the [Secretary of State] for filing articles of conversion, which must include:

(A) a statement that the limited partnership has been converted into another organization;

(B) the name and form of the organization and the jurisdiction of its governing statute;

(C) the date the conversion is effective under the governing statute of the converted organization;

(D) a statement that the conversion was approved as required by this [Act];

(E)   a statement that the conversion was approved as required by the governing statute of the converted organization; and

(F)   if the converted organization is a foreign organization not authorized to transact business in this State, the street and mailing address of an office which the [Secretary of State] may use for the purposes of Section 1105(c); and

(2)   if the converting organization is not a converting limited partnership, the converting organization shall deliver to the [Secretary of State] for filing a certificate of limited partnership, which must include, in addition to the information required by Section 201:

(A)   a statement that the limited partnership was converted from another organization;

(B)   the name and form of the organization and the jurisdiction of its governing statute; and

(C)   a statement that the conversion was approved in a manner that complied with the organization's governing statute.

(b)   A conversion becomes effective:

(1)   if the converted organization is a limited partnership, when the certificate of limited partnership takes effect; and

(2)   if the converted organization is not a limited partnership, as provided by the governing statute of the converted organization.

COMMENT

Subsection (b)—The effective date of a conversion is determined under the governing statute of the converted organization.

§ 1105.   Effect of Conversion

(a)   An organization that has been converted pursuant to this [article] is for all purposes the same entity that existed before the conversion.

(b)   When a conversion takes effect:

(1)   all property owned by the converting organization remains vested in the converted organization;

(2)   all debts, liabilities, and other obligations of the converting organization continue as obligations of the converted organization;

(3)   an action or proceeding pending by or against the converting organization may be continued as if the conversion had not occurred;

(4)   except as prohibited by other law, all of the rights, privileges, immunities, powers, and purposes of the converting organization remain vested in the converted organization;

(5)   except as otherwise provided in the plan of conversion, the terms and conditions of the plan of conversion take effect; and

(6)   except as otherwise agreed, the conversion does not dissolve a converting limited partnership for the purposes of [Article] 8.

(c)   A converted organization that is a foreign organization consents to the jurisdiction of the courts of this State to enforce any obligation owed by the converting limited partnership, if before the conversion the converting limited partnership was subject to suit in this State on the obligation. A converted organization that is a foreign organization and not authorized to transact business in this State appoints the [Secretary of State] as its agent for service of process for purposes of enforcing an obligation under this subsection. Service on the [Secretary of State] under this subsection is made in the same manner and with the same consequences as in Section 117(c) and (d).

COMMENT

Subsection (a)—A conversion changes an entity's legal type, but does not create a new entity.

Subsection (b)—Unlike a merger, a conversion involves a single entity, and the conversion therefore does not transfer any of the entity's rights or obligations.

§ 1106. Merger

(a)   A limited partnership may merge with one or more other constituent organizations pursuant to this section and Sections 1107 through 1109 and a plan of merger, if:

(1)   the governing statute of each the other organizations authorizes the merger;

(2)   the merger is not prohibited by the law of a jurisdiction that enacted any of those governing statutes; and

(3)   each of the other organizations complies with its governing statute in effecting the merger.

(b)   A plan of merger must be in a record and must include:

(1)   the name and form of each constituent organization;

(2)   the name and form of the surviving organization and, if the surviving organization is to be created by the merger, a statement to that effect;

(3)   the terms and conditions of the merger, including the manner and basis for converting the interests in each constituent organization into any combination of money, interests in the surviving organization, and other consideration;

(4)   if the surviving organization is to be created by the merger, the surviving organization's organizational documents; and

(5)   if the surviving organization is not to be created by the merger, any amendments to be made by the merger to the surviving organization's organizational documents.

COMMENT

For this Act to apply to a merger, at least one of the constituent organizations must be a limited partnership subject to this Act. The partners of any such limited partnership are subject to the duties and obligations stated in this Act, including Sections 304 (informational rights of limited partners), 305(b) (limited partner's obligation of good faith and fair dealing), 407 (informational rights of general partners), and 408 (general partner duties).

Subsection (a)(2)—Given the very broad definition of "organization," Section 1101(8), this Act authorizes mergers involving non-profit organizations. This provision is intended as an additional safeguard for that context.

Subsection (b)(3)—A plan of merger may provide that some persons with interests in a constituent organization will receive interests in the surviving organization, while other persons with interests in the same constituent organization will receive some other form of consideration. Thus, a "squeeze out" merger is possible. As noted above, the duties and obligations stated in this Act apply to the partners of a constituent organization that is a limited partnership subject to this Act. Those duties would apply to the process and terms under which a squeeze out merger occurs.

If a constituent organization is a limited partnership, the plan of merger will determine the fate of any interests held by mere transferees. This Act does not state any duty or obligation owed by a constituent limited partnership or its partners to mere transferees. That issue is a matter for other law.

§ 1107. Action on Plan of Merger by Constituent Limited Partnership

(a)   Subject to Section 1110, a plan of merger must be consented to by all the partners of a constituent limited partnership.

(b)   Subject to Section 1110 and any contractual rights, after a merger is approved, and at any time before a filing is made under Section 1108, a constituent limited partnership may amend the plan or abandon the planned merger:

(1)   as provided in the plan; and

(2)   except as prohibited by the plan, with the same consent as was required to approve the plan.

COMMENT

Section 1110 imposes special consent requirements for transactions which might make a partner personally liable for entity debts. The partnership agreement may not restrict the rights provided by Section 1110. *See* Section 110(b)(12).

Subsection (a)—Like many of the rules stated in this Act, this subsection's requirement of unanimous consent is a default rule. Subject only to Section 1110, the partnership agreement may state a different quantum of consent or provide a completely different approval mechanism. Varying this subsection's rule means that a partner might be subject to a merger (including a "squeeze out" merger) without consent and with no appraisal remedy. The partners of a constituent limited partnership are subject to the duties and obligations stated in this Act, and those duties would apply to the process and terms under which the merger occurs. However, if the partnership agreement allows for a merger with less than unanimous consent, the mere fact a partner objects to a merger does not mean that the partners favoring, arranging, consenting to or effecting the merger have breached a duty under this Act.

§ 1108. Filings Required for Merger; Effective Date

(a)   After each constituent organization has approved a merger, articles of merger must be signed on behalf of:

(1)   each preexisting constituent limited partnership, by each general partner listed in the certificate of limited partnership; and

(2)   each other preexisting constituent organization, by an authorized representative.

(b)   The articles of merger must include:

(1)   the name and form of each constituent organization and the jurisdiction of its governing statute;

(2)   the name and form of the surviving organization, the jurisdiction of its governing statute, and, if the surviving organization is created by the merger, a statement to that effect;

(3)   the date the merger is effective under the governing statute of the surviving organization;

(4)   if the surviving organization is to be created by the merger:

(A)   if it will be a limited partnership, the limited partnership's certificate of limited partnership; or

(B)   if it will be an organization other than a limited partnership, the organizational document that creates the organization;

(5)   if the surviving organization preexists the merger, any amendments provided for in the plan of merger for the organizational document that created the organization;

(6)   a statement as to each constituent organization that the merger was approved as required by the organization's governing statute;

(7) if the surviving organization is a foreign organization not authorized to transact business in this State, the street and mailing address of an office which the [Secretary of State] may use for the purposes of Section 1109(b); and

(8) any additional information required by the governing statute of any constituent organization.

(c) Each constituent limited partnership shall deliver the articles of merger for filing in the [office of the Secretary of State].

(d) A merger becomes effective under this [article]:

(1) if the surviving organization is a limited partnership, upon the later of:

(i) compliance with subsection (c); or

(ii) subject to Section 206(c), as specified in the articles of merger; or

(2) if the surviving organization is not a limited partnership, as provided by the governing statute of the surviving organization.

COMMENT

Subsection (b)—The effective date of a merger is determined under the governing statute of the surviving organization.

§ 1109. Effect of Merger

(a) When a merger becomes effective:

(1) the surviving organization continues or comes into existence;

(2) each constituent organization that merges into the surviving organization ceases to exist as a separate entity;

(3) all property owned by each constituent organization that ceases to exist vests in the surviving organization;

(4) all debts, liabilities, and other obligations of each constituent organization that ceases to exist continue as obligations of the surviving organization;

(5) an action or proceeding pending by or against any constituent organization that ceases to exist may be continued as if the merger had not occurred;

(6) except as prohibited by other law, all of the rights, privileges, immunities, powers, and purposes of each constituent organization that ceases to exist vest in the surviving organization;

(7) except as otherwise provided in the plan of merger, the terms and conditions of the plan of merger take effect; and

(8) except as otherwise agreed, if a constituent limited partnership ceases to exist, the merger does not dissolve the limited partnership for the purposes of [Article] 8;

(9) if the surviving organization is created by the merger:

(A) if it is a limited partnership, the certificate of limited partnership becomes effective; or

(B) if it is an organization other than a limited partnership, the organizational document that creates the organization becomes effective; and

(10) if the surviving organization preexists the merger, any amendments provided for in the articles of merger for the organizational document that created the organization become effective.

(b) A surviving organization that is a foreign organization consents to the jurisdiction of the courts of this State to enforce any obligation owed by a constituent organization, if before the merger the constituent organization was subject to suit in this State on the obligation. A surviving organization that is a foreign organization and not authorized to transact business in this State appoints the [Secretary of State] as its agent for service of process for the purposes of enforcing an obligation under this subsection. Service on the [Secretary of State] under this subsection is made in the same manner and with the same consequences as in Section 117(c) and (d).

§ 1110.   Restrictions on Approval of Conversions and Mergers and on Relinquishing LLLP Status

(a)   If a partner of a converting or constituent limited partnership will have personal liability with respect to a converted or surviving organization, approval and amendment of a plan of conversion or merger are ineffective without the consent of the partner, unless:

(1)   the limited partnership's partnership agreement provides for the approval of the conversion or merger with the consent of fewer than all the partners; and

(2)   the partner has consented to the provision of the partnership agreement.

(b)   An amendment to a certificate of limited partnership which deletes a statement that the limited partnership is a limited liability limited partnership is ineffective without the consent of each general partner unless:

(1)   the limited partnership's partnership agreement provides for the amendment with the consent of less than all the general partners; and

(2)   each general partner that does not consent to the amendment has consented to the provision of the partnership agreement.

(c)   A partner does not give the consent required by subsection (a) or (b) merely by consenting to a provision of the partnership agreement which permits the partnership agreement to be amended with the consent of fewer than all the partners.

COMMENT

This section imposes special consent requirements for transactions that might make a partner personally liable for entity debts. The partnership agreement may not restrict the rights provided by this section. *See* Section 110(b)(12).

Subsection (c)—This subsection prevents circumvention of the consent requirements of subsections (a) and (b).

Example: As initially . . . consented to, the partnership agreement of a limited partnership leaves in place the Act's rule requiring unanimous consent for a conversion or merger. The partnership agreement does provide, however, that the agreement may be amended with the affirmative vote of general partners owning 2/3 of the rights to receive distributions as general partners and of limited partners owning 2/3 of the rights to receive distributions as limited partners. The required vote is obtained for an amendment that permits approval of a conversion or merger by the same vote necessary to amend the partnership agreement. Partner X votes for the amendment. Partner Y votes against. Partner Z does not vote.

Subsequently the limited partnership proposes to convert to a limited partnership (not an LLLP) organized under the laws of another state, with Partners X, Y and Z each receiving interests as general partners. Under the amended partnership agreement, approval of the conversion does not require unanimous consent. However, since after the conversion, Partners X, Y and Z will each have "personal liability with respect to [the] converted . . . organization," Section 1110(a) applies.

As a result, the approval of the plan of conversion will require the consent of Partner Y and Partner Z. They did not consent to the amendment that provided for non-unanimous approval of a conversion or merger. Their initial consent to the partnership agreement, with its provision permitting non-unanimous consent for amendments, does <u>not</u> satisfy the consent requirement of Subsection 1110(a)(2).

In contrast, Partner X's consent is not required. Partner X lost its Section 1110(a) veto right by consenting directly to the amendment to the partnership agreement which permitted non-unanimous consent to a conversion or merger.

§ 1111.   Liability of General Partner After Conversion or Merger

(a)   A conversion or merger under this [article] does not discharge any liability under Sections 404 and 607 of a person that was a general partner in or dissociated as a general partner from a converting or constituent limited partnership, but:

(1)   the provisions of this [Act] pertaining to the collection or discharge of the liability continue to apply to the liability;

(2)   for the purposes of applying those provisions, the converted or surviving organization is deemed to be the converting or constituent limited partnership; and

(3)   if a person is required to pay any amount under this subsection:

(A)   the person has a right of contribution from each other person that was liable as a general partner under Section 404 when the obligation was incurred and has not been released from the obligation under Section 607; and

(B)   the contribution due from each of those persons is in proportion to the right to receive distributions in the capacity of general partner in effect for each of those persons when the obligation was incurred.

(b)   In addition to any other liability provided by law:

(1)   a person that immediately before a conversion or merger became effective was a general partner in a converting or constituent limited partnership that was not a limited liability limited partnership is personally liable for each obligation of the converted or surviving organization arising from a transaction with a third party after the conversion or merger becomes effective, if, at the time the third party enters into the transaction, the third party:

(A)   does not have notice of the conversion or merger; and

(B)   reasonably believes that:

(i)   the converted or surviving business is the converting or constituent limited partnership;

(ii)   the converting or constituent limited partnership is not a limited liability limited partnership; and

(iii)   the person is a general partner in the converting or constituent limited partnership; and

(2)   a person that was dissociated as a general partner from a converting or constituent limited partnership before the conversion or merger became effective is personally liable for each obligation of the converted or surviving organization arising from a transaction with a third party after the conversion or merger becomes effective, if:

(A)   immediately before the conversion or merger became effective the converting or surviving limited partnership was a not a limited liability limited partnership; and

(B)   at the time the third party enters into the transaction less than two years have passed since the person dissociated as a general partner and the third party:

(i)   does not have notice of the dissociation;

(ii)   does not have notice of the conversion or merger; and

(iii)   reasonably believes that the converted or surviving organization is the converting or constituent limited partnership, the converting or constituent limited partnership is not a limited liability limited partnership, and the person is a general partner in the converting or constituent limited partnership.

COMMENT

This section extrapolates the approach of Section 607 into the context of a conversion or merger involving a limited partnership.

Subsection (a)—This subsection pertains to general partner liability for obligations which a limited partnership incurred before a conversion or merger. Following RUPA and the UPA, this Act leaves to other law the question of when a limited partnership obligation is incurred.

If the converting or constituent limited partnership was a limited liability limited partnership at all times before the conversion or merger, this subsection will not apply because no person will have any liability under Section 404 or 607.

Subsection (b)—This subsection pertains to entity obligations incurred after a conversion or merger and creates lingering exposure to personal liability for general partners and persons previously dissociated as general partners. In contrast to subsection (a)(3), this subsection does not provide for contribution among persons personally liable under this section for the same entity obligation. That issue is left for other law.

Subsection (b)(1)—If the converting or constituent limited partnership was a limited liability limited partnership immediately before the conversion or merger, there is no lingering exposure to personal liability under this subsection.

Subsection (b)(1)(A)—A person might have notice under Section 103(d)(4) or (5) as well as under Section 103(b).

Subsection (b)(2)(B)(i)—A person might have notice under Section 103(d)(1) as well as under Section 103(b).

Subsection (b)(2)(B)(ii)—A person might have notice under Section 103(d)(4) or (5) as well as under Section 103(b).

§ 1112. Power of General Partners and Persons Dissociated as General Partners to Bind Organization After Conversion or Merger

(a) An act of a person that immediately before a conversion or merger became effective was a general partner in a converting or constituent limited partnership binds the converted or surviving organization after the conversion or merger becomes effective, if:

(1) before the conversion or merger became effective, the act would have bound the converting or constituent limited partnership under Section 402; and

(2) at the time the third party enters into the transaction, the third party:

(A) does not have notice of the conversion or merger; and

(B) reasonably believes that the converted or surviving business is the converting or constituent limited partnership and that the person is a general partner in the converting or constituent limited partnership.

(b) An act of a person that before a conversion or merger became effective was dissociated as a general partner from a converting or constituent limited partnership binds the converted or surviving organization after the conversion or merger becomes effective, if:

(1) before the conversion or merger became effective, the act would have bound the converting or constituent limited partnership under Section 402 if the person had been a general partner; and

(2) at the time the third party enters into the transaction, less than two years have passed since the person dissociated as a general partner and the third party:

(A) does not have notice of the dissociation;

(B)   does not have notice of the conversion or merger; and

(C)   reasonably believes that the converted or surviving organization is the converting or constituent limited partnership and that the person is a general partner in the converting or constituent limited partnership.

(c)   If a person having knowledge of the conversion or merger causes a converted or surviving organization to incur an obligation under subsection (a) or (b), the person is liable:

(1)   to the converted or surviving organization for any damage caused to the organization arising from the obligation; and

(2)   if another person is liable for the obligation, to that other person for any damage caused to that other person arising from the liability.

COMMENT

This section extrapolates the approach of Section 606 into the context of a conversion or merger involving a limited partnership.

Subsection (a)(2)(A)—A person might have notice under Section 103(d)(4) or (5) as well as under Section 103(b).

Subsection (b)(2)(A)—A person might have notice under Section 103(d)(1) as well as under Section 103(b).

Subsection (b)(2)(B)—A person might have notice under Section 103(d)(4) or (5) as well as under Section 103(b).

§ 1113.   [Article] not Exclusive

This [article] does not preclude an entity from being converted or merged under other law.

[ARTICLE] 12.   MISCELLANEOUS PROVISIONS

§ 1201.   Uniformity of Application and Construction

In applying and construing this Uniform Act, consideration must be given to the need to promote uniformity of the law with respect to its subject matter among States that enact it.

§ 1202.   Severability Clause

If any provision of this [Act] or its application to any person or circumstance is held invalid, the invalidity does not affect other provisions or applications of this [Act] which can be given effect without the invalid provision or application, and to this end the provisions of this [Act] are severable.

§ 1203.   Relation to Electronic Signatures in Global and National Commerce Act

This [Act] modifies, limits, or supersedes the federal Electronic Signatures in Global and National Commerce Act, 15 U.S.C. Section 7001 *et seq.*, but this [Act] does not modify, limit, or supersede Section 101(c) of that Act or authorize electronic delivery of any of the notices described in Section 103(b) of that act.

§ 1204.   Effective Date

This [Act] takes effect [effective date].

COMMENT

Section 1206 specifies how this Act affects domestic limited partnerships, with special provisions pertaining to domestic limited partnerships formed before the Act's effective date. Section 1206 contains no comparable provisions for foreign limited partnerships. Therefore, once this Act is effective, it applies immediately to all foreign limited partnerships, whether formed before or after the Act's effective date.

§ 1205. Repeals

Effective [all-inclusive date], the following acts and parts of acts are repealed: [the State Limited Partnership Act as amended and in effect immediately before the effective date of this [Act]].

§ 1206. Application to Existing Relationships

(a)   Before [all-inclusive date], this [Act] governs only:

(1)   a limited partnership formed on or after [the effective date of this [Act]]; and

(2)   except as otherwise provided in subsections (c) and (d), a limited partnership formed before [the effective date of this [Act]] which elects, in the manner provided in its partnership agreement or by law for amending the partnership agreement, to be subject to this [Act].

(b)   Except as otherwise provided in subsection (c), on and after [all-inclusive date] this [Act] governs all limited partnerships.

(c)   With respect to a limited partnership formed before [the effective date of this [Act]], the following rules apply except as the partners otherwise elect in the manner provided in the partnership agreement or by law for amending the partnership agreement:

(1)   Section 104(c) does not apply and the limited partnership has whatever duration it had under the law applicable immediately before [the effective date of this [Act]].

(2)   the limited partnership is not required to amend its certificate of limited partnership to comply with Section 201(a)(4).

(3)   Sections 601 and 602 do not apply and a limited partner has the same right and power to dissociate from the limited partnership, with the same consequences, as existed immediately before [the effective date of this [Act]].

(4)   Section 603(4) does not apply.

(5)   Section 603(5) does not apply and a court has the same power to expel a general partner as the court had immediately before [the effective date of this [Act]].

(6)   Section 801(3) does not apply and the connection between a person's dissociation as a general partner and the dissolution of the limited partnership is the same as existed immediately before [the effective date of this [Act]].

(d)   With respect to a limited partnership that elects pursuant to subsection (a)(2) to be subject to this [Act], after the election takes effect the provisions of this [Act] relating to the liability of the limited partnership's general partners to third parties apply:

(1)   before [all-inclusive date], to:

(A)   a third party that had not done business with the limited partnership in the year before the election took effect; and

(B)   a third party that had done business with the limited partnership in the year before the election took effect only if the third party knows or has received a notification of the election; and

(2)   on and after [all-inclusive date], to all third parties, but those provisions remain inapplicable to any obligation incurred while those provisions were inapplicable under paragraph (1)(B).

Legislative Note: *In a State that has previously amended its existing limited partnership statute to provide for limited liability limited partnerships (LLLPs), this Act should include transition provisions* *specifically applicable to preexisting limited liability limited partnerships. The precise wording of those provisions must depend on the wording of the State's previously enacted LLLP provisions. However, the following principles apply generally:*

1.   In Sections 806(b)(5) and 807(b)(4) (notice by dissolved limited partnership to claimants), the phrase "the limited partnership has been throughout its existence a limited liability limited partnership" should be revised to encompass a limited partnership that was a limited liability limited partnership under the State's previously enacted LLLP provisions.

2.   Section 1206(d) should provide that, if a preexisting limited liability limited partnership elects to be subject to this Act, this Act's provisions relating to the liability of general partners to third parties apply immediately to all third parties, regardless of whether a third party has previously done business with the limited liability limited partnership.

3.   A preexisting limited liability limited partnership that elects to be subject to this Act should have to comply with Sections 201(a)(4) (requiring the certificate of limited partnership to state whether the limited partnership is a limited liability limited partnership) and 108(c) (establishing name requirements for a limited liability limited partnership).

4.   As for Section 1206(b) (providing that, after a transition period, this Act applies to all preexisting limited partnerships):

a.   if a State's previously enacted LLLP provisions have requirements essentially the same as Sections 201(a)(4) and 108(c), preexisting limited liability limited partnerships should automatically retain LLLP status under this Act.

b.   if a State's previously enacted LLLP provisions have name requirements essentially the same as Section 108(c) and provide that a public filing other than the certificate of limited partnership establishes a limited partnership's status as a limited liability limited partnership:

i.   that filing can be deemed to an amendment to the certificate of limited partnership to comply with Section 201(a)(4), and

ii.   preexisting limited liability limited partnerships should automatically retain LLLP status under this Act.

c.   if a State's previously enacted LLLP provisions do not have name requirements essentially the same as Section 108(c), it will be impossible both to enforce Section 108(c) and provide for automatic transition to LLLP status under this Act.

COMMENT

Source: RUPA Section 1206.

This section pertains exclusively to domestic limited partnerships—i.e., to limited partnerships formed under this Act or a predecessor statute enacted by the same jurisdiction. For foreign limited partnerships, *see* the Comment to Section 1204.

This Act governs all limited partnerships formed on or after the Act's effective date. As for pre-existing limited partnerships, this section establishes an optional "elect in" period and a mandatory, all-inclusive date. The "elect in" period runs from the effective date, stated in Section 1204, until the all-inclusive date, stated in both subsection(a) and (b).

During the "elect in" period, a pre-existing limited partnership may elect to become subject to this Act. Subsection (d) states certain important consequences for a limited partnership that elects in. Beginning on the all-inclusive date, each pre-existing limited partnership that has not previously elected in becomes subject to this Act by operation of law.

Subsection (c)—This subsection specifies six provisions of this Act which never automatically apply to any pre-existing limited partnership. Except for subsection (c)(2), the list refers to provisions governing the relationship of the partners *inter se* and considered too different than predecessor law to be fairly applied to a preexisting limited partnership without the consent of its partners. Each of these *inter se* provisions is subject to change in the partnership agreement. However, many pre-existing limited partnerships may have taken for granted the analogous provisions of predecessor law and may therefore not have addressed the issues in their partnership agreements.

Subsection (c)(1)—Section 104(c) provides that a limited partnership has a perpetual duration.

Subsection (c)(2)—Section 201(a)(4) requires the certificate of limited partnership to state "whether the limited partnership is a limited liability limited partnership." The requirement is intended to force the organizers of a limited partnership to decide whether the limited partnership is to be an LLLP and therefore is inapposite to pre-existing limited partnerships. Moreover, applying the requirement to pre-existing limited partnerships would create a significant administrative burden both for limited partnerships and the filing officer and probably would result in many pre-existing limited partnerships being in violation of the requirement.

Subsection (c)(3)—Section 601 and 602 concern a person's dissociation as a limited partner.

Subsection (c)(4)—Section 603(4) provides for the expulsion of a general partner by the unanimous consent of the other partners in specified circumstances.

Subsection (c)(5)—Section 603(5) provides for the expulsion of a general partner by a court in specified circumstances.

Subsection (c)(6)—Section 801(3) concerns the continuance or dissolution of a limited partnership following a person's dissociation as a general partner.

Subsection (d)—Following RUPA Section 1206(c), this subsection limits the efficacy of the Act's liability protections for partners of an "electing in" limited partnership. The limitation:

- applies only to the benefit of "a third party that had done business with the limited partnership in the year before the election took effect," and

- ceases to apply when "the third party knows or has received a notification of the election" or on the "all-inclusive" date, whichever occurs first.

If the limitation causes a provision of this Act to be inapplicable with regard to a third party, the comparable provision of predecessor law applies.

Example: A pre-existing limited partnership elects to be governed by this Act before the "all-inclusive" date. Two months before the election, Third Party provided services to the limited partnership. Third Party neither knows nor has received a notification of the election. Until the "all inclusive" date, with regard to Third Party, Section 303's full liability shield does not apply to each limited partner. Instead, each limited partner has the liability shield applicable under predecessor law.

Subsection (d)(2)—To the extent subsection (d) causes a provision of this Act to be inapplicable when an obligation is incurred, the inapplicability continues as to that obligation even after the "all inclusive" date.

§ 1207. Savings Clause

This [Act] does not affect an action commenced, proceeding brought, or right accrued before this [Act] takes effect.

G. UNIFORM LIMITED PARTNERSHIP ACT (2013)

(with Selected Comments)

Table of Sections

[ARTICLE] 1.   GENERAL PROVISIONS

[ARTICLE] 2.   FORMATION; CERTIFICATE OF LIMITED PARTNERSHIP AND OTHER FILINGS

UNIFORM LIMITED PARTNERSHIP ACT (2013)

UNIFORM LIMITED PARTNERSHIP ACT (2013)

[ARTICLE] 1.   GENERAL PROVISIONS

§ 101.   Short Title

This [act] may be cited as the Uniform Limited Partnership Act.

§ 102.   Definitions

In this [act]:

(1)   "Certificate of limited partnership" means the certificate required by Section 201. The term includes the certificate as amended or restated.

(2)   "Contribution", except in the phrase "right of contribution", means property or a benefit described in Section 501 which is provided by a person to a limited partnership to become a partner or in the person's capacity as a partner.

(3)   "Debtor in bankruptcy" means a person that is the subject of:

(A)   an order for relief under Title 11 of the United States Code or a comparable order under a successor statute of general application; or

408

(B)   a comparable order under federal, state, or foreign law governing insolvency.

(4)   "Distribution" means a transfer of money or other property from a limited partnership to a person on account of a transferable interest or in the person's capacity as a partner. The term:

(A)   includes:

(i)   a redemption or other purchase by a limited partnership of a transferable interest; and

(ii)   a transfer to a partner in return for the partner's relinquishment of any right to participate as a partner in the management or conduct of the partnership's activities and affairs or to have access to records or other information concerning the partnership's activities and affairs; and

(B)   does not include amounts constituting reasonable compensation for present or past service or payments made in the ordinary course of business under a bona fide retirement plan or other bona fide benefits program.

(5)   "Foreign limited liability limited partnership" means a foreign limited partnership whose general partners have limited liability for the debts, obligations, or other liabilities of the foreign partnership under a provision similar to Section 404(c).

(6)   "Foreign limited partnership" means an unincorporated entity formed under the law of a jurisdiction other than this state which would be a limited partnership if formed under the law of this state. The term includes a foreign limited liability limited partnership.

(7)   "General partner" means a person that:

(A)   has become a general partner under Section 401 or was a general partner in a partnership when the partnership became subject to this [act] under Section 112; and

(B)   has not dissociated as a general partner under Section 603.

(8)   "Jurisdiction", used to refer to a political entity, means the United States, a state, a foreign country, or a political subdivision of a foreign country.

(9)   "Jurisdiction of formation" means the jurisdiction whose law governs the internal affairs of an entity.

(10)   "Limited liability limited partnership", except in the phrase "foreign limited liability limited partnership" and in [Article] 11, means a limited partnership whose certificate of limited partnership states that the partnership is a limited liability limited partnership.

(11)   "Limited partner" means a person that:

(A)   has become a limited partner under Section 301 or was a limited partner in a limited partnership when the partnership became subject to this [act] under Section 112; and

(B)   has not dissociated under Section 601.

(12)   "Limited partnership", except in the phrase "foreign limited partnership" and in [Article] 11, means an entity formed under this [act] or which becomes subject to this [act] under [Article] 11 or Section 112. The term includes a limited liability limited partnership.

(13)   "Partner" means a limited partner or general partner.

(14)   "Partnership agreement" means the agreement, whether or not referred to as a partnership agreement and whether oral, implied, in a record, or in any combination thereof, of all the partners of a limited partnership concerning the matters described in Section 105(a). The term includes the agreement as amended or restated.

(15)   "Person" means an individual, business corporation, nonprofit corporation, partnership, limited partnership, limited liability company, [general cooperative association,] limited cooperative

association, unincorporated nonprofit association, statutory trust, business trust, common-law business trust, estate, trust, association, joint venture, public corporation, government or governmental subdivision, agency, or instrumentality, or any other legal or commercial entity.

(16) "Principal office" means the principal executive office of a limited partnership or foreign limited partnership, whether or not the office is located in this state.

(17) "Property" means all property, whether real, personal, or mixed or tangible or intangible, or any right or interest therein.

(18) "Record", used as a noun, means information that is inscribed on a tangible medium or that is stored in an electronic or other medium and is retrievable in perceivable form.

(19) "Registered agent" means an agent of a limited partnership or foreign limited partnership which is authorized to receive service of any process, notice, or demand required or permitted by law to be served on the partnership.

(20) "Registered foreign limited partnership" means a foreign limited partnership that is registered to do business in this state pursuant to a statement of registration filed by the [Secretary of State].

(21) "Required information" means the information that a limited partnership is required to maintain under Section 108.

(22) "Sign" means, with present intent to authenticate or adopt a record:

   (A)   to execute or adopt a tangible symbol; or

   (B)   to attach to or logically associate with the record an electronic symbol, sound, or process.

(23) "State" means a state of the United States, the District of Columbia, Puerto Rico, the United States Virgin Islands, or any territory or insular possession subject to the jurisdiction of the United States.

(24) "Transfer" includes:

   (A)   an assignment;

   (B)   a conveyance;

   (C)   a sale;

   (D)   a lease;

   (E)   an encumbrance, including a mortgage or security interest;

   (F)   a gift; and

   (G)   a transfer by operation of law.

(25) "Transferable interest" means the right, as initially owned by a person in the person's capacity as a partner, to receive distributions from a limited partnership, whether or not the person remains a partner or continues to own any part of the right. The term applies to any fraction of the interest, by whomever owned.

(26) "Transferee" means a person to which all or part of a transferable interest has been transferred, whether or not the transferor is a partner. The term includes a person that owns a transferable interest under Section 602(a)(3) or 605(a)(4).

§ 103.   Knowledge; Notice

(a)   A person knows a fact if the person:

   (1)   has actual knowledge of it; or

   (2)   is deemed to know it under law other than this [act].

(b)   A person has notice of a fact if the person:

(1)   has reason to know the fact from all the facts known to the person at the time in question; or

(2)   is deemed to have notice of the fact under subsection (c) or (d).

(c)   A certificate of limited partnership on file in the office of the [Secretary of State] is notice that the partnership is a limited partnership and the persons designated in the certificate as general partners are general partners. Except as otherwise provided in subsection (d), the certificate is not notice of any other fact.

(d)   A person not a partner is deemed to have notice of:

(1)   a person's dissociation as a general partner 90 days after an amendment to the certificate of limited partnership which states that the other person has dissociated becomes effective or 90 days after a statement of dissociation pertaining to the other person becomes effective, whichever occurs first;

(2)   a limited partnership's:

(A)   dissolution 90 days after an amendment to the certificate of limited partnership stating that the limited partnership is dissolved becomes effective;

(B)   termination 90 days after a statement of termination under Section 802(b)(2)(F) becomes effective; and

(C)   participation in a merger, interest exchange, conversion, or domestication, 90 days after articles of merger, interest exchange, conversion, or domestication under [Article] 11 become effective.

(e)   Subject to Section 210(f), a person notifies another person of a fact by taking steps reasonably required to inform the other person in ordinary course, whether or not those steps cause the other person to know the fact.

(f)   A general partner's knowledge or notice of a fact relating to the limited partnership is effective immediately as knowledge of or notice to the partnership, except in the case of a fraud on the partnership committed by or with the consent of the general partner. A limited partner's knowledge or notice of a fact relating to the partnership is not effective as knowledge of or notice to the partnership.

§ 104.   Governing Law

The law of this state governs:

(1)   the internal affairs of a limited partnership; and

(2)   the liability of a partner as partner for a debt, obligation, or other liability of a limited partnership.

§ 105.   Partnership Agreement; Scope, Function, and Limitations

(a)   Except as otherwise provided in subsections (c) and (d), the partnership agreement governs:

(1)   relations among the partners as partners and between the partners and the limited partnership;

(2)   the activities and affairs of the partnership and the conduct of those activities and affairs; and

(3)   the means and conditions for amending the partnership agreement.

(b)   To the extent the partnership agreement does not provide for a matter described in subsection (a), this [act] governs the matter.

(c)   A partnership agreement may not:

(1)   vary the law applicable under Section 104;

(2)   vary a limited partnership's capacity under Section 111 to sue and be sued in its own name;

(3)   vary any requirement, procedure, or other provision of this [act] pertaining to:

     (A)   registered agents; or

     (B)   the [Secretary of State], including provisions pertaining to records authorized or required to be delivered to the [Secretary of State] for filing under this [act];

(4)   vary the provisions of Section 204;

(5)   vary the right of a general partner under Section 406(b)(2) to vote on or consent to an amendment to the certificate of limited partnership which deletes a statement that the limited partnership is a limited liability limited partnership;

(6)   alter or eliminate the duty of loyalty or the duty of care except as otherwise provided in subsection (d);

(7)   eliminate the contractual obligation of good faith and fair dealing under Sections 305(a) and 409(d), but the partnership agreement may prescribe the standards, if not manifestly unreasonable, by which the performance of the obligation is to be measured;

(8)   relieve or exonerate a person from liability for conduct involving bad faith, willful or intentional misconduct, or knowing violation of law;

(9)   vary the information required under Section 108 or unreasonably restrict the duties and rights under Section 304 or 407, but the partnership agreement may impose reasonable restrictions on the availability and use of information obtained under those sections and may define appropriate remedies, including liquidated damages, for a breach of any reasonable restriction on use;

(10)   vary the grounds for expulsion specified in Section 603(5)(B);

(11)   vary the power of a person to dissociate as a general partner under Section 604(a), except to require that the notice under Section 603(1) be in a record;

(12)   vary the causes of dissolution specified in Section 801(a)(6);

(13)   vary the requirement to wind up the partnership's activities and affairs as specified in Section 802(a), (b)(1), and (d);

(14)   unreasonably restrict the right of a partner to maintain an action under [Article] 9;

(15)   vary the provisions of Section 905, but the partnership agreement may provide that the partnership may not have a special litigation committee;

(16)   vary the right of a partner to approve a merger, interest exchange, conversion, or domestication under Section 1123(a)(2), 1133(a)(2), 1143(a)(2), or 1153(a)(2);

(17)   vary the required contents of a plan of merger under Section 1122(a), plan of interest exchange under Section 1132(a), plan of conversion under Section 1142(a), or plan of domestication under Section 1152(a); or

(18)   except as otherwise provided in Sections 106 and 107(b), restrict the rights under this [act] of a person other than a partner.

(d)   Subject to subsection (c)(8), without limiting other terms that may be included in a partnership agreement, the following rules apply:

(1)   The partnership agreement may:

(A) specify the method by which a specific act or transaction that would otherwise violate the duty of loyalty may be authorized or ratified by one or more disinterested and independent persons after full disclosure of all material facts; and

(B) alter the prohibition in Section 504(a)(2) so that the prohibition requires only that the partnership's total assets not be less than the sum of its total liabilities.

(2) If not manifestly unreasonable, the partnership agreement may:

(A) alter or eliminate the aspects of the duty of loyalty stated in Section 409(b);

(B) identify specific types or categories of activities that do not violate the duty of loyalty;

(C) alter the duty of care, but may not authorize conduct involving bad faith, willful or intentional misconduct, or knowing violation of law; and

(D) alter or eliminate any other fiduciary duty.

(e) The court shall decide as a matter of law whether a term of a partnership agreement is manifestly unreasonable under subsection (c)(7) or (d)(2). The court:

(1) shall make its determination as of the time the challenged term became part of the partnership agreement and by considering only circumstances existing at that time; and

(2) may invalidate the term only if, in light of the purposes, activities, and affairs of the limited partnership, it is readily apparent that:

(A) the objective of the term is unreasonable; or

(B) the term is an unreasonable means to achieve its objective.

COMMENT

The Harmonization Project rewrote this section to conform, for the most part, to the corresponding section of ULLCA (2006) (Last Amended).

Principal Provisions of the Act Concerning the Partnership Agreement

The partnership agreement is pivotal to a limited partnership, and Sections 105 through 107 are pivotal to this act. They must be read together, along with Section 102(14) (defining the partnership agreement).

This Section performs five essential functions. Subsection (a) establishes the primacy of the partnership agreement in establishing relations *inter se* the limited partnership and its partners. Subsection (b) recognizes this act as comprising mostly default rules—*i.e.*, gap fillers for issues as to which the partnership agreement provides no rule. Subsection (c) lists the few mandatory provisions of the act. Subsection (d) lists some provisions frequently found in partnership agreements, authorizing some provisions unconditionally and other provisions so long as "not manifestly unreasonable." Subsection (e) delineates in detail both the meaning of "not manifestly unreasonable" and the information relevant to a determining a claim that a provision of a partnership agreement is manifestly unreasonable.

Section 106 details the effect of a partnership agreement on the limited partnership and on persons becoming partners. Section 107 concerns the effect of a partnership agreement on third parties.

Role and Inevitability of Partnership Agreement

"A limited partnership is a creature of both statute and contract." *Cantor Fitzgerald, L.P. Cantor*, CIV.A. 18101, 2001 WL 1456494 at *5 (Del. Ch. Nov. 5, 2001); *Gottsacker v. Monnier*, 281 Wis. 2d 361, 370, 697 N.W.2d 436, 440 (2005) (stating that "from the partnership form, the LLC borrows . . . internal governance by contract"), and Section 102(14) delineates a very broad scope for "partnership agreement." As a result, once a limited partnership comes into existence and has at least one general partner and one limited partner, a partnership agreement necessarily exists. See Section 102(14), cmt. Accordingly, this act refers to "the partnership agreement" rather than "a partnership agreement." This phrasing should not, however, be read to require a limited partnership or its partners to take any formal action to adopt a partnership agreement.

Subject only to Subsections (c) and (d), the partnership agreement has plenary power to structure and regulate the relations of the partners *inter se*. Although the certificate of limited partnership is a limited partnership's foundational document, among the partners the partnership agreement controls.

The partnership agreement is the exclusive consensual process for modifying this act's various default rules pertaining to relationships *inter se* the partners and between the partners and the limited partnership. Section 105(b). The partnership agreement also has power over "[t]he obligations of a limited partnership and its partners to a person in the person's capacity as a transferee or a person dissociated as a partner." Section 107(b). For the relationship between the partnership agreement and certificate of limited partnership, see Section 107(d).

The Partnership Agreement and the Fiduciary and Other Duties of the General Partner

One of the most complex questions in the law of unincorporated business organizations is the extent to which an agreement among the organization's owners can affect the fiduciary and other duties of those who manage the organization—in the case of a limited partnership, the general partner (or partners). As explained in detail in the comment to Subsection (d)(3), this act rejects the notion that a contract can completely transform an inherently fiduciary relationship into a merely arm's length association. Within that limitation, however, this section provides substantial power to the partnership agreement to reshape, limit, and eliminate fiduciary and other managerial duties.

Subsection (a) recognizes that the partnership agreement is the map to the parties' deal and that any claim by a partner of managerial misconduct must be assessed first under the relevant terms of the partnership agreement. Subsection (d) specifically validates arrangements commonly used to reshape managerial duties and limit the consequences of breaching those duties. Subsection (c) contains relevant limitations, but those limitations: (i) must be read together with Subsection (d); and (ii) do not preclude the partnership agreement fundamentally redesigning the duties applicable to the general partners. For the act's design of those duties, see Sections 304, 407, and 409.

Subsection (a)—This subsection describes the very broad scope of a limited partnership's partnership agreement, which includes all matters constituting "internal affairs." Compare Section 105(a), with Section 104(1) (using the phrase "internal affairs" in stating a choice of law rule). This broad grant of authority is subject to the restrictions stated in Subsection (c), including the broad restriction stated in Paragraph (c)(18) (concerning the rights of third parties under this act).

Subsection (a)(1)—This paragraph encompasses all the rights and duties of each partner, including rights and duties pertaining to transactions under Article 11.

Subsection (a)(3)—Under this provision, the partnership agreement can control both the quantum of consent required (*e.g.*, majority of partners) and the means by which the consent is manifested (*e.g.*, prohibiting modifications except when consented to in writing). *See also* Section 107(a), cmt.

If the partnership agreement does not address the issue, this act provides the rule. Section 407(b)(4)(C) (requiring the affirmative vote or consent of all the partners) and 407(c)(3)(C) (same). Under Section 111 (supplemental principles of law), the parol evidence rule will apply to a written partnership agreement when appropriate under contract law.

Subsection (b)—To the extent the partnership agreement does not determine an inter se matter, this act determines the matter. The partnership agreement may vary any provision of this act pertaining to *inter se* matters, except as provided in Subsections (c) and (d).

Sometimes—but not always—the Comments to this act refer to a variable provision as a "default rule" and a non-waivable provision as "mandatory." These references are merely to draw attention to the default/mandatory distinction in particular contexts and have neither the intent nor the power to affect the default/mandatory status of provisions of this act whose comments lack a comparable reference.

Subsection (c)—This subsection lists provisions of this act whose respective effects cannot be varied or may be varied subject to a stated limitation. For historical reasons, this subsection uses the words "vary" and "alter" interchangeably. No difference in meaning is intended.

If a person claims that a term of the partnership agreement violates this subsection, as a matter of ordinary procedural law the burden of proof is on the person making the claim.

Subsection (c)(1)—Section 104 states that this act provides the law applicable to: (i) the internal affairs of a limited partnership formed under this act; and (ii) the liability of partners for obligations of the limited partnership. The organizers of a limited partnership make this choice of law by choosing to form a limited partnership under this act. Domestication to another jurisdiction will re-set the choice of law, *see* Sections 1151–56, but the partnership agreement cannot. The partnership agreement may incorporate wholesale and by reference the provisions of another jurisdiction's limited partnership statute, but that approach raises complex drafting issues—*e.g.*, how to address future revisions to that statute—and in any event is subject to the strictures of Section 105(c) and (d). *See also* Section 104(1), cmt.

Subsection (c) contains no parallel prohibition on varying Section 1001 (stating the governing law for foreign limited partnerships), because a prohibition is unnecessary. As a matter of fundamental contract law, an agreement among partners of one limited partnership is powerless to govern the affairs of another limited partnership.

Subsection (c)(2)—Under this act, a limited partnership is emphatically an entity, and the partners lack the power to alter that characteristic.

Subsection (c)(3)—This prohibition is arguably implicit in Subsection (c)(18) (affecting rights of third parties under this act) but is stated expressly to avoid any doubt.

Subsection (c)(4)—This provision means that the partnership agreement cannot affect the right of an "aggrieved" person to seek the court's help when "a person required by this [act] to sign a record or deliver a record to the filing office for filing under this [act] does not do so." Section 204(a).

Subsection (c)(5)—Because deleting the specified statement exposes each general partner to unlimited liability for each debt, liability, or other obligation of the limited partnership accrued after the deletion: (i) Section 406(b)(2) gives each general partner veto power; and (ii) this subsection makes that power non-waivable.

Subsection (c)(6)—This limitation is less powerful than might first appear, because Subsection (d) specifically authorizes substantial alterations to the duties of loyalty and care, including restricting and substantially eliminating those duties.

Subsection (c)(7)—Sections 305(a) and 409(d) refer to the "contractual obligation of good faith and fair dealing," which contract law implies in every contract. The partnership agreement cannot eliminate this obligation, neither in whole (*i.e.*, generally) nor in part (*i.e.*, as applicable to specified situations).

However, a partnership agreement may "prescribe the standards . . . by which the performance of the obligation is to be measured."

EXAMPLE: The partnership agreement of a limited partnership gives the general partner the discretion to cause the limited partnership to enter into contracts with affiliates of the general partner (so-called "Conflict Transactions"). The agreement further provides: "When causing the Limited Partnership to enter into a Conflict Transaction, the general partner complies with Section 409(d) of [this act] if a disinterested person, knowledgeable in the subject matter, states in writing that the terms and conditions of the Transaction are equivalent to the terms and conditions that would be agreed to by persons at arm's length in comparable circumstances." This provision "prescribe[s] the standards by which the performance of the [Section 409(d)] obligation is to be measured."

EXAMPLE: Same facts as the previous example, except that, during the performance of a Conflict Transaction, the general partner causes the limited partnership to waive material protections under the applicable contract. The standard stated in the previous example is inapposite to this conduct. Section 409(d) therefore applies to the conduct without any direct contractual delineation. (However, other terms of the agreement may be relevant to determining whether the conduct violates Section 409(d). See Section 409(d), cmt.)

EXAMPLE: The partnership agreement of a limited partnership gives the general partner "sole discretion" to make various decisions. The agreement further provides: "Whenever this agreement requires or permits a general partner to make a decision that has the potential to benefit one class of partners to the detriment of another class, the general partner complies with Section 409(d) of [this act] if the general partner makes the decision with:

    a.   the honest belief that the decision:

        i.   serves the best interests of the Limited Partnership; or

        ii.   at least does not injure or otherwise disserve those interests; and

    b.   the reasonable belief that the decision breaches no partner's rights under this agreement."

This provision "prescribe[s] the standards by which the performance of the [Section 409(d)] obligation is to be measured." Compare Section 105(c)(7), with *Nemec v. Shrader*, 991 A.2d 1120 (Del. 2010) (considering such a situation in the context of the right to call preferred stock and deciding by a 3–2 vote that exercising the call did not breach the implied covenant of good faith and fair dealing).

A partnership agreement that seeks to prescribe standards for measuring the contractual obligation of good faith and fair dealing under Section 409(d) should expressly refer to the obligation. *See Gerber v. Enter. Prods. Hldgs., LLC*, 67 A.3d 400, 418 (Del. 2013) (distinguishing between the implied contractual covenant and an express contractual obligation of "good faith" as stated in a limited partnership agreement).

For an explanation of the function and role of the covenant of good faith and fair dealing, see Section 409(d), comment. For the rules delimiting the "not manifestly unreasonable" requirement, see Subsection (e).

Subsection (c)(8)—These restrictions are ubiquitous in the law of business entities and, in conjunction with other provisions of this section, control the otherwise very broad power of a partnership agreement to affect fiduciary and other duties. The restrictions are central to the raft of exculpatory provisions that sprung up in corporate statutes in response to *Smith v. Van Gorkum*, 488 A.2d 858 (Del. 1985). Delaware led the response with DEL. CODE ANN. tit. 8, § 102(b)(7), and a number of LLC statutes have similar provisions. *E.g.* GA. CODE ANN. § 14–11–305(4)(A) (2011). For an extreme example, see VA. CODE ANN. § 13.1–1025 (B) (2012). In this context, "conduct" includes both acts and omissions. BLACK'S LAW DICTIONARY (9th ed. 2009) (defining conduct as "[p]ersonal behavior, whether by action or inaction").

The term "bad faith" has multiple meanings, and the context determines which meaning applies. In the context of the duty of loyalty, "bad faith" includes conduct motivated by ill will or other intent purposely to harm another person. The concept also includes conduct from which a person derives an improper personal benefit. *See, e.g., Mroz v. Hoaloha Na Eha, Inc.*, 410 F. Supp. 2d 919, 936–37 (D. Haw. 2005) (denying a motion to dismiss a claim that "the Majority Partners" were personally liable for the partnership's wrongful termination of the plaintiff; quoting the complaint as alleging that "the Majority Partners, individually and as a group, acted with malice and/or ill will, and or with an intent to serve their own personal interests and/or without an intent to serve company interests, and/or outside of the scope of their authority and/or without justification"); *BOGNC, LLC v. Cornelius NC Self-Storage LLC*, 10 CVS 19072, 2013 WL 1867065 at *9 (N.C. Super. [Business Court] May 1, 2013) (noting that "no . . . [exculpatory] provision may limit a manager's liability for acts known to be in conflict with the interests of the limited liability company, or for acts from which the manager derived an improper personal benefit") (citing N.C. GEN. STAT. § 57C–3–32(b)); *Lasica v. Savers Grp. of Minnesota, LLC*, A12-0092, 2012 WL 3553246 at *2 (Minn. Ct. App. Aug. 20, 2012) (noting that an "individual seeking indemnification [under statute providing for indemnification)] must have acted in good faith and must not have received an improper personal benefit") (citing MINN. STAT. § 322B.69, subds. 2(a)(2), (3) (2010)).

In the context of the duty of care, the concept of bad faith comes primarily from corporate law and means an extreme breach of the duty—*i.e.*, "the failure to exercise "*honest judgment* in the lawful and legitimate furtherance of corporate purposes." *Deblinger v. Sani-Pine Products Co., Inc.*, 107 A.D.3d 659, 661, 967 N.Y.S.2d 394 (2013) (quoting *Auerbach v. Bennett*, 47 N.Y.2d 619, 629, 393 N.E.2d 994 (1979) (emphasis added) (internal quotation marks omitted).

Thus, when a plaintiff alleges bad faith as pertaining to the duty of care, "[t]he burden . . . is to show irrationality: a plaintiff must demonstrate that no reasonable business person could possibly authorize the action in good faith. Put positively, the decision must go so far beyond the bounds of reasonable business judgment that its only explanation is bad faith." *In re Tower Air, Inc.*, 416 F.3d 229, 238 (3d Cir. 2005) (discussing then prevailing Delaware law) (citation omitted). *See also KDW Restructuring & Liquidation*

Servs. LLC v. Greenfield, 874 F. Supp. 2d 213, 226 (S.D.N.Y. 2012) (referring to a lack of "a rationale corporate purpose" and "a disregard for the duty to examine all available information—*information that was readily at hand*") (emphasis added).

With regard to both the duty of loyalty and the duty of care, "bad faith" is entirely distinct from the meaning of "good faith" in the contractual covenant of good faith and fair dealing. *See* Section 409(d), cmt.

Subsection (c)(8) pertains to indirect as well as direct efforts to "relieve or exonerate" and thus limits how far a partnership agreement can go in providing for indemnification. *See* Section 408(b) (stating a default rule for indemnification).

Although this paragraph does not expressly address contracts between a limited partnership and a general partner, the stated constraints must also apply to such contracts. If not, those constraints are effectively meaningless.

EXAMPLE: A limited partnership enters into a management contract with its general partner, and the contract provides the general partner exoneration for liability to the limited partnership even for willful and intentional misconduct. Most likely, contract law will treat the provision as against public policy and therefore unenforceable. RESTATEMENT (SECOND) OF CONTRACTS § 195(1) (1981) ("A term exempting a party from tort liability for harm caused intentionally or recklessly is unenforceable on grounds of public policy."). If not, a court should hold the provision unenforceable to avoid evisceration of Subsection (c)(8). (Or, the court could invoke the policy expressed in Subsection (c)(8) as grounds for holding the provision unenforceable under contract law.)

Subsection (c)(9)—Although phrased as a restriction, this provision grants substantial power to the partnership agreement.

EXAMPLE: The partnership agreement of a limited partnership states "No limited partner may have access to information constituting a trade secret of the Partnership." This restriction is reasonable.

The information required under Section 108 is skeletal, and the partnership agreement can impose reasonable limitations on access to and use of other information.

The act also empowers the limited partnership "as a matter within the ordinary course of its activities and affairs [to] impose reasonable restrictions and conditions on access to and use of information" obtained under Section 304 or 407. *See* Sections 304(j) and 407(j), cmts.

In determining whether a restriction is reasonable, a court might consider: (i) the danger or other problem the restriction seeks to avoid; (ii) the purpose for which the information is sought; and (iii) whether, in light of both the problem and the purpose, the restriction is reasonably tailored. Under this act, general and limited partners have sharply different roles. A restriction that is reasonable as to a limited partner is not necessarily reasonable as to a general partner. Restricting a limited partner's access to or use of the names and addresses of other limited partners is not per se unreasonable.

Subsection (c)(11)—A partnership agreement certainly may make a person's dissociation as a general partner a breach of contract, but eliminating even the *power* to dissociate would contradict the essence of the limited partnership. General partners in a limited partnership are analogous to partners in a general partnership, and the relationship among general partners is at its core a *voluntary* association.

Moreover, general partners in a limited partnership provide services not only as fiduciaries but also pursuant to a contract. *See* Section 105, cmt. (Role and Inevitability of Partnership Agreement). Only in exceptional circumstances does a party to a contract lack the power to breach, and such circumstances do not exist as to general partners of a limited partnership. Indeed, courts will not enjoin a person to remain in an ongoing contractual relationship that involves trust and confidence. E. ALLAN FARNSWORTH, CONTRACTS § 12.7 at 781 (3rd ed. 1999) ("A court will not grant specific performance of a contract to provide a service that is personal in nature. This refusal . . . is based [in part] of the undesirability of compelling the continuance of personal relations after disputes have arisen and confidence and loyalty have been shaken and the undesirability, in some instances, of imposing what might seem like involuntary servitude.") (footnote omitted).

For two reasons this act treats limited partners quite differently. First, to make possible the act a suitable vehicle for family limited partnerships, "[a] person does not have a right to dissociate as a limited partner before the completion of the winding up of the limited partnership." Section 601(a). *See also* Prefatory Note to 2011 Act, *"The Act's Overall Approach."*

Second, the partnership agreement may eliminate a limited partner's power to dissociate, because limited partners do not resemble contract obligors. Limited partners *qua* limited partners provide no services to the limited partnership, and therefore the analysis stated in the second paragraph of this comment does not apply. Moreover, limited partners have no fiduciary duties, Section 305(b), and therefore the analysis stated in the first paragraph of this comment is inapposite as well.

Subsection (c)(12)—The partnership agreement may not change the stated grounds for judicial dissolution but may determine the forum in which a claim for dissolution under Section 801(a)(6) is determined. For example, arbitration and forum selection clauses are commonplace in business relationships in general and in partnership agreements in particular.

The approach of this paragraph differs from the law of Delaware. *See Huatuco v. Satellite Healthcare*, CV 8465-VCG, 2013 WL 6460898 at *1 and n.2 (Del. Ch. Dec. 9, 2013) (stating that "the right to judicial dissolution is a default right which the parties may eschew by contract" but reserving the question of "[w]hether the parties may, by contract, divest this Court of its authority to order a dissolution in all circumstances, even where it appears manifest that equity so requires—leaving, for instance, irreconcilable members locked away together forever like some alternative entity version of Sartre's *Huis Clos*").

Subsection (c)(13)—The cited provisions comprise the non-waivable aspects of winding up a dissolved limited partnership. The other provisions of Section 802 are default rules.

Subsection (c)(14)—Article 9 delineates a partner's rights to bring direct and derivative actions. It would be unreasonable to frustrate these rights but not unreasonable to channel their exercise. For example, the partnership agreement might select a forum, require pre-suit mediation, provide for arbitration of both direct and derivative claims, or override Section 902 and require "universal demand" in all derivative cases. Similarly, it is not unreasonable to provide for liquidated damages consonant with the law of contracts. In contrast, it would be unreasonable for a partnership agreement to both: (i) require a would-be derivative plaintiff to make demand regardless of futility; and (ii) bar taking the claim to court no matter how long the general partners ponder the demand.

Subsection (c)(15)—A partnership agreement may not alter the act's rules for a special litigation committee but may preclude entirely the use of such a committee.

Subsection (c)(16)—Section 1123(a)(1), 1133(a)(1), 1143(a)(1), and 1153(a)(1) each requires the consent or the affirmative vote of all partners. The partnership agreement may modify these requirements. In contrast, under the sections stated in this subsection:

- each partner is protected from being merged, exchanged, converted, or domesticated "into" the status of a partner in a general partnership that is not a limited liability partnership (or a comparable "unshielded" position in some other organization) without the member having directly consented to either:

  o   the merger, interest exchange, conversion, or domestication; or

  o   a partnership agreement provision that permits such transactions to occur with less than unanimous consent of the partners; and

- merely consenting to a partnership agreement provision that permits amendment of the agreement with less than unanimous consent of the partners does not qualify as the requisite direct consent.

Subsection (c)(17)—Because these plans are the basic "deal documents" for each of the organic transactions contemplated in Article 11, the partnership agreement may not vary the contents of these plans.

Subsection (c)(18)—This limitation pertains only to "the rights under this [act] of" third parties other than partners. Moreover, the limitation is subject to two substantial exceptions: Section 106 (pertaining to the partnership agreement's relationship to the limited partnership itself and to persons becoming partners) and Section 107(b) (pertaining to the partnership agreement's power over the rights of transferees).

Subsection (d)—The partnership agreement has plenipotentiary power over the matters described in Subsection (a), except as specifically limited by Subsections (c). However, for the convenience of practitioners and the courts, Paragraphs 1 and 2 list various terms often found in partnership agreements. No negative inference should be drawn about terms not listed; the listing is provided "without limiting other terms that may be included in a partnership agreement."

Paragraph 2 lists arrangements subject to the "not manifestly unreasonable standard." Subsection (e) delineates that standard. The same standard applies to terms of a partnership agreement which seek to "prescribe the standards . . . by which the performance of the [contractual] obligation [of good faith and fair dealing] is to be measured." Subsection (c)(7).

Subsection (d)(1)(A)—An arrangement *not* involving "one or more disinterested and independent persons" acting "after full disclosure of all material facts" would "alter . . . the aspects of the duty of loyalty stated in Section 409(b)" and would therefore be subject to the "not manifestly unreasonable standard" of Subsection (d)(2)(A).

For the meaning of "material" as applied to information, see Section 409(f), comment.

Subsection (d)(1)(B)—Section 504(a)(2) prohibits distributions:

- *not merely* when, after the distribution, "the partnership's total assets would be less than the sum of its total liabilities,"

- *but also* when, after the distribution, the assets would less than the total liabilities "plus the amount that would be needed, if the partnership were to be dissolved and wound up at the time of the distribution, to satisfy the preferential rights upon dissolution and winding up of partners and transferees whose preferential rights are superior to those of persons receiving the distribution."

The second part of the solvency test pertains to preferential rights to distributions, is thus a matter *inter se* the partners and any transferees, and is therefore subject to change in the partnership agreement.

In contrast, the first part of the solvency test protects third parties—creditors of the limited partnership—and therefore cannot be changed by the partnership agreement. Section 105(c)(18). Likewise, the partnership agreement cannot change solvency test stated in Section 504(a)(1) (that "the partnership would not be able to pay its debts as they become due in the ordinary course of the partnership's activities and affairs").

Section (d)(2)—This act rejects the ultra-contractarian notion that fiduciary duty within a business organization is merely a set of default rules and seeks instead to balance the virtues of "freedom of contract" against the dangers that inescapably exist when some have power over the interests of others.

Nonetheless, a properly drafted partnership agreement may substantially alter and even eliminate fiduciary duties. Two important limitations exist. First, arrangements subject to this subsection may not be "manifestly unreasonable." *See* Subsection (e) (delineating this standard).

Second, the partnership agreement may not transform the relationship inter se the general partners to the limited partnership and limited partners into an entirely arm's length arrangement. For example, displacement of fiduciary duties is effective only to the extent that the displacement is stated clearly and with particularity. This rule is fundamental in the jurisprudence of fiduciary duty. *See, e.g., Paige Capital Mgmt., LLC v. Lerner Master Fund, LLC*, Civ. A. No. 5502-CS, 2011 WL 3505355 at *31 (Del. Ch. Aug. 8 2011) (stating that, even under a statute that "permits the waiver of fiduciary duties . . . such waivers must be set forth clearly"); *Kelly v. Blum*, Civ. A. No. 4516-VCP, 2010 WL 629850, at *10 n.70 (Del. Ch. Feb. 24, 2010) ("Having been granted great contractual freedom by the LLC Act, drafters of or parties to an LLC agreement should be expected to provide . . . clear and unambiguous provisions when they desire to expand, restrict or eliminate the operation of traditional fiduciary duties"). It would therefore be manifestly unreasonable for a partnership agreement to negate this rule.

Although Subsection (d)(2) does not expressly address contracts between a limited partnership and general partner, the stated constraints must also apply to such contracts. If not, those constraints are effectively meaningless.

EXAMPLE: A limited partnership enters into a management contract with its sole general partner, and the contract provides that the duties of loyalty stated in Section 409(b) are entirely eliminated. If the partnership agreement were to so provide, the provision would be subject to the "manifestly unreasonable standard." Section 105(d)(2)(A). Absent the authorization provided by Section 105(d)(2)(A), the management contract's attempt to waive fiduciary duties may be unenforceable as a matter of public policy and contract law. *See Neubauer v. Goldfarb*, 108 Cal. App. 4th 47, 57, 133 Cal. Rptr. 2d 218 (2003) (stating that "waiver of corporate directors' and majority shareholders' fiduciary duties to minority shareholders in private close corporations is against public policy and a contract provision in a buy-sell agreement purporting to effect such a waiver is void"). If not, a court should hold the provision unenforceable nonetheless so as to avoid eviscerating Subsection (d)(2).

Subsection (d)(2)(A)—Subject to the "not manifestly unreasonable" standard, this paragraph empowers the partnership agreement to eliminate *all* aspects of the duty of loyalty listed in Section 409(b). The obligation of good faith and fair dealing, Section 409(d), would remain. See Subsection (c)(6). As to any other, uncodified aspects of the duty of loyalty, see Subsection (d)(2)(D) (empowering the partnership agreement to "alter or eliminate any other fiduciary duty").

EXAMPLE: Joint Venture Limited Partnership ("JV") is a limited partnership, with two general partners, Kappa, Inc. ("Kappa") and Lambda, LLC ("Lambda"). The partnership agreement provides that:

- JV is managed by a "board" consisting of one person appointed by Kappa and one person appointed by Lambda;
- each appointee:
  - owes fiduciary and any other duties exclusively to the general partner that made the appointment; and
  - owes no duties to:
    - the other general partner;
    - the limited partners; and
    - the limited partnership itself.

The "not manifestly unreasonable" standard applies to these provisions under Subsection (d)(2)(A) and (D), and the provisions are not manifestly unreasonable. Note that the provisions do not affect the duties of Kappa and Lambda as general partners.

EXAMPLE: ABC Limited Partnership ("ABC") is a limited partnership with three general partners. ABC has two entirely separate lines of business, the Alpha business and the Beta business. Under ABC's partnership agreement:

- General Partner 1's responsibilities pertain exclusively to the Alpha business, while responsibility for:
  - the Beta business is allocated exclusively to General Partner 2; and
  - ABC's overall operations is allocated exclusively to General Partner 3.
- General Partner 2's responsibilities pertain exclusively to the Beta business, while responsibility for:
  - the Alpha business is allocated exclusively to General Partner 1; and
  - ABC's overall operations is allocated exclusively to General Partner 3.
- General Partner 1 has no fiduciary duties pertaining to the Beta business.
- General Partner 2 has no fiduciary duties pertaining to the Alpha business.

The "not manifestly unreasonable" standard applies to these provisions under Subsection (d)(2)(A) and (D), and the provisions are not manifestly unreasonable.

Subsection (d)(2)(B)—Under this paragraph, a partnership agreement might provide that an affiliate of a general partner will provide compensated services to the limited partnership at a price not exceeding market price, or that a general partner may pursue opportunities that otherwise would be partnership opportunities. Such arrangements are commonplace and permissible.

Subsection (d)(2)(C)—In this context, "conduct" includes both acts and omissions. Black's Law Dictionary (9th ed. 2009), conduct (defining conduct as "[p]ersonal behavior, whether by action or inaction"). Subject to the "not manifestly unreasonable" standard and the bedrock requirements stated here and in Subsection (c)(8), the partnership agreement can reduce the duty of care substantially. In particular, the partnership agreement can eliminate the aspects of the duty of care pertaining to gross negligence and recklessness.

This provision replicates in a particular context the general rule stated in Subsection (c)(8). For the meaning of "bad faith" in the context of the duty of care, see Subsection (c)(8), comment.

Subsection (e)—The "not manifestly unreasonable" concept became part of uniform business entity statutes when UPA (1997) imported the concept from the Uniform Commercial Code. (In the current version of the Uniform Commercial Code, the concept appears in Section 1–302(b).)

This subsection provides rules for applying the concept, specifying:

- who decides the issue of "manifestly unreasonable"
  - "the court . . . as a matter of law," Subsection (e);
- the framework for determining the issue
  - determination to be made "in light of the purposes, activities, and affairs of the limited partnership," Subsection (e)(2);
- the temporal setting for determining the issue
  - "determination [to be made] as of the time the challenged term became part of the partnership agreement," Subsection (e)(1); and
- what information is admissible for determining the issue
  - "only circumstances existing" when "the challenged term became part of the partnership agreement," Subsection (e)(1).

The subsection also provides a very demanding standard for persons claiming that a term of a partnership agreement is "manifestly unreasonable." "The court . . . may invalidate the term only if, in light of the purposes, activities, and affairs of the limited partnership it is *readily apparent* that: (A) the objective of the term is unreasonable; or (B) the term is an unreasonable means to achieve the term's objective." Subsection (e)(2) (emphasis added).

Subsection (e) is fundamental to this act, because: (i) this act generally defers to the agreement among the partners; and (ii) Subsection (e) safeguards the partnership agreement in at least four ways:

- Determining manifest unreasonableness inter se partners of an organization is a different task than doing so in a commercial context, where concepts like "usages of trade" are available to inform the analysis. Each business organization must be understood in its own terms and context.
- If loosely applied, the concept of "manifestly unreasonable" would permit a court to rewrite the partners' agreement, which would destroy the balance this act seeks to establish between freedom of contract and fiduciary duty.
- Case law has not adequately delineated the concept. *See, e.g., In re Brobeck, Phleger & Harrison LLP*, 408 B.R. 318, 335 (Bankr. N.D. Cal. 2009) ("RUPA [UPA (1997)] does not define what is 'manifestly unreasonable' and the parties have not cited, nor can the court locate, a decision that defines the term. Absent case law or even a dictionary definition, the court must rely on its common sense to recognize something as manifestly unreasonable.").
- In the context of statutes permitting stock transfer restrictions unless "manifestly unreasonable," courts have often ignored the word "manifestly." *See, e.g., Brandt v. Somerville*, 692 N.W.2d 144,

152 (N.D. 2005) (stating that "in close corporations, a majority of courts have sustained restrictions that are determined to be reasonable in light of the relevant circumstances"); *Roof Depot, Inc. v. Ohman*, 638 N.W.2d 782, 786 (Minn. Ct. App. 2002) (stating that "the restrictions [on share transfer] are not 'manifestly unreasonable' because they are reasonable means to ensure that the management and control of the business remains in the group of investors or with people well known to them"); *Castriota v. Castriota*, 268 N.J. Super. 417, 423–24, 633 A.2d 1024, 1027–28 (App. Div. 1993) ("We are obliged to apply the statute in a manner consonant with its essential purpose to permit reasonable restrictions upon alienation.").

Subsection (e)(1)—The significance of the phrase "as of the time the term as challenged became part of the partnership agreement" is best shown by example.

EXAMPLE: When a particular limited partnership comes into existence, its business plan is quite unusual and its success depends on the willingness of a particular individual to serve as the limited partnership's sole general partner. This individual has a rare combination of skills, experiences, and contacts, which are particularly appropriate for the partnership's start-up. In order to induce the individual to accept the position of sole general partner, the other partners are willing to have the partnership agreement significantly limit the general partner's fiduciary duties. Several years later, when the limited partnership's operations have turned prosaic and the general partner's talents and background are not nearly so crucial, a limited partner challenges the fiduciary duty limitations as manifestly unreasonable. The relevant time under Subsection (e)(1) is when the limited partnership began. Subsequent developments are not relevant, except as they might inferentially bear on the circumstances in existence at the relevant time.

EXAMPLE: As initially adopted, a partnership agreement identifies a category of decisions ordinarily subject to the duty of loyalty and provides that "the general partner's sole, reasonable discretion" satisfies the duty. A year later, the agreement is amended to delete the word "reasonable." Later, a partner claims that, without the word "reasonable," the provision is manifestly unreasonable. The relevant time under Subsection (e)(1) is when the agreement was amended, not when the agreement was initially adopted.

Subsection (e)(2)—If a person claims that a term of the partnership agreement is manifestly unreasonable under Subsections (c)(7) or (d)(2), as a matter of ordinary procedural law the person making the claim has the burden of proof.

§ 106.　Partnership Agreement; Effect on Limited Partnership and Person Becoming Partner; Preformation Agreement

(a)　A limited partnership is bound by and may enforce the partnership agreement, whether or not the partnership has itself manifested assent to the agreement.

(b)　A person that becomes a partner is deemed to assent to the partnership agreement.

(c)　Two or more persons intending to become the initial partners of a limited partnership may make an agreement providing that upon the formation of the partnership the agreement will become the partnership agreement.

§ 107.　Partnership Agreement; Effect on Third Parties and Relationship to Records Effective on Behalf of Limited Partnership

(a)　A partnership agreement may specify that its amendment requires the approval of a person that is not a party to the agreement or the satisfaction of a condition. An amendment is ineffective if its adoption does not include the required approval or satisfy the specified condition.

(b)　The obligations of a limited partnership and its partners to a person in the person's capacity as a transferee or person dissociated as a partner are governed by the partnership agreement. Subject only to a court order issued under Section 703(b)(2) to effectuate a charging order, an amendment to the partnership agreement made after a person becomes a transferee or is dissociated as a partner:

(1)   is effective with regard to any debt, obligation, or other liability of the partnership or its partners to the person in the person's capacity as a transferee or person dissociated as a partner; and

(2)   is not effective to the extent the amendment imposes a new debt, obligation, or other liability on the transferee or person dissociated as a partner.

(c)   If a record delivered by a limited partnership to the [Secretary of State] for filing becomes effective and contains a provision that would be ineffective under Section 105(c) or (d)(2) if contained in the partnership agreement, the provision is ineffective in the record.

(d)   Subject to subsection (c), if a record delivered by a limited partnership to the [Secretary of State] for filing becomes effective and conflicts with a provision of the partnership agreement:

(1)   the agreement prevails as to partners, persons dissociated as partners, and transferees; and

(2)   the record prevails as to other persons to the extent they reasonably rely on the record.

§ 108.   Required Information

A limited partnership shall maintain at its principal office the following information:

(1)   a current list showing the full name and last known street and mailing address of each partner, separately identifying the general partners, in alphabetical order, and the limited partners, in alphabetical order;

(2)   a copy of the initial certificate of limited partnership and all amendments to and restatements of the certificate, together with signed copies of any powers of attorney under which any certificate, amendment, or restatement has been signed;

(3)   a copy of any filed articles of merger, interest exchange, conversion, or domestication;

(4)   a copy of the partnership's federal, state, and local income tax returns and reports, if any, for the three most recent years;

(5)   a copy of any partnership agreement made in a record and any amendment made in a record to any partnership agreement;

(6)   a copy of any financial statement of the partnership for the three most recent years;

(7)   a copy of the three most recent [annual] [biennial] reports delivered by the partnership to the [Secretary of State] pursuant to Section 212;

(8)   a copy of any record made by the partnership during the past three years of any consent given by or vote taken of any partner pursuant to this [act] or the partnership agreement; and

(9)   unless contained in a partnership agreement made in a record, a record stating:

(A)   a description and statement of the agreed value of contributions other than money made and agreed to be made by each partner;

(B)   the times at which, or events on the happening of which, any additional contributions agreed to be made by each partner are to be made;

(C)   for any person that is both a general partner and a limited partner, a specification of what transferable interest the person owns in each capacity; and

(D)   any events upon the happening of which the partnership is to be dissolved and its activities and affairs wound up.

§ 109.   Dual Capacity

A person may be both a general partner and a limited partner. A person that is both a general and limited partner has the rights, powers, duties, and obligations provided by this [act] and the partnership agreement in each of those capacities. When the person acts as a general partner, the person is subject to the obligations, duties, and restrictions under this [act] and the partnership agreement for general partners. When the person acts as a limited partner, the person is subject to the obligations, duties, and restrictions under this [act] and the partnership agreement for limited partners.

§ 110.   Nature, Purpose, and Duration of Limited Partnership

(a)   A limited partnership is an entity distinct from its partners. A limited partnership is the same entity regardless of whether its certificate states that the limited partnership is a limited liability limited partnership.

(b)   A limited partnership may have any lawful purpose, regardless of whether for profit.

(c)   A limited partnership has perpetual duration.

§ 111.   Powers

A limited partnership has the capacity to sue and be sued in the name of the partnership and the power to do all things necessary or convenient to carry on the partnership's activities and affairs.

§ 112.   Application to Existing Relationships

(a)   Before [all-inclusive date], this [act] governs only:

(1)   a limited partnership formed on or after [the effective date of this [act]]; and

(2)   except as otherwise provided in subsections (c) and (d), a limited partnership formed before [the effective date of this [act]] which elects, in the manner provided in its partnership agreement or by law for amending the partnership agreement, to be subject to this [act].

(b)   Except as otherwise provided in subsections (c) and (d), on and after [all-inclusive date] this [act] governs all limited partnerships.

(c)   With respect to a limited partnership formed before [the effective date of this [act]], the following rules apply except as the partners otherwise elect in the manner provided in the partnership agreement or by law for amending the partnership agreement:

(1)   Section 110(c) does not apply and the limited partnership has whatever duration it had under the law applicable immediately before [the effective date of this [act]].

(2)   the limited partnership is not required to amend its certificate of limited partnership to comply with Section 201(b)(5).

(3)   Sections 601 and 602 do not apply and a limited partner has the same right and power to dissociate from the limited partnership, with the same consequences, as existed immediately before [the effective date of this [act]].

(4)   Section 603(4) does not apply.

(5)   Section 603(5) does not apply and a court has the same power to expel a general partner as the court had immediately before [the effective date of this [act]].

(6)   Section 801(a)(3) does not apply and the connection between a person's dissociation as a general partner and the dissolution of the limited partnership is the same as existed immediately before [the effective date of this [act]].

(d)   With respect to a limited partnership that elects pursuant to subsection (a)(2) to be subject to this [act], after the election takes effect the provisions of this [act] relating to the liability of the limited partnership's general partners to third parties apply:

(1)   before [all-inclusive date], to:

(A)   a third party that had not done business with the limited partnership in the year before the election took effect; and

(B)   a third party that had done business with the limited partnership in the year before the election took effect only if the third party knows or has been notified of the election; and

(2)   on and after [all-inclusive date], to all third parties, but those provisions remain inapplicable to any obligation incurred while those provisions were inapplicable under paragraph (1)(B).

Legislative Note: *Subsection 112(c) presupposes that this act is replacing ULPA (1976) (Last Amended 1985). If this act is replacing a substantially different limited partnership act, the enacting jurisdiction should consider whether: (i) this act makes material changes to the "default" (or "gap filler") rules of the predecessor statute; and (ii) if so, whether Subsection (c) should carry forward any of those rules for pre-existing limited partnerships. In this assessment, the focus is on pre-existing limited partnerships that have left default rules in place, whether advisedly or not. The central question is whether, for such limited partnerships, expanding Subsection (c) is necessary to prevent material changes to the partners' "deal."*

In an enacting jurisdiction that has previously amended its existing limited partnership statute to provide for limited liability limited partnerships (LLLPs), this act should include transition provisions specifically applicable to pre-existing limited liability limited partnerships. The precise wording of those provisions must depend on the wording of the State's previously enacted LLLP provisions. However, the following principles apply generally:

1.   In Sections 806(b)(5) and 807(b)(4) (notice by dissolved limited partnership to claimants), the phrase "the limited partnership has been throughout its existence a limited liability limited partnership" should be revised to encompass a limited partnership that was a limited liability limited partnership under the State's previously enacted LLLP provisions.

2.   Section 112(d) should provide that, if a pre-existing limited liability limited partnership elects to be subject to this act, this act's provisions relating to the liability of general partners to third parties apply immediately to all third parties, regardless of whether a third party has previously done business with the limited liability limited partnership.

3.   A pre-existing limited liability limited partnership that elects to be subject to this act should have to comply with Sections 201(b)(5) (requiring the certificate of limited partnership to state whether the limited partnership is a limited liability limited partnership) and 114(c) (establishing name requirements for a limited liability limited partnership).

4.   As for Section 112(b) (providing that, after a transition period, this act applies to all preexisting limited partnerships):

a.   if a State's previously enacted LLLP provisions have requirements essentially the same as Sections 201(b)(5) and 114(c), pre-existing limited liability limited partnerships should automatically retain LLLP status under this act.

b.   if a State's previously enacted LLLP provisions have name requirements essentially the same as Section 114(c) and provide that a public filing other than the certificate of limited partnership establishes a limited partnership's status as a limited liability limited partnership:

i.   that filing can be deemed to an amendment to the certificate of limited partnership to comply with Section 201(b)(5), and ii.   pre-existing limited liability limited partnerships should automatically retain LLLP status under this act.

      c.   if a State's previously enacted LLLP provisions do not have name requirements essentially the same as Section 114(c), it will be impossible both to enforce Section 114(c) and provide for automatic transition to LLLP status under this act.

It is recommended that the "all-inclusive" date should be at least one year after the effective date of this act, Section 1206, but no more than two years.

§ 113.   Supplemental Principles of Law

    Unless displaced by particular provisions of this [act], the principles of law and equity supplement this [act].

§ 114.   Permitted Names

    (a)   The name of a limited partnership may contain the name of any partner.

    (b)   The name of a limited partnership that is not a limited liability limited partnership must contain the phrase "limited partnership" or the abbreviation "LP" or "L.P." and may not contain the phrase "limited liability limited partnership" or the abbreviation "LLLP" or "L.L.L.P.".

    (c)   The name of a limited liability limited partnership must contain the phrase "limited liability limited partnership" or the abbreviation "LLLP" or "L.L.L.P." and must not contain the abbreviation "LP" or "L.P.".

    (d)   Except as otherwise provided in subsection (g), the name of a limited partnership, and the name under which a foreign limited partnership may register to do business in this state, must be distinguishable on the records of the [Secretary of State] from any:

      (1)   name of an existing person whose formation required the filing of a record by the [Secretary of State] and which is not at the time administratively dissolved;

      (2)   name of a limited liability partnership whose statement of qualification is in effect;

      (3)   name under which a person is registered to do business in this state by the filing of a record by the [Secretary of State];

      (4)   name reserved under Section 115 or other law of this state providing for the reservation of a name by the filing of a record by the [Secretary of State];

      (5)   name registered under Section 116 or other law of this state providing for the registration of a name by the filing of a record by the [Secretary of State]; and

      (6)   name registered under [this state's assumed or fictitious name statute].

    (e)   If a person consents in a record to the use of its name and submits an undertaking in a form satisfactory to the [Secretary of State] to change its name to a name that is distinguishable on the records of the [Secretary of State] from any name in any category of names in subsection (d), the name of the consenting person may be used by the person to which the consent was given.

    (f)   Except as otherwise provided in subsection (g), in determining whether a name is the same as or not distinguishable on the records of the [Secretary of State] from the name of another person, words, phrases, or abbreviations indicating the type of person, such as "corporation", "corp.", "incorporated", "Inc.", "professional corporation", "PC", "P.C.", "professional association", "PA", "P.A.", "Limited", "Ltd.", "limited partnership", "LP", "L.P.", "limited liability partnership", "LLP", "L.L.P.", "registered limited liability partnership", "RLLP", "R.L.L.P.", "limited liability limited partnership", "LLLP", "L.L.L.P.", "registered limited liability limited partnership", "RLLLP", "R.L.L.L.P.", "limited liability company", "LLC", "L.L.C.", "limited cooperative association", "limited cooperative", "LCA", or "L.C.A." may not be taken into account.

(g)   A person may consent in a record to the use of a name that is not distinguishable on the records of the [Secretary of State] from its name except for the addition of a word, phrase, or abbreviation indicating the type of person as provided in subsection (f). In such a case, the person need not change its name pursuant to subsection (e).

(h)   The name of a limited partnership or foreign limited partnership may not contain the words [insert prohibited words or words that may be used only with approval by an appropriate state agency].

(i)   A limited partnership or foreign limited partnership may use a name that is not distinguishable from a name described in subsection (d)(1) through (6) if the partnership delivers to the [Secretary of State] a certified copy of a final judgment of a court of competent jurisdiction establishing the right of the partnership to use the name in this state.

§ 115.   Reservation of Name

(a)   A person may reserve the exclusive use of a name that complies with Section 114 by delivering an application to the [Secretary of State] for filing. The application must state the name and address of the applicant and the name to be reserved. If the [Secretary of State] finds that the name is available, the [Secretary of State] shall reserve the name for the applicant's exclusive use for [120] days.

(b)   The owner of a reserved name may transfer the reservation to another person by delivering to the [Secretary of State] a signed notice in a record of the transfer which states the name and address of the person to which the reservation is being transferred.

§ 116.   Registration of Name

(a)   A foreign limited partnership not registered to do business in this state under [Article] 10 may register its name, or an alternate name adopted pursuant to Section 1006, if the name is distinguishable on the records of the [Secretary of State] from the names that are not available under Section 114.

(b)   To register its name or an alternate name adopted pursuant to Section 1006, a foreign limited partnership must deliver to the [Secretary of State] for filing an application stating the partnership's name, the jurisdiction and date of its formation, and any alternate name adopted pursuant to Section 1006. If the [Secretary of State] finds that the name applied for is available, the [Secretary of State] shall register the name for the applicant's exclusive use.

(c)   The registration of a name under this section is effective for [one year] after the date of registration.

(d)   A foreign limited partnership whose name registration is effective may renew the registration for successive [one-year] periods by delivering, not earlier than [three months] before the expiration of the registration, to the [Secretary of State] for filing a renewal application that complies with this section. When filed, the renewal application renews the registration for a succeeding [one-year] period.

(e)   A foreign limited partnership whose name registration is effective may register as a foreign limited partnership under the registered name or consent in a signed record to the use of that name by another person that is not an individual.

§ 117.   Registered Agent

(a)   Each limited partnership and each registered foreign limited partnership shall designate and maintain a registered agent in this state. The designation of a registered agent is an affirmation of fact by the limited partnership or registered foreign limited partnership that the agent has consented to serve.

(b)   A registered agent for a limited partnership or registered foreign limited partnership must have a place of business in this state.

(c)   The only duties under this [act] of a registered agent that has complied with this [act] are:

(1)   to forward to the limited partnership or registered foreign limited partnership at the address most recently supplied to the agent by the partnership or foreign partnership any process, notice, or demand pertaining to the partnership or foreign partnership which is served on or received by the agent;

(2)   if the registered agent resigns, to provide the notice required by Section 119(c) to the partnership or foreign partnership at the address most recently supplied to the agent by the partnership or foreign partnership; and

(3)   to keep current the information with respect to the agent in the certificate of limited partnership.

§ 118.   Change of Registered Agent or Address for Registered Agent by Limited Partnership

(a)   A limited partnership or registered foreign limited partnership may change its registered agent or the address of its registered agent by delivering to the [Secretary of State] for filing a statement of change that states:

(1)   the name of the partnership or foreign partnership; and

(2)   the information that is to be in effect as a result of the filing of the statement of change.

(b)   The general or limited partners of a limited partnership need not approve the [delivery to the Secretary of State] for filing of:

(1)   a statement of change under this section; or

(2)   a similar filing changing the registered agent or registered office, if any, of the partnership in any other jurisdiction.

(c)   A statement of change under this section designating a new registered agent is an affirmation of fact by the limited partnership or registered foreign limited partnership that the agent has consented to serve.

(d)   As an alternative to using the procedure in this section, a limited partnership may amend its certificate of limited partnership.

§ 119.   Resignation of Registered Agent

(a)   A registered agent may resign as an agent for a limited partnership or registered foreign limited partnership by delivering to the [Secretary of State] for filing a statement of resignation that states:

(1)   the name of the partnership or foreign partnership;

(2)   the name of the agent;

(3)   that the agent resigns from serving as registered agent for the partnership or foreign partnership; and

(4)   the address of the partnership or foreign partnership to which the agent will send the notice required by subsection (c).

(b)   A statement of resignation takes effect on the earlier of:

(1)   the 31st day after the day on which it is filed by the [Secretary of State]; or

(2)   the designation of a new registered agent for the limited partnership or registered foreign limited partnership.

(c)   A registered agent promptly shall furnish to the limited partnership or registered foreign limited partnership notice in a record of the date on which a statement of resignation was filed.

(d)   When a statement of resignation takes effect, the registered agent ceases to have responsibility under this [act] for any matter thereafter tendered to it as agent for the limited partnership or registered foreign limited partnership. The resignation does not affect any contractual rights the partnership or foreign partnership has against the agent or that the agent has against the partnership or foreign partnership.

(e)   A registered agent may resign with respect to a limited partnership or registered foreign limited partnership whether or not the partnership or foreign partnership is in good standing.

§ 120.   Change of Name or Address by Registered Agent

(a)   If a registered agent changes its name or address, the agent may deliver to the [Secretary of State] for filing a statement of change that states:

(1)   the name of the limited partnership or registered foreign limited partnership represented by the registered agent;

(2)   the name of the agent as currently shown in the records of the [Secretary of State] for the partnership or foreign partnership;

(3)   if the name of the agent has changed, its new name; and

(4)   if the address of the agent has changed, its new address.

(b)   A registered agent promptly shall furnish notice to the represented limited partnership or registered foreign limited partnership of the filing by the [Secretary of State] of the statement of change and the changes made by the statement.

Legislative Note: Many registered agents act in that capacity for many entities, and the Model Registered Agents Act (2006) (Last Amended 2013) provides a streamlined method through which a commercial registered agent can make a single filing to change its information for all represented entities. The single filing does not prevent an enacting state from assessing filing fees on the basis of the number of entity records affected. Alternatively the fees can be set on an incremental sliding fee or capitated amount based upon potential economies of costs for a bulk filing.

§ 121.   Service of Process, Notice, or Demand

(a)   A limited partnership or registered foreign limited partnership may be served with any process, notice, or demand required or permitted by law by serving its registered agent.

(b)   If a limited partnership or registered foreign limited partnership ceases to have a registered agent, or if its registered agent cannot with reasonable diligence be served, the partnership or foreign partnership may be served by registered or certified mail, return receipt requested, or by similar commercial delivery service, addressed to the partnership or foreign partnership at its principal office. The address of the principal office must be as shown in the partnership's or foreign partnership's most recent [annual] [biennial] report filed by the [Secretary of State]. Service is effected under this subsection on the earliest of:

(1)   the date the partnership or foreign partnership receives the mail or delivery by the commercial delivery service;

(2)   the date shown on the return receipt, if signed by the partnership or foreign partnership; or

(3)   five days after its deposit with the United States Postal Service, or with the commercial delivery service, if correctly addressed and with sufficient postage or payment.

(c)   If process, notice, or demand cannot be served on a limited partnership or registered foreign limited partnership pursuant to subsection (a) or (b), service may be made by handing a copy to the individual in charge of any regular place of business or activity of the partnership or foreign partnership if the individual served is not a plaintiff in the action.

(d)   Service of process, notice, or demand on a registered agent must be in a written record.

(e)   Service of process, notice, or demand may be made by other means under law other than this [act].

§ 122.   Delivery of Record

(a)   Except as otherwise provided in this [act], permissible means of delivery of a record include delivery by hand, mail, conventional commercial practice, and electronic transmission.

(b)   Delivery to the [Secretary of State] is effective only when a record is received by the [Secretary of State].

§ 123.   Reservation of Power to Amend or Repeal

The [legislature of this state] has power to amend or repeal all or part of this [act] at any time, and all limited partnerships and foreign limited partnerships subject to this [act] are governed by the amendment or repeal.

[ARTICLE] 2.   FORMATION; CERTIFICATE OF LIMITED PARTNERSHIP AND OTHER FILINGS

§ 201.   Formation of Limited Partnership; Certificate of Limited Partnership

(a)   To form a limited partnership, a person must deliver a certificate of limited partnership to the [Secretary of State] for filing.

(b)   A certificate of limited partnership must state:

(1)   the name of the limited partnership, which must comply with Section 114;

(2)   the street and mailing addresses of the partnership's principal office;

(3)   the name and street and mailing addresses in this state of the partnership's registered agent;

(4)   the name and street and mailing addresses of each general partner; and

(5)   whether the limited partnership is a limited liability limited partnership.

(c)   A certificate of limited partnership may contain statements as to matters other than those required by subsection (b), but may not vary or otherwise affect the provisions specified in Section 105(c) and (d) in a manner inconsistent with that section.

(d)   A limited partnership is formed when:

(1)   the certificate of limited partnership becomes effective:

(2)   at least two persons have become partners;

(3)   at least one person has become a general partner; and

(4)   at least one person has become a limited partner.

§ 202. Amendment or Restatement of Certificate of Limited Partnership

(a)   A certificate of limited partnership may be amended or restated at any time.

(b)   To amend its certificate of limited partnership, a limited partnership must deliver to the [Secretary of State] for filing an amendment stating:

    (1)   the name of the partnership;

    (2)   the date of filing of its initial certificate; and

    (3)   the text of the amendment.

(c)   To restate its certificate of limited partnership, a limited partnership must deliver to the [Secretary of State] for filing a restatement, designated as such in its heading.

(d)   A limited partnership shall promptly deliver to the [Secretary of State] for filing an amendment to a certificate of limited partnership to reflect:

    (1)   the admission of a new general partner;

    (2)   the dissociation of a person as a general partner; or

    (3)   the appointment of a person to wind up the limited partnership's activities and affairs under Section 802(c) or (d).

(e)   If a general partner knows that any information in a filed certificate of limited partnership was inaccurate when the certificate was filed or has become inaccurate due to changed circumstances, the general partner shall promptly:

    (1)   cause the certificate to be amended; or

    (2)   if appropriate, deliver to the [Secretary of State] for filing a statement of change under Section 118 or a statement of correction under Section 209.

§ 203. Signing of Records to be Delivered for Filing to [Secretary of State]

(a)   A record delivered to the [Secretary of State] for filing pursuant to this [act] must be signed as follows:

    (1)   An initial certificate of limited partnership must be signed by all general partners listed in the certificate.

    (2)   An amendment to the certificate of limited partnership adding or deleting a statement that the limited partnership is a limited liability limited partnership must be signed by all general partners listed in the certificate.

    (3)   An amendment to the certificate of limited partnership designating as general partner a person admitted under Section 801(a)(3)(B) following the dissociation of a limited partnership's last general partner must be signed by that person.

    (4)   An amendment to the certificate of limited partnership required by Section 802(c) following the appointment of a person to wind up the dissolved limited partnership's activities and affairs must be signed by that person.

    (5)   Any other amendment to the certificate of limited partnership must be signed by:

        (A)   at least one general partner listed in the certificate;

        (B)   each person designated in the amendment as a new general partner; and

        (C)   each person that the amendment indicates has dissociated as a general partner, unless:

            (i)   the person is deceased or a guardian or general conservator has been appointed for the person and the amendment so states; or

(ii)   the person has previously delivered to the [Secretary of State] for filing a statement of dissociation.

(6)   A restated certificate of limited partnership must be signed by at least one general partner listed in the certificate, and, to the extent the restated certificate effects a change under any other paragraph of this subsection, the certificate must be signed in a manner that satisfies that paragraph.

(7)   A statement of termination must be signed by all general partners listed in the certificate of limited partnership or, if the certificate of a dissolved limited partnership lists no general partners, by the person appointed pursuant to Section 802(c) or (d) to wind up the dissolved limited partnership's activities and affairs.

(8)   Any other record delivered by a limited partnership to the [Secretary of State] for filing must be signed by at least one general partner listed in the certificate of limited partnership.

(9)   A statement by a person pursuant to Section 605(a)(3) stating that the person has dissociated as a general partner must be signed by that person.

(10) A statement of negation by a person pursuant to Section 306 must be signed by that person.

(11) Any other record delivered on behalf of a person to the [Secretary of State] for filing must be signed by that person.

(b)   Any record delivered for filing under this [act] may be signed by an agent. Whenever this [act] requires a particular individual to sign a record and the individual is deceased or incompetent, the record may be signed by a legal representative of the individual.

(c)   A person that signs a record as an agent or legal representative thereby affirms as a fact that the person is authorized to sign the record.

§ 204.   Signing and Filing Pursuant to Judicial Order

(a)   If a person required by this [act] to sign a record or deliver a record to the [Secretary of State] for filing under this [act] does not do so, any other person that is aggrieved may petition [the appropriate court] to order:

(1)   the person to sign the record;

(2)   the person to deliver the record to the [Secretary of State] for filing; or

(3)   the [Secretary of State] to file the record unsigned.

(b)   If a petitioner under subsection (a) is not the limited partnership or foreign limited partnership to which the record pertains, the petitioner shall make the partnership or foreign partnership a party to the action.

(c)   A record filed under subsection (a)(3) is effective without being signed.

§ 205.   Liability for Inaccurate Information in Filed Record

(a)   If a record delivered to the [Secretary of State] for filing under this [act] and filed by the [Secretary of State] contains inaccurate information, a person that suffers loss by reliance on the information may recover damages for the loss from:

(1)   a person that signed the record, or caused another to sign it on the person's behalf, and knew the information to be inaccurate at the time the record was signed; and

(2)   a general partner if:

(A)   the record was delivered for filing on behalf of the partnership; and

(B) the general partner knew or had notice of the inaccuracy for a reasonably sufficient time before the information was relied upon so that, before the reliance, the general partner reasonably could have:

(i) effected an amendment under Section 202;

(ii) filed a petition under Section 204; or

(iii) delivered to the [Secretary of State] for filing a statement of change under Section 118 or a statement of correction under Section 209.

(b) An individual who signs a record authorized or required to be filed under this [act] affirms under penalty of perjury that the information stated in the record is accurate.

§ 206. Filing Requirements

(a) To be filed by the [Secretary of State] pursuant to this [act], a record must be received by the [Secretary of State], must comply with this [act], and satisfy the following:

(1) The filing of the record must be required or permitted by this [act].

(2) The record must be physically delivered in written form unless and to the extent the [Secretary of State] permits electronic delivery of records.

(3) The words in the record must be in English, and numbers must be in Arabic or Roman numerals, but the name of an entity need not be in English if written in English letters or Arabic or Roman numerals.

(4) The record must be signed by a person authorized or required under this [act] to sign the record.

(5) The record must state the name and capacity, if any, of each individual who signed it, either on behalf of the individual or the person authorized or required to sign the record, but need not contain a seal, attestation, acknowledgment, or verification.

(b) If law other than this [act] prohibits the disclosure by the [Secretary of State] of information contained in a record delivered to the [Secretary of State] for filing, the [Secretary of State] shall file the record if the record otherwise complies with this [act] but may redact the information.

(c) When a record is delivered to the [Secretary of State] for filing, any fee required under this [act] and any fee, tax, interest, or penalty required to be paid under this [act] or law other than this [act] must be paid in a manner permitted by the [Secretary of State] or by that law.

(d) The [Secretary of State] may require that a record delivered in written form be accompanied by an identical or conformed copy.

(e) The [Secretary of State] may provide forms for filings required or permitted to be made by this [act], but, except as otherwise provided in subsection (f), their use is not required.

(f) The [Secretary of State] may require that a cover sheet for a filing be on a form prescribed by the [Secretary of State].

§ 207. Effective Date and Time

Except as otherwise provided in Section 208 and subject to Section 209(d), a record filed under this [act] is effective:

(1) on the date and at the time of its filing by the [Secretary of State], as provided in Section 210(b);

(2) on the date of filing and at the time specified in the record as its effective time, if later than the time under paragraph (1);

(3)   at a specified delayed effective date and time, which may not be more than 90 days after the date of filing; or

(4)   if a delayed effective date is specified, but no time is specified, at 12:01 a.m. on the date specified, which may not be more than 90 days after the date of filing.

§ 208.   Withdrawal of Filed Record Before Effectiveness

(a)   Except as otherwise provided in Sections 1124, 1134, 1144, and 1154, a record delivered to the [Secretary of State] for filing may be withdrawn before it takes effect by delivering to the [Secretary of State] for filing a statement of withdrawal.

(b)   A statement of withdrawal must:

(1)   be signed by each person that signed the record being withdrawn, except as otherwise agreed by those persons;

(2)   identify the record to be withdrawn; and

(3)   if signed by fewer than all the persons that signed the record being withdrawn, state that the record is withdrawn in accordance with the agreement of all the persons that signed the record.

(c)   On filing by the [Secretary of State] of a statement of withdrawal, the action or transaction evidenced by the original record does not take effect.

§ 209.   Correcting Filed Record

(a)   A person on whose behalf a filed record was delivered to the [Secretary of State] for filing may correct the record if:

(1)   the record at the time of filing was inaccurate;

(2)   the record was defectively signed; or

(3)   the electronic transmission of the record to the [Secretary of State] was defective.

(b)   To correct a filed record, a person on whose behalf the record was delivered to the [Secretary of State] must deliver to the [Secretary of State] for filing a statement of correction.

(c)   A statement of correction:

(1)   may not state a delayed effective date;

(2)   must be signed by the person correcting the filed record;

(3)   must identify the filed record to be corrected;

(4)   must specify the inaccuracy or defect to be corrected; and

(5)   must correct the inaccuracy or defect.

(d)   A statement of correction is effective as of the effective date of the filed record that it corrects except for purposes of Section 103(d) and as to persons relying on the uncorrected filed record and adversely affected by the correction. For those purposes and as to those persons, the statement of correction is effective when filed.

§ 210.   Duty of [Secretary of State] to File; Review of Refusal to File; Delivery of Record by [Secretary of State]

(a)   The [Secretary of State] shall file a record delivered to the [Secretary of State] for filing which satisfies this [act]. The duty of the [Secretary of State] under this section is ministerial.

(b)   When the [Secretary of State] files a record, the [Secretary of State] shall record it as filed on the date and at the time of its delivery. After filing a record, the [Secretary of State] shall deliver to the person that submitted the record a copy of the record with an acknowledgment of the date and time of filing.

(c)   If the [Secretary of State] refuses to file a record, the [Secretary of State] shall, not later than [15] business days after the record is delivered:

(1)   return the record or notify the person that submitted the record of the refusal; and

(2)   provide a brief explanation in a record of the reason for the refusal.

(d)   If the [Secretary of State] refuses to file a record, the person that submitted the record may petition [the appropriate court] to compel filing of the record. The record and the explanation of the [Secretary of State] of the refusal to file must be attached to the petition. The court may decide the matter in a summary proceeding.

(e)   The filing of or refusal to file a record does not:

(1)   affect the validity or invalidity of the record in whole or in part; or

(2)   create a presumption that the information contained in the record is correct or incorrect.

(f)   Except as otherwise provided by Section 121 or by law other than this [act], the [Secretary of State] may deliver any record to a person by delivering it:

(1)   in person to the person that submitted it;

(2)   to the address of the person's registered agent;

(3)   to the principal office of the person; or

(4)   to another address the person provides to the [Secretary of State] for delivery.

§ 211.   Certificate of Good Standing or Registration

(a)   On request of any person, the [Secretary of State] shall issue a certificate of good standing for a limited partnership or a certificate of registration for a registered foreign limited partnership.

(b)   A certificate under subsection (a) must state:

(1)   the limited partnership's name or the registered foreign limited partnership's name used in this state;

(2)   in the case of a limited partnership:

(A)   that a certificate of limited partnership has been filed and has taken effect;

(B)   the date the certificate became effective;

(C)   the period of the partnership's duration if the records of the [Secretary of State] reflect that its period of duration is less than perpetual; and

(D)   that:

(i)   no statement of administrative dissolution, or statement of termination has been filed;

(ii)   the records of the [Secretary to State] do not otherwise reflect that the partnership has been dissolved or terminated; and

(iii)   a proceeding is not pending under Section 811;

(3)   in the case of a registered foreign limited partnership, that it is registered to do business in this state;

(4)   that all fees, taxes, interest, and penalties owed to this state by the limited partnership or the foreign partnership and collected through the [Secretary of State] have been paid, if:

(A) payment is reflected in the records of the [Secretary of State]; and

(B) nonpayment affects the good standing or registration of the partnership or foreign partnership;

(5) that the most recent [annual] [biennial] report required by Section 212 has been delivered to the [Secretary of State] for filing; and

(6) other facts reflected in the records of the [Secretary of State] pertaining to the limited partnership or foreign limited partnership which the person requesting the certificate reasonably requests.

(c) Subject to any qualification stated in the certificate, a certificate issued by the [Secretary of State] under subsection (a) may be relied on as conclusive evidence of the facts stated in the certificate.

§ 212.   [Annual] [Biennial] Report for [Secretary of State]

(a) A limited partnership or registered foreign limited partnership shall deliver to the [Secretary of State] for filing [an annual] [a biennial] report that states:

(1) the name of the partnership or foreign partnership;

(2) the name and street and mailing addresses of its registered agent in this state;

(3) the street and mailing addresses of its principal office;

(4) the name of at least one general partner; and

(5) in the case of a foreign partnership, its jurisdiction of formation and any alternate name adopted under Section 1006(a).

(b) Information in the [annual] [biennial] report must be current as of the date the report is signed by the limited partnership or registered foreign limited partnership.

(c) The first [annual] [biennial] report must be delivered to the [Secretary of State] for filing after [January 1] and before [April 1] of the year following the calendar year in which the limited partnership's certificate of limited partnership became effective or the registered foreign limited partnership registered to do business in this state. Subsequent [annual] [biennial] reports must be delivered to the [Secretary of State] for filing after [January 1] and before [April 1] of each [second] calendar year thereafter.

(d) If [an annual] [a biennial] report does not contain the information required by this section, the [Secretary of State] promptly shall notify the reporting limited partnership or registered foreign limited partnership in a record and return the report for correction.

(e) If [an annual] [a biennial] report contains the name or address of a registered agent which differs from the information shown in the records of the [Secretary of State] immediately before the report becomes effective, the differing information is considered a statement of change under Section 118.

[ARTICLE] 3.   LIMITED PARTNERS

§ 301.   Becoming Limited Partner

(a) Upon formation of a limited partnership, a person becomes a limited partner as agreed among the persons that are to be the initial partners.

(b) After formation, a person becomes a limited partner:

(1) as provided in the partnership agreement;

(2) as the result of a transaction effective under [Article] 11;

(3) with the affirmative vote or consent of all the partners; or

(4)   as provided in Section 801(a)(4) or (a)(5).

(c)   A person may become a limited partner without:

(1)   acquiring a transferable interest; or

(2)   making or being obligated to make a contribution to the limited partnership.

§ 302.   No Agency Power of Limited Partner as Limited Partner

(a)   A limited partner is not an agent of a limited partnership solely by reason of being a limited partner.

(b)   A person's status as a limited partner does not prevent or restrict law other than this [act] from imposing liability on a limited partnership because of the person's conduct.

§ 303.   No Liability as Limited Partner for Limited Partnership Obligations

(a)   A debt, obligation, or other liability of a limited partnership is not the debt, obligation, or other liability of a limited partner. A limited partner is not personally liable, directly or indirectly, by way of contribution or otherwise, for a debt, obligation, or other liability of the partnership solely by reason of being or acting as a limited partner, even if the limited partner participates in the management and control of the limited partnership. This subsection applies regardless of the dissolution of the partnership.

(b)   The failure of a limited partnership to observe formalities relating to the exercise of its powers or management of its activities and affairs is not a ground for imposing liability on a limited partner for a debt, obligation, or other liability of the partnership.

§ 304.   Rights to Information of Limited Partner and Person Dissociated as Limited Partner

(a)   On 10 days' demand, made in a record received by the limited partnership, a limited partner may inspect and copy required information during regular business hours in the limited partnership's principal office. The limited partner need not have any particular purpose for seeking the information.

(b)   During regular business hours and at a reasonable location specified by the limited partnership, a limited partner may inspect and copy information regarding the activities, affairs, financial condition, and other circumstances of the limited partnership as is just and reasonable if:

(1)   the limited partner seeks the information for a purpose reasonably related to the partner's interest as a limited partner;

(2)   the limited partner makes a demand in a record received by the limited partnership, describing with reasonable particularity the information sought and the purpose for seeking the information; and

(3)   the information sought is directly connected to the limited partner's purpose.

(c)   Not later than 10 days after receiving a demand pursuant to subsection (b), the limited partnership shall inform in a record the limited partner that made the demand of:

(1)   what information the partnership will provide in response to the demand and when and where the partnership will provide the information; and

(2)   the partnership's reasons for declining, if the partnership declines to provide any demanded information.

(d)   Whenever this [act] or a partnership agreement provides for a limited partner to vote on or give or withhold consent to a matter, before the vote is cast or consent is given or withheld, the limited partnership shall, without demand, provide the limited partner with all information that is known to the partnership and is material to the limited partner's decision.

(e)   Subject to subsection (j), on 10 days' demand made in a record received by a limited partnership, a person dissociated as a limited partner may have access to information to which the person was entitled while a limited partner if:

> (1)   the information pertains to the period during which the person was a limited partner;
>
> (2)   the person seeks the information in good faith; and
>
> (3)   the person satisfies the requirements imposed on a limited partner by subsection (b).

(f)   A limited partnership shall respond to a demand made pursuant to subsection (e) in the manner provided in subsection (c).

(g)   A limited partnership may charge a person that makes a demand under this section reasonable costs of copying, limited to the costs of labor and material.

(h)   A limited partner or person dissociated as a limited partner may exercise the rights under this section through an agent or, in the case of an individual under legal disability, a legal representative. Any restriction or condition imposed by the partnership agreement or under subsection (j) applies both to the agent or legal representative and to the limited partner or person dissociated as a limited partner.

(i)   Subject to Section 704, the rights under this section do not extend to a person as transferee.

(j)   In addition to any restriction or condition stated in its partnership agreement, a limited partnership, as a matter within the ordinary course of its activities and affairs, may impose reasonable restrictions and conditions on access to and use of information to be furnished under this section, including designating information confidential and imposing nondisclosure and safeguarding obligations on the recipient. In a dispute concerning the reasonableness of a restriction under this subsection, the partnership has the burden of proving reasonableness.

§ 305.   Limited Duties of Limited Partners

(a)   A limited partner shall discharge any duties to the partnership and the other partners under the partnership agreement and exercise any rights under this [act] or the partnership agreement consistently with the contractual obligation of good faith and fair dealing.

(b)   Except as otherwise provided in subsection (a), a limited partner does not have any duty to the limited partnership or to any other partner solely by reason of acting as a limited partner.

(c)   If a limited partner enters into a transaction with a limited partnership, the limited partner's rights and obligations arising from the transaction are the same as those of a person that is not a partner.

§ 306.   Person Erroneously Believing Self to be Limited Partner

(a)   Except as otherwise provided in subsection (b), a person that makes an investment in a business enterprise and erroneously but in good faith believes that the person has become a limited partner in the enterprise is not liable for the enterprise's obligations by reason of making the investment, receiving distributions from the enterprise, or exercising any rights of or appropriate to a limited partner, if, on ascertaining the mistake, the person:

> (1)   causes an appropriate certificate of limited partnership, amendment, or statement of correction to be signed and delivered to the [Secretary of State] for filing; or
>
> (2)   withdraws from future participation as an owner in the enterprise by signing and delivering to the [Secretary of State] for filing a statement of negation under this section.

(b)   A person that makes an investment described in subsection (a) is liable to the same extent as a general partner to any third party that enters into a transaction with the enterprise, believing in good faith that the person is a general partner, before the [Secretary of State] files a statement of negation, certificate of limited partnership, amendment, or statement of correction to show that the person is not a general partner.

(c) If a person makes a diligent effort in good faith to comply with subsection (a)(1) and is unable to cause the appropriate certificate of limited partnership, amendment, or statement of correction to be signed and delivered to the [Secretary of State] for filing, the person has the right to withdraw from the enterprise pursuant to subsection (a)(2) even if the withdrawal would otherwise breach an agreement with others that are or have agreed to become co-owners of the enterprise.

[ARTICLE] 4.   GENERAL PARTNERS

§ 401.   Becoming General Partner

(a) Upon formation of a limited partnership, a person becomes a general partner as agreed among the persons that are to be the initial partners.

(b) After formation of a limited partnership, a person becomes a general partner:

(1) as provided in the partnership agreement;

(2) as the result of a transaction effective under [Article] 11;

(3) with the affirmative vote or consent of all the partners; or

(4) as provided in Section 801(a)(3)(B).

(c) A person may become a general partner without:

(1) acquiring a transferable interest; or

(2) making or being obligated to make a contribution to the partnership.

§ 402.   General Partner Agent of Limited Partnership

(a) Each general partner is an agent of the limited partnership for the purposes of its activities and affairs. An act of a general partner, including the signing of a record in the partnership's name, for apparently carrying on in the ordinary course the partnership's activities and affairs or activities and affairs of the kind carried on by the partnership binds the partnership, unless the general partner did not have authority to act for the partnership in the particular matter and the person with which the general partner was dealing knew or had notice that the general partner lacked authority.

(b) An act of a general partner which is not apparently for carrying on in the ordinary course the limited partnership's activities and affairs or activities and affairs of the kind carried on by the partnership binds the partnership only if the act was actually authorized by all the other partners.

§ 403.   Limited Partnership Liable for General Partner's Actionable Conduct

(a) A limited partnership is liable for loss or injury caused to a person, or for a penalty incurred, as a result of a wrongful act or omission, or other actionable conduct, of a general partner acting in the ordinary course of activities and affairs of the partnership or with the actual or apparent authority of the partnership.

(b) If, in the course of a limited partnership's activities and affairs or while acting with actual or apparent authority of the partnership, a general partner receives or causes the partnership to receive money or property of a person not a partner, and the money or property is misapplied by a general partner, the partnership is liable for the loss.

§ 404.   General Partner's Liability

(a)   Except as otherwise provided in subsections (b) and (c), all general partners are liable jointly and severally for all debts, obligations, and other liabilities of the limited partnership unless otherwise agreed by the claimant or provided by law.

(b)   A person that becomes a general partner is not personally liable for a debt, obligation, or other liability of the limited partnership incurred before the person became a general partner.

(c)   A debt, obligation, or other liability of a limited partnership incurred while the partnership is a limited liability limited partnership is solely the debt, obligation, or other liability of the limited liability limited partnership. A general partner is not personally liable, directly or indirectly, by way of contribution or otherwise, for a debt, obligation, or other liability of the limited liability limited partnership solely by reason of being or acting as a general partner. This subsection applies:

(1)   despite anything inconsistent in the partnership agreement that existed immediately before the vote or consent required to become a limited liability limited partnership under Section 406(b)(2); and

(2)   regardless of the dissolution of the partnership.

(d)   The failure of a limited liability limited partnership to observe formalities relating to the exercise of its powers or management of its activities and affairs is not a ground for imposing liability on a general partner for a debt, obligation, or other liability of the partnership.

(e)   An amendment of a certificate of limited partnership which deletes a statement that the limited partnership is a limited liability limited partnership does not affect the limitation in this section on the liability of a general partner for a debt, obligation, or other liability of the limited partnership incurred before the amendment became effective.

§ 405.   Actions by and Against Partnership and Partners

(a)   To the extent not inconsistent with Section 404, a general partner may be joined in an action against the limited partnership or named in a separate action.

(b)   A judgment against a limited partnership is not by itself a judgment against a general partner. A judgment against a partnership may not be satisfied from a general partner's assets unless there is also a judgment against the general partner.

(c)   A judgment creditor of a general partner may not levy execution against the assets of the general partner to satisfy a judgment based on a claim against the limited partnership, unless the partner is personally liable for the claim under Section 404 and:

(1)   a judgment based on the same claim has been obtained against the limited partnership and a writ of execution on the judgment has been returned unsatisfied in whole or in part;

(2)   the partnership is a debtor in bankruptcy;

(3)   the general partner has agreed that the creditor need not exhaust partnership assets;

(4)   a court grants permission to the judgment creditor to levy execution against the assets of a general partner based on a finding that partnership assets subject to execution are clearly insufficient to satisfy the judgment, that exhaustion of assets is excessively burdensome, or that the grant of permission is an appropriate exercise of the court's equitable powers; or

(5)   liability is imposed on the general partner by law or contract independent of the existence of the partnership.

§ 406.   Management Rights of General Partner

(a)   Each general partner has equal rights in the management and conduct of the limited partnership's activities and affairs. Except as otherwise provided in this [act], any matter relating to the activities and affairs of the partnership is decided exclusively by the general partner or, if there is more than one general partner, by a majority of the general partners.

(b)   The affirmative vote or consent of all the partners is required to:

(1)   amend the partnership agreement;

(2)   amend the certificate of limited partnership to add or delete a statement that the limited partnership is a limited liability limited partnership; and

(3)   sell, lease, exchange, or otherwise dispose of all, or substantially all, of the limited partnership's property, with or without the good will, other than in the usual and regular course of the limited partnership's activities and affairs.

(c)   A limited partnership shall reimburse a general partner for an advance to the partnership beyond the amount of capital the general partner agreed to contribute.

(d)   A payment or advance made by a general partner which gives rise to a limited partnership obligation under subsection (c) or Section 408(a) constitutes a loan to the limited partnership which accrues interest from the date of the payment or advance.

(e)   A general partner is not entitled to remuneration for services performed for the limited partnership.

§ 407.   Rights to Information of General Partner and Person Dissociated as General Partner

(a)   A general partner may inspect and copy required information during regular business hours in the limited partnership's principal office, without having any particular purpose for seeking the information.

(b)   On reasonable notice, a general partner may inspect and copy during regular business hours, at a reasonable location specified by the limited partnership, any record maintained by the partnership regarding the partnership's activities, affairs, financial condition, and other circumstances, to the extent the information is material to the general partner's rights and duties under the partnership agreement or this [act].

(c)   A limited partnership shall furnish to each general partner:

(1)   without demand, any information concerning the partnership's activities, affairs, financial condition, and other circumstances which the partnership knows and is material to the proper exercise of the general partner's rights and duties under the partnership agreement or this [act], except to the extent the partnership can establish that it reasonably believes the general partner already knows the information; and

(2)   on demand, any other information concerning the partnership's activities, affairs, financial condition, and other circumstances, except to the extent the demand or the information demanded is unreasonable or otherwise improper under the circumstances.

(d)   The duty to furnish information under subsection (c) also applies to each general partner to the extent the general partner knows any of the information described in subsection (b).

(e)   Subject to subsection (j), on 10 days' demand made in a record received by a limited partnership, a person dissociated as a general partner may have access to the information and records described in subsections (a) and (b) at the locations specified in those subsections if:

(1)   the information or record pertains to the period during which the person was a general partner;

(2)   the person seeks the information or record in good faith; and

(3)   the person satisfies the requirements imposed on a limited partner by Section 304(b).

(f)   A limited partnership shall respond to a demand made pursuant to subsection (e) in the manner provided in Section 304(c).

(g)   A limited partnership may charge a person that makes a demand under this section the reasonable costs of copying, limited to the costs of labor and material.

(h)   A general partner or person dissociated as a general partner may exercise the rights under this section through an agent or, in the case of an individual under legal disability, a legal representative. Any restriction or condition imposed by the partnership agreement or under subsection (j) applies both to the agent or legal representative and to the general partner or person dissociated as a general partner.

(i)   The rights under this section do not extend to a person as transferee, but if:

(1)   a general partner dies, Section 704 applies; and

(2)   an individual dissociates as a general partner under Section 603(6)(B) or (C), the legal representative of the individual may exercise the rights under subsection (c) of a person dissociated as a general partner.

(j)   In addition to any restriction or condition stated in its partnership agreement, a limited partnership, as a matter within the ordinary course of its activities and affairs, may impose reasonable restrictions and conditions on access to and use of information to be furnished under this section, including designating information confidential and imposing nondisclosure and safeguarding obligations on the recipient. In a dispute concerning the reasonableness of a restriction under this subsection, the partnership has the burden of proving reasonableness.

§ 408.   Reimbursement; Indemnification; Advancement; and Insurance

(a)   A limited partnership shall reimburse a general partner for any payment made by the general partner in the course of the general partner's activities on behalf of the partnership, if the general partner complied with Sections 406, 409, and 504 in making the payment.

(b)   A limited partnership shall indemnify and hold harmless a person with respect to any claim or demand against the person and any debt, obligation, or other liability incurred by the person by reason of the person's former or present capacity as a general partner, if the claim, demand, debt, obligation, or other liability does not arise from the person's breach of Section 406, 409, or 504.

(c)   In the ordinary course of its activities and affairs, a limited partnership may advance reasonable expenses, including attorney's fees and costs, incurred by a person in connection with a claim or demand against the person by reason of the person's former or present capacity as a general partner, if the person promises to repay the partnership if the person ultimately is determined not to be entitled to be indemnified under subsection (b).

(d)   A limited partnership may purchase and maintain insurance on behalf of a general partner against liability asserted against or incurred by the general partner in that capacity or arising from that status even if, under Section 105(c)(8), the partnership agreement could not eliminate or limit the person's liability to the partnership for the conduct giving rise to the liability.

§ 409.   Standards of Conduct for General Partners

(a)   A general partner owes to the limited partnership and, subject to Section 901, the other partners the duties of loyalty and care stated in subsections (b) and (c).

(b)   The fiduciary duty of loyalty of a general partner includes the duties:

(1)   to account to the limited partnership and hold as trustee for it any property, profit, or benefit derived by the general partner:

(A)   in the conduct or winding up of the partnership's activities and affairs;

(B)   from a use by the general partner of the partnership's property; or

(C)   from the appropriation of a partnership opportunity;

(2)   to refrain from dealing with the partnership in the conduct or winding up of the partnership's activities and affairs as or on behalf of a person having an interest adverse to the partnership; and

(3)   to refrain from competing with the partnership in the conduct or winding up of the partnership's activities and affairs.

(c)   The duty of care of a general partner in the conduct or winding up of the limited partnership's activities and affairs is to refrain from engaging in grossly negligent or reckless conduct, willful or intentional misconduct, or knowing violation of law.

(d)   A general partner shall discharge the duties and obligations under this [act] or under the partnership agreement and exercise any rights consistently with the contractual obligation of good faith and fair dealing.

(e)   A general partner does not violate a duty or obligation under this [act] or under the partnership agreement solely because the general partner's conduct furthers the general partner's own interest.

(f)   All the partners of a limited partnership may authorize or ratify, after full disclosure of all material facts, a specific act or transaction by a general partner that otherwise would violate the duty of loyalty.

(g)   It is a defense to a claim under subsection (b)(2) and any comparable claim in equity or at common law that the transaction was fair to the limited partnership.

(h)   If, as permitted by subsection (f) or the partnership agreement, a general partner enters into a transaction with the limited partnership which otherwise would be prohibited by subsection (b)(2), the general partner's rights and obligations arising from the transaction are the same as those of a person that is not a general partner.

COMMENT

ULPA (2001) derived this section from UPA (1997) § 404. The 2011 and 2013 Harmonization amendments made one major substantive change; they "un-cabined" fiduciary duty. UPA (1997) § 404 had deviated substantially from UPA (1914) by purporting to codify all fiduciary duties owed by partners. This approach had a number of problems. Most notably, the exhaustive list of fiduciary duties left no room for the fiduciary duty owed by partners to each other—*i.e.*, "the punctilio of an honor the most sensitive." *Meinhard v. Salmon*, 164 N.E. 545, 546 (N.Y. 1928). Although UPA (1997) § 404(b) purported to state "[a] partner's duty of loyalty to the partnership *and the other partners*" (emphasis added), the three listed duties each protected the partnership and not the partners.

The 2011 and 2013 Harmonization amendments "un-cabined" fiduciary duty in both partnership acts, thereby harmonizing them to ULLCA (2006). As harmonized, this section states some of the core aspects of the fiduciary duty of loyalty, provides a duty of care, and incorporates the contractual obligation of good faith and fair dealing. The duties stated in this section are subject to the limited partnership agreement, but Section 105(c) and (d) contain important limitations on the power of the partnership agreement to affect fiduciary and other duties and the obligation of good faith and fair dealing.

For the effect of dissociation on a person's duties under this section, see Sections 602(a)(2) (limited partners) and 605(a)(2) (general partners).

Subsection (a)—This subsection recognizes two core managerial duties but, unlike UPA (1997) and ULPA (2001), does not purport to be exhaustive. For example, many cases characterize a manager's duty to disclose as a fiduciary duty. *E.g.*, *Lonergan v. EPE Holdings, LLC*, 5 A.3d 1008, 1023 (Del. Ch. 2010) (stating that "in the limited partnership context, absent contractual modification, a general partner owes fiduciary duties that include a duty of full disclosure") (quotation marks and citation omitted); *Exxon Corp. v. Burglin*, 4 F.3d 1294, 1298 (5th Cir. 1993) ("Under Alaska law, a general partner stands in a fiduciary relationship with the limited partnership and thereby owes 'a fiduciary duty . . . to disclose information concerning partnership affairs.' ") (quoting *Parker v. Northern Mixing Co.*, 756 P.2d 881, 894 (Alaska 1988)).

Subsection (b)—This subsection states three core aspects of the fiduciary duty of loyalty: (i) not "usurping" partnership opportunities or otherwise wrongly benefiting from the limited partnership's operations or property; (ii) avoiding conflict of interests in dealing with the limited partnership (whether directly or on behalf of another); and (iii) refraining from competing with the limited partnership. Essentially the same duties exist in agency law and under the law of all types of business organizations.

The duties apply beginning with "the conduct of the partnership's activities and affairs," which by definition cannot exist before the partnership does; thus the stated duties do not apply to pre-formation activities.

The duties stated in this subsection comprise a default rule. Under Section 105(d)(3)(A): "If not manifestly unreasonable, the partnership agreement may . . . alter or eliminate the aspects of the duty of loyalty stated in Section 409(b)."

Subsection (b)(1)—The phrase "hold as trustee" dates back to UPA (1914) § 21 and reflects the availability of disgorgement remedies, such as a constructive trust. In contrast to an actual trustee, a person subject to this duty does not: (i) face the special obstacles to consent characteristic of trust law; or (ii) enjoy protection for decisions taken in reliance on the governing instrument and other sources of information. *Cf.* Uniform Statutory Trust Entity Act (2009) (Last Amended 2013) § 506 ("A trustee [of a statutory trust] . . . is not liable to the trust or to a beneficial owner for breach of any duty, *including a fiduciary duty*, to the extent the breach results from reasonable reliance on: (1) a term of the governing instrument; (2) a record of the statutory trust; or (3) an opinion, report, or statement of another person that the person to which the opinion, report, or statement is made or delivered reasonably believes is within the other person's professional or expert competence and is made or delivered to the trustee.") (emphasis added).

Subsection (b)(1)(A)—This provision is consistent with a basic principle of agency law—namely, that an agent may not benefit at all from the performance of the agency unless the principal consents. RESTATEMENT (THIRD) OF AGENCY § 8.06, cmt. c. (2006). Typically, however, the limited partnership agreement legitimizes particular benefits—*e.g.*, a management fee paid to a general partner in addition to that partner's share of distributions. Also, an agreed allocation of distributions takes those benefits outside the reach of this provision.

Subsection (b)(1)(B)—For the expansive meaning of "property," see Section 102(17). The term includes confidential information.

Subsection (b)(1)(C)—This act does not specify what constitutes "a partnership opportunity," but ample case law exists. *See, e.g., In re Monetary Grp.*, 159 B.R. 964 (M.D. Fla. 1990) (discussing the usurpation of a limited partnership opportunity"), *aff'd in part, rev'd in part*, 2 F.3d 1098 (11th Cir. 1993); *Lichtyger v. Franchard Corp.*, 18 N.Y.2d 528, 223 N.E.2d 869, 873 (1966) ("There is no basis or warrant for distinguishing the fiduciary relationship of corporate director and shareholder from that of general partner and limited partner.")

In the context of winding up, the scope of partnership opportunities inevitably narrows.

In most, if not all, situations, usurping a partnership opportunity also breaches the duty not to compete, Paragraph (b)(3), but not *vice versa*.

Subsection (b)(2)—In this context, the phrase "adverse interest" is a term of art, meaning "to be on the other side of the table" in some dealing with the limited partnership. Absent informed consent by the limited partnership, this duty is breached by the mere existence of the conflict of interest; the limited partnership need not prove that the outcome of the dealing was adverse to the partnership. *But see* Subsection (g) (permitting the defense of fairness).

Subsection (b)(3)—Although competition is often thought of in terms of potential customers, this duty applies equally to competition for resources, including employees.

Subsection (c)—This act no longer refers to the duty of care as a fiduciary duty, because: the duty of care applies in many non-fiduciary situations; and (ii) breach of the duty of care is remediable only in damages while breach of a fiduciary duty gives rise also to equitable remedies, including disgorgement, constructive trust, and rescission.

The change in label is consistent with the RESTATEMENT (THIRD) OF AGENCY § 8.02 (2006), which refers to the agent's "fiduciary duty" to act loyally, but eschews the word "fiduciary" when stating the agent's duties of "care, competence, and diligence." *Id.* § 8.08. However, the label change is merely semantics; no change is the law is intended.

The partnership agreement can raise the standard of care, or subject to Sections 105(c)(8) and (d)(2)(C), lower it. A person's practical exposure for breaching the duty of care involves not only the standard of care but also any partnership agreement provision that: (i) exonerates the person from liability for breach of the duty of care, Section 105(c)(8); or (ii) entitles the person to indemnification despite such breach, Section 408(b), comment.

Subsection (d)—This subsection refers to the "*contractual* obligation of good faith and fair dealing" (emphasis added) and thereby invokes the implied obligation that exists in every contract. *See* RESTATEMENT (SECOND) CONTRACTS § 205 (1981) ("Every contract imposes upon each party a duty of good faith and fair dealing in its performance and its enforcement."). The adjective ("contractual") should help avoid decisions like *Phelps v. Frampton*, 2007 MT 263, 339 Mont. 330, 342–43, 170 P.3d 474, 483 (2007) (holding that Montana's version of UPA (1997) creates a statutory obligation of good faith and fair dealing separate from the implied contractual covenant).

At first glance, it may seem strange to apply a contractual obligation to statutory duties and rights— *i.e.*, duties and rights "under this [act]." However, for the most part those duties and rights apply to relationships *inter se* the partners and the limited partnership and function only to the extent not displaced by the partnership agreement. Those statutory default rules are thus intended to function like a contract; applying the contractual notion of good faith and fair dealing therefore makes sense.

The contractual obligation of "good faith" has nothing to do with the corporate concept of good faith that for years bedeviled courts and attorneys trying to understand: (i) Delaware's famous corporate law exoneration provision; and (ii) that provision's exception "for acts or omissions not in good faith." DEL. CODE ANN. tit. 8, § 102(b)(7) (2012). In that context, good faith is an aspect of the duty of loyalty. *See Stone ex rel. AmSouth Bancorporation v. Ritter*, 911 A.2d 362, 369–70 (Del. 2006).

Likewise, the contractual obligation of good faith and fair dealing has nothing to do with the "utmost good faith" sometimes used to describe the fiduciary duties that owners of closely held businesses owe each other. *See, e.g., Meinhard v. Salmon*, 249 N.Y. 458, 477, 164 N.E. 545, 551 (1928) ("[W]here parties engage in a joint enterprise each owes to the other the duty of the utmost good faith in all that relates to their common venture. Within its scope they stand in a fiduciary relationship."); *Donahue v. Rodd Electrotype Co. of New England, Inc.*, 367 Mass. 578, 593, 328 N.E.2d 505, 515 (1975) ("[S]tockholders in the close corporation owe one another substantially the same fiduciary duty in the operation of the enterprise that partners owe to one another. In our previous decisions, we have defined the standard of duty owed by partners to one another as the utmost good faith and loyalty.") (footnotes omitted) (citations omitted) (internal quotations omitted).

To the contrary, the contractual obligation of good faith and fair dealing is not a fiduciary duty, does not command altruism or self-abnegation, and does not prevent a general partner from acting in the general partner's own self-interest:

"Fair dealing" is not akin to the fair process component of entire fairness, *i.e.*, whether the fiduciary acted fairly when engaging in the challenged transaction as measured by duties of loyalty and care . . . It is rather a commitment to deal "fairly" in the sense of consistently with the terms of the parties' agreement and its purpose. Likewise "good faith" does not envision loyalty to the contractual counterparty, but rather faithfulness to the scope, purpose, and terms of the parties' contract. Both necessarily turn on the contract itself and what the parties would have agreed upon had the issue arisen when they were bargaining originally.

Gerber v. Enter. Products Holdings, LLC, 67 A.3d 400, 418–19 (Del. 2013) (quoting *ASB Allegiance Real Estate Fund v. Scion Breckenridge Managing Member, LLC*, 50 A.3d 434, 440–42 (Del. Ch. 2012), *aff'd in part, rev'd in part on other grounds*, 68 A.3d 665 (Del. 2013)) (footnotes omitted) (citations omitted) (internal quotations omitted). *See also* Subsection (e).

Courts should not use the contractual obligation to change ex post facto the parties' or this act's allocation of risk and power. To the contrary, the obligation should be used only to protect agreed-upon arrangements from conduct that is manifestly beyond what a reasonable person could have contemplated when the arrangements were made.

The partnership agreement or this act may grant discretion to a general partner, and the contractual obligation of good faith and fair dealing is especially salient when discretion is at issue. However, a general partner may properly exercise discretion even though another partner (whether general or limited) suffers as a consequence. Conduct does not violate the obligation of good faith and fair dealing merely because that conduct substantially prejudices a party. Indeed, parties allocate risk precisely because prejudice may occur.

The exercise of discretion constitutes a breach of the obligation of good faith and fair dealing only when the party claiming breach shows that the conduct has no honestly-held purpose that legitimately comports with the parties' agreed-upon arrangements:

> An implied covenant claim . . . looks to the past. It is not a free-floating duty unattached to the underlying legal documents. It does not ask what duty the law should impose on the parties given their relationship at the time of the wrong, but *rather what the parties would have agreed to themselves had they considered the issue in their original bargaining positions at the time of contracting.*

Gerber v. Enter. Prods. Holdings, LLC, 67 A.3d 400, 418 (Del. 2013) (quoting *ASB Allegiance Real Estate Fund v. Scion Breckenridge Managing Member, LLC*, 50 A.3d 434, 440–42 (Del. Ch. 2012), *aff'd in part, rev'd in part on other grounds*, 68 A.3d 665 (Del. 2013)) (emphasis added) (footnotes omitted) (citations omitted) (internal quotations omitted by *Gerber*).

In sum, the purpose of the contractual obligation of good faith and fair dealing is to protect the arrangement the partners have chosen for themselves, not to restructure that arrangement under the guise of safeguarding it.

As to the power of the partnership agreement to affect the contractual obligation of good faith and fair dealing, see Section 105(c)(7) (prohibiting elimination but allowing the agreement to "prescribe the standards, if not manifestly unreasonable, by which the performance of the obligation is to be measured"). For examples, see Section 105(c)(7), comment. As to whether the obligation stated in this subsection applies to the benefit of transferees, see Section 107(b), comment.

Subsection (e)—A general partner in a limited partnership has at least two different roles: (i) as a party to the limited partnership agreement, with rights and obligations under that agreement; and (ii) as manager or co-manager of the enterprise. This provision pertains to the first role. A general partner's exercise of rights under the partnership agreement is subject to the obligation of good faith and fair dealing, Subsection (d), but a general partner does not breach that contractual obligation "solely because the general partner's conduct furthers the general partner's own interest." In contrast, this provision is ineffective with regard to a general partner's duties as manager or co-manager. For example, a general partner's liability under Section 409(b)(3) (prohibiting competition) is not "solely because the general partner's conduct furthers the general partner's own interest." Rather, the liability results from the breach of a specific obligation—*i.e.*, the codified aspect of the duty of loyalty that prohibits competition.

Subsection (f)—Here and elsewhere in this act, information "is material if there is a substantial likelihood that a reasonable [decision maker] would consider it important in deciding how to vote" or take other action under this act or the partnership agreements. *See TSC Industries, Inc. v. Northway, Inc.*, 426 U.S. 438, 449, 96 S.Ct. 2126, 2132 (1976).

The partnership agreement can provide additional or different methods of authorization or ratification, subject to the strictures of Section 105(c)(5), (d)(1), and (d)(3)(A)(B) and (D).

Subsection (g)—This subsection codifies judge-made law applicable to all business entities. *See, e.g., Lonergan v. EPE Holdings, LLC*, 5 A.3d 1008, 1019 (Del. Ch. 2010) (discussing "entire fairness" in the context of a limited partnership"); *Gottsacker v. Monnier*, 281 Wis. 2d 361, 379, 697 N.W.2d 436, 444 (Wisc. 2005) (referring to "a willful failure to deal fairly with the LLC or its other members"); *Kahn v. Lynch Commc'n Sys., Inc.*, 638 A.2d 1110, 1116 (Del. 1994) (discussing "entire fairness" in the context of a corporation's merger with an affiliate).

Subsection (h)—This subsection is the modern, reformulated version of a language that sought to overturn the now-defunct notion that debts to partners were categorically inferior to debts to non-partner creditors. *See, e.g.,* ULPA (2001) § 112 ("A partner may lend money to and transact other business with the limited partnership and has the same rights and obligations with respect to the loan or other transaction as a person that is not a partner."). The reformulation makes clear that this provision has nothing to do with the fiduciary duty pertaining to conflict of interests. *See BT-I v. Equitable Life Assurance Soc'y of the United States,* 75 Cal. App. 4th 1406, 1415, 89 Cal. Rptr. 2d 811 (1999) (examining the prior formulation, explaining its history and stating "[w]e cannot discern anything in the purpose of [the prior formulation] that suggests an intent to affect a general partner's fiduciary duty to limited partners").

This subsection states a default rule. The partnership agreement may provide that debt to a general partner (or general partners generally) is subordinate to other partnership obligations. The agreement that creates the debt may do likewise.

[ARTICLE] 5. CONTRIBUTIONS AND DISTRIBUTIONS

§ 501. Form of Contribution

A contribution may consist of property transferred to, services performed for, or another benefit provided to the limited partnership or an agreement to transfer property to, perform services for, or provide another benefit to the partnership.

§ 502. Liability for Contribution

(a) A person's obligation to make a contribution to a limited partnership is not excused by the person's death, disability, termination, or other inability to perform personally.

(b) If a person does not fulfill an obligation to make a contribution other than money, the person is obligated at the option of the limited partnership to contribute money equal to the value, as stated in the required information, of the part of the contribution which has not been made.

(c) The obligation of a person to make a contribution may be compromised only by the affirmative vote or consent of all the partners. If a creditor of a limited partnership extends credit or otherwise acts in reliance on an obligation described in subsection (a) without knowledge or notice of a compromise under this subsection, the creditor may enforce the obligation.

§ 503. Sharing of and Right to Distributions Before Dissolution

(a) Any distribution made by a limited partnership before its dissolution and winding up must be shared among the partners on the basis of the value, as stated in the required information when the limited partnership decides to make the distribution, of the contributions the limited partnership has received from each partner, except to the extent necessary to comply with a transfer effective under Section 702 or charging order in effect under Section 703.

(b) A person has a right to a distribution before the dissolution and winding up of a limited partnership only if the partnership decides to make an interim distribution. A person's dissociation does not entitle the person to a distribution.

(c) A person does not have a right to demand or receive a distribution from a limited partnership in any form other than money. Except as otherwise provided in Section 810(f), a partnership may distribute an asset in kind only if each part of the asset is fungible with each other part and each person receives a percentage of the asset equal in value to the person's share of distributions.

(d) If a partner or transferee becomes entitled to receive a distribution, the partner or transferee has the status of, and is entitled to all remedies available to, a creditor of the limited partnership with respect to the distribution. However, the partnership's obligation to make a distribution is subject to offset for any amount owed to the partnership by the partner or a person dissociated as a partner on whose account the distribution is made.

§ 504.   Limitations on Distributions

(a) A limited partnership may not make a distribution, including a distribution under Section 810, if after the distribution:

(1) the partnership would not be able to pay its debts as they become due in the ordinary course of the partnership's activities and affairs; or

(2) the partnership's total assets would be less than the sum of its total liabilities plus the amount that would be needed, if the partnership were to be dissolved and wound up at the time of the distribution, to satisfy the preferential rights upon dissolution and winding up of partners and transferees whose preferential rights are superior to the rights of persons receiving the distribution.

(b) A limited partnership may base a determination that a distribution is not prohibited under subsection (a) on:

(1) financial statements prepared on the basis of accounting practices and principles that are reasonable in the circumstances; or

(2) a fair valuation or other method that is reasonable under the circumstances.

(c) Except as otherwise provided in subsection (e), the effect of a distribution under subsection (a) is measured:

(1) in the case of a distribution as defined in Section 102(4)(A), as of the earlier of:

(A) the date money or other property is transferred or debt is incurred by the limited partnership; or

(B) the date the person entitled to the distribution ceases to own the interest or right being acquired by the partnership in return for the distribution;

(2) in the case of any other distribution of indebtedness, as of the date the indebtedness is distributed; and

(3) in all other cases, as of the date:

(A) the distribution is authorized, if the payment occurs not later than 120 days after that date; or

(B) the payment is made, if the payment occurs more than 120 days after the distribution is authorized.

(d) A limited partnership's indebtedness to a partner or transferee incurred by reason of a distribution made in accordance with this section is at parity with the partnership's indebtedness to its general, unsecured creditors, except to the extent subordinated by agreement.

(e) A limited partnership's indebtedness, including indebtedness issued as a distribution, is not a liability for purposes of subsection (a) if the terms of the indebtedness provide that payment of principal and interest is made only if and to the extent that payment of a distribution could then be made under this section. If the indebtedness is issued as a distribution, each payment of principal or interest is treated as a distribution, the effect of which is measured on the date the payment is made.

(f) In measuring the effect of a distribution under Section 810, the liabilities of a dissolved limited partnership do not include any claim that has been disposed of under Section 806, 807, or 808.

§ 505.   Liability for Improper Distributions

(a) If a general partner consents to a distribution made in violation of Section 504 and in consenting to the distribution fails to comply with Section 409, the general partner is personally liable to the limited partnership for the amount of the distribution which exceeds the amount that could have been distributed without the violation of Section 504.

(b)   A person that receives a distribution knowing that the distribution violated Section 504 is personally liable to the limited partnership but only to the extent that the distribution received by the person exceeded the amount that could have been properly paid under Section 504.

(c)   A general partner against which an action is commenced because the general partner is liable under subsection (a) may:

(1)   implead any other person that is liable under subsection (a) and seek to enforce a right of contribution from the person; and

(2)   implead any person that received a distribution in violation of subsection (b) and seek to enforce a right of contribution from the person in the amount the person received in violation of subsection (b).

(d)   An action under this section is barred unless commenced not later than two years after the distribution.

[ARTICLE] 6.   DISSOCIATION

§ 601.   Dissociation as Limited Partner

(a)   A person does not have a right to dissociate as a limited partner before the completion of the winding up of the limited partnership.

(b)   A person is dissociated as a limited partner when:

(1)   the limited partnership knows or has notice of the person's express will to withdraw as a limited partner, but, if the person has specified a withdrawal date later than the date the partnership knew or had notice, on that later date;

(2)   an event stated in the partnership agreement as causing the person's dissociation as a limited partner occurs;

(3)   the person is expelled as a limited partner pursuant to the partnership agreement;

(4)   the person is expelled as a limited partner by the affirmative vote or consent of all the other partners if:

(A)   it is unlawful to carry on the limited partnership's activities and affairs with the person as a limited partner;

(B)   there has been a transfer of all the person's transferable interest in the partnership, other than:

(i)   a transfer for security purposes; or

(ii)   a charging order in effect under Section 703 which has not been foreclosed;

(C)   the person is an entity and:

(i)   the partnership notifies the person that it will be expelled as a limited partner because the person has filed a statement of dissolution or the equivalent, the person has been administratively dissolved, the person's charter or the equivalent has been revoked, or the person's right to conduct business has been suspended by the person's jurisdiction of formation; and

(ii)   not later than 90 days after the notification, the statement of dissolution or the equivalent has not been withdrawn, rescinded, or revoked, the person has not been reinstated, or the person's charter or the equivalent or right to conduct business has not been reinstated; or

(D)   the person is an unincorporated entity that has been dissolved and whose activities and affairs are being would up;

(5)   on application by the limited partnership or a partner in a direct action under Section 901, the person is expelled as a limited partner by judicial order because the person:

(A)   has engaged or is engaging in wrongful conduct that has affected adversely and materially, or will affect adversely and materially, the partnership's activities and affairs;

(B)   has committed willfully or persistently, or is committing willfully and persistently, a material breach of the partnership agreement or the contractual obligation of good faith and fair dealing under Section 305(a); or

(C)   has engaged or is engaging in conduct relating to the partnership's activities and affairs which makes it not reasonably practicable to carry on the activities and affairs with the person as a limited partner;

(6)   in the case of an individual, the individual dies;

(7)   in the case of a person that is a testamentary or inter vivos trust or is acting as a limited partner by virtue of being a trustee of such a trust, the trust's entire transferable interest in the limited partnership is distributed;

(8)   in the case of a person that is an estate or is acting as a limited partner by virtue of being a personal representative of an estate, the estate's entire transferable interest in the limited partnership is distributed;

(9)   in the case of a person that is not an individual, the existence of the person terminates;

(10)   the limited partnership participates in a merger under [Article] 11 and:

(A)   the partnership is not the surviving entity; or

(B)   otherwise as a result of the merger, the person ceases to be a limited partner;

(11)   the limited partnership participates in an interest exchange under [Article] 11 and, as a result of the interest exchange, the person ceases to be a limited partner;

(12)   the limited partnership participates in a conversion under [Article] 11;

(13)   the limited partnership participates in a domestication under [Article] 11 and, as a result of the domestication, the person ceases to be a limited partner; or

(14)   the limited partnership dissolves and completes winding up.

§ 602.   Effect of Dissociation as Limited Partner

(a)   If a person is dissociated as a limited partner:

(1)   subject to Section 704, the person does not have further rights as a limited partner;

(2)   the person's contractual obligation of good faith and fair dealing as a limited partner under Section 305(a) ends with regard to matters arising and events occurring after the person's dissociation; and

(3)   subject to Section 704 and [Article] 11, any transferable interest owned by the person in the person's capacity as a limited partner immediately before dissociation is owned by the person solely as a transferee.

(b)   A person's dissociation as a limited partner does not of itself discharge the person from any debt, obligation, or other liability to the limited partnership or the other partners which the person incurred while a limited partner.

§ 603.   Dissociation as General Partner

A person is dissociated as a general partner when:

(1)   the limited partnership knows or has notice of the person's express will to withdraw as a general partner, but, if the person has specified a withdrawal date later than the date the partnership knew or had notice, on that later date;

(2)   an event stated in the partnership agreement as causing the person's dissociation as a general partner occurs;

(3)   the person is expelled as a general partner pursuant to the partnership agreement;

(4)   the person is expelled as a general partner by the affirmative vote or consent of all the other partners if:

(A)   it is unlawful to carry on the limited partnership's activities and affairs with the person as a general partner;

(B)   there has been a transfer of all the person's transferable interest in the partnership, other than:

(i)   a transfer for security purposes; or

(ii)   a charging order in effect under Section 703 which has not been foreclosed;

(C)   the person is an entity and:

(i)   the partnership notifies the person that it will be expelled as a general partner because the person has filed a statement of dissolution or the equivalent, the person has been administratively dissolved, the person's charter or the equivalent has been revoked, or the person's right to conduct business has been suspended by the person's jurisdiction of formation; and

(ii)   not later than 90 days after the notification, the statement of dissolution or the equivalent has not been withdrawn, rescinded, or revoked, the person has not been reinstated, or the person's charter or the equivalent or right to conduct business has not been reinstated; or

(D)   the person is an unincorporated entity that has been dissolved and whose activities and affairs are being would up;

(5)   on application by the limited partnership or a partner in a direct action under Section 901, the person is expelled as a general partner by judicial order because the person:

(A)   has engaged or is engaging in wrongful conduct that has affected adversely and materially, or will affect adversely and materially, the partnership's activities and affairs;

(B)   has committed willfully or persistently, or is committing willfully or persistently, a material breach of the partnership agreement or a duty or obligation under Section 409; or

(C)   has engaged or is engaging in conduct relating to the partnership's activities and affairs which makes it not reasonably practicable to carry on the activities and affairs of the limited partnership with the person as a general partner;

(6)   in the case of an individual:

(A)   the individual dies;

(B)   a guardian or general conservator for the individual is appointed; or

(C)   a court orders that the individual has otherwise become incapable of performing the individual's duties as a general partner under this [act] or the partnership agreement;

(7)   the person:

(A)   becomes a debtor in bankruptcy;

(B)   executes an assignment for the benefit of creditors; or

(C)   seeks, consents to, or acquiesces in the appointment of a trustee, receiver, or liquidator of the person or of all or substantially all the person's property;

(8)   in the case of a person that is a testamentary or inter vivos trust or is acting as a general partner by virtue of being a trustee of such a trust, the trust's entire transferable interest in the limited partnership is distributed;

(9)   in the case of a person that is an estate or is acting as a general partner by virtue of being a personal representative of an estate, the estate's entire transferable interest in the limited partnership is distributed;

(10) in the case of a person that is not an individual, the existence of the person terminates;

(11) the limited partnership participates in a merger under [Article] 11 and:

(A)   the partnership is not the surviving entity; or

(B)   otherwise as a result of the merger, the person ceases to be a general partner;

(12) the limited partnership participates in an interest exchange under [Article] 11 and, as a result of the interest exchange, the person ceases to be a general partner;

(13) the limited partnership participates in a conversion under [Article] 11;

(14) the limited partnership participates in a domestication under [Article] 11 and, as a result of the domestication, the person ceases to be a general partner; or

(15) the limited partnership dissolves and completes winding up.

§ 604.   Power to Dissociate as General Partner; Wrongful Dissociation

(a)   A person has the power to dissociate as a general partner at any time, rightfully or wrongfully, by withdrawing as a general partner by express will under Section 603(1).

(b)   A person's dissociation as a general partner is wrongful only if the dissociation:

(1)   is in breach of an express provision of the partnership agreement; or

(2)   occurs before the completion of the winding up of the limited partnership, and:

(A)   the person withdraws as a general partner by express will;

(B)   the person is expelled as a general partner by judicial order under Section 603(5);

(C)   the person is dissociated as a general partner under Section 603(7); or

(D)   in the case of a person that is not a trust other than a business trust, an estate, or an individual, the person is expelled or otherwise dissociated as a general partner because it willfully dissolved or terminated.

(c)   A person that wrongfully dissociates as a general partner is liable to the limited partnership and, subject to Section 901, to the other partners for damages caused by the dissociation. The liability is in addition to any debt, obligation, or other liability of the general partner to the partnership or the other partners.

§ 605.   Effect of Dissociation as General Partner

(a)   If a person is dissociated as a general partner:

(1)   the person's right to participate as a general partner in the management and conduct of the limited partnership's activities and affairs terminates;

(2)   the person's duties and obligations as a general partner under Section 409 end with regard to matters arising and events occurring after the person's dissociation;

(3) the person may sign and deliver to the [Secretary of State] for filing a statement of dissociation pertaining to the person and, at the request of the limited partnership, shall sign an amendment to the certificate of limited partnership which states that the person has dissociated as a general partner; and

(4) subject to Section 704 and [Article] 11, any transferable interest owned by the person in the person's capacity as a general partner immediately before dissociation is owned by the person solely as a transferee.

(b) A person's dissociation as a general partner does not of itself discharge the person from any debt, obligation, or other liability to the limited partnership or the other partners which the person incurred while a general partner.

§ 606. Power to Bind and Liability of Person Dissociated as General Partner

(a) After a person is dissociated as a general partner and before the limited partnership is merged out of existence, converted, or domesticated under [Article] 11, or dissolved, the partnership is bound by an act of the person only if:

(1) the act would have bound the partnership under Section 402 before the dissociation; and

(2) at the time the other party enters into the transaction:

(A) less than two years has passed since the dissociation; and

(B) the other party does not know or have notice of the dissociation and reasonably believes that the person is a general partner.

(b) If a limited partnership is bound under subsection (a), the person dissociated as a general partner which caused the partnership to be bound is liable:

(1) to the partnership for any damage caused to the partnership arising from the obligation incurred under subsection (a); and

(2) if a general partner or another person dissociated as a general partner is liable for the obligation, to the general partner or other person for any damage caused to the general partner or other person arising from the liability.

§ 607. Liability of Person Dissociated as General Partner to Other Persons

(a) A person's dissociation as a general partner does not of itself discharge the person's liability as a general partner for a debt, obligation, or other liability of the limited partnership incurred before dissociation. Except as otherwise provided in subsections (b) and (c), the person is not liable for a partnership obligation incurred after dissociation.

(b) A person whose dissociation as a general partner results in a dissolution and winding up of the limited partnership's activities and affairs is liable on an obligation incurred by the partnership under Section 805 to the same extent as a general partner under Section 404.

(c) A person that is dissociated as a general partner without the dissociation resulting in a dissolution and winding up of the limited partnership's activities and affairs is liable on a transaction entered into by the partnership after the dissociation only if:

(1) a general partner would be liable on the transaction; and

(2) at the time the other party enters into the transaction:

(A) less than two years has passed since the dissociation; and

(B) the other party does not have knowledge or notice of the dissociation and reasonably believes that the person is a general partner.

(d) By agreement with a creditor of a limited partnership and the partnership, a person dissociated as a general partner may be released from liability for a debt, obligation, or other liability of the partnership.

(e) A person dissociated as a general partner is released from liability for a debt, obligation, or other liability of the limited partnership if the partnership's creditor, with knowledge or notice of the person's dissociation as a general partner but without the person's consent, agrees to a material alteration in the nature or time of payment of the debt, obligation, or other liability.

[ARTICLE] 7.   TRANSFERABLE INTERESTS AND RIGHTS OF TRANSFEREES AND CREDITORS

§ 701.   Nature of Transferable Interest

A transferable interest is personal property.

§ 702.   Transfer of Transferable Interest

(a) A transfer, in whole or in part, of a transferable interest:

(1) is permissible;

(2) does not by itself cause a person's dissociation as a partner or a dissolution and winding up of the limited partnership's activities and affairs; and

(3) subject to Section 704, does not entitle the transferee to:

(A) participate in the management or conduct of the partnership's activities and affairs; or

(B) except as otherwise provided in subsection (c), have access to required information, records, or other information concerning the partnership's activities and affairs.

(b) A transferee has the right to receive, in accordance with the transfer, distributions to which the transferor would otherwise be entitled.

(c) In a dissolution and winding up of a limited partnership, a transferee is entitled to an account of the partnership's transactions only from the date of dissolution.

(d) A transferable interest may be evidenced by a certificate of the interest issued by a limited partnership in a record, and, subject to this section, the interest represented by the certificate may be transferred by a transfer of the certificate.

(e) A limited partnership need not give effect to a transferee's rights under this section until the partnership knows or has notice of the transfer.

(f) A transfer of a transferable interest in violation of a restriction on transfer contained in the partnership agreement is ineffective if the intended transferee has knowledge or notice of the restriction at the time of transfer.

(g) Except as otherwise provided in Sections 601(b)(4)(B) and 603(4)(B), if a general or limited partner transfers a transferable interest, the transferor retains the rights of a general or limited partner other than the transferable interest transferred and retains all the duties and obligations of a general or limited partner.

(h) If a general or limited partner transfers a transferable interest to a person that becomes a general or limited partner with respect to the transferred interest, the transferee is liable for the transferor's obligations under Sections 502 and 505 known to the transferee when the transferee becomes a partner.

§ 703. Charging Order

(a) On application by a judgment creditor of a partner or transferee, a court may enter a charging order against the transferable interest of the judgment debtor for the unsatisfied amount of the judgment. A charging order constitutes a lien on a judgment debtor's transferable interest and requires the limited partnership to pay over to the person to which the charging order was issued any distribution that otherwise would be paid to the judgment debtor.

(b) To the extent necessary to effectuate the collection of distributions pursuant to a charging order in effect under subsection (a), the court may:

(1) appoint a receiver of the distributions subject to the charging order, with the power to make all inquiries the judgment debtor might have made; and

(2) make all other orders necessary to give effect to the charging order.

(c) Upon a showing that distributions under a charging order will not pay the judgment debt within a reasonable time, the court may foreclose the lien and order the sale of the transferable interest. The purchaser at the foreclosure sale obtains only the transferable interest, does not thereby become a partner, and is subject to Section 702.

(d) At any time before foreclosure under subsection (c), the partner or transferee whose transferable interest is subject to a charging order under subsection (a) may extinguish the charging order by satisfying the judgment and filing a certified copy of the satisfaction with the court that issued the charging order.

(e) At any time before foreclosure under subsection (c), a limited partnership or one or more partners whose transferable interests are not subject to the charging order may pay to the judgment creditor the full amount due under the judgment and thereby succeed to the rights of the judgment creditor, including the charging order.

(f) This [act] does not deprive any partner or transferee of the benefit of any exemption law applicable to the transferable interest of the partner or transferee.

(g) This section provides the exclusive remedy by which a person seeking in the capacity of a judgment creditor to enforce a judgment against a partner or transferee may satisfy the judgment from the judgment debtor's transferable interest.

§ 704. Power of Legal Representative of Deceased Partner

If a partner dies, the deceased partner's legal representative may exercise:

(1) the rights of a transferee provided in Section 702(c); and

(2) for the purposes of settling the estate, the rights of a current limited partner under Section 304.

[ARTICLE] 8.   DISSOLUTION AND WINDING UP

§ 801. Events Causing Dissolution

(a) A limited partnership is dissolved, and its activities and affairs must be wound up, upon the occurrence of any of the following:

(1) an event or circumstance that the partnership agreement states causes dissolution;

(2) the affirmative vote or consent of all general partners and of limited partners owning a majority of the rights to receive distributions as limited partners at the time the vote or consent is to be effective;

(3) after the dissociation of a person as a general partner:

(A) if the partnership has at least one remaining general partner, the affirmative vote or consent to dissolve the partnership not later than 90 days after the dissociation by partners owning a majority of the rights to receive distributions as partners at the time the vote or consent is to be effective; or

(B) if the partnership does not have a remaining general partner, the passage of 90 days after the dissociation, unless before the end of the period:

(i)   consent to continue the activities and affairs of the partnership and admit at least one general partner is given by limited partners owning a majority of the rights to receive distributions as limited partners at the time the consent is to be effective; and

(ii) at least one person is admitted as a general partner in accordance with the consent;

(4) the passage of 90 consecutive days after the dissociation of the partnership's last limited partner, unless before the end of the period the partnership admits at least one limited partner;

(5) the passage of 90 consecutive days during which the partnership has only one partner, unless before the end of the period:

(A) the partnership admits at least one person as a partner;

(B) if the previously sole remaining partner is only a general partner, the partnership admits the person as a limited partner; and

(C) if the previously sole remaining partner is only a limited partner, the partnership admits a person as a general partner;

(6) on application by a partner, the entry by [the appropriate court] of an order dissolving the partnership on the grounds that:

(A) the conduct of all or substantially all the partnership's activities and affairs is unlawful; or

(B) it is not reasonably practicable to carry on the partnership's activities and affairs in conformity with the certificate of limited partnership and partnership agreement; or

(7) the signing and filing of a statement of administrative dissolution by the [Secretary of State] under Section 811.

(b) If an event occurs that imposes a deadline on a limited partnership under subsection (a) and before the partnership has met the requirements of the deadline, another event occurs that imposes a different deadline on the partnership under subsection (a):

(1) the occurrence of the second event does not affect the deadline caused by the first event; and

(2) the partnership's meeting of the requirements of the first deadline does not extend the second deadline.

§ 802.   Winding Up

(a) A dissolved limited partnership shall wind up its activities and affairs and, except as otherwise provided in Section 803, the partnership continues after dissolution only for the purpose of winding up.

(b) In winding up its activities and affairs, the limited partnership:

(1) shall discharge the partnership's debts, obligations, and other liabilities, settle and close the partnership's activities and affairs, and marshal and distribute the assets of the partnership; and

(2)   may:

(A)   amend its certificate of limited partnership to state that the partnership is dissolved;

(B)   preserve the partnership activities, affairs, and property as a going concern for a reasonable time;

(C)   prosecute and defend actions and proceedings, whether civil, criminal, or administrative;

(D)   transfer the partnership's property;

(E)   settle disputes by mediation or arbitration;

(F)   deliver to the [Secretary of State] for filing a statement of termination stating the name of the partnership and that the partnership is terminated; and

(G)   perform other acts necessary or appropriate to the winding up.

(c)   If a dissolved limited partnership does not have a general partner, a person to wind up the dissolved partnership's activities and affairs may be appointed by the affirmative vote or consent of limited partners owning a majority of the rights to receive distributions as limited partners at the time the vote or consent is to be effective. A person appointed under this subsection:

(1)   has the powers of a general partner under Section 804 but is not liable for the debts, obligations, and other liabilities of the partnership solely by reason of having or exercising those powers or otherwise acting to wind up the dissolved partnership's activities and affairs; and

(2)   shall deliver promptly to the [Secretary of State] for filing an amendment to the partnership's certificate of limited partnership stating:

(A)   that the partnership does not have a general partner;

(B)   the name and street and mailing addresses of the person; and

(C)   that the person has been appointed pursuant to this subsection to wind up the partnership.

(d)   On the application of a partner, the [appropriate court] may order judicial supervision of the winding up of a dissolved limited partnership, including the appointment of a person to wind up the partnership's activities and affairs, if:

(1)   the partnership does not have a general partner and within a reasonable time following the dissolution no person has been appointed pursuant to subsection (c); or

(2)   the applicant establishes other good cause.

§ 803.   Rescinding Dissolution

(a)   A limited partnership may rescind its dissolution, unless a statement of termination applicable to the partnership has become effective, [the appropriate court] has entered an order under Section 801(a)(6) dissolving the partnership, or the [Secretary of State] has dissolved the partnership under Section 811.

(b)   Rescinding dissolution under this section requires:

(1)   the affirmative vote or consent of each partner; and

(2)   if the limited partnership has delivered to the [Secretary of State] for filing an amendment to the certificate of limited partnership stating that the partnership is dissolved and:

(A)   the amendment has not become effective, delivery to the [Secretary of State] for filing of a statement of withdrawal under Section 208 applicable to the amendment; or

(B)   the amendment has become effective, delivery to the [Secretary of State] for filing of an amendment to the certificate of limited partnership stating that dissolution has been rescinded under this section.

(c)   If a limited partnership rescinds its dissolution:

(1)   the partnership resumes carrying on its activities and affairs as if dissolution had never occurred;

(2)   subject to paragraph (3), any liability incurred by the partnership after the dissolution and before the rescission has become effective is determined as if dissolution had never occurred; and

(3)   the rights of a third party arising out of conduct in reliance on the dissolution before the third party knew or had notice of the rescission may not be adversely affected.

§ 804.   Power to Bind Partnership After Dissolution

(a)   A limited partnership is bound by a general partner's act after dissolution which:

(1)   is appropriate for winding up the partnership's activities and affairs; or

(2)   would have bound the partnership under Section 402 before dissolution if, at the time the other party enters into the transaction, the other party does not know or have notice of the dissolution.

(b)   A person dissociated as a general partner binds a limited partnership through an act occurring after dissolution if:

(1)   at the time the other party enters into the transaction:

(A)   less than two years has passed since the dissociation; and

(B)   the other party does not know or have notice of the dissociation and reasonably believes that the person is a general partner; and

(2)   the act:

(A)   is appropriate for winding up the partnership's activities and affairs; or

(B)   would have bound the partnership under Section 402 before dissolution and at the time the other party enters into the transaction the other party does not know or have notice of the dissolution.

§ 805.   Liability After Dissolution of General Partner and Person Dissociated as General Partner

(a)   If a general partner having knowledge of the dissolution causes a limited partnership to incur an obligation under Section 804(a) by an act that is not appropriate for winding up the partnership's activities and affairs, the general partner is liable:

(1)   to the partnership for any damage caused to the partnership arising from the obligation; and

(2)   if another general partner or a person dissociated as a general partner is liable for the obligation, to that other general partner or person for any damage caused to that other general partner or person arising from the liability.

(b)   If a person dissociated as a general partner causes a limited partnership to incur an obligation under Section 804(b), the person is liable:

(1)   to the partnership for any damage caused to the partnership arising from the obligation; and

(2) if a general partner or another person dissociated as a general partner is liable for the obligation, to the general partner or other person for any damage caused to the general partner or other person arising from the obligation.

§ 806. Known Claims Against Dissolved Limited Partnership

(a) Except as otherwise provided in subsection (d), a dissolved limited partnership may give notice of a known claim under subsection (b), which has the effect provided in subsection (c).

(b) A dissolved limited partnership may in a record notify its known claimants of the dissolution. The notice must:

(1) specify the information required to be included in a claim;

(2) state that a claim must be in writing and provide a mailing address to which the claim is to be sent;

(3) state the deadline for receipt of a claim, which may not be less than 120 days after the date the notice is received by the claimant;

(4) state that the claim will be barred if not received by the deadline; and

(5) unless the partnership has been throughout its existence a limited liability limited partnership, state that the barring of a claim against the partnership will also bar any corresponding claim against any general partner or person dissociated as a general partner which is based on Section 404.

(c) A claim against a dissolved limited partnership is barred if the requirements of subsection (b) are met and:

(1) the claim is not received by the specified deadline; or

(2) if the claim is timely received but rejected by the partnership:

(A) the partnership causes the claimant to receive a notice in a record stating that the claim is rejected and will be barred unless the claimant commences an action against the partnership to enforce the claim not later than 90 days after the claimant receives the notice; and

(B) the claimant does not commence the required action not later than 90 days after the claimant receives the notice.

(d) This section does not apply to a claim based on an event occurring after the date of dissolution or a liability that on that date is contingent.

§ 807. Other Claims Against Dissolved Limited Partnership

(a) A dissolved limited partnership may publish notice of its dissolution and request persons having claims against the partnership to present them in accordance with the notice.

(b) A notice under subsection (a) must:

(1) be published at least once in a newspaper of general circulation in the [county] in this state in which the dissolved limited partnership's principal office is located or, if the principal office is not located in this state, in the [county] in which the office of the partnership's registered agent is or was last located;

(2) describe the information required to be contained in a claim, state that the claim must be in writing, and provide a mailing address to which the claim is to be sent;

(3) state that a claim against the partnership is barred unless an action to enforce the claim is commenced not later than three years after publication of the notice; and

(4) unless the partnership has been throughout its existence a limited liability limited partnership, state that the barring of a claim against the partnership will also bar any corresponding claim against any general partner or person dissociated as a general partner which is based on Section 404.

(c) If a dissolved limited partnership publishes a notice in accordance with subsection (b), the claim of each of the following claimants is barred unless the claimant commences an action to enforce the claim against the partnership not later than three years after the publication date of the notice:

(1) a claimant that did not receive notice in a record under Section 806;

(2) a claimant whose claim was timely sent to the partnership but not acted on; and

(3) a claimant whose claim is contingent at, or based on an event occurring after, the date of dissolution.

(d) A claim not barred under this section or Section 806 may be enforced:

(1) against the dissolved limited partnership, to the extent of its undistributed assets;

(2) except as otherwise provided in Section 808, if assets of the partnership have been distributed after dissolution, against a partner or transferee to the extent of that person's proportionate share of the claim or of the partnership's assets distributed to the partner or transferee after dissolution, whichever is less, but a person's total liability for all claims under this paragraph may not exceed the total amount of assets distributed to the person after dissolution; and

(3) against any person liable on the claim under Sections 404 and 607.

§ 808.   Court Proceedings

(a) A dissolved limited partnership that has published a notice under Section 807 may file an application with [the appropriate court] in the [county] where the partnership's principal office is located or, if the principal office is not located in this state, where the office of its registered agent is or was last located, for a determination of the amount and form of security to be provided for payment of claims that are contingent, have not been made known to the partnership, or are based on an event occurring after the date of dissolution but which, based on the facts known to the partnership, are reasonably expected to arise after the date of dissolution. Security is not required for any claim that is or is reasonably anticipated to be barred under Section 807.

(b) Not later than 10 days after the filing of an application under subsection (a), the dissolved limited partnership shall give notice of the proceeding to each claimant holding a contingent claim known to the partnership.

(c) In a proceeding brought under this section, the court may appoint a guardian ad litem to represent all claimants whose identities are unknown. The reasonable fees and expenses of the guardian, including all reasonable expert witness fees, must be paid by the dissolved limited partnership.

(d) A dissolved limited partnership that provides security in the amount and form ordered by the court under subsection (a) satisfies the partnership's obligations with respect to claims that are contingent, have not been made known to the partnership, or are based on an event occurring after the date of dissolution, and such claims may not be enforced against a partner or transferee on account of assets received in liquidation.

§ 809.   Liability of General Partner and Person Dissociated as General Partner When Claim Against Limited Partnership Barred

If a claim against a dissolved limited partnership is barred under Section 806, 807, or 808, any corresponding claim under Section 404 or 607 is also barred.

§ 810. Disposition of Assets in Winding Up; When Contributions Required

(a)   In winding up its activities and affairs, a limited partnership shall apply its assets, including the contributions required by this section, to discharge the partnership's obligations to creditors, including partners that are creditors.

(b)   After a limited partnership complies with subsection (a), any surplus must be distributed in the following order, subject to any charging order in effect under Section 703:

(1)   to each person owning a transferable interest that reflects contributions made and not previously returned, an amount equal to the value of the unreturned contributions; and

(2)   among persons owning transferable interests in proportion to their respective rights to share in distributions immediately before the dissolution of the partnership.

(c)   If a limited partnership's assets are insufficient to satisfy all of its obligations under subsection (a), with respect to each unsatisfied obligation incurred when the partnership was not a limited liability limited partnership, the following rules apply:

(1)   Each person that was a general partner when the obligation was incurred and that has not been released from the obligation under Section 607 shall contribute to the partnership for the purpose of enabling the partnership to satisfy the obligation. The contribution due from each of those persons is in proportion to the right to receive distributions in the capacity of a general partner in effect for each of those persons when the obligation was incurred.

(2)   If a person does not contribute the full amount required under paragraph (1) with respect to an unsatisfied obligation of the partnership, the other persons required to contribute by paragraph (1) on account of the obligation shall contribute the additional amount necessary to discharge the obligation. The additional contribution due from each of those other persons is in proportion to the right to receive distributions in the capacity of a general partner in effect for each of those other persons when the obligation was incurred.

(3)   If a person does not make the additional contribution required by paragraph (2), further additional contributions are determined and due in the same manner as provided in that paragraph.

(d)   A person that makes an additional contribution under subsection (c)(2) or (3) may recover from any person whose failure to contribute under subsection (c)(1) or (2) necessitated the additional contribution. A person may not recover under this subsection more than the amount additionally contributed. A person's liability under this subsection may not exceed the amount the person failed to contribute.

(e)   All distributions made under subsections (b) and (c) must be paid in money.

§ 811. Administrative Dissolution

(a)   The [Secretary of State] may commence a proceeding under subsection (b) to dissolve a limited partnership administratively if the partnership does not:

(1)   pay any fee, tax, interest, or penalty required to be paid to the [Secretary of State] not later than [six months] after it is due;

(2)   deliver [an annual] [a biennial] report to the [Secretary of State] not later than [six months] after it is due; or

(3)   have a registered agent in this state for [60] consecutive days.

(b)   If the [Secretary of State] determines that one or more grounds exist for administratively dissolving a limited partnership, the [Secretary of State] shall serve the partnership with notice in a record of the [Secretary of State's] determination.

(c)   If a limited partnership, not later than [60] days after service of the notice under subsection (b), does not cure or demonstrate to the satisfaction of the [Secretary of State] the nonexistence of each ground determined by the [Secretary of State], the [Secretary of State] shall administratively dissolve the partnership by signing a statement of administrative dissolution that recites the grounds for dissolution and the effective date of dissolution. The [Secretary of State] shall file the statement and serve a copy on the partnership pursuant to Section 121.

(d)   A limited partnership that is administratively dissolved continues in existence as an entity but may not carry on any activities except as necessary to wind up its activities and affairs and liquidate its assets under Sections 802, 806, 807, 808, and 810, or to apply for reinstatement under Section 812.

(e)   The administrative dissolution of a limited partnership does not terminate the authority of its registered agent.

§ 812.   Reinstatement

(a)   A limited partnership that is administratively dissolved under Section 811 may apply to the [Secretary of State] for reinstatement [not later than [two] years after the effective date of dissolution]. The application must state:

(1)   the name of the partnership at the time of its administrative dissolution and, if needed, a different name that satisfies Section 114;

(2)   the address of the principal office of the partnership and the name and street and mailing addresses of its registered agent;

(3)   the effective date of the partnership's administrative dissolution; and

(4)   that the grounds for dissolution did not exist or have been cured.

(b)   To be reinstated, a limited partnership must pay all fees, taxes, interest, and penalties that were due to the [Secretary of State] at the time of the partnership's administrative dissolution and all fees, taxes, interest, and penalties that would have been due to the [Secretary of State] while the partnership was administratively dissolved.

(c)   If the [Secretary of State] determines that an application under subsection (a) contains the required information, is satisfied that the information is correct, and determines that all payments required to be made to the [Secretary of State] by subsection (b) have been made, the [Secretary of State] shall:

(1)   cancel the statement of administrative dissolution and prepare a statement of reinstatement that states the [Secretary of State's] determination and the effective date of reinstatement; and

(2)   file the statement of reinstatement and serve a copy on the limited partnership.

(d)   When reinstatement under this section has become effective, the following rules apply:

(1)   The reinstatement relates back to and takes effect as of the effective date of the administrative dissolution.

(2)   The limited partnership resumes carrying on its activities and affairs as if the administrative dissolution had not occurred.

(3)   The rights of a person arising out of an act or omission in reliance on the dissolution before the person knew or had notice of the reinstatement are not affected.

§ 813. Judicial Review of Denial of Reinstatement

(a) If the [Secretary of State] denies a limited partnership's application for reinstatement following administrative dissolution, the [Secretary of State] shall serve the partnership with a notice in a record that explains the reasons for the denial.

(b) A limited partnership may seek judicial review of denial of reinstatement in [the appropriate court] not later than [30] days after service of the notice of denial.

[ARTICLE] 9. ACTIONS BY PARTNERS

§ 901. Direct Action by Partner

(a) Subject to subsection (b), a partner may maintain a direct action against another partner or the limited partnership, with or without an accounting as to the partnership's activities and affairs, to enforce the partner's rights and otherwise protect the partner's interests, including rights and interests under the partnership agreement or this [act] or arising independently of the partnership relationship.

(b) A partner maintaining a direct action under this section must plead and prove an actual or threatened injury that is not solely the result of an injury suffered or threatened to be suffered by the limited partnership.

(c) A right to an accounting on a dissolution and winding up does not revive a claim barred by law.

§ 902. Derivative Action

A partner may maintain a derivative action to enforce a right of a limited partnership if:

(1) the partner first makes a demand on the general partners, requesting that they cause the partnership to bring an action to enforce the right, and the general partners do not bring the action within a reasonable time; or

(2) a demand under paragraph (1) would be futile.

§ 903. Proper Plaintiff

A derivative action to enforce a right of a limited partnership may be maintained only by a person that is a partner at the time the action is commenced and:

(1) was a partner when the conduct giving rise to the action occurred; or

(2) whose status as a partner devolved on the person by operation of law or pursuant to the terms of the partnership agreement from a person that was a partner at the time of the conduct.

§ 904. Pleading

In a derivative action, the complaint must state with particularity:

(1) the date and content of plaintiff's demand and the response to the demand by the general partner; or

(2) why demand should be excused as futile.

§ 905. Special Litigation Committee

(a) If a limited partnership is named as or made a party in a derivative proceeding, the partnership may appoint a special litigation committee to investigate the claims asserted in the proceeding and determine whether pursuing the action is in the best interests of the partnership. If the partnership appoints a special litigation committee, on motion by the committee made in the name of the partnership, except for good cause shown, the court shall stay discovery for the time reasonably necessary to permit the committee to make its investigation. This subsection does not prevent the court from:

(1)   enforcing a person's right to information under Section 304 or 407; or

(2)   granting extraordinary relief in the form of a temporary restraining order or preliminary injunction.

(b)   A special litigation committee must be composed of one or more disinterested and independent individuals, who may be partners.

(c)   A special litigation committee may be appointed:

(1)   by a majority of the general partners not named as parties in the proceeding; or

(2)   if all general partners are named as parties in the proceeding, by a majority of the general partners named as defendants.

(d)   After appropriate investigation, a special litigation committee may determine that it is in the best interests of the limited partnership that the proceeding:

(1)   continue under the control of the plaintiff;

(2)   continue under the control of the committee;

(3)   be settled on terms approved by the committee; or

(4)   be dismissed.

(e)   After making a determination under subsection (d), a special litigation committee shall file with the court a statement of its determination and its report supporting its determination and shall serve each party with a copy of the determination and report. The court shall determine whether the members of the committee were disinterested and independent and whether the committee conducted its investigation and made its recommendation in good faith, independently, and with reasonable care, with the committee having the burden of proof. If the court finds that the members of the committee were disinterested and independent and that the committee acted in good faith, independently, and with reasonable care, the court shall enforce the determination of the committee. Otherwise, the court shall dissolve the stay of discovery entered under subsection (a) and allow the action to continue under the control of the plaintiff.

§ 906.   Proceeds and Expenses

(a)   Except as otherwise provided in subsection (b):

(1)   any proceeds or other benefits of a derivative action, whether by judgment, compromise, or settlement, belong to the limited partnership and not to the plaintiff; and

(2)   if the plaintiff receives any proceeds, the plaintiff shall remit them immediately to the partnership.

(b)   If a derivative action is successful in whole or in part, the court may award the plaintiff reasonable expenses, including reasonable attorney's fees and costs, from the recovery of the limited partnership.

(c)   A derivative action on behalf of a limited partnership may not be voluntarily dismissed or settled without the court's approval.

[ARTICLE] 10.   FOREIGN LIMITED PARTNERSHIPS

§ 1001.   Governing Law

(a)   The law of the jurisdiction of formation of a foreign limited partnership governs:

(1)   the internal affairs of the partnership;

(2)   the liability of a partner as partner for a debt, obligation, or other liability of the partnership; and

(3)   the liability of a series of the partnership.

(b)   A foreign limited partnership is not precluded from registering to do business in this state because of any difference between the law of its jurisdiction of formation and the law of this state.

(c)   Registration of a foreign limited partnership to do business in this state does not authorize the foreign partnership to engage in any activities and affairs or exercise any power that a limited partnership may not engage in or exercise in this state.

§ 1002.   Registration to Do Business in This State

(a)   A foreign limited partnership may not do business in this state until it registers with the [Secretary of State] under this [article].

(b)   A foreign limited partnership doing business in this state may not maintain an action or proceeding in this state unless it is registered to do business in this state.

(c)   The failure of a foreign limited partnership to register to do business in this state does not impair the validity of a contract or act of the partnership or preclude it from defending an action or proceeding in this state.

(d)   A limitation on the liability of a general partner or limited partner of a foreign limited partnership is not waived solely because the partnership does business in this state without registering to do business in this state.

(e)   Section 1001(a) and (b) applies even if the foreign limited partnership fails to register under this [article].

§ 1003.   Foreign Registration Statement

To register to do business in this state, a foreign limited partnership must deliver a foreign registration statement to the [Secretary of State] for filing. The statement must state:

(1)   the name of the partnership and, if the name does not comply with Section 114, an alternate name adopted pursuant to Section 1006(a);

(2)   that the partnership is a foreign limited partnership;

(3)   the partnership's jurisdiction of formation;

(4)   the street and mailing addresses of the partnership's principal office and, if the law of the partnership's jurisdiction of formation requires the partnership to maintain an office in that jurisdiction, the street and mailing addresses of the required office; and

(5)   the name and street and mailing addresses of the partnership's registered agent in this state.

§ 1004.   Amendment of Foreign Registration Statement

A registered foreign limited partnership shall deliver to the [Secretary of State] for filing an amendment to its foreign registration statement if there is a change in:

(1)   the name of the partnership;

(2)   the partnership's jurisdiction of formation;

(3)   an address required by Section 1003(4); or

(4)   the information required by Section 1003(5).

§ 1005.   Activities Not Constituting Doing Business

(a)   Activities of a foreign limited partnership which do not constitute doing business in this state under this [article] include:

(1)   maintaining, defending, mediating, arbitrating, or settling an action or proceeding;

(2)   carrying on any activity concerning its internal affairs, including holding meetings of its partners;

(3)   maintaining accounts in financial institutions;

(4)   maintaining offices or agencies for the transfer, exchange, and registration of securities of the partnership or maintaining trustees or depositories with respect to those securities;

(5)   selling through independent contractors;

(6)   soliciting or obtaining orders by any means if the orders require acceptance outside this state before they become contracts;

(7)   creating or acquiring indebtedness, mortgages, or security interests in property;

(8)   securing or collecting debts or enforcing mortgages or security interests in property securing the debts and holding, protecting, or maintaining property;

(9)   conducting an isolated transaction that is not in the course of similar transactions;

(10) owning, without more, property; and

(11) doing business in interstate commerce.

(b)   A person does not do business in this state solely by being a partner of a foreign limited partnership that does business in this state.

(c)   This section does not apply in determining the contacts or activities that may subject a foreign limited partnership to service of process, taxation, or regulation under law of this state other than this [act].

§ 1006.   Noncomplying Name of Foreign Limited Partnership

(a)   A foreign limited partnership whose name does not comply with Section 114 may not register to do business in this state until it adopts, for the purpose of doing business in this state, an alternate name that complies with Section 114. A partnership that registers under an alternate name under this subsection need not comply with [this state's assumed or fictitious name statute]. After registering to do business in this state with an alternate name, a partnership shall do business in this state under:

(1)   the alternate name;

(2)   the partnership's name, with the addition of its jurisdiction of formation; or

(3)   a name the partnership is authorized to use under [this state's assumed or fictitious name statute].

(b)   If a registered foreign limited partnership changes its name to one that does not comply with Section 114, it may not do business in this state until it complies with subsection (a) by amending its registration to adopt an alternate name that complies with Section 114.

§ 1007. Withdrawal Deemed on Conversion to Domestic Filing Entity or Domestic Limited Liability Partnership

A registered foreign limited partnership that converts to a domestic limited liability partnership or to a domestic entity whose formation requires delivery of a record to the [Secretary of State] for filing is deemed to have withdrawn its registration on the effective date of the conversion.

§ 1008. Withdrawal on Dissolution or Conversion to Nonfiling Entity Other than Limited Liability Partnership

(a)   A registered foreign limited partnership that has dissolved and completed winding up or has converted to a domestic or foreign entity whose formation does not require the public filing of a record, other than a limited liability partnership, shall deliver a statement of withdrawal to the [Secretary of State] for filing. The statement must state:

(1)   in the case of a partnership that has completed winding up:

(A)   its name and jurisdiction of formation;

(B)   that the partnership surrenders its registration to do business in this state; and

(2)   in the case of a partnership that has converted:

(A)   the name of the converting partnership and its jurisdiction of formation;

(B)   the type of entity to which the partnership has converted and its jurisdiction of formation;

(C)   that the converted entity surrenders the converting partnership's registration to do business in this state and revokes the authority of the converting partnership's registered agent to act as registered agent in this state on behalf of the partnership or the converted entity; and

(D)   a mailing address to which service of process may be made under subsection (b).

(b)   After a withdrawal under this section has become effective, service of process in any action or proceeding based on a cause of action arising during the time the foreign limited partnership was registered to do business in this state may be made pursuant to Section 121.

§ 1009. Transfer of Registration

(a)   When a registered foreign limited partnership has merged into a foreign entity that is not registered to do business in this state or has converted to a foreign entity required to register with the [Secretary of State] to do business in this state, the foreign entity shall deliver to the [Secretary of State] for filing an application for transfer of registration. The application must state:

(1)   the name of the registered foreign limited partnership before the merger or conversion;

(2)   that before the merger or conversion the registration pertained to a foreign limited partnership;

(3)   the name of the applicant foreign entity into which the foreign limited partnership has merged or to which it has been converted and, if the name does not comply with Section 114, an alternate name adopted pursuant to Section 1006(a);

(4)   the type of entity of the applicant foreign entity and its jurisdiction of formation;

(5)   the street and mailing addresses of the principal office of the applicant foreign entity and, if the law of the entity's jurisdiction of formation requires the entity to maintain an office in that jurisdiction, the street and mailing addresses of that office; and

(6)   the name and street and mailing addresses of the applicant foreign entity's registered agent in this state.

(b)   When an application for transfer of registration takes effect, the registration of the foreign limited partnership to do business in this state is transferred without interruption to the foreign entity into which the partnership has merged or to which it has been converted.

§ 1010.   Termination of Registration

(a)   The [Secretary of State] may terminate the registration of a registered foreign limited partnership in the manner provided in subsections (b) and (c) if the partnership does not:

(1)   pay, not later than [60] days after the due date, any fee, tax, interest, or penalty required to be paid to the [Secretary of State] under this [act] or law other than this [act];

(2)   deliver to the [Secretary of State] for filing, not later than [60] days after the due date, [an annual] [a biennial] report required under Section 212;

(3)   have a registered agent as required by Section 117; or

(4)   deliver to the [Secretary of State] for filing a statement of a change under Section 118 not later than [30] days after a change has occurred in the name or address of the registered agent.

(b)   The [Secretary of State] may terminate the registration of a registered foreign limited partnership by:

(1)   filing a notice of termination or noting the termination in the records of the [Secretary of State]; and

(2)   delivering a copy of the notice or the information in the notation to the partnership's registered agent or, if the partnership does not have a registered agent, to the partnership's principal office.

(c)   The notice must state or the information in the notation must include:

(1)   the effective date of the termination, which must be at least [60] days after the date the [Secretary of State] delivers the copy; and

(2)   the grounds for termination under subsection (a).

(d)   The authority of the registered foreign limited partnership to do business in this state ceases on the effective date of the notice of termination or notation under subsection (b), unless before that date the partnership cures each ground for termination stated in the notice or notation. If the partnership cures each ground, the [Secretary of State] shall file a record so stating.

§ 1011.   Withdrawal of Registration of Registered Foreign Limited Partnership

(a)   A registered foreign limited partnership may withdraw its registration by delivering a statement of withdrawal to the [Secretary of State] for filing. The statement of withdrawal must state:

(1)   the name of the partnership and its jurisdiction of formation;

(2)   that the partnership is not doing business in this state and that it withdraws its registration to do business in this state;

(3)   that the partnership revokes the authority of its registered agent to accept service on its behalf in this state; and

(4)   an address to which service of process may be made under subsection (b).

(b)   After the withdrawal of the registration of a foreign limited partnership, service of process in any action or proceeding based on a cause of action arising during the time the partnership was registered to do business in this state may be made pursuant to Section 121.

§ 1012. Action by [Attorney General]

The [Attorney General] may maintain an action to enjoin a foreign limited partnership from doing business in this state in violation of this [article].

[ARTICLE] 11. MERGER, INTEREST EXCHANGE, CONVERSION, AND DOMESTICATION

[PART] 1. GENERAL PROVISIONS

§ 1101. Definitions

In this [article]:

(1) "Acquired entity" means the entity, all of one or more classes or series of interests of which are acquired in an interest exchange.

(2) "Acquiring entity" means the entity that acquires all of one or more classes or series of interests of the acquired entity in an interest exchange.

(3) "Conversion" means a transaction authorized by [Part] 4.

(4) "Converted entity" means the converting entity as it continues in existence after a conversion.

(5) "Converting entity" means the domestic entity that approves a plan of conversion pursuant to Section 1143 or the foreign entity that approves a conversion pursuant to the law of its jurisdiction of formation.

(6) "Distributional interest" means the right under an unincorporated entity's organic law and organic rules to receive distributions from the entity.

(7) "Domestic", with respect to an entity, means governed as to its internal affairs by the law of this state.

(8) "Domesticated limited partnership" means the domesticating limited partnership as it continues in existence after a domestication.

(9) "Domesticating limited partnership" means the domestic limited partnership that approves a plan of domestication pursuant to Section 1153 or the foreign limited partnership that approves a domestication pursuant to the law of its jurisdiction of formation.

(10) "Domestication" means a transaction authorized by [Part] 5.

(11) "Entity":

(A) means:

(i) a business corporation;

(ii) a nonprofit corporation;

(iii) a general partnership, including a limited liability partnership;

(iv) a limited partnership, including a limited liability limited partnership;

(v) a limited liability company;

[(vi) a general cooperative association;]

(vii) a limited cooperative association;

(viii) an unincorporated nonprofit association;

(ix) a statutory trust, business trust, or common-law business trust; or

469

     (x) any other person that has:

        (I) a legal existence separate from any interest holder of that person; or

        (II) the power to acquire an interest in real property in its own name; and

   (B) does not include:

     (i) an individual;

     (ii) a trust with a predominantly donative purpose or a charitable trust;

     (iii) an association or relationship that is not an entity listed in subparagraph A and is not a partnership under the rules stated in [Section 202(c) of the Uniform Partnership Act (1997) (Lasted Amended 2013)] [Section 7 of the Uniform Partnership Act (1914)] or a similar provision of the law of another jurisdiction;

     (iv) a decedent's estate; or

     (v) a government or a governmental subdivision, agency, or instrumentality.

(12) "Filing entity" means an entity whose formation requires the filing of a public organic record. The term does not include a limited liability partnership.

(13) "Foreign", with respect to an entity, means an entity governed as to its internal affairs by the law of a jurisdiction other than this state.

(14) "Governance interest" means a right under the organic law or organic rules of an unincorporated entity, other than as a governor, agent, assignee, or proxy, to:

   (A) receive or demand access to information concerning, or the books and records of, the entity;

   (B) vote for or consent to the election of the governors of the entity; or

   (C) receive notice of or vote on or consent to an issue involving the internal affairs of the entity.

(15) "Governor" means:

   (A) a director of a business corporation;

   (B) a director or trustee of a nonprofit corporation;

   (C) a general partner of a general partnership;

   (D) a general partner of a limited partnership;

   (E) a manager of a manager-managed limited liability company;

   (F) a member of a member-managed limited liability company;

   [(G) a director of a general cooperative association;]

   (H) a director of a limited cooperative association;

   (I) a manager of an unincorporated nonprofit association;

   (J) a trustee of a statutory trust, business trust, or common-law business trust; or

   (K) any other person under whose authority the powers of an entity are exercised and under whose direction the activities and affairs of the entity are managed pursuant to the organic law and organic rules of the entity.

(16) "Interest" means:

   (A) a share in a business corporation;

   (B) a membership in a nonprofit corporation;

(C)　a partnership interest in a general partnership;

(D)　a partnership interest in a limited partnership;

(E)　a membership interest in a limited liability company;

[(F)　a share in a general cooperative association;]

(G)　a member's interest in a limited cooperative association;

(H)　a membership in an unincorporated nonprofit association;

(I)　a beneficial interest in a statutory trust, business trust, or common-law business trust; or

(J)　a governance interest or distributional interest in any other type of unincorporated entity.

(17)　"Interest exchange" means a transaction authorized by [Part] 3.

(18)　"Interest holder" means:

(A)　a shareholder of a business corporation;

(B)　a member of a nonprofit corporation;

(C)　a general partner of a general partnership;

(D)　a general partner of a limited partnership;

(E)　a limited partner of a limited partnership;

(F)　a member of a limited liability company;

[(G)　a shareholder of a general cooperative association;]

(H)　a member of a limited cooperative association;

(I)　a member of an unincorporated nonprofit association;

(J)　a beneficiary or beneficial owner of a statutory trust, business trust, or common-law business trust; or

(K)　any other direct holder of an interest.

(19)　"Interest holder liability" means:

(A)　personal liability for a liability of an entity which is imposed on a person:

(i)　solely by reason of the status of the person as an interest holder; or

(ii)　by the organic rules of the entity which make one or more specified interest holders or categories of interest holders liable in their capacity as interest holders for all or specified liabilities of the entity; or

(B)　an obligation of an interest holder under the organic rules of an entity to contribute to the entity.

(20)　"Merger" means a transaction authorized by [Part] 2.

(21)　"Merging entity" means an entity that is a party to a merger and exists immediately before the merger becomes effective.

(22)　"Organic law" means the law of an entity's jurisdiction of formation governing the internal affairs of the entity.

(23)　"Organic rules" means the public organic record and private organic rules of an entity.

(24)　"Plan" means a plan of merger, plan of interest exchange, plan of conversion, or plan of domestication.

(25) "Plan of conversion" means a plan under Section 1142.

(26) "Plan of domestication" means a plan under Section 1152.

(27) "Plan of interest exchange" means a plan under Section 1132.

(28) "Plan of merger" means a plan under Section 1122.

(29) "Private organic rules" means the rules, whether or not in a record, that govern the internal affairs of an entity, are binding on all its interest holders, and are not part of its public organic record, if any. The term includes:

(A)   the bylaws of a business corporation;

(B)   the bylaws of a nonprofit corporation;

(C)   the partnership agreement of a general partnership;

(D)   the partnership agreement of a limited partnership;

(E)   the operating agreement of a limited liability company;

[(F)   the bylaws of a general cooperative association;]

(G)   the bylaws of a limited cooperative association;

(H)   the governing principles of an unincorporated nonprofit association; and

(I)   the trust instrument of a statutory trust or similar rules of a business trust or a common-law business trust.

(30) "Protected agreement" means:

(A)   a record evidencing indebtedness and any related agreement in effect on [the effective date of this [act]];

(B)   an agreement that is binding on an entity on [the effective date of this [act]];

(C)   the organic rules of an entity in effect on [the effective date of this [act]]; or

(D)   an agreement that is binding on any of the governors or interest holders of an entity on [the effective date of this [act]].

(31) "Public organic record" means the record the filing of which by the [Secretary of State] is required to form an entity and any amendment to or restatement of that record. The term includes:

(A)   the articles of incorporation of a business corporation;

(B)   the articles of incorporation of a nonprofit corporation;

(C)   the certificate of limited partnership of a limited partnership;

(D)   the certificate of organization of a limited liability company;

[(E)   the articles of incorporation of a general cooperative association;]

(F)   the articles of organization of a limited cooperative association; and

(G)   the certificate of trust of a statutory trust or similar record of a business trust.

(32) "Registered foreign entity" means a foreign entity that is registered to do business in this state pursuant to a record filed by the [Secretary of State].

(33) "Statement of conversion" means a statement under Section 1145.

(34) "Statement of domestication" means a statement under Section 1155.

(35) "Statement of interest exchange" means a statement under Section 1135.

(36) "Statement of merger" means a statement under Section 1125.

(37) "Surviving entity" means the entity that continues in existence after or is created by a merger.

(38) "Type of entity" means a generic form of entity:

(A) recognized at common law; or

(B) formed under an organic law, whether or not some entities formed under that organic law are subject to provisions of that law that create different categories of the form of entity.

§ 1102. Relationship of [Article] to Other Laws

(a) This [article] does not authorize an act prohibited by, and does not affect the application or requirements of, law other than this [article].

(b) A transaction effected under this [article] may not create or impair a right, duty, or obligation of a person under the statutory law of this state relating to a change in control, takeover, business combination, control-share acquisition, or similar transaction involving a domestic merging, acquired, converting, or domesticating business corporation unless:

(1) if the corporation does not survive the transaction, the transaction satisfies any requirements of the law; or

(2) if the corporation survives the transaction, the approval of the plan is by a vote of the shareholders or directors which would be sufficient to create or impair the right, duty, or obligation directly under the law.

§ 1103. Required Notice or Approval

(a) A domestic or foreign entity that is required to give notice to, or obtain the approval of, a governmental agency or officer of this state to be a party to a merger must give the notice or obtain the approval to be a party to an interest exchange, conversion, or domestication.

(b) Property held for a charitable purpose under the law of this state by a domestic or foreign entity immediately before a transaction under this [article] becomes effective may not, as a result of the transaction, be diverted from the objects for which it was donated, granted, devised, or otherwise transferred unless, to the extent required by or pursuant to the law of this state concerning cy pres or other law dealing with nondiversion of charitable assets, the entity obtains an appropriate order of [the appropriate court] [the Attorney General] specifying the disposition of the property.

(c) A bequest, devise, gift, grant, or promise contained in a will or other instrument of donation, subscription, or conveyance which is made to a merging entity that is not the surviving entity and which takes effect or remains payable after the merger inures to the surviving entity.

(d) A trust obligation that would govern property if transferred to a nonsurviving entity applies to property that is transferred to the surviving entity under this section.

Legislative Note: As an alternative to enacting Subsection (a), a state may identify each of its regulatory laws that requires prior approval for a merger of a regulated entity, decide whether regulatory approval should be required for an interest exchange, conversion, or domestication, and make amendments as appropriate to those laws.

As with Subsection (a), an adopting state may choose to amend its various laws with respect to the nondiversion of charitable property to cover the various transactions authorized by this act as an alternative to enacting Subsection (b).

§ 1104. Nonexclusivity

The fact that a transaction under this [article] produces a certain result does not preclude the same result from being accomplished in any other manner permitted by law other than this [article].

§ 1105. Reference to External Facts

A plan may refer to facts ascertainable outside the plan if the manner in which the facts will operate upon the plan is specified in the plan. The facts may include the occurrence of an event or a determination or action by a person, whether or not the event, determination, or action is within the control of a party to the transaction.

§ 1106. Appraisal Rights

An interest holder of a domestic merging, acquired, converting, or domesticating limited partnership is entitled to contractual appraisal rights in connection with a transaction under this [article] to the extent provided in:

(1)   the partnership agreement; or

(2)   the plan.

[§ 1107. Excluded Entities and Transactions

(a)   The following entities may not participate in a transaction under this [article]:

(1)

(2).

(b)   This [article] may not be used to effect a transaction that:

(1)

(2).]

Legislative Note: Subsection (a) may be used by states that have special statutes restricted to the organization of certain types of entities. A common example is banking statutes that prohibit banks from engaging in transactions other than pursuant to those statutes.

Nonprofit entities may participate in transactions under this act with for-profit entities, subject to compliance with Section 1103. If a state desires, however, to exclude entities with a charitable purpose or to exclude other types of entities from the scope of this act, that may be done by referring to those entities in Subsection (a).

Subsection (b) may be used to exclude certain types of transactions governed by more specific statutes. A common example is the conversion of an insurance company from mutual to stock form. There may be other types of transactions that vary greatly among the states.

[PART] 2. MERGER

§ 1121. Merger Authorized

(a)   By complying with this [part]:

(1)   one or more domestic limited partnerships may merge with one or more domestic or foreign entities into a domestic or foreign surviving entity; and

(2)   two or more foreign entities may merge into a domestic limited partnership.

(b)   By complying with the provisions of this [part] applicable to foreign entities, a foreign entity may be a party to a merger under this [part] or may be the surviving entity in such a merger if the merger is authorized by the law of the foreign entity's jurisdiction of formation.

§ 1122. Plan of Merger

(a)   A domestic limited partnership may become a party to a merger under this [part] by approving a plan of merger. The plan must be in a record and contain:

(1) as to each merging entity, its name, jurisdiction of formation, and type of entity;

(2) if the surviving entity is to be created in the merger, a statement to that effect and the entity's name, jurisdiction of formation, and type of entity;

(3) the manner of converting the interests in each party to the merger into interests, securities, obligations, money, other property, rights to acquire interests or securities, or any combination of the foregoing;

(4) if the surviving entity exists before the merger, any proposed amendments to:

(A) its public organic record, if any; and

(B) its private organic rules that are, or are proposed to be, in a record;

(5) if the surviving entity is to be created in the merger:

(A) its proposed public organic record, if any; and

(B) the full text of its private organic rules that are proposed to be in a record;

(6) the other terms and conditions of the merger; and

(7) any other provision required by the law of a merging entity's jurisdiction of formation or the organic rules of a merging entity.

(b) In addition to the requirements of subsection (a), a plan of merger may contain any other provision not prohibited by law.

§ 1123. Approval of Merger

(a) A plan of merger is not effective unless it has been approved:

(1) by a domestic merging limited partnership, by all the partners of the partnership entitled to vote on or consent to any matter; and

(2) in a record, by each partner of a domestic merging limited partnership which will have interest holder liability for debts, obligations, and other liabilities that are incurred_after the merger becomes effective, unless:

(A) the partnership agreement of the partnership provides in a record for the approval of a merger in which some or all of its partners become subject to interest holder liability by the affirmative vote or consent of fewer than all the partners; and

(B) the partner consented in a record to or voted for that provision of the partnership agreement or became a partner after the adoption of that provision.

(b) A merger involving a domestic merging entity that is not a limited partnership is not effective unless the merger is approved by that entity in accordance with its organic law.

(c) A merger involving a foreign merging entity is not effective unless the merger is approved by the foreign entity in accordance with the law of the foreign entity's jurisdiction of formation.

§ 1124. Amendment or Abandonment of Plan of Merger

(a) A plan of merger may be amended only with the consent of each party to the plan, except as otherwise provided in the plan.

(b) A domestic merging limited partnership may approve an amendment of a plan of merger:

(1) in the same manner as the plan was approved, if the plan does not provide for the manner in which it may be amended; or

(2)   by its partners in the manner provided in the plan, but a partner that was entitled to vote on or consent to approval of the merger is entitled to vote on or consent to any amendment of the plan that will change:

(A)   the amount or kind of interests, securities, obligations, money, other property, rights to acquire interests or securities, or any combination of the foregoing, to be received by the interest holders of any party to the plan;

(B)   the public organic record, if any, or private organic rules of the surviving entity that will be in effect immediately after the merger becomes effective, except for changes that do not require approval of the interest holders of the surviving entity under its organic law or organic rules; or

(C)   any other terms or conditions of the plan, if the change would adversely affect the partner in any material respect.

(c)   After a plan of merger has been approved and before a statement of merger becomes effective, the plan may be abandoned as provided in the plan. Unless prohibited by the plan, a domestic merging limited partnership may abandon the plan in the same manner as the plan was approved.

(d)   If a plan of merger is abandoned after a statement of merger has been delivered to the [Secretary of State] for filing and before the statement becomes effective, a statement of abandonment, signed by a party to the plan, must be delivered to the [Secretary of State] for filing before the statement of merger becomes effective. The statement of abandonment takes effect on filing, and the merger is abandoned and does not become effective. The statement of abandonment must contain:

(1)   the name of each party to the plan of merger;

(2)   the date on which the statement of merger was filed by the [Secretary of State]; and

(3)   a statement that the merger has been abandoned in accordance with this section.

§ 1125.   Statement of Merger; Effective Date of Merger

(a)   A statement of merger must be signed by each merging entity and delivered to the [Secretary of State] for filing.

(b)   A statement of merger must contain:

(1)   the name, jurisdiction of formation, and type of entity of each merging entity that is not the surviving entity;

(2)   the name, jurisdiction of formation, and type of entity of the surviving entity;

(3)   a statement that the merger was approved by each domestic merging entity, if any, in accordance with this [part] and by each foreign merging entity, if any, in accordance with the law of its jurisdiction of formation;

(4)   if the surviving entity exists before the merger and is a domestic filing entity, any amendment to its public organic record approved as part of the plan of merger;

(5)   if the surviving entity is created by the merger and is a domestic filing entity, its public organic record, as an attachment; and

(6)   if the surviving entity is created by the merger and is a domestic limited liability partnership, its statement of qualification, as an attachment.

(c)   In addition to the requirements of subsection (b), a statement of merger may contain any other provision not prohibited by law.

(d)   If the surviving entity is a domestic entity, its public organic record, if any, must satisfy the requirements of the law of this state, except that the public organic record does not need to be signed.

(e)   A plan of merger that is signed by all the merging entities and meets all the requirements of subsection (b) may be delivered to the [Secretary of State] for filing instead of a statement of merger and on filing has the same effect. If a plan of merger is filed as provided in this subsection, references in this [article] to a statement of merger refer to the plan of merger filed under this subsection.

(f)   If the surviving entity is a domestic limited partnership, the merger becomes effective when the statement of merger is effective. In all other cases, the merger becomes effective on the later of:

(1)   the date and time provided by the organic law of the surviving entity; and

(2)   when the statement is effective.

§ 1126.   Effect of Merger

(a)   When a merger becomes effective:

(1)   the surviving entity continues or comes into existence;

(2)   each merging entity that is not the surviving entity ceases to exist;

(3)   all property of each merging entity vests in the surviving entity without transfer, reversion, or impairment;

(4)   all debts, obligations, and other liabilities of each merging entity are debts, obligations, and other liabilities of the surviving entity;

(5)   except as otherwise provided by law or the plan of merger, all the rights, privileges, immunities, powers, and purposes of each merging entity vest in the surviving entity;

(6)   if the surviving entity exists before the merger:

(A)   all its property continues to be vested in it without transfer, reversion, or impairment;

(B)   it remains subject to all its debts, obligations, and other liabilities; and

(C)   all its rights, privileges, immunities, powers, and purposes continue to be vested in it;

(7)   the name of the surviving entity may be substituted for the name of any merging entity that is a party to any pending action or proceeding;

(8)   if the surviving entity exists before the merger:

(A)   its public organic record, if any, is amended to the extent provided in the statement of merger; and

(B)   its private organic rules that are to be in a record, if any, are amended to the extent provided in the plan of merger;

(9)   if the surviving entity is created by the merger, its private organic rules become effective and:

(A)   if it is a filing entity, its public organic record becomes effective; and

(B)   if it is a limited liability partnership, its statement of qualification becomes effective; and

(10)   the interests in each merging entity which are to be converted in the merger are converted, and the interest holders of those interests are entitled only to the rights provided to them under the plan of merger and to any appraisal rights they have under Section 1106 and the merging entity's organic law.

(b)   Except as otherwise provided in the organic law or organic rules of a merging entity, the merger does not give rise to any rights that an interest holder, governor, or third party would have upon a dissolution, liquidation, or winding up of the merging entity.

(c)   When a merger becomes effective, a person that did not have interest holder liability with respect to any of the merging entities and becomes subject to interest holder liability with respect to a domestic entity as a result of the merger has interest holder liability only to the extent provided by the organic law of that entity and only for those debts, obligations, and other liabilities that are incurred after the merger becomes effective.

(d)   When a merger becomes effective, the interest holder liability of a person that ceases to hold an interest in a domestic merging limited partnership with respect to which the person had interest holder liability is subject to the following rules:

(1)   The merger does not discharge any interest holder liability under this [act] to the extent the interest holder liability was incurred before the merger became effective.

(2)   The person does not have interest holder liability under this [act] for any debt, obligation, or other liability that is incurred after the merger becomes effective.

(3)   This [act] continues to apply to the release, collection, or discharge of any interest holder liability preserved under paragraph (1) as if the merger had not occurred.

(4)   The person has whatever rights of contribution from any other person as are provided by this [act], law other than this [act], or the partnership agreement of the domestic merging limited partnership with respect to any interest holder liability preserved under paragraph (1) as if the merger had not occurred.

(e)   When a merger becomes effective, a foreign entity that is the surviving entity may be served with process in this state for the collection and enforcement of any debts, obligations, or other liabilities of a domestic merging limited partnership as provided in Section 121.

(f)   When a merger becomes effective, the registration to do business in this state of any foreign merging entity that is not the surviving entity is canceled.

[PART] 3.   INTEREST EXCHANGE

§ 1131.   Interest Exchange Authorized

(a)   By complying with this [part]:

(1)   a domestic limited partnership may acquire all of one or more classes or series of interests of another domestic entity or a foreign entity in exchange for interests, securities, obligations, money, other property, rights to acquire interests or securities, or any combination of the foregoing; or

(2)   all of one or more classes or series of interests of a domestic limited partnership may be acquired by another domestic entity or a foreign entity in exchange for interests, securities, obligations, money, other property, rights to acquire interests or securities, or any combination of the foregoing.

(b)   By complying with the provisions of this [part] applicable to foreign entities, a foreign entity may be the acquiring or acquired entity in an interest exchange under this [part] if the interest exchange is authorized by the law of the foreign entity's jurisdiction of formation.

(c)   If a protected agreement contains a provision that applies to a merger of a domestic limited partnership but does not refer to an interest exchange, the provision applies to an interest exchange in which the domestic limited partnership is the acquired entity as if the interest exchange were a merger until the provision is amended after [the effective date of this [act]].

§ 1132. Plan of Interest Exchange

(a)   A domestic limited partnership may be the acquired entity in an interest exchange under this [part] by approving a plan of interest exchange. The plan must be in a record and contain:

(1)   the name of the acquired entity;

(2)   the name, jurisdiction of formation, and type of entity of the acquiring entity;

(3)   the manner of converting the interests in the acquired entity into interests, securities, obligations, money, other property, rights to acquire interests or securities, or any combination of the foregoing;

(4)   any proposed amendments to:

(A)   the certificate of limited partnership of the acquired entity; and

(B)   the partnership agreement of the acquired entity that are, or are proposed to be, in a record;

(5)   the other terms and conditions of the interest exchange; and

(6)   any other provision required by the law of this state or the partnership agreement of the acquired entity.

(b)   In addition to the requirements of subsection (a), a plan of interest exchange may contain any other provision not prohibited by law.

§ 1133. Approval of Interest Exchange

(a)   A plan of interest exchange is not effective unless it has been approved:

(1)   by all the partners of a domestic acquired limited partnership entitled to vote on or consent to any matter; and

(2)   in a record, by each partner of the domestic acquired limited partnership that will have interest holder liability for debts, obligations, and other liabilities that are incurred_after the interest exchange becomes effective, unless:

(A)   the partnership agreement of the partnership provides in a record for the approval of an interest exchange or a merger in which some or all its partners become subject to interest holder liability by the affirmative vote or consent of fewer than all of the partners; and

(B)   the partner consented in a record to or voted for that provision of the partnership agreement or became a partner after the adoption of that provision.

(b)   An interest exchange involving a domestic acquired entity that is not a limited partnership is not effective unless it is approved by the domestic entity in accordance with its organic law.

(c)   An interest exchange involving a foreign acquired entity is not effective unless it is approved by the foreign entity in accordance with the law of the foreign entity's jurisdiction of formation.

(d)   Except as otherwise provided in its organic law or organic rules, the interest holders of the acquiring entity are not required to approve the interest exchange.

§ 1134. Amendment or Abandonment of Plan of Interest Exchange

(a)   A plan of interest exchange may be amended only with the consent of each party to the plan, except as otherwise provided in the plan.

(b)   A domestic acquired limited partnership may approve an amendment of a plan of interest exchange:

(1)   in the same manner as the plan was approved, if the plan does not provide for the manner in which it may be amended; or

(2)   by its partners in the manner provided in the plan, but a partner that was entitled to vote on or consent to approval of the interest exchange is entitled to vote on or consent to any amendment of the plan that will change:

(A)   the amount or kind of interests, securities, obligations, money, other property, rights to acquire interests or securities, or any combination of the foregoing, to be received by any of the partners of the acquired partnership under the plan;

(B)   the certificate of limited partnership or partnership agreement of the acquired partnership that will be in effect immediately after the interest exchange becomes effective, except for changes that do not require approval of the partners of the acquired partnership under this [act] or the partnership agreement; or

(C)   any other terms or conditions of the plan, if the change would adversely affect the partner in any material respect.

(c)   After a plan of interest exchange has been approved and before a statement of interest exchange becomes effective, the plan may be abandoned as provided in the plan. Unless prohibited by the plan, a domestic acquired limited partnership may abandon the plan in the same manner as the plan was approved.

(d)   If a plan of interest exchange is abandoned after a statement of interest exchange has been delivered to the [Secretary of State] for filing and before the statement becomes effective, a statement of abandonment, signed by the acquired limited partnership, must be delivered to the [Secretary of State] for filing before the statement of interest exchange becomes effective. The statement of abandonment takes effect on filing, and the interest exchange is abandoned and does not become effective. The statement of abandonment must contain:

(1)   the name of the acquired partnership;

(2)   the date on which the statement of interest exchange was filed by the [Secretary of State]; and

(3)   a statement that the interest exchange has been abandoned in accordance with this section.

§ 1135.   Statement of Interest Exchange; Effective Date of Interest Exchange

(a)   A statement of interest exchange must be signed by a domestic acquired limited partnership and delivered to the [Secretary of State] for filing.

(b)   A statement of interest exchange must contain:

(1)   the name of the acquired limited partnership;

(2)   the name, jurisdiction of formation, and type of entity of the acquiring entity;

(3)   a statement that the plan of interest exchange was approved by the acquired limited partnership in accordance with this [part]; and

(4)   any amendments to the acquired limited partnership's certificate of limited partnership approved as part of the plan of interest exchange.

(c)   In addition to the requirements of subsection (b), a statement of interest exchange may contain any other provision not prohibited by law.

(d)   A plan of interest exchange that is signed by a domestic acquired limited partnership and meets all the requirements of subsection (b) may be delivered to the [Secretary of State] for filing instead of a statement of interest exchange and on filing has the same effect. If a plan of interest exchange is filed as provided in this subsection, references in this [article] to a statement of interest exchange refer to the plan of interest exchange filed under this subsection.

(e) An interest exchange becomes effective when the statement of interest exchange is effective.

§ 1136. Effect of Interest Exchange

(a) When an interest exchange in which the acquired entity is a domestic limited partnership becomes effective:

(1) the interests in the acquired partnership which are the subject of the interest exchange are converted, and the partners holding those interests are entitled only to the rights provided to them under the plan of interest exchange and to any appraisal rights they have under Section 1106;

(2) the acquiring entity becomes the interest holder of the interests in the acquired partnership stated in the plan of interest exchange to be acquired by the acquiring entity;

(3) the certificate of limited partnership of the acquired partnership is amended to the extent provided in the statement of interest exchange; and

(4) the provisions of the partnership agreement of the acquired partnership that are to be in a record, if any, are amended to the extent provided in the plan of interest exchange.

(b) Except as otherwise provided in the certificate of limited partnership or partnership agreement of a domestic acquired limited partnership, the interest exchange does not give rise to any rights that a partner or third party would have upon a dissolution, liquidation, or winding up of the acquired partnership.

(c) When an interest exchange becomes effective, a person that did not have interest holder liability with respect to a domestic acquired limited partnership and becomes subject to interest holder liability with respect to a domestic entity as a result of the interest exchange has interest holder liability only to the extent provided by the organic law of the entity and only for those debts, obligations, and other liabilities that are incurred after the interest exchange becomes effective.

(d) When an interest exchange becomes effective, the interest holder liability of a person that ceases to hold an interest in a domestic acquired limited partnership with respect to which the person had interest holder liability is subject to the following rules:

(1) The interest exchange does not discharge any interest holder liability under this [act] to the extent the interest holder liability was incurred before the interest exchange became effective.

(2) The person does not have interest holder liability under this [act] for any debt, obligation, or other liability that is incurred after the interest exchange becomes effective.

(3) This [act] continues to apply to the release, collection, or discharge of any interest holder liability preserved under paragraph (1) as if the interest exchange had not occurred.

(4) The person has whatever rights of contribution from any other person as are provided by this [act], law other than this [act], or the partnership agreement of the domestic acquired partnership with respect to any interest holder liability preserved under paragraph (1) as if the interest exchange had not occurred.

[PART] 4. CONVERSION

§ 1141. Conversion Authorized

(a) By complying with this [part], a domestic limited partnership may become:

(1) a domestic entity that is a different type of entity; or

(2)   a foreign entity that is a different type of entity, if the conversion is authorized by the law of the foreign entity's jurisdiction of formation.

(b)   By complying with the provisions of this [part] applicable to foreign entities, a foreign entity that is not a foreign limited partnership may become a domestic limited partnership if the conversion is authorized by the law of the foreign entity's jurisdiction of formation.

(c)   If a protected agreement contains a provision that applies to a merger of a domestic limited partnership but does not refer to a conversion, the provision applies to a conversion of the partnership as if the conversion were a merger until the provision is amended after [the effective date of this [act]].

§ 1142.   Plan of Conversion

(a)   A domestic limited partnership may convert to a different type of entity under this [part] by approving a plan of conversion. The plan must be in a record and contain:

(1)   the name of the converting limited partnership;

(2)   the name, jurisdiction of formation, and type of entity of the converted entity;

(3)   the manner of converting the interests in the converting limited partnership into interests, securities, obligations, money, other property, rights to acquire interests or securities, or any combination of the foregoing;

(4)   the proposed public organic record of the converted entity if it will be a filing entity;

(5)   the full text of the private organic rules of the converted entity which are proposed to be in a record;

(6)   the other terms and conditions of the conversion; and

(7)   any other provision required by the law of this state or the partnership agreement of the converting limited partnership.

(b)   In addition to the requirements of subsection (a), a plan of conversion may contain any other provision not prohibited by law.

§ 1143.   Approval of Conversion

(a)   A plan of conversion is not effective unless it has been approved:

(1)   by a domestic converting limited partnership, by all the partners of the limited partnership entitled to vote on or consent to any matter; and

(2)   in a record, by each partner of a domestic converting limited partnership which will have interest holder liability for debts, obligations, and other liabilities that are incurred after the conversion becomes effective, unless:

(A)   the partnership agreement of the partnership provides in a record for the approval of a conversion or a merger in which some or all of its partners become subject to interest holder liability by the affirmative vote or consent of fewer than all the partners; and

(B)   the partner voted for or consented in a record to that provision of the partnership agreement or became a partner after the adoption of that provision.

(b)   A conversion involving a domestic converting entity that is not a limited partnership is not effective unless it is approved by the domestic converting entity in accordance with its organic law.

(c)   A conversion of a foreign converting entity is not effective unless it is approved by the foreign entity in accordance with the law of the foreign entity's jurisdiction of formation.

§ 1144.   Amendment or Abandonment of Plan of Conversion

(a)   A plan of conversion of a domestic converting limited partnership may be amended:

(1) in the same manner as the plan was approved, if the plan does not provide for the manner in which it may be amended; or

(2) by its partners in the manner provided in the plan, but a partner that was entitled to vote on or consent to approval of the conversion is entitled to vote on or consent to any amendment of the plan that will change:

(A) the amount or kind of interests, securities, obligations, money, other property, rights to acquire interests or securities, or any combination of the foregoing, to be received by any of the partners of the converting partnership under the plan;

(B) the public organic record, if any, or private organic rules of the converted entity which will be in effect immediately after the conversion becomes effective, except for changes that do not require approval of the interest holders of the converted entity under its organic law or organic rules; or

(C) any other terms or conditions of the plan, if the change would adversely affect the partner in any material respect.

(b) After a plan of conversion has been approved by a domestic converting limited partnership and before a statement of conversion becomes effective, the plan may be abandoned as provided in the plan. Unless prohibited by the plan, a domestic converting limited partnership may abandon the plan in the same manner as the plan was approved.

(c) If a plan of conversion is abandoned after a statement of conversion has been delivered to the [Secretary of State] for filing and before the statement becomes effective, a statement of abandonment, signed by the converting entity, must be delivered to the [Secretary of State] for filing before the statement of conversion becomes effective. The statement of abandonment takes effect on filing, and the conversion is abandoned and does not become effective. The statement of abandonment must contain:

(1) the name of the converting limited partnership;

(2) the date on which the statement of conversion was filed by the [Secretary of State]; and

(3) a statement that the conversion has been abandoned in accordance with this section.

§ 1145. Statement of Conversion; Effective Date of Conversion

(a) A statement of conversion must be signed by the converting entity and delivered to the [Secretary of State] for filing.

(b) A statement of conversion must contain:

(1) the name, jurisdiction of formation, and type of entity of the converting entity;

(2) the name, jurisdiction of formation, and type of entity of the converted entity;

(3) if the converting entity is a domestic limited partnership, a statement that the plan of conversion was approved in accordance with this [part] or, if the converting entity is a foreign entity, a statement that the conversion was approved by the foreign entity in accordance with the law of its jurisdiction of formation;

(4) if the converted entity is a domestic filing entity, its public organic record, as an attachment; and

(5) if the converted entity is a domestic limited liability partnership, its statement of qualification, as an attachment.

(c) In addition to the requirements of subsection (b), a statement of conversion may contain any other provision not prohibited by law.

(d)   If the converted entity is a domestic entity, its public organic record, if any, must satisfy the requirements of the law of this state, except that the public organic record does not need to be signed.

(e)   A plan of conversion that is signed by a domestic converting limited partnership and meets all the requirements of subsection (b) may be delivered to the [Secretary of State] for filing instead of a statement of conversion and on filing has the same effect. If a plan of conversion is filed as provided in this subsection, references in this [article] to a statement of conversion refer to the plan of conversion filed under this subsection.

(f)   If the converted entity is a domestic limited partnership, the conversion becomes effective when the statement of conversion is effective. In all other cases, the conversion becomes effective on the later of:

(1)   the date and time provided by the organic law of the converted entity; and

(2)   when the statement is effective.

§ 1146.   Effect of Conversion

(a)   When a conversion becomes effective:

(1)   the converted entity is:

(A)   organized under and subject to the organic law of the converted entity; and

(B)   the same entity without interruption as the converting entity;

(2)   all property of the converting entity continues to be vested in the converted entity without transfer, reversion, or impairment;

(3)   all debts, obligations, and other liabilities of the converting entity continue as debts, obligations, and other liabilities of the converted entity;

(4)   except as otherwise provided by law or the plan of conversion, all the rights, privileges, immunities, powers, and purposes of the converting entity remain in the converted entity;

(5)   the name of the converted entity may be substituted for the name of the converting entity in any pending action or proceeding;

(6)   the certificate of limited partnership of the converted entity becomes effective;

(7)   the provisions of the partnership agreement of the converted entity which are to be in a record, if any, approved as part of the plan of conversion become effective; and

(8)   the interests in the converting entity are converted, and the interest holders of the converting entity are entitled only to the rights provided to them under the plan of conversion and to any appraisal rights they have under Section 1106.

(b)   Except as otherwise provided in the partnership agreement of a domestic converting limited partnership, the conversion does not give rise to any rights that a partner or third party would have upon a dissolution, liquidation, or winding up of the converting entity.

(c)   When a conversion becomes effective, a person that did not have interest holder liability with respect to the converting entity and becomes subject to interest holder liability with respect to a domestic entity as a result of the conversion has interest holder liability only to the extent provided by the organic law of the entity and only for those debts, obligations, and other liabilities that are incurred after the conversion becomes effective.

(d)   When a conversion becomes effective, the interest holder liability of a person that ceases to hold an interest in a domestic converting limited partnership with respect to which the person had interest holder liability is subject to the following rules:

(1)   The conversion does not discharge any interest holder liability under this [act] to the extent the interest holder liability was incurred before the conversion became effective.

(2) The person does not have interest holder liability under this [act] for any debt, obligation, or other liability that is incurred after the conversion becomes effective.

(3) This [act] continues to apply to the release, collection, or discharge of any interest holder liability preserved under paragraph (1) as if the conversion had not occurred.

(4) The person has whatever rights of contribution from any other person as are provided by this [act], law other than this [act], or the organic rules of the converting entity with respect to any interest holder liability preserved under paragraph (1) as if the conversion had not occurred.

(e) When a conversion becomes effective, a foreign entity that is the converted entity may be served with process in this state for the collection and enforcement of any of its debts, obligations, and other liabilities as provided in Section 121.

(f) If the converting entity is a registered foreign entity, its registration to do business in this state is canceled when the conversion becomes effective.

(g) A conversion does not require the entity to wind up its affairs and does not constitute or cause the dissolution of the entity.

[PART] 5. DOMESTICATION

§ 1151. Domestication Authorized

(a) By complying with this [part], a domestic limited partnership may become a foreign limited partnership if the domestication is authorized by the law of the foreign jurisdiction.

(b) By complying with the provisions of this [part] applicable to foreign limited partnerships, a foreign limited partnership may become a domestic limited partnership if the domestication is authorized by the law of the foreign limited partnership's jurisdiction of formation.

(c) If a protected agreement contains a provision that applies to a merger of a domestic limited partnership but does not refer to a domestication, the provision applies to a domestication of the limited partnership as if the domestication were a merger until the provision is amended after [the effective date of this [act]].

§ 1152. Plan of Domestication

(a) A domestic limited partnership may become a foreign limited partnership in a domestication by approving a plan of domestication. The plan must be in a record and contain:

(1) the name of the domesticating limited partnership;

(2) the name and jurisdiction of formation of the domesticated limited partnership;

(3) the manner of converting the interests in the domesticating limited partnership into interests, securities, obligations, money, other property, rights to acquire interests or securities, or any combination of the foregoing;

(4) the proposed certificate of limited partnership of the domesticated limited partnership;

(5) the full text of the provisions of the partnership agreement of the domesticated limited partnership, that are proposed to be in a record;

(6) the other terms and conditions of the domestication; and

(7) any other provision required by the law of this state or the partnership agreement of the domesticating limited partnership.

(b) In addition to the requirements of subsection (a), a plan of domestication may contain any other provision not prohibited by law.

§ 1153.   Approval of Domestication

(a)   A plan of domestication of a domestic domesticating limited partnership is not effective unless it has been approved:

(1)   by all the partners entitled to vote on or consent to any matter; and

(2)   in a record, by each partner that will have interest holder liability for debts, obligations, and other liabilities that are incurred after the domestication becomes effective, unless:

(A)   the partnership agreement of the domesticating partnership in a record provides for the approval of a domestication or merger in which some or all of its partners become subject to interest holder liability by the affirmative vote or consent of fewer than all the partners; and

(B)   the partner voted for or consented in a record to that provision of the partnership agreement or became a partner after the adoption of that provision.

(b)   A domestication of a foreign domesticating limited partnership is not effective unless it is approved in accordance with the law of the foreign limited partnership's jurisdiction of formation.

§ 1154.   Amendment or Abandonment of Plan of Domestication

(a)   A plan of domestication of a domestic domesticating limited partnership may be amended:

(1)   in the same manner as the plan was approved, if the plan does not provide for the manner in which it may be amended; or

(2)   by its partners in the manner provided in the plan, but a partner that was entitled to vote on or consent to approval of the domestication is entitled to vote on or consent to any amendment of the plan that will change:

(A)   the amount or kind of interests, securities, obligations, money, other property, rights to acquire interests or securities, or any combination of the foregoing, to be received by any of the partners of the domesticating limited partnership under the plan;

(B)   the certificate of limited partnership or partnership agreement of the domesticated limited partnership that will be in effect immediately after the domestication becomes effective, except for changes that do not require approval of the partners of the domesticated limited partnership under its organic law or partnership agreement; or

(C)   any other terms or conditions of the plan, if the change would adversely affect the partner in any material respect.

(b)   After a plan of domestication has been approved by a domestic domesticating limited partnership and before a statement of domestication becomes effective, the plan may be abandoned as provided in the plan. Unless prohibited by the plan, a domestic domesticating limited partnership may abandon the plan in the same manner as the plan was approved.

(c)   If a plan of domestication is abandoned after a statement of domestication has been delivered to the [Secretary of State] for filing and before the statement becomes effective, a statement of abandonment, signed by the domesticating limited partnership, must be delivered to the [Secretary of State] for filing before the statement of domestication becomes effective. The statement of abandonment takes effect on filing, and the domestication is abandoned and does not become effective. The statement of abandonment must contain:

(1)   the name of the domesticating limited partnership;

(2)   the date on which the statement of domestication was filed by the [Secretary of State]; and

(3)   a statement that the domestication has been abandoned in accordance with this section.

§ 1155.   Statement of Domestication; Effective Date of Domestication

(a)   A statement of domestication must be signed by the domesticating limited partnership and delivered to the [Secretary of State] for filing.

(b)   A statement of domestication must contain:

(1)   the name and jurisdiction of formation of the domesticating limited partnership;

(2)   the name and jurisdiction of formation of the domesticated limited partnership;

(3)   if the domesticating limited partnership is a domestic limited partnership, a statement that the plan of domestication was approved in accordance with this [part] or, if the domesticating limited partnership is a foreign limited partnership, a statement that the domestication was approved in accordance with the law of its jurisdiction of formation; and

(4)   the certificate of limited partnership of the domesticated limited partnership, as an attachment.

(c)   In addition to the requirements of subsection (b), a statement of domestication may contain any other provision not prohibited by law.

(d)   The certificate of limited partnership of a domesticated domestic limited partnership must satisfy the requirements of this [act], but the certificate does not need to be signed.

(e)   A plan of domestication that is signed by a domesticating domestic limited partnership and meets all the requirements of subsection (b) may be delivered to the [Secretary of State] for filing instead of a statement of domestication and on filing has the same effect. If a plan of domestication is filed as provided in this subsection, references in this [article] to a statement of domestication refer to the plan of domestication filed under this subsection.

(f)   If the domesticated entity is a domestic limited partnership, the domestication becomes effective when the statement of domestication is effective. If the domesticated entity is a foreign limited partnership, the domestication becomes effective on the later of:

(1)   the date and time provided by the organic law of the domesticated entity; and

(2)   when the statement is effective.

§ 1156.   Effect of Domestication

(a)   When a domestication becomes effective:

(1)   the domesticated entity is:

(A)   organized under and subject to the organic law of the domesticated entity[;] and

(B)   the same entity without interruption as the domesticating entity;

(2)   all property of the domesticating entity continues to be vested in the domesticated entity without transfer, reversion, or impairment;

(3)   all debts, obligations, and other liabilities of the domesticating entity continue as debts, obligations, and other liabilities of the domesticated entity;

(4)   except as otherwise provided by law or the plan of domestication, all the rights, privileges, immunities, powers, and purposes of the domesticating entity remain in the domesticated entity;

(5)   the name of the domesticated entity may be substituted for the name of the domesticating entity in any pending action or proceeding;

(6)   the certificate of limited partnership of the domesticated entity becomes effective;

(7)   the provisions of the partnership agreement of the domesticated entity that are to be in a record, if any, approved as part of the plan of domestication become effective; and

(8)   the interests in the domesticating entity are converted to the extent and as approved in connection with the domestication, and the partners of the domesticating entity are entitled only to the rights provided to them under the plan of domestication and to any appraisal rights they have under Section 1106.

(b)   Except as otherwise provided in the organic law or partnership agreement of the domesticating limited partnership, the domestication does not give rise to any rights that an partner or third party would have upon a dissolution, liquidation, or winding up of the domesticating partnership.

(c)   When a domestication becomes effective, a person that did not have interest holder liability with respect to the domesticating limited partnership and becomes subject to interest holder liability with respect to a domestic limited partnership as a result of the domestication has interest holder liability only to the extent provided by this [act] and only for those debts, obligations, and other liabilities that are incurred after the domestication becomes effective.

(d)   When a domestication becomes effective, the interest holder liability of a person that ceases to hold an interest in a domestic domesticating limited partnership with respect to which the person had interest holder liability is subject to the following rules:

(1)   The domestication does not discharge any interest holder liability under this [act] to the extent the interest holder liability was incurred before the domestication became effective.

(2)   A person does not have interest holder liability under this [act] for any debt, obligation, or other liability that is incurred after the domestication becomes effective.

(3)   This [act] continues to apply to the release, collection, or discharge of any interest holder liability preserved under paragraph (1) as if the domestication had not occurred.

(4)   A person has whatever rights of contribution from any other person as are provided by this [act], law other than this [act], or the partnership agreement of the domestic domesticating limited partnership with respect to any interest holder liability preserved under paragraph (1) as if the domestication had not occurred.

(e)   When a domestication becomes effective, a foreign limited partnership that is the domesticated partnership may be served with process in this state for the collection and enforcement of any of its debts, obligations, and other liabilities as provided in Section 121.

(f)   If the domesticating limited partnership is a registered foreign entity, the registration of the partnership is canceled when the domestication becomes effective.

(g)   A domestication does not require a domestic domesticating limited partnership to wind up its affairs and does not constitute or cause the dissolution of the partnership.

[ARTICLE] 12.   MISCELLANEOUS PROVISIONS

§ 1201.   Uniformity of Application and Construction

In applying and construing this uniform act, consideration must be given to the need to promote uniformity of the law with respect to its subject matter among states that enact it.

§ 1202.   Relation to Electronic Signatures in Global and National Commerce Act

This [act] modifies, limits, and supersedes the Electronic Signatures in Global and National Commerce Act, 15 U.S.C. Section 7001 et seq., but does not modify, limit, or supersede Section 101(c) of that act, 15 U.S.C. Section 7001(c), or authorize electronic delivery of any of the notices described in Section 103(b) of that act, 15 U.S.C. Section 7003(b).

§ 1203. Savings Clause

This [act] does not affect an action commenced, proceeding brought, or right accrued before [the effective date of this [act]].

§ 1204. Severability Clause

If any provision of this [act] or its application to any person or circumstance is held invalid, the invalidity does not affect other provisions or applications of this [act] which can be given effect without the invalid provision or application, and to this end the provisions of this [act] are severable.]

Legislative Note: Include this section only if this state lacks a general severability statute or decision by the highest court of this state stating a general rule of severability.

§ 1205. Repeals

The following are repealed:

(1) [the state limited partnership act as [amended, and as] in effect immediately before [the effective date of this [act]].

(2) . . . .

(3) . . . .

§ 1206. Effective Date

This [act] takes effect. . . .

§ 1203. Standing Rules.

This [act] does not increase or not commence a proceeding brought or [suit] accrued before the effective date of this [act].

§ 120. Effect of Filing Clause.

(1) An amendment of this [act] or its application to any person or circumstance is held invalid, the invalidity does not affect other provisions or applications of this [act] which can be given effect without the invalid provision or application, and to this end the provisions of this [act] are severable.

(2) Nothing in this [act] modifies, limits, or supersedes [section] ... or affects the validity of ... ... that are subject to [section] ...

§ 120. Repeals.

The following are repealed:

(1) [the Uniform Limited Partnership Act as amended at the date of enactment of this [act]];

(2) ...

(3) ...

§ 120. Effective Date.

This [act] takes effect ...

H. PARTNERSHIP FORMS

1. GENERAL PARTNERSHIP AGREEMENT

———————

Table of Contents

———————

THIS GENERAL PARTNERSHIP AGREEMENT dated as of the _____ day of _____ [date], by and between _____ and _____.

WHEREAS, the parties hereto, on this date, have agreed to form a general partnership; and

WHEREAS, the parties hereto, by this writing, desire to define the relative rights, duties and liabilities of the Partners in connection with such partnership.

NOW, THEREFORE, in consideration of the premises and the mutual promises hereinafter contained, the Partners hereby associate themselves and agree to form and do form a general partnership pursuant to the provisions of the [State] Uniform Partnership Act as amended, and the rights and liabilities of the Partners shall be as provided and set forth herein except as herein otherwise expressly provided.

ARTICLE 1.   DEFINITIONS

1.1) *Definitions.* Unless the context otherwise requires, when used in this Agreement, the terms listed in this Section shall have the following meanings:

(a)   "Assignment" means any sale, pledge, transfer, gift or other disposition, whether voluntary or by operation of law.

(b)   "Code" means the Internal Revenue Code of 1986, as amended from time to time, or corresponding provisions of subsequent laws.

(c)   "Partnership" means the _____ Partnership.

(d)   "Partnership Accountants" means such firm of accountants as may be selected by the Partners to prepare and/or audit the books of account of the Partnership.

(e)   "Partnership Interest" means the interest in the Partnership acquired and owned by each Partner.

GENERAL PARTNERSHIP AGREEMENT

(f) "Person" means any individual, partnership, corporation, trust, joint venture or association.

(g) "Prime Rate of Interest" means the prime rate of interest announced from time to time by [Bank].

(h) "Property" means the real property in _____ County, [State] legally described on Exhibit A attached hereto, together with all buildings and improvements constructed or located on such real property, all fixtures located in such buildings or on such real estate, and all easements and rights benefitting or appurtenant to such buildings or real property, all of which is subject to a contract for deed.

ARTICLE 2.   NAME, OFFICE, AND TERM

2.1) *Name of Partnership.* The name of the Partnership shall be _____.

2.2) *Principal Place of Business.* The office and principal place of business of the Partnership shall be _____ or such other place as the Partners shall, from time to time, determine.

2.3) *Term.* This Partnership shall commence as of the date hereof and shall continue for 40 years, unless sooner dissolved pursuant to the provisions of this Agreement or by operation of law.

ARTICLE 3.   POWERS AND PURPOSES

3.1) *Purpose.* The business purpose of the Partnership shall be to own and manage the Property. The Partnership may conduct other business activities only as the Partners may agree from time to time.

3.2) *Power of the Partnership.* The Partnership shall have the power to do any and all things necessary or desirable in the conduct of such business to the same extent and as fully as a natural person doing business as a sole proprietor, including, but not limited to, the power to borrow such funds (and to secure same by mortgage, deed of trust, collateral or otherwise) and to enter into such contracts (including a contract for deed) and to execute such instruments as may be necessary or appropriate to accomplish its business purpose.

ARTICLE 4.   PARTNERS

4.1) *Partners.* The Partners of the Partnership shall be _____.

ARTICLE 5.   CONTRIBUTIONS

5.1) *Partnership Interests.* _____ and _____ shall each have a 50% interest in the capital, income, profits, and assets of the Partnership. Such percentage interest is the Partner's "Percentage Interest" in the Partnership. Any changes to the Partners' Percentage Interest shall be reflected in an amendment to this Agreement.

5.2) *Initial Capital Contributions.* _____ and _____ will make an initial contribution to the capital of the Partnership in consideration for their Partnership Interests of their rights, title and interest in the Property, which _____ and _____ hereby acknowledge is owned 50% by _____ and 50% by _____.

5.3) *Additional Contributions.* The Partners agree to make additional contributions to the Partnership as follows:

(a) *Required Contributions.* Each Partner agrees to make additional capital contributions to the Partnership so as to equally share the holding costs of the Property and the out-of-pocket administrative and operating expenses of the Partnership. All such additional contributions shall be in proportion to the Partners' Percentage Interests, and all such contributions which are not in proportion to the Partners' Percentage Interests shall be deemed a loan to the Partnership and shall be repaid by the Partnership as set forth in Section 5.7. Any Partner who does not make such additional contributions within 90 days after the mailing of written notice of demand by the Partner who made such contribution shall be personally indebted to the Partnership for the amount of additional contributions not made, plus interest from the date of demand at the rate set forth in Section 5.7, and plus and costs of collection, including attorneys' fees. The Partnership may exercise any and all remedies available to it at law or equity to enforce such obligation. Without limiting any other remedies available to the Partnership, the amount of such obligation, including interest and costs, may be offset by the Partnership against any amount payable to the defaulting Partner as a distribution or upon such Partner's separation from the Partnership.

(b) *Voluntary Contributions.* The Partners shall make such additional capital contributions to the Partnership as the Partners agree upon from time to time. All such additional contributions shall be in proportion to the Partners' Percentage Interests, and all such additional contributions which are not made in proportion to the Partners' Percentage Interests shall be deemed a loan to the Partnership and shall be repaid by the Partnership as set forth in Section 5.7.

5.4) *Capital Accounts.* A separate capital account shall be maintained for each Partner and shall consist of such Partner's initial capital contribution to the Partnership. Each Partner's capital account shall be increased by (i) such Partner's share of Partnership income which is credited to capital, if any, and (ii) such Partner's additional capital contributions to the Partnership, if any. Each Partner's capital account shall be reduced by (i) distributions in reduction of capital, and (ii) such Partner's share of Partnership losses which are charged to capital. Capital accounts shall be maintained at all times in the same proportions as the Partner's Percentage Interests. Revaluation of Partnership capital may be made from time to time appropriate to the maintenance of such proportions.

5.5) *No Interest on Capital Contribution.* No interest shall be paid on the capital contributions of the Partners or upon any undrawn profits of any Partner which are credited to such Partner's capital account.

5.6) *Withdrawal of Capital Contributions.* A Partner shall not be entitled to withdraw any part of its capital contribution or to receive repayment of such Partner's capital contribution or to receive any distribution from the Partnership except as specifically provided herein. All distributions from the Partnership to the Partners shall be made in proportion to the Partners' respective Percentage Interests. To the extent any distribution to or withdrawal by a Partner in the capacity as a Partner is not so made, it shall be deemed a loan which such Partner is obligated to repay on demand at such rate as set forth in Section 5.7.

5.7) *Loans to Partnership.* Subject to the approval of all the Partners, any Partner may make loans to the Partnership from time to time for Partnership business. No such loan shall be treated as a contribution to the capital of the Partnership for any purposes hereunder, nor entitle such Partner to any increase in such Partner's share of the net income and loss of and cash distributions from the Partnership. The Partnership shall be obligated to such Partner for the amount of any such loans together with interest at an annual rate equal to 2% over the Prime Rate of Interest. The principal and interest on any loans to the Partnership pursuant to this Section shall be repaid before any distributions or cash or property to the Partners. No Partner shall have any obligation to make any such loan to the Partnership.

ARTICLE 6.   RIGHTS, POWERS, AND OBLIGATIONS OF PARTNERS

6.1) *Management.* Except as otherwise specifically provided in this Agreement, all Partnership decisions shall be made by the agreement of all of the Partners, but nothing in this Agreement shall be construed to prohibit or limit the authority of any Partner to transact any business for the Partnership which has been so authorized. Each Partner's voice in management shall be proportionate to such Partner's Percentage Interest. The Partners (acting solely and exclusively as provided in this Article) shall manage the affairs of the Partnership in a prudent and businesslike fashion, and shall use their best efforts to carry out the purposes and character of the business of the Partnership. Each Partner shall devote such of its time as it deems necessary to the management of the business of the Partnership, to the extent such management is entrusted to such Partner under the terms of this

GENERAL PARTNERSHIP AGREEMENT

Section, and neither Partner shall be compensated for services to the Partnership, except to the extent specifically authorized by the Partners from time to time.

6.2) *Managing Partner.* Notwithstanding the provisions of Section 6.1 or any other provision in this Agreement, the Partners may elect a Managing Partner who shall have the authority and power to take the following actions relating to the day-to-day operations of the Partnership: (i) deposit all receipts received by or on behalf of the Partnership; (ii) pay expenses and other obligations of the Partnership incurred in the ordinary course of business; (iii) perform such other actions specifically directed in this Agreement; and (iv) perform such other actions as may be directed by the Partners from time to time. The Partners choose _____ as the initial Managing Partner.

6.3) *Dealings Between Partnership and Partners.* The Partnership may contract or otherwise deal with a Partner or any affiliate of a Partner including loans to the Partnership (secured or unsecured), or the purchase or sale of property or services. In any such transaction between the Partnership and a Partner or such Partner's affiliates, the agreement shall be in writing and approved by unanimous consent of the Partners, and compensation paid or promised shall be reasonable and compensation for goods or services shall be paid only for goods or services actually furnished.

6.4) *Responsibilities to Partnership.* The Partners may have other business interests and may engage in any similar or other business or trade, profession, or employment whatsoever, including business interests relating to the development, construction, sale, syndication, operation, and disposition of commercial real estate projects.

6.5) *Restrictions in Operations.* No Partner shall make or endorse any note for the Partnership, or procure money or incur any debt for the Partnership, nor discount, assign, sell, transfer or pledge any significant assets of the Partnership, except as authorized by both Partners.

6.6) *Execution of Documents.* Any deed, mortgage, bill of sale, lease, or other instrument purporting to convey or encumber assets of the Partnership in whole or in part, or any other instrument on behalf of the Partnership, shall be signed by both Partners on behalf of the Partnership except as otherwise agreed by the Partners.

6.7) *Admission of Additional Partners.* Additional persons may be admitted to the Partnership as additional or substituted Partners upon the agreement of the Partners at such time, for such contributions, and upon such other terms and conditions as they may agree.

6.8) *Meetings.* A meeting of the Partners may be called by either Partner upon giving any form of actual notice, orally or in writing. The presence of both Partners shall constitute a quorum at any meeting and waiver of notice.

ARTICLE 7.   ACCOUNTING, RECORDS, AND REPORTS

7.1) *Fiscal Year.* The Partnership's fiscal year for financial reporting and for federal income tax purposes shall be the calendar year.

7.2) *Records and Accounting.* At all times during the existence of the Partnership, the Managing Partner shall keep or cause to be kept books and records of accounts utilizing the method of accounting selected by the Partners for federal income tax purposes which shall be adequate and appropriate for the Partnership's business, and in which each transaction of the Partnership shall be entered fully and accurately. Such books of account shall include such separate and additional accounts for each Partner as shall be necessary to reflect accurately the rights and interests of the respective Partners and shall specifically reflect the name, address, and interest held by each Partner for the purpose of determining recipients of cash contributions, reports and notices. All such books and records shall be maintained at the above-described principal place of business of the Partnership.

7.3) *Bank Accounts.* The Partnership bank account, in the name of the Partnership, shall be maintained by the Partnership, and all Partnership monies received by the Partnership shall be deposited in said bank account and may be withdrawn by check signed by such persons as the Partners decide.

7.4) *Right of Inspection: Lists of Partners.* One copy of the books of account described in Section 7.2, together with a copy of this Agreement and other relevant agreements and any amendments thereto, and one copy of every document relating to the ownership of, and condition of title to, the Property shall at all times be maintained at the office of the Partnership, and each Partner or his duly authorized representatives shall have access to and the right to inspect and copy them during normal business hours.

7.5) *Reports to Partners.*

(a) *Annual Reports.* The Managing Partner shall cause to be prepared within 75 days after the close of each fiscal year a report containing an unaudited cash flow statement, and an operating statement reflecting income and disbursements.

(b) *Financial Statements—Review.* If requested by any Partner, but not more than once per year, the Partners shall cause reviewed financial statements of the Partnership to be prepared by the Partnership Accountants with an opinion expressed therein. Such review shall be performed at the Partnership's expense.

7.6) *Tax Returns.* The Managing partner shall prepare or cause to be prepared by the Partnership Accountants and shall file on or before the due date (or any extension thereof any federal, state or local tax returns required to be filed by the Partnership. The Partners shall cause the Partnership to pay any taxes payable by the Partnership. The Partners shall also prepare or cause to be prepared by such Partnership Accountants an unaudited statement of each Partner's share of the Partnership's income, gains, losses, deductions and credits for use in the preparation of such Partner's tax returns for such fiscal year, as well as an estimate of such Partner's share of the Partnership's taxable losses or gains for the succeeding fiscal year for use in the preparation of its declaration of estimated federal income tax. _____ shall be the Tax Matters Partner ("TMP") as defined in Code Section 6231(a)(7), for purposes of Code Sections 6221 to 6233; provided, _____ shall provide all of the Partners with any and all notices received from any taxing authorities and shall not respond to any such notices nor settle any tax dispute without the approval and consent of the Partners. The designation of _____ as TMP shall be made in the first Partnership tax return of the Partnership.

7.7) *Section 754 Election.* Upon receipt of the written request of a Partner, the successor-in-interest of a Partner, or of the executors, administrators or legal representatives of a Partner, the Partners shall file on behalf of the Partnership an election under Section 754 of the Code permitting an adjustment to basis under Sections 734 and 743 of the Code.

ARTICLE 8. ALLOCATIONS AND DISTRIBUTIONS

8.1) *Allocation of Income.* The Partners agree that, both for income tax purposes (except as otherwise specifically provided in this Article 3) and for financial purposes, net income or loss, and all items of income, gain or receipt, and all items of loss, deduction and credit of the Partnership shall be allocated between the Partners in accordance with the Partners' respective Percentage Interests.

8.2) *Tax Basis.* For income tax purposes, income, gain, loss and deduction with respect to property contributed to the Partnership by a Partner shall be shared among Partners so as to take account of the variation, if any, between the basis of the property to the Partnership and its fair market value at the time of contribution in the manner provided in Section 704(c) of the Code, as amended.

8.3) *Distributions of Cash.* The "Cash Of The Partnership Available For Distribution" as herein defined shall be distributed at least quarterly to the Partners (or assignees of Partnership Interests), in the same ratio as such Partners or assignees shared in the allocation of income or loss pursuant to Section 8.1 above. Subject to Section 5.7, the Cash Of The Partnership Available For Distribution shall be that cash received by the Partnership from all sources, including from any refinancing of the Property, less cash disbursements of every kind, and less such reserves for accrued expenses and working capital requirements as the Partners in their reasonable discretion may from time to time set aside. Notwithstanding the foregoing, liquidating distributions upon dissolution of the Partnership shall be made in accordance with Section 10.3 hereof. All distributions from the Partnership to the Partners shall be made in proportion to the Partners' Percentage Interests.

8.4) *Allocation Between Assignor and Assignee.* In the case of an effective Assignment by a Partner of part or all of its Partnership Interest during any fiscal year, the taxable income or loss allocable to such Partnership Interest in respect to such fiscal year shall be allocated between the assignor and the assignee in proportion to the number of months during such fiscal year that each was the holder of such Partnership Interest, determined by reference to the date the Assignment thereof became effective.

8.5) *Sharing Liabilities.* The Partners agree that any economic losses sustained by them as a result of their status as Partners of the Partnership, and any liabilities or damages they may suffer or incur as a result, except as shall result from the wrongful or unauthorized acts of a Partner, shall be shared between them in accordance with their Percentage Interests.

8.6) *General Compliance with Section 704(b).* The capital accounts being maintained for the Partners and the allocations of Partnership items in Section 8.1 are intended to comply with Section 704(b) of the Code and applicable Treasury Regulations promulgated thereunder. If the partners determine that the manner in which such accounts are being maintained or such allocations are being made need to be modified to comply with the requirements of Section 704(b) of the Code and the applicable Treasury Regulations, the Partners may alter the method of maintaining such accounts and making such allocations and, if necessary, amend the Agreement accordingly; provided, any alteration in the method of maintaining such accounts and making such allocations and any amendment to the Agreement shall not materially alter the economic agreement among the Partners.

ARTICLE 9. ASSIGNMENT OF PARTNERSHIP INTERESTS

9.1) *Prohibition of Voluntary Sale or Assignment.* Except as otherwise provided herein, during the term of the Partnership, no Partner shall voluntarily sell, assign, transfer, set over, mortgage, pledge, hypothecate, or otherwise dispose of such Partner's Partnership Interest, in whole or in part, in the Partnership without the express written consent of the other Partner. Consent may be withheld for any reason or for no reason at all. Consent may also be conditioned upon any factors which the Partners deem necessary or desirable. No purported assignment of a Partnership Interest in violation of this Section 9.1(a) shall be valid or effective, and the Partnership may refuse to recognize any such purported assignment for any purpose.

ARTICLE 10. SEPARATION, DISSOLUTION, AND LIQUIDATION

10.1) *Separation of a Partner with Continuation of the Partnership.*

(a) The following events are referred to as an "involuntary transfer" of a Partner's (the "Assigning Partner") Partnership Interest:

(i) Death of a Partner,

(ii) Bankruptcy or insolvency of a Partner, or

(iii) Other involuntary transfer or assignment of a Partner's interest in the Partnership, including a transfer through levy, garnishment or foreclosure sale.

In the event of an involuntary transfer of an Assigning Partner's Partnership Interest as described above, the Partnership shall not for that reason dissolve or terminate but shall continue on the same terms and conditions herein provided as an existing Partnership if the other Partner (the "Remaining Partner") continues the business of the otherwise dissolved Partnership pursuant to [State] Statutes. The transferee of the Assigning Partner's Partnership Interest, including a judgment creditor, representative of the estate or the heirs of the deceased Partner, or the trustee in bankruptcy or other representative of the bankrupt Partner, shall succeed to the Partnership Interest of the Assigning Partner, subject to all the liabilities and obligations of the Assigning Partner under this Agreement, and shall be deemed an assignee of the Partnership

GENERAL PARTNERSHIP AGREEMENT

Interest of such partner in accordance with the provisions of the Uniform Partnership Act, and shall have such power as the Assigning Partner possessed to assign such Partnership Interest. Except as provided below, such creditor, personal representative or trustee shall not have the right to be substituted as a Partner but shall be entitled, as though it were a Partner, to receive distributions of cash and to be credited or debited with allocations of income or loss in the manner provided herein and to receive reports, but shall have no other rights of a Partner, and the consent of such creditor, personal representative or trustee shall not be required to approve any action of the Partnership. Notwithstanding the foregoing, upon the death of the Assigning Partner, the personal representative or beneficiary of the Assigning Partner's Partnership Interest shall have an option to become a Partner of the Partnership by delivering written notice of such exercise to the Remaining Partner, and, if the option is so exercised, such personal representative or beneficiary shall become a Partner of the Partnership with all of the rights and obligations of a Partner. Upon the request of the Remaining Partner, such personal representative or beneficiary shall execute such documents as may be requested to reflect his or her status as a Partner, including documents evidencing the assumption of liability for Partnership obligations. If the Remaining Partner does not elect to continue the business of the Partnership, then the affairs of the Partnership shall be wound up and terminated as provided in Sections 10.4 through 10.7 hereof.

(b)   For purposes of _____'s existing bankruptcy case, the provisions of this Section 10.1 shall not become effective unless the case is converted to a case under Chapter 7 of the Bankruptcy Code or a Chapter 11 trustee is duly appointed by order of the Court.

10.2) *Events Resulting in a Wrongful Dissolution of the Partnership.* The Partnership shall be considered dissolved if any Partner (or assignee thereof) unilaterally (i) withdraws from the Partnership, or (ii) otherwise attempts to end such Partner's affiliation with the Partnership or terminates the Partnership (including seeking a judicial decree pursuant to [State statute]), excluding those events specifically addressed in Section 10.1. Any Partner (or assignee thereof) that causes one of the events described in clauses (i) or (ii) above to occur shall be considered to have retired from the Partnership (and is referred to herein as the "Retiring Partner") wrongfully and thereby caused the wrongful dissolution of the Partnership. In the event of such a dissolution, the other Partner (the "Remaining Partner") shall be solely entitled to continue the business of the Partnership. If the Remaining Partner elects to continue the business of the Partnership, the Remaining Partner shall execute an agreement agreeing to hold the Retiring Partner harmless from any liabilities of the Partnership. The Retiring Partner shall accept this hold-harmless agreement in full satisfaction of such Retiring Partner's Partnership Interest.

If the Remaining Partner does not elect to continue the business of the Partnership, then the affairs of the Partnership shall be wound up and the Partnership terminated as provided in Sections 10.4 through 10.7 hereof. Notwithstanding the preceding sentence, the amount to which the Retiring Partner is entitled upon winding-up and termination shall be reduced by any damages caused by the wrongful dissolution of the Partnership.

10.3) *Events Resulting in the Non-Wrongful Dissolution of the Partnership.* The Partnership shall be dissolved upon the happening of any of the following events:

(a)   The sale or other disposition of all of the assets of the Partnership, except in the case of an installment sale of all of the assets of the Partnership, in which event the Partnership shall continue until the final installment payment; or

(b)   The approval of all Partners; or

(c)   The occurrence of any event which makes it unlawful for the business of the Partnership to be carried on or for the Partners to do it in a Partnership.

In the event of a non-wrongful dissolution, the business of the Partnership shall be wound up and terminated as provided in Sections 10.4 and 10.7 below.

GENERAL PARTNERSHIP AGREEMENT

10.4) *Final Statements.* Upon dissolution of the Partnership pursuant to Section 10.3 (or Sections 10. 1 or 10.2 in the event the Remaining Partner does not elect to continue the business), and again upon the completion of liquidation, statements shall be prepared by the Partnership's Accountants and furnished to the Partners and assignees of Partnership Interests. The statements furnished upon dissolution shall list the assets and liabilities of the Partnership, and the statement furnished upon completion of liquidation shall describe the disposition of the assets, the payment of or provision for liabilities, and the application of any remaining cash.

10.5) *Liquidation.* Upon the dissolution of the Partnership pursuant to Section 10.3 (or Sections 10.1 or 10.2 in the event the Remaining Partner does not elect to continue the business), the Partners or the person required by law to wind up the Partnership's affairs shall reduce the assets of the Partnership to cash. The partners shall continue to share net income or losses during liquidation in accordance with Section 8.1. Proceeds shall be applied in the following order of priority, after taking into account all capital account adjustments for the Partnership's taxable year during which such liquidation occurs, unless a court of appropriate jurisdiction should rule otherwise:

(a) to the payment of liabilities and obligations of the Partnership (excluding liabilities and other obligations to the Partners) and the expenses of liquidation;

(b) to the establishment of such reserves as the partners or such person may reasonably deem necessary for any contingent liabilities and obligations of the Partnership for such period as the Partners or such person shall deem advisable for the purpose of disbursing the reserves in payment of such liabilities or obligations and, at the expiration of such period, the balance of such reserves, if any, shall be distributed as hereinafter provided;

(c) to the repayment of any loans or advances that may have been made by any of the Partners or any affiliates thereof to the Partnership;

(d) the balance of such proceeds, if any, shall be distributed to the Partners and assignees of Partnership Interests pro rata in accordance with their respective Percentage Interests.

10.6) *Distribution in Kind.* If it does not appear to be in the best interest of the Partners that certain Partnership assets be converted into cash, and if an equitable pro rate distribution can be made, Partnership assets may be distributed in kind upon the approval of all of the Partners.

10.7) *Distribution in Event of Dissolution.* A Partner shall not be entitled to demand or to receive any Partnership property other than cash, and such Partner shall not be entitled to any distribution in dissolution of the Partnership until all liabilities owed by such partner to the Partnership have been paid and until any unpaid contributions to the Partnership owing by such Partner have been contributed.

ARTICLE 11.   IMPLEMENTATION PROVISIONS

11.1) *Conveyance to Partnership.* Simultaneous with the execution of this Agreement, _____ shall quit claim the Property to the Partnership, subject to the contract for deed. The Partners shall respectively be solely responsible for correcting any title matter affecting the Property which were caused by the action or inaction of the respective Partners.

11.2) *State Deed Tax.* The Partners shall be equally responsible for any State Deed Tax or other transfer and recording fees in connection with the conveyance of the Property to the Partnership.

ARTICLE 12.   MISCELLANEOUS

12.1) *Amendments.* This Agreement may be amended only by a writing signed by all Partners.

12.2) *Binding Effect.* This Partnership Agreement shall bind and inure to the benefit of the parties hereto and their respective heirs, representatives, successors and assigns.

12.3) *Separability.* In the event of any conflict between a provision of this Agreement and any provision of the Uniform Partnership Act not subject to variation by this Agreement, the provisions of

GENERAL PARTNERSHIP AGREEMENT

the Uniform Partnership Act shall govern. If one or more of the provisions of this Agreement or any application thereof shall be invalid, illegal or unenforceable in any respect, the validity, legality and enforceability of the remaining provisions and any other application thereof shall in no way be affected or impaired.

12.4) *Counterparts.* This Agreement may be executed in counterparts, all of which taken together shall constitute a single Agreement, or by the execution of a separate agreement under the terms of which the person executing such separate agreement specifically undertakes to be bound by the terms, provisions and agreements of this Agreement.

12.5) *Applicable Law.* All questions relating to the execution, validity, performance and interpretation of this Partnership Agreement shall be governed by the laws of the State of [State].

12.6) *Notices.* All notices provided for herein shall be in writing and shall be sent by first-class prepaid registered or certified mail to the Partnership at the Partnership's principal office and to the Partners at their respective address or, with respect to any Partner, to such other address regarding which the Partnership have been notified in writing. Upon a written request sent to the Partnership's principal office, a complete list of all Partners' names and addresses will be furnished to any Partner. The initial address of _____ is as follows:

_____

_____

_____

with a copy to:

_____

_____

_____

_____

The initial address of _____ is as follows:

_____

_____

_____

with a copy to:

_____

_____

_____

IN WITNESS WHEREOF, the parties hereto have executed this _____ General Partnership Agreement effective as of the day and year first above written.

_____

_____

2. LIMITED PARTNERSHIP AGREEMENT

Table of Contents

Agreement of Limited Partnership of
[Name] Limited Partnership
A [State] Limited Partnership

THIS AGREEMENT OF LIMITED PARTNERSHIP is made as of the day of _____, [Year], by and between [Name], as General Partner, and [Name], [Name], and such other Limited Partners as may be added pursuant to the terms hereof as Limited Partners.

ARTICLE I.   GENERAL PROVISIONS INFORMATION FOR CERTIFICATE

1.1   Formation of the Partnership. The General Partner and the Limited Partners hereby agree to form a limited partnership under the Act. The General Partner shall from time to time execute or cause to be executed all such certificates and other documents, and do or cause to be done all such filings, recordings, publishings, and other acts as the General Partner may deem necessary or appropriate to comply with the requirements of law for the formation and operation of the Partnership in all jurisdictions in which the Partnership shall desire to conduct business. The Partnership shall at all times be governed by the Act.

1.2   Name of the Partnership. The name of the Partnership is [Name], or such other name as shall be selected from time to time by the General Partner upon written notice to the Limited Partners.

1.3   Purpose. The purpose of the Partnership shall be to [Describe].

1.4   Office of the Partnership. The office of the Partnership required by the Revised Uniform Limited Partnership Act § 104 (RULPA) shall be located at [Address], or such other place or places in the state of [State] as the General Partner may from time to time designate by notice to the Limited Partners. In addition, the Partnership may maintain such other offices as the General Partner deems advisable.

1.5   Term. As provided in the Act, the formation of the Partnership shall occur upon the filing of a Certificate in the office of the Secretary [of State]. The Partnership shall continue until [Date], unless sooner dissolved and terminated upon the occurrence of any of the following events:

(a) The passage of ninety (90) days after the dissolution, merger, death, withdrawal, or adjudication of incompetency or bankruptcy of the last remaining General Partner, unless all of the Limited Partners consent in writing to continue the business of the Partnership pursuant to § 7.1;

(b) The sale, transfer, or other disposition of all or substantially all of the Partnership's assets as permitted by this Agreement; or

(c) The vote of the Majority of the Limited Partners to dissolve the Partnership;

provided, however, the Partnership shall not dissolve upon the dissolution, merger, withdrawal, death, or adjudication of incompetency or bankruptcy of less than all of the General Partners. The remaining General Partner hereby expressly agrees to continue the Partnership.

1.6 General Partner. The name and place of business of the General Partner is as follows: [*Describe*].

1.7 Amendment to Certificate of Limited Partnership. The General Partner shall cause an amendment to the Certificate to be filed in the office of the Secretary whenever the name of the Partnership is changed, the street address of the office of the Partnership required by RULPA § 104 is changed, the name or address of the General Partner is changed, an additional general partner is admitted to the Partnership, the address or name of the agent for service of process is changed, business is continued under RULPA § 801 after an event of withdrawal of a general partner, the date upon which the Partnership is to dissolve is changed, or a false or erroneous material statement has been discovered in the Certificate or any amendment thereto. The General Partner shall cause any amendment to the Certificate to be filed in the office of the Secretary. In addition, the General Partner shall take any other action that may be required or advisable to maintain the Partnership as a limited partnership existing under the Act.

1.8 Agent for Service of Process. The name and address of the agent for service of process of the Partnership shall be: [*Name, Address*].

ARTICLE II. DEFINITIONS

Unless otherwise expressly provided herein or unless the context otherwise requires, the terms with initial capital letters in this Partnership Agreement shall be defined as follows:

2.1 "Act" shall mean the [*State*] Revised Uniform Limited Partnership Act, codified at _____.

2.2 "Adjusted Capital Contribution" shall mean, with respect to each Partner as of a given date, such Partner's Capital Contribution pursuant to §§ 3.1 or 3.2 reduced by all Distributions made to such Partner or predecessor pursuant to § 4.1.1(a) and (b) prior to such date.

2.3 "Affiliate" shall mean any person or entity that directly, or indirectly through one or more intermediaries, controls or is controlled by, or is under common control with another person or entity.

2.4 "Agreement" shall mean this Agreement of Limited Partnership.

2.5 "Capital Account" shall mean the capital account to be maintained for each of the General Partners and each of the Limited Partners, which:

(a) Shall be increased by:

(1) The amount of money actually or deemed contributed by such Partner to the Partnership;

(2) The fair market value of the property contributed by such Partner to the Partnership (net of liabilities securing such contributed property that the Partnership is considered to assume or take subject to under IRC § 752); and

(3)   Allocations to such Partner of Partnership income and gain (or items thereof), including income and gain exempt from tax and income and gain described in Treasury Reg. § 1.704–1(b)(2)(iv)(g), but excluding income and gain described in Reg. § 1.704–1(b)(4)(i); and

(b)   Shall be decreased by:

(1)   The amount of money distributed to such Partner by the Partnership;

(2)   The fair market value of property distributed to such Partner by the Partnership (net of liabilities securing such distributed property that such Partner is considered to assume or take subject to under IRC § 752);

(3)   Allocations to such Partner of expenditures of partnerships of the type described in IRC § 705(a)(2)(B); and

(4)   Allocations of Partnership loss and deduction (or item thereof), including loss and deduction described in Reg. § 1.704–1(b)(2)(iv)(g), but excluding items described in (b)(3) above and loss or deduction described in Reg. § 1.704–1(b)(4)(i) or (iii); and

(c)   Shall be otherwise adjusted in accordance with the additional rules set forth in Reg. § 1.704–1(b)(2)(iv). For purposes of this Agreement, a Partner who has more than one interest in the Partnership shall have a single Capital Account that reflects all such interests, regardless of the class of interests owned by such Partner (*e.g.*, general or limited) and regardless of the time or manner in which such interests were acquired. It is the intent of the Partnership that the Capital Accounts of all Partners be determined and maintained in accordance with the principles of Reg. § 1.704–1(b) at all times throughout the full term of the Partnership.

2.6 **"Capital Contribution"** shall mean, with respect to each Partner, the amount contributed by such Partner to the capital of the Partnership as described in §§ 3.1 or 3.2.

2.7 **"Certificate"** shall mean the certificate of limited partnership and any amendment thereto described in § 1.7.

2.8 **"Code"** shall mean the Internal Revenue Code of 2002, as amended, or any corresponding provisions of succeeding law.

2.9 **"Distributable Cash"** shall mean, with respect to any fiscal period, all cash receipts received by the Partnership from operations in the ordinary course of business including, without limitation, income from invested Reserves, but after deducting Operating Cash Expenses, debt service, commitment fees, loan broker fees, and other payments made in connection with any loan to the Partnership or other loan secured by a lien on Partnership assets, capital expenditures of the Partnership, and amounts set aside for the creation or addition to Reserves. Distributable Cash does not include Capital Contributions.

2.10 **"Distributions"** shall refer to cash or to other property, from any source, distributed to the Limited Partners and the General Partners by the Partnership, but shall not include any payments to the General Partners made under the provisions of §§ 5.2 or 5.3.

2.11 **"General Partner"** shall mean [*Name*] or any other Person who may become a substitute or additional General Partner and who is elected or admitted hereto as a General Partner pursuant to the terms of this Agreement. Reference to a General Partner shall be to any one of the General Partners.

2.12 **"Interest"** shall mean the entire ownership interest of a Partner in the Partnership at a particular time, including the right of such Partner to any and all benefits to which a Partner may be entitled as provided in this Agreement, together with the obligations of such Partner to comply with all the terms and provisions of this Agreement.

2.13 **"Limited Partner"** shall refer to any Person who is admitted to the Partnership as a limited partner. Reference to a "Limited Partner" shall be to any one of the Limited Partners.

LIMITED PARTNERSHIP AGREEMENT

2.14 "Majority of the Limited Partners" shall mean the vote of Limited Partners who own, in the aggregate, more than 50% of the total outstanding Limited Partners' Interests. Each Limited Partner shall have a number of votes equal to the percentage described in § 4.2(c)(3).

2.15 "Operating Cash Expenses" shall mean, with respect to any fiscal period, the amount of cash disbursed in the ordinary course of operations of the Partnership during such period, including, without limitation, all cash expenses, such as legal and accounting fees, insurance premiums, taxes, and repair and maintenance expenses. Operating Cash Expenses shall not include expenditures paid out of Reserves.

2.16 "Partners" shall refer collectively to the General Partners and the Limited Partners, and reference to a "Partner" shall be to any one of the Partners.

2.17 "Partnership" shall refer to [*Name*], the partnership governed by this Agreement.

2.18 "Person" shall mean any individual, partnership, corporation, trust, or other entity.

2.19 "Refinancing" shall mean any refinancing or borrowing by the Partnership, secured by the Partnership's assets other than borrowings in the approximate amount of [*Dollars*] initially made to finance the Partnership.

2.20 "Reserves" shall mean, with respect to any fiscal period, funds set aside or amounts allocated during such period to reserves which may be maintained by the Partnership for working capital and to pay taxes, insurance, debt service, or other costs or expenses of the Partnership.

2.21 "Sale" means any transaction (other than the receipt of Capital Contributions) of the Partnership not in the ordinary course of business, including, without limitation, sales (including condemnations), exchanges, or other dispositions of real or personal property, recoveries of damage awards, and insurance proceeds (other than business interruption insurance proceeds), but excluding any Refinancing.

2.22 "Sale or Refinancing Proceeds," "Sale Proceeds," or **"Refinancing Proceeds"** as the context requires, means all cash receipts of the Partnership arising from a Sale or Refinancing, less the following:

(a) The amount necessary for the payment of all debts and obligations of the Partnership related to the particular Sale or Refinancing;

(b) The amount appropriate to provide Reserves to pay taxes, insurance, debt service, repairs, replacements or renewals, or other costs or expenses of the Partnership (including costs of improvements or additions in connection with the property).

2.23 "Substituted Limited Partner" shall mean the entity or individual to whom a Limited Partner has transferred all or a portion of its Interest under Article VII.

2.24 "Terminated Partner" means any General Partner who dies, becomes legally incapacitated, dissolves, is removed, or becomes bankrupt, and any Limited Partner who withdraws under the provisions of § 7.7.

2.25 "Treasury Regulations" shall mean the Regulations promulgated under the Code, as amended, including corresponding provisions of succeeding Regulations.

ARTICLE III.   CAPITAL CONTRIBUTIONS

3.1 Limited Partners. The Limited Partners have made Capital Contributions to the Partnership in the following amounts:

_____   _____   _____

_____   _____   _____

Receipt of such Capital Contributions is hereby acknowledged. No Limited Partner shall be required to make any additional Capital Contributions to the Partnership.

3.2 General Partner.

(a) *Initial Capital Contribution.* The General Partner has made a Capital Contribution to the Partnership in the amount of [*Dollars*].

(b) *Additional Capital Contributions.* The General Partner shall contribute in cash to the Partnership any amounts necessary or appropriate for the Partnership to pay, when due, any costs, expenses, or liabilities of the Partnership to the extent such costs or expenses are in excess of the cash receipts of the Partnership.

3.3 Interest. No Partner shall be entitled to receive interest on its Capital Contribution or Capital Account balance.

ARTICLE IV. ALLOCATION OF DISTRIBUTIONS, INCOME, LOSSES, AND OTHER ITEMS AMONG THE PARTNERS

4.1 Distributions to the Partners.

4.1.1 Cash Distributions.

(a) *From Operations.* Distributable Cash will be paid to the Partners in accordance with the percentage specified in § 4.2(c).

(b) *From Certain Sales or Refinancing Proceeds.* Distributions of Sale or Refinancing Proceeds other than in liquidation or Sale of all or substantially all Partnership property shall be made to the Partners in accordance with the following:

(i)   First, to the Partners in accordance with their Adjusted Capital Contributions.

(ii)   Second, to the Partners in accordance with the percentage specified in § 4.2(c).

(c) *In Liquidation.* Notwithstanding § 4.1.1(a) or (b), Distributions in liquidation of the Partnership and Sale Proceeds from the Sale of all or substantially all Partnership property shall be made to each Partner in the ratio that the positive Capital Account of each Partner, after adjustment for income or loss recognized by the Partnership in connection with such Sale and/or liquidation, bears to the sum of the positive Capital Accounts of all Partners (after such adjustment).

4.1.2 Distributions in Kind. Non-cash assets, if any, shall be distributed in a manner that reflects how cash proceeds from the Sale of such assets for fair market value would have been distributed (after any unrealized gain or loss attributable to such non-cash assets has been allocated among the Partners in accordance with § 4.2).

4.1.3 Deficit Balance. In the event of such Sale referred to in § 4.1.1(b) or of a liquidation as defined in Reg. § 1.704–1(b)(2)(ii)(g), the General Partner shall be required to contribute to the capital of the Partnership within the time period specified in § 4.1.4(b) an amount equal to the total of the negative balance in the General Partner's Capital Account, if any.

4.1.4 Timing.

(a)   The General Partner will make Distributions (other than Distributions in liquidation) for a calendar quarter, if any, within [*Number*] days of the end of such quarter to Partners of record as of that date, and such Distributions shall be deemed made as of the last day of such calendar quarter for all purposes. Distributions will be made without regard to Capital Accounts (except for Distributions pursuant to § 4.1.1(c)) or the number of days during the quarter that a person is a Partner.

(b)   The time and method of distributions described in § 4.1.1(c) and the deficit balance payment described in § 4.1.3 shall comply with Reg. § 1.704–1(b) or, as necessary, with any similar Regulations promulgated in the future, or if no such regulations apply, as soon as possible.

4.2 Allocation of Income and Losses.

LIMITED PARTNERSHIP AGREEMENT

(a) *Allocation of Income.* Except as provided in § 4.2(c), income and income exempt from federal income tax for each fiscal year of the Partnership shall be allocated as follows:

(i)   General Partner _____ %

(ii) Limited Partners _____ %

_____ %

(b) *Allocation of Losses.* Except as set forth in § 4.2(c) below, losses and expenditures not deductible in computing federal income tax for each fiscal year of the Partnership shall be allocated as follows:

(i)   General Partner _____ %

(ii) Limited Partners _____ %

_____ %

provided, however, in no event shall losses be allocated to any Limited Partner in an amount that would cause any deficit to his or her Capital Account to exceed zero. Any such losses shall be allocated to the General Partner.

(c) *Allocation of Gain on Sale or Disposition of Partnership Property.* Notwithstanding § 4.2(a), the gain from the Sale or disposition of all or substantially all of the property of the Partnership as computed for federal income tax purposes shall be allocated in the following manner and priority:

(1)   If any Partners have a deficit in their Capital Accounts, the gain shall be allocated among such Partners in the proportion which such deficits bear to each other until no Partner has a deficit in its Capital Account;

(2)   Second, to the Partners until the sum of the positive balance in each Partner's Capital Account equals the Adjusted Capital Contribution of such Partner;

(3)   Thereafter, to the Partners in accordance with the percentages specified below:

(i)   General Partner _____ %

(ii) Limited Partners _____ %

_____ %

(d) *Qualified Income Offset.* Notwithstanding anything contained herein to the contrary, if a Limited Partner unexpectedly receives an adjustment, allocation, or distribution described in Reg. § 1.704–1(b)(2)(ii)(d)(4), (5), and (6) that reduces its Capital Account balance below zero (computed after making all Capital Account adjustments for such fiscal year, debiting, as of the end of such fiscal year, adjustments, allocations, and distributions described in such clauses (4), (5) and (6) and crediting any amounts such Partner is obligated to restore or is deemed to be obligated to restore pursuant to the penultimate sentence of Reg. § 1.704–1(b)(4)(iv)(f)), then income of the Partnership shall be first allocated to such Limited Partners with deficit Capital Account balances in an amount and manner sufficient to eliminate such deficit balances as quickly as possible. This provision is intended to comply with Reg. § 1.704–1(b)(2)(ii) and shall be so interpreted and applied. Any allocation of income or gain pursuant to this § 4.2(d) shall be taken into account in computing subsequent allocations of income or gain pursuant to Article IV so that the net amount of income and gain allocated to the Partners, to the extent possible, equals the amounts that would have been allocated if no allocations under § 4.2(d) had occurred.

4.3 Determination of Income; Adjustments.

4.3.1 Computation of Income and Loss. The income and loss of the Partnership shall be determined at the end of each fiscal year of the Partnership and at such other time as the General

Partner shall determine. Except as provided in § 4.3.2, the income and loss of the Partnership shall be determined and calculated in accordance with federal income tax rules and principles.

4.3.2 Adjustments to Income and Loss. For purposes of computing income or loss on the disposition of a Partnership asset or for purposes of determining the cost recovery, depreciation, or amortization deduction with respect to any asset, the Partnership shall use such asset's book value determined in accordance with Reg. § 1.704–1(b). Consequently, each asset's book value shall be equal to its adjusted basis for federal income tax purposes except as follows:

(a) The initial book value of any asset contributed by a Partner to the Partnership shall be the gross fair market value of such asset;

(b) The book value of all Partnership assets shall be adjusted to equal their respective gross fair market values, as determined by the General Partner as of the following times: (1) the acquisition of an additional Interest in the Partnership by new or existing Partner in exchange for more than a *de minimis* capital contribution; (2) the distributions by the Partnership to a Partner of more than a *de minimis* amount of the Partnership property other than money; (3) the termination of the Partnership for federal income tax purposes pursuant to the IRC § 708(b)(1)(B); and (4) the liquidation of any Partner's Interest in the Partnership;

(c) If the book value of an asset has been determined pursuant to this § 4.3, such book value shall thereafter be used, and shall thereafter be adjusted by depreciation or amortization, if any, taken into account with respect to such asset, for purposes of computing income or loss.

4.4 Tax Allocations: IRC § 704(c). In accordance with IRC § 704(c) and the Treasury Regulations thereunder, income, gain, loss, and deduction with respect to any property contributed to the capital of the Partnership shall, solely for tax purposes, be allocated among the Partners so as to take account of any variation between the adjusted basis of such property to the Partnership for federal income tax purposes and its initial book value computed in accordance with § 4.3.2(a).

In the event the book value of any Partnership property is adjusted pursuant to § 4.3.2(b), subsequent allocations of income, gain, loss, and deduction with respect to such asset shall take account of any variation between the adjusted basis of such asset for federal income tax purposes and its book value in the same manner as IRC § 704(c) and the Treasury Regulations thereunder.

Subject to the restrictions set forth in § 9.5 below, any elections or other decisions relating to such allocations shall be made by the General Partner in any manner that reasonably reflects the purpose and intention of this Agreement. Allocations pursuant to this § 4.4 are solely for purposes of federal, state, and local taxes and shall not affect, or in any way be taken into account in computing, any Partner's Capital Account or share of income or loss, or distributions pursuant to any provision of this Agreement.

4.5 Allocation Between Assignor and Assignee. The portion of the income or losses of the Partnership for any fiscal year of the Partnership during which an Interest is assigned by a Partner (or by an Assignee or successor in Interest to a Partner), that is allocable with respect to such Interest, shall be apportioned between the assignor and the assignee of the Interest on the basis of actual performance of the Partnership during the months of the fiscal year that each is the owner thereof. The Partnership shall determine the portion of its income or loss attributable to each half-month of the fiscal year using a half-month convention and employing a reasonable interim closing of the books method.

ARTICLE V.   RIGHTS AND DUTIES OF THE GENERAL PARTNER

5.1 Management and Control. The General Partner shall have exclusive management and control of the business of the Partnership, and all decisions regarding the management and affairs of the Partnership shall be made by the General Partner. The General Partner shall have all the rights and powers of a general partner as provided in the Act and as otherwise provided by law. The signature or other action of the General Partner acting as such shall be the signature or other action of the

LIMITED PARTNERSHIP AGREEMENT

Partnership. Except as otherwise expressly provided in this Agreement, the General Partner is hereby granted the right, power, and authority to do on behalf of the Partnership all things which, in its sole judgment, are necessary, proper, or desirable to carry out the aforementioned duties and responsibilities, including but not limited to the right, power, and authority from time to time to do those things specified elsewhere in this Agreement and the following:

(a) To spend the capital and revenues of the Partnership in the furtherance of the business of the Partnership;

(b) To acquire, improve, manage, charter, operate, sell, transfer, exchange, encumber, pledge, and dispose of any real or personal property of the Partnership;

(c) To cause the Partnership to reimburse the General Partner for reasonable out-of-pocket expenses actually incurred by the General Partner in connection with the Partnership's business, including, but not limited to, any expense incurred in the organization of the Partnership or in connection with the offer and/or sale of Interests;

(d) Employ and dismiss from employment any and all employees, agents, independent contractors, attorneys, and accountants, including Affiliates of the General Partner;

(e) To enter into such agreements, contracts, and similar arrangements as the General Partner deems necessary or appropriate to accomplish the purposes of the Partnership;

(f) To borrow money on a secured or unsecured basis from individuals, banks, and other lending institutions in order to finance or refinance Partnership assets, to meet other Partnership obligations, to provide Partnership working capital, and for any other Partnership purpose; to execute promissory notes, deeds of trust, and assignments of Partnership property and such other security instruments as a lender of funds may require to secure repayment of such borrowing; to change, substitute, or amend such borrowing as, in its judgment, is in the best interest of the Partnership, and to execute any and all documents which may be required by the bank or other financial institution or other source to establish an escrow, trust agreement, or trust account with the bank, institution, or other source for the receipt of funds, sale proceeds, and other payments and the disbursements thereof to service such loan(s);

(g) To borrow monies from the General Partner or any Affiliate of the General Partner, for use by the Partnership in its operations, the aggregate amount of which shall become an obligation of the Partnership to the General Partner or such Affiliate, and shall be repaid with interest (at an annual rate not to exceed [Percent], not to exceed maximum rates under applicable usury laws) to the General Partner or such Affiliate out of gross receipts of the Partnership before any cash distributions to the Partners, with no prepayment charge or penalty permitted on such a loan, and such amounts shall constitute a loan by the General Partner or the Affiliate to the Partnership and not a Capital Contribution;

(h) To lend monies to any [person/Affiliate of the Partnership/General Partner/Affiliate of a General Partner] for [any purpose(s) related to the Partnership's operations and investments] upon any terms and conditions, provided that the same shall:

(1) As to loans secured by first liens on real estate and fixtures, not be (i) for an amount in excess of [Percent] of fair market value; (ii) based on a rate less than the then Applicable Federal Rate; or (iii) for a period of longer than [Number] years.

(2) As to loans secured by tangible personal property and accounts receivable less than [Number] days overdue, not be (i) for an amount in excess of [Percent] of fair market value; (ii) based on a rate less than the then Applicable Federal Rate; or (iii) for a period of longer than [Number] years.

(3) As to other loans, not be

(i) for an amount in excess of [Percent] of fair market value;

(ii) based on a rate less than the then Applicable Federal Rate; or

(iii) for a period of longer than [*Number*] years.

(i)   To purchase at the expense of the Partnership such liability, casualty, property, and other insurance as the General Partner in its sole discretion deems advisable to protect the partnership's assets against loss or claims of any nature; provided however, the General Partner shall not be liable to the Partnership or to other Partners for failure to purchase any insurance or if coverage should prove inadequate;

(j)   To the extent that funds of the Partnership are, in the General Partner's judgment, not required for the conduct of the Partnership's business, temporarily invest the excess funds in the manner set forth in § 10.2;

(k)   Sue and be sued, complain, defend, settle, or compromise with respect to any claim in favor of or against the Partnership, in the name and on behalf of the Partnership;

(*l*)   Prosecute and protect and defend or cause to be protected and defended all patents, patent rights, trade names, trademarks, and service marks, and all applications with respect thereto that may be held by the Partnership;

(m)   Enter into, execute, amend, supplement, acknowledge, and deliver any and all contracts, agreements, licenses, or other instruments necessary, proper, or desirable to carry out the purposes of the Partnership; and

(n)   Determine that any cash receipts of the Partnership shall be added to Distributable Cash.

5.2 Compensation; Reimbursement. The General Partner shall receive [*Describe*] compensation for performing its duties as General Partner under this Agreement. This provision shall not affect the General Partner's rights to receive its share of Distribution of Partnership funds as set forth in Article IV or § 8.3, or to receive reimbursement for amounts expended as set forth in § 5.1(c), or to receive compensation or other payments pursuant to contracts entered into as provided in § 5.3.

5.3 Contracts With the General Partner or Its Affiliates.

5.3.1 Contracts. Subject to the conditions set forth in § 5.3.2, the General Partner may, on behalf of the Partnership, enter into contracts with itself or any of the General Partner's Affiliates.

5.3.2 Conditions. Any agreements, contracts, and arrangements between the Partnership and the General Partner or any of its Affiliates whereby the General Partner or its Affiliates shall loan money or render any services to or from the Partnership or sell or lease goods to or from the Partnership, other than those described in the Offering Memorandum, shall be subject to the following conditions:

(a)   The compensation, price, or fee paid to the General Partner or any such Affiliate must be comparable and competitive with the compensation, price, or fee of any other Person who is rendering comparable services or selling or leasing comparable goods or borrowing or lending money which could reasonably be made available to the Partnership and shall be on competitive terms;

(b)   Any such agreements, contracts, and arrangements shall be embodied in a written contract which describes the subject matter thereof and all compensation to be paid therefor; and

(c)   Any such agreements, contracts, and arrangements must be approved by a majority vote of the Limited Partners.

5.3.3 Financing. The General Partner or its Affiliates may purchase property in its own name, and assume loans in connection therewith, and hold title thereto for the purpose of facilitating the acquisition of such property or the borrowing of money or obtaining financing for the Partnership if purchased for the Partnership for a price no greater than the cost of such property to the General Partner or such Affiliate, and provided there is no difference in the interest rates on the loans secured by the property at the time acquired by the General Partner or such Affiliate and the time acquired by the Partnership, nor any other benefit arising out of such transaction to the General Partner or such Affiliate apart from compensation otherwise permitted by this Agreement.

5.3.4 Validity. The validity of any transaction, agreement, or payment involving the Partnership and the General Partner or any Affiliate of the General Partner otherwise permitted by the terms of this Agreement shall not be affected by reason of the relationship between the Partnership and the General Partner or such Affiliate of the General Partner.

5.4 Right of Public to Rely on Authority of General Partner. Any person dealing with the Partnership or the General Partner may rely upon a certificate signed by the General Partner as to (a) the identity of any General Partner or Limited Partner hereof; (b) the existence or nonexistence of any fact or facts which constitute a condition precedent to acts by the General Partner or in any other manner germane to the affairs of the Partnership; (c) the persons who are authorized to execute and deliver any instrument or document of the Partnership; or (d) any act or failure to act by the Partnership or as to any other matter whatsoever involving the Partnership or any Partner.

5.5 Obligations of the General Partner. The General Partner shall:

(a) Devote to the Partnership and apply to the accomplishment of Partnership purposes so much of its time and attention as in its judgment is reasonably necessary to manage properly the affairs of the Partnership; *provided, however,* the General Partner is at all times specifically permitted to engage in any other business ventures and activities including such activities as may be deemed to be in competition with the Partnership and any conflict of interest which may result shall be resolved by the General Partner using its best business judgment;

(b) Cause the Partnership to have workmen's compensation, employer's liability, public liability, and property damage insurance in amounts required by law or believed by the General Partner to be adequate, whichever is greater;

(c) Maintain a Capital Account for each Partner;

(d) Cause the Partnership to carry out the obligations of the Partnership;

(e) Keep or cause to be kept the books and records required by § 9.1; and

(f) Prepare and deliver or cause to be prepared and delivered the reports required by §§ 9.2 and 9.3.

5.6 Good Faith. The General Partner shall manage and control the affairs of the Partnership to the best of its ability, and the General Partner shall use its best efforts to carry out the purposes of the Partnership for the benefit of all the Partners. In exercising its powers, the General Partner recognizes its fiduciary responsibilities to the Partnership. The General Partner shall have fiduciary responsibility for the safekeeping and use of all funds and assets of the Partnership, whether or not in its immediate possession and control. The General Partner shall not employ, or permit another to employ, such funds or assets in any manner except for the exclusive benefit of the Partnership.

5.7 Liability; Indemnification. In carrying out its duties and exercising its powers pursuant to this Agreement, the General Partner shall exercise reasonable skill, care, and business judgment. Neither the General Partner nor any of its agents shall be liable to the Partnership or the other Partners for any act or omission based upon errors of judgment, negligence, or other fault in connection with the business or affairs of the Partnership so long as the Person against whom liability is asserted acted in good faith on behalf of the Partnership and in a manner reasonably believed by such Person to be within the scope of his or her authority under this Agreement and in the best interests of the Partnership but only if such action or failure to act does not constitute gross negligence or willful misconduct. The Partnership agrees to indemnify the General Partner and its agents to the fullest extent permitted by law and to save and hold it and them harmless from and with respect to all (i) fees, costs, and expenses incurred in connection with or resulting from any claim, action, or demand against the General Partner, the Partnership, or any of the agents of either of them that arise out of or in any way relate to the Partnership, its properties, business, or affairs; and (ii) such claims, actions, and demands and any losses or damages resulting from such claims, actions, and demands, including amounts paid in settlement or compromise (if recommended by attorneys for the Partnership) of any such claim, action, or demand; *provided, however,* that this indemnification shall apply only so long as the person against whom a claim, action, or demand is asserted has acted in good faith on behalf of the Partnership or the General Partner and in a manner reasonably believed by such person to be within the scope of his or her authority under this Agreement and in the best interests of the Partnership, but only if such action or failure to act does not constitute gross negligence or willful misconduct. The termination of any action, suit, or proceeding by judgment, order, settlement, or upon a plea of *nolo contendere* or its equivalent, shall not of itself create a presumption that any person acted with gross negligence or willful misconduct.

5.8 Dissenting Limited Partners. The Limited Partners are aware that the terms of this Agreement permit certain amendments of the Agreement to be effective and certain other actions to be taken or omitted by or with respect to the Partnership, in each case with the approval of less than all of the Limited Partners. Each Limited Partner agrees that the General Partner, with full power of substitution, is hereby authorized and empowered to execute, acknowledge, make, swear to, verify, consent to, deliver, record, file, and/or publish, for and in the behalf, in the name, place, and stead of each such undersigned Limited Partner, any and all instruments and documents which may be necessary or appropriate to permit such amendment to be lawfully made or action lawfully taken or omitted, regardless of whether such Limited Partner has approved such amendment or action.

ARTICLE VI.   TERMINATION OF A GENERAL PARTNER

6.1   Death, Legal Incapacity, Dissolution, Removal, or Bankruptcy. The General Partner may *not* voluntarily withdraw as General Partner. Upon the death, legal incapacity, dissolution, removal, or bankruptcy of a General Partner, all of such Partner's rights and powers as a General Partner shall be terminated, except for any accrued rights to be compensated under § 5.2 and its rights under § 6.3, and such person shall cease to be a General Partner. Any of the remaining General Partners, if there are any, shall have the right to continue the business of the Partnership.

6.2   Removal of a General Partner. A majority of the Limited Partners may remove the General Partner. Written notice of such determination setting forth the effective date of such removal shall be served upon the General Partner, and as of the effective date, shall terminate all of such person's rights and powers as a General Partner. The Limited Partners may, at any time prior to the closing, revoke a notice of removal issued pursuant to this § 6.2. In that event, the Partnership shall not be obliged to purchase the Interest of the removed General Partner, and the Limited Partners shall reimburse the Partnership and the removed General Partner for any out-of-pocket costs incurred by the Partnership or the removed General Partner in obtaining the appraisal.

6.3   Interest of Terminated General Partner. In the event of the death, legal incapacity, dissolution, removal, or bankruptcy of a General Partner and if the business of the Partnership is not continued, then the Partnership shall be liquidated and terminated and the Partnership assets distributed in accordance with Article IV. Upon the death, legal incapacity, dissolution, removal, or bankruptcy of a General Partner and if the business of the Partnership is continued, then the Partnership shall purchase the Terminated Partner's Interest as follows:

(a)   *Price.* The purchase price for the Interest of the Terminated Partner shall be the fair market value of its Interest as determined herein. If the Partnership and the Terminated Partner (or its successor in interest) cannot agree on such fair market value within 90 days of the terminating event, an appraisal of the fair market value of the Partnership's assets shall be made by the procedure described in § 6.3(b). Promptly following completion of the appraisal, the Capital Accounts of the Partners shall be adjusted as if all assets of the Partnership had been sold or disposed of for an amount equal to the Appraised Market Value, determined according to § 6.3(b), and the resulting income or loss allocated pursuant to Article VIII. The fair market value for the Interest of the Terminated Partner will then be the positive balance, if any, of the Terminated Partner's Capital Account, as adjusted.

(b) *Appraisal Procedure.* The Terminated Partner (or its successor in interest) and the Partnership shall each engage and pay an appraiser to appraise the fair market value of the Partnership's assets based on an assumed all-cash sale of the assets as of the date of the terminating event. The Partnership's appraiser shall be that appraiser receiving the most votes from the Limited Partners pursuant to a meeting held, or other action taken by, the Limited Partners in accordance with Article XII. An average of the value established by the Terminated Partner's appraiser and the value established by the Partnership's appraiser shall be taken as the appraised market value of the Partnership's assets (the "Appraised Market Value").

(c) *Terms.* The purchase of the Terminated Partner's interest shall close within [*Number*] days after submission of the appraisers' written reports. The purchase price shall be paid in cash at closing, and the Terminated Partner shall assign and convey its Interest to the Partnership. The Partnership may, at its option, pay 25% of the applicable purchase price in cash at closing and the balance in three equal annual installments of principal and interest with interest at [*Percent*] per annum, commencing one year after closing.

6.4 Indemnity. A Terminated Partner shall be indemnified by all of the remaining Partners from any Partnership liabilities except to the extent any such liabilities arose prior to such purchase and sale of the selling Partner's interest and were not taken into account in determining the amount the Terminated Partner would receive pursuant to § 6.3(a) or arise subsequent to such purchase and sale and result from the negligence or misconduct of the selling Partner.

6.5 Termination of Executory Contracts With the General Partner or Affiliates. Upon removal of a General Partner, all executory contracts between the Partnership and the terminating General Partner or any Affiliate thereof (unless such Affiliate is also an Affiliate of a continuing General Partner) may be terminated by the Partnership effective upon 60 days' prior written notice of such termination to the party so terminated. The terminating General Partner or any Affiliate (unless such Affiliate is also an Affiliate of a continuing General Partner) thereof may also terminate and cancel any such executory contract effective upon 60 days' prior written notice of such termination and cancellation given to the Partnership.

ARTICLE VII. RIGHTS AND OBLIGATIONS OF LIMITED PARTNERS

7.1 No Participation in Management. No Limited Partner (other than the General Partner in case it is also a Limited Partner) shall take part in the management of the Partnership's business, transact any business in the Partnership's name, or have the power to sign documents or otherwise bind the Partnership. The Limited Partners shall, however, have the power to vote upon the following Partnership matters:

(a) Termination of the Partnership, in accordance with § 1.5(a) and (c);

(b) Amendment of the Agreement of Limited Partnership, in accordance with § 11.1;

(c) Removal of the General Partner, in accordance with § 6.2;

(d) Continuation of the Partnership after the resignation, removal, dissolution, or bankruptcy of the General Partner, in accordance with § 6.3(a);

(e) Approval of agreements, contracts, and arrangements between the Partnership and the General Partner or any of its Affiliates, in accordance with § 5.3.2(c);

(f) Audit of the balance sheet accompanying an annual report, in accordance with § 9.2(d).

7.2 Limitation of Liability. Pursuant to the Act, no Limited Partner shall have any personal liability whatever in his or her capacity as a Limited Partner for the debts of the Partnership or any of its losses beyond the amount contributed by him or her to the capital of the Partnership as set forth in § 3.1.

7.3 Transfer of a Limited Partner's Interest.

7.3.1 Requirements. Subject to any restrictions on transferability required by law or contained elsewhere in this Agreement, a Limited Partner may assign in writing his or her Interest, provided:

(a)   The assignee meets all of the requirements applicable to a Substituted Limited Partner and consents in writing in form satisfactory to the General Partner to be bound by the terms of this Agreement;

(b)   The General Partner consents in writing to the assignment, which consent shall be withheld only if such assignment does not comply with § 7.3.1(a) or if such assignment is to a tax-exempt entity, or if such assignment would jeopardize the status of the Partnership as a partnership for federal income tax purposes, would cause the Partnership to be terminated under IRC § 708, or would violate, or cause the Partnership to violate, any applicable law or governmental rule or regulation, including without limitation, any applicable federal or state securities law; and

(c)   if requested by the General Partner, an opinion from counsel for the Partnership is delivered to the General Partner stating that, in the opinion of said counsel, such assignment would not jeopardize the status of the Partnership as a partnership for federal income tax purposes, and would not violate, nor cause the Partnership to violate, any applicable law or governmental rule or regulation, including without limitation, any applicable federal or state securities law.

By executing this Agreement, each Limited Partner shall be deemed to have consented to any assignment consented to by the General Partner. Anything herein to the contrary notwithstanding, in no event shall an assignment be made to a minor (except in trust or pursuant to the Uniform Gifts to Minors Act) or to an incompetent.

7.3.2 Limited Liability. Each Limited Partner agrees that he or she will, upon request of the General Partner, execute such certificates or other documents and perform such acts as the General Partner deems appropriate after an assignment of that Limited Partner's Interest to preserve the limited liability status of the Partnership under the laws of the jurisdictions in which the Partnership is doing business. For purposes of this Section, any transfer of any Interest in the Partnership, whether voluntary or by operation of law, shall be considered an assignment.

7.3.3 Invalid Assignments. Any purported assignment of any Interest in the Partnership which is not made in compliance with this Agreement is hereby declared to be null and void and of no force or effect whatsoever.

7.3.4 Payment of Expenses. Each Limited Partner agrees that he or she will, prior to the time the General Partner consents to an assignment of any Interest by that Limited Partner, pay all reasonable expenses, including attorneys' fees, incurred by the Partnership in connection with such assignment.

7.3.5 Compliance with Applicable Statutes. Each of the Limited Partners, by executing this Agreement, hereby covenants and agrees that he or she will not, in any event, sell or distribute any Interest unless, in the opinion of counsel to the assignee (which counsel and opinion shall be satisfactory to counsel for the General Partner), such Interest may be legally sold or distributed in compliance with then-applicable federal and state statutes.

7.3.6 Rights of Assignor. Anything herein to the contrary notwithstanding, both the Partnership and the General Partner shall be entitled to treat the assignor of an Interest as the absolute owner thereof in all respects, and shall incur no liability for Distributions made in good faith to him or her, until such time as a written assignment that conforms to the requirements of this Article VII has been received by the Partnership and accepted by the General Partner.

7.4 Substituted Limited Partner.

7.4.1 Admission as Limited Partner—Consent by General Partner. The General Partner may, but need not, in its sole discretion, permit an assignee or transferee of the Interest of a Limited

Partner to be and become a Substituted Limited Partner in the Partnership entitled to all the rights and benefits under this Agreement of the transferor or assignor of such Interest; but no such assignee or transferee shall be or become a Substituted Limited Partner unless and until the General Partner in writing consents to the admission of such Person as a Substituted Limited Partner, which consent may be withheld in the absolute discretion of the General Partner. The Partners hereby consent and agree to such admission of a Substituted Limited Partner by the General Partner.

7.4.2 Documents and Expenses. Each substituted Limited Partner, as a condition to his or her admission as a Limited Partner, shall execute and acknowledge such instruments, in form and substance satisfactory to the General Partner, as the General Partner shall deem necessary or desirable to effectuate such admission and to confirm the agreement of the Substituted Limited Partner to be bound by all the terms and provisions of this Agreement with respect to the Interest acquired. All reasonable expenses, including attorneys' fees, incurred by the Partnership in this connection shall be borne by such Substituted Limited Partner.

7.4.3 Agreement Binding. Any Person who is admitted to the Partnership as a Substituted Limited Partner shall be subject to and bound by all the provisions of this Agreement as if originally a party to this Agreement.

7.4.4 Voting Rights. Unless and until an assignee of an Interest in the Partnership becomes a Substituted Limited Partner, such assignee shall not be entitled to vote with respect to such Interest.

7.4.5 Effective Date. The effective date of admission of a Substituted Limited Partner shall be the date designated by the General Partner in writing to the Substituted Limited Partner, which shall not be later than the first day of the month next following the date upon which the General Partner has given its written consent to such substitution.

7.5 Indemnification and Terms of Admission. Each Limited Partner shall indemnify and hold harmless the Partnership, the General Partner, and every Limited Partner against any claim, action, suit, or proceeding, whether civil, criminal, administrative, or investigative, by reason of or arising from any actual or alleged misrepresentation or misstatement of facts or omission to state facts by such Limited Partner in connection with the admission of a Substituted Limited Partner to the Partnership, against expenses for which the Partnership or such other Person has not otherwise been reimbursed (including attorneys' fees, judgments, fines, and amounts paid in settlement) actually and reasonably incurred by him or her in connection with such action, suit or proceeding.

7.6 Death or Incapacity of Limited Partner. The death, legal incapacity, bankruptcy, or dissolution of a Limited Partner shall not cause a dissolution of the Partnership, but the rights of such Limited Partner to share in the Income or Loss of the Partnership and to receive Distributions shall, on the occurrence of such an event, devolve on his or her personal representative, or in the event of the death of one whose Partnership Interest is held in joint tenancy, pass to the surviving joint tenants, subject to the terms and conditions of this Agreement. However, in no event shall such personal representative become a Substituted Limited Partner solely by reason of such capacity. The estate of the Limited Partner shall be liable for all the obligations of the deceased or incapacitated Limited Partner.

7.7 Withdrawal of Partner. A Limited Partner shall have the right to withdraw upon 30 days' notice to the Partnership, thereby becoming a Terminated Partner. The Partnership shall purchase the Terminated Partner's Interest under the terms provided in § 6.3(a), (b) and (c). The Terminated Partner shall be indemnified in accordance with § 6.4.

ARTICLE VIII. DISSOLUTION AND TERMINATION

8.1 Assumption of Agreements. No vote by the Partners to dissolve the Partnership pursuant to § 1.5(c) shall be effective unless, prior to or concurrently with such vote, there shall have been established procedures for the assumption of the Partnership's obligations under the agreements in force immediately prior to such vote regarding dissolution, and there shall have been an irrevocable appointment of an agent who shall be empowered to give and receive notices, reports, and payments

LIMITED PARTNERSHIP AGREEMENT

under such agreements and hold and exercise such other powers as are necessary to permit all other parties to such agreements to deal with such agent as if the agent were the sole owner of the Partnership's interest, which procedures are agreed to in writing by each of the other parties to such agreements.

8.2 Dissolution. The Partnership shall be dissolved upon the occurrence of any of the events identified in § 1.5. No Partner shall have the right to dissolve or terminate the Partnership for any reason other than as set forth in § 1.5 *or to withdraw voluntarily from the Partnership* other than as set forth in § 7.7, or to partition any property of the Partnership.

8.3 Distribution Upon Dissolution or Liquidation. Upon dissolution of the Partnership, the affairs of the Partnership shall be wound up and all of its debts and liabilities discharged in the order of priority as provided by law. If the Partnership is dissolved and wound up or is "liquidated" within the meaning of Reg. § 1.704–1(b)(2)(ii)(g), distributions shall be made in accordance with § 4.1.1(c). Each such distributee shall receive his or her share of the assets in cash or in kind, and the proportion of such share that is received in cash may vary, all as the General Partner in its sole discretion may decide.

8.4 Allocation of Income and Losses in Liquidation. Income and losses of the Partnership following the date of dissolution, including but not limited to income and losses upon the sale of all or substantially all of the Partnership assets, shall be determined in accordance with the provisions of § 4.3, and shall be credited or charged to the Capital Accounts of the Partners in the same manner as income and loss of the Partnership would have been credited or charged if there were no dissolution and liquidation.

8.5 Winding Up. The winding up of the affairs of the Partnership and the distribution of its assets shall be conducted exclusively by the General Partner, or if none, the Limited Partners who are hereby authorized to do all acts authorized by law for these purposes. Without limiting the generality of the foregoing, the General Partner, or if none, the Limited Partners, in carrying out such winding up and distribution, shall have full power and authority to sell all or any of the Partnership assets or to distribute the same in kind to the Partners subject to § 4.1.2. Any assets distributed in kind shall be subject to all operating agreements or other agreements relating thereto which shall survive the termination of the Partnership.

8.6 Cancellation. Upon compliance with the foregoing distribution plan, the General Partner, or if none, the Limited Partners, shall file a Certificate of Cancellation and the Partnership shall cease to exist.

ARTICLE IX. BOOKS, RECORDS, AND REPORTS

9.1 Books and Records. The General Partner shall keep at the Partnership's office the following Partnership documents required by RULPA § 104:

(a) A current list of the full name and last known business or residence address of each Partner, together with the capital contribution of each Partner;

(b) A copy of the Certificate and all amendments thereto, and executed copies of any powers of attorney pursuant to which any certificate has been executed;

(c) Copies of the Partnership's federal, state, and local income tax or information returns and reports, if any, for the six (6) most recent taxable years;

(d) Copies of this original Agreement and all Amendments to the Agreement;

(e) Financial statements of the Partnership for the six (6) most recent fiscal years; and

(f) The Partnership's books and records for at least the current and past three (3) fiscal years.

9.2 Delivery to Limited Partner and Inspection.

(a) Upon the request of a Limited Partner, the General Partner shall promptly deliver to the requesting Limited Partner, at the expense of the Partnership, a copy of the information required to be maintained by § 9.1(a), (b) or (d).

(b) Each Limited Partner has the right, upon reasonable request, to do each of the following:

(1) Inspect and copy during normal business hours any of the Partnership records required to be maintained by § 9.1; and

(2) Obtain from the General Partner, promptly after becoming available, a copy of the Partnership's federal, state, and local income tax or information returns for each year.

(c) The General Partner shall send to each Partner within 90 days after the end of each taxable year the information necessary for the Partner to complete its federal and state income tax or information returns.

(d) Within 120 days after the end of each fiscal year, the General Partner shall provide each Partner with an annual report containing

(1) a balance sheet as of the end of such fiscal year and statements of income or loss, Partners' equity, cash flow, and changes in financial position for such fiscal year which may, at the option of the General Partner, or will, upon request of a Majority of the Limited Partners, be audited;

(2) a statement describing the amount of all fees, compensation, and distributions paid by the Partnership for such fiscal year to the General Partner or any Affiliate of the General Partner;

(3) a statement of changes in Partners' Capital Accounts; and

(4) a report of the activities of the Partnership during such fiscal year.

(e) The General Partner shall, at the expense of the Partnership, prepare and file with appropriate state authorities and the SEC all reports required to be filed by the Partnership by the respective state's securities laws or said Commission, as the case may be.

9.3 Tax Returns. The General Partner, at the Partnership's expense, shall cause to be prepared tax returns for the Partnership and shall further cause such returns to be timely filed with the appropriate authorities.

9.4 Designation of Tax Matters Partner. The General Partner is hereby designated as the "Tax Matters Partner" under IRC § 6231(a)(7), to manage administrative tax proceedings conducted at the Partnership level by the Internal Revenue Service with respect to Partnership matters. Any Partner has the right to participate in such administrative proceedings relating to the determination of partnership items at the Partnership level. Expenses of such administrative proceedings undertaken by the Tax Matters Partner will be paid for out of Partnership assets. Each other Partner who elects to participate in such proceedings will be responsible for any expenses incurred by such Partner in connection with such participation. Further, the cost of any adjustments to a Partner and the cost of any resulting audits or adjustments of a Partner's tax return will be borne solely by the affected Partner.

9.5 Tax Elections. The General Partner shall have the authority to cause the Partnership to make any election required or permitted to be made for income tax purposes if the General Partner determines, in its sole judgment, that such election is in the best interests of the Partnership. Notwithstanding the foregoing, the General Partner may cause the Partnership to make, in accordance with IRC § 754 (1954), as amended (the "Code"), a timely election to adjust the basis of the Partnership property as described in IRC §§ 734 and 743 in the sole discretion of the General Partner.

LIMITED PARTNERSHIP AGREEMENT

ARTICLE X.   FISCAL AFFAIRS

10.1   Fiscal Year. The fiscal year of the Partnership shall be [*Describe*].

10.2   Partnership Funds. The funds of the Partnership shall be deposited in such bank account or accounts, or invested in such interest-bearing or non-interest-bearing investments, including, without limitation, checking and savings accounts, certificates of deposit, and time or demand deposits in commercial banks, banker's acceptances, securities issued by money market mutual funds, savings and loan association deposits, U.S. government securities and securities guaranteed by U.S. government agencies, as the General Partner shall, in its sole discretion, determine. Such funds shall not be commingled with funds of any other person. Withdrawals therefrom shall be made upon such signatures as the General Partner may designate.

10.3   Accounting Decisions. All decisions as to accounting principles, except as specifically provided to the contrary herein, shall be made by the General Partner.

10.4   Loans by the Partnership to the General Partner or Others. The Partnership shall not make any loans to the General Partner or to any other persons, except for purchase-money financing in connection with the sale of Partnership assets.

ARTICLE XI.   AMENDMENTS OF PARTNERSHIP DOCUMENTS

11.1   Amendments in General. Except as otherwise provided in this Agreement, this Agreement may be amended with the consent of the General Partner and by a majority vote of the Limited Partners.

11.2   Amendments Without Consent of Limited Partners. In addition to any amendments otherwise authorized herein, amendments may be made to this Agreement from time to time by the General Partner, without the consent of any of the Limited Partners: (i) to add to the duties or obligations of the General Partner or to surrender any right or power granted to the General Partner herein, for the benefit of the Limited Partners; (ii) to correct any error or resolve any ambiguity in or inconsistency among any of the provisions hereof, or to make any other provision with respect to matters or questions arising under this Agreement that is not inconsistent with the provisions of this Agreement; (iii) to delete or add any provision of this Agreement required to be so deleted or added by any state securities commission or similar governmental authority for the benefit or protection of the Limited Partners; and (iv) to add to or change the name of the Partnership.

11.3   Amendments Needing Consent of Affected Partners. Notwithstanding §§ 11.1 and 11.2, without the consent of the Partner or Partners to be adversely affected by an amendment to this Agreement, this Agreement may not be amended to (i) convert a Limited Partner's interest into a General Partner's interest; (ii) modify the limited liability of a Limited Partner; (iii) alter the interest of a Partner in income, gain, losses, deductions, credits, and Distributions; (iv) increase, add, or alter any obligation of any Partner; or (v) alter any provisions of Article IV or VI or this § 11.3.

11.4   Amendments After Change of Law. This Agreement and any other Partnership documents may be amended, if necessary, by the General Partner without the consent of the Limited Partners if there occurs any change that permits or requires an amendment of this Agreement under the Act or of any other Partnership document under applicable law, so long as no Partner is adversely affected (or consent is given by such Partner).

11.5   Limited Partners' Execution of Amendments. The Limited Partners hereby agree to execute an amendment to this Agreement whenever the execution of an amendment to this Agreement is requested by the General Partner and such amendment has been approved as required herein, and they agree to execute such other instruments and documents and to perform such other acts, as may be required to comply with the Act for the valid formation and existence of the Partnership as a limited partnership thereunder, whenever the execution or performance thereof shall be requested by the General Partner, all within 10 days after the request by the General Partner. In the event that any of the provisions of any such amendment to this Agreement shall be inconsistent with any of the provisions of this Agreement (if they are different documents), the provisions of this Agreement shall govern and control as among the parties.

ARTICLE XII.   MEETING AND VOTING RIGHTS

12.1   Notice of Meeting of Limited Partners.

12.1.1   Requirements for Calling Meeting. Upon the written request of holders of [*Percent*] or more of the Interests of the Limited Partners, the General Partner shall call a meeting of the Limited Partners. Notice of such meeting shall be given within thirty (30) days after, and the meeting shall be held within sixty (60) days after receipt of such request. The General Partner may also call a meeting of the Limited Partners on its own initiative by giving notice of such meeting not less than fourteen (14) and not more than sixty (60) days prior to the meeting. Any such notice shall state time, place, and, briefly, the purpose of the meeting, which shall be held at a reasonable time and place. Any Limited Partner may obtain a list of the names, addresses, and Interest owned by each Limited Partner upon written request to the General Partner. If a meeting is adjourned to another time or place, and if an announcement of the adjournment of time or place is made at the meeting, it shall not be necessary to give notice of the adjourned meeting. No notice of the time, place, or purpose of any meeting of Limited Partners need be given to any Limited Partner who attends in person or is represented by proxy, except for a Limited Partner attending a meeting for the express purpose of objecting at the beginning of the meeting to the transaction of any business on the ground that the meeting is not lawfully called or convened, or to any Limited Partner entitled to such notice who, in a writing executed and filed with the records of the meeting, either before or after the time thereof, waives such notice.

12.1.2   Record Date. For the purpose of determining the Limited Partners entitled to notice of, or to vote at, any meeting of the Limited Partners, or any adjournment or postponement thereof, or to vote by written consent without a meeting, the General Partner or the Limited Partners requesting such meeting or vote may fix, in advance, a date as the record date for any such determination of Limited Partners. Such date shall not be more than sixty (60) days nor less than ten (10) days before any such meeting or submission of a matter to the Limited Partners for a vote by written consent. If no record date is fixed for such determination of Limited Partners, the date on which notice of the meeting or submission of the matter to the Limited Partners for a vote by written consent is mailed should be the record date for such determination of Limited Partners.

12.2   Voting Rights and Procedure.

12.2.1   Voting Percentage. Each Limited Partner is entitled to a number of votes equal to the percentage described in § 4.2(c)(3).

12.2.2   Quorum. A Majority of the Limited Partners shall constitute a quorum at any meeting of the Partners.

12.2.3   Proxies. Each Limited Partner may authorize any person or persons to act for him or her by proxy with respect to any matter in which a Limited Partner is entitled to participate whether by waiving notice of any meeting or voting or participating at a meeting. Every proxy must be signed by the Limited Partner. No proxy shall be valid after the expiration of twelve (12) months from the date thereof unless otherwise provided in the proxy. Every proxy shall be revocable at the pleasure of the Limited Partner executing it, but the Partnership may rely on any properly executed proxy delivered to it until it receives written notice from the Limited Partner in question that said proxy has been revoked.

12.2.4   Action Taken Without Meeting. Any matter for which the approval or consent of the Limited Partners is required or for which the Limited Partners are authorized to take action under this Agreement or under applicable law may be approved or action may be taken by the Limited Partners without a meeting and shall be as valid and effective as action taken by the Limited Partners at a meeting assembled, if written consents to such action by the Limited Partners are signed by the

LIMITED PARTNERSHIP AGREEMENT

Limited Partners owning Interests constituting in the aggregate the Interest required to approve or otherwise authorize such action and such written consents are delivered to the General Partner.

12.2.5   Attendance. Personal presence of the Limited Partners shall not be required at any meeting, provided an effective written consent to or rejection of the action proposed to be taken at such meeting is submitted to the General Partner. Attendance by a Limited Partner and voting in person at any meeting shall revoke any written consents or rejections of such Limited Partner submitted with respect to action proposed to be taken at such meeting.

12.2.6   Conduct of Meeting. At each meeting of Limited Partners, the Limited Partners present or represented by proxy, by majority vote, may adopt such rules not inconsistent with the Agreement for the conduct of such meeting as they shall deem appropriate.

ARTICLE XIII.   POWER OF ATTORNEY

13.1   Power of Attorney.

13.1.1   General Partner. The Limited Partners, by their execution hereof, jointly and severally hereby make, constitute, and appoint the General Partner as their true and lawful agent and attorney-in-fact, with full power of substitutions, in their name, place, and stead to make, execute, sign, acknowledge, swear by, record, and file on behalf of them and on behalf of the Partnership (i) all certificates and other instruments deemed advisable by the General Partner to permit the Partnership to become or to continue as a limited partnership or partnership wherein the Limited Partners have limited liability in the jurisdiction where the Partnership may be doing business; (ii) all instruments that affect a change or modification of the Partnership in accordance with this Agreement, including without limitation the substitution of assignees as Substituted Limited Partners pursuant to § 7.4; (iii) all conveyances and other instruments deemed advisable by the General Partner to effect the dissolution and termination of the Partnership; (iv) all fictitious or assumed name certificates required or permitted to be filed on behalf of the Partnership; and (v) all other instruments which may be required or permitted by law to be filed on behalf of the Partnership.

13.1.2   In General. The foregoing power of attorney:

(a)   Is coupled with an interest and shall be irrevocable and survive the death or incapacity of each Limited Partner;

(b)   May be exercised by the General Partner either by signing separately as attorney-in-fact for each Limited Partner or, after listing all of the Limited Partners executing an instrument, by a signature acting as attorney-in-fact for all of them; and

(c)   Shall survive the delivery of an assignment by a Limited Partner of his or her Interest; except that, where the assignee of the Interest of such Limited Partner has been approved by the General Partner for admission to the Partnership as a Substituted Limited Partner, the power of attorney of the assignor shall survive the delivery of such assignment for the sole purpose of enabling the General Partner to execute, acknowledge, and file any instrument necessary to effect such substitution.

13.1.3   Other Instruments. Each Limited Partner shall execute and deliver to the General Partner, within five days after receipt of the General Partner's request therefor, such further designation, powers-of-attorney, and other instruments as the General Partner deems necessary.

13.1.4   Termination of Appointment. The appointment of the General Partner as attorney-in-fact pursuant to this power of attorney automatically shall terminate as to such entity or person at such time as it ceases to be the General Partner and from such time shall be effective only as to the substituted General Partner designated or elected pursuant to this Agreement.

LIMITED PARTNERSHIP AGREEMENT

ARTICLE XIV. MISCELLANEOUS

14.1 Notices. Any notice, offer, consent, or other communication required or permitted to be given or made hereunder shall be in writing and shall be deemed to have been sufficiently given or made when delivered personally to the party (or an officer of the party) to whom the same is directed, or (except in the event of a mail strike) five days after being mailed by first-class mail, postage prepaid, if to the Partnership, to the offices described in § 1.4, or if to a Partner, to the address set forth on Schedule A. Any Partner may change his or her address for the purpose of this Article by giving notice of such change to the Partnership, such change to become effective on the tenth (10th) day after such notice is given.

14.2 Governing Law; Successors; Severability. This Agreement shall be governed by the laws of the State of [*State*] as such laws are applied by [*State*] courts to agreements entered into and to be performed in [*State*] by and between residents of [*State*], and shall, subject to the restrictions on transferability set forth herein, bind and inure to the benefit of the heirs, executors, personal representatives, successors, and assigns of the parties hereto. If any provision of this Agreement shall be held to be invalid, the remainder of this Agreement shall not be affected thereby.

14.3 Entire Agreement. This Agreement constitutes the entire agreement between the parties; it supersedes any prior agreement or understanding among them, oral or written, all of which are hereby cancelled. This Agreement may not be modified or amended other than pursuant to Article XI.

14.4 Headings, etc. The headings in this Agreement are inserted for convenience of reference only and shall not affect interpretation of this Agreement. Wherever from the context it appears appropriate, each term stated in either the singular or the plural shall include the singular and the plural, and the pronouns stated in either the masculine or the neuter gender shall include the masculine, the feminine, and the neuter.

14.5 No Waiver. The failure of any Partner to seek redress for violation, or to insist on strict performance of any covenant or condition of this Agreement shall not prevent a subsequent act which would have constituted a violation from having the effect of an original violation.

14.6 Counterparts. This Agreement may be executed in several counterparts, each of which shall be deemed an original but all of which shall constitute one and the same instrument.

14.7 Other Business Ventures. Any Partner, or any shareholder, director, employee, Affiliate, or other Person holding a legal or beneficial interest in any entity which is a Partner, may engage in or possess an interest in other business ventures of every nature and description, independently or with others, whether such ventures are competitive with the Partnership or otherwise; neither the Partnership nor the Partners shall have any right by virtue of this Agreement in or to such independent ventures or to the income or profits derived therefrom.

14.8 Venue. In the event that any suit is brought arising out of or in connection with this Agreement, the parties consent to the jurisdiction of, and agree that sole venue will lie in the state and federal courts located in [*Describe*].

14.9 Further Assurance. The Limited Partners will execute and deliver such further instruments and do such further acts and things as may be required to carry out the intent and purpose of this Agreement.

14.10 Creditors. None of the provisions of this Agreement shall be for the benefit of or enforceable by any of the creditors of the Partnership or Partners.

14.11 Remedies. The rights and remedies of the Partners hereunder shall not be mutually exclusive, and the exercise of any right to which a Partner is entitled shall not preclude the exercise of any other right he or she may have.

LIMITED PARTNERSHIP AGREEMENT

14.12 Authority. Each individual executing this Agreement on behalf of a partnership, corporation, or other entity warrants that he or she is authorized to do so and that this Agreement will constitute the legally binding obligation of the entity which such person represents.

IN WITNESS WHEREOF, the parties have executed this Agreement as of the date first above written.

General Partner: Limited Partner:

_____   _____

By: _____   By: _____

Its _____   Its _____

[ATTACH SCHEDULE A. PARTNERS' ADDRESSES FOR NOTICE]

III. CORPORATIONS

A. MODEL BUSINESS CORPORATION ACT

(with Selected Comments)

———————

Table of Sections

CHAPTER 1.   GENERAL PROVISIONS

SUBCHAPTER A.   SHORT TITLE AND RESERVATION OF POWER

MODEL BUSINESS CORPORATION ACT

CHAPTER 2. INCORPORATION

CHAPTER 3. PURPOSES AND POWERS

CHAPTER 4. NAME

CHAPTER 5. OFFICE AND AGENT

CHAPTER 6. SHARES AND DISTRIBUTIONS

SUBCHAPTER A. SHARES

SUBCHAPTER B. ISSUANCE OF SHARES

SUBCHAPTER C. SUBSEQUENT ACQUISITION OF SHARES BY SHAREHOLDERS AND CORPORATION

MODEL BUSINESS CORPORATION ACT

MODEL BUSINESS CORPORATION ACT

CHAPTER 8.   DIRECTORS AND OFFICERS

SUBCHAPTER A.   BOARD OF DIRECTORS

SUBCHAPTER B.   MEETINGS AND ACTION OF THE BOARD

SUBCHAPTER C.   DIRECTORS

SUBCHAPTER D.   OFFICERS

SUBCHAPTER E.   INDEMNIFICATION AND ADVANCE FOR EXPENSES

SUBCHAPTER F.   DIRECTORS' CONFLICTING INTEREST TRANSACTIONS

MODEL BUSINESS CORPORATION ACT

CHAPTER 18. TRANSITION PROVISIONS

CHAPTER 1. GENERAL PROVISIONS

SUBCHAPTER A. SHORT TITLE AND RESERVATION OF POWER

§ 1.01 Short Title

This Act shall be known and may be cited as the "[name of state] Business Corporation Act."

§ 1.02 Reservation of Power to Amend or Repeal

The [name of state legislature] has power to amend or repeal all or part of this Act at any time and all domestic and foreign corporations subject to this Act are governed by the amendment or repeal.

SUBCHAPTER B. FILING DOCUMENTS

§ 1.20 Requirements for Documents; Extrinsic Facts

(a) A document must satisfy the requirements of this section, and of any other section that adds to or varies these requirements, to be entitled to filing by the secretary of state.

(b) This Act must require or permit filing the document in the office of the secretary of state.

(c) The document must contain the information required by this Act and may contain other information.

(d) The document must be typewritten or printed or, if electronically transmitted, it must be in a format that can be retrieved or reproduced in typewritten or printed form.

(e) The document must be in the English language. A corporate name need not be in English if written in English letters or Arabic or Roman numerals.

(f) The document must be signed:

    (1) by the chairman of the board of directors of a domestic or foreign corporation, by its president, or by another of its officers;

    (2) if directors have not been selected or the corporation has not been formed, by an incorporator; or

    (3) if the corporation is in the hands of a receiver, trustee, or other court-appointed fiduciary, by that fiduciary.

(g) The person executing the document shall sign it and state beneath or opposite the person's signature the person's name and the capacity in which the document is signed. The document may but need not contain a corporate seal, attestation, acknowledgment, or verification.

(h) If the secretary of state has prescribed a mandatory form for the document under section 1.21(a), the document must be in or on the prescribed form.

(i) The document must be delivered to the office of the secretary of state for filing. Delivery may be made by electronic transmission if and to the extent permitted by the secretary of state. If it is filed in typewritten or printed form and not transmitted electronically, the secretary of state may require one exact or conformed copy to be delivered with the document.

(j) When the document is delivered to the office of the secretary of state for filing, the correct filing fee, and any franchise tax, license fee, or penalty required by this Act or other law to be paid at the time of delivery for filing must be paid or provision for payment made in a manner permitted by the secretary of state.

(k) Whenever a provision of this Act permits any of the terms of a plan or a filed document to be dependent on facts objectively ascertainable outside the plan or filed document, the following provisions apply:

(1) The manner in which the facts will operate upon the terms of the plan or filed document must be set forth in the plan or filed document.

(2) The facts may include:

(i) any of the following that is available in a nationally recognized news or information medium either in print or electronically: statistical or market indices, market prices of any security or group of securities, interest rates, currency exchange rates, or similar economic or financial data;

(ii) a determination or action by any person or body, including the corporation or any other party to a plan or filed document; or

(iii) the terms of, or actions taken under, an agreement to which the corporation is a party, or any other agreement or document.

(3) As used in this subsection (k):

(i) "filed document" means a document filed by the secretary of state under any provision of this Act except chapter 15 or section 16.21; and

(ii) "plan" means a plan of domestication, conversion, merger, or share exchange.

(4) The following provisions of a plan or filed document may not be made dependent on facts outside the plan or filed document:

(i) the name and address of any person required in a filed document;

(ii) the registered office of any entity required in a filed document;

(iii) the registered agent of any entity required in a filed document;

(iv) the number of authorized shares and designation of each class or series of shares;

(v) the effective date of a filed document; and

(vi) any required statement in a filed document of the date on which the underlying transaction was approved or the manner in which that approval was given.

(5) If a provision of a filed document is made dependent on a fact ascertainable outside of the filed document, and that fact is neither ascertainable by reference to a source described in subsection (k)(2)(i) or a document that is a matter of public record, nor have the affected shareholders received notice of the fact from the corporation, then the corporation shall file with the secretary of state articles of amendment to the filed document setting forth the fact promptly after the time when the fact referred to is first ascertainable or thereafter changes. Articles of amendment under this subsection (k)(5) are deemed to be authorized by the authorization of the original filed document to which they relate and may be filed by the corporation without further action by the board of directors or the shareholders.

§ 1.21   Forms

(a)   The secretary of state may prescribe and furnish on request forms for: (i) an application for a certificate of existence, (ii) a foreign corporation's registration statement, (iii) a foreign corporation's statement of withdrawal, (iv) a foreign corporation's transfer of registration statement, and (v) the annual report. If the secretary of state so requires, use of these forms is mandatory.

(b)   The secretary of state may prescribe and furnish on request forms for other documents required or permitted to be filed by this Act but their use is not mandatory.

§ 1.22   Filing, Service, and Copying Fees

(a)   The secretary of state shall collect the following fees when the documents described in this subsection are delivered to the secretary of state for filing:

Document	Fee
Articles of incorporation	$_____.
Application for use of indistinguishable name	$_____.
Application for reserved name	$_____.
Notice of transfer of reserved name	$_____.
Application for registered name	$_____.
Application for renewal of registered name	$_____.
Corporation's statement of change of registered agent or registered office or both	$_____.
Agent's statement of change of registered office for each affected corporation not to exceed a total of $_____	$_____.
Agent's statement of resignation	No fee.
Articles of domestication	$_____.
Articles of conversion	$_____.
Amendment of articles of incorporation	$_____.
Restatement of articles of incorporation with amendment of articles	$_____.
Restatement of articles of incorporation without amendment of articles	$_____.
Articles of merger or share exchange	$_____.
Articles of dissolution	$_____.
Articles of revocation of dissolution	$_____.
Certificate of administrative dissolution	No fee.
Application for reinstatement following administrative dissolution	$_____.
Certificate of reinstatement	No fee.
Certificate of judicial dissolution	No fee.
Foreign registration statement	$_____.
Amendment of foreign registration statement	$_____.
Statement of withdrawal	$_____.

Transfer of foreign registration statement	$_____.
Notice of termination of registration	No fee.
Annual report	$_____.
Articles of correction	$_____.
Articles of validation	$_____.
Application for certificate of existence or foreign registration	$_____.
Any other document required or permitted to be filed by this Act	$_____.

(b)   The secretary of state shall collect a fee of $ _____ each time process is served on the secretary of state under this Act. The party to a proceeding causing service of process is entitled to recover this fee as costs if such party prevails in the proceeding.

(c)   The secretary of state shall collect the following fees for copying and certifying the copy of any filed document relating to a domestic or foreign corporation:

$ _____ a page for copying; and

$ _____ for the certificate.

§ 1.23   Effective Date of Filed Document

(a)   Except to the extent otherwise provided in section 1.24(c) and subchapter E of this chapter, a document accepted for filing is effective:

(1)   on the date and at the time of filing, as provided in section 1.25(b);

(2)   on the date of filing and at the time specified in the document as its effective time if later than the time under subsection (a)(1);

(3)   at a specified delayed effective date and time which may not be more than 90 days after filing; or

(4)   if a delayed effective date is specified, but no time is specified, at 12:01 a.m. on the date specified, which may not be more than 90 days after the date of filing.

(b)   If a filed document does not specify the time zone or place at which a date or time or both is to be determined, the date or time or both at which it becomes effective shall be those prevailing at the place of filing in this state.

§ 1.24   Correcting Filed Document

(a)   A document filed by the secretary of state pursuant to this Act may be corrected if (i) the document contains an inaccuracy, (ii) the document was defectively signed, attested, sealed, verified, or acknowledged, or (iii) the electronic transmission was defective.

(b)   A document is corrected:

(1)   by preparing articles of correction that

(i)   describe the document (including its filing date) or attach a copy of it to the articles of correction,

(ii)   specify the inaccuracy or defect to be corrected, and

(iii)   correct the inaccuracy or defect; and

(2)   by delivering the articles of correction to the secretary of state for filing.

(c)   Articles of correction are effective on the effective date of the document they correct except as to persons relying on the uncorrected document and adversely affected by the correction. As to those persons, articles of correction are effective when filed.

§ 1.25   Filing Duty of Secretary of State

(a)   If a document delivered to the office of the secretary of state for filing satisfies the requirements of section 1.20, the secretary of state shall file it.

(b)   The secretary of state files a document by recording it as filed on the date and time of receipt. After filing a document, the secretary of state shall return to the person who delivered the document for filing a copy of the document with an acknowledgement of the date and time of filing.

(c)   If the secretary of state refuses to file a document, it shall be returned to the person who delivered the document for filing within five days after the document was delivered, together with a brief, written explanation of the reason for the refusal.

(d)   The secretary of state's duty to file documents under this section is ministerial. The secretary of state's filing or refusing to file a document does not create a presumption that: (i) the document does or does not conform to the requirements of the Act; or (ii) the information contained in the document is correct or incorrect.

§ 1.26   Appeal from Secretary of State's Refusal to File Document

(a)   If the secretary of state refuses to file a document delivered for filing, the person that delivered the document for filing may petition [name or describe court] to compel its filing. The document and the explanation of the secretary of state of the refusal to file must be attached to the petition. The court may decide the matter in a summary proceeding.

(b)   The court may order the secretary of state to file the document or take other action the court considers appropriate.

(c)   The court's final decision may be appealed as in other civil proceedings.

§ 1.27   Evidentiary Effect of Copy of Filed Document

A certificate from the secretary of state delivered with a copy of a document filed by the secretary of state is conclusive evidence that the original document is on file with the secretary of state.

§ 1.28   Certificate of Existence or Registration

(a)   Any person may apply to the secretary of state to furnish a certificate of existence for a domestic corporation or a certificate of registration for a foreign corporation.

(b)   A certificate of existence sets forth:

(1)   the domestic corporation's corporate name;

(2)   that the domestic corporation is duly incorporated under the law of this state, the date of its incorporation, and the period of its duration if less than perpetual;

(3)   that all fees, taxes, and penalties owed to this state have been paid, if

(i)   payment is reflected in the records of the secretary of state and

(ii)   nonpayment affects the existence of the domestic corporation;

(4)   that its most recent annual report required by section 16.21 has been filed with the secretary of state;

(5)   that articles of dissolution have not been filed;

(6)   that the corporation is not administratively dissolved and a proceeding is not pending under section 14.21; and

(7)   other facts of record in the office of the secretary of state that may be requested by the applicant.

(c)   A certificate of registration sets forth:

(1)   the foreign corporation's name used in this state;

(2)   that the foreign corporation is registered to do business in this state;

(3)   that all fees, taxes, and penalties owed to this state have been paid, if

(i)   payment is reflected in the records of the secretary of state and

(ii)   nonpayment affects the registration of the foreign corporation;

(4)   that its most recent annual report required by section 16.21 has been filed with the secretary of state; and

(5)   other facts of record in the office of the secretary of state that may be requested by the applicant.

(d)   Subject to any qualification stated in the certificate, a certificate of existence or registration issued by the secretary of state may be relied upon as conclusive evidence of the facts stated in the certificate.

§ 1.29   Penalty for Signing False Document

(a)   A person commits an offense by signing a document that the person knows is false in any material respect with intent that the document be delivered to the secretary of state for filing.

(b)   An offense under this section is a [_____] misdemeanor [punishable by a fine of not to exceed $ _____].

SUBCHAPTER C.   SECRETARY OF STATE

§ 1.30   Powers

The secretary of state has the power reasonably necessary to perform the duties required of the secretary of state by this Act.

SUBCHAPTER D.   DEFINITIONS

§ 1.40   Act Definitions

In this Act, unless otherwise specified:

"Articles of incorporation" means the articles of incorporation described in section 2.02, all amendments to the articles of incorporation, and any other documents permitted or required to be delivered for filing by a domestic business corporation with the secretary of state under any provision of this Act that modify, amend, supplement, restate or replace the articles of incorporation. After an amendment of the articles of incorporation or any other document filed under this Act that restates the articles of incorporation in their entirety, the articles of incorporation shall not include any prior documents. When used with respect to a foreign corporation or a domestic or foreign nonprofit corporation, the "articles of incorporation" of such an entity means the document of such entity that is equivalent to the articles of incorporation of a domestic business corporation.

"Authorized shares" means the shares of all classes a domestic or foreign corporation is authorized to issue.

"Beneficial shareholder" means a person who owns the beneficial interest in shares, which may be a record shareholder or a person on whose behalf shares are registered in the name of an intermediary or nominee.

"Conspicuous" means so written, displayed, or presented that a reasonable person against whom the writing is to operate should have noticed it.

"Corporation," "domestic corporation," "business corporation" or "domestic business corporation" means a corporation for profit, which is not a foreign corporation, incorporated under this Act.

"Deliver" or "delivery" means any method of delivery used in conventional commercial practice, including delivery by hand, mail, commercial delivery, and, if authorized in accordance with section 1.41, by electronic transmission.

"Distribution" means a direct or indirect transfer of cash or other property (except a corporation's own shares) or incurrence of indebtedness by a corporation to or for the benefit of its shareholders in respect of any of its shares. A distribution may be in the form of a payment of a dividend; a purchase, redemption, or other acquisition of shares; a distribution of indebtedness; a distribution in liquidation; or otherwise.

"Document" means (i) any tangible medium on which information is inscribed, and includes handwritten, typed, printed or similar instruments, and copies of such instruments, or (ii) an electronic record.

"Domestic," with respect to an entity, means an entity governed as to its internal affairs by the law of this state.

"Effective date," when referring to a document accepted for filing by the secretary of state, means the time and date determined in accordance with section 1.23.

"Electronic" means relating to technology having electrical, digital, magnetic, wireless, optical, electromagnetic, or similar capabilities.

"Electronic record" means information that is stored in an electronic or other nontangible medium and is retrievable in paper form through an automated process used in conventional commercial practice, unless otherwise authorized in accordance with section 1.41(j).

"Electronic transmission" or "electronically transmitted" means any form or process of communication not directly involving the physical transfer of paper or another tangible medium, which (i) is suitable for the retention, retrieval, and reproduction of information by the recipient, and (ii) is retrievable in paper form by the recipient through an automated process used in conventional commercial practice, unless otherwise authorized in accordance with section 1.41(j).

"Eligible entity" means a domestic or foreign unincorporated entity or a domestic or foreign nonprofit corporation.

"Eligible interests" means interests or memberships.

"Employee" includes an officer but not a director. A director may accept duties that make the director also an employee.

"Entity" includes domestic and foreign business corporation; domestic and foreign nonprofit corporation; estate; trust; domestic and foreign unincorporated entity; and state, United States, and foreign government.

"Expenses" means reasonable expenses of any kind that are incurred in connection with a matter.

"Filing entity" means an unincorporated entity, other than a limited liability partnership, that is of a type that is created by filing a public organic record or is required to file a public organic record that evidences its creation.

"Foreign," with respect to an entity, means an entity governed as to its internal affairs by the organic law of a jurisdiction other than this state.

"Foreign corporation" or "foreign business corporation" means a corporation incorporated under a law other than the law of this state which would be a business corporation if incorporated under the law of this state.

"Foreign nonprofit corporation" means a corporation incorporated under a law other than the law of this state which would be a nonprofit corporation if incorporated under the law of this state.

"Foreign registration statement" means the foreign registration statement described in section 15.03.

"Governmental subdivision" includes authority, county, district, and municipality.

"Governor" means any person under whose authority the powers of an entity are exercised and under whose direction the activities and affairs of the entity are managed pursuant to the organic law governing the entity and its organic rules.

"Includes" and "including" denote a partial definition or a nonexclusive list.

"Individual" means a natural person.

"Interest" means either or both of the following rights under the organic law governing an unincorporated entity:

(i)   the right to receive distributions from the entity either in the ordinary course or upon liquidation; or

(ii)   the right to receive notice or vote on issues involving its internal affairs, other than as an agent, assignee, proxy or person responsible for managing its business and affairs.

"Interest holder" means a person who holds of record an interest.

"Interest holder liability" means:

(i)   personal liability for a debt, obligation, or other liability of a domestic or foreign corporation or eligible entity that is imposed on a person:

(A)   solely by reason of the person's status as a shareholder, member or interest holder; or

(B)   by the articles of incorporation of the domestic corporation or the organic rules of the eligible entity or foreign corporation that make one or more specified shareholders, members, or interest holders, or categories of shareholders, members, or interest holders, liable in their capacity as shareholders, members, or interest holders for all or specified liabilities of the corporation or eligible entity; or

(ii)   an obligation of a shareholder, member, or interest holder under the articles of incorporation of a domestic corporation or the organic rules of an eligible entity or foreign corporation to contribute to the entity.

For purposes of the foregoing, except as otherwise provided in the articles of incorporation of a domestic corporation or the organic law or organic rules of an eligible entity or a foreign corporation, interest holder liability arises under clause (i) when the corporation or eligible entity incurs the liability.

"Jurisdiction of formation" means the state or country the law of which includes the organic law governing a domestic or foreign corporation or eligible entity.

"Means" denotes an exhaustive definition.

"Membership" means the rights of a member in a domestic or foreign nonprofit corporation.

"Merger" means a transaction pursuant to section 11.02.

"Nonfiling entity" means an unincorporated entity that is of a type that is not created by filing a public organic record.

"Nonprofit corporation" or "domestic nonprofit corporation" means a corporation incorporated under the laws of this state and subject to the provisions of the [Model Nonprofit Corporation Act].

"Organic law" means the statute governing the internal affairs of a domestic or foreign business or nonprofit corporation or unincorporated entity.

"Organic rules" means the public organic record and private organic rules of a domestic or foreign corporation or eligible entity.

"Person" includes an individual and an entity.

"Principal office" means the office (in or out of this state) so designated in the annual report or foreign registration statement where the principal executive offices of a domestic or foreign corporation are located.

"Private organic rules" means (i) the bylaws of a domestic or foreign business or nonprofit corporation or (ii) the rules, regardless of whether in writing, that govern the internal affairs of an unincorporated entity, are binding on all its interest holders, and are not part of its public organic record, if any. Where private organic rules have been amended or restated, the term means the private organic rules as last amended or restated.

"Proceeding" includes civil suit and criminal, administrative, and investigatory action.

"Public organic record" means (i) the articles of incorporation of a domestic or foreign business or nonprofit corporation or (ii) the document, if any, the filing of which is required to create an unincorporated entity, or which creates the unincorporated entity and is required to be filed. Where a public organic record has been amended or restated, the term means the public organic record as last amended or restated.

"Record date" means the date fixed for determining the identity of the corporation's shareholders and their shareholdings for purposes of this Act. Unless another time is specified when the record date is fixed, the determination shall be made as of the close of business at the principal office of the corporation on the date so fixed.

"Record shareholder" means (i) the person in whose name shares are registered in the records of the corporation or (ii) the person identified as the beneficial owner of shares in a beneficial ownership certificate pursuant to section 7.23 on file with the corporation to the extent of the rights granted by such certificate.

"Registered foreign corporation" means a foreign corporation registered to do business in the state pursuant to chapter 15.

"Secretary" means the corporate officer to whom the board of directors has delegated responsibility under section 8.40(c) to maintain the minutes of the meetings of the board of directors and of the shareholders and for authenticating records of the corporation.

"Share exchange" means a transaction pursuant to section 11.03.

"Shareholder" means a record shareholder.

"Shares" means the units into which the proprietary interests in a domestic or foreign corporation are divided.

"Sign" or "signature" means, with present intent to authenticate or adopt a document:

    (i)   to execute or adopt a tangible symbol to a document, and includes any manual, facsimile, or conformed signature; or

(ii) to attach to or logically associate with an electronic transmission an electronic sound, symbol, or process, and includes an electronic signature in an electronic transmission.

"State," when referring to a part of the United States, includes a state and commonwealth (and their agencies and governmental subdivisions) and a territory and insular possession (and their agencies and governmental subdivisions) of the United States.

"Subscriber" means a person who subscribes for shares in a corporation, whether before or after incorporation.

"Type of entity" means a generic form of entity:

(i) recognized at common law; or

(ii) formed under an organic law, regardless of whether some entities formed under that law are subject to provisions of that law that create different categories of the form of entity.

"Unincorporated entity" means an organization or artificial legal person that either has a separate legal existence or has the power to acquire an estate in real property in its own name and that is not any of the following: a domestic or foreign business or nonprofit corporation, a series of a limited liability company or of another type of entity, an estate, a trust, a state, United States, or foreign government. The term includes a general partnership, limited liability company, limited partnership, business trust, joint stock association and unincorporated nonprofit association.

"United States" includes district, authority, bureau, commission, department, and any other agency of the United States.

"Unrestricted voting trust beneficial owner" means, with respect to any shareholder rights, a voting trust beneficial owner whose entitlement to exercise the shareholder right in question is not inconsistent with the voting trust agreement.

"Voting group" means all shares of one or more classes or series that under the articles of incorporation or this Act are entitled to vote and be counted together collectively on a matter at a meeting of shareholders. All shares entitled by the articles of incorporation or this Act to vote generally on the matter are for that purpose a single voting group.

"Voting power" means the current power to vote in the election of directors.

"Voting trust beneficial owner" means an owner of a beneficial interest in shares of the corporation held in a voting trust established pursuant to section 7.30(a).

"Writing" or "written" means any information in the form of a document.

OFFICIAL COMMENT

Section 1.40 contains definitions of terms used generally throughout the Act. Other subchapters and sections of the Act contain specialized definitions that are applicable only to those subchapters or sections.

Beneficial Shareholder

Because various provisions of the Act allow beneficial owners of shares to take actions as a shareholder even in the absence of a beneficial ownership certificate under section 7.23, the term "beneficial shareholder" has been defined in section 1.40.

The definition does not specify what interests are necessary for a person to be a beneficial shareholder, but consistent with section 8-207(a) of the Uniform Commercial Code, the Act contemplates that the corporation is entitled to treat the beneficial shareholder as having the full bundle of economic and voting rights associated with the shares. For this reason, the beneficial owner of shares in a voting trust has been defined separately in section 1.40 as a "voting trust beneficial owner."

Unlike section 7.23, which provides for a procedure to specify a beneficial owner in a beneficial ownership certificate, the definition of "beneficial shareholder" does not prescribe a procedure for establishing beneficial ownership. Where a court proceeding is involved, as it is, for example, in sections 7.41 (derivative proceeding), 13.30 (appraisal rights), and 14.30 (judicial dissolution), the court can determine what is necessary to establish beneficial ownership. In other situations, custom and practice and the reasonable requirements of the corporation should apply. Thus, a certification of a broker-dealer or other financial institution or a current account statement from such an institution often is sufficient to establish beneficial ownership. In the case of a public corporation, a filing with the Securities and Exchange Commission identifying beneficial ownership might be sufficient.

When shares of a public corporation are held, as explained in the Official Comment to section 7.23, indirectly in street name with a broker-dealer or other financial institution, which may in turn have the shares on deposit with Depository Trust Company ("DTC") as a clearing agency, a reference to shares in this Act is technically a reference to a "securities entitlement" under section 8–102(a)(17) of the Uniform Commercial Code, which is an undivided interest in a mass of shares held by the financial intermediary or on deposit with DTC. Nevertheless, the Act continues for convenience to refer to the interests as "shares," and thus references to shares should be read to include securities entitlements with respect to those shares.

Conspicuous

"Conspicuous" is defined in section 1.40 and is comparable to section 1–201(10) of the Uniform Commercial Code. The test is whether attention can reasonably be expected to be elicited.

Corporation, Domestic Corporation, Domestic Business Corporation, Business Corporation and Foreign Corporation

"Corporation," "domestic corporation," "business corporation," and "domestic business corporation," as defined in section 1.40, all mean the same thing and may be used interchangeably. The word "corporation," when used alone, refers only to a domestic corporation. In some instances, the phrase "domestic corporation" has been used to contrast it with a foreign corporation, a term also defined in section 1.40. The phrase "domestic business corporation" has been used on occasion to contrast it with a domestic nonprofit corporation. "Corporation" has been given special meanings in sections 5.01, 8.50 and 13.01.

Distribution

Section 1.40 defines "distribution" to include all transfers of cash or other property made by a corporation to any shareholder in respect of the corporation's shares, except mere changes in the unit of interest such as share dividends and share splits. Thus, a "distribution" includes the payment of a dividend, a purchase by a corporation of its own shares, a distribution of evidences of indebtedness or promissory notes of the corporation, and a distribution in voluntary or involuntary liquidation. If a corporation incurs indebtedness to shareholders in connection with a distribution (as in the case of a distribution of a debt instrument or an installment purchase of shares), the creation, incurrence, or distribution of the indebtedness is the event which constitutes the distribution rather than the subsequent payment of the debt by the corporation, except in the situation addressed in section 6.40(g).

The term "indirect" in the definition of "distribution" is intended to address transactions like the repurchase of parent company shares by a subsidiary whose actions are controlled by the parent. It also is intended to address any other transaction in which the substance is clearly the same as a typical dividend or share repurchase, no matter how structured or labeled.

The test for validity of distributions other than distributions in liquidation is set forth in section 6.40, and for distributions in liquidation in chapter 14.

Electronic Transmission

The terms "electronic," "electronic record," "electronic transmission" and "electronically transmitted" incorporate into the Act terminology from the Uniform Electronic Transmissions Act ("UETA") and the federal Electronic Signatures in Global and National Commerce Act ("E-Sign"). See Official Comment to section 1.41, Note on the Relationship Between Act Provisions on Electronic Technology and UETA and E-Sign. Electronic records and transmissions are intended to be broadly construed.

Entity

The term "entity," defined in section 1.40, appears in the definition of "person" in section 1.40 and covers all types of artificial persons. Estates and trusts and general partnerships are included even though they may not, in some jurisdictions, be considered artificial persons. "Trust," by itself, means a nonbusiness trust, such as a traditional testamentary or inter vivos trust. The term "entity" is broader than the term "unincorporated entity" which is also defined in section 1.40. See also the definitions in section 1.40 of "governmental subdivision," "state," and "United States." A form of co-ownership of property or sharing of returns from property that is not a partnership under the Uniform Partnership Act will not be an "unincorporated entity."

Expenses

The Act provides in a number of contexts that expenses relating to a proceeding incurred by a person shall or may be paid by another, through indemnification or by court order in specific contexts. See, for example, sections 7.46, 7.48, 8.53(a), 8.54, 13.31, 14.32(e), 16.04(c) and 16.05(c). Other than the requirement that expenses must be reasonable in the circumstances, the type or character of the expenses is not limited. Examples include such things as fees and disbursements of counsel, experts of all kinds, and jury and similar litigation consultants; travel, lodging, transcription, reproduction, photographic, video recording, communication, and delivery costs, whether included in the disbursements of counsel, experts, or consultants, or directly incurred; court costs; and premiums for posting required bonds.

Interest Holder Liability

The term "interest holder liability" is used in the context of provisions in chapters 9 and 11 that describe the effects on the personal liability of shareholders, members and interest holders when the entity in which they hold shares, memberships or interests is the subject of a transaction under those chapters. The term is also used in section 2.02 and chapter 10 with respect to the articles of incorporation and certain amendments to them. The term includes only liabilities that are imposed solely because of the person's status as a shareholder, member or interest holder, or by the organic rules of an entity on shareholders, members or interest holders. Liabilities that a shareholder, member or interest holder incurs by contract (other than a contract that is part of an entity's organic rules, such as a partnership agreement) are not included. Thus, for example, if a state's business corporation law were to make shareholders personally liable for unpaid wages, that liability would be an "interest holder liability." If, on the other hand, a shareholder were to contractually guarantee payment of an obligation of a corporation, that liability would not be an "interest holder liability."

Membership

"Membership" is defined in section 1.40 to refer only to the rights of a member in a nonprofit corporation. Although the owners of a limited liability company are generally referred to as "members," for purposes of the Act they are referred to as "interest holders" and what they own in the limited liability company is referred to in the Act as an "interest."

Organic Rules, Public Organic Record and Private Organic Rules

The term "organic rules" in section 1.40 includes both public organic records and private organic rules. The term "public organic record" includes such documents as the articles of incorporation of a business or nonprofit corporation, the certificate of limited partnership of a limited partnership, the articles of organization or certificate of formation of a limited liability company, the deed of trust of a business trust and comparable documents, however denominated, that are publicly filed to create other types of unincorporated entities. An election of limited liability partnership status is not of itself a public organic record because it does not create the underlying general or limited partnership by filing the election, although the election may be made part of the public organic record of the partnership by its organic law. The term "private organic rules" includes corporate bylaws, a partnership agreement of a general or limited partnership, an operating agreement of a limited liability company and comparable agreements, however denominated, of unincorporated types of other entities. Private organic rules of unincorporated entities are not required by the Act to be in writing, and therefore would include oral partnership agreements and oral operating agreements.

Person

The term "person" is defined in section 1.40 to include an individual or an entity. In the case of an individual the Act assumes that the person is competent to act in the matter under general state law independent of the corporation statute.

Principal Office

Many corporations maintain numerous offices, but there is usually one office, sometimes colloquially referred to as the home office or headquarters, where the principal corporate officers are located. The corporation must designate its principal office address in the annual report required by section 16.21, and a foreign corporation must also do so in its foreign registration statement. To clarify which corporate office is the principal office, the Act defines the office designated by the corporation in the annual report (or foreign registration statement) as the principal office of the corporation.

Secretary

The term "secretary" is defined in section 1.40 because the Act does not require the corporation to maintain any specific or titled officers. See section 8.40. However, some corporate officer, however titled, must perform the functions described in this definition, and various sections of the Act refer to that officer as the "secretary."

Shareholder and Record Shareholder

The term "shareholder" is usually used in the Act to mean a "record shareholder" as defined in section 1.40, but section 1.40 contemplates that definitions may be expanded or limited by the Act for purposes of specific provisions. The definition of "record shareholder" in section 1.40 includes a beneficial owner of shares named in a beneficial ownership certificate under section 7.23, but only to the extent of the rights granted the beneficial owner in the certificate—for example, the right to receive notice of, and vote at, shareholders' meetings. Various substantive sections of the Act also permit holders of voting trust certificates or beneficial owners of shares (not subject to a beneficial ownership certificate under section 7.23) to exercise some of the rights of a "shareholder." See, for example, section 7.40, which relates to derivative proceedings. Separate definitions of "voting trust beneficial owner," "unrestricted voting trust beneficial owner" and "beneficial shareholder" also appear in section 1.40.

Sign or Signature

The definition of "sign" or "signature" incorporates into the Act concepts and terminology from UETA and the federal E-Sign. Thus, the terms "sign" and "signature" include not only traditional forms of signing, such as manual, facsimile, or conformed signatures, but also electronic signatures in electronic transmissions. The intent of the Act is that any manifestation of an intention to sign or authenticate a document be accepted, although electronic transmissions having electronic signatures must comply with the requirements in the definition of "electronic transmission," including being retrievable in paper form by the recipient through an automated process unless otherwise authorized in accordance with section 1.41(j).

Unincorporated Entity

The term "unincorporated entity" is a subset of the broader term "entity" and includes an unincorporated nonprofit association. The Uniform Unincorporated Nonprofit Association Act gives an unincorporated nonprofit association the power to acquire an estate in real property and thus an unincorporated nonprofit association organized in a state that has adopted that act will be an "unincorporated entity." At common law, an unincorporated nonprofit association was not a legal entity and did not have the power to acquire real property.

As used in the definition of unincorporated entity, "business trust" includes any trust carrying on a business, such as a Massachusetts business trust, real estate investment trust, or other common law or statutory business trust. The term "unincorporated entity" (and thus the term "eligible entity") expressly excludes series of limited liability companies or of other types of entities, and estates and trusts (*i.e.*, trusts that are not business trusts), regardless of whether they would be considered artificial persons under the governing jurisdiction's law, to make it clear that they are not eligible to participate in a conversion under chapter 9 or a merger or share exchange under chapter 11.

Voting Group

Section 1.40 defines "voting group" for purposes of the Act as a matter of convenient reference. When the definition refers to shares entitled to vote "generally" on a matter, it signifies all shares entitled to vote together on the matter by the articles of incorporation or the Act, regardless of whether they also have the right to be counted or tabulated separately. "Voting groups" are thus the basic units of collective voting by shareholders, and voting by voting groups may provide essential protection to one or more classes or series of shares against actions that are detrimental to the rights or interests of that class or series.

The determination of which shares form part of a single voting group must be made from the provisions of the articles of incorporation and of the Act. In a few instances under the Act, the board of directors may establish the right to vote by voting groups. On most matters to be voted on by shareholders, only a single voting group, consisting of a class of voting or common shares, will be involved, and action on such a matter is effective when approved by that voting group pursuant to section 7.25. In other circumstances, the vote of multiple groups may be required. See sections 7.25 and 7.26.

Voting Power

Application of the definition of "voting power" turns on whether the relevant shares carry the power to vote in the election of directors as of the time for voting on the relevant transaction. If shares carry the power to vote in the election of directors only under a certain contingency, as is often the case with preferred stock, the shares would not carry voting power within the meaning of section 1.40 unless the contingency has occurred, and then only during the period when the voting rights are in effect. Shares that carry the power to vote for any directors as of the time to vote on the relevant transaction have the current power to vote in the election of directors within the meaning of the definition, even if the shares do not carry the power to vote for all directors.

Voting Trust Beneficial Owner and Unrestricted Voting Trust Beneficial Owner

Section 1.40 has a separate definition of "voting trust beneficial owner" because the number of such owners and value of their shares can enter into determinations under sections 13.02(b)(1) and 14.30(b)(ii). It also has a separate definition of "unrestricted voting trust beneficial owner" because rights are given under some provisions of the Act for a beneficial owner of shares deposited in a voting trust established under section 7.30 to take actions as a shareholder. These owners have the economic interest in the shares but the voting rights have been given to the voting trustee. In addition to the typical grant of voting rights, section 7.30 permits the voting trust agreement to confer on the voting trustee the right otherwise to act with respect to the shares, and thus could vest in the trustee the exclusive right to exercise statutory shareholder rights. The term "unrestricted voting trust beneficial owner" is used to distinguish from this possible limitation. If the voting trust agreement grants the trustee the exclusive right to act with respect to the shareholder right in question, then the voting trustee, and not the voting trust beneficial owner, may exercise those rights.

Writing or Written

"Writing" or "written" means information in the form of a "document," which in turn means any tangible medium on which information is inscribed, such as a paper instrument, as well as an electronic record. Thus, under the Act a written consent of shareholders under section 7.04, for example, may be in the form of paper or an electronic record.

§ 1.41   Notices and Other Communications

(a) A notice under this Act must be in writing unless oral notice is reasonable in the circumstances. Unless otherwise agreed between the sender and the recipient, words in a notice or other communication under this Act must be in English.

(b) A notice or other communication may be given by any method of delivery, except that electronic transmissions must be in accordance with this section. If the methods of delivery are impracticable, a notice or other communication may be given by means of a broad non-exclusionary distribution to the public (which may include a newspaper of general circulation in the area where published; radio, television, or other form of public broadcast communication; or other methods of distribution that the corporation has previously identified to its shareholders).

(c)   A notice or other communication to a domestic corporation or to a foreign corporation registered to do business in this state may be delivered to the corporation's registered agent at its registered office or to the secretary at the corporation's principal office shown in its most recent annual report or, in the case of a foreign corporation that has not yet delivered an annual report, in its foreign registration statement.

(d)   A notice or other communications may be delivered by electronic transmission if consented to by the recipient or if authorized by subsection (j).

(e)   Any consent under subsection (d) may be revoked by the person who consented by written or electronic notice to the person to whom the consent was delivered. Any such consent is deemed revoked if (i) the corporation is unable to deliver two consecutive electronic transmissions given by the corporation in accordance with such consent, and (ii) such inability becomes known to the secretary or an assistant secretary or to the transfer agent, or other person responsible for the giving of notice or other communications; provided, however, the inadvertent failure to treat such inability as a revocation shall not invalidate any meeting or other action.

(f)   Unless otherwise agreed between the sender and the recipient, an electronic transmission is received when:

(1)   it enters an information processing system that the recipient has designated or uses for the purposes of receiving electronic transmissions or information of the type sent, and from which the recipient is able to retrieve the electronic transmission; and

(2)   it is in a form capable of being processed by that system.

(g)   Receipt of an electronic acknowledgement from an information processing system described in subsection (f)(1) establishes that an electronic transmission was received but, by itself, does not establish that the content sent corresponds to the content received.

(h)   An electronic transmission is received under this section even if no person is aware of its receipt.

(i)   A notice or other communication, if in a comprehensible form or manner, is effective at the earliest of the following:

(1)   if in a physical form, the earliest of when it is actually received, or when it is left at:

(i)   a shareholder's address shown on the corporation's record of shareholders maintained by the corporation under section 16.01(d);

(ii)   a director's residence or usual place of business; or

(iii)   the corporation's principal office;

(2)   if mailed postage prepaid and correctly addressed to a shareholder, upon deposit in the United States mail;

(3)   if mailed by United States mail postage prepaid and correctly addressed to a recipient other than a shareholder, the earliest of when it is actually received, or:

(i)   if sent by registered or certified mail, return receipt requested, the date shown on the return receipt signed by or on behalf of the addressee; or

(ii)   five days after it is deposited in the United States mail;

(4)   if an electronic transmission, when it is received as provided in subsection (f); and

(5)   if oral, when communicated.

(j)   A notice or other communication may be in the form of an electronic transmission that cannot be directly reproduced in paper form by the recipient through an automated process used in conventional commercial practice only if (i) the electronic transmission is otherwise retrievable in perceivable form, and (ii) the sender and the recipient have consented in writing to the use of such form of electronic transmission.

(k) If this Act prescribes requirements for notices or other communications in particular circumstances, those requirements govern. If articles of incorporation or bylaws prescribe requirements for notices or other communications, not inconsistent with this section or other provisions of this Act, those requirements govern. The articles of incorporation or bylaws may authorize or require delivery of notices of meetings of directors by electronic transmission.

(*l*) In the event that any provisions of this Act are deemed to modify, limit, or supersede the federal Electronic Signatures in Global and National Commerce Act, 15 U.S.C. §§ 7001 et seq., the provisions of this Act shall control to the maximum extent permitted by section 102(a)(2) of that federal act.

(m) Whenever notice would otherwise be required to be given under any provision of this Act to a shareholder, the notice need not be given if:

(1) notices to shareholders of two consecutive annual meetings, and all notices of meetings during the period between such two consecutive annual meetings, have been sent, other than by electronic transmission, to such shareholder at such shareholder's address as shown on the records of the corporation and have been returned undeliverable or could not be delivered; or

(2) all, but not less than two, distributions to shareholders during a 12-month period, or two consecutive distributions to shareholders during a period of more than 12 months, have been sent to such shareholder at such shareholder's address as shown on the records of the corporation and have been returned undeliverable or could not be delivered.

If any shareholder to which this subsection (m) applies delivers to the corporation a written notice setting forth such shareholder's then-current address, the requirement that notice be given to such shareholder shall be reinstated.

§ 1.42 Number of Shareholders

(a) For purposes of this Act, the following identified as a shareholder in a corporation's current record of shareholders constitutes one shareholder:

(1) three or fewer co-owners;

(2) a corporation, partnership, trust, estate, or other entity; and

(3) the trustees, guardians, custodians, or other fiduciaries of a single trust, estate, or account.

(b) For purposes of this Act, shareholdings registered in substantially similar names constitute one shareholder if it is reasonable to believe that the names represent the same person.

§ 1.43 Qualified Director

(a) A "qualified director" is a director who, at the time action is to be taken under:

(1) section 2.02(b)(6), is not a director (i) to whom the limitation or elimination of the duty of an officer to offer potential business opportunities to the corporation would apply, or (ii) who has a material relationship with any other person to whom the limitation or elimination would apply;

(2) section 7.44, does not have (i) a material interest in the outcome of the proceeding, or (ii) a material relationship with a person who has such an interest;

(3) section 8.53 or 8.55, (i) is not a party to the proceeding, (ii) is not a director as to whom a transaction is a director's conflicting interest transaction or who sought a disclaimer of the corporation's interest in a business opportunity under section 8.70, which transaction or

disclaimer is challenged in the proceeding, and (iii) does not have a material relationship with a director described in either clause (i) or clause (ii) of this subsection (a)(3);

(4)   section 8.62, is not a director (i) as to whom the transaction is a director's conflicting interest transaction, or (ii) who has a material relationship with another director as to whom the transaction is a director's conflicting interest transaction; or

(5)   section 8.70, is not a director who (i) pursues or takes advantage of the business opportunity, directly, or indirectly through or on behalf of another person, or (ii) has a material relationship with a director or officer who pursues or takes advantage of the business opportunity, directly, or indirectly through or on behalf of another person.

(b)   For purposes of this section:

(1)   "material relationship" means a familial, financial, professional, employment or other relationship that would reasonably be expected to impair the objectivity of the director's judgment when participating in the action to be taken; and

(2)   "material interest" means an actual or potential benefit or detriment (other than one which would devolve on the corporation or the shareholders generally) that would reasonably be expected to impair the objectivity of the director's judgment when participating in the action to be taken.

(c)   The presence of one or more of the following circumstances shall not automatically prevent a director from being a qualified director:

(1)   nomination or election of the director to the current board by any director who is not a qualified director with respect to the matter (or by any person that has a material relationship with that director), acting alone or participating with others;

(2)   service as a director of another corporation of which a director who is not a qualified director with respect to the matter (or any individual who has a material relationship with that director), is or was also a director; or

(3)   with respect to action to be taken under section 7.44, status as a named defendant, as a director against whom action is demanded, or as a director who approved the conduct being challenged.

OFFICIAL COMMENT

The definition of the term "qualified director" identifies those directors: (i) who may take action on the dismissal of a derivative proceeding (section 7.44); (ii) who are eligible to make, in the first instance, the authorization and determination required in connection with the decision on a request for advance for expenses (section 8.53(c)) or for indemnification (sections 8.55(b) and (c)); (iii) who may authorize a director's conflicting interest transaction (section 8.62); (iv) who may disclaim the corporation's interest in a business opportunity (section 8.70(a)); and (v) who may make applicable the limitation or elimination of a duty of an officer to offer the corporation business opportunities before the officer or a related person of the officer pursues or takes the opportunity (section 2.02(b)(6)).

Although the term "qualified director" embraces the concept of independence, it does so only in relation to the director's interest or involvement in the specific situations to which the definition applies. The judicial decisions that have examined the qualifications of directors for such purposes have generally required that directors be both *disinterested,* in the sense of not having exposure to an actual or potential benefit or detriment arising out of the action being taken (as opposed to an actual or potential benefit or detriment to the corporation or all shareholders generally), and *independent,* in the sense of having no personal or other relationship with an interested director (*e.g.,* a director who is a party to a transaction with the corporation) that presents a reasonable likelihood that the director's objectivity will be impaired. The "qualified director" concept embraces both of those requirements, and its application is situation-specific; that is, "qualified director" determinations will depend upon the directly relevant facts and circumstances, and the disqualification of a director to act arises from factors that would reasonably be expected to impair the objectivity of the director's judgment. On the other hand, the concept does not suggest that a "qualified director" has or should have special expertise to act on the matter in question.

1. Disqualification Due to Conflicting Interest

The "qualified director" concept prescribes significant disqualifications, depending upon the purpose for which a director might be considered eligible to participate in the action to be taken. These disqualifications include the following:

- In the case of action under a provision adopted under the authority of section 2.02(b)(6) to limit or eliminate any duty of an officer to offer the corporation business opportunities, the definition excludes any director who is also an officer and to whom the provision would apply.

- In the case of action on dismissal of a derivative proceeding under section 7.44, the definition excludes any director who has a material interest in the outcome of the proceeding, such as where the proceeding involves a challenge to the validity of a transaction in which the director has a material financial interest.

- In the case of action to approve indemnification or advance of funds for expenses, the definition excludes any director who is a party to the proceeding (see section 8.50 for the definition of "party" and for the definition of "proceeding").

- In the case of action to approve a director's conflicting interest transaction, the definition excludes any director whose interest, knowledge or status results in the transaction being treated as a "director's conflicting interest transaction." See section 8.60 for the definition of "director's conflicting interest transaction."

- In the case of action under section 8.70(a) to disclaim corporate interest in a business opportunity, the definition excludes any director who directly or indirectly pursues or takes advantage of the business opportunity, or who has a material relationship with another director or officer who does so.

Whether a director has a material interest in the outcome of a proceeding in which the director does not have a conflicting personal interest is heavily fact-dependent. At one end of the spectrum, if a claim against a director is clearly frivolous or is not supported by particularized and well-pleaded facts, the director should not be deemed to have a "material interest in the outcome of the proceeding" within the meaning of section 1.43(a)(2), even though the director is named as a defendant. At the other end of the spectrum, a director normally should be deemed to have a "material interest in the outcome of the proceeding" within the meaning of section 1.43(a)(2) if a claim against the director is supported by particularized and well-pleaded facts which, if true, would be likely to give rise to a significant adverse outcome against the director.

2. Disqualification Due to Relationships with Interested Persons

In each context in which the "qualified director" definition applies, it also excludes any director who has a "material relationship" with another director (or, with respect to a provision applying to an officer under section 2.02(b)(6) or section 8.70, a "material relationship" with that officer) who is not disinterested for one or more of the reasons outlined in the preceding paragraph. Any relationship with such a person, whether the relationship is familial, financial, professional, employment or otherwise, is a "material relationship," as that term is defined in section 1.43(b)(1), if it would reasonably be expected to impair the objectivity of the director's judgment when voting or otherwise participating in action to be taken on a matter referred to in section 1.43(a). The determination of whether there is a "material relationship" should be based on the practicalities of the situation rather than on formalistic considerations. For example, a director employed by a corporation controlled by another director should be regarded as having an employment relationship with that director. On the other hand, a casual social acquaintance with another director should not be regarded as a disqualifying relationship.

The term "qualified director" is distinct from the generic term "independent director," which is not used in the Act. As a result, a director who might typically be viewed as an "independent director" may in some circumstances not be a "qualified director," and vice versa. See also the Official Comment to section 8.01.

3. Elimination of Automatic Disqualification in Certain Circumstances

Section 1.43(c) addresses three categories of circumstances that, if present alone or together, do not automatically prevent a director from being a qualified director:

- Subsection (c)(1) makes it clear that the participation of nonqualified directors (or interested shareholders or other interested persons) in the nomination or election of a director does not automatically prevent the director so nominated or elected from being qualified. Special litigation committees acting with regard to derivative litigation often consist of directors nominated or elected (after the alleged wrongful acts) by directors named as defendants in the action. In other settings, directors who are seeking indemnification, or who are interested in a director's conflicting interest transaction, may have participated in the nomination or election of an individual director who is otherwise a "qualified director."

- Subsection (c)(2) provides, in a similar fashion, that the mere fact that an individual director is or was a director of another corporation—on the board of which a director who is not a "qualified director" also serves or has served—does not automatically prevent qualification to act.

- Subsection (c)(3) confirms a number of decisions, involving dismissal of derivative proceedings, in which the court rejected a disqualification claim predicated on the mere fact that a director had been named as a defendant, was an individual against whom action has been demanded, or had approved the action being challenged. These cases have held that, where a director's approval of the challenged action is at issue, approval does not automatically make the director ineligible to act. On the other hand, for example, director approval of a challenged transaction, in combination with other particularized facts showing that the director's ability to act objectively on a proposal to dismiss a derivative proceeding is impaired by a material conflicting personal interest in the transaction, disqualifies a director from acting on the proposal to dismiss the proceeding.

The effect of section 1.43(c), while significant, is limited. It merely precludes an automatic inference of director disqualification from the circumstances specified in that subsection.

§ 1.44   Householding

(a)   A corporation has delivered written notice or any other report or statement under this Act, the articles of incorporation or the bylaws to all shareholders who share a common address if:

(1)   the corporation delivers one copy of the notice, report or statement to the common address;

(2)   the corporation addresses the notice, report or statement to those shareholders either as a group or to each of those shareholders individually or to the shareholders in a form to which each of those shareholders has consented; and

(3)   each of those shareholders consents to delivery of a single copy of such notice, report or statement to the shareholders' common address.

(b)   Any such consent described in subsections (a)(2) or (a)(3) shall be revocable by any of such shareholders who deliver written notice of revocation to the corporation. If such written notice of revocation is delivered, the corporation shall begin providing individual notices, reports or other statements to the revoking shareholder no later than 30 days after delivery of the written notice of revocation.

(c)   Any shareholder who fails to object by written notice to the corporation, within 60 days of written notice by the corporation of its intention to deliver single copies of notices, reports or statements to shareholders who share a common address as permitted by subsection (a), shall be deemed to have consented to receiving such single copy at the common address; provided that the notice of intention explains that consent may be revoked and the method for revoking.

SUBCHAPTER E.   RATIFICATION OF DEFECTIVE CORPORATE ACTIONS

§ 1.45   Definitions

In this subchapter:

"Corporate action" means any action taken by or on behalf of the corporation, including any action taken by the incorporator, the board of directors, a committee of the board of directors, an officer or agent of the corporation or the shareholders.

"Date of the defective corporate action" means the date (or the approximate date, if the exact date is unknown) the defective corporate action was purported to have been taken.

"Defective corporate action" means (i) any corporate action purportedly taken that is, and at the time such corporate action was purportedly taken would have been, within the power of the corporation, but is void or voidable due to a failure of authorization, and (ii) an overissue.

"Failure of authorization" means the failure to authorize, approve or otherwise effect a corporate action in compliance with the provisions of this Act, the articles of incorporation or bylaws, a corporate resolution or any plan or agreement to which the corporation is a party, if and to the extent such failure would render such corporate action void or voidable.

"Overissue" means the purported issuance of:

(i)   shares of a class or series in excess of the number of shares of a class or series the corporation has the power to issue under section 6.01 at the time of such issuance; or

(ii)   shares of any class or series that is not then authorized for issuance by the articles of incorporation.

"Putative shares" means the shares of any class or series (including shares issued upon exercise of rights, options, warrants or other securities convertible into shares of the corporation, or interests with respect to such shares) that were created or issued as a result of a defective corporate action, that (i) but for any failure of authorization would constitute valid shares, or (ii) cannot be determined by the board of directors to be valid shares.

"Valid shares" means the shares of any class or series that have been duly authorized and validly issued in accordance with this Act, including as a result of ratification or validation under this subchapter.

"Validation effective time" with respect to any defective corporate action ratified under this subchapter means the later of:

(i)   the time at which the ratification of the defective corporate action is approved by the shareholders, or if approval of shareholders is not required, the time at which the notice required by section 1.49 becomes effective in accordance with section 1.41; and

(ii)   the time at which any articles of validation filed in accordance with section 1.51 become effective.

The validation effective time shall not be affected by the filing or pendency of a judicial proceeding under section 1.52 or otherwise, unless otherwise ordered by the court.

§ 1.46   Defective Corporate Actions

(a)   A defective corporate action shall not be void or voidable if ratified in accordance with section 1.47 or validated in accordance with section 1.52.

(b)   Ratification under section 1.47 or validation under section 1.52 shall not be deemed to be the exclusive means of ratifying or validating any defective corporate action, and the absence or failure of ratification in accordance with this subchapter shall not, of itself, affect the validity or effectiveness of any corporate action properly ratified under common law or otherwise, nor shall it create a presumption that any such corporate action is or was a defective corporate action or void or voidable.

(c)   In the case of an overissue, putative shares shall be valid shares effective as of the date originally issued or purportedly issued upon:

(1)   the effectiveness under this subchapter and under chapter 10 of an amendment to the articles of incorporation authorizing, designating or creating such shares; or

(2)   the effectiveness of any other corporate action under this subchapter ratifying the authorization, designation or creation of such shares.

§ 1.47   Ratification of Defective Corporate Actions

(a)   To ratify a defective corporate action under this section (other than the ratification of an election of the initial board of directors under subsection (b)), the board of directors shall take action ratifying the action in accordance with section 1.48, stating:

(1)   the defective corporate action to be ratified and, if the defective corporate action involved the issuance of putative shares, the number and type of putative shares purportedly issued;

(2)   the date of the defective corporate action;

(3)   the nature of the failure of authorization with respect to the defective corporate action to be ratified; and

(4)   that the board of directors approves the ratification of the defective corporate action.

(b)   In the event that a defective corporate action to be ratified relates to the election of the initial board of directors of the corporation under section 2.05(a)(2), a majority of the persons who, at the time of the ratification, are exercising the powers of directors may take an action stating:

(1)   the name of the person or persons who first took action in the name of the corporation as the initial board of directors of the corporation;

(2)   the earlier of the date on which such persons first took such action or were purported to have been elected as the initial board of directors; and

(3)   that the ratification of the election of such person or persons as the initial board of directors is approved.

(c)   If any provision of this Act, the articles of incorporation or bylaws, any corporate resolution or any plan or agreement to which the corporation is a party in effect at the time action under subsection (a) is taken requires shareholder approval or would have required shareholder approval at the date of the occurrence of the defective corporate action, the ratification of the defective corporate action approved in the action taken by the directors under subsection (a) shall be submitted to the shareholders for approval in accordance with section 1.48.

(d)   Unless otherwise provided in the action taken by the board of directors under subsection (a), after the action by the board of directors has been taken and, if required, approved by the shareholders, the board of directors may abandon the ratification at any time before the validation effective time without further action of the shareholders.

§ 1.48   Action on Ratification

(a)   The quorum and voting requirements applicable to a ratifying action by the board of directors under section 1.47(a) shall be the quorum and voting requirements applicable to the corporate action proposed to be ratified at the time such ratifying action is taken.

(b)   If the ratification of the defective corporate action requires approval by the shareholders under section 1.47(c), and if the approval is to be given at a meeting, the corporation shall notify each holder of valid and putative shares, regardless of whether entitled to vote, as of the record date for notice of the meeting and as of the date of the occurrence of defective corporate action, provided that notice shall not be required to be given to holders of valid or putative shares whose identities or addresses for notice cannot be determined from the records of the corporation. The notice must state that the purpose, or one of the purposes, of the meeting, is to consider ratification of a defective corporate action and must be accompanied by (i) either a copy of the action taken by the board of directors in accordance with section 1.47(a) or the information required by sections 1.47(a)(1) through (a)(4), and (ii) a statement that any claim that the ratification of such defective corporate action and any putative shares issued as a result of such defective corporate action should not be effective, or should be effective only on certain conditions, shall be brought within 120 days from the applicable validation effective time.

(c) Except as provided in subsection (d) with respect to the voting requirements to ratify the election of a director, the quorum and voting requirements applicable to the approval by the shareholders required by section 1.47(c) shall be the quorum and voting requirements applicable to the corporate action proposed to be ratified at the time of such shareholder approval.

(d) The approval by shareholders to ratify the election of a director requires that the votes cast within the voting group favoring such ratification exceed the votes cast opposing such ratification of the election at a meeting at which a quorum is present.

(e) Putative shares on the record date for determining the shareholders entitled to vote on any matter submitted to shareholders under section 1.47(c) (and without giving effect to any ratification of putative shares that becomes effective as a result of such vote) shall neither be entitled to vote nor counted for quorum purposes in any vote to approve the ratification of any defective corporate action.

(f) If the approval under this section of putative shares would result in an overissue, in addition to the approval required by section 1.47, approval of an amendment to the articles of incorporation under chapter 10 to increase the number of shares of an authorized class or series or to authorize the creation of a class or series of shares so there would be no overissue shall also be required.

§ 1.49 Notice Requirements

(a) Unless shareholder approval is required under section 1.47(c), prompt notice of an action taken under section 1.47 shall be given to each holder of valid and putative shares, regardless of whether entitled to vote, as of (i) the date of such action by the board of directors and (ii) the date of the defective corporate action ratified, provided that notice shall not be required to be given to holders of valid and putative shares whose identities or addresses for notice cannot be determined from the records of the corporation.

(b) The notice must contain (i) either a copy of the action taken by the board of directors in accordance with section 1.47(a) or (b) or the information required by sections 1.47(a)(1) through (a)(4) or sections 1.47(b)(1) through (b)(3), as applicable, and (ii) a statement that any claim that the ratification of the defective corporate action and any putative shares issued as a result of such defective corporate action should not be effective, or should be effective only on certain conditions, shall be brought within 120 days from the applicable validation effective time.

(c) No notice under this section is required with respect to any action required to be submitted to shareholders for approval under section 1.47(c) if notice is given in accordance with section 1.48(b).

(d) A notice required by this section may be given in any manner permitted by section 1.41 and, for any corporation subject to the reporting requirements of Section 13 or 15(d) of the Securities Exchange Act of 1934, may be given by means of a filing or furnishing of such notice with the United States Securities and Exchange Commission.

§ 1.50   Effect of Ratification

From and after the validation effective time, and without regard to the 120-day period during which a claim may be brought under section 1.52:

(a)   Each defective corporate action ratified in accordance with section 1.47 shall not be void or voidable as a result of the failure of authorization identified in the action taken under section 1.47(a) or (b) and shall be deemed a valid corporate action effective as of the date of the defective corporate action;

(b)   The issuance of each putative share or fraction of a putative share purportedly issued pursuant to a defective corporate action identified in the action taken under section 1.47 shall not be void or voidable, and each such putative share or fraction of a putative share shall be deemed to be an identical share or fraction of a valid share as of the time it was purportedly issued; and

(c)   Any corporate action taken subsequent to the defective corporate action ratified in accordance with this subchapter in reliance on such defective corporate action having been validly effected and any subsequent defective corporate action resulting directly or indirectly from such original defective corporate action shall be valid as of the time taken.

§ 1.51   Filings

(a)   If the defective corporate action ratified under this subchapter would have required under any other section of this Act a filing in accordance with this Act, then, regardless of whether a filing was previously made in respect of such defective corporate action and in lieu of a filing otherwise required by this Act, the corporation shall file articles of validation in accordance with this section, and such articles of validation shall serve to amend or substitute for any other filing with respect to such defective corporate action required by this Act.

(b)   The articles of validation must set forth:

(1)   the defective corporate action that is the subject of the articles of validation (including, in the case of any defective corporate action involving the issuance of putative shares, the number and type of putative shares issued and the date or dates upon which such putative shares were purported to have been issued);

(2)   the date of the defective corporate action;

(3)   the nature of the failure of authorization in respect of the defective corporate action;

(4)   a statement that the defective corporate action was ratified in accordance with section 1.47, including the date on which the board of directors ratified such defective corporate action and the date, if any, on which the shareholders approved the ratification of such defective corporate action; and

(5)   the information required by subsection (c).

(c)   The articles of validation must also contain the following information:

(1)   if a filing was previously made in respect of the defective corporate action and no changes to such filing are required to give effect to the ratification of such defective corporate action in accordance with section 1.47, the articles of validation must set forth (i) the name, title and filing date of the filing previously made and any articles of correction to that filing and (ii) a statement that a copy of the filing previously made, together with any articles of correction to that filing, is attached as an exhibit to the articles of validation;

(2)   if a filing was previously made in respect of the defective corporate action and such filing requires any change to give effect to the ratification of such defective corporate action in accordance with section 1.47, the articles of validation must set forth (i) the name, title and filing date of the filing previously made and any articles of correction to that filing and (ii) a statement that a filing containing all of the information required to be included under the applicable section

or sections of the Act to give effect to such defective corporate action is attached as an exhibit to the articles of validation, and (iii) the date and time that such filing is deemed to have become effective; or

(3)   if a filing was not previously made in respect of the defective corporate action and the defective corporate action ratified under section 1.47 would have required a filing under any other section of the Act, the articles of validation must set forth (i) a statement that a filing containing all of the information required to be included under the applicable section or sections of the Act to give effect to such defective corporate action is attached as an exhibit to the articles of validation, and (ii) the date and time that such filing is deemed to have become effective.

§ 1.52   Judicial Proceedings Regarding Validity of Corporate Actions

(a)   Upon application by the corporation, any successor entity to the corporation, a director of the corporation, any shareholder, beneficial shareholder or unrestricted voting trust beneficial owner of the corporation, including any such shareholder, beneficial shareholder or unrestricted voting trust beneficial owner as of the date of the defective corporate action ratified under section 1.47, or any other person claiming to be substantially and adversely affected by a ratification under section 1.47, the [name or describe court] may:

(1)   determine the validity and effectiveness of any corporate action or defective corporate action;

(2)   determine the validity and effectiveness of any ratification under section 1.47;

(3)   determine the validity of any putative shares; and

(4)   modify or waive any of the procedures specified in section 1.47 or 1.48 to ratify a defective corporate action.

(b)   In connection with an action under this section, the court may make such findings or orders, and take into account any factors or considerations, regarding such matters as it deems proper under the circumstances.

(c)   Service of process of the application under subsection (a) on the corporation may be made in any manner provided by statute of this state or by rule of the applicable court for service on the corporation, and no other party need be joined in order for the court to adjudicate the matter. In an action filed by the corporation, the court may require notice of the action be provided to other persons specified by the court and permit such other persons to intervene in the action.

(d)   Notwithstanding any other provision of this section or otherwise under applicable law, any action asserting that the ratification of any defective corporate action and any putative shares issued as a result of such defective corporate action should not be effective, or should be effective only on certain conditions, shall be brought within 120 days of the validation effective time.

CHAPTER 2.   INCORPORATION

§ 2.01   Incorporators

One or more persons may act as the incorporator or incorporators of a corporation by delivering articles of incorporation to the secretary of state for filing.

§ 2.02   Articles of Incorporation

(a)   The articles of incorporation must set forth:

(1)   a corporate name for the corporation that satisfies the requirements of section 4.01;

(2)   the number of shares the corporation is authorized to issue;

    (3)   the street and mailing addresses of the corporation's initial registered office and the name of its initial registered agent at that office; and

    (4)   the name and address of each incorporator.

  (b)   The articles of incorporation may set forth:

    (1)   the names and addresses of the individuals who are to serve as the initial directors;

    (2)   provisions not inconsistent with law regarding:

        (i)   the purpose or purposes for which the corporation is organized;

        (ii)   managing the business and regulating the affairs of the corporation;

        (iii)   defining, limiting, and regulating the powers of the corporation, its board of directors, and shareholders;

        (iv)   a par value for authorized shares or classes of shares; or

        (v)   the imposition of interest holder liability on shareholders;

    (3)   any provision that under this Act is required or permitted to be set forth in the bylaws;

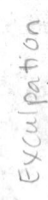

    (4)   a provision eliminating or limiting the liability of a director to the corporation or its shareholders for money damages for any action taken, or any failure to take any action, as a director, except liability for (i) the amount of a financial benefit received by a director to which the director is not entitled; (ii) an intentional infliction of harm on the corporation or the shareholders; (iii) a violation of section 8.32; or (iv) an intentional violation of criminal law;

    (5)   a provision permitting or making obligatory indemnification of a director for liability as defined in section 8.50 to any person for any action taken, or any failure to take any action, as a director, except liability for (i) receipt of a financial benefit to which the director is not entitled, (ii) an intentional infliction of harm on the corporation or the shareholders, (iii) a violation of section 8.32, or (iv) an intentional violation of criminal law; and

    (6)   a provision limiting or eliminating any duty of a director or any other person to offer the corporation the right to have or participate in any, or one or more classes or categories of, business opportunities, before the pursuit or taking of the opportunity by the director or other person; provided that any application of such a provision to an officer or a related person of that officer (i) also requires approval of that application by the board of directors, subsequent to the effective date of the provision, by action of qualified directors taken in compliance with the same procedures as are set forth in section 8.62, and (ii) may be limited by the authorizing action of the board.

  (c)   The articles of incorporation need not set forth any of the corporate powers enumerated in this Act.

  (d)   Provisions of the articles of incorporation may be made dependent upon facts objectively ascertainable outside the articles of incorporation in accordance with section 1.20(k).

  (e)   As used in this section, "related person" has the meaning specified in section 8.60.

§ 2.03   Incorporation

  (a)   Unless a delayed effective date is specified, the corporate existence begins when the articles of incorporation are filed.

  (b)   The secretary of state's filing of the articles of incorporation is conclusive proof that the incorporators satisfied all conditions precedent to incorporation except in a proceeding by the state to cancel or revoke the incorporation or involuntarily dissolve the corporation.

§2.04 Liability for Preincorporation Transactions

All persons purporting to act as or on behalf of a corporation, knowing there was no incorporation under this Act, are jointly and severally liable for all liabilities created while so acting.

OFFICIAL COMMENT

Ordinarily, only the filing of articles of incorporation should create the privilege of limited liability. Situations may arise, however, in which the protection of limited liability arguably should be recognized even though the simple incorporation process established by the Act has not been completed.

As a result, the Act imposes liability only on persons who act as or on behalf of corporations "knowing" that no corporation exists. In addition, section 2.04 does not foreclose the possibility that persons who urge defendants to execute contracts in the corporate name knowing that no steps to incorporate have been taken may be estopped to impose personal liability on individual defendants. This estoppel may be based on the inequity perceived when persons, unwilling or reluctant to enter into a commitment under their own name, are persuaded to use the name of a nonexistent corporation, and then are sought to be held personally liable under section 2.04 by the party advocating execution in the name of the corporation.

§2.05 Organization of Corporation

(a) After incorporation:

(1) if initial directors are named in the articles of incorporation, the initial directors shall hold an organizational meeting, at the call of a majority of the directors, to complete the organization of the corporation by appointing officers, adopting bylaws, and carrying on any other business brought before the meeting; or

(2) if initial directors are not named in the articles of incorporation, the incorporator or incorporators shall hold an organizational meeting at the call of a majority of the incorporators:

(i) to elect initial directors and complete the organization of the corporation; or

(ii) to elect a board of directors who shall complete the organization of the corporation.

(b) Action required or permitted by this Act to be taken by incorporators at an organizational meeting may be taken without a meeting if the action taken is evidenced by one or more written consents describing the action taken and signed by each incorporator.

(c) An organizational meeting may be held in or out of this state.

§2.06 Bylaws

(a) The incorporators or board of directors of a corporation shall adopt initial bylaws for the corporation.

(b) The bylaws of a corporation may contain any provision that is not inconsistent with law or the articles of incorporation.

(c) The bylaws may contain one or both of the following provisions:

(1) a requirement that if the corporation solicits proxies or consents with respect to an election of directors, the corporation include in its proxy statement and any form of its proxy or consent, to the extent and subject to such procedures or conditions as are provided in the bylaws, one or more individuals nominated by a shareholder in addition to individuals nominated by the board of directors; and

(2) a requirement that the corporation reimburse the expenses incurred by a shareholder in soliciting proxies or consents in connection with an election of directors, to the extent and subject to such procedures and conditions as are provided in the bylaws, provided that no bylaw so adopted shall apply to elections for which any record date precedes its adoption.

(d) Notwithstanding section 10.20(b)(2), the shareholders in amending, repealing, or adopting a bylaw described in subsection (c) may not limit the authority of the board of directors to amend or repeal any condition or procedure set forth in or to add any procedure or condition to such a bylaw to provide for a reasonable, practical, and orderly process.

OFFICIAL COMMENT

The responsibility for adopting the original bylaws is placed on the person or persons completing the organization of the corporation. Section 2.06(b) permits any bylaw provision that is not inconsistent with law or the articles of incorporation. This limitation precludes bylaw provisions that limit the managerial authority of directors established by section 8.01(b). For a list of provisions that may be included in the bylaws, see the Official Comment to section 2.02.

The power to amend or repeal bylaws, or adopt new bylaws after the organization of the corporation is completed, is addressed in sections 10.20, 10.21 and 10.22.

Section 2.06(c) expressly authorizes bylaws that require the corporation to include individuals nominated by shareholders for election as directors in its proxy statement and proxy cards (or consents) and that require the reimbursement by the corporation of expenses incurred by a shareholder in soliciting proxies (or consents) in an election of directors, in each case subject to such procedures or conditions as may be provided in the bylaws. Expenses reimbursed under section 2.06(c)(2) must be reasonable as contemplated in the definition of expenses set forth in section 1.40.

Examples of the procedures and conditions that may be included in bylaws contemplated by section 2.06(c) include provisions that relate to the ownership of shares (including requirements as to the duration of ownership); informational requirements; restrictions on the number of directors to be nominated or on the use of the provisions by shareholders seeking to acquire control; provisions requiring the nominating shareholder to indemnify the corporation; limitations on reimbursement based on the amount spent by the corporation or the proportion of votes cast for the nominee; and limitations concerning the election of directors by cumulative voting.

Section 2.06(c) clarifies that proxy access and expense reimbursement provisions do not infringe upon the scope of authority granted to the board of directors of a corporation under section 8.01(b). Section 2.06(c) underscores the model of corporate governance embodied by the Act and reflected in section 8.01, but recognizes that different corporations may wish to grant shareholders varying rights in selecting directors through the election process.

Section 2.06(d) limits the rule set forth in section 10.20(b)(2) that shareholder adopted bylaws may limit the authority of directors to amend bylaws, by specifying that such a limit will not apply absolutely to conditions and procedures set forth in access or reimbursement bylaws authorized by section 2.06(c). Section 2.06(d) allows directors to ensure that such bylaws adequately provide for a reasonable, practical, and orderly process, but is not intended to allow the board of directors to frustrate the purpose of a shareholder-adopted proxy access or expense reimbursement provision.

§ 2.07   Emergency Bylaws

(a) Unless the articles of incorporation provide otherwise, the board of directors may adopt bylaws to be effective only in an emergency defined in subsection (d). The emergency bylaws, which are subject to amendment or repeal by the shareholders, may make all provisions necessary for managing the corporation during the emergency, including:

    (1) procedures for calling a meeting of the board of directors;

    (2) quorum requirements for the meeting; and

    (3) designation of additional or substitute directors.

(b) All provisions of the regular bylaws not inconsistent with the emergency bylaws remain effective during the emergency. The emergency bylaws are not effective after the emergency ends.

(c) Corporate action taken in good faith in accordance with the emergency bylaws:

(1)   binds the corporation; and

(2)   may not be used to impose liability on a director, officer, employee, or agent of the corporation.

(d)   An emergency exists for purposes of this section if a quorum of the board of directors cannot readily be assembled because of some catastrophic event.

§ 2.08   Forum Selection Provisions

(a)   The articles of incorporation or the bylaws may require that any or all internal corporate claims shall be brought exclusively in any specified court or courts of this state and, if so specified, in any additional courts in this state or in any other jurisdictions with which the corporation has a reasonable relationship.

(b)   A provision of the articles of incorporation or bylaws adopted under subsection (a) shall not have the effect of conferring jurisdiction on any court or over any person or claim, and shall not apply if none of the courts specified by such provision has the requisite personal and subject matter jurisdiction. If the court or courts of this state specified in a provision adopted under subsection (a) do not have the requisite personal and subject matter jurisdiction and another court of this state does have such jurisdiction, then the internal corporate claim may be brought in such other court of this state, notwithstanding that such other court of this state is not specified in such provision, and in any other court specified in such provision that has the requisite jurisdiction.

(c)   No provision of the articles of incorporation or the bylaws may prohibit bringing an internal corporate claim in the courts of this state or require such claims to be determined by arbitration.

(d)   "Internal corporate claim" means, for the purposes of this section, (i) any claim that is based upon a violation of a duty under the laws of this state by a current or former director, officer, or shareholder in such capacity, (ii) any derivative action or proceeding brought on behalf of the corporation, (iii) any action asserting a claim arising pursuant to any provision of this Act or the articles of incorporation or bylaws, or (iv) any action asserting a claim governed by the internal affairs doctrine that is not included in (i) through (iii) above.

CHAPTER 3.   PURPOSES AND POWERS

§ 3.01   Purposes

(a)   Every corporation incorporated under this Act has the purpose of engaging in any lawful business unless a more limited purpose is set forth in the articles of incorporation.

(b)   A corporation engaging in a business that is subject to regulation under another statute of this state may incorporate under this Act only if permitted by, and subject to all limitations of, the other statute.

§ 3.02   General Powers

Unless its articles of incorporation provide otherwise, every corporation has perpetual duration and succession in its corporate name and has the same powers as an individual to do all things necessary or convenient to carry out its business and affairs, including power:

(a)   to sue and be sued, complain and defend in its corporate name;

(b)   to have a corporate seal, which may be altered at will, and to use it, or a facsimile of it, by impressing or affixing it or in any other manner reproducing it;

(c)   to make and amend bylaws, not inconsistent with its articles of incorporation or with the laws of this state, for managing the business and regulating the affairs of the corporation;

(d) to purchase, receive, lease, or otherwise acquire, and own, hold, improve, use, and otherwise deal with, real or personal property, or any legal or equitable interest in property, wherever located;

(e) to sell, convey, mortgage, pledge, lease, exchange, and otherwise dispose of all or any part of its property;

(f) to purchase, receive, subscribe for, or otherwise acquire, own, hold, vote, use, sell, mortgage, lend, pledge, or otherwise dispose of, and deal in and with shares or other interests in, or obligations of, any other entity;

(g) to make contracts and guarantees, incur liabilities, borrow money, issue its notes, bonds, and other securities and obligations (which may be convertible into or include the option to purchase other securities of the corporation), and secure any of its obligations by mortgage or pledge of any of its property, franchises, or income;

(h) to lend money, invest and reinvest its funds, and receive and hold real and personal property as security for repayment;

(i) to be a promoter, partner, member, associate, or manager of any partnership, joint venture, trust, or other entity;

(j) to conduct its business, locate offices, and exercise the powers granted by this Act within or without this state;

(k) to elect directors and appoint officers, employees, and agents of the corporation, define their duties, fix their compensation, and lend them money and credit;

(l) to pay pensions and establish pension plans, pension trusts, profit sharing plans, share bonus plans, share option plans, and benefit or incentive plans for any or all of its current or former directors, officers, employees, and agents;

(m) to make donations for the public welfare or for charitable, scientific, or educational purposes;

(n) to transact any lawful business that will aid governmental policy; and

(o) to make payments or donations, or do any other act, not inconsistent with law, that furthers the business and affairs of the corporation.

§ 3.03   Emergency Powers

(a) In anticipation of or during an emergency defined in subsection (d), the board of directors of a corporation may:

(1) modify lines of succession to accommodate the incapacity of any director, officer, employee, or agent; and

(2) relocate the principal office, designate alternative principal offices or regional offices, or authorize the officers to do so.

(b) During an emergency defined in subsection (d), unless emergency bylaws provide otherwise:

(1) notice of a meeting of the board of directors need be given only to those directors whom it is practicable to reach and may be given in any practicable manner; and

(2) one or more officers of the corporation present at a meeting of the board of directors may be deemed to be directors for the meeting, in order of rank and within the same rank in order of seniority, as necessary to achieve a quorum.

(c) Corporate action taken in good faith during an emergency under this section to further the ordinary business affairs of the corporation:

(1) binds the corporation; and

(2)   may not be used to impose liability on a director, officer, employee, or agent.

(d)   An emergency exists for purposes of this section if a quorum of the board of directors cannot readily be assembled because of some catastrophic event.

§ 3.04   Lack of Power to Act

(a)   Except as provided in subsection (b), the validity of corporate action may not be challenged on the ground that the corporation lacks or lacked power to act.

(b)   A corporation's power to act may be challenged:

(1)   in a proceeding by a shareholder against the corporation to enjoin the act;

(2)   in a proceeding by the corporation, directly, derivatively, or through a receiver, trustee, or other legal representative, against an incumbent or former director, officer, employee, or agent of the corporation; or

(3)   in a proceeding by the attorney general under section 14.30.

(c)   In a shareholder's proceeding under subsection (b)(1) to enjoin an unauthorized corporate act, the court may enjoin or set aside the act, if equitable and if all affected persons are parties to the proceeding, and may award damages for loss (other than anticipated profits) suffered by the corporation or another party because of enjoining the unauthorized act.

CHAPTER 4.   NAME

§ 4.01   Corporate Name

(a)   A corporate name:

(1)   must contain the word "corporation," "incorporated," "company," or "limited," or the abbreviation "corp.," "inc.," "co.," or "ltd.," or words or abbreviations of like import in another language; and

(2)   may not contain language stating or implying that the corporation is organized for a purpose other than that permitted by section 3.01 and its articles of incorporation.

(b)   Except as authorized by subsections (c) and (d), a corporate name must be distinguishable upon the records of the secretary of state from:

(1)   the corporate name of a corporation incorporated in this state which is not administratively dissolved;

(2)   a corporate name reserved or registered under section 4.02 or 4.03 or any similar provision of the law of this state;

(3)   the name of a foreign corporation registered to do business in this state or an alternate name adopted by a foreign corporation registered to do business in this state because its corporate name is unavailable;

(4)   the corporate name of a nonprofit corporation incorporated in this state which is not administratively dissolved;

(5)   the name of a foreign nonprofit corporation registered to do business in this state or an alternate name adopted by a foreign nonprofit corporation registered to conduct activities in this state because its real name is unavailable;

(6)   the name of a domestic filing entity or limited liability partnership which is not administratively dissolved;

(7) the name of a foreign unincorporated entity registered to do business in this state or an alternate name adopted by such an entity registered to conduct activities in this state because its real name is unavailable; and

(8) an assumed name registered under [state's assumed name statute].

(c) A corporation may apply to the secretary of state for authorization to use a name that is not distinguishable upon the secretary of state's records from one or more of the names described in subsection (b). The secretary of state shall authorize use of the name applied for if:

(1) the other corporation or unincorporated entity consents to the use in writing and submits an undertaking in form satisfactory to the secretary of state to change its name to a name that is distinguishable upon the records of the secretary of state from the name of the applying corporation; or

(2) the applicant delivers to the secretary of state a certified copy of the final judgment of a court of competent jurisdiction establishing the applicant's right to use the name applied for in this state.

(d) This Act does not control the use of fictitious names.

§ 4.02 Reserved Name

(a) A person may reserve the exclusive use of a corporate name, including a fictitious or alternate name for a foreign corporation whose corporate name is not available, by delivering an application to the secretary of state for filing. The application must set forth the name and address of the applicant and the name proposed to be reserved. If the secretary of state finds that the corporate name applied for is available, the secretary of state shall reserve the name for the applicant's exclusive use for a nonrenewable 120-day period.

(b) The owner of a reserved corporate name may transfer the reservation to another person by delivering to the secretary of state a signed notice of the transfer that states the name and address of the transferee.

§ 4.03 Registered Name

(a) A foreign corporation may register its corporate name (or its corporate name with the addition of any word or abbreviation listed in section 4.01(a)(1) if necessary for the corporate name to comply with section 4.01(a)(1)) if the name is distinguishable upon the records of the secretary of state from the corporate names that are not available under section 4.01(b).

(b) A foreign corporation registers its corporate name (or its corporate name with any addition permitted by subsection (a)) by delivering to the secretary of state for filing an application setting forth that name, the state or country and date of its incorporation, and a brief description of the nature of the business which is to be conducted in this state.

(c) The name is registered for the applicant's exclusive use upon the effective date of the application and for the remainder of the calendar year, unless renewed.

(d) A foreign corporation whose name registration is effective may renew it for successive years by delivering to the secretary of state for filing a renewal application, which complies with the requirements of subsection (b), between October 1 and December 31 of the preceding year. The renewal application when filed renews the registration for the following calendar year.

(e) A foreign corporation whose name registration is effective may thereafter (i) register to do business as a foreign corporation under the registered name (if it complies with section 4.01(a)(2)) or (ii) consent in writing to the use of that name by a domestic corporation thereafter incorporated under this Act or by another foreign corporation. The registration terminates when the domestic corporation is incorporated or the foreign corporation registers to do business under that name.

CHAPTER 5.   OFFICE AND AGENT

§ 5.01   Registered Office and Agent of Domestic and Registered Foreign Corporations

(a)   Each corporation shall continuously maintain in this state:

 (1)   a registered office that may be the same as any of its places of business; and

 (2)   a registered agent, which may be:

  (i)   an individual who resides in this state and whose business office is identical with the registered office; or

  (ii)   a domestic or foreign corporation or other eligible entity whose business office is identical with the registered office and, in the case of a foreign corporation or foreign eligible entity, is registered to do business in this state.

(b)   As used in this chapter, "corporation" means both a domestic corporation and a registered foreign corporation.

§ 5.02   Change of Registered Office or Registered Agent

(a)   A corporation may change its registered office or registered agent by delivering to the secretary of state for filing a statement of change that sets forth:

 (1)   the name of the corporation;

 (2)   the street and mailing addresses of its current registered office;

 (3)   if the current registered office is to be changed, the street and mailing addresses of the new registered office;

 (4)   the name of its current registered agent;

 (5)   if the current registered agent is to be changed, the name of the new registered agent and the new agent's written consent (either on the statement or attached to it) to the appointment; and

 (6)   that after the change or changes are made, the street and mailing addresses of its registered office and of the business office of its registered agent will be identical.

(b)   If the street or mailing address of a registered agent's business office changes, the agent shall change the street or mailing address of the registered office of any corporation for which the agent is the registered agent by delivering a signed written notice of the change to the corporation and delivering to the secretary of state for filing a signed statement that complies with the requirements of subsection (a) and states that the corporation has been notified of the change.

§ 5.03   Resignation of Registered Agent

(a)   A registered agent may resign as agent for a corporation by delivering to the secretary of state for filing a statement of resignation signed by the agent which states:

 (1)   the name of the corporation;

 (2)   the name of the agent;

 (3)   that the agent resigns from serving as registered agent for the corporation; and

 (4)   the address of the corporation to which the agent will deliver the notice required by subsection (c).

(b)   A statement of resignation takes effect on the earlier of:

 (1)   12:01 a.m. on the 31st day after the day on which it is filed by the secretary of state; or

(2)   the designation of a new registered agent for the corporation.

(c)   A registered agent promptly shall deliver to the corporation notice of the date on which a statement of resignation was delivered to the secretary of state for filing.

(d)   When a statement of resignation takes effect, the person that resigned ceases to have responsibility under this Act for any matter thereafter tendered to it as agent for the corporation. The resignation does not affect any contractual rights the corporation has against the agent or that the agent has against the corporation.

(e)   A registered agent may resign with respect to a corporation regardless of whether the corporation is in good standing.

§ 5.04   Service on Corporation

(a)   A corporation's registered agent is the corporation's agent for service of process, notice, or demand required or permitted by law to be served on the corporation.

(b)   If a corporation has no registered agent, or the agent cannot with reasonable diligence be served, the corporation may be served by registered or certified mail, return receipt requested, addressed to the secretary at the corporation's principal office. Service is perfected under this subsection at the earliest of:

(1)   the date the corporation receives the mail;

(2)   the date shown on the return receipt, if signed on behalf of the corporation; or

(3)   five days after its deposit in the U.S. mail, as evidenced by the postmark, if mailed postpaid and correctly addressed.

(c)   If process, notice, or demand (i) cannot be served on a corporation pursuant to subsection (a) or (b), or (ii) is to be served on a registered foreign corporation that has withdrawn its registration pursuant to section 15.07 or 15.09, or the registration of which has been terminated pursuant to section 15.11, then the secretary of state shall be an agent of the corporation upon whom process, notice, or demand may be served. Service of any process, notice, or demand on the secretary of state as agent for a corporation may be made by delivering to the secretary of state duplicate copies of the process, notice, or demand. If process, notice, or demand is served on the secretary of state, the secretary of state shall forward one of the copies by registered or certified mail, return receipt requested, to the corporation at the last address shown in the records of the secretary of state. Service is effected under this subsection (c) at the earliest of:

(1)   the date the corporation receives the process, notice, or demand;

(2)   the date shown on the return receipt, if signed on behalf of the corporation; or

(3)   five days after the process, notice, or demand is deposited with the United States mail by the secretary of state.

(d)   This section does not prescribe the only means, or necessarily the required means, of serving a corporation.

CHAPTER 6.   SHARES AND DISTRIBUTIONS

SUBCHAPTER A.   SHARES

§ 6.01   Authorized Shares

(a)   The articles of incorporation must set forth any classes of shares and series of shares within a class, and the number of shares of each class and series, that the corporation is authorized to issue. If more than one class or series of shares is authorized, the articles of incorporation must prescribe a distinguishing designation for each class or series and, before the issuance of shares of a class or series, describe the terms, including the preferences, rights, and limitations, of that class or series. Except to the extent varied as permitted by this section, all shares of a class or series must have terms, including preferences, rights, and limitations, that are identical with those of other shares of the same class or series.

(b)   The articles of incorporation must authorize:

(1)   one or more classes or series of shares that together have full voting rights, and

(2)   one or more classes or series of shares (which may be the same class, classes or series as those with voting rights) that together are entitled to receive the net assets of the corporation upon dissolution.

(c)   The articles of incorporation may authorize one or more classes or series of shares that:

(1)   have special, conditional, or limited voting rights, or no right to vote, except to the extent otherwise provided by this Act;

(2)   are redeemable or convertible as specified in the articles of incorporation:

(i)   at the option of the corporation, the shareholder, or another person or upon the occurrence of a specified event;

(ii)   for cash, indebtedness, securities, or other property; and

(iii) at prices and in amounts specified or determined in accordance with a formula;

(3)   entitle the holders to distributions calculated in any manner, including dividends that may be cumulative, noncumulative, or partially cumulative; or

(4)   have preference over any other class or series of shares with respect to distributions, including distributions upon the dissolution of the corporation.

(d)   Terms of shares may be made dependent upon facts objectively ascertainable outside the articles of incorporation in accordance with section 1.20(k).

(e)   Any of the terms of shares may vary among holders of the same class or series so long as such variations are expressly set forth in the articles of incorporation.

(f)   The description of the preferences, rights, and limitations of classes or series of shares in subsection (c) is not exhaustive.

§6.02   Terms of Class or Series Determined by Board of Directors

(a)   If the articles of incorporation so provide, the board of directors is authorized, without shareholder approval, to:

(1)   classify any unissued shares into one or more classes or into one or more series within a class;

(2)   reclassify any unissued shares of any class into one or more classes or into one or more series within one or more classes; or

(3)   reclassify any unissued shares of any series of any class into one or more classes or into one or more series within a class.

(b)   If the board of directors acts pursuant to subsection (a), it shall determine the terms, including the preferences, rights, and limitations, to the same extent permitted under section 6.01, of:

(1)   any class of shares before the issuance of any shares of that class, or

(2)   any series within a class before the issuance of any shares of that series.

(c)   Before issuing any shares of a class or series created under this section, the corporation shall deliver to the secretary of state for filing articles of amendment setting forth the terms determined under subsection (a).

§ 6.03   Issued and Outstanding Shares

(a)   A corporation may issue the number of shares of each class or series authorized by the articles of incorporation. Shares that are issued are outstanding shares until they are reacquired, redeemed, converted, or cancelled.

(b)   The reacquisition, redemption, or conversion of outstanding shares is subject to the limitations of subsection (c) and to section 6.40.

(c)   At all times that shares of the corporation are outstanding, one or more shares that together have full voting rights and one or more shares that together are entitled to receive the net assets of the corporation upon dissolution must be outstanding.

§ 6.04   Fractional Shares

(a)   A corporation may issue fractions of a share or in lieu of doing so may:

(1)   pay in cash the value of fractions of a share;

(2)   issue scrip in registered or bearer form entitling the holder to receive a full share upon surrendering enough scrip to equal a full share; or

(3)   arrange for disposition of fractional shares by the holders of such shares.

(b)   Each certificate representing scrip must be conspicuously labeled "scrip" and must contain the information required by section 6.25(b).

(c)   The holder of a fractional share is entitled to exercise the rights of a shareholder, including the rights to vote, to receive dividends and to receive distributions upon dissolution. The holder of scrip is not entitled to any of these rights unless the scrip provides for them.

(d)   The board of directors may authorize the issuance of scrip subject to any condition, including that:

(1)   the scrip will become void if not exchanged for full shares before a specified date; and

(2)   the shares for which the scrip is exchangeable may be sold and the proceeds paid to the scripholders.

SUBCHAPTER B.   ISSUANCE OF SHARES

§ 6.20   Subscription for Shares Before Incorporation

(a)   A subscription for shares entered into before incorporation is irrevocable for six months unless the subscription agreement provides a longer or shorter period or all the subscribers agree to revocation.

(b)   The board of directors may determine the payment terms of subscriptions for shares that were entered into before incorporation, unless the subscription agreement specifies them. A call for payment by the board of directors must be uniform so far as practicable as to all shares of the same class or series, unless the subscription agreement specifies otherwise.

(c)   Shares issued pursuant to subscriptions entered into before incorporation are fully paid and nonassessable when the corporation receives the consideration specified in the subscription agreement.

(d)   If a subscriber defaults in payment of cash or property under a subscription agreement entered into before incorporation, the corporation may collect the amount owed as any other debt.

Alternatively, unless the subscription agreement provides otherwise, the corporation may rescind the agreement and may sell the shares if the debt remains unpaid for more than 20 days after the corporation delivers a written demand for payment to the subscriber.

§ 6.21 Issuance of Shares

(a) The powers granted in this section to the board of directors may be reserved to the shareholders by the articles of incorporation.

(b) The board of directors may authorize shares to be issued for consideration consisting of any tangible or intangible property or benefit to the corporation, including cash, promissory notes, services performed, contracts for services to be performed, or other securities of the corporation.

(c) Before the corporation issues shares, the board of directors shall determine that the consideration received or to be received for shares to be issued is adequate. That determination by the board of directors is conclusive insofar as the adequacy of consideration for the issuance of shares relates to whether the shares are validly issued, fully paid, and nonassessable.

(d) When the corporation receives the consideration for which the board of directors authorized the issuance of shares, the shares issued therefor are fully paid and nonassessable.

(e) The corporation may place in escrow shares issued for a contract for future services or benefits or a promissory note, or make other arrangements to restrict the transfer of the shares, and may credit distributions in respect of the shares against their purchase price, until the services are performed, the benefits are received, or the note is paid. If the services are not performed, the benefits are not received, or the note is not paid, the shares escrowed or restricted and the distributions credited may be cancelled in whole or part.

(f) (1) An issuance of shares or other securities convertible into or rights exercisable for shares in a transaction or a series of integrated transactions requires approval of the shareholders, at a meeting at which a quorum consisting of a majority (or such greater number as the articles of incorporation may prescribe) of the votes entitled to be cast on the matter exists, if:

(i) the shares, other securities, or rights are to be issued for consideration other than cash or cash equivalents, and

(ii) the voting power of shares that are issued and issuable as a result of the transaction or series of integrated transactions will comprise more than 20% of the voting power of the shares of the corporation that were outstanding immediately before the transaction.

(2) In this subsection:

(i) For purposes of determining the voting power of shares issued and issuable as a result of a transaction or series of integrated transactions, the voting power of shares or other securities convertible into or rights exercisable for shares shall be the greater of (A) the voting power of the shares to be issued, or (B) the voting power of the shares that would be outstanding after giving effect to the conversion of convertible shares and other securities and the exercise of rights to be issued.

(ii) A series of transactions is integrated only if consummation of one transaction is made contingent on consummation of one or more of the other transactions.

OFFICIAL COMMENT

Because a statutory structure embodying "par value" and "stated capital" concepts does not protect creditors and senior security holders from payments to junior security holders, section 6.21 does not use these concepts.

1. Consideration

Because shares need not have a par value under section 6.21, there is no minimum price at which shares must be issued. Section 6.21(b) specifically validates "any tangible or intangible property or benefit to the corporation," as consideration for the present issue of shares, specifically including contracts for future services (including promoters' services) and promissory notes. The term "benefit" should be broadly construed also to include, for example, a reduction of a liability, a release of a claim, or intangible gain obtained by a corporation. Business judgment should determine what kind of property or benefit should be obtained for shares, and a determination by the directors meeting the requirements of section 8.30 to accept a specific kind of property or benefit for shares should be accepted and not circumscribed by artificial or arbitrary rules.

2. Board Determination of Adequacy

Protection of shareholders against abuse of the power granted to the board of directors to determine that shares should be issued for intangible property or benefit is provided by the requirements of section 8.30 applicable to a determination that the consideration received for shares is adequate.

In many instances, property or benefit received by the corporation will be of uncertain value; if the board of directors determines that the issuance of shares for the property or benefit is an appropriate transaction, that is sufficient under section 6.21. The board of directors does not have to make an explicit "adequacy" determination by formal resolution; that determination may be inferred from a determination to authorize the issuance of shares for a specified consideration. Likewise, section 6.21 does not require the board of directors to determine an exact value of the consideration to be entered on the books of the corporation.

The second sentence of section 6.21(c) describes the effect of the determination by the board of directors that consideration is adequate for the issuance of shares. That determination, without more, is conclusive to the extent that adequacy is relevant to the question whether the shares are validly issued, fully paid, and nonassessable. Whether shares are validly issued may depend on compliance with corporate procedural requirements, such as issuance within the amount authorized in the articles of incorporation or holding a directors' meeting upon proper notice and with a quorum present. The Act does not address the remedies that may be available for issuances that are subject to challenge. See subchapter E of chapter 1 regarding ratification of defective issuance of shares.

The Act also does not address whether validly issued shares may thereafter be cancelled on the grounds of fraud or bad faith if the shares are in the hands of the original shareholder or other persons who were aware of the circumstances under which they were issued when they acquired the shares. It also leaves to the Uniform Commercial Code other questions relating to the rights of persons other than the person acquiring the shares from the corporation. See the Official Comment to section 6.22.

Section 6.21(e) permits shares issued for contracts for future services or benefits or for promissory notes to be placed in escrow, or their transfer otherwise restricted, until the services are performed, the benefits are received or the notes are paid. In addition, any distributions on such shares may be credited against payment, or other agreed performance, of the consideration for the shares. Under section 6.21(e), if the corporation has restricted the transfer of the shares or placed them in escrow, it may cancel the shares and any credited distributions, in whole or in part, in the event of a failure of performance. This remedy is in the nature of a partial or complete rescission, and therefore rescission principles would be applicable.

Section 6.21 addresses only the corporation's cancellation remedy. It does not address whether other remedies may be available to the corporation, including a right to a deficiency against the nonperforming shareholder, or whether the shareholder may have any rights where the value of the shares subject to cancellation exceeds the value of the obligation remaining unperformed.

If the shares are issued without being restricted as provided in section 6.21(e), they are validly issued in so far as the adequacy of consideration is concerned. See section 6.22 and its Official Comment.

Section 6.24(c) provides express authority for delegation by the board of directors to officers for the issuance of shares as compensatory awards within limitations established by the board.

3. *Shareholder Approval Requirement for Certain Issuances*

The shareholder approval requirement of section 6.21(f) is generally patterned after the listing standards of national securities exchanges. The calculation of the 20% compares the maximum number of votes entitled to be cast by the shares to be issued or that could be outstanding after giving effect to the conversion of convertible securities and the exercise of rights being issued, with the actual number of votes entitled to be cast by outstanding shares before the transaction.

In making the 20% determination under section 6.21(f), shares that are issuable in a transaction of any kind, including a merger, share exchange, or acquisition of assets, on a contingent basis are counted as shares or securities to be issued as a result of the transaction. On the other hand, shares that are issuable under antidilution clauses, such as those designed to take account of future share splits or share dividends, are not counted as shares or securities to be issued as a result of the transaction, because they are issuable only as a result of a later corporate action authorizing the split or dividend. If a transaction involves an earn-out provision, under which the total amount of shares or securities to be issued will depend on future earnings or other performance measures, the maximum amount of shares or securities that can be issued under the earn-out must be included in the determination.

If the number of shares to be issued or issuable is not fixed, but is subject to a formula, the application of the test in section 6.21(f)(2)(i) requires a calculation of the maximum amount that could be issued under the formula, whether stated as a range or otherwise, in the governing agreement. Even if ultimate issuance of the maximum amount is unlikely, a vote will be required if the maximum amount would result in an issuance of more than 20% of the voting power of shares outstanding immediately before the transaction.

Shares that have or would have only contingent voting rights when issued or issuable are not shares that carry voting power for purposes of the calculation under section 6.21(f).

The vote required to approve issuances that fall within section 6.21(f) is the basic voting rule under the Act, set forth in section 7.25, that more shares must be voted in favor of the issuance than are voted against. This is the same voting rule that applies under chapter 9 for domestications and conversions, chapter 10 for amendments of the articles of incorporation, chapter 11 for mergers and share exchanges, chapter 12 for dispositions of assets that require shareholder approval, and chapter 14 for voluntary dissolutions. The quorum rule under section 6.21(f) is also the same as the quorum rule under chapters 9, 10, 11, 12, and 14.

Section 6.21(f) does not apply to an issuance for cash or cash equivalents, regardless of whether in connection with a public offering. "Cash equivalents" are generally short-term investments that are both readily convertible to known amounts of cash and present insignificant risk of changes in interest rates. Shares that are issued partly for cash or cash equivalents and partly for other consideration are "issued for consideration other than cash or cash equivalents" within the meaning of section 6.21(f).

The term "rights" in section 6.21(f) includes warrants, options, and rights of exchange, whether at the option of the holder, the corporation, or another person. The term "voting power" is defined in section 1.40 as the current power to vote in the election of directors. See also the Official Comment to that section. Because transactions are integrated within the meaning of section 6.21(f) only where consummation of one transaction is made contingent on consummation of one or more of the other transactions, transactions are not integrated for purposes of section 6.21(f) merely because they are proximate in time or because the kind of consideration for which the corporation issues shares is similar in each transaction.

Section 6.21(f) only applies to issuances for consideration. Accordingly, section 6.21(f) does not require shareholder approval for share dividends or for shareholder rights plans. See section 6.23 and its Official Comment.

Illustrations of the application of section 6.21(f) follow:

1.   C corporation, which has 2,000,000 shares of Class A voting common stock outstanding (carrying one vote per share), proposes to issue 600,000 shares of authorized but unissued Class B nonvoting common stock in exchange for a business owned by D Corporation. The proposed issuance does not require shareholder approval under section 6.21(f) because the Class B shares do not carry voting power.

2.   The facts being otherwise as stated in Illustration 1, C proposes to issue 600,000 additional shares of its Class A voting common stock. The proposed issuance requires shareholder approval under section

6.21(f) because the voting power carried by the shares to be issued will comprise more than 20% of the voting power of C's shares outstanding immediately before the issuance.

3.   The facts being otherwise as stated in Illustration 1, C proposes to issue 400,000 shares of authorized but unissued voting preferred stock, each share of which carries one vote and is convertible into 1.5 shares of Class A voting common stock. The proposed issuance requires shareholder approval under section 6.21(f). Although the voting power of the preferred shares to be issued will not comprise more than 20% of the voting power of C's shares outstanding immediately before the issuance, the voting power of the shares issuable upon conversion of the preferred shares will carry more than 20% of such voting power.

4.   The facts being otherwise as stated in Illustration 1, C proposes to issue 200,000 shares of its Class A voting common stock, and 100,000 shares of authorized but unissued nonvoting preferred stock, each share of which is convertible into 2.5 shares of C's Class A voting common stock. The proposed issuance requires shareholder approval under section 6.21(f) because the voting power of the Class A shares to be issued, after giving effect to the common stock that is issuable upon conversion of the preferred shares, would comprise more than 20% of the voting power of C's outstanding shares immediately before the issuance.

5.   The facts being otherwise as stated in Illustration 4, each share of the preferred stock is convertible into 1.2 shares of the Class A voting common stock. The proposed issuance does not require shareholder approval under section 6.21(f) because neither the voting power of the shares to be issued at the outset (200,000) nor the voting power of the shares that would be outstanding after giving effect to the common stock issuable upon conversion of the preferred shares (a total of 320,000) constitutes more than 20% of the voting power of C's outstanding shares immediately before the issuance.

6.   The facts being otherwise as stated in Illustration 1, C proposes to acquire businesses from Corporations G, H, and I for 200,000, 300,000, and 400,000 shares of Class A voting common stock, respectively, within a short period of time. None of the transactions is conditioned on the negotiation or completion of the other transactions. The proposed issuance of voting shares does not require shareholder approval, because the three transactions are not integrated within the meaning of section 6.21(f), and none of the transactions individually involves the issuance of more than 20% of the voting power of C's outstanding shares immediately before each issuance.

§ 6.22   Liability of Shareholders

(a)   A purchaser from a corporation of the corporation's own shares is not liable to the corporation or its creditors with respect to the shares except to pay the consideration for which the shares were authorized to be issued or specified in the subscription agreement.

(b)   A shareholder of a corporation is not personally liable for any liabilities of the corporation (including liabilities arising from acts of the corporation) except (i) to the extent provided in a provision of the articles of incorporation permitted by section 2.02(b)(2)(v), and (ii) that a shareholder may become personally liable by reason of the shareholder's own acts or conduct.

§ 6.23   Share Dividends

(a)   Unless the articles of incorporation provide otherwise, shares may be issued pro rata and without consideration to the corporation's shareholders or to the shareholders of one or more classes or series of shares. An issuance of shares under this subsection is a share dividend.

(b)   Shares of one class or series may not be issued as a share dividend in respect of shares of another class or series unless (i) the articles of incorporation so authorize, (ii) a majority of the votes entitled to be cast by the class or series to be issued approve the issue, or (iii) there are no outstanding shares of the class or series to be issued.

(c)   The board of directors may fix the record date for determining shareholders entitled to a share dividend, which date may not be retroactive. If the board of directors does not fix the record date for determining shareholders entitled to a share dividend, the record date is the date the board of directors authorizes the share dividend.

§ 6.24 Share Rights, Options, Warrants and Awards

(a) A corporation may issue rights, options, or warrants for the purchase of shares or other securities of the corporation. The board of directors shall determine (i) the terms and conditions upon which the rights, options, or warrants are issued and (ii) the terms, including the consideration for which the shares or other securities are to be issued. The authorization by the board of directors for the corporation to issue such rights, options, or warrants constitutes authorization of the issuance of the shares or other securities for which the rights, options or warrants are exercisable.

(b) The terms and conditions of such rights, options or warrants may include restrictions or conditions that:

(1) preclude or limit the exercise, transfer or receipt of such rights, options or warrants by any person or persons owning or offering to acquire a specified number or percentage of the outstanding shares or other securities of the corporation or by any transferee or transferees of any such person or persons, or

(2) invalidate or void such rights, options, or warrants held by any such person or persons or any such transferee or transferees.

(c) The board of directors may authorize one or more officers to (i) designate the recipients of rights, options, warrants, or other equity compensation awards that involve the issuance of shares and (ii) determine, within an amount and subject to any other limitations established by the board of directors and, if applicable, the shareholders, the number of such rights, options, warrants, or other equity compensation awards and the terms of such rights, options, warrants or awards to be received by the recipients, provided that an officer may not use such authority to designate himself or herself or any other persons as the board of directors may specify as a recipient of such rights, options, warrants, or other equity compensation awards.

OFFICIAL COMMENT

Section 6.24 specifically authorizes the creation of rights, options and warrants and confirms the broad discretion of the board of directors in determining the consideration to be received by the corporation for their issuance, including the creation of compensation plans for directors, officers, agents, and employees.

Section 6.24(a) does not require shareholder approval of rights, options, warrants or compensation plans. Of course, prior shareholder approval may be sought as a discretionary matter, or required to comply with the rules of national securities exchanges or to acquire federal income tax benefits that may be conditioned upon shareholder approval of such plans.

Section 6.24(b) confirms that the issuance of rights, options or warrants as part of a shareholder rights plan is permitted. The permissible scope of shareholder rights plans may, however, be limited by the courts.

Section 6.24(c) provides express authority for the delegation to officers of the designation of recipients of compensatory awards involving the issuance of shares, either directly or upon exercise of rights to acquire shares, and the determination of the amount and other terms of the awards, subject to any applicable limitations established by the board of directors or the shareholders. A board of directors (or a board committee with authority delegated to it under section 8.25, typically a compensation committee) may decide whether to exercise the authority under section 6.24(c) and, to the extent it does so, the board must specify the total amount that may be awarded and may impose any other limits it desires as part of the board's oversight of the award process. A board or committee delegating authority under section 6.24(c) would typically include appropriate limits. These limits might include, for example, the amount or range of shares to be awarded to different classes of employees, the timing and pricing of awards, and the vesting terms or other variable provisions of awards.

§ 6.25 Form and Content of Certificates

(a) Shares may, but need not, be represented by certificates. Unless this Act or another statute expressly provides otherwise, the rights and obligations of shareholders are identical regardless of whether their shares are represented by certificates.

(b)   At a minimum each share certificate must state on its face:

   (1)   the name of the corporation and that it is organized under the law of this state;

   (2)   the name of the person to whom issued; and

   (3)   the number and class of shares and the designation of the series, if any, the certificate represents.

(c)   If the corporation is authorized to issue different classes of shares or series of shares within a class, the front or back of each certificate must summarize (i) the preferences, rights, and limitations applicable to each class and series, (ii) any variations in preferences, rights, and limitations among the holders of the same class or series, and (iii) the authority of the board of directors to determine the terms of future classes or series. Alternatively, each certificate may state conspicuously on its front or back that the corporation will furnish the shareholder this information on request in writing and without charge.

(d)   Each share certificate must be signed by two officers designated in the bylaws.

(e)   If the person who signed a share certificate no longer holds office when the certificate is issued, the certificate is nevertheless valid.

§ 6.26   Shares Without Certificates

(a)   Unless the articles of incorporation or bylaws provide otherwise, the board of directors of a corporation may authorize the issuance of some or all of the shares of any or all of its classes or series without certificates. The authorization does not affect shares already represented by certificates until they are surrendered to the corporation.

(b)   Within a reasonable time after the issuance or transfer of shares without certificates, the corporation shall deliver to the shareholder a written statement of the information required on certificates by sections 6.25(b) and (c), and, if applicable, section 6.27.

§ 6.27   Restriction on Transfer of Shares

(a)   The articles of incorporation, the bylaws, an agreement among shareholders, or an agreement between shareholders and the corporation may impose restrictions on the transfer or registration of transfer of shares of the corporation. A restriction does not affect shares issued before the restriction was adopted unless the holders of the shares are parties to the restriction agreement or voted in favor of the restriction.

(b)   A restriction on the transfer or registration of transfer of shares is valid and enforceable against the holder or a transferee of the holder if the restriction is authorized by this section and its existence is noted conspicuously on the front or back of the certificate or is contained in the information statement required by section 6.26(b). Unless so noted or contained, a restriction is not enforceable against a person without knowledge of the restriction.

(c)   A restriction on the transfer or registration of transfer of shares is authorized:

   (1)   to maintain the corporation's status when it is dependent on the number or identity of its shareholders;

   (2)   to preserve exemptions under federal or state securities law; or

   (3)   for any other reasonable purpose.

(d)   A restriction on the transfer or registration of transfer of shares may:

   (1)   obligate the shareholder first to offer the corporation or other persons (separately, consecutively, or simultaneously) an opportunity to acquire the restricted shares;

   (2)   obligate the corporation or other persons (separately, consecutively, or simultaneously) to acquire the restricted shares;

(3)   require the corporation, the holders of any class or series of its shares, or other persons to approve the transfer of the restricted shares, if the requirement is not manifestly unreasonable; or

(4)   prohibit the transfer of the restricted shares to designated persons or classes of persons, if the prohibition is not manifestly unreasonable.

(e)   For purposes of this section, "shares" includes a security convertible into or carrying a right to subscribe for or acquire shares.

SUBCHAPTER C.   SUBSEQUENT ACQUISITION OF SHARES BY SHAREHOLDERS AND CORPORATION

§ 6.30   Shareholders' Preemptive Rights

(a)   The shareholders of a corporation do not have a preemptive right to acquire the corporation's unissued shares except to the extent the articles of incorporation so provide.

(b)   A statement included in the articles of incorporation that "the corporation elects to have preemptive rights" (or words of similar effect) means that the following principles apply except to the extent the articles of incorporation expressly provide otherwise:

(1)   The shareholders of the corporation have a preemptive right, granted on uniform terms and conditions prescribed by the board of directors to provide a fair and reasonable opportunity to exercise the right, to acquire proportional amounts of the corporation's [unissued] shares upon the decision of the board of directors to issue them.

(2)   A preemptive right may be waived by a shareholder. A waiver evidenced by a writing is irrevocable even though it is not supported by consideration.

(3)   There is no preemptive right with respect to:

(i)   shares issued as compensation to directors, officers, employees or agents of the corporation, its subsidiaries or affiliates;

(ii)   shares issued to satisfy conversion or option rights created to provide compensation to directors, officers, employees or agents of the corporation, its subsidiaries or affiliates;

(iii)   shares authorized in the articles of incorporation that are issued within six months from the effective date of incorporation; or

(iv)   shares sold otherwise than for cash.

(4)   Holders of shares of any class or series without voting power but with preferential rights to distributions have no preemptive rights with respect to shares of any class or series.

(5)   Holders of shares of any class or series with voting power but without preferential rights to distributions have no preemptive rights with respect to shares of any class or series with preferential rights to distributions unless the shares with preferential rights are convertible into or carry a right to subscribe for or acquire the shares without preferential rights.

(6)   Shares subject to preemptive rights that are not acquired by shareholders may be issued to any person for a period of one year after being offered to shareholders at a consideration set by the board of directors that is not lower than the consideration set for the exercise of preemptive rights. An offer at a lower consideration or after the expiration of one year is subject to the shareholders' preemptive rights.

(c)   For purposes of this section, "shares" includes a security convertible into or carrying a right to subscribe for or acquire shares.

§ 6.31   Corporation's Acquisition of Its Own Shares

(a)   A corporation may acquire its own shares, and shares so acquired constitute authorized but unissued shares.

(b)   If the articles of incorporation prohibit the reissue of the acquired shares, the number of authorized shares is reduced by the number of shares acquired.

SUBCHAPTER D.   DISTRIBUTIONS

§ 6.40   Distributions to Shareholders

(a)   A board of directors may authorize and the corporation may make distributions to its shareholders subject to restriction by the articles of incorporation and the limitation in subsection (c).

(b)   The board of directors may fix the record date for determining shareholders entitled to a distribution, which date may not be retroactive. If the board of directors does not fix a record date for determining shareholders entitled to a distribution (other than one involving a purchase, redemption, or other acquisition of the corporation's shares), the record date is the date the board of directors authorizes the distribution.

(c)   No distribution may be made if, after giving it effect:

    (1)   the corporation would not be able to pay its debts as they become due in the usual course of business; or

    (2)   the corporation's total assets would be less than the sum of its total liabilities plus (unless the articles of incorporation permit otherwise) the amount that would be needed, if the corporation were to be dissolved at the time of the distribution, to satisfy the preferential rights upon dissolution of shareholders whose preferential rights are superior to those receiving the distribution.

(d)   The board of directors may base a determination that a distribution is not prohibited under subsection (c) either on financial statements prepared on the basis of accounting practices and principles that are reasonable in the circumstances or on a fair valuation or other method that is reasonable in the circumstances.

(e)   Except as provided in subsection (g), the effect of a distribution under subsection (c) is measured:

    (1)   in the case of distribution by purchase, redemption, or other acquisition of the corporation's shares, as of the earlier of (i) the date cash or other property is transferred or debt to a shareholder is incurred by the corporation or (ii) the date the shareholder ceases to be a shareholder with respect to the acquired shares;

    (2)   in the case of any other distribution of indebtedness, as of the date the indebtedness is distributed; and

    (3)   in all other cases, as of (i) the date the distribution is authorized if the payment occurs within 120 days after the date of authorization or (ii) the date the payment is made if it occurs more than 120 days after the date of authorization.

(f)   A corporation's indebtedness to a shareholder incurred by reason of a distribution made in accordance with this section is at parity with the corporation's indebtedness to its general, unsecured creditors except to the extent subordinated by agreement.

(g)   Indebtedness of a corporation, including indebtedness issued as a distribution, is not considered a liability for purposes of determinations under subsection (c) if its terms provide that payment of principal and interest are made only if and to the extent that payment of a distribution to shareholders could then be made under this section. If such indebtedness is issued as a distribution, each payment of principal or interest is treated as a distribution, the effect of which is measured on the date the payment is actually made.

(h) This section shall not apply to distributions in liquidation under chapter 14.

OFFICIAL COMMENT

1. The Scope of Section 6.40

Section 6.40 imposes a single, uniform test on all distributions other than distributions in liquidation under chapter 14. Section 1.40 defines "distribution" broadly to include transfers of cash and other property (excluding a corporation's own shares) to a shareholder in respect of the corporation's shares. Examples of such transfers are cash or property dividends, payments by a corporation to purchase its own shares, and distributions of promissory notes or indebtedness. The financial provisions of the Act do not use the concept of surplus but do have restrictions on distributions built around both equity insolvency and balance sheet tests.

2. Equity Insolvency Test

"income sheet test"

In most cases involving a corporation operating as a going concern in the normal course, it will be apparent from information generally available that no particular inquiry concerning the equity insolvency test in section 6.40(c)(1) is needed. Although neither a balance sheet nor an income statement can be conclusive as to this test, the existence of significant shareholders' equity and normal operating conditions are of themselves a strong indication that no issue should arise under that test. In the case of a corporation having regularly audited financial statements, the absence of any qualification in the most recent auditor's opinion as to the corporation's status as a "going concern," coupled with a lack of subsequent adverse events, would normally be decisive.

It is only when circumstances indicate that the corporation is encountering difficulties or is in an uncertain position concerning its liquidity and operations that the board of directors or, more commonly, the officers or others upon whom they may place reliance under section 8.30(d), may need to address the issue. Because of the overall judgment required in evaluating the equity insolvency test, no "bright line" test is provided. However, in determining whether the equity insolvency test has been met, certain judgments or assumptions as to the future course of the corporation's business are customarily justified, absent clear evidence to the contrary. These include the likelihood that (i) based on existing and contemplated demand for the corporation's products or services, it will be able to generate funds over a period of time sufficient to satisfy its existing and reasonably anticipated obligations as they mature, and (ii) indebtedness which matures in the near-term will be refinanced where, on the basis of the corporation's financial condition and future prospects and the general availability of credit to businesses similarly situated, it is reasonable to assume that such refinancing may be accomplished. To the extent that the corporation may be subject to asserted or unasserted contingent liabilities, reasonable judgments as to the likelihood, amount, and time of any recovery against the corporation, after giving consideration to the extent to which the corporation is insured or otherwise protected against loss, may be utilized. There may be occasions when it would be useful to consider a cash flow analysis, based on a business forecast and budget, covering a sufficient period of time to permit a conclusion that known obligations of the corporation can reasonably be expected to be satisfied over the period of time that they will mature.

In exercising their judgment, the directors are entitled to rely, as provided in section 8.30(e), on information, opinions, reports, and statements prepared by others. Ordinarily, they should not be expected to become involved in the details of the various analyses or market or economic projections that may be relevant.

3. Balance Sheet Test

The determination of a corporation's assets and liabilities for purposes of the balance sheet test of section 6.40(c)(2) and the choice of the permissible basis on which to do so are left to the judgment of its board of directors. In making a judgment under section 6.40(d), the board may rely as provided in section 8.30(e) upon information, opinions, reports, and statements, including financial statements and other financial data, prepared or presented by public accountants or others.

Section 6.40 does not utilize particular accounting terminology of a technical nature or specify particular accounting concepts. In making determinations under this section, the board of directors may make judgments about accounting matters.

In a corporation with subsidiaries, the board of directors may rely on unconsolidated statements prepared on the basis of the equity method of accounting as to the corporation's investee corporations, including corporate joint ventures and subsidiaries, although other evidence would be relevant in the total determination. The board of directors is entitled to rely as provided by section 8.30(e) upon reasonably current financial statements in determining whether the balance sheet test of section 6.40(c)(2) has been met, unless the board has knowledge that makes such reliance unwarranted. Section 6.40 does not mandate the use of generally accepted accounting principles; it only requires the use of accounting practices and principles that are reasonable in the circumstances. Although corporations subject to registration under the Securities Exchange Act of 1934 must, and many other corporations in fact do, use financial statements prepared on the basis of generally accepted accounting principles, a great number of smaller or closely held corporations do not. Some of these corporations maintain records solely on a tax accounting basis and their financial statements are of necessity prepared on that basis. Others prepare financial statements that substantially reflect generally accepted accounting principles but may depart from them in some respects (*e.g.*, footnote disclosure). A statutory standard of reasonableness, rather than stipulating generally accepted accounting principles as the normative standard, is appropriate to achieve a reasonable degree of flexibility and to accommodate the needs of the many different types of business corporations which might be subject to these provisions, including in particular closely held corporations.

Section 6.40(d) specifically permits determinations to be made under section 6.40(c)(2) on the basis of a fair valuation or other method that is reasonable in the circumstances. The statute authorizes departures from historical cost accounting and permits the use of appraisal and current value methods to determine the amount available for distribution. No particular method of valuation is prescribed in the statute, as different methods may have validity depending upon the circumstances, including the type of enterprise and the purpose for which the determination is made. In most cases, a fair valuation method or a going concern basis would be appropriate if it is believed that the enterprise will continue as a going concern.

Ordinarily a corporation should not selectively revalue assets. It should consider the value of all of its material assets, regardless of whether they are reflected in the financial statements (*e.g.*, a valuable executory contract). Likewise, all of a corporation's material obligations should be considered and revalued to the extent appropriate and possible. In any event, section 6.40(d) calls for the application under section 6.40(c)(2) of a method of determining the aggregate amount of assets and liabilities that is reasonable in the circumstances.

The phrase "other method that is reasonable in the circumstances means that under section 6.40(c)(2) a wide variety of methods may be considered reasonable in a particular case even if any such method might not be a "fair valuation" or "current value" method.

4. *Relationship to the Federal Bankruptcy Code and Other Fraudulent Conveyance Statutes*

The Act establishes the validity of distributions from the corporate law standpoint under section 6.40 and determines the potential liability of directors for improper distributions under sections 8.30 and 8.32. The federal bankruptcy laws and state fraudulent conveyance statutes, on the other hand, are designed to enable the trustee or other representative to recapture for the benefit of creditors funds distributed to others in some circumstances. Accordingly, the tests of section 6.40 are different from the tests for insolvency under those statutes.

5. *Preferential Dissolution Rights and the Balance Sheet Test*

Section 6.40(c)(2) treats preferential dissolution rights of shares for distribution purposes as if they were liabilities for the sole purpose of determining the amount available for distributions. In making the calculation of the amount that must be added to the liabilities of the corporation to reflect the preferential dissolution rights, the assumption should be made that the preferential dissolution rights are to be established pursuant to the articles of incorporation as of the date of the distribution or proposed distribution. The amount so determined must include arrearages in preferential dividends if the articles of incorporation require that they be paid upon the dissolution of the corporation. In the case of shares having both preferential rights upon dissolution and other nonpreferential rights, only the preferential rights should be taken into account. The treatment of preferential dissolution rights of classes or series of shares set forth in section 6.40(c)(2) is applicable only to the balance sheet test and is not applicable to the equity insolvency test of section 6.40(c)(1). The treatment of preferential rights mandated by section 6.40(c)(2) may always be eliminated by an appropriate provision in the articles of incorporation.

6.   *Application to Acquisition of Shares*

In an acquisition of its shares, a corporation may transfer property or incur debt to the former holder of the shares. Share repurchase agreements involving payment for shares over a period of time are of special importance in closely held corporations. Section 6.40(e) provides a clear rule for this situation: the legality of the distribution must be measured at the time of the issuance or incurrence of the debt, not at a later date when the debt is actually paid, except as provided in section 6.40(g).

Section 6.40(g) provides that indebtedness need not be taken into account as a liability in determining whether the tests of section 6.40(c) have been met if the terms of the indebtedness provide that payments of principal or interest can be made only if and to the extent that payment of a distribution could then be made under section 6.40. This has the effect of making the holder of the indebtedness junior to all other creditors but senior to the holders of shares, not only during the time the corporation is operating but also upon dissolution and liquidation. It should be noted that the creation of such indebtedness, and the related limitations on payments of principal and interest, may create tax problems or raise other legal questions.

Although section 6.40(g) is applicable to all indebtedness meeting its tests, regardless of the circumstances of its issuance, it is anticipated that it will apply most frequently to permit the reacquisition of shares of the corporation at a time when the deferred purchase price exceeds the net worth of the corporation. This type of reacquisition may be necessary in the case of businesses in early stages of development or service businesses whose value derives principally from existing or prospective net income or cash flow rather than from net asset value. In such situations, net worth will usually be anticipated to grow over time from operations so that when payments in respect of the indebtedness are to be made the two insolvency tests will be satisfied. In the meantime, the fact that the indebtedness is outstanding will not prevent distributions that could be made under section 6.40(c) if the indebtedness were not counted in making the determination.

CHAPTER 7.   SHAREHOLDERS

SUBCHAPTER A.   MEETINGS

§ 7.01   Annual Meeting

(a)   Unless directors are elected by written consent in lieu of an annual meeting as permitted by section 7.04, a corporation shall hold a meeting of shareholders annually at a time stated in or fixed in accordance with the bylaws at which directors shall be elected.

(b)   Unless the board of directors determines to hold the meeting solely by means of remote communication in accordance with section 7.09(c), annual meetings may be held (i) in or out of this state at the place stated in or fixed in accordance with the bylaws, or (ii) if no place is stated or fixed in accordance with the bylaws, at the corporation's principal office.

(c)   The failure to hold an annual meeting at the time stated in or fixed in accordance with a corporation's bylaws does not affect the validity of any corporate action.

§ 7.02   Special Meeting

(a)   A corporation shall hold a special meeting of shareholders:

(1)   on call of its board of directors or the person or persons authorized to do so by the articles of incorporation or bylaws; or

(2)   if shareholders holding at least 10% of all the votes entitled to be cast on an issue proposed to be considered at the proposed special meeting sign, date, and deliver to the corporation one or more written demands for the meeting describing the purpose or purposes for

which it is to be held, provided that the articles of incorporation may fix a lower percentage or a higher percentage not exceeding 25% of all the votes entitled to be cast on any issue proposed to be considered. Unless otherwise provided in the articles of incorporation, a written demand for a special meeting may be revoked by a writing to that effect received by the corporation before the receipt by the corporation of demands sufficient in number to require the holding of a special meeting.

(b) If not otherwise fixed under section 7.03 or 7.07, the record date for determining shareholders entitled to demand a special meeting shall be the first date on which a signed shareholder demand is delivered to the corporation. No written demand for a special meeting shall be effective unless, within 60 days of the earliest date on which such a demand delivered to the corporation as required by this section was signed, written demands signed by shareholders holding at least the percentage of votes specified in or fixed in accordance with subsection (a)(2) have been delivered to the corporation.

(c) Unless the board of directors determines to hold the meeting solely by remote participation in accordance with section 7.09(c), special meetings of shareholders may be held (i) in or out of this state at the place stated in or fixed in accordance with the bylaws, or (ii) if no place is stated in or fixed in accordance with the bylaws, at the corporation's principal office.

(d) Only business within the purpose or purposes described in the meeting notice required by section 7.05(c) may be conducted at a special meeting of shareholders.

§ 7.03   Court-Ordered Meeting

(a) The [name or describe court] may summarily order a meeting to be held:

(1) on application of any shareholder of the corporation if an annual meeting was not held or action by written consent in lieu of an annual meeting did not become effective within the earlier of six months after the end of the corporation's fiscal year or 15 months after its last annual meeting; or

(2) on application of one or more shareholders who signed a demand for a special meeting valid under section 7.02, if:

(i) notice of the special meeting was not given within 30 days after the first day on which the requisite number of such demands have been delivered to the corporation; or

(ii) the special meeting was not held in accordance with the notice.

(b) The court may fix the time and place of the meeting, determine the shares entitled to participate in the meeting, specify a record date or dates for determining shareholders entitled to notice of and to vote at the meeting, prescribe the form and content of the meeting notice, fix the quorum required for specific matters to be considered at the meeting (or direct that the shares represented at the meeting constitute a quorum for action on those matters), and enter other orders necessary to accomplish the purpose or purposes of the meeting.

(c) For purposes of subsection (a)(1), "shareholder" means a record shareholder, a beneficial shareholder, and an unrestricted voting trust beneficial owner.

§ 7.04   Action Without Meeting

(a) Action required or permitted by this Act to be taken at a shareholders' meeting may be taken without a meeting if the action is taken by all the shareholders entitled to vote on the action. The action must be evidenced by one or more written consents bearing the date of signature and describing the action taken, signed by all the shareholders entitled to vote on the action and delivered to the corporation for filing by the corporation with the minutes or corporate records.

(b) The articles of incorporation may provide that any action required or permitted by this Act to be taken at a shareholders' meeting may be taken without a meeting, and without prior notice, if consents in writing setting forth the action so taken are signed by the holders of outstanding shares having not less than the minimum number of votes that would be required to authorize or take the action at a meeting at which all shares entitled to vote on the action were present and voted; provided, however, that if a corporation's articles of incorporation authorize shareholders to cumulate their votes when electing directors pursuant to section 7.28, directors may not be elected by less than unanimous written consent. A written consent must bear the date of signature of the shareholder who signs the consent and be delivered to the corporation for filing by the corporation with the minutes or corporate records.

(c)   If not otherwise fixed under section 7.07 and if prior action by the board of directors is not required respecting the action to be taken without a meeting, the record date for determining the shareholders entitled to take action without a meeting shall be the first date on which a signed written consent is delivered to the corporation. If not otherwise fixed under section 7.07 and if prior action by the board of directors is required respecting the action to be taken without a meeting, the record date shall be the close of business on the day the resolution of the board of directors taking such prior action is adopted. No written consent shall be effective to take the corporate action referred to therein unless, within 60 days of the earliest date on which a consent delivered to the corporation as required by this section was signed, written consents signed by sufficient shareholders to take the action have been delivered to the corporation. A written consent may be revoked by a writing to that effect delivered to the corporation before unrevoked written consents sufficient in number to take the corporate action have been delivered to the corporation.

(d)   A consent signed pursuant to the provisions of this section has the effect of a vote taken at a meeting and may be described as such in any document. Unless the articles of incorporation, bylaws or a resolution of the board of directors provides for a reasonable delay to permit tabulation of written consents, the action taken by written consent shall be effective when written consents signed by sufficient shareholders to take the action have been delivered to the corporation.

(e)   If this Act requires that notice of a proposed action be given to nonvoting shareholders and the action is to be taken by written consent of the voting shareholders, the corporation shall give its nonvoting shareholders written notice of the action not more than 10 days after (i) written consents sufficient to take the action have been delivered to the corporation, or (ii) such later date that tabulation of consents is completed pursuant to an authorization under subsection (d). The notice must reasonably describe the action taken and contain or be accompanied by the same material that, under any provision of this Act, would have been required to be sent to nonvoting shareholders in a notice of a meeting at which the proposed action would have been submitted to the shareholders for action.

(f)   If action is taken by less than unanimous written consent of the voting shareholders, the corporation shall give its nonconsenting voting shareholders written notice of the action not more than 10 days after (i) written consents sufficient to take the action have been delivered to the corporation, or (ii) such later date that tabulation of consents is completed pursuant to an authorization under subsection (d). The notice must reasonably describe the action taken and contain or be accompanied by the same material that, under any provision of this Act, would have been required to be sent to voting shareholders in a notice of a meeting at which the action would have been submitted to the shareholders for action.

(g)   The notice requirements in subsections (e) and (f) shall not delay the effectiveness of actions taken by written consent, and a failure to comply with such notice requirements shall not invalidate actions taken by written consent, provided that this subsection shall not be deemed to limit judicial power to fashion any appropriate remedy in favor of a shareholder adversely affected by a failure to give such notice within the required time period.

§ 7.05   Notice of Meeting

(a)   A corporation shall notify shareholders of the date, time, and place, if any, of each annual and special shareholders' meeting no fewer than 10 nor more than 60 days before the meeting date. If the board of directors has authorized participation by means of remote communication pursuant to section 7.09 for holders of any class or series of shares, the notice to the holders of such class or series of shares must describe the means of remote communication to be used. The notice must include the record date for determining the shareholders entitled to vote at the meeting, if such date is different from the record date for determining shareholders entitled to notice of the meeting. Unless this Act or the articles of incorporation require otherwise, the corporation is required to give notice only to shareholders entitled to vote at the meeting as of the record date for determining the shareholders entitled to notice of the meeting.

(b)   Unless this Act or the articles of incorporation require otherwise, the notice of an annual meeting of shareholders need not include a description of the purpose or purposes for which the meeting is called.

(c)   Notice of a special meeting of shareholders must include a description of the purpose or purposes for which the meeting is called.

(d)   If not otherwise fixed under section 7.03 or 7.07, the record date for determining shareholders entitled to notice of and to vote at an annual or special shareholders' meeting is the day before the first notice is delivered to shareholders.

(e)   Unless the bylaws require otherwise, if an annual or special shareholders' meeting is adjourned to a different date, time, or place, if any, notice need not be given of the new date, time, or place, if any, if the new date, time, or place, if any, is announced at the meeting before adjournment. If a new record date for the adjourned meeting is or must be fixed under section 7.07, however, notice of the adjourned meeting shall be given under this section to shareholders entitled to vote at such adjourned meeting as of the record date fixed for notice of such adjourned meeting.

§ 7.06   Waiver of Notice

(a)   A shareholder may waive any notice required by this Act or the articles of incorporation or bylaws, before or after the date and time stated in the notice. The waiver must be in writing, be signed by the shareholder entitled to the notice, and be delivered to the corporation for filing by the corporation with the minutes or corporate records.

(b)   A shareholder's attendance at a meeting:

(1)   waives objection to lack of notice or defective notice of the meeting, unless the shareholder at the beginning of the meeting objects to holding the meeting or transacting business at the meeting; and

(2)   waives objection to consideration of a particular matter at the meeting that is not within the purpose or purposes described in the meeting notice, unless the shareholder objects to considering the matter when it is presented.

§ 7.07   Record Date for Meeting

(a)   The bylaws may fix or provide the manner of fixing the record date or dates for one or more voting groups to determine the shareholders entitled to notice of a shareholders' meeting, to demand a special meeting, to vote, or to take any other action. If the bylaws do not fix or provide for fixing a record date, the board of directors may fix the record date.

(b)   A record date fixed under this section may not be more than 70 days before the meeting or action requiring a determination of shareholders and may not be retroactive.

(c)   A determination of shareholders entitled to notice of or to vote at a shareholders' meeting is effective for any adjournment of the meeting unless the board of directors fixes a new record date or dates, which it shall do if the meeting is adjourned to a date more than 120 days after the date fixed for the original meeting.

(d)   If a court orders a meeting adjourned to a date more than 120 days after the date fixed for the original meeting, it may provide that the original record date or dates continues in effect or it may fix a new record date or dates.

(e)   The record dates for a shareholders' meeting fixed by or in the manner provided in the bylaws or by the board of directors shall be the record date for determining shareholders entitled both to notice of and to vote at the shareholders' meeting, unless in the case of a record date fixed by the board of directors and to the extent not prohibited by the bylaws, the board, at the time it fixes the record date for shareholders entitled to notice of the meeting, fixes a later record date on or before the date of the meeting to determine the shareholders entitled to vote at the meeting.

§ 7.08   Conduct of the Meeting

(a)   At each meeting of shareholders, a chair shall preside. The chair shall be appointed as provided in the bylaws or, in the absence of such provision, by the board of directors.

(b)   The chair, unless the articles of incorporation or bylaws provide otherwise, shall determine the order of business and shall have the authority to establish rules for the conduct of the meeting.

(c)   Any rules adopted for, and the conduct of, the meeting shall be fair to shareholders.

(d)   The chair of the meeting shall announce at the meeting when the polls close for each matter voted upon. If no announcement is made, the polls shall be deemed to have closed upon the final adjournment of the meeting. After the polls close, no ballots, proxies or votes nor any revocations or changes to such ballots, proxies or votes may be accepted.

OFFICIAL COMMENT

Section 7.08 provides that, at any meeting of the shareholders, there shall be a chair who shall preside over the meeting. Inherent in the chair's power in section 7.08(b) to establish rules for the conduct of the meeting is the authority to require that the order of business be observed and that any discussion or comments from shareholders or their proxies be confined to the business item under discussion. The rules for conduct of the meeting may cover such subjects as the proper means for obtaining the floor, who shall have the right to address the meeting, the manner in which shareholders will be recognized to speak, time limits per speaker, the number of times a shareholder may address the meeting, and the person to whom questions should be addressed. The chair should be fair in determining the order of business and in establishing rules for the conduct of the meeting so as not to unfairly foreclose the right of shareholders— subject to the Act, the articles of incorporation and the bylaws—to raise items which are properly a subject for shareholder discussion or action at some point in the meeting before adjournment.

The Act provides that only business within the purpose or purposes described in the meeting notice may be conducted at a special shareholders' meeting. See sections 7.02(d) and 7.05(c). In addition, in order to raise a matter at an annual meeting (for example, to nominate an individual for election as a director or to propose a resolution for adoption), a shareholder may be required to comply with any advance notice provision in the articles of incorporation or bylaws. See the Official Comment to section 7.05.

§ 7.09   Remote Participation in Shareholders' Meetings; Meetings Held Solely by Remote Participation

(a)   Shareholders of any class or series of shares may participate in any meeting of shareholders by means of remote communication to the extent the board of directors authorizes such participation for such class or series. Participation as a shareholder by means of remote communication shall be subject to such guidelines and procedures as the board of directors adopts, and shall be in conformity with subsection (b).

(b)   Shareholders participating in a shareholders' meeting by means of remote communication shall be deemed present and may vote at such a meeting if the corporation has implemented reasonable measures:

(1)   to verify that each person participating remotely as a shareholder is a shareholder; and

(2)   to provide such shareholders a reasonable opportunity to participate in the meeting and to vote on matters submitted to the shareholders, including an opportunity to communicate, and to read or hear the proceedings of the meeting, substantially concurrently with such proceedings.

(c)   Unless the bylaws require the meeting of shareholders to be held at a place, the board of directors may determine that any meeting of shareholders shall not be held at any place and shall instead be held solely by means of remote communication, but only if the corporation implements the measures specified in subsection (b).

OFFICIAL COMMENT

Section 7.09 authorizes the board of directors to permit shareholders to participate in annual and special shareholders' meetings by means of remote communication, such as over the Internet or through telephone conference calls, subject to the conditions set forth in section 7.09(b) and any other guidelines and procedures that the board of directors adopts. This would include the use of electronic ballots to the extent authorized by the board of directors. This authorization extends as well to anyone to whom such shareholder has granted a proxy appointment. Section 7.09(a) ensures that the board of directors has the sole discretion to determine whether to allow shareholders to participate by means of remote communication.

Section 7.09 allows the board of directors to limit participation by means of remote communication to all shareholders of a particular class or series, but does not permit the board of directors to limit such participation to particular shareholders within a class or series. Section 7.09 is not intended to expand the rights to participate in meetings or otherwise alter the ability of the board of directors or the chair to conduct meetings, pursuant to section 7.08, in a manner that is fair. For example, many corporations limit shareholder comments and, if such practice is fair to shareholders consistent with section 7.08, such practice is not changed by section 7.09. The two requirements under section 7.09(b) reflect the minimum deemed necessary to safeguard the integrity of the shareholders' meeting. Section 7.09 specifically gives the board of directors the flexibility and discretion to adopt additional guidelines and procedures for allowing shareholders to participate in a meeting by means of remote communication.

To give corporations the flexibility to choose the most efficient means of remote communication, under section 7.09(a), the board of directors may require that shareholders communicate their desire to participate by a certain date and, if remote participation is not to be the exclusive means of shareholders participating in the meeting, may condition the provision of remote communication or the form of communication to be used on the affirmative response of a certain number or proportion of shareholders eligible to participate. If the board of directors authorizes shareholder participation by means of remote communication pursuant to this section, such authorization and the process for participating by remote means of communication must be included in the meeting notice required by section 7.05. Section 7.09(c) authorizes the board of directors to provide for a meeting of shareholders to be held solely by means of remote communication and to dispense with having a place for the meeting. This authority may be eliminated in a bylaw. If the bylaw is adopted by shareholders, it may only be amended by the shareholders unless the bylaw otherwise provides.

SUBCHAPTER B.   VOTING

§ 7.20   Shareholders' List for Meeting

(a)   After fixing a record date for a meeting, a corporation shall prepare an alphabetical list of the names of all its shareholders who are entitled to notice of a shareholders' meeting. If the board of directors fixes a different record date under section 7.07(e) to determine the shareholders entitled to vote at the meeting, a corporation also shall prepare an alphabetical list of the names of all its shareholders who are entitled to vote at the meeting. A list must be arranged by voting group (and within each voting group by class or series of shares) and show the address of and number of shares held by each shareholder. Nothing contained in this subsection shall require the corporation to include on such list the electronic mail address or other electronic contact information of a shareholder.

(b)   The shareholders' list for notice shall be available for inspection by any shareholder, beginning two business days after notice of the meeting is given for which the list was prepared and continuing through the meeting, (i) at the corporation's principal office or at a place identified in the meeting notice in the city where the meeting will be held or (ii) on a reasonably accessible electronic network, provided that the information required to gain access to such list is provided with the notice of the meeting. In the event that the corporation determines to make the list available on an electronic network, the corporation may take reasonable steps to ensure that such information is available only to shareholders of the corporation. A shareholders' list for voting shall be similarly available for inspection promptly after the record date for voting. A shareholder, or the shareholder's agent or attorney, is entitled on written demand to inspect and, subject to the requirements of section 16.02(c), to copy a list, during regular business hours and at the shareholder's expense, during the period it is available for inspection.

(c)   If the meeting is to be held at a place, the corporation shall make the list of shareholders entitled to vote available at the meeting, and any shareholder, or the shareholder's agent or attorney, is entitled to inspect the list at any time during the meeting or any adjournment. If the meeting is to be held solely by means of remote communication, then such list shall also be open to such inspection during the meeting on a reasonably accessible electronic network, and the information required to access such list shall be provided with the notice of the meeting.

(d)   If the corporation refuses to allow a shareholder, or the shareholder's agent or attorney, to inspect a shareholders' list before or at the meeting (or copy a list as permitted by subsection (b)), the [name or describe court], on application of the shareholder, may summarily order the inspection or copying at the corporation's expense and may postpone the meeting for which the list was prepared until the inspection or copying is complete.

(e)   Refusal or failure to prepare or make available the shareholders' list does not affect the validity of action taken at the meeting.

§ 7.21   Voting Entitlement of Shares

(a)   Except as provided in subsections (b) and (d) or unless the articles of incorporation provide otherwise, each outstanding share, regardless of class or series, is entitled to one vote on each matter voted on at a shareholders' meeting. Only shares are entitled to vote.

(b)   Shares of a corporation are not entitled to vote if they are owned by or otherwise belong to the corporation directly, or indirectly through an entity of which a majority of the voting power is held directly or indirectly by the corporation or which is otherwise controlled by the corporation.

(c)   Shares held by the corporation in a fiduciary capacity for the benefit of any person are entitled to vote unless they are held for the benefit of, or otherwise belong to, the corporation directly, or indirectly through an entity of which a majority of the voting power is held directly or indirectly by the corporation or which is otherwise controlled by the corporation.

(d)   Redeemable shares are not entitled to vote after delivery of written notice of redemption is effective and a sum sufficient to redeem the shares has been deposited with a bank, trust company, or other financial institution under an irrevocable obligation to pay the holders the redemption price on surrender of the shares.

(e)   For purposes of this section, "voting power" means the current power to vote in the election of directors of a corporation or to elect, select or appoint governors of another entity.

§ 7.22   Proxies

(a)   A shareholder may vote the shareholder's shares in person or by proxy.

(b)   A shareholder, or the shareholder's agent or attorney-in-fact, may appoint a proxy to vote or otherwise act for the shareholder by signing an appointment form, or by an electronic transmission. An electronic transmission must contain or be accompanied by information from which the recipient can determine the date of the transmission and that the transmission was authorized by the sender or the sender's agent or attorney-in-fact.

(c)   An appointment of a proxy is effective when a signed appointment form or an electronic transmission of the appointment is received by the inspector of election or the officer or agent of the corporation authorized to count votes. An appointment is valid for the term provided in the appointment form, and, if no term is provided, is valid for 11 months unless the appointment is irrevocable under subsection (d).

(d)   An appointment of a proxy is revocable unless the appointment form or electronic transmission states that it is irrevocable and the appointment is coupled with an interest. Appointments coupled with an interest include the appointment of:

   (1)   a pledgee;

   (2)   a person who purchased or agreed to purchase the shares;

   (3)   a creditor of the corporation who extended it credit under terms requiring the appointment;

   (4)   an employee of the corporation whose employment contract requires the appointment; or

   (5)   a party to a voting agreement created under section 7.31.

(e)   The death or incapacity of the shareholder appointing a proxy does not affect the right of the corporation to accept the proxy's authority unless notice of the death or incapacity is received by the secretary or other officer or agent authorized to tabulate votes before the proxy exercises authority under the appointment.

(f)   An appointment made irrevocable under subsection (d) is revoked when the interest with which it is coupled is extinguished.

(g)   Unless it otherwise provides, an appointment made irrevocable under subsection (d) continues in effect after a transfer of the shares and a transferee takes subject to the appointment, except that a transferee for value of shares subject to an irrevocable appointment may revoke the appointment if the transferee did not know of its existence when acquiring the shares and the existence of the irrevocable appointment was not noted conspicuously on the certificate representing the shares or on the information statement for shares without certificates.

(h)   Subject to section 7.24 and to any express limitation on the proxy's authority stated in the appointment form or electronic transmission, a corporation is entitled to accept the proxy's vote or other action as that of the shareholder making the appointment.

§ 7.23   Shares Held by Intermediaries and Nominees

(a)   A corporation's board of directors may establish a procedure under which a person on whose behalf shares are registered in the name of an intermediary or nominee may elect to be treated by the corporation as the record shareholder by filing with the corporation a beneficial ownership certificate. The terms, conditions, and limitations of this treatment shall be specified in the procedure. To the extent such person is treated under such procedure as having rights or privileges that the record shareholder otherwise would have, the record shareholder shall not have those rights or privileges.

(b)   The procedure must specify:

   (1)   the types of intermediaries or nominees to which it applies;

   (2)   the rights or privileges that the corporation recognizes in a person with respect to whom a beneficial ownership certificate is filed;

   (3)   the manner in which the procedure is selected which must include that the beneficial ownership certificate be signed or assented to by or on behalf of the record shareholder and the person on whose behalf the shares are held;

   (4)   the information that must be provided when the procedure is selected;

(5)   the period for which selection of the procedure is effective;

(6)   requirements for notice to the corporation with respect to the arrangement; and

(7)   the form and contents of the beneficial ownership certificate.

(c)   The procedure may specify any other aspects of the rights and duties created by the filing of a beneficial ownership certificate.

§ 7.24   Acceptance of Votes and Other Instruments

(a)   If the name signed on a vote, ballot, consent, waiver, shareholder demand, or proxy appointment corresponds to the name of a shareholder, the corporation, if acting in good faith, is entitled to accept the vote, ballot, consent, waiver, shareholder demand, or proxy appointment and give it effect as the act of the shareholder.

(b)   If the name signed on a vote, ballot, consent, waiver, shareholder demand, or proxy appointment does not correspond to the name of its shareholder, the corporation, if acting in good faith, is nevertheless entitled to accept the vote, ballot, consent, waiver, shareholder demand, or proxy appointment and give it effect as the act of the shareholder if:

(1)   the shareholder is an entity and the name signed purports to be that of an officer or agent of the entity;

(2)   the name signed purports to be that of an administrator, executor, guardian, or conservator representing the shareholder and, if the corporation requests, evidence of fiduciary status acceptable to the corporation has been presented with respect to the vote, ballot, consent, waiver, shareholder demand, or proxy appointment;

(3)   the name signed purports to be that of a receiver or trustee in bankruptcy of the shareholder and, if the corporation requests, evidence of this status acceptable to the corporation has been presented with respect to the vote, ballot, consent, waiver, shareholder demand, or proxy appointment;

(4)   the name signed purports to be that of a pledgee, beneficial owner, or attorney-in-fact of the shareholder and, if the corporation requests, evidence acceptable to the corporation of the signatory's authority to sign for the shareholder has been presented with respect to the vote, ballot, consent, waiver, shareholder demand, or proxy appointment; or

(5)   two or more persons are the shareholder as co-tenants or fiduciaries and the name signed purports to be the name of at least one of the co-owners and the person signing appears to be acting on behalf of all the co-owners.

(c)   The corporation is entitled to reject a vote, ballot, consent, waiver, shareholder demand, or proxy appointment if the person authorized to accept or reject such instrument, acting in good faith, has reasonable basis for doubt about the validity of the signature on it or about the signatory's authority to sign for the shareholder.

(d)   Neither the corporation or any person authorized by it, nor an inspector of election appointed under section 7.29, that accepts or rejects a vote, ballot, consent, waiver, shareholder demand, or proxy appointment in good faith and in accordance with the standards of this section 7.24 or section 7.22(b) is liable in damages to the shareholder for the consequences of the acceptance or rejection.

(e)   Corporate action based on the acceptance or rejection of a vote, ballot, consent, waiver, shareholder demand, or proxy appointment under this section is valid unless a court of competent jurisdiction determines otherwise.

(f)   If an inspector of election has been appointed under section 7.29, the inspector of election also has the authority to request information and make determinations under subsections (a), (b), and (c). Any determination made by the inspector of election under those subsections is controlling.

§ 7.25   Quorum and Voting Requirements for Voting Groups

(a)   Shares entitled to vote as a separate voting group may take action on a matter at a meeting only if a quorum of those shares exists with respect to that matter. Unless the articles of incorporation provide otherwise, shares representing a majority of the votes entitled to be cast on the matter by the voting group constitutes a quorum of that voting group for action on that matter. Whenever this Act requires a particular quorum for a specified action, the articles of incorporation may not provide for a lower quorum.

(b)   Once a share is represented for any purpose at a meeting, it is deemed present for quorum purposes for the remainder of the meeting and for any adjournment of that meeting unless a new record date is or must be fixed for that adjourned meeting.

(c)   If a quorum exists, action on a matter (other than the election of directors) by a voting group is approved if the votes cast within the voting group favoring the action exceed the votes cast opposing the action, unless the articles of incorporation require a greater number of affirmative votes.

(d)   An amendment of the articles of incorporation adding, changing, or deleting a quorum or voting requirement for a voting group greater than specified in subsection (a) or (c) is governed by section 7.27.

(e)   The election of directors is governed by section 7.28.

(f)   Whenever a provision of this Act provides for voting of classes or series as separate voting groups, the rules provided in section 10.04(c) for amendments of the articles of incorporation apply to that provision.

§ 7.26   Action by Single and Multiple Voting Groups

(a)   If the articles of incorporation or this Act provide for voting by a single voting group on a matter, action on that matter is taken when voted upon by that voting group as provided in section 7.25.

(b)   If the articles of incorporation or this Act provide for voting by two or more voting groups on a matter, action on that matter is taken only when voted upon by each of those voting groups counted separately as provided in section 7.25. Action may be taken by different voting groups on a matter at different times.

§ 7.27   Modifying Quorum or Voting Requirements

An amendment to the articles of incorporation that adds, changes, or deletes a quorum or voting requirement shall meet the same quorum requirement and be adopted by the same vote and voting groups required to take action under the quorum and voting requirements then in effect or proposed to be adopted, whichever is greater.

§ 7.28   Voting for Directors; Cumulative Voting

(a)   Unless otherwise provided in the articles of incorporation, directors are elected by a plurality of the votes cast by the shares entitled to vote in the election at a meeting at which a quorum is present.

(b)   Shareholders do not have a right to cumulate their votes for directors unless the articles of incorporation so provide.

(c)   A statement included in the articles of incorporation that "[all] [a designated voting group of] shareholders are entitled to cumulate their votes for directors" (or words of similar import) means that the shareholders designated are entitled to multiply the number of votes they are entitled to cast by the number of directors for whom they are entitled to vote and cast the product for a single candidate or distribute the product among two or more candidates.

(d)   Shares otherwise entitled to vote cumulatively may not be voted cumulatively at a particular meeting unless:

(1)   the meeting notice or proxy statement accompanying the notice states conspicuously that cumulative voting is authorized; or

(2)   a shareholder who has the right to cumulate the shareholder's votes gives notice to the corporation not less than 48 hours before the time set for the meeting of the shareholder's intent to cumulate votes during the meeting, and if one shareholder gives this notice all other shareholders in the same voting group participating in the election are entitled to cumulate their votes without giving further notice.

§ 7.29   Inspectors of Election

(a)   A corporation that has a class of equity securities registered pursuant to section 12 of the Securities Exchange Act of 1934 shall, and any other corporation may, appoint one or more inspectors to act at a meeting of shareholders in connection with determining voting results. Each inspector shall verify in writing that the inspector will faithfully execute the duties of inspector with strict impartiality and according to the best of the inspector's ability. An inspector may be an officer or employee of the corporation. The inspectors may appoint or retain other persons to assist the inspectors in the performance of the duties of inspector under subsection (b), and may rely on information provided by such persons and other persons, including those appointed to tabulate votes, unless the inspectors believe reliance is unwarranted.

(b)   The inspectors shall:

(1)   ascertain the number of shares outstanding and the voting power of each;

(2)   determine the shares represented at a meeting;

(3)   determine the validity of proxy appointments and ballots;

(4)   count the votes; and

(5)   make a written report of the results.

(c)   In performing their duties, the inspectors may examine (i) the proxy appointment forms and any other information provided in accordance with section 7.22(b), (ii) any envelope or related writing submitted with those appointment forms, (iii) any ballots, (iv) any evidence or other information specified in section 7.24 and (v) the relevant books and records of the corporation relating to its shareholders and their entitlement to vote, including any securities position list provided by a depository clearing agency.

(d)   The inspectors also may consider other information that they believe is relevant and reliable for the purpose of performing any of the duties assigned to them pursuant to subsection (b), including for the purpose of evaluating inconsistent, incomplete or erroneous information and reconciling information submitted on behalf of banks, brokers, their nominees or similar persons that indicates more votes being cast than a proxy authorized by the record shareholder is entitled to cast. If the inspectors consider other information allowed by this subsection, they shall in their report under subsection (b) specify the information considered by them, including the purpose or purposes for which the information was considered, the person or persons from whom they obtained the information, when the information was obtained, the means by which the information was obtained, and the basis for the inspectors' belief that such information is relevant and reliable.

(e)   Determinations of law by the inspectors of election are subject to de novo review by a court in a proceeding under section 7.49 or other judicial proceeding.

SUBCHAPTER C.   VOTING TRUSTS AND AGREEMENTS

§ 7.30   Voting Trusts

(a)   One or more shareholders may create a voting trust, conferring on a trustee the right to vote or otherwise act for them, by signing an agreement setting out the provisions of the trust (which may include anything consistent with its purpose) and transferring their shares to the trustee. When a voting trust agreement is signed, the trustee shall prepare a list of the names and addresses of all voting trust beneficial owners, together with the number and class of shares each transferred to the trust, and deliver copies of the list and agreement to the corporation at its principal office.

(b)   A voting trust becomes effective on the date the first shares subject to the trust are registered in the trustee's name.

(c)   Limits, if any, on the duration of a voting trust shall be as set forth in the voting trust. A voting trust that became effective when this Act provided a 10-year limit on its duration remains governed by the provisions of this section concerning duration then in effect, unless the voting trust is amended to provide otherwise by unanimous agreement of the parties to the voting trust.

§ 7.31   Voting Agreements

(a)   Two or more shareholders may provide for the manner in which they will vote their shares by signing an agreement for that purpose. A voting agreement created under this section is not subject to the provisions of section 7.30.

(b)   A voting agreement created under this section is specifically enforceable.

§ 7.32   Shareholder Agreements

(a)   An agreement among the shareholders of a corporation that complies with this section is effective among the shareholders and the corporation even though it is inconsistent with one or more other provisions of this Act in that it:

(1)   eliminates the board of directors or restricts the discretion or powers of the board of directors;

(2)   governs the authorization or making of distributions, regardless of whether they are in proportion to ownership of shares, subject to the limitations in section 6.40;

(3)   establishes who shall be directors or officers of the corporation, or their terms of office or manner of selection or removal;

(4)   governs, in general or in regard to specific matters, the exercise or division of voting power by or between the shareholders and directors or by or among any of them, including use of weighted voting rights or director proxies;

(5)   establishes the terms and conditions of any agreement for the transfer or use of property or the provision of services between the corporation and any shareholder, director, officer or employee of the corporation or among any of them;

(6)   transfers to one or more shareholders or other persons all or part of the authority to exercise the corporate powers or to manage the business and affairs of the corporation, including the resolution of any issue about which there exists a deadlock among directors or shareholders;

(7)   requires dissolution of the corporation at the request of one or more of the shareholders or upon the occurrence of a specified event or contingency; or

(8)   otherwise governs the exercise of the corporate powers or the management of the business and affairs of the corporation or the relationship among the shareholders, the directors and the corporation, or among any of them, and is not contrary to public policy.

(b)   An agreement authorized by this section shall be:

(1)   as set forth (i) in the articles of incorporation or bylaws and approved by all persons who are shareholders at the time of the agreement, or (ii) in a written agreement that is signed by all persons who are shareholders at the time of the agreement and is made known to the corporation; and

(2)   subject to amendment only by all persons who are shareholders at the time of the amendment, unless the agreement provides otherwise.

(c)   The existence of an agreement authorized by this section shall be noted conspicuously on the front or back of each certificate for outstanding shares or on the information statement required by section 6.26(b). If at the time of the agreement the corporation has shares outstanding represented by certificates, the corporation shall recall the outstanding certificates and issue substitute certificates that comply with this subsection. The failure to note the existence of the agreement on the certificate or information statement shall not affect the validity of the agreement or any action taken pursuant to it. Any purchaser of shares who, at the time of purchase, did not have knowledge of the existence of the agreement shall be entitled to rescission of the purchase. A purchaser shall be deemed to have knowledge of the existence of the agreement if its existence is noted on the certificate or information statement for the shares in compliance with this subsection and, if the shares are not represented by a certificate, the information statement is delivered to the purchaser at or before the time of purchase of the shares. An action to enforce the right of rescission authorized by this subsection shall be commenced within the earlier of 90 days after discovery of the existence of the agreement or two years after the time of purchase of the shares.

(d)   If the agreement ceases to be effective for any reason, the board of directors may, if the agreement is contained or referred to in the corporation's articles of incorporation or bylaws, adopt an amendment to the articles of incorporation or bylaws, without shareholder action, to delete the agreement and any references to it.

(e)   An agreement authorized by this section that limits the discretion or powers of the board of directors shall relieve the directors of, and impose upon the person or persons in whom such discretion or powers are vested, liability for acts or omissions imposed by law on directors to the extent that the discretion or powers of the directors are limited by the agreement.

(f)   The existence or performance of an agreement authorized by this section shall not be a ground for imposing personal liability on any shareholder for the acts or debts of the corporation even if the agreement or its performance treats the corporation as if it were a partnership or results in failure to observe the corporate formalities otherwise applicable to the matters governed by the agreement.

(g)   Incorporators or subscribers for shares may act as shareholders with respect to an agreement authorized by this section if no shares have been issued when the agreement is made.

(h)   Limits, if any, on the duration of an agreement authorized by this section must be set forth in the agreement. An agreement that became effective when this Act provided for a 10-year limit on duration of shareholder agreements, unless the agreement provided otherwise, remains governed by the provisions of this section concerning duration then in effect.

OFFICIAL COMMENT

Shareholders of some corporations, especially those that are closely held, frequently enter into agreements that govern the operation of the enterprise.

Section 7.32 provides, within the context of the traditional corporate structure, legal certainty to such agreements that embody various aspects of the business arrangement established by the shareholders to meet their business and personal needs. The subject matter of these arrangements includes governance of the entity, allocation of the economic return from the business, and other aspects of the relationships among shareholders, directors, and the corporation which are part of the business arrangement. Section 7.32 also recognizes that many of the corporate norms contained in the Act were designed with an eye towards corporations whose management and share ownership are distinct. These functions are often conjoined in some corporations, such as the close corporation. Thus, section 7.32 validates agreements among shareholders even when the agreements are inconsistent with the statutory norms contained in the Act.

Importantly, section 7.32 only addresses the parties to the shareholder agreement, their transferees, and the corporation, and does not have any binding legal effect on the state, creditors, or other third persons.

Section 7.32 supplements the other provisions of the Act. If an agreement is not in conflict with another section of the Act, no resort need be made to section 7.32 with its requirement of unanimity. For example, special provisions may be included in the articles of incorporation or bylaws with less than unanimous shareholder agreement so long as such provisions are not in conflict with other provisions of the Act. Similarly, section 7.32 would not have to be relied upon to validate typical buy-sell agreements among two or more shareholders or the covenants and other terms of a stock purchase agreement entered into in connection with the issuance of shares by a corporation.

1. Section 7.32(a)

An agreement authorized by section 7.32 is "not inconsistent with law" within the meaning of sections 2.02(b)(2) and 2.06(b) of the Act.

The range of agreements validated by section 7.32(a) is expansive though not unlimited. Section 7.32 defines the types of agreements that can be validated largely by illustration. The seven specific categories that are listed are designed to cover some of the most frequently used arrangements. There are numerous other arrangements that may be made, and section 7.32(a)(8) provides an additional category for any provisions that, in a manner inconsistent with any other provision of the Act, otherwise govern the exercise of the corporate powers or the management of the business and affairs of the corporation or the relationship between and among the shareholders, the directors, and the corporation or any of them, and are not contrary to public policy.

Section 7.32(a) validates virtually all types of shareholder agreements that, in practice, normally concern shareholders and their advisors. Given that breadth, any provision that may be contained in the articles of incorporation with a majority vote under sections 2.02(b)(2)(ii) and (iii), as well as under section 2.02(b)(4), may also be effective if contained in a shareholder agreement that complies with section 7.32.

The provisions of a shareholder agreement authorized by section 7.32(a) will often, in operation, conflict with the language of more than one section of the Act, and courts should in such cases construe all related sections of the Act flexibly and in a manner consistent with the underlying intent of the shareholder agreement. Thus, for example, in the case of an agreement that provides for weighted voting by directors, every reference in the Act to a majority or other proportion of directors should be construed to refer to a majority or other proportion of the votes of the directors.

Although the limits of section 7.32(a)(8) are left uncertain, there are provisions of the Act that may not be overridden if they reflect core principles of public policy with respect to corporate affairs. For example, a provision of a shareholder agreement that purports to eliminate all of the standards of conduct established under section 8.30 might be viewed as contrary to public policy and thus not validated under section 7.32(a)(8). Similarly, a provision that exculpates directors from liability more broadly than permitted by section 2.02(b)(4), or indemnifies them more broadly than permitted by section 2.02(b)(5), might not be validated under section 7.32 because of strong public policy reasons for the statutory limitations on the right to exculpate directors from liability and to indemnify them. The validity of some provisions may depend upon the circumstances. For example, a provision of a shareholder agreement that limited inspection rights under section 16.02 or the right to financial statements under section 16.20 might, as a general matter, be valid, but that provision might not be given effect if it prevented shareholders from obtaining information necessary to determine whether directors of the corporation have satisfied the standards of conduct under section 8.30. The foregoing are examples and are not intended to be exclusive.

As noted above, shareholder agreements otherwise validated by section 7.32 are not legally binding on the state, on creditors, or on other third parties. For example, an agreement that dispenses with the need to make corporate filings required by the Act would be ineffective. Similarly, an agreement among shareholders that provides that only the president has authority to enter into contracts for the corporation would not, without more, be binding against third parties, and ordinary principles of agency, including the concept of apparent authority, would continue to apply.

2. Section 7.32(b)

Section 7.32 minimizes the formal requirements for a shareholder agreement so as not to restrict unduly the shareholders' ability to take advantage of the flexibility the section provides. Thus, it is not necessary to "opt in" to a special class of close corporations to obtain the benefits of section 7.32. An agreement can be validated under section 7.32 whether it is set forth in the articles of incorporation, the bylaws or in a separate agreement, and regardless of whether section 7.32 is specifically referenced in the agreement. Where the corporation has a single shareholder, the requirement of an "agreement among the shareholders" is satisfied by the unilateral action of the shareholder in establishing the terms of the agreement, evidenced by provisions in the articles of incorporation or bylaws, or in a writing signed by the sole shareholder. Although a writing signed by all the shareholders is not required where the agreement is contained in articles of incorporation or bylaws unanimously approved, it may be desirable to have all the shareholders actually sign the instrument to establish unequivocally their agreement. Similarly, although transferees are bound by a valid shareholder agreement, subject to section 7.32(c), it may be desirable to obtain the affirmative written assent of the transferee at the time of the transfer. Section 7.32(b) also establishes and permits amendments by less than unanimous agreement if the shareholder agreement so provides.

Section 7.32(b) requires unanimous shareholder approval of the shareholder agreement regardless of entitlement to vote. Unanimity is required because an agreement authorized by section 7.32 can effect material organic changes in the corporation's operation and structure, and in the rights and obligations of shareholders.

The requirement that the shareholder agreement be made known to the corporation is the predicate for the requirement in section 7.32(c) that share certificates or information statements be legended to note the existence of the agreement. No specific form of notification is required and the agreement need not be filed with the corporation. In the case of shareholder agreements in the articles of incorporation or bylaws, the corporation will necessarily have notice. In the case of a shareholder agreement outside the articles of incorporation or bylaws, the requirement of signatures by all of the shareholders should in virtually all cases be sufficient to make the corporation aware of the agreement, as one or more signatories will normally also be a director or an officer.

3. Section 7.32(c)

Section 7.32(c) addresses the effect of a shareholder agreement on subsequent purchasers or transferees of shares. Typically, corporations with shareholder agreements also have restrictions on the transferability of the shares as authorized by section 6.27, thus lessening the practical effects of the problem in the context of voluntary transferees. Transferees of shares without knowledge of the agreement or those acquiring shares upon the death of an original participant in a close corporation may, however, be heavily affected. Weighing the burdens on transferees against the burdens on the remaining shareholders in the enterprise, section 7.32(c) affirms the continued validity of the shareholder agreement on all transferees, whether by purchase, gift, operation of law, or otherwise. Unlike restrictions on transfer, it may be impossible to enforce a shareholder agreement against less than all of the shareholders. Thus, under section 7.32, one who inherits shares subject to a shareholder agreement must continue to abide by the agreement. If that is not the desired result, care must be exercised at the initiation of the shareholder agreement to ensure a different outcome, such as providing for a buy-back upon death.

Where shares are transferred to a purchaser without knowledge of a shareholder agreement, the validity of the agreement is similarly unaffected, but the purchaser is afforded a rescission remedy against the seller. Under section 7.32(c), the time at which notice to a purchaser is relevant for purposes of determining entitlement to rescission is the time when a purchaser acquires the shares rather than when a commitment is made to acquire the shares. If the purchaser learns of the agreement after committing to purchase but before acquiring the shares, the purchaser may not proceed with the purchase and still obtain the benefit of the remedies in section 7.32(c). Under contract principles and the securities laws, a failure to disclose the existence of a shareholder agreement may constitute the omission of a material fact and may excuse performance of the commitment to purchase. The term "purchaser" includes a person acquiring shares upon initial issue or by transfer, and also includes a pledgee, for whom the time of purchase is the time the shares are pledged.

Section 7.32 addresses the underlying rights of shares and shareholders and the validity of shareholder action which redefines those rights, as contrasted with questions regarding entitlement to ownership of the security, competing ownership claims, and disclosure issues. Consistent with this dichotomy, the rights and remedies available to purchasers under section 7.32(c) are independent of those provided by contract law, Article 8 of the Uniform Commercial Code, the securities laws, and other laws outside the Act.

With respect to the related subject of restrictions on transferability of shares, note that section 7.32 does not directly address or validate such restrictions, which are governed instead by section 6.27 of the Act. However, if such restrictions are adopted as a part of a shareholder agreement that complies with the requirements of section 7.32, a court should apply the concept of reasonableness under section 6.27 in determining the validity of such restrictions.

Section 7.32(c) contains an affirmative requirement that the share certificate or information statement for the shares be legended to note the existence of a shareholder agreement. No specified form of legend is required, and a simple statement that "[t]he shares represented by this certificate are subject to a shareholder agreement" is sufficient. At that point, a purchaser must obtain a copy of the shareholder agreement from the transferor or proceed at the purchaser's peril. In the event a corporation fails to legend share certificates or information statements, a court may, in an appropriate case, imply a cause of action against the corporation in favor of an injured purchaser without knowledge of a shareholder agreement. The circumstances under which such a remedy would be implied, the proper measure of damages, and other attributes of and limitations on such an implied remedy are left to development in the courts.

A purchaser who has no actual knowledge of a shareholder agreement and is not charged with knowledge by virtue of a legend on the certificate or information statement has a rescission remedy against the transferor (which would be the corporation in the case of a new issue of shares).

If the shares are certificated and duly legended, a purchaser is charged with notice of the shareholder agreement even if the purchaser never saw the certificate. In the case of uncertificated shares, however, the purchaser is not charged with notice of the shareholder agreement unless a duly-legended information statement is delivered to the purchaser at or before the time of purchase. This different rule for uncertificated shares is intended to provide an additional safeguard to protect innocent purchasers, and is necessary because section 6.26(b) of the Act and Article 8 of the Uniform Commercial Code permit delivery of statements after a transfer of shares.

4.   Section 7.32(d)

Section 7.32(d) recognizes that the terms of a shareholder agreement may provide for its termination upon the happening of a specified event or condition. An example may be when the corporation undergoes an initial public offering. This approach is consistent with the broad freedom of contract provided to participants in such enterprises.

5.   Sections 7.32(e) through (g)

Section 7.32(e) provides a shift of liability from the directors to any person or persons in whom the discretion or powers otherwise exercised by the board of directors are vested under the shareholder agreement. A shareholder agreement which provides for such a shift of responsibility, with the concomitant shift of liability provided by subsection (e), could also provide for exculpation from that liability to the extent otherwise authorized by the Act. The transfer of liability provided by subsection (e) covers liabilities imposed on directors "by law," which is intended to include liabilities arising under the Act, the common law, and statutory law outside the Act.

Section 7.32(f) provides that shareholders shall not have personal liability for the debts of a corporation arising out of acts or omissions taken pursuant to a shareholder agreement validated by section 7.32. Section 7.32(g) authorizes shareholder agreements for corporations that are in the process of being organized and do not yet have shareholders.

6. Section 7.32(h)

Section 7.32 does not limit the duration of a shareholder agreement. This approach is consistent with the wide freedom of contract provided to participants in such enterprises. For agreements entered into during a time that section 7.32 provided for a 10-year term if no other time limit was specified, section 7.32(h) provides that its duration will be governed by the provisions of section 7.32 concerning duration in force at the time the agreement became effective. This would include, for example, both the default termination rule and the authority under former section 7.32(b)(2) that such an agreement's automatic 10-year term could be amended by all shareholders (unless the agreement had prohibited such amendment).

SUBCHAPTER D. DERIVATIVE PROCEEDINGS

§ 7.40 Subchapter Definitions

In this subchapter:

"Derivative proceeding" means a civil suit in the right of a domestic corporation or, to the extent provided in section 7.47, in the right of a foreign corporation.

"Shareholder" means a record shareholder, a beneficial shareholder, and an unrestricted voting trust beneficial owner.

§ 7.41 Standing

A shareholder may not commence or maintain a derivative proceeding unless the shareholder (i) was a shareholder of the corporation at the time of the act or omission complained of or became a shareholder through transfer by operation of law from one who was a shareholder at that time and (ii) fairly and adequately represents the interests of the corporation in enforcing the right of the corporation.

§ 7.42 Demand

No shareholder may commence a derivative proceeding until (i) a written demand has been made upon the corporation to take suitable action and (ii) 90 days have expired from the date delivery of the demand was made unless the shareholder has earlier been notified that the demand has been rejected by the corporation or unless irreparable injury to the corporation would result by waiting for the expiration of the 90-day period.

OFFICIAL COMMENT

Section 7.42 requires a written demand for two reasons. First, even though no director may be "qualified" (see section 1.43), the demand will give the corporation the opportunity to re-examine the act complained of in the light of a potential lawsuit and take corrective action. Second, the provision eliminates the time and expense of litigating whether demand is required. Requiring a demand in all cases does not impose an onerous burden given the relatively short waiting period and that this period may be shortened if irreparable injury to the corporation would result by waiting for the expiration of the 90-day period.

1. Form of Demand

Section 7.42 specifies only that the demand shall be in writing. Detailed pleading is not required given that the corporation can contact the shareholder for clarification if there are any questions, and cases have noted that a demand which sets forth the facts concerning share ownership and is sufficiently specific should apprise the corporation of the action sought to be taken and the grounds for that action so that the demand can be evaluated.

2. Upon Whom Demand Should Be Made

To ensure that the demand reaches the appropriate person for review, it should be addressed to the board of directors, chief executive officer, or secretary at the corporation's principal office. In most cases the board of directors will be the appropriate body to review the demand but there may be instances, such as a decision to sue a third party for an injury to the corporation, in which the taking of, or refusal to take, action would fall within the authority of an officer of the corporation.

3.   *The 90-Day Period*

The 90-day period in section 7.42 was chosen as a reasonable time within which the board of directors can meet, conduct the necessary inquiry into the charges, receive the results of the inquiry and make its decision. A fixed time period also eliminates litigation over what is or is not a reasonable time. If additional time is needed, the corporation may request counsel for the shareholder to delay filing suit until the inquiry has been completed or, if suit is commenced, the corporation can apply to the court for a stay under section 7.43.

Two exceptions are provided to the 90-day waiting period. The first exception is the situation where the shareholder has been notified of the rejection of the demand before the end of the 90 days. The standard under the second exception for irreparable injury to the corporation is intended to be the same as that governing the entry of a preliminary injunction. Other factors may also be considered, such as the possible expiration of the statute of limitations, although this would depend on the period of time during which the shareholder was aware of the grounds for the proceeding.

The shareholder bringing suit does not necessarily have to be the person making the demand. Only one demand need be made in order for the corporation to consider whether to take corrective action.

4.   *Response by the Corporation*

There is no obligation on the part of the corporation to respond to the demand. However, if the corporation, after receiving the demand, decides to institute litigation or, after a derivative proceeding has commenced, decides to assume control of the litigation, the shareholder's right to commence or control the proceeding normally ends unless it can be shown that the corporation will not adequately pursue the matter.

§ 7.43   Stay of Proceedings

If the corporation commences an inquiry into the allegations made in the demand or complaint, the court may stay any derivative proceeding for such period as the court deems appropriate.

§ 7.44   Dismissal

(a)   A derivative proceeding shall be dismissed by the court on motion by the corporation if one of the groups specified in subsection (b) or subsection (e) has determined in good faith, after conducting a reasonable inquiry upon which its conclusions are based, that the maintenance of the derivative proceeding is not in the best interests of the corporation.

(b)   Unless a panel is appointed pursuant to subsection (e), the determination in subsection (a) shall be made by:

(1)   a majority vote of qualified directors present at a meeting of the board of directors if the qualified directors constitute a quorum; or

(2)   a majority vote of a committee consisting of two or more qualified directors appointed by majority vote of qualified directors present at a meeting of the board of directors, regardless of whether such qualified directors constitute a quorum.

(c)   If a derivative proceeding is commenced after a determination has been made rejecting a demand by a shareholder, the complaint shall allege with particularity facts establishing either (1) that a majority of the board of directors did not consist of qualified directors at the time the determination was made or (2) that the requirements of subsection (a) have not been met.

(d)   If a majority of the board of directors consisted of qualified directors at the time the determination was made, the plaintiff shall have the burden of proving that the requirements of subsection (a) have not been met; if not, the corporation shall have the burden of proving that the requirements of subsection (a) have been met.

(e)   Upon motion by the corporation, the court may appoint a panel of one or more individuals to make a determination whether the maintenance of the derivative proceeding is in the best interests of the corporation. In such case, the plaintiff shall have the burden of proving that the requirements of subsection (a) have not been met.

OFFICIAL COMMENT

The procedures set forth in section 7.44 are not intended to be exclusive. Discretion is left with the courts to determine when a derivative action should be dismissed under circumstances other than those set forth in section 7.44. For example, as noted in the comment to section 7.42, there may be instances where a decision to commence an action falls within the authority of an officer of the corporation, depending upon the amount of the claim and the identity of the potential defendants.

1.   *The Persons Making the Determination and Timing*

The determination under section 7.44(b) that the maintenance of the proceeding is not in the best interests of the corporation can be made before commencement of the derivative action in response to a demand or after commencement of the action upon examination of the allegations of the complaint. Section 7.44(b) allows the determination to be made by "qualified directors" as defined in section 1.43. These provisions parallel the mechanics for authorizing an officer's pursuit of a business opportunity pursuant to a provision in the articles of incorporation (section 2.02(b)(6)), for determining entitlement to indemnification (section 8.55), for authorizing directors' conflicting interest transactions (section 8.62), and for renunciation of the corporation's interests in a business opportunity (section 8.70). Section 7.44(e) provides for the appointment of a panel only upon motion by the corporation. This would not, however, prevent the court on its own initiative from appointing a special master if permitted under applicable state rules of procedure.

This panel procedure may be desirable in a number of circumstances, particularly if there are no qualified directors available. In addition, even if there are qualified directors, they may not be in a position to conduct the inquiry.

2.   *Standards to Be Applied*

Section 7.44(a) contemplates that the court will examine the "good faith" of the persons making the determination. Both the determination and the inquiry in section 7.44(a) must be made in "good faith." Section 7.44(a) does not authorize the court to review the reasonableness of the determination to reject a demand or seek a dismissal. The "good faith" standard, which is also found in section 8.30 (general standards of conduct for directors) and 8.51 (authority to indemnify), is a subjective one, meaning "honestly or in an honest manner."

The word "inquiry"—rather than "investigation"—has been used to make it clear that the scope of the inquiry will depend upon the issues raised and the knowledge of the group making the determination with respect to those issues. In some cases, the issues may be within the knowledge of the group so that extensive additional investigation is not necessary. In other cases, the group may need to engage counsel and possibly other professionals to conduct an investigation and assist the group in its evaluation of the issues.

The phrase "upon which its conclusions are based" requires that the conclusions follow logically from the inquiry. The burden of convincing the court about this issue lies with whichever party has the burden under section 7.44(d). This phrase does not require the persons making the determination to prepare a written report that sets forth their determination and its bases, as circumstances will vary as to the need for such a report.

Section 7.44 is not intended to modify the general standards of conduct for directors set forth in section 8.30 but rather to make those standards more explicit in the derivative proceeding context. In this regard, the qualified directors making the determination would be entitled to rely on information and reports from other persons in accordance with section 8.30.

§ 7.45   Discontinuance or Settlement

A derivative proceeding may not be discontinued or settled without the court's approval. If the court determines that a proposed discontinuance or settlement will substantially affect the interests of the corporation's shareholders or a class or series of shareholders, the court shall direct that notice be given to the shareholders affected.

§ 7.46 Payment of Expenses

On termination of the derivative proceeding the court may:

 (1) order the corporation to pay the plaintiff's expenses incurred in the proceeding if it finds that the proceeding has resulted in a substantial benefit to the corporation;

 (2) order the plaintiff to pay any defendant's expenses incurred in defending the proceeding if it finds that the proceeding was commenced or maintained without reasonable cause or for an improper purpose; or

 (3) order a party to pay an opposing party's expenses incurred because of the filing of a pleading, motion or other paper, if it finds that the pleading, motion or other paper (i) was not well grounded in fact, after reasonable inquiry, or warranted by existing law or a good faith argument for the extension, modification or reversal of existing law or (ii) was interposed for an improper purpose, such as to harass or cause unnecessary delay or needless increase in the cost of litigation.

§ 7.47 Applicability to Foreign Corporations

In any derivative proceeding in the right of a foreign corporation, the matters covered by this subchapter shall be governed by the laws of the jurisdiction of incorporation of the foreign corporation except for sections 7.43, 7.45, and 7.46.

SUBCHAPTER E. PROCEEDING TO APPOINT CUSTODIAN OR RECEIVER

§ 7.48 Shareholder Action to Appoint a Custodian or Receiver

 (a) The [name or describe court] may appoint one or more persons to be custodians, or, if the corporation is insolvent, to be receivers, of and for a corporation in a proceeding by a shareholder where it is established that:

 (1) the directors are deadlocked in the management of the corporate affairs, the shareholders are unable to break the deadlock, and irreparable injury to the corporation is threatened or being suffered; or

 (2) the directors or those in control of the corporation are acting fraudulently and irreparable injury to the corporation is threatened or being suffered.

 (b) The court:

 (1) may issue injunctions, appoint a temporary custodian or temporary receiver with all the powers and duties the court directs, take other action to preserve the corporate assets wherever located, and carry on the business of the corporation until a full hearing is held;

 (2) shall hold a full hearing, after notifying all parties to the proceeding and any interested persons designated by the court, before appointing a custodian or receiver; and

 (3) has jurisdiction over the corporation and all of its property, wherever located.

 (c) The court may appoint an individual or domestic or foreign corporation (registered to do business in this state) as a custodian or receiver and may require the custodian or receiver to post bond, with or without sureties, in an amount the court directs.

 (d) The court shall describe the powers and duties of the custodian or receiver in its appointing order, which may be amended from time to time. Among other powers:

(1)   a custodian may exercise all of the powers of the corporation, through or in place of its board of directors, to the extent necessary to manage the business and affairs of the corporation; and

(2)   a receiver (i) may dispose of all or any part of the assets of the corporation wherever located, at a public or private sale, if authorized by the court; and (ii) may sue and defend in the receiver's own name as receiver in all courts of this state.

(e)   The court during a custodianship may redesignate the custodian a receiver, and during a receivership may redesignate the receiver a custodian, if doing so is in the best interests of the corporation.

(f)   The court from time to time during the custodianship or receivership may order compensation paid and expense disbursements or reimbursements made to the custodian or receiver from the assets of the corporation or proceeds from the sale of its assets.

(g)   In this section, "shareholder" means a record shareholder, a beneficial shareholder, and an unrestricted voting trust beneficial owner.

§7.49   Judicial Determination of Corporate Offices and Review of Elections and Shareholder Votes

(a)   Upon application of or in a proceeding commenced by a person specified in subsection (b), the [name or describe court] may determine:

(1)   the result or validity of the election, appointment, removal or resignation of a director or officer of the corporation;

(2)   the right of an individual to hold the office of director or officer of the corporation;

(3)   the result or validity of any vote by the shareholders of the corporation;

(4)   the right of a director to membership on a committee of the board of directors; and

(5)   the right of a person to nominate or an individual to be nominated as a candidate for election or appointment as a director of the corporation, and any right under a bylaw adopted pursuant to section 2.06(c) or any comparable right under any provision of the articles of incorporation, contract, or applicable law.

(b)   An application or proceeding pursuant to subsection (a) of this section may be filed or commenced by any of the following persons:

(1)   the corporation;

(2)   any record shareholder, beneficial shareholder or unrestricted voting trust beneficial owner of the corporation;

(3)   a director of the corporation, an individual claiming the office of director, or a director whose membership on a committee of the board of directors is contested, in each case who is seeking a determination of his or her right to such office or membership;

(4)   an officer of the corporation or an individual claiming to be an officer of the corporation, in each case who is seeking a determination of his or her right to such office; and

(5)   a person claiming a right covered by subsection (a)(5) and who is seeking a determination of such right.

(c)   In connection with any application or proceeding under subsection (a), the following shall be named as defendants, unless such person made the application or commenced the proceeding:

(1)   the corporation;

(2)   any individual whose right to office or membership on a committee of the board of directors is contested;

(3)　any individual claiming the office or membership at issue; and

(4)　any person claiming a right covered by subsection (a)(5) that is at issue.

(d)　In connection with any application or proceeding under subsection (a), service of process may be made upon each of the persons specified in subsection (c) either by:

(1)　service of process on the corporation addressed to such person in any manner provided by statute of this state or by rule of the applicable court for service on the corporation; or

(2)　service of process on the person in any manner provided by statute of this state or by rule of the applicable court.

(e)　When service of process is made upon a person other than the corporation by service upon the corporation pursuant to subsection (d)(1), the plaintiff and the corporation or its registered agent shall promptly provide written notice of such service, together with copies of all process and the application or complaint, to the person at the person's last known residence or business address, or as permitted by statute of this state or by rule of the applicable court.

(f)　In connection with any application or proceeding under subsection (a), the court shall dispose of the application or proceeding on an expedited basis and also may:

(1)　order such additional or further notice as the court deems proper under the circumstances;

(2)　order that additional persons be joined as parties to the proceeding if the court determines that such joinder is necessary for a just adjudication of matters before the court;

(3)　order an election or meeting be held in accordance with the provisions of section 7.03(b) or otherwise;

(4)　appoint a master to conduct an election or meeting;

(5)　enter temporary, preliminary or permanent injunctive relief;

(6)　resolve solely for the purpose of this proceeding any legal or factual issues necessary for the resolution of any of the matters specified in subsection (a), including the right and power of persons claiming to own shares to vote at any meeting of the shareholders; and

(7)　order such other relief as the court determines is equitable, just and proper.

(g)　It is not necessary to make shareholders a party to a proceeding or application pursuant to this section unless the shareholder is a required defendant under subsection (c)(4), relief is sought against the shareholder individually, or the court orders joinder pursuant to subsection (f)(2).

(h)　Nothing in this section limits, restricts, or abolishes the subject matter jurisdiction or powers of the court as existed before the enactment of this section, and an application or proceeding pursuant to this section is not the exclusive remedy or proceeding available with respect to the matters specified in subsection (a).

CHAPTER 8.　DIRECTORS AND OFFICERS

SUBCHAPTER A.　BOARD OF DIRECTORS

§ 8.01　Requirement for and Functions of Board of Directors

(a)　Except as may be provided in an agreement authorized under section 7.32, each corporation shall have a board of directors.

(b)　Except as may be provided in an agreement authorized under section 7.32, and subject to any limitation in the articles of incorporation permitted by section 2.02(b), all corporate powers shall be exercised by or under the authority of the board of directors, and the business and affairs of the corporation shall be managed by or under the direction, and subject to the oversight, of the board of directors.

OFFICIAL COMMENT

As provided in Section 8.01(a), the board of directors is the traditional form of governance, but the shareholders of a corporation may, in an agreement that satisfies the requirements of section 7.32, dispense with a board of directors and structure the corporation's management and governance to address specific needs of the enterprise.

In section 8.01(b), the phrase "by or under the direction, and subject to the oversight, of" encompasses the varying functions of boards of directors of different corporations. In some corporations, particularly closely held corporations, the board of directors may be involved in the day-to-day business and affairs and it may be reasonable to describe management as being "by" the board of directors. In many other corporations, including most public corporations, the business and affairs are managed "under the direction, and subject to the oversight, of" the board of directors, and operational management is delegated to executive officers and other professional managers.

Section 8.01(b) often is considered to constitute the heart of the governance provisions of the Act. Giving the board of directors the power, and the responsibility, to oversee and direct the business of the corporation permits separation of ownership of the corporation from control of its oversight and direction. The Act's broad grant of authority and responsibility to the board of directors constitutes the rejection of the concept that the directors, having been elected by the shareholders, merely serve as agents to implement the will of the shareholders. See section 8.30.

Section 8.01(b), in providing for corporate powers to be exercised under the direction of the board of directors, allows the board of directors to delegate to appropriate officers, employees or agents of the corporation authority to exercise powers and perform functions not required by law to be exercised or performed by the board of directors itself. Although such delegation does not relieve the board of directors from its responsibility to oversee the business and affairs of the corporation, directors are not personally responsible for actions or omissions of officers, employees, or agents of the corporation so long as the directors have relied reasonably and in good faith upon these officers, employees, or agents. See sections 8.30 and 8.31 and their Official Comments.

The scope of the board's oversight responsibility will vary depending on the nature of the corporation and its business. At least for public corporations, the board's responsibilities generally include oversight of the following:

- business performance, plans and strategy;
- management's assessment of major risks to which the corporation is or may be exposed;
- the performance and compensation of executive officers;
- policies and practices to foster the corporation's compliance with law and ethical conduct;
- management's preparation of the corporation's financial statements;
- management's design and assessment of effectiveness of the corporation's internal controls;
- plans for the succession of the chief executive officer and other executive officers;
- the composition of the board and of board committees; and
- whether the corporation has information and reporting systems in place to provide directors with appropriate information in a timely manner.

In giving attention to the composition of the board, directors of public corporations should consider the corporation's processes for obtaining and evaluating the views of shareholders, including processes for considering individuals proposed by shareholders as nominees for election as directors. Directors of public corporations also should take into account the important role of independent directors. When ownership is separated from responsibility for oversight and direction, as is the case with public corporations, having nonmanagement independent directors who participate actively in the board's oversight functions increases the likelihood that actions taken by the board, if challenged, will be given deference by the courts. The listing standards of most public securities markets have requirements for independent directors to serve on boards; in many cases, they must constitute a majority of the board, and certain board committees must be composed entirely of independent directors. The listing standards have differing rules as to what constitutes an independent director. The Act does not attempt to define "independent director." Ordinarily, an independent director may not be a present or recent member of senior management and must be free of significant professional, financial or similar relationships with the corporation, and the director and members of the director's immediate family must be free of similar relationships with the corporation's senior management. Judgment is required to determine independence in light of the particular circumstances, subject to any specific requirements of a listing standard. The qualifications for disinterestedness required of directors for specific purposes under the Act are similar, but not necessarily identical, to those that are prerequisites to independence. For the requirements for a director to be considered disinterested and qualified to act in those specified situations, see section 1.43. An individual who is an independent director may not be eligible to act in a particular case under those other provisions of the Act. Conversely, a director who is not independent (for example, a member of management) may be disinterested and qualified to act in a particular case.

Section 8.01(b) recognizes that the powers of the board of directors may be limited by express provisions in the articles of incorporation and in an agreement among all shareholders under section 7.32. In an agreement under section 7.32, board powers also may be assigned to others. Because all of the shareholders must approve a section 7.32 agreement, the only restriction on limiting or assigning board powers is that any limitation or assignment must be provided for in sections 7.32(a)(1) through (a)(7) or must not be contrary to public policy under section 7.32(a)(8). In contrast, as is provided in section 2.02(b)(2), any limitation on board powers in the articles of incorporation cannot be "inconsistent with law." As a result of this difference in standards, any such limitation under section 2.02 should not, for example, be inconsistent with requirements of section 8.30 regarding standards of conduct for directors or otherwise preclude the directors from fulfilling their duties to the corporation.

§ 8.02   Qualifications of Directors

(a) The articles of incorporation or bylaws may prescribe qualifications for directors or for nominees for directors. Qualifications must be reasonable as applied to the corporation and be lawful.

(b) A requirement that is based on a past, prospective, or current action, or expression of opinion, by a nominee or director that could limit the ability of a nominee or director to discharge his or her duties as a director is not a permissible qualification under this section. Notwithstanding the foregoing, qualifications may include not being or having been subject to specified criminal, civil, or regulatory sanctions or not having been removed as a director by judicial action or for cause.

(c) A director need not be a resident of this state or a shareholder unless the articles of incorporation or bylaws so prescribe.

(d) A qualification for nomination for director prescribed before a person's nomination shall apply to such person at the time of nomination. A qualification for nomination for director prescribed after a person's nomination shall not apply to such person with respect to such nomination.

(e) A qualification for director prescribed before a director has been elected or appointed may apply only at the time an individual becomes a director or may apply during a director's term. A qualification prescribed after a director has been elected or appointed shall not apply to that director before the end of that director's term.

§ 8.03   Number and Election of Directors

(a) A board of directors shall consist of one or more individuals, with the number specified in or fixed in accordance with the articles of incorporation or bylaws.

(b) The number of directors may be increased or decreased from time to time by amendment to, or in the manner provided in, the articles of incorporation or bylaws.

(c) Directors are elected at the first annual shareholders' meeting and at each annual shareholders' meeting thereafter unless elected by written consent in lieu of an annual meeting as permitted by section 7.04 or unless their terms are staggered under section 8.06.

§ 8.04   Election of Directors by Certain Classes or Series of Shares

If the articles of incorporation or action by the board of directors pursuant to section 6.02 authorize dividing the shares into classes or series, the articles of incorporation may also authorize the election of all or a specified number of directors by the holders of one or more authorized classes or series of shares. A class or series (or multiple classes or series) of shares entitled to elect one or more directors is a separate voting group for purposes of the election of directors.

§ 8.05   Terms of Directors Generally

(a) The terms of the initial directors of a corporation expire at the first shareholders' meeting at which directors are elected.

(b) The terms of all other directors expire at the next, or if their terms are staggered in accordance with section 8.06, at the applicable second or third, annual shareholders' meeting following their election, except to the extent (1) provided in section 10.22 if a bylaw electing to be governed by that section is in effect or (2) a shorter term is specified in the articles of incorporation in the event of a director nominee failing to receive a specified vote for election.

(c) A decrease in the number of directors does not shorten an incumbent director's term.

(d) The term of a director elected to fill a vacancy expires at the next shareholders' meeting at which directors are elected.

(e) Except to the extent otherwise provided in the articles of incorporation or under section 10.22 if a bylaw electing to be governed by that section is in effect, despite the expiration of a director's term, the director continues to serve until the director's successor is elected and qualifies or there is a decrease in the number of directors.

§ 8.06   Staggered Terms for Directors

The articles of incorporation may provide for staggering the terms of directors by dividing the total number of directors into two or three groups, with each group containing half or one-third of the total, as near as may be practicable. In that event, the terms of directors in the first group expire at the first annual shareholders' meeting after their election, the terms of the second group expire at the second annual shareholders' meeting after their election, and the terms of the third group, if any, expire at the third annual shareholders' meeting after their election. At each annual shareholders' meeting held thereafter, directors shall be elected for a term of two years or three years, as the case may be, to succeed those whose terms expire.

§ 8.07   Resignation of Directors

(a) A director may resign at any time by delivering a written notice of resignation to the board of directors, or its chair, or to the secretary.

(b) A resignation is effective as provided in section 1.41(i) unless the resignation provides for a delayed effectiveness, including effectiveness determined upon a future event or events. A resignation that is conditioned upon failing to receive a specified vote for election as a director may provide that it is irrevocable.

OFFICIAL COMMENT

In addition to permitting resignations effective at a date later than the date of delivery of the resignation, section 8.07(b) permits a director resignation to be conditioned upon "future events," which might include the director failing to achieve a specified vote for reelection, e.g., more votes "for" than "against" coupled with board acceptance of the resignation. Corporations and individual directors may thus give effect, in a manner subsequently enforceable by the corporation, to voting standards for the election of directors that exceed the plurality default standard in section 7.28. Section 8.07(b) also makes it clear that such arrangements do not contravene public policy. The express reference to the failure to receive a specified vote is not to be construed to address or negate the possible validity of other appropriate conditions for an irrevocable resignation.

Under section 8.10, a vacancy that will occur at a specific later date by reason of a resignation effective at a later date may be filled before the vacancy occurs, but the new director may not take office until the vacancy occurs. Because the individual tendering that resignation is still a member of the board, he or she may participate in all decisions until the specified date, including the choice of his or her successor under section 8.10.

§ 8.08   Removal of Directors by Shareholders

(a)   The shareholders may remove one or more directors with or without cause unless the articles of incorporation provide that directors may be removed only for cause.

(b)   If a director is elected by a voting group of shareholders, only the shareholders of that voting group may participate in the vote to remove that director.

(c)   A director may be removed if the number of votes cast to remove exceeds the number of votes cast not to remove the director, except to the extent the articles of incorporation or bylaws require a greater number; provided that if cumulative voting is authorized, a director may not be removed if, in the case of a meeting, the number of votes sufficient to elect the director under cumulative voting is voted against removal and, if action is taken by less than unanimous written consent, voting shareholders entitled to the number of votes sufficient to elect the director under cumulative voting do not consent to the removal.

(d)   A director may be removed by the shareholders only at a meeting called for the purpose of removing the director and the meeting notice must state that removal of the director is a purpose of the meeting.

§ 8.09   Removal of Directors by Judicial Proceeding

(a)   The [name or describe court] may remove a director from office or may order other relief, including barring the director from reelection for a period prescribed by the court, in a proceeding commenced by or in the right of the corporation if the court finds that (i) the director engaged in fraudulent conduct with respect to the corporation or its shareholders, grossly abused the position of director, or intentionally inflicted harm on the corporation; and (ii) considering the director's course of conduct and the inadequacy of other available remedies, removal or such other relief would be in the best interest of the corporation.

(b)   A shareholder proceeding on behalf of the corporation under subsection (a) shall comply with all of the requirements of subchapter 7D, except clause (i) of section 7.41.

§ 8.10   Vacancy on Board

(a)   Unless the articles of incorporation provide otherwise, if a vacancy occurs on a board of directors, including a vacancy resulting from an increase in the number of directors:

(1)   the shareholders may fill the vacancy;

(2)   the board of directors may fill the vacancy; or

(3)   if the directors remaining in office are less than a quorum, they may fill the vacancy by the affirmative vote of a majority of all the directors remaining in office.

(b)   If the vacant office was held by a director elected by a voting group of shareholders, only the holders of shares of that voting group are entitled to vote to fill the vacancy if it is filled by the shareholders, and only the remaining directors elected by that voting group, even if less than a quorum, are entitled to fill the vacancy if it is filled by the directors.

(c)   A vacancy that will occur at a specific later date (by reason of a resignation effective at a later date under section 8.07(b) or otherwise) may be filled before the vacancy occurs but the new director may not take office until the vacancy occurs.

§ 8.11   Compensation of Directors

Unless the articles of incorporation or bylaws provide otherwise, the board of directors may fix the compensation of directors.

SUBCHAPTER B.   MEETINGS AND ACTION OF THE BOARD

§ 8.20   Meetings

(a)   The board of directors may hold regular or special meetings in or out of this state.

(b)   Unless restricted by the articles of incorporation or bylaws, any or all directors may participate in any meeting of the board of directors through the use of any means of communication by which all directors participating may simultaneously hear each other during the meeting. A director participating in a meeting by this means is deemed to be present in person at the meeting.

§ 8.21   Action Without Meeting

(a)   Except to the extent that the articles of incorporation or bylaws require that action by the board of directors be taken at a meeting, action required or permitted by this Act to be taken by the board of directors may be taken without a meeting if each director signs a consent describing the action to be taken and delivers it to the corporation.

(b)   Action taken under this section is the act of the board of directors when one or more consents signed by all the directors are delivered to the corporation. The consent may specify a later time as the time at which the action taken is to be effective. A director's consent may be withdrawn by a revocation signed by the director and delivered to the corporation before delivery to the corporation of unrevoked written consents signed by all the directors.

(c)   A consent signed under this section has the effect of action taken at a meeting of the board of directors and may be described as such in any document.

§ 8.22   Notice of Meeting

(a)   Unless the articles of incorporation or bylaws provide otherwise, regular meetings of the board of directors may be held without notice of the date, time, place, or purpose of the meeting.

(b)   Unless the articles of incorporation or bylaws provide for a longer or shorter period, special meetings of the board of directors shall be preceded by at least two days' notice of the date, time, and place of the meeting. The notice need not describe the purpose of the special meeting unless required by the articles of incorporation or bylaws.

§ 8.23   Waiver of Notice

(a)   A director may waive any notice required by this Act, the articles of incorporation or the bylaws before or after the date and time stated in the notice. Except as provided by subsection (b), the waiver must be in writing, signed by the director entitled to the notice and delivered to the corporation for filing by the corporation with the minutes or corporate records.

(b)   A director's attendance at or participation in a meeting waives any required notice to the director of the meeting unless the director at the beginning of the meeting (or promptly upon arrival) objects to holding the meeting or transacting business at the meeting and does not after objecting vote for or assent to action taken at the meeting.

§ 8.24   Quorum and Voting

(a)   Unless the articles of incorporation or bylaws provide for a greater or lesser number or unless otherwise expressly provided in this Act, a quorum of a board of directors consists of a majority of the number of directors specified in or fixed in accordance with the articles of incorporation or bylaws.

(b)   The quorum of the board of directors specified in or fixed in accordance with the articles of incorporation or bylaws may not consist of less than one-third of the specified or fixed number of directors.

(c)   If a quorum is present when a vote is taken, the affirmative vote of a majority of directors present is the act of the board of directors unless the articles of incorporation or bylaws require the vote of a greater number of directors or unless otherwise expressly provided in this Act.

(d)   A director who is present at a meeting of the board of directors or a committee when corporate action is taken is deemed to have assented to the action taken unless: (i) the director objects at the beginning of the meeting (or promptly upon arrival) to holding it or transacting business at the meeting; (ii) the dissent or abstention from the action taken is entered in the minutes of the meeting; or (iii) the director delivers written notice of the director's dissent or abstention to the presiding officer of the meeting before its adjournment or to the corporation immediately after adjournment of the meeting. The right of dissent or abstention is not available to a director who votes in favor of the action taken.

§ 8.25   Committees of the Board

(a)   Unless this Act, the articles of incorporation or the bylaws provide otherwise, a board of directors may establish one or more board committees composed exclusively of one or more directors to perform functions of the board of directors.

(b)   The establishment of a board committee and appointment of members to it shall be approved by the greater of (i) a majority of all the directors in office when the action is taken or (ii) the number of directors required by the articles of incorporation or bylaws to take action under section 8.24, unless, in either case, this Act or the articles of incorporation provide otherwise.

(c)   Sections 8.20 through 8.24 apply to board committees and their members.

(d)   A board committee may exercise the powers of the board of directors under section 8.01, to the extent specified by the board of directors or in the articles of incorporation or bylaws, except that a board committee may not:

     (1)   authorize or approve distributions, except according to a formula or method, or within limits, prescribed by the board of directors;

     (2)   approve or propose to shareholders action that this Act requires be approved by shareholders;

     (3)   fill vacancies on the board of directors or, subject to subsection (e), on any board committees; or

     (4)   adopt, amend, or repeal bylaws.

(e)   The board of directors may appoint one or more directors as alternate members of any board committee to replace any absent or disqualified member during the member's absence or disqualification. If the articles of incorporation, the bylaws, or the resolution creating the board committee so provide, the member or members present at any board committee meeting and not disqualified from voting may, by unanimous action, appoint another director to act in place of an absent or disqualified member during that member's absence or disqualification.

OFFICIAL COMMENT

Section 8.25 deals only with board committees authorized to perform functions of the board of directors. The board of directors or management, independently of section 8.25, may establish non-board committees composed in whole or in part of directors, employees, or others to address matters in ways that do not constitute performing functions required to be performed by the board of directors under section 8.01, including acting in an advisory capacity.

Under section 8.25(a), except as otherwise provided by the Act, the articles of incorporation or the bylaws, a board committee may consist of a single director. This accommodates situations in which only one director may be present or available to make a decision on short notice, as well as situations in which it is unnecessary or inconvenient to have more than one member on a board committee or where only one board member is disinterested or independent with respect to a matter. Various other sections of the Act require the participation or approval of at least two qualified directors in order for the decision of the board or committee to have effect. (For the definition of "qualified director," see section 1.43.) These include a determination that maintenance of a derivative suit is not in the corporation's best interests (section 7.44(b)(2)), a determination that indemnification is permissible (section 8.55(b)(1)), an approval of a director's conflicting interest transaction (section 8.62(a)), and disclaimer of the corporation's interest in a business opportunity (section 8.70(a)).

The requirement of section 8.25(b) that, unless the Act or the articles of incorporation otherwise provide, a board committee may be created only by the affirmative vote of a majority of the board of directors then in office, or, if greater, by the number of directors required to take action by the articles of incorporation or bylaws, reflects the importance of the decision to invest board committees with power to act under section 8.25. Sections 7.44(b), 8.55(b), 8.62(a) and 8.70 contain exceptions to this rule.

The limitations in section 8.25(d)(1) through (4) are based on the principle that the listed actions so substantially affect the rights of shareholders or are so fundamental to the governance of the corporation that they should be determined by the full board and not delegated to a committee. On the other hand, section 8.25(d) allows board committees to take many actions that may be material, such as the authorization of long-term debt and capital investment or the issuance of shares.

Although section 8.25(d)(1) generally makes nondelegable the decision whether to authorize or approve distributions, including dividends, it does permit the delegation to a board committee of power to approve a distribution pursuant to a formula or method or within limits prescribed by the board of directors. Therefore, the board of directors could set a dollar range and timeframe for a prospective dividend and delegate to a board committee the authority to determine the exact amount and record and payment dates of the dividend. The board of directors also could establish certain conditions to the payment of a distribution and delegate to a board committee the power to determine whether the conditions have been satisfied.

Section 8.25(e) is a rule of convenience that permits the board of directors or the other board committee members to replace an absent or disqualified member during the time that the member is absent or disqualified. Unless otherwise provided or unless a quorum is no longer present, replacement of an absent or disqualified member of a committee is not necessary to permit the other committee members to continue to perform their duties.

§ 8.26 Submission of Matters for Shareholder Vote

A corporation may agree to submit a matter to a vote of its shareholders even if, after approving the matter, the board of directors determines it no longer recommends the matter.

OFFICIAL COMMENT

Section 8.26 authorizes a corporation to enter into an agreement, such as a merger agreement, containing a provision that requires a shareholder vote on the matter despite a subsequent change in the recommendation of the board of directors. Otherwise, a board is not required to submit a matter to the shareholders, even if it has been approved by the board. Section 8.26 also applies to the provisions of the Act that require the board of directors to approve a matter before recommending that the shareholders vote to approve it. Section 8.26 does not change the standards of conduct or liability applicable when considering whether to authorize such agreement by the corporation.

SUBCHAPTER C.   DIRECTORS

§ 8.30   Standards of Conduct for Directors

"loyalty"

(a)   Each member of the board of directors, when discharging the duties of a director, shall act: (i) in good faith, and (ii) in a manner the director reasonably believes to be in the best interests of the corporation.

"care"

(b)   The members of the board of directors or a board committee, when becoming informed in connection with their decision-making function or devoting attention to their oversight function, shall discharge their duties with the care that a person in a like position would reasonably believe appropriate under similar circumstances.

(c)   In discharging board or board committee duties, a director shall disclose, or cause to be disclosed, to the other board or committee members information not already known by them but known by the director to be material to the discharge of their decision-making or oversight functions, except that disclosure is not required to the extent that the director reasonably believes that doing so would violate a duty imposed under law, a legally enforceable obligation of confidentiality, or a professional ethics rule.

(d)   In discharging board or board committee duties, a director who does not have knowledge that makes reliance unwarranted is entitled to rely on the performance by any of the persons specified in subsection (f)(1) or subsection (f)(3) to whom the board may have delegated, formally or informally by course of conduct, the authority or duty to perform one or more of the board's functions that are delegable under applicable law.

(e)   In discharging board or board committee duties, a director who does not have knowledge that makes reliance unwarranted is entitled to rely on information, opinions, reports or statements, including financial statements and other financial data, prepared or presented by any of the persons specified in subsection (f).

(f)   A director is entitled to rely, in accordance with subsection (d) or (e), on:

(1)   one or more officers or employees of the corporation whom the director reasonably believes to be reliable and competent in the functions performed or the information, opinions, reports or statements provided;

(2)   legal counsel, public accountants, or other persons retained by the corporation as to matters involving skills or expertise the director reasonably believes are matters (i) within the particular person's professional or expert competence or (ii) as to which the particular person merits confidence; or

(3)   a board committee of which the director is not a member if the director reasonably believes the committee merits confidence.

OFFICIAL COMMENT

Section 8.30 sets standards of conduct for directors that focus on the manner in which directors make their decisions, not the correctness of the decisions made. Section 8.30 should be read in light of the basic role of directors set forth in section 8.01(b), which provides that the "business and affairs of a corporation shall be managed by or under the direction and subject to the oversight of the board of directors," as supplemented by various provisions of the Act assigning specific powers or responsibilities to the board. The standards of conduct for directors established by section 8.30 are analogous to those generally articulated by courts in evaluating director conduct, often referred to as the duties of care and loyalty.

Section 8.30 addresses standards of conduct—the level of performance expected of directors undertaking the role and responsibilities of the office of director. The section does not address the liability of a director, although exposure to liability may result from a failure to honor the standards of conduct required to be observed. The issue of director liability is addressed in sections 8.31 and 8.32. Section 8.30 does, however, play an important role in evaluating a director's conduct and the effectiveness of board action.

It has relevance in assessing, under section 8.31, the reasonableness of a director's belief. Similarly, it has relevance in assessing a director's timely attention to appropriate inquiry when particular facts and circumstances of significant concern materialize. It also serves as a frame of reference for determining, under section 8.32(a), liability for an unlawful distribution. Finally, section 8.30 compliance may influence a court's analysis where injunctive relief against a transaction is being sought. Directors act both individually and collectively as a board in performing their functions and discharging their duties. Section 8.30 addresses actions in both capacities.

Under the standards of section 8.30, the board may delegate or assign to appropriate officers or employees of the corporation the authority or duty to exercise powers that the law does not require the board to retain. Because the directors are entitled to rely on these persons absent knowledge making reliance unwarranted, the directors will not be in breach of the standards under section 8.30 as a result of their delegatees' actions or omissions so long as the board acted in good faith and complied with the other standards of conduct set forth in section 8.30 in delegating responsibility and, where appropriate, monitoring performance of the duties delegated. In addition, subsections (d), (e) and (f) permit a director to rely on enumerated third parties for specified purposes, although reliance is prohibited when a director has knowledge that makes reliance unwarranted. Section 8.30(a)'s standards of good faith and reasonable belief in the best interests of the corporation also apply to a director's reliance under subsections (d), (e) and (f).

1. Section 8.30(a)

Section 8.30(a) establishes the basic standards of conduct for all directors and its mandate governs all aspects of directors' conduct, including the requirements in other subsections. It includes concepts courts have used in defining the duty of loyalty. Two of the phrases used in section 8.30(a) deserve further comment:

- The phrase "reasonably believes" is both subjective and objective in character. Its first level of analysis is geared to what the particular director, acting in good faith, actually believes—not what objective analysis would lead another director (in a like position and acting in similar circumstances) to conclude. The second level of analysis is focused specifically on "reasonably." Although a director has wide discretion in gathering information and reaching conclusions, whether a director's belief is reasonable (*i.e.*, could—not would—a reasonable person in a like position and acting in similar circumstances, taking into account that director's knowledge and experience, have arrived at that belief) ultimately involves an overview that is objective in character.

- The phrase "best interests of the corporation" is key to an understanding of a director's duties. The term "corporation" is a surrogate for the business enterprise as well as a frame of reference encompassing the shareholder body. In determining the corporation's "best interests," the director has wide discretion in deciding how to weigh near-term opportunities versus long-term benefits as well as in making judgments where the interests of various groups of shareholders or other corporate constituencies may differ.

Section 8.30 operates as a "baseline" principle governing director conduct in circumstances uncomplicated by self-interest. The Act recognizes, however, that directors' personal interests may not always align with the corporation's best interests and provides procedures by which situations and transactions involving conflicts of interest can be processed. See subchapter D (derivative proceedings) of chapter 7 and subchapters E (indemnification and advance for expenses), F (directors' conflicting interest transactions), and G (business opportunities) of this chapter 8. Those procedures generally contemplate that the interested director will provide appropriate disclosure and will not be involved in taking action on the matter giving rise to the conflict of interest.

2. Section 8.30(b)

Section 8.30(b) establishes a general standard of care for directors in the context of their dealing with the board's decision-making and oversight functions. Although certain aspects will involve individual conduct (*e.g.*, preparation for meetings), these functions are generally performed by the board of directors through collective action, as recognized by the reference in subsection (b) to board and committee "members" and "their duties." In contrast with section 8.30(a)'s individual conduct mandate, section 8.30(b) has a two-fold thrust: it provides a standard of conduct for individual action and, more broadly, it states a conduct obligation—"shall discharge their duties"—concerning the degree of care to be used collectively by the directors when performing those functions. The standard is not what care a particular director might believe appropriate in the circumstances but what a person—in a like position and acting under similar circumstances—would reasonably believe to be appropriate. Thus, the degree of care that directors should employ under section 8.30(b) involves an objective standard.

The process by which a director becomes informed, in carrying out the decision-making and oversight functions, will vary. The directors' decision-making function is reflected in various sections of the Act, including: the issuance of shares (section 6.21); distributions (section 6.40); dismissal of derivative proceedings (section 7.44); indemnification (section 8.55); conflict of interest transaction authorization (section 8.62); articles of incorporation amendments (sections 10.02 and 10.03); bylaw amendments (section 10.20); mergers and share exchanges (section 11.04); asset dispositions (section 12.02); and dissolution (section 14.02). The directors' oversight function is established under section 8.01. In discharging the section 8.01 duties associated with the board's oversight function, the standard of care entails primarily a requirement of attention. In contrast with the board's decision-making function, which generally involves informed action at a point in time, the oversight function is concerned with a continuum and the attention of the directors accordingly involves participatory performance over a period of time.

Several of the phrases chosen to define the standard of conduct in section 8.30(b) deserve specific mention:

- The phrase "becoming informed," in the context of the decision-making function, refers to the process of gaining sufficient familiarity with the background facts and circumstances to make an informed judgment. Unless the circumstances would permit a reasonable director to conclude that he or she is already sufficiently informed, the standard of care requires every director to take steps to become informed about the background facts and circumstances before taking action on the matter at hand. The process typically involves review of written materials provided before or at the meeting and attention to or participation in the deliberations leading up to a vote. In addition to considering information and data on which a director is expressly entitled to rely under section 8.30(e), "becoming informed" can also involve consideration of information and data generated by other persons, for example, review of industry studies or research articles prepared by third parties. It can also involve direct communications, outside of the boardroom, with members of management or other directors. There is no one way for "becoming informed," and both the method and measure—"how to" and "how much"—are matters of reasonable judgment for the director to exercise.

- The phrase "devoting attention," in the context of the oversight function, refers to considering such matters as the corporation's information and reporting systems generally and not to an independent investigation into particular system inadequacies or noncompliance. Although directors typically give attention to future plans and trends as well as current activities, they should not be expected to anticipate any particular problems which the corporation may face except in those circumstances where something has occurred to make it obvious to the board that the corporation should be addressing a particular problem. The standard of care associated with the oversight function involves gaining assurances from management and advisers that appropriate systems have been established, such as those concerned with legal compliance, risk assessment or internal controls. Such assurances also should cover establishment of ongoing monitoring of the systems in place, with appropriate follow-up responses when alerted to the issues requiring attention.

- The reference to "person," without embellishment, is intended to avoid implying any qualifications, such as specialized expertise or experience requirements, beyond the basic attributes of common sense, practical wisdom, and informed judgment (however, see the last bullet below).

- The phrase "reasonably believe appropriate" refers to the array of possible options that a person possessing the basic attributes of common sense, practical wisdom and informed judgment would recognize to be available, in terms of the degree of care that might be appropriate, and from which a choice by such person would be made. The measure of care that such person might determine to be appropriate, in a given instance, would normally involve a selection from the range of options and any choice within the realm of reason would be an appropriate decision under the standard of care called for under section 8.30(b). However, a decision that is so removed from the realm of reason, or is so unreasonable, that it falls outside the permissible bounds of sound discretion, and thus is an abuse of discretion, will not satisfy the standard.

- The phrase "in a like position" recognizes that the "care" under consideration is that which would be used by the "person" if he or she were a director of the particular corporation.

- The combined phrase "in a like position . . . under similar circumstances" is intended to recognize that (i) the nature and extent of responsibilities will vary, depending upon such factors as the size, complexity, urgency, and location of activities carried on by the particular corporation, (ii) decisions must be made on the basis of the information known to the directors without the benefit of hindsight, and (iii) the special background, qualifications, and oversight responsibilities of a particular director may be relevant in evaluating that director's compliance with the standard of care.

3. Section 8.30(c)

A requirement to disclose to other directors information that a director knows to be material to the decision-making or oversight functions of the board of directors or a board committee is implicit in the standards of conduct set forth in sections 8.30(a) and (b), but section 8.30(c) makes this explicit. Thus, for example, when a member of the board of directors knows information that the director recognizes is material to a decision by the board but is not known to the other directors, the director is obligated to disclose that information to the other members of the board. Such disclosure can occur through direct statements in meetings of the board, or by any other timely means, including, for example, communicating the information to the chairman of the board or the chairman of a committee, or to the corporation's general counsel, and requesting that the recipient inform the other board or committee members of the information.

Section 8.30(c) recognizes that a duty of confidentiality to a third party can override a director's obligation to share with other directors information pertaining to a current corporate matter. In some circumstances, a duty of confidentiality to a third party may even prohibit disclosure of the nature or the existence of the duty itself. Ordinarily, however, a director who withholds material information based on a reasonable belief that a duty of confidentiality to a third party prohibits disclosure should advise the other directors of the existence and nature of that duty. Under the standards of conduct set forth in section 8.30(a), the withholding of material information may, depending on the nature of the material information and of the matter before the board of directors or a board committee, require that a director abstain or recuse himself or herself from all or a portion of the other directors' deliberation or vote on the matter to which the undisclosed information is material, or even resign as a director. See Official Comment to section 8.62.

In connection with a director's conflicting interest transaction, the required disclosure (as defined in section 8.60) that must be made under section 8.62(a) and the exceptions to the required disclosure in that context under section 8.62(b) have elements that parallel the disclosure obligation of directors under section 8.30(c). The demands of section 8.62, however, are more detailed and specific. They apply to just one situation—a director's conflicting interest transaction—while the requirements of section 8.30(c) apply generally to all other decision-making and oversight functions. For example, the specific requirements of section 8.62(a)(1) for deliberation and a vote outside the presence of the conflicted director are not imposed universally for all decision-making matters or for oversight matters that do not involve decisions. Although they may be different from the generally applicable provisions of section 8.30(c), the specific provisions of subchapter 8F control and are exclusive with respect to director conflicting interest transactions.

The requirement that a director disclose information to other directors as set forth in section 8.30(c) is different from any common law duty the board may have to cause the corporation to make disclosures to shareholders under certain circumstances. The Act does not seek to codify such a duty of disclosure, but leaves its existence and scope, the circumstances for its application, and the consequences of any failure to satisfy it, to be developed by courts on a case-by-case basis.

4. Section 8.30(d)

The delegation of authority and responsibility described in section 8.30(d) may take a variety of forms, including (i) formal action through a board resolution, (ii) implicit action through the election of corporate officers (*e.g.*, chief financial officer or controller) or the appointment of corporate managers (*e.g.*, credit manager), or (iii) informal action through a course of conduct (*e.g.*, involvement through corporate officers and managers in the management of a significant 50%-owned joint venture). Under section 8.30(d), a director may properly rely on those to whom authority has been delegated pursuant to section 8.30(d) respecting particular matters calling for specific action or attention in connection with the directors' decision-making function as well as matters on the board's continuing agenda, such as legal compliance and internal controls, in connection with the directors' oversight function. Delegation should be carried out in accordance with the standard of care set forth in section 8.30(b).

By identifying those persons upon whom a director may rely in connection with the discharge of duties, section 8.30(d) does not limit the ability of directors to delegate their powers under section 8.01(b) except where delegation is expressly prohibited by the Act or otherwise by applicable law. See section 8.25 and its Official Comment for discussion of delegation to committees of the authority of the board under section 8.01. By employing the concept of delegation, the Act does not limit the ability of directors to establish baseline principles as to management responsibilities. Specifically, section 8.01(b) provides that "all corporate powers shall be exercised by or under the authority of" the board, and a basic board function involves the allocation of management responsibilities and the related assignment (or delegation) of corporate powers. For example, a board can properly decide to retain a third party to assume responsibility for the administration of designated aspects of risk management for the corporation (*e.g.*, health insurance or disability claims).

Although the board of directors may delegate the authority or duty to perform one or more of its functions, delegation and reliance under section 8.30(d) may not alone constitute compliance with sections 8.30(a) and (b) and the action taken by the delegatee may not alone satisfy the directors or a noncommittee board member's section 8.01 responsibilities. On the other hand, failure of the board committee or the corporate officer or employee performing the function delegated to meet section 8.30(b)'s standard of care will not automatically result in violation by the board of section 8.01. Factors to be considered in determining whether a violation of section 8.01 has occurred will include the care used in the delegation to and supervision over the delegatee, and the amount of knowledge regarding the particular matter which is reasonably available to the particular director. Care in delegation and supervision includes appraisal of the capabilities and diligence of the delegatee in light of the subject and its relative importance and may be satisfied, in the usual case, by receipt of reports concerning the delegatee's activities. The enumeration of these factors is intended to emphasize that directors may not abdicate their responsibilities and avoid accountability simply by delegating authority to others. Rather, a director who is accountable for the acts of delegatees will fulfill the director's duties if the standards contained in section 8.30 are met.

5. Section 8.30(e)

Reliance under section 8.30(e) on a report, statement, opinion, or other information is permitted only if the director has read or heard orally presented the information, opinion, report or statement in question, or took other steps to become generally familiar with it. A director must comply with the general standard of care of section 8.30(b) in making a judgment as to the reliability and competence of the source of information upon which the director proposes to rely or, as appropriate, that it otherwise merits confidence.

6. Section 8.30(f)

In determining whether a corporate officer or employee is "reliable," for purposes of section 8.30(f)(1), the director would typically consider (i) the individual's background experience and scope of responsibility within the corporation in gauging the individual's familiarity and knowledge respecting the subject matter and (ii) the individual's record and reputation for honesty, care and ability in discharging responsibilities which he or she undertakes. In determining whether a person is "competent," the director would normally take into account the same considerations and, if expertise should be relevant, the director would consider the individual's technical skills as well. Recognition of the right of one director to rely on the expertise and experience of another director, in the context of board or committee deliberations, is unnecessary, for reliance on shared experience and wisdom of other board members is an implicit underpinning of collective board conduct. In relying on another member of the board, a director would quite properly take advantage of the colleague's knowledge and experience in becoming informed about the matter at hand before taking action; however, the director would be expected to exercise independent judgment when it comes time to vote.

Advisers on whom a director may rely under section 8.30(f)(2) include not only licensed professionals, such as lawyers, accountants, and engineers, but also those in other fields involving special experience and skills, such as investment bankers, geologists, management consultants, actuaries, and appraisers. The adviser could be an individual or an organization, such as a law or investment banking firm. Reliance on a nonmanagement director, who is specifically engaged (and, normally, additionally compensated) to undertake a special assignment or a particular consulting role, would fall within this outside adviser frame of reference. The concept of "expert competence" embraces a wide variety of qualifications and is not limited to the more precise and narrower recognition of experts under the Securities Act of 1933. In addition, a director may also rely on outside advisers where skills or expertise of a technical nature is not a prerequisite, or where the person's professional or expert competence has not been established, so long as the director reasonably believes the person merits confidence. For example, a board might choose to engage a private investigator to inquire into a particular matter (*e.g.*, follow up on rumors about a senior executive's alleged misconduct) and properly rely on the private investigator's report.

Section 8.30(f)(3) permits reliance on a board committee when it is submitting recommendations for action by the full board of directors as well as when it is performing supervisory or other functions in instances where neither the full board of directors nor the committee takes dispositive action. For example, the compensation committee typically reviews proposals and makes recommendations for action by the full board of directors. There also might be reliance upon an investigation undertaken by a board committee and reported to the full board, which forms the basis for a decision by the board of directors not to take dispositive action. Another example is reliance on a board committee, such as an audit committee with respect to the board's ongoing role of oversight of the accounting and auditing functions of the corporation. In addition, where reliance on information or materials prepared or presented by a board committee is not involved in connection with board action, a director may properly rely on oversight monitoring or dispositive action by a board committee (of which the director is not a member) empowered to act pursuant to authority delegated under section 8.25 or acting with the acquiescence of the board of directors. See the Official Comment to section 8.25. In parallel with section 8.30(f)(2)(ii), the concept of "confidence" is used instead of "competence" to avoid any inference that technical skills are a prerequisite. In the usual case, the appointment of committee members or the reconstitution of the membership of a standing committee (*e.g.*, the audit committee), following an annual shareholders' meeting, would alone manifest the noncommittee members' belief that the committee "merits confidence." Depending on the circumstances, the reliance contemplated by section 8.30(f)(3) is geared to the point in time when the board takes action or the period of time over which a committee is engaged in an oversight function; consequently, the judgment to be made (*i.e.*, whether a committee "merits confidence") will arise at varying points in time. Ordinarily, after making an initial judgment that a committee (of which a director is not a member) merits confidence, a director may continue to rely on that committee so long as the director has no reason to believe that confidence is no longer warranted.

7. *Application to Officers*

Section 8.30 generally deals only with directors. Section 8.42 and its Official Comment explain the extent to which the principles set forth in section 8.30 apply to officers.

§ 8.31 Standards of Liability for Directors

(a) A director shall not be liable to the corporation or its shareholders for any decision to take or not to take action, or any failure to take any action, as a director, unless the party asserting liability in a proceeding establishes that:

(1) no defense interposed by the director based on (i) any provision in the articles of incorporation authorized by section 2.02(b)(4) or by section 2.02(b)(6), or (ii) the protection afforded by section 8.61 (for action taken in compliance with section 8.62 or section 8.63), or (iii) the protection afforded by section 8.70, precludes liability; and

(2) the challenged conduct consisted or was the result of:

(i) action not in good faith; or

(ii) a decision

(A) which the director did not reasonably believe to be in the best interests of the corporation, or

(B) as to which the director was not informed to an extent the director reasonably believed appropriate in the circumstances; or

(iii) a lack of objectivity due to the director's familial, financial or business relationship with, or a lack of independence due to the director's domination or control by, another person having a material interest in the challenged conduct

(A) which relationship or which domination or control could reasonably be expected to have affected the director's judgment respecting the challenged conduct in a manner adverse to the corporation, and

(B) after a reasonable expectation to such effect has been established, the director shall not have established that the challenged conduct was reasonably believed by the director to be in the best interests of the corporation; or

(iv) a sustained failure of the director to devote attention to ongoing oversight of the business and affairs of the corporation, or a failure to devote timely attention, by making (or causing to be made) appropriate inquiry, when particular facts and circumstances of significant concern materialize that would alert a reasonably attentive director to the need for such inquiry; or

(v) receipt of a financial benefit to which the director was not entitled or any other breach of the director's duties to deal fairly with the corporation and its shareholders that is actionable under applicable law.

(b) The party seeking to hold the director liable:

(1) for money damages, shall also have the burden of establishing that:

(i)   harm to the corporation or its shareholders has been suffered, and

(ii) the harm suffered was proximately caused by the director's challenged conduct; or

(2) for other money payment under a legal remedy, such as compensation for the unauthorized use of corporate assets, shall also have whatever persuasion burden may be called for to establish that the payment sought is appropriate in the circumstances; or

(3) for other money payment under an equitable remedy, such as profit recovery by or disgorgement to the corporation, shall also have whatever persuasion burden may be called for to establish that the equitable remedy sought is appropriate in the circumstances.

(c) Nothing contained in this section shall (i) in any instance where fairness is at issue, such as consideration of the fairness of a transaction to the corporation under section 8.61(b)(3), alter the burden of proving the fact or lack of fairness otherwise applicable, (ii) alter the fact or lack of liability of a director under another section of this Act, such as the provisions governing the consequences of an unlawful distribution under section 8.32 or a transactional interest under section 8.61, or (iii) affect any rights to which the corporation or a shareholder may be entitled under another statute of this state or the United States.

OFFICIAL COMMENT

Boards of directors and corporate managers make numerous decisions that involve the balancing of risks and benefits for the enterprise. Although some decisions turn out to have been unwise or the result of a mistake of judgment, it is not reasonable to impose liability for an informed decision made in good faith which with the benefit of hindsight turns out to be wrong or unwise. Therefore, as a general rule, a director is not exposed to personal liability for injury or damage caused by an unwise decision and conduct conforming with the standards of section 8.30 will almost always be protected regardless of the end result. Moreover, the fact that a director's performance fails to meet the standards of section 8.30 does not in itself establish personal liability for damages that the corporation or its shareholders may have suffered as a consequence. Nevertheless, a director can be held liable for misfeasance or nonfeasance in performing his or her duties. Section 8.31 sets forth the standards of liability of directors as distinct from the standards of conduct set forth in section 8.30.

Courts have developed the broad common law concept of the business judgment rule. Although formulations vary, in basic principle, a board of directors generally enjoys a presumption of sound business judgment and its decisions will not be disturbed by a court substituting its own notions of what is or is not sound business judgment if the board's decisions can be attributed to any rational business purpose. It is also presumed that, in making a business decision, directors act in good faith, on an informed basis, and in the honest belief that the action taken is in the best interests of the corporation. The elements of the business judgment rule and the circumstances for its application continue to be developed and refined by courts. Accordingly, it would not be desirable to freeze the concept in a statute. Thus, section 8.31 does not codify the business judgment rule as a whole, although certain of its principal elements, relating to personal liability issues, are reflected in section 8.31(a)(2).

* * *

Note on Directors' Liability

A director's exposure to financial liability (*e.g.,* in a lawsuit for money damages suffered by the corporation or its shareholders claimed to have resulted from misfeasance or nonfeasance in connection with the performance of the director's duties) can be analyzed as follows:

- *Articles of incorporation limitations.* If the corporation's articles of incorporation contain a provision eliminating its directors' liability to the corporation or its shareholders for money damages, adopted pursuant to section 2.02(b)(4), there is no liability unless the director's conduct involves one of the exceptions prescribed in that section that preclude the elimination of liability. If the matter involves a director's taking of a business opportunity and an articles of incorporation provision has been adopted under section 2.02(b)(6) eliminating directors' duties with respect to those opportunities, there also will be no liability. See section 2.02 and its Official Comment.

- *Director's conflicting interest transaction safe harbor.* If the matter at issue involves a director's conflicting interest transaction (as defined in section 8.60) and a safe harbor procedure under section 8.61 involving action taken in compliance with section 8.62 or 8.63 has been properly implemented, there is no liability for the interested director arising out of the transaction. See subchapter 8F.

- *Business opportunities safe harbors.* Similarly, if the matter involves a director's pursuit or taking of a business opportunity, there is no liability for that director if (i) an applicable limitation or elimination of any duty to offer that business opportunity has been adopted pursuant to section 2.02(b)(6), or (ii) a safe harbor procedure under section 8.70 has been properly implemented, even if the articles of incorporation contain no provision under section 2.02(b)(6). See subchapter 8G.

- *Business judgment rule.* If a provision in the articles of incorporation adopted pursuant to section 2.02(b)(4) or (6) or a safe harbor procedure under section 8.61 or 8.70 does not shield the director's conduct from liability, the presumptions, standards of judicial review and procedural matters related to the business judgment rule may insulate the director from liability for conduct in connection with a corporate decision.

- *Damages and proximate cause.* If the business judgment rule does not shield the directors' decision-making from liability, as a general rule it must be established that money damages were suffered by the corporation or its shareholders and those damages resulted from and were legally caused by the challenged act or omission of the director.

- *Other liability for money payment.* Aside from a claim for damages, the director may have monetary liability for other reasons, for example, if corporate resources have been used without proper authorization, or a claim for disgorgement of short-swing trading profits under section 16(b) of the Securities Exchange Act of 1934.

- *Equitable profit recovery or disgorgement.* An equitable remedy compelling the disgorgement of the director's improper financial gain or entitling the corporation to profit recovery, where directors' duties have been breached, may require the payment of money by the director to the corporation.

- *Corporate indemnification.* If the director is monetarily liable, the director may be indemnified by the corporation for any payments made and expenses incurred, depending upon the circumstances. See subchapter 8E.

- *Insurance.* To the extent that corporate indemnification is not available, the director may be reimbursed for the money damages for which the director is accountable, together with proceeding-related expenses, if the claim and grounds for liability come within the coverage under directors' and officers' liability insurance that has been purchased by the corporation as authorized under section 8.57.

* * *

1. *Section 8.31(a)*

a.   **Section 8.31(a)(1)—Affirmative Defenses**

Under section 8.31(a)(1), if a provision in the articles of incorporation (i) (adopted pursuant to section 2.02(b)(4)) shelters the director from liability for money damages, or (ii) (adopted pursuant to section 2.02(b)(6)) limits or eliminates any duty to offer the particular business opportunity to the corporation, or if a safe harbor procedure under sections 8.61(b)(1) or (b)(2) or section 8.70(a)(1) shelters the director's conduct in connection with a conflicting interest transaction or the pursuit or taking of a business opportunity, and such defense applies to all claims in plaintiff's complaint, there is no need to consider further the application of section 8.31's standards of liability. In that event, the court would presumably grant the defendant director's motion for dismissal or summary judgment (or the equivalent) and the proceeding would be ended. If the defense applies to some but not all of plaintiff's claims, dismissal or summary judgment would presumably be granted with respect to those claims. Termination of the proceeding or dismissal of claims on the basis of a provision in the articles of incorporation or a safe harbor procedure will not automatically follow, however, if the party challenging the director's conduct can assert any of the valid bases for contesting the availability of the liability shelter. Absent such a challenge, the relevant shelter provision is self-executing and the individual director's exoneration from liability is automatic. Further, under both sections 8.61 and 8.70, the directors approving the conflicting interest transaction or approving a director's taking of the business opportunity will presumably be protected as well, because compliance with the relevant standards of conduct under section 8.30 is important for their action to be effective and because, as noted above, conduct meeting section 8.30's standards will almost always be protected.

If a claim of liability arising out of a challenged act or omission of a director is not resolved and disposed of under section 8.31(a)(1), section 8.31(a)(2) provides the basis for evaluating whether the conduct in question can be challenged. One of the elements in section 8.31(a)(2) must be established for a director to have liability under section 8.31.

b.   **Section 8.31(a)(2)(i)—Good Faith**

It is a basic standard under section 8.31(a)(2)(i) that a director's conduct in performing his or her duties be in good faith. If a director's conduct can be successfully challenged pursuant to other clauses of section 8.31(a)(2), there is a substantial likelihood that the conduct in question will also present an issue of good faith implicating section 8.31(a)(2)(i). Similarly, if section 8.31(a)(2) included only subsection (i), much of the conduct with which the other clauses are concerned could still be considered under that subsection, on the basis that such conduct evidenced the director's lack of good faith. Where conduct has not been found deficient on other grounds, decision-making outside the bounds of reasonable judgment can give rise to an inference of bad faith. That form of conduct, sometimes characterized as "reckless indifference" or "deliberate disregard," giving rise to an inference of bad faith can also raise a question whether the director could have reasonably believed that the best interests of the corporation would be served. These issues could arise, for example, in approval of conflicting interest transactions. See the Official Comment to section 8.61.

c.   **Section 8.31(a)(2)(ii)—Reasonable Belief**

Liability under section 8.31(a)(2)(ii) turns on a director's reasonable belief with respect to the nature of his or her decision and the degree to which he or she has become informed. In each case, the director must have an actual subjective belief and, so long as it is his or her honest and good faith belief, a director has wide discretion. There is also an objective element to be met, in that the director's belief must also be reasonable. The inquiry is similar to that in section 8.30(a)—could a reasonable person in a like position and acting in similar circumstances have arrived at that belief? In the rare case where a decision respecting the corporation's best interests is so removed from the realm of reason (*e.g.*, corporate waste), or a belief as to the sufficiency of the director's preparation to make an informed judgment is so unreasonable as to fall outside the permissible bounds of sound discretion (*e.g.*, if the director has undertaken no preparation and is completely uninformed), the director's judgment will not be sustained.

d.   Section 8.31(a)(2)(iii)—Lack of Objectivity or Independence

If the matter at issue involves a director's transactional interest, such as a "director's conflicting interest transaction" in which a "related person" is involved (see section 8.60), it will be governed by section 8.61; otherwise, a lack of objectivity due to a relationship's influence on the director's judgment will be evaluated, in the context of the pending challenge of director conduct, under section 8.31. If the matter at issue involves lack of independence, the proof of domination or control and its influence on the director's judgment will typically entail different (and perhaps more convincing) evidence than what may be involved in a lack of objectivity case. The variables are manifold, and the facts must be sorted out and weighed on a case-by-case basis. For example, the closeness or nature of the relationship with the person allegedly exerting influence on the director could be a factor. If the director is required under section 8.31(a)(2)(iii)(B) to establish that the action taken by him or her was reasonably believed to be in the best interests of the corporation, the inquiry will involve the elements of actual subjective belief and objective reasonableness similar to those found in section 8.31(a)(2)(ii) and section 8.30(a).

To call into question the director's objectivity or independence on the basis of a person's relationship with, or exertion of dominance over, the director, the person must have a material interest in the challenged conduct. In the typical case, analysis of another's interest would first consider the materiality of the transaction or conduct at issue—in most cases, any transaction or other action involving the attention of the board of directors or a board committee will cross the materiality threshold, but not always—and would then consider the materiality of that person's interest in the matter. The possibility that a director's judgment would be adversely affected by another's interest in a transaction or conduct that is not material, or another's immaterial interest in a transaction or conduct, is sufficiently remote that it should not be made subject to judicial review.

In situations where there may be a lack of objectivity, domination, a conflict of interest or divided loyalty, or even where there may be grounds for the issue to be raised, the better course to follow where board or committee action is required is usually for the director to disclose the facts and circumstances posing the possible issue, and then to withdraw from the meeting (or, in the alternative, to abstain from the deliberations and voting). The board members free of any possible taint may then take appropriate action as contemplated by section 8.30 (or section 8.61 if applicable). If this course is followed, the director's conduct respecting the matter in question should be beyond challenge.

e.   Section 8.31(a)(2)(iv)—Failure to Devote Attention

The director's role involves two fundamental components: the decision-making function and the oversight function. In contrast with the decision-making function, which generally involves action taken at a point in time, the oversight function under section 8.01(b) involves ongoing monitoring of the corporation's business and affairs over a period of time. Although the facts will be outcome-determinative, deficient conduct involving a sustained failure to exercise oversight—where found actionable—has typically been characterized by the courts in terms of abdication and continued neglect by a director to devote attention, not a brief distraction or temporary interruption. Also embedded in the oversight function is the need to inquire when suspicions are aroused. This need to inquire is not a component of ongoing oversight, and does not entail proactive vigilance, but arises under section 8.31(a)(2)(iv) when, and only when, particular facts and circumstances of material concern (*e.g.*, evidence of embezzlement at a high level or the discovery of significant inventory shortages) surface.

f.   Section 8.31(a)(2)(v)—Improper Financial Benefit and Other Breaches of Duties

Subchapter 8F deals in detail with directors' transactional interests. Its coverage of those interests is exclusive and its safe harbor procedures for director's conflicting interest transactions (as defined)—providing shelter from legal challenges based on interest conflicts, when properly observed—will establish a director's entitlement to any financial benefit gained from the transactional event. A director's conflicting interest transaction that is not protected by the fairness standard set forth in section 8.61(b)(3), pursuant to which the conflicted director may establish the transaction to have been fair to the corporation, would often involve receipt of a financial benefit to which the director was not entitled (*i.e.*, the transaction was not "fair" to the corporation). Unauthorized use of corporate assets, such as aircraft or hotel suites, would also provide a basis for the proper challenge of a director's conduct. There can be other forms of improper financial benefit not involving a transaction with the corporation or use of its facilities, such as where a director profits from unauthorized use of proprietary information.

There is no materiality threshold that applies to a financial benefit to which a director is not properly entitled. The Act observes this principle in several places, for example, the exception to liability elimination prescribed in section 2.02(b)(4)(i) and the indemnification restriction in section 8.51(d)(2), as well as the liability standard in section 8.31(a)(2)(v).

The second clause of section 8.31(a)(2)(v) is, in part, a catchall provision that implements the intention to make section 8.31 a generally inclusive provision but, at the same time, to recognize the existence of other breaches of common-law principles that can give rise to liability for directors. As developed in the case law, these actionable breaches may include unauthorized use of corporate property or information (which as noted above, might also be characterized as receipt of an improper financial benefit), unfair competition with the corporation or the taking of a corporate opportunity. In the case of corporate opportunity, if the director is alleged to have wrongfully diverted a business opportunity as to which the corporation had a prior right, the Act provides two possible safe harbors. First, any duty to offer the business opportunity to the corporation may have been limited or eliminated pursuant to a provision in the articles of incorporation authorized by section 2.02(b)(6). Second, section 8.70(a)(1) provides a safe harbor procedure for a director who wishes to pursue or take advantage of a business opportunity, regardless of whether such opportunity would be characterized as a "corporate opportunity" under existing case law. Note that section 8.70(b) provides that the fact that a director did not employ the safe harbor procedure of section 8.70(a)(1) does not create an implication that the opportunity should have first been presented to the corporation or alter the burden of proof otherwise applicable to establish a breach of the director's duty to the corporation.

2.   Section 8.31(b)

Whether a corporation or its shareholders have suffered harm and whether a particular director's conduct was the proximate cause of that harm may be affected by the collective nature of board action. Proper performance of the relevant duty through the action taken by the director's colleagues can overcome the consequences of his or her deficient conduct. For example, where a director's conduct can be challenged under section 8.31(a)(2)(ii)(B) by reason of having been uninformed about the decision or not reading the materials distributed before the meeting, or arriving late at the board meeting just in time for the vote but, nonetheless, voting in favor solely because the others were in favor—the favorable action by a quorum of properly informed directors would ordinarily protect the director against liability, either because there was no harm or the offending director's actions were not the proximate cause of the harm. Although the concept of "proximate cause" is a term of art that is basic to tort law, for purposes of section 8.31(b)(1), a useful approach for the concept's application would be that the challenged conduct must have been a "substantial factor in producing the harm."

3.   Section 8.31(c)

Section 8.31(c) expressly disclaims any shift of the burden of proof otherwise applicable where the question of the fairness of a transaction or other challenged conduct is at issue. This is the case whether the question of fairness arises under another section of the Act, such as section 8.61, under existing case law, under a judicial requirement in a particular instance or otherwise. Similarly, section 8.31 does not affect liability under other sections of the Act. It also does not foreclose any rights of the corporation or its shareholders under other laws, for example, rights of shareholders or the corporation under applicable federal securities laws. In addition, directors can have liability to persons other than the corporation and its shareholders, such as liability to employee benefit plan participants and beneficiaries (who may or may not be shareholders), if the directors are determined to be fiduciaries under other applicable laws, to government agencies for regulatory violations or to individuals claiming damages for injury governed by tort-law concepts (*e.g.*, libel or slander). Section 8.31 is not intended to change the standards applicable under these other laws or legal principles.

§ 8.32   Directors' Liability for Unlawful Distributions.

(a)   A director who votes for or assents to a distribution in excess of what may be authorized and made pursuant to section 6.40(a) or 14.09(a) is personally liable to the corporation for the amount of the distribution that exceeds what could have been distributed without violating section 6.40(a) or 14.09(a) if the party asserting liability establishes that when taking the action the director did not comply with section 8.30.

(b)   A director held liable under subsection (a) for an unlawful distribution is entitled to:

(1)   contribution from every other director who could be held liable under subsection (a) for the unlawful distribution; and

(2)   recoupment from each shareholder of the pro-rata portion of the amount of the unlawful distribution the shareholder accepted, knowing the distribution was made in violation of section 6.40(a) or 14.09(a).

(c)   A proceeding to enforce:

(1)   the liability of a director under subsection (a) is barred unless it is commenced within two years after the date (i) on which the effect of the distribution was measured under section 6.40(e) or (g), (ii) as of which the violation of section 6.40(a) occurred as the consequence of disregard of a restriction in the articles of incorporation, or (iii) on which the distribution of assets to shareholders under section 14.09(a) was made; or

(2)   contribution or recoupment under subsection (b) is barred unless it is commenced within one year after the liability of the claimant has been finally adjudicated under subsection (a).

SUBCHAPTER D.   OFFICERS

§ 8.40   Officers

(a)   A corporation has the officers described in its bylaws or appointed by the board of directors in accordance with the bylaws.

(b)   The board of directors may elect individuals to fill one or more offices of the corporation. An officer may appoint one or more officers if authorized by the bylaws or the board of directors.

(c)   The bylaws or the board of directors shall assign to an officer responsibility for maintaining and authenticating the records of the corporation required to be kept under section 16.01(a).

(d)   The same individual may simultaneously hold more than one office in a corporation.

§ 8.41   Functions of Officers

Each officer has the authority and shall perform the functions set forth in the bylaws or, to the extent consistent with the bylaws, the functions prescribed by the board of directors or by direction of an officer authorized by the board of directors to prescribe the functions of other officers.

§ 8.42   Standards of Conduct for Officers

(a)   An officer, when performing in such capacity, has the duty to act:

(1)   in good faith;

(2)   with the care that a person in a like position would reasonably exercise under similar circumstances; and

(3)   in a manner the officer reasonably believes to be in the best interests of the corporation.

(b)   The duty of an officer includes the obligation:

(1)　to inform the superior officer to whom, or the board of directors or the board committee to which, the officer reports of information about the affairs of the corporation known to the officer, within the scope of the officer's functions, and known to the officer to be material to such superior officer, board or committee; and

(2)　to inform his or her superior officer, or another appropriate person within the corporation, or the board of directors, or a board committee, of any actual or probable material violation of law involving the corporation or material breach of duty to the corporation by an officer, employee, or agent of the corporation, that the officer believes has occurred or is likely to occur.

(c)　In discharging his or her duties, an officer who does not have knowledge that makes reliance unwarranted is entitled to rely on:

(1)　the performance of properly delegated responsibilities by one or more employees of the corporation whom the officer reasonably believes to be reliable and competent in performing the responsibilities delegated; or

(2)　information, opinions, reports or statements, including financial statements and other financial data, prepared or presented by one or more employees of the corporation whom the officer reasonably believes to be reliable and competent in the matters presented or by legal counsel, public accountants, or other persons retained by the corporation as to matters involving skills or expertise the officer reasonably believes are matters (i) within the particular person's professional or expert competence or (ii) as to which the particular person merits confidence.

(d)　An officer shall not be liable to the corporation or its shareholders for any decision to take or not to take action, or any failure to take any action, as an officer, if the duties of the office are performed in compliance with this section. Whether an officer who does not comply with this section shall have liability will depend in such instance on applicable law, including those principles of section 8.31 that have relevance.

OFFICIAL COMMENT

Under section 8.42(a), an officer, when performing in such officer's official capacity, has to meet standards of conduct generally specified for directors under section 8.30. This section is not intended to modify, diminish or qualify the duties or standards of conduct that may be imposed upon specific officers by other law or regulation.

Common law has generally recognized a duty on the part of officers and key employees to disclose to their superiors material information relevant to the affairs of the corporation. This duty is implicit in, and embraced under, the broader standard of section 8.42(a), but section 8.42(b) sets forth this disclosure obligation explicitly. Section 8.42(b)(1) specifies that business information shall be transmitted through the officer's regular reporting channels. Section 8.42(b)(2) specifies the reporting responsibility differently with respect to actual or probable material violations of law or material breaches of duty. The use of the term "appropriate" in subsection (b)(2) accommodates any normative standard that the corporation may have prescribed for reporting potential violations of law or duty to a specified person, such as an ombudsperson, ethics officer, internal auditor, general counsel or the like, as well as situations where there is no designated person but the officer's immediate superior is not appropriate (for example, because the officer believes that individual is complicit in the unlawful activity or breach of duty).

Section 8.42(b)(1) should not be interpreted so broadly as to discourage efficient delegation of functions. It addresses the flow of information to the board of directors and to superior officers necessary to enable them to perform their decision-making and oversight functions. See the Official Comment to section 8.31. The officer's duties under subsection (b) may not be negated by agreement; however, their scope under section 8.42(b)(1) may be shaped by prescribing the scope of an officer's functional responsibilities.

With respect to the duties under section 8.42(b)(2), codes of conduct or codes of ethics may prescribe the circumstances in which and mechanisms by which officers and employees may discharge their duty to report material information to superior officers or the board of directors, or to other designated persons.

The term "material" modifying violations of law or breaches of duty in section 8.42(b)(2) denotes a qualitative as well as quantitative standard. It relates not only to the potential direct financial impact on the corporation, but also to the nature of the violation or breach. For example, an embezzlement of $10,000, or even less, would be material because of the seriousness of the offense, even though the amount involved would ordinarily not be material to the financial position or results of operations of the corporation.

The duty under section 8.42(b)(2) is triggered by an officer's subjective belief that a material violation of law or breach of duty actually or probably has occurred or is likely to occur. This duty is not triggered by objective knowledge concepts, such as whether the officer should have concluded that such misconduct was occurring. The subjectivity of the trigger under subsection (b)(2), however, does not excuse officers from their obligations under subsection (a) to act in good faith and with due care in the performance of the functions assigned to them, including oversight duties within their respective areas of responsibility. There may be occasions when the principles applicable under section 8.30(c) limiting the duty of disclosure by directors where a duty of confidentiality is overriding may also apply to officers. See the Official Comment to section 8.30(c).

An officer's ability to rely on others in meeting the standards prescribed in section 8.42 may be more limited, depending upon the circumstances of the particular case, than the measure and scope of reliance permitted a director under section 8.30, in view of the greater obligation the officer may have to be familiar with the affairs of the corporation. The proper delegation of responsibilities by an officer, separate and apart from the exercise of judgment as to the delegatee's reliability and competence, is concerned with the procedure employed. This will involve, in the usual case, sufficient communication such that the delegatee understands the scope of the assignment and, in turn, manifests to the officer a willingness and commitment to undertake its performance. The entitlement to rely upon employees assumes that a delegating officer will maintain a sufficient level of communication with the officer's subordinates to fulfill his or her supervisory responsibilities. The definition of "employee" in section 1.40 includes an officer; accordingly, section 8.42 contemplates the delegation of responsibilities to other officers as well as to non-officer employees.

Although under section 8.42(d), performance meeting that section's standards of conduct will eliminate an officer's exposure to any liability to the corporation or its shareholders, failure by an officer to meet that section's standards will not automatically result in liability. Deficient performance of duties by an officer, depending upon the facts and circumstances, will normally be dealt with through intracorporate disciplinary procedures, such as reprimand, compensation adjustment, delayed promotion, demotion or discharge. These procedures may be subject to (and limited by) the terms of an officer's employment agreement. See section 8.44.

In some cases, failure to observe relevant standards of conduct can give rise to an officer's liability to the corporation or its shareholders. A court review of challenged conduct will involve an evaluation of the particular facts and circumstances in light of applicable law. In this connection, section 8.42(d) recognizes that relevant principles of section 8.31, such as duties to deal fairly with the corporation and its shareholders and the challenger's burden of establishing proximately caused harm, should be taken into account. In addition, the business judgment rule will normally apply to decisions within an officer's discretionary authority. Liability to others can also arise from an officer's own acts or omissions (e.g., violations of law or tort claims) and, in some cases, an officer with supervisory responsibilities can have risk exposure in connection with the acts or omissions of others.

The Official Comment to section 8.30 supplements this Official Comment to the extent that it can be appropriately viewed as generally applicable to officers as well as directors.

§ 8.43 Resignation and Removal of Officers

(a) An officer may resign at any time by delivering a written notice to the board of directors, or its chair, or to the appointing officer or the secretary. A resignation is effective as provided in section 1.41(i) unless the notice provides for a delayed effectiveness, including effectiveness determined upon a future event or events. If effectiveness of a resignation is stated to be delayed and the board of directors or the appointing officer accepts the delay, the board of directors or the appointing officer may fill the pending vacancy before the delayed effectiveness but the new officer may not take office until the vacancy occurs.

(b)   An officer may be removed at any time with or without cause by: (i) the board of directors; (ii) the appointing officer, unless the bylaws or the board of directors provide otherwise; or (iii) any other officer if authorized by the bylaws or the board of directors.

(c)   In this section, "appointing officer" means the officer (including any successor to that officer) who appointed the officer resigning or being removed.

§ 8.44   Contract Rights of Officers

(a)   The election or appointment of an officer does not itself create contract rights.

(b)   An officer's removal does not affect the officer's contract rights, if any, with the corporation. An officer's resignation does not affect the corporation's contract rights, if any, with the officer.

SUBCHAPTER E.   INDEMNIFICATION AND ADVANCE FOR EXPENSES

§ 8.50   Subchapter Definitions

In this subchapter:

"Corporation" includes any domestic or foreign predecessor entity of a corporation in a merger.

"Director" or "officer" means an individual who is or was a director or officer, respectively, of a corporation or who, while a director or officer of the corporation, is or was serving at the corporation's request as a director, officer, manager, partner, trustee, employee, or agent of another entity or employee benefit plan. A director or officer is considered to be serving an employee benefit plan at the corporation's request if the individual's duties to the corporation also impose duties on, or otherwise involve services by, the individual to the plan or to participants in or beneficiaries of the plan. "Director" or "officer" includes, unless the context requires otherwise, the estate or personal representative of a director or officer.

"Liability" means the obligation to pay a judgment, settlement, penalty, fine (including an excise tax assessed with respect to an employee benefit plan), or expenses incurred with respect to a proceeding.

"Official capacity" means: (i) when used with respect to a director, the office of director in a corporation; and (ii) when used with respect to an officer, as contemplated in section 8.56, the office in a corporation held by the officer. "Official capacity" does not include service for any other domestic or foreign corporation or any joint venture, trust, employee benefit plan, or other entity.

"Party" means an individual who was, is, or is threatened to be made, a defendant or respondent in a proceeding.

"Proceeding" means any threatened, pending, or completed action, suit, or proceeding, whether civil, criminal, administrative, arbitrative, or investigative and whether formal or informal.

§ 8.51   Permissible Indemnification

(a)   Except as otherwise provided in this section, a corporation may indemnify an individual who is a party to a proceeding because the individual is a director against liability incurred in the proceeding if:

    (1)

        (i)   the director conducted himself or herself in good faith; and

        (ii)   the director reasonably believed:

(A)   in the case of conduct in an official capacity, that his or her conduct was in the best interests of the corporation; and

(B)   in all other cases, that his or her conduct was at least not opposed to the best interests of the corporation; and

(iii) in the case of any criminal proceeding, the director had no reasonable cause to believe his or her conduct was unlawful; or

(2)   the director engaged in conduct for which broader indemnification has been made permissible or obligatory under a provision of the articles of incorporation (as authorized by section 2.02(b)(5)).

(b)   A director's conduct with respect to an employee benefit plan for a purpose the director reasonably believed to be in the interests of the participants in, and the beneficiaries of, the plan is conduct that satisfies the requirement of subsection (a)(1)(ii)(B).

(c)   The termination of a proceeding by judgment, order, settlement, or conviction, or upon a plea of nolo contendere or its equivalent, is not, of itself, determinative that the director did not meet the relevant standard of conduct described in this section.

(d)   Unless ordered by a court under section 8.54(a)(3), a corporation may not indemnify a director:

(1)   in connection with a proceeding by or in the right of the corporation, except for expenses incurred in connection with the proceeding if it is determined that the director has met the relevant standard of conduct under subsection (a); or

(2)   in connection with any proceeding with respect to conduct for which the director was adjudged liable on the basis of receiving a financial benefit to which he or she was not entitled, regardless of whether it involved action in the director's official capacity.

OFFICIAL COMMENT

1. Section 8.51(a)

The standards for indemnification of directors contained in section 8.51(a) define the limits of the conduct for which discretionary indemnification is permitted under the Act, except to the extent that court-ordered indemnification is available under section 8.54(a)(3). Conduct that falls within these limits does not automatically entitle directors to indemnification, although a corporation may obligate itself to indemnify directors to the maximum extent permitted by applicable law. See section 8.58(a). Absent such an obligatory provision, section 8.52 defines much narrower circumstances in which directors are entitled as a matter of right to indemnification.

The standards of conduct in section 8.51(a) are not dependent on the type of proceeding in which the claim arises. These standards are closely related, but not identical, to the standards of conduct imposed by section 8.30 on directors when discharging the duties of a director: good faith, reasonable belief that the best interests of the corporation are being served, and appropriate care (*i.e.*, that which a person in a like position would reasonably believe appropriate under similar circumstances). As in the case of section 8.30, where the concept of good faith is also used, section 8.51 provides no definition for that term. The concept involves a subjective test, which would permit indemnification for an unwise decision or "a mistake of judgment," even though made negligently by objective standards. Section 8.51 also requires, as does section 8.30, a "reasonable" belief that conduct when acting in the director's official capacity was in the corporation's best interests. It then adds a provision, not found in section 8.30, relating to criminal proceedings that requires the director to have had no "reasonable cause" to believe that the conduct was unlawful. These both involve objective standards applicable to the director's belief concerning the effect of the conduct in question. Conduct includes both acts and omissions.

In section 8.51(a)(1)(ii)(B), the words "at least" qualify "not opposed to" and make clear that this standard is for conduct other than in an official capacity. Although this provision deals with indemnification by the corporation, a director serving another entity at the request of the corporation remains subject to the provisions of the law governing service to that other entity, including provisions dealing with conflicts of interest. Compare sections 8.60 through 8.63. Should indemnification from the requesting corporation be sought by a director for acts done while serving another entity, which acts involved breach of a duty owed to that other entity, nothing in section 8.51(a)(1)(ii)(B) would preclude the requesting corporation from considering, in assessing its own best interests, whether the fact that its director had engaged in a violation of the duty owed to the other entity was in fact "opposed to" the interests of the indemnifying corporation.

If the relevant standards are met, section 8.51 also permits indemnification in connection with a proceeding involving an alleged failure to satisfy legal standards other than the standards of conduct in section 8.30, *e.g.*, violations of antitrust, environmental or securities laws.

In addition to indemnification under section 8.51(a)(1), section 8.51(a)(2) permits indemnification under the standard of conduct set forth in a provision of the articles of incorporation adopted pursuant to section 2.02(b)(5). Based on such a provision, section 8.51(a)(2) permits indemnification in connection with claims by third parties and, through section 8.56, applies to officers as well as directors. (This goes beyond the scope of a provision of the articles of incorporation adopted pursuant to section 2.02(b)(4), which can only limit liability of directors against claims by the corporation or its shareholders.) Section 8.51(a)(2) is subject to the prohibition of subsection (d)(1) against indemnification of settlements and judgments in derivative suits, except as ordered by a court under section 8.54(a)(3). It is also subject to the prohibition of subsection (d)(2) against indemnification for receipt of an improper financial benefit; however, this prohibition is already subsumed in the exception contained in section 2.02(b)(5)(i).

2.　Section 8.51(b)

As discussed in the Official Comment to the definition of "director" or "officer" in section 8.50, ERISA requires that a "fiduciary" (as defined in ERISA) discharge the fiduciary's duties "solely in the interest" of the participants in and beneficiaries of an employee benefit plan. The standard in section 8.51(b) for indemnification of a director who is serving as a trustee or fiduciary for an employee benefit plan under ERISA is arguably an exception to the more general standard that conduct not in an official corporate capacity is indemnifiable if it is "at least not opposed to" the best interests of the corporation. However, a corporation that causes a director to undertake fiduciary duties in connection with an employee benefit plan should expect the director to act in the best interests of the plan's beneficiaries or participants. Thus, subsection (b) establishes and provides a standard for indemnification that is consistent with the statutory policies embodied in ERISA. See Official Comment to section 8.50(2).

3.　Section 8.51(c)

Section 8.51(c) rejects the argument that indemnification is automatically improper whenever a proceeding has been concluded on a basis that does not exonerate the director claiming indemnification. However, any judicial determination of substantive liability should be taken into account in determining whether the standards of section 8.51(a) were met. By the same token, it is clear that the termination of a proceeding by settlement or plea of no contest should not of itself create a presumption either that conduct met or did not meet the relevant standard of subsection (a) since a settlement or nolo plea may be agreed to for many reasons unrelated to the merits of the claim. On the other hand, a final determination of non-liability (including one based on a liability-limitation provision adopted under section 2.02(b)(4)) or an acquittal in a criminal case automatically entitles the director to indemnification of expenses under section 8.52.

4.　Section 8.51(d)

Section 8.51(d) does not permit indemnification of settlements and judgments in derivative proceedings which would give rise to a circularity in which the corporation receiving payment of damages by the director in the settlement or judgment (less attorneys' fees) would then immediately return the same amount to the director (including attorneys' fees) as indemnification. Thus, the corporation would be in a poorer economic position than if there had been no proceeding. Further, in many cases a director may be protected by a provision in the articles of incorporation under section 2.02(b)(4) limiting liability or because a proceeding was dismissed under section 7.44. The prohibition on indemnification of a settlement or a judgment in a derivative proceeding, however, does not extend to the related expenses incurred in the proceeding so long as the director meets the relevant standard of conduct set forth in section 8.51(a). In addition, indemnification and advance of expenses may be ordered by a court under section 8.54(a)(3) even if the relevant standard was not met.

Indemnification under section 8.51 is also prohibited if there has been an adjudication that a director received a financial benefit to which the director is not entitled, even if, for example, the director acted in a manner not opposed to the best interests of the corporation. For example, improper use of inside information for financial benefit should not be an action for which the corporation may elect to provide indemnification, even if the corporation was not thereby harmed. Given the express language of section 2.02(b)(5) establishing the limit of an indemnification provision contained in the articles of incorporation, a director found to have received an improper financial benefit would not be permitted indemnification under section 8.51(a)(2). Although it is unlikely that a director found to have received an improper financial benefit could meet the standard in section 8.51(a)(1)(ii)(B), this limitation is made explicit in section 8.51(d)(2). Section 8.54(a)(3) permits a director found liable in a proceeding referred to in section 8.51(d)(2) to petition a court for a judicial determination of entitlement to indemnification for expenses. The language of section 8.51(d)(2) parallels sections 2.02(b)(4)(i) and 2.02(b)(5)(i), and thus, the same standards should be used in interpreting the application of all three provisions. Although a settlement may create an obligation to pay money, it should not be construed for purposes of this subchapter as an adjudication of liability.

§ 8.52 Mandatory Indemnification

A corporation shall indemnify a director who was wholly successful, on the merits or otherwise, in the defense of any proceeding to which the director was a party because he or she was a director of the corporation against expenses incurred by the director in connection with the proceeding.

OFFICIAL COMMENT

Section 8.52 creates a right of indemnification in favor of the director who meets its requirements. Enforcement of this right by judicial proceeding is specifically contemplated by section 8.54(a)(1). Section 8.54(b) gives the director a right to recover expenses incurred in enforcing the director's right to indemnification under section 8.52.

The basic standard for mandatory indemnification is that the director has been "wholly successful, on the merits or otherwise," in the defense of the proceeding. A defendant is "wholly successful" only if the entire proceeding is disposed of on a basis which does not involve a finding of liability. A director who is precluded from mandatory indemnification by this requirement may still be entitled to permissible indemnification under section 8.51(a) or court-ordered indemnification under section 8.54(a)(3).

Although the standard "on the merits or otherwise" may result in an occasional defendant becoming entitled to indemnification because of procedural defenses not related to the merits, e.g., the statute of limitations or disqualification of the plaintiff, it is unreasonable to require a defendant with a valid procedural defense to undergo a possibly prolonged and expensive trial on the merits to establish eligibility for mandatory indemnification.

§ 8.53 Advance for Expenses

(a) A corporation may, before final disposition of a proceeding, advance funds to pay for or reimburse expenses incurred in connection with the proceeding by an individual who is a party to the proceeding because that individual is a director if the director delivers to the corporation a signed written undertaking of the director to repay any funds advanced if (i) the director is not entitled to mandatory indemnification under section 8.52 and (ii) it is ultimately determined under section 8.54 or section 8.55 that the director is not entitled to indemnification.

(b) The undertaking required by subsection (a) must be an unlimited general obligation of the director but need not be secured and may be accepted without reference to the financial ability of the director to make repayment.

(c) Authorizations under this section shall be made:

(1) by the board of directors:

(i)　if there are two or more qualified directors, by a majority vote of all the qualified directors (a majority of whom shall for such purpose constitute a quorum) or by a majority of the members of a committee consisting solely of two or more qualified directors appointed by such a vote; or

(ii)　if there are fewer than two qualified directors, by the vote necessary for action by the board of directors in accordance with section 8.24(c), in which authorization directors who are not qualified directors may participate; or

(2)　by the shareholders, but shares owned by or voted under the control of a director who at the time is not a qualified director may not be voted on the authorization.

§ 8.54　Court-Ordered Indemnification and Advance for Expenses

(a)　A director who is a party to a proceeding because he or she is a director may apply for indemnification or an advance for expenses to the court conducting the proceeding or to another court of competent jurisdiction. After receipt of an application and after giving any notice it considers necessary, the court shall:

(1)　order indemnification if the court determines that the director is entitled to mandatory indemnification under section 8.52;

(2)　order indemnification or advance for expenses if the court determines that the director is entitled to indemnification or advance for expenses pursuant to a provision authorized by section 8.58(a); or

(3)　order indemnification or advance for expenses if the court determines, in view of all the relevant circumstances, that it is fair and reasonable (i) to indemnify the director, or (ii) to advance expenses to the director, even if, in the case of (i) or (ii), he or she has not met the relevant standard of conduct set forth in section 8.51(a), failed to comply with section 8.53 or was adjudged liable in a proceeding referred to in section 8.51(d)(1) or (d)(2), but if the director was adjudged so liable indemnification shall be limited to expenses incurred in connection with the proceeding.

(b)　If the court determines that the director is entitled to indemnification under subsection (a)(1) or to indemnification or advance for expenses under subsection (a)(2), it shall also order the corporation to pay the director's expenses incurred in connection with obtaining court-ordered indemnification or advance for expenses. If the court determines that the director is entitled to indemnification or advance for expenses under subsection (a)(3), it may also order the corporation to pay the director's expenses to obtain court-ordered indemnification or advance for expenses.

§ 8.55　Determination and Authorization of Indemnification

(a)　A corporation may not indemnify a director under section 8.51 unless authorized for a specific proceeding after a determination has been made that indemnification is permissible because the director has met the relevant standard of conduct set forth in section 8.51.

(b)　The determination shall be made:

(1)　if there are two or more qualified directors, by the board of directors by a majority vote of all the qualified directors (a majority of whom shall for such purpose constitute a quorum), or by a majority of the members of a committee of two or more qualified directors appointed by such a vote;

(2)　by special legal counsel:

(i)　selected in the manner prescribed in subsection (b)(1); or

(ii)　if there are fewer than two qualified directors, selected by the board of directors (in which selection directors who are not qualified directors may participate); or

(3) by the shareholders, but shares owned by or voted under the control of a director who at the time is not a qualified director may not be voted on the determination.

(c) Authorization of indemnification shall be made in the same manner as the determination that indemnification is permissible except that if there are fewer than two qualified directors, or if the determination is made by special legal counsel, authorization of indemnification shall be made by those entitled to select special legal counsel under subsection (b)(2)(ii).

§ 8.56 Indemnification of Officers

(a) A corporation may indemnify and advance expenses under this subchapter to an officer who is a party to a proceeding because he or she is an officer

(1) to the same extent as a director; and

(2) if he or she is an officer but not a director, to such further extent as may be provided by the articles of incorporation or the bylaws, or by a resolution adopted or a contract approved by the board of directors or shareholders, except for

(i) liability in connection with a proceeding by or in the right of the corporation other than for expenses incurred in connection with the proceeding, or

(ii) liability arising out of conduct that constitutes

(A) receipt by the officer of a financial benefit to which he or she is not entitled,

(B) an intentional infliction of harm on the corporation or the shareholders, or

(C) an intentional violation of criminal law.

(b) Subsection (a)(2) shall apply to an officer who is also a director if he or she is made a party to the proceeding based on an act or omission solely as an officer.

(c) An officer who is not a director is entitled to mandatory indemnification under section 8.52, and may apply to a court under section 8.54 for indemnification or an advance for expenses, in each case to the same extent to which a director may be entitled to indemnification or advance for expenses under those sections.

§ 8.57 Insurance

A corporation may purchase and maintain insurance on behalf of an individual who is a director or officer of the corporation, or who, while a director or officer of the corporation, serves at the corporation's request as a director, officer, partner, trustee, employee, or agent of another domestic or foreign corporation or a joint venture, trust, employee benefit plan, or other entity, against liability asserted against or incurred by the individual in that capacity or arising from the individual's status as a director or officer, regardless of whether the corporation would have power to indemnify or advance expenses to the individual against the same liability under this subchapter.

§ 8.58 Variation by Corporate Action; Application of Subchapter

(a) A corporation may, by a provision in its articles of incorporation or bylaws or in a resolution adopted or a contract approved by the board of directors or shareholders, obligate itself in advance of the act or omission giving rise to a proceeding to provide indemnification in accordance with section 8.51 or advance funds to pay for or reimburse expenses in accordance with section 8.53. Any such obligatory provision shall be deemed to satisfy the requirements for authorization referred to in section 8.53(c) and in section 8.55(c). Any such provision that obligates the corporation to provide indemnification to the fullest extent permitted by law shall be deemed to obligate the corporation to advance funds to pay for or reimburse expenses in accordance with section 8.53 to the fullest extent permitted by law, unless the provision expressly provides otherwise.

(b) A right of indemnification or to advances for expenses created by this subchapter or under subsection (a) and in effect at the time of an act or omission shall not be eliminated or impaired with respect to such act or omission by an amendment of the articles of incorporation or bylaws or a resolution of the board of directors or shareholders, adopted after the occurrence of such act or omission, unless, in the case of a right created under subsection (a), the provision creating such right and in effect at the time of such act or omission explicitly authorizes such elimination or impairment after such act or omission has occurred.

(c) Any provision pursuant to subsection (a) shall not obligate the corporation to indemnify or advance expenses to a director of a predecessor of the corporation, pertaining to conduct with respect to the predecessor, unless otherwise expressly provided. Any provision for indemnification or advance for expenses in the articles of incorporation or bylaws, or a resolution of the board of directors or shareholders of a predecessor of the corporation in a merger or in a contract to which the predecessor is a party, existing at the time the merger takes effect, shall be governed by section 11.07(a)(4).

(d) Subject to subsection (b), a corporation may, by a provision in its articles of incorporation, limit any of the rights to indemnification or advance for expenses created by or pursuant to this subchapter.

(e) This subchapter does not limit a corporation's power to pay or reimburse expenses incurred by a director or an officer in connection with appearing as a witness in a proceeding at a time when he or she is not a party.

(f) This subchapter does not limit a corporation's power to indemnify, advance expenses to or provide or maintain insurance on behalf of an employee or agent.

OFFICIAL COMMENT

Section 8.58(a) authorizes a corporation to make obligatory the permissive provisions of subchapter E in advance of the conduct giving rise to the request for indemnification or advance for expenses. An obligatory provision satisfies the requirements for authorization in sections 8.53(c) and 8.55(c), but the requirements for determination of eligibility for indemnification in subsections (a) and (b) of those sections must still be met.

If a corporation provides for obligatory indemnification and not for obligatory advance for expenses, the provision should be reviewed to ensure that it properly reflects the intent in view of the third sentence of section 8.58(a). Also, a corporation should consider whether obligatory expense advance is intended for direct suits by the corporation as well as for derivative suits by shareholders in the right of the corporation. In the former case, assuming compliance with sections 8.53(a) and (b), the corporation could be required to fund the defense of a defendant director even where the board of directors has already concluded that the director has engaged in significant wrongdoing. See Official Comment to section 8.53.

Although section 8.58(d) permits a corporation to limit the right of the corporation to indemnify or advance expenses by a provision in its articles of incorporation, as provided in section 10.09, no such limitation will affect rights in existence when the provision becomes effective pursuant to section 1.23.

Subchapter E does not regulate the power of the corporation to indemnify or advance expenses to employees and agents. That subject is governed by the law of agency and related principles and frequently by contractual arrangements between the corporation and the employee or agent. Section 8.58(f) makes clear that, although indemnification, advance for expenses, and insurance for employees and agents are beyond the scope of subchapter E, the elaboration in subchapter E of standards and procedures for indemnification, expense advance, and insurance for directors and officers is not in any way intended to cast doubt on the power of the corporation to indemnify or advance expenses to or purchase and maintain insurance for employees and agents under section 3.02 or otherwise.

§ 8.59 Exclusivity of Subchapter

A corporation may provide indemnification or advance expenses to a director or an officer only as permitted by this subchapter.

SUBCHAPTER F.   DIRECTORS' CONFLICTING INTEREST TRANSACTIONS

INTRODUCTORY COMMENT

1.   *Overview.*

There are four basic elements in subchapter F.

First, subchapter F defines, with bright-line rules, the transactions that are to be treated as director's conflicting interest transactions.

Second, subchapter F provides that a director's transaction that is not within the statutory definition of a director's conflicting interest transaction is not subject to judicial review for fairness on the ground that it involved a conflict of interest (although circumstances that fall outside the statutory definition may afford the basis for a legal attack on the transaction on some other ground), even if the transaction involves some sort of conflict lying outside the statutory definition, such as a remote familial relationship.

Third, subchapter F provides that if a director's conflicting interest transaction is properly approved by disinterested (or "qualified") directors or shareholders, the transaction is insulated from judicial review for fairness (although, again, it might be open to attack on some basis other than the conflict).

Fourth, subchapter F also provides that if a director's conflicting interest transaction is properly approved by disinterested (or "qualified") directors or shareholders, the conflicted director may not be subject to an award of damages or other sanctions (although the director could be subject to claims on some basis other than the conflict).

Bright-line provisions of any kind represent a trade-off between the benefits of certainty and the danger that some transactions or conduct that fall outside the area circumscribed by the bright-lines may be so similar to the transactions and conduct that fall within the area that different treatment may seem anomalous. Subchapter F reflects the judgment that in corporate matters, where planning is critical, the clear and important efficiency gains that result from certainty through defining director's conflicting interest transactions exceed any potential and uncertain efficiency losses that might follow from excluding other director's transactions from judicial review for fairness on conflict-of-interest grounds.

2.   *Scope of Subchapter F*

Subchapter F addresses legal challenges based on director conflicts of interest only. Subchapter F does not undertake to define, regulate, or provide any form of procedure regarding other possible claims. For example, subchapter F does not address a claim that a controlling shareholder has violated a duty owed to the corporation or minority shareholders. So, although transactions between a corporation and a parent corporation or other controlling shareholder who owns less than all of its shares may give rise to the possibility of abuse of power by the controlling shareholder, subchapter F does not address proceedings brought on that basis because section 8.61 concerns only proceedings that are brought on the ground that a "director has an interest respecting the transaction."

Subchapter F applies only when there is a "transaction" by or with the corporation. For purposes of subchapter F, "transaction" generally connotes negotiations or consensual arrangements between the corporation and another party or parties that concern their respective and differing economic rights or interests—not a unilateral action by the corporation or a director. Whether safe harbor procedures of some kind might be available to the director and the corporation with respect to non-transactional matters is discussed in numbered part 3 of this Introductory Comment.

Subchapter F does not preclude the assertion of defenses, such as statute of limitations or failure of a condition precedent, that are based on grounds other than the defenses set forth in this subchapter.

The voting procedures and conduct standards prescribed in subchapter F deal solely with the complicating element presented by the director's conflicting interest in a transaction. A transaction that receives favorable directors' or shareholders' action complying with subchapter F may still fail to satisfy a different quorum requirement or to achieve a different vote than may be needed for substantive approval of the transaction under other applicable statutory provisions or under the articles of incorporation, and vice versa. (Under the Act, a corporation may set higher voting requirements and different quorum requirements in the articles of incorporation. See sections 2.02(b)(2) and 7.27). In addition, subchapter F does not shield misbehavior by a director or other person that is actionable under other provisions of the Act, such as section 8.31, or under other legal rules, regardless of whether the misbehavior is incident to a transaction with the corporation and regardless of whether the rule is one of corporate law.

Finally, certain corporate transactions or arrangements in which directors inherently have a special personal interest are of a unique character and are regulated by special procedural provisions of the Act. See sections 8.51 and 8.52 dealing with indemnification arrangements, and section 7.44 dealing with termination of derivative proceedings by board action. Any corporate transactions or arrangements affecting directors that are governed by such regulatory sections of the Act are not governed by subchapter F.

3. *Nontransactional Situations Involving Interest Conflicts*

A.   Corporate or Business Opportunity

Subchapter F does not apply by its terms to corporate or business opportunities because no transaction between the corporation and the director is involved in the taking of an opportunity. However, subchapter 8G provides, in effect, that the safe harbor procedures of section 8.62 or 8.63 may be employed, at the interested director's election, to protect the taking of a business opportunity that might be challenged under the corporate opportunity doctrine. Also, section 2.02(b)(6) permits a corporation to include in its articles of incorporation a provision that limits or eliminates the duty to present a business opportunity to the corporation.

B.   Other Situations

Many other kinds of situations can give rise to divergent economic interests between a director and the corporation. For example, a director's personal financial interests can be affected by a nontransactional policy decision of the board of directors, such as where it decides to establish a divisional headquarters in the director's small hometown. In other situations, simple inaction by a board might work to a director's personal advantage, or a flow of ongoing business relationships between a director and the corporation may, without centering upon any discrete "transaction," raise questions of possible favoritism, unfair dealing, or undue influence. If a director decides to engage in business activity that directly competes with the corporation's own business, the economic interest in that competing activity ordinarily will conflict with the best interests of the corporation and put in issue the breach of the director's duties to the corporation. Basic conflicts and improprieties can also arise out of a director's personal appropriation of corporate assets or improper use of corporate proprietary or inside information.

The circumstances in which such nontransactional conflict situations should be brought to the board of directors or shareholders for clearance, and the legal effect, if any, of such clearance, are matters for development under the common law and lie outside the ambit of subchapter F. Although these nontransactional situations are not covered by the provisions of subchapter F, a court may well recognize that the subchapter F procedures provide a useful analogy for dealing with such situations.

* * *

Note on Terms in Official Comments

In the Official Comments to subchapter F, the director who has a conflicting interest is for convenience referred to as "the director" or "D," and the corporation of which he or she is a director is referred to as "the corporation" or "X Co." A subsidiary of the corporation is referred to as "S Co." Another corporation dealing with X Co. is referred to as "Y Co."

§ 8.60   Subchapter Definitions

In this subchapter:

"Control" (including the term "controlled by") means (i) having the power, directly or indirectly, to elect or remove a majority of the members of the board of directors or other governing body of an entity, whether through the ownership of voting shares or interests, by contract, or otherwise, or (ii) being subject to a majority of the risk of loss from the entity's activities or entitled to receive a majority of the entity's residual returns.

"Director's conflicting interest transaction" means a transaction effected or proposed to be effected by the corporation (or by an entity controlled by the corporation)

(i) to which, at the relevant time, the director is a party;

(ii) respecting which, at the relevant time, the director had knowledge and a material financial interest known to the director; or

(iii) respecting which, at the relevant time, the director knew that a related person was a party or had a material financial interest.

"Fair to the corporation" means, for purposes of section 8.61(b)(3), that the transaction as a whole was beneficial to the corporation, taking into appropriate account whether it was (i) fair in terms of the director's dealings with the corporation, and (ii) comparable to what might have been obtainable in an arm's length transaction, given the consideration paid or received by the corporation.

"Material financial interest" means a financial interest in a transaction that would reasonably be expected to impair the objectivity of the director's judgment when participating in action on the authorization of the transaction.

"Related person" means:

(i) the individual's spouse;

(ii) a child, stepchild, grandchild, parent, step parent, grandparent, sibling, step sibling, half sibling, aunt, uncle, niece or nephew (or spouse of any such person) of the individual or of the individual's spouse;

(iii) a natural person living in the same home as the individual;

(iv) an entity (other than the corporation or an entity controlled by the corporation) controlled by the individual or any person specified above in this definition;

(v) a domestic or foreign (a) business or nonprofit corporation (other than the corporation or an entity controlled by the corporation) of which the individual is a director, (b) unincorporated entity of which the individual is a general partner or a member of the governing body, or (c) individual, trust or estate for whom or of which the individual is a trustee, guardian, personal representative or like fiduciary; or

(vi) a person that is, or an entity that is controlled by, an employer of the individual.

"Relevant time" means (i) the time at which directors' action respecting the transaction is taken in compliance with section 8.62, or (ii) if the transaction is not brought before the board of directors (or a committee) for action under section 8.62, at the time the corporation (or an entity controlled by the corporation) becomes legally obligated to consummate the transaction.

"Required disclosure" means disclosure of (i) the existence and nature of the director's conflicting interest, and (ii) all facts known to the director respecting the subject matter of the transaction that a director free of such conflicting interest would reasonably believe to be material in deciding whether to proceed with the transaction.

OFFICIAL COMMENT

The definitions set forth in section 8.60 apply only to subchapter F and section 2.02(b)(6) and, where relevant to subchapter G. They have no application elsewhere in the Act. (For the meaning and use of certain terms used below, such as "D," "X Co." and "Y Co.," see the Note on Terms at the end of the Introductory Comment of subchapter F.)

1. Director's Conflicting Interest Transaction

The definition of "director's conflicting interest transaction" in section 8.60 is the core concept underlying subchapter F. The definition operates preclusively in that, as used in section 8.61, it denies the power of a court to invalidate transactions or otherwise to remedy conduct on the ground that the director has a conflict of interest if it falls outside the statutory definition of "director's conflicting interest transaction."

a. Transaction

For purposes of subchapter F, "transaction" requires a bilateral (or multilateral) arrangement to which the corporation or an entity controlled by the corporation is a party. Subchapter F does not apply to transactions to which no such entity is a party. For example, a purchase or sale by the director of the corporation's shares on the open market or from or to a third party is not a "director's conflicting interest transaction" within the meaning of subchapter F.

b. Party to the Transaction—The Corporation or a Controlled Entity

In the usual case, the transaction would be effected by X Co. Assume, however, that X Co. controls the vote for directors of S Co. D wishes to sell a building D owns to X Co. and X Co. is willing to buy it. As a business matter, it makes no difference to X Co. whether it takes the title directly or indirectly through its subsidiary S Co. or some other entity that X Co. controls. The applicability of subchapter F does not depend upon that formal distinction, because the subchapter includes within its operative framework transactions by entities controlled by X Co. Thus, subchapter F would apply to a sale of the building by D to S Co.

c. Party to the Transaction—The Director or a Related Person

D can have a conflicting interest in only two ways.

First, a conflicting interest can arise under either clause (i) or (ii) of the definition of "director's conflicting interest transaction." This will be the case if, under clause (i), the transaction is between D and X Co. A conflicting interest also will arise under clause (ii) if D is not a party to the transaction, but knows about it and knows that he or she has a material financial interest in it. The personal economic stake of the director must be in the transaction itself—that is, the director's gain must flow directly from the transaction. A remote gain (for example, a future reduction in tax rates in the local community) is not enough to give rise to a conflicting interest under clause (ii) of the definition.

Second, a conflicting interest for D can arise under clause (iii) of the definition from the involvement in the transaction of a "related person" of D that is either a party to the transaction or has a "material financial interest" in it. "Related person" is defined in section 8.60.

Circumstances may arise where a director could have a conflicting interest under more than one clause of the definition. For example, if Y Co. is a party to or interested in the transaction with X Co. and Y Co. is a related person of D, the matter would fall under clause (iii), but D also may have a conflicting interest under clause (ii) if D's economic interest in Y Co. is sufficiently material and if the importance of the transaction to Y Co. is sufficiently material.

A director may have relationships and connections to persons and institutions that are not specified in clause (iii) of the definition. Such relationships and connections fall outside subchapter F because the categories of persons described in clause (iii) constitute the exclusive universe for purposes of subchapter F. For example, in a challenged transaction between X Co. and Y Co., suppose the court confronts the argument that D also is a major creditor of Y Co. and that creditor status in Y Co. gives D a conflicting interest. The court should rule that D's creditor status in Y Co. does not fit any category of the definition; and therefore, the conflict of interest claim must be rejected by reason of section 8.61(a). The result would be different if Y Co.'s debt to D were of such economic significance to D that it would either fall under clause (ii) of the definition or, if it placed D in control of Y Co., it would fall under clause (iii) (because Y Co. is a related person of D under clause (iv) of the definition). To explore the example further, if D is also a shareholder of Y Co., but D does not have a material financial interest in the transaction and does not control Y Co., no director's conflicting interest transaction arises and the transaction cannot be challenged on conflict of interest grounds. To avoid any appearance of impropriety, D, nonetheless, could consider recusal from the other directors' deliberations and voting on the transaction between X Co. and Y Co.

Any director's interest in a transaction that meets the criteria of the definition renders the transaction a "director's conflicting interest transaction." If the director's interest satisfies those criteria, subchapter F draws no distinction between a director's interest that clashes with the interests of the corporation and a director's interest that coincides with, or is parallel to, or even furthers the interests of the corporation.

Routine business transactions frequently occur between companies with overlapping directors. If X Co. and Y Co. have routine, frequent business dealings with terms dictated by competitive market forces, then even if a director of X Co. has a relevant relationship with Y Co., the transactions would almost always be defensible, regardless of approval by disinterested directors or shareholders, on the ground that they are "fair." For example, a common transaction involves a purchase of the corporation's products or services by Y Co., or perhaps by D or a related person, at prices normally charged by the corporation. In such circumstances, it usually will not be difficult for D to show that the transaction was on arms-length terms and was fair. Even a purchase by D of a product of X Co. at a usual "employee's discount," although technically assailable as a conflicting interest transaction, would customarily be viewed as a routine incident of the office of director and, thus, "fair" to the corporation.

2. Control

The definition of "control" in section 8.60 contains two independent clauses. The first clause addresses the ability to elect or remove a majority of the members of an entity's governing body. That power can arise, for example, from articles of incorporation or a shareholders' agreement. The second clause addresses economic interest in the entity and may include, among other circumstances, financial structures that do not have voting interests or a governing body in the traditional sense, such as special purpose entities.

3. Relevant Time

The definition of director's conflicting interest transaction requires that, except where he or she is a party, the director know of the transaction at the "relevant time" as defined in section 8.60. Where the director lacks such knowledge, the risk to the corporation that the director's judgment might be improperly influenced, or the risk of unfair dealing by the director, is not present. In a corporation of significant size, routine transactions in the ordinary course of business, which typically involve decision making at lower management levels, normally will not be known to the director and, if that is the case, will not meet the "knowledge" requirement of clauses (ii) or (iii) of the definition of director's conflicting interest transaction.

4. Material Financial Interest

The "interest" of a director or a related person in a transaction can be direct or indirect (*e.g.*, as an owner of an entity or a beneficiary of a trust or estate), but it must be financial for there to exist a "director's conflicting interest transaction." Thus, for example, an interest in a transaction between X Co. and a director's alma mater, or any other transaction involving X Co. and a party with which D might have emotional involvement but no financial interest, would not give rise to a director's conflicting interest transaction. Moreover, whether a financial interest is material does not turn on any assertion by the possibly conflicted director that the interest in question would not impair his or her objectivity if called upon to vote on the authorization of the transaction. Instead, assuming a court challenge asserting the materiality of the financial interest, the standard calls upon the trier of fact to determine whether the objectivity of the director would reasonably be expected to have been impaired by the financial interest when voting on the matter. Thus, the standard is objective, not subjective.

Under clause (ii) of the definition of "director's conflicting interest transaction," at the relevant time a director must have knowledge of his or her financial interest in the transaction in addition to knowing about the transaction itself. As a practical matter, a director could not be influenced by a financial interest about which that director had no knowledge. For example, the possibly conflicted director might know about X Co.'s transaction with Y Co., but might not know that his or her money manager recently established a significant position in Y Co. stock for the director's portfolio. In such circumstances, the transaction with Y Co. would not fall within clause (ii), notwithstanding the portfolio investment's significance. If the director did not know about the Y Co. portfolio investment, it could not reasonably be expected to impair the objectivity of that director's judgment.

Similarly, under clause (iii) of that definition, a director must know about his or her related person's financial interest in the transaction for the matter to give rise to a "material financial interest" as defined in section 8.60. If there is such knowledge and "interest" (*i.e.*, the financial interest could reasonably be expected to influence the director's judgment), then the matter involves a director's conflicting interest transaction.

5.   *Related Person*

Six categories of "related person" of the director are set out in the definition of that term. These categories are specific, exclusive and preemptive.

The first three categories involve closely related family, or near-family, individuals as specified in clauses (i) through (iii). These clauses are exclusive insofar as family relationships are concerned and include adoptive relationships. The references to a "spouse" include a common law spouse. Clause (iii) covers personal, as opposed to business, relationships; for example, clause (iii) does not cover a lessee.

Regarding the subcategories of persons described in clause (v) from the perspective of X Co., certain of D's relationships with other entities and D's fiduciary relationships are always a sensitive concern, separate and apart from whether D has a financial interest in the transaction. Clause (v) reflects the policy judgment that D cannot escape D's legal obligation to act in the best interests of another person for whom D has such a relationship and, accordingly, that such a relationship (without regard to any financial interest on D's part) should cause the relevant entity to have "related person" status.

The term "employer" as used in clause (vi) is not separately defined but should be interpreted in light of the purpose of subchapter F. The relevant inquiry is whether D, because of an employment relationship with an employer who has a significant stake in the outcome of the transaction, is likely to be influenced to act in the interest of that employer rather than in the interest of X Co.

References in the foregoing to "director" or "D" include the term "officer" where relevant in section 2.02(b)(6) and section 8.70.

6.   *Fair to the Corporation*

The term "fair" to the corporation in subchapter F has a special meaning. The transaction, viewed as a whole, must have been beneficial to the corporation.

In considering the "fairness" of the transaction, the court will be required to consider not only the market fairness of the terms of the deal—whether it is comparable to what might have been obtainable in an arm's length transaction—but also (as the board of directors would have been required to do) whether the transaction was one that was reasonably likely to yield favorable results (or reduce detrimental results). Thus, if a manufacturing company that lacks sufficient working capital allocates some of its scarce funds to purchase at a market price a sailing yacht owned by one of its directors, it will not be easy to persuade the court that the transaction was "fair" in the sense that it was reasonably made to further the business interests of the corporation. The fact that the price paid for the yacht was a "fair" market price, and that the full measure of disclosures made by the director is beyond challenge, may still not be enough to defend and uphold the transaction.

a.   Consideration and other terms of the transaction

The fairness of the consideration and other transaction terms are to be judged at the relevant time. See section 8.61(b)(3). The relevant inquiry is whether the consideration paid or received by the corporation or the benefit expected to be realized by the corporation was adequate in relation to the obligations assumed or received or other consideration provided by or to the corporation. If the issue in a transaction is the "fairness" of a price, "fair" is not to be taken to imply that there is one single "fair" price, all others being "unfair." Generally a "fair" price is any price within a range that an unrelated party might have been willing to pay or willing to accept, as the case may be, for the relevant property, asset, service or commitment, following a normal arm's-length business negotiation. The same approach applies not only to gauging the fairness of price, but also to the fairness evaluation of any other key term of the deal.

Although the "fair" criterion used to assess the consideration under section 8.61(b)(3) is also a range rather than a point, the width of that range may be narrower than would be the case in an arm's-length transaction. For example, the quality and completeness of disclosures, if any, made by the conflicted director that bear upon the consideration in question are relevant in determining whether the consideration paid or received by the corporation, although otherwise commercially reasonable, was "fair" for purposes of section 8.61(b)(3).

b.   Process of decision and the director's conduct

In some circumstances, the behavior of the director having the conflicting interest may affect the finding and content of "fairness." Fair dealing requires that the director make "required disclosure" at the "relevant time" (both as defined) even if the director plays no role in arranging or negotiating the terms of the transaction. One illustration of unfair dealing is the director's failure to disclose fully the director's interest or hidden defects known to the director regarding the transaction. Another illustration would be the exertion by the director of improper pressure upon the other directors or other parties that might be involved with the transaction. Whether a transaction can be successfully challenged by reason of deficient or improper conduct, notwithstanding the fairness of the economic terms, will turn on the court's evaluation of the conduct and its impact on the transaction.

7.   *Required Disclosure*

An important element of subchapter F's safe harbor procedures is that those acting for the corporation be able to make an informed judgment. As an example of "required disclosure" (as defined), if D knows that the land the corporation is proposing to buy from D is sinking into an abandoned coal mine, D must disclose not only D's interest in the transaction but also that the land is subsiding. As a director of X Co., D may not invoke the "buyer beware" doctrine. On the other hand, D does not have any obligation to reveal the price that D paid for the property 10 years ago, or the fact that D inherited the property, because that information is not material to the board's evaluation of the property and its business decision whether to proceed with the transaction. Further, although material facts respecting the subject of the transaction must be disclosed, D is not required to reveal personal or subjective information that bears upon D's negotiating position (such as, for example, D's urgent need for cash, or the lowest price D would be willing to accept). This is true even though such information would be highly relevant to the corporation's decision-making in that, if the information were known to the corporation, it could enable the corporation to hold out for more favorable terms.

§ 8.61   Judicial Action

(a)   A transaction effected or proposed to be effected by the corporation (or by an entity controlled by the corporation) may not be the subject of equitable relief, or give rise to an award of damages or other sanctions against a director of the corporation, in a proceeding by a shareholder or by or in the right of the corporation, on the ground that the director has an interest respecting the transaction, if it is not a director's conflicting interest transaction.

(b)   A director's conflicting interest transaction may not be the subject of equitable relief, or give rise to an award of damages or other sanctions against a director of the corporation, in a proceeding by a shareholder or by or in the right of the corporation, on the ground that the director has an interest respecting the transaction, if:

(1)   directors' action respecting the transaction was taken in compliance with section 8.62 at any time; or

(2)   shareholders' action respecting the transaction was taken in compliance with section 8.63 at any time; or

(3)   the transaction, judged according to the circumstances at the relevant time, is established to have been fair to the corporation.

OFFICIAL COMMENT

Section 8.61 is the operational section of subchapter F, as it prescribes the judicial consequences of the other sections. In general terms:

- If the section 8.62 or 8.63 procedures are complied with, or if it is established that at the relevant time a director's conflicting interest transaction was fair to the corporation, then a director's conflicting interest transaction is immune from attack by a shareholder or the corporation on the ground of an interest of the director. However, if the transaction is vulnerable to attack on some other ground, observance of subchapter F's procedures does not make it less so.

- If a transaction is *not* a director's conflicting interest transaction as defined in section 8.60, then the transaction may *not* be enjoined, rescinded, or made the basis of other sanction on the ground of a conflict of interest of a director, regardless of whether it went through the procedures of subchapter F. In that sense, subchapter F is specifically intended to be both comprehensive and exclusive.

- If a director's conflicting interest transaction that was not at any time the subject of action taken in compliance with section 8.62 or 8.63 is challenged on grounds of the director's conflicting interest, and is not shown to be fair to the corporation, then the court may take such remedial action as it considers appropriate under the applicable law of the jurisdiction.

1. Section 8.61(a)

Section 8.61(a) makes clear that the bright-line definition of "director's conflicting interest transaction" is exclusive with respect to a court's review of a director's interest in a transaction. So, for example, a transaction will not constitute a director's conflicting interest transaction and, therefore, will not be subject to judicial review on the ground that a director had an interest in the transaction, where the transaction is made with a relative of a director who is not one of the relatives specified in the definition of "related person," or on the ground of an alleged interest other than a material financial interest, such as a financial interest of the director that is not material, as defined in section 8.60, or a nonfinancial interest. If, however, there is reason to believe that the fairness of a transaction involving D could be questioned, D should subject the transaction to the safe harbor procedures of subchapter F. The procedures of section 8.62 (and, to a lesser extent, section 8.63) may be used for many transactions that lie outside the definitions of section 8.60.

2. Section 8.61(b)

Section 8.61(b)(1) provides a defense in a proceeding challenging a director's conflicting interest transaction if the procedures of section 8.62 have been properly followed.

The plaintiff may challenge the availability of that defense based on a failure to meet the specific requirements of section 8.62 or to conform with general standards of director conduct. For example, a challenge addressed to section 8.62 compliance might question whether the acting directors were "qualified directors" or might dispute the quality and completeness of the disclosures made by D to the qualified directors. If such a challenge is successful, the board action is ineffective for purposes of section 8.61(b)(1) and both D and the transaction may be subject to the full range of remedies that might apply, absent the safe harbor, unless the fairness of the transaction can be established under section 8.61(b)(3). The fact that a transaction has been nominally passed through safe harbor procedures does not preclude a subsequent challenge based on any failure to meet the requirements of section 8.62. A challenge to the effectiveness of board action for purposes of section 8.61(b)(1) might also assert that, although the conflicted director's conduct in connection with the process of approval by qualified directors may have been consistent with the statute's expectations, the qualified directors dealing with the matter did not act in good faith or on reasonable inquiry. The kind of relief that may be appropriate when qualified directors have approved a transaction but have not acted in good faith or have failed to become reasonably informed—and, again, where the fairness of the transaction has not been established under section 8.61(b)(3)—will depend heavily on the facts of the individual case.

Section 8.61(b)(2) regarding shareholders' approval of the transaction is the matching piece to section 8.61(b)(1) regarding directors' approval.

The language "at any time" in these provisions permits the directors or the shareholders to ratify a director's conflicting interest transaction after the fact for purposes of subchapter F.

Section 8.61(b)(3) permits a showing that a director's conflicting interest transaction was fair to the corporation even if there was no compliance with section 8.62 or 8.63. Under section 8.61(b)(3) the interested director has the burden of establishing that the transaction was fair.

* * *

Note on Directors' Compensation

Although directors' fees and other forms of director compensation are typically set by the board of directors and are specifically authorized by section 8.11 of the Act, they do involve a director's conflicting interest transaction in which most if not all of the directors may not be qualified directors. Therefore, board action on directors' compensation and benefits would be subject to judicial sanction if they are not favorably acted upon by shareholders pursuant to section 8.63 or if they are not in the circumstances fair to the corporation pursuant to section 8.61(b)(3).

§ 8.62   Directors' Action

(a)   Directors' action respecting a director's conflicting interest transaction is effective for purposes of section 8.61(b)(1) if the transaction has been authorized by the affirmative vote of a majority (but no fewer than two) of the qualified directors who voted on the transaction, after required disclosure by the conflicted director of information not already known by such qualified directors, or after modified disclosure in compliance with subsection (b), provided that:

(1)   the qualified directors have deliberated and voted outside the presence of and without the participation by any other director; and

(2)   where the action has been taken by a board committee, all members of the committee were qualified directors, and either (i) the committee was composed of all the qualified directors on the board of directors or (ii) the members of the committee were appointed by the affirmative vote of a majority of the qualified directors on the board of directors.

(b)   Notwithstanding subsection (a), when a transaction is a director's conflicting interest transaction only because a related person described in clause (v) or (vi) of the definition of "related person" in section 8.60 is a party to or has a material financial interest in the transaction, the conflicted director is not obligated to make required disclosure to the extent that the director reasonably believes that doing so would violate a duty imposed under law, a legally enforceable obligation of confidentiality, or a professional ethics rule, provided that the conflicted director discloses to the qualified directors voting on the transaction:

(1)   all information required to be disclosed that is not so violative,

(2)   the existence and nature of the director's conflicting interest, and

(3)   the nature of the conflicted director's duty not to disclose the confidential information.

(c)   A majority (but no fewer than two) of all the qualified directors on the board of directors, or on the board committee, constitutes a quorum for purposes of action that complies with this section.

(d)   Where directors' action under this section does not satisfy a quorum or voting requirement applicable to the authorization of the transaction by reason of the articles of incorporation or bylaws or a provision of law, independent action to satisfy those authorization requirements shall be taken by the board of directors or a board committee, in which action directors who are not qualified directors may participate.

OFFICIAL COMMENT

Section 8.62 provides the procedure for action by the board of directors or by a board committee under subchapter F. In the normal course this section, together with section 8.61(b), will be the key method for addressing directors' conflicting interest transactions. Any discussion of section 8.62 must have in mind the requirements that directors act in good faith and on reasonable inquiry. See section 8.30. Director action that does not comply with those requirements, even if otherwise in compliance with section 8.62, will be subject to challenge and not be given effect under section 8.62. See the Official Comment to section 8.61(b).

1.   *Section 8.62(a)*

The definition of "qualified director" in section 1.43(a)(4) excludes not only a director who is conflicted directly or because of a person specified in the categories of the "related person" definition in section 8.60, but also any director with a familial, financial, employment, professional or other relationship with *another director for whom the transaction is a director's conflicting interest transaction* that would be likely to impair the objectivity of the first director's judgment when participating in a vote on the transaction.

Action under section 8.62 may take the form of committee action meeting the requirements of subsection (a)(2). The requirements for effective committee action are intended to preclude the appointment as committee members of a favorably inclined minority from among all the qualified directors. With respect to required disclosure under subsection (a), if there is more than one conflicted director interested in the transaction, the need for required disclosure would apply to each.

2. Section 8.62(b)

Section 8.62(b) accommodates situations where a director who has a conflicting interest is not able to comply fully with the disclosure requirement of subsection (a) because of an extrinsic duty of confidentiality that such director reasonably believes to exist. The director may, for example, be prohibited from making full disclosure because of legal restrictions that happen to apply to the transaction (e.g., grand jury seal or national security statute) or professional ethics rule (e.g., attorney-client confidentiality). The most frequent use of subsection (b), however, will likely involve directors who have conflicting fiduciary obligations. If D is also a director of Y Co., D may have acquired confidential information from one or both directorships relevant to a transaction between X Co. and Y Co., that D cannot reveal to one without violating a fiduciary duty owed to the other. In such circumstances, subsection (b) enables the conflicting interest complication to be presented for consideration under subsection (a), and thereby enables X Co. (and Y Co.) and D to secure for the transaction the protection afforded by subchapter F even though D cannot, by reason of applicable law, confidentiality strictures or a professional ethics rule, make the full disclosure otherwise required.

To comply with section 8.62(b), D must meet all three requirements set forth in clauses (1), (2) and (3). D must then play no personal role in the board's (or committee's) ultimate deliberations or action. The purpose of subsection (b) is to make it clear that the provisions of subchapter F may be employed to "safe harbor" a transaction in circumstances where a conflicted director cannot, because of enforced fiduciary silence, disclose all the known facts. A director could, of course, encounter the same problem of mandated silence with regard to any matter that comes before the board; that is, the problem of forced silence is not linked at all to the problems of transactions involving a conflicting interest of a director. It could happen that at the same board meeting of X Co. at which D invokes subsection (b), another director who has no financial interest in the transaction might conclude that under applicable law he or she is bound to silence (because of attorney-client confidentiality, for example) and would under general principles of sound director conduct withdraw from participation in the board's deliberations and action. Of course, if D invokes subsection (b) and does not make disclosures that would otherwise be required under subsection (a) before leaving the meeting, the qualified directors may decline to act on the transaction out of concern that D knows (or may know) something they do not. On the other hand, if D is subject to an extrinsic duty of confidentiality but has no knowledge of material facts that should otherwise be disclosed, D would normally state just that and subsection (b) would be irrelevant. Having disclosed the existence and nature of the conflicting interest, D would thereby comply with the "required disclosure" as defined under section 8.60.

Although section 8.62(b) will apply to the recurring situation where transacting corporations have common directors (or where a director of one party is an officer of the other), it should not otherwise be read as attempting to address the scope, or mandate the consequences, of various silence-privileges.

Section 8.62(b) is available to D if a transaction is a director's conflicting interest transaction only because a related person described in clauses (v) or (vi) of the definition of that term in section 8.60 is a party to or has a material financial interest in the transaction. Its availability is so limited because in those instances a director owes a fiduciary duty to such a related person. If D or a related person of D other than a related person described in clauses (v) or (vi) of the definition of is a party to or has a material financial interest in the transaction, D's only options are satisfying the required disclosure obligation on an unrestricted basis, abandoning the transaction, or accepting the risk of establishing fairness under section 8.61(b)(3), if the transaction is challenged in a court proceeding.

Whenever a conflicted director proceeds in the manner provided in subsection (b), the other directors should recognize that the conflicted director may have information that, but for the narrow exception set forth in subsection (b), D would be required to reveal to the qualified directors who are acting on the transaction—information that could well indicate that the transaction would be either favorable or unfavorable for X Co.

3. Section 8.62(d)

Subsection 8.62(d) underscores the fact that the directors' voting procedures and requirements set forth in subsections (a) through (c) address only the director's conflicting interest. Thus, in any case where the quorum or voting requirements for substantive approval of a transaction differ from the quorum or voting requirements for "safe harbor" protection under section 8.62, the directors may find it necessary to conduct (and record in the minutes of the proceedings) two separate votes—one for section 8.62 purposes and the other for substantive approval purposes.

§ 8.63 Shareholders' Action

(a) Shareholders' action respecting a director's conflicting interest transaction is effective for purposes of section 8.61(b)(2) if a majority of the votes cast by the holders of all qualified shares are in favor of the transaction after (i) notice to shareholders describing the action to be taken respecting the transaction, (ii) provision to the corporation of the information referred to in subsection (b), and (iii) communication to the shareholders entitled to vote on the transaction of the information that is the subject of required disclosure, to the extent the information is not known by them. In the case of shareholders' action at a meeting, the shareholders entitled to vote shall be determined as of the record date for notice of the meeting.

(b) A director who has a conflicting interest respecting the transaction shall, before the shareholders' vote, inform the secretary or other officer or agent of the corporation authorized to tabulate votes, in writing, of the number of shares that the director knows are not qualified shares under subsection (c), and the identity of the holders of those shares.

(c) For purposes of this section: (i) "holder" means and "held by" refers to shares held by a record shareholder, a beneficial shareholder, and an unrestricted voting trust beneficial owner; and (ii) "qualified shares" means all shares entitled to be voted with respect to the transaction except for shares that the secretary or other officer or agent of the corporation authorized to tabulate votes either knows, or under subsection (b) is notified, are held by (A) a director who has a conflicting interest respecting the transaction or (B) a related person of the director (excluding a person described in clause (vi) of the definition of "related person" in section 8.60).

(d) A majority of the votes entitled to be cast by the holders of all qualified shares constitutes a quorum for purposes of compliance with this section. Subject to the provisions of subsection (e), shareholders' action that otherwise complies with this section is not affected by the presence of holders, or by the voting, of shares that are not qualified shares.

(e) If a shareholders' vote does not comply with subsection (a) solely because of a director's failure to comply with subsection (b), and if the director establishes that the failure was not intended to influence and did not in fact determine the outcome of the vote, the court may take such action respecting the transaction and the director, and may give such effect, if any, to the shareholders' vote, as the court considers appropriate in the circumstances.

(f) Where shareholders' action under this section does not satisfy a quorum or voting requirement applicable to the authorization of the transaction by reason of the articles of incorporation or the bylaws or a provision of law, independent action to satisfy those authorization requirements shall be taken by the shareholders, in which action shares that are not qualified shares may participate.

OFFICIAL COMMENT

Section 8.63 provides the machinery for shareholders' action that confers safe harbor protection for a director's conflicting interest transaction, just as section 8.62 provides the machinery for directors' action that confers subchapter F safe harbor protection for such a transaction.

1. Section 8.63(a)

Section 8.63(a) specifies the procedure required to confer effective safe harbor protection for a director's conflicting interest transaction through a vote of shareholders. In advance of the vote, three steps must be taken: (i) shareholders must be given timely and adequate notice describing the transaction; (ii) D must disclose the information called for in subsection (b); and (iii) required disclosure (as defined in section 8.60) must be made to the shareholders entitled to vote. Shareholder action that complies with subsection (a) may be taken at any time, before or after the corporation becomes legally obligated to complete the transaction.

Section 8.63 does not contain a "limited disclosure" provision that is comparable to section 8.62(b). Thus, the safe harbor protection of subchapter F is not available through shareholder action under section 8.63 in a case where D either remains silent or makes less than required disclosure because of an extrinsic duty of confidentiality

2. Section 8.63(b)

In many circumstances, the secretary or other person charged with counting votes on behalf of X Co. will have no way to know which of X Co.'s outstanding shares should be excluded from the vote. Section 8.63(b) (together with subsection (c)) therefore obligates a director who has a conflicting interest respecting the transaction, as a prerequisite to safe harbor protection by shareholder action, to provide information known to the director with respect to the shares that are not qualified.

If the person counting the votes knows, or is notified under subsection (b), that particular shares should be excluded but for some reason fails to exclude them from the count and their inclusion in the vote does not affect its outcome, the shareholders' vote will stand. If the improper inclusion determines the outcome, the shareholders' vote fails because it does not comply with subsection (a). Subsection (e) permits the court to take the appropriate action in cases where the notification under subsection (b) is defective but not determinative of the outcome of the vote.

3. Section 8.63(c)

The definition of "qualified shares" in section 8.63(c) does not exclude shares held by entities or persons described in clause (vi) of the definition of "related person" in section 8.60, *i.e.*, a person that is, or is an entity that is controlled by, an employer of D. If D is an employee of Y Co., that fact does not prevent Y Co. from exercising its usual rights to vote any shares it may hold in X Co. D may be unaware of, and would not necessarily monitor, whether his or her employer holds X Co. shares. Moreover, D will typically have no control over his or her employer and how it may vote its X Co. shares.

4. Section 8.63(e)

If D did not provide the information required under section 8.63(b), on its face the shareholders' action is not in compliance with subsection (a) and D has no safe harbor under subsection (a). In the absence of that safe harbor, D can be put to the burden of establishing the fairness of the transaction under section 8.61(b)(3).

That result is proper where D's failure to inform was determinative of the vote results or, worse, was part of a deliberate effort on D's part to influence the outcome. If, however, D's omission was not motivated by D's effort to influence the integrity of the voting process (for example, it was the result of D's negligence), and the voting of the unreported shares was not determinative of the outcome of the vote, then the court should be free to fashion an appropriate response to the situation in light of all the considerations at the time of its decision.

Despite the presumption of regularity customarily accorded the secretary's record, a plaintiff may go behind the secretary's record for purposes of subsection (e).

5. Section 8.63(f)

Section 8.63(f) underscores that the shareholders' voting procedures and requirements set forth in subsections (a) through (e) treat only the director's conflicting interest. A transaction that receives a shareholders' vote that complies with subchapter F may well fail to achieve a different vote or quorum that may be required for substantive approval of the transaction under other applicable statutory provisions or provisions contained in X Co.'s articles of incorporation or bylaws, and vice versa. Thus, in any case where the quorum or voting requirements for substantive approval of a transaction differ from the quorum or voting requirements for "safe harbor" protection under section 8.63, the corporation may find it necessary to conduct (and record in the minutes of the proceedings) two separate shareholder votes—one for section 8.63 purposes and the other for substantive approval purposes (or, if appropriate, conduct two separate tabulations of one vote).

SUBCHAPTER G. BUSINESS OPPORTUNITIES

§ 8.70 Business Opportunities

(a) If a director or officer pursues or takes advantage of a business opportunity directly, or indirectly through or on behalf of another person, that action may not be the subject of equitable relief, or give rise to an award of damages or other sanctions against the director, officer or other person, in a proceeding by or in the right of the corporation on the ground that the opportunity should have first been offered to the corporation, if

(1) before the director, officer or other person becomes legally obligated respecting the opportunity the director or officer brings it to the attention of the corporation and either:

(i) action by qualified directors disclaiming the corporation's interest in the opportunity is taken in compliance with the same procedures as are set forth in section 8.62, or

(ii) shareholders' action disclaiming the corporation's interest in the opportunity is taken in compliance with the procedures set forth in section 8.63,

in either case as if the decision being made concerned a director's conflicting interest transaction, except that, rather than making "required disclosure" as defined in section 8.60, the director or officer shall have made prior disclosure to those acting on behalf of the corporation of all material facts concerning the business opportunity known to the director or officer; or

(2) the duty to offer the corporation the business opportunity has been limited or eliminated pursuant to a provision of the articles of incorporation adopted (and where required, made effective by action of qualified directors) in accordance with section 2.02(b)(6).

(b) In any proceeding seeking equitable relief or other remedies based upon an alleged improper pursuit or taking advantage of a business opportunity by a director or officer, directly, or indirectly through or on behalf of another person, the fact that the director or officer did not employ the procedure described in subsection (a)(1)(i) or (ii) before pursuing or taking advantage of the opportunity shall not create an implication that the opportunity should have been first presented to the corporation or alter the burden of proof otherwise applicable to establish that the director or officer breached a duty to the corporation in the circumstances.

OFFICIAL COMMENT

Section 8.70(a)(1) provides a safe harbor for a director or officer weighing possible involvement with a prospective business opportunity that might constitute a "corporate opportunity." The phrase "directly, or indirectly through or on behalf of another person" recognizes the need to cover transactions pursued or effected either directly by the director or officer or indirectly through or on behalf of another person, which might be a related person as defined in section 8.60 or a person which is not a related person. By action of the board of directors or shareholders of the corporation under section 8.70(a)(1), the director or officer can obtain a disclaimer of the corporation's interest in the matter before proceeding with such involvement. In the alternative, the corporation may, among other things, (i) decline to disclaim its interest, (ii) delay a decision respecting granting a disclaimer pending receipt from the director or officer of additional information (or for any other reason), or (iii) attach conditions to the disclaimer it grants under section 8.70(a)(1).

The safe harbor provided under section 8.70(a)(1) may be utilized only for a specific business opportunity. A broader advance safe harbor for any, or one or more classes or categories of, business opportunities must meet the requirements of section 2.02(b)(6). Section 8.70(a)(2) confirms that if the duty of an officer or director to present an opportunity has been limited or eliminated by a provision in the articles of incorporation under section 2.02(b)(6) (and, in the case of officers, appropriate action by qualified directors as required by that section), a safe harbor exists in connection with the pursuit or taking of the opportunity. The common law doctrine of "corporate opportunity" has long been recognized as a part of the director's duty of loyalty and, under court decisions, extends to officers. See section 8.30(a) and its Official Comment. The doctrine recognizes that the corporation has a right prior to that of its directors or officers to act on certain business opportunities that come to the attention of the directors or officers. In such situations, a director or officer who acts on the opportunity for the benefit of the director or officer or another person without having first presented it to the corporation can be held to have "usurped" or "intercepted" a right of the corporation. A defendant director or officer who is found by a court to have violated the duty of loyalty in this regard, as well as related or other persons involved in the transaction, may be subject to damages or possible equitable remedies, including injunction, disgorgement or the imposition of a constructive trust in favor of the corporation. Although the doctrine's concept is easily described, whether it will be found to apply in a given case depends on the facts and circumstances of the particular situation and is thus frequently unpredictable.

In recognition that the corporation need not pursue every business opportunity of which it becomes aware, an opportunity coming within the doctrine's criteria that has been properly presented to and declined by the corporation may then be pursued or taken by the presenting director or officer without breach of the duty of loyalty.

The fact-intensive nature of the corporate opportunity doctrine resists statutory definition. Instead, subchapter G employs the broader notion of "business opportunity" that encompasses any opportunity, without regard to whether it would come within the judicial definition of a "corporate opportunity," as it may have been developed by courts in a jurisdiction. When properly employed, subchapter G provides a safe-harbor mechanism enabling a director or officer to pursue an opportunity directly, or indirectly through or on behalf of another person, free of possible challenge claiming conflict with the director's or officer's duty on the ground that the opportunity should first have been offered to the corporation. Section 8.70 is modeled on the safe-harbor and approval procedures of subchapter F pertaining to directors' conflicting interest transactions with, however, some modifications necessary to accommodate differences in the two matters addressed.

1. Section 8.70(a)(1)

Section 8.70(a)(1) describes the safe harbor available to a director or officer who elects to subject a business opportunity, regardless of whether the opportunity would be classified as a "corporate opportunity," to the disclosure and approval procedures set forth in that section. The safe harbor provided is as broad as that provided for a director's conflicting interest transaction in section 8.61. If the director or officer makes the prescribed disclosure of the facts specified and the corporation's interest in the opportunity is disclaimed by director action under subsection (a)(1)(i) or shareholder action under subsection (a)(1)(ii), the director or officer has foreclosed any claimed breach of the duty of loyalty and may not be subject to equitable relief, damages or other sanctions if the director or officer thereafter pursues or takes the opportunity for his or her own account or through or for the benefit of another person. As a general proposition, disclaimer by director action under subsection (a)(1)(i) must meet all of the requirements provided in section 8.62 with respect to a director's conflicting interest transaction and disclaimer by shareholder action under subsection (a)(1)(ii) must likewise meet all of the requirements for shareholder action under section 8.63. Note, however, several important differences.

First, in contrast to director or shareholder action under sections 8.62 and 8.63, which may be taken at any time, section 8.70(a)(1) requires that the director or officer present the opportunity and secure director or shareholder action disclaiming it *before* the director of officer or other person involved through or on behalf of the director or officer becomes legally obligated respecting the opportunity. The safe harbor concept contemplates that the corporation's decision maker will have full freedom of action in deciding whether the corporation should take over a proffered opportunity or disclaim the corporation's interest in it. If the director or officer could seek ratification after the legal obligation respecting the opportunity arises, the option of taking over the opportunity would, in most cases, be foreclosed to the corporation. The safe harbor's benefit is available only when the corporation can entertain the opportunity in a fully objective way.

The second difference relates to the necessary disclosure. Instead of employing section 8.60's definition of "required disclosure" which is incorporated in sections 8.62 and 8.63 and includes "the existence and nature of the director's conflicting interest," the disclosure obligation of section 8.70(a)(1) requires only that the director or officer reveal all material facts concerning the business opportunity known to the director or officer. The safe harbor procedure shields the director or officer even if a material fact regarding the business opportunity is not disclosed, so long as the proffering director or officer had no knowledge of that fact.

2. Section 8.70(b)

Section 8.70(b) reflects a fundamental difference between the coverage of subchapters F and G. Because subchapter F provides an exclusive definition of "director's conflicting interest transaction," any transaction meeting the definition that is not approved in accordance with the provisions of subchapter F is not entitled to its safe harbor. Unless the interested director can, upon challenge, establish the transaction's fairness, the director's conduct is presumptively actionable and subject to the full range of remedies that might otherwise be awarded by a court. In contrast, the concept of "business opportunity" under section 8.70 is not defined but is intended to be broader than what might be regarded as an actionable "corporate opportunity." This approach reflects the fact-intensive nature of the corporate opportunity doctrine, with the result that a director or officer may be inclined to seek safe harbor protection under section 8.70 before pursuing an opportunity that may or may not be a "corporate opportunity." Likewise, a director or officer may conclude that a business opportunity is not a "corporate opportunity" under applicable law and choose to pursue it without seeking a disclaimer by the corporation under subsection (a)(1). Accordingly, subsection (b) provides that a decision not to seek the safe harbor offered by subsection (a)(1) neither creates a negative implication nor alters the burden of proof in any subsequent proceeding seeking damages or equitable relief based upon an alleged improper taking of a "corporate opportunity."

CHAPTER 9. DOMESTICATION AND CONVERSION

INTRODUCTORY COMMENT

This chapter provides procedures by which a domestic corporation may become a foreign corporation or a different form of domestic or foreign entity and, conversely, a foreign corporation or an eligible entity may become a domestic corporation. These procedures are:

- **Domestication.** The procedures in subchapter 9B permit a corporation to change its state of incorporation, thus allowing a domestic corporation to become a foreign corporation or a foreign corporation to become a domestic corporation.

- **Conversion.** The procedures in subchapter 9C permit a domestic corporation to become a domestic or foreign eligible entity and also permit a domestic or foreign eligible entity to become a domestic corporation.

The provisions of this chapter apply only if a domestic corporation is present either immediately before or immediately after a domestication or conversion.

Note on Adoption: Some states may wish to generalize the provisions of this chapter so that they are not limited to transactions involving a domestic business corporation. For example, a state may wish to permit a domestic limited partnership to become a domestic limited liability company. The Model Entity Transactions Act prepared by the Uniform Law Commission is such a generalized statute. Some states have elected to include transactions that are described in chapter 9 as domestications in their definition of conversions and not to refer to domestication separately.

SUBCHAPTER A. PRELIMINARY PROVISIONS

§ 9.01 Definitions

As used in this chapter:

"Conversion" means a transaction pursuant to subchapter C.

"Converted entity" means the converting entity as it continues in existence after a conversion.

"Converting entity" means the domestic corporation or eligible entity that approves a plan of conversion pursuant to section 9.32 or the foreign eligible entity that approves a conversion pursuant to the organic law of the eligible entity.

"Domesticated corporation" means the domesticating corporation as it continues in existence after a domestication.

"Domesticating corporation" means the domestic corporation that approves a plan of domestication pursuant to section 9.21 or the foreign corporation that approves a domestication pursuant to the organic law of the foreign corporation.

"Domestication" means a transaction pursuant to subchapter B.

"Protected agreement" means:

(i)   a document evidencing indebtedness of a domestic corporation or eligible entity and any related agreement in effect immediately before the enactment date;

(ii)   an agreement that is binding on a domestic corporation or eligible entity immediately before the enactment date;

(iii) the articles of incorporation or bylaws of a domestic corporation or the organic rules of a domestic eligible entity, in each case in effect immediately before the enactment date; or

(iv)   an agreement that is binding on any of the shareholders, members, interest holders, directors or other governors of a domestic corporation or eligible entity, in their capacities as such, immediately before the enactment date.

For purposes of this definition and sections 9.20 and 9.30, "enactment date" means the first date on which the law of this state authorized a transaction having the effect of a domestication or a conversion, as applicable.

Note on adoption: When adopting the definition of "protected agreement," a state could consider setting out in the last sentence of the definition the actual dates when domestication and conversion statutes were first enacted in the state so those dates would be apparent on the face of the statute.

§ 9.02   Excluded Transactions [Optional]

This chapter may not be used to effect a transaction that:

(a)   [converts a company organized on the mutual principle to one organized on the basis of share ownership]; or

(b)   [other examples]

Note on adoption: A state should use this section to list those situations in which the state has enacted specific legislation governing the domestication or conversion of domestic corporations that engage in particular types of activities or that do business in a regulated industry. Mutual to share conversions (for instance, of an insurance company, bank, savings institution or credit union)) are examples of such transactions.

§ 9.03   Required Approvals [Optional]

If a domestic or foreign corporation or eligible entity may not be a party to a merger without the approval of the [attorney general], the [department of banking], the [department of insurance] or the [public utility commission], and the applicable statutes or regulations do not specifically deal with transactions under this chapter but do require such approval for mergers, a corporation or eligible entity shall not be a party to a transaction under this chapter without the prior approval of that agency or official.

Note on adoption: Section 9.03 is an optional provision that should be considered in states where corporations or other entities that conduct regulated activities, such as banking, insurance or the provision of public utility services, are incorporated or organized under general laws instead of under special laws applicable only to entities conducting the regulated activity. If this section is used, the list of officials and agencies should be conformed to the laws of the enacting state.

§ 9.04 Relationship of Chapter to Other Laws [Optional]

A transaction effected under this chapter may not create or impair a right, duty or obligation of a person under the statutory law of this state other than this chapter relating to a change in control, business combination, control-share acquisition, or similar transaction involving a domesticating or converting domestic corporation, unless the approval of the plan of domestication or conversion is by a vote of the shareholders or the board of directors which would be sufficient to create or impair the right, duty or obligation directly under that law.

SUBCHAPTER B. DOMESTICATION

§ 9.20 Domestication

(a) By complying with the provisions of this subchapter applicable to foreign corporations, a foreign corporation may become a domestic corporation if the domestication is permitted by the organic law of the foreign corporation.

(b) By complying with the provisions of this subchapter, a domestic corporation may become a foreign corporation pursuant to a plan of domestication if the domestication is permitted by the organic law of the foreign corporation.

(c) The plan of domestication must include:

    (1) the name of the domesticating corporation;

    (2) the name and jurisdiction of formation of the domesticated corporation;

    (3) the manner and basis of reclassifying the shares of the domesticating corporation into shares or other securities, obligations, rights to acquire shares or other securities, cash, other property, or any combination of the foregoing;

    (4) the proposed articles of incorporation and bylaws of the domesticated corporation; and

    (5) the other terms and conditions of the domestication.

(d) In addition to the requirements of subsection (c), a plan of domestication may contain any other provision not prohibited by law.

(e) The terms of a plan of domestication may be made dependent upon facts objectively ascertainable outside the plan in accordance with section 1.20(k).

(f) If a protected agreement of a domestic domesticating corporation in effect immediately before the domestication becomes effective contains a provision applying to a merger of the corporation and the agreement does not refer to a domestication of the corporation, the provision applies to a domestication of the corporation as if the domestication were a merger until such time as the provision is first amended after the enactment date.

§ 9.21 Action on a Plan of Domestication

In the case of a domestication of a domestic corporation into a foreign jurisdiction, the plan of domestication shall be adopted in the following manner:

    (a) The plan of domestication shall first be adopted by the board of directors.

(b)   The plan of domestication shall then be approved by the shareholders. In submitting the plan of domestication to the shareholders for approval, the board of directors shall recommend that the shareholders approve the plan, unless (i) the board of directors makes a determination that because of conflicts of interest or other special circumstances it should not make such a recommendation or (ii) section 8.26 applies. If either (i) or (ii) applies, the board shall inform the shareholders of the basis for its so proceeding.

(c)   The board of directors may set conditions for approval of the plan of domestication by the shareholders or the effectiveness of the plan of domestication.

(d)   If the approval of the shareholders is to be given at a meeting, the corporation shall notify each shareholder, regardless of whether entitled to vote, of the meeting of shareholders at which the plan of domestication is to be submitted for approval. The notice must state that the purpose, or one of the purposes, of the meeting is to consider the plan of domestication and must contain or be accompanied by a copy or summary of the plan. The notice must include or be accompanied by a copy of the articles of incorporation and the bylaws as they will be in effect immediately after the domestication.

(e)   Unless the articles of incorporation, or the board of directors acting pursuant to subsection (c), require a greater vote or a greater quorum, approval of the plan of domestication requires (i) the approval of the shareholders at a meeting at which a quorum exists consisting of a majority of the votes entitled to be cast on the plan, and, (ii) except as provided in subsection (f), the approval of each class or series of shares voting as a separate voting group at a meeting at which a quorum of the voting group exists consisting of a majority of the votes entitled to be cast on the plan by that voting group.

(f)   The articles of incorporation may expressly limit or eliminate the separate voting rights provided in subsection (e)(ii) as to any class or series of shares, except when the articles of incorporation of the foreign corporation resulting from the domestication include what would be in effect an amendment that would entitle the class or series to vote as a separate group under section 10.04 if it were a proposed amendment of the articles of incorporation of the domestic domesticating corporation.

(g)   If as a result of a domestication one or more shareholders of a domestic domesticating corporation would become subject to interest holder liability, approval of the plan of domestication shall require the signing in connection with the domestication, by each such shareholder, of a separate written consent to become subject to such interest holder liability, unless in the case of a shareholder that already has interest holder liability with respect to the domesticating corporation, the terms and conditions of the interest holder liability with respect to the domesticated corporation are substantially identical to those of the existing interest holder liability (other than for changes that eliminate or reduce such interest holder liability).

§ 9.22   Articles of Domestication; Effectiveness

(a)   After (i) a plan of domestication of a domestic corporation has been adopted and approved as required by this Act, or (ii) a foreign corporation that is the domesticating corporation has approved a domestication as required under its organic law, articles of domestication shall be signed by the domesticating corporation. The articles must set forth:

(1)   the name of the domesticating corporation and its jurisdiction of formation;

(2)   the name and jurisdiction of formation of the domesticated corporation; and

(3)   if the domesticating corporation is a domestic corporation, a statement that the plan of domestication was approved in accordance with this chapter or, if the domesticating corporation is a foreign corporation, a statement that the domestication was approved in accordance with its organic law.

(b)   If the domesticated corporation is a domestic corporation, the articles of domestication must attach articles of incorporation of the domesticated corporation that satisfy the requirements of section 2.02. Provisions that would not be required to be included in restated articles of incorporation may be omitted from the articles of incorporation attached to the articles of domestication.

(c)   The articles of domestication shall be delivered to the secretary of state for filing, and shall take effect at the effective date determined in accordance with section 1.23.

(d)   If the domesticated corporation is a domestic corporation, the domestication becomes effective when the articles of domestication are effective. If the domesticated corporation is a foreign corporation, the domestication becomes effective on the later of (i) the date and time provided by the organic law of the domesticated corporation, and (ii) when the articles of domestication are effective.

(e)   If the domesticating corporation is a foreign corporation that is registered to do business in this state under chapter 15, its registration statement shall be cancelled automatically when the domestication becomes effective.

§ 9.23   Amendment of Plan of Domestication; Abandonment

(a)   A plan of domestication of a domestic corporation may be amended:

(1)   in the same manner as the plan was approved, if the plan does not provide for the manner in which it may be amended; or

(2)   in the manner provided in the plan, except that a shareholder that was entitled to vote on or consent to approval of the plan is entitled to vote on or consent to any amendment of the plan that will change:

(i)   the amount or kind of shares or other securities, obligations, rights to acquire shares or other securities, cash, other property, or any combination of the foregoing, to be received by any of the shareholders of the domesticating corporation under the plan;

(ii)   the articles of incorporation or bylaws of the domesticated corporation that will be in effect immediately after the domestication becomes effective, except for changes that do not require approval of the shareholders of the domesticated corporation under its organic law or its proposed articles of incorporation or bylaws as set forth in the plan; or

(iii)   any of the other terms or conditions of the plan, if the change would adversely affect the shareholder in any material respect.

(b)   After a plan of domestication has been adopted and approved by a domestic corporation as required by this subchapter, and before the articles of domestication have become effective, the plan may be abandoned by the corporation without action by its shareholders in accordance with any procedures set forth in the plan or, if no such procedures are set forth in the plan, in the manner determined by the board of directors.

(c)   If a domestication is abandoned after the articles of domestication have been delivered to the secretary of state for filing but before the articles of domestication have become effective, articles of abandonment, signed by the domesticating corporation, must be delivered to the secretary of state for filing before the articles of domestication become effective. The articles of abandonment take effect upon filing, and the domestication shall be deemed abandoned and shall not become effective. The articles of abandonment must contain:

(1)   the name of the domesticating corporation;

(2)   the date on which the articles of domestication were filed by the secretary of state; and

(3)   a statement that the domestication has been abandoned in accordance with this section.

§ 9.24   Effect of Domestication

(a)   When a domestication becomes effective:

(1)   all property owned by, and every contract right possessed by, the domesticating corporation are the property and contract rights of the domesticated corporation without transfer, reversion or impairment;

(2)   all debts, obligations and other liabilities of the domesticating corporation are the debts, obligations and other liabilities of the domesticated corporation;

(3)   the name of the domesticated corporation may but need note be substituted for the name of the domesticating corporation in any pending proceeding;

(4)   the articles of incorporation and bylaws of the domesticated corporation become effective;

(5)   the shares of the domesticating corporation are reclassified into shares or other securities, obligations, rights to acquire shares or other securities, cash or other property in accordance with the terms of the domestication, and the shareholders of the domesticating corporation are entitled only to the rights provided to them by those terms and to any appraisal rights they may have under the organic law of the domesticating corporation; and

(6)   the domesticated corporation is:

(i)   incorporated under and subject to the organic law of the domesticated corporation;

(ii)   the same corporation without interruption as the domesticating corporation; and

(iii)   deemed to have been incorporated on the date the domesticating corporation was originally incorporated.

(b)   When a domestication of a domestic corporation into a foreign jurisdiction becomes effective, the domesticated corporation is deemed to:

(1)   appoint the secretary of state as its agent for service of process in a proceeding to enforce the rights of shareholders who exercise appraisal rights in connection with the domestication; and

(2)   agree that it will promptly pay the amount, if any, to which such shareholders are entitled under chapter 13.

(c)   Except as otherwise provided in the organic law or organic rules of a domesticating foreign corporation, the interest holder liability of a shareholder in a foreign corporation that is domesticated into this state who had interest holder liability in respect of such domesticating corporation before the domestication becomes effective shall be as follows:

(1)   The domestication does not discharge that prior interest holder liability with respect to any interest holder liabilities that arose before the domestication becomes effective.

(2)   The provisions of the organic law of the domesticating corporation shall continue to apply to the collection or discharge of any interest holder liabilities preserved by subsection (c)(1), as if the domestication had not occurred.

(3)   The shareholder shall have such rights of contribution from other persons as are provided by the organic law of the domesticating corporation with respect to any interest holder liabilities preserved by subsection (c)(1), as if the domestication had not occurred.

(4)   The shareholder shall not, by reason of such prior interest holder liability, have interest holder liability with respect to any interest holder liabilities that are incurred after the domestication becomes effective.

(d)   A shareholder who becomes subject to interest holder liability in respect of the domesticated corporation as a result of the domestication shall have such interest holder liability only in respect of interest holder liabilities that arise after the domestication becomes effective.

(e)   A domestication does not constitute or cause the dissolution of the domesticating corporation.

(f)   Property held for charitable purposes under the laws of this state by a domestic or foreign corporation immediately before a domestication shall not, as a result of the transaction, be diverted from the objects for which it was donated, granted, devised, or otherwise transferred except and to the extent permitted by or pursuant to the laws of this state addressing cy près or dealing with nondiversion of charitable assets.

(g)   A bequest, devise, gift, grant, or promise contained in a will or other instrument of donation, subscription, or conveyance which is made to the domesticating corporation and which takes effect or remains payable after the domestication inures to the domesticated corporation.

(h)   A trust obligation that would govern property if transferred to the domesticating corporation applies to property that is transferred to the domesticated corporation after the domestication takes effect.

SUBCHAPTER C.   NONPROFIT CONVERSION [OMITTED]

§ 9.30   Conversion

(a)   By complying with this chapter, a domestic corporation may become (i) a domestic eligible entity or (ii) a foreign eligible entity if the conversion is permitted by the organic law of the foreign entity.

(b)   By complying with this subchapter and applicable provisions of its organic law, a domestic eligible entity may become a domestic corporation. If procedures for the approval of a conversion are not provided by the organic law or organic rules of a domestic eligible entity, the conversion shall be adopted and approved in the same manner as a merger of that eligible entity. If the organic law or organic rules of a domestic eligible entity do not provide procedures for the approval of either a conversion or a merger, a plan of conversion may nonetheless be adopted and approved by the unanimous consent of all the interest holders of such eligible entity. In either such case, the conversion thereafter may be effected as provided in the other provisions of this subchapter; and for purposes of applying this chapter in such a case:

(1)   the eligible entity, its members or interest holders, eligible interests and organic rules taken together, shall be deemed to be a domestic business corporation, shareholders, shares and articles of incorporation, respectively and vice versa, as the context may require; and

(2)   if the business and affairs of the eligible entity are managed by a person or persons that are not identical to the members or interest holders, that person or persons shall be deemed to be the board of directors.

(c)   By complying with the provisions of this subchapter applicable to foreign entities, a foreign eligible entity may become a domestic corporation if the organic law of the foreign eligible entity permits it to become a business corporation in another jurisdiction.

(d)   If a protected agreement of a domestic converting corporation in effect immediately before the conversion becomes effective contains a provision applying to a merger of the corporation that is a converting entity and the agreement does not refer to a conversion of the corporation, the provision applies to a conversion of the corporation as if the conversion were a merger, until such time as the provision is first amended after the enactment date.

§ 9.31   Plan of Conversion

(a)   A domestic corporation may convert to a domestic or foreign eligible entity under this subchapter by approving a plan of conversion. The plan of conversion must include:

(1)   the name of the converting corporation;

(2)   the name, jurisdiction of formation and type of entity of the converted entity;

(3)   the manner and basis of converting the shares of the domestic corporation into eligible interests or other securities, obligations, rights to acquire eligible interests or other securities, cash, other property, or any combination of the foregoing;

(4)   the other terms and conditions of the conversion; and

(5)   the full text, as it will be in effect immediately after the conversion becomes effective, of the organic rules of the converted entity which are to be in writing.

(b)   In addition to the requirements of subsection (a), a plan of conversion may contain any other provision not prohibited by law.

(c)   The terms of a plan of conversion may be made dependent upon facts objectively ascertainable outside the plan in accordance with section 1.20(k).

§ 9.32   Action on a Plan of Conversion

In the case of a conversion of a domestic corporation to a domestic or foreign eligible entity, the plan of conversion shall be adopted in the following manner:

(a)   The plan of conversion shall first be adopted by the board of directors.

(b)   The plan of conversion shall then be approved by the shareholders. In submitting the plan of conversion to the shareholders for their approval, the board of directors must recommend that the shareholders approve the plan, unless (i) the board of directors makes a determination that because of conflicts of interest or other special circumstances it should not make such a recommendation, or (ii) section 8.26 applies. If either (i) or (ii) applies, the board of directors shall inform the shareholders of the basis for its so proceeding.

(c)   The board of directors may set conditions for approval of the plan of conversion by the shareholders or the effectiveness of the plan of conversion.

(d)   If the approval of the shareholders is to be given at a meeting, the corporation shall notify each shareholder, regardless of whether entitled to vote, of the meeting of shareholders at which the plan of conversion is to be submitted for approval. The notice must state that the purpose, or one of the purposes, of the meeting is to consider the plan of conversion and must contain or be accompanied by a copy or summary of the plan. The notice must include or be accompanied by a copy of the organic rules of the converted entity which are to be in writing as they will be in effect immediately after the conversion.

(e)   Unless the articles of incorporation, or the board of directors acting pursuant to subsection (c), require a greater vote or a greater quorum, approval of the plan of conversion requires (i) the approval of the shareholders at a meeting at which a quorum exists consisting of a majority of the votes entitled to be cast on the plan, and (ii) the approval of each class or series of shares voting as a separate voting group at a meeting at which a quorum of the voting group exists consisting of a majority of the votes entitled to be cast on the plan by that voting group.

(f)   If as a result of the conversion one or more shareholders of the converting domestic corporation would become subject to interest holder liability, approval of the plan of conversion shall require the signing in connection with the transaction, by each such shareholder, of a separate written consent to become subject to such interest holder liability.

§ 9.33 Articles of Conversion; Effectiveness

(a) After (i) a plan of conversion of a domestic corporation has been adopted and approved as required by this Act, or (ii) a domestic or foreign eligible entity that is the converting entity has approved a conversion as required under its organic law, articles of conversion shall be signed by the converting entity and must:

(1) state the name, jurisdiction of formation, and type of entity of the converting entity;

(2) state the name, jurisdiction of formation, and type of entity of the converted entity;

(3) if the converting entity is (i) a domestic corporation, state that the plan of conversion was approved in accordance with this subchapter; or (ii) an eligible entity, (A) state that the conversion was approved by the eligible entity in accordance with its organic law or (B) if the converting entity is a domestic eligible entity the organic law of which does not provide for approval of the conversion, state that the conversion was approved by the domestic eligible entity in accordance with this subchapter; and

(4) if the converted entity is (i) a domestic business corporation, or a domestic nonprofit corporation or filing entity, have attached the public organic record of the converted entity, except that provisions that would not be required to be included in a restated public organic record may be omitted; or (ii) a domestic limited liability partnership, have attached the filing required to become a limited liability partnership.

(b) If the converted entity is a domestic corporation, its articles of incorporation must satisfy the requirements of section 2.02, except that provisions that would not be required to be included in restated articles of incorporation may be omitted from the articles of incorporation. If the converted entity is a domestic eligible entity, its public organic record, if any, must satisfy the requirements of the organic law of this state, except that the public organic record does not need to be signed.

(c) The articles of conversion shall be delivered to the secretary of state for filing, and shall take effect at the effective date determined in accordance with section 1.23.

(d) If a converted entity is a domestic entity, the conversion becomes effective when the articles of conversion are effective. With respect to a conversion in which the converted entity is a foreign eligible entity, the conversion itself shall become effective at the later of (i) the date and time provided by the organic law of that eligible entity, and (ii) when the articles of conversion become effective.

(e) Articles of conversion under this section may be combined with any required conversion filing under the organic law of a domestic eligible entity that is the converting entity or converted entity if the combined filing satisfies the requirements of both this section and the other organic law.

(f) If the converting entity is a foreign eligible entity that is registered to do business in this state under a provision of law similar to chapter 15, its registration statement or other type of foreign qualification shall be cancelled automatically on the effective date of its conversion.

§ 9.34 Amendment of Plan of Conversion; Abandonment

(a) A plan of conversion of a converting entity that is a domestic corporation may be amended:

(1) in the same manner as the plan was approved, if the plan does not provide for the manner in which it may be amended; or

(2) in the manner provided in the plan, except that shareholders that were entitled to vote on or consent to approval of the plan are entitled to vote on or consent to any amendment of the plan that will change:

(i) the amount or kind of eligible interests or other securities, obligations, rights to acquire eligible interests or other securities, cash, other property, or any combination of the foregoing, to be received by any of the shareholders of the converting corporation under the plan;

        (ii) the organic rules of the converted entity that will be in effect immediately after the conversion becomes effective, except for changes that do not require approval of the eligible interest holders of the converted entity under its organic law or organic rules; or

        (iii) any other terms or conditions of the plan, if the change would adversely affect such shareholders in any material respect.

  (b) After a plan of conversion has been approved by a converting entity that is a domestic corporation in the manner required by this subchapter and before the articles of conversion become effective, the plan may be abandoned by the corporation without action by its shareholders in accordance with any procedures set forth in the plan or, if no such procedures are set forth in the plan, in the manner determined by the board of directors.

  (c) If a conversion is abandoned after the articles of conversion have been delivered to the secretary of state for filing and before the articles of conversion become effective, articles of abandonment, signed by the converting entity, must be delivered to the secretary of state for filing before the articles of conversion become effective. The articles of abandonment take effect on filing, and the conversion is abandoned and does not become effective. The articles of abandonment must contain:

    (1) the name of the converting entity;

    (2) the date on which the articles of conversion were filed by the secretary of state; and

    (3) a statement that the conversion has been abandoned in accordance with this section.

§ 9.35   Effect of Conversion

  (a) When a conversion becomes effective:

    (1) all property owned by, and every contract right possessed by, the converting entity remain the property and contract rights of the converted entity without transfer, reversion or impairment;

    (2) all debts, obligations and other liabilities of the converting entity remain the debts, obligations and other liabilities of the converted entity;

    (3) the name of the converted entity may but need not be substituted for the name of the converting entity in any pending action or proceeding;

    (4) if the converted entity is a filing entity or a domestic business corporation or a domestic or foreign nonprofit corporation, its public organic record and its private organic rules become effective;

    (5) if the converted entity is a nonfiling entity, its private organic rules become effective;

    (6) if the converted entity is a limited liability partnership, the filing required to become a limited liability partnership and its private organic rules become effective;

    (7) the shares or eligible interests of the converting entity are reclassified into shares, eligible interests or other securities, obligations, rights to acquire shares, eligible interests or other securities, cash, or other property in accordance with the terms of the conversion, and the shareholders or interest holders of the converting entity are entitled only to the rights provided to them by those terms and to any appraisal rights they may have under the organic law of the converting entity; and

    (8) the converted entity is:

        (i) incorporated or organized under and subject to the organic law of the converted entity;

        (ii) the same entity without interruption as the converting entity; and

    (iii) deemed to have been incorporated or otherwise organized on the date that the converting entity was originally incorporated or organized.

(b) When a conversion of a domestic corporation to a foreign eligible entity becomes effective, the converted entity is deemed to:

    (1) appoint the secretary of state as its agent for service of process in a proceeding to enforce the rights of shareholders who exercise appraisal rights in connection with the conversion; and

    (2) agree that it will promptly pay the amount, if any, to which such shareholders are entitled under chapter 13.

(c) Except as otherwise provided in the articles of incorporation of a domestic corporation or the organic law or organic rules of a foreign corporation or a domestic or foreign eligible entity, a shareholder or eligible interest holder who becomes subject to interest holder liability in respect of a domestic corporation or eligible entity as a result of the conversion shall have such interest holder liability only in respect of interest holder liabilities that arise after the conversion becomes effective.

(d) Except as otherwise provided in the organic law or the organic rules of the eligible entity, the interest holder liability of an interest holder in a converting eligible entity that converts to a domestic corporation who had interest holder liability in respect of such converting eligible entity before the conversion becomes effective shall be as follows:

    (1) The conversion does not discharge that prior interest holder liability with respect to any interest holder liabilities that arose before the conversion became effective.

    (2) The provisions of the organic law of the eligible entity shall continue to apply to the collection or discharge of any interest holder liabilities preserved by subsection (d)(1), as if the conversion had not occurred.

    (3) The eligible interest holder shall have such rights of contribution from other persons as are provided by the organic law of the eligible entity with respect to any interest holder liabilities preserved by subsection (d)(1), as if the conversion had not occurred.

    (4) The eligible interest holder shall not, by reason of such prior interest holder liability, have interest holder liability with respect to any interest holder liabilities that arise after the conversion becomes effective.

(e) A conversion does not require the converting entity to wind up its affairs and does not constitute or cause the dissolution or termination of the entity.

(f) Property held for charitable purposes under the laws of this state by a corporation or a domestic or foreign eligible entity immediately before a conversion shall not, as a result of the transaction, be diverted from the objects for which it was donated, granted, devised, or otherwise transferred except and to the extent permitted by or pursuant to the laws of this state addressing cy près or dealing with nondiversion of charitable assets.

(g) A bequest, devise, gift, grant, or promise contained in a will or other instrument of donation, subscription, or conveyance which is made to the converting entity and which takes effect or remains payable after the conversion inures to the converted entity.

(h) A trust obligation that would govern property if transferred to the converting entity applies to property that is transferred to the converted entity after the conversion takes effect.

CHAPTER 10.   AMENDMENT OF ARTICLES OF INCORPORATION AND BYLAWS

SUBCHAPTER A.   AMENDMENT OF ARTICLES OF INCORPORATION

§ 10.01   Authority to Amend

(a)   A corporation may amend its articles of incorporation at any time to add or change a provision that is required or permitted in the articles of incorporation as of the effective date of the amendment or to delete a provision that is not required to be contained in the articles of incorporation.

(b)   A shareholder of the corporation does not have a vested property right resulting from any provision in the articles of incorporation, including provisions relating to management, control, capital structure, dividend entitlement, or purpose or duration of the corporation.

§ 10.02   Amendment Before Issuance of Shares

If a corporation has not yet issued shares, its board of directors, or its incorporators if it has no board of directors, may adopt one or more amendments to the corporation's articles of incorporation.

§ 10.03   Amendment by Board of Directors and Shareholders

If a corporation has issued shares, an amendment to the articles of incorporation shall be adopted in the following manner:

(a)   The proposed amendment shall first be adopted by the board of directors.

(b)   Except as provided in sections 10.05, 10.07, and 10.08, the amendment shall then be approved by the shareholders. In submitting the proposed amendment to the shareholders for approval, the board of directors shall recommend that the shareholders approve the amendment, unless (i) the board of directors makes a determination that because of conflicts of interest or other special circumstances it should not make such a recommendation, or (ii) section 8.26 applies. If either (i) or (ii) applies, the board must inform the shareholders of the basis for its so proceeding.

(c)   The board of directors may set conditions for the approval of the amendment by the shareholders or the effectiveness of the amendment.

(d)   If the amendment is required to be approved by the shareholders, and the approval is to be given at a meeting, the corporation shall notify each shareholder, regardless of whether entitled to vote, of the meeting of shareholders at which the amendment is to be submitted for approval. The notice must state that the purpose, or one of the purposes, of the meeting is to consider the amendment. The notice must contain or be accompanied by a copy of the amendment.

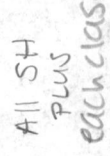

(e)   Unless the articles of incorporation, or the board of directors acting pursuant to subsection (c), require a greater vote or a greater quorum, approval of the amendment requires the approval of the shareholders at a meeting at which a quorum consisting of a majority of the votes entitled to be cast on the amendment exists, and, if any class or series of shares is entitled to vote as a separate group on the amendment, except as provided in section 10.04(c), the approval of each such separate voting group at a meeting at which a quorum of the voting group exists consisting of a majority of the votes entitled to be cast on the amendment by that voting group.

(f)   If as a result of an amendment of the articles of incorporation one or more shareholders of a domestic corporation would become subject to new interest holder liability, approval of the amendment requires the signing in connection with the amendment, by each such shareholder, of a separate written consent to become subject to such new interest holder liability, unless in the case of a shareholder that already has interest holder liability the terms and conditions of the new interest holder liability (i) are substantially identical to those of the existing interest holder liability, or (ii) are substantially identical to those of the existing interest holder liability (other than changes that eliminate or reduce such interest holder liability).

(g)   For purposes of subsection (f) and section 10.09, "new interest holder liability" means interest holder liability of a person resulting from an amendment of the articles of incorporation if (i) the person did not have interest holder liability before the amendment becomes effective, or (ii) the person had interest holder liability before the amendment becomes effective, the terms and conditions of which are changed when the amendment becomes effective.

§ 10.04   Voting on Amendments by Voting Groups

(a)   The holders of the outstanding shares of a class are entitled to vote as a separate voting group (if shareholder voting is otherwise required by this Act) on a proposed amendment to the articles of incorporation if the amendment would:

(1)   effect an exchange or reclassification of all or part of the shares of the class into shares of another class;

(2)   effect an exchange or reclassification, or create the right of exchange, of all or part of the shares of another class into shares of the class;

(3)   change the rights, preferences, or limitations of all or part of the shares of the class;

(4)   change the shares of all or part of the class into a different number of shares of the same class;

(5)   create a new class of shares having rights or preferences with respect to distributions that are prior or superior to the shares of the class;

(6)   increase the rights, preferences, or number of authorized shares of any class that, after giving effect to the amendment, have rights or preferences with respect to distributions that are prior or superior to the shares of the class;

(7)   limit or deny an existing preemptive right of all or part of the shares of the class; or

(8)   cancel or otherwise affect rights to distributions that have accumulated but not yet been authorized on all or part of the shares of the class.

(b)   If a proposed amendment would affect a series of a class of shares in one or more of the ways described in subsection (a), the holders of shares of that series are entitled to vote as a separate voting group on the proposed amendment.

(c)   If a proposed amendment that entitles the holders of two or more classes or series of shares to vote as separate voting groups under this section would affect those two or more classes or series in the same or a substantially similar way, the holders of shares of all the classes or series so affected shall vote together as a single voting group on the proposed amendment, unless otherwise provided in the articles of incorporation or added as a condition by the board of directors pursuant to section 10.03(c).

(d)   A class or series of shares is entitled to the voting rights granted by this section even if the articles of incorporation provide that the shares are nonvoting shares.

OFFICIAL COMMENT

Section 10.04(a) requires separate approval by voting groups for certain types of amendments to the articles of incorporation where the corporation has more than one class or series of shares outstanding. Even if a class or series of shares is described as "nonvoting" or the articles purport to make that class or series nonvoting "for all purposes," that class or series nonetheless has the voting rights provided by this section. Likewise, shares are entitled to vote as separate voting groups under this section even though the articles of incorporation purport to allow other classes or series of shares to vote as part of the same voting group. However, an amendment that does not require shareholder approval does not trigger the right to vote by voting groups under this section. This would include a determination by the board, pursuant to authority granted in the articles of incorporation, of the rights, preferences and limitations of any class before the issuance of any shares of that class, or of one or more series within a class before the issuance of any shares of that series. See sections 6.02(a) and (b).

The right to vote as a separate voting group provides a major protection for classes or series of shares with preferential rights, or classes or series of limited or nonvoting shares, against amendments that affect that class or series. This section, however, does not make the right to vote by a separate voting group dependent on an evaluation of whether the amendment is detrimental to that class or series; if the amendment is one of those described in section 10.04(a), the class or series is automatically entitled to vote as a separate voting group on the amendment.

An amendment that changes the number of shares owned by one or more shareholders of a class into a fraction of a share, through a "reverse split," falls within subsection (a)(4) and therefore requires approval by the class, voting as a separate voting group, whether the fractional share is to be issued or otherwise paid in cash under section 6.04. Sections 10.04(a)(5) and (6) refer to preferences with respect to distributions, including distributions in liquidation or dissolution. See section 1.40 and the Official Comment to section 1.40 under "Distributions."

Sections 7.25 and 7.26 set forth the mechanics of voting by multiple voting groups. Section 10.04(b) extends the privilege of voting as a separate voting group to a series of a class of shares if the series is affected in one or more of the ways described in subsection (a). Any distinguishing feature of a series, which an amendment affects or alters, should trigger the right of voting as a separate voting group for that series. However, if a proposed amendment that affects two or more classes or series of shares in the same or a substantially similar way, under subsection (c), the shares of all the class or series so affected must vote together, as a single voting group, unless otherwise provided in the articles of incorporation or a condition set by the board of directors pursuant to section 10.03(c).

The application of sections 10.04(b) and (c) may best be illustrated by the following examples, all of which assume there is no provision in the articles of incorporation providing otherwise and that the board has not set an additional voting condition.

First, assume there is a class of shares comprised of three series, each with different preferential dividend rights. A proposed amendment would reduce the rate of dividend applicable to the "Series A" shares and would change the dividend right of the "Series B" shares from a cumulative to a noncumulative right. The amendment would not affect the preferential dividend right of the "Series C" shares. Both Series A and B would be entitled to vote as separate voting groups on the proposed amendment; the holders of the Series C shares, not directly affected by the amendment, would not be entitled to vote unless the Series C shares are voting shares under the articles of incorporation, in which case the Series C shares would not vote as a separate voting group but would vote in the voting group consisting of all shares in the class, as well as in the voting group consisting of all shares with general voting rights under the articles of incorporation.

Second, if the proposed amendment would reduce the dividend right of Series A and change the dividend right of both Series B and C from a cumulative to a noncumulative right, the holders of Series A would be entitled to vote as a single voting group, and the holders of Series B and C would be required to vote together as a single, separate voting group.

Third, assume that a corporation has common stock and two classes of preferred stock. A proposed amendment would create a new class of senior preferred that would have priority in distribution rights over both the common stock and the existing classes of preferred stock. Because the creation of the new senior preferred would affect all three classes of stock in the same or a substantially similar way, all three classes would vote together as a single voting group on the proposed amendment.

§ 10.05   Amendment by Board of Directors

Unless the articles of incorporation provide otherwise, a corporation's board of directors may adopt amendments to the corporation's articles of incorporation without shareholder approval:

    (a)   to extend the duration of the corporation if it was incorporated at a time when limited duration was required by law;

(b)   to delete the names and addresses of the initial directors;

(c)   to delete the name and address of the initial registered agent or registered office, if a statement of change is on file with the secretary of state;

(d)   if the corporation has only one class of shares outstanding:

(1)   to change each issued and unissued authorized share of the class into a greater number of whole shares of that class; or

(2)   to increase the number of authorized shares of the class to the extent necessary to permit the issuance of shares as a share dividend;

(e)   to change the corporate name by substituting the word "corporation," "incorporated," "company," "limited," or the abbreviation "corp.," "inc.," "co.," or "ltd.," for a similar word or abbreviation in the name, or by adding, deleting, or changing a geographical attribution for the name;

(f)   to reflect a reduction in authorized shares, as a result of the operation of section 6.31(b), when the corporation has acquired its own shares and the articles of incorporation prohibit the reissue of the acquired shares;

(g)   to delete a class of shares from the articles of incorporation, as a result of the operation of section 6.31(b), when there are no remaining shares of the class because the corporation has acquired all shares of the class and the articles of incorporation prohibit the reissue of the acquired shares; or

(h)   to make any change expressly permitted by section 6.02(a) or (b) to be made without shareholder approval.

§ 10.06   Articles of Amendment

(a)   After an amendment to the articles of incorporation has been adopted and approved in the manner required by this Act and by the articles of incorporation, the corporation shall deliver to the secretary of state for filing articles of amendment, which must set forth:

(1)   the name of the corporation;

(2)   the text of each amendment adopted, or the information required by section 1.20(k)(5);

(3)   if an amendment provides for an exchange, reclassification, or cancellation of issued shares, provisions for implementing the amendment if not contained in the amendment itself, (which may be made dependent upon facts objectively ascertainable outside the articles of amendment in accordance with section 1.20(k)(5);

(4)   the date of each amendment's adoption; and

(5)   if an amendment:

(i)   was adopted by the incorporators or board of directors without shareholder approval, a statement that the amendment was duly adopted by the incorporators or by the board of directors, as the case may be, and that shareholder approval was not required;

(ii)   required approval by the shareholders, a statement that the amendment was duly approved by the shareholders in the manner required by this Act and by the articles of incorporation; or

(iii)   is being filed pursuant to section 1.20(k)(5), a statement to that effect.

(b)   Articles of amendment shall take effect at the effective date determined in accordance with section 1.23.

§ 10.07   Restated Articles of Incorporation

(a)   A corporation's board of directors may restate its articles of incorporation at any time, without shareholder approval, to consolidate all amendments into a single document.

(b)   If the restated articles include one or more new amendments that require shareholder approval, the amendments shall be adopted and approved as provided in section 10.03.

(c)   A corporation that restates its articles of incorporation shall deliver to the secretary of state for filing articles of restatement setting forth:

(1)   the name of the corporation;

(2)   the text of the restated articles of incorporation;

(3)   a statement that the restated articles consolidate all amendments into a single document; and

(4)   if a new amendment is included in the restated articles, the statements required under section 10.06 with respect to the new amendment.

(d)   Duly adopted restated articles of incorporation supersede the original articles of incorporation and all amendments to the articles of incorporation.

(e)   The secretary of state may certify restated articles of incorporation as the articles of incorporation currently in effect, without including the statements required by subsection (c)(4).

§ 10.08   Amendment Pursuant to Reorganization

(a)   A corporation's articles of incorporation may be amended without action by the board of directors or shareholders to carry out a plan of reorganization ordered or decreed by a court of competent jurisdiction under the authority of a law of the United States.

(b)   The individual or individuals designated by the court shall deliver to the secretary of state for filing articles of amendment setting forth:

(1)   the name of the corporation;

(2)   the text of each amendment approved by the court;

(3)   the date of the court's order or decree approving the articles of amendment;

(4)   the title of the reorganization proceeding in which the order or decree was entered; and

(5)   a statement that the court had jurisdiction of the proceeding under federal statute.

(c)   This section does not apply after entry of a final decree in the reorganization proceeding even though the court retains jurisdiction of the proceeding for limited purposes unrelated to consummation of the reorganization plan.

§ 10.09   Effect of Amendment

(a)   An amendment to the articles of incorporation does not affect a cause of action existing against or in favor of the corporation, a proceeding to which the corporation is a party, or the existing rights of persons other than the shareholders. An amendment changing a corporation's name does not affect a proceeding brought by or against the corporation in its former name.

(b)   A shareholder who becomes subject to new interest holder liability in respect of the corporation as a result of an amendment to the articles of incorporation shall have that new interest holder liability only in respect of interest holder liabilities that arise after the amendment becomes effective.

(c)   Except as otherwise provided in the articles of incorporation of the corporation, the interest holder liability of a shareholder who had interest holder liability in respect of the corporation before the amendment becomes effective and has new interest holder liability after the amendment becomes effective shall be as follows:

(1)   The amendment does not discharge that prior interest holder liability with respect to any interest holder liabilities that arose before the amendment becomes effective.

(2)   The provisions of the articles of incorporation of the corporation relating to interest holder liability as in effect immediately prior to the amendment shall continue to apply to the collection or discharge of any interest holder liabilities preserved by subsection (c)(1), as if the amendment had not occurred.

(3)   The shareholder shall have such rights of contribution from other persons as are provided by the articles of incorporation relating to interest holder liability as in effect immediately prior to the amendment with respect to any interest holder liabilities preserved by subsection (c)(1), as if the amendment had not occurred.

(4)   The shareholder shall not, by reason of such prior interest holder liability, have interest holder liability with respect to any interest holder liabilities that arise after the amendment becomes effective.

SUBCHAPTER B.   AMENDMENT OF BYLAWS

§ 10.20   Authority to Amend

(a)   A corporation's shareholders may amend or repeal the corporation's bylaws.

(b)   A corporation's board of directors may amend or repeal the corporation's bylaws, unless:

(1)   the articles of incorporation, section 10.21 or, if applicable, section 10.22 reserve that power exclusively to the shareholders in whole or part; or

(2)   except as provided in section 2.06(d), the shareholders in amending, repealing, or adopting a bylaw expressly provide that the board of directors may not amend, repeal, or adopt that bylaw.

(c)   A shareholder of the corporation does not have a vested property right resulting from any provision in the bylaws.

§ 10.21   Bylaw Increasing Quorum or Voting Requirement for Directors or Requiring a Meeting Place

(a)   A bylaw that increases a quorum or voting requirement for the board of directors may be amended or repealed:

(1)   if originally adopted by the shareholders, only by the shareholders, unless the bylaw otherwise provides; or

(2)   if adopted by the board of directors, either by the shareholders or by the board of directors.

(b)   A bylaw adopted or amended by the shareholders that increases a quorum or voting requirement for the board of directors may provide that it can be amended or repealed only by a specified vote of either the shareholders or the board of directors.

(c)   Action by the board of directors under subsection (a) to amend or repeal a bylaw that changes a quorum or voting requirement for the board of directors shall meet the same quorum requirement and be adopted by the same vote required to take action under the quorum and voting requirement then in effect or proposed to be adopted, whichever is greater.

§ 10.22 Bylaw Provisions Relating to the Election of Directors

(a) Unless the articles of incorporation (i) specifically prohibit the adoption of a bylaw pursuant to this section, (ii) alter the vote specified in section 7.28(a), or (iii) provide for cumulative voting, a corporation may elect in its bylaws to be governed in the election of directors as follows:

    (1) each vote entitled to be cast may be voted for or against up to that number of candidates that is equal to the number of directors to be elected, or a shareholder may indicate an abstention, but without cumulating the votes;

    (2) to be elected, a nominee shall have received a plurality of the votes cast by holders of shares entitled to vote in the election at a meeting at which a quorum is present, provided that a nominee who is elected but receives more votes against than for election shall serve as a director for a term that shall terminate on the date that is the earlier of (i) 90 days from the date on which the voting results are determined pursuant to section 7.29(b)(5) or (ii) the date on which an individual is selected by the board of directors to fill the office held by such director, which selection shall be deemed to constitute the filling of a vacancy by the board to which section 8.10 applies. Subject to subsection (a)(3), a nominee who is elected but receives more votes against than for election shall not serve as a director beyond the 90-day period referenced above; and

    (3) the board of directors may select any qualified individual to fill the office held by a director who received more votes against than for election.

(b) Subsection (a) does not apply to an election of directors by a voting group if (i) at the expiration of the time fixed under a provision requiring advance notification of director candidates, or (ii) absent such a provision, at a time fixed by the board of directors which is not more than 14 days before notice is given of the meeting at which the election is to occur, there are more candidates for election by the voting group than the number of directors to be elected, one or more of whom are properly proposed by shareholders. An individual shall not be considered a candidate for purposes of this subsection if the board of directors determines before the notice of meeting is given that such individual's candidacy does not create a bona fide election contest.

(c) A bylaw electing to be governed by this section may be repealed:

    (1) if originally adopted by the shareholders, only by the shareholders, unless the bylaw otherwise provides;

    (2) if adopted by the board of directors, by the board of directors or the shareholders.

OFFICIAL COMMENT

Section 10.22 is effective only if a corporation elects in a bylaw to be governed by its terms. The provisions of section 10.22 effectively modify the term and holdover provisions of section 8.05 pursuant to a limited exception for section 10.22 that is recognized in section 8.05. Accordingly, a bylaw provision that would seek to alter the term and holdover provision of section 8.05 that varied in any manner from section 10.22 would not be effective.

1. Section 10.22(a)

The rule in subsection (a) is straightforward if the nominees for director equal the number of directorships up for election. In that case, and by way of example, the holder of a single share could vote either for or against each director. In the unusual case that section 10.22(a) were applicable to a contested election notwithstanding the provisions of section 10.22(b) (*e.g.*, in the absence of an advance notice bylaw, a contest arises as a result of candidates for director being proposed subsequent to the determination date under section 10.22(b)), the holder of a share would have to choose whether to indicate opposition to a slate by voting in favor of a candidate on the preferred slate or by voting against a candidate on the disfavored slate, or to abstain. Because it would be in the interests of all contestants to explain in their proxy materials that against votes would not be counted in favor of any candidate in a contested election, the rational voter in a contested election might be expected to vote in favor of all candidates on the preferred slate to promote a simple plurality victory rather than voting against candidates on the disfavored slate. Nothing in section

10.22 would prevent the holder of more than one share from voting differently with respect to each share held.

Section 10.22(a) specifically contemplates that a corporate ballot for the election of directors would provide for "against" votes. Although there is no prohibition in the Act against a corporation offering shareholders the opportunity to vote "against" candidates at any time, unless the corporation elects to be governed by section 10.22 or the articles of incorporation are amended to make such a vote meaningful, an "against" vote is given no effect under the Act.

Section 10.22(a)(2) does not conflict with or alter the plurality voting default standard. However, because section 10.22 shortens the term of a director who is elected but receives more votes against election than in favor of election, a vacancy will exist if no action is taken to fill the vacancy before the expiration of the shortened term. As contemplated by section 8.10, that vacancy may be filled by shareholders or by the board of directors, unless the articles of incorporation provide otherwise. In the alternative, action could be taken by amendment to, or in the manner provided in, the articles of incorporation or bylaws to reduce the size of the board of directors. See section 8.03.

Under section 8.05(d), the director appointed to fill the vacancy would be up for reelection at the next annual meeting, even if the term for that directorship would otherwise have been for more than one year, as in the case of a staggered board.

There is also no limitation in section 10.22 or elsewhere in the Act on the power of either the board of directors or shareholders to fill a vacancy with the person who held such directorship before the vacancy arose.

2. Section 10.22(b)

Under section 10.22(b), when there are more candidates for election as directors by a voting group (as defined in section 1.40) than director positions to be filled, the resulting election contest would not be subject to the voting regime under section 10.22(a). Instead, it would be conducted by means of a plurality vote under section 7.28(a). Such plurality voting is appropriate in that circumstance because shareholders will have a choice between competing candidates.

The timing provided in clauses (i) and (ii) of subsection (b) for determining when section 10.22(a) does not apply to an election assures that the voting regime that will apply will be known in advance of the giving of notice, and that the disclosure of the voting rules and the proxy appointment form will be clear and reflect the applicable voting regime. The determination of how many candidates there are to fill the number of director positions up for election may be made by the board of directors. The board's determination of whether an individual shall not be considered a candidate for purposes of section 10.22(b) because the candidacy does not create a bona fide election contest must be made before notice of the meeting is given. The board of directors might choose, for example, to exercise this authority to preserve the voting regime under section 10.22(a) when it is clear that an individual has designated himself or herself as a candidate without intending to solicit votes or for the purpose of frustrating the availability of the section 10.22(a) voting regime.

The contested or uncontested nature of the election can change following the date for determining the voting regime that will apply. For example, an election that is contested at that date could become uncontested if a candidate withdraws. Conversely, unless the bylaws require advance notice of director nomination, an uncontested election could become contested before the vote is taken but after notice of the meeting has been given because there is no limitation on the ability of shareholders to nominate candidates for directorships up until the time nominations are closed at the meeting. Section 10.22(b) does not authorize changing the voting regime in those circumstances.

CHAPTER 11. MERGERS AND SHARE EXCHANGES

§ 11.01 Definitions

As used in this chapter:

"Acquired entity" means the domestic or foreign corporation or eligible entity that will have all of one or more classes or series of its shares or eligible interests acquired in a share exchange.

"Acquiring entity" means the domestic or foreign corporation or eligible entity that will acquire all of one or more classes or series of shares or eligible interests of the acquired entity in a share exchange.

"New interest holder liability" means interest holder liability of a person, resulting from a merger or share exchange, that is (i) in respect of an entity which is different from the entity in which the person held shares or eligible interests immediately before the merger or share exchange became effective; or (ii) in respect of the same entity as the one in which the person held shares or eligible interests immediately before the merger or share exchange became effective if (A) the person did not have interest holder liability immediately before the merger or share exchange became effective, or (B) the person had interest holder liability immediately before the merger or share exchange became effective, the terms and conditions of which were changed when the merger or share exchange became effective.

"Party to a merger" means any domestic or foreign corporation or eligible entity that will merge under a plan of merger but does not include a survivor created by the merger.

"Survivor" in a merger means the domestic or foreign corporation or eligible entity into which one or more other corporations or eligible entities are merged.

§ 11.02   Merger

(a) By complying with this chapter:

(1) one or more domestic business corporations may merge with one or more domestic or foreign business corporations or eligible entities pursuant to a plan of merger, resulting in a survivor; and

(2) two or more foreign business corporations or domestic or foreign eligible entities may merge, resulting in a survivor that is a domestic business corporation created in the merger.

(b) By complying with the provisions of this chapter applicable to foreign entities, a foreign business corporation or a foreign eligible entity may be a party to a merger with a domestic business corporation, or may be created as the survivor in a merger in which a domestic business corporation is a party, but only if the merger is permitted by the organic law of the foreign business corporation or eligible entity.

(c) If the organic law or organic rules of a domestic eligible entity do not provide procedures for the approval of a merger, a plan of merger may nonetheless be adopted and approved by the unanimous consent of all of the interest holders of such eligible entity, and the merger may thereafter by effected as provided in the other provisions of this chapter; and for the purposes of applying this chapter in such a case:

(1) the eligible entity, its members or interest holders, eligible interests and articles of incorporation or other organic rules taken together shall be deemed to be a domestic business corporation, shareholders, shares and articles of incorporation, respectively and vice versa as the context may require; and

(2) if the business and affairs of the eligible entity are managed by a person or persons that are not identical to the members or interest holders, that group shall be deemed to be the board of directors.

(d) The plan of merger must include:

(1) as to each party to the merger, its name, jurisdiction of formation, and type of entity;

(2) the survivor's name, jurisdiction of formation, and type of entity, and, if the survivor is to be created in the merger, a statement to that effect;

(3) the terms and conditions of the merger;

(4)   the manner and basis of converting the shares of each merging domestic or foreign business corporation and eligible interests of each merging domestic or foreign eligible entity into shares or other securities, eligible interests, obligations, rights to acquire shares, other securities or eligible interests, cash, other property, or any combination of the foregoing;

(5)   the articles of incorporation of any domestic or foreign business or nonprofit corporation, or the public organic record of any domestic or foreign unincorporated entity, to be created by the merger, or if a new domestic or foreign business or nonprofit corporation or unincorporated entity is not to be created by the merger, any amendments to the survivor's articles of incorporation or other public organic record; and

(6)   any other provisions required by the laws under which any party to the merger is organized or by which it is governed, or by the articles of incorporation or organic rules of any such party.

(e)   In addition to the requirements of subsection (d), a plan of merger may contain any other provision not prohibited by law.

(f)   Terms of a plan of merger may be made dependent on facts objectively ascertainable outside the plan in accordance with section 1.20(k).

(g)   A plan of merger may be amended only with the consent of each party to the merger, except as provided in the plan. A domestic party to a merger may approve an amendment to a plan:

(1)   in the same manner as the plan was approved, if the plan does not provide for the manner in which it may be amended; or

(2)   in the manner provided in the plan, except that shareholders, members, or interest holders that were entitled to vote on or consent to approval of the plan are entitled to vote on or consent to any amendment of the plan that will change:

(i)   the amount or kind of shares or other securities, eligible interests, obligations, rights to acquire shares, other securities or eligible interests, cash, or other property to be received under the plan by the shareholders, members, or interest holders of any party to the merger;

(ii)   the articles of incorporation of any domestic or foreign business or nonprofit corporation, or the organic rules of any unincorporated entity, that will be the survivor of the merger, except for changes permitted by section 10.05 or by comparable provisions of the organic law of any such foreign corporation or domestic or foreign nonprofit corporation or unincorporated entity; or

(iii)   any of the other terms or conditions of the plan if the change would adversely affect such shareholders, members, or interest holders in any material respect.

§ 11.03   Share Exchange

(a)   By complying with this chapter:

(1)   a domestic corporation may acquire all of the shares of one or more classes or series of shares of another domestic or foreign corporation, or all of the eligible interests of one or more classes or series of interests of a domestic or foreign eligible entity, in exchange for shares or other securities, eligible interests, obligations, rights to acquire shares or other securities or eligible interests, cash, other property, or any combination of the foregoing, pursuant to a plan of share exchange; or

(2)   all of the shares of one or more classes or series of shares of a domestic corporation may be acquired by another domestic or foreign corporation or eligible entity, in exchange for shares or other securities, eligible interests, obligations, rights to acquire shares or other securities or

eligible interests, cash, other property, or any combination of the foregoing, pursuant to a plan of share exchange.

(b)   A foreign corporation or eligible entity may be the acquired entity in a share exchange only if the share exchange is permitted by the organic law of that corporation or other entity.

(c)   If the organic law or organic rules of a domestic eligible entity does not provide procedures for the approval of a share exchange, a plan of share exchange may be adopted and approved, and the share exchange effected, in accordance with the procedures, if any, for a merger. If the organic law or organic rules of a domestic eligible entity does not provide procedures for the approval of either a share exchange or a merger, a plan of share exchange may nonetheless be adopted and approved by the unanimous consent of all of the interest holders of such eligible entity whose interests will be exchanged under the plan of share exchange, and the share exchange may thereafter be effected as provided in the other provisions of this chapter; and for purposes of applying this chapter in such a case:

(1)   the eligible entity, its interest holders, interests and articles of incorporation or other organic rules taken together shall be deemed to be a domestic business corporation, shareholders, shares and articles of incorporation, respectively and vice versa as the context may require; and

(2)   if the business and affairs of the eligible entity are managed by a person or persons that are not identical to the members or interest holders, that person or those persons shall be deemed to be the board of directors.

(d)   The plan of share exchange must include:

(1)   the name of each domestic or foreign corporation or other eligible entity the shares or eligible interests of which will be acquired and the name of the domestic or foreign corporation or eligible entity that will acquire those shares or eligible interests;

(2)   the terms and conditions of the share exchange;

(3)   the manner and basis of exchanging shares of a domestic or foreign corporation or eligible interests in a domestic or foreign eligible entity the shares or eligible interests of which will be acquired under the share exchange for shares or other securities, eligible interests, obligations, rights to acquire shares, other securities, or eligible interests, cash, other property, or any combination of the foregoing; and

(4)   any other provisions required by the organic law governing the acquired entity or its articles of incorporation or organic rules.

(e)   Terms of a plan of share exchange may be made dependent on facts objectively ascertainable outside the plan in accordance with section 1.20(k).

(f)   A plan of share exchange may be amended only with the consent of each party to the share exchange, except as provided in the plan. A domestic entity may approve an amendment to a plan:

(1)   in the same manner as the plan was approved, if the plan does not provide for the manner in which it may be amended; or

(2)   in the manner provided in the plan, except that shareholders, members, or interest holders that were entitled to vote on or consent to approval of the plan are entitled to vote on or consent to any amendment of the plan that will change:

(i)   the amount or kind of shares or other securities, eligible interests, obligations, rights to acquire shares, other securities or eligible interests, cash, or other property to be received under the plan by the shareholders, members or interest holders of the acquired entity; or

(ii)   any of the other terms or conditions of the plan if the change would adversely affect such shareholders, members or interest holders in any material respect.

OFFICIAL COMMENT

1. In General

It is often desirable to structure a corporate combination so that the separate existence of one or more parties to the combination does not cease although another corporation or other entity obtains ownership of the shares or interests of those parties. This objective is often particularly important in the formation of insurance and bank holding companies, but is not limited to those contexts. In the absence of the procedure authorized in section 11.03, this kind of result often can be accomplished only by a reverse triangular merger, which involves the formation by a corporation, A, of a new subsidiary, followed by a merger of that subsidiary into another party to the merger, B, effected through the exchange of A's securities for securities of B. Section 11.03 authorizes a more straightforward procedure to accomplish the same result.

Section 11.03 authorizes a share exchange—a transaction in which the acquiring entity acquires all of the shares or eligible interests of one or more classes or series of shares or eligible interests of the acquired entity. The shares or eligible interests of one or more other classes or series of the acquired entity may be excluded from the share exchange or may be included on different bases. Shares or eligible interests of the affected class or series of the acquired entity owned at the effective time of the share exchange by the acquiring entity (or any parent of the acquiring entity or by any wholly owned subsidiary of the acquiring entity or of any such parent, each as defined in section 11.04(k)), may also be excluded from the share exchange.

After the plan of share exchange is adopted and approved as required by section 11.04, it is binding on all holders of the shares or eligible interests of the class or series to be acquired. Section 11.03 does not limit the power of a domestic corporation to acquire shares of another corporation or interests in another entity in a transaction other than a share exchange. In contrast to mergers, the articles of incorporation or public organic record of a party to a share exchange may not be amended by a plan of share exchange. Such an amendment to the articles of incorporation may, however, be effected under chapter 10 as a separate element of a corporate combination that involves a share exchange.

2. Applicability to Foreign Corporations and Foreign and Domestic Eligible Entities

A foreign corporation or a foreign eligible entity may be an acquired entity in a share exchange authorized by chapter 11 only if the share exchange is permitted by the organic law of the foreign corporation or eligible entity. Whether and on what terms a foreign corporation or a foreign eligible entity is authorized to be a party to a share exchange is governed by its organic law. If a foreign corporation or eligible entity is so authorized, it must also comply with the applicable terms of chapter 11 in addition to the requirements of its organic law. For example, section 11.03(d) sets forth certain requirements for the content of a plan of share exchange.

With respect to a domestic eligible entity, if the law under which it is organized does not expressly authorize it to be a party to a share exchange under chapter 11, section 11.03(a) is intended to provide the necessary authority. In that case, section 11.03(c) provides procedures for adopting, approving and effecting a plan of share exchange.

3. Terms and Conditions of Share Exchange

Chapter 11 imposes no restrictions or limitations on the terms or conditions of a share exchange, except for those contained in section 11.03(f), and the requirement in section 11.03(a) that the acquiring entity must acquire all the shares or eligible interests of the acquired class or series of shares or eligible interests. However, shares or interests of the acquired class or series owned at the effective time of the share exchange by the acquiring entity or any of its parents or their wholly owned subsidiaries may be excluded from the exchange. The list in section 11.03(d) of provisions in a plan of share exchange is not exhaustive.

§ 11.04   Action on a Plan of Merger or Share Exchange

In the case of a domestic corporation that is a party to a merger or the acquired entity in a share exchange, the plan of merger or share exchange shall be adopted in the following manner:

(a)   The plan of merger or share exchange shall first be adopted by the board of directors.

(b)   Except as provided in subsections (h), (j) and (*l*) and in section 11.05, the plan of merger or share exchange shall then be approved by the shareholders. In submitting the plan of merger or share exchange to the shareholders for approval, the board of directors shall recommend that the shareholders approve the plan or, in the case of an offer referred to in subsection (j)(2), that the shareholders tender their shares to the offeror in response to the offer, unless (i) the board of directors makes a determination that because of conflicts of interest or other special circumstances it should not make such a recommendation or (ii) section 8.26 applies. If either (i) or (ii) applies, the board shall inform the shareholders of the basis for its so proceeding.

(c)   The board of directors may set conditions for the approval of the plan of merger or share exchange by the shareholders or the effectiveness of the plan of merger or share exchange.

(d)   If the plan of merger or share exchange is required to be approved by the shareholders, and if the approval is to be given at a meeting, the corporation shall notify each shareholder, regardless of whether entitled to vote, of the meeting of shareholders at which the plan is to be submitted for approval. The notice must state that the purpose, or one of the purposes, of the meeting is to consider the plan and must contain or be accompanied by a copy or summary of the plan. If the corporation is to be merged into an existing foreign or domestic corporation or eligible entity, the notice must also include or be accompanied by a copy or summary of the articles of incorporation and bylaws or the organic rules of that corporation or eligible entity. If the corporation is to be merged with a domestic or foreign corporation or eligible entity and a new domestic or foreign corporation or eligible entity is to be created pursuant to the merger, the notice must include or be accompanied by a copy or a summary of the articles of incorporation and bylaws or the organic rules of the new corporation or eligible entity.

(e)   Unless the articles of incorporation, or the board of directors acting pursuant to subsection (c), require a greater vote or a greater quorum, approval of the plan of merger or share exchange requires the approval of the shareholders at a meeting at which a quorum exists consisting of a majority of the votes entitled to be cast on the plan, and, if any class or series of shares is entitled to vote as a separate group on the plan of merger or share exchange, the approval of each such separate voting group at a meeting at which a quorum of the voting group is present consisting of a majority of the votes entitled to be cast on the merger or share exchange by that voting group.

(f)   Subject to subsection (g), separate voting by voting groups is required:

(1)   on a plan of merger, by each class or series of shares that:

(i)   are to be converted under the plan of merger into shares, other securities, eligible interests, obligations, rights to acquire shares, other securities or eligible interests, cash, other property, or any combination of the foregoing; or

(ii)   are entitled to vote as a separate group on a provision in the plan that constitutes a proposed amendment to the articles of incorporation of a surviving corporation that requires action by separate voting groups under section 10.04;

(2)   on a plan of share exchange, by each class or series of shares included in the exchange, with each class or series constituting a separate voting group; and

(3)   on a plan of merger or share exchange, if the voting group is entitled under the articles of incorporation to vote as a voting group to approve a plan of merger or share exchange, respectively.

(g)   The articles of incorporation may expressly limit or eliminate the separate voting rights provided in subsections (f)(1)(i) and (f)(2) as to any class or series of shares, except when the plan of merger or share exchange (i) includes what is or would be in effect an amendment subject to subsection (f)(1)(ii), and (ii) will not effect a substantive business combination.

(h)   Unless the articles of incorporation otherwise provide, approval by the corporation's shareholders of a plan of merger is not required if:

(1)   the corporation will survive the merger;

(2)   except for amendments permitted by section 10.05, its articles of incorporation will not be changed;

(3)   each shareholder of the corporation whose shares were outstanding immediately before the effective date of the merger or share exchange will hold the same number of shares, with identical preferences, rights and limitations, immediately after the effective date of the merger; and

(4)   the issuance in the merger of shares or other securities convertible into or rights exercisable for shares does not require a vote under section 6.21(f).

(i)   If as a result of a merger or share exchange one or more shareholders of a domestic corporation would become subject to new interest holder liability, approval of the plan of merger or share exchange requires the signing in connection with the transaction, by each such shareholder, of a separate written consent to become subject to such new interest holder liability, unless in the case of a shareholder that already has interest holder liability with respect to such domestic corporation, (i) the new interest holder liability is with respect to a domestic or foreign corporation (which may be a different or the same domestic corporation in which the person is a shareholder), and (ii) the terms and conditions of the new interest holder liability are substantially identical to those of the existing interest holder liability (other than for changes that eliminate or reduce such interest holder liability).

(j)   Unless the articles of incorporation otherwise provide, approval by the shareholders of a plan of merger or share exchange is not required if:

(1)   the plan of merger or share exchange expressly (i) permits or requires the merger or share exchange to be effected under this subsection and (ii) provides that, if the merger or share exchange is to be effected under this subsection, the merger or share exchange will be effected as soon as practicable following the satisfaction of the requirement set forth in subsection (j)(6);

(2)   another party to the merger, the acquiring entity in the share exchange, or a parent of another party to the merger or the acquiring entity in the share exchange, makes an offer to purchase, on the terms provided in the plan of merger or share exchange, any and all of the outstanding shares of the corporation that, absent this subsection, would be entitled to vote on the plan of merger or share exchange, except that the offer may exclude shares of the corporation that are owned at the commencement of the offer by the corporation, the offeror, or any parent of the offeror, or by any wholly owned subsidiary of any of the foregoing;

(3)   the offer discloses that the plan of merger or share exchange provides that the merger or share exchange will be effected as soon as practicable following the satisfaction of the requirement set forth in subsection (j)(6) and that the shares of the corporation that are not tendered in response to the offer will be treated as set forth in subsection (j)(8);

(4)   the offer remains open for at least 10 days;

(5)   the offeror purchases all shares properly tendered in response to the offer and not properly withdrawn;

(6)   the shares listed below are collectively entitled to cast at least the minimum number of votes on the merger or share exchange that, absent this subsection, would be required by this chapter and by the articles of incorporation for the approval of the merger or share exchange by the shareholders and by any other voting group entitled to vote on the merger or share exchange at a meeting at which all shares entitled to vote on the approval were present and voted:

(i)   shares purchased by the offeror in accordance with the offer;

(ii)   shares otherwise owned by the offeror or by any parent of the offeror or any wholly owned subsidiary of any of the foregoing; and

(iii) shares subject to an agreement that they are to be transferred, contributed or delivered to the offeror, any parent of the offeror, or any wholly owned subsidiary of any of the foregoing in exchange for shares or eligible interests in such offeror, parent or subsidiary;

(7) the offeror or a wholly owned subsidiary of the offeror merges with or into, or effects a share exchange in which it acquires shares of, the corporation; and

(8) each outstanding share of each class or series of shares of the corporation that the offeror is offering to purchase in accordance with the offer, and that is not purchased in accordance with the offer, is to be converted in the merger into, or into the right to receive, or is to be exchanged in the share exchange for, or for the right to receive, the same amount and kind of securities, eligible interests, obligations, rights, cash, or other property to be paid or exchanged in accordance with the offer for each share of that class or series of shares that is tendered in response to the offer, except that shares of the corporation that are owned by the corporation or that are described in clause (ii) or (iii) of subsection (j)(6) need not be converted into or exchanged for the consideration described in this subsection (j)(8).

(k) As used in subsection (j):

(1) "offer" means the offer referred to in subsection (j)(2);

(2) "offeror" means the person making the offer;

(3) "parent" of an entity means a person that owns, directly or indirectly (through one or more wholly owned subsidiaries), all of the outstanding shares of or eligible interests in that entity;

(4) shares tendered in response to the offer shall be deemed to have been "purchased" in accordance with the offer at the earliest time as of which (i) the offeror has irrevocably accepted those shares for payment and (ii) either (A) in the case of shares represented by certificates, the offeror, or the offeror's designated depository or other agent, has physically received the certificates representing those shares or (B) in the case of shares without certificates, those shares have been transferred into the account of the offeror or its designated depository or other agent, or an agent's message relating to those shares has been received by the offeror or its designated depository or other agent; and

(5) "wholly owned subsidiary" of a person means an entity of or in which that person owns, directly or indirectly (through one or more wholly owned subsidiaries), all of the outstanding shares or eligible interests.

(l) Unless the articles of incorporation otherwise provide,

(1) approval of a plan of share exchange by the shareholders of a domestic corporation is not required if the corporation is the acquiring entity in the share exchange; and

(2) shares not to be exchanged under the plan of share exchange are not entitled to vote on the plan.

§ 11.05   Merger Between Parent and Subsidiary or Between Subsidiaries

(a) A domestic or foreign parent entity that owns shares of a domestic corporation which carry at least 90% of the voting power of each class and series of the outstanding shares of the subsidiary that has voting power may (i) merge the subsidiary into itself (if it is a domestic or foreign corporation or eligible entity) or into another domestic or foreign corporation or eligible entity in which the parent entity owns at least 90% of the voting power of each class and series of the outstanding shares or eligible interests which have voting power, or (ii) merge itself (if it is a domestic or foreign corporation or eligible entity) into such subsidiary, in either case without the approval of the board of directors or shareholders of the subsidiary, unless the articles of incorporation or organic rules of the parent entity or the articles of incorporation of the subsidiary corporation otherwise provide. Section 11.04(i) applies to a merger under this section. The articles of merger relating to a merger under this section do not need to be signed by the subsidiary.

(b) A parent entity shall, within 10 days after the effective date of a merger approved under subsection (a), notify each of the subsidiary's shareholders that the merger has become effective.

(c) Except as provided in subsections (a) and (b), a merger between a parent entity and a domestic subsidiary corporation shall be governed by the provisions of chapter 11 applicable to mergers generally.

§ 11.06 Articles of Merger or Share Exchange

(a) After (i) a plan of merger has been adopted and approved as required by this Act, or (ii) if the merger is being effected under section 11.02(a)(2), the merger has been approved as required by the organic law governing the parties to the merger, then articles of merger shall be signed by each party to the merger except as provided in section 11.05(a). The articles must set forth:

(1) the name, jurisdiction of formation, and type of entity of each party to the merger;

(2) the name, jurisdiction of formation, and type of entity of the survivor;

(3) if the survivor of the merger is a domestic corporation and its articles of incorporation are amended, or if a new domestic corporation is created as a result of the merger:

(i) the amendments to the survivor's articles of incorporation; or

(ii) the articles of incorporation of the new corporation;

(4) if the survivor of the merger is a domestic eligible entity and its public organic record is amended, or if a new domestic eligible entity is created as a result of the merger:

(i) the amendments to the public organic record of the survivor; or

(ii) the public organic record of the new eligible entity;

(5) if the plan of merger required approval by the shareholders of a domestic corporation that is a party to the merger, a statement that the plan was duly approved by the shareholders and, if voting by any separate voting group was required, by each such separate voting group, in the manner required by this Act and the articles of incorporation;

(6) if the plan of merger or share exchange did not require approval by the shareholders of a domestic corporation that is a party to the merger, a statement to that effect;

(7) as to each foreign corporation that is a party to the merger, a statement that the participation of the foreign corporation was duly authorized as required by its organic law;

(8) as to each domestic or foreign eligible entity that is a party to the merger, a statement that the merger was approved in accordance with its organic law or section 11.02(c); and

(9) if the survivor is created by the merger and is a domestic limited liability partnership, the filing required to become a limited liability partnership, as an attachment.

(b) After a plan of share exchange in which the acquired entity is a domestic corporation or eligible entity has been adopted and approved as required by this Act, articles of share exchange shall be signed by the acquired entity and the acquiring entity. The articles shall set forth:

(1) the name of the acquired entity;

(2) the name, jurisdiction of formation, and type of entity of the domestic or foreign corporation or eligible entity that is the acquiring entity; and

(3) a statement that the plan of share exchange was duly approved by the acquired entity by:

(i)   the required vote or consent of each class or series of shares or eligible interests included in the exchange; and

(ii)   the required vote or consent of each other class or series of shares or eligible interests entitled to vote on approval of the exchange by the articles of incorporation or organic rules of the acquired entity or section 11.03(c).

(c)   In addition to the requirements of subsection (a) or (b), articles of merger or share exchange may contain any other provision not prohibited by law.

(d)   The articles of merger or share exchange shall be delivered to the secretary of state for filing and, subject to subsection (e), the merger or share exchange shall take effect at the effective date determined in accordance with section 1.23.

(e)   With respect to a merger in which one or more foreign entities is a party or a foreign entity created by the merger is the survivor, the merger itself shall become effective at the later of:

(1)   when all documents required to be filed in foreign jurisdictions to effect the merger have become effective, or

(2)   when the articles of merger take effect.

(f)   Articles of merger filed under this section may be combined with any filing required under the organic law governing any domestic eligible entity involved in the transaction if the combined filing satisfies the requirements of both this section and the other organic law.

§ 11.07   Effect of Merger or Share Exchange

(a)   When a merger becomes effective:

(1)   the domestic or foreign corporation or eligible entity that is designated in the plan of merger as the survivor continues or comes into existence, as the case may be;

(2)   the separate existence of every domestic or foreign corporation or eligible entity that is a party to the merger, other than the survivor, ceases;

(3)   all property owned by, and every contract right possessed by, each domestic or foreign corporation or eligible entity that is a party to the merger, other than the survivor, are the property and contract rights of the survivor without transfer, reversion or impairment;

(4)   all debts, obligations and other liabilities of each domestic or foreign corporation or eligible entity that is a party to the merger, other than the survivor, are debts, obligations or liabilities of the survivor;

(5)   the name of the survivor may, but need not be, substituted in any pending proceeding for the name of any party to the merger whose separate existence ceased in the merger;

(6)   if the survivor is a domestic entity, the articles of incorporation and bylaws or the organic rules of the survivor are amended to the extent provided in the plan of merger;

(7)   the articles of incorporation and bylaws or the organic rules of a survivor that is a domestic entity and is created by the merger become effective;

(8)   the shares of each domestic or foreign corporation that is a party to the merger, and the eligible interests in an eligible entity that is a party to a merger, that are to be converted in accordance with the terms of the merger into shares or other securities, eligible interests, obligations, rights to acquire shares, other securities, or eligible interests, cash, other property, or any combination of the foregoing, are converted, and the former holders of such shares or eligible interests are entitled only to the rights provided to them by those terms or to any rights they may have under chapter 13 or the organic law governing the eligible entity or foreign corporation;

(9) except as provided by law or the terms of the merger, all the rights, privileges, franchises, and immunities of each entity that is a party to the merger, other than the survivor, are the rights, privileges, franchises, and immunities of the survivor; and

(10) if the survivor exists before the merger:

(i) all the property and contract rights of the survivor remain its property and contract rights without transfer, reversion, or impairment;

(ii) the survivor remains subject to all its debts, obligations, and other liabilities; and

(iii) except as provided by law or the plan of merger, the survivor continues to hold all of its rights, privileges, franchises, and immunities.

(b) When a share exchange becomes effective, the shares or eligible interests in the acquired entity that are to be exchanged for shares or other securities, eligible interests, obligations, rights to acquire shares, other securities or eligible interests, cash, other property, or any combination of the foregoing, are entitled only to the rights provided to them in the plan of share exchange or to any rights they may have under chapter 13 or under the organic law governing the acquired entity.

(c) Except as otherwise provided in the articles of incorporation of a domestic corporation or the organic law governing or organic rules of a foreign corporation or a domestic or foreign eligible entity, the effect of a merger or share exchange on interest holder liability is as follows:

(1) A person who becomes subject to new interest holder liability in respect of an entity as a result of a merger or share exchange shall have that new interest holder liability only in respect of interest holder liabilities that arise after the merger or share exchange becomes effective.

(2) If a person had interest holder liability with respect to a party to the merger or the acquired entity before the merger or share exchange becomes effective with respect to shares or eligible interests of such party or acquired entity which were (i) exchanged in the merger or share exchange, (ii) were cancelled in the merger or (iii) the terms and conditions of which relating to interest holder liability were amended pursuant to the merger:

(i) The merger or share exchange does not discharge that prior interest holder liability with respect to any interest holder liabilities that arose before the merger or share exchange becomes effective.

(ii) The provisions of the organic law governing any entity for which the person had that prior interest holder liability shall continue to apply to the collection or discharge of any interest holder liabilities preserved by subsection (c)(2)(i), as if the merger or share exchange had not occurred.

(iii) The person shall have such rights of contribution from other persons as are provided by the organic law governing the entity for which the person had that prior interest holder liability with respect to any interest holder liabilities preserved by subsection (c)(2)(i), as if the merger or share exchange had not occurred.

(iv) The person shall not, by reason of such prior interest holder liability, have interest holder liability with respect to any interest holder liabilities that arise after the merger or share exchange becomes effective.

(3) If a person has interest holder liability both before and after a merger becomes effective with unchanged terms and conditions with respect to the entity that is the survivor by reason of owning the same shares or eligible interests before and after the merger becomes effective, the merger has no effect on such interest holder liability.

(4) A share exchange has no effect on interest holder liability related to shares or eligible interests of the acquired entity that were not exchanged in the share exchange.

(d) Upon a merger becoming effective, a foreign corporation, or a foreign eligible entity, that is the survivor of the merger is deemed to:

    (1)   appoint the secretary of state as its agent for service of process in a proceeding to enforce the rights of shareholders of each domestic corporation that is a party to the merger who exercise appraisal rights; and

    (2)   agree that it will promptly pay the amount, if any, to which such shareholders are entitled under chapter 13.

    (e)   Except as provided in the organic law governing a party to a merger or in its articles of incorporation or organic rules, the merger does not give rise to any rights that an interest holder, governor, or third party would have upon a dissolution, liquidation, or winding up of that party. The merger does not require a party to the merger to wind up its affairs and does not constitute or cause its dissolution or termination.

    (f)   Property held for a charitable purpose under the law of this state by a domestic or foreign corporation or eligible entity immediately before a merger becomes effective may not, as a result of the transaction, be diverted from the objects for which it was donated, granted, devised, or otherwise transferred except and to the extent permitted by or pursuant to the laws of this state addressing cy près or dealing with nondiversion of charitable assets.

    (g)   A bequest, devise, gift, grant, or promise contained in a will or other instrument of donation, subscription, or conveyance which is made to an entity that is a party to a merger that is not the survivor and which takes effect or remains payable after the merger inures to the survivor.

    (h)   A trust obligation that would govern property if transferred to a nonsurviving entity applies to property that is transferred to the survivor after a merger becomes effective

OFFICIAL COMMENT

Under section 11.07(a), in a merger the parties that merge become one. The survivor automatically becomes the owner of all real and personal property and becomes subject to all the liabilities, actual or contingent, of each other party to the merger. A merger is not a conveyance, transfer, or assignment. It does not give rise to claims of reverter or impairment of title based on a prohibited conveyance, transfer, or assignment. It does not give rise to a claim that a contract with a party to the merger is no longer in effect on the ground of nonassignability, unless the contract specifically addresses that issue. All pending proceedings involving either the survivor or a party whose separate existence ceased as a result of the merger are continued.

In contrast to a merger, a share exchange does not vest in the acquiring entity the assets of the acquired entity, or render the acquiring entity liable for the liabilities of the acquired entity. The statements in sections 11.07(a)(8) and 11.07(b) regarding the rights of former holders of shares or eligible interests are not intended to preclude an otherwise proper question concerning the validity of the merger or share exchange, or to override or otherwise affect any provisions of chapter 13 concerning the exclusiveness of rights under that chapter.

The deemed appointment and agreement in section 11.07(d) by a foreign survivor is based on the implied consent of such a foreign corporation, or foreign eligible entity, to the terms of chapter 11 by reason of entering into an agreement that is governed by this chapter.

Section 11.07(e) sets forth the impact of mergers and share exchanges on interest holder liability. Section 11.04(i) sets forth when approval of a merger or share exchange requires the consent of shareholders who would otherwise become subject to new interest holder liability.

§ 11.08 Abandonment of a Merger or Share Exchange

    (a)   After a plan of merger or share exchange has been adopted and approved as required by this chapter, and before articles of merger or share exchange have become effective, the plan may be abandoned by a domestic business corporation that is a party to the plan without action by its shareholders in accordance with any procedures set forth in the plan of merger or share exchange or, if no such procedures are set forth in the plan, in the manner determined by the board of directors.

(b)   If a merger or share exchange is abandoned under subsection (a) after articles of merger or share exchange have been delivered to the secretary of state for filing but before the merger or share exchange has become effective, a statement of abandonment signed by all the parties that signed the articles of merger or share exchange shall be delivered to the secretary of state for filing before the articles of merger or share exchange become effective. The statement shall take effect on filing and the merger or share exchange shall be deemed abandoned and shall not become effective. The statement of abandonment must contain:

(1)   the name of each party to the merger or the names of the acquiring and acquired entities in a share exchange;

(2)   the date on which the articles of merger or share exchange were filed by the secretary of state; and

(3)   a statement that the merger or share exchange has been abandoned in accordance with this section.

CHAPTER 12.   DISPOSITION OF ASSETS

§ 12.01   Disposition of Assets Not Requiring Shareholder Approval

No approval of the shareholders is required, unless the articles of incorporation otherwise provide:

(a)   to sell, lease, exchange, or otherwise dispose of any or all of the corporation's assets in the usual and regular course of business;

(b)   to mortgage, pledge, dedicate to the repayment of indebtedness (whether with or without recourse), or otherwise encumber any or all of the corporation's assets, regardless of whether in the usual and regular course of business;

(c)   to transfer any or all of the corporation's assets to one or more domestic or foreign corporations or other entities all of the shares or interests of which are owned by the corporation; or

(d)   to distribute assets pro rata to the holders of one or more classes or series of the corporation's shares.

OFFICIAL COMMENT

Section 12.01 specifies dispositions for which shareholder approval is not required, and section 12.02 specifies dispositions requiring shareholder approval.

Examples of dispositions in the usual and regular course of business under section 12.01(a) include the sale of a building that was the corporation's only major asset where the corporation was formed for the purpose of constructing and selling that building, the sale by a corporation of its only major business where the corporation was formed to buy and sell businesses and the proceeds of the sale are to be reinvested in the purchase of a new business, or sales of assets by an open- or closed-end investment company the portfolio of which turns over many times in short periods.

No shareholder approval is required for a transaction involving a pro rata distribution because it comes within section 12.01(d). An example is a spin-off in which shares of a subsidiary are distributed pro rata to the holders of one or more classes or series of shares. On the other hand, a non pro rata distribution—for example, a split-off in which shares of a subsidiary are distributed only to some shareholders in exchange for some or all of their shares—would require shareholder approval under section 12.02(a) if the disposition would leave the corporation without a significant continuing business activity. When the transaction involves a distribution in liquidation—for example, when two or more subsidiaries (whether they have existed previously or are newly formed) representing all of a dissolved corporation's business activities are distributed to shareholders (sometimes referred to as a split-up)—the transaction will be governed by chapter 14 (dissolution), not by chapter 12.

§ 12.02 Shareholder Approval of Certain Dispositions

(a) A sale, lease, exchange, or other disposition of assets, other than a disposition described in section 12.01, requires approval of the corporation's shareholders if the disposition would leave the corporation without a significant continuing business activity. A corporation will conclusively be deemed to have retained a significant continuing business activity if it retains a business activity that represented, for the corporation and its subsidiaries on a consolidated basis, at least (i) 25% of total assets at the end of the most recently completed fiscal year, and (ii) either 25% of either income from continuing operations before taxes or 25% of revenues from continuing operations, in each case, for the most recently completed fiscal year.

(b) To obtain the approval of the shareholders under subsection (a) the board of directors shall first adopt a resolution authorizing the disposition. The disposition shall then be approved by the shareholders. In submitting the disposition to the shareholders for approval, the board of directors shall recommend that the shareholders approve the disposition, unless (i) the board of directors makes a determination that because of conflicts of interest or other special circumstances it should not make such a recommendation, or (ii) section 8.26 applies. If either (i) or (ii) applies, the board shall inform the shareholders of the basis for its so proceeding.

(c) The board of directors may set conditions for the approval by the shareholders of a disposition or the effectiveness of the disposition.

(d) If a disposition is required to be approved by the shareholders under subsection (a), and if the approval is to be given at a meeting, the corporation shall notify each shareholder, regardless of whether entitled to vote, of the meeting of shareholders at which the disposition is to be submitted for approval. The notice must state that the purpose, or one of the purposes, of the meeting is to consider the disposition and must contain a description of the disposition, including the terms and conditions of the disposition and the consideration to be received by the corporation.

(e) Unless the articles of incorporation or the board of directors acting pursuant to subsection (c) require a greater vote or a greater quorum, the approval of a disposition by the shareholders shall require the approval of the shareholders at a meeting at which a quorum exists consisting of a majority of the votes entitled to be cast on the disposition.

(f) After a disposition has been approved by the shareholders under this chapter, and at any time before the disposition has been consummated, it may be abandoned by the corporation without action by the shareholders, subject to any contractual rights of other parties to the disposition.

(g) A disposition of assets in the course of dissolution under chapter 14 is not governed by this section.

(h) The assets of a direct or indirect consolidated subsidiary shall be deemed to be the assets of the parent corporation for the purposes of this section.

OFFICIAL COMMENT

1. In General

Section 12.02(a) requires shareholder approval for a sale, lease, exchange or other disposition of assets by a corporation that would leave the corporation without a significant continuing business activity, other than as provided in section 12.01. Whether a disposition leaves a corporation with a significant continuing business activity, within the meaning of section 12.02(a), depends on whether the corporation's remaining business activity is significant when compared to the corporation's business before the disposition. The 25% safe harbor provides a measure of certainty in making this determination. The safe-harbor test is applied to assets and to revenue or income for the fiscal year ended immediately before the decision by the board of directors to make the disposition in question.

If a corporation disposes of assets for the purpose of reinvesting the proceeds of the disposition in substantially the same business in a somewhat different form (for example, by selling the corporation's only plant for the purpose of buying or building a replacement plant), the disposition and reinvestment should be treated together, so that the transaction should not be deemed to leave the corporation without a significant continuing business activity.

In determining whether a disposition would leave a corporation without a significant continuing business activity, the test combines a parent corporation with subsidiaries that are or should be consolidated with it under applicable accounting principles. For example, if a corporation's only significant business is owned by a consolidated subsidiary, a sale of that business requires approval of the parent's shareholders under section 12.02. Correspondingly, if a corporation owns one significant business directly, and several other significant businesses through one or more wholly or almost wholly owned subsidiaries, a sale by the corporation of the single business it owns directly does not require shareholder approval under section 12.02 (for example, the 25% retention tests of section 12.02(a) are met).

If all or a large part of a corporation's assets are held for investment, the corporation actively manages those assets, and it has no other significant business, for purposes of chapter 12 the corporation should be considered to be in the business of investing in assets, so that a sale of most of those assets without a reinvestment should be considered a sale that would leave the corporation without a significant continuing business activity. In applying the 25% tests of section 12.02(a), an issue could arise if a corporation had more than one business activity, one or more of which might be traditional operating activities, such as manufacturing or distribution, and another of which might be considered managing investments in other securities or enterprises. If the activity constituting the management of investments is to be a continuing business activity as a result of the active engagement of the management of the corporation in that process and the 25% retention tests were met upon the disposition of the other businesses, shareholder approval would not be required.

A board of directors may determine that a retained continuing business falls within the 25% bright-line tests of the safe harbor in section 12.02(a) based either on accounting principles and practices that are reasonable in the circumstances or (in applying the asset test) on a fair valuation or other method that is reasonable in the circumstances in a manner similar to that described in section 6.40(d) and the Official Comment 4 to that section.

The use of the term "significant" and the specific 25% safe harbor test for purposes of this section do not imply a standard for the test of significance or materiality for any other purposes under the Act or otherwise.

2. Submission to Shareholders

When submitting a proposal to shareholders for a disposition of assets, the board of directors must recommend the disposition, subject to two exceptions in section 12.02(b). The board might exercise the exception under clause (i) where the number of directors having a conflicting interest makes it inadvisable for the board to recommend the disposition or where the board is evenly divided as to the merits of the proposal but is able to agree that shareholders should be permitted to consider it. Alternatively, the board of directors might exercise the exception under clause (ii), which recognizes that, under section 8.26, a board of directors may agree to submit a proposal for a disposition to a vote of shareholders even if, after approving the proposal, the board of directors determines that it no longer recommends the proposal.

Section 12.02(c) permits the board of directors to condition its submission to the shareholders of a proposal for a disposition of assets or the effectiveness of the disposition. Among the conditions that a board of directors might impose are that the proposal will not be deemed approved: (i) unless it is approved by a specified percentage of the shareholders, or by one or more specified classes or series of shares, voting as a separate voting group, or by a specified percentage of disinterested shareholders; or (ii) if shareholders holding more than a specified fraction of the outstanding shares exercise appraisal rights.

3. Quorum and Voting

Requirements concerning the timing and content of a notice of meeting, as required by section 12.02(d), are set out in section 7.05. Section 12.02(d) does not address the notice to be given to nonvoting or nonconsenting shareholders where the proposal is approved without a meeting by written consent. That requirement is imposed by section 7.04.

Section 12.02(e) sets forth quorum and voting requirements applicable to a shareholder vote to approve a disposition. In lieu of approval at a meeting, shareholder approval may be by written consent under the procedures set forth in section 7.04.

The Act does not mandate separate voting by voting groups on dispositions, because after a disposition under this chapter the rights of all classes or series of shares remain the same. Separate voting by voting groups may nevertheless be required if provided for in the articles of incorporation or by the board of directors, acting pursuant to section 12.02(c). Appraisal may be available to shareholders entitled to vote on the disposition. See chapter 13.

CHAPTER 13.   APPRAISAL RIGHTS

SUBCHAPTER A.   RIGHT TO APPRAISAL AND PAYMENT FOR SHARES

§ 13.01   Definitions

In this chapter:

"Affiliate" means a person that directly or indirectly through one or more intermediaries controls, is controlled by, or is under common control with another person or is a senior executive of such person. For purposes of section 13.02(b)(4), a person is deemed to be an affiliate of its senior executives.

"Corporation" means the domestic corporation that is the issuer of the shares held by a shareholder demanding appraisal and, for matters covered in sections 13.22 through 13.31, includes the survivor of a merger.

"Fair value" means the value of the corporation's shares determined:

    (i)   immediately before the effectiveness of the corporate action to which the shareholder objects;

    (ii)   using customary and current valuation concepts and techniques generally employed for similar businesses in the context of the transaction requiring appraisal; and

    (iii)   without discounting for lack of marketability or minority status except, if appropriate, for amendments to the articles of incorporation pursuant to section 13.02(a)(5).

"Interest" means interest from the date the corporate action becomes effective until the date of payment, at the rate of interest on judgments in this state on the effective date of the corporate action.

"Interested transaction" means a corporate action described in section 13.02(a), other than a merger pursuant to section 11.05, involving an interested person in which any of the shares or assets of the corporation are being acquired or converted. As used in this definition:

    (i)   "Interested person" means a person, or an affiliate of a person, who at any time during the one-year period immediately preceding approval by the board of directors of the corporate action:

        (A)   was the beneficial owner of 20% or more of the voting power of the corporation, other than as owner of excluded shares;

        (B)   had the power, contractually or otherwise, other than as owner of excluded shares, to cause the appointment or election of 25% or more of the directors to the board of directors of the corporation; or

        (C)   was a senior executive or director of the corporation or a senior executive of any affiliate of the corporation, and that senior executive or director will receive, as a result of the corporate action, a financial benefit not generally available to other shareholders as such, other than:

(I) employment, consulting, retirement, or similar benefits established separately and not as part of or in contemplation of the corporate action;

(II) employment, consulting, retirement, or similar benefits established in contemplation of, or as part of, the corporate action that are not more favorable than those existing before the corporate action or, if more favorable, that have been approved on behalf of the corporation in the same manner as is provided in section 8.62; or

(III) in the case of a director of the corporation who will, in the corporate action, become a director or governor of the acquiror or any of its affiliates, rights and benefits as a director or governor that are provided on the same basis as those afforded by the acquiror generally to other directors or governors of such entity or such affiliate.

(ii) "Beneficial owner" means any person who, directly or indirectly, through any contract, arrangement, or understanding, other than a revocable proxy, has or shares the power to vote, or to direct the voting of, shares; except that a member of a national securities exchange is not deemed to be a beneficial owner of securities held directly or indirectly by it on behalf of another person if the member is precluded by the rules of the exchange from voting without instruction on contested matters or matters that may affect substantially the rights or privileges of the holders of the securities to be voted. When two or more persons agree to act together for the purpose of voting their shares of the corporation, each member of the group formed thereby is deemed to have acquired beneficial ownership, as of the date of the agreement, of all shares having voting power of the corporation beneficially owned by any member of the group.

(iii) "Excluded shares" means shares acquired pursuant to an offer for all shares having voting power if the offer was made within one year before the corporate action for consideration of the same kind and of a value equal to or less than that paid in connection with the corporate action.

"Preferred shares" means a class or series of shares whose holders have preference over any other class or series of shares with respect to distributions.

"Senior executive" means the chief executive officer, chief operating officer, chief financial officer, and any individual in charge of a principal business unit or function.

"Shareholder" means a record shareholder, a beneficial shareholder, and a voting trust beneficial owner.

OFFICIAL COMMENT

1. Overview

Chapter 13 proceeds from the premise that judicial appraisal should be provided by statute only when two conditions co-exist. First, a proposed corporate action as approved by a majority will result in a fundamental change in the shares to be affected by the action. Second, uncertainty concerning the fair value of the affected shares may cause reasonable persons to differ about the fairness of the terms of the corporate action. Uncertainty is reduced, however, in the case of publicly traded shares. This explains both the market exception described below and the limits provided to that exception.

When these two conditions exist in connection with domestications and conversions under chapter 9, mergers and share exchanges under chapter 11, and dispositions of assets requiring shareholder approval under chapter 12, chapter 13 provides for appraisal rights. Each of these actions will result in a fundamental change in the shares that a disapproving shareholder may believe was not adequately compensated by the terms approved by the majority. Shareholders are not entitled to appraisal, however, if the change will not alter the terms of the class or series of securities that they hold. For example, statutory appraisal rights are not available for shares of any class or series of the surviving corporation in a merger that are not being changed in the merger or for shares of any class or series that is not included in a share exchange. Appraisal is also not triggered by a voluntary dissolution under chapter 14 because the dissolution does not affect liquidation rights of the shares of any class or series.

With the exception of reverse stock splits that result in cashing out some of the shares of a class or series, chapter 13 does not grant appraisal rights in connection with amendments to the articles of incorporation. This does not reflect a judgment that an amendment changing the terms of a particular class or series may not have significant economic effects. Rather, it reflects a judgment that distinguishing among different types of amendments for the purposes of statutory appraisal is necessarily arbitrary. Chapter 13 delineates in section 13.02(a)(5) a list of actions for which the corporation may voluntarily choose to provide appraisal. It also allows, under section 13.02(c), a provision in the articles of incorporation that eliminates, in whole or in part, statutory appraisal rights for preferred shares, subject to certain conditions.

Chapter 13 provides an exception to appraisal rights for publicly traded shares, referred to as the "market exception." This exception is available in those situations when shareholders are likely to receive fair value if they sell their shares in the market after the announcement of an appraisal-triggering transaction. For the market exception to apply under chapter 13, there must be a liquid market for the shares. The market exception does not apply where the appraisal-triggering action is a conflict transaction.

2. Definitions

Section 13.01 contains specialized definitions applicable only to chapter 13.

A. Corporation

The definition of "corporation" in section 13.01 includes, for purposes of the post-transaction matters covered in sections 13.22 through 13.31, a successor entity in a merger where the corporation is not the surviving entity. The definition does not include an acquiring entity in a share exchange or disposition of assets because the corporation whose shares or assets were acquired continues in existence in both of these instances and remains responsible for the appraisal obligations. Whether a foreign corporation or other form of domestic or foreign entity is subject to appraisal rights in connection with any of these transactions depends upon the applicable law of the relevant jurisdiction.

B. Fair value

Clause (i) of the definition of "fair value" in section 13.01 specifies that fair value is to be determined immediately before the effectiveness of the corporate action, which will be after the shareholder vote. Accordingly, section 13.01 permits consideration of changes in the value of the corporation's shares after the shareholder vote but before the effectiveness of the transaction, to the extent such changes are relevant. Similarly, in a two-step transaction culminating in a merger, fair value is determined immediately before the second step merger, taking into account any interim changes in value.

Clause (ii) of the definition of "fair value" in section 13.01 adopts the view that different transactions and different contexts may warrant different valuation methodologies. Customary valuation concepts and techniques will typically take into account numerous relevant factors, and will normally result in a range of values, not a particular single value. A court determining fair value under chapter 13 should give great deference to the aggregate consideration accepted or approved by a disinterested board of directors for an appraisal-triggering transaction.

Valuation discounts for lack of marketability or minority status are inappropriate in most appraisal actions, both because most transactions that trigger appraisal rights affect the corporation as a whole and because such discounts may give the majority the opportunity to take advantage of minority shareholders who have been forced against their will to accept the appraisal-triggering transaction. Clause (iii) of the definition of "fair value" adopts the view that appraisal should generally award a shareholder his or her proportional interest in the corporation after valuing the corporation as a whole, rather than the value of the shareholder's shares when valued alone.

C. Interest

The specification of the rate of interest on judgments, rather than a more subjective rate, eliminates a possible issue of contention and should facilitate voluntary settlements. Other state law determines whether interest is compound or simple.

D. Interested transaction

The term "interested transaction" addresses two groups of conflict transactions: those in subsections (i)(A) and (B) of the definition, which involve large shareholders; and those in subsection (i)(C), which involve senior executives and directors. The phrase "involving an interested person" as applied to subsections (i)(A) and (B) denotes participation beyond merely voting or participating on the same basis as other holders of securities of the same or a similar class or series. When a transaction fits within the definition of an interested transaction there are two consequences: the market exception will not be applicable, and the exclusion of other remedies under section 13.40 will not be applicable unless certain disinterested approvals have been obtained.

The definition of "beneficial owner" in subsection (ii) of the definition of "interested transaction" is used to identify possible conflict situations by deeming each member of a group that agrees to vote in concert to be a beneficial owner of all the voting shares owned by the members of the group. (In contrast, the term "beneficial shareholder," as defined in section 1.40, is used to identify those persons entitled to appraisal rights.) When an acquisition is effected in two steps (a tender offer followed by a merger) within one year, and the consideration in the merger is of the same kind and of at least the same value as that in the tender offer, the two-step acquisition is properly considered a single transaction for purposes of identifying conflict transactions, regardless of whether the second-step merger is governed by section 11.04 or 11.05. Therefore the shares acquired in such an offer (defined as "excluded shares" in subsection (iii)) are excluded in subsections (i)(A) and (B) from the determination of whether a person is an "interested person" for purposes of the second-step merger.

A reverse split in which small shareholders are cashed out will constitute an interested transaction if there is an affiliate of the corporation who satisfies the test in subsections (i)(A) or (B). In that case, the corporation itself will be considered an affiliate of the large shareholder and fall within the definition of "interested person," such that when the corporation acquires and cashes out the shares of the small shareholders the acquisition will be an interested transaction.

Subsection (i)(C) applies to management buyouts because management's participation in the buyout group is itself "a financial benefit not generally available to other shareholders." It also applies to transactions involving other types of economic benefits (excluding benefits afforded to shareholders generally) afforded to senior executives (as defined in section 13.01) and directors in specified conflict situations, unless specific objective or procedural standards are met. It would also apply to less common situations, such as where the vote of a director is manipulated by providing the director with special consideration to secure his or her vote in favor of the transaction. Section 13.01 specifically defines the term "affiliate" to include an entity of which a person is a senior executive. As a result of this definition, if a senior executive of the corporation is to continue and is to receive enumerated employment and other financial benefits after the transaction, exempting the transaction from the category of "interested transactions" will depend on meeting one of the three conditions specified in subsection (i)(C), for example:

- If an individual has an arrangement under which benefits will be triggered on a "change of control," such as accelerated vesting of options, retirement benefits, deferred compensation and similar items, or is afforded the opportunity to retire or leave the employ of the enterprise with more favorable economic results than would be the case absent a change of control, the existence of these arrangements would not mean that the transaction is an interested transaction if the arrangements had been established as a general condition of the individual's employment or continued employment, rather than in contemplation of the particular transaction.

- If such arrangements are established as part of, or as a condition of, the transaction, the transaction will still not be considered an interested transaction if the arrangements are either not more favorable to the officer or director than those already in existence or, if they treat the director or officer more favorably, are approved by "qualified" directors (*i.e.*, meeting the standard specified in section 1.43), in the same manner as provided for conflicting interest transactions generally with the corporation under section 8.62. This category would include arrangements with the corporation that have been negotiated as part of, or as a condition to, the transaction or arrangements with the acquiring company or one or more of its other subsidiaries.

- If a person who is a director of the corporation and, in connection with the transaction, is to become a director of the acquiror or its parent, or to continue as a director of the corporation when it becomes a subsidiary of the acquiror, the transaction will not be considered an interested transaction as long as that person will not be treated more favorably as a director than are other persons who are serving in the same director positions.

[E]. Senior executive

The definition of "senior executive" in section 13.01 encompasses the group of individuals in control of corporate information and the corporation's day-to-day operations. An employee of a subsidiary organization is a "senior executive" of the parent if the employee is "in charge of a principal business unit or function" of the parent and its subsidiaries on a combined or consolidated basis.

F. Shareholder

The definition of "shareholder" in section 13.01 encompasses beneficial shareholders and voting trust beneficial owners. This recognizes that these persons have or hold on behalf of others an economic interest in the shares. Use of the term "beneficial shareholder" for this purpose is to be contrasted with the use of the term "beneficial owner" in subsection (ii) of the definition of "interested transaction" to identify possible conflict situations. The distinction between "record shareholder" and "beneficial shareholder" appears primarily in section 13.03, which establishes the manner in which beneficial shareholders, and record shareholders who are acting on behalf of beneficial shareholders, perfect appraisal rights.

§ 13.02   Right to Appraisal

(a)   A shareholder is entitled to appraisal rights, and to obtain payment of the fair value of that shareholder's shares, in the event of any of the following corporate actions:

(1)   consummation of a merger to which the corporation is a party (i) if shareholder approval is required for the merger by section 11.04, or would be required but for the provisions of section 11.04(j), except that appraisal rights shall not be available to any shareholder of the corporation with respect to shares of any class or series that remain outstanding after consummation of the merger, or (ii) if the corporation is a subsidiary and the merger is governed by section 11.05;

(2)   consummation of a share exchange to which the corporation is a party the shares of which will be acquired, except that appraisal rights shall not be available to any shareholder of the corporation with respect to any class or series of shares of the corporation that is not acquired in the share exchange;

(3)   consummation of a disposition of assets pursuant to section 12.02 if the shareholder is entitled to vote on the disposition, except that appraisal rights shall not be available to any shareholder of the corporation with respect to shares of any class or series if (i) under the terms of the corporate action approved by the shareholders there is to be distributed to shareholders in cash the corporation's net assets, in excess of a reasonable amount reserved to meet claims of the type described in sections 14.06 and 14.07, (A) within one year after the shareholders' approval of the action and (B) in accordance with their respective interests determined at the time of distribution, and (ii) the disposition of assets is not an interested transaction;

(4)   an amendment of the articles of incorporation with respect to a class or series of shares that reduces the number of shares of a class or series owned by the shareholder to a fraction of a share if the corporation has the obligation or right to repurchase the fractional share so created;

(5)   any other merger, share exchange, disposition of assets or amendment to the articles of incorporation, in each case to the extent provided by the articles of incorporation, bylaws or a resolution of the board of directors;

(6)   consummation of a domestication pursuant to section 9.20 if the shareholder does not receive shares in the foreign corporation resulting from the domestication that have terms as favorable to the shareholder in all material respects, and represent at least the same percentage interest of the total voting rights of the outstanding shares of the foreign corporation, as the shares held by the shareholder before the domestication;

(7)   consummation of a conversion of the corporation to a nonprofit corporation pursuant to section 9.30; or

(8)   consummation of a conversion of the corporation to an unincorporated entity pursuant to section 9.30.

(b)   Notwithstanding subsection (a), the availability of appraisal rights under subsections (a)(1), (2), (3), (4), (6) and (8) shall be limited in accordance with the following provisions:

(1)   Appraisal rights shall not be available for the holders of shares of any class or series of shares which is:

(i)   a covered security under section 18(b)(1)(A) or (B) of the Securities Act of 1933;

(ii)   traded in an organized market and has at least 2,000 shareholders and a market value of at least $20 million (exclusive of the value of such shares held by the corporation's subsidiaries, senior executives and directors and by any beneficial shareholder and any voting trust beneficial owner owning more than 10% of such shares); or

(iii)   issued by an open end management investment company registered with the Securities and Exchange Commission under the Investment Company Act of 1940 and which may be redeemed at the option of the holder at net asset value.

(2)   The applicability of subsection (b)(1) shall be determined as of:

(i)   the record date fixed to determine the shareholders entitled to receive notice of the meeting of shareholders to act upon the corporate action requiring appraisal rights or, in the case of an offer made pursuant to section 11.04(j), the date of such offer; or

(ii)   if there is no meeting of shareholders and no offer made pursuant to section 11.04(j), the day before the consummation of the corporate action or effective date of the amendment of the articles of incorporation, as applicable.

(3)   Subsection (b)(1) shall not be applicable and appraisal rights shall be available pursuant to subsection (a) for the holders of any class or series of shares (i) who are required by the terms of the corporate action requiring appraisal rights to accept for such shares anything other than cash or shares of any class or any series of shares of any corporation, or any other proprietary interest of any other entity, that satisfies the standards set forth in subsection (b)(1) at the time the corporate action becomes effective, or (ii) in the case of the consummation of a disposition of assets pursuant to section 12.02, unless the cash, shares, or proprietary interests received in the disposition are, under the terms of the corporate action approved by the shareholders, to be distributed to the shareholders, as part of a distribution to shareholders of the net assets of the corporation in excess of a reasonable amount to meet claims of the type described in sections 14.06 and 14.07, (A) within one year after the shareholders' approval of the action, and (B) in accordance with their respective interests determined at the time of the distribution.

(4)   Subsection (b)(1) shall not be applicable and appraisal rights shall be available pursuant to subsection (a) for the holders of any class or series of shares where the corporate action is an interested transaction.

(c)   Notwithstanding any other provision of section 13.02, the articles of incorporation as originally filed or any amendment to the articles of incorporation may limit or eliminate appraisal rights for any class or series of preferred shares, except that (i) no such limitation or elimination shall be effective if the class or series does not have the right to vote separately as a voting group (alone or as part of a group) on the action or if the action is a conversion under section 9.30, or a merger having a similar effect as a conversion in which the converted entity is an eligible entity, and (ii) any such limitation or elimination contained in an amendment to the articles of incorporation that limits or eliminates appraisal rights for any of such shares that are outstanding immediately before the effective date of such amendment or that the corporation is or may be required to issue or sell thereafter pursuant to any conversion, exchange or other right existing immediately before the effective date of such amendment shall not apply to any corporate action that becomes effective within one year after the effective date of such amendment if such action would otherwise afford appraisal rights.

OFFICIAL COMMENT

1.　Transactions Requiring Appraisal Rights

Section 13.02(a) establishes the scope of appraisal rights by identifying those transactions that afford this right. Statutory appraisal is made available only for corporate actions that will result in a fundamental change in the shares to be affected by the action and then only when uncertainty concerning the fair value of the affected shares may cause reasonable differences about the fairness of the terms of the corporate action. The transactions that satisfy both of these criteria are set forth in section 13.02(a), subject to the exceptions set forth in section 13.02(b). In a two-step transaction authorized by section 11.04(j), shareholders at the time of the second step merger could have appraisal rights even though there is no shareholder vote. Shareholders who tender in response to the offer in the first step of such a transaction would not have appraisal rights; their tendering in response to the offer has the same effect on appraisal rights as if they had voted for the transaction.

Under section 13.02(b)(4), the reasons for granting appraisal rights in a reverse stock split in which shares are cashed out are similar to those for granting such rights in cases of cash-out mergers, as both transactions could compel affected shareholders to accept cash for their investment in an amount established by the corporation. Appraisal is afforded only for those shareholders of a class or series whose interest is so affected by the amendment. As provided in section 12.02(g), a disposition of assets by a corporation in the course of dissolution under chapter 14 is governed by that chapter, not chapter 12, and thus does not implicate appraisal rights.

An express grant of voluntary appraisal rights under section 13.02(a)(5) overrides any of the exceptions to the availability of appraisal rights in section 13.02(a). Any voluntary grant of appraisal rights by the corporation to the holders of one or more of its classes or series of shares in connection with a corporate action will automatically make all of the provisions of chapter 13 applicable to the corporation and such holders regarding that corporate action.

2.　Market Exception to Appraisal Rights

Chapter 13 provides a limited exception to appraisal rights for those situations where shareholders may either accept the appraisal-triggering corporate action or sell their shares in an organized market described in section 13.02(b)(1). For purposes of this chapter, the market exception is provided for a class or series of shares if two tests are satisfied: the market in which the shares are traded must be liquid, as described in section 13.02(b)(1), and the value of the shares established by the appraisal-triggering event must be the result of a process reasonably calculated to arrive at a price reflective of an arm's length transaction.

Because section 13.02(b)(3)(i) excludes from the market exception those transactions that require shareholders to accept anything other than cash or securities that also meet the liquidity tests of section 13.02(b)(1), shareholders are assured of receiving either appraisal rights, cash from the transaction, or shares or other proprietary interests in the survivor entity that are liquid. Section 13.02(b)(2) specifies the date on which the corporation must satisfy the requirements of section 13.02(b)(1) for the market exception to be applicable. Section 13.02(b)(4) recognizes that the market price of, or consideration for, shares of a corporation that proposes to engage in an interested transaction of the type listed in section 13.02(a) may be subject to influences where a corporation's management, controlling shareholders or directors have conflicting interests that could, if not dealt with appropriately, adversely affect the consideration that otherwise could have been expected. Section 13.02(b)(4) thus provides that the market exception will not apply in those instances where the transaction constitutes an interested transaction (as defined in section 13.01).

3.　Elimination of Appraisal Rights for Preferred Shares

Section 13.02(c) permits the corporation to eliminate or limit appraisal rights that would otherwise be available for the holders of one or more series or classes of preferred shares provided that the standards in that section are met. Chapter 13 does not permit the corporation to eliminate or limit the appraisal rights of common shares.

§ 13.03 Assertion of Rights by Nominees and Beneficial Shareholders

(a) A record shareholder may assert appraisal rights as to fewer than all the shares registered in the record shareholder's name but owned by a beneficial shareholder or a voting trust beneficial owner only if the record shareholder objects with respect to all shares of a class or series owned by the beneficial shareholder or the voting trust beneficial owner and notifies the corporation in writing of the name and address of each beneficial shareholder or voting trust beneficial owner on whose behalf appraisal rights are being asserted. The rights of a record shareholder who asserts appraisal rights for only part of the shares held of record in the record shareholder's name under this subsection shall be determined as if the shares as to which the record shareholder objects and the record shareholder's other shares were registered in the names of different record shareholders.

(b) A beneficial shareholder and a voting trust beneficial owner may assert appraisal rights as to shares of any class or series held on behalf of the shareholder only if such shareholder:

(1) submits to the corporation the record shareholder's written consent to the assertion of such rights no later than the date referred to in section 13.22(b)(2)(ii); and

(2) does so with respect to all shares of the class or series that are beneficially owned by the beneficial shareholder or the voting trust beneficial owner.

OFFICIAL COMMENT

Section 13.03 addresses the relationship between those who are entitled to assert appraisal rights and the widespread practice of nominee or street name ownership of publicly traded shares. Generally, a shareholder must demand appraisal for all the shares of a class or series which the shareholder owns. If a record shareholder is a nominee for several beneficial shareholders, some of whom wish to demand appraisal and some of whom do not, section 13.03(a) permits the record shareholder to assert appraisal rights with respect to a portion of the shares held of record by the record shareholder but only with respect to all the shares beneficially owned by a single person. The same rule applies to shares held by voting trustees. A shareholder who owns shares in more than one class or series, however, may assert appraisal rights for only some rather than all classes or series that the shareholder owns.

Voting trustees hold shares on behalf of voting trust beneficial owners and may want to or be required to pass the decision on asserting appraisal rights on to the voting trust beneficial owners. To make appraisal rights effective without burdening record shareholders, beneficial shareholders and voting trust beneficial owners are allowed to assert their own claims as provided in section 13.03(b). After the corporation has received the form of consent required by section 13.03(b)(1), the corporation must deal with the beneficial shareholder, or, in the case of a voting trust, the voting trust beneficial owner.

SUBCHAPTER B. PROCEDURE FOR EXERCISE OF APPRAISAL RIGHTS

§ 13.20 Notice of Appraisal Rights

(a) Where any corporate action specified in section 13.02(a) is to be submitted to a vote at a shareholders' meeting, the meeting notice (or where no approval of such action is required pursuant to section 11.04(j), the offer made pursuant to section 11.04(j)), must state that the corporation has concluded that appraisal rights are, are not or may be available under this chapter. If the corporation concludes that appraisal rights are or may be available, a copy of this chapter must accompany the meeting notice or offer sent to those record shareholders entitled to exercise appraisal rights.

(b) In a merger pursuant to section 11.05, the parent entity shall notify in writing all record shareholders of the subsidiary who are entitled to assert appraisal rights that the corporate action became effective. Such notice shall be sent within 10 days after the corporate action became effective and include the materials described in section 13.22.

(c)   Where any corporate action specified in section 13.02(a) is to be approved by written consent of the shareholders pursuant to section 7.04:

(1)   written notice that appraisal rights are, are not or may be available shall be sent to each record shareholder from whom a consent is solicited at the time consent of such shareholder is first solicited and, if the corporation has concluded that appraisal rights are or may be available, the notice must be accompanied by a copy of this chapter; and

(2)   written notice that appraisal rights are, are not or may be available must be delivered together with the notice to nonconsenting and nonvoting shareholders required by sections 7.04(e) and (f), may include the materials described in section 13.22 and, if the corporation has concluded that appraisal rights are or may be available, must be accompanied by a copy of this chapter.

(d)   Where corporate action described in section 13.02(a) is proposed, or a merger pursuant to section 11.05 is effected, the notice referred to in subsection (a) or (c), if the corporation concludes that appraisal rights are or may be available, and in subsection (b) must be accompanied by:

(1)   financial statements of the corporation that issued the shares that may be subject to appraisal, consisting of a balance sheet as of the end of a fiscal year ending not more than 16 months before the date of the notice, an income statement for that year, and a cash flow statement for that year; provided that, if such financial statements are not reasonably available, the corporation shall provide reasonably equivalent financial information; and

(2)   the latest interim financial statements of such corporation, if any.

(e)   The right to receive the information described in subsection (d) may be waived in writing by a shareholder before or after the corporate action.

OFFICIAL COMMENT

The notices required by sections 13.20(a), (b) and (c) are necessary because many shareholders do not know what appraisal rights they may have or how to assert them. Because appraisal is an "opt in" remedy, shareholders otherwise entitled to an appraisal of their shares by reason of corporate actions specified in section 13.02 must elect whether to seek that remedy or accept the results of that action.

Section 13.20(d) specifies certain disclosure requirements for corporate actions for which appraisal rights are provided. Disclosure of additional information may be necessary under common law disclosure duties.

By specifying certain disclosure requirements, section 13.20(d) reduces the risk, in the transactions to which it applies, of an uninformed shareholder decision whether to exercise appraisal rights. Section 13.31(b)(1) provides that a corporation may be liable for the fees and expenses of counsel and experts for the respective parties for failure to comply substantially with sections 13.20 and 13.24.

§ 13.21   Notice of Intent to Demand Payment and Consequences of Voting or Consenting

(a)   If a corporate action specified in section 13.02(a) is submitted to a vote at a shareholders' meeting, a shareholder who wishes to assert appraisal rights with respect to any class or series of shares:

(1)   shall deliver to the corporation, before the vote is taken, written notice of the shareholder's intent to demand payment if the proposed action is effectuated; and

(2)   shall not vote, or cause or permit to be voted, any shares of such class or series in favor of the proposed action.

(b)   If a corporate action specified in section 13.02(a) is to be approved by written consent, a shareholder who wishes to assert appraisal rights with respect to any class or series of shares shall not sign a consent in favor of the proposed action with respect to that class or series of shares.

(c)   If a corporate action specified in section 13.02(a) does not require shareholder approval pursuant to section 11.04(j), a shareholder who wishes to assert appraisal rights with respect to any class or series of shares (i) shall deliver to the corporation before the shares are purchased pursuant to the offer written notice of the shareholder's intent to demand payment if the proposed action is effected; and (ii) shall not tender, or cause or permit to be tendered, any shares of such class or series in response to such offer.

(d) A shareholder who fails to satisfy the requirements of subsection (a), (b) or (c) is not entitled to payment under this chapter.

§ 13.22 Appraisal Notice and Form

(a) If a corporate action requiring appraisal rights under section 13.02(a) becomes effective, the corporation shall deliver a written appraisal notice and form required by subsection (b) to all shareholders who satisfy the requirements of sections 13.21(a), (b) or (c). In the case of a merger under section 11.05, the parent shall deliver an appraisal notice and form to all record shareholders who may be entitled to assert appraisal rights.

(b) The appraisal notice shall be delivered no earlier than the date the corporate action specified in section 13.02(a) became effective, and no later than 10 days after such date, and must:

(1) supply a form that (i) specifies the first date of any announcement to shareholders made before the date the corporate action became effective of the principal terms of the proposed corporate action, and (ii) if such announcement was made, requires the shareholder asserting appraisal rights to certify whether beneficial ownership of those shares for which appraisal rights are asserted was acquired before that date, and (iii) requires the shareholder asserting appraisal rights to certify that such shareholder did not vote for or consent to the transaction as to the class or series of shares for which appraisal is sought;

(2) state:

(i) where the form shall be sent and where certificates for certificated shares shall be deposited and the date by which those certificates must be deposited, which date may not be earlier than the date by which the corporation must receive the required form under subsection (b)(2)(ii);

(ii) a date by which the corporation shall receive the form, which date may not be fewer than 40 nor more than 60 days after the date the subsection (a) appraisal notice is sent, and state that the shareholder shall have waived the right to demand appraisal with respect to the shares unless the form is received by the corporation by such specified date;

(iii) the corporation's estimate of the fair value of the shares;

(iv) that, if requested in writing, the corporation will provide, to the shareholder so requesting, within 10 days after the date specified in subsection (b)(2)(ii) the number of shareholders who return the forms by the specified date and the total number of shares owned by them; and

(v) the date by which the notice to withdraw under section 13.23 shall be received, which date shall be within 20 days after the date specified in subsection (b)(2)(ii); and

(3) be accompanied by a copy of this chapter.

§ 13.23 Perfection of Rights; Right to Withdraw

(a) A shareholder who receives notice pursuant to section 13.22 and who wishes to exercise appraisal rights shall sign and return the form sent by the corporation and, in the case of certificated shares, deposit the shareholder's certificates in accordance with the terms of the notice by the date referred to in the notice pursuant to section 13.22(b)(2)(ii). In addition, if applicable, the shareholder shall certify on the form whether the beneficial owner of such shares acquired beneficial ownership of the shares before the date required to be set forth in the notice pursuant to section 13.22(b)(1)(i). If a shareholder fails to make this certification, the corporation may elect to treat the shareholder's shares as after-acquired shares under section 13.25. Once a shareholder deposits that shareholder's certificates or, in the case of uncertificated shares, returns the signed forms, that shareholder loses all rights as a shareholder, unless the shareholder withdraws pursuant to subsection (b).

(b)   A shareholder who has complied with subsection (a) may nevertheless decline to exercise appraisal rights and withdraw from the appraisal process by so notifying the corporation in writing by the date set forth in the appraisal notice pursuant to section 13.22(b)(2)(v). A shareholder who fails to so withdraw from the appraisal process may not thereafter withdraw without the corporation's written consent.

(c)   A shareholder who does not sign and return the form and, in the case of certificated shares, deposit that shareholder's share certificates where required, each by the date set forth in the notice described in section 13.22(b), shall not be entitled to payment under this chapter.

§ 13.24   Payment

(a)   Except as provided in section 13.25, within 30 days after the form required by section 13.22(b)(2)(ii) is due, the corporation shall pay in cash to those shareholders who complied with section 13.23(a) the amount the corporation estimates to be the fair value of their shares, plus interest.

(b)   The payment to each shareholder pursuant to subsection (a) must be accompanied by:

(1) (i)   financial statements of the corporation that issued the shares to be appraised, consisting of a balance sheet as of the end of a fiscal year ending not more than 16 months before the date of payment, an income statement for that year, and a cash flow statement for that year; provided that, if such annual financial statements are not reasonably available, the corporation shall provide reasonably equivalent financial information, and (ii) the latest interim financial statements of such corporation, if any;

(2)   a statement of the corporation's estimate of the fair value of the shares, which estimate shall equal or exceed the corporation's estimate given pursuant to section 13.22(b)(2)(iii); and

(3)   a statement that shareholders described in subsection (a) have the right to demand further payment under section 13.26 and that if any such shareholder does not do so within the time period specified in section 13.26(b), such shareholder shall be deemed to have accepted the payment under subsection (a) in full satisfaction of the corporation's obligations under this chapter.

OFFICIAL COMMENT

Section 13.24 is applicable to shareholders who have complied with section 13.23(a) and to shareholders described in section 13.25(a) if the corporation so chooses. The corporation must, however, elect to treat all shareholders described in section 13.25(a) either under section 13.24 or under section 13.25; it may not treat some shareholders described in section 13.25(a) under section 13.24 but treat others under section 13.25.

The requirement of section 13.24 that the corporation pay its estimate of the fair value of the stock plus interest reflects a judgment that a difference of opinion over the total amount to be paid should not delay payment of the amount that is undisputed. Because a former shareholder must decide whether to accept that payment in full satisfaction, the corporation must include with the payment the information specified in section 13.24(b), which includes a reminder of the former shareholder's further rights.

Even though the information specified in section 13.24(b) was previously furnished under section 13.20(d) at the time notice of appraisal rights was given, it must still be furnished under section 13.24(b) at the time of payment. That information may need to be updated to satisfy the requirements of section 13.24(b).

§ 13.25   After-Acquired Shares

(a)   A corporation may elect to withhold payment required by section 13.24 from any shareholder who was required to, but did not certify that beneficial ownership of all of the shareholder's shares for which appraisal rights are asserted was acquired before the date set forth in the appraisal notice sent pursuant to section 13.22(b)(1).

(b)   If the corporation elected to withhold payment under subsection (a), it shall, within 30 days after the form required by section 13.22(b)(2)(ii) is due, notify all shareholders who are described in subsection (a):

    (1)   of the information required by section 13.24(b)(1);

    (2)   of the corporation's estimate of fair value pursuant to section 13.24(b)(2);

    (3)   that they may accept the corporation's estimate of fair value, plus interest, in full satisfaction of their demands or demand appraisal under section 13.26;

    (4)   that those shareholders who wish to accept such offer shall so notify the corporation of their acceptance of the corporation's offer within 30 days after receiving the offer; and

    (5)   that those shareholders who do not satisfy the requirements for demanding appraisal under section 13.26 shall be deemed to have accepted the corporation's offer.

(c)   Within 10 days after receiving the shareholder's acceptance pursuant to subsection (b)(4), the corporation shall pay in cash the amount it offered under subsection (b)(2) plus interest to each shareholder who agreed to accept the corporation's offer in full satisfaction of the shareholder's demand.

(d)   Within 40 days after delivering the notice described in subsection (b), the corporation shall pay in cash the amount it offered to pay under subsection (b)(2) plus interest to each shareholder described in subsection (b)(5).

§ 13.26   Procedure if Shareholder Dissatisfied with Payment or Offer

(a)   A shareholder paid pursuant to section 13.24 who is dissatisfied with the amount of the payment shall notify the corporation in writing of that shareholder's estimate of the fair value of the shares and demand payment of that estimate (less any payment under section 13.24) plus interest. A shareholder offered payment under section 13.25 who is dissatisfied with that offer shall reject the offer and demand payment of the shareholder's stated estimate of the fair value of the shares plus interest.

(b)   A shareholder who fails to notify the corporation in writing of that shareholder's demand to be paid the shareholder's stated estimate of the fair value plus interest under subsection (a) within 30 days after receiving the corporation's payment or offer of payment under section 13.24 or section 13.25, respectively, waives the right to demand payment under this section and shall be entitled only to the payment made or offered pursuant to those respective sections.

OFFICIAL COMMENT

A shareholder who is not content with the corporation's remittance under section 13.24, or offer of remittance under section 13.25, and wishes to pursue appraisal rights further must state in writing the amount the shareholder is willing to accept. A shareholder whose demand is deemed arbitrary, unreasonable or not in good faith, however, runs the risk of being assessed litigation expenses under section 13.31. These provisions are designed to encourage settlement without a judicial proceeding.

A shareholder to whom the corporation has made payment (or who has been offered payment under section 13.25) must make a supplemental demand within 30 days after receipt of the payment or offer of payment to permit the corporation to make an early decision on initiating appraisal proceedings. A failure to make such demand causes the shareholder to relinquish under section 13.26(b) anything beyond the amount the corporation paid or offered to pay.

SUBCHAPTER C.   JUDICIAL APPRAISAL OF SHARES

§ 13.30   Court Action

(a)   If a shareholder makes demand for payment under section 13.26 which remains unsettled, the corporation shall commence a proceeding within 60 days after receiving the payment demand and petition the court to determine the fair value of the shares and accrued interest. If the corporation does not commence the proceeding within the 60-day period, it shall pay in cash to each shareholder the amount the shareholder demanded pursuant to section 13.26 plus interest.

(b)   The corporation shall commence the proceeding in the [name or describe court].

(c)   The corporation shall make all shareholders (regardless of whether they are residents of this state) whose demands remain unsettled parties to the proceeding as in an action against their shares, and all parties shall be served with a copy of the petition. Nonresidents may be served by registered or certified mail or by publication as provided by law.

(d)   The jurisdiction of the court in which the proceeding is commenced under subsection (b) is plenary and exclusive. The court may appoint one or more persons as appraisers to receive evidence and recommend a decision on the question of fair value. The appraisers shall have the powers described in the order appointing them, or in any amendment to it. The shareholders demanding appraisal rights are entitled to the same discovery rights as parties in other civil proceedings. There shall be no right to a jury trial.

(e)   Each shareholder made a party to the proceeding is entitled to judgment (i) for the amount, if any, by which the court finds the fair value of the shareholder's shares exceeds the amount paid by the corporation to the shareholder for such shares, plus interest, or (ii) for the fair value, plus interest, of the shareholder's shares for which the corporation elected to withhold payment under section 13.25.

§ 13.31   Court Costs and Expenses

(a)   The court in an appraisal proceeding commenced under section 13.30 shall determine all court costs of the proceeding, including the reasonable compensation and expenses of appraisers appointed by the court. The court shall assess the court costs against the corporation, except that the court may assess court costs against all or some of the shareholders demanding appraisal, in amounts which the court finds equitable, to the extent the court finds such shareholders acted arbitrarily, vexatiously, or not in good faith with respect to the rights provided by this chapter.

(b)   The court in an appraisal proceeding may also assess the expenses of the respective parties in amounts the court finds equitable:

(1)   against the corporation and in favor of any or all shareholders demanding appraisal if the court finds the corporation did not substantially comply with the requirements of sections 13.20, 13.22, 13.24, or 13.25; or

(2)   against either the corporation or a shareholder demanding appraisal, in favor of any other party, if the court finds the party against whom expenses are assessed acted arbitrarily, vexatiously, or not in good faith with respect to the rights provided by this chapter.

(c)   If the court in an appraisal proceeding finds that the expenses incurred by any shareholder were of substantial benefit to other shareholders similarly situated and that such expenses should not be assessed against the corporation, the court may direct that such expenses be paid out of the amounts awarded the shareholders who were benefited.

(d)   To the extent the corporation fails to make a required payment pursuant to sections 13.24, 13.25, or 13.26, the shareholder may sue directly for the amount owed, and to the extent successful, shall be entitled to recover from the corporation all expenses of the suit.

SUBCHAPTER D.   OTHER REMEDIES

§ 13.40   Other Remedies Limited

(a)   The legality of a proposed or completed corporate action described in section 13.02(a) may not be contested, nor may the corporate action be enjoined, set aside or rescinded, in a legal or equitable proceeding by a shareholder after the shareholders have approved the corporate action.

(b)   Subsection (a) does not apply to a corporate action that:

(1)   was not authorized and approved in accordance with the applicable provisions of:

(i)   chapter 9, 10, 11, or 12;

(ii)   the articles of incorporation or bylaws; or

(iii)   the resolution of the board of directors authorizing the corporate action;

(2)   was procured as a result of fraud, a material misrepresentation, or an omission of a material fact necessary to make statements made, in light of the circumstances in which they were made, not misleading;

(3)   is an interested transaction, unless it has been recommended by the board of directors in the same manner as is provided in section 8.62 and has been approved by the shareholders in the same manner as is provided in section 8.63 as if the interested transaction were a director's conflicting interest transaction; or

(4)   is approved by less than unanimous consent of the voting shareholders pursuant to section 7.04 if:

(i)   the challenge to the corporate action is brought by a shareholder who did not consent and as to whom notice of the approval of the corporate action was not effective at least 10 days before the corporate action was effected; and

(ii)   the proceeding challenging the corporate action is commenced within 10 days after notice of the approval of the corporate action is effective as to the shareholder bringing the proceeding.

CHAPTER 14.   DISSOLUTION

SUBCHAPTER A.   VOLUNTARY DISSOLUTION

§ 14.01   Dissolution by Incorporators or Initial Directors

A majority of the incorporators or initial directors of a corporation that has not issued shares or has not commenced business may dissolve the corporation by delivering to the secretary of state for filing articles of dissolution that set forth:

(a)   the name of the corporation;

(b)   the date of its incorporation;

(c)   either (i) that none of the corporation's shares has been issued or (ii) that the corporation has not commenced business;

(d)   that no debt of the corporation remains unpaid;

(e)   that the net assets of the corporation remaining after winding up have been distributed to the shareholders, if shares were issued; and

(f)   that a majority of the incorporators or initial directors authorized the dissolution.

§ 14.02   Dissolution by Board of Directors and Shareholders

(a)   The board of directors may propose dissolution for submission to the shareholders by first adopting a resolution authorizing the dissolution.

(b)   For a proposal to dissolve to be adopted, it shall then be approved by the shareholders. In submitting the proposal to dissolve to the shareholders for approval, the board of directors shall recommend that the shareholders approve the dissolution, unless (i) the board of directors determines that because of conflict of interest or other special circumstances it should make no recommendation or (ii) section 8.26 applies. If either (i) or (ii) applies, the board shall inform the shareholders of the basis for its so proceeding.

(c)   The board of directors may set conditions for the approval of the proposal for dissolution by shareholders or the effectiveness of the dissolution.

(d)   If the approval of the shareholders is to be given at a meeting, the corporation shall notify each shareholder, regardless of whether entitled to vote, of the meeting of shareholders at which the dissolution is to be submitted for approval. The notice must state that the purpose, or one of the purposes, of the meeting is to consider dissolving the corporation.

(e)   Unless the articles of incorporation or the board of directors acting pursuant to subsection (c) require a greater vote, a greater quorum, or a vote by voting groups, adoption of the proposal to dissolve shall require the approval of the shareholders at a meeting at which a quorum exists consisting of a majority of the votes entitled to be cast on the proposal to dissolve.

§ 14.03   Articles of Dissolution

(a)   At any time after dissolution is authorized, the corporation may dissolve by delivering to the secretary of state for filing articles of dissolution setting forth:

(1)   the name of the corporation;

(2)   the date that dissolution was authorized; and

(3)   if dissolution was approved by the shareholders, a statement that the proposal to dissolve was duly approved by the shareholders in the manner required by this Act and by the articles of incorporation.

(b)   The articles of dissolution shall take effect at the effective date determined in accordance with section 1.23. A corporation is dissolved upon the effective date of its articles of dissolution.

(c)   For purposes of this subchapter, "dissolved corporation" means a corporation whose articles of dissolution have become effective and includes a successor entity to which the remaining assets of the corporation are transferred subject to its liabilities for purposes of liquidation.

§ 14.04   Revocation of Dissolution

(a)   A corporation may revoke its dissolution within 120 days after its effective date.

(b)   Revocation of dissolution shall be authorized in the same manner as the dissolution was authorized unless that authorization permitted revocation by action of the board of directors alone, in which event the board of directors may revoke the dissolution without shareholder action.

(c)   After the revocation of dissolution is authorized, the corporation may revoke the dissolution by delivering to the secretary of state for filing articles of revocation of dissolution, together with a copy of its articles of dissolution, that set forth:

(1)   the name of the corporation;

(2)   the effective date of the dissolution that was revoked;

(3)   the date that the revocation of dissolution was authorized;

(4)   if the corporation's board of directors (or incorporators) revoked the dissolution, a statement to that effect;

(5)   if the corporation's board of directors revoked a dissolution as authorized by the shareholders, a statement that revocation was permitted by action by the board of directors alone pursuant to that authorization; and

(6)   if shareholder action was required to revoke the dissolution, a statement that the revocation was duly approved by the shareholders in the manner required by this Act and by the articles of incorporation.

(d)   Revocation of dissolution is effective upon the effective date of the articles of revocation of dissolution.

(e)   When the revocation of dissolution is effective, it relates back to and takes effect as of the effective date of the dissolution and the corporation resumes carrying on its business as if dissolution had never occurred.

§ 14.05   Effect of Dissolution

(a)   A corporation that has dissolved continues its corporate existence but the dissolved corporation may not carry on any business except that appropriate to wind up and liquidate its business and affairs, including:

(1)   collecting its assets;

(2)   disposing of its properties that will not be distributed in kind to its shareholders;

(3)   discharging or making provision for discharging its liabilities;

(4)   making distributions of its remaining assets among its shareholders according to their interests; and

(5)   doing every other act necessary to wind up and liquidate its business and affairs.

(b)   Dissolution of a corporation does not:

(1)   transfer title to the corporation's property;

(2)   prevent transfer of its shares or securities;

(3)   subject its directors or officers to standards of conduct different from those prescribed in chapter 8;

(4)   change (i) quorum or voting requirements for its board of directors or shareholders; (ii) provisions for selection, resignation, or removal of its directors or officers or both; or (iii) provisions for amending its bylaws;

(5)   prevent commencement of a proceeding by or against the corporation in its corporate name;

(6)   abate or suspend a proceeding pending by or against the corporation on the effective date of dissolution; or

(7)   terminate the authority of the registered agent of the corporation.

(c)   A distribution in liquidation under this section may only be made by a dissolved corporation. For purposes of determining the shareholders entitled to receive a distribution in liquidation, the board of directors may fix a record date for determining shareholders entitled to a distribution in liquidation, which date may not be retroactive. If the board of directors does not fix a record date for determining shareholders entitled to a distribution in liquidation, the record date is the date the board of directors authorizes the distribution in liquidation.

§ 14.06 Known Claims Against Dissolved Corporation

(a)   A dissolved corporation may dispose of the known claims against it by notifying its known claimants in writing of the dissolution at any time after its effective date.

(b)   The written notice must:

(1)   describe information that must be included in a claim;

(2)   provide a mailing address where a claim may be sent;

(3)   state the deadline, which may not be fewer than 120 days after the written notice is effective, by which the dissolved corporation shall receive the claim; and

(4)   state that the claim will be barred if not received by the deadline.

(c)   A claim against the dissolved corporation is barred:

(1)   if a claimant who was given written notice under subsection (b) does not deliver the claim to the dissolved corporation by the deadline; or

(2)   if a claimant whose claim was rejected by the dissolved corporation does not commence a proceeding to enforce the claim within 90 days after the rejection notice is effective.

(d)   For purposes of this section, "claim" does not include a contingent liability or a claim based on an event occurring after the effective date of dissolution.

§ 14.07 Other Claims Against Dissolved Corporation

(a)   A dissolved corporation may publish notice of its dissolution and request that persons with claims against the dissolved corporation present them in accordance with the notice.

(b)   The notice must:

(1)   be published (i) one time in a newspaper of general circulation in the county where the dissolved corporation's principal office (or, if none in this state, its registered office) is or was last located or (ii) be posted conspicuously for at least 30 days on the dissolved corporation's website;

(2)   describe the information that must be included in a claim and provide a mailing address where the claim may be sent; and

(3)   state that a claim against the dissolved corporation will be barred unless a proceeding to enforce the claim is commenced within three years after the publication of the notice.

(c)   If the dissolved corporation publishes a notice in accordance with subsection (b), the claim of each of the following claimants is barred unless the claimant commences a proceeding to enforce the claim against the dissolved corporation within three years after the publication date of the notice:

(1)   a claimant who was not given written notice under section 14.06;

(2)   a claimant whose claim was timely sent to the dissolved corporation but not acted on by the corporation;

(3)   a claimant whose claim is contingent or based on an event occurring after the effective date of dissolution.

(d)   A claim that is not barred by section 14.06(c) or section 14.07(c) may be enforced:

(1)   against the dissolved corporation, to the extent of its undistributed assets; or

(2)   except as provided in section 14.08(d), if the assets have been distributed in liquidation, against a shareholder of the dissolved corporation to the extent of the shareholder's pro rata share of the claim or the corporate assets distributed to the shareholder in liquidation, whichever is less, but a shareholder's total liability for all claims under this section may not exceed the total amount of assets distributed to the shareholder.

§ 14.08   Court Proceedings

(a) A dissolved corporation that has published a notice under section 14.07 may file an application with the [name or describe court] for a determination of the amount and form of security to be provided for payment of claims that are contingent or have not been made known to the dissolved corporation or that are based on an event occurring after the effective date of dissolution but that, based on the facts known to the dissolved corporation, are reasonably estimated to arise after the effective date of dissolution. Provision need not be made for any claim that is or is reasonably anticipated to be barred under section 14.07(c).

(b) Within 10 days after the filing of the application, notice of the proceeding shall be given by the dissolved corporation to each claimant holding a contingent claim whose contingent claim is shown on the records of the dissolved corporation.

(c) The court may appoint a guardian ad litem to represent all claimants whose identities are unknown in any proceeding brought under this section. The reasonable fees and expenses of such guardian, including all reasonable expert witness fees, shall be paid by the dissolved corporation.

(d) Provision by the dissolved corporation for security in the amount and the form ordered by the court under section 14.08(a) shall satisfy the dissolved corporation's obligations with respect to claims that are contingent, have not been made known to the dissolved corporation or are based on an event occurring after the effective date of dissolution, and such claims may not be enforced against a shareholder who received assets in liquidation.

§ 14.09   Director Duties

(a) Directors shall cause the dissolved corporation to discharge or make reasonable provision for the payment of claims and make distributions in liquidation of assets to shareholders after payment or provision for claims.

(b) Directors of a dissolved corporation which has disposed of claims under sections 14.06, 14.07, or 14.08 shall not be liable for breach of section 14.09(a) with respect to claims against the dissolved corporation that are barred or satisfied under sections 14.06, 14.07 or 14.08.

SUBCHAPTER B.   ADMINISTRATIVE DISSOLUTION

§ 14.20   Grounds for Administrative Dissolution

The secretary of state may commence a proceeding under section 14.21 to dissolve a corporation administratively if:

(a) the corporation does not pay within 60 days after they are due any fees, taxes, interest or penalties imposed by this Act or other laws of this state;

(b) the corporation does not deliver its annual report to the secretary of state within 60 days after it is due;

(c) the corporation is without a registered agent or registered office in this state for 60 days or more;

(d) the secretary of state has not been notified within 60 days that the corporation's registered agent or registered office has been changed, that its registered agent has resigned, or that its registered office has been discontinued; or

(e) the corporation's period of duration stated in its articles of incorporation expires.

§ 14.21   Procedure for and Effect of Administrative Dissolution

(a)   If the secretary of state determines that one or more grounds exist under section 14.20 for dissolving a corporation, the secretary of state shall serve the corporation with written notice of such determination under section 5.04.

(b)   If the corporation does not correct each ground for dissolution or demonstrate to the reasonable satisfaction of the secretary of state that each ground determined by the secretary of state does not exist within 60 days after service of the notice under section 5.04, the secretary of state shall administratively dissolve the corporation by signing a certificate of dissolution that recites the ground or grounds for dissolution and its effective date. The secretary of state shall file the original of the certificate and serve a copy on the corporation under section 5.04.

(c)   A corporation administratively dissolved continues its corporate existence but may not carry on any business except that necessary to wind up and liquidate its business and affairs under section 14.05 and notify claimants under sections 14.06 and 14.07.

(d)   The administrative dissolution of a corporation does not terminate the authority of its registered agent.

§ 14.22   Reinstatement Following Administrative Dissolution

(a)   A corporation administratively dissolved under section 14.21 may apply to the secretary of state for reinstatement within two years after the effective date of dissolution. The application must:

(1)   state the name of the corporation and the effective date of its administrative dissolution;

(2)   state that the ground or grounds for dissolution either did not exist or have been eliminated;

(3)   state that the corporation's name satisfies the requirements of section 4.01; and

(4)   contain a certificate from the [taxing authority] reciting that all taxes owed by the corporation have been paid.

(b)   If the secretary of state determines that the application contains the information required by subsection (a) and that the information is correct, the secretary of state shall cancel the certificate of dissolution and prepare a certificate of reinstatement that recites such determination and the effective date of reinstatement, file the original of the certificate, and serve a copy on the corporation under section 5.04.

(c)   When the reinstatement is effective, it relates back to and takes effect as of the effective date of the administrative dissolution and the corporation resumes carrying on its business as if the administrative dissolution had never occurred.

§ 14.23   Appeal from Denial of Reinstatement

(a)   If the secretary of state denies a corporation's application for reinstatement following administrative dissolution, the secretary of state shall serve the corporation under section 5.04 with a written notice that explains the reason or reasons for denial.

(b)   The corporation may appeal the denial of reinstatement to the [name or describe court] within 30 days after service of the notice of denial is effected. The corporation appeals by petitioning the court to set aside the dissolution and attaching to the petition copies of the secretary of state's certificate of dissolution, the corporation's application for reinstatement, and the secretary of state's notice of denial.

(c)   The court may summarily order the secretary of state to reinstate the dissolved corporation or may take other action the court considers appropriate.

(d) The court's final decision may be appealed as in other civil proceedings.

SUBCHAPTER C. JUDICIAL DISSOLUTION

§ 14.30 Grounds for Judicial Dissolution

(a) The [name or describe court or courts] may dissolve a corporation:

    (1) in a proceeding by the attorney general if it is established that:

        (i) the corporation obtained its articles of incorporation through fraud; or

        (ii) the corporation has continued to exceed or abuse the authority conferred upon it by law;

    (2) in a proceeding by a shareholder if it is established that:

        (i) the directors are deadlocked in the management of the corporate affairs, the shareholders are unable to break the deadlock, and irreparable injury to the corporation is threatened or being suffered, or the business and affairs of the corporation can no longer be conducted to the advantage of the shareholders generally, because of the deadlock;

        (ii) the directors or those in control of the corporation have acted, are acting, or will act in a manner that is illegal, oppressive, or fraudulent;

        (iii) the shareholders are deadlocked in voting power and have failed, for a period that includes at least two consecutive annual meeting dates, to elect successors to directors whose terms have expired; or

        (iv) the corporate assets are being misapplied or wasted;

    (3) in a proceeding by a creditor if it is established that:

        (i) the creditor's claim has been reduced to judgment, the execution on the judgment returned unsatisfied, and the corporation is insolvent; or

        (ii) the corporation has admitted in writing that the creditor's claim is due and owing and the corporation is insolvent;

    (4) in a proceeding by the corporation to have its voluntary dissolution continued under court supervision; or

    (5) in a proceeding by a shareholder if the corporation has abandoned its business and has failed within a reasonable time to liquidate and distribute its assets and dissolve.

(b) Subsection (a)(2) shall not apply in the case of a corporation that, on the date of the filing of the proceeding, has shares which are:

        (i) a covered security under section 18(b)(1)(A) or (B) of the Securities Act of 1933; or

        (ii) not a covered security, but are held by at least 300 shareholders and the shares outstanding have a market value of at least $20 million (exclusive of the value of such shares held by the corporation's subsidiaries, senior executives, directors and beneficial shareholders and voting trust beneficial owners owning more than 10% of such shares).

(c) In subsection (a), "shareholder" means a record shareholder, a beneficial shareholder, and an unrestricted voting trust beneficial owner, and in subsection (b), "shareholder" means a record shareholder, a beneficial shareholder, and a voting trust beneficial owner.

OFFICIAL COMMENT

Section 14.30 provides grounds for the judicial dissolution of a corporation at the request of the state, a shareholder, a creditor, or when a corporation that has commenced voluntary dissolution seeks judicial oversight. Judicial oversight may be useful to protect the corporation from suits by creditors or shareholders.

Under this section, the court has discretion as to whether dissolution is appropriate even though the specified grounds for judicial dissolution exist.

1. Involuntary Dissolution by State

Section 14.30(a)(1) provides a means by which the state may ensure compliance with the fundamentals of corporate existence and prevent abuse. That section limits the power of the state in this regard to grounds that are reasonably related to this objective.

2. Involuntary Dissolution by Shareholders

Section 14.30(a)(2) provides for involuntary dissolution at the request of a shareholder under circumstances involving deadlock or significant abuse of power by controlling shareholders or directors. Section 14.30(c) extends the ability to seek judicial dissolution under section 14.30(a)(2) to beneficial shareholders and unrestricted voting trust beneficial owners, as these persons have, or hold on behalf of others, an economic interest in the shares. The remedy of judicial dissolution is available only for shareholders of corporations that do not meet the tests in section 14.30(b). Even for those corporations to which section 14.30(a)(2) applies, however, the court can take into account the number of shareholders and the nature of the trading market for the shares in deciding whether to exercise its discretion to order dissolution. Shareholders of corporations that meet the tests of section 14.30(b) may often have the ability to sell their shares if they are dissatisfied with current management or may seek other remedies under the Act. See, for example, sections 7.48(a) and 8.09. The grounds for dissolution under section 14.30(a)(2) are broader than those required to be shown for the appointment of a custodian or receiver under section 7.48(a). The difference is attributable to the different focus of the two proceedings. Although some of the circumstances listed in 14.30(a)(2), such as deadlock, may implicate the welfare of the corporation as a whole, the primary focus is on the effect of actions by those in control on the value of the complaining shareholder's individual investment. For example, "oppressive" behavior in section 14.30(a)(2)(ii) generally describes action directed against a particular shareholder. In contrast, the focus of protection in an action to appoint a custodian or receiver under section 7.48(a) is the corporate entity, and the remedy is intended to protect the interests of all shareholders, creditors and others who may have an interest therein. In other instances, action that is "illegal" or "fraudulent" under section 14.30(a)(2)(ii) may be severely prejudicial to the interests of an individual shareholder, whereas conduct that is illegal with respect to the entire corporation may be remedied by other causes of action under the Act.

Section 14.30(a)(5) provides a basis for a shareholder to obtain involuntary dissolution in the event the corporation has abandoned its business, but those in control of the corporation have delayed unreasonably in either liquidating and distributing its assets or completing the necessary procedures to dissolve the corporation

3. Involuntary Dissolution by Creditors

Creditors may obtain involuntary dissolution only when the corporation is insolvent and only in the limited circumstances set forth in section 14.30(a)(3). Typically, a proceeding under the federal bankruptcy laws is an alternative in these situations.

4. Judicial Supervision of Dissolution

A corporation that has commenced voluntary dissolution may petition a court to supervise its dissolution. Such an action may be appropriate to permit the orderly liquidation of the corporate assets and to protect the corporation from a multitude of creditors' suits or suits by dissatisfied shareholders.

§ 14.31   Procedure for Judicial Dissolution

(a) Venue for a proceeding by the attorney general to dissolve a corporation lies in [name or describe court]. Venue for a proceeding brought by any other party named in section 14.30(a) lies in [name or describe court].

(b) It is not necessary to make shareholders parties to a proceeding to dissolve a corporation unless relief is sought against them individually.

(c) A court in a proceeding brought to dissolve a corporation may issue injunctions, appoint a receiver or custodian during the proceeding with all powers and duties the court directs, take other action required to preserve the corporate assets wherever located, and carry on the business of the corporation until a full hearing can be held.

(d) Within 10 days of the commencement of a proceeding to dissolve a corporation under section 14.30(a)(2), the corporation shall deliver to all shareholders, other than the petitioner, a notice stating that the shareholders are entitled to avoid the dissolution of the corporation by electing to purchase the petitioner's shares under section 14.34 and accompanied by a copy of section 14.34.

§ 14.32   Receivership or Custodianship

(a) Unless an election to purchase has been filed under section 14.34, a court in a judicial proceeding brought to dissolve a corporation may appoint one or more receivers to wind up and liquidate, or one or more custodians to manage, the business and affairs of the corporation. The court shall hold a hearing, after notifying all parties to the proceeding and any interested persons designated by the court, before appointing a receiver or custodian. The court appointing a receiver or custodian has jurisdiction over the corporation and all of its property wherever located.

(b) The court may appoint an individual or a domestic or foreign corporation or eligible entity as a receiver or custodian, which, if a foreign corporation or foreign eligible entity, must be registered to do business in this state. The court may require the receiver or custodian to post bond, with or without sureties, in an amount the court directs.

(c) The court shall describe the powers and duties of the receiver or custodian in its appointing order, which may be amended from time to time. Among other powers:

(1) the receiver (i) may dispose of all or any part of the assets of the corporation wherever located, at a public or private sale; and (ii) may sue and defend in the receiver's own name as receiver of the corporation in all courts of this state;

(2) the custodian may exercise all of the powers of the corporation, through or in place of its board of directors, to the extent necessary to manage the affairs of the corporation in the best interests of its shareholders and creditors.

The receiver or custodian shall have such other powers and duties as the court may provide in the appointing order, which may be amended from time to time.

(d) The court during a receivership may redesignate the receiver a custodian and during a custodianship may redesignate the custodian a receiver.

(e) The court from time to time during the receivership or custodianship may order compensation paid and expenses paid or reimbursed to the receiver or custodian from the assets of the corporation or proceeds from the sale of the assets.

§ 14.33   Decree of Dissolution

(a) If after a hearing the court determines that one or more grounds for judicial dissolution described in section 14.30 exist, it may enter a decree dissolving the corporation and specifying the effective date of the dissolution, and the clerk of the court shall deliver a certified copy of the decree to the secretary of state for filing.

(b) After entering the decree of dissolution, the court shall direct the winding-up and liquidation of the corporation's business and affairs in accordance with section 14.05 and the notification of claimants in accordance with sections 14.06 and 14.07.

§ 14.34   Election to Purchase in Lieu of Dissolution

(a) In a proceeding under section 14.30(a)(2) to dissolve a corporation, the corporation may elect or, if it fails to elect, one or more shareholders may elect to purchase all shares owned by the petitioning shareholder at the fair value of the shares. An election pursuant to this section shall be irrevocable unless the court determines that it is equitable to set aside or modify the election.

(b)   An election to purchase pursuant to this section may be filed with the court at any time within 90 days after the filing of the petition under section 14.30(a)(2) or at such later time as the court in its discretion may allow. If the election to purchase is filed by one or more shareholders, the corporation shall, within 10 days thereafter, give written notice to all shareholders, other than the petitioner. The notice must state the name and number of shares owned by the petitioner and the name and number of shares owned by each electing shareholder and must advise the recipients of their right to join in the election to purchase shares in accordance with this section. Shareholders who wish to participate shall file notice of their intention to join in the purchase no later than 30 days after the effectiveness of the notice to them. All shareholders who have filed an election or notice of their intention to participate in the election to purchase thereby become parties to the proceeding and shall participate in the purchase in proportion to their ownership of shares as of the date the first election was filed, unless they otherwise agree or the court otherwise directs. After an election has been filed by the corporation or one or more shareholders, the proceeding under section 14.30(a)(2) may not be discontinued or settled, nor may the petitioning shareholder sell or otherwise dispose of his or her shares, unless the court determines that it would be equitable to the corporation and the shareholders, other than the petitioner, to permit such discontinuance, settlement, sale, or other disposition.

(c)   If, within 60 days of the filing of the first election, the parties reach agreement as to the fair value and terms of purchase of the petitioner's shares, the court shall enter an order directing the purchase of the petitioner's shares upon the terms and conditions agreed to by the parties.

(d)   If the parties are unable to reach an agreement as provided for in subsection (c), the court, upon application of any party, shall stay the proceedings under section 14.30(a)(2) and determine the fair value of the petitioner's shares as of the day before the date on which the petition under section 14.30(a)(2) was filed or as of such other date as the court deems appropriate under the circumstances.

(e)   Upon determining the fair value of the shares, the court shall enter an order directing the purchase upon such terms and conditions as the court deems appropriate, which may include payment of the purchase price in installments, where necessary in the interests of equity, provision for security to assure payment of the purchase price and any additional expenses as may have been awarded, and, if the shares are to be purchased by shareholders, the allocation of shares among them. In allocating the petitioner's shares among holders of different classes or series of shares, the court should attempt to preserve the existing distribution of voting rights among holders of different classes or series insofar as practicable and may direct that holders of a specific class or classes or series shall not participate in the purchase. Interest may be allowed at the rate and from the date determined by the court to be equitable, but if the court finds that the refusal of the petitioning shareholder to accept an offer of payment was arbitrary or otherwise not in good faith, no interest shall be allowed. If the court finds that the petitioning shareholder had probable grounds for relief under sections 14.30(a)(2)(ii) or (iv), it may award expenses to the petitioning shareholder.

(f)   Upon entry of an order under subsections (c) or (e), the court shall dismiss the petition to dissolve the corporation under section 14.30(a)(2), and the petitioning shareholder shall no longer have any rights or status as a shareholder of the corporation, except the right to receive the amounts awarded by the order of the court which shall be enforceable in the same manner as any other judgment.

(g)   The purchase ordered pursuant to subsection (e) shall be made within 10 days after the date the order becomes final.

(h)   Any payment by the corporation pursuant to an order under subsections (c) or (e), other than an award of expenses pursuant to subsection (e), is subject to the provisions of section 6.40.

SUBCHAPTER D.   MISCELLANEOUS

§ 14.40   Deposit with State Treasurer

Assets of a dissolved corporation that should be transferred to a creditor, claimant, or shareholder of the corporation who cannot be found or who is not competent to receive them shall be reduced to cash and deposited with the state treasurer or other appropriate state official for safekeeping. When the creditor, claimant, or shareholder furnishes satisfactory proof of entitlement to the amount deposited, the state treasurer or other appropriate state official shall pay such person or his or her representative that amount.

CHAPTER 15.   FOREIGN CORPORATIONS

§ 15.01   Governing Law

(a)   The law of the jurisdiction of formation of a foreign corporation governs:

(1)   the internal affairs of the foreign corporation; and

(2)   the interest holder liability of its shareholders.

(b)   A foreign corporation is not precluded from registering to do business in this state because of any difference between the law of the foreign corporation's jurisdiction of formation and the law of this state.

(c)   Registration of a foreign corporation to do business in this state does not permit the foreign corporation to engage in any business or affairs or exercise any power that a domestic corporation may not engage in or exercise in this state.

§ 15.02   Registration to Do Business in This State

(a)   A foreign corporation may not do business in this state until it registers with the secretary of state under this chapter.

(b)   A foreign corporation doing business in this state may not maintain a proceeding in any court of this state until it is registered to do business in this state.

(c)   The failure of a foreign corporation to register to do business in this state does not impair the validity of a contract or act of the foreign corporation or preclude it from defending a proceeding in this state.

(d)   A limitation on the liability of a shareholder or director of a foreign corporation is not waived solely because the foreign corporation does business in this state without registering.

(e)   Section 15.01(a) applies even if a foreign corporation fails to register under this chapter.

§ 15.03   Foreign Registration Statement

To register to do business in this state, a foreign corporation shall deliver a foreign registration statement to the secretary of state for filing. The registration statement must be signed by the foreign corporation and state:

(a)   the corporate name of the foreign corporation and, if the name does not comply with section 4.01, an alternate name as required by section 15.06;

(b)   the foreign corporation's jurisdiction of formation;

(c)   the street and mailing addresses of the foreign corporation's principal office and, if the law of the foreign corporation's jurisdiction of formation requires the foreign corporation to maintain an office in that jurisdiction, the street and mailing addresses of that office;

(d)　the street and mailing addresses of the foreign corporation's registered office in this state and the name of its registered agent at that office;

(e)　the names and business addresses of its directors and principal officers; and

(f)　a brief description of the nature of its business to be conducted in this state.

§ 15.04　Amendment of Foreign Registration Statement

A registered foreign corporation shall sign and deliver to the secretary of state for filing an amendment to its foreign registration statement if there is a change in:

(a)　its name or alternate name;

(b)　its jurisdiction of formation, unless its registration is deemed to have been withdrawn under section 15.08 or transferred under section 15.10; or

(c)　an address required by section 15.03(c).

§ 15.05　Activities Not Constituting Doing Business

(a)　Activities of a foreign corporation that do not constitute doing business in this state for purposes of this chapter include:

(1)　maintaining, defending, mediating, arbitrating, or settling a proceeding;

(2)　carrying on any activity concerning the internal affairs of the foreign corporation, including holding meetings of its shareholders or board of directors;

(3)　maintaining accounts in financial institutions;

(4)　maintaining offices or agencies for the transfer, exchange, and registration of securities of the foreign corporation or maintaining trustees or depositories with respect to those securities;

(5)　selling through independent contractors;

(6)　soliciting or obtaining orders by any means if the orders require acceptance outside this state before they become contracts;

(7)　creating or acquiring indebtedness, mortgages, or security interests in property;

(8)　securing or collecting debts or enforcing mortgages or security interests in property securing the debts, and holding, protecting, or maintaining property so acquired;

(9)　conducting an isolated transaction that is not in the course of similar transactions;

(10) owning, protecting and maintaining property; and

(11) doing business in interstate commerce.

(b)　This section does not apply in determining the contacts or activities that may subject a foreign corporation to service of process, taxation, or regulation under the laws of this state other than this Act.

§ 15.06　Noncomplying Name of Foreign Corporation

(a)　A foreign corporation whose name does not comply with section 4.01 may not register to do business in this state until it adopts, for the purpose of doing business in this state, an alternate name that complies with section 4.01 by filing a foreign registration statement under section 15.03, or if applicable, a transfer of registration statement under section 15.10, setting forth that alternate name. A foreign corporation adopting an alternate name as provided in this subsection need not file under this state's assumed or fictitious name statute with respect that alternate name. After registering to do business in this state with an alternate name, a foreign corporation shall do business in this state under:

(1)   the alternate name;

(2)   the foreign corporation's name, with the addition of its jurisdiction of formation; or

(3)   a name the foreign corporation is authorized to use under the assumed or fictitious name statute of this state.

(b)   If a registered foreign corporation changes its name after registration to a name that does not comply with section 4.01, it may not do business in this state until it complies with subsection (a) by amending its registration statement to adopt an alternate name that complies with section 4.01.

§ 15.07 Withdrawal of Registration of Registered Foreign Corporation

(a)   A registered foreign corporation may withdraw its registration by delivering a statement of withdrawal to the secretary of state for filing. The statement of withdrawal must be signed by the foreign corporation and state:

(1)   the name of the foreign corporation and its jurisdiction of formation;

(2)   that the foreign corporation is not doing business in this state and that it withdraws its registration to do business in this state;

(3)   that the foreign corporation revokes the authority of its registered agent in this state; and

(4)   an address to which process on the foreign corporation may be sent by the secretary of state under section 5.04(c).

(b)   After the withdrawal of the registration of a foreign corporation, service of process in any proceeding based on a cause of action arising during the time the entity was registered to do business in this state may be made as provided in section 5.04.

§ 15.08 Deemed Withdrawal Upon Domestication or Conversion to Certain Domestic Entities

A registered foreign corporation that domesticates to a domestic business corporation or converts to a domestic nonprofit corporation or any type of domestic filing entity or to a domestic limited liability partnership is deemed to have withdrawn its registration on the effectiveness of such event.

§ 15.09 Withdrawal Upon Dissolution or Conversion to Certain Nonfiling Entities

(a)   A registered foreign corporation that has dissolved and completed winding up or has converted to a domestic or foreign nonfiling entity other than a limited liability partnership shall deliver to the secretary of state for filing a statement of withdrawal. The statement must be signed by the dissolved corporation or the converted domestic or foreign nonfiling entity and state:

(1)   in the case of a foreign corporation that has completed winding up:

(i)   its name and jurisdiction of formation;

(ii)   that the foreign corporation withdraws its registration to do business in this state and revokes the authority of its registered agent to accept service on its behalf; and

(iii)   an address to which process on the foreign corporation may be sent by the secretary of state under section 5.04(c).

(2)   in the case of a foreign corporation that has converted to a domestic or foreign nonfiling entity other than a limited liability partnership:

(i)   the name of the converting foreign corporation and its jurisdiction of formation;

(ii)   the type of the nonfiling entity to which it has converted and its name and jurisdiction of formation;

(iii) that it withdraws its registration to do business in this state and revokes the authority of its registered agent to accept service on its behalf; and

(iv) an address to which process on the foreign corporation may be sent by the secretary of state under 5.04(c).

(b) After the withdrawal of the registration of a foreign corporation, service of process in any proceeding based on a cause of action arising during the time the entity was registered to do business in this state may be made as provided in section 5.04.

§ 15.10   Transfer of Registration

(a) If a registered foreign corporation merges into a nonregistered foreign corporation or converts to a foreign corporation required to register with the secretary of state to do business in this state, the foreign corporation shall deliver to the secretary of state for filing a transfer of registration statement. The transfer of registration statement must be signed by the surviving or converted foreign corporation and state:

(1) the name of the registered foreign corporation and its jurisdiction of formation before the merger or conversion;

(2) the name of the surviving or converted foreign corporation and its jurisdiction of formation after the merger or conversion and, if the name does not comply with section 4.01, an alternate name adopted pursuant to section 15.06; and

(3) the following information regarding the surviving or converted foreign corporation after the merger or conversion:

(i) the street and mailing addresses of the principal office of the foreign corporation and, if the law of the foreign corporation's jurisdiction of formation requires it to maintain an office in that jurisdiction, the street and mailing addresses of that office; and

(ii) the street and mailing addresses of the foreign corporation's registered office in this state and the name of its registered agent at that office.

(b) On the effective date of a transfer of registration statement as determined in accordance with section 1.23, the registration of the registered foreign corporation to do business in this state is transferred without interruption to the foreign corporation into which it has merged or to which it has been converted.

§ 15.11   Administrative Termination of Registration

(a) The secretary of state may terminate the registration of a registered foreign corporation in the manner provided in subsections (b) and (c) if:

(1) the foreign corporation does not pay within 60 days after they are due any fees, taxes, interest or penalties imposed by this Act or other laws of this state;

(2) the foreign corporation does not deliver its annual report to the secretary of state within 60 days after it is due;

(3) the foreign corporation is without a registered agent or registered office in this state for 60 days or more; or

(4) the secretary of state has not been notified within 60 days that the foreign corporation's registered agent or registered office has been changed, that its registered agent has resigned, or that its registered office has been discontinued.

(b) The secretary of state may terminate the registration of a registered foreign corporation by:

(1) filing a certificate of termination; and

(2) delivering a copy of the certificate of termination to the foreign corporation's registered agent or, if the foreign corporation does not have a registered agent, to the foreign corporation's principal office.

(c) The certificate of termination must state:

(1) the effective date of the termination, which must be not less than 60 days after the secretary of state delivers the copy of the certificate of termination as prescribed in subsection (b)(2); and

(2) the grounds for termination under subsection (a).

(d) The registration of a registered foreign corporation to do business in this state ceases on the effective date of the termination as set forth in the certificate of termination, unless before that date the foreign corporation cures each ground for termination stated in the certificate of termination. If the foreign corporation cures each ground, the secretary of state shall file a statement that the certificate of termination is withdrawn.

(e) After the effective date of the termination as set forth in the certificate of termination, service of process in any proceeding based on a cause of action arising during the time the entity was registered to do business in this state may be made as provided in section 5.04.

§ 15.12   Action by [Attorney General]

The [Attorney General] may maintain an action to enjoin a foreign corporation from doing business in this state in violation of this Act.

CHAPTER 16.   RECORDS AND REPORTS

SUBCHAPTER A.   RECORDS

§ 16.01   Corporate Records

(a) A corporation shall maintain the following records:

(1) its articles of incorporation as currently in effect;

(2) any notices to shareholders referred to in section 1.20(k)(5) specifying facts on which a filed document is dependent if those facts are not included in the articles of incorporation or otherwise available as specified in section 1.20(k)(5);

(3) its bylaws as currently in effect;

(4) all written communications within the past three years to shareholders generally;

(5) minutes of all meetings of, and records of all actions taken without a meeting by, its shareholders, its board of directors, and board committees established under section 8.25;

(6) a list of the names and business addresses of its current directors and officers; and

(7) its most recent annual report delivered to the secretary of state under section 16.21.

(b) A corporation shall maintain all annual financial statements prepared for the corporation for its last three fiscal years (or such shorter period of existence) and any audit or other reports with respect to such financial statements.

(c) A corporation shall maintain accounting records in a form that permits preparation of its financial statements.

(d) A corporation shall maintain a record of its current shareholders in alphabetical order by class or series of shares showing the address of, and the number and class or series of shares held by, each shareholder. Nothing contained in this subsection shall require the corporation to include in such record the electronic mail address or other electronic contact information of a shareholder.

(e)   A corporation shall maintain the records specified in this section in a manner so that they may be made available for inspection within a reasonable time.

§ 16.02   Inspection Rights of Shareholders

(a)   A shareholder of a corporation is entitled to inspect and copy, during regular business hours at the corporation's principal office, any of the records of the corporation described in section 16.01(a), excluding minutes of meetings of, and records of actions taken without a meeting by, the corporation's board of directors and board committees established under section 8.25, if the shareholder gives the corporation a signed written notice of the shareholder's demand at least five business days before the date on which the shareholder wishes to inspect and copy.

(b)   A shareholder of a corporation is entitled to inspect and copy, during regular business hours at a reasonable location specified by the corporation, any of the following records of the corporation if the shareholder meets the requirements of subsection (c) and gives the corporation a signed written notice of the shareholder's demand at least five business days before the date on which the shareholder wishes to inspect and copy:

(1)   the financial statements of the corporation maintained in accordance with section 16.01(b);

(2)   accounting records of the corporation;

(3)   excerpts from minutes of any meeting of, or records of any actions taken without a meeting by, the corporation's board of directors and board committees maintained in accordance with section 16.01(a); and

(4)   the record of shareholders maintained in accordance with section 16.01(d).

(c)   A shareholder may inspect and copy the records described in subsection (b) only if:

(1)   the shareholder's demand is made in good faith and for a proper purpose;

(2)   the shareholder's demand describes with reasonable particularity the shareholder's purpose and the records the shareholder desires to inspect; and

(3)   the records are directly connected with the shareholder's purpose.

(d)   The corporation may impose reasonable restrictions on the confidentiality, use or distribution of records described in subsection (b).

(e)   For any meeting of shareholders for which the record date for determining shareholders entitled to vote at the meeting is different than the record date for notice of the meeting, any person who becomes a shareholder subsequent to the record date for notice of the meeting and is entitled to vote at the meeting is entitled to obtain from the corporation upon request the notice and any other information provided by the corporation to shareholders in connection with the meeting, unless the corporation has made such information generally available to shareholders by posting it on its website or by other generally recognized means. Failure of a corporation to provide such information does not affect the validity of action taken at the meeting.

(f)   The right of inspection granted by this section may not be abolished or limited by a corporation's articles of incorporation or bylaws.

(g)   This section does not affect:

(1)   the right of a shareholder to inspect records under section 7.20 or, if the shareholder is in litigation with the corporation, to the same extent as any other litigant; or

(2)   the power of a court, independently of this Act, to compel the production of corporate records for examination and to impose reasonable restrictions as provided in section 16.04(c), provided that, in the case of production of records described in subsection (b) of this section at the request of a shareholder, the shareholder has met the requirements of subsection (c).

(h) For purposes of this section, "shareholder" means a record shareholder, a beneficial shareholder, and an unrestricted voting trust beneficial owner.

§ 16.03 Scope of Inspection Right

(a) A shareholder may appoint an agent or attorney to exercise the shareholder's inspection and copying rights under section 16.02.

(b) The corporation may, if reasonable, satisfy the right of a shareholder to copy records under section 16.02 by furnishing to the shareholder copies by photocopy or other means chosen by the corporation, including furnishing copies through an electronic transmission.

(c) The corporation may comply at its expense with a shareholder's demand to inspect the record of shareholders under section 16.02(b)(4) by providing the shareholder with a list of shareholders that was compiled no earlier than the date of the shareholder's demand.

(d) The corporation may impose a reasonable charge to cover the costs of providing copies of documents to the shareholder, which may be based on an estimate of such costs.

§ 16.04 Court-Ordered Inspection

(a) If a corporation does not allow a shareholder who complies with section 16.02(a) to inspect and copy any records required by that section to be available for inspection, the [name or describe court] may summarily order inspection and copying of the records demanded at the corporation's expense upon application of the shareholder.

(b) If a corporation does not within a reasonable time allow a shareholder who complies with section 16.02(b) to inspect and copy the records required by that section, the shareholder who complies with section 16.02(c) may apply to the [name or describe court] for an order to permit inspection and copying of the records demanded. The court shall dispose of an application under this subsection on an expedited basis.

(c) If the court orders inspection and copying of the records demanded under section 16.02(b), it may impose reasonable restrictions on their confidentiality, use or distribution by the demanding shareholder and it shall also order the corporation to pay the shareholder's expenses incurred to obtain the order unless the corporation establishes that it refused inspection in good faith because the corporation had:

(1) a reasonable basis for doubt about the right of the shareholder to inspect the records demanded; or

(2) required reasonable restrictions on the confidentiality, use or distribution of the records demanded to which the demanding shareholder had been unwilling to agree.

§ 16.05 Inspection Rights of Directors

(a) A director of a corporation is entitled to inspect and copy the books, records and documents of the corporation at any reasonable time to the extent reasonably related to the performance of the director's duties as a director, including duties as a member of a board committee, but not for any other purpose or in any manner that would violate any duty to the corporation.

(b) The [name or describe court] may order inspection and copying of the books, records and documents at the corporation's expense, upon application of a director who has been refused such inspection rights, unless the corporation establishes that the director is not entitled to such inspection rights. The court shall dispose of an application under this subsection on an expedited basis.

(c) If an order is issued, the court may include provisions protecting the corporation from undue burden or expense, and prohibiting the director from using information obtained upon exercise of the inspection rights in a manner that would violate a duty to the corporation, and may also order the corporation to reimburse the director for the director's expenses incurred in connection with the application.

OFFICIAL COMMENT

The purpose of section 16.05(a) is to confirm the principle that a director always is entitled to inspect books, records and documents to the extent reasonably related to the performance of the director's duties, provided that the requested inspection is not for an improper purpose and the director's use of the information obtained would not violate any duty to the corporation. In addition, section 16.05 sets forth a remedy for the director in circumstances where the corporation improperly denies the right of inspection.

Section 16.05(b) provides for a court order on an expedited basis because there is a presumption that significant latitude and discretion should be granted to the director, and the corporation has the burden of establishing that the director is not entitled to inspection of the documents requested. There may be circumstances where the director's inspection right might be denied, for example, when it would be contrary to the interest of the corporation because of adversity with the director, and the courts have broad discretion to address these circumstances. Section 16.05 does not directly deal with the ability of a director to inspect records of a subsidiary of which he or she is not also a director. A director's ability to inspect records of a subsidiary generally should be exercised through the parent's rights or power and section 16.05(a) does not independently provide that right or power to a director of the parent. In the case of wholly-owned subsidiaries, a director's ability to inspect should approximate his or her rights with respect to the parent.

SUBCHAPTER B.   REPORTS

§ 16.20   Financial Statements for Shareholders

(a)   Upon the written request of a shareholder, a corporation shall deliver or make available to such requesting shareholder by posting on its website or by other generally recognized means annual financial statements for the most recent fiscal year of the corporation for which annual financial statements have been prepared for the corporation. If financial statements have been prepared for the corporation on the basis of generally accepted accounting principles for such specified period, the corporation shall deliver or make available such financial statements to the requesting shareholder. If the annual financial statements to be delivered or made available to the requesting shareholder are audited or otherwise reported upon by a public accountant, the report shall also be delivered or made available to the requesting shareholder.

(b)   A corporation shall deliver, or make available and provide written notice of availability of, the financial statements required under subsection (a) to the requesting shareholder within five business days of delivery of such written request to the corporation.

(c)   A corporation may fulfill its responsibilities under this section by delivering the specified financial statements, or otherwise making them available, in any manner permitted by the applicable rules and regulations of the United States Securities and Exchange Commission.

(d)   Notwithstanding the provisions of subsections (a), (b) and (c) of this section:

(1)   as a condition to delivering or making available financial statements to a requesting shareholder, the corporation may require the requesting shareholder to agree to reasonable restrictions on the confidentiality, use and distribution of such financial statements; and

(2)   the corporation may, if it reasonably determines that the shareholder's request is not made in good faith or for a proper purpose, decline to deliver or make available such financial statements to that shareholder.

(e)   If a corporation does not respond to a shareholder's request for annual financial statements pursuant to this section in accordance with subsection (b) within five business days of delivery of such request to the corporation:

(1) The requesting shareholder may apply to the [name or describe court] for an order requiring delivery of or access to the requested financial statements. The court shall dispose of an application under this subsection on an expedited basis.

(2) If the court orders delivery or access to the requested financial statements, it may impose reasonable restrictions on their confidentiality, use or distribution.

(3) In such proceeding, if the corporation has declined to deliver or make available such financial statements because the shareholder had been unwilling to agree to restrictions proposed by the corporation on the confidentiality, use and distribution of such financials statements, the corporation shall have the burden of demonstrating that the restrictions proposed by the corporation were reasonable.

(4) In such proceeding, if the corporation has declined to deliver or make available such financial statements pursuant to section 16.20(d)(2), the corporation shall have the burden of demonstrating that it had reasonably determined that the shareholder's request was not made in good faith or for a proper purpose.

(5) If the court orders delivery or access to the requested financial statements it shall order the corporation to pay the shareholder's expenses incurred to obtain such order unless the corporation establishes that it had refused delivery or access to the requested financial statements because the shareholder had refused to agree to reasonable restrictions on the confidentiality, use or distribution of the financial statements or that the corporation had reasonably determined that the shareholder's request was not made in good faith or for a proper purpose.

OFFICIAL COMMENT

1. Section 16.20(a)

Although section 16.20 requires a corporation, upon the written request of a shareholder, to deliver or make available annual financial statements that have been prepared, it does not require a corporation to prepare financial statements. This recognizes that many small, closely held corporations do not regularly prepare formal financial statements unless required by banks, suppliers or other third parties.

Section 16.20 does not limit the financial statements to be delivered or made available to shareholders to financial statements prepared on the basis of generally accepted accounting principles. Many small corporations have never prepared financial statements on the basis of GAAP. "Cash basis" financial statements (often used in preparing the tax returns of small corporations) do not comply with GAAP. Smaller corporations that keep accrual basis records, and file their federal income tax returns on that basis, frequently do not make the adjustments that may be required to present their financial statements on a GAAP basis. Internally or externally prepared financial statements prepared on the basis of other accounting practices and principles that are reasonable in the circumstances, including tax returns filed with the U.S. Internal Revenue Service (if that is all that is prepared), will suffice for these types of corporations and they may satisfy their obligations under section 16.20 by delivering or making available the requested financial statements in whatever form that they have been prepared for other purposes. If a corporation does prepare financial statements on a GAAP basis for any purpose for the particular year, however, it must send or make available those statements to the requesting shareholder as provided by section 16.20(a).

The last sentence of section 16.20(a) requires that if the financial statements to be delivered or made available have been reported upon by a public accountant, that report must be furnished. Section 16.20(a) refers to a "public accountant." The same terminology is used in section 8.30 (standards of conduct for directors). In various states different terms are employed to identify those persons who are permitted under the state licensing requirements to act as professional accountants. Phrases like "independent public accountant," "certified public accountant," "public accountant," and others may be used. In adopting the term "public accountant," the Act uses the words in a general sense to refer to any class or classes of persons who, under the applicable requirements of a particular jurisdiction, are professionally entitled to practice accountancy.

Failure to comply with the requirements of section 16.20 does not adversely affect the existence or good standing of the corporation. Rather, failure to comply gives an aggrieved shareholder rights to compel compliance or to obtain damages, if they can be established, under general principles of law.

A shareholder may also seek access to the financial statements of the corporation through the inspection rights established in section 16.02.

2.   Section 16.20(d)

In establishing restrictions with respect to confidentiality, use or distribution that are reasonable under the circumstances, a corporation may consider a number of factors, including the potential competitive harm to the corporation and its other shareholders that could result if the confidential financial information were used to compete with the corporation or disclosed to third parties such as competitors. As provided in section 16.20(d)(2), a corporation may withhold delivery or making available its financial statements to a requesting shareholder if it reasonably determines that the shareholder's request is not made in good faith and for a proper purpose.

3.   Section 16.20(e)

If a corporation fails to comply with section 16.20(b) in a timely manner the judicial remedy of 16.20(e) directs the court to handle the proceeding on an expedited basis to discourage dilatory tactics to avoid or delay delivery or access to financial statements, but does not require the court to resolve these issues on a summary basis. Section 16.20(e), like section 16.04, establishes a sanction against unreasonable delay or refusal to deliver or provide access to financial statements by imposing on the corporation the shareholder's expenses in obtaining the court's order unless the corporation can establish that the shareholder had been unwilling to agree to reasonable restrictions on the confidentiality, use or distribution of the requested financial statements or the corporation had reasonably determined that the shareholder's request was not made in good faith or for a proper purpose.

§ 16.21   Annual Report for Secretary of State

(a)   Each domestic corporation shall deliver to the secretary of state for filing an annual report that sets forth:

(1)   the name of the corporation;

(2)   the street and mailing address of its registered office and the name of its registered agent at that office in this state;

(3)   the street and mailing address of its principal office;

(4)   the names and business addresses of its directors and principal officers;

(5)   a brief description of the nature of its business;

(6)   the total number of authorized shares, itemized by class and series, if any, within each class; and

(7)   the total number of issued and outstanding shares, itemized by class and series, if any, within each class.

(b)   Each foreign corporation registered to do business in this state shall deliver to the secretary of state for filing an annual report that sets forth:

(1)   the name of the foreign corporation and, if the name does not comply with section 4.01, an alternate name as required by section 15.06;

(2)   the foreign corporation's jurisdiction of formation;

(3)   the street and mailing addresses of the foreign corporation's principal office and, if the law of the foreign corporation's jurisdiction of formation requires the foreign corporation to maintain an office in that jurisdiction, the street and mailing addresses of that office;

(4)   the street and mailing addresses of the foreign corporation's registered office in this state and the name of its registered agent at that office;

(5)   the names and business addresses of its directors and principal officers; and

(6)   a brief description of the nature of its business conducted in this state.

(c)   Information in the annual report must be current as of the date the annual report is signed on behalf of the corporation.

(d)   The first annual report shall be delivered to the secretary of state between January 1 and April 1 of the year following the calendar year in which a domestic corporation was incorporated or a foreign corporation was registered to do business. Subsequent annual reports shall be delivered to the secretary of state between January 1 and April 1 of the following calendar years.

(e)   If an annual report does not contain the information required by this section, the secretary of state shall promptly notify the reporting domestic or foreign corporation in writing and return the report to it for correction. If the report is corrected to contain the information required by this section and delivered to the secretary of state within 30 days after the notice from the secretary of state becomes effective as determined in accordance with section 1.41, it is deemed to be timely filed.

CHAPTER 17.   BENEFIT CORPORATIONS

§ 17.01   Application of Chapter; Definitions

(a)   A corporation electing to become a benefit corporation under this chapter in the manner prescribed in this chapter is subject in all respects to the provisions of this Act, except to the extent this chapter imposes additional or different requirements, in which case such requirements apply. The inclusion of a provision in this chapter does not imply that a contrary or different rule of law applies to a corporation that is not a benefit corporation. This chapter does not affect a statute or rule of law that applies to a corporation that is not a benefit corporation.

(b)   As used in this chapter:

"Benefit corporation" means a corporation that includes in its articles of incorporation a statement that the corporation is subject to this chapter.

"Public benefit" means a positive effect, or reduction of negative effects, on one or more communities or categories of persons (other than shareholders solely in their capacity as shareholders) or on the environment, including effects of an artistic, charitable, economic, educational, cultural, literary, medical, religious, social, ecological, or scientific nature.

"Public benefit provision" means a provision in the articles of incorporation which states that the corporation shall pursue one or more identified public benefits.

"Responsible and sustainable manner" means a manner that:

(i)   pursues through the business of the corporation the creation of a positive effect on society and the environment, taken as a whole, that is material taking into consideration the corporation's size and the nature of its business; and

(ii)   considers, in addition to the interests of shareholders generally, the separate interests of stakeholders known to be affected by the conduct of the business of the corporation.

OFFICIAL COMMENT

Benefit Corporation

Chapter 17 does not create or imply any limitation on the factors or interests the board of directors of a corporation that is not a benefit corporation may take into account under section 8.30 of the Act.

Public Benefit

In addition to pursuing the creation of a positive effect on society and the environment, taken as a whole, the articles of incorporation of a benefit corporation may require a benefit corporation to pursue one or more identified public benefits. Public benefits are defined broadly. If the articles of incorporation include a public benefit provision, then directors also are required to act in a manner that pursues the identified public benefit or benefits in discharging their duties as provided in section 17.04. Pursuit of a public benefit may contribute to acting in a responsible and sustainable manner but, depending on the materiality to the corporation of the public benefit chosen, may or may not be sufficient by itself to satisfy that duty.

Responsible and Sustainable

The requirement in section 17.04(a) that directors act in a responsible and sustainable manner recognizes that corporate operations and business decisions may affect stakeholders other than shareholders. Such operations and decisions have the potential to affect, positively or negatively, critical resources, such as environmental capacities and social stability. The requirement that directors pursue, through the business of the corporation, creation of a positive effect on "society and the environment, taken as a whole" should be viewed in the context of the individual corporation and its ability to create a positive effect that is material considering its size and the nature of its business. It does not require the benefit corporation to create such an effect by itself. For many benefit corporations, pursuit of a positive effect may involve conduct that, in combination with similar conduct by others, can be expected to have a positive effect on society and the environment, taken as a whole. The requirement that the benefit be material makes clear that pursuit of more than a token or incidental benefit is required to satisfy the duty to act in a responsible and sustainable manner. The materiality requirement takes into account the size and nature of a business. It applies the same quantitative and qualitative considerations that would be applicable in other business contexts to determine whether an effect is "material" to the business of a particular corporation. The reference to "business of the corporation" encompasses both what the corporation does and how it conducts its business and operations.

Acting in a responsible and sustainable manner requires that directors consider the interests of shareholders as well as stakeholders known to be affected by the business of the corporation. Section 17.04(b) includes a nonexclusive list of stakeholder interests to be considered to the extent affected.

§ 17.02   Name; Share Certificates

(a) The name of a benefit corporation may contain the words "benefit corporation," the abbreviation "B.C.," or the designation "BC," any of which shall be deemed to satisfy the requirements of section 4.01(a)(1).

(b) Any share certificate issued by a benefit corporation, and any information statement delivered by a benefit corporation pursuant to section 6.26(b), must note conspicuously that the corporation is a benefit corporation subject to this chapter.

OFFICIAL COMMENT

A benefit corporation may, but need not, identify itself as such in its corporate name. In order to provide investors in a benefit corporation with notice they are investing in a corporation that does not operate solely for the benefit of its shareholders, share certificates and information statements evidencing shares in a benefit corporation must contain a legend identifying the corporation as a benefit corporation.

§ 17.03   Certain Amendments and Transactions; Votes Required

(a) Unless the articles of incorporation require a greater vote, in addition to any other approval of shareholders required under this Act, the approval of at least two-thirds of the votes entitled to be cast thereon, and, if any class or series of shares is entitled to vote as a separate group thereon, the approval of at least two-thirds of the votes entitled to be cast by that voting group, shall be required for a corporation that is not a benefit corporation to:

    (1) amend its articles of incorporation to include a statement that it is subject to this chapter; or

(2)   merge with or into, or enter into a share exchange with, another entity, or effect a domestication or conversion, if, as a result of the merger, share exchange, domestication, or conversion, the shares of any voting group would become, or be converted into or exchanged for the right to receive, shares of a benefit corporation or shares or interests in an entity subject to provisions of organic law analogous to those in this chapter; provided, however, that in the case of this subsection (a)(2), if the shares of one or more, but not all, voting groups are so affected, then only the shares in the voting groups so affected shall be entitled to cast votes under this subsection (a).

(b)   Unless the articles of incorporation require a greater vote, in addition to any other approval of shareholders required under this Act, the approval of at least two-thirds of the votes entitled to be cast thereon, and, if any class or series of shares is entitled to vote as a separate group thereon, the approval of at least two-thirds of the votes entitled to be cast by that voting group, shall be required for a benefit corporation to:

(1)   amend its articles of incorporation to eliminate a statement that the corporation is subject to this chapter; or

(2)   merge with or into, or enter into a share exchange with, another entity, or effect a domestication or conversion if, as a result of the merger, share exchange, domestication, or conversion, the shares of any voting group would become, or be converted into or exchanged for the right to receive, shares or interests in an entity that is neither a benefit corporation nor an entity subject to provisions of organic law analogous to those in this chapter; provided, however, that in the case of this subsection (b)(2), if the shares of one or more, but not all, voting groups are so affected, then only the shares in the voting groups so affected shall be entitled to cast votes under this subsection (b).

OFFICIAL COMMENT

Section 17.03 does not eliminate any vote otherwise required under the Act. Section 17.03(a) increases the shareholder vote otherwise required under the Act for amendments or transactions by which a corporation becomes a benefit corporation or shares of a corporation are converted into shares of a benefit corporation or interests in an analogous domestic entity (e.g., a benefit limited liability company) or foreign entity (e.g., a foreign benefit corporation or benefit limited liability company). The vote is increased because the change from ownership of shares of a corporation to those of a benefit corporation significantly changes the nature of the shareholder's investment. For the same reason, section 17.03(b) increases the shareholder vote requirement for amendments or transactions by which a benefit corporation ceases to be a benefit corporation or shares of a benefit corporation are converted into shares of a corporation that is not a benefit corporation or interests in a domestic or foreign entity that is not subject to provisions of organic law analogous to those of this chapter. When a transaction described in subsections (a)(2) or (b)(2) has the indicated effects on the shares of only some voting groups, the increased votes called for in subsections (a) and (b) apply only to shares in the affected voting groups.

§ 17.04   Duties of Directors

(a)   Each member of the board of directors of a benefit corporation, when discharging the duties of a director, shall act: (i) in a responsible and sustainable manner, and (ii) in a manner that pursues the public benefit or benefits identified in any public benefit provision.

(b)   In fulfilling the duties under subsection (a), a director shall consider, to the extent affected, in addition to the interests of shareholders generally, the separate interests of stakeholders known to be affected by the business of the corporation including:

(1)   the employees and work forces of the corporation, its subsidiaries, and its suppliers;

(2)   customers;

(3)   communities or society, including those of each community in which offices or facilities of the corporation, its subsidiaries, or its suppliers are located; and

(4) the local and global environment.

(c) A director of a benefit corporation shall not, by virtue of the duties imposed by subsections (a) and (b), owe any duty to a person other than the benefit corporation due to any interest of the person in the status of the corporation as a benefit corporation or in any public benefit provision.

(d) Unless otherwise provided in the articles of incorporation, the violation by a director of the duties imposed by subsections (a) and (b) shall not constitute an intentional infliction of harm on the corporation or the shareholders for purposes of sections 2.02(b)(4) and (5).

OFFICIAL COMMENT

Section 17.04 is the heart of the benefit corporation provisions. In addition to the duties imposed on directors of all corporations under section 8.30, section 17.04 requires directors of a benefit corporation to pursue through the business of the corporation a positive impact on society and the environment, taken as a whole, and to consider the interests of stakeholders in addition to the interests of shareholders generally. As noted in the Official Comment to section 17.01, the "business of the corporation" encompasses both what the corporation does and how it conducts its business and operations.

The list in section 17.04(b) of stakeholders to be considered is not exclusive, and stakeholders not specifically named but known to be affected by the corporation's business must be considered. The list is not a checklist and the interests of listed stakeholders need be considered only to the extent they are known to be affected by the decision in question. In considering the interests of stakeholders known to be affected, the extent to which an action or decision affects different stakeholders should also be considered.

The standards of director conduct and liability in sections 8.30 and 8.31 apply to actions of directors of a benefit corporation under sections 17.04(a) and (b). Likewise, the presumptions and standards of judicial review, including those related to the common law business judgment rule, described in the Official Comment to section 8.31, apply to director decisions under sections 17.04(a) and (b), including, as part of such decisions, the weighting and reconciliation of competing or inconsistent shareholder and stakeholder interests. A director being a shareholder of the corporation would not, by itself, be expected to constitute a material financial interest (as defined in section 8.60) when performing the duties of a director under sections 17.04(a) or (b), or prevent the business judgment rule from applying to decisions under sections 17.04(a) or (b). Thus, if directors take into account shareholder and relevant stakeholder interests, the business judgment rule would be expected to apply to any business decision that can rationally be viewed as being consistent with the board's duty to act in a responsible and sustainable manner and in furtherance of identified public benefit or benefits. This would be the case no matter how much weight is ultimately given to shareholder and to particular stakeholder interests.

For example, in exercising their duty to act in a responsible and sustainable manner, directors of a benefit corporation considering whether to close a facility would be required to consider the effects of closing the facility not only on shareholder interests but also on the separate interests of, among others, the workforce and community. However, after considering those effects, the directors, consistent with their duties under sections 17.04(a) and (b), could decide to close or not close the facility. This would be the case as long as their decision, taking those effects, and the interests of shareholders and other relevant stakeholders into account, can rationally be viewed as consistent with their duty to act in a responsible and sustainable manner, even if adverse to shareholder or stakeholder interests.

Sections 17.04(a) and (b) provide that all directors of a benefit corporation have the duty to act in a responsible and sustainable manner and does not provide for the creation of a "benefit director" with special duties. However, a benefit corporation may choose to assign oversight of responsibility and sustainability to a board committee. Many benefit corporations will have a chief sustainability officer or other officer with a similar role within management.

The provisions of section 17.04(c) make clear that benefit corporation duties may be enforced only by the corporation or by shareholders in a derivative proceeding brought under section 17.06.

Under section 17.04(d), if a corporation has a section 2.02(b)(4) provision in its articles of incorporation limiting the availability of money damages against directors except in certain enumerated circumstances, relief for violation of a director's duties under section 17.04 will be limited to non-monetary equitable relief, absent a financial benefit to a director to which the director is not entitled, an unlawful distribution, or an intentional violation of criminal law. Similarly, section 17.04(d) protects mandatory director indemnification rights granted in the articles of incorporation pursuant to section 2.02(b)(5) by providing that the limitations on indemnification of directors who intentionally harm either the corporation or shareholders are not applicable in the case of violations of sections 17.04(a) and (b).

§17.05 Annual Benefit Report

(a) No less than annually, a benefit corporation shall prepare a benefit report addressing the efforts of the corporation during the preceding year to operate in a responsible and sustainable manner, to pursue any public benefit or benefits identified in any public benefit provision, and to consider the interests described in section 17.04(b). The annual benefit report must include:

(1) the objectives that the board of directors has established for the corporation to operate in a responsible and sustainable manner, to pursue the public benefit or benefits identified in any public benefit provision, and to consider the interests described in section 17.04(b);

(2) the standards the board of directors has adopted to measure the corporation's progress in operating in a responsible and sustainable manner, in pursuing the public benefit or benefits identified in any public benefit provision, and in considering the interests described in section 17.04(b);

(3) if the articles of incorporation or bylaws require that the corporation use an independent third-party standard in reporting on the corporation's progress in operating in a responsible and sustainable manner, in pursuing the public benefit or benefits identified in any public benefit provision, or in considering the interests described in section 17.04(b), or if the board of directors has chosen to use such a standard, the applicable standard so required or chosen; and

(4) an assessment of the corporation's success in meeting the objectives and standards identified in subsections (a)(1) and (a)(2) and, if applicable, subsection (a)(3), and the basis for that assessment.

(b) The benefit corporation shall deliver to each shareholder, or make available and provide written notice to each shareholder of the availability of, the annual benefit report required by subsection (a) on or before the earlier of:

(1) 120 days following the end of the fiscal year of the benefit corporation; or

(2) the time that the benefit corporation delivers any other annual reports or annual financial statements to its shareholders.

(c) Any shareholder that has not received or been given access to an annual benefit report within the time required by subsection (b) may make a written request that the corporation deliver or make available the annual benefit report to the shareholder. If a benefit corporation does not deliver or make available an annual benefit report to the shareholder within five business days of receiving such request, the requesting shareholder may apply to the [name or describe court] for an order requiring delivery of or access to the annual benefit report. The court shall dispose of an action under this subsection (c) on an expedited basis.

(d) A benefit corporation shall post all of its annual benefit reports on the public portion of its website, if any. If a benefit corporation does not have a website, the benefit corporation shall provide a copy of its most recent annual benefit report, without charge, to any person that requests a copy in writing.

OFFICIAL COMMENT

The purpose of the annual benefit report is to provide a minimum level of visibility into the benefit corporation's efforts so that shareholders may determine how successful the corporation has been in operating in a responsible and sustainable manner and pursuing the public benefit or benefits identified in any public benefit provision.

Benefit corporations and their shareholders may find that measuring sustainability results against a third-party standard, as referenced in subsection (a)(3), provides added credibility to the corporation's sustainability efforts. A provision requiring measurement against a third-party standard may identify a particular third-party standard or may require that a third-party standard be utilized without specifying the particular third-party standard to be used. Absent such a provision in the articles of incorporation or bylaws, a benefit corporation is not required to measure its progress against a third-party standard, but is required to disclose the standard it has adopted to assess its progress in operating in a responsible and sustainable manner, in pursuing the public benefit or benefits identified in any public benefit provision, and in considering the interests described in section 17.04(b).

Section 17.05(c) provides a summary remedy to a shareholder that has not received or been given access to an annual benefit report after request, similar to the remedy provided under section 16.20(e)(1) for failure to provide financial statements upon request. Unlike section 16.20(e)(5), section 17.05(c) does not impose on the corporation the expenses incurred by the shareholder in a successful proceeding under section 17.05(e). However, such expenses could be awarded by a court in an appropriate case.

§ 17.06   Rights of Action

(a)   Except in a proceeding authorized under section 17.05(c) or this section, no person other than the corporation, or a shareholder in the right of the corporation pursuant to subsection (b), may bring an action or assert a claim with respect to the violation of any duty applicable to a benefit corporation or any of its directors under this chapter.

(b)   Except for a proceeding brought under section 17.05(c), a proceeding by a shareholder of a benefit corporation claiming violation of any duty applicable to a benefit corporation or any of its directors under this chapter:

(1)   must be brought in a derivative proceeding pursuant to subchapter 7D; and

(2)   may be brought only by a shareholder of the benefit corporation that at the time of the act or omission complained of either individually, or together with other shareholders bringing such action collectively, owned directly or indirectly at least five percent of a class of the corporation's outstanding shares or, in the case of a corporation with shares traded on an organized market as described in section 13.02(b)(1)(ii), either that percentage of shares or shares with a market value of at least $5 million at the time the proceeding is commenced.

(c)   A suit under subsection (b) may not be maintained if, during the pendency of the suit, the shareholder individually fails, or the shareholders collectively fail, to continue to own directly or indirectly the lesser of (i) the number of shares owned at the time the proceeding is commenced, (ii) a number of shares representing five percent of a class of the corporation's shares, or (iii) a number of shares with a market value of at least $5 million.

OFFICIAL COMMENT

In addition to the standing and demand requirements for bringing a derivative suit under sections 7.41 and 7.42, section 17.06(b) adds a minimum ownership threshold for shareholders to be permitted to bring a derivative proceeding for violation of the duties under chapter 17. The minimum ownership requirement does not apply in a suit under section 17.05(c) to receive or be given access to an annual benefit report. In addition, section 17.06(c) imposes a continuous ownership requirement for a shareholder to be able to maintain a derivative proceeding under section 17.06(b).

CHAPTER 18.   TRANSITION PROVISIONS

NOTE ON ADOPTION OF THE ACT

Chapter 18 addresses various transitional and interpretational issues that merit consideration by the legislature adopting the Act, especially as an entirety. This Note summarizes and explains some of those issues. Each adopting state will need to consider the differences between the Act and its existing corporation statute to determine if additional transitional provisions will be necessary.

Special Circumstances Warranting Delayed Effectiveness

The Act has been drafted to apply to domestic business corporations in existence on its effective date. See section 18.01. To the extent that some of the provisions of the Act differ in significant respects from earlier laws, it may be appropriate to delay the effective date of such provisions to give existing corporations adequate time to revise controlling corporate documents to take into account the provisions of the Act, or in unusual circumstances, to allow existing corporations to continue to be governed by a preexisting law until a later election to be governed by the pertinent provision of the Act. Two examples of such transitional problems are discussed below.

- Changes in Voting Requirements

  The Act, unlike some corporation statutes, requires by virtue of section 7.25 only that votes cast in favor exceed votes cast against, in a meeting at which a quorum is present, to approve transactions such as mergers, sale of substantially all the assets, important amendments to the articles of incorporation, and dissolution. When considering adoption of the Act's voting requirements, it is important to recognize that specific control arrangements may have been established on the assumption that the existing statutory voting requirements would not be reduced. Rather than defeat those reasonable assumptions by effectively eliminating a shareholder's power to veto changes when there was a higher statutory vote requirement, a state that adopts the Act's lesser voting requirement may wish to consider "grandfathering" existing corporations and afford them an option to elect to be governed by the new requirement.

- Increased Power of the Board of Directors

  The Act generally grants the board of directors authority to increase or decrease its own size without specific authority (section 8.03) unless the articles of incorporation restrict this power. Some corporation statutes do not grant this power to the board of directors unless express provision is made in the articles or bylaws. Corporations that have not granted this express power to the board of directors may in effect do so when they become subject to the Act, and a delayed effective date therefore may be appropriate.

Foreign Corporations

Although chapter 15 of the Act may change the rules applicable to foreign corporations in some states, these changes are not of a type that requires a transition period. It is therefore recommended that only a single effective date be provided for the application of the Act to foreign corporations and that delayed effective dates for specific provisions in this regard are unnecessary. See section 18.02.

Savings and Severability Provisions

The Act contains its own savings and severability provisions, in sections 18.03 and 18.04, respectively. If the state has a savings statute of general application, however, it may be unnecessary to adopt section 18.03. Likewise, if the state has a severability provision of general application, or if the state's highest court has established a general rule of severability, it may be unnecessary to adopt section 18.04.

Repeal

Although section 18.05 provides for repeal of previously enacted general corporation statutes that are specified, such repeal is generally unnecessary with regard to statutes providing special incorporation and regulatory provisions for corporations engaged in specific businesses, like banking and insurance. If these specialized statutes expressly incorporate by reference provisions from the general business corporation act, however, these statutes should be amended to refer specifically to the present Act rather than to an earlier statute; an appropriate provision would apply this Act to all these corporations except to the extent the specialized statute expressly provides that a different principle should apply.

§ 18.01   Application to Existing Domestic Corporations

This Act applies to all domestic corporations in existence on its effective date that were incorporated under any general statute of this state providing for incorporation of corporations for profit if power to amend or repeal the statute under which the corporation was incorporated was reserved.

§ 18.02   Application to Existing Foreign Corporations

A foreign corporation registered or authorized to do business in this state on the effective date of this Act is subject to this Act, is deemed to be registered to do business in this state, and is not required to file a foreign registration statement under this Act.

§ 18.03   Saving Provisions

(a)   Except as to procedural provisions, this Act does not affect a pending action or proceeding or a right accrued before the effective date of this Act, and a pending civil action or proceeding may be completed, and a right accrued may be enforced, as if this Act had not become effective.

(b)   If a penalty or punishment for violation of a statute or rule is reduced by this Act, the penalty, if not already imposed, shall be imposed in accordance with this Act.

§ 18.04   Severability

If any provision of this Act or its application to any person or circumstance is held invalid by a court of competent jurisdiction, the invalidity does not affect other provisions or applications of this Act that can be given effect without the invalid provision or application.

§ 18.05   Repeal

The following laws and parts of laws are repealed: [to be inserted by the adopting state].

B. PRIOR MODEL BUSINESS CORPORATION ACT PROVISIONS

In recent years, the Model Business Corporation Act has been amended in significant respects, although many jurisdictions have not adopted some or all of these amendments. This section contains some of the former provisions of the Act and the relevant Official Comments.

Table of Contents

CHAPTER 8

SUBCHAPTER C.   STANDARDS OF CONDUCT

CHAPTER 8

SUBCHAPTER C.   STANDARDS OF CONDUCT

§ 8.30   General Standards for Director Conduct

(a)   A director shall discharge his duties as a director, including his duties as a member of a committee:

(1)   In good faith;

(2)   with the care an ordinarily prudent person in a like position would exercise under similar circumstances; and

(3)   in a manner he reasonably believes to be in the best interests of the corporation.

(b)   In discharging his duties a director is entitled to rely on information, opinions, reports, or statements, including financial statements and other financial data, if prepared or presented by:

(1)   one or more officers or employees of the corporation whom the director reasonably believes to be reliable and competent in the matters presented;

(2)   legal counsel, public accountants, or other persons as to matters the director reasonably believes are within the person's professional or expert competence; or

(3)   a committee of the board of directors of which he is not a member if the director reasonably believes the committee merits confidence.

713

(c)   A director is not acting in good faith if he has knowledge concerning the matter in question that makes reliance otherwise permitted by subsection (b) unwarranted.

(d)   A director is not liable for any action taken as a director, or any failure to take any action, if he performed the duties of his office in compliance with this section.

§ 8.31   Director Conflict of Interest

(a)   A conflict of interest transaction is a transaction with the corporation in which a director of the corporation has a direct or indirect interest. A conflict of interest transaction is not voidable by the corporation solely because of the director's interest in the transaction if any one of the following is true:

   (1)   the material facts of the transaction and the director's interest were disclosed or known to the board of directors or a committee of the board of directors and the board of directors or committee authorized, approved, or ratified the transaction;

   (2)   the material facts of the transaction and the director's interest were disclosed or known to the shareholders entitled to vote and they authorized, approved, or ratified the transaction; or

   (3)   the transaction was fair to the corporation.

(b)   For purposes of this section, a director of the corporation has an indirect interest in a transaction if (1) another entity in which he has a material financial interest or in which he is a general partner is a party to the transaction or (2) another entity of which he is a director, officer, or trustee is a party to the transaction and the transaction is or should be considered by the board of directors of the corporation.

(c)   For purposes of subsection (a)(1), a conflict of interest transaction is authorized, approved, or ratified if it receives the affirmative vote of a majority of the directors on the board of directors (or on the committee) who have no direct or indirect interest in the transaction, but a transaction may not be authorized, approved, or ratified under this section by a single director. If a majority of the directors who have no direct or indirect interest in the transaction vote to authorize, approve, or ratify the transaction, a quorum is present for the purpose of taking action under this section. The presence of, or a vote cast by, a director with a direct or indirect interest in the transaction does not affect the validity of any action taken under subsection (a)(1) if the transaction is otherwise authorized, approved, or ratified as provided in that subsection.

(d)   For purposes of subsection (a)(2), a conflict of interest transaction is authorized, approved, or ratified if it receives the vote of a majority of the shares entitled to be counted under this subsection. Shares owned by or voted under the control of a director who has a direct or indirect interest in the transaction, and shares owned by or voted under the control of an entity described in subsection (b)(1), may not be counted in a vote of shareholders to determine whether to authorize, approve, or ratify a conflict of interest transaction under subsection (a)(2). The vote of those shares, however, is counted in determining whether the transaction is approved under other sections of this Act. A majority of the shares, whether or not present, that are entitled to be counted in a vote on the transaction under this subsection constitutes a quorum for the purpose of taking action under this section.

OFFICIAL COMMENT

1.   Conflict of Interest Transactions in General

Section 8.31 deals only with "conflict of interest" transactions by a director with the corporation, that is, transactions in which the director has an interest either (1) directly or (2) indirectly through an entity in which the director has a financial or managerial interest covered by section 8.31(b). A conflict of interest transaction does not include transactions in which the director participates in the transaction only as a shareholder and receives only a proportionate share of the advantage or benefit of the transaction. Section 8.31 deals only with conflict of interest transactions involving directors; it does not address analogous transactions entered into by officers, employees, or substantial or dominating shareholders unless they are also directors.

Section 8.31 rejects the common law view that all conflict of interest transactions entered into by directors are automatically voidable at the option of the corporation without regard to the fairness of the transaction or the manner in which the transaction was approved by the corporation. Section 8.31(a) makes any automatic rule of voidability inapplicable to transactions that are fair or that have been approved by directors or shareholders in the manner provided by the balance of section 8.31. The approval mechanisms set forth in section 8.31(c) and (d) relate only to the elimination of this automatic rule of voidability and do not address the manner in which the transactions must be approved under other sections of this Act. This is made clear by the express limitations in sections 8.31(c) and (d) that they are applicable only "for the purposes of this section" as well as the language of the second and third sentences of section 8.31(d).

The elimination of the automatic rule of voidability does not mean that all transactions that meet one or more of the tests set forth in section 8.31(a) are automatically valid. These transactions may be subject to attack on a variety of grounds independent of section 8.31—for example, that the transaction constituted waste, that it was not authorized by the appropriate corporate body, that it violated other sections of the Model Business Corporation Act, or that it was unenforceable under other common law principles. The sole purpose of section 8.31 is to sharply limit the common law principle of automatic voidability and in this respect section 8.31 follows earlier versions of the Model Act and the statutes of many states dealing with conflict of interest transactions.

* * *

2. *Requirements for Approval of Conflict of Interest Transactions*

Sections 8.31(c) and (d) provide special rules for determining whether the board of directors (or a committee thereof) or the shareholders have authorized, approved, or ratified a conflict of interest transaction so as to bring subsections (a)(1) or (a)(2) into play. Basically, these subsections require the transaction in question to be approved by an absolute majority of the directors (on the board of directors, or on the committee, as the case may be) or shares whose votes may be counted in determining whether the transaction should be authorized, approved, or ratified. If these votes are not obtained the transaction is tested under the fairness test of subsection (a)(3). The vote required for authorization, approval, or ratification of a conflict of interest transaction is more onerous than the standard applicable to normal voting requirements for approval of corporate actions—i.e., that a quorum be present and only the votes of directors or shares present or represented at that meeting be considered—because of the importance of assuring that conflict of interest transactions receive as broad consideration within the corporation as possible if independent review on the basis of fairness is to be avoided.

* * *

b. *Consideration by the Shareholders*

In some situations, the prohibition of section 8.31(d) will result in the conflict of interest issue being resolved by a majority of a minority of the shares. This will occur, for example, whenever a director who is the majority shareholder of the corporation is interested in a transaction. The vote on the conflict of interest issue under section 8.31, however, must be distinguished from the vote on the approval of the transaction itself under other sections of the Model Act, in which there is no prohibition against the voting of shares owned or controlled by an interested director. For example, if a parent corporation wishes to merge its 60-percent-owned subsidiary into itself, and the majority shareholder of the parent is a director of the subsidiary, the votes of the shares owned by the parent corporation may not be counted under section 8.31(d) (since the shares are owned by an entity which is a party to the transaction and which the director controls). The shares nevertheless may be voted on the merger proposal itself under chapter 11 of the Model Act, and the merger will, of course, normally be approved solely by the vote of the shares owned by the parent corporation. On the other hand, the test of section 8.31(a)(2) is not met unless the transaction is approved by at least a majority of the votes cast by the holders of the 40 percent of the shares not owned by the parent corporation. If this requirement is not met, the transaction may be evaluated under the fairness test of section 8.31(a)(3).

3.　Indirect Conflicts of Interest

Section 8.31 is applicable to "indirect" as well as direct conflicts; "indirect" is defined in section 8.31(b) to cover transactions between the corporation and an entity in which the director has a material financial interest or is a general partner. Further, section 8.31(b) covers indirect conflicts where the director is an officer or director of another entity (but does not have a material financial interest in the transaction) if the transaction is of sufficient importance that it is or should be considered by the board of directors of the corporation. The purpose of this last clause is to permit normal business transactions between large business entities that may have a common director to go forward without concern about the technical rules relating to conflict of interest unless the transaction is of such importance that it is or should be considered by the board of directors or the director may be deemed to have a material financial interest in the transaction. Thus, section 8.31 covers transactions between corporations with interlocking or common directors as well as the direct "interested director" transaction.

4.　"Fairness" of a Transaction

The fairness of a transaction for purposes of section 8.31 should be evaluated on the basis of the facts and circumstances as they were known or should have been known at the time the transaction was entered into. For example, the terms of a transaction subject to section 8.31 should normally be deemed "fair" if they are within the range that might have been entered into at arm's-length by disinterested persons.

5.　An "Interested" Director

The Model Act does not attempt to define precisely when a director should be viewed as "interested" for purposes of participating in the decision to adopt, approve, or ratify a conflict of interest transaction. Section 8.31(b) does, however, define one aspect of this concept—the "indirect" interest. For purposes of section 8.31 a director should normally be viewed as interested in a transaction if he or the immediate members of his family have a financial interest in the transaction or a relationship with the other parties to the transaction such that the relationship might reasonably be expected to affect his judgment in the particular matter in a manner adverse to the corporation.

CHAPTER 10.　AMENDMENT OF ARTICLES OF INCORPORATION AND BYLAWS

SUBCHAPTER B.　AMENDMENT OF BYLAWS

§ 10.20　Amendment by Board of Directors or Shareholders

(a)　A corporation's board of directors may amend or repeal the corporation's bylaws unless:

(1)　the articles of incorporation or this Act reserve this power exclusively to the shareholders in whole or part; or

(2)　the shareholders in amending or repealing a particular bylaw provide expressly that the board of directors may not amend or repeal that bylaw.

(b)　A corporation's shareholders may amend or repeal the corporation's bylaws even though the bylaws may also be amended or repealed by its board of directors.

OFFICIAL COMMENT

In the absence of a provision in the articles of incorporation, the power to amend or repeal bylaws is shared by the board of directors and shareholders. Amendment of bylaws by the board of directors is often simpler and more convenient than amendment by the shareholders and avoids the expense of calling a shareholders' meeting, a cost that [may] be significant in publicly held corporations. As used in this subchapter, "amendment" includes the adoption of a bylaw on a new subject as well as the alteration of existing bylaws.

Section 10.20(a) provides. however. that the power to amend or repeal bylaws may be reserved exclusively to the shareholders by an appropriate provision in the articles of incorporation. This option may appropriately be elected by a closely held corporation—for example, where control arrangements appear in the bylaws but one shareholder or group of shareholders has the power to name a majority of the board of directors. In such a corporation, the control arrangements may alternatively be placed in the articles of incorporation rather than the bylaws if there is no objection to making them a matter of public record.

Section 10.20(a)(1) provides that the power to amend or repeal the bylaws may be reserved to the shareholders "in whole or part." This language permits the reservation of power to be limited to specific articles or sections of the bylaws or to specific subjects or topics addressed in the bylaws. It is important that the areas reserved exclusively to the shareholders be delineated clearly and unambiguously.

Section 10.20(a)(2) permits the shareholders to adopt or amend a bylaw and reserve exclusively to themselves the power to amend or repeal it later. This reservation must be expressed in the action by the shareholders adopting or amending the bylaw. This option is also included for the benefit of closely held corporations.

Section 10.20(b) states that the power of shareholders to amend or repeal bylaws exists even though that power is shared with the board of directors. This section makes inapplicable the holdings of a few cases under differently phrased statutes that shareholders do not have a general or residual power to amend bylaws or that the power to amend bylaws may be vested exclusively in the board of directors. Under the Model Act the shareholders always have the power to amend or repeal the bylaws.

Section 10.21 and 10.22 limit the power of directors to adopt or amend supermajority provisions in bylaws.

CHAPTER 12.   SALE OF ASSETS

§ 12.01   Sale of Assets in Regular Course of Business and Mortgage of Assets

(a)   A corporation may, on the terms and conditions and for the consideration determined by the board of directors:

(1)   sell, lease, exchange, or otherwise dispose of all, or substantially all, of its property in the usual and regular course of business,

(2)   mortgage, pledge, dedicate to the repayment of indebtedness (whether with or without recourse), or otherwise encumber any or all of its property whether or not in the usual and regular course of business, or

(3)   transfer any or all of its property to a corporation all the shares of which are owned by the corporation.

(b)   Unless the articles of incorporation require it, approval by the shareholders of a transaction described in subsection (a) is not required.

OFFICIAL COMMENT

A sale of "all or substantially all" the corporate assets in the regular course of business is governed by section 12.01. Mortgages of all of the corporation's assets or redeployment of those assets through a wholly owned subsidiary are also covered by section 12.01. All other sales of "all or substantially all" the corporate assets are governed by section 12.02. Dispositions or transfers of property that do not involve "all or substantially all" the property of the corporation are not controlled by statute and may be approved by the board of directors (or authorized corporate officer) in the same manner as any other corporate transaction.

1.   The Meaning of "All or Substantially All"

The phrase "all or substantially all," chosen by the draftsmen of the Model Act, is intended to mean what it literally says, "all or substantially all." The phrase "substantially all" is synonymous with "nearly all" and was added merely to make it clear that the statutory requirements could not be avoided by retention of some minimal or nominal residue of the original assets. A sale of all the corporate assets other than cash or cash equivalents is normally the sale of "all or substantially all" of the corporation's property. A sale of several distinct manufacturing lines while retaining one or more lines is normally not a sale of "all or substantially all" even though the lines being sold are substantial and include a significant fraction of the corporation's former business. If the lines retained are viewed only as a temporary operation or as a pretext to avoid the "all or substantially all" requirements, however, the statutory requirements of chapter 12 must be complied with. Similarly, as sale of a plant but retention of operating assets (*e.g.* machinery and equipment), accounts receivable, good will, and the like with a view toward continuing the operation at another location is not a sale of "all or substantially all" the corporation's property.

Some court decisions have adopted a narrower construction of somewhat similar statutory language. These decisions should be viewed as resting on the diverse statutory language involved in those cases and should not be viewed as illustrating the meaning of "all or substantially all" intended by the draftsmen of the Model Act.

2.   Transfers of "All or Substantially All" of a Corporation's Assets That Do Not Require Shareholder Approval

Section 12.01 describes transfers or dispositions of "all or substantially all" the corporate assets that do not require shareholder approval unless the articles of incorporation require it. These transactions consist of (1) mortgages or pledges of all the corporation's property, whether or not the loan they secure is in the ordinary course of business, (2) transactions within the usual and regular course of business, and (3) transfers to wholly owned subsidiaries.

a.   Mortgages or Pledges

Mortgages or pledges of all the corporate assets may be demanded by lenders. They are essentially and substantively different from a sale or other disposition of assets even though they may take the form of a formal transfer of title to the mortgagee for security purposes, or of a dedication of assets to the repayment of indebtedness, as in the case of oil and gas production payments. The corporation remains in possession of the mortgaged property, may continue to use it for corporate purposes, in most cases must continue to manage the property, and may recover full title to the property by discharging the indebtedness.

b.   Sales in the Usual and Regular Course of Business

Most transfers of "all or substantially all" the corporate property (as defined above) are, almost by definition, not in the usual and regular course of business; sales by real estate corporations and by corporations organized to liquidate a business are examples of sales that may be included in this part of section 12.01(a). Typically, sales falling within the usual and regular course of business do not involve the sale of the corporate name or good will.

c.   Transfers to a Subsidiary

Section 12.01 provides that a transfer of property to a wholly owned subsidiary does not require a vote of shareholders. This provision, however, may not be used as a device to avoid a vote of shareholders by a multiple-step transaction.

§ 12.02   Sale of Assets Other Than in Regular Course of Business

(a)   A corporation may sell, lease, exchange, or otherwise dispose of all, or substantially all, of its property (with or without the good will), otherwise than in the usual and regular course of business, on the terms and conditions and for the consideration determined by the corporation's board of directors, if the board of directors proposes and its shareholders approve the proposed transaction.

(b)   For a transaction to be authorized:

(1)   the board of directors must recommend the proposed transaction to the shareholders unless the board of directors determines that because of conflict of interest or other special circumstances it should make no recommendation and communicates the basis for its determination to the shareholders with the submission of the proposed transaction; and

(2)   the shareholders entitled to vote must approve the transaction.

(c)   The board of directors may condition its submission of the proposed transaction on any basis.

(d)   The corporation shall notify each shareholder, whether or not entitled to vote, of the proposed shareholders' meeting in accordance with section 7.05. The notice must also state that the purpose, or one of the purposes, of the meeting is to consider the sale, lease, exchange, or other disposition of all, or substantially all, the property of the corporation and contain or be accompanied by a description of the transaction.

(e)   Unless the articles of incorporation or the board of directors (acting pursuant to subsection (c)) require a greater vote or a vote by voting groups, the transaction to be authorized must be approved by a majority of all the votes entitled to be cast on the transaction.

(f)   After a sale, lease, exchange, or other disposition of property is authorized, the transaction may be abandoned (subject to any contractual rights) without further shareholder action.

(g)   A transaction that constitutes a distribution is governed by section 6.40 and not by this section.

C. CALIFORNIA CORPORATIONS CODE

1. CALIFORNIA GENERAL CORPORATION LAW

(Selected Sections)

Table of Contents

CALIFORNIA GENERAL CORPORATION LAW

CHAPTER 21.   FOREIGN CORPORATIONS

CHAPTER 1.   GENERAL PROVISIONS AND DEFINITIONS

§ 114.   Financial Statements or Comparable Statements or Items

All references in this division to financial statements, balance sheets, income statements, and statements of cashflows, and all references to assets, liabilities, earnings, retained earnings, and similar accounting items of a corporation mean those financial statements or comparable statements or items prepared or determined in conformity with generally accepted accounting principles then applicable, fairly presenting in conformity with generally accepted accounting principles the matters that they purport to present, subject to any specific accounting treatment required by a particular section of this division. Unless otherwise expressly stated, all references in this division to financial statements mean, in the case of a corporation that has subsidiaries, consolidated statements of the corporation and each of its subsidiaries as are required to be included in the consolidated statements under generally accepted accounting principles then applicable and all references to accounting items mean the items determined on a consolidated basis in accordance with the consolidated financial statements. Financial statements other than annual statements may be condensed or otherwise presented as permitted by authoritative accounting pronouncements.

§ 158.   Close Corporation

(a)   "Close corporation" means a corporation, including a close social purpose corporation, whose articles contain, in addition to the provisions required by Section 202, a provision that all of the corporation's issued shares of all classes shall be held of record by not more than a specified number of persons, not exceeding 35, and a statement, "This corporation is a close corporation."

(b)   The special provisions referred to in subdivision (a) may be included in the articles by amendment, but if such amendment is adopted after the issuance of shares only by the affirmative vote of all of the issued and outstanding shares of all classes.

(c)   The special provisions referred to in subdivision (a) may be deleted from the articles by amendment, or the number of shareholders specified may be changed by amendment, but if such amendment is adopted after the issuance of shares, only by the affirmative vote of at least two-thirds of each class of the outstanding shares; provided, however, that the articles may provide for a lesser vote, but not less than a majority of the outstanding shares, or may deny a vote to any class, or both.

(d)   In determining the number of shareholders for the purposes of the provision in the articles authorized by this section, spouses and the personal representative of either shall be counted as one regardless of how shares may be held by either or both of them, a trust or personal representative of a decedent holding shares shall be counted as one regardless of the number of trustees or beneficiaries, and a partnership or corporation or business association holding shares shall be counted as one (except that any such trust or entity the primary purpose of which was the acquisition or voting of the shares shall be counted according to the number of beneficial interests therein).

(e)   A corporation shall cease to be a close corporation upon the filing of an amendment to its articles pursuant to subdivision (c) or, if it shall have more than the maximum number of holders of record of its shares specified in its articles as a result of an inter vivos transfer of shares which is not void under subdivision (d) of Section 418, the transfer of shares on distribution by will or pursuant to the laws of descent and distribution, the dissolution of a partnership or corporation or business association, or the termination of a trust which holds shares, by court decree upon dissolution of a marriage or otherwise by operation of law. Promptly upon acquiring more than the specified number of holders of record of its shares, a close corporation shall execute and file an amendment to its articles deleting the special provisions referred to in subdivision (a) and deleting any other provisions not permissible for a corporation which is not a close corporation, which amendment shall be promptly approved and filed by the board and need not be approved by the outstanding shares.

(f)   Nothing contained in this section shall invalidate any agreement among the shareholders to vote for the deletion from the articles of the special provisions referred to in subdivision (a) upon the lapse of a specified period of time or upon the occurrence of a certain event or condition or otherwise.

(g)   The following sections contain specific references to close corporations: Sections 186, 202, 204, 300, 418, 421, 1111, 1201, 1800, and 1904.

§ 160.   Control

(a)   Except as provided in subdivision (b), "control" means the possession, direct or indirect, of the power to direct or cause the direction of the management and policies of a corporation.

(b)   "Control" in Sections 181, 1001, and 1200 means the ownership directly or indirectly of shares or equity securities possessing more than 50 percent of the voting power of a domestic corporation, a foreign corporation, or another business entity.

§ 163.1   Cumulative Dividends in Arrears

For purposes of subdivision (b) of Section 500 and subdivision (b) of Section 506, "cumulative dividends in arrears" means only cumulative dividends that have not been paid as required on a scheduled payment date set forth in, or determined pursuant to, the articles of incorporation, regardless of whether those dividends had been declared prior to that scheduled payment date.

§ 166.   Distribution to Its Shareholders

"Distribution to its shareholders" means the transfer of cash or property by a corporation to its shareholders without consideration, whether by way of dividend or otherwise, except a dividend in shares of the corporation, or the purchase or redemption of its shares for cash or property, including the transfer, purchase, or redemption by a subsidiary of the corporation. The time of any distribution by way of dividend shall be the date of declaration thereof and the time of any distribution by purchase or redemption of shares shall be the date cash or property is transferred by the corporation, whether or not pursuant to a contract of an earlier date; provided, that where a debt obligation that is a security (as defined in Section 8102 of the Commercial Code) is issued in exchange for shares the time of the distribution is the date when the corporation acquires the shares in the exchange. In the case of a sinking fund payment, cash or property is transferred within the meaning of this section at the time that it is delivered to a trustee for the holders of preferred shares to be used for the redemption of the shares or physically segregated by the corporation in trust for that purpose. "Distribution to its shareholders" shall not include (a) satisfaction of a final judgment of a court or tribunal of appropriate jurisdiction ordering the rescission of the issuance of shares, (b) the rescission by a corporation of the issuance of it shares, if the board determines (with any director who is, or would be, a party to the transaction not being entitled to vote) that (1) it is reasonably likely that the holder or holders of the shares in question could legally enforce a claim for the rescission, (2) that the rescission is in the best interests of the corporation, and (3) the corporation is likely to be able to meet its liabilities (except those for which payment is otherwise adequately provided) as they mature, or (c) the repurchase by a corporation of its shares issued by it pursuant to Section 408, if the board determines (with any director who is, or would be, a party to the transaction not being entitled to vote) that (1) the repurchase is in the best interests of the corporation and that (2) the corporation is likely to be able to meet its liabilities (except those for which payment is otherwise adequately provided) as they mature.

§ 172. Liquidation Price; Liquidation Preference

"Liquidation price" or "liquidation preference" means amounts payable on shares of any class upon voluntary or involuntary dissolution, winding up or distribution of the entire assets of the corporation, including any cumulative dividends accrued and unpaid, in priority to shares of another class or classes.

§ 178. Proxy

"Proxy" means a written authorization signed or an electronic transmission authorized by a shareholder or the shareholder's attorney in fact giving another person or persons power to vote with respect to the shares of such shareholder. "Signed" for the purpose of this section means the placing of the shareholder's name or other authorization on the proxy (whether by manual signature, typewriting, telegraphic, or electronic transmission or otherwise) by the shareholder or the shareholder's attorney in fact.

A proxy may be transmitted by an oral telephonic transmission if it is submitted with information from which it may be determined that the proxy was authorized by the shareholder, or his or her attorney in fact.

§ 181. Reorganization

"Reorganization" means either:

(a) A merger pursuant to Chapter 11 (commencing with Section 1100) other than a short-form merger (a "merger reorganization").

(b) The acquisition by one domestic corporation, foreign corporation, or other business entity in exchange, in whole or in part, for its equity securities (or the equity securities of a domestic corporation, a foreign corporation, or another business entity which is in control of the acquiring entity) of equity securities of another domestic corporation, foreign corporation, or other business entity if, immediately after the acquisition, the acquiring entity has control of the other entity (an "exchange reorganization").

(c) The acquisition by one domestic corporation, foreign corporation, or other business entity in exchange in whole or in part for its equity securities (or the equity securities of a domestic corporation, a foreign corporation, or another business entity which is in control of the acquiring entity) or for its debt securities (or debt securities of a domestic corporation, foreign corporation, or other business entity which is in control of the acquiring entity) which are not adequately secured and which have a maturity date in excess of five years after the consummation of the reorganization, or both, of all or substantially all of the assets of another domestic corporation, foreign corporation, or other business entity (a "sale-of-assets reorganization").

§ 183.5 Share Exchange Tender Offer

"Share exchange tender offer" means any acquisition by one corporation in exchange in whole or in part for its equity securities (or the equity securities of a corporation which is in control of the acquiring corporation) of shares of another corporation, other than an exchange reorganization (subdivision (b) of Section 181).

§ 186. Shareholders' Agreement

"Shareholders' agreement" means a written agreement among all of the shareholders of a close corporation, or if a close corporation has only one shareholder between such shareholder and the corporation, as authorized by subdivision (b) of Section 300.

§ 194.   Vote

"Vote" includes authorization by written consent, subject to the provisions of subdivision (b) of Section 307 and subdivision (d) of Section 603.

§ 194.5   Voting Power

"Voting power" means the power to vote for the election of directors at the time any determination of voting power is made and does not include the right to vote upon the happening of some condition or event which has not yet occurred. In any case where different classes of shares are entitled to vote as separate classes for different members of the board, the determination of percentage of voting power shall be made on the basis of the percentage of the total number of authorized directors which the shares in question (whether of one or more classes) have the power to elect in an election at which all shares then entitled to vote for the election of any directors are voted.

§ 194.7   Voting Shift

"Voting shift" means a change, pursuant to or by operation of a provision of the articles, in the relative rights of the holders of one or more classes or series of shares, voting as one or more separate classes or series, to elect one or more directors.

* * *

CHAPTER 2.   ORGANIZATION AND BYLAWS

§ 204.   Articles of Incorporation; Optional Provisions

The articles of incorporation may set forth:

(a)   Any or all of the following provisions, which shall not be effective unless expressly provided in the articles:

(1)   Granting, with or without limitations, the power to levy assessments upon the shares or any class of shares.

(2)   Granting to shareholders preemptive rights to subscribe to any or all issues of shares or securities.

(3)   Special qualifications of persons who may be shareholders.

(4)   A provision limiting the duration of the corporation's existence to a specified date.

(5)   A provision requiring, for any or all corporate actions (except as provided in Section 303, subdivision (b) of Section 402.5, subdivision (c) of Section 708 and Section 1900) the vote of a larger proportion or of all of the shares of any class or series, or the vote or quorum for taking action of a larger proportion or of all of the directors, than is otherwise required by this division.

(6)   A provision limiting or restricting the business in which the corporation may engage or the powers which the corporation may exercise or both.

(7)   A provision conferring upon the holders of any evidences of indebtedness, issued or to be issued by the corporation, the right to vote in the election of directors and on any other matters on which shareholders may vote.

(8)   A provision conferring upon shareholders the right to determine the consideration for which shares shall be issued.

(9)   A provision requiring the approval of the shareholders (Section 153) or the approval of the outstanding shares (Section 152) for any corporate action, even though not otherwise required by this division.

(10) Provisions eliminating or limiting the personal liability of a director for monetary damages in an action brought by or in the right of the corporation for breach of a director's duties to the corporation and its shareholders, as set forth in Section 309, provided, however, that (A) such a provision may not eliminate or limit the liability of directors (i) for acts or omissions that involve intentional misconduct or a knowing and culpable violation of law, (ii) for acts or omissions that a director believes to be contrary to the best interests of the corporation or its shareholders or that involve the absence of good faith on the part of the director, (iii) for any transaction from which a director derived an improper personal benefit, (iv) for acts or omissions that show a reckless disregard for the director's duty to the corporation or its shareholders in circumstances in which the director was aware, or should have been aware, in the ordinary course of performing a director's duties, of a risk of serious injury to the corporation or its shareholders, (v) for acts or omissions that constitute an unexcused pattern of inattention that amounts to an abdication of the director's duty to the corporation or its shareholders, (vi) under Section 310, or (vii) under Section 316, (B) no such provision shall eliminate or limit the liability of a director for any act or omission occurring prior to the date when the provision becomes effective, and (C) no such provision shall eliminate or limit the liability of an officer for any act or omission as an officer, notwithstanding that the officer is also a director or that his or her actions, if negligent or improper, have been ratified by the directors.

(11) A provision authorizing, whether by bylaw, agreement, or otherwise, the indemnification of agents (as defined in Section 317) in excess of that expressly permitted by Section 317 for those agents of the corporation for breach of duty to the corporation and its stockholders, provided, however, that the provision may not provide for indemnification of any agent for any acts or omissions or transactions from which a director may not be relieved of liability as set forth in the exception to paragraph (10) or as to circumstances in which indemnity is expressly prohibited by Section 317.

Notwithstanding this subdivision, in the case of a close corporation any of the provisions referred to above may be validly included in a shareholders' agreement. Notwithstanding this subdivision, bylaws may require for all or any actions by the board the affirmative vote of a majority of the authorized number of directors. Nothing contained in this subdivision shall affect the enforceability, as between the parties thereto, of any lawful agreement not otherwise contrary to public policy.

(12)(A)   In the case of a corporation that does not have outstanding securities listed on the New York Stock Exchange, the NYSE Amex, the NASDAQ Global Market, or the NASDAQ Capital Market, a provision authorizing records administered by or on behalf of the corporation in which the names of all of the corporation's stockholders of record, the address and number of shares registered in the name of each of those stockholders, and all issuances and transfers of stock of the corporation to be recorded and kept on or by means of blockchain technology, provided that all of the following requirements are met:

(i)   The encrypted information in the records can be decrypted and converted into a clearly readable format within a reasonable period of time.

(ii)   The records can be used to prepare the list of shareholders.

(iii)   The records can be used to record information required to be included on stock certificates.

(iv)   The records can be used to record required transfers of stock.

(B)   For purposes of this paragraph, "blockchain technology" means a mathematically secured, chronological, and decentralized consensus ledger or database.

(b)   Reasonable restrictions upon the right to transfer or hypothecate shares of any class or classes or series, but no restriction shall be binding with respect to shares issued prior to the adoption of the restriction unless the holders of such shares voted in favor of the restriction.

(c)   The names and addresses of the persons appointed to act as initial directors.

(d) Any other provision, not in conflict with law, for the management of the business and for the conduct of the affairs of the corporation, including any provision which is required or permitted by this division to be stated in the bylaws.

(e) This section shall remain in effect only until January 1, 2022, and as of that date is repealed.

§ 204.5   Director Liability; Limiting Provision in Articles; Wording; Disclosure to Shareholders Regarding Provision

(a) If the articles of a corporation include a provision reading substantially as follows: "The liability of the directors of the corporation for monetary damages shall be eliminated to the fullest extent permissible under California law"; the corporation shall be considered to have adopted a provision as authorized by paragraph (10) of subdivision (a) of Section 204 and more specific wording shall not be required.

(b) This section shall not be construed as setting forth the exclusive method of adopting an article provision as authorized by paragraph (10) of subdivision (a) of Section 204.

(c) This section shall not change the otherwise applicable standards or duties to make full and fair disclosure to shareholders when approval of such a provision is sought.

§ 212.   Bylaws; Contents

(a) The bylaws shall set forth (unless such provision is contained in the articles, in which case it may only be changed by an amendment of the articles) the number of directors of the corporation; or that the number of directors shall be not less than a stated minimum nor more than a stated maximum (which in no case shall be greater than two times the stated minimum minus one); with the exact number of directors to be fixed, within the limits specified, by approval of the board or the shareholders (Section 153) in the manner provided in the bylaws, subject to paragraph (5) of subdivision (a) of Section 204. The number or minimum number of directors shall not be less than three; provided, however, that (1) before shares are issued, the number may be one, (2) before shares are issued, the number may be two, (3) so long as the corporation has only one shareholder, the number may be one, (4) so long as the corporation has only one shareholder, the number may be two, and (5) so long as the corporation has only two shareholders, the number may be two. After the issuance of shares, a bylaw specifying or changing a fixed number of directors or the maximum or minimum number or changing from a fixed to a variable board or vice versa may only be adopted by approval of the outstanding shares (Section 152); provided, however, that a bylaw or amendment of the articles reducing the fixed number or the minimum number of directors to a number less than five cannot be adopted if the votes cast against its adoption at a meeting or the shares not consenting in the case of action by written consent are equal to more than 16 $2/3$ percent of the outstanding shares entitled to vote.

(b) The bylaws may contain any provision, not in conflict with law or the articles for the management of the business and for the conduct of the affairs of the corporation, including, but not limited to:

(1) Any provision referred to in subdivision (b), (c) or (d) of Section 204.

(2) The time, place, and manner of calling, conducting, and giving notice of shareholders', directors', and committee meetings.

(3) The manner of execution, revocation, and use of proxies.

(4) The qualifications, duties, and compensation of directors; the time of their annual election; and the requirements of a quorum for directors' and committee meetings.

(5) The appointment and authority of committees of the board.

(6) The appointment, duties, compensation, and tenure of officers.

(7)   The mode of determination of holders of record of its shares.

(8)   The making of annual reports and financial statements to the shareholders.

(c)(1)   The bylaws may contain any provision, not in conflict with the articles, to manage and conduct the ordinary business affairs of the corporation effective only in an emergency as defined in Section 207, including, but not limited to, procedures for calling a board meeting, quorum requirements for a board meeting, and designation of additional or substitute directors.

(2)   During an emergency, the board may not take any action that requires the vote of the shareholders or otherwise is not in the corporation's ordinary course of business, unless the required vote of the shareholders was obtained prior to the emergency.

(3)   All provisions of the regular bylaws consistent with the emergency bylaws shall remain effective during the emergency, and the emergency bylaws shall not be effective after the emergency ends.

(4)   Corporate action taken in good faith in accordance with the emergency bylaws binds the corporation, and may not be used to impose liability on a

* * *

CHAPTER 3.   DIRECTORS AND MANAGEMENT

§ 300.   Powers of Board; Delegation; Close Corporations; Shareholders' Agreements; Validity; Liability; Failure to Observe Formalities

(a)   Subject to the provisions of this division and any limitations in the articles relating to action required to be approved by the shareholders (Section 153) or by the outstanding shares (Section 152), or by a less than majority vote of a class or series of preferred shares (Section 402.5), the business and affairs of the corporation shall be managed and all corporate powers shall be exercised by or under the direction of the board. The board may delegate the management of the day-to-day operation of the business of the corporation to a management company or other person provided that the business and affairs of the corporation shall be managed and all corporate powers shall be exercised under the ultimate direction of the board.

(b)   Notwithstanding subdivision (a) or any other provision of this division, but subject to subdivision (c), no shareholders' agreement, which relates to any phase of the affairs of a close corporation, including but not limited to management of its business, division of its profits or distribution of its assets on liquidation, shall be invalid as between the parties thereto on the ground that it so relates to the conduct of the affairs of the corporation as to interfere with the discretion of the board or that it is an attempt to treat the corporation as if it were a partnership or to arrange their relationships in a manner that would be appropriate only between partners. A transferee of shares covered by such an agreement which is filed with the secretary of the corporation for inspection by any prospective purchaser of shares, who has actual knowledge thereof or notice thereof by a notation on the certificate pursuant to Section 418, is bound by its provisions and is a party thereto for the purposes of subdivision (d). Original issuance of shares by the corporation to a new shareholder who does not become a party to the agreement terminates the agreement, except that if the agreement so provides it shall continue to the extent it is enforceable apart from this subdivision. The agreement may not be modified, extended or revoked without the consent of such a transferee, subject to any provision of the agreement permitting modification, extension or revocation by less than unanimous agreement of the parties. A transferor of shares covered by such an agreement ceases to be a party thereto upon ceasing to be a shareholder of the corporation unless the transferor is a party thereto other than as a shareholder. An agreement made pursuant to this subdivision shall terminate when the corporation ceases to be a close corporation, except that if the agreement so provides it shall continue to the extent it is enforceable apart from this subdivision. This subdivision does not apply to an agreement authorized by subdivision (a) of Section 706.

(c)   No agreement entered into pursuant to subdivision (b) may alter or waive any of the provisions of Sections 158, 417, 418, 500, 501, and 1111, subdivision (e) of Section 1201, Sections 2009, 2010, and 2011, or of Chapters 15 (commencing with Section 1500), 16 (commencing with Section 1600), 18 (commencing with Section 1800), and 22 (commencing with Section 2200). All other provisions of this division may be altered or waived as between the parties thereto in a shareholders' agreement, except the required filing of any document with the Secretary of State.

(d)   An agreement of the type referred to in subdivision (b) shall, to the extent and so long as the discretion or powers of the board in its management of corporate affairs is controlled by such agreement, impose upon each shareholder who is a party thereto liability for managerial acts performed or omitted by such person pursuant thereto that is otherwise imposed by this division upon directors, and the directors shall be relieved to that extent from such liability.

(e)   The failure of a close corporation to observe corporate formalities relating to meetings of directors or shareholders in connection with the management of its affairs, pursuant to an agreement authorized by subdivision (b), shall not be considered a factor tending to establish that the shareholders have personal liability for corporate obligations.

§ 301.   Directors; Election; Term

(a)   Except as provided in Section 301.5, at each annual meeting of shareholders, directors shall be elected to hold office until the next annual meeting. However, to effectuate a voting shift (Section 194.7) the articles may provide that directors hold office for a shorter term. The articles may provide for the election of one or more directors by the holders of the shares of any class or series voting as a class or series.

(b)   Each director, including a director elected to fill a vacancy, shall hold office until the expiration of the term for which elected and until a successor has been elected and qualified.

§ 301.5   Listed Corporations; Classes of Directors; Cumulative Voting; Election of Directors; Amendment of Articles and Bylaws

(a)   A listed corporation may, by amendment of its articles or bylaws, adopt provisions to divide the board of directors into two or three classes to serve for terms of two or three years respectively, or to eliminate cumulative voting, or both. After the issuance of shares, a corporation that is not a listed corporation may, by amendment of its articles or bylaws, adopt provisions to be effective when the corporation becomes a listed corporation to divide the board of directors into two or three classes to serve for terms of two or three years respectively, or to eliminate cumulative voting, or both. An article or bylaw amendment providing for division of the board of directors into classes, or any change in the number of classes, or the elimination of cumulative voting may only be adopted by the approval of the board and the outstanding shares (Section 152) voting as a single class, notwithstanding Section 903.

(b)   If the board of directors is divided into two classes pursuant to subdivision (a), the authorized number of directors shall be no less than six and one-half of the directors or as close an approximation as possible shall be elected at each annual meeting of shareholders. If the board of directors is divided into three classes, the authorized number of directors shall be no less than nine and one-third of the directors or as close an approximation as possible shall be elected at each annual meeting of shareholders. Directors of a listed corporation may be elected by classes at a meeting of shareholders at which an amendment to the articles or bylaws described in subdivision (a) is approved, but the extended terms for directors are contingent on that approval, and in the case of an amendment to the articles, the filing of any necessary amendment to the articles pursuant to Section 905 or 910.

(c)   If directors for more than one class are to be elected by the shareholders at any one meeting of shareholders and the election is by cumulative voting pursuant to Section 708, votes may be cumulated only for directors to be elected within each class.

(d)   For purposes of this section, a "listed corporation" means a corporation with outstanding shares listed on the New York Stock Exchange, the NYSE Amex, the NASDAQ Global Market, or the NASDAQ Capital Market.

(e)   Subject to subdivision (h), if a listed corporation having a board of directors divided into classes pursuant to subdivision (a) ceases to be a listed corporation for any reason, unless the articles of incorporation or bylaws of the corporation provide for the elimination of classes of directors at an earlier date or dates, the board of directors of the corporation shall cease to be divided into classes as to each class of directors on the date of the expiration of the term of the directors in that class and the term of each director serving at the time the corporation ceases to be a listed corporation (and the term of each director elected to fill a vacancy resulting from the death, resignation, or removal of any of those directors) shall continue until its expiration as if the corporation had not ceased to be a listed corporation.

(f)   Subject to subdivision (h), if a listed corporation having a provision in its articles or bylaws eliminating cumulative voting pursuant to subdivision (a) or permitting noncumulative voting in the election of directors pursuant to that subdivision, or both, ceases to be a listed corporation for any reason, the shareholders shall be entitled to cumulate their votes pursuant to Section 708 at any election of directors occurring while the corporation is not a listed corporation notwithstanding that provision in its articles of incorporation or bylaws.

(g)   Subject to subdivision (i), if a corporation that is not a listed corporation adopts amendments to its articles of incorporation or bylaws to divide its board of directors into classes or to eliminate cumulative voting, or both, pursuant to subdivision (a) and then becomes a listed corporation, unless the articles of incorporation or bylaws provide for those provisions to become effective at some other time and, in cases where classes of directors are provided for, identify the directors who, or the directorships that, are to be in each class or the method by which those directors or directorships are to be identified, the provisions shall become effective for the next election of directors after the corporation becomes a listed corporation at which all directors are to be elected.

(h)   If a corporation ceases to be a listed corporation on or after the record date for a meeting of shareholders and prior to the conclusion of the meeting, including the conclusion of the meeting after an adjournment or postponement that does not require or result in the setting of a new record date, then, solely for purposes of subdivisions (e) and (f), the corporation shall not be deemed to have ceased to be a listed corporation until the conclusion of the meeting of shareholders.

(i)   If a corporation becomes a listed corporation on or after the record date for a meeting of shareholders and prior to the conclusion of the meeting, including the conclusion of the meeting after an adjournment or postponement that does not require or result in the setting of a new record date, then, solely for purposes of subdivision (g), the corporation shall not be deemed to have become a listed corporation until the conclusion of the meeting of shareholders.

(j)   If an article amendment referred to in subdivision (a) is adopted by a listed corporation, the certificate of amendment shall include a statement of the facts showing that the corporation is a listed corporation within the meaning of subdivision (d). If an article or bylaw amendment referred to in subdivision (a) is adopted by a corporation which is not a listed corporation, the provision, as adopted, shall include the following statement or the substantial equivalent: "This provision shall become effective only when the corporation becomes a listed corporation within the meaning of Section 301.5 of the Corporations Code."

§ 303.   Directors; Removal Without Cause

(a)   Any or all of the directors may be removed without cause if the removal is approved by the outstanding shares (Section 152), subject to the following:

(1)   Except for a corporation to which paragraph (3) is applicable, no director may be removed (unless the entire board is removed) when the votes cast against removal, or not consenting in writing to the removal, would be sufficient to elect the director if voted cumulatively

at an election at which the same total number of votes were cast (or, if the action is taken by written consent, all shares entitled to vote were voted) and the entire number of directors authorized at the time of the director's most recent election were then being elected.

(2) When by the provisions of the articles the holders of the shares of any class or series, voting as a class or series, are entitled to elect one or more directors, any director so elected may be removed only by the applicable vote of the holders of the shares of that class or series.

(3) A director of a corporation whose board of directors is classified pursuant to Section 301.5 may not be removed if the votes cast against removal of the director, or not consenting in writing to the removal, would be sufficient to elect the director if voted cumulatively (without regard to whether shares may otherwise be voted cumulatively) at an election at which the same total number of votes were cast (or, if the action is taken by written consent, all shares entitled to vote were voted) and either the number of directors elected at the most recent annual meeting of shareholders, or if greater, the number of directors for whom removal is being sought, were then being elected.

(b) Any reduction of the authorized number of directors or amendment reducing the number of classes of directors does not remove any director prior to the expiration of the director's term of office.

(c) Except as provided in this section and Sections 302 and 304, a director may not be removed prior to the expiration of the director's term of office.

§ 307. Board Meetings; Notice; Participation; Use of Specified Electronic Communication Equipment; Quorum; Waiver of Meeting Requirement

(a) Unless otherwise provided in the articles or, subject to paragraph (5) of subdivision (a) of Section 204, in the bylaws, all of the following apply:

(1) Meetings of the board may be called by the chairperson of the board or the president or any vice president or the secretary or any two directors.

(2) Regular meetings of the board may be held without notice if the time and place of the meetings are fixed by the bylaws or the board. Special meetings of the board shall be held upon four days' notice by mail or 48 hours' notice delivered personally or by telephone, including a voice messaging system or by electronic transmission by the corporation (Section 20). The articles or bylaws may not dispense with notice of a special meeting. A notice, or waiver of notice, need not specify the purpose of any regular or special meeting of the board.

(3) Notice of a meeting need not be given to a director who provides a waiver of notice or a consent to holding the meeting or an approval of the minutes thereof in writing, whether before or after the meeting, or who attends the meeting without protesting, prior thereto or at its commencement, the lack of notice to that director. These waivers, consents and approvals shall be filed with the corporate records or made a part of the minutes of the meeting.

(4) A majority of the directors present, whether or not a quorum is present, may adjourn any meeting to another time and place. If the meeting is adjourned for more than 24 hours, notice of an adjournment to another time or place shall be given prior to the time of the adjourned meeting to the directors who were not present at the time of the adjournment.

(5) Meetings of the board may be held at a place within or without the state that has been designated in the notice of the meeting or, if not stated in the notice or there is no notice, designated in the bylaws or by resolution of the board.

(6) Members of the board may participate in a meeting through use of conference telephone, electronic video screen communication, or electronic transmission by and to the corporation (Sections 20 and 21). Participation in a meeting through use of conference telephone or electronic video screen communication pursuant to this subdivision constitutes presence in person at that meeting as long as all members participating in the meeting are able to hear one

another. Participation in a meeting through electronic transmission by and to the corporation (other than conference telephone and electronic video screen communication), pursuant to this subdivision constitutes presence in person at that meeting if both of the following apply:

(A) Each member participating in the meeting can communicate with all of the other members concurrently.

(B) Each member is provided the means of participating in all matters before the board, including, without limitation, the capacity to propose, or to interpose an objection to, a specific action to be taken by the corporation.

(7) A majority of the authorized number of directors constitutes a quorum of the board for the transaction of business. The articles or bylaws may not provide that a quorum shall be less than one-third the authorized number of directors or less than two, whichever is larger, unless the authorized number of directors is one, in which case one director constitutes a quorum.

(8) An act or decision done or made by a majority of the directors present at a meeting duly held at which a quorum is present is the act of the board, subject to the provisions of Section 310 and subdivision (e) of Section 317. The articles or bylaws may not provide that a lesser vote than a majority of the directors present at a meeting is the act of the board. A meeting at which a quorum is initially present may continue to transact business notwithstanding the withdrawal of directors, if any action taken is approved by at least a majority of the required quorum for that meeting.

(b) An action required or permitted to be taken by the board may be taken without a meeting, if all members of the board shall individually or collectively consent in writing to that action and if the number of members of the board serving at the time constitutes a quorum. The written consent or consents shall be filed with the minutes of the proceedings of the board. For purposes of this subdivision only, "all members of the board" shall include an "interested director" as described in subdivision (a) of Section 310 or a "common director" as described in subdivision (b) of Section 310 who abstains in writing from providing consent, where the disclosures required by Section 310 have been made to the noninterested or noncommon directors, as applicable, prior to their execution of the written consent or consents, the specified disclosures are conspicuously included in the written consent or consents executed by the noninterested or noncommon directors, and the noninterested or noncommon directors, as applicable, approve the action by a vote that is sufficient without counting the votes of the interested or common directors. If written consent is provided by the directors in accordance with the immediately preceding sentence and the disclosures made regarding the action that is the subject of the consent do not comply with the requirements of Section 310, the action that is the subject of the consent shall be deemed approved, but in any suit brought to challenge the action, the party asserting the validity of the action shall have the burden of proof in establishing that the action was just and reasonable to the corporation at the time it was approved.

(c) This section applies also to committees of the board and incorporators and action by those committees and incorporators, mutatis mutandis.

§ 309. Performance of Duties by Director; Liability

(a) A director shall perform the duties of a director, including duties as a member of any committee of the board upon which the director may serve, in good faith, in a manner such director believes to be in the best interests of the corporation and its shareholders and with such care, including reasonable inquiry, as an ordinarily prudent person in a like position would use under similar circumstances.

(b) In performing the duties of a director, a director shall be entitled to rely on information, opinions, reports or statements, including financial statements and other financial data, in each case prepared or presented by any of the following:

(1)   One or more officers or employees of the corporation whom the director believes to be reliable and competent in the matters presented.

(2)   Counsel, independent accountants or other persons as to matters which the director believes to be within such person's professional or expert competence.

(3)   A committee of the board upon which the director does not serve, as to matters within its designated authority, which committee the director believes to merit confidence,

so long as, in any such case, the director acts in good faith, after reasonable inquiry when the need therefor is indicated by the circumstances and without knowledge that would cause such reliance to be unwarranted.

(c)   A person who performs the duties of a director in accordance with subdivisions (a) and (b) shall have no liability based upon any alleged failure to discharge the person's obligations as a director. In addition, the liability of a director for monetary damages may be eliminated or limited in a corporation's articles to the extent provided in paragraph (10) of subdivision (a) of Section 204.

§ 310.   Contracts in Which Director Has Material Financial Interest; Validity

(a)   No contract or other transaction between a corporation and one or more of its directors, or between a corporation and any corporation, firm or association in which one or more of its directors has a material financial interest, is either void or voidable because such director or directors or such other corporation, firm or association are parties or because such director or directors are present at the meeting of the board or a committee thereof which authorizes, approves or ratifies the contract or transaction, if

(1)   The material facts as to the transaction and as to such director's interest are fully disclosed or known to the shareholders and such contract or transaction is approved by the shareholders (Section 153) in good faith, with the shares owned by the interested director or directors not being entitled to vote thereon, or

(2)   The material facts as to the transaction and as to such director's interest are fully disclosed or known to the board or committee, and the board or committee authorizes, approves or ratifies the contract or transaction in good faith by a vote sufficient without counting the vote of the interested director or directors and the contract or transaction is just and reasonable as to the corporation at the time it is authorized, approved or ratified, or

(3)   As to contracts or transactions not approved as provided in paragraph (1) or (2) of this subdivision, the person asserting the validity of the contract or transaction sustains the burden of proving that the contract or transaction was just and reasonable as to the corporation at the time it was authorized, approved or ratified.

A mere common directorship does not constitute a material financial interest within the meaning of this subdivision. A director is not interested within the meaning of this subdivision in a resolution fixing the compensation of another director as a director, officer or employee of the corporation, notwithstanding the fact that the first director is also receiving compensation from the corporation.

(b)   No contract or other transaction between a corporation and any corporation or association of which one or more of its directors are directors is either void or voidable because such director or directors are present at the meeting of the board or a committee thereof which authorizes, approves or ratifies the contract or transaction, if

(1)   The material facts as to the transaction and as to such director's other directorship are fully disclosed or known to the board or committee, and the board or committee authorizes, approves or ratifies the contract or transaction in good faith by a vote sufficient without counting the vote of the common director or directors or the contract or transaction is approved by the shareholders (Section 153) in good faith, or

(2)   As to contracts or transactions not approved as provided in paragraph (1) of this subdivision, the contract or transaction is just and reasonable as to the corporation at the time it is authorized, approved or ratified.

This subdivision does not apply to contracts or transactions covered by subdivision (a).

(c)   Interested or common directors may be counted in determining the presence of a quorum at a meeting of the board or a committee thereof which authorizes, approves or ratifies a contract or transaction.

§ 313.   Instrument in Writing and Assignment or Endorsement Thereof; Signatures; Validity

Subject to the provisions of subdivision (a) of Section 208, any note, mortgage, evidence of indebtedness, contract, share certificate, initial transaction statement or written statement, conveyance, or other instrument in writing, and any assignment or endorsement thereof, executed or entered into between any corporation and any other person, when signed by the chairperson of the board, the president or any vice president and the secretary, any assistant secretary, the chief financial officer or any assistant treasurer of such corporation, is not invalidated as to the corporation by any lack of authority of the signing officers in the absence of actual knowledge on the part of the other person that the signing officers had no authority to execute the same.

§ 317.   Indemnification of Agent of Corporation in Proceedings or Actions

(a)   For the purposes of this section, "agent" means any person who is or was a director, officer, employee or other agent of the corporation, or is or was serving at the request of the corporation as a director, officer, employee or agent of another foreign or domestic corporation, partnership, joint venture, trust or other enterprise, or was a director, officer, employee or agent of a foreign or domestic corporation which was a predecessor corporation of the corporation or of another enterprise at the request of the predecessor corporation; "proceeding" means any threatened, pending or completed action or proceeding, whether civil, criminal, administrative or investigative; and "expenses" includes without limitation attorneys' fees and any expenses of establishing a right to indemnification under subdivision (d) or paragraph (4) of subdivision (e).

(b)   A corporation shall have power to indemnify any person who was or is a party or is threatened to be made a party to any proceeding (other than an action by or in the right of the corporation to procure a judgment in its favor) by reason of the fact that the person is or was an agent of the corporation, against expenses, judgments, fines, settlements, and other amounts actually and reasonably incurred in connection with the proceeding if that person acted in good faith and in a manner the person reasonably believed to be in the best interests of the corporation and, in the case of a criminal proceeding, had no reasonable cause to believe the conduct of the person was unlawful. The termination of any proceeding by judgment, order, settlement, conviction, or upon a plea of nolo contendere or its equivalent shall not, of itself, create a presumption that the person did not act in good faith and in a manner which the person reasonably believed to be in the best interests of the corporation or that the person had reasonable cause to believe that the person's conduct was unlawful.

(c)   A corporation shall have power to indemnify any person who was or is a party or is threatened to be made a party to any threatened, pending, or completed action by or in the right of the corporation to procure a judgment in its favor by reason of the fact that the person is or was an agent of the corporation, against expenses actually and reasonably incurred by that person in connection with the defense or settlement of the action if the person acted in good faith, in a manner the person believed to be in the best interests of the corporation and its shareholders.

No indemnification shall be made under this subdivision for any of the following:

(1)   In respect of any claim, issue or matter as to which the person shall have been adjudged to be liable to the corporation in the performance of that person's duty to the corporation and its shareholders, unless and only to the extent that the court in which the proceeding is or was

pending shall determine upon application that, in view of all the circumstances of the case, the person is fairly and reasonably entitled to indemnity for expenses and then only to the extent that the court shall determine.

(2) Of amounts paid in settling or otherwise disposing of a pending action without court approval.

(3) Of expenses incurred in defending a pending action which is settled or otherwise disposed of without court approval.

(d) To the extent that an agent of a corporation has been successful on the merits in defense of any proceeding referred to in subdivision (b) or (c) or in defense of any claim, issue, or matter therein, the agent shall be indemnified against expenses actually and reasonably incurred by the agent in connection therewith.

(e) Except as provided in subdivision (d), any indemnification under this section shall be made by the corporation only if authorized in the specific case, upon a determination that indemnification of the agent is proper in the circumstances because the agent has met the applicable standard of conduct set forth in subdivision (b) or (c), by any of the following:

(1) A majority vote of a quorum consisting of directors who are not parties to such proceeding.

(2) If such a quorum of directors is not obtainable, by independent legal counsel in a written opinion.

(3) Approval of the shareholders (Section 153), with the shares owned by the person to be indemnified not being entitled to vote thereon.

(4) The court in which the proceeding is or was pending upon application made by the corporation or the agent or the attorney or other person rendering services in connection with the defense, whether or not the application by the agent, attorney or other person is opposed by the corporation.

(f) Expenses incurred in defending any proceeding may be advanced by the corporation prior to the final disposition of the proceeding upon receipt of an undertaking by or on behalf of the agent to repay that amount if it shall be determined ultimately that the agent is not entitled to be indemnified as authorized in this section. The provisions of subdivision (a) of Section 315 do not apply to advances made pursuant to this subdivision.

(g) The indemnification authorized by this section shall not be deemed exclusive of any additional rights to indemnification for breach of duty to the corporation and its shareholders while acting in the capacity of a director or officer of the corporation to the extent the additional rights to indemnification are authorized in an article provision adopted pursuant to paragraph (11) of subdivision (a) of Section 204. The indemnification provided by this section for acts, omissions, or transactions while acting in the capacity of, or while serving as, a director or officer of the corporation but not involving breach of duty to the corporation and its shareholders shall not be deemed exclusive of any other rights to which those seeking indemnification may be entitled under any bylaw, agreement, vote of shareholders or disinterested directors, or otherwise, to the extent the additional rights to indemnification are authorized in the articles of the corporation. An article provision authorizing indemnification "in excess of that otherwise permitted by Section 317" or "to the fullest extent permissible under California law" or the substantial equivalent thereof shall be construed to be both a provision for additional indemnification for breach of duty to the corporation and its shareholders as referred to in, and with the limitations required by, paragraph (11) of subdivision (a) of Section 204 and a provision for additional indemnification as referred to in the second sentence of this subdivision. The rights to indemnity hereunder shall continue as to a person who has ceased to be a director, officer, employee, or agent and shall inure to the benefit of the heirs, executors, and administrators of the person. Nothing contained in this section shall affect any right to indemnification to which persons other than the directors and officers may be entitled by contract or otherwise.

(h) No indemnification or advance shall be made under this section, except as provided in subdivision (d) or paragraph (4) of subdivision (e), in any circumstance where it appears:

(1) That it would be inconsistent with a provision of the articles, bylaws, a resolution of the shareholders, or an agreement in effect at the time of the accrual of the alleged cause of action asserted in the proceeding in which the expenses were incurred or other amounts were paid, which prohibits or otherwise limits indemnification.

(2) That it would be inconsistent with any condition expressly imposed by a court in approving a settlement.

(i) A corporation shall have power to purchase and maintain insurance on behalf of any agent of the corporation against any liability asserted against or incurred by the agent in that capacity or arising out of the agent's status as such whether or not the corporation would have the power to indemnify the agent against that liability under this section. The fact that a corporation owns all or a portion of the shares of the company issuing a policy of insurance shall not render this subdivision inapplicable if either of the following conditions are satisfied: (1) if the articles authorize indemnification in excess of that authorized in this section and the insurance provided by this subdivision is limited as indemnification is required to be limited by paragraph (11) of subdivision (a) of Section 204; or (2)(A) the company issuing the insurance policy is organized, licensed, and operated in a manner that complies with the insurance laws and regulations applicable to its jurisdiction of organization, (B) the company issuing the policy provides procedures for processing claims that do not permit that company to be subject to the direct control of the corporation that purchased that policy, and (C) the policy issued provides for some manner of risk sharing between the issuer and purchaser of the policy, on one hand, and some unaffiliated person or persons, on the other, such as by providing for more than one unaffiliated owner of the company issuing the policy or by providing that a portion of the coverage furnished will be obtained from some unaffiliated insurer or reinsurer.

(j) This section does not apply to any proceeding against any trustee, investment manager, or other fiduciary of an employee benefit plan in that person's capacity as such, even though the person may also be an agent as defined in subdivision (a) of the employer corporation. A corporation shall have power to indemnify such a trustee, investment manager, or other fiduciary to the extent permitted by subdivision (f) of Section 207.

* * *

CHAPTER 4.   SHARES AND SHARE CERTIFICATES

§ 409.   Issuance of Shares; Consideration; Liability to Call; Determination by Shareholders; Valuation of Property Other Than Money by Board Resolution

(a) Shares may be issued:

(1) For such consideration as is determined from time to time by the board, or by the shareholders if the articles so provide, consisting of any or all of the following: money paid; labor done; services actually rendered to the corporation or for its benefit or in its formation or reorganization; debts or securities canceled; and tangible or intangible property actually received either by the issuing corporation or by a wholly owned subsidiary; but neither promissory notes of the purchaser (unless adequately secured by collateral other than the shares acquired or unless permitted by Section 408) nor future services shall constitute payment or part payment for shares of the corporation; or

(2) As a share dividend or upon a stock split, reverse stock split, reclassification of outstanding shares into shares of another class, conversion of outstanding shares into shares of another class, exchange of outstanding shares for shares of another class or other change affecting outstanding shares.

(b)   Except as provided in subdivision (d), shares issued as provided in this section or Section 408 shall be declared and taken to be fully paid stock and not liable to any further call nor shall the holder thereof be liable for any further payments under the provisions of this division. In the absence of fraud in the transaction, the judgment of the directors as to the value of the consideration for shares shall be conclusive.

(c)   If the articles reserve to the shareholders the right to determine the consideration for the issue of any shares, such determination shall be made by approval of the outstanding shares (Section 152).

(d)   A corporation may issue the whole or any part of its shares as partly paid and subject to call for the remainder of the consideration to be paid therefor. On the certificate issued to represent any such partly paid shares or, for uncertificated securities, on the initial transaction statement for such partly paid shares, the total amount of the consideration to be paid therefor and the amount paid thereon shall be stated. Upon the declaration of any dividend on fully paid shares, the corporation shall declare a dividend upon partly paid shares of the same class, but only upon the basis of the percentage of the consideration actually paid thereon.

(e)   The board shall state by resolution its determination of the fair value to the corporation in monetary terms of any consideration other than money for which shares are issued. This subdivision does not affect the accounting treatment of any transaction, which shall be in conformity with generally accepted accounting principles.

§ 410.   Liability for Full Agreed Consideration; Time of Payment

(a)   Every subscriber to shares and every person to whom shares are originally issued is liable to the corporation for the full consideration agreed to be paid for the shares.

(b)   The full agreed consideration for shares shall be paid prior to or concurrently with the issuance thereof, unless the shares are issued as partly paid pursuant to subdivision (d) of Section 409, in which case the consideration shall be paid in accordance with the agreement of subscription or purchase.

§ 414.   Creditor's Remedy to Reach Liability Due Corporation on Shares

(a)   No action shall be brought by or on behalf of any creditor to reach and apply the liability, if any, of a shareholder to the corporation to pay the amount due on such shareholder's shares unless final judgment has been rendered in favor of the creditor against the corporation and execution has been returned unsatisfied in whole or in part or unless such proceedings would be useless.

(b)   All creditors of the corporation, with or without reducing their claims to judgment, may intervene in any such creditor's action to reach and apply unpaid subscriptions and any or all shareholders who hold partly paid shares may be joined in such action. Several judgments may be rendered for and against the parties to the action or in favor of a receiver for the benefit of the respective parties thereto.

(c)   All amounts paid by any shareholder in any such action shall be credited on the unpaid balance due the corporation upon such shareholder's shares.

* * *

CHAPTER 5.   DIVIDENDS AND REACQUISITIONS OF SHARES

§ 500.   **Distributions; Retained Earnings or Assets Remaining After Completion; Exemption of Broker-Dealer Licensee Meeting Certain Net Capital Requirements**

(a)   Neither a corporation nor any of its subsidiaries shall make any distribution to the corporation's shareholders (Section 166) unless the board of directors has determined in good faith either of the following:

(1)   The amount of retained earnings of the corporation immediately prior to the distribution equals or exceeds the sum of (A) the amount of the proposed distribution plus (B) the preferential dividends arrears amount.

(2)   Immediately after the distribution, the value of the corporation's assets would equal or exceed the sum of its total liabilities plus the preferential rights amount.

(b)   For the purpose of applying paragraph (1) of subdivision (a) to a distribution by a corporation, "preferential dividends arrears amount" means the amount, if any, of cumulative dividends in arrears on all shares having a preference with respect to payment of dividends over the class or series to which the applicable distribution is being made, provided that if the articles of incorporation provide that a distribution can be made without regard to preferential dividends arrears amount, then the preferential dividends arrears amount shall be zero. For the purpose of applying paragraph (2) of subdivision (a) to a distribution by a corporation, "preferential rights amount" means the amount that would be needed if the corporation were to be dissolved at the time of the distribution to satisfy the preferential rights, including accrued but unpaid dividends, of other shareholders upon dissolution that are superior to the rights of the shareholders receiving the distribution, provided that if the articles of incorporation provide that a distribution can be made without regard to any preferential rights, then the preferential rights amount shall be zero. In the case of a distribution of cash or property in payment by the corporation in connection with the purchase of its shares, (1) there shall be added to retained earnings all amounts that had been previously deducted therefrom with respect to obligations incurred in connection with the corporation's repurchase of its shares and reflected on the corporation's balance sheet, but not in excess of the principal of the obligations that remain unpaid immediately prior to the distribution and (2) there shall be deducted from liabilities all amounts that had been previously added thereto with respect to the obligations incurred in connection with the corporation's repurchase of its shares and reflected on the corporation's balance sheet, but not in excess of the principal of the obligations that will remain unpaid after the distribution, provided that no addition to retained earnings or deduction from liabilities under this subdivision shall occur on account of any obligation that is a distribution to the corporation's shareholders (Section 166) at the time the obligation is incurred.

(c)   The board of directors may base a determination that a distribution is not prohibited under subdivision (a) or under Section 501 on any of the following:

(1)   Financial statements prepared on the basis of accounting practices and principles that are reasonable under the circumstances.

(2)   A fair valuation.

(3)   Any other method that is reasonable under the circumstances.

(d)   The effect of a distribution under paragraph (1) or (2) of subdivision (a) is measured as of the date the distribution is authorized if the payment occurs within 120 days after the date of authorization.

(e)(1)   If terms of indebtedness provide that payment of principal and interest is to be made only if, and to the extent that, payment of a distribution to shareholders could then be made under this section, indebtedness of a corporation, including indebtedness issued as a distribution, is not a liability for purposes of determinations made under paragraph (2) of subdivision (a).

(2) If indebtedness is issued as a distribution, each payment of principal or interest on the indebtedness shall be treated as a distribution, the effect of which is measured on the date the payment of the indebtedness is actually made.

(f) This section does not apply to a corporation licensed as a broker-dealer under Chapter 2 (commencing with Section 25210) of Part 3 of Division 1 of Title 4, if immediately after giving effect to any distribution the corporation is in compliance with the net capital rules of the Commissioner of Business Oversight and the Securities and Exchange Commission.

§ 501.   Inability to Meet Liabilities as They Mature; Prohibition of Distribution

Neither a corporation nor any of its subsidiaries shall make any distribution to the corporation's shareholders (Section 166) if the corporation or the subsidiary making the distribution is, or as a result thereof would be, likely to be unable to meet its liabilities (except those whose payment is otherwise adequately provided for) as they mature.

§ 503.   Purchase or Redemption of Shares of Deceased Shareholder from Insurance Proceeds; Application of Provisions Relating to Prohibited Distributions

(a) The provisions of Sections 500 and 501 shall not apply to a purchase or redemption of shares of a deceased shareholder from the proceeds of insurance on the life of that shareholder in excess of the total amount of all premiums paid by the corporation for that insurance, in order to carry out the provisions of an agreement between the corporation and that shareholder to purchase or redeem those shares upon the death of the shareholder.

(b) The provisions of Sections 500 and 501 shall not apply to the purchase or redemption of shares of a disabled shareholder from the proceeds of disability insurance applicable to the disabled shareholder in excess of the total amount of all premiums paid by the corporation for the insurance, in order to carry out the provisions of an agreement between the corporation and the shareholder to purchase or redeem shares upon the disability of the shareholder as defined within that policy. For the purposes of this subdivision, "disability insurance" means an agreement of indemnification against the insured's loss of the ability to work due to accident or illness.

§ 506.   Receipt of Prohibited Dividend; Liability of Shareholder; Suit by Creditors or Other Shareholders; Fraudulent Transfers

(a) Any shareholder who receives any distribution prohibited by this chapter with knowledge of facts indicating the impropriety thereof is liable to the corporation for the benefit of all of the creditors or shareholders entitled to institute an action under subdivision (b) for the amount so received by the shareholder with interest thereon at the legal rate on judgments until paid, but not exceeding the liabilities of the corporation owed to nonconsenting creditors at the time of the violation and the injury suffered by nonconsenting shareholders, as the case may be. For purposes of determining the value of any noncash property received in a distribution described in the preceding sentence, the shareholder receiving that illegal distribution shall be liable to the corporation for an amount equal to the fair market value of the property at the time of the illegal distribution plus interest thereon from the date of the distribution at the legal rate on judgments until paid, together with all reasonably incurred costs of appraisal or other valuation, if any, of that property, but not exceeding the liabilities of the corporation owed to nonconsenting creditors at the time of the violation and the injury suffered by nonconsenting shareholders, as the case may be.

(b) Suit may be brought in the name of the corporation to enforce the liability (1) to creditors arising under subdivision (a) for a violation of Section 500 or 501 against any or all shareholders liable by any one or more creditors of the corporation whose debts or claims arose prior to the time of the distribution to shareholders and who have not consented thereto, whether or not they have reduced their claims to judgment, or (2) to shareholders arising under subdivision (a) for a violation of Section 500 against any or all shareholders liable by one or more holders of shares having preferential rights with respect to cumulative dividends in arrears, in the case of a violation of paragraph (1) of subdivision (a) of Section 500, or upon dissolution, in the case of a violation of paragraph (2) of subdivision (a) of Section 500, in each case who have not consented to the applicable distribution, without regard to the provisions in Section 800, and in each case to the extent the applicable shares with preferential rights were outstanding at the time of the distribution; provided that holders of shares of preferential rights shall not have the right to bring suit in the name of the corporation under this subdivision unless the preferential dividends arrears amount, in the case of a violation of paragraph (1) of subdivision (a) of Section 500, or the preferential rights amount, in the case of a violation of paragraph (2) of subdivision (a) of Section 500, was greater than zero. A cause of action with respect to an obligation to return a distribution pursuant to this section shall be extinguished unless the action is brought within four years after the date the distribution is made.

(c)   Any shareholder sued under this section may implead all other shareholders liable under this section and may compel contribution, either in that action or in an independent action against shareholders not joined in that action.

(d)   Nothing contained in this section affects any liability which any shareholder may have under Chapter 1 (commencing with Section 3439) of Title 2 of Part 2 of Division 4 of the Civil Code.

* * *

CHAPTER 6.   SHAREHOLDERS' MEETINGS AND CONSENTS

§ 604.   Proxies or Written Consents; Contents; Form

(a)   Any form of proxy or written consent distributed to 10 or more shareholders of a corporation with outstanding shares held of record by 100 or more persons shall afford an opportunity on the proxy or form of written consent to specify a choice between approval and disapproval of each matter or group of related matters intended to be acted upon at the meeting for which the proxy is solicited or by such written consent, other than elections to office, and shall provide, subject to reasonable specified conditions, that where the person solicited specifies a choice with respect to any such matter the shares will be voted in accordance therewith.

(b)   In any election of directors, any form of proxy in which the directors to be voted upon are named therein as candidates and which is marked by a shareholder "withhold" or otherwise marked in a manner indicating that the authority to vote for the election of directors is withheld shall not be voted for the election of a director.

(c)   Failure to comply with this section shall not invalidate any corporate action taken, but may be the basis for challenging any proxy at a meeting and the superior court may compel compliance therewith at the suit of any shareholder.

(d)   This section does not apply to any corporation with an outstanding class of securities registered under Section 12 of the Securities Exchange Act of 1934 or whose securities are exempted from such registration by Section 12(g)(2) of that act.

* * *

CHAPTER 7.   VOTING OF SHARES

§ 705.   Proxies; Validity; Expiration; Revocation; Irrevocable Proxies

(a)   Every person entitled to vote shares may authorize another person or persons to act by proxy with respect to such shares. Any proxy purporting to be executed in accordance with the provisions of this division shall be presumptively valid.

(b)   No proxy shall be valid after the expiration of 11 months from the date thereof unless otherwise provided in the proxy. Every proxy continues in full force and effect until revoked by the person executing it prior to the vote pursuant thereto, except as otherwise provided in this section.

Such revocation may be effected by a writing delivered to the corporation stating that the proxy is revoked or by a subsequent proxy executed by the person executing the prior proxy and presented to the meeting, or as to any meeting by attendance at such meeting and voting in person by the person executing the proxy. The dates contained on the forms of proxy presumptively determine the order of execution, regardless of the postmark dates on the envelopes in which they are mailed.

(c)   A proxy is not revoked by the death or incapacity of the maker unless, before the vote is counted, written notice of such death or incapacity is received by the corporation.

(d)   Except when other provision shall have been made by written agreement between the parties, the recordholder of shares which such person holds as pledgee or otherwise as security or which belong to another shall issue to the pledgor or to the owner of such shares, upon demand therefor and payment of necessary expenses thereof, a proxy to vote or take other action thereon.

(e)   A proxy which states that it is irrevocable is irrevocable for the period specified therein (notwithstanding subdivision (c)) when it is held by any of the following or a nominee of any of the following:

(1)   A pledgee.

(2)   A person who has purchased or agreed to purchase or holds an option to purchase the shares or a person who has sold a portion of such person's shares in the corporation to the maker of the proxy.

(3)   A creditor or creditors of the corporation or the shareholder who extended or continued credit to the corporation or the shareholder in consideration of the proxy if the proxy states that it was given in consideration of such extension or continuation of credit and the name of the person extending or continuing credit.

(4)   A person who has contracted to perform services as an employee of the corporation, if a proxy is required by the contract of employment and if the proxy states that it was given in consideration of such contract of employment, the name of the employee and the period of employment contracted for.

(5)   A person designated by or under an agreement under Section 706.

(6)   A beneficiary of a trust with respect to shares held by the trust.

Notwithstanding the period of irrevocability specified, the proxy becomes revocable when the pledge is redeemed, the option or agreement to purchase is terminated or the seller no longer owns any shares of the corporation or dies, the debt of the corporation or the shareholder is paid, the period of employment provided for in the contract of employment has terminated, the agreement under Section 706 has terminated, or the person ceases to be a beneficiary of the trust. In addition to the foregoing clauses (1) through (5), a proxy may be made irrevocable (notwithstanding subdivision (c)) if it is given to secure the performance of a duty or to protect a title, either legal or equitable, until the happening of events which, by its terms, discharge the obligations secured by it.

(f)   A proxy may be revoked, notwithstanding a provision making it irrevocable, by a transferee of shares without knowledge of the existence of the provision unless the existence of the proxy and its irrevocability appears, in the case of certificated securities, on the certificate representing such shares, or in the case of uncertificated securities, on the initial transaction statement and written statements.

§ 706.   Agreement Between Two or More Shareholders of a Corporation; Voting Trust Agreements

(a)   Notwithstanding any other provision of this division, an agreement between two or more shareholders of a corporation, if in writing and signed by the parties thereto, may provide that in exercising any voting rights the shares held by them shall be voted as provided by the agreement, or as the parties may agree or as determined in accordance with a procedure agreed upon by them, and the parties may but need not transfer the shares covered by such an agreement to a third party or parties with authority to vote them in accordance with the terms of the agreement. Such an agreement shall not be denied specific performance by a court on the ground that the remedy at law is adequate or on other grounds relating to the jurisdiction of a court of equity.

(b)   Shares in any corporation may be transferred by written agreement to trustees in order to confer upon them the right to vote and otherwise represent the shares for such period of time, not exceeding 10 years, as may be specified in the agreement. The validity of a voting trust agreement, otherwise lawful, shall not be affected during a period of 10 years from the date when it was created or last extended as hereinafter provided by the fact that under its terms it will or may last beyond such 10-year period. At any time within two years prior to the time of expiration of any voting trust agreement as originally fixed or as last extended as provided in this subdivision, one or more beneficiaries under the voting trust agreement may, by written agreement and with the written consent of the voting trustee or trustees, extend the duration of the voting trust agreement with respect to their shares for an additional period not exceeding 10 years from the expiration date of the trust as originally fixed or as last extended as provided in this subdivision. A duplicate of the voting trust agreement and any extension thereof shall be filed with the secretary of the corporation and shall be open to inspection by a shareholder, a holder of a voting trust certificate or the agent of either, upon the same terms as the record of shareholders of the corporation is open to inspection.

(c)   No agreement made pursuant to subdivision (a) shall be held to be invalid or unenforceable on the ground that it is a voting trust that does not comply with subdivision (b) or that it is a proxy that does not comply with Section 705.

(d)   This section shall not invalidate any voting or other agreement among shareholders or any irrevocable proxy complying with subdivision (e) of Section 705, which agreement or proxy is not otherwise illegal.

§ 708.   Directors; Cumulative Voting; Election by Ballot

(a)   Except as provided in Sections 301.5 and 708.5, every shareholder complying with subdivision (b) and entitled to vote at any election of directors may cumulate such shareholder's votes and give one candidate a number of votes equal to the number of directors to be elected multiplied by the number of votes to which the shareholder's shares are normally entitled, or distribute the shareholder's votes on the same principle among as many candidates as the shareholder thinks fit.

(b)   No shareholder shall be entitled to cumulate votes (i.e., cast for any candidate a number of votes greater than the number of votes that the shareholder normally is entitled to cast) unless the candidate or candidates' names have been placed in nomination prior to the voting and the shareholder has given notice at the meeting prior to the voting of the shareholder's intention to cumulate the shareholder's votes. If any one shareholder has given that notice, all shareholders may cumulate their votes for candidates in nomination.

(c)   Except as provided in Section 708.5, in any election of directors, the candidates receiving the highest number of affirmative votes of the shares entitled to be voted for them up to the number of directors to be elected by those shares are elected; votes against the director and votes withheld shall have no legal effect.

(d)   Subdivision (a) applies to the shareholders of any mutual water company organized or existing for the purpose of delivering water to its shareholders at cost on lands located within the boundaries of one or more reclamation districts now or hereafter legally existing in this state and created by or formed under the provisions of any statute of this state, but does not otherwise apply to the shareholders of mutual water companies unless their articles or bylaws so provide.

(e)   Elections for directors need not be by ballot unless a shareholder demands election by ballot at the meeting and before the voting begins or unless the bylaws so require.

§ 708.5   Director Election; Approval of Shareholders Required; Term of Incumbent Director When Not Approved in Uncontested Election; Board Vacancy

(a)   For purposes of this section, the following definitions shall apply:

(1)   "Uncontested election" means an election of directors in which, at the expiration of the time fixed under the articles of incorporation or bylaws requiring advance notification of director candidates or, absent such a provision in the articles of incorporation or bylaws, at a time fixed by the board of directors that is not more than 14 days before notice is given of the meeting at which the election is to occur, the number of candidates for election does not exceed the number of directors to be elected by the shareholders at that election.

(2)   "Listed corporation" means a domestic corporation that qualifies as a listed corporation under subdivision (d) of Section 301.5.

(b)   Notwithstanding paragraph (5) of subdivision (a) of Section 204, a listed corporation that has eliminated cumulative voting pursuant to subdivision (a) of Section 301.5 may amend its articles of incorporation or bylaws to provide that, in an uncontested election, approval of the shareholders, as specified in Section 153, shall be required to elect a director.

(c)   Notwithstanding subdivision (b) of Section 301, if an incumbent director fails to be elected by approval of the shareholders (Section 153) in an uncontested election of a listed corporation that has amended its articles of incorporation or bylaws pursuant to subdivision (b), then, unless the incumbent director has earlier resigned, the term of the incumbent director shall end on the date that is the earlier of 90 days after the date on which the voting results are determined pursuant to Section 707 or the date on which the board of directors selects a person to fill the office held by that director pursuant to subdivision (d).

(d)   Any vacancy on the board of directors resulting from any failure of a candidate to be elected by approval of the shareholders (Section 153) in an uncontested election of a listed corporation that has amended its articles of incorporation or bylaws pursuant to subdivision (b) shall be filled in accordance with the procedures set forth in Section 305.

§ 710.   Supermajority Vote Required; Approval

(a)   This section applies to a corporation with outstanding shares held of record by 100 or more persons (determined as provided in Section 605) that files an amendment of articles or certificate of determination containing a "supermajority vote" provision on or after January 1, 1989. This section shall not apply to a corporation that files an amendment of articles or certificate of determination on or after January 1, 1994, if, at the time of filing, the corporation has (1) outstanding shares of more than one class or series of stock, (2) no class of equity securities registered under Section 12(b) or 12(g) of the Securities Exchange Act of 1934, and (3) outstanding shares held of record by fewer than 300 persons determined as provided by Section 605.

(b)   A "supermajority vote" is a requirement set forth in the articles or in a certificate of determination authorized under any provision of this division that specified corporate action or actions be approved by a larger proportion of the outstanding shares than a majority, or by a larger proportion of the outstanding shares of a class or series than a majority, but no supermajority vote that is subject to this section shall require a vote in excess of 66 ⅔ percent of the outstanding shares or 66 ⅔ percent of the outstanding shares of any class or series of those shares.

(c)   An amendment of the articles or a certificate of determination that includes a supermajority vote requirement shall be approved by at least as large a proportion of the outstanding shares (Section 152) as is required pursuant to that amendment or certificate of determination for the approval of the specified corporate action or actions.

(d)   The amendments made to this section by the act amending this section in the 2001–02 Regular Session shall not affect the rights of minority shareholders existing under law.

§ 711. **Maintenance by Holding Legal Owners and Disclosure to Persons on Whose Behalf Shares Are Voted; Charges; Actions to Enforce Section; Payment of Costs and Attorney's Fees; Commencement of Duties on Jan. 1, 1990**

(a) The Legislature finds and declares that:

Many of the residents of this state are the legal and beneficial owners or otherwise the ultimate beneficiaries of shares of stock of domestic and foreign corporations, title to which may be held by a variety of intermediate owners as defined in subdivision (b). The informed and active involvement of such beneficial owners and beneficiaries in holding legal owners and, through them, management, accountable in their exercise of corporate power is essential to the interest of those beneficiaries and beneficial owners and to the economy and well-being of this state.

The purpose of this section is to serve the public interest by ensuring that voting records are maintained and disclosed as provided in this section. In the event that by statute or regulation pursuant to the federal Employee Retirement Income Security Act of 1974 (29 U.S.C. Sec. 1001 *et seq.*), there are imposed upon investment managers as defined in Sec. 2(38) thereof, duties substantially the same as those set forth in this section, compliance with those statutory or regulatory requirements by persons subject to this section shall be deemed to fulfill the obligations contained in this section.

This section shall be construed liberally to achieve that purpose.

(b) For purposes of this section, a person on whose behalf shares are voted includes, but is not limited to:

(1) A participant or beneficiary of an employee benefit plan with regard to shares held for the benefit of the participant or beneficiary.

(2) A shareholder, beneficiary, or contract owner of any entity (or of any portfolio of any entity) as defined in Section 3(a) of the federal Investment Company Act of 1940 (15 U.S.C. Sec. 80a–1 *et seq.*), as amended, to the extent the entity (or portfolio) holds the shares for which the record is requested.

(c) For the purposes of this section, a person on whose behalf shares are voted does not include:

(1) A person who possesses the right to terminate or withdraw from the shareholder, contract owner, participant, or beneficiary relationship with any entity (or any portfolio of any entity) defined in subdivision (b). This exclusion does not apply in the event the right of termination or withdrawal cannot be exercised without automatic imposition of a tax penalty. The right to substitute a relationship with an entity or portfolio, the shares of which are voted by or subject to the direction of the investment adviser (as defined in Section 2 of the federal Investment Company Act of 1940 (15 U.S.C. Sec. 80a–1 *et seq.*), as amended), of the prior entity or portfolio, or an affiliate of the investment adviser, shall not be deemed to be a right of termination or withdrawal within the meaning of this subdivision.

(2) A person entitled to receive information about a trust pursuant to Section 16061 of the Probate Code.

(3) A beneficiary, participant, contract owner, or shareholder whose interest is funded through the general assets of a life insurance company authorized to conduct business in this state.

(d) Every person possessing the power to vote shares of stock on behalf of another shall maintain a record of the manner in which the shares were voted. The record shall be maintained for a period of 12 consecutive months from the effective date of the vote.

(e) Upon a reasonable written request, the person possessing the power to vote shares of stock on behalf of another, or a designated agent, shall disclose the voting record with respect to any matter involving a specific security or securities in accordance with the following procedures:

(1) Except as set forth in paragraph (2), disclosure shall be made to the person making the request. The person making the disclosure may require identification sufficient to identify the person making the request as a person on whose behalf the shares were voted. A request for identification, if made, shall be reasonable, shall be made promptly, and may include a request for the person's social security number.

(2) If the person possessing the power to vote shares on behalf of another holds that power pursuant to an agreement entered into with a party other than the person making the request for disclosure, the person maintaining and disclosing the record pursuant to this section may, instead, make the requested disclosure to that party. Disclosure to that party shall be deemed compliance with the disclosure requirement of this section. If disclosure is made to that party and not to the person making the request, subdivision (i) shall not apply. However, nothing herein shall prohibit that party and the person possessing the power to vote on shares from entering into an agreement between themselves for the payment or assessment of a reasonable charge to defray expenses of disclosing the record.

(f) Where the entity subject to the requirements of this section is organized as a unit investment trust as defined in Section 4(2) of the federal Investment Company Act of 1940 (15 U.S.C. Sec. 80a–1 et seq.), the open-ended investment companies underlying the unit investment trust shall promptly make available their proxy voting records to the unit investment trust upon evidence of a bona fide request for voting record information pursuant to subdivision (e).

(g) Signing a proxy on another's behalf and forwarding it for disposition or receiving voting instructions does not constitute the power to vote. A person forwarding proxies or receiving voting instructions shall disclose the identity of the person having the power to vote shares upon reasonable written request by a person entitled to request a voting record under subdivision (c).

(h) For purposes of this section, if one or more persons has the power to vote shares on behalf of another, unless a governing instrument provides otherwise, the person or persons may designate an agent who shall maintain and disclose the record in accordance with subdivisions (b) and (c).

(i) Except as provided in paragraph (2) of subdivision (e), or as otherwise provided by law or a governing instrument, a person maintaining and disclosing a record pursuant to this section may assess a reasonable charge to the requesting person in order to defray expenses of disclosing the record in accordance with subdivision (e). Disclosure shall be made within a reasonable period after payment is received.

(j) Upon the petition of any person who successfully brings an action pursuant to or to enforce this section, the court may award costs and reasonable attorney's fees if the court finds that the defendant willfully violated this section.

(k) The obligation to maintain and disclose a voting record in accordance with subdivisions (b) and (c) shall commence January 1, 1990.

* * *

CHAPTER 8. SHAREHOLDER DERIVATIVE ACTIONS

§ 800.   Conditions; Security; Motion for Order; Determination

(a) As used in this section, "corporation" includes an unincorporated association; "board" includes the managing body of an unincorporated association; "shareholder" includes a member of an unincorporated association; and "shares" includes memberships in an unincorporated association.

(b) No action may be instituted or maintained in right of any domestic or foreign corporation by any holder of shares or of voting trust certificates of the corporation unless both of the following conditions exist:

(1) The plaintiff alleges in the complaint that plaintiff was a shareholder, of record or beneficially, or the holder of voting trust certificates at the time of the transaction or any part thereof of which plaintiff complains or that plaintiff's shares or voting trust certificates thereafter devolved upon plaintiff by operation of law from a holder who was a holder at the time of the transaction or any part thereof complained of; provided, that any shareholder who does not meet these requirements may nevertheless be allowed in the discretion of the court to maintain the action on a preliminary showing to and determination by the court, by motion and after a hearing, at which the court shall consider such evidence, by affidavit or testimony, as it deems material, that (i) there is a strong prima facie case in favor of the claim asserted on behalf of the corporation, (ii) no other similar action has been or is likely to be instituted, (iii) the plaintiff acquired the shares before there was disclosure to the public or to the plaintiff of the wrongdoing of which plaintiff complains, (iv) unless the action can be maintained the defendant may retain a gain derived from defendant's willful breach of a fiduciary duty, and (v) the requested relief will not result in unjust enrichment of the corporation or any shareholder of the corporation; and

(2) The plaintiff alleges in the complaint with particularity plaintiff's efforts to secure from the board such action as plaintiff desires, or the reasons for not making such effort, and alleges further that plaintiff has either informed the corporation or the board in writing of the ultimate facts of each cause of action against each defendant or delivered to the corporation or the board a true copy of the complaint which plaintiff proposes to file.

(c) In any action referred to in subdivision (b), at any time within 30 days after service of summons upon the corporation or upon any defendant who is an officer or director of the corporation, or held such office at the time of the acts complained of, the corporation or the defendant may move the court for an order, upon notice and hearing, requiring the plaintiff to furnish a bond as hereinafter provided. The motion shall be based upon one or both of the following grounds:

(1) That there is no reasonable possibility that the prosecution of the cause of action alleged in the complaint against the moving party will benefit the corporation or its shareholders.

(2) That the moving party, if other than the corporation, did not participate in the transaction complained of in any capacity.

The court on application of the corporation or any defendant may, for good cause shown, extend the 30-day period for an additional period or periods not exceeding 60 days.

(d) At the hearing upon any motion pursuant to subdivision (c), the court shall consider such evidence, written or oral, by witnesses or affidavit, as may be material (1) to the ground or grounds upon which the motion is based, or (2) to a determination of the probable reasonable expenses, including attorneys' fees, of the corporation and the moving party which will be incurred in the defense of the action. If the court determines, after hearing the evidence adduced by the parties, that the moving party has established a probability in support of any of the grounds upon which the motion is based, the court shall fix the amount of the bond, not to exceed fifty thousand dollars ($50,000), to be furnished by the plaintiff for reasonable expenses, including attorneys' fees, which may be incurred by the moving party and the corporation in connection with the action, including expenses for which the corporation may become liable pursuant to Section 317. A ruling by the court on the motion shall not be a determination of any issue in the action or of the merits thereof. If the court, upon the motion, makes a determination that a bond shall be furnished by the plaintiff as to any one or more defendants, the action shall be dismissed as to the defendant or defendants, unless the bond required by the court has been furnished within such reasonable time as may be fixed by the court.

(e) If the plaintiff shall, either before or after a motion is made pursuant to subdivision (c), or any order or determination pursuant to the motion, furnish a bond in the aggregate amount of fifty thousand dollars ($50,000) to secure the reasonable expenses of the parties entitled to make the motion, the plaintiff has complied with the requirements of this section and with any order for a bond theretofore made, and any such motion then pending shall be dismissed and no further or additional bond shall be required.

(f)   If a motion is filed pursuant to subdivision (c), no pleadings need be filed by the corporation or any other defendant and the prosecution of the action shall be stayed until 10 days after the motion has been disposed of.

* * *

CHAPTER 10.   SALES OF ASSETS

§ 1001.   Disposition of Substantially All Assets; Approval

(a)   A corporation may sell, lease, convey, exchange, transfer, or otherwise dispose of all or substantially all of its assets when the principal terms are approved by the board, and, unless the transaction is in the usual and regular course of its business, approved by the outstanding shares (Section 152), either before or after approval by the board and before or after the transaction. A transaction constituting a reorganization (Section 181) is subject to the provisions of Chapter 12 (commencing with Section 1200) and not this section (other than subdivision (d)). A transaction constituting a conversion (Section 161.9) is subject to the provisions of Chapter 11.5 (commencing with Section 1150) and not this section.

(b)   Notwithstanding approval of the outstanding shares (Section 152), the board may abandon the proposed transaction without further action by the shareholders, subject to the contractual rights, if any, of third parties.

(c)   The sale, lease, conveyance, exchange, transfer, or other disposition may be made upon those terms and conditions and for that consideration as the board may deem in the best interests of the corporation. The consideration may be money, securities, or other property.

(d)   If the acquiring party in a transaction pursuant to subdivision (a) of this section or subdivision (g) of Section 2001 is in control of or under common control with the disposing corporation, the principal terms of the sale must be approved by at least 90 percent of the voting power of the disposing corporation unless the disposition is to a domestic or foreign corporation or other business entity in consideration of the nonredeemable common shares or nonredeemable equity securities of the acquiring party or its parent.

(e)   Subdivision (d) does not apply to any transaction if the Commissioner of Business Oversight, the Insurance Commissioner, or the Public Utilities Commission has approved the terms and conditions of the transaction and the fairness of those terms and conditions pursuant to Section 25142, Section 696.5 of the Financial Code, Section 838.5 of the Insurance Code, or Section 822 of the Public Utilities Code.

* * *

CHAPTER 11.   MERGER

§ 1101.   Agreement of Merger; Approval of Boards; Contents

The board of each corporation which desires to merge shall approve an agreement of merger. The constituent corporations shall be parties to the agreement of merger and other persons, including a parent party (Section 1200), may be parties to the agreement of merger. The agreement shall state all of the following:

(a)   The terms and conditions of the merger.

(b)   The amendments, subject to Sections 900 and 907, to the articles of the surviving corporation to be effected by the merger, if any. If any amendment changes the name of the surviving corporation the new name may be the same as or similar to the name of a disappearing domestic or foreign corporation, subject to subdivision (b) of Section 201.

(c)   The name and place of incorporation of each constituent corporation and which of the constituent corporations is the surviving corporation.

(d)   The manner of converting the shares of each of the constituent corporations into shares or other securities of the surviving corporation and, if any shares of any of the constituent corporations are not to be converted solely into shares or other securities of the surviving corporation, the cash, rights, securities, or other property which the holders of those shares are to receive in exchange for the shares, which cash, rights, securities, or other property may be in addition to or in lieu of shares or other securities of the surviving corporation, or that the shares are canceled without consideration.

(e)   Other details or provisions as are desired, if any, including, without limitation, a provision for the payment of cash in lieu of fractional shares or for any other arrangement with respect thereto consistent with the provisions of Section 407.

Each share of the same class or series of any constituent corporation (other than the cancellation of shares held by a constituent corporation or its parent or a wholly owned subsidiary of either in another constituent corporation) shall, unless all shareholders of the class or series consent and except as provided in Section 407, be treated equally with respect to any distribution of cash, rights, securities, or other property. Notwithstanding subdivision (d), except in a short-form merger, and in the merger of a corporation into its subsidiary in which it owns at least 90 percent of the outstanding shares of each class, the nonredeemable common shares or nonredeemable equity securities of a constituent corporation may be converted only into nonredeemable common shares of the surviving party or a parent party if a constituent corporation or its parent owns, directly or indirectly, prior to the merger shares of another constituent corporation representing more than 50 percent of the voting power of the other constituent corporation prior to the merger, unless all of the shareholders of the class consent and except as provided in Section 407.

* * *

CHAPTER 12.   REORGANIZATIONS

§ 1200.   Approval by Board

A reorganization (Section 181) or a share exchange tender offer (Section 183.5) shall be approved by the board of:

(a)   Each constituent corporation in a merger reorganization;

(b)   The acquiring corporation in an exchange reorganization;

(c)   The acquiring corporation and the corporation whose property and assets are acquired in a sale-of-assets reorganization;

(d)   The acquiring corporation in a share exchange tender offer (Section 183.5); and

(e)   The corporation in control of any constituent or acquiring domestic or foreign corporation or other business entity under subdivision (a), (b) or (c) and whose equity securities are issued, transferred, or exchanged in the reorganization (a "parent party").

§ 1201.   Shareholder Approval; Board Abandonment

(a)   The principal terms of a reorganization shall be approved by the outstanding shares (Section 152) of each class of each corporation the approval of whose board is required under Section 1200, except as provided in subdivision (b) and except that (unless otherwise provided in the articles) no approval of any class of outstanding preferred shares of the surviving or acquiring corporation or parent party shall be required if the rights, preferences, privileges, and restrictions granted to or imposed upon that class of shares remain unchanged (subject to the provisions of subdivision (c)). For the purpose of this subdivision, two classes of common shares differing only as to voting rights shall be considered as a single class of shares.

(b)   No approval of the outstanding shares (Section 152) is required by subdivision (a) in the case of any corporation if that corporation, or its shareholders immediately before the reorganization, or both, shall own (immediately after the reorganization) equity securities, other than any warrant or right to subscribe to or purchase those equity securities, of the surviving or acquiring corporation or a parent party (subdivision (d) of Section 1200) possessing more than five-sixths of the voting power of the surviving or acquiring corporation or parent party. In making the determination of ownership by the shareholders of a corporation, immediately after the reorganization, of equity securities pursuant to the preceding sentence, equity securities which they owned immediately before the reorganization as shareholders of another party to the transaction shall be disregarded. For the purpose of this section only, the voting power of a corporation shall be calculated by assuming the conversion of all equity securities convertible (immediately or at some future time) into shares entitled to vote but not assuming the exercise of any warrant or right to subscribe to or purchase those shares.

(c)   Notwithstanding subdivision (b), the principal terms of a reorganization shall be approved by the outstanding shares (Section 152) of the surviving corporation in a merger reorganization if any amendment is made to its articles that would otherwise require that approval.

(d)   Notwithstanding subdivision (b), the principal terms of a reorganization shall be approved by the outstanding shares (Section 152) of any class of a corporation that is a party to a merger or sale-of-assets reorganization if holders of shares of that class receive shares of the surviving or acquiring corporation or parent party having different rights, preferences, privileges, or restrictions than those surrendered. Shares in a foreign corporation received in exchange for shares in a domestic corporation have different rights, preferences, privileges, and restrictions within the meaning of the preceding sentence.

(e)   Notwithstanding subdivisions (a) and (b), the principal terms of a reorganization shall be approved by the affirmative vote of at least two-thirds of each class, or a greater vote if required in the articles, of the outstanding shares (Section 152) of any close corporation if the reorganization would result in their receiving shares of a corporation that is not a close corporation. However, the articles may provide for a lesser vote, but not less than a majority of the outstanding shares of each class.

(f)   Notwithstanding subdivisions (a) and (b), the principal terms of a reorganization shall be approved by at least two-thirds of each class, or a greater vote if required in the articles, of the outstanding shares (Section 152) of a corporation that is a party to a merger reorganization if holders of shares receive shares of a surviving social purpose corporation in the merger.

(g)   Notwithstanding subdivisions (a) and (b), the principal terms of a reorganization shall be approved by the outstanding shares (Section 152) of any class of a corporation that is a party to a merger reorganization if holders of shares of that class receive interests of a surviving other business entity in the merger.

(h)   Notwithstanding subdivisions (a) and (b), the principal terms of a reorganization shall be approved by all shareholders of any class or series if, as a result of the reorganization, the holders of that class or series become personally liable for any obligations of a party to the reorganization, unless all holders of that class or series have the dissenters' rights provided in Chapter 13 (commencing with Section 1300).

(i)   Any approval required by this section may be given before or after the approval by the board. Notwithstanding approval required by this section, the board may abandon the proposed reorganization without further action by the shareholders, subject to the contractual rights, if any, of third parties.

§ 1201.5   Share Exchange Tender Offer; Approval of Principal Terms

(a)   The principal terms of a share exchange tender offer (Section 183.5) shall be approved by the outstanding shares (Section 152) of each class of the corporation making the tender offer or whose shares are to be used in the tender offer, except as provided in subdivision (b) and except that (unless otherwise provided in the articles) no approval of any class of outstanding preferred shares of either corporation shall be required, if the rights, preferences, privileges, and restrictions granted to or imposed upon that class of shares remain unchanged. For the purpose of this subdivision, two classes of common shares differing only as to voting rights shall be considered as a single class of shares.

(b) No approval of the outstanding shares (Section 152) is required by subdivision (a) in the case of any corporation if the corporation, or its shareholders immediately before the tender offer, or both, shall own (immediately after the completion of the share exchange proposed in the tender offer) equity securities, (other than any warrant or right to subscribe to or purchase the equity securities), of the corporation making the tender offer or of the corporation whose shares were used in the tender offer, possessing more than five-sixths of the voting power of either corporation. In making the determination of ownership by the shareholders of a corporation, immediately after the tender offer, of equity securities pursuant to the preceding sentence, equity securities which they owned immediately before the tender offer as shareholders of another party to the transaction shall be disregarded. For the purpose of this section only, the voting power of a corporation shall be calculated by assuming the conversion of all equity securities convertible (immediately or at some future time) into shares entitled to vote but not assuming the exercise of any warrant or right to subscribe to, or purchase, shares.

§ 1202. Terms of Merger Reorganization or Sale-of-Assets Reorganization; Approval by Shareholders; Foreign Corporations

(a) In addition to the requirements of Section 1201, the principal terms of a merger reorganization shall be approved by all the outstanding shares of a corporation if the agreement of merger provides that all the outstanding shares of that corporation are canceled without consideration in the merger.

(b) In addition to the requirements of Section 1201, if the terms of a merger reorganization or sale-of-assets reorganization provide that a class or series of preferred shares is to have distributed to it a lesser amount than would be required by applicable article provisions, the principal terms of the reorganization shall be approved by the same percentage of outstanding shares of that class or series which would be required to approve an amendment of the article provisions to provide for the distribution of that lesser amount.

(c) If a parent party within the meaning of Section 1200 is a foreign corporation (other than a foreign corporation to which subdivision (a) of Section 2115 is applicable), any requirement or lack of a requirement for approval by the outstanding shares of the foreign corporation shall be based, not on the application of Sections 1200 and 1201, but on the application of the laws of the state or place of incorporation of the foreign corporation.

§ 1203. Interested Party Proposal or Tender Offer to Shareholders; Affirmative Opinion; Delivery; Approval; Later Proposal or Tender Offer; Withdrawal of Vote, Consent, or Proxy; Procedures

(a) If a tender offer, including a share exchange tender offer (Section 183.5), or a written proposal for approval of a reorganization subject to Section 1200 or for a sale of assets subject to subdivision (a) of Section 1001 is made to some or all of a corporation's shareholders by an interested party (herein referred to as an "Interested Party Proposal"), an affirmative opinion in writing as to the fairness of the consideration to the shareholders of that corporation shall be delivered as follows:

(1) If no shareholder approval or acceptance is required for the consummation of the transaction, the opinion shall be delivered to the corporation's board of directors not later than the time that consummation of the transaction is authorized and approved by the board of directors.

(2) If a tender offer is made to the corporation's shareholders, the opinion shall be delivered to the shareholders at the time that the tender offer is first made in writing to the shareholders. However, if the tender offer is commenced by publication and tender offer materials are

subsequently mailed or otherwise distributed to the shareholders, the opinion may be omitted in that publication if the opinion is included in the materials distributed to the shareholders.

(3)   If a shareholders' meeting is to be held to vote on approval of the transaction, the opinion shall be delivered to the shareholders with the notice of the meeting (Section 601).

(4)   If consents of all shareholders entitled to vote are solicited in writing (Section 603), the opinion shall be delivered at the same time as that solicitation.

(5)   If the consents of all shareholders are not solicited in writing, the opinion shall be delivered to each shareholder whose consent is solicited prior to that shareholder's consent being given, and to all other shareholders at the time they are given the notice required by subdivision (b) of Section 603.

For purposes of this section, the term "interested party" means a person who is a party to the transaction and (A) directly or indirectly controls the corporation that is the subject of the tender offer or proposal, (B) is, or is directly or indirectly controlled by, an officer or director of the subject corporation, or (C) is an entity in which a material financial interest (subdivision (a) of Section 310) is held by any director or executive officer of the subject corporation. For purposes of the preceding sentence, "any executive officer" means the president, any vice president in charge of a principal business unit, division, or function such as sales, administration, research, development, or finance, and any other officer or other person who performs a policymaking function or has the same duties as those of a president or vice president. The opinion required by this subdivision shall be provided by a person who is not affiliated with the offeror and who, for compensation, engages in the business of advising others as to the value of properties, businesses, or securities. The fact that the opining person previously has provided services to the offeror or a related entity or is simultaneously engaged in providing advice or assistance with respect to the proposed transaction in a manner which makes its compensation contingent on the success of the proposed transaction shall not, for those reasons, be deemed to affiliate the opining person with the offeror. Nothing in this subdivision shall limit the applicability of the standards of review of the transaction in the event of a challenge thereto under Section 310 or subdivision (c) of Section 1312.

This subdivision shall not apply to an Interested Party Proposal if the corporation that is the subject thereof does not have shares held of record by 100 or more persons (determined as provided in Section 605), or if the transaction has been qualified under Section 25113 or 25121 and no order under Section 25140 or subdivision (a) of Section 25143 is in effect with respect to that qualification.

(b)   If a tender of shares or a vote or written consent is being sought pursuant to an Interested Party Proposal and a later tender offer or written proposal for a reorganization subject to Section 1200 or sale of assets subject to subdivision (a) of Section 1001 that would require a vote or written consent of shareholders is made to the corporation or its shareholders (herein referred to as a "Later Proposal") by any other person at least 10 days prior to the date for acceptance of the tendered shares or the vote or notice of shareholder approval on the Interested Party Proposal, then each of the following shall apply:

(1)   The shareholders shall be informed of the Later Proposal and any written material provided for this purpose by the later offeror shall be forwarded to the shareholders at that offeror's expense.

(2)   The shareholders shall be afforded a reasonable opportunity to withdraw any vote, consent, or proxy previously given before the vote or written consent on the Interested Party Proposal becomes effective, or a reasonable time to withdraw any tendered shares before the purchase of the shares pursuant to the Interested Party Proposal. For purposes of this subdivision, a delay of 10 days from the notice or publication of the Later Proposal shall be deemed to provide a reasonable opportunity or time to effect that withdrawal.

* * *

CHAPTER 13. DISSENTERS' RIGHTS

§ 1300. Reorganization or Short-Form Merger; Dissenting Shares; Corporate Purchase at Fair Market Value; Definitions

(a) If the approval of the outstanding shares (Section 152) of a corporation is required for a reorganization under subdivisions (a) and (b) or subdivision (e) or (f) of Section 1201, each shareholder of the corporation entitled to vote on the transaction and each shareholder of a subsidiary corporation in a short-form merger may, by complying with this chapter, require the corporation in which the shareholder holds shares to purchase for cash at their fair market value the shares owned by the shareholder which are dissenting shares as defined in subdivision (b). The fair market value shall be determined as of the day of, and immediately prior to, the first announcement of the terms of the proposed reorganization or short-form merger, excluding any appreciation or depreciation in consequence of the proposed reorganization or short-form merger, as adjusted for any stock split, reverse stock split, or share dividend that becomes effective thereafter.

(b) As used in this chapter, "dissenting shares" means shares to which all of the following apply:

(1) That were not, immediately prior to the reorganization or short-form merger, listed on any national securities exchange certified by the Commissioner of Business Oversight under subdivision (o) of Section 25100, and the notice of meeting of shareholders to act upon the reorganization summarizes this section and Sections 1301, 1302, 1303, and 1304; provided, however, that this provision does not apply to any shares with respect to which there exists any restriction on transfer imposed by the corporation or by any law or regulation; and provided, further, that this provision does not apply to any shares where the holder of those shares is required, by the terms of the reorganization or short-form merger, to accept for the shares anything except: (A) shares of any other corporation, which shares, at the time the reorganization or short-form merger is effective, are listed on any national securities exchange certified by the Commissioner of Business Oversight under subdivision (o) of Section 25100; (B) cash in lieu of fractional shares described in the foregoing subparagraph (A); or (C) any combination of the shares and cash in lieu of fractional shares described in the foregoing subparagraphs (A) and (B).

(2) That were outstanding on the date for the determination of shareholders entitled to vote on the reorganization and (A) were not voted in favor of the reorganization or, (B) if described in paragraph (1), were voted against the reorganization, or were held of record on the effective date of a short-form merger; provided, however, that subparagraph (A) rather than subparagraph (B) of this paragraph applies in any case where the approval required by Section 1201 is sought by written consent rather than at a meeting.

(3) That the dissenting shareholder has demanded that the corporation purchase at their fair market value, in accordance with Section 1301.

(4) That the dissenting shareholder has submitted for endorsement, in accordance with Section 1302.

(c) As used in this chapter, "dissenting shareholder" means the recordholder of dissenting shares and includes a transferee of record.

§ 1312. Right of Dissenting Shareholder to Attack, Set Aside or Rescind Merger or Reorganization; Restraining Order or Injunction; Conditions

(a) No shareholder of a corporation who has a right under this chapter to demand payment of cash for the shares held by the shareholder shall have any right at law or in equity to attack the validity of the reorganization or short-form merger, or to have the reorganization or short-form merger set aside or rescinded, except in an action to test whether the number of shares required to authorize or approve the reorganization have been legally voted in favor thereof; but any holder of shares of a class whose terms and provisions specifically set forth the amount to be paid in respect to them in the event of a reorganization or short-form merger is entitled to payment in accordance with those terms and provisions or, if the principal terms of the reorganization are approved pursuant to subdivision (b) of Section 1202, is entitled to payment in accordance with the terms and provisions of the approved reorganization.

(b) If one of the parties to a reorganization or short-form merger is directly or indirectly controlled by, or under common control with, another party to the reorganization or short-form merger, subdivision (a) shall not apply to any shareholder of such party who has not demanded payment of cash for such shareholder's shares pursuant to this chapter; but if the shareholder institutes any action to attack the validity of the reorganization or short-form merger or to have the reorganization or short-form merger set aside or rescinded, the shareholder shall not thereafter have any right to demand payment of cash for the shareholder's shares pursuant to this chapter. The court in any action attacking the validity of the reorganization or short-form merger or to have the reorganization or short-form merger set aside or rescinded shall not restrain or enjoin the consummation of the transaction except upon 10 days' prior notice to the corporation and upon a determination by the court that clearly no other remedy will adequately protect the complaining shareholder or the class of shareholders of which such shareholder is a member.

(c) If one of the parties to a reorganization or short-form merger is directly or indirectly controlled by, or under common control with, another party to the reorganization or short-form merger, in any action to attack the validity of the reorganization or short-form merger or to have the reorganization or short-form merger set aside or rescinded, (1) a party to a reorganization or short-form merger which controls another party to the reorganization or short-form merger shall have the burden of proving that the transaction is just and reasonable as to the shareholders of the controlled party, and (2) a person who controls two or more parties to a reorganization shall have the burden of proving that the transaction is just and reasonable as to the shareholders of any party so controlled.

* * *

CHAPTER 19. VOLUNTARY DISSOLUTION

§ 1900. Election by Shareholders; Required Vote; Election by Board; Grounds

(a) Any corporation may elect voluntarily to wind up and dissolve by the vote of shareholders holding shares representing 50 percent or more of the voting power.

(b) Any corporation which comes within one of the following descriptions may elect by approval by the board to wind up and dissolve:

(1) A corporation as to which an order for relief has been entered under Chapter 7 of the federal bankruptcy law.

(2) A corporation which has disposed of all of its assets and has not conducted any business for a period of five years immediately preceding the adoption of the resolution electing to dissolve the corporation.

(3) A corporation which has issued no shares.

* * *

CHAPTER 21. FOREIGN CORPORATIONS

§ 2115. Foreign Corporations Subject to Corporate Laws of State; Tests to Determine Subject Corporations; Laws Applicable; Time of Application

(a) A foreign corporation (other than a foreign association or foreign nonprofit corporation but including a foreign parent corporation even though it does not itself transact intrastate business) is subject to the requirements of subdivision (b) commencing on the date specified in subdivision (d) and continuing until the date specified in subdivision (e) if:

(1)   The average of the property factor, the payroll factor, and the sales factor (as defined in Sections 25129, 25132, and 25134 of the Revenue and Taxation Code) with respect to it is more than 50 percent during its latest full income year and

(2)   more than one-half of its outstanding voting securities are held of record by persons having addresses in this state appearing on the books of the corporation on the record date for the latest meeting of shareholders held during its latest full income year or, if no meeting was held during that year, on the last day of the latest full income year. The property factor, payroll factor, and sales factor shall be those used in computing the portion of its income allocable to this state in its franchise tax return or, with respect to corporations the allocation of whose income is governed by special formulas or that are not required to file separate or any tax returns, which would have been so used if they were governed by this three-factor formula. The determination of these factors with respect to any parent corporation shall be made on a consolidated basis, including in a unitary computation (after elimination of intercompany transactions) the property, payroll, and sales of the parent and all of its subsidiaries in which it owns directly or indirectly more than 50 percent of the outstanding shares entitled to vote for the election of directors, but deducting a percentage of the property, payroll, and sales of any subsidiary equal to the percentage minority ownership, if any, in the subsidiary. For the purpose of this subdivision, any securities held to the knowledge of the issuer in the names of broker-dealers, nominees for broker-dealers (including clearing corporations), or banks, associations, or other entities holding securities in a nominee name or otherwise on behalf of a beneficial owner (collectively "nominee holders"), shall not be considered outstanding. However, if the foreign corporation requests all nominee holders to certify, with respect to all beneficial owners for whom securities are held, the number of shares held for those beneficial owners having addresses (as shown on the records of the nominee holder) in this state and outside of this state, then all shares so certified shall be considered outstanding and held of record by persons having addresses either in this state or outside of this state as so certified, provided that the certification so provided shall be retained with the record of shareholders and made available for inspection and copying in the same manner as is provided in Section 1600 with respect to that record. A current list of beneficial owners of a foreign corporation's securities provided to the corporation by one or more nominee holders or their agent pursuant to the requirements of Rule 14b–1(b)(3) or 14b–2(b)(3) as adopted on January 6, 1992, promulgated under the Securities Exchange Act of 1934, shall constitute an acceptable certification with respect to beneficial owners for the purposes of this subdivision.

(b)   Except as provided in subdivision (c), the following chapters and sections of this division shall apply to a foreign corporation as defined in subdivision (a) (to the exclusion of the law of the jurisdiction in which it is incorporated):

Chapter 1 (general provisions and definitions), to the extent applicable to the following provisions;

Section 301 (annual election of directors);

Section 303 (removal of directors without cause);

Section 304 (removal of directors by court proceedings);

Section 305, subdivision (c) (filling of director vacancies where less than a majority in office elected by shareholders);

Section 309 (directors' standard of care);

Section 316 (excluding paragraph (3) of subdivision (a) and paragraph (3) of subdivision (f)) (liability of directors for unlawful distributions);

Section 317 (indemnification of directors, officers, and others);

Sections 500 to 505, inclusive (limitations on corporate distributions in cash or property);

Section 506 (liability of shareholder who receives unlawful distribution);

Section 600, subdivisions (b) and (c) (requirement for annual shareholders' meeting and remedy if same not timely held);

Section 708, subdivisions (a), (b), and (c) (shareholder's right to cumulate votes at any election of directors);

Section 710 (supermajority vote requirement);

Section 1001, subdivision (d) (limitations on sale of assets);

Section 1101 (provisions following subdivision (e)) (limitations on mergers);

Section 1151 (first sentence only) (limitations on conversions);

Section 1152 (requirements of conversions);

Chapter 12 (commencing with Section 1200) (reorganizations);

Chapter 13 (commencing with Section 1300) (dissenters' rights);

Sections 1500 and 1501 (records and reports);

Section 1508 (action by Attorney General);

Chapter 16 (commencing with Section 1600) (rights of inspection).

(c)   This section does not apply to any corporation (1) with outstanding securities listed on the New York Stock Exchange, the NYSE Amex, the NASDAQ Global Market, or the NASDAQ Capital Market, or (2) if all of its voting shares (other than directors' qualifying shares) are owned directly or indirectly by a corporation or corporations not subject to this section.

(d)   For purposes of subdivision (a), the requirements of subdivision (b) shall become applicable to a foreign corporation only upon the first day of the first income year of the corporation (1) commencing on or after the 135th day of the income year immediately following the latest income year with respect to which the tests referred to in subdivision (a) have been met or (2) commencing on or after the entry of a final order by a court of competent jurisdiction declaring that those tests have been met.

(e)   For purposes of subdivision (a), the requirements of subdivision (b) shall cease to be applicable to a foreign corporation (1) at the end of the first income year of the corporation immediately following the latest income year with respect to which at least one of the tests referred to in subdivision (a) is not met or (2) at the end of the income year of the corporation during which a final order has been entered by a court of competent jurisdiction declaring that one of those tests is not met, provided that a contrary order has not been entered before the end of the income year.

(f)   Any foreign corporation that is subject to the requirements of subdivision (b) shall advise any shareholder of record, any officer, director, employee, or other agent (within the meaning of Section 317) and any creditor of the corporation in writing, within 30 days of receipt of written request for that information, whether or not it is subject to subdivision (b) at the time the request is received. Any party who obtains a final determination by a court of competent jurisdiction that the corporation failed to provide to the party information required to be provided by this subdivision or provided the party information of the kind required to be provided by this subdivision that was incorrect, then the court, in its discretion, shall have the power to include in its judgment recovery by the party from the corporation of all court costs and reasonable attorneys' fees incurred in that legal proceeding to the extent they relate to obtaining that final determination.

2. CALIFORNIA CORPORATE SECURITIES LAW OF 1968

(Selected Sections)

Table of Contents

PART 5. FRAUDULENT AND PROHIBITED PRACTICES

§ 25402   Purchase or Sale of Securities by Person Having Access to Material Information Not Available to Public Through Special Relationship With Issuer

It is unlawful for an issuer or any person who is an officer, director or controlling person of an issuer or any other person whose relationship to the issuer gives him access, directly or indirectly, to material information about the issuer not generally available to the public, to purchase or sell any security of the issuer in this state at a time when he knows material information about the issuer gained from such relationship which would significantly affect the market price of that security and which is not generally available to the public, and which he knows is not intended to be so available, unless he has reason to believe that the person selling to or buying from him is also in possession of the information.

PART 6. ENFORCEMENT

CHAPTER 1. CIVIL LIABILITY

§ 25502.5   Liability of Violator of Insider Trading Prohibitions to Issuer; Allegation by Shareholder of Issuer; Consideration by Board

(a)   Any person other than the issuer who violates Section 25402 shall be liable to the issuer of the security purchased or sold in violation of Section 25402 for damages in an amount up to three times the difference between the price at which the security was purchased or sold and the market value which the security would have had at the time of the purchase or sale if the information known to the defendant had been publicly disseminated prior to that time and a reasonable time had elapsed for the market to absorb the information and shall be liable to the issuer of the security or to a person who institutes an action under this section in the right of the issuer of the security for reasonable costs and attorney's fees.

(b)   The amounts recoverable under this section by the issuer shall be reduced by any amount paid by the defendant in a proceeding brought by the Securities and Exchange Commission with

757

respect to the same transaction or transactions under the federal Insider Trading Sanctions Act of 1984 (15 U.S.C. Secs. 78a, 78c, 78o, 78t, 78u, and 78ff) or any other act regardless of whether the amount was paid pursuant to a judgment or settlement or paid before or after the filing of an action by the plaintiff against the defendant. If a proceeding has been commenced by the Securities and Exchange Commission but has not been finally resolved, the court shall delay entering a judgment for the plaintiff under this section until that proceeding is resolved.

(c)   If any shareholder of an issuer alleges to the board that there has been a violation of this section, the board shall be required to consider the allegation in good faith, and if the allegation involves misconduct by any director, that director shall not be entitled to vote on any matter involving the allegation. However, that director may be counted in determining the presence of a quorum at a meeting of the board or a committee of the board.

(d)   This section shall only apply to issuers who have total assets in excess of one million dollars ($1,000,000) and have a class of equity security held of record by 500 or more persons.

D. DELAWARE GENERAL CORPORATION LAW

Delaware Code, Title 8, Chapter 1

Table of Contents

SUBCHAPTER I. FORMATION

SUBCHAPTER II. POWERS

SUBCHAPTER III. REGISTERED OFFICE AND REGISTERED AGENT

SUBCHAPTER IV. DIRECTORS AND OFFICERS

DELAWARE GENERAL CORPORATION LAW

144. Interested directors; quorum.
145. Indemnification of officers, directors, employees and agents; insurance.
146. Submission of matters for stockholder vote.

SUBCHAPTER V.   STOCK AND DIVIDENDS

151. Classes and series of stock; redemption; rights.
152. Issuance of stock; lawful consideration; fully paid stock.
153. Consideration for stock.
154. Determination of amount of capital; capital, surplus and net assets defined.
155. Fractions of shares.
156. Partly paid shares.
157. Rights and options respecting stock.
158. Stock certificates; uncertificated shares.
159. Shares of stock; personal property, transfer and taxation.
160. Corporation's powers respecting ownership, voting, etc., of its own stock; rights of stock called for redemption.
161. Issuance of additional stock; when and by whom.
162. Liability of stockholder or subscriber for stock not paid in full.
163. Payment for stock not paid in full.
164. Failure to pay for stock; remedies.
165. Revocability of preincorporation subscriptions.
166. Formalities required of stock subscriptions.
167. Lost, stolen or destroyed stock certificates; issuance of new certificate or uncertificated shares.
168. Judicial proceedings to compel issuance of new certificate or uncertificated shares.
169. Situs of ownership of stock.
170. Dividends; payment; wasting asset corporations.
171. Special purpose reserves.
172. Liability of directors and committee members as to dividends or stock redemption.
173. Declaration and payment of dividends.
174. Liability of directors for unlawful payment of dividend or unlawful stock purchase or redemption; exoneration from liability; contribution among directors; subrogation.

SUBCHAPTER VI.   STOCK TRANSFERS

201. Transfer of stock, stock certificates and uncertificated stock.
202. Restrictions on transfer and ownership of securities.
203. Business combinations with interested stockholders.
204. Ratification of defective corporate acts and stock.
205. Proceedings regarding validity of defective corporate acts and stock.

SUBCHAPTER VII.   MEETINGS, ELECTIONS, VOTING AND NOTICE

211. Meetings of stockholders.
212. Voting rights of stockholders; proxies; limitations.
213. Fixing date for determination of stockholders of record.
214. Cumulative voting.
215. Voting rights of members of nonstock corporations; quorum; proxies.
216. Quorum and required vote for stock corporations.
217. Voting rights of fiduciaries, pledgors and joint owners of stock.
218. Voting trusts and other voting agreements.
219. List of stockholders entitled to vote; penalty for refusal to produce; stock ledger.
220. Inspection of books and records.
221. Voting, inspection and other rights of bondholders and debenture holders.

760

DELAWARE GENERAL CORPORATION LAW

SUBCHAPTER I.   FORMATION

§ 101.   Incorporators; how corporation formed; purposes.

(a)   Any person, partnership, association or corporation, singly or jointly with others, and without regard to such person's or entity's residence, domicile or state of incorporation, may incorporate or organize a corporation under this chapter by filing with the Division of Corporations in the Department of State a certificate of incorporation which shall be executed, acknowledged and filed in accordance with § 103 of this title.

(b)   A corporation may be incorporated or organized under this chapter to conduct or promote any lawful business or purposes, except as may otherwise be provided by the Constitution or other law of this State.

(c)   Corporations for constructing, maintaining and operating public utilities, whether in or outside of this State, may be organized under this chapter, but corporations for constructing, maintaining and operating public utilities within this State shall be subject to, in addition to this chapter, the special provisions and requirements of Title 26 applicable to such corporations.

§ 102.   Contents of certificate of incorporation.

(a)   The certificate of incorporation shall set forth:

(1)   The name of the corporation, which (i) shall contain 1 of the words "association," "company," "corporation," "club," "foundation," "fund," "incorporated," "institute," "society," "union," "syndicate," or "limited," (or abbreviations thereof, with or without punctuation), or words (or abbreviations thereof, with or without punctuation) of like import of foreign countries or jurisdictions (provided they are written in roman characters or letters); provided, however, that the Division of Corporations in the Department of State may waive such requirement (unless it determines that such name is, or might otherwise appear to be, that of a natural person) if such corporation executes, acknowledges and files with the Secretary of State in accordance with § 103 of this title a certificate stating that its total assets, as defined in § 503(i) of this title, are not less than $10,000,000, or, in the sole discretion of the Division of Corporations in the Department of State, if the corporation is both a nonprofit nonstock corporation and an association of professionals, (ii) shall be such as to distinguish it upon the records in the office of the Division of Corporations in the Department of State from the names that are reserved on such records and from the names on such records of each other corporation, partnership, limited partnership, limited liability company, registered series of a limited liability company or statutory trust organized or registered as a domestic or foreign corporation, partnership, limited partnership, limited liability company, registered series of a limited liability company or statutory trust under the laws of this State, except with the written consent of the person who has reserved such name or such other foreign corporation or domestic or foreign partnership, limited partnership, limited

liability company, registered series of a limited liability company or statutory trust, executed, acknowledged and filed with the Secretary of State in accordance with § 103 of this title, or except that, without prejudicing any rights of the person who has reserved such name or such other foreign corporation or domestic or foreign partnership, limited partnership, limited liability company, registered series of a limited liability company or statutory trust, the Division of Corporations in the Department of State may waive such requirement if the corporation demonstrates to the satisfaction of the Secretary of State that the corporation or a predecessor entity previously has made substantial use of such name or a substantially similar name, that the corporation has made reasonable efforts to secure such written consent, and that such waiver is in the interest of the State, (iii) except as permitted by § 395 of this title, shall not contain the word "trust," and (iv) shall not contain the word "bank," or any variation thereof, except for the name of a bank reporting to and under the supervision of the State Bank Commissioner of this State or a subsidiary of a bank or savings association (as those terms are defined in the Federal Deposit Insurance Act, as amended, at 12 U.S.C. § 1813), or a corporation regulated under the Bank Holding Company Act of 1956, as amended, 12 U.S.C. § 1841 et seq., or the Home Owners' Loan Act, as amended, 12 U.S.C. § 1461 et seq.; provided, however, that this section shall not be construed to prevent the use of the word "bank," or any variation thereof, in a context clearly not purporting to refer to a banking business or otherwise likely to mislead the public about the nature of the business of the corporation or to lead to a pattern and practice of abuse that might cause harm to the interests of the public or the State as determined by the Division of Corporations in the Department of State;

(2)   The address (which shall be stated in accordance with § 131(c) of this title) of the corporation's registered office in this State, and the name of its registered agent at such address;

(3)   The nature of the business or purposes to be conducted or promoted. It shall be sufficient to state, either alone or with other businesses or purposes, that the purpose of the corporation is to engage in any lawful act or activity for which corporations may be organized under the General Corporation Law of Delaware, and by such statement all lawful acts and activities shall be within the purposes of the corporation, except for express limitations, if any;

(4)   If the corporation is to be authorized to issue only 1 class of stock, the total number of shares of stock which the corporation shall have authority to issue and the par value of each of such shares, or a statement that all such shares are to be without par value. If the corporation is to be authorized to issue more than 1 class of stock, the certificate of incorporation shall set forth the total number of shares of all classes of stock which the corporation shall have authority to issue and the number of shares of each class and shall specify each class the shares of which are to be without par value and each class the shares of which are to have par value and the par value of the shares of each such class. The certificate of incorporation shall also set forth a statement of the designations and the powers, preferences and rights, and the qualifications, limitations or restrictions thereof, which are permitted by § 151 of this title in respect of any class or classes of stock or any series of any class of stock of the corporation and the fixing of which by the certificate of incorporation is desired, and an express grant of such authority as it may then be desired to grant to the board of directors to fix by resolution or resolutions any thereof that may be desired but which shall not be fixed by the certificate of incorporation. The foregoing provisions of this paragraph shall not apply to nonstock corporations. In the case of nonstock corporations, the fact that they are not authorized to issue capital stock shall be stated in the certificate of incorporation. The conditions of membership, or other criteria for identifying members, of nonstock corporations shall likewise be stated in the certificate of incorporation or the bylaws. Nonstock corporations shall have members, but failure to have members shall not affect otherwise valid corporate acts or work a forfeiture or dissolution of the corporation. Nonstock corporations may provide for classes or groups of members having relative rights, powers and duties, and may make provision for the future creation of additional classes or groups of members having such relative rights, powers and duties as may from time to time be established, including rights, powers and duties senior to existing classes and groups of members. Except as otherwise

provided in this chapter, nonstock corporations may also provide that any member or class or group of members shall have full, limited, or no voting rights or powers, including that any member or class or group of members shall have the right to vote on a specified transaction even if that member or class or group of members does not have the right to vote for the election of the members of the governing body of the corporation. Voting by members of a nonstock corporation may be on a per capita, number, financial interest, class, group, or any other basis set forth. The provisions referred to in the 3 preceding sentences may be set forth in the certificate of incorporation or the bylaws. If neither the certificate of incorporation nor the bylaws of a nonstock corporation state the conditions of membership, or other criteria for identifying members, the members of the corporation shall be deemed to be those entitled to vote for the election of the members of the governing body pursuant to the certificate of incorporation or bylaws of such corporation or otherwise until thereafter otherwise provided by the certificate of incorporation or the bylaws;

(5)　The name and mailing address of the incorporator or incorporators;

(6)　If the powers of the incorporator or incorporators are to terminate upon the filing of the certificate of incorporation, the names and mailing addresses of the persons who are to serve as directors until the first annual meeting of stockholders or until their successors are elected and qualify.

(b)　In addition to the matters required to be set forth in the certificate of incorporation by subsection (a) of this section, the certificate of incorporation may also contain any or all of the following matters:

(1)　Any provision for the management of the business and for the conduct of the affairs of the corporation, and any provision creating, defining, limiting and regulating the powers of the corporation, the directors, and the stockholders, or any class of the stockholders, or the governing body, members, or any class or group of members of a nonstock corporation; if such provisions are not contrary to the laws of this State. Any provision which is required or permitted by any section of this chapter to be stated in the bylaws may instead be stated in the certificate of incorporation;

(2)　The following provisions, in haec verba, (i), for a corporation other than a nonstock corporation, viz:

"Whenever a compromise or arrangement is proposed between this corporation and its creditors or any class of them and/or between this corporation and its stockholders or any class of them, any court of equitable jurisdiction within the State of Delaware may, on the application in a summary way of this corporation or of any creditor or stockholder thereof or on the application of any receiver or receivers appointed for this corporation under § 291 of Title 8 of the Delaware Code or on the application of trustees in dissolution or of any receiver or receivers appointed for this corporation under § 279 of Title 8 of the Delaware Code order a meeting of the creditors or class of creditors, and/or of the stockholders or class of stockholders of this corporation, as the case may be, to be summoned in such manner as the said court directs. If a majority in number representing three fourths in value of the creditors or class of creditors, and/or of the stockholders or class of stockholders of this corporation, as the case may be, agree to any compromise or arrangement and to any reorganization of this corporation as consequence of such compromise or arrangement, the said compromise or arrangement and the said reorganization shall, if sanctioned by the court to which the said application has been made, be binding on all the creditors or class of creditors, and/or on all the stockholders or class of stockholders, of this corporation, as the case may be, and also on this corporation"; or

(ii), for a nonstock corporation, viz:

"Whenever a compromise or arrangement is proposed between this corporation and its creditors or any class of them and/or between this corporation and its members or any class of them, any court of equitable jurisdiction within the State of Delaware may, on the application in a summary way of this corporation or of any creditor or member thereof or on the application of any receiver or receivers appointed for this corporation under § 291 of Title 8 of the Delaware Code or on the application of trustees in dissolution or of any receiver or receivers appointed for this corporation under § 279 of Title 8 of the Delaware Code order a meeting of the creditors or class of creditors, and/or of the members or class of members of this corporation, as the case may be, to be summoned in such manner as the said court directs. If a majority in number representing three fourths in value of the creditors or class of creditors, and/or of the members or class of members of this corporation, as the case may be, agree to any compromise or arrangement and to any reorganization of this corporation as consequence of such compromise or arrangement, the said compromise or arrangement and the said reorganization shall, if sanctioned by the court to which the said application has been made, be binding on all the creditors or class of creditors, and/or on all the members or class of members, of this corporation, as the case may be, and also on this corporation";

(3) Such provisions as may be desired granting to the holders of the stock of the corporation, or the holders of any class or series of a class thereof, the preemptive right to subscribe to any or all additional issues of stock of the corporation of any or all classes or series thereof, or to any securities of the corporation convertible into such stock. No stockholder shall have any preemptive right to subscribe to an additional issue of stock or to any security convertible into such stock unless, and except to the extent that, such right is expressly granted to such stockholder in the certificate of incorporation. All such rights in existence on July 3, 1967, shall remain in existence unaffected by this paragraph unless and until changed or terminated by appropriate action which expressly provides for the change or termination;

(4) Provisions requiring for any corporate action, the vote of a larger portion of the stock or of any class or series thereof, or of any other securities having voting power, or a larger number of the directors, than is required by this chapter;

(5) A provision limiting the duration of the corporation's existence to a specified date; otherwise, the corporation shall have perpetual existence;

(6) A provision imposing personal liability for the debts of the corporation on its stockholders to a specified extent and upon specified conditions; otherwise, the stockholders of a corporation shall not be personally liable for the payment of the corporation's debts except as they may be liable by reason of their own conduct or acts;

(7) A provision eliminating or limiting the personal liability of a director to the corporation or its stockholders for monetary damages for breach of fiduciary duty as a director, provided that such provision shall not eliminate or limit the liability of a director: (i) For any breach of the director's duty of loyalty to the corporation or its stockholders; (ii) for acts or omissions not in good faith or which involve intentional misconduct or a knowing violation of law; (iii) under § 174 of this title; or (iv) for any transaction from which the director derived an improper personal benefit. No such provision shall eliminate or limit the liability of a director for any act or omission occurring prior to the date when such provision becomes effective. All references in this paragraph to a director shall also be deemed to refer to such other person or persons, if any, who, pursuant to a provision of the certificate of incorporation in accordance with § 141(a) of this title, exercise or perform any of the powers or duties otherwise conferred or imposed upon the board of directors by this title.

(c) It shall not be necessary to set forth in the certificate of incorporation any of the powers conferred on corporations by this chapter.

(d) Except for provisions included pursuant to paragraphs (a)(1), (a)(2), (a)(5), (a)(6), (b)(2), (b)(5), (b)(7) of this section, and provisions included pursuant to paragraph (a)(4) of this section specifying the classes, number of shares, and par value of shares a corporation other than a nonstock corporation is authorized to issue, any provision of the certificate of incorporation may be made dependent upon facts ascertainable outside such instrument, provided that the manner in which such facts shall operate upon the provision is clearly and explicitly set forth therein. The term "facts," as used in this subsection, includes, but is not limited to, the occurrence of any event, including a determination or action by any person or body, including the corporation.

(e) The exclusive right to the use of a name that is available for use by a domestic or foreign corporation may be reserved by or on behalf of:

(1) Any person intending to incorporate or organize a corporation with that name under this chapter or contemplating such incorporation or organization;

(2) Any domestic corporation or any foreign corporation qualified to do business in the State of Delaware, in either case, intending to change its name or contemplating such a change;

(3) Any foreign corporation intending to qualify to do business in the State of Delaware and adopt that name or contemplating such qualification and adoption; and

(4) Any person intending to organize a foreign corporation and have it qualify to do business in the State of Delaware and adopt that name or contemplating such organization, qualification and adoption.

The reservation of a specified name may be made by filing with the Secretary of State an application, executed by the applicant, certifying that the reservation is made by or on behalf of a domestic corporation, foreign corporation or other person described in paragraphs (e)(1)–(4) of this section above, and specifying the name to be reserved and the name and address of the applicant. If the Secretary of State finds that the name is available for use by a domestic or foreign corporation, the Secretary shall reserve the name for the use of the applicant for a period of 120 days. The same applicant may renew for successive 120-day periods a reservation of a specified name by filing with the Secretary of State, prior to the expiration of such reservation (or renewal thereof), an application for renewal of such reservation, executed by the applicant, certifying that the reservation is renewed by or on behalf of a domestic corporation, foreign corporation or other person described in paragraphs (e)(1)–(4) of this section above and specifying the name reservation to be renewed and the name and address of the applicant. The right to the exclusive use of a reserved name may be transferred to any other person by filing in the office of the Secretary of State a notice of the transfer, executed by the applicant for whom the name was reserved, specifying the name reservation to be transferred and the name and address of the transferee. The reservation of a specified name may be cancelled by filing with the Secretary of State a notice of cancellation, executed by the applicant or transferee, specifying the name reservation to be cancelled and the name and address of the applicant or transferee. Unless the Secretary of State finds that any application, application for renewal, notice of transfer, or notice of cancellation filed with the Secretary of State as required by this subsection does not conform to law, upon receipt of all filing fees required by law the Secretary of State shall prepare and return to the person who filed such instrument a copy of the filed instrument with a notation thereon of the action taken by the Secretary of State. A fee as set forth in § 391 of this title shall be paid at the time of the reservation of any name, at the time of the renewal of any such reservation and at the time of the filing of a notice of the transfer or cancellation of any such reservation.

(f) The certificate of incorporation may not contain any provision that would impose liability on a stockholder for the attorneys' fees or expenses of the corporation or any other party in connection with an internal corporate claim, as defined in § 115 of this title.

§ 103. **Execution, acknowledgment, filing, recording and effective date of original certificate of incorporation and other instruments; exceptions.**

(a) Whenever any instrument is to be filed with the Secretary of State or in accordance with this section or chapter, such instrument shall be executed as follows:

(1) The certificate of incorporation, and any other instrument to be filed before the election of the initial board of directors if the initial directors were not named in the certificate of incorporation, shall be signed by the incorporator or incorporators (or, in the case of any such

other instrument, such incorporator's or incorporators' successors and assigns). If any incorporator is not available then any such other instrument may be signed, with the same effect as if such incorporator had signed it, by any person for whom or on whose behalf such incorporator, in executing the certificate of incorporation, was acting directly or indirectly as employee or agent, provided that such other instrument shall state that such incorporator is not available and the reason therefor, that such incorporator in executing the certificate of incorporation was acting directly or indirectly as employee or agent for or on behalf of such person, and that such person's signature on such instrument is otherwise authorized and not wrongful.

    (2)   All other instruments shall be signed:

        a.   By any authorized officer of the corporation; or

        b.   If it shall appear from the instrument that there are no such officers, then by a majority of the directors or by such directors as may be designated by the board; or

        c.   If it shall appear from the instrument that there are no such officers or directors, then by the holders of record, or such of them as may be designated by the holders of record, of a majority of all outstanding shares of stock; or

        d.   By the holders of record of all outstanding shares of stock.

(b)   Whenever this chapter requires any instrument to be acknowledged, such requirement is satisfied by either:

    (1)   The formal acknowledgment by the person or 1 of the persons signing the instrument that it is such person's act and deed or the act and deed of the corporation, and that the facts stated therein are true. Such acknowledgment shall be made before a person who is authorized by the law of the place of execution to take acknowledgments of deeds. If such person has a seal of office such person shall affix it to the instrument.

    (2)   The signature, without more, of the person or persons signing the instrument, in which case such signature or signatures shall constitute the affirmation or acknowledgment of the signatory, under penalties of perjury, that the instrument is such person's act and deed or the act and deed of the corporation, and that the facts stated therein are true.

(c)   Whenever any instrument is to be filed with the Secretary of State or in accordance with this section or chapter, such requirement means that:

    (1)   The signed instrument shall be delivered to the office of the Secretary of State;

    (2)   All taxes and fees authorized by law to be collected by the Secretary of State in connection with the filing of the instrument shall be tendered to the Secretary of State; and

    (3)   Upon delivery of the instrument, the Secretary of State shall record the date and time of its delivery. Upon such delivery and tender of the required taxes and fees, the Secretary of State shall certify that the instrument has been filed in the Secretary of State's office by endorsing upon the signed instrument the word "Filed", and the date and time of its filing. This endorsement is the "filing date" of the instrument, and is conclusive of the date and time of its filing in the absence of actual fraud. The Secretary of State shall file and index the endorsed instrument. Except as provided in paragraph (c)(4) of this section and in subsection (i) of this section, such filing date of an instrument shall be the date and time of delivery of the instrument.

    (4)   Upon request made upon or prior to delivery, the Secretary of State may, to the extent deemed practicable, establish as the filing date of an instrument a date and time after its delivery. If the Secretary of State refuses to file any instrument due to an error, omission or other imperfection, the Secretary of State may hold such instrument in suspension, and in such event, upon delivery of a replacement instrument in proper form for filing and tender of the required taxes and fees within 5 business days after notice of such suspension is given to the filer, the Secretary of State shall establish as the filing date of such instrument the date and time that

would have been the filing date of the rejected instrument had it been accepted for filing. The Secretary of State shall not issue a certificate of good standing with respect to any corporation with an instrument held in suspension pursuant to this subsection. The Secretary of State may establish as the filing date of an instrument the date and time at which information from such instrument is entered pursuant to paragraph (c)(8) of this section if such instrument is delivered on the same date and within 4 hours after such information is entered.

(5)   The Secretary of State, acting as agent for the recorders of each of the counties, shall collect and deposit in a separate account established exclusively for that purpose a county assessment fee with respect to each filed instrument and shall thereafter weekly remit from such account to the recorder of each of the said counties the amount or amounts of such fees as provided for in paragraph (c)(6) of this section or as elsewhere provided by law. Said fees shall be for the purposes of defraying certain costs incurred by the counties in merging the information and images of such filed documents with the document information systems of each of the recorder's offices in the counties and in retrieving, maintaining and displaying such information and images in the offices of the recorders and at remote locations in each of such counties. In consideration for its acting as the agent for the recorders with respect to the collection and payment of the county assessment fees, the Secretary of State shall retain and pay over to the General Fund of the State an administrative charge of 1 percent of the total fees collected.

(6)   The assessment fee to the counties shall be $24 for each 1-page instrument filed with the Secretary of State in accordance with this section and $9.00 for each additional page for instruments with more than 1 page. The recorder's office to receive the assessment fee shall be the recorder's office in the county in which the corporation's registered office in this State is, or is to be, located, except that an assessment fee shall not be charged for either a certificate of dissolution qualifying for treatment under § 391(a)(5)b. of this title or a document filed in accordance with subchapter XVI of this chapter.

(7)   The Secretary of State, acting as agent, shall collect and deposit in a separate account established exclusively for that purpose a courthouse municipality fee with respect to each filed instrument and shall thereafter monthly remit funds from such account to the treasuries of the municipalities designated in § 301 of Title 10. Said fees shall be for the purposes of defraying certain costs incurred by such municipalities in hosting the primary locations for the Delaware courts. The fee to such municipalities shall be $20 for each instrument filed with the Secretary of State in accordance with this section. The municipality to receive the fee shall be the municipality designated in § 301 of Title 10 in the county in which the corporation's registered office in this State is, or is to be, located, except that a fee shall not be charged for a certificate of dissolution qualifying for treatment under § 391(a)(5)b. of this title, a resignation of agent without appointment of a successor under § 136 of this title, or a document filed in accordance with subchapter XVI of this chapter.

(8)   The Secretary of State shall cause to be entered such information from each instrument as the Secretary of State deems appropriate into the Delaware Corporation Information System or any system which is a successor thereto in the office of the Secretary of State, and such information and a copy of each such instrument shall be permanently maintained as a public record on a suitable medium. The Secretary of State is authorized to grant direct access to such system to registered agents subject to the execution of an operating agreement between the Secretary of State and such registered agent. Any registered agent granted such access shall demonstrate the existence of policies to ensure that information entered into the system accurately reflects the content of instruments in the possession of the registered agent at the time of entry.

(d)   Any instrument filed in accordance with subsection (c) of this section shall be effective upon its filing date. Any instrument may provide that it is not to become effective until a specified time subsequent to the time it is filed, but such time shall not be later than a time on the ninetieth day after the date of its filing. If any instrument filed in accordance with subsection (c) of this section provides for a future effective date or time and if the transaction is terminated or its terms are amended to change the future effective date or time prior to the future effective date or time, the instrument shall be terminated or amended by the filing, prior to the future effective date or time set forth in such instrument, of a certificate of termination or amendment of the original instrument, executed in accordance with subsection (a) of this section, which shall identify the instrument which has been terminated or amended and shall state that the instrument has been terminated or the manner in which it has been amended.

(e) If another section of this chapter specifically prescribes a manner of executing, acknowledging or filing a specified instrument or a time when such instrument shall become effective which differs from the corresponding provisions of this section, then such other section shall govern.

(f) Whenever any instrument authorized to be filed with the Secretary of State under any provision of this title, has been so filed and is an inaccurate record of the corporate action therein referred to, or was defectively or erroneously executed, sealed or acknowledged, the instrument may be corrected by filing with the Secretary of State a certificate of correction of the instrument which shall be executed, acknowledged and filed in accordance with this section. The certificate of correction shall specify the inaccuracy or defect to be corrected and shall set forth the portion of the instrument in corrected form. In lieu of filing a certificate of correction the instrument may be corrected by filing with the Secretary of State a corrected instrument which shall be executed, acknowledged and filed in accordance with this section. The corrected instrument shall be specifically designated as such in its heading, shall specify the inaccuracy or defect to be corrected, and shall set forth the entire instrument in corrected form. An instrument corrected in accordance with this section shall be effective as of the date the original instrument was filed, except as to those persons who are substantially and adversely affected by the correction and as to those persons the instrument as corrected shall be effective from the filing date.

(g) Notwithstanding that any instrument authorized to be filed with the Secretary of State under this title is when filed inaccurately, defectively or erroneously executed, sealed or acknowledged, or otherwise defective in any respect, the Secretary of State shall have no liability to any person for the preclearance for filing, the acceptance for filing or the filing and indexing of such instrument by the Secretary of State.

(h) Any signature on any instrument authorized to be filed with the Secretary of State under this title may be a facsimile, a conformed signature or an electronically transmitted signature.

(i)(1) If:

a. Together with the actual delivery of an instrument and tender of the required taxes and fees, there is delivered to the Secretary of State a separate affidavit (which in its heading shall be designated as an "affidavit of extraordinary condition") attesting, on the basis of personal knowledge of the affiant or a reliable source of knowledge identified in the affidavit, that an earlier effort to deliver such instrument and tender such taxes and fees was made in good faith, specifying the nature, date and time of such good faith effort and requesting that the Secretary of State establish such date and time as the filing date of such instrument; or

b. Upon the actual delivery of an instrument and tender of the required taxes and fees, the Secretary of State in the Secretary's discretion provides a written waiver of the requirement for such an affidavit stating that it appears to the Secretary of State that an earlier effort to deliver such instrument and tender such taxes and fees was made in good faith and specifying the date and time of such effort; and

c. The Secretary of State determines that an extraordinary condition existed at such date and time, that such earlier effort was unsuccessful as a result of the existence of such extraordinary condition, and that such actual delivery and tender were made within a reasonable period (not to exceed 2 business days) after the cessation of such extraordinary condition, then the Secretary of State may establish such date and time as the filing date of such instrument. No fee shall be paid to the Secretary of State for receiving an affidavit of extraordinary condition.

(2)   For purposes of this subsection, an "extraordinary condition" means: any emergency resulting from an attack on, invasion or occupation by foreign military forces of, or disaster, catastrophe, war or other armed conflict, revolution or insurrection, or rioting or civil commotion in, the United States or a locality in which the Secretary of State conducts its business or in which the good faith effort to deliver the instrument and tender the required taxes and fees is made, or the immediate threat of any of the foregoing; or any malfunction or outage of the electrical or telephone service to the Secretary of State's office, or weather or other condition in or about a locality in which the Secretary of State conducts its business, as a result of which the Secretary of State's office is not open for the purpose of the filing of instruments under this chapter or such filing cannot be effected without extraordinary effort. The Secretary of State may require such proof as it deems necessary to make the determination required under paragraph (i)(1)c. of this section, and any such determination shall be conclusive in the absence of actual fraud.

(3)   If the Secretary of State establishes the filing date of an instrument pursuant to this subsection, the date and time of delivery of the affidavit of extraordinary condition or the date and time of the Secretary of State's written waiver of such affidavit shall be endorsed on such affidavit or waiver and such affidavit or waiver, so endorsed, shall be attached to the filed instrument to which it relates. Such filed instrument shall be effective as of the date and time established as the filing date by the Secretary of State pursuant to this subsection, except as to those persons who are substantially and adversely affected by such establishment and, as to those persons, the instrument shall be effective from the date and time endorsed on the affidavit of extraordinary condition or written waiver attached thereto.

(j)   Notwithstanding any other provision of this chapter, it shall not be necessary for any corporation to amend its certificate of incorporation, or any other document, that has been filed prior to August 1, 2011, to comply with § 131(c) of this title, provided that any certificate or other document filed under this chapter on or after August 1, 2011, and changing the address of a registered office shall comply with § 131(c) of this title.

§ 104.   Certificate of incorporation; definition.

The term "certificate of incorporation," as used in this chapter, unless the context requires otherwise, includes not only the original certificate of incorporation filed to create a corporation but also all other certificates, agreements of merger or consolidation, plans of reorganization, or other instruments, howsoever designated, which are filed pursuant to § 102, §§ 133–136, § 151, §§ 241–243, § 245, §§ 251–258, §§ 263–264, § 267, § 303, §§ 311–313, or any other section of this title, and which have the effect of amending or supplementing in some respect a corporation's certificate of incorporation.

§ 105.   Certificate of incorporation and other certificates; evidence.

A copy of a certificate of incorporation, or a restated certificate of incorporation, or of any other certificate which has been filed in the office of the Secretary of State as required by any provision of this title shall, when duly certified by the Secretary of State, be received in all courts, public offices and official bodies as prima facie evidence of:

(1)   Due execution, acknowledgment and filing of the instrument;

(2)   Observance and performance of all acts and conditions necessary to have been observed and performed precedent to the instrument becoming effective; and

(3)   Any other facts required or permitted by law to be stated in the instrument.

§ 106. Commencement of corporate existence.

Upon the filing with the Secretary of State of the certificate of incorporation, executed and acknowledged in accordance with § 103 of this title, the incorporator or incorporators who signed the certificate, and such incorporator's or incorporators' successors and assigns, shall, from the date of such filing, be and constitute a body corporate, by the name set forth in the certificate, subject to § 103(d) of this title and subject to dissolution or other termination of its existence as provided in this chapter.

§ 107. Powers of incorporators.

If the persons who are to serve as directors until the first annual meeting of stockholders have not been named in the certificate of incorporation, the incorporator or incorporators, until the directors are elected, shall manage the affairs of the corporation and may do whatever is necessary and proper to perfect the organization of the corporation, including the adoption of the original bylaws of the corporation and the election of directors.

§ 108. Organization meeting of incorporators or directors named in certificate of incorporation.

(a) After the filing of the certificate of incorporation an organization meeting of the incorporator or incorporators, or of the board of directors if the initial directors were named in the certificate of incorporation, shall be held, either within or without this State, at the call of a majority of the incorporators or directors, as the case may be, for the purposes of adopting bylaws, electing directors (if the meeting is of the incorporators) to serve or hold office until the first annual meeting of stockholders or until their successors are elected and qualify, electing officers if the meeting is of the directors, doing any other or further acts to perfect the organization of the corporation, and transacting such other business as may come before the meeting.

(b) The persons calling the meeting shall give to each other incorporator or director, as the case may be, at least 2 days' notice thereof in writing or by electronic transmission by any usual means of communication, which notice shall state the time, place and purposes of the meeting as fixed by the persons calling it. Notice of the meeting need not be given to anyone who attends the meeting or who waives notice either before or after the meeting.

(c) Any action permitted to be taken at the organization meeting of the incorporators or directors, as the case may be, may be taken without a meeting if each incorporator or director, where there is more than 1, or the sole incorporator or director where there is only 1, consents thereto in writing or by electronic transmission. Any person (whether or not then an incorporator or director) may provide, whether through instruction to an agent or otherwise, that a consent to action will be effective at a future time (including a time determined upon the happening of an event), no later than 60 days after such instruction is given or such provision is made and such consent shall be deemed to have been given for purposes of this subsection at such effective time so long as such person is then an incorporator or director, as the case may be, and did not revoke the consent prior to such time. Any such consent shall be revocable prior to its becoming effective.

(d) If any incorporator is not available to act, then any person for whom or on whose behalf the incorporator was acting directly or indirectly as employee or agent, may take any action that such incorporator would have been authorized to take under this section or § 107 of this title; provided that any instrument signed by such other person, or any record of the proceedings of a meeting in which such person participated, shall state that such incorporator is not available and the reason therefor, that such incorporator was acting directly or indirectly as employee or agent for or on behalf of such person, and that such person's signature on such instrument or participation in such meeting is otherwise authorized and not wrongful.

§ 109.   Bylaws.

(a)   The original or other bylaws of a corporation may be adopted, amended or repealed by the incorporators, by the initial directors of a corporation other than a nonstock corporation or initial members of the governing body of a nonstock corporation if they were named in the certificate of incorporation, or, before a corporation other than a nonstock corporation has received any payment for any of its stock, by its board of directors. After a corporation other than a nonstock corporation has received any payment for any of its stock, the power to adopt, amend or repeal bylaws shall be in the stockholders entitled to vote. In the case of a nonstock corporation, the power to adopt, amend or repeal bylaws shall be in its members entitled to vote. Notwithstanding the foregoing, any corporation may, in its certificate of incorporation, confer the power to adopt, amend or repeal bylaws upon the directors or, in the case of a nonstock corporation, upon its governing body. The fact that such power has been so conferred upon the directors or governing body, as the case may be, shall not divest the stockholders or members of the power, nor limit their power to adopt, amend or repeal bylaws.

(b)   The bylaws may contain any provision, not inconsistent with law or with the certificate of incorporation, relating to the business of the corporation, the conduct of its affairs, and its rights or powers or the rights or powers of its stockholders, directors, officers or employees. The bylaws may not contain any provision that would impose liability on a stockholder for the attorneys' fees or expenses of the corporation or any other party in connection with an internal corporate claim, as defined in § 115 of this title.

§ 110.   Emergency bylaws and other powers in emergency.

(a)   The board of directors of any corporation may adopt emergency bylaws, subject to repeal or change by action of the stockholders, which shall notwithstanding any different provision elsewhere in this chapter or in Chapters 3 [repealed] and 5 [repealed] of Title 26, or in Chapter 7 of Title 5, or in the certificate of incorporation or bylaws, be operative during any emergency resulting from an attack on the United States or on a locality in which the corporation conducts its business or customarily holds meetings of its board of directors or its stockholders, or during any nuclear or atomic disaster, or during the existence of any catastrophe, or other similar emergency condition, as a result of which a quorum of the board of directors or a standing committee thereof cannot readily be convened for action. The emergency bylaws may make any provision that may be practical and necessary for the circumstances of the emergency, including provisions that:

(1)   A meeting of the board of directors or a committee thereof may be called by any officer or director in such manner and under such conditions as shall be prescribed in the emergency bylaws;

(2)   The director or directors in attendance at the meeting, or any greater number fixed by the emergency bylaws, shall constitute a quorum; and

(3)   The officers or other persons designated on a list approved by the board of directors before the emergency, all in such order of priority and subject to such conditions and for such period of time (not longer than reasonably necessary after the termination of the emergency) as may be provided in the emergency bylaws or in the resolution approving the list, shall, to the extent required to provide a quorum at any meeting of the board of directors, be deemed directors for such meeting.

(b)   The board of directors, either before or during any such emergency, may provide, and from time to time modify, lines of succession in the event that during such emergency any or all officers or agents of the corporation shall for any reason be rendered incapable of discharging their duties.

(c)   The board of directors, either before or during any such emergency, may, effective in the emergency, change the head office or designate several alternative head offices or regional offices, or authorize the officers so to do.

(d)   No officer, director or employee acting in accordance with any emergency bylaws shall be liable except for wilful misconduct.

(e)   To the extent not inconsistent with any emergency bylaws so adopted, the bylaws of the corporation shall remain in effect during any emergency and upon its termination the emergency bylaws shall cease to be operative.

(f)   Unless otherwise provided in emergency bylaws, notice of any meeting of the board of directors during such an emergency may be given only to such of the directors as it may be feasible to reach at the time and by such means as may be feasible at the time, including publication or radio.

(g)   To the extent required to constitute a quorum at any meeting of the board of directors during such an emergency, the officers of the corporation who are present shall, unless otherwise provided in emergency bylaws, be deemed, in order of rank and within the same rank in order of seniority, directors for such meeting.

(h)   Nothing contained in this section shall be deemed exclusive of any other provisions for emergency powers consistent with other sections of this title which have been or may be adopted by corporations created under this chapter.

§ 111.   Jurisdiction to interpret, apply, enforce or determine the validity of corporate instruments and provisions of this title. [For application of this section, see 80 Del. Laws, c. 265, § 17]

(a)   Any civil action to interpret, apply, enforce or determine the validity of the provisions of:

(1)   The certificate of incorporation or the bylaws of a corporation;

(2)   Any instrument, document or agreement (i) by which a corporation creates or sells, or offers to create or sell, any of its stock, or any rights or options respecting its stock, or (ii) to which a corporation and 1 or more holders of its stock are parties, and pursuant to which any such holder or holders sell or offer to sell any of such stock, or (iii) by which a corporation agrees to sell, lease or exchange any of its property or assets, and which by its terms provides that 1 or more holders of its stock approve of or consent to such sale, lease or exchange;

(3)   Any written restrictions on the transfer, registration of transfer or ownership of securities under § 202 of this title;

(4)   Any proxy under § 212 or § 215 of this title;

(5)   Any voting trust or other voting agreement under § 218 of this title;

(6)   Any agreement, certificate of merger or consolidation, or certificate of ownership and merger governed by §§ 251–253, §§ 255–258, §§ 263–264, or § 267 of this title;

(7)   Any certificate of conversion under § 265 or § 266 of this title;

(8)   Any certificate of domestication, transfer or continuance under § 388, § 389 or § 390 of this title; or

(9)   Any other instrument, document, agreement, or certificate required by any provision of this title;

may be brought in the Court of Chancery, except to the extent that a statute confers exclusive jurisdiction on a court, agency or tribunal other than the Court of Chancery.

(b)   Any civil action to interpret, apply or enforce any provision of this title may be brought in the Court of Chancery.

§ 112.   Access to proxy solicitation materials.

The bylaws may provide that if the corporation solicits proxies with respect to an election of directors, it may be required, to the extent and subject to such procedures or conditions as may be provided in the bylaws, to include in its proxy solicitation materials (including any form of proxy it distributes), in addition to individuals nominated by the board of directors, 1 or more individuals nominated by a stockholder. Such procedures or conditions may include any of the following:

(1) A provision requiring a minimum record or beneficial ownership, or duration of ownership, of shares of the corporation's capital stock, by the nominating stockholder, and defining beneficial ownership to take into account options or other rights in respect of or related to such stock;

(2) A provision requiring the nominating stockholder to submit specified information concerning the stockholder and the stockholder's nominees, including information concerning ownership by such persons of shares of the corporation's capital stock, or options or other rights in respect of or related to such stock;

(3) A provision conditioning eligibility to require inclusion in the corporation's proxy solicitation materials upon the number or proportion of directors nominated by stockholders or whether the stockholder previously sought to require such inclusion;

(4) A provision precluding nominations by any person if such person, any nominee of such person, or any affiliate or associate of such person or nominee, has acquired or publicly proposed to acquire shares constituting a specified percentage of the voting power of the corporation's outstanding voting stock within a specified period before the election of directors;

(5) A provision requiring that the nominating stockholder undertake to indemnify the corporation in respect of any loss arising as a result of any false or misleading information or statement submitted by the nominating stockholder in connection with a nomination; and

(6) Any other lawful condition.

§ 113.   Proxy expense reimbursement.

(a) The bylaws may provide for the reimbursement by the corporation of expenses incurred by a stockholder in soliciting proxies in connection with an election of directors, subject to such procedures or conditions as the bylaws may prescribe, including:

(1) Conditioning eligibility for reimbursement upon the number or proportion of persons nominated by the stockholder seeking reimbursement or whether such stockholder previously sought reimbursement for similar expenses;

(2) Limitations on the amount of reimbursement based upon the proportion of votes cast in favor of 1 or more of the persons nominated by the stockholder seeking reimbursement, or upon the amount spent by the corporation in soliciting proxies in connection with the election;

(3) Limitations concerning elections of directors by cumulative voting pursuant to § 214 of this title; or

(4) Any other lawful condition.

(b) No bylaw so adopted shall apply to elections for which any record date precedes its adoption.

§ 114.   Application of chapter to nonstock corporations.

(a) Except as otherwise provided in subsections (b) and (c) of this section, the provisions of this chapter and of chapter 5 of this title shall apply to nonstock corporations in the manner specified in the following paragraphs (a)(1)–(4) of this section:

(1) All references to stockholders of the corporation shall be deemed to refer to members of the corporation;

(2) All references to the board of directors of the corporation shall be deemed to refer to the governing body of the corporation;

(3) All references to directors or to members of the board of directors of the corporation shall be deemed to refer to members of the governing body of the corporation; and

(4) All references to stock, capital stock, or shares thereof of a corporation authorized to issue capital stock shall be deemed to refer to memberships of a nonprofit nonstock corporation and to membership interests of any other nonstock corporation.

(b) Subsection (a) of this section shall not apply to:

(1) Sections 102(a)(4), (b)(1) and (2), 109(a), 114, 141, 154, 215, 228, 230(b), 241, 242, 253, 254, 255, 256, 257, 258, 271, 276, 311, 312, 313, 390, and 503 of this title, which apply to nonstock corporations by their terms;

(2) Sections 102(f), 109(b) (last sentence), 151, 152, 153, 155, 156, 157(d), 158, 161, 162, 163, 164, 165, 166, 167, 168, 203, 211, 212, 213, 214, 216, 219, 222, 231, 243, 244, 251, 252, 267, 274, 275, 324, 364, 366(a), 391 and 502(a)(5) of this title; and

(3) Subchapter XIV and subchapter XVI of this chapter.

(c) In the case of a nonprofit nonstock corporation, subsection (a) of this section shall not apply to:

(1) The sections and subchapters listed in subsection (b) of this section;

(2) Sections 102(b)(3), 111(a)(2) and (3), 144(a)(2), 217, 218(a) and (b), and 262 of this title; and

(3) Subchapter V, subchapter VI (other than §§ 204 and 205 of this title) and subchapter XV of this chapter.

(d) For purposes of this chapter:

(1) A "charitable nonstock corporation" is any nonprofit nonstock corporation that is exempt from taxation under § 501(c)(3) of the United States Internal Revenue Code [26 U.S.C. § 501(c)(3)], or any successor provisions.

(2) A "membership interest" is, unless otherwise provided in a nonstock corporation's certificate of incorporation, a member's share of the profits and losses of a nonstock corporation, or a member's right to receive distributions of the nonstock corporation's assets, or both;

(3) A "nonprofit nonstock corporation" is a nonstock corporation that does not have membership interests; and

(4) A "nonstock corporation" is any corporation organized under this chapter that is not authorized to issue capital stock.

§ 115. Forum selection provisions.

The certificate of incorporation or the bylaws may require, consistent with applicable jurisdictional requirements, that any or all internal corporate claims shall be brought solely and exclusively in any or all of the courts in this State, and no provision of the certificate of incorporation or the bylaws may prohibit bringing such claims in the courts of this State. "Internal corporate claims" means claims, including claims in the right of the corporation, (i) that are based upon a violation of a duty by a current or former director or officer or stockholder in such capacity, or (ii) as to which this title confers jurisdiction upon the Court of Chancery.

§ 116. Document form, signature and delivery.

(a) Except as provided in subsection (b) of this section, without limiting the manner in which any act or transaction may be documented, or the manner in which a document may be signed or delivered:

(1) Any act or transaction contemplated or governed by this chapter or the certificate of incorporation or bylaws may be provided for in a document, and an electronic transmission shall be deemed the equivalent of a written document. "Document" means:

     a.   Any tangible medium on which information is inscribed, and includes handwritten, typed, printed or similar instruments, and copies of such instruments; and

     b.   An electronic transmission.

(2) Whenever this chapter or the certificate of incorporation or bylaws requires or permits a signature, the signature may be a manual, facsimile, conformed or electronic signature. "Electronic signature" means an electronic symbol or process that is attached to, or logically associated with, a document and executed or adopted by a person with an intent to authenticate or adopt the document.

(3) Unless otherwise agreed between the sender and recipient, an electronic transmission shall be deemed delivered to a person for purposes of this chapter and the certificate of incorporation and bylaws when it enters an information processing system that the person has designated for the purpose of receiving electronic transmissions of the type delivered, so long as the electronic transmission is in a form capable of being processed by that system and such person is able to retrieve the electronic transmission. Whether a person has so designated an information processing system is determined by the certificate of incorporation, the bylaws or from the context and surrounding circumstances, including the parties' conduct. An electronic transmission is delivered under this section even if no person is aware of its receipt. Receipt of an electronic acknowledgement from an information processing system establishes that an electronic transmission was received but, by itself, does not establish that the content sent corresponds to the content received.

This chapter shall not prohibit 1 or more persons from conducting a transaction in accordance with Chapter 12A of Title 6 so long as the part or parts of the transaction that are governed by this chapter are documented, signed and delivered in accordance with this subsection or otherwise in accordance with this chapter. This subsection shall apply solely for purposes of determining whether an act or transaction has been documented, and the document has been signed and delivered, in accordance with this chapter, the certificate of incorporation and the bylaws.

(b) Subsection (a) of this section shall not apply to:

     (1) A document filed with or submitted to the Secretary of State, the Register in Chancery, or a court or other judicial or governmental body of this State;

     (2) A document comprising part of the stock ledger;

     (3) A certificate representing a security;

     (4) Any document expressly referenced as a notice (or waiver of notice) by this chapter, the certificate of incorporation or bylaws;

     (5) A consent in lieu of a meeting given by a director, stockholder or incorporator;

     (6) A ballot to vote on actions at a meeting of stockholders; and

     (7) An act or transaction effected pursuant to § 280 of this title or subchapters III, XIII or XVI of this chapter.

The foregoing shall not create any presumption about the lawful means to document a matter addressed by this subsection, or the lawful means to sign or deliver a document addressed by this subsection. A provision of the certificate of incorporation or bylaws shall not limit the application of subsection (a) of this section unless the provision expressly restricts one or more of the means of documenting an act or transaction, or of signing or delivering a document, permitted by subsection (a) of this section.

(c) In the event that any provision of this chapter is deemed to modify, limit or supersede the Electronic Signatures in Global and National Commerce Act, (15 U.S.C. § 7001 et. seq.), the provisions of this chapter shall control to the fullest extent permitted by § 7002(a)(2) of such act [15 U.S.C. § 7002(a)(2)].

SUBCHAPTER II. POWERS

§ 121. General powers.

(a) In addition to the powers enumerated in § 122 of this title, every corporation, its officers, directors and stockholders shall possess and may exercise all the powers and privileges granted by this chapter or by any other law or by its certificate of incorporation, together with any powers incidental thereto, so far as such powers and privileges are necessary or convenient to the conduct, promotion or attainment of the business or purposes set forth in its certificate of incorporation.

(b) Every corporation shall be governed by the provisions and be subject to the restrictions and liabilities contained in this chapter.

§ 122. Specific powers.

Every corporation created under this chapter shall have power to:

(1) Have perpetual succession by its corporate name, unless a limited period of duration is stated in its certificate of incorporation;

(2) Sue and be sued in all courts and participate, as a party or otherwise, in any judicial, administrative, arbitrative or other proceeding, in its corporate name;

(3) Have a corporate seal, which may be altered at pleasure, and use the same by causing it or a facsimile thereof, to be impressed or affixed or in any other manner reproduced;

(4) Purchase, receive, take by grant, gift, devise, bequest or otherwise, lease, or otherwise acquire, own, hold, improve, employ, use and otherwise deal in and with real or personal property, or any interest therein, wherever situated, and to sell, convey, lease, exchange, transfer or otherwise dispose of, or mortgage or pledge, all or any of its property and assets, or any interest therein, wherever situated;

(5) Appoint such officers and agents as the business of the corporation requires and to pay or otherwise provide for them suitable compensation;

(6) Adopt, amend and repeal bylaws;

(7) Wind up and dissolve itself in the manner provided in this chapter;

(8) Conduct its business, carry on its operations and have offices and exercise its powers within or without this State;

(9) Make donations for the public welfare or for charitable, scientific or educational purposes, and in time of war or other national emergency in aid thereof;

(10) Be an incorporator, promoter or manager of other corporations of any type or kind;

(11) Participate with others in any corporation, partnership, limited partnership, joint venture or other association of any kind, or in any transaction, undertaking or arrangement which the participating corporation would have power to conduct by itself, whether or not such participation involves sharing or delegation of control with or to others;

(12) Transact any lawful business which the corporation's board of directors shall find to be in aid of governmental authority;

(13) Make contracts, including contracts of guaranty and suretyship, incur liabilities, borrow money at such rates of interest as the corporation may determine, issue its notes, bonds

and other obligations, and secure any of its obligations by mortgage, pledge or other encumbrance of all or any of its property, franchises and income, and make contracts of guaranty and suretyship which are necessary or convenient to the conduct, promotion or attainment of the business of (a) a corporation all of the outstanding stock of which is owned, directly or indirectly, by the contracting corporation, or (b) a corporation which owns, directly or indirectly, all of the outstanding stock of the contracting corporation, or (c) a corporation all of the outstanding stock of which is owned, directly or indirectly, by a corporation which owns, directly or indirectly, all of the outstanding stock of the contracting corporation, which contracts of guaranty and suretyship shall be deemed to be necessary or convenient to the conduct, promotion or attainment of the business of the contracting corporation, and make other contracts of guaranty and suretyship which are necessary or convenient to the conduct, promotion or attainment of the business of the contracting corporation;

(14) Lend money for its corporate purposes, invest and reinvest its funds, and take, hold and deal with real and personal property as security for the payment of funds so loaned or invested;

(15) Pay pensions and establish and carry out pension, profit sharing, stock option, stock purchase, stock bonus, retirement, benefit, incentive and compensation plans, trusts and provisions for any or all of its directors, officers and employees, and for any or all of the directors, officers and employees of its subsidiaries;

(16) Provide insurance for its benefit on the life of any of its directors, officers or employees, or on the life of any stockholder for the purpose of acquiring at such stockholder's death shares of its stock owned by such stockholder.

(17) Renounce, in its certificate of incorporation or by action of its board of directors, any interest or expectancy of the corporation in, or in being offered an opportunity to participate in, specified business opportunities or specified classes or categories of business opportunities that are presented to the corporation or 1 or more of its officers, directors or stockholders.

§ 123.   Powers respecting securities of other corporations or entities.

Any corporation organized under the laws of this State may guarantee, purchase, take, receive, subscribe for or otherwise acquire; own, hold, use or otherwise employ; sell, lease, exchange, transfer or otherwise dispose of; mortgage, lend, pledge or otherwise deal in and with, bonds and other obligations of, or shares or other securities or interests in, or issued by, any other domestic or foreign corporation, partnership, association or individual, or by any government or agency or instrumentality thereof. A corporation while owner of any such securities may exercise all the rights, powers and privileges of ownership, including the right to vote.

§ 124.   Effect of lack of corporate capacity or power; ultra vires.

No act of a corporation and no conveyance or transfer of real or personal property to or by a corporation shall be invalid by reason of the fact that the corporation was without capacity or power to do such act or to make or receive such conveyance or transfer, but such lack of capacity or power may be asserted:

(1) In a proceeding by a stockholder against the corporation to enjoin the doing of any act or acts or the transfer of real or personal property by or to the corporation. If the unauthorized acts or transfer sought to be enjoined are being, or are to be, performed or made pursuant to any contract to which the corporation is a party, the court may, if all of the parties to the contract are parties to the proceeding and if it deems the same to be equitable, set aside and enjoin the performance of such contract, and in so doing may allow to the corporation or to the other parties to the contract, as the case may be, such compensation as may be equitable for the loss or damage sustained by any of them which may result from the action of the court in setting aside and enjoining the performance of such contract, but anticipated profits to be derived from the performance of the contract shall not be awarded by the court as a loss or damage sustained;

(2) In a proceeding by the corporation, whether acting directly or through a receiver, trustee or other legal representative, or through stockholders in a representative suit, against an incumbent or former officer or director of the corporation, for loss or damage due to such incumbent or former officer's or director's unauthorized act;

(3) In a proceeding by the Attorney General to dissolve the corporation, or to enjoin the corporation from the transaction of unauthorized business.

§ 125. Conferring academic or honorary degrees.

No corporation organized after April 18, 1945, shall have power to confer academic or honorary degrees unless the certificate of incorporation or an amendment thereof shall so provide and unless the certificate of incorporation or an amendment thereof prior to its being filed in the office of the Secretary of State shall have endorsed thereon the approval of the Department of Education of this State. No corporation organized before April 18, 1945, any provision in its certificate of incorporation to the contrary notwithstanding, shall possess the power aforesaid without first filing in the office of the Secretary of State a certificate of amendment so providing, the filing of which certificate of amendment in the office of the Secretary of State shall be subject to prior approval of the Department of Education, evidenced as hereinabove provided. Approval shall be granted only when it appears to the reasonable satisfaction of the Department of Education that the corporation is engaged in conducting a bona fide institution of higher learning, giving instructions in arts and letters, science or the professions, or that the corporation proposes, in good faith, to engage in that field and has or will have the resources, including personnel, requisite for the conduct of an institution of higher learning. Upon dissolution, all such corporations shall comply with § 8530 of Title 14. Notwithstanding any provision herein to the contrary, no corporation shall have the power to conduct a private business or trade school unless the certificate of incorporation or an amendment thereof, prior to its being filed in the office of the Secretary of State, shall have endorsed thereon the approval of the Department of Education pursuant to Chapter 85 of Title 14.

Notwithstanding the foregoing provisions, any corporation conducting a law school, which has its principal place of operation in Delaware, and which intends to meet the standards of approval of the American Bar Association, may, after it has been in actual operation for not less than 1 year, retain at its own expense a dean or dean emeritus of a law school fully approved by the American Bar Association to make an on-site inspection and report concerning the progress of the corporation toward meeting the standards for approval by the American Bar Association. Such dean or dean emeritus shall be chosen by the Attorney General from a panel of 3 deans whose names are presented to the Attorney General as being willing to serve. One such dean on this panel shall be nominated by the trustees of said law school corporation; another dean shall be nominated by a committee of the Student Bar Association of said law school; and the other dean shall be nominated by a committee of lawyers who are parents of students attending such law school. If any of the above-named groups cannot find a dean, it may substitute 2 full professors of accredited law schools for the dean it is entitled to nominate, and in such a case if the Attorney General chooses 1 of such professors, such professor shall serve the function of a dean as herein prescribed. If the dean so retained shall report in writing that, in such dean's professional judgment, the corporation is attempting, in good faith, to comply with the standards for approval of the American Bar Association and is making reasonable progress toward meeting such standards, the corporation may file a copy of the report with the Secretary of Education and with the Attorney General. Any corporation which complies with these provisions by filing such report shall be deemed to have temporary approval from the State and shall be entitled to amend its certificate of incorporation to authorize the granting of standard academic law degrees. Thereafter, until the law school operated by the corporation is approved by the American Bar Association, the corporation shall file once during each academic year a new report, in the same manner as the first report. If, at any time, the corporation fails to file such a report, or if the dean retained to render such report states that, in such dean's opinion, the corporation is not continuing to make reasonable progress toward accreditation, the Attorney General, at the request of the Secretary of Education, may file a complaint in the Court of Chancery to suspend said temporary approval and degree-granting power until a further report is filed by a dean or dean emeritus of an accredited law school that the school has resumed its progress towards meeting the standards for approval. Upon approval of the law school by the American Bar Association, temporary approval shall become final, and shall no longer be subject to suspension or vacation under this section.

§ 126.   Banking power denied.

(a)   No corporation organized under this chapter shall possess the power of issuing bills, notes, or other evidences of debt for circulation as money, or the power of carrying on the business of receiving deposits of money.

(b)   Corporations organized under this chapter to buy, sell and otherwise deal in notes, open accounts and other similar evidences of debt, or to loan money and to take notes, open accounts and other similar evidences of debt as collateral security therefor, shall not be deemed to be engaging in the business of banking.

§ 127.   Private foundation; powers and duties.

A corporation of this State which is a private foundation under the United States internal revenue laws and whose certificate of incorporation does not expressly provide that this section shall not apply to it is required to act or to refrain from acting so as not to subject itself to the taxes imposed by 26 U.S.C. § 4941 (relating to taxes on self-dealing), § 4942 (relating to taxes on failure to distribute income), § 4943 (relating to taxes on excess business holdings), § 4944 (relating to taxes on investments which jeopardize charitable purpose), or § 4945 (relating to taxable expenditures), or corresponding provisions of any subsequent United States internal revenue law.

SUBCHAPTER III.   REGISTERED OFFICE AND REGISTERED AGENT

§ 131.   Registered office in State; principal office or place of business in State.

(a)   Every corporation shall have and maintain in this State a registered office which may, but need not be, the same as its place of business.

(b)   Whenever the term "corporation's principal office or place of business in this State" or "principal office or place of business of the corporation in this State," or other term of like import, is or has been used in a corporation's certificate of incorporation, or in any other document, or in any statute, it shall be deemed to mean and refer to, unless the context indicates otherwise, the corporation's registered office required by this section; and it shall not be necessary for any corporation to amend its certificate of incorporation or any other document to comply with this section.

(c)   As contained in any certificate of incorporation or other document filed with the Secretary of State under this chapter, the address of a registered office shall include the street, number, city, county and postal code.

§ 132.   Registered agent in State; resident agent.

(a)   Every corporation shall have and maintain in this State a registered agent, which agent may be any of:

(1)   The corporation itself;

(2)   An individual resident in this State;

(3)   A domestic corporation (other than the corporation itself), a domestic partnership (whether general (including a limited liability partnership) or limited (including a limited liability limited partnership)), a domestic limited liability company or a domestic statutory trust; or

(4)   A foreign corporation, a foreign partnership (whether general (including a limited liability partnership) or limited (including a limited liability limited partnership)), a foreign limited liability company or a foreign statutory trust.

(b)   Every registered agent for a domestic corporation or a foreign corporation shall:

(1)   If an entity, maintain a business office in this State which is generally open, or if an individual, be generally present at a designated location in this State, at sufficiently frequent times to accept service of process and otherwise perform the functions of a registered agent;

(2)   If a foreign entity, be authorized to transact business in this State;

(3)   Accept service of process and other communications directed to the corporations for which it serves as registered agent and forward same to the corporation to which the service or communication is directed;

(4)   Forward to the corporations for which it serves as registered agent the annual report required by § 502 of this title or an electronic notification of same in a form satisfactory to the Secretary of State ("Secretary"); and

(5)   Satisfy and adhere to regulations established by the Secretary regarding the verification of both the identity of the entity's contacts and individuals for which the registered agent maintains a record for the reduction of risk of unlawful business purposes.

(c)   Any registered agent who at any time serves as registered agent for more than 50 entities (a "commercial registered agent"), whether domestic or foreign, shall satisfy and comply with the following qualifications.

(1)   A natural person serving as a commercial registered agent shall:

a.   Maintain a principal residence or a principal place of business in this State;

b.   Maintain a Delaware business license;

c.   Be generally present at a designated location within this State during normal business hours to accept service of process and otherwise perform the functions of a registered agent as specified in subsection (b) of this section;

d.   Provide the Secretary upon request with such information identifying and enabling communication with such commercial registered agent as the Secretary shall require; and

e.   Satisfy and adhere to regulations established by the Secretary regarding the verification of both the identity of the entity's contacts and individuals for which the natural person maintains a record for the reduction of risk of unlawful business purposes.

(2)   A domestic or foreign corporation, a domestic or foreign partnership (whether general (including a limited liability partnership) or limited (including a limited liability limited partnership)), a domestic or foreign limited liability company, or a domestic or foreign statutory trust serving as a commercial registered agent shall:

a.   Have a business office within this State which is generally open during normal business hours to accept service of process and otherwise perform the functions of a registered agent as specified in subsection (b) of this section;

b.   Maintain a Delaware business license;

c.   Have generally present at such office during normal business hours an officer, director or managing agent who is a natural person;

d.   Provide the Secretary upon request with such information identifying and enabling communication with such commercial registered agent as the Secretary shall require; and

e.   Satisfy and adhere to regulations established by the Secretary regarding the verification of both the identity of the entity's contacts and individuals for which it maintains a record for the reduction of risk of unlawful business purposes.

(3)   For purposes of this subsection and paragraph (f)(2)a. of this section, a commercial registered agent shall also include any registered agent which has an officer, director or managing agent in common with any other registered agent or agents if such registered agents at any time during such common service as officer, director or managing agent collectively served as registered agents for more than 50 entities, whether domestic or foreign.

(d)   Every corporation formed under the laws of this State or qualified to do business in this State shall provide to its registered agent and update from time to time as necessary the name, business address and business telephone number of a natural person who is an officer, director, employee, or designated agent of the corporation, who is then authorized to receive communications from the registered agent. Such person shall be deemed the communications contact for the corporation. Every registered agent shall retain (in paper or electronic form) the above information concerning the current communications contact for each corporation for which he, she or it serves as a registered agent. If the corporation fails to provide the registered agent with a current communications contact, the registered agent may resign as the registered agent for such corporation pursuant to § 136 of this title.

(e)   The Secretary is fully authorized to issue such regulations, as may be necessary or appropriate to carry out the enforcement of subsections (b), (c) and (d) of this section, and to take actions reasonable and necessary to assure registered agents' compliance with subsections (b), (c) and (d) of this section. Such actions may include refusal to file documents submitted by a registered agent, including the refusal to file any documents regarding an entity's formation.

(f)   Upon application of the Secretary, the Court of Chancery may enjoin any person or entity from serving as a registered agent or as an officer, director or managing agent of a registered agent.

(1)   Upon the filing of a complaint by the Secretary pursuant to this section, the Court may make such orders respecting such proceeding as it deems appropriate, and may enter such orders granting interim or final relief as it deems proper under the circumstances.

(2)   Any one or more of the following grounds shall be a sufficient basis to grant an injunction pursuant to this section:

a.   With respect to any registered agent who at any time within 1 year immediately prior to the filing of the Secretary's complaint is a commercial registered agent, failure after notice and warning to comply with the qualifications set forth in subsection (b) of this section and/or the requirements of subsection (c) or (d) of this section above;

b.   The person serving as a registered agent, or any person who is an officer, director or managing agent of an entity registered agent, has been convicted of a felony or any crime which includes an element of dishonesty or fraud or involves moral turpitude;

c.   The registered agent has engaged in conduct in connection with acting as a registered agent that is intended to or likely to deceive or defraud the public.

(3)   With respect to any order the court enters pursuant to this section with respect to an entity that has acted as a registered agent, the court may also direct such order to any person who has served as an officer, director, or managing agent of such registered agent. Any person who, on or after January 1, 2007, serves as an officer, director, or managing agent of an entity acting as a registered agent in this State shall be deemed thereby to have consented to the appointment of such registered agent as agent upon whom service of process may be made in any action brought pursuant to this section, and service as an officer, director, or managing agent of an entity acting as a registered agent in this State shall be a signification of the consent of such person that any process when so served shall be of the same legal force and validity as if served

upon such person within this State, and such appointment of the registered agent shall be irrevocable.

(4)   Upon the entry of an order by the Court enjoining any person or entity from acting as a registered agent, the Secretary shall mail or deliver notice of such order to each affected corporation at the address of its principal place of business as specified in its most recent franchise tax report or other record of the Secretary. If such corporation is a domestic corporation and fails to obtain and designate a new registered agent within 30 days after such notice is given, the Secretary shall declare the charter of such corporation forfeited. If such corporation is a foreign corporation, and fails to obtain and designate a new registered agent within 30 days after such notice is given, the Secretary shall forfeit its qualification to do business in this State. If the court enjoins a person or entity from acting as a registered agent as provided in this section and no new registered agent shall have been obtained and designated in the time and manner aforesaid, service of legal process against the corporation for which the registered agent had been acting shall thereafter be upon the Secretary in accordance with § 321 of this title. The Court of Chancery may, upon application of the Secretary on notice to the former registered agent, enter such orders as it deems appropriate to give the Secretary access to information in the former registered agent's possession in order to facilitate communication with the corporations the former registered agent served.

(g)   The Secretary is authorized to make a list of registered agents available to the public, and to establish such qualifications and issue such rules and regulations with respect to such listing as the Secretary deems necessary or appropriate.

(h)   Whenever the term "resident agent" or "resident agent in charge of a corporation's principal office or place of business in this State," or other term of like import which refers to a corporation's agent required by statute to be located in this State, is or has been used in a corporation's certificate of incorporation, or in any other document, or in any statute, it shall be deemed to mean and refer to, unless the context indicates otherwise, the corporation's registered agent required by this section; and it shall not be necessary for any corporation to amend its certificate of incorporation or any other document to comply with this section.

§ 133.   Change of location of registered office; change of registered agent.

Any corporation may, by resolution of its board of directors, change the location of its registered office in this State to any other place in this State. By like resolution, the registered agent of a corporation may be changed to any other person or corporation including itself. In either such case, the resolution shall be as detailed in its statement as is required by § 102(a)(2) of this title. Upon the adoption of such a resolution, a certificate certifying the change shall be executed, acknowledged, and filed in accordance with § 103 of this title.

§ 134.   Change of address or name of registered agent.

(a)   A registered agent may change the address of the registered office of the corporation or corporations for which the agent is a registered agent to another address in this State by filing with the Secretary of State a certificate, executed and acknowledged by such registered agent, setting forth the address at which such registered agent has maintained the registered office for each of the corporations for which it is a registered agent, and further certifying to the new address to which each such registered office will be changed on a given day, and at which new address such registered agent will thereafter maintain the registered office for each of the corporations for which it is a registered agent. Thereafter, or until further change of address, as authorized by law, the registered office in this State of each of the corporations for which the agent is a registered agent shall be located at the new address of the registered agent thereof as given in the certificate.

(b)   In the event of a change of name of any person or corporation acting as registered agent in this State, such registered agent shall file with the Secretary of State a certificate, executed and acknowledged by such registered agent, setting forth the new name of such registered agent, the name of such registered agent before it was changed, and the address at which such registered agent has maintained the registered office for each of the corporations for which it acts as a registered agent. A change of name of any person or corporation acting as a registered agent as a result of a merger or consolidation of the registered agent, with or into another person or corporation which succeeds to its assets by operation of law, shall be deemed a change of name for purposes of this section.

§ 135.   Resignation of registered agent coupled with appointment of successor.

The registered agent of 1 or more corporations may resign and appoint a successor registered agent by filing a certificate with the Secretary of State, stating the name and address of the successor agent, in accordance with § 102(a)(2) of this title. There shall be attached to such certificate a statement of each affected corporation ratifying and approving such change of registered agent. Each such statement shall be executed and acknowledged in accordance with § 103 of this title. Upon such filing, the successor registered agent shall become the registered agent of such corporations as have ratified and approved such substitution and the successor registered agent's address, as stated in such certificate, shall become the address of each such corporation's registered office in this State. The Secretary of State shall then issue a certificate that the successor registered agent has become the registered agent of the corporations so ratifying and approving such change and setting out the names of such corporations.

§ 136.   Resignation of registered agent not coupled with appointment of successor.

(a) The registered agent of a corporation, including a corporation which has become void pursuant to § 510 of this title, may resign without appointing a successor by filing a certificate of resignation with the Secretary of State, but such resignation shall not become effective until 30 days after the certificate is filed. The certificate shall be executed and acknowledged by the registered agent, shall contain a statement that written notice of resignation was given to the corporation at least 30 days prior to the filing of the certificate by mailing or delivering such notice to the corporation at its address last known to the registered agent and shall set forth the date of such notice. The certificate shall include such information last provided to the registered agent pursuant to § 132(d) of this title for a communications contact for the affected corporation. Such information regarding the communications contact shall not be deemed public. A certificate filed pursuant to this section must be on the form prescribed by the Secretary of State.

(b) After receipt of the notice of the resignation of its registered agent, provided for in subsection (a) of this section, the corporation for which such registered agent was acting shall obtain and designate a new registered agent to take the place of the registered agent so resigning in the same manner as provided in § 133 of this title for change of registered agent. If such corporation, being a corporation of this State, fails to obtain and designate a new registered agent as aforesaid prior to the expiration of the period of 30 days after the filing by the registered agent of the certificate of resignation, the Secretary of State shall declare the charter of such corporation forfeited. If such corporation, being a foreign corporation, fails to obtain and designate a new registered agent as aforesaid prior to the expiration of the period of 30 days after the filing by the registered agent of the certificate of resignation, the Secretary of State shall forfeit its authority to do business in this State.

(c) After the resignation of the registered agent shall have become effective as provided in this section and if no new registered agent shall have been obtained and designated in the time and manner aforesaid, service of legal process against the corporation for which the resigned registered agent had been acting shall thereafter be upon the Secretary of State in accordance with § 321 of this title.

SUBCHAPTER IV. DIRECTORS AND OFFICERS

§ 141. Board of directors; powers; number, qualifications, terms and quorum; committees; classes of directors; nonstock corporations; reliance upon books; action without meeting; removal.

(a) The business and affairs of every corporation organized under this chapter shall be managed by or under the direction of a board of directors, except as may be otherwise provided in this chapter or in its certificate of incorporation. If any such provision is made in the certificate of incorporation, the powers and duties conferred or imposed upon the board of directors by this chapter shall be exercised or performed to such extent and by such person or persons as shall be provided in the certificate of incorporation.

(b) The board of directors of a corporation shall consist of 1 or more members, each of whom shall be a natural person. The number of directors shall be fixed by, or in the manner provided in, the bylaws, unless the certificate of incorporation fixes the number of directors, in which case a change in the number of directors shall be made only by amendment of the certificate. Directors need not be stockholders unless so required by the certificate of incorporation or the bylaws. The certificate of incorporation or bylaws may prescribe other qualifications for directors. Each director shall hold office until such director's successor is elected and qualified or until such director's earlier resignation or removal. Any director may resign at any time upon notice given in writing or by electronic transmission to the corporation. A resignation is effective when the resignation is delivered unless the resignation specifies a later effective date or an effective date determined upon the happening of an event or events. A resignation which is conditioned upon the director failing to receive a specified vote for reelection as a director may provide that it is irrevocable. A majority of the total number of directors shall constitute a quorum for the transaction of business unless the certificate of incorporation or the bylaws require a greater number. Unless the certificate of incorporation provides otherwise, the bylaws may provide that a number less than a majority shall constitute a quorum which in no case shall be less than ⅓ of the total number of directors. The vote of the majority of the directors present at a meeting at which a quorum is present shall be the act of the board of directors unless the certificate of incorporation or the bylaws shall require a vote of a greater number.

(c)(1) All corporations incorporated prior to July 1, 1996, shall be governed by this paragraph (c)(1) of this section, provided that any such corporation may by a resolution adopted by a majority of the whole board elect to be governed by paragraph (c)(2) of this section, in which case this paragraph (c)(1) of this section shall not apply to such corporation. All corporations incorporated on or after July 1, 1996, shall be governed by paragraph (c)(2) of this section. The board of directors may, by resolution passed by a majority of the whole board, designate 1 or more committees, each committee to consist of 1 or more of the directors of the corporation. The board may designate 1 or more directors as alternate members of any committee, who may replace any absent or disqualified member at any meeting of the committee. The bylaws may provide that in the absence or disqualification of a member of a committee, the member or members present at any meeting and not disqualified from voting, whether or not the member or members present constitute a quorum, may unanimously appoint another member of the board of directors to act at the meeting in the place of any such absent or disqualified member. Any such committee, to the extent provided in the resolution of the board of directors, or in the bylaws of the corporation, shall have and may exercise all the powers and authority of the board of directors in the management of the business and affairs of the corporation, and may authorize the seal of the corporation to be affixed to all papers which may require it; but no such committee shall have the power or authority in reference to amending the certificate of incorporation (except that a committee may, to the extent authorized in the resolution or resolutions providing for the issuance of shares of stock adopted by the board of directors as provided in § 151(a) of this title, fix the designations and any of the preferences or rights of such shares relating to dividends, redemption, dissolution, any distribution of assets of the corporation or the conversion into, or the exchange of such shares for, shares of any other class or classes or any other series of the same or any other class or classes of stock of the corporation or fix the number of shares of any series of stock or authorize the increase or decrease of the shares of any series), adopting an agreement of merger or consolidation under § 251, § 252, § 254, § 255, § 256, § 257, § 258, § 263 or § 264 of this title, recommending to the stockholders the sale, lease or exchange of all or substantially all of the corporation's property and assets, recommending to the stockholders a dissolution of the corporation or a revocation of a dissolution, or amending the bylaws of the corporation; and, unless the resolution, bylaws or certificate of incorporation expressly so provides, no such committee shall have the power or authority to declare a dividend, to authorize the issuance of stock or to adopt a certificate of ownership and merger pursuant to § 253 of this title.

(2) The board of directors may designate 1 or more committees, each committee to consist of 1 or more of the directors of the corporation. The board may designate 1 or more directors as alternate members of any committee, who may replace any absent or disqualified member at any meeting of the committee. The bylaws may provide that in the absence or disqualification of a member of a committee, the member or members present at any meeting and not disqualified from voting, whether or not such member or members constitute a quorum, may unanimously appoint another member of the board of directors to act at the meeting in the place of any such absent or disqualified member. Any such committee, to the extent provided in the resolution of the board of directors, or in the bylaws of the corporation, shall have and may exercise all the powers and authority of the board of directors in the management of the business and affairs of the corporation, and may authorize the seal of the corporation to be affixed to all papers which may require it; but no such committee shall have the power or authority in reference to the following matter: (i) approving or adopting, or recommending to the stockholders, any action or matter (other than the election or removal of directors) expressly required by this chapter to be submitted to stockholders for approval or (ii) adopting, amending or repealing any bylaw of the corporation.

(3) Unless otherwise provided in the certificate of incorporation, the bylaws or the resolution of the board of directors designating the committee, a committee may create 1 or more subcommittees, each subcommittee to consist of 1 or more members of the committee, and delegate to a subcommittee any or all of the powers and authority of the committee. Except for references to committees and members of committees in subsection (c) of this section, every reference in this chapter to a committee of the board of directors or a member of a committee shall be deemed to include a reference to a subcommittee or member of a subcommittee.

(4) A majority of the directors then serving on a committee of the board of directors or on a subcommittee of a committee shall constitute a quorum for the transaction of business by the committee or subcommittee, unless the certificate of incorporation, the bylaws, a resolution of the board of directors or a resolution of a committee that created the subcommittee requires a greater or lesser number, provided that in no case shall a quorum be less than ⅓ of the directors then serving on the committee or subcommittee. The vote of the majority of the members of a committee or subcommittee present at a meeting at which a quorum is present shall be the act of the committee or subcommittee, unless the certificate of incorporation, the bylaws, a resolution of the board of directors or a resolution of a committee that created the subcommittee requires a greater number.

(d) The directors of any corporation organized under this chapter may, by the certificate of incorporation or by an initial bylaw, or by a bylaw adopted by a vote of the stockholders, be divided into 1, 2 or 3 classes; the term of office of those of the first class to expire at the first annual meeting held after such classification becomes effective; of the second class 1 year thereafter; of the third class 2 years thereafter; and at each annual election held after such classification becomes effective, directors shall be chosen for a full term, as the case may be, to succeed those whose terms expire. The certificate of incorporation or bylaw provision dividing the directors into classes may authorize the board of directors to assign members of the board already in office to such classes at the time such classification becomes effective. The certificate of incorporation may confer upon holders of any class or series of stock the right to elect 1 or more directors who shall serve for such term, and have such voting powers as shall be stated in the certificate of incorporation. The terms of office and voting powers of the directors elected separately by the holders of any class or series of stock may be greater than or less than those of any other director or class of directors. In addition, the certificate of incorporation may confer upon 1 or more directors, whether or not elected separately by the holders of any class or series of stock, voting powers greater than or less than those of other directors. Any such provision conferring greater or lesser voting power shall apply to voting in any committee, unless otherwise provided in the certificate of incorporation or bylaws. If the certificate of incorporation provides that 1 or more directors shall have more or less than 1 vote per director on any matter, every reference in this chapter to a majority or other proportion of the directors shall refer to a majority or other proportion of the votes of the directors.

(e)   A member of the board of directors, or a member of any committee designated by the board of directors, shall, in the performance of such member's duties, be fully protected in relying in good faith upon the records of the corporation and upon such information, opinions, reports or statements presented to the corporation by any of the corporation's officers or employees, or committees of the board of directors, or by any other person as to matters the member reasonably believes are within such other person's professional or expert competence and who has been selected with reasonable care by or on behalf of the corporation.

(f)   Unless otherwise restricted by the certificate of incorporation or bylaws, any action required or permitted to be taken at any meeting of the board of directors or of any committee thereof may be taken without a meeting if all members of the board or committee, as the case may be, consent thereto in writing, or by electronic transmission. Any person (whether or not then a director) may provide, whether through instruction to an agent or otherwise, that a consent to action will be effective at a future time (including a time determined upon the happening of an event), no later than 60 days after such instruction is given or such provision is made and such consent shall be deemed to have been given for purposes of this subsection at such effective time so long as such person is then a director and did not revoke the consent prior to such time. Any such consent shall be revocable prior to its becoming effective. After an action is taken, the consent or consents relating thereto shall be filed with the minutes of the proceedings of the board of directors, or the committee thereof, in the same paper or electronic form as the minutes are maintained.

(g)   Unless otherwise restricted by the certificate of incorporation or bylaws, the board of directors of any corporation organized under this chapter may hold its meetings, and have an office or offices, outside of this State.

(h)   Unless otherwise restricted by the certificate of incorporation or bylaws, the board of directors shall have the authority to fix the compensation of directors.

(i)   Unless otherwise restricted by the certificate of incorporation or bylaws, members of the board of directors of any corporation, or any committee designated by the board, may participate in a meeting of such board, or committee by means of conference telephone or other communications equipment by means of which all persons participating in the meeting can hear each other, and participation in a meeting pursuant to this subsection shall constitute presence in person at the meeting.

(j)   The certificate of incorporation of any nonstock corporation may provide that less than ⅓ of the members of the governing body may constitute a quorum thereof and may otherwise provide that the business and affairs of the corporation shall be managed in a manner different from that provided in this section. Except as may be otherwise provided by the certificate of incorporation, this section shall apply to such a corporation, and when so applied, all references to the board of directors, to members thereof, and to stockholders shall be deemed to refer to the governing body of the corporation, the members thereof and the members of the corporation, respectively; and all references to stock, capital stock, or shares thereof shall be deemed to refer to memberships of a nonprofit nonstock corporation and to membership interests of any other nonstock corporation.

(k)   Any director or the entire board of directors may be removed, with or without cause, by the holders of a majority of the shares then entitled to vote at an election of directors, except as follows:

(1)   Unless the certificate of incorporation otherwise provides, in the case of a corporation whose board is classified as provided in subsection (d) of this section, stockholders may effect such removal only for cause; or

(2)   In the case of a corporation having cumulative voting, if less than the entire board is to be removed, no director may be removed without cause if the votes cast against such director's removal would be sufficient to elect such director if then cumulatively voted at an election of the entire board of directors, or, if there be classes of directors, at an election of the class of directors of which such director is a part.

Whenever the holders of any class or series are entitled to elect 1 or more directors by the certificate of incorporation, this subsection shall apply, in respect to the removal without cause of a director or directors so elected, to the vote of the holders of the outstanding shares of that class or series and not to the vote of the outstanding shares as a whole.

§ 142.   Officers; titles, duties, selection, term; failure to elect; vacancies.

(a)   Every corporation organized under this chapter shall have such officers with such titles and duties as shall be stated in the bylaws or in a resolution of the board of directors which is not inconsistent with the bylaws and as may be necessary to enable it to sign instruments and stock certificates which comply with §§ 103(a)(2) and 158 of this title. One of the officers shall have the duty to record the proceedings of the meetings of the stockholders and directors in a book to be kept for that purpose. Any number of offices may be held by the same person unless the certificate of incorporation or bylaws otherwise provide.

(b)   Officers shall be chosen in such manner and shall hold their offices for such terms as are prescribed by the bylaws or determined by the board of directors or other governing body. Each officer shall hold office until such officer's successor is elected and qualified or until such officer's earlier resignation or removal. Any officer may resign at any time upon written notice to the corporation.

(c)   The corporation may secure the fidelity of any or all of its officers or agents by bond or otherwise.

(d)   A failure to elect officers shall not dissolve or otherwise affect the corporation.

(e)   Any vacancy occurring in any office of the corporation by death, resignation, removal or otherwise, shall be filled as the bylaws provide. In the absence of such provision, the vacancy shall be filled by the board of directors or other governing body.

§ 143.   Loans to employees and officers; guaranty of obligations of employees and officers.

Any corporation may lend money to, or guarantee any obligation of, or otherwise assist any officer or other employee of the corporation or of its subsidiary, including any officer or employee who is a director of the corporation or its subsidiary, whenever, in the judgment of the directors, such loan, guaranty or assistance may reasonably be expected to benefit the corporation. The loan, guaranty or other assistance may be with or without interest, and may be unsecured, or secured in such manner as the board of directors shall approve, including, without limitation, a pledge of shares of stock of the corporation. Nothing in this section contained shall be deemed to deny, limit or restrict the powers of guaranty or warranty of any corporation at common law or under any statute.

§ 144.   Interested directors; quorum.

(a)   No contract or transaction between a corporation and 1 or more of its directors or officers, or between a corporation and any other corporation, partnership, association, or other organization in which 1 or more of its directors or officers, are directors or officers, or have a financial interest, shall be void or voidable solely for this reason, or solely because the director or officer is present at or participates in the meeting of the board or committee which authorizes the contract or transaction, or solely because any such director's or officer's votes are counted for such purpose, if:

(1)   The material facts as to the director's or officer's relationship or interest and as to the contract or transaction are disclosed or are known to the board of directors or the committee, and the board or committee in good faith authorizes the contract or transaction by the affirmative votes of a majority of the disinterested directors, even though the disinterested directors be less than a quorum; or

(2)   The material facts as to the director's or officer's relationship or interest and as to the contract or transaction are disclosed or are known to the stockholders entitled to vote thereon, and the contract or transaction is specifically approved in good faith by vote of the stockholders; or

(3)   The contract or transaction is fair as to the corporation as of the time it is authorized, approved or ratified, by the board of directors, a committee or the stockholders.

(b)   Common or interested directors may be counted in determining the presence of a quorum at a meeting of the board of directors or of a committee which authorizes the contract or transaction.

§ 145.   Indemnification of officers, directors, employees and agents; insurance.

(a)   A corporation shall have power to indemnify any person who was or is a party or is threatened to be made a party to any threatened, pending or completed action, suit or proceeding, whether civil, criminal, administrative or investigative (other than an action by or in the right of the corporation) by reason of the fact that the person is or was a director, officer, employee or agent of the corporation, or is or was serving at the request of the corporation as a director, officer, employee or agent of another corporation, partnership, joint venture, trust or other enterprise, against expenses (including attorneys' fees), judgments, fines and amounts paid in settlement actually and reasonably incurred by the person in connection with such action, suit or proceeding if the person acted in good faith and in a manner the person reasonably believed to be in or not opposed to the best interests of the corporation, and, with respect to any criminal action or proceeding, had no reasonable cause to believe the person's conduct was unlawful. The termination of any action, suit or proceeding by judgment, order, settlement, conviction, or upon a plea of nolo contendere or its equivalent, shall not, of itself, create a presumption that the person did not act in good faith and in a manner which the person reasonably believed to be in or not opposed to the best interests of the corporation, and, with respect to any criminal action or proceeding, had reasonable cause to believe that the person's conduct was unlawful.

(b)   A corporation shall have power to indemnify any person who was or is a party or is threatened to be made a party to any threatened, pending or completed action or suit by or in the right of the corporation to procure a judgment in its favor by reason of the fact that the person is or was a director, officer, employee or agent of the corporation, or is or was serving at the request of the corporation as a director, officer, employee or agent of another corporation, partnership, joint venture, trust or other enterprise against expenses (including attorneys' fees) actually and reasonably incurred by the person in connection with the defense or settlement of such action or suit if the person acted in good faith and in a manner the person reasonably believed to be in or not opposed to the best interests of the corporation and except that no indemnification shall be made in respect of any claim, issue or matter as to which such person shall have been adjudged to be liable to the corporation unless and only to the extent that the Court of Chancery or the court in which such action or suit was brought shall determine upon application that, despite the adjudication of liability but in view of all the circumstances of the case, such person is fairly and reasonably entitled to indemnity for such expenses which the Court of Chancery or such other court shall deem proper.

(c)   To the extent that a present or former director or officer of a corporation has been successful on the merits or otherwise in defense of any action, suit or proceeding referred to in subsections (a) and (b) of this section, or in defense of any claim, issue or matter therein, such person shall be indemnified against expenses (including attorneys' fees) actually and reasonably incurred by such person in connection therewith.

(d)　Any indemnification under subsections (a) and (b) of this section (unless ordered by a court) shall be made by the corporation only as authorized in the specific case upon a determination that indemnification of the present or former director, officer, employee or agent is proper in the circumstances because the person has met the applicable standard of conduct set forth in subsections (a) and (b) of this section. Such determination shall be made, with respect to a person who is a director or officer of the corporation at the time of such determination:

(1)　By a majority vote of the directors who are not parties to such action, suit or proceeding, even though less than a quorum; or

(2)　By a committee of such directors designated by majority vote of such directors, even though less than a quorum; or

(3)　If there are no such directors, or if such directors so direct, by independent legal counsel in a written opinion; or

(4)　By the stockholders.

(e)　Expenses (including attorneys' fees) incurred by an officer or director of the corporation in defending any civil, criminal, administrative or investigative action, suit or proceeding may be paid by the corporation in advance of the final disposition of such action, suit or proceeding upon receipt of an undertaking by or on behalf of such director or officer to repay such amount if it shall ultimately be determined that such person is not entitled to be indemnified by the corporation as authorized in this section. Such expenses (including attorneys' fees) incurred by former directors and officers or other employees and agents of the corporation or by persons serving at the request of the corporation as directors, officers, employees or agents of another corporation, partnership, joint venture, trust or other enterprise may be so paid upon such terms and conditions, if any, as the corporation deems appropriate.

(f)　The indemnification and advancement of expenses provided by, or granted pursuant to, the other subsections of this section shall not be deemed exclusive of any other rights to which those seeking indemnification or advancement of expenses may be entitled under any bylaw, agreement, vote of stockholders or disinterested directors or otherwise, both as to action in such person's official capacity and as to action in another capacity while holding such office. A right to indemnification or to advancement of expenses arising under a provision of the certificate of incorporation or a bylaw shall not be eliminated or impaired by an amendment to the certificate of incorporation or the bylaws after the occurrence of the act or omission that is the subject of the civil, criminal, administrative or investigative action, suit or proceeding for which indemnification or advancement of expenses is sought, unless the provision in effect at the time of such act or omission explicitly authorizes such elimination or impairment after such action or omission has occurred.

(g)　A corporation shall have power to purchase and maintain insurance on behalf of any person who is or was a director, officer, employee or agent of the corporation, or is or was serving at the request of the corporation as a director, officer, employee or agent of another corporation, partnership, joint venture, trust or other enterprise against any liability asserted against such person and incurred by such person in any such capacity, or arising out of such person's status as such, whether or not the corporation would have the power to indemnify such person against such liability under this section.

(h)　For purposes of this section, references to "the corporation" shall include, in addition to the resulting corporation, any constituent corporation (including any constituent of a constituent) absorbed in a consolidation or merger which, if its separate existence had continued, would have had power and authority to indemnify its directors, officers, and employees or agents, so that any person who is or was a director, officer, employee or agent of such constituent corporation, or is or was serving at the request of such constituent corporation as a director, officer, employee or agent of another corporation, partnership, joint venture, trust or other enterprise, shall stand in the same position under this section with respect to the resulting or surviving corporation as such person would have with respect to such constituent corporation if its separate existence had continued.

(i)   For purposes of this section, references to "other enterprises" shall include employee benefit plans; references to "fines" shall include any excise taxes assessed on a person with respect to any employee benefit plan; and references to "serving at the request of the corporation" shall include any service as a director, officer, employee or agent of the corporation which imposes duties on, or involves services by, such director, officer, employee or agent with respect to an employee benefit plan, its participants or beneficiaries; and a person who acted in good faith and in a manner such person reasonably believed to be in the interest of the participants and beneficiaries of an employee benefit plan shall be deemed to have acted in a manner "not opposed to the best interests of the corporation" as referred to in this section.

(j)   The indemnification and advancement of expenses provided by, or granted pursuant to, this section shall, unless otherwise provided when authorized or ratified, continue as to a person who has ceased to be a director, officer, employee or agent and shall inure to the benefit of the heirs, executors and administrators of such a person.

(k)   The Court of Chancery is hereby vested with exclusive jurisdiction to hear and determine all actions for advancement of expenses or indemnification brought under this section or under any bylaw, agreement, vote of stockholders or disinterested directors, or otherwise. The Court of Chancery may summarily determine a corporation's obligation to advance expenses (including attorneys' fees).

§ 146.   Submission of matters for stockholder vote.

A corporation may agree to submit a matter to a vote of its stockholders whether or not the board of directors determines at any time subsequent to approving such matter that such matter is no longer advisable and recommends that the stockholders reject or vote against the matter.

SUBCHAPTER V.   STOCK AND DIVIDENDS

§ 151.   Classes and series of stock; redemption; rights.

(a)   Every corporation may issue 1 or more classes of stock or 1 or more series of stock within any class thereof, any or all of which classes may be of stock with par value or stock without par value and which classes or series may have such voting powers, full or limited, or no voting powers, and such designations, preferences and relative, participating, optional or other special rights, and qualifications, limitations or restrictions thereof, as shall be stated and expressed in the certificate of incorporation or of any amendment thereto, or in the resolution or resolutions providing for the issue of such stock adopted by the board of directors pursuant to authority expressly vested in it by the provisions of its certificate of incorporation. Any of the voting powers, designations, preferences, rights and qualifications, limitations or restrictions of any such class or series of stock may be made dependent upon facts ascertainable outside the certificate of incorporation or of any amendment thereto, or outside the resolution or resolutions providing for the issue of such stock adopted by the board of directors pursuant to authority expressly vested in it by its certificate of incorporation, provided that the manner in which such facts shall operate upon the voting powers, designations, preferences, rights and qualifications, limitations or restrictions of such class or series of stock is clearly and expressly set forth in the certificate of incorporation or in the resolution or resolutions providing for the issue of such stock adopted by the board of directors. The term "facts," as used in this subsection, includes, but is not limited to, the occurrence of any event, including a determination or action by any person or body, including the corporation. The power to increase or decrease or otherwise adjust the capital stock as provided in this chapter shall apply to all or any such classes of stock.

(b)   Any stock of any class or series may be made subject to redemption by the corporation at its option or at the option of the holders of such stock or upon the happening of a specified event; provided however, that immediately following any such redemption the corporation shall have outstanding 1 or more shares of 1 or more classes or series of stock, which share, or shares together, shall have full voting powers. Notwithstanding the limitation stated in the foregoing proviso:

(1)　Any stock of a regulated investment company registered under the Investment Company Act of 1940 [15 U.S.C. § 80a–1 et seq.], as heretofore or hereafter amended, may be made subject to redemption by the corporation at its option or at the option of the holders of such stock.

(2)　Any stock of a corporation which holds (directly or indirectly) a license or franchise from a governmental agency to conduct its business or is a member of a national securities exchange, which license, franchise or membership is conditioned upon some or all of the holders of its stock possessing prescribed qualifications, may be made subject to redemption by the corporation to the extent necessary to prevent the loss of such license, franchise or membership or to reinstate it.

Any stock which may be made redeemable under this section may be redeemed for cash, property or rights, including securities of the same or another corporation, at such time or times, price or prices, or rate or rates, and with such adjustments, as shall be stated in the certificate of incorporation or in the resolution or resolutions providing for the issue of such stock adopted by the board of directors pursuant to subsection (a) of this section.

(c)　The holders of preferred or special stock of any class or of any series thereof shall be entitled to receive dividends at such rates, on such conditions and at such times as shall be stated in the certificate of incorporation or in the resolution or resolutions providing for the issue of such stock adopted by the board of directors as hereinabove provided, payable in preference to, or in such relation to, the dividends payable on any other class or classes or of any other series of stock, and cumulative or noncumulative as shall be so stated and expressed. When dividends upon the preferred and special stocks, if any, to the extent of the preference to which such stocks are entitled, shall have been paid or declared and set apart for payment, a dividend on the remaining class or classes or series of stock may then be paid out of the remaining assets of the corporation available for dividends as elsewhere in this chapter provided.

(d)　The holders of the preferred or special stock of any class or of any series thereof shall be entitled to such rights upon the dissolution of, or upon any distribution of the assets of, the corporation as shall be stated in the certificate of incorporation or in the resolution or resolutions providing for the issue of such stock adopted by the board of directors as hereinabove provided.

(e)　Any stock of any class or of any series thereof may be made convertible into, or exchangeable for, at the option of either the holder or the corporation or upon the happening of a specified event, shares of any other class or classes or any other series of the same or any other class or classes of stock of the corporation, at such price or prices or at such rate or rates of exchange and with such adjustments as shall be stated in the certificate of incorporation or in the resolution or resolutions providing for the issue of such stock adopted by the board of directors as hereinabove provided.

(f)　If any corporation shall be authorized to issue more than 1 class of stock or more than 1 series of any class, the powers, designations, preferences and relative, participating, optional, or other special rights of each class of stock or series thereof and the qualifications, limitations or restrictions of such preferences and/or rights shall be set forth in full or summarized on the face or back of the certificate which the corporation shall issue to represent such class or series of stock, provided that, except as otherwise provided in § 202 of this title, in lieu of the foregoing requirements, there may be set forth on the face or back of the certificate which the corporation shall issue to represent such class or series of stock, a statement that the corporation will furnish without charge to each stockholder who so requests the powers, designations, preferences and relative, participating, optional, or other special rights of each class of stock or series thereof and the qualifications, limitations or restrictions of such preferences and/or rights. Within a reasonable time after the issuance or transfer of uncertificated stock, the registered owner thereof shall be given a notice, in writing or by electronic transmission, containing the information required to be set forth or stated on certificates pursuant to this section or § 156, § 202(a), § 218(a) or § 364 of this title or with respect to this section a statement that the corporation will furnish without charge to each stockholder who so requests the powers, designations, preferences and relative participating, optional or other special rights of each class of stock or series thereof and the qualifications, limitations or restrictions of such preferences and/or rights. Except as otherwise expressly provided by law, the rights and obligations of the holders of uncertificated stock and the rights and obligations of the holders of certificates representing stock of the same class and series shall be identical.

(g)   When any corporation desires to issue any shares of stock of any class or of any series of any class of which the powers, designations, preferences and relative, participating, optional or other rights, if any, or the qualifications, limitations or restrictions thereof, if any, shall not have been set forth in the certificate of incorporation or in any amendment thereto but shall be provided for in a resolution or resolutions adopted by the board of directors pursuant to authority expressly vested in it by the certificate of incorporation or any amendment thereto, a certificate of designations setting forth a copy of such resolution or resolutions and the number of shares of stock of such class or series as to which the resolution or resolutions apply shall be executed, acknowledged, filed and shall become effective, in accordance with § 103 of this title. Unless otherwise provided in any such resolution or resolutions, the number of shares of stock of any such series to which such resolution or resolutions apply may be increased (but not above the total number of authorized shares of the class) or decreased (but not below the number of shares thereof then outstanding) by a certificate likewise executed, acknowledged and filed setting forth a statement that a specified increase or decrease therein had been authorized and directed by a resolution or resolutions likewise adopted by the board of directors. In case the number of such shares shall be decreased the number of shares so specified in the certificate shall resume the status which they had prior to the adoption of the first resolution or resolutions. When no shares of any such class or series are outstanding, either because none were issued or because no issued shares of any such class or series remain outstanding, a certificate setting forth a resolution or resolutions adopted by the board of directors that none of the authorized shares of such class or series are outstanding, and that none will be issued subject to the certificate of designations previously filed with respect to such class or series, may be executed, acknowledged and filed in accordance with § 103 of this title and, when such certificate becomes effective, it shall have the effect of eliminating from the certificate of incorporation all matters set forth in the certificate of designations with respect to such class or series of stock. Unless otherwise provided in the certificate of incorporation, if no shares of stock have been issued of a class or series of stock established by a resolution of the board of directors, the voting powers, designations, preferences and relative, participating, optional or other rights, if any, or the qualifications, limitations or restrictions thereof, may be amended by a resolution or resolutions adopted by the board of directors. A certificate which:

(1)   States that no shares of the class or series have been issued;

(2)   Sets forth a copy of the resolution or resolutions; and

(3)   If the designation of the class or series is being changed, indicates the original designation and the new designation,

shall be executed, acknowledged and filed and shall become effective, in accordance with § 103 of this title. When any certificate filed under this subsection becomes effective, it shall have the effect of amending the certificate of incorporation; except that neither the filing of such certificate nor the filing of a restated certificate of incorporation pursuant to § 245 of this title shall prohibit the board of directors from subsequently adopting such resolutions as authorized by this subsection.

§ 152.   Issuance of stock; lawful consideration; fully paid stock.

The consideration, as determined pursuant to § 153(a) and (b) of this title, for subscriptions to, or the purchase of, the capital stock to be issued by a corporation shall be paid in such form and in such manner as the board of directors shall determine. The board of directors may authorize capital stock to be issued for consideration consisting of cash, any tangible or intangible property or any benefit to the corporation, or any combination thereof. The resolution authorizing the issuance of capital stock may provide that any stock to be issued pursuant to such resolution may be issued in 1 or more transactions in such numbers and at such times as are set forth in or determined by or in the manner set forth in the resolution, which may include a determination or action by any person or body, including the corporation, provided the resolution fixes a maximum number of shares that may be issued pursuant to such resolution, a time period during which such shares may be issued and a minimum amount of consideration for which such shares may be issued. The board of directors may determine the amount of consideration for which shares may be issued by setting a minimum amount of consideration or approving a formula by which the amount or minimum amount of consideration is determined. The formula may include or be made dependent upon facts ascertainable outside the formula, provided the manner in which such facts shall operate upon the formula is clearly and expressly set forth in the formula or in the resolution approving the formula. In the absence of actual fraud in the transaction, the judgment of the directors as to the value of such consideration shall be conclusive. The capital stock so issued shall be deemed to be fully paid and nonassessable stock upon receipt by the corporation of such consideration; provided, however, nothing contained herein shall prevent the board of directors from issuing partly paid shares under § 156 of this title.

§ 153.   Consideration for stock.

(a)   Shares of stock with par value may be issued for such consideration, having a value not less than the par value thereof, as determined from time to time by the board of directors, or by the stockholders if the certificate of incorporation so provides.

(b)   Shares of stock without par value may be issued for such consideration as is determined from time to time by the board of directors, or by the stockholders if the certificate of incorporation so provides.

(c)   Treasury shares may be disposed of by the corporation for such consideration as may be determined from time to time by the board of directors, or by the stockholders if the certificate of incorporation so provides.

(d)   If the certificate of incorporation reserves to the stockholders the right to determine the consideration for the issue of any shares, the stockholders shall, unless the certificate requires a greater vote, do so by a vote of a majority of the outstanding stock entitled to vote thereon.

§ 154.   Determination of amount of capital; capital, surplus and net assets defined.

Any corporation may, by resolution of its board of directors, determine that only a part of the consideration which shall be received by the corporation for any of the shares of its capital stock which it shall issue from time to time shall be capital; but, in case any of the shares issued shall be shares having a par value, the amount of the part of such consideration so determined to be capital shall be in excess of the aggregate par value of the shares issued for such consideration having a par value, unless all the shares issued shall be shares having a par value, in which case the amount of the part of such consideration so determined to be capital need be only equal to the aggregate par value of such shares. In each such case the board of directors shall specify in dollars the part of such consideration which shall be capital. If the board of directors shall not have determined (1) at the time of issue of any shares of the capital stock of the corporation issued for cash or (2) within 60 days after the issue of any shares of the capital stock of the corporation issued for consideration other than cash what part of the consideration for such shares shall be capital, the capital of the corporation in respect of such shares shall be an amount equal to the aggregate par value of such shares having a par value, plus the amount of the consideration for such shares without par value. The amount of the consideration so determined to be capital in respect of any shares without par value shall be the stated capital of such shares. The capital of the corporation may be increased from time to time by resolution of the board of directors directing that a portion of the net assets of the corporation in excess of the amount so determined to be capital be transferred to the capital account. The board of directors may direct that the portion of such net assets so transferred shall be treated as capital in respect of any shares of the corporation of any designated class or classes. The excess, if any, at any given time, of the net assets of the corporation over the amount so determined to be capital shall be surplus. Net assets means the amount by which total assets exceed total liabilities. Capital and surplus are not liabilities for this purpose. Notwithstanding anything in this section to the contrary, for purposes of this section and §§ 160 and 170 of this title, the capital of any nonstock corporation shall be deemed to be zero.

§ 155. Fractions of shares.

A corporation may, but shall not be required to, issue fractions of a share. If it does not issue fractions of a share, it shall (1) arrange for the disposition of fractional interests by those entitled thereto, (2) pay in cash the fair value of fractions of a share as of the time when those entitled to receive such fractions are determined or (3) issue scrip or warrants in registered form (either represented by a certificate or uncertificated) or in bearer form (represented by a certificate) which shall entitle the holder to receive a full share upon the surrender of such scrip or warrants aggregating a full share. A certificate for a fractional share or an uncertificated fractional share shall, but scrip or warrants shall not unless otherwise provided therein, entitle the holder to exercise voting rights, to receive dividends thereon and to participate in any of the assets of the corporation in the event of liquidation. The board of directors may cause scrip or warrants to be issued subject to the conditions that they shall become void if not exchanged for certificates representing the full shares or uncertificated full shares before a specified date, or subject to the conditions that the shares for which scrip or warrants are exchangeable may be sold by the corporation and the proceeds thereof distributed to the holders of scrip or warrants, or subject to any other conditions which the board of directors may impose.

§ 156. Partly paid shares.

Any corporation may issue the whole or any part of its shares as partly paid and subject to call for the remainder of the consideration to be paid therefor. Upon the face or back of each stock certificate issued to represent any such partly paid shares, or upon the books and records of the corporation in the case of uncertificated partly paid shares, the total amount of the consideration to be paid therefor and the amount paid thereon shall be stated. Upon the declaration of any dividend on fully paid shares, the corporation shall declare a dividend upon partly paid shares of the same class, but only upon the basis of the percentage of the consideration actually paid thereon.

§ 157. Rights and options respecting stock.

(a) Subject to any provisions in the certificate of incorporation, every corporation may create and issue, whether or not in connection with the issue and sale of any shares of stock or other securities of the corporation, rights or options entitling the holders thereof to acquire from the corporation any shares of its capital stock of any class or classes, such rights or options to be evidenced by or in such instrument or instruments as shall be approved by the board of directors.

(b) The terms upon which, including the time or times which may be limited or unlimited in duration, at or within which, and the consideration (including a formula by which such consideration may be determined) for which any such shares may be acquired from the corporation upon the exercise of any such right or option, shall be such as shall be stated in the certificate of incorporation, or in a resolution adopted by the board of directors providing for the creation and issue of such rights or options, and, in every case, shall be set forth or incorporated by reference in the instrument or instruments evidencing such rights or options. A formula by which such consideration may be determined may include or be made dependent upon facts ascertainable outside the formula, provided the manner in which such facts shall operate upon the formula is clearly and expressly set forth in the formula or in the resolution approving the formula. In the absence of actual fraud in the transaction, the judgment of the directors as to the consideration for the issuance of such rights or options and the sufficiency thereof shall be conclusive.

(c) The board of directors may, by a resolution adopted by the board, authorize 1 or more officers of the corporation to do 1 or both of the following: (i) designate officers and employees of the corporation or of any of its subsidiaries to be recipients of such rights or options created by the corporation, and (ii) determine the number of such rights or options to be received by such officers and employees; provided, however, that the resolution so authorizing such officer or officers shall specify the total number of rights or options such officer or officers may so award. The board of directors may not authorize an officer to designate himself or herself as a recipient of any such rights or options.

(d)   In case the shares of stock of the corporation to be issued upon the exercise of such rights or options shall be shares having a par value, the consideration so to be received therefor shall have a value not less than the par value thereof. In case the shares of stock so to be issued shall be shares of stock without par value, the consideration therefor shall be determined in the manner provided in § 153 of this title.

§ 158.   Stock certificates; uncertificated shares.

The shares of a corporation shall be represented by certificates, provided that the board of directors of the corporation may provide by resolution or resolutions that some or all of any or all classes or series of its stock shall be uncertificated shares. Any such resolution shall not apply to shares represented by a certificate until such certificate is surrendered to the corporation. Every holder of stock represented by certificates shall be entitled to have a certificate signed by, or in the name of, the corporation by any 2 authorized officers of the corporation representing the number of shares registered in certificate form. Any or all the signatures on the certificate may be a facsimile. In case any officer, transfer agent or registrar who has signed or whose facsimile signature has been placed upon a certificate shall have ceased to be such officer, transfer agent or registrar before such certificate is issued, it may be issued by the corporation with the same effect as if such person were such officer, transfer agent or registrar at the date of issue. A corporation shall not have power to issue a certificate in bearer form.

§ 159.   Shares of stock; personal property, transfer and taxation.

The shares of stock in every corporation shall be deemed personal property and transferable as provided in Article 8 of subtitle I of Title 6. No stock or bonds issued by any corporation organized under this chapter shall be taxed by this State when the same shall be owned by nonresidents of this State, or by foreign corporations. Whenever any transfer of shares shall be made for collateral security, and not absolutely, it shall be so expressed in the entry of transfer if, when the certificates are presented to the corporation for transfer or uncertificated shares are requested to be transferred, both the transferor and transferee request the corporation to do so.

§ 160.   Corporation's powers respecting ownership, voting, etc., of its own stock; rights of stock called for redemption.

(a)   Every corporation may purchase, redeem, receive, take or otherwise acquire, own and hold, sell, lend, exchange, transfer or otherwise dispose of, pledge, use and otherwise deal in and with its own shares; provided, however, that no corporation shall:

(1)   Purchase or redeem its own shares of capital stock for cash or other property when the capital of the corporation is impaired or when such purchase or redemption would cause any impairment of the capital of the corporation, except that a corporation other than a nonstock corporation may purchase or redeem out of capital any of its own shares which are entitled upon any distribution of its assets, whether by dividend or in liquidation, to a preference over another class or series of its stock, or, if no shares entitled to such a preference are outstanding, any of its own shares, if such shares will be retired upon their acquisition and the capital of the corporation reduced in accordance with §§ 243 and 244 of this title. Nothing in this subsection shall invalidate or otherwise affect a note, debenture or other obligation of a corporation given by it as consideration for its acquisition by purchase, redemption or exchange of its shares of stock if at the time such note, debenture or obligation was delivered by the corporation its capital was not then impaired or did not thereby become impaired;

(2)   Purchase, for more than the price at which they may then be redeemed, any of its shares which are redeemable at the option of the corporation; or

(3)   a.   In the case of a corporation other than a nonstock corporation, redeem any of its shares, unless their redemption is authorized by § 151(b) of this title and then only in accordance with such section and the certificate of incorporation, or

b.   In the case of a nonstock corporation, redeem any of its membership interests, unless their redemption is authorized by the certificate of incorporation and then only in accordance with the certificate of incorporation.

(b)   Nothing in this section limits or affects a corporation's right to resell any of its shares theretofore purchased or redeemed out of surplus and which have not been retired, for such consideration as shall be fixed by the board of directors.

(c)   Shares of its own capital stock belonging to the corporation or to another corporation, if a majority of the shares entitled to vote in the election of directors of such other corporation is held, directly or indirectly, by the corporation, shall neither be entitled to vote nor be counted for quorum purposes. Nothing in this section shall be construed as limiting the right of any corporation to vote stock, including but not limited to its own stock, held by it in a fiduciary capacity.

(d)   Shares which have been called for redemption shall not be deemed to be outstanding shares for the purpose of voting or determining the total number of shares entitled to vote on any matter on and after the date on which notice of redemption has been sent to holders thereof and a sum sufficient to redeem such shares has been irrevocably deposited or set aside to pay the redemption price to the holders of the shares upon surrender of certificates therefor.

§ 161.   Issuance of additional stock; when and by whom.

The directors may, at any time and from time to time, if all of the shares of capital stock which the corporation is authorized by its certificate of incorporation to issue have not been issued, subscribed for, or otherwise committed to be issued, issue or take subscriptions for additional shares of its capital stock up to the amount authorized in its certificate of incorporation.

§ 162.   Liability of stockholder or subscriber for stock not paid in full.

(a)   When the whole of the consideration payable for shares of a corporation has not been paid in, and the assets shall be insufficient to satisfy the claims of its creditors, each holder of or subscriber for such shares shall be bound to pay on each share held or subscribed for by such holder or subscriber the sum necessary to complete the amount of the unpaid balance of the consideration for which such shares were issued or are to be issued by the corporation.

(b)   The amounts which shall be payable as provided in subsection (a) of this section may be recovered as provided in § 325 of this title, after a writ of execution against the corporation has been returned unsatisfied as provided in said § 325.

(c)   Any person becoming an assignee or transferee of shares or of a subscription for shares in good faith and without knowledge or notice that the full consideration therefor has not been paid shall not be personally liable for any unpaid portion of such consideration, but the transferor shall remain liable therefor.

(d)   No person holding shares in any corporation as collateral security shall be personally liable as a stockholder but the person pledging such shares shall be considered the holder thereof and shall be so liable. No executor, administrator, guardian, trustee or other fiduciary shall be personally liable as a stockholder, but the estate or funds held by such executor, administrator, guardian, trustee or other fiduciary in such fiduciary capacity shall be liable.

(e)   No liability under this section or under § 325 of this title shall be asserted more than 6 years after the issuance of the stock or the date of the subscription upon which the assessment is sought.

(f)   In any action by a receiver or trustee of an insolvent corporation or by a judgment creditor to obtain an assessment under this section, any stockholder or subscriber for stock of the insolvent corporation may appear and contest the claim or claims of such receiver or trustee.

§ 163.   Payment for stock not paid in full.

The capital stock of a corporation shall be paid for in such amounts and at such times as the directors may require. The directors may, from time to time, demand payment, in respect of each share of stock not fully paid, of such sum of money as the necessities of the business may, in the judgment of the board of directors, require, not exceeding in the whole the balance remaining unpaid on said stock, and such sum so demanded shall be paid to the corporation at such times and by such installments as the directors shall direct. The directors shall give notice of the time and place of such payments, which notice shall be given at least 30 days before the time for such payment, to each holder of or subscriber for stock which is not fully paid at such holder's or subscriber's last known address.

§ 164.   Failure to pay for stock; remedies.

When any stockholder fails to pay any installment or call upon such stockholder's stock which may have been properly demanded by the directors, at the time when such payment is due, the directors may collect the amount of any such installment or call or any balance thereof remaining unpaid, from the said stockholder by an action at law, or they shall sell at public sale such part of the shares of such delinquent stockholder as will pay all demands then due from such stockholder with interest and all incidental expenses, and shall transfer the shares so sold to the purchaser, who shall be entitled to a certificate therefor.

Notice of the time and place of such sale and of the sum due on each share shall be given by advertisement at least 1 week before the sale, in a newspaper of the county in this State where such corporation's registered office is located, and such notice shall be mailed by the corporation to such delinquent stockholder at such stockholder's last known post-office address, at least 20 days before such sale.

If no bidder can be had to pay the amount due on the stock, and if the amount is not collected by an action at law, which may be brought within the county where the corporation has its registered office, within 1 year from the date of the bringing of such action at law, the said stock and the amount previously paid in by the delinquent stockholder on the stock shall be forfeited to the corporation.

§ 165.   Revocability of preincorporation subscriptions.

Unless otherwise provided by the terms of the subscription, a subscription for stock of a corporation to be formed shall be irrevocable, except with the consent of all other subscribers or the corporation, for a period of 6 months from its date.

§ 166.   Formalities required of stock subscriptions.

A subscription for stock of a corporation, whether made before or after the formation of a corporation, shall not be enforceable against a subscriber, unless in writing and signed by the subscriber or by such subscriber's agent.

§ 167.   Lost, stolen or destroyed stock certificates; issuance of new certificate or uncertificated shares.

A corporation may issue a new certificate of stock or uncertificated shares in place of any certificate theretofore issued by it, alleged to have been lost, stolen or destroyed, and the corporation may require the owner of the lost, stolen or destroyed certificate, or such owner's legal representative to give the corporation a bond sufficient to indemnify it against any claim that may be made against it on account of the alleged loss, theft or destruction of any such certificate or the issuance of such new certificate or uncertificated shares.

§ 168.   Judicial proceedings to compel issuance of new certificate or uncertificated shares.

(a)   If a corporation refuses to issue new uncertificated shares or a new certificate of stock in place of a certificate theretofore issued by it, or by any corporation of which it is the lawful successor, alleged to have been lost, stolen or destroyed, the owner of the lost, stolen or destroyed certificate or such owner's legal representatives may apply to the Court of Chancery for an order requiring the corporation to show cause why it should not issue new uncertificated shares or a new certificate of stock in place of the certificate so lost, stolen or destroyed. Such application shall be by a complaint which shall state the name of the corporation, the number and date of the certificate, if known or ascertainable by the plaintiff, the number of shares of stock represented thereby and to whom issued, and a statement of the circumstances attending such loss, theft or destruction. Thereupon the court shall make an order requiring the corporation to show cause at a time and place therein designated, why it should not issue new uncertificated shares or a new certificate of stock in place of the one described in the complaint. A copy of the complaint and order shall be served upon the corporation at least 5 days before the time designated in the order.

(b)   If, upon hearing, the court is satisfied that the plaintiff is the lawful owner of the number of shares of capital stock, or any part thereof, described in the complaint, and that the certificate therefor has been lost, stolen or destroyed, and no sufficient cause has been shown why new uncertificated shares or a new certificate should not be issued in place thereof, it shall make an order requiring the corporation to issue and deliver to the plaintiff new uncertificated shares or a new certificate for such shares. In its order the court shall direct that, prior to the issuance and delivery to the plaintiff of such new uncertificated shares or a new certificate, the plaintiff give the corporation a bond in such form and with such security as to the court appears sufficient to indemnify the corporation against any claim that may be made against it on account of the alleged loss, theft or destruction of any such certificate or the issuance of such new uncertificated shares or new certificate. No corporation which has issued uncertificated shares or a certificate pursuant to an order of the court entered hereunder shall be liable in an amount in excess of the amount specified in such bond.

§ 169.   Situs of ownership of stock.

For all purposes of title, action, attachment, garnishment and jurisdiction of all courts held in this State, but not for the purpose of taxation, the situs of the ownership of the capital stock of all corporations existing under the laws of this State, whether organized under this chapter or otherwise, shall be regarded as in this State.

§ 170.   Dividends; payment; wasting asset corporations.

(a)   The directors of every corporation, subject to any restrictions contained in its certificate of incorporation, may declare and pay dividends upon the shares of its capital stock either:

(1)   Out of its surplus, as defined in and computed in accordance with §§ 154 and 244 of this title; or

(2)   In case there shall be no such surplus, out of its net profits for the fiscal year in which the dividend is declared and/or the preceding fiscal year.

If the capital of the corporation, computed in accordance with §§ 154 and 244 of this title, shall have been diminished by depreciation in the value of its property, or by losses, or otherwise, to an amount less than the aggregate amount of the capital represented by the issued and outstanding stock of all classes having a preference upon the distribution of assets, the directors of such corporation shall not declare and pay out of such net profits any dividends upon any shares of any classes of its capital stock until the deficiency in the amount of capital represented by the issued and outstanding stock of all classes having a preference upon the distribution of assets shall have been repaired. Nothing in this subsection shall invalidate or otherwise affect a note, debenture or other obligation of the corporation paid by it as a dividend on shares of its stock, or any payment made thereon, if at the time such note, debenture or obligation was delivered by the corporation, the corporation had either surplus or net profits as provided in (a)(1) or (2) of this section from which the dividend could lawfully have been paid.

(b)   Subject to any restrictions contained in its certificate of incorporation, the directors of any corporation engaged in the exploitation of wasting assets (including but not limited to a corporation engaged in the exploitation of natural resources or other wasting assets, including patents, or engaged primarily in the liquidation of specific assets) may determine the net profits derived from the exploitation of such wasting assets or the net proceeds derived from such liquidation without taking into consideration the depletion of such assets resulting from lapse of time, consumption, liquidation or exploitation of such assets.

§ 171.   Special purpose reserves.

The directors of a corporation may set apart out of any of the funds of the corporation available for dividends a reserve or reserves for any proper purpose and may abolish any such reserve.

§ 172.   Liability of directors and committee members as to dividends or stock redemption.

A member of the board of directors, or a member of any committee designated by the board of directors, shall be fully protected in relying in good faith upon the records of the corporation and upon such information, opinions, reports or statements presented to the corporation by any of its officers or employees, or committees of the board of directors, or by any other person as to matters the director reasonably believes are within such other person's professional or expert competence and who has been selected with reasonable care by or on behalf of the corporation, as to the value and amount of the assets, liabilities and/or net profits of the corporation or any other facts pertinent to the existence and amount of surplus or other funds from which dividends might properly be declared and paid, or with which the corporation's stock might properly be purchased or redeemed.

§ 173.   Declaration and payment of dividends.

No corporation shall pay dividends except in accordance with this chapter. Dividends may be paid in cash, in property, or in shares of the corporation's capital stock. If the dividend is to be paid in shares of the corporation's theretofore unissued capital stock the board of directors shall, by resolution, direct that there be designated as capital in respect of such shares an amount which is not less than the aggregate par value of par value shares being declared as a dividend and, in the case of shares without par value being declared as a dividend, such amount as shall be determined by the board of directors. No such designation as capital shall be necessary if shares are being distributed by a corporation pursuant to a split-up or division of its stock rather than as payment of a dividend declared payable in stock of the corporation.

§ 174.   Liability of directors for unlawful payment of dividend or unlawful stock purchase or redemption; exoneration from liability; contribution among directors; subrogation.

(a)   In case of any wilful or negligent violation of § 160 or § 173 of this title, the directors under whose administration the same may happen shall be jointly and severally liable, at any time within 6 years after paying such unlawful dividend or after such unlawful stock purchase or redemption, to the corporation, and to its creditors in the event of its dissolution or insolvency, to the full amount of the dividend unlawfully paid, or to the full amount unlawfully paid for the purchase or redemption of the corporation's stock, with interest from the time such liability accrued. Any director who may have been absent when the same was done, or who may have dissented from the act or resolution by which the same was done, may be exonerated from such liability by causing his or her dissent to be entered on the books containing the minutes of the proceedings of the directors at the time the same was done, or immediately after such director has notice of the same.

(b) Any director against whom a claim is successfully asserted under this section shall be entitled to contribution from the other directors who voted for or concurred in the unlawful dividend, stock purchase or stock redemption.

(c) Any director against whom a claim is successfully asserted under this section shall be entitled, to the extent of the amount paid by such director as a result of such claim, to be subrogated to the rights of the corporation against stockholders who received the dividend on, or assets for the sale or redemption of, their stock with knowledge of facts indicating that such dividend, stock purchase or redemption was unlawful under this chapter, in proportion to the amounts received by such stockholders respectively.

SUBCHAPTER VI. STOCK TRANSFERS

§ 201. Transfer of stock, stock certificates and uncertificated stock.

Except as otherwise provided in this chapter, the transfer of stock and the certificates of stock which represent the stock or uncertificated stock shall be governed by Article 8 of subtitle I of Title 6. To the extent that any provision of this chapter is inconsistent with any provision of subtitle I of Title 6, this chapter shall be controlling.

§ 202. Restrictions on transfer and ownership of securities.

(a) A written restriction or restrictions on the transfer or registration of transfer of a security of a corporation, or on the amount of the corporation's securities that may be owned by any person or group of persons, if permitted by this section and noted conspicuously on the certificate or certificates representing the security or securities so restricted or, in the case of uncertificated shares, contained in the notice or notices given pursuant to § 151(f) of this title, may be enforced against the holder of the restricted security or securities or any successor or transferee of the holder including an executor, administrator, trustee, guardian or other fiduciary entrusted with like responsibility for the person or estate of the holder. Unless noted conspicuously on the certificate or certificates representing the security or securities so restricted or, in the case of uncertificated shares, contained in the notice or notices given pursuant to § 151(f) of this title, a restriction, even though permitted by this section, is ineffective except against a person with actual knowledge of the restriction.

(b) A restriction on the transfer or registration of transfer of securities of a corporation, or on the amount of a corporation's securities that may be owned by any person or group of persons, may be imposed by the certificate of incorporation or by the bylaws or by an agreement among any number of security holders or among such holders and the corporation. No restrictions so imposed shall be binding with respect to securities issued prior to the adoption of the restriction unless the holders of the securities are parties to an agreement or voted in favor of the restriction.

(c) A restriction on the transfer or registration of transfer of securities of a corporation or on the amount of such securities that may be owned by any person or group of persons is permitted by this section if it:

(1) Obligates the holder of the restricted securities to offer to the corporation or to any other holders of securities of the corporation or to any other person or to any combination of the foregoing, a prior opportunity, to be exercised within a reasonable time, to acquire the restricted securities; or

(2) Obligates the corporation or any holder of securities of the corporation or any other person or any combination of the foregoing, to purchase the securities which are the subject of an agreement respecting the purchase and sale of the restricted securities; or

(3) Requires the corporation or the holders of any class or series of securities of the corporation to consent to any proposed transfer of the restricted securities or to approve the proposed transferee of the restricted securities, or to approve the amount of securities of the corporation that may be owned by any person or group of persons; or

(4) Obligates the holder of the restricted securities to sell or transfer an amount of restricted securities to the corporation or to any other holders of securities of the corporation or to any other person or to any combination of the foregoing, or causes or results in the automatic sale or transfer of an amount of restricted securities to the corporation or to any other holders of securities of the corporation or to any other person or to any combination of the foregoing; or

(5) Prohibits or restricts the transfer of the restricted securities to, or the ownership of restricted securities by, designated persons or classes of persons or groups of persons, and such designation is not manifestly unreasonable.

(d) Any restriction on the transfer or the registration of transfer of the securities of a corporation, or on the amount of securities of a corporation that may be owned by a person or group of persons, for any of the following purposes shall be conclusively presumed to be for a reasonable purpose:

(1) Maintaining any local, state, federal or foreign tax advantage to the corporation or its stockholders, including without limitation:

    a. Maintaining the corporation's status as an electing small business corporation under subchapter S of the United States Internal Revenue Code [26 U.S.C. § 1371 et seq.], or

    b. Maintaining or preserving any tax attribute (including without limitation net operating losses), or

    c. Qualifying or maintaining the qualification of the corporation as a real estate investment trust pursuant to the United States Internal Revenue Code or regulations adopted pursuant to the United States Internal Revenue Code, or

(2) Maintaining any statutory or regulatory advantage or complying with any statutory or regulatory requirements under applicable local, state, federal or foreign law.

(e) Any other lawful restriction on transfer or registration of transfer of securities, or on the amount of securities that may be owned by any person or group of persons, is permitted by this section.

§ 203. Business combinations with interested stockholders.

(a) Notwithstanding any other provisions of this chapter, a corporation shall not engage in any business combination with any interested stockholder for a period of 3 years following the time that such stockholder became an interested stockholder, unless:

(1) Prior to such time the board of directors of the corporation approved either the business combination or the transaction which resulted in the stockholder becoming an interested stockholder;

(2) Upon consummation of the transaction which resulted in the stockholder becoming an interested stockholder, the interested stockholder owned at least 85% of the voting stock of the corporation outstanding at the time the transaction commenced, excluding for purposes of determining the voting stock outstanding (but not the outstanding voting stock owned by the interested stockholder) those shares owned (i) by persons who are directors and also officers and (ii) employee stock plans in which employee participants do not have the right to determine confidentially whether shares held subject to the plan will be tendered in a tender or exchange offer; or

(3) At or subsequent to such time the business combination is approved by the board of directors and authorized at an annual or special meeting of stockholders, and not by written consent, by the affirmative vote of at least 66 2/3% of the outstanding voting stock which is not owned by the interested stockholder.

(b) The restrictions contained in this section shall not apply if:

(1)   The corporation's original certificate of incorporation contains a provision expressly electing not to be governed by this section;

(2)   The corporation, by action of its board of directors, adopts an amendment to its bylaws within 90 days of February 2, 1988, expressly electing not to be governed by this section, which amendment shall not be further amended by the board of directors;

(3)   The corporation, by action of its stockholders, adopts an amendment to its certificate of incorporation or bylaws expressly electing not to be governed by this section; provided that, in addition to any other vote required by law, such amendment to the certificate of incorporation or bylaws must be adopted by the affirmative vote of a majority of the outstanding stock entitled to vote thereon. In the case of a corporation that both (i) has never had a class of voting stock that falls within any of the 2 categories set out in paragraph (b)(4) of this section, and (ii) has not elected by a provision in its original certificate of incorporation or any amendment thereto to be governed by this section, such amendment shall become effective upon (i) in the case of an amendment to the certificate of incorporation, the date and time at which the certificate filed in accordance with § 103 of this title becomes effective thereunder or (ii) in the case of an amendment to the bylaws, the date of the adoption of such amendment. In all other cases, an amendment adopted pursuant to this paragraph shall become effective (i) in the case of an amendment to the certificate of incorporation, 12 months after the date and time at which the certificate filed in accordance with § 103 of this title becomes effective thereunder or (ii) in the case of an amendment to the bylaws, 12 months after the date of the adoption of such amendment, and, in either case, the election not to be governed by this section shall not apply to any business combination between such corporation and any person who became an interested stockholder of such corporation on or before (A) in the case of an amendment to the certificate of incorporation, the date and time at which the certificate filed in accordance with § 103 of this title becomes effective thereunder; or (B) in the case of an amendment to the bylaws, the date of the adoption of such amendment. A bylaw amendment adopted pursuant to this paragraph shall not be further amended by the board of directors;

(4)   The corporation does not have a class of voting stock that is: (i) Listed on a national securities exchange; or (ii) held of record by more than 2,000 stockholders, unless any of the foregoing results from action taken, directly or indirectly, by an interested stockholder or from a transaction in which a person becomes an interested stockholder;

(5)   A stockholder becomes an interested stockholder inadvertently and (i) as soon as practicable divests itself of ownership of sufficient shares so that the stockholder ceases to be an interested stockholder; and (ii) would not, at any time within the 3-year period immediately prior to a business combination between the corporation and such stockholder, have been an interested stockholder but for the inadvertent acquisition of ownership;

(6)   The business combination is proposed prior to the consummation or abandonment of and subsequent to the earlier of the public announcement or the notice required hereunder of a proposed transaction which (i) constitutes 1 of the transactions described in the second sentence of this paragraph; (ii) is with or by a person who either was not an interested stockholder during the previous 3 years or who became an interested stockholder with the approval of the corporation's board of directors or during the period described in paragraph (b)(7) of this section; and (iii) is approved or not opposed by a majority of the members of the board of directors then in office (but not less than 1) who were directors prior to any person becoming an interested stockholder during the previous 3 years or were recommended for election or elected to succeed such directors by a majority of such directors. The proposed transactions referred to in the preceding sentence are limited to (x) a merger or consolidation of the corporation (except for a merger in respect of which, pursuant to § 251(f) of this title, no vote of the stockholders of the corporation is required); (y) a sale, lease, exchange, mortgage, pledge, transfer or other disposition (in 1 transaction or a series of transactions), whether as part of a dissolution or otherwise, of assets of the corporation or of any direct or indirect majority-owned subsidiary of the corporation

(other than to any direct or indirect wholly-owned subsidiary or to the corporation) having an aggregate market value equal to 50% or more of either that aggregate market value of all of the assets of the corporation determined on a consolidated basis or the aggregate market value of all the outstanding stock of the corporation; or (z) a proposed tender or exchange offer for 50% or more of the outstanding voting stock of the corporation. The corporation shall give not less than 20 days' notice to all interested stockholders prior to the consummation of any of the transactions described in clause (x) or (y) of the second sentence of this paragraph; or

(7)   The business combination is with an interested stockholder who became an interested stockholder at a time when the restrictions contained in this section did not apply by reason of any of paragraphs (b)(1) through (4) of this section, provided, however, that this paragraph (b)(7) shall not apply if, at the time such interested stockholder became an interested stockholder, the corporation's certificate of incorporation contained a provision authorized by the last sentence of this subsection (b).

Notwithstanding paragraphs (b)(1), (2), (3) and (4) of this section, a corporation may elect by a provision of its original certificate of incorporation or any amendment thereto to be governed by this section; provided that any such amendment to the certificate of incorporation shall not apply to restrict a business combination between the corporation and an interested stockholder of the corporation if the interested stockholder became such before the date and time at which the certificate filed in accordance with § 103 of this title becomes effective thereunder.

(c)   As used in this section only, the term:

(1)   "Affiliate" means a person that directly, or indirectly through 1 or more intermediaries, controls, or is controlled by, or is under common control with, another person.

(2)   "Associate," when used to indicate a relationship with any person, means: (i) Any corporation, partnership, unincorporated association or other entity of which such person is a director, officer or partner or is, directly or indirectly, the owner of 20% or more of any class of voting stock; (ii) any trust or other estate in which such person has at least a 20% beneficial interest or as to which such person serves as trustee or in a similar fiduciary capacity; and (iii) any relative or spouse of such person, or any relative of such spouse, who has the same residence as such person.

(3)   "Business combination," when used in reference to any corporation and any interested stockholder of such corporation, means:

(i)   Any merger or consolidation of the corporation or any direct or indirect majority-owned subsidiary of the corporation with (A) the interested stockholder, or (B) with any other corporation, partnership, unincorporated association or other entity if the merger or consolidation is caused by the interested stockholder and as a result of such merger or consolidation subsection (a) of this section is not applicable to the surviving entity;

(ii)   Any sale, lease, exchange, mortgage, pledge, transfer or other disposition (in 1 transaction or a series of transactions), except proportionately as a stockholder of such corporation, to or with the interested stockholder, whether as part of a dissolution or otherwise, of assets of the corporation or of any direct or indirect majority-owned subsidiary of the corporation which assets have an aggregate market value equal to 10% or more of either the aggregate market value of all the assets of the corporation determined on a consolidated basis or the aggregate market value of all the outstanding stock of the corporation;

(iii)   Any transaction which results in the issuance or transfer by the corporation or by any direct or indirect majority-owned subsidiary of the corporation of any stock of the corporation or of such subsidiary to the interested stockholder, except: (A) Pursuant to the exercise, exchange or conversion of securities exercisable for, exchangeable for or convertible into stock of such corporation or any such subsidiary which securities were outstanding prior to the time that the interested stockholder became such; (B) pursuant to a merger under § 251(g) of this title; (C) pursuant to a dividend or distribution paid or made, or the exercise, exchange or conversion of securities exercisable for, exchangeable for or convertible into stock of such corporation or any such subsidiary which security is distributed, pro rata to all holders of a class or series of stock of such corporation subsequent to the time the interested stockholder became such; (D) pursuant to an exchange offer by the corporation to purchase stock made on the same terms to all holders of said stock; or (E) any issuance or transfer of stock by the corporation; provided however, that in no case under items (C)–(E) of this subparagraph shall there be an increase in the interested stockholder's proportionate share of the stock of any class or series of the corporation or of the voting stock of the corporation;

(iv) Any transaction involving the corporation or any direct or indirect majority-owned subsidiary of the corporation which has the effect, directly or indirectly, of increasing the proportionate share of the stock of any class or series, or securities convertible into the stock of any class or series, of the corporation or of any such subsidiary which is owned by the interested stockholder, except as a result of immaterial changes due to fractional share adjustments or as a result of any purchase or redemption of any shares of stock not caused, directly or indirectly, by the interested stockholder; or

(v) Any receipt by the interested stockholder of the benefit, directly or indirectly (except proportionately as a stockholder of such corporation), of any loans, advances, guarantees, pledges or other financial benefits (other than those expressly permitted in paragraphs (c)(3)(i)–(iv) of this section) provided by or through the corporation or any direct or indirect majority-owned subsidiary.

(4) "Control," including the terms "controlling," "controlled by" and "under common control with," means the possession, directly or indirectly, of the power to direct or cause the direction of the management and policies of a person, whether through the ownership of voting stock, by contract or otherwise. A person who is the owner of 20% or more of the outstanding voting stock of any corporation, partnership, unincorporated association or other entity shall be presumed to have control of such entity, in the absence of proof by a preponderance of the evidence to the contrary; Notwithstanding the foregoing, a presumption of control shall not apply where such person holds voting stock, in good faith and not for the purpose of circumventing this section, as an agent, bank, broker, nominee, custodian or trustee for 1 or more owners who do not individually or as a group have control of such entity.

(5) "Interested stockholder" means any person (other than the corporation and any direct or indirect majority-owned subsidiary of the corporation) that (i) is the owner of 15% or more of the outstanding voting stock of the corporation, or (ii) is an affiliate or associate of the corporation and was the owner of 15% or more of the outstanding voting stock of the corporation at any time within the 3-year period immediately prior to the date on which it is sought to be determined whether such person is an interested stockholder, and the affiliates and associates of such person; provided, however, that the term "interested stockholder" shall not include (x) any person who (A) owned shares in excess of the 15% limitation set forth herein as of, or acquired such shares pursuant to a tender offer commenced prior to, December 23, 1987, or pursuant to an exchange offer announced prior to the aforesaid date and commenced within 90 days thereafter and either (I) continued to own shares in excess of such 15% limitation or would have but for action by the corporation or (II) is an affiliate or associate of the corporation and so continued (or so would have continued but for action by the corporation) to be the owner of 15% or more of the outstanding voting stock of the corporation at any time within the 3-year period immediately prior to the date on which it is sought to be determined whether such a person is an interested stockholder or (B) acquired said shares from a person described in item (A) of this paragraph by gift, inheritance or in a transaction in which no consideration was exchanged; or (y) any person whose ownership of shares in excess of the 15% limitation set forth herein is the result of action taken solely by the corporation; provided that such person shall be an interested stockholder if thereafter such person acquires additional shares of voting stock of the corporation, except as a result of further

corporate action not caused, directly or indirectly, by such person. For the purpose of determining whether a person is an interested stockholder, the voting stock of the corporation deemed to be outstanding shall include stock deemed to be owned by the person through application of paragraph (9) of this subsection but shall not include any other unissued stock of such corporation which may be issuable pursuant to any agreement, arrangement or understanding, or upon exercise of conversion rights, warrants or options, or otherwise.

(6)   "Person" means any individual, corporation, partnership, unincorporated association or other entity.

(7)   "Stock" means, with respect to any corporation, capital stock and, with respect to any other entity, any equity interest.

(8)   "Voting stock" means, with respect to any corporation, stock of any class or series entitled to vote generally in the election of directors and, with respect to any entity that is not a corporation, any equity interest entitled to vote generally in the election of the governing body of such entity. Every reference to a percentage of voting stock shall refer to such percentage of the votes of such voting stock.

(9)   "Owner," including the terms "own" and "owned," when used with respect to any stock, means a person that individually or with or through any of its affiliates or associates:

(i)   Beneficially owns such stock, directly or indirectly; or

(ii)   Has (A) the right to acquire such stock (whether such right is exercisable immediately or only after the passage of time) pursuant to any agreement, arrangement or understanding, or upon the exercise of conversion rights, exchange rights, warrants or options, or otherwise; provided, however, that a person shall not be deemed the owner of stock tendered pursuant to a tender or exchange offer made by such person or any of such person's affiliates or associates until such tendered stock is accepted for purchase or exchange; or (B) the right to vote such stock pursuant to any agreement, arrangement or understanding; provided, however, that a person shall not be deemed the owner of any stock because of such person's right to vote such stock if the agreement, arrangement or understanding to vote such stock arises solely from a revocable proxy or consent given in response to a proxy or consent solicitation made to 10 or more persons; or

(iii)   Has any agreement, arrangement or understanding for the purpose of acquiring, holding, voting (except voting pursuant to a revocable proxy or consent as described in item (B) of subparagraph (ii) of this paragraph), or disposing of such stock with any other person that beneficially owns, or whose affiliates or associates beneficially own, directly or indirectly, such stock.

(d)   No provision of a certificate of incorporation or bylaw shall require, for any vote of stockholders required by this section, a greater vote of stockholders than that specified in this section.

(e)   The Court of Chancery is hereby vested with exclusive jurisdiction to hear and determine all matters with respect to this section.

§ 204.   Ratification of defective corporate acts and stock. [For application of this section, see 80 Del. Laws, c. 40, § 16, and 81 Del. Laws, c. 354, § 16]

(a)   Subject to subsection (f) of this section, no defective corporate act or putative stock shall be void or voidable solely as a result of a failure of authorization if ratified as provided in this section or validated by the Court of Chancery in a proceeding brought under § 205 of this title.

(b)(1)   In order to ratify 1 or more defective corporate acts pursuant to this section (other than the ratification of an election of the initial board of directors pursuant to paragraph (b)(2) of this section), the board of directors of the corporation shall adopt resolutions stating:

(A)   The defective corporate act or acts to be ratified;

(B) The date of each defective corporate act or acts;

(C) If such defective corporate act or acts involved the issuance of shares of putative stock, the number and type of shares of putative stock issued and the date or dates upon which such putative shares were purported to have been issued;

(D) The nature of the failure of authorization in respect of each defective corporate act to be ratified; and

(E) That the board of directors approves the ratification of the defective corporate act or acts.

Such resolutions may also provide that, at any time before the validation effective time in respect of any defective corporate act set forth therein, notwithstanding the approval of the ratification of such defective corporate act by stockholders, the board of directors may abandon the ratification of such defective corporate act without further action of the stockholders. The quorum and voting requirements applicable to the ratification by the board of directors of any defective corporate act shall be the quorum and voting requirements applicable to the type of defective corporate act proposed to be ratified at the time the board adopts the resolutions ratifying the defective corporate act; provided that if the certificate of incorporation or bylaws of the corporation, any plan or agreement to which the corporation was a party or any provision of this title, in each case as in effect as of the time of the defective corporate act, would have required a larger number or portion of directors or of specified directors for a quorum to be present or to approve the defective corporate act, such larger number or portion of such directors or such specified directors shall be required for a quorum to be present or to adopt the resolutions to ratify the defective corporate act, as applicable, except that the presence or approval of any director elected, appointed or nominated by holders of any class or series of which no shares are then outstanding, or by any person that is no longer a stockholder, shall not be required.

(2) In order to ratify a defective corporate act in respect of the election of the initial board of directors of the corporation pursuant to § 108 of this title, a majority of the persons who, at the time the resolutions required by this paragraph (b)(2) of this section are adopted, are exercising the powers of directors under claim and color of an election or appointment as such may adopt resolutions stating:

(A) The name of the person or persons who first took action in the name of the corporation as the initial board of directors of the corporation;

(B) The earlier of the date on which such persons first took such action or were purported to have been elected as the initial board of directors; and

(C) That the ratification of the election of such person or persons as the initial board of directors is approved.

(c) Each defective corporate act ratified pursuant to paragraph (b)(1) of this section shall be submitted to stockholders for approval as provided in subsection (d) of this section, unless:

(1)(A) No other provision of this title, and no provision of the certificate of incorporation or bylaws of the corporation, or of any plan or agreement to which the corporation is a party, would have required stockholder approval of such defective corporate act to be ratified, either at the time of such defective corporate act or at the time the board of directors adopts the resolutions ratifying such defective corporate act pursuant to paragraph (b)(1) of this section; and

(B) Such defective corporate act did not result from a failure to comply with § 203 of this title; or

(2) As of the record date for determining the stockholders entitled to vote on the ratification of such defective corporate act, there are no shares of valid stock outstanding and entitled to vote thereon, regardless of whether there then exist any shares of putative stock.

(d) If the ratification of a defective corporate act is required to be submitted to stockholders for approval pursuant to subsection (c) of this section, due notice of the time, place, if any, and purpose of the meeting shall be given at least 20 days before the date of the meeting to each holder of valid stock and putative stock, whether voting or nonvoting, at the address of such holder as it appears or most recently appeared, as appropriate, on the records of the corporation. The notice shall also be given to the holders of record of valid stock and putative stock, whether voting or nonvoting, as of the time of the defective corporate act (or, in the case of any defective corporate act that involved the establishment of a record date for notice of or voting at any meeting of stockholders, for action by written consent of stockholders in lieu of a meeting, or for any other purpose, the record date for notice of or voting at such meeting, the record date for action by written consent, or the record date for such other action, as the case may be), other than holders whose identities or addresses cannot be determined from the records of the corporation. The notice shall contain a copy of the resolutions adopted by the board of directors pursuant to paragraph (b)(1) of this section or the information required by paragraphs (b)(1)(A) through (E) of this section and a statement that any claim that the defective corporate act or putative stock ratified hereunder is void or voidable due to the failure of authorization, or that the Court of Chancery should declare in its discretion that a ratification in accordance with this section not be effective or be effective only on certain conditions must be brought within 120 days from the applicable validation effective time. At such meeting, the quorum and voting requirements applicable to ratification of such defective corporate act shall be the quorum and voting requirements applicable to the type of defective corporate act proposed to be ratified at the time of the approval of the ratification, except that:

(1)   If the certificate of incorporation or bylaws of the corporation, any plan or agreement to which the corporation was a party or any provision of this title in effect as of the time of the defective corporate act would have required a larger number or portion of stock or of any class or series thereof or of specified stockholders for a quorum to be present or to approve the defective corporate act, the presence or approval of such larger number or portion of stock or of such class or series thereof or of such specified stockholders shall be required for a quorum to be present or to approve the ratification of the defective corporate act, as applicable, except that the presence or approval of shares of any class or series of which no shares are then outstanding, or of any person that is no longer a stockholder, shall not be required;

(2)   The approval by stockholders of the ratification of the election of a director shall require the affirmative vote of the majority of shares present at the meeting and entitled to vote on the election of such director, except that if the certificate of incorporation or bylaws of the corporation then in effect or in effect at the time of the defective election require or required a larger number or portion of stock or of any class or series thereof or of specified stockholders to elect such director, the affirmative vote of such larger number or portion of stock or of any class or series thereof or of such specified stockholders shall be required to ratify the election of such director, except that the presence or approval of shares of any class or series of which no shares are then outstanding, or of any person that is no longer a stockholder, shall not be required; and

(3)   In the event of a failure of authorization resulting from failure to comply with the provisions of § 203 of this title, the ratification of the defective corporate act shall require the vote set forth in § 203(a)(3) of this title, regardless of whether such vote would have otherwise been required.

Shares of putative stock on the record date for determining stockholders entitled to vote on any matter submitted to stockholders pursuant to subsection (c) of this section (and without giving effect to any ratification that becomes effective after such record date) shall neither be entitled to vote nor counted for quorum purposes in any vote to ratify any defective corporate act.

(e)   If a defective corporate act ratified pursuant to this section would have required under any other section of this title the filing of a certificate in accordance with § 103 of this title, then, whether or not a certificate was previously filed in respect of such defective corporate act and in lieu of filing the certificate otherwise required by this title, the corporation shall file a certificate of validation with respect to such defective corporate act in accordance with § 103 of this title. A separate certificate of validation shall be required for each defective corporate act requiring the filing of a certificate of validation under this section, except that (i) 2 or more defective corporate acts may be included in a single certificate of validation if the corporation filed, or to comply with this title would have filed, a single certificate under another provision of this title to effect such acts, and (ii) 2 or more overissues of shares of any class, classes or series of stock may be included in a single certificate of validation, provided that the increase in the number of authorized shares of each such class or series set forth in the certificate of validation shall be effective as of the date of the first such overissue. The certificate of validation shall set forth:

(1) Each defective corporate act that is the subject of the certificate of validation (including, in the case of any defective corporate act involving the issuance of shares of putative stock, the number and type of shares of putative stock issued and the date or dates upon which such putative shares were purported to have been issued), the date of such defective corporate act, and the nature of the failure of authorization in respect of such defective corporate act;

(2) A statement that such defective corporate act was ratified in accordance with this section, including the date on which the board of directors ratified such defective corporate act and the date, if any, on which the stockholders approved the ratification of such defective corporate act; and

(3) Information required by 1 of the following paragraphs:

a. If a certificate was previously filed under § 103 of this title in respect of such defective corporate act and no changes to such certificate are required to give effect to such defective corporate act in accordance with this section, the certificate of validation shall set forth (x) the name, title and filing date of the certificate previously filed and of any certificate of correction thereto and (y) a statement that a copy of the certificate previously filed, together with any certificate of correction thereto, is attached as an exhibit to the certificate of validation;

b. If a certificate was previously filed under § 103 of this title in respect of the defective corporate act and such certificate requires any change to give effect to the defective corporate act in accordance with this section (including a change to the date and time of the effectiveness of such certificate), the certificate of validation shall set forth (x) the name, title and filing date of the certificate so previously filed and of any certificate of correction thereto, (y) a statement that a certificate containing all of the information required to be included under the applicable section or sections of this title to give effect to the defective corporate act is attached as an exhibit to the certificate of validation, and (z) the date and time that such certificate shall be deemed to have become effective pursuant to this section; or

c. If a certificate was not previously filed under § 103 of this title in respect of the defective corporate act and the defective corporate act ratified pursuant to this section would have required under any other section of this title the filing of a certificate in accordance with § 103 of this title, the certificate of validation shall set forth (x) a statement that a certificate containing all of the information required to be included under the applicable section or sections of this title to give effect to the defective corporate act is attached as an exhibit to the certificate of validation, and (y) the date and time that such certificate shall be deemed to have become effective pursuant to this section.

A certificate attached to a certificate of validation pursuant to paragraph (e)(3)b. or c. of this section need not be separately executed and acknowledged and need not include any statement required by any other section of this title that such instrument has been approved and adopted in accordance with the provisions of such other section.

(f) From and after the validation effective time, unless otherwise determined in an action brought pursuant to § 205 of this title:

(1) Subject to the last sentence of subsection (d) of this section, each defective corporate act ratified in accordance with this section shall no longer be deemed void or voidable as a result of

the failure of authorization described in the resolutions adopted pursuant to subsection (b) of this section and such effect shall be retroactive to the time of the defective corporate act; and

(2) Subject to the last sentence of subsection (d) of this section, each share or fraction of a share of putative stock issued or purportedly issued pursuant to any such defective corporate act shall no longer be deemed void or voidable and shall be deemed to be an identical share or fraction of a share of outstanding stock as of the time it was purportedly issued.

(g) In respect of each defective corporate act ratified by the board of directors pursuant to subsection (b) of this section, prompt notice of the ratification shall be given to all holders of valid stock and putative stock, whether voting or nonvoting, as of the date the board of directors adopts the resolutions approving such defective corporate act, or as of a date within 60 days after such date of adoption, as established by the board of directors, at the address of such holder as it appears or most recently appeared, as appropriate, on the records of the corporation. The notice shall also be given to the holders of record of valid stock and putative stock, whether voting or nonvoting, as of the time of the defective corporate act, other than holders whose identities or addresses cannot be determined from the records of the corporation. The notice shall contain a copy of the resolutions adopted pursuant to subsection (b) of this section or the information specified in paragraphs (b)(1)(A) through (E) or paragraphs (b)(2)(A) through (C) of this section, as applicable, and a statement that any claim that the defective corporate act or putative stock ratified hereunder is void or voidable due to the failure of authorization, or that the Court of Chancery should declare in its discretion that a ratification in accordance with this section not be effective or be effective only on certain conditions must be brought within 120 days from the later of the validation effective time or the time at which the notice required by this subsection is given. Notwithstanding the foregoing, (i) no such notice shall be required if notice of the ratification of the defective corporate act is to be given in accordance with subsection (d) of this section, and (ii) in the case of a corporation that has a class of stock listed on a national securities exchange, the notice required by this subsection and the second sentence of subsection (d) of this section may be deemed given if disclosed in a document publicly filed by the corporation with the Securities and Exchange Commission pursuant to § 13, § 14 or § 15(d) (15 U.S.C. § 78m, § 77n or § 78o(d)) of the Securities Exchange Act of 1934, as amended, and the rules and regulations promulgated thereunder, or the corresponding provisions of any subsequent United States federal securities laws, rules or regulations. If any defective corporate act has been approved by stockholders acting pursuant to § 228 of this title, the notice required by this subsection may be included in any notice required to be given pursuant to § 228(e) of this title and, if so given, shall be sent to the stockholders entitled thereto under § 228(e) and to all holders of valid and putative stock to whom notice would be required under this subsection if the defective corporate act had been approved at a meeting other than any stockholder who approved the action by consent in lieu of a meeting pursuant to § 228 of this title or any holder of putative stock who otherwise consented thereto in writing. Solely for purposes of subsection (d) of this section and this subsection, notice to holders of putative stock, and notice to holders of valid stock and putative stock as of the time of the defective corporate act, shall be treated as notice to holders of valid stock for purposes of §§ 222 and 228, 229, 230, 232 and 233 of this title.

(h) As used in this section and in § 205 of this title only, the term:

(1) "Defective corporate act" means an overissue, an election or appointment of directors that is void or voidable due to a failure of authorization, or any act or transaction purportedly taken by or on behalf of the corporation that is, and at the time such act or transaction was purportedly taken would have been, within the power of a corporation under subchapter II of this chapter (without regard to the failure of authorization identified in § 204(b)(1)(D) of this title), but is void or voidable due to a failure of authorization;

(2) "Failure of authorization" means: (i) the failure to authorize or effect an act or transaction in compliance with (A) the provisions of this title, (B) the certificate of incorporation or bylaws of the corporation, or (C) any plan or agreement to which the corporation is a party or the disclosure set forth in any proxy or consent solicitation statement, if and to the extent such

failure would render such act or transaction void or voidable; or (ii) the failure of the board of directors or any officer of the corporation to authorize or approve any act or transaction taken by or on behalf of the corporation that would have required for its due authorization the approval of the board of directors or such officer;

    (3)   "Overissue" means the purported issuance of:

        a.   Shares of capital stock of a class or series in excess of the number of shares of such class or series the corporation has the power to issue under § 161 of this title at the time of such issuance; or

        b.   Shares of any class or series of capital stock that is not then authorized for issuance by the certificate of incorporation of the corporation;

    (4)   "Putative stock" means the shares of any class or series of capital stock of the corporation (including shares issued upon exercise of options, rights, warrants or other securities convertible into shares of capital stock of the corporation, or interests with respect thereto that were created or issued pursuant to a defective corporate act) that:

        a.   But for any failure of authorization, would constitute valid stock; or

        b.   Cannot be determined by the board of directors to be valid stock;

    (5)   "Time of the defective corporate act" means the date and time the defective corporate act was purported to have been taken;

    (6)   "Validation effective time" with respect to any defective corporate act ratified pursuant to this section means the latest of:

        a.   The time at which the defective corporate act submitted to the stockholders for approval pursuant to subsection (c) of this section is approved by such stockholders or if no such vote of stockholders is required to approve the ratification of the defective corporate act, the time at which the board of directors adopts the resolutions required by paragraph (b)(1) or (b)(2) of this section;

        b.   Where no certificate of validation is required to be filed pursuant to subsection (e) of this section, the time, if any, specified by the board of directors in the resolutions adopted pursuant to paragraph (b)(1) or (b)(2) of this section, which time shall not precede the time at which such resolutions are adopted; and

        c.   The time at which any certificate of validation filed pursuant to subsection (e) of this section shall become effective in accordance with § 103 of this title.

    (7)   "Valid stock" means the shares of any class or series of capital stock of the corporation that have been duly authorized and validly issued in accordance with this title.

In the absence of actual fraud in the transaction, the judgment of the board of directors that shares of stock are valid stock or putative stock shall be conclusive, unless otherwise determined by the Court of Chancery in a proceeding brought pursuant to § 205 of this title.

    (i)   Ratification under this section or validation under § 205 of this title shall not be deemed to be the exclusive means of ratifying or validating any act or transaction taken by or on behalf of the corporation, including any defective corporate act, or any issuance of stock, including any putative stock, or of adopting or endorsing any act or transaction taken by or in the name of the corporation prior to the commencement of its existence, and the absence or failure of ratification in accordance with either this section or validation under § 205 of this title shall not, of itself, affect the validity or effectiveness of any act or transaction or the issuance of any stock properly ratified under common law or otherwise, nor shall it create a presumption that any such act or transaction is or was a defective corporate act or that such stock is void or voidable.

§ 205. Proceedings regarding validity of defective corporate acts and stock. [For application of this section, see 80 Del. Laws, c. 40, § 16]

(a) Subject to subsection (f) of this section, upon application by the corporation, any successor entity to the corporation, any member of the board of directors, any record or beneficial holder of valid stock or putative stock, any record or beneficial holder of valid or putative stock as of the time of a defective corporate act ratified pursuant to § 204 of this title, or any other person claiming to be substantially and adversely affected by a ratification pursuant to § 204 of this title, the Court of Chancery may:

(1) Determine the validity and effectiveness of any defective corporate act ratified pursuant to § 204 of this title;

(2) Determine the validity and effectiveness of the ratification of any defective corporate act pursuant to § 204 of this title;

(3) Determine the validity and effectiveness of any defective corporate act not ratified or not ratified effectively pursuant to § 204 of this title;

(4) Determine the validity of any corporate act or transaction and any stock, rights or options to acquire stock; and

(5) Modify or waive any of the procedures set forth in § 204 of this title to ratify a defective corporate act.

(b) In connection with an action under this section, the Court of Chancery may:

(1) Declare that a ratification in accordance with and pursuant to § 204 of this title is not effective or shall only be effective at a time or upon conditions established by the Court;

(2) Validate and declare effective any defective corporate act or putative stock and impose conditions upon such validation by the Court;

(3) Require measures to remedy or avoid harm to any person substantially and adversely affected by a ratification pursuant to § 204 of this title or from any order of the Court pursuant to this section, excluding any harm that would have resulted if the defective corporate act had been valid when approved or effectuated;

(4) Order the Secretary of State to accept an instrument for filing with an effective time specified by the Court, which effective time may be prior or subsequent to the time of such order, provided that the filing date of such instrument shall be determined in accordance with § 103(c)(3) of this title;

(5) Approve a stock ledger for the corporation that includes any stock ratified or validated in accordance with this section or with § 204 of this title;

(6) Declare that shares of putative stock are shares of valid stock or require a corporation to issue and deliver shares of valid stock in place of any shares of putative stock;

(7) Order that a meeting of holders of valid stock or putative stock be held and exercise the powers provided to the Court under § 227 of this title with respect to such a meeting;

(8) Declare that a defective corporate act validated by the Court shall be effective as of the time of the defective corporate act or at such other time as the Court shall determine;

(9) Declare that putative stock validated by the Court shall be deemed to be an identical share or fraction of a share of valid stock as of the time originally issued or purportedly issued or at such other time as the Court shall determine; and

(10) Make such other orders regarding such matters as it deems proper under the circumstances.

(c)   Service of the application under subsection (a) of this section upon the registered agent of the corporation shall be deemed to be service upon the corporation, and no other party need be joined in order for the Court of Chancery to adjudicate the matter. In an action filed by the corporation, the Court may require notice of the action be provided to other persons specified by the Court and permit such other persons to intervene in the action.

(d)   In connection with the resolution of matters pursuant to subsections (a) and (b) of this section, the Court of Chancery may consider the following:

(1)   Whether the defective corporate act was originally approved or effectuated with the belief that the approval or effectuation was in compliance with the provisions of this title, the certificate of incorporation or bylaws of the corporation;

(2)   Whether the corporation and board of directors has treated the defective corporate act as a valid act or transaction and whether any person has acted in reliance on the public record that such defective corporate act was valid;

(3)   Whether any person will be or was harmed by the ratification or validation of the defective corporate act, excluding any harm that would have resulted if the defective corporate act had been valid when approved or effectuated;

(4)   Whether any person will be harmed by the failure to ratify or validate the defective corporate act; and

(5)   Any other factors or considerations the Court deems just and equitable.

(e)   The Court of Chancery is hereby vested with exclusive jurisdiction to hear and determine all actions brought under this section.

(f)   Notwithstanding any other provision of this section, no action asserting:

(1)   That a defective corporate act or putative stock ratified in accordance with § 204 of this title is void or voidable due to a failure of authorization identified in the resolution adopted in accordance with 204(b) of this title; or

(2)   That the Court of Chancery should declare in its discretion that a ratification in accordance with § 204 of this title not be effective or be effective only on certain conditions,

may be brought after the expiration of 120 days from the later of the validation effective time and the time notice, if any, that is required to be given pursuant to § 204(g) of this title is given with respect to such ratification, except that this subsection shall not apply to an action asserting that a ratification was not accomplished in accordance with § 204 of this title or to any person to whom notice of the ratification was required to have been given pursuant to § 204(d) or (g) of this title, but to whom such notice was not given.

SUBCHAPTER VII.   MEETINGS, ELECTIONS, VOTING AND NOTICE

§ 211.   Meetings of stockholders.

(a)(1)   Meetings of stockholders may be held at such place, either within or without this State as may be designated by or in the manner provided in the certificate of incorporation or bylaws, or if not so designated, as determined by the board of directors. If, pursuant to this paragraph or the certificate of incorporation or the bylaws of the corporation, the board of directors is authorized to determine the place of a meeting of stockholders, the board of directors may, in its sole discretion, determine that the meeting shall not be held at any place, but may instead be held solely by means of remote communication as authorized by paragraph (a)(2) of this section.

(2)   If authorized by the board of directors in its sole discretion, and subject to such guidelines and procedures as the board of directors may adopt, stockholders and proxyholders not physically present at a meeting of stockholders may, by means of remote communication:

      a.   Participate in a meeting of stockholders; and

      b.   Be deemed present in person and vote at a meeting of stockholders, whether such meeting is to be held at a designated place or solely by means of remote communication, provided that (i) the corporation shall implement reasonable measures to verify that each person deemed present and permitted to vote at the meeting by means of remote communication is a stockholder or proxyholder, (ii) the corporation shall implement reasonable measures to provide such stockholders and proxyholders a reasonable opportunity to participate in the meeting and to vote on matters submitted to the stockholders, including an opportunity to read or hear the proceedings of the meeting substantially concurrently with such proceedings, and (iii) if any stockholder or proxyholder votes or takes other action at the meeting by means of remote communication, a record of such vote or other action shall be maintained by the corporation.

    (b)   Unless directors are elected by written consent in lieu of an annual meeting as permitted by this subsection, an annual meeting of stockholders shall be held for the election of directors on a date and at a time designated by or in the manner provided in the bylaws. Stockholders may, unless the certificate of incorporation otherwise provides, act by written consent to elect directors; provided, however, that, if such consent is less than unanimous, such action by written consent may be in lieu of holding an annual meeting only if all of the directorships to which directors could be elected at an annual meeting held at the effective time of such action are vacant and are filled by such action. Any other proper business may be transacted at the annual meeting.

    (c)   A failure to hold the annual meeting at the designated time or to elect a sufficient number of directors to conduct the business of the corporation shall not affect otherwise valid corporate acts or work a forfeiture or dissolution of the corporation except as may be otherwise specifically provided in this chapter. If the annual meeting for election of directors is not held on the date designated therefor or action by written consent to elect directors in lieu of an annual meeting has not been taken, the directors shall cause the meeting to be held as soon as is convenient. If there be a failure to hold the annual meeting or to take action by written consent to elect directors in lieu of an annual meeting for a period of 30 days after the date designated for the annual meeting, or if no date has been designated, for a period of 13 months after the latest to occur of the organization of the corporation, its last annual meeting or the last action by written consent to elect directors in lieu of an annual meeting, the Court of Chancery may summarily order a meeting to be held upon the application of any stockholder or director. The shares of stock represented at such meeting, either in person or by proxy, and entitled to vote thereat, shall constitute a quorum for the purpose of such meeting, notwithstanding any provision of the certificate of incorporation or bylaws to the contrary. The Court of Chancery may issue such orders as may be appropriate, including, without limitation, orders designating the time and place of such meeting, the record date or dates for determination of stockholders entitled to notice of the meeting and to vote thereat, and the form of notice of such meeting.

    (d)   Special meetings of the stockholders may be called by the board of directors or by such person or persons as may be authorized by the certificate of incorporation or by the bylaws.

    (e)   All elections of directors shall be by written ballot unless otherwise provided in the certificate of incorporation; if authorized by the board of directors, such requirement of a written ballot shall be satisfied by a ballot submitted by electronic transmission, provided that any such electronic transmission must either set forth or be submitted with information from which it can be determined that the electronic transmission was authorized by the stockholder or proxy holder.

§ 212.   Voting rights of stockholders; proxies; limitations.

    (a)   Unless otherwise provided in the certificate of incorporation and subject to § 213 of this title, each stockholder shall be entitled to 1 vote for each share of capital stock held by such stockholder. If the certificate of incorporation provides for more or less than 1 vote for any share, on any matter, every reference in this chapter to a majority or other proportion of stock, voting stock or shares shall refer to such majority or other proportion of the votes of such stock, voting stock or shares.

(b)   Each stockholder entitled to vote at a meeting of stockholders or to express consent or dissent to corporate action in writing without a meeting may authorize another person or persons to act for such stockholder by proxy, but no such proxy shall be voted or acted upon after 3 years from its date, unless the proxy provides for a longer period.

(c)   Without limiting the manner in which a stockholder may authorize another person or persons to act for such stockholder as proxy pursuant to subsection (b) of this section, the following shall constitute a valid means by which a stockholder may grant such authority:

(1)   A stockholder may execute a document authorizing another person or persons to act for such stockholder as proxy. Execution may be accomplished by the stockholder or such stockholder's authorized officer, director, employee or agent.

(2)   A stockholder may authorize another person or persons to act for such stockholder as proxy by transmitting or authorizing the transmission of an electronic transmission to the person who will be the holder of the proxy or to a proxy solicitation firm, proxy support service organization or like agent duly authorized by the person who will be the holder of the proxy to receive such transmission, provided that any such transmission must either set forth or be submitted with information from which it can be determined that the transmission was authorized by the stockholder. If it is determined that such transmissions are valid, the inspectors or, if there are no inspectors, such other persons making that determination shall specify the information upon which they relied.

(d)   Any copy, facsimile telecommunication or other reliable reproduction of the document (including any electronic transmission) created pursuant to subsection (c) of this section may be substituted or used in lieu of the original document for any and all purposes for which the original document could be used, provided that such copy, facsimile telecommunication or other reproduction shall be a complete reproduction of the entire original document.

(e)   A duly executed proxy shall be irrevocable if it states that it is irrevocable and if, and only as long as, it is coupled with an interest sufficient in law to support an irrevocable power. A proxy may be made irrevocable regardless of whether the interest with which it is coupled is an interest in the stock itself or an interest in the corporation generally.

§ 213.   Fixing date for determination of stockholders of record.

(a)   In order that the corporation may determine the stockholders entitled to notice of any meeting of stockholders or any adjournment thereof, the board of directors may fix a record date, which record date shall not precede the date upon which the resolution fixing the record date is adopted by the board of directors, and which record date shall not be more than 60 nor less than 10 days before the date of such meeting. If the board of directors so fixes a date, such date shall also be the record date for determining the stockholders entitled to vote at such meeting unless the board of directors determines, at the time it fixes such record date, that a later date on or before the date of the meeting shall be the date for making such determination. If no record date is fixed by the board of directors, the record date for determining stockholders entitled to notice of and to vote at a meeting of stockholders shall be at the close of business on the day next preceding the day on which notice is given, or, if notice is waived, at the close of business on the day next preceding the day on which the meeting is held. A determination of stockholders of record entitled to notice of or to vote at a meeting of stockholders shall apply to any adjournment of the meeting; provided, however, that the board of directors may fix a new record date for determination of stockholders entitled to vote at the adjourned meeting, and in such case shall also fix as the record date for stockholders entitled to notice of such adjourned meeting the same or an earlier date as that fixed for determination of stockholders entitled to vote in accordance with the foregoing provisions of this subsection (a) at the adjourned meeting.

(b)   In order that the corporation may determine the stockholders entitled to consent to corporate action in writing without a meeting, the board of directors may fix a record date, which record date shall not precede the date upon which the resolution fixing the record date is adopted by the board of directors, and which date shall not be more than 10 days after the date upon which the resolution fixing the record date is adopted by the board of directors. If no record date has been fixed by the board of directors, the record date for determining stockholders entitled to consent to corporate action in writing without a meeting, when no prior action by the board of directors is required by this chapter, shall be the first date on which a signed written consent setting forth the action taken or proposed to be taken is delivered to the corporation by delivery to its registered office in this State, its principal place of business or an officer or agent of the corporation having custody of the book in which proceedings of meetings of stockholders are recorded. Delivery made to a corporation's registered office shall be by hand or by certified or registered mail, return receipt requested. If no record date has been fixed by the board of directors and prior action by the board of directors is required by this chapter, the record date for determining stockholders entitled to consent to corporate action in writing without a meeting shall be at the close of business on the day on which the board of directors adopts the resolution taking such prior action.

(c)   In order that the corporation may determine the stockholders entitled to receive payment of any dividend or other distribution or allotment of any rights or the stockholders entitled to exercise any rights in respect of any change, conversion or exchange of stock, or for the purpose of any other lawful action, the board of directors may fix a record date, which record date shall not precede the date upon which the resolution fixing the record date is adopted, and which record date shall be not more than 60 days prior to such action. If no record date is fixed, the record date for determining stockholders for any such purpose shall be at the close of business on the day on which the board of directors adopts the resolution relating thereto.

§ 214.   Cumulative voting.

The certificate of incorporation of any corporation may provide that at all elections of directors of the corporation, or at elections held under specified circumstances, each holder of stock or of any class or classes or of a series or series thereof shall be entitled to as many votes as shall equal the number of votes which (except for such provision as to cumulative voting) such holder would be entitled to cast for the election of directors with respect to such holder's shares of stock multiplied by the number of directors to be elected by such holder, and that such holder may cast all of such votes for a single director or may distribute them among the number to be voted for, or for any 2 or more of them as such holder may see fit.

§ 215.   Voting rights of members of nonstock corporations; quorum; proxies.

(a)   Sections 211 through 214 and 216 of this title shall not apply to nonstock corporations, except that § 211(a) and (d) of this title and § 212(c), (d), and (e) of this title shall apply to such corporations, and, when so applied, all references therein to stockholders and to the board of directors shall be deemed to refer to the members and the governing body of a nonstock corporation, respectively; and all references to stock, capital stock, or shares thereof shall be deemed to refer to memberships of a nonprofit nonstock corporation and to membership interests of any other nonstock corporation.

(b)   Unless otherwise provided in the certificate of incorporation or the bylaws of a nonstock corporation, and subject to subsection (f) of this section, each member shall be entitled at every meeting of members to 1 vote on each matter submitted to a vote of members. A member may exercise such voting rights in person or by proxy, but no proxy shall be voted on after 3 years from its date, unless the proxy provides for a longer period.

(c)   Unless otherwise provided in this chapter, the certificate of incorporation or bylaws of a nonstock corporation may specify the number of members having voting power who shall be present or represented by proxy at any meeting in order to constitute a quorum for, and the votes that shall be necessary for, the transaction of any business. In the absence of such specification in the certificate of incorporation or bylaws of a nonstock corporation:

    (1)   One-third of the members of such corporation shall constitute a quorum at a meeting of such members;

    (2)   In all matters other than the election of the governing body of such corporation, the affirmative vote of a majority of such members present in person or represented by proxy at the meeting and entitled to vote on the subject matter shall be the act of the members, unless the vote of a greater number is required by this chapter;

    (3)   Members of the governing body shall be elected by a plurality of the votes of the members of the corporation present in person or represented by proxy at the meeting and entitled to vote thereon; and

    (4)   Where a separate vote by a class or group or classes or groups is required, a majority of the members of such class or group or classes or groups, present in person or represented by proxy, shall constitute a quorum entitled to take action with respect to that vote on that matter and, in all matters other than the election of members of the governing body, the affirmative vote of the majority of the members of such class or group or classes or groups present in person or represented by proxy at the meeting shall be the act of such class or group or classes or groups.

    (d)   If the election of the governing body of any nonstock corporation shall not be held on the day designated by the bylaws, the governing body shall cause the election to be held as soon thereafter as convenient. The failure to hold such an election at the designated time shall not work any forfeiture or dissolution of the corporation, but the Court of Chancery may summarily order such an election to be held upon the application of any member of the corporation. At any election pursuant to such order the persons entitled to vote in such election who shall be present at such meeting, either in person or by proxy, shall constitute a quorum for such meeting, notwithstanding any provision of the certificate of incorporation or the bylaws of the corporation to the contrary.

    (e)   If authorized by the governing body, any requirement of a written ballot shall be satisfied by a ballot submitted by electronic transmission, provided that any such electronic transmission must either set forth or be submitted with information from which it can be determined that the electronic transmission was authorized by the member or proxy holder.

    (f)   Except as otherwise provided in the certificate of incorporation, in the bylaws, or by resolution of the governing body, the record date for any meeting or corporate action shall be deemed to be the date of such meeting or corporate action; provided, however, that no record date may precede any action by the governing body fixing such record date.

§ 216.   Quorum and required vote for stock corporations.

Subject to this chapter in respect of the vote that shall be required for a specified action, the certificate of incorporation or bylaws of any corporation authorized to issue stock may specify the number of shares and/or the amount of other securities having voting power the holders of which shall be present or represented by proxy at any meeting in order to constitute a quorum for, and the votes that shall be necessary for, the transaction of any business, but in no event shall a quorum consist of less than 1/3 of the shares entitled to vote at the meeting, except that, where a separate vote by a class or series or classes or series is required, a quorum shall consist of no less than 1/3 of the shares of such class or series or classes or series. In the absence of such specification in the certificate of incorporation or bylaws of the corporation:

    (1)   A majority of the shares entitled to vote, present in person or represented by proxy, shall constitute a quorum at a meeting of stockholders;

    (2)   In all matters other than the election of directors, the affirmative vote of the majority of shares present in person or represented by proxy at the meeting and entitled to vote on the subject matter shall be the act of the stockholders;

    (3)   Directors shall be elected by a plurality of the votes of the shares present in person or represented by proxy at the meeting and entitled to vote on the election of directors; and

   (4)   Where a separate vote by a class or series or classes or series is required, a majority of the outstanding shares of such class or series or classes or series, present in person or represented by proxy, shall constitute a quorum entitled to take action with respect to that vote on that matter and, in all matters other than the election of directors, the affirmative vote of the majority of shares of such class or series or classes or series present in person or represented by proxy at the meeting shall be the act of such class or series or classes or series.

A bylaw amendment adopted by stockholders which specifies the votes that shall be necessary for the election of directors shall not be further amended or repealed by the board of directors.

§ 217.   Voting rights of fiduciaries, pledgors and joint owners of stock.

   (a)   Persons holding stock in a fiduciary capacity shall be entitled to vote the shares so held. Persons whose stock is pledged shall be entitled to vote, unless in the transfer by the pledgor on the books of the corporation such person has expressly empowered the pledgee to vote thereon, in which case only the pledgee, or such pledgee's proxy, may represent such stock and vote thereon.

   (b)   If shares or other securities having voting power stand of record in the names of 2 or more persons, whether fiduciaries, members of a partnership, joint tenants, tenants in common, tenants by the entirety or otherwise, or if 2 or more persons have the same fiduciary relationship respecting the same shares, unless the secretary of the corporation is given written notice to the contrary and is furnished with a copy of the instrument or order appointing them or creating the relationship wherein it is so provided, their acts with respect to voting shall have the following effect:

   (1)   If only 1 votes, such person's act binds all;

   (2)   If more than 1 vote, the act of the majority so voting binds all;

   (3)   If more than 1 vote, but the vote is evenly split on any particular matter, each faction may vote the securities in question proportionally, or any person voting the shares, or a beneficiary, if any, may apply to the Court of Chancery or such other court as may have jurisdiction to appoint an additional person to act with the persons so voting the shares, which shall then be voted as determined by a majority of such persons and the person appointed by the Court. If the instrument so filed shows that any such tenancy is held in unequal interests, a majority or even split for the purpose of this subsection shall be a majority or even split in interest.

§ 218.   Voting trusts and other voting agreements.

   (a)   One stockholder or 2 or more stockholders may by agreement in writing deposit capital stock of an original issue with or transfer capital stock to any person or persons, or entity or entities authorized to act as trustee, for the purpose of vesting in such person or persons, entity or entities, who may be designated voting trustee, or voting trustees, the right to vote thereon for any period of time determined by such agreement, upon the terms and conditions stated in such agreement. The agreement may contain any other lawful provisions not inconsistent with such purpose. After delivery of a copy of the agreement to the registered office of the corporation in this State or the principal place of business of the corporation, which copy shall be open to the inspection of any stockholder of the corporation or any beneficiary of the trust under the agreement daily during business hours, certificates of stock or uncertificated stock shall be issued to the voting trustee or trustees to represent any stock of an original issue so deposited with such voting trustee or trustees, and any certificates of stock or uncertificated stock so transferred to the voting trustee or trustees shall be surrendered and cancelled and new certificates or uncertificated stock shall be issued therefore to the voting trustee or trustees. In the certificate so issued, if any, it shall be stated that it is issued pursuant to such agreement, and that fact shall also be stated in the stock ledger of the corporation. The voting trustee or trustees may vote the stock so issued or transferred during the period specified in the agreement. Stock standing in the name of the voting trustee or trustees may be voted either in person or by proxy, and in voting the stock, the voting trustee or trustees shall incur no responsibility as stockholder, trustee or otherwise, except for their own individual malfeasance. In any case where 2 or more persons or entities are designated as voting trustees, and the right and method of voting any stock standing in their names at any meeting of the corporation are not fixed by the agreement appointing the trustees, the right to vote the stock and the manner of voting it at the meeting shall be determined by a majority of the trustees, or if they be equally divided as to the right and manner of voting the stock in any particular case, the vote of the stock in such case shall be divided equally among the trustees.

(b)   Any amendment to a voting trust agreement shall be made by a written agreement, a copy of which shall be delivered to the registered office of the corporation in this State or principal place of business of the corporation.

(c)   An agreement between 2 or more stockholders, if in writing and signed by the parties thereto, may provide that in exercising any voting rights, the shares held by them shall be voted as provided by the agreement, or as the parties may agree, or as determined in accordance with a procedure agreed upon by them.

(d)   This section shall not be deemed to invalidate any voting or other agreement among stockholders or any irrevocable proxy which is not otherwise illegal.

§ 219.   List of stockholders entitled to vote; penalty for refusal to produce; stock ledger.

(a)   The corporation shall prepare, at least 10 days before every meeting of stockholders, a complete list of the stockholders entitled to vote at the meeting; provided, however, if the record date for determining the stockholders entitled to vote is less than 10 days before the meeting date, the list shall reflect the stockholders entitled to vote as of the tenth day before the meeting date, arranged in alphabetical order, and showing the address of each stockholder and the number of shares registered in the name of each stockholder. Nothing contained in this section shall require the corporation to include electronic mail addresses or other electronic contact information on such list. Such list shall be open to the examination of any stockholder for any purpose germane to the meeting for a period of at least 10 days prior to the meeting: (i) on a reasonably accessible electronic network, provided that the information required to gain access to such list is provided with the notice of the meeting, or (ii) during ordinary business hours, at the principal place of business of the corporation. In the event that the corporation determines to make the list available on an electronic network, the corporation may take reasonable steps to ensure that such information is available only to stockholders of the corporation. If the meeting is to be held at a place, then a list of stockholders entitled to vote at the meeting shall be produced and kept at the time and place of the meeting during the whole time thereof and may be examined by any stockholder who is present. If the meeting is to be held solely by means of remote communication, then such list shall also be open to the examination of any stockholder during the whole time of the meeting on a reasonably accessible electronic network, and the information required to access such list shall be provided with the notice of the meeting.

(b)   If the corporation, or an officer or agent thereof, refuses to permit examination of the list by a stockholder, such stockholder may apply to the Court of Chancery for an order to compel the corporation to permit such examination. The burden of proof shall be on the corporation to establish that the examination such stockholder seeks is for a purpose not germane to the meeting. The Court may summarily order the corporation to permit examination of the list upon such conditions as the Court may deem appropriate, and may make such additional orders as may be appropriate, including, without limitation, postponing the meeting or voiding the results of the meeting.

(c)   For purposes of this chapter, "stock ledger" means 1 or more records administered by or on behalf of the corporation in which the names of all of the corporation's stockholders of record, the address and number of shares registered in the name of each such stockholder, and all issuances and transfers of stock of the corporation are recorded in accordance with § 224 of this title. The stock ledger shall be the only evidence as to who are the stockholders entitled by this section to examine the list required by this section or to vote in person or by proxy at any meeting of stockholders.

§ 220.   Inspection of books and records.

(a)   As used in this section:

(1)   "Stockholder" means a holder of record of stock in a stock corporation, or a person who is the beneficial owner of shares of such stock held either in a voting trust or by a nominee on behalf of such person.

(2)   "Subsidiary" means any entity directly or indirectly owned, in whole or in part, by the corporation of which the stockholder is a stockholder and over the affairs of which the corporation directly or indirectly exercises control, and includes, without limitation, corporations, partnerships, limited partnerships, limited liability partnerships, limited liability companies, statutory trusts and/or joint ventures.

(3)   "Under oath" includes statements the declarant affirms to be true under penalty of perjury under the laws of the United States or any state.

(b)   Any stockholder, in person or by attorney or other agent, shall, upon written demand under oath stating the purpose thereof, have the right during the usual hours for business to inspect for any proper purpose, and to make copies and extracts from:

(1)   The corporation's stock ledger, a list of its stockholders, and its other books and records; and

(2)   A subsidiary's books and records, to the extent that:

     a.   The corporation has actual possession and control of such records of such subsidiary; or

     b.   The corporation could obtain such records through the exercise of control over such subsidiary, provided that as of the date of the making of the demand:

         1.   The stockholder inspection of such books and records of the subsidiary would not constitute a breach of an agreement between the corporation or the subsidiary and a person or persons not affiliated with the corporation; and

         2.   The subsidiary would not have the right under the law applicable to it to deny the corporation access to such books and records upon demand by the corporation.

In every instance where the stockholder is other than a record holder of stock in a stock corporation, or a member of a nonstock corporation, the demand under oath shall state the person's status as a stockholder, be accompanied by documentary evidence of beneficial ownership of the stock, and state that such documentary evidence is a true and correct copy of what it purports to be. A proper purpose shall mean a purpose reasonably related to such person's interest as a stockholder. In every instance where an attorney or other agent shall be the person who seeks the right to inspection, the demand under oath shall be accompanied by a power of attorney or such other writing which authorizes the attorney or other agent to so act on behalf of the stockholder. The demand under oath shall be directed to the corporation at its registered office in this State or at its principal place of business.

(c)   If the corporation, or an officer or agent thereof, refuses to permit an inspection sought by a stockholder or attorney or other agent acting for the stockholder pursuant to subsection (b) of this section or does not reply to the demand within 5 business days after the demand has been made, the stockholder may apply to the Court of Chancery for an order to compel such inspection. The Court of Chancery is hereby vested with exclusive jurisdiction to determine whether or not the person seeking inspection is entitled to the inspection sought. The Court may summarily order the corporation to permit the stockholder to inspect the corporation's stock ledger, an existing list of stockholders, and its other books and records, and to make copies or extracts therefrom; or the Court may order the corporation to furnish to the stockholder a list of its stockholders as of a specific date on condition that the stockholder first pay to the corporation the reasonable cost of obtaining and furnishing such list and on such other conditions as the Court deems appropriate. Where the stockholder seeks to inspect the corporation's books and records, other than its stock ledger or list of stockholders, such stockholder shall first establish that:

    (1)   Such stockholder is a stockholder;

    (2)   Such stockholder has complied with this section respecting the form and manner of making demand for inspection of such documents; and

    (3)   The inspection such stockholder seeks is for a proper purpose.

Where the stockholder seeks to inspect the corporation's stock ledger or list of stockholders and establishes that such stockholder is a stockholder and has complied with this section respecting the form and manner of making demand for inspection of such documents, the burden of proof shall be upon the corporation to establish that the inspection such stockholder seeks is for an improper purpose. The Court may, in its discretion, prescribe any limitations or conditions with reference to the inspection, or award such other or further relief as the Court may deem just and proper. The Court may order books, documents and records, pertinent extracts therefrom, or duly authenticated copies thereof, to be brought within this State and kept in this State upon such terms and conditions as the order may prescribe.

    (d)   Any director shall have the right to examine the corporation's stock ledger, a list of its stockholders and its other books and records for a purpose reasonably related to the director's position as a director. The Court of Chancery is hereby vested with the exclusive jurisdiction to determine whether a director is entitled to the inspection sought. The Court may summarily order the corporation to permit the director to inspect any and all books and records, the stock ledger and the list of stockholders and to make copies or extracts therefrom. The burden of proof shall be upon the corporation to establish that the inspection such director seeks is for an improper purpose. The Court may, in its discretion, prescribe any limitations or conditions with reference to the inspection, or award such other and further relief as the Court may deem just and proper.

§ 221.   Voting, inspection and other rights of bondholders and debenture holders.

Every corporation may in its certificate of incorporation confer upon the holders of any bonds, debentures or other obligations issued or to be issued by the corporation the power to vote in respect to the corporate affairs and management of the corporation to the extent and in the manner provided in the certificate of incorporation and may confer upon such holders of bonds, debentures or other obligations the same right of inspection of its books, accounts and other records, and also any other rights, which the stockholders of the corporation have or may have by reason of this chapter or of its certificate of incorporation. If the certificate of incorporation so provides, such holders of bonds, debentures or other obligations shall be deemed to be stockholders, and their bonds, debentures or other obligations shall be deemed to be shares of stock, for the purpose of any provision of this chapter which requires the vote of stockholders as a prerequisite to any corporate action and the certificate of incorporation may divest the holders of capital stock, in whole or in part, of their right to vote on any corporate matter whatsoever, except as set forth in § 242(b)(2) of this title.

§ 222.   Notice of meetings and adjourned meetings.

    (a)   Whenever stockholders are required or permitted to take any action at a meeting, a notice of the meeting in the form of a writing or electronic transmission shall be given which shall state the place, if any, date and hour of the meeting, the means of remote communications, if any, by which stockholders and proxy holders may be deemed to be present in person and vote at such meeting, the record date for determining the stockholders entitled to vote at the meeting, if such date is different from the record date for determining stockholders entitled to notice of the meeting, and, in the case of a special meeting, the purpose or purposes for which the meeting is called.

(b)   Unless otherwise provided in this chapter, the notice of any meeting shall be given not less than 10 nor more than 60 days before the date of the meeting to each stockholder entitled to vote at such meeting as of the record date for determining the stockholders entitled to notice of the meeting.

(c)   When a meeting is adjourned to another time or place, unless the bylaws otherwise require, notice need not be given of the adjourned meeting if the time, place, if any, thereof, and the means of remote communications, if any, by which stockholders and proxy holders may be deemed to be present in person and vote at such adjourned meeting are announced at the meeting at which the adjournment is taken. At the adjourned meeting the corporation may transact any business which might have been transacted at the original meeting. If the adjournment is for more than 30 days, a notice of the adjourned meeting shall be given to each stockholder of record entitled to vote at the meeting. If after the adjournment a new record date for stockholders entitled to vote is fixed for the adjourned meeting, the board of directors shall fix a new record date for notice of such adjourned meeting in accordance with § 213(a) of this title, and shall give notice of the adjourned meeting to each stockholder of record entitled to vote at such adjourned meeting as of the record date fixed for notice of such adjourned meeting.

§ 223.   Vacancies and newly created directorships.

(a)   Unless otherwise provided in the certificate of incorporation or bylaws:

(1)   Vacancies and newly created directorships resulting from any increase in the authorized number of directors elected by all of the stockholders having the right to vote as a single class may be filled by a majority of the directors then in office, although less than a quorum, or by a sole remaining director;

(2)   Whenever the holders of any class or classes of stock or series thereof are entitled to elect 1 or more directors by the certificate of incorporation, vacancies and newly created directorships of such class or classes or series may be filled by a majority of the directors elected by such class or classes or series thereof then in office, or by a sole remaining director so elected.

If at any time, by reason of death or resignation or other cause, a corporation should have no directors in office, then any officer or any stockholder or an executor, administrator, trustee or guardian of a stockholder, or other fiduciary entrusted with like responsibility for the person or estate of a stockholder, may call a special meeting of stockholders in accordance with the certificate of incorporation or the bylaws, or may apply to the Court of Chancery for a decree summarily ordering an election as provided in § 211 or § 215 of this title.

(b)   In the case of a corporation the directors of which are divided into classes, any directors chosen under subsection (a) of this section shall hold office until the next election of the class for which such directors shall have been chosen, and until their successors shall be elected and qualified.

(c)   If, at the time of filling any vacancy or any newly created directorship, the directors then in office shall constitute less than a majority of the whole board (as constituted immediately prior to any such increase), the Court of Chancery may, upon application of any stockholder or stockholders holding at least 10 percent of the voting stock at the time outstanding having the right to vote for such directors, summarily order an election to be held to fill any such vacancies or newly created directorships, or to replace the directors chosen by the directors then in office as aforesaid, which election shall be governed by § 211 or § 215 of this title as far as applicable.

(d)   Unless otherwise provided in the certificate of incorporation or bylaws, when 1 or more directors shall resign from the board, effective at a future date, a majority of the directors then in office, including those who have so resigned, shall have power to fill such vacancy or vacancies, the vote thereon to take effect when such resignation or resignations shall become effective, and each director so chosen shall hold office as provided in this section in the filling of other vacancies.

§ 224.   Form of records.

Any records administered by or on behalf of the corporation in the regular course of its business, including its stock ledger, books of account, and minute books, may be kept on, or by means of, or be in the form of, any information storage device, method, or 1 or more electronic networks or databases (including 1 or more distributed electronic networks or databases), provided that the records so kept can be converted into clearly legible paper form within a reasonable time, and, with respect to the stock ledger, that the records so kept (i) can be used to prepare the list of stockholders specified in §§ 219 and 220 of this title, (ii) record the information specified in §§ 156, 159, 217(a) and 218 of this title, and (iii) record transfers of stock as governed by Article 8 of subtitle I of Title 6. Any corporation shall convert any records so kept into clearly legible paper form upon the request of any person entitled to inspect such records pursuant to any provision of this chapter. When records are kept in such manner, a clearly legible paper form prepared from or by means of the information storage device, method, or 1 or more electronic networks or databases (including 1 or more distributed electronic networks or databases) shall be valid and admissible in evidence, and accepted for all other purposes, to the same extent as an original paper record of the same information would have been, provided the paper form accurately portrays the record.

§ 225.   Contested election of directors; proceedings to determine validity.

(a)   Upon application of any stockholder or director, or any officer whose title to office is contested, the Court of Chancery may hear and determine the validity of any election, appointment, removal or resignation of any director or officer of any corporation, and the right of any person to hold or continue to hold such office, and, in case any such office is claimed by more than 1 person, may determine the person entitled thereto; and to that end make such order or decree in any such case as may be just and proper, with power to enforce the production of any books, papers and records of the corporation relating to the issue. In case it should be determined that no valid election has been held, the Court of Chancery may order an election to be held in accordance with § 211 or § 215 of this title. In any such application, service of copies of the application upon the registered agent of the corporation shall be deemed to be service upon the corporation and upon the person whose title to office is contested and upon the person, if any, claiming such office; and the registered agent shall forward immediately a copy of the application to the corporation and to the person whose title to office is contested and to the person, if any, claiming such office, in a postpaid, sealed, registered letter addressed to such corporation and such person at their post-office addresses last known to the registered agent or furnished to the registered agent by the applicant stockholder. The Court may make such order respecting further or other notice of such application as it deems proper under the circumstances.

(b)   Upon application of any stockholder or upon application of the corporation itself, the Court of Chancery may hear and determine the result of any vote of stockholders upon matters other than the election of directors or officers. Service of the application upon the registered agent of the corporation shall be deemed to be service upon the corporation, and no other party need be joined in order for the Court to adjudicate the result of the vote. The Court may make such order respecting notice of the application as it deems proper under the circumstances.

(c)   If 1 or more directors has been convicted of a felony in connection with the duties of such director or directors to the corporation, or if there has been a prior judgment on the merits by a court of competent jurisdiction that 1 or more directors has committed a breach of the duty of loyalty in connection with the duties of such director or directors to that corporation, then, upon application by the corporation, or derivatively in the right of the corporation by any stockholder, in a subsequent action brought for such purpose, the Court of Chancery may remove from office such director or directors if the Court determines that the director or directors did not act in good faith in performing the acts resulting in the prior conviction or judgment and judicial removal is necessary to avoid irreparable harm to the corporation. In connection with such removal, the Court may make such orders as are necessary to effect such removal. In any such application, service of copies of the application upon the registered agent of the corporation shall be deemed to be service upon the corporation and upon the director or directors whose removal is sought; and the registered agent shall forward immediately a copy of the application to the corporation and to such director or directors, in a postpaid, sealed, registered letter addressed to such corporation and such director or directors at their post office addresses last known to the registered agent or furnished to the registered agent by the applicant. The Court may make such order respecting further or other notice of such application as it deems proper under the circumstances.

§ 226.   Appointment of custodian or receiver of corporation on deadlock or for other cause.

(a)   The Court of Chancery, upon application of any stockholder, may appoint 1 or more persons to be custodians, and, if the corporation is insolvent, to be receivers, of and for any corporation when:

(1)   At any meeting held for the election of directors the stockholders are so divided that they have failed to elect successors to directors whose terms have expired or would have expired upon qualification of their successors; or

(2)   The business of the corporation is suffering or is threatened with irreparable injury because the directors are so divided respecting the management of the affairs of the corporation that the required vote for action by the board of directors cannot be obtained and the stockholders are unable to terminate this division; or

(3)   The corporation has abandoned its business and has failed within a reasonable time to take steps to dissolve, liquidate or distribute its assets.

(b)   A custodian appointed under this section shall have all the powers and title of a receiver appointed under § 291 of this title, but the authority of the custodian is to continue the business of the corporation and not to liquidate its affairs and distribute its assets, except when the Court shall otherwise order and except in cases arising under paragraph (a)(3) of this section or § 352(a)(2) of this title.

(c)   In the case of a charitable nonstock corporation, the applicant shall provide a copy of any application referred to in subsection (a) of this section to the Attorney General of the State of Delaware within 1 week of its filing with the Court of Chancery.

§ 227.   Powers of Court in elections of directors.

(a)   The Court of Chancery, in any proceeding instituted under § 211, § 215 or § 225 of this title may determine the right and power of persons claiming to own stock to vote at any meeting of the stockholders.

(b)   The Court of Chancery may appoint a Master to hold any election provided for in § 211, § 215 or § 225 of this title under such orders and powers as it deems proper; and it may punish any officer or director for contempt in case of disobedience of any order made by the Court; and, in case of disobedience by a corporation of any order made by the Court, may enter a decree against such corporation for a penalty of not more than $5,000.

§ 228.   Consent of stockholders or members in lieu of meeting [for application of section, see 81 Del. Laws, c. 86, § 40].

(a)   Unless otherwise provided in the certificate of incorporation, any action required by this chapter to be taken at any annual or special meeting of stockholders of a corporation, or any action which may be taken at any annual or special meeting of such stockholders, may be taken without a meeting, without prior notice and without a vote, if a consent or consents in writing, setting forth the action so taken, shall be signed by the holders of outstanding stock having not less than the minimum number of votes that would be necessary to authorize or take such action at a meeting at which all shares entitled to vote thereon were present and voted and shall be delivered to the corporation by delivery to its registered office in this State, its principal place of business or an officer or agent of the corporation having custody of the book in which proceedings of meetings of stockholders are recorded. Delivery made to a corporation's registered office shall be by hand or by certified or registered mail, return receipt requested.

(b)   Unless otherwise provided in the certificate of incorporation, any action required by this chapter to be taken at a meeting of the members of a nonstock corporation, or any action which may be taken at any meeting of the members of a nonstock corporation, may be taken without a meeting, without prior notice and without a vote, if a consent or consents in writing, setting forth the action so taken, shall be signed by members having not less than the minimum number of votes that would be necessary to authorize or take such action at a meeting at which all members having a right to vote thereon were present and voted and shall be delivered to the corporation by delivery to its registered office in this State, its principal place of business or an officer or agent of the corporation having custody of the book in which proceedings of meetings of members are recorded. Delivery made to a corporation's registered office shall be by hand or by certified or registered mail, return receipt requested.

(c)   No written consent shall be effective to take the corporate action referred to therein unless written consents signed by a sufficient number of holders or members to take action are delivered to the corporation in the manner required by this section within 60 days of the first date on which a written consent is so delivered to the corporation. Any person executing a consent may provide, whether through instruction to an agent or otherwise, that such a consent will be effective at a future time (including a time determined upon the happening of an event), no later than 60 days after such instruction is given or such provision is made, if evidence of such instruction or provision is provided to the corporation. Unless otherwise provided, any such consent shall be revocable prior to its becoming effective.

(d)(1)   An electronic transmission consenting to an action to be taken and transmitted by a stockholder, member or proxyholder, or by a person or persons authorized to act for a stockholder, member or proxyholder, shall be deemed to be written and signed for the purposes of this section, provided that any such electronic transmission sets forth or is delivered with information from which the corporation can determine (A) that the electronic transmission was transmitted by the stockholder, member or proxyholder or by a person or persons authorized to act for the stockholder, member or proxyholder and (B) the date on which such stockholder, member or proxyholder or authorized person or persons transmitted such electronic transmission. A consent given by electronic transmission is delivered to the corporation upon the earliest of: (i) when the consent enters an information processing system, if any, designated by the corporation for receiving consents, so long as the electronic transmission is in a form capable of being processed by that system and the corporation is able to retrieve that electronic transmission; (ii) when a paper reproduction of the consent is delivered to the corporation's principal place of business or an officer or agent of the corporation having custody of the book in which proceedings of meetings of stockholders or members are recorded; (iii) when a paper reproduction of the consent is delivered to the corporation's registered office in this State by hand or by certified or registered mail, return receipt requested; or (iv) when delivered in such other manner, if any, provided by resolution of the board of directors or governing body of the corporation. Whether the corporation has so designated an information processing system to receive consents is determined by the certificate of incorporation, the bylaws or from the context and surrounding circumstances, including the conduct of the corporation. A consent given by electronic transmission is delivered under this section even if no person is aware of its receipt. Receipt of an electronic acknowledgement from an information processing system establishes that a consent given by electronic transmission was received but, by itself, does not establish that the content sent corresponds to the content received.

(2)   Any copy, facsimile or other reliable reproduction of a consent in writing may be substituted or used in lieu of the original writing for any and all purposes for which the original writing could be used, provided that such copy, facsimile or other reproduction shall be a complete reproduction of the entire original writing.

(e)   Prompt notice of the taking of the corporate action without a meeting by less than unanimous written consent shall be given to those stockholders or members who have not consented in writing and who, if the action had been taken at a meeting, would have been entitled to notice of the meeting if the record date for notice of such meeting had been the date that written consents signed by a sufficient number of holders or members to take the action were delivered to the corporation as provided in this section. In the event that the action which is consented to is such as would have required the filing of a certificate under any other section of this title, if such action had been voted on by stockholders or by members at a meeting thereof, the certificate filed under such other section shall state, in lieu of any statement required by such section concerning any vote of stockholders or members, that written consent has been given in accordance with this section.

§ 229.   Waiver of notice.

Whenever notice is required to be given under any provision of this chapter or the certificate of incorporation or bylaws, a written waiver, signed by the person entitled to notice, or a waiver by electronic transmission by the person entitled to notice, whether before or after the time stated therein, shall be deemed equivalent to notice. Attendance of a person at a meeting shall constitute a waiver of notice of such meeting, except when the person attends a meeting for the express purpose of objecting at the beginning of the meeting, to the transaction of any business because the meeting is not lawfully called or convened. Neither the business to be transacted at, nor the purpose of, any regular or special meeting of the stockholders, directors or members of a committee of directors need be specified in any written waiver of notice or any waiver by electronic transmission unless so required by the certificate of incorporation or the bylaws.

§ 230.   Exception to requirements of notice.

(a)   Whenever notice is required to be given, under any provision of this chapter or of the certificate of incorporation or bylaws of any corporation, to any person with whom communication is unlawful, the giving of such notice to such person shall not be required and there shall be no duty to apply to any governmental authority or agency for a license or permit to give such notice to such person. Any action or meeting which shall be taken or held without notice to any such person with whom communication is unlawful shall have the same force and effect as if such notice had been duly given. In the event that the action taken by the corporation is such as to require the filing of a certificate under any of the other sections of this title, the certificate shall state, if such is the fact and if notice is required, that notice was given to all persons entitled to receive notice except such persons with whom communication is unlawful.

(b)   Whenever notice is required to be given, under any provision of this title or the certificate of incorporation or bylaws of any corporation, to any stockholder or, if the corporation is a nonstock corporation, to any member, to whom (1) notice of 2 consecutive annual meetings, and all notices of meetings or of the taking of action by written consent without a meeting to such person during the period between such 2 consecutive annual meetings, or (2) all, and at least 2, payments (if sent by first-class mail) of dividends or interest on securities during a 12-month period, have been mailed addressed to such person at such person's address as shown on the records of the corporation and have been returned undeliverable, the giving of such notice to such person shall not be required. Any action or meeting which shall be taken or held without notice to such person shall have the same force and effect as if such notice had been duly given. If any such person shall deliver to the corporation a written notice setting forth such person's then current address, the requirement that notice be given to such person shall be reinstated. In the event that the action taken by the corporation is such as to require the filing of a certificate under any of the other sections of this title, the certificate need not state that notice was not given to persons to whom notice was not required to be given pursuant to this subsection.

(c)   The exception in paragraph (b)(1) of this section to the requirement that notice be given shall not be applicable to any notice returned as undeliverable if the notice was given by electronic transmission. The exception in paragraph (b)(1) of this section to the requirement that notice be given shall not be applicable to any stockholder or member whose electronic mail address appears on the records of the corporation and to whom notice by electronic transmission is not prohibited by § 232 of this title.

§ 231.   Voting procedures and inspectors of elections.

(a)   The corporation shall, in advance of any meeting of stockholders, appoint 1 or more inspectors to act at the meeting and make a written report thereof. The corporation may designate 1 or more persons as alternate inspectors to replace any inspector who fails to act. If no inspector or alternate is able to act at a meeting of stockholders, the person presiding at the meeting shall appoint 1 or more inspectors to act at the meeting. Each inspector, before entering upon the discharge of the duties of inspector, shall take and sign an oath faithfully to execute the duties of inspector with strict impartiality and according to the best of such inspector's ability.

(b)   The inspectors shall:

(1)   Ascertain the number of shares outstanding and the voting power of each;

(2)   Determine the shares represented at a meeting and the validity of proxies and ballots;

(3)   Count all votes and ballots;

(4)   Determine and retain for a reasonable period a record of the disposition of any challenges made to any determination by the inspectors; and

(5)   Certify their determination of the number of shares represented at the meeting, and their count of all votes and ballots.

The inspectors may appoint or retain other persons or entities to assist the inspectors in the performance of the duties of the inspectors.

(c)   The date and time of the opening and the closing of the polls for each matter upon which the stockholders will vote at a meeting shall be announced at the meeting. No ballot, proxies or votes, nor any revocations thereof or changes thereto, shall be accepted by the inspectors after the closing of the polls unless the Court of Chancery upon application by a stockholder shall determine otherwise.

(d)   In determining the validity and counting of proxies and ballots, the inspectors shall be limited to an examination of the proxies, any envelopes submitted with those proxies, any information provided in accordance with § 211(e) or § 212(c)(2) of this title, or any information provided pursuant to § 211(a)(2)b.(i) or (iii) of this title, ballots and the regular books and records of the corporation, except that the inspectors may consider other reliable information for the limited purpose of reconciling proxies and ballots submitted by or on behalf of banks, brokers, their nominees or similar persons which represent more votes than the holder of a proxy is authorized by the record owner to cast or more votes than the stockholder holds of record. If the inspectors consider other reliable information for the limited purpose permitted herein, the inspectors at the time they make their certification pursuant to paragraph (b)(5) of this section shall specify the precise information considered by them including the person or persons from whom they obtained the information, when the information was obtained, the means by which the information was obtained and the basis for the inspectors' belief that such information is accurate and reliable.

(e)   Unless otherwise provided in the certificate of incorporation or bylaws, this section shall not apply to a corporation that does not have a class of voting stock that is:

(1)   Listed on a national securities exchange;

(2)   Authorized for quotation on an interdealer quotation system of a registered national securities association; or

(3)   Held of record by more than 2,000 stockholders.

§ 232.   Delivery of notice; notice by electronic transmission.

(a)   Without limiting the manner by which notice otherwise may be given effectively to stockholders, any notice to stockholders given by the corporation under any provision of this chapter, the certificate of incorporation, or the bylaws may be given in writing directed to the stockholder's mailing address (or by electronic transmission directed to the stockholder's electronic mail address, as applicable) as it appears on the records of the corporation and shall be given:

(1)   If mailed, when the notice is deposited in the U.S. mail, postage prepaid;

(2)   If delivered by courier service, the earlier of when the notice is received or left at such stockholder's address; or

(3)   If given by electronic mail, when directed to such stockholder's electronic mail address unless the stockholder has notified the corporation in writing or by electronic transmission of an objection to receiving notice by electronic mail or such notice is prohibited by subsection (e) of this section.

A notice by electronic mail must include a prominent legend that the communication is an important notice regarding the corporation.

(b)   Without limiting the manner by which notice otherwise may be given effectively to stockholders, but subject to subsection (e) of this section, any notice to stockholders given by the corporation under any provision of this chapter, the certificate of incorporation, or the bylaws shall be effective if given by a form of electronic transmission consented to by the stockholder to whom the notice is given. Any such consent shall be revocable by the stockholder by written notice or electronic transmission to the corporation.

(c)   Notice given pursuant to subsection (b) of this section shall be deemed given:

(1)   If by facsimile telecommunication, when directed to a number at which the stockholder has consented to receive notice;

(2)   If by a posting on an electronic network together with separate notice to the stockholder of such specific posting, upon the later of:

a.   Such posting; and

b.   The giving of such separate notice; and

(3)   If by any other form of electronic transmission, when directed to the stockholder.

(d)   For purposes of this chapter:

(1)   "Electronic transmission" means any form of communication, not directly involving the physical transmission of paper, including the use of, or participation in, 1 or more electronic networks or databases (including 1 or more distributed electronic networks or databases), that creates a record that may be retained, retrieved and reviewed by a recipient thereof, and that may be directly reproduced in paper form by such a recipient through an automated process;

(2)   "Electronic mail" means an electronic transmission directed to a unique electronic mail address (which electronic mail shall be deemed to include any files attached thereto and any information hyperlinked to a website if such electronic mail includes the contact information of an officer or agent of the corporation who is available to assist with accessing such files and information); and

(3)   "Electronic mail address" means a destination, commonly expressed as a string of characters, consisting of a unique user name or mailbox (commonly referred to as the "local part" of the address) and a reference to an internet domain (commonly referred to as the "domain part" of the address), whether or not displayed, to which electronic mail can be sent or delivered.

(e)   Notwithstanding the foregoing, a notice may not be given by an electronic transmission from and after the time that:

(1)   The corporation is unable to deliver by such electronic transmission 2 consecutive notices given by the corporation; and

(2)   Such inability becomes known to the secretary or an assistant secretary of the corporation or to the transfer agent, or other person responsible for the giving of notice, provided, however, the inadvertent failure to discover such inability shall not invalidate any meeting or other action.

(f)   An affidavit of the secretary or an assistant secretary or of the transfer agent or other agent of the corporation that notice has been given shall, in the absence of fraud, be prima facie evidence of the facts stated therein.

(g)   No provision of this section, except for paragraphs (a)(1), (d)(2) and (d)(3) of this section, shall apply to § 164, § 296, § 311, § 312, or § 324 of this title.

§ 233.   Notice to stockholders sharing an address.

(a)   Without limiting the manner by which notice otherwise may be given effectively to stockholders, any notice to stockholders given by the corporation under any provision of this chapter, the certificate of incorporation, or the bylaws shall be effective if given by a single written notice to stockholders who share an address if consented to by the stockholders at that address to whom such notice is given. Any such consent shall be revocable by the stockholder by written notice to the corporation.

(b)   Any stockholder who fails to object in writing to the corporation, within 60 days of having been given written notice by the corporation of its intention to send the single notice permitted under subsection (a) of this section, shall be deemed to have consented to receiving such single written notice.

(c)   [Repealed.]

(d)   This section shall not apply to § 164, § 296, § 311, § 312 or § 324 of this title.

SUBCHAPTER VIII.   AMENDMENT OF CERTIFICATE OF INCORPORATION; CHANGES IN CAPITAL AND CAPITAL STOCK

§ 241.   Amendment of certificate of incorporation before receipt of payment for stock.

(a)   Before a corporation has received any payment for any of its stock, it may amend its certificate of incorporation at any time or times, in any and as many respects as may be desired, so long as its certificate of incorporation as amended would contain only such provisions as it would be lawful and proper to insert in an original certificate of incorporation filed at the time of filing the amendment.

(b)   The amendment of a certificate of incorporation authorized by this section shall be adopted by a majority of the incorporators, if directors were not named in the original certificate of incorporation or have not yet been elected, or, if directors were named in the original certificate of incorporation or have been elected and have qualified, by a majority of the directors. A certificate setting forth the amendment and certifying that the corporation has not received any payment for any of its stock, or that the corporation has no members, as applicable, and that the amendment has been duly adopted in accordance with this section shall be executed, acknowledged and filed in accordance with § 103 of this title. Upon such filing, the corporation's certificate of incorporation shall be deemed to be amended accordingly as of the date on which the original certificate of incorporation became effective, except as to those persons who are substantially and adversely affected by the amendment and as to those persons the amendment shall be effective from the filing date.

(c)   This section will apply to a nonstock corporation before such a corporation has any members; provided, however, that all references to directors shall be deemed to be references to members of the governing body of the corporation.

§ 242. Amendment of certificate of incorporation after receipt of payment for stock; nonstock corporations.

(a) After a corporation has received payment for any of its capital stock, or after a nonstock corporation has members, it may amend its certificate of incorporation, from time to time, in any and as many respects as may be desired, so long as its certificate of incorporation as amended would contain only such provisions as it would be lawful and proper to insert in an original certificate of incorporation filed at the time of the filing of the amendment; and, if a change in stock or the rights of stockholders, or an exchange, reclassification, subdivision, combination or cancellation of stock or rights of stockholders is to be made, such provisions as may be necessary to effect such change, exchange, reclassification, subdivision, combination or cancellation. In particular, and without limitation upon such general power of amendment, a corporation may amend its certificate of incorporation, from time to time, so as:

(1) To change its corporate name; or

(2) To change, substitute, enlarge or diminish the nature of its business or its corporate powers and purposes; or

(3) To increase or decrease its authorized capital stock or to reclassify the same, by changing the number, par value, designations, preferences, or relative, participating, optional, or other special rights of the shares, or the qualifications, limitations or restrictions of such rights, or by changing shares with par value into shares without par value, or shares without par value into shares with par value either with or without increasing or decreasing the number of shares, or by subdividing or combining the outstanding shares of any class or series of a class of shares into a greater or lesser number of outstanding shares; or

(4) To cancel or otherwise affect the right of the holders of the shares of any class to receive dividends which have accrued but have not been declared; or

(5) To create new classes of stock having rights and preferences either prior and superior or subordinate and inferior to the stock of any class then authorized, whether issued or unissued; or

(6) To change the period of its duration; or

(7) To delete:

a. Such provisions of the original certificate of incorporation which named the incorporator or incorporators, the initial board of directors and the original subscribers for shares; and

b. Such provisions contained in any amendment to the certificate of incorporation as were necessary to effect a change, exchange, reclassification, subdivision, combination or cancellation of stock, if such change, exchange, reclassification, subdivision, combination or cancellation has become effective.

Any or all such changes or alterations may be effected by 1 certificate of amendment.

(b) Every amendment authorized by subsection (a) of this section shall be made and effected in the following manner:

(1) If the corporation has capital stock, its board of directors shall adopt a resolution setting forth the amendment proposed, declaring its advisability, and either calling a special meeting of the stockholders entitled to vote in respect thereof for the consideration of such amendment or directing that the amendment proposed be considered at the next annual meeting of the stockholders; provided, however, that unless otherwise expressly required by the certificate of incorporation, no meeting or vote of stockholders shall be required to adopt an amendment that effects only changes described in paragraph (a)(1) or (7) of this section. Such special or annual meeting shall be called and held upon notice in accordance with § 222 of this title. The notice

shall set forth such amendment in full or a brief summary of the changes to be effected thereby unless such notice constitutes a notice of internet availability of proxy materials under the rules promulgated under the Securities Exchange Act of 1934 [15 U.S.C. § 78a et seq.]. At the meeting a vote of the stockholders entitled to vote thereon shall be taken for and against any proposed amendment that requires adoption by stockholders. If no vote of stockholders is required to effect such amendment, or if a majority of the outstanding stock entitled to vote thereon, and a majority of the outstanding stock of each class entitled to vote thereon as a class has been voted in favor of the amendment, a certificate setting forth the amendment and certifying that such amendment has been duly adopted in accordance with this section shall be executed, acknowledged and filed and shall become effective in accordance with § 103 of this title.

(2)   The holders of the outstanding shares of a class shall be entitled to vote as a class upon a proposed amendment, whether or not entitled to vote thereon by the certificate of incorporation, if the amendment would increase or decrease the aggregate number of authorized shares of such class, increase or decrease the par value of the shares of such class, or alter or change the powers, preferences, or special rights of the shares of such class so as to affect them adversely. If any proposed amendment would alter or change the powers, preferences, or special rights of 1 or more series of any class so as to affect them adversely, but shall not so affect the entire class, then only the shares of the series so affected by the amendment shall be considered a separate class for the purposes of this paragraph. The number of authorized shares of any such class or classes of stock may be increased or decreased (but not below the number of shares thereof then outstanding) by the affirmative vote of the holders of a majority of the stock of the corporation entitled to vote irrespective of this subsection, if so provided in the original certificate of incorporation, in any amendment thereto which created such class or classes of stock or which was adopted prior to the issuance of any shares of such class or classes of stock, or in any amendment thereto which was authorized by a resolution or resolutions adopted by the affirmative vote of the holders of a majority of such class or classes of stock.

(3)   If the corporation is a nonstock corporation, then the governing body thereof shall adopt a resolution setting forth the amendment proposed and declaring its advisability. If a majority of all the members of the governing body shall vote in favor of such amendment, a certificate thereof shall be executed, acknowledged and filed and shall become effective in accordance with § 103 of this title. The certificate of incorporation of any nonstock corporation may contain a provision requiring any amendment thereto to be approved by a specified number or percentage of the members or of any specified class of members of such corporation in which event such proposed amendment shall be submitted to the members or to any specified class of members of such corporation in the same manner, so far as applicable, as is provided in this section for an amendment to the certificate of incorporation of a stock corporation; and in the event of the adoption thereof by such members, a certificate evidencing such amendment shall be executed, acknowledged and filed and shall become effective in accordance with § 103 of this title.

(4)   Whenever the certificate of incorporation shall require for action by the board of directors of a corporation other than a nonstock corporation or by the governing body of a nonstock corporation, by the holders of any class or series of shares or by the members, or by the holders of any other securities having voting power the vote of a greater number or proportion than is required by any section of this title, the provision of the certificate of incorporation requiring such greater vote shall not be altered, amended or repealed except by such greater vote.

(c)   The resolution authorizing a proposed amendment to the certificate of incorporation may provide that at any time prior to the effectiveness of the filing of the amendment with the Secretary of State, notwithstanding authorization of the proposed amendment by the stockholders of the corporation or by the members of a nonstock corporation, the board of directors or governing body may abandon such proposed amendment without further action by the stockholders or members.

§ 243.   Retirement of stock.

(a)   A corporation, by resolution of its board of directors, may retire any shares of its capital stock that are issued but are not outstanding.

(b)   Whenever any shares of the capital stock of a corporation are retired, they shall resume the status of authorized and unissued shares of the class or series to which they belong unless the certificate of incorporation otherwise provides. If the certificate of incorporation prohibits the reissuance of such shares, or prohibits the reissuance of such shares as a part of a specific series only, a certificate stating that reissuance of the shares (as part of the class or series) is prohibited identifying the shares and reciting their retirement shall be executed, acknowledged and filed and shall become effective in accordance with § 103 of this title. When such certificate becomes effective, it shall have the effect of amending the certificate of incorporation so as to reduce accordingly the number of authorized shares of the class or series to which such shares belong or, if such retired shares constitute all of the authorized shares of the class or series to which they belong, of eliminating from the certificate of incorporation all reference to such class or series of stock.

(c)   If the capital of the corporation will be reduced by or in connection with the retirement of shares, the reduction of capital shall be effected pursuant to § 244 of this title.

§ 244.   Reduction of capital.

(a)   A corporation, by resolution of its board of directors, may reduce its capital in any of the following ways:

(1)   By reducing or eliminating the capital represented by shares of capital stock which have been retired;

(2)   By applying to an otherwise authorized purchase or redemption of outstanding shares of its capital stock some or all of the capital represented by the shares being purchased or redeemed, or any capital that has not been allocated to any particular class of its capital stock;

(3)   By applying to an otherwise authorized conversion or exchange of outstanding shares of its capital stock some or all of the capital represented by the shares being converted or exchanged, or some or all of any capital that has not been allocated to any particular class of its capital stock, or both, to the extent that such capital in the aggregate exceeds the total aggregate par value or the stated capital of any previously unissued shares issuable upon such conversion or exchange; or

(4)   By transferring to surplus (i) some or all of the capital not represented by any particular class of its capital stock; (ii) some or all of the capital represented by issued shares of its par value capital stock, which capital is in excess of the aggregate par value of such shares; or (iii) some of the capital represented by issued shares of its capital stock without par value.

(b)   Notwithstanding the other provisions of this section, no reduction of capital shall be made or effected unless the assets of the corporation remaining after such reduction shall be sufficient to pay any debts of the corporation for which payment has not been otherwise provided. No reduction of capital shall release any liability of any stockholder whose shares have not been fully paid.

(c)   [Repealed.]

§ 245.   Restated certificate of incorporation.

(a)   A corporation may, whenever desired, integrate into a single instrument all of the provisions of its certificate of incorporation which are then in effect and operative as a result of there having theretofore been filed with the Secretary of State 1 or more certificates or other instruments pursuant to any of the sections referred to in § 104 of this title, and it may at the same time also further amend its certificate of incorporation by adopting a restated certificate of incorporation.

(b)   If the restated certificate of incorporation merely restates and integrates but does not further amend the certificate of incorporation, as theretofore amended or supplemented by any instrument that was filed pursuant to any of the sections mentioned in § 104 of this title, it may be adopted by the board of directors without a vote of the stockholders, or it may be proposed by the directors and submitted by them to the stockholders for adoption, in which case the procedure and vote required, if any, by § 242 of this title for amendment of the certificate of incorporation shall be applicable. If the restated certificate of incorporation restates and integrates and also further amends in any respect the certificate of incorporation, as theretofore amended or supplemented, it shall be proposed by the directors and adopted by the stockholders in the manner and by the vote prescribed by § 242 of this title or, if the corporation has not received any payment for any of its stock, in the manner and by the vote prescribed by § 241 of this title.

(c)   A restated certificate of incorporation shall be specifically designated as such in its heading. It shall state, either in its heading or in an introductory paragraph, the corporation's present name, and, if it has been changed, the name under which it was originally incorporated, and the date of filing of its original certificate of incorporation with the Secretary of State. A restated certificate shall also state that it was duly adopted in accordance with this section. If it was adopted by the board of directors without a vote of the stockholders (unless it was adopted pursuant to § 241 of this title or without a vote of members pursuant to 242(b)(3) of this title), it shall state that it only restates and integrates and does not further amend (except, if applicable, as permitted under § 242(a)(1) and § 242(b)(1) of this title) the provisions of the corporation's certificate of incorporation as theretofore amended or supplemented, and that there is no discrepancy between those provisions and the provisions of the restated certificate. A restated certificate of incorporation may omit (a) such provisions of the original certificate of incorporation which named the incorporator or incorporators, the initial board of directors and the original subscribers for shares, and (b) such provisions contained in any amendment to the certificate of incorporation as were necessary to effect a change, exchange, reclassification, subdivision, combination or cancellation of stock, if such change, exchange, reclassification, subdivision, combination or cancellation has become effective. Any such omissions shall not be deemed a further amendment.

(d)   A restated certificate of incorporation shall be executed, acknowledged and filed in accordance with § 103 of this title. Upon its filing with the Secretary of State, the original certificate of incorporation, as theretofore amended or supplemented, shall be superseded; thenceforth, the restated certificate of incorporation, including any further amendments or changes made thereby, shall be the certificate of incorporation of the corporation, but the original date of incorporation shall remain unchanged.

(e)   Any amendment or change effected in connection with the restatement and integration of the certificate of incorporation shall be subject to any other provision of this chapter, not inconsistent with this section, which would apply if a separate certificate of amendment were filed to effect such amendment or change.

§ 246.   [Reserved.]

SUBCHAPTER IX.   MERGER, CONSOLIDATION OR CONVERSION

§ 251.   Merger or consolidation of domestic corporations [For application of this section, see 79 Del. Laws, c. 327, § 8 and 80 Del. Laws, c. 265, § 17].

(a)   Any 2 or more corporations of this State may merge into a single surviving corporation, which may be any 1 of the constituent corporations or may consolidate into a new resulting corporation formed by the consolidation, pursuant to an agreement of merger or consolidation, as the case may be, complying and approved in accordance with this section.

(b)   The board of directors of each corporation which desires to merge or consolidate shall adopt a resolution approving an agreement of merger or consolidation and declaring its advisability. The agreement shall state:

(1)   The terms and conditions of the merger or consolidation;

(2)   The mode of carrying the same into effect;

(3)   In the case of a merger, such amendments or changes in the certificate of incorporation of the surviving corporation as are desired to be effected by the merger (which amendments or changes may amend and restate the certificate of incorporation of the surviving corporation in its entirety), or, if no such amendments or changes are desired, a statement that the certificate of incorporation of the surviving corporation shall be its certificate of incorporation;

(4)   In the case of a consolidation, that the certificate of incorporation of the resulting corporation shall be as is set forth in an attachment to the agreement;

(5)   The manner, if any, of converting the shares of each of the constituent corporations into shares or other securities of the corporation surviving or resulting from the merger or consolidation, or of cancelling some or all of such shares, and, if any shares of any of the constituent corporations are not to remain outstanding, to be converted solely into shares or other securities of the surviving or resulting corporation or to be cancelled, the cash, property, rights or securities of any other corporation or entity which the holders of such shares are to receive in exchange for, or upon conversion of such shares and the surrender of any certificates evidencing them, which cash, property, rights or securities of any other corporation or entity may be in addition to or in lieu of shares or other securities of the surviving or resulting corporation; and

(6)   Such other details or provisions as are deemed desirable, including, without limiting the generality of the foregoing, a provision for the payment of cash in lieu of the issuance or recognition of fractional shares, rights or other securities of the surviving or resulting corporation or of any other corporation or entity the shares, rights or other securities of which are to be received in the merger or consolidation, or for any other arrangement with respect thereto, consistent with § 155 of this title.

The agreement so adopted shall be executed by an authorized person, provided that if the agreement is filed, it shall be executed and acknowledged in accordance with § 103 of this title. Any of the terms of the agreement of merger or consolidation may be made dependent upon facts ascertainable outside of such agreement, provided that the manner in which such facts shall operate upon the terms of the agreement is clearly and expressly set forth in the agreement of merger or consolidation. The term "facts," as used in the preceding sentence, includes, but is not limited to, the occurrence of any event, including a determination or action by any person or body, including the corporation.

(c)   The agreement required by subsection (b) of this section shall be submitted to the stockholders of each constituent corporation at an annual or special meeting for the purpose of acting on the agreement. Due notice of the time, place and purpose of the meeting shall be given to each holder of stock, whether voting or nonvoting, of the corporation at the stockholder's address as it appears on the records of the corporation, at least 20 days prior to the date of the meeting. The notice shall contain a copy of the agreement or a brief summary thereof. At the meeting, the agreement shall be considered and a vote taken for its adoption or rejection. If a majority of the outstanding stock of the corporation entitled to vote thereon shall be voted for the adoption of the agreement, that fact shall be certified on the agreement by the secretary or assistant secretary of the corporation, provided that such certification on the agreement shall not be required if a certificate of merger or consolidation is filed in lieu of filing the agreement. If the agreement shall be so adopted and certified by each constituent corporation, it shall then be filed and shall become effective, in accordance with § 103 of this title. In lieu of filing the agreement of merger or consolidation required by this section, the surviving or resulting corporation may file a certificate of merger or consolidation, executed in accordance with § 103 of this title, which states:

(1) The name and state of incorporation of each of the constituent corporations;

(2) That an agreement of merger or consolidation has been approved, adopted, executed and acknowledged by each of the constituent corporations in accordance with this section;

(3) The name of the surviving or resulting corporation;

(4) In the case of a merger, such amendments or changes in the certificate of incorporation of the surviving corporation as are desired to be effected by the merger (which amendments or changes may amend and restate the certificate of incorporation of the surviving corporation in its entirety), or, if no such amendments or changes are desired, a statement that the certificate of incorporation of the surviving corporation shall be its certificate of incorporation;

(5) In the case of a consolidation, that the certificate of incorporation of the resulting corporation shall be as set forth in an attachment to the certificate;

(6) That the executed agreement of consolidation or merger is on file at an office of the surviving or resulting corporation, stating the address thereof; and

(7) That a copy of the agreement of consolidation or merger will be furnished by the surviving or resulting corporation, on request and without cost, to any stockholder of any constituent corporation.

(d) Any agreement of merger or consolidation may contain a provision that at any time prior to the time that the agreement (or a certificate in lieu thereof) filed with the Secretary of State becomes effective in accordance with § 103 of this title, the agreement may be terminated by the board of directors of any constituent corporation notwithstanding approval of the agreement by the stockholders of all or any of the constituent corporations; in the event the agreement of merger or consolidation is terminated after the filing of the agreement (or a certificate in lieu thereof) with the Secretary of State but before the agreement (or a certificate in lieu thereof) has become effective, a certificate of termination or merger or consolidation shall be filed in accordance with § 103 of this title. Any agreement of merger or consolidation may contain a provision that the boards of directors of the constituent corporations may amend the agreement at any time prior to the time that the agreement (or a certificate in lieu thereof) filed with the Secretary of State becomes effective in accordance with § 103 of this title, provided that an amendment made subsequent to the adoption of the agreement by the stockholders of any constituent corporation shall not (1) alter or change the amount or kind of shares, securities, cash, property and/or rights to be received in exchange for or on conversion of all or any of the shares of any class or series thereof of such constituent corporation, (2) alter or change any term of the certificate of incorporation of the surviving corporation to be effected by the merger or consolidation, or (3) alter or change any of the terms and conditions of the agreement if such alteration or change would adversely affect the holders of any class or series thereof of such constituent corporation; in the event the agreement of merger or consolidation is amended after the filing thereof with the Secretary of State but before the agreement has become effective, a certificate of amendment of merger or consolidation shall be filed in accordance with § 103 of this title.

(e) In the case of a merger, the certificate of incorporation of the surviving corporation shall automatically be amended to the extent, if any, that changes in the certificate of incorporation are set forth in the agreement of merger.

(f) Notwithstanding the requirements of subsection (c) of this section, unless required by its certificate of incorporation, no vote of stockholders of a constituent corporation surviving a merger shall be necessary to authorize a merger if (1) the agreement of merger does not amend in any respect the certificate of incorporation of such constituent corporation, (2) each share of stock of such constituent corporation outstanding immediately prior to the effective date of the merger is to be an identical outstanding or treasury share of the surviving corporation after the effective date of the merger, and (3) either no shares of common stock of the surviving corporation and no shares, securities or obligations convertible into such stock are to be issued or delivered under the plan of merger, or the authorized unissued shares or the treasury shares of common stock of the surviving corporation to be issued or delivered under the plan of merger plus those initially issuable upon conversion of any other shares, securities or obligations to be issued or delivered under such plan do not exceed 20% of the shares of common stock of such constituent corporation outstanding immediately prior to the effective date of the merger. No vote of stockholders of a constituent corporation shall be necessary to authorize a merger or consolidation if no shares of the stock of such corporation shall have been issued prior to the adoption by the board of directors of the resolution approving the agreement of merger or consolidation. If an agreement of merger is adopted by the constituent corporation surviving the merger, by action of its board of directors and without any vote of its stockholders pursuant to this subsection, the secretary or assistant secretary of that corporation shall certify on the agreement that the agreement has been adopted pursuant to this subsection and, (1) if it has been adopted pursuant to the first sentence of this subsection, that the conditions specified in that sentence have been satisfied, or (2) if it has been adopted pursuant to the second sentence of this subsection, that no shares of stock of such corporation were issued prior to the adoption by the board of directors of the resolution approving the agreement of merger or consolidation, provided that such certification on the agreement shall not be required if a certificate of merger or consolidation is filed in lieu of filing the agreement. The agreement so adopted and certified shall then be filed and shall become effective, in accordance with § 103 of this title. Such filing shall constitute a representation by the person who executes the agreement that the facts stated in the certificate remain true immediately prior to such filing.

(g) Notwithstanding the requirements of subsection (c) of this section, unless expressly required by its certificate of incorporation, no vote of stockholders of a constituent corporation shall be necessary to authorize a merger with or into a single direct or indirect wholly-owned subsidiary of such constituent corporation if: (1) such constituent corporation and the direct or indirect wholly-owned subsidiary of such constituent corporation are the only constituent entities to the merger; (2) each share or fraction of a share of the capital stock of the constituent corporation outstanding immediately prior to the effective time of the merger is converted in the merger into a share or equal fraction of share of capital stock of a holding company having the same designations, rights, powers and preferences, and the qualifications, limitations and restrictions thereof, as the share of stock of the constituent corporation being converted in the merger; (3) the holding company and the constituent corporation are corporations of this State and the direct or indirect wholly-owned subsidiary that is the other constituent entity to the merger is a corporation or limited liability company of this State; (4) the certificate of incorporation and by-laws of the holding company immediately following the effective time of the merger contain provisions identical to the certificate of incorporation and by-laws of the constituent corporation immediately prior to the effective time of the merger (other than provisions, if any, regarding the incorporator or incorporators, the corporate name, the registered office and agent, the initial board of directors and the initial subscribers for shares and such provisions contained in any amendment to the certificate of incorporation as were necessary to effect a change, exchange, reclassification, subdivision, combination or cancellation of stock, if such change, exchange, reclassification, subdivision, combination, or cancellation has become effective); (5) as a result of the merger the constituent corporation or its successor becomes or remains a direct or indirect wholly-owned subsidiary of the holding company; (6) the directors of the constituent corporation become or remain the directors of the holding company upon the effective time of the merger; (7) the organizational documents of the surviving entity immediately following the effective time of the merger contain provisions identical to the certificate of incorporation of the constituent corporation immediately prior to the effective time of the merger (other than provisions, if any, regarding the incorporator or incorporators, the corporate or entity name, the registered office and agent, the initial board of directors and the initial subscribers for shares, references to members rather than stockholders or shareholders, references to interests, units or the like rather than stock or shares, references to managers, managing members or other members of the governing body rather than directors and such provisions contained in any amendment to the certificate of incorporation as were necessary to effect a change, exchange, reclassification, subdivision, combination or cancellation of stock, if such change, exchange, reclassification, subdivision, combination or cancellation has become effective); provided, however, that (i) if the organizational documents of the surviving entity do not contain the following provisions, they shall be amended in the merger to contain provisions requiring that (A) any act or transaction by or involving the surviving entity, other than the election or removal of directors or managers, managing members or other members of the governing body of the surviving entity, that requires for its adoption under this chapter or its organizational documents the approval of the stockholders or members of the surviving entity shall, by specific reference to this subsection, require, in addition, the approval of the stockholders of the holding company (or any successor by merger), by the same vote as is required by this chapter and/or by the organizational documents of the surviving entity; provided, however, that for purposes of this clause (i)(A), any surviving entity that is not a corporation shall include in such amendment a requirement that the approval of the stockholders of the holding company be obtained for any act or transaction by or involving the surviving entity, other than the election or removal of directors or managers, managing members or other members of the governing body of the surviving entity, which would require the approval of the stockholders of the surviving entity if the surviving entity were a corporation subject to this chapter; (B) any amendment of the organizational documents of a surviving entity that is not a corporation, which amendment would, if adopted by a corporation subject to this chapter, be required to be included in the certificate of incorporation of such corporation, shall, by specific reference to this subsection, require, in addition, the approval of the stockholders of the holding company (or any successor by merger), by the same vote as is required by this chapter and/or by the organizational documents of the surviving entity; and (C) the business and affairs of a surviving entity that is not a corporation shall be managed by or under the direction of a board of directors, board of managers or other governing body consisting of individuals who are subject to the same fiduciary duties applicable to, and who are liable for breach of such duties to the same extent as, directors of a corporation subject to this chapter; and (ii) the organizational documents of the surviving entity may be amended in the merger (A) to reduce the number of classes and shares of capital stock or other equity interests or units that the surviving entity is authorized to issue and (B) to eliminate any provision authorized by § 141(d) of this title; and (8) the stockholders of the constituent corporation do not recognize gain or loss for United States federal income tax purposes as determined by the board of directors of the constituent corporation. Neither paragraph (g)(7)(i) of this section nor any provision of a surviving entity's organizational documents required by paragraph (g)(7)(i) of this section shall be deemed or construed to require approval of the stockholders of the holding company to elect or remove directors or managers, managing members or other members of the governing body of the surviving entity. The term "organizational documents", as used in paragraph (g)(7) of this section and in the preceding sentence, shall, when used in reference to a corporation, mean the certificate of incorporation of such corporation, and when used in reference to a limited liability company, mean the limited liability company agreement of such limited liability company.

As used in this subsection only, the term "holding company" means a corporation which, from its incorporation until consummation of a merger governed by this subsection, was at all times a direct or indirect wholly-owned subsidiary of the constituent corporation and whose capital stock is issued in such merger. From and after the effective time of a merger adopted by a constituent corporation by action of its board of directors and without any vote of stockholders pursuant to this subsection: (i) to the extent the restrictions of § 203 of this title applied to the constituent corporation and its stockholders at the effective time of the merger, such restrictions shall apply to the holding company and its stockholders immediately after the effective time of the merger as though it were the constituent corporation, and all shares of stock of the holding company acquired in the merger shall for purposes of § 203 of this title be deemed to have been acquired at the time that the shares of stock of the constituent corporation converted in the merger were acquired, and provided further that any stockholder who immediately prior to the effective time of the merger was not an interested stockholder within the meaning of § 203 of this title shall not solely by reason of the merger become an interested stockholder of the holding company, (ii) if the corporate name of the holding company immediately following the effective time of the merger is the same as the corporate name of the constituent corporation immediately prior to the effective time of the merger, the shares of capital stock of the holding company into which the shares of capital stock of the constituent corporation are converted in the merger shall be represented by the stock certificates that previously represented shares of capital stock of the constituent corporation and (iii) to the extent a stockholder of the constituent corporation immediately prior to the merger had standing to institute or maintain derivative litigation on behalf of the constituent corporation, nothing in this section shall be deemed to limit or extinguish such standing. If an agreement of merger is adopted by a constituent corporation by action of its board of directors and without any vote of stockholders pursuant to this subsection, the secretary or assistant secretary of the constituent corporation shall certify on the agreement that the agreement has been adopted pursuant to this subsection and that the conditions specified in the first sentence of this subsection have been satisfied, provided that such certification on the agreement shall not be required if a certificate of merger or consolidation is filed in lieu of filing the agreement. The agreement so adopted and certified shall then be filed and become effective, in accordance with § 103 of this title. Such filing shall constitute a representation by the person who executes the agreement that the facts stated in the certificate remain true immediately prior to such filing.

(h)   Notwithstanding the requirements of subsection (c) of this section, unless expressly required by its certificate of incorporation, no vote of stockholders of a constituent corporation that has a class or series of stock that is listed on a national securities exchange or held of record by more than 2,000 holders immediately prior to the execution of the agreement of merger by such constituent corporation shall be necessary to authorize a merger if:

(1)   The agreement of merger expressly:

a.   Permits or requires such merger to be effected under this subsection; and

b.   Provides that such merger shall be effected as soon as practicable following the consummation of the offer referred to in paragraph (h)(2) of this section if such merger is effected under this subsection;

(2)   A corporation consummates an offer for all of the outstanding stock of such constituent corporation on the terms provided in such agreement of merger that, absent this subsection, would be entitled to vote on the adoption or rejection of the agreement of merger; provided, however, that such offer may be conditioned on the tender of a minimum number or percentage of shares of the stock of such constituent corporation, or of any class or series thereof, and such offer may exclude any excluded stock and provided further that the corporation may consummate separate offers for separate classes or series of the stock of such constituent corporation;

a.–d. [Repealed.]

(3)   Immediately following the consummation of the offer referred to in paragraph (h)(2) of this section, the stock irrevocably accepted for purchase or exchange pursuant to such offer and received by the depository prior to expiration of such offer, together with the stock otherwise owned by the consummating corporation or its affiliates and any rollover stock, equals at least such percentage of the shares of stock of such constituent corporation, and of each class or series thereof, that, absent this subsection, would be required to adopt the agreement of merger by this chapter and by the certificate of incorporation of such constituent corporation;

(4)   The corporation consummating the offer referred to in paragraph (h)(2) of this section merges with or into such constituent corporation pursuant to such agreement; and

(5)   Each outstanding share (other than shares of excluded stock) of each class or series of stock of such constituent corporation that is the subject of and is not irrevocably accepted for purchase or exchange in the offer referred to in paragraph (h)(2) of this section is to be converted in such merger into, or into the right to receive, the same amount and kind of cash, property, rights or securities to be paid for shares of such class or series of stock of such constituent corporation irrevocably accepted for purchase or exchange in such offer.

(6)   As used in this section only, the term:

a.   "Affiliate" means, in respect of the corporation making the offer referred to in paragraph (h)(2) of this section, any person that (i) owns, directly or indirectly, all of the outstanding stock of such corporation or (ii) is a direct or indirect wholly-owned subsidiary of such corporation or of any person referred to in clause (i) of this definition;

b. "Consummates" (and with correlative meaning, "consummation" and "consummating") means irrevocably accepts for purchase or exchange stock tendered pursuant to an offer;

c. "Depository" means an agent, including a depository, appointed to facilitate consummation of the offer referred to in paragraph (h)(2) of this section;

d. "Excluded stock" means (i) stock of such constituent corporation that is owned at the commencement of the offer referred to in paragraph (h)(2) of this section by such constituent corporation, the corporation making the offer referred to in paragraph (h)(2) of this section, any person that owns, directly or indirectly, all of the outstanding stock of the corporation making such offer, or any direct or indirect wholly-owned subsidiary of any of the foregoing and (ii) rollover stock;

e. "Person" means any individual, corporation, partnership, limited liability company, unincorporated association or other entity;

f. "Received" (solely for purposes of paragraph (h)(3) of this section) means (a) with respect to certificated shares, physical receipt of a stock certificate accompanied by an executed letter of transmittal, (b) with respect to uncertificated shares held of record by a clearing corporation as nominee, transfer into the depository's account by means of an agent's message, and (c) with respect to uncertificated shares held of record by a person other than a clearing corporation as nominee, physical receipt of an executed letter of transmittal by the depository; provided, however, that shares shall cease to be "received" (i) with respect to certificated shares, if the certificate representing such shares was canceled prior to consummation of the offer referred to in paragraph (h)(2) of this section, or (ii) with respect to uncertificated shares, to the extent such uncertificated shares have been reduced or eliminated due to any sale of such shares prior to consummation of the offer referred to in paragraph (h)(2) of this section; and

g. "Rollover stock" means any shares of stock of such constituent corporation that are the subject of a written agreement requiring such shares to be transferred, contributed or delivered to the consummating corporation or any of its affiliates in exchange for stock or other equity interests in such consummating corporation or an affiliate thereof; provided, however, that such shares of stock shall cease to be rollover stock for purposes of paragraph (h)(3) of this section if, immediately prior to the time the merger becomes effective under this chapter, such shares have not been transferred, contributed or delivered to the consummating corporation or any of its affiliates pursuant to such written agreement.

If an agreement of merger is adopted without the vote of stockholders of a corporation pursuant to this subsection, the secretary or assistant secretary of the surviving corporation shall certify on the agreement that the agreement has been adopted pursuant to this subsection and that the conditions specified in this subsection (other than the condition listed in paragraph (h)(4) of this section) have been satisfied; provided that such certification on the agreement shall not be required if a certificate of merger is filed in lieu of filing the agreement. The agreement so adopted and certified shall then be filed and shall become effective, in accordance with § 103 of this title. Such filing shall constitute a representation by the person who executes the agreement that the facts stated in the certificate remain true immediately prior to such filing.

§ 252. Merger or consolidation of domestic and foreign corporations; service of process upon surviving or resulting corporation.

(a) Any 1 or more corporations of this State may merge or consolidate with 1 or more foreign corporations, unless the laws of the jurisdiction or jurisdictions under which such foreign corporation or corporations are organized prohibit such merger or consolidation. The constituent corporations may merge into a single surviving corporation, which may be any 1 of the constituent corporations, or they may consolidate into a new resulting corporation formed by the consolidation, which may be a corporation of the jurisdiction of organization of any 1 of the constituent corporations, pursuant to an agreement of merger or consolidation, as the case may be, complying and approved in accordance with this section.

(b)   All the constituent corporations shall enter into an agreement of merger or consolidation. The agreement shall state:

(1)   The terms and conditions of the merger or consolidation;

(2)   The mode of carrying the same into effect;

(3)   In the case of a merger in which the surviving corporation is a corporation of this State, such amendments or changes in the certificate of incorporation of the surviving corporation as are desired to be effected by the merger (which amendments or changes may amend and restate the certificate of incorporation of the surviving corporation in its entirety), or, if no such amendments or changes are desired, a statement that the certificate of incorporation of the surviving corporation shall be its certificate of incorporation;

(4)   In the case of a consolidation in which the resulting corporation is a corporation of this State, that the certificate of incorporation of the resulting corporation shall be as is set forth in an attachment to the agreement;

(5)   The manner, if any, of converting the shares of each of the constituent corporations into shares or other securities of the corporation surviving or resulting from the merger or consolidation, or of cancelling some or all of such shares, and, if any shares of any of the constituent corporations are not to remain outstanding, to be converted solely into shares or other securities of the surviving or resulting corporation or to be cancelled, the cash, property, rights or securities of any other corporation or entity which the holders of such shares are to receive in exchange for, or upon conversion of, such shares and the surrender of any certificates evidencing them, which cash, property, rights or securities of any other corporation or entity may be in addition to or in lieu of the shares or other securities of the surviving or resulting corporation;

(6)   Such other details or provisions as are deemed desirable, including, without limiting the generality of the foregoing, a provision for the payment of cash in lieu of the issuance or recognition of fractional shares, rights or other securities of the surviving or resulting corporation or of any other corporation or entity the shares, rights or other securities of which are to be received in the merger or consolidation, or for some other arrangement with respect thereto, consistent with § 155 of this title; and

(7)   Such other provisions or facts as shall be required to be set forth in an agreement of merger or consolidation (including any provision for amendment of the certificate of incorporation (or equivalent document) of a surviving or resulting foreign corporation) by the laws of each jurisdiction under which any of the foreign corporations are organized.

Any of the terms of the agreement of merger or consolidation may be made dependent upon facts ascertainable outside of such agreement, provided that the manner in which such facts shall operate upon the terms of the agreement is clearly and expressly set forth in the agreement of merger or consolidation. The term "facts," as used in the preceding sentence, includes, but is not limited to, the occurrence of any event, including a determination or action by any person or body, including the corporation.

(c)   The agreement shall be adopted, approved, certified, executed and acknowledged by each of the constituent corporations in accordance with the laws under which it is organized, and, in the case of a corporation of this State, in the same manner as is provided in § 251 of this title. The agreement shall be filed and shall become effective for all purposes of the laws of this State when and as provided in § 251 of this title with respect to the merger or consolidation of corporations of this State. In lieu of filing the agreement of merger or consolidation, the surviving or resulting corporation may file a certificate of merger or consolidation, executed in accordance with § 103 of this title, which states:

(1) The name and jurisdiction of organization of each of the constituent corporations;

(2) That an agreement of merger or consolidation has been approved, adopted, certified, executed and acknowledged by each of the constituent corporations in accordance with this subsection;

(3) The name of the surviving or resulting corporation;

(4) In the case of a merger in which the surviving corporation is a corporation of this State, such amendments or changes in the certificate of incorporation of the surviving corporation as are desired to be effected by the merger (which amendments or changes may amend and restate the certificate of incorporation of the surviving corporation in its entirety), or, if no such amendments or changes are desired, a statement that the certificate of incorporation of the surviving corporation shall be its certificate of incorporation;

(5) In the case of a consolidation in which the resulting corporation is a corporation of this State, that the certificate of incorporation of the resulting corporation shall be as is set forth in an attachment to the certificate;

(6) That the executed agreement of consolidation or merger is on file at an office of the surviving or resulting corporation and the address thereof;

(7) That a copy of the agreement of consolidation or merger will be furnished by the surviving or resulting corporation, on request and without cost, to any stockholder of any constituent corporation;

(8) If the corporation surviving or resulting from the merger or consolidation is a corporation of this State, the authorized capital stock of each constituent corporation which is not a corporation of this State; and

(9) The agreement, if any, required by subsection (d) of this section.

(d) If the corporation surviving or resulting from the merger or consolidation is a foreign corporation, it shall agree that it may be served with process in this State in any proceeding for enforcement of any obligation of any constituent corporation of this State, as well as for enforcement of any obligation of the surviving or resulting corporation arising from the merger or consolidation, including any suit or other proceeding to enforce the right of any stockholders as determined in appraisal proceedings pursuant to § 262 of this title, and shall irrevocably appoint the Secretary of State as its agent to accept service of process in any such suit or other proceedings and shall specify the address to which a copy of such process shall be mailed by the Secretary of State. Process may be served upon the Secretary of State under this subsection by means of electronic transmission but only as prescribed by the Secretary of State. The Secretary of State is authorized to issue such rules and regulations with respect to such service as the Secretary of State deems necessary or appropriate. In the event of such service upon the Secretary of State in accordance with this subsection, the Secretary of State shall forthwith notify such surviving or resulting corporation thereof by letter, directed to such surviving or resulting corporation at its address so specified, unless such surviving or resulting corporation shall have designated in writing to the Secretary of State a different address for such purpose, in which case it shall be mailed to the last address so designated. Such letter shall be sent by a mail or courier service that includes a record of mailing or deposit with the courier and a record of delivery evidenced by the signature of the recipient. Such letter shall enclose a copy of the process and any other papers served on the Secretary of State pursuant to this subsection. It shall be the duty of the plaintiff in the event of such service to serve process and any other papers in duplicate, to notify the Secretary of State that service is being effected pursuant to this subsection and to pay the Secretary of State the sum of $50 for the use of the State, which sum shall be taxed as part of the costs in the proceeding, if the plaintiff shall prevail therein. The Secretary of State shall maintain an alphabetical record of any such service setting forth the name of the plaintiff and the defendant, the title, docket number and nature of the proceeding in which process has been served, the fact that service has been effected pursuant to this subsection, the return date thereof, and the day and hour service was made. The Secretary of State shall not be required to retain such information longer than 5 years from receipt of the service of process.

(e) Section 251(d) of this title shall apply to any merger or consolidation under this section; § 251(e) of this title shall apply to a merger under this section in which the surviving corporation is a corporation of this State; and § 251(f) and (h) of this title shall apply to any merger under this section.

§ 253. Merger of parent corporation and subsidiary corporation or corporations.

(a) In any case in which: (1) at least 90% of the outstanding shares of each class of the stock of a corporation or corporations (other than a corporation which has in its certificate of incorporation the provision required by § 251(g)(7)(i) of this title), of which class there are outstanding shares that, absent this subsection, would be entitled to vote on such merger, is owned by a corporation of this State or a foreign corporation, and (2) 1 or more of such corporations is a corporation of this State, unless the laws of the jurisdiction or jurisdictions under which the foreign corporation or corporations are organized prohibit such merger, the parent corporation may either merge the subsidiary corporation or corporations into itself and assume all of its or their obligations, or merge itself, or itself and 1 or more of such other subsidiary corporations, into 1 of the subsidiary corporations by executing, acknowledging and filing, in accordance with § 103 of this title, a certificate of such ownership and merger setting forth a copy of the resolution of its board of directors to so merge and the date of the adoption; provided, however, that in case the parent corporation shall not own all the outstanding stock of all the subsidiary corporations, parties to a merger as aforesaid, the resolution of the board of directors of the parent corporation shall state the terms and conditions of the merger, including the securities, cash, property, or rights to be issued, paid, delivered or granted by the surviving corporation upon surrender of each share of the subsidiary corporation or corporations not owned by the parent corporation, or the cancellation of some or all of such shares. Any of the terms of the resolution of the board of directors to so merge may be made dependent upon facts ascertainable outside of such resolution, provided that the manner in which such facts shall operate upon the terms of the resolution is clearly and expressly set forth in the resolution. The term "facts," as used in the preceding sentence, includes, but is not limited to, the occurrence of any event, including a determination or action by any person or body, including the corporation. If the parent corporation be not the surviving corporation, the resolution shall include provision for the pro rata issuance of stock of the surviving corporation to the holders of the stock of the parent corporation on surrender of any certificates therefor, and the certificate of ownership and merger shall state that the proposed merger has been approved by a majority of the outstanding stock of the parent corporation entitled to vote thereon at a meeting duly called and held after 20 days' notice of the purpose of the meeting given to each such stockholder at the stockholder's address as it appears on the records of the corporation if the parent corporation is a corporation of this State or state that the proposed merger has been adopted, approved, certified, executed and acknowledged by the parent corporation in accordance with the laws under which it is organized if the parent corporation is a foreign corporation. If the surviving corporation is a foreign corporation:

(1) Section 252(d) of this title or § 258(c) of this title, as applicable, shall also apply to a merger under this section; and

(2) The terms and conditions of the merger shall obligate the surviving corporation to provide the agreement, and take the actions, required by § 252(d) of this title or § 258(c) of this title, as applicable.

(b) If the surviving corporation is a Delaware corporation, it may change its corporate name by the inclusion of a provision to that effect in the resolution of merger adopted by the directors of the parent corporation and set forth in the certificate of ownership and merger, and upon the effective date of the merger, the name of the corporation shall be so changed.

(c)   Section § 251(d) of this title shall apply to a merger under this section, and § 251(e) of this title shall apply to a merger under this section in which the surviving corporation is the subsidiary corporation and is a corporation of this State. References to "agreement of merger" in § 251(d) and (e) of this title shall mean for purposes of this subsection the resolution of merger adopted by the board of directors of the parent corporation. Any merger which effects any changes other than those authorized by this section or made applicable by this subsection shall be accomplished under § 251, § 252, § 257, or § 258 of this title. Section 262 of this title shall not apply to any merger effected under this section, except as provided in subsection (d) of this section.

(d)   In the event all of the stock of a subsidiary Delaware corporation party to a merger effected under this section is not owned by the parent corporation immediately prior to the merger, the stockholders of the subsidiary Delaware corporation party to the merger shall have appraisal rights as set forth in § 262 of this title.

(e)   This section shall apply to nonstock corporations if the parent corporation is such a corporation and is the surviving corporation of the merger; provided, however, that references to the directors of the parent corporation shall be deemed to be references to members of the governing body of the parent corporation, and references to the board of directors of the parent corporation shall be deemed to be references to the governing body of the parent corporation.

(f)   Nothing in this section shall be deemed to authorize the merger of a corporation with a charitable nonstock corporation, if the charitable status of such charitable nonstock corporation would thereby be lost or impaired.

§ 254.   Merger or consolidation of domestic corporation and joint-stock or other association.

(a)   The term "joint-stock association" as used in this section, includes any association of the kind commonly known as a joint-stock association or joint-stock company and any unincorporated association, trust or enterprise having members or having outstanding shares of stock or other evidences of financial or beneficial interest therein, whether formed or organized by agreement or under statutory authority or otherwise and whether formed or organized under the laws of this State or any other jurisdiction, but does not include a corporation, partnership or limited liability company. The term "stockholder" as used in this section, includes every member of such joint-stock association or holder of a share of stock or other evidence of financial or beneficial interest therein.

(b)   Any 1 or more corporations of this State may merge or consolidate with 1 or more joint-stock associations, unless the laws of the jurisdiction or jurisdictions under which such joint-stock association or associations are formed or organized prohibit such merger or consolidation. Such corporation or corporations and such 1 or more joint-stock associations may merge into a single surviving corporation or joint-stock association, which may be any 1 of such corporations or joint-stock associations, or they may consolidate into a new resulting corporation of this State or a joint-stock association, pursuant to an agreement of merger or consolidation, as the case may be, complying and approved in accordance with this section. The surviving or resulting entity may be organized for profit or not organized for profit, and if the surviving or resulting entity is a corporation, it may be a stock corporation of this State or a nonstock corporation of this State.

(c)   Each such corporation and joint-stock association shall enter into a written agreement of merger or consolidation. The agreement shall state:

(1)   The terms and conditions of the merger or consolidation;

(2)   The mode of carrying the same into effect;

(3)   In the case of a merger in which the surviving entity is a corporation of this State, such amendments or changes in the certificate of incorporation of the surviving corporation as are desired to be effected by the merger (which amendments or changes may amend and restate the certificate of incorporation of the surviving corporation in its entirety), or, if no such amendments

or changes are desired, a statement that the certificate of incorporation of the surviving corporation shall be its certificate of incorporation;

(4) In the case of a consolidation in which the resulting entity is a corporation of this State, that the certificate of incorporation of the resulting corporation shall be as is set forth in an attachment to the agreement;

(5) The manner, if any, of converting the shares of stock of each stock corporation, the interest of members of each nonstock corporation, and the shares, membership or financial or beneficial interests in each of the joint-stock associations into shares or other securities of a stock corporation or membership interests of a nonstock corporation or into shares, memberships or financial or beneficial interests of the joint-stock association surviving or resulting from such merger or consolidation, or of cancelling some or all of such shares, memberships or financial or beneficial interests, and, if any shares of any such stock corporation, any membership interests of any such nonstock corporation or any shares, memberships or financial or beneficial interests in any such joint-stock association are not to remain outstanding, to be converted solely into shares or other securities of the stock corporation or membership interests of the nonstock corporation or into shares, memberships or financial or beneficial interests of the joint-stock association surviving or resulting from such merger or consolidation or to be cancelled, the cash, property, rights or securities of any other corporation or entity which the holders of shares of any such stock corporation, membership interests of any such nonstock corporation, or shares, memberships or financial or beneficial interests of any such joint-stock association are to receive in exchange for, or upon conversion of such shares, membership interests or shares, memberships or financial or beneficial interests, and the surrender of any certificates evidencing them, which cash, property, rights or securities of any other corporation or entity may be in addition to or in lieu of shares or other securities of the stock corporation or membership interests of the nonstock corporation or shares, memberships or financial or beneficial interests of the joint-stock association surviving or resulting from such merger or consolidation;

(6) Such other details or provisions as are deemed desirable, including, without limiting the generality of the foregoing, a provision for the payment of cash in lieu of the issuance or recognition of fractional shares, rights, other securities or interests of the surviving or resulting entity or of fractional shares, rights, other securities or interests of any other corporation or entity the securities of which are to be received in the merger or consolidation, or for some other arrangement with respect thereto, consistent with § 155 of this title; and

(7) Such other provisions or facts as shall be required to be set forth in an agreement of merger or consolidation (including any provision for amendment of the governing documents of a surviving joint-stock association) or required to establish and maintain a joint-stock association by the laws under which the joint-stock association is formed or organized.

Any of the terms of the agreement of merger or consolidation may be made dependent upon facts ascertainable outside of such agreement, provided that the manner in which such facts shall operate upon the terms of the agreement is clearly and expressly set forth in the agreement of merger or consolidation. The term "facts," as used in the preceding sentence, includes, but is not limited to, the occurrence of any event, including a determination or action by any person or body, including the corporation.

(d) The agreement required by subsection (c) of this section shall be adopted, approved, certified, executed and acknowledged by each of the stock or nonstock corporations in the same manner as is provided in § 251 or § 255 of this title, respectively, and in the case of the joint-stock associations in accordance with the laws of the jurisdiction under which they are formed or organized. The agreement shall be filed and shall become effective for all purposes of the laws of this State when and as provided in § 251 of this title with respect to the merger or consolidation of corporations of this State. In lieu of filing the agreement of merger or consolidation, the surviving or resulting entity may file a certificate of merger or consolidation, executed in accordance with § 103 of this title, which states:

(1) The name, jurisdiction of formation or organization and type of entity of each of the constituent entities;

(2) That an agreement of merger or consolidation has been approved, adopted, certified, executed and acknowledged by each of the constituent entities in accordance with this subsection;

(3) The name of the surviving or resulting corporation or joint-stock association;

(4) In the case of a merger in which the surviving entity is a corporation of this State, such amendments or changes in the certificate of incorporation of the surviving corporation as are desired to be effected by the merger (which amendments or changes may amend and restate the certificate of incorporation of the surviving corporation in its entirety), or, if no such amendments or changes are desired, a statement that the certificate of incorporation of the surviving corporation shall be its certificate of incorporation;

(5) In the case of a consolidation in which the resulting entity is a corporation of this State, that the certificate of incorporation of the resulting corporation shall be as is set forth in an attachment to the certificate;

(6) That the executed agreement of consolidation or merger is on file at an office of the surviving or resulting corporation or joint-stock association and the address thereof;

(7) That a copy of the agreement of consolidation or merger will be furnished by the surviving or resulting corporation or joint-stock association, on request and without cost, to any stockholder or member of any constituent entity; and

(8) The agreement, if any, required by § 252(d) of this title.

(e) Sections 251(d), 251(e) to the extent the surviving entity is a corporation of this State, §§ 251(f), 252(d), 259 through 262 and 328 of this title shall, insofar as they are applicable, apply to mergers or consolidations between corporations and joint-stock associations; the word "corporation" where applicable, as used in those sections, being deemed to include joint-stock associations as defined herein. Where the surviving or resulting entity is a corporation, for purposes of the laws of this State, the personal liability, if any, of any stockholder of a joint-stock association existing at the time of such merger or consolidation shall not thereby be extinguished, shall remain personal to such stockholder and shall not become the liability of any subsequent transferee of any share of stock in such surviving or resulting corporation or of any other stockholder of such surviving or resulting corporation.

(f) Nothing in this section shall be deemed to authorize the merger of a charitable nonstock corporation or charitable joint-stock association into a stock corporation or joint-stock association if the charitable status of such nonstock corporation or joint-stock association would be thereby lost or impaired, but a stock corporation or a joint-stock association may be merged into a charitable nonstock corporation or charitable joint-stock association which shall continue as the surviving corporation or joint-stock association.

§ 255. Merger or consolidation of domestic nonstock corporations.

(a) Any 2 or more nonstock corporations of this State, whether or not organized for profit, may merge into a single surviving corporation, which may be any 1 of the constituent corporations, or they may consolidate into a new resulting nonstock corporation, whether or not organized for profit, formed by the consolidation, pursuant to an agreement of merger or consolidation, as the case may be, complying and approved in accordance with this section.

(b) Subject to subsection (d) of this section, the governing body of each corporation which desires to merge or consolidate shall adopt a resolution approving an agreement of merger or consolidation. The agreement shall state:

(1) The terms and conditions of the merger or consolidation;

(2) The mode of carrying the same into effect;

    (3)   In the case of a merger, such amendments or changes in the certificate of incorporation of the surviving corporation as are desired to be effected by the merger (which amendments or changes may amend and restate the certificate of incorporation of the surviving corporation in its entirety), or, if no such amendments or changes are desired, a statement that the certificate of incorporation of the surviving corporation shall be its certificate of incorporation;

    (4)   In the case of a consolidation, that the certificate of incorporation of the resulting corporation shall be as is set forth in an attachment to the agreement;

    (5)   The manner, if any, of converting the memberships or membership interests of each of the constituent corporations into memberships or membership interests of the corporation surviving or resulting from the merger or consolidation, or of cancelling some or all of such memberships or membership interests, and, if any memberships or membership interests of any of the constituent corporations are not to remain outstanding, to be converted solely into memberships or membership interests of the surviving or resulting corporation or to be cancelled, the cash, property, rights or securities of any other corporation or entity which the holders of such memberships or membership interests are to receive in exchange for, or upon conversion of, such memberships or membership interests, which cash, property, rights or securities of any other corporation or entity may be in addition to or in lieu of memberships or membership interests of the surviving or resulting corporation; and

    (6)   Such other details or provisions as are deemed desirable, including, without limiting the generality of the foregoing, a provision for the payment of cash in lieu of the issuance or recognition of fractional shares, rights or other securities of any other corporation or entity the shares, rights or other securities of which are to be received in the merger or consolidation, or for some other arrangement with respect thereto, consistent with § 155 of this title.

The agreement so adopted shall be executed by an authorized person, provided that if the agreement is filed, it shall be executed and acknowledged in accordance with § 103 of this title. Any of the terms of the agreement of merger or consolidation may be made dependent upon facts ascertainable outside of such agreement, provided that the manner in which such facts shall operate upon the terms of the agreement is clearly and expressly set forth in the agreement of merger or consolidation. The term "facts," as used in the preceding sentence, includes, but is not limited to, the occurrence of any event, including a determination or action by any person or body, including the corporation.

    (c)   Subject to subsection (d) of this section, the agreement shall be submitted to the members of each constituent corporation, at an annual or special meeting thereof for the purpose of acting on the agreement. Due notice of the time, place and purpose of the meeting shall be given to each member of each such corporation who has the right to vote for the election of the members of the governing body of the corporation and to each other member who is entitled to vote on the merger under the certificate of incorporation or the bylaws of such corporation, at the member's address as it appears on the records of the corporation, at least 20 days prior to the date of the meeting. The notice shall contain a copy of the agreement or a brief summary thereof. At the meeting the agreement shall be considered and a vote, in person or by proxy, taken for the adoption or rejection of the agreement. If the agreement is adopted by a majority of the members of each such corporation entitled to vote for the election of the members of the governing body of the corporation and any other members entitled to vote on the merger under the certificate of incorporation or the bylaws of such corporation, then that fact shall be certified on the agreement by the officer of each such corporation performing the duties ordinarily performed by the secretary or assistant secretary of a corporation, provided that such certification on the agreement shall not be required if a certificate of merger or consolidation is filed in lieu of filing the agreement. If the agreement shall be adopted and certified by each constituent corporation in accordance with this section, it shall be filed and shall become effective in accordance with § 103 of this title. The provisions set forth in the last sentence of § 251(c) of this title shall apply to a merger under this section, and the reference therein to "stockholder" shall be deemed to include "member" hereunder.

(d)   Notwithstanding subsection (b) or (c) of this section, if, under the certificate of incorporation or the bylaws of any 1 or more of the constituent corporations, there shall be no members who have the right to vote for the election of the members of the governing body of the corporation, or for the merger, other than the members of the governing body themselves, no further action by the governing body or the members of such corporation shall be necessary if the resolution approving an agreement of merger or consolidation has been adopted by a majority of all the members of the governing body thereof, and that fact shall be certified on the agreement in the same manner as is provided in the case of the adoption of the agreement by the vote of the members of a corporation, provided that such certification on the agreement shall not be required if a certificate of merger or consolidation is filed in lieu of filing the agreement, and thereafter the same procedure shall be followed to consummate the merger or consolidation.

(e)   Section 251(d) of this title shall apply to a merger under this section; provided, however, that references to the board of directors, to stockholders, and to shares of a constituent corporation shall be deemed to be references to the governing body of the corporation, to members of the corporation, and to memberships or membership interests, as applicable, respectively.

(f)   Section 251(e) of this title shall apply to a merger under this section.

(g)   Nothing in this section shall be deemed to authorize the merger of a charitable nonstock corporation into a nonstock corporation if such charitable nonstock corporation would thereby have its charitable status lost or impaired; but a nonstock corporation may be merged into a charitable nonstock corporation which shall continue as the surviving corporation.

§ 256.   Merger or consolidation of domestic and foreign nonstock corporations; service of process upon surviving or resulting corporation.

(a)   Any 1 or more nonstock corporations of this State may merge or consolidate with 1 or more foreign nonstock corporations, unless the laws of the jurisdiction or jurisdictions under which such foreign nonstock corporation or corporations are organized prohibit such merger or consolidation. The constituent corporations may merge into a single surviving corporation, which may be any 1 of the constituent corporations, or they may consolidate into a new resulting nonstock corporation formed by the consolidation, which may be a corporation of the jurisdiction of organization of any 1 of the constituent corporations, pursuant to an agreement of merger or consolidation, as the case may be, complying and approved in accordance with this section. The term "foreign nonstock corporation" means a nonstock corporation organized under the laws of any jurisdiction other than this State.

(b)   All the constituent corporations shall enter into an agreement of merger or consolidation. The agreement shall state:

(1)   The terms and conditions of the merger or consolidation;

(2)   The mode of carrying the same into effect;

(3)   In the case of a merger in which the surviving corporation is a corporation of this State, such amendments or changes in the certificate of incorporation of the surviving corporation as are desired to be effected by the merger (which amendments or changes may amend and restate the certificate of incorporation of the surviving corporation in its entirety), or, if no such amendments or changes are desired, a statement that the certificate of incorporation of the surviving corporation shall be its certificate of incorporation;

(4)   In the case of a consolidation in which the resulting corporation is a corporation of this State, that the certificate of incorporation of the resulting corporation shall be as is set forth in an attachment to the agreement;

(5)   The manner, if any, of converting the memberships or membership interests of each of the constituent corporations into memberships or membership interests of the corporation surviving or resulting from the merger or consolidation, or of cancelling some or all of such memberships or membership interests, and, if any memberships or membership interests of any

of the constituent corporations are not to remain outstanding, to be converted solely into memberships or membership interests of the surviving or resulting corporation or to be cancelled, the cash, property, rights or securities of any other corporation or entity which the holders of such memberships or membership interests are to receive in exchange for, or upon conversion of, such memberships or membership interests, which cash, property, rights or securities of any other corporation or entity may be in addition to or in lieu of memberships or membership interests of the surviving or resulting corporation;

(6)   Such other details or provisions as are deemed desirable, including, without limiting the generality of the foregoing, a provision for the payment of cash in lieu of the issuance or recognition of fractional shares, rights or other securities of any other corporation or entity the shares, rights or other securities of which are to be received in the merger or consolidation, or for some other arrangement with respect thereto, consistent with § 155 of this title; and

(7)   Such other provisions or facts as shall be required to be set forth in an agreement of merger or consolidation (including any provision for amendment of the certificate of incorporation (or equivalent document) of a surviving foreign nonstock corporation) by the laws of each jurisdiction under which any of the foreign nonstock corporations are organized.

Any of the terms of the agreement of merger or consolidation may be made dependent upon facts ascertainable outside of such agreement, provided that the manner in which such facts shall operate upon the terms of the agreement is clearly and expressly set forth in the agreement of merger or consolidation. The term "facts," as used in the preceding sentence, includes, but is not limited to, the occurrence of any event, including a determination or action by any person or body, including the corporation.

(c)   The agreement shall be adopted, approved, certified, executed and acknowledged by each of the constituent corporations in accordance with the laws under which it is organized and, in the case of a Delaware corporation, in the same manner as is provided in § 255 of this title. The agreement shall be filed and shall become effective for all purposes of the laws of this State when and as provided in § 255 of this title with respect to the merger of nonstock corporations of this State. Insofar as they may be applicable, the provisions set forth in the last sentence of § 252(c) of this title shall apply to a merger under this section, and the reference therein to "stockholder" shall be deemed to include "member" hereunder.

(d)   If the corporation surviving or resulting from the merger or consolidation is a foreign nonstock corporation, it shall agree that it may be served with process in this State in any proceeding for enforcement of any obligation of any constituent corporation of this State, as well as for enforcement of any obligation of the surviving or resulting corporation arising from the merger or consolidation and shall irrevocably appoint the Secretary of State as its agent to accept service of process in any suit or other proceedings and shall specify the address to which a copy of such process shall be mailed by the Secretary of State. Process may be served upon the Secretary of State under this subsection by means of electronic transmission but only as prescribed by the Secretary of State. The Secretary of State is authorized to issue such rules and regulations with respect to such service as the Secretary of State deems necessary or appropriate. In the event of such service upon the Secretary of State in accordance with this subsection, the Secretary of State shall forthwith notify such surviving or resulting corporation thereof by letter, directed to such corporation at its address so specified, unless such surviving or resulting corporation shall have designated in writing to the Secretary of State a different address for such purpose, in which case it shall be mailed to the last address so designated. Such letter shall be sent by a mail or courier service that includes a record of mailing or deposit with the courier and a record of delivery evidenced by the signature of the recipient. Such letter shall enclose a copy of the process and any other papers served upon the Secretary of State. It shall be the duty of the plaintiff in the event of such service to serve process and any other papers in duplicate, to notify the Secretary of State that service is being made pursuant to this subsection, and to pay the Secretary of State the sum of $50 for the use of the State, which sum shall be taxed as a part of the costs in the proceeding if the plaintiff shall prevail therein. The Secretary of State shall maintain an alphabetical record of any such service setting forth the name of the plaintiff and defendant, the title, docket number and nature of the proceeding in which process has been served upon the Secretary of State, the fact that service has been effected pursuant to this subsection, the return date thereof, and the day and hour when the service was made. The Secretary of State shall not be required to retain such information for a period longer than 5 years from receipt of the service of process.

(e)   Section § 251(e) of this title shall apply to a merger under this section if the corporation surviving the merger is a corporation of this State.

(f)   Section 251(d) of this title shall apply to a merger under this section; provided, however, that references to the board of directors, to stockholders, and to shares of a constituent corporation shall be deemed to be references to the governing body of the corporation, to members of the corporation, and to memberships or membership interests, as applicable, respectively.

(g)   Nothing in this section shall be deemed to authorize the merger of a charitable nonstock corporation into a nonstock corporation, if the charitable status of such charitable nonstock corporation would thereby be lost or impaired; but a nonstock corporation may be merged into a charitable nonstock corporation which shall continue as the surviving corporation.

§ 257.   Merger or consolidation of domestic stock and nonstock corporations.

(a)   Any 1 or more nonstock corporations of this State, whether or not organized for profit, may merge or consolidate with 1 or more stock corporations of this State, whether or not organized for profit. The constituent corporations may merge into a single surviving corporation, which may be any 1 of the constituent corporations, or they may consolidate into a new resulting corporation formed by the consolidation, pursuant to an agreement of merger or consolidation, as the case may be, complying and approved in accordance with this section. The surviving constituent corporation or the resulting corporation may be organized for profit or not organized for profit and may be a stock corporation or a nonstock corporation.

(b)   The board of directors of each stock corporation which desires to merge or consolidate and the governing body of each nonstock corporation which desires to merge or consolidate shall adopt a resolution approving an agreement of merger or consolidation. The agreement shall state:

(1)   The terms and conditions of the merger or consolidation;

(2)   The mode of carrying the same into effect;

(3)   In the case of a merger, such amendments or changes in the certificate of incorporation of the surviving corporation as are desired to be effected by the merger (which amendments or changes may amend and restate the certificate of incorporation of the surviving corporation in its entirety), or, if no such amendments or changes are desired, a statement that the certificate of incorporation of the surviving corporation shall be its certificate of incorporation;

(4)   In the case of a consolidation, that the certificate of incorporation of the resulting corporation shall be as is set forth in an attachment to the agreement;

(5)   The manner, if any, of converting the shares of stock of a stock corporation and the memberships or membership interests of a nonstock corporation into shares or other securities of a stock corporation or memberships or membership interests of a nonstock corporation surviving or resulting from such merger or consolidation or of cancelling some or all of such shares or memberships or membership interests, and, if any shares of any such stock corporation or memberships or membership interests of any such nonstock corporation are not to remain outstanding, to be converted solely into shares or other securities of the stock corporation or memberships or membership interests of the nonstock corporation surviving or resulting from such merger or consolidation or to be cancelled, the cash, property, rights or securities of any other corporation or entity which the holders of shares of any such stock corporation or memberships or membership interests of any such nonstock corporation are to receive in

exchange for, or upon conversion of such shares or memberships or membership interests, and the surrender of any certificates evidencing them, which cash, property, rights or securities of any other corporation or entity may be in addition to or in lieu of shares or other securities of any stock corporation or memberships or membership interests of any nonstock corporation surviving or resulting from such merger or consolidation; and

(6)   Such other details or provisions as are deemed desirable, including, without limiting the generality of the foregoing, a provision for the payment of cash in lieu of the issuance or recognition of fractional shares, rights or other securities of the surviving or resulting corporation or of any other corporation or entity the shares, rights or other securities of which are to be received in the merger or consolidation, or for some other arrangement with respect thereto, consistent with § 155 of this title.

Any of the terms of the agreement of merger or consolidation may be made dependent upon facts ascertainable outside of such agreement, provided that the manner in which such facts shall operate upon the terms of the agreement is clearly and expressly set forth in the agreement of merger or consolidation. The term "facts," as used in the preceding sentence, includes, but is not limited to, the occurrence of any event, including a determination or action by any person or body, including the corporation.

(c)   The agreement required by subsection (b) of this section, in the case of each constituent stock corporation, shall be adopted, approved, certified, executed and acknowledged by each constituent corporation in the same manner as is provided in § 251 of this title and, in the case of each constituent nonstock corporation, shall be adopted, approved, certified, executed and acknowledged by each of said constituent corporations in the same manner as is provided in § 255 of this title. The agreement shall be filed and shall become effective for all purposes of the laws of this State when and as provided in § 251 of this title with respect to the merger of stock corporations of this State. Insofar as they may be applicable, the provisions set forth in the last sentence of § 251(c) of this title shall apply to a merger under this section, and the reference therein to "stockholder" shall be deemed to include "member" hereunder.

(d)   Section 251(e) of this title shall apply to a merger under this section; § 251(d) of this title shall apply to any constituent stock corporation participating in a merger or consolidation under this section; and § 251(f) of this title shall apply to any constituent stock corporation participating in a merger under this section.

(e)   Section 251(d) of this title shall apply to a merger under this section; provided, however, that, for purposes of a constituent nonstock corporation, references to the board of directors, to stockholders, and to shares of a constituent corporation shall be deemed to be references to the governing body of the corporation, to members of the corporation, and to memberships or membership interests, as applicable, respectively.

(f)   Nothing in this section shall be deemed to authorize the merger of a charitable nonstock corporation into a stock corporation, if the charitable status of such nonstock corporation would thereby be lost or impaired; but a stock corporation may be merged into a charitable nonstock corporation which shall continue as the surviving corporation.

§ 258.   Merger or consolidation of domestic and foreign stock and nonstock corporations.

(a)   Any 1 or more corporations of this State, whether stock or nonstock corporations and whether or not organized for profit, may merge or consolidate with 1 or more foreign corporations, unless the laws of the jurisdiction or jurisdictions under which such foreign corporation or corporations are organized prohibit such merger or consolidation. The constituent corporations may merge into a single surviving corporation, which may be any 1 of the constituent corporations, or they may consolidate into a new resulting corporation formed by the consolidation, which may be a corporation of the jurisdiction of organization of any 1 of the constituent corporations, pursuant to an agreement of merger or consolidation, as the case may be, complying and approved in accordance with this section.

The surviving or resulting corporation may be either a domestic or foreign stock corporation or a domestic or foreign nonstock corporation, as shall be specified in the agreement of merger or consolidation required by subsection (b) of this section. For purposes of this section, the term "foreign corporation" includes a nonstock corporation organized under the laws of any jurisdiction other than this State.

(b) The method and procedure to be followed by the constituent corporations so merging or consolidating shall be as prescribed in § 257 of this title in the case of Delaware corporations. The agreement of merger or consolidation shall be as provided in § 257 of this title and also set forth such other provisions or facts as shall be required to be set forth in an agreement of merger or consolidation (including any provision for amendment of the certificate of incorporation (or equivalent document) of a surviving foreign corporation) by the laws of the jurisdiction or jurisdictions which are stated in the agreement to be the laws under which the foreign corporation or corporations are organized. The agreement, in the case of foreign corporations, shall be adopted, approved, certified, executed and acknowledged in accordance with the laws under which each is organized.

(c) The requirements of § 252(d) of this title as to the appointment of the Secretary of State to receive process and the manner of serving the same in the event the surviving or resulting corporation is a foreign corporation shall also apply to mergers or consolidations effected under this section and such appointment, if any, shall be included in the certificate of merger or consolidation, if any, filed pursuant to subsection (b) of this section. Section 251(e) of this title shall apply to mergers effected under this section if the surviving corporation is a corporation of this State; § 251(d) of this title shall apply to any constituent corporation participating in a merger or consolidation under this section (provided, however, that for purposes of a constituent nonstock corporation, references to the board of directors, to stockholders, and to shares shall be deemed to be references to the governing body of the corporation, to members of the corporation, and to memberships or membership interests of the corporation, as applicable, respectively); and § 251(f) of this title shall apply to any constituent stock corporation of this State participating in a merger under this section.

(d) Nothing in this section shall be deemed to authorize the merger of a charitable nonstock corporation into a stock corporation, if the charitable status of such nonstock corporation would thereby be lost or impaired; but a stock corporation may be merged into a charitable nonstock corporation which shall continue as the surviving corporation.

§ 259. Status, rights, liabilities, of constituent and surviving or resulting corporations following merger or consolidation.

(a) When any merger or consolidation shall have become effective under this chapter, for all purposes of the laws of this State the separate existence of all the constituent corporations, or of all such constituent corporations except the one into which the other or others of such constituent corporations have been merged, as the case may be, shall cease and the constituent corporations shall become a new corporation, or be merged into 1 of such corporations, as the case may be, possessing all the rights, privileges, powers and franchises as well of a public as of a private nature, and being subject to all the restrictions, disabilities and duties of each of such corporations so merged or consolidated; and all and singular, the rights, privileges, powers and franchises of each of said corporations, and all property, real, personal and mixed, and all debts due to any of said constituent corporations on whatever account, as well for stock subscriptions as all other things in action or belonging to each of such corporations shall be vested in the corporation surviving or resulting from such merger or consolidation; and all property, rights, privileges, powers and franchises, and all and every other interest shall be thereafter as effectually the property of the surviving or resulting corporation as they were of the several and respective constituent corporations, and the title to any real estate vested by deed or otherwise, under the laws of this State, in any of such constituent corporations, shall not revert or be in any way impaired by reason of this chapter; but all rights of creditors and all liens upon any property of any of said constituent corporations shall be preserved unimpaired, and all debts, liabilities and duties of the respective constituent corporations shall thenceforth attach to said surviving or resulting corporation, and may be enforced against it to the same extent as if said debts, liabilities and duties had been incurred or contracted by it.

(b)   In the case of a merger of banks or trust companies, without any order or action on the part of any court or otherwise, all appointments, designations, and nominations, and all other rights and interests as trustee, executor, administrator, registrar of stocks and bonds, guardian of estates, assignee, receiver, trustee of estates of persons mentally ill and in every other fiduciary capacity, shall be automatically vested in the corporation resulting from or surviving such merger; provided, however, that any party in interest shall have the right to apply to an appropriate court or tribunal for a determination as to whether the surviving corporation shall continue to serve in the same fiduciary capacity as the merged corporation, or whether a new and different fiduciary should be appointed.

§ 260.   Powers of corporation surviving or resulting from merger or consolidation; issuance of stock, bonds or other indebtedness.

When 2 or more corporations are merged or consolidated, the corporation surviving or resulting from the merger may issue bonds or other obligations, negotiable or otherwise, and with or without coupons or interest certificates thereto attached, to an amount sufficient with its capital stock to provide for all the payments it will be required to make, or obligations it will be required to assume, in order to effect the merger or consolidation. For the purpose of securing the payment of any such bonds and obligations, it shall be lawful for the surviving or resulting corporation to mortgage its corporate franchise, rights, privileges and property, real, personal or mixed. The surviving or resulting corporation may issue certificates of its capital stock or uncertificated stock if authorized to do so and other securities to the stockholders of the constituent corporations in exchange or payment for the original shares, in such amount as shall be necessary in accordance with the terms of the agreement of merger or consolidation in order to effect such merger or consolidation in the manner and on the terms specified in the agreement.

§ 261.   Effect of merger upon pending actions.

Any action or proceeding, whether civil, criminal or administrative, pending by or against any corporation which is a party to a merger or consolidation shall be prosecuted as if such merger or consolidation had not taken place, or the corporation surviving or resulting from such merger or consolidation may be substituted in such action or proceeding.

§ 262.   Appraisal rights [for application of this section, see 79 Del. Laws, c. 72, § 22; 79 Del. Laws, c. 122, § 12; 80 Del. Laws, c. 265, § 18; 81 Del. Laws, c. 354, § 17; and 82 Del. Laws, c. 45, § 23].

(a)   Any stockholder of a corporation of this State who holds shares of stock on the date of the making of a demand pursuant to subsection (d) of this section with respect to such shares, who continuously holds such shares through the effective date of the merger or consolidation, who has otherwise complied with subsection (d) of this section and who has neither voted in favor of the merger or consolidation nor consented thereto in writing pursuant to § 228 of this title shall be entitled to an appraisal by the Court of Chancery of the fair value of the stockholder's shares of stock under the circumstances described in subsections (b) and (c) of this section. As used in this section, the word "stockholder" means a holder of record of stock in a corporation; the words "stock" and "share" mean and include what is ordinarily meant by those words; and the words "depository receipt" mean a receipt or other instrument issued by a depository representing an interest in 1 or more shares, or fractions thereof, solely of stock of a corporation, which stock is deposited with the depository.

(b)   Appraisal rights shall be available for the shares of any class or series of stock of a constituent corporation in a merger or consolidation to be effected pursuant to § 251 (other than a merger effected pursuant to § 251(g) of this title), § 252, § 254, § 255, § 256, § 257, § 258, § 263 or § 264 of this title:

(1)   Provided, however, that, except as expressly provided in § 363(b) of this title, no appraisal rights under this section shall be available for the shares of any class or series of stock, which stock, or depository receipts in respect thereof, at the record date fixed to determine the stockholders entitled to receive notice of the meeting of stockholders to act upon the agreement of merger or consolidation (or, in the case of a merger pursuant to § 251(h), as of immediately prior to the execution of the agreement of merger), were either: (i) listed on a national securities exchange or (ii) held of record by more than 2,000 holders; and further provided that no appraisal rights shall be available for any shares of stock of the constituent corporation surviving a merger if the merger did not require for its approval the vote of the stockholders of the surviving corporation as provided in § 251(f) of this title.

(2)   Notwithstanding paragraph (b)(1) of this section, appraisal rights under this section shall be available for the shares of any class or series of stock of a constituent corporation if the holders thereof are required by the terms of an agreement of merger or consolidation pursuant to §§ 251, 252, 254, 255, 256, 257, 258, 263 and 264 of this title to accept for such stock anything except:

   a.   Shares of stock of the corporation surviving or resulting from such merger or consolidation, or depository receipts in respect thereof;

   b.   Shares of stock of any other corporation, or depository receipts in respect thereof, which shares of stock (or depository receipts in respect thereof) or depository receipts at the effective date of the merger or consolidation will be either listed on a national securities exchange or held of record by more than 2,000 holders;

   c.   Cash in lieu of fractional shares or fractional depository receipts described in the foregoing paragraphs (b)(2)a. and b. of this section; or

   d.   Any combination of the shares of stock, depository receipts and cash in lieu of fractional shares or fractional depository receipts described in the foregoing paragraphs (b)(2)a., b. and c. of this section.

(3)   In the event all of the stock of a subsidiary Delaware corporation party to a merger effected under § 253 or § 267 of this title is not owned by the parent immediately prior to the merger, appraisal rights shall be available for the shares of the subsidiary Delaware corporation.

(4)   In the event of an amendment to a corporation's certificate of incorporation contemplated by § 363(a) of this title, appraisal rights shall be available as contemplated by § 363(b) of this title, and the procedures of this section, including those set forth in subsections (d) and (e) of this section, shall apply as nearly as practicable, with the word "amendment" substituted for the words "merger or consolidation," and the word "corporation" substituted for the words "constituent corporation" and/or "surviving or resulting corporation."

(c)   Any corporation may provide in its certificate of incorporation that appraisal rights under this section shall be available for the shares of any class or series of its stock as a result of an amendment to its certificate of incorporation, any merger or consolidation in which the corporation is a constituent corporation or the sale of all or substantially all of the assets of the corporation. If the certificate of incorporation contains such a provision, the provisions of this section, including those set forth in subsections (d),(e), and (g) of this section, shall apply as nearly as is practicable.

(d)   Appraisal rights shall be perfected as follows:

   (1)   If a proposed merger or consolidation for which appraisal rights are provided under this section is to be submitted for approval at a meeting of stockholders, the corporation, not less than 20 days prior to the meeting, shall notify each of its stockholders who was such on the record date for notice of such meeting (or such members who received notice in accordance with § 255(c) of this title) with respect to shares for which appraisal rights are available pursuant to subsection (b) or (c) of this section that appraisal rights are available for any or all of the shares of the constituent corporations, and shall include in such notice a copy of this section and, if 1 of the

constituent corporations is a nonstock corporation, a copy of § 114 of this title. Each stockholder electing to demand the appraisal of such stockholder's shares shall deliver to the corporation, before the taking of the vote on the merger or consolidation, a written demand for appraisal of such stockholder's shares; provided that a demand may be delivered to the corporation by electronic transmission if directed to an information processing system (if any) expressly designated for that purpose in such notice. Such demand will be sufficient if it reasonably informs the corporation of the identity of the stockholder and that the stockholder intends thereby to demand the appraisal of such stockholder's shares. A proxy or vote against the merger or consolidation shall not constitute such a demand. A stockholder electing to take such action must do so by a separate written demand as herein provided. Within 10 days after the effective date of such merger or consolidation, the surviving or resulting corporation shall notify each stockholder of each constituent corporation who has complied with this subsection and has not voted in favor of or consented to the merger or consolidation of the date that the merger or consolidation has become effective; or

(2)   If the merger or consolidation was approved pursuant to § 228, § 251(h), § 253, or § 267 of this title, then either a constituent corporation before the effective date of the merger or consolidation or the surviving or resulting corporation within 10 days thereafter shall notify each of the holders of any class or series of stock of such constituent corporation who are entitled to appraisal rights of the approval of the merger or consolidation and that appraisal rights are available for any or all shares of such class or series of stock of such constituent corporation, and shall include in such notice a copy of this section and, if 1 of the constituent corporations is a nonstock corporation, a copy of § 114 of this title. Such notice may, and, if given on or after the effective date of the merger or consolidation, shall, also notify such stockholders of the effective date of the merger or consolidation. Any stockholder entitled to appraisal rights may, within 20 days after the date of giving such notice or, in the case of a merger approved pursuant to § 251(h) of this title, within the later of the consummation of the offer contemplated by § 251(h) of this title and 20 days after the date of giving such notice, demand in writing from the surviving or resulting corporation the appraisal of such holder's shares; provided that a demand may be delivered to the corporation by electronic transmission if directed to an information processing system (if any) expressly designated for that purpose in such notice. Such demand will be sufficient if it reasonably informs the corporation of the identity of the stockholder and that the stockholder intends thereby to demand the appraisal of such holder's shares. If such notice did not notify stockholders of the effective date of the merger or consolidation, either (i) each such constituent corporation shall send a second notice before the effective date of the merger or consolidation notifying each of the holders of any class or series of stock of such constituent corporation that are entitled to appraisal rights of the effective date of the merger or consolidation or (ii) the surviving or resulting corporation shall send such a second notice to all such holders on or within 10 days after such effective date; provided, however, that if such second notice is sent more than 20 days following the sending of the first notice or, in the case of a merger approved pursuant to § 251(h) of this title, later than the later of the consummation of the offer contemplated by § 251(h) of this title and 20 days following the sending of the first notice, such second notice need only be sent to each stockholder who is entitled to appraisal rights and who has demanded appraisal of such holder's shares in accordance with this subsection. An affidavit of the secretary or assistant secretary or of the transfer agent of the corporation that is required to give either notice that such notice has been given shall, in the absence of fraud, be prima facie evidence of the facts stated therein. For purposes of determining the stockholders entitled to receive either notice, each constituent corporation may fix, in advance, a record date that shall be not more than 10 days prior to the date the notice is given, provided, that if the notice is given on or after the effective date of the merger or consolidation, the record date shall be such effective date. If no record date is fixed and the notice is given prior to the effective date, the record date shall be the close of business on the day next preceding the day on which the notice is given.

(e)   Within 120 days after the effective date of the merger or consolidation, the surviving or resulting corporation or any stockholder who has complied with subsections (a) and (d) of this section hereof and who is otherwise entitled to appraisal rights, may commence an appraisal proceeding by filing a petition in the Court of Chancery demanding a determination of the value of the stock of all such stockholders. Notwithstanding the foregoing, at any time within 60 days after the effective date of the merger or consolidation, any stockholder who has not commenced an appraisal proceeding or joined that proceeding as a named party shall have the right to withdraw such stockholder's demand for appraisal and to accept the terms offered upon the merger or consolidation. Within 120 days after the effective date of the merger or consolidation, any stockholder who has complied with the requirements of subsections (a) and (d) of this section hereof, upon request given in writing (or by electronic transmission directed to an information processing system (if any) expressly designated for that purpose in the notice of appraisal), shall be entitled to receive from the corporation surviving the merger or resulting from the consolidation a statement setting forth the aggregate number of shares not voted in favor of the merger or consolidation (or, in the case of a merger approved pursuant to § 251(h) of this title, the aggregate number of shares (other than any excluded stock (as defined in § 251(h)(6)d. of this title)) that were the subject of, and were not tendered into, and accepted for purchase or exchange in, the offer referred to in § 251(h)(2)), and, in either case, with respect to which demands for appraisal have been received and the aggregate number of holders of such shares. Such statement shall be given to the stockholder within 10 days after such stockholder's request for such a statement is received by the surviving or resulting corporation or within 10 days after expiration of the period for delivery of demands for appraisal under subsection (d) of this section hereof, whichever is later. Notwithstanding subsection (a) of this section, a person who is the beneficial owner of shares of such stock held either in a voting trust or by a nominee on behalf of such person may, in such person's own name, file a petition or request from the corporation the statement described in this subsection.

(f) Upon the filing of any such petition by a stockholder, service of a copy thereof shall be made upon the surviving or resulting corporation, which shall within 20 days after such service file in the office of the Register in Chancery in which the petition was filed a duly verified list containing the names and addresses of all stockholders who have demanded payment for their shares and with whom agreements as to the value of their shares have not been reached by the surviving or resulting corporation. If the petition shall be filed by the surviving or resulting corporation, the petition shall be accompanied by such a duly verified list. The Register in Chancery, if so ordered by the Court, shall give notice of the time and place fixed for the hearing of such petition by registered or certified mail to the surviving or resulting corporation and to the stockholders shown on the list at the addresses therein stated. Such notice shall also be given by 1 or more publications at least 1 week before the day of the hearing, in a newspaper of general circulation published in the City of Wilmington, Delaware or such publication as the Court deems advisable. The forms of the notices by mail and by publication shall be approved by the Court, and the costs thereof shall be borne by the surviving or resulting corporation.

(g) At the hearing on such petition, the Court shall determine the stockholders who have complied with this section and who have become entitled to appraisal rights. The Court may require the stockholders who have demanded an appraisal for their shares and who hold stock represented by certificates to submit their certificates of stock to the Register in Chancery for notation thereon of the pendency of the appraisal proceedings; and if any stockholder fails to comply with such direction, the Court may dismiss the proceedings as to such stockholder. If immediately before the merger or consolidation the shares of the class or series of stock of the constituent corporation as to which appraisal rights are available were listed on a national securities exchange, the Court shall dismiss the proceedings as to all holders of such shares who are otherwise entitled to appraisal rights unless (1) the total number of shares entitled to appraisal exceeds 1% of the outstanding shares of the class or series eligible for appraisal, (2) the value of the consideration provided in the merger or consolidation for such total number of shares exceeds $1 million, or (3) the merger was approved pursuant to § 253 or § 267 of this title.

(h) After the Court determines the stockholders entitled to an appraisal, the appraisal proceeding shall be conducted in accordance with the rules of the Court of Chancery, including any rules specifically governing appraisal proceedings. Through such proceeding the Court shall determine the fair value of the shares exclusive of any element of value arising from the accomplishment or expectation of the merger or consolidation, together with interest, if any, to be paid upon the amount determined to be the fair value. In determining such fair value, the Court shall take into account all relevant factors. Unless the Court in its discretion determines otherwise for good cause shown, and except as provided in this subsection, interest from the effective date of the merger through the date of payment of the judgment shall be compounded quarterly and shall accrue at 5% over the Federal Reserve discount rate (including any surcharge) as established from time to time during the period between the effective date of the merger and the date of payment of the judgment. At any time before the entry of judgment in the proceedings, the surviving corporation may pay to each stockholder entitled to appraisal an amount in cash, in which case interest shall accrue thereafter as provided herein only upon the sum of (1) the difference, if any, between the amount so paid and the fair value of the shares as determined by the Court, and (2) interest theretofore accrued, unless paid at that time. Upon application by the surviving or resulting corporation or by any stockholder entitled to participate in the appraisal proceeding, the Court may, in its discretion, proceed to trial upon the appraisal prior to the final determination of the stockholders entitled to an appraisal. Any stockholder whose name appears on the list filed by the surviving or resulting corporation pursuant to subsection (f) of this section and who has submitted such stockholder's certificates of stock to the Register in Chancery, if such is required, may participate fully in all proceedings until it is finally determined that such stockholder is not entitled to appraisal rights under this section.

(i)   The Court shall direct the payment of the fair value of the shares, together with interest, if any, by the surviving or resulting corporation to the stockholders entitled thereto. Payment shall be so made to each such stockholder, in the case of holders of uncertificated stock forthwith, and the case of holders of shares represented by certificates upon the surrender to the corporation of the certificates representing such stock. The Court's decree may be enforced as other decrees in the Court of Chancery may be enforced, whether such surviving or resulting corporation be a corporation of this State or of any state.

(j)   The costs of the proceeding may be determined by the Court and taxed upon the parties as the Court deems equitable in the circumstances. Upon application of a stockholder, the Court may order all or a portion of the expenses incurred by any stockholder in connection with the appraisal proceeding, including, without limitation, reasonable attorney's fees and the fees and expenses of experts, to be charged pro rata against the value of all the shares entitled to an appraisal.

(k)   From and after the effective date of the merger or consolidation, no stockholder who has demanded appraisal rights as provided in subsection (d) of this section shall be entitled to vote such stock for any purpose or to receive payment of dividends or other distributions on the stock (except dividends or other distributions payable to stockholders of record at a date which is prior to the effective date of the merger or consolidation); provided, however, that if no petition for an appraisal shall be filed within the time provided in subsection (e) of this section, or if such stockholder shall deliver to the surviving or resulting corporation a written withdrawal of such stockholder's demand for an appraisal and an acceptance of the merger or consolidation, either within 60 days after the effective date of the merger or consolidation as provided in subsection (e) of this section or thereafter with the written approval of the corporation, then the right of such stockholder to an appraisal shall cease. Notwithstanding the foregoing, no appraisal proceeding in the Court of Chancery shall be dismissed as to any stockholder without the approval of the Court, and such approval may be conditioned upon such terms as the Court deems just; provided, however that this provision shall not affect the right of any stockholder who has not commenced an appraisal proceeding or joined that proceeding as a named party to withdraw such stockholder's demand for appraisal and to accept the terms offered upon the merger or consolidation within 60 days after the effective date of the merger or consolidation, as set forth in subsection (e) of this section.

(l)   The shares of the surviving or resulting corporation to which the shares of such objecting stockholders would have been converted had they assented to the merger or consolidation shall have the status of authorized and unissued shares of the surviving or resulting corporation.

§ 263.   Merger or consolidation of domestic corporations and partnerships.

(a)   Any 1 or more corporations of this State may merge or consolidate with 1 or more partnerships (whether general (including a limited liability partnership) or limited (including a limited liability limited partnership)), unless the laws of the jurisdiction or jurisdictions under which such partnership or partnerships are formed prohibit such merger or consolidation. Such corporation or corporations and such 1 or more partnerships may merge with or into a surviving corporation, which may be any 1 of such corporations, or they may merge with or into a surviving partnership, which may be any 1 of such partnerships, or they may consolidate into a new resulting corporation, which corporation shall be a corporation of this State, or a partnership formed pursuant to an agreement of merger or consolidation, as the case may be, complying and approved in accordance with this section. The term "partnership" as used in this section includes any partnership (whether general (including a limited liability partnership) or limited (including a limited liability limited partnership)) formed under the laws of this State or the laws of any other jurisdiction.

(b)   Each such corporation and partnership shall enter into a written agreement of merger or consolidation. The agreement shall state:

(1)   The terms and conditions of the merger or consolidation;

(2)   The mode of carrying the same into effect;

(3)   In the case of a merger in which the surviving entity is a corporation of this State, such amendments or changes in the certificate of incorporation of the surviving corporation as are desired to be effected by the merger (which amendments or changes may amend and restate the certificate of incorporation of the surviving corporation in its entirety), or, if no such amendments or changes are desired, a statement that the certificate of incorporation of the surviving corporation shall be its certificate of incorporation;

(4)   In the case of a consolidation in which the resulting entity is a corporation of this State, that the certificate of incorporation of the resulting corporation shall be as is set forth in an attachment to the agreement;

(5)   The manner, if any, of converting the shares of stock of each such corporation and the partnership interests of each such partnership into shares, partnership interests or other securities of the entity surviving or resulting from such merger or consolidation or of cancelling some or all of such shares or interests, and if any shares of any such corporation or any partnership interests of any such partnership are not to remain outstanding, to be converted solely into shares, partnership interests or other securities of the entity surviving or resulting from such merger or consolidation or to be cancelled, the cash, property, rights or securities of any other corporation or entity which the holders of such shares or partnership interests are to receive in exchange for, or upon conversion of such shares or partnership interests and the surrender of any certificates evidencing them, which cash, property, rights or securities of any other corporation or entity may be in addition to or in lieu of shares, partnership interests or other securities of the entity surviving or resulting from such merger or consolidation;

(6)   Such other details or provisions as are deemed desirable, including, without limiting the generality of the foregoing, a provision for the payment of cash in lieu of the issuance or recognition of fractional shares, rights, other securities or interests of the surviving or resulting corporation or partnership or of any other corporation or entity the shares, rights, other securities or interests of which are to be received in the merger or consolidation, or for some other arrangement with respect thereto, consistent with § 155 of this title; and

(7)   Such other provisions or facts as shall be required to be set forth in an agreement of merger or consolidation (including any provision for amendment of the partnership agreement and statement of partnership existence or certificate of limited partnership (or equivalent documents) of the surviving partnership) by the laws of each jurisdiction under which any of the partnerships are formed.

Any of the terms of the agreement of merger or consolidation may be made dependent upon facts ascertainable outside of such agreement, provided that the manner in which such facts shall operate upon the terms of the agreement is clearly and expressly set forth in the agreement of merger or consolidation. The term "facts," as used in the preceding sentence, includes, but is not limited to, the occurrence of any event, including a determination or action by any person or body, including the corporation.

(c) The agreement required by subsection (b) of this section shall be adopted, approved, certified, executed and acknowledged by each of the corporations in the same manner as is provided in § 251 or § 255 of this title and, in the case of the partnerships, in accordance with their partnership agreements and in accordance with the laws of the jurisdiction under which they are formed. If the surviving or resulting entity is a partnership, in addition to any other approvals, each stockholder of a merging corporation who will become a general partner of the surviving or resulting partnership must approve the agreement of merger or consolidation. The agreement shall be filed and shall become effective for all purposes of the laws of this State when and as provided in § 251 or § 255 of this title with respect to the merger or consolidation of corporations of this State. In lieu of filing the agreement of merger or consolidation, the surviving or resulting corporation or partnership may file a certificate of merger or consolidation, executed in accordance with § 103 of this title, if the surviving or resulting entity is a corporation, or by a general partner, if the surviving or resulting entity is a partnership, which states:

(1) The name, jurisdiction of formation or organization and type of entity of each of the constituent entities;

(2) That an agreement of merger or consolidation has been approved, adopted, certified, executed and acknowledged by each of the constituent entities in accordance with this subsection;

(3) The name of the surviving or resulting corporation or partnership;

(4) In the case of a merger in which a corporation is the surviving entity, such amendments or changes in the certificate of incorporation of the surviving corporation as are desired to be effected by the merger (which amendments or changes may amend and restate the certificate of incorporation of the surviving corporation in its entirety), or, if no such amendments or changes are desired, a statement that the certificate of incorporation of the surviving corporation shall be its certificate of incorporation;

(5) In the case of a consolidation in which a corporation is the resulting entity, that the certificate of incorporation of the resulting corporation shall be as is set forth in an attachment to the certificate;

(6) That the executed agreement of consolidation or merger is on file at an office of the surviving or resulting corporation or partnership and the address thereof;

(7) That a copy of the agreement of consolidation or merger will be furnished by the surviving or resulting entity, on request and without cost, to any stockholder of any constituent corporation or any partner of any constituent partnership; and

(8) The agreement, if any, required by subsection (d) of this section.

(d) If the entity surviving or resulting from the merger or consolidation is a partnership formed under the laws of a jurisdiction other than this State, it shall agree that it may be served with process in this State in any proceeding for enforcement of any obligation of any constituent corporation or partnership of this State, as well as for enforcement of any obligation of the surviving or resulting corporation or partnership arising from the merger or consolidation, including any suit or other proceeding to enforce the right of any stockholders as determined in appraisal proceedings pursuant to § 262 of this title, and shall irrevocably appoint the Secretary of State as its agent to accept service of process in any such suit or other proceedings and shall specify the address to which a copy of such process shall be mailed by the Secretary of State. Process may be served upon the Secretary of State under this subsection by means of electronic transmission but only as prescribed by the Secretary of

State. The Secretary of State is authorized to issue such rules and regulations with respect to such service as the Secretary of State deems necessary or appropriate. In the event of such service upon the Secretary of State in accordance with this subsection, the Secretary of State shall forthwith notify such surviving or resulting corporation or partnership thereof by letter, directed to such surviving or resulting corporation or partnership at its address so specified, unless such surviving or resulting corporation or partnership shall have designated in writing to the Secretary of State a different address for such purpose, in which case it shall be mailed to the last address so designated. Such letter shall be sent by a mail or courier service that includes a record of mailing or deposit with the courier and a record of delivery evidenced by the signature of the recipient. Such letter shall enclose a copy of the process and any other papers served on the Secretary of State pursuant to this subsection. It shall be the duty of the plaintiff in the event of such service to serve process and any other papers in duplicate, to notify the Secretary of State that service is being effected pursuant to this subsection and to pay the Secretary of State the sum of $50 for the use of the State, which sum shall be taxed as part of the costs in the proceeding, if the plaintiff shall prevail therein. The Secretary of State shall maintain an alphabetical record of any such service setting forth the name of the plaintiff and the defendant, the title, docket number and nature of the proceeding in which process has been served upon the Secretary of State, the fact that service has been effected pursuant to this subsection, the return date thereof, and the day and hour service was made. The Secretary of State shall not be required to retain such information longer than 5 years from receipt of the service of process.

(e)   Sections 251(d)–(f), 255(c) (second sentence) and (d)–(f), 259–261 and 328 of this title shall, insofar as they are applicable, apply to mergers or consolidations between corporations and partnerships.

(f)   Nothing in this section shall be deemed to authorize the merger of a charitable nonstock corporation into a partnership, if the charitable status of such nonstock corporation would thereby be lost or impaired; but a partnership may be merged into a charitable nonstock corporation which shall continue as the surviving corporation.

§ 264.   Merger or consolidation of domestic corporations and limited liability companies; service of process upon surviving or resulting corporation or limited liability company.

(a)   Any 1 or more corporations of this State may merge or consolidate with 1 or more limited liability companies, unless the laws of the jurisdiction or jurisdictions under which such limited liability company or limited liability companies are formed prohibit such merger or consolidation. Such corporation or corporations and such 1 or more limited liability companies may merge with or into a surviving corporation, which may be any 1 of such corporations, or they may merge with or into a surviving limited liability company, which may be any 1 of such limited liability companies, or they may consolidate into a new resulting corporation, which corporation shall be a corporation of this State, or a limited liability company formed pursuant to an agreement of merger or consolidation, as the case may be, complying and approved in accordance with this section. The term "limited liability company" as used in this section includes any limited liability company formed under the laws of this State or the laws of any other jurisdiction.

(b)   Each such corporation and limited liability company shall enter into a written agreement of merger or consolidation. The agreement shall state:

(1)   The terms and conditions of the merger or consolidation;

(2)   The mode of carrying the same into effect;

(3)   In the case of a merger in which the surviving entity is a corporation of this State, such amendments or changes in the certificate of incorporation of the surviving corporation as are desired to be effected by the merger (which amendments or changes may amend and restate the certificate of incorporation of the surviving corporation in its entirety), or, if no such amendments

or changes are desired, a statement that the certificate of incorporation of the surviving corporation shall be its certificate of incorporation;

(4)   In the case of a consolidation in which the resulting entity is a corporation of this State, that the certificate of incorporation of the resulting corporation shall be as is set forth in an attachment to the agreement;

(5)   The manner, if any, of converting the shares of stock of each such corporation and the limited liability company interests of each such limited liability company into shares, limited liability company interests or other securities of the entity surviving or resulting from such merger or consolidation or of cancelling some or all of such shares or interests, and if any shares of any such corporation or any limited liability company interests of any such limited liability company are not to remain outstanding, to be converted solely into shares, limited liability company interests or other securities of the entity surviving or resulting from such merger or consolidation or to be cancelled, the cash, property, rights or securities of any other corporation or entity which the holders of such shares or limited liability company interests are to receive in exchange for, or upon conversion of such shares or limited liability company interests and the surrender of any certificates evidencing them, which cash, property, rights or securities of any other corporation or entity may be in addition to or in lieu of shares, limited liability company interests or other securities of the entity surviving or resulting from such merger or consolidation;

(6)   Such other details or provisions as are deemed desirable, including, without limiting the generality of the foregoing, a provision for the payment of cash in lieu of the issuance or recognition of fractional shares, rights, other securities or interests of the surviving or resulting corporation or limited liability company or of any other corporation or entity the shares, rights, other securities or interests of which are to be received in the merger or consolidation, or for some other arrangement with respect thereto, consistent with § 155 of this title; and

(7)   Such other provisions or facts as shall be required to be set forth in an agreement of merger or consolidation (including any provision for amendment of the limited liability company agreement and certificate of formation (or equivalent documents) of the surviving limited liability company) by the laws of each jurisdiction under which any of the limited liability companies are formed.

Any of the terms of the agreement of merger or consolidation may be made dependent upon facts ascertainable outside of such agreement, provided that the manner in which such facts shall operate upon the terms of the agreement is clearly and expressly set forth in the agreement of merger or consolidation. The term "facts," as used in the preceding sentence, includes, but is not limited to, the occurrence of any event, including a determination or action by any person or body, including the corporation.

(c)   The agreement required by subsection (b) of this section shall be adopted, approved, certified, executed and acknowledged by each of the corporations in the same manner as is provided in § 251 or § 255 of this title and, in the case of the limited liability companies, in accordance with their limited liability company agreements and in accordance with the laws of the jurisdiction under which they are formed. The agreement shall be filed and shall become effective for all purposes of the laws of this State when and as provided in § 251 or § 255 of this title with respect to the merger or consolidation of corporations of this State. In lieu of filing the agreement of merger or consolidation, the surviving or resulting corporation or limited liability company may file a certificate of merger or consolidation, executed in accordance with § 103 of this title, if the surviving or resulting entity is a corporation, or by an authorized person, if the surviving or resulting entity is a limited liability company, which states:

(1)   The name and jurisdiction of formation or organization of each of the constituent entities;

(2)   That an agreement of merger or consolidation has been approved, adopted, certified, executed and acknowledged by each of the constituent entities in accordance with this subsection;

(3)   The name of the surviving or resulting corporation or limited liability company;

(4)   In the case of a merger in which a corporation is the surviving entity, such amendments or changes in the certificate of incorporation of the surviving corporation as are desired to be effected by the merger (which amendments or changes may amend and restate the certificate of incorporation of the surviving corporation in its entirety), or, if no such amendments or changes are desired, a statement that the certificate of incorporation of the surviving corporation shall be its certificate of incorporation;

(5)   In the case of a consolidation in which a corporation is the resulting entity, that the certificate of incorporation of the resulting corporation shall be as is set forth in an attachment to the certificate;

(6)   That the executed agreement of consolidation or merger is on file at an office of the surviving or resulting corporation or limited liability company and the address thereof;

(7)   That a copy of the agreement of consolidation or merger will be furnished by the surviving or resulting entity, on request and without cost, to any stockholder of any constituent corporation or any member of any constituent limited liability company; and

(8)   The agreement, if any, required by subsection (d) of this section.

(d)   If the entity surviving or resulting from the merger or consolidation is a limited liability company formed under the laws of a jurisdiction other than this State, it shall agree that it may be served with process in this State in any proceeding for enforcement of any obligation of any constituent corporation or limited liability company of this State, as well as for enforcement of any obligation of the surviving or resulting corporation or limited liability company arising from the merger or consolidation, including any suit or other proceeding to enforce the right of any stockholders as determined in appraisal proceedings pursuant to the provisions of § 262 of this title, and shall irrevocably appoint the Secretary of State as its agent to accept service of process in any such suit or other proceedings and shall specify the address to which a copy of such process shall be mailed by the Secretary of State. Process may be served upon the Secretary of State under this subsection by means of electronic transmission but only as prescribed by the Secretary of State. The Secretary of State is authorized to issue such rules and regulations with respect to such service as the Secretary of State deems necessary or appropriate. In the event of such service upon the Secretary of State in accordance with this subsection, the Secretary of State shall forthwith notify such surviving or resulting corporation or limited liability company thereof by letter, directed to such surviving or resulting corporation or limited liability company at its address so specified, unless such surviving or resulting corporation or limited liability company shall have designated in writing to the Secretary of State a different address for such purpose, in which case it shall be mailed to the last address so designated. Such letter shall be sent by a mail or courier service that includes a record of mailing or deposit with the courier and a record of delivery evidenced by the signature of the recipient. Such letter shall enclose a copy of the process and any other papers served on the Secretary of State pursuant to this subsection. It shall be the duty of the plaintiff in the event of such service to serve process and any other papers in duplicate, to notify the Secretary of State that service is being effected pursuant to this subsection and to pay the Secretary of State the sum of $50 for the use of the State, which sum shall be taxed as part of the costs in the proceeding, if the plaintiff shall prevail therein. The Secretary of State shall maintain an alphabetical record of any such service setting forth the name of the plaintiff and the defendant, the title, docket number and nature of the proceeding in which process has been served upon the Secretary of State, the fact that service has been effected pursuant to this subsection, the return date thereof, and the day and hour service was made. The Secretary of State shall not be required to retain such information longer than 5 years from receipt of the service of process.

(e)   Sections 251(d)–(f), 255(c) (second sentence) and (d)–(f), 259–261 and 328 of this title shall, insofar as they are applicable, apply to mergers or consolidations between corporations and limited liability companies.

(f)   Nothing in this section shall be deemed to authorize the merger of a charitable nonstock corporation into a limited liability company, if the charitable status of such nonstock corporation would thereby be lost or impaired; but a limited liability company may be merged into a charitable nonstock corporation which shall continue as the surviving corporation.

§ 265.   Conversion of other entities to a domestic corporation.

(a)   As used in this section, the term "other entity" means a limited liability company, statutory trust, business trust or association, real estate investment trust, common-law trust or any other unincorporated business including a partnership (whether general (including a limited liability partnership) or limited (including a limited liability limited partnership)), or a foreign corporation.

(b)   Any other entity may convert to a corporation of this State by complying with subsection (h) of this section and filing in the office of the Secretary of State:

(1)   A certificate of conversion to corporation that has been executed in accordance with subsection (i) of this section and filed in accordance with § 103 of this title; and

(2)   A certificate of incorporation that has been executed, acknowledged and filed in accordance with § 103 of this title.

Each of the certificates required by this subsection (b) shall be filed simultaneously in the office of the Secretary of State and, if such certificates are not to become effective upon their filing as permitted by § 103(d) of this title, then each such certificate shall provide for the same effective date or time in accordance with § 103(d) of this title.

(c)   The certificate of conversion to corporation shall state:

(1)   The date on which and jurisdiction where the other entity was first created, incorporated, formed or otherwise came into being and, if it has changed, its jurisdiction immediately prior to its conversion to a domestic corporation;

(2)   The name and type of entity of the other entity immediately prior to the filing of the certificate of conversion to corporation; and

(3)   The name of the corporation as set forth in its certificate of incorporation filed in accordance with subsection (b) of this section.

(4)   [Repealed.]

(d)   Upon the effective time of the certificate of conversion to corporation and the certificate of incorporation, the other entity shall be converted to a corporation of this State and the corporation shall thereafter be subject to all of the provisions of this title, except that notwithstanding § 106 of this title, the existence of the corporation shall be deemed to have commenced on the date the other entity commenced its existence in the jurisdiction in which the other entity was first created, formed, incorporated or otherwise came into being.

(e)   The conversion of any other entity to a corporation of this State shall not be deemed to affect any obligations or liabilities of the other entity incurred prior to its conversion to a corporation of this State or the personal liability of any person incurred prior to such conversion.

(f)   When an other entity has been converted to a corporation of this State pursuant to this section, the corporation of this State shall, for all purposes of the laws of the State of Delaware, be deemed to be the same entity as the converting other entity. When any conversion shall have become effective under this section, for all purposes of the laws of the State of Delaware, all of the rights, privileges and powers of the other entity that has converted, and all property, real, personal and mixed, and all debts due to such other entity, as well as all other things and causes of action belonging to such other entity, shall remain vested in the domestic corporation to which such other entity has converted and shall be the property of such domestic corporation and the title to any real property vested by deed or otherwise in such other entity shall not revert or be in any way impaired by reason of this chapter; but all rights of creditors and all liens upon any property of such other entity shall be preserved unimpaired, and all debts, liabilities and duties of the other entity that has converted shall remain attached to the corporation of this State to which such other entity has converted, and may be enforced against it to the same extent as if said debts, liabilities and duties had originally been incurred or contracted by it in its capacity as a corporation of this State. The rights, privileges, powers and interests in property of the other entity, as well as the debts, liabilities and duties of the other entity, shall not be deemed, as a consequence of the conversion, to have been transferred to the domestic corporation to which such other entity has converted for any purpose of the laws of the State of Delaware.

(g)   Unless otherwise agreed for all purposes of the laws of the State of Delaware or as required under applicable non-Delaware law, the converting other entity shall not be required to wind up its affairs or pay its liabilities and distribute its assets, and the conversion shall not be deemed to constitute a dissolution of such other entity and shall constitute a continuation of the existence of the converting other entity in the form of a corporation of this State.

(h)   Prior to filing a certificate of conversion to corporation with the office of the Secretary of State, the conversion shall be approved in the manner provided for by the document, instrument, agreement or other writing, as the case may be, governing the internal affairs of the other entity and the conduct of its business or by applicable law, as appropriate, and a certificate of incorporation shall be approved by the same authorization required to approve the conversion.

(i)   The certificate of conversion to corporation shall be signed by any person who is authorized to sign the certificate of conversion to corporation on behalf of the other entity.

(j)   In connection with a conversion hereunder, rights or securities of, or interests in, the other entity which is to be converted to a corporation of this State may be exchanged for or converted into cash, property, or shares of stock, rights or securities of such corporation of this State or, in addition to or in lieu thereof, may be exchanged for or converted into cash, property, or shares of stock, rights or securities of or interests in another domestic corporation or other entity or may be cancelled.

§ 266.   Conversion of a domestic corporation to other entities.

(a)   A corporation of this State may, upon the authorization of such conversion in accordance with this section, convert to a limited liability company, statutory trust, business trust or association, real estate investment trust, common-law trust or any other unincorporated business including a partnership (whether general (including a limited liability partnership) or limited (including a limited liability limited partnership)) or a foreign corporation.

(b)   The board of directors of the corporation which desires to convert under this section shall adopt a resolution approving such conversion, specifying the type of entity into which the corporation shall be converted and recommending the approval of such conversion by the stockholders of the corporation. Such resolution shall be submitted to the stockholders of the corporation at an annual or special meeting. Due notice of the time, and purpose of the meeting shall be given to each holder of stock, whether voting or nonvoting, of the corporation at the address of the stockholder as it appears on the records of the corporation, at least 20 days prior to the date of the meeting. At the meeting, the resolution shall be considered and a vote taken for its adoption or rejection. If all outstanding shares of stock of the corporation, whether voting or nonvoting, shall be voted for the adoption of the resolution, the conversion shall be authorized.

(1)–(4)   [Repealed.]

(c)   If a corporation shall convert in accordance with this section to another entity organized, formed or created under the laws of a jurisdiction other than the State of Delaware, the corporation shall file with the Secretary of State a certificate of conversion executed in accordance with § 103 of this title, which certifies:

(1)   The name of the corporation, and if it has been changed, the name under which it was originally incorporated;

(2)   The date of filing of its original certificate of incorporation with the Secretary of State;

(3)   The name and jurisdiction of the entity to which the corporation shall be converted;

(4)   That the conversion has been approved in accordance with the provisions of this section;

(5)   The agreement of the corporation that it may be served with process in the State of Delaware in any action, suit or proceeding for enforcement of any obligation of the corporation arising while it was a corporation of this State, and that it irrevocably appoints the Secretary of State as its agent to accept service of process in any such action, suit or proceeding; and

(6)   The address to which a copy of the process referred to in paragraph (c)(5) of this section shall be mailed to it by the Secretary of State. Process may be served upon the Secretary of State in accordance with paragraph (c)(5) of this section by means of electronic transmission but only as prescribed by the Secretary of State. The Secretary of State is authorized to issue such rules and regulations with respect to such service as the Secretary of State deems necessary or appropriate. In the event of such service upon the Secretary of State in accordance with paragraph (c)(5) of this section, the Secretary of State shall forthwith notify such corporation that has converted out of the State of Delaware by letter, directed to such corporation that has converted out of the State of Delaware at the address so specified, unless such corporation shall have designated in writing to the Secretary of State a different address for such purpose, in which case it shall be mailed to the last address designated. Such letter shall be sent by a mail or courier service that includes a record of mailing or deposit with the courier and a record of delivery evidenced by the signature of the recipient. Such letter shall enclose a copy of the process and any other papers served on the Secretary of State pursuant to this subsection. It shall be the duty of the plaintiff in the event of such service to serve process and any other papers in duplicate, to notify the Secretary of State that service is being effected pursuant to this subsection and to pay the Secretary of State the sum of $50 for the use of the State, which sum shall be taxed as part of the costs in the proceeding, if the plaintiff shall prevail therein. The Secretary of State shall maintain an alphabetical record of any such service setting forth the name of the plaintiff and the defendant, the title, docket number and nature of the proceeding in which process has been served, the fact that service has been effected pursuant to this subsection, the return date thereof, and the day and hour service was made. The Secretary of State shall not be required to retain such information longer than 5 years from receipt of the service of process.

(d)   Upon the filing in the Office of the Secretary of State of a certificate of conversion to non-Delaware entity in accordance with subsection (c) of this section or upon the future effective date or time of the certificate of conversion to non-Delaware entity and payment to the Secretary of State of all fees prescribed under this title, the Secretary of State shall certify that the corporation has filed all documents and paid all fees required by this title, and thereupon the corporation shall cease to exist as a corporation of this State at the time the certificate of conversion becomes effective in accordance with § 103 of this title. Such certificate of the Secretary of State shall be prima facie evidence of the conversion by such corporation out of the State of Delaware.

(e)   The conversion of a corporation out of the State of Delaware in accordance with this section and the resulting cessation of its existence as a corporation of this State pursuant to a certificate of conversion to non-Delaware entity shall not be deemed to affect any obligations or liabilities of the corporation incurred prior to such conversion or the personal liability of any person incurred prior to such conversion, nor shall it be deemed to affect the choice of law applicable to the corporation with respect to matters arising prior to such conversion.

(f)   Unless otherwise provided in a resolution of conversion adopted in accordance with this section, the converting corporation shall not be required to wind up its affairs or pay its liabilities and distribute its assets, and the conversion shall not constitute a dissolution of such corporation.

(g)   In connection with a conversion of a domestic corporation to another entity pursuant to this section, shares of stock, of the corporation of this State which is to be converted may be exchanged for or converted into cash, property, rights or securities of, or interests in, the entity to which the corporation of this State is being converted or, in addition to or in lieu thereof, may be exchanged for or converted into cash, property, shares of stock, rights or securities of, or interests in, another domestic corporation or other entity or may be cancelled.

(h)   When a corporation has been converted to another entity or business form pursuant to this section, the other entity or business form shall, for all purposes of the laws of the State of Delaware, be deemed to be the same entity as the corporation. When any conversion shall have become effective under this section, for all purposes of the laws of the State of Delaware, all of the rights, privileges and powers of the corporation that has converted, and all property, real, personal and mixed, and all debts due to such corporation, as well as all other things and causes of action belonging to such corporation, shall remain vested in the other entity or business form to which such corporation has converted and shall be the property of such other entity or business form, and the title to any real property vested by deed or otherwise in such corporation shall not revert or be in any way impaired by reason of this chapter; but all rights of creditors and all liens upon any property of such corporation shall be preserved unimpaired, and all debts, liabilities and duties of the corporation that has converted shall remain attached to the other entity or business form to which such corporation has converted, and may be enforced against it to the same extent as if said debts, liabilities and duties had originally been incurred or contracted by it in its capacity as such other entity or business form. The rights, privileges, powers and interest in property of the corporation that has converted, as well as the debts, liabilities and duties of such corporation, shall not be deemed, as a consequence of the conversion, to have been transferred to the other entity or business form to which such corporation has converted for any purpose of the laws of the State of Delaware.

(i)   No vote of stockholders of a corporation shall be necessary to authorize a conversion if no shares of the stock of such corporation shall have been issued prior to the adoption by the board of directors of the resolution approving the conversion.

(j)   Nothing in this section shall be deemed to authorize the conversion of a charitable nonstock corporation into another entity, if the charitable status of such charitable nonstock corporation would thereby be lost or impaired.

§ 267.   Merger of parent entity and subsidiary corporation or corporations.

(a)   In any case in which: (1) at least 90% of the outstanding shares of each class of the stock of a corporation or corporations (other than a corporation which has in its certificate of incorporation the provision required by § 251(g)(7)(i) of this title), of which class there are outstanding shares that, absent this subsection, would be entitled to vote on such merger, is owned by an entity, and (2) 1 or more of such corporations is a corporation of this State, unless the laws of the jurisdiction or jurisdictions under which such entity or such foreign corporations are formed or organized prohibit such merger, the entity having such stock ownership may either merge the corporation or corporations into itself and assume all of its or their obligations, or merge itself, or itself and 1 or more of such corporations, into 1 of the other corporations by (a) authorizing such merger in accordance with such entity's governing documents and the laws of the jurisdiction under which such entity is formed or organized and (b) acknowledging and filing with the Secretary of State, in accordance with § 103 of this title, a certificate of such ownership and merger certifying (i) that such merger was authorized in accordance with such entity's governing documents and the laws of the jurisdiction under which such entity is formed or organized, such certificate executed in accordance with such entity's governing documents and in accordance with the laws of the jurisdiction under which such entity is formed or organized and (ii) the type of entity of each constituent entity to the merger; provided, however, that in case the entity shall not own all the outstanding stock of all the corporations, parties to a merger as aforesaid, (A) the certificate of ownership and merger shall state the terms and conditions of the merger, including the securities, cash, property, or rights to be issued, paid, delivered or granted by the surviving constituent party upon surrender of each share of the corporation or corporations not owned by the entity, or the cancellation of some or all of such shares and (B) such terms and conditions of the merger may not result in a holder of stock in a corporation becoming a general partner in a surviving entity that is a partnership (other than a limited liability partnership or a limited liability limited partnership). Any of the terms of the merger may be made dependent upon facts ascertainable outside of the certificate of ownership and merger, provided that the manner in which such facts shall operate upon the terms of the merger is clearly and expressly set forth in the certificate of ownership and merger. The term "facts," as used in the preceding sentence, includes, but is not limited to, the occurrence of any event, including a determination or action by any person or body, including the entity. If the surviving constituent party is an entity formed or organized under the laws of a jurisdiction other than this State, (1) § 252(d) of this title shall also apply to a merger under this section; if the surviving constituent party is the entity, the word "corporation" where applicable, as used in § 252(d) of this title, shall be deemed to include an entity as defined herein; and (2) the terms and conditions of the merger shall obligate the surviving constituent party to provide the agreement, and take the actions, required by § 252(d) of this title.

(b)   Sections 259, 261, and 328 of this title shall, insofar as they are applicable, apply to a merger under this section, and §§ 260 and 251(e) of this title shall apply to a merger under this section in which the surviving constituent party is a corporation of this State. For purposes of this subsection, references to "agreement of merger" in § 251(e) of this title shall mean the terms and conditions of the merger set forth in the certificate of ownership and merger, and references to "corporation" in §§ 259–261 of this title, and § 328 of this title shall be deemed to include the entity, as applicable. Section 262 of this title shall not apply to any merger effected under this section, except as provided in subsection (c) of this section.

(c)   In the event all of the stock of a Delaware corporation party to a merger effected under this section is not owned by the entity immediately prior to the merger, the stockholders of such Delaware corporation party to the merger shall have appraisal rights as set forth in § 262 of this title.

(d)   As used in this section only, the term:

(1)   "Constituent party" means an entity or corporation to be merged pursuant to this section;

(2)   "Entity" means a partnership (whether general (including a limited liability partnership) or limited (including a limited liability limited partnership)), limited liability company, any association of the kind commonly known as a joint-stock association or joint-stock company and any unincorporated association, trust or enterprise having members or having outstanding shares of stock or other evidences of financial or beneficial interest therein, whether formed or organized by agreement or under statutory authority or otherwise and whether formed or organized under the laws of this State or the laws of any other jurisdiction; and

(3)   "Governing documents" means a partnership agreement, limited liability company agreement, articles of association or any other instrument containing the provisions by which an entity is formed or organized.

SUBCHAPTER X.   SALE OF ASSETS, DISSOLUTION AND WINDING UP

§ 271.   Sale, lease or exchange of assets; consideration; procedure.

(a)   Every corporation may at any meeting of its board of directors or governing body sell, lease or exchange all or substantially all of its property and assets, including its goodwill and its corporate franchises, upon such terms and conditions and for such consideration, which may consist in whole or in part of money or other property, including shares of stock in, and/or other securities of, any other corporation or corporations, as its board of directors or governing body deems expedient and for the best interests of the corporation, when and as authorized by a resolution adopted by the holders of a majority of the outstanding stock of the corporation entitled to vote thereon or, if the corporation is a nonstock corporation, by a majority of the members having the right to vote for the election of the members of the governing body and any other members entitled to vote thereon under the certificate of incorporation or the bylaws of such corporation, at a meeting duly called upon at least 20 days' notice. The notice of the meeting shall state that such a resolution will be considered.

(b) Notwithstanding authorization or consent to a proposed sale, lease or exchange of a corporation's property and assets by the stockholders or members, the board of directors or governing body may abandon such proposed sale, lease or exchange without further action by the stockholders or members, subject to the rights, if any, of third parties under any contract relating thereto.

(c) For purposes of this section only, the property and assets of the corporation include the property and assets of any subsidiary of the corporation. As used in this subsection, "subsidiary" means any entity wholly-owned and controlled, directly or indirectly, by the corporation and includes, without limitation, corporations, partnerships, limited partnerships, limited liability partnerships, limited liability companies, and/or statutory trusts. Notwithstanding subsection (a) of this section, except to the extent the certificate of incorporation otherwise provides, no resolution by stockholders or members shall be required for a sale, lease or exchange of property and assets of the corporation to a subsidiary.

But no appraisal rights. cf. 262; Hariton

§ 272. Mortgage or pledge of assets.

The authorization or consent of stockholders to the mortgage or pledge of a corporation's property and assets shall not be necessary, except to the extent that the certificate of incorporation otherwise provides.

§ 273. Dissolution of joint venture corporation having 2 stockholders.

(a) If the stockholders of a corporation of this State, having only 2 stockholders each of which own 50% of the stock therein, shall be engaged in the prosecution of a joint venture and if such stockholders shall be unable to agree upon the desirability of discontinuing such joint venture and disposing of the assets used in such venture, either stockholder may, unless otherwise provided in the certificate of incorporation of the corporation or in a written agreement between the stockholders, file with the Court of Chancery a petition stating that it desires to discontinue such joint venture and to dispose of the assets used in such venture in accordance with a plan to be agreed upon by both stockholders or that, if no such plan shall be agreed upon by both stockholders, the corporation be dissolved. Such petition shall have attached thereto a copy of the proposed plan of discontinuance and distribution and a certificate stating that copies of such petition and plan have been transmitted in writing to the other stockholder and to the directors and officers of such corporation. The petition and certificate shall be executed and acknowledged in accordance with § 103 of this title.

(b) Unless both stockholders file with the Court of Chancery:

(1) Within 3 months of the date of the filing of such petition, a certificate similarly executed and acknowledged stating that they have agreed on such plan, or a modification thereof, and

(2) Within 1 year from the date of the filing of such petition, a certificate similarly executed and acknowledged stating that the distribution provided by such plan had been completed,

the Court of Chancery may dissolve such corporation and may by appointment of 1 or more trustees or receivers with all the powers and title of a trustee or receiver appointed under § 279 of this title, administer and wind up its affairs. Either or both of the above periods may be extended by agreement of the stockholders, evidenced by a certificate similarly executed, acknowledged and filed with the Court of Chancery prior to the expiration of such period.

(c) In the case of a charitable nonstock corporation, the petitioner shall provide a copy of any petition referred to in subsection (a) of this section to the Attorney General of the State of Delaware within 1 week of its filing with the Court of Chancery.

§ 274.   Dissolution before issuance of shares or beginning of business; procedure.

If a corporation has not issued shares or has not commenced the business for which the corporation was organized, a majority of the incorporators, or, if directors were named in the certificate of incorporation or have been elected, a majority of the directors, may surrender all of the corporation's rights and franchises by filing in the office of the Secretary of State a certificate, executed and acknowledged by a majority of the incorporators or directors, stating: that no shares of stock have been issued or that the business or activity for which the corporation was organized has not been begun; the date of filing of the corporation's original certificate of incorporation with the Secretary of State; that no part of the capital of the corporation has been paid, or, if some capital has been paid, that the amount actually paid in for the corporation's shares, less any part thereof disbursed for necessary expenses, has been returned to those entitled thereto; that if the corporation has begun business but it has not issued shares, all debts of the corporation have been paid; that if the corporation has not begun business but has issued stock certificates, all issued stock certificates, if any, have been surrendered and cancelled; and that all rights and franchises of the corporation are surrendered. Upon such certificate becoming effective in accordance with § 103 of this title, the corporation shall be dissolved.

§ 275.   Dissolution generally; procedure.

(a)   If it should be deemed advisable in the judgment of the board of directors of any corporation that it should be dissolved, the board, after the adoption of a resolution to that effect by a majority of the whole board at any meeting called for that purpose, shall cause notice of the adoption of the resolution and of a meeting of stockholders to take action upon the resolution to be given to each stockholder entitled to vote thereon as of the record date for determining the stockholders entitled to notice of the meeting.

(b)   At the meeting a vote shall be taken upon the proposed dissolution. If a majority of the outstanding stock of the corporation entitled to vote thereon shall vote for the proposed dissolution, a certification of dissolution shall be filed with the Secretary of State pursuant to subsection (d) of this section.

(c)   Dissolution of a corporation may also be authorized without action of the directors if all the stockholders entitled to vote thereon shall consent in writing and a certificate of dissolution shall be filed with the Secretary of State pursuant to subsection (d) of this section.

(d)   If dissolution is authorized in accordance with this section, a certificate of dissolution shall be executed, acknowledged and filed, and shall become effective, in accordance with § 103 of this title. Such certificate of dissolution shall set forth:

(1)   The name of the corporation;

(2)   The date dissolution was authorized;

(3)   That the dissolution has been authorized by the board of directors and stockholders of the corporation, in accordance with subsections (a) and (b) of this section, or that the dissolution has been authorized by all of the stockholders of the corporation entitled to vote on a dissolution, in accordance with subsection (c) of this section;

(4)   The names and addresses of the directors and officers of the corporation; and

(5)   The date of filing of the corporation's original certificate of incorporation with the Secretary of State.

(e)   The resolution authorizing a proposed dissolution may provide that notwithstanding authorization or consent to the proposed dissolution by the stockholders, or the members of a nonstock corporation pursuant to § 276 of this title, the board of directors or governing body may abandon such proposed dissolution without further action by the stockholders or members.

(f)   Upon a certificate of dissolution becoming effective in accordance with § 103 of this title, the corporation shall be dissolved.

§ 276.   Dissolution of nonstock corporation; procedure.

(a)   Whenever it shall be desired to dissolve any nonstock corporation, the governing body shall perform all the acts necessary for dissolution which are required by § 275 of this title to be performed by the board of directors of a corporation having capital stock. If any members of a nonstock corporation are entitled to vote for the election of members of its governing body or are entitled to vote for dissolution under the certificate of incorporation or the bylaws of such corporation, such members shall perform all the acts necessary for dissolution which are contemplated by § 275 of this title to be performed by the stockholders of a corporation having capital stock, including dissolution without action of the members of the governing body if all the members of the corporation entitled to vote thereon shall consent in writing and a certificate of dissolution shall be filed with the Secretary of State pursuant to § 275(d) of this title. If there is no member entitled to vote thereon, the dissolution of the corporation shall be authorized at a meeting of the governing body, upon the adoption of a resolution to dissolve by the vote of a majority of members of its governing body then in office. In all other respects, the method and proceedings for the dissolution of a nonstock corporation shall conform as nearly as may be to the proceedings prescribed by § 275 of this title for the dissolution of corporations having capital stock.

(b)   If a nonstock corporation has not commenced the business for which the corporation was organized, a majority of the governing body or, if none, a majority of the incorporators may surrender all of the corporation rights and franchises by filing in the office of the Secretary of State a certificate, executed and acknowledged by a majority of the incorporators or governing body, conforming as nearly as may be to the certificate prescribed by § 274 of this title.

§ 277.   Payment of franchise taxes before dissolution, merger, transfer or conversion.

No corporation shall be dissolved, merged, transferred (without continuing its existence as a corporation of this State) or converted under this chapter until:

(1)   All franchise taxes due to or assessable by the State including all franchise taxes due or which would be due or assessable for the entire calendar month during which such dissolution, merger, transfer or conversion becomes effective have been paid by the corporation; and

(2)   All annual franchise tax reports including a final annual franchise tax report for the year in which such dissolution, merger, transfer or conversion becomes effective have been filed by the corporation;

notwithstanding the foregoing, if the Secretary of State certifies that an instrument to effect a dissolution, merger, transfer or conversion has been filed in the Secretary of State's office, such corporation shall be dissolved, merged, transferred or converted at the effective time of such instrument.

§ 278.   Continuation of corporation after dissolution for purposes of suit and winding up affairs.

All corporations, whether they expire by their own limitation or are otherwise dissolved, shall nevertheless be continued, for the term of 3 years from such expiration or dissolution or for such longer period as the Court of Chancery shall in its discretion direct, bodies corporate for the purpose of prosecuting and defending suits, whether civil, criminal or administrative, by or against them, and of enabling them gradually to settle and close their business, to dispose of and convey their property, to discharge their liabilities and to distribute to their stockholders any remaining assets, but not for the purpose of continuing the business for which the corporation was organized. With respect to any action, suit or proceeding begun by or against the corporation either prior to or within 3 years after the date of its expiration or dissolution, the action shall not abate by reason of the dissolution of the corporation;

the corporation shall, solely for the purpose of such action, suit or proceeding, be continued as a body corporate beyond the 3-year period and until any judgments, orders or decrees therein shall be fully executed, without the necessity for any special direction to that effect by the Court of Chancery.

Sections 279 through 282 of this title shall apply to any corporation that has expired by its own limitation, and when so applied, all references in those sections to a dissolved corporation or dissolution shall include a corporation that has expired by its own limitation and to such expiration, respectively.

§ 279.   Trustees or receivers for dissolved corporations; appointment; powers; duties.

When any corporation organized under this chapter shall be dissolved in any manner whatever, the Court of Chancery, on application of any creditor, stockholder or director of the corporation, or any other person who shows good cause therefor, at any time, may either appoint 1 or more of the directors of the corporation to be trustees, or appoint 1 or more persons to be receivers, of and for the corporation, to take charge of the corporation's property, and to collect the debts and property due and belonging to the corporation, with power to prosecute and defend, in the name of the corporation, or otherwise, all such suits as may be necessary or proper for the purposes aforesaid, and to appoint an agent or agents under them, and to do all other acts which might be done by the corporation, if in being, that may be necessary for the final settlement of the unfinished business of the corporation. The powers of the trustees or receivers may be continued as long as the Court of Chancery shall think necessary for the purposes aforesaid.

§ 280.   Notice to claimants; filing of claims.

(a)(1) After a corporation has been dissolved in accordance with the procedures set forth in this chapter, the corporation or any successor entity may give notice of the dissolution, requiring all persons having a claim against the corporation other than a claim against the corporation in a pending action, suit or proceeding to which the corporation is a party to present their claims against the corporation in accordance with such notice. Such notice shall state:

> a.   That all such claims must be presented in writing and must contain sufficient information reasonably to inform the corporation or successor entity of the identity of the claimant and the substance of the claim;

> b.   The mailing address to which such a claim must be sent;

> c.   The date by which such a claim must be received by the corporation or successor entity, which date shall be no earlier than 60 days from the date thereof; and

> d.   That such claim will be barred if not received by the date referred to in paragraph (a)(1)c. of this section; and

> e.   That the corporation or a successor entity may make distributions to other claimants and the corporation's stockholders or persons interested as having been such without further notice to the claimant; and

> f.   The aggregate amount, on an annual basis, of all distributions made by the corporation to its stockholders for each of the 3 years prior to the date the corporation dissolved.

Such notice shall also be published at least once a week for 2 consecutive weeks in a newspaper of general circulation in the county in which the office of the corporation's last registered agent in this State is located and in the corporation's principal place of business and, in the case of a corporation having $10,000,000 or more in total assets at the time of its dissolution, at least once in all editions of a daily newspaper with a national circulation. On or before the date of the first publication of such notice, the corporation or successor entity shall mail a copy of such notice by certified or registered mail, return receipt requested, to each known claimant of the corporation including persons with claims asserted against the corporation in a pending action, suit or proceeding to which the corporation is a party.

(2) Any claim against the corporation required to be presented pursuant to this subsection is barred if a claimant who was given actual notice under this subsection does not present the claim to the dissolved corporation or successor entity by the date referred to in paragraph (a)(1)c. of this section.

(3) A corporation or successor entity may reject, in whole or in part, any claim made by a claimant pursuant to this subsection by mailing notice of such rejection by certified or registered mail, return receipt requested, to the claimant within 90 days after receipt of such claim and, in all events, at least 150 days before the expiration of the period described in § 278 of this title; provided however, that in the case of a claim filed pursuant to § 295 of this title against a corporation or successor entity for which a receiver or trustee has been appointed by the Court of Chancery the time period shall be as provided in § 296 of this title, and the 30-day appeal period provided for in § 296 of this title shall be applicable. A notice sent by a corporation or successor entity pursuant to this subsection shall state that any claim rejected therein will be barred if an action, suit or proceeding with respect to the claim is not commenced within 120 days of the date thereof, and shall be accompanied by a copy of §§ 278–283 of this title and, in the case of a notice sent by a court-appointed receiver or trustee and as to which a claim has been filed pursuant to § 295 of this title, copies of §§ 295 and 296 of this title.

(4) A claim against a corporation is barred if a claimant whose claim is rejected pursuant to paragraph (a)(3) of this section does not commence an action, suit or proceeding with respect to the claim no later than 120 days after the mailing of the rejection notice.

(b)(1) A corporation or successor entity electing to follow the procedures described in subsection (a) of this section shall also give notice of the dissolution of the corporation to persons with contractual claims contingent upon the occurrence or nonoccurrence of future events or otherwise conditional or unmatured, and request that such persons present such claims in accordance with the terms of such notice. Provided however, that as used in this section and in § 281 of this title, the term "contractual claims" shall not include any implied warranty as to any product manufactured, sold, distributed or handled by the dissolved corporation. Such notice shall be in substantially the form, and sent and published in the same manner, as described in paragraph (a)(1) of this section.

(2) The corporation or successor entity shall offer any claimant on a contract whose claim is contingent, conditional or unmatured such security as the corporation or successor entity determines is sufficient to provide compensation to the claimant if the claim matures. The corporation or successor entity shall mail such offer to the claimant by certified or registered mail, return receipt requested, within 90 days of receipt of such claim and, in all events, at least 150 days before the expiration of the period described in § 278 of this title. If the claimant offered such security does not deliver in writing to the corporation or successor entity a notice rejecting the offer within 120 days after receipt of such offer for security, the claimant shall be deemed to have accepted such security as the sole source from which to satisfy the claim against the corporation.

(c)(1) A corporation or successor entity which has given notice in accordance with subsection (a) of this section shall petition the Court of Chancery to determine the amount and form of security that will be reasonably likely to be sufficient to provide compensation for any claim against the corporation which is the subject of a pending action, suit or proceeding to which the corporation is a party other than a claim barred pursuant to subsection (a) of this section.

(2) A corporation or successor entity which has given notice in accordance with subsections (a) and (b) of this section shall petition the Court of Chancery to determine the amount and form of security that will be sufficient to provide compensation to any claimant who has rejected the offer for security made pursuant to paragraph (b)(2) of this section.

(3)   A corporation or successor entity which has given notice in accordance with subsection (a) of this section shall petition the Court of Chancery to determine the amount and form of security which will be reasonably likely to be sufficient to provide compensation for claims that have not been made known to the corporation or that have not arisen but that, based on facts known to the corporation or successor entity, are likely to arise or to become known to the corporation or successor entity within 5 years after the date of dissolution or such longer period of time as the Court of Chancery may determine not to exceed 10 years after the date of dissolution. The Court of Chancery may appoint a guardian ad litem in respect of any such proceeding brought under this subsection. The reasonable fees and expenses of such guardian, including all reasonable expert witness fees, shall be paid by the petitioner in such proceeding.

(d)   The giving of any notice or making of any offer pursuant to this section shall not revive any claim then barred or constitute acknowledgment by the corporation or successor entity that any person to whom such notice is sent is a proper claimant and shall not operate as a waiver of any defense or counterclaim in respect of any claim asserted by any person to whom such notice is sent.

(e)   As used in this section, the term "successor entity" shall include any trust, receivership or other legal entity governed by the laws of this State to which the remaining assets and liabilities of a dissolved corporation are transferred and which exists solely for the purposes of prosecuting and defending suits, by or against the dissolved corporation, enabling the dissolved corporation to settle and close the business of the dissolved corporation, to dispose of and convey the property of the dissolved corporation, to discharge the liabilities of the dissolved corporation and to distribute to the dissolved corporation's stockholders any remaining assets, but not for the purpose of continuing the business for which the dissolved corporation was organized.

(f)   The time periods and notice requirements of this section shall, in the case of a corporation or successor entity for which a receiver or trustee has been appointed by the Court of Chancery, be subject to variation by, or in the manner provided in, the Rules of the Court of Chancery.

(g)   In the case of a nonstock corporation, any notice referred to in the last sentence of paragraph (a)(3) of this section shall include a copy of § 114 of this title. In the case of a nonprofit nonstock corporation, provisions of this section regarding distributions to members shall not apply to the extent that those provisions conflict with any other applicable law or with that corporation's certificate of incorporation or bylaws.

§ 281.   Payment and distribution to claimants and stockholders.

(a)   A dissolved corporation or successor entity which has followed the procedures described in § 280 of this title:

(1)   Shall pay the claims made and not rejected in accordance with § 280(a) of this title,

(2)   Shall post the security offered and not rejected pursuant to § 280(b)(2) of this title,

(3)   Shall post any security ordered by the Court of Chancery in any proceeding under § 280(c) of this title, and

(4)   Shall pay or make provision for all other claims that are mature, known and uncontested or that have been finally determined to be owing by the corporation or such successor entity.

Such claims or obligations shall be paid in full and any such provision for payment shall be made in full if there are sufficient assets. If there are insufficient assets, such claims and obligations shall be paid or provided for according to their priority, and, among claims of equal priority, ratably to the extent of assets legally available therefor. Any remaining assets shall be distributed to the stockholders of the dissolved corporation; provided, however, that such distribution shall not be made before the expiration of 150 days from the date of the last notice of rejections given pursuant to § 280(a)(3) of this title. In the absence of actual fraud, the judgment of the directors of the dissolved corporation or the governing persons of such successor entity as to the provision made for the payment of all obligations under paragraph (a)(4) of this section shall be conclusive.

(b)   A dissolved corporation or successor entity which has not followed the procedures described in § 280 of this title shall, prior to the expiration of the period described in § 278 of this title, adopt a plan of distribution pursuant to which the dissolved corporation or successor entity (i) shall pay or make reasonable provision to pay all claims and obligations, including all contingent, conditional or unmatured contractual claims known to the corporation or such successor entity, (ii) shall make such provision as will be reasonably likely to be sufficient to provide compensation for any claim against the corporation which is the subject of a pending action, suit or proceeding to which the corporation is a party and (iii) shall make such provision as will be reasonably likely to be sufficient to provide compensation for claims that have not been made known to the corporation or that have not arisen but that, based on facts known to the corporation or successor entity, are likely to arise or to become known to the corporation or successor entity within 10 years after the date of dissolution. The plan of distribution shall provide that such claims shall be paid in full and any such provision for payment made shall be made in full if there are sufficient assets. If there are insufficient assets, such plan shall provide that such claims and obligations shall be paid or provided for according to their priority and, among claims of equal priority, ratably to the extent of assets legally available therefor. Any remaining assets shall be distributed to the stockholders of the dissolved corporation.

(c)   Directors of a dissolved corporation or governing persons of a successor entity which has complied with subsection (a) or (b) of this section shall not be personally liable to the claimants of the dissolved corporation.

(d)   As used in this section, the term "successor entity" has the meaning set forth in § 280(e) of this title.

(e)   The term "priority," as used in this section, does not refer either to the order of payments set forth in paragraph (a)(1)–(4) of this section or to the relative times at which any claims mature or are reduced to judgment.

(f)   In the case of a nonprofit nonstock corporation, provisions of this section regarding distributions to members shall not apply to the extent that those provisions conflict with any other applicable law or with that corporation's certificate of incorporation or bylaws.

§ 282.   Liability of stockholders of dissolved corporations.

(a)   A stockholder of a dissolved corporation the assets of which were distributed pursuant to § 281(a) or (b) of this title shall not be liable for any claim against the corporation in an amount in excess of such stockholder's pro rata share of the claim or the amount so distributed to such stockholder, whichever is less.

(b)   A stockholder of a dissolved corporation the assets of which were distributed pursuant to § 281(a) of this title shall not be liable for any claim against the corporation on which an action, suit or proceeding is not begun prior to the expiration of the period described in § 278 of this title.

(c)   The aggregate liability of any stockholder of a dissolved corporation for claims against the dissolved corporation shall not exceed the amount distributed to such stockholder in dissolution.

§ 283.   Jurisdiction.

The Court of Chancery shall have jurisdiction of any application prescribed in this subchapter and of all questions arising in the proceedings thereon, and may make such orders and decrees and issue injunctions therein as justice and equity shall require.

§ 284.   Revocation or forfeiture of charter; proceedings.

(a)   Upon motion by the Attorney General, the Court of Chancery shall have jurisdiction to revoke or forfeit the charter of any corporation for abuse, misuse or nonuse of its corporate powers, privileges or franchises. The Attorney General shall proceed for this purpose by complaint in the Court of Chancery.

(b)   The Court of Chancery shall have power, by appointment of trustees, receivers or otherwise, to administer and wind up the affairs of any corporation whose charter shall be revoked or forfeited by the Court of Chancery under this section, and to make such orders and decrees with respect thereto as shall be just and equitable respecting its affairs and assets and the rights of its stockholders and creditors.

(c)   No proceeding shall be instituted under this section for nonuse of any corporation's powers, privileges or franchises during the first 2 years after its incorporation.

§ 285.   Dissolution or forfeiture of charter by decree of court; filing.

Whenever any corporation is dissolved or its charter forfeited by decree or judgment of the Court of Chancery, the decree or judgment shall be forthwith filed by the Register in Chancery of the county in which the decree or judgment was entered, in the office of the Secretary of State, and a note thereof shall be made by the Secretary of State on the corporation's charter or certificate of incorporation and on the index thereof.

SUBCHAPTER XI.   INSOLVENCY; RECEIVERS AND TRUSTEES

§ 291.   Receivers for insolvent corporations; appointment and powers.

Whenever a corporation shall be insolvent, the Court of Chancery, on the application of any creditor or stockholder thereof, may, at any time, appoint 1 or more persons to be receivers of and for the corporation, to take charge of its assets, estate, effects, business and affairs, and to collect the outstanding debts, claims, and property due and belonging to the corporation, with power to prosecute and defend, in the name of the corporation or otherwise, all claims or suits, to appoint an agent or agents under them, and to do all other acts which might be done by the corporation and which may be necessary or proper. The powers of the receivers shall be such and shall continue so long as the Court shall deem necessary.

§ 292.   Title to property; filing order of appointment; exception.

(a)   Trustees or receivers appointed by the Court of Chancery of and for any corporation, and their respective survivors and successors, shall, upon their appointment and qualification or upon the death, resignation or discharge of any co-trustee or co-receiver, be vested by operation of law and without any act or deed, with the title of the corporation to all of its property, real, personal or mixed of whatsoever nature, kind, class or description, and wheresoever situate, except real estate situate outside this State.

(b)   Trustees or receivers appointed by the Court of Chancery shall, within 20 days from the date of their qualification, file in the office of the recorder in each county in this State, in which any real estate belonging to the corporation may be situated, a certified copy of the order of their appointment and evidence of their qualification.

(c)   This section shall not apply to receivers appointed pendente lite.

§ 293.   Notices to stockholders and creditors.

All notices required to be given to stockholders and creditors in any action in which a receiver or trustee for a corporation was appointed shall be given by the Register in Chancery, unless otherwise ordered by the Court of Chancery.

§ 294.   Receivers or trustees; inventory; list of debts and report.

Trustees or receivers shall, as soon as convenient, file in the office of the Register in Chancery of the county in which the proceeding is pending, a full and complete itemized inventory of all the assets of the corporation which shall show their nature and probable value, and an account of all debts due from and to it, as nearly as the same can be ascertained. They shall make a report to the Court of their proceedings, whenever and as often as the Court shall direct.

§ 295.   Creditors' proofs of claims; when barred; notice.

All creditors shall make proof under oath of their respective claims against the corporation, and cause the same to be filed in the office of the Register in Chancery of the county in which the proceeding is pending within the time fixed by and in accordance with the procedure established by the rules of the Court of Chancery. All creditors and claimants failing to do so, within the time limited by this section, or the time prescribed by the order of the Court, may, by direction of the Court, be barred from participating in the distribution of the assets of the corporation. The Court may also prescribe what notice, by publication or otherwise, shall be given to the creditors of the time fixed for the filing and making proof of claims.

§ 296.   Adjudication of claims; appeal.

(a) The Register in Chancery, immediately upon the expiration of the time fixed for the filing of claims, in compliance with § 295 of this title, shall notify the trustee or receiver of the filing of the claims, and the trustee or receiver, within 30 days after receiving the notice, shall inspect the claims, and if the trustee or receiver or any creditor shall not be satisfied with the validity or correctness of the same, or any of them, the trustee or receiver shall forthwith notify the creditors whose claims are disputed of such trustee's or receiver's decision. The trustee or receiver shall require all creditors whose claims are disputed to submit themselves to such examination in relation to their claims as the trustee or receiver shall direct, and the creditors shall produce such books and papers relating to their claims as shall be required. The trustee or receiver shall have power to examine, under oath or affirmation, all witnesses produced before such trustee or receiver touching the claims, and shall pass upon and allow or disallow the claims, or any part thereof, and notify the claimants of such trustee's or receiver's determination.

(b) Every creditor or claimant who shall have received notice from the receiver or trustee that such creditor's or claimant's claim has been disallowed in whole or in part may appeal to the Court of Chancery within 30 days thereafter. The Court, after hearing, shall determine the rights of the parties.

§ 297.   Sale of perishable or deteriorating property.

Whenever the property of a corporation is at the time of the appointment of a receiver or trustee encumbered with liens of any character, and the validity, extent or legality of any lien is disputed or brought in question, and the property of the corporation is of a character which will deteriorate in value pending the litigation respecting the lien, the Court of Chancery may order the receiver or trustee to sell the property of the corporation, clear of all encumbrances, at public or private sale, for the best price that can be obtained therefor, and pay the net proceeds arising from the sale thereof after deducting the costs of the sale into the Court, there to remain subject to the order of the Court, and to be disposed of as the Court shall direct.

§ 298.   Compensation, costs and expenses of receiver or trustee.

The Court of Chancery, before making distribution of the assets of a corporation among the creditors or stockholders thereof, shall allow a reasonable compensation to the receiver or trustee for such receiver's or trustee's services, and the costs and expenses incurred in and about the execution of such receiver's or trustee's trust, and the costs of the proceedings in the Court, to be first paid out of the assets.

§ 299.   Substitution of trustee or receiver as party; abatement of actions.

A trustee or receiver, upon application by such receiver or trustee in the court in which any suit is pending, shall be substituted as party plaintiff in the place of the corporation in any suit or proceeding which was so pending at the time of such receiver's or trustee's appointment. No action against a trustee or receiver of a corporation shall abate by reason of such receiver's or trustee's death, but, upon suggestion of the facts on the record, shall be continued against such receiver's or trustee's successor or against the corporation in case no new trustee or receiver is appointed.

§ 300.   Employee's lien for wages when corporation insolvent.

Whenever any corporation of this State, or any foreign corporation doing business in this State, shall become insolvent, the employees doing labor or service of whatever character in the regular employ of the corporation, shall have a lien upon the assets thereof for the amount of the wages due to them, not exceeding 2 months' wages respectively, which shall be paid prior to any other debt or debts of the corporation. The word "employee" shall not be construed to include any of the officers of the corporation.

§ 301.   Discontinuance of liquidation.

The liquidation of the assets and business of an insolvent corporation may be discontinued at any time during the liquidation proceedings when it is established that cause for liquidation no longer exists. In such event the Court of Chancery in its discretion, and subject to such condition as it may deem appropriate, may dismiss the proceedings and direct the receiver or trustee to redeliver to the corporation all of its remaining property and assets.

§ 302.   Compromise or arrangement between corporation and creditors or stockholders.

(a)   Whenever the provision permitted by § 102(b)(2) of this title is included in the original certificate of incorporation of any corporation, all persons who become creditors or stockholders thereof shall be deemed to have become such creditors or stockholders subject in all respects to that provision and the same shall be absolutely binding upon them. Whenever that provision is inserted in the certificate of incorporation of any such corporation by an amendment of its certificate all persons who become creditors or stockholders of such corporation after such amendment shall be deemed to have become such creditors or stockholders subject in all respects to that provision and the same shall be absolutely binding upon them.

(b)   The Court of Chancery may administer and enforce any compromise or arrangement made pursuant to the provision contained in § 102(b)(2) of this title and may restrain, pendente lite, all actions and proceedings against any corporation with respect to which the Court shall have begun the administration and enforcement of that provision and may appoint a temporary receiver for such corporation and may grant the receiver such powers as it deems proper, and may make and enforce such rules as it deems necessary for the exercise of such jurisdiction.

§ 303.   Proceeding under the Federal Bankruptcy Code of the United States; effectuation.

(a)   Any corporation of this State, an order for relief with respect to which has been entered pursuant to the Federal Bankruptcy Code, 11 U.S.C. § 101 et seq., or any successor statute, may put into effect and carry out any decrees and orders of the court or judge in such bankruptcy proceeding and may take any corporate action provided or directed by such decrees and orders, without further action by its directors or stockholders. Such power and authority may be exercised, and such corporate action may be taken, as may be directed by such decrees or orders, by the trustee or trustees of such corporation appointed or elected in the bankruptcy proceeding (or a majority thereof), or if none be appointed or elected and acting, by designated officers of the corporation, or by a representative appointed by the court or judge, with like effect as if exercised and taken by unanimous action of the directors and stockholders of the corporation.

(b)   Such corporation may, in the manner provided in subsection (a) of this section, but without limiting the generality or effect of the foregoing, alter, amend or repeal its bylaws; constitute or reconstitute and classify or reclassify its board of directors, and name, constitute or appoint directors and officers in place of or in addition to all or some of the directors or officers then in office; amend its certificate of incorporation, and make any change in its capital or capital stock, or any other amendment, change, or alteration, or provision, authorized by this chapter; be dissolved, transfer all or part of its assets, merge or consolidate as permitted by this chapter, in which case, however, no stockholder shall have any statutory right of appraisal of such stockholder's stock; change the location of its registered office, change its registered agent, and remove or appoint any agent to receive service of process; authorize and fix the terms, manner and conditions of, the issuance of bonds, debentures or other obligations, whether or not convertible into stock of any class, or bearing warrants or other evidences of optional rights to purchase or subscribe for stock of any class; or lease its property and franchises to any corporation, if permitted by law.

(c)   A certificate of any amendment, change or alteration, or of dissolution, or any agreement of merger or consolidation, made by such corporation pursuant to the foregoing provisions, shall be filed with the Secretary of State in accordance with § 103 of this title, and, subject to § 103(d) of this title, shall thereupon become effective in accordance with its terms and the provisions hereof. Such certificate, agreement of merger or other instrument shall be made, executed and acknowledged, as may be directed by such decrees or orders, by the trustee or trustees appointed or elected in the bankruptcy proceeding (or a majority thereof), or, if none be appointed or elected and acting, by the officers of the corporation, or by a representative appointed by the court or judge, and shall certify that provision for the making of such certificate, agreement or instrument is contained in a decree or order of a court or judge having jurisdiction of a proceeding under such Federal Bankruptcy Code or successor statute.

(d)   This section shall cease to apply to such corporation upon the entry of a final decree in the bankruptcy proceeding closing the case and discharging the trustee or trustees, if any; provided however, that the closing of a case and discharge of trustee or trustees, if any, will not affect the validity of any act previously performed pursuant to subsections (a) through (c) of this section.

(e)   On filing any certificate, agreement, report or other paper made or executed pursuant to this section, there shall be paid to the Secretary of State for the use of the State the same fees as are payable by corporations not in bankruptcy upon the filing of like certificates, agreements, reports or other papers.

SUBCHAPTER XII.   RENEWAL, REVIVAL, EXTENSION AND RESTORATION OF CERTIFICATE OF INCORPORATION OR CHARTER

§ 311.   Revocation of voluntary dissolution; restoration of expired certificate of incorporation.

(a)   At any time prior to the expiration of 3 years following the dissolution of a corporation pursuant to § 275 of this title or such longer period as the Court of Chancery may have directed pursuant to § 278 of this title, or at any time prior to the expiration of 3 years following the expiration of the time limited for the corporation's existence as provided in its certificate of incorporation or such longer period as the Court of Chancery may have directed pursuant to § 278 of this title, a corporation may revoke the dissolution theretofore effected by it or restore its certificate of incorporation after it has expired by its own limitation in the following manner:

(1)   For purposes of this section, the term "stockholders" shall mean the stockholders of record on the date the dissolution became effective or the date of expiration by limitation.

(2)   The board of directors shall adopt a resolution recommending that the dissolution be revoked in the case of a dissolution or that the certificate of incorporation be restored in the case of an expiration by limitation and directing that the question of the revocation or restoration be submitted to a vote at a special meeting of stockholders.

(3)   Notice of the special meeting of stockholders shall be given in accordance with § 222 of this title to each of the stockholders.

(4)   At the meeting a vote of the stockholders shall be taken on a resolution to revoke the dissolution in the case of a dissolution or to restore the certificate of incorporation in the case of an expiration by limitation. If a majority of the stock of the corporation which was outstanding and entitled to vote upon a dissolution at the time of its dissolution, in the case of a revocation of dissolution, or which was outstanding and entitled to vote upon an amendment to the certificate of incorporation to change the period of the corporation's duration at the time of its expiration by limitation, in the case of a restoration, shall be voted for the resolution, a certificate of revocation of dissolution or a certificate of restoration shall be executed, acknowledged and filed in accordance with § 103 of this title, which shall be specifically designated as a certificate of revocation of dissolution or a certificate of restoration in its heading and shall state:

a.   The name of the corporation;

b.   The address (which shall be stated in accordance with § 131(c) of this title) of the corporation's registered office in this State, and the name of its registered agent at such address;

c.   The names and respective addresses of its officers;

d.   The names and respective addresses of its directors;

e.   That a majority of the stock of the corporation which was outstanding and entitled to vote upon a dissolution at the time of its dissolution have voted in favor of a resolution to revoke the dissolution, in the case of a revocation of dissolution, or that a majority of the stock of the corporation which was outstanding and entitled to vote upon an amendment to the certificate of incorporation to change the period of the corporation's duration at the time of its expiration by limitation, in the case of a restoration, have voted in favor of a resolution to restore the certificate of incorporation; or, if it be the fact, that, in lieu of a meeting and vote of stockholders, the stockholders have given their written consent to the revocation or restoration in accordance with § 228 of this title; and

f.   In the case of a restoration, the new specified date limiting the duration of the corporation's existence or that the corporation shall have perpetual existence.

(b)   Upon the effective time of the filing in the office of the Secretary of State of the certificate of revocation of dissolution or the certificate of restoration, the revocation of the dissolution or the restoration of the corporation shall become effective and the corporation may again carry on its business.

(c)   Upon the effectiveness of the revocation of the dissolution or the restoration of the corporation as provided in subsection (b) of this section, the provisions of § 211(c) of this title shall govern, and the period of time the corporation was in dissolution or was expired by limitation shall be included within the calculation of the 30-day and 13-month periods to which § 211(c) of this title refers. An election of directors, however, may be held at the special meeting of stockholders to which subsection (a) of this section refers, and in that event, that meeting of stockholders shall be deemed an annual meeting of stockholders for purposes of § 211(c) of this title.

(d)   If after the dissolution became effective or after the expiration by limitation any other corporation organized under the laws of this State shall have adopted the same name as the corporation, or shall have adopted a name so nearly similar thereto as not to distinguish it from the corporation, or any foreign corporation shall have qualified to do business in this State under the same name as the corporation or under a name so nearly similar thereto as not to distinguish it from the corporation, then, in such case, the corporation shall not be reinstated under the same name which it bore when its dissolution became effective or it expired by limitation, but shall adopt and be reinstated or restored under some other name, and in such case the certificate to be filed under this section shall set forth the name borne by the corporation at the time its dissolution became effective or it expired by limitation and the new name under which the corporation is to be reinstated or restored.

(e)   Nothing in this section shall be construed to affect the jurisdiction or power of the Court of Chancery under § 279 or § 280 of this title.

(f)   At any time prior to the expiration of 3 years following the dissolution of a nonstock corporation pursuant to § 276 of this title or such longer period as the Court of Chancery may have directed pursuant to § 278 of this title, or at any time prior to the expiration of 3 years following the expiration of the time limited for a nonstock corporation's existence as provided in its certificate of incorporation or such longer period as the Court of Chancery may have directed pursuant to § 278 of this title, a nonstock corporation may revoke the dissolution thereofore effected by it or restore its certificate of incorporation after it has expired by limitation in a manner analogous to that by which the dissolution was authorized or, in the case of a restoration, in the manner in which an amendment to the certificate of incorporation to change the period of the corporation's duration would have been authorized at the time of its expiration by limitation including (i) if applicable, a vote of the members entitled to vote, if any, on the dissolution or the amendment and (ii) the filing of a certificate of revocation of dissolution or a certificate of restoration containing information comparable to that required by paragraph (a)(4) of this section. Notwithstanding the foregoing, only subsections (b), (d), and (e) of this section shall apply to nonstock corporations.

(g)   Any corporation that revokes its dissolution or restores its certificate of incorporation pursuant to this section shall file all annual franchise tax reports that the corporation would have had to file if it had not dissolved or expired and shall pay all franchise taxes that the corporation would have had to pay if it had not dissolved or expired. No payment made pursuant to this subsection shall reduce the amount of franchise tax due under Chapter 5 of this title for the year in which such revocation or restoration is effected.

§ 312.   Revival of certificate of incorporation.

(a)   As used in this section, the term "certificate of incorporation" includes the charter of a corporation organized under any special act or any law of this State.

(b)   Any corporation whose certificate of incorporation has become forfeited or void pursuant to this title or whose certificate of incorporation has been revived, but, through failure to comply strictly with the provisions of this chapter, the validity of whose revival has been brought into question, may at any time procure a revival of its certificate of incorporation, together with all the rights, franchises, privileges and immunities and subject to all of its duties, debts and liabilities which had been secured or imposed by its original certificate of incorporation and all amendments thereto, by complying with the requirements of this section. Notwithstanding the foregoing, this section shall not be applicable to a corporation whose certificate of incorporation has been revoked or forfeited pursuant to § 284 of this title.

(c)   The revival of the certificate of incorporation may be procured as authorized by the board of directors or members of the governing body of the corporation in accordance with subsection (h) of this section and by executing, acknowledging and filing a certificate of revival in accordance with § 103 of this title.

(d)   The certificate required by subsection (c) of this section shall state:

(1)   The date of filing of the corporation's original certificate of incorporation; the name under which the corporation was originally incorporated; the name of the corporation at the time its certificate of incorporation became forfeited or void pursuant to this title; and the new name under which the corporation is to be revived to the extent required by subsection (f) of this section;

(2)   The address (which shall be stated in accordance with § 131(c) of this title) of the corporation's registered office in this State and the name of its registered agent at such address;

(3)   That the corporation desiring to be revived and so reviving its certificate of incorporation was organized under the laws of this State;

881

(4) The date when the certificate of incorporation became forfeited or void pursuant to this title, or that the validity of any revival has been brought into question; and

(5) That the certificate of revival is filed by authority of the board of directors or members of the governing body of the corporation in accordance with subsection (h) of this section.

(e) Upon the filing of the certificate in accordance with § 103 of this title the corporation shall be revived with the same force and effect as if its certificate of incorporation had not been forfeited or void pursuant to this title. Such revival shall validate all contracts, acts, matters and things made, done and performed within the scope of its certificate of incorporation by the corporation, its directors or members of its governing body, officers, agents and stockholders or members during the time when its certificate of incorporation was forfeited or void pursuant to this title, with the same force and effect and to all intents and purposes as if the certificate of incorporation had at all times remained in full force and effect. All real and personal property, rights and credits, which belonged to the corporation at the time its certificate of incorporation became forfeited or void pursuant to this title and which were not disposed of prior to the time of its revival, and all real and personal property, rights and credits acquired by the corporation after its certificate of incorporation became forfeited or void pursuant to this title shall be vested in the corporation, after its revival, as if its certificate of incorporation had at all times remained in full force and effect, and the corporation after its revival shall be as exclusively liable for all contracts, acts, matters and things made, done or performed in its name and on its behalf by its directors or members of its governing body, officers, agents and stockholders or members prior to its revival, as if its certificate of incorporation had at all times remained in full force and effect.

(f) If, since the certificate of incorporation became forfeited or void pursuant to this title, any other corporation organized under the laws of this State shall have adopted the same name as the corporation sought to be revived or shall have adopted a name so nearly similar thereto as not to distinguish it from the corporation to be revived or any foreign corporation qualified in accordance with § 371 of this title shall have adopted the same name as the corporation sought to be revived or shall have adopted a name so nearly similar thereto as not to distinguish it from the corporation to be revived, then in such case the corporation to be revived shall not be revived under the same name which it bore when its certificate of incorporation became forfeited or void pursuant to this title, but shall be revived under some other name as set forth in the certificate to be filed pursuant to subsection (c) of this section.

(g) Any corporation that revives its certificate of incorporation under this chapter shall pay to this State a sum equal to all franchise taxes, penalties and interest thereon due at the time its certificate of incorporation became forfeited or void pursuant to this title; provided, however, that any corporation that revives its certificate of incorporation under this chapter whose certificate of incorporation has been forfeited or void for more than 5 years shall, in lieu of the payment of the franchise taxes and penalties otherwise required by this subsection, pay a sum equal to 3 times the amount of the annual franchise tax that would be due and payable by such corporation for the year in which the revival is effected, computed at the then current rate of taxation. No payment made pursuant to this subsection shall reduce the amount of franchise tax due under Chapter 5 of this title for the year in which the revival is effected.

(h) For purposes of this section and § 502(a) of this title, the board of directors or governing body of the corporation shall be comprised of the persons, who, but for the certificate of incorporation having become forfeited or void pursuant to this title, would be the duly elected or appointed directors or members of the governing body of the corporation. The requirement for authorization by the board of directors under subsection (c) of this section shall be satisfied if a majority of the directors or members of the governing body then in office, even though less than a quorum, or the sole director or member of the governing body then in office, authorizes the revival of the certificate of incorporation of the corporation and the filing of the certificate required by subsection (c) of this section. In any case where there shall be no directors of the corporation available for the purposes aforesaid, the stockholders may elect a full board of directors, as provided by the bylaws of the corporation, and the board so elected may then authorize the revival of the certificate of incorporation of the corporation and the filing of the certificate required by subsection (c) of this section. A special meeting of the stockholders for the purpose of electing directors may be called by any officer or stockholder upon notice given in accordance with § 222 of this title. For purposes of this section, the bylaws shall be the bylaws of the corporation that, but for the certificate of incorporation having become forfeited or void pursuant to this title, would be the duly adopted bylaws of the corporation.

(i) After a revival of the certificate of incorporation of the corporation shall have been effected, the provisions of § 211(c) of this title shall govern and the period of time during which the certificate of incorporation of the corporation was forfeited or void pursuant to this title shall be included within the calculation of the 30-day and 13-month periods to which § 211(c) of this title refers. A special meeting of stockholders held in accordance with subsection (h) of this section shall be deemed an annual meeting of stockholders for purposes of § 211(c) of this title.

(j) Except as otherwise provided in § 313 of this title, whenever it shall be desired to revive the certificate of incorporation of any nonstock corporation, the governing body shall perform all the acts necessary for the revival of the certificate of incorporation of the corporation which are performed by the board of directors in the case of a corporation having capital stock, and the members of any nonstock corporation who are entitled to vote for the election of members of its governing body and any other members entitled to vote for dissolution under the certificate of incorporation or the bylaws of such corporation, shall perform all the acts necessary for the revival of the certificate of incorporation of the corporation which are performed by the stockholders in the case of a corporation having capital stock. Except as otherwise provided in § 313 of this title, in all other respects, the procedure for the revival of the certificate of incorporation of a nonstock corporation shall conform, as nearly as may be applicable, to the procedure prescribed in this section for the revival of the certificate of incorporation of a corporation having capital stock; provided, however, that subsection (i) of this section shall not apply to nonstock corporations.

§ 313. Revival of certificate of incorporation or charter of exempt corporations.

(a) Every exempt corporation whose certificate of incorporation or charter has become forfeited, pursuant to § 136(b) of this title for failure to obtain a registered agent, or inoperative and void, by operation of § 510 of this title for failure to file annual franchise tax reports required, and for failure to pay taxes or penalties from which it would have been exempt if the reports had been filed, shall be deemed to have filed all the reports and be relieved of all the taxes and penalties, upon satisfactory proof submitted to the Secretary of State of its right to be classified as an exempt corporation pursuant to § 501(b) of this title, and upon filing with the Secretary of State a certificate of revival in manner and form as required by § 312 of this title.

(b) Upon the filing by the corporation of the proof of classification as required by subsection (a) of this section, the filing of the certificate of revival and payment of the required filing fees, the corporation shall be revived with the same force and effect as provided in § 312(e) of this title for other corporations.

(c) As used in this section, the term "exempt corporation" shall have the meaning given to it in § 501(b) of this title. Nothing contained in this section relieves any exempt corporation from filing the annual report required by § 502 of this title.

§ 314. Status of corporation.

Any corporation desiring to renew, extend and continue its corporate existence shall, upon complying with applicable constitutional provisions of this State, continue as provided in its certificate effecting the foregoing as a corporation and shall, in addition to the rights, privileges and immunities conferred by its charter, possess and enjoy all the benefits of this chapter, which are applicable to the nature of its business, and shall be subject to the restrictions and liabilities by this chapter imposed on such corporations.

SUBCHAPTER XIII.   SUITS AGAINST CORPORATIONS,
DIRECTORS, OFFICERS OR STOCKHOLDERS

§ 321.   Service of process on corporations.

(a)   Service of legal process upon any corporation of this State shall be made by delivering a copy personally to any officer or director of the corporation in this State, or the registered agent of the corporation in this State, or by leaving it at the dwelling house or usual place of abode in this State of any officer, director or registered agent (if the registered agent be an individual), or at the registered office or other place of business of the corporation in this State. If the registered agent be a corporation, service of process upon it as such agent may be made by serving, in this State, a copy thereof on the president, vice-president, secretary, assistant secretary or any director of the corporate registered agent. Service by copy left at the dwelling house or usual place of abode of any officer, director or registered agent, or at the registered office or other place of business of the corporation in this State, to be effective must be delivered thereat at least 6 days before the return date of the process, and in the presence of an adult person, and the officer serving the process shall distinctly state the manner of service in such person's return thereto. Process returnable forthwith must be delivered personally to the officer, director or registered agent.

(b)   In case the officer whose duty it is to serve legal process cannot by due diligence serve the process in any manner provided for by subsection (a) of this section, it shall be lawful to serve the process against the corporation upon the Secretary of State, and such service shall be as effectual for all intents and purposes as if made in any of the ways provided for in subsection (a) of this section. Process may be served upon the Secretary of State under this subsection by means of electronic transmission but only as prescribed by the Secretary of State. The Secretary of State is authorized to issue such rules and regulations with respect to such service as the Secretary of State deems necessary or appropriate. In the event that service is effected through the Secretary of State in accordance with this subsection, the Secretary of State shall forthwith notify the corporation by letter, directed to the corporation at its principal place of business as it appears on the records relating to such corporation on file with the Secretary of State or, if no such address appears, at its last registered office. Such letter shall be sent by a mail or courier service that includes a record of mailing or deposit with the courier and a record of delivery evidenced by the signature of the recipient. Such letter shall enclose a copy of the process and any other papers served on the Secretary of State pursuant to this subsection. It shall be the duty of the plaintiff in the event of such service to serve process and any other papers in duplicate, to notify the Secretary of State that service is being effected pursuant to this subsection, and to pay the Secretary of State the sum of $50 for the use of the State, which sum shall be taxed as part of the costs in the proceeding if the plaintiff shall prevail therein. The Secretary of State shall maintain an alphabetical record of any such service setting forth the name of the plaintiff and defendant, the title, docket number and nature of the proceeding in which process has been served upon the Secretary of State, the fact that service has been effected pursuant to this subsection, the return date thereof, and the day and hour when the service was made. The Secretary of State shall not be required to retain such information for a period longer than 5 years from receipt of the service of process.

(c)   Service upon corporations may also be made in accordance with § 3111 of Title 10 or any other statute or rule of court.

§ 322.   Failure of corporation to obey order of court; appointment of receiver.

Whenever any corporation shall refuse, fail or neglect to obey any order or decree of any court of this State within the time fixed by the court for its observance, such refusal, failure or neglect shall be a sufficient ground for the appointment of a receiver of the corporation by the Court of Chancery. If the corporation be a foreign corporation, such refusal, failure or neglect shall be a sufficient ground for the appointment of a receiver of the assets of the corporation within this State.

§ 323.   **Failure of corporation to obey writ of mandamus; quo warranto proceedings for forfeiture of charter.**

If any corporation fails to obey the mandate of any peremptory writ of mandamus issued by a court of competent jurisdiction of this State for a period of 30 days after the serving of the writ upon the corporation in any manner as provided by the laws of this State for the service of writs, any party in interest in the proceeding in which the writ of mandamus issued may file a statement of such fact prepared by such party or such party's attorney with the Attorney General of this State, and it shall thereupon be the duty of the Attorney General to forthwith commence proceedings of quo warranto against the corporation in a court of competent jurisdiction, and the court, upon competent proof of such state of facts and proper proceedings had in such proceeding in quo warranto, shall decree the charter of the corporation forfeited.

§ 324.   **Attachment of shares of stock or any option, right or interest therein; procedure; sale; title upon sale; proceeds.**

(a)   The shares of any person in any corporation with all the rights thereto belonging, or any person's option to acquire the shares, or such person's right or interest in the shares, may be attached under this section for debt, or other demands, if such person appears on the books of the corporation to hold or own such shares, option, right or interest. So many of the shares, or so much of the option, right or interest therein may be sold at public sale to the highest bidder, as shall be sufficient to satisfy the debt, or other demand, interest and costs, upon an order issued therefor by the court from which the attachment process issued, and after such notice as is required for sales upon execution process. Except as to an uncertificated security as defined in § 8–102 of Title 6, the attachment is not laid and no order of sale shall issue unless § 8–112 of Title 6 has been satisfied. No order of sale shall be issued until after final judgment shall have been rendered in any case. If the debtor lives out of the county, a copy of the order shall be sent by registered or certified mail, return receipt requested, to such debtor's last known address, and shall also be published in a newspaper published in the county of such debtor's last known residence, if there be any, 10 days before the sale; and if the debtor be a nonresident of this State shall be mailed as aforesaid and published at least twice for 2 successive weeks, the last publication to be at least 10 days before the sale, in a newspaper published in the county where the attachment process issued. If the shares of stock or any of them or the option to acquire shares or any such right or interest in shares, or any part of them, be so sold, any assignment, or transfer thereof, by the debtor, after attachment, shall be void.

(b)   When attachment process issues for shares of stock, or any option to acquire such or any right or interest in such, a certified copy of the process shall be left in this State with any officer or director, or with the registered agent of the corporation. Within 20 days after service of the process, the corporation shall serve upon the plaintiff a certificate of the number of shares held or owned by the debtor in the corporation, with the number or other marks distinguishing the same, or in the case the debtor appears on the books of the corporation to have an option to acquire shares of stock or any right or interest in any shares of stock of the corporation, there shall be served upon the plaintiff within 20 days after service of the process a certificate setting forth any such option, right or interest in the shares of the corporation in the language and form in which the option, right or interest appears on the books of the corporation, anything in the certificate of incorporation or bylaws of the corporation to the contrary notwithstanding. Service upon a corporate registered agent may be made in the manner provided in § 321 of this title.

(c)   If, after sale made and confirmed, a certified copy of the order of sale and return and the stock certificate, if any, be left with any officer or director or with the registered agent of the corporation, the purchaser shall be thereby entitled to the shares or any option to acquire shares or any right or interest in shares so purchased, and all income, or dividends which may have been declared, or become payable thereon since the attachment laid. Such sale, returned and confirmed, shall transfer the shares or the option to acquire shares or any right or interest in shares sold to the purchaser, as fully as if the debtor, or defendant, had transferred the same to such purchaser according to the certificate of incorporation or bylaws of the corporation, anything in the certificate of incorporation or bylaws to the contrary notwithstanding. The court which issued the levy and confirmed the sale shall have the power to make an order compelling the corporation, the shares of which were sold, to issue new certificates or uncertificated shares to the purchaser at the sale and to cancel the registration of the shares attached on the books of the corporation upon the giving of an open end bond by such purchaser adequate to protect such corporation.

(d)   The money arising from the sale of the shares or from the sale of the option or right or interest shall be applied and paid, by the public official receiving the same, as by law is directed as to the sale of personal property in cases of attachment.

§ 325.   Actions against officers, directors or stockholders to enforce liability of corporation; unsatisfied judgment against corporation.

(a)   When the officers, directors or stockholders of any corporation shall be liable by the provisions of this chapter to pay the debts of the corporation, or any part thereof, any person to whom they are liable may have an action, at law or in equity, against any 1 or more of them, and the complaint shall state the claim against the corporation, and the ground on which the plaintiff expects to charge the defendants personally.

(b)   No suit shall be brought against any officer, director or stockholder for any debt of a corporation of which such person is an officer, director or stockholder, until judgment be obtained therefor against the corporation and execution thereon returned unsatisfied.

§ 326.   Action by officer, director or stockholder against corporation for corporate debt paid.

When any officer, director or stockholder shall pay any debt of a corporation for which such person is made liable by the provisions of this chapter, such person may recover the amount so paid in an action against the corporation for money paid for its use, and in such action only the property of the corporation shall be liable to be taken, and not the property of any stockholder.

§ 327.   Stockholder's derivative action; allegation of stock ownership.

In any derivative suit instituted by a stockholder of a corporation, it shall be averred in the complaint that the plaintiff was a stockholder of the corporation at the time of the transaction of which such stockholder complains or that such stockholder's stock thereafter devolved upon such stockholder by operation of law.

§ 328.   Effect of liability of corporation on impairment of certain transactions.

The liability of a corporation of this State, or the stockholders, directors or officers thereof, or the rights or remedies of the creditors thereof, or of persons doing or transacting business with the corporation, shall not in any way be lessened or impaired by the sale of its assets, or by the increase or decrease in the capital stock of the corporation, or by its merger or consolidation with 1 or more corporations or by any change or amendment in its certificate of incorporation.

§ 329.   Defective organization of corporation as defense.

(a)   No corporation of this State and no person sued by any such corporation shall be permitted to assert the want of legal organization as a defense to any claim.

(b)   This section shall not be construed to prevent judicial inquiry into the regularity or validity of the organization of a corporation, or its lawful possession of any corporate power it may assert in any other suit or proceeding where its corporate existence or the power to exercise the corporate rights it asserts is challenged, and evidence tending to sustain the challenge shall be admissible in any such suit or proceeding.

§ 330.   Usury; pleading by corporation.

No corporation shall plead any statute against usury in any court of law or equity in any suit instituted to enforce the payment of any bond, note or other evidence of indebtedness issued or assumed by it.

SUBCHAPTER XIV.   CLOSE CORPORATIONS; SPECIAL PROVISIONS

§ 341.   Law applicable to close corporation.

(a)   This subchapter applies to all close corporations, as defined in § 342 of this title. Unless a corporation elects to become a close corporation under this subchapter in the manner prescribed in this subchapter, it shall be subject in all respects to this chapter, except this subchapter.

(b)   This chapter shall be applicable to all close corporations, as defined in § 342 of this title, except insofar as this subchapter otherwise provides.

§ 342.   Close corporation defined; contents of certificate of incorporation.

(a)   A close corporation is a corporation organized under this chapter whose certificate of incorporation contains the provisions required by § 102 of this title and, in addition, provides that:

(1)   All of the corporation's issued stock of all classes, exclusive of treasury shares, shall be represented by certificates and shall be held of record by not more than a specified number of persons, not exceeding 30; and

(2)   All of the issued stock of all classes shall be subject to 1 or more of the restrictions on transfer permitted by § 202 of this title; and

(3)   The corporation shall make no offering of any of its stock of any class which would constitute a "public offering" within the meaning of the United States Securities Act of 1933 [15 U.S.C. § 77a et seq.] as it may be amended from time to time.

(b)   The certificate of incorporation of a close corporation may set forth the qualifications of stockholders, either by specifying classes of persons who shall be entitled to be holders of record of stock of any class, or by specifying classes of persons who shall not be entitled to be holders of stock of any class or both.

(c)   For purposes of determining the number of holders of record of the stock of a close corporation, stock which is held in joint or common tenancy or by the entireties shall be treated as held by 1 stockholder.

§ 343.   Formation of a close corporation.

A close corporation shall be formed in accordance with §§ 101, 102 and 103 of this title, except that:

(1)   Its certificate of incorporation shall contain a heading stating the name of the corporation and that it is a close corporation; and

(2)   Its certificate of incorporation shall contain the provisions required by § 342 of this title.

§ 344.   Election of existing corporation to become a close corporation.

Any corporation organized under this chapter may become a close corporation under this subchapter by executing, acknowledging and filing, in accordance with § 103 of this title, a certificate of amendment of its certificate of incorporation which shall contain a statement that it elects to become a close corporation, the provisions required by § 342 of this title to appear in the certificate of incorporation of a close corporation, and a heading stating the name of the corporation and that it is a close corporation. Such amendment shall be adopted in accordance with the requirements of § 241 or

242 of this title, except that it must be approved by a vote of the holders of record of at least 2/3 of the shares of each class of stock of the corporation which are outstanding.

§ 345.   Limitations on continuation of close corporation status.

A close corporation continues to be such and to be subject to this subchapter until:

(1) It files with the Secretary of State a certificate of amendment deleting from its certificate of incorporation the provisions required or permitted by § 342 of this title to be stated in the certificate of incorporation to qualify it as a close corporation; or

(2) Any 1 of the provisions or conditions required or permitted by § 342 of this title to be stated in a certificate of incorporation to qualify a corporation as a close corporation has in fact been breached and neither the corporation nor any of its stockholders takes the steps required by § 348 of this title to prevent such loss of status or to remedy such breach.

§ 346.   Voluntary termination of close corporation status by amendment of certificate of incorporation; vote required.

(a) A corporation may voluntarily terminate its status as a close corporation and cease to be subject to this subchapter by amending its certificate of incorporation to delete therefrom the additional provisions required or permitted by § 342 of this title to be stated in the certificate of incorporation of a close corporation. Any such amendment shall be adopted and shall become effective in accordance with § 242 of this title, except that it must be approved by a vote of the holders of record of at least 2/3 of the shares of each class of stock of the corporation which are outstanding.

(b) The certificate of incorporation of a close corporation may provide that on any amendment to terminate its status as a close corporation, a vote greater than 2/3 or a vote of all shares of any class shall be required; and if the certificate of incorporation contains such a provision, that provision shall not be amended, repealed or modified by any vote less than that required to terminate the corporation's status as a close corporation.

§ 347.   Issuance or transfer of stock of a close corporation in breach of qualifying conditions.

(a) If stock of a close corporation is issued or transferred to any person who is not entitled under any provision of the certificate of incorporation permitted by § 342(b) of this title to be a holder of record of stock of such corporation, and if the certificate for such stock conspicuously notes the qualifications of the persons entitled to be holders of record thereof, such person is conclusively presumed to have notice of the fact of such person's ineligibility to be a stockholder.

(b) If the certificate of incorporation of a close corporation states the number of persons, not in excess of 30, who are entitled to be holders of record of its stock, and if the certificate for such stock conspicuously states such number, and if the issuance or transfer of stock to any person would cause the stock to be held by more than such number of persons, the person to whom such stock is issued or transferred is conclusively presumed to have notice of this fact.

(c) If a stock certificate of any close corporation conspicuously notes the fact of a restriction on transfer of stock of the corporation, and the restriction is one which is permitted by § 202 of this title, the transferee of the stock is conclusively presumed to have notice of the fact that such person has acquired stock in violation of the restriction, if such acquisition violates the restriction.

(d) Whenever any person to whom stock of a close corporation has been issued or transferred has, or is conclusively presumed under this section to have, notice either:

(1) That such person is a person not eligible to be a holder of stock of the corporation, or

(2)   That transfer of stock to such person would cause the stock of the corporation to be held by more than the number of persons permitted by its certificate of incorporation to hold stock of the corporation, or

(3)   That the transfer of stock is in violation of a restriction on transfer of stock,

the corporation may, at its option, refuse to register transfer of the stock into the name of the transferee.

(e)   Subsection (d) of this section shall not be applicable if the transfer of stock, even though otherwise contrary to subsection (a), (b) or (c) of this section has been consented to by all the stockholders of the close corporation, or if the close corporation has amended its certificate of incorporation in accordance with § 346 of this title.

(f)   The term "transfer," as used in this section, is not limited to a transfer for value.

(g)   The provisions of this section do not in any way impair any rights of a transferee regarding any right to rescind the transaction or to recover under any applicable warranty express or implied.

§ 348.   Involuntary termination of close corporation status; proceeding to prevent loss of status.

(a)   If any event occurs as a result of which 1 or more of the provisions or conditions included in a close corporation's certificate of incorporation pursuant to § 342 of this title to qualify it as a close corporation has been breached, the corporation's status as a close corporation under this subchapter shall terminate unless:

(1)   Within 30 days after the occurrence of the event, or within 30 days after the event has been discovered, whichever is later, the corporation files with the Secretary of State a certificate, executed and acknowledged in accordance with § 103 of this title, stating that a specified provision or condition included in its certificate of incorporation pursuant to § 342 of this title to qualify it as a close corporation has ceased to be applicable, and furnishes a copy of such certificate to each stockholder; and

(2)   The corporation concurrently with the filing of such certificate takes such steps as are necessary to correct the situation which threatens its status as a close corporation, including, without limitation, the refusal to register the transfer of stock which has been wrongfully transferred as provided by § 347 of this title, or a proceeding under subsection (b) of this section.

(b)   The Court of Chancery, upon the suit of the corporation or any stockholder, shall have jurisdiction to issue all orders necessary to prevent the corporation from losing its status as a close corporation, or to restore its status as a close corporation by enjoining or setting aside any act or threatened act on the part of the corporation or a stockholder which would be inconsistent with any of the provisions or conditions required or permitted by § 342 of this title to be stated in the certificate of incorporation of a close corporation, unless it is an act approved in accordance with § 346 of this title. The Court of Chancery may enjoin or set aside any transfer or threatened transfer of stock of a close corporation which is contrary to the terms of its certificate of incorporation or of any transfer restriction permitted by § 202 of this title, and may enjoin any public offering, as defined in § 342 of this title, or threatened public offering of stock of the close corporation.

§ 349.   Corporate option where a restriction on transfer of a security is held invalid.

If a restriction on transfer of a security of a close corporation is held not to be authorized by § 202 of this title, the corporation shall nevertheless have an option, for a period of 30 days after the judgment setting aside the restriction becomes final, to acquire the restricted security at a price which is agreed upon by the parties, or if no agreement is reached as to price, then at the fair value as determined by the Court of Chancery. In order to determine fair value, the Court may appoint an appraiser to receive evidence and report to the Court such appraiser's findings and recommendation as to fair value.

§ 350.   Agreements restricting discretion of directors.

A written agreement among the stockholders of a close corporation holding a majority of the outstanding stock entitled to vote, whether solely among themselves or with a party not a stockholder, is not invalid, as between the parties to the agreement, on the ground that it so relates to the conduct of the business and affairs of the corporation as to restrict or interfere with the discretion or powers of the board of directors. The effect of any such agreement shall be to relieve the directors and impose upon the stockholders who are parties to the agreement the liability for managerial acts or omissions which is imposed on directors to the extent and so long as the discretion or powers of the board in its management of corporate affairs is controlled by such agreement.

§ 351.   Management by stockholders.

The certificate of incorporation of a close corporation may provide that the business of the corporation shall be managed by the stockholders of the corporation rather than by a board of directors. So long as this provision continues in effect:

    (1)   No meeting of stockholders need be called to elect directors;

    (2)   Unless the context clearly requires otherwise, the stockholders of the corporation shall be deemed to be directors for purposes of applying provisions of this chapter; and

    (3)   The stockholders of the corporation shall be subject to all liabilities of directors.

Such a provision may be inserted in the certificate of incorporation by amendment if all incorporators and subscribers or all holders of record of all of the outstanding stock, whether or not having voting power, authorize such a provision. An amendment to the certificate of incorporation to delete such a provision shall be adopted by a vote of the holders of a majority of all outstanding stock of the corporation, whether or not otherwise entitled to vote. If the certificate of incorporation contains a provision authorized by this section, the existence of such provision shall be noted conspicuously on the face or back of every stock certificate issued by such corporation.

§ 352.   Appointment of custodian for close corporation.

    (a)   In addition to § 226 of this title respecting the appointment of a custodian for any corporation, the Court of Chancery, upon application of any stockholder, may appoint 1 or more persons to be custodians, and, if the corporation is insolvent, to be receivers, of any close corporation when:

    (1)   Pursuant to § 351 of this title the business and affairs of the corporation are managed by the stockholders and they are so divided that the business of the corporation is suffering or is threatened with irreparable injury and any remedy with respect to such deadlock provided in the certificate of incorporation or bylaws or in any written agreement of the stockholders has failed; or

    (2)   The petitioning stockholder has the right to the dissolution of the corporation under a provision of the certificate of incorporation permitted by § 355 of this title.

    (b)   In lieu of appointing a custodian for a close corporation under this section or § 226 of this title the Court of Chancery may appoint a provisional director, whose powers and status shall be as provided in § 353 of this title if the Court determines that it would be in the best interest of the corporation. Such appointment shall not preclude any subsequent order of the Court appointing a custodian for such corporation.

§ 353.   Appointment of a provisional director in certain cases.

    (a)   Notwithstanding any contrary provision of the certificate of incorporation or the bylaws or agreement of the stockholders, the Court of Chancery may appoint a provisional director for a close corporation if the directors are so divided respecting the management of the corporation's business and affairs that the votes required for action by the board of directors cannot be obtained with the consequence that the business and affairs of the corporation can no longer be conducted to the advantage of the stockholders generally.

(b)   An application for relief under this section must be filed (1) by at least one half of the number of directors then in office, (2) by the holders of at least one third of all stock then entitled to elect directors, or, (3) if there be more than 1 class of stock then entitled to elect 1 or more directors, by the holders of two thirds of the stock of any such class; but the certificate of incorporation of a close corporation may provide that a lesser proportion of the directors or of the stockholders or of a class of stockholders may apply for relief under this section.

(c)   A provisional director shall be an impartial person who is neither a stockholder nor a creditor of the corporation or of any subsidiary or affiliate of the corporation, and whose further qualifications, if any, may be determined by the Court of Chancery. A provisional director is not a receiver of the corporation and does not have the title and powers of a custodian or receiver appointed under §§ 226 and 291 of this title. A provisional director shall have all the rights and powers of a duly elected director of the corporation, including the right to notice of and to vote at meetings of directors, until such time as such person shall be removed by order of the Court of Chancery or by the holders of a majority of all shares then entitled to vote to elect directors or by the holders of two thirds of the shares of that class of voting shares which filed the application for appointment of a provisional director. A provisional director's compensation shall be determined by agreement between such person and the corporation subject to approval of the Court of Chancery, which may fix such person's compensation in the absence of agreement or in the event of disagreement between the provisional director and the corporation.

(d)   Even though the requirements of subsection (b) of this section relating to the number of directors or stockholders who may petition for appointment of a provisional director are not satisfied, the Court of Chancery may nevertheless appoint a provisional director if permitted by § 352(b) of this title.

§ 354.   Operating corporation as partnership.

No written agreement among stockholders of a close corporation, nor any provision of the certificate of incorporation or of the bylaws of the corporation, which agreement or provision relates to any phase of the affairs of such corporation, including but not limited to the management of its business or declaration and payment of dividends or other division of profits or the election of directors or officers or the employment of stockholders by the corporation or the arbitration of disputes, shall be invalid on the ground that it is an attempt by the parties to the agreement or by the stockholders of the corporation to treat the corporation as if it were a partnership or to arrange relations among the stockholders or between the stockholders and the corporation in a manner that would be appropriate only among partners.

§ 355.   Stockholders' option to dissolve corporation.

(a)   The certificate of incorporation of any close corporation may include a provision granting to any stockholder, or to the holders of any specified number or percentage of shares of any class of stock, an option to have the corporation dissolved at will or upon the occurrence of any specified event or contingency. Whenever any such option to dissolve is exercised, the stockholders exercising such option shall give written notice thereof to all other stockholders. After the expiration of 30 days following the sending of such notice, the dissolution of the corporation shall proceed as if the required number of stockholders having voting power had consented in writing to dissolution of the corporation as provided by § 228 of this title.

(b)   If the certificate of incorporation as originally filed does not contain a provision authorized by subsection (a) of this section, the certificate may be amended to include such provision if adopted by the affirmative vote of the holders of all the outstanding stock, whether or not entitled to vote, unless the certificate of incorporation specifically authorizes such an amendment by a vote which shall be not less than 2/3 of all the outstanding stock whether or not entitled to vote.

(c)   Each stock certificate in any corporation whose certificate of incorporation authorizes dissolution as permitted by this section shall conspicuously note on the face thereof the existence of the provision. Unless noted conspicuously on the face of the stock certificate, the provision is ineffective.

§ 356.   Effect of this subchapter on other laws.

This subchapter shall not be deemed to repeal any statute or rule of law which is or would be applicable to any corporation which is organized under this chapter but is not a close corporation.

SUBCHAPTER XV.   PUBLIC BENEFIT CORPORATIONS

§ 361.   Law applicable to public benefit corporations; how formed.

This subchapter applies to all public benefit corporations, as defined in § 362 of this title. If a corporation elects to become a public benefit corporation under this subchapter in the manner prescribed in this subchapter, it shall be subject in all respects to the provisions of this chapter, except to the extent this subchapter imposes additional or different requirements, in which case such requirements shall apply.

§ 362.   Public benefit corporation defined; contents of certificate of incorporation.

(a)   A "public benefit corporation" is a for-profit corporation organized under and subject to the requirements of this chapter that is intended to produce a public benefit or public benefits and to operate in a responsible and sustainable manner. To that end, a public benefit corporation shall be managed in a manner that balances the stockholders' pecuniary interests, the best interests of those materially affected by the corporation's conduct, and the public benefit or public benefits identified in its certificate of incorporation. In the certificate of incorporation, a public benefit corporation shall:

(1)   Identify within its statement of business or purpose pursuant to § 102(a)(3) of this title 1 or more specific public benefits to be promoted by the corporation; and

(2)   State within its heading that it is a public benefit corporation.

(b)   "Public benefit" means a positive effect (or reduction of negative effects) on 1 or more categories of persons, entities, communities or interests (other than stockholders in their capacities as stockholders) including, but not limited to, effects of an artistic, charitable, cultural, economic, educational, environmental, literary, medical, religious, scientific or technological nature. "Public benefit provisions" means the provisions of a certificate of incorporation contemplated by this subchapter.

(c)   The name of the public benefit corporation may contain the words "public benefit corporation," or the abbreviation "P.B.C.," or the designation "PBC," which shall be deemed to satisfy the requirements of § 102(a)(1)(i) of this title. If the name does not contain such language, the corporation shall, prior to issuing unissued shares of stock or disposing of treasury shares, provide notice to any person to whom such stock is issued or who acquires such treasury shares that it is a public benefit corporation; provided that such notice need not be provided if the issuance or disposal is pursuant to an offering registered under the Securities Act of 1933 [15 U.S.C. § 77r et seq.] or if, at the time of issuance or disposal, the corporation has a class of securities that is registered under the Securities Exchange Act of 1934 [15 U.S.C. § 78a et seq.].

§ 363. Certain amendments and mergers; votes required; appraisal rights. [For application of this section, see 80 Del. Laws, c. 40, § 16]

(a) Notwithstanding any other provisions of this chapter, a corporation that is not a public benefit corporation, may not, without the approval of 2/3 of the outstanding stock of the corporation entitled to vote thereon:

(1) Amend its certificate of incorporation to include a provision authorized by § 362(a)(1) of this title; or

(2) Merge or consolidate with or into another entity if, as a result of such merger or consolidation, the shares in such corporation would become, or be converted into or exchanged for the right to receive, shares or other equity interests in a domestic or foreign public benefit corporation or similar entity.

The restrictions of this section shall not apply prior to the time that the corporation has received payment for any of its capital stock, or in the case of a nonstock corporation, prior to the time that it has members.

(b) Any stockholder of a corporation that is not a public benefit corporation that holds shares of stock of such corporation immediately prior to the effective time of:

(1) An amendment to the corporation's certificate of incorporation to include a provision authorized by § 362(a)(1) of this title; or

(2) A merger or consolidation that would result in the conversion of the corporation's stock into or exchange of the corporation's stock for the right to receive shares or other equity interests in a domestic or foreign public benefit corporation or similar entity;

and has neither voted in favor of such amendment or such merger or consolidation nor consented thereto in writing pursuant to § 228 of this title, shall be entitled to an appraisal by the Court of Chancery of the fair value of the stockholder's shares of stock; provided, however, that no appraisal rights under this section shall be available for the shares of any class or series of stock, which stock, or depository receipts in respect thereof, at the record date fixed to determine the stockholders entitled to receive notice of the meeting of stockholders to act upon the agreement of merger or consolidation, or amendment, were either: (i) listed on a national securities exchange or (ii) held of record by more than 2,000 holders, unless, in the case of a merger or consolidation, the holders thereof are required by the terms of an agreement of merger or consolidation to accept for such stock anything except (A) shares of stock of any other corporation, or depository receipts in respect thereof, which shares of stock (or depository receipts in respect thereof) or depository receipts at the effective date of the merger or consolidation will be either listed on a national securities exchange or held of record by more than 2,000 holders; (B) cash in lieu of fractional shares or fractional depository receipts described in the foregoing clause (A); or (C) any combination of the shares of stock, depository receipts and cash in lieu of fractional shares or fractional depository receipts described in the foregoing clauses (A) and (B).

(c) Notwithstanding any other provisions of this chapter, a corporation that is a public benefit corporation may not, without the approval of 2/3 of the outstanding stock of the corporation entitled to vote thereon:

(1) Amend its certificate of incorporation to delete or amend a provision authorized by § 362(a)(1) or § 366(c) of this title; or

(2) Merge or consolidate with or into another entity if, as a result of such merger or consolidation, the shares in such corporation would become, or be converted into or exchanged for the right to receive, shares or other equity interests in a domestic or foreign corporation that is not a public benefit corporation or similar entity and the certificate of incorporation (or similar governing instrument) of which does not contain the identical provisions identifying the public benefit or public benefits pursuant to § 362(a) of this title or imposing requirements pursuant to § 366(c) of this title.

(d)   Notwithstanding the foregoing, a nonprofit nonstock corporation may not be a constituent corporation to any merger or consolidation governed by this section.

§ 364.   Stock certificates; notices regarding uncertificated stock.

Any stock certificate issued by a public benefit corporation shall note conspicuously that the corporation is a public benefit corporation formed pursuant to this subchapter. Any notice given by a public benefit corporation pursuant to § 151(f) of this title shall state conspicuously that the corporation is a public benefit corporation formed pursuant to this subchapter.

§ 365.   Duties of directors.

(a)   The board of directors shall manage or direct the business and affairs of the public benefit corporation in a manner that balances the pecuniary interests of the stockholders, the best interests of those materially affected by the corporation's conduct, and the specific public benefit or public benefits identified in its certificate of incorporation.

(b)   A director of a public benefit corporation shall not, by virtue of the public benefit provisions or § 362(a) of this title, have any duty to any person on account of any interest of such person in the public benefit or public benefits identified in the certificate of incorporation or on account of any interest materially affected by the corporation's conduct and, with respect to a decision implicating the balance requirement in subsection (a) of this section, will be deemed to satisfy such director's fiduciary duties to stockholders and the corporation if such director's decision is both informed and disinterested and not such that no person of ordinary, sound judgment would approve.

(c)   The certificate of incorporation of a public benefit corporation may include a provision that any disinterested failure to satisfy this section shall not, for the purposes of § 102(b)(7) or § 145 of this title, constitute an act or omission not in good faith, or a breach of the duty of loyalty.

§ 366.   Periodic statements and third-party certification.

(a)   A public benefit corporation shall include in every notice of a meeting of stockholders a statement to the effect that it is a public benefit corporation formed pursuant to this subchapter.

(b)   A public benefit corporation shall no less than biennially provide its stockholders with a statement as to the corporation's promotion of the public benefit or public benefits identified in the certificate of incorporation and of the best interests of those materially affected by the corporation's conduct. The statement shall include:

(1)   The objectives the board of directors has established to promote such public benefit or public benefits and interests;

(2)   The standards the board of directors has adopted to measure the corporation's progress in promoting such public benefit or public benefits and interests;

(3)   Objective factual information based on those standards regarding the corporation's success in meeting the objectives for promoting such public benefit or public benefits and interests; and

(4)   An assessment of the corporation's success in meeting the objectives and promoting such public benefit or public benefits and interests.

(c)   The certificate of incorporation or bylaws of a public benefit corporation may require that the corporation:

(1)   Provide the statement described in subsection (b) of this section more frequently than biennially;

(2)   Make the statement described in subsection (b) of this section available to the public; and/or

(3)   Use a third-party standard in connection with and/or attain a periodic third-party certification addressing the corporation's promotion of the public benefit or public benefits identified in the certificate of incorporation and/or the best interests of those materially affected by the corporation's conduct.

§ 367.   Derivative suits.

Stockholders of a public benefit corporation owning individually or collectively, as of the date of instituting such derivative suit, at least 2% of the corporation's outstanding shares or, in the case of a corporation with shares listed on a national securities exchange, the lesser of such percentage or shares of at least $2,000,000 in market value, may maintain a derivative lawsuit to enforce the requirements set forth in § 365(a) of this title.

§ 368.   No effect on other corporations.

This subchapter shall not affect a statute or rule of law that is applicable to a corporation that is not a public benefit corporation, except as provided in § 363 of this title.

SUBCHAPTER XVI.   FOREIGN CORPORATIONS

§ 371.   Definition; qualification to do business in State; procedure.

(a)   As used in this chapter, the words "foreign corporation" mean a corporation organized under the laws of any jurisdiction other than this State.

(b)   No foreign corporation shall do any business in this State, through or by branch offices, agents or representatives located in this State, until it shall have paid to the Secretary of State of this State for the use of this State, $80, and shall have filed in the office of the Secretary of State:

(1)   A certificate, as of a date not earlier than 6 months prior to the filing date, issued by an authorized officer of the jurisdiction of its incorporation evidencing its corporate existence. If such certificate is in a foreign language, a translation thereof, under oath of the translator, shall be attached thereto;

(2)   A statement executed by an authorized officer of each corporation setting forth (i) the name and address of its registered agent in this State, which agent may be any of the foreign corporation itself, an individual resident in this State, a domestic corporation, a domestic partnership (whether general (including a limited liability partnership) or limited (including a limited liability limited partnership)), a domestic limited liability company, a domestic statutory trust, a foreign corporation (other than the foreign corporation itself), a foreign partnership (whether general (including a limited liability partnership) or limited (including a limited liability limited partnership)), a foreign limited liability company or a foreign statutory trust, (ii) a statement, as of a date not earlier than 6 months prior to the filing date, of the assets and liabilities of the corporation, and (iii) the business it proposes to do in this State, and a statement that it is authorized to do that business in the jurisdiction of its incorporation. The statement shall be acknowledged in accordance with § 103 of this title.

(c)   The certificate of the Secretary of State, under seal of office, of the filing of the certificates required by subsection (b) of this section, shall be delivered to the registered agent upon the payment to the Secretary of State of the fee prescribed for such certificates, and the certificate shall be prima facie evidence of the right of the corporation to do business in this State; provided, that the Secretary of State shall not issue such certificate unless the name of the corporation is such as to distinguish it upon the records in the office of the Division of Corporations in the Department of State from the names that are reserved on such records and from the names on such records of each other corporation, partnership, limited partnership, limited liability company or statutory trust organized or registered as a domestic or foreign corporation, partnership, limited partnership, limited liability company or statutory trust under the laws of this State, except with the written consent of the person who has reserved such name or such other corporation, partnership, limited partnership, limited liability company or statutory trust, executed, acknowledged and filed with the Secretary of State in accordance with § 103 of this title. If the name of the foreign corporation conflicts with the name of a corporation, partnership, limited partnership, limited liability company or statutory trust organized under the laws of this State, or a name reserved for a corporation, partnership, limited partnership, limited liability company or statutory trust to be organized under the laws of this State, or a name reserved or registered as that of a foreign corporation, partnership, limited partnership, limited liability company or statutory trust under the laws of this State, the foreign corporation may qualify to do business if it adopts an assumed name which shall be used when doing business in this State as long as the assumed name is authorized for use by this section.

§ 372. Additional requirements in case of change of name, change of business purpose or merger or consolidation.

(a) Every foreign corporation admitted to do business in this State which shall change its corporate name, or enlarge, limit or otherwise change the business which it proposes to do in this State, shall, within 30 days after the time said change becomes effective, file with the Secretary of State a certificate, which shall set forth:

(1) The name of the foreign corporation as it appears on the records of the Secretary of State of this State;

(2) The jurisdiction of its incorporation;

(3) The date it was authorized to do business in this State;

(4) If the name of the foreign corporation has been changed, a statement of the name relinquished, a statement of the new name and a statement that the change of name has been effected under the laws of the jurisdiction of its incorporation and the date the change was effected;

(5) If the business it proposes to do in this State is to be enlarged, limited or otherwise changed, a statement reflecting such change and a statement that it is authorized to do in the jurisdiction of its incorporation the business which it proposes to do in this State.

(b) Whenever a foreign corporation authorized to transact business in this State shall be the survivor of a merger permitted by the laws of the state or country in which it is incorporated, it shall, within 30 days after the merger becomes effective, file a certificate, issued by the proper officer of the state or country of its incorporation, attesting to the occurrence of such event. If the merger has changed the corporate name of such foreign corporation or has enlarged, limited or otherwise changed the business it proposes to do in this State, it shall also comply with subsection (a) of this section.

(c) Whenever a foreign corporation authorized to transact business in this State ceases to exist because of a statutory merger or consolidation, it shall comply with § 381 of this title.

(d) The Secretary of State shall be paid, for the use of the State, $50 for filing and indexing each certificate required by subsection (a) or (b) of this section, and in the event of a change of name an additional $50 shall be paid for a certificate to be issued as evidence of filing the change of name.

§ 373. Exceptions to requirements.

(a) No foreign corporation shall be required to comply with §§ 371 and 372 of this title, under any of the following conditions:

(1) If it is in the mail order or a similar business, merely receiving orders by mail or otherwise in pursuance of letters, circulars, catalogs or other forms of advertising, or solicitation, accepting the orders outside this State, and filling them with goods shipped into this State;

(2) If it employs salespersons, either resident or traveling, to solicit orders in this State, either by display of samples or otherwise (whether or not maintaining sales offices in this State),

all orders being subject to approval at the offices of the corporation without this State, and all goods applicable to the orders being shipped in pursuance thereof from without this State to the vendee or to the seller or such seller's agent for delivery to the vendee, and if any samples kept within this State are for display or advertising purposes only, and no sales, repairs or replacements are made from stock on hand in this State;

(3)   If it sells, by contract consummated outside this State, and agrees, by the contract, to deliver into this State, machinery, plants or equipment, the construction, erection or installation of which within this State requires the supervision of technical engineers or skilled employees performing services not generally available, and as a part of the contract of sale agrees to furnish such services, and such services only, to the vendee at the time of construction, erection or installation;

(4)   If its business operations within this State, although not falling within the terms of paragraphs (a)(1), (2) and (3) of this section or any of them, are nevertheless wholly interstate in character;

(5)   If it is an insurance company doing business in this State;

(6)   If it creates, as borrower or lender, or acquires, evidences of debt, mortgages or liens on real or personal property;

(7)   If it secures or collects debts or enforces any rights in property securing the same.

(b)   This section shall have no application to the question of whether any foreign corporation is subject to service of process and suit in this State under § 382 of this title or any other law of this State.

§ 374.   Annual report.

Annually on or before June 30, a foreign corporation doing business in this State shall file a report with the Secretary of State. The report shall be made on a form designated by the Secretary of State and shall be signed by the corporation's president, secretary, treasurer or other proper officer duly authorized so to act, or by any of its directors, or if filing an initial report by any incorporator in the event its board of directors shall not have been elected. The fact that an individual's name is signed on a certification attached to a corporate report shall be prima facie evidence that such individual is authorized to certify the report on behalf of the corporation; however the official title or position of the individual signing the corporate report shall be designated. The report shall contain the following information:

(1)   The location of its registered office in this State, which shall include the street, number, city and postal code;

(2)   The name of the agent upon whom service of process against the corporation may be served;

(3)   The location of the principal place of business of the corporation, which shall include the street, number, city, state or foreign country; and

(4)   The names and addresses of all the directors as of the filing date of the report and the name and address of the officer who signs the report.

If any officer or director of a foreign corporation required to file an annual report with the Secretary of State shall knowingly make any false statement in the report, such officer or director shall be guilty of perjury.

§ 375.   Failure to file report.

Upon the failure, neglect or refusal of any foreign corporation to file an annual report as required by § 374 of this title, the Secretary of State may, in the Secretary of State's discretion, investigate the reasons therefor and shall terminate the right of the foreign corporation to do business within this State upon failure of the corporation to file an annual report within any 2-year period.

§ 376.   Service of process upon qualified foreign corporations.

(a)   All process issued out of any court of this State, all orders made by any court of this State, all rules and notices of any kind required to be served on any foreign corporation which has qualified to do business in this State may be served on the registered agent of the corporation designated in accordance with § 371 of this title, or, if there be no such agent, then on any officer, director or other agent of the corporation then in this State.

(b)   In case the officer whose duty it is to serve legal process cannot by due diligence serve the process in any manner provided for by subsection (a) of this section, it shall be lawful to serve the process against the corporation upon the Secretary of State, and such service shall be as effectual for all intents and purposes as if made in any of the ways provided for in subsection (a) of this section. Process may be served upon the Secretary of State under this subsection by means of electronic transmission but only as prescribed by the Secretary of State. The Secretary of State is authorized to issue such rules and regulations with respect to such service as the Secretary of State deems necessary or appropriate. In the event that service is effected through the Secretary of State in accordance with this subsection, the Secretary of State shall forthwith notify the corporation by letter, directed to the corporation at its principal place of business as it appears on the last annual report filed pursuant to § 374 of this title or, if no such address appears, at its last registered office. Such letter shall be sent by a mail or courier service that includes a record of mailing or deposit with the courier and a record of delivery evidenced by the signature of the recipient. Such letter shall enclose a copy of the process and any other papers served upon the Secretary of State pursuant to this subsection. It shall be the duty of the plaintiff in the event of such service to serve process and any other papers in duplicate, to notify the Secretary of State that service is being effected pursuant to this subsection, and to pay the Secretary of State the sum of $50 for the use of the State, which sum shall be taxed as a part of the costs in the proceeding if the plaintiff shall prevail therein. The Secretary of State shall maintain an alphabetical record of any such service setting forth the name of the plaintiff and the defendant, the title, docket number and nature of the proceeding in which process has been served upon the Secretary of State, the fact that service has been effected pursuant to this subsection, the return date thereof, and the day and hour when the service was made. The Secretary of State shall not be required to retain such information for a period longer than 5 years from receipt of such service.

§ 377.   Change of registered agent.

(a)   Any foreign corporation, which has qualified to do business in this State, may change its registered agent and substitute another registered agent by filing a certificate with the Secretary of State, acknowledged in accordance with § 103 of this title, setting forth:

(1)   The name and address of its registered agent designated in this State upon whom process directed to said corporation may be served; and

(2)   A revocation of all previous appointments of agent for such purposes.

Such registered agent shall comply with § 371(b)(2)(i) of this title.

(b)   Any individual or entity designated by a foreign corporation as its registered agent for service of process may resign by filing with the Secretary of State a signed statement that the registered agent is unwilling to continue to act as the registered agent of the corporation for service of process, including in the statement the post-office address of the main or headquarters office of the foreign corporation, but such resignation shall not become effective until 30 days after the statement is filed. The statement shall be acknowledged by the registered agent and shall contain a representation that written notice of resignation was given to the corporation at least 30 days prior to the filing of the statement by mailing or delivering such notice to the corporation at its address given in the statement.

(c)   If any agent designated and certified as required by § 371 of this title shall die or remove from this State, or resign, then the foreign corporation for which the agent had been so designated and certified shall, within 10 days after the death, removal or resignation of its agent, substitute, designate and certify to the Secretary of State, the name of another registered agent for the purposes of this subchapter, and all process, orders, rules and notices mentioned in § 376 of this title may be served on or given to the substituted agent with like effect as is prescribed in that section.

(d)   A foreign corporation whose qualification to do business in this State has been forfeited pursuant to § 132(f)(4) or § 136(b) of this title may be reinstated by filing a certificate of reinstatement with the Secretary of State, acknowledged in accordance with § 103 of this title, setting forth:

(1)   The name of the foreign corporation;

(2)   The effective date of the forfeiture; and

(3)   The name and address of the foreign corporation's registered agent required to be maintained by § 132 of this title.

(e)   Upon the filing of a certificate of reinstatement in accordance with subsection (d) of this section, the qualification of the foreign corporation to do business in this State shall be reinstated with the same force and effect as if it had not been forfeited pursuant to this title.

§ 378.   Penalties for noncompliance.

Any foreign corporation doing business of any kind in this State without first having complied with any section of this subchapter applicable to it, shall be fined not less than $200 nor more than $500 for each such offense. Any agent of any foreign corporation that shall do any business in this State for any foreign corporation before the foreign corporation has complied with any section of this subchapter applicable to it, shall be fined not less than $100 nor more than $500 for each such offense.

§ 379.   Banking powers denied.

(a)   No foreign corporation shall, within the limits of this State, by any implication or construction, be deemed to possess the power of discounting bills, notes or other evidence of debt, of receiving deposits, of buying and selling bills of exchange, or of issuing bills, notes or other evidences of debt upon loan for circulation as money, anything in its charter or articles of incorporation to the contrary notwithstanding, except as otherwise provided in subchapter VII of Chapter 7 or in Chapter 14 of Title 5.

(b)   All certificates issued by the Secretary of State under § 371 of this title shall expressly set forth the limitations and restrictions contained in this section.

§ 380.   Foreign corporation as fiduciary in this State.

A corporation organized and doing business under the laws of the District of Columbia or of any state of the United States other than Delaware, duly authorized by its certificate of incorporation or bylaws so to act, may be appointed by any last will and testament or other testamentary writing, probated within this State, or by a deed of trust, mortgage or other agreement, as executor, guardian, trustee or other fiduciary, and may act as such within this State, when and to the extent that the laws of the District of Columbia or of the state in which the foreign corporation is organized confer like powers upon corporations organized and doing business under the laws of this State.

§ 381.   Withdrawal of foreign corporation from State; procedure; service of process on Secretary of State.

(a)   Any foreign corporation which shall have qualified to do business in this State under § 371 of this title, may surrender its authority to do business in this State and may withdraw therefrom by filing with the Secretary of State:

(1) A certificate executed in accordance with § 103 of this title, stating that it surrenders its authority to transact business in the state and withdraws therefrom; and stating the address to which the Secretary of State may mail any process against the corporation that may be served upon the Secretary of State, or

(2) A copy of an order or decree of dissolution made by any court of competent jurisdiction or other competent authority of the State or other jurisdiction of its incorporation, certified to be a true copy under the hand of the clerk of the court or other official body, and the official seal of the court or official body or clerk thereof, together with a certificate executed in accordance with paragraph (a)(1) of this section, stating the address to which the Secretary of State may mail any process against the corporation that may be served upon the Secretary of State.

(b) The Secretary of State shall, upon payment to the Secretary of State of the fees prescribed in § 391 of this title, issue a sufficient number of certificates, under the Secretary of State's hand and official seal, evidencing the surrender of the authority of the corporation to do business in this State and its withdrawal therefrom. One of the certificates shall be furnished to the corporation withdrawing and surrendering its right to do business in this State.

(c) Upon the issuance of the certificates by the Secretary of State, the appointment of the registered agent of the corporation in this State, upon whom process against the corporation may be served, shall be revoked, and the corporation shall be deemed to have consented that service of process in any action, suit or proceeding based upon any cause of action arising in this State, during the time the corporation was authorized to transact business in this State, may thereafter be made by service upon the Secretary of State. Process may be served upon the Secretary of State under this subsection by means of electronic transmission but only as prescribed by the Secretary of State. The Secretary of State is authorized to issue such rules and regulations with respect to such service as the Secretary of State deems necessary or appropriate.

(d) In the event of service upon the Secretary of State in accordance with subsection (c) of this section, the Secretary of State shall forthwith notify the corporation by letter, directed to the corporation at the address stated in the certificate which was filed by the corporation with the Secretary of State pursuant to subsection (a) of this section. Such letter shall be sent by a mail or courier service that includes a record of mailing or deposit with the courier and a record of delivery evidenced by the signature of the recipient. Such letter shall enclose a copy of the process and any other papers served upon the Secretary of State. It shall be the duty of the plaintiff in the event of such service to serve process and any other papers in duplicate, to notify the Secretary of State that service is being made pursuant to this subsection, and to pay the Secretary of State the sum of $50 for the use of the State, which sum shall be taxed as part of the cost of the action, suit or proceeding if the plaintiff shall prevail therein. The Secretary of State shall maintain an alphabetical record of such service setting forth the name of the plaintiff and defendant, the title, docket number and nature of the proceeding in which the process has been served upon the Secretary of State, the fact that service has been effected pursuant to this subsection, the return date thereof, and the day and hour when the service was made. The Secretary of State shall not be required to retain such information for a period longer than 5 years from receipt of the service of process.

§ 382. Service of process on nonqualifying foreign corporations.

(a) Any foreign corporation which shall transact business in this State without having qualified to do business under § 371 of this title shall be deemed to have thereby appointed and constituted the Secretary of State of this State its agent for the acceptance of legal process in any civil action, suit or proceeding against it in any state or federal court in this State arising or growing out of any business transacted by it within this State. If any foreign corporation consents in writing to be subject to the jurisdiction of any state or federal court in this State for any civil action, suit or proceeding against it arising or growing out of any business or matter, and if the agreement or instrument setting forth such consent does not otherwise provide a manner of service of legal process in any such civil action, suit or proceeding against it, such foreign corporation shall be deemed to have thereby appointed and constituted the Secretary of State of this State its agent for the acceptance of legal process in any such civil action, suit or proceeding against it. The transaction of business in this State by such corporation and/or such consent by such corporation to the jurisdiction of any state or federal court in this State without provision for a manner of service of legal process shall be a signification of the agreement of such corporation that any process served upon the Secretary of State when so served shall be of the same legal force and validity as if served upon an authorized officer or agent personally within this State. Process may be served upon the Secretary of State under this subsection by means of electronic transmission but only as prescribed by the Secretary of State. The Secretary of State is authorized to issue such rules and regulations with respect to such service as the Secretary of State deems necessary or appropriate.

(b)   Section 373 of this title shall not apply in determining whether any foreign corporation is transacting business in this State within the meaning of this section; and "the transaction of business" or "business transacted in this State," by any such foreign corporation, whenever those words are used in this section, shall mean the course or practice of carrying on any business activities in this State, including, without limiting the generality of the foregoing, the solicitation of business or orders in this State. This section shall not apply to any insurance company doing business in this State.

(c)   In the event of service upon the Secretary of State in accordance with subsection (a) of this section, the Secretary of State shall forthwith notify the corporation thereof by letter, directed to the corporation at the address furnished to the Secretary of State by the plaintiff in such action, suit or proceeding. Such letter shall be sent by a mail or courier service that includes a record of mailing or deposit with the courier and a record of delivery evidenced by the signature of the recipient. Such letter shall enclose a copy of the process and any other papers served upon the Secretary of State. It shall be the duty of the plaintiff in the event of such service to serve process and any other papers in duplicate, to notify the Secretary of State that service is being made pursuant to this subsection, and to pay the Secretary of State the sum of $50 for the use of the State, which sum shall be taxed as a part of the costs in the proceeding if the plaintiff shall prevail therein. The Secretary of State shall maintain an alphabetical record of any such process setting forth the name of the plaintiff and defendant, the title, docket number and nature of the proceeding in which process has been served upon the Secretary of State, the fact that service has been effected pursuant to this subsection, the return date thereof, and the day and hour when the service was made. The Secretary of State shall not be required to retain such information for a period longer than 5 years from receipt of the service of process.

§ 383.   Actions by and against unqualified foreign corporations.

(a)   A foreign corporation which is required to comply with §§ 371 and 372 of this title and which has done business in this State without authority shall not maintain any action or special proceeding in this State unless and until such corporation has been authorized to do business in this State and has paid to the State all fees, penalties and franchise taxes for the years or parts thereof during which it did business in this State without authority. This prohibition shall not apply to any successor in interest of such foreign corporation.

(b)   The failure of a foreign corporation to obtain authority to do business in this State shall not impair the validity of any contract or act of the foreign corporation or the right of any other party to the contract to maintain any action or special proceeding thereon, and shall not prevent the foreign corporation from defending any action or special proceeding in this State.

§ 384.   Foreign corporations doing business without having qualified; injunctions.

The Court of Chancery shall have jurisdiction to enjoin any foreign corporation, or any agent thereof, from transacting any business in this State if such corporation has failed to comply with any section of this subchapter applicable to it or if such corporation has secured a certificate of the Secretary of State under § 371 of this title on the basis of false or misleading representations. The

Attorney General shall, upon the Attorney General's own motion or upon the relation of proper parties, proceed for this purpose by complaint in any county in which such corporation is doing business.

§ 385.   Filing of certain instruments with recorder of deeds not required.

No instrument that is required to be filed with the Secretary of State of this State by this subchapter need be filed with the recorder of deeds of any county of this State in order to comply with this subchapter.

SUBCHAPTER XVII.   DOMESTICATION AND TRANSFER

§ 388.   Domestication of non-United States entities.

(a)   As used in this section, the term:

(1)   "Foreign jurisdiction" means any foreign country or other foreign jurisdiction (other than the United States, any state, the District of Columbia, or any possession or territory of the United States); and

(2)   "Non-United States entity" means a corporation, a limited liability company, a statutory trust, a business trust or association, a real estate investment trust, a common-law trust, or any other unincorporated business or entity, including a partnership (whether general (including a limited liability partnership) or limited (including a limited liability limited partnership)), formed, incorporated, created or that otherwise came into being under the laws of any foreign jurisdiction.

(b)   Any non-United States entity may become domesticated as a corporation in this State by complying with subsection (h) of this section and filing with the Secretary of State:

(1)   A certificate of corporate domestication which shall be executed in accordance with subsection (g) of this section and filed in accordance with § 103 of this title; and

(2)   A certificate of incorporation, which shall be executed, acknowledged and filed in accordance with § 103 of this title.

Each of the certificates required by this subsection (b) shall be filed simultaneously with the Secretary of State and, if such certificates are not to become effective upon their filing as permitted by § 103(d) of this title, then each such certificate shall provide for the same effective date or time in accordance with § 103(d) of this title.

(c)   The certificate of corporate domestication shall certify:

(1)   The date on which and jurisdiction where the non-United States entity was first formed, incorporated, created or otherwise came into being;

(2)   The name of the non-United States entity immediately prior to the filing of the certificate of corporate domestication;

(3)   The name of the corporation as set forth in its certificate of incorporation filed in accordance with subsection (b) of this section; and

(4)   The jurisdiction that constituted the seat, siege social, or principal place of business or central administration of the non-United States entity or any other equivalent thereto under applicable law, immediately prior to the filing of the certificate of corporate domestication; and

(5)   That the domestication has been approved in the manner provided for by the document, instrument, agreement or other writing, as the case may be, governing the internal affairs of the non-United States entity and the conduct of its business or by applicable non-Delaware law, as appropriate.

(d)   Upon the certificate of corporate domestication and the certificate of incorporation becoming effective in accordance with § 103 of this title, the non-United States entity shall be domesticated as a corporation in this State and the corporation shall thereafter be subject to all of the provisions of this title, except that notwithstanding § 106 of this title, the existence of the corporation shall be deemed to have commenced on the date the non-United States entity commenced its existence in the jurisdiction in which the non-United States entity was first formed, incorporated, created or otherwise came into being.

(e) The domestication of any non-United States entity as a corporation in this State shall not be deemed to affect any obligations or liabilities of the non-United States entity incurred prior to its domestication as a corporation in this State, or the personal liability of any person therefor.

(f) The filing of a certificate of corporate domestication shall not affect the choice of law applicable to the non-United States entity, except that, from the effective time of the domestication, the law of the State of Delaware, including this title, shall apply to the non-United States entity to the same extent as if the non-United States entity had been incorporated as a corporation of this State on that date.

(g) The certificate of corporate domestication shall be signed by any person who is authorized to sign the certificate of corporate domestication on behalf of the non-United States entity.

(h) Prior to the filing of a certificate of corporate domestication with the Secretary of State, the domestication shall be approved in the manner provided for by the document, instrument, agreement or other writing, as the case may be, governing the internal affairs of the non-United States entity and the conduct of its business or by applicable non-Delaware law, as appropriate, and the certificate of incorporation shall be approved by the same authorization required to approve the domestication.

(i) When a non-United States entity has become domesticated as a corporation pursuant to this section, for all purposes of the laws of the State of Delaware, the corporation shall be deemed to be the same entity as the domesticating non-United States entity and the domestication shall constitute a continuation of the existence of the domesticating non-United States entity in the form of a corporation of this State. When any domestication shall have become effective under this section, for all purposes of the laws of the State of Delaware, all of the rights, privileges and powers of the non-United States entity that has been domesticated, and all property, real, personal and mixed, and all debts due to such non-United States entity, as well as all other things and causes of action belonging to such non-United States entity, shall remain vested in the corporation to which such non-United States entity has been domesticated (and also in the non-United States entity, if and for so long as the non-United States entity continues its existence in the foreign jurisdiction in which it was existing immediately prior to the domestication) and shall be the property of such corporation (and also of the non-United States entity, if and for so long as the non-United States entity continues its existence in the foreign jurisdiction in which it was existing immediately prior to the domestication), and the title to any real property vested by deed or otherwise in such non-United States entity shall not revert or be in any way impaired by reason of this title; but all rights of creditors and all liens upon any property of such non-United States entity shall be preserved unimpaired, and all debts, liabilities and duties of the non-United States entity that has been domesticated shall remain attached to the corporation to which such non-United States entity has been domesticated (and also to the non-United States entity, if and for so long as the non-United States entity continues its existence in the foreign jurisdiction in which it was existing immediately prior to the domestication), and may be enforced against it to the same extent as if said debts, liabilities and duties had originally been incurred or contracted by it in its capacity as such corporation. The rights, privileges, powers and interests in property of the non-United States entity, as well as the debts, liabilities and duties of the non-United States entity, shall not be deemed, as a consequence of the domestication, to have been transferred to the corporation to which such non-United States entity has domesticated for any purpose of the laws of the State of Delaware.

(j) Unless otherwise agreed or otherwise required under applicable non-Delaware law, the domesticating non-United States entity shall not be required to wind up its affairs or pay its liabilities and distribute its assets, and the domestication shall not be deemed to constitute a dissolution of such non-United States entity. If, following domestication, a non-United States entity that has become domesticated as a corporation of this State continues its existence in the foreign jurisdiction in which it was existing immediately prior to domestication, the corporation and such non-United States entity shall, for all purposes of the laws of the State of Delaware, constitute a single entity formed, incorporated, created or otherwise having come into being, as applicable, and existing under the laws of the State of Delaware and the laws of such foreign jurisdiction.

(k) In connection with a domestication under this section, shares of stock, rights or securities of, or interests in, the non-United States entity that is to be domesticated as a corporation of this State may be exchanged for or converted into cash, property, or shares of stock, rights or securities of such corporation or, in addition to or in lieu thereof, may be exchanged for or converted into cash, property, or shares of stock, rights or securities of, or interests in, another corporation or other entity or may be cancelled.

§ 389. Temporary transfer of domicile into this State.

(a) As used in this section:

(1) The term "emergency condition" shall be deemed to include but not be limited to any of the following:

    a. War or other armed conflict;

    b. Revolution or insurrection;

    c. Invasion or occupation by foreign military forces;

    d. Rioting or civil commotion of an extended nature;

    e. Domination by a foreign power;

    f. Expropriation, nationalization or confiscation of a material part of the assets or property of the non-United States entity;

    g. Impairment of the institution of private property (including private property held abroad);

    h. The taking of any action under the laws of the United States whereby persons resident in the jurisdiction, the law of which governs the internal affairs of the non-United States entity, might be treated as "enemies" or otherwise restricted under laws of the United States relating to trading with enemies of the United States;

    i. The immediate threat of any of the foregoing; and

    j. Such other event which, under the law of the jurisdiction governing the internal affairs of the non-United States entity, permits the non-United States entity to transfer its domicile.

(2) The term "foreign jurisdiction" and the term "non-United States entity" shall have the same meanings as set forth in § 388(a) of this title.

(3) The terms "officers" and "directors" include, in addition to such persons, trustees, managers, partners and all other persons performing functions equivalent to those of officers and directors, however named or described in any relevant instrument.

(b) Any non-United States entity may, subject to and upon compliance with this section, transfer its domicile (which term, as used in this section, shall be deemed to refer in addition to the seat, siege social or principal place of business or central administration of such entity, or any other equivalent thereto under applicable law) into this State, and may perform the acts described in this section, so long as the law by which the internal affairs of such entity are governed does not expressly prohibit such transfer.

(c) Any non-United States entity that shall propose to transfer its domicile into this State shall submit to the Secretary of State for the Secretary of State's review, at least 30 days prior to the proposed transfer of domicile, the following:

(1)   A copy of its certificate of incorporation and bylaws (or the equivalent thereof under applicable law), certified as true and correct by the appropriate director, officer or government official;

(2)   A certificate issued by an authorized official of the jurisdiction the law of which governs the internal affairs of the non-United States entity evidencing its existence;

(3)   A list indicating the person or persons who, in the event of a transfer pursuant to this section, shall be the authorized officers and directors of the non-United States entity, together with evidence of their authority to act and their respective executed agreements in writing regarding service of process as set out in subsection (j) of this section;

(4)   A certificate executed by the appropriate officer or director of the non-United States entity, setting forth:

    a.   The name and address of its registered agent in this State;

    b.   A general description of the business in which it is engaged;

    c.   That the filing of such certificate has been duly authorized by any necessary action and does not violate the certificate of incorporation or bylaws (or equivalent thereof under applicable law) or any material agreement or instrument binding on such entity;

    d.   A list indicating the person or persons authorized to sign the written communications required by subsection (e) of this section;

    e.   An affirmance that such transfer is not expressly prohibited under the law by which the internal affairs of the non-United States entity are governed; and

    f.   An undertaking that any transfer of domicile into this State will take place only in the event of an emergency condition in the jurisdiction the law of which governs the internal affairs of the non-United States entity and that such transfer shall continue only so long as such emergency condition, in the judgment of the non-United States entity's management, so requires; and

(5)   The examination fee prescribed under § 391 of this title.

If any of the documents referred to in paragraphs (c)(1)–(5) of this section are not in English, a translation thereof, under oath of the translator, shall be attached thereto. If such documents satisfy the requirements of this section, and if the name of the non-United States entity meets the requirements of § 102(a)(1) of this title, the Secretary of State shall notify the non-United States entity that such documents have been accepted for filing, and the records of the Secretary of State shall reflect such acceptance and such notification. In addition, the Secretary of State shall enter the name of the non-United States entity on the Secretary of State's reserved list to remain there so long as the non-United States entity is in compliance with this section. No document submitted under this subsection shall be available for public inspection pursuant to Chapter 100 of Title 29 until, and unless, such entity effects a transfer of its domicile as provided in this section. The Secretary of State may waive the 30-day period and translation requirement provided for in this subsection upon request by such entity, supported by facts (including, without limitation, the existence of an emergency condition) justifying such waiver.

(d)   On or before March 1 in each year, prior to the transfer of its domicile as provided for in subsection (e) of this section, during any such transfer and, in the event that it desires to continue to be subject to a transfer of domicile under this section, after its domicile has ceased to be in this State, the non-United States entity shall file a certificate executed by an appropriate officer or director of the non-United States entity, certifying that the documents submitted pursuant to this section remain in full force and effect or attaching any amendments or supplements thereto and translated as required in subsection (c) of this section, together with the filing fee prescribed under § 391 of this title. In the event that any non-United States entity fails to file the required certificate on or before March 1 in each year, all certificates and filings made pursuant to this section shall become null and void on

March 2 in such year, and any proposed transfer thereafter shall be subject to all of the required submissions and the examination fee set forth in subsection (c) of this section.

(e)   If the Secretary of State accepts the documents submitted pursuant to subsection (c) of this section for filing, such entity may transfer its domicile to this State at any time by means of a written communication to such effect addressed to the Secretary of State, signed by 1 of the persons named on the list filed pursuant to paragraph (c)(4)d. of this section, and confirming that the statements made pursuant to paragraph (c)(4) of this section remain true and correct; provided, that if emergency conditions have affected ordinary means of communication, such notification may be made by telegram, telex, telecopy or other form of writing so long as a duly signed duplicate is received by the Secretary of State within 30 days thereafter. The records of the Secretary of State shall reflect the fact of such transfer. Upon the payment to the Secretary of State of the fee prescribed under § 391 of this title, the Secretary of State shall certify that the non-United States entity has filed all documents and paid all fees required by this title. Such certificate of the Secretary of State shall be prima facie evidence of transfer by such non-United States entity of its domicile into this State.

(f)   Except to the extent expressly prohibited by the laws of this State, from and after the time that a non-United States entity transfers its domicile to this State pursuant to this section, the non-United States entity shall have all of the powers which it had immediately prior to such transfer under the law of the jurisdiction governing its internal affairs and the directors and officers designated pursuant to paragraph (c)(3) of this section, and their successors, may manage the business and affairs of the non-United States entity in accordance with the laws of such jurisdiction. Any such activity conducted pursuant to this section shall not be deemed to be doing business within this State for purposes of § 371 of this title. Any reference in this section to the law of the jurisdiction governing the internal affairs of a non-United States entity which has transferred its domicile into this State shall be deemed to be a reference to such law as in effect immediately prior to the transfer of domicile.

(g)   For purposes of any action in the courts of this State, no non-United States entity which has obtained the certificate of the Secretary of State referred to in subsection (e) of this section shall be deemed to be an "enemy" person or entity for any purpose, including, without limitation, in relation to any claim of title to its assets, wherever located, or to its ability to institute suit in said courts.

(h)   The transfer by any non-United States entity of its domicile into this State shall not be deemed to affect any obligations or liabilities of such non-United States entity incurred prior to such transfer.

(i)   The directors of any non-United States entity which has transferred its domicile into this State may withhold from any holder of equity interests in such entity any amounts payable to such holder on account of dividends or other distributions, if the directors shall determine that such holder will not have the full benefit of such payment, so long as the directors shall make provision for the retention of such withheld payment in escrow or under some similar arrangement for the benefit of such holder.

(j)   All process issued out of any court of this State, all orders made by any court of this State and all rules and notices of any kind required to be served on any non-United States entity which has transferred its domicile into this State may be served on the non-United States entity pursuant to § 321 of this title in the same manner as if such entity were a corporation of this State. The directors of a non-United States entity which has transferred its domicile into this State shall agree in writing that they will be amenable to service of process by the same means as, and subject to the jurisdiction of the courts of this State to the same extent as are directors of corporations of this State, and such agreements shall be submitted to the Secretary of State for filing before the respective directors take office.

(k)   Any non-United States entity which has transferred its domicile into this State may voluntarily return to the jurisdiction the law of which governs its internal affairs by filing with the Secretary of State an application to withdraw from this State. Such application shall be accompanied by a resolution of the directors of the non-United States entity authorizing such withdrawal and by a certificate of the highest diplomatic or consular official of such jurisdiction accredited to the United States indicating the consent of such jurisdiction to such withdrawal. The application shall also contain, or be accompanied by, the agreement of the non-United States entity that it may be served with process in this State in any proceeding for enforcement of any obligation of the non-United States entity arising prior to its withdrawal from this State, which agreement shall include the appointment of the Secretary of State as the agent of the non-United States entity to accept service of process in any such proceeding and shall specify the address to which a copy of process served upon the Secretary of State shall be mailed. Upon the payment of any fees and taxes owed to this State, the Secretary of State shall file the application and the non-United States entity's domicile shall, as of the time of filing, cease to be in this State.

§ 390. Transfer, domestication or continuance of domestic corporations.

(a) Upon compliance with the provisions of this section, any corporation existing under the laws of this State may transfer to or domesticate or continue in any foreign jurisdiction and, in connection therewith, may elect to continue its existence as a corporation of this State. As used in this section, the term:

(1) "Foreign jurisdiction" means any foreign country, or other foreign jurisdiction (other than the United States, any state, the District of Columbia, or any possession or territory of the United States); and

(2) "Resulting entity" means the entity formed, incorporated, created or otherwise coming into being as a consequence of the transfer of the corporation to, or its domestication or continuance in, a foreign jurisdiction pursuant to this section.

(b) The board of directors of the corporation which desires to transfer to or domesticate or continue in a foreign jurisdiction shall adopt a resolution approving such transfer, domestication or continuance specifying the foreign jurisdiction to which the corporation shall be transferred or in which the corporation shall be domesticated or continued and, if applicable, that in connection with such transfer, domestication or continuance the corporation's existence as a corporation of this State is to continue and recommending the approval of such transfer or domestication or continuance by the stockholders of the corporation. Such resolution shall be submitted to the stockholders of the corporation at an annual or special meeting. Due notice of the time, place and purpose of the meeting shall be given to each holder of stock, whether voting or nonvoting, of the corporation at the address of the stockholder as it appears on the records of the corporation, at least 20 days prior to the date of the meeting. At the meeting, the resolution shall be considered and a vote taken for its adoption or rejection. If all outstanding shares of stock of the corporation, whether voting or nonvoting, shall be voted for the adoption of the resolution, the corporation shall file with the Secretary of State a certificate of transfer if its existence as a corporation of this State is to cease or a certificate of transfer and domestic continuance if its existence as a corporation of this State is to continue, executed in accordance with § 103 of this title, which certifies:

(1) The name of the corporation, and if it has been changed, the name under which it was originally incorporated.

(2) The date of filing of its original certificate of incorporation with the Secretary of State.

(3) The foreign jurisdiction to which the corporation shall be transferred or in which it shall be domesticated or continued and the name of the resulting entity.

(4) That the transfer, domestication or continuance of the corporation has been approved in accordance with the provisions of this section.

(5) In the case of a certificate of transfer, (i) that the existence of the corporation as a corporation of this State shall cease when the certificate of transfer becomes effective, and (ii) the agreement of the corporation that it may be served with process in this State in any proceeding for enforcement of any obligation of the corporation arising while it was a corporation of this State

which shall also irrevocably appoint the Secretary of State as its agent to accept service of process in any such proceeding and specify the address (which may not be that of the corporation's registered agent without the written consent of the corporation's registered agent, such consent to be filed along with the certificate of transfer) to which a copy of such process shall be mailed by the Secretary of State. Process may be served upon the Secretary of State under this subsection by means of electronic transmission but only as prescribed by the Secretary of State. The Secretary of State is authorized to issue such rules and regulations with respect to such service as the Secretary of State deems necessary or appropriate. In the event of service upon the Secretary of State in accordance with this subsection, the Secretary of State shall forthwith notify such corporation that has transferred out of the State of Delaware by letter, directed to such corporation that has transferred out of the State of Delaware at the address so specified, unless such corporation shall have designated in writing to the Secretary of State a different address for such purpose, in which case it shall be mailed to the last address designated. Such letter shall be sent by a mail or courier service that includes a record of mailing or deposit with the courier and a record of delivery evidenced by the signature of the recipient. Such letter shall enclose a copy of the process and any other papers served on the Secretary of State pursuant to this subsection. It shall be the duty of the plaintiff in the event of such service to serve process and any other papers in duplicate, to notify the Secretary of State that service is being effected pursuant to this subsection and to pay the Secretary of State the sum of $50 for the use of the State, which sum shall be taxed as part of the costs in the proceeding, if the plaintiff shall prevail therein. The Secretary of State shall maintain an alphabetical record of any such service setting forth the name of the plaintiff and the defendant, the title, docket number and nature of the proceeding in which process has been served, the fact that service has been effected pursuant to this subsection, the return date thereof, and the day and hour service was made. The Secretary of State shall not be required to retain such information longer than 5 years from receipt of the service of process.

(6)   In the case of a certificate of transfer and domestic continuance, that the corporation will continue to exist as a corporation of this State after the certificate of transfer and domestic continuance becomes effective.

(c)   Upon the filing of a certificate of transfer in accordance with subsection (b) of this section and payment to the Secretary of State of all fees prescribed under this title, the Secretary of State shall certify that the corporation has filed all documents and paid all fees required by this title, and thereupon the corporation shall cease to exist as a corporation of this State at the time the certificate of transfer becomes effective in accordance with § 103 of this title. Such certificate of the Secretary of State shall be prima facie evidence of the transfer, domestication or continuance by such corporation out of this State.

(d)   The transfer, domestication or continuance of a corporation out of this State in accordance with this section and the resulting cessation of its existence as a corporation of this State pursuant to a certificate of transfer shall not be deemed to affect any obligations or liabilities of the corporation incurred prior to such transfer, domestication or continuance, the personal liability of any person incurred prior to such transfer, domestication or continuance, or the choice of law applicable to the corporation with respect to matters arising prior to such transfer, domestication or continuance. Unless otherwise agreed or otherwise provided in the certificate of incorporation, the transfer, domestication or continuance of a corporation out of the State of Delaware in accordance with this section shall not require such corporation to wind up its affairs or pay its liabilities and distribute its assets under this title and shall not be deemed to constitute a dissolution of such corporation.

(e)   If a corporation files a certificate of transfer and domestic continuance, after the time the certificate of transfer and domestic continuance becomes effective, the corporation shall continue to exist as a corporation of this State, and the law of the State of Delaware, including this title, shall apply to the corporation to the same extent as prior to such time. So long as a corporation continues to exist as a corporation of the State of Delaware following the filing of a certificate of transfer and domestic continuance, the continuing corporation and the resulting entity shall, for all purposes of the laws of the State of Delaware, constitute a single entity formed, incorporated, created or otherwise having come into being, as applicable, and existing under the laws of the State of Delaware and the laws of the foreign jurisdiction.

(f) When a corporation has transferred, domesticated or continued pursuant to this section, for all purposes of the laws of the State of Delaware, the resulting entity shall be deemed to be the same entity as the transferring, domesticating or continuing corporation and shall constitute a continuation of the existence of such corporation in the form of the resulting entity. When any transfer, domestication or continuance shall have become effective under this section, for all purposes of the laws of the State of Delaware, all of the rights, privileges and powers of the corporation that has transferred, domesticated or continued, and all property, real, personal and mixed, and all debts due to such corporation, as well as all other things and causes of action belonging to such corporation, shall remain vested in the resulting entity (and also in the corporation that has transferred, domesticated or continued, if and for so long as such corporation continues its existence as a corporation of this State) and shall be the property of such resulting entity (and also of the corporation that has transferred, domesticated or continued, if and for so long as such corporation continues its existence as a corporation of this State), and the title to any real property vested by deed or otherwise in such corporation shall not revert or be in any way impaired by reason of this title; but all rights of creditors and all liens upon any property of such corporation shall be preserved unimpaired, and all debts, liabilities and duties of such corporation shall remain attached to the resulting entity (and also to the corporation that has transferred, domesticated or continued, if and for so long as such corporation continues its existence as a corporation of this State), and may be enforced against it to the same extent as if said debts, liabilities and duties had originally been incurred or contracted by it in its capacity as such resulting entity. The rights, privileges, powers and interests in property of the corporation, as well as the debts, liabilities and duties of the corporation, shall not be deemed, as a consequence of the transfer, domestication or continuance, to have been transferred to the resulting entity for any purpose of the laws of the State of Delaware.

(g) In connection with a transfer, domestication or continuance under this section, shares of stock of the transferring, domesticating or continuing corporation may be exchanged for or converted into cash, property, or shares of stock, rights or securities of, or interests in, the resulting entity or, in addition to or in lieu thereof, may be exchanged for or converted into cash, property, or shares of stock, rights or securities of, or interests in, another corporation or other entity or may be cancelled.

(h) No vote of the stockholders of a corporation shall be necessary to authorize a transfer, domestication or continuance if no shares of the stock of such corporation shall have been issued prior to the adoption by the board of directors of the resolution approving the transfer, domestication or continuance.

(i) Whenever it shall be desired to transfer to or domesticate or continue in any foreign jurisdiction any nonstock corporation, the governing body shall perform all the acts necessary to effect a transfer, domestication or continuance which are required by this section to be performed by the board of directors of a corporation having capital stock. If the members of a nonstock corporation are entitled to vote for the election of members of its governing body or are entitled under the certificate of incorporation or the bylaws of such corporation to vote on such transfer, domestication or continuance or on a merger, consolidation, or dissolution of the corporation, they, and any other holder of any membership interest in the corporation, shall perform all the acts necessary to effect a transfer, domestication or continuance which are required by this section to be performed by the stockholders of a corporation having capital stock. If there is no member entitled to vote thereon, nor any other holder of any membership interest in the corporation, the transfer, domestication or continuance of the corporation shall be authorized at a meeting of the governing body, upon the adoption of a resolution to transfer or domesticate or continue by the vote of a majority of members of its governing body then in office. In all other respects, the method and proceedings for the transfer, domestication or continuance of a nonstock corporation shall conform as nearly as may be to the proceedings prescribed by this section for the transfer, domestication or continuance of corporations having capital stock. In the case of a charitable nonstock corporation, due notice of the corporation's intent to effect a transfer, domestication or continuance shall be mailed to the Attorney General of the State of Delaware 10 days prior to the date of the proposed transfer, domestication or continuance.

SUBCHAPTER XVIII.   MISCELLANEOUS PROVISIONS

§ 391.   Amounts payable to Secretary of State upon filing certificate or other paper.

(a)   The following fees and penalties shall be collected by and paid to the Secretary of State, for the use of the State:

(1)   Upon the receipt for filing of an original certificate of incorporation, the fee shall be computed on the basis of $0.02 for each share of authorized capital stock having par value up to and including 20,000 shares, $0.01 for each share in excess of 20,000 shares up to and including 200,000 shares, and ²/₅ of a $0.01 for each share in excess of 200,000 shares; $0.01 for each share of authorized capital stock without par value up to and including 20,000 shares, ¹/₂ of $0.01 for each share in excess of 20,000 shares up to and including 2,000,000 shares, and ²/₅ of $0.01 for each share in excess of 2,000,000 shares. In no case shall the amount paid be less than $15. For the purpose of computing the fee on par value stock each $100 unit of the authorized capital stock shall be counted as 1 assessable share.

(2)   Upon the receipt for filing of a certificate of amendment of certificate of incorporation, or a certificate of amendment of certificate of incorporation before payment of capital, or a restated certificate of incorporation, increasing the authorized capital stock of a corporation, the fee shall be an amount equal to the difference between the fee computed at the foregoing rates upon the total authorized capital stock of the corporation including the proposed increase, and the fee computed at the foregoing rates upon the total authorized capital stock excluding the proposed increase. In no case shall the amount paid be less than $30.

(3)   Upon the receipt for filing of a certificate of amendment of certificate of incorporation before payment of capital and not involving an increase of authorized capital stock, or an amendment to the certificate of incorporation not involving an increase of authorized capital stock, or a restated certificate of incorporation not involving an increase of authorized capital stock, or a certificate of retirement of stock, the fee to be paid shall be $30. For all other certificates relating to corporations, not otherwise provided for, the fee to be paid shall be $5.00. In the case of exempt corporations no fee shall be paid under this paragraph.

(4)   Upon the receipt for filing of a certificate of merger or consolidation of 2 or more corporations, the fee shall be an amount equal to the difference between the fee computed at the foregoing rates upon the total authorized capital stock of the corporation created by the merger or consolidation, and the fee so computed upon the aggregate amount of the total authorized capital stock of the constituent corporations. In no case shall the amount paid be less than $75. The foregoing fee shall be in addition to any tax or fee required under any other law of this State to be paid by any constituent entity that is not a corporation in connection with the filing of the certificate of merger or consolidation.

(5)   Upon the receipt for filing of a certificate of dissolution, there shall be paid to and collected by the Secretary of State a fee of:

a.   Forty dollars; or

b.   Ten dollars in the case of a certificate of dissolution which certifies that:

1.   The corporation has no assets and has ceased transacting business; and

2.   The corporation, for each year since its incorporation in this State, has been required to pay only the minimum franchise tax then prescribed by § 503 of this title; and

3. The corporation has paid all franchise taxes and fees due to or assessable by this State through the end of the year in which said certificate of dissolution is filed.

(6) Upon the receipt for filing of a certificate of reinstatement of a foreign corporation or a certificate of surrender and withdrawal from the State by a foreign corporation, there shall be collected by and paid to the Secretary of State a fee of $10.

(7) For receiving and filing and/or indexing any certificate, affidavit, agreement or any other paper provided for by this chapter, for which no different fee is specifically prescribed, a fee of $115 in each case shall be paid to the Secretary of State. The fee in the case of a certificate of incorporation filed as required by § 102 of this title shall be $25. For entering information from each instrument into the Delaware Corporation Information System in accordance with § 103(c)(8) of this title, the fee shall be $5.00.

a. A certificate of dissolution which meets the criteria stated in paragraph (a)(5)b. of this section shall not be subject to such fee; and

b. A certificate of incorporation filed in accordance with § 102 of this title shall be subject to a fee of $25.

(8) For receiving and filing and/or indexing the annual report of a foreign corporation doing business in this State, a fee of $125 shall be paid. In the event of neglect, refusal or failure on the part of any foreign corporation to file the annual report with the Secretary of State on or before June 30 each year, the corporation shall pay a penalty of $125.

(9) For recording and indexing articles of association and other papers required by this chapter to be recorded by the Secretary of State, a fee computed on the basis of $0.01 a line shall be paid.

(10) For certifying copies of any paper on file provided by this chapter, a fee of $50 shall be paid for each copy certified. In addition, a fee of $2.00 per page shall be paid in each instance where the Secretary of State provides the copies of the document to be certified.

(11) For issuing any certificate of the Secretary of State other than a certification of a copy under paragraph (a)(10) of this section, or a certificate that recites all of a corporation's filings with the Secretary of State, a fee of $50 shall be paid for each certificate. For issuing any certificate of the Secretary of State that recites all of a corporation's filings with the Secretary of State, a fee of $175 shall be paid for each certificate. For issuing any certificate via the Division's online services, a fee of up to $175 shall be paid for each certificate.

(12) For filing in the office of the Secretary of State any certificate of change of location or change of registered agent, as provided in § 133 of this title, there shall be collected by and paid to the Secretary of State a fee of $50, provided that no fee shall be charged pursuant to § 103(c)(6) and (c)(7) of this title.

(13) For filing in the office of the Secretary of State any certificate of change of address or change of name of registered agent, as provided in § 134 of this title, there shall be collected by and paid to the Secretary of State a fee of $50, plus the same fees for receiving, filing, indexing, copying and certifying the same as are charged in the case of filing a certificate of incorporation.

(14) For filing in the office of the Secretary of State any certificate of resignation of a registered agent and appointment of a successor, as provided in § 135 of this title, there shall be collected by and paid to the Secretary of State a fee of $50.

(15) For filing in the office of the Secretary of State, any certificate of resignation of a registered agent without appointment of a successor, as provided in §§ 136 and 377 of this title, there shall be collected by and paid to the Secretary of State a fee of $2.00 for each corporation whose registered agent has resigned by such certificate.

(16) For preparing and providing a written report of a record search, a fee of [up to $100] shall be paid.

(17) For preclearance of any document for filing, a fee of $250 shall be paid.

(18) For receiving and filing and/or indexing an annual franchise tax report of a corporation provided for by § 502 of this title, a fee of $25 shall be paid by exempt corporations and a fee of $50 shall be paid by all other corporations.

(19) For receiving and filing and/or indexing by the Secretary of State of a certificate of domestication and certificate of incorporation prescribed in § 388(d) of this title, a fee of $165, plus the fee payable upon the receipt for filing of an original certificate of incorporation, shall be paid.

(20) For receiving, reviewing and filing and/or indexing by the Secretary of State of the documents prescribed in § 389(c) of this title, a fee of $10,000 shall be paid.

(21) For receiving, reviewing and filing and/or indexing by the Secretary of State of the documents prescribed in § 389(d) of this title, an annual fee of $2,500 shall be paid.

(22) Except as provided in this section, the fees of the Secretary of State shall be as provided for in § 2315 of Title 29.

(23) In the case of exempt corporations, the total fees payable to the Secretary of State upon the filing of a Certificate of Change of Registered Agent and/or Registered Office or a Certificate of Revival shall be $5.00 and such filings shall be exempt from any fees or assessments pursuant to the requirements of § 103(c)(6) and (c)(7) of this title.

(24) For accepting a corporate name reservation application, an application for renewal of a corporate name reservation, or a notice of transfer or cancellation of a corporate name reservation, there shall be collected by and paid to the Secretary of State a fee of up to $75.

(25) For receiving and filing and/or indexing by the Secretary of State of a certificate of transfer or a certificate of continuance prescribed in § 390 of this title, a fee of $1,000 shall be paid.

(26) For receiving and filing and/or indexing by the Secretary of State of a certificate of conversion and certificate of incorporation prescribed in § 265 of this title, a fee of $115, plus the fee payable upon the receipt for filing of an original certificate of incorporation, shall be paid.

(27) For receiving and filing and/or indexing by the Secretary of State of a certificate of conversion prescribed in § 266 of this title, a fee of $165 shall be paid.

(28) For receiving and filing and/or indexing by the Secretary of State of a certificate of validation prescribed in § 204 of this title, a fee of $2,500 shall be paid; provided, that if the certificate of validation has the effect of increasing the authorized capital stock of a corporation, an additional fee, calculated in accordance with paragraph (a)(2) of this section, shall also be paid.

(b)(1)   For the purpose of computing the fee prescribed in paragraphs (a)(1), (2), (4) and (28) of this section the authorized capital stock of a corporation shall be considered to be the total number of shares which the corporation is authorized to issue, whether or not the total number of shares that may be outstanding at any 1 time be limited to a less number.

(2) For the purpose of computing the fee prescribed in paragraphs (a)(2), (3) and (28) of this section, a certificate of amendment of certificate of incorporation, or an amended certificate of incorporation before payment of capital, or a restated certificate of incorporation, or a certificate of validation, shall be considered as increasing the authorized capital stock of a corporation provided it involves an increase in the number of shares, or an increase in the par value of shares, or a change of shares with par value into shares without par value, or a change of shares without par value into shares with par value, or any combination of 2 or more of the above changes, and provided further that the fee computed at the rates set forth in paragraph (a)(1) of this section upon the total authorized capital stock of the corporation including the proposed change or changes exceeds the fee so computed upon the total authorized stock of the corporation excluding such change or changes.

(c)   The Secretary of State may issue photocopies or electronic image copies of instruments on file, as well as instruments, documents and other papers not on file, and for all such photocopies or electronic image copies which are not certified by the Secretary of State, a fee of $10 shall be paid for the first page and $2.00 for each additional page. Notwithstanding Delaware's Freedom of Information Act (Chapter 100 of Title 29) or any other provision of law granting access to public records, the Secretary of State upon request shall issue only photocopies or electronic image copies of public records in exchange for the fees described in this section, and in no case shall the Secretary of State be required to provide copies (or access to copies) of such public records (including without limitation bulk data, digital copies of instruments, documents and other papers, databases or other information) in an electronic medium or in any form other than photocopies or electronic image copies of such public records in exchange, as applicable, for the fees described in this section or § 2318 of Title 29 for each such record associated with a file number.

(d)   No fees for the use of the State shall be charged or collected from any corporation incorporated for the drainage and reclamation of lowlands or for the amendment or renewal of the charter of such corporation.

(e)   The Secretary of State may in the Secretary of State's discretion permit the extension of credit for the fees required by this section upon such terms as the Secretary of State shall deem to be appropriate.

(f)   The Secretary of State shall retain from the revenue collected from the fees required by this section a sum sufficient to provide at all times a fund of at least $500, but not more than $1,500, from which the Secretary of State may refund any payment made pursuant to this section to the extent that it exceeds the fees required by this section. The fund shall be deposited in the financial institution which is the legal depository of state moneys to the credit of the Secretary of State and shall be disbursable on order of the Secretary of State.

(g)   The Secretary of State may in the Secretary of State's discretion charge a fee of $60 for each check received for payment of any fee or tax under Chapter 1 or Chapter 6 of this title that is returned due to insufficient funds or as the result of a stop payment order.

(h)   In addition to those fees charged under subsections (a) and (c) of this section, there shall be collected by and paid to the Secretary of State the following:

(1)   For all services described in subsection (a) of this section that are requested to be completed within 30 minutes on the same day as the day of the request, an additional sum of up to $7,500 and for all services described in subsections (a) and (c) of this section that are requested to be completed within 1 hour on the same day as the day of the request, an additional sum of up to $1,000 and for all services described in subsections (a) and (c) of this section that are requested to be completed within 2 hours on the same day as the day of the request, an additional sum of up to $500; and

(2)   For all services described in subsections (a) and (c) of this section that are requested to be completed within the same day as the day of the request, an additional sum of up to $300; and

(3)   For all services described in subsections (a) and (c) of this section that are requested to be completed within a 24-hour period from the time of the request, an additional sum of up to $150.

The Secretary of State shall establish (and may from time to time alter or amend) a schedule of specific fees payable pursuant to this subsection.

(i)   A domestic corporation or a foreign corporation registered to do business in this State that files with the Secretary of State any instrument or certificate, and in connection therewith, neglects, refuses or fails to pay any fee or tax under Chapter 1 or Chapter 6 of this title shall, after written demand therefor by the Secretary of State by mail addressed to such domestic corporation or foreign corporation in care of its registered agent in this State, cease to be in good standing as a domestic corporation or registered as a foreign corporation in this State on the ninetieth day following the date of mailing of such demand, unless such fee or tax and, if applicable, the fee provided for in subsection (g) of this section are paid in full prior to the ninetieth day following the date of mailing of such demand. A domestic corporation that has ceased to be in good standing or a foreign corporation that has ceased to be registered by reason of the neglect, refusal or failure to pay any such fee or tax shall be restored to and have the status of a domestic corporation in good standing or a foreign corporation that is registered in this State upon the payment of the fee or tax which such domestic corporation or foreign corporation neglected, refused or failed to pay together with the fee provided for in subsection (g) of this section, if applicable. The Secretary of State shall not accept for filing any instrument authorized to be filed with the Secretary of State under this title in respect of any domestic corporation that is not in good standing or any foreign corporation that has ceased to be registered by reason of the neglect, refusal or failure to pay any such fee or tax, and shall not issue any certificate of good standing with respect to such domestic corporation or foreign corporation, unless and until such domestic corporation or foreign corporation shall have been restored to and have the status of a domestic corporation in good standing or a foreign corporation duly registered in this State.

(j)   As used in this section, the term "exempt corporation" shall have the meaning given to it in § 501(b) of this title.

§ 392.   [Reserved.]

§ 393.   Rights, liabilities and duties under prior statutes.

All rights, privileges and immunities vested or accrued by and under any laws enacted prior to the adoption or amendment of this chapter, all suits pending, all rights of action conferred, and all duties, restrictions, liabilities and penalties imposed or required by and under laws enacted prior to the adoption or amendment of this chapter, shall not be impaired, diminished or affected by this chapter.

§ 394.   Reserved power of State to amend or repeal chapter; chapter part of corporation's charter or certificate of incorporation.

This chapter may be amended or repealed, at the pleasure of the General Assembly, but any amendment or repeal shall not take away or impair any remedy under this chapter against any corporation or its officers for any liability which shall have been previously incurred. This chapter and all amendments thereof shall be a part of the charter or certificate of incorporation of every corporation except so far as the same are inapplicable and inappropriate to the objects of the corporation.

§ 395.   Corporations using "trust" in name, advertisements and otherwise; restrictions; violations and penalties; exceptions.

(a)   Except as provided below in subsection (d) of this section, every corporation of this State using the word "trust" as part of its name, except a corporation regulated under the Bank Holding Company Act of 1956, 12 U.S.C. § 1841 et seq., or § 10 of the Home Owners' Loan Act, 12 U.S.C. § 1467a et seq., as those statutes shall from time to time be amended, shall be under the supervision of the State Bank Commissioner of this State and shall make not less than 2 reports during each year to the Commissioner, according to the form which shall be prescribed by the Commissioner, verified by the oaths or affirmations of the president or vice-president, and the treasurer or secretary of the corporation, and attested by the signatures of at least 3 directors.

(b)   Except as provided below in subsection (d) of this section, no corporation of this State shall use the word "trust" as part of its name, except a corporation reporting to and under the supervision of the State Bank Commissioner of this State or a corporation regulated under the Bank Holding Company Act of 1956, 12 U.S.C. § 1841 et seq., or § 10 of the Home Owners' Loan Act, 12 U.S.C. § 1467a et seq., as those statutes shall from time to time be amended. Except as provided below in subsection (d) of this section, the name of any such corporation shall not be amended so as to include the word "trust" unless such corporation shall report to and be under the supervision of the

Commissioner, or unless it is regulated under the Bank Holding Company Act of 1956 or the Savings and Loan Holding Company Act.

(c)   No corporation of this State, except corporations reporting to and under the supervision of the State Bank Commissioner of this State or corporations regulated under the Bank Holding Company Act of 1956, 12 U.S.C. § 1841 et seq., or § 10 of the Home Owners' Loan Act, 12 U.S.C. § 1467a et seq., as those statutes shall from time to time be amended, shall advertise or put forth any sign as a trust company, or in any way solicit or receive deposits or transact business as a trust company.

(d)   The requirements and restrictions set forth above in subsections (a) and (b) of this section shall not apply to, and shall not be construed to prevent the use of the word "trust" as part of the name of, a corporation that is not subject to the supervision of the State Bank Commissioner of this State and that is not regulated under the Bank Holding Company Act of 1956, 12 U.S.C. § 1841 et seq., or § 10 of the Home Owners' Loan Act, 12 U.S.C. § 1467a et seq., where use of the word "trust" as part of such corporation's name clearly:

(1)   Does not refer to a trust business;

(2)   Is not likely to mislead the public into believing that the nature of the business of the corporation includes activities that fall under the supervision of the State Bank Commissioner of this State or that are regulated under the Bank Holding Company Act of 1956, 12 U.S.C. § 1841 et seq., or § 10 of the Home Owners' Loan Act, 12 U.S.C. § 1467a et seq.; and

(3)   Will not otherwise lead to a pattern and practice of abuse that might cause harm to the interests of the public or the State, as determined by the Director of the Division of Corporations and the State Bank Commissioner.

§ 396.   Publication of chapter by Secretary of State; distribution.

The Secretary of State may have printed, from time to time as the Secretary of State deems necessary, pamphlet copies of this chapter, and the Secretary of State shall dispose of the copies to persons and corporations desiring the same for a sum not exceeding the cost of printing. The money received from the sale of the copies shall be disposed of as are other fees of the office of the Secretary of State. Nothing in this section shall prevent the free distribution of single pamphlet copies of this chapter by the Secretary of State, for the printing of which provision is made from time to time by joint resolution of the General Assembly.

§ 397.   Penalty for unauthorized publication of chapter.

Whoever prints or publishes this chapter without the authority of the Secretary of State of this State, shall be fined not more than $500 or imprisoned not more than 3 months, or both.

§ 398.   Short title.

This chapter shall be known and may be identified and referred to as the "General Corporation Law of the State of Delaware."

E. NEW YORK BUSINESS CORPORATION LAW

(Selected Sections)

Table of Contents

ARTICLE 10.   NON-JUDICIAL DISSOLUTION

ARTICLE 11.   JUDICIAL DISSOLUTION

ARTICLE 13.   FOREIGN CORPORATIONS

ARTICLE 5.   CORPORATE FINANCE

§ 504.   Consideration and Payment for Shares

(a)   Consideration for the issue of shares shall consist of money or other property, tangible or intangible; labor or services actually received by or performed for the corporation or for its benefit or in its formation or reorganization; a binding obligation to pay the purchase price or the subscription price in cash or other property; a binding obligation to perform services having an agreed value; or a combination thereof. In the absence of fraud in the transaction, the judgment of the board or shareholders, as the case may be, as to the value of the consideration received for shares shall be conclusive.

(b)   *Repealed.*

(c)   Shares with par value may be issued for such consideration, not less than the par value thereof, as is fixed from time to time by the board.

(d)   Shares without par value may be issued for such consideration as is fixed from time to time by the board unless the certificate of incorporation reserves to the shareholders the right to fix the consideration. If such right is reserved as to any shares, a vote of the shareholders shall either fix the consideration to be received for the shares or authorize the board to fix such consideration.

(e)   Treasury shares may be disposed of by a corporation on such terms and conditions as are fixed from time to time by the board.

(f)   Upon distribution of authorized but unissued shares to shareholders, that part of the surplus of a corporation which is concurrently transferred to stated capital shall be the consideration for the issue of such shares.

(g)   In the event of a conversion of bonds or shares into shares, or in the event of an exchange of bonds or shares for shares, with or without par value, the consideration for the shares so issued in exchange or conversion shall be the sum of (1) either the principal sum of, and accrued interest on, the bonds so exchanged or converted, or the stated capital then represented by the shares so exchanged or converted, plus (2) any additional consideration paid to the corporation for the new shares, plus (3) any stated capital not theretofore allocated to any designated class or series which is thereupon allocated to the new shares, plus (4) any surplus thereupon transferred to stated capital and allocated to the new shares.

(h)   Certificates for shares may not be issued until the amount of the consideration therefor determined to be stated capital pursuant to section 506 (Determination of stated capital) has been paid in the form of cash, services rendered, personal or real property or a combination thereof and consideration for the balance (if any) complying with paragraph (a) of this section has been provided, except as provided in paragraphs (e) and (f) of section 505 (Rights and options to purchase shares; issue of rights and options to directors, officers and employees).

(i)   When the consideration for shares has been provided in compliance with paragraph (h) of this section, the subscriber shall be entitled to all the rights and privileges of a holder of such shares and to a certificate representing his shares, and such shares shall be fully paid and nonassessable.

(j)   Notwithstanding that such shares may be fully paid and nonassessable, the corporation may place in escrow shares issued for a binding obligation to pay cash or other property or to perform future services, or make other arrangements to restrict the transfer of the shares, and may credit distributions in respect of the shares against the obligation, until the obligation is performed. If the obligation is not performed in whole or in part, the corporation may pursue such remedies as are provided in the instrument evidencing the obligation or a related agreement or under law.

§ 505.   Rights and Options to Purchase Shares; Issue of Rights and Options to Directors, Officers and Employees

(a)(1)   Except as otherwise provided in this section or in the certificate of incorporation, a corporation may create and issue, whether or not in connection with the issue and sale of any of its shares or bonds, rights or options entitling the holders thereof to purchase from the corporation, upon such consideration, terms and conditions as may be fixed by the board, shares of any class or series, whether authorized but unissued shares, treasury shares or shares to be purchased or acquired or assets of the corporation.

(2)(i)   In the case of a domestic corporation that has a class of voting stock registered with the Securities and Exchange Commission pursuant to section twelve of the Exchange Act, the terms and conditions of such rights or options may include, without limitation, restrictions or conditions that preclude or limit the exercise, transfer or receipt of such rights or options by an interested shareholder or any transferee of any such interested shareholder or that invalidate or void such rights or options held by any such interested shareholder or any such transferee. For the purpose of this subparagraph, the terms "voting stock", "Exchange Act" and "interested shareholder" shall have the same meanings as set forth in section nine hundred twelve of this chapter;

(ii)   Determinations of the board of directors whether to impose, enforce or waive or otherwise render ineffective such limitations or conditions as are permitted by clause (i) of this subparagraph shall be subject to judicial review in an appropriate proceeding in which the courts formulate or apply appropriate standards in order to insure that such limitations or conditions are imposed, enforced or waived in the best long-term interests and short-term interests of the corporation and its shareholders considering, without limitation, the prospects for potential growth, development, productivity and profitability of the corporation.

(b)   The consideration for shares to be purchased under any such right or option shall comply with the requirements of section 504 (Consideration and payment for shares).

(c)   The terms and conditions of such rights or options, including the time or times at or within which and the price or prices at which they may be exercised and any limitations upon transferability, shall be set forth or incorporated by reference in the instrument or instruments evidencing such rights or options.

(d)   The issue of such rights or options to one or more directors, officers or employees of the corporation or a subsidiary or affiliate thereof, as an incentive to service or continued service with the corporation, a subsidiary or affiliate thereof, or to a trustee on behalf of such directors, officers or employees, shall be authorized as required by the policies of all stock exchanges or automated quotation systems on which the corporation's shares are listed or authorized for trading, or if the corporation's shares are not so listed or authorized, by a majority of the votes cast at a meeting of shareholders by the holders of shares entitled to vote thereon, or authorized by and consistent with a plan adopted by such vote of shareholders. If, under the certificate of incorporation, there are preemptive rights to any of the shares to be thus subject to rights or options to purchase, either such issue or such plan, if any shall also be approved by the vote or written consent of the holders of a majority of the shares entitled to exercise preemptive rights with respect to such shares and such vote or written consent shall operate to release the preemptive rights with respect thereto of the holders of all the shares that were entitled to exercise such preemptive rights.

In the absence of preemptive rights, nothing in this paragraph shall require shareholder approval for the issuance of rights or options to purchase shares of the corporation in substitution for, or upon the assumption of, rights or options issued by another corporation, if such substitution or assumption is in connection with such other corporation's merger or consolidation with, or the acquisition of its shares or all or part of its assets by, the corporation or its subsidiary.

(e)   A plan adopted by the shareholders for the issue of rights or options to directors, officers or employees shall include the material terms and conditions upon which such rights or options are to be issued, such as, but without limitation thereof, any restrictions on the number of shares that eligible individuals may have the right or option to purchase, the method of administering the plan, the terms and conditions of payment for shares in full or in installments, the issue of certificates for shares to be paid for in installments, any limitations upon the transferability of such shares and the voting and dividend rights to which the holders of such shares may be entitled, though the full amount of the consideration therefor has not been paid; provided that under this section no certificate for shares shall be delivered to a shareholder, prior to full payment therefor, unless the fact that the shares are partly paid is noted conspicuously on the face or back of such certificate.

(f)   If there is shareholder approval for the issue of rights or options to individual directors, officers or employees, but not under an approved plan under paragraph (e), the terms and conditions of issue set forth in paragraph (e) shall be permissible except that the grantees of such rights or options shall not be granted voting or dividend rights until the consideration for the shares to which they are entitled under such rights or options has been fully paid.

(g)   If there is shareholder approval for the issue of rights and options, such approval may provide that the board is authorized by certificate of amendment under section 805 (Certificate of amendment; contents) to increase the authorized shares of any class or series to such number as will be sufficient, when added to the previously authorized but unissued shares of such class or series, to satisfy any such rights or options entitling the holders thereof to purchase from the corporation authorized but unissued shares of such class or series.

(h)   In the absence of fraud in the transaction, the judgment of the board shall be conclusive as to the adequacy of the consideration, tangible or intangible, received or to be received by the corporation for the issue of rights or options for the purchase from the corporation of its shares.

(i)   The provisions of this section are inapplicable to the rights of the holders of convertible shares or bonds to acquire shares upon the exercise of conversion privileges under section 519 (Convertible shares and bonds).

§ 510.   Dividends or Other Distributions in Cash or Property

(a)   A corporation may declare and pay dividends or make other distributions in cash or its bonds or its property, including the shares or bonds of other corporations, on its outstanding shares, except when currently the corporation is insolvent or would thereby be made insolvent, or when the declaration, payment or distribution would be contrary to any restrictions contained in the certificate of incorporation.

(b)   Dividends may be declared or paid and other distributions may be made either (1) out of surplus, so that the net assets of the corporation remaining after such declaration, payment or distribution shall at least equal the amount of its stated capital, or (2) in case there shall be no such surplus, out of its net profits for the fiscal year in which the dividend is declared and/or the preceding fiscal year. If the capital of the corporation shall have been diminished by depreciation in the value of its property or by losses or otherwise to an amount less than the aggregate amount of the stated capital represented by the issued and outstanding shares of all classes having a preference upon the distribution of assets, the directors of such corporation shall not declare and pay out of such net profits any dividends upon any shares until the deficiency in the amount of stated capital represented by the issued and outstanding shares of all classes having a preference upon the distribution of assets shall have been repaired. A corporation engaged in the exploitation of natural resources or other wasting assets, including patents, or formed primarily for the liquidation of specific assets, may declare and pay dividends or make other distributions in excess of its surplus, computed after taking due account of depletion and amortization, to the extent that the cost of the wasting or specific assets has been recovered by depletion reserves, amortization or sale, if the net assets remaining after such dividends or distributions are sufficient to cover the liquidation preferences of shares having such preferences in involuntary liquidation.

(c)   *Repealed.*

§ 513.   Purchase, Redemption and Certain Other Transactions by a Corporation With Respect to Its Own Shares

(a)   Notwithstanding any authority contained in the certificate of incorporation, the shares of a corporation may not be purchased by the corporation, or, if redeemable, convertible or exchangeable shares, may not be redeemed, converted or exchanged, in each case for or into cash, other property, indebtedness or other securities of the corporation (other than shares of the corporation and rights to acquire such shares) if the corporation is then insolvent or would thereby be made insolvent. Shares may be purchased or redeemed only out of surplus.

(b)   When its redeemable, convertible or exchangeable shares are purchased by the corporation within the period during which such shares may be redeemed, converted or exchanged at the option of the corporation, the purchase price thereof shall not exceed the applicable redemption, conversion or exchange price stated in the certificate of incorporation. Upon a redemption, conversion or exchange, the amount payable by the corporation for shares having a cumulative preference on dividends may include the stated redemption, conversion or exchange price plus accrued dividends to the next dividend date following the date of redemption, conversion or exchange of such shares.

(c)   No domestic corporation which is subject to the provisions of section nine hundred twelve of this chapter shall purchase or agree to purchase more than ten percent of the stock of the corporation from a shareholder for more than the market value thereof unless such purchase or agreement to purchase is approved by the affirmative vote of the board of directors and a majority of the votes of all outstanding shares entitled to vote thereon at a meeting of shareholders unless the certificate of incorporation requires a greater percentage of the votes of the outstanding shares to approve.

The provisions of this paragraph shall not apply when the corporation offers to purchase shares from all holders of stock or for stock which the holder has been the beneficial owner of for more than two years.

The terms "stock", "beneficial owner", and "market value" shall be as defined in section nine hundred twelve of this chapter.

§ 514.   Agreements for Purchase by a Corporation of Its Own Shares

(a)   An agreement for the purchase by a corporation of its own shares shall be enforceable by the shareholder and the corporation to the extent such purchase is permitted at the time of purchase by section 513 (Purchase or redemption by a corporation of its own shares).

(b)   The possibility that a corporation may not be able to purchase its shares under section 513 shall not be a ground for denying to either party specific performance of an agreement for the purchase by a corporation of its own shares, if at the time for performance the corporation can purchase all or part of such shares under section 513.

ARTICLE 6. SHAREHOLDERS

§ 601. By-Laws

(a) The initial by-laws of a corporation shall be adopted by its incorporator or incorporators at the organization meeting. Thereafter, subject to section 613 (Limitations on right to vote), by-laws may be adopted, amended or repealed by a majority of the votes cast by the shares at the time entitled to vote in the election of any directors. When so provided in the certificate of incorporation or a by-law adopted by the shareholders, by-laws may also be adopted, amended or repealed by the board by such vote as may be therein specified, which may be greater than the vote otherwise prescribed by this chapter, but any by-law adopted by the board may be amended or repealed by the shareholders entitled to vote thereon as herein provided. Any reference in this chapter to a "by-law adopted by the shareholders" shall include a by-law adopted by the incorporator or incorporators.

(b) The by-laws may contain any provision relating to the business of the corporation, the conduct of its affairs, its rights or powers or the rights or powers of its shareholders, directors or officers, not inconsistent with this chapter or any other statute of this state or the certificate of incorporation.

§ 609. Proxies

(a) Every shareholder entitled to vote at a meeting of shareholders or to express consent or dissent without a meeting may authorize another person or persons to act for him by proxy.

(b) No proxy shall be valid after the expiration of eleven months from the date thereof unless otherwise provided in the proxy. Every proxy shall be revocable at the pleasure of the shareholder executing it, except as otherwise provided in this section.

(c) The authority of the holder of a proxy to act shall not be revoked by the incompetence or death of the shareholder who executed the proxy unless, before the authority is exercised, written notice of an adjudication of such incompetence or of such death is received by the corporate officer responsible for maintaining the list of shareholders.

(d) Except when other provision shall have been made by written agreement between the parties, the record holder of shares which he holds as pledgee or otherwise as security or which belong to another, shall issue to the pledgor or to such owner of such shares, upon demand therefor and payment of necessary expenses thereof, a proxy to vote or take other action thereon.

(e) A shareholder shall not sell his vote or issue a proxy to vote to any person for any sum of money or anything of value, except as authorized in this section and section 620 (Agreements as to voting; provision in certificate of incorporation as to control of directors); provided, however, that this paragraph shall not apply to votes, proxies or consents given by holders of preferred shares in connection with a proxy or consent solicitation made available on identical terms to all holders of shares of the same class or series and remaining open for acceptance for at least twenty business days.

(f) A proxy which is entitled "irrevocable proxy" and which states that it is irrevocable, is irrevocable when it is held by any of the following or a nominee of any of the following:

    (1) A pledgee;

    (2) A person who has purchased or agreed to purchase the shares;

    (3) A creditor or creditors of the corporation who extend or continue credit to the corporation in consideration of the proxy if the proxy states that it was given in consideration of such extension or continuation of credit, the amount thereof, and the name of the person extending or continuing credit;

(4)   A person who has contracted to perform services as an officer of the corporation, if a proxy is required by the contract of employment, if the proxy states that it was given in consideration of such contract of employment, the name of the employee and the period of employment contracted for;

(5)   A person designated by or under an agreement under paragraph (a) of section 620.

(g)   Notwithstanding a provision in a proxy, stating that it is irrevocable, the proxy becomes revocable after the pledge is redeemed, or the debt of the corporation is paid, or the period of employment provided for in the contract of employment has terminated, or the agreement under paragraph (a) of section 620 has terminated; and, in a case provided for in subparagraphs (f)(3) or (4), becomes revocable three years after the date of the proxy or at the end of the period, if any, specified therein, whichever period is less, unless the period of irrevocability is renewed from time to time by the execution of a new irrevocable proxy as provided in this section. This paragraph does not affect the duration of a proxy under paragraph (b).

(h)   A proxy may be revoked, notwithstanding a provision making it irrevocable, by a purchaser of shares without knowledge of the existence of the provision unless the existence of the proxy and its irrevocability is noted conspicuously on the face or back of the certificate representing such shares.

(i)   Without limiting the manner in which a shareholder may authorize another person or persons to act for him as proxy pursuant to paragraph (a) of this section, the following shall constitute a valid means by which a shareholder may grant such authority.

(1)   A shareholder may execute a writing authorizing another person or persons to act from him as proxy. Execution may be accomplished by the shareholder or the shareholder's authorized officer, director, employee or agent signing such writing or causing his or her signature to be affixed to such writing by any reasonable means including, but not limited to, by facsimile signature.

(2)   A shareholder may authorize another person or persons to act for the shareholder as proxy by transmitting or authorizing the transmission of a telegram, cablegram or other means of electronic transmission to the person who will be the holder of the proxy or to a proxy solicitation firm, proxy support service organization or like agent duly authorized by the person who will be the holder of the proxy to receive such transmission, provided that any such telegram, cablegram or other means of electronic transmission must either set forth or be submitted with information from which it can be reasonably determined that the telegram, cablegram or other electronic transmission was authorized by the shareholder. If it is determined that such telegrams, cablegrams or other electronic transmissions are valid, the inspectors or, if there are no inspectors, such other persons making that determination shall specify the nature of the information upon which they relied.

(j)   Any copy, facsimile telecommunication or other reliable reproduction of the writing or transmission created pursuant to paragraph (i) of this section may be substituted or used in lieu of the original writing or transmission for any and all purposes for which the original writing or transmission could be used, provided that such copy, facsimile telecommunication or other reproduction shall be a complete reproduction of the entire original writing or transmission.

§ 616.   Greater Requirement as to Quorum and Vote of Shareholders

(a)   The certificate of incorporation may contain provisions specifying either or both of the following:

(1)   That the proportion of votes of shares, or the proportion of votes of shares of any class or series thereof, the holders of which shall be present in person or by proxy at any meeting of shareholders, including a special meeting for election of directors under section 603 (Special meeting for election of directors), in order to constitute a quorum for the transaction of any business or of any specified item of business, including amendments to the certificate of

incorporation, shall be greater than the proportion prescribed by this chapter in the absence of such provision.

(2)   That the proportion of votes of shares, or votes of shares of a particular class or series of shares, that shall be necessary at any meeting of shareholders for the transaction of any business or of any specified item of business, including amendments to the certificate of incorporation, shall be greater than the proportion prescribed by this chapter in the absence of such provision.

(b)   An amendment of the certificate of incorporation which changes or strikes out a provision permitted by this section, shall be authorized at a meeting of shareholders by two-thirds of the votes of the shares entitled to vote thereon, or of such greater proportion of votes of shares, or votes of shares of a particular class or series of shares, as may be provided specifically in the certificate of incorporation for changing or striking out a provision permitted by this section.

(c)   If the certificate of incorporation of any corporation contains a provision authorized by this section, the existence of such provision shall be noted conspicuously on the face or back of every certificate for shares issued by such corporation, except that this requirement shall not apply to any corporation having any class of any equity security registered pursuant to Section twelve of the Securities Exchange Act of 1934, as amended.

§ 620.   Agreements as to Voting; Provision in Certificate of Incorporation as to Control of Directors

(a)   An agreement between two or more shareholders, if in writing and signed by the parties thereto, may provide that in exercising any voting rights, the shares held by them shall be voted as therein provided, or as they may agree, or as determined in accordance with a procedure agreed upon by them.

(b)   A provision in the certificate of incorporation otherwise prohibited by law because it improperly restricts the board in its management of the business of the corporation, or improperly transfers to one or more shareholders or to one or more persons or corporations to be selected by him or them, all or any part of such management otherwise within the authority of the board under this chapter, shall nevertheless be valid:

(1)   If all the incorporators or holders of record of all outstanding shares, whether or not having voting power, have authorized such provision in the certificate of incorporation or an amendment thereof; and

(2)   If, subsequent to the adoption of such provision, shares are transferred or issued only to persons who had knowledge or notice thereof or consented in writing to such provision.

(c)   A provision authorized by paragraph (b) shall be valid only so long as no shares of the corporation are listed on a national securities exchange or regularly quoted in an over-the-counter market by one or more members of a national or affiliated securities association.

(d)(1)   Except as provided in paragraph (e), an amendment to strike out a provision authorized by paragraph (b) shall be authorized at a meeting of shareholders by (A) (i) for any corporation in existence on the effective date of subparagraph (2) of this paragraph, two-thirds of the votes of the shares entitled to vote thereon and (ii) for any corporation in existence on the effective date of this clause the certificate of incorporation of which expressly provides such and for any corporation incorporated after the effective date of subparagraph (2) of this paragraph, a majority of the votes of the shares entitled to vote thereon or (B) in either case, by such greater proportion of votes of shares as may be required by the certificate of incorporation for that purpose.

(2)   Any corporation may adopt an amendment of the certificate of incorporation in accordance with the applicable clause or subclause of subparagraph (1) of this paragraph to provide that any further amendment of the certificate of incorporation that strikes out a provision authorized by paragraph (b) of this section shall be authorized at a meeting of the shareholders

by a specified proportion of votes of the shares, or votes of a particular class or series of shares, entitled to vote thereon, provided that such proportion may not be less than a majority.

(e) Alternatively, if a provision authorized by paragraph (b) shall have ceased to be valid under this section, the board may authorize a certificate of amendment under section 805 (Certificate of amendment; contents) striking out such provision. Such certificate shall set forth the event by reason of which the provision ceased to be valid.

(f) The effect of any such provision authorized by paragraph (b) shall be to relieve the directors and impose upon the shareholders authorizing the same or consenting thereto the liability for managerial acts or omissions that is imposed on directors by this chapter to the extent that and so long as the discretion or powers of the board in its management of corporate affairs is controlled by any such provision.

(g) If the certificate of incorporation of any corporation contains a provision authorized by paragraph (b), the existence of such provision shall be noted conspicuously on the face or back of every certificate for shares issued by such corporation.

§ 622. Preemptive Rights

(a) As used in this section, the term:

(1) "Unlimited dividend rights" means the right without limitation as to amount either to all or to a share of the balance of current or liquidating dividends after the payment of dividends on any shares entitled to a preference.

(2) "Equity shares" means shares of any class, whether or not preferred as to dividends or assets, which have unlimited dividend rights.

(3) "Voting rights" means the right to vote for the election of one or more directors, excluding a right so to vote which is dependent on the happening of an event specified in the certificate of incorporation which would change the voting rights of any class of shares.

(4) "Voting shares" means shares of any class which have voting rights, but does not include bonds on which voting rights are conferred under section 518 (Corporate bonds).

(5) "Preemptive right" means the right to purchase shares or other securities to be issued or subjected to rights or options to purchase, as such right is defined in this section.

(b)(1) With respect to any corporation incorporated prior to the effective date of subparagraph (2) of this paragraph, except as otherwise provided in the certificate of incorporation, and except as provided in this section, the holders of equity shares of any class, in case of the proposed issuance by the corporation of, or the proposed granting by the corporation of rights or options to purchase, its equity shares of any class or any shares or other securities convertible into or carrying rights or options to purchase its equity shares of any class, shall, if the issuance of the equity shares proposed to be issued or issuable upon exercise of such rights or options or upon conversion of such other securities would adversely affect the unlimited dividend rights of such holders, have the right during a reasonable time and on reasonable conditions, both to be fixed by the board, to purchase such shares or other securities in such proportions as shall be determined as provided in this section.

(2) With respect to any corporation incorporated on or after the effective date of this subparagraph, the holders of such shares shall not have any preemptive right, except as otherwise expressly provided in the certificate of incorporation.

(c) Except as otherwise provided in the certificate of incorporation, and except as provided in this section, the holders of voting shares of any class having any preemptive right under this paragraph on the date immediately prior to the effective date of subparagraph (2) of paragraph (b) of this section, in case of the proposed issuance by the corporation of, or the proposed granting by the corporation of rights or options to purchase, its voting shares of any class or any shares or other securities convertible into or carrying rights or options to purchase its voting shares of any class, shall, if the issuance of the voting shares proposed to be issued or issuable upon exercise of such rights or options or upon conversion of such other securities would adversely affect the voting rights of such holders, have the right during a reasonable time and on reasonable conditions, both to be fixed by the board, to purchase such shares or other securities in such proportions as shall be determined as provided in this section.

(d) The preemptive right provided for in paragraphs (b) and (c) shall entitle shareholders having such rights to purchase the shares or other securities to be offered or optioned for sale as nearly as practicable in such proportions as would, if such preemptive right were exercised, preserve the relative unlimited dividend rights and voting rights of such holders and at a price or prices not less favorable than the price or prices at which such shares or other securities are proposed to be offered for sale to others, without deduction of such reasonable expenses of and compensation for the sale, underwriting or purchase of such shares or other securities by underwriters or dealers as may lawfully be paid by the corporation. In case each of the shares entitling the holders thereof to preemptive rights does not confer the same unlimited dividend right or voting right, the board shall apportion the shares or other securities to be offered or optioned for sale among the shareholders having preemptive rights to purchase them in such proportions as in the opinion of the board shall preserve as far as practicable the relative unlimited dividend rights and voting rights of the holders at the time of such offering. The apportionment made by the board shall, in the absence of fraud or bad faith, be binding upon all shareholders.

(e) Unless otherwise provided in the certificate of incorporation, shares or other securities offered for sale or subjected to rights or options to purchase shall not be subject to preemptive rights under paragraph (b) or (c) of this section if they:

(1) Are to be issued by the board to effect a merger or consolidation or offered or subjected to rights or options for consideration other than cash;

(2) Are to be issued or subjected to rights or options under paragraph (d) of section 505 (Rights and options to purchase shares; issue of rights and options to directors, officers and employees);

(3) Are to be issued to satisfy conversion or option rights theretofore granted by the corporation;

(4) Are treasury shares;

(5) Are part of the shares or other securities of the corporation authorized in its original certificate of incorporation and are issued, sold or optioned within two years from the date of filing such certificate; or

(6) Are to be issued under a plan of reorganization approved in a proceeding under any applicable act of congress relating to reorganization of corporations.

(f) Shareholders of record entitled to preemptive rights on the record date fixed by the board under section 604 (Fixing record date), or, if no record date is fixed, then on the record date determined under section 604, and no others shall be entitled to the right defined in this section.

(g) The board shall cause to be given to each shareholder entitled to purchase shares or other securities in accordance with this section, a notice directed to him in the manner provided in section 605 (Notice of meetings of shareholders) setting forth the time within which and the terms and conditions upon which the shareholder may purchase such shares or other securities and also the apportionment made of the right to purchase among the shareholders entitled to preemptive rights. Such notice shall be given personally or by mail at least fifteen days prior to the expiration of the period during which the shareholder shall have the right to purchase. All shareholders entitled to preemptive rights to whom notice shall have been given as aforesaid shall be deemed conclusively to have had a reasonable time in which to exercise their preemptive rights.

(h)   Shares or other securities which have been offered to shareholders having preemptive rights to purchase and which have not been purchased by them within the time fixed by the board may thereafter, for a period of not exceeding one year following the expiration of the time during which shareholders might have exercised such preemptive rights, be issued, sold or subjected to rights or options to any other person or persons at a price, without deduction of such reasonable expenses of and compensation for the sale, underwriting or purchase of such shares by underwriters or dealers as may lawfully be paid by the corporation, not less than that at which they were offered to such shareholders. Any such shares or other securities not so issued, sold or subjected to rights or options to others during such one year period shall thereafter again be subject to the preemptive rights of shareholders.

(i)   Except as otherwise provided in the certificate of incorporation and except as provided in this section, no holder of any shares of any class shall as such holder have any preemptive right to purchase any other shares or securities of any class which at any time may be sold or offered for sale by the corporation. Unless otherwise provided in the certificate of incorporation, holders of bonds on which voting rights are conferred under section 518 shall have no preemptive rights.

§ 624.   Books and Records; Right of Inspection, Prima Facie Evidence

(a)   Each corporation shall keep correct and complete books and records of account and shall keep minutes of the proceedings of its shareholders, board and executive committee, if any, and shall keep at the office of the corporation in this state or at the office of its transfer agent or registrar in this state, a record containing the names and addresses of all shareholders, the number and class of shares held by each and the dates when they respectively became the owners of record thereof. Any of the foregoing books, minutes or records may be in written form or in any other form capable of being converted into written form within a reasonable time.

(b)   Any person who shall have been a shareholder of record of a corporation upon at least five days' written demand shall have the right to examine in person or by agent or attorney, during usual business hours, its minutes of the proceedings of its shareholders and record of shareholders and to make extracts therefrom for any purpose reasonably related to such person's interest as a shareholder. Holders of voting trust certificates representing shares of the corporation shall be regarded as shareholders for the purpose of this section. Any such agent or attorney shall be authorized in a writing that satisfies the requirements of a writing under paragraph (b) of section 609 (Proxies). A corporation requested to provide information pursuant to this paragraph shall make available such information in written form and in any other format in which such information is maintained by the corporation and shall not be required to provide such information in any other format. If a request made pursuant to this paragraph includes a request to furnish information regarding beneficial owners, the corporation shall make available such information in its possession regarding beneficial owners as is provided to the corporation by a registered broker or dealer or a bank, association or other entity that exercises fiduciary powers in connection with the forwarding of information to such owners. The corporation shall not be required to obtain information about beneficial owners not in its possession.

(c)   An inspection authorized by paragraph (b) may be denied to such shareholder or other person upon his refusal to furnish to the corporation, its transfer agent or registrar an affidavit that such inspection is not desired for a purpose which is in the interest of a business or object other than the business of the corporation and that he has not within five years sold or offered for sale any list of shareholders of any corporation of any type or kind, whether or not formed under the laws of this state, or aided or abetted any person in procuring any such record of shareholders for any such purpose.

(d)   Upon refusal by the corporation or by an officer or agent of the corporation to permit an inspection of the minutes of the proceedings of its shareholders or of the record of shareholders as herein provided, the person making the demand for inspection may apply to the supreme court in the judicial district where the office of the corporation is located, upon such notice as the court may direct, for an order directing the corporation, its officer or agent to show cause why an order should not be granted permitting such inspection by the applicant. Upon the return day of the order to show cause, the court shall hear the parties summarily, by affidavit or otherwise, and if it appears that the applicant is qualified and entitled to such inspection, the court shall grant an order compelling such inspection and awarding such further relief as to the court may seem just and proper.

(e)   Upon the written request of any shareholder, the corporation shall give or mail to such shareholder an annual balance sheet and profit and loss statement for the preceding fiscal year, and, if any interim balance sheet or profit and loss statement has been distributed to its shareholders or otherwise made available to the public, the most recent such interim balance sheet or profit and loss statement. The corporation shall be allowed a reasonable time to prepare such annual balance sheet and profit and loss statement.

(f)   Nothing herein contained shall impair the power of courts to compel the production for examination of the books and records of a corporation.

(g)   The books and records specified in paragraph (a) shall be prima facie evidence of the facts therein stated in favor of the plaintiff in any action or special proceeding against such corporation or any of its officers, directors or shareholders.

§ 625.   Infant Shareholders and Bondholders

(a)   A corporation may treat an infant who holds shares or bonds of such corporation as having capacity to receive and to empower others to receive dividends, interest, principal and other payments and distributions, to vote or express consent or dissent, in person or by proxy, and to make elections and exercise rights relating to such shares or bonds, unless, in the case of shares, the corporate officer responsible for maintaining the list of shareholders or the transfer agent of the corporation or, in the case of bonds, the treasurer or paying officer or agent has received written notice that such holder is an infant.

(b)   An infant holder of shares or bonds of a corporation who has received or empowered others to receive payments or distributions, voted or expressed consent or dissent, or made an election or exercised a right relating thereto, shall have no right thereafter to disaffirm or avoid, as against the corporation, any such act on his part, unless prior to such receipt, vote, consent, dissent, election or exercise, as to shares, the corporate officer responsible for maintaining the list of shareholders or its transfer agent or, in the case of bonds, the treasurer or paying officer had received written notice that such holder was an infant.

(c)   This section does not limit any other statute which authorizes any corporation to deal with an infant or limits the right of an infant to disaffirm his acts.

§ 626.   Shareholders' Derivative Action Brought in the Right of the Corporation to Procure a Judgment in Its Favor

(a)   An action may be brought in the right of a domestic or foreign corporation to procure a judgment in its favor, by a holder of shares or of voting trust certificates of the corporation or of a beneficial interest in such shares or certificates.

(b)   In any such action, it shall be made to appear that the plaintiff is such a holder at the time of bringing the action and that he was such a holder at the time of the transaction of which he complains, or that his shares or his interest therein devolved upon him by operation of law.

(c)   In any such action, the complaint shall set forth with particularity the efforts of the plaintiff to secure the initiation of such action by the board or the reasons for not making such effort.

(d)   Such action shall not be discontinued, compromised or settled, without the approval of the court having jurisdiction of the action. If the court shall determine that the interests of the shareholders or any class or classes thereof will be substantially affected by such discontinuance, compromise, or settlement, the court, in its discretion, may direct that notice, by publication or otherwise, shall be given to the shareholders or class or classes thereof whose interest it determines will be so affected; if notice is so directed to be given, the court may determine which one or more of the parties to the action shall bear the expense of giving the same, in such amount as the court shall determine and find to be reasonable in the circumstances, and the amount of such expense shall be awarded as special costs of the action and recoverable in the same manner as statutory taxable costs.

(e)   If the action on behalf of the corporation was successful, in whole or in part, or if anything was received by the plaintiff or plaintiffs or a claimant or claimants as the result of a judgment, compromise or settlement of an action or claim, the court may award the plaintiff or plaintiffs, claimant or claimants, reasonable expenses, including reasonable attorney's fees, and shall direct him or them to account to the corporation for the remainder of the proceeds so received by him or them. This paragraph shall not apply to any judgment rendered for the benefit of injured shareholders only and limited to a recovery of the loss or damage sustained by them.

§ 627.   Security for Expenses in Shareholders' Derivative Action Brought in the Right of the Corporation to Procure a Judgment in Its Favor

In any action specified in section 626 (Shareholders' derivative action brought in the right of the corporation to procure a judgment in its favor), unless the plaintiff or plaintiffs hold five percent or more of any class of the outstanding shares or hold voting trust certificates or a beneficial interest in shares representing five percent or more of any class of such shares, or the shares, voting trust certificates and beneficial interest of such plaintiff or plaintiffs have a fair value in excess of fifty thousand dollars, the corporation in whose right such action is brought shall be entitled at any stage of the proceedings before final judgment to require the plaintiff or plaintiffs to give security for the reasonable expenses, including attorney's fees, which may be incurred by it in connection with such action and by the other parties defendant in connection therewith for which the corporation may become liable under this chapter, under any contract or otherwise under law, to which the corporation shall have recourse in such amount as the court having jurisdiction of such action shall determine upon the termination of such action. The amount of such security may thereafter from time to time be increased or decreased in the discretion of the court having jurisdiction of such action upon showing that the security provided has or may become inadequate or excessive.

§ 630.   Liability of Shareholders for Wages Due to Laborers, Servants or Employees

(a)   The ten largest shareholders, as determined by the fair value of their beneficial interest as of the beginning of the period during which the unpaid services referred to in this section are performed, of every domestic corporation or of any foreign corporation, when the unpaid services were performed in the state, no shares of which are listed on a national securities exchange or regularly quoted in an over-the-counter market by one or more members of a national or an affiliated securities association, shall jointly and severally be personally liable for all debts, wages or salaries due and owing to any of its laborers, servants or employees other than contractors, for services performed by them for such corporation. Before such laborer, servant or employee shall charge such shareholder for such services, he shall give notice in writing to such shareholder that he intends to hold him liable under this section. Such notice shall be given within one hundred and eighty days after termination of such services, except that if, within such period, the laborer, servant or employee demands an examination of the record of shareholders under paragraph (b) of section 624 (Books and records; right of inspection, prima facie evidence) of this article, such notice may be given within sixty days after he has been given the opportunity to examine the record of shareholders. An action to enforce such liability shall be commenced within ninety days after the return of an execution unsatisfied against the corporation upon a judgment recovered against it for such services. The provisions of this paragraph shall not apply to an investment company registered as such under an act of congress entitled "Investment Company Act of 1940."

(b)   For the purposes of this section, wages or salaries shall mean all compensation and benefits payable by an employer to or for the account of the employee for personal services rendered by such employee. These shall specifically include but not be limited to salaries, overtime, vacation, holiday and severance pay; employer contributions to or payments of insurance or welfare benefits; employer contributions to pension or annuity funds; and any other moneys properly due or payable for services rendered by such employee.

(c) A shareholder who has paid more than his pro rata share under this section shall be entitled to contribution pro rata from the other shareholders liable under this section with respect to the excess so paid, over and above his pro rata share, and may sue them jointly or severally or any number of them to recover the amount due from them. Such recovery may be had in a separate action. As used in this paragraph, "pro rata" means in proportion to beneficial share interest. Before a shareholder may claim contribution from other shareholders under this paragraph, he shall, unless they have been given notice by a laborer, servant or employee under paragraph (a), give them notice in writing that he intends to hold them so liable to him. Such notice shall be given by him within twenty days after the date that notice was given to him by a laborer, servant or employee under paragraph (a).

ARTICLE 7. DIRECTORS AND OFFICERS

§ 709. Greater Requirement as to Quorum and Vote of Directors

(a) The certificate of incorporation may contain provisions specifying either or both of the following:

(1) That the proportion of directors that shall constitute a quorum for the transaction of business or of any specified item of business shall be greater than the proportion prescribed by this chapter in the absence of such provision.

(2) That the proportion of votes of directors that shall be necessary for the transaction of business or of any specified item of business shall be greater than the proportion prescribed by this chapter in the absence of such provision.

(b)(1) An amendment of the certificate of incorporation which changes or strikes out a provision permitted by this section shall be authorized at a meeting of shareholders by (A) (i) for any corporation in existence on the effective date of subparagraph (2) of this paragraph, two-thirds of the votes of all outstanding shares entitled to vote thereon, and (ii) for any corporation in existence on the effective date of this clause the certificate of incorporation of which expressly provides such and for any corporation incorporated after the effective date of subparagraph (2) of this paragraph, a majority of the votes of all outstanding shares entitled to vote thereon or (B) in either case, such greater proportion of votes of shares, or votes of a class or series of shares, as may be provided specifically in the certificate of incorporation for changing or striking out a provision permitted by this section.

(2) Any corporation may adopt an amendment of the certificate of incorporation in accordance with any applicable clause or subclause of subparagraph (1) of this paragraph to provide that any further amendment of the certificate of incorporation that changes or strikes out a provision permitted by this section shall be authorized at a meeting of the shareholders by a specified proportion of the votes of the shares, or particular class or series of shares, entitled to vote thereon, provided that such proportion may not be less than a majority.

(c) *Repealed.*

§ 713. Interested Directors

(a) No contract or other transaction between a corporation and one or more of its directors, or between a corporation and any other corporation, firm, association or other entity in which one or more of its directors are directors or officers, or have a substantial financial interest, shall be either void or voidable for this reason alone or by reason alone that such director or directors are present at the meeting of the board, or of a committee thereof, which approves such contract or transaction, or that his or their votes are counted for such purpose:

(1) If the material facts as to such director's interest in such contract or transaction and as to any such common directorship, officership or financial interest are disclosed in good faith or

known to the board or committee, and the board or committee approves such contract or transaction by a vote sufficient for such purpose without counting the vote of such interested director or, if the votes of the disinterested directors are insufficient to constitute an act of the board as defined in section 708 (Action by the board), by unanimous vote of the disinterested directors; or

(2)   If the material facts as to such director's interest in such contract or transaction and as to any such common directorship, officership or financial interest are disclosed in good faith or known to the shareholders entitled to vote thereon, and such contract or transaction is approved by vote of such shareholders.

(b)   If a contract or other transaction between a corporation and one or more of its directors, or between a corporation and any other corporation, firm, association or other entity in which one or more of its directors are directors or officers, or have a substantial financial interest, is not approved in accordance with paragraph (a), the corporation may avoid the contract or transaction unless the party or parties thereto shall establish affirmatively that the contract or transaction was fair and reasonable as to the corporation at the time it was approved by the board, a committee or the shareholders.

(c)   Common or interested directors may be counted in determining the presence of a quorum at a meeting of the board or of a committee which approves such contract or transaction.

(d)   The certificate of incorporation may contain additional restrictions on contracts or transactions between a corporation and its directors and may provide that contracts or transactions in violation of such restrictions shall be void or voidable by the corporation.

(e)   Unless otherwise provided in the certificate of incorporation or the by-laws, the board shall have authority to fix the compensation of directors for services in any capacity.

§ 715.   Officers

(a)   The board may elect or appoint a president, one or more vice-presidents, a secretary and a treasurer, and such other officers as it may determine, or as may be provided in the by-laws.

(b)   The certificate of incorporation may provide that all officers or that specified officers shall be elected by the shareholders instead of by the board.

(c)   Unless otherwise provided in the certificate of incorporation or the by-laws, all officers shall be elected or appointed to hold office until the meeting of the board following the next annual meeting of shareholders or, in the case of officers elected by the shareholders, until the next annual meeting of shareholders.

(d)   Each officer shall hold office for the term for which he is elected or appointed, and until his successor has been elected or appointed and qualified.

(e)   Any two or more offices may be held by the same person. When all of the issued and outstanding stock of the corporation is owned by one person, such person may hold all or any combination of offices.

(f)   The board may require any officer to give security for the faithful performance of his duties.

(g)   All officers as between themselves and the corporation shall have such authority and perform such duties in the management of the corporation as may be provided in the by-laws or, to the extent not so provided, by the board.

(h)   An officer shall perform his duties as an officer in good faith and with that degree of care which an ordinarily prudent person in a like position would use under similar circumstances. In performing his duties, an officer shall be entitled to rely on information, opinions, reports or statements including financial statements and other financial data, in each case prepared or presented by:

(1)   one or more other officers or employees of the corporation or of any other corporation of which at least fifty percentum of the outstanding shares of stock entitling the holders thereof to vote for the election of directors is owned directly or indirectly by the corporation, whom the officer believes to be reliable and competent in the matters presented, or

(2)   counsel, public accountants or other persons as to matters which the officer believes to be within such person's professional or expert competence, so long as in so relying he shall be acting in good faith and with such degree of care, but he shall not be considered to be acting in good faith if he has knowledge concerning the matter in question that would cause such reliance to be unwarranted. A person who so performs his duties shall have no liability by reason of being or having been an officer of the corporation.

§ 716.   Removal of Officers

(a)   Any officer elected or appointed by the board may be removed by the board with or without cause. An officer elected by the shareholders may be removed, with or without cause, only by vote of the shareholders, but his authority to act as an officer may be suspended by the board for cause.

(b)   The removal of an officer without cause shall be without prejudice to his contract rights, if any. The election or appointment of an officer shall not of itself create contract rights.

(c)   An action to procure a judgment removing an officer for cause may be brought by the attorney-general or by ten percent of the votes of the outstanding shares, whether or not entitled to vote. The court may bar from re-election or reappointment any officer so removed for a period fixed by the court.

§ 717.   Duty of Directors

(a)   A director shall perform his duties as a director, including his duties as a member of any committee of the board upon which he may serve, in good faith and with that degree of care which an ordinarily prudent person in a like position would use under similar circumstances. In performing his duties, a director shall be entitled to rely on information, opinions, reports or statements including financial statements and other financial data, in each case prepared or presented by:

(1)   one or more officers or employees of the corporation or of any other corporation of which at least fifty percentum of the outstanding shares of stock entitling the holders thereof to vote for the election of directors is owned directly or indirectly by the corporation, whom the director believes to be reliable and competent in the matters presented,

(2)   counsel, public accountants or other persons as to matters which the director believes to be within such person's professional or expert competence, or

(3)   a committee of the board upon which he does not serve, duly designated in accordance with a provision of the certificate of incorporation or the by-laws, as to matters within its designated authority, which committee the director believes to merit confidence, so long as in so relying he shall be acting in good faith and with such degree of care, but he shall not be considered to be acting in good faith if he has knowledge concerning the matter in question that would cause such reliance to be unwarranted. A person who so performs his duties shall have no liability by reason of being or having been a director of the corporation.

(b)   In taking action, including, without limitation, action which may involve or relate to a change or potential change in the control of the corporation, a director shall be entitled to consider, without limitation, (1) both the long-term and the short-term interests of the corporation and its shareholders and (2) the effects that the corporation's actions may have in the short-term or in the long-term upon any of the following:

(i)   the prospects for potential growth, development, productivity and profitability of the corporation;

(ii)   the corporation's current employees;

(iii)   the corporation's retired employees and other beneficiaries receiving or entitled to receive retirement, welfare or similar benefits from or pursuant to any plan sponsored, or agreement entered into, by the corporation;

(iv)   the corporation's customers and creditors; and

(v)   the ability of the corporation to provide, as a going concern, goods, services, employment opportunities and employment benefits and otherwise to contribute to the communities in which it does business.

Nothing in this paragraph shall create any duties owed by any director to any person or entity to consider or afford any particular weight to any of the foregoing or abrogate any duty of the directors, either statutory or recognized by common law or court decisions.

For purposes of this paragraph, "control" shall mean the possession, directly or indirectly, of the power to direct or cause the direction of the management and policies of the corporation, whether through the ownership of voting stock, by contract, or otherwise.

§ 719.   Liability of Directors in Certain Cases

(a)   Directors of a corporation who vote for or concur in any of the following corporate actions shall be jointly and severally liable to the corporation for the benefit of its creditors or shareholders, to the extent of any injury suffered by such persons, respectively, as a result of such action:

(1)   The declaration of any dividend or other distribution to the extent that it is contrary to the provisions of paragraphs (a) and (b) of section 510 (Dividends or other distributions in cash or property).

(2)   The purchase of the shares of the corporation to the extent that it is contrary to the provisions of section 513 (Purchase or redemption by a corporation of its own shares).

(3)   The distribution of assets to shareholders after dissolution of the corporation without paying or adequately providing for all known liabilities of the corporation, excluding any claims not filed by creditors within the time limit set in a notice given to creditors under articles 10 (Nonjudicial dissolution) or 11 (Judicial dissolution).

(4)   The making of any loan contrary to section 714 (Loans to directors).

(b)   A director who is present at a meeting of the board, or any committee thereof, when action specified in paragraph (a) is taken shall be presumed to have concurred in the action unless his dissent thereto shall be entered in the minutes of the meeting, or unless he shall submit his written dissent to the person acting as the secretary of the meeting before the adjournment thereof, or shall deliver or send by registered mail such dissent to the secretary of the corporation promptly after the adjournment of the meeting. Such right to dissent shall not apply to a director who voted in favor of such action. A director who is absent from a meeting of the board, or any committee thereof, when such action is taken shall be presumed to have concurred in the action unless he shall deliver or send by registered mail his dissent thereto to the secretary of the corporation or shall cause such dissent to be filed with the minutes of the proceedings of the board or committee within a reasonable time after learning of such action.

(c)   Any director against whom a claim is successfully asserted under this section shall be entitled to contribution from the other directors who voted for or concurred in the action upon which the claim is asserted.

(d)   Directors against whom a claim is successfully asserted under this section shall be entitled, to the extent of the amounts paid by them to the corporation as a result of such claims:

(1)   Upon payment to the corporation of any amount of an improper dividend or distribution, to be subrogated to the rights of the corporation against shareholders who received

such dividend or distribution with knowledge of facts indicating that it was not authorized by section 510, in proportion to the amounts received by them respectively.

(2)   Upon payment to the corporation of any amount of the purchase price of an improper purchase of shares, to have the corporation rescind such purchase of shares and recover for their benefit, but at their expense, the amount of such purchase price from any seller who sold such shares with knowledge of facts indicating that such purchase of shares by the corporation was not authorized by section 513.

(3)   Upon payment to the corporation of the claim of any creditor by reason of a violation of subparagraph (a)(3), to be subrogated to the rights of the corporation against shareholders who received an improper distribution of assets.

(4)   Upon payment to the corporation of the amount of any loan made contrary to section 714, to be subrogated to the rights of the corporation against a director who received the improper loan.

(e)   A director shall not be liable under this section if, in the circumstances, he performed his duty to the corporation under paragraph (a) of section 717.

(f)   This section shall not affect any liability otherwise imposed by law upon any director.

§ 720.   Action Against Directors and Officers for Misconduct

(a)   An action may be brought against one or more directors or officers of a corporation to procure a judgment for the following relief:

(1)   Subject to any provision of the certificate of incorporation authorized pursuant to paragraph (b) of section 402, to compel the defendant to account for his official conduct in the following cases:

(A)   The neglect of, or failure to perform, or other violation of his duties in the management and disposition of corporate assets committed to his charge.

(B)   The acquisition by himself, transfer to others, loss or waste of corporate assets due to any neglect of, or failure to perform, or other violation of his duties.

(C)   In the case of directors or officers of a benefit corporation organized under article seventeen of this chapter: (i) the failure to pursue the general public benefit purpose of a benefit corporation or any specific public benefit set forth in its certificate of incorporation; (ii) the failure by a benefit corporation to deliver or post an annual report as required by section seventeen hundred eight of article seventeen of this chapter; or (iii) the neglect of, or failure to perform, or other violation of his or her duties or standard of conduct under article seventeen of this chapter.

(2)   To set aside an unlawful conveyance, assignment or transfer of corporate assets, where the transferee knew of its unlawfulness.

(3)   To enjoin a proposed unlawful conveyance, assignment or transfer of corporate assets, where there is sufficient evidence that it will be made.

(b)   An action may be brought for the relief provided in this section, and in paragraph (a) of section 719 (Liability of directors in certain cases) by a corporation, or a receiver, trustee in bankruptcy, officer, director or judgment creditor thereof, or, under section 626 (Shareholders' derivative action brought in the right of the corporation to procure a judgment in its favor), by a shareholder, voting trust certificate holder, or the owner of a beneficial interest in shares thereof.

(c)   This section shall not affect any liability otherwise imposed by law upon any director or officer.

§ 721. Nonexclusivity of Statutory Provisions for Indemnification of Directors and Officers

The indemnification and advancement of expenses granted pursuant to, or provided by, this article shall not be deemed exclusive of any other rights to which a director or officer seeking indemnification or advancement of expenses may be entitled, whether contained in the certificate of incorporation or the by-laws or, when authorized by such certificate of incorporation or by-laws, (i) a resolution of shareholders, (ii) a resolution of directors, or (iii) an agreement providing for such indemnification, provided that no indemnification may be made to or on behalf of any director or officer if a judgment or other final adjudication adverse to the director or officer establishes that his acts were committed in bad faith or were the result of active and deliberate dishonesty and were material to the cause of action so adjudicated, or that he personally gained in fact a financial profit or other advantage to which he was not legally entitled. Nothing contained in this article shall affect any rights to indemnification to which corporate personnel other than directors and officers may be entitled by contract or otherwise under law.

§ 722. Authorization for Indemnification of Directors and Officers

(a) A corporation may indemnify any person made, or threatened to be made, a party to an action or proceeding (other than one by or in the right of the corporation to procure a judgment in its favor), whether civil or criminal, including an action by or in the right of any other corporation of any type or kind, domestic or foreign, or any partnership, joint venture, trust, employee benefit plan or other enterprise, which any director or officer of the corporation served in any capacity at the request of the corporation, by reason of the fact that he, his testator or intestate, was a director or officer of the corporation, or served such other corporation, partnership, joint venture, trust, employee benefit plan or other enterprise in any capacity, against judgments, fines, amounts paid in settlement and reasonable expenses, including attorneys' fees actually and necessarily incurred as a result of such action or proceeding, or any appeal therein, if such director or officer acted, in good faith, for a purpose which he reasonably believed to be in, or, in the case of service for any other corporation or any partnership, joint venture, trust, employee benefit plan or other enterprise, not opposed to, the best interests of the corporation and, in criminal actions or proceedings, in addition, had no reasonable cause to believe that his conduct was unlawful.

(b) The termination of any such civil or criminal action or proceeding by judgment, settlement, conviction or upon a plea of nolo contendere, or its equivalent, shall not in itself create a presumption that any such director or officer did not act, in good faith, for a purpose which he reasonably believed to be in, or, in the case of service for any other corporation or any partnership, joint venture, trust, employee benefit plan or other enterprise, not opposed to, the best interests of the corporation or that he had reasonable cause to believe that his conduct was unlawful.

(c) A corporation may indemnify any person made, or threatened to be made, a party to an action by or in the right of the corporation to procure a judgment in its favor by reason of the fact that he, his testator or intestate, is or was a director or officer of the corporation, or is or was serving at the request of the corporation as a director or officer of any other corporation of any type or kind, domestic or foreign, of any partnership, joint venture, trust, employee benefit plan or other enterprise, against amounts paid in settlement and reasonable expenses, including attorneys' fees, actually and necessarily incurred by him in connection with the defense or settlement of such action, or in connection with an appeal therein, if such director or officer acted, in good faith, for a purpose which he reasonably believed to be in, or, in the case of service for any other corporation or any partnership, joint venture, trust, employee benefit plan or other enterprise, not opposed to, the best interests of the corporation, except that no indemnification under this paragraph shall be made in respect of (1) a threatened action, or a pending action which is settled or otherwise disposed of, or (2) any claim, issue or matter as to which such person shall have been adjudged to be liable to the corporation, unless and only to the extent that the court in which the action was brought, or, if no action was brought, any court of competent jurisdiction, determines upon application that, in view of all the circumstances of the case, the person is fairly and reasonably entitled to indemnity for such portion of the settlement amount and expenses as the court deems proper.

(d) For the purpose of this section, a corporation shall be deemed to have requested a person to serve an employee benefit plan where the performance by such person of his duties to the corporation also imposes duties on, or otherwise involves services by, such person to the plan or participants or beneficiaries of the plan; excise taxes assessed on a person with respect to an employee benefit plan pursuant to applicable law shall be considered fines; and action taken or omitted by a person with respect to an employee benefit plan in the performance of such person's duties for a purpose reasonably believed by such person to be in the interest of the participants and beneficiaries of the plan shall be deemed to be for a purpose which is not opposed to the best interests of the corporation.

§ 723. Payment of Indemnification Other Than by Court Award

(a) A person who has been successful, on the merits or otherwise, in the defense of a civil or criminal action or proceeding of the character described in section 722 shall be entitled to indemnification as authorized in such section.

(b) Except as provided in paragraph (a), any indemnification under section 722 or otherwise permitted by section 721, unless ordered by a court under section 724 (Indemnification of directors and officers by a court), shall be made by the corporation, only if authorized in the specific case:

    (1) By the board acting by a quorum consisting of directors who are not parties to such action or proceeding upon a finding that the director or officer has met the standard of conduct set forth in section 722 or established pursuant to section 721, as the case may be, or,

    (2) If a quorum under subparagraph (1) is not obtainable or, even if obtainable, a quorum of disinterested directors so directs;

        (A) By the board upon the opinion in writing of independent legal counsel that indemnification is proper in the circumstances because the applicable standard of conduct set forth in such sections has been met by such director or officer, or

        (B) By the shareholders upon a finding that the director or officer has met the applicable standard of conduct set forth in such sections.

(c) Expenses incurred in defending a civil or criminal action or proceeding may be paid by the corporation in advance of the final disposition of such action or proceeding upon receipt of an undertaking by or on behalf of such director or officer to repay such amount as, and to the extent, required by paragraph (a) of section 725.

§ 724. Indemnification of Directors and Officers by a Court

(a) Notwithstanding the failure of a corporation to provide indemnification, and despite any contrary resolution of the board or of the shareholders in the specific case under section 723 (Payment of indemnification other than by court award), indemnification shall be awarded by a court to the extent authorized under section 722 (Authorization for indemnification of directors and officers), and paragraph (a) of section 723. Application therefor may be made, in every case, either:

    (1) In the civil action or proceeding in which the expenses were incurred or other amounts were paid, or

    (2) To the supreme court in a separate proceeding, in which case the application shall set forth the disposition of any previous application made to any court for the same or similar relief and also reasonable cause for the failure to make application for such relief in the action or proceeding in which the expenses were incurred or other amounts were paid.

(b) The application shall be made in such manner and form as may be required by the applicable rules of court or, in the absence thereof, by direction of a court to which it is made. Such application shall be upon notice to the corporation. The court may also direct that notice be given at the expense of the corporation to the shareholders and such other persons as it may designate in such manner as it may require.

(c) Where indemnification is sought by judicial action, the court may allow a person such reasonable expenses, including attorneys' fees, during the pendency of the litigation as are necessary in connection with his defense therein, if the court shall find that the defendant has by his pleadings or during the course of the litigation raised genuine issues of fact or law.

§ 725. Other Provisions Affecting Indemnification of Directors and Officers

(a) All expenses incurred in defending a civil or criminal action or proceeding which are advanced by the corporation under paragraph (c) of section 723 (Payment of indemnification other than by court award) or allowed by a court under paragraph (c) of section 724 (Indemnification of directors and officers by a court) shall be repaid in case the person receiving such advancement or allowance is ultimately found, under the procedure set forth in this article, not to be entitled to indemnification or, where indemnification is granted, to the extent the expenses so advanced by the corporation or allowed by the court exceed the indemnification to which he is entitled.

(b) No indemnification, advancement or allowance shall be made under this article in any circumstance where it appears:

(1) That the indemnification would be inconsistent with the law of the jurisdiction of incorporation of a foreign corporation which prohibits or otherwise limits such indemnification;

(2) That the indemnification would be inconsistent with a provision of the certificate of incorporation, a by-law, a resolution of the board or of the shareholders, an agreement or other proper corporate action, in effect at the time of the accrual of the alleged cause of action asserted in the threatened or pending action or proceeding in which the expenses were incurred or other amounts were paid, which prohibits or otherwise limits indemnification; or

(3) If there has been a settlement approved by the court, that the indemnification would be inconsistent with any condition with respect to indemnification expressly imposed by the court in approving the settlement.

(c) If any expenses or other amounts are paid by way of indemnification, otherwise than by court order or action by the shareholders, the corporation shall, not later than the next annual meeting of shareholders unless such meeting is held within three months from the date of such payment, and, in any event, within fifteen months from the date of such payment, mail to its shareholders of record at the time entitled to vote for the election of directors a statement specifying the persons paid, the amounts paid, and the nature and status at the time of such payment of the litigation or threatened litigation.

(d) If any action with respect to indemnification of directors and officers is taken by way of amendment of the by-laws, resolution of directors, or by agreement, then the corporation shall, not later than the next annual meeting of shareholders, unless such meeting is held within three months from the date of such action, and, in any event, within fifteen months from the date of such action, mail to its shareholders of record at the time entitled to vote for the election of directors a statement specifying the action taken.

(e) Any notification required to be made pursuant to the foregoing paragraph (c) or (d) of this section by any domestic mutual insurer shall be satisfied by compliance with the corresponding provisions of section one thousand two hundred sixteen of the insurance law.

(f) The provisions of this article relating to indemnification of directors and officers and insurance therefor shall apply to domestic corporations and foreign corporations doing business in this state, except as provided in section 1320 (Exemption from certain provisions).

§ 726.   Insurance for Indemnification of Directors and Officers

(a)   Subject to paragraph (b), a corporation shall have power to purchase and maintain insurance:

(1)   To indemnify the corporation for any obligation which it incurs as a result of the indemnification of directors and officers under the provisions of this article, and

(2)   To indemnify directors and officers in instances in which they may be indemnified by the corporation under the provisions of this article, and

(3)   To indemnify directors and officers in instances in which they may not otherwise be indemnified by the corporation under the provisions of this article provided the contract of insurance covering such directors and officers provides, in a manner acceptable to the superintendent of financial services, for a retention amount and for co-insurance.

(b)   No insurance under paragraph (a) may provide for any payment, other than cost of defense, to or on behalf of any director or officer:

(1)   if a judgment or other final adjudication adverse to the insured director or officer establishes that his acts of active and deliberate dishonesty were material to the cause of action so adjudicated, or that he personally gained in fact a financial profit or other advantage to which he was not legally entitled, or

(2)   in relation to any risk the insurance of which is prohibited under the insurance law of this state.

(c)   Insurance under any or all subparagraphs of paragraph (a) may be included in a single contract or supplement thereto. Retrospective rated contracts are prohibited.

(d)   The corporation shall, within the time and to the persons provided in paragraph (c) of section 725 (Other provisions affecting indemnification of directors or officers), mail a statement in respect of any insurance it has purchased or renewed under this section, specifying the insurance carrier, date of the contract, cost of the insurance, corporate positions insured, and a statement explaining all sums, not previously reported in a statement to shareholders, paid under any indemnification insurance contract.

(e)   This section is the public policy of this state to spread the risk of corporate management, notwithstanding any other general or special law of this state or of any other jurisdiction including the federal government.

ARTICLE 9.   MERGER OR CONSOLIDATION; GUARANTEE; DISPOSITION OF ASSETS; SHARE EXCHANGES

§ 912.   Requirements Relating to Certain Business Combinations

(a)   For the purposes of this section:

(1)   "Affiliate" means a person that directly, or indirectly through one or more intermediaries, controls, or is controlled by, or is under common control with, a specified person.

(2)   "Announcement date", when used in reference to any business combination, means the date of the first public announcement of the final, definitive proposal for such business combination.

(3)   "Associate", when used to indicate a relationship with any person, means (A) any corporation or organization of which such person is an officer or partner or is, directly or indirectly, the beneficial owner of ten percent or more of any class of voting stock, (B) any trust or other estate in which such person has a substantial beneficial interest or as to which such person serves as trustee or in a similar fiduciary capacity, and (C) any relative or spouse of such person, or any relative of such spouse, who has the same home as such person.

(4) "Beneficial owner", when used with respect to any stock, means a person:

(A) that, individually or with or through any of its affiliates or associates, beneficially owns such stock, directly or indirectly; or

(B) that, individually or with or through any of its affiliates or associates, has (i) the right to acquire such stock (whether such right is exercisable immediately or only after the passage of time), pursuant to any agreement, arrangement or understanding (whether or not in writing), or upon the exercise of conversion rights, exchange rights, warrants or options, or otherwise; provided, however, that a person shall not be deemed the beneficial owner of stock tendered pursuant to a tender or exchange offer made by such person or any of such person's affiliates or associates until such tendered stock is accepted for purchase or exchange; or (ii) the right to vote such stock pursuant to any agreement, arrangement or understanding (whether or not in writing); provided, however, that a person shall not be deemed the beneficial owner of any stock under this item if the agreement, arrangement or understanding to vote such stock (X) arises solely from a revocable proxy or consent given in response to a proxy or consent solicitation made in accordance with the applicable rules and regulations under the Exchange Act and (Y) is not then reportable on a Schedule 13D under the Exchange Act (or any comparable or successor report); or

(C) that has any agreement, arrangement or understanding (whether or not in writing), for the purpose of acquiring, holding, voting (except voting pursuant to a revocable proxy or consent as described in item (ii) of clause (B) of this subparagraph), or disposing of such stock with any other person that beneficially owns, or whose affiliates or associates beneficially own, directly or indirectly, such stock.

(5) "Business combination", when used in reference to any domestic corporation and any interested shareholder of such corporation, means:

(A) any merger or consolidation of such corporation or any subsidiary of such corporation with (i) such interested shareholder or (ii) any other corporation (whether or not itself an interested shareholder of such corporation) which is, or after such merger or consolidation would be, an affiliate or associate of such interested shareholder;

(B) any sale, lease, exchange, mortgage, pledge, transfer or other disposition (in one transaction or a series of transactions) to or with such interested shareholder or any affiliate or associate of such interested shareholder of assets of such corporation or any subsidiary of such corporation (i) having an aggregate market value equal to ten percent or more of the aggregate market value of all the assets, determined on a consolidated basis, of such corporation, (ii) having an aggregate market value equal to ten percent or more of the aggregate market value of all the outstanding stock of such corporation, or (iii) representing ten percent or more of the earning power or net income determined on a consolidated basis, of such corporation;

(C) the issuance or transfer by such corporation or any subsidiary of such corporation (in one transaction or a series of transactions) of any stock of such corporation or any subsidiary of such corporation which has an aggregate market value equal to five percent or more of the aggregate market value of all the outstanding stock of such corporation to such interested shareholder or any affiliate or associate of such interested shareholder except pursuant to the exercise of warrants or rights to purchase stock offered, or a dividend or distribution paid or made, pro rata to all shareholders of such corporation;

(D) the adoption of any plan or proposal for the liquidation or dissolution of such corporation proposed by, or pursuant to any agreement, arrangement or understanding (whether or not in writing) with, such interested shareholder or any affiliate or associate of such interested shareholder;

(E)   any reclassification of securities (including, without limitation, any stock split, stock dividend, or other distribution of stock in respect of stock, or any reverse stock split), or recapitalization of such corporation, or any merger or consolidation of such corporation with any subsidiary of such corporation, or any other transaction (whether or not with or into or otherwise involving such interested shareholder), proposed by, or pursuant to any agreement, arrangement or understanding (whether or not in writing) with, such interested shareholder or any affiliate or associate of such interested shareholder, which has the effect, directly or indirectly, of increasing the proportionate share of the outstanding shares of any class or series of voting stock or securities convertible into voting stock of such corporation or any subsidiary of such corporation which is directly or indirectly owned by such interested shareholder or any affiliate or associate of such interested shareholder, except as a result of immaterial changes due to fractional share adjustments; or

(F)   any receipt by such interested shareholder or any affiliate or associate of such interested shareholder of the benefit, directly or indirectly (except proportionately as a shareholder of such corporation) of any loans, advances, guarantees, pledges or other financial assistance or any tax credits or other tax advantages provided by or through such corporation.

(6)   "Common stock" means any stock other than preferred stock.

(7)   "Consummation date", with respect to any business combination, means the date of consummation of such business combination, or, in the case of a business combination as to which a shareholder vote is taken, the later of the business day prior to the vote or twenty days prior to the date of consummation of such business combination.

(8)   "Control", including the terms "controlling", "controlled by" and "under common control with", means the possession, directly or indirectly, of the power to direct or cause the direction of the management and policies of a person, whether through the ownership of voting stock, by contract, or otherwise. A person's beneficial ownership of ten percent or more of a corporation's outstanding voting stock shall create a presumption that such person has control of such corporation. Notwithstanding the foregoing, a person shall not be deemed to have control of a corporation if such person holds voting stock, in good faith and not for the purpose of circumventing this section, as an agent, bank, broker, nominee, custodian or trustee for one or more beneficial owners who do not individually or as a group have control of such corporation.

(9)   "Exchange Act" means the Act of Congress known as the Securities Exchange Act of 1934, as the same has been or hereafter may be amended from time to time.

(10)   "Interested shareholder", when used in reference to any domestic corporation, means any person (other than such corporation or any subsidiary of such corporation) that

(A)(i)   is the beneficial owner, directly or indirectly, of twenty percent or more of the outstanding voting stock of such corporation; or

(ii)   is an affiliate or associate of such corporation and at any time within the five-year period immediately prior to the date in question was the beneficial owner, directly or indirectly, of twenty percent or more of the then outstanding voting stock of such corporation; provided that

(B)   for the purpose of determining whether a person is an interested shareholder, the number of shares of voting stock of such corporation deemed to be outstanding shall include shares deemed to be beneficially owned by the person through application of subparagraph four of this paragraph but shall not include any other unissued shares of voting stock of such corporation which may be issuable pursuant to any agreement, arrangement or understanding, or upon exercise of conversion rights, warrants or options, or otherwise.

(11)   "Market value", when used in reference to stock or property of any domestic corporation, means:

(A) in the case of stock, the highest closing sale price during the thirty-day period immediately preceding the date in question of a share of such stock on the composite tape for New York stock exchange-listed stocks, or, if such stock is not quoted on such composite tape or if such stock is not listed on such exchange, on the principal United States securities exchange registered under the Exchange Act on which such stock is listed, or, if such stock is not listed on any such exchange, the highest closing bid quotation with respect to a share of such stock during the thirty-day period preceding the date in question on the National Association of Securities Dealers, Inc. Automated Quotations System or any system then in use, or if no such quotations are available, the fair market value on the date in question of a share of such stock as determined by the board of directors of such corporation in good faith; and

(B) in the case of property other than cash or stock, the fair market value of such property on the date in question as determined by the board of directors of such corporation in good faith.

(12) "Preferred stock" means any class or series of stock of a domestic corporation which under the by-laws or certificate of incorporation of such corporation is entitled to receive payment of dividends prior to any payment of dividends on some other class or series of stock, or is entitled in the event of any voluntary liquidation, dissolution or winding up of the corporation to receive payment or distribution of a preferential amount before any payments or distributions are received by some other class or series of stock.

(13) *Repealed*.

(14) "Stock" means:

(A) any stock or similar security, any certificate of interest, any participation in any profit sharing agreement, any voting trust certificate, or any certificate of deposit for stock; and

(B) any security convertible, with or without consideration, into stock, or any warrant, call or other option or privilege of buying stock without being bound to do so, or any other security carrying any right to acquire, subscribe to or purchase stock.

(15) "Stock acquisition date", with respect to any person and any domestic corporation, means the date that such person first becomes an interested shareholder of such corporation.

(16) "Subsidiary" of any person means any other corporation of which a majority of the voting stock is owned, directly or indirectly, by such person.

(17) "Voting stock" means shares of capital stock of a corporation entitled to vote generally in the election of directors.

(b) Notwithstanding anything to the contrary contained in this chapter (except the provisions of paragraph (d) of this section), no domestic corporation shall engage in any business combination with any interested shareholder of such corporation for a period of five years following such interested shareholder's stock acquisition date unless such business combination or the purchase of stock made by such interested shareholder on such interested shareholder's stock acquisition date is approved by the board of directors of such corporation prior to such interested shareholder's stock acquisition date. If a good faith proposal is made in writing to the board of directors of such corporation regarding a business combination, the board of directors shall respond, in writing, within thirty days or such shorter period, if any, as may be required by the Exchange Act, setting forth its reasons for its decision regarding such proposal. If a good faith proposal to purchase stock is made in writing to the board of directors of such corporation, the board of directors, unless it responds affirmatively in writing within thirty days or such shorter period, if any, as may be required by the Exchange Act, shall be deemed to have disapproved such stock purchase.

(c)   Notwithstanding anything to the contrary contained in this chapter (except the provisions of paragraphs (b) and (d) of this section), no domestic corporation shall engage at any time in any business combination with any interested shareholder of such corporation other than a business combination specified in any one of subparagraph (1), (2) or (3):

(1)   A business combination approved by the board of directors of such corporation prior to such interested shareholder's stock acquisition date, or where the purchase of stock made by such interested shareholder on such interested shareholder's stock acquisition date had been approved by the board of directors of such corporation prior to such interested shareholder's stock acquisition date.

(2)   A business combination approved by the affirmative vote of the holders of a majority of the outstanding voting stock not beneficially owned by such interested shareholder or any affiliate or associate of such interested shareholder at a meeting called for such purpose no earlier than five years after such interested shareholder's stock acquisition date.

(3)   A business combination that meets all of the following conditions:

(A)   The aggregate amount of the cash and the market value as of the consummation date of consideration other than cash to be received per share by holders of outstanding shares of common stock of such corporation in such business combination is at least equal to the higher of the following:

(i)   the highest per share price paid by such interested shareholder at a time when he was the beneficial owner, directly or indirectly, of five percent or more of the outstanding voting stock of such corporation, for any shares of common stock of the same class or series acquired by it (X) within the five-year period immediately prior to the announcement date with respect to such business combination, or (Y) within the five-year period immediately prior to, or in, the transaction in which such interested shareholder became an interested shareholder, whichever is higher; plus, in either case, interest compounded annually from the earliest date on which such highest per share acquisition price was paid through the consummation date at the rate for one-year United States treasury obligations from time to time in effect; less the aggregate amount of any cash dividends paid, and the market value of any dividends paid other than in cash, per share of common stock since such earliest date, up to the amount of such interest; and

(ii)   the market value per share of common stock on the announcement date with respect to such business combination or on such interested shareholder's stock acquisition date, whichever is higher; plus interest compounded annually from such date through the consummation date at the rate for one-year United States treasury obligations from time to time in effect; less the aggregate amount of any cash dividends paid, and the market value of any dividends paid other than in cash, per share of common stock since such date, up to the amount of such interest.

(B)   The aggregate amount of the cash and the market value as of the consummation date of consideration other than cash to be received per share by holders of outstanding shares of any class or series of stock, other than common stock, of such corporation is at least equal to the highest of the following (whether or not such interested shareholder has previously acquired any shares of such class or series of stock):

(i)   the highest per share price paid by such interested shareholder at a time when he was the beneficial owner, directly or indirectly, of five percent or more of the outstanding voting stock of such corporation, for any shares of such class or series of stock acquired by it (X) within the five-year period immediately prior to the announcement date with respect to such business combination, or (Y) within the five-year period immediately prior to, or in, the transaction in which such interested shareholder became an interested shareholder, whichever is higher; plus, in either case, interest compounded annually from the earliest date on which such highest per share acquisition price was paid through the consummation date at the rate for one-year United States treasury obligations from time to time in effect; less the aggregate amount of any cash dividends paid, and the market value of any dividends paid other than in cash, per share of such class or series of stock since such earliest date, up to the amount of such interest;

(ii)   the highest preferential amount per share to which the holders of shares of such class or series of stock are entitled in the event of any voluntary liquidation, dissolution or winding up of such corporation, plus the aggregate amount of any dividends declared or due as to which such holders are entitled prior to payment of dividends on some other class or series of stock (unless the aggregate amount of such dividends is included in such preferential amount); and

(iii)   the market value per share of such class or series of stock on the announcement date with respect to such business combination or on such interested shareholder's stock acquisition date, whichever is higher; plus interest compounded annually from such date through the consummation date at the rate for one-year United States treasury obligations from time to time in effect; less the aggregate amount of any cash dividends paid, and the market value of any dividends paid other than in cash, per share of such class or series of stock since such date, up to the amount of such interest.

(C)   The consideration to be received by holders of a particular class or series of outstanding stock (including common stock) of such corporation in such business combination is in cash or in the same form as the interested shareholder has used to acquire the largest number of shares of such class or series of stock previously acquired by it, and such consideration shall be distributed promptly.

(D)   The holders of all outstanding shares of stock of such corporation not beneficially owned by such interested shareholder immediately prior to the consummation of such business combination are entitled to receive in such business combination cash or other consideration for such shares in compliance with clauses (A), (B) and (C) of this subparagraph.

(E)   After such interested shareholder's stock acquisition date and prior to the consummation date with respect to such business combination, such interested shareholder has not become the beneficial owner of any additional shares of voting stock of such corporation except:

(i)   as part of the transaction which resulted in such interested shareholder becoming an interested shareholder;

(ii)   by virtue of proportionate stock splits, stock dividends or other distributions of stock in respect of stock not constituting a business combination under clause (E) of subparagraph five of paragraph (a) of this section;

(iii)   through a business combination meeting all of the conditions of paragraph (b) of this section and this paragraph; or

(iv)   through purchase by such interested shareholder at any price which, if such price had been paid in an otherwise permissible business combination the announcement date and consummation date of which were the date of such purchase, would have satisfied the requirements of clauses (A), (B) and (C) of this subparagraph.

(d)   The provisions of this section shall not apply:

(1)   to any business combination of a domestic corporation that does not have a class of voting stock registered with the Securities and Exchange Commission pursuant to section twelve of the Exchange Act, unless the certificate of incorporation provides otherwise; or

(2)   to any business combination of a domestic corporation whose certificate of incorporation has been amended to provide that such corporation shall be subject to the provisions of this section, which did not have a class of voting stock registered with the Securities and Exchange Commission pursuant to section twelve of the Exchange Act on the effective date of such amendment, and which is a business combination with an interested shareholder whose stock acquisition date is prior to the effective date of such amendment; or

(3)   to any business combination of a domestic corporation (i) the original certificate of incorporation of which contains a provision expressly electing not to be governed by this section, or (ii) which adopts an amendment to such corporation's by-laws prior to March thirty-first, nineteen hundred eighty-six, expressly electing not to be governed by this section, or (iii) which adopts an amendment to such corporation's by-laws, approved by the affirmative vote of a majority of votes of the outstanding voting stock of such corporation, excluding the voting stock of interested shareholders and their affiliates and associates, expressly electing not to be governed by this section, provided that such amendment to the by-laws shall not be effective until eighteen months after such vote of such corporation's shareholders and shall not apply to any business combination of such corporation with an interested shareholder whose stock acquisition date is on or prior to the effective date of such amendment; or

(4)   to any business combination of a domestic corporation with an interested shareholder of such corporation which became an interested shareholder inadvertently, if such interested shareholder (i) as soon as practicable, divests itself of a sufficient amount of the voting stock of such corporation so that it no longer is the beneficial owner, directly or indirectly, of twenty percent or more of the outstanding voting stock of such corporation, and (ii) would not at any time within the five-year period preceding the announcement date with respect to such business combination have been an interested shareholder but for such inadvertent acquisition; or

(5)   to any business combination with an interested shareholder who was the beneficial owner, directly or indirectly, of five percent or more of the outstanding voting stock of such corporation on October thirtieth, nineteen hundred eighty-five, and remained so to such interested shareholder's stock acquisition date.

ARTICLE 10.   NON-JUDICIAL DISSOLUTION

§ 1002.   Dissolution Under Provision in Certificate of Incorporation

(a)   The certificate of incorporation may contain a provision that any shareholder, or the holders of any specified number or proportion of shares or votes of shares, or of any specified number or proportion of shares or votes of shares of any class or series thereof, may require the dissolution of the corporation at will or upon the occurrence of a specified event. If the certificate of incorporation contains such a provision, a certificate of dissolution under section 1003 (Certificate of dissolution; contents) may be signed, verified and delivered to the department of state as provided in section 104 (Certificate; requirements, signing, filing, effectiveness) when authorized by a holder or holders of the number or proportion of shares or votes of shares specified in such provision, given in such manner as may be specified therein, or if no manner is specified therein, when authorized on written consent signed by such holder or holders; or such certificate may be signed, verified and delivered to the department by such holder or holders or by such of them as are designated by them.

(b)   An amendment of the certificate of incorporation which adds a provision permitted by this section, or which changes or strikes out such a provision, shall be authorized at a meeting of shareholders by vote of all outstanding shares, whether or not otherwise entitled to vote on any amendment, or of such lesser proportion of shares and of such class or series of shares, but not less than a majority of all outstanding shares entitled to vote on any amendment, as may be provided specifically in the certificate of incorporation for adding, changing or striking out a provision permitted by this section.

(c)   If the certificate of incorporation of any corporation contains a provision authorized by this section, the existence of such provision shall be noted conspicuously on the face or back of every certificate for shares issued by such corporation.

ARTICLE 11.   JUDICIAL DISSOLUTION

§ 1104.   Petition in Case of Deadlock Among Directors or Shareholders

(a)   Except as otherwise provided in the certificate of incorporation under section 613 (Limitations on right to vote), the holders of shares representing one-half of the votes of all outstanding shares of a corporation entitled to vote in an election of directors may present a petition for dissolution on one or more of the following grounds:

(1)   That the directors are so divided respecting the management of the corporation's affairs that the votes required for action by the board cannot be obtained.

(2)   That the shareholders are so divided that the votes required for the election of directors cannot be obtained.

(3)   That there is internal dissension and two or more factions of shareholders are so divided that dissolution would be beneficial to the shareholders.

(b)   If the certificate of incorporation provides that the proportion of votes required for action by the board, or the proportion of votes of shareholders required for election of directors, shall be greater than that otherwise required by this chapter, such a petition may be presented by the holders of shares representing more than one-third of the votes of all outstanding shares entitled to vote on non-judicial dissolution under section 1001 (Authorization of dissolution).

(c)   Notwithstanding any provision in the certificate of incorporation, any holder of shares entitled to vote at an election of directors of a corporation, may present a petition for its dissolution on the ground that the shareholders are so divided that they have failed, for a period which includes at least two consecutive annual meeting dates, to elect successors to directors whose terms have expired or would have expired upon the election and qualification of their successors.

§ 1104–a.   Petition for Judicial Dissolution Under Special Circumstances

(a)   The holders of shares representing twenty percent or more of the votes of all outstanding shares of a corporation, other than a corporation registered as an investment company under an act of congress entitled "Investment Company Act of 1940", no shares of which are listed on a national securities exchange or regularly quoted in an over-the-counter market by one or more members of a national or an affiliated securities association, entitled to vote in an election of directors may present a petition of dissolution on one or more of the following grounds:

(1)   The directors or those in control of the corporation have been guilty of illegal, fraudulent or oppressive actions toward the complaining shareholders;

(2)   The property or assets of the corporation are being looted, wasted, or diverted for non-corporate purposes by its directors, officers or those in control of the corporation.

(b)   The court, in determining whether to proceed with involuntary dissolution pursuant to this section, shall take into account:

(1)   Whether liquidation of the corporation is the only feasible means whereby the petitioners may reasonably expect to obtain a fair return on their investment; and

(2)   Whether liquidation of the corporation is reasonably necessary for the protection of the rights and interests of any substantial number of shareholders or of the petitioners.

(c)   In addition to all other disclosure requirements, the directors or those in control of the corporation, no later than thirty days after the filing of a petition hereunder, shall make available for inspection and copying to the petitioners under reasonable working conditions the corporate financial books and records for the three preceding years.

(d)   The court may order stock valuations be adjusted and may provide for a surcharge upon the directors or those in control of the corporation upon a finding of wilful or reckless dissipation or transfer of assets or corporate property without just or adequate compensation therefor.

§ 1111.   Judgment or Final Order of Dissolution

(a)   In an action or special proceeding under this article if, in the court's discretion, it shall appear that the corporation should be dissolved, it shall make a judgment or final order dissolving the corporation.

(b)   In making its decision, the court shall take into consideration the following criteria:

(1)   In an action brought by the attorney-general, the interest of the public is of paramount importance.

(2)   In a special proceeding brought by directors or shareholders, the benefit to the shareholders of a dissolution is of paramount importance.

(3)   In a special proceeding brought under section 1104 (Petition in case of deadlock among directors or shareholders) or section 1104–a (Petition for judicial dissolution under special circumstances) dissolution is not to be denied merely because it is found that the corporate business has been or could be conducted at a profit.

(c)   If the judgment or final order shall provide for a dissolution of the corporation, the court may, in its discretion, provide therein for the distribution of the property of the corporation to those entitled thereto according to their respective rights.

(d)   The clerk of the court or such other person as the court may direct shall transmit certified copies of the judgment or final order of dissolution to the department of state and to the clerk of the county in which the office of the corporation was located at the date of the judgment or order. Upon filing by the department of state, the corporation shall be dissolved.

(e)   The corporation shall promptly thereafter transmit a certified copy of the judgment or final order to the clerk of each other county in which its certificate of incorporation was filed.

§ 1118.   Purchase of Petitioner's Shares; Valuation

(a)   In any proceeding brought pursuant to section eleven hundred four-a of this chapter, any other shareholder or shareholders or the corporation may, at any time within ninety days after the filing of such petition or at such later time as the court in its discretion may allow, elect to purchase the shares owned by the petitioners at their fair value and upon such terms and conditions as may be approved by the court, including the conditions of paragraph (c) herein. An election pursuant to this section shall be irrevocable unless the court, in its discretion, for just and equitable considerations, determines that such election be revocable.

(b)   If one or more shareholders or the corporation elect to purchase the shares owned by the petitioner but are unable to agree with the petitioner upon the fair value of such shares, the court, upon the application of such prospective purchaser or purchasers or the petitioner, may stay the proceedings brought pursuant to section 1104–a of this chapter and determine the fair value of the petitioner's shares as of the day prior to the date on which such petition was filed, exclusive of any element of value arising from such filing but giving effect to any adjustment or surcharge found to be appropriate in the proceeding under section 1104–a of this chapter. In determining the fair value of the petitioner's shares, the court, in its discretion, may award interest from the date the petition is filed to the date of payment for the petitioner's share at an equitable rate upon judicially determined fair value of his shares.

(c)   In connection with any election to purchase pursuant to this section:

(1)   If such election is made beyond ninety days after the filing of the petition, and the court allows such petition, the court, in its discretion, may award the petitioner his reasonable expenses incurred in the proceeding prior to such election, including reasonable attorneys' fees;

(2)   The court, in its discretion, may require, at any time prior to the actual purchase of petitioner's shares, the posting of a bond or other acceptable security in an amount sufficient to secure petitioner for the fair value of his shares.

ARTICLE 13.   FOREIGN CORPORATIONS

§ 1317.   Liabilities of Directors and Officers of Foreign Corporations

(a)   Except as otherwise provided in this chapter, the directors and officers of a foreign corporation doing business in this state are subject, to the same extent as directors and officers of a domestic corporation, to the provisions of:

(1)   Section 719 (Liability of directors in certain cases) except subparagraph (a)(3) thereof, and

(2)   Section 720 (Action against directors and officers for misconduct.)

(b)   Any liability imposed by paragraph (a) may be enforced in, and such relief granted by, the courts in this state, in the same manner as in the case of a domestic corporation.

§ 1318.   Liability of Foreign Corporations for Failure to Disclose Required Information

A foreign corporation doing business in this state shall, in the same manner as a domestic corporation, disclose to its shareholders of record who are residents of this state the information required under paragraph (c) of section 510 (Dividends or other distributions in cash or property), paragraphs (f) and (g) of section 511 (Share distributions and changes), paragraph (d) of section 515 (Reacquired shares), paragraph (c) of section 516 (Reduction of stated capital in certain cases), and shall be liable as provided in section 520 (Liability for failure to disclose required information) for failure to comply in good faith with these requirements.

§ 1319.   Applicability of Other Provisions

(a)   In addition to articles 1 (Short title; definitions; application; certificates; miscellaneous) and 3 (Corporate name and service of process) and the other sections of article 13 (foreign corporations), the following provisions, to the extent provided therein, shall apply to a foreign corporation doing business in this state, its directors, officers and shareholders:

(1)   Section 623 (Procedure to enforce shareholder's right to receive payment for shares).

(2)   Section 626 (Shareholders' derivative action brought in the right of the corporation to procure a judgment in its favor).

(3)   Section 627 (Security for expenses in shareholders' derivative action brought in the right of the corporation to procure a judgment in its favor).

(4)   Section 630 (Liability of shareholders for wages due to laborers, servants or employees).

(5)   Sections 721 (Nonexclusivity of statutory provisions for indemnification of directors and officers) through 726 (Insurance for indemnification of directors and officers), inclusive.

(6)   Section 808 (Reorganization under act of congress).

(7)   Section 907 (Merger or consolidation of domestic and foreign corporations).

§ 1320. Exemption from Certain Provisions

(a)   Notwithstanding any other provision of this chapter, a foreign corporation doing business in this state which is authorized under this article, its directors, officers and shareholders, shall be exempt from the provisions of paragraph (e) of section 1316 (Voting trust records), subparagraph (a)(1) of section 1317 (Liabilities of directors and officers of foreign corporations), section 1318 (Liability of foreign corporations for failure to disclose required information) and subparagraph (a)(4) of section 1319 (Applicability of other provisions) if when such provision would otherwise apply:

(1)   Shares of such corporation were listed on a national securities exchange, or

(2)   Less than one-half of the total of its business income for the preceding three fiscal years, or such portion thereof as the foreign corporation was in existence, was allocable to this state for franchise tax purposes under the tax law.

F. CORPORATION FORMS

Table of Forms

---

1. DELAWARE FORMS

A. MORRIS, NICHOLS, ARSHT & TUNNELL FORM CERTIFICATE OF INCORPORATION*

CERTIFICATE OF INCORPORATION
OF
NEWCO, INC.

FIRST: The name of the corporation is Newco, Inc. (hereinafter referred to as the "Corporation").

SECOND: The address of the registered office of the Corporation in the State of Delaware is Corporation Trust Center, 1209 Orange Street, in the City of Wilmington, County of New Castle. The name of the registered agent of the Corporation at that address is The Corporation Trust Company.

THIRD: The purpose of the Corporation is to engage in any lawful act or activity for which a corporation may be organized under the Delaware General Corporation Law.

FOURTH: A. The total number of shares of all classes of stock which the Corporation shall have authority to issue is _____ (_____), consisting of _____ (_____) shares of Common Stock, par value one cent ($.01) per share (the "Common Stock") and _____ (_____) shares of Preferred Stock, par value one cent ($.01) per share (the "Preferred Stock").

B.   The board of directors is authorized, subject to any limitations prescribed by law, to provide for the issuance of shares of Preferred Stock in series, and by filing a certificate pursuant to the applicable law of the State of Delaware (such certificate being hereinafter referred to as a "Preferred Stock Designation"), to establish from time to time the number of shares to be included in each such series, and to fix the designation, powers, preferences, and rights of the shares of each such series and any qualifications, limitations or restrictions thereof. The number of authorized shares of Preferred Stock may be increased or decreased (but not below the number of shares thereof then outstanding) by the affirmative vote of the holders of a majority of the Common Stock, without a vote of the holders of the Preferred Stock, or of any series thereof, unless a vote of any such holders is required pursuant to the terms of any Preferred Stock Designation.

C.   Each outstanding share of Common Stock shall entitle the holder thereof to one vote on each matter properly submitted to the stockholders of the Corporation for their vote; *provided, however,* that, except as otherwise required by law, holders of Common Stock shall not be entitled to vote on any amendment to this Certificate of Incorporation (including any Certificate of Designations relating to any series of Preferred Stock) that relates solely to the terms of one or more outstanding series of

---

*   Thanks to Frederick H. Alexander, a member of Morris, Nichols, Arsht & Tunnell, for furnishing the Delaware Form Certificate of Incorporation and By-Laws.

Preferred Stock if the holders of such affected series are entitled, either separately or together as a class with the holders of one or more other such series, to vote thereon pursuant to this Certificate of Incorporation (including any Certificate of Designations relating to any series of Preferred Stock).

FIFTH: The following provisions are inserted for the management of the business and the conduct of the affairs of the Corporation, and for further definition, limitation and regulation of the powers of the Corporation and of its directors and stockholders:

A.   The business and affairs of the Corporation shall be managed by or under the direction of the board of directors. In addition to the powers and authority expressly conferred upon them by statute or by this Certificate of Incorporation or the by-laws of the Corporation, the directors are hereby empowered to exercise all such powers and do all such acts and things as may be exercised or done by the Corporation.

B.   The directors of the Corporation need not be elected by written ballot unless the by-laws so provide.

C.   Any action required or permitted to be taken by the stockholders of the Corporation must be effected at a duly called annual or special meeting of stockholders of the Corporation and may not be effected by any consent in writing by such stockholders.

D.   Special meetings of stockholders of the Corporation may be called only by the board of directors acting pursuant to a resolution adopted by a majority of the Whole Board. For purposes of this Certificate of Incorporation, the term "Whole Board" shall mean the total number of authorized directors whether or not there exist any vacancies in previously authorized directorships.

SIXTH: A. Subject to the rights of the holders of any series of Preferred Stock to elect additional directors under specified circumstances, the number of directors shall be fixed from time to time exclusively by the board of directors pursuant to a resolution adopted by a majority of the Whole Board. The directors, other than those who may be elected by the holders of any series of Preferred Stock under specified circumstances, shall be divided into three classes, with the term of office of the first class to expire at the Corporation's first annual meeting of stockholders, the term of office of the second class to expire at the Corporation's second annual meeting of stockholders and the term of office of the third class to expire at the Corporation's third annual meeting of stockholders, with each director to hold office until his or her successor shall have been duly elected and qualified. At each annual meeting of stockholders, directors elected to succeed those directors whose terms expire shall be elected for a term of office to expire at the third succeeding annual meeting of stockholders after their election, with each director to hold office until his or her successor shall have been duly elected and qualified.

B.   Subject to the rights of the holders of any series of Preferred Stock then outstanding, newly created directorships resulting from any increase in the authorized number of directors or any vacancies in the board of directors resulting from death, resignation, retirement, disqualification, removal from office or other cause shall, unless otherwise required by law or by resolution of the board of directors, be filled only by a majority vote of the directors then in office, though less than a quorum (and not by stockholders), and directors so chosen shall serve for a term expiring at the annual meeting of stockholders at which the term of office of the class to which they have been chosen expires or until such director's successor shall have been duly elected and qualified. No decrease in the authorized number of directors shall shorten the term of any incumbent director.

C.   Advance notice of stockholder nominations for the election of directors and of business to be brought by stockholders before any meeting of the stockholders of the Corporation shall be given in the manner provided in the by-laws of the Corporation.

D.   Subject to the rights of the holders of any series of Preferred Stock then outstanding, any director, or the entire board of directors, may be removed from office at any time, but only for cause and only by the affirmative vote of the holders of at least _____ percent (__%) of the voting power of

CERTIFICATE OF INCORPORATION

all of the then-outstanding shares of capital stock of the Corporation entitled to vote generally in the election of directors, voting together as a single class.

SEVENTH: The board of directors is expressly empowered to adopt, amend or repeal by-laws of the Corporation. Any adoption, amendment or repeal of the by-laws of the Corporation by the board of directors shall require the approval of a majority of the Whole Board. The stockholders shall also have power to adopt, amend or repeal the by-laws of the Corporation; provided, however, that, in addition to any vote of the holders of any class or series of stock of the Corporation required by law or by this Certificate of Incorporation, the affirmative vote of the holders of at least _____ percent (__%) of the voting power of all of the then-outstanding shares of the capital stock of the Corporation entitled to vote generally in the election of directors, voting together as a single class, shall be required to adopt, amend or repeal any provision of the by-laws of the Corporation.

EIGHTH: A director of the Corporation shall not be personally liable to the Corporation or its stockholders for monetary damages for breach of fiduciary duty as a director, except for liability (i) for any breach of the director's duty of loyalty to the Corporation or its stockholders, (ii) for acts or omissions not in good faith or which involve intentional misconduct or a knowing violation of law, (iii) under Section 174 of the Delaware General Corporation Law, or (iv) for any transaction from which the director derived an improper personal benefit. If the Delaware General Corporation Law is amended to authorize corporate action further eliminating or limiting the personal liability of directors, then the liability of a director of the Corporation shall be eliminated or limited to the fullest extent permitted by the Delaware General Corporation Law, as so amended.

Any repeal or modification of the foregoing paragraph by the stockholders of the Corporation shall not adversely affect any right or protection of a director of the Corporation existing at the time of such repeal or modification.

NINTH: The Corporation reserves the right to amend or repeal any provision contained in this Certificate of Incorporation in the manner prescribed by the laws of the State of Delaware and all rights conferred upon stockholders are granted subject to this reservation; provided, however, that, notwithstanding any other provision of this Certificate of Incorporation or any provision of law that might otherwise permit a lesser vote or no vote, but in addition to any vote of the holders of any class or series of the stock of this corporation required by law or by this Certificate of Incorporation, the affirmative vote of the holders of at least _____ percent (__%) of the voting power of all of the then-outstanding shares of the capital stock of the Corporation entitled to vote generally in the election of Directors, voting together as a single class, shall be required to amend or repeal this Article NINTH, Sections C or D of Article FIFTH, Article SIXTH, Article SEVENTH, or Article EIGHTH.

TENTH: The incorporator is _____, whose mailing address is _____.

I, THE UNDERSIGNED, being the incorporator, for the purpose of forming a corporation under the laws of the State of Delaware do make, file and record this Certificate of Incorporation, do certify that the facts herein stated are true, and, accordingly, have hereto set my hand this ___ day of _____, 2000.

_____

CONTINUING DIRECTOR PROVISION

ARTICLE _____

The board of directors is expressly authorized to cause the Corporation to issue rights pursuant to Section 157 of the Delaware General Corporation Law and, in that connection, to enter into any agreements necessary or convenient for such issuance[, and to enter into other agreements necessary and convenient to the conduct of the business of the corporation]. Any such agreement may include provisions limiting, in certain circumstances, the ability of the board of directors of the Corporation to redeem the securities issued pursuant thereto or to take other action thereunder or in connection therewith unless there is a specified number or percentage of Continuing Directors then in office.

BYLAWS

Pursuant to Section 141(a) of the Delaware General Corporation Law, the Continuing Directors shall have the power and authority to make all decisions and determinations, and exercise or perform such other acts, that any such agreement provides that such Continuing Directors shall make, exercise or perform. For purposes of this Article _____ and any such agreement, the term, "Continuing Directors," shall mean (1) those directors who were members of the board of directors of the Corporation at the time the Corporation entered into such agreement and any director who subsequently becomes a member of the board of directors, if such director's nomination for election to the board of directors is recommended or approved by the majority vote of the Continuing Directors then in office and (2) such other members of the board of directors, if any, designated in, or in the manner provided in, such agreement as Continuing Directors.

IF THE CONTINUING DIRECTOR PROVISION IS ADOPTED, THE SECTION 102(B)(7) PROVISION OF THE CORPORATION SHOULD BE AMENDED TO ADD:

All references in this Article _____ to a director shall also be deemed to refer to any such director acting in his or her capacity as a Continuing Director.

B. MORRIS, NICHOLS, ARSHT & TUNNELL FORM BYLAWS

BYLAWS OF NEWCO, INC.
ARTICLE I—STOCKHOLDERS

Section 1.   Annual Meeting.

(1)   An annual meeting of the stockholders, for the election of directors to succeed those whose terms expire and for the transaction of such other business as may properly come before the meeting, shall be held at such place, on such date, and at such time as the Board of Directors shall each year fix, which date shall be within thirteen (13) months of the last annual meeting of stockholders.

(2)   Nominations of persons for election to the Board of Directors and the proposal of business to be transacted by the stockholders may be made at an annual meeting of stockholders (a) pursuant to the Corporation's notice with respect to such meeting, (b) by or at the direction of the Board of Directors or (c) by any stockholder of record of the Corporation who was a stockholder of record at the time of the giving of the notice provided for in the following paragraph, who is entitled to vote at the meeting and who has complied with the notice procedures set forth in this section.

(3)   For nominations or other business to be properly brought before an annual meeting by a stockholder pursuant to clause (c) of the foregoing paragraph, (1) the stockholder must have given timely notice thereof in writing to the Secretary of the Corporation, (2) such business must be a proper matter for stockholder action under the General Corporation Law of the State of Delaware, (3) if the stockholder, or the beneficial owner on whose behalf any such proposal or nomination is made, has provided the Corporation with a Solicitation Notice, as that term is defined in subclause (c)(iii) of this paragraph, such stockholder or beneficial owner must, in the case of a proposal, have delivered a proxy statement and form of proxy to holders of at least the percentage of the Corporation's voting shares required under applicable law to carry any such proposal, or, in the case of a nomination or nominations, have delivered a proxy statement and form of proxy to holders of a percentage of the Corporation's voting shares reasonably believed by such stockholder or beneficial holder to be sufficient to elect the nominee or nominees proposed to be nominated by such stockholder, and must, in either case, have included in such materials the Solicitation Notice and (4) if no Solicitation Notice relating thereto has been timely provided pursuant to this section, the stockholder or beneficial owner proposing such business or nomination must not have solicited a number of proxies sufficient to have required the delivery of such a Solicitation Notice under this section. To be timely, a stockholder's notice shall be delivered to the Secretary at the principal executive offices of the Corporation not less than 45 or more than 75 days prior to the first anniversary (the "Anniversary") of the date on which the Corporation first mailed its proxy materials for the preceding year's annual meeting of stockholders; provided, however, that if the date of the annual meeting is advanced more than 30 days

prior to or delayed by more than 30 days after the anniversary of the preceding year's annual meeting, notice by the stockholder to be timely must be so delivered not later than the close of business on the later of (i) the 90th day prior to such annual meeting or (ii) the 10th day following the day on which public announcement of the date of such meeting is first made. Such stockholder's notice shall set forth (a) as to each person whom the stockholder proposes to nominate for election or reelection as a director all information relating to such person as would be required to be disclosed in solicitations of proxies for the election of such nominees as directors pursuant to Regulation 14A under the Securities Exchange Act of 1934, as amended (the "Exchange Act"), and such person's written consent to serve as a director if elected; (b) as to any other business that the stockholder proposes to bring before the meeting, a brief description of such business, the reasons for conducting such business at the meeting and any material interest in such business of such stockholder and the beneficial owner, if any, on whose behalf the proposal is made; (c) as to the stockholder giving the notice and the beneficial owner, if any, on whose behalf the nomination or proposal is made (i) the name and address of such stockholder, as they appear on the Corporation's books, and of such beneficial owner, (ii) the class and number of shares of the Corporation that are owned beneficially and of record by such stockholder and such beneficial owner, and (iii) whether either such stockholder or beneficial owner intends to deliver a proxy statement and form of proxy to holders of, in the case of a proposal, at least the percentage of the Corporation's voting shares required under applicable law to carry the proposal or, in the case of a nomination or nominations, a sufficient number of holders of the Corporation's voting shares to elect such nominee or nominees (an affirmative statement of such intent, a "Solicitation Notice").

(4)   Notwithstanding anything in the second sentence of the third paragraph of this Section 1 to the contrary, in the event that the number of directors to be elected to the Board of Directors is increased and there is no public announcement naming all of the nominees for director or specifying the size of the increased Board of Directors made by the Corporation at least 55 days prior to the Anniversary, a stockholder's notice required by this Bylaw shall also be considered timely, but only with respect to nominees for any new positions created by such increase, if it shall be delivered to the Secretary at the principal executive offices of the Corporation not later than the close of business on the 10th day following the day on which such public announcement is first made by the Corporation.

(5)   Only persons nominated in accordance with the procedures set forth in this Section 1 shall be eligible to serve as directors and only such business shall be conducted at an annual meeting of stockholders as shall have been brought before the meeting in accordance with the procedures set forth in this section. The chairman of the meeting shall have the power and the duty to determine whether a nomination or any business proposed to be brought before the meeting has been made in accordance with the procedures set forth in these By-Laws and, if any proposed nomination or business is not in compliance with these By-Laws, to declare that such defectively proposed business or nomination shall not be presented for stockholder action at the meeting and shall be disregarded.

(6)   For purposes of these By-Laws, "public announcement" shall mean disclosure in a press release reported by the Dow Jones News Service, Associated Press or a comparable national news service or in a document publicly filed by the Corporation with the Securities and Exchange Commission pursuant to Section 13, 14 or 15(d) of the Exchange Act.

(7)   Notwithstanding the foregoing provisions of this Section 1, a stockholder shall also comply with all applicable requirements of the Exchange Act and the rules and regulations thereunder with respect to matters set forth in this Section 1. Nothing in this Section 1 shall be deemed to affect any rights of stockholders to request inclusion of proposals in the Corporation's proxy statement pursuant to Rule 14a–8 under the Exchange Act.

Section 2.   Special Meetings.

(1)   Special meetings of the stockholders, other than those required by statute, may be called at any time by the Board of Directors acting pursuant to a resolution adopted by a majority of the Whole Board. For purposes of these By-Laws, the term "Whole Board" shall mean the total number of

authorized directors whether or not there exist any vacancies in previously authorized directorships. The Board of Directors may postpone or reschedule any previously scheduled special meeting.

(2) Only such business shall be conducted at a special meeting of stockholders as shall have been brought before the meeting pursuant to the Corporation's notice of meeting. Nominations of persons for election to the Board of Directors may be made at a special meeting of stockholders at which directors are to be elected pursuant to the Corporation's notice of meeting (a) by or at the direction of the Board of Directors or (b) by any stockholder of record of the Corporation who is a stockholder of record at the time of giving of notice provided for in this paragraph, who shall be entitled to vote at the meeting and who complies with the notice procedures set forth in Section 1 of this Article I. Nominations by stockholders of persons for election to the Board of Directors may be made at such a special meeting of stockholders if the stockholder's notice required by the third paragraph of Section 1 of this Article I shall be delivered to the Secretary at the principal executive offices of the Corporation not later than the close of business on the later of the 90th day prior to such special meeting or the 10th day following the day on which public announcement is first made of the date of the special meeting and of the nominees proposed by the Board of Directors to be elected at such meeting.

(3) Notwithstanding the foregoing provisions of this Section 2, a stockholder shall also comply with all applicable requirements of the Exchange Act and the rules and regulations thereunder with respect to matters set forth in this Section 2. Nothing in this Section 2 shall be deemed to affect any rights of stockholders to request inclusion of proposals in the Corporation's proxy statement pursuant to Rule 14a–8 under the Exchange Act.

Section 3.   Notice of Meetings.

Notice of the place, if any, date, and time of all meetings of the stockholders, and the means of remote communications, if any, by which stockholders and proxyholders may be deemed to be present in person and vote at such meeting, shall be given, not less than ten (10) nor more than sixty (60) days before the date on which the meeting is to be held, to each stockholder entitled to vote at such meeting, except as otherwise provided herein or required by law (meaning, here and hereinafter, as required from time to time by the Delaware General Corporation Law or the Certificate of Incorporation of the Corporation).

When a meeting is adjourned to another time or place, notice need not be given of the adjourned meeting if the time and place, if any, thereof, and the means of remote communications, if any, by which stockholders and proxyholders may be deemed to be present in person and vote at such adjourned meeting are announced at the meeting at which the adjournment is taken; provided, however, that if the date of any adjourned meeting is more than thirty (30) days after the date for which the meeting was originally noticed, or if a new record date is fixed for the adjourned meeting, notice of the place, if any, date, and time of the adjourned meeting and the means of remote communications, if any, by which stockholders and proxyholders may be deemed to be present in person and vote at such adjourned meeting, shall be given in conformity herewith. At any adjourned meeting, any business may be transacted which might have been transacted at the original meeting.

Section 4.   Quorum.

At any meeting of the stockholders, the holders of a majority of all of the shares of the stock entitled to vote at the meeting, present in person or by proxy, shall constitute a quorum for all purposes, unless or except to the extent that the presence of a larger number may be required by law. Where a separate vote by a class or classes or series is required, a majority of the shares of such class or classes or series present in person or represented by proxy shall constitute a quorum entitled to take action with respect to that vote on that matter.

If a quorum shall fail to attend any meeting, the chairman of the meeting may adjourn the meeting to another place, if any, date, or time.

BYLAWS

Section 5. Organization.

Such person as the Board of Directors may have designated or, in the absence of such a person, the Chairman of the Board or, in his or her absence, the President of the Corporation or, in his or her absence, such person as may be chosen by the holders of a majority of the shares entitled to vote who are present, in person or by proxy, shall call to order any meeting of the stockholders and act as chairman of the meeting. In the absence of the Secretary of the Corporation, the secretary of the meeting shall be such person as the chairman of the meeting appoints.

Section 6. Conduct of Business.

The chairman of any meeting of stockholders shall determine the order of business and the procedure at the meeting, including such regulation of the manner of voting and the conduct of discussion as seem to him or her in order. The chairman shall have the power to adjourn the meeting to another place, if any, date and time. The date and time of the opening and closing of the polls for each matter upon which the stockholders will vote at the meeting shall be announced at the meeting.

Section 7. Proxies and Voting.

At any meeting of the stockholders, every stockholder entitled to vote may vote in person or by proxy authorized by an instrument in writing or by a transmission permitted by law filed in accordance with the procedure established for the meeting. Any copy, facsimile telecommunication or other reliable reproduction of the writing or transmission created pursuant to this paragraph may be substituted or used in lieu of the original writing or transmission for any and all purposes for which the original writing or transmission could be used, provided that such copy, facsimile telecommunication or other reproduction shall be a complete reproduction of the entire original writing or transmission.

The Corporation may, and to the extent required by law, shall, in advance of any meeting of stockholders, appoint one or more inspectors to act at the meeting and make a written report thereof. The Corporation may designate one or more alternate inspectors to replace any inspector who fails to act. If no inspector or alternate is able to act at a meeting of stockholders, the person presiding at the meeting may, and to the extent required by law, shall, appoint one or more inspectors to act at the meeting. Each inspector, before entering upon the discharge of his or her duties, shall take and sign an oath faithfully to execute the duties of inspector with strict impartiality and according to the best of his or her ability. Every vote taken by ballots shall be counted by a duly appointed inspector or inspectors.

All elections shall be determined by a plurality of the votes cast, and except as otherwise required by law, all other matters shall be determined by a majority of the votes cast affirmatively or negatively.

Section 8. Stock List.

A complete list of stockholders entitled to vote at any meeting of stockholders, arranged in alphabetical order for each class of stock and showing the address of each such stockholder and the number of shares registered in his or her name, shall be open to the examination of any such stockholder for a period of at least 10 days prior to the meeting in the manner provided by law.

The stock list shall also be open to the examination of any stockholder during the whole time of the meeting as provided by law. This list shall presumptively determine the identity of the stockholders entitled to vote at the meeting and the number of shares held by each of them.

BYLAWS

ARTICLE II—BOARD OF DIRECTORS

Section 1.   Number, Election and Term of Directors.

Subject to the rights of the holders of any series of preferred stock to elect directors under specified circumstances, the number of directors shall be fixed from time to time exclusively by the Board of Directors pursuant to a resolution adopted by a majority of the Whole Board. The directors, other than those who may be elected by the holders of any series of preferred stock under specified circumstances, shall be divided, with respect to the time for which they severally hold office, into three classes with the term of office of the first class to expire at the Corporation's first annual meeting of stockholders, the term of office of the second class to expire at the Corporation's second annual meeting of stockholders and the term of office of the third class to expire at the Corporation's third annual meeting of stockholders, with each director to hold office until his or her successor shall have been duly elected and qualified. At each annual meeting of stockholders, commencing with the first annual meeting, (i) directors elected to succeed those directors whose terms then expire shall be elected for a term of office to expire at the third succeeding annual meeting of stockholders after their election, with each director to hold office until his or her successor shall have been duly elected and qualified, and (ii) if authorized by a resolution of the Board of Directors, directors may be elected to fill any vacancy on the Board of Directors, regardless of how such vacancy shall have been created.

Section 2.   Newly Created Directorships and Vacancies.

Subject to the rights of the holders of any series of preferred stock then outstanding, newly created directorships resulting from any increase in the authorized number of directors or any vacancies in the Board of Directors resulting from death, resignation, retirement, disqualification, removal from office or other cause shall, unless otherwise required by law or by resolution of the Board of Directors, be filled only by a majority vote of the directors then in office, though less than a quorum (and not by stockholders), and directors so chosen shall serve for a term expiring at the annual meeting of stockholders at which the term of office of the class to which they have been elected expires or until such director's successor shall have been duly elected and qualified. No decrease in the number of authorized directors shall shorten the term of any incumbent director.

Section 3.   Regular Meetings.

Regular meetings of the Board of Directors shall be held at such place or places, on such date or dates, and at such time or times as shall have been established by the Board of Directors and publicized among all directors. A notice of each regular meeting shall not be required.

Section 4.   Special Meetings.

Special meetings of the Board of Directors may be called by the Chairman of the Board, the President or by a majority of the Whole Board and shall be held at such place, on such date, and at such time as they or he or she shall fix. Notice of the place, date, and time of each such special meeting shall be given to each director by whom it is not waived by mailing written notice not less than five (5) days before the meeting or by telephone or by telegraphing or telexing or by facsimile or electronic transmission of the same not less than twenty-four (24) hours before the meeting. Unless otherwise indicated in the notice thereof, any and all business may be transacted at a special meeting.

Section 5.   Quorum.

At any meeting of the Board of Directors, a majority of the total number of the Whole Board shall constitute a quorum for all purposes. If a quorum shall fail to attend any meeting, a majority of those present may adjourn the meeting to another place, date, or time, without further notice or waiver thereof.

Section 6.   Participation in Meetings by Conference Telephone.

Members of the Board of Directors, or of any committee thereof, may participate in a meeting of such Board of Directors or committee by means of conference telephone or other communications equipment by means of which all persons participating in the meeting can hear each other and such participation shall constitute presence in person at such meeting.

Section 7.   Conduct of Business.

At any meeting of the Board of Directors, business shall be transacted in such order and manner as the Board of Directors may from time to time determine, and all matters shall be determined by the vote of a majority of the directors present, except as otherwise provided herein or required by law. Action may be taken by the Board of Directors without a meeting if all members thereof consent thereto in writing or by electronic transmission, and the writing or writings or electronic transmission or transmissions are filed with the minutes of proceedings of the Board of Directors. Such filing shall be in paper form if the minutes are maintained in paper form and shall be in electronic form if the minutes are maintained in electronic form.

Section 8.   Compensation of Directors.

Unless otherwise restricted by the certificate of incorporation, the Board of Directors shall have the authority to fix the compensation of the directors. The directors may be paid their expenses, if any, of attendance at each meeting of the Board of Directors and may be paid a fixed sum for attendance at each meeting of the Board of Directors or paid a stated salary or paid other compensation as director. No such payment shall preclude any director from serving the Corporation in any other capacity and receiving compensation therefor. Members of special or standing committees may be allowed compensation for attending committee meetings.

ARTICLE III—COMMITTEES

Section 1.   Committees of the Board of Directors.

The Board of Directors may from time to time designate committees of the Board of Directors, with such lawfully delegable powers and duties as it thereby confers, to serve at the pleasure of the Board of Directors and shall, for those committees and any others provided for herein, elect a director or directors to serve as the member or members, designating, if it desires, other directors as alternate members who may replace any absent or disqualified member at any meeting of the committee. In the absence or disqualification of any member of any committee and any alternate member in his or her place, the member or members of the committee present at the meeting and not disqualified from voting, whether or not he or she or they constitute a quorum, may by unanimous vote appoint another member of the Board of Directors to act at the meeting in the place of the absent or disqualified member.

Section 2.   Conduct of Business.

Each committee may determine the procedural rules for meeting and conducting its business and shall act in accordance therewith, except as otherwise provided herein or required by law. Adequate provision shall be made for notice to members of all meetings; one-third (1/3) of the members shall constitute a quorum unless the committee shall consist of one (1) or two (2) members, in which event one (1) member shall constitute a quorum; and all matters shall be determined by a majority vote of the members present. Action may be taken by any committee without a meeting if all members thereof consent thereto in writing or by electronic transmission, and the writing or writings or electronic transmission or transmissions are filed with the minutes of the proceedings of such committee. Such filing shall be in paper form if the minutes are maintained in paper form and shall be in electronic form if the minutes are maintained in electronic form.

BYLAWS

ARTICLE IV—OFFICERS

Section 1. Generally.

The officers of the Corporation shall consist of a Chairman of the Board, a President, one or more Vice Presidents, a Secretary, a Treasurer and such other officers as may from time to time be appointed by the Board of Directors. Officers shall be elected by the Board of Directors, which shall consider that subject at its first meeting after every annual meeting of stockholders. Each officer shall hold office until his or her successor is elected and qualified or until his or her earlier resignation or removal. Any number of offices may be held by the same person. The salaries of officers elected by the Board of Directors shall be fixed from time to time by the Board of Directors or by such officers as may be designated by resolution of the Board of Directors.

Section 2. Chairman of the Board.

The Chairman of the Board shall be the chief executive officer of the Corporation. Subject to the provisions of these By-laws and to the direction of the Board of Directors, he or she shall have the responsibility for the general management and control of the business and affairs of the Corporation and shall perform all duties and have all powers which are commonly incident to the office of chief executive or which are delegated to him or her by the Board of Directors. He or she shall have power to sign all stock certificates, contracts and other instruments of the Corporation which are authorized and shall have general supervision and direction of all of the other officers, employees and agents of the Corporation.

Section 3. President.

The President shall be the chief operating officer of the Corporation. He or she shall have general responsibility for the management and control of the operations of the Corporation and shall perform all duties and have all powers which are commonly incident to the office of chief operating officer or which are delegated to him or her by the Board of Directors. Subject to the direction of the Board of Directors and the Chairman of the Board, the President shall have power to sign all stock certificates, contracts and other instruments of the Corporation which are authorized and shall have general supervision of all of the other officers (other than the Chairman of the Board or any Vice Chairman), employees and agents of the Corporation.

Section 4. Vice President.

Each Vice President shall have such powers and duties as may be delegated to him or her by the Board of Directors. One (1) Vice President shall be designated by the Board of Directors to perform the duties and exercise the powers of the President in the event of the President's absence or disability.

Section 5. Treasurer.

The Treasurer shall have the responsibility for maintaining the financial records of the Corporation. He or she shall make such disbursements of the funds of the Corporation as are authorized and shall render from time to time an account of all such transactions and of the financial condition of the Corporation. The Treasurer shall also perform such other duties as the Board of Directors may from time to time prescribe.

Section 6. Secretary.

The Secretary shall issue all authorized notices for, and shall keep minutes of, all meetings of the stockholders and the Board of Directors. He or she shall have charge of the corporate books and shall perform such other duties as the Board of Directors may from time to time prescribe.

Section 7.   Delegation of Authority.

The Board of Directors may from time to time delegate the powers or duties of any officer to any other officers or agents, notwithstanding any provision hereof.

Section 8.   Removal.

Any officer of the Corporation may be removed at any time, with or without cause, by the Board of Directors.

Section 9.   Action with Respect to Securities of Other Corporations.

Unless otherwise directed by the Board of Directors, the President or any officer of the Corporation authorized by the President shall have power to vote and otherwise act on behalf of the Corporation, in person or by proxy, at any meeting of stockholders of or with respect to any action of stockholders of any other Corporation in which this Corporation may hold securities and otherwise to exercise any and all rights and powers which this Corporation may possess by reason of its ownership of securities in such other Corporation.

ARTICLE V—STOCK

Section 1.   Certificates of Stock.

Each stockholder shall be entitled to a certificate signed by, or in the name of the Corporation by, the President or a Vice President, and by the Secretary or an Assistant Secretary, or the Treasurer or an Assistant Treasurer, certifying the number of shares owned by him or her. Any or all of the signatures on the certificate may be by facsimile.

Section 2.   Transfers of Stock.

Transfers of stock shall be made only upon the transfer books of the Corporation kept at an office of the Corporation or by transfer agents designated to transfer shares of the stock of the Corporation. Except where a certificate is issued in accordance with Section 4 of Article V of these By-laws, an outstanding certificate for the number of shares involved shall be surrendered for cancellation before a new certificate is issued therefor.

Section 3.   Record Date.

In order that the Corporation may determine the stockholders entitled to notice of or to vote at any meeting of stockholders, or to receive payment of any dividend or other distribution or allotment of any rights or to exercise any rights in respect of any change, conversion or exchange of stock or for the purpose of any other lawful action, the Board of Directors may, except as otherwise required by law, fix a record date, which record date shall not precede the date on which the resolution fixing the record date is adopted and which record date shall not be more than sixty (60) nor less than ten (10) days before the date of any meeting of stockholders, nor more than sixty (60) days prior to the time for such other action as hereinbefore described; provided, however, that if no record date is fixed by the Board of Directors, the record date for determining stockholders entitled to notice of or to vote at a meeting of stockholders shall be at the close of business on the day next preceding the day on which notice is given or, if notice is waived, at the close of business on the day next preceding the day on which the meeting is held, and, for determining stockholders entitled to receive payment of any dividend or other distribution or allotment of rights or to exercise any rights of change, conversion or exchange of stock or for any other purpose, the record date shall be at the close of business on the day on which the Board of Directors adopts a resolution relating thereto.

A determination of stockholders of record entitled to notice of or to vote at a meeting of stockholders shall apply to any adjournment of the meeting; provided, however, that the Board of Directors may fix a new record date for the adjourned meeting.

Section 4.   Lost, Stolen or Destroyed Certificates.

In the event of the loss, theft or destruction of any certificate of stock, another may be issued in its place pursuant to such regulations as the Board of Directors may establish concerning proof of such loss, theft or destruction and concerning the giving of a satisfactory bond or bonds of indemnity.

Section 5.   Regulations.

The issue, transfer, conversion and registration of certificates of stock shall be governed by such other regulations as the Board of Directors may establish.

ARTICLE VI—NOTICES

Section 1.   Notices.

If mailed, notice to stockholders shall be deemed given when deposited in the mail, postage prepaid, directed to the stockholder at such stockholder's address as it appears on the records of the Corporation. Without limiting the manner by which notice otherwise may be given effectively to stockholders, any notice to stockholders may be given by electronic transmission in the manner provided in Section 232 of the Delaware General Corporation Law.

Section 2.   Waivers.

A written waiver of any notice, signed by a stockholder or director, or waiver by electronic transmission by such person, whether given before or after the time of the event for which notice is to be given, shall be deemed equivalent to the notice required to be given to such person. Neither the business nor the purpose of any meeting need be specified in such a waiver. Attendance at any meeting shall constitute waiver of notice except attendance for the sole purpose of objecting to the timeliness of notice.

ARTICLE VII—MISCELLANEOUS

Section 1.   Facsimile Signatures.

In addition to the provisions for use of facsimile signatures elsewhere specifically authorized in these By-laws, facsimile signatures of any officer or officers of the Corporation may be used whenever and as authorized by the Board of Directors or a committee thereof.

Section 2.   Corporate Seal.

The Board of Directors may provide a suitable seal, containing the name of the Corporation, which seal shall be in the charge of the Secretary. If and when so directed by the Board of Directors or a committee thereof, duplicates of the seal may be kept and used by the Treasurer or by an Assistant Secretary or Assistant Treasurer.

Section 3.   Reliance upon Books, Reports and Records.

Each director, each member of any committee designated by the Board of Directors, and each officer of the Corporation shall, in the performance of his or her duties, be fully protected in relying in good faith upon the books of account or other records of the Corporation and upon such information, opinions, reports or statements presented to the Corporation by any of its officers or employees, or committees of the Board of Directors so designated, or by any other person as to matters which such director or committee member reasonably believes are within such other person's professional or expert competence and who has been selected with reasonable care by or on behalf of the Corporation.

Section 4.   Fiscal Year.

The fiscal year of the Corporation shall be as fixed by the Board of Directors.

Section 5.   Time Periods.

In applying any provision of these By-laws which requires that an act be done or not be done a specified number of days prior to an event or that an act be done during a period of a specified number of days prior to an event, calendar days shall be used, the day of the doing of the act shall be excluded, and the day of the event shall be included.

ARTICLE VIII—INDEMNIFICATION OF DIRECTORS AND OFFICERS

Section 1.   Right to Indemnification.

Each person who was or is made a party or is threatened to be made a party to or is otherwise involved in any action, suit or proceeding, whether civil, criminal, administrative or investigative (hereinafter a "proceeding"), by reason of the fact that he or she is or was a director or an officer of the Corporation or is or was serving at the request of the Corporation as a director, officer or trustee of another corporation or of a partnership, joint venture, trust or other enterprise, including service with respect to an employee benefit plan (hereinafter an "indemnitee"), whether the basis of such proceeding is alleged action in an official capacity as a director, officer or trustee or in any other capacity while serving as a director, officer or trustee, shall be indemnified and held harmless by the Corporation to the fullest extent authorized by the Delaware General Corporation Law, as the same exists or may hereafter be amended (but, in the case of any such amendment, only to the extent that such amendment permits the Corporation to provide broader indemnification rights than such law permitted the Corporation to provide prior to such amendment), against all expense, liability and loss (including attorneys' fees, judgments, fines, ERISA excise taxes or penalties and amounts paid in settlement) reasonably incurred or suffered by such indemnitee in connection therewith; provided, however, that, except as provided in Section 3 of this Article VIII with respect to proceedings to enforce rights to indemnification, the Corporation shall indemnify any such indemnitee in connection with a proceeding (or part thereof) initiated by such indemnitee only if such proceeding (or part thereof) was authorized by the Board of Directors of the Corporation.

Section 2.   Right to Advancement of Expenses.

In addition to the right to indemnification conferred in Section 1 of this Article VIII, an indemnitee shall also have the right to be paid by the Corporation the expenses (including attorney's fees) incurred in defending any such proceeding in advance of its final disposition (hereinafter an "advancement of expenses"); provided, however, that, if the Delaware General Corporation Law requires, an advancement of expenses incurred by an indemnitee in his or her capacity as a director or officer (and not in any other capacity in which service was or is rendered by such indemnitee, including, without limitation, service to an employee benefit plan) shall be made only upon delivery to the Corporation of an undertaking (hereinafter an "undertaking"), by or on behalf of such indemnitee, to repay all amounts so advanced if it shall ultimately be determined by final judicial decision from which there is no further right to appeal (hereinafter a "final adjudication") that such indemnitee is not entitled to be indemnified for such expenses under this Section 2 or otherwise.

Section 3.   Right of Indemnitee to Bring Suit.

If a claim under Section 1 or 2 of this Article VIII is not paid in full by the Corporation within sixty (60) days after a written claim has been received by the Corporation, except in the case of a claim for an advancement of expenses, in which case the applicable period shall be twenty (20) days, the indemnitee may at any time thereafter bring suit against the Corporation to recover the unpaid amount of the claim. If successful in whole or in part in any such suit, or in a suit brought by the Corporation to recover an advancement of expenses pursuant to the terms of an undertaking, the indemnitee shall be entitled to be paid also the expense of prosecuting or defending such suit. In (i) any suit brought by the indemnitee to enforce a right to indemnification hereunder (but not in a suit brought by the indemnitee to enforce a right to an advancement of expenses) it shall be a defense that, and (ii) in any suit brought by the Corporation to recover an advancement of expenses pursuant to the terms of an undertaking, the Corporation shall be entitled to recover such expenses upon a final adjudication that, the indemnitee has not met any applicable standard for indemnification set forth in the Delaware General Corporation Law. Neither the failure of the Corporation (including its directors who are not parties to such action, a committee of such directors, independent legal counsel, or its stockholders) to have made a determination prior to the commencement of such suit that indemnification of the indemnitee is proper in the circumstances because the indemnitee has met the applicable standard of conduct set forth in the Delaware General Corporation Law, nor an actual determination by the Corporation (including its directors who are not parties to such action, a committee of such directors, independent legal counsel, or its stockholders) that the indemnitee has not met such applicable standard of conduct, shall create a presumption that the indemnitee has not met the applicable standard of conduct or, in the case of such a suit brought by the indemnitee, be a defense to such suit. In any suit brought by the indemnitee to enforce a right to indemnification or to an advancement of expenses hereunder, or brought by the Corporation to recover an advancement of expenses pursuant to the terms of an undertaking, the burden of proving that the indemnitee is not entitled to be indemnified, or to such advancement of expenses, under this Article VIII or otherwise shall be on the Corporation.

Section 4.   Non-Exclusivity of Rights.

The rights to indemnification and to the advancement of expenses conferred in this Article VIII shall not be exclusive of any other right which any person may have or hereafter acquire under any statute, the Corporation's Certificate of Incorporation, By-laws, agreement, vote of stockholders or directors or otherwise.

Section 5.   Insurance.

The Corporation may maintain insurance, at its expense, to protect itself and any director, officer, employee or agent of the Corporation or another corporation, partnership, joint venture, trust or other enterprise against any expense, liability or loss, whether or not the Corporation would have the power to indemnify such person against such expense, liability or loss under the Delaware General Corporation Law.

Section 6.   Indemnification of Employees and Agents of the Corporation.

The Corporation may, to the extent authorized from time to time by the Board of Directors, grant rights to indemnification and to the advancement of expenses to any employee or agent of the Corporation to the fullest extent of the provisions of this Article with respect to the indemnification and advancement of expenses of directors and officers of the Corporation.

Section 7.   Nature of Rights.

The rights conferred upon indemnitees in this Article VIII shall be contract rights and such rights shall continue as to an indemnitee who has ceased to be a director, officer or trustee and shall inure to the benefit of the indemnitee's heirs, executors and administrators. Any amendment, alteration or repeal of this Article VIII that adversely affects any right of an indemnitee or its successors shall be prospective only and shall not limit or eliminate any such right with respect to any proceeding involving any occurrence or alleged occurrence of any action or omission to act that took place prior to such amendment or repeal.

BYLAWS

ARTICLE IX—AMENDMENTS

In furtherance and not in limitation of the powers conferred by law, the Board of Directors is expressly authorized to adopt, amend and repeal these By-Laws subject to the power of the holders of capital stock of the Corporation to adopt, amend or repeal the By-Laws; provided, however, that, with respect to the power of holders of capital stock to adopt, amend and repeal By-Laws of the Corporation, notwithstanding any other provision of these By-Laws or any provision of law which might otherwise permit a lesser vote or no vote, but in addition to any affirmative vote of the holders of any particular class or series of the capital stock of the Corporation required by law, these By-Laws or any preferred stock, the affirmative vote of the holders of at least _____ percent of the voting power of all of the then-outstanding shares entitled to vote generally in the election of directors, voting together as a single class, shall be required to adopt, amend or repeal any provision of these By-Laws.

2. BAKER & McKENZIE/RICHARDS, LAYTON & FINGER POISON PILL DOCUMENTS

Date:	March ___, 2002
To:	The Board of Directors of XYZ, Inc.
Re:	Stockholder Rights Plan

We have been asked to advise the Board of Directors of XYZ, Inc. (the "Company") in connection with the possible implementation of a stockholder rights plan ("Rights Plan"). We believe the Board of Directors should consider adopting such a plan for the following reasons: First, the Company may be considered an attractive target for an unsolicited takeover proposal. The price of the Company's common stock has declined from a 52-week high of $___ to a recent trading range of $___. The current trading prices do not reflect the prospective impact of certain of the Company's initiatives, such as the implementation of expense controls, the anticipated roll-out of new product lines, and the benefits of increased research and development expenditures. Management anticipates the benefits of the initiatives to drop to the bottom line and eventually lead to increased gross revenues. Second, in light of the declines this year in stock prices, approximately 140 companies adopted stockholder rights plans during the first half of 2001, an increase, according to Thompson Financial Securities Data, of 45% over the same period in 2000. Additionally, investment bankers view such plans as low cost insurance for takeover protections in today's environment of plunging stock prices. A properly designed Rights Plan will assist the Board of Directors in establishing a "level playing field" for negotiations with prospective acquirors. Consequently, we believe that the Board of Directors should consider the adoption of a stockholder rights plan as an important component of its stockholder protection strategy.

An effectively implemented, properly designed Rights Plan gives the Board of Directors a powerful tool to deal with a prospective acquiror to make certain that any proposed transaction is, in the Board's view, in the best interest of the Company and its stockholders. While a Rights Plan will not, and is not intended to, prohibit a person from initiating or completing an acquisition of the Company, it is intended to strengthen the ability of the Board of Directors to fulfill its fiduciary duties to take actions which are in the best interests of stockholders.

In connection with any decision with respect to the Company's adoption of a Rights Plan, we recommend that the Board consider the documents attached hereto. These documents consist of the following:

1. Overview Memorandum;

2. Questions and Answers Regarding the Rights Plan;

3. Summary of the Terms of the Proposed Rights Plan;

4. Summary of Financial Accounting and Tax Consequences;

5. Illustration of Dilution;

6. Form of Letter to Stockholders; and

7. Form of Press Release.

If, after consideration of the materials included with this memorandum, the Board wishes to proceed with the possible implementation of a Rights Plan, we advise the Board to obtain the advice and counsel of its financial advisors regarding, among other things, the current mergers and acquisitions environment and the effect on the price of the Company's common stock as a result of the implementation of a Rights Plan. We would also then provide the Board with a copy of the proposed Rights Plan.

POISON PILL DOCUMENTS

OVERVIEW

We believe it is appropriate for XYZ, Inc. (the "Company") to consider whether to adopt a stockholder rights plan (a "Rights Plan"). An effectively implemented, properly designed Rights Plan gives the Board of Directors a powerful tool to deal with a prospective acquiror to make certain that any proposed transaction is, in the Board's view, in the best interests of the Company and its stockholders. The first Rights Plan was adopted by Crown Zellerbach Corporation in July 1984. Today, more than 2,300 Rights Plans are currently in effect.

A Rights Plan is designed to deter certain types of takeover tactics and to otherwise encourage third parties interested in acquiring a company to negotiate with its Board of Directors. In particular, a Rights Plan is intended to help (i) reduce the risk of coercive two-tiered, front-end loaded or partial offers which may not offer fair value to all stockholders; (ii) mitigate against market accumulators who through open market and/or private purchases may achieve a position of substantial influence or control without paying to selling or remaining stockholders a fair control premium; (iii) deter market accumulators who are simply interested in putting the Company "into play"; and (iv) preserve the Board of Directors' bargaining power and flexibility to deal with third-party acquirors and to otherwise seek to maximize values for all stockholders.

While a Rights Plan will not, and is not intended to, insulate the Company from all takeover attempts, it is intended to strengthen the ability of the Board of Directors to fulfill its fiduciary duties to take actions which are in the best interests of stockholders. Thus, for example, the Rights Plan should help substantially in deterring attempts to take over the Company on terms which are determined by the Board of Directors not to be acceptable. A Rights Plan, however, is not designed to deter a proxy contest or a fair offer for the whole Company. Also, a Rights Plan may have little effect on a bidder which is well financed and prepared to pay a fair price for all shares in cash.

This memorandum discusses legal and financial considerations relating to the adoption of a Rights Plan, and also briefly describes the terms of a Rights Plan which we recommend for consideration. Tab 3 hereto contains a summary of the terms of the plan we would recommend that the Board consider.

DISCUSSION

I.   *General Considerations*

Board adoption. A Rights Plan may be authorized and implemented by Board action without any stockholder vote. Following the adoption of a Rights Plan, a press release would be issued and a letter describing the plan would be sent to stockholders. Copies of proposed forms of press release and letter to stockholders are attached at Tab 7 and Tab 6, respectively.

Modification by Board. As more fully described in the section below entitled "Basic Terms," the Board is given substantial flexibility to amend the Rights Plan. In addition, the rights may be redeemed for nominal consideration prior to their becoming irrevocable.

Reasons for adopting a Rights Plan. Stockholder Rights Plans are basically designed to deter unfair takeover tactics and otherwise to encourage third parties interested in acquiring a company to negotiate with its Board of Directors. In particular, Rights Plans similar to the plan recommended for consideration by the Company are intended to put the Board of Directors in a better position in dealing with the types of activities and tactics described in clauses (i) through (iv) in the second paragraph under "Overview" above.

Standards and procedures. In connection with considering the adoption of a Rights Plan, the Board of Directors should follow certain standards and procedures, including, among others:

1.   The Board should consider the perceived threats to the Company and its stockholders of coercive or unfair offers and accumulation programs;

2. The Rights Plan should be tailored so that it is reasonable in relation to the threats posed. Rights Plans should not be designed to bar an offer which the Board deems beneficial to stockholders;

3. The Board should receive advice from its legal and financial advisors concerning the current takeover environment, particularly circumstances peculiar to the Company and its industry, the financial and market impact of adoption of a Rights Plan, and the legality of the plan under applicable Delaware law;

4. The Board should be provided with and review the documents constituting the particular Rights Plan under consideration and a reasonable summary (as included herein) thereof;

5. The Board's legal and financial advisors should discuss with the Board the plan's terms, purposes and effects, and the factors relevant to its adoption. The Board's independent directors should be actively involved; and

6. Sufficient time for full review and informed decision-making should be taken.

Financial and tax effects. The adoption of a Rights Plan should have no impact on earnings per share and should not otherwise affect the financial statements of the Company until the rights trade separately and are "in the money."

The distribution of rights pursuant to a Rights Plan should not be taxable to the Company or to stockholders. However, stockholders may, depending upon the circumstances, recognize taxable income in the event that the rights become exercisable for common stock (or other consideration) of the Company or for common stock of the acquiring company. The Company's redemption of the rights also will be a taxable event to stockholders. A memorandum describing certain financial accounting and tax consequences of the adoption of a Rights Plan is included under Tab 4.

II. *Basic Terms*

The following is a general description of the stockholder Rights Plan which we recommend for consideration by the Company's Board. However, the terms of this Rights Plan can be varied to address any specific concerns that the Company or its Board may have. Set forth under "Common Variations" below are summaries of certain common provisions that other companies have included in their Rights Plans.

To implement the Rights Plan, the Board of Directors would authorize a dividend to all holders of the Company's common stock of one "right" for each share of common stock outstanding (the "Common Stock"). Each right would initially entitle its registered holder to purchase from the Company a fraction of a share of a new series of preferred stock of the Company (which is intended to be essentially the economic equivalent of the Common Stock), at an initial price intended to reflect the long-term trading value of a share of Common Stock over the term of the plan (the "Purchase Price"). Premiums over current market used by other companies have generally been in the 300–500% range, but the Purchase Price selected for the Company should be specifically determined based on advice from the Company's financial advisors.

Until a person acquires beneficial ownership of 15% or more of the outstanding Common Stock (thereby becoming an "Acquiring Person") or commences a tender offer that would result in his owning 15% or more of the outstanding Common Stock, the rights (i) are evidenced by the Common Stock certificates, (ii) may be transferred with and only with the Common Stock and (iii) are not exercisable. Upon the occurrence of any such events the rights become exercisable and separate certificates are distributed to the holders of record of the Common Stock; thereafter, the Common Stock and the rights trade separately.

The rights expire after a period of time from the date of issuance, unless earlier redeemed by the Company (as described below). We recommend 10 years as the term of the rights. The Board of Directors of the Company generally may redeem the rights at a nominal price (*i.e.*, $0.001 per right) until someone becomes an Acquiring Person.

POISON PILL DOCUMENTS

If any person becomes an Acquiring Person, each holder of a right (other than the Acquiring Person and its affiliates and associates) thereafter has the right to receive, upon exercise of the right at the Purchase Price, Common Stock (or, under certain circumstances, a combination of cash, Common Stock, other securities or other assets) having a value of two times such Purchase Price.

If anyone becomes an Acquiring Person and the Company then (i) engages in a merger or other business combination transaction with another person in which the Common Stock are changed or exchanged, or (ii) sells or transfers 50% or more of its assets or earning power to another person or persons, each right (other than rights of the Acquiring Person and its affiliates and associates, which will have become void) thereafter entitles the holder of such right to receive, upon exercise of the right at the Purchase Price, Common Stock of such other person (or, in certain circumstances, of an affiliate of such other person) having a value of two times such Purchase Price.

At any time after any person becomes an Acquiring Person and prior to the earlier of one of the events described in clause (i) or (ii) in the previous paragraph or the acquisition by any person of 50% or more of the outstanding Common Stock, the Board of Directors may exchange the rights (other than rights held by the Acquiring Person and its affiliates or associates, which will have become void), in whole or in part, for Common Stock (or fractional shares of preferred stock having essentially equivalent rights, preferences and privileges) having a value per right equal to the difference between the value of the Common Stock receivable upon exercise of the right and the Purchase Price.

Until a right is exercised, holders have no stockholder rights (such as voting rights or rights to receive dividends). The terms of the rights, other than the redemption price, may be amended by the Board of Directors in any manner as long as the rights are redeemable. Thereafter, the terms of the rights may be amended in any manner, as long as the amendment does not adversely affect the interests of holders of rights.

III. *Common Variations*

Although most modern Rights Plans contain the provisions described under "Basic Terms" above, a number of variations have developed. Set forth below is a general discussion of two of the most common variations.

Many Rights Plans contain provisions that provide that a person does not become an "Acquiring Person" by acquiring beneficial ownership of 15% or more of the outstanding Common Stock if such person acquires such stock pursuant to a "Permitted Offer." Permitted Offer is often defined to mean a tender or exchange offer for all outstanding Common Stock at a price and on terms determined by the Board to be fair to stockholders and otherwise in the best interest of the Company and its stockholders. Sometimes, "Permitted Offer" is even more broadly defined to include the acquisition of shares pursuant to any transaction approved by the Board of Directors. Although these provisions may appear sensible, they are unnecessary in most modern Rights Plans for two reasons. First, many Rights Plans, including the one we recommend, provide that the Board of Directors can amend the Rights Plan in any respect, other than to change the redemption price, at any time prior to the time an Acquiring Person becomes such. Second, since the redemption price of the rights is generally a nominal amount (*i.e.*, $.001 per right), the Board can redeem the rights if and when it believes an acquisition transaction is in the best interests of the Company and its stockholders.

Some Rights Plans also have a so-called "back-door" redemption clause, which allows the Board to redeem the rights after an Acquiring Person has become such. The advocates of this provision believe that it gives the Board more room to negotiate with a hostile acquiror. On the other hand, the inclusion of such a provision creates an incentive for an aggressive acquiror to cross the triggering threshold, thereby forcing the Board, and not the acquiror, to make the final decision on whether or not the rights will dilute the acquiror. For this reason, our recommended Rights Plan does not include such a "back-door" redemption clause.

POISON PILL DOCUMENTS

CONCLUSION

In summary, a Rights Plan is a flexible vehicle by which a company, by considering a variety of different structures, options and variations and by tailoring the plan to address the Company's individual needs and objectives, can provide significant protection to its stockholders. We recommend that XYZ, Inc. consider the adoption of a Rights Plan as an important component of its stockholder protection strategy.

QUESTIONS AND ANSWERS ABOUT STOCKHOLDER RIGHTS PLANS

1. *What is the purpose of a Stockholder Rights Plan?*

A stockholder rights plan ("Rights Plan") is designed to deter certain types of takeover tactics and to otherwise encourage third parties interested in acquiring the Company to negotiate with its Board of Directors. In particular, a Rights Plan is intended to help (i) reduce the risk of coercive two-tiered, front-end loaded or partial offers which may not offer fair value to all stockholders; (ii) mitigate against market accumulators who through open market and/or private purchases may achieve a position of substantial influence or control without paying to selling or remaining stockholders a fair control premium; (iii) deter market accumulators who are simply interested in putting the Company "into play"; and (iv) preserve the Board of Directors' bargaining power and flexibility to deal with third-party acquirors and to otherwise seek to maximize values for all stockholders.

While a Rights Plan will not, and is not intended, to insulate the Company from all takeovers, it is intended to strengthen the ability of the Board of Directors to fulfill its fiduciary duties to take actions which are in the best interests of stockholders. Thus, for example, the Rights Plan should help substantially in deterring attempts to take over the Company on terms which are determined by the Board of Directors not to be acceptable. A Rights Plan, however, is not designed to deter a proxy contest or a fair offer for the whole Company. Also, a Rights Plan may have little effect on a bidder which is well financed and prepared to pay a fair price for all shares in cash.

A Rights Plan is intended to achieve these goals by confronting a potential acquiror of the Company's common stock (the "Common Stock") with the possibility that the Company's stockholders will be able to dilute substantially the acquiror's equity interest by exercising "Rights" (which are issued under the Rights Plan) to buy additional stock in the Company—*or in certain cases, stock of the acquiror*—at a substantial discount.

2. *How many companies have Rights Plans?*

Since the first Rights Plan was adopted by Crown Zellerbach Corporation in July 1984, such plans have become commonplace in Delaware. Today, more than 2,300 Rights Plans are currently in effect. Many Fortune 500 companies have adopted Rights Plans. In addition, there is not a single state that does not permit their adoption.

3. *Why have so many companies considered the adoption of Rights Plans?*

In November 1985, the Delaware Supreme Court upheld a Rights Plan adopted by Household International as a legitimate action taken by a Board of Directors to protect its stockholders from coercive takeover tactics. In addition, a number of courts and state legislatures have recognized the potential benefits that a Rights Plan offers to assist a board of directors in protecting the best interests of all stockholders.

4. *How does the Board of Directors go about implementing a Rights Plan?*

If the Board of Directors, after fully considering a Rights Plan with the advice and the assistance of its legal and financial advisors, determines that the Rights Plan is in the best interests of the Company and its stockholders, the Board would declare a dividend distribution of one Right for each outstanding share of the Company's Common Stock. Each Right initially would be attached to each share of Common Stock and would entitle the holder of such Right to purchase 1/1000th of a share of a new series of preferred stock at a price which is designed to reflect the projected long-term value of the Company's Common Stock over the term of the Plan (*e.g.*, typically 3 to 5 times the current market price of the Common Stock when the Rights Plan is adopted). One one-thousandth of a share of preferred stock is intended to be the economic equivalent of one share of Common Stock. However, upon the occurrence of a "Flip-in" or "Flip-over" Event (described below), each Right would become the right to purchase Common Stock of the Company or, in certain circumstances, the acquiring person, at a substantial discount.

5. *Why are shares of preferred stock rather than Common Stock used in the Rights Plan?*

Although the dividend, liquidation, voting and other rights of the preferred stock are designed so that each 1/1000th of a share of preferred stock would have rights similar to one share of Common Stock, preferred stock is used so that the Company's authorized Common Stock could be used for other purposes and would not have to be reserved for issuance upon exercise of the Rights. In addition, since each full share of preferred stock is sufficient to cover the exercise of 1000 Rights, many fewer shares of preferred stock would have to be reserved.

6. *Will the adoption of a Rights Plan affect earnings per share or be a taxable event?*

Since the purchase price under the Rights greatly exceeds the market price of the Common Stock, the adoption of the Rights Plan should not be dilutive and should not affect reported earnings per share. In addition, the distribution of the Rights should not be a taxable event for either the Company or the stockholders receiving the Rights.

7. *When do the Rights first become exercisable?*

At the time the Rights Plan is adopted, the Rights are neither exercisable nor traded separately from the Common Stock. In fact, at the time of adoption of the Rights Plan, the Common Stock certificates represent both the outstanding Common Stock and the outstanding Rights.

The Rights will detach from the Common Stock (that is, Rights Certificates will be distributed and will trade separately) and become exercisable shortly after (i) any person or group acquires beneficial ownership of 15% or more of the outstanding Common Stock or (ii) any person or group commences a tender or exchange offer which would result in that person or group beneficially owning 15% or more of the outstanding Common Stock. The date on which the Rights detach is referred to as the Distribution Date.

8. *Is it likely that many Rights would be exercised following the Distribution Date?*

Until such time as the market price of the Common Stock rises above the exercise price of the Rights, it is highly unlikely that any holder of Rights would exercise such Rights. However, if a "Flip-in Event" or a "Flip-over Event" (described below) were to occur, the Rights would become valuable and entitle the holder to purchase Common Stock of the Company or common stock of the acquiror, as the case may be, at a substantial discount.

9. *What are the "Flip-in" or "Flip-over" events and what rights are created by the occurrence of such events?*

Flip-in Events   –   A Flip-in Event would be deemed to have occurred if any person becomes the beneficial owner of more than a specified percentage of the outstanding Common Stock (*i.e.*, 15%).

Upon the occurrence of a Flip-in Event, each holder of a Right, other than Rights held by an Acquiring Person, will thereafter be entitled to purchase Common Stock of the Company (or in certain circumstances cash, property or other securities of the Company) with a value at the time of such Flip-in Event of two times the then exercise price of the Rights. Since an Acquiring Person will not be entitled to exercise its Rights following the occurrence of a Flip-in Event, its equity interest in the Company would be substantially diluted.

Flip-over Events   –   A Flip-over Event will be deemed to have occurred if following the acquisition of 15% or more of the Common Stock by any person:

(i)   the Company is acquired in a merger or other business combination;

(ii)   the Company is the continuing or surviving corporation in a merger in which all or part of the Common Stock is exchanged for stock, cash or other property; or

(iii)   50% or more of the Company's assets or earning power is sold or otherwise transferred in one transaction or a series of related transactions.

The Flip-over Events are designed to avoid circumvention of the Flip-in rights and to make any second-step transaction economically prohibitive and thereby deter two-tiered or partial offers. Upon the occurrence of a Flip-over Event, each Right would entitle its holder to purchase common stock of the acquiring person with a value of twice the then exercise price of the Rights.

10.   *When do the Rights expire?*

Unless redeemed or exchanged earlier by the Company, the Rights would expire ten years from the date of issuance. The ten year period has been selected by most companies to provide a meaningful period of protection.

11.   *May the Board of Directors redeem the Rights and at what price?*

In general, the Board of Directors may redeem the Rights at any time prior to the time some person or group acquires beneficial ownership of, or announces its intention to commence, or commences, a tender or exchange offer with respect to, 15% or more of the outstanding Common Stock. The redemption price is $0.001 per Right.

In addition to the stated period for redemption, at any time prior to the date on which the Rights would otherwise become nonredeemable, the Board of Directors may amend the Rights Plan to extend the period for redemption.

12.   *Under what circumstances might the Board of Directors wish to redeem the Rights?*

As described earlier, the Rights Plan is intended to enable the Board of Directors to respond to unsolicited acquisition proposals in a manner which is in the best interests of the Company and its stockholders. Accordingly, if there is a proposed takeover which the Board deems advantageous, the Board would be in a position to redeem the outstanding Rights at a nominal consideration. In addition, it is always possible that the circumstances relating to a particular unsolicited takeover and/or future developments in the takeover area, including future judicial decisions, might suggest at some future time that a Board of Directors consider the desirability of redeeming the outstanding Rights.

13.   *Will the Board of Directors be able to amend the provisions of the Rights once the Rights Plan has been adopted?*

The Rights Plan provides the Board with significant flexibility to amend the terms of the Rights Plan. For so long as the Rights are redeemable, the Board may, without the approval of any holder of Rights, supplement or amend any provision of the Rights Plan other than to change the redemption price. At any time when the rights are not redeemable, the Board may amend the Rights Plan in any manner that does not adversely affect the holders of Rights.

14.   *May additional Rights be issued after the date the Rights Plan is adopted, including in connection with Common Stock issuances upon the exercise of stock options and convertible security conversions?*

Prior to the Distribution Date, all Common Stock issued by the Company would have Rights attached.

After the Distribution Date, in general, the Company would issue Rights in connection with the Common Stock issued upon the exercise of stock options or under any employee plan or arrangement, or upon the exercise, conversion or exchange of securities issued by the Company prior to the Distribution Date.

POISON PILL DOCUMENTS

15. *Where will the Rights be traded?*

Since the Rights prior to the Distribution Date are deemed to be represented by the Common Stock certificates, the Rights will initially be listed and traded on the same exchanges on which the Common Stock are listed and traded. However, prior to the Distribution Date, there will be no separate trading market for the Rights.

16. *What will happen if the Company does not have sufficient Common Stock to issue following the occurrence of either a "Flip-in" or a "Flip-over" event?*

The Rights Plan provides that, following a "Flip-in" event, the Company would be required to reduce the purchase price or to substitute, if necessary, cash, preferred stock, debt securities or other property with a value equal to the Common Stock which would otherwise be issuable.

This should not be a problem following a "Flip-over" event since, under the terms of the Rights Plan, the Company may not engage in a transaction (*e.g.*, a merger) constituting a "Flip-over" event unless the acquiring person has sufficient common stock authorized to permit the full exercise of the Rights.

17. *What impact would the adoption of the Rights Plan have on the Business Judgment Rule and future actions of the Board under the Plan?*

Following the adoption of the Rights Plan, the Board of Directors would of course continue to be required to exercise its duties with due care and loyalty and would continue to act as fiduciaries for the Company's stockholders. In this regard, it should be noted that future decisions with respect to a redemption of the Rights, like all other decisions in the takeover area, may prove difficult. In addition, although the business judgment rule should apply to all future decisions (including redemption) it is possible that a court in reviewing all the facts and circumstances (including the existence of a Rights Plan) may subject a Board's decision to greater scrutiny.

18. *Are there any disadvantages to adopting a Rights Plan?*

The primary disadvantage would be that, if and when the Rights became nonredeemable, the Company would lose flexibility in engaging in transactions qualifying as "Flip-over" events. Even though this is a disadvantage, it is necessary to achieve the deterrent effect of the Rights Plan. In addition, a number of institutional investors have submitted stockholder proposals requesting that the Rights Plans be redeemed or submitted to a stockholder vote.

19. *Why do some stockholders oppose Rights Plans?*

Opponents of Rights Plans have asserted that the effect of a Rights Plan is to usurp the right of stockholders to consider third party offers for their shares. Opponents also assert that the primary motivation in adopting Rights Plans is entrenchment of management.

SUMMARY OF THE TERMS OF THE PROPOSED RIGHTS PLAN

20. *Effectiveness.* The Rights Plan shall be effective as of the date of the Rights Agreement for all shares of the Company's common stock (the "Common Stock") outstanding on the established Record Date and for all Common Stock issued prior to the earliest of the Distribution Date (as defined below), the redemption of the Rights, the exchange of the Rights or the expiration of the Rights. In addition, in certain limited circumstances, Rights may be issued with respect to shares of Common Stock issued after the Distribution Date.

21. *Right Certificates.* Right Certificates shall be distributed to stockholders as soon as practicable after the Distribution Date. Until the Distribution Date, Rights shall be evidenced by certificates for Common Stock.

22. *Term.* The rights will expire on the tenth anniversary of the date of the Rights Agreement unless earlier redeemed or exchanged by the Company as provided below.

POISON PILL DOCUMENTS

23. *Exercisability*. Initially, the Rights will not be exercisable. The Rights shall become exercisable upon the earlier of (i) the tenth calendar day after the first public announcement that a person or group (other than the Company, any of its subsidiaries or any employee stock plan of the Company), together with its affiliates and associates, has acquired, or obtained the right to acquire, beneficial ownership of 15% or more of the outstanding Common Stock (such person or group being called an "Acquiring Person"), or (ii) the tenth business day after the commencement of, or first public announcement of an intention to commence, a tender or exchange offer which would result in a person or group obtaining beneficial ownership of 15% or more of the outstanding Common Stock (the earlier of such dates being called the "Distribution Date"). The timing of the Distribution Date is in some cases subject to extension by the Board of Directors. After the Distribution Date, the Rights shall be exercisable by the registered holders of the Right Certificates. Each Right shall be exercisable for 1/1000th of a share of Series A Junior Participating Preferred Stock (the "Series A Preferred Stock") (as described below), subject to adjustment. The exercise price with respect to each Right shall be $___, subject to adjustment.

24. *Detachability*. Prior to the Distribution Date, the Rights shall be transferable only with the related Common Stock certificates and shall automatically be transferred with such certificates. After the Distribution Date, the Rights shall be separately transferable, and the Company will provide Right Certificates to all holders of Common Stock.

25. *Terms of Series A Preferred Stock*. The terms of the Series A Preferred Stock have been designed so that each 1/1000th of a share of Series A Preferred Stock will have economic attributes (*i.e.*, participation in dividends and liquidation and voting rights) substantially equivalent to one whole share of the Common Stock of the Company. In addition, the Series A Preferred Stock have certain minimum dividend and liquidation preferences. See Exhibit A for a more detailed description of the Series A Preferred Stock.

26. *The Flip-In Provision*. In the event that a person becomes an Acquiring Person (a "Flip-In Event"), the holder of each Right (other than the Acquiring Person, its affiliates and associates and certain transferees thereof) will thereafter have the right to receive, upon exercise thereof, for the exercise price, in lieu of shares of Series A Preferred Stock, that number of Common Stock which at the time of such transaction would have a market value of twice the exercise price. The Company may at its option substitute 1/1000ths of a share of Series A Preferred Stock for some or all of the Common Stock so issuable. In the event there is insufficient Common Stock to permit exercise in full of Rights, the Company must issue shares of Series A Preferred Stock, cash, property or other securities of the Company with an aggregate value equal to twice the exercise price. Upon the occurrence of any such Flip-In Event, any Rights that are owned by an Acquiring Person, its affiliates and certain transferees thereof shall become null and void.

27. *The Flip-Over Provision*. In the event that, from and after a Flip-In Event, (a) the Company is acquired in a merger or other business combination, (b) the Company is the continuing or surviving corporation in a merger in which all or part of the Company's Common Stock is exchanged for stock, cash or other property, or (c) 50% or more of the Company's assets, or assets accounting for 50% or more of its net income, are sold, leased, exchanged or otherwise transferred (in one or more transactions), proper provision shall be made so that each holder of a Right (other than the Acquiring Person, its affiliates and associates and certain transferees thereof whose Rights became void) shall thereafter have the right to receive, upon the exercise thereof, for the exercise price, that number of shares of common stock of the acquiring company which at the time of such transaction would have a market value of twice the exercise price.

28. *Redemption*. The Rights are redeemable by the Board of Directors at a redemption price of $.001 per Right (the "Redemption Price") any time prior to the earlier of (i) the time that an Acquiring Person becomes such, or (ii) the expiration date. Immediately upon the action of the Board electing to redeem the Rights, and without any further action and without any notice, the right to exercise the Rights will terminate and the only right of the holders of Rights will be to receive the Redemption Price.

29. *Exchange.* At any time after a Flip-In Event, but prior to a Flip-Over Event or the time that any person becomes the beneficial owner of 50% or more of the outstanding Common Stock, the Board may exchange each Right for a number of shares of Common Stock (or fractional shares of Series A Preferred Stock or similar securities) having a value equal to the difference between the market value of the shares of Common Stock receivable upon exercise of the Right and the exercise price of the Right.

30. *Amendment.* For so long as the Rights are redeemable, the Company may, without the approval of any holder of the Rights, supplement or amend any provision of the Rights Agreement. At any time when the Rights are not redeemable, the Company may amend the Rights in any manner that does not adversely affect the holders of Rights. In no event may any supplement or amendment be made which changes the Redemption Price.

31. *Voting.* The holder of a Right, as such, will have no rights as a stockholder of the Company, including, without limitation, the right to vote or to receive dividends.

EXHIBIT A

DESCRIPTION OF SERIES A JUNIOR PARTICIPATING
PREFERRED STOCK

32. *Designation, Par Value, and Ranking.* The Company will be authorized to issue shares of Series A Junior Participating Preferred Stock, par value $.001 per share ("Series A Preferred Stock"). The Series A Preferred Stock has the following features.

33. *Dividends.* The holders of Series A Preferred Stock are entitled to receive quarterly cumulative dividends in an amount per share equal to the greater of $10.00 or 1000 times the dividends declared on the Common Stock since the preceding quarterly dividend payment date, or with respect to the first quarterly dividend payment date, since the date of issuance. Noncash dividends are payable in kind in a per share amount equal to 1000 times any noncash dividends paid per share of Common Stock.

34. *Voting Rights.* Holders of Series A Preferred Stock are entitled to vote on each matter on which holders of Common Stock are entitled to vote, and shall have 1000 votes per share.

35. *Certain Restrictions.* Whenever quarterly dividends or distributions on the Series A Preferred Stock are in arrears, the Company's right to declare or pay dividends or other distributions on or to redeem or purchase any shares of stock ranking junior to or on a parity with the Series A Preferred Stock is subject to certain restrictions.

36. *Liquidation Rights.* Upon any liquidation, dissolution or winding up of the Corporation, whether voluntary or involuntary, the holders of shares of Series A Preferred Stock will be entitled to receive, before any distribution is made to holders of shares of Common Stock or any other stock ranking junior to the Series A Preferred Stock, a minimum of $1000 per share, plus an amount equal to any accrued dividends and distribution thereon whether or not declared, to the date of payment, and will be entitled to an aggregate payment of 1000 times the amount per share distributed to the holders of Common Stock.

37. *Redemption.* The shares of Series A Preferred Stock are not subject to redemption by the Company.

38. *Amalgamation, Merger, etc.* In the event of an amalgamation, merger or similar transaction in which the Common Stock are exchanged for or converted into other securities, cash or any other property, the shares of Series A Preferred Stock will be similarly exchanged or converted in an amount per share equal to 1000 times the amount per share of securities, cash or other property into which each share of Common Stock is changed or converted.

39. *Adjustment of Participation Rights.* In the event that, after the date of the Rights Agreement, a dividend in Common Stock is paid on the Common Stock, or the Common Stock is

subdivided or combined, then the rights of the Series A Preferred Stock with respect to voting and participation in dividends, liquidation and merger consideration will automatically be adjusted proportionately.

40. *Rank.* The Series A Preferred Stock will rank senior to the Common Stock and, unless otherwise provided, junior to all future series of preferred stock.

FINANCIAL ACCOUNTING AND TAX CONSEQUENCES

Financial Accounting Consequences:

- No income statement impact unless and until the Rights become exercisable and are "in the money."

- Adoption of a Plan should have no balance sheet impact.

- Pooling considerations should no longer be relevant in light of the approval in June 2001 by the Financial Accounting Standards Board ("FASB") of its statements mandating the use of the purchase method of accounting for all business combinations commenced after June 30, 2001.

- The price paid to redeem Rights will be a charge to equity.

- Exercise of Rights and exchange of Rights for Common Stock will be treated as a capital transaction.

Tax Considerations:

- Distribution of Rights should not result in taxable income to the distributee or to the Company.

- When the Rights subsequently separate but are still "out of the money," there still should not be any taxable income to the distributee or the Company.

- If and when the Rights "flip-in" to the Company's Common Stock, it is again likely that there will not be any taxable event to the holder or the Company (although there is some possibility of taxability to holders of Rights if the "flip-in" can be linked to dividends received by the holders of the Company's Common Stock within three years of either side of the "flip-in" event). In addition, the "flip-in" could be taxable to holders of Rights if the Company has outstanding convertible securities with anti-dilution provisions which do not completely adjust for the "flip-in" of the Rights. In either case, the IRS could argue that the "flip-in" constitutes a taxable dividend to holders of Rights under the stock dividend rules of § 305 of the I.R.C. It also is possible that the "flip-in" event may be construed as a taxable exchange of a warrant to buy preferred stock (if the Rights were initially exercisable for preferred stock) for a warrant to buy Common Stock.

- If the Rights "flip-over" and become exercisable for Common Stock of the Acquiror, the holder would recognize a taxable gain (capital gain if the Right and the underlying stock are held as capital assets) equal to the difference between the holder's basis in the Right and the fair market value of the "new" Right.

- If the Company redeems the Rights prior to the time the Rights separate from the Company's Common Stock, the payment of the redemption price to Stockholders will in all likelihood be dividend income. If the Company redeems the Rights after the time the Rights separate from the Common Stock, it is not entirely clear whether the payment of the redemption price to holders of Rights will be taxable to holders of Rights as capital gain or ordinary income but, in any event, should not be dividend income.

- The Internal Revenue Service has ruled privately that Rights do not constitute "other property" or "boot" for purposes of the reorganization provisions of the Internal Revenue Code. Thus, the fact that Rights are to be issued with the Company's Common Stock as part of an acquisition by the Company should not restrict the Company's ability to consummate those forms of tax-free reorganizations that do not permit boot.

POISON PILL DOCUMENTS

ILLUSTRATION OF DILUTION

The following hypothetical example illustrates the "economic hurt" or "poison" inherent in the Rights Plan.

Assume the Company has 1,000 shares outstanding and a person purchases 15% or more of the outstanding shares, thereby becoming an "Acquiring Person" and triggering the "flip-in." Assume further the market price of the Company's Common Stock is $1 per share and the exercise price of the Rights is $4 per share.

Dilution in Voting. If all stockholders other than the Acquiring Person (whose Rights become void if there is a "flip-in") exercised their Rights, the Acquiring Person's voting power would be diluted down from 15% (*i.e.*, 150 shares owned out of 1,000 shares outstanding) to 1.92% (*i.e.*, 150 shares owned out of 7,800 shares outstanding).

The 7,800 shares outstanding assumes that stockholders exercise all their rights by paying $4 in cash for each Right. Such an exercise of Rights would, after the "flip-in", entitle all stockholders (other than an Acquiring Person) to purchase 8 shares of stock for each Right. That is, they are entitled to use the $4 exercise price to purchase shares equal to $8 in value. This would result in the issuance of 6,800 additional shares (850 Rights times 8 shares per Right). Since there were already 1,000 shares outstanding the new total outstanding becomes 7,800 shares.

Economic Dilution. In the same example described above, the economic dilution for the Acquiring Person is quite substantial (assuming the Acquiring Person's stock was worth $1 per share—*i.e.*, the market value immediately before the "flip-in" occurs), the Acquiring Person's shares fall in value by approximately 43.6% (from $1 per share to $0.564 per share).

This results from the following hypothetical analysis. Assume that the aggregate market value of the Company was $1,000 immediately before the "flip-in" (*i.e.*, 1,000 shares at $1 per share). The issuance of 6,800 additional shares upon exercise of the 850 Rights held by all stockholders other than the Acquiring Person added $3,400 in cash to the value of the Company (*i.e.*, 850 Rights times $4 per Right). This would increase the total value of the Company to $4,400, which results in a hypothetical value of $0.564 for each of the 7,800 outstanding shares.

FORM OF LETTER TO STOCKHOLDERS

——— ———, 2002

Dear XYZ, Inc. Stockholder:

The Board of Directors has announced the adoption of a Stockholder Rights Plan. This letter describes the Plan and explains our reasons for adopting it. Also, we are enclosing a document entitled "Summary of Rights to Purchase Common Stock Shares of XYZ, Inc." which provides more detailed information about the Rights Plan, and we urge you to read it carefully.

The Plan is intended to protect your interests in the event XYZ, Inc. ("Company") is confronted with an unsolicited takeover attempt or certain types of unfair takeover tactics. Specifically, the Plan contains provisions designed to deter a gradual accumulation of shares in the open market, a partial or two-tiered tender offer that does not treat all stockholders equally, the acquisition in the open market or otherwise of shares constituting control without offering fair value to all stockholders, or other abusive takeover tactics which the Board believes are not in the best interests of the Company's stockholders. These tactics unfairly pressure stockholders, squeeze them out of their investment without giving them any real choice, and deprive them of the full value of their shares.

A large number of other companies have Rights Plans similar to the one we have adopted. We consider the Rights Plan to be the best available means of protecting your right to retain your equity investment in Company and the full value of that investment, while not foreclosing a fair acquisition bid for the Company.

POISON PILL DOCUMENTS

The Plan is not intended to prevent a takeover of the Company and will not do so. The mere declaration of the rights dividend should not affect any prospective offeror willing to make an all cash offer at a full and fair price or willing to negotiate with the Board of Directors, and will not interfere with a merger or other business combination transaction approved by your Board of Directors.

Prior to adopting the Rights Plan, the Board of Directors was concerned that a person or company could acquire control of the Company without paying a fair premium for control and without offering a fair price to all stockholders, and that, if a competitor acquired control of the Company, the competitor would have a conflict of interest with respect to the Company and could use any acquired influence over or control of the Company to the detriment of the other stockholders of the Company. The Board believes that such results would not be in the best interests of all stockholders.

The Rights may be redeemed by the Company at $0.001 per Right up to the time any person or group has acquired 15% or more of the Company's shares, and thus they should not interfere with any merger or other business combination approved by the Board of Directors.

Issuance of the Rights does not in any way weaken the financial strength of the Company or interfere with its business plan. The issuance of the Rights has no dilutive effect, will not affect reported earnings per share, is not taxable to the Company or to you, and will not change the way in which you can currently trade the Company's shares. As explained in detail below, the Rights will only be exercisable if and when an event occurs which triggers their effectiveness. They will then operate to protect you against being deprived of your right to share in the full measure of the Company's long-term potential.

The Board was aware when it acted that some people have advanced arguments that securities of the type we are issuing deter legitimate acquisition proposals. We carefully considered these views and concluded that the arguments are speculative and do not justify leaving stockholders without this protection against unfair treatment by an acquiror—who, after all, is seeking his own company's advantage, not yours. The Board believes that the Rights represent a sound and reasonable means of addressing the complex issues of corporate policy created by the current takeover environment.

The Rights will be issued to stockholders of record on _____ ___, 2002, and will expire in ten years. Initially, the Rights will not be exercisable, certificates will not be sent to you, and the Rights will automatically trade with the Common Stock. However, ten days after a person or group either acquires 15% or more of the Company's Common Stock or commences a tender or exchange offer that would result in such person or group owning 15% or more of the outstanding shares (even if no purchases actually occur), the Rights will become exercisable and separate certificates representing the Rights will be distributed. We expect that the Rights will begin to trade independently from the Common Stock at that time. At no time will the Rights have any voting power.

Each Right initially will entitle the holder thereof to buy from the Company one unit of a share of preferred stock for $_____. If, however, any person acquires 15% or more of the Company's Common Stock, each Right not owned by such 15%-or-more stockholder would become exercisable for the number of Common Stock of the Company (or in certain circumstances cash, property or other securities) having at that time a market value of two times the then current exercise price of the Right. If the Company is acquired in a merger or other business combination, or sells 50% or more of its assets or earning power to another person, at any time after a person acquires 15% or more of the Company's Common Stock, the Rights will entitle the holder thereof to buy a number of Common Stock of the acquiring company having a market value of twice the then current exercise price of each Right.

At any time after a person acquires 15% or more of the Company's Common Stock and prior to the earlier of the time (i) the Company is acquired in a merger or other business combination, (ii) the Company is the continuing or surviving corporation in a merger and all or part of the Company's Common Stock is exchanged for stock, cash or other property, or (iii) the Company sells 50% or more of its assets or earning power to another person, the Company may exchange each Right (other than Rights owned by a 15% or more stockholder which shall have become void) for a number of Common Stock of the Company (or in certain circumstances preferred stock of the Company) having a value equal to the difference between the market value of the Common Stock receivable upon exercise of the Right and the exercise price of the Right.

While, as noted above, the distribution of the Rights will not be taxable to you or the Company, stockholders may, depending upon the circumstances, recognize taxable income when the Rights become exercisable.

Maximizing long-term stockholder value is the major goal of the Company's management and Board of Directors.

Sincerely,

Chairman of the Board

FOR IMMEDIATE RELEASE

CONTACT:

_____ 2002

XYZ, INC. ADOPTS
STOCKHOLDER RIGHTS PLAN

New York, New York—XYZ, Inc. ("XYZ") announced today that on _____, 2002, its Board of Directors adopted a Stockholder Rights Plan in which rights will be distributed as a dividend at the rate of one Right for each share of common stock, par value $0.001 per share, of XYZ (the "Common Stock") held by stockholders of record as of the close of business on _____ ___, 2002. The Rights Plan is designed to deter certain types of unfair takeover tactics and to prevent an acquiror from gaining control of XYZ without offering a fair price to all of XYZ's stockholders. The Rights will expire on _____, 2011.

Each Right initially will entitle stockholders to buy one one-thousandth of a share of Series A Junior Participating Preferred Stock Shares of XYZ, for $_____. The Rights will be exercisable only if a person or group acquires beneficial ownership of 15% or more of XYZ's Common Stock or commences a tender or exchange offer upon consummation of which such person or group would beneficially own 15% or more of XYZ's Common Stock.

If any person becomes the beneficial owner of 15% or more of XYZ's Common Stock, then each Right not owned by the 15%-or-more stockholder or related parties will entitle its holder to purchase, at the Right's then current exercise price, shares of XYZ's Common Stock (or in certain circumstances, cash, property, or other securities) having a value of twice the Right's then current exercise price. In addition, if after any person has become a 15%-or-more stockholder, XYZ is involved in a merger or other business combination transaction with another person in which XYZ does not survive or in which its Common Stock is changed or exchanged, or sells 50% or more of its assets or earning power to another person, each Right not owned by the 15%-or-more stockholder or related parties will entitle its holder to purchase, at the Right's then current exercise price, shares of common stock of such other person having a value of twice the Right's then current exercise price.

At any time after a person acquires 15% or more of XYZ's Common Stock and prior to the earlier of the time (i) XYZ is involved in a merger or other business combination transaction with another person in which XYZ does not survive or in which its Common Stock is changed or exchanged, (ii) XYZ is the continuing or surviving corporation in a merger and all or part of its Common Stock is exchanged for stock, cash or other property, or (iii) XYZ sells 50% or more of its assets or earning power to another person, XYZ may exchange each Right (other than Rights owned by the 15%-or-more stockholder which shall have become void) for a number of shares of Common Stock of XYZ (or in certain circumstances shares of preferred stock of XYZ) having a value equal to the difference between the market value of the shares of Common Stock receivable upon exercise of the Rights and the exercise price of the Right.

XYZ will generally be entitled to redeem the Rights at $0.001 per Right at any time until a 15% position has been acquired.

POISON PILL DOCUMENTS

Details of the Stockholder Rights Plan are outlined in a letter which will be mailed to all stockholders.

About XYZ (www.XYZ.com)

[description of XYZ business]

The statements in this release regarding projected results are preliminary and "forward-looking statements" within the meaning of the Private Securities Litigation Reform Act of 1995. In addition, this report contains other forward-looking statements including statements regarding the Company's or third parties' expectations, predictions, views, opportunities, plans, strategies, beliefs, and statements of similar effect. The forward-looking statements in this report are subject to a variety of risks and uncertainties. Actual results could differ materially. Factors that could cause actual results to differ include but are not limited to the following: [description of factors].

IV. LIMITED LIABILITY COMPANIES

A. REVISED UNIFORM LIMITED LIABILITY COMPANY ACT (2006)

Table of Contents

[ARTICLE] 1

GENERAL PROVISIONS

[ARTICLE] 2

FORMATION; CERTIFICATE OF ORGANIZATION AND OTHER FILINGS

[ARTICLE] 3

RELATIONS OF MEMBERS AND MANAGERS TO PERSONS DEALING WITH LIMITED LIABILITY COMPANY

REVISED UNIFORM LIMITED LIABILITY
COMPANY ACT (2006)

REVISED UNIFORM LIMITED LIABILITY
COMPANY ACT (2006)

REVISED UNIFORM LIMITED LIABILITY
COMPANY ACT (2006)

REVISED UNIFORM LIMITED LIABILITY COMPANY ACT

PREFATORY NOTE

Background to this Act:
Developments since the Conference Considered and Approved
the Original Uniform Limited Liability Company Act (ULLCA)

The Uniform Limited Liability Company Act ("ULLCA") was conceived in 1992 and first adopted by the Conference in 1994. By that time nearly every state had adopted an LLC statute, and those statutes varied considerably in both form and substance. Many of those early statutes were based on the first version of the ABA Model Prototype LLC Act.

ULLCA's drafting relied substantially on the then recently adopted Revised Uniform Partnership Act ("RUPA"), and this reliance was especially heavy with regard to member-managed LLCs. ULLCA's provisions for manager-managed LLCs comprised an amalgam fashioned from the 1985 Revised Uniform Limited Partnership Act ("RULPA") and the Model Business Corporation Act ("MBCA"). ULLCA's provisions were also significantly influenced by the then-applicable federal tax classification regulations, which classified an unincorporated organization as a corporation if the organization more nearly resembled a corporation than a partnership. Those same regulations also made the tax classification of single-member LLCs problematic.

Much has changed. All states and the District of Columbia have adopted LLC statutes, and many LLC statutes have been substantially amended several times. LLC filings are significant in every U.S. jurisdiction, and in many states new LLC filings approach or even outnumber new corporate filings on an annual basis. Manager-managed LLCs have become a significant factor in non-publicly-traded capital markets, and increasing numbers of states provide for mergers and conversions involving LLCs and other unincorporated entities.

In 1997, the tax classification context changed radically, when the IRS' "check-the-box" regulations became effective. Under these regulations, an "unincorporated" business entity is taxed either as a partnership or disregarded entity (depending upon the number of owners) unless it elects to be taxed as a corporation. Exceptions exist (*e.g.*, entities whose interests are publicly-traded), but, in general, tax classification concerns no longer constrain the structure of LLCs and the content of LLC statutes. Single-member LLCs, once suspect because novel and of uncertain tax status, are now popular both for sole proprietorships and as corporate subsidiaries.

In 1995, the Conference amended RUPA to add "full-shield" LLP provisions, and today every state has some form of LLP legislation (either through a RUPA adoption or shield-related revisions to a UPA-based statute). While some states still provide only a "partial shield" for LLPs, many states have adopted "full shield" LLP provisions. In full-shield jurisdictions, LLPs and member-managed LLCs offer entrepreneurs very similar attributes and, in the case of professional service organizations, LLPs may dominate the field.

ULLCA was revised in 1996 in anticipation of the "check the box" regulations and has been adopted in a number of states. In many non-ULLCA states, the LLC statute includes RUPA-like provisions. However, state LLC laws are far from uniform.

Eighteen years have passed since the IRS issued its gate-opening Revenue Ruling 88–76, declaring that a Wyoming LLC would be taxed as a partnership despite the entity's corporate-like liability shield. More than eight years have passed since the IRS opened the gate still further with the "check the box" regulations. It is an opportune moment to identify the best elements of the myriad "first generation" LLC statutes and to infuse those elements into a new, "second generation" uniform act.

Noteworthy Provisions of the New Act

The Revised Uniform Limited Company Act is drafted to replace a state's current LLC statute, whether or not that statute is based on ULLCA. The new Act's noteworthy provisions concern:

REVISED UNIFORM LIMITED LIABILITY
COMPANY ACT (2006)

- the operating agreement
- fiduciary duty
- the ability to "pre-file" a certificate of organization without having a member at the time of the filing
- the power of a member or manager to bind the limited liability company
- default rules on management structure
- charging orders
- a remedy for oppressive conduct
- derivative claims and special litigation committees
- organic transactions—mergers, conversions, and domestications

The Operating Agreement: Like the partnership agreement in a general or limited partnership, an LLC's operating agreement serves as the foundational contract among the entity's owners. RUPA pioneered the notion of centralizing all statutory provisions pertaining to the foundational contract, and—like ULLCA and ULPA (2001)—the new Act continues that approach. However, because an operating agreement raises issues too numerous and complex to include easily in a single section, the new Act uses three related sections to address the operating agreement:

- Section 110—scope, function, and limitations;
- Section 111—effect on limited liability company and persons becoming members; preformation agreement; and
- Section 112—effect on third parties and relationship to records effective on behalf of limited liability company.

The new Act also contains a number of substantive innovations concerning the operating agreement, including:

- better delineating the extent to which the operating agreement can define, alter, or even eliminate aspects of fiduciary duty;
- expressly authorizing the operating agreement to relieve members and managers from liability for money damages arising from breach of duty, subject to specific limitations; and
- stating specific rules for applying the statutory phrase "manifestly unreasonable" and thereby providing clear guidance for courts considering whether to invalidate operating agreement provisions that address fiduciary duty and other sensitive matters.

Fiduciary Duty: RUPA also pioneered the idea of codifying partners' fiduciary duties in order to protect the partnership agreement from judicial second-guessing. This approach—to "cabin in" (or corral) fiduciary duty—was followed in ULLCA and ULPA (2001). In contrast, the new Act recognizes that, at least in the realm of limited liability companies:

- the "cabin in" approach creates more problems than it solves ([e.g.,] by putting inordinate pressure on the concept of "good faith and fair dealing"); and
- the better way to protect the operating agreement from judicial second-guessing is to:
    * increase and clarify the power of the operating agreement to define or re-shape fiduciary duties (including the power to eliminate aspects of fiduciary duties); and
    * provide some guidance to courts when a person seeks to escape an agreement by claiming its provisions are "manifestly unreasonable."

Accordingly, the new Act codifies major fiduciary duties but does not purport to do so exhaustively. *See* Section 409.

REVISED UNIFORM LIMITED LIABILITY
COMPANY ACT (2006)

<u>The Ability to "Pre-File" a Certificate of Organization</u>: The Comments to Section 201 explain in detail how the new Act resolves the difficult question of the "shelf LLC"—i.e., an LLC formed without having at least one member upon formation. In short, the Act: (i) permits an organizer to file a certificate of organization without a person "waiting in the wings" to become a member upon formation; but (ii) provides that the LLC is not formed until and unless at least one person becomes a member and the organizer makes a second filing stating that the LLC has at least one member.

<u>The Power of a Member or Manager to Bind the Limited Liability Company</u>: In 1914, the original Uniform Partnership Act codified a particular type of apparent authority by position, providing that "[t]he act of every partner . . . for apparently carrying on in the usual way the business of the partnership binds the partnership. . . ." This concept of "statutory apparent authority" applies by linkage in the 1916 Uniform Limited Partnership Act and the 1976/85 Revised Uniform Limited Partnership Act and appears in RUPA, ULLCA, ULPA (2001), and almost every LLC statute in the United States.

The concept makes good sense for general and limited partnerships. A third party dealing with either type of partnership can know by the formal name of the entity and by a person's status as general or limited partner whether the person has the power to bind the entity.

The concept does not make sense for modern LLC law, because: (i) an LLC's status as member-managed or manager-managed is not apparent from the LLC's name (creating traps for unwary third parties); and (ii) although most LLC statutes provide templates for member-management and manager-management, variability of management structure is a key strength of the LLC as a form of business organization.

The new Act recognizes that "statutory apparent authority" is an attribute of partnership formality that does not belong in an LLC statute. Section 301(a) provides that "a member is not an agent of the limited liability company solely by reason of being a member." Other law—most especially the law of agency—will handle power-to-bind questions.

Although conceptually innovative, this approach will not significantly alter the commercial reality that exists between limited liability companies and third parties, because:

1. The vast majority of interactions between limited liability companies and "third parties" are quotidian and transpire without agency law issues being recognized by the parties, let alone disputed.

2. When a limited liability company enters into a major transaction with a sophisticated third party, the third party never relies on statutory apparent authority to determine that the person purporting to act for the limited liability company has the authority to do so.

3. Most LLCs use employees to carry out most of the LLC's dealings with third parties. In that context, the agency power of members and managers is usually irrelevant. (If an employee's authority is contested and the employee "reports to" a member or manager, the member or manager's authority will be relevant to determining the employee's authority. However, in that situation, agency law principles will suffice to delineate the manager or member's supervisory authority.)

4. Very few current LLC statutes contain rules for attributing to an LLC the wrongful acts of the LLC's members or managers. *Compare* RUPA § 305. In this realm, this Act merely acknowledges pre-existing reality.

5. As explained in detail in the Comments to section 301 and 407(c), agency law principles are well-suited to the tasks resulting from the "de-codification" of apparent authority by position.

The moment is opportune for this reform. The newly-issued Restatement (Third) of Agency gives substantial attention to the power of an enterprise's participants to bind the enterprise. In addition, the new Act has "souped up" RUPA's statement of authority to permit an LLC to publicly file a statement of authority for a position (not merely a particular person). Statements of authority will enable LLCs to provide reliable documentation of authority to enter into transactions without having to disclose to third parties the entirety of the operating agreement. (The new Act also has eliminated prolix provisions that sought to restate agency law rules on notice and knowledge.)

<u>Default Rules on Management Structure</u>: The new Act retains the manager-managed and member-managed constructs as options for members to use in configuring their *inter se* relationship, and the operating agreement is the vehicle by which the members make and state their choice of management structure. Given the elimination of statutory apparent authority, it is unnecessary and could be confusing to require the articles of organization to state the members' determination on this point.

<u>Charging Orders</u>: The charging order mechanism: (i) dates back to the 1914 Uniform Partnership Act and the English Partnership Act of 1890; and (ii) is an essential part of the "pick your partner" approach that is fundamental to the law of unincorporated businesses. The new Act continues the charging order mechanism, but modernizes the statutory language so that the language (and its protections against outside interference in an LLC's activities) can be readily understood.

<u>A Remedy for Oppressive Conduct</u>: Reflecting case law developments around the country, the new Act permits a member (but not a transferee) to seek a court order "dissolving the company on the grounds that the managers or those members in control of the company . . . have acted or are acting in a manner that is oppressive and was, is, or will be directly harmful to the [member]." Section 701(5)(B). This provision is necessary given the perpetual duration of an LLC formed under this Act, Section 104(c), and this Act's elimination of the "put right" provided by ULLCA, § 701.

<u>Derivative Claims and Special Litigation Committees</u>: The new Act contains modern provisions addressing derivative litigation, including a provision authorizing special litigation committees and subjecting their composition and conduct to judicial review.

<u>Organic Transactions—Mergers, Conversions, and Domestications</u>: The new Act has comprehensive, self-contained provisions for these transactions, including "inter-species" transactions.

No Provision for "Series" LLCs

The new Act also has a very noteworthy omission; it does not authorize "series LLCs." Under a series approach, a single limited liability company may establish and contain within itself separate series. Each series is treated as an enterprise separate from each other and from the LLC itself. Each series has associated with it specified members, assets, and obligations, and—due to what have been called "internal shields"—the obligations of one series are not the obligation of any other series or of the LLC.

Delaware pioneered the series concept, and the concept has apparently been quite useful in structuring certain types of investment funds and in arranging complex financing. Other states have followed Delaware's lead, but a number of difficult and substantial questions remain unanswered, including:

- *conceptual*—How can a series be—and expect to be treated as—a separate legal person for liability and other purposes if the series is defined as part of another legal person?

- *bankruptcy*—Bankruptcy law has not recognized the series as a separate legal person. If a series becomes insolvent, will the entire LLC and the other series become part of the bankruptcy proceedings? Will a bankruptcy court consolidate the assets and liabilities of the separate series?

- *efficacy of the internal shields in the courts of other states*—Will the internal shields be respected in the courts of states whose LLC statutes do not recognize series? Most LLC statutes provide that "foreign law governs" the liability of members of a foreign LLC. However, those provisions do not apply to the series question, because those provisions pertain to the liability of a member for the obligations of the LLC. For a series LLC, the pivotal question is entirely different—namely, whether some assets of an LLC should be immune from some of the creditors of the LLC.

- *tax treatment*—Will the IRS and the states treat each series separately? Will separate returns be filed? May one series "check the box" for corporate tax classification and the others not?

- *securities law*—Given the panoply of unanswered questions, what types of disclosures must be made when a membership interest is subject to securities law?

The Drafting Committee considered a series proposal at its February 2006 meeting, but, after serious discussion, no one was willing to urge adoption of the proposal, even for the limited purposes of further discussion. Given the availability of well-established alternate structures (*e.g.*, multiple single member LLCs, an LLC "holding company" with LLC subsidiaries), it made no sense for the Act to endorse the complexities and risks of a series approach.

REVISED UNIFORM LIMITED LIABILITY COMPANY ACT

[ARTICLE] 1

GENERAL PROVISIONS

§ 101. Short Title

This [act] may be cited as the Revised Uniform Limited Liability Company Act.

Comment

This Act is drafted to replace a state's current LLC statute, whether or not that statute is based on the original Uniform Limited Liability Company Act. Section 1104 contains transition provisions.

§ 102. Definitions

In this [act]:

(1) "Certificate of organization" means the certificate required by Section 201. The term includes the certificate as amended or restated.

(2) "Contribution" means any benefit provided by a person to a limited liability company:

(A) in order to become a member upon formation of the company and in accordance with an agreement between or among the persons that have agreed to become the initial members of the company;

(B) in order to become a member after formation of the company and in accordance with an agreement between the person and the company; or

(C) in the person's capacity as a member and in accordance with the operating agreement or an agreement between the member and the company.

(3) "Debtor in bankruptcy" means a person that is the subject of:

(A) an order for relief under Title 11 of the United States Code or a successor statute of general application; or

(B) a comparable order under federal, state, or foreign law governing insolvency.

(4) "Designated office" means:

(A) the office that a limited liability company is required to designate and maintain under Section 113; or

(B) the principal office of a foreign limited liability company.

(5) "Distribution", except as otherwise provided in Section 405(g), means a transfer of money or other property from a limited liability company to another person on account of a transferable interest.

(6) "Effective", with respect to a record required or permitted to be delivered to the [Secretary of State] for filing under this [act], means effective under Section 205(c).

(7) "Foreign limited liability company" means an unincorporated entity formed under the law of a jurisdiction other than this state and denominated by that law as a limited liability company.

(8) "Limited liability company", except in the phrase "foreign limited liability company", means an entity formed under this [act].

(9) "Manager" means a person that under the operating agreement of a manager-managed limited liability company is responsible, alone or in concert with others, for performing the management functions stated in Section 407(c).

(10) "Manager-managed limited liability company" means a limited liability company that qualifies under Section 407(a).

(11) "Member" means a person that has become a member of a limited liability company under Section 401 and has not dissociated under Section 602.

(12) "Member-managed limited liability company" means a limited liability company that is not a manager-managed limited liability company.

(13) "Operating agreement" means the agreement, whether or not referred to as an operating agreement and whether oral, in a record, implied, or in any combination thereof, of all the members of a limited liability company, including a sole member, concerning the matters described in Section 110(a). The term includes the agreement as amended or restated.

(14) "Organizer" means a person that acts under Section 201 to form a limited liability company.

(15) "Person" means an individual, corporation, business trust, estate, trust, partnership, limited liability company, association, joint venture, public corporation, government or governmental subdivision, agency, or instrumentality, or any other legal or commercial entity.

(16) "Principal office" means the principal executive office of a limited liability company or foreign limited liability company, whether or not the office is located in this state.

(17) "Record" means information that is inscribed on a tangible medium or that is stored in an electronic or other medium and is retrievable in perceivable form.

(18) "Sign" means, with the present intent to authenticate or adopt a record:

    (A) to execute or adopt a tangible symbol; or

    (B) to attach to or logically associate with the record an electronic symbol, sound, or process.

(19) "State" means a state of the United States, the District of Columbia, Puerto Rico, the United States Virgin Islands, or any territory or insular possession subject to the jurisdiction of the United States.

(20) "Transfer" includes an assignment, conveyance, deed, bill of sale, lease, mortgage, security interest, encumbrance, gift, and transfer by operation of law.

(21) "Transferable interest" means the right, as originally associated with a person's capacity as a member, to receive distributions from a limited liability company in accordance with the operating agreement, whether or not the person remains a member or continues to own any part of the right.

(22) "Transferee" means a person to which all or part of a transferable interest has been transferred, whether or not the transferor is a member.

Comment

This Section contains definitions for terms used throughout the Act, while Section 1001 contains definitions specific to Article 10's provisions on mergers, conversions and domestications. Section 405(g) contains an exception to the definition of "distribution," which is specific to Section 405.

Paragraph (1) [Certificate of organization]—The original ULLCA and most other LLC statutes use "articles of organization" rather than "certificate of organization." This Act purposely uses the latter term to signal that: (i) the certificate merely reflects the existence of an LLC (rather than being the locus for important governance rules); and (ii) this document is significantly different from articles of *incorporation*, which have a substantially greater power to affect *inter se* rules for the corporate entity and its owners. For the relationship between the certificate of organization and the operating agreement, *see* Section 112(d).

Paragraph (2) [Contribution]—This definition serves to distinguish capital contributions from other circumstances under which a member or would-be member might provide benefits to a limited liability company (*e.g.*, providing services to the LLC as an employee or independent contractor, leasing property to the LLC). The definition contemplates three typical situations in which contributions are made, and for each situation establishes two "markers" to identify capital contributions—the purpose for which the contributor makes the contribution and the agreement that contemplates the contribution:

circumstance	purpose/cause of providing benefits	the relevant agreement
pre-formation deal among would-be initial members [Paragraph 2(A)]	in order to become initial member(s)	agreement among would-be initial members
deal between an existing LLC and would-be member [Paragraph 2(B)]	in order to become a member	agreement between the LLC and the would-be member
member contribution [Paragraph 2(C)]	in member's capacity as a member	operating agreement or an agreement between the member and the LLC

This definition does not encompass capital raised from transferees, which is sometimes provided for in operating agreements. In such circumstances, the default rules for liquidating distributions should be altered accordingly. *See* Section 708(b)(1) ("referring to contributions made by a member and not previously returned").

Paragraph (7) [Foreign limited liability company]—Some statutes have elaborate definitions addressing the question of whether a non-U.S. entity is a "foreign limited liability company." The NY statute, for example, defines a "foreign limited liability company" as:

> an unincorporated organization formed under the laws of any jurisdiction, including any foreign country, other than the laws of this state (i) that is not authorized to do business in this state under any other law of this state and (ii) of which some or all of the persons who are entitled (A) to receive a distribution of the assets thereof upon the dissolution of the organization or otherwise or (B) to exercise voting rights with respect to an interest in the organization have, or are entitled or authorized to have, under the laws of such other jurisdiction, limited liability for the contractual obligations or other liabilities of the organization.

N.Y. LIMIT LIAB Co. LAW § 102(k) (McKinney 2006). ULLCA § 101(8) takes a similar but less complex approach ("an unincorporated entity organized under laws other than the laws of this State which afford limited liability to its owners comparable to the liability under Section 303 and is not required to obtain a certificate of authority to transact business under any law of this State other than this [Act]"). This Act follows Delaware's still simpler approach. DEL. CODE ANN. tit. 6, § 18–101(4) (2006) ("denominated as such").

Paragraph (8) [Limited liability company]—This definition makes no reference to a limited liability company having members upon formation, but Section 201 does. For a detailed discussion of the "shelf LLC" issue, *see* the Comment to Section 201.

Paragraph (9) [Manager]—The Act uses the word "manager" as a term of art, whose applicability is confined to manager-managed LLCs. The phrase "manager-managed" is itself a term of art, referring only to an LLC whose operating agreement refers to the LLC as such. Paragraph 10 (defining "manager-managed limited liability company"). Thus, for purposes of this Act, if the members of a *member*-managed LLC delegate plenipotentiary management authority to one person (whether or not a member), this Act's references to "manager" do not apply to that person.

This approach does have the potential for confusion, but confusion around the term "manager" is common to almost all LLC statutes. The confusion stems from the choice to define "manager" as a term of art in a way that can be at odds with other, common usages of the word. For example, a member-managed LLC might well have an "office manager" or a "property manager." Moreover, in a manager-managed LLC, the "property manager" is not likely to be a manager as the term is used in many LLC statutes. *See, e.g., Brown v. MR Group, LLC*, 278 Wis.2d 760, 768–9, 693 N.W.2d 138, 143 (Wis.App. 2005) (rejecting a party's urging to use the dictionary definition of "manager" in determining coverage of a policy applicable to a limited liability company and its "managers" and relying instead on the meaning of the term under the Wisconsin LLC act).

Under this Act, the category of "person" is not limited to individuals. Therefore, a "manager" need not be a natural person. After a person ceases to be a manager, the term "manager" continues to apply to the person's conduct while a manager. *See* Section 407(c)(7).

Paragraph (10) [Manager-managed]—This Act departs from most LLC statutes (including the original ULLCA) by authorizing a private agreement (the operating agreement) rather than a public document (certificate or articles of organization) to establish an LLC's status as a manager-managed limited liability company. Using the operating agreement makes sense, because under this Act managerial structure creates no statutory power to bind the entity. *See* Section 301 (eliminating statutory apparent authority). The only direct consequences of manager-managed status are *inter se*—principally the triggering of a set of rules concerning management structure, fiduciary duty, and information rights. Sections 407–410. The management structure rules are entirely default provisions—subject to change in whole or in part by the operating agreement. The operating agreement can also significantly affect the duty and rights provisions. Section 110.

For pre-existing limited liability companies that eventually become subject to this Act, Section 1104(c) provides that "language in the limited liability company's articles of organization designating the company's management structure will operate as if that language were in the operating agreement." For limited liability companies formed under this Act, the typical method to select manager-managed status will be an explicit provision of the operating agreement. However, a reference in the certificate of organization to manager-management might be evidence of the contents of the operating agreement. *See* Comment to Section 112(b).

An LLC that is "manager-managed" under this definition does not cease to be so simply because the members fail to designate anyone to act as a manager. In that situation, absent additional facts, the LLC is manager-managed and the manager position is vacant. Non-manager members who exercise managerial functions during the vacancy (or at any other time) will have duties as determined by other law, most particularly the law of agency.

Paragraph 10(A) and (B)—In these paragraphs, the phrases "manager-managed" and "managed by managers" are "magic words"—i.e., for either subparagraph to apply, the operating agreement must include precisely the required language. However, the word "expressly" does not mean "in writing" or "in a record." This Act permits operating agreements to be oral (in whole or in part), and an oral provision of an operating agreement could contain the magic words. This Act also recognizes that provisions of an operating agreement may be reflected in patterns of conduct.

Oral and implied agreements invite memory problems and "swearing matches." Section 110(a)(4) empowers the operating agreement to determine "the means and conditions for the amending the operating agreement."

Paragraph 10(C)—In contrast to Paragraphs 10(A) and (B), this provision does not contain "magic words" and considers instead all terms of the operating agreement that expressly refer to management by managers.

Paragraph [(11)] [Member]—After a person has been dissociated as a member, Section 602, the term "member" continues to apply to the person's conduct while a member. *See* Section 603(b).

Paragraph [(12)] [Member-managed limited liability company]—A limited liability company that does not effectively designate itself a manager-member limited liability company will operate, subject to any contrary provisions in the operating agreement, under statutory rules providing for management by the members. Section 407(a). For a discussion of potential confusion relating to the term "manager", *see* the Comment to Paragraph 9 (Manager).

Paragraph (13) [Operating Agreement]—This definition must be read in conjunction with Sections 110 through 112, which further describe the operating agreement. An operating agreement is a contract, and therefore all statutory language pertaining to the operating agreement must be understood in the context of the law of contracts.

The definition in Paragraph 13 is very broad and recognizes a wide scope of authority for the operating agreement: "the matters described in Section 110(a)." Those matters include not only all relations *inter se* the members and the limited liability company but also all "activities of the company and the conduct of those activities." Section 110(a)(3). Moreover, the definition puts no limits on the form of the operating agreement. To the contrary, the definition contains the phrase "whether oral, in a record, implied, or in any combination thereof".

This Act states no rule as to whether the statute of frauds applies to an oral operating agreement. Case law suggests that an oral agreement to form a partnership or joint venture with a term exceeding one year is within the statute. *E.g. Abbott v. Hurst*, 643 So.2d 589, 592 (Ala. 1994) ("Partnership agreements, like other contracts, are subject to the Statute of Frauds. A contract of partnership for a term exceeding one year is within the Statute of Frauds and is void unless it is in writing; however, a contract establishing a partnership terminable at the will of any partner is generally held to be capable of performance by its terms within one year of its making and, therefore, to be outside the Statute of Frauds.") (citations omitted); *Pemberton v. Ladue Realty & Const. Co.*, 362 Mo. 768, 770–71, 244 S.W.2d 62, 64 (Mo. 1951) (rejecting plaintiff's contention that mere part performance sufficed to take the oral agreement outside the statute and holding that partnership was therefore at will); *Ebker v. Tan Jay Int'l, Ltd.*, 739 F.2d 812, 827–28 (2d Cir.1984) (same analysis with regard to a joint venture). However, it is not possible to form an LLC without someone signing and delivering to the filing officer a certificate of organization in record form, Section 201(a), and the Act itself then establishes the LLC's duration. Subject to the operating agreement, that duration is perpetual. Section 104(c). An oral provision of an operating agreement calling for performance that extends beyond a year might be within the one-year provision—*e.g.*, an oral agreement that a particular member will serve (and be permitted to serve) as manager for three years.

An oral provision of an operating agreement which involves the transfer of land, whether by or to the LLC, might come within the land provision of the statute of frauds. *Froiseth v. Nowlin*, 156 Wash. 314, 316, 287 P. 55. 56 (Wash. 1930) ("[The land provision] applies to an oral contract to transfer or convey partnership real property, and the interest of the other partners therein, to one partner as an individual, as well as to a parol contract by one of the parties to convey certain land owned by him individually to the partnership, or to another partner, or to put it into the partnership stock.") (quoting 27 CORPUS JURIS 220).

In contrast, the fact that a limited liability company owns or deals in real property does not bring within the land provision agreements pertaining to the LLC's membership interests. Interests in a limited liability company are personal property and reflect no direct interest in the entity's assets. Re-ULLCA §§ 501 & 102(21). Thus, the real property issues pertaining to the LLC's ownership of land do not "flow through" to the members and membership interests. *See, e.g.*, *Wooten v. Marshall*, 153 F. Supp. 759, 763–764 (S.D. N.Y. 1957) (involving an "oral agreement for a joint venture concerning the purchase, exploitation and eventual disposition of this 160 acre tract" and stating "[t]he real property acquired and dealt with by the venturers takes on the character of personal property as between the partners in the enterprise, and hence is not covered by [the Statute of Frauds].")

The operating agreement may comprise a number of separate documents (or records), however denominated, unless the operating agreement itself provides otherwise. Section 110(a)(4). Absent a contrary provision in the operating agreement, a threshold qualification for status as part of the "operating agreement" is the assent of all the persons then members. An agreement among less than all of the members might well be enforceable among those members as parties, but would not be part of the operating agreement.

An agreement to form an LLC is not itself an operating agreement. The term "operating agreement" presupposes the existence of members, and a person cannot have "member" status until the LLC exists. However, the Act's very broad definition of "operating agreement" means that, as soon as a limited liability company has any members, the limited liability company has an operating agreement. For example, suppose: (i) two persons orally and informally agree to join their activities in some way through the mechanism of an LLC, (ii) they form the LLC or cause it to be formed, and (iii) without further ado or agreement, they become the LLC's initial members. The LLC has an operating agreement. "[A]ll the members" have agreed on who the members are, and that agreement—no matter how informal or rudimentary—is an agreement "concerning the matters described in Section 110(a)." (To the extent the agreement does not provide the *inter se* "rules of the game," this Act "fills in the gaps." Section 110(b).)

The same result follows when a person becomes the sole initial member of an LLC. It is not plausible that the person would lack any understanding or intention with regard to the LLC. That understanding or intention constitutes an "agreement of all the members of the limited liability company, including a sole member."

It may seem oxymoronic to refer an "agreement of . . . a sole member," but this approach is common in LLC statutes. *See, e.g.*, ARIZ. REV. STAT. ANN. § 29–601(14)(b) (2006) (defining operating agreement to mean "in the case of a limited liability company that has a single member, any written or oral statement of the member made in good faith"); COLO. REV. STAT. ANN. § 7–80–102(11)(b)(I) (West 2006) (defining operating agreement to include, in the case of a single member LLC "[a]ny writing, without regard to whether such writing otherwise constitutes an agreement . . . signed by the sole member"); N.H. REV. STAT. ANN. § 304–c:1(VI) (2006) (defining limited liability company agreement to include "a document adopted by the sole member"); OR. REV. STAT. ANN. § 63.431(2) (2005) (vesting the "power to adopt, alter, amend or repeal an operating agreement of . . . a single member limited liability company, in the sole member of the limited liability company"); R.I. GEN. LAWS § 7–16–2(19) (2005) (stating that the term operating agreement "includes a document adopted by the sole member of a limited liability company that has only one member"); and WASH. REV. CODE ANN. § 25.15.005(5) (West 2006) (defining limited liability company agreement to include "any written statement of the sole member").

This re-definition of "agreement" is a function of "path dependence." By the time single-member LLCs became widely accepted, almost all LLC statutes were premised on the LLC's key organic document being the operating agreement. Because a key function of the operating agreement is to override statutory default rules, it was necessary to make clear that a sole member could make an operating agreement. Such an agreement may also be of interest to third parties, because the operating agreement binds the LLC. Section 111(a).

In light of Paragraph 13's broad definition, it is possible to argue that any activity involving unanimous consent of the members becomes part of the operating agreement. For example, if pursuant to an operating agreement all the members consent to the redemption of one-half of the managing-member's transferable interest, does that action constitute an addition to the agreement?

Typically, such questions will turn on the practical issue of whether the unanimous consent pertained solely to a single event (now past) or also to future circumstances (now in controversy) rather than on the semantic question of whether the operating agreement has been amended. Occasionally, however, the amendment *vel non* question could have practical import. For example, if the operating agreement entitles a non-member to approve (or veto) amendments, *see* Section 112(a), the members and the non-member might see the matter quite differently.

Careful drafting of veto provisions can help avoid controversy—*e.g.*, by defining with specificity the type of decisions subject to the veto. On the question of how far a written (or "in a record") operating agreement can go to prevent oral or implied-in-fact terms, *see* Section 110(a)(4).

If it is necessary for a court to decide whether the contents of a matter approved by unanimous consent have become part of the operating agreement, the court should rely on principles of contract interpretation and look:

- first, at the manifestations of the members, including:
    - the manifestations made to give the unanimous consent; and

- any terms of the operating agreement (*e.g.*, terms specifying how matters become part of the operating agreement); and

- second, at whether, viewed from the perspective of a reasonable person in the position of the members giving consent, the consent was intended to incorporate the matter into the ongoing "rules of the game" or merely take some particular action as already permitted by those rules.

Of course, if all the members have the same understanding, the reasonableness *vel non* of that understanding is irrelevant and the shared meaning governs. *See* RESTATEMENT (SECOND) OF CONTRACTS, § 201(1) (1981).

Paragraph (14) [Organizer]—If an LLC is to have one or more members when the filing officer files the certificate of organization, the organizer: (i) acts on behalf of the person or persons who will become the LLC's initial members, Section 401(a) and (b); and (ii) has no function other than to compose, sign, and deliver to the filing officer for filing the certificate of organization. Section 201(a). If an LLC is to have its first member sometime *after* the filing officer files the certificate of organization, the organizer has the power to admit the initial member or members, Section 401(c), and to sign and deliver for filing the notice of initial membership described in Section 201(e)(1). Whether in this latter category of circumstances the organizer acts on behalf of the initial member or members is determined under ordinary principles of agency law and depends on the facts of each situation.

Paragraph (20) [Transfer]—The reference to "transfer by operation of law" is significant in connection with Section 502 (Transfer of Transferable Interest). That section severely restricts a transferee's rights (absent the consent of the members), and this definition makes those restrictions applicable, for example, to transfers ordered by a family court as part of a divorce proceeding and transfers resulting from the death of a member. The restrictions also apply to transfers in the context of a member's bankruptcy, except to the extent that bankruptcy law supersedes this Act.

Paragraph (21) [Transferee]—"Transferee" has displaced "assignee" as the Conference's term of art.

§ 103. Knowledge; Notice

(a) A person knows a fact when the person:

    (1) has actual knowledge of it; or

    (2) is deemed to know it under subsection (d)(1) or law other than this [act].

(b) A person has notice of a fact when the person:

    (1) has reason to know the fact from all of the facts known to the person at the time in question; or

    (2) is deemed to have notice of the fact under subsection (d)(2).

(c) A person notifies another of a fact by taking steps reasonably required to inform the other person in ordinary course, whether or not the other person knows the fact.

(d) A person that is not a member is deemed:

    (1) to know of a limitation on authority to transfer real property as provided in Section 302(g); and

    (2) to have notice of a limited liability company's:

        (A) dissolution, 90 days after a statement of dissolution under Section 702(b)(2)(A) becomes effective;

        (B) termination, 90 days after a statement of termination Section 702(b)(2)(F) becomes effective; and

        (C) merger, conversion, or domestication, 90 days after articles of merger, conversion, or domestication under [Article] 10 become effective.

Comment

This section is substantially slimmer than the corresponding provisions of previous uniform acts pertaining to business organizations (RUPA, ULLCA, and ULPA (2001)). Each of those acts borrowed heavily from the comparable UCC provisions. For the most part, this Act relies instead on generally applicable principles of agency law, and therefore this section is mostly confined to rules specifically tailored to this Act.

Several facets of this section warrant particular note. First, and most fundamentally, because this Act does not provide for "statutory apparent authority," *see* Section 301, this section contains no special rules for attributing to an LLC information possessed, communicated to, or communicated by a member or manager.

Second, the section contains no generally applicable provisions determining when an organization is charged with knowledge or notice, because those imputation rules: (i) comprise core topics within the law of agency; (ii) are very complicated; (iii) should not have any different content under this Act than in other circumstances; and (iv) are the subject of considerable attention in the new Restatement (Third) of Agency.

Third, this Act does not define "notice" to include "knowledge." Although conceptualizing the latter as giving the former makes logical sense and has a long pedigree, that conceptualization is counter-intuitive for the non-*aficionado*. In ordinary usage, notice has a meaning separate from knowledge. This Act follows ordinary usage and therefore contains some references to "knowledge or notice."

Subsection (a)(2)—In this context, the most important source of "law other than this [act]" is the common law of agency.

Subsection (b)(1)—The "facts known to the person at the time in question" include facts the person is deemed to know under subsection (a)(2).

Subsection (d)(2)—Under this Act, the power to bind a limited liability company to a third party is primarily a matter of agency law. Section 301, Comment. The constructive notice provided under this paragraph will be relevant if a third party makes a claim under agency law that someone who purported to act on behalf of a limited liability company had the apparent authority to do so.

§ 104. Nature, Purpose, and Duration of Limited Liability Company

(a) A limited liability company is an entity distinct from its members.

(b) A limited liability company may have any lawful purpose, regardless of whether for profit.

(c) A limited liability company has perpetual duration.

Legislative Note: This state should consider whether to amend statutes protecting the public interest in organizations formed for charitable or similar purposes.

Comment

Subsection (a)—The "separate entity" characteristic is fundamental to a limited liability company and is inextricably connected to both the liability shield, Section 304, and the charging order provision, Section 503.

Subsection (b)—The phrase "any lawful purpose, regardless of whether for profit" means that: (i) a limited liability company need not have any business purpose; and (ii) the issue of profit *vel non* is irrelevant to the question of whether a limited liability company has been validly formed. Although some LLC statutes continue to require a business purpose, this Act follows the current trend and takes a more expansive approach.

The expansive approach comports both with the original ULLCA and with ULPA (2001). *See* ULLCA §§ 112(a) (captioned with reference to "Nature of Business" and permitting "any lawful purpose, subject to any law of this State governing or regulating business") and 101(3) (defining "Business" as including "every trade, occupation, profession, and other lawful purpose, whether or not carried on for profit"); ULPA (2001) § 104(b) (permitting a limited partnership to be organized for any "lawful" purpose). *Compare* UPA § 6 (defining a general partnership as organized for profit), RUPA § 101(6) (same), and RULPA (1976/85) § 106 (delineating the "Nature of [a limited partnership's] Business" by linking back to "any business that a partnership without limited partners may carry on").

The subsection does not bar a limited liability company from being organized to carry on charitable activities, and this act does not include any protective provisions pertaining to charitable purposes. Those protections must be (and typically are) found in other law, although sometimes that "other law" appears within a state's non-profit corporation statute. *See, e.g.,* MINN. STAT. § 317A.811 (2006) (providing restrictions on charitable organizations that seek to "dissolve, merge, or consolidate, or to transfer all or substantially all of their assets" but imposing those restrictions only on "corporations," which are elsewhere defined as corporations incorporated under the non-profit corporation act).

Subsection (c)—In this context, the word "perpetual" is a misnomer, albeit one commonplace in LLC statutes. Like all current LLC statutes, this Act provides several consent-based avenues to override perpetuity: a term specified in the operating agreement; an event specified in the operating agreement; member consent. Section 701 (events causing dissolution). In this context, "perpetuity" actually means that the Act does not require a definite term and creates no nexus between the dissociation of a member and the dissolution of the entity. (The dissociation of an LLC's last remaining member does threaten dissolution). Section 701(a)(3) (stating, as a default rule, that a limited liability company dissolves "upon . . . the passage of 90 consecutive days during which the limited liability company has no members").

An operating agreement is not a publicly-filed document, which means that the public record pertaining to a limited liability company will not necessarily reveal whether a limited liability company actually has a perpetual duration. *Accord* ULPA (2001) § 104, comment to subsection (c) ("The partnership agreement has the power to vary this subsection [which provides for perpetual duration], either by stating a definite term or by specifying an event or events which cause dissolution . . . . . [The limited partnership act] also recognizes several other occurrences that cause dissolution. Thus, the public record pertaining to a limited partnership will not necessarily reveal whether the limited partnership actually has a perpetual duration.")

§ 105.   Powers

A limited liability company has the capacity to sue and be sued in its own name and the power to do all things necessary or convenient to carry on its activities.

Comment

Following ULPA (2001), § 105, this Act omits as unnecessary any detailed list of specific powers. *Compare* ULLCA § 112 (containing a detailed list).

The capacity to sue and be sued is mentioned specifically so that Section 110(c)(1) can prohibit the operating agreement from varying that capacity. An LLC's standing to enforce the operating agreement is a separate matter, which is covered by Section 111(a) (stating, as a default rule, that the limited liability company "may enforce the operating agreement").

§ 106.   Governing Law

The law of this state governs:

(1)   the internal affairs of a limited liability company; and

(2)   the liability of a member as member and a manager as manager for the debts, obligations, or other liabilities of a limited liability company.

Comment

Paragraph (1)—Like any other legal concept, "internal affairs" may be indeterminate at its edges. However, the concept certainly includes interpretation and enforcement of the operating agreement, relations among the members as members; relations between the limited liability company and a member as a member, relations between a manager-managed limited liability company and a manager, and relations between a manager of a manager-managed limited liability company and the members as members. *Compare* RESTATEMENT (SECOND) OF CONFLICT OF LAWS § 302, cmt. a (defining "internal affairs" with reference to a corporation as "the relations inter se of the corporation, its shareholders, directors, officers or agents").

The operating agreement cannot alter this provision. Section 110(c)(2). However, an operating agreement may lawfully incorporate by reference the provisions of another state's LLC statute. If done correctly, this incorporation makes the foreign statutory language part of the operating agreement, and the incorporated terms (together with the rest of the operating agreement) then govern the members (and those claiming through the members) to the extent not prohibited by this Act. *See* Section 110. This approach does not switch the limited liability company's governing law to that of another state, but instead takes the provisions of another state's law and incorporates them by reference into the contract among the members.

Paragraph (2)—This paragraph certainly encompasses Section 304 (the liability shield) but does not necessarily encompass a claim that a member or manager is liable to a third party for (i) having purported to bind a limited liability company to the third party; or (ii) having committed a tort against the third party while acting on the limited liability company's behalf or in the course of the company's business. That liability is not by status (i.e., not "as member . . . [or] as manager") but rather results from function or conduct. Contrast Section 301(b) (stating that, although this Act does not make a member as member the agent of a limited liability company, other law may make an LLC liable for the conduct of a member).

This paragraph is stated separately from Paragraph (1), because it can be argued that the liability of members and managers to third parties is not an internal affair. *See, e.g.,* RESTATEMENT (SECOND) OF CONFLICT OF LAWS, § 307 (treating shareholders' liability separately from the internal affairs doctrine). A few cases subsume owner/manager liability into internal affairs, but many do not. *See, e.g., Kalb, Voorhis & Co. v. American Fin. Corp.,* 8 F.3d 130, 132 (2nd Cir. 1993). In any event, the rule stated in this paragraph is correct. All sensible authorities agree that, except in extraordinary circumstances, "shield-related" issues should be determined according to the law of the state of organization.

§ 107. Supplemental Principles of Law

Unless displaced by particular provisions of this [act], the principles of law and equity supplement this [act].

§ 108. Name

(a) The name of a limited liability company must contain the words "limited liability company" or "limited company" or the abbreviation "L.L.C.", "LLC", "L.C.", or "LC". "Limited" may be abbreviated as "Ltd.", and "company" may be abbreviated as "Co.".

(b) Unless authorized by subsection (c), the name of a limited liability company must be distinguishable in the records of the [Secretary of State] from:

(1) the name of each person that is not an individual and that is incorporated, organized, or authorized to transact business in this state;

(2) the limited liability company name stated in each certificate of organization that contains the statement as provided in Section 201(b)(3) and that has not lapsed; and

(3) each name reserved under Section 109 and [cite other state laws allowing the reservation or registration of business names, including fictitious or assumed name statutes].

(c) A limited liability company may apply to the [Secretary of State] for authorization to use a name that does not comply with subsection (b). The [Secretary of State] shall authorize use of the name applied for if, as to each noncomplying name:

(1) the present user, registrant, or owner of the noncomplying name consents in a signed record to the use and submits an undertaking in a form satisfactory to the [Secretary of State] to change the noncomplying name to a name that complies with subsection (b) and is distinguishable in the records of the [Secretary of State] from the name applied for; or

(2) the applicant delivers to the [Secretary of State] a certified copy of the final judgment of a court establishing the applicant's right to use in this state the name applied for.

(d)   Subject to Section 805, this section applies to a foreign limited liability company transacting business in this state which has a certificate of authority to transact business in this state or which has applied for a certificate of authority.

Comment

Subsection (a) is taken verbatim from ULLCA § 105(a). Except for subsection (b)(2), the rest of the section is taken from ULPA (2001) § 108.

Subsection (b)(2)—This language is necessary to protect a name contained in a filed certificate of organization that has not become effective because there are no members. If a statement of membership is not thereafter timely filed, "the certificate lapses and is void," thereby freeing the name. Section 201(e)(1).

§ 109.   Reservation of Name

(a)   A person may reserve the exclusive use of the name of a limited liability company, including a fictitious or assumed name for a foreign limited liability company whose name is not available, by delivering an application to the [Secretary of State] for filing. The application must state the name and address of the applicant and the name proposed to be reserved. If the [Secretary of State] finds that the name applied for is available, it must be reserved for the applicant's exclusive use for a 120-day period.

(b)   The owner of a name reserved for a limited liability company may transfer the reservation to another person by delivering to the [Secretary of State] for filing a signed notice of the transfer which states the name and address of the transferee.

Comment

Source: ULLCA, § 106.

Subsection (a)—Although 120-day reservation period is non-renewable, this subsection does not prevent a person from seeking successive 120-day periods of reservation.

§ 110.   Operating Agreement; Scope, Function, and Limitations

(a)   Except as otherwise provided in subsections (b) and (c), the operating agreement governs:

(1)   relations among the members as members and between the members and the limited liability company;

(2)   the rights and duties under this [act] of a person in the capacity of manager;

(3)   the activities of the company and the conduct of those activities; and

(4)   the means and conditions for amending the operating agreement.

(b)   To the extent the operating agreement does not otherwise provide for a matter described in subsection (a), this [act] governs the matter.

(c)   An operating agreement may not:

(1)   vary a limited liability company's capacity under Section 105 to sue and be sued in its own name;

(2)   vary the law applicable under Section 106;

(3)   vary the power of the court under Section 204;

(4)   subject to subsections (d) through (g), eliminate the duty of loyalty, the duty of care, or any other fiduciary duty;

(5)   subject to subsections (d) through (g), eliminate the contractual obligation of good faith and fair dealing under Section 409(d);

(6)   unreasonably restrict the duties and rights stated in Section 410;

(7)   vary the power of a court to decree dissolution in the circumstances specified in Section 701(a)(4) and (5);

(8)   vary the requirement to wind up a limited liability company's business as specified in Section 702(a) and (b)(1);

(9)   unreasonably restrict the right of a member to maintain an action under [Article] 9;

(10) restrict the right to approve a merger, conversion, or domestication under Section 1014 to a member that will have personal liability with respect to a surviving, converted, or domesticated organization; or

(11) except as otherwise provided in Section 112(b), restrict the rights under this [act] of a person other than a member or manager.

(d)   If not manifestly unreasonable, the operating agreement may:

(1)   restrict or eliminate the duty:

(A)   as required in Section 409(b)(1) and (g), to account to the limited liability company and to hold as trustee for it any property, profit, or benefit derived by the member in the conduct or winding up of the company's business, from a use by the member of the company's property, or from the appropriation of a limited liability company opportunity;

(B)   as required in Section 409(b)(2) and (g), to refrain from dealing with the company in the conduct or winding up of the company's business as or on behalf of a party having an interest adverse to the company; and

(C)   as required by Section 409(b)(3) and (g), to refrain from competing with the company in the conduct of the company's business before the dissolution of the company;

(2)   identify specific types or categories of activities that do not violate the duty of loyalty;

(3)   alter the duty of care, except to authorize intentional misconduct or knowing violation of law;

(4)   alter any other fiduciary duty, including eliminating particular aspects of that duty; and

(5)   prescribe the standards by which to measure the performance of the contractual obligation of good faith and fair dealing under Section 409(d).

(e)   The operating agreement may specify the method by which a specific act or transaction that would otherwise violate the duty of loyalty may be authorized or ratified by one or more disinterested and independent persons after full disclosure of all material facts.

(f)   To the extent the operating agreement of a member-managed limited liability company expressly relieves a member of a responsibility that the member would otherwise have under this [act] and imposes the responsibility on one or more other members, the operating agreement may, to the benefit of the member that the operating agreement relieves of the responsibility, also eliminate or limit any fiduciary duty that would have pertained to the responsibility.

(g)   The operating agreement may alter or eliminate the indemnification for a member or manager provided by Section 408(a) and may eliminate or limit a member or manager's liability to the limited liability company and members for money damages, except for:

(1)   breach of the duty of loyalty;

(2)   a financial benefit received by the member or manager to which the member or manager is not entitled;

(3)   a breach of a duty under Section 406;

(4) intentional infliction of harm on the company or a member; or

(5) an intentional violation of criminal law.

(h) The court shall decide any claim under subsection (d) that a term of an operating agreement is manifestly unreasonable. The court:

(1) shall make its determination as of the time the challenged term became part of the operating agreement and by considering only circumstances existing at that time; and

(2) may invalidate the term only if, in light of the purposes and activities of the limited liability company, it is readily apparent that:

(A) the objective of the term is unreasonable; or

(B) the term is an unreasonable means to achieve the provision's objective.

Comment

The operating agreement is pivotal to a limited liability company, and Sections 110 through 112 are pivotal to this Act. They must be read together, along with Section 102(13) (defining the operating agreement).

One of the most complex questions in the law of unincorporated business organizations is the extent to which an agreement among the organization's owners can affect the law of fiduciary duty. This section gives special attention to that question and is organized as follows:

Subsection (a)	grants broad, *general* authority to the operating agreement
Subsection (b)	establishes this Act as comprising the "default rules" ("gap fillers") for matters within the purview of the operating agreement but not addressed by the operating agreement
Subsection (c)	states restrictions on the power of the operating agreement, especially but not exclusively with regard to fiduciary duties and the contractual obligation of good faith
Subsection (d)	contains *specific* grants of authority for the operating agreement with regard to fiduciary duty and the contractual obligation of good faith; expressed so as to state restrictions on those specific grants—including the "if not manifestly unreasonable" standard
Subsection (e)	specifically grants the operating agreement the power to provide mechanisms for approving or ratifying conduct that would otherwise violate the duty of loyalty; expressed so as to state restrictions on those mechanism—full disclosure and disinterested and independent decision makers
Subsection (f)	specifically authorizes the operating agreement to divest a member of fiduciary duty with regard to a matter if the operating agreement is also divesting the person of responsibility for the matter (and imposing that responsibility on one or more other members)
Subsection (g)	contains *specific* grants of authority for the operating agreement with regard to indemnification and exculpatory provisions; expressed so as to state restrictions on those specific grants
Subsection (h)	provides rules for applying the "not manifestly unreasonable" standard established by subsection (d)

A limited liability company is as much a creature of contract as of statute, and Section 102(13) delineates a very broad scope for "operating agreement." As a result, once an LLC comes into existence and has a member, the LLC necessarily has an operating agreement. *See* Comment to Section 102(13). Accordingly, this Act refers to "the operating agreement" rather than "an operating agreement."

This phrasing should not, however, be read to require a limited liability company or its members to take any formal action to adopt an operating agreement. *Compare* CAL. CORP. CODE § 17050(a) (West 2006) ("In order to form a limited liability company, one or more persons shall execute and file articles of organization with, and on a form prescribed by, the Secretary of State and, either before or after the filing of articles of organization, the members shall have entered into an operating agreement.")

The operating agreement is the exclusive consensual process for modifying this Act's various default rules pertaining to relationships *inter se* the members and between the members and the limited liability company. Section 110(b). The operating agreement also has power over "the rights and duties under this [act] of a person in the capacity of manager," subsection (a)(2), and "the obligations of a limited liability company and its members to a person in the person's capacity as a transferee or dissociated member." Section 112(b).

Subsection (a)—This section describes the very broad scope of a limited liability company's operating agreement, which includes all matters constituting "internal affairs." *Compare* Section 106(1) (using the phrase "internal affairs" in stating a choice of law rule). This broad grant of authority is subject to the restrictions stated in subsection (c), including the broad restriction stated in paragraph (c)(11) (concerning the rights under this Act of third parties).

Subsection (a)(1)—Under this Act, a limited liability company is emphatically an entity, and the members lack the power to alter that characteristic.

Subsection (a)(2)—Under this paragraph, the operating agreement has the power to affect the rights and duties of managers (including non-member managers). Because the term "[o]perating agreement. . . . includes the agreement as amended or restated," Section 102(13), this paragraph gives the members the ongoing power to define the role of an LLC's managers. Power is not the same as right, however, and exercising the power provided by this paragraph might constitute a breach of a separate contract between the LLC and the manager. A non-member manager might also have rights under Section 112(a).

Subsection (a)(4)—If the operating agreement does not address this matter, under subsection (b) this Act provides the rule. The rule appears in Section 407(b)(5) and 407(c)(4)(D) (unanimous consent).

This Act does not specially authorize the operating agreement to limit the sources in which terms of the operating agreement might be found or limit amendments to specified modes (*e.g.*, prohibiting modifications except when consented to in writing). *Compare* UCC § 2–209(2) (authorizing such prohibitions in a "signed agreement" for the sale of goods). However, this Paragraph (a)(4) could be read to encompass such authorization. Also, under Section 107 the parol evidence rule will apply to a written operating agreement containing an appropriate merger provision.

Subsection (c)—If a person claims that a term of the operating agreement violates this subsection, as a matter of ordinary procedural law the burden is on the person making the claim.

Subsection (c)(4)—This limitation is less powerful than might first appear, because subsections (d) through (g) specifically authorize significantly alterations to fiduciary duty. The reference to "or any other fiduciary duty" is necessary because the Act has "un-cabined" fiduciary duty. *See* Comment to Section 409.

Subsection (c)(9)—Arbitration and forum selection provisions are commonplace in business agreements, and this paragraph's restrictions do not reflect any special hostility to or skepticism of such provisions.

Subsection (c)(10)—Under Section 1014:

- each member is protected from being merged, converted, or domesticated "into" the status of an unshielded general partner (or comparable position) without the member having *directly* consented to either:

    - the merger, conversion, or domestication; or

    - an operating agreement provision that permits such transactions to occur with less than unanimous consent of the members; and

- merely consenting to an operating agreement provision that permits amendment of the operating agreement with less than unanimous consent of the members does not qualify as the requisite direct consent.

The sole function of subsection (c)(10) is to protect Section 1014 by denying the operating agreement the power to restrict or otherwise undercut the protections of Section 1014.

Subsection (c)(11)—This limitation pertains only to "the rights under this[act] of" third parties. The extent to which an operating agreement can affect other rights of third parties is a question for other law, particularly the law of contracts.

Subsection (d)—Delaware recently amended its LLC statute to permit an operating agreement to fully "eliminate" fiduciary duty within an LLC. This Act rejects the ultra-contractarian notion that fiduciary duty within a business organization is merely a set of default rule and seeks instead to balance the virtues of "freedom of contract" against the dangers that inescapably exist when some have power over the interests of others. As one source has explained:

> The open-ended nature of fiduciary duty reflects the law's long-standing recognition that devious people can smell a loophole a mile away. For centuries, the law has assumed that (1) power creates opportunities for abuse and (2) the devious creativity of those in power may outstrip the prescience of those trying, through ex ante contract drafting, to constrain that combination of power and creativity.

CARTER G. BISHOP AND DANIEL S. KLEINBERGER, LIMITED LIABILITY COMPANIES: TAX AND BUSINESS LAW, ¶ 14.05[4][a][ii]

Subsection (h) contains rules for applying the "not manifestly unreasonable" standard.

Subsection (d)(1)—Subject to the "not manifestly unreasonable" standard, this paragraph empowers the operating agreement to eliminate <u>all</u> aspects of the duty of loyalty listed in Section 409. The contractual obligation of good faith would remain, *see* subsections(c)(5) and (d)(5), as would any other, uncodified aspects of the duty of loyalty. *See* Comment to Section 409 (explaining the decision to "un-cabin" fiduciary duty). *See also* subsection (d)(4) (empowering the operating agreement to "alter any other fiduciary duty, including eliminating particular aspects of that duty").

Subsection (d)(3)—The operating agreement's power to affect this Act's duty of care both parallels and differs from the agreement's power to affect this Act's duty of loyalty as well as any other fiduciary duties not codified in the statute. With regard to all fiduciary duties, the operating agreement is subject to the "manifestly unreasonable" standard. The differences concern: (i) the extent of the operating agreement's power to restrict the duty; and (ii) the power of the operating agreement to provide indemnity or exculpation for persons subject to the duty.

duty	extent of operating agreement's power to restrict the duty (subject to the "manifestly unreasonable" standard) § 110(d)(1), (3) and (4)	power of the operating agreement to provide indemnity or exculpation w/r/t breach of the duty § 110(g)
loyalty	restrict or completely eliminate	none
care	alter, but not eliminate; specifically may not authorize intentional misconduct or knowing violation of law	complete
other fiduciary duties, not codified in the statute	restrict or completely eliminate Section 110(4)	complete

Subsection (e)—Section 409(f) states the Act's default rule for authorization or ratification—unanimous consent. This subsection specifically empowers the operating agreement to provide alternate mechanisms but, in doing so, imposes significant restrictions—namely, any alternate mechanism must involve full disclosure to, and the disinterestedness and independence of, the decision makers. These restrictions are consonant with ordinary notions of authorization and ratification.

This Act provides four separate methods through which those with management power in a limited liability company can proceed with conduct that would otherwise violate the duty of loyalty:

Method	Statutory Authority
The operating agreement might eliminate the duty or otherwise permit the conduct, without need for further authorization or ratification.	Section 110(d)(1) and (2)
The conduct might be authorized or ratified by all the members after full disclosure.	Section 409(f)
The operating agreement might establish a mechanism other than the informed consent for authorizing or ratifying the conduct.	Section 110(e)
In the case of self-dealing the conduct might be successfully defended as being or having been fair to the limited liability company.	Section 409(e)

Subsection (f)—This subsection is intended to make clear that—regardless of the strictures stated elsewhere in this section—in the specified circumstances the operating agreement can entirely strip away the pertinent fiduciary duties.

Subsection (g)—This subsection specifically empowers the operating agreement to address matters of indemnification and exculpation but subjects that power to stated limitations. Those limitations are drawn from the raft of exculpatory provisions that sprung up in corporate statutes in response to *Smith v. Van Gorkum*, 488 A.2d 858 (Del. 1985). Delaware led the response with DEL. CODE ANN. tit. 8, § 102(b)(7) (2006), and a number of LLC statutes have similar provisions. *E.g.* GA. CODE ANN. § 14–11–305(4)(A) (West 2006); IDAHO CODE ANN. § 53–624(1) (2006). For an extreme example, *see* VA. CODE ANN. § 13.1–1025 (West 2006) (establishing limits of monetary liability as the default rule).

The restrictions stated in paragraphs (1) through (5) apply both to indemnification and exculpation. The power to "alter or eliminate the indemnification provided by Section 408(a)" includes the power to expand or reduce that indemnification.

Subsection (g)(4)—Due to this paragraph, an exculpatory provision cannot shield against a member's claim of oppression. *See* Section 701(a)(5)(B) and (b).

Subsection (h)—The "not manifestly unreasonable standard" became part of uniform business entity statutes when RUPA imported the concept from the Uniform Commercial Code. This subsection provides rules for applying that standard, which are necessary because:

- Determining unreasonableness *inter se* owners of an organization is a different task than doing so in a commercial context, where concepts like "usages of trade" are available to inform the analysis. Each business organization must be understood in its own terms and context.

- If loosely applied, the standard would permit a court to rewrite the members' agreement, which would destroy the balance this Act seeks to establish between freedom of contract and fiduciary duty.

- Case law research indicates that courts have tended to disregard the significance of the word "manifestly."

- Some decisions have considered reasonableness as of the time of the complaint, which means that a prospectively reasonable allocation of risk could be overturned because it functioned as agreed.

If a person claims that a term of the operating agreement in manifestly unreasonable under subsections (d) and (h), as a matter of ordinary procedural law the burden is on the person making the claim.

Subsection (h)(1)—The significance of the phrase "as of the time the term as challenged became part of the operating agreement" is best shown by example.

EXAMPLE: An LLC's operating agreement as initially adopted includes a provision subjecting a matter to "the manager's sole, reasonable discretion." A year later, the agreement is amended to delete the word "reasonable." Later, a member claims that, without the word "reasonable," the provision is manifestly unreasonable. The relevant time under subsection (h)(1) is when the agreement was amended, not when the agreement was initially adopted.

EXAMPLE: When a particular manager-managed LLC comes into existence, its business plan is quite unusual and its success depends on the willingness of a particular individual to serve as the LLC's sole manager. This individual has a rare combination of skills, experiences, and contacts, which are particularly appropriate for the LLC's start-up. In order to induce the individual to accept the position of sole manager, the members are willing to have the operating agreement significantly limit the manager's fiduciary duties. Several years later, when the LLC's operations have turned prosaic and the manager's talents and background are not nearly so crucial, a member challenges the fiduciary duty limitations as manifestly unreasonable. The relevant time under subsection (h)(1) is when the LLC began. Subsequent developments are not relevant, except as they might inferentially bear on the circumstances in existence at the relevant time.

§ 111. Operating Agreement; Effect on Limited Liability Company and Persons Becoming Members; Pre-Formation Agreement

(a) A limited liability company is bound by and may enforce the operating agreement, whether or not the company has itself manifested assent to the operating agreement.

(b) A person that becomes a member of a limited liability company is deemed to assent to the operating agreement.

(c) Two or more persons intending to become the initial members of a limited liability company may make an agreement providing that upon the formation of the company the agreement will become the operating agreement. One person intending to become the initial member of a limited liability company may assent to terms providing that upon the formation of the company the terms will become the operating agreement.

Comment

Subsection (a)—This subsection does not consider whether a limited liability company is an indispensable party to a suit concerning the operating agreement. That is a question of procedural law, which can determine whether federal diversity jurisdiction exists.

Subsection (b)—Given the possibility of oral and implied-in-fact components to the operating agreement, *see* Comment to Section 110(a)(4), a person becoming a member of an existing limited liability company should take precautions to ascertain fully the contents of the operating agreement.

Subsection (c)—The second sentence refers to "assent to terms" rather than "make an agreement" because, under venerable principles of contract law, an agreement presupposes at least two parties. This Act specifically defines the operating agreement to include a sole member, Section 102(13), but a preformation arrangement is not an operating agreement. An operating agreement is among "members," and, under this Act, the earliest a person can become a member is upon the formation of the limited liability company. Section 401.

§ 112. Operating Agreement; Effect on Third Parties and Relationship to Records Effective on Behalf of Limited Liability Company

(a) An operating agreement may specify that its amendment requires the approval of a person that is not a party to the operating agreement or the satisfaction of a condition. An amendment is ineffective if its adoption does not include the required approval or satisfy the specified condition.

(b) The obligations of a limited liability company and its members to a person in the person's capacity as a transferee or dissociated member are governed by the operating agreement. Subject only to any court order issued under Section 503(b)(2) to effectuate a charging order, an amendment to the operating agreement made after a person becomes a transferee or dissociated member is effective with regard to any debt, obligation, or other liability of the limited liability company or its members to the person in the person's capacity as a transferee or dissociated member.

(c)   If a record that has been delivered by a limited liability company to the [Secretary of State] for filing and has become effective under this [act] contains a provision that would be ineffective under Section 110(c) if contained in the operating agreement, the provision is likewise ineffective in the record.

(d)   Subject to subsection (c), if a record that has been delivered by a limited liability company to the [Secretary of State] for filing and has become effective under this [act] conflicts with a provision of the operating agreement:

>   (1)   the operating agreement prevails as to members, dissociated members, transferees, and managers; and

>   (2)   the record prevails as to other persons to the extent they reasonably rely on the record.

Comment

Subsection (a)—This subsection, derived from DEL. CODE ANN. tit. 6, § 18–302(e), permits a non-member to have veto rights over amendments to the operating agreement. Such veto rights are likely to be sought by lenders but may also be attractive to non-member managers.

> EXAMPLE: A non-member manager enters into a management contract with the LLC, and that agreement provides in part that the LLC may remove the manager without cause only with the consent of members holding 2/3 of the profits interests. The operating agreement contains a parallel provision, but the non-member manager is not a party to the operating agreement. Later the LLC members amend the operating agreement to change the quantum to a simple majority and thereafter purport to remove the manager without cause. Although the LLC has undoubtedly breached its contract with the manager and subjected itself to a damage claim, the LLC has the power under Section 110(a)(2) to effect the removal—unless the operating agreement provided the non-member manager a veto right over changes in the quantum provision.

The subsection does not refer to member veto rights because, unless otherwise provided in the operating agreement, the consent of each member is necessary to effect an amendment. Section 407(b)(5) and (c)(4)(D).

Subsection (b)—The law of unincorporated business organizations is only beginning to grapple in a modern way with the tension between the rights of an organization's owners to carry on their activities as they see fit (or have agreed) and the rights of transferees of the organization's economic interests. (Such transferees can include the heirs of business founders as well as former owners who are "locked in" as transferees of their own interests. *See* Section 603(a)(3).).

If the law categorically favors the owners, there is a serious risk of expropriation and other abuse. On the other hand, if the law grants former owners and other transferees the right to seek judicial protection, that specter can "freeze the deal" as of the moment an owner leaves the enterprise or a third party obtains an economic interest.

Bauer v. Blomfield Co. / Holden Joint Venture, 849 P.2d 1365 (Alaska 1993) illustrates this point nicely. The case arose after all the partners had approved a commission arrangement with a third party and the arrangement dried up all the partnership profits. When an assignee of a partnership interest objected, the court majority flatly rejected not only the claim but also the assignee's right to assert the claim. A mere assignee "was not entitled to complain about a decision made with the consent of all the partners." *Id.* at 1367. A footnote explained, "We are unwilling to hold that partners owe a duty of good faith and fair dealing to assignees of a partner's interest." *Id.* at 1367, n. 2.

The dissent, invoking the law of contracts, asserted that the majority had turned the statutory protection of the partners' management prerogatives into an instrument for abuse of assignees:

It is a well-settled principle of contract law that an assignee steps into the shoes of an assignor as to the rights assigned. Today, the court summarily dismisses this principle in a footnote and leaves the assignee barefoot. . . .

As interpreted by the court, the [partnership] statute now allows partners to deprive an assignee of profits to which he is entitled by law for whatever outrageous motive or reason. The court's opinion essentially leaves the assignee of a partnership interest without remedy to enforce his right.

Id. at 1367–8 (Matthews, J., dissenting).

The *Bauer* majority is consistent with the limited but long-standing case law in this area (all of it pertaining to partnerships rather than LLCs). This subsection follows the *Bauer* majority and other cases by expressly subjecting transferees and dissociated members to operating agreement amendments made after the transfer or dissociation. *Compare* UPA § 32(2) (permitting an assignee to seek judicial dissolution of an at-will general partnership at any time and of a partnership for a term or undertaking if partnership continues in existence after the completion of the term or undertaking); RUPA § 801(6) (same except adding the requirement that the court determine that dissolution is equitable); ULLCA, § 801(5) (same as RUPA); ULLCA, § 801(4) (permitting a dissociated member to seek dissolution on the grounds *inter alia* of oppressive conduct). *See also* UCC §§ 9–405(a) and (b) and RESTATEMENT (SECOND) OF CONTRACTS § 338 (1981) (recognizing a duty of good faith applicable to the modification of a contract when an assignment of contract is in effect).

The issue of whether, in extreme and sufficiently harsh circumstances, transferees might be able to claim some type of duty or obligation to protect against expropriation, is a question for other law.

Subsection (d)—A limited liability company is a creature of contract as well as a creature of statute. It will be possible, albeit improvident, for the operating agreement to be inconsistent with the certificate of organization or other public filings pertaining to the limited liability company. For those circumstances, this subsection provides rules for determining which source of information prevails.

For members, managers and transferees, the operating agreement is paramount. For third parties seeking to invoke the public record, actual knowledge of that record is necessary and notice, deemed notice, and deemed knowledge under Section 103 are irrelevant. A third party wishing to enforce the public record over the operating agreement must show reasonable reliance on the public record, and reliance presupposes knowledge.

The mere fact that a term is present in a publicly-filed record and not in the operating agreement, or *vice versa*, does not automatically establish a conflict. This subsection does not expressly cover a situation in which (i) one of the specified filed records contains information in addition to, but not inconsistent with, the operating agreement, and (ii) a person, other than a member or transferee, reasonably relies on the additional information. However, the policy reflected in this subsection seems equally applicable to that situation.

Section 110(a)(4) might also be relevant to the subject matter of this subsection. Absent a contrary provision in the operating agreement, language in an LLC's certificate of organization might be evidence of the members' agreement and might thereby constitute or at least imply a term of the operating agreement.

This subsection does not apply to records delivered to the [Secretary of State] for filing on behalf of persons other than a limited liability company.

§ 113.   Office and Agent for Service of Process

(a)   A limited liability company shall designate and continuously maintain in this state:

   (1)   an office, which need not be a place of its activity in this state; and

   (2)   an agent for service of process.

(b)   A foreign limited liability company that has a certificate of authority under Section 802 shall designate and continuously maintain in this state an agent for service of process.

(c)   An agent for service of process of a limited liability company or foreign limited liability company must be an individual who is a resident of this state or other person with authority to transact business in this state.

Comment

Source: ULPA (2001), § 114.

§ 114.   Change of Designated Office or Agent for Service of Process

(a)   A limited liability company or foreign limited liability company may change its designated office, its agent for service of process, or the address of its agent for service of process by delivering to the [Secretary of State] for filing a statement of change containing:

(1)   the name of the company;

(2)   the street and mailing addresses of its current designated office;

(3)   if the current designated office is to be changed, the street and mailing addresses of the new designated office;

(4)   the name and street and mailing addresses of its current agent for service of process; and

(5)   if the current agent for service of process or an address of the agent is to be changed, the new information.

(b)   Subject to Section 205(c), a statement of change is effective when filed by the [Secretary of State].

Comment

Source—ULPA (2001) § 115, which is based on ULLCA § 109.

Subsection (a)—This subsection uses "may" rather than "shall" because other avenues exist. A limited liability company may also change the information by amending its certificate of organization, Section 202, or through its annual report. Section 209(e). A foreign limited liability company may use its annual report. Section 209(e). However, neither a limited liability company nor a foreign limited liability company may wait for the annual report if the information described in the public record becomes inaccurate. See Sections 207 (imposing liability for false information in record) and 116(b) (providing for substitute service).

§ 115.   Resignation of Agent for Service of Process

(a)   To resign as an agent for service of process of a limited liability company or foreign limited liability company, the agent must deliver to the [Secretary of State] for filing a statement of resignation containing the company name and stating that the agent is resigning.

(b)   The [Secretary of State] shall file a statement of resignation delivered under subsection (a) and mail or otherwise provide or deliver a copy to the designated office of the limited liability company or foreign limited liability company and another copy to the principal office of the company if the mailing addresses of the principal office appears in the records of the [Secretary of State] and is different from the mailing address of the designated office.

(c)   An agency for service of process terminates on the earlier of:

(1)   the 31st day after the [Secretary of State] files the statement of resignation;

(2)   when a record designating a new agent for service of process is delivered to the [Secretary of State] for filing on behalf of the limited liability company and becomes effective.

Comment

Source—ULPA (2001) § 116, which is based on ULLCA § 110.

§ 116. Service of Process

(a)   An agent for service of process appointed by a limited liability company or foreign limited liability company is an agent of the company for service of any process, notice, or demand required or permitted by law to be served on the company.

(b)   If a limited liability company or foreign limited liability company does not appoint or maintain an agent for service of process in this state or the agent for service of process cannot with reasonable diligence be found at the agent's street address, the [Secretary of State] is an agent of the company upon whom process, notice, or demand may be served.

(c)   Service of any process, notice, or demand on the [Secretary of State] as agent for a limited liability company or foreign limited liability company may be made by delivering to the [Secretary of State] duplicate copies of the process, notice, or demand. If a process, notice, or demand is served on the [Secretary of State], the [Secretary of State] shall forward one of the copies by registered or certified mail, return receipt requested, to the company at its designated office.

(d)   Service is effected under subsection (c) at the earliest of:

(1)   the date the limited liability company or foreign limited liability company receives the process, notice, or demand;

(2)   the date shown on the return receipt, if signed on behalf of the company; or

(3)   five days after the process, notice, or demand is deposited with the United States Postal Service, if correctly addressed and with sufficient postage.

(e)   The [Secretary of State] shall keep a record of each process, notice, and demand served pursuant to this section and record the time of, and the action taken regarding, the service.

(f)   This section does not affect the right to serve process, notice, or demand in any other manner provided by law.

Comment

Source—ULPA (2001) § 117, which is based on ULLCA § 111.

[ARTICLE] 2

FORMATION; CERTIFICATE OF ORGANIZATION AND OTHER FILINGS

§ 201. Formation of Limited Liability Company; Certificate of Organization

(a)   One or more persons may act as organizers to form a limited liability company by signing and delivering to the [Secretary of State] for filing a certificate of organization.

(b)   A certificate of organization must state:

(1)   the name of the limited liability company, which must comply with Section 108;

(2)   the street and mailing addresses of the initial designated office and the name and street and mailing addresses of the initial agent for service of process of the company; and

(3)   if the company will have no members when the [Secretary of State] files the certificate, a statement to that effect.

(c)   Subject to Section 112(c), a certificate of organization may also contain statements as to matters other than those required by subsection (b). However, a statement in a certificate of organization is not effective as a statement of authority.

(d)   Unless the filed certificate of organization contains the statement as provided in subsection (b)(3), the following rules apply:

(1)   A limited liability company is formed when the [Secretary of State] has filed the certificate of organization and the company has at least one member, unless the certificate states a delayed effective date pursuant to Section 205(c).

(2)   If the certificate states a delayed effective date, a limited liability company is not formed if, before the certificate takes effect, a statement of cancellation is signed and delivered to the [Secretary of State] for filing and the [Secretary of State] files the certificate.

(3)   Subject to any delayed effective date and except in a proceeding by this state to dissolve a limited liability company, the filing of the certificate of organization by the [Secretary of State] is conclusive proof that the organizer satisfied all conditions to the formation of a limited liability company.

(e)   If a filed certificate of organization contains a statement as provided in subsection (b)(3), the following rules apply:

(1)   The certificate lapses and is void unless, within [90] days from the date the [Secretary of State] files the certificate, an organizer signs and delivers to the [Secretary of State] for filing a notice stating:

(A)   that the limited liability company has at least one member; and

(B)   the date on which a person or persons became the company's initial member or members.

(2)   If an organizer complies with paragraph (1), a limited liability company is deemed formed as of the date of initial membership stated in the notice delivered pursuant to paragraph (1).

(3)   Except in a proceeding by this state to dissolve a limited liability company, the filing of the notice described in paragraph (1) by the [Secretary of State] is conclusive proof that the organizer satisfied all conditions to the formation of a limited liability company.

Legislative Note: Enacting jurisdictions should consider revising their "name statutes" generally, to protect "the limited liability company name stated in each certificate of organization that contains the statement as provided in Section 201(b)(3)." Section 108(b)(2).

Comment

No topic received more attention or generated more debate in the drafting process for this Act than the question of the "shelf LLC"—i.e., an LLC formed without having at least one member upon formation. Reasonable minds differed (occasionally intensely) as to whether the "shelf" approach (i) is necessary to accommodate current business practices; and (ii) somehow does conceptual violence to the partnership antecedents of the limited liability company.

The 2006 Annual Meeting Draft provided for a "limited shelf"—a shelf that lacked capacity to conduct any substantive activities:

(a)   Except as otherwise provided in subsection (b), a limited liability company has the capacity to sue and be sued in its own name and the power to do all things necessary or convenient to carry on its activities.

(b)   Until a limited liability company has or has had at least one member, the company lacks the capacity to do any act or carry on any activity except:

(1)   delivering to the [Secretary of State] for filing a statement of change under Sections 114, an amendment to the certificate under Section 202, a statement of correction under Section 206, an annual report under section 209, and a statement of termination under Section 702(b)(2)(F);

(2)   admitting a member under section 401; and

(3)   dissolving under Section 701.

(c)   A limited liability company that has or has had at least one member may ratify an act or activity that occurred when the company lacked capacity under subsection (b).

However, when the Conference considered the 2006 Annual Meeting Draft, the Drafting Committee itself proposed an amendment, and the Conference agreed. A product of intense discussion and compromise with several ABA Advisors, the amendment substituted a double filing and "embryonic certificate" approach. An organizer may deliver for filing a certificate of organization without the company having any members and the filing officer will file the certificate, but:

- the certificate as delivered to the filing officer must acknowledge that situation, Subsection (a)(3);

- the limited liability company is not formed until and unless the organizer timely delivers to the filing officer a notice that the company has at least one member, Subsection (e)(1); and

- if the organizer does not timely deliver the required notice, the certificate lapses and is void. *Id.*

The Conference recommends a 90-day "window" for filing the notice, which must state "the date on which a person or persons became the company's initial member or members." When the filing officer files that notice, the company is deemed formed as of the date stated in the notice. Subsection (e)(2).

Thus under this Act, the delivery to the filing officer of a certificate of organization has different consequences, depending on whether the certificate contains the "no members" statement as provided by subsection (b)(3).

does the certificate contain the "no members" statement under subsection (b)(3)	by delivering the certificate for filing, what is the organizer affirming, per Section 207(c), about members	effect of the filing officer filing the certificate	logical relationship of the filed certificate to the formation of the LLC
no	that the LLC will have at least one member upon formation	LLC is formed, subject to any delayed effective date	necessary and sufficient
yes	that the LLC will have no members when the filing officer files the certificate	the document is part of the public record, protects the name, and starts the 90-day clock ticking	necessary but not sufficient

Subsection (b)—This Act does not require the certificate of organization to designate whether the limited liability company is manager-managed or member-managed. Under this Act, those characterizations pertain principally to *inter se* relations, and the Act therefore looks to the operating agreement to make the characterization. *See* Sections 102(10) and (12); 407(a).

Subsection (d)—This subsection states the "pathway" through which a limited liability company is formed if the certificate of organization does not contain a statement as provided in subsection (b)(3)—i.e., if the limited liability company will have at least one member when the filing officer files the certificate.

Subsection (e)—This subsection states the "pathway" through which a limited liability company is formed if the certificate of organization contains a statement as provided in subsection (b)(3)—i.e., if the limited liability company will not have at least one member when the filing officer files the certificate.

This pathway requires a second filing in order to form the limited liability company: "a notice stating (A) that the limited liability company has at least one member; and (B) the date on which a person or persons became the company's initial member or members." Subsection (e)(1).

In this pathway, a certificate of organization may not itself state a delayed effective date, Section 205(c), because:

- the reason to state a delayed effective date in a certificate of organization is to set the date on which the limited liability company is formed, Section 205(c); and

- when a certificate contains a statement as provided in subsection (b)(3), this Act mandates when (if at all) the limited liability company is deemed formed—i.e., "as of the date of initial membership stated in the notice delivered" to the filing officer as the second filing. Subsection (e)(2).

§ 202. Amendment or Restatement of Certificate of Organization

(a) A certificate of organization may be amended or restated at any time.

(b) To amend its certificate of organization, a limited liability company must deliver to the [Secretary of State] for filing an amendment stating:

(1) the name of the company;

(2) the date of filing of its certificate of organization; and

(3) the changes the amendment makes to the certificate as most recently amended or restated.

(c) To restate its certificate of organization, a limited liability company must deliver to the [Secretary of State] for filing a restatement, designated as such in its heading, stating:

(1) in the heading or an introductory paragraph, the company's present name and the date of the filing of the company's initial certificate of organization;

(2) if the company's name has been changed at any time since the company's formation, each of the company's former names; and

(3) the changes the restatement makes to the certificate as most recently amended or restated.

(d) Subject to Sections 112(c) and 205(c), an amendment to or restatement of a certificate of organization is effective when filed by the [Secretary of State].

(e) If a member of a member-managed limited liability company, or a manager of a manager-managed limited liability company, knows that any information in a filed certificate of organization was inaccurate when the certificate was filed or has become inaccurate owing to changed circumstances, the member or manager shall promptly:

(1) cause the certificate to be amended; or

(2) if appropriate, deliver to the [Secretary of State] for filing a statement of change under Section 114 or a statement of correction under Section 206.

Comment

Subsection (e)—This subsection is taken from ULPA (2001) § 202(c), which imposes the responsibility on general partners. The original ULLCA had no comparable provision.

This subsection imposes an obligation directly on the members and managers rather than on the limited liability company. A member or manager's failure to meet the obligation exposes the member or manager to liability to third parties under Section 207(a)(2) and might constitute a breach of the member or manager's duties under Section 409(c) and (g)(1). In addition, an aggrieved person may seek a remedy under Section 204 (Signing and Filing Pursuant to Judicial Order).

Like other provisions of the Act requiring records to be delivered to the filing officer for filing, this section is not subject to change by the operating agreement. *See* Section 110(c)(11) (precluding the operating agreement from "restrict[ing] the rights under this [act] of a person other than a member or manager").

§ 203.   Signing of Records to be Delivered for Filing to [Secretary of State]

(a)   A record delivered to the [Secretary of State] for filing pursuant to this [act] must be signed as follows:

(1)   Except as otherwise provided in paragraphs (2) through (4), a record signed on behalf of a limited liability company must be signed by a person authorized by the company.

(2)   A limited liability company's initial certificate of organization must be signed by at least one person acting as an organizer.

(3)   A notice under Section 201(e)(1) must be signed by an organizer.

(4)   A record filed on behalf of a dissolved limited liability company that has no members must be signed by the person winding up the company's activities under Section 702(c) or a person appointed under Section 702(d) to wind up those activities.

(5)   A statement of cancellation under Section 201(d)(2) must be signed by each organizer that signed the initial certificate of organization, but a personal representative of a deceased or incompetent organizer may sign in the place of the decedent or incompetent.

(6)   A statement of denial by a person under Section 303 must be signed by that person.

(7)   Any other record must be signed by the person on whose behalf the record is delivered to the [Secretary of State].

(b)   Any record filed under this [act] may be signed by an agent.

Comment

Subsection (b)—This subsection does not require that the agent's authority be memorialized in a writing or other record. However, a person signing as an agent "thereby affirms under penalties of perjury that [the assertion of agent status is] . . . accurate." Section 207(c).

§ 204.   Signing and Filing Pursuant to Judicial Order

(a)   If a person required by this [act] to sign a record or deliver a record to the [Secretary of State] for filing under [this act] does not do so, any other person that is aggrieved may petition the [appropriate court] to order:

(1)   the person to sign the record;

(2)   the person to deliver the record to the [Secretary of State] for filing; or

(3)   the [Secretary of State] to file the record unsigned.

(b)   If a petitioner under subsection (a) is not the limited liability company or foreign limited liability company to which the record pertains, the petitioner shall make the company a party to the action.

Comment

Source—ULPA (2001) § 205, which is based on RULPA § 205, which was the source of ULLCA § 210.

Subsection (a)(3)—A record filed under this paragraph is effective without being signed.

§ 205.   Delivery to and Filing of Records by [Secretary of State]; Effective Time and Date

(a)   A record authorized or required to be delivered to the [Secretary of State] for filing under this [act] must be captioned to describe the record's purpose, be in a medium permitted by the [Secretary of State], and be delivered to the [Secretary of State]. If the filing fees have been paid, unless the [Secretary of State] determines that a record does not comply with the filing requirements of this [act], the [Secretary of State] shall file the record and:

(1)   for a statement of denial under Section 303, send a copy of the filed statement and a receipt for the fees to the person on whose behalf the statement was delivered for filing and to the limited liability company; and

(2)   for all other records, send a copy of the filed record and a receipt for the fees to the person on whose behalf the record was filed.

(b)   Upon request and payment of the requisite fee, the [Secretary of State] shall send to the requester a certified copy of a requested record.

(c)   Except as otherwise provided in Sections 115 and 206 and except for a certificate of organization that contains a statement as provided in Section 201(b)(3), a record delivered to the [Secretary of State] for filing under this [act] may specify an effective time and a delayed effective date. Subject to Sections 115, 201(d)(1), and 206, a record filed by the [Secretary of State] is effective:

(1)   if the record does not specify either an effective time or a delayed effective date, on the date and at the time the record is filed as evidenced by the [Secretary of State's] endorsement of the date and time on the record;

(2)   if the record specifies an effective time but not a delayed effective date, on the date the record is filed at the time specified in the record;

(3)   if the record specifies a delayed effective date but not an effective time, at 12:01 a.m. on the earlier of:

(A)   the specified date; or

(B)   the 90th day after the record is filed; or

(4)   if the record specifies an effective time and a delayed effective date, at the specified time on the earlier of:

(A)   the specified date; or

(B)   the 90th day after the record is filed.

Comment

Source—ULPA (2001) § 206, which was based on ULLCA § 206.

This Act uses the concept of "filing" to refer to the official act of the [Secretary of State], which is typically preceded by a person "delivering" some record "to the [Secretary of State] for filing."

Subsection (c)(3)(B) and 4(B)—If a person delivers to the Secretary of State for filing a record that contains an over-long delay in the effective date, the Secretary of State: (i) will not reject the record; and (ii) is neither required nor authorized to inform the person that this Act will truncate the period of delay specified in the record.

§ 206.   Correcting Filed Record

(a)   A limited liability company or foreign limited liability company may deliver to the [Secretary of State] for filing a statement of correction to correct a record previously delivered by the company to the [Secretary of State] and filed by the [Secretary of State], if at the time of filing the record contained inaccurate information or was defectively signed.

(b)   A statement of correction under subsection (a) may not state a delayed effective date and must:

(1)   describe the record to be corrected, including its filing date, or attach a copy of the record as filed;

(2)   specify the inaccurate information and the reason it is inaccurate or the manner in which the signing was defective; and

(3)   correct the defective signature or inaccurate information.

(c)   When filed by the [Secretary of State], a statement of correction under subsection (a) is effective retroactively as of the effective date of the record the statement corrects, but the statement is effective when filed:

(1)   for the purposes of Section 103(d); and

(2)   as to persons that previously relied on the uncorrected record and would be adversely affected by the retroactive effect.

Comment

Source—ULPA (2001) § 207, which was based on ULLCA § 207.

§ 207.   Liability for Inaccurate Information in Filed Record

(a)   If a record delivered to the [Secretary of State] for filing under this [act] and filed by the [Secretary of State] contains inaccurate information, a person that suffers a loss by reliance on the information may recover damages for the loss from:

(1)   a person that signed the record, or caused another to sign it on the person's behalf, and knew the information to be inaccurate at the time the record was signed; and

(2)   subject to subsection (b), a member of a member-managed limited liability company or the manager of a manager-managed limited liability company, if:

(A)   the record was delivered for filing on behalf of the company; and

(B)   the member or manager had notice of the inaccuracy for a reasonably sufficient time before the information was relied upon so that, before the reliance, the member or manager reasonably could have:

(i)   effected an amendment under Section 202;

(ii)   filed a petition under Section 204; or

(iii)   delivered to the [Secretary of State] for filing a statement of change under Section 114 or a statement of correction under Section 206.

(b)   To the extent that the operating agreement of a member-managed limited liability company expressly relieves a member of responsibility for maintaining the accuracy of information contained in records delivered on behalf of the company to the [Secretary of State] for filing under this [act] and imposes that responsibility on one or more other members, the liability stated in subsection (a)(2) applies to those other members and not to the member that the operating agreement relieves of the responsibility.

(c)   An individual who signs a record authorized or required to be filed under this [act] affirms under penalty of perjury that the information stated in the record is accurate.

Comment

Source: ULPA (2001) § 208, which expanded on ULLCA § 209.

Section (a)(2)(B)—This subparagraph implies that doing any of the acts listed in clauses (i) through (iii) will preclude liability arising from subsequent reliance. In this connection, Clause (a)(2)(B)(ii) warrants special attention, because that act (filing a petition in court) can occur without any immediate effect on the records relevant to a limited liability company maintained by the filing officer. The other clauses refer to acts that (assuming no filing backlog) affect that public record immediately.

§ 208.   Certificate of Existence or Authorization

(a)   The [Secretary of State], upon request and payment of the requisite fee, shall furnish to any person a certificate of existence for a limited liability company if the records filed in the [office of the Secretary of State] show that the company has been formed under Section 201 and the [Secretary of State] has not filed a statement of termination pertaining to the company. A certificate of existence must state:

(1)   the company's name;

(2)   that the company was duly formed under the laws of this state and the date of formation;

(3)   whether all fees, taxes, and penalties due under this [act] or other law to the [Secretary of State] have been paid;

(4)   whether the company's most recent annual report required by Section 209 has been filed by the [Secretary of State];

(5)   whether the [Secretary of State] has administratively dissolved the company;

(6)   whether the company has delivered to the [Secretary of State] for filing a statement of dissolution;

(7)   that a statement of termination has not been filed by the [Secretary of State]; and

(8)   other facts of record in the [office of the Secretary of State] which are specified by the person requesting the certificate.

(b)   The [Secretary of State], upon request and payment of the requisite fee, shall furnish to any person a certificate of authorization for a foreign limited liability company if the records filed in the [office of the Secretary of State] show that the [Secretary of State] has filed a certificate of authority, has not revoked the certificate of authority, and has not filed a notice of cancellation. A certificate of authorization must state:

(1)   the company's name and any alternate name adopted under Section 805(a) for use in this state;

(2)   that the company is authorized to transact business in this state;

(3)   whether all fees, taxes, and penalties due under this [act] or other law to the [Secretary of State] have been paid;

(4)   whether the company's most recent annual report required by Section 209 has been filed by the [Secretary of State];

(5)   that the [Secretary of State] has not revoked the company's certificate of authority and has not filed a notice of cancellation; and

(6)   other facts of record in the [office of the Secretary of State] which are specified by the person requesting the certificate.

(c)   Subject to any qualification stated in the certificate, a certificate of existence or certificate of authorization issued by the [Secretary of State] is conclusive evidence that the limited liability company is in existence or the foreign limited liability company is authorized to transact business in this state.

Comment

Source—ULPA (2001), § 209, which was based on ULLCA, § 208.

The information provided in a certificate of existence or authorization is, of course, current only as of the date of the certificate.

§ 209. Annual Report for [Secretary of State]

(a) Each year, a limited liability company or a foreign limited liability company authorized to transact business in this state shall deliver to the [Secretary of State] for filing a report that states:

(1) the name of the company;

(2) the street and mailing addresses of the company's designated office and the name and street and mailing addresses of its agent for service of process in this state;

(3) the street and mailing addresses of its principal office; and

(4) in the case of a foreign limited liability company, the state or other jurisdiction under whose law the company is formed and any alternate name adopted under Section 805(a).

(b) Information in an annual report under this section must be current as of the date the report is delivered to the [Secretary of State] for filing.

(c) The first annual report under this section must be delivered to the [Secretary of State] between [January 1 and April 1] of the year following the calendar year in which a limited liability company was formed or a foreign limited liability company was authorized to transact business. A report must be delivered to the [Secretary of State] between [January 1 and April 1] of each subsequent calendar year.

(d) If an annual report under this section does not contain the information required in subsection (a), the [Secretary of State] shall promptly notify the reporting limited liability company or foreign limited liability company and return the report to it for correction. If the report is corrected to contain the information required in subsection (a) and delivered to the [Secretary of State] within 30 days after the effective date of the notice, it is timely delivered.

(e) If an annual report under this section contains an address of a designated office or the name or address of an agent for service of process which differs from the information shown in the records of the [Secretary of State] immediately before the annual report becomes effective, the differing information in the annual report is considered a statement of change under Section 114.

Comment

Source—ULPA (2001) § 210, which was based on ULLCA § 211.

A limited liability company that fails to comply with this section is subject to administrative dissolution. Section 705(a)(2). A foreign limited liability company that fails to comply with this section is subject to having its certificate of authority revoked. Section 806(a)(2).

[ARTICLE] 3

RELATIONS OF MEMBERS AND MANAGERS TO PERSONS DEALING WITH LIMITED LIABILITY COMPANY

§ 301. No Agency Power of Member as Member

(a) A member is not an agent of a limited liability company solely by reason of being a member.

(b) A person's status as a member does not prevent or restrict law other than this [act] from imposing liability on a limited liability company because of the person's conduct.

Comment

Subsection (a)—Most LLC statutes, including the original ULLCA, provide for what might be termed "statutory apparent authority" for members in a member-managed limited liability company and managers in a manager-managed limited liability company. This approach codifies the common law notion of apparent authority by position and dates back at least to the original, 1914 Uniform Partnership Act. UPA, § 9 provided that "the act of every partner . . . for apparently carrying on in the usual way the business of the partnership . . . binds the partnership," and that formulation has been essentially followed by RUPA, § 301, ULLCA, § 301, ULPA (2001), § 402, and myriad state LLC statutes.

This Act rejects the statutory apparent authority approach, for reasons summarized in a "Progress Report on the Revised Uniform Limited Liability Company Act," published in the March 2006 issue of the newsletter of the ABA Committee on Partnerships and Unincorporated Business Organizations:

> The concept [of statutory apparent authority] still makes sense both for general and limited partnerships. A third party dealing with either type of partnership can know by the formal name of the entity and by a person's status as general or limited partner whether the person has the power to bind the entity.
>
> Most LLC statutes have attempted to use the same approach but with a fundamentally important (and problematic) distinction. An LLC's status as member-managed or manager-managed determines whether members or managers have the statutory power to bind. But an LLC's status as member- or manager-managed is not apparent from the LLC's name. A third party must check the public record, which may reveal that the LLC is manager-managed, which in turn means a member as member has no power to bind the LLC. As a result, a provision that originated in 1914 as a protection for third parties can, in the LLC context, easily function as a trap for the unwary. The problem is exacerbated by the almost infinite variety of management structures permissible in and used by LLCs.
>
> The new Act cuts through this problem by simply eliminating statutory apparent authority.

PUBOGRAM, Vol. XXIII, no. 2 at 9–10.

Codifying power to bind according to position makes sense only for organizations that have well-defined, well-known, and almost paradigmatic management structures. Because:

- flexibility of management structure is a hallmark of the limited liability company; and

- an LLC's name gives no signal as to the organization's structure,

it makes no sense to:

- require each LLC to publicly select between two statutorily preordained structures (i.e., manager-managed/member-managed); and then

- link a "statutory power to bind" to each of those two structures.

Under this Act, other law—most especially the law of agency—will handle power-to-bind questions. *See* the Comment to subsection (b).

This subsection does not address the power to bind of a manager in a manager-managed LLC, although this Act does consider a manager's management responsibilities. *See* Section 407(c) (allocating management authority, subject to the operating agreement). For a discussion of how agency law will approach the actual and apparent authority of managers, *see* Section 407(c), cmt.

Subsection (b)—As the "flip side" to subsection (a), this subsection expressly preserves the power of other law to hold an LLC directly or vicariously liable on account of conduct by a person who happens to be a member. For example, given the proper set of circumstances: (i) a member might have actual or apparent authority to bind an LLC to a contract; (ii) the doctrine of *respondeat superior* might make an LLC liable for the tortious conduct of a member (i.e., in some circumstances a member acts as a "servant" of the LLC); and (iii) an LLC might be liable for negligently supervising a member who is acting on behalf of the LLC. A person's status as a member does not weigh against these or any other relevant theories of law.

Moreover, subsection (a) does not prevent member status from being relevant to one or more elements of an "other law" theory. The most categorical example concerns the authority of a non-manager member of a manager-managed LLC.

EXAMPLE: A vendor knows that an LLC is manager-managed but chooses to accept the signature of a person whom the vendor knows is merely a member of the LLC. Assuring the vendor that the LLC will stand by the member's commitment, the member states, "It's such a simple matter; no one will mind." The member genuinely believes the statement, and the vendor accepts the assurance.

The person's status as a mere member will undermine a claim of apparent authority. RESTATEMENT (THIRD) OF AGENCY § 2.03, cmt. d (2006) (explaining the "reasonable belief" element of a claim of apparent authority, and role played by context, custom, and the supposed agent's position in an organization). Likewise, the member will have no actual authority. Absent additional facts, section 407(c)(1) (vesting all management authority in the managers) renders the member's belief unreasonable. RESTATEMENT (THIRD) OF AGENCY § 2.01, cmt. c (2006) (explaining the "reasonable belief" element of a claim of actual authority).

In general, a member's actual authority to act for an LLC will depend fundamentally on the operating agreement.

EXAMPLE: Rachael and Sam, who have known each other for years, decide to go into business arranging musical tours. They fill out and electronically sign a one page form available on the website of the Secretary of State and become the organizers of MMT, LLC. They are the only members of the LLC, and their understanding of who will do what in managing the enterprise is based on several lengthy, late-night conversations that preceded the LLC's formation. Sam is to "get the acts," and Rachael is to manage the tour logistics. There is no written operating agreement.

In the terminology of this Act, MMT, LLC is member-managed, Section 407(a), and the understanding reached in the late night conversations has become part of the LLC's operating agreement. Section 111(c). In agency law terms, the operating agreement constitutes a manifestation by the LLC to Rachael and Sam concerning the scope of their respective authority to act on behalf of the LLC. RESTATEMENT (THIRD) OF AGENCY § 2.01, cmt. c (2006) (explaining that a person's actual authority depends first on some manifestation attributable to the principal and stating: "Actual authority is a consequence of a principal's expressive conduct toward an agent, through which the principal manifests assent to be affected by the agent's action, and the agent's reasonable understanding of the principal's manifestation.")

Circumstances outside the operating agreement can also be relevant to determining the scope of a member's actual authority.

EXAMPLE: Homeworks, LLC is a manager-managed LLC with three members. The LLC's written operating agreement:

- specifies in considerable detail the management responsibilities of Margaret, the LLC's manager-member, and also states that Margaret is responsible for "the day-to-day operations" of the company;

- puts Garrett, a non-manager member, in charge of the LLC's transportation department; and

- specifies no management role for Brooksley, the third member.

When the LLC's chief financial officer quits suddenly, Margaret asks Brooksley, a CPA, to "step in until we can hire a replacement."

Under the operating agreement, Margaret's request to Brooksley is within Margaret's actual authority and is a manifestation attributable to the LLC. If Brooksley manifests assent to Margaret's request, Brooksley will have the actual authority to act as the LLC's CFO.

In the unlikely event that two or more people form a member-managed LLC without any understanding of how to allocate management responsibility between or among them, agency law, operating in the context the Act's "gap fillers" on management responsibility, will produce the following result:

A single member of a multi-member, member-managed LLC:

- has no actual authority to commit the LLC to any matter "outside the ordinary course of the activities of the company," section 407(b)(3); and

- has the actual authority to commit the LLC to any matter "in the ordinary course of the activities of the company," section 407(b)(2), unless the member has reason to know that other members might disagree or the member has some other reason to know that consultation with fellow members is appropriate.

For an explanation of this result, *see* Section 407(c), cmt., which provides a detailed agency law analysis in the context of a multi-manager, manager-managed LLC whose operating agreement is silent on the analogous question.

The common law of agency will also determine the apparent authority of a member of a member-managed LLC, and in that analysis what the particular third party knows or has reason to know about the management structure and business practices of the particular LLC will always be relevant. RESTATEMENT (THIRD) OF AGENCY § 3.03, cmt. b (2006) ("A principal may also make a manifestation by placing an agent in a defined position in an organization . . . . Third parties who interact with the principal through the agent will naturally and reasonably assume that the agent has authority to do acts consistent with the agent's position . . . unless they have notice of facts suggesting that this may not be so.")

Under section 301(a), however, the mere fact that a person is a member of a member-managed limited liability company cannot *by itself* establish apparent authority by position. A course of dealing, however, may easily change the analysis:

EXAMPLE: David is a one of two members of DS, LLC, a member-managed LLC. David orders paper clips on behalf of the LLC, signing the purchase agreement, "David, as a member of DS, LLC." The vendor accepts the order, sends an invoice to the LLC's address, and in due course receives a check drawn on the LLC's bank account. When David next places an order with the vendor, the LLC's payment of the first order is a manifestation that the vendor may use in establishing David's apparent authority to place the second order.

§ 302. Statement of Authority

(a) A limited liability company may deliver to the [Secretary of State] for filing a statement of authority. The statement:

(1) must include the name of the company and the street and mailing addresses of its designated office;

(2) with respect to any position that exists in or with respect to the company, may state the authority, or limitations on the authority, of all persons holding the position to:

(A) execute an instrument transferring real property held in the name of the company; or

(B) enter into other transactions on behalf of, or otherwise act for or bind, the company; and

(3) may state the authority, or limitations on the authority, of a specific person to:

(A) execute an instrument transferring real property held in the name of the company; or

(B) enter into other transactions on behalf of, or otherwise act for or bind, the company.

(b) To amend or cancel a statement of authority filed by the [Secretary of State] under Section 205(a), a limited liability company must deliver to the [Secretary of State] for filing an amendment or cancellation stating:

(1) the name of the company;

(2) the street and mailing addresses of the company's designated office;

(3) the caption of the statement being amended or canceled and the date the statement being affected became effective; and

(4) the contents of the amendment or a declaration that the statement being affected is canceled.

(c) A statement of authority affects only the power of a person to bind a limited liability company to persons that are not members.

(d)   Subject to subsection (c) and Section 103(d) and except as otherwise provided in subsections (f), (g), and (h), a limitation on the authority of a person or a position contained in an effective statement of authority is not by itself evidence of knowledge or notice of the limitation by any person.

(e)   Subject to subsection (c), a grant of authority not pertaining to transfers of real property and contained in an effective statement of authority is conclusive in favor of a person that gives value in reliance on the grant, except to the extent that when the person gives value:

(1)   the person has knowledge to the contrary;

(2)   the statement has been canceled or restrictively amended under subsection (b); or

(3)   a limitation on the grant is contained in another statement of authority that became effective after the statement containing the grant became effective.

(f)   Subject to subsection (c), an effective statement of authority that grants authority to transfer real property held in the name of the limited liability company and that is recorded by certified copy in the office for recording transfers of the real property is conclusive in favor of a person that gives value in reliance on the grant without knowledge to the contrary, except to the extent that when the person gives value:

(1)   the statement has been canceled or restrictively amended under subsection (b) and a certified copy of the cancellation or restrictive amendment has been recorded in the office for recording transfers of the real property; or

(2)   a limitation on the grant is contained in another statement of authority that became effective after the statement containing the grant became effective and a certified copy of the later-effective statement is recorded in the office for recording transfers of the real property.

(g)   Subject to subsection (c), if a certified copy of an effective statement containing a limitation on the authority to transfer real property held in the name of a limited liability company is recorded in the office for recording transfers of that real property, all persons are deemed to know of the limitation.

(h)   Subject to subsection (i), an effective statement of dissolution or termination is a cancellation of any filed statement of authority for the purposes of subsection (f) and is a limitation on authority for the purposes of subsection (g).

(i)   After a statement of dissolution becomes effective, a limited liability company may deliver to the [Secretary of State] for filing and, if appropriate, may record a statement of authority that is designated as a post-dissolution statement of authority. The statement operates as provided in subsections (f) and (g).

(j)   Unless earlier canceled, an effective statement of authority is canceled by operation of law five years after the date on which the statement, or its most recent amendment, becomes effective. This cancellation operates without need for any recording under subsection (f) or (g).

(k)   An effective statement of denial operates as a restrictive amendment under this section and may be recorded by certified copy for the purposes of subsection (f)(1).

Comment

This section is derived from and builds on RUPA, § 303, and, like that provision is conceptually divided into two realms: statements pertaining to the power to transfer interests in the LLC's real property and statements pertaining to other matters. In the latter realm, statements are filed only in the records of the [Secretary of State], operate only to the extent the statements are actually known. Section 302(d) and (e).

As to interests in real property, in contrast, this section: (i) requires double-filing—with the [Secretary of State] and in the appropriate land records; and (ii) provides for constructive knowledge of statements limiting authority. Thus, a properly filed and recorded statement can protect the limited liability company, Section 302(g), and, in order for a statement pertaining to real property to be a sword in the hands of a third party, the statement must have been both filed and properly recorded. Section 302(f).

Subsection (a)(2)—This paragraph permits a statement to designate authority by position (or office) rather than by specific person. This type of a statement will enable LLCs to provide evidence of ongoing authority to enter into transactions without having to disclose to third parties the entirety of the operating agreement.

Here and elsewhere in the section, the phrase "real property" includes interests in real property, such as mortgages, easements, etc.

Subsection (b)—For the requirement that the original statement, like any other record, be appropriately captioned, *see* Section 205(a).

Subsection (c)—This subsection contains a very important limitation—i.e., that this section's rules do not operate *viz a viz* members. The text of RUPA, § 303 makes this very important point only obliquely, but the Comment to that section is unequivocal:

It should be emphasized that Section 303 concerns the authority of partners to bind the partnership to third persons. As among the partners, the authority of a partner to take any action is governed by the partnership agreement, or by the provisions of RUPA governing the relations among partners, and is not affected by the filing or recording of a statement of partnership authority.

RUPA § 303, comment 4.

However, like any other record delivered for filing on behalf of an LLC, a statement of authority might be some evidence of the contents of the operating agreement. *See* Comment to Section 112(d).

Subsection (d)—The phrase "by itself" is important, because the existence of a limitation could be evidence if, for example, the person in question reviewed the public record at a time when the limitation was of record.

Subsection (e)(1)—What happens if a statement of authority conflicts with the contents of an LLC's certificate of organization? The contents of the certificate are not statements of authority, Section 201(c), so the information in the certificate does not directly figure into the operation of this section. However, if the person claiming to rely on a statement of authority had read the certificate's conflicting information before giving value, that fact might be evidence that person gave value with "knowledge to the contrary" of the statement.

§ 303. Statement of Denial

A person named in a filed statement of authority granting that person authority may deliver to the [Secretary of State] for filing a statement of denial that:

(1) provides the name of the limited liability company and the caption of the statement of authority to which the statement of denial pertains; and

(2) denies the grant of authority.

Comment

For the effect of a statement of denial, *see* Section 302(k).

§ 304. Liability of Members and Managers

(a) The debts, obligations, or other liabilities of a limited liability company, whether arising in contract, tort, or otherwise:

(1) are solely the debts, obligations, or other liabilities of the company; and

(2) do not become the debts, obligations, or other liabilities of a member or manager solely by reason of the member acting as a member or manager acting as a manager.

(b) The failure of a limited liability company to observe any particular formalities relating to the exercise of its powers or management of its activities is not a ground for imposing liability on the members or managers for the debts, obligations, or other liabilities of the company.

Comment

Subsection (a)(2)—This paragraph shields members and managers only against the debts, obligations and liabilities of the limited liability company and is irrelevant to claims seeking to hold a member or manager directly liable on account of the member's or manager's own conduct.

EXAMPLE: A manager personally guarantees a debt of a limited liability company. Subsection (a)(2) is irrelevant to the manager's liability as guarantor.

EXAMPLE: A member purports to bind a limited liability company while lacking any agency law power to do so. The limited liability company is not bound, but the member is liable for having breached the "warranty of authority" (an agency law doctrine). Subsection (a)(2) does not apply. The liability is not *for* a "debt[ ], obligation[ ], [or] liabilit[y] of a limited liability company," but rather is the member's direct liability resulting because the limited liability company is *not* indebted, obligated or liable. RESTATEMENT (THIRD) OF AGENCY § 6.10 (2006).

EXAMPLE: A manager of a limited liability company defames a third party in circumstances that render the limited liability company vicariously liable under agency law. Under subsection (a)(2), the third party cannot hold the manager accountable for the *company's* liability, but that protection is immaterial. The manager is the tortfeasor and in that role is directly liable to the third party.

Subsection (a)(2) pertains only to claims by third parties and is irrelevant to claims by a limited liability company against a member or manager and *vice versa. See e.g.* Sections 408 (pertaining to a limited liability company's obligation to indemnify a member or manager), 409 (pertaining to management duties) and 901 (pertaining to a member's rights to bring a direct claim against a limited liability company).

Subsection (b)—This subsection pertains to the equitable doctrine of "piercing the veil"—i.e., conflating an entity and its owners to hold one liable for the obligations of the other. The doctrine of "piercing the corporate veil" is well-established, and courts regularly (and sometimes almost reflexively) apply that doctrine to limited liability companies. In the corporate realm, "disregard of corporate formalities" is a key factor in the piercing analysis. In the realm of LLCs, that factor is inappropriate, because informality of organization and operation is both common and desired.

This subsection does not preclude consideration of another key piercing factor—disregard by an entity's owners of the entity's economic separateness from the owners.

EXAMPLE: The operating agreement of a three-member, member-managed limited liability company requires formal monthly meetings of the members. Each of the members works in the LLC's business, and they consult each other regularly. They have forgotten or ignore the requirement of monthly meetings. Under subsection (b), that fact is irrelevant to a piercing claim.

EXAMPLE: The sole owner of a limited liability company uses a car titled in the company's name for personal purposes and writes checks on the company's account to pay for personal expenses. These facts are relevant to a piercing claim; they pertain to economic separateness, not subsection (b) formalities.

This subsection has no relevance to a member's claim of oppression under Section 701(a)(5)(B). In some circumstances, disregard of agreed-upon formalities can be a "freeze out" mechanism. Likewise, this section has no relevance to a member's claim that the disregard of agreed-upon formalities is a breach of the operating agreement.

Provisions of regulatory law may impose liability by status on a member or manager. *See* CARTER G. BISHOP AND DANIEL S. KLEINBERGER, LIMITED LIABILITY COMPANIES: TAX AND BUSINESS LAW, ¶ 6.04(4) (Statutory Liability).

[ARTICLE] 4

RELATIONS OF MEMBERS TO EACH OTHER
AND TO LIMITED LIABILITY COMPANY

§ 401. Becoming Member

(a) If a limited liability company is to have only one member upon formation, the person becomes a member as agreed by that person and the organizer of the company. That person and the organizer may be, but need not be, different persons. If different, the organizer acts on behalf of the initial member.

(b) If a limited liability company is to have more than one member upon formation, those persons become members as agreed by the persons before the formation of the company. The organizer acts on behalf of the persons in forming the company and may be, but need not be, one of the persons.

(c) If a filed certificate of organization contains the statement required by Section 201(b)(3), a person becomes an initial member of the limited liability company with the consent of a majority of the organizers. The organizers may consent to more than one person simultaneously becoming the company's initial members.

(d) After formation of a limited liability company, a person becomes a member:

(1) as provided in the operating agreement;

(2) as the result of a transaction effective under [Article] 10;

(3) with the consent of all the members; or

(4) if, within 90 consecutive days after the company ceases to have any members:

(A) the last person to have been a member, or the legal representative of that person, designates a person to become a member; and

(B) the designated person consents to become a member.

(e) A person may become a member without acquiring a transferable interest and without making or being obligated to make a contribution to the limited liability company.

Comment

Most LLC statutes address in separate provisions: (i) how an LLC obtains its initial member or members; and (ii) how additional persons might later become members. This Act follows that approach. Subsections (a) and (b) address the most common circumstances under which a limited liability company is formed—with one or more persons becoming members upon formation. Subsection (c) addresses how a person becomes the initial member of an LLC whose certificate of organization was filed without there being any members. Subsection (d) addresses how persons become members after an LLC has had at least one member.

For a discussion of the concept of a "shelf LLC" and this Act's requirement that a limited liability company have at least one member upon formation, *see* the Comment to Section 201.

Subsection (d)(4)—The personal representative of the last member may designate her-, him-, or itself as the new member.

Subsection (e)—To accommodate business practices and also because a limited liability company need not have a business purpose, this subsection permits so-called "non-economic members."

§ 402. Form of Contribution

A contribution may consist of tangible or intangible property or other benefit to a limited liability company, including money, services performed, promissory notes, other agreements to contribute money or property, and contracts for services to be performed.

Comment

Source—ULPA (2001) § 501, which derived from ULLCA § 401.

§ 403. Liability for Contributions

(a) A person's obligation to make a contribution to a limited liability company is not excused by the person's death, disability, or other inability to perform personally. If a person does not make a required contribution, the person or the person's estate is obligated to contribute money equal to the value of the part of the contribution which has not been made, at the option of the company.

(b) A creditor of a limited liability company which extends credit or otherwise acts in reliance on an obligation described in subsection (a) may enforce the obligation.

Comment

Source: ULLCA § 402, which is taken from RULPA § 502(b), which also gave rise to ULPA (2001) § 502.

Subsection (a)—The reference to "perform personally" is not limited to individuals but rather may refer to any legal person (including an entity) that has a non-delegable duty.

§ 404. Sharing of and Right to Distributions Before Dissolution

(a) Any distributions made by a limited liability company before its dissolution and winding up must be in equal shares among members and dissociated members, except to the extent necessary to comply with any transfer effective under Section 502 and any charging order in effect under Section 503.

(b) A person has a right to a distribution before the dissolution and winding up of a limited liability company only if the company decides to make an interim distribution. A person's dissociation does not entitle the person to a distribution.

(c) A person does not have a right to demand or receive a distribution from a limited liability company in any form other than money. Except as otherwise provided in Section 708(c), a limited liability company may distribute an asset in kind if each part of the asset is fungible with each other part and each person receives a percentage of the asset equal in value to the person's share of distributions.

(d) If a member or transferee becomes entitled to receive a distribution, the member or transferee has the status of, and is entitled to all remedies available to, a creditor of the limited liability company with respect to the distribution.

Comment

This Act follows both the original ULLCA and ULPA (2001) in omitting any default rule for allocation of losses. The Comment to ULPA (2001), § 503 explains that omission as follows:

This Act has no provision allocating profits and losses among the partners. Instead, the Act directly apportions the right to receive distributions. Nearly all limited partnerships will choose to allocate profits and losses in order to comply with applicable tax, accounting and other regulatory requirements. Those requirements, rather than this Act, are the proper source of guidance for that profit and loss allocation.

Subsection (b)—The second sentence of this subsection accords with Section 603(a)(3)—upon dissociation a person is treated as a mere transferee of its own transferable interest. Like most *inter se* rules in this Act, this one is subject to the operating agreement. *See* Comment to Section 603(a)(3).

§ 405. Limitations on Distribution

(a) A limited liability company may not make a distribution if after the distribution:

(1)   the company would not be able to pay its debts as they become due in the ordinary course of the company's activities; or

(2)   the company's total assets would be less than the sum of its total liabilities plus the amount that would be needed, if the company were to be dissolved, wound up, and terminated at the time of the distribution, to satisfy the preferential rights upon dissolution, winding up, and termination of members whose preferential rights are superior to those of persons receiving the distribution.

(b)   A limited liability company may base a determination that a distribution is not prohibited under subsection (a) on financial statements prepared on the basis of accounting practices and principles that are reasonable in the circumstances or on a fair valuation or other method that is reasonable under the circumstances.

(c)   Except as otherwise provided in subsection (f), the effect of a distribution under subsection (a) is measured:

(1)   in the case of a distribution by purchase, redemption, or other acquisition of a transferable interest in the company, as of the date money or other property is transferred or debt incurred by the company; and

(2)   in all other cases, as of the date:

(A)   the distribution is authorized, if the payment occurs within 120 days after that date; or

(B)   the payment is made, if the payment occurs more than 120 days after the distribution is authorized.

(d)   A limited liability company's indebtedness to a member incurred by reason of a distribution made in accordance with this section is at parity with the company's indebtedness to its general, unsecured creditors.

(e)   A limited liability company's indebtedness, including indebtedness issued in connection with or as part of a distribution, is not a liability for purposes of subsection (a) if the terms of the indebtedness provide that payment of principal and interest are made only to the extent that a distribution could be made to members under this section.

(f)   If indebtedness is issued as a distribution, each payment of principal or interest on the indebtedness is treated as a distribution, the effect of which is measured on the date the payment is made.

(g)   In subsection (a), "distribution" does not include amounts constituting reasonable compensation for present or past services or reasonable payments made in the ordinary course of business under a bona fide retirement plan or other benefits program.

Comment

Source—ULPA (2001) § 508, which was derived from ULLCA § 406, which was in turn derived from MBCA § 6.40.

Subsection (b)—This subsection appears to involve a pure standard of ordinary care, in contrast with the more complicated approach stated in Section 409(c).

Subsection (g)—This exception applies only for the purposes of this section. *See* the Comment to Section 503(b)(2). The exception is derived from existing statutory provisions. *See, e.g.*, DEL. CODE ANN., tit. 6, § 18–607(a) (2006) and VA. CODE ANN. § 13.1–1035(E) (West 2006). *See also In re Tri-River Trading, LLC*, 329 B.R. 252, 266 (8th Cir. BAP 2005), aff'd. 452 F.3d 756 (8th Cir. 2006) ("We know of no principle of law which suggests that a manager of a company is required to give up agreed upon salary to pay creditors when business turns bad.")

§ 406.   Liability for Improper Distributions

(a)   Except as otherwise provided in subsection (b), if a member of a member-managed limited liability company or manager of a manager-managed limited liability company consents to a distribution made in violation of Section 405 and in consenting to the distribution fails to comply with Section 409, the member or manager is personally liable to the company for the amount of the distribution that exceeds the amount that could have been distributed without the violation of Section 405.

(b)   To the extent the operating agreement of a member-managed limited liability company expressly relieves a member of the authority and responsibility to consent to distributions and imposes that authority and responsibility on one or more other members, the liability stated in subsection (a) applies to the other members and not the member that the operating agreement relieves of authority and responsibility.

(c)   A person that receives a distribution knowing that the distribution to that person was made in violation of Section 405 is personally liable to the limited liability company but only to the extent that the distribution received by the person exceeded the amount that could have been properly paid under Section 405.

(d)   A person against which an action is commenced because the person is liable under subsection (a) may:

(1)   implead any other person that is subject to liability under subsection (a) and seek to compel contribution from the person; and

(2)   implead any person that received a distribution in violation of subsection (c) and seek to compel contribution from the person in the amount the person received in violation of subsection (c).

(e)   An action under this section is barred if not commenced within two years after the distribution.

Comment

Source—Same derivation as Section 405.

Liability under this section is not affected by a person ceasing to be a member, manager or transferee after the time that the liability attaches.

Subsection (b)—The operating agreement could not accomplish the "switch" in liability provided by this subsection, because the "switch" implicates the rights of third parties under this Act. Section 110(c)(11).

Subsections (c) and (d)(2)—Liability could apply to a person who receives a distribution under a charging order, but only if the person meets the knowledge requirement. That situation is very unlikely unless the person with the charging order is also a member or manager.

§ 407.   Management of Limited Liability Company

(a)   A limited liability company is a member-managed limited liability company unless the operating agreement:

(1)   expressly provides that:

(A)   the company is or will be "manager-managed";

(B)   the company is or will be "managed by managers"; or

(C)   management of the company is or will be "vested in managers"; or

(2)   includes words of similar import.

(b)   In a member-managed limited liability company, the following rules apply:

(1) The management and conduct of the company are vested in the members.

(2) Each member has equal rights in the management and conduct of the company's activities.

(3) A difference arising among members as to a matter in the ordinary course of the activities of the company may be decided by a majority of the members.

(4) An act outside the ordinary course of the activities of the company may be undertaken only with the consent of all members.

(5) The operating agreement may be amended only with the consent of all members.

(c) In a manager-managed limited liability company, the following rules apply:

(1) Except as otherwise expressly provided in this [act], any matter relating to the activities of the company is decided exclusively by the managers.

(2) Each manager has equal rights in the management and conduct of the activities of the company.

(3) A difference arising among managers as to a matter in the ordinary course of the activities of the company may be decided by a majority of the managers.

(4) The consent of all members is required to:

(A) sell, lease, exchange, or otherwise dispose of all, or substantially all, of the company's property, with or without the good will, outside the ordinary course of the company's activities;

(B) approve a merger, conversion, or domestication under [Article] 10;

(C) undertake any other act outside the ordinary course of the company's activities; and

(D) amend the operating agreement.

(5) A manager may be chosen at any time by the consent of a majority of the members and remains a manager until a successor has been chosen, unless the manager at an earlier time resigns, is removed, or dies, or, in the case of a manager that is not an individual, terminates. A manager may be removed at any time by the consent of a majority of the members without notice or cause.

(6) A person need not be a member to be a manager, but the dissociation of a member that is also a manager removes the person as a manager. If a person that is both a manager and a member ceases to be a manager, that cessation does not by itself dissociate the person as a member.

(7) A person's ceasing to be a manager does not discharge any debt, obligation, or other liability to the limited liability company or members which the person incurred while a manager.

(d) An action requiring the consent of members under this [act] may be taken without a meeting, and a member may appoint a proxy or other agent to consent or otherwise act for the member by signing an appointing record, personally or by the member's agent.

(e) The dissolution of a limited liability company does not affect the applicability of this section. However, a person that wrongfully causes dissolution of the company loses the right to participate in management as a member and a manager.

(f) This [act] does not entitle a member to remuneration for services performed for a member-managed limited liability company, except for reasonable compensation for services rendered in winding up the activities of the company.

Comment

Subsection (a)—This subsection follows implicitly from the definitions of "manager-managed" and "member-managed" limited liability companies, Section 102(10) and (12), but is included here for the sake of clarity. Although this Act has eliminated the link between management structure and statutory apparent authority, Section 301, the Act retains the manager-managed and member-managed constructs as options for members to use to structure their *inter se* relationship.

Subsection (b)—The subsection states default rules that, under Section 110, are subject to the operating agreement.

Subsection (c)—Like subsection (b), this subsection states default rules that, under Section 110, are subject to the operating agreement. For example, a limited liability company's operating agreement might state "This company is manager-managed," Section 102(10)(i), while providing that managers must submit specified ordinary matters for review by the members.

The actual authority of an LLC's manager or managers is a question of agency law and depends fundamentally on the contents of the operating agreement and any separate management contract between the LLC and its manager or managers. These agreements are the primary source of the manifestations of the LLC (as principal) from which a manager (as agent) will form the reasonable beliefs that delimit the scope of the manager's actual authority. RESTATEMENT (THIRD) OF AGENCY § 3.01 (2006). *See also* RESTATEMENT (SECOND) OF AGENCY §§ 15, 26.

Other information may be relevant as well, such as the course of dealing within the LLC, unless the operating agreement effectively precludes consideration of that information. *See* Section 110(a)(4) (stating that the operating agreement governs "the means and conditions for amending the operating agreement") and the comment to that subparagraph, which states that:

[Although this] Act does not specially authorize the operating agreement to limit the sources in which terms of the operating agreement might be found or limit amendments to specified modes ... Paragraph (a)(4) could be read to encompass such authorization. Also, under Section 107 the parol evidence rule will apply to a written operating agreement containing an appropriate merger provision.

If the operating agreement and a management contract conflict, the reasonable manager will know that the operating agreement controls the extent of the manager's rightful authority to act for the LLC—despite any contract claims the manager might have. *See* Section 111(a)(2) (stating that the operating agreement governs "the rights and duties under this [act] of a person in the capacity of manager") and the comment to that paragraph, which states:

Because the term "[o]perating agreement. . . . includes the agreement as amended or restated," Section 102(13), this paragraph gives the members the ongoing power to define the role of an LLC's managers. Power is not the same as right, however, and exercising the power provided by this paragraph might constitute a breach of a separate contract between the LLC and the manager.

See also RESTATEMENT (THIRD) OF AGENCY § 8.13, cmt. b (2006) and RESTATEMENT (SECOND) OF AGENCY, § 432, cmt. b (stating that, when a principal's instructions to an agent contravene a contract between the principal and agent, the agent may have a breach of contract claim but has no right to act contrary to the principal's instructions).

If (i) an LLC's operating agreement merely states that the LLC is manager-managed and does not further specify the managerial responsibilities, and (ii) the LLC has only one manager, the actual authority analysis is simple. In that situation, this subsection:

- serves as "gap filler" to the operating agreement; and thereby

- constitutes the LLC's manifestation to the manager as to the scope of the manager's authority; and thereby

- delimits the manager's actual authority, subject to whatever subsequent manifestations the LLC may make to the manager (*e.g.*, by a vote of the members, or an amendment of the operating agreement).

If the operating agreement states only that the LLC is manager-managed and the LLC has more than one manager, the question of actual authority has an additional aspect. It is necessary to determine what actual authority any one manager has to act alone.

Paragraphs (c)(2), (3), and (4) combine to provide the answer. A single manager of a multi-manager LLC:

- has no actual authority to commit the LLC to any matter "outside the ordinary course of the activities of the company," paragraph (c)(4)(C), or any matter encompassed in paragraph (c)(4); and

- has the actual authority to commit the LLC to any matter "in the ordinary course of the activities of the company," paragraph (c)(3), unless the manager has reason to know that other managers might disagree or the manager has some other reason to know that consultation with fellow managers is appropriate.

The first point follows self-evidently from the language of paragraphs (c)(3) and (c)(4). In light of that language, no manager could reasonably believe to the contrary (unless the operating agreement provided otherwise).

The second point follows because:

- Subsection (c) serves as the gap-filler manifestation from the LLC to its managers, and subsection (c) does not require managers of a multi-manager LLC to act only in concert or after consultation.

- To the contrary, subject to the operating agreement:

  - paragraph (c)(2) expressly provides that "each manager has equal rights in the management and conduct of the activities of the company," and

  - paragraph (c)(3) suggests that several (as well as joint) activity is appropriate on ordinary matters, so long as the manager acting in the matter has no reason to believe that the matter will be controversial among the managers and therefore requires a decision under paragraph (c)(3).

While the individual members of a corporate board of directors lack actual authority to bind the corporation, 2 WILLIAM MEADE FLETCHER, FLETCHER CYCLOPEDIA OF THE LAW OF CORPORATIONS, § 392 (noting "the overwhelming weight of authority"), subsection (c) does not describe "board" management. Instead, subsection (c) provides management rules derived from those that govern the members of a general partnership and multiple general partners of a limited partnership. RUPA, § 401 and ULPA (2001), § 406.

The common law of agency will also determine the apparent authority of an LLC's manager or managers, and in that analysis what the particular third party knows or has reason to know about the management structure and business practices of the particular LLC will always be relevant. RESTATEMENT (THIRD) OF AGENCY § 3.03 cmt. d (2006) ("The nature of an organization's business or activity is relevant to whether a third party could reasonably believe that a [manager] is authorized to commit the organization to a particular transaction.").

As a general matter, however—i.e., as to the apparent authority of the position of LLC manager under this Act—courts may view the position as clothing its occupants with the apparent authority to take actions that reasonably appear within the ordinary course of the company's business. The actual authority analysis stated above supports that proposition; absent a reason to believe to the contrary, a third party could reasonably believe a manager to possess the authority contemplated by the gap-fillers of the statute. *But see* Section 102(9), cmt. (stating that "confusion around the term 'manager' is common to almost all LLC statutes").

Subsection (c)(5)—Under the default rule stated in this paragraph, dissolution of an entity that is a manager does not end the entity's status as manager. Contrast Section 602(4)(D) (referring to the expulsion of a member that is a partnership or limited liability company and authorizing the other members to expel, by unanimous consent, the dissolved partnership or limited liability company).

An LLC does not cease to be "manager-managed" simply because no managers are in place. In that situation, absent additional facts, the LLC is manager-managed and the manager position is vacant. Non-manager members who exercise managerial functions during the vacancy (or at any other time) will have duties as determined by other law, most particularly the law of agency.

Subsection (c)(7)—The obligation to safeguard trade secrets and other confidential or propriety information is incurred when the person is a manager, and a subsequent cessation does not entitle the person to usurp the information or use it to the prejudice of the LLC after the cessation.

Subsection (e)—Under the default rules of this Act, it is not possible for a person to wrongfully cause dissolution (as distinguished from wrongfully dissociating). *Compare* Section 701 with Section 601(b). However, the operating agreement might contemplate wrongful dissolution, and this subsection would then apply—unless the operating provides otherwise. Under the second sentence of this subsection, a person might lose the rights to act as a manager without automatically and formally ceasing to be denominated as a manager.

Subsection (f)—This provision traces back to the 1914 Uniform Partnership Act, § 18(f) and is included for fear that its absence might be misinterpreted as implying a contrary rule.

This Act does not provide for remuneration to a manager of a manager-managed LLC. That issue is for the operating agreement, or a separate agreement between the LLC and the manager. A manager seeking compensation will have the burden of proving an agreement. For a case demonstrating how *not* to establish an agreement, *see Jandrain v. Lovald*, 351 B.R. 679 (D. S.D. 2006).

§ 408.   Indemnification and Insurance

(a)   A limited liability company shall reimburse for any payment made and indemnify for any debt, obligation, or other liability incurred by a member of a member-managed company or the manager of a manager-managed company in the course of the member's or manager's activities on behalf of the company, if, in making the payment or incurring the debt, obligation, or other liability, the member or manager complied with the duties stated in Sections 405 and 409.

(b)   A limited liability company may purchase and maintain insurance on behalf of a member or manager of the company against liability asserted against or incurred by the member or manager in that capacity or arising from that status even if, under Section 110(g), the operating agreement could not eliminate or limit the person's liability to the company for the conduct giving rise to the liability.

Comment

Subsection (a)—This subsection states a default rule, which corresponds to the default rules on management duties. In the default mode, the correspondence is appropriate, because otherwise the statutory rule on indemnification could undercut or even vitiate the statutory rules on duty. Both this subsection and the rules on duty are subject to the operating agreement.

This subsection does not expressly require a limited liability company to provide advances to cover expenses. However, in some jurisdictions the indemnity obligation might be interpreted to include an obligation to make advances.

This subsection concerns only managers of manager-managed limited liability companies and members of member-managed companies. The definite article in the phrases "the member's" [paragraph (1)] and "the member" [paragraph (2)] refers back to the original phrase "A limited liability company shall reimburse ... and indemnify ... a member of a member-managed company...." A limited liability company's obligation, if any, to reimburse or indemnify others (including non-managing members of a manager-managed LLC and LLC employees) is a question for other law, including the law of agency.

Subsection (b)—In contrast to subsection (a), this subsection encompasses all members, not just members in a member-managed LLC.

This subsection's language is very broad and authorizes an LLC to purchase insurance to cover, *e.g.*, a manager's intentional misconduct. It is unlikely that such insurance would be available. For restrictions on the power of an operating agreement to provide for indemnification, *see* Section 110, particularly subsection (g).

§ 409. Standards of Conduct for Members and Managers

(a) A member of a member-managed limited liability company owes to the company and, subject to Section 901(b), the other members the fiduciary duties of loyalty and care stated in subsections (b) and (c).

(b) The duty of loyalty of a member in a member-managed limited liability company includes the duties:

(1) to account to the company and to hold as trustee for it any property, profit, or benefit derived by the member:

(A) in the conduct or winding up of the company's activities;

(B) from a use by the member of the company's property; or

(C) from the appropriation of a limited liability company opportunity;

(2) to refrain from dealing with the company in the conduct or winding up of the company's activities as or on behalf of a person having an interest adverse to the company; and

(3) to refrain from competing with the company in the conduct of the company's activities before the dissolution of the company.

(c) Subject to the business judgment rule, the duty of care of a member of a member-managed limited liability company in the conduct and winding up of the company's activities is to act with the care that a person in a like position would reasonably exercise under similar circumstances and in a manner the member reasonably believes to be in the best interests of the company. In discharging this duty, a member may rely in good faith upon opinions, reports, statements, or other information provided by another person that the member reasonably believes is a competent and reliable source for the information.

(d) A member in a member-managed limited liability company or a manager-managed limited liability company shall discharge the duties under this [act] or under the operating agreement and exercise any rights consistently with the contractual obligation of good faith and fair dealing.

(e) It is a defense to a claim under subsection (b)(2) and any comparable claim in equity or at common law that the transaction was fair to the limited liability company.

(f) All of the members of a member-managed limited liability company or a manager-managed limited liability company may authorize or ratify, after full disclosure of all material facts, a specific act or transaction that otherwise would violate the duty of loyalty.

(g) In a manager-managed limited liability company, the following rules apply:

(1) Subsections (a), (b), (c), and (e) apply to the manager or managers and not the members.

(2) The duty stated under subsection (b)(3) continues until winding up is completed.

(3) Subsection (d) applies to the members and managers.

(4) Subsection (f) applies only to the members.

(5) A member does not have any fiduciary duty to the company or to any other member solely by reason of being a member.

Comment

This section follows the structure of many LLC acts, first stating the duties of members in a member-managed limited liability company and then using that statement and a "switching" mechanism, subsection (g), to allocate duties in a manager-managed company. The duties stated in this section are subject to the operating agreement, but Section 110 contains important limitations on the power of the operating agreement to affect fiduciary duties and the obligation of good faith.

This section contains several noteworthy developments in the law of unincorporated business organizations:

- fiduciary duty is "uncabined"—*see* the Comment to subsections (a) and (b);

- the duty of care is not set at gross negligence—*see* the Comment to subsection (c); and

- the statutory endorsement of self-interest is omitted—*see* the Comment to section (e)

The standards, duties, and obligations of this Section are subject to delineation, restriction, and, to some extent, elimination by the operating agreement. *See* Section 110.

Subsections (a) and (b)—Until the promulgation of RUPA, it was almost axiomatic that: (i) fiduciary duties reflect judge-made law; and (ii) statutory formulations can express some of that law but do not exhaustively codify it. The original UPA was a prime example of this approach.

In an effort to respect freedom of contract, bolster predictability, and protect partnership agreements from second-guessing, the Conference decided that RUPA should fence or "cabin in" all fiduciary duties within a statutory formulation. That decision was followed without re-consideration in ULLCA and ULPA (2001).

This Act takes a different approach. After lengthy discussion in the drafting committee and on the floor of the 2006 Annual Meeting, the Conference decided that: (i) the "corral" created by RUPA does not fit in the very complex and variegated world of LLCs; and (ii) it is impracticable to cabin all LLC-related fiduciary duties within a statutory formulation.

As a result, this Act: (i) eschews "only" and "limited to"—the words RUPA used in an effort to exhaustively codify fiduciary duty; (ii) codifies the core of the fiduciary duty of loyalty; but (iii) does not purport to discern every possible category of overreaching. One important consequence is to allow courts to continue to use fiduciary duty concepts to police disclosure obligations in member-to-member and member-LLC transactions.

Subsection (c)—Although ULLCA, § 409(c) followed RUPA, § 404(c) and provided a gross negligence standard of care, at least a plurality of LLC statutes use an ordinary care standard. Sandra K. Miller, *The Role of the Court in Balancing Contractual Freedom With the Need For Mandatory Constraints on Opportunistic and Abusive Conduct in the LLC*, 152 U. PA. L. REV 1609, 1658 (May 2004) (containing two tables characterizing the standard of care under LLC statutes: 21 states with "good faith prudent person" language and 19 states using "gross negligence or willful misconduct" language); Elizabeth S. Miller and Thomas E. Rutledge, *The Duty of Finest Loyalty and Reasonable Decisions: The Business Judgment Rule in Unincorporated Business Organizations*, 30 DEL. J. CORP. L. 343, 366–368 (2005) (stating that "[a]pproximately eighteen state LLC statutes parallel language formerly used in the MBCA and require managers and managing members to act in good faith and exercise the care of an ordinarily prudent person in a like position under similar circumstances"). *See also* William J. Callison, *"The Law Does Not Perfectly Comprehend. . . .": The Inadequacy of the Gross Negligence Duty of Care Standard in Unincorporated Business Organizations*, 94 KY. L.J. 451, 452 (2005–2006) ("examin[ing] the gross negligence standard and find[ing] it wanting, particularly as it has intruded, largely unexamined and by drafting osmosis, into subsequent uniform acts governing limited partnerships and limited liability companies").

In some circumstances, an unadorned standard of ordinary care is appropriate for those in charge of a business organization or similar, non-business enterprise. In others, the proper application of the duty of care must take into account the difficulties inherent in establishing an enterprise's most fundamental policies, supervising the enterprise's overall activities, or making complex business judgments. Corporate law subdivides circumstances somewhat according to the formal role exercised by the person whose conduct is later challenged (*e.g.*, distinguishing the duties of directors from the duties of officers). LLC law cannot follow that approach, because a hallmark of the LLC entity is its structural flexibility.

This subsection, therefore, seeks "the best of both worlds"—stating a standard of ordinary care but subjecting that standard to the business judgment rule to the extent circumstances warrant. The content and force of the business judgment rule vary across jurisdictions, and therefore the meaning of this subsection may vary from jurisdiction to jurisdiction.

That result is intended. In any jurisdiction, the business judgment rule's application will vary depending on the nature of the challenged conduct. There is, for example, very little (if any) judgment involved when a person with managerial power acts (or fails to act) on an essentially ministerial matter. Moreover, under the law of many jurisdictions, the business judgment rule applies similarly across the range of business organizations. That is, the doctrine is sufficiently broad and conceptual so that the formality of organizational choice is less important in shaping the application of the rule than are the nature of the challenged conduct and the responsibilities and authority of the person whose conduct is being challenged.

This Act seeks therefore to invoke rather than unsettle whatever may be each jurisdiction's approach to the business judgment rule.

Subsection (d)—This subsection refers to the "*contractual* obligation of good faith and fair dealing" to emphasize that the obligation is not an invitation to re-write agreements among the members. As explained in the Comment to ULPA (2001), § 305(b):

> The obligation of good faith and fair dealing is not a fiduciary duty, does not command altruism or self-abnegation, and does not prevent a partner from acting in the partner's own self-interest. Courts should not use the obligation to change ex post facto the parties' or this Act's allocation of risk and power. To the contrary, in light of the nature of a limited partnership, the obligation should be used only to protect agreed-upon arrangements from conduct that is manifestly beyond what a reasonable person could have contemplated when the arrangements were made. . . . In sum, the purpose of the obligation of good faith and fair dealing is to protect the arrangement the partners have chosen for themselves, not to restructure that arrangement under the guise of safeguarding it.

At first glance, it may seem strange to apply a contractual obligation to statutory duties and rights— i.e., duties and rights "under this [act]." However, for the most part those duties and rights apply to relationships *inter se* the members and the LLC and function only to the extent not displaced by the operating agreement. In the contract-based organization that is an LLC, those statutory default rules are intended to function like a contract. Therefore, applying the contractual notion of good faith makes sense.

As to whether the obligation stated in this subsection applies to transferees, *see* the Comment to Section 112(b).

Subsection (e)—Section 409 omits a noteworthy provision, which, beginning with RUPA, has been standard in the uniform business entity acts. RUPA, ULLCA, ULPA (2001) each placed the following language in the subsection following the formulation of the obligation of good faith:

> A member . . . does not violate a duty or obligation under this [act] or under the operating agreement merely because the member's conduct furthers the member's own interest.

This language is inappropriate in the complex and variegated world of LLCs. As a proposition of contract law, the language is axiomatic and therefore unnecessary. In the context of fiduciary duty, the language is at best incomplete, at worst wrong, and in any event confusing.

This Act's subsection (e) takes a very different approach, stating a well-established principle of judge-made law. Despite Section 107, the statement is not surplusage. Given this Act's very detailed treatment of fiduciary duties and especially the Act's very detailed treatment of the power of the operating agreement to modify fiduciary duties, the statement is important because its absence might be confusing. (An *ex post* fairness justification is not the same as an *ex ante* agreement to modify, but the topics are sufficiently close for a danger of the affirmative pregnant.)

This Act also omits, as anachronistic and potentially confusing, any provision resembling ULLCA, § 409(f) ("A member of a member-managed company may lend money to and transact other business with the company. As to each loan or transaction, the rights and obligations of the member are the same as those of a person who is not a member, subject to other applicable law.") *See also* ULPA (2001), § 112 ("A partner may lend money to and transact other business with the limited partnership and has the same rights and obligations with respect to the loan or other transaction as a person that is not a partner.")

Those provisions originated to combat the notion that debts to partners were categorically inferior to debts to non-partner creditors. That notion has never been part of LLC law, and so a modern uniform LLC act need not include language combating the notion. Moreover, to the uninitiated the language can be confusing, because the words might: (i) seem to undercut the duty of loyalty, which they do not; and (ii) deflect attention from bankruptcy law and the law of fraudulent transfer, which assuredly can look askance at transactions between an entity and an "insider."

Subsection (f)—The operating agreement can provide additional or different methods of authorization or ratification, subject to the strictures of Section 110(e). *See* the Comment to that subsection.

Subsection (g)—This is the "switching" mechanism, referred to in the introduction to this Comment.

Subsection (g)(2)—On the assumption that the members of a manager-managed LLC are dependent on the manager, this paragraph extends the duty longer than in a member-managed LLC.

Subsection (g)(5)—This paragraph merely negates a claim of fiduciary duty that is exclusively status-based and does not immunize misconduct.

EXAMPLE: Although a limited liability company is manager-managed, one member who is not a manager owns a controlling interest and effectively, albeit indirectly, controls the company's activities. A member owning a minority interest brings an action for dissolution under Section 701(a)(5)(B) (oppression by "the managers or those members in control of the company"). The court wishes to understand a claim as one alleging a breach of fiduciary duty by the controlling member. Subsection (g)(5) does not preclude that approach.

§ 410. Right of Members, Managers, and Dissociated Members to Information

(a) In a member-managed limited liability company, the following rules apply:

(1) On reasonable notice, a member may inspect and copy during regular business hours, at a reasonable location specified by the company, any record maintained by the company regarding the company's activities, financial condition, and other circumstances, to the extent the information is material to the member's rights and duties under the operating agreement or this [act].

(2) The company shall furnish to each member:

(A) without demand, any information concerning the company's activities, financial condition, and other circumstances which the company knows and is material to the proper exercise of the member's rights and duties under the operating agreement or this [act], except to the extent the company can establish that it reasonably believes the member already knows the information; and

(B) on demand, any other information concerning the company's activities, financial condition, and other circumstances, except to the extent the demand or information demanded is unreasonable or otherwise improper under the circumstances.

(3) The duty to furnish information under paragraph (2) also applies to each member to the extent the member knows any of the information described in paragraph (2).

(b) In a manager-managed limited liability company, the following rules apply:

(1) The informational rights stated in subsection (a) and the duty stated in subsection (a)(3) apply to the managers and not the members.

(2) During regular business hours and at a reasonable location specified by the company, a member may obtain from the company and inspect and copy full information regarding the activities, financial condition, and other circumstances of the company as is just and reasonable if:

(A) the member seeks the information for a purpose material to the member's interest as a member;

(B) the member makes a demand in a record received by the company, describing with reasonable particularity the information sought and the purpose for seeking the information; and

(C)   the information sought is directly connected to the member's purpose.

(3)   Within 10 days after receiving a demand pursuant to paragraph (2)(B), the company shall in a record inform the member that made the demand:

(A)   of the information that the company will provide in response to the demand and when and where the company will provide the information; and

(B)   if the company declines to provide any demanded information, the company's reasons for declining.

(4)   Whenever this [act] or an operating agreement provides for a member to give or withhold consent to a matter, before the consent is given or withheld, the company shall, without demand, provide the member with all information that is known to the company and is material to the member's decision.

(c)   On 10 days' demand made in a record received by a limited liability company, a dissociated member may have access to information to which the person was entitled while a member if the information pertains to the period during which the person was a member, the person seeks the information in good faith, and the person satisfies the requirements imposed on a member by subsection (b)(2). The company shall respond to a demand made pursuant to this subsection in the manner provided in subsection (b)(3).

(d)   A limited liability company may charge a person that makes a demand under this section the reasonable costs of copying, limited to the costs of labor and material.

(e)   A member or dissociated member may exercise rights under this section through an agent or, in the case of an individual under legal disability, a legal representative. Any restriction or condition imposed by the operating agreement or under subsection (g) applies both to the agent or legal representative and the member or dissociated member.

(f)   The rights under this section do not extend to a person as transferee.

(g)   In addition to any restriction or condition stated in its operating agreement, a limited liability company, as a matter within the ordinary course of its activities, may impose reasonable restrictions and conditions on access to and use of information to be furnished under this section, including designating information confidential and imposing nondisclosure and safeguarding obligations on the recipient. In a dispute concerning the reasonableness of a restriction under this subsection, the company has the burden of proving reasonableness.

Comment

This section is derived from ULPA (2001), §§ 304 (rights to information of limited partners and former limited partners) and 407 (same re: general partners and former general partners). The rules stated here are what might be termed "quasi-default rules"—subject to some change by the operating agreement. Section 110(c)(6) (prohibiting unreasonable restrictions on the information rights stated in this section).

Although the rights and duties stated in this section are extensive, they may not necessarily be exhaustive. In some situations, some courts have seen owners' information rights as reflecting a fiduciary duty of those with management power. This Act's statement of fiduciary duties is not exhaustive. *See* Comment to Section 409 (explaining that this Act does not seek to "cabin in" all fiduciary duties). In contrast, the operating agreement has considerable "cabining in" power of its own. Section 110(d)(4).

Subsection (a)—Paragraph 1 states the rule pertaining to information memorialized in "records maintained by the company". Paragraph 2 applies to information not in such a record. Appropriately, paragraph (2) sets a more demanding standard for those seeking information.

Subsection (a)(2) and (3)—In appropriate circumstances, violation of either or both of these provisions might cause a court to enjoin or even rescind action taken by the LLC, especially when the violation has interfered with an approval or veto mechanism involving member consent. *E.g., Blue Chip Emerald LLC v. Allied Partners Inc.*, 299 A.D.2d 278, 279–280 (N.Y. App. Div. 2002) (invoking partnership law precedent as reflecting a duty of full disclosure and holding that "[a]bsent such full disclosure, the transaction is voidable)."

Subsection (a)(2)—Violation of this paragraph could give rise to a claim for damages against a member or manager [*see* subsection (b)(1)] who breaches the duties stated in Section 409 in causing or suffering the LLC to violate this paragraph.

Subsection (a)(3)—A member's violation of this paragraph is actionable in damages without need to show a violation of a duty stated in Section 409.

Subsection (b)(1)—This is a switching provision. A manager's violation of the duty stated in subsection (a)(3) is actionable in damages without need to show a violation of a duty stated in Section 409.

Subsection (b)(2)—This paragraph refers to "information" rather than "records maintained by the company"—compare subsection (a)—so in some circumstances the company might have an obligation to memorialize information. Such circumstances will likely be rare or at least unusual. Section 410 generally concerns providing existing information, not creating it. In any event, a member does not trigger the company's obligation under this paragraph merely by satisfying subparagraphs (A) through (C). The member must also satisfy the "just and reasonable" requirement.

Subsection (c)—This section does not control the rights of the estate of a member who dissociates by dying. In that circumstance, Section 504 controls.

Subsection (g)—The phrase "as a matter within the ordinary course of its activities" means that a mere majority consent is needed to impose a restriction or condition. *See* Section 407(b)(3) and (c)(3). This approach is necessary, lest a requesting member (or manager-member) have the power to block imposition of a reasonable restriction or condition needed to prevent the requestor from abusing the LLC.

The burden of proof under this subsection contrasts with the burden of proof when someone claims that a term of an operating agreement violates Section 110(c)(6). Under that subsection, as a matter of ordinary procedural law, the burden is on the person making the claim.

[ARTICLE] 5

TRANSFERABLE INTERESTS AND RIGHTS
OF TRANSFEREES AND CREDITORS

§ 501.   Nature of Transferable Interest

A transferable interest is personal property.

Comment

Source—This Article most directly follows ULPA (2001), Article 7, because ULPA (2001) reflects the Conference's most recent thinking on the issues addressed here. However, ULPA (2001), Article 7 is quite similar in substance to ULLCA, Article 5, and both those Articles derive from Article 5 of RUPA.

Whether a transferable interest pledged as security is governed by Article 8 or 9 of the Uniform Commercial Code depends on the facts and the rules stated in those Articles.

This Act does not include ULLCA § 501(a), which provided: "A member is not a co-owner of, and has no transferable interest in, property of a limited liability company." That language was a vestige of the "aggregate" notion of the law of general partnerships, and in a modern LLC statute would be at least surplusage and perhaps confusing as well.

§ 502.   Transfer of Transferable Interest

(a)   A transfer, in whole or in part, of a transferable interest:

(1)   is permissible;

(2)   does not by itself cause a member's dissociation or a dissolution and winding up of the limited liability company's activities; and

(3)   subject to Section 504, does not entitle the transferee to:

(A)   participate in the management or conduct of the company's activities; or

(B)   except as otherwise provided in subsection (c), have access to records or other information concerning the company's activities.

(b)   A transferee has the right to receive, in accordance with the transfer, distributions to which the transferor would otherwise be entitled.

(c)   In a dissolution and winding up of a limited liability company, a transferee is entitled to an account of the company's transactions only from the date of dissolution.

(d)   A transferable interest may be evidenced by a certificate of the interest issued by the limited liability company in a record, and, subject to this section, the interest represented by the certificate may be transferred by a transfer of the certificate.

(e)   A limited liability company need not give effect to a transferee's rights under this section until the company has notice of the transfer.

(f)   A transfer of a transferable interest in violation of a restriction on transfer contained in the operating agreement is ineffective as to a person having notice of the restriction at the time of transfer.

(g)   Except as otherwise provided in Section 602(4)(B), when a member transfers a transferable interest, the transferor retains the rights of a member other than the interest in distributions transferred and retains all duties and obligations of a member.

(h)   When a member transfers a transferable interest to a person that becomes a member with respect to the transferred interest, the transferee is liable for the member's obligations under Sections 403 and 406(c) known to the transferee when the transferee becomes a member.

Comment

One of the most fundamental characteristics of LLC law is its fidelity to the "pick your partner" principle. This section is the core of the Act's provisions reflecting and protecting that principle.

A member's rights in a limited liability company are bifurcated into economic rights (the transferable interest) and governance rights (including management rights, consent rights, rights to information, rights to seek judicial intervention). Unless the operating agreement otherwise provides, a member acting without the consent of all other members lacks both the power and the right to: (i) bestow membership on a non-member, Section 401(d); or (ii) transfer to a non-member anything other than some or all of the member's transferable interest. Section 502(a)(3). However, consistent with current law, a member may transfer governance rights to another member without obtaining consent from the other members. Thus, this Act does not itself protect members from control shifts that result from transfers among members (as distinguished from transfers to non-members who seek thereby to become members).

This section applies regardless of whether the transferor is a member, a transferee of a member, a transferee of a transferee, etc. *See* Section 102(21) (defining "transferable interest" in terms of a right "originally associated with a person's capacity as a member" regardless of "whether or not the person remains a member or continues to own any part of the right").

Subsection (a)—The definition of "transfer," Section 102(20), and this subsection's reference to "in whole or in part" combine to mean that this section encompasses not only unconditional, permanent, and complete transfers but also temporary, contingent, and partial ones as well. Thus, for example, a charging order under Section 504 effects a transfer of part of the judgment debtor's transferable interest, as does the pledge of a transferable interest as collateral for a loan and the gift of a life-interest in a member's rights to distribution.

Subsection (a)(2)—Section 602(4)(B) creates a risk of dissociation via expulsion when a member transfers all of the member's transferable interest.

Subsection (a)(3)—Mere transferees have no right to intrude as the members carry on their activities as members. When a member dies, other law may effect a transfer of the member's interest to the member's estate or personal representative. Section 504 contains special rules applicable to that situation.

Subsection (b)—Amounts due under this subsection are of course subject to offset for any amount owed to the limited liability company by the member or dissociated member on whose account the distribution is made. As to whether an LLC may properly offset for claims against a transferor that was never a member is matter for other law, specifically the law of contracts dealing with assignments.

Subsection (d)—The use of certificates can raise issues relating to Articles 8 and 9 of the Uniform Commercial Code.

§ 503. Charging Order

(a) On application by a judgment creditor of a member or transferee, a court may enter a charging order against the transferable interest of the judgment debtor for the unsatisfied amount of the judgment. A charging order constitutes a lien on a judgment debtor's transferable interest and requires the limited liability company to pay over to the person to which the charging order was issued any distribution that would otherwise be paid to the judgment debtor.

(b) To the extent necessary to effectuate the collection of distributions pursuant to a charging order in effect under subsection (a), the court may:

(1) appoint a receiver of the distributions subject to the charging order, with the power to make all inquiries the judgment debtor might have made; and

(2) make all other orders necessary to give effect to the charging order.

(c) Upon a showing that distributions under a charging order will not pay the judgment debt within a reasonable time, the court may foreclose the lien and order the sale of the transferable interest. The purchaser at the foreclosure sale obtains only the transferable interest, does not thereby become a member, and is subject to Section 502.

(d) At any time before foreclosure under subsection (c), the member or transferee whose transferable interest is subject to a charging order under subsection (a) may extinguish the charging order by satisfying the judgment and filing a certified copy of the satisfaction with the court that issued the charging order.

(e) At any time before foreclosure under subsection (c), a limited liability company or one or more members whose transferable interests are not subject to the charging order may pay to the judgment creditor the full amount due under the judgment and thereby succeed to the rights of the judgment creditor, including the charging order.

(f) This [act] does not deprive any member or transferee of the benefit of any exemption laws applicable to the member's or transferee's transferable interest.

(g) This section provides the exclusive remedy by which a person seeking to enforce a judgment against a member or transferee may, in the capacity of judgment creditor, satisfy the judgment from the judgment debtor's transferable interest.

Comment

Charging order provisions appear in various forms in UPA, ULPA, RULPA, RUPA, ULLCA, and ULPA (2001). This section builds on those acts, while: (i) modernizing the language: (ii) making explicit certain points that have been at best implicit; and (iii) seeking to delineate more precisely the types of extraordinary circumstances that would have to exist before a court enforcing a charging order would be justified in interfering with an LLC's management or activities.

This section balances the needs of a judgment creditor of a member or transferee with the needs of the limited liability company and the members. The section achieves that balance by allowing the judgment creditor to collect on the judgment through the transferable interest of the judgment debtor while prohibiting interference in the management and activities of the limited liability company.

Under this section, the judgment creditor of a member or transferee is entitled to a charging order against the relevant transferable interest. While in effect, that order entitles the judgment creditor to whatever distributions would otherwise be due to the member or transferee whose interest is subject to the order. However, the judgment creditor has no say in the timing or amount of those distributions. The charging order does not entitle the judgment creditor to accelerate any distributions or to otherwise interfere with the management and activities of the limited liability company.

The operating agreement has no power to alter the provisions of this section to the prejudice of third parties. Section 110(c)(11).

Subsection (a)—The phrase "judgment debtor" encompasses both members and transferees. As a matter of civil procedure and due process, an application for a charging order must be served both on the limited liability company and the member or transferee whose transferable interest is to be charged.

Subsection (b)—Paragraph (2) refers to "other orders" rather than "additional orders". Therefore, given appropriate circumstances, a court may invoke either paragraph (1) or (2) or both.

Subsection (b)(1)—The receiver contemplated here is not a receiver for the limited liability company, but rather a receiver for the distributions. The principal advantage provided by this paragraph is an expanded right to information. However, that right goes no further than "the extent necessary to effectuate the collections of distributions pursuant to a charging order."

Subsection (b)(2)—This paragraph must be understood in the context of the balance described in the introduction to this section's Comment. In particular, the court's power to make orders "that the circumstances may of the case may require" is limited to "giv[ing] effect to the charging order."

Example: A judgment creditor with a charging order believes that the limited liability company should invest less of its surplus in operations, leaving more funds for distributions. The creditor moves the court for an order directing the limited liability company to restrict re-investment. Subsection (b)(2) does not authorize the court to grant the motion.

Example: A judgment creditor with a judgment for $10,000 against a member obtains a charging order against the member's transferable interest. Having been properly served with the order, the limited liability company nonetheless fails to comply and makes a $3000 distribution to the member. The court has the power to order the limited liability company to pay $3000 to the judgment creditor to "give effect to the charging order."

Under subsection (b)(2), the court also has the power to decide whether a particular payment is a distribution, because that decision determines whether the payment is part of a transferable interest subject to a charging order. To the extent a payment is not a distribution, it is not part of the transferable interest and is not subject to subsection (g). The payment is therefore subject to whatever other creditor remedies may apply.

Section 405(g) states a special exception to the definition of "distribution," but that exception applies only "[f]or purposes of subsection (a)" of Section 405. Therefore, whether a charging order applies to "amounts constituting reasonable compensation for present or past services or reasonable payments made in the ordinary course of business under a bona fide retirement plan or other benefits program," Section 405(g), is a question determined under this section, without regard to Section 405(g). To date, case law is scant, but there is authority holding that compensation is a distribution. *PB Real Estate, Inc. v. Dem II Properties*, 719 A.2d 73, 75 (Conn. App. Ct. 1998) (rejecting the defendants' claim that the payments at issue were merely compensation for their services to their law firm, which was organized as an LLC; noting that the defendants' characterization was at odds with the firm's business records and tax returns; holding that the payments received were distributions subject to the charging order).

This Act has no specific rules for determining the fate or effect of a charging order when the limited liability company undergoes a merger, conversion, or domestication under [Article] 10. In the proper circumstances, such an organic change might trigger an order under subsection (b)(2).

Subsection (c)—The phrase "that distributions under the charging order will not pay the judgment debt within a reasonable period of time" comes from case law. *See, e.g., Nigri v. Lotz*, 453 S.E.2d 780, 783 (Ga. Ct. App. 1995).

Subsection (e)—This Act jettisons the confusing concept of redemption and substitutes an approach that more closely parallels the modern, real-world possibility of the LLC or its members buying the underlying judgment (and thereby dispensing with any interference the judgment creditor might seek to inflict on the LLC). When possible, buying the judgment remains superior to the mechanism provided by this subsection, because: (i) this subsection requires full satisfaction of the underlying judgment, (ii) while the LLC or the other members might be able to buy the judgment for less than face value. On the other hand, this subsection operates without need for the judgment creditor's consent, so it remains a valuable protection in the event a judgment creditor seeks to do mischief to the LLC.

Whether an LLC's decision to invoke this subsection is "ordinary course" or "outside the ordinary course," Section 407(b)(3) and (4) and (c)(3) and (4)(C), depends on the circumstances. However, the involvement of this subsection does not by itself make the decision "outside the ordinary course."

Subsection (g)—This subsection does not override Article 9, which may provide different remedies for a secured creditor acting in that capacity. A secured creditor with a judgment might decide to proceed under Article 9 alone, under this section alone, or under both Article 9 and this section. In the last-mentioned circumstance, the constraints of this section would apply to the charging order but not to the Article 9 remedies.

This subsection is not intended to prevent a court from effecting a "reverse pierce" where appropriate. In a reverse pierce, the court conflates the entity and its owner to hold the entity liable for a debt of the owner. *Litchfield Asset Mgmt. Corp. v. Howell*, 799 A.2d 298, 312 (Conn. App. Ct. 2002) (approving a reverse pierce where a judgment debtor had established a limited liability company in a patent attempt frustrate the judgment creditor).

§ 504. Power of Personal Representative of Deceased Member

If a member dies, the deceased member's personal representative or other legal representative may exercise the rights of a transferee provided in Section 502(c) and, for the purposes of settling the estate, the rights of a current member under Section 410.

Comment

Source: ULPA (2001) § 704.

Section 410 pertains only to information rights.

[ARTICLE] 6

MEMBER'S DISSOCIATION

§ 601. Member's Power to Dissociate; Wrongful Dissociation

(a) A person has the power to dissociate as a member at any time, rightfully or wrongfully, by withdrawing as a member by express will under Section 602(1).

(b) A person's dissociation from a limited liability company is wrongful only if the dissociation:

(1) is in breach of an express provision of the operating agreement; or

(2) occurs before the termination of the company and:

(A) the person withdraws as a member by express will;

(B) the person is expelled as a member by judicial order under Section 602(5);

(C) the person is dissociated under Section 602(7)(A) by becoming a debtor in bankruptcy; or

(D)   in the case of a person that is not a trust other than a business trust, an estate, or an individual, the person is expelled or otherwise dissociated as a member because it willfully dissolved or terminated.

(c)   A person that wrongfully dissociates as a member is liable to the limited liability company and, subject to Section 901, to the other members for damages caused by the dissociation. The liability is in addition to any other debt, obligation, or other liability of the member to the company or the other members.

Comment

Source—ULPA (2001) § 604, which is based on RUPA Section 602. ULLCA § 602 is functionally identical in some respects but is not a good overall source, because that section presupposes the term/at-will paradigm.

§ 602.   Events Causing Dissociation

A person is dissociated as a member from a limited liability company when:

(1)   the company has notice of the person's express will to withdraw as a member, but, if the person specified a withdrawal date later than the date the company had notice, on that later date;

(2)   an event stated in the operating agreement as causing the person's dissociation occurs;

(3)   the person is expelled as a member pursuant to the operating agreement;

(4)   the person is expelled as a member by the unanimous consent of the other members if:

(A)   it is unlawful to carry on the company's activities with the person as a member;

(B)   there has been a transfer of all of the person's transferable interest in the company, other than:

(i)   a transfer for security purposes; or

(ii)   a charging order in effect under Section 503 which has not been foreclosed;

(C)   the person is a corporation and, within 90 days after the company notifies the person that it will be expelled as a member because the person has filed a certificate of dissolution or the equivalent, its charter has been revoked, or its right to conduct business has been suspended by the jurisdiction of its incorporation, the certificate of dissolution has not been revoked or its charter or right to conduct business has not been reinstated; or

(D)   the person is a limited liability company or partnership that has been dissolved and whose business is being wound up;

(5)   on application by the company, the person is expelled as a member by judicial order because the person:

(A)   has engaged, or is engaging, in wrongful conduct that has adversely and materially affected, or will adversely and materially affect, the company's activities;

(B)   has willfully or persistently committed, or is willfully and persistently committing, a material breach of the operating agreement or the person's duties or obligations under Section 409; or

(C)   has engaged in, or is engaging, in conduct relating to the company's activities which makes it not reasonably practicable to carry on the activities with the person as a member;

(6)   in the case of a person who is an individual:

(A)   the person dies; or

(B) in a member-managed limited liability company:

(i) a guardian or general conservator for the person is appointed; or

(ii) there is a judicial order that the person has otherwise become incapable of performing the person's duties as a member under [this act] or the operating agreement;

(7) in a member-managed limited liability company, the person:

(A) becomes a debtor in bankruptcy;

(B) executes an assignment for the benefit of creditors; or

(C) seeks, consents to, or acquiesces in the appointment of a trustee, receiver, or liquidator of the person or of all or substantially all of the person's property;

(8) in the case of a person that is a trust or is acting as a member by virtue of being a trustee of a trust, the trust's entire transferable interest in the company is distributed;

(9) in the case of a person that is an estate or is acting as a member by virtue of being a personal representative of an estate, the estate's entire transferable interest in the company is distributed;

(10) in the case of a member that is not an individual, partnership, limited liability company, corporation, trust, or estate, the termination of the member;

(11) the company participates in a merger under [Article] 10, if:

(A) the company is not the surviving entity; or

(B) otherwise as a result of the merger, the person ceases to be a member;

(12) the company participates in a conversion under [Article] 10;

(13) the company participates in a domestication under [Article] 10, if, as a result of the domestication, the person ceases to be a member; or

(14) the company terminates.

Comment

Source—ULLCA § 601; RUPA Section 601; ULPA (2001) §§ 601 and 603.

Paragraph (4)(B)—Under this paragraph (unless the operating agreement provides otherwise), a member's transferee can protect itself from the vulnerability of "bare transferee" status by obligating the member/transferor to retain a 1% interest and then to exercise its governance rights (including the right to bring a derivative suit) to protect the transferee's interests.

§ 603. Effect of Person's Dissociation as Member

(a) When a person is dissociated as a member of a limited liability company:

(1) the person's right to participate as a member in the management and conduct of the company's activities terminates;

(2) if the company is member-managed, the person's fiduciary duties as a member end with regard to matters arising and events occurring after the person's dissociation; and

(3) subject to Section 504 and [Article] 10, any transferable interest owned by the person immediately before dissociation in the person's capacity as a member is owned by the person solely as a transferee.

(b) A person's dissociation as a member of a limited liability company does not of itself discharge the person from any debt, obligation, or other liability to the company or the other members which the person incurred while a member.

Comment

Source—ULPA (2001) § 605, which was drawn from RUPA Section 603(b).

Subsection (a)—This provision makes no reference to power-to-bind matters, because the Act provides that a member *qua* member has no power to bind the LLC. Section 301.

Subsection (a)(2)—This provision applies only when the limited liability company is member-managed, because in a manager-managed LLC these duties do not apply to a member *qua* member. Section 409(g)(5).

Subsection (a)(3)—This paragraph accords with Section 404(b)—dissociation does not entitle a person to any distribution. Like most *inter se* rules in this Act, this one is subject to the operating agreement. For example, the operating agreement has the power to provide for the buy out of a person's transferable interest in connection with the person's dissociation.

Subsection (b)—In a member-managed limited liability company, the obligation to safeguard trade secrets and other confidential or proprietary information is incurred when a person is a member. A subsequent dissociation does not entitle the person to usurp the information or use it to the prejudice of the LLC after the dissociation. (In a manager-managed LLC, any obligations of a non-manager member *viz a viz* proprietary information would be a matter for the operating agreement, the obligation of good faith, or other law.)

[ARTICLE] 7

DISSOLUTION AND WINDING UP

§ 701. Events Causing Dissolution

(a) A limited liability company is dissolved, and its activities must be wound up, upon the occurrence of any of the following:

(1) an event or circumstance that the operating agreement states causes dissolution;

(2) the consent of all the members;

(3) the passage of 90 consecutive days during which the company has no members;

(4) on application by a member, the entry by [appropriate court] of an order dissolving the company on the grounds that:

(A) the conduct of all or substantially all of the company's activities is unlawful; or

(B) it is not reasonably practicable to carry on the company's activities in conformity with the certificate of organization and the operating agreement; or

(5) on application by a member, the entry by [appropriate court] of an order dissolving the company on the grounds that the managers or those members in control of the company:

(A) have acted, are acting, or will act in a manner that is illegal or fraudulent; or

(B) have acted or are acting in a manner that is oppressive and was, is, or will be directly harmful to the applicant.

(b) In a proceeding brought under subsection (a)(5), the court may order a remedy other than dissolution.

Comment

Subsection(a)(4)—The standard stated here is conventional, and this subsection (a)(4) is non-waivable. Section 110(c)(7).

Subsection (a)(5)—ULLCA § 801(4)(v) contains a comparable provision, although that provision also gives standing to dissociated members. Even in non-ULLCA states, courts have begun to apply close corporation "oppression" doctrine to LLCs.

This provision's reference to "those members in control of the company" implies that such members have a duty to avoid acting oppressively toward fellow members.

Subsection (a)(5) is non-waivable. *See* Section 110(c)(7).

Subsection (b)—In the close corporation context, many courts have reached this position without express statutory authority, most often with regard to court-ordered buyouts of oppressed shareholders. This subsection saves courts and litigants the trouble of re-inventing that wheel in the LLC context. However, unlike, subsection (a)(4) and (5), subsection (b) can be overridden by the operating agreement. Thus, the members may agree to a restrict or eliminate a court's power to craft a lesser remedy, even to the extent of confining the court (and themselves) to the all-or-nothing remedy of dissolution.

§ 702.   Winding Up

(a)   A dissolved limited liability company shall wind up its activities, and the company continues after dissolution only for the purpose of winding up.

(b)   In winding up its activities, a limited liability company:

(1)   shall discharge the company's debts, obligations, or other liabilities, settle and close the company's activities, and marshal and distribute the assets of the company; and

(2)   may:

(A)   deliver to the [Secretary of State] for filing a statement of dissolution stating the name of the company and that the company is dissolved;

(B)   preserve the company activities and property as a going concern for a reasonable time;

(C)   prosecute and defend actions and proceedings, whether civil, criminal, or administrative;

(D)   transfer the company's property;

(E)   settle disputes by mediation or arbitration;

(F)   deliver to the [Secretary of State] for filing a statement of termination stating the name of the company and that the company is terminated; and

(G)   perform other acts necessary or appropriate to the winding up.

(c)   If a dissolved limited liability company has no members, the legal representative of the last person to have been a member may wind up the activities of the company. If the person does so, the person has the powers of a sole manager under Section 407(c) and is deemed to be a manager for the purposes of Section 304(a)(2).

(d)   If the legal representative under subsection (c) declines or fails to wind up the company's activities, a person may be appointed to do so by the consent of transferees owning a majority of the rights to receive distributions as transferees at the time the consent is to be effective. A person appointed under this subsection:

(1)   has the powers of a sole manager under Section 407(c) and is deemed to be a manager for the purposes of Section 304(a)(2); and

(2)   shall promptly deliver to the [Secretary of State] for filing an amendment to the company's certificate of organization to:

(A)   state that the company has no members;

(B)   state that the person has been appointed pursuant to this subsection to wind up the company; and

(C)   provide the street and mailing addresses of the person.

(e) The [appropriate court] may order judicial supervision of the winding up of a dissolved limited liability company, including the appointment of a person to wind up the company's activities:

(1) on application of a member, if the applicant establishes good cause;

(2) on the application of a transferee, if:

(A) the company does not have any members;

(B) the legal representative of the last person to have been a member declines or fails to wind up the company's activities; and

(C) within a reasonable time following the dissolution a person has not been appointed pursuant to subsection (d); or

(3) in connection with a proceeding under Section 701(a)(4) or (5).

Comment

Source—ULPA (2001) § 803, which was based on RUPA Sections 802 and 803.

Because under this Act the power to bind a limited liability company to a third party is primarily a matter of agency law, Section 301, Comment, this Act has no need of provisions delineating the effect of dissolution on a member or manager's power to bind.

Subsection (b)(2)(A) and (F)—For the constructive notice effect of a statement of dissolution or termination, *see* Section 103(d)(2)(A) and (B).

§ 703. Known Claims Against Dissolved Limited Liability Company

(a) Except as otherwise provided in subsection (d), a dissolved limited liability company may give notice of a known claim under subsection (b), which has the effect as provided in subsection (c).

(b) A dissolved limited liability company may in a record notify its known claimants of the dissolution. The notice must:

(1) specify the information required to be included in a claim;

(2) provide a mailing address to which the claim is to be sent;

(3) state the deadline for receipt of the claim, which may not be less than 120 days after the date the notice is received by the claimant; and

(4) state that the claim will be barred if not received by the deadline.

(c) A claim against a dissolved limited liability company is barred if the requirements of subsection (b) are met and:

(1) the claim is not received by the specified deadline; or

(2) if the claim is timely received but rejected by the company:

(A) the company causes the claimant to receive a notice in a record stating that the claim is rejected and will be barred unless the claimant commences an action against the company to enforce the claim within 90 days after the claimant receives the notice; and

(B) the claimant does not commence the required action within the 90 days.

(d) This section does not apply to a claim based on an event occurring after the effective date of dissolution or a liability that on that date is contingent.

Comment

Source—ULPA (2001) § 806, which was based on ULLCA § 807, which in turn was based on MBCA § 14.06.

§ 704. Other Claims Against Dissolved Limited Liability Company

(a) A dissolved limited liability company may publish notice of its dissolution and request persons having claims against the company to present them in accordance with the notice.

(b) The notice authorized by subsection (a) must:

(1) be published at least once in a newspaper of general circulation in the [county] in this state in which the dissolved limited liability company's principal office is located or, if it has none in this state, in the [county] in which the company's designated office is or was last located;

(2) describe the information required to be contained in a claim and provide a mailing address to which the claim is to be sent; and

(3) state that a claim against the company is barred unless an action to enforce the claim is commenced within five years after publication of the notice.

(c) If a dissolved limited liability company publishes a notice in accordance with subsection (b), unless the claimant commences an action to enforce the claim against the company within five years after the publication date of the notice, the claim of each of the following claimants is barred:

(1) a claimant that did not receive notice in a record under Section 703;

(2) a claimant whose claim was timely sent to the company but not acted on; and

(3) a claimant whose claim is contingent at, or based on an event occurring after, the effective date of dissolution.

(d) A claim not barred under this section may be enforced:

(1) against a dissolved limited liability company, to the extent of its undistributed assets; and

(2) if assets of the company have been distributed after dissolution, against a member or transferee to the extent of that person's proportionate share of the claim or of the assets distributed to the member or transferee after dissolution, whichever is less, but a person's total liability for all claims under this paragraph does not exceed the total amount of assets distributed to the person after dissolution.

Comment

Source—ULPA (2001) § 807, which was based on ULLCA § 808, which in turn was based on MBCA § 14.07.

Subsection (d)(2)—Liability under this paragraph extends to those who have received distributions under a charging order. *See* Comment to 502(a) (explaining that the beneficiary of a charging order is a transferee). Unlike Section 406(c) (recapture of improper interim distributions), this paragraph contains no "knowledge" element.

§ 705. Administrative Dissolution

(a) The [Secretary of State] may dissolve a limited liability company administratively if the company does not:

(1) pay, within 60 days after the due date, any fee, tax, or penalty due to the [Secretary of State] under this [act] or law other than this [act]; or

(2) deliver, within 60 days after the due date, its annual report to the [Secretary of State].

(b) If the [Secretary of State] determines that a ground exists for administratively dissolving a limited liability company, the [Secretary of State] shall file a record of the determination and serve the company with a copy of the filed record.

(c) If within 60 days after service of the copy pursuant to subsection (b) a limited liability company does not correct each ground for dissolution or demonstrate to the reasonable satisfaction of the [Secretary of State] that each ground determined by the [Secretary of State] does not exist, the [Secretary of State] shall dissolve the company administratively by preparing, signing, and filing a declaration of dissolution that states the grounds for dissolution. The [Secretary of State] shall serve the company with a copy of the filed declaration.

(d) A limited liability company that has been administratively dissolved continues in existence but, subject to Section 706, may carry on only activities necessary to wind up its activities and liquidate its assets under Sections 702 and 708 and to notify claimants under Sections 703 and 704.

(e) The administrative dissolution of a limited liability company does not terminate the authority of its agent for service of process.

Comment

Source—ULPA (2001) § 809, which was based on ULLCA §§ 809 and 810. *See also* RMBCA §§ 14.20 and 14.21.

§ 706. Reinstatement Following Administrative Dissolution

(a) A limited liability company that has been administratively dissolved may apply to the [Secretary of State] for reinstatement within two years after the effective date of dissolution. The application must be delivered to the [Secretary of State] for filing and state:

(1) the name of the company and the effective date of its dissolution;

(2) that the grounds for dissolution did not exist or have been eliminated; and

(3) that the company's name satisfies the requirements of Section 108.

(b) If the [Secretary of State] determines that an application under subsection (a) contains the required information and that the information is correct, the [Secretary of State] shall prepare a declaration of reinstatement that states this determination, sign and file the original of the declaration of reinstatement, and serve the limited liability company with a copy.

(c) When a reinstatement becomes effective, it relates back to and takes effect as of the effective date of the administrative dissolution and the limited liability company may resume its activities as if the dissolution had not occurred.

Comment

Source—ULPA (2001) § 810, which was based on ULLCA § 811. *See also* RMBCA Section 14.22.

§ 707. Appeal From Rejection of Reinstatement

(a) If the [Secretary of State] rejects a limited liability company's application for reinstatement following administrative dissolution, the [Secretary of State] shall prepare, sign, and file a notice that explains the reason for rejection and serve the company with a copy of the notice.

(b) Within 30 days after service of a notice of rejection of reinstatement under subsection (a), a limited liability company may appeal from the rejection by petitioning the [appropriate court] to set aside the dissolution. The petition must be served on the [Secretary of State] and contain a copy of the [Secretary of State's] declaration of dissolution, the company's application for reinstatement, and the [Secretary of State's] notice of rejection.

(c) The court may order the [Secretary of State] to reinstate a dissolved limited liability company or take other action the court considers appropriate.

Comment

Source—ULPA (2001) § 811, which was based on ULLCA § 812.

This section uses "rejection" rather than "denial" (the word used by both ULPA (2001) and ULLCA). The change is to avoid confusion with a "statement of denial" under Section 302.

§ 708. Distribution of Assets in Winding Up Limited Liability Company's Activities

(a) In winding up its activities, a limited liability company must apply its assets to discharge its obligations to creditors, including members that are creditors.

(b) After a limited liability company complies with subsection (a), any surplus must be distributed in the following order, subject to any charging order in effect under Section 503:

(1) to each person owning a transferable interest that reflects contributions made by a member and not previously returned, an amount equal to the value of the unreturned contributions; and

(2) in equal shares among members and dissociated members, except to the extent necessary to comply with any transfer effective under Section 502.

(c) If a limited liability company does not have sufficient surplus to comply with subsection (b)(1), any surplus must be distributed among the owners of transferable interests in proportion to the value of their respective unreturned contributions.

(d) All distributions made under subsections (b) and (c) must be paid in money.

Comment

Source: ULLCA § 806, restyled.

Subsection (a)—This section is mostly not a default rule. *See* Section 110(c)(11) (stating that "except as provided in Section 112(b), [the operating agreement may not] restrict the rights under this [act] of a person other than a member or manager"). However, if the creditors are willing, a dissolved limited liability company may certainly make agreements with them specifying the terms under which the LLC will "discharge its obligations to creditors."

Subsections (b), (c) and (d)—These subsection provide default rules. Distributions under these subsections (or otherwise under the operating agreement) are subject to Section 503 (charging orders).

[ARTICLE] 8

FOREIGN LIMITED LIABILITY COMPANIES

§ 801. Governing Law

(a) The law of the state or other jurisdiction under which a foreign limited liability company is formed governs:

(1) the internal affairs of the company; and

(2) the liability of a member as member and a manager as manager for the debts, obligations, or other liabilities of the company.

(b) A foreign limited liability company may not be denied a certificate of authority by reason of any difference between the law of the jurisdiction under which the company is formed and the law of this state.

(c) A certificate of authority does not authorize a foreign limited liability company to engage in any business or exercise any power that a limited liability company may not engage in or exercise in this state.

Comment

Subsection (a)—This Section parallels the formulation stated in Section 106 for a domestic limited liability company.

Subsection (a)(2)—This provision does not pertain to the "internal shields" of a foreign "series" LLC, because those shields do not concern the liability of members or managers for the obligations of the LLC. Instead, those shields seek to protect specified assets of the LLC (associated with one series) from being available to satisfy specified obligations of the LLC (associated with another series). *See* the Prefatory Note, *No Provision for "Series" LLCs*.

§ 802. Application for Certificate of Authority

(a) A foreign limited liability company may apply for a certificate of authority to transact business in this state by delivering an application to the [Secretary of State] for filing. The application must state:

(1) the name of the company and, if the name does not comply with Section 108, an alternate name adopted pursuant to Section 805(a);

(2) the name of the state or other jurisdiction under whose law the company is formed;

(3) the street and mailing addresses of the company's principal office and, if the law of the jurisdiction under which the company is formed requires the company to maintain an office in that jurisdiction, the street and mailing addresses of the required office; and

(4) the name and street and mailing addresses of the company's initial agent for service of process in this state.

(b) A foreign limited liability company shall deliver with a completed application under subsection (a) a certificate of existence or a record of similar import signed by the [Secretary of State] or other official having custody of the company's publicly filed records in the state or other jurisdiction under whose law the company is formed.

Comment

Source—ULPA (2001) § 902, which was based on ULLCA § 1002.

§ 803. Activities Not Constituting Transacting Business

(a) Activities of a foreign limited liability company which do not constitute transacting business in this state within the meaning of this [article] include:

(1) maintaining, defending, or settling an action or proceeding;

(2) carrying on any activity concerning its internal affairs, including holding meetings of its members or managers;

(3) maintaining accounts in financial institutions;

(4) maintaining offices or agencies for the transfer, exchange, and registration of the company's own securities or maintaining trustees or depositories with respect to those securities;

(5) selling through independent contractors;

(6) soliciting or obtaining orders, whether by mail or electronic means or through employees or agents or otherwise, if the orders require acceptance outside this state before they become contracts;

(7) creating or acquiring indebtedness, mortgages, or security interests in real or personal property;

(8)   securing or collecting debts or enforcing mortgages or other security interests in property securing the debts and holding, protecting, or maintaining property so acquired;

(9)   conducting an isolated transaction that is completed within 30 days and is not in the course of similar transactions; and

(10) transacting business in interstate commerce.

(b)   For purposes of this [article], the ownership in this state of income-producing real property or tangible personal property, other than property excluded under subsection (a), constitutes transacting business in this state.

(c)   This section does not apply in determining the contacts or activities that may subject a foreign limited liability company to service of process, taxation, or regulation under law of this state other than this [act].

Comment

Source—ULPA (2001) § 903, which was based on ULLCA § 1003.

§ 804.   Filing of Certificate of Authority

Unless the [Secretary of State] determines that an application for a certificate of authority does not comply with the filing requirements of this [act], the [Secretary of State], upon payment of all filing fees, shall file the application of a foreign limited liability company, prepare, sign, and file a certificate of authority to transact business in this state, and send a copy of the filed certificate, together with a receipt for the fees, to the company or its representative.

Comment

Source—ULPA (2001) § 904, which was based on ULLCA § 1004 and RULPA § 903.

§ 805.   Noncomplying Name of Foreign Limited Liability Company

(a)   A foreign limited liability company whose name does not comply with Section 108 may not obtain a certificate of authority until it adopts, for the purpose of transacting business in this state, an alternate name that complies with Section 108. A foreign limited liability company that adopts an alternate name under this subsection and obtains a certificate of authority with the alternate name need not comply with [fictitious or assumed name statute]. After obtaining a certificate of authority with an alternate name, a foreign limited liability company shall transact business in this state under the alternate name unless the company is authorized under [fictitious or assumed name statute] to transact business in this state under another name.

(b)   If a foreign limited liability company authorized to transact business in this state changes its name to one that does not comply with Section 108, it may not thereafter transact business in this state until it complies with subsection (a) and obtains an amended certificate of authority.

Comment

Source—ULPA (2001) § 905, which was based on ULLCA § 1005.

§ 806.   Revocation of Certificate of Authority

(a)   A certificate of authority of a foreign limited liability company to transact business in this state may be revoked by the [Secretary of State] in the manner provided in subsections (b) and (c) if the company does not:

(1)   pay, within 60 days after the due date, any fee, tax, or penalty due to the [Secretary of State] under this [act] or law other than this [act];

(2)   deliver, within 60 days after the due date, its annual report required under Section 209;

(3) appoint and maintain an agent for service of process as required by Section 113(b); or

(4) deliver for filing a statement of a change under Section 114 within 30 days after a change has occurred in the name or address of the agent.

(b) To revoke a certificate of authority of a foreign limited liability company, the [Secretary of State] must prepare, sign, and file a notice of revocation and send a copy to the company's agent for service of process in this state, or if the company does not appoint and maintain a proper agent in this state, to the company's designated office. The notice must state:

(1) the revocation's effective date, which must be at least 60 days after the date the [Secretary of State] sends the copy; and

(2) the grounds for revocation under subsection (a).

(c) The authority of a foreign limited liability company to transact business in this state ceases on the effective date of the notice of revocation unless before that date the company cures each ground for revocation stated in the notice filed under subsection (b). If the company cures each ground, the [Secretary of State] shall file a record so stating.

Comment

Source—ULPA (2001) § 906, which was based on ULLCA § 1006.

§ 807.   Cancellation of Certificate of Authority

To cancel its certificate of authority to transact business in this state, a foreign limited liability company must deliver to the [Secretary of State] for filing a notice of cancellation stating the name of the company and that the company desires to cancel its certificate of authority. The certificate is canceled when the notice becomes effective.

§ 808.   Effect of Failure to Have Certificate of Authority

(a) A foreign limited liability company transacting business in this state may not maintain an action or proceeding in this state unless it has a certificate of authority to transact business in this state.

(b) The failure of a foreign limited liability company to have a certificate of authority to transact business in this state does not impair the validity of a contract or act of the company or prevent the company from defending an action or proceeding in this state.

(c) A member or manager of a foreign limited liability company is not liable for the debts, obligations, or other liabilities of the company solely because the company transacted business in this state without a certificate of authority.

(d) If a foreign limited liability company transacts business in this state without a certificate of authority or cancels its certificate of authority, it appoints the [Secretary of State] as its agent for service of process for rights of action arising out of the transaction of business in this state.

Comment

Source—ULPA (2001) § 907, which was based on RULPA § 907(d) and ULLCA § 1008.

§ 809.   Action by [Attorney General]

The [Attorney General] may maintain an action to enjoin a foreign limited liability company from transacting business in this state in violation of this [article].

Comment

Source—ULPA (2001) § 908, which was based on RULPA § 908 and ULLCA § 1009.

[ARTICLE] 9

ACTIONS BY MEMBERS

§ 901.   Direct Action by Member

(a)   Subject to subsection (b), a member may maintain a direct action against another member, a manager, or the limited liability company to enforce the member's rights and otherwise protect the member's interests, including rights and interests under the operating agreement or this [act] or arising independently of the membership relationship.

(b)   A member maintaining a direct action under this section must plead and prove an actual or threatened injury that is not solely the result of an injury suffered or threatened to be suffered by the limited liability company.

Comment

Subsection (a)—Source: ULPA (2001) § 1001(a), which was based on RUPA Section 405(b). The subsection has been somewhat re-styled from the ULPA version, and the phrase "for legal or equitable relief" has been deleted as unnecessary. ULPA's reference to "with or without an accounting" has been deleted because the reference: (i) was to the partnership remedy of accounting, which reflected the aggregate nature of a partnership and is inapposite for an *entity* such as an LLC; and (ii) generated some confusion with the equitable claim for an accounting (in the nature of a constructive trust). The "entity-analog" to the partnership-as-aggregate notion of an accounting is the distinction between a direct and derivative claim.

The last phrase of this subsection ("or arising independently . . .") comes from RUPA § 405(b)(3), does not create any new rights, obligations, or remedies, and is included merely to emphasize that a person's membership in an LLC does not preclude the person from enforcing rights existing "independently or the membership relationship."

Subsection (b)—Source: ULPA (2001) § 1001(b). The Comment to that subsection explains:

In ordinary contractual situations it is axiomatic that each party to a contract has standing to sue for breach of that contract. Within a limited partnership, however, different circumstances may exist. A partner does not have a direct claim against another partner merely because the other partner has breached the operating agreement. Likewise a partner's violation of this Act does not automatically create a direct claim for every other partner. To have standing in his, her, or its own right, a partner plaintiff must be able to show a harm that occurs independently of the harm caused or threatened to be caused to the limited partnership.

§ 902.   Derivative Action

A member may maintain a derivative action to enforce a right of a limited liability company if:

(1)   the member first makes a demand on the other members in a member-managed limited liability company, or the managers of a manager-managed limited liability company, requesting that they cause the company to bring an action to enforce the right, and the managers or other members do not bring the action within a reasonable time; or

(2)   a demand under paragraph (1) would be futile.

Comment

Source—ULPA (2001) § 1002, which was a re-styled version RULPA § 1001.

§ 903.   Proper Plaintiff

(a)   Except as otherwise provided in subsection (b), a derivative action under Section 902 may be maintained only by a person that is a member at the time the action is commenced and remains a member while the action continues.

(b)   If the sole plaintiff in a derivative action dies while the action is pending, the court may permit another member of the limited liability company to be substituted as plaintiff.

Comment

This section abandons the traditional "contemporaneous ownership" rule, on the theory that the protections of that rule are unnecessary given the closely-held nature of most limited liability companies and the built-in, statutory restrictions on persons becoming members.

Subsection (b)—This subsection will be inapposite if the limited liability company has only two members, one of whom is the derivative plaintiff. In that limited circumstance, the plaintiff's death would cause the derivative action to abate. The "pick your partner" principal enshrined in Section 502 would prevent the decedent's heirs from succeeding to plaintiff status in the derivative action. This Act does not take a position on whether the death of member abates a <u>direct</u> claim against the LLC or a fellow member.

§ 904.   Pleading

In a derivative action under Section 902, the complaint must state with particularity:

(1)   the date and content of the plaintiff's demand and the response to the demand by the managers or other members; or

(2)   if a demand has not been made, the reasons a demand under Section 902(1) would be futile.

Comment

Source—ULPA (2001) § 1004, which was a re-styled version RULPA § 1003.

§ 905.   Special Litigation Committee

(a)   If a limited liability company is named as or made a party in a derivative proceeding, the company may appoint a special litigation committee to investigate the claims asserted in the proceeding and determine whether pursuing the action is in the best interests of the company. If the company appoints a special litigation committee, on motion by the committee made in the name of the company, except for good cause shown, the court shall stay discovery for the time reasonably necessary to permit the committee to make its investigation. This subsection does not prevent the court from enforcing a person's right to information under Section 410 or, for good cause shown, granting extraordinary relief in the form of a temporary restraining order or preliminary injunction.

(b)   A special litigation committee may be composed of one or more disinterested and independent individuals, who may be members.

(c)   A special litigation committee may be appointed:

(1)   in a member-managed limited liability company:

(A)   by the consent of a majority of the members not named as defendants or plaintiffs in the proceeding; and

(B)   if all members are named as defendants or plaintiffs in the proceeding, by a majority of the members named as defendants; or

(2)   in a manager-managed limited liability company:

(A)   by a majority of the managers not named as defendants or plaintiffs in the proceeding; and

(B)   if all managers are named as defendants or plaintiffs in the proceeding, by a majority of the managers named as defendants.

(d)   After appropriate investigation, a special litigation committee may determine that it is in the best interests of the limited liability company that the proceeding:

    (1)   continue under the control of the plaintiff;

    (2)   continue under the control of the committee;

    (3)   be settled on terms approved by the committee; or

    (4)   be dismissed.

    (e)   After making a determination under subsection (d), a special litigation committee shall file with the court a statement of its determination and its report supporting its determination, giving notice to the plaintiff. The court shall determine whether the members of the committee were disinterested and independent and whether the committee conducted its investigation and made its recommendation in good faith, independently, and with reasonable care, with the committee having the burden of proof. If the court finds that the members of the committee were disinterested and independent and that the committee acted in good faith, independently, and with reasonable care, the court shall enforce the determination of the committee. Otherwise, the court shall dissolve the stay of discovery entered under subsection (a) and allow the action to proceed under the direction of the plaintiff.

Comment

    Although special litigation committees are best known in the corporate field, they are no more inherently corporate than derivative litigation or the notion that an organization is a person distinct from its owners. An "SLC" can serve as an ADR mechanism, help protect an agreed upon arrangement from strike suits, protect the interests of members who are neither plaintiffs nor defendants (if any), and bring to any judicial decision the benefits of a specially tailored business judgment.

    This section's approach corresponds to established law in most jurisdictions, modified to fit the typical governance structures of a limited liability company.

    Subsection (a)—On the availability of Section 410 remedies pending the SLC's investigation, *compare Kaufman v. Computer Assoc. Int'l, Inc.*, No. Civ.A. 699-N, 2005 WL 3470589 at *1 (Del.Ch. Dec. 21, 2005, as revised) (presenting "the question of whether to stay a books and records action under 8 Del. C. § 220 at the request of a special litigation committee when a derivative action encompassing substantially the same allegations of wrongdoing filed by different plaintiffs is pending in another jurisdiction;" concluding "[f]or reasons that have much to do with the light burden imposed by the plaintiff's demand in this case . . . that the special litigation committee's motion to stay the books and records action should be denied").

    Subsection (d)—The standard stated for judicial review of the SLC determination follows *Auerbach v. Bennett*, 47 N.Y.2d 619, 419 N.Y.S.2d 920 (N.Y. 1979) rather than *Zapata Corp. v. Maldonado*, 430 A.2d 779 (Del. 1981), because the latter's reference to a court's business judgment has generally not been followed in other states.

    Houle Low, 407 Mass. 810, 822, 556 N.E.2d 51, 58 (Mass. 1990) contains an excellent explanation of the court's role in reviewing an SLC decision:

> The value of a special litigation committee is coextensive with the extent to which that committee truly exercises business judgment. In order to ensure that special litigation committees do act for the [entity]'s best interest, a good deal of judicial oversight is necessary in each case. At the same time, however, courts must be careful not to usurp the committee's valuable role in exercising business judgment . . . . . [A] special litigation committee must be independent, unbiased, and act in good faith. Moreover, such a committee must conduct a thorough and careful analysis regarding the plaintiff's derivative suit, . . . The burden of proving that these procedural requirements have been met must rest, in all fairness, on the party capable of making that proof—the [entity].

For a discussion of how a court should approach the question of independence, *see Einhorn v. Culea*, 612 N.W.2d 78, 91 (Wis.2000).

§ 906.   Proceeds and Expenses

    (a)   Except as otherwise provided in subsection (b):

(1)   any proceeds or other benefits of a derivative action under Section 902, whether by judgment, compromise, or settlement, belong to the limited liability company and not to the plaintiff; and

(2)   if the plaintiff receives any proceeds, the plaintiff shall remit them immediately to the company.

(b)   If a derivative action under Section 902 is successful in whole or in part, the court may award the plaintiff reasonable expenses, including reasonable attorney's fees and costs, from the recovery of the limited liability company.

Comment

Source—ULPA (2001) § 1005, which was a re-styled version RULPA § 1004.

[ARTICLE] 10

MERGER, CONVERSION, AND DOMESTICATION

§ 1001.   Definitions

In this [article]:

(1)   "Constituent limited liability company" means a constituent organization that is a limited liability company.

(2)   "Constituent organization" means an organization that is party to a merger.

(3)   "Converted organization" means the organization into which a converting organization converts pursuant to Sections 1006 through 1009.

(4)   "Converting limited liability company" means a converting organization that is a limited liability company.

(5)   "Converting organization" means an organization that converts into another organization pursuant to Section 1006.

(6)   "Domesticated company" means the company that exists after a domesticating foreign limited liability company or limited liability company effects a domestication pursuant to Sections 1010 through 1013.

(7)   "Domesticating company" means the company that effects a domestication pursuant to Sections 1010 through 1013.

(8)   "Governing statute" means the statute that governs an organization's internal affairs.

(9)   "Organization" means a general partnership, including a limited liability partnership, limited partnership, including a limited liability limited partnership, limited liability company, business trust, corporation, or any other person having a governing statute. The term includes a domestic or foreign organization regardless of whether organized for profit.

(10) "Organizational documents" means:

(A)   for a domestic or foreign general partnership, its partnership agreement;

(B)   for a limited partnership or foreign limited partnership, its certificate of limited partnership and partnership agreement;

(C)   for a domestic or foreign limited liability company, its certificate or articles of organization and operating agreement, or comparable records as provided in its governing statute;

(D)   for a business trust, its agreement of trust and declaration of trust;

(E) for a domestic or foreign corporation for profit, its articles of incorporation, bylaws, and other agreements among its shareholders which are authorized by its governing statute, or comparable records as provided in its governing statute; and

(F) for any other organization, the basic records that create the organization and determine its internal governance and the relations among the persons that own it, have an interest in it, or are members of it.

(11) "Personal liability" means liability for a debt, obligation, or other liability of an organization which is imposed on a person that co-owns, has an interest in, or is a member of the organization:

(A) by the governing statute solely by reason of the person co-owning, having an interest in, or being a member of the organization; or

(B) by the organization's organizational documents under a provision of the governing statute authorizing those documents to make one or more specified persons liable for all or specified debts, obligations, or other liabilities of the organization solely by reason of the person or persons co-owning, having an interest in, or being a member of the organization.

(12) "Surviving organization" means an organization into which one or more other organizations are merged whether the organization preexisted the merger or was created by the merger.

Comment

This article is based on Article 11 of ULPA (2001) and differs principally in treating domestications as a separate type of organic transaction rather than as a subset of conversions.

§ 1002. Merger

(a) A limited liability company may merge with one or more other constituent organizations pursuant to this section, Sections 1003 through 1005, and a plan of merger, if:

(1) the governing statute of each of the other organizations authorizes the merger;

(2) the merger is not prohibited by the law of a jurisdiction that enacted any of the governing statutes; and

(3) each of the other organizations complies with its governing statute in effecting the merger.

(b) A plan of merger must be in a record and must include:

(1) the name and form of each constituent organization;

(2) the name and form of the surviving organization and, if the surviving organization is to be created by the merger, a statement to that effect;

(3) the terms and conditions of the merger, including the manner and basis for converting the interests in each constituent organization into any combination of money, interests in the surviving organization, and other consideration;

(4) if the surviving organization is to be created by the merger, the surviving organization's organizational documents that are proposed to be in a record; and

(5) if the surviving organization is not to be created by the merger, any amendments to be made by the merger to the surviving organization's organizational documents that are, or are proposed to be, in a record.

§ 1003. Action on Plan of Merger by Constituent Limited Liability Company

(a) Subject to Section 1014, a plan of merger must be consented to by all the members of a constituent limited liability company.

(b)   Subject to Section 1014 and any contractual rights, after a merger is approved, and at any time before articles of merger are delivered to the [Secretary of State] for filing under Section 1004, a constituent limited liability company may amend the plan or abandon the merger:

(1)   as provided in the plan; or

(2)   except as otherwise prohibited in the plan, with the same consent as was required to approve the plan.

§ 1004.   Filings Required for Merger; Effective Date

(a)   After each constituent organization has approved a merger, articles of merger must be signed on behalf of:

(1)   each constituent limited liability company, as provided in Section 203(a); and

(2)   each other constituent organization, as provided in its governing statute.

(b)   Articles of merger under this section must include:

(1)   the name and form of each constituent organization and the jurisdiction of its governing statute;

(2)   the name and form of the surviving organization, the jurisdiction of its governing statute, and, if the surviving organization is created by the merger, a statement to that effect;

(3)   the date the merger is effective under the governing statute of the surviving organization;

(4)   if the surviving organization is to be created by the merger:

(A)   if it will be a limited liability company, the company's certificate of organization; or

(B)   if it will be an organization other than a limited liability company, the organizational document that creates the organization that is in a public record;

(5)   if the surviving organization preexists the merger, any amendments provided for in the plan of merger for the organizational document that created the organization that are in a public record;

(6)   a statement as to each constituent organization that the merger was approved as required by the organization's governing statute;

(7)   if the surviving organization is a foreign organization not authorized to transact business in this state, the street and mailing addresses of an office that the [Secretary of State] may use for the purposes of Section 1005(b); and

(8)   any additional information required by the governing statute of any constituent organization.

(c)   Each constituent limited liability company shall deliver the articles of merger for filing in the [office of the Secretary of State].

(d)   A merger becomes effective under this [article]:

(1)   if the surviving organization is a limited liability company, upon the later of:

(A)   compliance with subsection (c); or

(B)   subject to Section 205(c), as specified in the articles of merger; or

(2)   if the surviving organization is not a limited liability company, as provided by the governing statute of the surviving organization.

§ 1005. Effect of Merger

(a) When a merger becomes effective:

(1)   the surviving organization continues or comes into existence;

(2)   each constituent organization that merges into the surviving organization ceases to exist as a separate entity;

(3)   all property owned by each constituent organization that ceases to exist vests in the surviving organization;

(4)   all debts, obligations, or other liabilities of each constituent organization that ceases to exist continue as debts, obligations, or other liabilities of the surviving organization;

(5)   an action or proceeding pending by or against any constituent organization that ceases to exist may be continued as if the merger had not occurred;

(6)   except as prohibited by other law, all of the rights, privileges, immunities, powers, and purposes of each constituent organization that ceases to exist vest in the surviving organization;

(7)   except as otherwise provided in the plan of merger, the terms and conditions of the plan of merger take effect; and

(8)   except as otherwise agreed, if a constituent limited liability company ceases to exist, the merger does not dissolve the limited liability company for the purposes of [Article] 7;

(9)   if the surviving organization is created by the merger:

(A)   if it is a limited liability company, the certificate of organization becomes effective; or

(B)   if it is an organization other than a limited liability company, the organizational document that creates the organization becomes effective; and

(10) if the surviving organization preexisted the merger, any amendments provided for in the articles of merger for the organizational document that created the organization become effective.

(b)   A surviving organization that is a foreign organization consents to the jurisdiction of the courts of this state to enforce any debt, obligation, or other liability owed by a constituent organization, if before the merger the constituent organization was subject to suit in this state on the debt, obligation, or other liability. A surviving organization that is a foreign organization and not authorized to transact business in this state appoints the [Secretary of State] as its agent for service of process for the purposes of enforcing a debt, obligation, or other liability under this subsection. Service on the [Secretary of State] under this subsection must be made in the same manner and has the same consequences as in Section 116(c) and (d).

§ 1006. Conversion

(a)   An organization other than a limited liability company or a foreign limited liability company may convert to a limited liability company, and a limited liability company may convert to an organization other than a foreign limited liability company pursuant to this section, Sections 1007 through 1009, and a plan of conversion, if:

(1)   the other organization's governing statute authorizes the conversion;

(2)   the conversion is not prohibited by the law of the jurisdiction that enacted the other organization's governing statute; and

(3)   the other organization complies with its governing statute in effecting the conversion.

(b)   A plan of conversion must be in a record and must include:

(1)   the name and form of the organization before conversion;

(2)   the name and form of the organization after conversion;

(3)   the terms and conditions of the conversion, including the manner and basis for converting interests in the converting organization into any combination of money, interests in the converted organization, and other consideration; and

(4)   the organizational documents of the converted organization that are, or are proposed to be, in a record.

§ 1007.   Action on Plan of Conversion by Converting Limited Liability Company

(a)   Subject to Section 1014, a plan of conversion must be consented to by all the members of a converting limited liability company.

(b)   Subject to Section 1014 and any contractual rights, after a conversion is approved, and at any time before articles of conversion are delivered to the [Secretary of State] for filing under Section 1008, a converting limited liability company may amend the plan or abandon the conversion:

(1)   as provided in the plan; or

(2)   except as otherwise prohibited in the plan, by the same consent as was required to approve the plan.

§ 1008.   Filings Required for Conversion; Effective Date

(a)   After a plan of conversion is approved:

(1)   a converting limited liability company shall deliver to the [Secretary of State] for filing articles of conversion, which must be signed as provided in Section 203(a) and must include:

(A)   a statement that the limited liability company has been converted into another organization;

(B)   the name and form of the organization and the jurisdiction of its governing statute;

(C)   the date the conversion is effective under the governing statute of the converted organization;

(D)   a statement that the conversion was approved as required by this [act];

(E)   a statement that the conversion was approved as required by the governing statute of the converted organization; and

(F)   if the converted organization is a foreign organization not authorized to transact business in this state, the street and mailing addresses of an office which the [Secretary of State] may use for the purposes of Section 1009(c); and

(2)   if the converting organization is not a converting limited liability company, the converting organization shall deliver to the [Secretary of State] for filing a certificate of organization, which must include, in addition to the information required by Section 201(b):

(A)   a statement that the converted organization was converted from another organization;

(B)   the name and form of that converting organization and the jurisdiction of its governing statute; and

(C)   a statement that the conversion was approved in a manner that complied with the converting organization's governing statute.

(b)   A conversion becomes effective:

(1) if the converted organization is a limited liability company, when the certificate of organization takes effect; and

(2) if the converted organization is not a limited liability company, as provided by the governing statute of the converted organization.

§ 1009. Effect of Conversion

(a) An organization that has been converted pursuant to this [article] is for all purposes the same entity that existed before the conversion.

(b) When a conversion takes effect:

(1) all property owned by the converting organization remains vested in the converted organization;

(2) all debts, obligations, or other liabilities of the converting organization continue as debts, obligations, or other liabilities of the converted organization;

(3) an action or proceeding pending by or against the converting organization may be continued as if the conversion had not occurred;

(4) except as prohibited by law other than this [act], all of the rights, privileges, immunities, powers, and purposes of the converting organization remain vested in the converted organization;

(5) except as otherwise provided in the plan of conversion, the terms and conditions of the plan of conversion take effect; and

(6) except as otherwise agreed, the conversion does not dissolve a converting limited liability company for the purposes of [Article] 7.

(c) A converted organization that is a foreign organization consents to the jurisdiction of the courts of this state to enforce any debt, obligation, or other liability for which the converting limited liability company is liable if, before the conversion, the converting limited liability company was subject to suit in this state on the debt, obligation, or other liability. A converted organization that is a foreign organization and not authorized to transact business in this state appoints the [Secretary of State] as its agent for service of process for purposes of enforcing a debt, obligation, or other liability under this subsection. Service on the [Secretary of State] under this subsection must be made in the same manner and has the same consequences as in Section 116(c) and (d).

§ 1010. Domestication

(a) A foreign limited liability company may become a limited liability company pursuant to this section, Sections 1011 through 1013, and a plan of domestication, if:

(1) the foreign limited liability company's governing statute authorizes the domestication;

(2) the domestication is not prohibited by the law of the jurisdiction that enacted the governing statute; and

(3) the foreign limited liability company complies with its governing statute in effecting the domestication.

(b) A limited liability company may become a foreign limited liability company pursuant to this section, Sections 1011 through 1013, and a plan of domestication, if:

(1) the foreign limited liability company's governing statute authorizes the domestication;

(2) the domestication is not prohibited by the law of the jurisdiction that enacted the governing statute; and

(3)   the foreign limited liability company complies with its governing statute in effecting the domestication.

(c)   A plan of domestication must be in a record and must include:

(1)   the name of the domesticating company before domestication and the jurisdiction of its governing statute;

(2)   the name of the domesticated company after domestication and the jurisdiction of its governing statute;

(3)   the terms and conditions of the domestication, including the manner and basis for converting interests in the domesticating company into any combination of money, interests in the domesticated company, and other consideration; and

(4)   the organizational documents of the domesticated company that are, or are proposed to be, in a record.

§ 1011.   Action on Plan of Domestication by Domesticating Limited Liability Company

(a)   A plan of domestication must be consented to:

(1)   by all the members, subject to Section 1014, if the domesticating company is a limited liability company; and

(2)   as provided in the domesticating company's governing statute, if the company is a foreign limited liability company.

(b)   Subject to any contractual rights, after a domestication is approved, and at any time before articles of domestication are delivered to the [Secretary of State] for filing under Section 1012, a domesticating limited liability company may amend the plan or abandon the domestication:

(1)   as provided in the plan; or

(2)   except as otherwise prohibited in the plan, by the same consent as was required to approve the plan.

§ 1012.   Filings Required for Domestication; Effective Date

(a)   After a plan of domestication is approved, a domesticating company shall deliver to the [Secretary of State] for filing articles of domestication, which must include:

(1)   a statement, as the case may be, that the company has been domesticated from or into another jurisdiction;

(2)   the name of the domesticating company and the jurisdiction of its governing statute;

(3)   the name of the domesticated company and the jurisdiction of its governing statute;

(4)   the date the domestication is effective under the governing statute of the domesticated company;

(5)   if the domesticating company was a limited liability company, a statement that the domestication was approved as required by this [act];

(6)   if the domesticating company was a foreign limited liability company, a statement that the domestication was approved as required by the governing statute of the other jurisdiction; and

(7)   if the domesticated company was a foreign limited liability company not authorized to transact business in this state, the street and mailing addresses of an office that the [Secretary of State] may use for the purposes of Section 1013(b).

(b)   A domestication becomes effective:

(1) when the certificate of organization takes effect, if the domesticated company is a limited liability company; and

(2) according to the governing statute of the domesticated company, if the domesticated organization is a foreign limited liability company.

§ 1013. Effect of Domestication

(a) When a domestication takes effect:

(1) the domesticated company is for all purposes the company that existed before the domestication;

(2) all property owned by the domesticating company remains vested in the domesticated company;

(3) all debts, obligations, or other liabilities of the domesticating company continue as debts, obligations, or other liabilities of the domesticated company;

(4) an action or proceeding pending by or against a domesticating company may be continued as if the domestication had not occurred;

(5) except as prohibited by other law, all of the rights, privileges, immunities, powers, and purposes of the domesticating company remain vested in the domesticated company;

(6) except as otherwise provided in the plan of domestication, the terms and conditions of the plan of domestication take effect; and

(7) except as otherwise agreed, the domestication does not dissolve a domesticating limited liability company for the purposes of [Article] 7.

(b) A domesticated company that is a foreign limited liability company consents to the jurisdiction of the courts of this state to enforce any debt, obligation, or other liability owed by the domesticating company, if, before the domestication, the domesticating company was subject to suit in this state on the debt, obligation, or other liability. A domesticated company that is a foreign limited liability company and not authorized to transact business in this state appoints the [Secretary of State] as its agent for service of process for purposes of enforcing a debt, obligation, or other liability under this subsection. Service on the [Secretary of State] under this subsection must be made in the same manner and has the same consequences as in Section 116(c) and (d).

(c) If a limited liability company has adopted and approved a plan of domestication under Section 1010 providing for the company to be domesticated in a foreign jurisdiction, a statement surrendering the company's certificate of organization must be delivered to the [Secretary of State] for filing setting forth:

(1) the name of the company;

(2) a statement that the certificate of organization is being surrendered in connection with the domestication of the company in a foreign jurisdiction;

(3) a statement the domestication was approved as required by this [act]; and

(4) the jurisdiction of formation of the domesticated foreign limited liability company.

§ 1014. Restrictions on Approval of Mergers, Conversions, and Domestications

(a) If a member of a constituent, converting, or domesticating limited liability company will have personal liability with respect to a surviving, converted, or domesticated organization, approval or amendment of a plan of merger, conversion, or domestication is ineffective without the consent of the member, unless:

(1) the company's operating agreement provides for approval of a merger, conversion, or domestication with the consent of fewer than all the members; and

(2)   the member has consented to the provision of the operating agreement.

(b)   A member does not give the consent required by subsection (a) merely by consenting to a provision of the operating agreement that permits the operating agreement to be amended with the consent of fewer than all the members.

§ 1015.   [Article] Not Exclusive

This [article] does not preclude an entity from being merged, converted, or domesticated under law other than this [act].

[ARTICLE] 11

MISCELLANEOUS PROVISIONS

§ 1101.   Uniformity of Application and Construction

In applying and construing this uniform act, consideration must be given to the need to promote uniformity of the law with respect to its subject matter among states that enact it.

§ 1102.   Relation to Electronic Signatures in Global and National Commerce Act

This [act] modifies, limits, and supersedes the federal Electronic Signatures in Global and National Commerce Act, 15 U.S.C. Section 7001 *et seq.*, but does not modify, limit, or supersede Section 101(c) of that act, 15 U.S.C. Section 7001(c), or authorize electronic delivery of any of the notices described in Section 103(b) of that act, 15 U.S.C. Section 7003(b).

§ 1103.   Savings Clause

This [act] does not affect an action commenced, proceeding brought, or right accrued before this [act] takes effect.

§ 1104.   Application to Existing Relationships

(a)   Before [all-inclusive date], this [act] governs only:

(1)   a limited liability company formed on or after [the effective date of this act]; and

(2)   except as otherwise provided in subsection (c), a limited liability company formed before [the effective date of this act] which elects, in the manner provided in its operating agreement or by law for amending the operating agreement, to be subject to this [act].

(b)   Except as otherwise provided in subsection (c), on and after [all-inclusive date] this [act] governs all limited liability companies.

(c)   For the purposes applying this [act] to a limited liability company formed before [the effective date of this act]:

(1)   the company's articles of organization are deemed to be the company's certificate of organization; and

(2)   for the purposes of applying Section 102(10) and subject to Section 112(d), language in the company's articles of organization designating the company's management structure operates as if that language were in the operating agreement.

Legislative Note: It is recommended that the "all-inclusive" date should be at least one year after the date of enactment but no longer than two years.

Each enacting jurisdiction should consider whether: (i) this Act makes material changes to the "default" (or "gap filler") rules of jurisdiction's predecessor statute; and (ii) if so, whether subsection (c) should carry forward any of those rules for pre-existing limited liability companies. In this assessment, the focus is on pre-existing limited liability companies that have left default rules in place, whether advisedly or not. The central question is whether, for such limited liability companies, expanding subsection (c) is necessary to prevent material changes to the members' "deal."

For an example of this type of analysis in the context of another business entity act, see the Uniform Limited Partnership Act (2001), § 1206(c).

Section 301 (de-codifying statutory apparent authority) does not require any special transition provisions, because: (i) applying the law of agency, as explained in the Comments to Sections 301 and 407, will produce appropriate results; and (ii) the notion of "lingering apparent authority" will protect any third party that has previously relied on the statutory apparent authority of a member of a particular member-managed LLC or a manager of a particular manager-managed LLC. RESTATEMENT (THIRD) OF AGENCY *§ 3.11, cmt. c (2006).*

It is unnecessary to expand subsection (c) of this Act if the state's predecessor act is the original Uniform Limited Liability Company Act, revised to provide for perpetual duration.

Comment

Subsection (c)—When a pre-existing limited liability company becomes subject to this Act, the company ceases to be governed by the predecessor act, including whatever requirements that act might have imposed for the contents of the articles of organization.

§ 1105. Repeals

Effective [all-inclusive date], the following acts and parts of acts are repealed: [the state limited liability company act, as amended, and in effect immediately before the effective date of this act].

§ 1106. Effective Date

This [act] takes effect on. . . .

B. REVISED UNIFORM LIMITED LIABILITY COMPANY ACT (2013)

(with Selected Comments)

Table of Contents

[ARTICLE] 1

GENERAL PROVISIONS

[ARTICLE] 2

FORMATION; CERTIFICATE OF ORGANIZATION AND OTHER FILINGS

REVISED UNIFORM LIMITED LIABILITY
COMPANY ACT (2013)

REVISED UNIFORM LIMITED LIABILITY
COMPANY ACT (2013)

[ARTICLE] 1

GENERAL PROVISIONS

§ 101.   **Short Title**

This [act] may be cited as the Uniform Limited Liability Company Act.

§ 102. Definitions

In this [act]:

(1) "Certificate of organization" means the certificate required by Section 201. The term includes the certificate as amended or restated.

(2) "Contribution", except in the phrase "right of contribution", means property or a benefit described in Section 402 which is provided by a person to a limited liability company to become a member or in the person's capacity as a member.

(3) "Debtor in bankruptcy" means a person that is the subject of:

(A) an order for relief under Title 11 of the United States Code or a comparable order under a successor statute of general application; or

(B) a comparable order under federal, state, or foreign law governing insolvency.

(4) "Distribution" means a transfer of money or other property from a limited liability company to a person on account of a transferable interest or in the person's capacity as a member. The term:

(A) includes:

(i) a redemption or other purchase by a limited liability company of a transferable interest; and

(ii) a transfer to a member in return for the member's relinquishment of any right to participate as a member in the management or conduct of the company's activities and affairs or to have access to records or other information concerning the company's activities and affairs; and

(B) does not include amounts constituting reasonable compensation for present or past service or payments made in the ordinary course of business under a bona fide retirement plan or other bona fide benefits program.

(5) "Foreign limited liability company" means an unincorporated entity formed under the law of a jurisdiction other than this state which would be a limited liability company if formed under the law of this state.

(6) "Jurisdiction", used to refer to a political entity, means the United States, a state, a foreign county, or a political subdivision of a foreign country.

(7) "Jurisdiction of formation" means the jurisdiction whose law governs the internal affairs of an entity.

(8) "Limited liability company", except in the phrase "foreign limited liability company" and in [Article] 10, means an entity formed under this [act] or which becomes subject to this [act] under [Article] 10 or Section 110.

(9) "Manager" means a person that under the operating agreement of a manager-managed limited liability company is responsible, alone or in concert with others, for performing the management functions stated in Section 407(c).

(10) "Manager-managed limited liability company" means a limited liability company that qualifies under Section 407(a).

(11) "Member" means a person that:

(A) has become a member of a limited liability company under Section 401 or was a member in a company when the company became subject to this [act] under Section 110; and

(B) has not dissociated under Section 602.

(12) "Member-managed limited liability company" means a limited liability company that is not a manager-managed limited liability company.

(13) "Operating agreement" means the agreement, whether or not referred to as an operating agreement and whether oral, implied, in a record, or in any combination thereof, of all the members of a limited liability company, including a sole member, concerning the matters described in Section 105(a). The term includes the agreement as amended or restated.

(14) "Organizer" means a person that acts under Section 201 to form a limited liability company.

(15) "Person" means an individual, business corporation, nonprofit corporation, partnership, limited partnership, limited liability company, [general cooperative association,] limited cooperative association, unincorporated nonprofit association, statutory trust, business trust, common-law business trust, estate, trust, association, joint venture, public corporation, government or governmental subdivision, agency, or instrumentality, or any other legal or commercial entity.

(16) "Principal office" means the principal executive office of a limited liability company or foreign limited liability company, whether or not the office is located in this state.

(17) "Property" means all property, whether real, personal, or mixed or tangible or intangible, or any right or interest therein.

(18) "Record", used as a noun, means information that is inscribed on a tangible medium or that is stored in an electronic or other medium and is retrievable in perceivable form.

(19) "Registered agent" means an agent of a limited liability company or foreign limited liability company which is authorized to receive service of any process, notice, or demand required or permitted by law to be served on the company.

(20) "Registered foreign limited liability company" means a foreign limited liability company that is registered to do business in this state pursuant to a statement of registration filed by the [Secretary of State].

(21) "Sign" means, with present intent to authenticate or adopt a record:

    (A) to execute or adopt a tangible symbol; or

    (B) to attach to or logically associate with the record an electronic symbol, sound, or process.

(22) "State" means a state of the United States, the District of Columbia, Puerto Rico, the United States Virgin Islands, or any territory or insular possession subject to the jurisdiction of the United States.

(23) "Transfer" includes:

    (A) an assignment;

    (B) a conveyance;

    (C) a sale;

    (D) a lease;

    (E) an encumbrance, including a mortgage or security interest;

    (F) a gift; and

    (G) a transfer by operation of law.

(24) "Transferable interest" means the right, as initially owned by a person in the person's capacity as a member, to receive distributions from a limited liability company, whether or not the person remains a member or continues to own any part of the right. The term applies to any fraction of the interest, by whomever owned.

(25) "Transferee" means a person to which all or part of a transferable interest has been transferred, whether or not the transferor is a member. The term includes a person that owns a transferable interest under Section 603(a)(3).

§ 103. Knowledge; Notice

(a) A person knows a fact if the person:

   (1) has actual knowledge of it; or

   (2) is deemed to know it under subsection (d)(1) or law other than this [act].

(b) A person has notice of a fact if the person:

   (1) has reason to know the fact from all the facts known to the person at the time in question; or

   (2) is deemed to have notice of the fact under subsection (d)(2).

(c) Subject to Section 210(f), a person notifies another person of a fact by taking steps reasonably required to inform the other person in ordinary course, whether or not those steps cause the other person to know the fact.

(d) A person not a member is deemed:

   (1) to know of a limitation on authority to transfer real property as provided in Section 302(g); and

   (2) to have notice of a limited liability company's:

      (A) dissolution 90 days after a statement of dissolution under Section 702(b)(2)(A) becomes effective;

      (B) termination 90 days after a statement of termination under Section 702(b)(2)(F) becomes effective; and

      (C) participation in a merger, interest exchange, conversion, or domestication, 90 days after articles of merger, interest exchange, conversion, or domestication under [Article] 10 become effective.

§ 104. Governing Law

The law of this state governs:

   (1) the internal affairs of a limited liability company; and

   (2) the liability of a member as member and a manager as manager for a debt, obligation, or other liability of a limited liability company.

§ 105. Operating Agreement; Scope, Function, and Limitations

(a) Except as otherwise provided in subsections (c) and (d), the operating agreement governs:

   (1) relations among the members as members and between the members and the limited liability company;

   (2) the rights and duties under this [act] of a person in the capacity of manager;

   (3) the activities and affairs of the company and the conduct of those activities and affairs; and

   (4) the means and conditions for amending the operating agreement.

(b) To the extent the operating agreement does not provide for a matter described in subsection (a), this [act] governs the matter.

(c) An operating agreement may not:

   (1) vary the law applicable under Section 104;

(2)   vary a limited liability company's capacity under Section 109 to sue and be sued in its own name;

(3)   vary any requirement, procedure, or other provision of this [act] pertaining to:

(A)   registered agents; or

(B)   the [Secretary of State], including provisions pertaining to records authorized or required to be delivered to the [Secretary of State] for filing under this [act];

(4)   vary the provisions of Section 204;

(5)   alter or eliminate the duty of loyalty or the duty of care, except as otherwise provided in subsection (d);

(6)   eliminate the contractual obligation of good faith and fair dealing under Section 409(d), but the operating agreement may prescribe the standards, if not manifestly unreasonable, by which the performance of the obligation is to be measured;

(7)   relieve or exonerate a person from liability for conduct involving bad faith, willful or intentional misconduct, or knowing violation of law;

(8)   unreasonably restrict the duties and rights under Section 410, but the operating agreement may impose reasonable restrictions on the availability and use of information obtained under that section and may define appropriate remedies, including liquidated damages, for a breach of any reasonable restriction on use;

(9)   vary the causes of dissolution specified in Section 701(a)(4);

(10) vary the requirement to wind up the company's activities and affairs as specified in Section 702(a), (b)(1), and (e);

(11) unreasonably restrict the right of a member to maintain an action under [Article] 8;

(12) vary the provisions of Section 805, but the operating agreement may provide that the company may not have a special litigation committee;

(13) vary the right of a member to approve a merger, interest exchange, conversion, or domestication under Section 1023(a)(2), 1033(a)(2), 1043(a)(2), or 1053(a)(2);

(14) vary the required contents of a plan of merger under Section 1022(a), plan of interest exchange under Section 1032(a), plan of conversion under Section 1042(a), or plan of domestication under Section 1052(a); or

(15) except as otherwise provided in Sections 106 and 107(b), restrict the rights under this [act] of a person other than a member or manager.

(d)   Subject to subsection (c)(7), without limiting other terms that may be included in an operating agreement, the following rules apply:

(1)   The operating agreement may:

(A)   specify the method by which a specific act or transaction that would otherwise violate the duty of loyalty may be authorized or ratified by one or more disinterested and independent persons after full disclosure of all material facts; and

(B)   alter the prohibition in Section 405(a)(2) so that the prohibition requires only that the company's total assets not be less than the sum of its total liabilities.

(2)   To the extent the operating agreement of a member-managed limited liability company expressly relieves a member of a responsibility that the member otherwise would have under this [act] and imposes the responsibility on one or more other members, the agreement also may eliminate or limit any fiduciary duty of the member relieved of the responsibility which would have pertained to the responsibility.

(3)   If not manifestly unreasonable, the operating agreement may:

(A)   alter or eliminate the aspects of the duty of loyalty stated in Section 409(b) and (i);

(B)   identify specific types or categories of activities that do not violate the duty of loyalty;

(C)   alter the duty of care, but may not authorize conduct involving bad faith, willful or intentional misconduct, or knowing violation of law; and

(D)   alter or eliminate any other fiduciary duty.

(e)   The court shall decide as a matter of law whether a term of an operating agreement is manifestly unreasonable under subsection (c)(6) or (d)(3). The court:

(1)   shall make its determination as of the time the challenged term became part of the operating agreement and by considering only circumstances existing at that time; and

(2)   may invalidate the term only if, in light of the purposes, activities, and affairs of the limited liability company, it is readily apparent that:

(A)   the objective of the term is unreasonable; or

(B)   the term is an unreasonable means to achieve the term's objective.

COMMENT

Principal Provisions of the Act Concerning the Operating Agreement

The operating agreement is pivotal to a limited liability company, and Sections 105 through 107 are pivotal to this act. They must be read together, along with Section 102(13) (defining the operating agreement).

This section performs five essential functions. Subsection (a) establishes the primacy of the operating agreement in establishing relations *inter se* the limited liability company, its member or members, and any manager. Subsection (b) recognizes this act as comprising mostly default rules—*i.e.*, gap fillers for issues as to which the operating agreement provides no rule. Subsection (c) lists the few mandatory provisions of the act. Subsection (d) lists some provisions frequently found in operating agreements, authorizing some unconditionally and others so long as "not manifestly unreasonable." Subsection (e) delineates in detail both the meaning of "not manifestly unreasonable" and the information relevant to a determining a claim that a provision of an operating agreement is manifestly unreasonable.

Section 106 details the effect of an operating agreement on the limited liability company and on persons becoming members of an LLC. Section 107 concerns the effect of an operating agreement on third parties.

Role and Inevitability of Operating Agreement

A limited liability company is as much a creature of contract as of statute, *TravelCenters of Am., L.L.C. v. Brog*, CIV.A. 3516-CC, 2008 WL 1746987, at *1 (Del. Ch. Apr. 3, 2008) (stating that "limited liability companies are creatures of contract"); *Gottsacker v. Monnier*, 281 Wis. 2d 361, 370, 697 N.W.2d 436, 440 (2005) (stating that "from the partnership form, the LLC borrows . . . internal governance by contract"), and Section 102(13) delineates a very broad scope for "operating agreement." As a result, once an LLC comes into existence and has a member, the LLC necessarily has an operating agreement. *See* the comment to Section 102(13). Accordingly, this act refers to "the operating agreement" rather than "an operating agreement." This phrasing should not, however, be read to require a limited liability company or its members to take any formal action to adopt an operating agreement.

The operating agreement is the exclusive consensual process for modifying this act's various default rules pertaining to relationships *inter se* the members and between the members and the limited liability company. Section 105(b). The operating agreement also has power over "the rights and duties under this [act] of a person in the capacity of manager," Subsection (a)(2), and "the obligations of a limited liability company and its members to a person in the person's capacity as a transferee or person dissociated as a member," Section 107(b). For the relationship between the operating agreement and certificate of formation, see Section 107(d).

The Operating Agreement and the Fiduciary and Other Duties of Those Who Manage

One of the most complex questions in the law of unincorporated business organizations is the extent to which an agreement among the organization's owners can affect the fiduciary and other duties of those who manage the organization (e.g., members in a member-managed LLC; managers in a manager-managed LLC). As explained in detail in the comment to Subsection (d)(3), this act rejects the notion that a contract can completely transform an inherently fiduciary relationship into a merely arm's length association. Within that limitation, however, this section provides substantial power to the operating agreement to reshape, limit, and eliminate fiduciary and other managerial duties.

Subsection (a) recognizes that the operating agreement is the map to the parties' deal and that any claim by a member of managerial misconduct must be assessed first under the relevant terms of the operating agreement. Subsection (d) specifically validates arrangements commonly used to reshape managerial duties and limit the consequences of breaching those duties. Subsection (c) contains relevant limitations, but those limitations: (i) must be read together with subsection (d); and (ii) do not preclude the operating agreement fundamentally redesigning the duties applicable to those who manage the organization. For the act's design of those duties, see Sections 409 and 410.

Subsection (a)—This section describes the very broad scope of a limited liability company's operating agreement, which includes all matters constituting "internal affairs." *Compare* Subsection (a), *with* Section 104(1) (using the phrase "internal affairs" in stating a choice of law rule). This broad grant of authority is subject to the restrictions stated in Subsection (c), including the broad restriction stated in Paragraph (c)(15) (concerning the rights of third parties under this act).

Subsection (a)(1)—This paragraph encompasses all the rights and duties of each member, including rights and duties pertaining to transactions under Article 10.

Subsection (a)(2)—Under this paragraph, the operating agreement has the power to affect the rights and duties of managers (including non-member managers). Because the term "[o]perating agreement . . . includes the agreement as amended or restated," Section 102(13), this paragraph gives the members the ongoing power to define the role of an LLC's managers. Power is not the same as right, however, and exercising the power provided by this paragraph might constitute a breach of a separate contract between the LLC and the manager. A non-member manager might also have rights under Section 107(a).

Subsection (a)(4)—Under this provision, the operating agreement can control both the quantum of consent required (*e.g.*, majority of members) and the means by which the consent is manifested (*e.g.*, prohibiting modifications except when consented to in writing). *See* the comment to Section 107(a).

If the operating agreement does not address the issue, this act provides the rule. Section 407(b)(4)(C) and 407(c)(3)(C) each require the affirmative vote or consent of all the members. Under Section 111 (supplemental principles of law), the parol evidence rule will apply to a written operating agreement when appropriate under contract law.

Subsection (b)—To the extent the operating agreement does not determine an inter se matter, this act determines the matter. The operating agreement may vary any provision of this act pertaining to *inter se* matters, except as provided in Subsections (c) and (d).

Sometimes—but not always—the Comments to this act refer to a variable provision as a "default rule" and a non-waivable provision as "mandatory." These references are merely to draw attention to the default/mandatory distinction in particular contexts and have neither the intent nor the power to affect the default/mandatory status of provisions of this act whose comments lack a comparable reference.

Subsection (c)—This subsection lists provisions of this act whose respective effects cannot be varied or may be varied subject to a stated limitation. For historical reasons, this subsection uses the words "vary" and "alter" interchangeably. No difference in meaning is intended.

If a person claims that a term of the operating agreement violates this subsection, as a matter of ordinary procedural law the burden of proof is on the person making the claim.

Subsection (c)(1)—Section 104 states that this act provides the law applicable to: (i) the internal affairs of an LLC formed under this act; and (ii) the liability of members and managers for obligations of the LLC. The organizers of an LLC make this choice of law by choosing to form an LLC under this act.

Domestication to another jurisdiction will re-set the choice of law, see Sections 1051–56, but the operating agreement cannot, *see* the comment to Section 104(1).

Subsection (c) contains no parallel prohibition on varying Section 901 (stating the governing law for foreign limited liability companies), because a prohibition is unnecessary. As a matter of fundamental contract law, an agreement among members of one limited liability company is powerless to govern the affairs of another limited liability company.

Subsection (c)(2)—Under this act, a limited liability company is emphatically an entity, and the members lack the power to alter that characteristic.

Subsection (c)(3)—This prohibition is arguably implicit in Subsection (c)(15) (affecting rights of third parties under this act) but is specifically noted to avoid doubt.

Subsection (c)(4)—This provision means that the operating agreement cannot affect the right of an "aggrieved" person to seek the court's help when "a person required by this [act] to sign a record or deliver a record to the [Secretary of State] for filing under this [act] does not do so." Section 204(a).

Subsection (c)(5)—This limitation is less powerful than might first appear, because Subsection (d) specifically authorizes substantial alterations to the duties of loyalty and care, including restricting and substantially eliminating those duties.

Subsection (c)(6)—Section 409(d) refers to the "contractual obligation of good faith and fair dealing," which contract law implies in every contract. The operating agreement cannot eliminate this obligation, neither in whole (*i.e.*, generally) nor in part (*i.e.*, as applicable to specified situations).

However, an operating agreement may "prescribe the standards . . . by which the performance of the obligation is to be measured."

EXAMPLE: The operating agreement of a manager-managed LLC gives the manager the discretion to cause the LLC to enter into contracts with affiliates of the manager (so-called "Conflict Transactions"). The agreement further provides: "When causing the Company to enter into a Conflict Transaction, the manager complies with Section 409(d) of [this act] if a disinterested person, knowledgeable in the subject matter, states in writing that the terms and conditions of the Conflict Transaction are equivalent to the terms and conditions that would be agreed to by persons at arm's length in comparable circumstances." This provision "prescribe[s] the standards by which the performance of the [Section 409(d)] obligation is to be measured."

EXAMPLE: Same facts as the previous example, except that, during the performance of a Conflict Transaction, the manager causes the LLC to waive material protections under the applicable contract. The standard stated in the previous example is inapposite to this conduct. Section 409(d) therefore applies to the conduct without any direct contractual delineation. (However, other terms of the agreement may be relevant to determining whether the conduct violates Section 409(d). See the comment to Section 409(d).)

EXAMPLE: The operating agreement of a manager-managed LLC gives the manager "sole discretion" to make various decisions. The agreement further provides: "Whenever this agreement requires or permits a manager to make a decision that has the potential to benefit one class of members to the detriment of another class, the manager complies with Section 409(d) of [this act] if the manager makes the decision with:

a.   the honest belief that the decision:

i.   serves the best interests of the LLC; or

ii.   at least does not injure or otherwise disserve those interests; and

b.   the reasonable belief that the decision breaches no member's rights under this agreement."

This provision "prescribe[s] the standards by which the performance of the [Section 409(d)] obligation is to be measured." *Compare* Section 105(c)(6), *with Nemec v. Shrader*, 991 A.2d 1120 (Del. 2010) (considering such a situation in the context of the right to call preferred stock and deciding by a 3–2 vote that exercising the call did not breach the implied covenant of good faith and fair dealing).

An operating agreement that seeks to prescribe standards for measuring the contractual obligation of good faith and fair dealing under Section 409(d) should expressly refer to the obligation. *See Gerber v. Enter. Prods. Hldgs., L.L.C.*, 67 A.3d 400, 418 (Del. 2013) (distinguishing between the implied contractual covenant and an express contractual obligation of "good faith" as stated in a limited partnership agreement).

For an explanation of the function and role of the covenant of good faith and fair dealing, see Section 409(d), comment. For the rules delimiting the "not manifestly unreasonable" requirement, see Subsection (e).

Subsection (c)(7)—These restrictions are ubiquitous in the law of business entities and, in conjunction with other provisions of this section, control the otherwise very broad power of an operating agreement to affect fiduciary and other duties. The restrictions are central to the raft of exculpatory provisions that sprung up in corporate statutes in response to *Smith v. Van Gorkum*, 488 A.2d 858 (Del. 1985), *overruled on other grounds by Gantler v. Stephens*, 965 A.2d 695 (Del. 2009). Delaware led the response with DEL. CODE ANN. tit. 8, § 102(b)(7), and a number of LLC statutes have similar provisions. *E.g.*, GA. CODE ANN. § 14–11–305(4)(A) (2011). For an extreme example, *see* VA. CODE ANN. § 13.1–1025 (B) (2012). In this context, "conduct" includes both acts and omissions. BLACK'S LAW DICTIONARY (9th ed. 2009) (defining conduct as "[p]ersonal behavior, whether by action or inaction").

The term "bad faith" has multiple meanings, and the context determines which meaning applies. In the context of the duty of loyalty, "bad faith" includes conduct motivated by ill will or other intent purposely to harm another person. The concept also includes conduct from which a person derives an improper personal benefit. *See, e.g., Mroz v. Hoaloha Na Eha, Inc.*, 410 F. Supp. 2d 919, 936–37 (D. Haw. 2005) (denying a motion to dismiss a claim that "the Majority Partners" were personally liable for the partnership's wrongful termination of the plaintiff; quoting the complaint as alleging that "the Majority Partners, individually and as a group, acted with malice and/or ill will, and/or with an intent to serve their own personal interests and/or without an intent to serve company interests, and/or outside of the scope of their authority and/or without justification"); *BOGNC, L.L.C. v. Cornelius NC Self-Storage L.L.C.*, 10 CVS 19072, 2013 WL 1867065, at *9 (N.C. Super. [Business Court] May 1, 2013) (noting that "no . . . [exculpatory] provision may limit a manager's liability for acts known to be in conflict with the interests of the limited liability company, or for acts from which the manager derived an improper personal benefit") (citing N.C. GEN. STAT. § 57C–3–32(b)); *Lasica v. Savers Grp. of Minn., L.L.C.*, A12-0092, 2012 WL 3553246, at *2 (Minn. Ct. App. Aug. 20, 2012) (noting that an "individual seeking indemnification [under statute providing for indemnification] must have acted in good faith and must not have received an improper personal benefit") (citing MINN. STAT. § 322B.699, subdivs. 2(a)(2), (3) (2010)).

In the context of the duty of care, the concept of bad faith comes primarily from corporate law and means an extreme breach of the duty (i.e., "the failure to exercise "honest judgment in the lawful and legitimate furtherance of corporate purposes." *Deblinger v. Sani-Pine Products Co., Inc.*, 107 A.D.3d 659, 661, 967 N.Y.S.2d 394 (2013) (quoting *Auerbach v. Bennett*, 47 N.Y.2d 619, 629, 393 N.E.2d 994 (1979)) (emphasis added) (internal quotation marks omitted).

Thus, when a plaintiff alleges bad faith as pertaining to the duty of care, "[t]he burden . . . is to show irrationality: a plaintiff must demonstrate that no reasonable business person could possibly authorize the action in good faith. Put positively, the decision must go so far beyond the bounds of reasonable business judgment that its only explanation is bad faith." *In re Tower Air, Inc.*, 416 F.3d 229, 238 (3d Cir. 2005) (discussing then prevailing Delaware law) (citation [omitted]); *see also KDW Restructuring & Liquidation Servs. LLC v. Greenfield*, 874 F. Supp. 2d 213, 226 (S.D.N.Y. 2012) (referring to a lack of "a rationale corporate purpose" and "a disregard for the duty to examine all available information—*information that was readily at hand*") (emphasis added).

With regard to both the duty of loyalty and the duty of care, "bad faith" is entirely distinct from the meaning of "good faith" in the contractual covenant of good faith and fair dealing. See the comment to Section 409(d).

Subsection (c)(7) pertains to indirect as well as direct efforts to "relieve or exonerate" and thus limits how far an operating agreement can go in providing for indemnification. *See* Section 408(b) (stating a default rule for indemnification). Also, in accordance with this paragraph, an exculpatory provision cannot shield against a member's claim of oppression. *See* Section 701(a)(4)(C).

Although this paragraph does not expressly address contracts between an LLC and a member or manager, the stated constraints must also apply to such contracts. If not, those constraints are effectively meaningless.

EXAMPLE: A manager-managed LLC enters into a management contract with its sole manager, and the contract provides the manager exoneration for liability to the LLC even for willful and intentional misconduct. Most likely, contract law will treat the provision as against public policy and therefore unenforceable. RESTATEMENT (SECOND) OF CONTRACTS § 195(1) (1981) ("A term exempting a party from tort liability for harm caused intentionally or recklessly is unenforceable on grounds of public policy."). If not, a court should hold the provision unenforceable to avoid evisceration of Subsection (c)(7). (Or, the court could invoke the policy expressed in Subsection (c)(7) as grounds for holding the provision unenforceable under contract law.)

Subsection (c)(8)—Although phrased as a restriction, this provision grants substantial power to the operating agreement.

EXAMPLE: A law firm operates as a limited liability company, and the operating agreement provides that a "Compensation Committee" periodically decides each member's compensation. The agreement also states that only members who are on the Compensation Committee may have access to the Committee's compensation decisions pertaining to other members. This restriction is reasonable.

The act also empowers the LLC "as a matter within the ordinary course of its activities and affairs [to] impose reasonable restrictions and conditions on access to and use of information" obtained under Section 410. *See* Section 410(h).

In determining whether a restriction is reasonable, a court might consider: (i) the danger or other problem the restriction seeks to avoid; (ii) the purpose for which the information is sought; and (iii) whether, in light of both the problem and the purpose, the restriction is reasonably tailored. In addition, a restriction that is reasonable viz-a-viz a non-managing member in a manager-managed LLC might be unreasonable viz-a-viz a managing member or in the context of a member-managed LLC.

Subsection (c)(9)—The operating agreement may not change the stated grounds for judicial dissolution but may determine the forum in which a claim for dissolution under Section 701(a)(4) is determined. For example, arbitration and forum selection clauses are commonplace in business relationships in general and in operating agreements in particular.

The approach of this paragraph differs from the law of Delaware. *Huatuco v. Satellite Healthcare*, CV 8465-VCG, 2013 WL 6460898, at *1, n.2 (Del. Ch. Dec. 9, 2013) (stating that "the right to judicial dissolution is a default right which the parties may eschew by contract" but reserving the question of "[w]hether the parties may, by contract, divest this Court of its authority to order a dissolution in all circumstances, even where it appears manifest that equity so requires—leaving, for instance, irreconcilable members locked away together forever like some alternative entity version of Sartre's *Huis Clos*").

Subsection (c)(10)—The cited provisions comprise the non-waivable aspects of winding up a dissolved limited liability company. The other provisions of Section 702 are default rules.

Subsection (c)(11)—Article 8 delineates a member's rights to bring direct and derivative actions. It would be unreasonable to frustrate these rights but not unreasonable to channel their exercise. For example, the operating agreement might select a forum, require pre-suit mediation, provide for arbitration of both direct and derivative claims, or override Section 802 and require "universal demand" in all derivative cases. Similarly, it is not unreasonable to provide for liquidated damages consonant with the law of contracts. In contrast, it would be unreasonable for an operating agreement to both: (i) require a would-be derivative plaintiff to make demand regardless of futility; and (ii) bar taking the claim to court no matter how long the management group ponders the demand.

Subsection (c)(12)—An operating agreement may not alter the act's rules for a special litigation committee but may preclude entirely the use of such a committee.

Subsection (c)(13)—Section 1023(a)(1), 1033(a)(1), 1043(a)(1), and 1053(a)(1) each requires the consent or the affirmative vote of all members. The operating agreement may modify these requirements. In contrast, under the sections stated in this subsection:

- each member is protected from being merged, exchanged, converted, or domesticated "into" the status of a partner in a general partnership that is not a limited liability partnership (or a comparable "unshielded" position in some other organization) without the member having directly consented to either:

  o the merger, interest exchange, conversion, or domestication; or

  o an operating agreement provision that permits such transactions to occur with less than unanimous consent of the members; and

- merely consenting to an operating agreement provision that permits amendment of the agreement with less than unanimous consent of the members does not qualify as the requisite direct consent.

Subsection (c)(14)—Because these plans are the basic "deal documents" for each of the organic transactions contemplated in Article 10, the operating agreement may not vary the contents of these plans.

Subsection (c)(15)—This limitation pertains only to "the rights under this [act] of" third parties other than members and managers. Moreover, the limitation is subject to two substantial exceptions: Section 106 (pertaining to the operating agreement's relationship to the limited liability company itself and to persons becoming members) and Section 107(b) (pertaining to the operating agreement's power over the rights of transferees).

Subsection (d)—The operating agreement has plenipotentiary power over the matters described in Subsection (a), except as specifically limited by Subsections (c) and (d)(3). However, for the convenience of practitioners and the courts. Paragraphs 1 and 2 list various terms often found in operating agreements. No negative inference should be drawn about terms not listed; the listing is provided "without limiting other terms that may be included in an operating agreement."

Paragraph 3 lists terms subject to the "not manifestly unreasonable" standard. Subsection (e) delineates that standard. The same standard applies to terms of an operating agreement which seek to "prescribe the standards . . . by which the performance of the [Section 409(d)] obligation [of good faith and fair dealing] is to be measured." Subsection (c)(6).

Subsection (d)(1)(A)—An arrangement *not* involving "one or more disinterested and independent persons" acting "after full disclosure of all material facts" would "alter . . . the aspects of the duty of loyalty stated in Section 409(b) and (i)" and would therefore be subject to the "not manifestly unreasonable standard" of Subsection (d)(3)(A).

For the meaning of "material" as applied to information, see Section 409(f), comment.

Subsection (d)(1)(B)—Section 405(a)(2) prohibits distributions:

- *not merely* when, after the distribution, "the company's total assets would be less than the sum of its total liabilities,"

- *but also* when, after the distribution, the assets would less than the total liabilities "plus the amount that would be needed, if the company were to be dissolved and wound up at the time of the distribution, to satisfy the preferential rights upon dissolution and winding up of members and transferees whose preferential rights are superior to those of persons receiving the distribution."

The second part of the solvency test pertains to preferential rights to distributions, is thus a matter *inter se* the members and any transferees, and is therefore subject to change in the operating agreement.

In contrast, the first part of the solvency test protects third parties—creditors of the LLC—and therefore cannot be changed by the operating agreement. Subsection (c)(15). Likewise, the operating agreement cannot change the solvency test stated in Section 405(a)(1) (providing that "the company would not be able to pay its debts as they become due in the ordinary course of the company's activities and affairs").

Subsection (d)(2)—This provision is limited to member-managed limited liability companies on the premise that: (i) managers are collectively responsible; and (ii) managers may properly delegate a duty but the delegation does not discharge the duty. However, in a manager-managed LLC (as well as in a member-managed LLC), subject to Subsection (d)(3) the operating agreement may alter or even eliminate fiduciary duties.

EXAMPLE: ABC LLC ("ABC") is a member-managed LLC. ABC has two entirely separate lines of business, the Alpha business and the Beta business. Under ABC's operating agreement:

- Member 1's responsibilities pertain exclusively to the Alpha business, while responsibility for:
  - the Beta business is allocated exclusively to Member 2; and
  - ABC's overall operations is allocated exclusively to Member 3.
- Member 2's responsibilities pertain exclusively to the Beta business, while responsibility for:
  - the Alpha business is allocated exclusively to Member 1; and
  - ABC's overall operations is allocated exclusively to Member 3.
- Member 1 has no fiduciary duties pertaining to the Beta business.
- Member 2 has no fiduciary duties pertaining to the Alpha business.

The elimination of Member 1's fiduciary duties with regard to the Beta business and Member 2's fiduciary duties with regard to the Alpha business are enforceable, without regard to the "manifestly unreasonable" standard of Subsection (d)(3).

Subsection (d)(3)—This act rejects the ultra-contractarian notion that fiduciary duty within a business organization is merely a set of default rules and seeks instead to balance the virtues of "freedom of contract" against the dangers that inescapably exist when some persons have power over the interests of others. *Cf.* Leo E. Strine, Jr. J. Travis Laster, *The Siren Song of Unlimited Contractual Freedom*, ELGAR HANDBOOK ON ALTERNATIVE ENTITIES (Eds. Mark Lowenstein and Robert Hillman), forthcoming 2014, Edward Elgar Publishing 2014) (noting that an "argument often made in favor of [Delaware] alternative entity statutes is that they allow for the elimination of fiduciary duties and the establishment of a purely contractual relationship between entity managers and investors" and stating that "[a]s judges who have seen our fair share of alternative entity disputes, we do not immediately grasp why this would be seen as a compelling advantage"); available at SSRN: http://ssrn.com/abstract=2481039, at 9–10 (footnote omitted).

Under this act, a properly drafted operating agreement may substantially alter and even eliminate fiduciary duties. However, two important limitations exist.

First, arrangements subject to this subsection may not be "manifestly unreasonable." See Subsection (e) (delineating this standard).

Second, the operating agreement may not transform the relationship inter se members, managers, and the LLC into an entirely arm's length arrangement. For example, displacement of fiduciary duties is effective only to the extent that the displacement is stated clearly and with particularity. This rule is fundamental in the jurisprudence of fiduciary duty. *See, e.g., Paige Capital Mgmt, L.L.C. v. Lerner Master Fund, L.L.C.*, Civ. A. No. 5502-CS, 2011 WL 3505355, at *31 (Del. Ch. Aug. 8, 2011) (Del. Ch. 2011) (stating that, even under a statute that "permits the waiver of fiduciary duties . . . such waivers must be set forth clearly"); *Kelly v. Blum*, Civ. A. No. 4516-VCP, 2010 WL 629850, at *10, n.70 (Del. Ch. Feb. 24, 2010) ("Having been granted great contractual freedom by the LLC Act, drafters of or parties to an LLC agreement should be expected to provide . . . clear and unambiguous provisions when they desire to expand, restrict or eliminate the operation of traditional fiduciary duties"). It would therefore be manifestly unreasonable for an operating agreement to negate this rule.

Although Subsection (d)(3) does not expressly address contracts between an LLC and a member or manager, the stated constraints must also apply to such contracts. If not, those constraints are effectively meaningless.

EXAMPLE: A manager-managed LLC enters into a management contract with its sole manager, and the contract provides that the duties of loyalty stated in Section 409(b) and (i) are entirely eliminated. If the operating agreement were to so provide, the provision would be subject to the "manifestly unreasonable standard." Section 105(d)(3)(A). Absent the authorization provided by Section

105(d)(3)(A), the management contract's attempt to waive fiduciary duties may be unenforceable as a matter of public policy and contract law. *See Neubauer v. Goldfarb*, 108 Cal. App. 4th 47, 57, 133 Cal. Rptr. 2d 218 (2003) (stating that "waiver of corporate directors' and majority shareholders' fiduciary duties to minority shareholders in private close corporations is against public policy and a contract provision in a buy-sell agreement purporting to effect such a waiver is void"). If not, a court should hold the provision unenforceable nonetheless so as to avoid eviscerating Subsection (d)(3).

Subsection (d)(3)(A)—Subject to the "not manifestly unreasonable" standard, this paragraph empowers the operating agreement to eliminate *all* aspects of the duty of loyalty listed in Section 409(b). The obligation of good faith and fair dealing, Section 409(d), would remain. See Subsection (c)(6). As to any other, uncodified aspects of the duty of loyalty, see Subsection (d)(3)(D) (empowering the operating agreement to "alter or eliminate any other fiduciary duty").

EXAMPLE: Joint Venture LLC ("JV") is a manager-managed limited liability company, with two members, Kappa, Inc. ("Kappa") and Lambda, LLC ("Lambda"). The operating agreement provides that:

- JV is managed by a "board of managers" consisting of one person appointed by Kappa and one person appointed by Lambda;

- each appointee:

  o owes fiduciary and any other duties exclusively to the member that made the appointment; and

  o owes no duties to the other member and the limited liability company.

The "not manifestly unreasonable" standard applies to these provisions under Subsection (d)(3)(A) and (D), and the provisions are not manifestly unreasonable. Note that the provisions do not affect the duties of Kappa and Lambda to:

- the limited liability company, under applicable case law (pertaining to the obligations of owners of an entity who control the entity indirectly); and

- each other, under applicable case law and Section 701(a)(4)(C)(ii) (providing for judicial dissolution when "the managers or those members in control of the company . . . have acted or are acting in a manner that is oppressive and was, is, or will be directly harmful to the [member seeking dissolution").

EXAMPLE: ABC LLC ("ABC") is a manager-managed limited liability company with three managers and two entirely separate lines of business, the Alpha business and the Beta business. Under ABC's operating agreement:

- Manager 1's responsibilities pertain exclusively to the Alpha business; responsibility for:

  o the Beta business is allocated exclusively to Manager 2; and

  o ABC's overall operations is allocated exclusively to Manager 3.

- Manager 2's responsibilities pertain exclusively to the Beta business; responsibility for:

  o the Alpha business is allocated exclusively to Manager 1; and

  o ABC's overall operations is allocated exclusively to Manager 3.

- Manager 1 has no fiduciary duties pertaining to the Beta business.

- Manager 2 has no fiduciary duties pertaining to the Alpha business.

The "not manifestly unreasonable" standard applies to these provisions under Subsection (d)(3)(A) and (D), and the provisions are not manifestly unreasonable.

Subsection (d)(3)(B)—Under this paragraph, an operating agreement might provide that an affiliate of a manager of a manager-managed LLC will provide compensated services to the LLC at a price not exceeding market price, or that the manager may pursue opportunities that otherwise would be company opportunities. Such arrangements are commonplace and permissible.

Subsection (d)(3)(C)—In this context, "conduct" includes both acts and omissions. BLACK'S LAW DICTIONARY (9th ed. 2009) (defining conduct as "[p]ersonal behavior, whether by action or inaction"). Subject to the "not manifestly unreasonable" standard and the bedrock requirements stated here and in Subsection (c)(7), the operating agreement can reduce the duty of care substantially. In particular, the operating agreement can eliminate the aspects of the duty of care pertaining to gross negligence and recklessness.

This provision replicates in a particular context the general rule stated in Subsection (c)(7). For the meaning of "bad faith" in the context of the duty of care, see Subsection (c)(7), comment.

Subsection (e)—The "not manifestly unreasonable" concept became part of uniform business entity statutes when UPA (1997) imported the concept from the Uniform Commercial Code. (In the current version of the Uniform Commercial Code, the concept appears in Section 1–302(b).)

This subsection provides rules for applying the concept, specifying:

- who decides the issue of "manifestly unreasonable"
  - "the court . . . as a matter of law," Subsection (e);
- the framework for determining the issue
  - determination to be made "in light of the purposes, activities, and affairs of the limited liability company," Subsection (e)(2);
- the temporal setting for determining the issue
  - "determination [to be made] as of the time the challenged term became part of the operating agreement," Subsection (e)(1); and
- what information is admissible for determining the issue
  - "only circumstances existing" when "the challenged term became part of the operating agreement," Subsection (e)(1).

The subsection also provides a very demanding standard for persons claiming that a term of an operating agreement is "manifestly unreasonable." "The court . . . may invalidate the term only if, in light of the purposes, activities, and affairs of the limited liability company, it is *readily apparent* that: (A) the objective of the term is unreasonable; or (B) the term is an unreasonable means to achieve the term's objective." Subsection (e)(2) (emphasis added).

Subsection (e) is fundamental to this act, because: (i) this act generally defers to the agreement among the members; and (ii) Subsection (e) safeguards the operating agreement in at least four ways:

- Determining manifest unreasonableness *inter se* owners of an organization is a different task than doing so in a commercial context, where concepts like "usages of trade" are available to inform the analysis. Each business organization must be understood in its own terms and context.

- If loosely applied, the concept of "manifestly unreasonable" would permit a court to rewrite the members' agreement, which would destroy the balance this act seeks to establish between freedom of contract and fiduciary duty.

- Case law has not adequately delineated the concept. *See, e.g., In re Brobeck, Phleger & Harrison L.L.P.*, 408 B.R. 318, 335 (Bankr. N.D. Cal. 2009) ("RUPA [UPA (1997)] does not define what is 'manifestly unreasonable' and the parties have not cited, nor can the court locate, a decision that defines the term. Absent case law or even a dictionary definition, the court must rely on its common sense to recognize something as manifestly unreasonable.").

- In the context of statutes permitting stock transfer restrictions unless "manifestly unreasonable," courts have often ignored the word "manifestly." *See, e.g., Brandt v. Somerville*, 692 N.W.2d 144, 152 (N.D. 2005) (stating that "in close corporations, a majority of courts have sustained restrictions that are determined to be reasonable in light of the relevant circumstances"); *Roof Depot, Inc. v. Ohman*, 638 N.W.2d 782, 786 (Minn. Ct. App. 2002) (stating that "the restrictions [on share transfer] are not 'manifestly unreasonable' because they are reasonable means to ensure that the management and control of the business remains in the group of investors or with people well known to them"); *Castriota v. Castriota*, 633 A.2d 1024, 1027–28 (App. Div. 1993) ("We are obliged to apply the statute in a manner consonant with its essential purpose to permit reasonable restrictions upon alienation.").

Subsection (e)(1)—The significance of the phrase "as of the time the term as challenged became part of the operating agreement" is best shown by example.

EXAMPLE: When a particular manager-managed LLC comes into existence, its business plan is quite unusual and its success depends on the willingness of a particular individual to serve as the LLC's sole manager. This individual has a rare combination of skills, experiences, and contacts, which are particularly appropriate for the LLC's start-up. In order to induce the individual to accept the position of sole manager, the members are willing to have the operating agreement significantly limit the manager's fiduciary duties. Several years later, when the LLC's operations have turned prosaic and the manager's talents and background are not nearly so crucial, a member challenges the fiduciary duty limitations as manifestly unreasonable. The relevant time under Subsection (e)(1) is when the LLC began. Subsequent developments are not relevant, except as they might inferentially bear on the circumstances in existence at the relevant time.

EXAMPLE: As initially adopted, an operating agreement identifies a category of decisions ordinarily subject to the duty of loyalty and provides that "the manager's sole, reasonable discretion" satisfies the duty. A year later, the agreement is amended to delete the word "reasonable." Later, a member claims that, without the word "reasonable," the provision is manifestly unreasonable. The relevant time under Subsection (e)(1) is when the agreement was amended, not when the agreement was initially adopted.

Subsection (e)(2)—If a person claims that a term of the operating agreement is manifestly unreasonable under Subsections (c)(6) or (d)(3), as a matter of ordinary procedural law the person making the claim has the burden of proof.

§ 106. Operating Agreement; Effect on Limited Liability Company and Person Becoming Member; Preformation Agreement

(a) A limited liability company is bound by and may enforce the operating agreement, whether or not the company has itself manifested assent to the operating agreement.

(b) A person that becomes a member is deemed to assent to the operating agreement.

(c) Two or more persons intending to become the initial members of a limited liability company may make an agreement providing that upon the formation of the company the agreement will become the operating agreement. One person intending to become the initial member of a limited liability company may assent to terms providing that upon the formation of the company the terms will become the operating agreement.

§ 107. Operating Agreement; Effect on Third Parties and Relationship to Records Effective on Behalf of Limited Liability Company

(a) An operating agreement may specify that its amendment requires the approval of a person that is not a party to the agreement or the satisfaction of a condition. An amendment is ineffective if its adoption does not include the required approval or satisfy the specified condition.

(b) The obligations of a limited liability company and its members to a person in the person's capacity as a transferee or a person dissociated as a member are governed by the operating agreement. Subject only to a court order issued under Section 503(b)(2) to effectuate a charging order, an amendment to the operating agreement made after a person becomes a transferee or is dissociated as a member:

(1) is effective with regard to any debt, obligation, or other liability of the limited liability company or its members to the person in the person's capacity as a transferee or person dissociated as a member; and

(2) is not effective to the extent the amendment imposes a new debt, obligation, or other liability on the transferee or person dissociated as a member.

(c)   If a record delivered by a limited liability company to the [Secretary of State] for filing becomes effective and contains a provision that would be ineffective under Section 105(c) or (d)(3) if contained in the operating agreement, the provision is ineffective in the record.

(d)   Subject to subsection (c), if a record delivered by a limited liability company to the [Secretary of State] for filing becomes effective and conflicts with a provision of the operating agreement:

(1)   the agreement prevails as to members, persons dissociated as members, transferees, and managers; and

(2)   the record prevails as to other persons to the extent they reasonably rely on the record.

§ 108.   Nature, Purpose, and Duration of Limited Liability Company

(a)   A limited liability company is an entity distinct from its member or members.

(b)   A limited liability company may have any lawful purpose, regardless of whether for profit.

(c)   A limited liability company has perpetual duration.

§ 109.   Powers

A limited liability company has the capacity to sue and be sued in its own name and the power to do all things necessary or convenient to carry on its activities and affairs.

§ 110.   Application to Existing Relationships

(a)   Before [all-inclusive date], this [act] governs only:

(1)   a limited liability company formed on or after [the effective date of this [act]]; and

(2)   except as otherwise provided in subsection (c), a limited liability company formed before [the effective date of this [act]] which elects, in the manner provided in its operating agreement or by law for amending the operating agreement, to be subject to this [act].

(b)   Except as otherwise provided in subsection (c), on and after [all-inclusive date] this [act] governs all limited liability companies.

(c)   For purposes of applying this [act] to a limited liability company formed before [the effective date of this [act]]:

(1)   the company's articles of organization are deemed to be the company's certificate of organization; and

(2)   for purposes of applying Section 102(10) and subject to Section 107(d), language in the company's articles of organization designating the company's management structure operates as if that language were in the operating agreement.

Legislative Note:

For states that have previously enacted ULLCA (2006):

For these states this section is unnecessary. There is no need for a delayed effective date, even with regard to pre-existing limited liability companies.

For states that have not previously enacted ULLCA (2006):

Each enacting jurisdiction should consider whether: (i) this act makes material changes to the "default" (or "gap filler") rules of a predecessor statute; and (ii) if so, whether Subsection (c) should carry forward any of those rules for pre-existing limited liability companies. In this assessment, the focus is on pre-existing limited liability companies that have left default rules in place, whether advisedly or not. The central question is whether, for such limited liability companies, expanding Subsection (c) is necessary to prevent material changes to the members' "deal."

Section 301 (de-codifying statutory apparent authority) does not require any special transition provisions, because: (i) applying the law of agency, as explained in the Comments to Sections 301 and 407, will produce appropriate results; and (ii) the notion of "lingering apparent authority" will protect any third party that has previously relied on the statutory apparent authority of a member of a particular member-managed LLC or a manager of a particular manager-managed LLC. RESTATEMENT (THIRD) OF AGENCY § 3.11, cmt. c (2006).

It is recommended that the "all-inclusive" date should be at least one year after the effective date of this act, Section 1106, but no more than two years.

§ 111.   Supplemental Principles of Law

Unless displaced by particular provisions of this [act], the principles of law and equity supplement this [act].

§ 112.   Permitted Names

(a)   The name of a limited liability company must contain the phrase "limited liability company" or "limited company" or the abbreviation "L.L.C.", "LLC", "L.C.", or "LC". "Limited" may be abbreviated as "Ltd.", and "company" may be abbreviated as "Co.".

(b)   Except as otherwise provided in subsection (d), the name of a limited liability company, and the name under which a foreign limited liability company may register to do business in this state, must be distinguishable on the records of the [Secretary of State] from any:

(1)   name of an existing person whose formation required the filing of a record by the [Secretary of State] and which is not at the time administratively dissolved;

(2)   name of a limited liability partnership whose statement of qualification is in effect;

(3)   name under which a person is registered to do business in this state by the filing of a record by the [Secretary of State];

(4)   name reserved under Section 113 or other law of this state providing for the reservation of a name by the filing of a record by the [Secretary of State];

(5)   name registered under Section 114 or other law of this state providing for the registration of a name by the filing of a record by the [Secretary of State]; and

(6)   name registered under [this state's assumed or fictitious name statute].

(c)   If a person consents in a record to the use of its name and submits an undertaking in a form satisfactory to the [Secretary of State] to change its name to a name that is distinguishable on the records of the [Secretary of State] from any name in any category of names in subsection (b), the name of the consenting person may be used by the person to which the consent was given.

(d)   Except as otherwise provided in subsection (e), in determining whether a name is the same as or not distinguishable on the records of the [Secretary of State] from the name of another person, words, phrases, or abbreviations indicating a type of person, such as "corporation", "corp.", "incorporated", "Inc.", "professional corporation", "P.C.", "PC", "professional association", "P.A.", "PA", "Limited", "Ltd.", "limited partnership", "L.P.", "LP", "limited liability partnership", "L.L.P.", "LLP", "registered limited liability partnership", "R.L.L.P.", "RLLP", "limited liability limited partnership", "L.L.L.P.", "LLLP", "registered limited liability limited partnership", "R.L.L.L.P.", "RLLLP", "limited liability company", "L.L.C.", "LLC", "limited cooperative association", "limited cooperative", or "L.C.A.", or "LCA" may not be taken into account.

(e)   A person may consent in a record to the use of a name that is not distinguishable on the records of the [Secretary of State] from its name except for the addition of a word, phrase, or abbreviation indicating the type of person as provided in subsection (d). In such a case, the person need not change its name pursuant to subsection (c).

(f)   The name of a limited liability company or foreign limited liability company may not contain the words [insert prohibited word or words that may be used only with approval by an appropriate state agency].

(g)   A limited liability company or foreign limited liability company may use a name that is not distinguishable from a name described in subsection (b)(1) through (6) if the company delivers to the [Secretary of State] a certified copy of a final judgment of a court of competent jurisdiction establishing the right of the company to use the name in this state.

§ 113.   Reservation of Name

(a)   A person may reserve the exclusive use of a name that complies with Section 112 by delivering an application to the [Secretary of State] for filing. The application must state the name and address of the applicant and the name to be reserved. If the [Secretary of State] finds that the name is available, the [Secretary of State] shall reserve the name for the applicant's exclusive use for [120] days.

(b)   The owner of a reserved name may transfer the reservation to another person by delivering to the [Secretary of State] a signed notice in a record of the transfer which states the name and address of the person to which the reservation is being transferred.

§ 114.   Registration of Name

(a)   A foreign limited liability company not registered to do business in this state under [Article] 9 may register its name, or an alternate name adopted pursuant to Section 906, if the name is distinguishable on the records of the [Secretary of State] from the names that are not available under Section 112.

(b)   To register its name or an alternate name adopted pursuant to Section 906, a foreign limited liability company must deliver to the [Secretary of State] for filing an application stating the company's name, the jurisdiction and date of its formation, and any alternate name adopted pursuant to Section 906. If the [Secretary of State] finds that the name applied for is available, the [Secretary of State] shall register the name for the applicant's exclusive use.

(c)   The registration of a name under this section is effective for [one year] after the date of registration.

(d)   A foreign limited liability company whose name registration is effective may renew the registration for successive [one-year] periods by delivering, not earlier than [three months] before the expiration of the registration, to the [Secretary of State] for filing a renewal application that complies with this section. When filed, the renewal application renews the registration for a succeeding [one-year] period.

(e)   A foreign limited liability company whose name registration is effective may register as a foreign limited liability company under the registered name or consent in a signed record to the use of that name by another person that is not an individual.

§ 115.   Registered Agent

(a)   Each limited liability company and each registered foreign limited liability company shall designate and maintain a registered agent in this state. The designation of a registered agent is an affirmation of fact by the limited liability company or registered foreign limited liability company that the agent has consented to serve.

(b)   A registered agent for a limited liability company or registered foreign limited liability company must have a place of business in this state.

(c)   The only duties under this [act] of a registered agent that has complied with this [act] are:

(1) to forward to the limited liability company or registered foreign limited liability company at the address most recently supplied to the agent by the company or foreign company any process, notice, or demand pertaining to the company or foreign company which is served on or received by the agent;

(2) if the registered agent resigns, to provide the notice required by Section 117(c) to the company or foreign company at the address most recently supplied to the agent by the company or foreign company; and

(3) to keep current the information with respect to the agent in the certificate of organization or foreign registration statement.

§ 116. Change of Registered Agent or Address for Registered Agent by Limited Liability Company

(a) A limited liability company or registered foreign limited liability company may change its registered agent or the address of its registered agent by delivering to the [Secretary of State] for filing a statement of change that states:

(1) the name of the company or foreign company; and

(2) the information that is to be in effect as a result of the filing of the statement of change.

(b) The members or managers of a limited liability company need not approve the delivery to the [Secretary of State] filing of:

(1) a statement of change under this section; or

(2) a similar filing changing the registered agent or registered office, if any, of the company in any other jurisdiction.

(c) A statement of change under this section designating a new registered agent is an affirmation of fact by the limited liability company or registered foreign limited liability company that the agent has consented to serve.

(d) As an alternative to using the procedure in this section, a limited liability company may amend its certificate of organization.

§ 117. Resignation of Registered Agent

(a) A registered agent may resign as an agent for a limited liability company or registered foreign limited liability company by delivering to the [Secretary of State] for filing a statement of resignation that states:

(1) the name of the company or foreign company;

(2) the name of the agent;

(3) that the agent resigns from serving as registered agent for the company or foreign company; and

(4) the address of the company or foreign company to which the agent will send the notice required by subsection (c).

(b) A statement of resignation takes effect on the earlier of:

(1) the 31st day after the day on which it is filed by the [Secretary of State]; or

(2) the designation of a new registered agent for the limited liability company or registered foreign limited liability company.

(c) A registered agent promptly shall furnish to the limited liability company or registered foreign limited liability company notice in a record of the date on which a statement of resignation was filed.

(d) When a statement of resignation takes effect, the registered agent ceases to have responsibility under this [act] for any matter thereafter tendered to it as agent for the limited liability company or registered foreign limited liability company. The resignation does not affect any contractual rights the company or foreign company has against the agent or that the agent has against the company or foreign company.

(e) A registered agent may resign with respect to a limited liability company or registered foreign limited liability company whether or not the company or foreign company is in good standing.

§ 118.   Change of Name or Address by Registered Agent

(a) If a registered agent changes its name or address, the agent may deliver to the [Secretary of State] for filing a statement of change that states:

(1) the name of the limited liability company or registered foreign limited liability company represented by the registered agent;

(2) the name of the agent as currently shown in the records of the [Secretary of State] for the company or foreign company;

(3) if the name of the agent has changed, its new name; and

(4) if the address of the agent has changed, its new address.

(b) A registered agent promptly shall furnish notice to the represented limited liability company or registered foreign limited liability company of the filing by the [Secretary of State] of the statement of change and the changes made by the statement.

Legislative Note: Many registered agents act in that capacity for many entities, and the Model Registered Agents Act (2006) (Last Amended 2013) provides a streamlined method through which a commercial registered agent can make a single filing to change its information for all represented entities. The single filing does not prevent an enacting state from assessing filing fees on the basis of the number of entity records affected. Alternatively the fees can be set on an incremental sliding fee or capitated amount based upon potential economies of costs for a bulk filing.

§ 119.   Service of Process, Notice, or Demand

(a) A limited liability company or registered foreign limited liability company may be served with any process, notice, or demand required or permitted by law by serving its registered agent.

(b) If a limited liability company or registered foreign limited liability company ceases to have a registered agent, or if its registered agent cannot with reasonable diligence be served, the company or foreign company may be served by registered or certified mail, return receipt requested, or by similar commercial delivery service, addressed to the company or foreign company at its principal office. The address of the principal office must be as shown on the company's or foreign company's most recent [annual] [biennial] report filed by the [Secretary of State]. Service is effected under this subsection on the earliest of:

(1) the date the company or foreign company receives the mail or delivery by the commercial delivery service;

(2) the date shown on the return receipt, if signed by the company or foreign company; or

(3) five days after its deposit with the United States Postal Service, or with the commercial delivery service, if correctly addressed and with sufficient postage or payment.

(c) If process, notice, or demand cannot be served on a limited liability company or registered foreign limited liability company pursuant to subsection (a) or (b), service may be made by handing a copy to the individual in charge of any regular place of business or activity of the company or foreign company if the individual served is not a plaintiff in the action.

(d) Service of process, notice, or demand on a registered agent must be in a written record.

(e) Service of process, notice, or demand may be made by other means under law other than this [act].

§ 120. Delivery of Record

(a) Except as otherwise provided in this [act], permissible means of delivery of a record include delivery by hand, mail, conventional commercial practice, and electronic transmission.

(b) Delivery to the [Secretary of State] is effective only when a record is received by the [Secretary of State].

§ 121. Reservation of Power to Amend or Repeal

The [legislature of this state] has power to amend or repeal all or part of this [act] at any time, and all limited liability companies and foreign limited liability companies subject to this [act] are governed by the amendment or repeal.

[ARTICLE] 2

FORMATION; CERTIFICATE OF ORGANIZATION AND OTHER FILINGS

§ 201. Formation of Limited Liability Company; Certificate of Organization

(a) One or more persons may act as organizers to form a limited liability company by delivering to the [Secretary of State] for filing a certificate of organization.

(b) A certificate of organization must state:

(1) the name of the limited liability company, which must comply with Section 112;

(2) the street and mailing addresses of the company's principal office; and

(3) the name and street and mailing addresses in this state of the company's registered agent.

(c) A certificate of organization may contain statements as to matters other than those required by subsection (b), but may not vary or otherwise affect the provisions specified in Section 105(c) and (d) in a manner inconsistent with that section. However, a statement in a certificate of organization is not effective as a statement of authority.

(d) A limited liability company is formed when the certificate of organization becomes effective and at least one person has become a member.

§ 202. Amendment or Restatement of Certificate of Organization

(a) A certificate of organization may be amended or restated at any time.

(b) To amend its certificate of organization, a limited liability company must deliver to the [Secretary of State] for filing an amendment stating:

(1) the name of the company;

(2) the date of filing of its initial certificate; and

(3) the text of the amendment.

(c) To restate its certificate of organization, a limited liability company must deliver to the [Secretary of State] for filing a restatement, designated as such in its heading.

(d) If a member of a member-managed limited liability company, or a manager of a manager-managed limited liability company, knows that any information in a filed certificate of organization was inaccurate when the certificate was filed or has become inaccurate due to changed circumstances, the member or manager shall promptly:

(1)   cause the certificate to be amended; or

(2)   if appropriate, deliver to the [Secretary of State] for filing a statement of change under Section 116 or a statement of correction under Section 209.

§ 203.   Signing of Records to be Delivered for Filing to [Secretary of State]

(a)   A record delivered to the [Secretary of State] for filing pursuant to this [act] must be signed as follows:

(1)   Except as otherwise provided in paragraphs (2) and (3), a record signed by a limited liability company must be signed by a person authorized by the company.

(2)   A company's initial certificate of organization must be signed by at least one person acting as an organizer.

(3)   A record delivered on behalf of a dissolved company that has no member must be signed by the person winding up the company's activities and affairs under Section 702(c) or a person appointed under Section 702(d) to wind up the activities and affairs.

(4)   A statement of denial by a person under Section 303 must be signed by that person.

(5)   Any other record delivered on behalf of a person to the [Secretary of State] for filing must be signed by that person.

(b)   A record delivered for filing under this [act] may be signed by an agent. Whenever this [act] requires a particular individual to sign a record and the individual is deceased or incompetent, the record may be signed by a legal representative of the individual.

(c)   A person that signs a record as an agent or legal representative affirms as a fact that the person is authorized to sign the record.

§ 204.   Signing and Filing Pursuant to Judicial Order

(a)   If a person required by this [act] to sign a record or deliver a record to the [Secretary of State] for filing under this [act] does not do so, any other person that is aggrieved may petition [the appropriate court] to order:

(1)   the person to sign the record;

(2)   the person to deliver the record to the [Secretary of State] for filing; or

(3)   the [Secretary of State] to file the record unsigned.

(b)   If a petitioner under subsection (a) is not the limited liability company or foreign limited liability company to which the record pertains, the petitioner shall make the company or foreign company a party to the action.

(c)   A record filed under subsection (a)(3) is effective without being signed.

§ 205.   Liability for Inaccurate Information in Filed Record

(a)   If a record delivered to the [Secretary of State] for filing under this [act] and filed by the [Secretary of State] contains inaccurate information, a person that suffers loss by reliance on the information may recover damages for the loss from:

(1)   a person that signed the record, or caused another to sign it on the person's behalf, and knew the information to be inaccurate at the time the record was signed; and

(2)   subject to subsection (b), a member of a member-managed limited liability company or a manager of a manager-managed limited liability company if:

(A)   the record was delivered for filing on behalf of the company; and

(B)   the member or manager knew or had notice of the inaccuracy for a reasonably sufficient time before the information was relied upon so that, before the reliance, the member or manager reasonably could have:

(i)   effected an amendment under Section 202;

(ii)   filed a petition under Section 204; or

(iii)   delivered to the [Secretary of State] for filing a statement of change under Section 116 or a statement of correction under Section 209.

(b)   To the extent the operating agreement of a member-managed limited liability company expressly relieves a member of responsibility for maintaining the accuracy of information contained in records delivered on behalf of the company to the [Secretary of State] for filing under this [act] and imposes that responsibility on one or more other members, the liability stated in subsection (a)(2) applies to those other members and not to the member that the operating agreement relieves of the responsibility.

(c)   An individual who signs a record authorized or required to be filed under this [act] affirms under penalty of perjury that the information stated in the record is accurate.

§ 206.   Filing Requirements

(a)   To be filed by the [Secretary of State] pursuant to this [act], a record must be received by the [Secretary of State], comply with this [act], and satisfy the following:

(1)   The filing of the record must be required or permitted by this [act].

(2)   The record must be physically delivered in written form unless and to the extent the [Secretary of State] permits electronic delivery of records.

(3)   The words in the record must be in English, and numbers must be in Arabic or Roman numerals, but the name of an entity need not be in English if written in English letters or Arabic or Roman numerals.

(4)   The record must be signed by a person authorized or required under this [act] to sign the record.

(5)   The record must state the name and capacity, if any, of each individual who signed it, either on behalf of the individual or the person authorized or required to sign the record, but need not contain a seal, attestation, acknowledgment, or verification.

(b)   If law other than this [act] prohibits the disclosure by the [Secretary of State] of information contained in a record delivered to the [Secretary of State] for filing, the [Secretary of State] shall file the record if the record otherwise complies with this [act] but may redact the information.

(c)   When a record is delivered to the [Secretary of State] for filing, any fee required under this [act] and any fee, tax, interest, or penalty required to be paid under this [act] or law other than this [act] must be paid in a manner permitted by the [Secretary of State] or by that law.

(d)   The [Secretary of State] may require that a record delivered in written form be accompanied by an identical or conformed copy.

(e)   The [Secretary of State] may provide forms for filings required or permitted to be made by this [act], but, except as otherwise provided in subsection (f), their use is not required.

(f)   The [Secretary of State] may require that a cover sheet for a filing be on a form prescribed by the [Secretary of State].

§ 207.   Effective Date and Time

Except as otherwise provided in Section 208 and subject to Section 209(d), a record filed under this [act] is effective:

(1)   on the date and at the time of its filing by the [Secretary of State], as provided in Section 210(b);

(2)   on the date of filing and at the time specified in the record as its effective time, if later than the time under paragraph (1);

(3)   at a specified delayed effective date and time, which may not be more than 90 days after the date of filing; or

(4)   if a delayed effective date is specified, but no time is specified, at 12:01 a.m. on the date specified, which may not be more than 90 days after the date of filing.

§ 208.   Withdrawal of Filed Record Before Effectiveness

(a)   Except as otherwise provided in Sections 1024, 1034, 1044, and 1054, a record delivered to the [Secretary of State] for filing may be withdrawn before it takes effect by delivering to the [Secretary of State] for filing a statement of withdrawal.

(b)   A statement of withdrawal must:

(1)   be signed by each person that signed the record being withdrawn, except as otherwise agreed by those persons;

(2)   identify the record to be withdrawn; and

(3)   if signed by fewer than all the persons that signed the record being withdrawn, state that the record is withdrawn in accordance with the agreement of all the persons that signed the record.

(c)   On filing by the [Secretary of State] of a statement of withdrawal, the action or transaction evidenced by the original record does not take effect.

§ 209.   Correcting Filed Record

(a)   A person on whose behalf a filed record was delivered to the [Secretary of State] for filing may correct the record if:

(1)   the record at the time of filing was inaccurate;

(2)   the record was defectively signed; or

(3)   the electronic transmission of the record to the [Secretary of State] was defective.

(b)   To correct a filed record, a person on whose behalf the record was delivered to the [Secretary of State] must deliver to the [Secretary of State] for filing a statement of correction.

(c)   A statement of correction:

(1)   may not state a delayed effective date;

(2)   must be signed by the person correcting the filed record;

(3)   must identify the filed record to be corrected;

(4)   must specify the inaccuracy or defect to be corrected; and

(5)   must correct the inaccuracy or defect.

(d)   A statement of correction is effective as of the effective date of the filed record that it corrects except for purposes of Section 103(d) and as to persons relying on the uncorrected filed record and adversely affected by the correction. For those purposes and as to those persons, the statement of correction is effective when filed.

§ 210. Duty of [Secretary of State] to File; Review of Refusal to File; Delivery of Record by [Secretary of State]

(a)   The [Secretary of State] shall file a record delivered to the [Secretary of State] for filing which satisfies this [act]. The duty of the [Secretary of State] under this section is ministerial.

(b)   When the [Secretary of State] files a record, the [Secretary of State] shall record it as filed on the date and at the time of its delivery. After filing a record, the [Secretary of State] shall deliver to the person that submitted the record a copy of the record with an acknowledgment of the date and time of filing and, in the case of a statement of denial, also to the limited liability company to which the statement pertains.

(c)   If the [Secretary of State] refuses to file a record, the [Secretary of State] shall, not later than [15] business days after the record is delivered:

(1)   return the record or notify the person that submitted the record of the refusal; and

(2)   provide a brief explanation in a record of the reason for the refusal.

(d)   If the [Secretary of State] refuses to file a record, the person that submitted the record may petition [the appropriate court] to compel filing of the record. The record and the explanation of the [Secretary of State] of the refusal to file must be attached to the petition. The court may decide the matter in a summary proceeding.

(e)   The filing of or refusal to file a record does not:

(1)   affect the validity or invalidity of the record in whole or in part; or

(2)   create a presumption that the information contained in the record is correct or incorrect.

(f)   Except as otherwise provided by Section 119 or by law other than this [act], the [Secretary of State] may deliver any record to a person by delivering it:

(1)   in person to the person that submitted it;

(2)   to the address of the person's registered agent;

(3)   to the principal office of the person; or

(4)   to another address the person provides to the [Secretary of State] for delivery.

§ 211. Certificate of Good Standing or Registration

(a)   On request of any person, the [Secretary of State] shall issue a certificate of good standing for a limited liability company or a certificate of registration for a registered foreign limited liability company.

(b)   A certificate under subsection (a) must state:

(1)   the limited liability company's name or the registered foreign limited liability company's name used in this state;

(2)   in the case of a limited liability company:

(A)   that a certificate of organization has been filed and has taken effect;

(B)   the date the certificate became effective;

(C)   the period of the company's duration if the records of the [Secretary of State] reflect that its period of duration is less than perpetual; and

(D) that:

(i) no statement of dissolution, statement of administrative dissolution, or statement of termination has been filed;

(ii) the records of the [Secretary to State] do not otherwise reflect that the company has been dissolved or terminated; and

(iii) a proceeding is not pending under Section 708;

(3) in the case of a registered foreign limited liability company, that it is registered to do business in this state;

(4) that all fees, taxes, interest, and penalties owed to this state by the limited liability company or foreign limited liability company and collected through the [Secretary of State] have been paid, if:

(A) payment is reflected in the records of the [Secretary of State]; and

(B) nonpayment affects the good standing or registration of the company or foreign company;

(5) that the most recent [annual] [biennial] report required by Section 212 has been delivered to the [Secretary of State] for filing; and

(6) other facts reflected in the records of the [Secretary of State] pertaining to the limited liability company or foreign limited liability company which the person requesting the certificate reasonably requests.

(c) Subject to any qualification stated in the certificate, a certificate issued by the [Secretary of State] under subsection (a) may be relied on as conclusive evidence of the facts stated in the certificate.

§ 212. [Annual] [Biennial] Report for [Secretary of State]

(a) A limited liability company or registered foreign limited liability company shall deliver to the [Secretary of State] for filing [an annual] [a biennial] report that states:

(1) the name of the company or foreign company;

(2) the name and street and mailing addresses of its registered agent in this state;

(3) the street and mailing addresses of its principal office;

(4) if the company is member managed, the name of at least one member;

(5) if the company is manager managed, the name of at least one manager; and

(6) in the case of a foreign company, its jurisdiction of formation and any alternate name adopted under Section 906(a).

(b) Information in the [annual] [biennial] report must be current as of the date the report is signed by the limited liability company or registered foreign limited liability company.

(c) The first [annual] [biennial] report must be delivered to the [Secretary of State] for filing after [January 1] and before [April 1] of the year following the calendar year in which the limited liability company's certificate of organization became effective or the registered foreign limited liability company registered to do business in this state. Subsequent [annual] [biennial] reports must be delivered to the [Secretary of State] for filing after [January 1] and before [April 1] of each [second] calendar year thereafter.

(d) If [an annual] [a biennial] report does not contain the information required by this section, the [Secretary of State] promptly shall notify the reporting limited liability company or registered foreign limited liability company in a record and return the report for correction.

(e) If [an annual] [a biennial] report contains the name or address of a registered agent which differs from the information shown in the records of the [Secretary of State] immediately before the report becomes effective, the differing information in the report is considered a statement of change under Section 116.

[ARTICLE] 3

RELATIONS OF MEMBERS AND MANAGERS TO PERSONS DEALING WITH LIMITED LIABILITY COMPANY

§ 301.   No Agency Power of Member as Member

(a)   A member is not an agent of a limited liability company solely by reason of being a member.

(b)   A person's status as a member does not prevent or restrict law other than this [act] from imposing liability on a limited liability company because of the person's conduct.

§ 302.   Statement of Limited Liability Company Authority

(a)   A limited liability company may deliver to the [Secretary of State] for filing a statement of authority. The statement:

(1)   must include the name of the company and the name and street and mailing addresses of its registered agent;

(2)   with respect to any position that exists in or with respect to the company, may state the authority, or limitations on the authority, of all persons holding the position to:

(A)   sign an instrument transferring real property held in the name of the company; or

(B)   enter into other transactions on behalf of, or otherwise act for or bind, the company; and

(3)   may state the authority, or limitations on the authority, of a specific person to:

(A)   sign an instrument transferring real property held in the name of the company; or

(B)   enter into other transactions on behalf of, or otherwise act for or bind, the company.

(b)   To amend or cancel a statement of authority filed by the [Secretary of State], a limited liability company must deliver to the [Secretary of State] for filing an amendment or cancellation stating:

(1)   the name of the company;

(2)   the name and street and mailing addresses of the company's registered agent;

(3)   the date the statement being affected became effective; and

(4)   the contents of the amendment or a declaration that the statement is canceled.

(c)   A statement of authority affects only the power of a person to bind a limited liability company to persons that are not members.

(d)   Subject to subsection (c) and Section 103(d), and except as otherwise provided in subsections (f), (g), and (h), a limitation on the authority of a person or a position contained in an effective statement of authority is not by itself evidence of any person's knowledge or notice of the limitation.

(e)   Subject to subsection (c), a grant of authority not pertaining to transfers of real property and contained in an effective statement of authority is conclusive in favor of a person that gives value in reliance on the grant, except to the extent that when the person gives value:

(1)   the person has knowledge to the contrary;

(2)   the statement has been canceled or restrictively amended under subsection (b); or

(3)   a limitation on the grant is contained in another statement of authority that became effective after the statement containing the grant became effective.

(f)   Subject to subsection (c), an effective statement of authority that grants authority to transfer real property held in the name of the limited liability company, a certified copy of which statement is recorded in the office for recording transfers of the real property, is conclusive in favor of a person that gives value in reliance on the grant without knowledge to the contrary, except to the extent that when the person gives value:

(1)   the statement has been canceled or restrictively amended under subsection (b), and a certified copy of the cancellation or restrictive amendment has been recorded in the office for recording transfers of the real property; or

(2)   a limitation on the grant is contained in another statement of authority that became effective after the statement containing the grant became effective, and a certified copy of the later-effective statement is recorded in the office for recording transfers of the real property.

(g)   Subject to subsection (c), if a certified copy of an effective statement containing a limitation on the authority to transfer real property held in the name of a limited liability company is recorded in the office for recording transfers of that real property, all persons are deemed to know of the limitation.

(h)   Subject to subsection (i), an effective statement of dissolution or termination is a cancellation of any filed statement of authority for the purposes of subsection (f) and is a limitation on authority for the purposes of subsection (g).

(i)   After a statement of dissolution becomes effective, a limited liability company may deliver to the [Secretary of State] for filing and, if appropriate, may record a statement of authority that is designated as a post-dissolution statement of authority. The statement operates as provided in subsections (f) and (g).

(j)   Unless earlier canceled, an effective statement of authority is canceled by operation of law five years after the date on which the statement, or its most recent amendment, becomes effective. This cancellation operates without need for any recording under subsection (f) or (g).

(k)   An effective statement of denial operates as a restrictive amendment under this section and may be recorded by certified copy for purposes of subsection (f)(1).

§ 303.   Statement of Denial

A person named in a filed statement of authority granting that person authority may deliver to the [Secretary of State] for filing a statement of denial that:

(1)   provides the name of the limited liability company and the caption of the statement of authority to which the statement of denial pertains; and

(2)   denies the grant of authority.

§ 304.   Liability of Members and Managers

(a)   A debt, obligation, or other liability of a limited liability company is solely the debt, obligation, or other liability of the company. A member or manager is not personally liable, directly or indirectly, by way of contribution or otherwise, for a debt, obligation, or other liability of the company solely by reason of being or acting as a member or manager. This subsection applies regardless of the dissolution of the company.

(b)   The failure of a limited liability company to observe formalities relating to the exercise of its powers or management of its activities and affairs is not a ground for imposing liability on a member or manager for a debt, obligation, or other liability of the company.

REVISED UNIFORM LIMITED LIABILITY
COMPANY ACT (2013)

[ARTICLE] 4

RELATIONS OF MEMBERS TO EACH OTHER
AND TO LIMITED LIABILITY COMPANY

§ 401. Becoming Member

(a) If a limited liability company is to have only one member upon formation, the person becomes a member as agreed by that person and the organizer of the company. That person and the organizer may be, but need not be, different persons. If different, the organizer acts on behalf of the initial member.

(b) If a limited liability company is to have more than one member upon formation, those persons become members as agreed by the persons before the formation of the company. The organizer acts on behalf of the persons in forming the company and may be, but need not be, one of the persons.

(c) After formation of a limited liability company, a person becomes a member:

   (1) as provided in the operating agreement;

   (2) as the result of a transaction effective under [Article] 10;

   (3) with the affirmative vote or consent of all the members; or

   (4) as provided in Section 701(a)(3).

(d) A person may become a member without:

   (1) acquiring a transferable interest; or

   (2) making or being obligated to make a contribution to the limited liability company.

§ 402. Form of Contribution

A contribution may consist of property transferred to, services performed for, or another benefit provided to the limited liability company or an agreement to transfer property to, perform services for, or provide another benefit to the company.

§ 403. Liability for Contributions

(a) A person's obligation to make a contribution to a limited liability company is not excused by the person's death, disability, termination, or other inability to perform personally.

(b) If a person does not fulfill an obligation to make a contribution other than money, the person is obligated at the option of the limited liability company to contribute money equal to the value of the part of the contribution which has not been made.

(c) The obligation of a person to make a contribution may be compromised only by the affirmative vote or consent of all the members. If a creditor of a limited liability company extends credit or otherwise acts in reliance on an obligation described in subsection (a) without knowledge or notice of a compromise under this subsection, the creditor may enforce the obligation.

§ 404. Sharing of and Right to Distributions Before Dissolution

(a) Any distribution made by a limited liability company before its dissolution and winding up must be in equal shares among members and persons dissociated as members, except to the extent necessary to comply with a transfer effective under Section 502 or charging order in effect under Section 503.

(b) A person has a right to a distribution before the dissolution and winding up of a limited liability company only if the company decides to make an interim distribution. A person's dissociation does not entitle the person to a distribution.

(c)   A person does not have a right to demand or receive a distribution from a limited liability company in any form other than money. Except as otherwise provided in Section 707(d), a company may distribute an asset in kind only if each part of the asset is fungible with each other part and each person receives a percentage of the asset equal in value to the person's share of distributions.

(d)   If a member or transferee becomes entitled to receive a distribution, the member or transferee has the status of, and is entitled to all remedies available to, a creditor of the limited liability company with respect to the distribution. However, the company's obligation to make a distribution is subject to offset for any amount owed to the company by the member or a person dissociated as a member on whose account the distribution is made.

§ 405. Limitations on Distributions

(a)   A limited liability company may not make a distribution, including a distribution under Section 707, if after the distribution:

(1)   the company would not be able to pay its debts as they become due in the ordinary course of the company's activities and affairs; or

(2)   the company's total assets would be less than the sum of its total liabilities plus the amount that would be needed, if the company were to be dissolved and wound up at the time of the distribution, to satisfy the preferential rights upon dissolution and winding up of members and transferees whose preferential rights are superior to the rights of persons receiving the distribution.

(b)   A limited liability company may base a determination that a distribution is not prohibited under subsection (a) on:

(1)   financial statements prepared on the basis of accounting practices and principles that are reasonable in the circumstances; or

(2)   a fair valuation or other method that is reasonable under the circumstances.

(c)   Except as otherwise provided in subsection (e), the effect of a distribution under subsection (a) is measured:

(1)   in the case of a distribution as defined in Section 102(4)(A), as of the earlier of:

(A)   the date money or other property is transferred or debt is incurred by the limited liability company; or

(B)   the date the person entitled to the distribution ceases to own the interest or right being acquired by the company in return for the distribution;

(2)   in the case of any other distribution of indebtedness, as of the date the indebtedness is distributed; and

(3)   in all other cases, as of the date:

(A)   the distribution is authorized, if the payment occurs not later than 120 days after that date; or

(B)   the payment is made, if the payment occurs more than 120 days after the distribution is authorized.

(d)   A limited liability company's indebtedness to a member or transferee incurred by reason of a distribution made in accordance with this section is at parity with the company's indebtedness to its general, unsecured creditors, except to the extent subordinated by agreement.

(e)   A limited liability company's indebtedness, including indebtedness issued as a distribution, is not a liability for purposes of subsection (a) if the terms of the indebtedness provide that payment of principal and interest is made only if and to the extent that payment of a distribution could then be made under this section. If the indebtedness is issued as a distribution, each payment of principal or interest is treated as a distribution, the effect of which is measured on the date the payment is made.

(f) In measuring the effect of a distribution under Section 707, the liabilities of a dissolved limited liability company do not include any claim that has been disposed of under Section 704, 705, or 706.

§ 406. Liability for Improper Distributions

(a) Except as otherwise provided in subsection (b), if a member of a member-managed limited liability company or manager of a manager-managed limited liability company consents to a distribution made in violation of Section 405 and in consenting to the distribution fails to comply with Section 409, the member or manager is personally liable to the company for the amount of the distribution which exceeds the amount that could have been distributed without the violation of Section 405.

(b) To the extent the operating agreement of a member-managed limited liability company expressly relieves a member of the authority and responsibility to consent to distributions and imposes that authority and responsibility on one or more other members, the liability stated in subsection (a) applies to the other members and not the member that the operating agreement relieves of the authority and responsibility.

(c) A person that receives a distribution knowing that the distribution violated Section 405 is personally liable to the limited liability company but only to the extent that the distribution received by the person exceeded the amount that could have been properly paid under Section 405.

(d) A person against which an action is commenced because the person is liable under subsection (a) may:

(1) implead any other person that is liable under subsection (a) and seek to enforce a right of contribution from the person; and

(2) implead any person that received a distribution in violation of subsection (c) and seek to enforce a right of contribution from the person in the amount the person received in violation of subsection (c).

(e) An action under this section is barred unless commenced not later than two years after the distribution.

§ 407. Management of Limited Liability Company

(a) A limited liability company is a member-managed limited liability company unless the operating agreement:

(1) expressly provides that:

(A) the company is or will be "manager-managed";

(B) the company is or will be "managed by managers"; or

(C) management of the company is or will be "vested in managers"; or

(2) includes words of similar import.

(b) In a member-managed limited liability company, the following rules apply:

(1) Except as expressly provided in this [act], the management and conduct of the company are vested in the members.

(2) Each member has equal rights in the management and conduct of the company's activities and affairs.

(3)   A difference arising among members as to a matter in the ordinary course of the activities and affairs of the company may be decided by a majority of the members.

(4)   The affirmative vote or consent of all the members is required to:

(A)   undertake an act outside the ordinary course of the activities and affairs of the company; or

(B)   amend the operating agreement.

(c)   In a manager-managed limited liability company, the following rules apply:

(1)   Except as expressly provided in this [act], any matter relating to the activities and affairs of the company is decided exclusively by the manager, or, if there is more than one manager, by a majority of the managers.

(2)   Each manager has equal rights in the management and conduct of the company's activities and affairs.

(3)   The affirmative vote or consent of all members is required to:

(A)   undertake an act outside the ordinary course of the company's activities and affairs; or

(B)   amend the operating agreement.

(4)   A manager may be chosen at any time by the affirmative vote or consent of a majority of the members and remains a manager until a successor has been chosen, unless the manager at an earlier time resigns, is removed, or dies, or, in the case of a manager that is not an individual, terminates. A manager may be removed at any time by the affirmative vote or consent of a majority of the members without notice or cause.

(5)   A person need not be a member to be a manager, but the dissociation of a member that is also a manager removes the person as a manager. If a person that is both a manager and a member ceases to be a manager, that cessation does not by itself dissociate the person as a member.

(6)   A person's ceasing to be a manager does not discharge any debt, obligation, or other liability to the limited liability company or members which the person incurred while a manager.

(d)   An action requiring the vote or consent of members under this [act] may be taken without a meeting, and a member may appoint a proxy or other agent to vote, consent, or otherwise act for the member by signing an appointing record, personally or by the member's agent.

(e)   The dissolution of a limited liability company does not affect the applicability of this section. However, a person that wrongfully causes dissolution of the company loses the right to participate in management as a member and a manager.

(f)   A limited liability company shall reimburse a member for an advance to the company beyond the amount of capital the member agreed to contribute.

(g)   A payment or advance made by a member which gives rise to a limited liability company obligation under subsection (f) or Section 408(a) constitutes a loan to the company which accrues interest from the date of the payment or advance.

(h)   A member is not entitled to remuneration for services performed for a member-managed limited liability company, except for reasonable compensation for services rendered in winding up the activities of the company.

§ 408.   Reimbursement; Indemnification; Advancement; and Insurance

(a)   A limited liability company shall reimburse a member of a member-managed company or the manager of a manager-managed company for any payment made by the member or manager in the course of the member's or manager's activities on behalf of the company, if the member or manager complied with Sections 405, 407, and 409 in making the payment.

(b)   A limited liability company shall indemnify and hold harmless a person with respect to any claim or demand against the person and any debt, obligation, or other liability incurred by the person by reason of the person's former or present capacity as a member or manager, if the claim, demand, debt, obligation, or other liability does not arise from the person's breach of Section 405, 407, or 409.

(c)   In the ordinary course of its activities and affairs, a limited liability company may advance reasonable expenses, including attorney's fees and costs, incurred by a person in connection with a claim or demand against the person by reason of the person's former or present capacity as a member or manager, if the person promises to repay the company if the person ultimately is determined not to be entitled to be indemnified under subsection (b).

(d)   A limited liability company may purchase and maintain insurance on behalf of a member or manager against liability asserted against or incurred by the member or manager in that capacity or arising from that status even if, under Section 105(c)(7), the operating agreement could not eliminate or limit the person's liability to the company for the conduct giving rise to the liability.

§ 409.   Standards of Conduct for Members and Managers

(a)   A member of a member-managed limited liability company owes to the company and, subject to Section 801, the other members the duties of loyalty and care stated in subsections (b) and (c).

(b)   The fiduciary duty of loyalty of a member in a member-managed limited liability company includes the duties:

(1)   to account to the company and hold as trustee for it any property, profit, or benefit derived by the member:

(A)   in the conduct or winding up of the company's activities and affairs;

(B)   from a use by the member of the company's property; or

(C)   from the appropriation of a company opportunity;

(2)   to refrain from dealing with the company in the conduct or winding up of the company's activities and affairs as or on behalf of a person having an interest adverse to the company; and

(3)   to refrain from competing with the company in the conduct of the company's activities and affairs before the dissolution of the company.

(c)   The duty of care of a member of a member-managed limited liability company in the conduct or winding up of the company's activities and affairs is to refrain from engaging in grossly negligent or reckless conduct, willful or intentional misconduct, or knowing violation of law.

(d)   A member shall discharge the duties and obligations under this [act] or under the operating agreement and exercise any rights consistently with the contractual obligation of good faith and fair dealing.

(e)   A member does not violate a duty or obligation under this [act] or under the operating agreement solely because the member's conduct furthers the member's own interest.

(f)   All the members of a member-managed limited liability company or a manager-managed limited liability company may authorize or ratify, after full disclosure of all material facts, a specific act or transaction that otherwise would violate the duty of loyalty.

(g)   It is a defense to a claim under subsection (b)(2) and any comparable claim in equity or at common law that the transaction was fair to the limited liability company.

(h)   If, as permitted by subsection (f) or (i)(6) or the operating agreement, a member enters into a transaction with the limited liability company which otherwise would be prohibited by subsection (b)(2), the member's rights and obligations arising from the transaction are the same as those of a person that is not a member.

(i)   In a manager-managed limited liability company, the following rules apply:

    (1)   Subsections (a), (b), (c), and (g) apply to the manager or managers and not the members.

    (2)   The duty stated under subsection (b)(3) continues until winding up is completed.

    (3)   Subsection (d) applies to managers and members.

    (4)   Subsection (e) applies only to members.

    (5)   The power to ratify under subsection (f) applies only to the members.

    (6)   Subject to subsection (d), a member does not have any duty to the company or to any other member solely by reason of being a member.

COMMENT

This section states some of the core aspects of the fiduciary duty of loyalty, provides a duty of care, and incorporates the contractual obligation of good faith and fair dealing. The section follows the structure of many LLC acts, first stating the duties of members in a member-managed limited liability company and then using that statement and a "switching" mechanism, Subsection (i), to allocate duties in a manager-managed company. The duties stated in this section are subject to the operating agreement, but Section 105(c) and (d) contain important limitations on the power of the operating agreement to affect fiduciary and other duties and the obligation of good faith and fair dealing.

For the effect of dissociation on a person's duties under this section, see Section 603(a)(2).

Subsection (a)—This subsection recognizes two core managerial duties but, unlike some earlier uniform acts, does not purport to state all managerial duties. Indeed, many cases characterize a manager's duty to disclose as a fiduciary duty. *E.g., Salm v. Feldstein*, 20 A.D.3d 469, 470, 799 N.Y.S.2d 104, 105 (N.Y. App. Div. 2005) (stating that, "[a]s the managing member of the [limited liability] company and as a co-member with the plaintiff, the defendant owed the plaintiff a fiduciary duty to make full disclosure of all material facts"); *Metro Commc'n Corp. BVI v. Advanced Mobilecomm Technologies Inc.*, 854 A.2d 121, 156 n. 78 (Del. Ch. 2004) (referring to "certain standards governing the disclosure-related duties of the fiduciaries of Delaware business entities;" noting that "[t]hese standards have been mostly articulated in the corporate context but the corporate standards often serve as the default rule in the alternative entity context").

Subsection (b)—This subsection states three core aspects of the fiduciary duty of loyalty: (i) not "usurping" company opportunities or otherwise wrongly benefiting from the company's operations or property; (ii) avoiding conflict of interests in dealing with the company (whether directly or on behalf of another); and (iii) refraining from competing with the company. Essentially the same duties exist in agency law and under the law of all types of business organizations.

The subsection applies beginning with "the conduct of the company's activities and affairs," which by definition cannot exist before the company exists; thus the stated duties do not apply to pre-formation activities. In some circumstances, comparable duties might arise from other law, particular the law of agency. *See, e.g.*, Section 401(a) and (b) (stating that the organizer acts "on behalf of others").

The stated duties comprise a default rule. Under Section 105(d)(3)(A): "If not manifestly unreasonable, the operating agreement may . . . alter or eliminate the aspects of the duty of loyalty stated in Section 409(b)."

Subsection (b)(1)—The phrase "hold as trustee" dates back to UPA (1914) § 21 and reflects the availability of disgorgement remedies, such as a constructive trust. In contrast to an actual trustee, a person subject to this duty does not: (i) face the special obstacles to consent characteristic of trust law; or (ii) enjoy protection for decisions taken in reliance on the governing instrument and other sources of information. *Cf.* UNIFORM STATUTORY TRUST ENTITY ACT (2009) (Last Amended 2013) § 506 ("A trustee [of a statutory trust] . . . is not liable to the trust or to a beneficial owner for breach of any duty, *including a fiduciary duty*, to the extent the breach results from reasonable reliance on: (i) a term of the governing instrument; (ii) a record of the statutory trust; or (iii) an opinion, report, or statement of another person that the person to which the opinion, report, or statement is made or delivered reasonably believes is within the other person's professional or expert competence and is made or delivered to the trustee . . . .") (emphasis added).

Subsection (b)(1)(A)—This provision is consistent with a basic principle of agency law—namely, that an agent may not benefit at all from the performance of the agency unless the principal consents. RESTATEMENT (THIRD) OF AGENCY § 8.06, cmt. c (2006). Typically, however, the operating agreement will legitimize particular benefits—*e.g.*, a management fee paid to a managing member in addition to that member's share of distributions. Also, an agreed allocation of distributions takes those benefits outside the reach of this provision.

Subsection (b)(1)(B)—For the expansive meaning of "property," see Section 102(17). The term includes confidential information.

Subsection (b)(1)(C)—This act does not specify what constitutes "a company opportunity," but ample case law exists. *See, e.g., Ebenezer United Methodist Church v. Riverwalk Development Phase, II, LLC*, 45 A.3d 883, 887 (Md. App. 2012) (discussing the "interest or reasonable expectancy test"); *In re McCook Metals, L.L.C.*, 319 B.R. 570, 596 (Bkrtcy. N.D.Ill. 2005) (discussing the "line of business test").

This duty continues through winding up, although in that context the scope of company opportunities inevitably narrows.

In most, if not all, situations, usurping a company opportunity also breaches the duty not to compete, Paragraph (b)(3), but not vice versa.

Subsection (b)(2)—In this context, the phrase "adverse interest" is a term of art, meaning "to be on the other side of the table" in some dealing with the limited liability company. Absent informed consent by the LLC, this duty is breached by the mere existence of the conflict of interest; the LLC need not prove that the outcome of the dealing was adverse to the LLC. *But see* Subsection (g) (permitting the defense of fairness). This duty continues through winding up.

Subsection (b)(3)—Although competition is often thought of in terms of potential customers, this duty applies equally to competition for resources, including employees. The duty not to compete continues longer in a manager-managed LLC. *See* Subsection (i)(2).

Subsection (c)—ULLCA (2006) § 409(c) stated a different rule: "Subject to the business judgment rule, the duty of care of a member of a member-managed limited liability company in the conduct and winding up of the company's activities is to act with the care that a person in a like position would reasonably exercise under similar circumstances and in a manner the member reasonably believes to be in the best interests of the company." As part of the Harmonization Project, the ULLCA duty of care was conformed to the duty of care stated in ULPA (2001) and UPA (1997).

Neither this act nor the two harmonized partnership acts refer to the duty of care as a fiduciary duty, because: (i) the duty of care applies in many non-fiduciary situations; and (ii) breach of the duty of care is remediable only in damages while breach of a fiduciary duty gives rise also to equitable remedies, including disgorgement, constructive trust, and rescission. *See* ULPA (2001) (Last Amended 2013) § 409(c) and UPA (1997) (Last Amended 2013) § 409(c).

The change in label is consistent with the RESTATEMENT (THIRD) OF AGENCY § 8.02 (2006), which refers to the agent's "fiduciary duty to act loyally," but eschews the word "fiduciary" when stating the agent's duties of "care, competence, and diligence." *Id.* § 8.08. However, the change in label is merely semantics; no change in the law is intended.

The operating agreement can raise the standard of care, or subject to Sections 105(c)(7) and (d)(3)(C), lower it. A person's practical exposure for breaching the duty of care involves not only the standard of care but also any operating agreement provision that: (i) exonerates the person from liability for breach of the duty of care, Section 105(c)(7); or (ii) entitles the person to indemnification despite such breach, Section 408(b), comment.

Subsection (d)—This subsection refers to the "contractual obligation of good faith and fair dealing" (emphasis added) and thereby invokes the implied obligation that exists in every contract. *See* RESTATEMENT (SECOND) CONTRACTS § 205 (1981) ("Every contract imposes upon each party a duty of good faith and fair dealing in its performance and its enforcement."). The adjective ("contractual") should help avoid decisions like *Phelps v. Frampton*, 2007 MT 263, 339 Mont. 330, 342–43, 170 P.3d 474, 483 (2007) (holding that Montana's version of UPA (1997) creates a statutory obligation of good faith and fair dealing separate from the implied contractual covenant).

At first glance, it may seem strange to apply a contractual obligation to statutory duties and rights— *i.e.*, duties and rights "under this [act]." However, for the most part those duties and rights apply to relationships *inter se* the members and the LLC and function only to the extent not displaced by the operating agreement. These statutory default rules are intended in essence to function like a contract; applying the contractual notion of good faith and fair dealing therefore makes sense.

The contractual obligation of "good faith" has nothing to do with the corporate concept of good faith that for years bedeviled courts and attorneys trying to understand: (i) Delaware's famous corporate law exoneration provision; and (ii) that provision's exception "for acts or omissions not in good faith." DEL. CODE ANN. tit. 8, § 102(b)(7) (2012). In that context, good faith is an aspect of the duty of loyalty. *See Stone ex rel. AmSouth Bancorporation v. Ritter*, 911 A.2d 362, 369–70 (Del. 2006).

Likewise, the contractual obligation of good faith and fair dealing has nothing to do with the "utmost good faith" sometimes used to describe the fiduciary duties that owners of closely held businesses owe each other. *See, e.g., Meinhard v. Salmon*, 249 N.Y. 458, 477, 164 N.E. 545, 551 (1928) ("[W]here parties engage in a joint enterprise each owes to the other the duty of the utmost good faith in all that relates to their common venture. Within its scope they stand in a fiduciary relationship."); *Donahue v. Rodd Electrotype Co. of New England, Inc.*, 367 Mass. 578, 593, 328 N.E.2d 505, 515 (1975) ("[S]tockholders in the close corporation owe one another substantially the same fiduciary duty in the operation of the enterprise1 that partners owe to one another. In our previous decisions, we have defined the standard of duty owed by partners to one another as the utmost good faith and loyalty.") (footnotes omitted) (citations omitted) (internal quotations omitted).

To the contrary, the contractual obligation of good faith and fair dealing is not a fiduciary duty, does not command altruism or self-abnegation, and does not prevent a member from acting in the member's own self-interest:

"Fair dealing" is not akin to the fair process component of entire fairness, *i.e.*, whether the fiduciary acted fairly when engaging in the challenged transaction as measured by duties of loyalty and care . . . . It is rather a commitment to deal "fairly" in the sense of consistently with the terms of the parties' agreement and its purpose. Likewise "good faith" does not envision loyalty to the contractual counterparty, but rather faithfulness to the scope, purpose, and terms of the parties' contract. Both necessarily turn on the contract itself and what the parties would have agreed upon had the issue arisen when they were bargaining originally.

Gerber v. Enter. Products Holdings, LLC, 67 A.3d 400, 418–19 (Del. 2013) (quoting *ASB Allegiance Real Estate Fund v. Scion Breckenridge Managing Member, LLC*, 50 A.3d 434, 440–42 (Del. Ch. 2012), *aff'd in part, rev'd in part on other grounds*, 68 A.3d 665 (Del. 2013)) (footnotes omitted) (citations omitted) (internal quotations omitted without ellipsis by *Gerber*). *See also* Subsection (e).

Courts should not use the contractual obligation to change *ex post facto* the parties' or this act's allocation of risk and power. To the contrary, the obligation should be used only to protect agreed-upon arrangements from conduct that is manifestly beyond what a reasonable person could have contemplated when the arrangements were made.

The operating agreement or this act may grant discretion to a member or manager, and the contractual obligation of good faith and fair dealing is especially salient when discretion is at issue. However, a member or manager may properly exercise discretion even though another member suffers as a consequence. Conduct does not violate the obligation of good faith and fair dealing merely because that conduct substantially prejudices a party. Indeed, parties allocate risk precisely because prejudice may occur.

The exercise of discretion constitutes a breach of the obligation of good faith and fair dealing only when the party claiming breach shows that the conduct has no honestly-held purpose that legitimately comports with the parties' agreed-upon arrangements:

An implied covenant claim ... looks to the past. It is not a free-floating duty unattached to the underlying legal documents. It does not ask what duty the law should impose on the parties given their relationship at the time of the wrong, but *rather what the parties would have agreed to themselves had they considered the issue in their original bargaining positions at the time of contracting.*

Gerber v. Enter. Prods. Holdings, LLC, 67 A.3d 400, 418 (Del. 2013) (quoting *ASB Allegiance Real Estate Fund v. Scion Breckenridge Managing Member, LLC*, 50 A.3d 434, 440–42 (Del. Ch. 2012), *aff'd in part, rev'd in part on other grounds*, 68 A.3d 665 (Del. 2013)) (emphasis added) (footnotes omitted) (citations omitted) (internal quotations omitted without ellipsis by *Gerber*).

In sum, the purpose of the contractual obligation of good faith and fair dealing is to protect the arrangement the members have chosen for themselves, not to restructure that arrangement under the guise of safeguarding it.

As to the power of the operating agreement to affect the contractual obligation of good faith and fair dealing, see Section 105(c)(6) (prohibiting elimination but allowing the agreement to "prescribe standards, if not manifestly unreasonable, by which the performance of the obligation is to be measured"). For examples, see Section 105(c)(6), comment. As to whether the obligation stated in this subsection applies to transferees, see Section 107(b), comment.

Subsection (e)—A member in a member-managed LLC has at least two different roles: (i) as a party to the operating agreement, with rights and obligations under that agreement; and (ii) as manager or co-manager of the enterprise. This provision pertains to the first role. A member's exercise of rights under the operating agreement is subject to the obligation of good faith and fair dealing, Subsection (d), but a person does not breach that contractual obligation "solely because the [person's exercise of rights] furthers the [person's] own interest." In contrast, this provision is ineffective with regard to a member's duties as manager or co-manager. For example, a member's liability under Section 409(b)(3) (prohibiting competition) is not "solely because the member's conduct furthers the member's own interest." Rather, the liability results from the breach of a specific obligation—*i.e.*, the codified aspect of the duty of loyalty that prohibits competition.

With regard to a manager-managed LLC: (i) the same analysis applies to a member that is a manager; and (ii) with regard to a non-managing member the analysis as to contractual rights applies and the analysis as to managerial duties is inapposite.

Subsection (f)—Here and elsewhere in this act, information "is material if there is a substantial likelihood that a reasonable [decision maker] would consider it important in deciding how to vote" or take other action under this act or the operating agreements. *TSC Industries, Inc. v. Northway, Inc.*, 426 U.S. 438, 449, 96 S.Ct. 2126, 2132 (1976).

The operating agreement can provide additional or different methods of authorization or ratification, subject to the strictures of Section 105(c)(5), (d)(1), and (d)(3)(A)(B) and (D).

Subsection (g)—This subsection codifies judge-made law applicable to all business entities. *See, e.g., Gottsacker v. Monnier*, 281 Wis. 2d 361, 379, 697 N.W.2d 436, 444 (Wisc. 2005) (referring to "a willful failure to deal fairly with the LLC or its other members"); *Lonergan v. EPE Holdings, LLC*, 5 A.3d 1008, 1019 (Del. Ch. 2010) (discussing "entire fairness" in the context of a limited partnership"); *Kahn v. Lynch Commc'n Sys., Inc.*, 638 A.2d 1110, 1116 (Del. 1994) (discussing "entire fairness" in the context of a corporation's merger with an affiliate); *Lonergan v. EPE Holdings, LLC*, 5 A.3d 1008, 1019 (Del. Ch. 2010) (discussing "entire fairness" in the context of a limited partnership").

Subsection (h)—This subsection is the modern, reformulated version of a language that sought to overturn the now-defunct notion that debts to owners were categorically inferior to debts to non-owner creditors. *See, e.g.*, ULPA (2001) § 112 ("A partner may lend money to and transact other business with the limited partnership and has the same rights and obligations with respect to the loan or other transaction as a person that is not a partner."). The reformulation makes clear that this provision has nothing to do with the fiduciary duty pertaining to conflict of interests. *See BT-I v. Equitable Life Assurance Soc'y of the United States*, 75 Cal. App. 4th 1406, 1415, 89 Cal. Rptr. 2d 811 (1999) (examining the prior formulation, explaining its history and stating "[w]e cannot discern anything in the purpose of [the prior formulation] that suggests an intent to affect a general partner's fiduciary duty to limited partners").

This subsection states a default rule. The operating agreement may provide that debt to a member (or members generally) is subordinate to other limited liability company obligations. The agreement that creates the debt may do likewise.

Subsection (i)—This is the "switching" mechanism, referred to in the introduction to this comment. The list does not include Subsection (h).

Subsection (i)(1)—This provision switches most managerial duties to the managers and away from members. Of course, if a member is a manager, the duties apply to the member-manager in the person's capacity of manager.

Subsection (i)(2)—On the assumption that the members of a manager-managed LLC are dependent on the manager, this paragraph extends the duty not to compete longer than in a member-managed LLC.

Subsection (i)(3)—The contractual obligation of good faith and fair dealing applies to members regardless of whether they are managers; non-managing members have rights and perhaps duties under the operating agreement and under this act. As to non-member managers, the operating agreement (and the corresponding obligation of good faith and fair dealing) are relevant regardless of whether the manager is party to the agreement. *See* Section 105(a)(2) (stating that the operating agreement "governs . . . the rights and duties under this [act] of a person in the capacity of manager"). Also, non-member managers will have rights and obligations under this act, which per Subsection (d) are also subject to the obligation of good faith and fair dealing.

Subsection (i)(4)—As explained in the comment to Subsection (e), that provision does not apply to the managerial function.

Subsection (i)(5)—The power to ratify belongs to the entity's owners; thus Subsection (f) does not switch from members to managers.

Subsection (i)(6)—This paragraph merely negates a claim of fiduciary duty that is exclusively status-based and does not immunize misconduct.

EXAMPLE: Although a limited liability company is manager-managed, one member who is not a manager owns a controlling interest and effectively, albeit indirectly, controls the company's activities. A member owning a minority interest brings an action for dissolution under Section 701(a)(4)(C)(ii) (oppression by "the managers or those members in control of the company"). This paragraph does not prevent the court from construing the claim as alleging a breach of fiduciary duty by the controlling member.

§ 410.   Rights to Information of Member, Manager, and Person Dissociated as Member

(a)   In a member-managed limited liability company, the following rules apply:

(1)   On reasonable notice, a member may inspect and copy during regular business hours, at a reasonable location specified by the company, any record maintained by the company regarding the company's activities, affairs, financial condition, and other circumstances, to the extent the information is material to the member's rights and duties under the operating agreement or this [act].

(2)   The company shall furnish to each member:

(A)   without demand, any information concerning the company's activities, affairs, financial condition, and other circumstances which the company knows and is material to the proper exercise of the member's rights and duties under the operating agreement or this [act], except to the extent the company can establish that it reasonably believes the member already knows the information; and

(B)   on demand, any other information concerning the company's activities, affairs, financial condition, and other circumstances, except to the extent the demand for the information demanded is unreasonable or otherwise improper under the circumstances.

(3)   The duty to furnish information under paragraph (2) also applies to each member to the extent the member knows any of the information described in paragraph (2).

(b)   In a manager-managed limited liability company, the following rules apply:

(1)   The informational rights stated in subsection (a) and the duty stated in subsection (a)(3) apply to the managers and not the members.

(2)   During regular business hours and at a reasonable location specified by the company, a member may inspect and copy information regarding the activities, affairs, financial condition, and other circumstances of the company as is just and reasonable if:

(A)   the member seeks the information for a purpose reasonably related to the member's interest as a member;

(B)   the member makes a demand in a record received by the company, describing with reasonable particularity the information sought and the purpose for seeking the information; and

(C)   the information sought is directly connected to the member's purpose.

(3)   Not later than 10 days after receiving a demand pursuant to paragraph (2)(B), the company shall inform in a record the member that made the demand of:

(A)   what information the company will provide in response to the demand and when and where the company will provide the information; and

(B)   the company's reasons for declining, if the company declines to provide any demanded information.

(4)   Whenever this [act] or an operating agreement provides for a member to vote on or give or withhold consent to a matter, before the vote is cast or consent is given or withheld, the company shall, without demand, provide the member with all information that is known to the company and is material to the member's decision.

(c)   Subject to subsection (h), on 10 days' demand made in a record received by a limited liability company, a person dissociated as a member may have access to the information to which the person was entitled while a member if:

(1)   the information pertains to the period during which the person was a member;

(2)   the person seeks the information in good faith; and

(3)   the person satisfies the requirements imposed on a member by subsection (b)(2).

(d)   A limited liability company shall respond to a demand made pursuant to subsection (c) in the manner provided in subsection (b)(3).

(e)   A limited liability company may charge a person that makes a demand under this section the reasonable costs of copying, limited to the costs of labor and material.

(f)   A member or person dissociated as a member may exercise the rights under this section through an agent or, in the case of an individual under legal disability, a legal representative. Any restriction or condition imposed by the operating agreement or under subsection (h) applies both to the agent or legal representative and to the member or person dissociated as a member.

(g)   Subject to Section 504, the rights under this section do not extend to a person as transferee.

(h)   In addition to any restriction or condition stated in its operating agreement, a limited liability company, as a matter within the ordinary course of its activities and affairs, may impose reasonable restrictions and conditions on access to and use of information to be furnished under this section, including designating information confidential and imposing nondisclosure and safeguarding obligations on the recipient. In a dispute concerning the reasonableness of a restriction under this subsection, the company has the burden of proving reasonableness.

[ARTICLE] 5

TRANSFERABLE INTERESTS AND RIGHTS
OF TRANSFEREES AND CREDITORS

§ 501. Nature of Transferable Interest

A transferable interest is personal property.

§ 502. Transfer of Transferable Interest

(a) Subject to Section 503(f), a transfer, in whole or in part, of a transferable interest:

(1) is permissible;

(2) does not by itself cause a person's dissociation as a member or a dissolution and winding up of the limited liability company's activities and affairs; and

(3) subject to Section 504, does not entitle the transferee to:

(A) participate in the management or conduct of the company's activities and affairs; or

(B) except as otherwise provided in subsection (c), have access to records or other information concerning the company's activities and affairs.

(b) A transferee has the right to receive, in accordance with the transfer, distributions to which the transferor would otherwise be entitled.

(c) In a dissolution and winding up of a limited liability company, a transferee is entitled to an account of the company's transactions only from the date of dissolution.

(d) A transferable interest may be evidenced by a certificate of the interest issued by a limited liability company in a record, and, subject to this section, the interest represented by the certificate may be transferred by a transfer of the certificate.

(e) A limited liability company need not give effect to a transferee's rights under this section until the company knows or has notice of the transfer.

(f) A transfer of a transferable interest in violation of a restriction on transfer contained in the operating agreement is ineffective if the intended transferee has knowledge or notice of the restriction at the time of transfer.

(g) Except as otherwise provided in Section 602(5)(B), if a member transfers a transferable interest, the transferor retains the rights of a member other than the transferable interest transferred and retains all the duties and obligations of a member.

(h) If a member transfers a transferable interest to a person that becomes a member with respect to the transferred interest, the transferee is liable for the member's obligations under Sections 403 and 406 known to the transferee when the transferee becomes a member.

§ 503. Charging Order

(a) On application by a judgment creditor of a member or transferee, a court may enter a charging order against the transferable interest of the judgment debtor for the unsatisfied amount of the judgment. Except as otherwise provided in subsection (f), a charging order constitutes a lien on a judgment debtor's transferable interest and requires the limited liability company to pay over to the person to which the charging order was issued any distribution that otherwise would be paid to the judgment debtor.

(b) To the extent necessary to effectuate the collection of distributions pursuant to a charging order in effect under subsection (a), the court may:

(1)   appoint a receiver of the distributions subject to the charging order, with the power to make all inquiries the judgment debtor might have made; and

(2)   make all other orders necessary to give effect to the charging order.

(c)   Upon a showing that distributions under a charging order will not pay the judgment debt within a reasonable time, the court may foreclose the lien and order the sale of the transferable interest. Except as otherwise provided in subsection (f), the purchaser at the foreclosure sale obtains only the transferable interest, does not thereby become a member, and is subject to Section 502.

(d)   At any time before foreclosure under subsection (c), the member or transferee whose transferable interest is subject to a charging order under subsection (a) may extinguish the charging order by satisfying the judgment and filing a certified copy of the satisfaction with the court that issued the charging order.

(e)   At any time before foreclosure under subsection (c), a limited liability company or one or more members whose transferable interests are not subject to the charging order may pay to the judgment creditor the full amount due under the judgment and thereby succeed to the rights of the judgment creditor, including the charging order.

(f)   If a court orders foreclosure of a charging order lien against the sole member of a limited liability company:

(1)   the court shall confirm the sale;

(2)   the purchaser at the sale obtains the member's entire interest, not only the member's transferable interest;

(3)   the purchaser thereby becomes a member; and

(4)   the person whose interest was subject to the foreclosed charging order is dissociated as a member.

(g)   This [act] does not deprive any member or transferee of the benefit of any exemption law applicable to the transferable interest of the member or transferee.

(h)   This section provides the exclusive remedy by which a person seeking in the capacity of judgment creditor to enforce a judgment against a member or transferee may satisfy the judgment from the judgment debtor's transferable interest.

§ 504.   Power of Legal Representative of Deceased Member

If a member dies, the deceased member's legal representative may exercise:

(1)   the rights of a transferee provided in Section 502(c); and

(2)   for the purposes of settling the estate, the rights the deceased member had under Section 410.

[ARTICLE] 6

DISSOCIATION

§ 601.   Power to Dissociate as Member; Wrongful Dissociation

(a)   A person has the power to dissociate as a member at any time, rightfully or wrongfully, by withdrawing as a member by express will under Section 602(1).

(b)   A person's dissociation as a member is wrongful only if the dissociation:

(1)   is in breach of an express provision of the operating agreement; or

(2)   occurs before the completion of the winding up of the limited liability company and:

   (A)   the person withdraws as a member by express will;

   (B)   the person is expelled as a member by judicial order under Section 602(6);

   (C)   the person is dissociated under Section 602(8); or

   (D)   in the case of a person that is not a trust other than a business trust, an estate, or an individual, the person is expelled or otherwise dissociated as a member because it willfully dissolved or terminated.

(c)   A person that wrongfully dissociates as a member is liable to the limited liability company and, subject to Section 801, to the other members for damages caused by the dissociation. The liability is in addition to any debt, obligation, or other liability of the member to the company or the other members.

§ 602.   Events Causing Dissociation

A person is dissociated as a member when:

(1)   the limited liability company knows or has notice of the person's express will to withdraw as a member, but, if the person has specified a withdrawal date later than the date the company knew or had notice, on that later date;

(2)   an event stated in the operating agreement as causing the person's dissociation occurs;

(3)   the person's entire interest is transferred in a foreclosure sale under Section 503(f);

(4)   the person is expelled as a member pursuant to the operating agreement;

(5)   the person is expelled as a member by the affirmative vote or consent of all the other members if:

   (A)   it is unlawful to carry on the limited liability company's activities and affairs with the person as a member;

   (B)   there has been a transfer of all the person's transferable interest in the company, other than:

      (i)   a transfer for security purposes; or

      (ii)   a charging order in effect under Section 503 which has not been foreclosed;

   (C)   the person is an entity and:

      (i)   the company notifies the person that it will be expelled as a member because the person has filed a statement of dissolution or the equivalent, the person has been administratively dissolved, the person's charter or the equivalent has been revoked, or the person's right to conduct business has been suspended by the person's jurisdiction of formation; and

      (ii)   not later than 90 days after the notification, the statement of dissolution or the equivalent has not been withdrawn, rescinded, or revoked, the person has not been reinstated, or the person's charter or the equivalent or right to conduct business has not been reinstated; or

   (D)   the person is an unincorporated entity that has been dissolved and whose activities and affairs are being wound up;

(6)   on application by the limited liability company or a member in a direct action under Section 801, the person is expelled as a member by judicial order because the person:

   (A)   has engaged or is engaging in wrongful conduct that has affected adversely and materially, or will affect adversely and materially, the company's activities and affairs;

(B) has committed willfully or persistently, or is committing willfully or persistently, a material breach of the operating agreement or a duty or obligation under Section 409; or

(C) has engaged or is engaging in conduct relating to the company's activities and affairs which makes it not reasonably practicable to carry on the activities and affairs with the person as a member;

(7) in the case of an individual:

(A) the individual dies; or

(B) in a member-managed limited liability company:

(i) a guardian or general conservator for the individual is appointed; or

(ii) a court orders that the individual has otherwise become incapable of performing the individual's duties as a member under this [act] or the operating agreement;

(8) in a member-managed limited liability company, the person:

(A) becomes a debtor in bankruptcy;

(B) signs an assignment for the benefit of creditors; or

(C) seeks, consents to, or acquiesces in the appointment of a trustee, receiver, or liquidator of the person or of all or substantially all the person's property;

(9) in the case of a person that is a testamentary or inter vivos trust or is acting as a member by virtue of being a trustee of such a trust, the trust's entire transferable interest in the limited liability company is distributed;

(10) in the case of a person that is an estate or is acting as a member by virtue of being a personal representative of an estate, the estate's entire transferable interest in the limited liability company is distributed;

(11) in the case of a person that is not an individual, the existence of the person terminates;

(12) the limited liability company participates in a merger under [Article] 10 and:

(A) the company is not the surviving entity; or

(B) otherwise as a result of the merger, the person ceases to be a member;

(13) the limited liability company participates in an interest exchange under [Article] 10 and, as a result of the interest exchange, the person ceases to be a member;

(14) the limited liability company participates in a conversion under [Article] 10;

(15) the limited liability company participates in a domestication under [Article] 10 and, as a result of the domestication, the person ceases to be a member; or

(16) the limited liability company dissolves and completes winding up.

§ 603. Effect of Dissociation

(a) If a person is dissociated as a member:

(1) the person's right to participate as a member in the management and conduct of the limited liability company's activities and affairs terminates;

(2) the person's duties and obligations under Section 409 as a member end with regard to matters arising and events occurring after the person's dissociation; and

(3) subject to Section 504 and [Article] 10, any transferable interest owned by the person in the person's capacity as a member immediately before dissociation is owned by the person solely as a transferee.

(b)   A person's dissociation as a member does not of itself discharge the person from any debt, obligation, or other liability to the limited liability company or the other members which the person incurred while a member.

[ARTICLE] 7

DISSOLUTION AND WINDING UP

§ 701.   Events Causing Dissolution

(a)   A limited liability company is dissolved, and its activities and affairs must be wound up, upon the occurrence of any of the following:

(1)   an event or circumstance that the operating agreement states causes dissolution;

(2)   the affirmative vote or consent of all the members;

(3)   the passage of 90 consecutive days during which the company has no members unless before the end of the period:

(A)   consent to admit at least one specified person as a member is given by transferees owning the rights to receive a majority of distributions as transferees at the time the consent is to be effective; and

(B)   at least one person becomes a member in accordance with the consent;

(4)   on application by a member, the entry by [the appropriate court] of an order dissolving the company on the grounds that:

(A)   the conduct of all or substantially all the company's activities and affairs is unlawful;

(B)   it is not reasonably practicable to carry on the company's activities and affairs in conformity with the certificate of organization and the operating agreement; or

(C)   the managers or those members in control of the company:

(i)   have acted, are acting, or will act in a manner that is illegal or fraudulent; or

(ii)   have acted or are acting in a manner that is oppressive and was, is, or will be directly harmful to the applicant; or

(5)   the signing and filing of a statement of administrative dissolution by the [Secretary of State] under Section 708.

(b)   In a proceeding brought under subsection (a)(4)(C), the court may order a remedy other than dissolution.

§ 702.   Winding Up

(a)   A dissolved limited liability company shall wind up its activities and affairs and, except as otherwise provided in Section 703, the company continues after dissolution only for the purpose of winding up.

(b)   In winding up its activities and affairs, a limited liability company:

(1)   shall discharge the company's debts, obligations, and other liabilities, settle and close the company's activities and affairs, and marshal and distribute the assets of the company; and

(2)   may:

(A)   deliver to the [Secretary of State] for filing a statement of dissolution stating the name of the company and that the company is dissolved;

(B)   preserve the company activities, affairs, and property as a going concern for a reasonable time;

(C)   prosecute and defend actions and proceedings, whether civil, criminal, or administrative;

(D)   transfer the company's property;

(E)   settle disputes by mediation or arbitration;

(F)   deliver to the [Secretary of State] for filing a statement of termination stating the name of the company and that the company is terminated; and

(G)   perform other acts necessary or appropriate to the winding up.

(c)   If a dissolved limited liability company has no members, the legal representative of the last person to have been a member may wind up the activities and affairs of the company. If the person does so, the person has the powers of a sole manager under Section 407(c) and is deemed to be a manager for the purposes of Section 304(a).

(d)   If the legal representative under subsection (c) declines or fails to wind up the limited liability company's activities and affairs, a person may be appointed to do so by the consent of transferees owning a majority of the rights to receive distributions as transferees at the time the consent is to be effective. A person appointed under this subsection:

(1)   has the powers of a sole manager under Section 407(c) and is deemed to be a manager for the purposes of Section 304(a); and

(2)   shall deliver promptly to the [Secretary of State] for filing an amendment to the company's certificate of organization stating:

(A)   that the company has no members;

(B)   the name and street and mailing addresses of the person; and

(C)   that the person has been appointed pursuant to this subsection to wind up the company.

(e)   [The appropriate court] may order judicial supervision of the winding up of a dissolved limited liability company, including the appointment of a person to wind up the company's activities and affairs:

(1)   on the application of a member, if the applicant establishes good cause;

(2)   on the application of a transferee, if:

(A)   the company does not have any members;

(B)   the legal representative of the last person to have been a member declines or fails to wind up the company's activities; and

(C)   within a reasonable time following the dissolution a person has not been appointed pursuant to subsection (c); or

(3)   in connection with a proceeding under Section 701(a)(4).

§ 703.   Rescinding Dissolution

(a)   A limited liability company may rescind its dissolution, unless a statement of termination applicable to the company has become effective, [the appropriate court] has entered an order under Section 701(a)(4) dissolving the company, or the [Secretary of State] has dissolved the company under Section 708.

(b)   Rescinding dissolution under this section requires:

(1)   the affirmative vote or consent of each member; and

(2)   if the limited liability company has delivered to the [Secretary of State] for filing a statement of dissolution and:

(A)   the statement has not become effective, delivery to the [Secretary of State] for filing of a statement of withdrawal under Section 208 applicable to the statement of dissolution; or

(B)   if the statement of dissolution has become effective, delivery to the [Secretary of State] for filing of a statement of rescission stating the name of the company and that dissolution has been rescinded under this section.

(c)   If a limited liability company rescinds its dissolution:

(1)   the company resumes carrying on its activities and affairs as if dissolution had never occurred;

(2)   subject to paragraph (3), any liability incurred by the company after the dissolution and before the rescission has becomes effective is determined as if dissolution had never occurred; and

(3)   the rights of a third party arising out of conduct in reliance on the dissolution before the third party knew or had notice of the rescission may not be adversely affected.

§ 704.   Known Claims Against Dissolved Limited Liability Company

(a)   Except as otherwise provided in subsection (d), a dissolved limited liability company may give notice of a known claim under subsection (b), which has the effect provided in subsection (c).

(b)   A dissolved limited liability company may in a record notify its known claimants of the dissolution. The notice must:

(1)   specify the information required to be included in a claim;

(2)   state that a claim must be in writing and provide a mailing address to which the claim is to be sent;

(3)   state the deadline for receipt of a claim, which may not be less than 120 days after the date the notice is received by the claimant; and

(4)   state that the claim will be barred if not received by the deadline.

(c)   A claim against a dissolved limited liability company is barred if the requirements of subsection (b) are met and:

(1)   the claim is not received by the specified deadline; or

(2)   if the claim is timely received but rejected by the company:

(A)   the company causes the claimant to receive a notice in a record stating that the claim is rejected and will be barred unless the claimant commences an action against the company to enforce the claim not later than 90 days after the claimant receives the notice; and

(B)   the claimant does not commence the required action not later than 90 days after the claimant receives the notice.

(d)   This section does not apply to a claim based on an event occurring after the date of dissolution or a liability that on that date is contingent.

§ 705. Other Claims Against Dissolved Limited Liability Company

(a)   A dissolved limited liability company may publish notice of its dissolution and request persons having claims against the company to present them in accordance with the notice.

(b)   A notice under subsection (a) must:

(1)   be published at least once in a newspaper of general circulation in the [county] in this state in which the dissolved limited liability company's principal office is located or, if the principal office is not located in this state, in the [county] in which the office of the company's registered agent is or was last located;

(2)   describe the information required to be contained in a claim, state that the claim must be in writing, and provide a mailing address to which the claim is to be sent; and

(3)   state that a claim against the company is barred unless an action to enforce the claim is commenced not later than three years after publication of the notice.

(c)   If a dissolved limited liability company publishes a notice in accordance with subsection (b), the claim of each of the following claimants is barred unless the claimant commences an action to enforce the claim against the company not later than three years after the publication date of the notice:

(1)   a claimant that did not receive notice in a record under Section 704;

(2)   a claimant whose claim was timely sent to the company but not acted on; and

(3)   a claimant whose claim is contingent at, or based on an event occurring after, the date of dissolution.

(d)   A claim not barred under this section or Section 704 may be enforced:

(1)   against a dissolved limited liability company, to the extent of its undistributed assets; and

(2)   except as otherwise provided in Section 706, if assets of the company have been distributed after dissolution, against a member or transferee to the extent of that person's proportionate share of the claim or of the company's assets distributed to the member or transferee after dissolution, whichever is less, but a person's total liability for all claims under this paragraph may not exceed the total amount of assets distributed to the person after dissolution.

§ 706. Court Proceedings

(a)   A dissolved limited liability company that has published a notice under Section 705 may file an application with [the appropriate court] in the [county] where the company's principal office is located or, if the principal office is not located in this state, where the office of its registered agent is or was last located, for a determination of the amount and form of security to be provided for payment of claims that are reasonably expected to arise after the date of dissolution based on facts known to the company and:

(1)   at the time of application:

(A)   are contingent; or

(B)   have not been made known to the company; or

(2)   are based on an event occurring after the date of dissolution.

(b)   Security is not required for any claim that is or is reasonably anticipated to be barred under Section 705.

(c)   Not later than 10 days after the filing of an application under subsection (a), the dissolved limited liability company shall give notice of the proceeding to each claimant holding a contingent claim known to the company.

(d)   In a proceeding under this section, the court may appoint a guardian ad litem to represent all claimants whose identities are unknown. The reasonable fees and expenses of the guardian, including all reasonable expert witness fees, must be paid by the dissolved limited liability company.

(e)   A dissolved limited liability company that provides security in the amount and form ordered by the court under subsection (a) satisfies the company's obligations with respect to claims that are contingent, have not been made known to the company, or are based on an event occurring after the date of dissolution, and such claims may not be enforced against a member or transferee on account of assets received in liquidation.

§ 707.   Disposition of Assets in Winding Up

(a)   In winding up its activities and affairs, a limited liability company shall apply its assets to discharge the company's obligations to creditors, including members that are creditors.

(b)   After a limited liability company complies with subsection (a), any surplus must be distributed in the following order, subject to any charging order in effect under Section 503:

(1)   to each person owning a transferable interest that reflects contributions made and not previously returned, an amount equal to the value of the unreturned contributions; and

(2)   among persons owning transferable interests in proportion to their respective rights to share in distributions immediately before the dissolution of the company.

(c)   If a limited liability company does not have sufficient surplus to comply with subsection (b)(1), any surplus must be distributed among the owners of transferable interests in proportion to the value of the respective unreturned contributions.

(d)   All distributions made under subsections (b) and (c) must be paid in money.

§ 708.   Administrative Dissolution

(a)   The [Secretary of State] may commence a proceeding under subsection (b) to dissolve a limited liability company administratively if the company does not:

(1)   pay any fee, tax, interest, or penalty required to be paid to the [Secretary of State] not later than [six months] after it is due;

(2)   deliver [an annual] [a biennial] report to the [Secretary of State] not later than [six months] after it is due; or

(3)   have a registered agent in this state for [60] consecutive days.

(b)   If the [Secretary of State] determines that one or more grounds exist for administratively dissolving a limited liability company, the [Secretary of State] shall serve the company with notice in a record of the [Secretary of State's] determination.

(c)   If a limited liability company, not later than [60] days after service of the notice under subsection (b), does not cure or demonstrate to the satisfaction of the [Secretary of State] the nonexistence of each ground determined by the [Secretary of State], the [Secretary of State] shall administratively dissolve the company by signing a statement of administrative dissolution that recites the grounds for dissolution and the effective date of dissolution. The [Secretary of State] shall file the statement and serve a copy on the company pursuant to Section 210.

(d)   A limited liability company that is administratively dissolved continues in existence as an entity but may not carry on any activities except as necessary to wind up its activities and affairs and liquidate its assets under Sections 702, 704, 705, 706, and 707, or to apply for reinstatement under Section 709.

(e)   The administrative dissolution of a limited liability company does not terminate the authority of its registered agent.

§ 709.   Reinstatement

(a)   A limited liability company that is administratively dissolved under Section 708 may apply to the [Secretary of State] for reinstatement [not later than [two] years after the effective date of dissolution]. The application must state:

(1)   the name of the company at the time of its administrative dissolution and, if needed, a different name that satisfies Section 112;

(2)   the address of the principal office of the company and the name and street and mailing addresses of its registered agent;

(3)   the effective date of the company's administrative dissolution; and

(4)   that the grounds for dissolution did not exist or have been cured.

(b)   To be reinstated, a limited liability company must pay all fees, taxes, interest, and penalties that were due to the [Secretary of State] at the time of the company's administrative dissolution and all fees, taxes, interest, and penalties that would have been due to the [Secretary of State] while the company was administratively dissolved.

(c)   If the [Secretary of State] determines that an application under subsection (a) contains the required information, is satisfied that the information is correct, and determines that all payments required to be made to the [Secretary of State] by subsection (b) have been made, the [Secretary of State] shall:

(1)   cancel the statement of administrative dissolution and prepare a statement of reinstatement that states the [Secretary of State's] determination and the effective date of reinstatement; and

(2)   file the statement of reinstatement and serve a copy on the limited liability company.

(d)   When reinstatement under this section has become effective, the following rules apply:

(1)   The reinstatement relates back to and takes effect as of the effective date of the administrative dissolution.

(2)   The limited liability company resumes carrying on its activities and affairs as if the administrative dissolution had not occurred.

(3)   The rights of a person arising out of an act or omission in reliance on the dissolution before the person knew or had notice of the reinstatement are not affected.

§ 710.   Judicial Review of Denial of Reinstatement

(a)   If the [Secretary of State] denies a limited liability company's application for reinstatement following administrative dissolution, the [Secretary of State] shall serve the company with a notice in a record that explains the reasons for the denial.

(b)   A limited liability company may seek judicial review of denial of reinstatement in [the appropriate court] not later than [30] days after service of the notice of denial.

[ARTICLE] 8

ACTIONS BY MEMBERS

§ 801. Direct Action by Member

(a) Subject to subsection (b), a member may maintain a direct action against another member, a manager, or the limited liability company to enforce the member's rights and protect the member's interests, including rights and interests under the operating agreement or this [act] or arising independently of the membership relationship.

(b) A member maintaining a direct action under this section must plead and prove an actual or threatened injury that is not solely the result of an injury suffered or threatened to be suffered by the limited liability company.

§ 802. Derivative Action

A member may maintain a derivative action to enforce a right of a limited liability company if:

(1) the member first makes a demand on the other members in a member-managed limited liability company, or the managers of a manager-managed limited liability company, requesting that they cause the company to bring an action to enforce the right, and the managers or other members do not bring the action within a reasonable time; or

(2) a demand under paragraph (1) would be futile.

§ 803. Proper Plaintiff

A derivative action to enforce a right of a limited liability company may be maintained only by a person that is a member at the time the action is commenced and:

(1) was a member when the conduct giving rise to the action occurred; or

(2) whose status as a member devolved on the person by operation of law or pursuant to the terms of the operating agreement from a person that was a member at the time of the conduct.

§ 804. Pleading

In a derivative action, the complaint must state with particularity:

(1) the date and content of plaintiff's demand and the response to the demand by the managers or other members; or

(2) why demand should be excused as futile.

§ 805. Special Litigation Committee

(a) If a limited liability company is named as or made a party in a derivative proceeding, the company may appoint a special litigation committee to investigate the claims asserted in the proceeding and determine whether pursuing the action is in the best interests of the company. If the company appoints a special litigation committee, on motion by the committee made in the name of the company, except for good cause shown, the court shall stay discovery for the time reasonably necessary to permit the committee to make its investigation. This subsection does not prevent the court from:

(1) enforcing a person's right to information under Section 410; or

(2) granting extraordinary relief in the form of a temporary restraining order or preliminary injunction.

(b) A special litigation committee must be composed of one or more disinterested and independent individuals, who may be members.

(c)   A special litigation committee may be appointed:

    (1)   in a member-managed limited liability company:

        (A)   by the affirmative vote or consent of a majority of the members not named as parties in the proceeding; or

        (B)   if all members are named as parties in the proceeding, by a majority of the members named as defendants; or

    (2)   in a manager-managed limited liability company:

        (A)   by a majority of the managers not named as parties in the proceeding; or

        (B)   if all managers are named as parties in the proceeding, by a majority of the managers named as defendants.

(d)   After appropriate investigation, a special litigation committee may determine that it is in the best interests of the limited liability company that the proceeding:

    (1)   continue under the control of the plaintiff;

    (2)   continue under the control of the committee;

    (3)   be settled on terms approved by the committee; or

    (4)   be dismissed.

(e)   After making a determination under subsection (d), a special litigation committee shall file with the court a statement of its determination and its report supporting its determination and shall serve each party with a copy of the determination and report. The court shall determine whether the members of the committee were disinterested and independent and whether the committee conducted its investigation and made its recommendation in good faith, independently, and with reasonable care, with the committee having the burden of proof. If the court finds that the members of the committee were disinterested and independent and that the committee acted in good faith, independently, and with reasonable care, the court shall enforce the determination of the committee. Otherwise, the court shall dissolve the stay of discovery entered under subsection (a) and allow the action to continue under the control of the plaintiff.

§ 806.   Proceeds and Expenses

(a)   Except as otherwise provided in subsection (b):

    (1)   any proceeds or other benefits of a derivative action, whether by judgment, compromise, or settlement, belong to the limited liability company and not to the plaintiff; and

    (2)   if the plaintiff receives any proceeds, the plaintiff shall remit them immediately to the company.

(b)   If a derivative action is successful in whole or in part, the court may award the plaintiff reasonable expenses, including reasonable attorney's fees and costs, from the recovery of the limited liability company.

(c)   A derivative action on behalf of a limited liability company may not be voluntarily dismissed or settled without the court's approval.

[ARTICLE] 9

FOREIGN LIMITED LIABILITY COMPANIES

§ 901.   Governing Law

(a)   The law of the jurisdiction of formation of a foreign limited liability company governs:

(1)   the internal affairs of the company;

(2)   the liability of a member as member and a manager as manager for a debt, obligation, or other liability of the company; and

(3)   the liability of a series of the company.

(b)   A foreign limited liability company is not precluded from registering to do business in this state because of any difference between the law of its jurisdiction of formation and the law of this state.

(c)   Registration of a foreign limited liability company to do business in this state does not authorize the foreign company to engage in any activities and affairs or exercise any power that a limited liability company may not engage in or exercise in this state.

§ 902.   Registration to do Business in This State

(a)   A foreign limited liability company may not do business in this state until it registers with the [Secretary of State] under this [article].

(b)   A foreign limited liability company doing business in this state may not maintain an action or proceeding in this state unless it is registered to do business in this state.

(c)   The failure of a foreign limited liability company to register to do business in this state does not impair the validity of a contract or act of the company or preclude it from defending an action or proceeding in this state.

(d)   A limitation on the liability of a member or manager of a foreign limited liability company is not waived solely because the company does business in this state without registering to do business in this state.

(e)   Section 901(a) and (b) applies even if a foreign limited liability company fails to register under this [article].

§ 903.   Foreign Registration Statement

To register to do business in this state, a foreign limited liability company must deliver a foreign registration statement to the [Secretary of State] for filing. The statement must state:

(1)   the name of the company and, if the name does not comply with Section 112, an alternate name adopted pursuant to Section 906(a);

(2)   that the company is a foreign limited liability company;

(3)   the company's jurisdiction of formation;

(4)   the street and mailing addresses of the company's principal office and, if the law of the company's jurisdiction of formation requires the company to maintain an office in that jurisdiction, the street and mailing addresses of the required office; and

(5)   the name and street and mailing addresses of the company's registered agent in this state.

§ 904.   Amendment of Foreign Registration Statement

A registered foreign limited liability company shall deliver to the [Secretary of State] for filing an amendment to its foreign registration statement if there is a change in:

(1) the name of the company;

(2) the company's jurisdiction of formation;

(3) an address required by Section 903(4); or

(4) the information required by Section 903(5).

§ 905. Activities Not Constituting Doing Business

(a) Activities of a foreign limited liability company which do not constitute doing business in this state under this [article] include:

(1) maintaining, defending, mediating, arbitrating, or settling an action or proceeding;

(2) carrying on any activity concerning its internal affairs, including holding meetings of its members or managers;

(3) maintaining accounts in financial institutions;

(4) maintaining offices or agencies for the transfer, exchange, and registration of securities of the company or maintaining trustees or depositories with respect to those securities;

(5) selling through independent contractors;

(6) soliciting or obtaining orders by any means if the orders require acceptance outside this state before they become contracts;

(7) creating or acquiring indebtedness, mortgages, or security interests in property;

(8) securing or collecting debts or enforcing mortgages or security interests in property securing the debts and holding, protecting, or maintaining property;

(9) conducting an isolated transaction that is not in the course of similar transactions;

(10) owning, without more, property; and

(11) doing business in interstate commerce.

(b) A person does not do business in this state solely by being a member or manager of a foreign limited liability company that does business in this state.

(c) This section does not apply in determining the contacts or activities that may subject a foreign limited liability company to service of process, taxation, or regulation under law of this state other than this [act].

§ 906. Noncomplying Name of Foreign Limited Liability Company

(a) A foreign limited liability company whose name does not comply with Section 112 may not register to do business in this state until it adopts, for the purpose of doing business in this state, an alternate name that complies with Section 112. A company that registers under an alternate name under this subsection need not comply with [this state's assumed or fictitious name statute]. After registering to do business in this state with an alternate name, a company shall do business in this state under:

(1) the alternate name;

(2) the company's name, with the addition of its jurisdiction of formation; or

(3) a name the company is authorized to use under [this state's assumed or fictitious name statute].

(b) If a registered foreign limited liability company changes its name to one that does not comply with Section 112, it may not do business in this state until it complies with subsection (a) by amending its registration to adopt an alternate name that complies with Section 112.

§ 907.   Withdrawal Deemed on Conversion to Domestic Filing Entity or Domestic Limited Liability Partnership

A registered foreign limited liability company that converts to a domestic limited liability partnership or to a domestic entity whose formation requires delivery of a record to the [Secretary of State] for filing is deemed to have withdrawn its registration on the effective date of the conversion.

§ 908.   Withdrawal on Dissolution or Conversion to Nonfiling Entity Other than Limited Liability Partnership

(a)   A registered foreign limited liability company that has dissolved and completed winding up or has converted to a domestic or foreign entity whose formation does not require the public filing of a record, other than a limited liability partnership, shall deliver a statement of withdrawal to the [Secretary of State] for filing. The statement must state:

(1)   in the case of a company that has completed winding up:

(A)   its name and jurisdiction of formation;

(B)   that the company surrenders its registration to do business in this state; and

(2)   in the case of a company that has converted:

(A)   the name of the converting company and its jurisdiction of formation;

(B)   the type of entity to which the company has converted and its jurisdiction of formation;

(C)   that the converted entity surrenders the converting company's registration to do business in this state and revokes the authority of the converting company's registered agent to act as registered agent in this state on behalf of the company or the converted entity; and

(D)   a mailing address to which service of process may be made under subsection (b).

(b)   After a withdrawal under this section has become effective, service of process in any action or proceeding based on a cause of action arising during the time the foreign limited liability company was registered to do business in this state may be made pursuant to Section 119.

§ 909.   Transfer of Registration

(a)   When a registered foreign limited liability company has merged into a foreign entity that is not registered to do business in this state or has converted to a foreign entity required to register with the [Secretary of State] to do business in this state, the foreign entity shall deliver to the [Secretary of State] for filing an application for transfer of registration. The application must state:

(1)   the name of the registered foreign limited liability company before the merger or conversion;

(2)   that before the merger or conversion the registration pertained to a foreign limited liability company;

(3)   the name of the applicant foreign entity into which the foreign limited liability company has merged or to which it has been converted and, if the name does not comply with Section 112, an alternate name adopted pursuant to Section 906(a);

(4)   the type of entity of the applicant foreign entity and its jurisdiction of formation;

(5)   the street and mailing addresses of the principal office of the applicant foreign entity and, if the law of the entity's jurisdiction of formation requires the entity to maintain an office in that jurisdiction, the street and mailing addresses of that office; and

(6)   the name and street and mailing addresses of the applicant foreign entity's registered agent in this state.

(b) When an application for transfer of registration takes effect, the registration of the foreign limited liability company to do business in this state is transferred without interruption to the foreign entity into which the company has merged or to which it has been converted.

§ 910. Termination of Registration

(a) The [Secretary of State] may terminate the registration of a registered foreign limited liability company in the manner provided in subsections (b) and (c) if the company does not:

(1) pay, not later than [60] days after the due date, any fee, tax, interest, or penalty required to be paid to the [Secretary of State] under this [act] or law other than this [act];

(2) deliver to the [Secretary of State] for filing, not later than [60] days after the due date, [an annual] [a biennial] report required under Section 212;

(3) have a registered agent as required by Section 115; or

(4) deliver to the [Secretary of State] for filing a statement of a change under Section 116 not later than [30] days after a change has occurred in the name or address of the registered agent.

(b) The [Secretary of State] may terminate the registration of a registered foreign limited liability company by:

(1) filing a notice of termination or noting the termination in the records of the [Secretary of State]; and

(2) delivering a copy of the notice or the information in the notation to the company's registered agent or, if the company does not have a registered agent, to the company's principal office.

(c) The notice must state or the information in the notation must include:

(1) the effective date of the termination, which must be at least [60] days after the date the [Secretary of State] delivers the copy; and

(2) the grounds for termination under subsection (a).

(d) The authority of a registered foreign limited liability company to do business in this state ceases on the effective date of the notice of termination or notation under subsection (b), unless before that date the company cures each ground for termination stated in the notice or notation. If the company cures each ground, the [Secretary of State] shall file a record so stating.

§ 911. Withdrawal of Registration of Registered Foreign Limited Liability Company

(a) A registered foreign limited liability company may withdraw its registration by delivering a statement of withdrawal to the [Secretary of State] for filing. The statement of withdrawal must state:

(1) the name of the company and its jurisdiction of formation;

(2) that the company is not doing business in this state and that it withdraws its registration to do business in this state;

(3) that the company revokes the authority of its registered agent to accept service on its behalf in this state; and

(4) an address to which service of process may be made under subsection (b).

(b) After the withdrawal of the registration of a foreign limited liability company, service of process in any action or proceeding based on a cause of action arising during the time the company was registered to do business in this state may be made pursuant to Section 119.

§ 912.   Action by [Attorney General]

The [Attorney General] may maintain an action to enjoin a foreign limited liability company from doing business in this state in violation of this [article].

[ARTICLE] 10

MERGER, INTEREST EXCHANGE, CONVERSION, AND DOMESTICATION

[PART] 1

GENERAL PROVISIONS

§ 1001.   Definitions

In this [article]:

(1) "Acquired entity" means the entity, all of one or more classes or series of interests of which are acquired in an interest exchange.

(2) "Acquiring entity" means the entity that acquires all of one or more classes or series of interests of the acquired entity in an interest exchange.

(3) "Conversion" means a transaction authorized by [Part] 4.

(4) "Converted entity" means the converting entity as it continues in existence after a conversion.

(5) "Converting entity" means the domestic entity that approves a plan of conversion pursuant to Section 1043 or the foreign entity that approves a conversion pursuant to the law of its jurisdiction of formation.

(6) "Distributional interest" means the right under an unincorporated entity's organic law and organic rules to receive distributions from the entity.

(7) "Domestic", with respect to an entity, means governed as to its internal affairs by the law of this state.

(8) "Domesticated limited liability company" means the domesticating limited liability company as it continues in existence after a domestication.

(9) "Domesticating limited liability company" means the domestic limited liability company that approves a plan of domestication pursuant to Section 1053 or the foreign limited liability company that approves a domestication pursuant to the law of its jurisdiction of formation.

(10) "Domestication" means a transaction authorized by [Part] 5.

(11) "Entity":

(A) means:

(i)   a business corporation;

(ii)   a nonprofit corporation;

(iii) a general partnership, including a limited liability partnership;

(iv)   a limited partnership, including a limited liability limited partnership;

(v)   a limited liability company;

[(vi) a general cooperative association;]

(vii) a limited cooperative association;

(viii) an unincorporated nonprofit association;

      (ix) a statutory trust, business trust, or common-law business trust; or

      (x) any other person that has:

         (I) a legal existence separate from any interest holder of that person; or

         (II) the power to acquire an interest in real property in its own name; and

  (B) does not include:

      (i) an individual;

      (ii) a trust with a predominantly donative purpose or a charitable trust;

      (iii) an association or relationship that is not an entity listed in subparagraph A and is not a partnership under the rules stated in [Section 202(c) of the Uniform Partnership Act (1997) (Last Amended 2013)] [Section 7 of the Uniform Partnership Act (1914)] or a similar provision of the law of another jurisdiction;

      (iv) a decedent's estate; or

      (v) a government or a governmental subdivision, agency, or instrumentality.

  (12) "Filing entity" means an entity whose formation requires the filing of a public organic record. The term does not include a limited liability partnership.

  (13) "Foreign", with respect to an entity, means an entity governed as to its internal affairs by the law of a jurisdiction other than this state.

  (14) "Governance interest" means a right under the organic law or organic rules of an unincorporated entity, other than as a governor, agent, assignee, or proxy, to:

  (A) receive or demand access to information concerning, or the books and records of, the entity;

  (B) vote for or consent to the election of the governors of the entity; or

  (C) receive notice of or vote on or consent to an issue involving the internal affairs of the entity.

  (15) "Governor" means:

  (A) a director of a business corporation;

  (B) a director or trustee of a nonprofit corporation;

  (C) a general partner of a general partnership;

  (D) a general partner of a limited partnership;

  (E) a manager of a manager-managed limited liability company;

  (F) a member of a member-managed limited liability company;

  [(G) a director of a general cooperative association;]

  (H) a director of a limited cooperative association;

  (I) a manager of an unincorporated nonprofit association;

  (J) a trustee of a statutory trust, business trust, or common-law business trust; or

  (K) any other person under whose authority the powers of an entity are exercised and under whose direction the activities and affairs of the entity are managed pursuant to the organic law and organic rules of the entity.

  (16) "Interest" means:

  (A) a share in a business corporation;

(B) a membership in a nonprofit corporation;

(C) a partnership interest in a general partnership;

(D) a partnership interest in a limited partnership;

(E) a membership interest in a limited liability company;

[(F) a share in a general cooperative association;]

(G) a member's interest in a limited cooperative association;

(H) a membership in an unincorporated nonprofit association;

(I) a beneficial interest in a statutory trust, business trust, or common-law business trust; or

(J) a governance interest or distributional interest in any other type of unincorporated entity.

(17) "Interest exchange" means a transaction authorized by [Part] 3.

(18) "Interest holder" means:

(A) a shareholder of a business corporation;

(B) a member of a nonprofit corporation;

(C) a general partner of a general partnership;

(D) a general partner of a limited partnership;

(E) a limited partner of a limited partnership;

(F) a member of a limited liability company;

[(G) a shareholder of a general cooperative association;]

(H) a member of a limited cooperative association;

(I) a member of an unincorporated nonprofit association;

(J) a beneficiary or beneficial owner of a statutory trust, business trust, or common-law business trust; or

(K) any other direct holder of an interest.

(19) "Interest holder liability" means:

(A) personal liability for a liability of an entity which is imposed on a person:

(i) solely by reason of the status of the person as an interest holder; or

(ii) by the organic rules of the entity which make one or more specified interest holders or categories of interest holders liable in their capacity as interest holders for all or specified liabilities of the entity; or

(B) an obligation of an interest holder under the organic rules of an entity to contribute to the entity.

(20) "Merger" means a transaction authorized by [Part] 2.

(21) "Merging entity" means an entity that is a party to a merger and exists immediately before the merger becomes effective.

(22) "Organic law" means the law of an entity's jurisdiction of formation governing the internal affairs of the entity.

(23) "Organic rules" means the public organic record and private organic rules of an entity.

(24) "Plan" means a plan of merger, plan of interest exchange, plan of conversion, or plan of domestication.

(25) "Plan of conversion" means a plan under Section 1042.

(26) "Plan of domestication" means a plan under Section 1052.

(27) "Plan of interest exchange" means a plan under Section 1032.

(28) "Plan of merger" means a plan under Section 1022.

(29) "Private organic rules" means the rules, whether or not in a record, that govern the internal affairs of an entity, are binding on all its interest holders, and are not part of its public organic record, if any. The term includes:

    (A) the bylaws of a business corporation;

    (B) the bylaws of a nonprofit corporation;

    (C) the partnership agreement of a general partnership;

    (D) the partnership agreement of a limited partnership;

    (E) the operating agreement of a limited liability company;

    [(F) the bylaws of a general cooperative association;]

    (G) the bylaws of a limited cooperative association;

    (H) the governing principles of an unincorporated nonprofit association; and

    (I) the trust instrument of a statutory trust or similar rules of a business trust or common-law business trust.

(30) "Protected agreement" means:

    (A) a record evidencing indebtedness and any related agreement in effect on [the effective date of this [act]];

    (B) an agreement that is binding on an entity on [the effective date of this [act]];

    (C) the organic rules of an entity in effect on [the effective date of this [act]]; or

    (D) an agreement that is binding on any of the governors or interest holders of an entity on [the effective date of this [act]].

(31) "Public organic record" means the record the filing of which by the [Secretary of State] is required to form an entity and any amendment to or restatement of that record. The term includes:

    (A) the articles of incorporation of a business corporation;

    (B) the articles of incorporation of a nonprofit corporation;

    (C) the certificate of limited partnership of a limited partnership;

    (D) the certificate of organization of a limited liability company;

    [(E) the articles of incorporation of a general cooperative association;]

    (F) the articles of organization of a limited cooperative association; and

    (G) the certificate of trust of a statutory trust or similar record of a business trust.

(32) "Registered foreign entity" means a foreign entity that is registered to do business in this state pursuant to a record filed by the [Secretary of State].

(33) "Statement of conversion" means a statement under Section 1045.

(34) "Statement of domestication" means a statement under Section 1055.

(35) "Statement of interest exchange" means a statement under Section 1035.

(36) "Statement of merger" means a statement under Section 1025.

(37) "Surviving entity" means the entity that continues in existence after or is created by a merger.

(38) "Type of entity" means a generic form of entity:

(A) recognized at common law; or

(B) formed under an organic law, whether or not some entities formed under that organic law are subject to provisions of that law that create different categories of the form of entity.

§ 1002. Relationship of [Article] to Other Laws

(a) This [article] does not authorize an act prohibited by, and does not affect the application or requirements of, law other than this [article].

(b) A transaction effected under this [article] may not create or impair a right, duty or obligation of a person under the statutory law of this state other than this [article] relating to a change in control, takeover, business combination, control-share acquisition, or similar transaction involving a domestic merging, acquired, converting, or domesticating business corporation unless:

(1) if the corporation does not survive the transaction, the transaction satisfies any requirements of the law; or

(2) if the corporation survives the transaction, the approval of the plan is by a vote of the shareholders or directors which would be sufficient to create or impair the right, duty, or obligation directly under the law.

§ 1003. Required Notice or Approval

(a) A domestic or foreign entity that is required to give notice to, or obtain the approval of, a governmental agency or officer of this state to be a party to a merger must give the notice or obtain the approval to be a party to an interest exchange, conversion, or domestication.

(b) Property held for a charitable purpose under the law of this state by a domestic or foreign entity immediately before a transaction under this [article] becomes effective may not, as a result of the transaction, be diverted from the objects for which it was donated, granted, devised, or otherwise transferred unless, to the extent required by or pursuant to the law of this state concerning cy pres or other law dealing with nondiversion of charitable assets, the entity obtains an appropriate order of [the appropriate court] [the Attorney General] specifying the disposition of the property.

(c) A bequest, devise, gift, grant, or promise contained in a will or other instrument of donation, subscription, or conveyance which is made to a merging entity that is not the surviving entity and which takes effect or remains payable after the merger inures to the surviving entity.

(d) A trust obligation that would govern property if transferred to a nonsurviving entity applies to property that is transferred to the surviving entity under this section.

Legislative Note: As an alternative to enacting Subsection (a), a state may identify each of its regulatory laws that requires prior approval for a merger of a regulated entity, decide whether regulatory approval should be required for an interest exchange, conversion, or domestication, and make amendments as appropriate to those laws.

As with Subsection (a), an adopting state may choose to amend its various laws with respect to the nondiversion of charitable property to cover the various transactions authorized by this act as an alternative to enacting Subsection (b).

§ 1004. Nonexclusivity

The fact that a transaction under this [article] produces a certain result does not preclude the same result from being accomplished in any other manner permitted by law other than this [article].

§ 1005. Reference to External Facts

A plan may refer to facts ascertainable outside the plan if the manner in which the facts will operate upon the plan is specified in the plan. The facts may include the occurrence of an event or a determination or action by a person, whether or not the event, determination, or action is within the control of a party to the transaction.

§ 1006. Appraisal Rights

An interest holder of a domestic merging, acquired, converting, or domesticating limited liability company is entitled to contractual appraisal rights in connection with a transaction under this [article] to the extent provided in:

(1) the operating agreement; or

(2) the plan.

[§ 1007. Excluded Entities and Transactions

(a) The following entities may not participate in a transaction under this [article]:

(1)

(2).

(b) This [article] may not be used to effect a transaction that:

(1)

(2).]

Legislative Note: Subsection (a) may be used by states that have special statutes restricted to the organization of certain types of entities. A common example is banking statutes that prohibit banks from engaging in transactions other than pursuant to those statutes.

Nonprofit entities may participate in transactions under this act with for-profit entities, subject to compliance with Section 1003. If a state desires, however, to exclude entities with a charitable purpose or to exclude other types of entities from the scope of this article, that may be done by referring to those entities in Subsection (a).

Subsection (b) may be used to exclude certain types of transactions governed by more specific statutes. A common example is the conversion of an insurance company from mutual to stock form. There may be other types of transactions that vary greatly among the states.

[PART] 2

MERGER

§ 1021. Merger Authorized

(a) By complying with this [part]:

(1) one or more domestic limited liability companies may merge with one or more domestic or foreign entities into a domestic or foreign surviving entity; and

(2) two or more foreign entities may merge into a domestic limited liability company.

(b)   By complying with the provisions of this [part] applicable to foreign entities, a foreign entity may be a party to a merger under this [part] or may be the surviving entity in such a merger if the merger is authorized by the law of the foreign entity's jurisdiction of formation.

§ 1022.   Plan of Merger

(a)   A domestic limited liability company may become a party to a merger under this [part] by approving a plan of merger. The plan must be in a record and contain:

(1)   as to each merging entity, its name, jurisdiction of formation, and type of entity;

(2)   if the surviving entity is to be created in the merger, a statement to that effect and the entity's name, jurisdiction of formation, and type of entity;

(3)   the manner of converting the interests in each party to the merger into interests, securities, obligations, money, other property, rights to acquire interests or securities, or any combination of the foregoing;

(4)   if the surviving entity exists before the merger, any proposed amendments to:

(A)   its public organic record, if any; and

(B)   its private organic rules that are, or are proposed to be, in a record;

(5)   if the surviving entity is to be created in the merger:

(A)   its proposed public organic record, if any; and

(B)   the full text of its private organic rules that are proposed to be in a record;

(6)   the other terms and conditions of the merger; and

(7)   any other provision required by the law of a merging entity's jurisdiction of formation or the organic rules of a merging entity.

(b)   In addition to the requirements of subsection (a), a plan of merger may contain any other provision not prohibited by law.

§ 1023.   Approval of Merger

(a)   A plan of merger is not effective unless it has been approved:

(1)   by a domestic merging limited liability company, by all the members of the company entitled to vote on or consent to any matter; and

(2)   in a record, by each member of a domestic merging limited liability company which will have interest holder liability for debts, obligations, and other liabilities that are incurred after the merger becomes effective, unless:

(A)   the operating agreement of the company provides in a record for the approval of a merger in which some or all of its members become subject to interest holder liability by the affirmative vote or consent of fewer than all the members; and

(B)   the member consented in a record to or voted for that provision of the operating agreement or became a member after the adoption of that provision.

(b)   A merger involving a domestic merging entity that is not a limited liability company is not effective unless the merger is approved by that entity in accordance with its organic law.

(c)   A merger involving a foreign merging entity is not effective unless the merger is approved by the foreign entity in accordance with the law of the foreign entity's jurisdiction of formation.

§ 1024. Amendment or Abandonment of Plan of Merger

(a) A plan of merger may be amended only with the consent of each party to the plan, except as otherwise provided in the plan.

(b) A domestic merging limited liability company may approve an amendment of a plan of merger:

(1) in the same manner as the plan was approved, if the plan does not provide for the manner in which it may be amended; or

(2) by its managers or members in the manner provided in the plan, but a member that was entitled to vote on or consent to approval of the merger is entitled to vote on or consent to any amendment of the plan that will change:

(A) the amount or kind of interests, securities, obligations, money, other property, rights to acquire interests or securities, or any combination of the foregoing, to be received by the interest holders of any party to the plan;

(B) the public organic record, if any, or private organic rules of the surviving entity that will be in effect immediately after the merger becomes effective, except for changes that do not require approval of the interest holders of the surviving entity under its organic law or organic rules; or

(C) any other terms or conditions of the plan, if the change would adversely affect the member in any material respect.

(c) After a plan of merger has been approved and before a statement of merger becomes effective, the plan may be abandoned as provided in the plan. Unless prohibited by the plan, a domestic merging limited liability company may abandon the plan in the same manner as the plan was approved.

(d) If a plan of merger is abandoned after a statement of merger has been delivered to the [Secretary of State] for filing and before the statement becomes effective, a statement of abandonment, signed by a party to the plan, must be delivered to the [Secretary of State] for filing before the statement of merger becomes effective. The statement of abandonment takes effect on filing, and the merger is abandoned and does not become effective. The statement of abandonment must contain:

(1) the name of each party to the plan of merger;

(2) the date on which the statement of merger was filed by the [Secretary of State]; and

(3) a statement that the merger has been abandoned in accordance with this section.

§ 1025. Statement of Merger; Effective Date of Merger

(a) A statement of merger must be signed by each merging entity and delivered to the [Secretary of State] for filing.

(b) A statement of merger must contain:

(1) the name, jurisdiction of formation, and type of entity of each merging entity that is not the surviving entity;

(2) the name, jurisdiction of formation, and type of entity of the surviving entity;

(3) a statement that the merger was approved by each domestic merging entity, if any, in accordance with this [part] and by each foreign merging entity, if any, in accordance with the law of its jurisdiction of formation;

(4) if the surviving entity exists before the merger and is a domestic filing entity, any amendment to its public organic record approved as part of the plan of merger;

(5) if the surviving entity is created by the merger and is a domestic filing entity, its public organic record, as an attachment; and

(6) if the surviving entity is created by the merger and is a domestic limited liability partnership, its statement of qualification, as an attachment.

(c) In addition to the requirements of subsection (b), a statement of merger may contain any other provision not prohibited by law.

(d) If the surviving entity is a domestic entity, its public organic record, if any, must satisfy the requirements of the law of this state, except that the public organic record does not need to be signed.

(e) A plan of merger that is signed by all the merging entities and meets all the requirements of subsection (b) may be delivered to the [Secretary of State] for filing instead of a statement of merger and on filing has the same effect. If a plan of merger is filed as provided in this subsection, references in this [article] to a statement of merger refer to the plan of merger filed under this subsection.

(f) If the surviving entity is a domestic limited liability company, the merger becomes effective when the statement of merger is effective. In all other cases, the merger becomes effective on the later of:

(1) the date and time provided by the organic law of the surviving entity; and

(2) when the statement is effective.

§ 1026. Effect of Merger

(a) When a merger becomes effective:

(1) the surviving entity continues or comes into existence;

(2) each merging entity that is not the surviving entity ceases to exist;

(3) all property of each merging entity vests in the surviving entity without transfer, reversion, or impairment;

(4) all debts, obligations, and other liabilities of each merging entity are debts, obligations, and other liabilities of the surviving entity;

(5) except as otherwise provided by law or the plan of merger, all the rights, privileges, immunities, powers, and purposes of each merging entity vest in the surviving entity;

(6) if the surviving entity exists before the merger:

(A) all its property continues to be vested in it without transfer, reversion, or impairment;

(B) it remains subject to all its debts, obligations, and other liabilities; and

(C) all its rights, privileges, immunities, powers, and purposes continue to be vested in it;

(7) the name of the surviving entity may be substituted for the name of any merging entity that is a party to any pending action or proceeding;

(8) if the surviving entity exists before the merger:

(A) its public organic record, if any, is amended to the extent provided in the statement of merger; and

(B) its private organic rules that are to be in a record, if any, are amended to the extent provided in the plan of merger;

(9) if the surviving entity is created by the merger, its private organic rules are effective and:

(A)   if it is a filing entity, its public organic record becomes effective; and

(B)   if it is a limited liability partnership, its statement of qualification becomes effective; and

(10) the interests in each merging entity which are to be converted in the merger are converted, and the interest holders of those interests are entitled only to the rights provided to them under the plan of merger and to any appraisal rights they have under Section 1006 and the merging entity's organic law.

(b)   Except as otherwise provided in the organic law or organic rules of a merging entity, the merger does not give rise to any rights that an interest holder, governor, or third party would have upon a dissolution, liquidation, or winding up of the merging entity.

(c)   When a merger becomes effective, a person that did not have interest holder liability with respect to any of the merging entities and becomes subject to interest holder liability with respect to a domestic entity as a result of the merger has interest holder liability only to the extent provided by the organic law of that entity and only for those debts, obligations, and other liabilities that are incurred after the merger becomes effective.

(d)   When a merger becomes effective, the interest holder liability of a person that ceases to hold an interest in a domestic merging limited liability company with respect to which the person had interest holder liability is subject to the following rules:

(1)   The merger does not discharge any interest holder liability under this [act] to the extent the interest holder liability was incurred before the merger became effective.

(2)   The person does not have interest holder liability under this [act] for any debt, obligation, or other liability that is incurred after the merger becomes effective.

(3)   This [act] continues to apply to the release, collection, or discharge of any interest holder liability preserved under paragraph (1) as if the merger had not occurred.

(4)   The person has whatever rights of contribution from any other person as are provided by this [act], law other than this [act], or the operating agreement of the domestic merging limited liability company with respect to any interest holder liability preserved under paragraph (1) as if the merger had not occurred.

(e)   When a merger becomes effective, a foreign entity that is the surviving entity may be served with process in this state for the collection and enforcement of any debts, obligations, or other liabilities of a domestic merging limited liability company as provided in Section 119.

(f)   When a merger becomes effective, the registration to do business in this state of any foreign merging entity that is not the surviving entity is canceled.

[PART] 3

INTEREST EXCHANGE

§ 1031.   Interest Exchange Authorized

(a)   By complying with this [part]:

(1)   a domestic limited liability company may acquire all of one or more classes or series of interests of another domestic entity or a foreign entity in exchange for interests, securities, obligations, money, other property, rights to acquire interests or securities, or any combination of the foregoing; or

(2)   all of one or more classes or series of interests of a domestic limited liability company may be acquired by another domestic entity or a foreign entity in exchange for interests,

securities, obligations, money, other property, rights to acquire interests or securities, or any combination of the foregoing.

(b)   By complying with the provisions of this [part] applicable to foreign entities, a foreign entity may be the acquiring or acquired entity in an interest exchange under this [part] if the interest exchange is authorized by the law of the foreign entity's jurisdiction of formation.

(c)   If a protected agreement contains a provision that applies to a merger of a domestic limited liability company but does not refer to an interest exchange, the provision applies to an interest exchange in which the domestic limited liability company is the acquired entity as if the interest exchange were a merger until the provision is amended after [the effective date of this [act]].

§ 1032.   Plan of Interest Exchange

(a)   A domestic limited liability company may be the acquired entity in an interest exchange under this [part] by approving a plan of interest exchange. The plan must be in a record and contain:

(1)   the name of the acquired entity;

(2)   the name, jurisdiction of formation, and type of entity of the acquiring entity;

(3)   the manner of converting the interests in the acquired entity into interests, securities, obligations, money, other property, rights to acquire interests or securities, or any combination of the foregoing;

(4)   any proposed amendments to:

(A)   the certificate of organization of the acquired entity; and

(B)   the operating agreement of the acquired entity that are, or are proposed to be, in a record;

(5)   the other terms and conditions of the interest exchange; and

(6)   any other provision required by the law of this state or the operating agreement of the acquired entity.

(b)   In addition to the requirements of subsection (a), a plan of interest exchange may contain any other provision not prohibited by law.

§ 1033.   Approval of Interest Exchange

(a)   A plan of interest exchange is not effective unless it has been approved:

(1)   by all the members of a domestic acquired limited liability company entitled to vote on or consent to any matter; and

(2)   in a record, by each member of the domestic acquired limited liability company that will have interest holder liability for debts, obligations, and other liabilities that are incurred after the interest exchange becomes effective, unless:

(A)   the operating agreement of the company provides in a record for the approval of an interest exchange or a merger in which some or all of its members become subject to interest holder liability by the affirmative vote or consent of fewer than all the members; and

(B)   the member consented in a record to or voted for that provision of the operating agreement or became a member after the adoption of that provision.

(b)   An interest exchange involving a domestic acquired entity that is not a limited liability company is not effective unless it is approved by the domestic entity in accordance with its organic law.

(c)   An interest exchange involving a foreign acquired entity is not effective unless it is approved by the foreign entity in accordance with the law of the foreign entity's jurisdiction of formation.

(d)   Except as otherwise provided in its organic law or organic rules, the interest holders of the acquiring entity are not required to approve the interest exchange.

§ 1034.   Amendment or Abandonment of Plan of Interest Exchange

(a)   A plan of interest exchange may be amended only with the consent of each party to the plan, except as otherwise provided in the plan.

(b)   A domestic acquired limited liability company may approve an amendment of a plan of interest exchange:

(1)   in the same manner as the plan was approved, if the plan does not provide for the manner in which it may be amended; or

(2)   by its managers or members in the manner provided in the plan, but a member that was entitled to vote on or consent to approval of the interest exchange is entitled to vote on or consent to any amendment of the plan that will change:

(A)   the amount or kind of interests, securities, obligations, money, other property, rights to acquire interests or securities, or any combination of the foregoing, to be received by any of the members of the acquired company under the plan;

(B)   the certificate of organization or operating agreement of the acquired company that will be in effect immediately after the interest exchange becomes effective, except for changes that do not require approval of the members of the acquired company under this [act] or the operating agreement; or

(C)   any other terms or conditions of the plan, if the change would adversely affect the member in any material respect.

(c)   After a plan of interest exchange has been approved and before a statement of interest exchange becomes effective, the plan may be abandoned as provided in the plan. Unless prohibited by the plan, a domestic acquired limited liability company may abandon the plan in the same manner as the plan was approved.

(d)   If a plan of interest exchange is abandoned after a statement of interest exchange has been delivered to the [Secretary of State] for filing and before the statement becomes effective, a statement of abandonment, signed by the acquired limited liability company, must be delivered to the [Secretary of State] for filing before the statement of interest exchange becomes effective. The statement of abandonment takes effect on filing, and the interest exchange is abandoned and does not become effective. The statement of abandonment must contain:

(1)   the name of the acquired company;

(2)   the date on which the statement of interest exchange was filed by the [Secretary of State]; and

(3)   a statement that the interest exchange has been abandoned in accordance with this section.

§ 1035.   Statement of Interest Exchange; Effective Date of Interest Exchange

(a)   A statement of interest exchange must be signed by a domestic acquired limited liability company and delivered to the [Secretary of State] for filing.

(b)   A statement of interest exchange must contain:

(1)   the name of the acquired limited liability company;

(2)   the name, jurisdiction of formation, and type of entity of the acquiring entity;

(3)   a statement that the plan of interest exchange was approved by the acquired company in accordance with this [part]; and

(4)   any amendments to the acquired company's certificate of organization approved as part of the plan of interest exchange.

(c)   In addition to the requirements of subsection (b), a statement of interest exchange may contain any other provision not prohibited by law.

(d)   A plan of interest exchange that is signed by a domestic acquired limited liability company and meets all the requirements of subsection (b) may be delivered to the [Secretary of State] for filing instead of a statement of interest exchange and on filing has the same effect. If a plan of interest exchange is filed as provided in this subsection, references in this [article] to a statement of interest exchange refer to the plan of interest exchange filed under this subsection.

(e)   An interest exchange becomes effective when the statement of interest exchange is effective.

§ 1036.   Effect of Interest Exchange

(a)   When an interest exchange in which the acquired entity is a domestic limited liability company becomes effective:

(1)   the interests in the acquired company which are the subject of the interest exchange are converted, and the members holding those interests are entitled only to the rights provided to them under the plan of interest exchange and to any appraisal rights they have under Section 1006;

(2)   the acquiring entity becomes the interest holder of the interests in the acquired company stated in the plan of interest exchange to be acquired by the acquiring entity;

(3)   the certificate of organization of the acquired company is amended to the extent provided in the statement of interest exchange; and

(4)   the provisions of the operating agreement of the acquired company that are to be in a record, if any, are amended to the extent provided in the plan of interest exchange.

(b)   Except as otherwise provided in the operating agreement of a domestic acquired limited liability company, the interest exchange does not give rise to any rights that a member, manager, or third party would have upon a dissolution, liquidation, or winding up of the acquired company.

(c)   When an interest exchange becomes effective, a person that did not have interest holder liability with respect to a domestic acquired limited liability company and becomes subject to interest holder liability with respect to a domestic entity as a result of the interest exchange has interest holder liability only to the extent provided by the organic law of the entity and only for those debts, obligations, and other liabilities that are incurred after the interest exchange becomes effective.

(d)   When an interest exchange becomes effective, the interest holder liability of a person that ceases to hold an interest in a domestic acquired limited liability company with respect to which the person had interest holder liability is subject to the following rules:

(1)   The interest exchange does not discharge any interest holder liability under this [act] to the extent the interest holder liability was incurred before the interest exchange became effective.

(2)   The person does not have interest holder liability under this [act] for any debt, obligation, or other liability that is incurred after the interest exchange becomes effective.

(3)   This [act] continues to apply to the release, collection, or discharge of any interest holder liability preserved under paragraph (1) as if the interest exchange had not occurred.

(4)   The person has whatever rights of contribution from any other person as are provided by this [act], law other than this [act], or the operating agreement of the acquired company with

respect to any interest holder liability preserved under paragraph (1) as if the interest exchange had not occurred.

[PART] 4

CONVERSION

§ 1041. Conversion Authorized

(a) By complying with this [part], a domestic limited liability company may become:

(1) a domestic entity that is a different type of entity; or

(2) a foreign entity that is a different type of entity, if the conversion is authorized by the law of the foreign entity's jurisdiction of formation.

(b) By complying with the provisions of this [part] applicable to foreign entities, a foreign entity that is not a foreign limited liability company may become a domestic limited liability company if the conversion is authorized by the law of the foreign entity's jurisdiction of formation.

(c) If a protected agreement contains a provision that applies to a merger of a domestic limited liability company but does not refer to a conversion, the provision applies to a conversion of the company as if the conversion were a merger until the provision is amended after [the effective date of this [act]].

§ 1042. Plan of Conversion

(a) A domestic limited liability company may convert to a different type of entity under this [part] by approving a plan of conversion. The plan must be in a record and contain:

(1) the name of the converting limited liability company;

(2) the name, jurisdiction of formation, and type of entity of the converted entity;

(3) the manner of converting the interests in the converting limited liability company into interests, securities, obligations, money, other property, rights to acquire interests or securities, or any combination of the foregoing;

(4) the proposed public organic record of the converted entity if it will be a filing entity;

(5) the full text of the private organic rules of the converted entity which are proposed to be in a record;

(6) the other terms and conditions of the conversion; and

(7) any other provision required by the law of this state or the operating agreement of the converting limited liability company.

(b) In addition to the requirements of subsection (a), a plan of conversion may contain any other provision not prohibited by law.

§ 1043. Approval of Conversion

(a) A plan of conversion is not effective unless it has been approved:

(1) by a domestic converting limited liability company, by all the members of the limited liability company entitled to vote on or consent to any matter; and

(2) in a record, by each member of a domestic converting limited liability company which will have interest holder liability for debts, obligations, and other liabilities that are incurred after the conversion becomes effective, unless:

(A) the operating agreement of the company provides in a record for the approval of a conversion or a merger in which some or all of its members become subject to interest holder liability by the affirmative vote or consent of fewer than all the members; and

(B) the member voted for or consented in a record to that provision of the operating agreement or became a member after the adoption of that provision.

(b) A conversion involving a domestic converting entity that is not a limited liability company is not effective unless it is approved by the domestic converting entity in accordance with its organic law.

(c) A conversion of a foreign converting entity is not effective unless it is approved by the foreign entity in accordance with the law of the foreign entity's jurisdiction of formation.

§ 1044. Amendment or Abandonment of Plan of Conversion

(a) A plan of conversion of a domestic converting limited liability company may be amended:

(1) in the same manner as the plan was approved, if the plan does not provide for the manner in which it may be amended; or

(2) by its managers or members in the manner provided in the plan, but a member that was entitled to vote on or consent to approval of the conversion is entitled to vote on or consent to any amendment of the plan that will change:

(A) the amount or kind of interests, securities, obligations, money, other property, rights to acquire interests or securities, or any combination of the foregoing, to be received by any of the members of the converting company under the plan;

(B) the public organic record, if any, or private organic rules of the converted entity which will be in effect immediately after the conversion becomes effective, except for changes that do not require approval of the interest holders of the converted entity under its organic law or organic rules; or

(C) any other terms or conditions of the plan, if the change would adversely affect the member in any material respect.

(b) After a plan of conversion has been approved by a domestic converting limited liability company and before a statement of conversion becomes effective, the plan may be abandoned as provided in the plan. Unless prohibited by the plan, a domestic converting limited liability company may abandon the plan in the same manner as the plan was approved.

(c) If a plan of conversion is abandoned after a statement of conversion has been delivered to the [Secretary of State] for filing and before the statement becomes effective, a statement of abandonment, signed by the converting entity, must be delivered to the [Secretary of State] for filing before the statement of conversion becomes effective. The statement of abandonment takes effect on filing, and the conversion is abandoned and does not become effective. The statement of abandonment must contain:

(1) the name of the converting limited liability company;

(2) the date on which the statement of conversion was filed by the [Secretary of State]; and

(3) a statement that the conversion has been abandoned in accordance with this section.

§ 1045. Statement of Conversion; Effective Date of Conversion

(a) A statement of conversion must be signed by the converting entity and delivered to the [Secretary of State] for filing.

(b) A statement of conversion must contain:

(1) the name, jurisdiction of formation, and type of entity of the converting entity;

(2)   the name, jurisdiction of formation, and type of entity of the converted entity;

(3)   if the converting entity is a domestic limited liability company, a statement that the plan of conversion was approved in accordance with this [part] or, if the converting entity is a foreign entity, a statement that the conversion was approved by the foreign entity in accordance with the law of its jurisdiction of formation;

(4)   if the converted entity is a domestic filing entity, its public organic record, as an attachment; and

(5)   if the converted entity is a domestic limited liability partnership, its statement of qualification, as an attachment.

(c)   In addition to the requirements of subsection (b), a statement of conversion may contain any other provision not prohibited by law.

(d)   If the converted entity is a domestic entity, its public organic record, if any, must satisfy the requirements of the law of this state, except that the public organic record does not need to be signed.

(e)   A plan of conversion that is signed by a domestic converting limited liability company and meets all the requirements of subsection (b) may be delivered to the [Secretary of State] for filing instead of a statement of conversion and on filing has the same effect. If a plan of conversion is filed as provided in this subsection, references in this [article] to a statement of conversion refer to the plan of conversion filed under this subsection.

(f)   If the converted entity is a domestic limited liability company, the conversion becomes effective when the statement of conversion is effective. In all other cases, the conversion becomes effective on the later of:

(1)   the date and time provided by the organic law of the converted entity; and

(2)   when the statement is effective.

§ 1046.   Effect of Conversion

(a)   When a conversion becomes effective:

(1)   the converted entity is:

(A)   organized under and subject to the organic law of the converted entity; and

(B)   the same entity without interruption as the converting entity;

(2)   all property of the converting entity continues to be vested in the converted entity without transfer, reversion, or impairment;

(3)   all debts, obligations, and other liabilities of the converting entity continue as debts, obligations, and other liabilities of the converted entity;

(4)   except as otherwise provided by law or the plan of conversion, all the rights, privileges, immunities, powers, and purposes of the converting entity remain in the converted entity;

(5)   the name of the converted entity may be substituted for the name of the converting entity in any pending action or proceeding;

(6)   the certificate of organization of the converted entity becomes effective;

(7)   the provisions of the operating agreement of the converted entity which are to be in a record, if any, approved as part of the plan of conversion become effective; and

(8)   the interests in the converting entity are converted, and the interest holders of the converting entity are entitled only to the rights provided to them under the plan of conversion and to any appraisal rights they have under Section 1006.

(b)   Except as otherwise provided in the operating agreement of a domestic converting limited liability company, the conversion does not give rise to any rights that a member, manager, or third party would have upon a dissolution, liquidation, or winding up of the converting entity.

(c)   When a conversion becomes effective, a person that did not have interest holder liability with respect to the converting entity and becomes subject to interest holder liability with respect to a domestic entity as a result of the conversion has interest holder liability only to the extent provided by the organic law of the entity and only for those debts, obligations, and other liabilities that are incurred after the conversion becomes effective.

(d)   When a conversion becomes effective, the interest holder liability of a person that ceases to hold an interest in a domestic converting limited liability company with respect to which the person had interest holder liability is subject to the following rules:

(1)   The conversion does not discharge any interest holder liability under this [act] to the extent the interest holder liability was incurred before the conversion became effective;

(2)   The person does not have interest holder liability under this [act] for any debt, obligation, or other liability that arises after the conversion becomes effective.

(3)   This [act] continues to apply to the release, collection, or discharge of any interest holder liability preserved under paragraph (1) as if the conversion had not occurred.

(4)   The person has whatever rights of contribution from any other person as are provided by this [act], law other than this [act], or the organic rules of the converting entity with respect to any interest holder liability preserved under paragraph (1) as if the conversion had not occurred.

(e)   When a conversion becomes effective, a foreign entity that is the converted entity may be served with process in this state for the collection and enforcement of any of its debts, obligations, and other liabilities as provided in Section 119.

(f)   If the converting entity is a registered foreign entity, its registration to do business in this state is canceled when the conversion becomes effective.

(g)   A conversion does not require the entity to wind up its affairs and does not constitute or cause the dissolution of the entity.

[PART] 5

DOMESTICATION

§ 1051.   Domestication Authorized

(a)   By complying with this [part], a domestic limited liability company may become a foreign limited liability company if the domestication is authorized by the law of the foreign jurisdiction.

(b)   By complying with the provisions of this [part] applicable to foreign limited liability companies, a foreign limited liability company may become a domestic limited liability company if the domestication is authorized by the law of the foreign limited liability company's jurisdiction of formation.

(c)   If a protected agreement contains a provision that applies to a merger of a domestic limited liability company but does not refer to a domestication, the provision applies to a domestication of the limited liability company as if the domestication were a merger until the provision is amended after [the effective date of this [act]].

§ 1052.   Plan of Domestication

(a)   A domestic limited liability company may become a foreign limited liability company in a domestication by approving a plan of domestication. The plan must be in a record and contain:

(1)   the name of the domesticating limited liability company;

(2)   the name and jurisdiction of formation of the domesticated limited liability company;

(3)   the manner of converting the interests in the domesticating limited liability company into interests, securities, obligations, money, other property, rights to acquire interests or securities, or any combination of the foregoing;

(4)   the proposed certificate of organization of the domesticated limited liability company;

(5)   the full text of the provisions of the operating agreement of the domesticated limited liability company that are proposed to be in a record;

(6)   the other terms and conditions of the domestication; and

(7)   any other provision required by the law of this state or the operating agreement of the domesticating limited liability company.

(b)   In addition to the requirements of subsection (a), a plan of domestication may contain any other provision not prohibited by law.

§ 1053.   Approval of Domestication

(a)   A plan of domestication of a domestic domesticating limited liability company is not effective unless it has been approved:

(1)   by all the members entitled to vote on or consent to any matter; and

(2)   in a record, by each member that will have interest holder liability for debts, obligations, and other liabilities that are incurred after the domestication becomes effective, unless:

(A)   the operating agreement of the domesticating company in a record provides for the approval of a domestication or merger in which some or all of its members become subject to interest holder liability by the affirmative vote or consent of fewer than all the members; and

(B)   the member voted for or consented in a record to that provision of the operating agreement or became a member after the adoption of that provision.

(b)   A domestication of a foreign domesticating limited liability company is not effective unless it is approved in accordance with the law of the foreign limited liability company's jurisdiction of formation.

§ 1054.   Amendment or Abandonment of Plan of Domestication

(a)   A plan of domestication of a domestic domesticating limited liability company may be amended:

(1)   in the same manner as the plan was approved, if the plan does not provide for the manner in which it may be amended; or

(2)   by its managers or members in the manner provided in the plan, but a member that was entitled to vote on or consent to approval of the domestication is entitled to vote on or consent to any amendment of the plan that will change:

(A)   the amount or kind of interests, securities, obligations, money, other property, rights to acquire interests or securities, or any combination of the foregoing, to be received by any of the members of the domesticating limited liability company under the plan;

(B)   the certificate of organization or operating agreement of the domesticated limited liability company that will be in effect immediately after the domestication becomes effective, except for changes that do not require approval of the members of the domesticated limited liability company under its organic law or operating agreement; or

(C)   any other terms or conditions of the plan, if the change would adversely affect the member in any material respect.

(b)   After a plan of domestication has been approved by a domestic domesticating limited liability company and before a statement of domestication becomes effective, the plan may be abandoned as provided in the plan. Unless prohibited by the plan, a domestic domesticating limited liability company may abandon the plan in the same manner as the plan was approved.

(c)   If a plan of domestication is abandoned after a statement of domestication has been delivered to the [Secretary of State] for filing and before the statement becomes effective, a statement of abandonment, signed by the domesticating limited liability company, must be delivered to the [Secretary of State] for filing before the statement of domestication becomes effective. The statement of abandonment takes effect on filing, and the domestication is abandoned and does not become effective. The statement of abandonment must contain:

(1)   the name of the domesticating limited liability company;

(2)   the date on which the statement of domestication was filed by the [Secretary of State]; and

(3)   a statement that the domestication has been abandoned in accordance with this section.

§ 1055.   Statement of Domestication; Effective Date of Domestication

(a)   A statement of domestication must be signed by the domesticating limited liability company and delivered to the [Secretary of State] for filing.

(b)   A statement of domestication must contain:

(1)   the name and jurisdiction of formation of the domesticating limited liability company;

(2)   the name and jurisdiction of formation of the domesticated limited liability company;

(3)   if the domesticating limited liability company is a domestic limited liability company, a statement that the plan of domestication was approved in accordance with this [part] or, if the domesticating limited liability company is a foreign limited liability company, a statement that the domestication was approved in accordance with the law of its jurisdiction of formation; and

(4)   the certificate of organization of the domesticated limited liability company, as an attachment.

(c)   In addition to the requirements of subsection (b), a statement of domestication may contain any other provision not prohibited by law.

(d)   The certificate of organization of a domestic domesticated limited liability company must satisfy the requirements of this [act], but the certificate does not need to be signed.

(e)   A plan of domestication that is signed by a domesticating domestic limited liability company and meets all the requirements of subsection (b) may be delivered to the [Secretary of State] for filing instead of a statement of domestication and on filing has the same effect. If a plan of domestication is filed as provided in this subsection, references in this [article] to a statement of domestication refer to the plan of domestication filed under this subsection.

(f)   If the domesticated entity is a domestic limited liability company, the domestication becomes effective when the statement of domestication is effective. If the domesticated entity is a foreign limited liability company, the domestication becomes effective on the later of:

(1)   the date and time provided by the organic law of the domesticated entity; and

(2)   when the statement is effective.

§ 1056. Effect of Domestication

(a)   When a domestication becomes effective:

(1)   the domesticated entity is:

(A)   organized under and subject to the organic law of the domesticated entity; and

(B)   the same entity without interruption as the domesticating entity;

(2)   all property of the domesticating entity continues to be vested in the domesticated entity without transfer, reversion, or impairment;

(3)   all debts, obligations, and other liabilities of the domesticating entity continue as debts, obligations, and other liabilities of the domesticated entity;

(4)   except as otherwise provided by law or the plan of domestication, all the rights, privileges, immunities, powers, and purposes of the domesticating entity remain in the domesticated entity;

(5)   the name of the domesticated entity may be substituted for the name of the domesticating entity in any pending action or proceeding;

(6)   the certificate of organization of the domesticated entity becomes effective;

(7)   the provisions of the operating agreement of the domesticated entity that are to be in a record, if any, approved as part of the plan of domestication become effective; and

(8)   the interests in the domesticating entity are converted to the extent and as approved in connection with the domestication, and the members of the domesticating entity are entitled only to the rights provided to them under the plan of domestication and to any appraisal rights they have under Section 1006.

(b)   Except as otherwise provided in the organic law or operating agreement of the domesticating limited liability company, the domestication does not give rise to any rights that a member, manager, or third party would otherwise have upon a dissolution, liquidation, or winding up of the domesticating company.

(c)   When a domestication becomes effective, a person that did not have interest holder liability with respect to the domesticating limited liability company and becomes subject to interest holder liability with respect to a domestic company as a result of the domestication has interest holder liability only to the extent provided by this [act] and only for those debts, obligations, and other liabilities that are incurred after the domestication becomes effective.

(d)   When a domestication becomes effective, the interest holder liability of a person that ceases to hold an interest in a domestic domesticating limited liability company with respect to which the person had interest holder liability is subject to the following rules:

(1)   The domestication does not discharge any interest holder liability under this [act] to the extent the interest holder liability was incurred before the domestication became effective.

(2)   A person does not have interest holder liability under this [act] for any debt, obligation, or other liability that is incurred after the domestication becomes effective.

(3)   This [act] continues to apply to the release, collection, or discharge of any interest holder liability preserved under paragraph (1) as if the domestication had not occurred.

(4)   A person has whatever rights of contribution from any other person as are provided by this [act], law other than this [act], or the operating agreement of the domestic domesticating limited liability company with respect to any interest holder liability preserved under paragraph (1) as if the domestication had not occurred.

(e)   When a domestication becomes effective, a foreign limited liability company that is the domesticated company may be served with process in this state for the collection and enforcement of any of its debts, obligations, and other liabilities as provided in Section 119.

(f)   If the domesticating limited liability company is a registered foreign entity, the registration of the company is canceled when the domestication becomes effective.

(g)   A domestication does not require a domestic domesticating limited liability company to wind up its affairs and does not constitute or cause the dissolution of the company.

[ARTICLE] 11
MISCELLANEOUS PROVISIONS

§ 1101.   Uniformity of Application and Construction

In applying and construing this uniform act, consideration must be given to the need to promote uniformity of the law with respect to its subject matter among states that enact it.

§ 1102.   Relation to Electronic Signatures in Global and National Commerce Act

This [act] modifies, limits, and supersedes the Electronic Signatures in Global and National Commerce Act, 15 U.S.C. Section 7001 et seq., but does not modify, limit, or supersede Section 101(c) of that act, 15 U.S.C. Section 7001(c), or authorize electronic delivery of any of the notices described in Section 103(b) of that act, 15 U.S.C. Section 7003(b).

§ 1103.   Savings Clause

This [act] does not affect an action commenced, proceeding brought, or right accrued before [the effective date of this [act]].

§ 1104.   Severability Clause

If any provision of this [act] or its application to any person or circumstance is held invalid, the invalidity does not affect other provisions or applications of this [act] which can be given effect without the invalid provision or application, and to this end the provisions of this [act] are severable.]

Legislative Note: Include this section only if this state lacks a general severability statute or decision by the highest court of this state stating a general rule of severability.

§ 1105.   Repeals

The following are repealed:

(1)   [the state limited liability company act, as [amended, and as] in effect immediately before [the effective date of this [act]];

(2)   . . . .

(3)   . . . .

§ 1106.   Effective Date

This [act] takes effect . . . .

C. DELAWARE LIMITED LIABILITY COMPANY ACT

Delaware Code, Title 6, Chapter 18

Table of Contents

SUBCHAPTER I. GENERAL PROVISIONS

SUBCHAPTER II. FORMATION; CERTIFICATE OF FORMATION

1145

DELAWARE LIMITED LIABILITY COMPANY ACT

SUBCHAPTER III. MEMBERS

SUBCHAPTER IV. MANAGERS

SUBCHAPTER V. FINANCE

SUBCHAPTER VI. DISTRIBUTIONS AND RESIGNATION

SUBCHAPTER VII. ASSIGNMENT OF LIMITED LIABILITY COMPANY INTERESTS

SUBCHAPTER VIII. DISSOLUTION

SUBCHAPTER IX.   FOREIGN LIMITED LIABILITY COMPANIES

SUBCHAPTER X.   DERIVATIVE ACTIONS

SUBCHAPTER XI.   MISCELLANEOUS

SUBCHAPTER XII.   STATUTORY PUBLIC BENEFIT LIMITED LIABILITY COMPANIES

SUBCHAPTER I.   GENERAL PROVISIONS

§ 18–101.   Definitions.

As used in this chapter unless the context otherwise requires:

(1)   "Bankruptcy" means an event that causes a person to cease to be a member as provided in § 18–304 of this title.

(2)   "Certificate of formation" means the certificate referred to in § 18–201 of this title, and the certificate as amended.

(3)   "Contribution" means any cash, property, services rendered or a promissory note or other obligation to contribute cash or property or to perform services, which a person contributes to a limited liability company in the person's capacity as a member.

(4)   "Document" means:

a.   Any tangible medium on which information is inscribed, and includes handwritten, typed, printed or similar instruments, and copies of such instruments; and

b.   An electronic transmission.

(5)   "Electronic transmission" means any form of communication not directly involving the physical transmission of paper, including the use of, or participation in, 1 or more electronic networks or databases (including 1 or more distributed electronic networks or databases), that creates a record that may be retained, retrieved and reviewed by a recipient thereof and that may be directly reproduced in paper form by such a recipient through an automated process.

(6)   "Foreign limited liability company" means a limited liability company formed under the laws of any state or under the laws of any foreign country or other foreign jurisdiction. When used in this title in reference to a foreign limited liability company, the terms "limited liability company agreement," "limited liability company interest," "manager" or "member" shall mean a limited liability company agreement, limited liability company interest, manager or member, respectively, under the laws of the state or foreign country or other foreign jurisdiction under which the foreign limited liability company is formed.

(7)   "Knowledge" means a person's actual knowledge of a fact, rather than the person's constructive knowledge of the fact.

(8)   "Limited liability company" and "domestic limited liability company" means a limited liability company formed under the laws of the State of Delaware and having 1 or more members.

(9)   "Limited liability company agreement" means any agreement (whether referred to as a limited liability company agreement, operating agreement or otherwise), written, oral or implied, of the member or members as to the affairs of a limited liability company and the conduct of its business. A member or manager of a limited liability company or an assignee of a limited liability company interest is bound by the limited liability company agreement whether or not the member or manager or assignee executes the limited liability company agreement. A limited liability company is not required to execute its limited liability company agreement. A limited liability company is bound by its limited liability company agreement whether or not the limited liability company executes the limited liability company agreement. A limited liability company agreement of a limited liability company having only 1 member shall not be unenforceable by reason of there being only 1 person who is a party to the limited liability company agreement. A limited liability company agreement is not subject to any statute of frauds (including § 2714 of this title). A limited liability company agreement may provide rights to any person, including a person who is not a party to the limited liability company agreement, to the extent set forth therein. A written limited liability company agreement or another written agreement or writing:

a.   May provide that a person shall be admitted as a member of a limited liability company, or shall become an assignee of a limited liability company interest or other rights or powers of a member to the extent assigned:

1.   If such person (or a representative authorized by such person orally, in writing or by other action such as payment for a limited liability company interest)

executes the limited liability company agreement or any other writing evidencing the intent of such person to become a member or assignee; or

    2.   Without such execution, if such person (or a representative authorized by such person orally, in writing or by other action such as payment for a limited liability company interest) complies with the conditions for becoming a member or assignee as set forth in the limited liability company agreement or any other writing; and

    b.   Shall not be unenforceable by reason of its not having been signed by a person being admitted as a member or becoming an assignee as provided in paragraph (7)a. of this section, or by reason of its having been signed by a representative as provided in this chapter.

(10) "Limited liability company interest" means a member's share of the profits and losses of a limited liability company and a member's right to receive distributions of the limited liability company's assets.

(11) "Liquidating trustee" means a person carrying out the winding up of a limited liability company.

(12) "Manager" means a person who is named as a manager of a limited liability company in, or designated as a manager of a limited liability company pursuant to, a limited liability company agreement or similar instrument under which the limited liability company is formed, and includes a manager of the limited liability company generally and a manager associated with a series of the limited liability company. Unless the context otherwise requires, references in this chapter to a manager (including references in this chapter to a manager of a limited liability company) shall be deemed to be references to a manager of the limited liability company generally and to a manager associated with a series with respect to such series.

(13) "Member" means a person who is admitted to a limited liability company as a member as provided in § 18–301 of this title, and includes a member of the limited liability company generally and a member associated with a series of the limited liability company. Unless the context otherwise requires, references in this chapter to a member (including references in this chapter to a member of a limited liability company) shall be deemed to be references to a member of the limited liability company generally and to a member associated with a series with respect to such series.

(14) "Person" means a natural person, partnership (whether general or limited), limited liability company, trust (including a common law trust, business trust, statutory trust, voting trust or any other form of trust), estate, association (including any group, organization, co-tenancy, plan, board, council or committee), corporation, government (including a country, state, county or any other governmental subdivision, agency or instrumentality), custodian, nominee or any other individual or entity (or series thereof) in its own or any representative capacity, in each case, whether domestic or foreign.

(15) "Personal representative" means, as to a natural person, the executor, administrator, guardian, conservator or other legal representative thereof and, as to a person other than a natural person, the legal representative or successor thereof.

(16) "Protected series" means a designated series of members, managers, limited liability company interests or assets that is established in accordance with § 18–215(b) of this title.

(17) "Registered series" means a designated series of members, managers, limited liability company interests or assets that is formed in accordance with § 18–218 of this title.

(18) "Series" means a designated series of members, managers, limited liability company interests or assets that is a protected series or a registered series, or that is neither a protected series nor a registered series.

(19) "State" means the District of Columbia or the Commonwealth of Puerto Rico or any state, territory, possession or other jurisdiction of the United States other than the State of Delaware.

§ 18–102.   Name set forth in certificate.

The name of each limited liability company as set forth in its certificate of formation:

(1) Shall contain the words "Limited Liability Company" or the abbreviation "L.L.C." or the designation "LLC";

(2) May contain the name of a member or manager;

(3) Must be such as to distinguish it upon the records in the office of the Secretary of State from the name on such records of any corporation, partnership, limited partnership, statutory trust, limited liability company, registered series of a limited liability company or registered series of a limited partnership reserved, registered, formed or organized under the laws of the State of Delaware or qualified to do business or registered as a foreign corporation, foreign limited partnership, foreign statutory trust, foreign partnership, or foreign limited liability company in the State of Delaware; provided however, that a limited liability company may register under any name which is not such as to distinguish it upon the records in the office of the Secretary of State from the name on such records of any domestic or foreign corporation, partnership, limited partnership, statutory trust, registered series of a limited liability company, registered series of a limited partnership or foreign limited liability company reserved, registered, formed or organized under the laws of the State of Delaware with the written consent of the other corporation, partnership, limited partnership, statutory trust, registered series of a limited liability company, registered series of a limited partnership or foreign limited liability company, which written consent shall be filed with the Secretary of State; provided further, that, if on July 31, 2011, a limited liability company is registered (with the consent of another limited liability company) under a name which is not such as to distinguish it upon the records in the office of the Secretary of State from the name on such records of such other domestic limited liability company, it shall not be necessary for any such limited liability company to amend its certificate of formation to comply with this subsection;

(4) May contain the following words: "Company," "Association," "Club," "Foundation," "Fund," "Institute," "Society," "Union," "Syndicate," "Limited", "Public Benefit" or "Trust" (or abbreviations of like import); and

(5) Shall not contain the word "bank," or any variation thereof, except for the name of a bank reporting to and under the supervision of the State Bank Commissioner of this State or a subsidiary of a bank or savings association (as those terms are defined in the Federal Deposit Insurance Act, as amended, at 12 U.S.C. § 1813), or a limited liability company regulated under the Bank Holding Company Act of 1956, as amended, 12 U.S.C. § 1841 et seq., or the Home Owners' Loan Act, as amended, 12 U.S.C. § 1461 et seq.; provided, however, that this section shall not be construed to prevent the use of the word "bank," or any variation thereof, in a context clearly not purporting to refer to a banking business or otherwise likely to mislead the public about the nature of the business of the limited liability company or to lead to a pattern and practice of abuse that might cause harm to the interests of the public or this State as determined by the Division of Corporations in the Department of State.

§ 18–103.   Reservation of name.

(a) The exclusive right to the use of a name may be reserved by:

(1) Any person intending to organize a limited liability company under this chapter and to adopt that name;

(2)   Any person intending to form a registered series of a limited liability company under this chapter and to adopt that name in accordance with § 18–218(e) of this title;

(3)   Any domestic limited liability company or any foreign limited liability company registered in the State of Delaware which, in either case, proposes to change its name;

(4)   Any foreign limited liability company intending to register in the State of Delaware and adopt that name; and

(5)   Any person intending to organize a foreign limited liability company and intending to have it register in the State of Delaware and adopt that name.

(b)   The reservation of a specified name shall be made by filing with the Secretary of State an application, executed by the applicant, specifying the name to be reserved and the name and address of the applicant. If the Secretary of State finds that the name is available for use by a domestic or foreign limited liability company, the Secretary shall reserve the name for the exclusive use of the applicant for a period of 120 days. Once having so reserved a name, the same applicant may again reserve the same name for successive 120-day periods. The right to the exclusive use of a reserved name may be transferred to any other person by filing in the office of the Secretary of State a notice of the transfer, executed by the applicant for whom the name was reserved, specifying the name to be transferred and the name and address of the transferee. The reservation of a specified name may be canceled by filing with the Secretary of State a notice of cancellation, executed by the applicant or transferee, specifying the name reservation to be canceled and the name and address of the applicant or transferee. Unless the Secretary of State finds that any application, notice of transfer, or notice of cancellation filed with the Secretary of State as required by this subsection does not conform to law, upon receipt of all filing fees required by law the Secretary shall prepare and return to the person who filed such instrument a copy of the filed instrument with a notation thereon of the action taken by the Secretary of State.

(c)   A fee as set forth in § 18–1105(a)(1) of this title shall be paid at the time of the initial reservation of any name, at the time of the renewal of any such reservation and at the time of the filing of a notice of the transfer or cancellation of any such reservation.

§ 18–104.   Registered office; registered agent.

(a)   Each limited liability company shall have and maintain in the State of Delaware:

(1)   A registered office, which may but need not be a place of its business in the State of Delaware; and

(2)   A registered agent for service of process on the limited liability company, having a business office identical with such registered office, which agent may be any of:

a.   The limited liability company itself,

b.   An individual resident in the State of Delaware,

c.   A domestic limited liability company (other than the limited liability company itself), a domestic corporation, a domestic partnership (whether general (including a limited liability partnership) or limited (including a limited liability limited partnership)), or a domestic statutory trust, or

d.   A foreign corporation, a foreign partnership (whether general (including a limited liability partnership) or limited (including a limited liability limited partnership)), a foreign limited liability company, or a foreign statutory trust.

(b)   A registered agent may change the address of the registered office of the limited liability company(ies) for which it is registered agent to another address in the State of Delaware by paying a fee as set forth in § 18–1105(a)(2) of this title and filing with the Secretary of State a certificate, executed by such registered agent, setting forth the address at which such registered agent has maintained the registered office for each of the limited liability companies for which it is a registered agent, and further certifying to the new address to which each such registered office will be changed on a given day, and at which new address such registered agent will thereafter maintain the registered office for each of the limited liability companies for which it is a registered agent. Upon the filing of such certificate, the Secretary of State shall furnish to the registered agent a certified copy of the same under the Secretary's hand and seal of office, and thereafter, or until further change of address, as authorized by law, the registered office in the State of Delaware of each of the limited liability companies for which the agent is a registered agent shall be located at the new address of the registered agent thereof as given in the certificate. In the event of a change of name of any person acting as a registered agent of a limited liability company, such registered agent shall file with the Secretary of State a certificate executed by such registered agent setting forth the new name of such registered agent, the name of such registered agent before it was changed, and the address at which such registered agent has maintained the registered office for each of the limited liability companies for which it is a registered agent, and shall pay a fee as set forth in § 18–1105(a)(2) of this title. Upon the filing of such certificate, the Secretary of State shall furnish to the registered agent a certified copy of the certificate under the Secretary of State's own hand and seal of office. A change of name of any person acting as a registered agent of a limited liability company as a result of a merger or consolidation of the registered agent with or into another person which succeeds to its assets and liabilities by operation of law shall be deemed a change of name for purposes of this section. Filing a certificate under this section shall be deemed to be an amendment of the certificate of formation of each limited liability company affected thereby, and each such limited liability company shall not be required to take any further action with respect thereto to amend its certificate of formation under § 18–202 of this title. Any registered agent filing a certificate under this section shall promptly, upon such filing, deliver a copy of any such certificate to each limited liability company affected thereby.

(c)   The registered agent of 1 or more limited liability companies may resign and appoint a successor registered agent by paying a fee as set forth in § 18–1105(a)(2) of this title and filing a certificate with the Secretary of State stating that it resigns and the name and address of the successor registered agent. There shall be attached to such certificate a statement of each affected limited liability company ratifying and approving such change of registered agent. Upon such filing, the successor registered agent shall become the registered agent of such limited liability companies as have ratified and approved such substitution, and the successor registered agent's address, as stated in such certificate, shall become the address of each such limited liability company's registered office in the State of Delaware. The Secretary of State shall then issue a certificate that the successor registered agent has become the registered agent of the limited liability companies so ratifying and approving such change and setting out the names of such limited liability companies. Filing of such certificate of resignation shall be deemed to be an amendment of the certificate of formation of each limited liability company affected thereby, and each such limited liability company shall not be required to take any further action with respect thereto to amend its certificate of formation under § 18–202 of this title.

(d)   The registered agent of a limited liability company, including a limited liability company whose certificate of formation has been cancelled pursuant to § 18–1108 of this title, may resign without appointing a successor registered agent by paying a fee as set forth in § 18–1105(a)(2) of this title and filing a certificate of resignation with the Secretary of State, but such resignation shall not become effective until 30 days after the certificate is filed. The certificate shall contain a statement that written notice of resignation was given to the limited liability company at least 30 days prior to the filing of the certificate by mailing or delivering such notice to the limited liability company at its address last known to the registered agent and shall set forth the date of such notice. The certificate shall include such information last provided to the registered agent pursuant to subsection (g) of this section of this title for a communications contact for the limited liability company. Such information regarding the communications contact shall not be deemed public. A certificate filed pursuant to this subsection must be on the form prescribed by the Secretary of State. After receipt of the notice of the resignation of its registered agent, the limited liability company for which such registered agent was acting shall obtain and designate a new registered agent, to take the place of the registered agent so resigning. If such limited liability company fails to obtain and designate a new registered agent as aforesaid prior to the expiration of the period of 30 days after the filing by the registered agent of the certificate of resignation, the certificate of formation of such limited liability company shall be canceled. After the resignation of the registered agent shall have become effective as provided in this section and if no new registered agent shall have been obtained and designated in the time and manner aforesaid, service of legal process against each limited liability company (and each protected series and each registered series thereof) for which the resigned registered agent had been acting shall thereafter be upon the Secretary of State in accordance with § 18–105 of this title.

(e)   Every registered agent shall:

(1)   If an entity, maintain a business office in the State of Delaware which is generally open, or if an individual, be generally present at a designated location in the State of Delaware, at sufficiently frequent times to accept service of process and otherwise perform the functions of a registered agent;

(2)   If a foreign entity, be authorized to transact business in the State of Delaware;

(3)   Accept service of process and other communications directed to the limited liability companies (and any protected series or registered series thereof) and foreign limited liability companies for which it serves as registered agent and forward same to the limited liability company or foreign limited liability company to which the service or communication is directed;

(4)   Forward to the limited liability companies and foreign limited liability companies for which it serves as registered agent the statement for the annual tax for such limited liability company (and each registered series thereof) or such foreign limited liability company, as applicable, as described in § 18–1107 of this title or an electronic notification of same in a form satisfactory to the Secretary of State; and

(5)   Satisfy and adhere to regulations established by the Secretary regarding the verification of both the identity of the entity's contacts and individuals for which the registered agent maintains a record for the reduction of risk of unlawful business purposes.

(f)   Any registered agent who at any time serves as registered agent for more than 50 entities (a "commercial registered agent"), whether domestic or foreign, shall satisfy and comply with the following qualifications:

(1)   A natural person serving as a commercial registered agent shall:

a.   Maintain a principal residence or a principal place of business in the State of Delaware;

b.   Maintain a Delaware business license;

c.   Be generally present at a designated location within the State of Delaware during normal business hours to accept service of process and otherwise perform the functions of a registered agent as specified in subsection (e) of this section;

d.   Provide the Secretary of State upon request with such information identifying and enabling communication with such commercial registered agent as the Secretary of State shall require; and

e.   Satisfy and adhere to regulations established by the Secretary regarding the verification of both the identity of the entity's contacts and individuals for which the natural person maintains a record for the reduction of risk of unlawful business purposes.

(2)   A domestic or foreign corporation, a domestic or foreign partnership (whether general (including a limited liability partnership) or limited (including a limited liability limited partnership)), a domestic or foreign limited liability company, or a domestic or foreign statutory trust serving as a commercial registered agent shall:

    a.   Have a business office within the State of Delaware which is generally open during normal business hours to accept service of process and otherwise perform the functions of a registered agent as specified in subsection (e) of this section;

    b.   Maintain a Delaware business license;

    c.   Have generally present at such office during normal business hours an officer, director or managing agent who is a natural person;

    d.   Provide the Secretary of State upon request with such information identifying and enabling communication with such commercial registered agent as the Secretary of State shall require; and

    e.   Satisfy and adhere to regulations established by the Secretary regarding the verification of both the identity of the entity's contacts and individuals for which it maintains a record for the reduction of risk of unlawful business purposes.

    (3)   For purposes of this subsection and paragraph (i)(2)a. of this section, a commercial registered agent shall also include any registered agent which has an officer, director or managing agent in common with any other registered agent or agents if such registered agents at any time during such common service as officer, director or managing agent collectively served as registered agents for more than 50 entities, whether domestic or foreign.

    (g)   Every domestic limited liability company and every foreign limited liability company qualified to do business in the State of Delaware shall provide to its registered agent and update from time to time as necessary the name, business address and business telephone number of a natural person who is a member, manager, officer, employee or designated agent of the domestic or foreign limited liability company who is then authorized to receive communications from the registered agent. Such person shall be deemed the communications contact for the domestic or foreign limited liability company. A domestic limited liability company, upon receipt of a request by the communications contact delivered in writing or by electronic transmission, shall provide the communications contact with the name, business address and business telephone number of a natural person who has access to the record required to be maintained pursuant to § 18–305(h) of this title. Every registered agent shall retain (in paper or electronic form) the above information concerning the current communications contact for each domestic limited liability company and each foreign limited liability company for which that registered agent serves as registered agent. If the domestic or foreign limited liability company fails to provide the registered agent with a current communications contact, the registered agent may resign as the registered agent for such domestic or foreign limited liability company pursuant to this section.

    (h)   The Secretary of State is fully authorized to issue such regulations, as may be necessary or appropriate to carry out the enforcement of subsections (e), (f) and (g) of this section, and to take actions reasonable and necessary to assure registered agents' compliance with subsections (e), (f) and (g) of this section. Such actions may include refusal to file documents submitted by a registered agent, including the refusal to file any documents regarding an entity's formation.

    (i)   Upon application of the Secretary of State, the Court of Chancery may enjoin any person or entity from serving as a registered agent or as an officer, director or managing agent of a registered agent.

    (1)   Upon the filing of a complaint by the Secretary of State pursuant to this section, the court may make such orders respecting such proceeding as it deems appropriate, and may enter such orders granting interim or final relief as it deems proper under the circumstances.

    (2)   Any 1 or more of the following grounds shall be a sufficient basis to grant an injunction pursuant to this section:

    a.   With respect to any registered agent who at any time within 1 year immediately prior to the filing of the Secretary of State's complaint is a commercial registered agent, failure after notice and warning to comply with the qualifications set forth in subsection (e) of this section and/or the requirements of subsection (f) or (g) of this section above;

    b.   The person serving as a registered agent, or any person who is an officer, director or managing agent of an entity registered agent, has been convicted of a felony or any crime which includes an element of dishonesty or fraud or involves moral turpitude; or

    c.   The registered agent has engaged in conduct in connection with acting as a registered agent that is intended to or likely to deceive or defraud the public.

(3)   With respect to any order the court enters pursuant to this section with respect to an entity that has acted as a registered agent, the Court may also direct such order to any person who has served as an officer, director or managing agent of such registered agent. Any person who, on or after January 1, 2007, serves as an officer, director or managing agent of an entity acting as a registered agent in the State of Delaware shall be deemed thereby to have consented to the appointment of such registered agent as agent upon whom service of process may be made in any action brought pursuant to this section, and service as an officer, director or managing agent of an entity acting as a registered agent in the State of Delaware shall be a signification of the consent of such person that any process when so served shall be of the same legal force and validity as if served upon such person within the State of Delaware, and such appointment of the registered agent shall be irrevocable.

(4)   Upon the entry of an order by the Court enjoining any person or entity from acting as a registered agent, the Secretary of State shall mail or deliver notice of such order to each affected domestic or foreign limited liability company:

    a.   That has specified the address of a place of business in a record of the Secretary of State, to the address specified, or

    b.   An address of which the Secretary of State has obtained from the domestic or foreign limited liability company's former registered agent, to the address obtained.

If such a domestic limited liability company fails to obtain and designate a new registered agent within 30 days after such notice is given, the certificate of formation of such limited liability company shall be canceled. If such a foreign limited liability company fails to obtain and designate a new registered agent within 30 days after such notice is given, such foreign limited liability company shall not be permitted to do business in the State of Delaware and its registration shall be canceled. If any other affected domestic limited liability company fails to obtain and designate a new registered agent within 60 days after entry of an order by the Court enjoining such limited liability company's registered agent from acting as a registered agent, the certificate of formation of such limited liability company shall be canceled. If any other affected foreign limited liability company fails to obtain and designate a new registered agent within 60 days after entry of an order by the Court enjoining such foreign limited liability company's registered agent from acting as a registered agent, such foreign limited liability company shall not be permitted to do business in the State of Delaware and its registration shall be canceled. If the Court enjoins a person or entity from acting as a registered agent as provided in this section and no new registered agent shall have been obtained and designated in the time and manner aforesaid, service of legal process against the domestic or foreign limited liability company for which the registered agent had been acting shall thereafter be upon the Secretary of State in accordance with § 18–105 or § 18–911 of this title. The Court of Chancery may, upon application of the Secretary of State on notice to the former registered agent, enter such orders as it deems appropriate to give the Secretary of State access to information in the former registered agent's possession in order to facilitate communication with the domestic and foreign limited liability companies the former registered agent served.

(j)   The Secretary of State is authorized to make a list of registered agents available to the public, and to establish such qualifications and issue such rules and regulations with respect to such listing as the Secretary of State deems necessary or appropriate.

(k) As contained in any certificate of formation, application for registration as a foreign limited liability company, or other document filed in the office of the Secretary of State under this chapter, the address of a registered agent or registered office shall include the street, number, city and postal code.

§ 18–105. Service of process on domestic limited liability companies and protected series or registered series thereof.

(a) Service of legal process upon any domestic limited liability company or any protected series or registered series thereof shall be made by delivering a copy personally to any manager of the limited liability company in the State of Delaware, or the registered agent of the limited liability company in the State of Delaware, or by leaving it at the dwelling house or usual place of abode in the State of Delaware of any such manager or registered agent (if the registered agent be an individual), or at the registered office or other place of business of the limited liability company in the State of Delaware. If service of legal process is made upon the registered agent of the limited liability company in the State of Delaware on behalf of any such protected series or registered series, such process shall include the name of the limited liability company and the name of such protected series or registered series. If the registered agent be a corporation, service of process upon it as such may be made by serving, in the State of Delaware, a copy thereof on the president, vice-president, secretary, assistant secretary or any director of the corporate registered agent. Service by copy left at the dwelling house or usual place of abode of a manager or registered agent, or at the registered office or other place of business of the limited liability company in the State of Delaware, to be effective, must be delivered thereat at least 6 days before the return date of the process, and in the presence of an adult person, and the officer serving the process shall distinctly state the manner of service in the officer's return thereto. Process returnable forthwith must be delivered personally to the manager or registered agent.

(b) In case the officer whose duty it is to serve legal process cannot by due diligence serve the process in any manner provided for by subsection (a) of this section, it shall be lawful to serve the process against the limited liability company or any protected series or registered series thereof upon the Secretary of State, and such service shall be as effectual for all intents and purposes as if made in any of the ways provided for in subsection (a) of this section. If service of legal process is made upon the Secretary of State on behalf of any such protected series or registered series, such process shall include the name of the limited liability company and the name of such protected series or registered series. Process may be served upon the Secretary of State under this subsection by means of electronic transmission but only as prescribed by the Secretary of State. The Secretary of State is authorized to issue such rules and regulations with respect to such service as the Secretary of State deems necessary or appropriate. In the event that service is effected through the Secretary of State in accordance with this subsection, the Secretary of State shall forthwith notify the limited liability company by letter, directed to the limited liability company at its address as it appears on the records relating to such limited liability company on file with the Secretary of State or, if no such address appears, at its last registered office. Such letter shall be sent by a mail or courier service that includes a record of mailing or deposit with the courier and a record of delivery evidenced by the signature of the recipient. Such letter shall enclose a copy of the process and any other papers served on the Secretary of State pursuant to this subsection. It shall be the duty of the plaintiff in the event of such service to serve process and any other papers in duplicate, to notify the Secretary of State that service is being effected pursuant to this subsection, and to pay the Secretary of State the sum of $50 for the use of the State of Delaware, which sum shall be taxed as part of the costs in the proceeding if the plaintiff shall prevail therein. The Secretary of State shall maintain an alphabetical record of any such service setting forth the name of the plaintiff and defendant, the title, docket number and nature of the proceeding in which process has been served upon the Secretary, the fact that service has been effected pursuant to this subsection, the return date thereof, and the day and hour when the service was made. The Secretary of State shall not be required to retain such information for a period longer than 5 years from the Secretary's receipt of the service of process.

§ 18–106.   Nature of business permitted; powers.

(a)   A limited liability company may carry on any lawful business, purpose or activity, whether or not for profit, with the exception of the business of banking as defined in § 126 of Title 8.

(b)   A limited liability company shall possess and may exercise all the powers and privileges granted by this chapter or by any other law or by its limited liability company agreement, together with any powers incidental thereto, including such powers and privileges as are necessary or convenient to the conduct, promotion or attainment of the business, purposes or activities of the limited liability company.

(c)   Notwithstanding any provision of this chapter to the contrary, without limiting the general powers enumerated in subsection (b) of this section, a limited liability company shall, subject to such standards and restrictions, if any, as are set forth in its limited liability company agreement, have the power and authority to make contracts of guaranty and suretyship and enter into interest rate, basis, currency, hedge or other swap agreements or cap, floor, put, call, option, exchange or collar agreements, derivative agreements, or other agreements similar to any of the foregoing.

(d)   Unless otherwise provided in a limited liability company agreement, a limited liability company has the power and authority to grant, hold or exercise a power of attorney, including an irrevocable power of attorney.

§ 18–107.   Business transactions of member or manager with the limited liability company.

Except as provided in a limited liability company agreement, a member or manager may lend money to, borrow money from, act as a surety, guarantor or endorser for, guarantee or assume 1 or more obligations of, provide collateral for, and transact other business with, a limited liability company and, subject to other applicable law, has the same rights and obligations with respect to any such matter as a person who is not a member or manager.

§ 18–108.   Indemnification.

Subject to such standards and restrictions, if any, as are set forth in its limited liability company agreement, a limited liability company may, and shall have the power to, indemnify and hold harmless any member or manager or other person from and against any and all claims and demands whatsoever.

§ 18–109.   Service of process on managers and liquidating trustees.

(a)   A manager or a liquidating trustee of a limited liability company may be served with process in the manner prescribed in this section in all civil actions or proceedings brought in the State of Delaware involving or relating to the business of the limited liability company or a violation by the manager or the liquidating trustee of a duty to the limited liability company or any member of the limited liability company, whether or not the manager or the liquidating trustee is a manager or a liquidating trustee at the time suit is commenced. A manager's or a liquidating trustee's serving as such constitutes such person's consent to the appointment of the registered agent of the limited liability company (or, if there is none, the Secretary of State) as such person's agent upon whom service of process may be made as provided in this section. Such service as a manager or a liquidating trustee shall signify the consent of such manager or liquidating trustee that any process when so served shall be of the same legal force and validity as if served upon such manager or liquidating trustee within the State of Delaware and such appointment of the registered agent (or, if there is none, the Secretary of State) shall be irrevocable. As used in this subsection (a) and in subsections (b), (c) and (d) of this section, the term "manager" refers (i) to a person who is a manager as defined in § 18–101 of this title and (ii) to a person, whether or not a member of a limited liability company, who, although not a "manager" as defined in § 18–101 of this title, participates materially in the management of the limited liability company; provided however, that the power to elect or otherwise select or to participate in the election or selection of a person to be a "manager" as defined in § 18–101 of this title shall not, by itself, constitute participation in the management of the limited liability company.

(b)   Service of process shall be effected by serving the registered agent (or, if there is none, the Secretary of State) with 1 copy of such process in the manner provided by law for service of writs of summons. In the event service is made under this subsection upon the Secretary of State, the plaintiff shall pay to the Secretary of State the sum of $50 for the use of the State of Delaware, which sum shall be taxed as part of the costs of the proceeding if the plaintiff shall prevail therein. In addition, the Prothonotary or the Register in Chancery of the court in which the civil action or proceeding is pending shall, within 7 days of such service, deposit in the United States mails, by registered mail, postage prepaid, true and attested copies of the process, together with a statement that service is being made pursuant to this section, addressed to such manager or liquidating trustee at the registered office of the limited liability company and at the manager's or liquidating trustee's address last known to the party desiring to make such service.

(c)   In any action in which any such manager or liquidating trustee has been served with process as hereinabove provided, the time in which a defendant shall be required to appear and file a responsive pleading shall be computed from the date of mailing by the Prothonotary or the Register in Chancery as provided in subsection (b) of this section; however, the court in which such action has been commenced may order such continuance or continuances as may be necessary to afford such manager or liquidating trustee reasonable opportunity to defend the action.

(d)   In a written limited liability company agreement or other writing, a manager or member may consent to be subject to the nonexclusive jurisdiction of the courts of, or arbitration in, a specified jurisdiction, or the exclusive jurisdiction of the courts of the State of Delaware, or the exclusivity of arbitration in a specified jurisdiction or the State of Delaware, and to be served with legal process in the manner prescribed in such limited liability company agreement or other writing. Except by agreeing to arbitrate any arbitrable matter in a specified jurisdiction or in the State of Delaware, a member who is not a manager may not waive its right to maintain a legal action or proceeding in the courts of the State of Delaware with respect to matters relating to the organization or internal affairs of a limited liability company.

(e)   Nothing herein contained limits or affects the right to serve process in any other manner now or hereafter provided by law. This section is an extension of and not a limitation upon the right otherwise existing of service of legal process upon nonresidents.

(f)   The Court of Chancery and the Superior Court may make all necessary rules respecting the form of process, the manner of issuance and return thereof and such other rules which may be necessary to implement this section and are not inconsistent with this section.

§ 18–110.   Contested matters relating to managers; contested votes.

(a)   Upon application of any member or manager, the Court of Chancery may hear and determine the validity of any admission, election, appointment, removal or resignation of a manager of a limited liability company, and the right of any person to become or continue to be a manager of a limited liability company, and, in case the right to serve as a manager is claimed by more than 1 person, may determine the person or persons entitled to serve as managers; and to that end make such order or decree in any such case as may be just and proper, with power to enforce the production of any books, papers and records of the limited liability company relating to the issue. In any such application, the limited liability company shall be named as a party and service of copies of the application upon the registered agent of the limited liability company shall be deemed to be service upon the limited liability company and upon the person or persons whose right to serve as a manager is contested and upon the person or persons, if any, claiming to be a manager or claiming the right to be a manager; and the registered agent shall forward immediately a copy of the application to the limited liability company and to the person or persons whose right to serve as a manager is contested and to the person or persons, if any, claiming to be a manager or the right to be a manager, in a postpaid, sealed, registered letter addressed to such limited liability company and such person or persons at their post-office addresses last known to the registered agent or furnished to the registered agent by the applicant member or manager. The Court may make such order respecting further or other notice of such application as it deems proper under these circumstances.

(b)   Upon application of any member or manager, the Court of Chancery may hear and determine the result of any vote of members or managers upon matters as to which the members or managers of the limited liability company, or any class or group of members or managers, have the right to vote pursuant to the limited liability company agreement or other agreement or this chapter (other than the admission, election, appointment, removal or resignation of managers). In any such application, the limited liability company shall be named as a party and service of the application upon the registered agent of the limited liability company shall be deemed to be service upon the limited liability company, and no other party need be joined in order for the Court to adjudicate the result of the vote. The Court may make such order respecting further or other notice of such application as it deems proper under these circumstances.

(c)   As used in this section, the term "manager" refers to a person:

(1)   Who is a "manager" as defined in § 18–101 of this title; and

(2)   Whether or not a member of a limited liability company, who, although not a "manager" as defined in § 18–101 of this title, participates materially in the management of the limited liability company;

provided however, that the power to elect or otherwise select or to participate in the election or selection of a person to be a "manager" as defined in § 18–101 of this title shall not, by itself, constitute participation in the management of the limited liability company.

(d)   Nothing herein contained limits or affects the right to serve process in any other manner now or hereafter provided by law. This section is an extension of and not a limitation upon the right otherwise existing of service of legal process upon nonresidents.

§ 18–111.   Interpretation and enforcement of limited liability company agreement.

Any action to interpret, apply or enforce the provisions of a limited liability company agreement, or the duties, obligations or liabilities of a limited liability company to the members or managers of the limited liability company, or the duties, obligations or liabilities among members or managers and of members or managers to the limited liability company, or the rights or powers of, or restrictions on, the limited liability company, members or managers, or any provision of this chapter, or any other instrument, document, agreement or certificate contemplated by any provision of this chapter, may be brought in the Court of Chancery.

As used in this section, the term "manager" refers to a person:

(1)   Who is a "manager" as defined in § 18–101 of this title; and

(2)   Whether or not a member of a limited liability company, who, although not a "manager" as defined in § 18–101 of this title, participates materially in the management of the limited liability company;

provided however, that the power to elect or otherwise select or to participate in the election or selection of a person to be a "manager" as defined in § 18–101 of this title shall not, by itself, constitute participation in the management of the limited liability company.

§ 18–112.   Judicial cancellation of certificate of formation; proceedings.

(a)   Upon motion by the Attorney General, the Court of Chancery shall have jurisdiction to cancel the certificate of formation of any domestic limited liability company for abuse or misuse of its limited liability company powers, privileges or existence. The Attorney General shall proceed for this purpose in the Court of Chancery.

(b)   The Court of Chancery shall have power, by appointment of trustees, receivers or otherwise, to administer and wind up the affairs of any domestic limited liability company whose certificate of formation shall be canceled by the Court of Chancery under this section, and to make such orders and decrees with respect thereto as shall be just and equitable respecting its affairs and assets and the rights of its members and creditors.

§ 18–113.   Document form, signature and delivery.

(a)   Except as provided in subsection (b) of this section, without limiting the manner in which any act or transaction may be documented, or the manner in which a document may be signed or delivered:

(1)   Any act or transaction contemplated or governed by this chapter or the limited liability company agreement may be provided for in a document, and an electronic transmission is the equivalent of a written document.

(2)   Whenever this chapter or the limited liability company agreement requires or permits a signature, the signature may be a manual, facsimile, conformed or electronic signature. "Electronic signature" means an electronic symbol or process that is attached to, or logically associated with, a document and executed or adopted by a person with an intent to authenticate or adopt the document.

(3)   Unless otherwise provided in the limited liability company agreement or agreed between the sender and recipient, an electronic transmission is delivered to a person for purposes of this chapter and the limited liability company agreement when it enters an information processing system that the person has designated for the purpose of receiving electronic transmissions of the type delivered, so long as the electronic transmission is in a form capable of being processed by that system and such person is able to retrieve the electronic transmission. Whether a person has so designated an information processing system is determined by the limited liability company agreement or from the context and surrounding circumstances, including the parties' conduct. An electronic transmission is delivered under this section even if no person is aware of its receipt. Receipt of an electronic acknowledgement from an information processing system establishes that an electronic transmission was received but, by itself, does not establish that the content sent corresponds to the content received.

This chapter shall not prohibit 1 or more persons from conducting a transaction in accordance with Chapter 12A of this title so long as the part or parts of the transaction that are governed by this chapter are documented, signed and delivered in accordance with this subsection or otherwise in accordance with this chapter. This subsection shall apply solely for purposes of determining whether an act or transaction has been documented, and the document has been signed and delivered, in accordance with this chapter and the limited liability company agreement.

(b)   Subsection (a) of this section shall not apply to:

(1)   A document filed with or submitted to the Secretary of State, the Register in Chancery, or a court or other judicial or governmental body of this State;

(2)   A certificate of limited liability company interest; and

(3)   An act or transaction effected pursuant to § 18–104, § 18–105, or § 18–109 or subchapter IX or X of this title.

The foregoing shall not create any presumption about the lawful means to document a matter addressed by this subsection, or the lawful means to sign or deliver a document addressed by this subsection. A provision of the limited liability company agreement shall not limit the application of subsection (a) of this section unless the provision expressly restricts one or more of the means of documenting an act or transaction, or of signing or delivering a document, permitted by subsection (a) of this section.

(c)   In the event that any provision of this chapter is deemed to modify, limit or supersede the Electronic Signatures in Global and National Commerce Act, 15 U.S.C. § 7001 et. seq., the provisions of this chapter shall control to the fullest extent permitted by § 7002(a)(2) of such act [15 U.S.C. § 7002(a)(2)].

SUBCHAPTER II.   FORMATION; CERTIFICATE OF FORMATION

§ 18–201.   Certificate of formation.

(a)   In order to form a limited liability company, 1 or more authorized persons must execute a certificate of formation. The certificate of formation shall be filed in the office of the Secretary of State and set forth:

(1)   The name of the limited liability company;

(2)   The address of the registered office and the name and address of the registered agent for service of process required to be maintained by § 18–104 of this title; and

(3)   Any other matters the members determine to include therein.

(b)   A limited liability company is formed at the time of the filing of the initial certificate of formation in the office of the Secretary of State or at any later date or time specified in the certificate of formation if, in either case, there has been substantial compliance with the requirements of this section. A limited liability company formed under this chapter shall be a separate legal entity, the existence of which as a separate legal entity shall continue until cancellation of the limited liability company's certificate of formation.

(c)   The filing of the certificate of formation in the office of the Secretary of State shall make it unnecessary to file any other documents under Chapter 31 of this title.

(d)   A limited liability company agreement shall be entered into or otherwise existing either before, after or at the time of the filing of a certificate of formation and, whether entered into or otherwise existing before, after or at the time of such filing, may be made effective as of the effective time of such filing or at such other time or date as provided in or reflected by the limited liability company agreement.

(e)   A certificate of formation substantially complies with § 18–201(a)(2) of this title if it contains the name of the registered agent and the address of the registered office even if the certificate of formation does not expressly designate such person as the registered agent or such address as the registered office or the address of the registered agent.

§ 18–202.   Amendment to certificate of formation.

(a)   A certificate of formation is amended by filing a certificate of amendment thereto in the office of the Secretary of State. The certificate of amendment shall set forth:

(1)   The name of the limited liability company; and

(2)   The amendment to the certificate of formation.

(b)   A manager or, if there is no manager, then any member who becomes aware that any statement in a certificate of formation was false when made, or that any matter described has changed making the certificate of formation false in any material respect, shall promptly amend the certificate of formation.

(c)   A certificate of formation may be amended at any time for any other proper purpose.

(d)   Unless otherwise provided in this chapter or unless a later effective date or time (which shall be a date or time certain) is provided for in the certificate of amendment, a certificate of amendment shall be effective at the time of its filing with the Secretary of State.

§ 18–203.   Cancellation of certificate.

(a)   A certificate of formation shall be canceled upon the dissolution and the completion of winding up of a limited liability company, or as provided in § 18–104(d), § 18–104 (i)(4), § 18–112 or § 18–1108 of this title, or upon the filing of a certificate of merger or consolidation or a certificate of ownership and merger if the limited liability company is not the surviving or resulting entity in a merger or consolidation or upon the future effective date or time of a certificate of merger or consolidation or a certificate of ownership and merger if the limited liability company is not the surviving or resulting entity in a merger or consolidation, or upon the filing of a certificate of transfer or upon the future effective date or time of a certificate of transfer, or upon the filing of a certificate of conversion to non-Delaware entity or upon the future effective date or time of a certificate of conversion to non-Delaware entity or upon the filing of a certificate of division if the limited liability company is a dividing company that is not a surviving company or upon the future effective date or time of a certificate of division if the limited liability company is a dividing company that is not a surviving company. A certificate of cancellation shall be filed in the office of the Secretary of State to accomplish the cancellation of a certificate of formation upon the dissolution and the completion of winding up of a limited liability company and shall set forth:

(1)   The name of the limited liability company;

(2)   The date of filing of its certificate of formation;

(3)   If the limited liability company has formed 1 or more registered series whose certificate of registered series has not been canceled prior to the filing of the certificate of cancellation, the name of each such registered series;

(4)   The future effective date or time (which shall be a date or time certain) of cancellation if it is not to be effective upon the filing of the certificate; and

(5)   Any other information the person filing the certificate of cancellation determines.

(b)   A certificate of cancellation that is filed in the office of the Secretary of State prior to the dissolution or the completion of winding up of a limited liability company may be corrected as an erroneously executed certificate of cancellation by filing with the office of the Secretary of State a certificate of correction of such certificate of cancellation in accordance with § 18–211 of this title.

(c)   The Secretary of State shall not issue a certificate of good standing with respect to a limited liability company (or any registered series thereof) if its certificate of formation is canceled.

§ 18–204.   Execution.

(a)   Each certificate required by this subchapter to be filed in the office of the Secretary of State shall be executed by 1 or more authorized persons or, in the case of a certificate of conversion to limited liability company or certificate of limited liability company domestication, by any person authorized to execute such certificate on behalf of the other entity or non-United States entity, respectively, except that a certificate of merger or consolidation filed by a surviving or resulting other business entity shall be executed by any person authorized to execute such certificate on behalf of such other business entity.

(b)   Unless otherwise provided in a limited liability company agreement, any person may sign any certificate or amendment thereof or enter into a limited liability company agreement or amendment thereof by an agent, including an attorney-in-fact. An authorization, including a power of attorney, to sign any certificate or amendment thereof or to enter into a limited liability company agreement or amendment thereof need not be in writing, need not be sworn to, verified or acknowledged, and need not be filed in the office of the Secretary of State, but if in writing, must be retained by the limited liability company.

(c)   For all purposes of the laws of the State of Delaware, unless otherwise provided in a limited liability company agreement, a power of attorney or proxy with respect to a limited liability company granted to any person shall be irrevocable if it states that it is irrevocable and it is coupled with an interest sufficient in law to support an irrevocable power or proxy. Such irrevocable power of attorney or proxy, unless otherwise provided therein or in a limited liability company agreement, shall not be affected by subsequent death, disability, incapacity, dissolution, termination of existence or bankruptcy of, or any other event concerning, the principal. A power of attorney or proxy with respect to matters relating to the organization, internal affairs or termination of a limited liability company or granted by a person as a member or an assignee of a limited liability company interest or by a person seeking to become a member or an assignee of a limited liability company interest and, in either case, granted to the limited liability company, a manager or member thereof, or any of their respective officers, directors, managers, members, partners, trustees, employees or agents shall be deemed coupled with an interest sufficient in law to support an irrevocable power or proxy. The provisions of this subsection shall not be construed to limit the enforceability of a power of attorney or proxy that is part of a limited liability company agreement.

(d) The execution of a certificate by a person who is authorized by this chapter to execute such certificate constitutes an oath or affirmation, under the penalties of perjury in the third degree, that, to the best of such person's knowledge and belief, the facts stated therein are true.

§ 18–205. Execution, amendment or cancellation by judicial order.

(a) If a person required to execute a certificate required by this subchapter fails or refuses to do so, any other person who is adversely affected by the failure or refusal may petition the Court of Chancery to direct the execution of the certificate. If the Court finds that the execution of the certificate is proper and that any person so designated has failed or refused to execute the certificate, it shall order the Secretary of State to record an appropriate certificate.

(b) If a person required to execute a limited liability company agreement or amendment thereof fails or refuses to do so, any other person who is adversely affected by the failure or refusal may petition the Court of Chancery to direct the execution of the limited liability company agreement or amendment thereof. If the Court finds that the limited liability company agreement or amendment thereof should be executed and that any person required to execute the limited liability company agreement or amendment thereof has failed or refused to do so, it shall enter an order granting appropriate relief.

§ 18–206. Filing.

(a) The signed copy of any certificate authorized to be filed under this chapter shall be delivered to the Secretary of State. A person who executes a certificate as an agent or fiduciary need not exhibit evidence of that person's authority as a prerequisite to filing. Any signature on any certificate authorized to be filed with the Secretary of State under any provision of this chapter may be a facsimile, a conformed signature or an electronically transmitted signature. Upon delivery of any certificate, the Secretary of State shall record the date and time of its delivery. Unless the Secretary of State finds that any certificate does not conform to law, upon receipt of all filing fees required by law the Secretary of State shall:

(1) Certify that any certificate authorized to be filed under this chapter has been filed in the Secretary of State's office by endorsing upon the signed certificate the word "Filed," and the date and time of the filing. This endorsement is conclusive of the date and time of its filing in the absence of actual fraud. Except as provided in paragraph (a)(5) or (a)(6) of this section, such date and time of filing of a certificate shall be the date and time of delivery of the certificate;

(2) File and index the endorsed certificate;

(3) Prepare and return to the person who filed it or that person's representative a copy of the signed certificate, similarly endorsed, and shall certify such copy as a true copy of the signed certificate; and

(4) Cause to be entered such information from the certificate as the Secretary of State deems appropriate into the Delaware Corporation Information System or any system which is a successor thereto in the office of the Secretary of State, and such information and a copy of such certificate shall be permanently maintained as a public record on a suitable medium. The Secretary of State is authorized to grant direct access to such system to registered agents subject to the execution of an operating agreement between the Secretary of State and such registered agent. Any registered agent granted such access shall demonstrate the existence of policies to ensure that information entered into the system accurately reflects the content of certificates in the possession of the registered agent at the time of entry.

(5) Upon request made upon or prior to delivery, the Secretary of State may, to the extent deemed practicable, establish as the date and time of filing of a certificate a date and time after its delivery. If the Secretary of State refuses to file any certificate due to an error, omission or other imperfection, the Secretary of State may hold such certificate in suspension, and in such event, upon delivery of a replacement certificate in proper form for filing and tender of the required fees within 5 business days after notice of such suspension is given to the filer, the Secretary of State shall establish as the date and time of filing of such certificate the date and time that would have been the date and time of filing of the rejected certificate had it been accepted for filing. The Secretary of State shall not issue a certificate of good standing with respect to any limited liability company or registered series with a certificate held in suspension pursuant to this subsection. The Secretary of State may establish as the date and time of filing of a certificate the date and time at which information from such certificate is entered pursuant to paragraph (a)(4) of this section if such certificate is delivered on the same date and within 4 hours after such information is entered.

(6) If:

a. Together with the actual delivery of a certificate and tender of the required fees, there is delivered to the Secretary of State a separate affidavit (which in its heading shall be designated as an affidavit of extraordinary condition) attesting, on the basis of personal knowledge of the affiant or a reliable source of knowledge identified in the affidavit, that an earlier effort to deliver such certificate and tender such fees was made in good faith, specifying the nature, date and time of such good faith effort and requesting that the Secretary of State establish such date and time as the date and time of filing of such certificate; or

b. Upon the actual delivery of a certificate and tender of the required fees, the Secretary of State in the Secretary of State's own discretion provides a written waiver of the requirement for such an affidavit stating that it appears to the Secretary of State that an earlier effort to deliver such certificate and tender such fees was made in good faith and specifying the date and time of such effort; and

c. The Secretary of State determines that an extraordinary condition existed at such date and time, that such earlier effort was unsuccessful as a result of the existence of such extraordinary condition, and that such actual delivery and tender were made within a reasonable period (not to exceed 2 business days) after the cessation of such extraordinary condition, then the Secretary of State may establish such date and time as the date and time of filing of such certificate. No fee shall be paid to the Secretary of State for receiving an affidavit of extraordinary condition. For purposes of this subsection, an extraordinary condition means: any emergency resulting from an attack on, invasion or occupation by foreign military forces of, or disaster, catastrophe, war or other armed conflict, revolution or insurrection or rioting or civil commotion in, the United States or a locality in which the Secretary of State conducts its business or in which the good faith effort to deliver the certificate and tender the required fees is made, or the immediate threat of any of the foregoing; or any malfunction or outage of the electrical or telephone service to the Secretary of State's office, or weather or other condition in or about a locality in which the Secretary of State conducts its business, as a result of which the Secretary of State's office is not open for the purpose of the filing of certificates under this chapter or such filing cannot be effected without extraordinary effort. The Secretary of State may require such proof as it deems necessary to make the determination required under this paragraph (a)(6)c., and any such determination shall be conclusive in the absence of actual fraud. If the Secretary of State establishes the date and time of filing of a certificate pursuant to this subsection, the date and time of delivery of the affidavit of extraordinary condition or the date and time of the Secretary of State's written waiver of such affidavit shall be endorsed on such affidavit or waiver and such affidavit or waiver, so endorsed, shall be attached to the filed certificate to which it relates. Such filed certificate shall be effective as of the date and time established as the date and time of filing by the Secretary of State pursuant to this subsection, except as to those persons who are substantially and adversely affected by such establishment and, as to those persons, the certificate shall be effective from the date and time endorsed on the affidavit of extraordinary condition or written waiver attached thereto.

(b) Notwithstanding any other provision of this chapter, any certificate filed under this chapter shall be effective at the time of its filing with the Secretary of State or at any later date or time (not later than a time on the one hundred and eightieth day after the date of its filing if such date of filing is on or after January 1, 2012) specified in the certificate. Upon the filing of a certificate of amendment (or judicial decree of amendment), certificate of correction, corrected certificate or restated certificate in the office of the Secretary of State, or upon the future effective date or time of a certificate of amendment (or judicial decree thereof) or restated certificate, as provided for therein, the certificate of formation or certificate of registered series, as applicable, shall be amended, corrected or restated as set forth therein. Upon the filing of a certificate of cancellation (or a judicial decree thereof), a certificate of merger or consolidation or a certificate of ownership and merger or a certificate of division which acts as a certificate of cancellation, a certificate of transfer, a certificate of conversion to a non-Delaware entity, or a certificate of conversion of registered series to protected series, or upon the future effective date or time of a certificate of cancellation (or a judicial decree thereof), a certificate of merger or consolidation or a certificate of ownership and merger or a certificate of division which acts as a certificate of cancellation, a certificate of transfer, a certificate of conversion to a non-Delaware entity, or a certificate of conversion of registered series to protected series, as provided for therein, or as specified in § 18–104(d), § 18–104(i)(4), § 18–112 or § 18–1108 of this title, the certificate of formation or certificate of registered series, as applicable, is canceled. Upon the filing of a certificate of limited liability company domestication or upon the future effective date or time of a certificate of limited liability company domestication, the entity filing the certificate of limited liability company domestication is domesticated as a limited liability company with the effect provided in § 18–212 of this title. Upon the filing of a certificate of conversion to limited liability company or upon the future effective date or time of a certificate of conversion to limited liability company, the entity filing the certificate of conversion to limited liability company is converted to a limited liability company with the effect provided in § 18–214 of this title. Upon the filing of a certificate of conversion of protected series to registered series, or upon the future effective date or time of a certificate of conversion of protected series to registered series, the protected series with respect to which such filing is made is converted to a registered series with the effect provided in § 18–219 of this title. Upon the filing of a certificate of conversion of registered series to protected series, or upon the future effective date or time of a certificate of conversion of registered series to protected series, the registered series filing such certificate is converted to a protected series with the effect provided in § 18–220 of this title. Upon the filing of a certificate of revival, a limited liability company or a registered series is revived with the effect provided in § 18–1109 or § 18–1110 of this title. Upon the filing of a certificate of transfer and domestic continuance, or upon the future effective date or time of a certificate of transfer and domestic continuance, as provided for therein, the limited liability company filing the certificate of transfer and domestic continuance shall continue to exist as a limited liability company of the State of Delaware with the effect provided in § 18–213 of this title.

(c) If any certificate filed in accordance with this chapter provides for a future effective date or time and if, prior to such future effective date or time set forth in such certificate, the transaction is terminated or its terms are amended to change the future effective date or time or any other matter described in such certificate so as to make such certificate false or inaccurate in any respect, such certificate shall, prior to the future effective date or time set forth in such certificate, be terminated or amended by the filing of a certificate of termination or certificate of amendment of such certificate, executed in accordance with § 18-204 of this title, which shall identify the certificate which has been terminated or amended and shall state that the certificate has been terminated or the manner in which it has been amended. Upon the filing of a certificate of amendment of a certificate with a future effective date or time, the certificate identified in such certificate of amendment is amended. Upon the filing of a certificate of termination of a certificate with a future effective date or time, the certificate identified in such certificate of termination is terminated.

(d)   A fee as set forth in § 18-1105(a)(3) of this title shall be paid at the time of the filing of a certificate of formation, a certificate of registered series, a certificate of amendment, a certificate of correction, a certificate of amendment of a certificate with a future effective date or time, a certificate of termination of a certificate with a future effective date or time, a certificate of cancellation, a certificate of merger or consolidation, a certificate of ownership and merger, a restated certificate, a corrected certificate, a certificate of conversion to limited liability company, a certificate of conversion to a non-Delaware entity, a certificate of conversion of protected series to registered series, a certificate of conversion of registered series to protected series, a certificate of transfer, a certificate of transfer and domestic continuance, a certificate of limited liability company domestication, a certificate of division or a certificate of revival.

(e)   The Secretary of State, acting as agent, shall collect and deposit in a separate account established exclusively for that purpose, a courthouse municipality fee with respect to each filed instrument and shall thereafter monthly remit funds from such account to the treasuries of the municipalities designated in § 301 of Title 10. Said fees shall be for the purposes of defraying certain costs incurred by such municipalities in hosting the primary locations for the Delaware Courts. The fee to such municipalities shall be $ 20 for each instrument filed with the Secretary of State in accordance with this section. The municipality to receive the fee shall be the municipality designated in § 301 of Title 10 in the county in which the limited liability company's registered office in this State is, or is to be, located, except that a fee shall not be charged for a document filed in accordance with subchapter IX of this chapter.

(f)   A fee as set forth in § 18-1105(a)(4) of this title shall be paid for a certified copy of any paper on file as provided for by this chapter, and a fee as set forth in § 18-1105(a)(5) of this title shall be paid for each page copied.

(g)   Notwithstanding any other provision of this chapter, it shall not be necessary for any limited liability company or foreign limited liability company to amend its certificate of formation, its application for registration as a foreign limited liability company, or any other document that has been filed in the office of the Secretary of State prior to August 1, 2011, to comply with § 18-104(k) of this title; notwithstanding the foregoing, any certificate or other document filed under this chapter on or after August 1, 2011, and changing the address of a registered agent or registered office shall comply with § 18-104(k) of this title.

§ 18-207.   Notice.

The fact that a certificate of formation is on file in the office of the Secretary of State is notice that the entity formed in connection with the filing of the certificate of formation is a limited liability company formed under the laws of the State of Delaware and is notice of all other facts set forth therein which are required to be set forth in a certificate of formation by § 18-201(a)(1) and (2) or § 18-1202 of this title and which are permitted to be set forth in a certificate of formation by § 18-215(b) or § 18-218(b) of this title. The fact that a certificate of registered series is on file in the office of the Secretary of State is notice that the registered series named in such certificate of registered series has been formed pursuant to § 18-218 of this title and is notice of all other facts set forth therein which are required to be set forth in a certificate of registered series by § 18-218(d) of this title.

§ 18–208. Restated certificate.

(a) *Restated certificate of formation.*—

(1) A limited liability company may, whenever desired, integrate into a single instrument all of the provisions of its certificate of formation which are then in effect and operative as a result of there having theretofore been filed with the Secretary of State 1 or more certificates or other instruments pursuant to any of the sections referred to in this subchapter, and it may at the same time also further amend its certificate of formation by adopting a restated certificate of formation.

(2) If a restated certificate of formation merely restates and integrates but does not further amend the initial certificate of formation, as theretofore amended or supplemented by any instrument that was executed and filed pursuant to any of the sections in this subchapter, it shall be specifically designated in its heading as a "Restated Certificate of Formation" together with such other words as the limited liability company may deem appropriate and shall be executed by an authorized person and filed as provided in § 18–206 of this title in the office of the Secretary of State. If a restated certificate restates and integrates and also further amends in any respect the certificate of formation, as theretofore amended or supplemented, it shall be specifically designated in its heading as an "Amended and Restated Certificate of Formation" together with such other words as the limited liability company may deem appropriate and shall be executed by at least 1 authorized person, and filed as provided in § 18–206 of this title in the office of the Secretary of State.

(3) A restated certificate of formation shall state, either in its heading or in an introductory paragraph, the limited liability company's present name, and, if it has been changed, the name under which it was originally filed, and the date of filing of its original certificate of formation with the Secretary of State, and the future effective date or time (which shall be a date or time certain) of the restated certificate if it is not to be effective upon the filing of the restated certificate. A restated certificate shall also state that it was duly executed and is being filed in accordance with this section. If a restated certificate only restates and integrates and does not further amend a limited liability company's certificate of formation as theretofore amended or supplemented and there is no discrepancy between those provisions and the restated certificate, it shall state that fact as well.

(4) Upon the filing of a restated certificate of formation with the Secretary of State, or upon the future effective date or time of a restated certificate of formation as provided for therein, the initial certificate of formation, as theretofore amended or supplemented, shall be superseded; thenceforth, the restated certificate of formation, including any further amendment or changes made thereby, shall be the certificate of formation of the limited liability company, but the original effective date of formation shall remain unchanged.

(5) Any amendment or change effected in connection with the restatement and integration of the certificate of formation shall be subject to any other provision of this chapter, not inconsistent with this section, which would apply if a separate certificate of amendment were filed to effect such amendment or change.

(b) *Restated certificate of registered series.*—

(1) A registered series of a limited liability company may, whenever desired, integrate into a single instrument all of the provisions of its certificate of registered series which are then in effect and operative as a result of there having theretofore been filed with the Secretary of State 1 or more certificates or other instruments pursuant to any of the sections referred to in this subchapter, and it may at the same time also further amend its certificate of registered series by adopting a restated certificate of registered series.

(2) If a restated certificate of registered series merely restates and integrates but does not further amend the initial certificate of registered series, as theretofore amended or supplemented by any instrument that was executed and filed pursuant to any of the sections in this subchapter,

it shall be specifically designated in its heading as a "Restated Certificate of Registered Series" together with such other words as the registered series may deem appropriate and shall be executed by an authorized person and filed as provided in § 18–206 of this title in the office of the Secretary of State. If a restated certificate restates and integrates and also further amends in any respect the certificate of registered series as theretofore amended or supplemented, it shall be specifically designated in its heading as an "Amended and Restated Certificate of Registered Series" together with such other words as the registered series may deem appropriate and shall be executed by at least 1 authorized person, and filed as provided in § 18–206 of this title in the office of the Secretary of State.

(3) A restated certificate of registered series shall state, either in its heading or in an introductory paragraph, the name of the limited liability company, the present name of the registered series, and, if the name of the registered series has been changed, the name under which it was originally filed, and the date of filing of its original certificate of registered series with the Secretary of State, and the future effective date or time (which shall be a date or time certain) of the restated certificate of registered series if it is not to be effective upon the filing of the restated certificate of registered series. A restated certificate shall also state that it was duly executed and is being filed in accordance with this section. If a restated certificate only restates and integrates and does not further amend a certificate of registered series, as theretofore amended or supplemented and there is no discrepancy between those provisions and the restated certificate, it shall state that fact as well.

(4) Upon the filing of a restated certificate of registered series with the Secretary of State, or upon the future effective date or time of a restated certificate of registered series as provided for therein, the initial certificate of registered series, as theretofore amended or supplemented, shall be superseded; thenceforth, the restated certificate of registered series, including any further amendment or changes made thereby, shall be the certificate of registered series of such registered series, but the original effective date of formation of the registered series, as applicable, shall remain unchanged.

(5) Any amendment or change effected in connection with the restatement and integration of a certificate of registered series shall be subject to any other provision of this chapter, not inconsistent with this section, which would apply if a separate certificate of amendment were filed to effect such amendment or change.

§ 18–209.   Merger and consolidation.

(a) As used in this section and in §§ 18–204, 18–217, 18–219, 18–220 and 18–221 of this title, "other business entity" means a corporation, a statutory trust, a business trust, an association, a real estate investment trust, a common-law trust, or any other incorporated or unincorporated business or entity, including a partnership (whether general (including a limited liability partnership) or limited (including a limited liability limited partnership)), and a foreign limited liability company, but excluding a domestic limited liability company. As used in this section and in §§ 18–210 and 18–301 of this title, "plan of merger" means a writing approved by a domestic limited liability company, in the form of resolutions or otherwise, that states the terms and conditions of a merger under subsection (i) of this section.

(b) Pursuant to an agreement of merger or consolidation, 1 or more domestic limited liability companies may merge or consolidate with or into 1 or more domestic limited liability companies or 1 or more other business entities formed or organized under the laws of the State of Delaware or any other state or the United States or any foreign country or other foreign jurisdiction, or any combination thereof, with such domestic limited liability company or other business entity as the agreement shall provide being the surviving or resulting domestic limited liability company or other business entity. Unless otherwise provided in the limited liability company agreement, an agreement of merger or consolidation or a plan of merger shall be approved by each domestic limited liability company which is to merge or consolidate by members who own more than 50 percent of the then current percentage or other interest in the profits of the domestic limited liability company owned by all of the members. In connection with a merger or consolidation hereunder, rights or securities of, or interests in, a domestic limited liability company or other business entity which is a constituent party to the merger or consolidation may be exchanged for or converted into cash, property, rights or securities of, or interests in, the surviving or resulting domestic limited liability company or other business entity or, in addition to or in lieu thereof, may be exchanged for or converted into cash, property, rights or securities of, or interests in, a domestic limited liability company or other business entity which is not the surviving or resulting limited liability company or other business entity in the merger or consolidation, may remain outstanding or may be canceled. Notwithstanding prior approval, an agreement of merger or consolidation or a plan of merger may be terminated or amended pursuant to a provision for such termination or amendment contained in the agreement of merger or consolidation or plan of merger. Unless otherwise provided in a limited liability company agreement, a limited liability company whose original certificate of formation was filed with the Secretary of State and effective on or prior to July 31, 2015, shall continue to be governed by the second sentence of this subsection as in effect on July 31, 2015.

(c)   Except in the case of a merger under subsection (i) of this section, if a domestic limited liability company is merging or consolidating under this section, the domestic limited liability company or other business entity surviving or resulting in or from the merger or consolidation shall file a certificate of merger or consolidation executed by 1 or more authorized persons on behalf of the domestic limited liability company when it is the surviving or resulting entity in the office of the Secretary of State. The certificate of merger or consolidation shall state:

(1)   The name, jurisdiction of formation or organization and type of entity of each of the domestic limited liability companies and other business entities which is to merge or consolidate;

(2)   That an agreement of merger or consolidation has been approved and executed by each of the domestic limited liability companies and other business entities which is to merge or consolidate;

(3)   The name of the surviving or resulting domestic limited liability company or other business entity;

(4)   In the case of a merger in which a domestic limited liability company is the surviving entity, such amendments, if any, to the certificate of formation of the surviving domestic limited liability company to change its name, registered office or registered agent as are desired to be effected by the merger;

(5)   The future effective date or time (which shall be a date or time certain) of the merger or consolidation if it is not to be effective upon the filing of the certificate of merger or consolidation;

(6)   That the agreement of merger or consolidation is on file at a place of business of the surviving or resulting domestic limited liability company or other business entity, and shall state the address thereof;

(7)   That a copy of the agreement of merger or consolidation will be furnished by the surviving or resulting domestic limited liability company or other business entity, on request and without cost, to any member of any domestic limited liability company or any person holding an interest in any other business entity which is to merge or consolidate; and

(8)   If the surviving or resulting entity is not a domestic limited liability company, or a corporation, partnership (whether general (including a limited liability partnership) or limited (including a limited liability limited partnership)) or statutory trust organized under the laws of the State of Delaware, a statement that such surviving or resulting other business entity agrees that it may be served with process in the State of Delaware in any action, suit or proceeding for the enforcement of any obligation of any domestic limited liability company which is to merge or consolidate, irrevocably appointing the Secretary of State as its agent to accept service of process

in any such action, suit or proceeding and specifying the address to which a copy of such process shall be mailed to it by the Secretary of State. Process may be served upon the Secretary of State under this subsection by means of electronic transmission but only as prescribed by the Secretary of State. The Secretary of State is authorized to issue such rules and regulations with respect to such service as the Secretary of State deems necessary or appropriate. In the event of service hereunder upon the Secretary of State, the procedures set forth in § 18–911(c) of this title shall be applicable, except that the plaintiff in any such action, suit or proceeding shall furnish the Secretary of State with the address specified in the certificate of merger or consolidation provided for in this section and any other address which the plaintiff may elect to furnish, together with copies of such process as required by the Secretary of State, and the Secretary of State shall notify such surviving or resulting other business entity at all such addresses furnished by the plaintiff in accordance with the procedures set forth in § 18–911(c) of this title.

(d)   Unless a future effective date or time is provided in a certificate of merger or consolidation, or in the case of a merger under subsection (i) of this section in a certificate of ownership and merger, in which event a merger or consolidation shall be effective at any such future effective date or time, a merger or consolidation shall be effective upon the filing in the office of the Secretary of State of a certificate of merger or consolidation or a certificate of ownership and merger.

(e)   A certificate of merger or consolidation or a certificate of ownership and merger shall act as a certificate of cancellation for a domestic limited liability company which is not the surviving or resulting entity in the merger or consolidation. A certificate of merger that sets forth any amendment in accordance with paragraph (c)(4) of this section shall be deemed to be an amendment to the certificate of formation of the limited liability company, and the limited liability company shall not be required to take any further action to amend its certificate of formation under § 18–202 of this title with respect to such amendments set forth in the certificate of merger. Whenever this section requires the filing of a certificate of merger or consolidation, such requirement shall be deemed satisfied by the filing of an agreement of merger or consolidation containing the information required by this section to be set forth in the certificate of merger or consolidation.

(f)   An agreement of merger or consolidation or a plan of merger approved in accordance with subsection (b) of this section may:

(1)   Effect any amendment to the limited liability company agreement; or

(2)   Effect the adoption of a new limited liability company agreement, for a limited liability company if it is the surviving or resulting limited liability company in the merger or consolidation.

Any amendment to a limited liability company agreement or adoption of a new limited liability company agreement made pursuant to the foregoing sentence shall be effective at the effective time or date of the merger or consolidation and shall be effective notwithstanding any provision of the limited liability company agreement relating to amendment or adoption of a new limited liability company agreement, other than a provision that by its terms applies to an amendment to the limited liability company agreement or the adoption of a new limited liability company agreement, in either case, in connection with a merger or consolidation. The provisions of this subsection shall not be construed to limit the accomplishment of a merger or of any of the matters referred to herein by any other means provided for in a limited liability company agreement or other agreement or as otherwise permitted by law, including that the limited liability company agreement of any constituent limited liability company to the merger or consolidation (including a limited liability company formed for the purpose of consummating a merger or consolidation) shall be the limited liability company agreement of the surviving or resulting limited liability company.

(g)   When any merger or consolidation shall have become effective under this section, for all purposes of the laws of the State of Delaware, all of the rights, privileges and powers of each of the domestic limited liability companies and other business entities that have merged or consolidated, and all property, real, personal and mixed, and all debts due to any of said domestic limited liability companies and other business entities, as well as all other things and causes of action belonging to each of such domestic limited liability companies and other business entities, shall be vested in the surviving or resulting domestic limited liability company or other business entity, and shall thereafter be the property of the surviving or resulting domestic limited liability company or other business entity as they were of each of the domestic limited liability companies and other business entities that have merged or consolidated, and the title to any real property vested by deed or otherwise, under the laws of the State of Delaware, in any of such domestic limited liability companies and other business entities, shall not revert or be in any way impaired by reason of this chapter; but all rights of creditors and all liens upon any property of any of said domestic limited liability companies and other business entities shall be preserved unimpaired, and all debts, liabilities and duties of each of the said domestic limited liability companies and other business entities that have merged or consolidated shall thenceforth attach to the surviving or resulting domestic limited liability company or other business entity, and may be enforced against it to the same extent as if said debts, liabilities and duties had been incurred or contracted by it. Unless otherwise agreed, a merger or consolidation of a domestic limited liability company, including a domestic limited liability company which is not the surviving or resulting entity in the merger or consolidation, shall not require such domestic limited liability company to wind up its affairs under § 18–803 of this title or pay its liabilities and distribute its assets under § 18–804 of this title, and the merger or consolidation shall not constitute a dissolution of such limited liability company.

(h)   A limited liability company agreement may provide that a domestic limited liability company shall not have the power to merge or consolidate as set forth in this section.

(i)   In any case in which (i) at least 90% of the outstanding shares of each class of the stock of a corporation or corporations (other than a corporation which has in its certificate of incorporation the provision required by § 251(g)(7)(i) of Title 8), of which class there are outstanding shares that, absent § 267(a) of Title 8, would be entitled to vote on such merger, is owned by a domestic limited liability company, (ii) 1 or more of such corporations is a corporation of the State of Delaware, and (iii) any corporation that is not a corporation of the State of Delaware is a corporation of any other state or the District of Columbia or another jurisdiction, the laws of which do not forbid such merger, the domestic limited liability company having such stock ownership may either merge the corporation or corporations into itself and assume all of its or their obligations, or merge itself, or itself and 1 or more of such corporations, into 1 of the other corporations, pursuant to a plan of merger. If a domestic limited liability company is causing a merger under this subsection, the domestic limited liability company shall file a certificate of ownership and merger executed by 1 or more authorized persons on behalf of the domestic limited liability company in the office of the Secretary of State. The certificate of ownership and merger shall certify that such merger was authorized in accordance with the domestic limited liability company's limited liability company agreement and this chapter, and if the domestic limited liability company shall not own all the outstanding stock of all the corporations that are parties to the merger, shall state the terms and conditions of the merger, including the securities, cash, property, or rights to be issued, paid, delivered or granted by the surviving domestic limited liability company or corporation upon surrender of each share of the corporation or corporations not owned by the domestic limited liability company, or the cancellation of some or all of such shares. If a corporation surviving a merger under this subsection is not a corporation organized under the laws of the State of Delaware, then the terms and conditions of the merger shall obligate such corporation to agree that it may be served with process in the State of Delaware in any proceeding for enforcement of any obligation of the domestic limited liability company or any obligation of any constituent corporation of the State of Delaware, as well as for enforcement of any obligation of the surviving corporation, including any suit or other proceeding to enforce the right of any stockholders as determined in appraisal proceedings pursuant to § 262 of Title 8, and to irrevocably appoint the Secretary of State as its agent to accept service of process in any such suit or other proceedings, and to specify the address to which a copy of such process shall be mailed by the Secretary of State. Process may be served upon the Secretary of State under this subsection by means of electronic transmission but only as prescribed by the Secretary of State. The Secretary of State is authorized to issue such rules and regulations with respect to such service as the Secretary of State deems necessary or appropriate. In the event of such service upon the Secretary of State in accordance with this subsection, the Secretary of State shall forthwith notify such surviving corporation thereof by letter, directed to such surviving corporation at its address so specified, unless such surviving corporation shall have designated in writing to the Secretary of State a different address for such purpose, in which case it shall be mailed to the last address so designated. Such letter shall be sent by a mail or courier service that includes a record of mailing or deposit with the courier and a record of delivery evidenced by the signature of the recipient. Such letter shall enclose a copy of the process and any other papers served on the Secretary of State pursuant to this subsection. It shall be the duty of the plaintiff in the event of such service to serve process and any other papers in duplicate, to notify the Secretary of State that service is being effected pursuant to this subsection and to pay the Secretary of State the sum of $50 for the use of the State of Delaware, which sum shall be taxed as part of the costs in the proceeding, if the plaintiff shall prevail therein. The Secretary of State shall maintain an alphabetical record of any such service setting forth the name of the plaintiff and the defendant, the title, docket number and nature of the proceeding in which process has been served, the fact that service has been effected pursuant to this subsection, the return date thereof, and the day and hour service was made. The Secretary of State shall not be required to retain such information longer than 5 years from receipt of the service of process.

§ 18–210.   Contractual appraisal rights.

A limited liability company agreement or an agreement of merger or consolidation or a plan of merger or a plan of division may provide that contractual appraisal rights with respect to a limited liability company interest or another interest in a limited liability company shall be available for any class or group or series of members or limited liability company interests in connection with any amendment of a limited liability company agreement, any merger or consolidation in which the limited liability company or a registered series of the limited liability company is a constituent party to the merger or consolidation, any division of the limited liability company, any conversion of the limited liability company to another business form, any conversion of a protected series of the limited liability company to a registered series of such limited liability company, any conversion of a registered series of the limited liability company to a protected series of such limited liability company, any transfer to or domestication or continuance in any jurisdiction by the limited liability company, or the sale of all or substantially all of the limited liability company's assets. The Court of Chancery shall have jurisdiction to hear and determine any matter relating to any such appraisal rights.

§ 18–211.   Certificate of correction.

(a)   Whenever any certificate authorized to be filed with the office of the Secretary of State under any provision of this chapter has been so filed and is an inaccurate record of the action therein referred to, or was defectively or erroneously executed, such certificate may be corrected by filing with the office of the Secretary of State a certificate of correction of such certificate. The certificate of correction shall specify the inaccuracy or defect to be corrected, shall set forth the portion of the certificate in corrected form, and shall be executed and filed as required by this chapter. The certificate of correction shall be effective as of the date the original certificate was filed, except as to those persons who are substantially and adversely affected by the correction, and as to those persons the certificate of correction shall be effective from the filing date.

(b)   In lieu of filing a certificate of correction, a certificate may be corrected by filing with the Secretary of State a corrected certificate which shall be executed and filed as if the corrected certificate were the certificate being corrected, and a fee equal to the fee payable to the Secretary of State for a certificate of correction as prescribed by § 18–1105 of this title shall be paid and collected by the Secretary of State for the use of the State of Delaware in connection with the filing of the corrected certificate. The corrected certificate shall be specifically designated as such in its heading, shall specify the inaccuracy or defect to be corrected and shall set forth the entire certificate in corrected form. A certificate corrected in accordance with this section shall be effective as of the date the original certificate was filed, except as to those persons who are substantially and adversely affected by the correction and as to those persons the certificate as corrected shall be effective from the filing date.

§ 18–212.   Domestication of non-United States entities.

(a)   As used in this section and in § 18–204 of this title, "non-United States entity" means a foreign limited liability company (other than 1 formed under the laws of a state) or a corporation, a statutory trust, a business trust, an association, a real estate investment trust, a common-law trust or any other incorporated or unincorporated business or entity, including a partnership (whether general (including a limited liability partnership) or limited (including a limited liability limited partnership)) formed, incorporated, created or that otherwise came into being under the laws of any foreign country or other foreign jurisdiction (other than any state).

(b)   Any non-United States entity may become domesticated as a limited liability company in the State of Delaware by complying with subsection (g) of this section and filing in the office of the Secretary of State in accordance with § 18–206 of this title:

     (1)   A certificate of limited liability company domestication that has been executed in accordance with § 18–204 of this title; and

     (2)   A certificate of formation that complies with § 18–201 of this title and has been executed by 1 or more authorized persons in accordance with § 18–204 of this title.

Each of the certificates required by this subsection (b) shall be filed simultaneously in the office of the Secretary of State and, if such certificates are not to become effective upon their filing as permitted by § 18–206(b) of this title, then each such certificate shall provide for the same effective date or time in accordance with § 18–206(b) of this title.

(c)   The certificate of limited liability company domestication shall state:

     (1)   The date on which and jurisdiction where the non-United States entity was first formed, incorporated, created or otherwise came into being;

     (2)   The name of the non-United States entity immediately prior to the filing of the certificate of limited liability company domestication;

     (3)   The name of the limited liability company as set forth in the certificate of formation filed in accordance with subsection (b) of this section;

     (4)   The future effective date or time (which shall be a date or time certain) of the domestication as a limited liability company if it is not to be effective upon the filing of the certificate of limited liability company domestication and the certificate of formation;

     (5)   The jurisdiction that constituted the seat, siege social, or principal place of business or central administration of the non-United States entity, or any other equivalent thereto under applicable law, immediately prior to the filing of the certificate of limited liability company domestication; and

     (6)   That the domestication has been approved in the manner provided for by the document, instrument, agreement or other writing, as the case may be, governing the internal affairs of the non-United States entity and the conduct of its business or by applicable non-Delaware law, as appropriate.

(d)   Upon the filing in the office of the Secretary of State of the certificate of limited liability company domestication and the certificate of formation or upon the future effective date or time of the certificate of limited liability company domestication and the certificate of formation, the non-United States entity shall be domesticated as a limited liability company in the State of Delaware and the limited liability company shall thereafter be subject to all of the provisions of this chapter, except that notwithstanding § 18–201 of this title, the existence of the limited liability company shall be deemed to have commenced on the date the non-United States entity commenced its existence in the jurisdiction in which the non-United States entity was first formed, incorporated, created or otherwise came into being.

(e)   The domestication of any non-United States entity as a limited liability company in the State of Delaware shall not be deemed to affect any obligations or liabilities of the non-United States entity incurred prior to its domestication as a limited liability company in the State of Delaware, or the personal liability of any person therefor.

(f)   The filing of a certificate of limited liability company domestication shall not affect the choice of law applicable to the non-United States entity, except that from the effective date or time of the domestication, the law of the State of Delaware, including the provisions of this chapter, shall apply to the non-United States entity to the same extent as if the non-United States entity had been formed as a limited liability company on that date.

(g)   Prior to the filing of a certificate of limited liability company domestication with the Office of the Secretary of State, the domestication shall be approved in the manner provided for by the document, instrument, agreement or other writing, as the case may be, governing the internal affairs of the non-United States entity and the conduct of its business or by applicable non-Delaware law, as appropriate, and a limited liability company agreement shall be approved by the same authorization required to approve the domestication.

(h)   When any domestication shall have become effective under this section, for all purposes of the laws of the State of Delaware, all of the rights, privileges and powers of the non-United States entity that has been domesticated, and all property, real, personal and mixed, and all debts due to such non-United States entity, as well as all other things and causes of action belonging to such non-United States entity, shall remain vested in the domestic limited liability company to which such non-United States entity has been domesticated (and also in the non-United States entity, if and for so long as the non-United States entity continues its existence in the foreign jurisdiction in which it was existing immediately prior to the domestication) and shall be the property of such domestic limited liability company (and also of the non-United States entity, if and for so long as the non-United States entity continues its existence in the foreign jurisdiction in which it was existing immediately prior to the domestication), and the title to any real property vested by deed or otherwise in such non-United States entity shall not revert or be in any way impaired by reason of this chapter; but all rights of creditors and all liens upon any property of such non-United States entity shall be preserved unimpaired, and all debts, liabilities and duties of the non-United States entity that has been domesticated shall remain attached to the domestic limited liability company to which such non-United States entity has been domesticated (and also to the non-United States entity, if and for so long as the non-United States entity continues its existence in the foreign jurisdiction in which it was existing immediately prior to the domestication), and may be enforced against it to the same extent as if said debts, liabilities and duties had originally been incurred or contracted by it in its capacity as a domestic limited liability company. The rights, privileges, powers and interests in property of the non-United States entity, as well as the debts, liabilities and duties of the non-United States entity, shall not be deemed, as a consequence of the domestication, to have been transferred to the domestic limited liability company to which such non-United States entity has domesticated for any purpose of the laws of the State of Delaware.

(i)   When a non-United States entity has become domesticated as a limited liability company pursuant to this section, for all purposes of the laws of the State of Delaware, the limited liability company shall be deemed to be the same entity as the domesticating non-United States entity and the domestication shall constitute a continuation of the existence of the domesticating non-United States entity in the form of a domestic limited liability company. Unless otherwise agreed, for all purposes of the laws of the State of Delaware, the domesticating non-United States entity shall not be required to wind up its affairs or pay its liabilities and distribute its assets, and the domestication shall not be deemed to constitute a dissolution of such non-United States entity. If, following domestication, a non-United States entity that has become domesticated as a limited liability company continues its existence in the foreign country or other foreign jurisdiction in which it was existing immediately prior to domestication, the limited liability company and such non-United States entity shall, for all purposes of the laws of the State of Delaware, constitute a single entity formed, incorporated, created or otherwise having come into being, as applicable, and existing under the laws of the State of Delaware and the laws of such foreign country or other foreign jurisdiction.

(j)   In connection with a domestication hereunder, rights or securities of, or interests in, the non-United States entity that is to be domesticated as a domestic limited liability company may be exchanged for or converted into cash, property, rights or securities of, or interests in, such domestic limited liability company or, in addition to or in lieu thereof, may be exchanged for or converted into cash, property, rights or securities of, or interests in, another domestic limited liability company or other entity, may remain outstanding or may be canceled.

§ 18–213.   Transfer or continuance of domestic limited liability companies.

(a)   Upon compliance with this section, any limited liability company may transfer to or domesticate or continue in any jurisdiction, other than any state, and, in connection therewith, may elect to continue its existence as a limited liability company in the State of Delaware.

(b)   If the limited liability company agreement specifies the manner of authorizing a transfer or domestication or continuance described in subsection (a) of this section, the transfer or domestication or continuance shall be authorized as specified in the limited liability company agreement. If the limited liability company agreement does not specify the manner of authorizing a transfer or domestication or continuance described in subsection (a) of this section and does not prohibit such a transfer or domestication or continuance, the transfer or domestication or continuance shall be authorized in the same manner as is specified in the limited liability company agreement for authorizing a merger or consolidation that involves the limited liability company as a constituent party to the merger or consolidation. If the limited liability company agreement does not specify the manner of authorizing a transfer or domestication or continuance described in subsection (a) of this section or a merger or consolidation that involves the limited liability company as a constituent party and does not prohibit such a transfer or domestication or continuance, the transfer or domestication or continuance shall be authorized by the approval by members who own more than 50 percent of the then current percentage or other interest in the profits of the domestic limited liability company owned by all of the members. If a transfer or domestication or continuance described in subsection (a) of this section shall be authorized as provided in this subsection (b), a certificate of transfer if the limited liability company's existence as a limited liability company of the State of Delaware is to cease, or a certificate of transfer and domestic continuance if the limited liability company's existence as a limited liability company in the State of Delaware is to continue, executed in accordance with § 18–204 of this title, shall be filed in the office of the Secretary of State in accordance with 18–206 of this title. The certificate of transfer or the certificate of transfer and domestic continuance shall state:

(1)   The name of the limited liability company and, if it has been changed, the name under which its certificate of formation was originally filed;

(2)   The date of the filing of its original certificate of formation with the Secretary of State;

(3)   The jurisdiction to which the limited liability company shall be transferred or in which it shall be domesticated or continued and the name of the entity or business form formed, incorporated, created or that otherwise comes into being as a consequence of the transfer of the limited liability company to, or its domestication or continuance in, such foreign jurisdiction;

(4)   The future effective date or time (which shall be a date or time certain) of the transfer to or domestication or continuance in the jurisdiction specified in paragraph (b)(3) of this section if it is not to be effective upon the filing of the certificate of transfer or the certificate of transfer and domestic continuance;

(5)   That the transfer or domestication or continuance of the limited liability company has been approved in accordance with this section;

(6)   In the case of a certificate of transfer, (i) that the existence of the limited liability company as a limited liability company of the State of Delaware shall cease when the certificate

of transfer becomes effective, and (ii) the agreement of the limited liability company that it may be served with process in the State of Delaware in any action, suit or proceeding for enforcement of any obligation of the limited liability company arising while it was a limited liability company of the State of Delaware, and that it irrevocably appoints the Secretary of State as its agent to accept service of process in any such action, suit or proceeding;

(7)   The address (which may not be that of the limited liability company's registered agent without the written consent of the limited liability company's registered agent, such consent to be filed with the certificate of transfer) to which a copy of the process referred to in paragraph (b)(6) of this section shall be mailed to it by the Secretary of State. Process may be served upon the Secretary of State under paragraph (b)(6) of this section by means of electronic transmission but only as prescribed by the Secretary of State. The Secretary of State is authorized to issue such rules and regulations with respect to such service as the Secretary of State deems necessary or appropriate. In the event of service hereunder upon the Secretary of State, the procedures set forth in § 18–911(c) of this title shall be applicable, except that the plaintiff in any such action, suit or proceeding shall furnish the Secretary of State with the address specified in this subsection and any other address that the plaintiff may elect to furnish, together with copies of such process as required by the Secretary of State, and the Secretary of State shall notify the limited liability company that has transferred or domesticated or continued out of the State of Delaware at all such addresses furnished by the plaintiff in accordance with the procedures set forth in § 18–911(c) of this title; and

(8)   In the case of a certificate of transfer and domestic continuance, that the limited liability company will continue to exist as a limited liability company of the State of Delaware after the certificate of transfer and domestic continuance becomes effective.

Unless otherwise provided in a limited liability company agreement, a limited liability company whose original certificate of formation was filed with the Secretary of State and effective on or prior to July 31, 2015, shall continue to be governed by the third sentence of this subsection as in effect on July 31, 2015.

(c)   Upon the filing in the office of the Secretary of State of the certificate of transfer or upon the future effective date or time of the certificate of transfer and payment to the Secretary of State of all fees prescribed in this chapter, the Secretary of State shall certify that the limited liability company has filed all documents and paid all fees required by this chapter, and thereupon the limited liability company shall cease to exist as a limited liability company of the State of Delaware. Such certificate of the Secretary of State shall be prima facie evidence of the transfer or domestication or continuance by such limited liability company out of the State of Delaware.

(d)   The transfer or domestication or continuance of a limited liability company out of the State of Delaware in accordance with this section and the resulting cessation of its existence as a limited liability company of the State of Delaware pursuant to a certificate of transfer shall not be deemed to affect any obligations or liabilities of the limited liability company incurred prior to such transfer or domestication or continuance or the personal liability of any person incurred prior to such transfer or domestication or continuance, nor shall it be deemed to affect the choice of law applicable to the limited liability company with respect to matters arising prior to such transfer or domestication or continuance. Unless otherwise agreed, the transfer or domestication or continuance of a limited liability company out of the State of Delaware in accordance with this section shall not require such limited liability company to wind up its affairs under § 18–803 of this title or pay its liabilities and distribute its assets under § 18–804 of this title and shall not be deemed to constitute a dissolution of such limited liability company.

(e)   If a limited liability company files a certificate of transfer and domestic continuance, after the time the certificate of transfer and domestic continuance becomes effective, the limited liability company shall continue to exist as a limited liability company of the State of Delaware, and the laws of the State of Delaware, including this chapter, shall apply to the limited liability company to the same extent as prior to such time. So long as a limited liability company continues to exist as a limited liability company of the State of Delaware following the filing of a certificate of transfer and domestic continuance, the continuing domestic limited liability company and the entity or business form formed, incorporated, created or that otherwise came into being as a consequence of the transfer of the limited liability company to, or its domestication or continuance in, a foreign country or other foreign jurisdiction shall, for all purposes of the laws of the State of Delaware, constitute a single entity formed, incorporated, created or otherwise having come into being, as applicable, and existing under the laws of the State and the laws of such foreign country or other foreign jurisdiction.

(f)   In connection with a transfer or domestication or continuance of a domestic limited liability company to or in another jurisdiction pursuant to subsection (a) of this section, rights or securities of, or interests in, such limited liability company may be exchanged for or converted into cash, property, rights or securities of, or interests in, the entity or business form in which the limited liability company will exist in such other jurisdiction as a consequence of the transfer or domestication or continuance or, in addition to or in lieu thereof, may be exchanged for or converted into cash, property, rights or securities of, or interests in, another entity or business form, may remain outstanding or may be canceled.

(g)   When a limited liability company has transferred or domesticated or continued out of the State of Delaware pursuant to this section, the transferred or domesticated or continued entity or business form shall, for all purposes of the laws of the State of Delaware, be deemed to be the same entity as the limited liability company and shall constitute a continuation of the existence of such limited liability company in the form of the transferred or domesticated or continued entity or business form. When any transfer or domestication or continuance of a limited liability company out of the State of Delaware shall have become effective under this section, for all purposes of the laws of the State of Delaware, all of the rights, privileges and powers of the limited liability company that has transferred or domesticated or continued, and all property, real, personal and mixed, and all debts due to such limited liability company, as well as all other things and causes of action belonging to such limited liability company, shall remain vested in the transferred or domesticated or continued entity or business form (and also in the limited liability company that has transferred, domesticated or continued, if and for so long as such limited liability company continues its existence as a domestic limited liability company) and shall be the property of such transferred or domesticated or continued entity or business form (and also of the limited liability company that has transferred, domesticated or continued, if and for so long as such limited liability company continues its existence as a domestic limited liability company), and the title to any real property vested by deed or otherwise in such limited liability company shall not revert or be in any way impaired by reason of this chapter; but all rights of creditors and all liens upon any property of such limited liability company shall be preserved unimpaired, and all debts, liabilities and duties of the limited liability company that has transferred or domesticated or continued shall remain attached to the transferred or domesticated or continued entity or business form (and also to the limited liability company that has transferred, domesticated or continued, if and for so long as such limited liability company continues its existence as a domestic limited liability company), and may be enforced against it to the same extent as if said debts, liabilities and duties had originally been incurred or contracted by it in its capacity as the transferred or domesticated or continued entity or business form. The rights, privileges, powers and interests in property of the limited liability company that has transferred or domesticated or continued, as well as the debts, liabilities and duties of such limited liability company, shall not be deemed, as a consequence of the transfer or domestication or continuance out of the State of Delaware, to have been transferred to the transferred or domesticated or continued entity or business form for any purpose of the laws of the State of Delaware.

(h)   A limited liability company agreement may provide that a domestic limited liability company shall not have the power to transfer, domesticate or continue as set forth in this section.

§ 18–214.   Conversion of certain entities to a limited liability company.

(a)   As used in this section and in § 18–204 of this title, the term "other entity" means a corporation, a statutory trust, a business trust, an association, a real estate investment trust, a common-law trust or any other incorporated or unincorporated business or entity, including a partnership (whether general (including a limited liability partnership) or limited (including a limited liability limited partnership)) or a foreign limited liability company.

(b) Any other entity may convert to a domestic limited liability company by complying with subsection (h) of this section and filing in the office of the Secretary of State in accordance with § 18–206 of this title:

(1) A certificate of conversion to limited liability company that has been executed in accordance with § 18–204 of this title; and

(2) A certificate of formation that complies with § 18–201 of this title and has been executed by 1 or more authorized persons in accordance with § 18–204 of this title.

Each of the certificates required by this subsection (b) shall be filed simultaneously in the office of the Secretary of State and, if such certificates are not to become effective upon their filing as permitted by § 18–206(b) of this title, then each such certificate shall provide for the same effective date or time in accordance with § 18–206(b) of this title.

(c) The certificate of conversion to limited liability company shall state:

(1) The date on which and jurisdiction where the other entity was first created, incorporated, formed or otherwise came into being and, if it has changed, its jurisdiction immediately prior to its conversion to a domestic limited liability company;

(2) The name and type of entity of the other entity immediately prior to the filing of the certificate of conversion to limited liability company;

(3) The name of the limited liability company as set forth in its certificate of formation filed in accordance with subsection (b) of this section; and

(4) The future effective date or time (which shall be a date or time certain) of the conversion to a limited liability company if it is not to be effective upon the filing of the certificate of conversion to limited liability company and the certificate of formation.

(d) Upon the filing in the office of the Secretary of State of the certificate of conversion to limited liability company and the certificate of formation or upon the future effective date or time of the certificate of conversion to limited liability company and the certificate of formation, the other entity shall be converted into a domestic limited liability company and the limited liability company shall thereafter be subject to all of the provisions of this chapter, except that notwithstanding § 18–201 of this title, the existence of the limited liability company shall be deemed to have commenced on the date the other entity commenced its existence in the jurisdiction in which the other entity was first created, formed, incorporated or otherwise came into being.

(e) The conversion of any other entity into a domestic limited liability company shall not be deemed to affect any obligations or liabilities of the other entity incurred prior to its conversion to a domestic limited liability company or the personal liability of any person incurred prior to such conversion.

(f) When any conversion shall have become effective under this section, for all purposes of the laws of the State of Delaware, all of the rights, privileges and powers of the other entity that has converted, and all property, real, personal and mixed, and all debts due to such other entity, as well as all other things and causes of action belonging to such other entity, shall remain vested in the domestic limited liability company to which such other entity has converted and shall be the property of such domestic limited liability company, and the title to any real property vested by deed or otherwise in such other entity shall not revert or be in any way impaired by reason of this chapter; but all rights of creditors and all liens upon any property of such other entity shall be preserved unimpaired, and all debts, liabilities and duties of the other entity that has converted shall remain attached to the domestic limited liability company to which such other entity has converted, and may be enforced against it to the same extent as if said debts, liabilities and duties had originally been incurred or contracted by it in its capacity as a domestic limited liability company. The rights, privileges, powers and interests in property of the other entity, as well as the debts, liabilities and duties of the other entity, shall not be deemed, as a consequence of the conversion, to have been transferred to the domestic limited liability company to which such other entity has converted for any purpose of the laws of the State of Delaware.

(g)   Unless otherwise agreed, for all purposes of the laws of the State of Delaware, the converting other entity shall not be required to wind up its affairs or pay its liabilities and distribute its assets, and the conversion shall not be deemed to constitute a dissolution of such other entity. When an other entity has been converted to a limited liability company pursuant to this section, for all purposes of the laws of the State of Delaware, the limited liability company shall be deemed to be the same entity as the converting other entity and the conversion shall constitute a continuation of the existence of the converting other entity in the form of a domestic limited liability company.

(h)   Prior to filing a certificate of conversion to limited liability company with the office of the Secretary of State, the conversion shall be approved in the manner provided for by the document, instrument, agreement or other writing, as the case may be, governing the internal affairs of the other entity and the conduct of its business or by applicable law, as appropriate and a limited liability company agreement shall be approved by the same authorization required to approve the conversion.

(i)   In connection with a conversion hereunder, rights or securities of or interests in the other entity which is to be converted to a domestic limited liability company may be exchanged for or converted into cash, property, or rights or securities of or interests in such domestic limited liability company or, in addition to or in lieu thereof, may be exchanged for or converted into cash, property, or rights or securities of or interests in another domestic limited liability company or other entity, may remain outstanding or may be canceled.

(j)   The provisions of this section shall not be construed to limit the accomplishment of a change in the law governing, or the domicile of, an other entity to the State of Delaware by any other means provided for in a limited liability company agreement or other agreement or as otherwise permitted by law, including by the amendment of a limited liability company agreement or other agreement.

§ 18–215.   Series of members, managers, limited liability company interests or assets.

(a)   A limited liability company agreement may establish or provide for the establishment of 1 or more designated series of members, managers, limited liability company interests or assets. Any such series may have separate rights, powers or duties with respect to specified property or obligations of the limited liability company or profits and losses associated with specified property or obligations, and any such series may have a separate business purpose or investment objective. No provision of subsection (b) of this section or § 18–218 of this title shall be construed to limit the application of the principle of freedom of contract to a series that is not a protected series or a registered series. Other than pursuant to §§ 18–219, 18–220 and 18–221, a series may not merge, convert or consolidate pursuant to any section of this title or any other statute of this State.

(b)   A series established in accordance with the following sentence is a protected series. Notwithstanding anything to the contrary set forth in this chapter or under other applicable law, in the event that a limited liability company agreement establishes or provides for the establishment of 1 or more series, and to the extent the records maintained for any such series account for the assets associated with such series separately from the other assets of the limited liability company, or any other series thereof, and if the limited liability company agreement so provides, and if notice of the limitation on liabilities of a series as referenced in this subsection is set forth in the certificate of formation of the limited liability company, then the debts, liabilities, obligations and expenses incurred, contracted for or otherwise existing with respect to such series shall be enforceable against the assets of such series only, and not against the assets of the limited liability company generally or any other series thereof, and, unless otherwise provided in the limited liability company agreement, none of the debts, liabilities, obligations and expenses incurred, contracted for or otherwise existing with respect to the limited liability company generally or any other series thereof shall be enforceable against the assets of such series. Neither the preceding sentence nor any provision pursuant thereto in a limited liability company agreement or certificate of formation shall (i) restrict a protected series or limited liability company on behalf of a protected series from agreeing in the limited liability company agreement or otherwise that any or all of the debts, liabilities, obligations and expenses incurred, contracted for or otherwise existing with respect to the limited liability company generally or any other series thereof shall be enforceable against the assets of such protected series or (ii) restrict a limited liability company from agreeing in the limited liability company agreement or otherwise that any or all of the debts, liabilities, obligations and expenses incurred, contracted for or otherwise existing with respect to a protected series shall be enforceable against the assets of the limited liability company generally. A limited liability company agreement does not need to use the term protected when referencing series or refer to this section. Assets associated with a protected series may be held directly or indirectly, including in the name of such series, in the name of the limited liability company, through a nominee or otherwise. Records maintained for a protected series that reasonably identify its assets, including by specific listing, category, type, quantity, computational or allocational formula or procedure (including a percentage or share of any asset or assets) or by any other method where the identity of such assets is objectively determinable, will be deemed to account for the assets associated with such series separately from the other assets of the limited liability company, or any other series thereof. Notice in a certificate of formation of the limitation on liabilities of a protected series as referenced in this subsection shall be sufficient for all purposes of this subsection whether or not the limited liability company has established any protected series when such notice is included in the certificate of formation, and there shall be no requirement that (i) any specific protected series of the limited liability company be referenced in such notice, or (ii) such notice use the term protected when referencing series or include a reference to this section. The fact that a certificate of formation that contains the foregoing notice of the limitation on liabilities of a protected series is on file in the office of the Secretary of State shall constitute notice of such limitation on liabilities of a protected series. As used in this chapter, a reference to assets of a protected series includes assets associated with such series, a reference to assets associated with a protected series includes assets of such series, a reference to members or managers of a protected series includes members or managers associated with such series, and a reference to members or managers associated with a protected series includes members or managers of such series. The following shall apply to a protected series:

(1)　A protected series may carry on any lawful business, purpose or activity, whether or not for profit, with the exception of the business of banking as defined in § 126 of Title 8. Unless otherwise provided in a limited liability company agreement, a protected series shall have the power and capacity to, in its own name, contract, hold title to assets (including real, personal and intangible property), grant liens and security interests, and sue and be sued.

(2)　Except as otherwise provided by this chapter, no member or manager of a protected series shall be obligated personally for any debt, obligation or liability of such series, whether arising in contract, tort or otherwise, solely by reason of being a member or acting as manager of such series. Notwithstanding the preceding sentence, under a limited liability company agreement or under another agreement, a member or manager may agree to be obligated personally for any or all of the debts, obligations and liabilities of 1 or more protected series.

(3)　A limited liability company agreement may provide for classes or groups of members or managers associated with a protected series having such relative rights, powers and duties as the limited liability company agreement may provide, and may make provision for the future creation in the manner provided in the limited liability company agreement of additional classes or groups of members or managers associated with such series having such relative rights, powers and duties as may from time to time be established, including rights, powers and duties senior to existing classes and groups of members or managers associated with such series. A limited liability company agreement may provide for the taking of an action, including the amendment of the limited liability company agreement, without the vote or approval of any member or manager or class or group of members or managers, including an action to create under the provisions of the limited liability company agreement a class or group of a protected series of limited liability company interests that was not previously outstanding. A limited liability company agreement may provide that any member or class or group of members associated with a protected series shall have no voting rights.

(4)   A limited liability company agreement may grant to all or certain identified members or managers or a specified class or group of the members or managers associated with a protected series the right to vote separately or with all or any class or group of the members or managers associated with such series, on any matter. Voting by members or managers associated with a protected series may be on a per capita, number, financial interest, class, group or any other basis.

(5)   Unless otherwise provided in a limited liability company agreement, the management of a protected series shall be vested in the members associated with such series in proportion to the then current percentage or other interest of members in the profits of such series owned by all of the members associated with such series, the decision of members owning more than 50 percent of the said percentage or other interest in the profits controlling; provided, however, that if a limited liability company agreement provides for the management of a protected series, in whole or in part, by a manager, the management of such series, to the extent so provided, shall be vested in the manager who shall be chosen in the manner provided in the limited liability company agreement. The manager of a protected series shall also hold the offices and have the responsibilities accorded to the manager as set forth in a limited liability company agreement. A protected series may have more than 1 manager. Subject to § 18–602 of this title, a manager shall cease to be a manager with respect to a protected series as provided in a limited liability company agreement. Except as otherwise provided in a limited liability company agreement, any event under this chapter or in a limited liability company agreement that causes a manager to cease to be a manager with respect to a protected series shall not, in itself, cause such manager to cease to be a manager of the limited liability company or with respect to any other series thereof.

(6)   Notwithstanding § 18–606 of this title, but subject to paragraphs (b)(7) and (b)(10) of this section, and unless otherwise provided in a limited liability company agreement, at the time a member of a protected series becomes entitled to receive a distribution with respect to such series, the member has the status of, and is entitled to all remedies available to, a creditor of such series, with respect to the distribution. A limited liability company agreement may provide for the establishment of a record date with respect to allocations and distributions with respect to a protected series.

(7)   Notwithstanding § 18–607(a) of this title, a limited liability company may make a distribution with respect to a protected series. A limited liability company shall not make a distribution with respect to a protected series to a member to the extent that at the time of the distribution, after giving effect to the distribution, all liabilities of such series, other than liabilities to members on account of their limited liability company interests with respect to such series and liabilities for which the recourse of creditors is limited to specified property of such series, exceed the fair value of the assets associated with such series, except that the fair value of property of such series that is subject to a liability for which the recourse of creditors is limited shall be included in the assets associated with such series only to the extent that the fair value of that property exceeds that liability. For purposes of the immediately preceding sentence, the term "distribution" shall not include amounts constituting reasonable compensation for present or past services or reasonable payments made in the ordinary course of business pursuant to a bona fide retirement plan or other benefits program. A member who receives a distribution in violation of this paragraph (b)(7), and who knew at the time of the distribution that the distribution violated this paragraph (b)(7), shall be liable to the protected series for the amount of the distribution. A member who receives a distribution in violation of this paragraph (b)(7), and who did not know at the time of the distribution that the distribution violated this paragraph (b)(7), shall not be liable for the amount of the distribution. Subject to § 18–607(c) of this title, which shall apply to any distribution made with respect to a protected series under this

paragraph (b)(7), this paragraph (b)(7) shall not affect any obligation or liability of a member under an agreement or other applicable law for the amount of a distribution.

(8) Unless otherwise provided in the limited liability company agreement, a member shall cease to be associated with a protected series and to have the power to exercise any rights or powers of a member with respect to such series upon the assignment of all of the member's limited liability company interest with respect to such series. Except as otherwise provided in a limited liability company agreement, any event under this chapter or a limited liability company agreement that causes a member to cease to be associated with a protected series shall not, in itself, cause such member to cease to be associated with any other series or terminate the continued membership of a member in the limited liability company or cause the termination of the protected series, regardless of whether such member was the last remaining member associated with such series.

(9) Subject to § 18–801 of this title, except to the extent otherwise provided in the limited liability company agreement, a protected series may be terminated and its affairs wound up without causing the dissolution of the limited liability company. The termination of a protected series shall not affect the limitation on liabilities of such series provided by this subsection (b). A protected series is terminated and its affairs shall be wound up upon the dissolution of the limited liability company under § 18–801 of this title or otherwise upon the first to occur of the following:

a. At the time specified in the limited liability company agreement;

b. Upon the happening of events specified in the limited liability company agreement;

c. Unless otherwise provided in the limited liability company agreement, upon the vote or consent of members associated with such series who own more than 2/3 of the then-current percentage or other interest in the profits of such series of the limited liability company owned by all of the members associated with such series; or

d. The termination of such series under paragraph (b)(11) of this section.

Unless otherwise provided in a limited liability company agreement, a limited liability company whose original certificate of formation was filed with the Secretary of State and effective on or prior to July 31, 2015, shall continue to be governed by paragraph (k)(3) of this section as in effect on July 31, 2015 (except that "affirmative" and "written" shall be deleted from such paragraph (k)(3) of this section).

(10) Notwithstanding § 18–803(a) of this title, unless otherwise provided in the limited liability company agreement, a manager associated with a protected series who has not wrongfully terminated such series or, if none, the members associated with such series or a person approved by the members associated with such series, in either case, by members who own more than 50 percent of the then current percentage or other interest in the profits of such series owned by all of the members associated with such series, may wind up the affairs of such series; but the Court of Chancery, upon cause shown, may wind up the affairs of a protected series upon application of any member or manager associated with such series, or the member's personal representative or assignee, and in connection therewith, may appoint a liquidating trustee. The persons winding up the affairs of a protected series may, in the name of the limited liability company and for and on behalf of the limited liability company and such series, take all actions with respect to such series as are permitted under § 18–803(b) of this title. The persons winding up the affairs of a protected series shall provide for the claims and obligations of such series and distribute the assets of such series as provided in § 18–804 of this title, which section shall apply to the winding up and distribution of assets of a protected series. Actions taken in accordance with this paragraph (b)(10) shall not affect the liability of members and shall not impose liability on a liquidating trustee. Unless otherwise provided in a limited liability company agreement, a limited liability company whose original certificate of formation was filed with the Secretary of

State and effective on or prior to July 31, 2015, shall continue to be governed by the first sentence of this paragraph (b)(10) as in effect on July 31, 2015.

(11) On application by or for a member or manager associated with a protected series, the Court of Chancery may decree termination of such series whenever it is not reasonably practicable to carry on the business of such series in conformity with a limited liability company agreement.

(12) For all purposes of the laws of the State of Delaware, a protected series is an association, regardless of the number of members or managers, if any, of such series.

(c) If a foreign limited liability company that is registering to do business in the State of Delaware in accordance with § 18–902 of this title is governed by a limited liability company agreement that establishes or provides for the establishment of designated series of members, managers, limited liability company interests or assets having separate rights, powers or duties with respect to specified property or obligations of the foreign limited liability company or profits and losses associated with specified property or obligations, that fact shall be so stated on the application for registration as a foreign limited liability company. In addition, the foreign limited liability company shall state on such application whether the debts, liabilities and obligations incurred, contracted for or otherwise existing with respect to a particular series, if any, shall be enforceable against the assets of such series only, and not against the assets of the foreign limited liability company generally or any other series thereof, and whether any of the debts, liabilities, obligations and expenses incurred, contracted for or otherwise existing with respect to the foreign limited liability company generally or any other series thereof shall be enforceable against the assets of such series.

§ 18–216.   Approval of conversion of a limited liability company.

(a) Upon compliance with this section, a domestic limited liability company may convert to a corporation, a statutory trust, a business trust, an association, a real estate investment trust, a common-law trust or any other incorporated or unincorporated business or entity, including a partnership (whether general (including a limited liability partnership) or limited (including a limited liability limited partnership)) or a foreign limited liability company.

(b) If the limited liability company agreement specifies the manner of authorizing a conversion of the limited liability company, the conversion shall be authorized as specified in the limited liability company agreement. If the limited liability company agreement does not specify the manner of authorizing a conversion of the limited liability company and does not prohibit a conversion of the limited liability company, the conversion shall be authorized in the same manner as is specified in the limited liability company agreement for authorizing a merger or consolidation that involves the limited liability company as a constituent party to the merger or consolidation. If the limited liability company agreement does not specify the manner of authorizing a conversion of the limited liability company or a merger or consolidation that involves the limited liability company as a constituent party and does not prohibit a conversion of the limited liability company, the conversion shall be authorized by the approval by members who own more than 50 percent of the then current percentage or other interest in the profits of the domestic limited liability company owned by all of the members. Unless otherwise provided in a limited liability company agreement, a limited liability company whose original certificate of formation was filed with the Secretary of State and effective on or prior to July 31, 2015, shall continue to be governed by the third sentence of this subsection as in effect on July 31, 2015.

(c) Unless otherwise agreed, the conversion of a domestic limited liability company to another entity or business form pursuant to this section shall not require such limited liability company to wind up its affairs under § 18–803 of this title or pay its liabilities and distribute its assets under § 18–804 of this title, and the conversion shall not constitute a dissolution of such limited liability company. When a limited liability company has converted to another entity or business form pursuant to this section, for all purposes of the laws of the State of Delaware, the other entity or business form shall be deemed to be the same entity as the converting limited liability company and the conversion shall constitute a continuation of the existence of the limited liability company in the form of such other entity or business form.

(d)   In connection with a conversion of a domestic limited liability company to another entity or business form pursuant to this section, rights or securities of or interests in the domestic limited liability company which is to be converted may be exchanged for or converted into cash, property, rights or securities of or interests in the entity or business form into which the domestic limited liability company is being converted or, in addition to or in lieu thereof, may be exchanged for or converted into cash, property, rights or securities of or interests in another entity or business form, may remain outstanding or may be canceled.

(e)   If a limited liability company shall convert in accordance with this section to another entity or business form organized, formed or created under the laws of a jurisdiction other than the State of Delaware, a certificate of conversion to non-Delaware entity executed in accordance with § 18–204 of this title, shall be filed in the office of the Secretary of State in accordance with § 18–206 of this title. The certificate of conversion to non-Delaware entity shall state:

(1)   The name of the limited liability company and, if it has been changed, the name under which its certificate of formation was originally filed;

(2)   The date of filing of its original certificate of formation with the Secretary of State;

(3)   The jurisdiction in which the entity or business form, to which the limited liability company shall be converted, is organized, formed or created, and the name of such entity or business form;

(4)   The future effective date or time (which shall be a date or time certain) of the conversion if it is not to be effective upon the filing of the certificate of conversion to non-Delaware entity;

(5)   That the conversion has been approved in accordance with this section;

(6)   The agreement of the limited liability company that it may be served with process in the State of Delaware in any action, suit or proceeding for enforcement of any obligation of the limited liability company arising while it was a limited liability company of the State of Delaware, and that it irrevocably appoints the Secretary of State as its agent to accept service of process in any such action, suit or proceeding;

(7)   The address to which a copy of the process referred to in paragraph (e)(6) of this section shall be mailed to it by the Secretary of State. Process may be served upon the Secretary of State under paragraph (e)(6) of this section by means of electronic transmission but only as prescribed by the Secretary of State. The Secretary of State is authorized to issue such rules and regulations with respect to such service as the Secretary of State deems necessary or appropriate. In the event of service hereunder upon the Secretary of State, the procedures set forth in § 18–911(c) of this title shall be applicable, except that the plaintiff in any such action, suit or proceeding shall furnish the Secretary of State with the address specified in this subdivision and any other address that the plaintiff may elect to furnish, together with copies of such process as required by the Secretary of State, and the Secretary of State shall notify the limited liability company that has converted out of the State of Delaware at all such addresses furnished by the plaintiff in accordance with the procedures set forth in § 18–911(c) of this title.

(f)   Upon the filing in the office of the Secretary of State of the certificate of conversion to non-Delaware entity or upon the future effective date or time of the certificate of conversion to non-Delaware entity and payment to the Secretary of State of all fees prescribed in this chapter, the Secretary of State shall certify that the limited liability company has filed all documents and paid all fees required by this chapter, and thereupon the limited liability company shall cease to exist as a limited liability company of the State of Delaware. Such certificate of the Secretary of State shall be prima facie evidence of the conversion by such limited liability company out of the State of Delaware.

(g) The conversion of a limited liability company out of the State of Delaware in accordance with this section and the resulting cessation of its existence as a limited liability company of the State of Delaware pursuant to a certificate of conversion to non-Delaware entity shall not be deemed to affect any obligations or liabilities of the limited liability company incurred prior to such conversion or the personal liability of any person incurred prior to such conversion, nor shall it be deemed to affect the choice of law applicable to the limited liability company with respect to matters arising prior to such conversion.

(h) When any conversion shall have become effective under this section, for all purposes of the laws of the State of Delaware, all of the rights, privileges and powers of the limited liability company that has converted, and all property, real, personal and mixed, and all debts due to such limited liability company, as well as all other things and causes of action belonging to such limited liability company, shall remain vested in the other entity or business form to which such limited liability company has converted and shall be the property of such other entity or business form, and the title to any real property vested by deed or otherwise in such limited liability company shall not revert or be in any way impaired by reason of this chapter; but all rights of creditors and all liens upon any property of such limited liability company shall be preserved unimpaired, and all debts, liabilities and duties of the limited liability company that has converted shall remain attached to the other entity or business form to which such limited liability company has converted, and may be enforced against it to the same extent as if said debts, liabilities and duties had originally been incurred or contracted by it in its capacity as such other entity or business form. The rights, privileges, powers and interests in property of the limited liability company that has converted, as well as the debts, liabilities and duties of such limited liability company, shall not be deemed, as a consequence of the conversion, to have been transferred to the other entity or business form to which such limited liability company has converted for any purpose of the laws of the State of Delaware.

(i) A limited liability company agreement may provide that a domestic limited liability company shall not have the power to convert as set forth in this section.

§ 18–217. Division of a limited liability company.

(a) As used in this section and §§ 18–203, 18–301 and 18–1203:

(1) "Dividing company" means the domestic limited liability company that is effecting a division in the manner provided in this section.

(2) "Division" means the division of a dividing company into 2 or more domestic limited liability companies in accordance with this section.

(3) "Division company" means a surviving company, if any, and each resulting company.

(4) "Division contact" means, in connection with any division, a natural person who is a Delaware resident, any division company in such division or any other domestic limited liability company or other business entity as defined in § 18–209 of this title formed or organized under the laws of the State of Delaware, which division contact shall maintain a copy of the plan of division for a period of 6 years from the effective date of the division and shall comply with paragraph (g)(3) of this section.

(5) "Organizational documents" means the certificate of formation and limited liability company agreement of a domestic limited liability company.

(6) "Resulting company" means a domestic limited liability company formed as a consequence of a division.

(7) "Surviving company" means a dividing company that survives the division.

(b) Pursuant to a plan of division, any domestic limited liability company may, in the manner provided in this section, be divided into 2 or more domestic limited liability companies. The division of a domestic limited liability company in accordance with this section and, if applicable, the resulting cessation of the existence of the dividing company pursuant to a certificate of division shall not be deemed to affect the personal liability of any person incurred prior to such division with respect to matters arising prior to such division, nor shall it be deemed to affect the validity or enforceability of any obligations or liabilities of the dividing company incurred prior to such division; provided, that the obligations and liabilities of the dividing company shall be allocated to and vested in, and valid and enforceable obligations of, such division company or companies to which such obligations and liabilities have been allocated pursuant to the plan of division, as provided in subsection (l) of this section. Each resulting company in a division shall be formed in compliance with the requirements of this chapter and subsection (i) of this section.

(c)   If the limited liability company agreement of the dividing company specifies the manner of adopting a plan of division, the plan of division shall be adopted as specified in the limited liability company agreement. If the limited liability company agreement of the dividing company does not specify the manner of adopting a plan of division and does not prohibit a division of the limited liability company, the plan of division shall be adopted in the same manner as is specified in the limited liability company agreement for authorizing a merger or consolidation that involves the limited liability company as a constituent party to the merger or consolidation. If the limited liability company agreement of the dividing company does not specify the manner of adopting a plan of division or authorizing a merger or consolidation that involves the limited liability company as a constituent party and does not prohibit a division of the limited liability company, the adoption of a plan of division shall be authorized by the approval by members who own more than 50 percent of the then current percentage or other interest in the profits of the dividing company owned by all of the members. Notwithstanding prior approval, a plan of division may be terminated or amended pursuant to a provision for such termination or amendment contained in the plan of division.

(d)   Unless otherwise provided in a plan of division, the division of a domestic limited liability company pursuant to this section shall not require such limited liability company to wind up its affairs under § 18–803 of this title or pay its liabilities and distribute its assets under § 18–804 of this title, and the division shall not constitute a dissolution of such limited liability company.

(e)   In connection with a division under this section, rights or securities of, or interests in, the dividing company may be exchanged for or converted into cash, property, rights or securities of, or interests in, the surviving company or any resulting company or, in addition to or in lieu thereof, may be exchanged for or converted into cash, property, rights or securities of, or interests in, a domestic limited liability company or any other business entity which is not a division company or may be canceled or remain outstanding (if the dividing company is a surviving company).

(f)   A plan of division adopted in accordance with subsection (c) of this section:

(1)   May effect any amendment to the limited liability company agreement of the dividing company if it is a surviving company in the division; or

(2)   May effect the adoption of a new limited liability company agreement for the dividing company if it is a surviving company in the division; and

(3)   Shall effect the adoption of a limited liability company agreement for each resulting company.

Any amendment to a limited liability company agreement or adoption of a new limited liability company agreement for the dividing company, if it is a surviving company in the division, or adoption of a limited liability company agreement for each resulting company made pursuant to the foregoing sentence shall be effective at the effective time or date of the division. Any amendment to a limited liability company agreement or adoption of a limited liability company agreement for the dividing company, if it is a surviving company in the division, shall be effective notwithstanding any provision in the limited liability company agreement of the dividing company relating to amendment or adoption of a new limited liability company agreement, other than a provision that by its terms applies to an amendment to the limited liability company agreement or the adoption of a new limited liability company agreement, in either case, in connection with a division, merger or consolidation.

(g)   If a domestic limited liability company is dividing under this section, the dividing company shall adopt a plan of division which shall set forth:

(1)   The terms and conditions of the division, including:

a.   Any conversion or exchange of the limited liability company interests of the dividing company into or for limited liability company interests or other securities or obligations of any division company or cash, property or rights or securities or obligations of or interests in any other business entity or domestic limited liability company which is not a division company, or that the limited liability company interests of the dividing company shall remain outstanding or be canceled, or any combination of the foregoing; and

b.   The allocation of assets, property, rights, series, debts, liabilities and duties of the dividing company among the division companies;

(2)   The name of each resulting company and, if the dividing company will survive the division, the name of the surviving company;

(3)   The name and business address of a division contact which shall have custody of a copy of the plan of division. The division contact, or any successor division contact, shall serve for a period of 6 years following the effective date of the division. During such 6-year period the division contact shall provide, without cost, to any creditor of the dividing company, within 30 days following the division contact's receipt of a written request from any creditor of the dividing company, the name and business address of the division company to which the claim of such creditor was allocated pursuant to the plan of division; and

(4)   Any other matters that the dividing company determines to include therein.

(h)   If a domestic limited liability company divides under this section, the dividing company shall file a certificate of division executed by 1 or more authorized persons on behalf of such dividing company in the office of the Secretary of State in accordance with § 18–204 of this title and a certificate of formation that complies with § 18–201 of this title for each resulting company executed by 1 or more authorized persons in accordance with § 18–204 of this title. The certificate of division shall state:

(1)   The name of the dividing company and, if it has been changed, the name under which its certificate of formation was originally filed and whether the dividing company is a surviving company;

(2)   The date of filing of the dividing company's original certificate of formation with the Secretary of State;

(3)   The name of each division company;

(4)   The name and business address of the division contact required by paragraph (g)(3) of this section;

(5)   The future effective date or time (which shall be a date or time certain) of the division if it is not to be effective upon the filing of the certificate of division;

(6)   That the division has been approved in accordance with this section;

(7)   That the plan of division is on file at a place of business of such division company as is specified therein, and shall state the address thereof; and

(8)   That a copy of the plan of division will be furnished by such division company as is specified therein, on request and without cost, to any member of the dividing company.

(i)   The certificate of division and each certificate of formation for each resulting company required by subsection (h) of this section shall be filed simultaneously in the office of the Secretary of State and, if such certificates are not to become effective upon their filing as permitted by § 18–206(b) of this title, then each such certificate shall provide for the same effective date or time in accordance with § 18–206(b) of this title. Concurrently with the effective date or time of a division, the limited liability company agreement of each resulting company shall become effective.

(j) A certificate of division shall act as a certificate of cancellation for a dividing company which is not a surviving company.

(k) A limited liability company agreement may provide that a domestic limited liability company shall not have the power to divide as set forth in this section.

(*l*) Upon the division of a domestic limited liability company becoming effective:

(1) The dividing company shall be divided into the distinct and independent resulting companies named in the plan of division, and, if the dividing company is not a surviving company, the existence of the dividing company shall cease.

(2) For all purposes of the laws of the State of Delaware, all of the rights, privileges and powers, and all the property, real, personal and mixed, of the dividing company and all debts due on whatever account to it, as well as all other things and other causes of action belonging to it, shall without further action be allocated to and vested in the applicable division company in such a manner and basis and with such effect as is specified in the plan of division, and the title to any real property or interest therein allocated to and vested in any division company shall not revert or be in any way impaired by reason of the division.

(3) Each division company shall, from and after effectiveness of the certificate of division, be liable as a separate and distinct domestic limited liability company for such debts, liabilities and duties of the dividing company as are allocated to such division company pursuant to the plan of division in the manner and on the basis provided in paragraph (g)(1)b. of this section.

(4) Each of the debts, liabilities and duties of the dividing company shall without further action be allocated to and be the debts, liabilities and duties of such division company as is specified in the plan of division as having such debts, liabilities and duties allocated to it, in such a manner and basis and with such effect as is specified in the plan of division, and no other division company shall be liable therefor, so long as the plan of division does not constitute a fraudulent transfer under applicable law, and all liens upon any property of the dividing company shall be preserved unimpaired, and all debts, liabilities and duties of the dividing company shall remain attached to the division company to which such debts, liabilities and duties have been allocated in the plan of division, and may be enforced against such division company to the same extent as if said debts, liabilities and duties had originally been incurred or contracted by it in its capacity as a domestic limited liability company.

(5) In the event that any allocation of assets, debts, liabilities and duties to division companies in accordance with a plan of division is determined by a court of competent jurisdiction to constitute a fraudulent transfer, each division company shall be jointly and severally liable on account of such fraudulent transfer notwithstanding the allocations made in the plan of division; provided, however, the validity and effectiveness of the division are not otherwise affected thereby.

(6) Debts and liabilities of the dividing company that are not allocated by the plan of division shall be the joint and several debts and liabilities of all of the division companies.

(7) It shall not be necessary for a plan of division to list each individual asset, property, right, series, debt, liability or duty of the dividing company to be allocated to a division company so long as the assets, property, rights, series, debts, liabilities or duties so allocated are reasonably identified by any method where the identity of such assets, property, rights, series, debts, liabilities or duties is objectively determinable.

(8) The rights, privileges, powers and interests in property of the dividing company that have been allocated to a division company, as well as the debts, liabilities and duties of the dividing company that have been allocated to such division company pursuant to a plan of

division, shall remain vested in each such division company and shall not be deemed, as a result of the division, to have been assigned or transferred to such division company for any purpose of the laws of the State of Delaware.

(9) Any action or proceeding pending against a dividing company may be continued against the surviving company as if the division did not occur, but subject to paragraph (*l*)(4) of this section, and against any resulting company to which the asset, property, right, series, debt, liability or duty associated with such action or proceeding was allocated pursuant to the plan of division by adding or substituting such resulting company as a party in the action or proceeding.

(m) In applying the provisions of this chapter on distributions, a direct or indirect allocation of property or liabilities in a division is not deemed a distribution for purposes of this chapter.

(n) The provisions of this section shall not be construed to limit the means of accomplishing a division by any other means provided for in a limited liability company agreement or other agreement or as otherwise permitted by this chapter or as otherwise permitted by law.

(o) All limited liability companies formed on or after August 1, 2018, shall be governed by this section. All limited liability companies formed prior to August 1, 2018, shall be governed by this section; provided, that if the dividing company is a party to any written contract, indenture or other agreement entered into prior to August 1, 2018, that, by its terms, restricts, conditions or prohibits the consummation of a merger or consolidation by the dividing company with or into another party, or the transfer of assets by the dividing company to another party, then such restriction, condition or prohibition shall be deemed to apply to a division as if it were a merger, consolidation or transfer of assets, as applicable.

§ 18–218.   Registered series of members, managers, limited liability company interests or assets.

(a) If a limited liability company agreement provides for the establishment or formation of 1 or more series, then a registered series may be formed by complying with this § 18–218. A limited liability company agreement does not need to use the term registered when referencing series or refer to this § 18–218, and a reference in a limited liability company agreement for a registered series, including a registered series resulting from the conversion of a protected series to a registered series, may continue to refer to § 18–215 of this title, which reference shall be deemed a reference to this § 18–218 with respect to such registered series. A registered series is formed by the filing of a certificate of registered series in the office of the Secretary of State.

(b) Notice of the limitation on liabilities of a registered series as referenced in subsection (c) of this section shall be set forth in the certificate of formation of the limited liability company. Notice in a certificate of formation of the limitation on liabilities of a registered series as referenced in subsection (c) of this section shall be sufficient for all purposes of this subsection whether or not the limited liability company has formed any registered series when such notice is included in the certificate of formation, and there shall be no requirement that (i) any specific registered series of the limited liability company be referenced in such notice, (ii) such notice use the term registered when referencing series or include a reference to this § 18–218, or (iii) the certificate of formation be amended if it includes a reference to § 18–215 of this title. Any reference to § 18–215 of this title in a certificate of formation of a limited liability company that has one or more registered series shall be deemed a reference to this § 18–218 with respect to such registered series. The fact that a certificate of formation that contains the foregoing notice of the limitation on liabilities of a series is on file in the office of the Secretary of State shall constitute notice of such limitation on liabilities of a registered series.

(c) Notwithstanding anything to the contrary set forth in this chapter or under other applicable law, to the extent the records maintained for a registered series account for the assets associated with such series separately from the other assets of the limited liability company, or any other series thereof, then the debts, liabilities, obligations and expenses incurred, contracted for or otherwise existing with respect to such series shall be enforceable against the assets of such series only, and not against the assets of the limited liability company generally or any other series thereof, and, unless otherwise provided in the limited liability company agreement, none of the debts, liabilities, obligations and expenses incurred, contracted for or otherwise existing with respect to the limited liability company generally or any other series thereof shall be enforceable against the assets of such series. Neither the preceding sentences nor any provision pursuant thereto in a limited liability company agreement, certificate of formation or certificate of registered series shall (i) restrict a registered series or limited liability company on behalf of a registered series from agreeing in the limited liability company agreement or otherwise that any or all of the debts, liabilities, obligations and expenses incurred, contracted for or otherwise existing with respect to the limited liability company generally or any other series thereof shall be enforceable against the assets of such registered series or (ii) restrict a limited liability company from agreeing in the limited liability company agreement or otherwise that any or all of the debts, liabilities, obligations and expenses incurred, contracted for or otherwise existing with respect to a registered series shall be enforceable against the assets of the limited liability company generally. Assets associated with a registered series may be held directly or indirectly, including in the name of such series, in the name of the limited liability company, through a nominee or otherwise. Records maintained for a registered series that reasonably identify its assets, including by specific listing, category, type, quantity, computational or allocational formula or procedure (including a percentage or share of any asset or assets) or by any other method where the identity of such assets is objectively determinable, will be deemed to account for the assets associated with such series separately from the other assets of the limited liability company, or any other series thereof. As used in this chapter, a reference to assets of a registered series includes assets associated with such series, a reference to assets associated with a registered series includes assets of such series, a reference to members or managers of a registered series includes members or managers associated with such series, and a reference to members or managers associated with a registered series includes members or managers of such series. The following shall apply to a registered series:

(1)   A registered series may carry on any lawful business, purpose or activity, whether or not for profit, with the exception of the business of banking as defined in § 126 of Title 8. Unless otherwise provided in a limited liability company agreement, a registered series shall have the power and capacity to, in its own name, contract, hold title to assets (including real, personal and intangible property), grant liens and security interests, and sue and be sued.

(2)   Except as otherwise provided by this chapter, no member or manager of a registered series shall be obligated personally for any debt, obligation or liability of such series, whether arising in contract, tort or otherwise, solely by reason of being a member or acting as manager of such series. Notwithstanding the preceding sentence, under a limited liability company agreement or under another agreement, a member or manager may agree to be obligated personally for any or all of the debts, obligations and liabilities of 1 or more registered series.

(3)   A limited liability company agreement may provide for classes or groups of members or managers associated with a registered series having such relative rights, powers and duties as the limited liability company agreement may provide, and may make provision for the future creation in the manner provided in the limited liability company agreement of additional classes or groups of members or managers associated with such series having such relative rights, powers and duties as may from time to time be established, including rights, powers and duties senior to existing classes and groups of members or managers associated with such series. A limited liability company agreement may provide for the taking of an action, including the amendment of the limited liability company agreement, without the vote or approval of any member or manager or class or group of members or managers, including an action to create under the provisions of the limited liability company agreement a class or group of a registered series of limited liability company interests that was not previously outstanding. A limited liability company agreement may provide that any member or class or group of members associated with a registered series shall have no voting rights.

(4)   A limited liability company agreement may grant to all or certain identified members or managers or a specified class or group of the members or managers associated with a registered

series the right to vote separately or with all or any class or group of the members or managers associated with such series, on any matter. Voting by members or managers associated with a registered series may be on a per capita, number, financial interest, class, group or any other basis.

(5)   Unless otherwise provided in a limited liability company agreement, the management of a registered series shall be vested in the members associated with such series in proportion to the then current percentage or other interest of members in the profits of such series owned by all of the members associated with such series, the decision of members owning more than 50 percent of the said percentage or other interest in the profits controlling; provided, however, that if a limited liability company agreement provides for the management of a registered series, in whole or in part, by a manager, the management of such series, to the extent so provided, shall be vested in the manager who shall be chosen in the manner provided in the limited liability company agreement. The manager of a registered series shall also hold the offices and have the responsibilities accorded to the manager as set forth in a limited liability company agreement. A registered series may have more than 1 manager. Subject to § 18–602 of this title, a manager shall cease to be a manager with respect to a registered series as provided in a limited liability company agreement. Except as otherwise provided in a limited liability company agreement, any event under this chapter or in a limited liability company agreement that causes a manager to cease to be a manager with respect to a registered series shall not, in itself, cause such manager to cease to be a manager of the limited liability company or with respect to any other series thereof.

(6)   Notwithstanding § 18–606 of this title, but subject to paragraphs (c)(7) and (c)(10) of this section, and unless otherwise provided in a limited liability company agreement, at the time a member of a registered series becomes entitled to receive a distribution with respect to such series, the member has the status of, and is entitled to all remedies available to, a creditor of such series, with respect to the distribution. A limited liability company agreement may provide for the establishment of a record date with respect to allocations and distributions with respect to a registered series.

(7)   Notwithstanding § 18–607(a) of this title, a limited liability company may make a distribution with respect to a registered series. A limited liability company shall not make a distribution with respect to a registered series to a member to the extent that at the time of the distribution, after giving effect to the distribution, all liabilities of such series, other than liabilities to members on account of their limited liability company interests with respect to such series and liabilities for which the recourse of creditors is limited to specified property of such series, exceed the fair value of the assets associated with such series, except that the fair value of property of such series that is subject to a liability for which the recourse of creditors is limited shall be included in the assets associated with such series only to the extent that the fair value of that property exceeds that liability. For purposes of the immediately preceding sentence, the term "distribution" shall not include amounts constituting reasonable compensation for present or past services or reasonable payments made in the ordinary course of business pursuant to a bona fide retirement plan or other benefits program. A member who receives a distribution in violation of this subsection, and who knew at the time of the distribution that the distribution violated this subsection, shall be liable to the registered series for the amount of the distribution. A member who receives a distribution in violation of this subsection, and who did not know at the time of the distribution that the distribution violated this subsection, shall not be liable for the amount of the distribution. Subject to § 18–607(c) of this title, which shall apply to any distribution made with respect to a registered series under this subsection, this subsection shall not affect any obligation or liability of a member under an agreement or other applicable law for the amount of a distribution.

(8)   Unless otherwise provided in the limited liability company agreement, a member shall cease to be associated with a registered series and to have the power to exercise any rights or powers of a member with respect to such series upon the assignment of all of the member's limited

liability company interest with respect to such series. Except as otherwise provided in a limited liability company agreement, any event under this chapter or a limited liability company agreement that causes a member to cease to be associated with a registered series shall not, in itself, cause such member to cease to be associated with any other series or terminate the continued membership of a member in the limited liability company or cause the dissolution of the registered series, regardless of whether such member was the last remaining member associated with such series.

(9)   Subject to § 18–801 of this title, except to the extent otherwise provided in the limited liability company agreement, a registered series may be dissolved and its affairs wound up without causing the dissolution of the limited liability company. The dissolution of a registered series shall not affect the limitation on liabilities of such series provided by this subsection (c). A registered series is dissolved and its affairs shall be wound up upon the dissolution of the limited liability company under § 18–801 of this title or otherwise upon the first to occur of the following:

    a.   At the time specified in the limited liability company agreement;

    b.   Upon the happening of events specified in the limited liability company agreement;

    c.   Unless otherwise provided in the limited liability company agreement, upon the vote or consent of members associated with such series who own more than 2/3 of the then-current percentage or other interest in the profits of such series of the limited liability company owned by all of the members associated with such series; or

    d.   The dissolution of such series under paragraph (c)(11) of this section.

(10)   Notwithstanding § 18–803(a) of this title, unless otherwise provided in the limited liability company agreement, a manager associated with a registered series who has not wrongfully dissolved such series or, if none, the members associated with such series or a person approved by the members associated with such series, in either case, by members who own more than 50 percent of the then current percentage or other interest in the profits of such series owned by all of the members associated with such series, may wind up the affairs of such series; but the Court of Chancery, upon cause shown, may wind up the affairs of a registered series upon application of any member or manager associated with such series, or the member's personal representative or assignee, and in connection therewith, may appoint a liquidating trustee. The persons winding up the affairs of a registered series may, in the name of the limited liability company and for and on behalf of the limited liability company and such series, take all actions with respect to such series as are permitted under § 18–803(b) of this title. The persons winding up the affairs of a registered series shall provide for the claims and obligations of such series and distribute the assets of such series as provided in § 18–804 of this title, which section shall apply to the winding up and distribution of assets of a registered series. Actions taken in accordance with this subsection shall not affect the liability of members and shall not impose liability on a liquidating trustee.

(11)   On application by or for a member or manager associated with a registered series, the Court of Chancery may decree dissolution of such series whenever it is not reasonably practicable to carry on the business of such series in conformity with a limited liability company agreement.

(12)   For all purposes of the laws of the State of Delaware, a registered series is an association, regardless of the number of members or managers, if any, of such series.

(d)   In order to form a registered series of a limited liability company, a certificate of registered series must be filed in accordance with this subsection.

    (1)   A certificate of registered series:

      a.   Shall set forth:

        1.   The name of the limited liability company; and

2.   The name of the registered series.

b.   May include any other matter that the members of such registered series determine to include therein.

(2)   A certificate of registered series shall be executed in accordance with § 18–204 of this title and shall be filed in the office of the Secretary of State in accordance with § 18–206 of this title. A certificate of registered series shall be effective as of the effective time of such filing unless a later effective date or time (which shall be a date or time certain) is provided for in the certificate of registered series. A certificate of registered series is not an amendment to the certificate of formation of the limited liability company. The filing of a certificate of registered series in the office of the Secretary of State shall make it unnecessary to file any other documents under Chapter 31 of this title.

(3)   A certificate of registered series is amended by filing a certificate of amendment thereto in the office of the Secretary of State. The certificate of amendment of certificate of registered series shall set forth:

a.   The name of the limited liability company;

b.   The name of the registered series; and

c.   The amendment to the certificate of registered series.

(4)   A manager of a registered series or, if there is no manager, then any member of a registered series who becomes aware that any statement in a certificate of registered series filed with respect to such registered series was false when made, or that any matter described therein has changed making the certificate of registered series false in any material respect, shall promptly amend the certificate of registered series.

(5)   A certificate of registered series may be amended at any time for any other proper purpose.

(6)   Unless otherwise provided in this chapter or unless a later effective date or time (which shall be a date or time certain) is provided for in the certificate of amendment of certificate of registered series, a certificate of amendment of certificate of registered series shall be effective at the time of its filing with the Secretary of State.

(7)   A certificate of registered series shall be canceled upon the cancellation of the certificate of formation of the limited liability company named in the certificate of registered series, or upon the filing of a certificate of cancellation of the certificate of registered series or upon the future effective date or time of a certificate of cancellation of the certificate of registered series, or as provided in § 18–1108(b) of this title, or upon the filing of a certificate of merger or consolidation of registered series if the registered series is not the surviving or resulting registered series in a merger or consolidation or upon the future effective date or time of a certificate of merger or consolidation of registered series if the registered series is not the surviving or resulting registered series in a merger or consolidation, or upon the filing of a certificate of conversion of registered series to protected series or upon the future effective date or time of a certificate of conversion of registered series to protected series. A certificate of cancellation of the certificate of registered series may be filed at any time, and shall be filed, in the office of the Secretary of State to accomplish the cancellation of a certificate of registered series upon the dissolution of a registered series for which a certificate of registered series was filed and completion of the winding up of such registered series. A certificate of cancellation of the certificate of registered series shall set forth:

a.   The name of the limited liability company;

b.   The name of the registered series;

c.   The date of filing of the certificate of registered series;

d.   The future effective date or time (which shall be a date or time certain) of cancellation if it is not to be effective upon the filing of the certificate of cancellation; and

e.   Any other information the person filing the certificate of cancellation of the certificate of registered series determines.

(8)   A certificate of cancellation of the certificate of registered series that is filed in the office of the Secretary of State prior to the dissolution or the completion of winding up of a registered series may be corrected as an erroneously executed certificate of cancellation of the certificate of registered series by filing with the office of the Secretary of State a certificate of correction of such certificate of cancellation of the certificate of registered series in accordance with § 18–211 of this title.

(9)   The Secretary of State shall not issue a certificate of good standing with respect to a registered series if its certificate of registered series is canceled or the limited liability company has ceased to be in good standing.

(e)   The name of each registered series as set forth in its certificate of registered series:

(1)   Shall begin with the name of the limited liability company, including any word, abbreviation or designation required by § 18–102 of this title;

(2)   May contain the name of a member or manager;

(3)   Must be such as to distinguish it upon the records in the office of the Secretary of State from the name on such records of any corporation, partnership, limited partnership, statutory trust, limited liability company or registered series reserved, registered, formed or organized under the laws of the State of Delaware or qualified to do business or registered as a foreign corporation, foreign limited partnership, foreign statutory trust, foreign partnership or foreign limited liability company in the State of Delaware; provided, however, that a registered series may register under any name which is not such as to distinguish it upon the records in the office of the Secretary of State from the name on such records of any domestic or foreign corporation, partnership, limited partnership, statutory trust, registered series or foreign limited liability company reserved, registered, formed or organized under the laws of the State of Delaware with the written consent of the other corporation, partnership, limited partnership, statutory trust, registered series or foreign limited liability company, which written consent shall be filed with the Secretary of State;

(4)   May contain the following words: "Company," "Association," "Club," "Foundation," "Fund," "Institute," "Society," "Union," "Syndicate," "Limited," "Public Benefit" or "Trust" (or abbreviations of like import); and

(5)   Shall not contain the word "bank," or any variation thereof, except for the name of a bank reporting to and under the supervision of the State Bank Commissioner of this State or a subsidiary of a bank or savings association (as those terms are defined in the Federal Deposit Insurance Act, as amended, at 12 U.S.C. § 1813), or a limited liability company regulated under the Bank Holding Company Act of 1956, as amended, 12 U.S.C. § 1841 et seq., or the Home Owners' Loan Act, as amended, 12 U.S.C. § 1461 et seq.; provided, however, that this section shall not be construed to prevent the use of the word "bank," or any variation thereof, in a context clearly not purporting to refer to a banking business or otherwise likely to mislead the public about the nature of the business of the limited liability company or the registered series, or to lead to a pattern and practice of abuse that might cause harm to the interests of the public or this State as determined by the Division of Corporations in the Department of State.

§ 18–219.   **Approval of conversion of a protected series of a domestic limited liability company to a registered series of such domestic limited liability company.**

(a)   A protected series of a domestic limited liability company may convert to a registered series of such domestic limited liability company by complying with this section and filing in the office of the Secretary of State in accordance with § 18–206 of this title:

(1)   A certificate of conversion of protected series to registered series that has been executed in accordance with § 18–204 of this title; and

(2)   A certificate of registered series that complies with § 18–218(d) of this title and has been executed by 1 or more authorized persons in accordance with § 18–204 of this title.

Each of the certificates required by this subsection (a) shall be filed simultaneously in the office of the Secretary of State and, if such certificates are not to become effective upon their filing as permitted by § 18–206(b) of this title, then each such certificate shall provide for the same effective date or time in accordance with § 18–206(b) of this title.

An existing series may not become a registered series other than pursuant to this section.

(b)   If the limited liability company agreement specifies the manner of authorizing a conversion of a protected series of such limited liability company to a registered series of such limited liability company, the conversion of a protected series to a registered series shall be authorized as specified in the limited liability company agreement. If the limited liability company agreement does not specify the manner of authorizing a conversion of a protected series of such limited liability company to a registered series of such limited liability company and does not prohibit a conversion of a protected series to a registered series, the conversion shall be authorized by members of such protected series who own more than 50 percent of the then current percentage or other interest in the profits of such protected series owned by all of the members of such protected series.

(c)   Unless otherwise agreed, the conversion of a protected series of a limited liability company to a registered series of such limited liability company pursuant to this section shall not require such limited liability company or such protected series of such limited liability company to wind up its affairs under § 18–803 or § 18–215 of this title or pay its liabilities and distribute its assets under § 18–804 or § 18–215 of this title, and the conversion of a protected series of a limited liability company to a registered series of such limited liability company shall not constitute a dissolution of such limited liability company or a termination of such protected series. When a protected series of a limited liability company has converted to a registered series of such limited liability company pursuant to this section, for all purposes of the laws of the State of Delaware, the registered series shall be deemed to be the same series as the converting protected series and the conversion shall constitute a continuation of the existence of the protected series in the form of such registered series.

(d)   In connection with a conversion of a protected series of a limited liability company to a registered series of such limited liability company pursuant to this section, rights or securities of or interests in the protected series which is to be converted may be exchanged for or converted into cash, property, rights or securities of or interests in the registered series into which the protected series is being converted or, in addition to or in lieu thereof, may be exchanged for or converted into cash, property, rights or securities of or interests in any other business entity, may remain outstanding or may be canceled.

(e)   If a protected series shall convert to a registered series in accordance with this section, a certificate of conversion of protected series to registered series executed in accordance with § 18–204 of this title shall be filed in the office of the Secretary of State in accordance with § 18–206 of this title. The certificate of conversion of protected series to registered series shall state:

(1)   The name of the limited liability company and, if it has been changed, the name under which its certificate of formation was originally filed;

(2)   The name of the protected series and, if it has been changed, the name of the protected series as originally established;

(3)   The name of the registered series as set forth in its certificate of registered series filed in accordance with subsection (a) of this section;

(4)   The date of filing of the original certificate of formation of the limited liability company with the Secretary of State;

(5)   The date on which the protected series was established;

(6)   The future effective date or time (which shall be a date or time certain) of the conversion if it is not to be effective upon the filing of the certificate of conversion of protected series to registered series; and

(7)   That the conversion has been approved in accordance with this section.

(f)   A copy of the certificate of conversion of protected series to registered series certified by the Secretary of State shall be prima facie evidence of the conversion by such protected series to a registered series of such limited liability company.

(g)   When any conversion shall have become effective under this section, for all purposes of the laws of the State of Delaware, all of the rights, privileges and powers of the protected series that has converted, and all property, real, personal and mixed, and all debts due to such protected series, as well as all other things and causes of action belonging to such protected series, shall remain vested in the registered series to which such protected series has converted and shall be the property of such registered series, and the title to any real property vested by deed or otherwise in such protected series shall not revert or be in any way impaired by reason of this chapter; but all rights of creditors and all liens upon any property of such protected series shall be preserved unimpaired, and all debts, liabilities and duties of the protected series that has converted shall remain attached to the registered series to which such protected series has converted, and may be enforced against it to the same extent as if said debts, liabilities and duties had originally been incurred or contracted by it in its capacity as such registered series. The rights, privileges, powers and interests in property of the protected series that has converted, as well as the debts, liabilities and duties of such protected series, shall not be deemed, as a consequence of the conversion, to have been transferred to the registered series to which such protected series of such limited liability company has converted for any purpose of the laws of the State of Delaware.

(h)   A limited liability company agreement may provide that a protected series of a limited liability company shall not have the power to convert to a registered series of such limited liability company as set forth in this section.

§ 18–220.   **Approval of conversion of a registered series of a domestic limited liability company to a protected series of such domestic limited liability company.**

(a)   Upon compliance with this section, a registered series of a domestic limited liability company may convert to a protected series of such domestic limited liability company. An existing registered series may not become a protected series other than pursuant to this section.

(b)   If the limited liability company agreement specifies the manner of authorizing a conversion of a registered series of such limited liability company to a protected series of such limited liability company, the conversion of a registered series to a protected series shall be authorized as specified in the limited liability company agreement. If the limited liability company agreement does not specify the manner of authorizing a conversion of a registered series of such limited liability company to a protected series of such limited liability company and does not prohibit a conversion of a registered series to a protected series, the conversion shall be authorized by members of such registered series who own more than 50 percent of the then current percentage or other interest in the profits of such registered series owned by all of the members of such registered series.

(c)   Unless otherwise agreed, the conversion of a registered series of a limited liability company to a protected series of such limited liability company pursuant to this section shall not require such limited liability company or such registered series of such limited liability company to wind up its affairs under § 18–803 or § 18–218 of this title or pay its liabilities and distribute its assets under § 18–804 or § 18–218 of this title, and the conversion of a registered series of a limited liability company to a protected series of such limited liability company shall not constitute a dissolution of such limited liability company or of such registered series. When a registered series of a limited liability company has converted to a protected series of such limited liability company pursuant to this section, for all purposes of the laws of the State of Delaware, the protected series shall be deemed to be the same series as the converting registered series and the conversion shall constitute a continuation of the existence of the registered series in the form of such protected series.

(d)   In connection with a conversion of a registered series of a limited liability company to protected series of such limited liability company pursuant to this section, rights or securities of or interests in the registered series which is to be converted may be exchanged for or converted into cash, property, rights or securities of or interests in the protected series into which the registered series is being converted or, in addition to or in lieu thereof, may be exchanged for or converted into cash, property, rights or securities of or interests in any other business entity, may remain outstanding or may be canceled.

(e)   If a registered series shall convert to a protected series in accordance with this section, a certificate of conversion of registered series to protected series executed in accordance with § 18–204 of this title shall be filed in the office of the Secretary of State in accordance with § 18–206 of this title. The certificate of conversion of registered series to protected series shall state:

(1)   The name of the limited liability company and, if it has been changed, the name under which its certificate of formation was originally filed;

(2)   The date of filing of the original certificate of formation of the limited liability company with the Secretary of State;

(3)   The name of the registered series and, if it has been changed, the name under which its certificate of registered series was originally filed;

(4)   The date of filing of its original certificate of registered series with the Secretary of State;

(5)   The future effective date or time (which shall be a date or time certain) of the conversion if it is not to be effective upon the filing of the certificate of conversion of registered series to protected series; and

(6)   That the conversion has been approved in accordance with this section.

(f)   Upon the filing in the office of the Secretary of State of the certificate of conversion of registered series to protected series or upon the future effective date or time of the certificate of conversion of registered series to protected series and payment to the Secretary of State of all fees prescribed in this chapter, the Secretary of State shall certify that the registered series has filed all documents and paid all fees required by this chapter. Such certificate of the Secretary of State shall be prima facie evidence of the conversion by such registered series to a protected series of such limited liability company.

(g)   When any conversion shall have become effective under this section, for all purposes of the laws of the State of Delaware, all of the rights, privileges and powers of the registered series that has converted, and all property, real, personal and mixed, and all debts due to such registered series, as well as all other things and causes of action belonging to such registered series, shall remain vested in the protected series to which such registered series has converted and shall be the property of such protected series, and the title to any real property vested by deed or otherwise in such registered series shall not revert or be in any way impaired by reason of this chapter; but all rights of creditors and all liens upon any property of such registered series shall be preserved unimpaired, and all debts, liabilities and duties of the registered series that has converted shall remain attached to the protected series to which such registered series has converted, and may be enforced against it to the same extent as if said debts, liabilities and duties had originally been incurred or contracted by it in its capacity as such protected series. The rights, privileges, powers and interests in property of the registered series that has converted, as well as the debts, liabilities and duties of such registered series, shall not be deemed, as a consequence of the conversion, to have been transferred to the protected series to which such registered series of such limited liability company has converted for any purpose of the laws of the State of Delaware.

(h)   A limited liability company agreement may provide that a registered series of a limited liability company shall not have the power to convert to a protected series of such limited liability company as set forth in this section.

§ 18–221.   Merger and consolidation of registered series.

(a)   Pursuant to an agreement of merger or consolidation, 1 or more registered series may merge or consolidate with or into 1 or more other registered series of the same limited liability company with such registered series as the agreement shall provide being the surviving or resulting registered series. Unless otherwise provided in the limited liability company agreement, an agreement of merger or consolidation shall be approved by each registered series which is to merge or consolidate by members of such registered series who own more than 50 percent of the then current percentage or other interest in the profits of such registered series owned by all of the members of such registered series. In connection with a merger or consolidation hereunder, rights or securities of, or interests in, a registered series which is a constituent party to the merger or consolidation may be exchanged for or converted into cash, property, rights or securities of, or interests in, the surviving or resulting registered series or, in addition to or in lieu thereof, may be exchanged for or converted into cash, property, rights or securities of, or interests in, a domestic limited liability company or other business entity which is not the surviving or resulting registered series in the merger or consolidation, may remain outstanding or may be canceled. Notwithstanding prior approval, an agreement of merger or consolidation may be terminated or amended pursuant to a provision for such termination or amendment contained in the agreement of merger or consolidation.

(b)   If a registered series is merging or consolidating under this section, the registered series surviving or resulting in or from the merger or consolidation shall file a certificate of merger or consolidation of registered series executed by 1 or more authorized persons on behalf of the registered series when it is the surviving or resulting registered series in the office of the Secretary of State. The certificate of merger or consolidation of registered series shall state:

(1)   The name of each registered series which is to merge or consolidate and the name of the limited liability company that formed such registered series;

(2)   That an agreement of merger or consolidation has been approved and executed by or on behalf of each registered series which is to merge or consolidate;

(3)   The name of the surviving or resulting registered series;

(4)   Such amendment, if any, to the certificate of registered series of the registered series that is the surviving registered series to change the name of the surviving registered series, as is desired to be effected by the merger;

(5)   The future effective date or time (which shall be a date or time certain) of the merger or consolidation if it is not to be effective upon the filing of the certificate of merger or consolidation of registered series;

(6)   That the agreement of merger or consolidation is on file at a place of business of the surviving or resulting registered series or the limited liability company that formed such registered series, and shall state the address thereof; and

(7)   That a copy of the agreement of merger or consolidation will be furnished by the surviving or resulting registered series, on request and without cost, to any member of any registered series which is to merge or consolidate.

(c)   Unless a future effective date or time is provided in a certificate of merger or consolidation of registered series, a merger or consolidation pursuant to this section shall be effective upon the filing in the office of the Secretary of State of a certificate of merger or consolidation of registered series.

(d)   A certificate of merger or consolidation of registered series shall act as a certificate of cancellation of the certificate of registered series of the registered series which is not the surviving or resulting registered series in the merger or consolidation. A certificate of merger or consolidation of registered series that sets forth any amendment in accordance with paragraph (b)(4) of this section shall be deemed to be an amendment to the certificate of registered series of the surviving registered series, and no further action shall be required to amend the certificate of registered series of the surviving registered series under § 18–218 of this title with respect to such amendments set forth in such certificate of merger or consolidation. Whenever this section requires the filing of a certificate of merger or consolidation of registered series, such requirement shall be deemed satisfied by the filing of an agreement of merger or consolidation containing the information required by this section to be set forth in such certificate of merger or consolidation.

(e)   An agreement of merger or consolidation approved in accordance with subsection (a) of this section may effect any amendment to the limited liability company agreement relating solely to the registered series that are constituent parties to the merger or consolidation.

Any amendment to a limited liability company agreement relating solely to the registered series that are constituent parties to the merger or consolidation made pursuant to the foregoing sentence shall be effective at the effective time or date of the merger or consolidation and shall be effective notwithstanding any provision of the limited liability company agreement relating to amendment of the limited liability company agreement, other than a provision that by its terms applies to an amendment to the limited liability company agreement in connection with a merger or consolidation. The provisions of this subsection shall not be construed to limit the accomplishment of a merger or of any of the matters referred to herein by any other means provided for in a limited liability company agreement or other agreement or as otherwise permitted by law, including that the limited liability company agreement relating to any constituent registered series to the merger or consolidation (including a registered series formed for the purpose of consummating a merger or consolidation) shall be the limited liability company agreement of the surviving or resulting registered series.

(f)   When any merger or consolidation shall have become effective under this section, for all purposes of the laws of the State of Delaware, all of the rights, privileges and powers of each of the registered series that have merged or consolidated, and all property, real, personal and mixed, and all debts due to any of said registered series, as well as all other things and causes of action belonging to each of such registered series, shall be vested in the surviving or resulting registered series, and shall thereafter be the property of the surviving or resulting registered series as they were of each of the registered series that have merged or consolidated, and the title to any real property vested by deed or otherwise, under the laws of the State of Delaware, in any of such registered series, shall not revert or be in any way impaired by reason of this chapter; but all rights of creditors and all liens upon any property of any of said registered series shall be preserved unimpaired, and all debts, liabilities and duties of each of the said registered series that have merged or consolidated shall thenceforth attach to the surviving or resulting registered series, and may be enforced against it to the same extent as if said debts, liabilities and duties had been incurred or contracted by it. Unless otherwise agreed, a merger or consolidation of a registered series of a limited liability company, including a registered series which is not the surviving or resulting registered series in the merger or consolidation, shall not require such registered series to wind up its affairs under § 18–218 of this title, or pay its liabilities and distribute its assets under § 18–218 of this title and the merger or consolidation shall not constitute a dissolution of such registered series.

(g)   A limited liability company agreement may provide that a registered series of such limited liability company shall not have the power to merge or consolidate as set forth in this section.

SUBCHAPTER III.   MEMBERS

§ 18–301.   Admission of members.

(a)   In connection with the formation of a limited liability company, a person is admitted as a member of the limited liability company upon the later to occur of:

(1)   The formation of the limited liability company; or

(2)   The time provided in and upon compliance with the limited liability company agreement or, if the limited liability company agreement does not so provide, when the person's admission is reflected in the records of the limited liability company.

(b)   After the formation of a limited liability company, a person is admitted as a member of the limited liability company:

(1)   In the case of a person who is not an assignee of a limited liability company interest, including a person acquiring a limited liability company interest directly from the limited liability company and a person to be admitted as a member of the limited liability company without acquiring a limited liability company interest in the limited liability company at the time provided in and upon compliance with the limited liability company agreement or, if the limited liability company agreement does not so provide, upon the consent of all members and when the person's admission is reflected in the records of the limited liability company;

(2)   In the case of an assignee of a limited liability company interest, as provided in § 18–704(a) of this title and at the time provided in and upon compliance with the limited liability company agreement or, if the limited liability company agreement does not so provide, when any such person's permitted admission is reflected in the records of the limited liability company;

(3)   In the case of a person being admitted as a member of a surviving or resulting limited liability company pursuant to a merger or consolidation approved in accordance with § 18–209(b) of this title, as provided in the limited liability company agreement of the surviving or resulting limited liability company or in the agreement of merger or consolidation or plan of merger, and in the event of any inconsistency, the terms of the agreement of merger or consolidation or plan of merger shall control; and in the case of a person being admitted as a member of a limited liability company pursuant to a merger or consolidation in which such limited liability company is not the surviving or resulting limited liability company in the merger or consolidation, as provided in the limited liability company agreement of such limited liability company; or

(4)   In the case of a person being admitted as a member of a division company pursuant to a division approved in accordance with § 18–217(c) of this title, as provided in the limited liability company agreement of such division company or in the plan of division, and in the event of any inconsistency, the terms of the plan of division shall control; and in the case of a person being admitted as a member of a limited liability company pursuant to a division in which such limited liability company is not a division company in the division, as provided in the limited liability company agreement of such limited liability company.

(c)   In connection with the domestication of a non-United States entity (as defined in § 18–212 of this title) as a limited liability company in the State of Delaware in accordance with § 18–212 of this title or the conversion of an other entity (as defined in § 18–214 of this title) to a domestic limited liability company in accordance with § 18–214 of this title, a person is admitted as a member of the limited liability company as provided in the limited liability company agreement.

(d)   A person may be admitted to a limited liability company as a member of the limited liability company and may receive a limited liability company interest in the limited liability company without making a contribution or being obligated to make a contribution to the limited liability company.

Unless otherwise provided in a limited liability company agreement, a person may be admitted to a limited liability company as a member of the limited liability company without acquiring a limited liability company interest in the limited liability company. Unless otherwise provided in a limited liability company agreement, a person may be admitted as the sole member of a limited liability company without making a contribution or being obligated to make a contribution to the limited liability company or without acquiring a limited liability company interest in the limited liability company.

(e) Unless otherwise provided in a limited liability company agreement or another agreement, a member shall have no preemptive right to subscribe to any additional issue of limited liability company interests or another interest in a limited liability company.

§18-302. Classes and voting.

(a) A limited liability company agreement may provide for classes or groups of members having such relative rights, powers and duties as the limited liability company agreement may provide, and may make provision for the future creation in the manner provided in the limited liability company agreement of additional classes or groups of members having such relative rights, powers and duties as may from time to time be established, including rights, powers and duties senior to existing classes and groups of members. A limited liability company agreement may provide for the taking of an action, including the amendment of the limited liability company agreement, without the vote or approval of any member or class or group of members, including an action to create under the provisions of the limited liability company agreement a class or group of limited liability company interests that was not previously outstanding. A limited liability company agreement may provide that any member or class or group of members shall have no voting rights.

(b) A limited liability company agreement may grant to all or certain identified members or a specified class or group of the members the right to vote separately or with all or any class or group of the members or managers, on any matter. Voting by members may be on a per capita, number, financial interest, class, group or any other basis.

(c) A limited liability company agreement may set forth provisions relating to notice of the time, place or purpose of any meeting at which any matter is to be voted on by any members, waiver of any such notice, action by consent without a meeting, the establishment of a record date, quorum requirements, voting in person or by proxy, or any other matter with respect to the exercise of any such right to vote.

(d) Unless otherwise provided in a limited liability company agreement, meetings of members may be held by means of conference telephone or other communications equipment by means of which all persons participating in the meeting can hear each other, and participation in a meeting pursuant to this subsection shall constitute presence in person at the meeting. Unless otherwise provided in a limited liability company agreement, on any matter that is to be voted on, consented to or approved by members, the members may take such action without a meeting, without prior notice and without a vote if consented to or approved, in writing, by electronic transmission or by any other means permitted by law, by members having not less than the minimum number of votes that would be necessary to authorize or take such action at a meeting at which all members entitled to vote thereon were present and voted. Unless otherwise provided in a limited liability company agreement, if a person (whether or not then a member) consenting as a member to any matter provides that such consent will be effective at a future time (including a time determined upon the happening of an event), then such person shall be deemed to have consented as a member at such future time so long as such person is then a member. Unless otherwise provided in a limited liability company agreement, on any matter that is to be voted on by members, the members may vote in person or by proxy, and such proxy may be granted in writing, by means of electronic transmission or as otherwise permitted by applicable law. Unless otherwise provided in a limited liability company agreement, a consent transmitted by electronic transmission by a member or by a person or persons authorized to act for a member shall be deemed to be written and signed for purposes of this subsection.

(e)   If a limited liability company agreement provides for the manner in which it may be amended, including by requiring the approval of a person who is not a party to the limited liability company agreement or the satisfaction of conditions, it may be amended only in that manner or as otherwise permitted by law, including as permitted by § 18–209(f) of this title (provided that the approval of any person may be waived by such person and that any such conditions may be waived by all persons for whose benefit such conditions were intended). Unless otherwise provided in a limited liability company agreement, a supermajority amendment provision shall only apply to provisions of the limited liability company agreement that are expressly included in the limited liability company agreement. As used in this section, "supermajority amendment provision" means any amendment provision set forth in a limited liability company agreement requiring that an amendment to a provision of the limited liability company agreement be adopted by no less than the vote or consent required to take action under such latter provision.

(f)   If a limited liability company agreement does not provide for the manner in which it may be amended, the limited liability company agreement may be amended with the approval of all of the members or as otherwise permitted by law, including as permitted by § 18–209(f) of this title. This subsection shall only apply to a limited liability company whose original certificate of formation was filed with the Secretary of State on or after January 1, 2012.

§ 18–303.   Liability to third parties.

(a)   Except as otherwise provided by this chapter, the debts, obligations and liabilities of a limited liability company, whether arising in contract, tort or otherwise, shall be solely the debts, obligations and liabilities of the limited liability company, and no member or manager of a limited liability company shall be obligated personally for any such debt, obligation or liability of the limited liability company solely by reason of being a member or acting as a manager of the limited liability company.

(b)   Notwithstanding the provisions of subsection (a) of this section, under a limited liability company agreement or under another agreement, a member or manager may agree to be obligated personally for any or all of the debts, obligations and liabilities of the limited liability company.

§ 18–304.   Events of bankruptcy.

A person ceases to be a member of a limited liability company upon the happening of any of the following events:

(1)   Unless otherwise provided in a limited liability company agreement, or with the consent of all members, a member:

a.   Makes an assignment for the benefit of creditors;

b.   Files a voluntary petition in bankruptcy;

c.   Is adjudged a bankrupt or insolvent, or has entered against the member an order for relief, in any bankruptcy or insolvency proceeding;

d.   Files a petition or answer seeking for the member any reorganization, arrangement, composition, readjustment, liquidation, dissolution or similar relief under any statute, law or regulation;

e.   Files an answer or other pleading admitting or failing to contest the material allegations of a petition filed against the member in any proceeding of this nature;

f.   Seeks, consents to or acquiesces in the appointment of a trustee, receiver or liquidator of the member or of all or any substantial part of the member's properties; or

(2)   Unless otherwise provided in a limited liability company agreement, or with the consent of all members, 120 days after the commencement of any proceeding against the member seeking reorganization, arrangement, composition, readjustment, liquidation, dissolution or

similar relief under any statute, law or regulation, if the proceeding has not been dismissed, or if within 90 days after the appointment without the member's consent or acquiescence of a trustee, receiver or liquidator of the member or of all or any substantial part of the member's properties, the appointment is not vacated or stayed, or within 90 days after the expiration of any such stay, the appointment is not vacated.

§ 18–305.   Access to and confidentiality of information; records.

(a)   Each member of a limited liability company, in person or by attorney or other agent, has the right, subject to such reasonable standards (including standards governing what information and documents are to be furnished at what time and location and at whose expense) as may be set forth in a limited liability company agreement or otherwise established by the manager or, if there is no manager, then by the members, to obtain from the limited liability company from time to time upon reasonable demand for any purpose reasonably related to the member's interest as a member of the limited liability company:

(1)   True and full information regarding the status of the business and financial condition of the limited liability company;

(2)   Promptly after becoming available, a copy of the limited liability company's federal, state and local income tax returns for each year;

(3)   A current list of the name and last known business, residence or mailing address of each member and manager;

(4)   A copy of any written limited liability company agreement and certificate of formation and all amendments thereto, together with executed copies of any written powers of attorney pursuant to which the limited liability company agreement and any certificate and all amendments thereto have been executed;

(5)   True and full information regarding the amount of cash and a description and statement of the agreed value of any other property or services contributed by each member and which each member has agreed to contribute in the future, and the date on which each became a member; and

(6)   Other information regarding the affairs of the limited liability company as is just and reasonable.

(b)   Each manager shall have the right to examine all of the information described in subsection (a) of this section for a purpose reasonably related to the position of manager.

(c)   The manager of a limited liability company shall have the right to keep confidential from the members, for such period of time as the manager deems reasonable, any information which the manager reasonably believes to be in the nature of trade secrets or other information the disclosure of which the manager in good faith believes is not in the best interest of the limited liability company or could damage the limited liability company or its business or which the limited liability company is required by law or by agreement with a third party to keep confidential.

(d)   A limited liability company may maintain its records in other than a written form, including on, by means of, or in the form of any information storage device, method, or 1 or more electronic networks or databases (including 1 or more distributed electronic networks or databases), if such form is capable of conversion into written form within a reasonable time.

(e)   Any demand under this section shall be in writing and shall state the purpose of such demand. In every instance where an attorney or other agent shall be the person who seeks the right to obtain the information described in subsection (a) of this section, the demand shall be accompanied by a power of attorney or such other writing which authorizes the attorney or other agent to so act on behalf of the member.

(f)   Any action to enforce any right arising under this section shall be brought in the Court of Chancery. If the limited liability company refuses to permit a member, or attorney or other agent acting for the member, to obtain or a manager to examine the information described in subsection (a) of this section or does not reply to the demand that has been made within 5 business days (or such shorter or longer period of time as is provided for in a limited liability company agreement but not longer than 30 business days) after the demand has been made, the demanding member or manager may apply to the Court of Chancery for an order to compel such disclosure. The Court of Chancery is hereby vested with exclusive jurisdiction to determine whether or not the person seeking such information is entitled to the information sought. The Court of Chancery may summarily order the limited liability company to permit the demanding member to obtain or manager to examine the information described in subsection (a) of this section and to make copies or abstracts therefrom, or the Court of Chancery may summarily order the limited liability company to furnish to the demanding member or manager the information described in subsection (a) of this section on the condition that the demanding member or manager first pay to the limited liability company the reasonable cost of obtaining and furnishing such information and on such other conditions as the Court of Chancery deems appropriate. When a demanding member seeks to obtain or a manager seeks to examine the information described in subsection (a) of this section, the demanding member or manager shall first establish:

(1)   That the demanding member or manager has complied with the provisions of this section respecting the form and manner of making demand for obtaining or examining of such information, and

(2)   That the information the demanding member or manager seeks is reasonably related to the member's interest as a member or the manager's position as a manager, as the case may be.

The Court of Chancery may, in its discretion, prescribe any limitations or conditions with reference to the obtaining or examining of information, or award such other or further relief as the Court of Chancery may deem just and proper. The Court of Chancery may order books, documents and records, pertinent extracts therefrom, or duly authenticated copies thereof, to be brought within the State of Delaware and kept in the State of Delaware upon such terms and conditions as the order may prescribe.

(g)   The rights of a member or manager to obtain information as provided in this section may be restricted in an original limited liability company agreement or in any subsequent amendment approved or adopted by all of the members or in compliance with any applicable requirements of the limited liability company agreement. The provisions of this subsection shall not be construed to limit the ability to impose restrictions on the rights of a member or manager to obtain information by any other means permitted under this chapter.

(h)   A limited liability company shall maintain a current record that identifies the name and last known business, residence or mailing address of each member and manager.

§ 18–306.   Remedies for breach of limited liability company agreement by member.

A limited liability company agreement may provide that:

(1)   A member who fails to perform in accordance with, or to comply with the terms and conditions of, the limited liability company agreement shall be subject to specified penalties or specified consequences; and

(2)   At the time or upon the happening of events specified in the limited liability company agreement, a member shall be subject to specified penalties or specified consequences.

Such specified penalties or specified consequences may include and take the form of any penalty or consequence set forth in § 18–502(c) of this title.

SUBCHAPTER IV.   MANAGERS

§ 18–401.   Admission of managers.

A person may be named or designated as a manager of the limited liability company as provided in § 18–101(12) of this title.

§ 18–402.   Management of limited liability company.

Unless otherwise provided in a limited liability company agreement, the management of a limited liability company shall be vested in its members in proportion to the then current percentage or other interest of members in the profits of the limited liability company owned by all of the members, the decision of members owning more than 50 percent of the said percentage or other interest in the profits controlling; provided however, that if a limited liability company agreement provides for the management, in whole or in part, of a limited liability company by a manager, the management of the limited liability company, to the extent so provided, shall be vested in the manager who shall be chosen in the manner provided in the limited liability company agreement. The manager shall also hold the offices and have the responsibilities accorded to the manager by or in the manner provided in a limited liability company agreement. Subject to § 18–602 of this title, a manager shall cease to be a manager as provided in a limited liability company agreement. A limited liability company may have more than 1 manager. Unless otherwise provided in a limited liability company agreement, each member and manager has the authority to bind the limited liability company.

§ 18–403.   Contributions by a manager.

A manager of a limited liability company may make contributions to the limited liability company and share in the profits and losses of, and in distributions from, the limited liability company as a member. A person who is both a manager and a member has the rights and powers, and is subject to the restrictions and liabilities, of a manager and, except as provided in a limited liability company agreement, also has the rights and powers, and is subject to the restrictions and liabilities, of a member to the extent of the manager's participation in the limited liability company as a member.

§ 18–404.   Classes and voting.

(a)   A limited liability company agreement may provide for classes or groups of managers having such relative rights, powers and duties as the limited liability company agreement may provide, and may make provision for the future creation in the manner provided in the limited liability company agreement of additional classes or groups of managers having such relative rights, powers and duties as may from time to time be established, including rights, powers and duties senior to existing classes and groups of managers. A limited liability company agreement may provide for the taking of an action, including the amendment of the limited liability company agreement, without the vote or approval of any manager or class or group of managers, including an action to create under the provisions of the limited liability company agreement a class or group of limited liability company interests that was not previously outstanding.

(b)   A limited liability company agreement may grant to all or certain identified managers or a specified class or group of the managers the right to vote, separately or with all or any class or group of managers or members, on any matter. Voting by managers may be on a per capita, number, financial interest, class, group or any other basis.

(c)   A limited liability company agreement may set forth provisions relating to notice of the time, place or purpose of any meeting at which any matter is to be voted on by any manager or class or group of managers, waiver of any such notice, action by consent without a meeting, the establishment of a record date, quorum requirements, voting in person or by proxy, or any other matter with respect to the exercise of any such right to vote.

(d)   Unless otherwise provided in a limited liability company agreement, meetings of managers may be held by means of conference telephone or other communications equipment by means of which all persons participating in the meeting can hear each other, and participation in a meeting pursuant to this subsection shall constitute presence in person at the meeting. Unless otherwise provided in a limited liability company agreement, on any matter that is to be voted on, consented to or approved by managers, the managers may take such action without a meeting, without prior notice and without a vote if consented to or approved, in writing, by electronic transmission or by any other means permitted by law, by managers having not less than the minimum number of votes that would be necessary to authorize or take such action at a meeting at which all managers entitled to vote thereon were present and voted. Unless otherwise provided in a limited liability company agreement, if a person (whether or not then a manager) consenting as a manager to any matter provides that such consent will be effective at a future time (including a time determined upon the happening of an event), then such person shall be deemed to have consented as a manager at such future time so long as such person is then a manager. Unless otherwise provided in a limited liability company agreement, on any matter that is to be voted on by managers, the managers may vote in person or by proxy, and such proxy may be granted in writing, by means of electronic transmission or as otherwise permitted by applicable law. Unless otherwise provided in a limited liability company agreement, a consent transmitted by electronic transmission by a manager or by a person or persons authorized to act for a manager shall be deemed to be written and signed for purposes of this subsection.

§ 18–405.   **Remedies for breach of limited liability company agreement by manager.**

A limited liability company agreement may provide that:

(1)   A manager who fails to perform in accordance with, or to comply with the terms and conditions of, the limited liability company agreement shall be subject to specified penalties or specified consequences; and

(2)   At the time or upon the happening of events specified in the limited liability company agreement, a manager shall be subject to specified penalties or specified consequences.

§ 18–406.   **Reliance on reports and information by member or manager.**

A member, manager or liquidating trustee of a limited liability company shall be fully protected in relying in good faith upon the records of the limited liability company and upon information, opinions, reports or statements presented by another manager, member or liquidating trustee, an officer or employee of the limited liability company, or committees of the limited liability company, members or managers, or by any other person as to matters the member, manager or liquidating trustees reasonably believes are within such other person's professional or expert competence, including information, opinions, reports or statements as to the value and amount of the assets, liabilities, profits or losses of the limited liability company, or the value and amount of assets or reserves or contracts, agreements or other undertakings that would be sufficient to pay claims and obligations of the limited liability company or to make reasonable provision to pay such claims and obligations, or any other facts pertinent to the existence and amount of assets from which distributions to members or creditors might properly be paid.

§ 18–407.   **Delegation of rights and powers to manage.**

Unless otherwise provided in the limited liability company agreement, a member or manager of a limited liability company has the power and authority to delegate to 1 or more other persons any or all of the member's or manager's, as the case may be, rights, powers and duties to manage and control the business and affairs of the limited liability company. Any such delegation may be to agents, officers and employees of a member or manager or the limited liability company, and by a management agreement or another agreement with, or otherwise to, other persons. Unless otherwise provided in the limited liability company agreement, such delegation by a member or manager shall be irrevocable if it states that it is irrevocable. Unless otherwise provided in the limited liability company agreement, such delegation by a member or manager of a limited liability company shall not cause the member or manager to cease to be a member or manager, as the case may be, of the limited liability company or cause the person to whom any such rights, powers and duties have been delegated to be a member or manager, as the case may be, of the limited liability company. No other provision of this chapter shall be construed to restrict a member's or manager's power and authority to delegate any or all of its rights, powers and duties to manage and control the business and affairs of the limited liability company.

SUBCHAPTER V.   FINANCE

§ 18–501.   Form of contribution.

The contribution of a member to a limited liability company may be in cash, property or services rendered, or a promissory note or other obligation to contribute cash or property or to perform services.

§ 18–502.   Liability for contribution.

(a)   Except as provided in a limited liability company agreement, a member is obligated to a limited liability company to perform any promise to contribute cash or property or to perform services, even if the member is unable to perform because of death, disability or any other reason. If a member does not make the required contribution of property or services, the member is obligated at the option of the limited liability company to contribute cash equal to that portion of the agreed value (as stated in the records of the limited liability company) of the contribution that has not been made. The foregoing option shall be in addition to, and not in lieu of, any other rights, including the right to specific performance, that the limited liability company may have against such member under the limited liability company agreement or applicable law.

(b)   Unless otherwise provided in a limited liability company agreement, the obligation of a member to make a contribution or return money or other property paid or distributed in violation of this chapter may be compromised only by consent of all the members. Notwithstanding the compromise, a creditor of a limited liability company who extends credit, after the entering into of a limited liability company agreement or an amendment thereto which, in either case, reflects the obligation, and before the amendment thereof to reflect the compromise, may enforce the original obligation to the extent that, in extending credit, the creditor reasonably relied on the obligation of a member to make a contribution or return. A conditional obligation of a member to make a contribution or return money or other property to a limited liability company may not be enforced unless the conditions of the obligation have been satisfied or waived as to or by such member. Conditional obligations include contributions payable upon a discretionary call of a limited liability company prior to the time the call occurs.

(c)   A limited liability company agreement may provide that the interest of any member who fails to make any contribution that the member is obligated to make shall be subject to specified penalties for, or specified consequences of, such failure. Such penalty or consequence may take the form of reducing or eliminating the defaulting member's proportionate interest in a limited liability company, subordinating the member's limited liability company interest to that of nondefaulting members, a forced sale of that limited liability company interest, forfeiture of the defaulting member's limited liability company interest, the lending by other members of the amount necessary to meet the defaulting member's commitment, a fixing of the value of the defaulting member's limited liability company interest by appraisal or by formula and redemption or sale of the limited liability company interest at such value, or other penalty or consequence.

§ 18–503.   Allocation of profits and losses.

The profits and losses of a limited liability company shall be allocated among the members, and among classes or groups of members, in the manner provided in a limited liability company agreement. If the limited liability company agreement does not so provide, profits and losses shall be allocated on the basis of the agreed value (as stated in the records of the limited liability company) of the contributions made by each member to the extent they have been received by the limited liability company and have not been returned.

§ 18–504.   Allocation of distributions.

Distributions of cash or other assets of a limited liability company shall be allocated among the members, and among classes or groups of members, in the manner provided in a limited liability company agreement. If the limited liability company agreement does not so provide, distributions shall be made on the basis of the agreed value (as stated in the records of the limited liability company) of the contributions made by each member to the extent they have been received by the limited liability company and have not been returned.

§ 18–505.   Defense of usury not available.

No obligation of a member or manager of a limited liability company to the limited liability company, or to a member or manager of the limited liability company, arising under the limited liability company agreement or a separate agreement or writing, and no note, instrument or other writing evidencing any such obligation of a member or manager, shall be subject to the defense of usury, and no member or manager shall interpose the defense of usury with respect to any such obligation in any action.

SUBCHAPTER VI.   DISTRIBUTIONS AND RESIGNATION

§ 18–601.   Interim distributions.

Except as provided in this subchapter, to the extent and at the times or upon the happening of the events specified in a limited liability company agreement, a member is entitled to receive from a limited liability company distributions before the member's resignation from the limited liability company and before the dissolution and winding up thereof.

§ 18–602.   Resignation of manager.

A manager may resign as a manager of a limited liability company at the time or upon the happening of events specified in a limited liability company agreement and in accordance with the limited liability company agreement. A limited liability company agreement may provide that a manager shall not have the right to resign as a manager of a limited liability company. Notwithstanding that a limited liability company agreement provides that a manager does not have the right to resign as a manager of a limited liability company, a manager may resign as a manager of a limited liability company at any time by giving written notice to the members and other managers. If the resignation of a manager violates a limited liability company agreement, in addition to any remedies otherwise available under applicable law, a limited liability company may recover from the resigning manager damages for breach of the limited liability company agreement and offset the damages against the amount otherwise distributable to the resigning manager.

§ 18–603.   Resignation of member.

A member may resign from a limited liability company only at the time or upon the happening of events specified in a limited liability company agreement and in accordance with the limited liability company agreement. Notwithstanding anything to the contrary under applicable law, unless a limited liability company agreement provides otherwise, a member may not resign from a limited liability company prior to the dissolution and winding up of the limited liability company. Notwithstanding anything to the contrary under applicable law, a limited liability company agreement may provide that a limited liability company interest may not be assigned prior to the dissolution and winding up of the limited liability company.

Unless otherwise provided in a limited liability company agreement, a limited liability company whose original certificate of formation was filed with the Secretary of State and effective on or prior to July 31, 1996, shall continue to be governed by this section as in effect on July 31, 1996.

§ 18–604.   Distribution upon resignation.

Except as provided in this subchapter, upon resignation any resigning member is entitled to receive any distribution to which such member is entitled under a limited liability company agreement and, if not otherwise provided in a limited liability company agreement, such member is entitled to receive, within a reasonable time after resignation, the fair value of such member's limited liability company interest as of the date of resignation based upon such member's right to share in distributions from the limited liability company.

§ 18–605.   Distribution in kind.

Except as provided in a limited liability company agreement, a member, regardless of the nature of the member's contribution, has no right to demand and receive any distribution from a limited liability company in any form other than cash. Except as provided in a limited liability company agreement, a member may not be compelled to accept a distribution of any asset in kind from a limited liability company to the extent that the percentage of the asset distributed exceeds a percentage of that asset which is equal to the percentage in which the member shares in distributions from the limited liability company. Except as provided in the limited liability company agreement, a member may be compelled to accept a distribution of any asset in kind from a limited liability company to the extent that the percentage of the asset distributed is equal to a percentage of that asset which is equal to the percentage in which the member shares in distributions from the limited liability company.

§ 18–606.   Right to distribution.

Subject to §§ 18–607 and 18–804 of this title, and unless otherwise provided in a limited liability company agreement, at the time a member becomes entitled to receive a distribution, the member has the status of, and is entitled to all remedies available to, a creditor of a limited liability company with respect to the distribution. A limited liability company agreement may provide for the establishment of a record date with respect to allocations and distributions by a limited liability company.

§ 18–607.   Limitations on distribution.

(a)   A limited liability company shall not make a distribution to a member to the extent that at the time of the distribution, after giving effect to the distribution, all liabilities of the limited liability company, other than liabilities to members on account of their limited liability company interests and liabilities for which the recourse of creditors is limited to specified property of the limited liability company, exceed the fair value of the assets of the limited liability company, except that the fair value of property that is subject to a liability for which the recourse of creditors is limited shall be included in the assets of the limited liability company only to the extent that the fair value of that property exceeds that liability. For purposes of this subsection (a), the term "distribution" shall not include amounts constituting reasonable compensation for present or past services or reasonable payments made in the ordinary course of business pursuant to a bona fide retirement plan or other benefits program.

(b)   A member who receives a distribution in violation of subsection (a) of this section, and who knew at the time of the distribution that the distribution violated subsection (a) of this section, shall be liable to a limited liability company for the amount of the distribution. A member who receives a distribution in violation of subsection (a) of this section, and who did not know at the time of the distribution that the distribution violated subsection (a) of this section, shall not be liable for the amount of the distribution. Subject to subsection (c) of this section, this subsection shall not affect any obligation or liability of a member under an agreement or other applicable law for the amount of a distribution.

(c)　Unless otherwise agreed, a member who receives a distribution from a limited liability company shall have no liability under this chapter or other applicable law for the amount of the distribution after the expiration of 3 years from the date of the distribution unless an action to recover the distribution from such member is commenced prior to the expiration of the said 3-year period and an adjudication of liability against such member is made in the said action.

SUBCHAPTER VII.　ASSIGNMENT OF LIMITED LIABILITY COMPANY INTERESTS

§ 18–701.　Nature of limited liability company interest.

A limited liability company interest is personal property. A member has no interest in specific limited liability company property.

§ 18–702.　Assignment of limited liability company interest.

(a)　A limited liability company interest is assignable in whole or in part except as provided in a limited liability company agreement. The assignee of a member's limited liability company interest shall have no right to participate in the management of the business and affairs of a limited liability company except as provided in a limited liability company agreement or, unless otherwise provided in the limited liability company agreement, upon the vote or consent of all of the members of the limited liability company.

(b)　Unless otherwise provided in a limited liability company agreement:

(1)　An assignment of a limited liability company interest does not entitle the assignee to become or to exercise any rights or powers of a member;

(2)　An assignment of a limited liability company interest entitles the assignee to share in such profits and losses, to receive such distribution or distributions, and to receive such allocation of income, gain, loss, deduction, or credit or similar item to which the assignor was entitled, to the extent assigned; and

(3)　A member ceases to be a member and to have the power to exercise any rights or powers of a member upon assignment of all of the member's limited liability company interest. Unless otherwise provided in a limited liability company agreement, the pledge of, or granting of a security interest, lien or other encumbrance in or against, any or all of the limited liability company interest of a member shall not cause the member to cease to be a member or to have the power to exercise any rights or powers of a member.

(c)　Unless otherwise provided in a limited liability company agreement, a member's interest in a limited liability company may be evidenced by a certificate of limited liability company interest issued by the limited liability company. A limited liability company agreement may provide for the assignment or transfer of any limited liability company interest represented by such a certificate and make other provisions with respect to such certificates. A limited liability company shall not have the power to issue a certificate of limited liability company interest in bearer form.

(d)　Unless otherwise provided in a limited liability company agreement and except to the extent assumed by agreement, until an assignee of a limited liability company interest becomes a member, the assignee shall have no liability as a member solely as a result of the assignment.

(e)　Unless otherwise provided in the limited liability company agreement, a limited liability company may acquire, by purchase, redemption or otherwise, any limited liability company interest or other interest of a member or manager in the limited liability company. Unless otherwise provided in the limited liability company agreement, any such interest so acquired by the limited liability company shall be deemed canceled.

§ 18–703. Member's limited liability company interest subject to charging order.

(a) On application by a judgment creditor of a member or of a member's assignee, a court having jurisdiction may charge the limited liability company interest of the judgment debtor to satisfy the judgment. To the extent so charged, the judgment creditor has only the right to receive any distribution or distributions to which the judgment debtor would otherwise have been entitled in respect of such limited liability company interest.

(b) A charging order constitutes a lien on the judgment debtor's limited liability company interest.

(c) This chapter does not deprive a member or member's assignee of a right under exemption laws with respect to the judgment debtor's limited liability company interest.

(d) The entry of a charging order is the exclusive remedy by which a judgment creditor of a member or a member's assignee may satisfy a judgment out of the judgment debtor's limited liability company interest and attachment, garnishment, foreclosure or other legal or equitable remedies are not available to the judgment creditor, whether the limited liability company has 1 member or more than 1 member.

(e) No creditor of a member or of a member's assignee shall have any right to obtain possession of, or otherwise exercise legal or equitable remedies with respect to, the property of the limited liability company.

(f) The Court of Chancery shall have jurisdiction to hear and determine any matter relating to any such charging order.

§ 18–704. Right of assignee to become member.

(a) An assignee of a limited liability company interest becomes a member:

(1) As provided in the limited liability company agreement;

(2) Unless otherwise provided in the limited liability company agreement, upon the vote or consent of all of the members of the limited liability company; or

(3) Unless otherwise provided in the limited liability company agreement by a specific reference to this subsection or otherwise provided in connection with the assignment, upon the voluntary assignment by the sole member of the limited liability company of all of the limited liability company interests in the limited liability company to a single assignee. An assignment will be voluntary for purposes of this subsection if it is consented to by the member at the time of the assignment and is not effected by foreclosure or other similar legal process.

(b) An assignee who has become a member has, to the extent assigned, the rights and powers, and is subject to the restrictions and liabilities, of a member under a limited liability company agreement and this chapter. Notwithstanding the foregoing, unless otherwise provided in a limited liability company agreement, an assignee who becomes a member is liable for the obligations of the assignor to make contributions as provided in § 18–502 of this title, but shall not be liable for the obligations of the assignor under subchapter VI of this chapter. However, the assignee is not obligated for liabilities, including the obligations of the assignor to make contributions as provided in § 18–502 of this title, unknown to the assignee at the time the assignee became a member and which could not be ascertained from a limited liability company agreement.

(c) Whether or not an assignee of a limited liability company interest becomes a member, the assignor is not released from liability to a limited liability company under subchapters V and VI of this chapter.

§ 18–705.   Powers of estate of deceased or incompetent member.

If a member who is an individual dies or a court of competent jurisdiction adjudges the member to be incompetent to manage the member's person or property, the member's personal representative may exercise all of the member's rights for the purpose of settling the member's estate or administering the member's property, including any power under a limited liability company agreement of an assignee to become a member. If a member is a corporation, trust or other entity and is dissolved or terminated, the powers of that member may be exercised by its personal representative.

SUBCHAPTER VIII.   DISSOLUTION

§ 18–801.   Dissolution.

(a)   A limited liability company is dissolved and its affairs shall be wound up upon the first to occur of the following:

(1)   At the time specified in a limited liability company agreement, but if no such time is set forth in the limited liability company agreement, then the limited liability company shall have a perpetual existence;

(2)   Upon the happening of events specified in a limited liability company agreement;

(3)   Unless otherwise provided in a limited liability company agreement, upon the vote or consent of members who own more than 2/3 of the then-current percentage or other interest in the profits of the limited liability company owned by all of the members;

(4)   At any time there are no members; provided, that the limited liability company is not dissolved and is not required to be wound up if:

a.   Unless otherwise provided in a limited liability company agreement, within 90 days or such other period as is provided for in the limited liability company agreement after the occurrence of the event that terminated the continued membership of the last remaining member, the personal representative of the last remaining member agrees to continue the limited liability company and to the admission of the personal representative of such member or its nominee or designee to the limited liability company as a member, effective as of the occurrence of the event that terminated the continued membership of the last remaining member; provided, that a limited liability company agreement may provide that the personal representative of the last remaining member shall be obligated to agree to continue the limited liability company and to the admission of the personal representative of such member or its nominee or designee to the limited liability company as a member, effective as of the occurrence of the event that terminated the continued membership of the last remaining member, or

b.   A member is admitted to the limited liability company in the manner provided for in the limited liability company agreement, effective as of the occurrence of the event that terminated the continued membership of the last remaining member, within 90 days or such other period as is provided for in the limited liability company agreement after the occurrence of the event that terminated the continued membership of the last remaining member, pursuant to a provision of the limited liability company agreement that specifically provides for the admission of a member to the limited liability company after there is no longer a remaining member of the limited liability company.

(5)   The entry of a decree of judicial dissolution under § 18–802 of this title.

Unless otherwise provided in a limited liability company agreement, a limited liability company whose original certificate of formation was filed with the Secretary of State and effective on or prior to July 31, 2015, shall continue to be governed by paragraph (a)(3) of this section as in effect on July 31, 2015 (except that "affirmative" and "written" shall be deleted from such paragraph (a)(3) of this section).

(b)   Unless otherwise provided in a limited liability company agreement, the death, retirement, resignation, expulsion, bankruptcy or dissolution of any member or the occurrence of an event that terminates the continued membership of any member shall not cause the limited liability company to be dissolved or its affairs to be wound up, and upon the occurrence of any such event, the limited liability company shall be continued without dissolution.

§ 18–802.   Judicial dissolution.

On application by or for a member or manager the Court of Chancery may decree dissolution of a limited liability company whenever it is not reasonably practicable to carry on the business in conformity with a limited liability company agreement.

§ 18–803.   Winding up.

(a)   Unless otherwise provided in a limited liability company agreement, a manager who has not wrongfully dissolved a limited liability company or, if none, the members or a person approved by the members, in either case, by members who own more than 50 percent of the then current percentage or other interest in the profits of the limited liability company owned by all of the members, may wind up the limited liability company's affairs; but the Court of Chancery, upon cause shown, may wind up the limited liability company's affairs upon application of any member or manager, or the member's personal representative or assignee, and in connection therewith, may appoint a liquidating trustee. Unless otherwise provided in a limited liability company agreement, a limited liability company whose original certificate of formation was filed with the Secretary of State and effective on or prior to July 31, 2015, shall continue to be governed by this subsection as in effect on July 31, 2015.

(b)   Upon dissolution of a limited liability company and until the filing of a certificate of cancellation as provided in § 18–203 of this title, the persons winding up the limited liability company's affairs may, in the name of, and for and on behalf of, the limited liability company, prosecute and defend suits, whether civil, criminal or administrative, gradually settle and close the limited liability company's business, dispose of and convey the limited liability company's property, discharge or make reasonable provision for the limited liability company's liabilities, and distribute to the members any remaining assets of the limited liability company, all without affecting the liability of members and managers and without imposing liability on a liquidating trustee.

§ 18–804.   Distribution of assets.

(a)   Upon the winding up of a limited liability company, the assets shall be distributed as follows:

(1)   To creditors, including members and managers who are creditors, to the extent otherwise permitted by law, in satisfaction of liabilities of the limited liability company (whether by payment or the making of reasonable provision for payment thereof) other than liabilities for which reasonable provision for payment has been made and liabilities for distributions to members and former members under § 18–601 or § 18–604 of this title;

(2)   Unless otherwise provided in a limited liability company agreement, to members and former members in satisfaction of liabilities for distributions under § 18–601 or § 18–604 of this title; and

(3)   Unless otherwise provided in a limited liability company agreement, to members first for the return of their contributions and second respecting their limited liability company interests, in the proportions in which the members share in distributions.

(b)   A limited liability company which has dissolved:

(1)   Shall pay or make reasonable provision to pay all claims and obligations, including all contingent, conditional or unmatured contractual claims, known to the limited liability company;

(2)   Shall make such provision as will be reasonably likely to be sufficient to provide compensation for any claim against the limited liability company which is the subject of a pending action, suit or proceeding to which the limited liability company is a party; and

(3)   Shall make such provision as will be reasonably likely to be sufficient to provide compensation for claims that have not been made known to the limited liability company or that have not arisen but that, based on facts known to the limited liability company, are likely to arise or to become known to the limited liability company within 10 years after the date of dissolution.

If there are sufficient assets, such claims and obligations shall be paid in full and any such provision for payment made shall be made in full. If there are insufficient assets, such claims and obligations shall be paid or provided for according to their priority and, among claims of equal priority, ratably to the extent of assets available therefor. Unless otherwise provided in the limited liability company agreement, any remaining assets shall be distributed as provided in this chapter. Any liquidating trustee winding up a limited liability company's affairs who has complied with this section shall not be personally liable to the claimants of the dissolved limited liability company by reason of such person's actions in winding up the limited liability company.

(c)   A member who receives a distribution in violation of subsection (a) of this section, and who knew at the time of the distribution that the distribution violated subsection (a) of this section, shall be liable to the limited liability company for the amount of the distribution. For purposes of the immediately preceding sentence, the term "distribution" shall not include amounts constituting reasonable compensation for present or past services or reasonable payments made in the ordinary course of business pursuant to a bona fide retirement plan or other benefits program. A member who receives a distribution in violation of subsection (a) of this section, and who did not know at the time of the distribution that the distribution violated subsection (a) of this section, shall not be liable for the amount of the distribution. Subject to subsection (d) of this section, this subsection shall not affect any obligation or liability of a member under an agreement or other applicable law for the amount of a distribution.

(d)   Unless otherwise agreed, a member who receives a distribution from a limited liability company to which this section applies shall have no liability under this chapter or other applicable law for the amount of the distribution after the expiration of 3 years from the date of the distribution unless an action to recover the distribution from such member is commenced prior to the expiration of the said 3-year period and an adjudication of liability against such member is made in the said action.

(e)   Section 18–607 of this title shall not apply to a distribution to which this section applies.

§ 18–805.   Trustees or receivers for limited liability companies; appointment; powers; duties.

When the certificate of formation of any limited liability company formed under this chapter shall be canceled by the filing of a certificate of cancellation pursuant to § 18–203 of this title, the Court of Chancery, on application of any creditor, member or manager of the limited liability company, or any other person who shows good cause therefor, at any time, may either appoint 1 or more of the managers of the limited liability company to be trustees, or appoint 1 or more persons to be receivers, of and for the limited liability company, to take charge of the limited liability company's property, and to collect the debts and property due and belonging to the limited liability company, with the power to prosecute and defend, in the name of the limited liability company, or otherwise, all such suits as may be necessary or proper for the purposes aforesaid, and to appoint an agent or agents under them, and to do all other acts which might be done by the limited liability company, if in being, that may be necessary for the final settlement of the unfinished business of the limited liability company. The powers of the trustees or receivers may be continued as long as the Court of Chancery shall think necessary for the purposes aforesaid.

§ 18–806.   Revocation of dissolution.

If a limited liability company agreement provides the manner in which a dissolution may be revoked, it may be revoked in that manner and, unless a limited liability company agreement prohibits revocation of dissolution, then notwithstanding the occurrence of an event set forth in § 18–801(a)(1), (2), (3) or (4) of this title, the limited liability company shall not be dissolved and its affairs shall not be wound up if, prior to the filing of a certificate of cancellation in the office of the Secretary of State, the limited liability company is continued, effective as of the occurrence of such event:

(1)   In the case of dissolution effected by the vote or consent of the members or other persons, pursuant to such vote or consent (and the approval of any members or other persons whose approval is required under the limited liability company agreement to revoke a dissolution contemplated by this paragraph);

(2)   In the case of dissolution under § 18–801(a)(1) or (2) of this title (other than a dissolution effected by the vote or consent of the members or other persons or the occurrence of an event that causes the last remaining member to cease to be a member), pursuant to such vote or consent that, pursuant to the terms of the limited liability company agreement, is required to amend the provision of the limited liability company agreement effecting such dissolution (and the approval of any members or other persons whose approval is required under the limited liability company agreement to revoke a dissolution contemplated by this paragraph); and

(3)   In the case of dissolution effected by the occurrence of an event that causes the last remaining member to cease to be a member, pursuant to the vote or consent of the personal representative of the last remaining member of the limited liability company or the assignee of all of the limited liability company interests in the limited liability company (and the approval of any other persons whose approval is required under the limited liability company agreement to revoke a dissolution contemplated by this paragraph).

If there is no remaining member of the limited liability company and the personal representative of the last remaining member or the assignee of all of the limited liability company interests in the limited liability company votes in favor of or consents to the continuation of the limited liability company, such personal representative or such assignee, as applicable, shall be required to agree to the admission of a nominee or designee as a member, effective as of the occurrence of the event that terminated the continued membership of the last remaining member. The provisions of this section shall not be construed to limit the accomplishment of a revocation of dissolution by other means permitted by law.

SUBCHAPTER IX.   FOREIGN LIMITED LIABILITY COMPANIES

§ 18–901.   Law governing.

(a)   Subject to the Constitution of the State of Delaware:

(1)   The laws of the state, territory, possession, or other jurisdiction or country under which a foreign limited liability company is organized govern its organization and internal affairs and the liability of its members and managers; and

(2)   A foreign limited liability company may not be denied registration by reason of any difference between those laws and the laws of the State of Delaware.

(b)   A foreign limited liability company shall be subject to § 18–106 of this title.

§ 18–902.   Registration required; application.

Before doing business in the State of Delaware, a foreign limited liability company shall register with the Secretary of State. In order to register, a foreign limited liability company shall submit to the Secretary of State:

(1)   A copy executed by an authorized person of an application for registration as a foreign limited liability company, setting forth:

    a.   The name of the foreign limited liability company and, if different, the name under which it proposes to register and do business in the State of Delaware;

    b.   The state, territory, possession or other jurisdiction or country where formed, the date of its formation and a statement from an authorized person that, as of the date of filing, the foreign limited liability company validly exists as a limited liability company under the laws of the jurisdiction of its formation;

    c.   The nature of the business or purposes to be conducted or promoted in the State of Delaware;

    d.   The address of the registered office and the name and address of the registered agent for service of process required to be maintained by § 18–904(b) of this title;

    e.   A statement that the Secretary of State is appointed the agent of the foreign limited liability company for service of process under the circumstances set forth in § 18–910(b) of this title; and

    f.   The date on which the foreign limited liability company first did, or intends to do, business in the State of Delaware.

(2)   A certificate, as of a date not earlier than 6 months prior to the filing date, issued by an authorized officer of the jurisdiction of its formation evidencing its existence. If such certificate is in a foreign language, a translation thereof, under oath of the translator, shall be attached thereto.

(3)   A fee as set forth in § 18–1105(a)(6) of this title shall be paid.

§ 18–903.   Issuance of registration.

(a)   If the Secretary of State finds that an application for registration conforms to law and all requisite fees have been paid, the Secretary shall:

(1)   Certify that the application has been filed by endorsing upon the original application the word "Filed", and the date and hour of the filing. This endorsement is conclusive of the date and time of its filing in the absence of actual fraud;

(2)   File and index the endorsed application.

(b)   The Secretary of State shall prepare and return to the person who filed the application or the person's representative a copy of the original signed application, similarly endorsed, and shall certify such copy as a true copy of the original signed application.

(c)   The filing of the application with the Secretary of State shall make it unnecessary to file any other documents under Chapter 31 of this title.

§ 18–904.   Name; registered office; registered agent.

(a)   A foreign limited liability company may register with the Secretary of State under any name (whether or not it is the name under which it is registered in the jurisdiction of its formation) that includes the words "Limited Liability Company" or the abbreviation "L.L.C." or the designation "LLC" and that could be registered by a domestic limited liability company; provided however, that a foreign limited liability company may register under any name which is not such as to distinguish it upon the records in the office of the Secretary of State from the name on such records of any domestic or foreign corporation, partnership, statutory trust, limited liability company or limited partnership reserved, registered, formed or organized under the laws of the State of Delaware with the written consent of the other corporation, partnership, statutory trust, limited liability company or limited partnership, which written consent shall be filed with the Secretary of State.

(b)   Each foreign limited liability company shall have and maintain in the State of Delaware:

(1)   A registered office which may but need not be a place of its business in the State of Delaware; and

(2)   A registered agent for service of process on the foreign limited liability company, having a business office identical with such registered office, which agent may be any of:

a.   An individual resident in the State of Delaware,

b.   A domestic limited liability company, a domestic corporation, a domestic partnership (whether general (including a limited liability partnership) or limited (including a limited liability limited partnership)), or a domestic statutory trust, or

c.   A foreign corporation, a foreign partnership (whether general (including a limited liability partnership) or limited (including a limited liability limited partnership)), a foreign limited liability company (other than the foreign limited liability company itself), or a foreign statutory trust.

(c)   A registered agent may change the address of the registered office of the foreign limited liability company or companies for which the agent is registered agent to another address in the State of Delaware by paying a fee as set forth in § 18–1105(a)(7) of this title and filing with the Secretary of State a certificate, executed by such registered agent, setting forth the address at which such registered agent has maintained the registered office for each of the foreign limited liability companies for which it is a registered agent, and further certifying to the new address to which each such registered office will be changed on a given day, and at which new address such registered agent will thereafter maintain the registered office for each of the foreign limited liability companies for which it is registered agent. Upon the filing of such certificate, the Secretary of State shall furnish to the registered agent a certified copy of the same under the Secretary's hand and seal of office, and thereafter, or until further change of address, as authorized by law, the registered office in the State of Delaware of each of the foreign limited liability companies for which the agent is a registered agent shall be located at the new address of the registered agent thereof as given in the certificate. In the event of a change of name of any person acting as a registered agent of a foreign limited liability company, such registered agent shall file with the Secretary of State a certificate, executed by such registered agent, setting forth the new name of such registered agent, the name of such registered agent before it was changed and the address at which such registered agent has maintained the registered office for each of the foreign limited liability companies for which it is registered agent, and shall pay a fee as set forth in § 18–1105(a)(7) of this title. Upon the filing of such certificate, the Secretary of State shall furnish to the registered agent a certified copy of the same under the Secretary of State's own hand and seal of office. A change of name of any person acting as a registered agent of a foreign limited liability company as a result of the merger or consolidation of the registered agent with or into another person which succeeds to its assets and liabilities by operation of law shall be deemed a change of name for purposes of this section. Filing a certificate under this section shall be deemed to be an amendment of the application of each foreign limited liability company affected thereby and each such foreign limited liability company shall not be required to take any further action with respect thereto to amend its application under § 18–905 of this title. Any registered agent filing a certificate under this section shall promptly, upon such filing, deliver a copy of any such certificate to each foreign limited liability company affected thereby.

(d)   The registered agent of 1 or more foreign limited liability companies may resign and appoint a successor registered agent by paying a fee as set forth in § 18–1105(a)(7) of this title and filing a certificate with the Secretary of State stating that it resigns and the name and address of the successor registered agent. There shall be attached to such certificate a statement of each affected foreign limited liability company ratifying and approving such change of registered agent. Upon such filing, the successor registered agent shall become the registered agent of such foreign limited liability companies as have ratified and approved such substitution and the successor registered agent's address, as stated in such certificate, shall become the address of each such foreign limited liability company's registered office in the State of Delaware. The Secretary of State shall then issue a certificate that the successor registered agent has become the registered agent of the foreign limited liability companies so ratifying and approving such change and setting out the names of such foreign limited liability companies. Filing of such certificate of resignation shall be deemed to be an amendment of the application of each foreign limited liability company affected thereby and each such foreign limited liability company shall not be required to take any further action with respect thereto to amend its application under § 18–905 of this title.

(e)   The registered agent of 1 or more foreign limited liability companies may resign without appointing a successor registered agent by paying a fee as set forth in § 18–1105(a)(7) of this title and filing a certificate of resignation with the Secretary of State, but such resignation shall not become effective until 30 days after the certificate is filed. The certificate shall contain a statement that written notice of resignation was given to each affected foreign limited liability company at least 30 days prior to the filing of the certificate by mailing or delivering such notice to the foreign limited liability company at its address last known to the registered agent and shall set forth the date of such notice. After receipt of the notice of the resignation of its registered agent, the foreign limited liability company for which such registered agent was acting shall obtain and designate a new registered agent to take the place of the registered agent so resigning. If such foreign limited liability company fails to obtain and designate a new registered agent as aforesaid prior to the expiration of the period of 30 days after the filing by the registered agent of the certificate of resignation, such foreign limited liability company shall not be permitted to do business in the State of Delaware and its registration shall be canceled. After the resignation of the registered agent shall have become effective as provided in this section and if no new registered agent shall have been obtained and designated in the time and manner aforesaid, service of legal process against each foreign limited liability company for which the resigned registered agent had been acting shall thereafter be upon the Secretary of State in accordance with § 18–911 of this title.

§ 18–905.   Amendments to application.

If any statement in the application for registration of a foreign limited liability company was false when made or any arrangements or other facts described have changed, making the application false in any respect, the foreign limited liability company shall promptly file in the office of the Secretary of State a certificate, executed by an authorized person, correcting such statement, together with a fee as set forth in § 18–1105(a)(6) of this title.

§ 18–906.   Cancellation of registration.

A foreign limited liability company may cancel its registration by filing with the Secretary of State a certificate of cancellation, executed by an authorized person, together with a fee as set forth in § 18–1105(a)(6) of this title. The registration of a foreign limited liability company shall be canceled as provided in §§ 18–104(i)(4), 18–904(e) and 18–1107(h) of this title. A cancellation does not terminate the authority of the Secretary of State to accept service of process on the foreign limited liability company with respect to causes of action arising out of the doing of business in the State of Delaware.

§ 18–907.   Doing business without registration.

(a)   A foreign limited liability company doing business in the State of Delaware may not maintain any action, suit or proceeding in the State of Delaware until it has registered in the State of Delaware, and has paid to the State of Delaware all fees and penalties for the years or parts thereof, during which it did business in the State of Delaware without having registered.

(b)   The failure of a foreign limited liability company to register in the State of Delaware does not impair:

(1)   The validity of any contract or act of the foreign limited liability company;

(2)   The right of any other party to the contract to maintain any action, suit or proceeding on the contract; or

(3)   Prevent the foreign limited liability company from defending any action, suit or proceeding in any court of the State of Delaware.

(c)   A member or a manager of a foreign limited liability company is not liable for the obligations of the foreign limited liability company solely by reason of the limited liability company's having done business in the State of Delaware without registration.

(d)   Any foreign limited liability company doing business in the State of Delaware without first having registered shall be fined and shall pay to the Secretary of State $200 for each year or part thereof during which the foreign limited liability company failed to register in the State of Delaware.

§ 18–908.   Foreign limited liability companies doing business without having qualified; injunctions.

The Court of Chancery shall have jurisdiction to enjoin any foreign limited liability company, or any agent thereof, from doing any business in the State of Delaware if such foreign limited liability company has failed to register under this subchapter or if such foreign limited liability company has secured a certificate of the Secretary of State under § 18–903 of this title on the basis of false or misleading representations. Upon the motion of the Attorney General or upon the relation of proper parties, the Attorney General shall proceed for this purpose by complaint in any county in which such foreign limited liability company is doing or has done business.

§ 18–909.   Execution; liability.

Section 18–204(d) of this title shall be applicable to foreign limited liability companies as if they were domestic limited liability companies.

§ 18–910.   Service of process on registered foreign limited liability companies.

(a)   Service of legal process upon any foreign limited liability company shall be made by delivering a copy personally to any managing or general agent or manager of the foreign limited liability company in the State of Delaware or the registered agent of the foreign limited liability company in the State of Delaware, or by leaving it at the dwelling house or usual place of abode in the State of Delaware of any such managing or general agent, manager or registered agent (if the registered agent be an individual), or at the registered office or other place of business of the foreign limited liability company in the State of Delaware. If the registered agent be a corporation, service of process upon it as such may be made by serving, in the State of Delaware, a copy thereof on the president, vice-president, secretary, assistant secretary or any director of the corporate registered agent. Service by copy left at the dwelling house or usual place of abode of any managing or general agent, manager or registered agent, or at the registered office or other place of business of the foreign limited liability company in the State of Delaware, to be effective must be delivered thereat at least 6 days before the return date of the process, and in the presence of an adult person, and the officer serving the process shall distinctly state the manner of service in the officer's return thereto. Process returnable forthwith must be delivered personally to the managing or general agent, manager or registered agent.

(b)   In case the officer whose duty it is to serve legal process cannot by due diligence serve the process in any manner provided for by subsection (a) of this section, it shall be lawful to serve the process against the foreign limited liability company upon the Secretary of State, and such service shall be as effectual for all intents and purposes as if made in any of the ways provided for in subsection (a) of this section. Process may be served upon the Secretary of State under this subsection by means of electronic transmission but only as prescribed by the Secretary of State. The Secretary of State is authorized to issue such rules and regulations with respect to such service as the Secretary of State deems necessary or appropriate. In the event that service is effected through the Secretary of State in accordance with this subsection, the Secretary of State shall forthwith notify the foreign limited liability company by letter, directed to the foreign limited liability company at its last registered office. Such letter shall be sent by a mail or courier service that includes a record of mailing or deposit with the courier and a record of delivery evidenced by the signature of the recipient. Such letter shall enclose a copy of the process and any other papers served on the Secretary of State pursuant to this subsection. It shall be the duty of the plaintiff in the event of such service to serve process and any other papers in duplicate, to notify the Secretary of State that service is being effected pursuant to this subsection, and to pay to the Secretary of State the sum of $50 for the use of the State of Delaware, which sum shall be taxed as a part of the costs in the proceeding if the plaintiff shall prevail therein. The Secretary of State shall maintain an alphabetical record of any such service setting forth the name of the plaintiff and defendant, the title, docket number and nature of the proceeding in which process has been served upon the Secretary, the fact that service has been effected pursuant to this subsection, the return date thereof and the day and hour when the service was made. The Secretary of State shall not be required to retain such information for a period longer than 5 years from the Secretary's receipt of the service of process.

§ 18–911.   Service of process on unregistered foreign limited liability companies.

(a) Any foreign limited liability company which shall do business in the State of Delaware without having registered under § 18–902 of this title shall be deemed to have thereby appointed and constituted the Secretary of State of the State of Delaware its agent for the acceptance of legal process in any civil action, suit or proceeding against it in any state or federal court in the State of Delaware arising or growing out of any business done by it within the State of Delaware. The doing of business in the State of Delaware by such foreign limited liability company shall be a signification of the agreement of such foreign limited liability company that any such process when so served shall be of the same legal force and validity as if served upon an authorized manager or agent personally within the State of Delaware. Process may be served upon the Secretary of State under this subsection by means of electronic transmission but only as prescribed by the Secretary of State. The Secretary of State is authorized to issue such rules and regulations with respect to such service as the Secretary of State deems necessary or appropriate.

(b) Whenever the words "doing business," "the doing of business" or "business done in this State," by any such foreign limited liability company are used in this section, they shall mean the course or practice of carrying on any business activities in the State of Delaware, including, without limiting the generality of the foregoing, the solicitation of business or orders in the State of Delaware.

(c) In the event of service upon the Secretary of State in accordance with subsection (a) of this section, the Secretary of State shall forthwith notify the foreign limited liability company thereof by letter, directed to the foreign limited liability company at the address furnished to the Secretary of State by the plaintiff in such action, suit or proceeding. Such letter shall be sent by a mail or courier service that includes a record of mailing or deposit with the courier and a record of delivery evidenced by the signature of the recipient. Such letter shall enclose a copy of the process and any other papers served upon the Secretary of State. It shall be the duty of the plaintiff in the event of such service to serve process and any other papers in duplicate, to notify the Secretary of State that service is being made pursuant to this subsection, and to pay to the Secretary of State the sum of $50 for the use of the State of Delaware, which sum shall be taxed as part of the costs in the proceeding, if the plaintiff shall prevail therein. The Secretary of State shall maintain an alphabetical record of any such process setting forth the name of the plaintiff and defendant, the title, docket number and nature of the proceeding in which process has been served upon the Secretary, the return date thereof, and the day and hour when the service was made. The Secretary of State shall not be required to retain such information for a period longer than 5 years from the receipt of the service of process.

§ 18–912.   Activities not constituting doing business.

(a) Activities of a foreign limited liability company in the State of Delaware that do not constitute doing business for the purpose of this subchapter include:

(1) Maintaining, defending or settling an action or proceeding;

(2) Holding meetings of its members or managers or carrying on any other activity concerning its internal affairs;

(3) Maintaining bank accounts;

(4) Maintaining offices or agencies for the transfer, exchange or registration of the limited liability company's own securities or maintaining trustees or depositories with respect to those securities;

(5) Selling through independent contractors;

(6) Soliciting or obtaining orders, whether by mail or through employees or agents or otherwise, if the orders require acceptance outside the State of Delaware before they become contracts;

(7) Selling, by contract consummated outside the State of Delaware, and agreeing, by the contract, to deliver into the State of Delaware, machinery, plants or equipment, the construction, erection or installation of which within the State of Delaware requires the supervision of technical engineers or skilled employees performing services not generally available, and as part of the contract of sale agreeing to furnish such services, and such services only, to the vendee at the time of construction, erection or installation;

(8) Creating, as borrower or lender, or acquiring indebtedness with or without a mortgage or other security interest in property;

(9) Collecting debts or foreclosing mortgages or other security interests in property securing the debts, and holding, protecting and maintaining property so acquired;

(10) Conducting an isolated transaction that is not 1 in the course of similar transactions;

(11) Doing business in interstate commerce; and

(12) Doing business in the State of Delaware as an insurance company.

(b) A person shall not be deemed to be doing business in the State of Delaware solely by reason of being a member or manager of a domestic limited liability company or a foreign limited liability company.

(c) This section does not apply in determining whether a foreign limited liability company is subject to service of process, taxation or regulation under any other law of the State of Delaware.

SUBCHAPTER X. DERIVATIVE ACTIONS

§ 18–1001.   Right to bring action.

A member or an assignee of a limited liability company interest may bring an action in the Court of Chancery in the right of a limited liability company to recover a judgment in its favor if managers or members with authority to do so have refused to bring the action or if an effort to cause those managers or members to bring the action is not likely to succeed.

§ 18–1002.   Proper plaintiff.

In a derivative action, the plaintiff must be a member or an assignee of a limited liability company interest at the time of bringing the action and:

(1) At the time of the transaction of which the plaintiff complains; or

(2)   The plaintiff's status as a member or an assignee of a limited liability company interest had devolved upon the plaintiff by operation of law or pursuant to the terms of a limited liability company agreement from a person who was a member or an assignee of a limited liability company interest at the time of the transaction.

§ 18–1003.   Complaint.

In a derivative action, the complaint shall set forth with particularity the effort, if any, of the plaintiff to secure initiation of the action by a manager or member or the reasons for not making the effort.

§ 18–1004.   Expenses.

If a derivative action is successful, in whole or in part, as a result of a judgment, compromise or settlement of any such action, the court may award the plaintiff reasonable expenses, including reasonable attorney's fees, from any recovery in any such action or from a limited liability company.

SUBCHAPTER XI.   MISCELLANEOUS

§ 18–1101.   Construction and application of chapter and limited liability company agreement.

(a)   The rule that statutes in derogation of the common law are to be strictly construed shall have no application to this chapter.

(b)   It is the policy of this chapter to give the maximum effect to the principle of freedom of contract and to the enforceability of limited liability company agreements.

(c)   To the extent that, at law or in equity, a member or manager or other person has duties (including fiduciary duties) to a limited liability company or to another member or manager or to another person that is a party to or is otherwise bound by a limited liability company agreement, the member's or manager's or other person's duties may be expanded or restricted or eliminated by provisions in the limited liability company agreement; provided, that the limited liability company agreement may not eliminate the implied contractual covenant of good faith and fair dealing.

(d)   Unless otherwise provided in a limited liability company agreement, a member or manager or other person shall not be liable to a limited liability company or to another member or manager or to another person that is a party to or is otherwise bound by a limited liability company agreement for breach of fiduciary duty for the member's or manager's or other person's good faith reliance on the provisions of the limited liability company agreement.

(e)   A limited liability company agreement may provide for the limitation or elimination of any and all liabilities for breach of contract and breach of duties (including fiduciary duties) of a member, manager or other person to a limited liability company or to another member or manager or to another person that is a party to or is otherwise bound by a limited liability company agreement; provided, that a limited liability company agreement may not limit or eliminate liability for any act or omission that constitutes a bad faith violation of the implied contractual covenant of good faith and fair dealing.

(f)   Unless the context otherwise requires, as used herein, the singular shall include the plural and the plural may refer to only the singular. The use of any gender shall be applicable to all genders. The captions contained herein are for purposes of convenience only and shall not control or affect the construction of this chapter.

(g)   Sections 9–406 and 9–408 of this title do not apply to any interest in a limited liability company, including all rights, powers and interests arising under a limited liability company agreement or this chapter. This provision prevails over §§ 9–406 and 9–408 of this title.

(h)   Action validly taken pursuant to 1 provision of this chapter shall not be deemed invalid solely because it is identical or similar in substance to an action that could have been taken pursuant to some other provision of this chapter but fails to satisfy 1 or more requirements prescribed by such other provision.

(i)   A limited liability company agreement that provides for the application of Delaware law shall be governed by and construed under the laws of the State of Delaware in accordance with its terms.

(j)   The provisions of this chapter shall apply whether a limited liability company has 1 member or more than 1 member.

§ 18-1102.   Short title.

This chapter may be cited as the "Delaware Limited Liability Company Act."

§ 18-1103.   Severability.

If any provision of this chapter or its application to any person or circumstances is held invalid, the invalidity does not affect other provisions or applications of the chapter which can be given effect without the invalid provision or application, and to this end, the provisions of this chapter are severable.

§ 18-1104.   Cases not provided for in this chapter.

In any case not provided for in this chapter, the rules of law and equity, including the rules of law and equity relating to fiduciary duties and the law merchant, shall govern.

§ 18-1105.   Fees.

(a)   No document required to be filed under this chapter shall be effective until the applicable fee required by this section is paid. The following fees shall be paid to and collected by the Secretary of State for the use of the State of Delaware:

(1)   Upon the receipt for filing of an application for reservation of name, an application for renewal of reservation or a notice of transfer or cancellation of reservation pursuant to § 18-103(b) of this title, a fee in the amount of $75.

(2)   Upon the receipt for filing of a certificate under § 18-104(b) of this title, a fee in the amount of $200, upon the receipt for filing of a certificate under § 18-104(c) of this title, a fee in the amount of $200, and upon the receipt for filing of a certificate under § 18-104(d) of this title, a fee in the amount of $2.00 for each limited liability company whose registered agent has resigned by such certificate.

(3)   Upon the receipt for filing of a certificate of formation under § 18-201 of this title or a certificate of registered series under § 18-218 of this title, a fee in the amount of $70 and upon the receipt for filing of a certificate of limited liability company domestication under § 18-212 of this title, a certificate of transfer or a certificate of transfer and domestic continuance under § 18-213 of this title, a certificate of conversion to limited liability company under § 18-214 of this title, a certificate of conversion to a non-Delaware entity under § 18-216 of this title, a certificate of amendment under § 18-202 or § 18-218(d)(3) of this title (except as otherwise provided in paragraph (a)(11) of this section), a certificate of cancellation under § 18-203 or § 18-218(d)(7) of this title, a certificate of merger or consolidation or a certificate of ownership and merger under § 18-209 of this title, a restated certificate of formation or a restated certificate of registered series under § 18-208 of this title, a certificate of amendment of a certificate with a future effective date or time under § 18-206(c) of this title, a certificate of termination of a certificate with a future effective date or time under § 18-206(c) of this title, a certificate of correction under § 18-211 of this title, a certificate of division under § 18-217 of this title, a certificate of conversion of protected series to registered series under § 18-219 of this title, a certificate of conversion of registered series to protected series under § 18-220 of this title, a certificate of merger or

consolidation of registered series under § 18–221 of this title or a certificate of revival under § 18–1109 or § 18–1110 of this title, a fee in the amount of $180, plus, in the case of a certificate of cancellation under § 18–203 of this title, a fee in the amount of $50 for each registered series of the limited liability company named in the certificate of cancellation.

(4)　For certifying copies of any paper on file as provided for by this chapter, a fee in the amount of $50 for each copy certified. In addition, a fee of $2.00 per page shall be paid in each instance where the Secretary of State provides the copies of the document to be certified.

(5)　The Secretary of State may issue photocopies or electronic image copies of instruments on file, as well as instruments, documents and other papers not on file, and for all such photocopies or electronic image copies which are not certified by the Secretary of State, a fee of $10 shall be paid for the first page and $2.00 for each additional page. Notwithstanding Delaware's Freedom of Information Act (Chapter 100 of Title 29) or other provision of law granting access to public records, the Secretary of State upon request shall issue only photocopies or electronic image copies of public records in exchange for the fees described in this section, and in no case shall the Secretary of State be required to provide copies (or access to copies) of such public records (including without limitation bulk data, digital copies of instruments, documents and other papers, databases or other information) in an electronic medium or in any form other than photocopies or electronic image copies of such public records in exchange, as applicable, for the fees described in this section or § 2318 of Title 29 for each such record associated with a file number.

(6)　Upon the receipt for filing of an application for registration as a foreign limited liability company under § 18–902 of this title, a certificate under § 18–905 of this title or a certificate of cancellation under § 18–906 of this title, a fee in the amount of $200.

(7)　Upon the receipt for filing of a certificate under § 18–904(c) of this title, a fee in the amount of $200, upon the receipt for filing of a certificate under § 18–904(d) of this title, a fee in the amount of $200, and upon the receipt for filing of a certificate under § 18–904(e) of this title, a fee in the amount of $2.00 for each foreign limited liability company whose registered agent has resigned by such certificate.

(8)　For preclearance of any document for filing, a fee in the amount of $250.

(9)　For preparing and providing a written report of a record search, a fee of up to $100.

(10)　For issuing any certificate of the Secretary of State, including but not limited to a certificate of good standing with respect to a limited liability company or a registered series thereof, other than a certification of a copy under paragraph (a)(4) of this section, a fee in the amount of $50, except that for issuing any certificate of the Secretary of State that recites all of the filings with the Secretary of State of a limited liability company or all of the filings of any registered series or that lists all of the registered series formed by a limited liability company, a fee of $175 shall be paid for each such certificate. For issuing any certificate via the Secretary of State's online services, a fee of up to $175 shall be paid for each certificate.

(11)　For receiving and filing and/or indexing any certificate, affidavit, agreement or any other paper provided for by this chapter, for which no different fee is specifically prescribed, a fee in the amount of $200. For filing any instrument submitted by a limited liability company or foreign limited liability company that only changes the registered office or registered agent and is specifically captioned as a certificate of amendment changing only the registered office or registered agent, a fee in the amount of $50 provided that no fee shall be charged pursuant to § 18–206(e) of this title.

(12)　The Secretary of State may in the Secretary of State's own discretion charge a fee of $60 for each check received for payment of any fee that is returned due to insufficient funds or the result of a stop payment order.

(b)   In addition to those fees charged under subsection (a) of this section, there shall be collected by and paid to the Secretary of State the following:

(1)   For all services described in subsection (a) of this section that are requested to be completed within 30 minutes on the same day as the day of the request, an additional sum of up to $7,500 and for all services described in subsection (a) of this section that are requested to be completed within 1 hour on the same day as the day of the request, an additional sum of up to $1,000 and for all services described in subsection (a) of this section that are requested to be completed within 2 hours on the same day of the request, an additional sum of up to $500;

(2)   For all services described in subsection (a) of this section that are requested to be completed within the same day as the day of the request, an additional sum of up to $300; and

(3)   For all services described in subsection (a) of this section that are requested to be completed within a 24-hour period from the time of the request, an additional sum of up to $150.

The Secretary of State shall establish (and may from time to time amend) a schedule of specific fees payable pursuant to this subsection.

(c)   The Secretary of State may in his or her discretion permit the extension of credit for the fees required by this section upon such terms as the secretary shall deem to be appropriate.

(d)   The Secretary of State shall retain from the revenue collected from the fees required by this section a sum sufficient to provide at all times a fund of at least $500, but not more than $1,500, from which the secretary may refund any payment made pursuant to this section to the extent that it exceeds the fees required by this section. The funds shall be deposited in a financial institution which is a legal depository of State of Delaware moneys to the credit of the Secretary of State and shall be disbursable on order of the Secretary of State.

(e)   Except as provided in this section, the fees of the Secretary of State shall be as provided in § 2315 of Title 29.

§ 18–1106.   Reserved power of State of Delaware to alter or repeal chapter.

All provisions of this chapter may be altered from time to time or repealed and all rights of members and managers are subject to this reservation. Unless expressly stated to the contrary in this chapter, all amendments of this chapter shall apply to limited liability companies and members and managers whether or not existing as such at the time of the enactment of any such amendment.

§ 18–1107.   Taxation of limited liability companies and registered series.

(a)   For purposes of any tax imposed by the State of Delaware or any instrumentality, agency or political subdivision of the State of Delaware, a domestic limited liability company or a foreign limited liability company qualified to do business in the State of Delaware shall be classified as a partnership unless classified otherwise for federal income tax purposes, in which case the domestic or foreign limited liability company shall be classified in the same manner as it is classified for federal income tax purposes. For purposes of any tax imposed by the State of Delaware or any instrumentality, agency or political subdivision of the State of Delaware, a member or an assignee of a member of a domestic limited liability company or a foreign limited liability company qualified to do business in the State of Delaware shall be treated as either a resident or nonresident partner unless classified otherwise for federal income tax purposes, in which case the member or assignee of a member shall have the same status as such member or assignee of a member has for federal income tax purposes.

(b)   Every domestic limited liability company and every foreign limited liability company registered to do business in the State of Delaware shall pay an annual tax, for the use of the State of Delaware, in the amount of $300. There shall be paid by or on behalf of each registered series of a domestic limited liability company an annual tax, for use of the State of Delaware, in the amount of $75 per registered series.

(c)   The annual tax for a domestic limited liability company shall be due and payable on the first day of June following the close of the calendar year or upon the cancellation of a certificate of formation. The annual tax for a registered series shall be due and payable on the first day of June following the close of the calendar year or upon the cancellation of a certificate of registered series. The annual tax for a foreign limited liability company shall be due and payable on the first day of June following the close of the calendar year or upon the cancellation of the certificate of registration. The Secretary of State shall receive the annual tax and pay over all taxes collected to the Department of Finance of the State of Delaware. If the annual tax remains unpaid after the due date, the tax shall bear interest at the rate of 1 and one-half percent for each month or portion thereof until fully paid.

(d)   The Secretary of State shall, at least 60 days prior to June 1 of each year, cause to be mailed to each domestic limited liability company and each registered series thereof and each foreign limited liability company required to comply with the provisions of this section in care of its registered agent in the State of Delaware an annual statement for the tax to be paid hereunder.

(e)   In the event of neglect, refusal or failure on the part of any domestic limited liability company, registered series or foreign limited liability company to pay the annual tax to be paid hereunder on or before June 1 in any year, such domestic limited liability company or foreign limited liability company shall pay the sum of $200, and such registered series shall pay the sum of $50, to be recovered by adding that amount to the annual tax and such additional sum shall become a part of the tax and shall be collected in the same manner and subject to the same penalties.

(f)   In case any domestic limited liability company, registered series or foreign limited liability company shall fail to pay the annual tax due within the time required by this section, and in case the agent in charge of the registered office of any domestic limited liability company or foreign limited liability company upon whom process against such domestic limited liability company or any protected series or registered series thereof or foreign limited liability company may be served shall die, resign, refuse to act as such, remove from the State of Delaware or cannot with due diligence be found, it shall be lawful while default continues to serve process against such domestic limited liability company or any protected series or registered series thereof or foreign limited liability company upon the Secretary of State. Such service upon the Secretary of State shall be made in the manner and shall have the effect stated in § 18–105 of this title in the case of a domestic limited liability company or any protected series or registered series thereof and § 18–910 of this title in the case of a foreign limited liability company and shall be governed in all respects by said sections.

(g)   The annual tax shall be a debt due from a domestic limited liability company, registered series or foreign limited liability company to the State of Delaware, for which an action at law may be maintained after the same shall have been in arrears for a period of 1 month. The tax shall also be a preferred debt in the case of insolvency.

(h)   A domestic limited liability company that neglects, refuses or fails to pay the annual tax when due shall cease to be in good standing as a domestic limited liability company and all registered series thereof shall also cease to be in good standing. A registered series that neglects, refuses or fails to pay the annual tax when due shall cease to be in good standing as a registered series. A foreign limited liability company that neglects, refuses or fails to pay the annual tax when due shall cease to be registered as a foreign limited liability company in the State of Delaware.

(i)   A domestic limited liability company or registered series that has ceased to be in good standing or a foreign limited liability company that has ceased to be registered by reason of the failure by the limited liability company, registered series or foreign limited liability company to pay an annual tax shall be restored to and have the status of a domestic limited liability company or registered series in good standing or a foreign limited liability company that is registered in the State of Delaware upon the payment of the annual tax and all penalties and interest thereon for each year for which such domestic limited liability company, registered series or foreign limited liability company neglected, refused or failed to pay an annual tax.

(j)   On the motion of the Attorney General or upon request of the Secretary of State, whenever any annual tax due under this chapter from any domestic limited liability company, registered series or foreign limited liability company shall have remained in arrears for a period of 3 months after the tax shall have become payable, the Attorney General may apply to the Court of Chancery, by petition in the name of the State of Delaware, on 5 days' notice to such domestic limited liability company, registered series or foreign limited liability company, which notice may be served in such manner as the Court may direct, for an injunction to restrain such domestic limited liability company, registered series or foreign limited liability company from the transaction of any business within the State of Delaware or elsewhere, until the payment of the annual tax, and all penalties and interest due thereon and the cost of the application which shall be fixed by the Court. The Court of Chancery may grant the injunction, if a proper case appears, and upon granting and service of the injunction, such domestic limited liability company, registered series or foreign limited liability company thereafter shall not transact any business until the injunction shall be dissolved.

(k)   A domestic limited liability company that has ceased to be in good standing by reason of the domestic limited liability company's neglect, refusal or failure to pay an annual tax shall remain a domestic limited liability company formed under this chapter, and each registered series thereof shall remain a registered series formed under this chapter, and each protected series thereof shall remain a protected series established under this chapter. A registered series that has ceased to be in good standing by reason of the registered series' neglect, refusal or failure to pay an annual tax shall remain a registered series formed under this chapter. The Secretary of State shall not accept for filing any certificate (except a certificate of resignation of a registered agent when a successor registered agent is not being appointed) required or permitted by this chapter to be filed in respect of any domestic limited liability company, registered series or foreign limited liability company if such domestic limited liability company, registered series or foreign limited liability company has neglected, refused or failed to pay an annual tax, and shall not issue any certificate of good standing with respect to such domestic limited liability company, registered series or foreign limited liability company, unless or until such domestic limited liability company, registered series or foreign limited liability company shall have been restored to and have the status of a domestic limited liability company or registered series in good standing or a foreign limited liability company duly registered in the State of Delaware.

(l)   A domestic limited liability company that has ceased to be in good standing (and each protected series and registered series thereof), a registered series that has ceased to be in good standing, or a foreign limited liability company that has ceased to be registered in the State of Delaware by reason of the domestic limited liability company's, registered series' or foreign limited liability company's neglect, refusal or failure to pay an annual tax may not maintain any action, suit or proceeding in any court of the State of Delaware until such domestic limited liability company, registered series or foreign limited liability company has been restored to and has the status of a domestic limited liability company, registered series or foreign limited liability company in good standing or duly registered in the State of Delaware. An action, suit or proceeding may not be maintained in any court of the State of Delaware by any successor or assignee of such domestic limited liability company (or any protected series or registered series thereof), registered series, or foreign limited liability company on any right, claim or demand arising out the transaction of business by such domestic limited liability company (or any protected series or registered series thereof) or registered series after the domestic limited liability company or registered series has ceased to be in good standing or a foreign limited liability company that has ceased to be registered in the State of Delaware until such domestic limited liability company, registered series or foreign limited liability company, or any person that has acquired all or substantially all of its assets, has paid any annual tax then due and payable, together with penalties and interest thereon.

(m)   The neglect, refusal or failure of a domestic limited liability company, registered series or foreign limited liability company to pay an annual tax shall not impair the validity of any contract, deed, mortgage, security interest, lien or act of such domestic limited liability company or any protected series or registered series thereof or foreign limited liability company or prevent such domestic limited liability company or any protected series or registered series thereof or foreign limited liability company from defending any action, suit or proceeding with any court of the State of Delaware.

(n)   A member or manager of a domestic limited liability company, registered series or foreign limited liability company is not liable for the debts, obligations or liabilities of such domestic limited liability company, registered series or foreign limited liability company solely by reason of the neglect, refusal or failure of such domestic limited liability company, registered series or foreign limited liability company to pay an annual tax or by reason of such domestic limited liability company, registered series or foreign limited liability company ceasing to be in good standing or duly registered. A protected series or registered series of a domestic limited liability company is not liable for the debts, obligations or liabilities of such domestic limited liability company or any other series thereof solely by reason of the neglect, refusal or failure of such domestic limited liability company or other series to pay an annual tax or by reason of such domestic limited liability company or other series ceasing to be in good standing.

§ 18–1108.   Cancellation of certificate of formation or certificate of registered series for failure to pay taxes.

(a)   The certificate of formation of a domestic limited liability company shall be canceled if the annual tax due under § 18–1107 of this title for the domestic limited liability company is not paid for a period of 3 years from the date it is due, such cancellation to be effective on the third anniversary of such due date.

(b)   The certificate of registered series shall be canceled if the annual tax due under § 18–1107 of this title is not paid for a period of 3 years from the date it is due, such cancellation to be effective on the third anniversary of such due date.

(c)   A list of those domestic limited liability companies and registered series whose certificates of formation or certificates of registered series were canceled on June 1 of such calendar year pursuant to § 18–1108(a) or § 18–1108(b) of this title shall be filed in the office of the Secretary of State. On or before October 31 of each calendar year, the Secretary of State shall publish such list on the Internet or on a similar medium for a period of 1 week and shall advertise the website or other address where such list can be accessed in at least 1 newspaper of general circulation in the State of Delaware.

§ 18–1109.   Revival of domestic limited liability company.

(a)   A domestic limited liability company whose certificate of formation has been canceled pursuant to § 18–104(d) or (i)(4) or § 18–1108(a) of this title may be revived by filing in the office of the Secretary of State a certificate of revival accompanied by the payment of the fee required by § 18–1105(a)(3) of this title and payment of the annual tax due under § 18–1107 of this title and all penalties and interest thereon due at the time of the cancellation of its certificate of formation. The certificate of revival shall set forth:

(1)   The name of the limited liability company at the time its certificate of formation was canceled and, if such name is not available at the time of revival, the name under which the limited liability company is to be revived;

(2)   The date of filing of the original certificate of formation of the limited liability company;

(3)   The address of the limited liability company's registered office in the State of Delaware and the name and address of the limited liability company's registered agent in the State of Delaware;

(4)   A statement that the certificate of revival is filed by 1 or more persons authorized to execute and file the certificate of revival to revive the limited liability company; and

(5)   Any other matters the persons executing the certificate of revival determine to include therein.

(b)   The certificate of revival shall be deemed to be an amendment to the certificate of formation of the limited liability company, and the limited liability company shall not be required to take any further action to amend its certificate of formation under § 18–202 of this title with respect to the matters set forth in the certificate of revival.

(c)   Upon the filing of a certificate of revival, a limited liability company and all registered series thereof that have been formed and whose certificate of registered series has not been canceled prior to the cancellation of the certificate of formation shall be revived with the same force and effect as if its certificate of formation had not been canceled pursuant to § 18–104(d), § 18–104(i)(4) or § 18–1108(a) of this title. Such revival shall validate all contracts, acts, matters and things made, done and performed by the limited liability company, its members, managers, employees and agents during the time when its certificate of formation was canceled pursuant to § 18–104(d), § 18–104(i)(4) or § 18–1108(a) of this title, with the same force and effect and to all intents and purposes as if the certificate of formation had remained in full force and effect. All real and personal property, and all rights and interests, which belonged to the limited liability company at the time its certificate of formation was canceled pursuant to § 18–104(d), § 18–104(i)(4) or § 18–1108(a) of this title or which were acquired by the limited liability company following the cancellation of its certificate of formation pursuant to § 18–104(d), § 18–104(i)(4) or § 18–1108(a) of this title, and which were not disposed of prior to the time of its revival, shall be vested in the limited liability company after its revival as fully as they were held by the limited liability company at, and after, as the case may be, the time its certificate of formation was canceled pursuant to § 18–104(d), § 18–104(i)(4) or § 18–1108(a) of this title. After its revival, the limited liability company shall be as exclusively liable for all contracts, acts, matters and things made, done or performed in its name and on its behalf by its members, managers, employees and agents prior to its revival as if its certificate of formation had at all times remained in full force and effect.

§ 18–1110.   Revival of a registered series.

(a)   A registered series whose certificate of registered series has been canceled pursuant to § 18–1108(b) of this title may be revived by filing in the office of the Secretary of State a certificate of revival of registered series accompanied by the payment of the fee required by § 18–1105(a)(3) of this title and payment of the annual tax due under § 18–1107 of this title and all penalties and interest thereon due at the time of the cancellation of its certificate of registered series. The certificate of revival of registered series shall set forth:

(1)   The name of the limited liability company at the time the certificate of registered series was canceled and, if such name has changed, the name of the limited liability company at the time of revival of the registered series;

(2)   The name of the registered series at the time the certificate of registered series was canceled and, if such name is not available at the time of revival, the name under which the registered series is to be revived;

(3)   The date of filing of the original certificate of registered series;

(4)   A statement that the certificate of revival of registered series is filed by 1 or more persons authorized to execute and file such certificate of revival to revive the registered series; and

(5)   Any other matters the persons executing the certificate of revival of registered series determine to include therein.

(b)   The certificate of revival of registered series shall be deemed to be an amendment to the certificate of registered series, and no further actions shall be required to amend its certificate of registered series under § 18–218(d)(3) of this title with respect to the matters set forth in such certificate of revival.

(c)   Upon the filing of a certificate of revival of registered series, a registered series shall be revived with the same force and effect as if its certificate of registered series had not been canceled pursuant to § 18–1108(b) of this title. Such revival shall validate all contracts, acts, matters and things made, done and performed by the registered series, its members, managers, employees and agents during the time when its certificate of registered series was canceled pursuant to § 18–1108(b) of this title, with the same force and effect and to all intents and purposes as if the certificate of registered series had remained in full force and effect. All real and personal property, and all rights and interests, which belonged to the registered series at the time its certificate of registered series was canceled pursuant to § 18–1108(b) of this title or which were acquired by the registered series following the cancellation of its certificate of registered series pursuant to § 18–1108(b) of this title, and which were not disposed of prior to the time of its revival, shall be vested in the registered series after its revival as fully as they were held by the registered series at, and after, as the case may be, the time its certificate of registered series was canceled pursuant to § 18–1108(b) of this title. After its revival, the registered series shall be as exclusively liable for all contracts, acts, matters and things made, done or performed in its name and on its behalf by its members, managers, employees and agents prior to its revival as if its certificate of registered series had at all times remained in full force and effect.

SUBCHAPTER XII.   STATUTORY PUBLIC BENEFIT LIMITED LIABILITY COMPANIES

§ 18–1201.   Law applicable to statutory public benefit limited liability companies; how formed.

This subchapter applies to all statutory public benefit limited liability companies, as defined in § 18–1202 of this title. If a limited liability company elects to become a statutory public benefit limited liability company under this subchapter in the manner prescribed in this subchapter, it shall be subject in all respects to the provisions of this chapter, except to the extent this subchapter imposes additional or different requirements, in which case such requirements shall apply, and notwithstanding § 18–1101 of this title or any other provision of this title, such requirements imposed by this subchapter may not be altered in the limited liability company agreement.

§ 18–1202.   Statutory public benefit limited liability company defined; contents of certificate of formation and limited liability company agreement.

(a)   A "statutory public benefit limited liability company" is a for-profit limited liability company formed under and subject to the requirements of this chapter that is intended to produce a public benefit or public benefits and to operate in a responsible and sustainable manner. To that end, a statutory public benefit limited liability company shall be managed in a manner that balances the members' pecuniary interests, the best interests of those materially affected by the limited liability company's conduct, and the public benefit or public benefits set forth in its certificate of formation. A statutory public benefit limited liability company shall state in the heading of its certificate of formation that it is a statutory public benefit limited liability company and shall set forth 1 or more specific public benefits to be promoted by the limited liability company in its certificate of formation. The limited liability company agreement of a statutory public benefit limited liability company may not contain any provision inconsistent with this subchapter.

(b)   "Public benefit" means a positive effect (or reduction of negative effects) on 1 or more categories of persons, entities, communities or interests (other than members in their capacities as members) including, but not limited to, effects of an artistic, charitable, cultural, economic, educational, environmental, literary, medical, religious, scientific or technological nature. "Public benefit provisions" means the provisions of a limited liability company agreement contemplated by this subchapter.

§ 18–1203.   Certain amendments and mergers; votes required.

Notwithstanding any other provision of this chapter, a statutory public benefit limited liability company may not, without the approval of members who own at least 2/3 of the then-current percentage or other interest in the profits of the limited liability company owned by all members:

(1)   Amend its certificate of formation to delete or amend a provision required by § 18–1202(a) of this title;

(2)   Merge or consolidate with or into another entity or divide into 2 or more domestic limited liability companies if, as a result of such merger, consolidation or division, the limited liability company interests in such limited liability company would become, or be converted into or exchanged for the right to receive, limited liability company interests or other equity interests in a domestic or foreign limited liability company or other entity that is not a statutory public benefit limited liability company or similar entity, the certificate of formation or limited liability company agreement (or similar governing document) of which does not contain provisions identifying a public benefit or public benefits comparable in all material respects to those set forth in the certificate of formation of such limited liability company as contemplated by § 18–1202(a) of this title; or

(3)   Cease to be a statutory public benefit limited liability company under the provisions of this subchapter.

§ 18–1204.   Duties of members or managers.

(a)   The members or managers or other persons with authority to manage or direct the business and affairs of a statutory public benefit limited liability company shall manage or direct the business and affairs of the statutory public benefit limited liability company in a manner that balances the pecuniary interests of the members, the best interests of those materially affected by the limited liability company's conduct, and the specific public benefit or public benefits set forth in its certificate of formation. Unless otherwise provided in a limited liability company agreement, no member, manager or other person with authority to manage or direct the business and affairs of the statutory public benefit limited liability company shall have any liability for monetary damages for the failure to manage or direct the business and affairs of the statutory public benefit limited liability company as provided in this subsection.

(b)   A member or manager of a statutory public benefit limited liability company or any other person with authority to manage or direct the business and affairs of the statutory public benefit limited liability company shall not, by virtue of the public benefit provisions or § 18–1202(a) of this title, have any duty to any person on account of any interest of such person in the public benefit or public benefits set forth in its certificate of formation or on account of any interest materially affected by the limited liability company's conduct and, with respect to a decision implicating the balance requirement in subsection (a) of this section, will be deemed to satisfy such person's fiduciary duties to members and the limited liability company if such person's decision is both informed and disinterested and not such that no person of ordinary, sound judgment would approve.

§ 18–1205.   Periodic statements and third-party certification.

A statutory public benefit limited liability company shall no less than biennially provide its members with a statement as to the limited liability company's promotion of the public benefit or public benefits set forth in its certificate of formation and as to the best interests of those materially affected by the limited liability company's conduct. The statement shall include:

(1)   The objectives that have been established to promote such public benefit or public benefits and interests;

(2)   The standards that have been adopted to measure the limited liability company's progress in promoting such public benefit or public benefits and interests;

(3)   Objective factual information based on those standards regarding the limited liability company's success in meeting the objectives for promoting such public benefit or public benefits and interests; and

(4)   An assessment of the limited liability company's success in meeting the objectives and promoting such public benefit or public benefits and interests.

§ 18–1206.   Derivative suits.

Members of a statutory public benefit limited liability company or assignees of limited liability company interests in a statutory public benefit limited liability company owning individually or collectively, as of the date of instituting such derivative suit, at least 2% of the then-current percentage or other interest in the profits of the limited liability company or, in the case of a limited liability company with limited liability company interests listed on a national securities exchange, the lesser of such percentage or limited liability company interests of at least $2,000,000 in market value, may maintain a derivative lawsuit to enforce the requirements set forth in § 18–1204(a) of this title.

§ 18–1207.   No effect on other limited liability companies.

This subchapter shall not affect a statute or rule of law that is applicable to a limited liability company that is not a statutory public benefit limited liability company.

§ 18–1208.   Accomplishment by other means.

The provisions of this subchapter shall not be construed to limit the accomplishment by any other means permitted by law of the formation or operation of a limited liability company that is formed or operated for a public benefit (including a limited liability company that is designated as a public benefit limited liability company) that is not a statutory public benefit limited liability company.

D. LIMITED LIABILITY COMPANY FORMS

Table of Forms

Forms
1.   Morrison & Foerster LLP Form Operating Agreement for Delaware Limited Liability Company

---

1.   MORRISON & FOERSTER LLP FORM OPERATING AGREEMENT FOR DELAWARE LIMITED LIABILITY COMPANY*

OPERATING AGREEMENT OF
XYZ PARTNERS, L.L.C.

THIS OPERATING AGREEMENT (the "Agreement") of XYZ Partners, L.L.C., a Delaware limited liability company (the "Company"), is made as of _____ ("Effective Date") by and among the Company and the Members (as defined below).

RECITALS:

WHEREAS, the Members desire to enter into this Agreement to provide for the operation and management of the Company.

NOW, THEREFORE, in consideration of the mutual covenants and agreements herein contained and other good and valuable consideration, the receipt and sufficiency of which are hereby acknowledged, the parties agree as follows:

SECTION 1.   FORMATION AND PURPOSE

1.1   Formation

1.1.1   The Members, by execution of this Agreement, form the Company as a limited liability company under and pursuant to the Delaware Limited Liability Company Act (the "Act"). For that purpose, the Members have caused the Company's Certificate of Formation to be executed and filed with the Secretary of State of the State of Delaware.

1.1.2   Each Member adopts this Agreement as the Operating Agreement of the Company, pursuant to the Act.

1.2   Subscription for Membership Interests

1.2.1   Each Member agrees to his status as a Member and subscribes for the acquisition of a Membership Interest, upon the terms and conditions set forth in this Agreement.

1.3   Name

The name of the Company is XYZ Partners, L.L.C. All Company business must be conducted in the name of the Company or such other names that comply with applicable law as the Board of Managers may select from time to time.

---

*   Thanks to Jack L. Lewis, Partner at Morrison & Foerster LLP, for providing this Form Operating Agreement.

OPERATING AGREEMENT

1.4 Governing Law

This Agreement and all issues regarding the rights and obligations of the Members, the construction, enforcement and interpretation hereof, and the formation, administration and termination of the Company shall be governed by the provisions of the Act and other applicable laws of the State of Delaware without reference to conflict of laws principles.

1.5 Purposes

The Company has been formed for the purposes of transacting any and all lawful business for which limited liability companies may be organized under the Act, and it is specifically contemplated that the activity of the Company shall consist solely of providing, through its Members, services under the Consulting Services Agreements, and such other activities as the Board of Managers shall have unanimously determined to be joint endeavors of the Members in which each Member will share equally in the resulting income and expense.

1.6 Foreign Qualification Governmental Filings

Prior to the Company's conducting business in any jurisdiction other than the State of Delaware, the Board of Managers, or Officers, if any, shall cause the Company to comply with all requirements necessary to qualify the Company as a foreign limited liability company in such jurisdiction. The Board of Managers, or Officers, if any shall execute, acknowledge, swear to and deliver all certificates and other instruments conforming to this Agreement that are necessary or appropriate to qualify, or, as appropriate, to continue or terminate such qualification of, the Company as a foreign limited liability company in all such jurisdictions in which the Company may conduct business.

SECTION 2. DEFINITIONS

2.1 Definitions

2.1.1 "Act" means the Delaware Limited Liability Company Act, as amended from time to time.

2.1.2 "Code" means the Internal Revenue Code of 1986, as amended, and any successor statute.

2.1.3 "Company" means XYZ Partners, L.L.C.

2.1.4 "Consulting Services Agreement" means, with respect to each of John Smith and Jane Jones, that certain Consulting Services Agreement dated _____, among such person, as named consultant thereunder, and ABC, Inc.

2.1.5 "Debt Instrument" means a promissory note or installment contractual obligation.

2.1.6 "Managers" means the individual(s) designated as Managers of the Company from time to time in accordance with the provisions of Section 4.1.1.

2.1.7 "Members" means those persons identified on *Exhibit A*, as such exhibit may be amended from time to time.

2.1.8 "Membership Interest" shall have the meaning ascribed to it in Section 3.1.2.

2.1.9 "Net Cash Flow" shall have the meaning ascribed to it in Section 6.1.1.

2.1.10 "Net Contributions" shall mean the amount of any capital contributions made by a Member.

2.1.11 "Officers" shall have the meaning ascribed to it in Section 4.1.1(b).

2.1.12 "Transfer" shall have the meaning ascribed to it in Section 9.2.1.

OPERATING AGREEMENT

2.2 Other Terms

Other terms used in this Agreement are defined in the context in which they are used and shall have the meanings there indicated.

SECTION 3. STATUS, RIGHTS AND OBLIGATIONS OF MEMBERS

3.1 Members

3.1.1 *Members.* The names of the Members of the Company and the notice address of each such Member are set forth on *Exhibit A* attached hereto.

3.1.2 *Membership Interests.* The Members agree that each Member's percentage of ownership interest in the Company (hereinafter referred to as a "Membership Interest") shall be as set forth on *Exhibit A*, as it may be amended from time to time pursuant to this Agreement.

3.2 Voting

Members shall vote in relative proportion to their respective Membership Interests. Any action requiring a vote, consent or approval of a "majority of the Members" shall be authorized if Members holding more than fifty percent (50%) of the outstanding Membership Interests entitled to vote, vote for, consent to or approve of, such action.

3.3 Meetings of Members

3.3.1 *Meetings.* Meetings of Members shall be held at such date, time and place as the Board of Managers may fix from time to time. Meetings of the Members may be called by the Board of Managers or by any Manager for the purpose of addressing any matters on which the Members may vote.

3.3.2 *Notice.* Written notice of a meeting of Members shall be sent or otherwise given to each Member not less than ten (10) nor more than sixty (60) days before the date of the meeting. The notice shall specify the place, date and hour of the meeting and the general nature of the business to be transacted. Notice of any meeting of Members shall be given in the manner prescribed by Section 10.4 hereof.

3.4 Action Without Meeting

Any action required or permitted to be taken at a meeting of the Members may be taken without a meeting if the action is approved by a majority of the Members. Each such action without a meeting shall be evidenced by one or more written consents to be filed with the Company's records. Such action shall be effective as of the date specified in the written consent(s). Prompt notice of the taking of such action without a meeting by less than unanimous written approval shall be given to those Members who have not approved of such action in writing.

3.5 Restricted Activities

3.5.1 *Use of Company Information.* Each Member covenants and agrees with the Company and the other Members that, except on behalf of the Company and as authorized by the Company, it will not use or permit others to use, disclose or divulge to others, copy or reproduce or remove from the custody and control of the Company any information relating to or used in the business and operations of the Company whether in written or unwritten form or in a form produced or stored by any magnetic, electrical or mechanical means or process, that is confidential information or a trade secret of the Company.

3.5.2 *Other Business Ventures.* Each Member may engage in or possess any interest in any other business of any nature and description, independently or with others, and neither the

Company nor the other Members shall have any rights in or to any such independent venture or the income or profits derived therefrom.

3.6 No Preemptive Rights.

No Member shall have any preemptive, preferential or other similar right with respect to

  (i)   additional capital contributions or loans to the Company; or

  (ii)   the issuance or sale of any Membership Interests by the Company.

SECTION 4. MANAGEMENT OF THE COMPANY

4.1 Management by Board of Managers

4.1.1 *Appointment and Replacement of Managers; Officers.*

  (a) *Number; Election.* The operation of the Company shall be managed by, and the responsibility for managing the business and affairs of the Company shall be delegated to, a Board of Managers consisting of not more than five (5) managers (as defined in Section 8–101 of the Act) (each a "Manager") appointed by a majority of the Members, each of whom shall be a natural person but who does not need to be a Member. The initial Managers of the Company shall be John Smith and Jane Jones.

  (b) *Officers.* The responsibility for managing the business and affairs of the Company may be delegated by the Board of Managers to such other persons as may be appointed by the Board of Managers. The Board of Managers of the Company may, from time to time as they deem advisable, appoint officers of the Company (the "Officers") and assign in writing titles (including, without limitation, President, Vice President, Secretary and Treasurer) to any such person. Unless the Board of Managers decides otherwise, if the title is one commonly used for officers of a business corporation formed under the Delaware General Corporation Law, the assignment of such title shall constitute the delegation to such person of the authorities and duties that are normally associated with that office. Any delegation pursuant to this Section 4 may be revoked at any time by the Board of Managers.

  (c) *Term; Resignation; Removal.* Each Manager shall hold office until his successor is elected and qualified or until his earlier resignation or removal. Any Manager may resign at any time upon written notice to the Company. Any Manager may be removed, with or without cause, by the vote of a majority of the Members.

  (d) *Filling of Vacancies.* Vacancies resulting from any increase in the authorized number of Managers and any vacancies on the Board of Managers resulting from death, resignation, disqualification, removal or other cause shall be filled by the affirmative vote of a majority of the remaining Managers, and the Managers so chosen shall hold office until the next annual election and until their successors are duly elected and shall qualify, or until their earlier resignation or removal.

4.1.2 *General Authority of the Board of Managers.*

  (a) Except to the extent that the approval of the Members (or Members holding a specified proportion of interests) is otherwise required by this Agreement or the Act, and subject to the conditions and limitations set forth elsewhere in this Section 4, the Board of Managers shall have full, complete and exclusive discretion to manage and control the business of the Company in furtherance of the purposes for which the Company is formed. The Board of Managers shall exercise its best efforts to promote and protect the interests of the Company and shall devote such time and attention as is reasonably necessary and appropriate to discharge such obligations.

(b)   In furtherance and not in limitation of the foregoing grant of authority, the Board of Managers (including any delegated Officer) is empowered on behalf of the Company to negotiate, execute and deliver such agreements, instruments, deeds, certificates and other documents as the Board of Managers deem necessary and appropriate in the Board of Managers' discretion to effect the purposes and interests of the Company.

(c)   All decisions made for and on behalf of the Company by the Board of Managers shall be binding upon the Company. No person dealing with the Company shall be required to determine the authority of the Board of Managers or any Officer to enter into any undertaking on behalf of the Company, nor to determine any fact or circumstance bearing upon the existence of such authority; *provided, however,* that nothing herein shall extinguish, limit, or condition the liability of the Board of Managers or any Officer to the Members to discharge their obligations in accordance with this Agreement and the Act.

4.1.3   *Meetings of the Board of Managers.*

(a)   *Place of Meetings.* The Board of Managers of the Company may hold meetings, both regular and special, either within or outside the State of Delaware.

(b)   *Regular Meetings.* Regular meetings of the Board of Managers may be held without other notice at such time and at such place as shall from time to time be determined by the Board of Managers.

(c)   *Special Meetings.* Special meetings of the Board of Managers may be called by any Manager or the President of the Company (if a President has been designated), on one day's notice to each Manager, either personally or by mail, facsimile, telegram or express courier.

(d)   *Quorum; Vote Required for Action.* At all meetings of the Board of Managers, a majority of the total number of Managers then in office shall constitute a quorum for the transaction of business and the act of a majority of the Managers present at any meeting at which there is a quorum shall be the act of the Board of Managers, except as may be otherwise specifically provided herein or in the Certificate of Formation. If a quorum shall not be present at any meeting of the Board of Managers, the Managers present may adjourn the meeting from time to time, without notice other than announcement at the meeting of the time and place of the adjourned meeting, until a quorum shall be present.

(e)   *Participation By Conference Telephone.* Managers may participate in a meeting of the Board of Managers by means of conference telephone or similar communications equipment by means of which all persons participating in the meeting can hear each other, and participation in a meeting pursuant to this subsection shall constitute presence in person at such meeting.

(f)   *Action Without Meeting.* Any action required or permitted to be taken at any meeting of the Board of Managers may be taken without a meeting, if a majority of the Managers then in office consent thereto in writing, and the writing or writings are filed with the minutes of proceedings of the Board of Managers.

4.1.4   *Limitations Upon Managers' Authority.*

(a)   Without first obtaining the unanimous written consent of the Members, the Board of Managers shall not:

(i)   Do any act in contravention of this Agreement;

(ii)   Do any act (other than a sale of all or any part of the assets of the Company) that would make it impossible to carry on the ordinary business of the Company;

      (iii) Admit a person as a Member of the Company other than in accordance with the terms of this Agreement; or

      (iv) Require any Member to contribute to the capital of the Company except as expressly provided in this Agreement.

    (b) The foregoing limitations are in addition to, and do not supersede any other limitations or prohibitions expressly imposed upon the Managers under this Agreement or by the Act.

    4.1.5 *Reimbursement.* All expenses incurred with respect to the organization, operation and management of the Company shall be borne by the Company. The Managers shall be entitled to reimbursement from the Company for direct expenses allocable to the organization, operation and management of the Company.

4.3 Managers and Affiliates Dealing With the Company

The Board of Managers may appoint, employ, contract or otherwise deal with any person, including persons with whom a Manager is affiliated, and persons in which a Manager has a financial interest, for transacting Company business, including any acts or services for the Company as the Managers may approve; *provided, however,* that fees or other payments and terms of any contract with such parties shall not be in excess of prevailing competitive rates for such transactions.

SECTION 5. CAPITAL CONTRIBUTIONS AND FINANCIAL OBLIGATIONS OF MEMBERS

5.1 Initial Capital Contributions

Contemporaneously with the execution of this Agreement, each Member shall make the initial cash capital contribution set opposite such Member's name in *Exhibit A*. Such capital shall be used by the Company to fund the operations of the Company and pay the expenses thereof. In addition, each Member shall, by execution of this Agreement, be deemed to have contributed to the Company all of such Member's right to receive payments under sections 4 and 5 of such Member's Consulting Services Agreement, and so much of section 8 of such agreement as may be relevant to Losses (within the meaning of such section) that are treated by the Members as incurred by the Company. After such contribution of rights, the Members shall be considered to receive any such payments under the Consulting Services Agreements as an agent of the Company, and consistent therewith shall pay over, assign to, or account to the Company for all such payments received thereunder. Such rights shall, at the time of contribution, be considered to have fair market value of zero, and no amount shall be reflected in such Member's capital account by reason of the contribution of such rights.

5.2 Additional Contributions

    5.2.1 The Board of Managers may arrange for the provision of such additional funds as are deemed necessary to conduct Company business. Such additional funds may be raised by loans to the Company from outside sources, or by loans or capital contributions to the Company from one or more Members.

    5.2.2 No Member shall be required to make any additional capital contributions to the Company, unless all the Members have agreed in writing that such capital contribution is or may be required on certain conditions.

5.3 No Interest Upon Capital Contributions

No Member shall be entitled to be paid interest by the Company on his capital contributions.

5.4 Return of Capital Contributions

No Member shall be entitled to withdraw any part of his capital contributions or his capital account or to receive any distribution from the Company, except as specifically provided in this Agreement. Except as otherwise provided herein, there shall be no obligation to return to any Member or withdrawn Member any part of such Member's capital contributions to the Company for so long as the Company continues in existence.

5.5 Loans Not to be Treated as Capital Contributions

Loans or advances by any Member to the Company shall not be considered capital contributions and shall not increase the capital account balance of the lending or advancing Member.

5.6 No Loans Required.

Except as provided in this Agreement, no Member shall be required under any circumstances to contribute or lend any money or property to the Company, except to the extent that such Member has agreed to do so in writing.

5.7 No Third Party Beneficiaries.

The provisions of this Agreement relating to the financial obligations of Members are not intended to be for the benefit of any creditor or other person (except Members) to whom any debts, liabilities or obligations are owed by (or who otherwise has any claim against) the Company or any of the Members; and, except for Members, no creditor or other person shall obtain any right under any of such provisions or shall by reason of any of such provisions make any claim with respect to any debt, liability or obligation (or otherwise) against the Company or any of the Members.

SECTION 6. DISTRIBUTIONS OF CASH AND PROPERTY

6.1 Distribution of Net Cash Flow and Mandatory Tax Distributions

6.1.1 *Net Cash Flow Defined.* The term "Net Cash Flow" for a fiscal year of the Company shall mean:

(a) All cash receipts as shown on the books of the Company (excluding, however, capital contributions from Members and net proceeds to the Company from the sale or the disposition of substantially all of the Company's assets), reduced by cash disbursements for Company purposes including interest and principal upon loans, and all cash reserves set aside by the Board of Managers that the Board of Managers deem necessary or appropriate to accomplish the Company business; *plus*

(b) Any other funds, including amounts previously set aside as reserves by the Board of Managers, deemed available by the Board of Managers for distribution as Net Cash Flow.

6.1.2 *Priority of Distribution.* Subject to Section 6.1.3, the Board of Managers shall determine what portion of the Net Cash Flow of the Company for a fiscal year shall be paid to Members as a distribution; provided that such distribution shall be paid out to the Members *pro rata* in accordance with their respective Membership Interests. The Board of Managers shall determine the timing of when such distributions shall be made to the Members.

6.1.3 *Mandatory Distributions for Taxes.* With respect to any fiscal year in which the Company has net income allocable to the Members in accordance with Section 7.2.2, the Board of Managers shall cause the Company to distribute to each Member pursuant to Section 6.1.2 an amount equal to not less than fifty percent (50%) of the net income so allocated to such Member with respect to such fiscal year; provided however, that in no event shall a distribution be required under this Section 6.1.3 in excess of the Company's Net Cash Flow for such fiscal year. Distributions required under this section 6.1.3 shall be made not later than the April 1 following the close of such fiscal year.

6.2 Distribution of the Proceeds of Dissolution

If the Company dissolves, the net proceeds of dissolution, including any accompanying sale of Company assets, shall be distributed in the following order of priority:

(a) First, toward the satisfaction of all outstanding debts and other obligations of the Company, including Members who are creditors.

(b) Then, *pro rata* among those Members with positive capital account balances, in proportion to their respective capital account balances, after adjustments for distributions under Sections 6.1 and tax allocations for the current fiscal year.

6.3 Distribution of Debt Instruments

6.3.1 In the event the Company sells any of its assets and all or a portion of the sales price is paid by a Debt Instrument, if such sale occurs in conjunction with the dissolution of the Company, all interest and principal received by the Company shall be treated as net proceeds of dissolution, and shall be distributed in accordance with Section 6.2 hereof.

6.3.2 In the event the Company holds a Debt Instrument as described in Section 6.3.1 and the Company either is dissolved in conjunction with the sale that gave rise to such Debt Instrument or dissolves prior to payment in full of such Debt Instrument, the Board of Managers shall assign such Debt Instrument to a trustee who shall collect all sums that may become due and payable under the Debt Instrument, who shall have the power and authority to act to enforce all rights of the holder of such Debt Instrument and who shall distribute such sums pursuant to the formula described in Section 6.2.

6.4 Distributions in Kind

6.4.1 No Member shall be entitled to demand and receive distributions other than in cash form, except for the distribution of rights under such Member's Consulting Services Agreement contemplated by Section 6.4.2 of this Agreement.

6.4.2 If any Company assets are distributed in kind, such assets shall be distributed to each Member, provided that, to the maximum extent possible, the rights of the Company to receive payments with respect to services, reimbursements or indemnification, under a Member's Consulting Services Agreement, to the extent arising after the event causing the Company's dissolution, shall be distributed to such Member. The amount by which the fair market value of any property to be distributed in kind to the Members exceeds or is less than the tax basis of such property shall, to the extent not otherwise recognized by the Company, be taken into account for purposes of allocation of gain or loss and distributions of proceeds to the Members under this Section 6 as if the property had been sold by the Company for its fair market value on the date of the distribution and the proceeds distributed. The fair market value of any property to be distributed in kind to the Members shall be determined by the Board of Managers in their reasonable discretion, except that any to be distributed in kind to the Members shall be valued as follows:

(a) If the securities are then traded on a national securities exchange, the NASDAQ National Market System (or a similar national quotation system) or the NASDAQ SmallCap Market, then the value shall be deemed to be the average of the closing prices of the securities on such exchange or system over the 30-day period ending three (3) days prior to the distribution; and

(b) If the securities are actively traded over-the-counter, then the value shall be deemed to be the average of the closing bid prices over the 30-day period ending three (3) days prior to the distribution; and

(c) If there is no active public trading market for the securities, then the value shall be the fair market value thereof, as determined in the reasonable discretion of the Board of Managers.

(d) Rights under any Member's Consulting Services Agreement distributed pursuant to Section 6.4.2, to the extent relating to payments for services or reimbursements for expenses or indemnifiable losses attributable to periods after the event causing the Company's distribution of such rights, shall be considered to have a fair market value of zero.

SECTION 7. FEDERAL AND STATE TAX MATTERS

7.1 Maintenance of Members' Capital Accounts

With respect to each Member, a separate "capital account" for such Member shall be established and maintained throughout the full term of the Company in accordance with applicable Treasury Regulations that must be complied with in order for the allocations of taxable profits and losses provided in this Agreement to have "economic effect" under applicable Treasury Regulations.

7.2 Allocations of Profits and Losses of the Company

Subject to Section 7.3 below, the Company's net income or loss for a fiscal year, computed in accordance with Treasury Regulations section 1.704–1(b)(2)(iv), shall be allocated among the Members for each fiscal year as follows:

7.2.1 *Net Loss.* The net loss (other than from a sale or disposition of all or substantially all of the Company's assets), if any, for a fiscal year of the Company shall be allocated to the Members in accordance with their respective Membership Interests.

7.2.2 *Net Income.* The net income (other than from a sale or disposition of all or substantially all of the Company's assets), if any, for a fiscal year of the Company shall be allocated to the Members in accordance with their respective Membership Interests.

7.2.3 *Net Loss from Sale of All or Substantially All of the Company Assets.* The net loss from a sale or other disposition of all or substantially all of the Company assets shall be allocated among the Members as follows:

(a) First, to the Members, if any, having positive capital account balances in excess of their Net Contributions amounts in proportion to such excess positive balances, until the balance in each such Member's capital account equals the amount of such Member's Net Contributions, or, if there is insufficient loss to accomplish this result, to cause such excess positive balances to be in the same ratio as the Members' respective Membership Interests;

(b) Second, to the Members, if any, having positive capital account balances, in proportion to such positive balances, until the balances in their capital accounts equal zero; and

(c) Thereafter, to the Members in accordance with their respective Membership Interests.

7.2.4 *Net Income from Sale of All or Substantially All of the Company Assets.* The net income from a sale or other disposition of all or substantially all of the Company assets shall be allocated among the Members as follows:

(a) First, to the Members, if any, having negative capital account balances, in proportion to such negative balances, until the balances in their capital accounts equal zero;

(b) Second, to the extent any Member has a positive capital account balance that is less than the amount of such Member's Net Contributions, to each such Member, in the amounts necessary, and in the ratio of such amounts, to cause the positive capital account balance of each such Member to be equal to the amount of such Member's Net Contributions;

(c) Third, to the Members in the amounts necessary, and in the ratio of such amounts, to cause their positive capital account balances in excess of the amounts of their respective Net Contributions to be in the same ratio as their respective Membership Interests; and

(d) Thereafter, to the Members in accordance with their respective Membership Interests.

7.3 Special Tax Allocations

Notwithstanding anything to the contrary contained above in Section 7.2:

7.3.1 The Company shall comply with Treasury Regulation Section 1.704–2 with respect to the allocation of deductions and minimum gain relating to nonrecourse debts of the Company.

7.3.2 No Member shall be allocated a net loss that would cause or increase a deficit balance in his capital account in excess of any actual or deemed obligation of such Member to restore deficits (as defined in Treasury Regulation Section 1.704–1(b)(2)(ii)(c)). If any Member shall receive with respect to the Company an adjustment, allocation or distribution in the nature described in Treasury Regulation Section 1.704–1(b)(2)(ii)(d)(4)–(6) that causes or increases a deficit in such Member's capital account, such Member shall be allocated items of income and gain in an amount and manner as will eliminate such deficit balance as quickly as possible. It is intended that this Section 8.3.2 shall constitute a "qualified income offset" within the meaning of Treasury Regulation Section 1.704–1(b)(2)(ii)(d)(3).

7.3.3 Any allocations required pursuant to Section 7.3.2 shall be taken into account in allocating net income and net loss pursuant to Section 7.2 above so that, to the extent possible, the net amount of such allocations shall be equal to the net amount that would have been allocated to each Member if the allocations pursuant to Section 7.3.2 had not occurred.

7.3.4 Any portion of any income, gain, loss or deduction with respect to property contributed to the Company by a Member (or revalued pursuant to Treasury Regulation section 1.704–1(b)(2)(iv)(f) shall be allocated among the Members in accordance with Code Section 704(c) and Treasury Regulation Section 1.704–3 so as to take account of the variation, if any, between the adjusted tax basis of such property to the Company and its fair market value at the time of the contributions).

7.3.5 In the event of the Transfer of all or any part of a Membership Interest (in accordance with the provisions of this Agreement) at any time other than the end of a fiscal year, the share of income or loss (in respect of the Membership Interest so transferred) shall be allocated between the transferor and the transferee in the same ratio as the number of days in such fiscal year before and after such Transfer. The provisions of this Section 7.3.5 shall not apply to any income or loss attributable to the sale or other disposition of all or substantially all of the Company assets, or to other extraordinary non-recurring items. Such income and loss shall be allocated to the owner of the Membership Interest as of the date of closing of the sale or other disposition, or, with respect to other extraordinary non-recurring items, the date the income is realized or the loss is incurred, as the case may be.

7.4 Tax Year and Accounting Matters

The taxable year of the Company shall be the calendar year. The Company shall adopt such methods of accounting, and file its tax returns on the methods of accounting, as determined by the

Board of Managers upon the advice of the certified public accounting firm servicing the books and records of the Company.

7.5 Tax Matters Partner

Jane Jones shall be the "Tax Matters Partner" for federal income tax purposes. All costs and expenses incurred by the Tax Matters Partner in performing her duties as such (including legal and accounting fees) shall be borne by the Company.

7.6 Tax Elections

The Tax Matters Partner, in the exercise of his reasonable discretion, may cause the Company to make or revoke all tax elections provided for under the Code.

SECTION 8.   TERM AND TERMINATION OF THE COMPANY

8.1 Term of the Company

The term of the Company commenced upon the filing of the Certificate of Formation, and shall continue until dissolved and terminated in accordance with this Agreement.

8.2 Events of Termination

The Company shall be dissolved upon the occurrence of any of the following events:

8.2.1   The unanimous written consent of the Members to dissolve and terminate the Company;

8.2.2   The sale, transfer or assignment of substantially all the assets of the Company;

8.2.3   Unless waived by unanimous written consent of the Members, the termination or amendment of any Member's Consulting Services Agreement affecting the payments to be made thereafter pursuant to sections 4, 5 or 8 of such agreement, unless such termination or amendment shall simultaneously and identically apply to every Member's Consulting Services Agreement;

8.2.4   The death, resignation, retirement, expulsion, bankruptcy or dissolution of a Member or occurrence of any other event that terminates the continued membership of a Member in the Company;

8.2.5   Entry of a decree of judicial dissolution; or

8.2.6   As otherwise required by Delaware law.

8.3 Conclusion of Affairs

In the event of the dissolution of the Company for any reason, the Board of Managers shall proceed promptly to wind up the affairs of and liquidate the Company. Except as otherwise provided in this Agreement, the Members shall continue to share distributions and tax allocations during the period of liquidation in the same manner as before the dissolution. The Board of Managers shall have reasonable discretion to determine the time, manner and terms of any sale or sales of Company property pursuant to such liquidation having due regard to the activity and the condition and relevant market and general financial and economic conditions and consistent with their fiduciary obligations to the Members.

8.4 Liquidating Distributions

After paying or providing for the payment of all debts or liabilities of the Company and all expenses of liquidation, and subject to the right of the Board of Managers to set up such reserves as they may deem reasonably necessary for any contingent or unforeseen liabilities or obligations of the Company, the proceeds of the liquidation and any other assets of the Company shall be distributed to

OPERATING AGREEMENT

or for the benefit of the Members in accordance with this Agreement. The Board of Managers shall have the right to distribute assets in kind, valued at the then fair market value of such assets (as determined in accordance with Section 6.4.2), as a liquidating distribution to the Members.

8.5 Termination

Within a reasonable time following the completion of the liquidation of the Company, the Board of Managers shall supply to each of the Members a statement that shall set forth the assets and the liabilities of the Company as of the date of complete liquidation and each Member's portion of the distributions pursuant to this Agreement. Upon completion of the liquidation of the Company and the distribution of all Company assets, the Company shall terminate and the Board of Managers shall have the authority to execute and file with the Delaware Secretary of State a Certificate of Cancellation of the Company, as well as any and all other documents required to effectuate the dissolution and termination of the Company.

SECTION 9.   ADMISSION, TRANSFERS, ADDITION, SUBSTITUTION, AND WITHDRAWAL OF MEMBERS

9.1 Admission

A new Member may be admitted to membership in the Company through the issuance by the Company of a Membership Interest directly to such new Member upon the unanimous written consent of the Members.

9.2 Restrictions on Transfers

9.2.1 Membership Interests (including "economic interest") may be assigned, sold, gifted, pledged, encumbered, mortgaged or otherwise transferred (a "Transfer") in whole or in part only upon the written consent of a majority of the Members; provided that no such Transfer shall be made unless the Company shall have been offered, and such offer remains unaccepted for 20 days, the opportunity to purchase such Member's Membership Interest at a price and on terms no less favorable than those of such proposed Transfer. 9.2.2 Unless waived by the Board of Managers, a Membership Interest shall not be Transferred in the absence of an opinion of counsel, satisfactory to the Board of Managers, that the transfer of the Membership Interest is exempt from the registration requirements under the Securities Act of 1933, as amended, or any applicable state securities laws.

9.3 Admission of Substituted or Additional Members

9.3.1 No person not a Member on the date of this Agreement shall become a Member hereunder under any of the provisions hereof unless such person shall expressly assume and agree to be bound by all of the terms and conditions of this Agreement. Each such person shall also cause to be delivered to the Company, at his, her or its sole cost and expense such documents or instruments as may be required in the discretion of the Board of Managers in order to effect such person's admission as an additional Member. Upon compliance with all provisions hereof applicable to such person becoming a Member, the Board of Managers are authorized to execute and deliver such amendments hereto as are necessary to constitute such person or entity a Member of the Company. Any transferee of a Membership Interest that has not been admitted as a substituted Member shall be an "assignee," entitled only to allocations of net profits, net losses and other tax items of the Company and to distributions from the Company, and shall not be entitled to vote or participate in the affairs and management of the Company.

9.3.2 A Member who has Transferred his Membership Interest shall cease to be a Member upon Transfer of the Member's entire Membership Interest and thereafter shall have no further powers, rights or privileges as a Member hereunder, but shall, unless otherwise relieved of such obligations by agreement of all the other Members or by operation of law, remain liable for all obligations and duties as a Member related to the time during which he was a Member.

9.3.3 The Company, each Member and any other person or persons having business with the Company need deal only with Members who are admitted as Members of the Company, and they shall not be required to deal with any other person by reason of a Transfer by a Member, except as otherwise provided in this Agreement. In the absence of the written consent provided in Section 9.2.1, any payment to an assigning Member shall acquit the Company and the Managers of all liability to any other persons who may be interested in such payment by reason of a Transfer by such Member.

9.3.4 No person shall have a perfected lien or security interest in a Membership Interest unless the creation of such interest is in accord with the provisions of this Agreement and the Company is notified of such interest and provided a copy of all documentation with respect thereto, including financing statements, prior to execution and filing.

9.3.5 Any Transfer not in accord with this Agreement shall be void.

9.3.6 Each Member agrees not to Transfer all or any part of his Membership Interest (or take or omit any action, that could result in a deemed Transfer) if such Transfer (either considered alone or in the aggregate with prior Transfers by other Members) would result in the Company being treated as a "publicly traded partnership" under Code Section 7704.

9.4 No Right to Withdraw

No Member shall have any right to voluntarily resign or otherwise withdraw from the Company without the unanimous written consent of the Members.

9.5 Effect of Withdrawal

On and as of the effective date of a Member's withdrawal from the Company under the provisions of this Agreement, such former Member shall cease to have any Membership Interest or any management or other rights, status or privileges of a Member, but such former Member shall not be released or discharged from any of the obligations of a Member under the provisions of this Agreement, unless agreed to and evidenced by the unanimous written consent of the Members.

SECTION 10. ADMINISTRATIVE PROVISIONS

10.1 Principal Office

10.1.1 The initial principal place of business and principal office of the Company shall be at _____. The Company may relocate the principal office and principal place of business and have such additional offices as the Managers may deem advisable.

10.1.2 The Managers shall have the power, on behalf of the Company, to designate, where required, a registered agent (or other agent for receipt of service of process) in each state or other jurisdiction in which the Company transacts business and to designate, to the extent required, an office, place of business or mailing address, within or without that state or other jurisdiction.

10.2 Bank Accounts

10.2.1 Funds of the Company shall be deposited in an account or accounts of a type, in form and name and in a bank(s) or other financial institution(s) that are participants in federal insurance programs as selected by the Board of Managers. The Board of Managers shall arrange for the appropriate conduct of such accounts. Funds may be withdrawn from such accounts only for bona fide and legitimate Company purposes and may from time to time be invested in such short-term securities, money market funds, certificates of deposit or other liquid assets as the Board of Managers deem appropriate.

10.2.2 The Members acknowledge that the Board of Managers may maintain Company funds in accounts, money market funds, certificates of deposit, other liquid assets in excess of the insurance provided by the Federal Deposit Insurance Corporation or other depository insurance institutions and that the Board of Managers shall not be accountable or liable for any loss of such funds resulting from failure or insolvency of the depository institution.

10.3 Books and Records

10.3.1 At all times during the term of the Company, the Board of Managers shall keep, or cause to be kept, full and faithful books of account, records and supporting documents, which shall reflect, completely, accurately and in reasonable detail, each transaction of the Company (including, without limitation, transactions with the Managers or affiliates). The books of account shall be maintained and tax returns prepared and filed in the method of accounting determined by the Board of Managers. The books of account, records and all documents and other writings of the Company shall be kept and maintained at the principal office of the Company. Each Member or his designated representative shall, upon reasonable notice to the Board of Managers, have access to such financial books, records and documents during reasonable business hours and may inspect and make copies of any of them at his own expense.

10.3.2 The Board of Managers shall cause the Company to keep at its principal office the following:

   (a) A current list of the full name and last known business address of each Member, in alphabetical order;

   (b) A copy of the Certificate of Formation and all articles of amendment and certificates of amendment thereto;

   (c) Copies of the Company's federal, state and local income tax returns and reports, if any, for the three (3) most recent years; and

   (d) Copies of this Agreement, as it may be amended, and of any financial statements of the Company for the three (3) most recent years.

10.4 Notices

All notices required or permitted hereunder shall be in writing and shall be deemed effectively given: (a) upon personal delivery to the party to be notified, (b) when sent by confirmed facsimile if sent during normal business hours of the recipient, if not, then on the next business day, (c) five (5) days after having been sent by registered or certified mail, return receipt requested, postage prepaid, or (d) one (1) business day after deposit with a nationally recognized overnight courier, specifying next day delivery, with written verification of receipt. All communications shall be sent to the Company at the address as set forth in Section 10.1.1 and to a Member at the Member's address set forth on *Exhibit A* attached hereto or at such other address as the Company or a Member may designate by ten (10) days advance written notice to the other parties hereto.

SECTION 11.   INDEMNIFICATION AND LIMITATION OF LIABILITY

11.1 Indemnification of Members and Managers

Except as provided in Section 11.3, every person who was or is a party or who is threatened to be made a party to any pending, completed, or impending action, suit, or proceeding of any kind, whether civil, criminal, administrative, arbitrative or investigative (whether or not by or in the right of the Company) by reason of (i) being or having been a Manager, Officer or Member of the Company; (ii) being or having been a member, manager, partner, officer, or director of any other entity at the request of the Company; or (iii) serving or having served in a representative capacity for the Company in connection with any partnership, joint venture, committee, trust, employee benefit plan or other enterprise, shall be indemnified by the Company against all expenses (including reasonable attorney fees), judgments, fines, penalties, awards, costs, amounts paid in settlement and liabilities of all kinds, actually incurred by him incidental to or resulting from such action, suit, or proceeding to the fullest extent permitted under the Act, without limiting any other indemnification rights to which he otherwise may be entitled. The Company may, but shall not be required to, purchase insurance on behalf of such person against liability asserted against or incurred by such person in his capacity as a Manager, Officer or Member whether or not the Company would have authority to indemnify him against the same liability under the provisions of this Section 11.1 or the Act.

11.2 Liability Limitation

Except as provided in Section 11.3, no Member or Manager shall have liability to the Company or other Members for monetary damages resulting from a single transaction, occurrence or isolated course of conduct.

11.3 Qualification of Indemnification

The indemnification rights and limitations on liabilities set forth in Sections 11.1 and 11.2 shall not apply to claims based upon gross negligence, any willful misconduct or intentional breach of the terms of this Agreement, or knowing violations of criminal law or any federal or state securities law, nor shall such indemnification rights preclude the Company or any Member from recovery for any loss or damage otherwise covered under any insurance policy or fidelity bonding. Nothing herein shall be deemed to prohibit or limit the Company's right to pay, or obtain insurance covering, the costs (including attorney fees) to defend an indemnitee, Member, Officer or Manager against any such claims, subject to a full reservation of rights to reimbursement in the event of a final adjudication adverse to such indemnitee, Member, Officer or Manager.

11.4 Advances for Expenses

Expenses (including reasonable attorney fees) incurred by or in respect of any such person in connection with any such action, suit or proceeding, whether civil, criminal, administrative, arbitrative or investigative, may be paid by the Company in advance of the final disposition thereof upon receipt of an undertaking by or on behalf of such person to repay such amount, unless it shall ultimately be determined that he is entitled to be indemnified by the Company, in which case reimbursement shall not be required.

11.5 Elimination of Liability

The Members acknowledge, agree and desire that, except as set forth in Section 11.3, the liability of any Member, Officer or Manager to the Company or to any of the other Members shall be eliminated, to the maximum extent possible, pursuant to the Act. The provisions of this Section 11 are in addition to, and not in substitution for, any other right to indemnity to which any person who is or may be indemnified by or pursuant to this Section 11 may otherwise be entitled, and to the powers otherwise accorded by law to the Company to indemnify any such person and to purchase and maintain insurance on behalf of any such person against any liability asserted against or incurred by him in any capacity referred to in this Section 11 or arising from his status as serving or having served in any such capacity (whether or not the Company would have the power to indemnify against such liability).

11.6 No Retroactive Effect of Amendment

No amendment or repeal of this Section 11 shall limit or eliminate the right to indemnification provided hereunder with respect to acts or omissions occurring before such amendment or repeal.

OPERATING AGREEMENT

SECTION 12.   MISCELLANEOUS PROVISIONS

12.1 Entire Agreement

This Agreement, including the exhibits attached hereto and incorporated herein by reference, constitutes the entire agreement of the Members with respect to the matters covered herein. This Agreement supersedes all prior agreements and oral understandings among the Members with respect to such matters.

12.2 Amendment; Form of Company

12.2.1 Except as provided by law or otherwise set forth herein, this Agreement may only be modified or amended by the written consent of a majority of the Members; *provided, however*, that *Exhibit A* hereto may be amended from time to time by the Board of Managers to the extent required to accurately reflect the then current status of the information contained thereon.

12.2.2 Without first obtaining the written consent of a majority of the Members, the Board of Managers shall not change or reorganize the Company into any other legal form.

12.3 Severability

Each provision of this Agreement shall be considered severable and if for any reason any provision or provisions hereof are determined to be invalid and contrary to existing or future law, such provision shall be deemed to be restated to reflect as nearly as possible the original intentions of the parties to this Agreement in accordance with applicable law. The remainder of this Agreement shall remain in full force and effect.

12.4 Successors

Except as expressly otherwise provided herein, this Agreement is binding upon, and inures to the benefit of, the parties hereto and their respective heirs, executors, administrators, personal and legal representatives, successors and assigns.

12.5 Counterparts

This Agreement may be executed in any number of counterparts, each of which shall be an original, but all of which together shall constitute one instrument, binding upon all parties hereto, notwithstanding that all such parties may not have executed the same counterpart.

IN WITNESS WHEREOF, the parties have executed this Agreement to be effective as of the Effective Date.

MEMBERS:

_____

John Smith

_____

Jane Jones

OPERATING AGREEMENT

EXHIBIT A

Name	Address	Membership Interest	Capital Contribution
John Smith	_____ _____	50%	$1,000
Jane Jones	_____ _____	50%	$1,000
TOTAL		100%	$2,000

V. FEDERAL SECURITIES LAW

A. SECURITIES ACT OF 1933

(Selected Sections)

15 U.S.C. §§ 77a *et seq.*

Table of Contents

Short Title

§ 77a [P.L. § 1]. This subchapter may be cited as the "Securities Act of 1933".

Definitions; Promotion of Efficiency, Competition, and Capital Formation

§ 77b [P.L. § 2]. (a) Definitions.—When used in this subchapter, unless the context otherwise requires—

(1) The term "security" means any note, stock, treasury stock, security future, security-based swap, bond, debenture, evidence of indebtedness, certificate of interest or participation in any profit-sharing agreement, collateral-trust certificate, preorganization certificate or subscription, transferable share, investment contract, voting-trust certificate, certificate of

1251

deposit for a security, fractional undivided interest in oil, gas, or other mineral rights, any put, call, straddle, option, or privilege on any security, certificate of deposit, or group or index of securities (including any interest therein or based on the value thereof), or any put, call, straddle, option, or privilege entered into on a national securities exchange relating to foreign currency, or, in general, any interest or instrument commonly known as a "security", or any certificate of interest or participation in, temporary or interim certificate for, receipt for, guarantee of, or warrant or right to subscribe to or purchase, any of the foregoing.

(2)   The term "person" means an individual, a corporation, a partnership, an association, a joint-stock company, a trust, any unincorporated organization, or a government or political subdivision thereof. As used in this paragraph the term "trust" shall include only a trust where the interest or interests of the beneficiary or beneficiaries are evidenced by a security.

(3)   The term "sale" or "sell" shall include every contract of sale or disposition of a security or interest in a security, for value. The term "offer to sell", "offer for sale", or "offer" shall include every attempt or offer to dispose of, or solicitation of an offer to buy, a security or interest in a security, for value. The terms defined in this paragraph and the term "offer to buy" as used in subsection (c) of section 77e of this title shall not include preliminary negotiations or agreements between an issuer (or any person directly or indirectly controlling or controlled by an issuer, or under direct or indirect common control with an issuer) and any underwriter or among underwriters who are or are to be in privity of contract with an issuer (or any person directly or indirectly controlling or controlled by an issuer, or under direct or indirect common control with an issuer). Any security given or delivered with, or as a bonus on account of, any purchase of securities or any other thing, shall be conclusively presumed to constitute a part of the subject of such purchase and to have been offered and sold for value. The issue or transfer of a right or privilege, when originally issued or transferred with a security, giving the holder of such security the right to convert such security into another security of the same issuer or of another person, or giving a right to subscribe to another security of the same issuer or of another person, which right cannot be exercised until some future date, shall not be deemed to be an offer or sale of such other security; but the issue or transfer of such other security upon the exercise of such right of conversion or subscription shall be deemed a sale of such other security. Any offer or sale of a security futures product by or on behalf of the issuer of the securities underlying the security futures product, an affiliate of the issuer, or an underwriter, shall constitute a contract for sale of, sale of, offer for sale, or offer to sell the underlying securities. Any offer or sale of a security-based swap by or on behalf of the issuer of the securities upon which such security-based swap is based or is referenced, an affiliate of the issuer, or an underwriter, shall constitute a contract for sale of, sale of, offer for sale, or offer to sell such securities. The publication or distribution by a broker or dealer of a research report about an emerging growth company that is the subject of a proposed public offering of the common equity securities of such emerging growth company pursuant to a registration statement that the issuer proposes to file, or has filed, or that is effective shall be deemed for purposes of paragraph (10) of this subsection and section 77e(c) of this title not to constitute an offer for sale or offer to sell a security, even if the broker or dealer is participating or will participate in the registered offering of the securities of the issuer. As used in this paragraph, the term "research report" means a written, electronic, or oral communication that includes information, opinions, or recommendations with respect to securities of an issuer or an analysis of a security or an issuer, whether or not it provides information reasonably sufficient upon which to base an investment decision.

(4)   The term "issuer" means every person who issues or proposes to issue any security; except that with respect to certificates of deposit, voting-trust certificates, or collateral-trust certificates, or with respect to certificates of interest or shares in an unincorporated investment trust not having a board of directors (or persons performing similar functions) or of the fixed, restricted management, or unit type, the term "issuer" means the person or persons performing the acts and assuming the duties of depositor or manager pursuant to the provisions of the trust or other agreement or instrument under which such securities are issued; except that in the case

of an unincorporated association which provides by its articles for limited liability of any or all of its members, or in the case of a trust, committee, or other legal entity, the trustees or members thereof shall not be individually liable as issuers of any security issued by the association, trust, committee, or other legal entity; except that with respect to equipment-trust certificates or like securities, the term "issuer" means the person by whom the equipment or property is or is to be used; and except that with respect to fractional undivided interests in oil, gas, or other mineral rights, the term "issuer" means the owner of any such right or of any interest in such right (whether whole or fractional) who creates fractional interests therein for the purpose of public offering.

(5) The term "Commission" means the Securities and Exchange Commission.

(6) The term "Territory" means Puerto Rico, the Virgin Islands, and the insular possessions of the United States.

(7) The term "interstate commerce" means trade or commerce in securities or any transportation or communication relating thereto among the several States or between the District of Columbia or any Territory of the United States and any State or other Territory, or between any foreign country and any State, Territory, or the District of Columbia, or within the District of Columbia.

(8) The term "registration statement" means the statement provided for in section 77f of this title, and includes any amendment thereto and any report, document, or memorandum filed as part of such statement or incorporated therein by reference.

(9) The term "write" or "written" shall include printed, lithographed, or any means of graphic communication.

(10) The term "prospectus" means any prospectus, notice, circular, advertisement, letter, or communication, written or by radio or television, which offers any security for sale or confirms the sale of any security; except that (a) a communication sent or given after the effective date of the registration statement (other than a prospectus permitted under subsection (b) of section 77j of this title) shall not be deemed a prospectus if it is proved that prior to or at the same time with such communication a written prospectus meeting the requirements of subsection (a) of section 77j of this title at the time of[1] such communication was sent or given to the person to whom the communication was made, and (b) a notice, circular, advertisement, letter, or communication in respect of a security shall not be deemed to be a prospectus if it states from whom a written prospectus meeting the requirements of section 77j of this title may be obtained and, in addition, does no more than identify the security, state the price thereof, state by whom orders will be executed, and contain such other information as the Commission, by rules or regulations deemed necessary or appropriate in the public interest and for the protection of investors, and subject to such terms and conditions as may be prescribed therein, may permit.

(11) The term "underwriter" means any person who has purchased from an issuer with a view to, or offers or sells for an issuer in connection with, the distribution of any security, or participates or has a direct or indirect participation in any such undertaking, or participates or has a participation in the direct or indirect underwriting of any such undertaking; but such term shall not include a person whose interest is limited to a commission from an underwriter or dealer not in excess of the usual and customary distributors' or sellers' commission. As used in this paragraph the term "issuer" shall include, in addition to an issuer, any person directly or indirectly controlling or controlled by the issuer, or any person under direct or indirect common control with the issuer.

(12) The term "dealer" means any person who engages either for all or part of his time, directly or indirectly, as agent, broker, or principal, in the business of offering, buying, selling, or otherwise dealing or trading in securities issued by another person.

---

[1] So in original.

(13) The term "insurance company" means a company which is organized as an insurance company, whose primary and predominant business activity is the writing of insurance or the reinsuring of risks underwritten by insurance companies, and which is subject to supervision by the insurance commissioner, or a similar official or agency, of a State or territory or the District of Columbia; or any receiver or similar official or any liquidating agent for such company, in his capacity as such.

(14) The term "separate account" means an account established and maintained by an insurance company pursuant to the laws of any State or territory of the United States, the District of Columbia, or of Canada or any province thereof, under which income, gains and losses, whether or not realized, from assets allocated to such account, are, in accordance with the applicable contract, credited to or charged against such account without regard to other income, gains, or losses of the insurance company.

(15) The term "accredited investor" shall mean—

(i)   a bank as defined in section 77c(a)(2) of this title whether acting in its individual or fiduciary capacity; an insurance company as defined in paragraph (13) of this subsection; an investment company registered under the Investment Company Act of 1940 [15 U.S.C. 80a–1 et seq.] or a business development company as defined in section 2(a)(48) of that Act [15 U.S.C. 80a–2(a)(48)]; a Small Business Investment Company licensed by the Small Business Administration; or an employee benefit plan, including an individual retirement account, which is subject to the provisions of the Employee Retirement Income Security Act of 1974 [29 U.S.C. 1001 et seq.], if the investment decision is made by a plan fiduciary, as defined in section 3(21) of such Act [29 U.S.C. 1002(21)], which is either a bank, insurance company, or registered investment adviser; or

(ii)   any person who, on the basis of such factors as financial sophistication, net worth, knowledge, and experience in financial matters, or amount of assets under management qualifies as an accredited investor under rules and regulations which the Commission shall prescribe.

(16) The terms "security future", "narrow-based security index", and "security futures product" have the same meanings as provided in section 78c(a)(55) of this title.

(17) The terms "swap" and "security-based swap" have the same meanings as in section 1a of title 7.

(18) The terms "purchase" or "sale" of a security-based swap shall be deemed to mean the execution, termination (prior to its scheduled maturity date), assignment, exchange, or similar transfer or conveyance of, or extinguishing of rights or obligations under, a security-based swap, as the context may require.

(19) The term "emerging growth company" means an issuer that had total annual gross revenues of less than $1,000,000,000 (as such amount is indexed for inflation every 5 years by the Commission to reflect the change in the Consumer Price Index for All Urban Consumers published by the Bureau of Labor Statistics, setting the threshold to the nearest 1,000,000) during its most recently completed fiscal year. An issuer that is an emerging growth company as of the first day of that fiscal year shall continue to be deemed an emerging growth company until the earliest of—

(A)   the last day of the fiscal year of the issuer during which it had total annual gross revenues of $1,000,000,000 (as such amount is indexed for inflation every 5 years by the Commission to reflect the change in the Consumer Price Index for All Urban Consumers published by the Bureau of Labor Statistics, setting the threshold to the nearest 1,000,000) or more;

(B)   the last day of the fiscal year of the issuer following the fifth anniversary of the date of the first sale of common equity securities of the issuer pursuant to an effective registration statement under this subchapter;

(C)   the date on which such issuer has, during the previous 3-year period, issued more than $1,000,000,000 in non-convertible debt; or

(D)   the date on which such issuer is deemed to be a "large accelerated filer", as defined in section 240.12b–2 of title 17, Code of Federal Regulations, or any successor thereto.

(b)   Consideration of promotion of efficiency, competition, and capital formation.—Whenever pursuant to this subchapter the Commission is engaged in rulemaking and is required to consider or determine whether an action is necessary or appropriate in the public interest, the Commission shall also consider, in addition to the protection of investors, whether the action will promote efficiency, competition, and capital formation.

Classes of Securities Under This Subchapter

§ 77c [P.L. § 3]. (a) Exempted securities.—Except as hereinafter expressly provided, the provisions of this subchapter shall not apply to any of the following classes of securities:

(1)   Reserved.

(2)   Any security issued or guaranteed by the United States or any territory thereof, or by the District of Columbia, or by any State of the United States, or by any political subdivision of a State or territory, or by any public instrumentality of one or more States or territories, or by any person controlled or supervised by and acting as an instrumentality of the Government of the United States pursuant to authority granted by the Congress of the United States; or any certificate of deposit for any of the foregoing; or any security issued or guaranteed by any bank; or any security issued by or representing an interest in or a direct obligation of a Federal Reserve bank; or any interest or participation in any common trust fund or similar fund that is excluded from the definition of the term "investment company" under section 3(c)(3) of the Investment Company Act of 1940 [15 U.S.C. 80a–3(c)(3)]; or any security which is an industrial development bond (as defined in section 103(c)(2)[1] of title 26) the interest on which is excludable from gross income under section 103(a)(1)[1] of title 26 if, by reason of the application of paragraph (4) or (6) of section 103(c)[1] of title 26 (determined as if paragraphs (4)(A), (5), and (7) were not included in such section 103(c)),[1] paragraph (1) of such section 103(c)[1] does not apply to such security; or any interest or participation in a single trust fund, or in a collective trust fund maintained by a bank, or any security arising out of a contract issued by an insurance company, which interest, participation, or security is issued in connection with (A) a stock bonus, pension, or profit-sharing plan which meets the requirements for qualification under section 401 of title 26, (B) an annuity plan which meets the requirements for the deduction of the employer's contributions under section 404(a)(2) of title 26, (C) a governmental plan as defined in section 414(d) of title 26 which has been established by an employer for the exclusive benefit of its employees or their beneficiaries for the purpose of distributing to such employees or their beneficiaries the corpus and income of the funds accumulated under such plan, if under such plan it is impossible, prior to the satisfaction of all liabilities with respect to such employees and their beneficiaries, for any part of the corpus or income to be used for, or diverted to, purposes other than the exclusive benefit of such employees or their beneficiaries, or (D) a church plan, company, or account that is excluded from the definition of an investment company under section 3(c)(14) of the Investment Company Act of 1940 [15 U.S.C. 80a–3(c)(14)], other than any plan described in subparagraph (A), (B), (C), or (D) of this paragraph (i) the contributions under which are held in a single trust fund or in a separate account maintained by an insurance company for a single employer and under which an amount in excess of the employer's contribution is allocated to the purchase of securities (other than interests or participations in the trust or separate account itself) issued by

---

[1]   See References in Text note below. [Not reproduced here.]

the employer or any company directly or indirectly controlling, controlled by, or under common control with the employer, (ii) which covers employees some or all of whom are employees within the meaning of section 401(c)(1) of title 26 (other than a person participating in a church plan who is described in section 414(e)(3)(B) of title 26), or (iii) which is a plan funded by an annuity contract described in section 403(b) of title 26 (other than a retirement income account described in section 403(b)(9) of title 26, to the extent that the interest or participation in such single trust fund or collective trust fund is issued to a church, a convention or association of churches, or an organization described in section 414(e)(3)(A) of title 26 establishing or maintaining the retirement income account or to a trust established by any such entity in connection with the retirement income account). The Commission, by rules and regulations or order, shall exempt from the provisions of section 77e of this title any interest or participation issued in connection with a stock bonus, pension, profit-sharing, or annuity plan which covers employees some or all of whom are employees within the meaning of section 401(c)(1) of title 26, if and to the extent that the Commission determines this to be necessary or appropriate in the public interest and consistent with the protection of investors and the purposes fairly intended by the policy and provisions of this subchapter. For purposes of this paragraph, a security issued or guaranteed by a bank shall not include any interest or participation in any collective trust fund maintained by a bank; and the term "bank" means any national bank, or banking institution organized under the laws of any State, territory, or the District of Columbia, the business of which is substantially confined to banking and is supervised by the State or territorial banking commission or similar official; except that in the case of a common trust fund or similar fund, or a collective trust fund, the term "bank" has the same meaning as in the Investment Company Act of 1940 [15 U.S.C. 80a–1 et seq.];

(3)   Any note, draft, bill of exchange, or banker's acceptance which arises out of a current transaction or the proceeds of which have been or are to be used for current transactions, and which has a maturity at the time of issuance of not exceeding nine months, exclusive of days of grace, or any renewal thereof the maturity of which is likewise limited;

(4)   Any security issued by a person organized and operated exclusively for religious, educational, benevolent, fraternal, charitable, or reformatory purposes and not for pecuniary profit, and no part of the net earnings of which inures to the benefit of any person, private stockholder, or individual, or any security of a fund that is excluded from the definition of an investment company under section 3(c)(10)(B) of the Investment Company Act of 1940 [15 U.S.C. 80a–3(c)(10)(B)];

(5)   Any security issued (A) by a savings and loan association, building and loan association, cooperative bank, homestead association, or similar institution, which is supervised and examined by State or Federal authority having supervision over any such institution; or (B) by (i) a farmer's cooperative organization exempt from tax under section 521 of title 26, (ii) a corporation described in section 501(c)(16) of title 26 and exempt from tax under section 501(a) of title 26, or (iii) a corporation described in section 501(c)(2) of title 26 which is exempt from tax under section 501(a) of title 26 and is organized for the exclusive purpose of holding title to property, collecting income therefrom, and turning over the entire amount thereof, less expenses, to an organization or corporation described in clause (i) or (ii);

(6)   Any interest in a railroad equipment trust. For purposes of this paragraph "interest in a railroad equipment trust" means any interest in an equipment trust, lease, conditional sales contract, or other similar arrangement entered into, issued, assumed, guaranteed by, or for the benefit of, a common carrier to finance the acquisition of rolling stock, including motive power;

(7)   Certificates issued by a receiver or by a trustee or debtor in possession in a case under title 11, with the approval of the court;

(8)   Any insurance or endowment policy or annuity contract or optional annuity contract, issued by a corporation subject to the supervision of the insurance commissioner, bank

commissioner, or any agency or officer performing like functions, of any State or Territory of the United States or the District of Columbia;

(9) Except with respect to a security exchanged in a case under title 11, any security exchanged by the issuer with its existing security holders exclusively where no commission or other remuneration is paid or given directly or indirectly for soliciting such exchange;

(10) Except with respect to a security exchanged in a case under title 11, any security which is issued in exchange for one or more bona fide outstanding securities, claims or property interests, or partly in such exchange and partly for cash, where the terms and conditions of such issuance and exchange are approved, after a hearing upon the fairness of such terms and conditions at which all persons to whom it is proposed to issue securities in such exchange shall have the right to appear, by any court, or by any official or agency of the United States, or by any State or Territorial banking or insurance commission or other governmental authority expressly authorized by law to grant such approval;

(11) Any security which is a part of an issue offered and sold only to persons resident within a single State or Territory, where the issuer of such security is a person resident and doing business within or, if a corporation, incorporated by and doing business within, such State or Territory.

(12) Any equity security issued in connection with the acquisition by a holding company of a bank under section 1842(a) of title 12 or a savings association under section 1467a(e) of title 12, if—

(A) the acquisition occurs solely as part of a reorganization in which security holders exchange their shares of a bank or savings association for shares of a newly formed holding company with no significant assets other than securities of the bank or savings association and the existing subsidiaries of the bank or savings association;

(B) the security holders receive, after that reorganization, substantially the same proportional share interests in the holding company as they held in the bank or savings association, except for nominal changes in shareholders' interests resulting from lawful elimination of fractional interests and the exercise of dissenting shareholders' rights under State or Federal law;

(C) the rights and interests of security holders in the holding company are substantially the same as those in the bank or savings association prior to the transaction, other than as may be required by law; and

(D) the holding company has substantially the same assets and liabilities, on a consolidated basis, as the bank or savings association had prior to the transaction.

For purposes of this paragraph, the term "savings association" means a savings association (as defined in section 1813(b) of title 12) the deposits of which are insured by the Federal Deposit Insurance Corporation.

(13) Any security issued by or any interest or participation in any church plan, company or account that is excluded from the definition of an investment company under section 3(c)(14) of the Investment Company Act of 1940 [15 U.S.C. 80a–3(c)(14)].

(14) Any security futures product that is—

(A) cleared by a clearing agency registered under section 78q–1 of this title or exempt from registration under subsection (b)(7) of such section 78q–1; and

(B) traded on a national securities exchange or a national securities association registered pursuant to section 78o–3(a) of this title.

(b) Additional exemptions.—

(1)   Small issues exemptive authority—The Commission may from time to time by its rules and regulations, and subject to such terms and conditions as may be prescribed therein, add any class of securities to the securities exempted as provided in this section, if it finds that the enforcement of this subchapter with respect to such securities is not necessary in the public interest and for the protection of investors by reason of the small amount involved or the limited character of the public offering; but no issue of securities shall be exempted under this subsection where the aggregate amount at which such issue is offered to the public exceeds $5,000,000.

(2)   Additional issues.—The Commission shall by rule or regulation add a class of securities to the securities exempted pursuant to this section in accordance with the following terms and conditions:

(A)   The aggregate offering amount of all securities offered and sold within the prior 12-month period in reliance on the exemption added in accordance with this paragraph shall not exceed $50,000,000.

(B)   The securities may be offered and sold publicly.

(C)   The securities shall not be restricted securities within the meaning of the Federal securities laws and the regulations promulgated thereunder.

(D)   The civil liability provision in section 77l(a)(2) of this title shall apply to any person offering or selling such securities.

(E)   The issuer may solicit interest in the offering prior to filing any offering statement, on such terms and conditions as the Commission may prescribe in the public interest or for the protection of investors.

(F)   The Commission shall require the issuer to file audited financial statements with the Commission annually.

(G)   Such other terms, conditions, or requirements as the Commission may determine necessary in the public interest and for the protection of investors, which may include—

(i)   a requirement that the issuer prepare and electronically file with the Commission and distribute to prospective investors an offering statement, and any related documents, in such form and with such content as prescribed by the Commission, including audited financial statements, a description of the issuer's business operations, its financial condition, its corporate governance principles, its use of investor funds, and other appropriate matters; and

(ii)   disqualification provisions under which the exemption shall not be available to the issuer or its predecessors, affiliates, officers, directors, underwriters, or other related persons, which shall be substantially similar to the disqualification provisions contained in the regulations adopted in accordance with section 926 of the Dodd-Frank Wall Street Reform and Consumer Protection Act (15 U.S.C. 77d note).

(3)   Limitation.—Only the following types of securities may be exempted under a rule or regulation adopted pursuant to paragraph (2): equity securities, debt securities, and debt securities convertible or exchangeable to equity interests, including any guarantees of such securities.

(4)   Periodic disclosures.—Upon such terms and conditions as the Commission determines necessary in the public interest and for the protection of investors, the Commission by rule or regulation may require an issuer of a class of securities exempted under paragraph (2) to make available to investors and file with the Commission periodic disclosures regarding the issuer, its business operations, its financial condition, its corporate governance principles, its use of investor funds, and other appropriate matters, and also may provide for the suspension and termination of such a requirement with respect to that issuer.

(5) Adjustment.—Not later than 2 years after April 5, 2012,1 and every 2 years thereafter, the Commission shall review the offering amount limitation described in paragraph (2)(A) and shall increase such amount as the Commission determines appropriate. If the Commission determines not to increase such amount, it shall report to the Committee on Financial Services of the House of Representatives and the Committee on Banking, Housing, and Urban Affairs of the Senate on its reasons for not increasing the amount.

(c) Securities issued by small investment company.—The Commission may from time to time by its rules and regulations and subject to such terms and conditions as may be prescribed therein, add to the securities exempted as provided in this section any class of securities issued by a small business investment company under the Small Business Investment Act of 1958 [15 U.S.C. 661 et seq.] if it finds, having regard to the purposes of that Act, that the enforcement of this subchapter with respect to such securities is not necessary in the public interest and for the protection of investors.

Exempted Transactions

§ 77d [P.L. § 4]. (a) In general

The provisions of section 77e of this title shall not apply to—

(1) transactions by any person other than an issuer, underwriter, or dealer.

(2) transactions by an issuer not involving any public offering.

(3) transactions by a dealer (including an underwriter no longer acting as an underwriter in respect of the security involved in such transaction), except—

(A) transactions taking place prior to the expiration of forty days after the first date upon which the security was bona fide offered to the public by the issuer or by or through an underwriter,

(B) transactions in a security as to which a registration statement has been filed taking place prior to the expiration of forty days after the effective date of such registration statement or prior to the expiration of forty days after the first date upon which the security was bona fide offered to the public by the issuer or by or through an underwriter after such effective date, whichever is later (excluding in the computation of such forty days any time during which a stop order issued under section 77h of this title is in effect as to the security), or such shorter period as the Commission may specify by rules and regulations or order, and

(C) transactions as to securities constituting the whole or a part of an unsold allotment to or subscription by such dealer as a participant in the distribution of such securities by the issuer or by or through an underwriter.

With respect to transactions referred to in clause (B), if securities of the issuer have not previously been sold pursuant to an earlier effective registration statement the applicable period, instead of forty days, shall be ninety days, or such shorter period as the Commission may specify by rules and regulations or order.

(4) brokers' transactions executed upon customers' orders on any exchange or in the over-the-counter market but not the solicitation of such orders.

(5) transactions involving offers or sales by an issuer solely to one or more accredited investors, if the aggregate offering price of an issue of securities offered in reliance on this paragraph does not exceed the amount allowed under section 77c(b)(1) of this title, if there is no advertising or public solicitation in connection with the transaction by the issuer or anyone acting on the issuer's behalf, and if the issuer files such notice with the Commission as the Commission shall prescribe.

(6) transactions involving the offer or sale of securities by an issuer (including all entities controlled by or under common control with the issuer), provided that—

(A) the aggregate amount sold to all investors by the issuer, including any amount sold in reliance on the exemption provided under this paragraph during the 12-month period preceding the date of such transaction, is not more than $1,000,000;

(B) the aggregate amount sold to any investor by an issuer, including any amount sold in reliance on the exemption provided under this paragraph during the 12-month period preceding the date of such transaction, does not exceed—

(i) the greater of $2,000 or 5 percent of the annual income or net worth of such investor, as applicable, if either the annual income or the net worth of the investor is less than $100,000; and

(ii) 10 percent of the annual income or net worth of such investor, as applicable, not to exceed a maximum aggregate amount sold of $100,000, if either the annual income or net worth of the investor is equal to or more than $100,000;

(C) the transaction is conducted through a broker or funding portal that complies with the requirements of section 77d–1(a) of this title; and

(D) the issuer complies with the requirements of section 77d–1(b) of this title.

(7) transactions meeting the requirements of subsection (d).

(b) Offers and sales exempt under 17 CFR 230.506

Offers and sales exempt under section 230.506 of title 17, Code of Federal Regulations (as revised pursuant to section 201 of the Jumpstart Our Business Startups Act) shall not be deemed public offerings under the Federal securities laws as a result of general advertising or general solicitation.

(c) Securities offered and sold in compliance with Rule 506 of Regulation D

(1) With respect to securities offered and sold in compliance with Rule 506 of Regulation D under this subchapter, no person who meets the conditions set forth in paragraph (2) shall be subject to registration as a broker or dealer pursuant to section 78o(a)(1) of this title,[1] solely because—

(A) that person maintains a platform or mechanism that permits the offer, sale, purchase, or negotiation of or with respect to securities, or permits general solicitations, general advertisements, or similar or related activities by issuers of such securities, whether online, in person, or through any other means;

(B) that person or any person associated with that person co-invests in such securities; or

(C) that person or any person associated with that person provides ancillary services with respect to such securities.

(2) The exemption provided in paragraph (1) shall apply to any person described in such paragraph if—

(A) such person and each person associated with that person receives no compensation in connection with the purchase or sale of such security;

(B) such person and each person associated with that person does not have possession of customer funds or securities in connection with the purchase or sale of such security; and

(C) such person is not subject to a statutory disqualification as defined in section 78c(a)(39) of this title[1] and does not have any person associated with that person subject to such a statutory disqualification.

---

[1] See References in Text note below. [Not reproduced here.]
[1] See References in Text note below. [Not reproduced here.]

(3)   For the purposes of this subsection, the term "ancillary services" means—

(A)   the provision of due diligence services, in connection with the offer, sale, purchase, or negotiation of such security, so long as such services do not include, for separate compensation, investment advice or recommendations to issuers or investors; and

(B)   the provision of standardized documents to the issuers and investors, so long as such person or entity does not negotiate the terms of the issuance for and on behalf of third parties and issuers are not required to use the standardized documents as a condition of using the service.

(d)   Certain accredited investor transactions

The transactions referred to in subsection (a)(7) are transactions meeting the following requirements:

(1)   Accredited investor requirement.—Each purchaser is an accredited investor, as that term is defined in section 230.501(a) of title 17, Code of Federal Regulations (or any successor regulation).

(2)   Prohibition on general solicitation or advertising.—Neither the seller, nor any person acting on the seller's behalf, offers or sells securities by any form of general solicitation or general advertising.

(3)   Information requirement.—In the case of a transaction involving the securities of an issuer that is neither subject to section 78m or 78o(d) of this title, nor exempt from reporting pursuant to section 240.12g3–2(b) of title 17, Code of Federal Regulations, nor a foreign government (as defined in section 230.405 of title 17, Code of Federal Regulations) eligible to register securities under Schedule B, the seller and a prospective purchaser designated by the seller obtain from the issuer, upon request of the seller, and the seller in all cases makes available to a prospective purchaser, the following information (which shall be reasonably current in relation to the date of resale under this section):

(A)   The exact name of the issuer and the issuer's predecessor (if any).

(B)   The address of the issuer's principal executive offices.

(C)   The exact title and class of the security.

(D)   The par or stated value of the security.

(E)   The number of shares or total amount of the securities outstanding as of the end of the issuer's most recent fiscal year.

(F)   The name and address of the transfer agent, corporate secretary, or other person responsible for transferring shares and stock certificates.

(G)   A statement of the nature of the business of the issuer and the products and services it offers, which shall be presumed reasonably current if the statement is as of 12 months before the transaction date.

(H)   The names of the officers and directors of the issuer.

(I)   The names of any persons registered as a broker, dealer, or agent that shall be paid or given, directly or indirectly, any commission or remuneration for such person's participation in the offer or sale of the securities.

(J)   The issuer's most recent balance sheet and profit and loss statement and similar financial statements, which shall—

(i)   be for such part of the 2 preceding fiscal years as the issuer has been in operation;

(ii) be prepared in accordance with generally accepted accounting principles or, in the case of a foreign private issuer, be prepared in accordance with generally accepted accounting principles or the International Financial Reporting Standards issued by the International Accounting Standards Board;

(iii) be presumed reasonably current if—

(I) with respect to the balance sheet, the balance sheet is as of a date less than 16 months before the transaction date; and

(II) with respect to the profit and loss statement, such statement is for the 12 months preceding the date of the issuer's balance sheet; and

(iv) if the balance sheet is not as of a date less than 6 months before the transaction date, be accompanied by additional statements of profit and loss for the period from the date of such balance sheet to a date less than 6 months before the transaction date.

(K) To the extent that the seller is a control person with respect to the issuer, a brief statement regarding the nature of the affiliation, and a statement certified by such seller that they have no reasonable grounds to believe that the issuer is in violation of the securities laws or regulations.

(4) *Issuers disqualified.*—The transaction is not for the sale of a security where the seller is an issuer or a subsidiary, either directly or indirectly, of the issuer.

(5) *Bad actor prohibition.*—Neither the seller, nor any person that has been or will be paid (directly or indirectly) remuneration or a commission for their participation in the offer or sale of the securities, including solicitation of purchasers for the seller is subject to an event that would disqualify an issuer or other covered person under Rule 506(d)(1) of Regulation D (17 CFR 230.506(d)(1)) or is subject to a statutory disqualification described under section 78c(a)(39) of this title.

(6) *Business requirement.*—The issuer is engaged in business, is not in the organizational stage or in bankruptcy or receivership, and is not a blank check, blind pool, or shell company that has no specific business plan or purpose or has indicated that the issuer's primary business plan is to engage in a merger or combination of the business with, or an acquisition of, an unidentified person.

(7) *Underwriter prohibition.*—The transaction is not with respect to a security that constitutes the whole or part of an unsold allotment to, or a subscription or participation by, a broker or dealer as an underwriter of the security or a redistribution.

(8) *Outstanding class requirement.*—The transaction is with respect to a security of a class that has been authorized and outstanding for at least 90 days prior to the date of the transaction.

(e) Additional requirements

(1) In general.—With respect to an exempted transaction described under subsection (a)(7):

(A) Securities acquired in such transaction shall be deemed to have been acquired in a transaction not involving any public offering.

(B) Such transaction shall be deemed not to be a distribution for purposes of section 77b(a)(11) of this title.

(C) Securities involved in such transaction shall be deemed to be restricted securities within the meaning of Rule 144 (17 CFR 230.144).

(2) Rule of construction.—The exemption provided by subsection (a)(7) shall not be the exclusive means for establishing an exemption from the registration requirements of section 77e of this title.

Prohibitions Relating to Interstate Commerce and the Mails

§ 77e [P.L. § 5]. (a) Sale or delivery after sale of unregistered securities.—Unless a registration statement is in effect as to a security, it shall be unlawful for any person, directly or indirectly—

(1) to make use of any means or instruments of transportation or communication in interstate commerce or of the mails to sell such security through the use or medium of any prospectus or otherwise; or

(2) to carry or cause to be carried through the mails or in interstate commerce, by any means or instruments of transportation, any such security for the purpose of sale or for delivery after sale.

(b) Necessity of prospectus meeting requirements of section 77j of this title.—It shall be unlawful for any person, directly or indirectly—

(1) to make use of any means or instruments of transportation or communication in interstate commerce or of the mails to carry or transmit any prospectus relating to any security with respect to which a registration statement has been filed under this subchapter, unless such prospectus meets the requirements of section 77j of this title; or

(2) to carry or cause to be carried through the mails or in interstate commerce any such security for the purpose of sale or for delivery after sale, unless accompanied or preceded by a prospectus that meets the requirements of subsection (a) of section 77j of this title.

(c) Necessity of filing registration statement.—It shall be unlawful for any person, directly or indirectly, to make use of any means or instruments of transportation or communication in interstate commerce or of the mails to offer to sell or offer to buy through the use or medium of any prospectus or otherwise any security, unless a registration statement has been filed as to such security, or while the registration statement is the subject of a refusal order or stop order or (prior to the effective date of the registration statement) any public proceeding or examination under section 77h of this title.

(d) Limitation.—Notwithstanding any other provision of this section, an emerging growth company or any person authorized to act on behalf of an emerging growth company may engage in oral or written communications with potential investors that are qualified institutional buyers or institutions that are accredited investors, as such terms are respectively defined in section 230.144A and section 230.501(a) of title 17, Code of Federal Regulations, or any successor thereto, to determine whether such investors might have an interest in a contemplated securities offering, either prior to or following the date of filing of a registration statement with respect to such securities with the Commission, subject to the requirement of subsection (b)(2).

(e) Security-based swaps.—Notwithstanding the provisions of section 77c or 77d of this title, unless a registration statement meeting the requirements of section 77j(a) of this title is in effect as to a security-based swap, it shall be unlawful for any person, directly or indirectly, to make use of any means or instruments of transportation or communication in interstate commerce or of the mails to offer to sell, offer to buy or purchase or sell a security-based swap to any person who is not an eligible contract participant as defined in section 1a(18) of title 7.

Registration of Securities

§ 77f [P.L. § 6]. (a) Method of registration.—Any security may be registered with the Commission under the terms and conditions hereinafter provided, by filing a registration statement in triplicate, at least one of which shall be signed by each issuer, its principal executive officer or officers, its principal financial officer, its comptroller or principal accounting officer, and the majority of its board of directors or persons performing similar functions (or, if there is no board of directors or persons performing similar functions, by the majority of the persons or board having the power of management of the issuer), and in case the issuer is a foreign or Territorial person by its duly authorized representative in the United States; except that when such registration statement relates to a security issued by a foreign government, or political subdivision thereof, it need be signed only by the underwriter of such security. Signatures of all such persons when written on the said registration statements shall be presumed to have been so written by authority of the person whose signature is so affixed and the burden of proof, in the event such authority shall be denied, shall be upon the party denying the same. The affixing of any signature without the authority of the purported signer shall constitute a violation of this subchapter. A registration statement shall be deemed effective only as to the securities specified therein as proposed to be offered.

(b)　Registration fee.—

(1)　Fee payment required—At the time of filing a registration statement, the applicant shall pay to the Commission a fee at a rate that shall be equal to $92 per $1,000,000 of the maximum aggregate price at which such securities are proposed to be offered, except that during fiscal year 2003 and any succeeding fiscal year such fee shall be adjusted pursuant to paragraph (2).

(2)　Annual adjustment—For each fiscal year, the Commission shall by order adjust the rate required by paragraph (1) for such fiscal year to a rate that, when applied to the baseline estimate of the aggregate maximum offering prices for such fiscal year, is reasonably likely to produce aggregate fee collections under this subsection that are equal to the target fee collection amount for such fiscal year.

(3)　Pro rata application—The rates per $1,000,000 required by this subsection shall be applied pro rata to amounts and balances of less than $1,000,000.

(4)　Review and effective date.—In exercising its authority under this subsection, the Commission shall not be required to comply with the provisions of section 553 of title 5. An adjusted rate prescribed under paragraph (2) and published under paragraph (5) shall not be subject to judicial review. An adjusted rate prescribed under paragraph (2) shall take effect on the first day of the fiscal year to which such rate applies.

(5)　Publication.—The Commission shall publish in the Federal Register notices of the rate applicable under this subsection and under sections 78m(e) and 78n(g)[1] of this title for each fiscal year not later than August 31 of the fiscal year preceding the fiscal year to which such rate applies, together with any estimates or projections on which such rate is based.

(6)　Definitions.—For purposes of this subsection:

(A)　Target fee collection amount.—The target fee collection amount for each fiscal year is determined according to the following table:

Fiscal year:	Target setting collection amount
2002	$377,000,000
2003	$435,000,000
2004	$467,000,000
2005	$570,000,000
2006	$689,000,000
2007	$214,000,000
2008	$234,000,000
2009	$284,000,000
2010	$334,000,000
2011	$394,000,000
2012	$425,000,000

---

[1]　See References in Text note below. [Not reproduced here.]

2013	$455,000,000
2014	$485,000,000
2015	$515,000,000
2016	$550,000,000
2017	$585,000,000
2018	$620,000,000
2019	$660,000,000
2020	$705,000,000
2021 and each fiscal year thereafter	An amount that is equal to the target fee collection amount for the prior fiscal year, adjusted by the rate of inflation.

(B) Baseline estimate of the aggregate maximum offering prices.—The baseline estimate of the aggregate maximum offering prices for any fiscal year is the baseline estimate of the aggregate maximum offering price at which securities are proposed to be offered pursuant to registration statements filed with the Commission during such fiscal year as determined by the Commission, after consultation with the Congressional Budget Office and the Office of Management and Budget, using the methodology required for projections pursuant to section 907 of title 2.

(c) Time registration effective.—The filing with the Commission of a registration statement, or of an amendment to a registration statement, shall be deemed to have taken place upon the receipt thereof, but the filing of a registration statement shall not be deemed to have taken place unless it is accompanied by a United States postal money order or a certified bank check or cash for the amount of the fee required under subsection (b) of this section.

(d) Information available to public.—The information contained in or filed with any registration statement shall be made available to the public under such regulations as the Commission may prescribe, and copies thereof, photostatic or otherwise, shall be furnished to every applicant at such reasonable charge as the Commission may prescribe.

(e) Emerging growth companies.—

(1) In general.—Any emerging growth company, prior to its initial public offering date, may confidentially submit to the Commission a draft registration statement, for confidential nonpublic review by the staff of the Commission prior to public filing, provided that the initial confidential submission and all amendments thereto shall be publicly filed with the Commission not later than 15 days before the date on which the issuer conducts a road show, as such term is defined in section 230.433(h)(4) of title 17, Code of Federal Regulations, or any successor thereto. An issuer that was an emerging growth company at the time it submitted a confidential registration statement or, in lieu thereof, a publicly filed registration statement for review under this subsection but ceases to be an emerging growth company thereafter shall continue to be treated as an emerging market growth company for the purposes of this subsection through the earlier of the date on which the issuer consummates its initial public offering pursuant to such registrations statement or the end of the 1-year period beginning on the date the company ceases to be an emerging growth company.

(2) Confidentiality.—Notwithstanding any other provision of this subchapter, the Commission shall not be compelled to disclose any information provided to or obtained by the Commission pursuant to this subsection. For purposes of section 552 of title 5, this subsection shall be considered a statute described in subsection (b)(3)(B) of such section 552. Information described in or obtained pursuant to this subsection shall be deemed to constitute confidential information for purposes of section 78x(b)(2) of this title.

Information Required in Registration Statement

§ 77g [P.L. § 7]. (a) Information required in registration statement

(1) In general.—The registration statement, when relating to a security other than a security issued by a foreign government, or political subdivision thereof, shall contain the information, and be accompanied by the documents, specified in Schedule A of section 77aa of this title, and when relating to a security issued by a foreign government, or political subdivision thereof, shall contain the information, and be accompanied by the documents, specified in Schedule B of section 77aa of this title; except that the Commission may by rules or regulations provide that any such information or document need not be included in respect of any class of issuers or securities if it finds that the requirement of such information or document is inapplicable to such class and that disclosure fully adequate for the protection of investors is otherwise required to be included within the registration statement. If any accountant, engineer, or appraiser, or any person whose profession gives authority to a statement made by him, is named as having prepared or certified any part of the registration statement, or is named as having prepared or certified a report or valuation for use in connection with the registration statement, the written consent of such person shall be filed with the registration statement. If any such person is named as having prepared or certified a report or valuation (other than a public official document or statement) which is used in connection with the registration statement, but is not named as having prepared or certified such report or valuation for use in connection with the registration statement, the written consent of such person shall be filed with the registration statement unless the Commission dispenses with such filing as impracticable or as involving undue hardship on the person filing the registration statement. Any such registration statement shall contain such other information, and be accompanied by such other documents, as the Commission may by rules or regulations require as being necessary or appropriate in the public interest or for the protection of investors.

(2) Treatment of emerging growth companies.—An emerging growth company—

(A) need not present more than 2 years of audited financial statements in order for the registration statement of such emerging growth company with respect to an initial public offering of its common equity securities to be effective, and in any other registration statement to be filed with the Commission, an emerging growth company need not present selected financial data in accordance with section 229.301 of title 17, Code of Federal Regulations, for any period prior to the earliest audited period presented in connection with its initial public offering; and

(B) may not be required to comply with any new or revised financial accounting standard until such date that a company that is not an issuer (as defined under section 7201 of this title) is required to comply with such new or revised accounting standard, if such standard applies to companies that are not issuers.

(b) Registration statement for blank check companies

(1) The Commission shall prescribe special rules with respect to registration statements filed by any issuer that is a blank check company. Such rules may, as the Commission determines necessary or appropriate in the public interest or for the protection of investors—

(A) require such issuers to provide timely disclosure, prior to or after such statement becomes effective under section 77h of this title, of (i) information regarding the company to be acquired and the specific application of the proceeds of the offering, or (ii) additional information necessary to prevent such statement from being misleading;

(B) place limitations on the use of such proceeds and the distribution of securities by such issuer until the disclosures required under subparagraph (A) have been made; and

(C) provide a right of rescission to shareholders of such securities.

(2) The Commission may, as it determines consistent with the public interest and the protection of investors, by rule or order exempt any issuer or class of issuers from the rules prescribed under paragraph (1).

(3) For purposes of paragraph (1) of this subsection, the term "blank check company" means any development stage company that is issuing a penny stock (within the meaning of section 78c(a)(51) of this title) and that—

(A) has no specific business plan or purpose; or

(B) has indicated that its business plan is to merge with an unidentified company or companies.

(c) Disclosure requirements.—

(1) In general.—The Commission shall adopt regulations under this subsection requiring each issuer of an asset-backed security to disclose, for each tranche or class of security, information regarding the assets backing that security.

(2) Content of regulations.—In adopting regulations under this subsection, the Commission shall—

(A) set standards for the format of the data provided by issuers of an asset-backed security, which shall, to the extent feasible, facilitate comparison of such data across securities in similar types of asset classes; and

(B) require issuers of asset-backed securities, at a minimum, to disclose asset-level or loan-level data, if such data are necessary for investors to independently perform due diligence, including—

(i) data having unique identifiers relating to loan brokers or originators;

(ii) the nature and extent of the compensation of the broker or originator of the assets backing the security; and

(iii) the amount of risk retention by the originator and the securitizer of such assets.

(d) Registration statement for asset-backed securities.—Not later than 180 days after July 21, 2010, the Commission shall issue rules relating to the registration statement required to be filed by any issuer of an asset-backed security (as that term is defined in section 78c(a)(77)[1] of this title) that require any issuer of an asset-backed security—

(1) to perform a review of the assets underlying the asset-backed security; and

(2) to disclose the nature of the review under paragraph (1).

Taking Effect of Registration Statements and Amendments Thereto

§ 77h [P.L. § 8]. (a) Effective date of registration statement.—Except as hereinafter provided, the effective date of a registration statement shall be the twentieth day after the filing thereof or such earlier date as the Commission may determine, having due regard to the adequacy of the information respecting the issuer theretofore available to the public, to the facility with which the nature of the securities to be registered, their relationship to the capital structure of the issuer and the rights of holders thereof can be understood, and to the public interest and the protection of investors. If any amendment to any such statement is filed prior to the effective date of such statement, the registration statement shall be deemed to have been filed when such amendment was filed; except that an amendment filed with the consent of the Commission, prior to the effective date of the registration

---

[1] See References in Text note below. [Not reproduced here.]

statement, or filed pursuant to an order of the Commission, shall be treated as a part of the registration statement.

(b) Incomplete or inaccurate registration statement.—If it appears to the Commission that a registration statement is on its face incomplete or inaccurate in any material respect, the Commission may, after notice by personal service or the sending of confirmed telegraphic notice not later than ten days after the filing of the registration statement, and opportunity for hearing (at a time fixed by the Commission) within ten days after such notice by personal service or the sending of such telegraphic notice, issue an order prior to the effective date of registration refusing to permit such statement to become effective until it has been amended in accordance with such order. When such statement has been amended in accordance with such order the Commission shall so declare and the registration shall become effective at the time provided in subsection (a) of this section or upon the date of such declaration, whichever date is the later.

(c) Effective date of amendment to registration statement.—An amendment filed after the effective date of the registration statement, if such amendment, upon its face, appears to the Commission not to be incomplete or inaccurate in any material respect, shall become effective on such date as the Commission may determine, having due regard to the public interest and the protection of investors.

(d) Untrue statements or omissions in registration statement.—If it appears to the Commission at any time that the registration statement includes any untrue statement of a material fact or omits to state any material fact required to be stated therein or necessary to make the statements therein not misleading, the Commission may, after notice by personal service or the sending of confirmed telegraphic notice, and after opportunity for hearing (at a time fixed by the Commission) within fifteen days after such notice by personal service or the sending of such telegraphic notice, issue a stop order suspending the effectiveness of the registration statement. When such statement has been amended in accordance with such stop order, the Commission shall so declare and thereupon the stop order shall cease to be effective.

(e) Examination for issuance of stop order.—The Commission is empowered to make an examination in any case in order to determine whether a stop order should issue under subsection (d) of this section. In making such examination the Commission or any officer or officers designated by it shall have access to and may demand the production of any books and papers of, and may administer oaths and affirmations to and examine, the issuer, underwriter, or any other person, in respect of any matter relevant to the examination, and may, in its discretion, require the production of a balance sheet exhibiting the assets and liabilities of the issuer, or its income statement, or both, to be certified to by a public or certified accountant approved by the Commission. If the issuer or underwriter shall fail to cooperate, or shall obstruct or refuse to permit the making of an examination, such conduct shall be proper ground for the issuance of a stop order.

(f) Notice requirements.—Any notice required under this section shall be sent to or served on the issuer, or, in case of a foreign government or political subdivision thereof, to or on the underwriter, or, in the case of a foreign or Territorial person, to or on its duly authorized representative in the United States named in the registration statement, properly directed in each case of telegraphic notice to the address given in such statement.

Cease-and-Desist Proceedings

§ 77h–1 [P.L. § 8A]. (a) Authority of Commission.—If the Commission finds, after notice and opportunity for hearing, that any person is violating, has violated, or is about to violate any provision of this subchapter, or any rule or regulation thereunder, the Commission may publish its findings and enter an order requiring such person, and any other person that is, was, or would be a cause of the violation, due to an act or omission the person knew or should have known would contribute to such violation, to cease and desist from committing or causing such violation and any future violation of the same provision, rule, or regulation. Such order may, in addition to requiring a person to cease and desist from committing or causing a violation, require such person to comply, or to take steps to effect compliance, with such provision, rule, or regulation, upon such terms and conditions and within such time as the Commission may specify in such order. Any such order may, as the Commission deems appropriate, require future compliance or steps to effect future compliance, either permanently or for such period of time as the Commission may specify, with such provision, rule, or regulation with respect to any security, any issuer, or any other person.

(b) Hearing.—The notice instituting proceedings pursuant to subsection (a) of this section shall fix a hearing date not earlier than 30 days nor later than 60 days after service of the notice unless an earlier or a later date is set by the Commission with the consent of any respondent so served.

(c) Temporary order.—

(1) In general.—Whenever the Commission determines that the alleged violation or threatened violation specified in the notice instituting proceedings pursuant to subsection (a) of this section, or the continuation thereof, is likely to result in significant dissipation or conversion of assets, significant harm to investors, or substantial harm to the public interest, including, but not limited to, losses to the Securities Investor Protection Corporation, prior to the completion of the proceedings, the Commission may enter a temporary order requiring the respondent to cease and desist from the violation or threatened violation and to take such action to prevent the violation or threatened violation and to prevent dissipation or conversion of assets, significant harm to investors, or substantial harm to the public interest as the Commission deems appropriate pending completion of such proceeding. Such an order shall be entered only after notice and opportunity for a hearing, unless the Commission determines that notice and hearing prior to entry would be impracticable or contrary to the public interest. A temporary order shall become effective upon service upon the respondent and, unless set aside, limited, or suspended by the Commission or a court of competent jurisdiction, shall remain effective and enforceable pending the completion of the proceedings.

(2) Applicability.—This subsection shall apply only to a respondent that acts, or, at the time of the alleged misconduct acted, as a broker, dealer, investment adviser, investment company, municipal securities dealer, government securities broker, government securities dealer, or transfer agent, or is, or was at the time of the alleged misconduct, an associated person of, or a person seeking to become associated with, any of the foregoing.

(d) Review of temporary orders.—

(1) Commission review.—At any time after the respondent has been served with a temporary cease-and-desist order pursuant to subsection (c) of this section, the respondent may apply to the Commission to have the order set aside, limited, or suspended. If the respondent has been served with a temporary cease-and-desist order entered without a prior Commission hearing, the respondent may, within 10 days after the date on which the order was served, request a hearing on such application and the Commission shall hold a hearing and render a decision on such application at the earliest possible time.

(2) Judicial review.—Within—

(A) 10 days after the date the respondent was served with a temporary cease-and-desist order entered with a prior Commission hearing, or

(B) 10 days after the Commission renders a decision on an application and hearing under paragraph (1), with respect to any temporary cease-and-desist order entered without a prior Commission hearing,

the respondent may apply to the United States district court for the district in which the respondent resides or has its principal place of business, or for the District of Columbia, for an order setting aside, limiting, or suspending the effectiveness or enforcement of the order, and the court shall have jurisdiction to enter such an order. A respondent served with a temporary cease-and-desist order entered without a prior Commission hearing may not apply to the court except after hearing and decision by the Commission on the respondent's application under paragraph (1) of this subsection.

(3) No automatic stay of temporary order.—The commencement of proceedings under paragraph (2) of this subsection shall not, unless specifically ordered by the court, operate as a stay of the Commission's order.

(4) Exclusive review.—Section 77i(a) of this title shall not apply to a temporary order entered pursuant to this section.

(e) Authority to enter order requiring accounting and disgorgement.—In any cease-and-desist proceeding under subsection (a) of this section, the Commission may enter an order requiring accounting and disgorgement, including reasonable interest. The Commission is authorized to adopt rules, regulations, and orders concerning payments to investors, rates of interest, periods of accrual, and such other matters as it deems appropriate to implement this subsection.

(f) Authority of the Commission to prohibit persons from serving as officers or directors.—In any cease-and-desist proceeding under subsection (a) of this section, the Commission may issue an order to prohibit, conditionally or unconditionally, and permanently or for such period of time as it shall determine, any person who has violated section 77q(a)(1) of this title or the rules or regulations thereunder, from acting as an officer or director of any issuer that has a class of securities registered pursuant to section 78l of this title, or that is required to file reports pursuant to section 78o(d) of this title, if the conduct of that person demonstrates unfitness to serve as an officer or director of any such issuer.

(g) Authority to impose money penalties.—

(1) Grounds.—In any cease-and-desist proceeding under subsection (a), the Commission may impose a civil penalty on a person if the Commission finds, on the record, after notice and opportunity for hearing, that—

(A) such person—

(i) is violating or has violated any provision of this subchapter, or any rule or regulation issued under this subchapter; or

(ii) is or was a cause of the violation of any provision of this subchapter, or any rule or regulation thereunder; and

(B) such penalty is in the public interest.

(2) Maximum amount of penalty.—

(A) First tier.—The maximum amount of a penalty for each act or omission described in paragraph (1) shall be $7,500 for a natural person or $75,000 for any other person.

(B) Second tier.—Notwithstanding subparagraph (A), the maximum amount of penalty for each such act or omission shall be $75,000 for a natural person or $375,000 for any other person, if the act or omission described in paragraph (1) involved fraud, deceit, manipulation, or deliberate or reckless disregard of a regulatory requirement.

(C) Third tier.—Notwithstanding subparagraphs (A) and (B), the maximum amount of penalty for each such act or omission shall be $150,000 for a natural person or $725,000 for any other person, if—

(i) the act or omission described in paragraph (1) involved fraud, deceit, manipulation, or deliberate or reckless disregard of a regulatory requirement; and

(ii) such act or omission directly or indirectly resulted in—

(I) substantial losses or created a significant risk of substantial losses to other persons; or

(II) substantial pecuniary gain to the person who committed the act or omission.

(3) Evidence concerning ability to pay.—In any proceeding in which the Commission may impose a penalty under this section, a respondent may present evidence of the ability of the respondent to pay such penalty. The Commission may, in its discretion, consider such evidence in determining whether such penalty is in the public interest. Such evidence may relate to the extent of the ability of the respondent to continue in business and the collectability of a penalty, taking into account any other claims of the United States or third parties upon the assets of the respondent and the amount of the assets of the respondent.

Court Review of Orders

§ 77i [P.L. § 9]. (a) Any person aggrieved by an order of the Commission may obtain a review of such order in the court of appeals of the United States, within any circuit wherein such person resides or has his principal place of business, or in the United States Court of Appeals for the District of Columbia, by filing in such Court, within sixty days after the entry of such order, a written petition praying that the order of the Commission be modified or be set aside in whole or in part. A copy of such petition shall be forthwith transmitted by the clerk of the court to the Commission, and thereupon the Commission shall file in the court the record upon which the order complained of was entered, as provided in section 2112 of title 28. No objection to the order of the Commission shall be considered by the court unless such objection shall have been urged before the Commission. The finding of the Commission as to the facts, if supported by evidence, shall be conclusive. If either party shall apply to the court for leave to adduce additional evidence, and shall show to the satisfaction of the court that such additional evidence is material and that there were reasonable grounds for failure to adduce such evidence in the hearing before the Commission, the court may order such additional evidence to be taken before the Commission and to be adduced upon the hearing in such manner and upon such terms and conditions as to the court may seem proper. The Commission may modify its findings as to the facts, by reason of the additional evidence so taken, and it shall file such modified or new findings, which, if supported by evidence, shall be conclusive, and its recommendation, if any, for the modification or setting aside of the original order. The jurisdiction of the court shall be exclusive and its judgment and decree, affirming, modifying, or setting aside, in whole or in part, any order of the Commission, shall be final, subject to review by the Supreme Court of the United States upon certiorari or certification as provided in section 1254 of title 28.

(b) The commencement of proceedings under subsection (a) of this section shall not, unless specifically ordered by the court, operate as a stay of the Commission's order.

Information Required in Prospectus

§ 77j [P.L. § 10]. (a) Information in registration statement; documents not required

Except to the extent otherwise permitted or required pursuant to this subsection or subsections (c), (d), or (e) of this section—

(1) a prospectus relating to a security other than a security issued by a foreign government or political subdivision thereof, shall contain the information contained in the registration statement, but it need not include the documents referred to in paragraphs (28) to (32), inclusive, of schedule A of section 77aa of this title;

(2) a prospectus relating to a security issued by a foreign government or political subdivision thereof shall contain the information contained in the registration statement, but it need not include the documents referred to in paragraphs (13) and (14) of schedule B of section 77aa of this title;

(3) notwithstanding the provisions of paragraphs (1) and (2) of this subsection when a prospectus is used more than nine months after the effective date of the registration statement, the information contained therein shall be as of a date not more than sixteen months prior to

such use, so far as such information is known to the user of such prospectus or can be furnished by such user without unreasonable effort or expense;

(4)   there may be omitted from any prospectus any of the information required under this subsection which the Commission may by rules or regulations designate as not being necessary or appropriate in the public interest or for the protection of investors.

(b)   Summarizations and omissions allowed by rules and regulations.—In addition to the prospectus permitted or required in subsection (a) of this section, the Commission shall by rules or regulations deemed necessary or appropriate in the public interest or for the protection of investors permit the use of a prospectus for the purposes of subsection (b)(1) of section 77e of this title which omits in part or summarizes information in the prospectus specified in subsection (a) of this section. A prospectus permitted under this subsection shall, except to the extent the Commission by rules or regulations deemed necessary or appropriate in the public interest or for the protection of investors otherwise provides, be filed as part of the registration statement but shall not be deemed a part of such registration statement for the purposes of section 77k of this title. The Commission may at any time issue an order preventing or suspending the use of a prospectus permitted under this subsection, if it has reason to believe that such prospectus has not been filed (if required to be filed as part of the registration statement) or includes any untrue statement of a material fact or omits to state any material fact required to be stated therein or necessary to make the statements therein, in the light of the circumstances under which such prospectus is or is to be used, not misleading. Upon issuance of an order under this subsection, the Commission shall give notice of the issuance of such order and opportunity for hearing by personal service or the sending of confirmed telegraphic notice. The Commission shall vacate or modify the order at any time for good cause or if such prospectus has been filed or amended in accordance with such order.

(c)   Additional information required by rules and regulations.—Any prospectus shall contain such other information as the Commission may by rules or regulations require as being necessary or appropriate in the public interest or for the protection of investors.

(d)   Classification of prospectuses.—In the exercise of its powers under subsections (a), (b), or (c) of this section, the Commission shall have authority to classify prospectuses according to the nature and circumstances of their use or the nature of the security, issue, issuer, or otherwise, and, by rules and regulations and subject to such terms and conditions as it shall specify therein, to prescribe as to each class the form and contents which it may find appropriate and consistent with the public interest and the protection of investors.

(e)   Information in conspicuous part of prospectus.—The statements or information required to be included in a prospectus by or under authority of subsections (a), (b), (c), or (d) of this section, when written, shall be placed in a conspicuous part of the prospectus and, except as otherwise permitted by rules or regulations, in type as large as that used generally in the body of the prospectus.

(f)   Prospectus consisting of radio or television broadcast.—In any case where a prospectus consists of a radio or television broadcast, copies thereof shall be filed with the Commission under such rules and regulations as it shall prescribe. The Commission may by rules and regulations require the filing with it of forms and prospectuses used in connection with the offer or sale of securities registered under this subchapter.

Civil Liabilities on Account of False Registration Statement

§ 77k [P.L. § 11]. (a) Persons possessing cause of action; persons liable.—In case any part of the registration statement, when such part became effective, contained an untrue statement of a material fact or omitted to state a material fact required to be stated therein or necessary to make the statements therein not misleading, any person acquiring such security (unless it is proved that at the time of such acquisition he knew of such untruth or omission) may, either at law or in equity, in any court of competent jurisdiction, sue—

(1)   every person who signed the registration statement;

(2)   every person who was a director of (or person performing similar functions) or partner in the issuer at the time of the filing of the part of the registration statement with respect to which his liability is asserted;

(3)   every person who, with his consent, is named in the registration statement as being or about to become a director, person performing similar functions, or partner;

(4)   every accountant, engineer, or appraiser, or any person whose profession gives authority to a statement made by him, who has with his consent been named as having prepared or certified any part of the registration statement, or as having prepared or certified any report or valuation which is used in connection with the registration statement, with respect to the statement in such registration statement, report, or valuation, which purports to have been prepared or certified by him;

(5)   every underwriter with respect to such security.

If such person acquired the security after the issuer has made generally available to its security holders an earning[s] statement covering a period of at least twelve months beginning after the effective date of the registration statement, then the right of recovery under this subsection shall be conditioned on proof that such person acquired the security relying upon such untrue statement in the registration statement or relying upon the registration statement and not knowing of such omission, but such reliance may be established without proof of the reading of the registration statement by such person.

(b)   Persons exempt from liability upon proof of issues.—Notwithstanding the provisions of subsection (a) of this section no person, other than the issuer, shall be liable as provided therein who shall sustain the burden of proof—

(1)   that before the effective date of the part of the registration statement with respect to which his liability is asserted (A) he had resigned from or had taken such steps as are permitted by law to resign from, or ceased or refused to act in, every office, capacity, or relationship in which he was described in the registration statement as acting or agreeing to act, and (B) he had advised the Commission and the issuer in writing that he had taken such action and that he would not be responsible for such part of the registration statement; or

(2)   that if such part of the registration statement became effective without his knowledge, upon becoming aware of such fact he forthwith acted and advised the Commission, in accordance with paragraph (1) of this subsection, and, in addition, gave reasonable public notice that such part of the registration statement had become effective without his knowledge; or

(3)   that—

(A)   as regards any part of the registration statement not purporting to be made on the authority of an expert, and not purporting to be a copy of or extract from a report or valuation of an expert, and not purporting to be made on the authority of a public official document or statement, he had, after reasonable investigation, reasonable ground to believe and did believe, at the time such part of the registration statement became effective, that the statements therein were true and that there was no omission to state a material fact required to be stated therein or necessary to make the statements therein not misleading; and

(B)   as regards any part of the registration statement purporting to be made upon his authority as an expert or purporting to be a copy of or extract from a report or valuation of himself as an expert,

(i)   he had, after reasonable investigation, reasonable ground to believe and did believe, at the time such part of the registration statement became effective, that the statements therein were true and that there was no omission to state a material fact required to be stated therein or necessary to make the statements therein not misleading, or

(ii)   such part of the registration statement did not fairly represent his statement as an expert or was not a fair copy of or extract from his report or valuation as an expert; and

(C)   as regards any part of the registration statement purporting to be made on the authority of an expert (other than himself) or purporting to be a copy of or extract from a report or valuation of an expert (other than himself), he had no reasonable ground to believe and did not believe, at the time such part of the registration statement became effective, that the statements therein were untrue or that there was an omission to state a material fact required to be stated therein or necessary to make the statements therein not misleading, or that such part of the registration statement did not fairly represent the statement of the expert or was not a fair copy of or extract from the report or valuation of the expert; and

(D)   as regards any part of the registration statement purporting to be a statement made by an official person or purporting to be a copy of or extract from a public official document, he had no reasonable ground to believe and did not believe, at the time such part of the registration statement became effective, that the statements therein were untrue, or that there was an omission to state a material fact required to be stated therein or necessary to make the statements therein not misleading, or that such part of the registration statement did not fairly represent the statement made by the official person or was not a fair copy of or extract from the public official document.

(c)   Standard of reasonableness.—In determining, for the purpose of paragraph (3) of subsection (b) of this section, what constitutes reasonable investigation and reasonable ground for belief, the standard of reasonableness shall be that required of a prudent man in the management of his own property.

(d)   Effective date of registration statement with regard to underwriters.—If any person becomes an underwriter with respect to the security after the part of the registration statement with respect to which his liability is asserted has become effective, then for the purposes of paragraph (3) of subsection (b) of this section such part of the registration statement shall be considered as having become effective with respect to such person as of the time when he became an underwriter.

(e)   Measure of damages; undertaking for payment of costs.—The suit authorized under subsection (a) of this section may be to recover such damages as shall represent the difference between the amount paid for the security (not exceeding the price at which the security was offered to the public) and

(1)   the value thereof as of the time such suit was brought, or

(2)   the price at which such security shall have been disposed of in the market before suit, or

(3)   the price at which such security shall have been disposed of after suit but before judgment if such damages shall be less than the damages representing the difference between the amount paid for the security (not exceeding the price at which the security was offered to the public) and the value thereof as of the time such suit was brought:

Provided, That if the defendant proves that any portion or all of such damages represents other than the depreciation in value of such security resulting from such part of the registration statement, with respect to which his liability is asserted, not being true or omitting to state a material fact required to be stated therein or necessary to make the statements therein not misleading, such portion of or all such damages shall not be recoverable. In no event shall any underwriter (unless such underwriter shall have knowingly received from the issuer for acting as an underwriter some benefit, directly or indirectly, in which all other underwriters similarly situated did not share in proportion to their respective interests in the underwriting) be liable in any suit or as a consequence of suits authorized under subsection (a) of this section for damages in excess of the total price at which the securities underwritten by him and distributed to the public were offered to the public. In any suit under this or any other section of this subchapter the court may, in its discretion, require an undertaking for the payment of the costs of such suit, including reasonable attorney's fees, and if judgment shall be rendered against a party litigant, upon the motion of the other party litigant, such costs may be assessed in favor of such party litigant (whether or not such undertaking has been required) if the court believes the suit or the defense to have been without merit, in an amount sufficient to reimburse him for the reasonable expenses incurred by him, in connection with such suit, such costs to be taxed in the manner usually provided for taxing of costs in the court in which the suit was heard.

(f)   Joint and several liability; liability of outside director.—

(1)   Except as provided in paragraph (2), all or any one or more of the persons specified in subsection (a) of this section shall be jointly and severally liable, and every person who becomes liable to make any payment under this section may recover contribution as in cases of contract from any person who, if sued separately, would have been liable to make the same payment, unless the person who has become liable was, and the other was not, guilty of fraudulent misrepresentation.

(2)(A)   The liability of an outside director under subsection (e) of this section shall be determined in accordance with section 78u–4(f) of this title.

(B)   For purposes of this paragraph, the term "outside director" shall have the meaning given such term by rule or regulation of the Commission.

(g)   Offering price to public as maximum amount recoverable.—In no case shall the amount recoverable under this section exceed the price at which the security was offered to the public.

Civil Liabilities Arising in Connection with Prospectuses and Communications

§ 77l [P.L. § 12]. (a) In general.—Any person who—

(1)   offers or sells a security in violation of section 77e of this title, or

(2)   offers or sells a security (whether or not exempted by the provisions of section 77c of this title, other than paragraphs (2) and (14) of subsection (a) of said section), by the use of any means or instruments of transportation or communication in interstate commerce or of the mails, by means of a prospectus or oral communication, which includes an untrue statement of a material fact or omits to state a material fact necessary in order to make the statements, in the light of the circumstances under which they were made, not misleading (the purchaser not knowing of such untruth or omission), and who shall not sustain the burden of proof that he did not know, and in the exercise of reasonable care could not have known, of such untruth or omission,

shall be liable, subject to subsection (b) of this section, to the person purchasing such security from him, who may sue either at law or in equity in any court of competent jurisdiction, to recover the consideration paid for such security with interest thereon, less the amount of any income received thereon, upon the tender of such security, or for damages if he no longer owns the security.

(b)   Loss causation.—In an action described in subsection (a)(2) of this section, if the person who offered or sold such security proves that any portion or all of the amount recoverable under subsection (a)(2) of this section represents other than the depreciation in value of the subject security resulting from such part of the prospectus or oral communication, with respect to which the liability of that person is asserted, not being true or omitting to state a material fact required to be stated therein or necessary to make the statement not misleading, then such portion or amount, as the case may be, shall not be recoverable.

Limitation of Actions

§ 77m [P.L. § 13]. No action shall be maintained to enforce any liability created under section 77k or 77*l*(a)(2) of this title unless brought within one year after the discovery of the untrue statement or the omission, or after such discovery should have been made by the exercise of reasonable diligence, or, if the action is to enforce a liability created under section 77*l*(a)(1) of this title, unless brought within one year after the violation upon which it is based. In no event shall any such action be brought to enforce a liability created under section 77k or 77*l*(a)(1) of this title more than three years after the security was bona fide offered to the public, or under section 77*l*(a)(2) of this title more than three years after the sale.

Contrary Stipulations Void

§ 77n [P.L. § 14]. Any condition, stipulation, or provision binding any person acquiring any security to waive compliance with any provision of this subchapter or of the rules and regulations of the Commission shall be void.

Liability of Controlling Persons

§ 77o [P.L. § 15]. (a) Controlling persons.—Every person who, by or through stock ownership, agency, or otherwise, or who, pursuant to or in connection with an agreement or understanding with one or more other persons by or through stock ownership, agency, or otherwise, controls any person liable under sections 77k or 77*l* of this title, shall also be liable jointly and severally with and to the same extent as such controlled person to any person to whom such controlled person is liable, unless the controlling person had no knowledge of or reasonable ground to believe in the existence of the facts by reason of which the liability of the controlled person is alleged to exist.

(b) Prosecution of persons who aid and abet violations.—For purposes of any action brought by the Commission under subparagraph (b) or (d) of section 77t of this title, any person that knowingly or recklessly provides substantial assistance to another person in violation of a provision of this subchapter, or of any rule or regulation issued under this subchapter, shall be deemed to be in violation of such provision to the same extent as the person to whom such assistance is provided.

Fraudulent Interstate Transactions

§ 77q [P.L. § 17]. (a) Use of interstate commerce for purpose of fraud or deceit.—It shall be unlawful for any person in the offer or sale of any securities (including security-based swaps) or any security-based swap agreement (as defined in section 78c(a)(78)[1] of this title) by the use of any means or instruments of transportation or communication in interstate commerce or by use of the mails, directly or indirectly—

(1) to employ any device, scheme, or artifice to defraud, or

(2) to obtain money or property by means of any untrue statement of a material fact or any omission to state a material fact necessary in order to make the statements made, in light of the circumstances under which they were made, not misleading; or

(3) to engage in any transaction, practice, or course of business which operates or would operate as a fraud or deceit upon the purchaser.

(b) Use of interstate commerce for purpose of offering for sale.—It shall be unlawful for any person, by the use of any means or instruments of transportation or communication in interstate commerce or by the use of the mails, to publish, give publicity to, or circulate any notice, circular, advertisement, newspaper, article, letter, investment service, or communication which, though not purporting to offer a security for sale, describes such security for a consideration received or to be

---

[1]   See References in Text note below. [Not reproduced here.]

received, directly or indirectly, from an issuer, underwriter, or dealer, without fully disclosing the receipt, whether past or prospective, of such consideration and the amount thereof.

(c) Exemptions of section 77c not applicable to this section.—The exemptions provided in section 77c of this title shall not apply to the provisions of this section.

(d) Authority with respect to security-based swap agreements.—The authority of the Commission under this section with respect to security-based swap agreements (as defined in section 78c(a)(78) of this title) shall be subject to the restrictions and limitations of section 77b–1(b) of this title.

Exemption from State Regulation of Securities Offerings

§ 77r [P.L. § 18]. (a) Scope of exemption

Except as otherwise provided in this section, no law, rule, regulation, or order, or other administrative action of any State or any political subdivision thereof—

(1) requiring, or with respect to, registration or qualification of securities, or registration or qualification of securities transactions, shall directly or indirectly apply to a security that—

(A) is a covered security; or

(B) will be a covered security upon completion of the transaction;

(2) shall directly or indirectly prohibit, limit, or impose any conditions upon the use of—

(A) with respect to a covered security described in subsection (b), any offering document that is prepared by or on behalf of the issuer; or

(B) any proxy statement, report to shareholders, or other disclosure document relating to a covered security or the issuer thereof that is required to be and is filed with the Commission or any national securities organization registered under section 78o–3 of this title, except that this subparagraph does not apply to the laws, rules, regulations, or orders, or other administrative actions of the State of incorporation of the issuer; or

(3) shall directly or indirectly prohibit, limit, or impose conditions, based on the merits of such offering or issuer, upon the offer or sale of any security described in paragraph (1).

(b) Covered securities

For purposes of this section, the following are covered securities:

(1) Exclusive Federal registration of nationally traded securities

A security is a covered security if such security is—

(A) a security designated as qualified for trading in the national market system pursuant to section 78k–1(a)(2) of this title that is listed, or authorized for listing, on a national securities exchange (or tier or segment thereof); or

(B) a security of the same issuer that is equal in seniority or that is a senior security to a security described in subparagraph (A).

(2) Exclusive Federal registration of investment companies

A security is a covered security if such security is a security issued by an investment company that is registered, or that has filed a registration statement, under the Investment Company Act of 1940 [15 U.S.C. 80a–1 et seq.].

(3) Sales to qualified purchasers

A security is a covered security with respect to the offer or sale of the security to qualified purchasers, as defined by the Commission by rule. In prescribing such rule, the Commission may define the term "qualified purchaser" differently with respect to different categories of securities, consistent with the public interest and the protection of investors.

(4) Exemption in connection with certain exempt offerings

A security is a covered security with respect to a transaction that is exempt from registration under this subchapter pursuant to—

(A) paragraph (1) or (3) of section 77d[1] of this title, and the issuer of such security files reports with the Commission pursuant to section 78m or 78o(d) of this title;

(B) section 77d(4)[1] of this title;

(C) section 77d(6)[1] of this title;

(D) a rule or regulation adopted pursuant to section 77c(b)(2) of this title and such security is—

(i) offered or sold on a national securities exchange; or

(ii) offered or sold to a qualified purchaser, as defined by the Commission pursuant to paragraph (3) with respect to that purchase or sale;

(E) section 77c(a) of this title, other than the offer or sale of a security that is exempt from such registration pursuant to paragraph (4), (10), or (11) of such section, except that a municipal security that is exempt from such registration pursuant to paragraph (2) of such section is not a covered security with respect to the offer or sale of such security in the State in which the issuer of such security is located;

(F) Commission rules or regulations issued under section 77d(2)[1] of this title, except that this subparagraph does not prohibit a State from imposing notice filing requirements that are substantially similar to those required by rule or regulation under section 77d(2)[1] of this title that are in effect on September 1, 1996; or

(G) section 77d(a)(7) of this title.

(c) Preservation of authority

(1) Fraud authority

Consistent with this section, the securities commission (or any agency or office performing like functions) of any State shall retain jurisdiction under the laws of such State to investigate and bring enforcement actions, in connection with securities or securities transactions[2]

(A) with respect to—

(i) fraud or deceit; or

(ii) unlawful conduct by a broker, dealer, or funding portal; and

(B) in connection to[3] a transaction described under section 77d(6)[1] of this title, with respect to—

(i) fraud or deceit; or

(ii) unlawful conduct by a broker, dealer, funding portal, or issuer.

(2) Preservation of filing requirements

---

[1] See References in Text note below. [Not reproduced here.]

[2] So in original. The comma after "enforcement actions" probably should be a hyphen and the words "in connection with securities or securities transactions" probably should be part of subpar. (A).

[3] So in original. Probably should be "with".

[1] See References in Text note below. [Not reproduced here.]

(A)   Notice filings permitted

Nothing in this section prohibits the securities commission (or any agency or office performing like functions) of any State from requiring the filing of any document filed with the Commission pursuant to this subchapter, together with annual or periodic reports of the value of securities sold or offered to be sold to persons located in the State (if such sales data is not included in documents filed with the Commission), solely for notice purposes and the assessment of any fee, together with a consent to service of process and any required fee.

(B)   Preservation of fees

(i)   In general

Until otherwise provided by law, rule, regulation, or order, or other administrative action of any State or any political subdivision thereof, adopted after October 11, 1996, filing or registration fees with respect to securities or securities transactions shall continue to be collected in amounts determined pursuant to State law as in effect on the day before October 11, 1996.

(ii)   Schedule

The fees required by this subparagraph shall be paid, and all necessary supporting data on sales or offers for sales required under subparagraph (A), shall be reported on the same schedule as would have been applicable had the issuer not relied on the exemption provided in subsection (a).

(C)   Availability of preemption contingent on payment of fees

(i)   In general

During the period beginning on October 11, 1996, and ending 3 years after October 11, 1996, the securities commission (or any agency or office performing like functions) of any State may require the registration of securities issued by any issuer who refuses to pay the fees required by subparagraph (B).

(ii)   Delays

For purposes of this subparagraph, delays in payment of fees or underpayments of fees that are promptly remedied shall not constitute a refusal to pay fees.

(D)   Fees not permitted on listed securities

Notwithstanding subparagraphs (A), (B), and (C), no filing or fee may be required with respect to any security that is a covered security pursuant to subsection (b)(1), or will be such a covered security upon completion of the transaction, or is a security of the same issuer that is equal in seniority or that is a senior security to a security that is a covered security pursuant to subsection (b)(1).

(F)[4]   Fees not permitted on crowdfunded securities

Notwithstanding subparagraphs (A), (B), and (C), no filing or fee may be required with respect to any security that is a covered security pursuant to subsection (b)(4)(B), or will be such a covered security upon completion of the transaction, except for the securities commission (or any agency or office performing like functions) of the State of the principal place of business of the issuer, or any State in which purchasers of 50 percent or greater of the aggregate amount of the issue are residents, provided that for purposes of this subparagraph, the term "State" includes the District of Columbia and the territories of the United States.

(3)   Enforcement of requirements

---

[4]   So in original. No subpar. (E) has been enacted.

Nothing in this section shall prohibit the securities commission (or any agency or office performing like functions) of any State from suspending the offer or sale of securities within such State as a result of the failure to submit any filing or fee required under law and permitted under this section.

(d)   Definitions

For purposes of this section, the following definitions shall apply:

(1)   Offering document

The term "offering document"—

(A)   has the meaning given the term "prospectus" in section 77b(a)(10) of this title, but without regard to the provisions of subparagraphs (a) and (b) of that section; and

(B)   includes a communication that is not deemed to offer a security pursuant to a rule of the Commission.

(2)   Prepared by or on behalf of the issuer

Not later than 6 months after October 11, 1996, the Commission shall, by rule, define the term "prepared by or on behalf of the issuer" for purposes of this section.

(3)   State

The term "State" has the same meaning as in section 78c of this title.

(4)   Senior security

The term "senior security" means any bond, debenture, note, or similar obligation or instrument constituting a security and evidencing indebtedness, and any stock of a class having priority over any other class as to distribution of assets or payment of dividends.

Special Powers of Commission

§ 77s [P.L. § 19]. (a) Rules and regulations.—The Commission shall have authority from time to time to make, amend, and rescind such rules and regulations as may be necessary to carry out the provisions of this subchapter, including rules and regulations governing registration statements and prospectuses for various classes of securities and issuers, and defining accounting, technical, and trade terms used in this subchapter. Among other things, the Commission shall have authority, for the purposes of this subchapter, to prescribe the form or forms in which required information shall be set forth, the items or details to be shown in the balance sheet and earning statement, and the methods to be followed in the preparation of accounts, in the appraisal or valuation of assets and liabilities, in the determination of depreciation and depletion, in the differentiation of recurring and nonrecurring income, in the differentiation of investment and operating income, and in the preparation, where the Commission deems it necessary or desirable, of consolidated balance sheets or income accounts of any person directly or indirectly controlling or controlled by the issuer, or any person under direct or indirect common control with the issuer. The rules and regulations of the Commission shall be effective upon publication in the manner which the Commission shall prescribe. No provision of this subchapter imposing any liability shall apply to any act done or omitted in good faith in conformity with any rule or regulation of the Commission, notwithstanding that such rule or regulation may, after such act or omission, be amended or rescinded or be determined by judicial or other authority to be invalid for any reason.

(b)   Recognition of accounting standards.—

(1)   In general.—In carrying out its authority under subsection (a) of this section and under section 13(b) of the Securities Exchange Act of 1934 [15 U.S.C. 78m(b)], the Commission may recognize, as "generally accepted" for purposes of the securities laws, any accounting principles established by a standard setting body—

(A) that—

(i) is organized as a private entity;

(ii) has, for administrative and operational purposes, a board of trustees (or equivalent body) serving in the public interest, the majority of whom are not, concurrent with their service on such board, and have not been during the 2-year period preceding such service, associated persons of any registered public accounting firm;

(iii) is funded as provided in section 7219 of this title;

(iv) has adopted procedures to ensure prompt consideration, by majority vote of its members, of changes to accounting principles necessary to reflect emerging accounting issues and changing business practices; and

(v) considers, in adopting accounting principles, the need to keep standards current in order to reflect changes in the business environment, the extent to which international convergence on high quality accounting standards is necessary or appropriate in the public interest and for the protection of investors; and

(B) that the Commission determines has the capacity to assist the Commission in fulfilling the requirements of subsection (a) of this section and section 13(b) of the Securities Exchange Act of 1934 [15 U.S.C. 78m(b)], because, at a minimum, the standard setting body is capable of improving the accuracy and effectiveness of financial reporting and the protection of investors under the securities laws.

(2) Annual report.—A standard setting body described in paragraph (1) shall submit an annual report to the Commission and the public, containing audited financial statements of that standard setting body.

(c) Production of evidence.—For the purpose of all investigations which, in the opinion of the Commission, are necessary and proper for the enforcement of this subchapter, any member of the Commission or any officer or officers designated by it are empowered to administer oaths and affirmations, [subpoena] witnesses, take evidence, and require the production of any books, papers, or other documents which the Commission deems relevant or material to the inquiry. Such attendance of witnesses and the production of such documentary evidence may be required from any place in the United States or any Territory at any designated place of hearing.

(d) Federal and State cooperation.—

(1) The Commission is authorized to cooperate with any association composed of duly constituted representatives of State governments whose primary assignment is the regulation of the securities business within those States, and which, in the judgment of the Commission, could assist in effectuating greater uniformity in Federal-State securities matters. The Commission shall, at its discretion, cooperate, coordinate, and share information with such an association for the purposes of carrying out the policies and projects set forth in paragraphs (2) and (3).

(2) It is the declared policy of this subsection that there should be greater Federal and State cooperation in securities matters, including.—

(A) maximum effectiveness of regulation,

(B) maximum uniformity in Federal and State regulatory standards,

(C) minimum interference with the business of capital formation, and

(D) a substantial reduction in costs and paperwork to diminish the burdens of raising investment capital (particularly by small business) and to diminish the costs of the administration of the Government programs involved.

(3)   The purpose of this subsection is to engender cooperation between the Commission, any such association of State securities officials, and other duly constituted securities associations in the following areas:

(A)   the sharing of information regarding the registration or exemption of securities issues applied for in the various States;

(B)   the development and maintenance of uniform securities forms and procedures; and

(C)   the development of a uniform exemption from registration for small issuers which can be agreed upon among several States or between the States and the Federal Government. The Commission shall have the authority to adopt such an exemption as agreed upon for Federal purposes. Nothing in this chapter shall be construed as authorizing preemption of State law.

(4)   In order to carry out these policies and purposes, the Commission shall conduct an annual conference as well as such other meetings as are deemed necessary, to which representatives from such securities associations, securities self-regulatory organizations, agencies, and private organizations involved in capital formation shall be invited to participate.

(5)   For fiscal year 1982, and for each of the three succeeding fiscal years, there are authorized to be appropriated such amounts as may be necessary and appropriate to carry out the policies, provisions, and purposes of this subsection. Any sums so appropriated shall remain available until expended.

(6)   Notwithstanding any other provision of law, neither the Commission nor any other person shall be required to establish any procedures not specifically required by the securities laws, as that term is defined in section 3(a)(47) of the Securities Exchange Act of 1934 [15 U.S.C. 78c(a)(47)], or by chapter 5 of title 5, in connection with cooperation, coordination, or consultation with—

(A)   any association referred to in paragraph (1) or (3) or any conference or meeting referred to in paragraph (4), while such association, conference, or meeting is carrying out activities in furtherance of the provisions of this subsection; or

(B)   any forum, agency, or organization, or group referred to in section 80c–1 of this title, while such forum, agency, organization, or group is carrying out activities in furtherance of the provisions of such section 80c–1.

As used in this paragraph, the terms "association", "conference", "meeting", "forum", "agency", "organization", and "group" include any committee, subgroup, or representative of such entities.

(e)   Evaluation of rules or programs.—For the purpose of evaluating any rule or program of the Commission issued or carried out under any provision of the securities laws, as defined in section 3 of the Securities Exchange Act of 1934 (15 U.S.C. 78c), and the purposes of considering, proposing, adopting, or engaging in any such rule or program or developing new rules or programs, the Commission may—

(1)   gather information from and communicate with investors or other members of the public;

(2)   engage in such temporary investor testing programs as the Commission determines are in the public interest or would protect investors; and

(3)   consult with academics and consultants, as necessary to carry out this subsection.

(f)   Rule of construction.—For purposes of the Paperwork Reduction Act (44 U.S.C. 3501 et seq.), any action taken under subsection (e) shall not be construed to be a collection of information.

(g)   Funding for the GASB.—

(1) In general.—The Commission may, subject to the limitations imposed by section 15B of the Securities Exchange Act of 1934 (15 U.S.C. 78o–4), require a national securities association registered under the Securities Exchange Act of 1934 [15 U.S.C. 78a et seq.] to establish—

(A) a reasonable annual accounting support fee to adequately fund the annual budget of the Governmental Accounting Standards Board (referred to in this subsection as the "GASB"); and

(B) rules and procedures, in consultation with the principal organizations representing State governors, legislators, local elected officials, and State and local finance officers, to provide for the equitable allocation, assessment, and collection of the accounting support fee established under subparagraph (A) from the members of the association, and the remittance of all such accounting support fees to the Financial Accounting Foundation.

(2) Annual budget.—For purposes of this subsection, the annual budget of the GASB is the annual budget reviewed and approved according to the internal procedures of the Financial Accounting Foundation.

(3) Use of funds.—Any fees or funds collected under this subsection shall be used to support the efforts of the GASB to establish standards of financial accounting and reporting recognized as generally accepted accounting principles applicable to State and local governments of the United States.

(4) Limitation on fee.—The annual accounting support fees collected under this subsection for a fiscal year shall not exceed the recoverable annual budgeted expenses of the GASB (which may include operating expenses, capital, and accrued items).

(5) Rules of construction.—

(A) Fees not public monies.—Accounting support fees collected under this subsection and other receipts of the GASB shall not be considered public monies of the United States.

(B) Limitation on authority of the Commission.—Nothing in this subsection shall be construed to—

(i) provide the Commission or any national securities association direct or indirect oversight of the budget or technical agenda of the GASB; or

(ii) affect the setting of generally accepted accounting principles by the GASB.

(C) Noninterference with States.—Nothing in this subsection shall be construed to impair or limit the authority of a State or local government to establish accounting and financial reporting standards.

Jurisdiction of Offenses and Suits

§ 77v [P.L. § 22]. (a) Federal and State courts; venue; service of process; review; removal; costs.— The district courts of the United States and the United States courts of any Territory shall have jurisdiction of offenses and violations under this subchapter and under the rules and regulations promulgated by the Commission in respect thereto, and, concurrent with State and Territorial courts, except as provided in section 77p of this title with respect to covered class actions, of all suits in equity and actions at law brought to enforce any liability or duty created by this subchapter. Any such suit or action may be brought in the district wherein the defendant is found or is an inhabitant or transacts business, or in the district where the offer or sale took place, if the defendant participated therein, and process in such cases may be served in any other district of which the defendant is an inhabitant or wherever the defendant may be found. In any action or proceeding instituted by the Commission under this subchapter in a United States district court for any judicial district, a subpoena issued to compel the attendance of a witness or the production of documents or tangible things (or both) at a hearing or trial may be served at any place within the United States. Rule 45(c)(3)(A)(ii) of the Federal Rules of Civil Procedure shall not apply to a subpoena issued under the preceding sentence. Judgments and decrees so rendered shall be subject to review as provided in sections 1254, 1291, 1292, and 1294 of title 28. Except as provided in section 77p(c) of this title, no case arising under this subchapter and brought in any State court of competent jurisdiction shall be removed to any court of the United States. No costs shall be assessed for or against the Commission in any proceeding under this subchapter brought by or against it in the Supreme Court or such other courts.

(b)   Contumacy or refusal to obey [subpoena]; contempt.—In case of contumacy or refusal to obey a [subpoena] issued to any person, any of the said United States courts, within the jurisdiction of which said person guilty of contumacy or refusal to obey is found or resides, upon application by the Commission may issue to such person an order requiring such person to appear before the Commission, or one of its examiners designated by it, there to produce documentary evidence if so ordered, or there to give evidence touching the matter in question; and any failure to obey such order of the court may be punished by said court as a contempt thereof.

(c)   Extraterritorial jurisdiction.—The district courts of the United States and the United States courts of any Territory shall have jurisdiction of an action or proceeding brought or instituted by the Commission or the United States alleging a violation of section 77q(a) of this title involving—

(1)   conduct within the United States that constitutes significant steps in furtherance of the violation, even if the securities transaction occurs outside the United States and involves only foreign investors; or

(2)   conduct occurring outside the United States that has a foreseeable substantial effect within the United States.

SCHEDULE OF INFORMATION REQUIRED
IN REGISTRATION STATEMENT

§ 77aa [P.L. Schedule A]

Schedule A

(1)   The name under which the issuer is doing or intends to do business;

(2)   the name of the State or other sovereign power under which the issuer is organized;

(3)   the location of the issuer's principal business office, and if the issuer is a foreign or territorial person, the name and address of its agent in the United States authorized to receive notice;

(4)   the names and addresses of the directors or persons performing similar functions, and the chief executive, financial and accounting officers, chosen or to be chosen if the issuer be a corporation, association, trust, or other entity; of all partners, if the issuer be a partnership; and of the issuer, if the issuer be an individual; and of the promoters in the case of a business to be formed, or formed within two years prior to the filing of the registration statement;

(5)   the names and addresses of the underwriters;

(6)   the names and addresses of all persons, if any, owning of record or beneficially, if known, more than 10 per centum of any class of stock of the issuer, or more than 10 per centum in the aggregate of the outstanding stock of the issuer as of a date within twenty days prior to the filing of the registration statement;

(7)   the amount of securities of the issuer held by any person specified in paragraphs (4), (5), and (6) of this schedule, as of a date within twenty days prior to the filing of the registration statement, and, if possible, as of one year prior thereto, and the amount of the securities, for which the registration statement is filed, to which such persons have indicated their intention to subscribe;

(8)   the general character of the business actually transacted or to be transacted by the issuer;

(9)   a statement of the capitalization of the issuer, including the authorized and outstanding amounts of its capital stock and the proportion thereof paid up, the number and classes of shares in

which such capital stock is divided, par value thereof, or if it has no par value, the stated or assigned value thereof, a description of the respective voting rights, preferences, conversion and exchange rights, rights to dividends, profits, or capital of each class, with respect to each other class, including the retirement and liquidation rights or values thereof;

(10) a statement of the securities, if any, covered by options outstanding or to be created in connection with the security to be offered, together with the names and addresses of all persons, if any, to be allotted more than 10 per centum in the aggregate of such options;

(11) the amount of capital stock of each class issued or included in the shares of stock to be offered;

(12) the amount of the funded debt outstanding and to be created by the security to be offered, with a brief description of the date, maturity, and character of such debt, rate of interest, character of amortization provisions, and the security, if any, therefor. If substitution of any security is permissible, a summarized statement of the conditions under which such substitution is permitted. If substitution is permissible without notice, a specific statement to that effect;

(13) the specific purposes in detail and the approximate amounts to be devoted to such purposes, so far as determinable, for which the security to be offered is to supply funds, and if the funds are to be raised in part from other sources, the amounts thereof and the sources thereof, shall be stated;

(14) the remuneration, paid or estimated to be paid, by the issuer or its predecessor, directly or indirectly, during the past year and ensuing year to (a) the directors or persons performing similar functions, and (b) its officers and other persons, naming them wherever such remuneration exceeded $25,000 during any such year;

(15) the estimated net proceeds to be derived from the security to be offered;

(16) the price at which it is proposed that the security shall be offered to the public or the method by which such price is computed and any variation therefrom at which any portion of such security is proposed to be offered to any persons or classes of persons, other than the underwriters, naming them or specifying the class. A variation in price may be proposed prior to the date of the public offering of the security, but the Commission shall immediately be notified of such variation;

(17) all commissions or discounts paid or to be paid, directly or indirectly, by the issuer to the underwriters in respect of the sale of the security to be offered. Commissions shall include all cash, securities, contracts, or anything else of value, paid, to be set aside, disposed of, or understandings with or for the benefit of any other persons in which any underwriter is interested, made, in connection with the sale of such security. A commission paid or to be paid in connection with the sale of such security by a person in which the issuer has an interest or which is controlled or directed by, or under common control with, the issuer shall be deemed to have been paid by the issuer. Where any such commission is paid the amount of such commission paid to each underwriter shall be stated;

(18) the amount or estimated amounts, itemized in reasonable detail, of expenses, other than commissions specified in paragraph (17) of this schedule, incurred or borne by or for the account of the issuer in connection with the sale of the security to be offered or properly chargeable thereto, including legal, engineering, certification, authentication, and other charges;

(19) the net proceeds derived from any security sold by the issuer during the two years preceding the filing of the registration statement, the price at which such security was offered to the public, and the names of the principal underwriters of such security;

(20) any amount paid within two years preceding the filing of the registration statement or intended to be paid to any promoter and the consideration for any such payment;

(21) the names and addresses of the vendors and the purchase price of any property, or good will, acquired or to be acquired, not in the ordinary course of business, which is to be defrayed in whole or in part from the proceeds of the security to be offered, the amount of any commission payable to any person in connection with such acquisition, and the name or names of such person or persons, together

with any expense incurred or to be incurred in connection with such acquisition, including the cost of borrowing money to finance such acquisition;

(22) full particulars of the nature and extent of the interest, if any, of every director, principal executive officer, and of every stockholder holding more than 10 per centum of any class of stock or more than 10 per centum in the aggregate of the stock of the issuer, in any property acquired, not in the ordinary course of business of the issuer, within two years preceding the filing of the registration statement or proposed to be acquired at such date;

(23) the names and addresses of counsel who have passed on the legality of the issue;

(24) dates of and parties to, and the general effect concisely stated of every material contract made, not in the ordinary course of business, which contract is to be executed in whole or in part at or after the filing of the registration statement or which contract has been made not more than two years before such filing. Any management contract or contract providing for special bonuses or profit-sharing arrangements, and every material patent or contract for a material patent right, and every contract by or with a public utility company or an affiliate thereof, providing for the giving or receiving of technical or financial advice or service (if such contract may involve a charge to any party thereto at a rate in excess of $2,500 per year in cash or securities or anything else of value), shall be deemed a material contract;

(25) a balance sheet as of a date not more than ninety days prior to the date of the filing of the registration statement showing all of the assets of the issuer, the nature and cost thereof, whenever determinable, in such detail and in such form as the Commission shall prescribe (with intangible items segregated), including any loan in excess of $20,000 to any officer, director, stockholder or person directly or indirectly controlling or controlled by the issuer, or person under direct or indirect common control with the issuer. All the liabilities of the issuer in such detail and such form as the Commission shall prescribe, including surplus of the issuer showing how and from what sources such surplus was created, all as of a date not more than ninety days prior to the filing of the registration statement. If such statement be not certified by an independent public or certified accountant, in addition to the balance sheet required to be submitted under this schedule, a similar detailed balance sheet of the assets and liabilities of the issuer, certified by an independent public or certified accountant, of a date not more than one year prior to the filing of the registration statement, shall be submitted;

(26) a profit and loss statement of the issuer showing earnings and income, the nature and source thereof, and the expenses and fixed charges in such detail and such form as the Commission shall prescribe for the latest fiscal year for which such statement is available and for the two preceding fiscal years, year by year, or, if such issuer has been in actual business for less than three years, then for such time as the issuer has been in actual business, year by year. If the date of the filing of the registration statement is more than six months after the close of the last fiscal year, a statement from such closing date to the latest practicable date. Such statement shall show what the practice of the issuer has been during the three years or lesser period as to the character of the charges, dividends or other distributions made against its various surplus accounts, and as to depreciation, depletion, and maintenance charges, in such detail and form as the Commission shall prescribe, and if stock dividends or avails from the sale of rights have been credited to income, they shall be shown separately with a statement of the basis upon which the credit is computed. Such statement shall also differentiate between any recurring and nonrecurring income and between any investment and operating income. Such statement shall be certified by an independent public or certified accountant;

(27) if the proceeds, or any part of the proceeds, of the security to be issued is to be applied directly or indirectly to the purchase of any business, a profit and loss statement of such business certified by an independent public or certified accountant, meeting the requirements of paragraph (26) of this schedule, for the three preceding fiscal years, together with a balance sheet, similarly certified, of such business, meeting the requirements of paragraph (25) of this schedule of a date not more than ninety days prior to the filing of the registration statement or at the date such business was acquired by the issuer if the business was acquired by the issuer more than ninety days prior to the filing of the registration statement;

(28) a copy of any agreement or agreements (or, if identical agreements are used, the forms thereof) made with any underwriter, including all contracts and agreements referred to in paragraph (17) of this schedule;

(29) a copy of the opinion or opinions of counsel in respect to the legality of the issue, with a translation of such opinion, when necessary, into the English language;

(30) a copy of all material contracts referred to in paragraph (24) of this schedule, but no disclosure shall be required of any portion of any such contract if the Commission determines that disclosure of such portion would impair the value of the contract and would not be necessary for the protection of the investors;

(31) unless previously filed and registered under the provisions of this subchapter, and brought up to date, (a) a copy of its articles of incorporation, with all amendments thereof and of its existing bylaws or instruments corresponding thereto, whatever the name, if the issuer be a corporation; (b) copy of all instruments by which the trust is created or declared, if the issuer is a trust; (c) a copy of its articles of partnership or association and all other papers pertaining to its organization, if the issuer is a partnership, unincorporated association, joint-stock company, or any other form of organization; and

(32) a copy of the underlying agreements or indentures affecting any stock, bonds, or debentures offered or to be offered.

In case of certificates of deposit, voting trust certificates, collateral trust certificates, certificates of interest or shares in unincorporated investment trusts, equipment trust certificates, interim or other receipts for certificates, and like securities, the Commission shall establish rules and regulations requiring the submission of information of a like character applicable to such cases, together with such other information as it may deem appropriate and necessary regarding the character, financial or otherwise, of the actual issuer of the securities and/or the person performing the acts and assuming the duties of depositor or manager.

§ 77aa [P.L. Schedule B]

Schedule B

(1)   Name of borrowing government or subdivision thereof;

(2)   specific purposes in detail and the approximate amounts to be devoted to such purposes, so far as determinable, for which the security to be offered is to supply funds, and if the funds are to be raised in part from other sources, the amounts thereof and the sources thereof, shall be stated;

(3)   the amount of the funded debt and the estimated amount of the floating debt outstanding and to be created by the security to be offered, excluding intergovernmental debt, and a brief description of the date, maturity, character of such debt, rate of interest, character of amortization provisions, and the security, if any, therefor. If substitution of any security is permissible, a statement of the conditions under which such substitution is permitted. If substitution is permissible without notice, a specific statement to that effect;

(4)   whether or not the issuer or its predecessor has, within a period of twenty years prior to the filing of the registration statement, defaulted on the principal or interest of any external security, excluding intergovernmental debt, and, if so, the date, amount, and circumstances of such default, and the terms of the succeeding arrangement, if any;

(5)   the receipts, classified by source, and the expenditures, classified by purpose, in such detail and form as the Commission shall prescribe for the latest fiscal year for which such information is available and the two preceding fiscal years, year by year;

(6)   the names and addresses of the underwriters;

(7)   the name and address of its authorized agent, if any, in the United States;

(8)   the estimated net proceeds to be derived from the sale in the United States of the security to be offered;

(9)   the price at which it is proposed that the security shall be offered in the United States to the public or the method by which such price is computed. A variation in price may be proposed prior to the date of the public offering of the security, but the Commission shall immediately be notified of such variation;

(10) all commissions paid or to be paid, directly or indirectly, by the issuer to the underwriters in respect of the sale of the security to be offered. Commissions shall include all cash, securities, contracts, or anything else of value, paid, to be set aside, disposed of, or understandings with or for the benefit of any other persons in which the underwriter is interested, made, in connection with the sale of such security. Where any such commission is paid, the amount of such commission paid to each underwriter shall be stated;

(11) the amount or estimated amounts, itemized in reasonable detail, of expenses, other than the commissions specified in paragraph (10) of this schedule, incurred or borne by or for the account of the issuer in connection with the sale of the security to be offered or properly chargeable thereto, including legal, engineering, certification, and other charges;

(12) the names and addresses of counsel who have passed upon the legality of the issue;

(13) a copy of any agreement or agreements made with any underwriter governing the sale of the security within the United States; and

(14) an agreement of the issuer to furnish a copy of the opinion or opinions of counsel in respect to the legality of the issue, with a translation, where necessary, into the English language. Such opinion shall set out in full all laws, decrees, ordinances, or other acts of Government under which the issue of such security has been authorized.

B. SECURITIES EXCHANGE ACT OF 1934

(Selected Sections)

15 U.S.C. §§ 78a *et seq.*

Table of Contents

TITLE I—REGULATION OF SECURITIES EXCHANGES

78*oo* [P.L. § 38].   Federal National Mortgage Association, Federal Home Loan Mortgage Corporation, Federal Home Loan Banks.

TITLE 1—REGULATION OF SECURITIES EXCHANGES

Short Title

§ 78a [P.L. § 1]. This chapter may be cited as the "Securities Exchange Act of 1934."

Necessity for Regulation

§ 78b [P.L. § 2]. For the reasons hereinafter enumerated, transactions in securities as commonly conducted upon securities exchanges and over-the-counter markets are effected with a national public interest which makes it necessary to provide for regulation and control of such transactions and of practices and matters related thereto, including transactions by officers, directors, and principal security holders, to require appropriate reports, to remove impediments to and perfect the mechanisms of a national market system for securities and a national system for the clearance and settlement of securities transactions and the safeguarding of securities and funds related thereto, and to impose requirements necessary to make such regulation and control reasonably complete and effective, in order to protect interstate commerce, the national credit, the Federal taxing power, to protect and make more effective the national banking system and Federal Reserve System, and to insure the maintenance of fair and honest markets in such transactions:

(1)   Such transactions (a) are carried on in large volume by the public generally and in large part originate outside the States in which the exchanges and over-the-counter markets are located and/or are effected by means of the mails and instrumentalities of interstate commerce; (b) constitute an important part of the current of interstate commerce; (c) involve in large part the securities of issuers engaged in interstate commerce; (d) involve the use of credit, directly affect the financing of trade, industry, and transportation in interstate commerce, and directly affect and influence the volume of interstate commerce; and affect the national credit.

(2)   The prices established and offered in such transactions are generally disseminated and quoted throughout the United States and foreign countries and constitute a basis for determining and establishing the prices at which securities are bought and sold, the amount of certain taxes owing to the United States and to the several States by owners, buyers, and sellers of securities, and the value of collateral for bank loans.

(3)   Frequently the prices of securities on such exchanges and markets are susceptible to manipulation and control, and the dissemination of such prices gives rise to excessive speculation, resulting in sudden and unreasonable fluctuations in the prices of securities which (a) cause alternately unreasonable expansion and unreasonable contraction of the volume of credit available for trade, transportation, and industry in interstate commerce, (b) hinder the proper appraisal of the value of securities and thus prevent a fair calculation of taxes owing to the United States and to the several States by owners, buyers, and sellers of securities, and (c) prevent the fair valuation of collateral for bank loans and/or obstruct the effective operation of the national banking system and Federal Reserve System.

(4)   National emergencies, which produce widespread unemployment and the dislocation of trade, transportation, and industry, and which burden interstate commerce and adversely affect the general welfare, are precipitated, intensified, and prolonged by manipulation and sudden and unreasonable fluctuations of security prices and by excessive speculation on such exchanges and markets, and to meet such emergencies the Federal Government is put to such great expense as to burden the national credit.

Definitions and Application

§ 78c [P.L. § 3]. (a) Definitions.—When used in this chapter, unless the context otherwise requires—

(1)   The term "exchange" means any organization, association, or group of persons, whether incorporated or unincorporated, which constitutes, maintains, or provides a market place or facilities for bringing together purchasers and sellers of securities or for otherwise performing with respect to securities the functions commonly performed by a stock exchange as that term is generally understood, and includes the market place and the market facilities maintained by such exchange.

(2)   The term "facility" when used with respect to an exchange includes its premises, tangible or intangible property whether on the premises or not, any right to the use of such premises or property or any service thereof for the purpose of effecting or reporting a transaction on an exchange (including, among other things, any system of communication to or from the exchange, by ticker or otherwise, maintained by or with the consent of the exchange), and any right of the exchange to the use of any property or service.

(3)(A)   The term "member" when used with respect to a national securities exchange means (i) any natural person permitted to effect transactions on the floor of the exchange without the services of another person acting as broker, (ii) any registered broker or dealer with which such a natural person is associated, (iii) any registered broker or dealer permitted to designate as a representative such a natural person, and (iv) any other registered broker or dealer which agrees to be regulated by such exchange and with respect to which the exchange undertakes to enforce compliance with the provisions of this chapter, the rules and regulations thereunder, and its own rules. For purposes of sections 78f(b)(1), 78f(b)(4), 78f(b)(6), 78f(b)(7), 78f(d), 78q(d), 78s(d), 78s(e), 78s(g), 78s(h), and 78u of this title, the term "member" when used with respect to a national securities exchange also means, to the extent of the rules of the exchange specified by the Commission, any person required by the Commission to comply with such rules pursuant to section 78f(f) of this title.

(B)   The term "member" when used with respect to a registered securities association means any broker or dealer who agrees to be regulated by such association and with respect to whom the association undertakes to enforce compliance with the provisions of this chapter, the rules and regulations thereunder, and its own rules.

(4)   Broker.—

(A)   In general.—The term "broker" means any person engaged in the business of effecting transactions in securities for the account of others.

(B)   Exception for certain bank activities.—A bank shall not be considered to be a broker because the bank engages in any one or more of the following activities under the conditions described:

(i)   Third party brokerage arrangements.—The bank enters into a contractual or other written arrangement with a broker or dealer registered under this chapter under which the broker or dealer offers brokerage services on or off the premises of the bank if—

(I)   such broker or dealer is clearly identified as the person performing the brokerage services;

(II)   the broker or dealer performs brokerage services in an area that is clearly marked and, to the extent practicable, physically separate from the routine deposit-taking activities of the bank;

(III) any materials used by the bank to advertise or promote generally the availability of brokerage services under the arrangement clearly indicate that the brokerage services are being provided by the broker or dealer and not by the bank;

(IV) any materials used by the bank to advertise or promote generally the availability of brokerage services under the arrangement are in compliance with the Federal securities laws before distribution;

(V)   bank employees (other than associated persons of a broker or dealer who are qualified pursuant to the rules of a self-regulatory organization) perform only clerical or ministerial functions in connection with brokerage transactions including scheduling appointments with the associated persons of a broker or dealer, except that bank employees may forward customer funds or securities and may describe in general terms the types of investment vehicles available from the bank and the broker or dealer under the arrangement;

(VI) bank employees do not receive incentive compensation for any brokerage transaction unless such employees are associated persons of a broker or dealer and are qualified pursuant to the rules of a self-regulatory organization, except that the bank employees may receive compensation for the referral of any customer if the compensation is a nominal one-time cash fee of a fixed dollar amount and the payment of the fee is not contingent on whether the referral results in a transaction;

(VII) such services are provided by the broker or dealer on a basis in which all customers that receive any services are fully disclosed to the broker or dealer;

(VIII) the bank does not carry a securities account of the customer except as permitted under clause (ii) or (viii) of this subparagraph; and

(IX) the bank, broker, or dealer informs each customer that the brokerage services are provided by the broker or dealer and not by the bank and that the securities are not deposits or other obligations of the bank, are not guaranteed by the bank, and are not insured by the Federal Deposit Insurance Corporation.

(ii)   Trust activities.—The bank effects transactions in a trustee capacity, or effects transactions in a fiduciary capacity in its trust department or other department that is regularly examined by bank examiners for compliance with fiduciary principles and standards, and—

(I)   is chiefly compensated for such transactions, consistent with fiduciary principles and standards, on the basis of an administration or annual fee (payable on a monthly, quarterly, or other basis), a percentage of assets under management, or a flat or capped per order processing fee equal to not more than the cost incurred by the bank in connection with executing securities transactions for trustee and fiduciary customers, or any combination of such fees; and

(II)   does not publicly solicit brokerage business, other than by advertising that it effects transactions in securities in conjunction with advertising its other trust activities.

(iii)   Permissible securities transactions.—The bank effects transactions in—

(I)   commercial paper, bankers acceptances, or commercial bills;

(II)   exempted securities;

(III) qualified Canadian government obligations as defined in section 24 of title 12, in conformity with section 78o–5 of this title and the rules and regulations thereunder, or obligations of the North American Development Bank; or

(IV) any standardized, credit enhanced debt security issued by a foreign government pursuant to the March 1989 plan of then Secretary of the Treasury Brady, used by such foreign government to retire outstanding commercial bank loans.

(iv) Certain stock purchase plans.—

(I) Employee benefit plans.—The bank effects transactions, as part of its transfer agency activities, in the securities of an issuer as part of any pension, retirement, profit-sharing, bonus, thrift, savings, incentive, or other similar benefit plan for the employees of that issuer or its affiliates (as defined in section 1841 of title 12), if the bank does not solicit transactions or provide investment advice with respect to the purchase or sale of securities in connection with the plan.

(II) Dividend reinvestment plans.—The bank effects transactions, as part of its transfer agency activities, in the securities of an issuer as part of that issuer's dividend reinvestment plan, if—

(aa) the bank does not solicit transactions or provide investment advice with respect to the purchase or sale of securities in connection with the plan; and

(bb) the bank does not net shareholders' buy and sell orders, other than for programs for odd-lot holders or plans registered with the Commission.

(III) Issuer plans.—The bank effects transactions, as part of its transfer agency activities, in the securities of an issuer as part of a plan or program for the purchase or sale of that issuer's shares, if—

(aa) the bank does not solicit transactions or provide investment advice with respect to the purchase or sale of securities in connection with the plan or program; and

(bb) the bank does not net shareholders' buy and sell orders, other than for programs for odd-lot holders or plans registered with the Commission.

(IV) Permissible delivery of materials.—The exception to being considered a broker for a bank engaged in activities described in subclauses (I), (II), and (III) will not be affected by delivery of written or electronic plan materials by a bank to employees of the issuer, shareholders of the issuer, or members of affinity groups of the issuer, so long as such materials are—

(aa) comparable in scope or nature to that permitted by the Commission as of November 12, 1999; or

(bb) otherwise permitted by the Commission.

(v) Sweep accounts.—The bank effects transactions as part of a program for the investment or reinvestment of deposit funds into any no-load, open-end management investment company registered under the Investment Company Act of 1940 [15 U.S.C. 80a–1 et seq.] that holds itself out as a money market fund.

(vi) Affiliate transactions.—The bank effects transactions for the account of any affiliate of the bank (as defined in section 1841 of title 12) other than—

(I) a registered broker or dealer; or

(II) an affiliate that is engaged in merchant banking, as described in section 1843(k)(4)(H) of title 12.

(vii) Private securities offerings.—The bank—

(I)   effects sales as part of a primary offering of securities not involving a public offering, pursuant to section 3(b), 4(2),[1] or 4(5)[1] of the Securities Act of 1933 [15 U.S.C. 77c(b), 77d(a)(2), 77d(a)(5)] or the rules and regulations issued thereunder;

(II)   at any time after the date that is 1 year after November 12, 1999, is not affiliated with a broker or dealer that has been registered for more than 1 year in accordance with this chapter, and engages in dealing, market making, or underwriting activities, other than with respect to exempted securities; and

(III) if the bank is not affiliated with a broker or dealer, does not effect any primary offering described in subclause (I) the aggregate amount of which exceeds 25 percent of the capital of the bank, except that the limitation of this subclause shall not apply with respect to any sale of government securities or municipal securities.

(viii) Safekeeping and custody activities.—

(I)   In general.—The bank, as part of customary banking activities—

(aa) provides safekeeping or custody services with respect to securities, including the exercise of warrants and other rights on behalf of customers;

(bb) facilitates the transfer of funds or securities, as a custodian or a clearing agency, in connection with the clearance and settlement of its customers' transactions in securities;

(cc) effects securities lending or borrowing transactions with or on behalf of customers as part of services provided to customers pursuant to division (aa) or (bb) or invests cash collateral pledged in connection with such transactions;

(dd) holds securities pledged by a customer to another person or securities subject to purchase or resale agreements involving a customer, or facilitates the pledging or transfer of such securities by book entry or as otherwise provided under applicable law, if the bank maintains records separately identifying the securities and the customer; or

(ee) serves as a custodian or provider of other related administrative services to any individual retirement account, pension, retirement, profit sharing, bonus, thrift savings, incentive, or other similar benefit plan.

(II) Exception for carrying broker activities.-The exception to being considered a broker for a bank engaged in activities described in subclause (I) shall not apply if the bank, in connection with such activities, acts in the United States as a carrying broker (as such term, and different formulations thereof, are used in section 78o(c)(3) of this title and the rules and regulations thereunder) for any broker or dealer, unless such carrying broker activities are engaged in with respect to government securities (as defined in paragraph (42) of this subsection).

(ix) Identified banking products.—The bank effects transactions in identified banking products as defined in section 206 of the Gramm-Leach-Bliley Act.

(x)   Municipal securities.—The bank effects transactions in municipal securities.

(xi) De minimis exception.—The bank effects, other than in transactions referred to in clauses (i) through (x), not more than 500 transactions in securities in any calendar

---

[1] See References in Text note below. [Not reproduced here.]

year, and such transactions are not effected by an employee of the bank who is also an employee of a broker or dealer.

(C) Execution by broker or dealer.—The exception to being considered a broker for a bank engaged in activities described in clauses (ii), (iv), and (viii) of subparagraph (B) shall not apply if the activities described in such provisions result in the trade in the United States of any security that is a publicly traded security in the United States, unless—

(i) the bank directs such trade to a registered broker or dealer for execution;

(ii) the trade is a cross trade or other substantially similar trade of a security that—

(I) is made by the bank or between the bank and an affiliated fiduciary; and

(II) is not in contravention of fiduciary principles established under applicable Federal or State law; or

(iii) the trade is conducted in some other manner permitted under rules, regulations, or orders as the Commission may prescribe or issue.

(D) Fiduciary capacity.—For purposes of subparagraph (B)(ii), the term "fiduciary capacity" means—

(i) in the capacity as trustee, executor, administrator, registrar of stocks and bonds, transfer agent, guardian, assignee, receiver, or custodian under a uniform gift to minor act, or as an investment adviser if the bank receives a fee for its investment advice;

(ii) in any capacity in which the bank possesses investment discretion on behalf of another; or

(iii) in any other similar capacity.

(E) Exception for entities subject to section 78o(e).1.—The term "broker" does not include a bank that—

(i) was, on the day before November 12, 1999, subject to section 78o(e) 1 of this title; and

(ii) is subject to such restrictions and requirements as the Commission considers appropriate.

(F) Joint rulemaking required.—The Commission and the Board of Governors of the Federal Reserve System shall jointly adopt a single set of rules or regulations to implement the exceptions in subparagraph (B).

(5) Dealer.—

(A) In general.—The term "dealer" means any person engaged in the business of buying and selling securities (not including security-based swaps, other than security-based swaps with or for persons that are not eligible contract participants) for such person's own account through a broker or otherwise.

(B) Exception for person not engaged in the business of dealing.—The term "dealer" does not include a person that buys or sells securities (not including security-based swaps, other than security-based swaps with or for persons that are not eligible contract participants) for such person's own account, either individually or in a fiduciary capacity, but not as a part of a regular business.

(C) Exception for certain bank activities.—A bank shall not be considered to be a dealer because the bank engages in any of the following activities under the conditions described:

(i) *Permissible securities transactions.*—The bank buys or sells—

(I)   commercial paper, bankers acceptances, or commercial bills;

(II) exempted securities;

(III) qualified Canadian government obligations as defined in section 24 of title 12, in conformity with section 78*o*–5 of this title and the rules and regulations thereunder, or obligations of the North American Development Bank; or

(IV) any standardized, credit enhanced debt security issued by a foreign government pursuant to the March 1989 plan of then Secretary of the Treasury Brady, used by such foreign government to retire outstanding commercial bank loans.

(ii) *Investment, trustee, and fiduciary transactions.*—The bank buys or sells securities for investment purposes—

(I)   for the bank; or

(II) for accounts for which the bank acts as a trustee or fiduciary.

(iii) *Asset-backed transactions.*—The bank engages in the issuance or sale to qualified investors, through a grantor trust or other separate entity, of securities backed by or representing an interest in notes, drafts, acceptances, loans, leases, receivables, other obligations (other than securities of which the bank is not the issuer), or pools of any such obligations predominantly originated by—

(I)   the bank;

(II) an affiliate of any such bank other than a broker or dealer; or

(III) a syndicate of banks of which the bank is a member, if the obligations or pool of obligations consists of mortgage obligations or consumer-related receivables.

(iv) *Identified banking products.*—The bank buys or sells identified banking products, as defined in section 206 of the Gramm-Leach-Bliley Act.

(6)   The term "bank" means (A) a banking institution organized under the laws of the United States or a Federal savings association, as defined in section 1462(5) 1 of title 12, (B) a member bank of the Federal Reserve System, (C) any other banking institution or savings association, as defined in section 1462(4) 1 of title 12, whether incorporated or not, doing business under the laws of any State or of the United States, a substantial portion of the business of which consists of receiving deposits or exercising fiduciary powers similar to those permitted to national banks under the authority of the Comptroller of the Currency pursuant to section 92a of title 12, and which is supervised and examined by State or Federal authority having supervision over banks or savings associations, and which is not operated for the purpose of evading the provisions of this chapter, and (D) a receiver, conservator, or other liquidating agent of any institution or firm included in clauses (A), (B), or (C) of this paragraph.

(7)   The term "director" means any director of a corporation or any person performing similar functions with respect to any organization, whether incorporated or unincorporated.

(8)   The term "issuer" means any person who issues or proposes to issue any security; except that with respect to certificates of deposit for securities, voting-trust certificates, or collateral-trust certificates, or with respect to certificates of interest or shares in an unincorporated investment trust not having a board of directors or of the fixed, restricted management, or unit type, the term "issuer" means the person or persons performing the acts and assuming the duties of depositor or manager pursuant to the provisions of the trust or other agreement or instrument under which such securities are issued; and except that with respect to equipment-trust

certificates or like securities, the term "issuer" means the person by whom the equipment or property is, or is to be, used.

(9) The term "person" means a natural person, company, government, or political subdivision, agency, or instrumentality of a government.

(10) The term "security" means any note, stock, treasury stock, security future, security-based swap, bond, debenture, certificate of interest or participation in any profit-sharing agreement or in any oil, gas, or other mineral royalty or lease, any collateral-trust certificate, preorganization certificate or subscription, transferable share, investment contract, voting-trust certificate, certificate of deposit for a security, any put, call, straddle, option, or privilege on any security, certificate of deposit, or group or index of securities (including any interest therein or based on the value thereof), or any put, call, straddle, option, or privilege entered into on a national securities exchange relating to foreign currency, or in general, any instrument commonly known as a "security"; or any certificate of interest or participation in, temporary or interim certificate for, receipt for, or warrant or right to subscribe to or purchase, any of the foregoing; but shall not include currency or any note, draft, bill of exchange, or banker's acceptance which has a maturity at the time of issuance of not exceeding nine months, exclusive of days of grace, or any renewal thereof the maturity of which is likewise limited.

(11) The term "equity security" means any stock or similar security; or any security future on any such security; or any security convertible, with or without consideration, into such a security, or carrying any warrant or right to subscribe to or purchase such a security; or any such warrant or right; or any other security which the Commission shall deem to be of similar nature and consider necessary or appropriate, by such rules and regulations as it may prescribe in the public interest or for the protection of investors, to treat as an equity security.

(12)(A) The term "exempted security" or "exempted securities" includes—

    (i)   government securities, as defined in paragraph (42) of this subsection;

    (ii)   municipal securities, as defined in paragraph (29) of this subsection;

    (iii)   any interest or participation in any common trust fund or similar fund that is excluded from the definition of the term "investment company" under section 3(c)(3) of the Investment Company Act of 1940 [15 U.S.C. 80a–3(c)(3)];

    (iv)   any interest or participation in a single trust fund, or a collective trust fund maintained by a bank, or any security arising out of a contract issued by an insurance company, which interest, participation, or security is issued in connection with a qualified plan as defined in subparagraph (C) of this paragraph;

    (v)   any security issued by or any interest or participation in any pooled income fund, collective trust fund, collective investment fund, or similar fund that is excluded from the definition of an investment company under section 3(c)(10)(B) of the Investment Company Act of 1940 [15 U.S.C. 80a–3(c)(10)(B)];

    (vi)   solely for purposes of sections 78*l*, 78m, 78n, and 78p of this title, any security issued by or any interest or participation in any church plan, company, or account that is excluded from the definition of an investment company under section 3(c)(14) of the Investment Company Act of 1940 [15 U.S.C. 80a–3(c)(14)]; and

    (vii)   such other securities (which may include, among others, unregistered securities, the market in which is predominantly intrastate) as the Commission may, by such rules and regulations as it deems consistent with the public interest and the protection of investors, either unconditionally or upon specified terms and conditions or for stated periods, exempt from the operation of any one or more provisions of this chapter which by their terms do not apply to an "exempted security" or to "exempted securities".

(B)(i) Notwithstanding subparagraph (A)(i) of this paragraph, government securities shall not be deemed to be "exempted securities" for the purposes of section 78q–1 of this title.

(ii) Notwithstanding subparagraph (A)(ii) of this paragraph, municipal securities shall not be deemed to be "exempted securities" for the purposes of sections 78o and 78q–1 of this title.

(C) For purposes of subparagraph (A)(iv) of this paragraph, the term "qualified plan" means (i) a stock bonus, pension, or profit-sharing plan which meets the requirements for qualification under section 401 of title 26, (ii) an annuity plan which meets the requirements for the deduction of the employer's contribution under section 404(a)(2) of title 26, (iii) a governmental plan as defined in section 414(d) of title 26 which has been established by an employer for the exclusive benefit of its employees or their beneficiaries for the purpose of distributing to such employees or their beneficiaries the corpus and income of the funds accumulated under such plan, if under such plan it is impossible, prior to the satisfaction of all liabilities with respect to such employees and their beneficiaries, for any part of the corpus or income to be used for, or diverted to, purposes other than the exclusive benefit of such employees or their beneficiaries, or (iv) a church plan, company, or account that is excluded from the definition of an investment company under section 3(c)(14) of the Investment Company Act of 1940 [15 U.S.C. 80a–3(c)(14)], other than any plan described in clause (i), (ii), or (iii) of this subparagraph which (I) covers employees some or all of whom are employees within the meaning of section 401(c) of title 26, or (II) is a plan funded by an annuity contract described in section 403(b) of title 26.

(13) The terms "buy" and "purchase" each include any contract to buy, purchase, or otherwise acquire. For security futures products, such term includes any contract, agreement, or transaction for future delivery. For security-based swaps, such terms include the execution, termination (prior to its scheduled maturity date), assignment, exchange, or similar transfer or conveyance of, or extinguishing of rights or obligations under, a security-based swap, as the context may require.

(14) The terms "sale" and "sell" each include any contract to sell or otherwise dispose of. For security futures products, such term includes any contract, agreement, or transaction for future delivery. For security-based swaps, such terms include the execution, termination (prior to its scheduled maturity date), assignment, exchange, or similar transfer or conveyance of, or extinguishing of rights or obligations under, a security-based swap, as the context may require.

(15) The term "Commission" means the Securities and Exchange Commission established by section 78d of this title.

(16) The term "State" means any State of the United States, the District of Columbia, Puerto Rico, the Virgin Islands, or any other possession of the United States.

(17) The term "interstate commerce" means trade, commerce, transportation, or communication among the several States, or between any foreign country and any State, or between any State and any place or ship outside thereof. The term also includes intrastate use of (A) any facility of a national securities exchange or of a telephone or other interstate means of communication, or (B) any other interstate instrumentality.

(18) The term "person associated with a broker or dealer" or "associated person of a broker or dealer" means any partner, officer, director, or branch manager of such broker or dealer (or any person occupying a similar status or performing similar functions), any person directly or indirectly controlling, controlled by, or under common control with such broker or dealer, or any employee of such broker or dealer, except that any person associated with a broker or dealer whose functions are solely clerical or ministerial shall not be included in the meaning of such term for purposes of section 78o(b) of this title (other than paragraph (6) thereof).

(19) The terms "investment company", "affiliated person", "insurance company", "separate account", and "company" have the same meanings as in the Investment Company Act of 1940.

(20) The terms "investment adviser" and "underwriter" have the same meanings as in the Investment Advisers Act of 1940.

* * *

(26) The term "self-regulatory organization" means any national securities exchange, registered securities association, or registered clearing agency, or (solely for purposes of sections 78s(b), 78s(c), and 78w(b) of this title) the Municipal Securities Rulemaking Board established by section 78o–4 of this title.

* * *

(38) The term "market maker" means any specialist permitted to act as a dealer, any dealer acting in the capacity of block positioner, and any dealer who, with respect to a security, holds himself out (by entering quotations in an inter-dealer communications system or otherwise) as being willing to buy and sell such security for his own account on a regular or continuous basis.

(39) A person is subject to a "statutory disqualification" with respect to membership or participation in, or association with a member of, a self-regulatory organization, if such person—

(A) has been and is expelled or suspended from membership or participation in, or barred or suspended from being associated with a member of, any self-regulatory organization, foreign equivalent of a self-regulatory organization, foreign or international securities exchange, contract market designated pursuant to section 5 of the Commodity Exchange Act (7 U.S.C. 7), or any substantially equivalent foreign statute or regulation, or futures association registered under section 17 of such Act (7 U.S.C. 21), or any substantially equivalent foreign statute or regulation, or has been and is denied trading privileges on any such contract market or foreign equivalent;

(B) is subject to—

(i) an order of the Commission, other appropriate regulatory agency, or foreign financial regulatory authority—

(I) denying, suspending for a period not exceeding 12 months, or revoking his registration as a broker, dealer, municipal securities dealer, government securities broker, government securities dealer, security-based swap dealer, or major security-based swap participant or limiting his activities as a foreign person performing a function substantially equivalent to any of the above; or

(II) barring or suspending for a period not exceeding 12 months his being associated with a broker, dealer, municipal securities dealer, government securities broker, government securities dealer, security-based swap dealer, major security-based swap participant, or foreign person performing a function substantially equivalent to any of the above;

(ii) an order of the Commodity Futures Trading Commission denying, suspending, or revoking his registration under the Commodity Exchange Act (7 U.S.C. 1 et seq.); or

(iii) an order by a foreign financial regulatory authority denying, suspending, or revoking the person's authority to engage in transactions in contracts of sale of a commodity for future delivery or other instruments traded on or subject to the rules of a contract market, board of trade, or foreign equivalent thereof;

(C) by his conduct while associated with a broker, dealer, municipal securities dealer, government securities broker, government securities dealer, security-based swap dealer, or major security-based swap participant, or while associated with an entity or person required to be registered under the Commodity Exchange Act, has been found to be a cause of any effective suspension, expulsion, or order of the character described in subparagraph (A) or (B) of this paragraph, and in entering such a suspension, expulsion, or order, the Commission, an appropriate regulatory agency, or any such self-regulatory organization shall have jurisdiction to find whether or not any person was a cause thereof;

(D)   by his conduct while associated with any broker, dealer, municipal securities dealer, government securities broker, government securities dealer, security-based swap dealer, major security-based swap participant, or any other entity engaged in transactions in securities, or while associated with an entity engaged in transactions in contracts of sale of a commodity for future delivery or other instruments traded on or subject to the rules of a contract market, board of trade, or foreign equivalent thereof, has been found to be a cause of any effective suspension, expulsion, or order by a foreign or international securities exchange or foreign financial regulatory authority empowered by a foreign government to administer or enforce its laws relating to financial transactions as described in subparagraph (A) or (B) of this paragraph;

(E)   has associated with him any person who is known, or in the exercise of reasonable care should be known, to him to be a person described by subparagraph (A), (B), (C), or (D) of this paragraph; or

(F)   has committed or omitted any act, or is subject to an order or finding, enumerated in subparagraph (D), (E), (H), or (G) of paragraph (4) of section 78o(b) of this title, has been convicted of any offense specified in subparagraph (B) of such paragraph (4) or any other felony within ten years of the date of the filing of an application for membership or participation in, or to become associated with a member of, such self-regulatory organization, is enjoined from any action, conduct, or practice specified in subparagraph (C) of such paragraph (4), has willfully made or caused to be made in any application for membership or participation in, or to become associated with a member of, a self-regulatory organization, report required to be filed with a self-regulatory organization, or proceeding before a self-regulatory organization, any statement which was at the time, and in the light of the circumstances under which it was made, false or misleading with respect to any material fact, or has omitted to state in any such application, report, or proceeding any material fact which is required to be stated therein.

* * *

(50) The term "foreign securities authority" means any foreign government, or any governmental body or regulatory organization empowered by a foreign government to administer or enforce its laws as they relate to securities matters.

* * *

(58) Audit committee.—The term "audit committee" means—

(A)   a committee (or equivalent body) established by and amongst the board of directors of an issuer for the purpose of overseeing the accounting and financial reporting processes of the issuer and audits of the financial statements of the issuer; and

(B)   if no such committee exists with respect to an issuer, the entire board of directors of the issuer.

(59) Registered public accounting firm.—The term "registered public accounting firm" has the same meaning as in section 2 of the Sarbanes-Oxley Act of 2002 [15 U.S.C. 7201].

* * *

Securities and Exchange Commission

§ 78d [P.L. § 4]. (a) Establishment; composition; limitations on commissioners; terms of office.—There is hereby established a Securities and Exchange Commission (hereinafter referred to as the "Commission") to be composed of five commissioners to be appointed by the President by and with the advice and consent of the Senate. Not more than three of such commissioners shall be members of the same political party, and in making appointments members of different political parties shall be appointed alternately as nearly as may be practicable. No commissioner shall engage in any other business, vocation, or employment than that of serving as commissioner, nor shall any commissioner participate, directly or indirectly, in any stock-market operations or transactions of a character subject to regulation by the Commission pursuant to this chapter. Each commissioner shall hold office for a term of five years and until his successor is appointed and has qualified, except that he shall not so continue to serve beyond the expiration of the next session of Congress subsequent to the expiration of said fixed term of office, and except (1) any commissioner appointed to fill a vacancy occurring prior to the expiration of the term for which his predecessor was appointed shall be appointed for the remainder of such term, and (2) the terms of office of the commissioners first taking office after June 6, 1934, shall expire as designated by the President at the time of nomination, one at the end of one year, one at the end of two years, one at the end of three years, one at the end of four years, and one at the end of five years, after June 6, 1934.

* * *

Delegation of Functions by Commission

§ 78d–1 [P.L. § 4A]. (a) Authorization; functions delegable; eligible persons; application of other laws.—In addition to its existing authority, the Securities and Exchange Commission shall have the authority to delegate, by published order or rule, any of its functions to a division of the Commission, an individual Commissioner, an administrative law judge, or an employee or employee board, including functions with respect to hearing, determining, ordering, certifying, reporting, or otherwise acting as to any work, business, or matter. Nothing in this section shall be deemed to supersede the provisions of section 556(b) of title 5, or to authorize the delegation of the function of rulemaking as defined in subchapter II of chapter 5 of title 5, with reference to general rules as distinguished from rules of particular applicability, or of the making of any rule pursuant to section 78s(c) of this title.

(b) Right of review; procedure.—With respect to the delegation of any of its functions, as provided in subsection (a) of this section, the Commission shall retain a discretionary right to review the action of any such division of the Commission, individual Commissioner, administrative law judge, employee, or employee board, upon its own initiative or upon petition of a party to or intervenor in such action, within such time and in such manner as the Commission by rule shall prescribe. The vote of one member of the Commission shall be sufficient to bring any such action before the Commission for review. A person or party shall be entitled to review by the Commission if he or it is adversely affected by action at a delegated level which (1) denies any request for action pursuant to section 77h(a) or section 77h(c) of this title or the first sentence of section 78l(d) of this title; (2) suspends trading in a security pursuant to section 78l(k) of this title; or (3) is pursuant to any provision of this chapter in a case of adjudication, as defined in section 551 of title 5, not required by this chapter to be determined on the record after notice and opportunity for hearing (except to the extent there is involved a matter described in section 554(a)(1) through (6) of such title 5).

(c) Finality of delegated action.—If the right to exercise such review is declined, or if no such review is sought within the time stated in the rules promulgated by the Commission, then the action of any such division of the Commission, individual Commissioner, administrative law judge, employee, or employee board, shall, for all purposes, including appeal or review thereof, be deemed the action of the Commission.

Transfer of Functions with Respect to Assignment of Personnel to Chairman

§ 78d–2 [P.L. § 4B]. In addition to the functions transferred by the provisions of Reorganization Plan Numbered 10 of 1950 (64 Stat. 1265), there are hereby transferred from the Commission to the Chairman of the Commission the functions of the Commission with respect to the assignment of Commission personnel, including Commissioners, to perform such functions as may have been delegated by the Commission to the Commission personnel, including Commissioners, pursuant to section 78d–1 of this title.

Appearance and Practice Before the Commission

§ 78d–3 [P.L. § 4C]. (a) Authority to censure.—The Commission may censure any person, or deny, temporarily or permanently, to any person the privilege of appearing or practicing before the Commission in any way, if that person is found by the Commission, after notice and opportunity for hearing in the matter—

(1)   not to possess the requisite qualifications to represent others;

(2)   to be lacking in character or integrity, or to have engaged in unethical or improper professional conduct; or

(3)   to have willfully violated, or willfully aided and abetted the violation of, any provision of the securities laws or the rules and regulations issued thereunder.

(b)   Definition.—With respect to any registered public accounting firm or associated person, for purposes of this section, the term "improper professional conduct" means—

(1)   intentional or knowing conduct, including reckless conduct, that results in a violation of applicable professional standards; and

(2)   negligent conduct in the form of—

(A)   a single instance of highly unreasonable conduct that results in a violation of applicable professional standards in circumstances in which the registered public accounting firm or associated person knows, or should know, that heightened scrutiny is warranted; or

(B)   repeated instances of unreasonable conduct, each resulting in a violation of applicable professional standards, that indicate a lack of competence to practice before the Commission.

Transactions on Unregistered Exchanges

§ 78e [P.L. § 5]. It shall be unlawful for any broker, dealer, or exchange, directly or indirectly, to make use of the mails or any means or instrumentality of interstate commerce for the purpose of using any facility of an exchange within or subject to the jurisdiction of the United States to effect any transaction in a security, or to report any such transaction, unless such exchange (1) is registered as national securities exchange under section 78f of this title, or (2) is exempted from such registration upon application by the exchange because, in the opinion of the Commission, by reason of the limited volume of transactions effected on such exchange, it is not practicable and not necessary or appropriate in the public interest or for the protection of investors to require such registration.

National Securities Exchanges

§ 78f [P.L. § 6]. (a) Registration; application.—An exchange may be registered as a national securities exchange under the terms and conditions hereinafter provided in this section and in accordance with the provisions of section 78s(a) of this title, by filing with the Commission an application for registration in such form as the Commission, by rule, may prescribe containing the rules of the exchange and such other information and documents as the Commission, by rule, may prescribe as necessary or appropriate in the public interest or for the protection of investors.

(b)   Determination by Commission requisite to registration of applicant as a national securities exchange.—An exchange shall not be registered as a national securities exchange unless the Commission determines that—

(1)   Such exchange is so organized and has the capacity to be able to carry out the purposes of this chapter and to comply, and (subject to any rule or order of the Commission pursuant to section 78q(d) or 78s(g)(2) of this title) to enforce compliance by its members and persons associated with its members, with the provisions of this chapter, the rules and regulations thereunder, and the rules of the exchange.

(2)   Subject to the provisions of subsection (c) of this section, the rules of the exchange provide that any registered broker or dealer or natural person associated with a registered broker or dealer may become a member of such exchange and any person may become associated with a member thereof.

(3)   The rules of the exchange assure a fair representation of its members in the selection of its directors and administration of its affairs and provide that one or more directors shall be representative of issuers and investors and not be associated with a member of the exchange, broker, or dealer.

(4)   The rules of the exchange provide for the equitable allocation of reasonable dues, fees, and other charges among its members and issuers and other persons using its facilities.

(5)   The rules of the exchange are designed to prevent fraudulent and manipulative acts and practices, to promote just and equitable principles of trade, to foster cooperation and coordination with persons engaged in regulating, clearing, settling, processing information with respect to, and facilitating transactions in securities, to remove impediments to and perfect the mechanism of a free and open market and a national market system, and, in general, to protect investors and the public interest; and are not designed to permit unfair discrimination between customers, issuers, brokers, or dealers, or to regulate by virtue of any authority conferred by this chapter matters not related to the purposes of this chapter or the administration of the exchange.

(6)   The rules of the exchange provide that (subject to any rule or order of the Commission pursuant to section 78q(d) or 78s(g)(2) of this title) its members and persons associated with its members shall be appropriately disciplined for violation of the provisions of this chapter, the rules or regulations thereunder, or the rules of the exchange, by expulsion, suspension, limitation of activities, functions, and operations, fine, censure, being suspended or barred from being associated with a member, or any other fitting sanction.

(7)   The rules of the exchange are in accordance with the provisions of subsection (d) of this section, and in general, provide a fair procedure for the disciplining of members and persons associated with members, the denial of membership to any person seeking membership therein, the barring of any person from becoming associated with a member thereof, and the prohibition or limitation by the exchange of any person with respect to access to services offered by the exchange or a member thereof.

(8)   The rules of the exchange do not impose any burden on competition not necessary or appropriate in furtherance of the purposes of this chapter.

(9)(A) The rules of the exchange prohibit the listing of any security issued in a limited partnership rollup transaction (as such term is defined in paragraphs (4) and (5) of section 78n(h) of this title), unless such transaction was conducted in accordance with procedures designed to protect the rights of limited partners, including—

(i)   the right of dissenting limited partners to one of the following:

(I)   an appraisal and compensation;

(II) retention of a security under substantially the same terms and conditions as the original issue;

(III) approval of the limited partnership rollup transaction by not less than 75 percent of the outstanding securities of each of the participating limited partnerships;

(IV) the use of a committee of limited partners that is independent, as determined in accordance with rules prescribed by the exchange, of the general partner or sponsor, that has been approved by a majority of the outstanding units of each of the participating limited partnerships, and that has such authority as is necessary to protect the interest of limited partners, including the authority to hire independent advisors, to negotiate with the general partner or sponsor on behalf of the limited partners, and to make a recommendation to the limited partners with respect to the proposed transaction; or

(V) other comparable rights that are prescribed by rule by the exchange and that are designed to protect dissenting limited partners;

(ii) the right not to have their voting power unfairly reduced or abridged;

(iii) the right not to bear an unfair portion of the costs of a proposed limited partnership rollup transaction that is rejected; and

(iv) restrictions on the conversion of contingent interests or fees into non-contingent interests or fees and restrictions on the receipt of a non-contingent equity interest in exchange for fees for services which have not yet been provided.

(B) As used in this paragraph, the term "dissenting limited partner" means a person who, on the date on which soliciting material is mailed to investors, is a holder of a beneficial interest in a limited partnership that is the subject of a limited partnership rollup transaction, and who casts a vote against the transaction and complies with procedures established by the exchange, except that for purposes of an exchange or tender offer, such person shall file an objection in writing under the rules of the exchange during the period during which the offer is outstanding.

(10)(A) The rules of the exchange prohibit any member that is not the beneficial owner of a security registered under section 78*l* of this title from granting a proxy to vote the security in connection with a shareholder vote described in subparagraph (B), unless the beneficial owner of the security has instructed the member to vote the proxy in accordance with the voting instructions of the beneficial owner.

(B) A shareholder vote described in this subparagraph is a shareholder vote with respect to the election of a member of the board of directors of an issuer, executive compensation, or any other significant matter, as determined by the Commission, by rule, and does not include a vote with respect to the uncontested election of a member of the board of directors of any investment company registered under the Investment Company Act of 1940 [15 U.S.C. 80a–1 et seq.].

(C) Nothing in this paragraph shall be construed to prohibit a national securities exchange from prohibiting a member that is not the beneficial owner of a security registered under section 78*l* of this title from granting a proxy to vote the security in connection with a shareholder vote not described in subparagraph (A).

(c) Denial of membership in national exchanges; denial of association with member; conditions; limitation of membership.—

(1) A national securities exchange shall deny membership to (A) any person, other than a natural person, which is not a registered broker or dealer or (B) any natural person who is not, or is not associated with, a registered broker or dealer.

(2) A national securities exchange may, and in cases in which the Commission, by order, directs as necessary or appropriate in the public interest or for the protection of investors shall,

deny membership to any registered broker or dealer or natural person associated with a registered broker or dealer, and bar from becoming associated with a member any person, who is subject to a statutory disqualification. A national securities exchange shall file notice with the Commission not less than thirty days prior to admitting any person to membership or permitting any person to become associated with a member, if the exchange knew, or in the exercise of reasonable care should have known, that such person was subject to a statutory disqualification. The notice shall be in such form and contain such information as the Commission, by rule, may prescribe as necessary or appropriate in the public interest or for the protection of investors.

* * *

(d) Discipline of national securities exchange members and persons associated with members; summary proceedings.—(1) In any proceeding by a national securities exchange to determine whether a member or person associated with a member should be disciplined (other than a summary proceeding pursuant to paragraph (3) of this subsection), the exchange shall bring specific charges, notify such member or person of, and give him an opportunity to defend against, such charges, and keep a record. . . .

* * *

(e) Commissions, allowances, discounts, and other fees.—(1) On and after June 4, 1975, no national securities exchange may impose any schedule or fix rates of commissions, allowances, discounts, or other fees to be charged by its members. . . .

* * *

(f) Compliance of non-members with exchange rules.—The Commission, by rule or order, as it deems necessary or appropriate in the public interest and for the protection of investors, to maintain fair and orderly markets, or to assure equal regulation, may require—

(1) any person not a member or a designated representative of a member of a national securities exchange effecting transactions on such exchange without the services of another person acting as a broker, or

(2) any broker or dealer not a member of a national securities exchange effecting transactions on such exchange on a regular basis,

to comply with such rules of such exchange as the Commission may specify.

(g) Notice registration of security futures product exchanges.

(1) Registration required.—An exchange that lists or trades security futures products may register as a national securities exchange solely for the purposes of trading security futures products if—

(A) the exchange is a board of trade, as that term is defined by the Commodity Exchange Act (7 U.S.C. 1a(2)) [7 U.S.C. 1 et seq.], that has been designated a contract market by the Commodity Futures Trading Commission and such designation is not suspended by order of the Commodity Futures Trading Commission; and

(B) such exchange does not serve as a market place for transactions in securities other than—

(i) security futures products; or

(ii) futures on exempted securities or groups or indexes of securities or options thereon that have been authorized under section 2(a)(1)(C) of the Commodity Exchange Act [7 U.S.C. 2(a)(1)(C)].

(2) Registration by notice filing.

(A) Form and content.—An exchange required to register only because such exchange lists or trades security futures products may register for purposes of this section by filing with the Commission a written notice in such form as the Commission, by rule, may prescribe containing the rules of the exchange and such other information and documents concerning such exchange, comparable to the information and documents required for national securities exchanges under subsection (a) of this section, as the Commission, by rule, may prescribe as necessary or appropriate in the public interest or for the protection of investors. If such exchange has filed documents with the Commodity Futures Trading Commission, to the extent that such documents contain information satisfying the Commission's informational requirements, copies of such documents may be filed with the Commission in lieu of the required written notice.

(B)   Immediate effectiveness.—Such registration shall be effective contemporaneously with the submission of notice, in written or electronic form, to the Commission, except that such registration shall not be effective if such registration would be subject to suspension or revocation.

(C)   Termination.—Such registration shall be terminated immediately if any of the conditions for registration set forth in this subsection are no longer satisfied.

(3)   Public availability.—The Commission shall promptly publish in the Federal Register an acknowledgment of receipt of all notices the Commission receives under this subsection and shall make all such notices available to the public.

(4)   Exemption of exchanges from specified provisions.

(A)   Transaction exemptions.—An exchange that is registered under paragraph (1) of this subsection shall be exempt from, and shall not be required to enforce compliance by its members with, and its members shall not, solely with respect to those transactions effected on such exchange in security futures products, be required to comply with, the following provisions of this chapter and the rules thereunder:

(i)   Subsections (b)(2), (b)(3), (b)(4), (b)(7), (b)(9), (c), (d), and (e) of this section.

(ii)   Section 78h of this title.

(iii)   Section 78k of this title.

(iv)   Subsections (d), (f), and (k)[1] of section 78q of this title.

(v)   Subsections (a), (f), and (h) of section 78s of this title.

(B)   Rule change exemptions.—An exchange that registered under paragraph (1) of this subsection shall also be exempt from submitting proposed rule changes pursuant to section 78s(b) of this title, except that—

(i)   such exchange shall file proposed rule changes related to higher margin levels, fraud or manipulation, recordkeeping, reporting, listing standards, or decimal pricing for security futures products, sales practices for security futures products for persons who effect transactions in security futures products, or rules effectuating such exchange's obligation to enforce the securities laws pursuant to section 78s(b)(7) of this title;

(ii)   such exchange shall file pursuant to sections 78s(b)(1) and 78s(b)(2) of this title proposed rule changes related to margin, except for changes resulting in higher margin levels; and

(iii)   such exchange shall file pursuant to section 78s(b)(1) of this title proposed rule changes that have been abrogated by the Commission pursuant to section 78s(b)(7)(C) of this title.

---

[1]   See References in Text note below. [Not reproduced here.]

(5) Trading in security futures products.

(A) In general.—Subject to subparagraph (B), it shall be unlawful for any person to execute or trade a security futures product until the later of.—

(i) 1 year after December 21, 2000; or

(ii) such date that a futures association registered under section 17 of the Commodity Exchange Act [7 U.S.C. 21] has met the requirements set forth in section 78o–3(k)(2) of this title.

(B) Principal-to-principal transactions.—Notwithstanding subparagraph (A), a person may execute or trade a security futures product transaction if—

(i) the transaction is entered into—

(I) on a principal-to-principal basis between parties trading for their own accounts or as described in section 1a(18)(B)(ii) of the Commodity Exchange Act [7 U.S.C. 1a(18)(B)(ii)]; and

(II) only between eligible contract participants (as defined in subparagraphs (A), (B)(ii), and (C) of such section 1a(18) [7 U.S.C. 1a(18)(A), (B)(ii), (C)]) at the time at which the persons enter into the agreement, contract, or transaction; and

(ii) the transaction is entered into on or after the later of—

(I) 8 months after December 21, 2000; or

(II) such date that a futures association registered under section 17 of the Commodity Exchange Act [7 U.S.C. 21] has met the requirements set forth in section 78o–3(k)(2) of this title.

* * *

Manipulation of Security Prices

§ 78i [P.L. § 9]. (a) Transactions relating to purchase or sale of security.—It shall be unlawful for any person, directly or indirectly, by the use of the mails or any means or instrumentality of interstate commerce, or of any facility of any national securities exchange, or for any member of a national securities exchange—

(1) For the purpose of creating a false or misleading appearance of active trading in any security other than a government security, or a false or misleading appearance with respect to the market for any such security, (A) to effect any transaction in such security which involves no change in the beneficial ownership thereof, or (B) to enter an order or orders for the purchase of such security with the knowledge that an order or orders of substantially the same size, at substantially the same time, and at substantially the same price, for the sale of any such security, has been or will be entered by or for the same or different parties, or (C) to enter any order or orders for the sale of any such security with the knowledge that an order or orders of substantially the same size, at substantially the same time, and at substantially the same price, for the purchase of such security, has been or will be entered by or for the same or different parties.

(2) To effect, alone or with 1 or more other persons, a series of transactions in any security registered on a national securities exchange, any security not so registered, or in connection with any security-based swap or security-based swap agreement with respect to such security creating actual or apparent active trading in such security, or raising or depressing the price of such security, for the purpose of inducing the purchase or sale of such security by others.

(3) If a dealer, broker, security-based swap dealer, major security-based swap participant, or other person selling or offering for sale or purchasing or offering to purchase the security, a security-based swap, or a security-based swap agreement with respect to such security, to induce the purchase or sale of any security registered on a national securities exchange, any security not

so registered, any security-based swap, or any security-based swap agreement with respect to such security by the circulation or dissemination in the ordinary course of business of information to the effect that the price of any such security will or is likely to rise or fall because of market operations of any 1 or more persons conducted for the purpose of raising or depressing the price of such security.

(4)   If a dealer, broker, security-based swap dealer, major security-based swap participant, or other person selling or offering for sale or purchasing or offering to purchase the security, a security-based swap, or security-based swap agreement with respect to such security, to make, regarding any security registered on a national securities exchange, any security not so registered, any security-based swap, or any security-based swap agreement with respect to such security, for the purpose of inducing the purchase or sale of such security, such security-based swap, or such security-based swap agreement any statement which was at the time and in the light of the circumstances under which it was made, false or misleading with respect to any material fact, and which that person knew or had reasonable ground to believe was so false or misleading.

(5)   For a consideration, received directly or indirectly from a broker, dealer, security-based swap dealer, major security-based swap participant, or other person selling or offering for sale or purchasing or offering to purchase the security, a security-based swap, or security-based swap agreement with respect to such security, to induce the purchase of any security registered on a national securities exchange, any security not so registered, any security-based swap, or any security-based swap agreement with respect to such security by the circulation or dissemination of information to the effect that the price of any such security will or is likely to rise or fall because of the market operations of any 1 or more persons conducted for the purpose of raising or depressing the price of such security.

(6)   To effect either alone or with one or more other persons any series of transactions for the purchase and/or sale of any security other than a government security for the purpose of pegging, fixing, or stabilizing the price of such security in contravention of such rules and regulations as the Commission may prescribe as necessary or appropriate in the public interest or for the protection of investors.

(b)   Transactions relating to puts, calls, straddles, options, futures, or security-based swaps.—
It shall be unlawful for any person to effect, in contravention of such rules and regulations as the Commission may prescribe as necessary or appropriate in the public interest or for the protection of investors—

(1)   any transaction in connection with any security whereby any party to such transaction acquires—

(A)   any put, call, straddle, or other option or privilege of buying the security from or selling the security to another without being bound to do so;

(B)   any security futures product on the security; or

(C)   any security-based swap involving the security or the issuer of the security;

(2)   any transaction in connection with any security with relation to which such person has, directly or indirectly, any interest in any—

(A)   such put, call, straddle, option, or privilege;

(B)   such security futures product; or

(C)   such security-based swap; or

(3)   any transaction in any security for the account of any person who such person has reason to believe has, and who actually has, directly or indirectly, any interest in any—

(A)   such put, call, straddle, option, or privilege;

    (B)   such security futures product with relation to such security; or

    (C)   any security-based swap involving such security or the issuer of such security.

    (c)   Endorsement or guarantee of puts, calls, straddles, or options.—It shall be unlawful for any broker, dealer, or member of a national securities exchange directly or indirectly to endorse or guarantee the performance of any put, call, straddle, option, or privilege in relation to any security other than a government security, in contravention of such rules and regulations as the Commission may prescribe as necessary or appropriate in the public interest or for the protection of investors.

    (d)   Transactions relating to short sales of securities.—It shall be unlawful for any person, directly or indirectly, by the use of the mails or any means or instrumentality of interstate commerce, or of any facility of any national securities exchange, or for any member of a national securities exchange to effect, alone or with one or more other persons, a manipulative short sale of any security. The Commission shall issue such other rules as are necessary or appropriate to ensure that the appropriate enforcement options and remedies are available for violations of this subsection in the public interest or for the protection of investors.

    (e)   Registered warrant, right, or convertible security not included in "put", "call", "straddle", or "option".—The terms "put", "call", "straddle", "option", or "privilege" as used in this section shall not include any registered warrant, right, or convertible security.

    (f)   Persons liable; suits at law or in equity.—Any person who willfully participates in any act or transaction in violation of subsections (a), (b), or (c) of this section, shall be liable to any person who shall purchase or sell any security at a price which was affected by such act or transaction, and the person so injured may sue in law or in equity in any court of competent jurisdiction to recover the damages sustained as a result of any such act or transaction. In any such suit the court may, in its discretion, require an undertaking for the payment of the costs of such suit, and assess reasonable costs, including reasonable attorneys' fees, against either party litigant. Every person who becomes liable to make any payment under this subsection may recover contribution as in cases of contract from any person who, if joined in the original suit, would have been liable to make the same payment. No action shall be maintained to enforce any liability created under this section, unless brought within one year after the discovery of the facts constituting the violation and within three years after such violation.

    (g)   Subsection (a) not applicable to exempted securities.—The provisions of subsection (a) of this section shall not apply to an exempted security.

    (h)   Foreign currencies and security futures products.

    (1)   Notwithstanding any other provision of law, the Commission shall have the authority to regulate the trading of any put, call, straddle, option, or privilege on any security, certificate of deposit, or group or index of securities (including any interest therein or based on the value thereof), or any put, call, straddle, option, or privilege entered into on a national securities exchange relating to foreign currency (but not, with respect to any of the foregoing, an option on a contract for future delivery other than a security futures product).

    (2)   Notwithstanding the Commodity Exchange Act [7 U.S.C. 1 et seq.], the Commission shall have the authority to regulate the trading of any security futures product to the extent provided in the securities laws.

    (i)   Limitations on practices that affect market volatility.—It shall be unlawful for any person, by the use of the mails or any means or instrumentality of interstate commerce or of any facility of any national securities exchange, to use or employ any act or practice in connection with the purchase or sale of any equity security in contravention of such rules or regulations as the Commission may adopt, consistent with the public interest, the protection of investors, and the maintenance of fair and orderly markets—

(1) to prescribe means reasonably designed to prevent manipulation of price levels of the equity securities market or a substantial segment thereof; and

(2) to prohibit or constrain, during periods of extraordinary market volatility, any trading practice in connection with the purchase or sale of equity securities that the Commission determines (A) has previously contributed significantly to extraordinary levels of volatility that have threatened the maintenance of fair and orderly markets; and (B) is reasonably certain to engender such levels of volatility if not prohibited or constrained.

In adopting rules under paragraph (2), the Commission shall, consistent with the purposes of this subsection, minimize the impact on the normal operations of the market and a natural person's freedom to buy or sell any equity security.

* * *

Manipulative and Deceptive Devices

§ 78j [P.L. § 10]. It shall be unlawful for any person, directly or indirectly, by the use of any means or instrumentality of interstate commerce or of the mails, or of any facility of any national securities exchange—

(a)(1) To effect a short sale, or to use or employ any stop-loss order in connection with the purchase or sale, of any security other than a government security, in contravention of such rules and regulations as the Commission may prescribe as necessary or appropriate in the public interest or for the protection of investors.

(2) Paragraph (1) of this subsection shall not apply to security futures products.

(b) To use or employ, in connection with the purchase or sale of any security registered on a national securities exchange or any security not so registered, or any securities-based swap agreement[1] any manipulative or deceptive device or contrivance in contravention of such rules and regulations as the Commission may prescribe as necessary or appropriate in the public interest or for the protection of investors.

* * *

Audit Requirements

§ 78j–1 [P.L. § 10A]. (a) In general.—Each audit required pursuant to this chapter of the financial statements of an issuer by a registered public accounting firm shall include, in accordance with generally accepted auditing standards, as may be modified or supplemented from time to time by the Commission—

(1) procedures designed to provide reasonable assurance of detecting illegal acts that would have a direct and material effect on the determination of financial statement amounts;

(2) procedures designed to identify related party transactions that are material to the financial statements or otherwise require disclosure therein; and

(3) an evaluation of whether there is substantial doubt about the ability of the issuer to continue as a going concern during the ensuing fiscal year.

(b) Required response to audit discoveries.

(1) Investigation and report to management.—If, in the course of conducting an audit pursuant to this chapter to which subsection (a) of this section applies, the registered public accounting firm detects or otherwise becomes aware of information indicating that an illegal act (whether or not perceived to have a material effect on the financial statements of the issuer) has

---

[1] So in original. Probably should be followed by a comma.

or may have occurred, the firm shall, in accordance with generally accepted auditing standards, as may be modified or supplemented from time to time by the Commission—

(A)(i)   determine whether it is likely that an illegal act has occurred; and

(ii)   if so, determine and consider the possible effect of the illegal act on the financial statements of the issuer, including any contingent monetary effects, such as fines, penalties, and damages; and

(B)   as soon as practicable, inform the appropriate level of the management of the issuer and assure that the audit committee of the issuer, or the board of directors of the issuer in the absence of such a committee, is adequately informed with respect to illegal acts that have been detected or have otherwise come to the attention of such firm in the course of the audit, unless the illegal act is clearly inconsequential.

(2)   Response to failure to take remedial action.—If, after determining that the audit committee of the board of directors of the issuer, or the board of directors of the issuer in the absence of an audit committee, is adequately informed with respect to illegal acts that have been detected or have otherwise come to the attention of the firm in the course of the audit of such firm, the registered public accounting firm concludes that—

(A)   the illegal act has a material effect on the financial statements of the issuer;

(B)   the senior management has not taken, and the board of directors has not caused senior management to take, timely and appropriate remedial actions with respect to the illegal act; and

(C)   the failure to take remedial action is reasonably expected to warrant departure from a standard report of the auditor, when made, or warrant resignation from the audit engagement;

the registered public accounting firm shall, as soon as practicable, directly report its conclusions to the board of directors.

(3)   Notice to Commission; response to failure to notify.—An issuer whose board of directors receives a report under paragraph (2) shall inform the Commission by notice not later than 1 business day after the receipt of such report and shall furnish the registered public accounting firm making such report with a copy of the notice furnished to the Commission. If the registered public accounting firm fails to receive a copy of the notice before the expiration of the required 1-business-day period, the registered public accounting firm shall—

(A)   resign from the engagement; or

(B)   furnish to the Commission a copy of its report (or the documentation of any oral report given) not later than 1 business day following such failure to receive notice.

(4)   Report after resignation.—If a registered public accounting firm resigns from an engagement under paragraph (3)(A), the firm shall, not later than 1 business day following the failure by the issuer to notify the Commission under paragraph (3), furnish to the Commission a copy of the report of the firm (or the documentation of any oral report given).

(c)   Auditor liability limitation.—No registered public accounting firm shall be liable in a private action for any finding, conclusion, or statement expressed in a report made pursuant to paragraph (3) or (4) of subsection (b) of this section, including any rule promulgated pursuant thereto.

(d)   Civil penalties in cease-and-desist proceedings.—If the Commission finds, after notice and opportunity for hearing in a proceeding instituted pursuant to section 78u–3 of this title, that a registered public accounting firm has willfully violated paragraph (3) or (4) of subsection (b) of this section, the Commission may, in addition to entering an order under section 78u–3 of this title, impose a civil penalty against the registered public accounting firm and any other person that the Commission finds was a cause of such violation. The determination to impose a civil penalty and the amount of the penalty shall be governed by the standards set forth in section 78u–2 of this title.

(e) Preservation of existing authority.—Except as provided in subsection (d) of this section, nothing in this section shall be held to limit or otherwise affect the authority of the Commission under this chapter.

(f) Definitions.—As used in this section, the term "illegal act" means an act or omission that violates any law, or any rule or regulation having the force of law. As used in this section, the term "issuer" means an issuer (as defined in section 78c of this title), the securities of which are registered under section 78l of this title, or that is required to file reports pursuant to section 78o(d) of this title, or that files or has filed a registration statement that has not yet become effective under the Securities Act of 1933 (15 U.S.C. 77a et seq.), and that it has not withdrawn.

(g) Prohibited activities.—Except as provided in subsection (h) of this section, it shall be unlawful for a registered public accounting firm (and any associated person of that firm, to the extent determined appropriate by the Commission) that performs for any issuer any audit required by this chapter or the rules of the Commission under this chapter or, beginning 180 days after the date of commencement of the operations of the Public Company Accounting Oversight Board established under section 7211 of this title (in this section referred to as the "Board"), the rules of the Board, to provide to that issuer, contemporaneously with the audit, any non-audit service, including—

(1) bookkeeping or other services related to the accounting records or financial statements of the audit client;

(2) financial information systems design and implementation;

(3) appraisal or valuation services, fairness opinions, or contribution-in-kind reports;

(4) actuarial services;

(5) internal audit outsourcing services;

(6) management functions or human resources;

(7) broker or dealer, investment adviser, or investment banking services;

(8) legal services and expert services unrelated to the audit; and

(9) any other service that the Board determines, by regulation, is impermissible.

(h) Preapproval required for non-audit services.—A registered public accounting firm may engage in any non-audit service, including tax services, that is not described in any of paragraphs (1) through (9) of subsection (g) of this section for an audit client, only if the activity is approved in advance by the audit committee of the issuer, in accordance with subsection (i) of this section.

(i) Preapproval requirements.

(1) In general.—(A) Audit committee action.—All auditing services (which may entail providing comfort letters in connection with securities underwritings or statutory audits required for insurance companies for purposes of State law) and non-audit services, other than as provided in subparagraph (B), provided to an issuer by the auditor of the issuer shall be preapproved by the audit committee of the issuer.

(B) De minimis exception.—The preapproval requirement under subparagraph (A) is waived with respect to the provision of non-audit services for an issuer, if—

(i) the aggregate amount of all such non-audit services provided to the issuer constitutes not more than 5 percent of the total amount of revenues paid by the issuer to its auditor during the fiscal year in which the non-audit services are provided;

(ii) such services were not recognized by the issuer at the time of the engagement to be non-audit services; and

(iii) such services are promptly brought to the attention of the audit committee of the issuer and approved prior to the completion of the audit by the audit committee or by 1 or more members of the audit committee who are members of the board of directors to whom authority to grant such approvals has been delegated by the audit committee.

(2) Disclosure to investors.—Approval by an audit committee of an issuer under this subsection of a non-audit service to be performed by the auditor of the issuer shall be disclosed to investors in periodic reports required by section 78m(a) of this title.

(3) Delegation authority.—The audit committee of an issuer may delegate to 1 or more designated members of the audit committee who are independent directors of the board of directors, the authority to grant preapprovals required by this subsection. The decisions of any member to whom authority is delegated under this paragraph to preapprove an activity under this subsection shall be presented to the full audit committee at each of its scheduled meetings.

(4) Approval of audit services for other purposes.—In carrying out its duties under subsection (m)(2) of this section, if the audit committee of an issuer approves an audit service within the scope of the engagement of the auditor, such audit service shall be deemed to have been preapproved for purposes of this subsection.

(j) Audit partner rotation.—It shall be unlawful for a registered public accounting firm to provide audit services to an issuer if the lead (or coordinating) audit partner (having primary responsibility for the audit), or the audit partner responsible for reviewing the audit, has performed audit services for that issuer in each of the 5 previous fiscal years of that issuer.

(k) Reports to audit committees.—Each registered public accounting firm that performs for any issuer any audit required by this chapter shall timely report to the audit committee of the issuer—

(1) all critical accounting policies and practices to be used;

(2) all alternative treatments of financial information within generally accepted accounting principles that have been discussed with management officials of the issuer, ramifications of the use of such alternative disclosures and treatments, and the treatment preferred by the registered public accounting firm; and

(3) other material written communications between the registered public accounting firm and the management of the issuer, such as any management letter or schedule of unadjusted differences.

(l) Conflicts of interest.—It shall be unlawful for a registered public accounting firm to perform for an issuer any audit service required by this chapter, if a chief executive officer, controller, chief financial officer, chief accounting officer, or any person serving in an equivalent position for the issuer, was employed by that registered independent public accounting firm and participated in any capacity in the audit of that issuer during the 1-year period preceding the date of the initiation of the audit.

(m) Standards relating to audit committees.

(1) Commission rules.—(A) In general.—Effective not later than 270 days after July 30, 2002, the Commission shall, by rule, direct the national securities exchanges and national securities associations to prohibit the listing of any security of an issuer that is not in compliance with the requirements of any portion of paragraphs (2) through (6).

(B) Opportunity to cure defects.—The rules of the Commission under subparagraph (A) shall provide for appropriate procedures for an issuer to have an opportunity to cure any defects that would be the basis for a prohibition under subparagraph (A), before the imposition of such prohibition.

(2) Responsibilities relating to registered public accounting firms.—The audit committee of each issuer, in its capacity as a committee of the board of directors, shall be directly responsible for the appointment, compensation, and oversight of the work of any registered public accounting firm employed by that issuer (including resolution of disagreements between management and the auditor regarding financial reporting) for the purpose of preparing or issuing an audit report

or related work, and each such registered public accounting firm shall report directly to the audit committee.

(3) Independence.—(A) In general.—Each member of the audit committee of the issuer shall be a member of the board of directors of the issuer, and shall otherwise be independent.

(B) Criteria.—In order to be considered to be independent for purposes of this paragraph, a member of an audit committee of an issuer may not, other than in his or her capacity as a member of the audit committee, the board of directors, or any other board committee—

(i)   accept any consulting, advisory, or other compensatory fee from the issuer; or

(ii) be an affiliated person of the issuer or any subsidiary thereof.

(C) Exemption authority.—The Commission may exempt from the requirements of subparagraph (B) a particular relationship with respect to audit committee members, as the Commission determines appropriate in light of the circumstances.

(4) Complaints.—Each audit committee shall establish procedures for—

(A) the receipt, retention, and treatment of complaints received by the issuer regarding accounting, internal accounting controls, or auditing matters; and

(B) the confidential, anonymous submission by employees of the issuer of concerns regarding questionable accounting or auditing matters.

(5) Authority to engage advisers.—Each audit committee shall have the authority to engage independent counsel and other advisers, as it determines necessary to carry out its duties.

(6) Funding.—Each issuer shall provide for appropriate funding, as determined by the audit committee, in its capacity as a committee of the board of directors, for payment of compensation—

(A) to the registered public accounting firm employed by the issuer for the purpose of rendering or issuing an audit report; and

(B) to any advisers employed by the audit committee under paragraph (5).

Compensation Committees

§ 78j–3 [P.L. § 10C]. (a) Independence of compensation committees.

(1) Listing standards.—The Commission shall, by rule, direct the national securities exchanges and national securities associations to prohibit the listing of any equity security of an issuer, other than an issuer that is a controlled company, limited partnership, company in bankruptcy proceedings, open-ended management investment company that is registered under the Investment Company Act of 1940 [15 U.S.C. 80a–1 et seq.], or a foreign private issuer that provides annual disclosures to shareholders of the reasons that the foreign private issuer does not have an independent compensation committee, that does not comply with the requirements of this subsection.

(2) Independence of compensation committees.—The rules of the Commission under paragraph (1) shall require that each member of the compensation committee of the board of directors of an issuer be—

(A) a member of the board of directors of the issuer; and

(B) independent.

(3) Independence.—The rules of the Commission under paragraph (1) shall require that, in determining the definition of the term "independence" for purposes of paragraph (2), the

national securities exchanges and the national securities associations shall consider relevant factors, including—

(A) the source of compensation of a member of the board of directors of an issuer, including any consulting, advisory, or other compensatory fee paid by the issuer to such member of the board of directors; and

(B) whether a member of the board of directors of an issuer is affiliated with the issuer, a subsidiary of the issuer, or an affiliate of a subsidiary of the issuer.

(4) Exemption authority.—The rules of the Commission under paragraph (1) shall permit a national securities exchange or a national securities association to exempt a particular relationship from the requirements of paragraph (2), with respect to the members of a compensation committee, as the national securities exchange or national securities association determines is appropriate, taking into consideration the size of an issuer and any other relevant factors.

(b) Independence of compensation consultants and other compensation committee advisers.

(1) In general.—The compensation committee of an issuer may only select a compensation consultant, legal counsel, or other adviser to the compensation committee after taking into consideration the factors identified by the Commission under paragraph (2).

(2) Rules.—The Commission shall identify factors that affect the independence of a compensation consultant, legal counsel, or other adviser to a compensation committee of an issuer. Such factors shall be competitively neutral among categories of consultants, legal counsel, or other advisers and preserve the ability of compensation committees to retain the services of members of any such category, and shall include—

(A) the provision of other services to the issuer by the person that employs the compensation consultant, legal counsel, or other adviser;

(B) the amount of fees received from the issuer by the person that employs the compensation consultant, legal counsel, or other adviser, as a percentage of the total revenue of the person that employs the compensation consultant, legal counsel, or other adviser;

(C) the policies and procedures of the person that employs the compensation consultant, legal counsel, or other adviser that are designed to prevent conflicts of interest;

(D) any business or personal relationship of the compensation consultant, legal counsel, or other adviser with a member of the compensation committee; and

(E) any stock of the issuer owned by the compensation consultant, legal counsel, or other adviser.

(c) Compensation committee authority relating to compensation consultants.

(1) Authority to retain compensation consultant.—(A) In general.—The compensation committee of an issuer, in its capacity as a committee of the board of directors, may, in its sole discretion, retain or obtain the advice of a compensation consultant.

(B) Direct responsibility of compensation committee.—The compensation committee of an issuer shall be directly responsible for the appointment, compensation, and oversight of the work of a compensation consultant.

(C) Rule of construction.—This paragraph may not be construed—

(i) to require the compensation committee to implement or act consistently with the advice or recommendations of the compensation consultant; or

(ii) to affect the ability or obligation of a compensation committee to exercise its own judgment in fulfillment of the duties of the compensation committee.

(2)   Disclosure.—In any proxy or consent solicitation material for an annual meeting of the shareholders (or a special meeting in lieu of the annual meeting) occurring on or after the date that is 1 year after July 21, 2010, each issuer shall disclose in the proxy or consent material, in accordance with regulations of the Commission, whether—

(A)   the compensation committee of the issuer retained or obtained the advice of a compensation consultant; and

(B)   the work of the compensation consultant has raised any conflict of interest and, if so, the nature of the conflict and how the conflict is being addressed.

(d)   Authority to engage independent legal counsel and other advisers.—(1) In general.—The compensation committee of an issuer, in its capacity as a committee of the board of directors, may, in its sole discretion, retain and obtain the advice of independent legal counsel and other advisers.

(2)   Direct responsibility of compensation committee.—The compensation committee of an issuer shall be directly responsible for the appointment, compensation, and oversight of the work of independent legal counsel and other advisers.

(3)   Rule of construction.—This subsection may not be construed—

(A)   to require a compensation committee to implement or act consistently with the advice or recommendations of independent legal counsel or other advisers under this subsection; or

(B)   to affect the ability or obligation of a compensation committee to exercise its own judgment in fulfillment of the duties of the compensation committee.

(e)   Compensation of compensation consultants, independent legal counsel, and other advisers.—Each issuer shall provide for appropriate funding, as determined by the compensation committee in its capacity as a committee of the board of directors, for payment of reasonable compensation—

(1)   to a compensation consultant; and

(2)   to independent legal counsel or any other adviser to the compensation committee.

(f)   Commission rules.—(1) In general.—Not later than 360 days after July 21, 2010, the Commission shall, by rule, direct the national securities exchanges and national securities associations to prohibit the listing of any security of an issuer that is not in compliance with the requirements of this section.

(2)   Opportunity to cure defects.—The rules of the Commission under paragraph (1) shall provide for appropriate procedures for an issuer to have a reasonable opportunity to cure any defects that would be the basis for the prohibition under paragraph (1), before the imposition of such prohibition.

(3)   Exemption authority.—(A) In general.—The rules of the Commission under paragraph (1) shall permit a national securities exchange or a national securities association to exempt a category of issuers from the requirements under this section, as the national securities exchange or the national securities association determines is appropriate.

(B)   Considerations.—In determining appropriate exemptions under subparagraph (A), the national securities exchange or the national securities association shall take into account the potential impact of the requirements of this section on smaller reporting issuers.

(g)   Controlled company exemption.—(1) In general.—This section shall not apply to any controlled company.

(2)   Definition.—For purposes of this section, the term "controlled company" means an issuer—

(A) that is listed on a national securities exchange or by a national securities association; and

(B) that holds an election for the board of directors of the issuer in which more than 50 percent of the voting power is held by an individual, a group, or another issuer.

Recovery of Erroneously Awarded Compensation Policy

§ 78j–4 [P.L. § 10D]. (a) Listing standards.—The Commission shall, by rule, direct the national securities exchanges and national securities associations to prohibit the listing of any security of an issuer that does not comply with the requirements of this section.

(b) Recovery of funds.—The rules of the Commission under subsection (a) shall require each issuer to develop and implement a policy providing—

(1) for disclosure of the policy of the issuer on incentive-based compensation that is based on financial information required to be reported under the securities laws; and

(2) that, in the event that the issuer is required to prepare an accounting restatement due to the material noncompliance of the issuer with any financial reporting requirement under the securities laws, the issuer will recover from any current or former executive officer of the issuer who received incentive-based compensation (including stock options awarded as compensation) during the 3-year period preceding the date on which the issuer is required to prepare an accounting restatement, based on the erroneous data, in[1] excess of what would have been paid to the executive officer under the accounting restatement.

Registration Requirements for Securities

§ 78l [P.L. § 12]. (a) General requirement of registration.—It shall be unlawful for any member, broker, or dealer to effect any transaction in any security (other than an exempted security) on a national securities exchange unless a registration is effective as to such security for such exchange in accordance with the provisions of this chapter and the rules and regulations thereunder. The provisions of this subsection shall not apply in respect of a security futures product traded on a national securities exchange.

(b) Procedure for registration; information.—A security may be registered on a national securities exchange by the issuer filing an application with the exchange (and filing with the Commission such duplicate originals thereof as the Commission may require), which application shall contain—

(1) Such information, in such detail, as to the issuer and any person directly or indirectly controlling or controlled by, or under direct or indirect common control with, the issuer, and any guarantor of the security as to principal or interest or both, as the Commission may by rules and regulations require, as necessary or appropriate in the public interest or for the protection of investors, in respect of the following:

(A) the organization, financial structure, and nature of the business;

(B) the terms, position, rights, and privileges of the different classes of securities outstanding;

(C) the terms on which their securities are to be, and during the preceding three years have been, offered to the public or otherwise;

(D) the directors, officers, and underwriters, and each security holder of record holding more than 10 per centum of any class of any equity security of the issuer (other than an exempted security), their remuneration and their interests in the securities of, and their

---

[1] So in original. Probably should be "compensation in".

material contracts with, the issuer and any person directly or indirectly controlling or controlled by, or under direct or indirect common control with, the issuer;

   (E)   remuneration to others than directors and officers exceeding $20,000 per annum;

   (F)   bonus and profit-sharing arrangements;

   (G)   management and service contracts;

   (H)   options existing or to be created in respect of their securities;

   (I)   material contracts, not made in the ordinary course of business, which are to be executed in whole or in part at or after the filing of the application or which were made not more than two years before such filing, and every material patent or contract for a material patent right shall be deemed a material contract;

   (J)   balance sheets for not more than the three preceding fiscal years, certified if required by the rules and regulations of the Commission by a registered public accounting firm;

   (K)   profit and loss statements for not more than the three preceding fiscal years, certified if required by the rules and regulations of the Commission by a registered public accounting firm; and

   (L)   any further financial statements which the Commission may deem necessary or appropriate for the protection of investors.

   (2)   Such copies of articles of incorporation, bylaws, trust indentures, or corresponding documents by whatever name known, underwriting arrangements, and other similar documents of, and voting trust agreements with respect to, the issuer and any person directly or indirectly controlling or controlled by, or under direct or indirect common control with, the issuer as the Commission may require as necessary or appropriate for the proper protection of investors and to insure fair dealing in the security.

   (3)   Such copies of material contracts, referred to in paragraph (1)(I) above, as the Commission may require as necessary or appropriate for the proper protection of investors and to insure fair dealing in the security.

   (c)   Additional or alternative information.—If in the judgment of the Commission any information required under subsection (b) of this section is inapplicable to any specified class or classes of issuers, the Commission shall require in lieu thereof the submission of such other information of comparable character as it may deem applicable to such class of issuers.

   (d)   Effective date of registration; withdrawal of registration.—If the exchange authorities certify to the Commission that the security has been approved by the exchange for listing and registration, the registration shall become effective thirty days after the receipt of such certification by the Commission or within such shorter period of time as the Commission may determine. A security registered with a national securities exchange may be withdrawn or stricken from listing and registration in accordance with the rules of the exchange and, upon such terms as the Commission may deem necessary to impose for the protection of investors, upon application by the issuer or the exchange to the Commission; whereupon the issuer shall be relieved from further compliance with the provisions of this section and section 78m of this title and any rules or regulations under such sections as to the securities so withdrawn or stricken. An unissued security may be registered only in accordance with such rules and regulations as the Commission may prescribe as necessary or appropriate in the public interest or for the protection of investors.

* * *

   (f)   Unlisted trading privileges for security originally listed on another national exchange.

(1)(A)   Notwithstanding the preceding subsections of this section, any national securities exchange, in accordance with the requirements of this subsection and the rules hereunder, may extend unlisted trading privileges to—

(i)   any security that is listed and registered on a national securities exchange, subject to subparagraph (B); and

(ii)   any security that is otherwise registered pursuant to this section, or that would be required to be so registered except for the exemption from registration provided in subparagraph (B) or (G) of subsection (g)(2) of this section, subject to subparagraph (E) of this paragraph.

(B)   A national securities exchange may not extend unlisted trading privileges to a security described in subparagraph (A)(i) during such interval, if any, after the commencement of an initial public offering of such security, as is or may be required pursuant to subparagraph (C).

(C)   Not later than 180 days after October 22, 1994, the Commission shall prescribe, by rule or regulation, the duration of the interval referred to in subparagraph (B), if any, as the Commission determines to be necessary or appropriate for the maintenance of fair and orderly markets, the protection of investors and the public interest, or otherwise in furtherance of the purposes of this chapter. Until the earlier of the effective date of such rule or regulation or 240 days after October 22, 1994, such interval shall begin at the opening of trading on the day on which such security commences trading on the national securities exchange with which such security is registered and end at the conclusion of the next day of trading.

(D)   The Commission may prescribe, by rule or regulation such additional procedures or requirements for extending unlisted trading privileges to any security as the Commission deems necessary or appropriate for the maintenance of fair and orderly markets, the protection of investors and the public interest, or otherwise in furtherance of the purposes of this chapter.

(E)   No extension of unlisted trading privileges to securities described in subparagraph (A)(ii) may occur except pursuant to a rule, regulation, or order of the Commission approving such extension or extensions. In promulgating such rule or regulation or in issuing such order, the Commission—

(i)   shall find that such extension or extensions of unlisted trading privileges is consistent with the maintenance of fair and orderly markets, the protection of investors and the public interest, and otherwise in furtherance of the purposes of this chapter;

(ii)   shall take account of the public trading activity in such securities, the character of such trading, the impact of such extension on the existing markets for such securities, and the desirability of removing impediments to and the progress that has been made toward the development of a national market system; and

(iii)   shall not permit a national securities exchange to extend unlisted trading privileges to such securities if any rule of such national securities exchange would unreasonably impair the ability of a dealer to solicit or effect transactions in such securities for its own account, or would unreasonably restrict competition among dealers in such securities or between such dealers acting in the capacity of market makers who are specialists and such dealers who are not specialists.

(F)   An exchange may continue to extend unlisted trading privileges in accordance with this paragraph only if the exchange and the subject security continue to satisfy the requirements for eligibility under this paragraph, including any rules and regulations issued by the Commission pursuant to this paragraph, except that unlisted trading privileges may continue with regard to securities which had been admitted on such exchange prior to July

1, 1964, notwithstanding the failure to satisfy such requirements. If unlisted trading privileges in a security are discontinued pursuant to this subparagraph, the exchange shall cease trading in that security, unless the exchange and the subject security thereafter satisfy the requirements of this paragraph and the rules issued hereunder.

(G)   For purposes of this paragraph—

(i)   a security is the subject of an initial public offering if—

(I)   the offering of the subject security is registered under the Securities Act of 1933 [15 U.S.C. 77a et seq.]; and

(II)   the issuer of the security, immediately prior to filing the registration statement with respect to the offering, was not subject to the reporting requirements of section 78m or 78o(d) of this title; and

(ii)   an initial public offering of such security commences at the opening of trading on the day on which such security commences trading on the national securities exchange with which such security is registered.

(2)(A)   At any time within 60 days of commencement of trading on an exchange of a security pursuant to unlisted trading privileges, the Commission may summarily suspend such unlisted trading privileges on the exchange. Such suspension shall not be reviewable under section 78y of this title and shall not be deemed to be a final agency action for purposes of section 704 of title 5. Upon such suspension—

(i)   the exchange shall cease trading in the security by the close of business on the date of such suspension, or at such time as the Commission may prescribe by rule or order for the maintenance of fair and orderly markets, the protection of investors and the public interest, or otherwise in furtherance of the purposes of this chapter; and

(ii)   if the exchange seeks to extend unlisted trading privileges to the security, the exchange shall file an application to reinstate its ability to do so with the Commission pursuant to such procedures as the Commission may prescribe by rule or order for the maintenance of fair and orderly markets, the protection of investors and the public interest, or otherwise in furtherance of the purposes of this chapter.

(B)   A suspension under subparagraph (A) shall remain in effect until the Commission, by order, grants approval of an application to reinstate, as described in subparagraph (A)(ii).

(C)   A suspension under subparagraph (A) shall not affect the validity or force of an extension of unlisted trading privileges in effect prior to such suspension.

(D)   The Commission shall not approve an application by a national securities exchange to reinstate its ability to extend unlisted trading privileges to a security unless the Commission finds, after notice and opportunity for hearing, that the extension of unlisted trading privileges pursuant to such application is consistent with the maintenance of fair and orderly markets, the protection of investors and the public interest, and otherwise in furtherance of the purposes of this chapter. If the application is made to reinstate unlisted trading privileges to a security described in paragraph (1)(A)(ii), the Commission—

(i)   shall take account of the public trading activity in such security, the character of such trading, the impact of such extension on the existing markets for such a security, and the desirability of removing impediments to and the progress that has been made toward the development of a national market system; and

(ii)   shall not grant any such application if any rule of the national securities exchange making application under this subsection would unreasonably impair the ability of a dealer to solicit or effect transactions in such security for its own account, or would unreasonably restrict competition among dealers in such security or between such dealers acting in the capacity of marketmakers who are specialists and such dealers who are not specialists.

(3) Notwithstanding paragraph (2), the Commission shall by rules and regulations suspend unlisted trading privileges in whole or in part for any or all classes of securities for a period not exceeding twelve months, if it deems such suspension necessary or appropriate in the public interest or for the protection of investors or to prevent evasion of the purposes of this chapter.

(4) On the application of the issuer of any security for which unlisted trading privileges on any exchange have been continued or extended pursuant to this subsection, or of any broker or dealer who makes or creates a market for such security, or of any other person having a bona fide interest in the question of termination or suspension of such unlisted trading privileges, or on its own motion, the Commission shall by order terminate, or suspend for a period not exceeding twelve months, such unlisted trading privileges for such security if the Commission finds, after appropriate notice and opportunity for hearing, that such termination or suspension is necessary or appropriate in the public interest or for the protection of investors.

(5) In any proceeding under this subsection in which appropriate notice and opportunity for hearing are required, notice of not less than ten days to the applicant in such proceeding, to the issuer of the security involved, to the exchange which is seeking to continue or extend or has continued or extended unlisted trading privileges for such security, and to the exchange, if any, on which such security is listed and registered, shall be deemed adequate notice, and any broker or dealer who makes or creates a market for such security, and any other person having a bona fide interest in such proceeding, shall upon application be entitled to be heard.

(6) Any security for which unlisted trading privileges are continued or extended pursuant to this subsection shall be deemed to be registered on a national securities exchange within the meaning of this chapter. The powers and duties of the Commission under this chapter shall be applicable to the rules of an exchange in respect of any such security. The Commission may, by such rules and regulations as it deems necessary or appropriate in the public interest or for the protection of investors, either unconditionally or upon specified terms and conditions, or for stated periods, exempt such securities from the operation of any provision of section 78m, 78n, or 78p of this title.

(g) Registration of securities by issuer; exemptions.

(1) Every issuer which is engaged in interstate commerce, or in a business affecting interstate commerce, or whose securities are traded by use of the mails or any means or instrumentality of interstate commerce shall—

(A) within 120 days after the last day of its first fiscal year ended on which the issuer has total assets exceeding $10,000,000 and a class of equity security (other than an exempted security) held of record by either—

(i) 2,000 persons, or

(ii) 500 persons who are not accredited investors (as such term is defined by the Commission), and

(B) in the case of an issuer that is a bank, a savings and loan holding company (as defined in section 1467a of title 12), or a bank holding company, as such term is defined in section 1841 of title 12, not later than 120 days after the last day of its first fiscal year ended after the effective date of this subsection, on which the issuer has total assets exceeding $10,000,000 and a class of equity security (other than an exempted security) held of record by 2,000 or more persons,

register such security by filing with the Commission a registration statement (and such copies thereof as the Commission may require) with respect to such security containing such information and documents as the Commission may specify comparable to that which is required in an application to register a security pursuant to subsection (b) of this section. Each such registration statement shall become effective sixty days after filing with the Commission or within such shorter period as the Commission may direct. Until such registration statement becomes effective it shall not be deemed filed for the purposes of section 78r of this title. Any issuer may register any class of equity security not required to be registered by filing a registration statement pursuant to the provisions of this paragraph. The Commission is authorized to extend the date upon which any issuer or class of issuers is required to register a security pursuant to the provisions of this paragraph.

(2)   The provisions of this subsection shall not apply in respect of—

(A)   any security listed and registered on a national securities exchange.

(B)   any security issued by an investment company registered pursuant to section 80a–8 of this title.

(C)   any security, other than permanent stock, guaranty stock, permanent reserve stock, or any similar certificate evidencing nonwithdrawable capital, issued by a savings and loan association, building and loan association, cooperative bank, homestead association, or similar institution, which is supervised and examined by State or Federal authority having supervision over any such institution.

(D)   any security of an issuer organized and operated exclusively for religious, educational, benevolent, fraternal, charitable, or reformatory purposes and not for pecuniary profit, and no part of the net earnings of which inures to the benefit of any private shareholder or individual; or any security of a fund that is excluded from the definition of an investment company under section 80a–3(c)(10)(B) of this title.

(E)   any security of an issuer which is a "cooperative association" as defined in the Agricultural Marketing Act, approved June 15, 1929, as amended [12 U.S.C. 1141 et seq.], or a federation of such cooperative associations, if such federation possesses no greater powers or purposes than cooperative associations so defined.

(F)   any security issued by a mutual or cooperative organization which supplies a commodity or service primarily for the benefit of its members and operates not for pecuniary profit, but only if the security is part of a class issuable only to persons who purchase commodities or services from the issuer, the security is transferable only to a successor in interest or occupancy of premises serviced or to be served by the issuer, and no dividends are payable to the holder of the security.

(G)   any security issued by an insurance company if all of the following conditions are met:

(i)   Such insurance company is required to and does file an annual statement with the Commissioner of Insurance (or other officer or agency performing a similar function) of its domiciliary State, and such annual statement conforms to that prescribed by the National Association of Insurance Commissioners or in the determination of such State commissioner, officer or agency substantially conforms to that so prescribed.

(ii)   Such insurance company is subject to regulation by its domiciliary State of proxies, consents, or authorizations in respect of securities issued by such company and such regulation conforms to that prescribed by the National Association of Insurance Commissioners.

(iii) After July 1, 1966, the purchase and sales of securities issued by such insurance company by beneficial owners, directors, or officers of such company are subject to regulation (including reporting) by its domiciliary State substantially in the manner provided in section 78p of this title.

(H) any interest or participation in any collective trust funds maintained by a bank or in a separate account maintained by an insurance company which interest or participation is issued in connection with (i) a stock-bonus, pension, or profit-sharing plan which meets the requirements for qualification under section 401 of title 26, (ii) an annuity plan which meets the requirements for deduction of the employer's contribution under section 404(a)(2) of title 26, or (iii) a church plan, company, or account that is excluded from the definition of an investment company under section 80a–3(c)(14) of this title.

(3) The Commission may by rules or regulations or, on its own motion, after notice and opportunity for hearing, by order, exempt from this subsection any security of a foreign issuer, including any certificate of deposit for such a security, if the Commission finds that such exemption is in the public interest and is consistent with the protection of investors.

(4) Registration of any class of security pursuant to this subsection shall be terminated ninety days, or such shorter period as the Commission may determine, after the issuer files a certification with the Commission that the number of holders of record of such class of security is reduced to less than 300 persons, or, in the case of a bank, a savings and loan holding company (as defined in section 1467a of title 12), or a bank holding company, as such term is defined in section 1841 of title 12, 1,200 persons. . . .

* * *

(h) Exemption by rules and regulations from certain provisions of section.—The Commission may by rules and regulations, or upon application of an interested person, by order, after notice and opportunity for hearing, exempt in whole or in part any issuer or class of issuers from the provisions of subsection (g) of this section or from section 78m, 78n, or 78o(d) of this title or may exempt from section 78p of this title any officer, director, or beneficial owner of securities of any issuer, any security of which is required to be registered pursuant to subsection (g) hereof, upon such terms and conditions and for such period as it deems necessary or appropriate, if the Commission finds, by reason of the number of public investors, amount of trading interest in the securities, the nature and extent of the activities of the issuer, income or assets of the issuer, or otherwise, that such action is not inconsistent with the public interest or the protection of investors. . . .

(i) Securities issued by banks.—In respect of any securities issued by banks and savings associations the deposits of which are insured in accordance with the Federal Deposit Insurance Act [12 U.S.C. 1811 et seq.], the powers, functions, and duties vested in the Commission to administer and enforce this section and sections 78j–1(m), 78m, 78n(a), 78n(c), 78n(d), 78n(f), and 78p of this title, and sections 7241, 7242, 7243, 7244, 7261(b), 7262, 7264, and 7265 of this title, (1) with respect to national banks and Federal savings associations, the accounts of which are insured by the Federal Deposit Insurance Corporation[3] are vested in the Comptroller of the Currency, (2) with respect to all other member banks of the Federal Reserve System are vested in the Board of Governors of the Federal Reserve System, and (3) with respect to all other insured banks and State savings associations, the accounts of which are insured by the Federal Deposit Insurance Corporation, are vested in the Federal Deposit Insurance Corporation. The Comptroller of the Currency, the Board of Governors of the Federal Reserve System, and the Federal Deposit Insurance Corporation shall have the power to make such rules and regulations as may be necessary for the execution of the functions vested in them as provided in this subsection. In carrying out their responsibilities under this subsection, the agencies named in the first sentence of this subsection shall issue substantially similar regulations to regulations and rules issued by the Commission under this section and sections 78j–1(m), 78m, 78n(a), 78n(c), 78n(d), 78n(f), and 78p of this title, and sections 7241, 7242, 7243, 7244, 7261(b), 7262, 7264, and 7265 of this title, unless they find that implementation of substantially similar regulations with respect to insured banks and insured institutions are not necessary or appropriate in the public interest or for protection of investors, and publish such findings, and the detailed reasons therefor, in the Federal Register. Such regulations of the above-named agencies, or the reasons for failure to

---

[3] So in original. Probably should be followed by a comma.

publish such substantially similar regulations to those of the Commission, shall be published in the Federal Register within 120 days of October 28, 1974, and, thereafter, within 60 days of any changes made by the Commission in its relevant regulations and rules.

(j)   Denial, suspension, or revocation of registration; notice and hearing.—The Commission is authorized, by order, as it deems necessary or appropriate for the protection of investors to deny, to suspend the effective date of, to suspend for a period not exceeding twelve months, or to revoke the registration of a security, if the Commission finds, on the record after notice and opportunity for hearing, that the issuer, of such security has failed to comply with any provision of this chapter or the rules and regulations thereunder. No member of a national securities exchange, broker, or dealer shall make use of the mails or any means or instrumentality of interstate commerce to effect any transaction in, or to induce the purchase or sale of, any security the registration of which has been and is suspended or revoked pursuant to the preceding sentence.

(k)   Trading suspensions; emergency authority.

(1)   Trading suspensions.—If in its opinion the public interest and the protection of investors so require, the Commission is authorized by order—

(A)   summarily to suspend trading in any security (other than an exempted security) for a period not exceeding 10 business days, and

(B)   summarily to suspend all trading on any national securities exchange or otherwise, in securities other than exempted securities, for a period not exceeding 90 calendar days.

The action described in subparagraph (B) shall not take effect unless the Commission notifies the President of its decision and the President notifies the Commission that the President does not disapprove of such decision. If the actions described in subparagraph (A) or (B) involve a security futures product, the Commission shall consult with and consider the views of the Commodity Futures Trading Commission.

(2)   Emergency orders.—(A) In general—The Commission, in an emergency, may by order summarily take such action to alter, supplement, suspend, or impose requirements or restrictions with respect to any matter or action subject to regulation by the Commission or a self-regulatory organization under the securities laws, as the Commission determines is necessary in the public interest and for the protection of investors—

(i)   to maintain or restore fair and orderly securities markets (other than markets in exempted securities);

(ii)   to ensure prompt, accurate, and safe clearance and settlement of transactions in securities (other than exempted securities); or

(iii)   to reduce, eliminate, or prevent the substantial disruption by the emergency of—

(I)   securities markets (other than markets in exempted securities), investment companies, or any other significant portion or segment of such markets; or

(II)   the transmission or processing of securities transactions (other than transactions in exempted securities).

(B)   Effective period.—An order of the Commission under this paragraph shall continue in effect for the period specified by the Commission, and may be extended. Except as provided in subparagraph (C), an order of the Commission under this paragraph may not continue in effect for more than 10 business days, including extensions.

(C)   Extension.—An order of the Commission under this paragraph may be extended to continue in effect for more than 10 business days if, at the time of the extension, the

Commission finds that the emergency still exists and determines that the continuation of the order beyond 10 business days is necessary in the public interest and for the protection of investors to attain an objective described in clause (i), (ii), or (iii) of subparagraph (A). In no event shall an order of the Commission under this paragraph continue in effect for more than 30 calendar days.

(D) Security futures.—If the actions described in subparagraph (A) involve a security futures product, the Commission shall consult with and consider the views of the Commodity Futures Trading Commission.

(E) Exemption.—In exercising its authority under this paragraph, the Commission shall not be required to comply with the provisions of—

(i) section 78s(c) of this title; or

(ii) section 553 of title 5.

(3) Termination of emergency actions by President.—The President may direct that action taken by the Commission under paragraph (1)(B) or paragraph (2) of this subsection shall not continue in effect.

(4) Compliance with orders.—No member of a national securities exchange, broker, or dealer shall make use of the mails or any means or instrumentality of interstate commerce to effect any transaction in, or to induce the purchase or sale of, any security in contravention of an order of the Commission under this subsection unless such order has been stayed, modified, or set aside as provided in paragraph (5) of this subsection or has ceased to be effective upon direction of the President as provided in paragraph (3).

(5) Limitations on review of orders.—An order of the Commission pursuant to this subsection shall be subject to review only as provided in section 78y(a) of this title. Review shall be based on an examination of all the information before the Commission at the time such order was issued. The reviewing court shall not enter a stay, writ of mandamus, or similar relief unless the court finds, after notice and hearing before a panel of the court, that the Commission's action is arbitrary, capricious, an abuse of discretion, or otherwise not in accordance with law.

(6) Consultation.—Prior to taking any action described in paragraph (1)(B), the Commission shall consult with and consider the views of the Secretary of the Treasury, the Board of Governors of the Federal Reserve System, and the Commodity Futures Trading Commission, unless such consultation is impracticable in light of the emergency.

(7) Definition.—For purposes of this subsection, the term "emergency" means—

(A) a major market disturbance characterized by or constituting—

(i) sudden and excessive fluctuations of securities prices generally, or a substantial threat thereof, that threaten fair and orderly markets; or

(ii) a substantial disruption of the safe or efficient operation of the national system for clearance and settlement of transactions in securities, or a substantial threat thereof; or

(B) a major disturbance that substantially disrupts, or threatens to substantially disrupt—

(i) the functioning of securities markets, investment companies, or any other significant portion or segment of the securities markets; or

(ii) the transmission or processing of securities transactions.

(*l*) Issuance of any security in contravention of rules and regulations; application to annuity contracts and variable life policies.—It shall be unlawful for an issuer, any class of whose securities is registered pursuant to this section or would be required to be so registered except for the exemption from registration provided by subsection (g)(2)(B) or (g)(2)(G) of this section, by the use of any means or instrumentality of interstate commerce, or of the mails, to issue, either originally or upon transfer, any of such securities in a form or with a format which contravenes such rules and regulations as the Commission may prescribe as necessary or appropriate for the prompt and accurate clearance and settlement of transactions in securities. The provisions of this subsection shall not apply to variable annuity contracts or variable life policies issued by an insurance company or its separate accounts.

Periodical and Other Reports

§ 78m [P.L. § 13]. (a) Reports by issuer of security; contents.—Every issuer of a security registered pursuant to section 78l of this title shall file with the Commission, in accordance with such rules and regulations as the Commission may prescribe as necessary or appropriate for the proper protection of investors and to insure fair dealing in the security—

(1) such information and documents (and such copies thereof) as the Commission shall require to keep reasonably current the information and documents required to be included in or filed with an application or registration statement filed pursuant to section 78l of this title, except that the Commission may not require the filing of any material contract wholly executed before July 1, 1962.

(2) such annual reports (and such copies thereof), certified if required by the rules and regulations of the Commission by independent public accountants, and such quarterly reports (and such copies thereof), as the Commission may prescribe.

Every issuer of a security registered on a national securities exchange shall also file a duplicate original of such information, documents, and reports with the exchange. In any registration statement, periodic report, or other reports to be filed with the Commission, an emerging growth company need not present selected financial data in accordance with section 229.301 of title 17, Code of Federal Regulations, for any period prior to the earliest audited period presented in connection with its first registration statement that became effective under this chapter or the Securities Act of 1933 [15 U.S.C. 77a et seq.] and, with respect to any such statement or reports, an emerging growth company may not be required to comply with any new or revised financial accounting standard until such date that a company that is not an issuer (as defined under section 7201 of this title) is required to comply with such new or revised accounting standard, if such standard applies to companies that are not issuers.

(b)   Form of report; books, records, and internal accounting; directives.

(1)   The Commission may prescribe, in regard to reports made pursuant to this chapter, the form or forms in which the required information shall be set forth, the items or details to be shown in the balance sheet and the earnings statement, and the methods to be followed in the preparation of reports, in the appraisal or valuation of assets and liabilities, in the determination of depreciation and depletion, in the differentiation of recurring and nonrecurring income, in the differentiation of investment and operating income, and in the preparation, where the Commission deems it necessary or desirable, of separate and/or consolidated balance sheets or income accounts of any person directly or indirectly controlling or controlled by the issuer, or any person under direct or indirect common control with the issuer; but in the case of the reports of any person whose methods of accounting are prescribed under the provisions of any law of the United States, or any rule or regulation thereunder, the rules and regulations of the Commission with respect to reports shall not be inconsistent with the requirements imposed by such law or rule or regulation in respect of the same subject matter (except that such rules and regulations of the Commission may be inconsistent with such requirements to the extent that the Commission determines that the public interest or the protection of investors so requires).

(2)   Every issuer which has a class of securities registered pursuant to section 78l of this title and every issuer which is required to file reports pursuant to section 78o(d) of this title shall—

(A) make and keep books, records, and accounts, which, in reasonable detail, accurately and fairly reflect the transactions and dispositions of the assets of the issuer;

(B) devise and maintain a system of internal accounting controls sufficient to provide reasonable assurances that—

(i) transactions are executed in accordance with management's general or specific authorization;

(ii) transactions are recorded as necessary (I) to permit preparation of financial statements in conformity with generally accepted accounting principles or any other criteria applicable to such statements, and (II) to maintain accountability for assets;

(iii) access to assets is permitted only in accordance with management's general or specific authorization; and

(iv) the recorded accountability for assets is compared with the existing assets at reasonable intervals and appropriate action is taken with respect to any differences; and

(C) notwithstanding any other provision of law, pay the allocable share of such issuer of a reasonable annual accounting support fee or fees, determined in accordance with section 7219 of this title.

(3)(A) With respect to matters concerning the national security of the United States, no duty or liability under paragraph (2) of this subsection shall be imposed upon any person acting in cooperation with the head of any Federal department or agency responsible for such matters if such act in cooperation with such head of a department or agency was done upon the specific, written directive of the head of such department or agency pursuant to Presidential authority to issue such directives. Each directive issued under this paragraph shall set forth the specific facts and circumstances with respect to which the provisions of this paragraph are to be invoked. Each such directive shall, unless renewed in writing, expire one year after the date of issuance.

(B) Each head of a Federal department or agency of the United States who issues a directive pursuant to this paragraph shall maintain a complete file of all such directives and shall, on October 1 of each year, transmit a summary of matters covered by such directives in force at any time during the previous year to the Permanent Select Committee on Intelligence of the House of Representatives and the Select Committee on Intelligence of the Senate.

(4) No criminal liability shall be imposed for failing to comply with the requirements of paragraph (2) of this subsection except as provided in paragraph (5) of this subsection.

(5) No person shall knowingly circumvent or knowingly fail to implement a system of internal accounting controls or knowingly falsify any book, record, or account described in paragraph (2).

(6) Where an issuer which has a class of securities registered pursuant to section 78l of this title or an issuer which is required to file reports pursuant to section 78o(d) of this title holds 50 per centum or less of the voting power with respect to a domestic or foreign firm, the provisions of paragraph (2) require only that the issuer proceed in good faith to use its influence, to the extent reasonable under the issuer's circumstances, to cause such domestic or foreign firm to devise and maintain a system of internal accounting controls consistent with paragraph (2). Such circumstances include the relative degree of the issuer's ownership of the domestic or foreign firm and the laws and practices governing the business operations of the country in which such firm is located. An issuer which demonstrates good faith efforts to use such influence shall be conclusively presumed to have complied with the requirements of paragraph (2).

(7)   For the purpose of paragraph (2) of this subsection, the terms "reasonable assurances" and "reasonable detail" mean such level of detail and degree of assurance as would satisfy prudent officials in the conduct of their own affairs.

(c)   Alternative reports.—If in the judgment of the Commission any report required under subsection (a) of this section is inapplicable to any specified class or classes of issuers, the Commission shall require in lieu thereof the submission of such reports of comparable character as it may deem applicable to such class or classes of issuers.

(d)   Reports by persons acquiring more than five per centum of certain classes of securities.

(1)   Any person who, after acquiring directly or indirectly the beneficial ownership of any equity security of a class which is registered pursuant to section 78l of this title, or any equity security of an insurance company which would have been required to be so registered except for the exemption contained in section 78l(g)(2)(G) of this title, or any equity security issued by a closed-end investment company registered under the Investment Company Act of 1940 [15 U.S.C. 80a–1 et seq.] or any equity security issued by a Native Corporation pursuant to section 1629c(d)(6) of title 43, or otherwise becomes or is deemed to become a beneficial owner of any of the foregoing upon the purchase or sale of a security-based swap that the Commission may define by rule, and is directly or indirectly the beneficial owner of more than 5 per centum of such class shall, within ten days after such acquisition or within such shorter time as the Commission may establish by rule, file with the Commission, a statement containing such of the following information, and such additional information, as the Commission may by rules and regulations, prescribe as necessary or appropriate in the public interest or for the protection of investors—

(A)   the background, and identity, residence, and citizenship of, and the nature of such beneficial ownership by, such person and all other persons by whom or on whose behalf the purchases have been or are to be effected;

(B)   the source and amount of the funds or other consideration used or to be used in making the purchases, and if any part of the purchase price is represented or is to be represented by funds or other consideration borrowed or otherwise obtained for the purpose of acquiring, holding, or trading such security, a description of the transaction and the names of the parties thereto, except that where a source of funds is a loan made in the ordinary course of business by a bank, as defined in section 78c(a)(6) of this title, if the person filing such statement so requests, the name of the bank shall not be made available to the public;

(C)   if the purpose of the purchases or prospective purchases is to acquire control of the business of the issuer of the securities, any plans or proposals which such persons may have to liquidate such issuer, to sell its assets to or merge it with any other persons, or to make any other major change in its business or corporate structure;

(D)   the number of shares of such security which are beneficially owned, and the number of shares concerning which there is a right to acquire, directly or indirectly, by (i) such person, and (ii) by each associate of such person, giving the background, identity, residence, and citizenship of each such associate; and

(E)   information as to any contracts, arrangements, or understandings with any person with respect to any securities of the issuer, including but not limited to transfer of any of the securities, joint ventures, loan or option arrangements, puts or calls, guaranties of loans, guaranties against loss or guaranties of profits, division of losses or profits, or the giving or withholding of proxies, naming the persons with whom such contracts, arrangements, or understandings have been entered into, and giving the details thereof.

(2)   If any material change occurs in the facts set forth in the statement filed with the Commission, an amendment shall be filed with the Commission, in accordance with such rules and regulations as the Commission may prescribe as necessary or appropriate in the public interest or for the protection of investors.

(3)   When two or more persons act as a partnership, limited partnership, syndicate, or other group for the purpose of acquiring, holding, or disposing of securities of an issuer, such syndicate or group shall be deemed a "person" for the purposes of this subsection.

(4)   In determining, for purposes of this subsection, any percentage of a class of any security, such class shall be deemed to consist of the amount of the outstanding securities of such class, exclusive of any securities of such class held by or for the account of the issuer or a subsidiary of the issuer.

(5)   The Commission, by rule or regulation or by order, may permit any person to file in lieu of the statement required by paragraph (1) of this subsection or the rules and regulations thereunder, a notice stating the name of such person, the number of shares of any equity securities subject to paragraph (1) which are owned by him, the date of their acquisition and such other information as the Commission may specify, if it appears to the Commission that such securities were acquired by such person in the ordinary course of his business and were not acquired for the purpose of and do not have the effect of changing or influencing the control of the issuer nor in connection with or as a participant in any transaction having such purpose or effect.

(6)   The provisions of this subsection shall not apply to—

(A)   any acquisition or offer to acquire securities made or proposed to be made by means of a registration statement under the Securities Act of 1933 [15 U.S.C. 77a et seq.];

(B)   any acquisition of the beneficial ownership of a security which, together with all other acquisitions by the same person of securities of the same class during the preceding twelve months, does not exceed 2 per centum of that class;

(C)   any acquisition of an equity security by the issuer of such security;

(D)   any acquisition or proposed acquisition of a security which the Commission, by rules or regulations or by order, shall exempt from the provisions of this subsection as not entered into for the purpose of, and not having the effect of, changing or influencing the control of the issuer or otherwise as not comprehended within the purposes of this subsection.

(e)   Purchase of securities by issuer.

(1)   It shall be unlawful for an issuer which has a class of equity securities registered pursuant to section 78l of this title, or which is a closed-end investment company registered under the Investment Company Act of 1940 [15 U.S.C. 80a–1 et seq.], to purchase any equity security issued by it if such purchase is in contravention of such rules and regulations as the Commission, in the public interest or for the protection of investors, may adopt (A) to define acts and practices which are fraudulent, deceptive, or manipulative, and (B) to prescribe means reasonably designed to prevent such acts and practices. Such rules and regulations may require such issuer to provide holders of equity securities of such class with such information relating to the reasons for such purchase, the source of funds, the number of shares to be purchased, the price to be paid for such securities, the method of purchase, and such additional information, as the Commission deems necessary or appropriate in the public interest or for the protection of investors, or which the Commission deems to be material to a determination whether such security should be sold.

(2)   For the purpose of this subsection, a purchase by or for the issuer or any person controlling, controlled by, or under common control with the issuer, or a purchase subject to control of the issuer or any such person, shall be deemed to be a purchase by the issuer. The Commission shall have power to make rules and regulations implementing this paragraph in the public interest and for the protection of investors, including exemptive rules and regulations covering situations in which the Commission deems it unnecessary or inappropriate that a purchase of the type described in this paragraph shall be deemed to be a purchase by the issuer for purposes of some or all of the provisions of paragraph (1) of this subsection.

(3)   At the time of filing such statement as the Commission may require by rule pursuant to paragraph (1) of this subsection, the person making the filing shall pay to the Commission a fee at a rate that, subject to paragraph (4), is equal to $92 per $1,000,000 of the value of securities proposed to be purchased. The fee shall be reduced with respect to securities in an amount equal to any fee paid with respect to any securities issued in connection with the proposed transaction under section 6(b) of the Securities Act of 1933 [15 U.S.C. 77f(b)], or the fee paid under that section shall be reduced in an amount equal to the fee paid to the Commission in connection with such transaction under this paragraph.

* * *

(f)   Reports by institutional investment managers.—(1) Every institutional investment manager which uses the mails, or any means or instrumentality of interstate commerce in the course of its business as an institutional investment manager and which exercises investment discretion with respect to accounts holding equity securities of a class described in subsection (d)(1) of this section or otherwise becomes or is deemed to become a beneficial owner of any security of a class described in subsection (d)(1) upon the purchase or sale of a security-based swap that the Commission may define by rule, having an aggregate fair market value on the last trading day in any of the preceding twelve months of at least $100,000,000 or such lesser amount (but in no case less than $10,000,000) as the Commission, by rule, may determine, shall file reports with the Commission in such form, for such periods, and at such times after the end of such periods as the Commission, by rule, may prescribe, but in no event shall such reports be filed for periods longer than one year or shorter than one quarter. Such reports shall include for each such equity security held on the last day of the reporting period by accounts (in aggregate or by type as the Commission, by rule, may prescribe) with respect to which the institutional investment manager exercises investment discretion (other than securities held in amounts which the Commission, by rule, determines to be insignificant for purposes of this subsection), the name of the issuer and the title, class, CUSIP number, number of shares or principal amount, and aggregate fair market value of each such security. Such reports may also include for accounts (in aggregate or by type) with respect to which the institutional investment manager exercises investment discretion such of the following information as the Commission, by rule, prescribes—

(A)   the name of the issuer and the title, class, CUSIP number, number of shares or principal amount, and aggregate fair market value or cost or amortized cost of each other security (other than an exempted security) held on the last day of the reporting period by such accounts;

(B)   the aggregate fair market value or cost or amortized cost of exempted securities (in aggregate or by class) held on the last day of the reporting period by such accounts;

(C)   the number of shares of each equity security of a class described in subsection (d)(1) of this section held on the last day of the reporting period by such accounts with respect to which the institutional investment manager possesses sole or shared authority to exercise the voting rights evidenced by such securities;

(D)   the aggregate purchases and aggregate sales during the reporting period of each security (other than an exempted security) effected by or for such accounts; and

(E)   with respect to any transaction or series of transactions having a market value of at least $500,000 or such other amount as the Commission, by rule, may determine, effected during the reporting period by or for such accounts in any equity security of a class described in subsection (d)(1) of this section—

(i)   the name of the issuer and the title, class, and CUSIP number of the security;

(ii)   the number of shares or principal amount of the security involved in the transaction;

(iii)   whether the transaction was a purchase or sale;

(iv)   the per share price or prices at which the transaction was effected;

(v)   the date or dates of the transaction;

(vi)   the date or dates of the settlement of the transaction;

(vii)   the broker or dealer through whom the transaction was effected;

(viii) the market or markets in which the transaction was effected; and

(ix)   such other related information as the Commission, by rule, may prescribe.

* * *

(6)(A)   For purposes of this subsection the term "institutional investment manager" includes any person, other than a natural person, investing in or buying and selling securities for its own account, and any person exercising investment discretion with respect to the account of any other person.

* * *

(g)   Statement of equity security ownership.

(1)   Any person who is directly or indirectly the beneficial owner of more than 5 per centum of any security of a class described in subsection (d)(1) of this section or otherwise becomes or is deemed to become a beneficial owner of any security of a class described in subsection (d)(1) upon the purchase or sale of a security-based swap that the Commission may define by rule shall file with the Commission a statement setting forth, in such form and at such time as the Commission may, by rule, prescribe—

(A)   such person's identity, residence, and citizenship; and

(B)   the number and description of the shares in which such person has an interest and the nature of such interest.

(2)   If any material change occurs in the facts set forth in the statement filed with the Commission, an amendment shall be filed with the Commission, in accordance with such rules and regulations as the Commission may prescribe as necessary or appropriate in the public interest or for the protection of investors.

(3)   When two or more persons act as a partnership, limited partnership, syndicate, or other group for the purpose of acquiring, holding, or disposing of securities of an issuer, such syndicate or group shall be deemed a "person" for the purposes of this subsection.

(4)   In determining, for purposes of this subsection, any percentage of a class of any security, such class shall be deemed to consist of the amount of the outstanding securities of such class, exclusive of any securities of such class held by or for the account of the issuer or a subsidiary of the issuer.

(5)   In exercising its authority under this subsection, the Commission shall take such steps as it deems necessary or appropriate in the public interest or for the protection of investors (A) to achieve centralized reporting of information regarding ownership, (B) to avoid unnecessarily duplicative reporting by and minimize the compliance burden on persons required to report, and (C) to tabulate and promptly make available the information contained in any report filed pursuant to this subsection in a manner which will, in the view of the Commission, maximize the usefulness of the information to other Federal and State agencies and the public.

(6)   The Commission may, by rule or order, exempt, in whole or in part, any person or class of persons from any or all of the reporting requirements of this subsection as it deems necessary or appropriate in the public interest or for the protection of investors.

(h)   Large trader reporting

(1) Identification requirements for large traders.—For the purpose of monitoring the impact on the securities markets of securities transactions involving a substantial volume or a large fair market value or exercise value and for the purpose of otherwise assisting the Commission in the enforcement of this chapter, each large trader shall—

(A) provide such information to the Commission as the Commission may by rule or regulation prescribe as necessary or appropriate, identifying such large trader and all accounts in or through which such large trader effects such transactions; and

(B) identify, in accordance with such rules or regulations as the Commission may prescribe as necessary or appropriate, to any registered broker or dealer by or through whom such large trader directly or indirectly effects securities transactions, such large trader and all accounts directly or indirectly maintained with such broker or dealer by such large trader in or through which such transactions are effected.

(2) Recordkeeping and reporting requirements for brokers and dealers.—Every registered broker or dealer shall make and keep for prescribed periods such records as the Commission by rule or regulation prescribes as necessary or appropriate in the public interest, for the protection of investors, or otherwise in furtherance of the purposes of this chapter, with respect to securities transactions that equal or exceed the reporting activity level effected directly or indirectly by or through such registered broker or dealer of or for any person that such broker or dealer knows is a large trader, or any person that such broker or dealer has reason to know is a large trader on the basis of transactions in securities effected by or through such broker or dealer. Such records shall be available for reporting to the Commission, or any self-regulatory organization that the Commission shall designate to receive such reports, on the morning of the day following the day the transactions were effected, and shall be reported to the Commission or a self-regulatory organization designated by the Commission immediately upon request by the Commission or such a self-regulatory organization. Such records and reports shall be in a format and transmitted in a manner prescribed by the Commission (including, but not limited to, machine readable form).

(3) Aggregation rules.—The Commission may prescribe rules or regulations governing the manner in which transactions and accounts shall be aggregated for the purpose of this subsection, including aggregation on the basis of common ownership or control.

(4) Examination of broker and dealer records.—All records required to be made and kept by registered brokers and dealers pursuant to this subsection with respect to transactions effected by large traders are subject at any time, or from time to time, to such reasonable periodic, special, or other examinations by representatives of the Commission as the Commission deems necessary or appropriate in the public interest, for the protection of investors, or otherwise in furtherance of the purposes of this chapter.

(5) Factors to be considered in Commission actions.—In exercising its authority under this subsection, the Commission shall take into account—

(A) existing reporting systems;

(B) the costs associated with maintaining information with respect to transactions effected by large traders and reporting such information to the Commission or self-regulatory organizations; and

(C) the relationship between the United States and international securities markets.

(6) Exemptions.—The Commission, by rule, regulation, or order, consistent with the purposes of this chapter, may exempt any person or class of persons or any transaction or class of transactions, either conditionally or upon specified terms and conditions or for stated periods, from the operation of this subsection, and the rules and regulations thereunder.

(7) Authority of Commission to limit disclosure of information.—Notwithstanding any other provision of law, the Commission shall not be compelled to disclose any information

required to be kept or reported under this subsection. Nothing in this subsection shall authorize the Commission to withhold information from Congress, or prevent the Commission from complying with a request for information from any other Federal department or agency requesting information for purposes within the scope of its jurisdiction, or complying with an order of a court of the United States in an action brought by the United States or the Commission. For purposes of section 552 of title 5, this subsection shall be considered a statute described in subsection (b)(3)(B) of such section 552.

(8) Definitions.—For purposes of this subsection—

(A) the term "large trader" means every person who, for his own account or an account for which he exercises investment discretion, effects transactions for the purchase or sale of any publicly traded security or securities by use of any means or instrumentality of interstate commerce or of the mails, or of any facility of a national securities exchange, directly or indirectly by or through a registered broker or dealer in an aggregate amount equal to or in excess of the identifying activity level;

(B) the term "publicly traded security" means any equity security (including an option on individual equity securities, and an option on a group or index of such securities) listed, or admitted to unlisted trading privileges, on a national securities exchange, or quoted in an automated interdealer quotation system;

(C) the term "identifying activity level" means transactions in publicly traded securities at or above a level of volume, fair market value, or exercise value as shall be fixed from time to time by the Commission by rule or regulation, specifying the time interval during which such transactions shall be aggregated;

(D) the term "reporting activity level" means transactions in publicly traded securities at or above a level of volume, fair market value, or exercise value as shall be fixed from time to time by the Commission by rule, regulation, or order, specifying the time interval during which such transactions shall be aggregated; and

(E) the term "person" has the meaning given in section 78c(a)(9) of this title and also includes two or more persons acting as a partnership, limited partnership, syndicate, or other group, but does not include a foreign central bank.

(i) Accuracy of financial reports.—Each financial report that contains financial statements, and that is required to be prepared in accordance with (or reconciled to) generally accepted accounting principles under this chapter and filed with the Commission shall reflect all material correcting adjustments that have been identified by a registered public accounting firm in accordance with generally accepted accounting principles and the rules and regulations of the Commission.

(j) Off-balance sheet transactions.—Not later than 180 days after July 30, 2002, the Commission shall issue final rules providing that each annual and quarterly financial report required to be filed with the Commission shall disclose all material off-balance sheet transactions, arrangements, obligations (including contingent obligations), and other relationships of the issuer with unconsolidated entities or other persons, that may have a material current or future effect on financial condition, changes in financial condition, results of operations, liquidity, capital expenditures, capital resources, or significant components of revenues or expenses.

(k) Prohibition on personal loans to executives.

(1) In general.—It shall be unlawful for any issuer (as defined in section 7201 of this title), directly or indirectly, including through any subsidiary, to extend or maintain credit, to arrange for the extension of credit, or to renew an extension of credit, in the form of a personal loan to or for any director or executive officer (or equivalent thereof) of that issuer. An extension of credit maintained by the issuer on July 30, 2002, shall not be subject to the provisions of this subsection, provided that there is no material modification to any term of any such extension of credit or any renewal of any such extension of credit on or after July 30, 2002.

(2) Limitation.—Paragraph (1) does not preclude any home improvement and manufactured home loans (as that term is defined in section 1464 of title 12), consumer credit (as defined in section 1602 of this title), or any extension of credit under an open end credit plan (as defined in section 1602 of this title), or a charge card (as defined in section 1637(c)(4)(e) of this title), or any extension of credit by a broker or dealer registered under section 78o of this title to an employee of that broker or dealer to buy, trade, or carry securities, that is permitted under rules or regulations of the Board of Governors of the Federal Reserve System pursuant to section 78g of this title (other than an extension of credit that would be used to purchase the stock of that issuer), that is—

(A) made or provided in the ordinary course of the consumer credit business of such issuer;

(B) of a type that is generally made available by such issuer to the public; and

(C) made by such issuer on market terms, or terms that are no more favorable than those offered by the issuer to the general public for such extensions of credit.

(3) Rule of construction for certain loans.—Paragraph (1) does not apply to any loan made or maintained by an insured depository institution (as defined in section 3 of the Federal Deposit Insurance Act (12 U.S.C. 1813)), if the loan is subject to the insider lending restrictions of section 375b of title 12.

(*l*) Real time issuer disclosures.—Each issuer reporting under subsec. (a) of this section or section 78o(d) of this title shall disclose to the public on a rapid and current basis such additional information concerning material changes in the financial condition or operations of the issuer, in plain English, which may include trend and qualitative information and graphic presentations, as the Commission determines, by rule, is necessary or useful for the protection of investors and in the public interest.

* * *

Proxies

§ 78n [P.L. § 14]. (a) Solicitation of proxies in violation of rules and regulations.

(1) It shall be unlawful for any person, by the use of the mails or by any means or instrumentality of interstate commerce or of any facility of a national securities exchange or otherwise, in contravention of such rules and regulations as the Commission may prescribe as necessary or appropriate in the public interest or for the protection of investors, to solicit or to permit the use of his name to solicit any proxy or consent or authorization in respect of any security (other than an exempted security) registered pursuant to section 78*l* of this title.

(2) The rules and regulations prescribed by the Commission under paragraph (1) may include—

(A) a requirement that a solicitation of proxy, consent, or authorization by (or on behalf of) an issuer include a nominee submitted by a shareholder to serve on the board of directors of the issuer; and

(B) a requirement that an issuer follow a certain procedure in relation to a solicitation described in subparagraph (A).

(b) Giving or refraining from giving proxy in respect of any security carried for account of customer.

(1) It shall be unlawful for any member of a national securities exchange, or any broker or dealer registered under this chapter, or any bank, association, or other entity that exercises fiduciary powers, in contravention of such rules and regulations as the Commission may prescribe as necessary or appropriate in the public interest or for the protection of investors, to give, or to refrain from giving a proxy, consent, authorization, or information statement in respect of any

security registered pursuant to section 78*l* of this title, or any security issued by an investment company registered under the Investment Company Act of 1940 [15 U.S.C. 80a–1 et seq.], and carried for the account of a customer.

(2)   With respect to banks, the rules and regulations prescribed by the Commission under paragraph (1) shall not require the disclosure of the names of beneficial owners of securities in an account held by the bank on December 28, 1985, unless the beneficial owner consents to the disclosure. The provisions of this paragraph shall not apply in the case of a bank which the Commission finds has not made a good faith effort to obtain such consent from such beneficial owners.

(c)   Information to holders of record prior to annual or other meeting.—Unless proxies, consents, or authorizations in respect of a security registered pursuant to section 78*l* of this title, or a security issued by an investment company registered under the Investment Company Act of 1940 [15 U.S.C. 80a–1 et seq.], are solicited by or on behalf of the management of the issuer from the holders of record of such security in accordance with the rules and regulations prescribed under subsection (a) of this section, prior to any annual or other meeting of the holders of such security, such issuer shall, in accordance with rules and regulations prescribed by the Commission, file with the Commission and transmit to all holders of record of such security information substantially equivalent to the information which would be required to be transmitted if a solicitation were made, but no information shall be required to be filed or transmitted pursuant to this subsection before July 1, 1964.

(d)   Tender offer by owner of more than five per centum of class of securities; exceptions.

(1)   It shall be unlawful for any person, directly or indirectly, by use of the mails or by any means or instrumentality of interstate commerce or of any facility of a national securities exchange or otherwise, to make a tender offer for, or a request or invitation for tenders of, any class of any equity security which is registered pursuant to section 78*l* of this title, or any equity security of an insurance company which would have been required to be so registered except for the exemption contained in section 78*l*(g)(2)(G) of this title, or any equity security issued by a closed-end investment company registered under the Investment Company Act of 1940 [15 U.S.C. 80a–1 et seq.], if, after consummation thereof, such person would, directly or indirectly, be the beneficial owner of more than 5 per centum of such class, unless at the time copies of the offer or request or invitation are first published or sent or given to security holders such person has filed with the Commission a statement containing such of the information specified in section 78m(d) of this title, and such additional information as the Commission may by rules and regulations prescribe as necessary or appropriate in the public interest or for the protection of investors. All requests or invitations for tenders or advertisements making a tender offer or requesting or inviting tenders of such a security shall be filed as a part of such statement and shall contain such of the information contained in such statement as the Commission may by rules and regulations prescribe. Copies of any additional material soliciting or requesting such tender offers subsequent to the initial solicitation or request shall contain such information as the Commission may by rules and regulations prescribe as necessary or appropriate in the public interest or for the protection of investors, and shall be filed with the Commission not later than the time copies of such material are first published or sent or given to security holders. Copies of all statements, in the form in which such material is furnished to security holders and the Commission, shall be sent to the issuer not later than the date such material is first published or sent or given to any security holders.

(2)   When two or more persons act as a partnership, limited partnership, syndicate, or other group for the purpose of acquiring, holding, or disposing of securities of an issuer, such syndicate or group shall be deemed a "person" for purposes of this subsection.

(3)   In determining, for purposes of this subsection, any percentage of a class of any security, such class shall be deemed to consist of the amount of the outstanding securities of such class, exclusive of any securities of such class held by or for the account of the issuer or a subsidiary of the issuer.

(4)   Any solicitation or recommendation to the holders of such a security to accept or reject a tender offer or request or invitation for tenders shall be made in accordance with such rules and regulations as the Commission may prescribe as necessary or appropriate in the public interest or for the protection of investors.

(5)   Securities deposited pursuant to a tender offer or request or invitation for tenders may be withdrawn by or on behalf of the depositor at any time until the expiration of seven days after the time definitive copies of the offer or request or invitation are first published or sent or given to security holders, and at any time after sixty days from the date of the original tender offer or request or invitation, except as the Commission may otherwise prescribe by rules, regulations, or order as necessary or appropriate in the public interest or for the protection of investors.

(6)   Where any person makes a tender offer, or request or invitation for tenders, for less than all the outstanding equity securities of a class, and where a greater number of securities is deposited pursuant thereto within ten days after copies of the offer or request or invitation are first published or sent or given to security holders than such person is bound or willing to take up and pay for, the securities taken up shall be taken up as nearly as may be pro rata, disregarding fractions, according to the number of securities deposited by each depositor. The provisions of this subsection shall also apply to securities deposited within ten days after notice of an increase in the consideration offered to security holders, as described in paragraph (7), is first published or sent or given to security holders.

(7)   Where any person varies the terms of a tender offer or request or invitation for tenders before the expiration thereof by increasing the consideration offered to holders of such securities, such person shall pay the increased consideration to each security holder whose securities are taken up and paid for pursuant to the tender offer or request or invitation for tenders whether or not such securities have been taken up by such person before the variation of the tender offer or request or invitation.

(8)   The provisions of this subsection shall not apply to any offer for, or request or invitation for tenders of, any security—

   (A)   if the acquisition of such security, together with all other acquisitions by the same person of securities of the same class during the preceding twelve months, would not exceed 2 per centum of that class;

   (B)   by the issuer of such security; or

   (C)   which the Commission, by rules or regulations or by order, shall exempt from the provisions of this subsection as not entered into for the purpose of, and not having the effect of, changing or influencing the control of the issuer or otherwise as not comprehended within the purposes of this subsection.

(e)   Untrue statement of material fact or omission of fact with respect to tender offer.—It shall be unlawful for any person to make any untrue statement of a material fact or omit to state any material fact necessary in order to make the statements made, in the light of the circumstances under which they are made, not misleading, or to engage in any fraudulent, deceptive, or manipulative acts or practices, in connection with any tender offer or request or invitation for tenders, or any solicitation of security holders in opposition to or in favor of any such offer, request, or invitation. The Commission shall, for the purposes of this subsection, by rules and regulations define, and prescribe means reasonably designed to prevent, such acts and practices as are fraudulent, deceptive, or manipulative.

(f)   Election or designation of majority of directors of issuer by owner of more than five per centum of class of securities at other than meeting of security holders.—If, pursuant to any arrangement or understanding with the person or persons acquiring securities in a transaction subject to subsection (d) of this section or subsection (d) of section 78m of this title, any persons are to be elected or designated as directors of the issuer, otherwise than at a meeting of security holders, and the persons so elected or designated will constitute a majority of the directors of the issuer, then, prior to the time any such person takes office as a director, and in accordance with rules and regulations prescribed by the Commission, the issuer shall file with the Commission, and transmit to all holders of record of securities of the issuer who would be entitled to vote at a meeting for election of directors, information substantially equivalent to the information which would be required by subsection (a) or (c) of this section to be transmitted if such person or persons were nominees for election as directors at a meeting of such security holders.

* * *

(i) Disclosure of pay versus performance.—The Commission shall, by rule, require each issuer to disclose in any proxy or consent solicitation material for an annual meeting of the shareholders of the issuer a clear description of any compensation required to be disclosed by the issuer under section 229.402 of title 17, Code of Federal Regulations (or any successor thereto), including, for any issuer other than an emerging growth company, information that shows the relationship between executive compensation actually paid and the financial performance of the issuer, taking into account any change in the value of the shares of stock and dividends of the issuer and any distributions. The disclosure under this subsection may include a graphic representation of the information required to be disclosed.

(j) Disclosure of hedging by employees and directors.—The Commission shall, by rule, require each issuer to disclose in any proxy or consent solicitation material for an annual meeting of the shareholders of the issuer whether any employee or member of the board of directors of the issuer, or any designee of such employee or member, is permitted to purchase financial instruments (including prepaid variable forward contracts, equity swaps, collars, and exchange funds) that are designed to hedge or offset any decrease in the market value of equity securities—

(1) granted to the employee or member of the board of directors by the issuer as part of the compensation of the employee or member of the board of directors; or

(2) held, directly or indirectly, by the employee or member of the board of directors.

Shareholder Approval of Executive Compensation

§ 78n–1 [P.L. § 14A]. (a) Separate resolution required.

(1) In general.—Not less frequently than once every 3 years, a proxy or consent or authorization for an annual or other meeting of the shareholders for which the proxy solicitation rules of the Commission require compensation disclosure shall include a separate resolution subject to shareholder vote to approve the compensation of executives, as disclosed pursuant to section 229.402 of title 17, Code of Federal Regulations, or any successor thereto.

(2) Frequency of vote.—Not less frequently than once every 6 years, a proxy or consent or authorization for an annual or other meeting of the shareholders for which the proxy solicitation rules of the Commission require compensation disclosure shall include a separate resolution subject to shareholder vote to determine whether votes on the resolutions required under paragraph (1) will occur every 1, 2, or 3 years.

(3) Effective date.—The proxy or consent or authorization for the first annual or other meeting of the shareholders occurring after the end of the 6-month period beginning on July 21, 2010, shall include—

(A) the resolution described in paragraph (1); and

(B) a separate resolution subject to shareholder vote to determine whether votes on the resolutions required under paragraph (1) will occur every 1, 2, or 3 years.

(b) Shareholder approval of golden parachute compensation.

(1) Disclosure.—In any proxy or consent solicitation material (the solicitation of which is subject to the rules of the Commission pursuant to subsection (a)) for a meeting of the shareholders occurring after the end of the 6-month period beginning on July 21, 2010, at which

shareholders are asked to approve an acquisition, merger, consolidation, or proposed sale or other disposition of all or substantially all the assets of an issuer, the person making such solicitation shall disclose in the proxy or consent solicitation material, in a clear and simple form in accordance with regulations to be promulgated by the Commission, any agreements or understandings that such person has with any named executive officers of such issuer (or of the acquiring issuer, if such issuer is not the acquiring issuer) concerning any type of compensation (whether present, deferred, or contingent) that is based on or otherwise relates to the acquisition, merger, consolidation, sale, or other disposition of all or substantially all of the assets of the issuer and the aggregate total of all such compensation that may (and the conditions upon which it may) be paid or become payable to or on behalf of such executive officer.

(2)   Shareholder approval.—Any proxy or consent or authorization relating to the proxy or consent solicitation material containing the disclosure required by paragraph (1) shall include a separate resolution subject to shareholder vote to approve such agreements or understandings and compensation as disclosed, unless such agreements or understandings have been subject to a shareholder vote under subsection (a).

(c)   Rule of construction.—The shareholder vote referred to in subsections (a) and (b) shall not be binding on the issuer or the board of directors of an issuer, and may not be construed—

(1)   as overruling a decision by such issuer or board of directors;

(2)   to create or imply any change to the fiduciary duties of such issuer or board of directors;

(3)   to create or imply any additional fiduciary duties for such issuer or board of directors; or

(4)   to restrict or limit the ability of shareholders to make proposals for inclusion in proxy materials related to executive compensation.

(d)   Disclosure of votes.—Every institutional investment manager subject to section 78m(f) of this title shall report at least annually how it voted on any shareholder vote pursuant to subsections (a) and (b), unless such vote is otherwise required to be reported publicly by rule or regulation of the Commission.

(e)   Exemption.—(1) In general.—The Commission may, by rule or order, exempt any other issuer or class of issuers from the requirement under subsection (a) or (b). In determining whether to make an exemption under this subsection, the Commission shall take into account, among other considerations, whether the requirements under subsections (a) and (b) disproportionately burdens[1] small issuers.

(2)   Treatment of emerging growth companies.

(A)   In general.—An emerging growth company shall be exempt from the requirements of subsections (a) and (b).

(B)   Compliance after termination of emerging growth company treatment.—An issuer that was an emerging growth company but is no longer an emerging growth company shall include the first separate resolution described under subsection (a)(1) not later than the end of—

(i)   in the case of an issuer that was an emerging growth company for less than 2 years after the date of first sale of common equity securities of the issuer pursuant to an effective registration statement under the Securities Act of 1933 [15 U.S.C. 77a et seq.], the 3-year period beginning on such date; and

(ii)   in the case of any other issuer, the 1-year period beginning on the date the issuer is no longer an emerging growth company.

---

[1]   So in original. Probably should be "burden".

Corporate Governance

§ 78n–2 [P.L. § 14B]. Not later than 180 days after July 21, 2010, the Commission shall issue rules that require an issuer to disclose in the annual proxy sent to investors the reasons why the issuer has chosen—

(1)   the same person to serve as chairman of the board of directors and chief executive officer (or in equivalent positions); or

(2)   different individuals to serve as chairman of the board of directors and chief executive officer (or in equivalent positions of the issuer).

Directors, Officers, and Principal Stockholders

§ 78p [P.L. § 16]. (a) Disclosures required.

(1)   Directors, officers, and principal stockholders required to file.—Every person who is directly or indirectly the beneficial owner of more than 10 percent of any class of any equity security (other than an exempted security) which is registered pursuant to section 78l of this title, or who is a director or an officer of the issuer of such security, shall file the statements required by this subsection with the Commission.

(2)   Time of filing—The statements required by this subsection shall be filed—

(A)   at the time of the registration of such security on a national securities exchange or by the effective date of a registration statement filed pursuant to section 78l(g) of this title;

(B)   within 10 days after he or she becomes such beneficial owner, director, or officer, or within such shorter time as the Commission may establish by rule;

(C)   if there has been a change in such ownership, or if such person shall have purchased or sold a security-based swap agreement involving such equity security, before the end of the second business day following the day on which the subject transaction has been executed, or at such other time as the Commission shall establish, by rule, in any case in which the Commission determines that such 2-day period is not feasible.

(3)   Contents of statements.—A statement filed—

(A)   under subparagraph (A) or (B) of paragraph (2) shall contain a statement of the amount of all equity securities of such issuer of which the filing person is the beneficial owner; and

(B)   under subparagraph (C) of such paragraph shall indicate ownership by the filing person at the date of filing, any such changes in such ownership, and such purchases and sales of the security-based swap agreements or security-based swaps as have occurred since the most recent such filing under such subparagraph.

(4)   Electronic filing and availability.—Beginning not later than 1 year after July 30, 2002—

(A)   a statement filed under subparagraph (C) of paragraph (2) shall be filed electronically;

(B)   the Commission shall provide each such statement on a publicly accessible Internet site not later than the end of the business day following that filing; and

(C)   the issuer (if the issuer maintains a corporate website) shall provide that statement on that corporate website, not later than the end of the business day following that filing.

(b)   Profits from purchase and sale of security within six months.—For the purpose of preventing the unfair use of information which may have been obtained by such beneficial owner, director, or officer by reason of his relationship to the issuer, any profit realized by him from any purchase and sale, or any sale and purchase, of any equity security of such issuer (other than an exempted security) or a security-based swap agreement involving any such equity security within any period of less than six months, unless such security or security-based swap agreement was acquired in good faith in connection with a debt previously contracted, shall inure to and be recoverable by the issuer, irrespective of any intention on the part of such beneficial owner, director, or officer in entering into such transaction of holding the security or security-based swap agreement purchased or of not repurchasing the security or security-based swap agreement sold for a period exceeding six months. Suit to recover such profit may be instituted at law or in equity in any court of competent jurisdiction by the issuer, or by the owner of any security of the issuer in the name and in behalf of the issuer if the issuer shall fail or refuse to bring such suit within sixty days after request or shall fail diligently to prosecute the same thereafter; but no such suit shall be brought more than two years after the date such profit was realized. This subsection shall not be construed to cover any transaction where such beneficial owner was not such both at the time of the purchase and sale, or the sale and purchase, of the security or security-based swap agreement or a security-based swap involved, or any transaction or transactions which the Commission by rules and regulations may exempt as not comprehended within the purpose of this subsection.

(c)   Conditions for sale of security by beneficial owner, director, or officer.—It shall be unlawful for any such beneficial owner, director, or officer, directly or indirectly, to sell any equity security of such issuer (other than an exempted security), if the person selling the security or his principal (1) does not own the security sold, or (2) if owning the security, does not deliver it against such sale within twenty days thereafter, or does not within five days after such sale deposit it in the mails or other usual channels of transportation; but no person shall be deemed to have violated this subsection if he proves that notwithstanding the exercise of good faith he was unable to make such delivery or deposit within such time, or that to do so would cause undue inconvenience or expense.

(d)   Securities held in investment account, transactions in ordinary course of business, and establishment of primary or secondary market.—The provisions of subsection (b) of this section shall not apply to any purchase and sale, or sale and purchase, and the provisions of subsection (c) of this section shall not apply to any sale, of an equity security not then or theretofore held by him in an investment account, by a dealer in the ordinary course of his business and incident to the establishment or maintenance by him of a primary or secondary market (otherwise than on a national securities exchange or an exchange exempted from registration under section 78e of this title) for such security. The Commission may, by such rules and regulations as it deems necessary or appropriate in the public interest, define and prescribe terms and conditions with respect to securities held in an investment account and transactions made in the ordinary course of business and incident to the establishment or maintenance of a primary or secondary market.

(e)   Application of section to foreign or domestic arbitrage transactions.—The provisions of this section shall not apply to foreign or domestic arbitrage transactions unless made in contravention of such rules and regulations as the Commission may adopt in order to carry out the purposes of this section.

* * *

Records and Reports

§ 78q [P.L. § 17]. (a) Rules and regulations.

(1)   Every national securities exchange, member thereof, broker or dealer who transacts a business in securities through the medium of any such member, registered securities association, registered broker or dealer, registered municipal securities dealer municipal advisor,,[1] registered securities information processor, registered transfer agent, nationally recognized statistical rating organization, and registered clearing agency and the Municipal Securities Rulemaking

---

[1]   So in original.

Board shall make and keep for prescribed periods such records, furnish such copies thereof, and make and disseminate such reports as the Commission, by rule, prescribes as necessary or appropriate in the public interest, for the protection of investors, or otherwise in furtherance of the purposes of this chapter. Any report that a nationally recognized statistical rating organization is required by Commission rules under this paragraph to make and disseminate to the Commission shall be deemed furnished to the Commission.

(2)   Every registered clearing agency shall also make and keep for prescribed periods such records, furnish such copies thereof, and make and disseminate such reports, as the appropriate regulatory agency for such clearing agency, by rule, prescribes as necessary or appropriate for the safeguarding of securities and funds in the custody or control of such clearing agency or for which it is responsible.

(3)   Every registered transfer agent shall also make and keep for prescribed periods such records, furnish such copies thereof, and make such reports as the appropriate regulatory agency for such transfer agent, by rule, prescribes as necessary or appropriate in furtherance of the purposes of section 78q–1 of this title.

(b)   Records subject to examination.

(1)   Procedures for cooperation with other agencies.—All records of persons described in subsection (a) of this section are subject at any time, or from time to time, to such reasonable periodic, special, or other examinations by representatives of the Commission and the appropriate regulatory agency for such persons as the Commission or the appropriate regulatory agency for such persons deems necessary or appropriate in the public interest, for the protection of investors, or otherwise in furtherance of the purposes of this chapter: Provided, however, That the Commission shall, prior to conducting any such examination of a—

(A)   registered clearing agency, registered transfer agent, or registered municipal securities dealer for which it is not the appropriate regulatory agency, give notice to the appropriate regulatory agency for such clearing agency, transfer agent, or municipal securities dealer of such proposed examination and consult with such appropriate regulatory agency concerning the feasibility and desirability of coordinating such examination with examinations conducted by such appropriate regulatory agency with a view to avoiding unnecessary regulatory duplication or undue regulatory burdens for such clearing agency, transfer agent, or municipal securities dealer. . . .

* * *

(4)   Rules of construction.—

* * *

(C)   Nothing in the proviso in paragraph (1) shall be construed to impair or limit (other than by the requirement of prior consultation) the power of the Commission under this subsection to examine any clearing agency, transfer agent, or municipal securities dealer or to affect in any way the power of the Commission under any other provision of this chapter or otherwise to inspect, examine, or investigate any such clearing agency, transfer agent, or municipal securities dealer.

(c)   Copies of reports filed with other regulatory agencies.

(1)   Every clearing agency, transfer agent, and municipal securities dealer for which the Commission is not the appropriate regulatory agency shall (A) file with the appropriate regulatory agency for such clearing agency, transfer agent, or municipal securities dealer a copy of any application, notice, proposal, report, or document filed with the Commission by reason of its being a clearing agency, transfer agent, or municipal securities dealer and (B) file with the Commission a copy of any application, notice, proposal, report, or document filed with such appropriate regulatory agency by reason of its being a clearing agency, transfer agent, or municipal securities dealer. The Municipal Securities Rulemaking Board shall file with each

agency enumerated in section 78c(a)(34)(A) of this title copies of every proposed rule change filed with the Commission pursuant to section 78s(b) of this title.

(2)   The appropriate regulatory agency for a clearing agency, transfer agent, or municipal securities dealer for which the Commission is not the appropriate regulatory agency shall file with the Commission notice of the commencement of any proceeding and a copy of any order entered by such appropriate regulatory agency against any clearing agency, transfer agent, municipal securities dealer, or person associated with a transfer agent or municipal securities dealer, and the Commission shall file with such appropriate regulatory agency, if any, notice of the commencement of any proceeding and a copy of any order entered by the Commission against the clearing agency, transfer agent, or municipal securities dealer, or against any person associated with a transfer agent or municipal securities dealer for which the agency is the appropriate regulatory agency.

(3)   The Commission and the appropriate regulatory agency for a clearing agency, transfer agent, or municipal securities dealer for which the Commission is not the appropriate regulatory agency shall each notify the other and make a report of any examination conducted by it of such clearing agency, transfer agent, or municipal securities dealer, and, upon request, furnish to the other a copy of such report and any data supplied to it in connection with such examination.

(4)   The Commission or the appropriate regulatory agency may specify that documents required to be filed pursuant to this subsection with the Commission or such agency, respectively, may be retained by the originating clearing agency, transfer agent, or municipal securities dealer, or filed with another appropriate regulatory agency. The Commission or the appropriate regulatory agency (as the case may be) making such a specification shall continue to have access to the document on request.

(d)   Self-regulatory organizations.

(1)   The Commission, by rule or order, as it deems necessary or appropriate in the public interest and for the protection of investors, to foster cooperation and coordination among self-regulatory organizations, or to remove impediments to and foster the development of a national market system and national system for the clearance and settlement of securities transactions, may—

(A)   with respect to any person who is a member of or participant in more than one self-regulatory organization, relieve any such self-regulatory organization of any responsibility under this chapter (i) to receive regulatory reports from such person, (ii) to examine such person for compliance, or to enforce compliance by such person, with specified provisions of this chapter, the rules and regulations thereunder, and its own rules, or (iii) to carry out other specified regulatory functions with respect to such person, and

(B)   allocate among self-regulatory organizations the authority to adopt rules with respect to matters as to which, in the absence of such allocation, such self-regulatory organizations share authority under this chapter.

In making any such rule or entering any such order, the Commission shall take into consideration the regulatory capabilities and procedures of the self-regulatory organizations, availability of staff, convenience of location, unnecessary regulatory duplication, and such other factors as the Commission may consider germane to the protection of investors, cooperation and coordination among self-regulatory organizations, and the development of a national market system and a national system for the clearance and settlement of securities transactions. The Commission, by rule or order, as it deems necessary or appropriate in the public interest and for the protection of investors, may require any self-regulatory organization relieved of any responsibility pursuant to this paragraph, and any person with respect to whom such responsibility relates, to take such steps as are specified in any such rule or order to notify customers of, and persons doing business with, such person of the limited nature of such self-regulatory organization's responsibility for such person's acts, practices, and course of business.

(2)   A self-regulatory organization shall furnish copies of any report of examination of any person who is a member of or a participant in such self-regulatory organization to any other self-regulatory organization of which such person is a member or in which such person is a participant upon the request of such person, such other self-regulatory organization, or the Commission.

(e)   Balance sheet and income statement; other financial statements and information.

(1)(A)   Every registered broker or dealer shall annually file with the Commission a balance sheet and income statement certified by a[5] independent public accounting firm, or by a registered public accounting firm if the firm is required to be registered under the Sarbanes-Oxley Act of 2002,,[1] prepared on a calendar or fiscal year basis, and such other financial statements (which shall, as the Commission specifies, be certified) and information concerning its financial condition as the Commission, by rule may prescribe as necessary or appropriate in the public interest or for the protection of investors.

(B)   Every registered broker and dealer shall annually send to its customers its certified balance sheet and such other financial statements and information concerning its financial condition as the Commission, by rule, may prescribe pursuant to subsection (a) of this section.

(C)   The Commission, by rule or order, may conditionally or unconditionally exempt any registered broker or dealer, or class of such brokers or dealers, from any provision of this paragraph if the Commission determines that such exemption is consistent with the public interest and the protection of investors.

(2)   The Commission, by rule, as it deems necessary or appropriate in the public interest or for the protection of investors, may prescribe the form and content of financial statements filed pursuant to this chapter and the accounting principles and accounting standards used in their preparation.

(f)   Missing, lost, counterfeit, and stolen securities.

(1)   Every national securities exchange, member thereof, registered securities association, broker, dealer, municipal securities dealer, government securities broker, government securities dealer, registered transfer agent, registered clearing agency, participant therein, member of the Federal Reserve System, and bank whose deposits are insured by the Federal Deposit Insurance Corporation shall—

(A)   report to the Commission or other person designated by the Commission and, in the case of securities issued pursuant to chapter 31 of title 31, to the Secretary of the Treasury such information about securities that are missing, lost, counterfeit, stolen, or cancelled, in such form and within such time as the Commission, by rule, determines is necessary or appropriate in the public interest or for the protection of investors; such information shall be available on request for a reasonable fee, to any such exchange, member, association, broker, dealer, municipal securities dealer, government securities broker, government securities dealer, transfer agent, clearing agency, participant, member of the Federal Reserve System, or insured bank, and such other persons as the Commission, by rule, designates; and

(B)   make such inquiry with respect to information reported pursuant to this subsection as the Commission, by rule, prescribes as necessary or appropriate in the public interest or for the protection of investors, to determine whether securities in their custody or control, for which they are responsible, or in which they are effecting, clearing, or settling a transaction have been reported as missing, lost, counterfeit, stolen, cancelled, or reported in such other manner as the Commission, by rule, may prescribe.

---

[5]   So in original. Probably should be "an".
[1]   So in original.

(2)   Every member of a national securities exchange, broker, dealer, registered transfer agent, registered clearing agency, registered securities information processor, national securities exchange, and national securities association shall require that each of its partners, directors, officers, and employees be fingerprinted and shall submit such fingerprints, or cause the same to be submitted, to the Attorney General of the United States for identification and appropriate processing. The Commission, by rule, may exempt from the provisions of this paragraph upon specified terms, conditions, and periods, any class of partners, directors, officers, or employees of any such member, broker, dealer, transfer agent, clearing agency, securities information processor, national securities exchange, or national securities association, if the Commission finds that such action is not inconsistent with the public interest or the protection of investors. Notwithstanding any other provision of law, in providing identification and processing functions, the Attorney General shall provide the Commission and self-regulatory organizations designated by the Commission with access to all criminal history record information.

(3)(A)   In order to carry out the authority under paragraph (1) above, the Commission or its designee may enter into agreement with the Attorney General to use the facilities of the National Crime Information Center ("NCIC") to receive, store, and disseminate information in regard to missing, lost, counterfeit, or stolen securities and to permit direct inquiry access to NCIC's file on such securities for the financial community.

(B)   In order to carry out the authority under paragraph (1) of this subsection, the Commission or its designee and the Secretary of the Treasury shall enter into an agreement whereby the Commission or its designee will receive, store, and disseminate information in the possession, and which comes into the possession, of the Department of the Treasury in regard to missing, lost, counterfeit, or stolen securities.

(4)   In regard to paragraphs (1), (2), and (3), above insofar as such paragraphs apply to any bank or member of the Federal Reserve System, the Commission may delegate its authority to:

(A)   the Comptroller of the Currency as to national banks;

(B)   the Federal Reserve Board in regard to any member of the Federal Reserve System which is not a national bank; and

(C)   the Federal Deposit Insurance Corporation for any State bank which is insured by the Federal Deposit Insurance Corporation but which is not a member of the Federal Reserve System.

(5)   The Commission shall encourage the insurance industry to require their insured to report expeditiously instances of missing, lost, counterfeit, or stolen securities to the Commission or to such other person as the Commission may, by rule, designate to receive such information.

(g)   Persons extending credit.—Any broker, dealer, or other person extending credit who is subject to the rules and regulations prescribed by the Board of Governors of the Federal Reserve System pursuant to this chapter shall make such reports to the Board as it may require as necessary or appropriate to enable it to perform the functions conferred upon it by this chapter. If any such broker, dealer, or other person shall fail to make any such report or fail to furnish full information therein, or, if in the judgment of the Board it is otherwise necessary, such broker, dealer, or other person shall permit such inspections to be made by the Board with respect to the business operations of such broker, dealer, or other person as the Board may deem necessary to enable it to obtain the required information.

(h)   Risk assessment for holding company systems.

(1)   Obligations to obtain, maintain, and report information.—Every person who is (A) a registered broker or dealer, or (B) a registered municipal securities dealer for which the Commission is the appropriate regulatory agency, shall obtain such information and make and keep such records as the Commission by rule prescribes concerning the registered person's policies, procedures, or systems for monitoring and controlling financial and operational risks to

it resulting from the activities of any of its associated persons, other than a natural person. Such records shall describe, in the aggregate, each of the financial and securities activities conducted by, and the customary sources of capital and funding of, those of its associated persons whose business activities are reasonably likely to have a material impact on the financial or operational condition of such registered person, including its net capital, its liquidity, or its ability to conduct or finance its operations. The Commission, by rule, may require summary reports of such information to be filed with the Commission no more frequently than quarterly.

(2) Authority to require additional information.—If, as a result of adverse market conditions or based on reports provided to the Commission pursuant to paragraph (1) of this subsection or other available information, the Commission reasonably concludes that it has concerns regarding the financial or operational condition of (A) any registered broker or dealer, or (B) any registered municipal securities dealer, government securities broker, or government securities dealer for which the Commission is the appropriate regulatory agency, the Commission may require the registered person to make reports concerning the financial and securities activities of any of such person's associated persons, other than a natural person, whose business activities are reasonably likely to have a material impact on the financial or operational condition of such registered person. The Commission, in requiring reports pursuant to this paragraph, shall specify the information required, the period for which it is required, the time and date on which the information must be furnished, and whether the information is to be furnished directly to the Commission or to a self-regulatory organization with primary responsibility for examining the registered person's financial and operational condition.

(3) Special provisions with respect to associated persons subject to Federal banking agency regulation.

(A) Cooperation in implementation.—In developing and implementing reporting requirements pursuant to paragraph (1) of this subsection with respect to associated persons subject to examination by or reporting requirements of a Federal banking agency, the Commission shall consult with and consider the views of each such Federal banking agency. If a Federal banking agency comments in writing on a proposed rule of the Commission under this subsection that has been published for comment, the Commission shall respond in writing to such written comment before adopting the proposed rule. The Commission shall, at the request of the Federal banking agency, publish such comment and response in the Federal Register at the time of publishing the adopted rule.

(B) Use of banking agency reports.—A registered broker, dealer, or municipal securities dealer shall be in compliance with any recordkeeping or reporting requirement adopted pursuant to paragraph (1) of this subsection concerning an associated person that is subject to examination by or reporting requirements of a Federal banking agency if such broker, dealer, or municipal securities dealer utilizes for such recordkeeping or reporting requirement copies of reports filed by the associated person with the Federal banking agency pursuant to section 161 of title 12, subchapter VIII of chapter 3 of title 12, section 1817(a) of title 12, section 1467a(b) of title 12, or section 1847 of title 12. The Commission may, however, by rule adopted pursuant to paragraph (1), require any broker, dealer, or municipal securities dealer filing such reports with the Commission to obtain, maintain, or report supplemental information if the Commission makes an explicit finding that such supplemental information is necessary to inform the Commission regarding potential risks to such broker, dealer, or municipal securities dealer. Prior to requiring any such supplemental information, the Commission shall first request the Federal banking agency to expand its reporting requirements to include such information.

(C) Procedure for requiring additional information.—Prior to making a request pursuant to paragraph (2) of this subsection for information with respect to an associated person that is subject to examination by or reporting requirements of a Federal banking agency, the Commission shall—

(i)   notify such agency of the information required with respect to such associated person; and

(ii)   consult with such agency to determine whether the information required is available from such agency and for other purposes, unless the Commission determines that any delay resulting from such consultation would be inconsistent with ensuring the financial and operational condition of the broker, dealer, municipal securities dealer, government securities broker, or government securities dealer or the stability or integrity of the securities markets.

(D)   Exclusion for examination reports.—Nothing in this subsection shall be construed to permit the Commission to require any registered broker or dealer, or any registered municipal securities dealer, government securities broker, or government securities dealer for which the Commission is the appropriate regulatory agency, to obtain, maintain, or furnish any examination report of any Federal banking agency or any supervisory recommendations or analysis contained therein.

(E)   Confidentiality of information provided.—No information provided to or obtained by the Commission from any Federal banking agency pursuant to a request by the Commission under subparagraph (C) of this paragraph regarding any associated person which is subject to examination by or reporting requirements of a Federal banking agency may be disclosed to any other person (other than a self-regulatory organization), without the prior written approval of the Federal banking agency. Nothing in this subsection shall authorize the Commission to withhold information from Congress, or prevent the Commission from complying with a request for information from any other Federal department or agency requesting the information for purposes within the scope of its jurisdiction, or complying with an order of a court of the United States in an action brought by the United States or the Commission.

(F)   Notice to banking agencies concerning financial and operational condition concerns.—The Commission shall notify the Federal banking agency of any concerns of the Commission regarding significant financial or operational risks resulting from the activities of any registered broker or dealer, or any registered municipal securities dealer, government securities broker, or government securities dealer for which the Commission is the appropriate regulatory agency, to any associated person thereof which is subject to examination by or reporting requirements of the Federal banking agency.

(G)   "Federal banking agency" defined.—For purposes of this paragraph, the term "Federal banking agency" shall have the same meaning as the term "appropriate Federal bank agency" in section 1813(q) of title 12.

(4)   Exemptions.—The Commission by rule or order may exempt any person or class of persons, under such terms and conditions and for such periods as the Commission shall provide in such rule or order, from the provisions of this subsection, and the rules thereunder. In granting such exemptions, the Commission shall consider, among other factors—

(A)   whether information of the type required under this subsection is available from a supervisory agency (as defined in section 3401(6)[6] of title 12), a State insurance commission or similar State agency, the Commodity Futures Trading Commission, or a similar foreign regulator;

(B)   the primary business of any associated person;

(C)   the nature and extent of domestic or foreign regulation of the associated person's activities;

(D)   the nature and extent of the registered person's securities activities; and

---

[6]   See References in Text note below. [Not reproduced here.]

(E) with respect to the registered person and its associated persons, on a consolidated basis, the amount and proportion of assets devoted to, and revenues derived from, activities in the United States securities markets.

(5) Authority to limit disclosure of information.—Notwithstanding any other provision of law, the Commission shall not be compelled to disclose any information required to be reported under this subsection, or any information supplied to the Commission by any domestic or foreign regulatory agency that relates to the financial or operational condition of any associated person of a registered broker, dealer, government securities broker, government securities dealer, or municipal securities dealer. Nothing in this subsection shall authorize the Commission to withhold information from Congress, or prevent the Commission from complying with a request for information from any other Federal department or agency requesting the information for purposes within the scope of its jurisdiction, or complying with an order of a court of the United States in an action brought by the United States or the Commission. For purposes of section 552 of title 5, this subsection shall be considered a statute described in subsection (b)(3)(B) of such section 552. In prescribing regulations to carry out the requirements of this subsection, the Commission shall designate information described in or obtained pursuant to subparagraph (B) or (C) of paragraph (3) of this subsection as confidential information for purposes of section 78x(b)(2) of this title.

(i) Authority to limit disclosure of information.—Notwithstanding any other provision of law, the Commission shall not be compelled to disclose any information required to be reported under subsection (h) or (i)[6] of this section or any information supplied to the Commission by any domestic or foreign regulatory agency that relates to the financial or operational condition of any associated person of a broker or dealer, investment bank holding company, or any affiliate of an investment bank holding company. Nothing in this subsection shall authorize the Commission to withhold information from Congress, or prevent the Commission from complying with a request for information from any other Federal department or agency or any self-regulatory organization requesting the information for purposes within the scope of its jurisdiction, or complying with an order of a court of the United States in an action brought by the United States or the Commission. For purposes of section 552 of title 5, this subsection shall be considered a statute described in subsection (b)(3)(B) of such section 552. In prescribing regulations to carry out the requirements of this subsection, the Commission shall designate information described in or obtained pursuant to subparagraphs (A), (B), and (C) of subsection (i)(5)[6] of this section as confidential information for purposes of section 78x(b)(2) of this title.

(j) Coordination of examining authorities.

(1) Elimination of duplication.—The Commission and the examining authorities, through cooperation and coordination of examination and oversight activities, shall eliminate any unnecessary and burdensome duplication in the examination process.

(2) Coordination of examinations.—The Commission and the examining authorities shall share such information, including reports of examinations, customer complaint information, and other nonpublic regulatory information, as appropriate to foster a coordinated approach to regulatory oversight of brokers and dealers that are subject to examination by more than one examining authority.

(3) Examinations for cause.—At any time, any examining authority may conduct an examination for cause of any broker or dealer subject to its jurisdiction.

(4) Confidentiality.—(A) In general.—Section 78x of this title shall apply to the sharing of information in accordance with this subsection. The Commission shall take appropriate action under section 78x(c) of this title to ensure that such information is not inappropriately disclosed.

---

[6] See References in Text note below. [Not reproduced here.]

(B) *Appropriate disclosure not prohibited.*—Nothing in this paragraph authorizes the Commission or any examining authority to withhold information from the Congress, or prevent the Commission or any examining authority from complying with a request for information from any other Federal department or agency requesting the information for purposes within the scope of its jurisdiction, or complying with an order of a court of the United States in an action brought by the United States or the Commission.

(5) *"Examining authority" defined.*—For purposes of this subsection, the term "examining authority" means a self-regulatory organization registered with the Commission under this chapter (other than a registered clearing agency) with the authority to examine, inspect, and otherwise oversee the activities of a registered broker or dealer.

Liability for Misleading Statements

§ 78r [P.L. § 18]. (a) *Persons liable; persons entitled to recover; defense of good faith; suit at law or in equity; costs, etc.*—Any person who shall make or cause to be made any statement in any application, report, or document filed pursuant to this chapter or any rule or regulation thereunder or any undertaking contained in a registration statement as provided in subsection (d) of section 78o of this title, which statement was at the time and in the light of the circumstances under which it was made false or misleading with respect to any material fact, shall be liable to any person (not knowing that such statement was false or misleading) who, in reliance upon such statement, shall have purchased or sold a security at a price which was affected by such statement, for damages caused by such reliance, unless the person sued shall prove that he acted in good faith and had no knowledge that such statement was false or misleading. A person seeking to enforce such liability may sue at law or in equity in any court of competent jurisdiction. In any such suit the court may, in its discretion, require an undertaking for the payment of the costs of such suit, and assess reasonable costs, including reasonable attorneys' fees, against either party litigant.

(b) *Contribution.*—Every person who becomes liable to make payment under this section may recover contribution as in cases of contract from any person who, if joined in the original suit, would have been liable to make the same payment.

(c) *Period of limitations.*—No action shall be maintained to enforce any liability created under this section unless brought within one year after the discovery of the facts constituting the cause of action and within three years after such cause of action accrued.

Liability of Controlling Persons and Persons Who Aid and Abet Violations

§ 78t [P.L. § 20]. (a) *Joint and several liability; good faith defense.*—Every person who, directly or indirectly, controls any person liable under any provision of this chapter or of any rule or regulation thereunder shall also be liable jointly and severally with and to the same extent as such controlled person to any person to whom such controlled person is liable (including to the Commission in any action brought under paragraph (1) or (3) of section 78u(d) of this title), unless the controlling person acted in good faith and did not directly or indirectly induce the act or acts constituting the violation or cause of action.

(b) *Unlawful activity through or by means of any other person.*—It shall be unlawful for any person, directly or indirectly, to do any act or thing which it would be unlawful for such person to do under the provisions of this chapter or any rule or regulation thereunder through or by means of any other person.

(c) *Hindering, delaying, or obstructing the making or filing of any document, report, or information.*—It shall be unlawful for any director or officer of, or any owner of any securities issued by, any issuer required to file any document, report, or information under this chapter or any rule or regulation thereunder without just cause to hinder, delay, or obstruct the making or filing of any such document, report, or information.

(d)   Liability for trading in securities while in possession of material nonpublic information.—Wherever communicating, or purchasing or selling a security while in possession of, material nonpublic information would violate, or result in liability to any purchaser or seller of the security under any provisions of this chapter, or any rule or regulation thereunder, such conduct in connection with a purchase or sale of a put, call, straddle, option, privilege or security-based swap agreement with respect to such security or with respect to a group or index of securities including such security, shall also violate and result in comparable liability to any purchaser or seller of that security under such provision, rule, or regulation.

(e)   Prosecution of persons who aid and abet violations.—For purposes of any action brought by the Commission under paragraph (1) or (3) of section 78u(d) of this title, any person that knowingly or recklessly provides substantial assistance to another person in violation of a provision of this chapter, or of any rule or regulation issued under this chapter, shall be deemed to be in violation of such provision to the same extent as the person to whom such assistance is provided.

* * *

Liability to Contemporaneous Traders for Insider Trading

§ 78t–1 [P.L. § 20A]. (a) Private rights of action based on contemporaneous trading.—Any person who violates any provision of this chapter or the rules or regulations thereunder by purchasing or selling a security while in possession of material, nonpublic information shall be liable in an action in any court of competent jurisdiction to any person who, contemporaneously with the purchase or sale of securities that is the subject of such violation, has purchased (where such violation is based on a sale of securities) or sold (where such violation is based on a purchase of securities) securities of the same class.

(b)   Limitations on liability.

(1)   Contemporaneous trading actions limited to profit gained or loss avoided.—The total amount of damages imposed under subsection (a) of this section shall not exceed the profit gained or loss avoided in the transaction or transactions that are the subject of the violation.

(2)   Offsetting disgorgements against liability.—The total amount of damages imposed against any person under subsection (a) of this section shall be diminished by the amounts, if any, that such person may be required to disgorge, pursuant to a court order obtained at the instance of the Commission, in a proceeding brought under section 78u(d) of this title relating to the same transaction or transactions.

(3)   Controlling person liability.—No person shall be liable under this section solely by reason of employing another person who is liable under this section, but the liability of a controlling person under this section shall be subject to section 78t(a) of this title.

(4)   Statute of limitations.—No action may be brought under this section more than 5 years after the date of the last transaction that is the subject of the violation.

(c)   Joint and several liability for communicating.—Any person who violates any provision of this chapter or the rules or regulations thereunder by communicating material, nonpublic information shall be jointly and severally liable under subsection (a) of this section with, and to the same extent as, any person or persons liable under subsection (a) of this section to whom the communication was directed.

(d)   Authority not to restrict other express or implied rights of action.—Nothing in this section shall be construed to limit or condition the right of any person to bring an action to enforce a requirement of this chapter or the availability of any cause of action implied from a provision of this chapter.

(e)   Provisions not to affect public prosecutions.—This section shall not be construed to bar or limit in any manner any action by the Commission or the Attorney General under any other provision of this chapter, nor shall it bar or limit in any manner any action to recover penalties, or to seek any other order regarding penalties.

Investigations and Actions

§ 78u [P.L. § 21]. (a) Authority and discretion of Commission to investigate violations.

(1)   The Commission may, in its discretion, make such investigations as it deems necessary to determine whether any person has violated, is violating, or is about to violate any provision of this chapter, the rules or regulations thereunder, the rules of a national securities exchange or registered securities association of which such person is a member or a person associated, or, as to any act or practice, or omission to act, while associated with a member, formerly associated with a member, the rules of a registered clearing agency in which such person is a participant, or, as to any act or practice, or omission to act, while a participant, was a participant, the rules of the Public Company Accounting Oversight Board, of which such person is a registered public accounting firm, a person associated with such a firm, or, as to any act, practice, or omission to act, while associated with such firm, a person formerly associated with such a firm, or the rules of the Municipal Securities Rulemaking Board, and may require or permit any person to file with it a statement in writing, under oath or otherwise as the Commission shall determine, as to all the facts and circumstances concerning the matter to be investigated. The Commission is authorized in its discretion, to publish information concerning any such violations, and to investigate any facts, conditions, practices, or matters which it may deem necessary or proper to aid in the enforcement of such provisions, in the prescribing of rules and regulations under this chapter, or in securing information to serve as a basis for recommending further legislation concerning the matters to which this chapter relates.

(2)   On request from a foreign securities authority, the Commission may provide assistance in accordance with this paragraph if the requesting authority states that the requesting authority is conducting an investigation which it deems necessary to determine whether any person has violated, is violating, or is about to violate any laws or rules relating to securities matters that the requesting authority administers or enforces. The Commission may, in its discretion, conduct such investigation as the Commission deems necessary to collect information and evidence pertinent to the request for assistance. Such assistance may be provided without regard to whether the facts stated in the request would also constitute a violation of the laws of the United States. In deciding whether to provide such assistance, the Commission shall consider whether (A) the requesting authority has agreed to provide reciprocal assistance in securities matters to the Commission; and (B) compliance with the request would prejudice the public interest of the United States.

(b)   Attendance of witnesses; production of records.—For the purpose of any such investigation, or any other proceeding under this chapter, any member of the Commission or any officer designated by it is empowered to administer oaths and affirmations, [subpoena] witnesses, compel their attendance, take evidence, and require the production of any books, papers, correspondence, memoranda, or other records which the Commission deems relevant or material to the inquiry. Such attendance of witnesses and the production of any such records may be required from any place in the United States or any State at any designated place of hearing.

(c)   Judicial enforcement of investigative power of Commission; refusal to obey [subpoena]; criminal sanctions.—In case of contumacy by, or refusal to obey a [subpoena] issued to, any person, the Commission may invoke the aid of any court of the United States within the jurisdiction of which such investigation or proceeding is carried on, or where such person resides or carries on business, in requiring the attendance and testimony of witnesses and the production of books, papers, correspondence, memoranda, and other records. And such court may issue an order requiring such person to appear before the Commission or member or officer designated by the Commission, there to produce records, if so ordered, or to give testimony touching the matter under investigation or in question; and any failure to obey such order of the court may be punished by such court as a contempt thereof. All process in any such case may be served in the judicial district whereof such person is an inhabitant or wherever he may be found. Any person who shall, without just cause, fail or refuse to attend and testify or to answer any lawful inquiry or to produce books, papers, correspondence, memoranda, and other records, if in his power so to do, in obedience to the [subpoena] of the Commission, shall be guilty of a misdemeanor and, upon conviction, shall be subject to a fine of not more than $1,000 or to imprisonment for a term of not more than one year, or both.

(d) Injunction proceedings; authority of court to prohibit persons from serving as officers and directors; money penalties in civil actions.

(1) Whenever it shall appear to the Commission that any person is engaged or is about to engage in acts or practices constituting a violation of any provision of this chapter, the rules or regulations thereunder, the rules of a national securities exchange or registered securities association of which such person is a member or a person associated with a member, the rules of a registered clearing agency in which such person is a participant, the rules of the Public Company Accounting Oversight Board, of which such person is a registered public accounting firm or a person associated with such a firm, or the rules of the Municipal Securities Rulemaking Board, it may in its discretion bring an action in the proper district court of the United States, the United States District Court for the District of Columbia, or the United States courts of any territory or other place subject to the jurisdiction of the United States, to enjoin such acts or practices, and upon a proper showing a permanent or temporary injunction or restraining order shall be granted without bond. The Commission may transmit such evidence as may be available concerning such acts or practices as may constitute a violation of any provision of this chapter or the rules or regulations thereunder to the Attorney General, who may, in his discretion, institute the necessary criminal proceedings under this chapter.

(2) Authority of Court To Prohibit Persons From Serving as Officers and Directors.—In any proceeding under paragraph (1) of this subsection, the court may prohibit, conditionally or unconditionally, and permanently or for such period of time as it shall determine, any person who violated section 78j(b) of this title or the rules or regulations thereunder from acting as an officer or director of any issuer that has a class of securities registered pursuant to section 78*l* of this title or that is required to file reports pursuant to section 78o(d) of this title if the person's conduct demonstrates unfitness to serve as an officer or director of any such issuer.

(3) Money Penalties in Civil Actions.

(A) Authority of commission.—Whenever it shall appear to the Commission that any person has violated any provision of this chapter, the rules or regulations thereunder, or a cease-and-desist order entered by the Commission pursuant to section 78u–3 of this title, other than by committing a violation subject to a penalty pursuant to section 78u–1 of this title, the Commission may bring an action in a United States district court to seek, and the court shall have jurisdiction to impose, upon a proper showing, a civil penalty to be paid by the person who committed such violation.

(B) Amount of penalty.

(i) First tier.-The amount of the penalty shall be determined by the court in light of the facts and circumstances. For each violation, the amount of the penalty shall not exceed the greater of (I) $5,000 for a natural person or $50,000 for any other person, or (II) the gross amount of pecuniary gain to such defendant as a result of the violation.

(ii) Second tier.-Notwithstanding clause (i), the amount of penalty for each such violation shall not exceed the greater of (I) $50,000 for a natural person or $250,000 for any other person, or (II) the gross amount of pecuniary gain to such defendant as a result of the violation, if the violation described in subparagraph (A) involved fraud, deceit, manipulation, or deliberate or reckless disregard of a regulatory requirement.

(iii) Third tier.-Notwithstanding clauses (i) and (ii), the amount of penalty for each such violation shall not exceed the greater of (I) $100,000 for a natural person or $500,000 for any other person, or (II) the gross amount of pecuniary gain to such defendant as a result of the violation, if—

(aa) the violation described in subparagraph (A) involved fraud, deceit, manipulation, or deliberate or reckless disregard of a regulatory requirement; and

(bb) such violation directly or indirectly resulted in substantial losses or created a significant risk of substantial losses to other persons.

(C) Procedures for collection.

(i)   Payment of penalty to treasury.—A penalty imposed under this section shall be payable into the Treasury of the United States, except as otherwise provided in section 7246 of this title and section 78u–6 of this title.

(ii) Collection of penalties.—If a person upon whom such a penalty is imposed shall fail to pay such penalty within the time prescribed in the court's order, the Commission may refer the matter to the Attorney General who shall recover such penalty by action in the appropriate United States district court.

(iii) Remedy not exclusive.—The actions authorized by this paragraph may be brought in addition to any other action that the Commission or the Attorney General is entitled to bring.

(iv) Jurisdiction and venue.—For purposes of section 78aa of this title, actions under this paragraph shall be actions to enforce a liability or a duty created by this chapter.

(D) Special provisions relating to a violation of a cease-and-desist order.—In an action to enforce a cease-and-desist order entered by the Commission pursuant to section 78u–3 of this title, each separate violation of such order shall be a separate offense, except that in the case of a violation through a continuing failure to comply with the order, each day of the failure to comply shall be deemed a separate offense.

(4) Prohibition of attorneys' fees paid from commission disgorgement funds.—Except as otherwise ordered by the court upon motion by the Commission, or, in the case of an administrative action, as otherwise ordered by the Commission, funds disgorged as the result of an action brought by the Commission in Federal court, or as a result of any Commission administrative action, shall not be distributed as payment for attorneys' fees or expenses incurred by private parties seeking distribution of the disgorged funds.

(5) Equitable Relief.—In any action or proceeding brought or instituted by the Commission under any provision of the securities laws, the Commission may seek, and any Federal court may grant, any equitable relief that may be appropriate or necessary for the benefit of investors.

(6) Authority of a court to prohibit persons from participating in an offering of penny stock.

(A) In general.—In any proceeding under paragraph (1) against any person participating in, or, at the time of the alleged misconduct who was participating in, an offering of penny stock, the court may prohibit that person from participating in an offering of penny stock, conditionally or unconditionally, and permanently or for such period of time as the court shall determine.

(B) Definition.—For purposes of this paragraph, the term "person participating in an offering of penny stock" includes any person engaging in activities with a broker, dealer, or issuer for purposes of issuing, trading, or inducing or attempting to induce the purchase or sale of, any penny stock. The Commission may, by rule or regulation, define such term to include other activities, and may, by rule, regulation, or order, exempt any person or class of persons, in whole or in part, conditionally or unconditionally, from inclusion in such term.

(e) Mandamus.—Upon application of the Commission the district courts of the United States and the United States courts of any territory or other place subject to the jurisdiction of the United States shall have jurisdiction to issue writs of mandamus, injunctions, and orders commanding (1) any person to comply with the provisions of this chapter, the rules, regulations, and orders thereunder, the rules of a national securities exchange or registered securities association of which such person is a member or person associated with a member, the rules of a registered clearing agency in which such person is a participant, the rules of the Public Company Accounting Oversight Board, of which such person is a registered public accounting firm or a person associated with such a firm, the rules of the Municipal Securities Rulemaking Board, or any undertaking contained in a registration statement as provided in subsection (d) of section 78o of this title, (2) any national securities exchange or registered securities association to enforce compliance by its members and persons associated with its members with the provisions of this chapter, the rules, regulations, and orders thereunder, and the rules of such exchange or association, or (3) any registered clearing agency to enforce compliance by its participants with the provisions of the rules of such clearing agency.

(f) Rules of self-regulatory organizations or Board.—Notwithstanding any other provision of this chapter, the Commission shall not bring any action pursuant to subsection (d) or (e) of this section against any person for violation of, or to command compliance with, the rules of a self-regulatory organization or the Public Company Accounting Oversight Board unless it appears to the Commission that (1) such self-regulatory organization or the Public Company Accounting Oversight Board is unable or unwilling to take appropriate action against such person in the public interest and for the protection of investors, or (2) such action is otherwise necessary or appropriate in the public interest or for the protection of investors.

(g) Consolidation of actions; consent of Commission.—Notwithstanding the provisions of section 1407(a) of title 28, or any other provision of law, no action for equitable relief instituted by the Commission pursuant to the securities laws shall be consolidated or coordinated with other actions not brought by the Commission, even though such other actions may involve common questions of fact, unless such consolidation is consented to by the Commission.

(h) Access to records.

(1) The Right to Financial Privacy Act of 1978 [12 U.S.C. 3401 et seq.] shall apply with respect to the Commission, except as otherwise provided in this subsection.

(2) Notwithstanding section 1105 or 1107 of the Right to Financial Privacy Act of 1978 [12 U.S.C. 3405 or 3407], the Commission may have access to and obtain copies of, or the information contained in financial records of a customer from a financial institution without prior notice to the customer upon an ex parte showing to an appropriate United States district court that the Commission seeks such financial records pursuant to a [subpoena] issued in conformity with the requirements of section 19(b)[1] of the Securities Act of 1933, section 21(b) of the Securities Exchange Act of 1934 [15 U.S.C. 78u(b)], section 42(b) of the Investment Company Act of 1940 [15 U.S.C. 80a–41(b)], or section 209(b) of the Investment Advisers Act of 1940 [15 U.S.C. 80b–9(b)], and that the Commission has reason to believe that—

(A) delay in obtaining access to such financial records, or the required notice, will result in—

(i) flight from prosecution;

(ii) destruction of or tampering with evidence;

(iii) transfer of assets or records outside the territorial limits of the United States;

(iv) improper conversion of investor assets; or

---

[1] See References in Text note below. [Not reproduced here.]

(v)   impeding the ability of the Commission to identify or trace the source or disposition of funds involved in any securities transaction;

(B)   such financial records are necessary to identify or trace the record or beneficial ownership interest in any security;

(C)   the acts, practices or course of conduct under investigation involve—

(i)   the dissemination of materially false or misleading information concerning any security, issuer, or market, or the failure to make disclosures required under the securities laws, which remain uncorrected; or

(ii)   a financial loss to investors or other persons protected under the securities laws which remains substantially uncompensated; or

(D)   the acts, practices or course of conduct under investigation—

(i)   involve significant financial speculation in securities; or

(ii)   endanger the stability of any financial or investment intermediary.

* * *

Civil Penalties for Insider Trading

§ 78u–1 [P.L. § 21A]. (a) Authority to impose civil penalties.

(1)   Judicial actions by Commission authorized.—Whenever it shall appear to the Commission that any person has violated any provision of this chapter or the rules or regulations thereunder by purchasing or selling a security or security-based swap agreement while in possession of material, nonpublic information in, or has violated any such provision by communicating such information in connection with, a transaction on or through the facilities of a national securities exchange or from or through a broker or dealer, and which is not part of a public offering by an issuer of securities other than standardized options or security futures products, the Commission—

(A)   may bring an action in a United States district court to seek, and the court shall have jurisdiction to impose, a civil penalty to be paid by the person who committed such violation; and

(B)   may, subject to subsection (b)(1) of this section, bring an action in a United States district court to seek, and the court shall have jurisdiction to impose, a civil penalty to be paid by a person who, at the time of the violation, directly or indirectly controlled the person who committed such violation.

(2)   Amount of penalty for person who committed violation.—The amount of the penalty which may be imposed on the person who committed such violation shall be determined by the court in light of the facts and circumstances, but shall not exceed three times the profit gained or loss avoided as a result of such unlawful purchase, sale, or communication.

(3)   Amount of penalty for controlling person.—The amount of the penalty which may be imposed on any person who, at the time of the violation, directly or indirectly controlled the person who committed such violation, shall be determined by the court in light of the facts and circumstances, but shall not exceed the greater of $1,000,000, or three times the amount of the profit gained or loss avoided as a result of such controlled person's violation. If such controlled person's violation was a violation by communication, the profit gained or loss avoided as a result of the violation shall, for purposes of this paragraph only, be deemed to be limited to the profit gained or loss avoided by the person or persons to whom the controlled person directed such communication.

(b)   Limitations on liability.

(1) Liability of controlling persons.—No controlling person shall be subject to a penalty under subsection (a)(1)(B) of this section unless the Commission establishes that—

(A) such controlling person knew or recklessly disregarded the fact that such controlled person was likely to engage in the act or acts constituting the violation and failed to take appropriate steps to prevent such act or acts before they occurred; or

(B) such controlling person knowingly or recklessly failed to establish, maintain, or enforce any policy or procedure required under section 78o(f)[1] of this title or section 80b–4a of this title and such failure substantially contributed to or permitted the occurrence of the act or acts constituting the violation.

(2) Additional restrictions on liability.—No person shall be subject to a penalty under subsection (a) of this section solely by reason of employing another person who is subject to a penalty under such subsection, unless such employing person is liable as a controlling person under paragraph (1) of this subsection. Section 78t(a) of this title shall not apply to actions under subsection (a) of this section.

(c) Authority of Commission.—The Commission, by such rules, regulations, and orders as it considers necessary or appropriate in the public interest or for the protection of investors, may exempt, in whole or in part, either unconditionally or upon specific terms and conditions, any person or transaction or class of persons or transactions from this section.

(d) Procedures for collection.

(1) Payment of penalty to Treasury.—A penalty imposed under this section shall be payable into the Treasury of the United States, except as otherwise provided in section 7246 of this title and section 78u–6 of this title.

(2) Collection of penalties.—If a person upon whom such a penalty is imposed shall fail to pay such penalty within the time prescribed in the court's order, the Commission may refer the matter to the Attorney General who shall recover such penalty by action in the appropriate United States district court.

(3) Remedy not exclusive.—The actions authorized by this section may be brought in addition to any other actions that the Commission or the Attorney General are entitled to bring.

(4) Jurisdiction and venue.—For purposes of section 78aa of this title, actions under this section shall be actions to enforce a liability or a duty created by this chapter.

(5) Statute of limitations.—No action may be brought under this section more than 5 years after the date of the purchase or sale. This section shall not be construed to bar or limit in any manner any action by the Commission or the Attorney General under any other provision of this chapter, nor shall it bar or limit in any manner any action to recover penalties, or to seek any other order regarding penalties, imposed in an action commenced within 5 years of such transaction.

(e) Definition.—For purposes of this section, "profit gained" or "loss avoided" is the difference between the purchase or sale price of the security and the value of that security as measured by the trading price of the security a reasonable period after public dissemination of the nonpublic information.

(f) Limitation on Commission authority.—The authority of the Commission under this section with respect to security-based swap agreements shall be subject to the restrictions and limitations of section 78c–1(b) of this title.

(g) Duty of Members and employees of Congress.

---

[1] See References in Text note below. [Not reproduced here.]

(1) In general.—Subject to the rule of construction under section 10 of the STOCK Act and solely for purposes of the insider trading prohibitions arising under this chapter, including section 78j(b) of this title and Rule 10b–5 thereunder, each Member of Congress or employee of Congress owes a duty arising from a relationship of trust and confidence to the Congress, the United States Government, and the citizens of the United States with respect to material, nonpublic information derived from such person's position as a Member of Congress or employee of Congress or gained from the performance of such person's official responsibilities.

(2) Definitions.—In this subsection—

(A) the term "Member of Congress" means a member of the Senate or House of Representatives, a Delegate to the House of Representatives, and the Resident Commissioner from Puerto Rico; and

(B) the term "employee of Congress" means—

(i) any individual (other than a Member of Congress), whose compensation is disbursed by the Secretary of the Senate or the Chief Administrative Officer of the House of Representatives; and

(ii) any other officer or employee of the legislative branch (as defined in section 109(11) of the Ethics in Government Act of 1978 (5 U.S.C. App. 109(11))).

(3) Rule of construction.—Nothing in this subsection shall be construed to impair or limit the construction of the existing antifraud provisions of the securities laws or the authority of the Commission under those provisions.

(h) Duty of other Federal officials.

(1) In general.—Subject to the rule of construction under section 10 of the STOCK Act and solely for purposes of the insider trading prohibitions arising under this chapter, including section 78j(b) of this title, and Rule 10b–5 thereunder, each executive branch employee, each judicial officer, and each judicial employee owes a duty arising from a relationship of trust and confidence to the United States Government and the citizens of the United States with respect to material, nonpublic information derived from such person's position as an executive branch employee, judicial officer, or judicial employee or gained from the performance of such person's official responsibilities.

(2) Definitions.—In this subsection—

(A) the term "executive branch employee"—

(i) has the meaning given the term "employee" under section 2105 of title 5;

(ii) includes—

(I) the President;

(II) the Vice President; and

(III) an employee of the United States Postal Service or the Postal Regulatory Commission;

(B) the term "judicial employee" has the meaning given that term in section 109(8) of the Ethics in Government Act of 1978 (5 U.S.C. App. 109(8)); and

(C) the term "judicial officer" has the meaning given that term under section 109(10) of the Ethics in Government Act of 1978 (5 U.S.C. App. 109(10)).

(3) Rule of construction.—Nothing in this subsection shall be construed to impair or limit the construction of the existing antifraud provisions of the securities laws or the authority of the Commission under those provisions.

(i)   Participation in initial public offerings.—An individual described in section 101(f) of the Ethics in Government Act of 1978 may not purchase securities that are the subject of an initial public offering (within the meaning given such term in section 78l(f)(1)(G)(i) of this title) in any manner other than is available to members of the public generally.

Civil Remedies in Administrative Proceedings

§ 78u–2 [P.L. § 21B]. (a) Commission authority to assess money penalties.

(1)   In general.—In any proceeding instituted pursuant to sections 78o(b)(4), 78o(b)(6), 78o–6, 78o–4, 78o–5, 78o–7, or 78q–1 of this title against any person, the Commission or the appropriate regulatory agency may impose a civil penalty if it finds, on the record after notice and opportunity for hearing, that such penalty is in the public interest and that such person—

(A)   has willfully violated any provision of the Securities Act of 1933 [15 U.S.C. 77a et seq.], the Investment Company Act of 1940 [15 U.S.C. 80a–1 et seq.], the Investment Advisers Act of 1940 [15 U.S.C. 80b–1 et seq.], or this chapter, or the rules or regulations thereunder, or the rules of the Municipal Securities Rulemaking Board;

(B)   has willfully aided, abetted, counseled, commanded, induced, or procured such a violation by any other person;

(C)   has willfully made or caused to be made in any application for registration or report required to be filed with the Commission or with any other appropriate regulatory agency under this chapter, or in any proceeding before the Commission with respect to registration, any statement which was, at the time and in the light of the circumstances under which it was made, false or misleading with respect to any material fact, or has omitted to state in any such application or report any material fact which is required to be stated therein; or . . . .

* * *

(b)   Maximum amount of penalty.

(1)   First tier.—The maximum amount of penalty for each act or omission described in subsection (a) of this section shall be $5,000 for a natural person or $50,000 for any other person.

(2)   Second tier.—Notwithstanding paragraph (1), the maximum amount of penalty for each such act or omission shall be $50,000 for a natural person or $250,000 for any other person if the act or omission described in subsection (a) of this section involved fraud, deceit, manipulation, or deliberate or reckless disregard of a regulatory requirement.

(3)   Third tier.—Notwithstanding paragraphs (1) and (2), the maximum amount of penalty for each such act or omission shall be $100,000 for a natural person or $500,000 for any other person if—

(A)   the act or omission described in subsection (a) of this section involved fraud, deceit, manipulation, or deliberate or reckless disregard of a regulatory requirement; and

(B)   such act or omission directly or indirectly resulted in substantial losses or created a significant risk of substantial losses to other persons or resulted in substantial pecuniary gain to the person who committed the act or omission.

(c)   Determination of public interest.—In considering under this section whether a penalty is in the public interest, the Commission or the appropriate regulatory agency may consider—

(1)   whether the act or omission for which such penalty is assessed involved fraud, deceit, manipulation, or deliberate or reckless disregard of a regulatory requirement;

(2)   the harm to other persons resulting either directly or indirectly from such act or omission;

(3)   the extent to which any person was unjustly enriched, taking into account any restitution made to persons injured by such behavior;

(4)   whether such person previously has been found by the Commission, another appropriate regulatory agency, or a self-regulatory organization to have violated the Federal securities laws, State securities laws, or the rules of a self-regulatory organization, has been enjoined by a court of competent jurisdiction from violations of such laws or rules, or has been convicted by a court of competent jurisdiction of violations of such laws or of any felony or misdemeanor described in section 78o(b)(4)(B) of this title;

(5)   the need to deter such person and other persons from committing such acts or omissions; and

(6)   such other matters as justice may require.

(d)   Evidence concerning ability to pay.—In any proceeding in which the Commission or the appropriate regulatory agency may impose a penalty under this section, a respondent may present evidence of the respondent's ability to pay such penalty. The Commission or the appropriate regulatory agency may, in its discretion, consider such evidence in determining whether such penalty is in the public interest. Such evidence may relate to the extent of such person's ability to continue in business and the collectability of a penalty, taking into account any other claims of the United States or third parties upon such person's assets and the amount of such person's assets.

(e)   Authority to enter order requiring accounting and disgorgement.—In any proceeding in which the Commission or the appropriate regulatory agency may impose a penalty under this section, the Commission or the appropriate regulatory agency may enter an order requiring accounting and disgorgement, including reasonable interest. The Commission is authorized to adopt rules, regulations, and orders concerning payments to investors, rates of interest, periods of accrual, and such other matters as it deems appropriate to implement this subsection.

(f)   Security-based swaps.

(1)   Clearing agency.—Any clearing agency that knowingly or recklessly evades or participates in or facilitates an evasion of the requirements of section 78c–3 of this title shall be liable for a civil money penalty in twice the amount otherwise available for a violation of section 78c–3 of this title.

(2)   Security-based swap dealer or major security-based swap participant.—Any security-based swap dealer or major security-based swap participant that knowingly or recklessly evades or participates in or facilitates an evasion of the requirements of section 78c–3 of this title shall be liable for a civil money penalty in twice the amount otherwise available for a violation of section 78c–3 of this title.

Cease-and-Desist Proceedings

§ 78u–3 [P.L. § 21C]. (a) Authority of Commission.—If the Commission finds, after notice and opportunity for hearing, that any person is violating, has violated, or is about to violate any provision of this chapter, or any rule or regulation thereunder, the Commission may publish its findings and enter an order requiring such person, and any other person that is, was, or would be a cause of the violation, due to an act or omission the person knew or should have known would contribute to such violation, to cease and desist from committing or causing such violation and any future violation of the same provision, rule, or regulation. Such order may, in addition to requiring a person to cease and desist from committing or causing a violation, require such person to comply, or to take steps to effect compliance, with such provision, rule, or regulation, upon such terms and conditions and within such time as the Commission may specify in such order. Any such order may, as the Commission deems appropriate, require future compliance or steps to effect future compliance, either permanently or for such period of time as the Commission may specify, with such provision, rule, or regulation with respect to any security, any issuer, or any other person.

(b) Hearing.—The notice instituting proceedings pursuant to subsection (a) of this section shall fix a hearing date not earlier than 30 days nor later than 60 days after service of the notice unless an earlier or a later date is set by the Commission with the consent of any respondent so served.

(c) Temporary order.

(1) In general.—Whenever the Commission determines that the alleged violation or threatened violation specified in the notice instituting proceedings pursuant to subsection (a) of this section, or the continuation thereof, is likely to result in significant dissipation or conversion of assets, significant harm to investors, or substantial harm to the public interest, including, but not limited to, losses to the Securities Investor Protection Corporation, prior to the completion of the proceedings, the Commission may enter a temporary order requiring the respondent to cease and desist from the violation or threatened violation and to take such action to prevent the violation or threatened violation and to prevent dissipation or conversion of assets, significant harm to investors, or substantial harm to the public interest as the Commission deems appropriate pending completion of such proceedings. Such an order shall be entered only after notice and opportunity for a hearing, unless the Commission determines that notice and hearing prior to entry would be impracticable or contrary to the public interest. A temporary order shall become effective upon service upon the respondent and, unless set aside, limited, or suspended by the Commission or a court of competent jurisdiction, shall remain effective and enforceable pending the completion of the proceedings.

(2) Applicability.—Paragraph (1) shall apply only to a respondent that acts, or, at the time of the alleged misconduct acted, as a broker, dealer, investment adviser, investment company, municipal securities dealer, government securities broker, government securities dealer, registered public accounting firm (as defined in section 7201 of this title), or transfer agent, or is, or was at the time of the alleged misconduct, an associated person of, or a person seeking to become associated with, any of the foregoing.

(3) Temporary freeze.

(A) In general.—(i) Issuance of temporary order.—Whenever, during the course of a lawful investigation involving possible violations of the Federal securities laws by an issuer of publicly traded securities or any of its directors, officers, partners, controlling persons, agents, or employees, it shall appear to the Commission that it is likely that the issuer will make extraordinary payments (whether compensation or otherwise) to any of the foregoing persons, the Commission may petition a Federal district court for a temporary order requiring the issuer to escrow, subject to court supervision, those payments in an interest-bearing account for 45 days.

(ii) Standard.—A temporary order shall be entered under clause (i), only after notice and opportunity for a hearing, unless the court determines that notice and hearing prior to entry of the order would be impracticable or contrary to the public interest.

(iii) Effective period.—A temporary order issued under clause (i) shall—

(I) become effective immediately;

(II) be served upon the parties subject to it; and

(III) unless set aside, limited or suspended by a court of competent jurisdiction, shall remain effective and enforceable for 45 days.

(iv) Extensions authorized.—The effective period of an order under this subparagraph may be extended by the court upon good cause shown for not longer than 45 additional days, provided that the combined period of the order shall not exceed 90 days.

(B) Process on determination of violations.

(i)   Violations charged.—If the issuer or other person described in subparagraph (A) is charged with any violation of the Federal securities laws before the expiration of the effective period of a temporary order under subparagraph (A) (including any applicable extension period), the order shall remain in effect, subject to court approval, until the conclusion of any legal proceedings related thereto, and the affected issuer or other person, shall have the right to petition the court for review of the order.

(ii) Violations not charged.—If the issuer or other person described in subparagraph (A) is not charged with any violation of the Federal securities laws before the expiration of the effective period of a temporary order under subparagraph (A) (including any applicable extension period), the escrow shall terminate at the expiration of the 45-day effective period (or the expiration of any extension period, as applicable), and the disputed payments (with accrued interest) shall be returned to the issuer or other affected person.

(d)   Review of temporary orders.

(1)   Commission review.—At any time after the respondent has been served with a temporary cease-and-desist order pursuant to subsection (c) of this section, the respondent may apply to the Commission to have the order set aside, limited, or suspended. If the respondent has been served with a temporary cease-and-desist order entered without a prior Commission hearing, the respondent may, within 10 days after the date on which the order was served, request a hearing on such application and the Commission shall hold a hearing and render a decision on such application at the earliest possible time.

(2)   Judicial review.—Within—

(A)   10 days after the date the respondent was served with a temporary cease-and-desist order entered with a prior Commission hearing, or

(B)   10 days after the Commission renders a decision on an application and hearing under paragraph (1), with respect to any temporary cease-and-desist order entered without a prior Commission hearing,

the respondent may apply to the United States district court for the district in which the respondent resides or has its principal place of business, or for the District of Columbia, for an order setting aside, limiting, or suspending the effectiveness or enforcement of the order, and the court shall have jurisdiction to enter such an order. A respondent served with a temporary cease-and-desist order entered without a prior Commission hearing may not apply to the court except after hearing and decision by the Commission on the respondent's application under paragraph (1) of this subsection.

(3)   No automatic stay of temporary order.—The commencement of proceedings under paragraph (2) of this subsection shall not, unless specifically ordered by the court, operate as a stay of the Commission's order.

(4)   Exclusive review.—Section 78y of this title shall not apply to a temporary order entered pursuant to this section.

(e)   Authority to enter order requiring accounting and disgorgement.—In any cease-and-desist proceeding under subsection (a) of this section, the Commission may enter an order requiring accounting and disgorgement, including reasonable interest. The Commission is authorized to adopt rules, regulations, and orders concerning payments to investors, rates of interest, periods of accrual, and such other matters as it deems appropriate to implement this subsection.

(f)   Authority of the Commission to prohibit persons from serving as officers or directors.—In any cease-and-desist proceeding under subsection (a) of this section, the Commission may issue an order to prohibit, conditionally or unconditionally, and permanently or for such period of time as it shall determine, any person who has violated section 78j(b) of this title or the rules or regulations thereunder, from acting as an officer or director of any issuer that has a class of securities registered pursuant to section 78*l* of this title, or that is required to file reports pursuant to section 78*o*(d) of this title, if the conduct of that person demonstrates unfitness to serve as an officer or director of any such issuer.

Private Securities Litigation

§ 78u–4 [P.L. § 21D]. (a) Private class actions.

(1)   In general.—The provisions of this subsection shall apply in each private action arising under this chapter that is brought as a plaintiff class action pursuant to the Federal Rules of Civil Procedure.

(2)   Certification filed with complaint.

(A)   In general.—Each plaintiff seeking to serve as a representative party on behalf of a class shall provide a sworn certification, which shall be personally signed by such plaintiff and filed with the complaint, that—

(i)   states that the plaintiff has reviewed the complaint and authorized its filing;

(ii)   states that the plaintiff did not purchase the security that is the subject of the complaint at the direction of plaintiff's counsel or in order to participate in any private action arising under this chapter;

(iii)   states that the plaintiff is willing to serve as a representative party on behalf of a class, including providing testimony at deposition and trial, if necessary;

(iv)   sets forth all of the transactions of the plaintiff in the security that is the subject of the complaint during the class period specified in the complaint;

(v)   identifies any other action under this chapter, filed during the 3-year period preceding the date on which the certification is signed by the plaintiff, in which the plaintiff has sought to serve as a representative party on behalf of a class; and

(vi)   states that the plaintiff will not accept any payment for serving as a representative party on behalf of a class beyond the plaintiff's pro rata share of any recovery, except as ordered or approved by the court in accordance with paragraph (4).

(B)   Nonwaiver of attorney-client privilege.—The certification filed pursuant to subparagraph (A) shall not be construed to be a waiver of the attorney-client privilege.

(3)   Appointment of lead plaintiff.

(A)   Early notice to class members.

(i)   In general.—Not later than 20 days after the date on which the complaint is filed, the plaintiff or plaintiffs shall cause to be published, in a widely circulated national business-oriented publication or wire service, a notice advising members of the purported plaintiff class—

(I)   of the pendency of the action, the claims asserted therein, and the purported class period; and

(II)   that, not later than 60 days after the date on which the notice is published, any member of the purported class may move the court to serve as lead plaintiff of the purported class.

(ii)   Multiple actions.—If more than one action on behalf of a class asserting substantially the same claim or claims arising under this chapter is filed, only the plaintiff or plaintiffs in the first filed action shall be required to cause notice to be published in accordance with clause (i).

(iii) Additional notices may be required under Federal rules.—Notice required under clause (i) shall be in addition to any notice required pursuant to the Federal Rules of Civil Procedure.

(B) Appointment of lead plaintiff.

(i) In general.—Not later than 90 days after the date on which a notice is published under subparagraph (A)(i), the court shall consider any motion made by a purported class member in response to the notice, including any motion by a class member who is not individually named as a plaintiff in the complaint or complaints, and shall appoint as lead plaintiff the member or members of the purported plaintiff class that the court determines to be most capable of adequately representing the interests of class members (hereafter in this paragraph referred to as the "most adequate plaintiff") in accordance with this subparagraph.

(ii) Consolidated actions.—If more than one action on behalf of a class asserting substantially the same claim or claims arising under this chapter has been filed, and any party has sought to consolidate those actions for pretrial purposes or for trial, the court shall not make the determination required by clause (i) until after the decision on the motion to consolidate is rendered. As soon as practicable after such decision is rendered, the court shall appoint the most adequate plaintiff as lead plaintiff for the consolidated actions in accordance with this paragraph.

(iii) Rebuttable presumption.

(I) In general.—Subject to subclause (II), for purposes of clause (i), the court shall adopt a presumption that the most adequate plaintiff in any private action arising under this chapter is the person or group of persons that—

(aa) has either filed the complaint or made a motion in response to a notice under subparagraph (A)(i);

(bb) in the determination of the court, has the largest financial interest in the relief sought by the class; and

(cc) otherwise satisfies the requirements of Rule 23 of the Federal Rules of Civil Procedure.

(II) Rebuttal evidence.—The presumption described in subclause (I) may be rebutted only upon proof by a member of the purported plaintiff class that the presumptively most adequate plaintiff—

(aa) will not fairly and adequately protect the interests of the class; or

(bb) is subject to unique defenses that render such plaintiff incapable of adequately representing the class.

(iv) Discovery.—For purposes of this subparagraph, discovery relating to whether a member or members of the purported plaintiff class is the most adequate plaintiff may be conducted by a plaintiff only if the plaintiff first demonstrates a reasonable basis for a finding that the presumptively most adequate plaintiff is incapable of adequately representing the class.

(v) Selection of lead counsel.—The most adequate plaintiff shall, subject to the approval of the court, select and retain counsel to represent the class.

(vi) Restrictions on professional plaintiffs.—Except as the court may otherwise permit, consistent with the purposes of this section, a person may be a lead plaintiff, or an officer, director, or fiduciary of a lead plaintiff, in no more than 5 securities class actions brought as plaintiff class actions pursuant to the Federal Rules of Civil Procedure during any 3-year period.

(4)   Recovery by plaintiffs.—The share of any final judgment or of any settlement that is awarded to a representative party serving on behalf of a class shall be equal, on a per share basis, to the portion of the final judgment or settlement awarded to all other members of the class. Nothing in this paragraph shall be construed to limit the award of reasonable costs and expenses (including lost wages) directly relating to the representation of the class to any representative party serving on behalf of a class.

(5)   Restrictions on settlements under seal.—The terms and provisions of any settlement agreement of a class action shall not be filed under seal, except that on motion of any party to the settlement, the court may order filing under seal for those portions of a settlement agreement as to which good cause is shown for such filing under seal. For purposes of this paragraph, good cause shall exist only if publication of a term or provision of a settlement agreement would cause direct and substantial harm to any party.

(6)   Restrictions on payment of attorneys' fees and expenses.—Total attorneys' fees and expenses awarded by the court to counsel for the plaintiff class shall not exceed a reasonable percentage of the amount of any damages and prejudgment interest actually paid to the class.

(7)   Disclosure of settlement terms to class members.—Any proposed or final settlement agreement that is published or otherwise disseminated to the class shall include each of the following statements, along with a cover page summarizing the information contained in such statements:

(A)   Statement of plaintiff recovery.—The amount of the settlement proposed to be distributed to the parties to the action, determined in the aggregate and on an average per share basis.

(B)   Statement of potential outcome of case.

(i)   Agreement on amount of damages.—If the settling parties agree on the average amount of damages per share that would be recoverable if the plaintiff prevailed on each claim alleged under this chapter, a statement concerning the average amount of such potential damages per share.

(ii)   Disagreement on amount of damages.—If the parties do not agree on the average amount of damages per share that would be recoverable if the plaintiff prevailed on each claim alleged under this chapter, a statement from each settling party concerning the issue or issues on which the parties disagree.

(iii)   Inadmissibility for certain purposes.—A statement made in accordance with clause (i) or (ii) concerning the amount of damages shall not be admissible in any Federal or State judicial action or administrative proceeding, other than an action or proceeding arising out of such statement.

(C)   Statement of attorneys' fees or costs sought.—If any of the settling parties or their counsel intend to apply to the court for an award of attorneys' fees or costs from any fund established as part of the settlement, a statement indicating which parties or counsel intend to make such an application, the amount of fees and costs that will be sought (including the amount of such fees and costs determined on an average per share basis), and a brief explanation supporting the fees and costs sought. Such information shall be clearly summarized on the cover page of any notice to a party of any proposed or final settlement agreement.

(D)   Identification of lawyers' representatives.—The name, telephone number, and address of one or more representatives of counsel for the plaintiff class who will be reasonably available to answer questions from class members concerning any matter contained in any notice of settlement published or otherwise disseminated to the class.

(E) Reasons for settlement.—A brief statement explaining the reasons why the parties are proposing the settlement.

(F) Other information.—Such other information as may be required by the court.

(8) Security for payment of costs in class actions.—In any private action arising under this chapter that is certified as a class action pursuant to the Federal Rules of Civil Procedure, the court may require an undertaking from the attorneys for the plaintiff class, the plaintiff class, or both, or from the attorneys for the defendant, the defendant, or both, in such proportions and at such times as the court determines are just and equitable, for the payment of fees and expenses that may be awarded under this subsection.

(9) Attorney conflict of interest.—If a plaintiff class is represented by an attorney who directly owns or otherwise has a beneficial interest in the securities that are the subject of the litigation, the court shall make a determination of whether such ownership or other interest constitutes a conflict of interest sufficient to disqualify the attorney from representing the plaintiff class.

(b) Requirements for securities fraud actions.

(1) Misleading statements and omissions.—In any private action arising under this chapter in which the plaintiff alleges that the defendant—

(A) made an untrue statement of a material fact; or

(B) omitted to state a material fact necessary in order to make the statements made, in the light of the circumstances in which they were made, not misleading;

the complaint shall specify each statement alleged to have been misleading, the reason or reasons why the statement is misleading, and, if an allegation regarding the statement or omission is made on information and belief, the complaint shall state with particularity all facts on which that belief is formed.

(2) Required state of mind.

(A) In general.—Except as provided in subparagraph (B), in any private action arising under this chapter in which the plaintiff may recover money damages only on proof that the defendant acted with a particular state of mind, the complaint shall, with respect to each act or omission alleged to violate this chapter, state with particularity facts giving rise to a strong inference that the defendant acted with the required state of mind.

(B) Exception.—In the case of an action for money damages brought against a credit rating agency or a controlling person under this chapter, it shall be sufficient, for purposes of pleading any required state of mind in relation to such action, that the complaint state with particularity facts giving rise to a strong inference that the credit rating agency knowingly or recklessly failed—

(i) to conduct a reasonable investigation of the rated security with respect to the factual elements relied upon by its own methodology for evaluating credit risk; or

(ii) to obtain reasonable verification of such factual elements (which verification may be based on a sampling technique that does not amount to an audit) from other sources that the credit rating agency considered to be competent and that were independent of the issuer and underwriter.

(3) Motion to dismiss; stay of discovery.

(A) Dismissal for failure to meet pleading requirements.—In any private action arising under this chapter, the court shall, on the motion of any defendant, dismiss the complaint if the requirements of paragraphs (1) and (2) are not met.

(B)　Stay of discovery.—In any private action arising under this chapter, all discovery and other proceedings shall be stayed during the pendency of any motion to dismiss, unless the court finds upon the motion of any party that particularized discovery is necessary to preserve evidence or to prevent undue prejudice to that party.

(C)　Preservation of evidence.

(i)　In general.—During the pendency of any stay of discovery pursuant to this paragraph, unless otherwise ordered by the court, any party to the action with actual notice of the allegations contained in the complaint shall treat all documents, data compilations (including electronically recorded or stored data), and tangible objects that are in the custody or control of such person and that are relevant to the allegations, as if they were the subject of a continuing request for production of documents from an opposing party under the Federal Rules of Civil Procedure.

(ii)　Sanction for willful violation.—A party aggrieved by the willful failure of an opposing party to comply with clause (i) may apply to the court for an order awarding appropriate sanctions.

(D)　Circumvention of stay of discovery.—Upon a proper showing, a court may stay discovery proceedings in any private action in a State court, as necessary in aid of its jurisdiction, or to protect or effectuate its judgments, in an action subject to a stay of discovery pursuant to this paragraph.

(4)　Loss causation.—In any private action arising under this chapter, the plaintiff shall have the burden of proving that the act or omission of the defendant alleged to violate this chapter caused the loss for which the plaintiff seeks to recover damages.

(c)　Sanctions for abusive litigation.

(1)　Mandatory review by court.—In any private action arising under this chapter, upon final adjudication of the action, the court shall include in the record specific findings regarding compliance by each party and each attorney representing any party with each requirement of Rule 11(b) of the Federal Rules of Civil Procedure as to any complaint, responsive pleading, or dispositive motion.

(2)　Mandatory sanctions.—If the court makes a finding under paragraph (1) that a party or attorney violated any requirement of Rule 11(b) of the Federal Rules of Civil Procedure as to any complaint, responsive pleading, or dispositive motion, the court shall impose sanctions on such party or attorney in accordance with Rule 11 of the Federal Rules of Civil Procedure. Prior to making a finding that any party or attorney has violated Rule 11 of the Federal Rules of Civil Procedure, the court shall give such party or attorney notice and an opportunity to respond.

(3)　Presumption in favor of attorneys' fees and costs.

(A)　In general.—Subject to subparagraphs (B) and (C), for purposes of paragraph (2), the court shall adopt a presumption that the appropriate sanction—

(i)　for failure of any responsive pleading or dispositive motion to comply with any requirement of Rule 11(b) of the Federal Rules of Civil Procedure is an award to the opposing party of the reasonable attorneys' fees and other expenses incurred as a direct result of the violation; and

(ii)　for substantial failure of any complaint to comply with any requirement of Rule 11(b) of the Federal Rules of Civil Procedure is an award to the opposing party of the reasonable attorneys' fees and other expenses incurred in the action.

(B)　Rebuttal evidence.—The presumption described in subparagraph (A) may be rebutted only upon proof by the party or attorney against whom sanctions are to be imposed that—

(i)   the award of attorneys' fees and other expenses will impose an unreasonable burden on that party or attorney and would be unjust, and the failure to make such an award would not impose a greater burden on the party in whose favor sanctions are to be imposed; or

(ii)   the violation of Rule 11(b) of the Federal Rules of Civil Procedure was de minimis.

(C)   Sanctions.—If the party or attorney against whom sanctions are to be imposed meets its burden under subparagraph (B), the court shall award the sanctions that the court deems appropriate pursuant to Rule 11 of the Federal Rules of Civil Procedure.

(d)   Defendant's right to written interrogatories.—In any private action arising under this chapter in which the plaintiff may recover money damages, the court shall, when requested by a defendant, submit to the jury a written interrogatory on the issue of each such defendant's state of mind at the time the alleged violation occurred.

(e)   Limitation on damages.

(1)   In general.—Except as provided in paragraph (2), in any private action arising under this chapter in which the plaintiff seeks to establish damages by reference to the market price of a security, the award of damages to the plaintiff shall not exceed the difference between the purchase or sale price paid or received, as appropriate, by the plaintiff for the subject security and the mean trading price of that security during the 90-day period beginning on the date on which the information correcting the misstatement or omission that is the basis for the action is disseminated to the market.

(2)   Exception.—In any private action arising under this chapter in which the plaintiff seeks to establish damages by reference to the market price of a security, if the plaintiff sells or repurchases the subject security prior to the expiration of the 90-day period described in paragraph (1), the plaintiff's damages shall not exceed the difference between the purchase or sale price paid or received, as appropriate, by the plaintiff for the security and the mean trading price of the security during the period beginning immediately after dissemination of information correcting the misstatement or omission and ending on the date on which the plaintiff sells or repurchases the security.

(3)   "Mean trading price" defined.—For purposes of this subsection, the "mean trading price" of a security shall be an average of the daily trading price of that security, determined as of the close of the market each day during the 90-day period referred to in paragraph (1).

(f)   Proportionate liability.

(1)   Applicability.—Nothing in this subsection shall be construed to create, affect, or in any manner modify, the standard for liability associated with any action arising under the securities laws.

(2)   Liability for damages.

(A)   Joint and several liability.—Any covered person against whom a final judgment is entered in a private action shall be liable for damages jointly and severally only if the trier of fact specifically determines that such covered person knowingly committed a violation of the securities laws.

(B)   Proportionate liability.

(i)   In general.—Except as provided in subparagraph (A), a covered person against whom a final judgment is entered in a private action shall be liable solely for the portion of the judgment that corresponds to the percentage of responsibility of that covered person, as determined under paragraph (3).

(ii) Recovery by and costs of covered person.—In any case in which a contractual relationship permits, a covered person that prevails in any private action may recover the attorney's fees and costs of that covered person in connection with the action.

(3) Determination of responsibility

(A) In general.—In any private action, the court shall instruct the jury to answer special interrogatories, or if there is no jury, shall make findings, with respect to each covered person and each of the other persons claimed by any of the parties to have caused or contributed to the loss incurred by the plaintiff, including persons who have entered into settlements with the plaintiff or plaintiffs, concerning—

(i) whether such person violated the securities laws;

(ii) the percentage of responsibility of such person, measured as a percentage of the total fault of all persons who caused or contributed to the loss incurred by the plaintiff; and

(iii) whether such person knowingly committed a violation of the securities laws.

(B) Contents of special interrogatories or findings.—The responses to interrogatories, or findings, as appropriate, under subparagraph (A) shall specify the total amount of damages that the plaintiff is entitled to recover and the percentage of responsibility of each covered person found to have caused or contributed to the loss incurred by the plaintiff or plaintiffs.

(C) Factors for consideration.—In determining the percentage of responsibility under this paragraph, the trier of fact shall consider—

(i) the nature of the conduct of each covered person found to have caused or contributed to the loss incurred by the plaintiff or plaintiffs; and

(ii) the nature and extent of the causal relationship between the conduct of each such person and the damages incurred by the plaintiff or plaintiffs.

(4) Uncollectible share.

(A) In general.—Notwithstanding paragraph (2)(B), upon[1] motion made not later than 6 months after a final judgment is entered in any private action, the court determines that all or part of the share of the judgment of the covered person is not collectible against that covered person, and is also not collectible against a covered person described in paragraph (2)(A), each covered person described in paragraph (2)(B) shall be liable for the uncollectible share as follows:

(i) Percentage of net worth.—Each covered person shall be jointly and severally liable for the uncollectible share if the plaintiff establishes that—

(I) the plaintiff is an individual whose recoverable damages under the final judgment are equal to more than 10 percent of the net worth of the plaintiff; and

(II) the net worth of the plaintiff is equal to less than $200,000.

(ii) Other plaintiffs.—With respect to any plaintiff not described in subclauses (I) and (II) of clause (i), each covered person shall be liable for the uncollectible share in proportion to the percentage of responsibility of that covered person, except that the total liability of a covered person under this clause may not exceed 50 percent of the proportionate share of that covered person, as determined under paragraph (3)(B).

(iii) Net worth.—For purposes of this subparagraph, net worth shall be determined as of the date immediately preceding the date of the purchase or sale (as

---

[1] So in original. Probably should be preceded by "if,".

applicable) by the plaintiff of the security that is the subject of the action, and shall be equal to the fair market value of assets, minus liabilities, including the net value of the investments of the plaintiff in real and personal property (including personal residences).

(B) Overall limit.—In no case shall the total payments required pursuant to subparagraph (A) exceed the amount of the uncollectible share.

(C) Covered persons subject to contribution.—A covered person against whom judgment is not collectible shall be subject to contribution and to any continuing liability to the plaintiff on the judgment.

(5) Right of contribution.—To the extent that a covered person is required to make an additional payment pursuant to paragraph (4), that covered person may recover contribution—

(A) from the covered person originally liable to make the payment;

(B) from any covered person liable jointly and severally pursuant to paragraph (2)(A);

(C) from any covered person held proportionately liable pursuant to this paragraph who is liable to make the same payment and has paid less than his or her proportionate share of that payment; or

(D) from any other person responsible for the conduct giving rise to the payment that would have been liable to make the same payment.

(6) Nondisclosure to jury.—The standard for allocation of damages under paragraphs (2) and (3) and the procedure for reallocation of uncollectible shares under paragraph (4) shall not be disclosed to members of the jury.

(7) Settlement discharge.

(A) In general.—A covered person who settles any private action at any time before final verdict or judgment shall be discharged from all claims for contribution brought by other persons. Upon entry of the settlement by the court, the court shall enter a bar order constituting the final discharge of all obligations to the plaintiff of the settling covered person arising out of the action. The order shall bar all future claims for contribution arising out of the action—

(i) by any person against the settling covered person; and

(ii) by the settling covered person against any person, other than a person whose liability has been extinguished by the settlement of the settling covered person.

(B) Reduction.—If a covered person enters into a settlement with the plaintiff prior to final verdict or judgment, the verdict or judgment shall be reduced by the greater of—

(i) an amount that corresponds to the percentage of responsibility of that covered person; or

(ii) the amount paid to the plaintiff by that covered person.

(8) Contribution.—A covered person who becomes jointly and severally liable for damages in any private action may recover contribution from any other person who, if joined in the original action, would have been liable for the same damages. A claim for contribution shall be determined based on the percentage of responsibility of the claimant and of each person against whom a claim for contribution is made.

(9) Statute of limitations for contribution.—In any private action determining liability, an action for contribution shall be brought not later than 6 months after the entry of a final, nonappealable judgment in the action, except that an action for contribution brought by a covered person who was required to make an additional payment pursuant to paragraph (4) may be brought not later than 6 months after the date on which such payment was made.

(10) Definitions.—For purposes of this subsection—

(A) a covered person "knowingly commits a violation of the securities laws"—

(i) with respect to an action that is based on an untrue statement of material fact or omission of a material fact necessary to make the statement not misleading, if—

(I) that covered person makes an untrue statement of a material fact, with actual knowledge that the representation is false, or omits to state a fact necessary in order to make the statement made not misleading, with actual knowledge that, as a result of the omission, one of the material representations of the covered person is false; and

(II) persons are likely to reasonably rely on that misrepresentation or omission; and

(ii) with respect to an action that is based on any conduct that is not described in clause (i), if that covered person engages in that conduct with actual knowledge of the facts and circumstances that make the conduct of that covered person a violation of the securities laws;

(B) reckless conduct by a covered person shall not be construed to constitute a knowing commission of a violation of the securities laws by that covered person;

(C) the term "covered person" means—

(i) a defendant in any private action arising under this chapter; or

(ii) a defendant in any private action arising under section 77k of this title, who is an outside director of the issuer of the securities that are the subject of the action; and

(D) the term "outside director" shall have the meaning given such term by rule or regulation of the Commission.

Application of Safe Harbor for Forward-Looking Statements

§ 78u–5 [P.L. § 21E]. (a) Applicability.—This section shall apply only to a forward-looking statement made by—

(1) an issuer that, at the time that the statement is made, is subject to the reporting requirements of section 78m(a) of this title or section 78o(d) of this title;

(2) a person acting on behalf of such issuer;

(3) an outside reviewer retained by such issuer making a statement on behalf of such issuer; or

(4) an underwriter, with respect to information provided by such issuer or information derived from information provided by such issuer.

(b) Exclusions.—Except to the extent otherwise specifically provided by rule, regulation, or order of the Commission, this section shall not apply to a forward-looking statement—

(1) that is made with respect to the business or operations of the issuer, if the issuer—

(A) during the 3-year period preceding the date on which the statement was first made—

(i) was convicted of any felony or misdemeanor described in clauses (i) through (iv) of section 78o(b)(4)(B) of this title; or

(ii) has been made the subject of a judicial or administrative decree or order arising out of a governmental action that—

        (I)   prohibits future violations of the antifraud provisions of the securities laws;

        (II)   requires that the issuer cease and desist from violating the antifraud provisions of the securities laws; or

        (III)   determines that the issuer violated the antifraud provisions of the securities laws;

    (B)   makes the forward-looking statement in connection with an offering of securities by a blank check company;

    (C)   issues penny stock;

    (D)   makes the forward-looking statement in connection with a rollup transaction; or

    (E)   makes the forward-looking statement in connection with a going private transaction; or

(2)   that is—(A) included in a financial statement prepared in accordance with generally accepted accounting principles;

    (B)   contained in a registration statement of, or otherwise issued by, an investment company;

    (C)   made in connection with a tender offer;

    (D)   made in connection with an initial public offering;

    (E)   made in connection with an offering by, or relating to the operations of, a partnership, limited liability company, or a direct participation investment program; or

    (F)   made in a disclosure of beneficial ownership in a report required to be filed with the Commission pursuant to section 78m(d) of this title.

(c)   Safe harbor.

(1)   In general.—Except as provided in subsection (b) of this section, in any private action arising under this chapter that is based on an untrue statement of a material fact or omission of a material fact necessary to make the statement not misleading, a person referred to in subsection (a) of this section shall not be liable with respect to any forward-looking statement, whether written or oral, if and to the extent that—

    (A)   the forward-looking statement is—

        (i)   identified as a forward-looking statement, and is accompanied by meaningful cautionary statements identifying important factors that could cause actual results to differ materially from those in the forward-looking statement; or

        (ii)   immaterial; or

    (B)   the plaintiff fails to prove that the forward-looking statement—

        (i)   if made by a natural person, was made with actual knowledge by that person that the statement was false or misleading; or

        (ii)   if made by a business entity;[1] was—

        (I)   made by or with the approval of an executive officer of that entity; and

        (II)   made or approved by such officer with actual knowledge by that officer that the statement was false or misleading.

---

[1]   So in original. The semicolon probably should be a comma.

(2) Oral forward-looking statements.—In the case of an oral forward-looking statement made by an issuer that is subject to the reporting requirements of section 78m(a) of this title or section 78o(d) of this title, or by a person acting on behalf of such issuer, the requirement set forth in paragraph (1)(A) shall be deemed to be satisfied—

(A) if the oral forward-looking statement is accompanied by a cautionary statement—

(i) that the particular oral statement is a forward-looking statement; and

(ii) that the actual results might differ materially from those projected in the forward-looking statement; and

(B) if—(i) the oral forward-looking statement is accompanied by an oral statement that additional information concerning factors that could cause actual results to materially differ from those in the forward-looking statement is contained in a readily available written document, or portion thereof;

(ii) the accompanying oral statement referred to in clause (i) identifies the document, or portion thereof, that contains the additional information about those factors relating to the forward-looking statement; and

(iii) the information contained in that written document is a cautionary statement that satisfies the standard established in paragraph (1)(A).

(3) Availability.—Any document filed with the Commission or generally disseminated shall be deemed to be readily available for purposes of paragraph (2).

(4) Effect on other safe harbors.—The exemption provided for in paragraph (1) shall be in addition to any exemption that the Commission may establish by rule or regulation under subsection (g) of this section.

(d) Duty to update.—Nothing in this section shall impose upon any person a duty to update a forward-looking statement.

(e) Dispositive motion.—On any motion to dismiss based upon subsection (c)(1) of this section, the court shall consider any statement cited in the complaint and any cautionary statement accompanying the forward-looking statement, which are not subject to material dispute, cited by the defendant.

(f) Stay pending decision on motion.—In any private action arising under this chapter, the court shall stay discovery (other than discovery that is specifically directed to the applicability of the exemption provided for in this section) during the pendency of any motion by a defendant for summary judgment that is based on the grounds that—

(1) the statement or omission upon which the complaint is based is a forward-looking statement within the meaning of this section; and

(2) the exemption provided for in this section precludes a claim for relief.

(g) Exemption authority.—In addition to the exemptions provided for in this section, the Commission may, by rule or regulation, provide exemptions from or under any provision of this chapter, including with respect to liability that is based on a statement or that is based on projections or other forward-looking information, if and to the extent that any such exemption is consistent with the public interest and the protection of investors, as determined by the Commission.

(h) Effect on other authority of Commission.—Nothing in this section limits, either expressly or by implication, the authority of the Commission to exercise similar authority or to adopt similar rules and regulations with respect to forward-looking statements under any other statute under which the Commission exercises rulemaking authority.

(i) Definitions.—For purposes of this section, the following definitions shall apply:

(1) Forward-looking statement.—The term "forward-looking statement" means.—

(A) a statement containing a projection of revenues, income (including income loss), earnings (including earnings loss) per share, capital expenditures, dividends, capital structure, or other financial items;

(B) a statement of the plans and objectives of management for future operations, including plans or objectives relating to the products or services of the issuer;

(C) a statement of future economic performance, including any such statement contained in a discussion and analysis of financial condition by the management or in the results of operations included pursuant to the rules and regulations of the Commission;

(D) any statement of the assumptions underlying or relating to any statement described in subparagraph (A), (B), or (C);

(E) any report issued by an outside reviewer retained by an issuer, to the extent that the report assesses a forward-looking statement made by the issuer; or

(F) a statement containing a projection or estimate of such other items as may be specified by rule or regulation of the Commission.

(2) Investment company.—The term "investment company" has the same meaning as in section 80a–3(a) of this title.

(3) Going private transaction.—The term "going private transaction" has the meaning given that term under the rules or regulations of the Commission issued pursuant to section 78m(e) of this title.

(4) Person acting on behalf of an issuer.—The term "person acting on behalf of an issuer" means any officer, director, or employee of such issuer.

(5) Other terms.—The terms "blank check company", "rollup transaction", "partnership", "limited liability company", "executive officer of an entity" and "direct participation investment program", have the meanings given those terms by rule or regulation of the Commission.

Unlawful Representations

§ 78z [P.L. § 26]. No action or failure to act by the Commission or the Board of Governors of the Federal Reserve System, in the administration of this chapter shall be construed to mean that the particular authority has in any way passed upon the merits of, or given approval to, any security or any transaction or transactions therein, nor shall such action or failure to act with regard to any statement or report filed with or examined by such authority pursuant to this chapter or rules and regulations thereunder, be deemed a finding by such authority that such statement or report is true and accurate on its face or that it is not false or misleading. It shall be unlawful to make, or cause to be made, to any prospective purchaser or seller of a security any representation that any such action or failure to act by any such authority is to be so construed or has such effect.

Jurisdiction of Offenses and Suits

§ 78aa [P.L. § 27]. (a) In general.—The district courts of the United States and the United States courts of any Territory or other place subject to the jurisdiction of the United States shall have exclusive jurisdiction of violations of this chapter or the rules and regulations thereunder, and of all suits in equity and actions at law brought to enforce any liability or duty created by this chapter or the rules and regulations thereunder. Any criminal proceeding may be brought in the district wherein any act or transaction constituting the violation occurred. Any suit or action to enforce any liability or duty created by this chapter or rules and regulations thereunder, or to enjoin any violation of such chapter or rules and regulations, may be brought in any such district or in the district wherein the defendant is found or is an inhabitant or transacts business, and process in such cases may be served in any other district of which the defendant is an inhabitant or wherever the defendant may be found. In any action or proceeding instituted by the Commission under this chapter in a United States district court for any judicial district, a subpoena issued to compel the attendance of a witness or the production of documents or tangible things (or both) at a hearing or trial may be served at any place within the United States. Rule 45(c)(3)(A)(ii) of the Federal Rules of Civil Procedure shall not apply to a subpoena issued under the preceding sentence. Judgments and decrees so rendered shall be subject to review as provided in sections 1254, 1291, 1292, and 1294 of title 28. No costs shall be assessed for or against the Commission in any proceeding under this chapter brought by or against it in the Supreme Court or such other courts.

(b) Extraterritorial jurisdiction.—The district courts of the United States and the United States courts of any Territory shall have jurisdiction of an action or proceeding brought or instituted by the Commission or the United States alleging a violation of the antifraud provisions of this chapter involving—

(1) conduct within the United States that constitutes significant steps in furtherance of the violation, even if the securities transaction occurs outside the United States and involves only foreign investors; or

(2) conduct occurring outside the United States that has a foreseeable substantial effect within the United States.

Special Provision Relating to Statute of Limitations on Private Causes of Action

§ 78aa–1 [P.L. § 27A]. (a) Effect on pending causes of action.—The limitation period for any private civil action implied under section 78j(b) of this title that was commenced on or before June 19, 1991, shall be the limitation period provided by the laws applicable in the jurisdiction, including principles of retroactivity, as such laws existed on June 19, 1991.

(b) Effect on dismissed causes of action.—Any private civil action implied under section 78j(b) of this title that was commenced on or before June 19, 1991—

(1) which was dismissed as time barred subsequent to June 19, 1991, and

(2) which would have been timely filed under the limitation period provided by the laws applicable in the jurisdiction, including principles of retroactivity, as such laws existed on June 19, 1991,

shall be reinstated on motion by the plaintiff not later than 60 days after December 19, 1991.

Effect on Existing Law

§ 78bb [P.L. § 28]. (a) Limitation on judgments.

(1) In general.—No person permitted to maintain a suit for damages under the provisions of this chapter shall recover, through satisfaction of judgment in 1 or more actions, a total amount in excess of the actual damages to that person on account of the act complained of. Except as otherwise specifically provided in this chapter, nothing in this chapter shall affect the jurisdiction of the securities commission (or any agency or officer performing like functions) of any State over any security or any person insofar as it does not conflict with the provisions of this chapter or the rules and regulations under this chapter.

(2) Rule of construction.—Except as provided in subsection (f), the rights and remedies provided by this chapter shall be in addition to any and all other rights and remedies that may exist at law or in equity.

(3) State bucket shop laws.—No State law which prohibits or regulates the making or promoting of wagering or gaming contracts, or the operation of "bucket shops" or other similar or related activities, shall invalidate—

(A) any put, call, straddle, option, privilege, or other security subject to this chapter (except any security that has a pari-mutuel payout or otherwise is determined by the Commission, acting by rule, regulation, or order, to be appropriately subject to such laws), or apply to any activity which is incidental or related to the offer, purchase, sale, exercise, settlement, or closeout of any such security;

(B) any security-based swap between eligible contract participants; or

(C) any security-based swap effected on a national securities exchange registered pursuant to section 78f(b) of this title.

(4) Other State provisions.—No provision of State law regarding the offer, sale, or distribution of securities shall apply to any transaction in a security-based swap or a security futures product, except that this paragraph may not be construed as limiting any State antifraud law of general applicability. A security-based swap may not be regulated as an insurance contract under any provision of State law.

(b) Modification of disciplinary procedures.—Nothing in this chapter shall be construed to modify existing law with regard to the binding effect (1) on any member of or participant in any self-regulatory organization of any action taken by the authorities of such organization to settle disputes between its members or participants, (2) on any municipal securities dealer or municipal securities broker of any action taken pursuant to a procedure established by the Municipal Securities Rulemaking Board to settle disputes between municipal securities dealers and municipal securities brokers, or (3) of any action described in paragraph (1) or (2) on any person who has agreed to be bound thereby.

(c) Continuing validity of disciplinary sanctions.—The stay, setting aside, or modification pursuant to section 78s(e) of this title of any disciplinary sanction imposed by a self-regulatory organization on a member thereof, person associated with a member, or participant therein, shall not affect the validity or force of any action taken as a result of such sanction by the self-regulatory organization prior to such stay, setting aside, or modification: Provided, That such action is not inconsistent with the provisions of this chapter or the rules or regulations thereunder. The rights of any person acting in good faith which arise out of any such action shall not be affected in any way by such stay, setting aside, or modification.

(d) Physical location of facilities of registered clearing agencies or registered transfer agents not to subject changes in beneficial or record ownership of securities to State or local taxes.—No State or political subdivision thereof shall impose any tax on any change in beneficial or record ownership of securities effected through the facilities of a registered clearing agency or registered transfer agent or any nominee thereof or custodian therefor or upon the delivery or transfer of securities to or through or receipt from such agency or agent or any nominee thereof or custodian therefor, unless such change in beneficial or record ownership or such transfer or delivery or receipt would otherwise be taxable by such State or political subdivision if the facilities of such registered clearing agency, registered transfer agent, or any nominee thereof or custodian therefor were not physically located in the taxing State or political subdivision. No State or political subdivision thereof shall impose any tax on securities which are deposited in or retained by a registered clearing agency, registered transfer agent, or any nominee thereof or custodian therefor, unless such securities would otherwise be taxable by such State or political subdivision if the facilities of such registered clearing agency, registered transfer agent, or any nominee thereof or custodian therefor were not physically located in the taxing State or political subdivision.

(e) Exchange, broker, and dealer commissions; brokerage and research services.

(1) No person using the mails, or any means or instrumentality of interstate commerce, in the exercise of investment discretion with respect to an account shall be deemed to have acted unlawfully or to have breached a fiduciary duty under State or Federal law unless expressly provided to the contrary by a law enacted by the Congress or any State subsequent to June 4, 1975, solely by reason of his having caused the account to pay a member of an exchange, broker, or dealer an amount of commission for effecting a securities transaction in excess of the amount of commission another member of an exchange, broker, or dealer would have charged for effecting that transaction, if such person determined in good faith that such amount of commission was

reasonable in relation to the value of the brokerage and research services provided by such member, broker, or dealer, viewed in terms of either that particular transaction or his overall responsibilities with respect to the accounts as to which he exercises investment discretion. This subsection is exclusive and plenary insofar as conduct is covered by the foregoing, unless otherwise expressly provided by contract: Provided, however, That nothing in this subsection shall be construed to impair or limit the power of the Commission under any other provision of this chapter or otherwise.

(2) A person exercising investment discretion with respect to an account shall make such disclosure of his policies and practices with respect to commissions that will be paid for effecting securities transactions, at such times and in such manner, as the appropriate regulatory agency, by rule, may prescribe as necessary or appropriate in the public interest or for the protection of investors.

(3) For purposes of this subsection a person provides brokerage and research services insofar as he—

(A) furnishes advice, either directly or through publications or writings, as to the value of securities, the advisability of investing in, purchasing, or selling securities, and the availability of securities or purchasers or sellers of securities;

(B) furnishes analyses and reports concerning issuers, industries, securities, economic factors and trends, portfolio strategy, and the performance of accounts; or

(C) effects securities transactions and performs functions incidental thereto (such as clearance, settlement, and custody) or required in connection therewith by rules of the Commission or a self-regulatory organization of which such person is a member or person associated with a member or in which such person is a participant.

(4) The provisions of this subsection shall not apply with regard to securities that are security futures products.

(f) Limitations on remedies.

(1) Class action limitations.—No covered class action based upon the statutory or common law of any State or subdivision thereof may be maintained in any State or Federal court by any private party alleging—

(A) a misrepresentation or omission of a material fact in connection with the purchase or sale of a covered security; or

(B) that the defendant used or employed any manipulative or deceptive device or contrivance in connection with the purchase or sale of a covered security.

(2) Removal of covered class actions.—Any covered class action brought in any State court involving a covered security, as set forth in paragraph (1), shall be removable to the Federal district court for the district in which the action is pending, and shall be subject to paragraph (1).

(3) Preservation of certain actions.

(A) Actions under State law of State of incorporation

(i) Actions preserved.—Notwithstanding paragraph (1) or (2), a covered class action described in clause (ii) of this subparagraph that is based upon the statutory or common law of the State in which the issuer is incorporated (in the case of a corporation) or organized (in the case of any other entity) may be maintained in a State or Federal court by a private party.

(ii) Permissible actions.—A covered class action is described in this clause if it involves—

(I)   the purchase or sale of securities by the issuer or an affiliate of the issuer exclusively from or to holders of equity securities of the issuer; or

(II)   any recommendation, position, or other communication with respect to the sale of securities of an issuer that—

(aa) is made by or on behalf of the issuer or an affiliate of the issuer to holders of equity securities of the issuer; and

(bb) concerns decisions of such equity holders with respect to voting their securities, acting in response to a tender or exchange offer, or exercising dissenters' or appraisal rights.

(B)   State actions.

(i)   In general.—Notwithstanding any other provision of this subsection, nothing in this subsection may be construed to preclude a State or political subdivision thereof or a State pension plan from bringing an action involving a covered security on its own behalf, or as a member of a class comprised solely of other States, political subdivisions, or State pension plans that are named plaintiffs, and that have authorized participation, in such action.

(ii) State pension plan defined.—For purposes of this subparagraph, the term "State pension plan" means a pension plan established and maintained for its employees by the government of a State or political subdivision thereof, or by any agency or instrumentality thereof.

(C)   Actions under contractual agreements between issuers and indenture trustees.—Notwithstanding paragraph (1) or (2), a covered class action that seeks to enforce a contractual agreement between an issuer and an indenture trustee may be maintained in a State or Federal court by a party to the agreement or a successor to such party.

(D)   Remand of removed actions.—In an action that has been removed from a State court pursuant to paragraph (2), if the Federal court determines that the action may be maintained in State court pursuant to this subsection, the Federal court shall remand such action to such State court.

(4)   Preservation of State jurisdiction.—The securities commission (or any agency or office performing like functions) of any State shall retain jurisdiction under the laws of such State to investigate and bring enforcement actions.

(5)   Definitions.—For purposes of this subsection, the following definitions shall apply:

(A)   Affiliate of the issuer.—The term "affiliate of the issuer" means a person that directly or indirectly, through one or more intermediaries, controls or is controlled by or is under common control with, the issuer.

(B)   Covered class action.—The term "covered class action" means—

(i)   any single lawsuit in which—

(I)   damages are sought on behalf of more than 50 persons or prospective class members, and questions of law or fact common to those persons or members of the prospective class, without reference to issues of individualized reliance on an alleged misstatement or omission, predominate over any questions affecting only individual persons or members; or

(II)   one or more named parties seek to recover damages on a representative basis on behalf of themselves and other unnamed parties similarly situated, and questions of law or fact common to those persons or members of the prospective class predominate over any questions affecting only individual persons or members; or

(ii)   any group of lawsuits filed in or pending in the same court and involving common questions of law or fact, in which—

(I)   damages are sought on behalf of more than 50 persons; and

(II)   the lawsuits are joined, consolidated, or otherwise proceed as a single action for any purpose.

(C)   Exception for derivative actions.—Notwithstanding subparagraph (B), the term "covered class action" does not include an exclusively derivative action brought by one or more shareholders on behalf of a corporation.

(D)   Counting of certain class members.—For purposes of this paragraph, a corporation, investment company, pension plan, partnership, or other entity, shall be treated as one person or prospective class member, but only if the entity is not established for the purpose of participating in the action.

(E)   Covered security.—The term "covered security" means a security that satisfies the standards for a covered security specified in paragraph (1) or (2) of section 18(b) of the Securities Act of 1933 [15 U.S.C. 77r(b)], at the time during which it is alleged that the misrepresentation, omission, or manipulative or deceptive conduct occurred, except that such term shall not include any debt security that is exempt from registration under the Securities Act of 1933 [15 U.S.C. 77a et seq.] pursuant to rules issued by the Commission under section 4(2)[1] of that Act [15 U.S.C. 77d(a)(2)].

(F)   Rule of construction.—Nothing in this paragraph shall be construed to affect the discretion of a State court in determining whether actions filed in such court should be joined, consolidated, or otherwise allowed to proceed as a single action.

Validity of Contracts

§ 78cc [P.L. § 29]. (a) Waiver provisions.—Any condition, stipulation, or provision binding any person to waive compliance with any provision of this chapter or of any rule or regulation thereunder, or of any rule of a self-regulatory organization, shall be void.

(b)   Contract provisions in violation of chapter.—Every contract made in violation of any provision of this chapter or of any rule or regulation thereunder, and every contract (including any contract for listing a security on an exchange) heretofore or hereafter made, the performance of which involves the violation of, or the continuance of any relationship or practice in violation of, any provision of this chapter or any rule or regulation thereunder, shall be void (1) as regards the rights of any person who, in violation of any such provision, rule, or regulation, shall have made or engaged in the performance of any such contract, and (2) as regards the rights of any person who, not being a party to such contract, shall have acquired any right thereunder with actual knowledge of the facts by reason of which the making or performance of such contract was in violation of any such provision, rule, or regulation: Provided, (A) That no contract shall be void by reason of this subsection because of any violation of any rule or regulation prescribed pursuant to paragraph (3) of subsection (c) of section 78o of this title, and (B) that no contract shall be deemed to be void by reason of this subsection in any action maintained in reliance upon this subsection, by any person to or for whom any broker or dealer sells, or from or for whom any broker or dealer purchases, a security in violation of any rule or regulation prescribed pursuant to paragraph (1) or (2) of subsection (c) of section 78o of this title, unless such action is brought within one year after the discovery that such sale or purchase involves such violation and within three years after such violation. The Commission may, in a rule or regulation prescribed pursuant to such paragraph (2) of such section 78o(c) of this title, designate such rule or regulation, or portion thereof, as a rule or regulation, or portion thereof, a contract in violation of which shall not be void by reason of this subsection.

---

[1]   See References in Text note below. [Not reproduced here.]

(c)   Validity of loans, extensions of credit, and creation of liens; actual knowledge of violation.—Nothing in this chapter shall be construed (1) to affect the validity of any loan or extension of credit (or any extension or renewal thereof) made or of any lien created prior or subsequent to the enactment of this chapter, unless at the time of the making of such loan or extension of credit (or extension or renewal thereof) or the creating of such lien, the person making such loan or extension of credit (or extension or renewal thereof) or acquiring such lien shall have actual knowledge of facts by reason of which the making of such loan or extension of credit (or extension or renewal thereof) or the acquisition of such lien is a violation of the provisions of this chapter or any rule or regulation thereunder, or (2) to afford a defense to the collection of any debt or obligation or the enforcement of any lien by any person who shall have acquired such debt, obligation, or lien in good faith for value and without actual knowledge of the violation of any provision of this chapter or any rule or regulation thereunder affecting the legality of such debt, obligation, or lien.

Prohibited Foreign Trade Practices by Issuers

§ 78dd–1 [P.L. § 30A]. (a) Prohibition.—It shall be unlawful for any issuer which has a class of securities registered pursuant to section 78*l* of this title or which is required to file reports under section 78*o*(d) of this title, or for any officer, director, employee, or agent of such issuer or any stockholder thereof acting on behalf of such issuer, to make use of the mails or any means or instrumentality of interstate commerce corruptly in furtherance of an offer, payment, promise to pay, or authorization of the payment of any money, or offer, gift, promise to give, or authorization of the giving of anything of value to—

(1)   any foreign official for purposes of—

(A)(i)   influencing any act or decision of such foreign official in his official capacity, (ii) inducing such foreign official to do or omit to do any act in violation of the lawful duty of such official, or (iii) securing any improper advantage; or

(B)   inducing such foreign official to use his influence with a foreign government or instrumentality thereof to affect or influence any act or decision of such government or instrumentality,

in order to assist such issuer in obtaining or retaining business for or with, or directing business to, any person;

(2)   any foreign political party or official thereof or any candidate for foreign political office for purposes of—

(A)(i)   influencing any act or decision of such party, official, or candidate in its or his official capacity, (ii) inducing such party, official, or candidate to do or omit to do an act in violation of the lawful duty of such party, official, or candidate, or (iii) securing any improper advantage; or

(B)   inducing such party, official, or candidate to use its or his influence with a foreign government or instrumentality thereof to affect or influence any act or decision of such government or instrumentality,

in order to assist such issuer in obtaining or retaining business for or with, or directing business to, any person; or

(3)   any person, while knowing that all or a portion of such money or thing of value will be offered, given, or promised, directly or indirectly, to any foreign official, to any foreign political party or official thereof, or to any candidate for foreign political office, for purposes of—

(A)(i)   influencing any act or decision of such foreign official, political party, party official, or candidate in his or its official capacity, (ii) inducing such foreign official, political party, party official, or candidate to do or omit to do any act in violation of the lawful duty of such foreign official, political party, party official, or candidate, or (iii) securing any improper advantage; or

(B)   inducing such foreign official, political party, party official, or candidate to use his or its influence with a foreign government or instrumentality thereof to affect or influence any act or decision of such government or instrumentality,

in order to assist such issuer in obtaining or retaining business for or with, or directing business to, any person.

(b)   Exception for routine governmental action.—Subsections (a) and (g) of this section shall not apply to any facilitating or expediting payment to a foreign official, political party, or party official the purpose of which is to expedite or to secure the performance of a routine governmental action by a foreign official, political party, or party official.

(c)   Affirmative defenses.—It shall be an affirmative defense to actions under subsection (a) or (g) of this section that—

(1)   the payment, gift, offer, or promise of anything of value that was made, was lawful under the written laws and regulations of the foreign official's, political party's, party official's, or candidate's country; or

(2)   the payment, gift, offer, or promise of anything of value that was made, was a reasonable and bona fide expenditure, such as travel and lodging expenses, incurred by or on behalf of a foreign official, party, party official, or candidate and was directly related to—

(A)   the promotion, demonstration, or explanation of products or services; or

(B)   the execution or performance of a contract with a foreign government or agency thereof.

(d)   Guidelines by Attorney General.—Not later than one year after August 23, 1988, the Attorney General, after consultation with the Commission, the Secretary of Commerce, the United States Trade Representative, the Secretary of State, and the Secretary of the Treasury, and after obtaining the views of all interested persons through public notice and comment procedures, shall determine to what extent compliance with this section would be enhanced and the business community would be assisted by further clarification of the preceding provisions of this section and may, based on such determination and to the extent necessary and appropriate, issue—

(1)   guidelines describing specific types of conduct, associated with common types of export sales arrangements and business contracts, which for purposes of the Department of Justice's present enforcement policy, the Attorney General determines would be in conformance with the preceding provisions of this section; and

(2)   general precautionary procedures which issuers may use on a voluntary basis to conform their conduct to the Department of Justice's present enforcement policy regarding the preceding provisions of this section.

The Attorney General shall issue the guidelines and procedures referred to in the preceding sentence in accordance with the provisions of subchapter II of chapter 5 of title 5 and those guidelines and procedures shall be subject to the provisions of chapter 7 of that title.

(e)   Opinions of Attorney General.—(1) The Attorney General, after consultation with appropriate departments and agencies of the United States and after obtaining the views of all interested persons through public notice and comment procedures, shall establish a procedure to provide responses to specific inquiries by issuers concerning conformance of their conduct with the Department of Justice's present enforcement policy regarding the preceding provisions of this section. The Attorney General shall, within 30 days after receiving such a request, issue an opinion in response to that request. The opinion shall state whether or not certain specified prospective conduct would, for purposes of the Department of Justice's present enforcement policy, violate the preceding provisions of this section. Additional requests for opinions may be filed with the Attorney General regarding other specified prospective conduct that is beyond the scope of conduct specified in previous requests. In any action brought under the applicable provisions of this section, there shall be a rebuttable presumption that conduct, which is specified in a request by an issuer and for which the Attorney General has issued an opinion that such conduct is in conformity with the Department of Justice's present enforcement policy, is in compliance with the preceding provisions of this section. Such a presumption may be rebutted by a preponderance of the evidence. In considering the presumption for purposes of this paragraph, a court shall weigh all relevant factors, including but not limited to whether the information submitted to the Attorney General was accurate and complete and whether it was within the scope of the conduct specified in any request received by the Attorney General. The Attorney General shall establish the procedure required by this paragraph in accordance with the provisions of subchapter II of chapter 5 of title 5 and that procedure shall be subject to the provisions of chapter 7 of that title.

(2)   Any document or other material which is provided to, received by, or prepared in the Department of Justice or any other department or agency of the United States in connection with a request by an issuer under the procedure established under paragraph (1), shall be exempt from disclosure under section 552 of title 5 and shall not, except with the consent of the issuer, be made publicly available, regardless of whether the Attorney General responds to such a request or the issuer withdraws such request before receiving a response.

(3)   Any issuer who has made a request to the Attorney General under paragraph (1) may withdraw such request prior to the time the Attorney General issues an opinion in response to such request. Any request so withdrawn shall have no force or effect.

(4)   The Attorney General shall, to the maximum extent practicable, provide timely guidance concerning the Department of Justice's present enforcement policy with respect to the preceding provisions of this section to potential exporters and small businesses that are unable to obtain specialized counsel on issues pertaining to such provisions. Such guidance shall be limited to responses to requests under paragraph (1) concerning conformity of specified prospective conduct with the Department of Justice's present enforcement policy regarding the preceding provisions of this section and general explanations of compliance responsibilities and of potential liabilities under the preceding provisions of this section.

(f)   Definitions.—For purposes of this section:

(1)(A)   The term "foreign official" means any officer or employee of a foreign government or any department, agency, or instrumentality thereof, or of a public international organization, or any person acting in an official capacity for or on behalf of any such government or department, agency, or instrumentality, or for or on behalf of any such public international organization.

(B)   For purposes of subparagraph (A), the term "public international organization" means—

(i)   an organization that is designated by Executive order pursuant to section 288 of title 22; or

(ii)   any other international organization that is designated by the President by Executive order for the purposes of this section, effective as of the date of publication of such order in the Federal Register.

(2)(A)   A person's state of mind is "knowing" with respect to conduct, a circumstance, or a result if—

(i)   such person is aware that such person is engaging in such conduct, that such circumstance exists, or that such result is substantially certain to occur; or

(ii)   such person has a firm belief that such circumstance exists or that such result is substantially certain to occur.

(B)   When knowledge of the existence of a particular circumstance is required for an offense, such knowledge is established if a person is aware of a high probability of the existence of such circumstance, unless the person actually believes that such circumstance does not exist.

(3)(A) The term "routine governmental action" means only an action which is ordinarily and commonly performed by a foreign official in—

(i) obtaining permits, licenses, or other official documents to qualify a person to do business in a foreign country;

(ii) processing governmental papers, such as visas and work orders;

(iii) providing police protection, mail pick-up and delivery, or scheduling inspections associated with contract performance or inspections related to transit of goods across country;

(iv) providing phone service, power and water supply, loading and unloading cargo, or protecting perishable products or commodities from deterioration; or

(v) actions of a similar nature.

(B) The term "routine governmental action" does not include any decision by a foreign official whether, or on what terms, to award new business to or to continue business with a particular party, or any action taken by a foreign official involved in the decisionmaking process to encourage a decision to award new business to or continue business with a particular party.

(g) Alternative jurisdiction.—(1) It shall also be unlawful for any issuer organized under the laws of the United States, or a State, territory, possession, or commonwealth of the United States or a political subdivision thereof and which has a class of securities registered pursuant to section 78l of this title or which is required to file reports under section 78o(d) of this title, or for any United States person that is an officer, director, employee, or agent of such issuer or a stockholder thereof acting on behalf of such issuer, to corruptly do any act outside the United States in furtherance of an offer, payment, promise to pay, or authorization of the payment of any money, or offer, gift, promise to give, or authorization of the giving of anything of value to any of the persons or entities set forth in paragraphs (1), (2), and (3) of subsection (a) of this section for the purposes set forth therein, irrespective of whether such issuer or such officer, director, employee, agent, or stockholder makes use of the mails or any means or instrumentality of interstate commerce in furtherance of such offer, gift, payment, promise, or authorization.

(2) As used in this subsection, the term "United States person" means a national of the United States (as defined in section 1101 of title 8) or any corporation, partnership, association, joint-stock company, business trust, unincorporated organization, or sole proprietorship organized under the laws of the United States or any State, territory, possession, or commonwealth of the United States, or any political subdivision thereof.

Prohibited Foreign Trade Practices by Domestic Concerns

§ 78dd–2 [P.L. § 104]. (a) Prohibition.—It shall be unlawful for any domestic concern, other than an issuer which is subject to section 78dd–1 of this title, or for any officer, director, employee, or agent of such domestic concern or any stockholder thereof acting on behalf of such domestic concern, to make use of the mails or any means or instrumentality of interstate commerce corruptly in furtherance of an offer, payment, promise to pay, or authorization of the payment of any money, or offer, gift, promise to give, or authorization of the giving of anything of value to—

(1) any foreign official for purposes of—

(A)(i) influencing any act or decision of such foreign official in his official capacity, (ii) inducing such foreign official to do or omit to do any act in violation of the lawful duty of such official, or (iii) securing any improper advantage; or

(B) inducing such foreign official to use his influence with a foreign government or instrumentality thereof to affect or influence any act or decision of such government or instrumentality,

in order to assist such domestic concern in obtaining or retaining business for or with, or directing business to, any person;

(2) any foreign political party or official thereof or any candidate for foreign political office for purposes of—

(A)(i) influencing any act or decision of such party, official, or candidate in its or his official capacity, (ii) inducing such party, official, or candidate to do or omit to do an act in violation of the lawful duty of such party, official, or candidate, or (iii) securing any improper advantage; or

(B) inducing such party, official, or candidate to use its or his influence with a foreign government or instrumentality thereof to affect or influence any act or decision of such government or instrumentality,

in order to assist such domestic concern in obtaining or retaining business for or with, or directing business to, any person; or

(3) any person, while knowing that all or a portion of such money or thing of value will be offered, given, or promised, directly or indirectly, to any foreign official, to any foreign political party or official thereof, or to any candidate for foreign political office, for purposes of—

(A)(i) influencing any act or decision of such foreign official, political party, party official, or candidate in his or its official capacity, (ii) inducing such foreign official, political party, party official, or candidate to do or omit to do any act in violation of the lawful duty of such foreign official, political party, party official, or candidate, or (iii) securing any improper advantage; or

(B) inducing such foreign official, political party, party official, or candidate to use his or its influence with a foreign government or instrumentality thereof to affect or influence any act or decision of such government or instrumentality,

in order to assist such domestic concern in obtaining or retaining business for or with, or directing business to, any person.

(b) Exception for routine governmental action.—Subsections (a) and (i) of this section shall not apply to any facilitating or expediting payment to a foreign official, political party, or party official the purpose of which is to expedite or to secure the performance of a routine governmental action by a foreign official, political party, or party official.

(c) Affirmative defenses.—It shall be an affirmative defense to actions under subsection (a) or (i) of this section that—

(1) the payment, gift, offer, or promise of anything of value that was made, was lawful under the written laws and regulations of the foreign official's, political party's, party official's, or candidate's country; or

(2) the payment, gift, offer, or promise of anything of value that was made, was a reasonable and bona fide expenditure, such as travel and lodging expenses, incurred by or on behalf of a foreign official, party, party official, or candidate and was directly related to—

(A) the promotion, demonstration, or explanation of products or services; or

(B) the execution or performance of a contract with a foreign government or agency thereof.

(d) Injunctive relief.

(1)   When it appears to the Attorney General that any domestic concern to which this section applies, or officer, director, employee, agent, or stockholder thereof, is engaged, or about to engage, in any act or practice constituting a violation of subsection (a) or (i) of this section, the Attorney General may, in his discretion, bring a civil action in an appropriate district court of the United States to enjoin such act or practice, and upon a proper showing, a permanent injunction or a temporary restraining order shall be granted without bond.

(2)   For the purpose of any civil investigation which, in the opinion of the Attorney General, is necessary and proper to enforce this section, the Attorney General or his designee are empowered to administer oaths and affirmations, subpoena witnesses, take evidence, and require the production of any books, papers, or other documents which the Attorney General deems relevant or material to such investigation. The attendance of witnesses and the production of documentary evidence may be required from any place in the United States, or any territory, possession, or commonwealth of the United States, at any designated place of hearing.

(3)   In case of contumacy by, or refusal to obey a subpoena issued to, any person, the Attorney General may invoke the aid of any court of the United States within the jurisdiction of which such investigation or proceeding is carried on, or where such person resides or carries on business, in requiring the attendance and testimony of witnesses and the production of books, papers, or other documents. Any such court may issue an order requiring such person to appear before the Attorney General or his designee, there to produce records, if so ordered, or to give testimony touching the matter under investigation. Any failure to obey such order of the court may be punished by such court as a contempt thereof. All process in any such case may be served in the judicial district in which such person resides or may be found. The Attorney General may make such rules relating to civil investigations as may be necessary or appropriate to implement the provisions of this subsection.

(e)   Guidelines by Attorney General.—Not later than 6 months after August 23, 1988, the Attorney General, after consultation with the Securities and Exchange Commission, the Secretary of Commerce, the United States Trade Representative, the Secretary of State, and the Secretary of the Treasury, and after obtaining the views of all interested persons through public notice and comment procedures, shall determine to what extent compliance with this section would be enhanced and the business community would be assisted by further clarification of the preceding provisions of this section and may, based on such determination and to the extent necessary and appropriate, issue—

(1)   guidelines describing specific types of conduct, associated with common types of export sales arrangements and business contracts, which for purposes of the Department of Justice's present enforcement policy, the Attorney General determines would be in conformance with the preceding provisions of this section; and

(2)   general precautionary procedures which domestic concerns may use on a voluntary basis to conform their conduct to the Department of Justice's present enforcement policy regarding the preceding provisions of this section.

The Attorney General shall issue the guidelines and procedures referred to in the preceding sentence in accordance with the provisions of subchapter II of chapter 5 of title 5 and those guidelines and procedures shall be subject to the provisions of chapter 7 of that title.

(f)   Opinions of Attorney General.

(1)   The Attorney General, after consultation with appropriate departments and agencies of the United States and after obtaining the views of all interested persons through public notice and comment procedures, shall establish a procedure to provide responses to specific inquiries by domestic concerns concerning conformance of their conduct with the Department of Justice's present enforcement policy regarding the preceding provisions of this section. The Attorney General shall, within 30 days after receiving such a request, issue an opinion in response to that request. The opinion shall state whether or not certain specified prospective conduct would, for purposes of the Department of Justice's present enforcement policy, violate the preceding

provisions of this section. Additional requests for opinions may be filed with the Attorney General regarding other specified prospective conduct that is beyond the scope of conduct specified in previous requests. In any action brought under the applicable provisions of this section, there shall be a rebuttable presumption that conduct, which is specified in a request by a domestic concern and for which the Attorney General has issued an opinion that such conduct is in conformity with the Department of Justice's present enforcement policy, is in compliance with the preceding provisions of this section. Such a presumption may be rebutted by a preponderance of the evidence. In considering the presumption for purposes of this paragraph, a court shall weigh all relevant factors, including but not limited to whether the information submitted to the Attorney General was accurate and complete and whether it was within the scope of the conduct specified in any request received by the Attorney General. The Attorney General shall establish the procedure required by this paragraph in accordance with the provisions of subchapter II of chapter 5 of title 5 and that procedure shall be subject to the provisions of chapter 7 of that title.

(2) Any document or other material which is provided to, received by, or prepared in the Department of Justice or any other department or agency of the United States in connection with a request by a domestic concern under the procedure established under paragraph (1), shall be exempt from disclosure under section 552 of title 5 and shall not, except with the consent of the domestic concern, be made publicly available, regardless of whether the Attorney General responds to such a request or the domestic concern withdraws such request before receiving a response.

(3) Any domestic concern who has made a request to the Attorney General under paragraph (1) may withdraw such request prior to the time the Attorney General issues an opinion in response to such request. Any request so withdrawn shall have no force or effect.

(4) The Attorney General shall, to the maximum extent practicable, provide timely guidance concerning the Department of Justice's present enforcement policy with respect to the preceding provisions of this section to potential exporters and small businesses that are unable to obtain specialized counsel on issues pertaining to such provisions. Such guidance shall be limited to responses to requests under paragraph (1) concerning conformity of specified prospective conduct with the Department of Justice's present enforcement policy regarding the preceding provisions of this section and general explanations of compliance responsibilities and of potential liabilities under the preceding provisions of this section.

(g) Penalties.

(1)(A) Any domestic concern that is not a natural person and that violates subsection (a) or (i) of this section shall be fined not more than $2,000,000.

(B) Any domestic concern that is not a natural person and that violates subsection (a) or (i) of this section shall be subject to a civil penalty of not more than $10,000 imposed in an action brought by the Attorney General.

(2)(A) Any natural person that is an officer, director, employee, or agent of a domestic concern, or stockholder acting on behalf of such domestic concern, who willfully violates subsection (a) or (i) of this section shall be fined not more than $100,000 or imprisoned not more than 5 years, or both.

(B) Any natural person that is an officer, director, employee, or agent of a domestic concern, or stockholder acting on behalf of such domestic concern, who violates subsection (a) or (i) of this section shall be subject to a civil penalty of not more than $10,000 imposed in an action brought by the Attorney General.

(3) Whenever a fine is imposed under paragraph (2) upon any officer, director, employee, agent, or stockholder of a domestic concern, such fine may not be paid, directly or indirectly, by such domestic concern.

(h) Definitions.—For purposes of this section:

(1) The term "domestic concern" means—

(A) any individual who is a citizen, national, or resident of the United States; and

(B) any corporation, partnership, association, joint-stock company, business trust, unincorporated organization, or sole proprietorship which has its principal place of business in the United States, or which is organized under the laws of a State of the United States or a territory, possession, or commonwealth of the United States.

(2)(A) The term "foreign official" means any officer or employee of a foreign government or any department, agency, or instrumentality thereof, or of a public international organization, or any person acting in an official capacity for or on behalf of any such government or department, agency, or instrumentality, or for or on behalf of any such public international organization.

(B) For purposes of subparagraph (A), the term "public international organization" means—

(i) an organization that is designated by Executive order pursuant to section 288 of title 22; or

(ii) any other international organization that is designated by the President by Executive order for the purposes of this section, effective as of the date of publication of such order in the Federal Register.

(3)(A) A person's state of mind is "knowing" with respect to conduct, a circumstance, or a result if—

(i) such person is aware that such person is engaging in such conduct, that such circumstance exists, or that such result is substantially certain to occur; or

(ii) such person has a firm belief that such circumstance exists or that such result is substantially certain to occur.

(B) When knowledge of the existence of a particular circumstance is required for an offense, such knowledge is established if a person is aware of a high probability of the existence of such circumstance, unless the person actually believes that such circumstance does not exist.

(4)(A) The term "routine governmental action" means only an action which is ordinarily and commonly performed by a foreign official in—

(i) obtaining permits, licenses, or other official documents to qualify a person to do business in a foreign country;

(ii) processing governmental papers, such as visas and work orders;

(iii) providing police protection, mail pick-up and delivery, or scheduling inspections associated with contract performance or inspections related to transit of goods across country;

(iv) providing phone service, power and water supply, loading and unloading cargo, or protecting perishable products or commodities from deterioration; or

(v) actions of a similar nature.

(B) The term "routine governmental action" does not include any decision by a foreign official whether, or on what terms, to award new business to or to continue business with a particular party, or any action taken by a foreign official involved in the decision-making process to encourage a decision to award new business to or continue business with a particular party.

(5)   The term "interstate commerce" means trade, commerce, transportation, or communication among the several States, or between any foreign country and any State or between any State and any place or ship outside thereof, and such term includes the intrastate use of—

    (A)   a telephone or other interstate means of communication, or

    (B)   any other interstate instrumentality.

(i)   Alternative jurisdiction.

(1)   It shall also be unlawful for any United States person to corruptly do any act outside the United States in furtherance of an offer, payment, promise to pay, or authorization of the payment of any money, or offer, gift, promise to give, or authorization of the giving of anything of value to any of the persons or entities set forth in paragraphs (1), (2), and (3) of subsection (a) of this section, for the purposes set forth therein, irrespective of whether such United States person makes use of the mails or any means or instrumentality of interstate commerce in furtherance of such offer, gift, payment, promise, or authorization.

(2)   As used in this subsection, the term "United States person" means a national of the United States (as defined in section 1101 of title 8) or any corporation, partnership, association, joint-stock company, business trust, unincorporated organization, or sole proprietorship organized under the laws of the United States or any State, territory, possession, or commonwealth of the United States, or any political subdivision thereof.

Penalties

§ 78ff [P.L. § 32]. (a) Willful violations; false and misleading statements.—Any person who willfully violates any provision of this chapter (other than section 78dd–1 of this title), or any rule or regulation thereunder the violation of which is made unlawful or the observance of which is required under the terms of this chapter, or any person who willfully and knowingly makes, or causes to be made, any statement in any application, report, or document required to be filed under this chapter or any rule or regulation thereunder or any undertaking contained in a registration statement as provided in subsection (d) of section 78o of this title, or by any self-regulatory organization in connection with an application for membership or participation therein or to become associated with a member thereof which statement was false or misleading with respect to any material fact, shall upon conviction be fined not more than $5,000,000, or imprisoned not more than 20 years, or both, except that when such person is a person other than a natural person, a fine not exceeding $25,000,000 may be imposed; but no person shall be subject to imprisonment under this section for the violation of any rule or regulation if he proves that he had no knowledge of such rule or regulation.

(b)   Failure to file information, documents, or reports.—Any issuer which fails to file information, documents, or reports required to be filed under subsection (d) of section 78o of this title or any rule or regulation thereunder shall forfeit to the United States the sum of $100 for each and every day such failure to file shall continue. Such forfeiture, which shall be in lieu of any criminal penalty for such failure to file which might be deemed to arise under subsection (a) of this section, shall be payable into the Treasury of the United States and shall be recoverable in a civil suit in the name of the United States.

(c)   Violations by issuers, officers, directors, stockholders, employees, or agents of issuers.

(1)(A)   Any issuer that violates subsection (a) or (g) of section 78dd–1 of this title shall be fined not more than $2,000,000.

    (B)   Any issuer that violates subsection (a) or (g) of section 78dd–1 of this title shall be subject to a civil penalty of not more than $10,000 imposed in an action brought by the Commission.

(2)(A)   Any officer, director, employee, or agent of an issuer, or stockholder acting on behalf of such issuer, who willfully violates subsection (a) or (g) of section 78dd–1 of this title shall be fined not more than $100,000, or imprisoned not more than 5 years, or both.

(B)   Any officer, director, employee, or agent of an issuer, or stockholder acting on behalf of such issuer, who violates subsection (a) or (g) of section 78dd–1 of this title shall be subject to a civil penalty of not more than $10,000 imposed in an action brought by the Commission.

(3)   Whenever a fine is imposed under paragraph (2) upon any officer, director, employee, agent, or stockholder of an issuer, such fine may not be paid, directly or indirectly, by such issuer.

Federal National Mortgage Association, Federal Home Loan Mortgage Corporation, Federal Home Loan Banks

§ 78oo [P.L. § 38]. (a) Federal National Mortgage Association and Federal Home Loan Mortgage Corporation.—No class of equity securities of the Federal National Mortgage Association or the Federal Home Loan Mortgage Corporation shall be treated as an exempted security for purposes of section 78l, 78m, 78n, or 78p of this title.

(b)   Federal Home Loan Banks.

(1)   Registration.—Each Federal Home Loan Bank shall register a class of its common stock under section 78l(g) of this title, not later than 120 days after July 30, 2008, and shall thereafter maintain such registration and be treated for purposes of this chapter as an "issuer", the securities of which are required to be registered under section 78l of this title, regardless of the number of members holding such stock at any given time.

(2)   Standards relating to audit committees.—Each Federal Home Loan Bank shall comply with the rules issued by the Commission under section 78j–1(m) of this title.

(c)   Definitions.—For purposes of this section, the following definitions shall apply:

(1)   Federal Home Loan Bank; member.—The terms "Federal Home Loan Bank" and "member", have the same meanings as in section 1422 of title 12.

(2)   Federal National Mortgage Association.—The term "Federal National Mortgage Association" means the corporation created by the Federal National Mortgage Association Charter Act [12 U.S.C. 1716 et seq.].

(3)   Federal Home Loan Mortgage Corporation.—The term "Federal Home Loan Mortgage Corporation" means the corporation created by the Federal Home Loan Mortgage Corporation Act [12 U.S.C. 1451 et seq.].

C. RULES UNDER THE SECURITIES ACT OF 1933

(Selected)

17 C.F.R. §§ 230.100 *et seq.*

Table of Contents*

---

* Although this table of contents lists rule numbers, the rules themselves are printed with their CFR sections (§ 230.[rule number]). For example, Rule 134 is § 230.134.

GENERAL REQUIREMENTS

FORM AND CONTENT OF PROSPECTUSES

FILINGS; FEES; EFFECTIVE DATE

AMENDMENTS; WITHDRAWALS

REGULATION D—RULES GOVERNING THE LIMITED OFFER AND SALE OF SECURITIES WITHOUT REGISTRATION UNDER THE SECURITIES ACT OF 1933

---

§ 230.134   Communications Not Deemed a Prospectus.

Except as provided in paragraphs (e) and (g) of this section, the terms "prospectus" as defined in section 2(a)(10) of the Act or "free writing prospectus" as defined in Rule 405 (§ 230.405) shall not include a communication limited to the statements required or permitted by this section, provided that the communication is published or transmitted to any person only after a registration statement relating to the offering that includes a prospectus satisfying the requirements of section 10 of the Act (except as otherwise permitted in paragraph (a) of this section) has been filed.

(a)   Such communication may include any one or more of the following items of information, which need not follow the numerical sequence of this paragraph, provided that, except as to paragraphs (a)(4) through (6) of this section, the prospectus included in the filed registration statement does not have to include a price range otherwise required by rule:

    (1)   Factual information about the legal identity and business location of the issuer limited to the following: the name of the issuer of the security, the address, phone number, and e-mail address of the issuer's principal offices and contact for investors, the issuer's country of organization, and the geographic areas in which it conducts business;

(2) The title of the security or securities and the amount or amounts being offered, which title may include a designation as to whether the securities are convertible, exercisable, or exchangeable, and as to the ranking of the securities;

(3) A brief indication of the general type of business of the issuer, limited to the following:

(i) In the case of a manufacturing company, the general type of manufacturing, the principal products or classes of products manufactured, and the segments in which the company conducts business;

(ii) In the case of a public utility company, the general type of services rendered, a brief indication of the area served, and the segments in which the company conducts business;

(iii) In the case of an asset-backed issuer, the identity of key parties, such as sponsor, depositor, issuing entity, servicer or servicers, and trustee, the asset class of the transaction, and the identity of any credit enhancement or other support; and

(iv) In the case of any other type of company, a corresponding statement;

(4) The price of the security, or if the price is not known, the method of its determination or the *bona fide* estimate of the price range as specified by the issuer or the managing underwriter or underwriters;

(5) In the case of a fixed income security, the final maturity and interest rate provisions or, if the final maturity or interest rate provisions are not known, the probable final maturity or interest rate provisions, as specified by the issuer or the managing underwriter or underwriters;

(6) In the case of a fixed income security with a fixed (non-contingent) interest rate provision, the yield or, if the yield is not known, the probable yield range, as specified by the issuer or the managing underwriter or underwriters and the yield of fixed income securities with comparable maturity and security rating;

(7) A brief description of the intended use of proceeds of the offering, if then disclosed in the prospectus that is part of the filed registration statement;

(8) The name, address, phone number, and e-mail address of the sender of the communication and the fact that it is participating, or expects to participate, in the distribution of the security;

(9) The type of underwriting, if then included in the disclosure in the prospectus that is part of the filed registration statement;

(10) The names of underwriters participating in the offering of the securities, and their additional roles, if any, within the underwriting syndicate;

(11) The anticipated schedule for the offering (including the approximate date upon which the proposed sale to the public will begin) and a description of marketing events (including the dates, times, locations, and procedures for attending or otherwise accessing them);

(12) A description of the procedures by which the underwriters will conduct the offering and the procedures for transactions in connection with the offering with the issuer or an underwriter or participating dealer (including procedures regarding account-opening and submitting indications of interest and conditional offers to buy), and procedures regarding directed share plans and other participation in offerings by officers, directors, and employees of the issuer;

(13) Whether, in the opinion of counsel, the security is a legal investment for savings banks, fiduciaries, insurance companies, or similar investors under the laws of any State or Territory or the District of Columbia, and the permissibility or status of the investment under the Employee Retirement Income Security Act of 1974 [29 U.S.C. 1001 *et seq.*];

(14) Whether, in the opinion of counsel, the security is exempt from specified taxes, or the extent to which the issuer has agreed to pay any tax with respect to the security or measured by the income therefrom;

(15) Whether the security is being offered through rights issued to security holders, and, if so, the class of securities the holders of which will be entitled to subscribe, the subscription ratio, the actual or proposed record date, the date upon which the rights were issued or are expected to be issued, the actual or anticipated date upon which they will expire, and the approximate subscription price, or any of the foregoing;

(16) Any statement or legend required by any state law or administrative authority;

(17) [Reserved]

(18) The names of selling security holders, if then disclosed in the prospectus that is part of the filed registration statement;

(19) The names of securities exchanges or other securities markets where any class of the issuer's securities are, or will be, listed;

(20) The ticker symbols, or proposed ticker symbols, of the issuer's securities;

(21) The CUSIP number as defined in Rule 17Ad–19(a)(5) of the Securities Exchange Act of 1934 (§ 240.17Ad–19(a)(5) of this chapter) assigned to the securities being offered; and

(22) Information disclosed in order to correct inaccuracies previously contained in a communication permissibly made pursuant to this section.

(b) Except as provided in paragraph (c) of this section, every communication used pursuant to this section shall contain the following:

(1) If the registration statement has not yet become effective, the following statement:

A registration statement relating to these securities has been filed with the Securities and Exchange Commission but has not yet become effective. These securities may not be sold nor may offers to buy be accepted prior to the time the registration statement becomes effective; and

(2) The name and address of a person or persons from whom a written prospectus for the offering meeting the requirements of section 10 of the Act (other than a free writing prospectus as defined in Rule 405) including as to the identified paragraphs above a price range where required by rule, may be obtained.

(c) Any of the statements or information specified in paragraph (b) of this section may, but need not, be contained in a communication which:

(1) Does no more than state from whom and include the uniform resource locator (URL) where a written prospectus meeting the requirements of section 10 of the Act (other than a free writing prospectus as defined in Rule 405) may be obtained, identify the security, state the price thereof and state by whom orders will be executed; or

(2) Is accompanied or preceded by a prospectus or a summary prospectus, other than a free writing prospectus as defined in Rule 405, which meets the requirements of section 10 of the Act, including a price range where required by rule, at the date of such preliminary communication.

(d) A communication sent or delivered to any person pursuant to this section which is accompanied or preceded by a prospectus which meets the requirements of section 10 of the Act (other than a free writing prospectus as defined in Rule 405), including a price range where required by rule, at the date of such communication, may solicit from the recipient of the communication an offer to buy the security or request the recipient to indicate whether he or she might be interested in the security, if the communication contains substantially the following statement:

No offer to buy the securities can be accepted and no part of the purchase price can be received until the registration statement has become effective, and any such offer may be withdrawn or revoked, without obligation or commitment of any kind, at any time prior to notice of its acceptance given after the effective date.

Provided, that such statement need not be included in such a communication to a dealer.

(e)   A section 10 prospectus included in any communication pursuant to this section shall remain a prospectus for all purposes under the Act.

(f)   The provision in paragraphs (c)(2) and (d) of this section that a prospectus that meets the requirements of section 10 of the Act precede or accompany a communication will be satisfied if such communication is an electronic communication containing an active hyperlink to such prospectus.

(g)   This section does not apply to a communication relating to an investment company registered under the Investment Company Act of 1940 (15 U.S.C. 80a–1 *et seq.*) or a business development company as defined in section 2(a)(48) of the Investment Company Act of 1940 (15 U.S.C. 80a–2(a)(48))

§ 230.135   Notice of Proposed Registered Offerings.

(a)   *When notice is not an offer.* For purposes of section 5 of the Act (15 U.S.C. 77e) only, an issuer or a selling security holder (and any person acting on behalf of either of them) that publishes through any medium a notice of a proposed offering to be registered under the Act will not be deemed to offer its securities for sale through that notice if:

(1)   *Legend.* The notice includes a statement to the effect that it does not constitute an offer of any securities for sale; and

(2)   *Limited notice content.* The notice otherwise includes no more than the following information:

(i)   The name of the issuer;

(ii)   The title, amount and basic terms of the securities offered;

(iii)   The amount of the offering, if any, to be made by selling security holders;

(iv)   The anticipated timing of the offering;

(v)   A brief statement of the manner and the purpose of the offering, without naming the underwriters;

(vi)   Whether the issuer is directing its offering to only a particular class of purchasers;

(vii)   Any statements or legends required by the laws of any state or foreign country or administrative authority; and

(viii) In the following offerings, the notice may contain additional information, as follows:

(A)   *Rights offering.* In a rights offering to existing security holders:

(*1*)   The class of security holders eligible to subscribe;

(*2*)   The subscription ratio and expected subscription price;

(*3*)   The proposed record date;

(*4*)   The anticipated issuance date of the rights; and

(*5*)   The subscription period or expiration date of the rights offering.

(B)   *Offering to employees.* In an offering to employees of the issuer or an affiliated company:

(*1*)   The name of the employer;

(*2*)   The class of employees being offered the securities;

(*3*)   The offering price; and

(*4*)   The duration of the offering period.

(C) *Exchange offer.* In an exchange offer:

(*1*) . The basic terms of the exchange offer;

(*2*)   The name of the subject company;

(*3*)   The subject class of securities sought in the exchange offer.

(D) *Rule 145(a) offering.* In a § 230.145(a) offering:

(*1*)   The name of the person whose assets are to be sold in exchange for the securities to be offered;

(*2*)   The names of any other parties to the transaction;

(*3*)   A brief description of the business of the parties to the transaction;

(*4*)   The date, time and place of the meeting of security holders to vote on or consent to the transaction; and

(*5*)   A brief description of the transaction and the basic terms of the transaction.

(b) *Corrections of misstatements about the offering.* A person that publishes a notice in reliance on this section may issue a notice that contains no more information than is necessary to correct inaccuracies published about the proposed offering.

Note to § 230.135: Communications under this section relating to business combination transactions must be filed as required by § 230.425(b).

§ 230.137   Publications or Distributions of Research Reports by Brokers or Dealers That are Not Participating in an Issuer's Registered Distribution of Securities.

Under the following conditions, the terms "offers," "participates," or "participation" in section 2(a)(11) of the Act shall not be deemed to apply to the publication or distribution of research reports with respect to the securities of an issuer which is the subject of an offering pursuant to a registration statement that the issuer proposes to file, or has filed, or that is effective:

(a) The broker or dealer (and any affiliate) that has distributed the report and, if different, the person (and any affiliate) that has published the report have not participated, are not participating, and do not propose to participate in the distribution of the securities that are or will be the subject of the registered offering.

(b) In connection with the publication or distribution of the research report, the broker or dealer (and any affiliate) that has distributed the report and, if different, the person (and any affiliate) that has published the report are not receiving and have not received consideration directly or indirectly from, and are not acting under any direct or indirect arrangement or understanding with:

(1)   The issuer of the securities;

(2)   A selling security holder;

(3)   Any participant in the distribution of the securities that are or will be the subject of the registration statement; or

(4)   Any other person interested in the securities that are or will be the subject of the registration statement.

Instruction to § 230.137(b): This paragraph (b) does not preclude payment of:

1.   The regular price being paid by the broker or dealer for independent research, so long as the conditions of this paragraph (b) are satisfied; or

2.   The regular subscription or purchase price for the research report.

(c)   The broker or dealer publishes or distributes the research report in the regular course of its business.

(d)   The issuer is not and during the past three years neither the issuer nor any of its predecessors was:

(1)   A blank check company as defined in Rule 419(a)(2) (§ 230.419(a)(2));

(2)   A shell company, other than a business combination related shell company, each as defined in Rule 405 (§ 230.405); or

(3)   An issuer for an offering of penny stock as defined in Rule 3a51–1 of the Securities Exchange Act of 1934 (§ 240.3a51–1 of this chapter).

(e)   *Definition of research report.* For purposes of this section, *research report* means a written communication, as defined in Rule 405, that includes information, opinions, or recommendations with respect to securities of an issuer or an analysis of a security or an issuer, whether or not it provides information reasonably sufficient upon which to base an investment decision.

§ 230.138   Publications or Distributions of Research Reports by Brokers or Dealers About Securities Other Than Those They Are Distributing.

(a)   *Registered offerings.* Under the following conditions, a broker's or dealer's publication or distribution of research reports about securities of an issuer shall be deemed for purposes of sections 2(a)(10) and 5(c) of the Act not to constitute an offer for sale or offer to sell a security which is the subject of an offering pursuant to a registration statement that the issuer proposes to file, or has filed, or that is effective, even if the broker or dealer is participating or will participate in the registered offering of the issuer's securities:

(1)(i)   The research report relates solely to the issuer's common stock, or debt securities or preferred stock convertible into its common stock, and the offering involves solely the issuer's non-convertible debt securities or non-convertible, non-participating preferred stock; or

(ii)   The research report relates solely to the issuer's non-convertible debt securities or non-convertible, non-participating preferred stock, and the offering involves solely the issuer's common stock, or debt securities or preferred stock convertible into its common stock.

Instruction to paragraph (a)(1): If the issuer has filed a shelf registration statement under Rule 415(a)(1)(x) (§ 230.415(a)(1)(x)) or pursuant to General Instruction I.D. of Form S-3 or General Instruction I.C. of Form F-3 (§ 239.13 or § 239.33 of this chapter) with respect to multiple classes of securities, the conditions of paragraph (a)(1) of this section must be satisfied for the offering in which the broker or dealer is participating or will participate.

(2)   The issuer as of the date of reliance on this section:

(i)   Is required to file reports, and has filed all periodic reports required during the preceding 12 months (or such shorter time that the issuer was required to file such reports) on Forms 10-K (§ 249.310 of this chapter), 10-Q (§ 249.308a of this chapter), and 20-F (§ 249.220f of this chapter) pursuant to Section 13 or Section 15(d) of the Securities Exchange Act of 1934 (15 U.S.C. 78m or 78o(d)); or

(ii) Is a foreign private issuer that:

(A) Meets all of the registrant requirements of Form F-3 other than the reporting history provisions of General Instructions I.A.1. and I.A.2(a) of Form F-3;

(B) Either:

(*1*) Satisfies the public float threshold in General Instruction I.B.1. of Form F-3; or

(*2*) Is issuing non-convertible securities, other than common equity, and the issuer meets the provisions of General Instruction I.B.2. of Form F-3 (referenced in 17 CFR 239.33 of this chapter); and

(C) Either:

(*1*) Has its equity securities trading on a designated offshore securities market as defined in Rule 902(b) (§ 230.902(b)) and has had them so traded for at least 12 months; or

(*2*) Has a worldwide market value of its outstanding common equity held by non-affiliates of $700 million or more.

(*3*) The broker or dealer publishes or distributes research reports on the types of securities in question in the regular course of its business; and

(*4*) The issuer is not, and during the past three years neither the issuer nor any of its predecessors was:

(*i*) A blank check company as defined in Rule 419(a)(2) (§ 230.419(a)(2));

(*ii*) A shell company, other than a business combination related shell company, each as defined in Rule 405 (§ 230.405); or

(*iii*) An issuer for an offering of penny stock as defined in Rule 3a51–1 of the Securities Exchange Act of 1934 (§ 240.3a51–1 of this chapter).

(b) *Rule 144A offerings.* If the conditions in paragraph (a) of this section are satisfied, a broker's or dealer's publication or distribution of a research report shall not be considered an offer for sale or an offer to sell a security or general solicitation or general advertising, in connection with an offering relying on Rule 144A (§ 230.144A).

(c) *Regulation S offerings.* If the conditions in paragraph (a) of this section are satisfied, a broker's or dealer's publication or distribution of a research report shall not:

(1) Constitute directed selling efforts as defined in Rule 902(c) (§ 230.902(c)) for offerings under Regulation S (§ 230.901 through § 230.905); or

(2) Be inconsistent with the offshore transaction requirement in Rule 902(h) (§ 230.902(h)) for offerings under Regulation S.

(d) *Definition of research report.* For purposes of this section, research report means a written communication, as defined in Rule 405, that includes information, opinions, or recommendations with respect to securities of an issuer or an analysis of a security or an issuer, whether or not it provides information reasonably sufficient upon which to base an investment decision.

§ 230.139 Publications or Distributions of Research Reports by Brokers or Dealers Distributing Securities.

(a) *Registered offerings.* Under the conditions of paragraph (a)(1) or (2) of this section, a broker's or dealer's publication or distribution of a research report about an issuer or any of its securities shall be deemed for purposes of sections 2(a)(10) and 5(c) of the Act not to constitute an offer for sale or offer to sell a security that is the subject of an offering pursuant to a registration statement that the issuer proposes to file, or has filed, or that is effective, even if the broker or dealer is participating or will participate in the registered offering of the issuer's securities. For purposes of the Fair Access to Investment Research Act of 2017 [Pub. L. 115–66, 131 Stat. 1196 (2017)], a safe harbor has been established for covered investment fund research reports, and the specific terms of that safe harbor are set forth in § 230.139b.

(1) *Issuer-specific research reports.* (i) The issuer either:

(A)(*1*)   At the later of the time of filing its most recent Form S-3 (§ 239.13 of this chapter) or Form F-3 (§ 239.33 of this chapter) or the time of its most recent amendment to such registration statement for purposes of complying with section 10(a)(3) of the Act or, if no Form S-3 or Form F-3 has been filed, at the date of reliance on this section, meets the registrant requirements of such Form S-3 or Form F-3 and:

(*i*)   At such date, meets the minimum float provisions of General Instruction I.B.1 of such Forms; or

(*ii*)   At the date of reliance on this section, is, or if a registration statement has not been filed, will be, offering non-convertible securities, other than common equity, and meets the requirements for the General Instruction I.B.2. of Form S-3 or Form F-3 (referenced in 17 CFR 239.13 and 17 CFR 239.33 of this chapter); or

(*iii*) At the date of reliance on this section is a well-known seasoned issuer as defined in Rule 405 (§ 230.405), other than a majority-owned subsidiary that is a well-known seasoned issuer by virtue of paragraph (1)(ii) of the definition of well-known seasoned issuer in Rule 405; and

(*2*)   As of the date of reliance on this section, has filed all periodic reports required during the preceding 12 months on Forms 10-K (§ 249.310 of this chapter), 10-Q (§ 249.308a of this chapter), and 20-F (§ 249.220f of this chapter) pursuant to section 13 or section 15(d) of the Securities Exchange Act of 1934 (15 U.S.C. 78m or 78*o*(d)); or

(B)   Is a foreign private issuer that as of the date of reliance on this section:

(*1*)   Meets all of the registrant requirements of Form F-3 other than the reporting history provisions of General Instructions I.A.1. and I.A.2(a) of Form F-3;

(*2*)   Either:

(*i*)   Satisfies the public float threshold in General Instruction I.B.1. of Form F-3; or

(*ii*)   Is issuing non-convertible securities, other than common equity, and meets the provisions of General Instruction I.B.2. of Form F-3 (referenced in 17 CFR 239.33 of this chapter); and

(*3*)   Either:

(*i*)   Has its equity securities trading on a designated offshore securities market as defined in Rule 902(b) (§ 230.902(b)) and has had them so traded for at least 12 months; or

(*ii*)   Has a worldwide market value of its outstanding common equity held by non-affiliates of $700 million or more;

(ii)   The issuer is not and during the past three years neither the issuer nor any of its predecessors was:

(A)   A blank check company as defined in Rule 419(a)(2) (§ 230.419(a)(2));

(B) A shell company, other than a business combination related shell company, each as defined in Rule 405 (§ 230.405); or

(C) An issuer for an offering of penny stock as defined in Rule 3a51–1 of the Securities Exchange Act of 1934 (§ 240.3a51–1 of this chapter); and

(iii) The broker or dealer publishes or distributes research reports in the regular course of its business and such publication or distribution does not represent the initiation of publication of research reports about such issuer or its securities or reinitiation of such publication following discontinuation of publication of such research reports.

(2) *Industry reports.* (i) The issuer is required to file reports pursuant to section 13 or section 15(d) of the Securities Exchange Act of 1934 or satisfies the conditions in paragraph (a)(1)(i)(B) of this section;

(ii) The condition in paragraph (a)(1)(ii) of this section is satisfied;

(iii) The research report includes similar information with respect to a substantial number of issuers in the issuer's industry or sub-industry, or contains a comprehensive list of securities currently recommended by the broker or dealer;

(iv) The analysis regarding the issuer or its securities is given no materially greater space or prominence in the publication than that given to other securities or issuers; and

(v) The broker or dealer publishes or distributes research reports in the regular course of its business and, at the time of the publication or distribution of the research report, is including similar information about the issuer or its securities in similar reports.

(b) *Rule 144A offerings.* If the conditions in paragraph (a)(1) or (a)(2) of this section are satisfied, a broker's or dealer's publication or distribution of a research report shall not be considered an offer for sale or an offer to sell a security or general solicitation or general advertising, in connection with an offering relying on Rule 144A (§ 230.144A).

(c) *Regulation S offerings.* If the conditions in paragraph (a)(1) or (a)(2) of this section are satisfied, a broker's or dealer's publication or distribution of a research report shall not:

(1) Constitute directed selling efforts as defined in Rule 902(c) (§ 230.902(c)) for offerings under Regulation S (§§ 230.901 through 230.905); or

(2) Be inconsistent with the offshore transaction requirement in Rule 902(h) (§ 230.902(h)) for offerings under Regulation S.

(d) *Definition of research report.* For purposes of this section, *research report* means a written communication, as defined in Rule 405, that includes information, opinions, or recommendations with respect to securities of an issuer or an analysis of a security or an issuer, whether or not it provides information reasonably sufficient upon which to base an investment decision.

Instruction to § 230.139. Projections. A projection constitutes an analysis or information falling within the definition of research report. When a broker or dealer publishes or distributes projections of an issuer's sales or earnings in reliance on paragraph (a)(2) of this section, it must:

1. Have previously published or distributed projections on a regular basis in order to satisfy the "regular course of its business" condition;

2. At the time of publishing or disseminating a research report, be publishing or distributing projections with respect to that issuer; and

3. For purposes of paragraph (a)(2)(iii) of this section, include projections covering the same or similar periods with respect to either a substantial number of issuers in the issuer's industry or sub-industry or substantially all issuers represented in the comprehensive list of securities contained in the research report.

§ 230.144 Persons Deemed Not to Be Engaged in a Distribution and Therefore Not Underwriters.

Preliminary Note. Certain basic principles are essential to an understanding of the registration requirements in the Securities Act of 1933 (the Act or the Securities Act) and the purposes underlying Rule 144:

1. If any person sells a non-exempt security to any other person, the sale must be registered unless an exemption can be found for the transaction.

2. Section 4(1) of the Securities Act provides one such exemption for a transaction "by a person other than an issuer, underwriter, or dealer." Therefore, an understanding of the term "underwriter" is important in determining whether or not the Section 4(1) exemption from registration is available for the sale of the securities.

The term "underwriter" is broadly defined in Section 2(a)(11) of the Securities Act to mean any person who has purchased from an issuer with a view to, or offers or sells for an issuer in connection with, the distribution of any security, or participates, or has a direct or indirect participation in any such undertaking, or participates or has a participation in the direct or indirect underwriting of any such undertaking. The interpretation of this definition traditionally has focused on the words "with a view to" in the phrase "purchased from an issuer with a view to * * * distribution." An investment banking firm which arranges with an issuer for the public sale of its securities is clearly an "underwriter" under that section. However, individual investors who are not professionals in the securities business also may be "underwriters" if they act as links in a chain of transactions through which securities move from an issuer to the public.

Since it is difficult to ascertain the mental state of the purchaser at the time of an acquisition of securities, prior to and since the adoption of Rule 144, subsequent acts and circumstances have been considered to determine whether the purchaser took the securities "with a view to distribution" at the time of the acquisition. Emphasis has been placed on factors such as the length of time the person held the securities and whether there has been an unforeseeable change in circumstances of the holder. Experience has shown, however, that reliance upon such factors alone has led to uncertainty in the application of the registration provisions of the Act.

The Commission adopted Rule 144 to establish specific criteria for determining whether a person is not engaged in a distribution. Rule 144 creates a safe harbor from the Section 2(a)(11) definition of "underwriter." A person satisfying the applicable conditions of the Rule 144 safe harbor is deemed not to be engaged in a distribution of the securities and therefore not an underwriter of the securities for purposes of Section 2(a)(11). Therefore, such a person is deemed not to be an underwriter when determining whether a sale is eligible for the Section 4(1) exemption for "transactions by any person other than an issuer, underwriter, or dealer." If a sale of securities complies with all of the applicable conditions of Rule 144:

1. Any affiliate or other person who sells restricted securities will be deemed not to be engaged in a distribution and therefore not an underwriter for that transaction;

2. Any person who sells restricted or other securities on behalf of an affiliate of the issuer will be deemed not to be engaged in a distribution and therefore not an underwriter for that transaction; and

3. The purchaser in such transaction will receive securities that are not restricted securities.

Rule 144 is not an exclusive safe harbor. A person who does not meet all of the applicable conditions of Rule 144 still may claim any other available exemption under the Act for the sale of the securities. The Rule 144 safe harbor is not available to any person with respect to any transaction or series of transactions that, although in technical compliance with Rule 144, is part of a plan or scheme to evade the registration requirements of the Act.

(a) *Definitions.* The following definitions shall apply for the purposes of this section.

(1) An *affiliate* of an issuer is a person that directly, or indirectly through one or more intermediaries, controls, or is controlled by, or is under common control with, such issuer.

(2) The term *person* when used with reference to a person for whose account securities are to be sold in reliance upon this section includes, in addition to such person, all of the following persons:

(i) Any relative or spouse of such person, or any relative of such spouse, any one of whom has the same home as such person;

(ii) Any trust or estate in which such person or any of the persons specified in paragraph (a)(2)(i) of this section collectively own 10 percent or more of the total beneficial interest or of which any of such persons serve as trustee, executor or in any similar capacity; and

(iii) Any corporation or other organization (other than the issuer) in which such person or any of the persons specified in paragraph (a)(2)(i) of this section are the beneficial owners collectively of 10 percent or more of any class of equity securities or 10 percent or more of the equity interest.

(3) The term *restricted securities* means:

(i) Securities acquired directly or indirectly from the issuer, or from an affiliate of the issuer, in a transaction or chain of transactions not involving any public offering;

(ii) Securities acquired from the issuer that are subject to the resale limitations of § 230.502(d) under Regulation D or § 230.701(c);

(iii) Securities acquired in a transaction or chain of transactions meeting the requirements of § 230.144A;

(iv) Securities acquired from the issuer in a transaction subject to the conditions of Regulation CE (§ 230.1001);

(v) Equity securities of domestic issuers acquired in a transaction or chain of transactions subject to the conditions of § 230.901 or § 230.903 under Regulation S (§ 230.901 through § 230.905, and Preliminary Notes);

(vi) Securities acquired in a transaction made under § 230.801 to the same extent and proportion that the securities held by the security holder of the class with respect to which the rights offering was made were, as of the record date for the rights offering, "restricted securities" within the meaning of this paragraph (a)(3);

(vii) Securities acquired in a transaction made under § 230.802 to the same extent and proportion that the securities that were tendered or exchanged in the exchange offer or business combination were "restricted securities" within the meaning of this paragraph (a)(3); and

(viii) Securities acquired from the issuer in a transaction subject to an exemption under section 4(5) (15 U.S.C. 77d(5)) of the Act.

(4) The term *debt securities* means:

(i) Any security other than an equity security as defined in § 230.405;

(ii) Non-participatory preferred stock, which is defined as non-convertible capital stock, the holders of which are entitled to a preference in payment of dividends and in distribution of assets on liquidation, dissolution, or winding up of the issuer, but are not entitled to participate in residual earnings or assets of the issuer; and

(iii) Asset-backed securities, as defined in § 229.1101 of this chapter.

(b) *Conditions to be met.* Subject to paragraph (i) of this section, the following conditions must be met:

(1) *Non-affiliates.* (i) If the issuer of the securities is, and has been for a period of at least 90 days immediately before the sale, subject to the reporting requirements of section 13 or 15(d) of the Securities Exchange Act of 1934 (the Exchange Act), any person who is not an affiliate of the issuer at the time of the sale, and has not been an affiliate during the preceding three months, who sells restricted securities of the issuer for his or her own account shall be deemed not to be an underwriter of those securities within the meaning of section 2(a)(11) of the Act if all of the conditions of paragraphs (c)(1) and (d) of this section are met. The requirements of paragraph (c)(1) of this section shall not apply to restricted securities sold for the account of a person who is not an affiliate of the issuer at the time of the sale and has not been an affiliate during the preceding three months, provided a period of one year has elapsed since the later of the date the securities were acquired from the issuer or from an affiliate of the issuer.

(ii) If the issuer of the securities is not, or has not been for a period of at least 90 days immediately before the sale, subject to the reporting requirements of section 13 or 15(d) of the Exchange Act, any person who is not an affiliate of the issuer at the time of the sale, and has not been an affiliate during the preceding three months, who sells restricted securities of the issuer for his or her own account shall be deemed not to be an underwriter of those securities within the meaning of section 2(a)(11) of the Act if the condition of paragraph (d) of this section is met.

(2) *Affiliates or persons selling on behalf of affiliates.* Any affiliate of the issuer, or any person who was an affiliate at any time during the 90 days immediately before the sale, who sells restricted securities, or any person who sells restricted or any other securities for the account of an affiliate of the issuer of such securities, or any person who sells restricted or any other securities for the account of a person who was an affiliate at any time during the 90 days immediately before the sale, shall be deemed not to be an underwriter of those securities within the meaning of section 2(a)(11) of the Act if all of the conditions of this section are met.

(c) *Current public information.* Adequate current public information with respect to the issuer of the securities must be available. Such information will be deemed to be available only if the applicable condition set forth in this paragraph is met:

(1) *Reporting issuers.* The issuer is, and has been for a period of at least 90 days immediately before the sale, subject to the reporting requirements of section 13 or 15(d) of the Exchange Act and has:

(i) Filed all required reports under section 13 or 15(d) of the Exchange Act, as applicable, during the 12 months preceding such sale (or for such shorter period that the issuer was required to file such reports), other than Form 8-K reports (§ 249.308 of this chapter); and

(ii) Submitted electronically every Interactive Data File (§ 232.11 of this chapter) required to be submitted pursuant to § 232.405 of this chapter, during the 12 months preceding such sale (or for such shorter period that the issuer was required to submit such files); or

(2) *Non-reporting issuers.* If the issuer is not subject to the reporting requirements of section 13 or 15(d) of the Exchange Act, there is publicly available the information concerning the issuer specified in paragraphs (a)(5)(i) to (xiv), inclusive, and paragraph (a)(5)(xvi) of § 240.15c2-11 of this chapter, or, if the issuer is an insurance company, the information specified in section 12(g)(2)(G)(i) of the Exchange Act (15 U.S.C. 78 *l* (g)(2)(G)(i)).

Note to § 230.144(c): With respect to paragraph (c)(1), the person can rely upon:

1. A statement in whichever is the most recent report, quarterly or annual, required to be filed and filed by the issuer that such issuer has:

a.   Filed all reports required under section 13 or 15(d) of the Exchange Act, as applicable, during the preceding 12 months (or for such shorter period that the issuer was required to file such reports), other than Form 8-K reports (§ 249.308 of this chapter), and has been subject to such filing requirements for the past 90 days; and

b.   Submitted electronically and posted on its corporate Web site, if any, every Interactive Data File (§ 232.11 of this chapter) required to be submitted and posted pursuant to Rule 405 of Regulation S–T (§ 232.405 of this chapter), during the preceding 12 months (or for such shorter period that the issuer was required to submit and post such files); or

2.   A written statement from the issuer that it has complied with such reporting, submission or posting requirements.

3.   Neither type of statement may be relied upon, however, if the person knows or has reason to believe that the issuer has not complied with such requirements.

(d) *Holding period for restricted securities.* If the securities sold are restricted securities, the following provisions apply:

(1) *General rule.* (i) If the issuer of the securities is, and has been for a period of at least 90 days immediately before the sale, subject to the reporting requirements of section 13 or 15(d) of the Exchange Act, a minimum of six months must elapse between the later of the date of the acquisition of the securities from the issuer, or from an affiliate of the issuer, and any resale of such securities in reliance on this section for the account of either the acquiror or any subsequent holder of those securities.

(ii) If the issuer of the securities is not, or has not been for a period of at least 90 days immediately before the sale, subject to the reporting requirements of section 13 or 15(d) of the Exchange Act, a minimum of one year must elapse between the later of the date of the acquisition of the securities from the issuer, or from an affiliate of the issuer, and any resale of such securities in reliance on this section for the account of either the acquiror or any subsequent holder of those securities.

(iii) If the acquiror takes the securities by purchase, the holding period shall not begin until the full purchase price or other consideration is paid or given by the person acquiring the securities from the issuer or from an affiliate of the issuer.

(2) *Promissory notes, other obligations or installment contracts.* Giving the issuer or affiliate of the issuer from whom the securities were purchased a promissory note or other obligation to pay the purchase price, or entering into an installment purchase contract with such seller, shall not be deemed full payment of the purchase price unless the promissory note, obligation or contract:

(i)   Provides for full recourse against the purchaser of the securities;

(ii)   Is secured by collateral, other than the securities purchased, having a fair market value at least equal to the purchase price of the securities purchased; and

(iii) Shall have been discharged by payment in full prior to the sale of the securities.

(3) *Determination of holding period.* The following provisions shall apply for the purpose of determining the period securities have been held:

(i) *Stock dividends, splits and recapitalizations.* Securities acquired from the issuer as a dividend or pursuant to a stock split, reverse split or recapitalization shall be deemed to have been acquired at the same time as the securities on which the dividend or, if more than one, the initial dividend was paid, the securities involved in the split or reverse split, or the securities surrendered in connection with the recapitalization.

(ii) *Conversions and exchanges.* If the securities sold were acquired from the issuer solely in exchange for other securities of the same issuer, the newly acquired securities shall be deemed to have been acquired at the same time as the securities surrendered for conversion or exchange, even if the securities surrendered were not convertible or exchangeable by their terms.

Note to § 230.144(d)(3)(ii): If the surrendered securities originally did not provide for cashless conversion or exchange by their terms and the holder provided consideration, other than solely securities of the same issuer, in connection with the amendment of the surrendered securities to permit cashless conversion or exchange, then the newly acquired securities shall be deemed to have been acquired at the same time as such amendment to the surrendered securities, so long as, in the conversion or exchange, the securities sold were acquired from the issuer solely in exchange for other securities of the same issuer.

(iii) *Contingent issuance of securities.* Securities acquired as a contingent payment of the purchase price of an equity interest in a business, or the assets of a business, sold to the issuer or an affiliate of the issuer shall be deemed to have been acquired at the time of such sale if the issuer or affiliate was then committed to issue the securities subject only to conditions other than the payment of further consideration for such securities. An agreement entered into in connection with any such purchase to remain in the employment of, or not to compete with, the issuer or affiliate or the rendering of services pursuant to such agreement shall not be deemed to be the payment of further consideration for such securities.

(iv) *Pledged securities.* Securities which are bona-fide pledged by an affiliate of the issuer when sold by the pledgee, or by a purchaser, after a default in the obligation secured by the pledge, shall be deemed to have been acquired when they were acquired by the pledgor, except that if the securities were pledged without recourse they shall be deemed to have been acquired by the pledgee at the time of the pledge or by the purchaser at the time of purchase.

(v) *Gifts of securities.* Securities acquired from an affiliate of the issuer by gift shall be deemed to have been acquired by the donee when they were acquired by the donor.

(vi) *Trusts.* Where a trust settlor is an affiliate of the issuer, securities acquired from the settlor by the trust, or acquired from the trust by the beneficiaries thereof, shall be deemed to have been acquired when such securities were acquired by the settlor.

(vii) *Estates.* Where a deceased person was an affiliate of the issuer, securities held by the estate of such person or acquired from such estate by the estate beneficiaries shall be deemed to have been acquired when they were acquired by the deceased person, except that no holding period is required if the estate is not an affiliate of the issuer or if the securities are sold by a beneficiary of the estate who is not such an affiliate.

Note to § 230.144(d)(3)(vii): While there is no holding period or amount limitation for estates and estate beneficiaries which are not affiliates of the issuer, paragraphs (c) and (h) of this section apply to securities sold by such persons in reliance upon this section.

(viii) *Rule 145(a) transactions.* The holding period for securities acquired in a transaction specified in § 230.145(a) shall be deemed to commence on the date the securities were acquired by the purchaser in such transaction, except as otherwise provided in paragraphs (d)(3)(ii) and (ix) of this section.

(ix) *Holding company formations.* Securities acquired from the issuer in a transaction effected solely for the purpose of forming a holding company shall be deemed to have been acquired at the same time as the securities of the predecessor issuer exchanged in the holding company formation where:

(A) The newly formed holding company's securities were issued solely in exchange for the securities of the predecessor company as part of a reorganization of the predecessor company into a holding company structure;

(B) Holders received securities of the same class evidencing the same proportional interest in the holding company as they held in the predecessor, and the rights and interests of the holders of such securities are substantially the same as those they possessed as holders of the predecessor company's securities; and

(C) Immediately following the transaction, the holding company has no significant assets other than securities of the predecessor company and its existing subsidiaries and has substantially the same assets and liabilities on a consolidated basis as the predecessor company had before the transaction.

(x) *Cashless exercise of options and warrants.* If the securities sold were acquired from the issuer solely upon cashless exercise of options or warrants issued by the issuer, the newly acquired securities shall be deemed to have been acquired at the same time as the exercised options or warrants, even if the options or warrants exercised originally did not provide for cashless exercise by their terms.

Note 1 to § 230.144(d)(3)(x): If the options or warrants originally did not provide for cashless exercise by their terms and the holder provided consideration, other than solely securities of the same issuer, in connection with the amendment of the options or warrants to permit cashless exercise, then the newly acquired securities shall be deemed to have been acquired at the same time as such amendment to the options or warrants so long as the exercise itself was cashless.

Note 2 to § 230.144(d)(3)(x): If the options or warrants are not purchased for cash or property and do not create any investment risk to the holder, as in the case of employee stock options, the newly acquired securities shall be deemed to have been acquired at the time the options or warrants are exercised, so long as the full purchase price or other consideration for the newly acquired securities has been paid or given by the person acquiring the securities from the issuer or from an affiliate of the issuer at the time of exercise.

(e) *Limitation on amount of securities sold.* Except as hereinafter provided, the amount of securities sold for the account of an affiliate of the issuer in reliance upon this section shall be determined as follows:

(1) If any securities are sold for the account of an affiliate of the issuer, regardless of whether those securities are restricted, the amount of securities sold, together with all sales of securities of the same class sold for the account of such person within the preceding three months, shall not exceed the greatest of:

(i) One percent of the shares or other units of the class outstanding as shown by the most recent report or statement published by the issuer, or

(ii) The average weekly reported volume of trading in such securities on all national securities exchanges and/or reported through the automated quotation system of a registered securities association during the four calendar weeks preceding the filing of notice required by paragraph (h), or if no such notice is required the date of receipt of the order to execute the transaction by the broker or the date of execution of the transaction directly with a market maker, or

(iii) The average weekly volume of trading in such securities reported pursuant to an *effective transaction reporting plan* or an *effective national market system plan* as those terms are defined in § 242.600 of this chapter during the four-week period specified in paragraph (e)(1)(ii) of this section.

(2) If the securities sold are debt securities, then the amount of debt securities sold for the account of an affiliate of the issuer, regardless of whether those securities are restricted, shall not exceed the greater of the limitation set forth in paragraph (e)(1) of this section or, together with all sales of securities of the same tranche (or class when the securities are non-participatory preferred stock) sold for the account of such person within the preceding three months, ten

percent of the principal amount of the tranche (or class when the securities are non-participatory preferred stock) attributable to the securities sold.

(3) *Determination of amount.* For the purpose of determining the amount of securities specified in paragraph (e)(1) of this section and, as applicable, paragraph (e)(2) of this section, the following provisions shall apply:

(i) Where both convertible securities and securities of the class into which they are convertible are sold, the amount of convertible securities sold shall be deemed to be the amount of securities of the class into which they are convertible for the purpose of determining the aggregate amount of securities of both classes sold;

(ii) The amount of securities sold for the account of a pledgee of those securities, or for the account of a purchaser of the pledged securities, during any period of three months within six months (or within one year if the issuer of the securities is not, or has not been for a period of at least 90 days immediately before the sale, subject to the reporting requirements of section 13 or 15(d) of the Exchange Act) after a default in the obligation secured by the pledge, and the amount of securities sold during the same three-month period for the account of the pledgor shall not exceed, in the aggregate, the amount specified in paragraph (e)(1) or (2) of this section, whichever is applicable;

Note to § 230.144(e)(3)(ii): Sales by a pledgee of securities pledged by a borrower will not be aggregated under paragraph (e)(3)(ii) with sales of the securities of the same issuer by other pledgees of such borrower in the absence of concerted action by such pledgees.

(iii) The amount of securities sold for the account of a donee of those securities during any three-month period within six months (or within one year if the issuer of the securities is not, or has not been for a period of at least 90 days immediately before the sale, subject to the reporting requirements of section 13 or 15(d) of the Exchange Act) after the donation, and the amount of securities sold during the same three-month period for the account of the donor, shall not exceed, in the aggregate, the amount specified in paragraph (e)(1) or (2) of this section, whichever is applicable;

(iv) Where securities were acquired by a trust from the settlor of the trust, the amount of such securities sold for the account of the trust during any three-month period within six months (or within one year if the issuer of the securities is not, or has not been for a period of at least 90 days immediately before the sale, subject to the reporting requirements of section 13 or 15(d) of the Exchange Act) after the acquisition of the securities by the trust, and the amount of securities sold during the same three-month period for the account of the settlor, shall not exceed, in the aggregate, the amount specified in paragraph (e)(1) or (2) of this section, whichever is applicable;

(v) The amount of securities sold for the account of the estate of a deceased person, or for the account of a beneficiary of such estate, during any three-month period and the amount of securities sold during the same three-month period for the account of the deceased person prior to his death shall not exceed, in the aggregate, the amount specified in paragraph (e)(1) or (2) of this section, whichever is applicable: *Provided,* that no limitation on amount shall apply if the estate or beneficiary of the estate is not an affiliate of the issuer;

(vi) When two or more affiliates or other persons agree to act in concert for the purpose of selling securities of an issuer, all securities of the same class sold for the account of all such persons during any three-month period shall be aggregated for the purpose of determining the limitation on the amount of securities sold;

(vii) The following sales of securities need not be included in determining the amount of securities to be sold in reliance upon this section:

(A) Securities sold pursuant to an effective registration statement under the Act;

(B) Securities sold pursuant to an exemption provided by Regulation A (§ 230.251 through § 230.263) under the Act;

(C) Securities sold in a transaction exempt pursuant to section 4 of the Act (15 U.S.C. 77d) and not involving any public offering; and

(D) Securities sold offshore pursuant to Regulation S (§ 230.901 through § 230.905, and Preliminary Notes) under the Act.

(f) *Manner of sale.* (1) The securities shall be sold in one of the following manners:

(i) *Brokers' transactions* within the meaning of section 4(4) of the Act;

(ii) Transactions directly with a *market maker*, as that term is defined in section 3(a)(38) of the Exchange Act; or

(iii) *Riskless principal transactions* where:

(A) The offsetting trades must be executed at the same price (exclusive of an explicitly disclosed markup or markdown, commission equivalent, or other fee);

(B) The transaction is permitted to be reported as riskless under the rules of a self-regulatory organization; and

(C) The requirements of paragraphs (g)(2) (applicable to any markup or markdown, commission equivalent, or other fee), (g)(3), and (g)(4) of this section are met.

Note to § 230.144(f)(1): For purposes of this paragraph, a *riskless principal transaction* means a principal transaction where, after having received from a customer an order to buy, a broker or dealer purchases the security as principal in the market to satisfy the order to buy or, after having received from a customer an order to sell, sells the security as principal to the market to satisfy the order to sell.

(2) The person selling the securities shall not:

(i) Solicit or arrange for the solicitation of orders to buy the securities in anticipation of or in connection with such transaction, or

(ii) Make any payment in connection with the offer or sale of the securities to any person other than the broker or dealer who executes the order to sell the securities.

(3) Paragraph (f) of this section shall not apply to:

(i) Securities sold for the account of the estate of a deceased person or for the account of a beneficiary of such estate provided the estate or estate beneficiary is not an affiliate of the issuer; or

(ii) Debt securities.

(g) *Brokers' transactions.* The term *brokers' transactions* in section 4(4) of the Act shall for the purposes of this rule be deemed to include transactions by a broker in which such broker:

(1) Does no more than execute the order or orders to sell the securities as agent for the person for whose account the securities are sold;

(2) Receives no more than the usual and customary broker's commission;

(3) Neither solicits nor arranges for the solicitation of customers' orders to buy the securities in anticipation of or in connection with the transaction; *Provided,* that the foregoing shall not preclude:

(i) Inquiries by the broker of other brokers or dealers who have indicated an interest in the securities within the preceding 60 days;

(ii) Inquiries by the broker of his customers who have indicated an unsolicited bona fide interest in the securities within the preceding 10 business days;

(iii) The publication by the broker of bid and ask quotations for the security in an inter-dealer quotation system provided that such quotations are incident to the maintenance of a bona fide inter-dealer market for the security for the broker's own account and that the broker has published bona fide bid and ask quotations for the security in an inter-dealer quotation system on each of at least twelve days within the preceding thirty calendar days with no more than four business days in succession without such two-way quotations; or

(iv) The publication by the broker of bid and ask quotations for the security in an alternative trading system, as defined in § 242.300 of this chapter, provided that the broker has published bona fide bid and ask quotations for the security in the alternative trading system on each of the last twelve business days; and

Note to § 230.144(g)(3)(ii): The broker should obtain and retain in his files written evidence of indications of bona fide unsolicited interest by his customers in the securities at the time such indications are received.

(4) After reasonable inquiry is not aware of circumstances indicating that the person for whose account the securities are sold is an underwriter with respect to the securities or that the transaction is a part of a distribution of securities of the issuer. Without limiting the foregoing, the broker shall be deemed to be aware of any facts or statements contained in the notice required by paragraph (h) of this section.

Notes: (i) The broker, for his own protection, should obtain and retain in his files a copy of the notice required by paragraph (h) of this section.

(ii) The reasonable inquiry required by paragraph (g)(3) of this section should include, but not necessarily be limited to, inquiry as to the following matters:

(*a*) The length of time the securities have been held by the person for whose account they are to be sold. If practicable, the inquiry should include physical inspection of the securities;

(*b*) The nature of the transaction in which the securities were acquired by such person;

(*c*) The amount of securities of the same class sold during the past 3 months by all persons whose sales are required to be taken into consideration pursuant to paragraph (e) of this section;

(*d*) Whether such person intends to sell additional securities of the same class through any other means;

(*e*) Whether such person has solicited or made any arrangement for the solicitation of buy orders in connection with the proposed sale of securities;

(*f*) Whether such person has made any payment to any other person in connection with the proposed sale of the securities; and

(*g*) The number of shares or other units of the class outstanding, or the relevant trading volume.

(h) *Notice of proposed sale.* (1) If the amount of securities to be sold in reliance upon this rule during any period of three months exceeds 5,000 shares or other units or has an aggregate sale price in excess of $50,000, three copies of a notice on Form 144 (§ 239.144 of this chapter) shall be filed with the Commission. If such securities are admitted to trading on any national securities exchange, one copy of such notice also shall be transmitted to the principal exchange on which such securities are admitted.

(2) The Form 144 shall be signed by the person for whose account the securities are to be sold and shall be transmitted for filing concurrently with either the placing with a broker of an order to execute a sale of securities in reliance upon this rule or the execution directly with a market maker of such a sale. Neither the filing of such notice nor the failure of the Commission

to comment on such notice shall be deemed to preclude the Commission from taking any action that it deems necessary or appropriate with respect to the sale of the securities referred to in such notice. The person filing the notice required by this paragraph shall have a bona fide intention to sell the securities referred to in the notice within a reasonable time after the filing of such notice.

(i)   *Unavailability to securities of issuers with no or nominal operations and no or nominal non-cash assets.* (1) This section is not available for the resale of securities initially issued by an issuer defined below:

(i)   An issuer, other than a business combination related shell company, as defined in § 230.405, or an asset-backed issuer, as defined in Item 1101(b) of Regulation AB (§ 229.1101(b) of this chapter), that has:

(A)   No or nominal operations; and

(B)   Either:

(*1*)   No or nominal assets;

(*2*)   Assets consisting solely of cash and cash equivalents; or

(*3*)   Assets consisting of any amount of cash and cash equivalents and nominal other assets; or

(ii)   An issuer that has been at any time previously an issuer described in paragraph (i)(1)(i).

(2)   Notwithstanding paragraph (i)(1), if the issuer of the securities previously had been an issuer described in paragraph (i)(1)(i) but has ceased to be an issuer described in paragraph (i)(1)(i); is subject to the reporting requirements of section 13 or 15(d) of the Exchange Act; has filed all reports and other materials required to be filed by section 13 or 15(d) of the Exchange Act, as applicable, during the preceding 12 months (or for such shorter period that the issuer was required to file such reports and materials), other than Form 8-K reports (§ 249.308 of this chapter); and has filed current "Form 10 information" with the Commission reflecting its status as an entity that is no longer an issuer described in paragraph (i)(1)(i), then those securities may be sold subject to the requirements of this section after one year has elapsed from the date that the issuer filed "Form 10 information" with the Commission.

(3)   The term "Form 10 information" means the information that is required by Form 10 or Form 20-F (§ 249.210 or § 249.220f of this chapter), as applicable to the issuer of the securities, to register under the Exchange Act each class of securities being sold under this rule. The issuer may provide the Form 10 information in any filing of the issuer with the Commission. The Form 10 information is deemed filed when the initial filing is made with the Commission.

§ 230.144A   Private Resales of Securities to Institutions.

Preliminary Notes:

1.   This section relates solely to the application of section 5 of the Act and not to antifraud or other provisions of the federal securities laws.

2.   Attempted compliance with this section does not act as an exclusive election; any seller hereunder may also claim the availability of any other applicable exemption from the registration requirements of the Act.

3.   In view of the objective of this section and the policies underlying the Act, this section is not available with respect to any transaction or series of transactions that, although in technical compliance with this section, is part of a plan or scheme to evade the registration provisions of the Act. In such cases, registration under the Act is required.

4.   Nothing in this section obviates the need for any issuer or any other person to comply with the securities registration or broker-dealer registration requirements of the Securities Exchange Act of 1934 (the *Exchange Act*), whenever such requirements are applicable.

5.   Nothing in this section obviates the need for any person to comply with any applicable state law relating to the offer or sale of securities.

6.   Securities acquired in a transaction made pursuant to the provisions of this section are deemed to be *restricted securities* within the meaning of § 230.144(a)(3) of this chapter.

7.   The fact that purchasers of securities from the issuer thereof may purchase such securities with a view to reselling such securities pursuant to this section will not affect the availability to such issuer of an exemption under section 4(a)(2) of the Act, or Regulation D under the Act, from the registration requirements of the Act.

(a)   *Definitions.* (1) For purposes of this section, *qualified institutional buyer* shall mean:

(i)   Any of the following entities, acting for its own account or the accounts of other qualified institutional buyers, that in the aggregate owns and invests on a discretionary basis at least $100 million in securities of issuers that are not affiliated with the entity:

(A)   Any *insurance company* as defined in section 2(a)(13) of the Act;

Note: A purchase by an insurance company for one or more of its separate accounts, as defined by section 2(a)(37) of the Investment Company Act of 1940 (the "Investment Company Act"), which are neither registered under section 8 of the Investment Company Act nor required to be so registered, shall be deemed to be a purchase for the account of such insurance company.

(B)   Any *investment company* registered under the Investment Company Act or any *business development company* as defined in section 2(a)(48) of that Act;

(C)   Any *Small Business Investment Company* licensed by the U.S. Small Business Administration under section 301(c) or (d) of the Small Business Investment Act of 1958;

(D)   Any *plan* established and maintained by a state, its political subdivisions, or any agency or instrumentality of a state or its political subdivisions, for the benefit of its employees;

(E)   Any *employee benefit plan* within the meaning of title I of the Employee Retirement Income Security Act of 1974;

(F)   Any trust fund whose trustee is a bank or trust company and whose participants are exclusively plans of the types identified in paragraph (a)(1)(i) (D) or (E) of this section, except trust funds that include as participants individual retirement accounts or H.R. 10 plans.

(G)   Any *business development company* as defined in section 202(a)(22) of the Investment Advisers Act of 1940;

(H)   Any organization described in section 501(c)(3) of the Internal Revenue Code, corporation (other than a bank as defined in section 3(a)(2) of the Act or a savings and loan association or other institution referenced in section 3(a)(5)(A) of the Act or a foreign bank or savings and loan association or equivalent institution), partnership, or Massachusetts or similar business trust; and

(I)   Any *investment adviser* registered under the Investment Advisers Act.

(ii)   Any *dealer* registered pursuant to section 15 of the Exchange Act, acting for its own account or the accounts of other qualified institutional buyers, that in the aggregate owns and invests on a discretionary basis at least $10 million of securities of issuers that are not affiliated with the dealer, *Provided,* That securities constituting the whole or a part of an unsold allotment to or subscription by a dealer as a participant in a public offering shall not be deemed to be owned by such dealer;

(iii) Any *dealer* registered pursuant to section 15 of the Exchange Act acting in a riskless principal transaction on behalf of a qualified institutional buyer;

Note: A registered dealer may act as agent, on a non-discretionary basis, in a transaction with a qualified institutional buyer without itself having to be a qualified institutional buyer.

(iv) Any investment company registered under the Investment Company Act, acting for its own account or for the accounts of other qualified institutional buyers, that is part of a family of investment companies which own in the aggregate at least $100 million in securities of issuers, other than issuers that are affiliated with the investment company or are part of such family of investment companies. *Family of investment companies* means any two or more investment companies registered under the Investment Company Act, except for a unit investment trust whose assets consist solely of shares of one or more registered investment companies, that have the same investment adviser (or, in the case of unit investment trusts, the same depositor), Provided That, for purposes of this section:

(A) Each series of a series company (as defined in Rule 18f–2 under the Investment Company Act [17 CFR 270.18f–2]) shall be deemed to be a separate investment company; and

(B) Investment companies shall be deemed to have the same adviser (or depositor) if their advisers (or depositors) are majority-owned subsidiaries of the same parent, or if one investment company's adviser (or depositor) is a majority-owned subsidiary of the other investment company's adviser (or depositor);

(v) Any entity, all of the equity owners of which are qualified institutional buyers, acting for its own account or the accounts of other qualified institutional buyers; and

(vi) Any *bank* as defined in section 3(a)(2) of the Act, any savings and loan association or other institution as referenced in section 3(a)(5)(A) of the Act, or any foreign bank or savings and loan association or equivalent institution, acting for its own account or the accounts of other qualified institutional buyers, that in the aggregate owns and invests on a discretionary basis at least $100 million in securities of issuers that are not affiliated with it and that has an audited net worth of at least $25 million as demonstrated in its latest annual financial statements, as of a date not more than 16 months preceding the date of sale under the Rule in the case of a U.S. bank or savings and loan association, and not more than 18 months preceding such date of sale for a foreign bank or savings and loan association or equivalent institution.

(2) In determining the aggregate amount of securities owned and invested on a discretionary basis by an entity, the following instruments and interests shall be excluded: bank deposit notes and certificates of deposit; loan participations; repurchase agreements; securities owned but subject to a repurchase agreement; and currency, interest rate and commodity swaps.

(3) The aggregate value of securities owned and invested on a discretionary basis by an entity shall be the cost of such securities, except where the entity reports its securities holdings in its financial statements on the basis of their market value, and no current information with respect to the cost of those securities has been published. In the latter event, the securities may be valued at market for purposes of this section.

(4) In determining the aggregate amount of securities owned by an entity and invested on a discretionary basis, securities owned by subsidiaries of the entity that are consolidated with the entity in its financial statements prepared in accordance with generally accepted accounting principles may be included if the investments of such subsidiaries are managed under the direction of the entity, except that, unless the entity is a reporting company under section 13 or 15(d) of the Exchange Act, securities owned by such subsidiaries may not be included if the entity

itself is a majority-owned subsidiary that would be included in the consolidated financial statements of another enterprise.

(5) For purposes of this section, *riskless principal transaction* means a transaction in which a dealer buys a security from any person and makes a simultaneous offsetting sale of such security to a qualified institutional buyer, including another dealer acting as riskless principal for a qualified institutional buyer.

(6) For purposes of this section, *effective conversion premium* means the amount, expressed as a percentage of the security's conversion value, by which the price at issuance of a convertible security exceeds its conversion value.

(7) For purposes of this section, *effective exercise premium* means the amount, expressed as a percentage of the warrant's exercise value, by which the sum of the price at issuance and the exercise price of a warrant exceeds its exercise value.

(b) *Sales by persons other than issuers or dealers.* Any person, other than the issuer or a dealer, who offers or sells securities in compliance with the conditions set forth in paragraph (d) of this section shall be deemed not to be engaged in a distribution of such securities and therefore not to be an underwriter of such securities within the meaning of sections 2(a)(11) and 4(a)(1) of the Act.

(c) *Sales by dealers.* Any dealer who offers or sells securities in compliance with the conditions set forth in paragraph (d) of this section shall be deemed not to be a participant in a distribution of such securities within the meaning of section 4(a)(3)(C) of the Act and not to be an underwriter of such securities within the meaning of section 2(a)(11) of the Act, and such securities shall be deemed not to have been offered to the public within the meaning of section 4(a)(3)(A) of the Act.

(d) *Conditions to be met.* To qualify for exemption under this section, an offer or sale must meet the following conditions:

(1) The securities are sold only to a qualified institutional buyer or a purchaser that the seller and any person acting on behalf of the seller reasonably believe is a qualified institutional buyer. In determining whether a prospective purchaser is a qualified institutional buyer, the seller and any person acting on its behalf shall be entitled to rely upon the following non-exclusive methods of establishing the prospective purchaser's ownership and discretionary investments of securities:

(i) The prospective purchaser's most recent publicly available financial statements, *Provided* That such statements present the information as of a date within 16 months preceding the date of sale of securities under this section in the case of a U.S. purchaser and within 18 months preceding such date of sale for a foreign purchaser;

(ii) The most recent publicly available information appearing in documents filed by the prospective purchaser with the Commission or another United States federal, state, or local governmental agency or self-regulatory organization, or with a foreign governmental agency or self-regulatory organization, *Provided* That any such information is as of a date within 16 months preceding the date of sale of securities under this section in the case of a U.S. purchaser and within 18 months preceding such date of sale for a foreign purchaser;

(iii) The most recent publicly available information appearing in a recognized securities manual, *Provided* That such information is as of a date within 16 months preceding the date of sale of securities under this section in the case of a U.S. purchaser and within 18 months preceding such date of sale for a foreign purchaser; or

(iv) A certification by the chief financial officer, a person fulfilling an equivalent function, or other executive officer of the purchaser, specifying the amount of securities owned and invested on a discretionary basis by the purchaser as of a specific date on or since the close of the purchaser's most recent fiscal year, or, in the case of a purchaser that is a member of a family of investment companies, a certification by an executive officer of the investment adviser specifying the amount of securities owned by the family of investment companies as of a specific date on or since the close of the purchaser's most recent fiscal year;

(2)   The seller and any person acting on its behalf takes reasonable steps to ensure that the purchaser is aware that the seller may rely on the exemption from the provisions of section 5 of the Act provided by this section;

(3)   The securities offered or sold:

(i)   Were not, when issued, of the same class as securities listed on a national securities exchange registered under section 6 of the Exchange Act or quoted in a U.S. automated inter-dealer quotation system; *Provided,* That securities that are convertible or exchangeable into securities so listed or quoted at the time of issuance and that had an effective conversion premium of less than 10 percent, shall be treated as securities of the class into which they are convertible or exchangeable; and that warrants that may be exercised for securities so listed or quoted at the time of issuance, for a period of less than 3 years from the date of issuance, or that had an effective exercise premium of less than 10 percent, shall be treated as securities of the class to be issued upon exercise; and *Provided further,* That the Commission may from time to time, taking into account then-existing market practices, designate additional securities and classes of securities that will not be deemed of the same class as securities listed on a national securities exchange or quoted in a U.S. automated inter-dealer quotation system; and

(ii)   Are not securities of an open-end investment company, unit investment trust or face-amount certificate company that is or is required to be registered under section 8 of the Investment Company Act; and

(4)(i)   In the case of securities of an issuer that is neither subject to section 13 or 15(d) of the Exchange Act, nor exempt from reporting pursuant to Rule 12g3–2(b) (§ 240.12g3–2(b) of this chapter) under the Exchange Act, nor a foreign government as defined in Rule 405 (§ 230.405 of this chapter) eligible to register securities under Schedule B of the Act, the holder and a prospective purchaser designated by the holder have the right to obtain from the issuer, upon request of the holder, and the prospective purchaser has received from the issuer, the seller, or a person acting on either of their behalf, at or prior to the time of sale, upon such prospective purchaser's request to the holder or the issuer, the following information (which shall be reasonably current in relation to the date of resale under this section): a very brief statement of the nature of the business of the issuer and the products and services it offers; and the issuer's most recent balance sheet and profit and loss and retained earnings statements, and similar financial statements for such part of the two preceding fiscal years as the issuer has been in operation (the financial statements should be audited to the extent reasonably available).

(ii)   The requirement that the information be *reasonably current* will be presumed to be satisfied if:

(A)   The balance sheet is as of a date less than 16 months before the date of resale, the statements of profit and loss and retained earnings are for the 12 months preceding the date of such balance sheet, and if such balance sheet is not as of a date less than 6 months before the date of resale, it shall be accompanied by additional statements of profit and loss and retained earnings for the period from the date of such balance sheet to a date less than 6 months before the date of resale; and

(B)   The statement of the nature of the issuer's business and its products and services offered is as of a date within 12 months prior to the date of resale; or

(C)   With regard to foreign private issuers, the required information meets the timing requirements of the issuer's home country or principal trading markets.

(e)   Offers and sales of securities pursuant to this section shall be deemed not to affect the availability of any exemption or safe harbor relating to any previous or subsequent offer or sale of such securities by the issuer or any prior or subsequent holder thereof.

§ 230.145   **Reclassification of Securities, Mergers, Consolidations and Acquisitions of Assets.**

Preliminary Note: Rule 145 (§ 230.145 of this chapter) is designed to make available the protection provided by registration under the Securities Act of 1933, as amended (Act), to persons who are offered securities in a business combination of the type described in paragraphs (a) (1), (2) and (3) of the rule. The thrust of the rule is that an *offer, offer to sell, offer for sale*, or *sale* occurs when there is submitted to security holders a plan or agreement pursuant to which such holders are required to elect, on the basis of what is in substance a new investment decision, whether to accept a new or different security in exchange for their existing security. Rule 145 embodies the Commission's determination that such transactions are subject to the registration requirements of the Act, and that the previously existing *no-sale* theory of Rule 133 is no longer consistent with the statutory purposes of the Act. See Release No. 33–5316 (October 6, 1972) [37 FR 23631]. Securities issued in transactions described in paragraph (a) of Rule 145 may be registered on Form S-4 or F-4 (§ 239.25 or § 239.34 of this chapter) or Form N-14 (§ 239.23 of this chapter) under the Act.

Transactions for which statutory exemptions under the Act, including those contained in sections 3(a)(9), (10), (11) and 4(a)(2), are otherwise available are not affected by Rule 145. Reference is made to Rule 153a (§ 230.153a of this chapter) describing the prospectus delivery required in a transaction of the type referred to in Rule 145. A reclassification of securities covered by Rule 145 would be exempt from registration pursuant to section 3(a)(9) or (11) of the Act if the conditions of either of these sections are satisfied.

(a)   *Transactions within this section.* An *offer, offer to sell, offer for sale,* or *sale* shall be deemed to be involved, within the meaning of section 2(3) of the Act, so far as the security holders of a corporation or other person are concerned where, pursuant to statutory provisions of the jurisdiction under which such corporation or other person is organized, or pursuant to provisions contained in its certificate of incorporation or similar controlling instruments, or otherwise, there is submitted for the vote or consent of such security holders a plan or agreement for:

(1)   *Reclassifications.* A reclassification of securities of such corporation or other person, other than a stock split, reverse stock split, or change in par value, which involves the substitution of a security for another security;

(2)   *Mergers of consolidations.* A statutory merger or consolidation or similar plan or acquisition in which securities of such corporation or other person held by such security holders will become or be exchanged for securities of any person, unless the sole purpose of the transaction is to change an issuer's domicile solely within the United States; or

(3)   *Transfers of assets.* A transfer of assets of such corporation or other person, to another person in consideration of the issuance of securities of such other person or any of its affiliates, if:

(i)   Such plan or agreement provides for dissolution of the corporation or other person whose security holders are voting or consenting; or

(ii)   Such plan or agreement provides for a pro rata or similar distribution of such securities to the security holders voting or consenting; or

(iii)   The board of directors or similar representatives of such corporation or other person, adopts resolutions relative to paragraph (a)(3) (i) or (ii) of this section within 1 year after the taking of such vote or consent; or

(iv)   The transfer of assets is a part of a preexisting plan for distribution of such securities, notwithstanding paragraph (a)(3) (i), (ii), or (iii) of this section.

(b) *Communications before a Registration Statement is filed.* Communications made in connection with or relating to a transaction described in paragraph (a) of this section that will be registered under the Act may be made under § 230.135, § 230.165 or § 230.166.

(c) *Persons and parties deemed to be underwriters.* For purposes of this section, if any party to a transaction specified in paragraph (a) of this section is a shell company, other than a business combination related shell company, as those terms are defined in § 230.405, any party to that transaction, other than the issuer, or any person who is an affiliate of such party at the time such transaction is submitted for vote or consent, who publicly offers or sells securities of the issuer acquired in connection with any such transaction, shall be deemed to be engaged in a distribution and therefore to be an underwriter thereof within the meaning of Section 2(a)(11) of the Act.

(d) *Resale provisions for persons and parties deemed underwriters.* Notwithstanding the provisions of paragraph (c), a person or party specified in that paragraph shall not be deemed to be engaged in a distribution and therefore not to be an underwriter of securities acquired in a transaction specified in paragraph (a) that was registered under the Act if:

(1) The issuer has met the requirements applicable to an issuer of securities in paragraph (i)(2) of § 230.144; and

(2) One of the following three conditions is met:

(i) Such securities are sold by such person or party in accordance with the provisions of paragraphs (c), (e), (f), and (g) of § 230.144 and at least 90 days have elapsed since the date the securities were acquired from the issuer in such transaction; or

(ii) Such person or party is not, and has not been for at least three months, an affiliate of the issuer, and at least six months, as determined in accordance with paragraph (d) of § 230.144, have elapsed since the date the securities were acquired from the issuer in such transaction, and the issuer meets the requirements of paragraph (c) of § 230.144; or

(iii) Such person or party is not, and has not been for at least three months, an affiliate of the issuer, and at least one year, as determined in accordance with paragraph (d) of § 230.144, has elapsed since the date the securities were acquired from the issuer in such transaction.

Note to § 230.145(c) and (d): Paragraph (d) is not available with respect to any transaction or series of transactions that, although in technical compliance with the rule, is part of a plan or scheme to evade the registration requirements of the Act.

(e) *Definitions.* (1) The term *affiliate* as used in paragraphs (c) and (d) of this section shall have the same meaning as the definition of that term in § 230.144.

(2) The term *party* as used in paragraphs (c) and (d) of this section shall mean the corporations, business entities, or other persons, other than the issuer, whose assets or capital structure are affected by the transactions specified in paragraph (a) of this section.

(3) The term *person* as used in paragraphs (c) and (d) of this section, when used in reference to a person for whose account securities are to be sold, shall have the same meaning as the definition of that term in paragraph (a)(2) of § 230.144.

§ 230.147   Intrastate Offers and Sales.

(a) This section shall not raise any presumption that the exemption provided by section 3(a)(11) of the Act (15 U.S.C. 77c(a)(11)) is not available for transactions by an issuer which do not satisfy all of the provisions of this section.

(b) *Manner of offers and sales.* An issuer, or any person acting on behalf of the issuer, shall be deemed to conduct an offering in compliance with section 3(a)(11) of the Act (15 U.S.C. 77c(a)(11)), where offers and sales are made only to persons resident within the same state or territory in which the issuer is resident and doing business, within the meaning of section 3(a)(11) of the Act, so long as the issuer complies with the provisions of paragraphs (c), (d), and (f) through (h) of this section.

(c)   *Nature of the issuer.* The issuer of the securities shall at the time of any offers and sales be a person resident and doing business within the state or territory in which all of the offers and sales are made.

(1)   The issuer shall be deemed to be a resident of the state or territory in which:

(i)   It is incorporated or organized, and it has its principal place of business, if a corporation, limited partnership, trust or other form of business organization that is organized under state or territorial law. The issuer shall be deemed to have its principal place of business in a state or territory in which the officers, partners or managers of the issuer primarily direct, control and coordinate the activities of the issuer;

(ii)   It has its principal place of business, as defined in paragraph (c)(1)(i) of this section, if a general partnership or other form of business organization that is not organized under any state or territorial law;

(iii)   Such person's principal residence is located, if an individual.

Instruction to paragraph (c)(1): An issuer that has previously conducted an intrastate offering pursuant to this section (§ 230.147) or Rule 147A (§ 230.147A) may not conduct another intrastate offering pursuant to this section (§ 230.147) in a different state or territory, until the expiration of the time period specified in paragraph (e) of this section (§ 230.147(e)) or paragraph (e) of Rule 147A (§ 230.147A(e)), calculated on the basis of the date of the last sale in such offering.

(2)   The issuer shall be deemed to be doing business within a state or territory if the issuer satisfies at least one of the following requirements:

(i)   The issuer derived at least 80% of its consolidated gross revenues from the operation of a business or of real property located in or from the rendering of services within such state or territory;

Instruction to paragraph (c)(2)(i): Revenues must be calculated based on the issuer's most recent fiscal year, if the first offer of securities pursuant to this section is made during the first six months of the issuer's current fiscal year, and based on the first six months of the issuer's current fiscal year or during the twelve-month fiscal period ending with such six-month period, if the first offer of securities pursuant to this section is made during the last six months of the issuer's current fiscal year.

(ii)   The issuer had at the end of its most recent semi-annual fiscal period prior to an initial offer of securities in any offering or subsequent offering pursuant to this section, at least 80% of its assets and those of its subsidiaries on a consolidated basis located within such state or territory;

(iii)   The issuer intends to use and uses at least 80% of the net proceeds to the issuer from sales made pursuant to this section (§ 230.147) in connection with the operation of a business or of real property, the purchase of real property located in, or the rendering of services within such state or territory; or

(iv)   A majority of the issuer's employees are based in such state or territory.

(d)   *Residence of offerees and purchasers.* Offers and sales of securities pursuant to this section (§ 230.147) shall be made only to residents of the state or territory in which the issuer is resident, as determined pursuant to paragraph (c) of this section, or who the issuer reasonably believes, at the time of the offer and sale, are residents of the state or territory in which the issuer is resident. For purposes of determining the residence of offerees and purchasers:

(1)   A corporation, partnership, limited liability company, trust or other form of business organization shall be deemed to be a resident of a state or territory if, at the time of the offer and

sale to it, it has its principal place of business, as defined in paragraph (c)(1)(i) of this section, within such state or territory.

Instruction to paragraph (d)(1): A trust that is not deemed by the law of the state or territory of its creation to be a separate legal entity is deemed to be a resident of each state or territory in which its trustee is, or trustees are, resident.

(2)   Individuals shall be deemed to be residents of a state or territory if such individuals have, at the time of the offer and sale to them, their principal residence in the state or territory.

(3)   A corporation, partnership, trust or other form of business organization, which is organized for the specific purpose of acquiring securities offered pursuant to this section (§ 230.147), shall not be a resident of a state or territory unless all of the beneficial owners of such organization are residents of such state or territory.

Instruction to paragraph (d): Obtaining a written representation from purchasers of in-state residency status will not, without more, be sufficient to establish a reasonable belief that such purchasers are in-state residents.

(e)   *Limitation on resales.* For a period of six months from the date of the sale by the issuer of a security pursuant to this section (§ 230.147), any resale of such security shall be made only to persons resident within the state or territory in which the issuer was resident, as determined pursuant to paragraph (c) of this section, at the time of the sale of the security by the issuer.

Instruction to paragraph (e): In the case of convertible securities, resales of either the convertible security, or if it is converted, the underlying security, could be made during the period described in paragraph (e) only to persons resident within such state or territory. For purposes of this paragraph (e), a conversion in reliance on section 3(a)(9) of the Act (15 U.S.C. 77c(a)(9)) does not begin a new period.

(f)   *Precautions against interstate sales.* (1) The issuer shall, in connection with any securities sold by it pursuant to this section:

(i)   Place a prominent legend on the certificate or other document evidencing the security stating that: "Offers and sales of these securities were made under an exemption from registration and have not been registered under the Securities Act of 1933. For a period of six months from the date of the sale by the issuer of these securities, any resale of these securities (or the underlying securities in the case of convertible securities) shall be made only to persons resident within the state or territory of [identify the name of the state or territory in which the issuer was resident at the time of the sale of the securities by the issuer].";

(ii)   Issue stop transfer instructions to the issuer's transfer agent, if any, with respect to the securities, or, if the issuer transfers its own securities, make a notation in the appropriate records of the issuer; and

(iii)   Obtain a written representation from each purchaser as to his or her residence.

(2)   The issuer shall, in connection with the issuance of new certificates for any of the securities that are sold pursuant to this section (§ 230.147) that are presented for transfer during the time period specified in paragraph (e), take the steps required by paragraphs (f)(1)(i) and (ii) of this section.

(3)   The issuer shall, at the time of any offer or sale by it of a security pursuant to this section (§ 230.147), prominently disclose to each offeree in the manner in which any such offer is communicated and to each purchaser of such security in writing a reasonable period of time before the date of sale, the following: "Sales will be made only to residents of [identify the name of the state or territory in which the issuer was resident at the time of the sale of the securities by the issuer]. Offers and sales of these securities are made under an exemption from registration and have not been registered under the Securities Act of 1933. For a period of six months from the

date of the sale by the issuer of the securities, any resale of the securities (or the underlying securities in the case of convertible securities) shall be made only to persons resident within the state or territory of [identify the name of the state or territory in which the issuer was resident at the time of the sale of the securities by the issuer]."

(g) *Integration with other offerings.* Offers or sales made in reliance on this section will not be integrated with:

(1) Offers or sales of securities made prior to the commencement of offers and sales of securities pursuant to this section (§ 230.147); or

(2) Offers or sales made after completion of offers and sales of securities pursuant to this section (§ 230.147) that are:

(i) Registered under the Act, except as provided in paragraph (h) of this section (§ 230.147);

(ii) Exempt from registration under Regulation A (§§ 230.251 through 230.263);

(iii) Exempt from registration under Rule 701 (§ 230.701);

(iv) Made pursuant to an employee benefit plan;

(v) Exempt from registration under Regulation S (§§ 230.901 through 230.905);

(vi) Exempt from registration under section 4(a)(6) of the Act (15 U.S.C. 77d(a)(6)); or

(vii) Made more than six months after the completion of an offering conducted pursuant to this section (§ 230.147).

Instruction to paragraph (g): If none of the safe harbors applies, whether subsequent offers and sales of securities will be integrated with any securities offered or sold pursuant to this section (§ 230.147) will depend on the particular facts and circumstances.

(h) *Offerings limited to qualified institutional buyers and institutional accredited investors.* Where an issuer decides to register an offering under the Act after making offers in reliance on this section (§ 230.147) limited only to qualified institutional buyers and institutional accredited investors referenced in section 5(d) of the Act, such offers will not be subject to integration with any subsequent registered offering. If the issuer makes offers in reliance on this section (§ 230.147) to persons other than qualified institutional buyers and institutional accredited investors referenced in section 5(d) of the Act, such offers will not be subject to integration if the issuer (and any underwriter, broker, dealer, or agent used by the issuer in connection with the proposed offering) waits at least 30 calendar days between the last such offer made in reliance on this section (§ 230.147) and the filing of the registration statement with the Commission.

§ 230.147A   Intrastate Sales Exemption.

(a) *Scope of the exemption.* Offers and sales by or on behalf of an issuer of its securities made in accordance with this section (§ 230.147A) are exempt from section 5 of the Act (15 U.S.C. 77e). This exemption is not available to an issuer that is an investment company registered or required to be registered under the Investment Company Act of 1940 (15 U.S.C. 80a–1 *et seq.*).

(b) *Manner of offers and sales.* An issuer, or any person acting on behalf of the issuer, may rely on this exemption to make offers and sales using any form of general solicitation and general advertising, so long as the issuer complies with the provisions of paragraphs (c), (d), and (f) through (h) of this section.

(c) *Nature of the issuer.* The issuer of the securities shall at the time of any offers and sales be a person resident and doing business within the state or territory in which all of the sales are made.

(1) The issuer shall be deemed to be a resident of the state or territory in which it has its principal place of business. The issuer shall be deemed to have its principal place of business in

a state or territory in which the officers, partners or managers of the issuer primarily direct, control and coordinate the activities of the issuer.

(2)   The issuer shall be deemed to be doing business within a state or territory if the issuer satisfies at least one of the following requirements:

(i)   The issuer derived at least 80% of its consolidated gross revenues from the operation of a business or of real property located in or from the rendering of services within such state or territory;

Instruction to paragraph (c)(2)(i): Revenues must be calculated based on the issuer's most recent fiscal year, if the first offer of securities pursuant to this section is made during the first six months of the issuer's current fiscal year, and based on the first six months of the issuer's current fiscal year or during the twelve-month fiscal period ending with such six-month period, if the first offer of securities pursuant to this section is made during the last six months of the issuer's current fiscal year.

(ii)   The issuer had at the end of its most recent semi-annual fiscal period prior to an initial offer of securities in any offering or subsequent offering pursuant to this section, at least 80% of its assets and those of its subsidiaries on a consolidated basis located within such state or territory;

(iii)   The issuer intends to use and uses at least 80% of the net proceeds to the issuer from sales made pursuant to this section (§ 230.147A) in connection with the operation of a business or of real property, the purchase of real property located in, or the rendering of services within such state or territory; or

(iv)   A majority of the issuer's employees are based in such state or territory.

Instruction to paragraph (c): An issuer that has previously conducted an intrastate offering pursuant to this section (§ 230.147A) or Rule 147 (§ 230.147) may not conduct another intrastate offering pursuant to this section (§ 230.147A) in a different state or territory, until the expiration of the time period specified in paragraph (e) of this section (§ 230.147A(e)) or paragraph (e) of Rule 147 (§ 230.147(e)), calculated on the basis of the date of the last sale in such offering.

(d)   *Residence of purchasers.* Sales of securities pursuant to this section (§ 230.147A) shall be made only to residents of the state or territory in which the issuer is resident, as determined pursuant to paragraph (c) of this section, or who the issuer reasonably believes, at the time of sale, are residents of the state or territory in which the issuer is resident. For purposes of determining the residence of purchasers:

(1)   A corporation, partnership, limited liability company, trust or other form of business organization shall be deemed to be a resident of a state or territory if, at the time of sale to it, it has its principal place of business, as defined in paragraph (c)(1) of this section, within such state or territory.

Instruction to paragraph (d)(1): A trust that is not deemed by the law of the state or territory of its creation to be a separate legal entity is deemed to be a resident of each state or territory in which its trustee is, or trustees are, resident.

(2)   Individuals shall be deemed to be residents of a state or territory if such individuals have, at the time of sale to them, their principal residence in the state or territory.

(3)   A corporation, partnership, trust or other form of business organization, which is organized for the specific purpose of acquiring securities offered pursuant to this section (§ 230.147A), shall not be a resident of a state or territory unless all of the beneficial owners of such organization are residents of such state or territory.

Instruction to paragraph (d): Obtaining a written representation from purchasers of in-state residency status will not, without more, be sufficient to establish a reasonable belief that such purchasers are in-state residents.

(e) *Limitation on resales.* For a period of six months from the date of the sale by the issuer of a security pursuant to this section (§ 230.147A), any resale of such security shall be made only to persons resident within the state or territory in which the issuer was resident, as determined pursuant to paragraph (c) of this section, at the time of the sale of the security by the issuer.

Instruction to paragraph (e): In the case of convertible securities, resales of either the convertible security, or if it is converted, the underlying security, could be made during the period described in paragraph (e) only to persons resident within such state or territory. For purposes of this paragraph (e), a conversion in reliance on section 3(a)(9) of the Act (15 U.S.C. 77c(a)(9)) does not begin a new period.

(f) *Precautions against interstate sales.* (1) The issuer shall, in connection with any securities sold by it pursuant to this section:

(i) Place a prominent legend on the certificate or other document evidencing the security stating that: "Offers and sales of these securities were made under an exemption from registration and have not been registered under the Securities Act of 1933. For a period of six months from the date of the sale by the issuer of these securities, any resale of these securities (or the underlying securities in the case of convertible securities) shall be made only to persons resident within the state or territory of [identify the name of the state or territory in which the issuer was resident at the time of the sale of the securities by the issuer].";

(ii) Issue stop transfer instructions to the issuer's transfer agent, if any, with respect to the securities, or, if the issuer transfers its own securities, make a notation in the appropriate records of the issuer; and

(iii) Obtain a written representation from each purchaser as to his or her residence.

(2) The issuer shall, in connection with the issuance of new certificates for any of the securities that are sold pursuant to this section (§ 230.147A) that are presented for transfer during the time period specified in paragraph (e), take the steps required by paragraphs (f)(1)(i) and (ii) of this section.

(3) The issuer shall, at the time of any offer or sale by it of a security pursuant to this section (§ 230.147A), prominently disclose to each offeree in the manner in which any such offer is communicated and to each purchaser of such security in writing a reasonable period of time before the date of sale, the following: "Sales will be made only to residents of the state or territory of [identify the name of the state or territory in which the issuer was resident at the time of the sale of the securities by the issuer]. Offers and sales of these securities are made under an exemption from registration and have not been registered under the Securities Act of 1933. For a period of six months from the date of the sale by the issuer of the securities, any resale of the securities (or the underlying securities in the case of convertible securities) shall be made only to persons resident within the state or territory of [identify the name of the state or territory in which the issuer was resident at the time of the sale of the securities by the issuer]."

(g) *Integration with other offerings.* Offers or sales made in reliance on this section will not be integrated with:

(1) Offers or sales of securities made prior to the commencement of offers and sales of securities pursuant to this section (§ 230.147A); or

(2) Offers or sales of securities made after completion of offers and sales of securities pursuant to this section (§ 230.147A) that are:

(i) Registered under the Act, except as provided in paragraph (h) of this section (§ 230.147A);

(ii) Exempt from registration under Regulation A (§§ 230.251 through 230.263);

(iii) Exempt from registration under Rule 701 (§ 230.701);

    (iv) Made pursuant to an employee benefit plan;

    (v) Exempt from registration under Regulation S (§§ 230.901 through 230.905);

    (vi) Exempt from registration under section 4(a)(6) of the Act (15 U.S.C. 77d(a)(6)); or

    (vii) Made more than six months after the completion of an offering conducted pursuant to this section (§ 230.147A).

Instruction to paragraph (g): If none of the safe harbors applies, whether subsequent offers and sales of securities will be integrated with any securities offered or sold pursuant to this section (§ 230.147A) will depend on the particular facts and circumstances.

    (h) *Offerings limited to qualified institutional buyers and institutional accredited investors.* Where an issuer decides to register an offering under the Act after making offers in reliance on this section (§ 230.147A) limited only to qualified institutional buyers and institutional accredited investors referenced in section 5(d) of the Act, such offers will not be subject to integration with any subsequent registered offering. If the issuer makes offers in reliance on this section (§ 230.147A) to persons other than qualified institutional buyers and institutional accredited investors referenced in section 5(d) of the Act, such offers will not be subject to integration if the issuer (and any underwriter, broker, dealer, or agent used by the issuer in connection with the proposed offering) waits at least 30 calendar days between the last such offer made in reliance on this section (§ 230.147A) and the filing of the registration statement with the Commission.

§ 230.149   Definition of "Exchanged" in Section 3(a)(9), for Certain Transactions.

    The term *exchanged* in section 3(a)(9) (sec. 202(c), 48 Stat. 906; 15 U.S.C. 77c(9)) shall be deemed to include the issuance of a security in consideration of the surrender, by the existing security holders of the issuer, of outstanding securities of the issuer, notwithstanding the fact that the surrender of the outstanding securities may be required by the terms of the plans of exchange to be accompanied by such payment in cash by the security holder as may be necessary to effect an equitable adjustment, in respect of dividends or interest paid or payable on the securities involved in the exchange, as between such security holder and other security holders of the same class accepting the offer of exchange.

§ 230.150   Definition of "Commission or Other Remuneration" in Section 3(a)(9), For Certain Transactions.

    The term *commission or other remuneration* in section 3(a)(9) of the Act shall not include payments made by the issuer, directly or indirectly, to its security holders in connection with an exchange of securities for outstanding securities, when such payments are part of the terms of the offer of exchange.

§ 230.152   Definition of "Transactions By an Issuer Not Involving any Public Offering" in Section 4(2), for Certain Transactions.

    The phrase *transactions by an issuer not involving any public offering* in section 4(a)(2)(48 Stat. 77, sec. 203(a), 48 Stat. 906; 15 U.S.C. 77d) shall be deemed to apply to transactions not involving any public offering at the time of said transactions although subsequently thereto the issuer decides to make a public offering and/or files a registration statement.

§ 230.155   Integration of Abandoned Offerings.

    Compliance with paragraph (b) or (c) of this section provides a non-exclusive safe harbor from integration of private and registered offerings. Because of the objectives of Rule 155 and the policies underlying the Act, Rule 155 is not available to any issuer for any transaction or series of transactions that, although in technical compliance with the rule, is part of a plan or scheme to evade the registration requirements of the Act.

(a) *Definition of terms.* For the purposes of this section only, a *private offering* means an unregistered offering of securities that is exempt from registration under Section 4(a)(2) or 4(5) of the Act (15 U.S.C. 77d(2) and 77d(5)) or Rule 506 of Regulation D (§ 230.506).

(b) *Abandoned private offering followed by a registered offering.* A private offering of securities will not be considered part of an offering for which the issuer later files a registration statement if:

(1)   No securities were sold in the private offering;

(2)   The issuer and any person(s) acting on its behalf terminate all offering activity in the private offering before the issuer files the registration statement;

(3)   The Section 10(a) final prospectus and any Section 10 preliminary prospectus used in the registered offering disclose information about the abandoned private offering, including:

(i)   The size and nature of the private offering;

(ii)   The date on which the issuer abandoned the private offering;

(iii)   That any offers to buy or indications of interest given in the private offering were rejected or otherwise not accepted; and

(iv)   That the prospectus delivered in the registered offering supersedes any offering materials used in the private offering; and

(4)   The issuer does not file the registration statement until at least 30 calendar days after termination of all offering activity in the private offering, unless the issuer and any person acting on its behalf offered securities in the private offering only to persons who were (or who the issuer reasonably believes were):

(i)   Accredited investors (as that term is defined in § 230.501(a)); or

(ii)   Persons who satisfy the knowledge and experience standard of § 230.506(b)(2)(ii).

(c) *Abandoned registered offering followed by a private offering.* An offering for which the issuer filed a registration statement will not be considered part of a later commenced private offering if:

(1)   No securities were sold in the registered offering;

(2)   The issuer withdraws the registration statement under § 230.477;

(3)   Neither the issuer nor any person acting on the issuer's behalf commences the private offering earlier than 30 calendar days after the effective date of withdrawal of the registration statement under § 230.477;

(4)   The issuer notifies each offeree in the private offering that:

(i)   The offering is not registered under the Act;

(ii)   The securities will be "restricted securities" (as that term is defined in § 230.144(a)(3)) and may not be resold unless they are registered under the Act or an exemption from registration is available;

(iii)   Purchasers in the private offering do not have the protection of Section 11 of the Act (15 U.S.C. 77k); and

(iv)   A registration statement for the abandoned offering was filed and withdrawn, specifying the effective date of the withdrawal; and

(5)   Any disclosure document used in the private offering discloses any changes in the issuer's business or financial condition that occurred after the issuer filed the registration statement that are material to the investment decision in the private offering.

§ 230.175   Liability for Certain Statements by Issuers.

(a)   A statement within the coverage of paragraph (b) of this section which is made by or on behalf of an issuer or by an outside reviewer retained by the issuer shall be deemed not to be a fraudulent statement (as defined in paragraph (d) of this section), unless it is shown that such statement was made or reaffirmed without a reasonable basis or was disclosed other than in good faith.

(b)   This rule applies to the following statements:

(1)   A forward-looking statement (as defined in paragraph (c) of this section) made in a document filed with the Commission, in Part I of a quarterly report on Form 10-Q, (§ 249.308a of this chapter), or in an annual report to security holders meeting the requirements of Rule 14a–3(b) and (c) or 14c–3(a) and (b) under the Securities Exchange Act of 1934 (§§ 240.14a–3(b) and (c) or 240.14c–3(a) and (b) of this chapter), a statement reaffirming such forward-looking statement after the date the document was filed or the annual report was made publicly available, or a forward-looking statement made before the date the document was filed or the date the annual report was publicly available if such statement is reaffirmed in a filed document, in Part I of a quarterly report on Form 10-Q, or in an annual report made publicly available within a reasonable time after the making of such forward-looking statement; *Provided,* that

(i)   At the time such statements are made or reaffirmed, either the issuer is subject to the reporting requirements of section 13(a) or 15(d) of the Securities Exchange Act of 1934 and has complied with the requirements of Rule 13a–1 or 15d–1 (§§ 239.13a–1 or 239.15d–1 of this chapter) thereunder, if applicable, to file its most recent annual report on Form 10-K, Form 20-F, or Form 40-F; or if the issuer is not subject to the reporting requirements of Section 13(a) or 15(d) of the Securities Exchange Act of 1934, the statements are made in a registration statement filed under the Act, offering statement or solicitation of interest, written document or broadcast script under Regulation A or pursuant to sections 12(b) or (g) of the Securities Exchange Act of 1934; and

(ii)   The statements are not made by or on behalf of an issuer that is an investment company registered under the Investment Company Act of 1940; and

(2)   Information that is disclosed in a document filed with the Commission, in Part I of a quarterly report on Form 10-Q (§ 249.308a of this chapter) or in an annual report to shareholders meeting the requirements of Rules 14a–3 (b) and (c) or 14c–3 (a) and (b) under the Securities Exchange Act of 1934 (§§ 240.14a–3(b) and (c) or 240.14c–3(a) and (b) of this chapter) and that relates to:

(i)   The effects of changing prices on the business enterprise, presented voluntarily or pursuant to Item 303 of Regulation S–K (§ 229.303 of this chapter), "Management's Discussion and Analysis of Financial Condition and Results of Operations," Item 5 of Form 20-F (§ 249.220(f) of this chapter), "Operating and Financial Review and Prospects," Item 302 of Regulation S–K (§ 229.302 of this chapter), "Supplementary Financial Information," or Rule 3–20(c) of Regulation S–X (§ 210.3–20(c) of this chapter); or

(ii)   The value of proved oil and gas reserves (such as a standardized measure of discounted future net cash flows relating to proved oil and gas reserves as set forth in FASB ASC paragraphs 932–235–50–29 through 932–235–50–36) (Extractive Activities—Oil and Gas Topic) presented voluntarily or pursuant to Item 302 of Regulation S–K (§ 229.302 of this chapter).

(c)   For the purpose of this rule, the term *forward-looking statement* shall mean and shall be limited to:

(1)   A statement containing a projection of revenues, income (loss), earnings (loss) per share, capital expenditures, dividends, capital structure or other financial items;

1422

(2) A statement of management's plans and objectives for future operations;

(3) A statement of future economic performance contained in management's discussion and analysis of financial condition and results of operations included pursuant to Item 303 of Regulation S–K (§ 229.303 of this chapter) or Item 9 of Form 20-F; or Item 5 of Form 20-F.

(4) Disclosed statements of the assumptions underlying or relating to any of the statements described in paragraphs (c) (1), (2), or (3) of this section.

(d) For the purpose of this rule the term *fraudulent statement* shall mean a statement which is an untrue statement of a material fact, a statement false or misleading with respect to any material fact, an omission to state a material fact necessary to make a statement not misleading, or which constitutes the employment of a manipulative, deceptive, or fraudulent device, contrivance, scheme, transaction, act, practice, course of business, or an artifice to defraud, as those terms are used in the Securities Act of 1933 or the rules or regulations promulgated thereunder.

§ 230.176 Circumstances Affecting the Determination of What Constitutes Reasonable Investigation and Reasonable Grounds for Belief Under Section 11 of the Securities Act.

In determining whether or not the conduct of a person constitutes a reasonable investigation or a reasonable ground for belief meeting the standard set forth in section 11(c), relevant circumstances include, with respect to a person other than the issuer.

(a) The type of issuer;

(b) The type of security;

(c) The type of person;

(d) The office held when the person is an officer;

(e) The presence or absence of another relationship to the issuer when the person is a director or proposed director;

(f) Reasonable reliance on officers, employees, and others whose duties should have given them knowledge of the particular facts (in the light of the functions and responsibilities of the particular person with respect to the issuer and the filing);

(g) When the person is an underwriter, the type of underwriting arrangement, the role of the particular person as an underwriter and the availability of information with respect to the registrant; and

(h) Whether, with respect to a fact or document incorporated by reference, the particular person had any responsibility for the fact or document at the time of the filing from which it was incorporated.

REGULATION A—CONDITIONAL SMALL ISSUES EXEMPTION

§ 230.251 Scope of Exemption.

(a) *Tier 1 and Tier 2.* A public offer or sale of eligible securities, as defined in Rule 261 (§ 230.261), pursuant to Regulation A shall be exempt under section 3(b) from the registration requirements of the Securities Act of 1933 (the "Securities Act") (15 U.S.C. 77a et seq.).

(1) Tier 1. Offerings pursuant to Regulation A in which the sum of all cash and other consideration to be received for the securities being offered ("aggregate offering price") plus the gross proceeds for all securities sold pursuant to other offering statements within the 12 months before the start of and during the current offering of securities ("aggregate sales") does not exceed $20,000,000, including not more than $6,000,000 offered by all selling securityholders that are affiliates of the issuer ("Tier 1 offerings").

(2) Tier 2. Offerings pursuant to Regulation A in which the sum of the aggregate offering price and aggregate sales does not exceed $50,000,000, including not more than $15,000,000 offered by all selling securityholders that are affiliates of the issuer ("Tier 2 offerings").

(3) *Additional limitation on secondary sales in first year.* The portion of the aggregate offering price attributable to the securities of selling securityholders shall not exceed 30% of the aggregate offering price of a particular offering in:

(i) The issuer's first offering pursuant to Regulation A; or

(ii) Any subsequent Regulation A offering that is qualified within one year of the qualification date of the issuer's first offering.

Note to paragraph (a). Where a mixture of cash and non-cash consideration is to be received, the aggregate offering price must be based on the price at which the securities are offered for cash. Any portion of the aggregate offering price or aggregate sales attributable to cash received in a foreign currency must be translated into United States currency at a currency exchange rate in effect on, or at a reasonable time before, the date of the sale of the securities. If securities are not offered for cash, the aggregate offering price or aggregate sales must be based on the value of the consideration as established by bona fide sales of that consideration made within a reasonable time, or, in the absence of sales, on the fair value as determined by an accepted standard. Valuations of non-cash consideration must be reasonable at the time made. If convertible securities or warrants are being offered and such securities are convertible, exercisable, or exchangeable within one year of the offering statement's qualification or at the discretion of the issuer, the underlying securities must also be qualified and the aggregate offering price must include the actual or maximum estimated conversion, exercise, or exchange price of such securities.

(b) *Issuer.* The issuer of the securities:

(1) Is an entity organized under the laws of the United States or Canada, or any State, Province, Territory or possession thereof, or the District of Columbia, with its principal place of business in the United States or Canada;

(2) [Reserved]

(3) Is not a development stage company that either has no specific business plan or purpose, or has indicated that its business plan is to merge with or acquire an unidentified company or companies;

(4) Is not an investment company registered or required to be registered under the Investment Company Act of 1940 (15 U.S.C. 80a–1 et seq.) or a business development company as defined in section 2(a)(48) of the Investment Company Act of 1940 (15 U.S.C. 80a–2(a)(48));

(5) Is not issuing fractional undivided interests in oil or gas rights, or a similar interest in other mineral rights;

(6) Is not, and has not been, subject to any order of the Commission entered pursuant to Section 12(j) (15 U.S.C. 78l(j)) of the Securities Exchange Act of 1934 (the "Exchange Act") (15 U.S.C. 78a et seq.) within five years before the filing of the offering statement;

(7) Has filed with the Commission all reports required to be filed, if any, pursuant to Rule 257 (§ 230.257) during the two years before the filing of the offering statement (or for such shorter period that the issuer was required to file such reports); and

(8) Is not disqualified under Rule 262 (§ 230.262).

(c) *Integration with other offerings.* Offers or sales made in reliance on this Regulation A will not be integrated with:

(1) Prior offers or sales of securities; or

(2)   Subsequent offers or sales of securities that are:

(i)   Registered under the Securities Act, except as provided in Rule 255(e) (§ 230.255(e));

(ii)   Exempt from registration under Rule 701 (§ 230.701);

(iii)   Made pursuant to an employee benefit plan;

(iv)   Exempt from registration under Regulation S (§§ 230.901 through 203.905);

(v)   Made more than six months after the completion of the Regulation A offering; or

(vi)   Exempt from registration under Section 4(a)(6) of the Securities Act (15 U.S.C. 77d(a)(6)).

Note to paragraph (c). If these safe harbors do not apply, whether subsequent offers and sales of securities will be integrated with the Regulation A offering will depend on the particular facts and circumstances.

(d)   *Offering conditions*—(1) *Offers.* (i) Except as allowed by Rule 255 (§ 230.255), no offer of securities may be made unless an offering statement has been filed with the Commission.

(ii)   After the offering statement has been filed, but before it is qualified:

(A)   Oral offers may be made;

(B)   Written offers pursuant to Rule 254 (§ 230.254) may be made; and

(C)   Solicitations of interest and other communications pursuant to Rule 255 (§ 230.255) may be made.

(iii) Offers may be made after the offering statement has been qualified, but any written offers must be accompanied with or preceded by the most recent offering circular filed with the Commission for such offering.

(2)   *Sales.* (i) No sale of securities may be made:

(A)   Until the offering statement has been qualified;

(B)   By issuers that are not currently required to file reports pursuant to Rule 257(b) (§ 230.257(b)), until a Preliminary Offering Circular is delivered at least 48 hours before the sale to any person that before qualification of the offering statement had indicated an interest in purchasing securities in the offering, including those persons that responded to an issuer's solicitation of interest materials; and

(C)   In a Tier 2 offering of securities that are not listed on a registered national securities exchange upon qualification, unless the purchaser is either an accredited investor (as defined in Rule 501 (§ 230.501)) or the aggregate purchase price to be paid by the purchaser for the securities (including the actual or maximum estimated conversion, exercise, or exchange price for any underlying securities that have been qualified) is no more than ten percent (10%) of the greater of such purchaser's:

(*1*)   Annual income or net worth if a natural person (with annual income and net worth for such natural person purchasers determined as provided in Rule 501 (§ 230.501)); or

(*2*)   Revenue or net assets for such purchaser's most recently completed fiscal year end if a non-natural person.

Note to paragraph (d)(2)(i)(C). When securities underlying warrants or convertible securities are being qualified pursuant to Tier 2 of Regulation A one year or more after the qualification of an offering for which investment limitations previously applied, purchasers of the underlying securities for which investment limitations would apply at that later date may determine compliance with the ten percent

(10%) investment limitation using the conversion, exercise, or exchange price to acquire the underlying securities at that later time without aggregating such price with the price of the overlying warrants or convertible securities.

(D) The issuer may rely on a representation of the purchaser when determining compliance with the ten percent (10%) investment limitation in this paragraph (d)(2)(i)(C), provided that the issuer does not know at the time of sale that any such representation is untrue.

(ii) In a transaction that represents a sale by the issuer or an underwriter, or a sale by a dealer within 90 calendar days after qualification of the offering statement, each underwriter or dealer selling in such transaction must deliver to each purchaser from it, not later than two business days following the completion of such sale, a copy of the Final Offering Circular, subject to the following provisions:

(A) If the sale was by the issuer and was not effected by or through an underwriter or dealer, the issuer is responsible for delivering the Final Offering Circular as if the issuer were an underwriter;

(B) For continuous or delayed offerings pursuant to paragraph (d)(3) of this section, the 90 calendar day period for dealers shall commence on the day of the first bona fide offering of securities under such offering statement;

(C) If the security is listed on a registered national securities exchange, no offering circular need be delivered by a dealer more than 25 calendar days after the later of the qualification date of the offering statement or the first date on which the security was bona fide offered to the public;

(D) No offering circular need be delivered by a dealer if the issuer is subject, immediately prior to the time of the filing of the offering statement, to the reporting requirements of Rule 257(b) (§ 230.257(b)); and

(E) The Final Offering Circular delivery requirements set forth in paragraph (d)(2)(ii) of this section may be satisfied by delivering a notice to the effect that the sale was made pursuant to a qualified offering statement that includes the uniform resource locator ("URL"), which, in the case of an electronic-only offering, must be an active hyperlink, where the Final Offering Circular, or the offering statement of which such Final Offering Circular is part, may be obtained on the Commission's Electronic Data Gathering, Analysis and Retrieval System ("EDGAR") and contact information sufficient to notify a purchaser where a request for a Final Offering Circular can be sent and received in response.

(3) *Continuous or delayed offerings.* (i) Continuous or delayed offerings may be made under this Regulation A, so long as the offering statement pertains only to:

(A) Securities that are to be offered or sold solely by or on behalf of a person or persons other than the issuer, a subsidiary of the issuer, or a person of which the issuer is a subsidiary;

(B) Securities that are to be offered and sold pursuant to a dividend or interest reinvestment plan or an employee benefit plan of the issuer;

(C) Securities that are to be issued upon the exercise of outstanding options, warrants, or rights;

(D) Securities that are to be issued upon conversion of other outstanding securities;

(E) Securities that are pledged as collateral; or

(F) Securities the offering of which will be commenced within two calendar days after the qualification date, will be made on a continuous basis, may continue for a period in excess of 30 calendar days from the date of initial qualification, and will be offered in an amount that, at the time the offering statement is qualified, is reasonably expected to be offered and sold within two years from the initial qualification date. These securities may be offered and sold only if not more than three years have elapsed since the initial qualification date of the offering statement under which they are being offered and sold; provided, however, that if a new offering statement has been filed pursuant to this paragraph (d)(3)(i)(F), securities covered by the prior offering statement may continue to be offered and sold until the earlier of the qualification date of the new offering statement or 180 calendar days after the third anniversary of the initial qualification date of the prior offering statement. Before the end of such three-year period, an issuer may file a new offering statement covering the securities. The new offering statement must include all the information that would be required at that time in an offering statement relating to all offerings that it covers. Before the qualification date of the new offering statement, the issuer may include as part of such new offering statement any unsold securities covered by the earlier offering statement by identifying on the cover page of the new offering circular, or the latest amendment, the amount of such unsold securities being included. The offering of securities on the earlier offering statement will be deemed terminated as of the date of qualification of the new offering statement. Securities may be sold pursuant to this paragraph (d)(3)(i)(F) only if the issuer is current in its annual and semiannual filings pursuant to Rule 257(b) (§ 230.257(b)), at the time of such sale.

(ii) At the market offerings, by or on behalf of the issuer or otherwise, are not permitted under this Regulation A. As used in this paragraph (d)(3)(ii), the term *at the market offering* means an offering of equity securities into an existing trading market for outstanding shares of the same class at other than a fixed price.

(e) *Confidential treatment.* A request for confidential treatment may be made under Rule 406 (§ 230.406) for information required to be filed, and Rule 83 (§ 200.83) for information not required to be filed.

(f) *Electronic filing.* Documents filed or otherwise provided to the Commission pursuant to this Regulation A must be submitted in electronic format by means of EDGAR in accordance with the EDGAR rules set forth in Regulation S–T (17 CFR part 232).

§ 230.252   Offering Statement.

(a) *Documents to be included.* The offering statement consists of the contents required by Form 1-A (§ 239.90 of this chapter) and any other material information necessary to make the required statements, in light of the circumstances under which they are made, not misleading.

(b) *Paper, printing, language and pagination.* Except as otherwise specified in this rule, the requirements for offering statements are the same as those specified in Rule 403 (§ 230.403) for registration statements under the Act. No fee is payable to the Commission upon either the submission or filing of an offering statement on Form 1-A, or any amendment to an offering statement.

(c) *Signatures.* The issuer, its principal executive officer, principal financial officer, principal accounting officer, and a majority of the members of its board of directors or other governing body, must sign the offering statement in the manner prescribed by Form 1-A. If a signature is by a person on behalf of any other person, evidence of authority to sign must be filed, except where an executive officer signs for the issuer.

(d) *Non-public submission.* An issuer whose securities have not been previously sold pursuant to a qualified offering statement under this Regulation A or an effective registration statement under the Securities Act may submit a draft offering statement to the Commission for non-public review by the staff of the Commission before public filing, provided that the offering statement shall not be qualified less than 21 calendar days after the public filing with the Commission of:

(1) The initial non-public submission;

(2) All non-public amendments; and

(3) All non-public correspondence submitted by or on behalf of the issuer to the Commission staff regarding such submissions (subject to any separately approved confidential treatment request under Rule 251(e) (§ 230.251(e)).

(e) *Qualification.* An offering statement and any amendment thereto can be qualified only at such date and time as the Commission may determine.

(f) *Amendments.* (1)(i) Amendments to an offering statement must be signed and filed with the Commission in the same manner as the initial filing. Amendments to an offering statement must be filed under cover of Form 1-A and must be numbered consecutively in the order in which filed.

(ii) Every amendment that includes amended audited financial statements must include the consent of the certifying accountant to the use of such accountant's certification in connection with the amended financial statements in the offering statement or offering circular and to being named as having audited such financial statements.

(iii) Amendments solely relating to Part III of Form 1-A must comply with the requirements of paragraph (f)(1)(i) of this section, except that such amendments may be limited to Part I of Form 1-A, an explanatory note, and all of the information required by Part III of Form 1-A.

(2) Post-qualification amendments must be filed in the following circumstances for ongoing offerings:

(i) At least every 12 months after the qualification date to include the financial statements that would be required by Form 1-A as of such date; or

(ii) To reflect any facts or events arising after the qualification date of the offering statement (or the most recent post-qualification amendment thereof) which, individually or in the aggregate, represent a fundamental change in the information set forth in the offering statement.

§ 230.253   Offering Circular.

(a) *Contents.* An offering circular must include the information required by Form 1-A for offering circulars.

(b) *Information that may be omitted.* Notwithstanding paragraph (a) of this section, a qualified offering circular may omit information with respect to the public offering price, underwriting syndicate (including any material relationships between the issuer or selling securityholders and the unnamed underwriters, brokers or dealers), underwriting discounts or commissions, discounts or commissions to dealers, amount of proceeds, conversion rates, call prices and other items dependent upon the offering price, delivery dates, and terms of the securities dependent upon the offering date; provided, that the following conditions are met:

(1) The securities to be qualified are offered for cash.

(2) The outside front cover page of the offering circular includes a bona fide estimate of the range of the maximum offering price and the maximum number of shares or other units of securities to be offered or a bona fide estimate of the principal amount of debt securities offered, subject to the following conditions:

(i) The range must not exceed $2 for offerings where the upper end of the range is $10 or less or 20% if the upper end of the price range is over $10; and

(ii) The upper end of the range must be used in determining the aggregate offering price under Rule 251(a) (§ 230.251(a)).

(3) The offering statement does not relate to securities to be offered by competitive bidding.

(4) The volume of securities (the number of equity securities or aggregate principal amount of debt securities) to be offered may not be omitted in reliance on this paragraph (b).

Note to paragraph (b). A decrease in the volume of securities offered or a change in the bona fide estimate of the offering price range from that indicated in the offering circular filed as part of a qualified offering statement may be disclosed in the offering circular filed with the Commission pursuant to Rule 253(g) (§ 230.253(g)), so long as the decrease in the volume of securities offered or change in the price range would not materially change the disclosure contained in the offering statement at qualification. Notwithstanding the foregoing, any decrease in the volume of securities offered and any deviation from the low or high end of the price range may be reflected in the offering circular supplement filed with the Commission pursuant to Rule 253(g)(1) or (3) (§ 230.253(g)(1) or (3)) if, in the aggregate, the decrease in volume and/or change in price represent no more than a 20% change from the maximum aggregate offering price calculable using the information in the qualified offering statement. In no circumstances may this paragraph be used to offer securities where the maximum aggregate offering price would result in the offering exceeding the limit set forth in Rule 251(a) (§ 230.251(a)) or if the change would result in a Tier 1 offering becoming a Tier 2 offering. An offering circular supplement may not be used to increase the volume of securities being offered. Additional securities may only be offered pursuant to a new offering statement or post-qualification amendment qualified by the Commission.

(c) *Filing of omitted information.* The information omitted from the offering circular in reliance upon paragraph (b) of this section must be contained in an offering circular filed with the Commission pursuant to paragraph (g) of this section; except that if such offering circular is not so filed by the later of 15 business days after the qualification date of the offering statement or 15 business days after the qualification of a post-qualification amendment thereto that contains an offering circular, the information omitted in reliance upon paragraph (b) of this section must be contained in a qualified post-qualification amendment to the offering statement.

(d) *Presentation of information.* (1) Information in the offering circular must be presented in a clear, concise and understandable manner and in a type size that is easily readable. Repetition of information should be avoided; cross-referencing of information within the document is permitted.

(2) Where an offering circular is distributed through an electronic medium, issuers may satisfy legibility requirements applicable to printed documents by presenting all required information in a format readily communicated to investors.

(e) *Date.* An offering circular must be dated approximately as of the date it was filed with the Commission.

(f) *Cover page legend.* The cover page of every offering circular must display the following statement highlighted by prominent type or in another manner:

The United States Securities and Exchange Commission does not pass upon the merits of or give its approval to any securities offered or the terms of the offering, nor does it pass upon the accuracy or completeness of any offering circular or other solicitation materials. These securities are offered pursuant to an exemption from registration with the Commission; however, the Commission has not made an independent determination that the securities offered are exempt from registration.

(g) *Offering circular supplements.* (1) An offering circular that discloses information previously omitted from the offering circular in reliance upon Rule 253(b) (§ 230.253(b)) must be filed with the Commission no later than two business days following the earlier of the date of determination of the offering price or the date such offering circular is first used after qualification in connection with a public offering or sale.

(2) An offering circular that reflects information other than that covered in paragraph (g)(1) of this section that constitutes a substantive change from or addition to the information set forth in the last offering circular filed with the Commission must be filed with the Commission no later than five business days after the date it is first used after qualification in connection with a public offering or sale. If an offering circular filed pursuant to this paragraph (g)(2) consists of an offering circular supplement attached to an offering circular that previously had been filed or was not required to be filed pursuant to paragraph (g) of this section because it did not contain substantive changes from an offering circular that previously was filed, only the offering circular supplement need be filed under paragraph (g) of this section, provided that the cover page of the offering circular supplement identifies the date(s) of the related offering circular and any offering circular supplements thereto that together constitute the offering circular with respect to the securities currently being offered or sold.

(3) An offering circular that discloses information, facts or events covered in both paragraphs (g)(1) and (2) of this section must be filed with the Commission no later than two business days following the earlier of the date of the determination of the offering price or the date it is first used after qualification in connection with a public offering or sale.

(4) An offering circular required to be filed pursuant to paragraph (g) of this section that is not filed within the time frames specified in paragraphs (g)(1) through (3) of this section, as applicable, must be filed pursuant to this paragraph (g)(4) as soon as practicable after the discovery of such failure to file.

(5) Each offering circular filed under this section must contain in the upper right corner of the cover page the paragraphs of paragraphs (g)(1) through (4) of this section under which the filing is made, and the file number of the offering statement to which the offering circular relates.

§ 230.254　　Preliminary Offering Circular.

After the filing of an offering statement, but before its qualification, written offers of securities may be made if they meet the following requirements:

(a) *Outside front cover page.* The outside front cover page of the material bears the caption Preliminary Offering Circular, the date of issuance, and the following legend, which must be highlighted by prominent type or in another manner:

An offering statement pursuant to Regulation A relating to these securities has been filed with the Securities and Exchange Commission. Information contained in this Preliminary Offering Circular is subject to completion or amendment. These securities may not be sold nor may offers to buy be accepted before the offering statement filed with the Commission is qualified. This Preliminary Offering Circular shall not constitute an offer to sell or the solicitation of an offer to buy nor may there be any sales of these securities in any state in which such offer, solicitation or sale would be unlawful before registration or qualification under the laws of any such state. We may elect to satisfy our obligation to deliver a Final Offering Circular by sending you a notice within two business days after the completion of our sale to you that contains the URL where the Final Offering Circular or the offering statement in which such Final Offering Circular was filed may be obtained.

(b) *Other contents.* The Preliminary Offering Circular contains substantially the information required to be in an offering circular by Form 1-A (§ 239.90 of this chapter), except that certain information may be omitted under Rule 253(b) (§ 230.253(b)) subject to the conditions set forth in such rule.

(c) *Filing.* The Preliminary Offering Circular is filed as a part of the offering statement.

§ 230.255　　Solicitations of Interest and Other Communications.

(a) *Solicitation of interest.* At any time before the qualification of an offering statement, including before the non-public submission or public filing of such offering statement, an issuer or any person authorized to act on behalf of an issuer may communicate orally or in writing to determine whether there is any interest in a contemplated securities offering. Such communications are deemed to be an offer of a security for sale for purposes of the antifraud provisions of the federal securities laws. No solicitation or acceptance of money or other consideration, nor of any commitment, binding or otherwise, from any person is permitted until qualification of the offering statement.

(b) *Conditions.* The communications must:

(1) State that no money or other consideration is being solicited, and if sent in response, will not be accepted;

(2) State that no offer to buy the securities can be accepted and no part of the purchase price can be received until the offering statement is qualified, and any such offer may be withdrawn or revoked, without obligation or commitment of any kind, at any time before notice of its acceptance given after the qualification date;

(3) State that a person's indication of interest involves no obligation or commitment of any kind; and

(4) After the public filing of the offering statement:

(i) State from whom a copy of the most recent version of the Preliminary Offering Circular may be obtained, including a phone number and address of such person;

(ii) Provide the URL where such Preliminary Offering Circular, or the offering statement in which such Preliminary Offering Circular was filed, may be obtained; or

(iii) Include a complete copy of the Preliminary Offering Circular.

(c) *Indications of interest.* Any written communication under this rule may include a means by which a person may indicate to the issuer that such person is interested in a potential offering. This issuer may require the name, address, telephone number, and/or email address in any response form included pursuant to this paragraph (c).

(d) *Revised solicitations of interest.* If solicitation of interest materials are used after the public filing of the offering statement and such solicitation of interest materials contain information that is inaccurate or inadequate in any material respect, revised solicitation of interest materials must be redistributed in a substantially similar manner as such materials were originally distributed. Notwithstanding the foregoing in this paragraph (d), if the only information that is inaccurate or inadequate is contained in a Preliminary Offering Circular provided with the solicitation of interest materials pursuant to paragraphs (b)(4)(i) or (ii) of this section, no such redistribution is required in the following circumstances:

(1) in the case of paragraph (b)(4)(i) of this section, the revised Preliminary Offering Circular will be provided to any persons making new inquiries and will be recirculated to any persons making any previous inquiries; or

(2) in the case of paragraph (b)(4)(ii) of this section, the URL continues to link directly to the most recent Preliminary Offering Circular or to the offering statement in which such revised Preliminary Offering Circular was filed.

(e) *Abandoned offerings.* Where an issuer decides to register an offering under the Securities Act after soliciting interest in a contemplated, but subsequently abandoned, Regulation A offering, the abandoned Regulation A offering would not be subject to integration with the registered offering if the issuer engaged in solicitations of interest pursuant to this rule only to qualified institutional buyers and institutional accredited investors permitted by Section 5(d) of the Securities Act. If the issuer engaged in solicitations of interest to persons other than qualified institutional buyers and institutional accredited investors, an abandoned Regulation A offering would not be subject to integration if the issuer (and any underwriter, broker, dealer, or agent used by the issuer in connection with the proposed offering) waits at least 30 calendar days between the last such solicitation of interest in the Regulation A offering and the filing of the registration statement with the Commission.

§ 230.256   Definition of "Qualified Purchaser".

For purposes of Section 18(b)(3) of the Securities Act [15 U.S.C. 77r(b)(3)], a "qualified purchaser" means any person to whom securities are offered or sold pursuant to a Tier 2 offering of this Regulation A.

§ 230.257   Periodic and Current Reporting; Exit Report.

(a) *Tier 1: Exit report.* Each issuer that has filed an offering statement for a Tier 1 offering that has been qualified pursuant to this Regulation A must file an exit report on Form 1-Z (§ 239.94 of this chapter) not later than 30 calendar days after the termination or completion of the offering.

(b) *Tier 2: Periodic and current reporting.* Each issuer that has filed an offering statement for a Tier 2 offering that has been qualified pursuant to this Regulation A must file with the Commission the following periodic and current reports:

(1) *Annual reports.* An annual report on Form 1-K (§ 239.91 of this chapter) for the fiscal year in which the offering statement became qualified and for any fiscal year thereafter, unless the issuer's obligation to file such annual report is suspended under paragraph (d) of this section. Annual reports must be filed within the period specified in Form 1-K.

(2) *Special financial report.* (i) A special financial report on Form 1-K or Form 1-SA if the offering statement did not contain the following:

(A) Audited financial statements for the issuer's most recent fiscal year (or for the life of the issuer if less than a full fiscal year) preceding the fiscal year in which the issuer's offering statement became qualified; or

(B) unaudited financial statements covering the first six months of the issuer's current fiscal year if the offering statement was qualified during the last six months of that fiscal year.

(ii) The special financial report described in paragraph (b)(2)(i)(A) of this section must be filed under cover of Form 1-K within 120 calendar days after the qualification date of the offering statement and must include audited financial statements for such fiscal year or other period specified in that paragraph, as the case may be. The special financial report described in paragraph (b)(2)(i)(B) of this section must be filed under cover of Form 1-SA within 90 calendar days after the qualification date of the offering statement and must include the semiannual financial statements for the first six months of the issuer's fiscal year, which may be unaudited.

(iii) A special financial report must be signed in accordance with the requirements of the form on which it is filed.

(3) *Semiannual report.* A semiannual report on Form 1-SA (§ 239.92 of this chapter) within the period specified in Form 1-SA. Semiannual reports must cover the first six months of each fiscal year of the issuer, commencing with the first six months of the fiscal year immediately following the most recent fiscal year for which full financial statements were included in the offering statement, or, if the offering statement included financial statements for the first six months of the fiscal year following the most recent full fiscal year, for the first six months of the following fiscal year.

(4) *Current reports.* Current reports on Form 1-U (§ 239.93 of this chapter) with respect to the matters and within the period specified in that form, unless substantially the same information has been previously reported to the Commission by the issuer under cover of Form 1-K or Form 1-SA.

(5) *Reporting by successor issuers.* Where in connection with a succession by merger, consolidation, exchange of securities, acquisition of assets or otherwise, securities of any issuer that is not required to file reports pursuant to paragraph (b) of this section are issued to the

holders of any class of securities of another issuer that is required to file such reports, the duty to file reports pursuant to paragraph (b) of this section shall be deemed to have been assumed by the issuer of the class of securities so issued. The successor issuer must, after the consummation of the succession, file reports in accordance with paragraph (b) of this section, unless that issuer is exempt from filing such reports or the duty to file such reports is terminated or suspended under paragraph (d) of this section.

(6) *Exchange Act reporting requirements.* The duty to file reports under this rule shall be deemed to have been met if the issuer is subject to the reporting requirements of Section 13 or 15(d) of the Exchange Act (15 U.S.C. 78m or 15 U.S.C. 78o) and, as of each Form 1-K and Form 1-SA due date, has filed all reports required to be filed by Section 13 or 15(d) of the Exchange Act (15 U.S.C. 78m or 15 U.S.C. 78o) during the 12 months (or such shorter period that the registrant was required to file such reports) preceding such due date.

(7) [Effective Jan. 4, 2021] *Exemption for subsidiary issuers of guaranteed securities and subsidiary guarantors.* Any issuer of a guaranteed security, or guarantor of a security, that is permitted to omit financial statements by Item (b)(7)(i) of Part F/S of Form 1-A (referenced in § 239.90), Item 7(g)(1) of Part II of Form 1-K (referenced in § 239.91), and Item 3(e) of Form 1-SA (referenced in § 239.92), is exempt from the requirements of this paragraph (b).

(c) *Amendments.* All amendments to the reports described in paragraphs (a) and (b) of this section must be filed under cover of the form amended, marked with the letter A to designate the document as an amendment, e.g., "1–K/A," and in compliance with pertinent requirements applicable to such reports. Amendments filed pursuant to this paragraph (c) must set forth the complete text of each item as amended, but need not include any items that were not amended. Amendments must be numbered sequentially and be filed separately for each report amended. Amendments must be signed on behalf of the issuer by a duly authorized representative of the issuer. An amendment to any report required to include certifications as specified in the applicable form must include new certifications by the appropriate persons.

(d) *Suspension of duty to file reports.*

(1) [Reserved]

(2) The duty to file reports under paragraph (b) of this section with respect to a class of securities held of record (as defined in Rule 12g5–1 (§ 240.12g5–1 of this chapter)) by less than 300 persons, or less than 1,200 persons for a bank (as defined in Section 3(a)(6) of the Exchange Act (15 U.S.C. 78c(a)(6)), or a bank holding company (as defined in section 2 of the Bank Holding Company Act of 1956 (12 U.S.C. 1841)), shall be suspended for such class of securities immediately upon filing with the Commission an exit report on Form 1-Z (§ 239.94 of this chapter) if the issuer of such class has filed all reports due pursuant to this rule before the date of such Form 1-Z filing for the shorter of:

(i) The period since the issuer became subject to such reporting obligation; or

(ii) Its most recent three fiscal years and the portion of the current year preceding the date of filing Form 1-Z.

(3) For the purposes of paragraph (d)(2) of this section, the term class shall be construed to include all securities of an issuer that are of substantially similar character and the holders of which enjoy substantially similar rights and privileges. If the Form 1-Z is subsequently withdrawn or if it is denied because the issuer was ineligible to use the form, the issuer must, within 60 calendar days, file with the Commission all reports which would have been required if such exit report had not been filed. If the suspension resulted from the issuer's merger into, or consolidation with, another issuer or issuers, the notice must be filed by the successor issuer.

(4) The ability to suspend reporting, as described in paragraph (d)(2) of this section, is not available for any class of securities if:

(i)   During that fiscal year a Tier 2 offering statement was qualified;

(ii)   The issuer has not filed an annual report under this rule or the Exchange Act for the fiscal year in which a Tier 2 offering statement was qualified; or

(iii)   Offers or sales of securities of that class are being made pursuant to a Tier 2 Regulation A offering.

(e)   *Termination of duty to file reports.* If the duty to file reports is deemed to have been met pursuant to paragraph (b)(6) of this section and such status ends because the issuer terminates or suspends its duty to file reports under the Exchange Act, the issuer's obligation to file reports under paragraph (b) of this section shall:

(1)   Automatically terminate if the issuer is eligible to suspend its duty to file reports under paragraphs (d)(2) and (3) of this section; or

(2)   Recommence with the report covering the most recent financial period after that included in any effective registration statement or filed Exchange Act report.

(f)   [Effective Mar. 30, 2020 through July 15, 2020] *Temporary relief from ongoing reporting requirements.* (1) An issuer that is not able to meet a filing deadline for any report or form required to be filed by § 230.252(f)(2)(i) or paragraphs (a) through (c) of this section during the period from and including March 26, 2020, to May 31, 2020, due to circumstances relating to coronavirus disease 2019 (COVID-19) shall be deemed to have satisfied the filing deadline for such report or form if:

(i)   The issuer promptly discloses on its public website or provides direct notification to its investors that it is relying on this paragraph (f); and

(ii)   The issuer files such report or form with the Commission no later than 45 days after the original filing deadline of the report or form.

(2)   In any report or form filed pursuant to paragraph (f)(1)(ii) of this section, the issuer must disclose that it is relying on this paragraph (f) and state the reasons why, in good faith, it could not file such report or form on a timely basis.

§ 230.258   Suspension of the Exemption.

(a)   *Suspension.* The Commission may at any time enter an order temporarily suspending a Regulation A exemption if it has reason to believe that:

(1)   No exemption is available or any of the terms, conditions or requirements of Regulation A have not been complied with;

(2)   The offering statement, any sales or solicitation of interest material, or any report filed pursuant to Rule 257 (§ 230.257) contains any untrue statement of a material fact or omits to state a material fact necessary in order to make the statements made, in light of the circumstances under which they are made, not misleading;

(3)   The offering is being made or would be made in violation of section 17 of the Securities Act;

(4)   An event has occurred after the filing of the offering statement that would have rendered the exemption hereunder unavailable if it had occurred before such filing;

(5)   Any person specified in Rule 262(a) (§ 230.262(a)) has been indicted for any crime or offense of the character specified in Rule 262(a)(1) (§ 230.262(a)(1)), or any proceeding has been initiated for the purpose of enjoining any such person from engaging in or continuing any conduct or practice of the character specified in Rule 262(a)(2) (§ 230.262(a)(2)), or any proceeding has been initiated for the purposes of Rule 262(a)(3)–(8) (§ 230.262(a)(3) through (8)); or

(6)   The issuer or any promoter, officer, director, or underwriter has failed to cooperate, or has obstructed or refused to permit the making of an investigation by the Commission in connection with any offering made or proposed to be made in reliance on Regulation A.

(b)   *Notice and hearing.* Upon the entry of an order under paragraph (a) of this section, the Commission will promptly give notice to the issuer, any underwriter, and any selling securityholder:

(1)   That such order has been entered, together with a brief statement of the reasons for the entry of the order; and

(2)   That the Commission, upon receipt of a written request within 30 calendar days after the entry of the order, will, within 20 calendar days after receiving the request, order a hearing at a place to be designated by the Commission.

(c)   *Suspension order.* If no hearing is requested and none is ordered by the Commission, an order entered under paragraph (a) of this section shall become permanent on the 30th calendar day after its entry and shall remain in effect unless or until it is modified or vacated by the Commission. Where a hearing is requested or is ordered by the Commission, the Commission will, after notice of and opportunity for such hearing, either vacate the order or enter an order permanently suspending the exemption.

(d)   *Permanent suspension.* The Commission may, at any time after notice of and opportunity for hearing, enter an order permanently suspending the exemption for any reason upon which it could have entered a temporary suspension order under paragraph (a) of this section. Any such order shall remain in effect until vacated by the Commission.

(e)   *Notice procedures.* All notices required by this rule must be given by personal service, registered or certified mail to the addresses given by the issuer, any underwriter and any selling securityholder in the offering statement.

§ 230.259   Withdrawal or Abandonment of Offering Statements.

(a)   *Withdrawal.* If none of the securities that are the subject of an offering statement has been sold and such offering statement is not the subject of a proceeding under Rule 258 (§ 230.258), the offering statement may be withdrawn with the Commission's consent. The application for withdrawal must state the reason the offering statement is to be withdrawn and must be signed by an authorized representative of the issuer. Any withdrawn document will remain in the Commission's files, as well as the related request for withdrawal.

(b)   *Abandonment.* When an offering statement has been on file with the Commission for nine months without amendment and has not become qualified, the Commission may, in its discretion, declare the offering statement abandoned. If the offering statement has been amended, the nine-month period shall be computed from the date of the latest amendment.

§ 230.260   Insignificant Deviations From a Term, Condition or Requirement of Regulation A.

(a)   *Failure to comply.* A failure to comply with a term, condition or requirement of Regulation A will not result in the loss of the exemption from the requirements of section 5 of the Securities Act for any offer or sale to a particular individual or entity, if the person relying on the exemption establishes that:

(1)   The failure to comply did not pertain to a term, condition or requirement directly intended to protect that particular individual or entity;

(2)   The failure to comply was insignificant with respect to the offering as a whole, provided that any failure to comply with Rule 251(a), (b), and (d)(1) and (3) (§ 230.251(a), (b), and (d)(1) and (3)) shall be deemed to be significant to the offering as a whole; and

(3)   A good faith and reasonable attempt was made to comply with all applicable terms, conditions and requirements of Regulation A.

(b)   *Action by Commission.* A transaction made in reliance upon Regulation A must comply with all applicable terms, conditions and requirements of the regulation. Where an exemption is established only through reliance upon paragraph (a) of this section, the failure to comply shall nonetheless be actionable by the Commission under section 20 of the Securities Act.

(c)   *Suspension.* This provision provides no relief or protection from a proceeding under Rule 258 (§ 230.258).

§ 230.261   Definitions.

As used in this Regulation A, all terms have the same meanings as in Rule 405 (§ 230.405), except that all references to *registrant* in those definitions shall refer to the issuer of the securities to be offered and sold under Regulation A. In addition, these terms have the following meanings:

(a)   *Affiliated issuer.* An affiliate (as defined in Rule 501 (§ 230.501)) of the issuer that is issuing securities in the same offering.

(b)   *Business day.* Any day except Saturdays, Sundays or United States federal holidays.

(c)   *Eligible securities.* Equity securities, debt securities, and securities convertible or exchangeable to equity interests, including any guarantees of such securities, but not including asset-backed securities as such term is defined in Item 1101(c) of Regulation AB.

(d)   *Final order.* A written directive or declaratory statement issued by a federal or state agency described in Rule 262(a)(3) (§ 230.262(a)(3)) under applicable statutory authority that provides for notice and an opportunity for hearing, which constitutes a final disposition or action by that federal or state agency.

(e)   *Final offering circular.* The more recent of: the current offering circular contained in a qualified offering statement; and any offering circular filed pursuant to Rule 253(g) (§ 230.253(g)). If, however, the issuer is relying on Rule 253(b) ((§ 230.253(b)), the Final Offering Circular is the most recent of the offering circular filed pursuant to Rule 253(g)(1) or (3) (§ 230.253(g)(1) or (3)) and any subsequent offering circular filed pursuant to Rule 253(g) (§ 230.253(g)).

(f)   *Offering statement.* An offering statement prepared pursuant to Regulation A.

(g)   *Preliminary offering circular.* The offering circular described in Rule 254 (§ 230.254).

§ 230.262   Disqualification Provisions.

(a)   *Disqualification events.* No exemption under this Regulation A shall be available for a sale of securities if the issuer; any predecessor of the issuer; any affiliated issuer; any director, executive officer, other officer participating in the offering, general partner or managing member of the issuer; any beneficial owner of 20% or more of the issuer's outstanding voting equity securities, calculated on the basis of voting power; any promoter connected with the issuer in any capacity at the time of filing, any offer after qualification, or such sale; any person that has been or will be paid (directly or indirectly) remuneration for solicitation of purchasers in connection with such sale of securities; any general partner or managing member of any such solicitor; or any director, executive officer or other officer participating in the offering of any such solicitor or general partner or managing member of such solicitor:

(1)   Has been convicted, within ten years before the filing of the offering statement (or five years, in the case of issuers, their predecessors and affiliated issuers), of any felony or misdemeanor:

(i)   In connection with the purchase or sale of any security;

(ii)   Involving the making of any false filing with the Commission; or

(iii) Arising out of the conduct of the business of an underwriter, broker, dealer, municipal securities dealer, investment adviser or paid solicitor of purchasers of securities;

(2) Is subject to any order, judgment or decree of any court of competent jurisdiction, entered within five years before the filing of the offering statement, that, at the time of such filing, restrains or enjoins such person from engaging or continuing to engage in any conduct or practice:

(i) In connection with the purchase or sale of any security;

(ii) Involving the making of any false filing with the Commission; or

(iii) Arising out of the conduct of the business of an underwriter, broker, dealer, municipal securities dealer, investment adviser or paid solicitor of purchasers of securities;

(3) Is subject to a final order (as defined in Rule 261 (§ 230.261)) of a state securities commission (or an agency or officer of a state performing like functions); a state authority that supervises or examines banks, savings associations, or credit unions; a state insurance commission (or an agency or officer of a state performing like functions); an appropriate federal banking agency; the U.S. Commodity Futures Trading Commission; or the National Credit Union Administration that:

(i) At the time of the filing of the offering statement, bars the person from:

(A) Association with an entity regulated by such commission, authority, agency, or officer;

(B) Engaging in the business of securities, insurance or banking; or

(C) Engaging in savings association or credit union activities; or

(ii) Constitutes a final order based on a violation of any law or regulation that prohibits fraudulent, manipulative, or deceptive conduct entered within ten years before such filing of the offering statement;

(4) Is subject to an order of the Commission entered pursuant to section 15(b) or 15B(c) of the Securities Exchange Act of 1934 (15 U.S.C. 78o(b) or 78o–4(c)) or section 203(e) or (f) of the Investment Advisers Act of 1940 (15 U.S.C. 80b–3(e) or (f)) that, at the time of the filing of the offering statement:

(i) Suspends or revokes such person's registration as a broker, dealer, municipal securities dealer or investment adviser;

(ii) Places limitations on the activities, functions or operations of such person; or

(iii) Bars such person from being associated with any entity or from participating in the offering of any penny stock;

(5) Is subject to any order of the Commission entered within five years before the filing of the offering statement that, at the time of such filing, orders the person to cease and desist from committing or causing a violation or future violation of:

(i) Any scienter-based anti-fraud provision of the federal securities laws, including without limitation section 17(a)(1) of the Securities Act of 1933 (15 U.S.C. 77q(a)(1)), section 10(b) of the Securities Exchange Act of 1934 (15 U.S.C. 78j(b)) and 17 CFR 240.10b–5, section 15(c)(1) of the Securities Exchange Act of 1934 (15 U.S.C. 78o(c)(1)) and section 206(1) of the Investment Advisers Act of 1940 (15 U.S.C. 80b–6(1)), or any other rule or regulation thereunder; or

(ii) Section 5 of the Securities Act of 1933 (15 U.S.C. 77e).

(6) Is suspended or expelled from membership in, or suspended or barred from association with a member of, a registered national securities exchange or a registered national or affiliated

securities association for any act or omission to act constituting conduct inconsistent with just and equitable principles of trade;

(7) Has filed (as a registrant or issuer), or was or was named as an underwriter in, any registration statement or offering statement filed with the Commission that, within five years before the filing of the offering statement, was the subject of a refusal order, stop order, or order suspending the Regulation A exemption, or is, at the time of such filing, the subject of an investigation or proceeding to determine whether a stop order or suspension order should be issued; or

(8) Is subject to a United States Postal Service false representation order entered within five years before the filing of the offering statement, or is, at the time of such filing, subject to a temporary restraining order or preliminary injunction with respect to conduct alleged by the United States Postal Service to constitute a scheme or device for obtaining money or property through the mail by means of false representations.

(b) *Transition, waivers, reasonable care exception.* Paragraph (a) of this section shall not apply:

(1) With respect to any order under § 230.262(a)(3) or (5) that occurred or was issued before June 19, 2015;

(2) Upon a showing of good cause and without prejudice to any other action by the Commission, if the Commission determines that it is not necessary under the circumstances that an exemption be denied;

(3) If, before the filing of the offering statement, the court or regulatory authority that entered the relevant order, judgment or decree advises in writing (whether contained in the relevant judgment, order or decree or separately to the Commission or its staff) that disqualification under paragraph (a) of this section should not arise as a consequence of such order, judgment or decree; or

(4) If the issuer establishes that it did not know and, in the exercise of reasonable care, could not have known that a disqualification existed under paragraph (a) of this section.

Note to paragraph (b)(4). An issuer will not be able to establish that it has exercised reasonable care unless it has made, in light of the circumstances, factual inquiry into whether any disqualifications exist. The nature and scope of the factual inquiry will vary based on the facts and circumstances concerning, among other things, the issuer and the other offering participants.

(c) *Affiliated issuers.* For purposes of paragraph (a) of this section, events relating to any affiliated issuer that occurred before the affiliation arose will be not considered disqualifying if the affiliated entity is not:

(1) In control of the issuer; or

(2) Under common control with the issuer by a third party that was in control of the affiliated entity at the time of such events.

(d) *Disclosure of prior "bad actor" events.* The issuer must include in the offering circular a description of any matters that would have triggered disqualification under paragraphs (a)(3) and (5) of this section but occurred before June 19, 2015. The failure to provide such information shall not prevent an issuer from relying on Regulation A if the issuer establishes that it did not know and, in the exercise of reasonable care, could not have known of the existence of the undisclosed matter or matters.

§ 230.263   Consent to Service of Process.

(a) If the issuer is not organized under the laws of any of the states or territories of the United States of America, it shall furnish to the Commission a written irrevocable consent and power of attorney on Form F-X (§ 239.42 of this chapter) at the time of filing the offering statement required by Rule 252 (§ 230.252).

(b) Any change to the name or address of the agent for service of the issuer shall be communicated promptly to the Commission through amendment of the requisite form and referencing the file number of the relevant offering statement.

REGULATION C—REGISTRATION

§ 230.400   Application of §§ 230.400 to 230.494, Inclusive.

Sections 230.400 to 230.494 shall govern every registration of securities under the Act, except that any provision in a form, or an item of Regulation S–K (17 CFR 229.001 *et seq.*) referred to in such form, covering the same subject matter as any such rule shall be controlling unless otherwise specifically provided in §§ 230.400 to 230.494.

GENERAL REQUIREMENTS

§ 230.404   Preparation of Registration Statement.

(a) A registration statement shall consist of the facing sheet of the applicable form; a prospectus containing the information called for by Part I of such form; the information, list of exhibits, undertakings and signatures required to be set forth in Part II of such form; financial statements and schedules; exhibits; any other information or documents filed as part of the registration statement; and all documents or information incorporated by reference in the foregoing (whether or not required to be filed).

(b) All general instructions, instructions to items of the form, and instructions as to financial statements, exhibits, or prospectuses are to be omitted from the registration statement in all cases.

(c) The prospectus shall contain the information called for by all of the items of Part I of the applicable form, except that unless otherwise specified, no reference need be made to inapplicable items, and negative answers to any item in Part I may be omitted. A copy of the prospectus may be filed as a part of the registration statement in lieu of furnishing the information in item-and-answer form. Wherever a copy of the prospectus is filed in lieu of information in item-and-answer form, the text of the items of the form is to be omitted from the registration statement, as well as from the prospectus, except to the extent provided in paragraph (d) of this rule.

(d) Where any items of a form call for information not required to be included in the prospectus, generally Part II of such form, the text of such items, including the numbers and captions thereof, together with the answers thereto shall be filed with the prospectus under cover of the facing sheet of the form as a part of the registration statement. However, the text of such items may be omitted provided the answers are so prepared as to indicate the coverage of the item without the necessity of reference to the text of the item. If any such item is inapplicable, or the answer thereto is in the negative, a statement to that effect shall be made. Any financial statements not required to be included in the prospectus shall also be filed as a part of the registration statement proper, unless incorporated by reference pursuant to Rule 411 (§ 230.411).

§ 230.405   Definitions of Terms.

Unless the context otherwise requires, all terms used in §§ 230.400 to 230.494, inclusive, or in the forms for registration have the same meanings as in the Act and in the general rules and regulations. In addition, the following definitions apply, unless the context otherwise requires:

Affiliate. An *affiliate* of, or person *affiliated* with, a specified person, is a person that directly, or indirectly through one or more intermediaries, controls or is controlled by, or is under common control with, the person specified.

Amount. The term *amount,* when used in regard to securities, means the principal amount if relating to evidences of indebtedness, the number of shares if relating to shares, and the number of units if relating to any other kind of security.

Associate. The term *associate,* when used to indicate a relationship with any person, means (1) a corporation or organization (other than the registrant or a majority-owned subsidiary of the registrant) of which such person is an officer or partner or is, directly or indirectly, the beneficial owner of 10 percent or more of any class of equity securities, (2) any trust or other estate in which such person has a substantial beneficial interest or as to which such person serves as trustee or in a similar capacity, and (3) any relative or spouse of such person, or any relative of such spouse, who has the same home as such person or who is a director or officer of the registrant or any of its parents or subsidiaries.

Automatic shelf registration statement. The term *automatic shelf registration statement* means a registration statement filed on Form S-3 or Form F-3 (§ 239.13 or § 239.33 of this chapter) by a well-known seasoned issuer pursuant to General Instruction I.D. or I.C. of such forms, respectively.

Business combination related shell company. The term *business combination related shell company* means a shell company (as defined in § 230.405) that is:

(1) Formed by an entity that is not a shell company solely for the purpose of changing the corporate domicile of that entity solely within the United States; or

(2) Formed by an entity that is not a shell company solely for the purpose of completing a business combination transaction (as defined in § 230.165(f)) among one or more entities other than the shell company, none of which is a shell company.

Business development company. The term *business development company* refers to a company which has elected to be regulated as a business development company under sections 55 through 65 of the Investment Company Act of 1940.

Certified. The term *certified,* when used in regard to financial statements, means examined and reported upon with an opinion expressed by an independent public or certified public accountant.

Charter. The term *charter* includes articles of incorporation, declarations of trust, articles of association or partnership, or any similar instrument, as amended, affecting (either with or without filing with any governmental agency) the organization or creation of an incorporated or unincorporated person.

Common equity. The term *common equity* means any class of common stock or an equivalent interest, including but not limited to a unit of beneficial interest in a trust or a limited partnership interest.

Commission. The term *Commission* means the Securities and Exchange Commission.

Control. The term *control* (including the terms *controlling, controlled by* and *under common control with*) means the possession, direct or indirect, of the power to direct or cause the direction of the management and policies of a person, whether through the ownership of voting securities, by contract, or otherwise.

Depositary share. The term *depositary share* means a security, evidenced by an American Depositary Receipt, that represents a foreign security or a multiple of or fraction thereof deposited with a depositary.

Director. The term *director* means any director of a corporation or any person performing similar functions with respect to any organization whether incorporated or unincorporated.

* * *

Emerging growth company.

(1) The term *emerging growth company* means an issuer that had total annual gross revenues of less than $1,070,000,000 during its most recently completed fiscal year.

(2)   An issuer that is an emerging growth company as of the first day of that fiscal year shall continue to be deemed an emerging growth company until the earliest of:

(i)   The last day of the fiscal year of the issuer during which it had total annual gross revenues of $1,070,000,000 or more;

(ii)   The last day of the fiscal year of the issuer following the fifth anniversary of the date of the first sale of common equity securities of the issuer pursuant to an effective registration statement under the Securities Act of 1933;

(iii)   The date on which such issuer has, during the previous three year period, issued more than $1,000,000,000 in non-convertible debt; or

(iv)   The date on which such issuer is deemed to be a large accelerated filer, as defined in Rule 12b–2 of the Exchange Act (§ 240.12b–2 of this chapter).

Employee. The term *employee* does not include a director, trustee, or officer.

Employee benefit plan. The term *employee benefit plan* means any written purchase, savings, option, bonus, appreciation, profit sharing, thrift, incentive, pension or similar plan or written compensation contract solely for employees, directors, general partners, trustees (where the registrant is a business trust), officers, or consultants or advisors. However, consultants or advisors may participate in an employee benefit plan only if:

(1)   They are natural persons;

(2)   They provide *bona fide* services to the registrant; and

(3)   The services are not in connection with the offer or sale of securities in a capital-raising transaction, and do not directly or indirectly promote or maintain a market for the registrant's securities.

Equity security. The term *equity security* means any stock or similar security, certificate of interest or participation in any profit sharing agreement, preorganization certificate or subscription, transferable share, voting trust certificate or certificate of deposit for an equity security, limited partnership interest, interest in a joint venture, or certificate of interest in a business trust; any security future on any such security; or any security convertible, with or without consideration into such a security, or carrying any warrant or right to subscribe to or purchase such a security; or any such warrant or right; or any put, call, straddle, or other option or privilege of buying such a security from or selling such a security to another without being bound to do so.

Executive officer. The term *executive officer,* when used with reference to a registrant, means its president, any vice president of the registrant in charge of a principal business unit, division or function (such as sales, administration or finance), any other officer who performs a policy making function or any other person who performs similar policy making functions for the registrant. Executive officers of subsidiaries may be deemed executive officers of the registrant if they perform such policy making functions for the registrant.

Fiscal year. The term *fiscal year* means the annual accounting period or, if no closing date has been adopted, the calendar year ending on December 31.

* * *

Material. The term *material,* when used to qualify a requirement for the furnishing of information as to any subject, limits the information required to those matters to which there is a substantial likelihood that a reasonable investor would attach importance in determining whether to purchase the security registered.

Officer. The term *officer* means a president, vice president, secretary, treasurer or principal financial officer, comptroller or principal accounting officer, and any person routinely performing corresponding functions with respect to any organization whether incorporated or unincorporated.

Parent. A *parent* of a specified person is an affiliate controlling such person directly, or indirectly through one or more intermediaries.

Predecessor. The term *predecessor* means a person the major portion of the business and assets of which another person acquired in a single succession, or in a series of related successions in each of which the acquiring person acquired the major portion of the business and assets of the acquired person.

Principal underwriter. The term *principal underwriter* means an underwriter in privity of contract with the issuer of the securities as to which he is underwriter, the term *issuer* having the meaning given in sections 2(4) and 2(11) of the Act.

Promoter. (1) The term *promoter* includes:

(i)   Any person who, acting alone or in conjunction with one or more other persons, directly or indirectly takes initiative in founding and organizing the business or enterprise of an issuer; or

(ii)   Any person who, in connection with the founding and organizing of the business or enterprise of an issuer, directly or indirectly receives in consideration of services or property, or both services and property, 10 percent or more of any class of securities of the issuer or 10 percent or more of the proceeds from the sale of any class of such securities. However, a person who receives such securities or proceeds either solely as underwriting commissions or solely in consideration of property shall not be deemed a promoter within the meaning of this paragraph if such person does not otherwise take part in founding and organizing the enterprise.

(2)   All persons coming within the definition of *promoter* in paragraph (1) of this definition may be referred to as *founders* or *organizers* or by another term provided that such term is reasonably descriptive of those persons' activities with respect to the issuer.

Prospectus. Unless otherwise specified or the context otherwise requires, the term *prospectus* means a prospectus meeting the requirements of section 10(a) of the Act.

Registrant. The term *registrant* means the issuer of the securities for which the registration statement is filed.

Share. The term *share* means a share of stock in a corporation or unit of interest in an unincorporated person.

Shell company. The term *shell company* means a registrant, other than an asset-backed issuer as defined in Item 1101(b) of Regulation AB (§ 229.1101(b) of this chapter), that has:

(1)   No or nominal operations; and

(2)   Either:

(i)   No or nominal assets;

(ii)   Assets consisting solely of cash and cash equivalents; or

(iii)   Assets consisting of any amount of cash and cash equivalents and nominal other assets.

Note: For purposes of this definition, the determination of a registrant's assets (including cash and cash equivalents) is based solely on the amount of assets that would be reflected on the registrant's balance sheet prepared in accordance with generally accepted accounting principles on the date of that determination.

* * *

Smaller reporting company. As used in this part, the term *smaller reporting company* means an issuer that is not an investment company, an asset-backed issuer (as defined in § 229.1101 of this chapter), or a majority-owned subsidiary of a parent that is not a smaller reporting company and that:

(1)   Had a public float of less than $250 million; or

(2)   Had annual revenues of less than $100 million and either:

    (i)   No public float; or

    (ii)   A public float of less than $700 million.

(3)   Whether an issuer is a smaller reporting company is determined on an annual basis.

    (i)   For issuers that are required to file reports under section 13(a) or 15(d) of the Exchange Act:

    (A) Public float is measured as of the last business day of the issuer's most recently completed second fiscal quarter and computed by multiplying the aggregate worldwide number of shares of its voting and non-voting common equity held by non-affiliates by the price at which the common equity was last sold, or the average of the bid and asked prices of common equity, in the principal market for the common equity;

    (B) Annual revenues are as of the most recently completed fiscal year for which audited financial statements are available; and

    (C) An issuer must reflect the determination of whether it came within the definition of smaller reporting company in its quarterly report on Form 10-Q for the first fiscal quarter of the next year, indicating on the cover page of that filing, and in subsequent filings for that fiscal year, whether it is a smaller reporting company, except that, if a determination based on public float indicates that the issuer is newly eligible to be a smaller reporting company, the issuer may choose to reflect this determination beginning with its first quarterly report on Form 10-Q following the determination, rather than waiting until the first fiscal quarter of the next year.

    (ii)   For determinations based on an initial registration statement under the Securities Act or Exchange Act for shares of its common equity:

    (A) Public float is measured as of a date within 30 days of the date of the filing of the registration statement and computed by multiplying the aggregate worldwide number of shares of its voting and non-voting common equity held by non-affiliates before the registration plus, in the case of a Securities Act registration statement, the number of shares of its voting and non-voting common equity included in the registration statement by the estimated public offering price of the shares;

    (B) Annual revenues are as of the most recently completed fiscal year for which audited financial statements are available; and

    (C) The issuer must reflect the determination of whether it came within the definition of smaller reporting company in the registration statement and must appropriately indicate on the cover page of the filing, and subsequent filings for the fiscal year in which the filing is made, whether it is a smaller reporting company. The issuer must re-determine its status at the end of its second fiscal quarter and then reflect any change in status as provided in paragraph (3)(i)(C) of this definition. In the case of a determination based on an initial Securities Act registration statement, an issuer that was not determined to be a smaller reporting company has the option to re-determine its status at the conclusion of the offering covered by the registration statement based on the actual offering price and number of shares sold.

    (iii) Once an issuer determines that it does not qualify for smaller reporting company status because it exceeded one or more of the current thresholds, it will remain unqualified unless when making its annual determination either:

    (A) It determines that its public float was less than $200 million; or

(B) It determines that its public float and its annual revenues meet the requirements for subsequent qualification included in the following chart:

Prior annual revenues	Prior public float	
	None or less than $700 million	$700 million or more
Less than $100 million	Neither threshold exceeded	Public float—Less than $560 million; and
		Revenues—Less than $100 million.
$100 million or more	Public float—None or less than $700 million; and	Public float—Less than $560 million; and
	Revenues—Less than $80 million	Revenues—Less than $80 million.

INSTRUCTION 1 TO DEFINITION OF "SMALLER REPORTING COMPANY": A registrant that qualifies as a smaller reporting company under the public float thresholds identified in paragraphs (1) and (3)(iii)(A) of this definition will qualify as a smaller reporting company regardless of its revenues.

INSTRUCTION 2 TO DEFINITION OF "SMALLER REPORTING COMPANY": A foreign private issuer is not eligible to use the requirements for smaller reporting companies unless it uses the forms and rules designated for domestic issuers and provides financial statements prepared in accordance with U.S. Generally Accepted Accounting Principles.

Subsidiary. A *subsidiary* of a specified person is an affiliate controlled by such person directly, or indirectly through one or more intermediaries. (*See also majority owned subsidiary, significant subsidiary, totally held subsidiary,* and *wholly owned subsidiary.*)

Succession. The term *succession* means the direct acquisition of the assets comprising a going business, whether by merger, consolidation, purchase, or other direct transfer. The term does not include the acquisition of control of a business unless followed by the direct acquisition of its assets. The terms *succeed* and *successor* have meanings correlative to the foregoing.

* * *

Voting securities. The term *voting securities* means securities the holders of which are presently entitled to vote for the election of directors.

* * *

§ 230.408   Additional Information.

(a) In addition to the information expressly required to be included in a registration statement, there shall be added such further material information, if any, as may be necessary to make the required statements, in the light of the circumstances under which they are made, not misleading.

(b) Notwithstanding paragraph (a) of this section, unless otherwise required to be included in the registration statement, the failure to include in a registration statement information included in a free writing prospectus will not, solely by virtue of inclusion of the information in a free writing prospectus (as defined in Rule 405 (§ 230.405)), be considered an omission of material information required to be included in the registration statement.

§ 230.415   Delayed or Continuous Offering and Sale of Securities.

(a) Securities may be registered for an offering to be made on a continuous or delayed basis in the future, *Provided,* That:

(1) The registration statement pertains only to:

(i) Securities which are to be offered or sold solely by or on behalf of a person or persons other than the registrant, a subsidiary of the registrant or a person of which the registrant is a subsidiary;

(ii) Securities which are to be offered and sold pursuant to a dividend or interest reinvestment plan or an employee benefit plan of the registrant;

(iii) Securities which are to be issued upon the exercise of outstanding options, warrants or rights;

(iv) Securities which are to be issued upon conversion of other outstanding securities;

(v) Securities which are pledged as collateral;

(vi) Securities which are registered on Form F-6 (§ 239.36 of this chapter);

(vii) Asset-backed securities (as defined in 17 CFR 229.1101(c)) registered (or qualified to be registered) on Form SF-3 (§ 239.45 of this chapter) which are to be offered and sold on an immediate or delayed basis by or on behalf of the registrant;

Instruction to paragraph (a)(1)(vii): The requirements of General Instruction I.B.1 of Form SF-3 (§ 239.45 of this chapter) must be met for any offerings of an asset-backed security (as defined in 17 CFR 229.1101(c)) registered in reliance on this paragraph (a)(1)(vii).

(viii) Securities which are to be issued in connection with business combination transactions;

(ix) Securities, other than asset-backed securities (as defined in 17 CFR 229.1101(c)), the offering of which will be commenced promptly, will be made on a continuous basis and may continue for a period in excess of 30 days from the date of initial effectiveness;

(x) Securities registered (or qualified to be registered) on Form S-3 or Form F-3 (§ 239.13 or § 239.33 of this chapter) which are to be offered and sold on an immediate, continuous or delayed basis by or on behalf of the registrant, a majority-owned subsidiary of the registrant or a person of which the registrant is a majority-owned subsidiary; or

(xi) Shares of common stock which are to be offered and sold on a delayed or continuous basis by or on behalf of a registered closed-end management investment company or business development company that makes periodic repurchase offers pursuant to § 270.23c–3 of this chapter.

(xii) Asset-backed securities (as defined in 17 CFR 229.1101(c)) that are to be offered and sold on a continuous basis if the offering is commenced promptly and being conducted on the condition that the consideration paid for such securities will be promptly refunded to the purchaser unless:

(A) All of the securities being offered are sold at a specified price within a specified time; and

(B) The total amount due to the seller is received by him by a specified date.

(2) Securities in paragraph (a)(1)(viii) of this section and securities in paragraph (a)(1)(ix) of this section that are not registered on Form S-3 or Form F-3 (§ 239.13 or § 239.33 of this chapter) may only be registered in an amount which, at the time the registration statement becomes effective, is reasonably expected to be offered and sold within two years from the initial effective date of the registration.

(3) The registrant furnishes the undertakings required by Item 512(a) of Regulation S–K (§ 229.512(a) of this chapter), except that a registrant that is an investment company filing on Form N-2 must furnish the undertakings required by Item 34.4 of Form N-2 (§ 239.14 and § 274.11a–1 of this chapter).

(4)   In the case of a registration statement pertaining to an at the market offering of equity securities by or on behalf of the registrant, the offering must come within paragraph (a)(1)(x) of this section. As used in this paragraph, the term "at the market offering" means an offering of equity securities into an existing trading market for outstanding shares of the same class at other than a fixed price.

(5)   Securities registered on an automatic shelf registration statement and securities described in paragraphs (a)(1)(vii), (ix), and (x) of this section may be offered and sold only if not more than three years have elapsed since the initial effective date of the registration statement under which they are being offered and sold, *provided, however,* that if a new registration statement has been filed pursuant to paragraph (a)(6) of this section:

(i)   If the new registration statement is an automatic shelf registration statement, it shall be immediately effective pursuant to Rule 462(e) (§ 230.462(e)); or

(ii)   If the new registration statement is not an automatic shelf registration statement:

(A)   Securities covered by the prior registration statement may continue to be offered and sold until the earlier of the effective date of the new registration statement or 180 days after the third anniversary of the initial effective date of the prior registration statement; and

(B)   A continuous offering of securities covered by the prior registration statement that commenced within three years of the initial effective date may continue until the effective date of the new registration statement if such offering is permitted under the new registration statement.

(6)   Prior to the end of the three-year period described in paragraph (a)(5) of this section, an issuer may file a new registration statement covering securities described in such paragraph (a)(5) of this section, which may, if permitted, be an automatic shelf registration statement. The new registration statement and prospectus included therein must include all the information that would be required at that time in a prospectus relating to all offering(s) that it covers. Prior to the effective date of the new registration statement (including at the time of filing in the case of an automatic shelf registration statement), the issuer may include on such new registration statement any unsold securities covered by the earlier registration statement by identifying on the bottom of the facing page of the new registration statement or latest amendment thereto the amount of such unsold securities being included and any filing fee paid in connection with such unsold securities, which will continue to be applied to such unsold securities. The offering of securities on the earlier registration statement will be deemed terminated as of the date of effectiveness of the new registration statement.

(b)   This section shall not apply to any registration statement pertaining to securities issued by a face-amount certificate company or redeemable securities issued by an open-end management company or unit investment trust under the Investment Company Act of 1940 or any registration statement filed by any foreign government or political subdivision thereof.

FORM AND CONTENT OF PROSPECTUSES

§ 230.421   Presentation of Information in Prospectuses.

(a)   The information required in a prospectus need not follow the order of the items or other requirements in the form. Such information shall not, however, be set forth in such fashion as to obscure any of the required information or any information necessary to keep the required information from being incomplete or misleading. Where an item requires information to be given in a prospectus in tabular form it shall be given in substantially the tabular form specified in the item.

(b)   You must present the information in a prospectus in a clear, concise and understandable manner. You must prepare the prospectus using the following standards:

(1) Present information in clear, concise sections, paragraphs, and sentences. Whenever possible, use short, explanatory sentences and bullet lists;

(2) Use descriptive headings and subheadings;

(3) Avoid frequent reliance on glossaries or defined terms as the primary means of explaining information in the prospectus. Define terms in a glossary or other section of the document only if the meaning is unclear from the context. Use a glossary only if it facilitates understanding of the disclosure; and

(4) Avoid legal and highly technical business terminology.

Note to § 230.421(b): In drafting the disclosure to comply with this section, you should avoid the following:

1. Legalistic or overly complex presentations that make the substance of the disclosure difficult to understand;

2. Vague "boilerplate" explanations that are imprecise and readily subject to different interpretations;

3. Complex information copied directly from legal documents without any clear and concise explanation of the provision(s); and

4. Disclosure repeated in different sections of the document that increases the size of the document but does not enhance the quality of the information.

(c) All information required to be included in a prospectus shall be clearly understandable without the necessity of referring to the particular form or to the general rules and regulations. Except as to financial statements and information required in a tabular form, the information set forth in a prospectus may be expressed in condensed or summarized form. In lieu of repeating information in the form of notes to financial statements, references may be made to other parts of the prospectus where such information is set forth.

(d)(1) To enhance the readability of the prospectus, you must use plain English principles in the organization, language, and design of the front and back cover pages, the summary, and the risk factors section.

(2) You must draft the language in these sections so that at a minimum it substantially complies with each of the following plain English writing principles:

(i) Short sentences;

(ii) Definite, concrete, everyday words;

(iii) Active voice;

(iv) Tabular presentation or bullet lists for complex material, whenever possible;

(v) No legal jargon or highly technical business terms; and

(vi) No multiple negatives.

(3) In designing these sections or other sections of the prospectus, you may include pictures, logos, charts, graphs, or other design elements so long as the design is not misleading and the required information is clear. You are encouraged to use tables, schedules, charts and graphic illustrations of the results of operations, balance sheet, or other financial data that present the data in an understandable manner. Any presentation must be consistent with the financial statements and non-financial information in the prospectus. You must draw the graphs and charts to scale. Any information you provide must not be misleading.

Instruction to § 230.421: You should read Securities Act Release No. 33–7497 (January 28, 1998) for information on plain English principles.

§ 230.430   Prospectus for Use Prior to Effective Date.

(a) A form of prospectus filed as a part of the registration statement shall be deemed to meet the requirements of section 10 of the Act for the purpose of section 5(b)(1) thereof prior to the effective date of the registration statement, provided such form of prospectus contains substantially the information required by the Act and the rules and regulations thereunder to be included in a prospectus meeting the requirements of section 10(a) of the Act for the securities being registered, or contains substantially that information except for the omission of information with respect to the offering price, underwriting discounts or commissions, discounts or commissions to dealers, amount of proceeds, conversion rates, call prices, or other matters dependent upon the offering price. Every such form of prospectus shall be deemed to have been filed as a part of the registration statement for the purpose of section 7 of the Act.

(b) A form of prospectus filed as part of a registration statement on Form N-1A (§ 239.15A and § 274.11A of this chapter), Form N-2 (§ 239.14 and § 274.11a–1 of this chapter), Form N-3 (§ 239.17a and § 274.11b of this chapter), Form N-4 (§ 239.17b and § 274.11c of this chapter), or Form N-6 (§ 239.17c and § 274.11d of this chapter) shall be deemed to meet the requirements of Section 10 of the Act (15 U.S.C. 77j) for the purpose of Section 5(b)(1) thereof (15 U.S.C. 77e(b)(1)) prior to the effective date of the registration statement, provided that:

(1) Such form of prospectus meets the requirements of paragraph (a) of this section; and

(2) Such registration statement contains a form of Statement of Additional Information that is made available to persons receiving such prospectus upon written or oral request, and without charge, unless the form of prospectus contains the information otherwise required to be disclosed in the form of Statement of Additional Information. Every such form of prospectus shall be deemed to have been filed as part of the registration statement for the purpose of section 7 of the Act.

§ 230.431   Summary Prospectuses.

(a) A summary prospectus prepared and filed (except a summary prospectus filed by an open-end management investment company registered under the Investment Company Act of 1940) as part of a registration statement in accordance with this section shall be deemed to be a prospectus permitted under section 10(b) of the Act (15 U.S.C. 77j(b)) for the purposes of section 5(b)(1) of the Act (15 U.S.C. 77e(b)(1)) if the form used for registration of the securities to be offered provides for the use of a summary prospectus and the following conditions are met:

(1)(i) The registrant is organized under the laws of the United States or any State or Territory or the District of Columbia and has its principal business operations in the United States or its territories; or

(ii) The registrant is a foreign private issuer eligible to use Form F-2 (§ 239.32 of this chapter);

(2) The registrant has a class of securities registered pursuant to section 12(b) of the Securities Exchange Act of 1934 or has a class of equity securities registered pursuant to section 12(g) of that Act or is required to file reports pursuant to section 15(d) of that Act;

(3) The registrant: (i) Has been subject to the requirements of section 12 or 15(d) of the Securities Exchange Act of 1934 and has filed all the material required to be filed pursuant to sections 13, 14 or 15(d) of that Act for a period of at least thirty-six calendar months immediately preceding the filing of the registration statement; and (ii) has filed in a timely manner all reports required to be filed during the twelve calendar months and any portion of a month immediately preceding the filing of the registration statement and, if the registrant has used (during the twelve calendar months and any portion of a month immediately preceding the filing of the registration statement) Rule 12b–25(b) under the Securities Exchange Act of 1934 (§ 240.12b–25

of this chapter) with respect to a report or portion of a report, that report or portion thereof has actually been filed within the time period prescribed by that Rule; and

(4)   Neither the registrant nor any of its consolidated or unconsolidated subsidiaries has, since the end of its last fiscal year for which certified financial statements of the registrant and its consolidated subsidiaries were included in a report filed pursuant to section 13(a) or 15(d) of the Securities Exchange Act of 1934: (i) failed to pay any dividend or sinking fund installment on preferred stock; or (ii) defaulted on any installment or installments on indebtedness for borrowed money, or on any rental on one or more long term leases, which defaults in the aggregate are material to the financial position of the registrant and its consolidated and unconsolidated subsidiaries, taken as a whole.

(b)   A summary prospectus shall contain the information specified in the instructions as to summary prospectuses in the form used for registration of the securities to be offered. Such prospectus may include any other information the substance of which is contained in the registration statement except as otherwise specifically provided in the instructions as to summary prospectuses in the form used for registration. It shall not include any information the substance of which is not contained in the registration statement except that a summary prospectus may contain any information specified in Rule 134(a) (§ 230.134(a)). No reference need be made to inapplicable terms and negative answers to any item of the form may be omitted.

(c)   All information included in a summary prospectus, other than the statement required by paragraph (e) of this section, may be expressed in such condensed or summarized form as may be appropriate in the light of the circumstances under which the prospectus is to be used. The information need not follow the numerical sequence of the items of the form used for registration. Every summary prospectus shall be dated approximately as of the date of its first use.

(d)   When used prior to the effective date of the registration statement, a summary prospectus shall be captioned a "Preliminary Summary Prospectus" and shall comply with the applicable requirements relating to a preliminary prospectus.

(e)   A statement to the following effect shall be prominently set forth in conspicuous print at the beginning or at the end of every summary prospectus:

"Copies of a more complete prospectus may be obtained from" (Insert name(s), address(es) and telephone number(s)).

Copies of a summary prospectus filed with the Commission pursuant to paragraph (g) of this section may omit the names of persons from whom the complete prospectus may be obtained.

(f)   Any summary prospectus published in a newspaper, magazine or other periodical need only be set in type at least as large as 7 point modern type. Nothing in this rule shall prevent the use of reprints of a summary prospectus published in a newspaper, magazine, or other periodical, if such reprints are clearly legible.

(g)   Eight copies of every proposed summary prospectus shall be filed as a part of the registration statement, or as an amendment thereto, at least 5 days (exclusive of Saturdays, Sundays and holidays) prior to the use thereof, or prior to the release for publication by any newspaper, magazine or other person, whichever is earlier. The Commission may, however, in its discretion, authorize such use or publication prior to the expiration of the 5-day period upon a written request for such authorization. Within 7 days after the first use or publication thereof, 5 additional copies shall be filed in the exact form in which it was used or published.

§ 230.432   Additional Information Required to Be Included in Prospectuses Relating to Tender Offers.

Notwithstanding the provisions of any form for the registration of securities under the Act, any prospectus relating to securities to be offered in connection with a tender offer for, or a request or invitation for tenders of, securities subject to either § 240.13e–4 or section 14(d) of the Securities

Exchange Act of 1934 (15 U.S.C. 78n(d)) must include the information required by § 240.13e–4(d)(1) or § 240.14d–6(d)(1) of this chapter, as applicable, in all tender offers, requests or invitations that are published, sent or given to security holders.

FILINGS; FEES; EFFECTIVE DATE

§ 230.460   Distribution of Preliminary Prospectus.

(a)   Pursuant to the statutory requirement that the Commission in ruling upon requests for acceleration of the effective date of a registration statement shall have due regard to the adequacy of the information respecting the issuer theretofore available to the public, the Commission may consider whether the persons making the offering have taken reasonable steps to make the information contained in the registration statement conveniently available to underwriters and dealers who it is reasonably anticipated will be invited to participate in the distribution of the security to be offered or sold.

(b)(1)   As a minimum, reasonable steps to make the information conveniently available would involve the distribution, to each underwriter and dealer who it is reasonably anticipated will be invited to participate in the distribution of the security, a reasonable time in advance of the anticipated effective date of the registration statement, of as many copies of the proposed form of preliminary prospectus permitted by Rule 430 (§ 230.430) as appears to be reasonable to secure adequate distribution of the preliminary prospectus.

(2)   In the case of a registration statement filed by a closed-end investment company on Form N-2 (§ 239.14 and § 274.11a–1 of this chapter), reasonable steps to make information conveniently available would involve distribution of a sufficient number of copies of the Statement of Additional Information required by § 230.430(b) as it appears to be reasonable to secure their adequate distribution either to each underwriter or dealer who it is reasonably anticipated will be invited to participate in the distribution of the security, or to the underwriter, dealer or other source named on the cover page of the preliminary prospectus as being the person investors should contact in order to obtain the Statement of Additional Information.

(c)   The granting of acceleration will not be conditioned upon

(1)   The distribution of a preliminary prospectus in any state where such distribution would be illegal; or

(2)   The distribution of a preliminary prospectus (i) in the case of a registration statement relating solely to securities to be offered at competitive bidding, provided the undertaking in Item 512(d)(1) of Regulation S–K (§ 229.512(d)(2) of this chapter) is included in the registration statement and distribution of prospectuses pursuant to such undertaking is made prior to the publication or distribution of the invitation for bids, or

(ii)   In the case of a registration statement relating to a security issued by a face-amount certificate company or a redeemable security issued by an open-end management company or unit investment trust if any other security of the same class is currently being offered or sold, pursuant to an effective registration statement by the issuer or by or through an underwriter, or

(iii)   In the case of an offering of subscription rights unless it is contemplated that the distribution will be made through dealers and the underwriters intend to make the offering during the stockholders' subscription period, in which case copies of the preliminary prospectus must be distributed to dealers prior to the effective date of the registration statement in the same fashion as is required in the case of other offerings through underwriters, or

(iv)   In the case of a registration statement pertaining to a security to be offered pursuant to an exchange offer or transaction described in Rule 145 (§ 230.145).

§ 230.461   Acceleration of Effective Date.

(a)   Requests for acceleration of the effective date of a registration statement shall be made by the registrant and the managing underwriters of the proposed issue, or, if there are no managing underwriters, by the principal underwriters of the proposed issue, and shall state the date upon which it is desired that the registration statement shall become effective. Such requests may be made in writing or orally, provided that, if an oral request is to be made, a letter indicating that fact and stating that the registrant and the managing or principal underwriters are aware of their obligations under the Act must accompany the registration statement for a pre-effective amendment (thereto) at the time of filing with the Commission. Written requests may be sent to the Commission by facsimile transmission. If, by reason of the expected arrangement in connection with the offering, it is to be requested that the registration statement shall become effective at a particular hour of the day, the Commission must be advised to that effect not later than the second business day before the day which it is desired that the registration statement shall become effective. A person's request for acceleration will be considered confirmation of such person's awareness of the person's obligations under the Act. Not later than the time of filing the last amendment prior to the effective date of the registration statement, the registrant shall inform the Commission as to whether or not the amount of compensation to be allowed or paid to the underwriters and any other arrangements among the registrant, the underwriters and other broker dealers participating in the distribution, as described in the registration statement, have been reviewed to the extent required by the National Association of Securities Dealers, Inc. and such Association has issued a statement expressing no objections to the compensation and other arrangements.

(b)   Having due regard to the adequacy of information respecting the registrant theretofore available to the public, to the facility with which the nature of the securities to be registered, their relationship to the capital structure of the registrant issuer and the rights of holders thereof can be understood, and to the public interest and the protection of investors, as provided in section 8(a) of the Act, it is the general policy of the Commission, upon request, as provided in paragraph (a) of this section, to permit acceleration of the effective date of the registration statement as soon as possible after the filing of appropriate amendments, if any. In determining the date on which a registration statement shall become effective, the following are included in the situations in which the Commission considers that the statutory standards of section 8(a) may not be met and may refuse to accelerate the effective date:

(1)   Where there has not been a bona fide effort to make the prospectus reasonably concise, readable, and in compliance with the plain English requirements of Rule 421(d) of Regulation C (17 CFR 230.421(d)) in order to facilitate an understanding of the information in the prospectus.

(2)   Where the form of preliminary prospectus, which has been distributed by the issuer or underwriter, is found to be inaccurate or inadequate in any material respect, until the Commission has received satisfactory assurance that appropriate correcting material has been sent to all underwriters and dealers who received such preliminary prospectus or prospectuses in quantity sufficient for their information and the information of others to whom the inaccurate or inadequate material was sent.

(3)   Where the Commission is currently making an investigation of the issuer, a person controlling the issuer, or one of the underwriters, if any, of the securities to be offered, pursuant to any of the Acts administered by the Commission.

(4)   Where one or more of the underwriters, although firmly committed to purchase securities covered by the registration statement, is subject to and does not meet the financial responsibility requirements of Rule 15c3–1 under the Securities Exchange Act of 1934 (§ 240.15c3–1 of this chapter). For the purposes of this paragraph underwriters will be deemed to be firmly committed even though the obligation to purchase is subject to the usual conditions as to receipt of opinions of counsel, accountants, etc., the accuracy of warranties or representations, the happening of calamities or the occurrence of other events the determination of which is not expressed to be in the sole or absolute discretion of the underwriters.

(5)   Where there have been transactions in securities of the registrant by persons connected with or proposed to be connected with the offering which may have artificially affected or may artificially affect the market price of the security being offered.

(6)   Where the amount of compensation to be allowed or paid to the underwriters and any other arrangements among the registrant, the underwriters and other broker dealers participating in the distribution, as described in the registration statement, if required to be reviewed by the National Association of Securities Dealers, Inc. (NASD), have been reviewed by the NASD and the NASD has not issued a statement expressing no objections to the compensation and other arrangements.

(7)   Where, in the case of a significant secondary offering at the market, the registrant, selling security holders and underwriters have not taken sufficient measures to insure compliance with Regulation M (§§ 242.100 through 242.105 of this chapter).

(c)   Insurance against liabilities arising under the Act, whether the cost of insurance is borne by the registrant, the insured or some other person, will not be considered a bar to acceleration, unless the registrant is a registered investment company or a business development company and the cost of such insurance is borne by other than an insured officer or director of the registrant. In the case of such a registrant, the Commission may refuse to accelerate the effective date of the registration statement when the registrant is organized or administered pursuant to any instrument (including a contract for insurance against liabilities arising under the Act) that protects or purports to protect any director or officer of the company against any liability to the company or its security holders to which he or she would otherwise be subject by reason of willful misfeasance, bad faith, gross negligence or reckless disregard of the duties involved in the conduct of his or her office.

AMENDMENTS; WITHDRAWALS

§ 230.473   Delaying Amendments.

(a)   An amendment in the following form filed with a registration statement, or as an amendment to a registration statement which has not become effective, shall be deemed, for the purpose of section 8(a) of the Act, to be filed on such date or dates as may be necessary to delay the effective date of such registration statement (1) until the registrant shall file a further amendment which specifically states as provided in paragraph (b) of this section that such registration statement shall thereafter become effective in accordance with section 8(a) of the Act, or (2) until the registration statement shall become effective on such date as the Commission, acting pursuant to section 8(a), may determine:

The registrant hereby amends this registration statement on such date or dates as may be necessary to delay its effective date until the registrant shall file a further amendment which specifically states that this registration statement shall thereafter become effective in accordance with section 8(a) of the Securities Act of 1933 or until the registration statement shall become effective on such date as the Commission acting pursuant to said section 8(a), may determine.

(b)   An amendment which for the purpose of paragraph (a)(1) of this section specifically states that a registration statement shall thereafter become effective in accordance with section 8(a) of the Act, shall be in the following form:

This registration statement shall hereafter become effective in accordance with the provisions of section 8(a) of the Securities Act of 1933.

(c)   An amendment pursuant to paragraph (a) of this section which is filed with a registration statement shall be set forth on the facing page thereof following the calculation of the registration fee. Any such amendment filed after the filing of the registration statement, any amendment altering the proposed date of public sale of the securities being registered, or any amendment filed pursuant to paragraph (b) of this section may be made by telegram, letter or facsimile transmission. Each such telegraphic amendment shall be confirmed in writing within a reasonable time by the filing of a signed copy of the amendment. Such confirmation shall not be deemed an amendment.

(d)   No amendments pursuant to paragraph (a) of this section may be filed with a registration statement on Form F-7, F-8 or F-80 (§ 239.37, § 239.38 or § 239.41 of this chapter); on Form F-9 or F-10 (§ 239.39 or § 239.40 of this chapter) relating to an offering being made contemporaneously in the United States and the issuer's home jurisdiction; on Form S-8 (§ 239.16b of this chapter); on Form S-3 or F-3 (§ 239.13 or § 239.33 of this chapter) relating to a dividend or interest reinvestment plan; on Form S-3 or Form F-3 relating to an automatic shelf registration statement; or on Form S-4 (§ 239.25 of this chapter) complying with General Instruction G of that Form.

REGULATION D—RULES GOVERNING THE LIMITED OFFER AND SALE OF SECURITIES WITHOUT REGISTRATION UNDER THE SECURITIES ACT OF 1933

§ 230.500   Use of Regulation D.

Users of Regulation D (§§ 230.500 *et seq.*) should note the following:

(a)   Regulation D relates to transactions exempted from the registration requirements of section 5 of the Securities Act of 1933 (the Act) (15 U.S.C.77a *et seq.,* as amended). Such transactions are not exempt from the antifraud, civil liability, or other provisions of the federal securities laws. Issuers are reminded of their obligation to provide such further material information, if any, as may be necessary to make the information required under Regulation D, in light of the circumstances under which it is furnished, not misleading.

(b)   Nothing in Regulation D obviates the need to comply with any applicable state law relating to the offer and sale of securities. Regulation D is intended to be a basic element in a uniform system of federal-state limited offering exemptions consistent with the provisions of sections 18 and 19(c) of the Act (15 U.S.C. 77r and 77(s)(c)). In those states that have adopted Regulation D, or any version of Regulation D, special attention should be directed to the applicable state laws and regulations, including those relating to registration of persons who receive remuneration in connection with the offer and sale of securities, to disqualification of issuers and other persons associated with offerings based on state administrative orders or judgments, and to requirements for filings of notices of sales.

(c)   Attempted compliance with any rule in Regulation D does not act as an exclusive election; the issuer can also claim the availability of any other applicable exemption. For instance, an issuer's failure to satisfy all the terms and conditions of rule 506(b) (§ 230.506(b)) shall not raise any presumption that the exemption provided by section 4(a)(2) of the Act (15 U.S.C. 77d(2)) is not available.

(d)   Regulation D is available only to the issuer of the securities and not to any affiliate of that issuer or to any other person for resales of the issuer's securities. Regulation D provides an exemption only for the transactions in which the securities are offered or sold by the issuer, not for the securities themselves.

(e)   Regulation D may be used for business combinations that involve sales by virtue of rule 145(a) (§ 230.145(a)) or otherwise.

(f)   In view of the objectives of Regulation D and the policies underlying the Act, Regulation D is not available to any issuer for any transaction or chain of transactions that, although in technical compliance with Regulation D, is part of a plan or scheme to evade the registration provisions of the Act. In such cases, registration under the Act is required.

(g)   Securities offered and sold outside the United States in accordance with Regulation S (§ 230.901 through 905) need not be registered under the Act. *See* Release No. 33–6863. Regulation S may be relied upon for such offers and sales even if coincident offers and sales are made in accordance with Regulation D inside the United States. Thus, for example, persons who are offered and sold securities in accordance with Regulation S would not be counted in the calculation of the number of purchasers under Regulation D. Similarly, proceeds from such sales would not be included in the aggregate offering price. The provisions of this paragraph (g), however, do not apply if the issuer elects to rely solely on Regulation D for offers or sales to persons made outside the United States.

§ 230.501   Definitions and Terms Used in Regulation D.

As used in Regulation D (§ 230.500 *et seq.* of this chapter), the following terms shall have the meaning indicated:

(a) *Accredited investor. Accredited investor* shall mean any person who comes within any of the following categories, or who the issuer reasonably believes comes within any of the following categories, at the time of the sale of the securities to that person:

(1)   Any bank as defined in section 3(a)(2) of the Act, or any savings and loan association or other institution as defined in section 3(a)(5)(A) of the Act whether acting in its individual or fiduciary capacity; any broker or dealer registered pursuant to section 15 of the Securities Exchange Act of 1934; any insurance company as defined in section 2(a)(13) of the Act; any investment company registered under the Investment Company Act of 1940 or a business development company as defined in section 2(a)(48) of that Act; any Small Business Investment Company licensed by the U.S. Small Business Administration under section 301(c) or (d) of the Small Business Investment Act of 1958; any plan established and maintained by a state, its political subdivisions, or any agency or instrumentality of a state or its political subdivisions, for the benefit of its employees, if such plan has total assets in excess of $5,000,000; any employee benefit plan within the meaning of the Employee Retirement Income Security Act of 1974 if the investment decision is made by a plan fiduciary, as defined in section 3(21) of such act, which is either a bank, savings and loan association, insurance company, or registered investment adviser, or if the employee benefit plan has total assets in excess of $5,000,000 or, if a self-directed plan, with investment decisions made solely by persons that are accredited investors;

(2)   Any private business development company as defined in section 202(a)(22) of the Investment Advisers Act of 1940;

(3)   Any organization described in section 501(c)(3) of the Internal Revenue Code, corporation, Massachusetts or similar business trust, or partnership, not formed for the specific purpose of acquiring the securities offered, with total assets in excess of $5,000,000;

(4)   Any director, executive officer, or general partner of the issuer of the securities being offered or sold, or any director, executive officer, or general partner of a general partner of that issuer;

(5)   Any natural person whose individual net worth, or joint net worth with that person's spouse, exceeds $1,000,000.

(i)   Except as provided in paragraph (a)(5)(ii) of this section, for purposes of calculating net worth under this paragraph (a)(5):

(A)   The person's primary residence shall not be included as an asset;

(B)   Indebtedness that is secured by the person's primary residence, up to the estimated fair market value of the primary residence at the time of the sale of securities, shall not be included as a liability (except that if the amount of such indebtedness outstanding at the time of sale of securities exceeds the amount outstanding 60 days before such time, other than as a result of the acquisition of the primary residence, the amount of such excess shall be included as a liability); and

(C)   Indebtedness that is secured by the person's primary residence in excess of the estimated fair market value of the primary residence at the time of the sale of securities shall be included as a liability;

(ii) Paragraph (a)(5)(i) of this section will not apply to any calculation of a person's net worth made in connection with a purchase of securities in accordance with a right to purchase such securities, provided that:

(A) Such right was held by the person on July 20, 2010;

(B) The person qualified as an accredited investor on the basis of net worth at the time the person acquired such right; and

(C) The person held securities of the same issuer, other than such right, on July 20, 2010.

(6) Any natural person who had an individual income in excess of $200,000 in each of the two most recent years or joint income with that person's spouse in excess of $300,000 in each of those years and has a reasonable expectation of reaching the same income level in the current year;

(7) Any trust, with total assets in excess of $5,000,000, not formed for the specific purpose of acquiring the securities offered, whose purchase is directed by a sophisticated person as described in § 230.506(b)(2)(ii); and

(8) Any entity in which all of the equity owners are accredited investors.

(b) *Affiliate*. An *affiliate* of, or person *affiliated* with, a specified person shall mean a person that directly, or indirectly through one or more intermediaries, controls or is controlled by, or is under common control with, the person specified.

(c) *Aggregate offering price*. *Aggregate offering price* shall mean the sum of all cash, services, property, notes, cancellation of debt, or other consideration to be received by an issuer for issuance of its securities. Where securities are being offered for both cash and non-cash consideration, the aggregate offering price shall be based on the price at which the securities are offered for cash. Any portion of the aggregate offering price attributable to cash received in a foreign currency shall be translated into United States currency at the currency exchange rate in effect at a reasonable time prior to or on the date of the sale of the securities. If securities are not offered for cash, the aggregate offering price shall be based on the value of the consideration as established by bona fide sales of that consideration made within a reasonable time, or, in the absence of sales, on the fair value as determined by an accepted standard. Such valuations of non-cash consideration must be reasonable at the time made.

(d) *Business combination*. *Business combination* shall mean any transaction of the type specified in paragraph (a) of Rule 145 under the Act (17 CFR 230.145) and any transaction involving the acquisition by one issuer, in exchange for all or a part of its own or its parent's stock, of stock of another issuer if, immediately after the acquisition, the acquiring issuer has control of the other issuer (whether or not it had control before the acquisition).

(e) *Calculation of number of purchasers*. For purposes of calculating the number of purchasers under § 230.506(b) only, the following shall apply:

(1) The following purchasers shall be excluded:

(i) Any relative, spouse or relative of the spouse of a purchaser who has the same primary residence as the purchaser;

(ii) Any trust or estate in which a purchaser and any of the persons related to him as specified in paragraph (e)(1)(i) or (e)(1)(iii) of this section collectively have more than 50 percent of the beneficial interest (excluding contingent interests);

(iii) Any corporation or other organization of which a purchaser and any of the persons related to him as specified in paragraph (e)(1)(i) or (e)(1)(ii) of this section collectively are beneficial owners of more than 50 percent of the equity securities (excluding directors' qualifying shares) or equity interests; and

(iv) Any accredited investor.

(2) A corporation, partnership or other entity shall be counted as one purchaser. If, however, that entity is organized for the specific purpose of acquiring the securities offered and is not an accredited investor under paragraph (a)(8) of this section, then each beneficial owner of equity securities or equity interests in the entity shall count as a separate purchaser for all provisions of Regulation D (§§ 230.501–230.508), except to the extent provided in paragraph (e)(1) of this section.

(3) A non-contributory employee benefit plan within the meaning of Title I of the Employee Retirement Income Security Act of 1974 shall be counted as one purchaser where the trustee makes all investment decisions for the plan.

Note: The issuer must satisfy all the other provisions of Regulation D for all purchasers whether or not they are included in calculating the number of purchasers. Clients of an investment adviser or customers of a broker or dealer shall be considered the "purchasers" under Regulation D regardless of the amount of discretion given to the investment adviser or broker or dealer to act on behalf of the client or customer.

(f) *Executive officer. Executive officer* shall mean the president, any vice president in charge of a principal business unit, division or function (such as sales, administration or finance), any other officer who performs a policy making function, or any other person who performs similar policy making functions for the issuer. Executive officers of subsidiaries may be deemed executive officers of the issuer if they perform such policy making functions for the issuer.

(g) *Final order.* Final order shall mean a written directive or declaratory statement issued by a federal or state agency described in § 230.506(d)(1)(iii) under applicable statutory authority that provides for notice and an opportunity for hearing, which constitutes a final disposition or action by that federal or state agency.

(h) *Issuer.* The definition of the term issuer in section 2(a)(4) of the Act shall apply, except that in the case of a proceeding under the Federal Bankruptcy Code (11 U.S.C. 101 *et seq.*), the trustee or debtor in possession shall be considered the issuer in an offering under a plan or reorganization, if the securities are to be issued under the plan.

(i) *Purchaser representative. Purchaser representative* shall mean any person who satisfies all of the following conditions or who the issuer reasonably believes satisfies all of the following conditions:

(1) Is not an affiliate, director, officer or other employee of the issuer, or beneficial owner of 10 percent or more of any class of the equity securities or 10 percent or more of the equity interest in the issuer, except where the purchaser is:

(i) A relative of the purchaser representative by blood, marriage or adoption and not more remote than a first cousin;

(ii) A trust or estate in which the purchaser representative and any persons related to him as specified in paragraph (i)(1)(i) or (i)(1)(iii)* of this section collectively have more than 50 percent of the beneficial interest (excluding contingent interest) or of which the purchaser representative serves as trustee, executor, or in any similar capacity; or

(iii) A corporation or other organization of which the purchaser representative and any persons related to him as specified in paragraph (i)(1)(i) or (i)(1)(ii)** of this section collectively are the beneficial owners of more than 50 percent of the equity securities (excluding directors' qualifying shares) or equity interests;

---

 * The text of the rule cites to (h)(1)(i) and (h)(1)(iii), but that is presumably an error.
 ** The text of the rule cites to (h)(1)(i) and (h)(1)(ii), but that is presumably an error.

(2)   Has such knowledge and experience in financial and business matters that he is capable of evaluating, alone, or together with other purchaser representatives of the purchaser, or together with the purchaser, the merits and risks of the prospective investment;

(3)   Is acknowledged by the purchaser in writing, during the course of the transaction, to be his purchaser representative in connection with evaluating the merits and risks of the prospective investment; and

(4)   Discloses to the purchaser in writing a reasonable time prior to the sale of securities to that purchaser any material relationship between himself or his affiliates and the issuer or its affiliates that then exists, that is mutually understood to be contemplated, or that has existed at any time during the previous two years, and any compensation received or to be received as a result of such relationship.

Note 1 to 230.501: A person acting as a purchaser representative should consider the applicability of the registration and antifraud provisions relating to brokers and dealers under the Securities Exchange Act of 1934 (*Exchange Act*) (15 U.S.C. 78a *et seq.*, as amended) and relating to investment advisers under the Investment Advisers Act of 1940.

Note 2 to 230.501: The acknowledgment required by paragraph (h)(3) and the disclosure required by paragraph (h)(4) of this section must be made with specific reference to each prospective investment. Advance blanket acknowledgment, such as for *all securities transactions* or *all private placements*, is not sufficient.

Note 3 to 230.501: Disclosure of any material relationships between the purchaser representative or his affiliates and the issuer or its affiliates does not relieve the purchaser representative of his obligation to act in the interest of the purchaser.

§ 230.502   General Conditions to Be Met.

The following conditions shall be applicable to offers and sales made under Regulation D (§ 230.500 *et seq.* of this chapter):

(a)   *Integration.* All sales that are part of the same Regulation D offering must meet all of the terms and conditions of Regulation D. Offers and sales that are made more than six months before the start of a Regulation D offering or are made more than six months after completion of a Regulation D offering will not be considered part of that Regulation D offering, so long as during those six month periods there are no offers or sales of securities by or for the issuer that are of the same or a similar class as those offered or sold under Regulation D, other than those offers or sales of securities under an employee benefit plan as defined in rule 405 under the Act (17 CFR 230.405).

Note: The term *offering* is not defined in the Act or in Regulation D. If the issuer offers or sells securities for which the safe harbor rule in paragraph (a) of this § 230.502 is unavailable, the determination as to whether separate sales of securities are part of the same offering (*i.e.*, are considered *integrated*) depends on the particular facts and circumstances. Generally, transactions otherwise meeting the requirements of an exemption will not be integrated with simultaneous offerings being made outside the United States in compliance with Regulation S. *See* Release No. 33–6863.

The following factors should be considered in determining whether offers and sales should be integrated for purposes of the exemptions under Regulation D:

(a)   Whether the sales are part of a single plan of financing;

(b)   Whether the sales involve issuance of the same class of securities;

(c)   Whether the sales have been made at or about the same time;

(d)   Whether the same type of consideration is being received; and

(e)   Whether the sales are made for the same general purpose.

See Release 33–4552 (November 6, 1962) [27 FR 11316].

(b) *Information requirements—*(1) *When information must be furnished.* If the issuer sells securities under § 230.506(b) to any purchaser that is not an accredited investor, the issuer shall furnish the information specified in paragraph (b)(2) of this section to such purchaser a reasonable time prior to sale. The issuer is not required to furnish the specified information to purchasers when it sells securities under § 230.504, or to any accredited investor.

Note: When an issuer provides information to investors pursuant to paragraph (b)(1), it should consider providing such information to accredited investors as well, in view of the anti-fraud provisions of the federal securities laws.

(2) *Type of information to be furnished.* (i) If the issuer is not subject to the reporting requirements of section 13 or 15(d) of the Exchange Act, at a reasonable time prior to the sale of securities the issuer shall furnish to the purchaser, to the extent material to an understanding of the issuer, its business and the securities being offered:

(A) *Non-financial statement information.* If the issuer is eligible to use Regulation A (§ 230.251–263), the same kind of information as would be required in Part II of Form 1-A (§ 239.90 of this chapter). If the issuer is not eligible to use Regulation A, the same kind of information as required in Part I of a registration statement filed under the Securities Act on the form that the issuer would be entitled to use.

(B) *Financial statement information—*(1) *Offerings up to $2,000,000.* The information required in Article 8 of Regulation S–X (§ 210.8 of this chapter), except that only the issuer's balance sheet, which shall be dated within 120 days of the start of the offering, must be audited.

(2) *Offerings up to $7,500,000.* The financial statement information required in Form S-1 (§ 239.10 of this chapter) for smaller reporting companies. If an issuer, other than a limited partnership, cannot obtain audited financial statements without unreasonable effort or expense, then only the issuer's balance sheet, which shall be dated within 120 days of the start of the offering, must be audited. If the issuer is a limited partnership and cannot obtain the required financial statements without unreasonable effort or expense, it may furnish financial statements that have been prepared on the basis of Federal income tax requirements and examined and reported on in accordance with generally accepted auditing standards by an independent public or certified accountant.

(3) *Offerings over $7,500,000.* The financial statement as would be required in a registration statement filed under the Act on the form that the issuer would be entitled to use. If an issuer, other than a limited partnership, cannot obtain audited financial statements without unreasonable effort or expense, then only the issuer's balance sheet, which shall be dated within 120 days of the start of the offering, must be audited. If the issuer is a limited partnership and cannot obtain the required financial statements without unreasonable effort or expense, it may furnish financial statements that have been prepared on the basis of Federal income tax requirements and examined and reported on in accordance with generally accepted auditing standards by an independent public or certified accountant.

(C) If the issuer is a foreign private issuer eligible to use Form 20-F (§ 249.220f of this chapter), the issuer shall disclose the same kind of information required to be included in a registration statement filed under the Act on the form that the issuer would be entitled to use. The financial statements need be certified only to the extent required by paragraph (b)(2)(i) (B) (*1*), (*2*) or (*3*) of this section, as appropriate.

(ii)   If the issuer is subject to the reporting requirements of section 13 or 15(d) of the Exchange Act, at a reasonable time prior to the sale of securities the issuer shall furnish to the purchaser the information specified in paragraph (b)(2)(ii)(A) or (B) of this section, and in either event the information specified in paragraph (b)(2)(ii)(C) of this section:

(A)   The issuer's annual report to shareholders for the most recent fiscal year, if such annual report meets the requirements of Rules 14a–3 or 14c–3 under the Exchange Act (§ 240.14a–3 or § 240.14c–3 of this chapter), the definitive proxy statement filed in connection with that annual report, and if requested by the purchaser in writing, a copy of the issuer's most recent Form 10-K (§ 249.310 of this chapter) under the Exchange Act.

(B)   The information contained in an annual report on Form 10-K (§ 249.310 of this chapter) under the Exchange Act or in a registration statement on Form S-1 (§ 239.11 of this chapter) or S-11 (§ 239.18 of this chapter) under the Act or on Form 10 (§ 249.210 of this chapter) under the Exchange Act, whichever filing is the most recent required to be filed.

(C)   The information contained in any reports or documents required to be filed by the issuer under sections 13(a), 14(a), 14(c), and 15(d) of the Exchange Act since the distribution or filing of the report or registration statement specified in paragraphs (b)(2)(ii) (A) or (B), and a brief description of the securities being offered, the use of the proceeds from the offering, and any material changes in the issuer's affairs that are not disclosed in the documents furnished.

(D)   If the issuer is a foreign private issuer, the issuer may provide in lieu of the information specified in paragraph (b)(2)(ii) (A) or (B) of this section, the information contained in its most recent filing on Form 20-F or Form F-1 (§ 239.31 of the chapter).

(iii)   Exhibits required to be filed with the Commission as part of a registration statement or report, other than an annual report to shareholders or parts of that report incorporated by reference in a Form 10-K report, need not be furnished to each purchaser that is not an accredited investor if the contents of material exhibits are identified and such exhibits are made available to a purchaser, upon his or her written request, a reasonable time before his or her purchase.

(iv)   At a reasonable time prior to the sale of securities to any purchaser that is not an accredited investor in a transaction under § 230.506(b), the issuer shall furnish to the purchaser a brief description in writing of any material written information concerning the offering that has been provided by the issuer to any accredited investor but not previously delivered to such unaccredited purchaser. The issuer shall furnish any portion or all of this information to the purchaser, upon his written request a reasonable time prior to his purchase.

(v)   The issuer shall also make available to each purchaser at a reasonable time prior to his purchase of securities in a transaction under § 230.506(b) the opportunity to ask questions and receive answers concerning the terms and conditions of the offering and to obtain any additional information which the issuer possesses or can acquire without unreasonable effort or expense that is necessary to verify the accuracy of information furnished under paragraph (b)(2)(i) or (ii) of this section.

(vi)   For business combinations or exchange offers, in addition to information required by Form S-4 (17 CFR 239.25), the issuer shall provide to each purchaser at the time the plan is submitted to security holders, or, with an exchange, during the course of the transaction and prior to sale, written information about any terms or arrangements of the proposed transactions that are materially different from those for all other security holders. For purposes of this subsection, an issuer which is not subject to the reporting requirements of section 13 or 15(d) of the Exchange Act may satisfy the requirements of Part I.B. or C. of Form S-4 by compliance with paragraph (b)(2)(i) of this § 230.502.

(vii) At a reasonable time prior to the sale of securities to any purchaser that is not an accredited investor in a transaction under § 230.506(b), the issuer shall advise the purchaser of the limitations on resale in the manner contained in paragraph (d)(2) of this section. Such disclosure may be contained in other materials required to be provided by this paragraph.

(c) *Limitation on manner of offering.* Except as provided in § 230.504(b)(1) or § 230.506(c), neither the issuer nor any person acting on its behalf shall offer or sell the securities by any form of general solicitation or general advertising, including, but not limited to, the following:

(1) Any advertisement, article, notice or other communication published in any newspaper, magazine, or similar media or broadcast over television or radio; and

(2) Any seminar or meeting whose attendees have been invited by any general solicitation or general advertising; *Provided, however,* that publication by an issuer of a notice in accordance with § 230.135c or filing with the Commission by an issuer of a notice of sales on Form D (17 CFR 239.500) in which the issuer has made a good faith and reasonable attempt to comply with the requirements of such form, shall not be deemed to constitute general solicitation or general advertising for purposes of this section; *Provided further,* that, if the requirements of § 230.135e are satisfied, providing any journalist with access to press conferences held outside of the United States, to meetings with issuer or selling security holder representatives conducted outside of the United States, or to written press-related materials released outside the United States, at or in which a present or proposed offering of securities is discussed, will not be deemed to constitute general solicitation or general advertising for purposes of this section.

(d) *Limitations on resale.* Except as provided in § 230.504(b)(1), securities acquired in a transaction under Regulation D shall have the status of securities acquired in a transaction under section 4(a)(2) of the Act and cannot be resold without registration under the Act or an exemption therefrom. The issuer shall exercise reasonable care to assure that the purchasers of the securities are not underwriters within the meaning of section 2(a)(11) of the Act, which reasonable care may be demonstrated by the following:

(1) Reasonable inquiry to determine if the purchaser is acquiring the securities for himself or for other persons;

(2) Written disclosure to each purchaser prior to sale that the securities have not been registered under the Act and, therefore, cannot be resold unless they are registered under the Act or unless an exemption from registration is available; and

(3) Placement of a legend on the certificate or other document that evidences the securities stating that the securities have not been registered under the Act and setting forth or referring to the restrictions on transferability and sale of the securities.

While taking these actions will establish the requisite reasonable care, it is not the exclusive method to demonstrate such care. Other actions by the issuer may satisfy this provision. In addition, § 230.502(b)(2)(vii) requires the delivery of written disclosure of the limitations on resale to investors in certain instances.

§ 230.503   Filing of Notice of Sales.

(a) *When notice of sales on Form D is required and permitted to be filed.* (1) An issuer offering or selling securities in reliance on § 230.504 or § 230.506 must file with the Commission a notice of sales containing the information required by Form D (17 CFR 239.500) for each new offering of securities no later than 15 calendar days after the first sale of securities in the offering, unless the end of that period falls on a Saturday, Sunday or holiday, in which case the due date would be the first business day following.

(2)   An issuer may file an amendment to a previously filed notice of sales on Form D at any time.

(3)   An issuer must file an amendment to a previously filed notice of sales on Form D for an offering:

(i)   To correct a material mistake of fact or error in the previously filed notice of sales on Form D, as soon as practicable after discovery of the mistake or error;

(ii)   To reflect a change in the information provided in the previously filed notice of sales on Form D, as soon as practicable after the change, except that no amendment is required to reflect a change that occurs after the offering terminates or a change that occurs solely in the following information:

(A)   The address or relationship to the issuer of a related person identified in response to Item 3 of the notice of sales on Form D;

(B)   An issuer's revenues or aggregate net asset value;

(C)   The minimum investment amount, if the change is an increase, or if the change, together with all other changes in that amount since the previously filed notice of sales on Form D, does not result in a decrease of more than 10%;

(D)   Any address or state(s) of solicitation shown in response to Item 12 of the notice of sales on Form D;

(E)   The total offering amount, if the change is a decrease, or if the change, together with all other changes in that amount since the previously filed notice of sales on Form D, does not result in an increase of more than 10%;

(F)   The amount of securities sold in the offering or the amount remaining to be sold;

(G)   The number of non-accredited investors who have invested in the offering, as long as the change does not increase the number to more than 35;

(H)   The total number of investors who have invested in the offering; or

(I)   The amount of sales commissions, finders' fees or use of proceeds for payments to executive officers, directors or promoters, if the change is a decrease, or if the change, together with all other changes in that amount since the previously filed notice of sales on Form D, does not result in an increase of more than 10%; and

(iii)   Annually, on or before the first anniversary of the filing of the notice of sales on Form D or the filing of the most recent amendment to the notice of sales on Form D, if the offering is continuing at that time.

(4)   An issuer that files an amendment to a previously filed notice of sales on Form D must provide current information in response to all requirements of the notice of sales on Form D regardless of why the amendment is filed.

(b)   *How notice of sales on Form D must be filed and signed.* (1) A notice of sales on Form D must be filed with the Commission in electronic format by means of the Commission's Electronic Data Gathering, Analysis, and Retrieval System (EDGAR) in accordance with EDGAR rules set forth in Regulation S–T (17 CFR Part 232).

(2)   Every notice of sales on Form D must be signed by a person duly authorized by the issuer.

§ 230.504   Exemption for Limited Offerings and Sales of Securities Not Exceeding $5,000,000.

(a) *Exemption.* Offers and sales of securities that satisfy the conditions in paragraph (b) of this § 230.504 by an issuer that is not:

(1) Subject to the reporting requirements of section 13 or 15(d) of the Exchange Act,;

(2) An investment company; or

(3) A development stage company that either has no specific business plan or purpose or has indicated that its business plan is to engage in a merger or acquisition with an unidentified company or companies, or other entity or person, shall be exempt from the provision of section 5 of the Act under section 3(b) of the Act.

(b) *Conditions to be met—*(1) *General conditions.* To qualify for exemption under this § 230.504, offers and sales must satisfy the terms and conditions of §§ 230.501 and 230.502 (a), (c) and (d), except that the provisions of § 230.502 (c) and (d) will not apply to offers and sales of securities under this § 230.504 that are made:

(i) Exclusively in one or more states that provide for the registration of the securities, and require the public filing and delivery to investors of a substantive disclosure document before sale, and are made in accordance with those state provisions;

(ii) In one or more states that have no provision for the registration of the securities or the public filing or delivery of a disclosure document before sale, if the securities have been registered in at least one state that provides for such registration, public filing and delivery before sale, offers and sales are made in that state in accordance with such provisions, and the disclosure document is delivered before sale to all purchasers (including those in the states that have no such procedure); or

(iii) Exclusively according to state law exemptions from registration that permit general solicitation and general advertising so long as sales are made only to "accredited investors" as defined in § 230.501(a).

(2) The aggregate offering price for an offering of securities under this § 230.504, as defined in § 230.501(c), shall not exceed $5,000,000, less the aggregate offering price for all securities sold within the twelve months before the start of and during the offering of securities under this § 230.504, in violation of section 5(a) of the Securities Act.

Instruction to paragraph (b)(2): If a transaction under § 230.504 fails to meet the limitation on the aggregate offering price, it does not affect the availability of this § 230.504 for the other transactions considered in applying such limitation. For example, if an issuer sold $5,000,000 of its securities on January 1, 2014 under this § 230.504 and an additional $500,000 of its securities on July 1, 2014, this § 230.504 would not be available for the later sale, but would still be applicable to the January 1, 2014 sale.

(3) *Disqualifications.* No exemption under this section shall be available for the securities of any issuer if such issuer would be subject to disqualification under § 230.506(d) on or after January 20, 2017; provided that disclosure of prior "bad actor" events shall be required in accordance with § 230.506(e).

Instruction to paragraph (b)(3): For purposes of disclosure of prior "bad actor" events pursuant to § 230.506(e), an issuer shall furnish to each purchaser, a reasonable time prior to sale, a description in writing of any matters that would have triggered disqualification under this paragraph (b)(3) but occurred before January 20, 2017.

§ 230.506   Exemption for Limited Offers and Sales Without Regard to Dollar Amount of Offering.

(a) *Exemption.* Offers and sales of securities by an issuer that satisfy the conditions in paragraph (b) or (c) of this section shall be deemed to be transactions not involving any public offering within the meaning of section 4(a)(2) of the Act.

(b) *Conditions to be met in offerings subject to limitation on manner of offering*—(1) *General conditions.* To qualify for an exemption under this section, offers and sales must satisfy all the terms and conditions of §§ 230.501 and 230.502.

(2) *Specific conditions*—(i) *Limitation on number of purchasers.* There are no more than or the issuer reasonably believes that there are no more than 35 purchasers of securities from the issuer in any offering under paragraph (b) of this section.

Note to paragraph (b)(2)(i): See § 230.501(e) for the calculation of the number of purchasers and § 230.502(a) for what may or may not constitute an offering under paragraph (b) of this section.

(ii) *Nature of purchasers.* Each purchaser who is not an accredited investor either alone or with his purchaser representative(s) has such knowledge and experience in financial and business matters that he is capable of evaluating the merits and risks of the prospective investment, or the issuer reasonably believes immediately prior to making any sale that such purchaser comes within this description.

(c) *Conditions to be met in offerings not subject to limitation on manner of offering*—(1) *General conditions.* To qualify for exemption under this section, sales must satisfy all the terms and conditions of §§ 230.501 and 230.502(a) and (d).

(2) *Specific conditions*—(i) *Nature of purchasers.* All purchasers of securities sold in any offering under paragraph (c) of this section are accredited investors.

(ii) *Verification of accredited investor status.* The issuer shall take reasonable steps to verify that purchasers of securities sold in any offering under paragraph (c) of this section are accredited investors. The issuer shall be deemed to take reasonable steps to verify if the issuer uses, at its option, one of the following non-exclusive and non-mandatory methods of verifying that a natural person who purchases securities in such offering is an accredited investor; provided, however, that the issuer does not have knowledge that such person is not an accredited investor:

(A) In regard to whether the purchaser is an accredited investor on the basis of income, reviewing any Internal Revenue Service form that reports the purchaser's income for the two most recent years (including, but not limited to, Form W-2, Form 1099, Schedule K-1 to Form 1065, and Form 1040) and obtaining a written representation from the purchaser that he or she has a reasonable expectation of reaching the income level necessary to qualify as an accredited investor during the current year;

(B) In regard to whether the purchaser is an accredited investor on the basis of net worth, reviewing one or more of the following types of documentation dated within the prior three months and obtaining a written representation from the purchaser that all liabilities necessary to make a determination of net worth have been disclosed:

(1) With respect to assets: Bank statements, brokerage statements and other statements of securities holdings, certificates of deposit, tax assessments, and appraisal reports issued by independent third parties; and

(2) With respect to liabilities: A consumer report from at least one of the nationwide consumer reporting agencies; or

(C)   Obtaining a written confirmation from one of the following persons or entities that such person or entity has taken reasonable steps to verify that the purchaser is an accredited investor within the prior three months and has determined that such purchaser is an accredited investor:

   (1)   A registered broker-dealer;

   (2)   An investment adviser registered with the Securities and Exchange Commission;

   (3)   A licensed attorney who is in good standing under the laws of the jurisdictions in which he or she is admitted to practice law; or

   (4)   A certified public accountant who is duly registered and in good standing under the laws of the place of his or her residence or principal office.

(D)   In regard to any person who purchased securities in an issuer's Rule 506(b) offering as an accredited investor prior to September 23, 2013 and continues to hold such securities, for the same issuer's Rule 506(c) offering, obtaining a certification by such person at the time of sale that he or she qualifies as an accredited investor.

Instructions to paragraph (c)(2)(ii)(A) through (D) of this section:

1.   The issuer is not required to use any of these methods in verifying the accredited investor status of natural persons who are purchasers. These methods are examples of the types of non-exclusive and non-mandatory methods that satisfy the verification requirement in § 230.506(c)(2)(ii).

2.   In the case of a person who qualifies as an accredited investor based on joint income with that person's spouse, the issuer would be deemed to satisfy the verification requirement in § 230.506(c)(2)(ii)(A) by reviewing copies of Internal Revenue Service forms that report income for the two most recent years in regard to, and obtaining written representations from, both the person and the spouse.

3.   In the case of a person who qualifies as an accredited investor based on joint net worth with that person's spouse, the issuer would be deemed to satisfy the verification requirement in § 230.506(c)(2)(ii)(B) by reviewing such documentation in regard to, and obtaining written representations from, both the person and the spouse.

(d)   *"Bad Actor" disqualification.* (1) No exemption under this section shall be available for a sale of securities if the issuer; any predecessor of the issuer; any affiliated issuer; any director, executive officer, other officer participating in the offering, general partner or managing member of the issuer; any beneficial owner of 20% or more of the issuer's outstanding voting equity securities, calculated on the basis of voting power; any promoter connected with the issuer in any capacity at the time of such sale; any investment manager of an issuer that is a pooled investment fund; any person that has been or will be paid (directly or indirectly) remuneration for solicitation of purchasers in connection with such sale of securities; any general partner or managing member of any such investment manager or solicitor; or any director, executive officer or other officer participating in the offering of any such investment manager or solicitor or general partner or managing member of such investment manager or solicitor:

   (i)   Has been convicted, within ten years before such sale (or five years, in the case of issuers, their predecessors and affiliated issuers), of any felony or misdemeanor:

   (A)   In connection with the purchase or sale of any security;

   (B)   Involving the making of any false filing with the Commission; or

   (C)   Arising out of the conduct of the business of an underwriter, broker, dealer, municipal securities dealer, investment adviser or paid solicitor of purchasers of securities;

(ii) Is subject to any order, judgment or decree of any court of competent jurisdiction, entered within five years before such sale, that, at the time of such sale, restrains or enjoins such person from engaging or continuing to engage in any conduct or practice:

(A) In connection with the purchase or sale of any security;

(B) Involving the making of any false filing with the Commission; or

(C) Arising out of the conduct of the business of an underwriter, broker, dealer, municipal securities dealer, investment adviser or paid solicitor of purchasers of securities;

(iii) Is subject to a final order of a state securities commission (or an agency or officer of a state performing like functions); a state authority that supervises or examines banks, savings associations, or credit unions; a state insurance commission (or an agency or officer of a state performing like functions); an appropriate federal banking agency; the U.S. Commodity Futures Trading Commission; or the National Credit Union Administration that:

(A) At the time of such sale, bars the person from:

(1) Association with an entity regulated by such commission, authority, agency, or officer;

(2) Engaging in the business of securities, insurance or banking; or

(3) Engaging in savings association or credit union activities; or

(B) Constitutes a final order based on a violation of any law or regulation that prohibits fraudulent, manipulative, or deceptive conduct entered within ten years before such sale;

(iv) Is subject to an order of the Commission entered pursuant to section 15(b) or 15B(c) of the Securities Exchange Act of 1934 (15 U.S.C. 78*o*(b) or 78*o*–4(c)) or section 203(e) or (f) of the Investment Advisers Act of 1940 (15 U.S.C. 80b–3(e) or (f)) that, at the time of such sale:

(A) Suspends or revokes such person's registration as a broker, dealer, municipal securities dealer or investment adviser;

(B) Places limitations on the activities, functions or operations of such person; or

(C) Bars such person from being associated with any entity or from participating in the offering of any penny stock;

(v) Is subject to any order of the Commission entered within five years before such sale that, at the time of such sale, orders the person to cease and desist from committing or causing a violation or future violation of:

(A) Any scienter-based anti-fraud provision of the federal securities laws, including without limitation section 17(a)(1) of the Securities Act of 1933 (15 U.S.C. 77q(a)(1)), section 10(b) of the Securities Exchange Act of 1934 (15 U.S.C. 78j(b)) and 17 CFR 240.10b–5, section 15(c)(1) of the Securities Exchange Act of 1934 (15 U.S.C. 78*o*(c)(1)) and section 206(1) of the Investment Advisers Act of 1940 (15 U.S.C. 80b–6(1)), or any other rule or regulation thereunder; or

(B) Section 5 of the Securities Act of 1933 (15 U.S.C. 77e).

(vi) Is suspended or expelled from membership in, or suspended or barred from association with a member of, a registered national securities exchange or a registered national or affiliated securities association for any act or omission to act constituting conduct inconsistent with just and equitable principles of trade;

(vii) Has filed (as a registrant or issuer), or was or was named as an underwriter in, any registration statement or Regulation A offering statement filed with the Commission that, within five years before such sale, was the subject of a refusal order, stop order, or order suspending the

Regulation A exemption, or is, at the time of such sale, the subject of an investigation or proceeding to determine whether a stop order or suspension order should be issued; or

(viii) Is subject to a United States Postal Service false representation order entered within five years before such sale, or is, at the time of such sale, subject to a temporary restraining order or preliminary injunction with respect to conduct alleged by the United States Postal Service to constitute a scheme or device for obtaining money or property through the mail by means of false representations.

(2)   Paragraph (d)(1) of this section shall not apply:

(i)   With respect to any conviction, order, judgment, decree, suspension, expulsion or bar that occurred or was issued before September 23, 2013;

(ii)   Upon a showing of good cause and without prejudice to any other action by the Commission, if the Commission determines that it is not necessary under the circumstances that an exemption be denied;

(iii)   If, before the relevant sale, the court or regulatory authority that entered the relevant order, judgment or decree advises in writing (whether contained in the relevant judgment, order or decree or separately to the Commission or its staff) that disqualification under paragraph (d)(1) of this section should not arise as a consequence of such order, judgment or decree; or

(iv)   If the issuer establishes that it did not know and, in the exercise of reasonable care, could not have known that a disqualification existed under paragraph (d)(1) of this section.

Instruction to paragraph (d)(2)(iv). An issuer will not be able to establish that it has exercised reasonable care unless it has made, in light of the circumstances, factual inquiry into whether any disqualifications exist. The nature and scope of the factual inquiry will vary based on the facts and circumstances concerning, among other things, the issuer and the other offering participants.

(3)   For purposes of paragraph (d)(1) of this section, events relating to any affiliated issuer that occurred before the affiliation arose will be not considered disqualifying if the affiliated entity is not:

(i)   In control of the issuer; or

(ii)   Under common control with the issuer by a third party that was in control of the affiliated entity at the time of such events.

(e)   *Disclosure of prior "bad actor" events.* The issuer shall furnish to each purchaser, a reasonable time prior to sale, a description in writing of any matters that would have triggered disqualification under paragraph (d)(1) of this section but occurred before September 23, 2013. The failure to furnish such information timely shall not prevent an issuer from relying on this section if the issuer establishes that it did not know and, in the exercise of reasonable care, could not have known of the existence of the undisclosed matter or matters.

Instruction to paragraph (e). An issuer will not be able to establish that it has exercised reasonable care unless it has made, in light of the circumstances, factual inquiry into whether any disqualifications exist. The nature and scope of the factual inquiry will vary based on the facts and circumstances concerning, among other things, the issuer and the other offering participants.

§ 230.507   Disqualifying Provision Relating to Exemptions Under §§ 230.504 and 230.506.

(a)   No exemption under § 230.504 or § 230.506 shall be available for an issuer if such issuer, any of its predecessors or affiliates have been subject to any order, judgment, or decree of any court of competent jurisdiction temporarily, preliminary or permanently enjoining such person for failure to comply with § 230.503.

(b)   Paragraph (a) of this section shall not apply if the Commission determines, upon a showing of good cause, that it is not necessary under the circumstances that the exemption be denied.

§ 230.508   Insignificant Deviations From a Term, Condition or Requirement of Regulation D.

(a)   A failure to comply with a term, condition or requirement of § 230.504 or § 230.506 will not result in the loss of the exemption from the requirements of section 5 of the Act for any offer or sale to a particular individual or entity, if the person relying on the exemption shows:

(1)   The failure to comply did not pertain to a term, condition or requirement directly intended to protect that particular individual or entity; and

(2)   The failure to comply was insignificant with respect to the offering as a whole, provided that any failure to comply with paragraph (c) of § 230.502, paragraph (b)(2) of § 230.504 and paragraph (b)(2)(i) of § 230.506 shall be deemed to be significant to the offering as a whole; and

(3)   A good faith and reasonable attempt was made to comply with all applicable terms, conditions and requirements of § 230.504 or § 230.506.

(b)   A transaction made in reliance on § 230.504 or § 230.506 shall comply with all applicable terms, conditions and requirements of Regulation D. Where an exemption is established only through reliance upon paragraph (a) of this section, the failure to comply shall nonetheless be actionable by the Commission under section 20 of the Act.

D. RULES UNDER THE SECURITIES EXCHANGE ACT OF 1934

(Selected)

17 C.F.R. §§ 240.0–1 *et seq.*

---

*Table of Contents**

---

* Although this table of contents lists rule numbers, the rules themselves are printed with their CFR sections (§ 240.[rule number]). For example, Rule 3b–2 is § 240.3b–2.

1934 ACT RULES

REPURCHASES BY ISSUERS

REPORTS BY INSTITUTIONAL MANAGERS

SOLICITATION OF PROXIES

TENDER OFFERS

RULES RELATING TO OVER-THE-COUNTER MARKETS

REPORTS OF DIRECTORS, OFFICERS, AND PRINCIPAL SHAREHOLDERS

EXEMPTION OF CERTAIN TRANSACTIONS FROM SECTION 16(b)

DEFINITIONS

§ 240.3b–2. Definition of "Officer"

The term officer means a president, vice president, secretary, treasury or principal financial officer, comptroller or principal accounting officer, and any person routinely performing corresponding functions with respect to any organization whether incorporated or unincorporated.

MANIPULATIVE AND DECEPTIVE DEVICES AND CONTRIVANCES

§ 240.10b–5. Employment of Manipulative and Deceptive Devices

It shall be unlawful for any person, directly or indirectly, by the use of any means or instrumentality of interstate commerce, or of the mails or of any facility of any national securities exchange,

(a) To employ any device, scheme, or artifice to defraud,

(b) To make any untrue statement of a material fact or to omit to state a material fact necessary in order to make the statements made, in the light of the circumstances under which they were made, not misleading, or

(c) To engage in any act, practice, or course of business which operates or would operate as a fraud or deceit upon any person,

in connection with the purchase or sale of any security.

§ 240.10b5–1.   Trading "On the Basis of" Material Nonpublic Information in Insider Trading Cases

Preliminary Note to § 240.10b5–1

This provision defines when a purchase or sale constitutes trading "on the basis of" material nonpublic information in insider trading cases brought under Section 10(b) of the Act and Rule 10b–5 thereunder. The law of insider trading is otherwise defined by judicial opinions construing Rule 10b–5, and Rule 10b5–1 does not modify the scope of insider trading law in any other respect.

(a)   General. The "manipulative and deceptive devices" prohibited by Section 10(b) of the Act (15 U.S.C. 78j) and § 240.10b–5 thereunder include, among other things, the purchase or sale of a security of any issuer, on the basis of material nonpublic information about that security or issuer, in breach of a duty of trust or confidence that is owed directly, indirectly, or derivatively, to the issuer of that security or the shareholders of that issuer, or to any other person who is the source of the material nonpublic information.

(b)   Definition of "on the basis of." Subject to the affirmative defenses in paragraph (c) of this section, a purchase or sale of a security of an issuer is "on the basis of" material nonpublic information about that security or issuer if the person making the purchase or sale was aware of the material nonpublic information when the person made the purchase or sale.

(c)   Affirmative defenses. (1)(i) Subject to paragraph (c)(1)(ii) of this section, a person's purchase or sale is not "on the basis of" material nonpublic information if the person making the purchase or sale demonstrates that:

(A)   Before becoming aware of the information, the person had:

(1)   Entered into a binding contract to purchase or sell the security,

(2)   Instructed another person to purchase or sell the security for the instructing person's account, or

(3)   Adopted a written plan for trading securities;

(B)   The contract, instruction, or plan described in paragraph (c)(1)(i)(A) of this Section:

(1)   Specified the amount of securities to be purchased or sold and the price at which and the date on which the securities were to be purchased or sold;

(2)   Included a written formula or algorithm, or computer program, for determining the amount of securities to be purchased or sold and the price at which and the date on which the securities were to be purchased or sold; or

(3)   Did not permit the person to exercise any subsequent influence over how, when, or whether to effect purchases or sales; provided, in addition, that any other person who, pursuant to the contract, instruction, or plan, did exercise such influence must not have been aware of the material nonpublic information when doing so; and

(C)   The purchase or sale that occurred was pursuant to the contract, instruction, or plan. A purchase or sale is not "pursuant to a contract, instruction, or plan" if, among other things, the person who entered into the contract, instruction, or plan altered or deviated from the contract, instruction, or plan to purchase or sell securities (whether by changing the amount, price, or timing of the purchase or sale), or entered into or altered a corresponding or hedging transaction or position with respect to those securities.

(ii)   Paragraph (c)(1)(i) of this section is applicable only when the contract, instruction, or plan to purchase or sell securities was given or entered into in good faith and not as part of a plan or scheme to evade the prohibitions of this section.

(iii)   This paragraph (c)(1)(iii) defines certain terms as used in paragraph (c) of this Section.

(A) Amount. "Amount" means either a specified number of shares or other securities or a specified dollar value of securities.

(B) Price. "Price" means the market price on a particular date or a limit price, or a particular dollar price.

(C) Date. "Date" means, in the case of a market order, the specific day of the year on which the order is to be executed (or as soon thereafter as is practicable under ordinary principles of best execution). "Date" means, in the case of a limit order, a day of the year on which the limit order is in force.

(2) A person other than a natural person also may demonstrate that a purchase or sale of securities is not "on the basis of" material nonpublic information if the person demonstrates that:

(i) The individual making the investment decision on behalf of the person to purchase or sell the securities was not aware of the information; and

(ii) The person had implemented reasonable policies and procedures, taking into consideration the nature of the person's business, to ensure that individuals making investment decisions would not violate the laws prohibiting trading on the basis of material nonpublic information. These policies and procedures may include those that restrict any purchase, sale, and causing any purchase or sale of any security as to which the person has material nonpublic information, or those that prevent such individuals from becoming aware of such information.

§ 240.10b5–2. Duties of Trust or Confidence in Misappropriation Insider Trading Cases

Preliminary Note to § 240.10b5–2

This section provides a non-exclusive definition of circumstances in which a person has a duty of trust or confidence for purposes of the "misappropriation" theory of insider trading under Section 10(b) of the Act and Rule 10b–5. The law of insider trading is otherwise defined by judicial opinions construing Rule 10b–5, and Rule 10b5–2 does not modify the scope of insider trading law in any other respect.

(a) Scope of Rule. This section shall apply to any violation of Section 10(b) of the Act (15 U.S.C. 78j(b)) and § 240.10b–5 thereunder that is based on the purchase or sale of securities on the basis of, or the communication of, material nonpublic information misappropriated in breach of a duty of trust or confidence.

(b) Enumerated "duties of trust or confidence." For purposes of this section, a "duty of trust or confidence" exists in the following circumstances, among others:

(1) Whenever a person agrees to maintain information in confidence;

(2) Whenever the person communicating the material nonpublic information and the person to whom it is communicated have a history, pattern, or practice of sharing confidences, such that the recipient of the information knows or reasonably should know that the person communicating the material nonpublic information expects that the recipient will maintain its confidentiality; or

(3) Whenever a person receives or obtains material nonpublic information from his or her spouse, parent, child, or sibling; provided, however, that the person receiving or obtaining the information may demonstrate that no duty of trust or confidence existed with respect to the information, by establishing that he or she neither knew nor reasonably should have known that the person who was the source of the information expected that the person would keep the information confidential, because of the parties' history, pattern, or practice of sharing and maintaining confidences, and because there was no agreement or understanding to maintain the confidentiality of the information.

* * *

§ 240.10b–18.   Purchases of Certain Equity Securities by the Issuer and Others

Preliminary Notes to § 240.10b–18

1.   Section 240.10b–18 provides an issuer (and its affiliated purchasers) with a "safe harbor" from liability for manipulation under sections 9(a)(2) of the Act and § 240.10b–5 under the Act solely by reason of the manner, timing, price, and volume of their repurchases when they repurchase the issuer's common stock in the market in accordance with the section's manner, timing, price, and volume conditions. As a safe harbor, compliance with § 240.10b–18 is voluntary. To come within the safe harbor, however, an issuer's repurchases must satisfy (on a daily basis) each of the section's four conditions. Failure to meet any one of the four conditions will remove all of the issuer's repurchases from the safe harbor for that day. The safe harbor, moreover, is not available for repurchases that, although made in technical compliance with the section, are part of a plan or scheme to evade the federal securities laws.

2.   Regardless of whether the repurchases are effected in accordance with § 240.10b–18, reporting issuers must report their repurchasing activity as required by Item 703 of Regulations S–K and S–B (17 CFR 229.703 and 228.703) and Item 15(e) of Form 20-F (17 CFR 249.220f) (regarding foreign private issuers), and closed-end management investment companies that are registered under the Investment Company Act of 1940 must report their repurchasing activity as required by Item 8 of Form N-CSR (17 CFR 249.331; 17 CFR 274.128).

(a)   Definitions. Unless otherwise provided, all terms used in this section shall have the same meaning as in the Act. In addition, the following definitions shall apply:

(1)   ADTV means the average daily trading volume reported for the security during the four calendar weeks preceding the week in which the Rule 10b–18 purchase is to be effected.

(2)   Affiliate means any person that directly or indirectly controls, is controlled by, or is under common control with, the issuer.

(3)   Affiliated purchaser means:

(i)   A person acting, directly or indirectly, in concert with the issuer for the purpose of acquiring the issuer's securities; or

(ii)   An affiliate who, directly or indirectly, controls the issuer's purchases of such securities, whose purchases are controlled by the issuer, or whose purchases are under common control with those of the issuer; Provided, however, that "affiliated purchaser" shall not include a broker, dealer, or other person solely by reason of such broker, dealer, or other person effecting Rule 10b–18 purchases on behalf of the issuer or for its account, and shall not include an officer or director of the issuer solely by reason of that officer or director's participation in the decision to authorize Rule 10b–18 purchases by or on behalf of the issuer.

(4)   Agent independent of the issuer has the meaning contained in § 242.100 of this chapter.

(5)   Block means a quantity of stock that either:

(i)   Has a purchase price of $200,000 or more; or

(ii)   Is at least 5,000 shares and has a purchase price of at least $50,000; or

(iii)   Is at least 20 round lots of the security and totals 150 percent or more of the trading volume for that security or, in the event that trading volume data are unavailable, is at least 20 round lots of the security and totals at least one-tenth of one percent (.001) of the outstanding shares of the security, exclusive of any shares owned by any affiliate; Provided, however, That a block under paragraph (a)(5)(i), (ii), and (iii) shall not include any amount a broker or dealer, acting as principal, has accumulated for the purpose of sale or resale to the issuer or to any affiliated purchaser of the issuer if the issuer or such affiliated purchaser knows or has reason to know that such amount was accumulated for such purpose, nor shall it include any amount that a broker or dealer has sold short to the issuer or to any affiliated purchaser of the issuer if the issuer or such affiliated purchaser knows or has reason to know that the sale was a short sale.

(6) *Consolidated system* means a consolidated transaction or quotation reporting system that collects and publicly disseminates on a current and continuous basis transaction or quotation information in common equity securities pursuant to an effective transaction reporting plan or an effective national market system plan (as those terms are defined in § 242.600 of this chapter).

(7) *Market-wide trading suspension* means a market-wide trading halt of 30 minutes or more that is:

(i) Imposed pursuant to the rules of a national securities exchange or a national securities association in response to a market-wide decline during a single trading session; or

(ii) Declared by the Commission pursuant to its authority under section 12(k) of the Act (15 U.S.C. 78 l (k)).

(8) *Plan* has the meaning contained in § 242.100 of this chapter.

(9) *Principal market* for a security means the single securities market with the largest reported trading volume for the security during the six full calendar months preceding the week in which the Rule 10b–18 purchase is to be effected.

(10) *Public float value* has the meaning contained in § 242.100 of this chapter.

(11) *Purchase price* means the price paid per share as reported, exclusive of any commission paid to a broker acting as agent, or commission equivalent, mark-up, or differential paid to a dealer.

(12) *Riskless principal transaction* means a transaction in which a broker or dealer after having received an order from an issuer to buy its security, buys the security as principal in the market at the same price to satisfy the issuer's buy order. The issuer's buy order must be effected at the same price per-share at which the broker or dealer bought the shares to satisfy the issuer's buy order, exclusive of any explicitly disclosed markup or markdown, commission equivalent, or other fee. In addition, only the first leg of the transaction, when the broker or dealer buys the security in the market as principal, is reported under the rules of a self-regulatory organization or under the Act. For purposes of this section, the broker or dealer must have written policies and procedures in place to assure that, at a minimum, the issuer's buy order was received prior to the offsetting transaction; the offsetting transaction is allocated to a riskless principal account or the issuer's account within 60 seconds of the execution; and the broker or dealer has supervisory systems in place to produce records that enable the broker or dealer to accurately and readily reconstruct, in a time-sequenced manner, all orders effected on a riskless principal basis.

(13) *Rule 10b–18 purchase* means a purchase (or any bid or limit order that would effect such purchase) of an issuer's common stock (or an equivalent interest, including a unit of beneficial interest in a trust or limited partnership or a depository share) by or for the issuer or any affiliated purchaser (including riskless principal transactions). However, it does not include any purchase of such security:

(i) Effected during the applicable restricted period of a distribution that is subject to § 242.102 of this chapter;

(ii) Effected by or for an issuer plan by an agent independent of the issuer;

(iii) Effected as a fractional share purchase (a fractional interest in a security) evidenced by a script certificate, order form, or similar document;

(iv) Effected during the period from the time of public announcement (as defined in § 230.165(f)) of a merger, acquisition, or similar transaction involving a recapitalization, until the earlier of the completion of such transaction or the completion of the vote by target shareholders. This exclusion does not apply to Rule 10b–18 purchases:

(A)   Effected during such transaction in which the consideration is solely cash and there is no valuation period; or

(B)   Where:

(1)   The total volume of Rule 10b–18 purchases effected on any single day does not exceed the lesser of 25% of the security's four-week ADTV or the issuer's average daily Rule 10b–18 purchases during the three full calendar months preceding the date of the announcement of such transaction;

(2)   The issuer's block purchases effected pursuant to paragraph (b)(4) of this section do not exceed the average size and frequency of the issuer's block purchases effected pursuant to paragraph (b)(4) of this section during the three full calendar months preceding the date of the announcement of such transaction; and

(3)   Such purchases are not otherwise restricted or prohibited;

(v)   Effected pursuant to § 240.13e–1;

(vi)   Effected pursuant to a tender offer that is subject to § 240.13e–4 or specifically excepted from § 240.13e–4; or

(vii)   Effected pursuant to a tender offer that is subject to section 14(d) of the Act (15 U.S.C. 78n(d)) and the rules and regulations thereunder.

(b)   Conditions to be met. Rule 10b–18 purchases shall not be deemed to have violated the anti-manipulation provisions of sections 9(a)(2) or 10(b) of the Act (15 U.S.C. 78i(a)(2) or 78j(b)), or § 240.10b–5 under the Act, solely by reason of the time, price, or amount of the Rule 10b–18 purchases, or the number of brokers or dealers used in connection with such purchases, if the issuer or affiliated purchaser of the issuer effects the Rule 10b–18 purchases according to each of the following conditions:

(1)   One broker or dealer. Rule 10b–18 purchases must be effected from or through only one broker or dealer on any single day; Provided, however, that:

(i)   The "one broker or dealer" condition shall not apply to Rule 10b–18 purchases that are not solicited by or on behalf of the issuer or its affiliated purchaser(s);

(ii)   Where Rule 10b–18 purchases are effected by or on behalf of more than one affiliated purchaser of the issuer (or the issuer and one or more of its affiliated purchasers) on a single day, the issuer and all affiliated purchasers must use the same broker or dealer; and

(iii)   Where Rule 10b–18 purchases are effected on behalf of the issuer by a broker-dealer that is not an electronic communication network (ECN) or other alternative trading system (ATS), that broker-dealer can access ECN or other ATS liquidity in order to execute repurchases on behalf of the issuer (or any affiliated purchaser of the issuer) on that day.

(2)   Time of purchases. Rule 10b–18 purchases must not be:

(i)   The opening (regular way) purchase reported in the consolidated system;

(ii)   Effected during the 10 minutes before the scheduled close of the primary trading session in the principal market for the security, and the 10 minutes before the scheduled close of the primary trading session in the market where the purchase is effected, for a security that has an ADTV value of $1 million or more and a public float value of $150 million or more; and

(iii)   Effected during the 30 minutes before the scheduled close of the primary trading session in the principal market for the security, and the 30 minutes before the scheduled close of the primary trading session in the market where the purchase is effected, for all other securities;

(iv) However, for purposes of this section, Rule 10b–18 purchases may be effected following the close of the primary trading session until the termination of the period in which last sale prices are reported in the consolidated system so long as such purchases are effected at prices that do not exceed the lower of the closing price of the primary trading session in the principal market for the security and any lower bids or sale prices subsequently reported in the consolidated system, and all of this section's conditions are met. However, for purposes of this section, the issuer may use one broker or dealer to effect Rule 10b–18 purchases during this period that may be different from the broker or dealer that it used during the primary trading session. However, the issuer's Rule 10b–18 purchase may not be the opening transaction of the session following the close of the primary trading session.

(3) Price of purchases. Rule 10b–18 purchases must be effected at a purchase price that:

(i) Does not exceed the highest independent bid or the last independent transaction price, whichever is higher, quoted or reported in the consolidated system at the time the Rule 10b–18 purchase is effected;

(ii) For securities for which bids and transaction prices are not quoted or reported in the consolidated system, Rule 10b–18 purchases must be effected at a purchase price that does not exceed the highest independent bid or the last independent transaction price, whichever is higher, displayed and disseminated on any national securities exchange or on any inter-dealer quotation system (as defined in § 240.15c2–11) that displays at least two priced quotations for the security, at the time the Rule 10b–18 purchase is effected; and

(iii) For all other securities, Rule 10b–18 purchases must be effected at a price no higher than the highest independent bid obtained from three independent dealers.

(4) Volume of purchases. The total volume of Rule 10b–18 purchases effected by or for the issuer and any affiliated purchasers effected on any single day must not exceed 25 percent of the ADTV for that security; However, once each week, in lieu of purchasing under the 25 percent of ADTV limit for that day, the issuer or an affiliated purchaser of the issuer may effect one block purchase if:

(i) No other Rule 10b–18 purchases are effected that day, and

(ii) The block purchase is not included when calculating a security's four week ADTV under this section.

(c) Alternative conditions. The conditions of paragraph (b) of this section shall apply in connection with Rule 10b–18 purchases effected during a trading session following the imposition of a market-wide trading suspension, except:

(1) That the time of purchases condition in paragraph (b)(2) of this section shall not apply, either:

(i) From the reopening of trading until the scheduled close of trading on the day that the market-wide trading suspension is imposed; or

(ii) At the opening of trading on the next trading day until the scheduled close of trading that day, if a market-wide trading suspension was in effect at the close of trading on the preceding day; and

(2) The volume of purchases condition in paragraph (b)(4) of this section is modified so that the amount of Rule 10b–18 purchases must not exceed 100 percent of the ADTV for that security.

(d) Other purchases. No presumption shall arise that an issuer or an affiliated purchaser has violated the anti-manipulation provisions of sections 9(a)(2) or 10(b) of the Act (15 U.S.C. 78i(a)(2) or

78j(b)), or § 240.10b–5 under the Act, if the Rule 10b–18 purchases of such issuer or affiliated purchaser do not meet the conditions specified in paragraph (b) or (c) of this section.

* * *

REPORTS UNDER SECTION 10A

§ 240.10A–2.   Auditor Independence

It shall be unlawful for an auditor not to be independent under § 210.2–01(c)(2)(iii)(B), (c)(4), (c)(6), (c)(7), and § 210.2–07.

* * *

§ 240.10A–3.   Listing Standards Relating to Audit Committees

(a)   Pursuant to section 10A(m) of the Act (15 U.S.C. 78j–1(m)) and section 3 of the Sarbanes-Oxley Act of 2002 (15 U.S.C. 7202):

(1)   National securities exchanges. The rules of each national securities exchange registered pursuant to section 6 of the Act (15 U.S.C. 78f) must, in accordance with the provisions of this section, prohibit the initial or continued listing of any security of an issuer that is not in compliance with the requirements of any portion of paragraph (b) or (c) of this section.

(2)   National securities associations. The rules of each national securities association registered pursuant to section 15A of the Act (15 U.S.C. 78o–3) must, in accordance with the provisions of this section, prohibit the initial or continued listing in an automated inter-dealer quotation system of any security of an issuer that is not in compliance with the requirements of any portion of paragraph (b) or (c) of this section.

(3)   Opportunity to cure defects. The rules required by paragraphs (a)(1) and (a)(2) of this section must provide for appropriate procedures for a listed issuer to have an opportunity to cure any defects that would be the basis for a prohibition under paragraph (a) of this section, before the imposition of such prohibition. Such rules also may provide that if a member of an audit committee ceases to be independent in accordance with the requirements of this section for reasons outside the member's reasonable control, that person, with notice by the issuer to the applicable national securities exchange or national securities association, may remain an audit committee member of the listed issuer until the earlier of the next annual shareholders meeting of the listed issuer or one year from the occurrence of the event that caused the member to be no longer independent.

(4)   Notification of noncompliance. The rules required by paragraphs (a)(1) and (a)(2) of this section must include a requirement that a listed issuer must notify the applicable national securities exchange or national securities association promptly after an executive officer of the listed issuer becomes aware of any material noncompliance by the listed issuer with the requirements of this section.

(5)   Implementation. (i) The rules of each national securities exchange or national securities association meeting the requirements of this section must be operative, and listed issuers must be in compliance with those rules, by the following dates:

(A)   July 31, 2005 for foreign private issuers and smaller reporting companies (as defined in § 240.12b–2); and

(B)   For all other listed issuers, the earlier of the listed issuer's first annual shareholders meeting after January 15, 2004, or October 31, 2004.

(ii)   Each national securities exchange and national securities association must provide to the Commission, no later than July 15, 2003, proposed rules or rule amendments that comply with this section.

(iii) Each national securities exchange and national securities association must have final rules or rule amendments that comply with this section approved by the Commission no later than December 1, 2003.

(b) Required standards. (1) Independence. (i) Each member of the audit committee must be a member of the board of directors of the listed issuer, and must otherwise be independent; provided that, where a listed issuer is one of two dual holding companies, those companies may designate one audit committee for both companies so long as each member of the audit committee is a member of the board of directors of at least one of such dual holding companies.

(ii) Independence requirements for non-investment company issuers. In order to be considered to be independent for purposes of this paragraph (b)(1), a member of an audit committee of a listed issuer that is not an investment company may not, other than in his or her capacity as a member of the audit committee, the board of directors, or any other board committee:

(A) Accept directly or indirectly any consulting, advisory, or other compensatory fee from the issuer or any subsidiary thereof, provided that, unless the rules of the national securities exchange or national securities association provide otherwise, compensatory fees do not include the receipt of fixed amounts of compensation under a retirement plan (including deferred compensation) for prior service with the listed issuer (provided that such compensation is not contingent in any way on continued service); or

(B) Be an affiliated person of the issuer or any subsidiary thereof.

(iii) Independence requirements for investment company issuers. In order to be considered to be independent for purposes of this paragraph (b)(1), a member of an audit committee of a listed issuer that is an investment company may not, other than in his or her capacity as a member of the audit committee, the board of directors, or any other board committee:

(A) Accept directly or indirectly any consulting, advisory, or other compensatory fee from the issuer or any subsidiary thereof, provided that, unless the rules of the national securities exchange or national securities association provide otherwise, compensatory fees do not include the receipt of fixed amounts of compensation under a retirement plan (including deferred compensation) for prior service with the listed issuer (provided that such compensation is not contingent in any way on continued service); or

(B) Be an "interested person" of the issuer as defined in section 2(a)(19) of the Investment Company Act of 1940 (15 U.S.C. 80a–2(a)(19)).

(iv) Exemptions from the independence requirements. (A) For an issuer listing securities pursuant to a registration statement under section 12 of the Act (15 U.S.C. 78*l*), or for an issuer that has a registration statement under the Securities Act of 1933 (15 U.S.C. 77a *et seq.*) covering an initial public offering of securities to be listed by the issuer, where in each case the listed issuer was not, immediately prior to the effective date of such registration statement, required to file reports with the Commission pursuant to section 13(a) or 15(d) of the Act (15 U.S.C. 78m(a) or 78*o*(d)):

(1) All but one of the members of the listed issuer's audit committee may be exempt from the independence requirements of paragraph (b)(1)(ii) of this section for 90 days from the date of effectiveness of such registration statement; and

(2) A minority of the members of the listed issuer's audit committee may be exempt from the independence requirements of paragraph (b)(1)(ii) of this section for one year from the date of effectiveness of such registration statement.

(B) An audit committee member that sits on the board of directors of a listed issuer and an affiliate of the listed issuer is exempt from the requirements of paragraph (b)(1)(ii)(B) of this section if the member, except for being a director on each such board of directors, otherwise meets the independence requirements of paragraph (b)(1)(ii) of this section for each such entity, including the receipt of only ordinary-course compensation for serving as a member of the board of directors, audit committee or any other board committee of each such entity.

(C) An employee of a foreign private issuer who is not an executive officer of the foreign private issuer is exempt from the requirements of paragraph (b)(1)(ii) of this section if the employee is elected or named to the board of directors or audit committee of the foreign private issuer pursuant to the issuer's governing law or documents, an employee collective bargaining or similar agreement or other home country legal or listing requirements.

(D) An audit committee member of a foreign private issuer may be exempt from the requirements of paragraph (b)(1)(ii)(B) of this section if that member meets the following requirements:

(1) The member is an affiliate of the foreign private issuer or a representative of such an affiliate;

(2) The member has only observer status on, and is not a voting member or the chair of, the audit committee; and

(3) Neither the member nor the affiliate is an executive officer of the foreign private issuer.

(E) An audit committee member of a foreign private issuer may be exempt from the requirements of paragraph (b)(1)(ii)(B) of this section if that member meets the following requirements:

(1) The member is a representative or designee of a foreign government or foreign governmental entity that is an affiliate of the foreign private issuer; and

(2) The member is not an executive officer of the foreign private issuer.

(F) In addition to paragraphs (b)(1)(iv)(A) through (E) of this section, the Commission may exempt from the requirements of paragraphs (b)(1)(ii) or (b)(1)(iii) of this section a particular relationship with respect to audit committee members, as the Commission determines appropriate in light of the circumstances.

(2) Responsibilities relating to registered public accounting firms. The audit committee of each listed issuer, in its capacity as a committee of the board of directors, must be directly responsible for the appointment, compensation, retention and oversight of the work of any registered public accounting firm engaged (including resolution of disagreements between management and the auditor regarding financial reporting) for the purpose of preparing or issuing an audit report or performing other audit, review or attest services for the listed issuer, and each such registered public accounting firm must report directly to the audit committee.

(3) Complaints. Each audit committee must establish procedures for:

(i) The receipt, retention, and treatment of complaints received by the listed issuer regarding accounting, internal accounting controls, or auditing matters; and

(ii) The confidential, anonymous submission by employees of the listed issuer of concerns regarding questionable accounting or auditing matters.

(4) Authority to engage advisers. Each audit committee must have the authority to engage independent counsel and other advisers, as it determines necessary to carry out its duties.

(5) Funding. Each listed issuer must provide for appropriate funding, as determined by the audit committee, in its capacity as a committee of the board of directors, for payment of:

(i)   Compensation to any registered public accounting firm engaged for the purpose of preparing or issuing an audit report or performing other audit, review or attest services for the listed issuer;

(ii)   Compensation to any advisers employed by the audit committee under paragraph (b)(4) of this section; and

(iii)   Ordinary administrative expenses of the audit committee that are necessary or appropriate in carrying out its duties.

(c)   General exemptions. (1) At any time when an issuer has a class of securities that is listed on a national securities exchange or national securities association subject to the requirements of this section, the listing of other classes of securities of the listed issuer on a national securities exchange or national securities association is not subject to the requirements of this section.

(2)   At any time when an issuer has a class of common equity securities (or similar securities) that is listed on a national securities exchange or national securities association subject to the requirements of this section, the listing of classes of securities of a direct or indirect consolidated subsidiary or an at least 50% beneficially owned subsidiary of the issuer (except classes of equity securities, other than non-convertible, non-participating preferred securities, of such subsidiary) is not subject to the requirements of this section.

(3)   The listing of securities of a foreign private issuer is not subject to the requirements of paragraphs (b)(1) through (b)(5) of this section if the foreign private issuer meets the following requirements:

(i)   The foreign private issuer has a board of auditors (or similar body), or has statutory auditors, established and selected pursuant to home country legal or listing provisions expressly requiring or permitting such a board or similar body;

(ii)   The board or body, or statutory auditors is required under home country legal or listing requirements to be either:

(A)   Separate from the board of directors; or

(B)   Composed of one or more members of the board of directors and one or more members that are not also members of the board of directors;

(iii)   The board or body, or statutory auditors, are not elected by management of such issuer and no executive officer of the foreign private issuer is a member of such board or body, or statutory auditors;

(iv)   Home country legal or listing provisions set forth or provide for standards for the independence of such board or body, or statutory auditors, from the foreign private issuer or the management of such issuer;

(v)   Such board or body, or statutory auditors, in accordance with any applicable home country legal or listing requirements or the issuer's governing documents, are responsible, to the extent permitted by law, for the appointment, retention and oversight of the work of any registered public accounting firm engaged (including, to the extent permitted by law, the resolution of disagreements between management and the auditor regarding financial reporting) for the purpose of preparing or issuing an audit report or performing other audit, review or attest services for the issuer; and

(vi)   The audit committee requirements of paragraphs (b)(3), (b)(4) and (b)(5) of this section apply to such board or body, or statutory auditors, to the extent permitted by law.

(4)   The listing of a security futures product cleared by a clearing agency that is registered pursuant to section 17A of the Act (15 U.S.C. 78q–1) or that is exempt from the registration requirements of section 17A pursuant to paragraph (b)(7)(A) of such section is not subject to the requirements of this section.

(5)   The listing of a standardized option, as defined in § 240.9b–1(a)(4), issued by a clearing agency that is registered pursuant to section 17A of the Act (15 U.S.C. 78q–1) is not subject to the requirements of this section.

(6)   The listing of securities of the following listed issuers are not subject to the requirements of this section:

(i)   Asset-Backed Issuers (as defined in § 229.1101 of this chapter);

(ii)   Unit investment trusts (as defined in 15 U.S.C. 80a–4(2)); and

(iii) Foreign governments (as defined in § 240.3b–4(a)).

(7)   The listing of securities of a listed issuer is not subject to the requirements of this section if:

(i)   The listed issuer, as reflected in the applicable listing application, is organized as a trust or other unincorporated association that does not have a board of directors or persons acting in a similar capacity; and

(ii)   The activities of the listed issuer that is described in paragraph (c)(7)(i) of this section are limited to passively owning or holding (as well as administering and distributing amounts in respect of) securities, rights, collateral or other assets on behalf of or for the benefit of the holders of the listed securities.

(d)   Disclosure. Any listed issuer availing itself of an exemption from the independence standards contained in paragraph (b)(1)(iv) of this section (except paragraph (b)(1)(iv)(B) of this section), the general exemption contained in paragraph (c)(3) of this section or the last sentence of paragraph (a)(3) of this section, must:

(1)   Disclose its reliance on the exemption and its assessment of whether, and if so, how, such reliance would materially adversely affect the ability of the audit committee to act independently and to satisfy the other requirements of this section in any proxy or information statement for a meeting of shareholders at which directors are elected that is filed with the Commission pursuant to the requirements of section 14 of the Act (15 U.S.C. 78n); and

(2)   Disclose the information specified in paragraph (d)(1) of this section in, or incorporate such information by reference from such proxy or information statement filed with the Commission into, its annual report filed with the Commission pursuant to the requirements of section 13(a) or 15(d) of the Act (15 U.S.C. 78m(a) or 78o(d)).

(e)   Definitions. Unless the context otherwise requires, all terms used in this section have the same meaning as in the Act. In addition, unless the context otherwise requires, the following definitions apply for purposes of this section:

(1)(i)   The term affiliate of, or a person affiliated with, a specified person, means a person that directly, or indirectly through one or more intermediaries, controls, or is controlled by, or is under common control with, the person specified.

(ii)(A)   A person will be deemed not to be in control of a specified person for purposes of this section if the person:

(1)   Is not the beneficial owner, directly or indirectly, of more than 10% of any class of voting equity securities of the specified person; and

(2)   Is not an executive officer of the specified person.

(B)   Paragraph (e)(1)(ii)(A) of this section only creates a safe harbor position that a person does not control a specified person. The existence of the safe harbor does not create a presumption in any way that a person exceeding the ownership requirement in paragraph (e)(1)(ii)(A)(1) of this section controls or is otherwise an affiliate of a specified person.

(iii) The following will be deemed to be affiliates:

(A) An executive officer of an affiliate;

(B) A director who also is an employee of an affiliate;

(C) A general partner of an affiliate; and

(D) A managing member of an affiliate.

(iv) For purposes of paragraph (e)(1)(i) of this section, dual holding companies will not be deemed to be affiliates of or persons affiliated with each other by virtue of their dual holding company arrangements with each other, including where directors of one dual holding company are also directors of the other dual holding company, or where directors of one or both dual holding companies are also directors of the businesses jointly controlled, directly or indirectly, by the dual holding companies (and, in each case, receive only ordinary-course compensation for serving as a member of the board of directors, audit committee or any other board committee of the dual holding companies or any entity that is jointly controlled, directly or indirectly, by the dual holding companies).

(2) In the case of foreign private issuers with a two-tier board system, the term board of directors means the supervisory or non-management board.

(3) In the case of a listed issuer that is a limited partnership or limited liability company where such entity does not have a board of directors or equivalent body, the term board of directors means the board of directors of the managing general partner, managing member or equivalent body.

(4) The term control (including the terms controlling, controlled by and under common control with) means the possession, direct or indirect, of the power to direct or cause the direction of the management and policies of a person, whether through the ownership of voting securities, by contract, or otherwise.

(5) The term dual holding companies means two foreign private issuers that:

(i) Are organized in different national jurisdictions;

(ii) Collectively own and supervise the management of one or more businesses which are conducted as a single economic enterprise; and

(iii) Do not conduct any business other than collectively owning and supervising such businesses and activities reasonably incidental thereto.

(6) The term executive officer has the meaning set forth in § 240.3b–7.

(7) The term foreign private issuer has the meaning set forth in § 240.3b–4(c).

(8) The term indirect acceptance by a member of an audit committee of any consulting, advisory or other compensatory fee includes acceptance of such a fee by a spouse, a minor child or stepchild or a child or stepchild sharing a home with the member or by an entity in which such member is a partner, member, an officer such as a managing director occupying a comparable position or executive officer, or occupies a similar position (except limited partners, non-managing members and those occupying similar positions who, in each case, have no active role in providing services to the entity) and which provides accounting, consulting, legal, investment banking or financial advisory services to the issuer or any subsidiary of the issuer.

(9) The terms listed and listing refer to securities listed on a national securities exchange or listed in an automated inter-dealer quotation system of a national securities association or to issuers of such securities.

Instructions to § 240.10A-3

1.   The requirements in paragraphs (b)(2) through (b)(5), (c)(3)(v) and (c)(3)(vi) of this section do not conflict with, and do not affect the application of, any requirement or ability under a listed issuer's governing law or documents or other home country legal or listing provisions that requires or permits shareholders to ultimately vote on, approve or ratify such requirements. The requirements instead relate to the assignment of responsibility as between the audit committee and management. In such an instance, however, if the listed issuer provides a recommendation or nomination regarding such responsibilities to shareholders, the audit committee of the listed issuer, or body performing similar functions, must be responsible for making the recommendation or nomination.

2.   The requirements in paragraphs (b)(2) through (b)(5), (c)(3)(v), (c)(3)(vi) and Instruction 1 of this section do not conflict with any legal or listing requirement in a listed issuer's home jurisdiction that prohibits the full board of directors from delegating such responsibilities to the listed issuer's audit committee or limits the degree of such delegation. In that case, the audit committee, or body performing similar functions, must be granted such responsibilities, which can include advisory powers, with respect to such matters to the extent permitted by law, including submitting nominations or recommendations to the full board.

3.   The requirements in paragraphs (b)(2) through (b)(5), (c)(3)(v) and (c)(3)(vi) of this section do not conflict with any legal or listing requirement in a listed issuer's home jurisdiction that vests such responsibilities with a government entity or tribunal. In that case, the audit committee, or body performing similar functions, must be granted such responsibilities, which can include advisory powers, with respect to such matters to the extent permitted by law.

4.   For purposes of this section, the determination of a person's beneficial ownership must be made in accordance with § 240.13d-3.

* * *

REGISTRATION AND REPORTING

§ 240.12b-2.   Definitions

Unless the context otherwise requires, the following terms, when used in the rules contained in this regulation or in Regulation 13A or 15D or in the forms for statements and reports filed pursuant to sections 12, 13 or 15(d) of the act, shall have the respective meanings indicated in this rule:

Accelerated filer and large accelerated filer—(1) *Accelerated filer.* The term *accelerated filer* means an issuer after it first meets the following conditions as of the end of its fiscal year:

(i)   The issuer had an aggregate worldwide market value of the voting and non-voting common equity held by its non-affiliates of $75 million or more, but less than $700 million, as of the last business day of the issuer's most recently completed second fiscal quarter;

(ii)   The issuer has been subject to the requirements of section 13(a) or 15(d) of the Act (15 U.S.C. 78m or 78o(d)) for a period of at least twelve calendar months; and

(iii) The issuer has filed at least one annual report pursuant to section 13(a) or 15(d) of the Act; and

(iv)   The issuer is not eligible to use the requirements for smaller reporting companies under the revenue test in paragraph (2) or (3)(iii)(B) of the "smaller reporting company" definition in this section, as applicable.

(2)   *Large accelerated filer.* The term *large accelerated filer* means an issuer after it first meets the following conditions as of the end of its fiscal year:

(i)   The issuer had an aggregate worldwide market value of the voting and non-voting common equity held by its non-affiliates of $700 million or more, as of the last business day of the issuer's most recently completed second fiscal quarter;

(ii)   The issuer has been subject to the requirements of section 13(a) or 15(d) of the Act for a period of at least twelve calendar months; and

(iii)   The issuer has filed at least one annual report pursuant to section 13(a) or 15(d) of the Act; and

(iv)   The issuer is not eligible to use the requirements for smaller reporting companies under the revenue test in paragraph (2) or (3)(iii)(B) of the "smaller reporting company" definition in this section, as applicable.

(3)   *Entering and exiting accelerated filer and large accelerated filer status.*

(i)   The determination at the end of the issuer's fiscal year for whether a non-accelerated filer becomes an accelerated filer, or whether a non-accelerated filer or accelerated filer becomes a large accelerated filer, governs the deadlines for the annual report to be filed for that fiscal year, the quarterly and annual reports to be filed for the subsequent fiscal year and all annual and quarterly reports to be filed thereafter while the issuer remains an accelerated filer or large accelerated filer.

(ii)   Once an issuer becomes an accelerated filer, it will remain an accelerated filer unless: The issuer determines, at the end of a fiscal year, that the aggregate worldwide market value of the voting and non-voting common equity held by its non-affiliates was less than $60 million, as of the last business day of the issuer's most recently completed second fiscal quarter; or it determines that it is eligible to use the requirements for smaller reporting companies under the revenue test in paragraph (2) or (3)(iii)(B) of the "smaller reporting company" definition in this section, as applicable. An issuer that makes either of these determinations becomes a non-accelerated filer. The issuer will not become an accelerated filer again unless it subsequently meets the conditions in paragraph (1) of this definition.

(iii)   Once an issuer becomes a large accelerated filer, it will remain a large accelerated filer unless: It determines, at the end of a fiscal year, that the aggregate worldwide market value of the voting and non-voting common equity held by its non-affiliates ("aggregate worldwide market value") was less than $560 million, as of the last business day of the issuer's most recently completed second fiscal quarter or it determines that it is eligible to use the requirements for smaller reporting companies under the revenue test in paragraph (2) or (3)(iii)(B) of the "smaller reporting company" definition in this section, as applicable. If the issuer's aggregate worldwide market value was $60 million or more, but less than $560 million, as of the last business day of the issuer's most recently completed second fiscal quarter, and it is not eligible to use the requirements for smaller reporting companies under the revenue test in paragraph (2) or (3)(iii)(B) of the "smaller reporting company" definition in this section, as applicable, it becomes an accelerated filer. If the issuer's aggregate worldwide market value was less than $60 million, as of the last business day of the issuer's most recently completed second fiscal quarter, or it is eligible to use the requirements for smaller reporting companies under the revenue test in paragraph (2) or (3)(iii)(B) of the "smaller reporting company" definition in this section, it becomes a non-accelerated filer. An issuer will not become a large accelerated filer again unless it subsequently meets the conditions in paragraph (2) of this definition.

(iv)   The determination at the end of the issuer's fiscal year for whether an accelerated filer becomes a non-accelerated filer, or a large accelerated filer becomes an accelerated filer or a non-accelerated filer, governs the deadlines for the annual report to be filed for that fiscal year, the quarterly and annual reports to be filed for the subsequent fiscal year and all annual and quarterly reports to be filed thereafter while the issuer remains an accelerated filer or non-accelerated filer.

NOTE TO PARAGRAPHS (1), (2) AND (3): The aggregate worldwide market value of the issuer's outstanding voting and non-voting common equity shall be computed by use of the price at which the common equity was last sold, or the average of the bid and asked prices of such common equity, in the principal market for such common equity.

(4)   For purposes of paragraphs (1), (2), and (3) of this definition only, a business development company is considered to be eligible to use the requirements for smaller reporting companies under the revenue test in paragraph (2) or (3)(iii)(B) of the "smaller reporting company" definition in this section, provided that the business development company meets the requirements of the test using annual investment income under Rule 6–07.1 of Regulation S-X (17 CFR 210.6–07.1) as the measure of its "annual revenues" for purposes of the test.

* * *

Emerging growth company. (1) The term *emerging growth company* means an issuer that had total annual gross revenues of less than $1,070,000,000 during its most recently completed fiscal year.

(2)   An issuer that is an emerging growth company as of the first day of that fiscal year shall continue to be deemed an emerging growth company until the earliest of:

(i)   The last day of the fiscal year of the issuer during which it had total annual gross revenues of $1,070,000,000 or more;

(ii)   The last day of the fiscal year of the issuer following the fifth anniversary of the date of the first sale of common equity securities of the issuer pursuant to an effective registration statement under the Securities Act of 1933;

(iii)   The date on which such issuer has, during the previous three year period, issued more than $1,000,000,000 in non-convertible debt; or

(iv)   The date on which such issuer is deemed to be a large accelerated filer, as defined in Rule 12b–2 (§ 240.12b–2 of this chapter).

* * *

Smaller reporting company. As used in this part, the term *smaller reporting company* means an issuer that is not an investment company, an asset-backed issuer (as defined in § 229.1101 of this chapter), or a majority-owned subsidiary of a parent that is not a smaller reporting company and that:

(1)   Had a public float of less than $250 million; or

(2)   Had annual revenues of less than $100 million and either:

(i)   No public float; or

(ii)   A public float of less than $700 million.

(3)   Whether an issuer is a smaller reporting company is determined on an annual basis.

(i)   For issuers that are required to file reports under section 13(a) or 15(d) of the Exchange Act:

(A)   Public float is measured as of the last business day of the issuer's most recently completed second fiscal quarter and computed by multiplying the aggregate worldwide number of shares of its voting and non-voting common equity held by non-affiliates by the price at which the common equity was last sold, or the average of the bid and asked prices of common equity, in the principal market for the common equity;

(B)   Annual revenues are as of the most recently completed fiscal year for which audited financial statements are available; and

(C)   An issuer must reflect the determination of whether it came within the definition of smaller reporting company in its quarterly report on Form 10-Q for the first fiscal quarter of the next year, indicating on the cover page of that filing, and in subsequent filings for that fiscal year, whether it is a smaller reporting company, except that, if a determination based on public float indicates that the issuer is newly eligible to be a smaller reporting company, the issuer may choose to reflect this determination beginning with its first quarterly report on Form 10-Q following the determination, rather than waiting until the first fiscal quarter of the next year.

(ii)   For determinations based on an initial registration statement under the Securities Act or Exchange Act for shares of its common equity:

(A)   Public float is measured as of a date within 30 days of the date of the filing of the registration statement and computed by multiplying the aggregate worldwide number of shares of its voting and non-voting common equity held by non-affiliates before the registration plus, in the case of a Securities Act registration statement, the number of shares of its voting and non-voting common equity included in the registration statement by the estimated public offering price of the shares;

(B)   Annual revenues are as of the most recently completed fiscal year for which audited financial statements are available; and

(C)   The issuer must reflect the determination of whether it came within the definition of smaller reporting company in the registration statement and must appropriately indicate on the cover page of the filing, and subsequent filings for the fiscal year in which the filing is made, whether it is a smaller reporting company. The issuer must re-determine its status at the end of its second fiscal quarter and then reflect any change in status as provided in paragraph (3)(i)(C) of this definition. In the case of a determination based on an initial Securities Act registration statement, an issuer that was not determined to be a smaller reporting company has the option to re-determine its status at the conclusion of the offering covered by the registration statement based on the actual offering price and number of shares sold.

(iii)   Once an issuer determines that it does not qualify for smaller reporting company status because it exceeded one or more of the current thresholds, it will remain unqualified unless when making its annual determination either:

(A)   It determines that its public float was less than $200 million; or

(B)   It determines that its public float and its annual revenues meet the requirements for subsequent qualification included in the following chart:

Prior annual revenues	Prior public float	
	None or less than $700 million	**$700 million or more**
Less than $100 million	Neither threshold exceeded	Public float—Less than $560 million; and
		Revenues—Less than $100 million.
$100 million or more	Public float—None or less than $700 million; and	Public float—Less than $560 million; and
	Revenues—Less than $80 million	Revenues—Less than $80 million.

INSTRUCTION 1 TO DEFINITION OF "SMALLER REPORTING COMPANY": A registrant that qualifies as a smaller reporting company under the public float thresholds identified in paragraphs (1) and (3)(iii)(A) of this definition will qualify as a smaller reporting company regardless of its revenues.

INSTRUCTION 2 TO DEFINITION OF "SMALLER REPORTING COMPANY": A foreign private issuer is not eligible to use the requirements for smaller reporting companies unless it uses the forms and rules designated for domestic issuers and provides financial statements prepared in accordance with U.S. Generally Accepted Accounting Principles.

* * *

EXTENSIONS AND TEMPORARY EXEMPTIONS; DEFINITIONS

§ 240.12g–1.   Registration of Securities; Exemption from Section 12(g)

An issuer is not required to register a class of equity securities pursuant to section 12(g)(1) of the Act (15 U.S.C. 78*l*(g)(1)) if on the last day of its most recent fiscal year:

(a)   The issuer had total assets not exceeding $10 million; or

(b)(1)   The class of equity securities was held of record by fewer than 2,000 persons and fewer than 500 of those persons were not accredited investors (as such term is defined in § 230.501(a) of this chapter, determined as of such day rather than at the time of the sale of the securities); or

(2)   The class of equity securities was held of record by fewer than 2,000 persons in the case of a bank; a savings and loan holding company, as such term is defined in section 10 of the Home Owners' Loan Act (12 U.S.C. 1461); or a bank holding company, as such term is defined in section 2 of the Bank Holding Company Act of 1956 (12 U.S.C. 1841).

REPORTS OF ISSUERS OF SECURITIES REGISTERED PURSUANT TO SECTION 12

§ 240.13a–1.   Requirements of Annual Reports

Every issuer having securities registered pursuant to section 12 of the Act (15 U.S.C. 78 l) shall file an annual report on the appropriate form authorized or prescribed therefor for each fiscal year after the last full fiscal year for which financial statements were filed in its registration statement. Annual reports shall be filed within the period specified in the appropriate form.

* * *

§ 240.13a–11.   Current Reports on Form 8-K

(a)   * * * [E]very registrant subject to § 240.13a–1 shall file a current report on Form 8-K within the period specified in that form unless substantially the same information as that required by Form 8-K has been previously reported by the registrant.

* * *

§ 240.13a–13.   Quarterly Reports on Form 10-Q

(a)   * * * [E]very issuer that has securities registered pursuant to section 12 of the Act and is required to file annual reports pursuant to section 13 of the Act, and has filed or intends to file such reports on Form 10-K (§ 249.310 of this chapter), shall file a quarterly report on Form 10-Q (§ 249.308a of this chapter) within the period specified in General Instruction A.1. to that form for each of the first three quarters of each fiscal year of the issuer, commencing with the first fiscal quarter following the most recent fiscal year for which full financial statements were included in the registration statement, or, if the registration statement included financial statements for an interim period subsequent to the most recent fiscal year end meeting the requirements of Article 10 of Regulation S–X and Rule 8–03 of Regulation S–X for smaller reporting companies, for the first fiscal quarter subsequent to the quarter reported upon in the registration statement. The first quarterly report of the issuer shall be filed either within 45 days after the effective date of the registration statement or on or before the date on which such report would have been required to be filed if the issuer has been required to file reports on Form 10-Q as of its last fiscal quarter, whichever is later.

* * *

§ 240.13a–14.   **Certification of Disclosure in Annual and Quarterly Reports**

(a)   Each report, including transition reports, filed on Form 10-Q, Form 10-K, Form 20-F or Form 40-F (§ 249.308a, § 249.310, § 249.220f or § 249.240f of this chapter) under Section 13(a) of the Act (15 U.S.C. 78m(a)), other than a report filed by an Asset-Backed Issuer (as defined in § 229.1101 of this chapter) or a report on Form 20-F filed under § 240.13a–19, must include certifications in the form specified in the applicable exhibit filing requirements of such report and such certifications must be filed as an exhibit to such report. Each principal executive and principal financial officer of the issuer, or persons performing similar functions, at the time of filing of the report must sign a certification. The principal executive and principal financial officers of an issuer may omit the portion of the introductory language in paragraph 4 as well as language in paragraph 4(b) of the certification that refers to the certifying officers' responsibility for designing, establishing and maintaining internal control over financial reporting for the issuer until the issuer becomes subject to the internal control over financial reporting requirements in § 240.13a–15 or § 240.15d–15.

(b)   Each periodic report containing financial statements filed by an issuer pursuant to section 13(a) of the Act (15 U.S.C. 78m(a)) must be accompanied by the certifications required by Section 1350 of Chapter 63 of Title 18 of the United States Code (18 U.S.C. 1350) and such certifications must be furnished as an exhibit to such report as specified in the applicable exhibit requirements for such report. Each principal executive and principal financial officer of the issuer (or equivalent thereof) must sign a certification. This requirement may be satisfied by a single certification signed by an issuer's principal executive and principal financial officers.

(c)   A person required to provide a certification specified in paragraph (a), (b) or (d) of this section may not have the certification signed on his or her behalf pursuant to a power of attorney or other form of confirming authority.

(d)   Each annual report and transition report filed on Form 10-K (§ 249.310 of this chapter) by an asset-backed issuer under section 13(a) of the Act (15 U.S.C. 78m(a)) must include a certification in the form specified in the applicable exhibit filing requirements of such report and such certification must be filed as an exhibit to such report. Terms used in paragraphs (d) and (e) of this section have the same meaning as in Item 1101 of Regulation AB (§ 229.1101 of this chapter).

(e)   With respect to asset-backed issuers, the certification required by paragraph (d) of this section must be signed by either:

(1)   The senior officer in charge of securitization of the depositor if the depositor is signing the report; or

(2)   The senior officer in charge of the servicing function of the servicer if the servicer is signing the report on behalf of the issuing entity. If multiple servicers are involved in servicing the pool assets, the senior officer in charge of the servicing function of the master servicer (or entity performing the equivalent function) must sign if a representative of the servicer is to sign the report on behalf of the issuing entity.

(f)   The certification requirements of this section do not apply to an Interactive Data File, as defined in § 232.11 of this chapter (Rule 11 of Regulation S–T).

§ 240.13a–15.   **Controls and Procedures**

(a)   Every issuer that has a class of securities registered pursuant to section 12 of the Act (15 U.S.C. 78*l*), other than an Asset-Backed Issuer (as defined in § 229.1101 of this chapter), a small business investment company registered on Form N-5 (§§ 239.24 and 274.5 of this chapter), or a unit investment trust as defined in section 4(2) of the Investment Company Act of 1940 (15 U.S.C. 80a–4(2)), must maintain disclosure controls and procedures (as defined in paragraph (e) of this section) and, if the issuer either had been required to file an annual report pursuant to section 13(a) or 15(d) of the Act (15 U.S.C. 78m(a) or 78o(d)) for the prior fiscal year or had filed an annual report with the Commission for the prior fiscal year, internal control over financial reporting (as defined in paragraph (f) of this section).

(b) Each such issuer's management must evaluate, with the participation of the issuer's principal executive and principal financial officers, or persons performing similar functions, the effectiveness of the issuer's disclosure controls and procedures, as of the end of each fiscal quarter, except that management must perform this evaluation:

(1) In the case of a foreign private issuer (as defined in § 240.3b–4) as of the end of each fiscal year; and

(2) In the case of an investment company registered under section 8 of the Investment Company Act of 1940 (15 U.S.C. 80a–8), within the 90-day period prior to the filing date of each report requiring certification under § 270.30a–2 of this chapter.

(c) The management of each such issuer, that either had been required to file an annual report pursuant to section 13(a) or 15(d) of the Act (15 U.S.C. 78m(a) or 78o(d)) for the prior fiscal year or previously had filed an annual report with the Commission for the prior fiscal year, other than an investment company registered under section 8 of the Investment Company Act of 1940, must evaluate, with the participation of the issuer's principal executive and principal financial officers, or persons performing similar functions, the effectiveness, as of the end of each fiscal year, of the issuer's internal control over financial reporting. The framework on which management's evaluation of the issuer's internal control over financial reporting is based must be a suitable, recognized control framework that is established by a body or group that has followed due-process procedures, including the broad distribution of the framework for public comment. Although there are many different ways to conduct an evaluation of the effectiveness of internal control over financial reporting to meet the requirements of this paragraph, an evaluation that is conducted in accordance with the interpretive guidance issued by the Commission in Release No. 34–55929 will satisfy the evaluation required by this paragraph.

(d) The management of each such issuer that either had been required to file an annual report pursuant to section 13(a) or 15(d) of the Act (15 U.S.C. 78m(a) or 78o(d)) for the prior fiscal year or had filed an annual report with the Commission for the prior fiscal year, other than an investment company registered under section 8 of the Investment Company Act of 1940 (15 U.S.C. 80a–8), must evaluate, with the participation of the issuer's principal executive and principal financial officers, or persons performing similar functions, any change in the issuer's internal control over financial reporting, that occurred during each of the issuer's fiscal quarters, or fiscal year in the case of a foreign private issuer, that has materially affected, or is reasonably likely to materially affect, the issuer's internal control over financial reporting.

(e) For purposes of this section, the term disclosure controls and procedures means controls and other procedures of an issuer that are designed to ensure that information required to be disclosed by the issuer in the reports that it files or submits under the Act (15 U.S.C. 78a *et seq.*) is recorded, processed, summarized and reported, within the time periods specified in the Commission's rules and forms. Disclosure controls and procedures include, without limitation, controls and procedures designed to ensure that information required to be disclosed by an issuer in the reports that it files or submits under the Act is accumulated and communicated to the issuer's management, including its principal executive and principal financial officers, or persons performing similar functions, as appropriate to allow timely decisions regarding required disclosure.

(f) The term internal control over financial reporting is defined as a process designed by, or under the supervision of, the issuer's principal executive and principal financial officers, or persons performing similar functions, and effected by the issuer's board of directors, management and other personnel, to provide reasonable assurance regarding the reliability of financial reporting and the preparation of financial statements for external purposes in accordance with generally accepted accounting principles and includes those policies and procedures that:

(1) Pertain to the maintenance of records that in reasonable detail accurately and fairly reflect the transactions and dispositions of the assets of the issuer;

(2) Provide reasonable assurance that transactions are recorded as necessary to permit preparation of financial statements in accordance with generally accepted accounting principles, and that receipts and expenditures of the issuer are being made only in accordance with authorizations of management and directors of the issuer; and

(3) Provide reasonable assurance regarding prevention or timely detection of unauthorized acquisition, use or disposition of the issuer's assets that could have a material effect on the financial statements.

* * *

§ 240.13a–20.   Plain English Presentation of Specified Information

(a) Any information included or incorporated by reference in a report filed under section 13(a) of the Act (15 U.S.C. 78m(a)) that is required to be disclosed pursuant to Item 402, 403, 404 or 407 of Regulation S–K (§ 229.402, § 229.403, § 229.404 or § 229.407 of this chapter) must be presented in a clear, concise and understandable manner. You must prepare the disclosure using the following standards:

(1) Present information in clear, concise sections, paragraphs and sentences;

(2) Use short sentences;

(3) Use definite, concrete, everyday words;

(4) Use the active voice;

(5) Avoid multiple negatives;

(6) Use descriptive headings and subheadings;

(7) Use a tabular presentation or bullet lists for complex material, wherever possible;

(8) Avoid legal jargon and highly technical business and other terminology;

(9) Avoid frequent reliance on glossaries or defined terms as the primary means of explaining information. Define terms in a glossary or other section of the document only if the meaning is unclear from the context. Use a glossary only if it facilitates understanding of the disclosure; and

(10) In designing the presentation of the information you may include pictures, logos, charts, graphs and other design elements so long as the design is not misleading and the required information is clear. You are encouraged to use tables, schedules, charts and graphic illustrations that present relevant data in an understandable manner, so long as such presentations are consistent with applicable disclosure requirements and consistent with other information in the document. You must draw graphs and charts to scale. Any information you provide must not be misleading.

* * *

REPORTS BY BENEFICIAL OWNERS

§ 240.13d–1.   Filing of Schedules 13D and 13G

(a) Any person who, after acquiring directly or indirectly the beneficial ownership of any equity security of a class which is specified in paragraph (i) of this section, is directly or indirectly the beneficial owner of more than five percent of the class shall, within 10 days after the acquisition, file with the Commission, a statement containing the information required by Schedule 13D (§ 240.13d–101).

(b)(1)   A person who would otherwise be obligated under paragraph (a) of this section to file a statement on Schedule 13D (§ 240.13d–101) may, in lieu thereof, file with the Commission, a short-form statement on Schedule 13G (§ 240.13d–102), Provided, That:

    (i)   Such person has acquired such securities in the ordinary course of his business and not with the purpose nor with the effect of changing or influencing the control of the issuer, nor in connection with or as a participant in any transaction having such purpose or effect, including any transaction subject to § 240.13d–3(b), other than activities solely in connection with a nomination under § 240.14a–11;

* * *

    (2)   The Schedule 13G filed pursuant to paragraph (b)(1) of this section shall be filed within 45 days after the end of the calendar year in which the person became obligated under paragraph (b)(1) of this section to report the person's beneficial ownership as of the last day of the calendar year, Provided, That it shall not be necessary to file a Schedule 13G unless the percentage of the class of equity security specified in paragraph (i) of this section beneficially owned as of the end of the calendar year is more than five percent; However, if the person's direct or indirect beneficial ownership exceeds 10 percent of the class of equity securities prior to the end of the calendar year, the initial Schedule 13G shall be filed within 10 days after the end of the first month in which the person's direct or indirect beneficial ownership exceeds 10 percent of the class of equity securities, computed as of the last day of the month.

* * *

§ 240.13d–2.   Filing of Amendments to Schedules 13D or 13G

(a)   If any material change occurs in the facts set forth in the Schedule 13D (§ 240.13d–101) required by § 240.13d–1(a), including, but not limited to, any material increase or decrease in the percentage of the class beneficially owned, the person or persons who were required to file the statement shall promptly file or cause to be filed with the Commission an amendment disclosing that change. An acquisition or disposition of beneficial ownership of securities in an amount equal to one percent or more of the class of securities shall be deemed "material" for purposes of this section; acquisitions or dispositions of less than those amounts may be material, depending upon the facts and circumstances.

* * *

§ 240.13d–3.   Determination of Beneficial Owner

(a)   For the purposes of sections 13(d) and 13(g) of the Act a beneficial owner of a security includes any person who, directly or indirectly, through any contract, arrangement, understanding, relationship, or otherwise has or shares:

    (1)   Voting power which includes the power to vote, or to direct the voting of, such security; and/or,

    (2)   Investment power which includes the power to dispose, or to direct the disposition of, such security.

(b)   Any person who, directly or indirectly, creates or uses a trust, proxy, power of attorney, pooling arrangement or any other contract, arrangement, or device with the purpose of effect of divesting such person of beneficial ownership of a security or preventing the vesting of such beneficial ownership as part of a plan or scheme to evade the reporting requirements of section 13(d) or (g) of the Act shall be deemed for purposes of such sections to be the beneficial owner of such security.

(c)   All securities of the same class beneficially owned by a person, regardless of the form which such beneficial ownership takes, shall be aggregated in calculating the number of shares beneficially owned by such person.

(d)   Notwithstanding the provisions of paragraphs (a) and (c) of this rule:

(1)(i)   A person shall be deemed to be the beneficial owner of a security, subject to the provisions of paragraph (b) of this rule, if that person has the right to acquire beneficial ownership of such security, as defined in Rule 13d–3(a) (§ 240.13d–3(a)) within sixty days, including but not limited to any right to acquire: (A) Through the exercise of any option, warrant or right; (B) through the conversion of a security; (C) pursuant to the power to revoke a trust, discretionary account, or similar arrangement; or (D) pursuant to the automatic termination of a trust, discretionary account or similar arrangement; provided, however, any person who acquires a security or power specified in paragraphs (d)(1)(i)(A), (B) or (C), of this section, with the purpose or effect of changing or influencing the control of the issuer, or in connection with or as a participant in any transaction having such purpose or effect, immediately upon such acquisition shall be deemed to be the beneficial owner of the securities which may be acquired through the exercise or conversion of such security or power. Any securities not outstanding which are subject to such options, warrants, rights or conversion privileges shall be deemed to be outstanding for the purpose of computing the percentage of outstanding securities of the class owned by such person but shall not be deemed to be outstanding for the purpose of computing the percentage of the class by any other person.

(ii)   Paragraph (d)(1)(i) of this section remains applicable for the purpose of determining the obligation to file with respect to the underlying security even though the option, warrant, right or convertible security is of a class of equity security, as defined in § 240.13d–1(i), and may therefore give rise to a separate obligation to file.

(2)   A member of a national securities exchange shall not be deemed to be a beneficial owner of securities held directly or indirectly by it on behalf of another person solely because such member is the record holder of such securities and, pursuant to the rules of such exchange, may direct the vote of such securities, without instruction, on other than contested matters or matters that may affect substantially the rights or privileges of the holders of the securities to be voted, but is otherwise precluded by the rules of such exchange from voting without instruction.

(3)   A person who in the ordinary course of his business is a pledgee of securities under a written pledge agreement shall not be deemed to be the beneficial owner of such pledged securities until the pledgee has taken all formal steps necessary which are required to declare a default and determines that the power to vote or to direct the vote or to dispose or to direct the disposition of such pledged securities will be exercised, provided, that:

(i)   The pledgee agreement is bona fide and was not entered into with the purpose nor with the effect of changing or influencing the control of the issuer, nor in connection with any transaction having such purpose or effect, including any transaction subject to Rule 13d–3(b);

(ii)   The pledgee is a person specified in Rule 13d–1(b)(ii), including persons meeting the conditions set forth in paragraph (G) thereof; and

(iii)   The pledgee agreement, prior to default, does not grant to the pledgee;

(A)   The power to vote or to direct the vote of the pledged securities; or

(B)   The power to dispose or direct the disposition of the pledged securities, other than the grant of such power(s) pursuant to a pledge agreement under which credit is extended subject to regulation T (12 CFR 220.1 to 220.8) and in which the pledgee is a broker or dealer registered under section 15 of the act.

(4)   A person engaged in business as an underwriter of securities who acquires securities through his participation in good faith in a firm commitment underwriting registered under the Securities Act of 1933 shall not be deemed to be the beneficial owner of such securities until the expiration of forty days after the date of such acquisition.

§ 240.13d–4.   Disclaimer of Beneficial Ownership

Any person may expressly declare in any statement filed that the filing of such statement shall not be construed as an admission that such person is, for the purposes of sections 13(d) or 13(g) of the Act, the beneficial owner of any securities covered by the statement.

§ 240.13d–5.   Acquisition of Securities

(a)   A person who becomes a beneficial owner of securities shall be deemed to have acquired such securities for purposes of section 13(d)(1) of the Act, whether such acquisition was through purchase or otherwise. However, executors or administrators of a decedent's estate generally will be presumed not to have acquired beneficial ownership of the securities in the decedent's estate until such time as such executors or administrators are qualified under local law to perform their duties.

(b)(1)   When two or more persons agree to act together for the purpose of acquiring, holding, voting or disposing of equity securities of an issuer, the group formed thereby shall be deemed to have acquired beneficial ownership, for purposes of sections 13(d) and (g) of the Act, as of the date of such agreement, of all equity securities of that issuer beneficially owned by any such persons.

(2)   Notwithstanding the previous paragraph, a group shall be deemed not to have acquired any equity securities beneficially owned by the other members of the group solely by virtue of their concerted actions relating to the purchase of equity securities directly from an issuer in a transaction not involving a public offering: Provided, That:

(i)   All the members of the group are persons specified in Rule 13d–1(b)(1)(ii);

(ii)   The purchase is in the ordinary course of each member's business and not with the purpose nor with the effect of changing or influencing control of the issuer, nor in connection with or as a participant in any transaction having such purpose or effect, including any transaction subject to Rule 13d–3(b);

(iii)   There is no agreement among, or between any members of the group to act together with respect to the issuer or its securities except for the purpose of facilitating the specific purchase involved; and

(iv)   The only actions among or between any members of the group with respect to the issuer or its securities subsequent to the closing date of the non-public offering are those which are necessary to conclude ministerial matters directly related to the completion of the offer or sale of the securities.

§ 240.13d–6.   Exemption of Certain Acquisitions

The acquisition of securities of an issuer by a person who, prior to such acquisition, was a beneficial owner of more than five percent of the outstanding securities of the same class as those acquired shall be exempt from section 13(d) of the Act: Provided, That:

(a)   The acquisition is made pursuant to preemptive subscription rights in an offering made to all holders of securities of the class to which the preemptive subscription rights pertain;

(b)   Such person does not acquire additional securities except through the exercise of his pro rata share of the preemptive subscription rights; and

(c)   The acquisition is duly reported, if required, pursuant to section 16(a) of the Act and the rules and regulations thereunder.

§ 240.13d–7.   Dissemination

One copy of the Schedule filed pursuant to §§ 240.13d–1 and 240.13d–2 shall be sent to the issuer of the security at its principal executive office by registered or certified mail. A copy of Schedules filed pursuant to §§ 240.13d–1(a) and 240.13d–2(a) shall also be sent to each national securities exchange where the security is traded.

* * *

REPURCHASES BY ISSUERS

§ 240.13e–1.   Purchase of Securities by the Issuer During a Third-Party Tender Offer

An issuer that has received notice that it is the subject of a tender offer made under Section 14(d)(1) of the Act (15 U.S.C. 78n), that has commenced under § 240.14d–2 must not purchase any of its equity securities during the tender offer unless the issuer first:

(a)   Files a statement with the Commission containing the following information:

(1)   The title and number of securities to be purchased;

(2)   The names of the persons or classes of persons from whom the issuer will purchase the securities;

(3)   The name of any exchange, inter-dealer quotation system or any other market on or through which the securities will be purchased;

(4)   The purpose of the purchase;

(5)   Whether the issuer will retire the securities, hold the securities in its treasury, or dispose of the securities. If the issuer intends to dispose of the securities, describe how it intends to do so; and

(6)   The source and amount of funds or other consideration to be used to make the purchase. If the issuer borrows any funds or other consideration to make the purchase or enters any agreement for the purpose of acquiring, holding, or trading the securities, describe the transaction and agreement and identify the parties; and

(b)   Pays the fee required by § 240.0–11 when it files the initial statement.

(c)   This section does not apply to periodic repurchases in connection with an employee benefit plan or other similar plan of the issuer so long as the purchases are made in the ordinary course and not in response to the tender offer.

Instruction to § 240.13e–1:

File eight copies if paper filing is permitted.

§ 240.13e–3.   Going Private Transactions by Certain Issuers or Their Affiliates

(a)   Definitions. Unless indicated otherwise or the context otherwise requires, all terms used in this section and in Schedule 13E–3 [§ 240.13e–100] shall have the same meaning as in the Act or elsewhere in the General Rules and Regulations thereunder. In addition, the following definitions apply:

(1)   An affiliate of an issuer is a person that directly or indirectly through one or more intermediaries controls, is controlled by, or is under common control with such issuer. For the purposes of this section only, a person who is not an affiliate of an issuer at the commencement of such person's tender offer for a class of equity securities of such issuer will not be deemed an affiliate of such issuer prior to the stated termination of such tender offer and any extensions thereof;

(2)   The term purchase means any acquisition for value including, but not limited to, (i) any acquisition pursuant to the dissolution of an issuer subsequent to the sale or other disposition of substantially all the assets of such issuer to its affiliate, (ii) any acquisition pursuant to a merger,

(iii) any acquisition of fractional interests in connection with a reverse stock split, and (iv) any acquisition subject to the control of an issuer or an affiliate of such issuer;

(3) A Rule 13e-3 transaction is any transaction or series of transactions involving one or more of the transactions described in paragraph (a)(3)(i) of this section which has either a reasonable likelihood or a purpose of producing, either directly or indirectly, any of the effects described in paragraph (a)(3)(ii) of this section;

(i) The transactions referred to in paragraph (a)(3) of this section are:

(A) A purchase of any equity security by the issuer of such security or by an affiliate of such issuer;

(B) A tender offer for or request or invitation for tenders of any equity security made by the issuer of such class of securities or by an affiliate of such issuer; or

(C) A solicitation subject to Regulation 14A [§§ 240.14a-1 to 240.14b-1] of any proxy, consent or authorization of, or a distribution subject to Regulation 14C [§§ 240.14c-1 to 14c-101] of information statements to, any equity security holder by the issuer of the class of securities or by an affiliate of such issuer, in connection with: a merger, consolidation, reclassification, recapitalization, reorganization or similar corporate transaction of an issuer or between an issuer (or its subsidiaries) and its affiliate; a sale of substantially all the assets of an issuer to its affiliate or group of affiliates; or a reverse stock split of any class of equity securities of the issuer involving the purchase of fractional interests.

(ii) The effects referred to in paragraph (a)(3) of this section are:

(A) Causing any class of equity securities of the issuer which is subject to section 12(g) or section 15(d) of the Act to become eligible for termination of registration under Rule 12g-4 (§ 240.12g-4) or Rule 12h-6 (§ 240.12h-6), or causing the reporting obligations with respect to such class to become eligible for termination under Rule 12h-6 (§ 240.12h-6); or suspension under Rule 12h-3 (§ 240.12h-3) or section 15(d); or

(B) Causing any class of equity securities of the issuer which is either listed on a national securities exchange or authorized to be quoted in an inter-dealer quotation system of a registered national securities association to be neither listed on any national securities exchange nor authorized to be quoted on an inter-dealer quotation system of any registered national securities association.

(4) An unaffiliated security holder is any security holder of an equity security subject to a Rule 13e-3 transaction who is not an affiliate of the issuer of such security.

(b) Application of section to an issuer (or an affiliate of such issuer) subject to section 12 of the Act.

(1) It shall be a fraudulent, deceptive or manipulative act or practice, in connection with a Rule 13e-3 transaction, for an issuer which has a class of equity securities registered pursuant to section 12 of the Act or which is a closed-end investment company registered under the Investment Company Act of 1940, or an affiliate of such issuer, directly or indirectly

(i) To employ any device, scheme or artifice to defraud any person;

(ii) To make any untrue statement of a material fact or to omit to state a material fact necessary in order to make the statements made, in light of the circumstances under which they were made, not misleading; or

(iii) To engage in any act, practice or course of business which operates or would operate as a fraud or deceit upon any person.

(2) As a means reasonably designed to prevent fraudulent, deceptive or manipulative acts or practices in connection with any Rule 13e-3 transaction, it shall be unlawful for an issuer

which has a class of equity securities registered pursuant to section 12 of the Act, or an affiliate of such issuer, to engage, directly or indirectly, in a Rule 13e–3 transaction unless:

(i) Such issuer or affiliate complies with the requirements of paragraphs (d), (e) and (f) of this section; and

(ii) The Rule 13e–3 transaction is not in violation of paragraph (b)(1) of this section.

(c) Application of section to an issuer (or an affiliate of such issuer) subject to section 15(d) of the Act.

(1) It shall be unlawful as a fraudulent, deceptive or manipulative act or practice for an issuer which is required to file periodic reports pursuant to Section 15(d) of the Act, or an affiliate of such issuer, to engage, directly or indirectly, in a Rule 13e–3 transaction unless such issuer or affiliate complies with the requirements of paragraphs (d), (e) and (f) of this section.

(2) An issuer or affiliate which is subject to paragraph (c)(1) of this section and which is soliciting proxies or distributing information statements in connection with a transaction described in paragraph (a)(3)(i)(A) of this section may elect to use the timing procedures for conducting a solicitation subject to Regulation 14A (§§ 240.14a–1 to 240.14b–1) or a distribution subject to Regulation 14C (§§ 240.14c–1 to 240.14c–101) in complying with paragraphs (d), (e) and (f) of this section, provided that if an election is made, such solicitation or distribution is conducted in accordance with the requirements of the respective regulations, including the filing of preliminary copies of soliciting materials or an information statement at the time specified in Regulation 14A or 14C, respectively.

(d) Material required to be filed. The issuer or affiliate engaging in a Rule 13e–3 transaction must file with the Commission:

(1) A Schedule 13E–3 (§ 240.13e–100), including all exhibits;

(2) An amendment to Schedule 13E–3 reporting promptly any material changes in the information set forth in the schedule previously filed; and

(3) A final amendment to Schedule 13E–3 reporting promptly the results of the Rule 13e–3 transaction.

(e) Disclosure of information to security holders.

(1) In addition to disclosing the information required by any other applicable rule or regulation under the federal securities laws, the issuer or affiliate engaging in a § 240.13e–3 transaction must disclose to security holders of the class that is the subject of the transaction, as specified in paragraph (f) of this section, the following:

(i) The information required by Item 1 of Schedule 13E–3 (§ 240.13e–100) (Summary Term Sheet);

(ii) The information required by Items 7, 8 and 9 of Schedule 13E–3, which must be prominently disclosed in a "Special Factors" section in the front of the disclosure document;

(iii) A prominent legend on the outside front cover page that indicates that neither the Securities and Exchange Commission nor any state securities commission has: approved or disapproved of the transaction; passed upon the merits or fairness of the transaction; or passed upon the adequacy or accuracy of the disclosure in the document. The legend also must make it clear that any representation to the contrary is a criminal offense;

(iv) The information concerning appraisal rights required by § 229.1016(f) of this chapter; and

(v) The information required by the remaining items of Schedule 13E–3, except for § 229.1016 of this chapter (exhibits), or a fair and adequate summary of the information.

Instructions to paragraph (e)(1):

1.   If the Rule 13e–3 transaction also is subject to Regulation 14A (§§ 240.14a–1 through 240.14b–2) or 14C (§§ 240.14c–1 through 240.14c–101), the registration provisions and rules of the Securities Act of 1933, Regulation 14D or § 240.13e–4, the information required by paragraph (e)(1) of this section must be combined with the proxy statement, information statement, prospectus or tender offer material sent or given to security holders.

2.   If the Rule 13e–3 transaction involves a registered securities offering, the legend required by § 229.501(b)(7) of this chapter must be combined with the legend required by paragraph (e)(1)(iii) of this section.

3.   The required legend must be written in clear, plain language.

(2)   If there is any material change in the information previously disclosed to security holders, the issuer or affiliate must disclose the change promptly to security holders as specified in paragraph (f)(1)(iii) of this section.

(f)   Dissemination of information to security holders.

(1)   If the Rule 13e–3 transaction involves a purchase as described in paragraph (a)(3)(i)(A) of this section or a vote, consent, authorization, or distribution of information statements as described in paragraph (a)(3)(i)(C) of this section, the issuer or affiliate engaging in the Rule 13e–3 transaction shall:

(i)   Provide the information required by paragraph (e) of this section: (A) In accordance with the provisions of any applicable Federal or State law, but in no event later than 20 days prior to: any such purchase; any such vote, consent or authorization; or with respect to the distribution of information statements, the meeting date, or if corporate action is to be taken by means of the written authorization or consent of security holders, the earliest date on which corporate action may be taken: Provided, however, That if the purchase subject to this section is pursuant to a tender offer excepted from Rule 13e–4 by paragraph (g)(5) of Rule 13e–4, the information required by paragraph (e) of this section shall be disseminated in accordance with paragraph (e) of Rule 13e–4 no later than 10 business days prior to any purchase pursuant to such tender offer, (B) to each person who is a record holder of a class of equity securities subject to the Rule 13e–3 transaction as of a date not more than 20 days prior to the date of dissemination of such information.

(ii)   If the issuer or affiliate knows that securities of the class of securities subject to the Rule 13e–3 transaction are held of record by a broker, dealer, bank or voting trustee or their nominees, such issuer or affiliate shall (unless Rule 14a–13(a) [§ 240.14a–13(a)] or 14c–7 [§ 240.14c–7] is applicable) furnish the number of copies of the information required by paragraph (e) of this section that are requested by such persons (pursuant to inquiries by or on behalf of the issuer or affiliate), instruct such persons to forward such information to the beneficial owners of such securities in a timely manner and undertake to pay the reasonable expenses incurred by such persons in forwarding such information; and

(iii)   Promptly disseminate disclosure of material changes to the information required by paragraph (d) of this section in a manner reasonably calculated to inform security holders.

(2)   If the Rule 13e–3 transaction is a tender offer or a request or invitation for tenders of equity securities which is subject to Regulation 14D [§§ 240.14d–1 to 240.14d–101] or Rule 13e–4 [§ 240.13e–4], the tender offer containing the information required by paragraph (e) of this section, and any material change with respect thereto, shall be published, sent or given in accordance with Regulation 14D or Rule 13e–4, respectively, to security holders of the class of securities being sought by the issuer or affiliate.

(g)   Exceptions. This section shall not apply to:

(1) Any Rule 13e–3 transaction by or on behalf of a person which occurs within one year of the date of termination of a tender offer in which such person was the bidder and became an affiliate of the issuer as a result of such tender offer: Provided, That the consideration offered to unaffiliated security holders in such Rule 13e–3 transaction is at least equal to the highest consideration offered during such tender offer and Provided further, That:

(i) If such tender offer was made for any or all securities of a class of the issuer;

(A) Such tender offer fully disclosed such person's intention to engage in a Rule 13e–3 transaction, the form and effect of such transaction and, to the extent known, the proposed terms thereof; and

(B) Such Rule 13e–3 transaction is substantially similar to that described in such tender offer; or

(ii) If such tender offer was made for less than all the securities of a class of the issuer:

(A) Such tender offer fully disclosed a plan of merger, a plan of liquidation or a similar binding agreement between such person and the issuer with respect to a Rule 13e–3 transaction; and

(B) Such Rule 13e–3 transaction occurs pursuant to the plan of merger, plan of liquidation or similar binding agreement disclosed in the bidder's tender offer.

(2) Any Rule 13e–3 transaction in which the security holders are offered or receive only an equity security Provided, That:

(i) Such equity security has substantially the same rights as the equity security which is the subject of the Rule 13e–3 transaction including, but not limited to, voting, dividends, redemption and liquidation rights except that this requirement shall be deemed to be satisfied if unaffiliated security holders are offered common stock;

(ii) Such equity security is registered pursuant to section 12 of the Act or reports are required to be filed by the issuer thereof pursuant to section 15(d) of the Act; and

(iii) If the security which is the subject of the Rule 13e–3 transaction was either listed on a national securities exchange or authorized to be quoted in an interdealer quotation system of a registered national securities association, such equity security is either listed on a national securities exchange or authorized to be quoted in an inter-dealer quotation system of a registered national securities association.

(3) [Reserved]

(4) Redemptions, calls or similar purchases of an equity security by an issuer pursuant to specific provisions set forth in the instrument(s) creating or governing that class of equity securities; or

(5) Any solicitation by an issuer with respect to a plan of reorganization under Chapter XI of the Bankruptcy Act, as amended, if made after the entry of an order approving such plan pursuant to section 1125(b) of that Act and after, or concurrently with, the transmittal of information concerning such plan as required by section 1125(b) of that Act.

(6) Any tender offer or business combination made in compliance with § 230.802 of this chapter, § 240.13e–4(h)(8) or § 240.14d–1(c) or any other kind of transaction that otherwise meets the conditions for reliance on the cross-border exemptions set forth in § 240.13e–4(h)(8), § 240.14d–1(c) or § 230.802 of this chapter except for the fact that it is not technically subject to those rules.

Instruction to § 240.13e–3(g)(6):

To the extent applicable, the acquiror must comply with the conditions set forth in § 230.802 of this chapter, and §§ 240.13e–4(h)(8) and 14d–1(c). If the acquiror publishes or otherwise disseminates an informational document to the holders of the subject securities in connection with the transaction, the acquiror must furnish an English translation of that informational document, including any amendments thereto, to the Commission under cover of Form CB (§ 239.800 of this chapter) by the first business day after publication or dissemination. If the acquiror is a foreign entity, it must also file a Form F-X (§ 239.42 of this chapter) with the Commission at the same time as the submission of the Form CB to appoint an agent for service in the United States.

§ 240.13e–4.   Tender Offers by Issuers

(a)   Definitions. Unless the context otherwise requires, all terms used in this section and in Schedule TO (§ 240.14d–100) shall have the same meaning as in the Act or elsewhere in the General Rules and Regulations thereunder. In addition, the following definitions shall apply:

(1)   The term issuer means any issuer which has a class of equity security registered pursuant to section 12 of the Act, or which is required to file periodic reports pursuant to section 15(d) of the Act, or which is a closed-end investment company registered under the Investment Company Act of 1940.

(2)   The term issuer tender offer refers to a tender offer for, or a request or invitation for tenders of, any class of equity security, made by the issuer of such class of equity security or by an affiliate of such issuer.

(3)   As used in this section and in Schedule TO (§ 240.14d–100), the term business day means any day, other than Saturday, Sunday, or a Federal holiday, and shall consist of the time period from 12:01 a.m. through 12:00 midnight Eastern Time. In computing any time period under this Rule or Schedule TO, the date of the event that begins the running of such time period shall be included except that if such event occurs on other than a business day such period shall begin to run on and shall include the first business day thereafter.

(4)   The term commencement means 12:01 a.m. on the date that the issuer or affiliate has first published, sent or given the means to tender to security holders. For purposes of this section, the means to tender includes the transmittal form or a statement regarding how the transmittal form may be obtained.

(5)   The term termination means the date after which securities may not be tendered pursuant to an issuer tender offer.

(6)   The term security holders means holders of record and beneficial owners of securities of the class of equity security which is the subject of an issuer tender offer.

(7)   The term security position listing means, with respect to the securities of any issuer held by a registered clearing agency in the name of the clearing agency or its nominee, a list of those participants in the clearing agency on whose behalf the clearing agency holds the issuer's securities and of the participants' respective positions in such securities as of a specified date.

(b)   Filing, disclosure and dissemination. As soon as practicable on the date of commencement of the issuer tender offer, the issuer or affiliate making the issuer tender offer must comply with:

(1)   The filing requirements of paragraph (c)(2) of this section;

(2)   The disclosure requirements of paragraph (d)(1) of this section; and

(3)   The dissemination requirements of paragraph (e) of this section.

(c)   Material required to be filed. The issuer or affiliate making the issuer tender offer must file with the Commission:

(1)   All written communications made by the issuer or affiliate relating to the issuer tender offer, from and including the first public announcement, as soon as practicable on the date of the communication;

(2)   A Schedule TO (§ 240.14d–100), including all exhibits;

(3)   An amendment to Schedule TO (§ 240.14d–100) reporting promptly any material changes in the information set forth in the schedule previously filed; and

(4)   A final amendment to Schedule TO (§ 240.14d–100) reporting promptly the results of the issuer tender offer.

Instructions to § 240.13e–4(c):

1.   Pre-commencement communications must be filed under cover of Schedule TO (§ 240.14d–100) and the box on the cover page of the schedule must be marked.

2.   Any communications made in connection with an exchange offer registered under the Securities Act of 1933 need only be filed under § 230.425 of this chapter and will be deemed filed under this section.

3.   Each pre-commencement written communication must include a prominent legend in clear, plain language advising security holders to read the tender offer statement when it is available because it contains important information. The legend also must advise investors that they can get the tender offer statement and other filed documents for free at the Commission's web site and explain which documents are free from the issuer.

4.   *See* §§ 230.135, 230.165 and 230.166 of this chapter for pre-commencement communications made in connection with registered exchange offers.

5.   "Public announcement" is any oral or written communication by the issuer, affiliate or any person authorized to act on their behalf that is reasonably designed to, or has the effect of, informing the public or security holders in general about the issuer tender offer.

(d)   Disclosure of tender offer information to security holders.

(1)   The issuer or affiliate making the issuer tender offer must disclose, in a manner prescribed by paragraph (e)(1) of this section, the following:

(i)   The information required by Item 1 of Schedule TO (§ 240.14d–100) (summary term sheet); and

(ii)   The information required by the remaining items of Schedule TO for issuer tender offers, except for Item 12 (exhibits), or a fair and adequate summary of the information.

(2)   If there are any material changes in the information previously disclosed to security holders, the issuer or affiliate must disclose the changes promptly to security holders in a manner specified in paragraph (e)(3) of this section.

(3)   If the issuer or affiliate disseminates the issuer tender offer by means of summary publication as described in paragraph (e)(1)(iii) of this section, the summary advertisement must not include a transmittal letter that would permit security holders to tender securities sought in the offer and must disclose at least the following information:

(i)   The identity of the issuer or affiliate making the issuer tender offer;

(ii)   The information required by § 229.1004(a)(1) and § 229.1006(a) of this chapter;

(iii)   Instructions on how security holders can obtain promptly a copy of the statement required by paragraph (d)(1) of this section, at the issuer or affiliate's expense; and

(iv)   A statement that the information contained in the statement required by paragraph (d)(1) of this section is incorporated by reference.

(e)   Dissemination of tender offers to security holders. An issuer tender offer will be deemed to be published, sent or given to security holders if the issuer or affiliate making the issuer tender offer complies fully with one or more of the methods described in this section.

(1)   For issuer tender offers in which the consideration offered consists solely of cash and/or securities exempt from registration under section 3 of the Securities Act of 1933 (15 U.S.C. 77c):

(i)   Dissemination of cash issuer tender offers by long-form publication: By making adequate publication of the information required by paragraph (d)(1) of this section in a newspaper or newspapers, on the date of commencement of the issuer tender offer.

(ii)   Dissemination of any issuer tender offer by use of stockholder and other lists:

(A) By mailing or otherwise furnishing promptly a statement containing the information required by paragraph (d)(1) of this section to each security holder whose name appears on the most recent stockholder list of the issuer;

(B) By contacting each participant on the most recent security position listing of any clearing agency within the possession or access of the issuer or affiliate making the issuer tender offer, and making inquiry of each participant as to the approximate number of beneficial owners of the securities sought in the offer that are held by the participant;

(C) By furnishing to each participant a sufficient number of copies of the statement required by paragraph (d)(1) of this section for transmittal to the beneficial owners; and

(D) By agreeing to reimburse each participant promptly for its reasonable expenses incurred in forwarding the statement to beneficial owners.

(iii) Dissemination of certain cash issuer tender offers by summary publication:

(A) If the issuer tender offer is not subject to § 240.13e–3, by making adequate publication of a summary advertisement containing the information required by paragraph (d)(3) of this section in a newspaper or newspapers, on the date of commencement of the issuer tender offer; and

(B) By mailing or otherwise furnishing promptly the statement required by paragraph (d)(1) of this section and a transmittal letter to any security holder who requests a copy of the statement or transmittal letter.

Instruction to paragraph (e)(1):

For purposes of paragraphs (e)(1)(i) and (e)(1)(iii) of this section, adequate publication of the issuer tender offer may require publication in a newspaper with a national circulation, a newspaper with metropolitan or regional circulation, or a combination of the two, depending upon the facts and circumstances involved.

(2)   For tender offers in which the consideration consists solely or partially of securities registered under the Securities Act of 1933, a registration statement containing all of the required information, including pricing information, has been filed and a preliminary prospectus or a prospectus that meets the requirements of Section 10(a) of the Securities Act (15 U.S.C. 77j(a)), including a letter of transmittal, is delivered to security holders. However, for going-private transactions (as defined by § 240.13e–3) and roll-up transactions (as described by Item 901 of Regulation S–K (§ 229.901 of this chapter)), a registration statement registering the securities to be offered must have become effective and only a prospectus that meets the requirements of Section 10(a) of the Securities Act may be delivered to security holders on the date of commencement.

Instructions to paragraph (e)(2):

1.   If the prospectus is being delivered by mail, mailing on the date of commencement is sufficient.

2.   A preliminary prospectus used under this section may not omit information under § 230.430 or § 230.430A of this chapter.

3. If a preliminary prospectus is used under this section and the issuer must disseminate material changes, the tender offer must remain open for the period specified in paragraph (e)(3) of this section.

4. If a preliminary prospectus is used under this section, tenders may be requested in accordance with § 230.162(a) of this chapter.

(3) If a material change occurs in the information published, sent or given to security holders, the issuer or affiliate must disseminate promptly disclosure of the change in a manner reasonably calculated to inform security holders of the change. In a registered securities offer where the issuer or affiliate disseminates the preliminary prospectus as permitted by paragraph (e)(2) of this section, the offer must remain open from the date that material changes to the tender offer materials are disseminated to security holders, as follows:

(i) Five business days for a prospectus supplement containing a material change other than price or share levels;

(ii) Ten business days for a prospectus supplement containing a change in price, the amount of securities sought, the dealer's soliciting fee, or other similarly significant change;

(iii) Ten business days for a prospectus supplement included as part of a post-effective amendment; and

(iv) Twenty business days for a revised prospectus when the initial prospectus was materially deficient.

(f) Manner of making tender offer.

(1) The issuer tender offer, unless withdrawn, shall remain open until the expiration of:

(i) At least twenty business days from its commencement; and

(ii) At least ten business days from the date that notice of an increase or decrease in the percentage of the class of securities being sought or the consideration offered or the dealer's soliciting fee to be given is first published, sent or given to security holders.

Provided, however, That, for purposes of this paragraph, the acceptance for payment by the issuer or affiliate of an additional amount of securities not to exceed two percent of the class of securities that is the subject of the tender offer shall not be deemed to be an increase. For purposes of this paragraph, the percentage of a class of securities shall be calculated in accordance with section 14(d)(3) of the Act.

(2) The issuer or affiliate making the issuer tender offer shall permit securities tendered pursuant to the issuer tender offer to be withdrawn:

(i) At any time during the period such issuer tender offer remains open; and

(ii) If not yet accepted for payment, after the expiration of forty business days from the commencement of the issuer tender offer.

(3) If the issuer or affiliate makes a tender offer for less than all of the outstanding equity securities of a class, and if a greater number of securities is tendered pursuant thereto than the issuer or affiliate is bound or willing to take up and pay for, the securities taken up and paid for shall be taken up and paid for as nearly as may be pro rata, disregarding fractions, according to the number of securities tendered by each security holder during the period such offer remains open; Provided, however, That this provision shall not prohibit the issuer or affiliate making the issuer tender offer from:

(i) Accepting all securities tendered by persons who own, beneficially or of record, an aggregate of not more than a specified number which is less than one hundred shares of such security and who tender all their securities, before prorating securities tendered by others; or

(ii)   Accepting by lot securities tendered by security holders who tender all securities held by them and who, when tendering their securities, elect to have either all or none or at least a minimum amount or none accepted, if the issuer or affiliate first accepts all securities tendered by security holders who do not so elect;

(4)   In the event the issuer or affiliate making the issuer tender increases the consideration offered after the issuer tender offer has commenced, such issuer or affiliate shall pay such increased consideration to all security holders whose tendered securities are accepted for payment by such issuer or affiliate.

(5)   The issuer or affiliate making the tender offer shall either pay the consideration offered, or return the tendered securities, promptly after the termination or withdrawal of the tender offer.

(6)   Until the expiration of at least ten business days after the date of termination of the issuer tender offer, neither the issuer nor any affiliate shall make any purchases, otherwise than pursuant to the tender offer, of:

(i)   Any security which is the subject of the issuer tender offer, or any security of the same class and series, or any right to purchase any such securities; and

(ii)   In the case of an issuer tender offer which is an exchange offer, any security being offered pursuant to such exchange offer, or any security of the same class and series, or any right to purchase any such security.

(7)   The time periods for the minimum offering periods pursuant to this section shall be computed on a concurrent as opposed to a consecutive basis.

(8)   No issuer or affiliate shall make a tender offer unless:

(i)   The tender offer is open to all security holders of the class of securities subject to the tender offer; and

(ii)   The consideration paid to any security holder for securities tendered in the tender offer is the highest consideration paid to any other security holder for securities tendered in the tender offer.

(9)   Paragraph (f)(8)(i) of this section shall not:

(i)   Affect dissemination under paragraph (e) of this section; or

(ii)   Prohibit an issuer or affiliate from making a tender offer excluding all security holders in a state where the issuer or affiliate is prohibited from making the tender offer by administrative or judicial action pursuant to a state statute after a good faith effort by the issuer or affiliate to comply with such statute.

(10) Paragraph (f)(8)(ii) of this section shall not prohibit the offer of more than one type of consideration in a tender offer, provided that:

(i)   Security holders are afforded equal right to elect among each of the types of consideration offered; and

(ii)   The highest consideration of each type paid to any security holder is paid to any other security holder receiving that type of consideration.

(11) If the offer and sale of securities constituting consideration offered in an issuer tender offer is prohibited by the appropriate authority of a state after a good faith effort by the issuer or affiliate to register or qualify the offer and sale of such securities in such state:

(i)   The issuer or affiliate may offer security holders in such state an alternative form of consideration; and

(ii)   Paragraph (f)(10) of this section shall not operate to require the issuer or affiliate to offer or pay the alternative form of consideration to security holders in any other state.

(12)(i)   Paragraph (f)(8)(ii) of this section shall not prohibit the negotiation, execution or amendment of an employment compensation, severance or other employee benefit arrangement, or payments made or to be made or benefits granted or to be granted according to such an arrangement, with respect to any security holder of the issuer, where the amount payable under the arrangement:

(A)   Is being paid or granted as compensation for past services performed, future services to be performed, or future services to be refrained from performing, by the security holder (and matters incidental thereto); and

(B)   Is not calculated based on the number of securities tendered or to be tendered in the tender offer by the security holder.

(ii)   The provisions of paragraph (f)(12)(i) of this section shall be satisfied and, therefore, pursuant to this non-exclusive safe harbor, the negotiation, execution or amendment of an arrangement and any payments made or to be made or benefits granted or to be granted according to that arrangement shall not be prohibited by paragraph (f)(8)(ii) of this section, if the arrangement is approved as an employment compensation, severance or other employee benefit arrangement solely by independent directors as follows:

(A)   The compensation committee or a committee of the board of directors that performs functions similar to a compensation committee of the issuer approves the arrangement, regardless of whether the issuer is a party to the arrangement, or, if an affiliate is a party to the arrangement, the compensation committee or a committee of the board of directors that performs functions similar to a compensation committee of the affiliate approves the arrangement; or

(B)   If the issuer's or affiliate's board of directors, as applicable, does not have a compensation committee or a committee of the board of directors that performs functions similar to a compensation committee or if none of the members of the issuer's or affiliate's compensation committee or committee that performs functions similar to a compensation committee is independent, a special committee of the board of directors formed to consider and approve the arrangement approves the arrangement; or

(C)   If the issuer or affiliate, as applicable, is a foreign private issuer, any or all members of the board of directors or any committee of the board of directors authorized to approve employment compensation, severance or other employee benefit arrangements under the laws or regulations of the home country approves the arrangement.

Instructions to paragraph (f)(12)(ii):

For purposes of determining whether the members of the committee approving an arrangement in accordance with the provisions of paragraph (f)(12)(ii) of this section are independent, the following provisions shall apply:

1.   If the issuer or affiliate, as applicable, is a listed issuer (as defined in § 240.10A–3 of this chapter) whose securities are listed either on a national securities exchange registered pursuant to section 6(a) of the Exchange Act (15 U.S.C. 78f(a)) or in an inter-dealer quotation system of a national securities association registered pursuant to section 15A(a) of the Exchange Act (15 U.S.C. 78o–3(a)) that has independence requirements for compensation committee members that have been approved by the Commission (as those requirements may be modified or supplemented), apply the issuer's or affiliate's definition of independence that it uses for determining that the members of the compensation committee are independent in compliance with the listing standards applicable to compensation committee members of the listed issuer.

2.   If the issuer or affiliate, as applicable, is not a listed issuer (as defined in § 240.10A–3 of this chapter), apply the independence requirements for compensation committee members of a national securities exchange registered pursuant to section 6(a) of the Exchange Act (15 U.S.C. 78f(a)) or an inter-dealer quotation system of a national securities association registered pursuant to section 15A(a) of the Exchange Act (15 U.S.C. 78o–3(a)) that have been approved by the Commission (as those requirements may be modified or supplemented). Whatever definition the issuer or affiliate, as applicable, chooses, it must apply that definition consistently to all members of the committee approving the arrangement.

3.   Notwithstanding Instructions 1 and 2 to paragraph (f)(12)(ii), if the issuer or affiliate, as applicable, is a closed-end investment company registered under the Investment Company Act of 1940, a director is considered to be independent if the director is not, other than in his or her capacity as a member of the board of directors or any board committee, an "interested person" of the investment company, as defined in section 2(a)(19) of the Investment Company Act of 1940 (15 U.S.C. 80a–2(a)(19)).

4.   If the issuer or affiliate, as applicable, is a foreign private issuer, apply either the independence standards set forth in Instructions 1 and 2 to paragraph (f)(12)(ii) or the independence requirements of the laws, regulations, codes or standards of the home country of the issuer or affiliate, as applicable, for members of the board of directors or the committee of the board of directors approving the arrangement.

5.   A determination by the issuer's or affiliate's board of directors, as applicable, that the members of the board of directors or the committee of the board of directors, as applicable, approving an arrangement in accordance with the provisions of paragraph (f)(12)(ii) are independent in accordance with the provisions of this instruction to paragraph (f)(12)(ii) shall satisfy the independence requirements of paragraph (f)(12)(ii).

Instruction to paragraph (f)(12):

The fact that the provisions of paragraph (f)(12) of this section extend only to employment compensation, severance and other employee benefit arrangements and not to other arrangements, such as commercial arrangements, does not raise any inference that a payment under any such other arrangement constitutes consideration paid for securities in a tender offer.

(13) Electronic filings. If the issuer or affiliate is an electronic filer, the minimum offering periods set forth in paragraph (f)(1) of this section shall be tolled for any period during which it fails to file in electronic format, absent a hardship exemption (§§ 232.201 and 232.202 of this chapter), the Schedule TO (§ 240.14d–100), the tender offer material specified in Item 1016(a)(1) of Regulation M–A (§ 229.1016(a)(1) of this chapter), and any amendments thereto. If such documents were filed in paper pursuant to a hardship exemption (*see* § 232.201 and § 232.202 of this chapter), the minimum offering periods shall be tolled for any period during which a required confirming electronic copy of such Schedule and tender offer material is delinquent.

* * *

(h) This section shall not apply to:

(1) Calls or redemptions of any security in accordance with the terms and conditions of its governing instruments;

(2) Offers to purchase securities evidenced by a scrip certificate, order form or similar document which represents a fractional interest in a share of stock or similar security;

(3) Offers to purchase securities pursuant to a statutory procedure for the purchase of dissenting security holders' securities;

(4) Any tender offer which is subject to section 14(d) of the Act;

(5) Offers to purchase from security holders who own an aggregate of not more than a specified number of shares that is less than one hundred: Provided, however, That:

(i)   The offer complies with paragraph (f)(8)(i) of this section with respect to security holders who own a number of shares equal to or less than the specified number of shares, except that an issuer can elect to exclude participants in a plan as that term is defined in § 242.100 of this chapter, or to exclude security holders who do not own their shares as of a specified date determined by the issuer; and

(ii)   The offer complies with paragraph (f)(8)(ii) of this section or the consideration paid pursuant to the offer is determined on the basis of a uniformly applied formula based on the market price of the subject security;

(6)   An issuer tender offer made solely to effect a rescission offer: Provided, however, That the offer is registered under the Securities Act of 1933 (15 U.S.C. 77a *et seq.*), and the consideration is equal to the price paid by each security holder, plus legal interest if the issuer elects to or is required to pay legal interest;

(7)   Offers by closed-end management investment companies to repurchase equity securities pursuant to § 270.23c–3 of this chapter;

(8)   Cross-border tender offers (Tier I). Any issuer tender offer (including any exchange offer) where the issuer is a foreign private issuer as defined in § 240.3b–4 if the following conditions are satisfied.

(i)   Except in the case of an issuer tender offer that is commenced during the pendency of a tender offer made by a third party in reliance on § 240.14d–1(c), U.S. holders do not hold more than 10 percent of the subject class sought in the offer (as determined under Instructions 2 or 3 to paragraph (h)(8) and paragraph (i) of this section);

(ii)   The issuer or affiliate must permit U.S. holders to participate in the offer on terms at least as favorable as those offered any other holder of the same class of securities that is the subject of the offer; however:

(A)   Registered exchange offers. If the issuer or affiliate offers securities registered under the Securities Act of 1933 (15 U.S.C. 77a *et seq.*), the issuer or affiliate need not extend the offer to security holders in those states or jurisdictions that prohibit the offer or sale of the securities after the issuer or affiliate has made a good faith effort to register or qualify the offer and sale of securities in that state or jurisdiction, except that the issuer or affiliate must offer the same cash alternative to security holders in any such state or jurisdiction that it has offered to security holders in any other state or jurisdiction.

(B)   Exempt exchange offers. If the issuer or affiliate offers securities exempt from registration under § 230.802 of this chapter, the issuer or affiliate need not extend the offer to security holders in those states or jurisdictions that require registration or qualification, except that the issuer or affiliate must offer the same cash alternative to security holders in any such state or jurisdiction that it has offered to security holders in any other state or jurisdiction.

(C)   Cash only consideration. The issuer or affiliate may offer U.S. holders cash only consideration for the tender of the subject securities, notwithstanding the fact that the issuer or affiliate is offering security holders outside the United States a consideration that consists in whole or in part of securities of the issuer or affiliate, if the issuer or affiliate has a reasonable basis for believing that the amount of cash is substantially equivalent to the value of the consideration offered to non-U.S. holders, and either of the following conditions are satisfied:

(1)   The offered security is a "margin security" within the meaning of Regulation T (12 CFR 220.2) and the issuer or affiliate undertakes to provide, upon the request of any U.S. holder or the Commission staff, the closing price and daily trading volume of the security on the principal trading market for the security as

of the last trading day of each of the six months preceding the announcement of the offer and each of the trading days thereafter; or

(2) If the offered security is not a "margin security" within the meaning of Regulation T (12 CFR 220.2), the issuer or affiliate undertakes to provide, upon the request of any U.S. holder or the Commission staff, an opinion of an independent expert stating that the cash consideration offered to U.S. holders is substantially equivalent to the value of the consideration offered security holders outside the United States.

(D) Disparate tax treatment. If the issuer or affiliate offers "loan notes" solely to offer sellers tax advantages not available in the United States and these notes are neither listed on any organized securities market nor registered under the Securities Act of 1933 (15 U.S.C. 77a et seq.), the loan notes need not be offered to U.S. holders.

(iii) Informational documents. (A) If the issuer or affiliate publishes or otherwise disseminates an informational document to the holders of the securities in connection with the issuer tender offer (including any exchange offer), the issuer or affiliate must furnish that informational document, including any amendments thereto, in English, to the Commission on Form CB (§ 249.480 of this chapter) by the first business day after publication or dissemination. If the issuer or affiliate is a foreign company, it must also file a Form F-X (§ 239.42 of this chapter) with the Commission at the same time as the submission of Form CB to appoint an agent for service in the United States.

(B) The issuer or affiliate must disseminate any informational document to U.S. holders, including any amendments thereto, in English, on a comparable basis to that provided to security holders in the home jurisdiction.

(C) If the issuer or affiliate disseminates by publication in its home jurisdiction, the issuer or affiliate must publish the information in the United States in a manner reasonably calculated to inform U.S. holders of the offer.

(iv) An investment company registered or required to be registered under the Investment Company Act of 1940 (15 U.S.C. 80a–1 et seq.), other than a registered closed-end investment company, may not use this paragraph (h)(8); or

(9) Any other transaction or transactions, if the Commission, upon written request or upon its own motion, exempts such transaction or transactions, either unconditionally, or on specified terms and conditions, as not constituting a fraudulent, deceptive or manipulative act or practice comprehended within the purpose of this section.

(i) Cross-border tender offers (Tier II). Any issuer tender offer (including any exchange offer) that meets the conditions in paragraph (i)(1) of this section shall be entitled to the exemptive relief specified in paragraph (i)(2) of this section, provided that such issuer tender offer complies with all the requirements of this section other than those for which an exemption has been specifically provided in paragraph (i)(2) of this section. In addition, any issuer tender offer (including any exchange offer) subject only to the requirements of section 14(e) of the Act and Regulation 14E (§§ 240.14e–1 through 240.14e–8) thereunder that meets the conditions in paragraph (i)(1) of this section also shall be entitled to the exemptive relief specified in paragraph (i)(2) of this section, to the extent needed under the requirements of Regulation 14E, so long as the tender offer complies with all requirements of Regulation 14E other than those for which an exemption has been specifically provided in paragraph (i)(2) of this section:

(1) Conditions. (i) The issuer is a foreign private issuer as defined in § 240.3b–4 and is not an investment company registered or required to be registered under the Investment Company Act of 1940 (15 U.S.C. 80a–1 et seq.), other than a registered closed-end investment company; and

(ii) Except in the case of an issuer tender offer commenced during the pendency of a tender offer made by a third party in reliance on § 240.14d–1(d), U.S. holders do not hold more than 40 percent of the class of securities sought in the offer (as determined in accordance with Instructions 2 or 3 to paragraphs (h)(8) and (i) of this section).

(2) Exemptions. The issuer tender offer shall comply with all requirements of this section other than the following:

(i) Equal treatment—loan notes. If the issuer or affiliate offers loan notes solely to offer sellers tax advantages not available in the United States and these notes are neither listed on any organized securities market nor registered under the Securities Act (15 U.S.C. 77a *et seq.*), the loan notes need not be offered to U.S. holders, notwithstanding paragraph (f)(8) and (h)(9) of this section.

(ii) Equal treatment—separate U.S. and foreign offers. Notwithstanding the provisions of paragraph (f)(8) of this section, an issuer or affiliate conducting an issuer tender offer meeting the conditions of paragraph (i)(1) of this section may separate the offer into multiple offers: one offer made to U.S. holders, which also may include all holders of American Depositary Shares representing interests in the subject securities, and one or more offers made to non-U.S. holders. The U.S. offer must be made on terms at least as favorable as those offered any other holder of the same class of securities that is the subject of the tender offers. U.S. holders may be included in the foreign offer(s) only where the laws of the jurisdiction governing such foreign offer(s) expressly preclude the exclusion of U.S. holders from the foreign offer(s) and where the offer materials distributed to U.S. holders fully and adequately disclose the risks of participating in the foreign offer(s).

(iii) Notice of extensions. Notice of extensions made in accordance with the requirements of the home jurisdiction law or practice will satisfy the requirements of § 240.14e–1(d).

(iv) Prompt payment. Payment made in accordance with the requirements of the home jurisdiction law or practice will satisfy the requirements of § 240.14e–1(c).

(v) Suspension of withdrawal rights during counting of tendered securities. The issuer or affiliate may suspend withdrawal rights required under paragraph (f)(2) of this section at the end of the offer and during the period that securities tendered into the offer are being counted, provided that:

(A) The issuer or affiliate has provided an offer period, including withdrawal rights, for a period of at least 20 U.S. business days;

(B) At the time withdrawal rights are suspended, all offer conditions have been satisfied or waived, except to the extent that the issuer or affiliate is in the process of determining whether a minimum acceptance condition included in the terms of the offer has been satisfied by counting tendered securities; and

(C) Withdrawal rights are suspended only during the counting process and are reinstated immediately thereafter, except to the extent that they are terminated through the acceptance of tendered securities.

(vi) Early termination of an initial offering period. An issuer or affiliate conducting an issuer tender offer may terminate an initial offering period, including a voluntary extension of that period, if at the time the initial offering period and withdrawal rights terminate, the following conditions are met:

(A) The initial offering period has been open for at least 20 U.S. business days;

(B) The issuer or affiliate has adequately discussed the possibility of and the impact of the early termination in the original offer materials;

(C) The issuer or affiliate provides a subsequent offering period after the termination of the initial offering period;

(D) All offer conditions are satisfied as of the time when the initial offering period ends; and

(E) The issuer or affiliate does not terminate the initial offering period or any extension of that period during any mandatory extension required under U.S. tender offer rules.

Instructions to paragraph (h)(8) and (i) of this section:

1.   Home jurisdiction means both the jurisdiction of the issuer's incorporation, organization or chartering and the principal foreign market where the issuer's securities are listed or quoted.

2.   U.S. holder means any security holder resident in the United States. To determine the percentage of outstanding securities held by U.S. holders:

i.   Calculate the U.S. ownership as of a date no more than 60 days before and no more than 30 days after the public announcement of the tender offer. If you are unable to calculate as of a date within these time frames, the calculation may be made as of the most recent practicable date before public announcement, but in no event earlier than 120 days before announcement;

ii.   Include securities underlying American Depositary Shares convertible or exchangeable into the securities that are the subject of the tender offer when calculating the number of subject securities outstanding, as well as the number held by U.S. holders. Exclude from the calculations other types of securities that are convertible or exchangeable into the securities that are the subject of the tender offer, such as warrants, options and convertible securities;

iii.   Use the method of calculating record ownership in § 240.12g3–2(a), except that your inquiry as to the amount of securities represented by accounts of customers resident in the United States may be limited to brokers, dealers, banks and other nominees located in the United States, your jurisdiction of incorporation, and the jurisdiction that is the primary trading market for the subject securities, if different than your jurisdiction of incorporation;

iv.   If, after reasonable inquiry, you are unable to obtain information about the amount of securities represented by accounts of customers resident in the United States, you may assume, for purposes of this definition, that the customers are residents of the jurisdiction in which the nominee has its principal place of business; and

v.   Count securities as beneficially owned by residents of the United States as reported on reports of beneficial ownership that are provided to you or publicly filed and based on information otherwise provided to you.

3.   If you are unable to conduct the analysis of U.S. ownership set forth in Instruction 2 above, U.S. holders will be presumed to hold 10 percent or less of the outstanding subject securities (40 percent for Tier II) so long as there is a primary trading market outside the United States, as defined in § 240.12h–6(f)(5) of this chapter, unless:

i.   Average daily trading volume of the subject securities in the United States for a recent twelve-month period ending on a date no more than 60 days before the public announcement of the tender offer exceeds 10 percent (or 40 percent) of the average daily trading volume of that class of securities on a worldwide basis for the same period; or

ii.   The most recent annual report or annual information filed or submitted by the issuer with securities regulators of the home jurisdiction or with the Commission or any jurisdiction in which the subject securities trade before the public announcement of the offer indicates that U.S. holders hold more than 10 percent (or 40 percent) of the outstanding subject class of securities; or

iii.   You know or have reason to know, before the public announcement of the offer, that the level of U.S. ownership of the subject securities exceeds 10 percent (or 40 percent) of such securities. As an example, you are deemed to know information about U.S. ownership of the subject class of securities that is publicly available and that appears in any filing with the

Commission or any regulatory body in the home jurisdiction and, if different, the non-U.S. jurisdiction in which the primary trading market for the subject class of securities is located. You are also deemed to know information obtained or readily available from any other source that is reasonably reliable, including from persons you have retained to advise you about the transaction, as well as from third-party information providers. These examples are not intended to be exclusive.

4. United States means the United States of America, its territories and possessions, any State of the United States, and the District of Columbia.

5. The exemptions provided by paragraphs (h)(8) and (i) of this section are not available for any securities transaction or series of transactions that technically complies with paragraph (h)(8) and (i) of this section but are part of a plan or scheme to evade the provisions of this section.

(j)(1) It shall be a fraudulent, deceptive or manipulative act or practice, in connection with an issuer tender offer, for an issuer or an affiliate of such issuer, in connection with an issuer tender offer:

(i) To employ any device, scheme or artifice to defraud any person;

(ii) To make any untrue statement of a material fact or to omit to state a material fact necessary in order to make the statements made, in the light of the circumstances under which they were made, not misleading; or

(iii) To engage in any act, practice or course of business which operates or would operate as a fraud or deceit upon any person.

(2) As a means reasonably designed to prevent fraudulent, deceptive or manipulative acts or practices in connection with any issuer tender offer, it shall be unlawful for an issuer or an affiliate of such issuer to make an issuer tender offer unless:

(i) Such issuer or affiliate complies with the requirements of paragraphs (b), (c), (d), (e) and (f) of this section; and

(ii) The issuer tender offer is not in violation of paragraph (j)(1) of this section.

REPORTS BY INSTITUTIONAL MANAGERS

§ 240.13f–1. **Reporting by Institutional Investment Managers of Information with Respect to Accounts Over Which They Exercise Investment Discretion**

(a)(1) Every institutional investment manager which exercises investment discretion with respect to accounts holding section 13(f) securities, as defined in paragraph (c) of this section, having an aggregate fair market value on the last trading day of any month of any calendar year of at least $100,000,000 shall file a report on Form 13F (§ 249.325 of this chapter) with the Commission within 45 days after the last day of such calendar year and within 45 days after the last day of each of the first three calendar quarters of the subsequent calendar year.

(2) An amendment to a Form 13F (§ 249.325 of this chapter) report, other than one reporting only holdings that were not previously reported in a public filing for the same period, must set forth the complete text of the Form 13F. Amendments must be numbered sequentially.

(b) For the purposes of this rule, "investment discretion" has the meaning set forth in section 3(a)(35) of the Act (15 U.S.C. 78c(a)(35)). An institutional investment manager shall also be deemed to exercise "investment discretion" with respect to all accounts over which any person under its control exercises investment discretion.

(c) For purposes of this rule "section 13(f) securities" shall mean equity securities of a class described in section 13(d)(1) of the Act that are admitted to trading on a national securities exchange or quoted on the automated quotation system of a registered securities association. In determining what classes of securities are section 13(f) securities, an institutional investment manager may rely on the most recent list of such securities published by the Commission pursuant to section 13(f)(4) of the Act (15 U.S.C. 78m(f)(4)). Only securities of a class on such list shall be counted in determining whether an institutional investment manager must file a report under this rule (§ 240.13f–1(a)) and only those securities shall be reported in such report. Where a person controls the issuer of a class of equity securities which are "section 13(f) securities" as defined in this rule, those securities shall not be deemed to be "section 13(f) securities" with respect to the controlling person, provided that such person does not otherwise exercise investment discretion with respect to accounts with fair market value of at least $100,000,000 within the meaning of paragraph (a) of this section.

* * *

SOLICITATION OF PROXIES

§ 240.14a–1.   Definitions

Unless the context otherwise requires, all terms used in this regulation have the same meanings as in the Act or elsewhere in the general rules and regulations thereunder. In addition, the following definitions apply unless the context otherwise requires:

(a)   Associate. The term "associate," used to indicate a relationship with any person, means:

(1)   Any corporation or organization (other than the registrant or a majority owned subsidiary of the registrant) of which such person is an officer or partner or is, directly or indirectly, the beneficial owner of 10 percent or more of any class of equity securities;

(2)   Any trust or other estate in which such person has a substantial beneficial interest or as to which such person serves as trustee or in a similar fiduciary capacity; and

(3)   Any relative or spouse of such person, or any relative of such spouse, who has the same home as such person or who is a director or officer of the registrant or any of its parents or subsidiaries.

(b)   Employee benefit plan. For purposes of §§ 240.14a–13, 240.14b–1 and 240.14b–2, the term "employee benefit plan" means any purchase, savings, option, bonus, appreciation, profit sharing, thrift, incentive, pension or similar plan primarily for employees, directors, trustees or officers.

(c)   Entity that exercises fiduciary powers. The term "entity that exercises fiduciary powers" means any entity that holds securities in nominee name or otherwise on behalf of a beneficial owner but does not include a clearing agency registered pursuant to section 17A of the Act or a broker or a dealer.

(d)   Exempt employee benefit plan securities. For purposes of §§ 240.14a–13, 240.14b–1 and 240.14b–2, the term "exempt employee benefit plan securities" means:

(1)   Securities of the registrant held by an employee benefit plan, as defined in paragraph (b) of this section, where such plan is established by the registrant; or

(2)   If notice regarding the current solicitation has been given pursuant to § 240.14a–13(a)(1)(ii)(C) or if notice regarding the current request for a list of names, addresses and securities positions of beneficial owners has been given pursuant to § 240.14a–13(b)(3), securities of the registrant held by an employee benefit plan, as defined in paragraph (b) of this section, where such plan is established by an affiliate of the registrant.

(e)   Last fiscal year. The term "last fiscal year" of the registrant means the last fiscal year of the registrant ending prior to the date of the meeting for which proxies are to be solicited or if the solicitation involves written authorizations or consents in lieu of a meeting, the earliest date they may be used to effect corporate action.

(f)   Proxy. The term "proxy" includes every proxy, consent or authorization within the meaning of section 14(a) of the Act. The consent or authorization may take the form of failure to object or to dissent.

(g)   Proxy statement. The term "proxy statement" means the statement required by § 240.14a–3(a) whether or not contained in a single document.

(h)   Record date. The term "record date" means the date as of which the record holders of securities entitled to vote at a meeting or by written consent or authorization shall be determined.

(i)   Record holder. For purposes of §§ 240.14a–13, 240.14b–1 and 240.14b–2, the term "record holder" means any broker, dealer, voting trustee, bank, association or other entity that exercises fiduciary powers which holds securities of record in nominee name or otherwise or as a participant in a clearing agency registered pursuant to section 17A of the Act.

(j)   Registrant. The term "registrant" means the issuer of the securities in respect of which proxies are to be solicited.

(k)   Respondent bank. For purposes of §§ 240.14a–13, 240.14b–1 and 240.14b–2, the term "respondent bank" means any bank, association or other entity that exercises fiduciary powers which holds securities on behalf of beneficial owners and deposits such securities for safekeeping with another bank, association or other entity that exercises fiduciary powers.

(*l*)   Solicitation. (1) The terms "solicit" and "solicitation" include:

(i)   Any request for a proxy whether or not accompanied by or included in a form of proxy;

(ii)   Any request to execute or not to execute, or to revoke, a proxy; or

(iii)   The furnishing of a form of proxy or other communication to security holders under circumstances reasonably calculated to result in the procurement, withholding or revocation of a proxy.

(2)   The terms do not apply, however, to:

(i)   The furnishing of a form of proxy to a security holder upon the unsolicited request of such security holder;

(ii)   The performance by the registrant of acts required by § 240.14a–7;

(iii)   The performance by any person of ministerial acts on behalf of a person soliciting a proxy; or

(iv)   A communication by a security holder who does not otherwise engage in a proxy solicitation (other than a solicitation exempt under § 240.14a–2) stating how the security holder intends to vote and the reasons therefor, provided that the communication:

(A)   Is made by means of speeches in public forums, press releases, published or broadcast opinions, statements, or advertisements appearing in a broadcast media, or newspaper, magazine or other bona fide publication disseminated on a regular basis,

(B)   Is directed to persons to whom the security holder owes a fiduciary duty in connection with the voting of securities of a registrant held by the security holder, or

(C)   Is made in response to unsolicited requests for additional information with respect to a prior communication by the security holder made pursuant to this paragraph (*l*)(2)(iv).

§ 240.14a–2.   Solicitations to Which § 240.14a–3 to § 240.14a–15 Apply

Sections 240.14a–3 to 240.14a–15, except as specified, apply to every solicitation of a proxy with respect to securities registered pursuant to section 12 of the Act (15 U.S.C. 78 l), whether or not trading in such securities has been suspended. To the extent specified below, certain of these sections also apply to roll-up transactions that do not involve an entity with securities registered pursuant to section 12 of the Act.

(a)   Sections 240.14a–3 to 240.14a–15 do not apply to the following:

(1)   Any solicitation by a person in respect to securities carried in his name or in the name of his nominee (otherwise than as voting trustee) or held in his custody, if such person—

(i)   Receives no commission or remuneration for such solicitation, directly or indirectly, other than reimbursement of reasonable expenses,

(ii)   Furnishes promptly to the person solicited (or such person's household in accordance with § 240.14a–3(e)(1)) a copy of all soliciting material with respect to the same subject matter or meeting received from all persons who shall furnish copies thereof for such purpose and who shall, if requested, defray the reasonable expenses to be incurred in forwarding such material, and

(iii)   In addition, does no more than impartially instruct the person solicited to forward a proxy to the person, if any, to whom the person solicited desires to give a proxy, or impartially request from the person solicited instructions as to the authority to be conferred by the proxy and state that a proxy will be given if no instructions are received by a certain date.

(2)   Any solicitation by a person in respect of securities of which he is the beneficial owner;

(3)   Any solicitation involved in the offer and sale of securities registered under the Securities Act of 1933: Provided, That this paragraph shall not apply to securities to be issued in any transaction of the character specified in paragraph (a) of Rule 145 under that Act;

(4)   Any solicitation with respect to a plan of reorganization under Chapter 11 of the Bankruptcy Reform Act of 1978, as amended, if made after the entry of an order approving the written disclosure statement concerning a plan of reorganization pursuant to section 1125 of said Act and after, or concurrently with, the transmittal of such disclosure statement as required by section 1125 of said Act;

(5)   [Reserved]

(6)   Any solicitation through the medium of a newspaper advertisement which informs security holders of a source from which they may obtain copies of a proxy statement, form of proxy and any other soliciting material and does no more than:

(i)   Name the registrant,

(ii)   State the reason for the advertisement, and

(iii)   Identify the proposal or proposals to be acted upon by security holders.

(b)   Sections 240.14a–3 to 240.14a–6 (other than paragraphs 14a–6(g) and 14a–6(p)), § 240.14a–8, § 240.14a–10, and §§ 240.14a–12 to 240.14a–15 do not apply to the following:

(1)   Any solicitation by or on behalf of any person who does not, at any time during such solicitation, seek directly or indirectly, either on its own or another's behalf, the power to act as proxy for a security holder and does not furnish or otherwise request, or act on behalf of a person who furnishes or requests, a form of revocation, abstention, consent or authorization. Provided, however, That the exemption set forth in this paragraph shall not apply to:

(i)   The registrant or an affiliate or associate of the registrant (other than an officer or director or any person serving in a similar capacity);

(ii)   An officer or director of the registrant or any person serving in a similar capacity engaging in a solicitation financed directly or indirectly by the registrant;

(iii)   An officer, director, affiliate or associate of a person that is ineligible to rely on the exemption set forth in this paragraph (other than persons specified in paragraph (b)(1)(i) of this section), or any person serving in a similar capacity;

(iv) Any nominee for whose election as a director proxies are solicited;

(v) Any person soliciting in opposition to a merger, recapitalization, reorganization, sale of assets or other extraordinary transaction recommended or approved by the board of directors of the registrant who is proposing or intends to propose an alternative transaction to which such person or one of its affiliates is a party;

(vi) Any person who is required to report beneficial ownership of the registrant's equity securities on a Schedule 13D (§ 240.13d–101), unless such person has filed a Schedule 13D and has not disclosed pursuant to Item 4 thereto an intent, or reserved the right, to engage in a control transaction, or any contested solicitation for the election of directors;

(vii) Any person who receives compensation from an ineligible person directly related to the solicitation of proxies, other than pursuant to § 240.14a–13;

(viii) Where the registrant is an investment company registered under the Investment Company Act of 1940 (15 U.S.C. 80a–1 *et seq.*), an "interested person" of that investment company, as that term is defined in section 2(a)(19) of the Investment Company Act (15 U.S.C. 80a–2);

(ix) Any person who, because of a substantial interest in the subject matter of the solicitation, is likely to receive a benefit from a successful solicitation that would not be shared pro rata by all other holders of the same class of securities, other than a benefit arising from the person's employment with the registrant; and

(x) Any person acting on behalf of any of the foregoing.

(2) Any solicitation made otherwise than on behalf of the registrant where the total number of persons solicited is not more than ten;

(3) The furnishing of proxy voting advice by any person (the "advisor") to any other person with whom the advisor has a business relationship, if:

(i) The advisor renders financial advice in the ordinary course of his business;

(ii) The advisor discloses to the recipient of the advice any significant relationship with the registrant or any of its affiliates, or a security holder proponent of the matter on which advice is given, as well as any material interests of the advisor in such matter;

(iii) The advisor receives no special commission or remuneration for furnishing the proxy voting advice from any person other than a recipient of the advice and other persons who receive similar advice under this subsection; and

(iv) The proxy voting advice is not furnished on behalf of any person soliciting proxies or on behalf of a participant in an election subject to the provisions of § 240.14a–12(c); and

(4) Any solicitation in connection with a roll-up transaction as defined in Item 901(c) of Regulation S–K (§ 229.901 of this chapter) in which the holder of a security that is the subject of a proposed roll-up transaction engages in preliminary communications with other holders of securities that are the subject of the same limited partnership roll-up transaction for the purpose of determining whether to solicit proxies, consents, or authorizations in opposition to the proposed limited partnership roll-up transaction; provided, however, that:

(i) This exemption shall not apply to a security holder who is an affiliate of the registrant or general partner or sponsor; and

(ii) This exemption shall not apply to a holder of five percent (5%) or more of the outstanding securities of a class that is the subject of the proposed roll-up transaction who engages in the business of buying and selling limited partnership interests in the secondary market unless that holder discloses to the persons to whom the communications are made such ownership interest and any relations of the holder to the parties of the transaction or to the transaction itself, as required by § 240.14a–6(n)(1) and specified in the Notice of

Exempt Preliminary Roll-up Communication (§ 240.14a–104). If the communication is oral, this disclosure may be provided to the security holder orally. Whether the communication is written or oral, the notice required by § 240.14a–6(n) and § 240.14a–104 shall be furnished to the Commission.

(5) Publication or distribution by a broker or a dealer of a research report in accordance with Rule 138 (§ 230.138 of this chapter) or Rule 139 (§ 230.139 of this chapter) during a transaction in which the broker or dealer or its affiliate participates or acts in a an advisory role.

(6) Any solicitation by or on behalf of any person who does not seek directly or indirectly, either on its own or another's behalf, the power to act as proxy for a shareholder and does not furnish or otherwise request, or act on behalf of a person who furnishes or requests, a form of revocation, abstention, consent, or authorization in an electronic shareholder forum that is established, maintained or operated pursuant to the provisions of § 240.14a–17, provided that the solicitation is made more than 60 days prior to the date announced by a registrant for its next annual or special meeting of shareholders. If the registrant announces the date of its next annual or special meeting of shareholders less than 60 days before the meeting date, then the solicitation may not be made more than two days following the date of the registrant's announcement of the meeting date. Participation in an electronic shareholder forum does not eliminate a person's eligibility to solicit proxies after the date that this exemption is no longer available, or is no longer being relied upon, provided that any such solicitation is conducted in accordance with this regulation.

* * *

§ 240.14a–3.   Information to Be Furnished to Security Holders

(a) No solicitation subject to this regulation shall be made unless each person solicited is concurrently furnished or has previously been furnished with:

(1) A publicly-filed preliminary or definitive proxy statement, in the form and manner described in § 240.14a–16, containing the information specified in Schedule 14A (§ 240.14a–101);

(2) A preliminary or definitive written proxy statement included in a registration statement filed under the Securities Act of 1933 on Form S-4 or F-4 (§ 239.25 or § 239.34 of this chapter) or Form N-14 (§ 239.23 of this chapter) and containing the information specified in such Form; or

(3) A publicly-filed preliminary or definitive proxy statement, not in the form and manner described in § 240.14a–16, containing the information specified in Schedule 14A (§ 240.14a–101), if:

(i) The solicitation relates to a business combination transaction as defined in § 230.165 of this chapter, as well as transactions for cash consideration requiring disclosure under Item 14 of § 240.14a–101.

(ii) The solicitation may not follow the form and manner described in § 240.14a–16 pursuant to the laws of the state of incorporation of the registrant;

(b) If the solicitation is made on behalf of the registrant, other than an investment company registered under the Investment Company Act of 1940, and relates to an annual (or special meeting in lieu of the annual) meeting of security holders, or written consent in lieu of such meeting, at which directors are to be elected, each proxy statement furnished pursuant to paragraph (a) of this section shall be accompanied or preceded by an annual report to security holders as follows:

(1) The report shall include, for the registrant and its subsidiaries, consolidated and audited balance sheets as of the end of the two most recent fiscal years and audited statements of income and cash flows for each of the three most recent fiscal years prepared in accordance with Regulation S–X (part 210 of this chapter), except that the provisions of Article 3 (other than

§§ 210.3–03(e), 210.3–04 and 210.3–20) and Article 11 shall not apply. Any financial statement schedules or exhibits or separate financial statements which may otherwise be required in filings with the Commission may be omitted. If the financial statements of the registrant and its subsidiaries consolidated in the annual report filed or to be filed with the Commission are not required to be audited, the financial statements required by this paragraph may be unaudited. A smaller reporting company may provide the information in Article 8 of Regulation S–X (§ 210.8 of this chapter) in lieu of the financial information required by this paragraph 9(b)(1).

Note 1 to paragraph (b)(1): If the financial statements for a period prior to the most recently completed fiscal year have been examined by a predecessor accountant, the separate report of the predecessor accountant may be omitted in the report to security holders, provided the registrant has obtained from the predecessor accountant a reissued report covering the prior period presented and the successor accountant clearly indicates in the scope paragraph of his or her report (a) that the financial statements of the prior period were examined by other accountants, (b) the date of their report, (c) the type of opinion expressed by the predecessor accountant and (d) the substantive reasons therefore, if it was other than unqualified. It should be noted, however, that the separate report of any predecessor accountant is required in filings with the Commission. If, for instance, the financial statements in the annual report to security holders are incorporated by reference in a Form 10-K, the separate report of a predecessor accountant shall be filed in Part II or in Part IV as a financial statement schedule.

Note 2 to paragraph (b)(1): For purposes of complying with § 240.14a–3, if the registrant has changed its fiscal closing date, financial statements covering two years and one period of 9 to 12 months shall be deemed to satisfy the requirements for statements of income and cash flows for the three most recent fiscal years.

(2)(i)   Financial statements and notes thereto shall be presented in roman type at least as large and as legible as 10-point modern type. If necessary for convenient presentation, the financial statements may be in roman type as large and as legible as 8-point modern type. All type shall be leaded at least 2 points.

(ii)   Where the annual report to security holders is delivered through an electronic medium, issuers may satisfy legibility requirements applicable to printed documents, such as type size and font, by presenting all required information in a format readily communicated to investors.

(3)   The report shall contain the supplementary financial information required by item 302 of Regulation S–K (§ 229.302 of this chapter).

(4)   The report shall contain information concerning changes in and disagreements with accountants on accounting and financial disclosure required by Item 304 of Regulation S–K (§ 229.304 of this chapter).

(5)(i)   The report shall contain the selected financial data required by Item 301 of Regulation S–K (§ 229.301 of this chapter).

(ii)   The report shall contain management's discussion and analysis of financial condition and results of operations required by Item 303 of Regulation S–K (§ 229.303 of this chapter).

(iii)   The report shall contain the quantitative and qualitative disclosures about market risk required by Item 305 of Regulation S–K (§ 229.305 of this chapter).

(6)   The report shall contain a brief description of the business done by the registrant and its subsidiaries during the most recent fiscal year which will, in the opinion of management, indicate the general nature and scope of the business of the registrant and its subsidiaries.

(7)   The report shall contain information relating to the registrant's industry segments, classes of similar products or services, foreign and domestic operations and exports sales required by paragraphs (b), (c)(1)(i) and (d) of Item 101 of Regulation S–K (§ 229.101 of this chapter).

(8)   The report shall identify each of the registrant's directors and executive officers, and shall indicate the principal occupation or employment of each such person and the name and principal business of any organization by which such person is employed.

(9)   The report shall contain the market price of and dividends on the registrant's common equity and related security holder matters required by Items 201(a), (b) and (c) of Regulation S–K (§ 229.201(a), (b) and (c) of this chapter). If the report precedes or accompanies a proxy statement or information statement relating to an annual meeting of security holders at which directors are to be elected (or special meeting or written consents in lieu of such meeting), furnish the performance graph required by Item 201(e) (§ 229.201(e) of this chapter).

(10) The registrant's proxy statement, or the report, shall contain an undertaking in bold face or otherwise reasonably prominent type to provide without charge to each person solicited upon the written request of any such person, a copy of the registrant's annual report on Form 10-K, including the financial statements and the financial statement schedules, required to be filed with the Commission pursuant to Rule 13a–1 (§ 240.13a–1 of this chapter) under the Act for the registrant's most recent fiscal year, and shall indicate the name and address (including title or department) of the person to whom such a written request is to be directed. In the discretion of management, a registrant need not undertake to furnish without charge copies of all exhibits to its Form 10-K, provided that the copy of the annual report on Form 10-K furnished without charge to requesting security holders is accompanied by a list briefly describing all the exhibits not contained therein and indicating that the registrant will furnish any exhibit upon the payment of a specified reasonable fee, which fee shall be limited to the registrant's reasonable expenses in furnishing such exhibit. If the registrant's annual report to security holders complies with all of the disclosure requirements of Form 10-K and is filed with the Commission in satisfaction of its Form 10-K filing requirements, such registrant need not furnish a separate Form 10-K to security holders who receive a copy of such annual report.

Note to paragraph (b)(10): Pursuant to the undertaking required by paragraph (b)(10) of this section, a registrant shall furnish a copy of its annual report on Form 10-K (§ 249.310 of this chapter) to a beneficial owner of its securities upon receipt of a written request from such person. Each request must set forth a good faith representation that, as of the record date for the solicitation requiring the furnishing of the annual report to security holders pursuant to paragraph (b) of this section, the person making the request was a beneficial owner of securities entitled to vote.

(11) Subject to the foregoing requirements, the report may be in any form deemed suitable by management and the information required by paragraphs (b)(5) to (10) of this section may be presented in an appendix or other separate section of the report, provided that the attention of security holders is called to such presentation.

Note: Registrants are encouraged to utilize tables, schedules, charts and graphic illustrations of present financial information in an understandable manner. Any presentation of financial information must be consistent with the data in the financial statements contained in the report and, if appropriate, should refer to relevant portions of the financial statements and notes thereto.

(12) [Reserved]

(13) Paragraph (b) of this section shall not apply, however, to solicitations made on behalf of the registrant before the financial statements are available if a solicitation is being made at the same time in opposition to the registrant and if the registrant's proxy statement includes an undertaking in bold face type to furnish such annual report to security holders to all persons being solicited at least 20 calendar days before the date of the meeting or, if the solicitation refers to a written consent or authorization in lieu of a meeting, at least 20 calendar days prior to the earliest date on which it may be used to effect corporate action.

(c)   Seven copies of the report sent to security holders pursuant to this rule shall be mailed to the Commission, solely for its information, not later than the date on which such report is first sent or given to security holders or the date on which preliminary copies, or definitive copies, if preliminary filing was not required, of solicitation material are filed with the Commission pursuant to Rule 14a-6, whichever date is later. The report is not deemed to be "soliciting material" or to be "filed" with the Commission or subject to this regulation otherwise than as provided in this Rule, or to the liabilities of section 18 of the Act, except to the extent that the registrant specifically requests that it be treated as a part of the proxy soliciting material or incorporates it in the proxy statement or other filed report by reference.

(d)   An annual report to security holders prepared on an integrated basis pursuant to General Instruction H to Form 10-K (§ 249.310 of this chapter) may also be submitted in satisfaction of this section. When filed as the annual report on Form 10-K, responses to the Items of that form are subject to section 18 of the Act notwithstanding paragraph (c) of this section.

(e)(1)(i)   A registrant will be considered to have delivered an annual report to security holders, proxy statement or Notice of Internet Availability of Proxy Materials, as described in § 240.14a–16, to all security holders of record who share an address if:

(A)   The registrant delivers one annual report to security holders, proxy statement or Notice of Internet Availability of Proxy Materials, as applicable, to the shared address;

(B)   The registrant addresses the annual report to security holders, proxy statement or Notice of Internet Availability of Proxy Materials, as applicable, to the security holders as a group (for example, "ABC Fund [or Corporation] Security Holders," "Jane Doe and Household," "The Smith Family"), to each of the security holders individually (for example, "John Doe and Richard Jones") or to the security holders in a form to which each of the security holders has consented in writing;

Note to paragraph (e)(1)(i)(B): Unless the registrant addresses the annual report to security holders, proxy statement or Notice of Internet Availability of Proxy Materials to the security holders as a group or to each of the security holders individually, it must obtain, from each security holder to be included in the household group, a separate affirmative written consent to the specific form of address the registrant will use.

(C)   The security holders consent, in accordance with paragraph (e)(1)(ii) of this section, to delivery of one annual report to security holders or proxy statement, as applicable;

(D)   With respect to delivery of the proxy statement or Notice of Internet Availability of Proxy Materials, the registrant delivers, together with or subsequent to delivery of the proxy statement, a separate proxy card for each security holder at the shared address; and

(E)   The registrant includes an undertaking in the proxy statement to deliver promptly upon written or oral request a separate copy of the annual report to security holders, proxy statement or Notice of Internet Availability of Proxy Materials, as applicable, to a security holder at a shared address to which a single copy of the document was delivered.

(ii) Consent—(A) Affirmative written consent. Each security holder must affirmatively consent, in writing, to delivery of one annual report to security holders or proxy statement, as applicable. A security holder's affirmative written consent will be considered valid only if the security holder has been informed of:

(1)   The duration of the consent;

(2)   The specific types of documents to which the consent will apply;

(3)   The procedures the security holder must follow to revoke consent; and

(4)   The registrant's obligation to begin sending individual copies to a security holder within thirty days after the security holder revokes consent.

(B)   Implied consent. The registrant need not obtain affirmative written consent from a security holder for purposes of paragraph (e)(1)(ii)(A) of this section if all of the following conditions are met:

(1)   The security holder has the same last name as the other security holders at the shared address or the registrant reasonably believes that the security holders are members of the same family;

(2)   The registrant has sent the security holder a notice at least 60 days before the registrant begins to rely on this section concerning delivery of annual reports to security holders, proxy statements or Notices of Internet Availability of Proxy Materials to that security holder. The notice must:

(i)   Be a separate written document;

(ii)   State that only one annual report to security holders, proxy statement or Notice of Internet Availability of Proxy Materials, as applicable, will be delivered to the shared address unless the registrant receives contrary instructions;

(iii)   Include a toll-free telephone number, or be accompanied by a reply form that is pre-addressed with postage provided, that the security holder can use to notify the registrant that the security holder wishes to receive a separate annual report to security holders, proxy statement or Notice of Internet Availability of Proxy Materials;

(iv)   State the duration of the consent;

(v)   Explain how a security holder can revoke consent;

(vi)   State that the registrant will begin sending individual copies to a security holder within thirty days after the security holder revokes consent; and

(vii)   Contain the following prominent statement, or similar clear and understandable statement, in bold-face type: "Important Notice Regarding Delivery of Security Holder Documents." This statement also must appear on the envelope in which the notice is delivered. Alternatively, if the notice is delivered separately from other communications to security holders, this statement may appear either on the notice or on the envelope in which the notice is delivered.

Note to paragraph (e)(1)(ii)(B)(2): The notice should be written in plain English. *See* § 230.421(d)(2) of this chapter for a discussion of plain English principles.

(3)   The registrant has not received the reply form or other notification indicating that the security holder wishes to continue to receive an individual copy of the annual report to security holders, proxy statement or Notice of Internet Availability of Proxy Materials, as applicable, within 60 days after the registrant sent the notice required by paragraph (e)(1)(ii)(B)(2) of this section; and

(4)   The registrant delivers the document to a post office box or residential street address.

Note to paragraph (e)(1)(ii)(B)(4): The registrant can assume that a street address is residential unless the registrant has information that indicates the street address is a business.

(iii) Revocation of consent. If a security holder, orally or in writing, revokes consent to delivery of one annual report to security holders, proxy statement or Notice of Internet Availability of Proxy Materials to a shared address, the registrant must begin sending individual copies to that security holder within 30 days after the registrant receives revocation of the security holder's consent.

(iv) Definition of address. Unless otherwise indicated, for purposes of this section, address means a street address, a post office box number, an electronic mail address, a facsimile telephone number or other similar destination to which paper or electronic documents are delivered, unless otherwise provided in this section. If the registrant has reason to believe that the address is a street address of a multi-unit building, the address must include the unit number.

Note to paragraph (e)(1): A person other than the registrant making a proxy solicitation may deliver a single proxy statement to security holders of record or beneficial owners who have separate accounts and share an address if: (a) the registrant or intermediary has followed the procedures in this section; and (b) the registrant or intermediary makes available the shared address information to the person in accordance with § 240.14a–7(a)(2)(i) and (ii).

(2) Notwithstanding paragraphs (a) and (b) of this section, unless state law requires otherwise, a registrant is not required to send an annual report to security holders, proxy statement or Notice of Internet Availability of Proxy Materials to a security holder if:

(i) An annual report to security holders and a proxy statement, or a Notice of Internet Availability of Proxy Materials, for two consecutive annual meetings; or

(ii) All, and at least two, payments (if sent by first class mail) of dividends or interest on securities, or dividend reinvestment confirmations, during a twelve month period, have been mailed to such security holder's address and have been returned as undeliverable. If any such security holder delivers or causes to be delivered to the registrant written notice setting forth his then current address for security holder communications purposes, the registrant's obligation to deliver an annual report to security holders, a proxy statement or a Notice of Internet Availability of Proxy Materials under this section is reinstated.

(f) The provisions of paragraph (a) of this section shall not apply to a communication made by means of speeches in public forums, press releases, published or broadcast opinions, statements, or advertisements appearing in a broadcast media, newspaper, magazine or other bona fide publication disseminated on a regular basis, provided that:

(1) No form of proxy, consent or authorization or means to execute the same is provided to a security holder in connection with the communication; and

(2) At the time the communication is made, a definitive proxy statement is on file with the Commission pursuant to § 240.14a–6(b).

§ 240.14a–4. Requirements as to Proxy

(a) The form of proxy (1) shall indicate in bold-face type whether or not the proxy is solicited on behalf of the registrant's board of directors or, if provided other than by a majority of the board of directors, shall indicate in bold-face type on whose behalf the solicitation is made;

(2) Shall provide a specifically designated blank space for dating the proxy card; and

(3) Shall identify clearly and impartially each separate matter intended to be acted upon, whether or not related to or conditioned on the approval of other matters, and whether proposed by the registrant or by security holders. No reference need be made, however, to proposals as to which discretionary authority is conferred pursuant to paragraph (c) of this section.

Note to paragraph (a)(3) (Electronic filers): Electronic filers shall satisfy the filing requirements of Rule 14a–6(a) or (b) (§ 240.14a–6(a) or (b)) with respect to the form of proxy by filing the form of proxy as an appendix at the end of the proxy statement. Forms of proxy shall not be filed as exhibits or separate documents within an electronic submission.

(b)(1)   Means shall be provided in the form of proxy whereby the person solicited is afforded an opportunity to specify by boxes a choice between approval or disapproval of, or abstention with respect to each separate matter referred to therein as intended to be acted upon, other than elections to office and votes to determine the frequency of shareholder votes on executive compensation pursuant to § 240.14a–21(b) of this chapter. A proxy may confer discretionary authority with respect to matters as to which a choice is not specified by the security holder provided that the form of proxy states in bold-face type how it is intended to vote the shares represented by the proxy in each such case.

(2)   A form of proxy that provides for the election of directors shall set forth the names of persons nominated for election as directors, including any person whose nomination by a shareholder or shareholder group satisfies the requirements of § 240.14a–11, an applicable state or foreign law provision, or a registrant's governing documents as they relate to the inclusion of shareholder director nominees in the registrant's proxy materials. Such form of proxy shall clearly provide any of the following means for security holders to withhold authority to vote for each nominee:

(i)   A box opposite the name of each nominee which may be marked to indicate that authority to vote for such nominee is withheld; or

(ii)   An instruction in bold-face type which indicates that the security holder may withhold authority to vote for any nominee by lining through or otherwise striking out the name of any nominee; or

(iii) Designated blank spaces in which the security holder may enter the names of nominees with respect to whom the security holder chooses to withhold authority to vote; or

(iv)   Any other similar means, provided that clear instructions are furnished indicating how the security holder may withhold authority to vote for any nominee.

Such form of proxy also may provide a means for the security holder to grant authority to vote for the nominees set forth, as a group, provided that there is a similar means for the security holder to withhold authority to vote for such group of nominees. Any such form of proxy which is executed by the security holder in such manner as not to withhold authority to vote for the election of any nominee shall be deemed to grant such authority, provided that the form of proxy so states in bold-face type. Means to grant authority to vote for any nominees as a group or to withhold authority for any nominees as a group may not be provided if the form of proxy includes one or more shareholder nominees in accordance with § 240.14a–11, an applicable state or foreign law provision, or a registrant's governing documents as they relate to the inclusion of shareholder director nominees in the registrant's proxy materials.

Instructions. 1. Paragraph (2) does not apply in the case of a merger, consolidation or other plan if the election of directors is an integral part of the plan.

2.   If applicable state law gives legal effect to votes cast against a nominee, then in lieu of, or in addition to, providing a means for security holders to withhold authority to vote, the registrant should provide a similar means for security holders to vote against each nominee.

(3)   A form of proxy which provides for a shareholder vote on the frequency of shareholder votes to approve the compensation of executives required by section 14A(a)(2) of the Securities Exchange Act of 1934 (15 U.S.C. 78n–1(a)(2)) shall provide means whereby the person solicited is afforded an opportunity to specify by boxes a choice among 1, 2 or 3 years, or abstain.

(c)   A proxy may confer discretionary authority to vote on any of the following matters:

(1)   For an annual meeting of shareholders, if the registrant did not have notice of the matter at least 45 days before the date on which the registrant first sent its proxy materials for the prior year's annual meeting of shareholders (or date specified by an advance notice provision),

and a specific statement to that effect is made in the proxy statement or form of proxy. If during the prior year the registrant did not hold an annual meeting, or if the date of the meeting has changed more than 30 days from the prior year, then notice must not have been received a reasonable time before the registrant sends its proxy materials for the current year.

(2)   In the case in which the registrant has received timely notice in connection with an annual meeting of shareholders (as determined under paragraph (c)(1) of this section), if the registrant includes, in the proxy statement, advice on the nature of the matter and how the registrant intends to exercise its discretion to vote on each matter. However, even if the registrant includes this information in its proxy statement, it may not exercise discretionary voting authority on a particular proposal if the proponent:

(i)   Provides the registrant with a written statement, within the time-frame determined under paragraph (c)(1) of this section, that the proponent intends to deliver a proxy statement and form of proxy to holders of at least the percentage of the company's voting shares required under applicable law to carry the proposal;

(ii)   Includes the same statement in its proxy materials filed under § 240.14a–6; and

(iii)   Immediately after soliciting the percentage of shareholders required to carry the proposal, provides the registrant with a statement from any solicitor or other person with knowledge that the necessary steps have been taken to deliver a proxy statement and form of proxy to holders of at least the percentage of the company's voting shares required under applicable law to carry the proposal.

(3)   For solicitations other than for annual meetings or for solicitations by persons other than the registrant, matters which the persons making the solicitation do not know, a reasonable time before the solicitation, are to be presented at the meeting, if a specific statement to that effect is made in the proxy statement or form of proxy.

(4)   Approval of the minutes of the prior meeting if such approval does not amount to ratification of the action taken at that meeting;

(5)   The election of any person to any office for which a bona fide nominee is named in the proxy statement and such nominee is unable to serve or for good cause will not serve.

(6)   Any proposal omitted from the proxy statement and form of proxy pursuant to § 240.14a–8 or § 240.14a–9 of this chapter.

(7)   Matters incident to the conduct of the meeting.

(d)   No proxy shall confer authority:

(1)   To vote for the election of any person to any office for which a bona fide nominee is not named in the proxy statement,

(2)   To vote at any annual meeting other than the next annual meeting (or any adjournment thereof) to be held after the date on which the proxy statement and form of proxy are first sent or given to security holders,

(3)   To vote with respect to more than one meeting (and any adjournment thereof) or more than one consent solicitation or

(4)   To consent to or authorize any action other than the action proposed to be taken in the proxy statement, or matters referred to in paragraph (c) of this rule. A person shall not be deemed to be a bona fide nominee and he shall not be named as such unless he has consented to being named in the proxy statement and to serve if elected. Provided, however, That nothing in this section 240.14a–4 shall prevent any person soliciting in support of nominees who, if elected, would constitute a minority of the board of directors, from seeking authority to vote for nominees named in the registrant's proxy statement, so long as the soliciting party:

(i)   Seeks authority to vote in the aggregate for the number of director positions then subject to election;

(ii)   Represents that it will vote for all the registrant nominees, other than those registrant nominees specified by the soliciting party;

(iii)   Provides the security holder an opportunity to withhold authority with respect to any other registrant nominee by writing the name of that nominee on the form of proxy; and

(iv)   States on the form of proxy and in the proxy statement that there is no assurance that the registrant's nominees will serve if elected with any of the soliciting party's nominees.

(e)   The proxy statement or form of proxy shall provide, subject to reasonable specified conditions, that the shares represented by the proxy will be voted and that where the person solicited specifies by means of a ballot provided pursuant to paragraph (b) of this section a choice with respect to any matter to be acted upon, the shares will be voted in accordance with the specifications so made.

(f)   No person conducting a solicitation subject to this regulation shall deliver a form of proxy, consent or authorization to any security holder unless the security holder concurrently receives, or has previously received, a definitive proxy statement that has been filed with the Commission pursuant to § 240.14a–6(b).

§ 240.14a–5.   Presentation of Information in Proxy Statement

(a)   The information included in the proxy statement shall be clearly presented and the statements made shall be divided into groups according to subject matter and the various groups of statements shall be preceded by appropriate headings. The order of items and sub-items in the schedule need not be followed. Where practicable and appropriate, the information shall be presented in tabular form. All amounts shall be stated in figures. Information required by more than one applicable item need not be repeated. No statement need be made in response to any item or sub-item which is inapplicable.

(b)   Any information required to be included in the proxy statement as to terms of securities or other subject matter which from a standpoint of practical necessity must be determined in the future may be stated in terms of present knowledge and intention. To the extent practicable, the authority to be conferred concerning each such matter shall be confined within limits reasonably related to the need for discretionary authority. Subject to the foregoing, information which is not known to the persons on whose behalf the solicitation is to be made and which it is not reasonably within the power of such persons to ascertain or procure may be omitted, if a brief statement of the circumstances rendering such information unavailable is made.

(c)   Any information contained in any other proxy soliciting material which has been furnished to each person solicited in connection with the same meeting or subject matter may be omitted from the proxy statement, if a clear reference is made to the particular document containing such information.

(d)(1)   All printed proxy statements shall be in roman type at least as large and as legible as 10-point modern type, except that to the extent necessary for convenient presentation financial statements and other tabular data, but not the notes thereto, may be in roman type at least as large and as legible as 8-point modern type. All such type shall be leaded at least 2 points.

(2)   Where a proxy statement is delivered through an electronic medium, issuers may satisfy legibility requirements applicable to printed documents, such as type size and font, by presenting all required information in a format readily communicated to investors.

(e)   All proxy statements shall disclose, under an appropriate caption, the following dates:

(1) The deadline for submitting shareholder proposals for inclusion in the registrant's proxy statement and form of proxy for the registrant's next annual meeting, calculated in the manner provided in § 240.14a–8(e)(Question 5);

(2) The date after which notice of a shareholder proposal submitted outside the processes of § 240.14a–8 is considered untimely, either calculated in the manner provided by § 240.14a–4(c)(1) or as established by the registrant's advance notice provision, if any, authorized by applicable state law; and

(3) The deadline for submitting nominees for inclusion in the registrant's proxy statement and form of proxy pursuant to § 240.14a–11, an applicable state or foreign law provision, or a registrant's governing documents as they relate to the inclusion of shareholder director nominees in the registrant's proxy materials for the registrant's next annual meeting of shareholders.

(f)   If the date of the next annual meeting is subsequently advanced or delayed by more than 30 calendar days from the date of the annual meeting to which the proxy statement relates, the registrant shall, in a timely manner, inform shareholders of such change, and the new dates referred to in paragraphs (e)(1) and (e)(2) of this section, by including a notice, under Item 5, in its earliest possible quarterly report on Form 10-Q (§ 249.308a of this chapter), or, in the case of investment companies, in a shareholder report under § 270.30d–1 of this chapter under the Investment Company Act of 1940, or, if impracticable, any means reasonably calculated to inform shareholders.

§ 240.14a–6.   Filing Requirements

(a)   Preliminary proxy statement. Five preliminary copies of the proxy statement and form of proxy shall be filed with the Commission at least 10 calendar days prior to the date definitive copies of such material are first sent or given to security holders, or such shorter period prior to that date as the Commission may authorize upon a showing of good cause thereunder. A registrant, however, shall not file with the Commission a preliminary proxy statement, form of proxy or other soliciting material to be furnished to security holders concurrently therewith if the solicitation relates to an annual (or special meeting in lieu of the annual) meeting, or for an investment company registered under the Investment Company Act of 1940 (15 U.S.C. 80a–1 *et seq.*) or a business development company, if the solicitation relates to any meeting of security holders at which the only matters to be acted upon are:

(1)   The election of directors;

(2)   The election, approval or ratification of accountant(s);

(3)   A security holder proposal included pursuant to Rule 14a–8 (§ 240.14a–8 of this chapter);

(4)   A shareholder nominee for director included pursuant to § 240.14a–11, an applicable state or foreign law provision, or a registrant's governing documents as they relate to the inclusion of shareholder director nominees in the registrant's proxy materials.

(5)   The approval or ratification of a plan as defined in paragraph (a)(6)(ii) of Item 402 of Regulation S–K (§ 229.402(a)(6)(ii) of this chapter) or amendments to such a plan;

(6)   With respect to an investment company registered under the Investment Company Act of 1940 or a business development company, a proposal to continue, without change, any advisory or other contract or agreement that previously has been the subject of a proxy solicitation for which proxy material was filed with the Commission pursuant to this section;

(7)   With respect to an open-end investment company registered under the Investment Company Act of 1940, a proposal to increase the number of shares authorized to be issued; and/or

(8)   A vote to approve the compensation of executives as required pursuant to section 14A(a)(1) of the Securities Exchange Act of 1934 (15 U.S.C. 78n–1(a)(1)) and § 240.14a–21(a) of this chapter, or pursuant to section 111(e)(1) of the Emergency Economic Stabilization Act of 2008 (12 U.S.C. 5221(e)(1)) and § 240.14a–20 of this chapter, a vote to determine the frequency of

shareholder votes to approve the compensation of executives as required pursuant to Section 14A(a)(2) of the Securities Exchange Act of 1934 (15 U.S.C. 78n–1(a)(2)) and § 240.14a–21(b) of this chapter, or any other shareholder advisory vote on executive compensation.

This exclusion from filing preliminary proxy material does not apply if the registrant comments upon or refers to a solicitation in opposition in connection with the meeting in its proxy material.

Note 1 to paragraph (a): The filing of revised material does not recommence the ten day time period unless the revised material contains material revisions or material new proposal(s) that constitute a fundamental change in the proxy material.

Note 2 to paragraph (a): The official responsible for the preparation of the proxy material should make every effort to verify the accuracy and completeness of the information required by the applicable rules. The preliminary material should be filed with the Commission at the earliest practicable date.

Note 3 to paragraph (a): Solicitation in Opposition. For purposes of the exclusion from filing preliminary proxy material, a "solicitation in opposition" includes: (a) Any solicitation opposing a proposal supported by the registrant; and (b) any solicitation supporting a proposal that the registrant does not expressly support, other than a security holder proposal included in the registrant's proxy material pursuant to Rule 14a–8 (§ 240.14a–8 of this chapter). The inclusion of a security holder proposal in the registrant's proxy material pursuant to Rule 14a–8 does not constitute a "solicitation in opposition," even if the registrant opposes the proposal and/or includes a statement in opposition to the proposal. The inclusion of a shareholder nominee in the registrant's proxy materials pursuant to § 240.14a–11, an applicable state or foreign law provision, or a registrant's governing documents as they relate to the inclusion of shareholder director nominees in the registrant's proxy materials does not constitute a "solicitation in opposition" for purposes of Rule 14a–6(a) (§ 240.14a–6(a)), even if the registrant opposes the shareholder nominee and solicits against the shareholder nominee and in favor of a registrant nominee.

Note 4 to paragraph (a): A registrant that is filing proxy material in preliminary form only because the registrant has commented on or referred to a solicitation in opposition should indicate that fact in a transmittal letter when filing the preliminary material with the Commission.

(b) Definitive proxy statement and other soliciting material. Eight definitive copies of the proxy statement, form of proxy and all other soliciting materials, in the same form as the materials sent to security holders, must be filed with the Commission no later than the date they are first sent or given to security holders. Three copies of these materials also must be filed with, or mailed for filing to, each national securities exchange on which the registrant has a class of securities listed and registered.

(c) Personal solicitation materials. If part or all of the solicitation involves personal solicitation, then eight copies of all written instructions or other materials that discuss, review or comment on the merits of any matter to be acted on, that are furnished to persons making the actual solicitation for their use directly or indirectly in connection with the solicitation, must be filed with the Commission no later than the date the materials are first sent or given to these persons.

(d) Release dates. All preliminary proxy statements and forms of proxy filed pursuant to paragraph (a) of this section shall be accompanied by a statement of the date on which definitive copies thereof filed pursuant to paragraph (b) of this section are intended to be released to security holders. All definitive material filed pursuant to paragraph (b) of this section shall be accompanied by a statement of the date on which copies of such material were released to security holders, or, if not released, the date on which copies thereof are intended to be released. All material filed pursuant to paragraph (c) of this section shall be accompanied by a statement of the date on which copies thereof were released to the individual who will make the actual solicitation or if not released, the date on which copies thereof are intended to be released.

(e)(1) Public availability of information. All copies of preliminary proxy statements and forms of proxy filed pursuant to paragraph (a) of this section shall be clearly marked "Preliminary Copies," and shall be deemed immediately available for public inspection unless confidential treatment is obtained pursuant to paragraph (e)(2) of this section.

(2) *Confidential treatment.* If action will be taken on any matter specified in Item 14 of Schedule 14A (§ 240.14a–101), all copies of the preliminary proxy statement and form of proxy filed under paragraph (a) of this section will be for the information of the Commission only and will not be deemed available for public inspection until filed with the Commission in definitive form so long as:

(i) The proxy statement does not relate to a matter or proposal subject to § 240.13e–3 or a roll-up transaction as defined in Item 901(c) of Regulation S–K (§ 229.901(c) of this chapter);

(ii) Neither the parties to the transaction nor any persons authorized to act on their behalf have made any public communications relating to the transaction except for statements where the content is limited to the information specified in § 230.135 of this chapter; and

(iii) The materials are filed in paper and marked "Confidential, For Use of the Commission Only." In all cases, the materials may be disclosed to any department or agency of the United States Government and to the Congress, and the Commission may make any inquiries or investigation into the materials as may be necessary to conduct an adequate review by the Commission.

Instruction to paragraph (e)(2): If communications are made publicly that go beyond the information specified in § 230.135 of this chapter, the preliminary proxy materials must be re-filed promptly with the Commission as public materials.

(f) *Communications not required to be filed.* Copies of replies to inquiries from security holders requesting further information and copies of communications which do no more than request that forms of proxy theretofore solicited be signed and returned need not be filed pursuant to this section.

(g) *Solicitations subject to § 240.14a–2(b)(1).* (1) Any person who:

(i) Engages in a solicitation pursuant to § 240.14a–2(b)(1), and

(ii) At the commencement of that solicitation owns beneficially securities of the class which is the subject of the solicitation with a market value of over $5 million,

shall furnish or mail to the Commission, not later than three days after the date the written solicitation is first sent or given to any security holder, five copies of a statement containing the information specified in the Notice of Exempt Solicitation (§ 240.14a–103) which statement shall attach as an exhibit all written soliciting materials. Five copies of an amendment to such statement shall be furnished or mailed to the Commission, in connection with dissemination of any additional communications, not later than three days after the date the additional material is first sent or given to any security holder. Three copies of the Notice of Exempt Solicitation and amendments thereto shall, at the same time the materials are furnished or mailed to the Commission, be furnished or mailed to each national securities exchange upon which any class of securities of the registrant is listed and registered.

(2) Notwithstanding paragraph (g)(1) of this section, no such submission need be made with respect to oral solicitations (other than with respect to scripts used in connection with such oral solicitations), speeches delivered in a public forum, press releases, published or broadcast opinions, statements, and advertisements appearing in a broadcast media, or a newspaper, magazine or other bona fide publication disseminated on a regular basis.

(h) *Revised material.* Where any proxy statement, form of proxy or other material filed pursuant to this section is amended or revised, two of the copies of such amended or revised material filed pursuant to this section (or in the case of investment companies registered under the Investment Company Act of 1940, three of such copies) shall be marked to indicate clearly and precisely the changes effected therein. If the amendment or revision alters the text of the material the changes in such text shall be indicated by means of underscoring or in some other appropriate manner.

(i)   Fees. At the time of filing the proxy solicitation material, the persons upon whose behalf the solicitation is made, other than investment companies registered under the Investment Company Act of 1940, shall pay to the Commission the following applicable fee:

(1)   For preliminary proxy material involving acquisitions, mergers, spinoffs, consolidations or proposed sales or other dispositions of substantially all the assets of the company, a fee established in accordance with Rule 0–11 (§ 240.0–11 of this chapter) shall be paid. No refund shall be given.

(2)   For all other proxy submissions and submissions made pursuant to § 240.14a–6(g), no fee shall be required.

(j)   Merger proxy materials. (1) Any proxy statement, form of proxy or other soliciting material required to be filed by this section that also is either

(i)   Included in a registration statement filed under the Securities Act of 1933 on Forms S-4 (§ 239.25 of this chapter), F-4 (§ 239.34 of this chapter) or N-14 (§ 239.23 of this chapter); or

(ii)   Filed under § 230.424, § 230.425 or § 230.497 of this chapter is required to be filed only under the Securities Act, and is deemed filed under this section.

(2)   Under paragraph (j)(1) of this section, the fee required by paragraph (i) of this section need not be paid.

(k)   Computing time periods. In computing time periods beginning with the filing date specified in Regulation 14A (§§ 240.14a–1 to 240.14b–1 of this chapter), the filing date shall be counted as the first day of the time period and midnight of the last day shall constitute the end of the specified time period.

* * *

§ 240.14a–7.   **Obligations of Registrants to Provide a List of, or Mail Soliciting Material to, Security Holders**

(a)   If the registrant has made or intends to make a proxy solicitation in connection with a security holder meeting or action by consent or authorization, upon the written request by any record or beneficial holder of securities of the class entitled to vote at the meeting or to execute a consent or authorization to provide a list of security holders or to mail the requesting security holder's materials, regardless of whether the request references this section, the registrant shall:

(1)   Deliver to the requesting security holder within five business days after receipt of the request:

(i)   Notification as to whether the registrant has elected to mail the security holder's soliciting materials or provide a security holder list if the election under paragraph (b) of this section is to be made by the registrant;

(ii)   A statement of the approximate number of record holders and beneficial holders, separated by type of holder and class, owning securities in the same class or classes as holders which have been or are to be solicited on management's behalf, or any more limited group of such holders designated by the security holder if available or retrievable under the registrant's or its transfer agent's security holder data systems; and

(iii)   The estimated cost of mailing a proxy statement, form of proxy or other communication to such holders, including to the extent known or reasonably available, the estimated costs of any bank, broker, and similar person through whom the registrant has solicited or intends to solicit beneficial owners in connection with the security holder meeting or action;

(2)   Perform the acts set forth in either paragraphs (a)(2)(i) or (a)(2)(ii) of this section, at the registrant's or requesting security holder's option, as specified in paragraph (b) of this section:

(i)   Send copies of any proxy statement, form of proxy, or other soliciting material, including a Notice of Internet Availability of Proxy Materials (as described in § 240.14a–16), furnished by the security holder to the record holders, including banks, brokers, and similar entities, designated by the security holder. A sufficient number of copies must be sent to the banks, brokers, and similar entities for distribution to all beneficial owners designated by the security holder. The security holder may designate only record holders and/or beneficial owners who have not requested paper and/ or e-mail copies of the proxy statement. If the registrant has received affirmative written or implied consent to deliver a single proxy statement to security holders at a shared address in accordance with the procedures in § 240.14a–3(e)(1), a single copy of the proxy statement or Notice of Internet Availability of Proxy Materials furnished by the security holder shall be sent to that address, provided that if multiple copies of the Notice of Internet Availability of Proxy Materials are furnished by the security holder for that address, the registrant shall deliver those copies in a single envelope to that address. The registrant shall send the security holder material with reasonable promptness after tender of the material to be sent, envelopes or other containers therefore, postage or payment for postage and other reasonable expenses of effecting such distribution. The registrant shall not be responsible for the content of the material; or

(ii)   Deliver the following information to the requesting security holder within five business days of receipt of the request:

(A)   A reasonably current list of the names, addresses and security positions of the record holders, including banks, brokers and similar entities holding securities in the same class or classes as holders which have been or are to be solicited on management's behalf, or any more limited group of such holders designated by the security holder if available or retrievable under the registrant's or its transfer agent's security holder data systems;

(B)   The most recent list of names, addresses and security positions of beneficial owners as specified in § 240.14a–13(b), in the possession, or which subsequently comes into the possession, of the registrant;

(C)   The names of security holders at a shared address that have consented to delivery of a single copy of proxy materials to a shared address, if the registrant has received written or implied consent in accordance with § 240.14a–3(e)(1); and

(D)   If the registrant has relied on § 240.14a–16, the names of security holders who have requested paper copies of the proxy materials for all meetings and the names of security holders who, as of the date that the registrant receives the request, have requested paper copies of the proxy materials only for the meeting to which the solicitation relates.

(iii)   All security holder list information shall be in the form requested by the security holder to the extent that such form is available to the registrant without undue burden or expense. The registrant shall furnish the security holder with updated record holder information on a daily basis or, if not available on a daily basis, at the shortest reasonable intervals; provided, however, that the registrant need not provide beneficial or record holder information more current than the record date for the meeting or action.

(b)(1)   The requesting security holder shall have the options set forth in paragraph (a)(2) of this section, and the registrant shall have corresponding obligations, if the registrant or general partner or sponsor is soliciting or intends to solicit with respect to:

(i)   A proposal that is subject to § 240.13e–3;

* * *

(2)   With respect to all other requests pursuant to this section, the registrant shall have the option to either mail the security holder's material or furnish the security holder list as set forth in this section.

(c)   At the time of a list request, the security holder making the request shall:

(1)   If holding the registrant's securities through a nominee, provide the registrant with a statement by the nominee or other independent third party, or a copy of a current filing made with the Commission and furnished to the registrant, confirming such holder's beneficial ownership; and

(2)   Provide the registrant with an affidavit, declaration, affirmation or other similar document provided for under applicable state law identifying the proposal or other corporate action that will be the subject of the security holder's solicitation or communication and attesting that:

(i)   The security holder will not use the list information for any purpose other than to solicit security holders with respect to the same meeting or action by consent or authorization for which the registrant is soliciting or intends to solicit or to communicate with security holders with respect to a solicitation commenced by the registrant; and

(ii)   The security holder will not disclose such information to any person other than a beneficial owner for whom the request was made and an employee or agent to the extent necessary to effectuate the communication or solicitation.

(d)   The security holder shall not use the information furnished by the registrant pursuant to paragraph (a)(2)(ii) of this section for any purpose other than to solicit security holders with respect to the same meeting or action by consent or authorization for which the registrant is soliciting or intends to solicit or to communicate with security holders with respect to a solicitation commenced by the registrant; or disclose such information to any person other than an employee, agent, or beneficial owner for whom a request was made to the extent necessary to effectuate the communication or solicitation. The security holder shall return the information provided pursuant to paragraph (a)(2)(ii) of this section and shall not retain any copies thereof or of any information derived from such information after the termination of the solicitation.

(e)   The security holder shall reimburse the reasonable expenses incurred by the registrant in performing the acts requested pursuant to paragraph (a) of this section.

Note 1 to § 240.14a–7. Reasonably prompt methods of distribution to security holders may be used instead of mailing. If an alternative distribution method is chosen, the costs of that method should be considered where necessary rather than the costs of mailing.

Note 2 to § 240.14a–7. When providing the information required by § 240.14a–7(a)(1)(ii), if the registrant has received affirmative written or implied consent to delivery of a single copy of proxy materials to a shared address in accordance with § 240.14a–3(e)(1), it shall exclude from the number of record holders those to whom it does not have to deliver a separate proxy statement.

§ 240.14a–8.   Shareholder Proposals

This section addresses when a company must include a shareholder's proposal in its proxy statement and identify the proposal in its form of proxy when the company holds an annual or special meeting of shareholders. In summary, in order to have your shareholder proposal included on a company's proxy card, and included along with any supporting statement in its proxy statement, you must be eligible and follow certain procedures. Under a few specific circumstances, the company is permitted to exclude your proposal, but only after submitting its reasons to the Commission. We structured this section in a question-and-answer format so that it is easier to understand. The references to "you" are to a shareholder seeking to submit the proposal.

(a)   Question 1: What is a proposal? A shareholder proposal is your recommendation or requirement that the company and/or its board of directors take action, which you intend to present at a meeting of the company's shareholders. Your proposal should state as clearly as possible the course of action that you believe the company should follow. If your proposal is placed on the company's proxy card, the company must also provide in the form of proxy means for shareholders to specify by boxes a choice between approval or disapproval, or abstention. Unless otherwise indicated, the word "proposal" as used in this section refers both to your proposal, and to your corresponding statement in support of your proposal (if any).

(b)   Question 2: Who is eligible to submit a proposal, and how do I demonstrate to the company that I am eligible?

(1)   In order to be eligible to submit a proposal, you must have continuously held at least $2,000 in market value, or 1%, of the company's securities entitled to be voted on the proposal at the meeting for at least one year by the date you submit the proposal. You must continue to hold those securities through the date of the meeting.

(2)   If you are the registered holder of your securities, which means that your name appears in the company's records as a shareholder, the company can verify your eligibility on its own, although you will still have to provide the company with a written statement that you intend to continue to hold the securities through the date of the meeting of shareholders. However, if like many shareholders you are not a registered holder, the company likely does not know that you are a shareholder, or how many shares you own. In this case, at the time you submit your proposal, you must prove your eligibility to the company in one of two ways:

(i)   The first way is to submit to the company a written statement from the "record" holder of your securities (usually a broker or bank) verifying that, at the time you submitted your proposal, you continuously held the securities for at least one year. You must also include your own written statement that you intend to continue to hold the securities through the date of the meeting of shareholders; or

(ii)   The second way to prove ownership applies only if you have filed a Schedule 13D (§ 240.13d–101), Schedule 13G (§ 240.13d–102), Form 3 (§ 249.103 of this chapter), Form 4 (§ 249.104 of this chapter) and/or Form 5 (§ 249.105 of this chapter), or amendments to those documents or updated forms, reflecting your ownership of the shares as of or before the date on which the one-year eligibility period begins. If you have filed one of these documents with the SEC, you may demonstrate your eligibility by submitting to the company:

(A)   A copy of the schedule and/or form, and any subsequent amendments reporting a change in your ownership level;

(B)   Your written statement that you continuously held the required number of shares for the one-year period as of the date of the statement; and

(C)   Your written statement that you intend to continue ownership of the shares through the date of the company's annual or special meeting.

(c)   Question 3: How many proposals may I submit? Each shareholder may submit no more than one proposal to a company for a particular shareholders' meeting.

(d)   Question 4: How long can my proposal be? The proposal, including any accompanying supporting statement, may not exceed 500 words.

(e)   Question 5: What is the deadline for submitting a proposal?

(1)   If you are submitting your proposal for the company's annual meeting, you can in most cases find the deadline in last year's proxy statement. However, if the company did not hold an annual meeting last year, or has changed the date of its meeting for this year more than 30 days

from last year's meeting, you can usually find the deadline in one of the company's quarterly reports on Form 10-Q (§ 249.308a of this chapter), or in shareholder reports of investment companies under § 270.30d–1 of this chapter of the Investment Company Act of 1940. In order to avoid controversy, shareholders should submit their proposals by means, including electronic means, that permit them to prove the date of delivery.

(2)   The deadline is calculated in the following manner if the proposal is submitted for a regularly scheduled annual meeting. The proposal must be received at the company's principal executive offices not less than 120 calendar days before the date of the company's proxy statement released to shareholders in connection with the previous year's annual meeting. However, if the company did not hold an annual meeting the previous year, or if the date of this year's annual meeting has been changed by more than 30 days from the date of the previous year's meeting, then the deadline is a reasonable time before the company begins to print and send its proxy materials.

(3)   If you are submitting your proposal for a meeting of shareholders other than a regularly scheduled annual meeting, the deadline is a reasonable time before the company begins to print and send its proxy materials.

(f)   Question 6: What if I fail to follow one of the eligibility or procedural requirements explained in answers to Questions 1 through 4 of this section?

(1)   The company may exclude your proposal, but only after it has notified you of the problem, and you have failed adequately to correct it. Within 14 calendar days of receiving your proposal, the company must notify you in writing of any procedural or eligibility deficiencies, as well as of the time frame for your response. Your response must be postmarked, or transmitted electronically, no later than 14 days from the date you received the company's notification. A company need not provide you such notice of a deficiency if the deficiency cannot be remedied, such as if you fail to submit a proposal by the company's properly determined deadline. If the company intends to exclude the proposal, it will later have to make a submission under § 240.14a–8 and provide you with a copy under Question 10 below, § 240.14a–8(j).

(2)   If you fail in your promise to hold the required number of securities through the date of the meeting of shareholders, then the company will be permitted to exclude all of your proposals from its proxy materials for any meeting held in the following two calendar years.

(g)   Question 7: Who has the burden of persuading the Commission or its staff that my proposal can be excluded? Except as otherwise noted, the burden is on the company to demonstrate that it is entitled to exclude a proposal.

(h)   Question 8: Must I appear personally at the shareholders' meeting to present the proposal?

(1)   Either you, or your representative who is qualified under state law to present the proposal on your behalf, must attend the meeting to present the proposal. Whether you attend the meeting yourself or send a qualified representative to the meeting in your place, you should make sure that you, or your representative, follow the proper state law procedures for attending the meeting and/or presenting your proposal.

(2)   If the company holds its shareholder meeting in whole or in part via electronic media, and the company permits you or your representative to present your proposal via such media, then you may appear through electronic media rather than traveling to the meeting to appear in person.

(3)   If you or your qualified representative fail to appear and present the proposal, without good cause, the company will be permitted to exclude all of your proposals from its proxy materials for any meetings held in the following two calendar years.

(i)   Question 9: If I have complied with the procedural requirements, on what other bases may a company rely to exclude my proposal?

(1)   Improper under state law: If the proposal is not a proper subject for action by shareholders under the laws of the jurisdiction of the company's organization;

Note to paragraph (i)(1): Depending on the subject matter, some proposals are not considered proper under state law if they would be binding on the company if approved by shareholders. In our experience, most proposals that are cast as recommendations or requests that the board of directors take specified action are proper under state law. Accordingly, we will assume that a proposal drafted as a recommendation or suggestion is proper unless the company demonstrates otherwise.

(2)   Violation of law: If the proposal would, if implemented, cause the company to violate any state, federal, or foreign law to which it is subject;

Note to paragraph (i)(2): We will not apply this basis for exclusion to permit exclusion of a proposal on grounds that it would violate foreign law if compliance with the foreign law would result in a violation of any state or federal law.

(3)   Violation of proxy rules: If the proposal or supporting statement is contrary to any of the Commission's proxy rules, including § 240.14a–9, which prohibits materially false or misleading statements in proxy soliciting materials;

(4)   Personal grievance; special interest: If the proposal relates to the redress of a personal claim or grievance against the company or any other person, or if it is designed to result in a benefit to you, or to further a personal interest, which is not shared by the other shareholders at large;

(5)   Relevance: If the proposal relates to operations which account for less than 5 percent of the company's total assets at the end of its most recent fiscal year, and for less than 5 percent of its net earnings and gross sales for its most recent fiscal year, and is not otherwise significantly related to the company's business;

(6)   Absence of power/authority: If the company would lack the power or authority to implement the proposal;

(7)   Management functions: If the proposal deals with a matter relating to the company's ordinary business operations;

(8)   Director elections: If the proposal:

(i)   Would disqualify a nominee who is standing for election;

(ii)   Would remove a director from office before his or her term expired;

(iii) Questions the competence, business judgment, or character of one or more nominees or directors;

(iv) Seeks to include a specific individual in the company's proxy materials for election to the board of directors; or

(v)   Otherwise could affect the outcome of the upcoming election of directors.

(9)   Conflicts with company's proposal: If the proposal directly conflicts with one of the company's own proposals to be submitted to shareholders at the same meeting;

Note to paragraph (i)(9): A company's submission to the Commission under this section should specify the points of conflict with the company's proposal.

(10)   Substantially implemented: If the company has already substantially implemented the proposal;

Note to paragraph (i)(10): A company may exclude a shareholder proposal that would provide an advisory vote or seek future advisory votes to approve the compensation of executives as disclosed pursuant to Item 402 of Regulation S–K (§ 229.402 of this chapter) or any successor to Item 402 (a "say-on-pay vote") or that relates to the frequency of say-on-pay votes, provided that in the most recent shareholder vote required by § 240.14a–21(b) of this chapter a single year (i.e., one, two, or three years) received approval of a majority of votes cast on the matter and the company has adopted a policy on the frequency of say-on-pay votes that is consistent with the choice of the majority of votes cast in the most recent shareholder vote required by § 240.14a–21(b) of this chapter.

(11) Duplication: If the proposal substantially duplicates another proposal previously submitted to the company by another proponent that will be included in the company's proxy materials for the same meeting;

(12) Resubmissions: If the proposal deals with substantially the same subject matter as another proposal or proposals that has or have been previously included in the company's proxy materials within the preceding 5 calendar years, a company may exclude it from its proxy materials for any meeting held within 3 calendar years of the last time it was included if the proposal received:

(i)   Less than 3% of the vote if proposed once within the preceding 5 calendar years;

(ii)   Less than 6% of the vote on its last submission to shareholders if proposed twice previously within the preceding 5 calendar years; or

(iii)   Less than 10% of the vote on its last submission to shareholders if proposed three times or more previously within the preceding 5 calendar years; and

(13) Specific amount of dividends: If the proposal relates to specific amounts of cash or stock dividends.

(j)   Question 10: What procedures must the company follow if it intends to exclude my proposal?

(1)   If the company intends to exclude a proposal from its proxy materials, it must file its reasons with the Commission no later than 80 calendar days before it files its definitive proxy statement and form of proxy with the Commission. The company must simultaneously provide you with a copy of its submission. The Commission staff may permit the company to make its submission later than 80 days before the company files its definitive proxy statement and form of proxy, if the company demonstrates good cause for missing the deadline.

(2)   The company must file six paper copies of the following:

(i)   The proposal;

(ii)   An explanation of why the company believes that it may exclude the proposal, which should, if possible, refer to the most recent applicable authority, such as prior Division letters issued under the rule; and

(iii)   A supporting opinion of counsel when such reasons are based on matters of state or foreign law.

(k)   Question 11: May I submit my own statement to the Commission responding to the company's arguments?

Yes, you may submit a response, but it is not required. You should try to submit any response to us, with a copy to the company, as soon as possible after the company makes its submission. This way, the Commission staff will have time to consider fully your submission before it issues its response. You should submit six paper copies of your response.

(l)   Question 12: If the company includes my shareholder proposal in its proxy materials, what information about me must it include along with the proposal itself?

(1)   The company's proxy statement must include your name and address, as well as the number of the company's voting securities that you hold. However, instead of providing that information, the company may instead include a statement that it will provide the information to shareholders promptly upon receiving an oral or written request.

(2)   The company is not responsible for the contents of your proposal or supporting statement.

(m)   Question 13: What can I do if the company includes in its proxy statement reasons why it believes shareholders should not vote in favor of my proposal, and I disagree with some of its statements?

(1)   The company may elect to include in its proxy statement reasons why it believes shareholders should vote against your proposal. The company is allowed to make arguments reflecting its own point of view, just as you may express your own point of view in your proposal's supporting statement.

(2)   However, if you believe that the company's opposition to your proposal contains materially false or misleading statements that may violate our anti-fraud rule, § 240.14a–9, you should promptly send to the Commission staff and the company a letter explaining the reasons for your view, along with a copy of the company's statements opposing your proposal. To the extent possible, your letter should include specific factual information demonstrating the inaccuracy of the company's claims. Time permitting, you may wish to try to work out your differences with the company by yourself before contacting the Commission staff.

(3)   We require the company to send you a copy of its statements opposing your proposal before it sends its proxy materials, so that you may bring to our attention any materially false or misleading statements, under the following timeframes:

(i)   If our no-action response requires that you make revisions to your proposal or supporting statement as a condition to requiring the company to include it in its proxy materials, then the company must provide you with a copy of its opposition statements no later than 5 calendar days after the company receives a copy of your revised proposal; or

(ii)   In all other cases, the company must provide you with a copy of its opposition statements no later than 30 calendar days before its files definitive copies of its proxy statement and form of proxy under § 240.14a–6.

§ 240.14a–9.   False or Misleading Statements

(a)   No solicitation subject to this regulation shall be made by means of any proxy statement, form of proxy, notice of meeting or other communication, written or oral, containing any statement which, at the time and in the light of the circumstances under which it is made, is false or misleading with respect to any material fact, or which omits to state any material fact necessary in order to make the statements therein not false or misleading or necessary to correct any statement in any earlier communication with respect to the solicitation of a proxy for the same meeting or subject matter which has become false or misleading.

(b)   The fact that a proxy statement, form of proxy or other soliciting material has been filed with or examined by the Commission shall not be deemed a finding by the Commission that such material is accurate or complete or not false or misleading, or that the Commission has passed upon the merits of or approved any statement contained therein or any matter to be acted upon by security holders. No representation contrary to the foregoing shall be made.

(c)   No nominee, nominating shareholder or nominating shareholder group, or any member thereof, shall cause to be included in a registrant's proxy materials, either pursuant to the Federal proxy rules, an applicable state or foreign law provision, or a registrant's governing documents as they relate to including shareholder nominees for director in a registrant's proxy materials, include in a notice on Schedule 14N (§ 240.14n–101), or include in any other related communication, any statement which, at the time and in the light of the circumstances under which it is made, is false or misleading with respect to any material fact, or which omits to state any material fact necessary in order to make the statements therein not false or misleading or necessary to correct any statement in any earlier communication with respect to a solicitation for the same meeting or subject matter which has become false or misleading.

Note: The following are some examples of what, depending upon particular facts and circumstances, may be misleading within the meaning of this section.

a.   Predictions as to specific future market values.

b.   Material which directly or indirectly impugns character, integrity or personal reputation, or directly or indirectly makes charges concerning improper, illegal or immoral conduct or associations, without factual foundation.

c.   Failure to so identify a proxy statement, form of proxy and other soliciting material as to clearly distinguish it from the soliciting material of any other person or persons soliciting for the same meeting or subject matter.

d.   Claims made prior to a meeting regarding the results of a solicitation.

§ 240.14a–10.   Prohibition of Certain Solicitations

No person making a solicitation which is subject to §§ 240.14a–1 to 240.14a–10 shall solicit:

(a)   Any undated or postdated proxy; or

(b)   Any proxy which provides that it shall be deemed to be dated as of any date subsequent to the date on which it is signed by the security holder.

§ 240.14a–12.   Solicitation Before Furnishing a Proxy Statement

(a)   Notwithstanding the provisions of § 240.14a–3(a), a solicitation may be made before furnishing security holders with a proxy statement meeting the requirements of § 240.14a–3(a) if:

(1)   Each written communication includes:

(i)   The identity of the participants in the solicitation (as defined in Instruction 3 to Item 4 of Schedule 14A (§ 240.14a–101)) and a description of their direct or indirect interests, by security holdings or otherwise, or a prominent legend in clear, plain language advising security holders where they can obtain that information; and

(ii)   A prominent legend in clear, plain language advising security holders to read the proxy statement when it is available because it contains important information. The legend also must explain to investors that they can get the proxy statement, and any other relevant documents, for free at the Commission's web site and describe which documents are available free from the participants; and

(2)   A definitive proxy statement meeting the requirements of § 240.14a–3(a) is sent or given to security holders solicited in reliance on this section before or at the same time as the forms of proxy, consent or authorization are furnished to or requested from security holders.

(b)   Any soliciting material published, sent or given to security holders in accordance with paragraph (a) of this section must be filed with the Commission no later than the date the material is first published, sent or given to security holders. Three copies of the material must at the same time be filed with, or mailed for filing to, each national securities exchange upon which any class of securities of the registrant is listed and registered. The soliciting material must include a cover page in the form set forth in Schedule 14A (§ 240.14a–101) and the appropriate box on the cover page must be marked. Soliciting material in connection with a registered offering is required to be filed only under § 230.424 or § 230.425 of this chapter, and will be deemed filed under this section.

(c)   Solicitations by any person or group of persons for the purpose of opposing a solicitation subject to this regulation by any other person or group of persons with respect to the election or removal of directors at any annual or special meeting of security holders also are subject to the following provisions:

(1) *Application of this rule to annual report to security holders.* Notwithstanding the provisions of § 240.14a–3 (b) and (c), any portion of the annual report to security holders referred to in § 240.14a–3(b) that comments upon or refers to any solicitation subject to this rule, or to any participant in the solicitation, other than the solicitation by the management, must be filed with the Commission as proxy material subject to this regulation. This must be filed in electronic format unless an exemption is available under Rules 201 or 202 of Regulation S–T (§ 232.201 or § 232.202 of this chapter).

(2) *Use of reprints or reproductions.* In any solicitation subject to this § 240.14a–12(c), soliciting material that includes, in whole or part, any reprints or reproductions of any previously published material must:

(i) State the name of the author and publication, the date of prior publication, and identify any person who is quoted without being named in the previously published material.

(ii) Except in the case of a public or official document or statement, state whether or not the consent of the author and publication has been obtained to the use of the previously published material as proxy soliciting material.

(iii) If any participant using the previously published material, or anyone on his or her behalf, paid, directly or indirectly, for the preparation or prior publication of the previously published material, or has made or proposes to make any payments or give any other consideration in connection with the publication or republication of the material, state the circumstances.

Instruction 1 to § 240.14a–12. If paper filing is permitted, file eight copies of the soliciting material with the Commission, except that only three copies of the material specified by § 240.14a–12(c)(1) need be filed.

Instruction 2 to § 240.14a–12. Any communications made under this section after the definitive proxy statement is on file but before it is disseminated also must specify that the proxy statement is publicly available and the anticipated date of dissemination.

Instruction 3 to § 240.14a–12. Inclusion of a nominee pursuant to § 240.14a–11, an applicable state or foreign law provision, or a registrant's governing documents as they relate to the inclusion of shareholder director nominees in the registrant's proxy materials, or solicitations by a nominating shareholder or nominating shareholder group that are made in connection with that nomination constitute solicitations in opposition subject to § 240.14a–12(c), except for purposes of § 240.14a–6(a).

§ 240.14a–13. Obligation of Registrants in Communicating with Beneficial Owners

(a) If the registrant knows that securities of any class entitled to vote at a meeting (or by written consents or authorizations if no meeting is held) with respect to which the registrant intends to solicit proxies, consents or authorizations are held of record by a broker, dealer, voting trustee, bank, association, or other entity that exercises fiduciary powers in nominee name or otherwise, the registrant shall:

(1) By first class mail or other equally prompt means:

(i) Inquire of each such record holder:

(A) Whether other persons are the beneficial owners of such securities and if so, the number of copies of the proxy and other soliciting material necessary to supply such material to such beneficial owners;

(B) In the case of an annual (or special meeting in lieu of the annual) meeting, or written consents in lieu of such meeting, at which directors are to be elected, the number of copies of the annual report to security holders necessary to supply such report to beneficial owners to whom such reports are to be distributed by such record holder or its nominee and not by the registrant;

(C)   If the record holder has an obligation under § 240.14b–1(b)(3) or § 240.14b–2(b)(4)(ii) and (iii), whether an agent has been designated to act on its behalf in fulfilling such obligation and, if so, the name and address of such agent; and

(D)   Whether it holds the registrant's securities on behalf of any respondent bank and, if so, the name and address of each such respondent bank; and

(ii)   Indicate to each such record holder:

(A)   Whether the registrant, pursuant to paragraph (c) of this section, intends to distribute the annual report to security holders to beneficial owners of its securities whose names, addresses and securities positions are disclosed pursuant to § 240.14b–1(b)(3) or § 240.14b–2(b)(4)(ii) and (iii);

(B)   The record date; and

(C)   At the option of the registrant, any employee benefit plan established by an affiliate of the registrant that holds securities of the registrant that the registrant elects to treat as exempt employee benefit plan securities;

(2)   Upon receipt of a record holder's or respondent bank's response indicating, pursuant to § 240.14b–2(b)(1)(i), the names and addresses of its respondent banks, within one business day after the date such response is received, make an inquiry of and give notification to each such respondent bank in the same manner required by paragraph (a)(1) of this section; Provided, however, the inquiry required by paragraphs (a)(1) and (a)(2) of this section shall not cover beneficial owners of exempt employee benefit plan securities;

(3)   Make the inquiry required by paragraph (a)(1) of this section at least 20 business days prior to the record date of the meeting of security holders, or

(i)   If such inquiry is impracticable 20 business days prior to the record date of a special meeting, as many days before the record date of such meeting as is practicable or,

(ii)   If consents or authorizations are solicited, and such inquiry is impracticable 20 business days before the earliest date on which they may be used to effect corporate action, as many days before that date as is practicable, or

(iii)   At such later time as the rules of a national securities exchange on which the class of securities in question is listed may permit for good cause shown; Provided, however, That if a record holder or respondent bank has informed the registrant that a designated office(s) or department(s) is to receive such inquiries, the inquiry shall be made to such designated office(s) or department(s); and

(4)   Supply, in a timely manner, each record holder and respondent bank of whom the inquiries required by paragraphs (a)(1) and (a)(2) of this section are made with copies of the proxy, other proxy soliciting material, and/or the annual report to security holders, in such quantities, assembled in such form and at such place(s), as the record holder or respondent bank may reasonably request in order to send such material to each beneficial owner of securities who is to be furnished with such material by the record holder or respondent bank; and

(5)   Upon the request of any record holder or respondent bank that is supplied with proxy soliciting material and/or annual reports to security holders pursuant to paragraph (a)(4) of this section, pay its reasonable expenses for completing the sending of such material to beneficial owners.

Note 1: If the registrant's list of security holders indicates that some of its securities are registered in the name of a clearing agency registered pursuant to Section 17A of the Act (*e.g.*, "Cede & Co.," nominee for the Depository Trust Company), the registrant shall make appropriate inquiry of the clearing agency and thereafter of the participants in such clearing agency who may hold on behalf of a beneficial owner or respondent bank, and shall comply with the above paragraph with respect to any such participant (*see* § 240.14a–1(i)).

Note 2: The attention of registrants is called to the fact that each broker, dealer, bank, association, and other entity that exercises fiduciary powers has an obligation pursuant to § 240.14b–1 and § 240.14b–2 (except as provided therein with respect to exempt employee benefit plan securities held in nominee name) and, with respect to brokers and dealers, applicable self-regulatory organization requirements to obtain and forward, within the time periods prescribed therein, (a) proxies (or in lieu thereof requests for voting instructions) and proxy soliciting materials to beneficial owners on whose behalf it holds securities, and (b) annual reports to security holders to beneficial owners on whose behalf it holds securities, unless the registrant has notified the record holder or respondent bank that it has assumed responsibility to send such material to beneficial owners whose names, addresses, and securities positions are disclosed pursuant to § 240.14b–1(b)(3) and § 240.14b–2(b)(4)(ii) and (iii).

Note 3: The attention of registrants is called to the fact that registrants have an obligation, pursuant to paragraph (d) of this section, to cause proxies (or in lieu thereof requests for voting instructions), proxy soliciting material and annual reports to security holders to be furnished, in a timely manner, to beneficial owners of exempt employee benefit plan securities.

(b)   Any registrant requesting pursuant to § 240.14b–1(b)(3) or § 240.14b–2(b)(4)(ii) and (iii) a list of names, addresses and securities positions of beneficial owners of its securities who either have consented or have not objected to disclosure of such information shall:

(1)   By first class mail or other equally prompt means, inquire of each record holder and each respondent bank identified to the registrant pursuant to § 240.14b–2(b)(4)(i) whether such record holder or respondent bank holds the registrant's securities on behalf of any respondent banks and, if so, the name and address of each such respondent bank;

(2)   Request such list to be compiled as of a date no earlier than five business days after the date the registrant's request is received by the record holder or respondent bank; Provided, however, That if the record holder or respondent bank has informed the registrant that a designated office(s) or department(s) is to receive such requests, the request shall be made to such designated office(s) or department(s);

(3)   Make such request to the following persons that hold the registrant's securities on behalf of beneficial owners: all brokers, dealers, banks, associations and other entities that exercises fiduciary powers; Provided however, such request shall not cover beneficial owners of exempt employee benefit plan securities as defined in § 240.14a–1(d)(1); and, at the option of the registrant, such request may give notice of any employee benefit plan established by an affiliate of the registrant that holds securities of the registrant that the registrant elects to treat as exempt employee benefit plan securities;

(4)   Use the information furnished in response to such request exclusively for purposes of corporate communications; and

(5)   Upon the request of any record holder or respondent bank to whom such request is made, pay the reasonable expenses, both direct and indirect, of providing beneficial owner information.

Note: A registrant will be deemed to have satisfied its obligations under paragraph (b) of this section by requesting consenting and non-objecting beneficial owner lists from a designated agent acting on behalf of the record holder or respondent bank and paying to that designated agent the reasonable expenses of providing the beneficial owner information.

(c)   A registrant, at its option, may send its annual report to security holders to the beneficial owners whose identifying information is provided by record holders and respondent banks, pursuant to § 240.14b–1(b)(3) or § 240.14b–2(b)(4)(ii) and (iii), provided that such registrant notifies the record holders and respondent banks, at the time it makes the inquiry required by paragraph (a) of this section, that the registrant will send the annual report to security holders to the beneficial owners so identified.

(d) If a registrant solicits proxies, consents or authorizations from record holders and respondent banks who hold securities on behalf of beneficial owners, the registrant shall cause proxies (or in lieu thereof requests or voting instructions), proxy soliciting material and annual reports to security holders to be furnished, in a timely manner, to beneficial owners of exempt employee benefit plan securities.

* * *

§ 240.14a–16.   Internet Availability of Proxy Materials

(a)(1) A registrant shall furnish a proxy statement pursuant to § 240.14a–3(a), or an annual report to security holders pursuant to § 240.14a–3(b), to a security holder by sending the security holder a Notice of Internet Availability of Proxy Materials, as described in this section, 40 calendar days or more prior to the security holder meeting date, or if no meeting is to be held, 40 calendar days or more prior to the date the votes, consents or authorizations may be used to effect the corporate action, and complying with all other requirements of this section.

(2) Unless the registrant chooses to follow the full set delivery option set forth in paragraph (n) of this section, it must provide the record holder or respondent bank with all information listed in paragraph (d) of this section in sufficient time for the record holder or respondent bank to prepare, print and send a Notice of Internet Availability of Proxy Materials to beneficial owners at least 40 calendar days before the meeting date.

(b)(1) All materials identified in the Notice of Internet Availability of Proxy Materials must be publicly accessible, free of charge, at the Web site address specified in the notice on or before the time that the notice is sent to the security holder and such materials must remain available on that Web site through the conclusion of the meeting of security holders.

(2) All additional soliciting materials sent to security holders or made public after the Notice of Internet Availability of Proxy Materials has been sent must be made publicly accessible at the specified Web site address no later than the day on which such materials are first sent to security holders or made public.

(3) The Web site address relied upon for compliance under this section may not be the address of the Commission's electronic filing system.

(4) The registrant must provide security holders with a means to execute a proxy as of the time the Notice of Internet Availability of Proxy Materials is first sent to security holders.

(c) The materials must be presented on the Web site in a format, or formats, convenient for both reading online and printing on paper.

(d) The Notice of Internet Availability of Proxy Materials must contain the following:

(1) A prominent legend in bold-face type that states "Important Notice Regarding the Availability of Proxy Materials for the Shareholder Meeting To Be Held on [insert meeting date]";

(2) An indication that the communication is not a form for voting and presents only an overview of the more complete proxy materials, which contain important information and are available on the Internet or by mail, and encouraging a security holder to access and review the proxy materials before voting;

(3) The Internet Web site address where the proxy materials are available;

(4) Instructions regarding how a security holder may request a paper or e-mail copy of the proxy materials at no charge, including the date by which they should make the request to

facilitate timely delivery, and an indication that they will not otherwise receive a paper or e-mail copy;

(5) The date, time, and location of the meeting, or if corporate action is to be taken by written consent, the earliest date on which the corporate action may be effected;

(6) A clear and impartial identification of each separate matter intended to be acted on and the soliciting person's recommendations, if any, regarding those matters, but no supporting statements;

(7) A list of the materials being made available at the specified Web site;

(8) A toll-free telephone number, an e-mail address, and an Internet Web site where the security holder can request a copy of the proxy statement, annual report to security holders, and form of proxy, relating to all of the registrant's future security holder meetings and for the particular meeting to which the proxy materials being furnished relate;

(9) Any control/identification numbers that the security holder needs to access his or her form of proxy;

(10) Instructions on how to access the form of proxy, provided that such instructions do not enable a security holder to execute a proxy without having access to the proxy statement and, if required by § 240.14a–3(b), the annual report to security holders; and

(11) Information on how to obtain directions to be able to attend the meeting and vote in person.

(e)(1) The Notice of Internet Availability of Proxy Materials may not be incorporated into, or combined with, another document, except that it may be incorporated into, or combined with, a notice of security holder meeting required under state law, unless state law prohibits such incorporation or combination.

(2) The Notice of Internet Availability of Proxy Materials may contain only the information required by paragraph (d) of this section and any additional information required to be included in a notice of security holders meeting under state law; provided that:

(i) The registrant must revise the information on the Notice of Internet Availability of Proxy Materials, including any title to the document, to reflect the fact that:

(A) The registrant is conducting a consent solicitation rather than a proxy solicitation; or

(B) The registrant is not soliciting proxy or consent authority, but is furnishing an information statement pursuant to § 240.14c–2; and

(ii) The registrant may include a statement on the Notice to educate security holders that no personal information other than the identification or control number is necessary to execute a proxy.

(f)(1) Except as provided in paragraph (h) of this section, the Notice of Internet Availability of Proxy Materials must be sent separately from other types of security holder communications and may not accompany any other document or materials, including the form of proxy.

(2) Notwithstanding paragraph (f)(1) of this section, the registrant may accompany the Notice of Internet Availability of Proxy Materials with:

(i) A pre-addressed, postage-paid reply card for requesting a copy of the proxy materials;

(ii) A copy of any notice of security holder meeting required under state law if that notice is not combined with the Notice of Internet Availability of Proxy Materials;

(iii) In the case of an investment company registered under the Investment Company Act of 1940, the company's prospectus, a summary prospectus that satisfies the requirements of § 230.498(b) of this chapter, a Notice under § 270.30e–3 of this chapter, or a report that is required to be transmitted to stockholders by section 30(e) of the Investment Company Act (15 U.S.C. 80a–29(e)) and the rules thereunder; and

(iv) An explanation of the reasons for a registrant's use of the rules detailed in this section and the process of receiving and reviewing the proxy materials and voting as detailed in this section.

(g) *Plain English.* (1) To enhance the readability of the Notice of Internet Availability of Proxy Materials, the registrant must use plain English principles in the organization, language, and design of the notice.

(2) The registrant must draft the language in the Notice of Internet Availability of Proxy Materials so that, at a minimum, it substantially complies with each of the following plain English writing principles:

(i) Short sentences;

(ii) Definite, concrete, everyday words;

(iii) Active voice;

(iv) Tabular presentation or bullet lists for complex material, whenever possible;

(v) No legal jargon or highly technical business terms; and

(vi) No multiple negatives.

(3) In designing the Notice of Internet Availability of Proxy Materials, the registrant may include pictures, logos, or similar design elements so long as the design is not misleading and the required information is clear.

(h) The registrant may send a form of proxy to security holders if:

(1) At least 10 calendar days or more have passed since the date it first sent the Notice of Internet Availability of Proxy Materials to security holders and the form of proxy is accompanied by a copy of the Notice of Internet Availability of Proxy Materials; or

(2) The form of proxy is accompanied or preceded by a copy, via the same medium, of the proxy statement and any annual report to security holders that is required by § 240.14a–3(b).

(i) The registrant must file a form of the Notice of Internet Availability of Proxy Materials with the Commission pursuant to § 240.14a–6(b) no later than the date that the registrant first sends the notice to security holders.

(j) *Obligation to provide copies.* (1) The registrant must send, at no cost to the record holder or respondent bank and by U.S. first class mail or other reasonably prompt means, a paper copy of the proxy statement, information statement, annual report to security holders, and form of proxy (to the extent each of those documents is applicable) to any record holder or respondent bank requesting such a copy within three business days after receiving a request for a paper copy.

(2) The registrant must send, at no cost to the record holder or respondent bank and via e-mail, an electronic copy of the proxy statement, information statement, annual report to security holders, and form of proxy (to the extent each of those documents is applicable) to any record holder or respondent bank requesting such a copy within three business days after receiving a request for an electronic copy via e-mail.

(3) The registrant must provide copies of the proxy materials for one year after the conclusion of the meeting or corporate action to which the proxy materials relate, provided that, if the registrant receives the request after the conclusion of the meeting or corporate action to

which the proxy materials relate, the registrant need not send copies via First Class mail and need not respond to such request within three business days.

(4)   The registrant must maintain records of security holder requests to receive materials in paper or via e-mail for future solicitations and must continue to provide copies of the materials to a security holder who has made such a request until the security holder revokes such request.

(k)   Security holder information. (1) A registrant or its agent shall maintain the Internet Web site on which it posts its proxy materials in a manner that does not infringe on the anonymity of a person accessing such Web site.

(2)   The registrant and its agents shall not use any e-mail address obtained from a security holder solely for the purpose of requesting a copy of proxy materials pursuant to paragraph (j) of this section for any purpose other than to send a copy of those materials to that security holder. The registrant shall not disclose such information to any person other than an employee or agent to the extent necessary to send a copy of the proxy materials pursuant to paragraph (j) of this section.

(*l*)   A person other than the registrant may solicit proxies pursuant to the conditions imposed on registrants by this section, provided that:

(1)   A soliciting person other than the registrant is required to provide copies of its proxy materials only to security holders to whom it has sent a Notice of Internet Availability of Proxy Materials; and

(2)   A soliciting person other than the registrant must send its Notice of Internet Availability of Proxy Materials by the later of:

(i)   40 Calendar days prior to the security holder meeting date or, if no meeting is to be held, 40 calendar days prior to the date the votes, consents, or authorizations may be used to effect the corporate action; or

(ii)   The date on which it files its definitive proxy statement with the Commission, provided its preliminary proxy statement is filed no later than 10 calendar days after the date that the registrant files its definitive proxy statement.

(3)   Content of the soliciting person's Notice of Internet Availability of Proxy Materials. (i) If, at the time a soliciting person other than the registrant sends its Notice of Internet Availability of Proxy Materials, the soliciting person is not aware of all matters on the registrant's agenda for the meeting of security holders, the soliciting person's Notice on Internet Availability of Proxy Materials must provide a clear and impartial identification of each separate matter on the agenda to the extent known by the soliciting person at that time. The soliciting person's notice also must include a clear statement indicating that there may be additional agenda items of which the soliciting person is not aware and that the security holder cannot direct a vote for those items on the soliciting person's proxy card provided at that time.

(ii)   If a soliciting person other than the registrant sends a form of proxy not containing all matters intended to be acted upon, the Notice of Internet Availability of Proxy Materials must clearly state whether execution of the form of proxy will invalidate a security holder's prior vote on matters not presented on the form of proxy.

(m)   This section shall not apply to a proxy solicitation in connection with a business combination transaction, as defined in § 230.165 of this chapter, as well as transactions for cash consideration requiring disclosure under Item 14 of § 240.14a–101.

(n)   Full Set Delivery Option. (1) For purposes of this paragraph (n), the term full set of proxy materials shall include all of the following documents:

(i)   A copy of the proxy statement;

(ii)   A copy of the annual report to security holders if required by § 240.14a–3(b); and

(iii) A form of proxy.

(2) Notwithstanding paragraphs (e) and (f)(2) of this section, a registrant or other soliciting person may:

(i) Accompany the Notice of Internet Availability of Proxy Materials with a full set of proxy materials; or

(ii) Send a full set of proxy materials without a Notice of Internet Availability of Proxy Materials if all of the information required in a Notice of Internet Availability of Proxy Materials pursuant to paragraphs (d) and (n)(4) of this section is incorporated in the proxy statement and the form of proxy.

(3) A registrant or other soliciting person that sends a full set of proxy materials to a security holder pursuant to this paragraph (n) need not comply with

(i) The timing provisions of paragraphs (a) and (l)(2) of this section; and

(ii) The obligation to provide copies pursuant to paragraph (j) of this section.

(4) A registrant or other soliciting person that sends a full set of proxy materials to a security holder pursuant to this paragraph (n) need not include in its Notice of Internet Availability of Proxy Materials, proxy statement, or form of proxy the following disclosures:

(i) Instructions regarding the nature of the communication pursuant to paragraph (d)(2) of this section;

(ii) Instructions on how to request a copy of the proxy materials; and

(iii) Instructions on how to access the form of proxy pursuant to paragraph (d)(10) of this section.

§ 240.14a–17.   Electronic Shareholder Forums

(a) A shareholder, registrant, or third party acting on behalf of a shareholder or registrant may establish, maintain, or operate an electronic shareholder forum to facilitate interaction among the registrant's shareholders and between the registrant and its shareholders as the shareholder or registrant deems appropriate. Subject to paragraphs (b) and (c) of this section, the forum must comply with the federal securities laws, including Section 14(a) of the Act and its associated regulations, other applicable federal laws, applicable state laws, and the registrant's governing documents.

(b) No shareholder, registrant, or third party acting on behalf of a shareholder or registrant, by reason of establishing, maintaining, or operating an electronic shareholder forum, will be liable under the federal securities laws for any statement or information provided by another person to the electronic shareholder forum. Nothing in this section prevents or alters the application of the federal securities laws, including the provisions for liability for fraud, deception, or manipulation, or other applicable federal and state laws to the person or persons that provide a statement or information to an electronic shareholder forum.

(c) Reliance on the exemption in § 240.14a–2(b)(6) to participate in an electronic shareholder forum does not eliminate a person's eligibility to solicit proxies after the date that the exemption in § 240.14a–2(b)(6) is no longer available, or is no longer being relied upon, provided that any such solicitation is conducted in accordance with this regulation.

* * *

§ 240.14a–20.   Shareholder Approval of Executive Compensation of TARP Recipients

If a solicitation is made by a registrant that is a TARP recipient, as defined in section 111(a)(3) of the Emergency Economic Stabilization Act of 2008 (12 U.S.C. 5221(a)(3)), during the period in which any obligation arising from financial assistance provided under the TARP, as defined in section 3(8) of the Emergency Economic Stabilization Act of 2008 (12 U.S.C. 5202(8)), remains outstanding and the solicitation relates to an annual (or special meeting in lieu of the annual) meeting of security holders for which proxies will be solicited for the election of directors, as required pursuant to section 111(e)(1) of the Emergency Economic Stabilization Act of 2008 (12 U.S.C. 5221(e)(1)), the registrant shall provide a separate shareholder vote to approve the compensation of executives, as disclosed pursuant to Item 402 of Regulation S–K (§ 229.402 of this chapter), including the compensation discussion and analysis, the compensation tables, and any related material.

Note to § 240.14a–20: TARP recipients that are smaller reporting companies entitled to provide scaled disclosure pursuant to Item 402(*l*) of Regulation S–K are not required to include a compensation discussion and analysis in their proxy statements in order to comply with this section. In the case of these smaller reporting companies, the required vote must be to approve the compensation of executives as disclosed pursuant to Item 402(m) through (q) of Regulation S–K.

§ 240.14a–21.   Shareholder Approval of Executive Compensation, Frequency of Votes for Approval of Executive Compensation and Shareholder Approval of Golden Parachute Compensation

    (a)   If a solicitation is made by a registrant, other than an emerging growth company as defined in Rule 12b–2 (§ 240.12b–2), and the solicitation relates to an annual or other meeting of shareholders at which directors will be elected and for which the rules of the Commission require executive compensation disclosure pursuant to Item 402 of Regulation S–K (§ 229.402 of this chapter), the registrant shall, for the first annual or other meeting of shareholders on or after January 21, 2011, or for the first annual or other meeting of shareholders on or after January 21, 2013 if the registrant is a smaller reporting company, and thereafter no later than the annual or other meeting of shareholders held in the third calendar year after the immediately preceding vote under this subsection, include a separate resolution subject to shareholder advisory vote to approve the compensation of its named executive officers, as disclosed pursuant to Item 402 of Regulation S–K.

Instruction to paragraph (a):

    The registrant's resolution shall indicate that the shareholder advisory vote under this subsection is to approve the compensation of the registrant's named executive officers as disclosed pursuant to Item 402 of Regulation S–K (§ 229.402 of this chapter). The following is a non-exclusive example of a resolution that would satisfy the requirements of this subsection: "RESOLVED, that the compensation paid to the company's named executive officers, as disclosed pursuant to Item 402 of Regulation S–K, including the Compensation Discussion and Analysis, compensation tables and narrative discussion is hereby APPROVED."

    (b)   If a solicitation is made by a registrant, other than an emerging growth company as defined in Rule 12b–2 (§ 240.12b–2), and the solicitation relates to an annual or other meeting of shareholders at which directors will be elected and for which the rules of the Commission require executive compensation disclosure pursuant to Item 402 of Regulation S–K (§ 229.402 of this chapter), the registrant shall, for the first annual or other meeting of shareholders on or after January 21, 2011, or for the first annual or other meeting of shareholders on or after January 21, 2013 if the registrant is a smaller reporting company, and thereafter no later than the annual or other meeting of shareholders held in the sixth calendar year after the immediately preceding vote under this subsection, include a separate resolution subject to shareholder advisory vote as to whether the shareholder vote required by paragraph (a) of this section should occur every 1, 2 or 3 years. Registrants required to provide a separate shareholder vote pursuant to § 240.14a–20 of this chapter shall include the separate resolution required by this section for the first annual or other meeting of shareholders after the registrant has repaid all obligations arising from financial assistance provided under the TARP, as defined in section 3(8) of the Emergency Economic Stabilization Act of 2008 (12 U.S.C. 5202(8)), and thereafter no later than the annual or other meeting of shareholders held in the sixth calendar year after the immediately preceding vote under this subsection.

    (c)   If a solicitation is made by a registrant, other than an emerging growth company as defined in Rule 12b–2 (§ 240.12b–2), for a meeting of shareholders at which shareholders are asked to approve an acquisition, merger, consolidation or proposed sale or other disposition of all or substantially all the assets of the registrant, the registrant shall include a separate resolution subject to shareholder advisory vote to approve any agreements or understandings and compensation disclosed pursuant to Item 402(t) of Regulation S–K (§ 229.402(t) of this chapter), unless such agreements or understandings have been subject to a shareholder advisory vote under paragraph (a) of this section. Consistent with section 14A(b) of the Exchange Act (15 U.S.C. 78n–1(b)), any agreements or understandings between an acquiring company and the named executive officers of the registrant, where the registrant is not the acquiring company, are not required to be subject to the separate shareholder advisory vote under this paragraph.

Instructions to § 240.14a–21:

1.   Disclosure relating to the compensation of directors required by Item 402(k) (§ 229.402(k) of this chapter) and Item 402(r) of Regulation S–K (§ 229.402(r) of this chapter) is not subject to the shareholder vote required by paragraph (a) of this section. If a registrant includes disclosure pursuant to Item 402(s) of Regulation S–K (§ 229.402(s) of this chapter) about the registrant's compensation policies and practices as they relate to risk management and risk-taking incentives, these policies and practices would not be subject to the shareholder vote required by paragraph (a) of this section. To the extent that risk considerations are a material aspect of the registrant's compensation policies or decisions for named executive officers, the registrant is required to discuss them as part of its Compensation Discussion and Analysis under § 229.402(b) of this chapter, and therefore such disclosure would be considered by shareholders when voting on executive compensation.

2.   If a registrant includes disclosure of golden parachute compensation arrangements pursuant to Item 402(t) (§ 229.402(t) of this chapter) in an annual meeting proxy statement, such disclosure would be subject to the shareholder advisory vote required by paragraph (a) of this section.

3.   Registrants that are smaller reporting companies entitled to provide scaled disclosure in accordance with Item 402(l) of Regulation S–K (§ 229.402(l) of this chapter) are not required to include a Compensation Discussion and Analysis in their proxy statements in order to comply with this section. For smaller reporting companies, the vote required by paragraph (a) of this section must be to approve the compensation of the named executive officers as disclosed pursuant to Item 402(m) through (q) of Regulation S–K (§ 229.402(m) through (q) of this chapter).

4.   A registrant that has ceased being an emerging growth company shall include the first separate resolution described under § 240.14a–21(a) not later than the end of (i) in the case of a registrant that was an emerging growth company for less than two years after the date of first sale of common equity securities of the registrant pursuant to an effective registration statement under the Securities Act of 1933 (15 U.S.C 77a et seq.), the three-year period beginning on such date; and (ii) in the case of any other registrant, the one-year period beginning on the date the registrant is no longer an emerging growth company.

§ 240.14b–1.   **Obligation of Registered Brokers and Dealers in Connection with the Prompt Forwarding of Certain Communications to Beneficial Owners**

(a)   *Definitions.* Unless the context otherwise requires, all terms used in this section shall have the same meanings as in the Act and, with respect to proxy soliciting material, as in § 240.14a–1 thereunder and, with respect to information statements, as in § 240.14c–1 thereunder. In addition, as used in this section, the term "registrant" means:

(1)   The issuer of a class of securities registered pursuant to section 12 of the Act; or

(2)   An investment company registered under the Investment Company Act of 1940.

(b)   *Dissemination and beneficial owner information requirements.* A broker or dealer registered under Section 15 of the Act shall comply with the following requirements for disseminating certain communications to beneficial owners and providing beneficial owner information to registrants.

(1)   The broker or dealer shall respond, by first class mail or other equally prompt means, directly to the registrant no later than seven business days after the date it receives an inquiry made in accordance with § 240.14a–13(a) or § 240.14c–7(a) by indicting, by means of a search card or otherwise:

(i)   The approximate number of customers of the broker or dealer who are beneficial owners of the registrant's securities that are held of record by the broker, dealer, or its nominee;

(ii)   The number of customers of the broker or dealer who are beneficial owners of the registrant's securities who have objected to disclosure of their names, addresses, and securities positions if the registrant has indicated, pursuant to § 240.14a–13(a)(1)(ii)(A) or § 240.14c–7(a)(1)(ii)(A), that it will distribute the annual report to security holders to beneficial owners of its securities whose names, addresses and securities positions are disclosed pursuant to paragraph (b)(3) of this section; and

(iii)   The identity of the designated agent of the broker or dealer, if any, acting on its behalf in fulfilling its obligations under paragraph (b)(3) of this section; Provided, however, that if the broker or dealer has informed the registrant that a designated office(s) or department(s) is to receive such inquiries, receipt for purposes of paragraph (b)(1) of this section shall mean receipt by such designated office(s) or department(s).

(2)   The broker or dealer shall, upon receipt of the proxy, other proxy soliciting material, information statement, and/or annual report to security holders from the registrant or other soliciting person, forward such materials to its customers who are beneficial owners of the registrant's securities no later than five business days after receipt of the proxy material, information statement or annual report to security holders.

Note to paragraph (b)(2): At the request of a registrant, or on its own initiative so long as the registrant does not object, a broker or dealer may, but is not required to, deliver one annual report to security holders, proxy statement, information statement, or Notice of Internet Availability of Proxy Materials to more than one beneficial owner sharing an address if the requirements set forth in § 240.14a–3(e)(1) (with respect to annual reports to security holders, proxy statements, and Notices of Internet Availability of Proxy Materials) and § 240.14c–3(c) (with respect to annual reports to security holders, information statements, and Notices of Internet Availability of Proxy Materials) applicable to registrants, with the exception of § 240.14a–3(e)(1)(i)(E), are satisfied instead by the broker or dealer.

(3)   The broker or dealer shall, through its agent or directly:

(i)   Provide the registrant, upon the registrant's request, with the names, addresses, and securities positions, compiled as of a date specified in the registrant's request which is no earlier than five business days after the date the registrant's request is received, of its customers who are beneficial owners of the registrant's securities and who have not objected to disclosure of such information; Provided, however, that if the broker or dealer has informed the registrant that a designated office(s) or department(s) is to receive such requests, receipt shall mean receipt by such designated office(s) or department(s); and

(ii)   Transmit the data specified in paragraph (b)(3)(i) of this section to the registrant no later than five business days after the record date or other date specified by the registrant.

Note 1: Where a broker or dealer employs a designated agent to act on its behalf in performing the obligations imposed on the broker or dealer by paragraph (b)(3) of this section, the five business day time period for determining the date as of which the beneficial owner information is to be compiled is calculated from the date the designated agent receives the registrant's request. In complying with the registrant's request for beneficial owner information under paragraph (b)(3) of this section, a broker or dealer need only supply the registrant with the names, addresses, and securities positions of non-objecting beneficial owners.

Note 2: If a broker or dealer receives a registrant's request less than five business days before the requested compilation date, it must provide a list compiled as of a date that is no more than five business days after receipt and transmit the list within five business days after the compilation date.

(c)   Exceptions to dissemination and beneficial owner information requirements. A broker or dealer registered under section 15 of the Act shall be subject to the following with respect to its dissemination and beneficial owner information requirements.

(1)   With regard to beneficial owners of exempt employee benefit plan securities, the broker or dealer shall:

(i)   Not include information in its response pursuant to paragraph (b)(1) of this section or forward proxies (or in lieu thereof requests for voting instructions), proxy soliciting material, information statements, or annual reports to security holders pursuant to paragraph (b)(2) of this section to such beneficial owners; and

(ii)   Not include in its response, pursuant to paragraph (b)(3) of this section, data concerning such beneficial owners.

(2)   A broker or dealer need not satisfy:

(i)   Its obligations under paragraphs (b)(2), (b)(3) and (d) of this section if the registrant or other soliciting person, as applicable, does not provide assurance of reimbursement of the broker's or dealer's reasonable expenses, both direct and indirect, incurred in connection with performing the obligations imposed by paragraphs (b)(2), (b)(3) and (d) of this section; or

(ii)   Its obligation under paragraph (b)(2) of this section to forward annual reports to security holders to non-objecting beneficial owners identified by the broker or dealer, through its agent or directly, pursuant to paragraph (b)(3) of this section if the registrant notifies the broker or dealer pursuant to § 240.14a–13(c) or § 240.14c–7(c) that the registrant will send the annual report to security holders to such non-objecting beneficial owners identified by the broker or dealer and delivered in a list to the registrant pursuant to paragraph (b)(3) of this section.

(3)   In its response pursuant to paragraph (b)(1) of this section, a broker or dealer shall not include information about annual reports to security holders, proxy statements or information statements that will not be delivered to security holders sharing an address because of the broker or dealer's reliance on the procedures referred to in the Note to paragraph (b)(2) of this section.

(d)   Upon receipt from the soliciting person of all of the information listed in § 240.14a–16(d), the broker or dealer shall:

(1)   Prepare and send a Notice of Internet Availability of Proxy Materials containing the information required in paragraph (e) of this section to beneficial owners no later than:

(i)   With respect to a registrant, 40 calendar days prior to the security holder meeting date or, if no meeting is to be held, 40 calendar days prior to the date the votes, consents, or authorizations may be used to effect the corporate action; and

(ii)   With respect to a soliciting person other than the registrant, the later of:

(A)   40 calendar days prior to the security holder meeting date or, if no meeting is to be held, 40 calendar days prior to the date the votes, consents, or authorizations may be used to effect the corporate action; or

(B)   10 calendar days after the date that the registrant first sends its proxy statement or Notice of Internet Availability of Proxy Materials to security holders.

(2)   Establish a Web site at which beneficial owners are able to access the broker or dealer's request for voting instructions and, at the broker or dealer's option, establish a Web site at which beneficial owners are able to access the proxy statement and other soliciting materials, provided

that such Web sites are maintained in a manner consistent with paragraphs (b), (c), and (k) of § 240.14a–16;

(3)   Upon receipt of a request from the registrant or other soliciting person, send to security holders specified by the registrant or other soliciting person a copy of the request for voting instructions accompanied by a copy of the intermediary's Notice of Internet Availability of Proxy Materials 10 calendar days or more after the broker or dealer sends its Notice of Internet Availability of Proxy Materials pursuant to paragraph (d)(1); and

(4)   Upon receipt of a request for a copy of the materials from a beneficial owner:

(i)   Request a copy of the soliciting materials from the registrant or other soliciting person, in the form requested by the beneficial owner, within three business days after receiving the beneficial owner's request;

(ii)   Forward a copy of the soliciting materials to the beneficial owner, in the form requested by the beneficial owner, within three business days after receiving the materials from the registrant or other soliciting person; and

(iii)   Maintain records of security holder requests to receive a paper or e-mail copy of the proxy materials in connection with future proxy solicitations and provide copies of the proxy materials to a security holder who has made such a request for all securities held in the account of that security holder until the security holder revokes such request.

(5)   Notwithstanding any other provisions in this paragraph (d), if the broker or dealer receives copies of the proxy statement and annual report to security holders (if applicable) from the soliciting person with instructions to forward such materials to beneficial owners, the broker or dealer:

(i)   Shall either:

(A)   Prepare a Notice of Internet Availability of Proxy Materials and forward it with the proxy statement and annual report to security holders (if applicable); or

(B)   Incorporate any information required in the Notice of Internet Availability of Proxy Materials that does not appear in the proxy statement into the broker or dealer's request for voting instructions to be sent with the proxy statement and annual report (if applicable);

(ii)   Need not comply with the following provisions:

(A)   The timing provisions of paragraph (d)(1)(ii) of this section; and

(B)   Paragraph (d)(4) of this section; and

(iii)   Need not include in its Notice of Internet Availability of Proxy Materials or request for voting instructions the following disclosures:

(A)   Legends 1 and 3 in § 240.14a–16(d)(1); and

(B)   Instructions on how to request a copy of the proxy materials.

(e)   Content of Notice of Internet Availability of Proxy Materials. The broker or dealer's Notice of Internet Availability of Proxy Materials shall:

(1)   Include all information, as it relates to beneficial owners, required in a registrant's Notice of Internet Availability of Proxy Materials under § 240.14a–16(d), provided that the broker or dealer shall provide its own, or its agent's, toll-free telephone number, an e-mail address, and an Internet Web site to service requests for copies from beneficial owners;

(2)   Include a brief description, if applicable, of the rules that permit the broker or dealer to vote the securities if the beneficial owner does not return his or her voting instructions; and

(3)   Otherwise be prepared and sent in a manner consistent with paragraphs (e), (f), and (g) of § 240.14a–16.

§ 240.14b–2.   **Obligation of Banks, Associations and Other Entities That Exercise Fiduciary Powers in Connection with the Prompt Forwarding of Certain Communications to Beneficial Owners**

(a)   Definitions. Unless the context otherwise requires, all terms used in this section shall have the same meanings as in the Act and, with respect to proxy soliciting material, as in § 240.14a–1 thereunder and, with respect to information statements, as in § 240.14c–1 thereunder. In addition, as used in this section, the following terms shall apply:

(1)   The term bank means a bank, association, or other entity that exercises fiduciary powers.

(2)   The term beneficial owner includes any person who has or shares, pursuant to an instrument, agreement, or otherwise, the power to vote, or to direct the voting of a security.

Note 1: If more than one person shares voting power, the provisions of the instrument creating that voting power shall govern with respect to whether consent to disclosure of beneficial owner information has been given.

Note 2: If more than one person shares voting power or if the instrument creating that voting power provides that such power shall be exercised by different persons depending on the nature of the corporate action involved, all persons entitled to exercise such power shall be deemed beneficial owners; Provided, however, that only one such beneficial owner need be designated among the beneficial owners to receive proxies or requests for voting instructions, other proxy soliciting material, information statements, and/or annual reports to security holders, if the person so designated assumes the obligation to disseminate, in a timely manner, such materials to the other beneficial owners.

(3)   The term registrant means:

(i)   The issuer of a class of securities registered pursuant to section 12 of the Act; or

(ii)   An investment company registered under the Investment Company Act of 1940.

(b)   Dissemination and beneficial owner information requirements. A bank shall comply with the following requirements for disseminating certain communications to beneficial owners and providing beneficial owner information to registrants.

(1)   The bank shall:

(i)   Respond, by first class mail or other equally prompt means, directly to the registrant, no later than one business day after the date it receives an inquiry made in accordance with § 240.14a–13(a) or § 240.14c–7(a) by indicating the name and address of each of its respondent banks that holds the registrant's securities on behalf of beneficial owners, if any; and

(ii)   Respond, by first class mail or other equally prompt means, directly to the registrant no later than seven business days after the date it receives an inquiry made in accordance with § 240.14a–13(a) or § 240.14c–7(a) by indicating, by means of a search card or otherwise:

(A)   The approximate number of customers of the bank who are beneficial owners of the registrant's securities that are held of record by the bank or its nominee;

(B)   If the registrant has indicated, pursuant to § 240.14a–13(a)(1)(ii)(A) or § 240.14c–7(a)(1)(ii)(A), that it will distribute the annual report to security holders to beneficial owners of its securities whose names, addresses, and securities positions are disclosed pursuant to paragraphs (b)(4)(ii) and (iii) of this section:

(1)   With respect to customer accounts opened on or before December 28, 1986, the number of beneficial owners of the registrant's securities who have affirmatively consented to disclosure of their names, addresses, and securities positions; and

(2)   With respect to customer accounts opened after December 28, 1986, the number of beneficial owners of the registrant's securities who have not objected to disclosure of their names, addresses, and securities positions; and

(C)   The identity of its designated agent, if any, acting on its behalf in fulfilling its obligations under paragraphs (b)(4) (ii) and (iii) of this section;

Provided, however, that, if the bank or respondent bank has informed the registrant that a designated office(s) or department(s) is to receive such inquiries, receipt for purposes of paragraphs (b)(1)(i) and (ii) of this section shall mean receipt by such designated office(s) or department(s).

(2)   Where proxies are solicited, the bank shall, within five business days after the record date:

(i)   Execute an omnibus proxy, including a power of substitution, in favor of its respondent banks and forward such proxy to the registrant; and

(ii)   Furnish a notice to each respondent bank in whose favor an omnibus proxy has been executed that it has executed such a proxy, including a power of substitution, in its favor pursuant to paragraph (b)(2)(i) of this section.

(3)   Upon receipt of the proxy, other proxy soliciting material, information statement, and/or annual report to security holders from the registrant or other soliciting person, the bank shall forward such materials to each beneficial owner on whose behalf it holds securities, no later than five business days after the date it receives such material and, where a proxy is solicited, the bank shall forward, with the other proxy soliciting material and/or the annual report to security holders, either:

(i)   A properly executed proxy:

(A)   Indicating the number of securities held for such beneficial owner;

(B)   Bearing the beneficial owner's account number or other form of identification, together with instructions as to the procedures to vote the securities;

(C)   Briefly stating which other proxies, if any, are required to permit securities to be voted under the terms of the instrument creating that voting power or applicable state law; and

(D)   Being accompanied by an envelope addressed to the registrant or its agent, if not provided by the registrant; or

(ii)   A request for voting instructions (for which registrant's form of proxy may be used and which shall be voted by the record holder bank or respondent bank in accordance with the instructions received), together with an envelope addressed to the record holder bank or respondent bank.

Note to paragraph (b)(3): At the request of a registrant, or on its own initiative so long as the registrant does not object, a bank may, but is not required to, deliver one annual report to security holders, proxy statement, information statement, or Notice of Internet Availability of Proxy Materials to more than one beneficial owner sharing an address if the requirements set forth in § 240.14a–3(e)(1) (with respect to annual reports to security holders, proxy statements, and Notices of Internet Availability of Proxy Materials) and § 240.14c–3(c) (with respect to annual reports to security holders, information statements, and Notices of Internet Availability of Proxy Materials) applicable to registrants, with the exception of § 240.14a–3(e)(1)(i)(E), are satisfied instead by the bank.

(4)   The bank shall:

(i) Respond, by first class mail or other equally prompt means, directly to the registrant no later than one business day after the date it receives an inquiry made in accordance with § 240.14a–13(b)(1) or § 240.14c–7(b)(1) by indicating the name and address of each of its respondent banks that holds the registrant's securities on behalf of beneficial owners, if any;

(ii) Through its agent or directly, provide the registrant, upon the registrant's request, and within the time specified in paragraph (b)(4)(iii) of this section, with the names, addresses, and securities position, compiled as of a date specified in the registrant's request which is no earlier than five business days after the date the registrant's request is received, of:

(A) With respect to customer accounts opened on or before December 28, 1986, beneficial owners of the registrant's securities on whose behalf it holds securities who have consented affirmatively to disclosure of such information, subject to paragraph (b)(5) of this section; and

(B) With respect to customer accounts opened after December 28, 1986, beneficial owners of the registrant's securities on whose behalf it holds securities who have not objected to disclosure of such information;

Provided, however, that if the record holder bank or respondent bank has informed the registrant that a designated office(s) or department(s) is to receive such requests, receipt for purposes of paragraphs (b)(4) (i) and (ii) of this section shall mean receipt by such designated office(s) or department(s); and

(iii) Through its agent or directly, transmit the data specified in paragraph (b)(4)(ii) of this section to the registrant no later than five business days after the date specified by the registrant.

Note 1: Where a record holder bank or respondent bank employs a designated agent to act on its behalf in performing the obligations imposed on it by paragraphs (b)(4) (ii) and (iii) of this section, the five business day time period for determining the date as of which the beneficial owner information is to be compiled is calculated from the date the designated agent receives the registrant's request. In complying with the registrant's request for beneficial owner information under paragraphs (b)(4) (ii) and (iii) of this section, a record holder bank or respondent bank need only supply the registrant with the names, addresses and securities positions of affirmatively consenting and non-objecting beneficial owners.

Note 2: If a record holder bank or respondent bank receives a registrant's request less than five business days before the requested compilation date, it must provide a list compiled as of a date that is no more than five business days after receipt and transmit the list within five business days after the compilation date.

(5) For customer accounts opened on or before December 28, 1986, unless the bank has made a good faith effort to obtain affirmative consent to disclosure of beneficial owner information pursuant to paragraph (b)(4)(ii) of this section, the bank shall provide such information as to beneficial owners who do not object to disclosure of such information. A good faith effort to obtain affirmative consent to disclosure of beneficial owner information shall include, but shall not be limited to, making an inquiry:

(i) Phrased in neutral language, explaining the purpose of the disclosure and the limitations on the registrant's use thereof;

(ii) Either in at least one mailing separate from other account mailings or in repeated mailings; and

(iii) In a mailing that includes a return card, postage paid enclosure.

(c) Exceptions to dissemination and beneficial owner information requirements. The bank shall be subject to the following respect to its dissemination and beneficial owner requirements.

(1) With regard to beneficial owners of exempt employee benefit plan securities, the bank shall not:

(i) Include information in its response pursuant to paragraph (b)(1) of this section; or forward proxies (or in lieu thereof requests for voting instructions), proxy soliciting material, information statements, or annual reports to security holders pursuant to paragraph (b)(3) of this section to such beneficial owners; or

(ii) Include in its response pursuant to paragraphs (b)(4) and (b)(5) of this section data concerning such beneficial owners.

(2) The bank need not satisfy:

(i) Its obligations under paragraphs (b)(2), (b)(3), (b)(4) and (d) of this section if the registrant or other soliciting person, as applicable, does not provide assurance of reimbursement of its reasonable expenses, both direct and indirect, incurred in connection with performing the obligations imposed by paragraphs (b)(2), (b)(3), (b)(4) and (d) of this section; or

(ii) Its obligation under paragraph (b)(3) of this section to forward annual reports to security holders to consenting and non-objecting beneficial owners identified pursuant to paragraphs (b)(4) (ii) and (iii) of this section if the registrant notifies the record holder bank or respondent bank, pursuant to § 240.14a–13(c) or § 240.14c–7(c), that the registrant will send the annual report to security holders to beneficial owners whose names addresses and securities positions are disclosed pursuant to paragraphs (b)(4) (ii) and (iii) of this section.

(3) For the purposes of determining the fees which may be charged to registrants pursuant to § 240.14a–13(b)(5), § 240.14c–7(a)(5), and paragraph (c)(2) of this section for performing obligations under paragraphs (b)(2), (b)(3), and (b)(4) of this section, an amount no greater than that permitted to be charged by brokers or dealers for reimbursement of their reasonable expenses, both direct and indirect, incurred in connection with performing the obligations imposed by paragraphs (b)(2) and (b)(3) of § 240.14b–1, shall be deemed to be reasonable.

(4) In its response pursuant to paragraph (b)(1)(ii)(A) of this section, a bank shall not include information about annual reports to security holders, proxy statements or information statements that will not be delivered to security holders sharing an address because of the bank's reliance on the procedures referred to in the Note to paragraph (b)(3) of this section.

(d) Upon receipt from the soliciting person of all of the information listed in § 240.14a–16(d), the bank shall:

(1) Prepare and send a Notice of Internet Availability of Proxy Materials containing the information required in paragraph (e) of this section to beneficial owners no later than:

(i) With respect to a registrant, 40 calendar days prior to the security holder meeting date or, if no meeting is to be held, 40 calendar days prior to the date the votes, consents, or authorizations may be used to effect the corporate action; and

(ii) With respect to a soliciting person other than the registrant, the later of:

(A) 40 calendar days prior to the security holder meeting date or, if no meeting is to be held, 40 calendar days prior to the date the votes, consents, or authorizations may be used to effect the corporate action; or

(B) 10 calendar days after the date that the registrant first sends its proxy statement or Notice of Internet Availability of Proxy Materials to security holders.

(2) Establish a Web site at which beneficial owners are able to access the bank's request for voting instructions and, at the bank's option, establish a Web site at which beneficial owners are able to access the proxy statement and other soliciting materials, provided that such Web sites are maintained in a manner consistent with paragraphs (b), (c), and (k) of § 240.14a–16;

(3)   Upon receipt of a request from the registrant or other soliciting person, send to security holders specified by the registrant or other soliciting person a copy of the request for voting instructions accompanied by a copy of the intermediary's Notice of Internet Availability of Proxy Materials 10 days or more after the bank sends its Notice of Internet Availability of Proxy Materials pursuant to paragraph (d)(1); and

(4)   Upon receipt of a request for a copy of the materials from a beneficial owner:

(i)   Request a copy of the soliciting materials from the registrant or other soliciting person, in the form requested by the beneficial owner, within three business days after receiving the beneficial owner's request;

(ii)   Forward a copy of the soliciting materials to the beneficial owner, in the form requested by the beneficial owner, within three business days after receiving the materials from the registrant or other soliciting person; and

(iii)   Maintain records of security holder requests to receive a paper or e-mail copy of the proxy materials in connection with future proxy solicitations and provide copies of the proxy materials to a security holder who has made such a request for all securities held in the account of that security holder until the security holder revokes such request.

(5)   Notwithstanding any other provisions in this paragraph (d), if the bank receives copies of the proxy statement and annual report to security holders (if applicable) from the soliciting person with instructions to forward such materials to beneficial owners, the bank:

(i)   Shall either:

(A)   Prepare a Notice of Internet Availability of Proxy Materials and forward it with the proxy statement and annual report to security holders (if applicable); or

(B)   Incorporate any information required in the Notice of Internet Availability of Proxy Materials that does not appear in the proxy statement into the bank's request for voting instructions to be sent with the proxy statement and annual report (if applicable);

(ii)   Need not comply with the following provisions:

(A)   The timing provisions of paragraph (d)(1)(ii) of this section; and

(B)   Paragraph (d)(4) of this section; and

(iii)   Need not include in its Notice of Internet Availability of Proxy Materials or request for voting instructions the following disclosures:

(A)   Legends 1 and 3 in § 240.14a–16(d)(1); and

(B)   Instructions on how to request a copy of the proxy materials.

(e)   Content of Notice of Internet Availability of Proxy Materials. The bank's Notice of Internet Availability of Proxy Materials shall:

(1)   Include all information, as it relates to beneficial owners, required in a registrant's Notice of Internet Availability of Proxy Materials under § 240.14a–16(d), provided that the bank shall provide its own, or its agent's, toll-free telephone number, e-mail address, and Internet Web site to service requests for copies from beneficial owners; and

(2)   Otherwise be prepared and sent in a manner consistent with paragraphs (e), (f), and (g) of § 240.14a–16.

* * *

TENDER OFFERS

§ 240.14d–1. Scope of and Definitions Applicable to Regulations 14D and 14E

(a) Scope. Regulation 14D (§§ 240.14d–1 through 240.14d–101) shall apply to any tender offer that is subject to section 14(d)(1) of the Act (15 U.S.C. 78n(d)(1)), including, but not limited to, any tender offer for securities of a class described in that section that is made by an affiliate of the issuer of such class. Regulation 14E (§§ 240.14e–1 through 240.14e–8) shall apply to any tender offer for securities (other than exempted securities) unless otherwise noted therein.

* * *

(g) Definitions. Unless the context otherwise requires, all terms used in Regulation 14D and Regulation 14E have the same meaning as in the Act and in Rule 12b–2 (§ 240.12b–2) promulgated thereunder. In addition, for purposes of sections 14(d) and 14(e) of the Act and Regulations 14D and 14E, the following definitions apply:

(1) The term beneficial owner shall have the same meaning as that set forth in Rule 13d–3: Provided, however, That, except with respect to Rule 14d–3, Rule 14d–9(d), the term shall not include a person who does not have or share investment power or who is deemed to be a beneficial owner by virtue of Rule 13d–3(d)(1) (§ 240.13d–3(d)(1));

(2) The term bidder means any person who makes a tender offer or on whose behalf a tender offer is made: Provided, however, That the term does not include an issuer which makes a tender offer for securities of any class of which it is the issuer;

(3) The term business day means any day, other than Saturday, Sunday or a federal holiday, and shall consist of the time period from 12:01 a.m. through 12:00 midnight Eastern time. In computing any time period under section 14(d)(5) or section 14(d)(6) of the Act or under Regulation 14D or Regulation 14E, the date of the event which begins the running of such time period shall be included except that if such event occurs on other than a business day such period shall begin to run on and shall include the first business day thereafter; and

(4) The term initial offering period means the period from the time the offer commences until all minimum time periods, including extensions, required by Regulations 14D (§§ 240.14d–1 through 240.14d–103) and 14E (§§ 240.14e–1 through 240.14e–8) have been satisfied and all conditions to the offer have been satisfied or waived within these time periods.

(5) The term security holders means holders of record and beneficial owners of securities which are the subject of a tender offer;

(6) The term security position listing means, with respect to securities of any issuer held by a registered clearing agency in the name of the clearing agency or its nominee, a list of those participants in the clearing agency on whose behalf the clearing agency holds the issuer's securities and of the participants' respective positions in such securities as of a specified date.

(7) The term subject company means any issuer of securities which are sought by a bidder pursuant to a tender offer;

(8) The term subsequent offering period means the period immediately following the initial offering period meeting the conditions specified in § 240.14d–11.

(9) The term tender offer material means:

(i) The bidder's formal offer, including all the material terms and conditions of the tender offer and all amendments thereto;

(ii) The related transmittal letter (whereby securities of the subject company which are sought in the tender offer may be transmitted to the bidder or its depositary) and all amendments thereto; and

(iii) Press releases, advertisements, letters and other documents published by the bidder or sent or given by the bidder to security holders which, directly or indirectly, solicit, invite or request tenders of the securities being sought in the tender offer;

(h)   Signatures. Where the Act or the rules, forms, reports or schedules thereunder require a document filed with or furnished to the Commission to be signed, such document shall be manually signed, or signed using either typed signatures or duplicated or facsimile versions of manual signatures. Where typed, duplicated or facsimile signatures are used, each signatory to the filing shall manually sign a signature page or other document authenticating, acknowledging or otherwise adopting his or her signature that appears in the filing. Such document shall be executed before or at the time the filing is made and shall be retained by the filer for a period of five years. Upon request, the filer shall furnish to the Commission or its staff a copy of any or all documents retained pursuant to this section.

§ 240.14d–2.   Commencement of a Tender Offer

(a)   Date of commencement. A bidder will have commenced its tender offer for purposes of section 14(d) of the Act (15 U.S.C. 78n) and the rules under that section at 12:01 a.m. on the date when the bidder has first published, sent or given the means to tender to security holders. For purposes of this section, the means to tender includes the transmittal form or a statement regarding how the transmittal form may be obtained.

(b)   Pre-commencement communications. A communication by the bidder will not be deemed to constitute commencement of a tender offer if:

(1)   It does not include the means for security holders to tender their shares into the offer; and

(2)   All written communications relating to the tender offer, from and including the first public announcement, are filed under cover of Schedule TO (§ 240.14d–100) with the Commission no later than the date of the communication. The bidder also must deliver to the subject company and any other bidder for the same class of securities the first communication relating to the transaction that is filed, or required to be filed, with the Commission.

Instructions to paragraph (b)(2):

1.   The box on the front of Schedule TO indicating that the filing contains pre-commencement communications must be checked.

2.   Any communications made in connection with an exchange offer registered under the Securities Act of 1933 need only be filed under § 230.425 of this chapter and will be deemed filed under this section.

3.   Each pre-commencement written communication must include a prominent legend in clear, plain language advising security holders to read the tender offer statement when it is available because it contains important information. The legend also must advise investors that they can get the tender offer statement and other filed documents for free at the Commission's web site and explain which documents are free from the offeror.

4.   *See* §§ 230.135, 230.165 and 230.166 of this chapter for pre-commencement communications made in connection with registered exchange offers.

5.   "Public announcement" is any oral or written communication by the bidder, or any person authorized to act on the bidder's behalf, that is reasonably designed to, or has the effect of, informing the public or security holders in general about the tender offer.

(c)   Filing and other obligations triggered by commencement. As soon as practicable on the date of commencement, a bidder must comply with the filing requirements of § 240.14d–3(a), the dissemination requirements of § 240.14d–4(a) or (b), and the disclosure requirements of § 240.14d–6(a).

§ 240.14d–3.   Filing and Transmission of Tender Offer Statement

(a)   Filing and transmittal. No bidder shall make a tender offer if, after consummation thereof, such bidder would be the beneficial owner of more than 5 percent of the class of the subject company's securities for which the tender offer is made, unless as soon as practicable on the date of the commencement of the tender offer such bidder:

(1)   Files with the Commission a Tender Offer Statement on Schedule TO (§ 240.14d–100), including all exhibits thereto;

(2)   Delivers a copy of such Schedule TO, including all exhibits thereto:

(i)   To the subject company at its principal executive office; and

(ii)   To any other bidder, which has filed a Schedule TO with the Commission relating to a tender offer which has not yet terminated for the same class of securities of the subject company, at such bidder's principal executive office or at the address of the person authorized to receive notices and communications (which is disclosed on the cover sheet of such other bidder's Schedule TO);

(3)   Gives telephonic notice of the information required by Rule 14d–6(d)(2)(i) and (ii) (§ 240.14d–6(d)(2)(i) and (ii)) and mails by means of first class mail a copy of such Schedule TO, including all exhibits thereto:

(i)   To each national securities exchange where such class of the subject company's securities is registered and listed for trading (which may be based upon information contained in the subject company's most recent Annual Report on Form 10-K (§ 249.310 of this chapter) filed with the Commission unless the bidder has reason to believe that such information is not current), which telephonic notice shall be made when practicable before the opening of each such exchange; and

(ii)   To the National Association of Securities Dealers, Inc. ("NASD") if such class of the subject company's securities is authorized for quotation in the NASDAQ interdealer quotation system.

(b)   Post-commencement amendments and additional materials. The bidder making the tender offer must file with the Commission:

(1)   An amendment to Schedule TO (§ 240.14d–100) reporting promptly any material changes in the information set forth in the schedule previously filed and including copies of any additional tender offer materials as exhibits; and

(2)   A final amendment to Schedule TO (§ 240.14d–100) reporting promptly the results of the tender offer.

Instruction to paragraph (b): A copy of any additional tender offer materials or amendment filed under this section must be sent promptly to the subject company and to any exchange and/or NASD, as required by paragraph (a) of this section, but in no event later than the date the materials are first published, sent or given to security holders.

(c)   Certain announcements. Notwithstanding the provisions of paragraph (b) of this section, if the additional tender offer material or an amendment to Schedule TO discloses only the number of shares deposited to date, and/or announces an extension of the time during which shares may be tendered, then the bidder may file such tender offer material or amendment and send a copy of such tender offer material or amendment to the subject company, any exchange and/or the NASD, as required by paragraph (a) of this section, promptly after the date such tender offer material is first published or sent or given to security holders.

§ 240.14d–4.   Dissemination of Tender Offers to Security Holders

As soon as practicable on the date of commencement of a tender offer, the bidder must publish, send or give the disclosure required by § 240.14d–6 to security holders of the class of securities that is the subject of the offer, by complying with all of the requirements of any of the following:

(a)   Cash tender offers and exempt securities offers. For tender offers in which the consideration consists solely of cash and/or securities exempt from registration under section 3 of the Securities Act of 1933 (15 U.S.C. 77c):

(1)   Long-form publication. The bidder makes adequate publication in a newspaper or newspapers of long-form publication of the tender offer.

(2)   Summary publication. (i) If the tender offer is not subject to Rule 13e–3 (§ 240.13e–3), the bidder makes adequate publication in a newspaper or newspapers of a summary advertisement of the tender offer; and

(ii)   Mails by first class mail or otherwise furnishes with reasonable promptness the bidder's tender offer materials to any security holder who requests such tender offer materials pursuant to the summary advertisement or otherwise.

(3)   Use of stockholder lists and security position listings. Any bidder using stockholder lists and security position listings under § 240.14d–5 must comply with paragraph (a)(1) or (2) of this section on or before the date of the bidder's request under § 240.14d–5(a).

Instruction to paragraph (a): Tender offers may be published or sent or given to security holders by other methods, but with respect to summary publication and the use of stockholder lists and security position listings under § 240.14d–5, paragraphs (a)(2) and (a)(3) of this section are exclusive.

(b)   Registered securities offers. For tender offers in which the consideration consists solely or partially of securities registered under the Securities Act of 1933, a registration statement containing all of the required information, including pricing information, has been filed and a preliminary prospectus or a prospectus that meets the requirements of section 10(a) of the Securities Act (15 U.S.C. 77j(a)), including a letter of transmittal, is delivered to security holders. However, for going-private transactions (as defined by § 240.13e–3) and roll-up transactions (as described by Item 901 of Regulation S–K (§ 229.901 of this chapter)), a registration statement registering the securities to be offered must have become effective and only a prospectus that meets the requirements of section 10(a) of the Securities Act may be delivered to security holders on the date of commencement.

Instructions to paragraph (b):

1.   If the prospectus is being delivered by mail, mailing on the date of commencement is sufficient.

2.   A preliminary prospectus used under this section may not omit information under §§ 230.430 or 230.430A of this chapter.

3.   If a preliminary prospectus is used under this section and the bidder must disseminate material changes, the tender offer must remain open for the period specified in paragraph (d)(2) of this section.

4.   If a preliminary prospectus is used under this section, tenders may be requested in accordance with § 230.162(a) of this chapter.

(c)   Adequate publication. Depending on the facts and circumstances involved, adequate publication of a tender offer pursuant to this section may require publication in a newspaper with a national circulation or may only require publication in a newspaper with metropolitan or regional circulation or may require publication in a combination thereof: Provided, however, That publication in all editions of a daily newspaper with a national circulation shall be deemed to constitute adequate publication.

(d) Publication of changes and extension of the offer. (1) If a tender offer has been published or sent or given to security holders by one or more of the methods enumerated in this section, a material change in the information published or sent or given to security holders shall be promptly disseminated to security holders in a manner reasonably designed to inform security holders of such change; Provided, however, That if the bidder has elected pursuant to Rule 14d–5 (f)(1) of this section to require the subject company to disseminate amendments disclosing material changes to the tender offer materials pursuant to Rule 14d–5, the bidder shall disseminate material changes in the information published or sent or given to security holders at least pursuant to Rule 14d–5.

(2) In a registered securities offer where the bidder disseminates the preliminary prospectus as permitted by paragraph (b) of this section, the offer must remain open from the date that material changes to the tender offer materials are disseminated to security holders, as follows:

(i) Five business days for a prospectus supplement containing a material change other than price or share levels;

(ii) Ten business days for a prospectus supplement containing a change in price, the amount of securities sought, the dealer's soliciting fee, or other similarly significant change;

(iii) Ten business days for a prospectus supplement included as part of a post-effective amendment; and

(iv) Twenty business days for a revised prospectus when the initial prospectus was materially deficient.

§ 240.14d–5. Dissemination of Certain Tender Offers by the Use of Stockholder Lists and Security Position Listings

(a) Obligations of the subject company. Upon receipt by a subject company at its principal executive offices of a bidder's written request, meeting the requirements of paragraph (e) of this section, the subject company shall comply with the following sub-paragraphs.

(1) The subject company shall notify promptly transfer agents and any other person who will assist the subject company in complying with the requirements of this section of the receipt by the subject company of a request by a bidder pursuant to this section.

(2) The subject company shall promptly ascertain whether the most recently prepared stockholder list, written or otherwise, within the access of the subject company was prepared as of a date earlier than ten business days before the date of the bidder's request and, if so, the subject company shall promptly prepare or cause to be prepared a stockholder list as of the most recent practicable date which shall not be more than ten business days before the date of the bidder's request.

(3) The subject company shall make an election to comply and shall comply with all of the provisions of either paragraph (b) or paragraph (c) of this section. The subject company's election once made shall not be modified or revoked during the bidder's tender offer and extensions thereof.

(4) No later than the second business day after the date of the bidder's request, the subject company shall orally notify the bidder, which notification shall be confirmed in writing, of the subject company's election made pursuant to paragraph (a)(3) of this section. Such notification shall indicate (i) the approximate number of security holders of the class of securities being sought by the bidder and, (ii) if the subject company elects to comply with paragraph (b) of this section, appropriate information concerning the location for delivery of the bidder's tender offer materials and the approximate direct costs incidental to the mailing to security holders of the bidder's tender offer materials computed in accordance with paragraph (g)(2) of this section.

(b)   Mailing of tender offer materials by the subject company. A subject company which elects pursuant to paragraph (a)(3) of this section to comply with the provisions of this paragraph shall perform the acts prescribed by the following paragraphs.

(1)   The subject company shall promptly contact each participant named on the most recent security position listing of any clearing agency within the access of the subject company and make inquiry of each such participant as to the approximate number of beneficial owners of the subject company securities being sought in the tender offer held by each such participant.

(2)   No later than the third business day after delivery of the bidder's tender offer materials pursuant to paragraph (g)(1) of this section, the subject company shall begin to mail or cause to be mailed by means of first class mail a copy of the bidder's tender offer materials to each person whose name appears as a record holder of the class of securities for which the offer is made on the most recent stockholder list referred to in paragraph (a)(2) of this section. The subject company shall use its best efforts to complete the mailing in a timely manner but in no event shall such mailing be completed in a substantially greater period of time than the subject company would complete a mailing to security holders of its own materials relating to the tender offer.

(3)   No later than the third business day after the delivery of the bidder's tender offer materials pursuant to paragraph (g)(1) of this section, the subject company shall begin to transmit or cause to be transmitted a sufficient number of sets of the bidder's tender offer materials to the participants named on the security position listings described in paragraph (b)(1) of this section. The subject company shall use its best efforts to complete the transmittal in a timely manner but in no event shall such transmittal be completed in a substantially greater period of time than the subject company would complete a transmittal to such participants pursuant to security position listings of clearing agencies of its own material relating to the tender offer.

(4)   The subject company shall promptly give oral notification to the bidder, which notification shall be confirmed in writing, of the commencement of the mailing pursuant to paragraph (b)(2) of this section and of the transmittal pursuant to paragraph (b)(3) of this section.

(5)   During the tender offer and any extension thereof the subject company shall use reasonable efforts to update the stockholder list and shall mail or cause to be mailed promptly following each update a copy of the bidder's tender offer materials (to the extent sufficient sets of such materials have been furnished by the bidder) to each person who has become a record holder since the later of (i) the date of preparation of the most recent stockholder list referred to in paragraph (a)(2) of this section or (ii) the last preceding update.

(6)   If the bidder has elected pursuant to paragraph (f)(1) of this section to require the subject company to disseminate amendments disclosing material changes to the tender offer materials pursuant to this section, the subject company, promptly following delivery of each such amendment, shall mail or cause to be mailed a copy of each such amendment to each record holder whose name appears on the shareholder list described in paragraphs (a)(2) and (b)(5) of this section and shall transmit or cause to be transmitted sufficient copies of such amendment to each participant named on security position listings who received sets of the bidder's tender offer materials pursuant to paragraph (b)(3) of this section.

(7)   The subject company shall not include any communication other than the bidder's tender offer materials or amendments thereto in the envelopes or other containers furnished by the bidder.

(8)   Promptly following the termination of the tender offer, the subject company shall reimburse the bidder the excess, if any, of the amounts advanced pursuant to paragraph (f)(3)(iii) over the direct costs incidental to compliance by the subject company and its agents in performing the acts required by this section computed in accordance with paragraph (g)(2) of this section.

(c)   Delivery of stockholder lists and security position listings. A subject company which elects pursuant to paragraph (a)(3) of this section to comply with the provisions of this paragraph shall perform the acts prescribed by the following paragraphs.

(1)   No later than the third business day after the date of the bidder's request, the subject company must furnish to the bidder at the subject company's principal executive office a copy of the names and addresses of the record holders on the most recent stockholder list referred to in paragraph (a)(2) of this section; the names and addresses of participants identified on the most recent security position listing of any clearing agency that is within the access of the subject company; and the most recent list of names, addresses and security positions of beneficial owners as specified in § 240.14a–13(b), in the possession of the subject company, or that subsequently comes into its possession. All security holder list information must be in the format requested by the bidder to the extent the format is available to the subject company without undue burden or expense.

(2)   If the bidder has elected pursuant to paragraph (f)(1) of this section to require the subject company to disseminate amendments disclosing material changes to the tender offer materials, the subject company shall update the stockholder list by furnishing the bidder with the name and address of each record holder named on the stockholder list, and not previously furnished to the bidder, promptly after such information becomes available to the subject company during the tender offer and any extensions thereof.

(d)   Liability of subject company and others. Neither the subject company nor any affiliate or agent of the subject company nor any clearing agency shall be:

(1)   Deemed to have made a solicitation or recommendation respecting the tender offer within the meaning of section 14(d)(4) based solely upon the compliance or noncompliance by the subject company or any affiliate or agent of the subject company with one or more requirements of this section;

(2)   Liable under any provision of the Federal securities laws to the bidder or to any security holder based solely upon the inaccuracy of the current names or addresses on the stockholder list or security position listing, unless such inaccuracy results from a lack of reasonable care on the part of the subject company or any affiliate or agent of the subject company;

(3)   Deemed to be an "underwriter" within the meaning of section (2)(11) of the Securities Act of 1933 for any purpose of that Act or any rule or regulation promulgated thereunder based solely upon the compliance or noncompliance by the subject company or any affiliate or agent of the subject company with one or more of the requirements of this section;

(4)   Liable under any provision of the Federal securities laws for the disclosure in the bidder's tender offer materials, including any amendment thereto, based solely upon the compliance or noncompliance by the subject company or any affiliate or agent of the subject company with one or more of the requirements of this section.

(e)   Content of the bidder's request. The bidder's written request referred to in paragraph (a) of this section shall include the following:

(1)   The identity of the bidder;

(2)   The title of the class of securities which is the subject of the bidder's tender offer;

(3)   A statement that the bidder is making a request to the subject company pursuant to paragraph (a) of this section for the use of the stockholder list and security position listings for the purpose of disseminating a tender offer to security holders;

(4)   A statement that the bidder is aware of and will comply with the provisions of paragraph (f) of this section;

(5)   A statement as to whether or not it has elected pursuant to paragraph (f)(1) of this section to disseminate amendments disclosing material changes to the tender offer materials pursuant to this section; and

(6)   The name, address and telephone number of the person whom the subject company shall contact pursuant to paragraph (a)(4) of this section.

(f)   Obligations of the bidder. Any bidder who requests that a subject company comply with the provisions of paragraph (a) of this section shall comply with the following paragraphs.

(1)   The bidder shall make an election whether or not to require the subject company to disseminate amendments disclosing material changes to the tender offer materials pursuant to this section, which election shall be included in the request referred to in paragraph (a) of this section and shall not be revocable by the bidder during the tender offer and extensions thereof.

(2)   With respect to a tender offer subject to section 14(d)(1) of the Act in which the consideration consists solely of cash and/or securities exempt from registration under section 3 of the Securities Act of 1933, the bidder shall comply with the requirements of Rule 14d–4(a)(3).

(3)   If the subject company elects to comply with paragraph (b) of this section,

(i)   The bidder shall promptly deliver the tender offer materials after receipt of the notification from the subject company as provided in paragraph (a)(4) of this section;

(ii)   The bidder shall promptly notify the subject company of any amendment to the bidder's tender offer materials requiring compliance by the subject company with paragraph (b)(6) of this section and shall promptly deliver such amendment to the subject company pursuant to paragraph (g)(1) of this section;

(iii)   The bidder shall advance to the subject company an amount equal to the approximate cost of conducting mailings to security holders computed in accordance with paragraph (g)(2) of this section;

(iv)   The bidder shall promptly reimburse the subject company for the direct costs incidental to compliance by the subject company and its agents in performing the acts required by this section computed in accordance with paragraph (g)(2) of this section which are in excess of the amount advanced pursuant to paragraph (f)(2)(iii) of this section; and

(v)   The bidder shall mail by means of first class mail or otherwise furnish with reasonable promptness the tender offer materials to any security holder who requests such materials.

(4)   If the subject company elects to comply with paragraph (c) of this section,

(i)   The bidder shall use the stockholder list and security position listings furnished to the bidder pursuant to paragraph (c) of this section exclusively in the dissemination of tender offer materials to security holders in connection with the bidder's tender offer and extensions thereof;

(ii)   The bidder shall return the stockholder lists and security position listings furnished to the bidder pursuant to paragraph (c) of this section promptly after the termination of the bidder's tender offer;

(iii)   The bidder shall accept, handle and return the stockholder lists and security position listings furnished to the bidder pursuant to paragraph (c) of this section to the subject company on a confidential basis;

(iv)   The bidder shall not retain any stockholder list or security position listing furnished by the subject company pursuant to paragraph (c) of this section, or any copy thereof, nor retain any information derived from any such list or listing or copy thereof after the termination of the bidder's tender offer;

(v)   The bidder shall mail by means of first class mail, at its own expense, a copy of its tender offer materials to each person whose identity appears on the stockholder list as furnished and updated by the subject company pursuant to paragraphs (c)(1) and (2) of this section;

(vi) The bidder shall contact the participants named on the security position listing of any clearing agency, make inquiry of each participant as to the approximate number of sets of tender offer materials required by each such participant, and furnish, at its own expense, sufficient sets of tender offer materials and any amendment thereto to each such participant for subsequent transmission to the beneficial owners of the securities being sought by the bidder;

(vii) The bidder shall mail by means of first class mail or otherwise furnish with reasonable promptness the tender offer materials to any security holder who requests such materials; and

(viii) The bidder shall promptly reimburse the subject company for direct costs incidental to compliance by the subject company and its agents in performing the acts required by this section computed in accordance with paragraph (g)(2) of this section.

(g)   Delivery of materials, computation of direct costs. (1) Whenever the bidder is required to deliver tender offer materials or amendments to tender offer materials, the bidder shall deliver to the subject company at the location specified by the subject company in its notice given pursuant to paragraph (a)(4) of this section a number of sets of the materials or of the amendment, as the case may be, at least equal to the approximate number of security holders specified by the subject company in such notice, together with appropriate envelopes or other containers therefor: Provided, however, That such delivery shall be deemed not to have been made unless the bidder has complied with paragraph (f)(3)(iii) of this section at the time the materials or amendments, as the case may be, are delivered.

(2)   The approximate direct cost of mailing the bidder's tender offer materials shall be computed by adding (i) the direct cost incidental to the mailing of the subject company's last annual report to shareholders (excluding employee time), less the costs of preparation and printing of the report, and postage, plus (ii) the amount of first class postage required to mail the bidder's tender offer materials. The approximate direct costs incidental to the mailing of the amendments to the bidder's tender offer materials shall be computed by adding (iii) the estimated direct costs of preparing mailing labels, of updating shareholder lists and of third party handling charges plus (iv) the amount of first class postage required to mail the bidder's amendment. Direct costs incidental to the mailing of the bidder's tender offer materials and amendments thereto when finally computed may include all reasonable charges paid by the subject company to third parties for supplies or services, including costs attendant to preparing shareholder lists, mailing labels, handling the bidder's materials, contacting participants named on security position listings and for postage, but shall exclude indirect costs, such as employee time which is devoted to either contesting or supporting the tender offer on behalf of the subject company. The final billing for direct costs shall be accompanied by an appropriate accounting in reasonable detail.

Note to § 240.14d–5: Reasonably prompt methods of distribution to security holders may be used instead of mailing. If alternative methods are chosen, the approximate direct costs of distribution shall be computed by adding the estimated direct costs of preparing the document for distribution through the chosen medium (including updating of shareholder lists) plus the estimated reasonable cost of distribution through that medium. Direct costs incidental to the distribution of tender offer materials and amendments thereto may include all reasonable charges paid by the subject company to third parties for supplies or services, including costs attendant to preparing shareholder lists, handling the bidder's materials, and contacting participants named on security position listings, but shall not include indirect costs, such as employee time which is devoted to either contesting or supporting the tender offer on behalf of the subject company.

§ 240.14d–6.   Disclosure of Tender Offer Information to Security Holders

(a)   Information required on date of commencement. (1) Long-form publication. If a tender offer is published, sent or given to security holders on the date of commencement by means of long-form publication under § 240.14d–4(a)(1), the long-form publication must include the information required by paragraph (d)(1) of this section.

(2)   Summary publication. If a tender offer is published, sent or given to security holders on the date of commencement by means of summary publication under § 240.14d–4(a)(2):

(i)   The summary advertisement must contain at least the information required by paragraph (d)(2) of this section; and

(ii)   The tender offer materials furnished by the bidder upon request of any security holder must include the information required by paragraph (d)(1) of this section.

(3)   Use of stockholder lists and security position listings. If a tender offer is published, sent or given to security holders on the date of commencement by the use of stockholder lists and security position listings under § 240.14d–4(a)(3):

(i)   The summary advertisement must contain at least the information required by paragraph (d)(2) of this section; and

(ii)   The tender offer materials transmitted to security holders pursuant to such lists and security position listings and furnished by the bidder upon the request of any security holder must include the information required by paragraph (d)(1) of this section.

(4)   Other tender offers. If a tender offer is published or sent or given to security holders other than pursuant to § 240.14d–4(a), the tender offer materials that are published or sent or given to security holders on the date of commencement of such offer must include the information required by paragraph (d)(1) of this section.

(b)   Information required in other tender offer materials published after commencement. Except for tender offer materials described in paragraphs (a)(2)(ii) and (a)(3)(ii) of this section, additional tender offer materials published, sent or given to security holders after commencement must include:

(1)   The identities of the bidder and subject company;

(2)   The amount and class of securities being sought;

(3)   The type and amount of consideration being offered; and

(4)   The scheduled expiration date of the tender offer, whether the tender offer may be extended and, if so, the procedures for extension of the tender offer.

Instruction to paragraph (b): If the additional tender offer materials are summary advertisements, they also must include the information required by paragraphs (d)(2)(v) of this section.

(c)   Material changes. A material change in the information published or sent or given to security holders must be promptly disclosed to security holders in additional tender offer materials.

(d)   Information to be included. (1) Tender offer materials other than summary publication. The following information is required by paragraphs (a)(1), (a)(2)(ii), (a)(3)(ii) and (a)(4) of this section:

(i)   The information required by Item 1 of Schedule TO (§ 240.14d–100) (Summary Term Sheet); and

(ii)   The information required by the remaining items of Schedule TO (§ 240.14d–100) for third-party tender offers, except for Item 12 (exhibits) of Schedule TO (§ 240.14d–100), or a fair and adequate summary of the information.

(2)   Summary Publication. The following information is required in a summary advertisement under paragraphs (a)(2)(i) and (a)(3)(i) of this section:

(i)   The identity of the bidder and the subject company;

(ii)   The information required by Item 1004(a)(1) of Regulation M–A (§ 229.1004(a)(1) of this chapter);

(iii)   If the tender offer is for less than all of the outstanding securities of a class of equity securities, a statement as to whether the purpose or one of the purposes of the tender offer is to acquire or influence control of the business of the subject company;

(iv)   A statement that the information required by paragraph (d)(1) of this section is incorporated by reference into the summary advertisement;

(v)   Appropriate instructions as to how security holders may obtain promptly, at the bidder's expense, the bidder's tender offer materials; and

(vi)   In a tender offer published or sent or given to security holders by use of stockholder lists and security position listings under § 240.14d–4(a)(3), a statement that a request is being made for such lists and listings. The summary publication also must state that tender offer materials will be mailed to record holders and will be furnished to brokers, banks and similar persons whose name appears or whose nominee appears on the list of security holders or, if applicable, who are listed as participants in a clearing agency's security position listing for subsequent transmittal to beneficial owners of such securities. If the list furnished to the bidder also included beneficial owners pursuant to § 240.14d–5(c)(1) and tender offer materials will be mailed directly to beneficial holders, include a statement to that effect.

(3)   *No transmittal letter.* Neither the initial summary advertisement nor any subsequent summary advertisement may include a transmittal letter (the letter furnished to security holders for transmission of securities sought in the tender offer) or any amendment to the transmittal letter.

§ 240.14d–7.   Additional Withdrawal Rights

(a)   *Rights.* (1) In addition to the provisions of section 14(d)(5) of the Act, any person who has deposited securities pursuant to a tender offer has the right to withdraw any such securities during the period such offer request or invitation remains open.

(2)   *Exemption during subsequent offering period.* Notwithstanding the provisions of section 14(d)(5) of the Act (15 U.S.C. 78n(d)(5)) and paragraph (a) of this section, the bidder need not offer withdrawal rights during a subsequent offering period.

(b)   *Notice of withdrawal.* Notice of withdrawal pursuant to this section shall be deemed to be timely upon the receipt by the bidder's depositary of a written notice of withdrawal specifying the name(s) of the tendering stockholder(s), the number or amount of the securities to be withdrawn and the name(s) in which the certificate(s) is (are) registered, if different from that of the tendering security holder(s). A bidder may impose other reasonable requirements, including certificate numbers and a signed request for withdrawal accompanied by a signature guarantee, as conditions precedent to the physical release of withdrawn securities.

§ 240.14d–8.   Exemption from Statutory Pro Rata Requirements

Notwithstanding the pro rata provisions of section 14(d)(6) of the Act, if any person makes a tender offer or request or invitation for tenders, for less than all of the outstanding equity securities of a class, and if a greater number of securities are deposited pursuant thereto than such person is bound or willing to take up and pay for, the securities taken up and paid for shall be taken up and paid for as nearly as may be pro rata, disregarding fractions, according to the number of securities deposited by each depositor during the period such offer, request or invitation remains open.

§ 240.14d–9.   Recommendation or Solicitation by the Subject Company and Others

(a)   Pre-commencement communications. A communication by a person described in paragraph (e) of this section with respect to a tender offer will not be deemed to constitute a recommendation or solicitation under this section if:

(1)   The tender offer has not commenced under § 240.14d–2; and

(2)   The communication is filed under cover of Schedule 14D–9 (§ 240.14d–101) with the Commission no later than the date of the communication.

Instructions to paragraph (a)(2):

1.   The box on the front of Schedule 14D–9 (§ 240.14d–101) indicating that the filing contains pre-commencement communications must be checked.

2.   Any communications made in connection with an exchange offer registered under the Securities Act of 1933 need only be filed under § 230.425 of this chapter and will be deemed filed under this section.

3.   Each pre-commencement written communication must include a prominent legend in clear, plain language advising security holders to read the company's solicitation/recommendation statement when it is available because it contains important information. The legend also must advise investors that they can get the recommendation and other filed documents for free at the Commission's web site and explain which documents are free from the filer.

4.   *See* §§ 230.135, 230.165 and 230.166 of this chapter for pre-commencement communications made in connection with registered exchange offers.

(b)   Post-commencement communications. After commencement by a bidder under § 240.14d–2, no solicitation or recommendation to security holders may be made by any person described in paragraph (e) of this section with respect to a tender offer for such securities unless as soon as practicable on the date such solicitation or recommendation is first published or sent or given to security holders such person complies with the following:

(1)   Such person shall file with the Commission a Tender Offer Solicitation/ Recommendation Statement on Schedule 14D–9 (§ 240.14d–101), including all exhibits thereto; and

(2)   If such person is either the subject company or an affiliate of the subject company,

(i)   Such person shall hand deliver a copy of the Schedule 14D–9 to the bidder at its principal office or at the address of the person authorized to receive notices and communications (which is set forth on the cover sheet of the bidder's Schedule TO (§ 240.14d–100)) filed with the Commission; and

(ii)   Such person shall give telephonic notice (which notice to the extent possible shall be given prior to the opening of the market) of the information required by Items 1003(d) and 1012(a) of Regulation M–A (§ 229.1003(d) and § 229.1012(a)) and shall mail a copy of the Schedule to each national securities exchange where the class of securities is registered and listed for trading and, if the class is authorized for quotation in the NASDAQ interdealer quotation system, to the National Association of Securities Dealers, Inc. ("NASD").

(3)   If such person is neither the subject company nor an affiliate of the subject company,

(i)   Such person shall mail a copy of the schedule to the bidder at its principal office or at the address of the person authorized to receive notices and communications (which is set forth on the cover sheet of the bidder's Schedule TO (§ 240.14d–100) filed with the Commission); and

(ii)   Such person shall mail a copy of the Schedule to the subject company at its principal office.

(c)   Amendments. If any material change occurs in the information set forth in the Schedule 14D–9 (§ 240.14d–101) required by this section, the person who filed such Schedule 14D–9 shall:

(1)   File with the Commission an amendment on Schedule 14D–9 (§ 240.14d–101) disclosing such change promptly, but not later than the date such material is first published, sent or given to security holders; and

(2)   Promptly deliver copies and give notice of the amendment in the same manner as that specified in paragraph (b)(2) or (3) of this section, whichever is applicable; and

(3)   Promptly disclose and disseminate such change in a manner reasonably designed to inform security holders of such change.

(d)   Information required in solicitation or recommendation. Any solicitation or recommendation to holders of a class of securities referred to in section 14(d)(1) of the Act with respect to a tender offer for such securities shall include the name of the person making such solicitation or recommendation and the information required by Items 1 through 8 of Schedule 14D–9 (§ 240.14d–101) or a fair and adequate summary thereof: Provided, however, That such solicitation or recommendation may omit any of such information previously furnished to security holders of such class of securities by such person with respect to such tender offer.

(e)   Applicability. (1) Except as is provided in paragraphs (e)(2) and (f) of this section, this section shall only apply to the following persons:

(i)   The subject company, any director, officer, employee, affiliate or subsidiary of the subject company;

(ii)   Any record holder or beneficial owner of any security issued by the subject company, by the bidder, or by any affiliate of either the subject company or the bidder; and

(iii)   Any person who makes a solicitation or recommendation to security holders on behalf of any of the foregoing or on behalf of the bidder other than by means of a solicitation or recommendation to security holders which has been filed with the Commission pursuant to this section or Rule 14d–3 (§ 240.14d–3).

(2)   Notwithstanding paragraph (e)(1) of this section, this section shall not apply to the following persons:

(i)   A bidder who has filed a Schedule TO (§ 240.14d–100) pursuant to Rule 14d–3 (§ 240.14d–3);

(ii)   Attorneys, banks, brokers, fiduciaries or investment advisers who are not participating in a tender offer in more than a ministerial capacity and who furnish information and/or advice regarding such tender offer to their customers or clients on the unsolicited request of such customers or clients or solely pursuant to a contract or a relationship providing for advice to the customer or client to whom the information and/or advice is given.

(iii)   Any person specified in paragraph (e)(1) of this section if:

(A)   The subject company is the subject of a tender offer conducted under § 240.14d–1(c);

(B)   Any person specified in paragraph (e)(1) of this section furnishes to the Commission on Form CB (§ 249.480 of this chapter) the entire informational document it publishes or otherwise disseminates to holders of the class of securities in connection with the tender offer no later than the next business day after publication or dissemination;

(C)   Any person specified in paragraph (e)(1) of this section disseminates any informational document to U.S. holders, including any amendments thereto, in English, on a comparable basis to that provided to security holders in the issuer's home jurisdiction; and

(D) Any person specified in paragraph (e)(1) of this section disseminates by publication in its home jurisdiction, such person must publish the information in the United States in a manner reasonably calculated to inform U.S. security holders of the offer.

(f) *Stop-look-and-listen communication.* This section shall not apply to the subject company with respect to a communication by the subject company to its security holders which only:

(1) Identifies the tender offer by the bidder;

(2) States that such tender offer is under consideration by the subject company's board of directors and/or management;

(3) States that on or before a specified date (which shall be no later than 10 business days from the date of commencement of such tender offer) the subject company will advise such security holders of (i) whether the subject company recommends acceptance or rejection of such tender offer; expresses no opinion and remains neutral toward such tender offer; or is unable to take a position with respect to such tender offer and (ii) the reason(s) for the position taken by the subject company with respect to the tender offer (including the inability to take a position); and

(4) Requests such security holders to defer making a determination whether to accept or reject such tender offer until they have been advised of the subject company's position with respect thereto pursuant to paragraph (f)(3) of this section.

(g) *Statement of management's position.* A statement by the subject company's of its position with respect to a tender offer which is required to be published or sent or given to security holders pursuant to Rule 14e–2 shall be deemed to constitute a solicitation or recommendation within the meaning of this section and section 14(d)(4) of the Act.

§ 240.14d–10.   **Equal Treatment of Security Holders**

(a) No bidder shall make a tender offer unless:

(1) The tender offer is open to all security holders of the class of securities subject to the tender offer; and

(2) The consideration paid to any security holder for securities tendered in the tender offer is the highest consideration paid to any other security holder for securities tendered in the tender offer.

(b) Paragraph (a)(1) of this section shall not:

(1) Affect dissemination under Rule 14d–4 (§ 240.14d–4); or

(2) Prohibit a bidder from making a tender offer excluding all security holders in a state where the bidder is prohibited from making the tender offer by administrative or judicial action pursuant to a state statute after a good faith effort by the bidder to comply with such statute.

(c) Paragraph (a)(2) of this section shall not prohibit the offer of more than one type of consideration in a tender offer, Provided, That:

(1) Security holders are afforded equal right to elect among each of the types of consideration offered; and

(2) The highest consideration of each type paid to any security holder is paid to any other security holder receiving that type of consideration.

(d)(1) Paragraph (a)(2) of this section shall not prohibit the negotiation, execution or amendment of an employment compensation, severance or other employee benefit arrangement, or payments made or to be made or benefits granted or to be granted according to such an arrangement, with respect to any security holder of the subject company, where the amount payable under the arrangement:

(i) Is being paid or granted as compensation for past services performed, future services to be performed, or future services to be refrained from performing, by the security holder (and matters incidental thereto); and

(ii) Is not calculated based on the number of securities tendered or to be tendered in the tender offer by the security holder.

(2) The provisions of paragraph (d)(1) of this section shall be satisfied and, therefore, pursuant to this non-exclusive safe harbor, the negotiation, execution or amendment of an arrangement and any payments made or to be made or benefits granted or to be granted according to that arrangement shall not be prohibited by paragraph (a)(2) of this section, if the arrangement is approved as an employment compensation, severance or other employee benefit arrangement solely by independent directors as follows:

(i) The compensation committee or a committee of the board of directors that performs functions similar to a compensation committee of the subject company approves the arrangement, regardless of whether the subject company is a party to the arrangement, or, if the bidder is a party to the arrangement, the compensation committee or a committee of the board of directors that performs functions similar to a compensation committee of the bidder approves the arrangement; or

(ii) If the subject company's or bidder's board of directors, as applicable, does not have a compensation committee or a committee of the board of directors that performs functions similar to a compensation committee or if none of the members of the subject company's or bidder's compensation committee or committee that performs functions similar to a compensation committee is independent, a special committee of the board of directors formed to consider and approve the arrangement approves the arrangement; or

(iii) If the subject company or bidder, as applicable, is a foreign private issuer, any or all members of the board of directors or any committee of the board of directors authorized to approve employment compensation, severance or other employee benefit arrangements under the laws or regulations of the home country approves the arrangement.

Instructions to paragraph (d)(2): For purposes of determining whether the members of the committee approving an arrangement in accordance with the provisions of paragraph (d)(2) of this section are independent, the following provisions shall apply:

1. If the bidder or subject company, as applicable, is a listed issuer (as defined in § 240.10A–3 of this chapter) whose securities are listed either on a national securities exchange registered pursuant to section 6(a) of the Exchange Act (15 U.S.C. 78f(a)) or in an inter-dealer quotation system of a national securities association registered pursuant to section 15A(a) of the Exchange Act (15 U.S.C. 78o–3(a)) that has independence requirements for compensation committee members that have been approved by the Commission (as those requirements may be modified or supplemented), apply the bidder's or subject company's definition of independence that it uses for determining that the members of the compensation committee are independent in compliance with the listing standards applicable to compensation committee members of the listed issuer.

2. If the bidder or subject company, as applicable, is not a listed issuer (as defined in § 240.10A–3 of this chapter), apply the independence requirements for compensation committee members of a national securities exchange registered pursuant to section 6(a) of the Exchange Act (15 U.S.C. 78f(a)) or an inter-dealer quotation system of a national securities association registered pursuant to section 15A(a) of the Exchange Act (15 U.S.C. 78o–3(a)) that have been approved by the Commission (as those requirements may be modified or supplemented). Whatever definition the bidder or subject company, as applicable, chooses, it must apply that definition consistently to all members of the committee approving the arrangement.

3.   Notwithstanding Instructions 1 and 2 to paragraph (d)(2), if the bidder or subject company, as applicable, is a closed-end investment company registered under the Investment Company Act of 1940, a director is considered to be independent if the director is not, other than in his or her capacity as a member of the board of directors or any board committee, an "interested person" of the investment company, as defined in section 2(a)(19) of the Investment Company Act of 1940 (15 U.S.C. 80a–2(a)(19)).

4.   If the bidder or the subject company, as applicable, is a foreign private issuer, apply either the independence standards set forth in Instructions 1 and 2 to paragraph (d)(2) or the independence requirements of the laws, regulations, codes or standards of the home country of the bidder or subject company, as applicable, for members of the board of directors or the committee of the board of directors approving the arrangement.

5.   A determination by the bidder's or the subject company's board of directors, as applicable, that the members of the board of directors or the committee of the board of directors, as applicable, approving an arrangement in accordance with the provisions of paragraph (d)(2) are independent in accordance with the provisions of this instruction to paragraph (d)(2) shall satisfy the independence requirements of paragraph (d)(2).

Instruction to paragraph (d): The fact that the provisions of paragraph (d) of this section extend only to employment compensation, severance and other employee benefit arrangements and not to other arrangements, such as commercial arrangements, does not raise any inference that a payment under any such other arrangement constitutes consideration paid for securities in a tender offer.

(e)   If the offer and sale of securities constituting consideration offered in a tender offer is prohibited by the appropriate authority of a state after a good faith effort by the bidder to register or qualify the offer and sale of such securities in such state:

(1)   The bidder may offer security holders in such state an alternative form of consideration; and

(2)   Paragraph (c) of this section shall not operate to require the bidder to offer or pay the alternative form of consideration to security holders in any other state.

(f)   This section shall not apply to any tender offer with respect to which the Commission, upon written request or upon its own motion, either unconditionally or on specified terms and conditions, determines that compliance with this section is not necessary or appropriate in the public interest or for the protection of investors.

* * *

§ 240.14e–1.   Unlawful Tender Offer Practices

As a means reasonably designed to prevent fraudulent, deceptive or manipulative acts or practices within the meaning of section 14(e) of the Act, no person who makes a tender offer shall:

(a)   Hold such tender offer open for less than twenty business days from the date such tender offer is first published or sent to security holders; provided, however, that if the tender offer involves a roll-up transaction as defined in Item 901(c) of Regulation S–K (17 CFR 229.901(c)) and the securities being offered are registered (or authorized to be registered) on Form S-4 (17 CFR 229.25) or Form F-4 (17 CFR 229.34), the offer shall not be open for less than sixty calendar days from the date the tender offer is first published or sent to security holders;

(b)   Increase or decrease the percentage of the class of securities being sought or the consideration offered or the dealer's soliciting fee to be given in a tender offer unless such tender offer remains open for at least ten business days from the date that notice of such increase or decrease is first published or sent or given to security holders.

Provided, however, That, for purposes of this paragraph, the acceptance for payment of an additional amount of securities not to exceed two percent of the class of securities that is the subject of the tender offer shall not be deemed to be an increase. For purposes of this paragraph, the percentage of a class of securities shall be calculated in accordance with section 14(d)(3) of the Act.

(c)   Fail to pay the consideration offered or return the securities deposited by or on behalf of security holders promptly after the termination or withdrawal of a tender offer. This paragraph does not prohibit a bidder electing to offer a subsequent offering period under § 240.14d–11 from paying for securities during the subsequent offering period in accordance with that section.

(d)   Extend the length of a tender offer without issuing a notice of such extension by press release or other public announcement, which notice shall include disclosure of the approximate number of securities deposited to date and shall be issued no later than the earlier of: (i) 9:00 a.m. Eastern time, on the next business day after the scheduled expiration date of the offer or (ii), if the class of securities which is the subject of the tender offer is registered on one or more national securities exchanges, the first opening of any one of such exchanges on the next business day after the scheduled expiration date of the offer.

(e)   The periods of time required by paragraphs (a) and (b) of this section shall be tolled for any period during which the bidder has failed to file in electronic format, absent a hardship exemption (§§ 232.201 and 232.202 of this chapter), the Schedule TO Tender Offer Statement (§ 240.14d–100), any tender offer material required to be filed by Item 12 of that Schedule pursuant to paragraph (a) of Item 1016 of Regulation M–A (§ 229.1016(a) of this chapter), and any amendments thereto. If such documents were filed in paper pursuant to a hardship exemption (*see* § 232.201 and § 232.202(d)), the minimum offering periods shall be tolled for any period during which a required confirming electronic copy of such Schedule and tender offer material is delinquent.

§ 240.14e–2.   Position of Subject Company with Respect to a Tender Offer

(a)   *Position of subject company.* As a means reasonably designed to prevent fraudulent, deceptive or manipulative acts or practices within the meaning of section 14(e) of the Act, the subject company, no later than 10 business days from the date the tender offer is first published or sent or given, shall publish, send or give to security holders a statement disclosing that the subject company:

(1)   Recommends acceptance or rejection of the bidder's tender offer;

(2)   Expresses no opinion and is remaining neutral toward the bidder's tender offer; or

(3)   Is unable to take a position with respect to the bidder's tender offer. Such statement shall also include the reason(s) for the position (including the inability to take a position) disclosed therein.

(b)   *Material change.* If any material change occurs in the disclosure required by paragraph (a) of this section, the subject company shall promptly publish or send or give a statement disclosing such material change to security holders.

* * *

§ 240.14e–3.   Transactions in Securities on the Basis of Material, Nonpublic Information in the Context of Tender Offers

(a)   If any person has taken a substantial step or steps to commence, or has commenced, a tender offer (the "offering person"), it shall constitute a fraudulent, deceptive or manipulative act or practice within the meaning of section 14(e) of the Act for any other person who is in possession of material information relating to such tender offer which information he knows or has reason to know is nonpublic and which he knows or has reason to know has been acquired directly or indirectly from:

(1)   The offering person,

(2)   The issuer of the securities sought or to be sought by such tender offer, or

(3)   Any officer, director, partner or employee or any other person acting on behalf of the offering person or such issuer, to purchase or sell or cause to be purchased or sold any of such securities or any securities convertible into or exchangeable for any such securities or any option or right to obtain or to dispose of any of the foregoing securities, unless within a reasonable time prior to any purchase or sale such information and its source are publicly disclosed by press release or otherwise.

(b)   A person other than a natural person shall not violate paragraph (a) of this section if such person shows that:

(1)   The individual(s) making the investment decision on behalf of such person to purchase or sell any security described in paragraph (a) of this section or to cause any such security to be purchased or sold by or on behalf of others did not know the material, nonpublic information; and

(2)   Such person had implemented one or a combination of policies and procedures, reasonable under the circumstances, taking into consideration the nature of the person's business, to ensure that individual(s) making investment decision(s) would not violate paragraph (a) of this section, which policies and procedures may include, but are not limited to, (i) those which restrict any purchase, sale and causing any purchase and sale of any such security or (ii) those which prevent such individual(s) from knowing such information.

(c)   Notwithstanding anything in paragraph (a) of this section to contrary, the following transactions shall not be violations of paragraph (a) of this section:

(1)   Purchase(s) of any security described in paragraph (a) of this section by a broker or by another agent on behalf of an offering person; or

(2)   Sale(s) by any person of any security described in paragraph (a) of this section to the offering person.

(d)(1)   As a means reasonably designed to prevent fraudulent, deceptive or manipulative acts or practices within the meaning of section 14(e) of the Act, it shall be unlawful for any person described in paragraph (d)(2) of this section to communicate material, nonpublic information relating to a tender offer to any other person under circumstances in which it is reasonably foreseeable that such communication is likely to result in a violation of this section except that this paragraph shall not apply to a communication made in good faith,

(i)   To the officers, directors, partners or employees of the offering person, to its advisors or to other persons, involved in the planning, financing, preparation or execution of such tender offer;

(ii)   To the issuer whose securities are sought or to be sought by such tender offer, to its officers, directors, partners, employees or advisors or to other persons, involved in the planning, financing, preparation or execution of the activities of the issuer with respect to such tender offer; or

(iii)   To any person pursuant to a requirement of any statute or rule or regulation promulgated thereunder.

(2)   The persons referred to in paragraph (d)(1) of this section are:

(i)   The offering person or its officers, directors, partners, employees or advisors;

(ii)   The issuer of the securities sought or to be sought by such tender offer or its officers, directors, partners, employees or advisors;

(iii)   Anyone acting on behalf of the persons in paragraph (d)(2)(i) of this section or the issuer or persons in paragraph (d)(2)(ii) of this section; and

(iv)   Any person in possession of material information relating to a tender offer which information he knows or has reason to know is nonpublic and which he knows or has reason to know has been acquired directly or indirectly from any of the above.

§ 240.14e–4.   **Prohibited Transactions in Connection with Partial Tender Offers**

(a)   Definitions. For purposes of this section:

(1)   The amount of a person's "net long position" in a subject security shall equal the excess, if any, of such person's "long position" over such person's "short position." For the purposes of determining the net long position as of the end of the proration period and for tendering concurrently to two or more partial tender offers, securities that have been tendered in accordance with the rule and not withdrawn are deemed to be part of the person's long position.

(i)   Such person's long position is the amount of subject securities that such person:

(A)   Or his agent has title to or would have title to but for having lent such securities; or

(B)   Has purchased, or has entered into an unconditional contract, binding on both parties thereto, to purchase but has not yet received; or

(C)   Has exercised a standardized call option for; or

(D)   Has converted, exchanged, or exercised an equivalent security for; or

(E)   Is entitled to receive upon conversion, exchange, or exercise of an equivalent security.

(ii)   Such person's short position, is the amount of subject securities or subject securities underlying equivalent securities that such person:

(A)   Has sold, or has entered into an unconditional contract, binding on both parties thereto, to sell; or

(B)   Has borrowed; or

(C)   Has written a non-standardized call option, or granted any other right pursuant to which his shares may be tendered by another person; or

(D)   Is obligated to deliver upon exercise of a standardized call option sold on or after the date that a tender offer is first publicly announced or otherwise made known by the bidder to holders of the security to be acquired, if the exercise price of such option is lower than the highest tender offer price or stated amount of the consideration offered for the subject security. For the purpose of this paragraph, if one or more tender offers for the same security are ongoing on such date, the announcement date shall be that of the first announced offer.

(2)   The term equivalent security means:

(i)   Any security (including any option, warrant, or other right to purchase the subject security), issued by the person whose securities are the subject of the offer, that is immediately convertible into, or exchangeable or exercisable for, a subject security, or

(ii)   Any other right or option (other than a standardized call option) that entitles the holder thereof to acquire a subject security, but only if the holder thereof reasonably believes that the maker or writer of the right or option has title to and possession of the subject security and upon exercise will promptly deliver the subject security.

(3)   The term subject security means a security that is the subject of any tender offer or request or invitation for tenders.

(4)   For purposes of this rule, a person shall be deemed to "tender" a security if he:

(i)   Delivers a subject security pursuant to an offer,

(ii)   Causes such delivery to be made,

(iii)   Guarantees delivery of a subject security pursuant to a tender offer,

(iv) Causes a guarantee of such delivery to be given by another person, or

(v) Uses any other method by which acceptance of a tender offer may be made.

(5) The term partial tender offer means a tender offer or request or invitation for tenders for less than all of the outstanding securities subject to the offer in which tenders are accepted either by lot or on a pro rata basis for a specified period, or a tender offer for all of the outstanding shares that offers a choice of consideration in which tenders for different forms of consideration may be accepted either by lot or on a pro rata basis for a specified period.

(6) The term standardized call option means any call option that is traded on an exchange, or for which quotation information is disseminated in an electronic interdealer quotation system of a registered national securities association.

(b) It shall be unlawful for any person acting alone or in concert with others, directly or indirectly, to tender any subject security in a partial tender offer:

(1) For his own account unless at the time of tender, and at the end of the proration period or period during which securities are accepted by lot (including any extensions thereof), he has a net long position equal to or greater than the amount tendered in:

(i) The subject security and will deliver or cause to be delivered such security for the purpose of tender to the person making the offer within the period specified in the offer; or

(ii) An equivalent security and, upon the acceptance of his tender will acquire the subject security by conversion, exchange, or exercise of such equivalent security to the extent required by the terms of the offer, and will deliver or cause to be delivered the subject security so acquired for the purpose of tender to the person making the offer within the period specified in the offer; or

(2) For the account of another person unless the person making the tender:

(i) Possesses the subject security or an equivalent security, or

(ii) Has a reasonable belief that, upon information furnished by the person on whose behalf the tender is made, such person owns the subject security or an equivalent security and will promptly deliver the subject security or such equivalent security for the purpose of tender to the person making the tender.

(c) This rule shall not prohibit any transaction or transactions which the Commission, upon written request or upon its own motion, exempts, either unconditionally or on specified terms and conditions.

* * *

§ 240.14f-1.   Change in Majority of Directors

If, pursuant to any arrangement or understanding with the person or persons acquiring securities in a transaction subject to section 13(d) or 14(d) of the Act, any persons are to be elected or designated as directors of the issuer, otherwise than at a meeting of security holders, and the persons so elected or designated will constitute a majority of the directors of the issuer, then, not less than 10 days prior to the date any such person take office as a director, or such shorter period prior to that date as the Commission may authorize upon a showing of good cause therefor, the issuer shall file with the Commission and transmit to all holders of record of securities of the issuer who would be entitled to vote at a meeting for election of directors, information substantially equivalent to the information which would be required by Items 6 (a), (d) and (e), 7 and 8 of Schedule 14A of Regulation 14A (§ 240.14a-101 of this chapter) to be transmitted if such person or persons were nominees for election as directors at a meeting of such security holders. Eight copies of such information shall be filed with the Commission.

* * *

RULES RELATING TO OVER-THE-COUNTER MARKETS

§ 240.15c2–8.   Delivery of Prospectus

(a)   It shall constitute a deceptive act or practice, as those terms are used in section 15(c)(2) of the Act, for a broker or dealer to participate in a distribution of securities with respect to which a registration statement has been filed under the Securities Act of 1933 unless he complies with the requirements set forth in paragraphs (b) through (h) of this section. For the purposes of this section, a broker or dealer participating in the distribution shall mean any underwriter and any member or proposed member of the selling group.

(b)   In connection with an issue of securities, the issuer of which has not previously been required to file reports pursuant to sections 13(a) or 15(d) of the Securities Exchange Act of 1934, unless such issuer has been exempted from the requirement to file reports thereunder pursuant to section 12(h) of the Act, such broker or dealer shall deliver a copy of the preliminary prospectus to any person who is expected to receive a confirmation of sale at least 48 hours prior to the sending of such confirmation. *Provided, however,* this paragraph (b) shall apply to all issuances of asset-backed securities (as defined in § 229.1101(c) of this chapter) regardless of whether the issuer has previously been required to file reports pursuant to sections 13(a) or 15(d) of the Securities Exchange Act of 1934, or exempted from the requirement to file reports thereunder pursuant to section 12(h) of the Act (15 U.S.C. 78*l*).

(c)   Such broker or dealer shall take reasonable steps to furnish to any person who makes written request for a preliminary prospectus between the filing date and a reasonable time prior to the effective date of the registration statement to which such prospectus relates, a copy of the latest preliminary prospectus on file with the Commission. Reasonable steps shall include receiving an undertaking by the managing underwriter or underwriters to send such copy to the address given in the requests.

(d)   Such broker or dealer shall take reasonable steps to comply promptly with the written request of any person for a copy of the final prospectus relating to such securities during the period between the effective date of the registration statement and the later of either the termination of such distribution, or the expiration of the applicable 40- or 90-day period under section 4(3) of the Securities Act of 1933. Reasonable steps shall include receiving an undertaking by the managing underwriter or underwriters to send such copy to the address given in the requests. (The 40-day and 90-day periods referred to above shall be deemed to apply for purposes of this rule irrespective of the provisions of paragraphs (b) and (d) of § 230.174 of this chapter).

(e)   Such broker or dealer shall take reasonable steps (1) to make available a copy of the preliminary prospectus relating to such securities to each of his associated persons who is expected, prior to the effective date, to solicit customers' order for such securities before the making of any such solicitation by such associated persons and (2) to make available to each such associated person a copy of any amended preliminary prospectus promptly after the filing thereof.

(f)   Such broker or dealer shall take reasonable steps to make available a copy of the final prospectus relating to such securities to each of his associated persons who is expected, after the effective date, to solicit customers' orders for such securities prior to the making of any such solicitation by such associated persons, unless a preliminary prospectus which is substantially the same as the final prospectus except for matters relating to the price of the stocks, has been so made available.

(g)   If the broker or dealer is a managing underwriter of such distribution, he shall take reasonable steps to see to it that all other brokers or dealers participating in such distribution are promptly furnished with sufficient copies, as requested by them, of each preliminary prospectus, each amended preliminary prospectus and the final prospectus to enable them to comply with paragraphs (b), (c), (d), and (e) of this section.

(h)   If the broker or dealer is a managing underwriter of such distribution, he shall take reasonable steps to see that any broker or dealer participating in the distribution or trading in the registered security is furnished reasonable quantities of the final prospectus relating to such securities, as requested by him, in order to enable him to comply with the prospectus delivery requirements of section 5(b) (1) and (2) of the Securities Act of 1933.

(i)   This section shall not require the furnishing of prospectuses in any state where such furnishing would be unlawful under the laws of such state: Provided, however, That this provision is not to be construed to relieve a broker or dealer from complying with the requirements of section 5(b)(1) and (2) of the Securities Act of 1933.

§ 240.15c2–11.   Initiation or Resumption of Quotations Without Specific Information

Preliminary Note: Brokers and dealers may wish to refer to Securities Exchange Act Release No. 29094 (April 17, 1991), for a discussion of procedures for gathering and reviewing the information required by this rule and the requirement that a broker or dealer have a reasonable basis for believing that the information is accurate and obtained from reliable sources.

(a)   As a means reasonably designed to prevent fraudulent, deceptive, or manipulative acts or practices, it shall be unlawful for a broker or dealer to publish any quotation for a security or, directly or indirectly, to submit any such quotation for publication, in any quotation medium (as defined in this section) unless such broker or dealer has in its records the documents and information required by this paragraph (for purposes of this section, "paragraph (a) information"), and, based upon a review of the paragraph (a) information together with any other documents and information required by paragraph (b) of this section, has a reasonable basis under the circumstances for believing that the paragraph (a) information is accurate in all material respects, and that the sources of the paragraph (a) information are reliable. The information required pursuant to this paragraph is:

(1)   A copy of the prospectus specified by section 10(a) of the Securities Act of 1933 for an issuer that has filed a registration statement under the Securities Act of 1933, other than a registration statement on Form F-6, which became effective less than 90 calendar days prior to the day on which such broker or dealer publishes or submits the quotation to the quotation medium, Provided That such registration statement has not thereafter been the subject of a stop order which is still in effect when the quotation is published or submitted; or

(2)   A copy of the offering circular provided for under Regulation A under the Securities Act of 1933 for an issuer that has filed a notification under Regulation A and was authorized to commence the offering less than 40 calendar days prior to the day on which such broker or dealer publishes or submits the quotation to the quotation medium, Provided That the offering circular provided for under Regulation A has not thereafter become the subject of a suspension order which is still in effect when the quotation is published or submitted; or

(3)   A copy of the issuer's most recent annual report filed pursuant to section 13 or 15(d) of the Act or pursuant to Regulation A ((§§ 230.251 through 230.263 of this chapter), or a copy of the annual statement referred to in section 12(g)(2)(G)(i) of the Act in the case of an issuer required to file reports pursuant to section 13 or 15(d) of the Act or an issuer of a security covered by section 12(g)(2)(B) or (G) of the Act, together with any semiannual, quarterly and current reports that have been filed under the provisions of the Act or Regulation A by the issuer after such annual report or annual statement; provided, however, that until such issuer has filed its first annual report pursuant to section 13 or 15(d) of the Act or pursuant to Regulation A, or annual statement referred to in section 12(g)(2)(G)(i) of the Act, the broker or dealer has in its records a copy of the prospectus specified by section 10(a) of the Securities Act of 1933 included in a registration statement filed by the issuer under the Securities Act of 1933, other than a registration statement on Form F-6, or a copy of the offering circular specified by Regulation A included in an offering statement filed by the issuer under Regulation A, that became effective or was qualified within the prior 16 months, or a copy of any registration statement filed by the issuer under section 12 of the Act that became effective within the prior 16 months, together with any semiannual, quarterly and current reports filed thereafter under section 13 or 15(d) of the Act or Regulation A; and provided further, that the broker or dealer has a reasonable basis under the circumstances for believing that the issuer is current in filing annual, semiannual, quarterly,

and current reports filed pursuant to section 13 or 15(d) of the Act or Regulation A, or, in the case of an insurance company exempted from section 12(g) of the Act by reason of section 12(g)(2)(G) thereof, the annual statement referred to in section 12(g)(2)(G)(i) of the Act; or

(4)   The information that, since the beginning of its last fiscal year, the issuer has published pursuant to § 240.12g3–2(b), and which the broker or dealer shall make reasonably available upon the request of a person expressing an interest in a proposed transaction in the issuer's security with the broker or dealer, such as by providing the requesting person with appropriate instructions regarding how to obtain the information electronically; or

(5)   The following information, which shall be reasonably current in relation to the day the quotation is submitted and which the broker or dealer shall make reasonably available upon request to any person expressing an interest in a proposed transaction in the security with such broker or dealer:

(i)   The exact name of the issuer and its predecessor (if any);

(ii)   The address of its principal executive offices;

(iii)   The state of incorporation, if it is a corporation;

(iv)   The exact title and class of the security;

(v)   The par or stated value of the security;

(vi)   The number of shares or total amount of the securities outstanding as of the end of the issuer's most recent fiscal year;

(vii)   The name and address of the transfer agent;

(viii)   The nature of the issuer's business;

(ix)   The nature of products or services offered;

(x)   The nature and extent of the issuer's facilities;

(xi)   The name of the chief executive officer and members of the board of directors;

(xii)   The issuer's most recent balance sheet and profit and loss and retained earnings statements;

(xiii)   Similar financial information for such part of the 2 preceding fiscal years as the issuer or its predecessor has been in existence;

(xiv)   Whether the broker or dealer or any associated person is affiliated, directly or indirectly with the issuer;

(xv)   Whether the quotation is being published or submitted on behalf of any other broker or dealer, and, if so, the name of such broker or dealer; and

(xvi)   Whether the quotation is being submitted or published directly or indirectly on behalf of the issuer, or any director, officer or any person, directly or indirectly the beneficial owner of more than 10 percent of the outstanding units or shares of any equity security of the issuer, and, if so, the name of such person, and the basis for any exemption under the federal securities laws for any sales of such securities on behalf of such person.

If such information is made available to others upon request pursuant to this paragraph, such delivery, unless otherwise represented, shall not constitute a representation by such broker or dealer that such information is accurate, but shall constitute a representation by such broker or dealer that the information is reasonably current in relation to the day the quotation is submitted, that the broker or dealer has a reasonable basis under the circumstances for believing the information is accurate in all material respects, and that the information was obtained from sources which the broker or dealer has a reasonable basis for believing are reliable. This paragraph (a)(5) shall not apply to any security of an issuer included in paragraph (a)(3) of this section unless a report or statement of such issuer described in paragraph (a)(3) of this section is not reasonably available to the broker or dealer. A report or statement of an issuer described in paragraph (a)(3) of this section shall be "reasonably available" when such report or statement is filed with the Commission.

(b)   With respect to any security the quotation of which is within the provisions of this section, the broker or dealer submitting or publishing such quotation shall have in its records the following documents and information:

(1)   A record of the circumstances involved in the submission of publication of such quotation, including the identity of the person or persons for whom the quotation is being submitted or published and any information regarding the transactions provided to the broker or dealer by such person or persons;

(2)   A copy of any trading suspension order issued by the Commission pursuant to section 12(k) of the Act respecting any securities of the issuer or its predecessor (if any) during the 12 months preceding the date of the publication or submission of the quotation, or a copy of the public release issued by the Commission announcing such trading suspension order; and

(3)   A copy or a written record of any other material information (including adverse information) regarding the issuer which comes to the broker's or dealer's knowledge or possession before the publication or submission of the quotation.

(c)   The broker or dealer shall preserve the documents and information required under paragraphs (a) and (b) of this section for a period of not less than three years, the first two years in an easily accessible place.

(d)(1)   For any security of an issuer included in paragraph (a)(5) of this section, the broker or dealer submitting the quotation shall furnish to the interdealer quotation system (as defined in paragraph (e)(2) of this section), in such form as such system shall prescribe, at least 3 business days before the quotation is published or submitted, the information regarding the security and the issuer which such broker or dealer is required to maintain pursuant to said paragraph (a)(5) of this section.

(2)   For any security of an issuer included in paragraph (a)(3) of this section,

(i)   A broker-dealer shall be in compliance with the requirement to obtain current reports filed by the issuer if the broker-dealer obtains all current reports filed with the Commission by the issuer as of a date up to five business days in advance of the earlier of the date of submission of the quotation to the quotation medium and the date of submission of the information in paragraph (a) of this section pursuant to the applicable rule of the Financial Industry Regulatory Authority, Inc. or its successor organization; and

(ii)   A broker-dealer shall be in compliance with the requirement to obtain the annual, quarterly, and current reports filed by the issuer, if the broker-dealer has made arrangements to receive all such reports when filed by the issuer and it has regularly received reports from the issuer on a timely basis, unless the broker-dealer has a reasonable basis under the circumstances for believing that the issuer has failed to file a required report or has filed a report but has not sent it to the broker-dealer.

(e)   For purposes of this section:

(1)   Quotation medium shall mean any "interdealer quotation system" or any publication or electronic communications network or other device which is used by brokers or dealers to make known to others their interest in transactions in any security, including offers to buy or sell at a stated price or otherwise, or invitations of offers to buy or sell.

(2)   Interdealer quotation system shall mean any system of general circulation to brokers or dealers which regularly disseminates quotations of identified brokers or dealers.

(3)   Except as otherwise specified in this rule, quotation shall mean any bid or offer at a specified price with respect to a security, or any indication of interest by a broker or dealer in

receiving bids or offers from others for a security, or any indication by a broker or dealer that he wishes to advertise his general interest in buying or selling a particular security.

(4) Issuer, in the case of quotations for American Depositary Receipts, shall mean the issuer of the deposited shares represented by such American Depositary Receipts.

(f) The provisions of this section shall not apply to:

(1) The publication or submission of a quotation respecting a security admitted to trading on a national securities exchange and which is traded on such an exchange on the same day as, or on the business day next preceding, the day the quotation is published or submitted.

(2) The publication or submission by a broker or dealer, solely on behalf of a customer (other than a person acting as or for a dealer), of a quotation that represents the customer's indication of interest and does not involve the solicitation of the customer's interest; Provided, however, That this paragraph (f)(2) shall not apply to a quotation consisting of both a bid and an offer, each of which is at a specified price, unless the quotation medium specifically identifies the quotation as representing such an unsolicited customer interest.

(3)(i) The publication or submission, in an interdealer quotation system that specifically identifies as such unsolicited customer indications of interest of the kind described in paragraph (f)(2) of this section, of a quotation respecting a security which has been the subject of quotations (exclusive of any identified customer interests) in such a system on each of at least 12 days within the previous 30 calendar days, with no more than 4 business days in succession without a quotation; or

(ii) The publication or submission, in an interdealer quotation system that does not so identify any such unsolicited customer indications of interest, of a quotation respecting a security which has been the subject of both bid and ask quotations in an interdealer quotation system at specified prices on each of at least 12 days within the previous 30 calendar days, with no more than 4 business days in succession without such a two-way quotation;

(iii) A dealer acting in the capacity of market maker, as defined in section 3(a)(38) of the Act, that has published or submitted a quotation respecting a security in an interdealer quotation system and such quotation has qualified for an exception provided in this paragraph (f)(3), may continue to publish or submit quotations for such security in the interdealer quotation system without compliance with this section unless and until such dealer ceases to submit or publish a quotation or ceases to act in the capacity of market maker respecting such security.

(4) The publication or submission of a quotation respecting a municipal security.

(5) The publication or submission of a quotation respecting a Nasdaq security (as defined in § 242.600 of this chapter), and such security's listing is not suspended, terminated, or prohibited.

(g) The requirement in paragraph (a)(5) of this section that the information with respect to the issuer be "reasonably current" will be presumed to be satisfied, unless the broker or dealer has information to the contrary, if:

(1) The balance sheet is as of a date less than 16 months before the publication or submission of the quotation, the statements of profit and loss and retained earnings are for the 12 months preceding the date of such balance sheet, and if such balance sheet is not as of a date less than 6 months before the publication or submission of the quotation, it shall be accompanied by additional statements of profit and loss and retained earnings for the period from the date of such balance sheet to a date less than 6 months before the publication or submission of the quotation.

(2)   Other information regarding the issuer specified in paragraph (a)(5) of this section is as of a date within 12 months prior to the publication or submission of the quotation.

(h)   This section shall not prohibit any publication or submission of any quotation if the Commission, upon written request or upon its own motion, exempts such quotation either unconditionally or on specified terms and conditions, as not constituting a fraudulent, manipulative or deceptive practice comprehended within the purpose of this section.

* * *

§ 240.15c3–5.   Risk Management Controls for Brokers or Dealers with Market Access

(a)   For the purpose of this section:

(1)   The term market access shall mean:

(i)   Access to trading in securities on an exchange or alternative trading system as a result of being a member or subscriber of the exchange or alternative trading system, respectively; or

(ii)   Access to trading in securities on an alternative trading system provided by a broker-dealer operator of an alternative trading system to a non-broker-dealer.

(2)   The term regulatory requirements shall mean all federal securities laws, rules and regulations, and rules of self-regulatory organizations, that are applicable in connection with market access.

(b)   A broker or dealer with market access, or that provides a customer or any other person with access to an exchange or alternative trading system through use of its market participant identifier or otherwise, shall establish, document, and maintain a system of risk management controls and supervisory procedures reasonably designed to manage the financial, regulatory, and other risks of this business activity. Such broker or dealer shall preserve a copy of its supervisory procedures and a written description of its risk management controls as part of its books and records in a manner consistent with § 240.17a–4(e)(7). A broker-dealer that routes orders on behalf of an exchange or alternative trading system for the purpose of accessing other trading centers with protected quotations in compliance with Rule 611 of Regulation NMS (§ 242.611) for NMS stocks, or in compliance with a national market system plan for listed options, shall not be required to comply with this rule with regard to such routing services, except with regard to paragraph (c)(1)(ii) of this section.

(c)   The risk management controls and supervisory procedures required by paragraph (b) of this section shall include the following elements:

(1)   Financial risk management controls and supervisory procedures. The risk management controls and supervisory procedures shall be reasonably designed to systematically limit the financial exposure of the broker or dealer that could arise as a result of market access, including being reasonably designed to:

(i)   Prevent the entry of orders that exceed appropriate pre-set credit or capital thresholds in the aggregate for each customer and the broker or dealer and, where appropriate, more finely-tuned by sector, security, or otherwise by rejecting orders if such orders would exceed the applicable credit or capital thresholds; and

(ii)   Prevent the entry of erroneous orders, by rejecting orders that exceed appropriate price or size parameters, on an order-by-order basis or over a short period of time, or that indicate duplicative orders.

(2)   Regulatory risk management controls and supervisory procedures. The risk management controls and supervisory procedures shall be reasonably designed to ensure compliance with all regulatory requirements, including being reasonably designed to:

(i)　Prevent the entry of orders unless there has been compliance with all regulatory requirements that must be satisfied on a pre-order entry basis;

(ii)　Prevent the entry of orders for securities for a broker or dealer, customer, or other person if such person is restricted from trading those securities;

(iii)　Restrict access to trading systems and technology that provide market access to persons and accounts pre-approved and authorized by the broker or dealer; and

(iv)　Assure that appropriate surveillance personnel receive immediate post-trade execution reports that result from market access.

(d)　The financial and regulatory risk management controls and supervisory procedures described in paragraph (c) of this section shall be under the direct and exclusive control of the broker or dealer that is subject to paragraph (b) of this section.

(1)　Notwithstanding the foregoing, a broker or dealer that is subject to paragraph (b) of this section may reasonably allocate, by written contract, after a thorough due diligence review, control over specific regulatory risk management controls and supervisory procedures described in paragraph (c)(2) of this section to a customer that is a registered broker or dealer, provided that such broker or dealer subject to paragraph (b) of this section has a reasonable basis for determining that such customer, based on its position in the transaction and relationship with an ultimate customer, has better access than the broker or dealer to that ultimate customer and its trading information such that it can more effectively implement the specified controls or procedures.

(2)　Any allocation of control pursuant to paragraph (d)(1) of this section shall not relieve a broker or dealer that is subject to paragraph (b) of this section from any obligation under this section, including the overall responsibility to establish, document, and maintain a system of risk management controls and supervisory procedures reasonably designed to manage the financial, regulatory, and other risks of market access.

(e)　A broker or dealer that is subject to paragraph (b) of this section shall establish, document, and maintain a system for regularly reviewing the effectiveness of the risk management controls and supervisory procedures required by paragraphs (b) and (c) of this section and for promptly addressing any issues.

(1)　Among other things, the broker or dealer shall review, no less frequently than annually, the business activity of the broker or dealer in connection with market access to assure the overall effectiveness of such risk management controls and supervisory procedures. Such review shall be conducted in accordance with written procedures and shall be documented. The broker or dealer shall preserve a copy of such written procedures, and documentation of each such review, as part of its books and records in a manner consistent with § 240.17a–4(e)(7) and § 240.17a–4(b), respectively.

(2)　The Chief Executive Officer (or equivalent officer) of the broker or dealer shall, on an annual basis, certify that such risk management controls and supervisory procedures comply with paragraphs (b) and (c) of this section, and that the broker or dealer conducted such review, and such certifications shall be preserved by the broker or dealer as part of its books and records in a manner consistent with § 240.17a–4(b).

(f)　The Commission, by order, may exempt from the provisions of this section, either unconditionally or on specified terms and conditions, any broker or dealer, if the Commission determines that such exemption is necessary or appropriate in the public interest consistent with the protection of investors.

* * *

§ 240.15d–20.   Plain English Presentation of Specified Information

(a)   Any information included or incorporated by reference in a report filed under section 15(d) of the Act (15 U.S.C. 78o(d)) that is required to be disclosed pursuant to Item 402, 403, 404 or 407 of Regulation S–K (§ 229.402, § 229.403, § 229.404 or § 229.407 of this chapter) must be presented in a clear, concise and understandable manner. You must prepare the disclosure using the following standards:

(1)   Present information in clear, concise sections, paragraphs and sentences;

(2)   Use short sentences;

(3)   Use definite, concrete, everyday words;

(4)   Use the active voice;

(5)   Avoid multiple negatives;

(6)   Use descriptive headings and subheadings;

(7)   Use a tabular presentation or bullet lists for complex material, wherever possible;

(8)   Avoid legal jargon and highly technical business and other terminology;

(9)   Avoid frequent reliance on glossaries or defined terms as the primary means of explaining information. Define terms in a glossary or other section of the document only if the meaning is unclear from the context. Use a glossary only if it facilitates understanding of the disclosure; and

(10) In designing the presentation of the information you may include pictures, logos, charts, graphs and other design elements so long as the design is not misleading and the required information is clear. You are encouraged to use tables, schedules, charts and graphic illustrations that present relevant data in an understandable manner, so long as such presentations are consistent with applicable disclosure requirements and consistent with other information in the document. You must draw graphs and charts to scale. Any information you provide must not be misleading.

* * *

REPORTS OF DIRECTORS, OFFICERS, AND PRINCIPAL SHAREHOLDERS

§ 240.16a–1.   Definition of Terms

Terms defined in this rule shall apply solely to section 16 of the Act and the rules thereunder. These terms shall not be limited to section 16(a) of the Act but also shall apply to all other subsections under section 16 of the Act.

(a)   The term beneficial owner shall have the following applications:

(1)   Solely for purposes of determining whether a person is a beneficial owner of more than ten percent of any class of equity securities registered pursuant to section 12 of the Act, the term "beneficial owner" shall mean any person who is deemed a beneficial owner pursuant to section 13(d) of the Act and the rules thereunder; provided, however, that the following institutions or persons shall not be deemed the beneficial owner of securities of such class held for the benefit of third parties or in customer or fiduciary accounts in the ordinary course of business (or in the case of an employee benefit plan specified in paragraph (a)(1)(vi) of this section, of securities of such class allocated to plan participants where participants have voting power) as long as such shares are acquired by such institutions or persons without the purpose or effect of changing or influencing control of the issuer or engaging in any arrangement subject to Rule 13d–3(b) (§ 240.13d–3(b)):

(i)   A broker or dealer registered under section 15 of the Act (15 U.S.C. 78o);

(ii)   A bank as defined in section 3(a)(6) of the Act (15 U.S.C. 78c);

(iii)   An insurance company as defined in section 3(a)(19) of the Act (15 U.S.C. 78c);

(iv)   An investment company registered under section 8 of the Investment Company Act of 1940 (15 U.S.C. 80a–8);

(v)   Any person registered as an investment adviser under Section 203 of the Investment Advisers Act of 1940 (15 U.S.C. 80b–3) or under the laws of any state;

(vi)   An employee benefit plan as defined in Section 3(3) of the Employee Retirement Income Security Act of 1974, as amended, 29 U.S.C. 1001 *et seq.* ("ERISA") that is subject to the provisions of ERISA, or any such plan that is not subject to ERISA that is maintained primarily for the benefit of the employees of a state or local government or instrumentality, or an endowment fund;

(vii)   A parent holding company or control person, provided the aggregate amount held directly by the parent or control person, and directly and indirectly by their subsidiaries or affiliates that are not persons specified in § 240.16a–1 (a)(1)(i) through (x), does not exceed one percent of the securities of the subject class;

(viii)   A savings association as defined in Section 3(b) of the Federal Deposit Insurance Act (12 U.S.C. 1813);

(ix)   A church plan that is excluded from the definition of an investment company under section 3(c)(14) of the Investment Company Act of 1940 (15 U.S.C. 80a–30);

(x)   A non-U.S. institution that is the functional equivalent of any of the institutions listed in paragraphs (a)(1)(i) through (ix) of this section, so long as the non-U.S. institution is subject to a regulatory scheme that is substantially comparable to the regulatory scheme applicable to the equivalent U.S. institution and the non-U.S. institution is eligible to file a Schedule 13G pursuant to § 240.13d–1(b)(1)(ii)(J); and

(xi)   A group, provided that all the members are persons specified in § 240.16a–1 (a)(1)(i) through (x).

Note to paragraph (a): Pursuant to this section, a person deemed a beneficial owner of more than ten percent of any class of equity securities registered under section 12 of the Act would file a Form 3 (§ 249.103), but the securities holdings disclosed on Form 3, and changes in beneficial ownership reported on subsequent Forms 4 (§ 249.104) or 5 (§ 249.105), would be determined by the definition of "beneficial owner" in paragraph (a)(2) of this section.

(2)   Other than for purposes of determining whether a person is a beneficial owner of more than ten percent of any class of equity securities registered under Section 12 of the Act, the term beneficial owner shall mean any person who, directly or indirectly, through any contract, arrangement, understanding, relationship or otherwise, has or shares a direct or indirect pecuniary interest in the equity securities, subject to the following:

(i)   The term pecuniary interest in any class of equity securities shall mean the opportunity, directly or indirectly, to profit or share in any profit derived from a transaction in the subject securities.

(ii)   The term indirect pecuniary interest in any class of equity securities shall include, but not be limited to:

(A)   Securities held by members of a person's immediate family sharing the same household; provided, however, that the presumption of such beneficial ownership may be rebutted; *see also* § 240.16a–1(a)(4);

(B)   A general partner's proportionate interest in the portfolio securities held by a general or limited partnership. The general partner's proportionate interest, as evidenced by the partnership agreement in effect at the time of the transaction and the partnership's most recent financial statements, shall be the greater of:

(1) The general partner's share of the partnership's profits, including profits attributed to any limited partnership interests held by the general partner and any other interests in profits that arise from the purchase and sale of the partnership's portfolio securities; or

(2) The general partner's share of the partnership capital account, including the share attributable to any limited partnership interest held by the general partner.

(C) A performance-related fee, other than an asset-based fee, received by any broker, dealer, bank, insurance company, investment company, investment adviser, investment manager, trustee or person or entity performing a similar function; provided, however, that no pecuniary interest shall be present where:

(1) The performance-related fee, regardless of when payable, is calculated based upon net capital gains and/or net capital appreciation generated from the portfolio or from the fiduciary's overall performance over a period of one year or more; and

(2) Equity securities of the issuer do not account for more than ten percent of the market value of the portfolio. A right to a nonperformance-related fee alone shall not represent a pecuniary interest in the securities;

(D) A person's right to dividends that is separated or separable from the underlying securities. Otherwise, a right to dividends alone shall not represent a pecuniary interest in the securities;

(E) A person's interest in securities held by a trust, as specified in § 240.16a–8(b); and

(F) A person's right to acquire equity securities through the exercise or conversion of any derivative security, whether or not presently exercisable.

(iii) A shareholder shall not be deemed to have a pecuniary interest in the portfolio securities held by a corporation or similar entity in which the person owns securities if the shareholder is not a controlling shareholder of the entity and does not have or share investment control over the entity's portfolio.

(3) Where more than one person subject to section 16 of the Act is deemed to be a beneficial owner of the same equity securities, all such persons must report as beneficial owners of the securities, either separately or jointly, as provided in § 240.16a–3(j). In such cases, the amount of short-swing profit recoverable shall not be increased above the amount recoverable if there were only one beneficial owner.

(4) Any person filing a statement pursuant to section 16(a) of the Act may state that the filing shall not be deemed an admission that such person is, for purposes of section 16 of the Act or otherwise, the beneficial owner of any equity securities covered by the statement.

(5) The following interests are deemed not to confer beneficial ownership for purposes of section 16 of the Act:

(i) Interests in portfolio securities held by any investment company registered under the Investment Company Act of 1940 (15 U.S.C. 80a–1 *et seq.*); and

(ii) Interests in securities comprising part of a broad-based, publicly traded market basket or index of stocks, approved for trading by the appropriate federal governmental authority.

(b)   The term call equivalent position shall mean a derivative security position that increases in value as the value of the underlying equity increases, including, but not limited to, a long convertible security, a long call option, and a short put option position.

(c)   The term derivative securities shall mean any option, warrant, convertible security, stock appreciation right, or similar right with an exercise or conversion privilege at a price related to an equity security, or similar securities with a value derived from the value of an equity security, but shall not include:

(1)   Rights of a pledgee of securities to sell the pledged securities;

(2)   Rights of all holders of a class of securities of an issuer to receive securities pro rata, or obligations to dispose of securities, as a result of a merger, exchange offer, or consolidation involving the issuer of the securities;

(3)   Rights or obligations to surrender a security, or have a security withheld, upon the receipt or exercise of a derivative security or the receipt or vesting of equity securities, in order to satisfy the exercise price or the tax withholding consequences of receipt, exercise or vesting;

(4)   Interests in broad-based index options, broad-based index futures, and broad-based publicly traded market baskets of stocks approved for trading by the appropriate federal governmental authority;

(5)   Interests or rights to participate in employee benefit plans of the issuer;

(6)   Rights with an exercise or conversion privilege at a price that is not fixed; or

(7)   Options granted to an underwriter in a registered public offering for the purpose of satisfying over-allotments in such offering.

(d)   The term equity security of such issuer shall mean any equity security or derivative security relating to an issuer, whether or not issued by that issuer.

(e)   The term immediate family shall mean any child, stepchild, grandchild, parent, stepparent, grandparent, spouse, sibling, mother-in-law, father-in-law, son-in-law, daughter-in-law, brother-in-law, or sister-in-law, and shall include adoptive relationships.

(f)   The term "officer" shall mean an issuer's president, principal financial officer, principal accounting officer (or, if there is no such accounting officer, the controller), any vice-president of the issuer in charge of a principal business unit, division or function (such as sales, administration or finance), any other officer who performs a policy-making function, or any other person who performs similar policy-making functions for the issuer. Officers of the issuer's parent(s) or subsidiaries shall be deemed officers of the issuer if they perform such policy-making functions for the issuer. In addition, when the issuer is a limited partnership, officers or employees of the general partner(s) who perform policy-making functions for the limited partnership are deemed officers of the limited partnership. When the issuer is a trust, officers or employees of the trustee(s) who perform policy-making functions for the trust are deemed officers of the trust.

Note: "Policy-making function" is not intended to include policy-making functions that are not significant. If pursuant to Item 401(b) of Regulation S–K (§ 229.401(b)) the issuer identifies a person as an "executive officer," it is presumed that the Board of Directors has made that judgment and that the persons so identified are the officers for purposes of Section 16 of the Act, as are such other persons enumerated in this paragraph (f) but not in Item 401(b).

(g)   The term portfolio securities shall mean all securities owned by an entity, other than securities issued by the entity.

(h)   The term put equivalent position shall mean a derivative security position that increases in value as the value of the underlying equity decreases, including, but not limited to, a long put option and a short call option position.

§ 240.16a–2.   Persons and Transactions Subject to Section 16

Any person who is the beneficial owner, directly or indirectly, of more than ten percent of any class of equity securities ("ten percent beneficial owner") registered pursuant to section 12 of the Act (15 U.S.C. 78 l), any director or officer of the issuer of such securities, and any person specified in section 30(h) of the Investment Company Act of 1940 (15 U.S.C. 80a–29(h)), including any person specified in § 240.16a–8, shall be subject to the provisions of section 16 of the Act (15 U.S.C. 78p). The rules under section 16 of the Act apply to any class of equity securities of an issuer whether or not registered under section 12 of the Act. The rules under section 16 of the Act also apply to non-equity securities as provided by the Investment Company Act of 1940. With respect to transactions by persons subject to section 16 of the Act:

(a)   A transaction(s) carried out by a director or officer in the six months prior to the director or officer becoming subject to section 16 of the Act shall be subject to section 16 of the Act and reported on the first required Form 4 only if the transaction(s) occurred within six months of the transaction giving rise to the Form 4 filing obligation and the director or officer became subject to section 16 of the Act solely as a result of the issuer registering a class of equity securities pursuant to section 12 of the Act.

(b)   A transaction(s) following the cessation of director or officer status shall be subject to section 16 of the Act only if:

(1)   Executed within a period of less than six months of an opposite transaction subject to section 16(b) of the Act that occurred while that person was a director or officer; and

(2)   Not otherwise exempted from section 16(b) of the Act pursuant to the provisions of this chapter.

Note to paragraph (b): For purposes of this paragraph, an acquisition and a disposition each shall be an opposite transaction with respect to the other.

(c)   The transaction that results in a person becoming a ten percent beneficial owner is not subject to section 16 of the Act unless the person otherwise is subject to section 16 of the Act. A ten percent beneficial owner not otherwise subject to section 16 of the Act must report only those transactions conducted while the beneficial owner of more than ten percent of a class of equity securities of the issuer registered pursuant to section 12 of the Act.

(d)(1)   Transactions by a person or entity shall be exempt from the provisions of section 16 of the Act for the 12 months following appointment and qualification, to the extent such person or entity is acting as:

(i)   Executor or administrator of the estate of a decedent;

(ii)   Guardian or member of a committee for an incompetent;

(iii)   Receiver, trustee in bankruptcy, assignee for the benefit of creditors, conservator, liquidating agent, or other similar person duly authorized by law to administer the estate or assets of another person; or

(iv)   Fiduciary in a similar capacity.

(2)   Transactions by such person or entity acting in a capacity specified in paragraph (d)(1) of this section after the period specified in that paragraph shall be subject to section 16 of the Act only where the estate, trust or other entity is a beneficial owner of more than ten percent of any class of equity security registered pursuant to section 12 of the Act.

§ 240.16a–3.   Reporting Transactions and Holdings

(a)   Initial statements of beneficial ownership of equity securities required by section 16(a) of the Act shall be filed on Form 3. Statements of changes in beneficial ownership required by that section shall be filed on Form 4. Annual statements shall be filed on Form 5. At the election of the reporting person, any transaction required to be reported on Form 5 may be reported on an earlier filed Form 4. All such statements shall be prepared and filed in accordance with the requirements of the applicable form.

(b)   A person filing statements pursuant to section 16(a) of the Act with respect to any class of equity securities registered pursuant to section 12 of the Act need not file an additional statement on Form 3:

(1)   When an additional class of equity securities of the same issuer becomes registered pursuant to section 12 of the Act; or

(2)   When such person assumes a different or an additional relationship to the same issuer (for example, when an officer becomes a director).

(c)   Any issuer that has equity securities listed on more than one national securities exchange may designate one exchange as the only exchange with which reports pursuant to section 16(a) of the Act need be filed. Such designation shall be made in writing and shall be filed with the Commission and with each national securities exchange on which any equity security of the issuer is listed at the time of such election. The reporting person's obligation to file reports with each national securities exchange on which any equity security of the issuer is listed shall be satisfied by filing with the exchange so designated.

(d)   Any person required to file a statement with respect to securities of a single issuer under both section 16(a) of the Act (15 U.S.C. 78p(a)) and section 30(h) of the Investment Company Act of 1940 (15 U.S.C. 80a–29(h)) may file a single statement containing the required information, which will be deemed to be filed under both Acts.

(e)   [Reserved]

(f)(1)   A Form 5 shall be filed by every person who at any time during the issuer's fiscal year was subject to section 16 of the Act with respect to such issuer, except as provided in paragraph (f)(2) of this section. The Form shall be filed within 45 days after the issuer's fiscal year end, and shall disclose the following holdings and transactions not reported previously on Forms 3, 4 or 5:

(i)   All transactions during the most recent fiscal year that were exempt from section 16(b) of the Act, except:

(A)   Exercises and conversions of derivative securities exempt under either § 240.16b–3 or § 240.16b–6(b), and any transaction exempt under § 240.16b–3(d), § 240.16b–3(e), or § 240.16b–3(f) (these are required to be reported on Form 4);

(B)   Transactions exempt from section 16(b) of the Act pursuant to § 240.16b–3(c), which shall be exempt from section 16(a) of the Act; and

(C)   Transactions exempt from section 16(a) of the Act pursuant to another rule;

(ii)   Transactions that constituted small acquisitions pursuant to § 240.16a–6(a);

(iii)   All holdings and transactions that should have been reported during the most recent fiscal year, but were not; and

(iv)   With respect to the first Form 5 requirement for a reporting person, all holdings and transactions that should have been reported in each of the issuer's last two fiscal years but were not, based on the reporting person's reasonable belief in good faith in the completeness and accuracy of the information.

(2)   Notwithstanding the above, no Form 5 shall be required where all transactions otherwise required to be reported on the Form 5 have been reported before the due date of the Form 5.

Persons no longer subject to section 16 of the Act, but who were subject to the Section at any time during the issuer's fiscal year, must file a Form 5 unless paragraph (f)(2) is satisfied. *See also* § 240.16a–2(b) regarding the reporting obligations of persons ceasing to be officers or directors.

(g)(1)   A Form 4 must be filed to report: All transactions not exempt from section 16(b) of the Act; All transactions exempt from section 16(b) of the Act pursuant to § 240.16b–3(d), § 240.16b–3(e), or § 240.16b–3(f); and all exercises and conversions of derivative securities, regardless of whether exempt from section 16(b) of the Act. Form 4 must be filed before the end of the second business day following the day on which the subject transaction has been executed.

(2)   Solely for purposes of section 16(a)(2)(C) of the Act and paragraph (g)(1) of this section, the date on which the executing broker, dealer or plan administrator notifies the reporting person of the execution of the transaction is deemed the date of execution for a transaction where the following conditions are satisfied:

(i)   the transaction is pursuant to a contract, instruction or written plan for the purchase or sale of equity securities of the issuer (as defined in § 16a–1(d)) that satisfies the affirmative defense conditions of § 240.10b5–1(c) of this chapter; and

(ii)   the reporting person does not select the date of execution.

(3)   Solely for purposes of section 16(a)(2)(C) of the Act and paragraph (g)(1) of this section, the date on which the plan administrator notifies the reporting person that the transaction has been executed is deemed the date of execution for a discretionary transaction (as defined in § 16b–3(b)(1)) for which the reporting person does not select the date of execution.

(4)   In the case of the transactions described in paragraphs (g)(2) and (g)(3) of this section, if the notification date is later than the third business day following the trade date of the transaction, the date of execution is deemed to be the third business day following the trade date of the transaction.

(5)   At the option of the reporting person, transactions that are reportable on Form 5 may be reported on Form 4, so long as the Form 4 is filed no later than the due date of the Form 5 on which the transaction is otherwise required to be reported.

(h)   The date of filing with the Commission shall be the date of receipt by the Commission.

(i)   Signatures. Where Section 16 of the Act, or the rules or forms thereunder, require a document filed with or furnished to the Commission to be signed, such document shall be manually signed, or signed using either typed signatures or duplicated or facsimile versions of manual signatures. Where typed, duplicated or facsimile signatures are used, each signatory to the filing shall manually sign a signature page or other document authenticating, acknowledging or otherwise adopting his or her signature that appears in the filing. Such document shall be executed before or at the time the filing is made and shall be retained by the filer for a period of five years. Upon request, the filer shall furnish to the Commission or its staff a copy of any or all documents retained pursuant to this section.

(j)   Where more than one person subject to section 16 of the Act is deemed to be a beneficial owner of the same equity securities, all such persons must report as beneficial owners of the securities, either separately or jointly. Where persons in a group are deemed to be beneficial owners of equity securities pursuant to § 240.16a–1(a)(1) due to the aggregation of holdings, a single Form 3, 4 or 5 may be filed on behalf of all persons in the group. Joint and group filings must include all required information for each beneficial owner, and such filings must be signed by each beneficial owner, or on behalf of such owner by an authorized person.

* * *

§ 240.16a–4.   Derivative Securities

(a)   For purposes of section 16 of the Act, both derivative securities and the underlying securities to which they relate shall be deemed to be the same class of equity securities, except that the acquisition or disposition of any derivative security shall be separately reported.

(b)   The exercise or conversion of a call equivalent position shall be reported on Form 4 and treated for reporting purposes as:

   (1)   A purchase of the underlying security; and

   (2)   A closing of the derivative security position.

(c)   The exercise or conversion of a put equivalent position shall be reported on Form 4 and treated for reporting purposes as:

   (1)   A sale of the underlying security; and

   (2)   A closing of the derivative security position.

(d)   The disposition or closing of a long derivative security position, as a result of cancellation or expiration, shall be exempt from section 16(a) of the Act if exempt from section 16(b) of the Act pursuant to § 240.16b–6(d).

Note to § 240.16a–4: A purchase or sale resulting from an exercise or conversion of a derivative security may be exempt from section 16(b) of the Act pursuant to § 240.16b–3 or § 240.16b–6(b).

* * *

§ 240.16a–6.   Small Acquisitions

(a)   Any acquisition of an equity security or the right to acquire such securities, other than an acquisition from the issuer (including an employee benefit plan sponsored by the issuer), not exceeding $10,000 in market value shall be reported on Form 5, subject to the following conditions:

   (1)   Such acquisition, when aggregated with other acquisitions of securities of the same class (including securities underlying derivative securities, but excluding acquisitions exempted by rule from section 16(b) or previously reported on Form 4 or Form 5) within the prior six months, does not exceed a total of $10,000 in market value; and

   (2)   The person making the acquisition does not within six months thereafter make any disposition, other than by a transaction exempt from section 16(b) of the Act.

(b)   If an acquisition no longer qualifies for the reporting deferral in paragraph (a) of this section, all such acquisitions that have not yet been reported must be reported on Form 4 before the end of the second business day following the day on which the conditions of paragraph (a) of this section are no longer met.

§ 240.16a–7.   Transactions Effected in Connection with a Distribution

(a)   Any purchase and sale, or sale and purchase, of a security that is made in connection with the distribution of a substantial block of securities shall be exempt from the provisions of section 16(a) of the Act, to the extent specified in this rule, subject to the following conditions:

   (1)   The person effecting the transaction is engaged in the business of distributing securities and is participating in good faith, in the ordinary course of such business, in the distribution of such block of securities; and

   (2)   The security involved in the transaction is:

      (i)   Part of such block of securities and is acquired by the person effecting the transaction, with a view to distribution thereof, from the issuer or other person on whose behalf such securities are being distributed or from a person who is participating in good faith in the distribution of such block of securities; or

(ii) A security purchased in good faith by or for the account of the person effecting the transaction for the purpose of stabilizing the market price of securities of the class being distributed or to cover an over-allotment or other short position created in connection with such distribution.

(b) Each person participating in the transaction must qualify on an individual basis for an exemption pursuant to this section.

* * *

§ 240.16a–9. Stock Splits, Stock Dividends, and Pro Rata Rights

The following shall be exempt from section 16 of the Act:

(a) The increase or decrease in the number of securities held as a result of a stock split or stock dividend applying equally to all securities of a class, including a stock dividend in which equity securities of a different issuer are distributed; and

(b) The acquisition of rights, such as shareholder or pre-emptive rights, pursuant to a pro rata grant to all holders of the same class of equity securities registered under section 12 of the Act.

Note: The exercise or sale of a pro rata right shall be reported pursuant to § 240.16a–4 and the exercise shall be eligible for exemption from section 16(b) of the Act pursuant to § 240.16b–6(b).

§ 240.16a–10. Exemptions Under Section 16(a)

Except as provided in § 240.16a–6, any transaction exempted from the requirements of section 16(a) of the Act, insofar as it is otherwise subject to the provisions of section 16(b), shall be likewise exempt from section 16(b) of the Act.

* * *

EXEMPTION OF CERTAIN TRANSACTIONS FROM SECTION 16(b)

§ 240.16b–1. Transactions Approved by a Regulatory Authority

Any purchase and sale, or sale and purchase, of a security shall be exempt from section 16(b) of the Act, if the transaction is effected by an investment company registered under the Investment Company Act of 1940 (15 U.S.C. 80a–1 *et seq.*) and both the purchase and sale of such security have been exempted from the provisions of section 17(a) (15 U.S.C. 80a–17(a)) of the Investment Company Act of 1940, by rule or order of the Commission.

* * *

§ 240.16b–3. Transactions Between an Issuer and Its Officers or Directors

(a) General. A transaction between the issuer (including an employee benefit plan sponsored by the issuer) and an officer or director of the issuer that involves issuer equity securities shall be exempt from section 16(b) of the Act if the transaction satisfies the applicable conditions set forth in this section.

(b) Definitions. (1) A Discretionary Transaction shall mean a transaction pursuant to an employee benefit plan that:

(i) Is at the volition of a plan participant;

(ii) Is not made in connection with the participant's death, disability, retirement or termination of employment;

(iii) Is not required to be made available to a plan participant pursuant to a provision of the Internal Revenue Code; and

(iv) Results in either an intra-plan transfer involving an issuer equity securities fund, or a cash distribution funded by a volitional disposition of an issuer equity security.

(2) An Excess Benefit Plan shall mean an employee benefit plan that is operated in conjunction with a Qualified Plan, and provides only the benefits or contributions that would be provided under a Qualified Plan but for any benefit or contribution limitations set forth in the Internal Revenue Code of 1986, or any successor provisions thereof.

(3)(i) A Non-Employee Director shall mean a director who:

(A) Is not currently an officer (as defined in § 240.16a–1(f)) of the issuer or a parent or subsidiary of the issuer, or otherwise currently employed by the issuer or a parent or subsidiary of the issuer;

(B) Does not receive compensation, either directly or indirectly, from the issuer or a parent or subsidiary of the issuer, for services rendered as a consultant or in any capacity other than as a director, except for an amount that does not exceed the dollar amount for which disclosure would be required pursuant to § 229.404(a) of this chapter; and

(C) Does not possess an interest in any other transaction for which disclosure would be required pursuant to § 229.404(a) of this chapter.

(ii) Notwithstanding paragraph (b)(3)(i) of this section, a Non-Employee Director of a closed-end investment company shall mean a director who is not an "interested person" of the issuer, as that term is defined in Section 2(a)(19) of the Investment Company Act of 1940.

(4) A Qualified Plan shall mean an employee benefit plan that satisfies the coverage and participation requirements of sections 410 and 401(a)(26) of the Internal Revenue Code of 1986, or any successor provisions thereof.

(5) A Stock Purchase Plan shall mean an employee benefit plan that satisfies the coverage and participation requirements of sections 423(b)(3) and 423(b)(5), or section 410, of the Internal Revenue Code of 1986, or any successor provisions thereof.

(c) Tax-conditioned plans. Any transaction (other than a Discretionary Transaction) pursuant to a Qualified Plan, an Excess Benefit Plan, or a Stock Purchase Plan shall be exempt without condition.

(d) Acquisitions from the issuer. Any transaction, other than a Discretionary Transaction, involving an acquisition from the issuer (including without limitation a grant or award), whether or not intended for a compensatory or other particular purpose, shall be exempt if:

(1) The transaction is approved by the board of directors of the issuer, or a committee of the board of directors that is composed solely of two or more Non-Employee Directors;

(2) The transaction is approved or ratified, in compliance with section 14 of the Act, by either: the affirmative votes of the holders of a majority of the securities of the issuer present, or represented, and entitled to vote at a meeting duly held in accordance with the applicable laws of the state or other jurisdiction in which the issuer is incorporated; or the written consent of the holders of a majority of the securities of the issuer entitled to vote; provided that such ratification occurs no later than the date of the next annual meeting of shareholders; or

(3) The issuer equity securities so acquired are held by the officer or director for a period of six months following the date of such acquisition, provided that this condition shall be satisfied with respect to a derivative security if at least six months elapse from the date of acquisition of the derivative security to the date of disposition of the derivative security (other than upon exercise or conversion) or its underlying equity security.

(e) Dispositions to the issuer. Any transaction, other than a Discretionary Transaction, involving the disposition to the issuer of issuer equity securities, whether or not intended for a compensatory or other particular purpose, shall be exempt, provided that the terms of such disposition are approved in advance in the manner prescribed by either paragraph (d)(1) or paragraph (d)(2) of this section.

(f) Discretionary Transactions. A Discretionary Transaction shall be exempt only if effected pursuant to an election made at least six months following the date of the most recent election, with respect to any plan of the issuer, that effected a Discretionary Transaction that was:

(1) An acquisition, if the transaction to be exempted would be a disposition; or

(2) A disposition, if the transaction to be exempted would be an acquisition.

Notes to § 240.16b–3:

Note (1): The exercise or conversion of a derivative security that does not satisfy the conditions of this section is eligible for exemption from section 16(b) of the Act to the extent that the conditions of § 240.16b–6(b) are satisfied.

Note (2): Section 16(a) reporting requirements applicable to transactions exempt pursuant to this section are set forth in § 240.16a–3(f) and (g) and § 240.16a–4.

Note (3): The approval conditions of paragraphs (d)(1), (d)(2) and (e) of this section require the approval of each specific transaction, and are not satisfied by approval of a plan in its entirety except for the approval of a plan pursuant to which the terms and conditions of each transaction are fixed in advance, such as a formula plan. Where the terms of a subsequent transaction (such as the exercise price of an option, or the provision of an exercise or tax withholding right) are provided for in a transaction as initially approved pursuant to paragraphs (d)(1), (d)(2) or (e), such subsequent transaction shall not require further specific approval.

Note (4): For purposes of determining a director's status under those portions of paragraph (b)(3)(i) that reference § 229.404(a) of this chapter, an issuer may rely on the disclosure provided under § 229.404(a) of this chapter for the issuer's most recent fiscal year contained in the most recent filing in which disclosure required under § 229.404(a) is presented. Where a transaction disclosed in that filing was terminated before the director's proposed service as a Non-Employee Director, that transaction will not bar such service. The issuer must believe in good faith that any current or contemplated transaction in which the director participates will not be required to be disclosed under § 229.404(a) of this chapter, based on information readily available to the issuer and the director at the time such director proposes to act as a Non-Employee Director. At such time as the issuer believes in good faith, based on readily available information, that a current or contemplated transaction with a director will be required to be disclosed under § 229.404(a) in a future filing, the director no longer is eligible to serve as a Non-Employee Director; provided, however, that this determination does not result in retroactive loss of a Rule 16b–3 exemption for a transaction previously approved by the director while serving as a Non-Employee Director consistent with this note. In making the determinations specified in this Note, the issuer may rely on information it obtains from the director, for example, pursuant to a response to an inquiry.

* * *

§ 240.16b–6.   Derivative Securities

(a) The establishment of or increase in a call equivalent position or liquidation of or decrease in a put equivalent position shall be deemed a purchase of the underlying security for purposes of section 16(b) of the Act, and the establishment of or increase in a put equivalent position or liquidation of or decrease in a call equivalent position shall be deemed a sale of the underlying securities for purposes of section 16(b) of the Act: Provided, however, That if the increase or decrease occurs as a result of the fixing of the exercise price of a right initially issued without a fixed price, where the date the price is fixed is not known in advance and is outside the control of the recipient, the increase or decrease shall be exempt from section 16(b) of the Act with respect to any offsetting transaction within the six months prior to the date the price is fixed.

(b)   The closing of a derivative security position as a result of its exercise or conversion shall be exempt from the operation of section 16(b) of the Act, and the acquisition of underlying securities at a fixed exercise price due to the exercise or conversion of a call equivalent position or the disposition of underlying securities at a fixed exercise price due to the exercise of a put equivalent position shall be exempt from the operation of section 16(b) of the Act: Provided, however, That the acquisition of underlying securities from the exercise of an out-of-the-money option, warrant, or right shall not be exempt unless the exercise is necessary to comport with the sequential exercise provisions of the Internal Revenue Code (26 U.S.C. 422A).

Note to paragraph (b): The exercise or conversion of a derivative security that does not satisfy the conditions of this section is eligible for exemption from section 16(b) of the Act to the extent that the conditions of § 240.16b–3 are satisfied.

(c)   In determining the short-swing profit recoverable pursuant to section 16(b) of the Act from transactions involving the purchase and sale or sale and purchase of derivative and other securities, the following rules apply:

(1)   Short-swing profits in transactions involving the purchase and sale or sale and purchase of derivative securities that have identical characteristics (*e.g.*, purchases and sales of call options of the same strike price and expiration date, or purchases and sales of the same series of convertible debentures) shall be measured by the actual prices paid or received in the short-swing transactions.

(2)   Short-swing profits in transactions involving the purchase and sale or sale and purchase of derivative securities having different characteristics but related to the same underlying security (*e.g.*, the purchase of a call option and the sale of a convertible debenture) or derivative securities and underlying securities shall not exceed the difference in price of the underlying security on the date of purchase or sale and the date of sale or purchase. Such profits may be measured by calculating the short-swing profits that would have been realized had the subject transactions involved purchases and sales solely of the derivative security that was purchased or solely of the derivative security that was sold, valued as of the time of the matching purchase or sale, and calculated for the lesser of the number of underlying securities actually purchased or sold.

(d)   Upon cancellation or expiration of an option within six months of the writing of the option, any profit derived from writing the option shall be recoverable under section 16(b) of the Act. The profit shall not exceed the premium received for writing the option. The disposition or closing of a long derivative security position, as a result of cancellation or expiration, shall be exempt from section 16(b) of the Act where no value is received from the cancellation or expiration.

§ 240.16b–7.   Mergers, Reclassifications, and Consolidations

(a)   The following transactions shall be exempt from the provisions of section 16(b) of the Act:

(1)   The acquisition of a security of a company, pursuant to a merger, reclassification or consolidation, in exchange for a security of a company that before the merger, reclassification or consolidation, owned 85 percent or more of either:

(i)   The equity securities of all other companies involved in the merger, reclassification or consolidation, or in the case of a consolidation, the resulting company; or

(ii)   The combined assets of all the companies involved in the merger, reclassification or consolidation, computed according to their book values before the merger, reclassification or consolidation as determined by reference to their most recent available financial statements for a 12 month period before the merger, reclassification or consolidation, or such shorter time as the company has been in existence.

(2)   The disposition of a security, pursuant to a merger, reclassification or consolidation, of a company that before the merger, reclassification or consolidation, owned 85 percent or more of either:

      (i)   The equity securities of all other companies involved in the merger, reclassification or consolidation or, in the case of a consolidation, the resulting company; or

      (ii)   The combined assets of all the companies undergoing merger, reclassification or consolidation, computed according to their book values before the merger, reclassification or consolidation as determined by reference to their most recent available financial statements for a 12 month period before the merger, reclassification or consolidation.

(b)   A merger within the meaning of this section shall include the sale or purchase of substantially all the assets of one company by another in exchange for equity securities which are then distributed to the security holders of the company that sold its assets.

(c)   The exemption provided by this section applies to any securities transaction that satisfies the conditions specified in this section and is not conditioned on the transaction satisfying any other conditions.

(d)   Notwithstanding the foregoing, if a person subject to section 16 of the Act makes any non-exempt purchase of a security in any company involved in the merger, reclassification or consolidation and any non-exempt sale of a security in any company involved in the merger, reclassification or consolidation within any period of less than six months during which the merger, reclassification or consolidation took place, the exemption provided by this section shall be unavailable to the extent of such purchase and sale.

* * *

E. FORMS UNDER THE SECURITIES ACT OF 1933

(Selected)

Table of Contents

FORM S-1

REGISTRATION STATEMENT UNDER THE SECURITIES ACT OF 1933

* * *

GENERAL INSTRUCTIONS

I. Eligibility Requirements for Use of Form S-1

This Form shall be used for the registration under the Securities Act of 1933 ("Securities Act"); of securities of all registrants for which no other form is authorized or prescribed, except that this Form shall not be used for securities of foreign governments or political subdivisions thereof or asset-backed securities, as defined in 17 CFR 229.1101(c).

II. Application of General Rules and Regulations

A. Attention is directed to the General Rules and Regulations under the Securities Act, particularly those comprising Regulation C (17 CFR 230.400 to 230.494) thereunder. That Regulation contains general requirements regarding the preparation and filing of the registration statement.

B. Attention is directed to Regulation S–K (17 CFR Part 229) for the requirements applicable to the content of the non-financial statement portions of registration statements under the Securities Act. Where this Form directs the registrant to furnish information required by Regulation S–K and the item of Regulation S–K so provides, information need only be furnished to the extent appropriate.

C. A registration statement filed (or submitted for confidential review) under Section 6 of the Securities Act (15 U.S.C. 77f) by an emerging growth company, defined in Section 2(a)(19) of the Securities Act (15 U.S.C. 77b(a)(19)), prior to an initial public offering may omit financial information for historical periods otherwise required by Regulation S–X (17 CFR Part 210) as of the time of filing (or confidential submission) of the registration statement, provided that:

1. The omitted financial information relates to a historical period that the registrant reasonably believes will not be required to be included in this Form at the time of the contemplated offering; and

2. Prior to the registrant distributing a preliminary prospectus to investors, the registration statement is amended to include all financial information required by Regulation S–X at the date of the amendment.

FORM S-1

III. Exchange Offers

If any of the securities being registered are to be offered in exchange for securities of any other issuer, the prospectus shall also include the information which would be required by item 11 if the securities of such other issuer were registered on this Form. There shall also be included the information concerning such securities of such other issuer which would be called for by Item 9 if such securities were being registered. In connection with this instruction, reference is made to Rule 409.

IV. Roll-up Transactions

If the securities to be registered on this Form will be issued in a roll-up transaction as defined in Item 901(c) of Regulation S–K (17 CFR 229.901(c)), attention is directed to the requirements of Form S-4 applicable to roll-up transactions, including, but not limited to, General Instruction I.

V. Registration of Additional Securities

With respect to the registration of additional securities for an offering pursuant to Rule 462(b) under the Securities Act, the registrant may file a registration statement consisting only of the following: the facing page; a statement that the contents of the earlier registration statement, identified by file number, are incorporated by reference; required opinions and consents; the signature page; and any price-related information omitted from the earlier registration statement in reliance on Rule 430A that the registrant chooses to include in the new registration statement. The information contained in such a Rule 462(b) registration statement shall be deemed to be a part of the earlier registration statement as of the date of effectiveness of the Rule 462(b) registration statement. Any opinion or consent required in the Rule 462(b) registration statement may be incorporated by reference from the earlier registration statement with respect to the offering, if: (i) such opinion or consent expressly provides for such incorporation; and (ii) such opinion relates to the securities registered pursuant to Rule 462(b). *See* Rule 439(b) under the Securities Act (17 CFR 230.439(b)).

VI. Offerings of Asset-Backed Securities.

The following applies if a registration statement on this Form S-1 is being used to register an offering of asset-backed securities. Terms used in this General Instruction VI. have the same meaning as in Item 1101 of Regulation AB (17 CFR 229.1101).

A. *Items that may be Omitted.*

Such registrants may omit the information called for by Item 11, Information with Respect to the Registrant.

B. *Substitute Information to be Included.*

In addition to the Items that are otherwise required by this Form, the registrant must furnish in the prospectus the information required by Items 1102 through 1120 of Regulation AB (17 CFR 229.1102 through 229.1120).

C. *Signatures.*

The registration statement must be signed by the depositor, the depositor's principal executive officer or officers, principal financial officer and controller or principal accounting officer, and by at least a majority of the depositor's board of directors or persons performing similar functions.

VII. Eligibility to Use Incorporation by Reference

If a registrant meets the following requirements in paragraphs A-F immediately prior to the time of filing a registration statement on this Form, it may elect to provide information required by Items 3 through 11 of this Form in accordance with Item 11A and Item 12 of this Form. Notwithstanding the foregoing, in the financial statements, incorporating by reference or cross-referencing to information outside of the financial statements is not permitted unless otherwise specifically permitted or required by the Commission's rules or by U.S. Generally Accepted Accounting Principles or International Financial Reporting Standards as issued by the International Accounting Standards Board, whichever is applicable.

FORM S-1

A. The registrant is subject to the requirement to file reports pursuant to Section 13 or Section 15(d) of the Securities Exchange Act of 1934 ("Exchange Act").

B. The registrant has filed all reports and other materials required to be filed by Sections 13(a), 14, or 15(d) of the Exchange Act during the preceding 12 months (or for such shorter period that the registrant was required to file such reports and materials).

C. The registrant has filed an annual report required under Section 13(a) or Section 15(d) of the Exchange Act for its most recently completed fiscal year.

D. The registrant is not:

    1. And during the past three years neither the registrant nor any of its predecessors was:

        (a) A blank check company as defined in Rule 419(a)(2) (§ 230.419(a)(2));

        (b) A shell company, other than a business combination related shell company, each as defined in Rule 405(§ 230.405); or

        (c) A registrant for an offering of penny stock as defined in Rule 3a51–1 of the Exchange Act (§ 240.3a51–1 of this chapter).

    2. Registering an offering that effectuates a business combination transaction as defined in Rule 165(f)(1) (§ 230.165(f)(1) of this chapter).

E. If a registrant is a successor registrant it shall be deemed to have satisfied conditions A., B., C., and D.2 above if:

    1. Its predecessor and it, taken together, do so, provided that the succession was primarily for the purpose of changing the state of incorporation of the predecessor or forming a holding company and that the assets and liabilities of the successor at the time of succession were substantially the same as those of the predecessor; or

    2. All predecessors met the conditions at the time of succession and the registrant has continued to do so since the succession.

F. The registrant makes its periodic and current reports filed pursuant to Section 13 or Section 15(d) of the Exchange Act that are incorporated by reference pursuant to Item 11A or Item 12 of this Form readily available and accessible on a Web site maintained by or for the registrant and containing information about the registrant.

PART I—INFORMATION REQUIRED IN PROSPECTUS

Item 1. Forepart of the Registration Statement and Outside Front Cover Page of Prospectus.

Set forth in the forepart of the registration statement and on the outside front cover page of the prospectus the information required by Item 501 of Regulation S–K (§ 229.501 of this chapter).

Item 2. Inside Front and Outside Back Cover Pages of Prospectus.

Set forth on the inside front cover page of the prospectus or, where permitted, on the outside back cover page, the information required by Item 502 of Regulation S–K (§ 229.502 of this chapter).

Item 3. Summary Information, Risk Factors and Ratio of Earnings to Fixed Charges.

Furnish the information required by Items 105 and 503 of Regulation S–K (§ 229.105 and § 229.503 of this chapter).

Item 4. Use of Proceeds.

Furnish the information required by Item 504 of Regulation S–K (§ 229.504 of this chapter).

FORM S-1

Item 5. Determination of Offering Price.

Furnish the information required by Item 505 of Regulation S–K (§ 229.505 of this chapter).

Item 6. Dilution.

Furnish the information required by Item 506 of Regulation S–K (§ 229.506 of this chapter).

Item 7. Selling Security Holders.

Furnish the information required by Item 507 of Regulation S–K (§ 229.507 of this chapter).

Item 8. Plan of Distribution.

Furnish the information required by Item 508 of Regulation S–K (§ 229.508 of this chapter).

Item 9. Description of Securities to be Registered.

Furnish the information required by Item 202 of Regulation S–K (§ 229.202 of this chapter).

Item 10. Interests of Named Experts and Counsel.

Furnish the information required by Item 509 of Regulation S–K (§ 229.509 of this chapter).

Item 11. Information with Respect to the Registrant.

Furnish the following information with respect to the registrant:

(a) Information required by Item 101 of Regulation S–K (§ 229.101 of this chapter), description of business;

(b) Information required by Item 102 of Regulation S–K (§ 229.102 of this chapter), description of property;

(c) Information required by Item 103 of Regulation S–K (§ 229.103 of this chapter), legal proceedings;

(d) Where common equity securities are being offered, information required by Item 201 of Regulation S–K (§ 229.201 of this chapter), market price of and dividends on the registrant's common equity and related stockholder matters;

(e) Financial statements meeting the requirements of Regulation S–X (17 CFR Part 210) (Schedules required under Regulation S–X shall be filed as "Financial Statement Schedules" pursuant to Item 15, Exhibits and Financial Statement Schedules, of this Form), as well as any financial information required by Rule 3–05 and Article 11 of Regulation S–X. A smaller reporting company may provide the information in Rule 8–04 and 8–05 of Regulation S–X in lieu of the financial information required by Rule 3–05 and Article 11 of Regulation S–X;

(f) Information required by Item 301 of Regulation S–K (§ 229.301 of this chapter), selected financial data;

(g) Information required by Item 302 of Regulation S–K (§ 229.302 of this chapter), supplementary financial information;

(h) Information required by Item 303 of Regulation S–K (§ 229.303 of this chapter), management's discussion and analysis of financial condition and results of operations;

(i) Information required by Item 304 of Regulation S–K (§ 229.304 of this chapter), changes in and disagreements with accountants on accounting and financial disclosure;

(j) Information required by Item 305 of Regulation S–K (§ 229.305 of this chapter), quantitative and qualitative disclosures about market risk[;]

(k) Information required by Item 401 of Regulation S–K (§ 229.401 of this chapter), directors and executive officers;

FORM S-1

(*l*)   Information required by Item 402 of Regulation S–K (§ 229.402 of this chapter), executive compensation, and information required by paragraph (e)(4) of Item 407 of Regulation S–K (§ 229.407 of this chapter), corporate governance;

(m) Information required by Item 403 of Regulation S–K (§ 229.403 of this chapter), security ownership of certain beneficial owners and management; and

(n) Information required by Item 404 of Regulation S–K (§ 229.404 of this chapter), transactions with related persons, promoters and certain control persons, and Item 407(a) of Regulation S–K (§ 229.407(a) of this chapter), corporate governance.

Item 11A. Material Changes.

If the registrant elects to incorporate information by reference pursuant to General Instruction VII., describe any and all material changes in the registrant's affairs which have occurred since the end of the latest fiscal year for which audited financial statements were included in the latest Form 10-K and that have not been described in a Form 10-Q or Form 8-K filed under the Exchange Act.

Item 12. Incorporation of Certain Information by Reference.

If the registrant elects to incorporate information by reference pursuant to General Instruction VII.:

(a)   It must specifically incorporate by reference into the prospectus contained in the registration statement the following documents by means of a statement to that effect in the prospectus listing all such documents:

(1)   The registrant's latest annual report on Form 10-K filed pursuant to Section 13(a) or Section 15(d) of the Exchange Act that contains financial statements for the registrant's latest fiscal year for which a Form 10-K was required to have been filed; and

(2)   All other reports filed pursuant to Section 13(a) or 15(d) of the Exchange Act or proxy or information statements filed pursuant to Section 14 of the Exchange Act since the end of the fiscal year covered by the annual report referred to in paragraph (a)(1) above.

Note to Item 12(a). Attention is directed to Rule 439 (§ 230.439) regarding consent to use of material incorporated by reference.

(b)   In addition to the incorporation by reference permitted pursuant to paragraph (a) of this Item, a smaller reporting company, as defined in Rule 405 (17 CFR 230.405), may elect to incorporate by reference information filed after the effective date of the registration statement. A smaller reporting company making this election must state in the prospectus contained in the registration statement that all documents subsequently filed by the registrant pursuant to Sections 13(a), 13(c), 14 or 15(d) of the Exchange Act, prior to the termination of the offering shall be deemed to be incorporated by reference into the prospectus.

(c)(1)   The registrant must state:

(i)   That it will provide to each person, including any beneficial owner, to whom a prospectus is delivered, a copy of any or all of the reports or documents that have been incorporated by reference in the prospectus contained in the registration statement but not delivered with the prospectus;

(ii) That it will provide these reports or documents upon written or oral request;

(iii) That it will provide these reports or documents at no cost to the requester;

(iv) The name, address, telephone number, and e-mail address, if any, to which the request for these reports or documents must be made; and

(v)   The registrant's Web site address, including the uniform resource locator (URL) where the incorporated reports and other documents may be accessed.

Note to Item 12(c)(1). If the registrant sends any of the information that is incorporated by reference in the prospectus contained in the registration statement to security holders, it also must send any exhibits that are specifically incorporated by reference in that information.

    (2)   The registrant must:

        (i)   Identify the reports and other information that it files with the SEC; and

        (ii)   State that the SEC maintains an Internet site that contains reports, proxy and information statements, and other information regarding issuers that file electronically with the SEC and state the address of that site (http://www.sec.gov).

Item 12A. Disclosure of Commission Position on Indemnification for Securities Act Liabilities.

Furnish the information required by Item 510 of Regulation S–K (§ 229.510 of this chapter).

PART II—INFORMATION NOT REQUIRED IN PROSPECTUS

Item 13. Other Expenses of Issuance and Distribution.

Furnish the information required by Item 511 of Regulation S–K (§ 229.511 of this chapter).

Item 14. Indemnification of Directors and Officers.

Furnish the information required by Item 702 of Regulation S–K (§ 229.702 of this chapter).

Item 15. Recent Sales of Unregistered Securities.

Furnish the information required by Item 701 of Regulation S–K (§ 229.701 of this chapter).

Item 16. Exhibits and Financial Statement Schedules.

    (a)   Subject to the rules regarding incorporation by reference, furnish the exhibits as required by Item 601 of Regulation S–K (§ 229.601 of this chapter).

    (b)   Furnish the financial statement schedules required by Regulation S–X (17 CFR Part 210) and Item 11(e) of this Form. These schedules shall be lettered or numbered in the manner described for exhibits in paragraph (a).

Item 17. Undertakings.

Furnish the undertakings required by Item 512 of Regulation S–K (§ 229.512 of this chapter).

***

FORM S-3

REGISTRATION STATEMENT UNDER THE SECURITIES ACT OF 1933

***

GENERAL INSTRUCTIONS

I.   Eligibility Requirements for Use of Form S-3

This instruction sets forth registrant requirements and transaction requirements for the use of Form S-3. Any registrant which meets the requirements of I.A. below ("Registrant Requirements") may use this Form for the registration of securities under the Securities Act of 1933 ("Securities Act") which are offered in any transaction specified in I.B. below ("Transaction Requirement") provided that the requirement applicable to the specified transaction are met. With respect to majority-owned subsidiaries, *see* Instruction I.C. below. With respect to well-known seasoned issuers and majority-owned subsidiaries of well-known seasoned issuers, *see* Instruction I.D. below.

FORM S-3

A.   **Registrant Requirements.** Registrants must meet the following conditions in order to use this Form S-3 for registration under the Securities Act of securities offered in the transactions specified in I. B. below:

1.   The registrant is organized under the laws of the United States or any State or Territory or the District of Columbia and has its principal business operations in the United States or its territories.

2.   The registrant has a class of securities registered pursuant to Section 12(b) of the Securities Exchange Act of 1934 ("Exchange Act") or a class of equity securities registered pursuant to Section 12(g) of the Exchange Act or is required to file reports pursuant to Section 15(d) of the Exchange Act.

3.   The registrant:

(a)   has been subject to the requirements of Section 12 or 15(d) of the Exchange Act and has filed all the material required to be filed pursuant to Section 13, 14 or 15(d) for a period of at least twelve calendar months immediately preceding the filing of the registration statement on this Form; and

(b)   has filed in a timely manner all reports required to be filed during the twelve calendar months and any portion of a month immediately preceding the filing of the registration statement, other than a report that is required solely pursuant to Item 1.01, 1.02, 1.04, 2.03, 2.04, 2.05, 2.06, 4.02(a) or 5.02(e) of Form 8–K (§ 249.308 of this chapter). If the registrant has used (during the twelve calendar months and any portion of a month immediately preceding the filing of the registration statement) Rule 12b–25(b) (§ 240.12b–25(b) of this chapter) under the Exchange Act with respect to a report or a portion of a report, that report or portion thereof has actually been filed within the time period prescribed by that rule.

4.   Neither the registrant nor any of its consolidated or unconsolidated subsidiaries have, since the end of the last fiscal year for which certified financial statements of the registrant and its consolidated subsidiaries were included in a report filed pursuant to Section 13(a) or 15(d) of the Exchange Act: (a) failed to pay any dividend or sinking fund installment on preferred stock; or (b) defaulted (i) on any installment or installments on indebtedness for borrowed money, or (ii) on any rental on one or more long term leases, which defaults in the aggregate are material to the financial position of the registrant and its consolidated and unconsolidated subsidiaries, taken as a whole.

* * *

B.   **Transaction Requirements.** Security offerings meeting any of the following conditions and made by a registrant meeting the Registrant Requirements specified in I.A. above may be registered on this Form:

1.   *Primary Offerings by Certain Registrants.* Securities to be offered for cash by or on behalf of a registrant, or outstanding securities to be offered for cash for the account of any person other than the registrant, including securities acquired by standby underwriters in connection with the call or redemption by the registrant of warrants or a class of convertible securities; *provided* that the aggregate market value of the voting and non-voting common equity held by non-affiliates of the registrant is $75 million or more.

Instruction. For the purposes of this Form, "common equity" is as defined in Securities Act Rule 405 (§ 230.405 of this chapter). The aggregate market value of the registrant's outstanding voting and non-voting common equity shall be computed by use of the price at which the common equity was last sold, or the average of the bid and asked prices of such common equity, in the principal market for such common equity as of a date within 60 days prior to the date of filing. *See* the definition of "affiliate" in Securities Act Rule 405., as of a date within 60 days prior to the date of filing. *See* the definition of "affiliate" in Securities Act Rule 405 (§ 230.405 of this chapter).

2.   *Primary Offerings of Non-Convertible Securities Other than Common Equity.* Non-convertible securities, other than common equity, to be offered for cash by or on behalf of a registrant, provided the registrant:

FORM S-3

(i) has issued (as of a date within 60 days prior to the filing of the registration statement) at least $1 billion in non-convertible securities, other than common equity, in primary offerings for cash, not exchange, registered under the Securities Act, over the prior three years; or

(ii) has outstanding (as of a date within 60 days prior to the filing of the registration statement) at least $750 million of non-convertible securities, other than common equity, issued in primary offerings for cash, not exchange, registered under the Securities Act; or

(iii) is a wholly-owned subsidiary of a well-known seasoned issuer (as defined in 17 CFR 230.405); or

(iv) is a majority-owned operating partnership of a real estate investment trust that qualifies as a well-known seasoned issuer (as defined in 17 CFR 230.405).

Instruction. For purposes of Instruction I.B.2(i) above, an insurance company, as defined in Section 2(a)(13) of the Securities Act, when using this Form to register offerings of securities subject to regulation under the insurance laws of any State or Territory of the United States or the District of Columbia ("insurance contracts"), may include purchase payments or premium payments for insurance contracts, including purchase payments or premium payments for variable insurance contracts (not including purchase payments or premium payments initially allocated to investment options that are not registered under the Securities Act), issued in offerings registered under the Securities Act over the prior three years. For purposes of Instruction I.B.2(ii) above, an insurance company, as defined in Section 2(a)(13) of the Securities Act, when using this Form to register offerings of insurance contracts, may include the contract value, as of the measurement date, of any outstanding insurance contracts, including variable insurance contracts (not including the value allocated as of the measurement date to investment options that are not registered under the Securities Act), issued in offerings registered under the Securities Act.

3. *Transactions Involving Secondary Offerings.* Outstanding securities to be offered for the account of any person other than the issuer, including securities acquired by standby underwriters in connection with the call or redemption by the issuer of warrants or a class of convertible securities, if securities of the same class are listed and registered on a national securities exchange or are quoted on the automated quotation system of a national securities association. (In addition, attention is directed to General Instruction C to Form S-8 (§ 239.16b) for the registration of employee benefit plan securities for resale.)

* * *

PART I

INFORMATION REQUIRED IN PROSPECTUS

Item 1. Forepart of the Registration Statement and Outside Front Cover Pages of Prospectus.

Set forth in the forepart of the registration statement and on the outside front cover page of the prospectus the information required by Item 501 of Regulation S–K (§ 229.501 of this chapter).

Item 2. Inside Front and Outside Back Cover Pages of Prospectus.

Set forth on the inside front cover page of the prospectus or, where permitted, on the outside back cover page, the information required by Item 502 of Regulation S–K (§ 229.502 of this chapter).

Item 3. Summary Information, Risk Factors and Ratio of Earnings to Fixed Charges.

Furnish the information required by Items 105 and 503 of Regulation S–K (§ 229.105 and § 229.503 of this chapter).

FORM S-3

Item 4.   Use of Proceeds.

Furnish the information required by Items 105 and 503 of Regulation S–K (§ 229.105 and § 229.503 of this chapter).

Item 5.   Determination of Offering Price.

Furnish the information required by Item 505 of Regulation S–K (§ 229.505 of this chapter).

Item 6.   Dilution.

Furnish the information required by Item 506 of Regulation S–K (§ 229.506 of this chapter).

Item 7.   Selling Security Holders.

Furnish the information required by Item 507 of Regulation S–K (§ 229.507 of this chapter).

Item 8.   Plan of Distribution.

Furnish the information required by Item 508 of Regulation S–K (§ 229.508 of this chapter).

Item 9.   Description of Securities to be Registered.

Furnish the information required by Item 202 of Regulation S–K (§ 229.202 of this chapter), unless capital stock is to be registered and securities of the same class are registered pursuant to Section 12 of the Exchange Act.

Item 10. Interests of Named Experts and Counsel.

Furnish the information required by Item 509 of Regulation S–K (§ 229.509 of this chapter).

Item 11. Material Changes.

(a)   Describe any and all material changes in the registrant's affairs which have occurred since the end of the latest fiscal year for which certified financial statements were included in the latest annual report to security holders and which have not been described in a report on Form 10-Q (§ 249.308a of this chapter) or Form 8-K (§ 249.308 of this chapter) filed under the Exchange Act.

(b)   Include in the prospectus, if not incorporated by reference therein from the reports filed under the Exchange Act specified in Item 12(a), a proxy or information statement filed pursuant to Section 14 of the Exchange Act, a prospectus previously filed pursuant to Rule 424(b) or (c) under the Securities Act (§ 230.424(b) or (c) of this chapter) or, where no prospectus is required to be filed pursuant to Rule 424(b), the prospectus included in the registration statement at effectiveness, or a Form 8-K filed during either of the two preceding years: (i) information required by Rule 3–05 and Article 11 of Regulation S-X (17 CFR Part 210); (ii) restated financial statements prepared in accordance with Regulation S-X if there has been a change in accounting principles or a correction in an error where such change or correction requires a material retroactive restatement of financial statements; (iii) restated financial statements prepared in accordance with Regulation S-X where a combination of entities under common control has been consummated subsequent to the most recent fiscal year and the transferred businesses, considered in the aggregate, are significant pursuant to Rule 11–01(b), or (iv) any financial information required because of a material disposition of assets outside the normal course of business.

Item 12. Incorporation of Certain Information by Reference.

(a)   The documents listed in (1) and (2) below shall be specifically incorporated by reference into the prospectus by means of a statement to that effect in the prospectus listing all such documents:

(1)   the registrant's latest annual report on Form 10-K (17 CFR 249.310) filed pursuant to Section 13(a) or 15(d) of the Exchange Act that contains financial statements for the registrant's latest fiscal year for which a Form 10-K was required to be filed; and

(2)   all other reports filed pursuant to Section 13(a) or 15(d) of the Exchange Act since the end of the fiscal year covered by the annual report referred to in (1) above; and

FORM S-3

(3)   if capital stock is to be registered and securities of the same class are registered under Section 12 of the Exchange Act, the description of such class of securities which is contained in a registration statement filed under the Exchange Act, including any amendment or reports filed for the purpose of updating such description.

(b)   The prospectus shall also state that all documents subsequently filed by the registrant pursuant to Sections 13(a), 13(c), 14 or 15(d) of the Exchange Act, prior to the termination of the offering shall be deemed to be incorporated by reference into the prospectus. *Instruction.* Attention is directed to Rule 439 (§ 230.439 of this chapter) regarding consent to use of material incorporated by reference.

(c)   (1) You must state

(i)   that you will provide to each person, including any beneficial owner, to whom a prospectus is delivered, a copy of any or all of the information that has been incorporated by reference in the prospectus but not delivered with the prospectus;

(ii)   that you will provide this information upon written or oral request;

(iii)   that you will provide this information at no cost to the requester; and

(iv)   the name, address, and telephone number to which the request for this information must be made.

Note to Item 12(c)(1). If you send any of the information that is incorporated by reference in the prospectus to security holders, you also must send any exhibits that are specifically incorporated by reference in that information.

(2)   You must

(i)   identify the reports and other information that you file with the SEC; and

(ii)   state that the SEC maintains an Internet site that contains reports, proxy and information statements, and other information regarding issuers that file electronically with the SEC and state the address of that site (http://www.sec.gov). Disclose your Internet address, if available.

(d)   Any information required in the prospectus in response to Item 3 through Item 11 of this Form may be included in the prospectus through documents filed pursuant to Section 13(a), 14, or 15(d) of the Exchange Act that are incorporated or deemed incorporated by reference into the prospectus that is part of the registration statement. Notwithstanding the foregoing, in the financial statements, incorporating by reference or cross-referencing to information outside of the financial statements is not permitted unless otherwise specifically permitted or required by the Commission's rules or by U.S. Generally Accepted Accounting Principles or International Financial Reporting Standards as issued by the International Accounting Standards Board, whichever is applicable.

Item 13. Disclosure of Commission Position on Indemnification for Securities Act Liabilities.

Furnish the information required by Item 510 of Regulation S–K (§ 229.510 of this chapter).

PART II

INFORMATION NOT REQUIRED IN PROSPECTUS

Item 14. Other Expenses of Issuance and Distribution.

Furnish the information required by Item 511 of Regulation S–K (§ 229.511 of this chapter).

Item 15. Indemnification of Directors and Officers.

Furnish the information required by Item 702 of Regulation S–K (§ 229.702 of this chapter).

FORM S-4

Item 16. Exhibits.

Subject to the rules regarding incorporation by reference, furnish the exhibits required by Item 601 of Regulation S–K (§ 229.601 of this chapter).

Item 17. Undertakings.

Furnish the undertakings required by Item 512 of Regulation S–K (§ 229.512 of this chapter).

* * *

FORM S-4

REGISTRATION STATEMENT UNDER THE SECURITIES ACT OF 1933

* * *

GENERAL INSTRUCTIONS

A. Rule as to Use of Form S-4.

1. This Form may be used for registration under the Securities Act of 1933 ("Securities Act") of securities to be issued (1) in a transaction of the type specified in paragraph (a) of Rule 145 (§ 230.145 of this chapter); (2) in a merger in which the applicable state law would not require the solicitation of the votes or consents of all of the security holders of the company being acquired; (3) in an exchange offer for securities of the issuer or another entity; (4) in a public reoffering or resale of any such securities acquired pursuant to this registration statement; or (5) in more than one of the kinds of transaction listed in (1) through (4) registered on one registration statement.

* * *

E. Compliance with Exchange Act Rules.

1. If a corporation or other person submits a proposal to its security holders entitled to vote on, or consent to, the transaction in which the securities being registered are to be issued, and such person's submission to its security holders is subject to Regulation 14A (§§ 240.14a–1) through 14b–1 of this chapter) or 14C (§§ 240.14c–1 through 14c–101 of this chapter) under the Exchange Act, then the provisions of such Regulations shall apply in all respects to such person's submission, except that (a) the prospectus may be in the form of a proxy or information statement and may contain the information required by this Form in lieu of that required by Schedule 14A (§ 240.14a–101) or 14C (§ 240.14c–101) of Regulation 14A or 14C under the Exchange Act; and (b) copies of the preliminary and definitive proxy or information statement, form of proxy or other material filed as a part of the registration statement shall be deemed filed pursuant to such person's obligations under such Regulations.

2. If the proxy or information material sent to security holders is not subject to Regulation 14A or 14C, all such material shall be filed as a part of the registration statement at the time the statement is filed or as an amendment thereto prior to the use of such material.

3. If the transaction in which the securities being registered are to be issued is subject to Section 13(e), 14(d) or 14(e) of the Exchange Act, the provisions of those sections and the rules and regulations thereunder shall apply to the transaction in addition to the provisions of this Form.

* * *

FORM S-4

PART I

INFORMATION REQUIRED IN THE PROSPECTUS

A. Information About the Transaction

Item 1. Forepart of Registration Statement and Outside Front Cover Page of Prospectus.

Set forth in the forepart of the registration statement and on the outside front cover page of the prospectus the information required by Item 501 of Regulation S–K (§ 229.501 of this chapter).

Item 2. Inside Front and Outside Back Cover Pages of Prospectus.

Provide the information required by Item 502 of Regulation S–K. In addition, on the inside front cover page, you must state

(1) that the prospectus incorporates important business and financial information about the company that is not included in or delivered with the document; and

(2) that this information is available without charge to security holders upon written or oral request. Give the name, address, and telephone number to which security holders must make this request. In addition, you must state that to obtain timely delivery, security holders must request the information no later than five business days before the date they must make their investment decision. Specify the date by which security holders must request this information. You must highlight this statement by print type or otherwise.

Note to Item 2. If you send any of the information that is incorporated by reference in the prospectus to security holders, you also must send any exhibits that are specifically incorporated by reference in that information.

Item 3. Risk Factors, Ratio of Earnings to Fixed Charges and Other Information.

Provide in the forepart of the prospectus a summary containing the information required by Items 105 and 503 of Regulation S–K (§ 229.105 and § 229.503 of this chapter) and the following:

(a) The name, complete mailing address (including the Zip Code), and telephone number (including the area code) of the principal executive offices of the registrant and the company being acquired;

(b) A brief description of the general nature of the business conducted by the registrant and by the company being acquired;

(c) A brief description of the transaction in which the securities being registered are to be offered;

(d) The information required by Item 301 of Regulation S–K (§ 229.301 of this chapter) (selected financial data) for (i) the registrant; (ii) the company being acquired; and (iii) if material, the registrant, on a pro forma basis, giving effect to the transaction. To the extent the information is required to be presented in the prospectus pursuant to Items 12, 14, 16 or 17, it need not be repeated pursuant to this Item;

(e) If material, the information required by Item 301 of Regulation S–K for the registrant on a pro forma basis, giving effect to the transaction. To the extent the information is required to be presented in the prospectus pursuant to Items 12 or 14, it need not be repeated pursuant to this Item.

(f) In comparative columnar form, historical and pro forma per share data of the registrant and historical and equivalent pro forma per share data of the company being acquired for the following items:

(1) book value per share as of the date financial data is presented pursuant to Item 301 of Regulation S–K (§ 229.301 of this chapter) (selected financial data);

(2)   Cash dividends declared per share for the periods for which financial data is presented pursuant to Item 301 of Regulation S–K (§ 229.301 of this chapter) (selected financial data);

(3)   income (loss) per share from continuing operations for the periods for which financial data is presented pursuant to Item 301 of Regulation S–K (§ 229.301 of this chapter) (selected financial data).

Instruction to paragraph (e) and (f).

For a business combination accounted for as a purchase, the financial information required by paragraphs (e) and (f) shall be presented only for the most recent fiscal year and interim period. For a business combination accounted for as a pooling, the financial information required by paragraphs (e) and (f) (except for information with regard to book value) shall be presented for the most recent three fiscal years and interim period. For a business combination accounted for as a pooling, information with regard to book value shall be presented as of the end of the most recent fiscal year and interim period. Equivalent pro forma per share amounts shall be calculated by multiplying the pro forma income (loss) per share before nonrecurring charges or credits directly attributable to the transaction, pro forma book value per share, and the pro forma dividends per share of the registrant by the exchange ratio so that the per share amounts are equated to the respective values for one share of the company being acquired.

(g)   In comparative columnar form, the market value of securities of the company being acquired (on an historical and equivalent per share basis) and the market value of the securities of the registrant (on an historical basis) as of the date preceding public announcement of the proposed transaction, or, if no such public announcement was made, as of the day preceding the day the agreement with respect to the transaction was entered into;

(h)   With respect to the registrant and the company being acquired, a brief statement comparing the percentage of outstanding shares entitled to vote held by directors, executive officers and their affiliates and the vote required for approval of the proposed transaction;

(i)   A statement as to whether any federal or state regulatory requirements must be complied with or approval must be obtained in connection with the transaction, and if so, the status of such compliance or approval;

(j)   A statement about whether or not dissenters' rights of appraisal exist, including a cross-reference to the information provided pursuant to Item 18 or 19 of this Form; and

(k)   A brief statement about the tax consequences of the transaction, or if appropriate, consisting of a cross-reference to the information provided pursuant to Item 4 of this Form.

Item 4.   Terms of the Transaction.

(a)   Furnish a summary of the material features of the proposed transaction. The summary shall include, where applicable:

(1)   A brief summary of the terms of the acquisition agreement;

(2)   The reasons of the registrant and of the company being acquired for engaging in the transaction;

(3)   The information required by Item 202 of Regulation S–K (§ 229.202 of this chapter), description of registrant's securities, unless: (i) the registrant would meet the requirements for use of Form S-3, (ii) capital stock is to be registered and (iii) securities of the same class are registered under Section 12 of the Exchange Act and (i) listed for trading or admitted to unlisted trading privileges on a national securities exchange; or (ii) are securities for which bid and offer quotations are reported in an automated quotations system operated by a national securities association;

(4)   An explanation of any material differences between the rights of security holders of the company being acquired and the rights of holders of the securities being offered;

(5) A brief statement as to the accounting treatment the transaction; and

(6) The federal income tax consequences of the transaction.

(b) If a report, opinion or appraisal materially relating to the transaction has been received from an outside party, and such report, opinion or appraisal is referred to in the prospectus, furnish the same information as would be required by Item 1015(b) of Regulation M–A (229.1015(b) of this chapter).

(c) Incorporate the acquisition agreement by reference into the prospectus by means of a statement to that effect.

Item 5. Pro Forma Financial Information.

Furnish financial information required by Article 11 of Regulation S–X (§ 210.11–01 et. sq. of this chapter) with respect to this transaction. A smaller reporting company may provide the information in Rule 8–05 of Regulation S–X (§ 210.8–05 of this chapter) in lieu of the financial information required by Article 11 of Regulation S–X.

* * *

Item 6. Material Contracts with the Company Being Acquired.

Describe any past, present or proposed material contracts, arrangements, understandings, relationships, negotiations or transactions during the periods for which financial statements are presented or incorporated by reference pursuant to Part I.B. or C. of this Form between the company being acquired or its affiliates and the registrant or its affiliates, such as those concerning: a merger, consolidation or acquisition; a tender offer or other acquisition of securities; an election of directors; or a sale or other transfer of a material amount of assets.

Item 7. Additional Information Required for Reoffering by Persons and Parties Deemed to Be Underwriters.

If any of the securities are to be reoffered to the public by any person or party who is deemed to be an underwriter thereof, furnish the following information in the prospectus, at the time it is being used for the reoffer of the securities to the extent it is not already furnished therein:

(a) The information required by Item 507 of Regulation S–K (§ 229.507 of this chapter), selling security holders; and

(b) Information with respect to the consummation of the transaction pursuant to which the securities were acquired and any material change in the registrant's affairs subsequent to the transaction.

Item 8. Interests of Named Experts and Counsel.

Furnish the information required by Item 509 of Regulation S–K (§ 229.509 of this chapter).

Item 9. Disclosure of Commission Position on Indemnification for Securities Act Liabilities.

Furnish the information required by Item 510 of Regulation S–K (§ 229.510 of this chapter).

B. Information About the Registrant

Item 10. Information with Respect to S-3 Registrants.

If the registrant meets the requirements for use of Form S-3 and elects to furnish information in accordance with the provisions of this Item, furnish information as required below:

(a) Describe any and all material changes in the registrant's affairs that have occurred since the end of the latest fiscal year for which audited financial statements were included in the latest annual report to security holders and that have not been described in a report on Form 10-Q (§ 249.308a of this chapter) or Form 8-K (§ 249.308 of this chapter) filed under the Exchange Act.

FORM S-4

* * *

Item 11. Incorporation of Certain Information by Reference.

If the registrant meets the requirements of Form S-3 and elects to furnish information in accordance with the provisions of Item 10 of this Form:

(a)   Incorporate by reference into the prospectus, by means of a statement to that effect listing all documents so incorporated, the documents listed in paragraphs (1), (2) and, if applicable, (3) below.

(1)   The registrant's latest annual report on Form 10-K (§ 249.310 of this chapter) filed pursuant to Section 13(a) or 15(d) of the Exchange Act which contains financial statements for the registrant's latest fiscal year for which a Form 10-K was required to be filed;

(2)   All other reports filed pursuant to Section 13(a) or 15(d) of the Exchange Act since the end of the fiscal year covered by the annual report referred to in Item 11(a)(1) of this Form; and

(3)   If capital stock is to be registered and securities of the same class are registered under Section 12 of the Exchange Act and: (i) listed for trading or admitted to unlisted trading privileges on a national securities exchange; or (ii) are securities for which bid and offer quotations are reported in an automated quotations system operated by a national securities association, the description of such class of securities which is contained in a registration statement filed under the Exchange Act, including any amendment or reports filed for the purpose of updating such description.

(b)   The prospectus also shall state that all documents subsequently filed by the registrant pursuant to Sections 13(a), 13(c), 14 or 15(d) of the Exchange Act, prior to one of the following dates, whichever is applicable, shall be deemed to be incorporated by reference into the prospectus:

(1)   If a meeting of security holders is to be held, the date on which such meeting is held;

(2)   If a meeting of security holders is not to be held, the date on which the transaction is consummated;

(3)   If securities of the registrant are being offered in exchange for securities of any other issuer, the date the offering is terminated; or

(4)   If securities are being offered in a reoffering or resale of securities acquired pursuant to this registration statement, the date the reoffering is terminated.

(c)   You must

(1)   identify the reports and other information that you file with the SEC; and

(2)   State that the SEC maintains an Internet site that contains reports, proxy and information statements, and other information regarding issuers that file electronically with the SEC and state the address of that site (http://www.sec.gov). Disclose your Internet address, if available.

Instruction. Attention is directed to Rule 439 (§ 230.439 of this chapter) regarding consent to the use of material incorporated by reference.

Item 12. Information with Respect to S-3 Registrants.

If the registrant meets the requirements for use of Form S-3 and elects to comply with this Item, furnish the information required by either paragraph (a) or paragraph (b) of this Item. The information required by paragraph (b) shall be furnished if the registrant satisfies the conditions of paragraph (c) of this Item.

(a)   If the registrant elects to deliver this prospectus together with a copy of either its latest Form 10-K filed pursuant to Sections 13(a) or 15(d) of the Exchange Act or its latest annual report to security holders, which at the time of original preparation met the requirements of either Rule 14a–3 or Rule 14c–3:

1609

FORM S-4

(1)   Indicate that the prospectus is accompanied by either a copy of the registrant's latest Form 10-K or a copy of its latest annual report to security holders, whichever the registrant elects to deliver pursuant to paragraph (a) of this Item.

(2)   Provide financial and other information with respect to the registrant in the form required by Part I of Form 10-Q as of the end of the most recent fiscal quarter which ended after the end of the latest fiscal year for which certified financial statements were included in the latest Form 10-K or the latest report to security holders (whichever the registrant elects to deliver pursuant to paragraph (a) of this Item), and more than forty-five days prior to the effective date of this registration statement (or as of a more recent date) by one of the following means:

(i)   including such information in the prospectus;

(ii)   providing without charge to each person to whom a prospectus is delivered a copy of the registrant's latest Form 10-Q; or

(iii)   providing without charge to each person to whom a prospectus is delivered a copy of the registrant's latest quarterly report that was delivered to its security holders and which included the required financial information.

(3)   If not reflected in the registrant's latest Form 10-K or its latest annual report to security holders (whichever the registrant elects to deliver pursuant to paragraph (a) of this Item) provide information required by Rule 3–05 (§ 210.3–05 of this chapter) and Article 11 (§ 210.11–01 through § 210.11[–]03 of this chapter) of Regulation S–X. Smaller reporting companies may provide the information required by Rule 8–04 and 8–05 of Regulation S–X.

(4)   Describe any and all material changes in the registrant's affairs which have occurred since the end of the latest fiscal year for which audited financial statements were included in the latest Form 10-K or the latest annual report to security holders (whichever the registrant elects to deliver pursuant to paragraph (a) of this Item) and that were not described in a Form 10-Q or quarterly report delivered with the prospectus in accordance with paragraphs (a)(2)(ii) or (iii) of this Item.

Instruction. Where the registrant elects to deliver the documents identified in paragraph (a) with a preliminary prospectus, such documents need not be redelivered with the final prospectus.

(b)   If the registrant does not elect to deliver its latest Form 10-K or its latest annual report to security holders:

(1)   Furnish a brief description of the business done by the registrant and its subsidiaries during the most recent fiscal year as required by Rule 14a–3 to be included in an annual report to security holders. The description also should take into account changes in the registrant's business that have occurred between the end of the latest fiscal year and the effective date of the registration statement.

(2)   Include financial statements and information as required by Rule 14a–3(b)(1) (240.14a–3(b)(1) of this chapter) to be included in an annual report to security holders. In addition, provide:

[(i)]   the interim financial information required by Rule 10–01 of Regulation S–X (§ 210.10–01 of this chapter) for a filing on Form 10-Q;

(ii)   financial information required by Rule 3–05 and Article 11 of Regulation S–X with respect to transactions other than that pursuant to which the securities being registered are to be issued;

(iii)   restated financial statements prepared in accordance with Regulation S–X if there has been a change in accounting principles or a correction of an error where such change or correction requires a material retroactive restatement of financial statements;

(iv)   Restated financial statements prepared in accordance with Regulation S–X where one or more business combinations accounted for by the pooling of interest method of accounting have been consummated subsequent to the most recent fiscal year and the acquired businesses, considered in the aggregate, are significant pursuant to Rule 11–01(b) of Regulation S–X; and

    (v)   Any financial information required because of a material disposition of assets outside of the normal course of business;

    (3)   Furnish the information required by the following:

    (i)   Item 101(b), (c)(1)(i) and (d) of Regulation S–K (§ 229.101 of this chapter), industry segments, classes of similar products or services, foreign and domestic operations and export sales;

    (ii)   where common equity securities are being offered, Item 201 of Regulation S–K (§ 229.201 of this chapter), market price of and dividends on the registrant's common equity and related stockholder matters;

    (iii)   Item 301 of Regulation S–K (§ 229.301 of this chapter), selected financial data;

    (iv)   Item 302 of Regulation S–K (§ 229.302 of this chapter), supplementary financial information;

    (v)   Item 303 of Regulation S–K (§ 229.303 of this chapter), management's discussion and analysis of financial condition and results of operations;

    (vi)   Item 304 of Regulation S–K (§ 229.304 of this chapter), changes in and disagreements with accountants on accounting and financial disclosure; and

    (vii) Item 305 of Regulation S–K (§ 229.305 of this chapter), quantitative and qualitative disclosures about market risk.

(c)   The registrant shall furnish the information required by paragraph (b) of this Item if;

    (1)   the registrant was required to make a material retroactive restatement of financial statements because of

    (i)   a change in accounting principles; or

    (ii)   a correction of an error; or

    (iii)   a combination under common control was effected subsequent to the most recent fiscal year and the acquired businesses considered in the aggregate meet the test of a significant subsidiary; OR

    (2)   the registrant engaged in a material disposition of assets outside the normal course of business; AND

    (3)   such restatement of financial statements or disposition of assets was not reflected in the registrant's latest annual report to security holders and/or its latest Form 10-K filed pursuant to Sections 13(a) or 15(d) of the Exchange Act.

Item 13. Incorporation of Certain Information by Reference.

If the registrant meets the requirements of Form S-3 and elects to furnish information in accordance with the provisions of Item 12 of this Form:

(a)   Incorporate by reference into the prospectus, means of a statement to that effect in the prospectus listing all documents so incorporated, the documents listed in paragraphs (1) and (2) of this Item and, if applicable, the portions of the documents listed in paragraphs (3) and (4) thereof.

    (1)   The registrant's latest annual report on Form 10-K filed pursuant to Section 13(a) or 15(d) of the Exchange Act which contains audited financial statements for the registrant's latest fiscal year for which a Form 10-K was required to be filed.

FORM S-4

(2)   All other reports filed pursuant to Section 13(a) or 15(d) of the Exchange Act since the end of the fiscal year covered by the annual report referred to in paragraph (a)(1) of this Item.

(3)   If the registrant elects to deliver its latest annual report to security holders pursuant to Item 12 of this Form, the information furnished in accordance with the following:

(i)   Item 101(b), (c)(1)(i) and (d) of Regulation S–K, segments, classes of similar products or services, foreign and domestic operations and export sales;

(ii)   Where common equity securities are being issued, Item 201 of Regulation S–K, market price of and dividends on the registrant's common equity and related stockholder matters;

(iii)   Item 301 of Regulation S–K, selected financial data;

(iv)   Item 302 of Regulation S–K, supplementary financial information;

(v)   Item 303 of Regulation S–K, management's discussion and analysis of financial condition and results of operations;

(vi)   Item 304 of Regulation S–K, changes in and disagreements with accountants on accounting and financial disclosure; and

(vii) Item 305 of Regulation S–K (§ 229.305 of this chapter) quantitative and qualitative disclosures about market risk.

(4)   If the registrant elects, pursuant to Item 12(a)(2)(iii) of this Form, to provide a copy of its latest quarterly report which was delivered to security holders, financial information equivalent to that required to be presented in Part I of Form 10-Q.

Instruction. Attention is directed to Rule 439 regarding consent to the use of material incorporated by reference.

(b)   The registrant also may state, if it so chooses, that specifically described portions of its annual or quarterly report to security holders, other than those portions required to be incorporated by reference pursuant to paragraphs (a)(3) and (4) of this Item, are not part of the registration statement. In such case, the description of portions that are not incorporated by reference or that are excluded shall be made with clarity and in reasonable detail.

(c)   *Electronic filings.* Electronic filers electing to deliver and incorporate by reference all, or any portion, of the quarterly or annual report to security holders pursuant to this Item shall file as an exhibit such quarterly or annual report to security holders, or such portion thereof that is incorporated by reference, in electronic format.

(d)   You must

(1)   identify the reports and other information that you file with the SEC; and

(2)   State that the SEC maintains an Internet site that contains reports, proxy and information statements, and other information regarding issuers that file electronically with the SEC and state the address of that site (http://www.sec.gov). Disclose your Internet address, if available.

Item 14. Information with Respect to Registrants Other Than S-3 Registrants.

If the registrant does not meet the requirements for use of Form or S-3, or otherwise elects to comply with this Item in lieu of Item 10 or 12, furnish the information required by:

(a)   Item 101 of Regulation S–K, description of business;

(b)   Item 102 of Regulation S–K, description of property;

(c)   Item 103 of Regulation S–K, legal proceedings;

FORM S-4

(d)   Where common equity securities are being issued, Item 201 of Regulation S–K, market price of and dividends on the registrant's common equity and related stockholder matters;

(e)   Financial statements meeting the requirements of Regulation S–X, (schedules required by Regulation S–X shall be filed as "Financial Statement Schedules" pursuant to Item 21 of this Form), as well as financial information required by Rule 3–05 and Article 11 of Regulation S–X with respect to transactions other than that pursuant to which the securities being registered are to be issued.

(f)   Item 301 of Regulation S–K, selected financial data;

(g)   Item 302 of Regulation S–K, supplementary financial information;

(h)   Item 303 of Regulation S–K, management's discussion and analysis of financial condition and results of operations;

(i)   Item 304 of Regulation S–K, changes in and disagreements with accountants on accounting and financial disclosure; and

(j)   Item 305 of Regulation S–K (§ 229.305 of this chapter), quantitative and qualitative disclosures about market risk.

C.   Information About the Company Being Acquired

Item 15. Information with Respect to S-3 Companies.

If the company being acquired meets the requirements for use of Form S-3 and compliance with this Item is elected, furnish the information that would be required by Items 10 and 11 of this Form if securities of such company were being registered.

Item 16. Information with Respect to S-3 Companies.

(a)   If the company being acquired meets the requirements for use of Form S-3 and elects to comply with this Item, furnish the information that would be required by Items 12 and 13 of this Form if securities of such company were being registered.

(b)   *Electronic filings.* In addition to satisfying the requirements of paragraph (a) of this Item, electronic filers that elect to deliver and incorporate by reference all, or any portion, of the quarterly or annual report to security holders of a company being acquired pursuant to this Item shall file as an exhibit such quarterly or annual report to security holders, or such portion thereof that is incorporated by reference, in electronic format.

Item 17. Information with Respect to Companies Other Than S-3 Companies.

If the company being acquired does not meet the requirements for use of Form S-3, or compliance with this Item is otherwise elected in lieu of Item 15 or 16, furnish the information required by paragraph (a) or (b) of this Item, whichever is applicable.

(a)   If the company being acquired is subject to the reporting requirements of Section 13(a) or 15(d) of the Exchange Act, or compliance with this subparagraph in lieu of subparagraph (b) of this Item is selected, furnish the information that would be required by Item 14 of this Form if the securities of such company were being registered; *however*, only those schedules required by Rules 12–15, 28 and 29 of Regulation S–X (§ 210.12–15, 28, 29 of this chapter) need be provided with respect to the company being acquired.

(b)   If the company being acquired is not subject to the reporting requirements of either Section 13(a) or 15(d) of the Exchange Act; or, because of Section 12(i) of the Exchange Act, has not furnished an annual report to security holders pursuant to Rule 14a–3 (§ 240.14a–3 of this chapter) or Rule 14c–3 (§ 240.14c–3 of this chapter) for its latest fiscal year; furnish the information that would be required by the following if securities of such company were being registered:

(1)   a brief description of the business done by the company which indicates the general nature and scope of the business;

(2)   Item 201 of Regulation S–K, market price of and dividends on the registrant's common equity and related stockholder matters;

(3)   Item 301 of Regulation S–K, selected financial data;

(4)   Item 302 of Regulation S–K, supplementary financial information;

(5)   Item 303 of Regulation S–K, management's discussion and analysis of financial condition and results of operations;

(6)   Item 304(b) of Regulation S–K (§ 229.304 of this chapter), changes in and disagreements with accountants on accounting and financial disclosure;

(7)   Financial statements that would be required in an annual report sent to security holders under Rules 14a–3(b)(1) and (b)(2) (§ 240.14b–3 of this chapter), if an annual report was required. If the registrant's security holders are not voting, the transaction is not a roll-up transaction (as described by Item 901 of Regulation S–K (§ 229.901 of this chapter)), and:

(i)   the company being acquired is significant to the registrant in excess of the 20% level as determined under § 210.3–05(b)(2), provide financial statements of the company being acquired for the latest fiscal year in conformity with GAAP. In addition, if the company being acquired has provided its security holders with financial statements prepared in conformity with GAAP for either or both of the two fiscal years before the latest fiscal year, provide the financial statements for those years; or

(ii)   the company being acquired is significant to the registrant at or below the 20% level, no financial information (including pro forma and comparative per share information) for the company being acquired need be provided.

Instructions:

1.   The financial statements required by this paragraph for the latest fiscal year need be audited only to the extent practicable. The financial statements for the fiscal years before the latest fiscal year need not be audited if they were not previously audited.

2.   If the financial statements required by this paragraph are prepared on the basis of a comprehensive body of accounting principles other than U.S. GAAP, provide a reconciliation to U.S. GAAP in accordance with Item 17 of Form 20-F (§ 249.220f of this chapter) unless a reconciliation is unavailable or not obtainable without unreasonable cost or expense. At a minimum, provide a narrative description of all material variations in accounting principles, practices and methods used in preparing the non-U.S. GAAP financial statements from those accepted in the U.S. when the financial statements are prepared on a basis other than U.S. GAAP.

3.   If this Form is used to register resales to the public by any person who is deemed an underwriter within the meaning of Rule 145(c) (§ 230.145(c) of this chapter) with respect to the securities being reoffered, the financial statements must be audited for the fiscal years required to be presented under paragraph (b)(2) of Rule 3–05 of Regulation S–X (17 CFR 210.3–05(b)(2)).

4.   In determining the significance of an acquisition for purposes of this paragraph, apply the tests prescribed in Rule 1–02(w) (§ 210.1–02(w) of this chapter).

(8)   the quarterly financial and other information as would have been required had the company being acquired been required to file Part I of Form 10-Q (§ 249.308a) for the most recent quarter for which such a report would have been on file at the time the registration statement becomes effective or for a period ending as of a more recent date.

(9)   schedules required by Rules 12–15, 28 and 29 of Regulation S–X.

(10) Item 305 of Regulation S–K (§ 229.305 of this chapter), quantitative and qualitative disclosures about market risk.

D.   Voting and Management Information

Item 18. Information if Proxies, Consents or Authorizations are to be Solicited.

(a)   If proxies, consents or authorizations are to be solicited, furnish the following information, except as provided by paragraph (b) of this Item:

(1)   The information required by Item 1 of Schedule 14A, date, time and place information;

(2)   The information required by Item 2 of Schedule 14A, revocability of proxy;

(3)   The information required by Item 3 of Schedule 14A, dissenters' rights of appraisal;

(4)   The information required by Item 4 of Schedule 14A, persons making the solicitation;

(5)   With respect to both the registrant and the company being acquired, the information required by:

(i)   Item 5 of Schedule 14A, interest of certain persons in matters to be acted upon; and

(ii)   Item 6 of Schedule 14A, voting securities and principal holders thereof;

(6)   The information required by Item 21 of Schedule 14A, vote required for approval; and

(7)   With respect to each person who will serve as a director or an executive officer of the surviving or acquiring company, the information required by:

(i)   Item 401 of Regulation S–K (§ 229.401 of this chapter), directors and executive officers;

(ii)   Item 402 of Regulation S–K (§ 229.402 of this chapter), executive compensation, and paragraph (e)(4) of Item 407 of Regulation S–K (§ 229.407(e)(4) of this chapter), corporate governance;

(iii)   Item 404 of Regulation S–K (§ 229.404 of this chapter), transactions with related persons, promoters and certain control persons, and Item 407(a) of Regulation S–K (§ 229.407(a) of this chapter), corporate governance.

(b)   If the registrant or the company being acquired meets the requirements for use of Form S-3, any information required by paragraphs (a)(5)(ii) and (7) of this Item with respect to such company may be incorporated by reference from its latest annual report on Form 10-K.

Item 19. Information if Proxies, Consents or Authorizations are not to be Solicited or in an Exchange Offer.

(a)   If the transaction is an exchange offer or if proxies, consents or authorizations are not to be solicited, furnish, where applicable, the following information, except as provided by paragraph (c) of this item;

(1)   The information required by Item 2 of Schedule 14C, statement that proxies are not to be solicited;

(2)   The date, time and place of the meeting of security holders, unless such information is otherwise disclosed in material furnished to security holders with the prospectus.

(3)   The information required by Item 3 of Schedule 14A, dissenters' rights of appraisal;

(4)   With respect to both the registrant and the company being acquired, a brief description of any material interest, direct or indirect, by security holdings or otherwise, of affiliates of the registrant and of the company being acquired, in the proposed transaction;

Instruction. This subparagraph shall not apply to any interest arising from the ownership of securities of the registrant where the security holder receives no extra or special benefit not shared on a pro rata basis by all other holders of the same class.

(5)   With respect to both the registrant and the company being acquired, the information required by Item 6 of Schedule 14A, voting securities and principal holders thereof;

(6)   The information required by Item 21 of Schedule 14A, vote required for approval;

(7)   With respect to each person who will serve as a director or an executive officer of the surviving or acquiring company the information required by:

(i)   Item 401 of Regulation S–K, directors and executive officers;

(ii)   Item 402 of Regulation S–K (§ 229.402 of this chapter), executive compensation, and paragraph (e)(4) of Item 407 of Regulation S–K (§ 229.407(e)(4) of this chapter), corporate governance;

(iii)   Item 404 of Regulation S–K (§ 229.404), transactions with related persons, promoters and certain controls persons, and Item 407(a) of Regulation S–K (§ 229.407(a)), corporate governance.

(b)   If the transaction is an exchange offer, furnish the information required by paragraphs (a)(4), (a)(5), and (a)(7) of this Item, except as provided by paragraph (c) of this Item.

(c)   If the registrant or the company being acquired meets the requirements for use of Form S-3, any information required by paragraphs (a)(5) and (7) of this Item with respect to such company may be incorporated by reference from its latest annual report on Form 10-K.

PART II

INFORMATION NOT REQUIRED IN PROSPECTUS

Item 20. Indemnification of Directors and Officers.

Furnish the information required by Item 702 of Regulation S–K (§ 229.702 of this chapter).

Item 21. Exhibits and Financial Statement Schedules.

(a)   Subject to the rules regarding incorporation by reference, furnish the exhibits as required by Item 601 of Regulation S–K (§ 229.601 of this chapter).

* * *

F. FORMS AND SCHEDULES UNDER THE SECURITIES EXCHANGE ACT OF 1934

(Selected)

FORM 8-K

GENERAL INSTRUCTIONS

A. Rule as to Use of Form 8-K.

1. Form 8-K shall be used for current reports under Section 13 or 15(d) of the Securities Exchange Act of 1934, filed pursuant to Rule 13a–11 or Rule 15d–11 and for reports of nonpublic information required to be disclosed by Regulation FD (17 CFR 243.100 and 243.101).

2. Form 8-K may be used by a registrant to satisfy its filing obligations pursuant to Rule 425 under the Securities Act, regarding written communications related to business combination transactions, or Rules 14a–12(b) or Rule 14d–2(b) under the Exchange Act, relating to soliciting materials and pre-commencement communications pursuant to tender offers, respectively, provided that the Form 8-K filing satisfies all the substantive requirements of those rules (other than the Rule 425(c) requirement to include certain specified information in any prospectus filed pursuant to such rule). Such filing is also deemed to be filed pursuant to any rule for which the box is checked. A registrant is not required to check the box in connection with Rule 14a–12(b) or Rule 14d–2(b) if the communication is filed pursuant to Rule 425. Communications filed pursuant to Rule 425 are deemed filed under the other applicable sections. *See* Note 2 to Rule 425, Rule 14a–12(b) and Instruction 2 to Rule 14d–2(b)(2).

B. Events to be Reported and Time for Filing of Reports.

1. A report on this form is required to be filed or furnished, as applicable, upon the occurrence of any one or more of the events specified in the items in Sections 1—6 and 9 of this form. Unless otherwise specified, a report is to be filed or furnished within four business days after occurrence of the event. If the event occurs on a Saturday, Sunday or holiday on which the Commission is not open for business, then the four business day period shall begin to run on, and include, the first business day thereafter. A registrant either furnishing a report on this form under Item 7.01 (Regulation FD Disclosure) or electing to file a report on this form under Item 8.01 (Other Events) solely to satisfy its obligations under Regulation FD (17 CFR 243.100 and 243.101) must furnish such report or make such filing, as applicable, in accordance with the requirements of Rule 100(a) of Regulation FD (17 CFR 243.100(a)), including the deadline for furnishing or filing such report. A report pursuant to Item 5.08 is to be filed within four business days after the registrant determines the anticipated meeting date.

2.   The information in a report furnished pursuant to Item 2.02 (Results of Operations and Financial Condition) or Item 7.01 (Regulation FD Disclosure) shall not be deemed to be "filed" for purposes of Section 18 of the Exchange Act or otherwise subject to the liabilities of that section, unless the registrant specifically states that the information is to be considered "filed" under the Exchange Act or incorporates it by reference into a filing under the Securities Act or the Exchange Act. If a report on Form 8-K contains disclosures under Item 2.02 or Item 7.01, whether or not the report contains disclosures regarding other items, all exhibits to such report relating to Item 2.02 or Item 7.01 will be deemed furnished, and not filed, unless the registrant specifies, under Item 9.01 (Financial Statements and Exhibits), which exhibits, or portions of exhibits, are intended to be deemed filed rather than furnished pursuant to this instruction.

3.   If the registrant previously has reported substantially the same information as required by this form, the registrant need not make an additional report of the information on this form. To the extent that an item calls for disclosure of developments concerning a previously reported event or transaction, any information required in the new report or amendment about the previously reported event or transaction may be provided by incorporation by reference to the previously filed report. The term previously reported is defined in Rule 12b–2 (17 CFR 240.12b–2).

4.   Copies of agreements, amendments or other documents or instruments required to be filed pursuant to Form 8-K are not required to be filed or furnished as exhibits to the Form 8-K unless specifically required to be filed or furnished by the applicable Item. This instruction does not affect the requirement to otherwise file such agreements, amendments or other documents or instruments, including as exhibits to registration statements and periodic reports pursuant to the requirements of Item 601 of Regulation S–K.

5.   When considering current reporting on this form, particularly of other events of material importance pursuant to Item 7.01 (Regulation FD Disclosure) and Item 8.01(Other Events), registrants should have due regard for the accuracy, completeness and currency of the information in registration statements filed under the Securities Act which incorporate by reference information in reports filed pursuant to the Exchange Act, including reports on this form.

6.   A registrant's report under Item 7.01 (Regulation FD Disclosure) or Item 8.01 (Other Events) will not be deemed an admission as to the materiality of any information in the report that is required to be disclosed solely by Regulation FD.

* * *

F.   Incorporation by Reference.

If the registrant makes available to its stockholders or otherwise publishes, within the period prescribed for filing the report, a press release or other document or statement containing information meeting some or all of the requirements of this form, the information called for may be incorporated by reference to such published document or statement, in answer or partial answer to any item or items of this form, provided copies thereof are filed as an exhibit to the report on this form.

* * *

INFORMATION TO BE INCLUDED IN THE REPORT

Section 1—Registrant's Business and Operations

Item 1.01   Entry into a Material Definitive Agreement.

(a)   If the registrant has entered into a material definitive agreement not made in the ordinary course of business of the registrant, or into any amendment of such agreement that is material to the registrant, disclose the following information:

(1)   the date on which the agreement was entered into or amended, the identity of the parties to the agreement or amendment and a brief description of any material relationship

between the registrant or its affiliates and any of the parties, other than in respect of the material definitive agreement or amendment; and

(2)   a brief description of the terms and conditions of the agreement or amendment that are material to the registrant.

(b)   For purposes of this Item 1.01, a <u>material definitive agreement</u> means an agreement that provides for obligations that are material to and enforceable against the registrant, or rights that are material to the registrant and enforceable by the registrant against one or more other parties to the agreement, in each case whether or not subject to conditions.

Instructions.

1.   Any material definitive agreement of the registrant not made in the ordinary course of the registrant's business must be disclosed under this Item 1.01. An agreement is deemed to be not made in the ordinary course of a registrant's business even if the agreement is such as ordinarily accompanies the kind of business conducted by the registrant if it involves the subject matter identified in Item 601(b)(10)(ii)(A)–(D) of Regulation S–K (17 CFR 229.601(b)(10)(ii)(A)–(D)). An agreement involving the subject matter identified in Item 601(b)(10)(iii)(A) or (B) need not be disclosed under this Item.

2.   A registrant must provide disclosure under this Item 1.01 if the registrant succeeds as a party to the agreement or amendment to the agreement by assumption or assignment (other than in connection with a merger or acquisition or similar transaction).

3.   With respect to asset-backed securities, as defined in Item 1101 of Regulation AB (17 CFR 229.1101), disclosure is required under this Item 1.01 regarding the entry into or an amendment to a definitive agreement that is material to the asset-backed securities transaction, even if the registrant is not a party to such agreement (*e.g.*, a servicing agreement with a servicer contemplated by Item 1108(a)(3) of Regulation AB (17 CFR 229.1108(a)(3))).

Item 1.02   Termination of a Material Definitive Agreement.

(a)   If a material definitive agreement which was not made in the ordinary course of business of the registrant and to which the registrant is a party is terminated otherwise than by expiration of the agreement on its stated termination date, or as a result of all parties completing their obligations under such agreement, and such termination of the agreement is material to the registrant, disclose the following information:

(1)   the date of the termination of the material definitive agreement, the identity of the parties to the agreement and a brief description of any material relationship between the registrant or its affiliates and any of the parties other than in respect of the material definitive agreement;

(2)   a brief description of the terms and conditions of the agreement that are material to the registrant;

(3)   a brief description of the material circumstances surrounding the termination; and

(4)   any material early termination penalties incurred by the registrant.

(b)   For purposes of this Item 1.02, the term <u>material definitive agreement</u> shall have the same meaning as set forth in Item 1.01(b).

Instructions.

1.   No disclosure is required solely by reason of this Item 1.02 during negotiations or discussions regarding termination of a material definitive agreement unless and until the agreement has been terminated.

FORM 8-K

2.　No disclosure is required solely by reason of this Item 1.02 if the registrant believes in good faith that the material definitive agreement has not been terminated, unless the registrant has received a notice of termination pursuant to the terms of agreement.

3.　With respect to asset-backed securities, as defined in Item 1101 of Regulation AB (17 CFR 229.1101), disclosure is required under this Item 1.02 regarding the termination of a definitive agreement that is material to the asset-backed securities transaction (otherwise than by expiration of the agreement on its stated termination date or as a result of all parties completing their obligations under such agreement), even if the registrant is not a party to such agreement (*e.g.*, a servicing agreement with a servicer contemplated by Item 1108(a)(3) of Regulation AB (17 CFR 229.1108(a)(3)).

Item 1.03　Bankruptcy or Receivership.

(a)　If a receiver, fiscal agent or similar officer has been appointed for a registrant or its parent, in a proceeding under the U.S. Bankruptcy Code or in any other proceeding under state or federal law in which a court or governmental authority has assumed jurisdiction over substantially all of the assets or business of the registrant or its parent, or if such jurisdiction has been assumed by leaving the existing directors and officers in possession but subject to the supervision and orders of a court or governmental authority, disclose the following information:

(1)　the name or other identification of the proceeding;

(2)　the identity of the court or governmental authority;

(3)　the date that jurisdiction was assumed; and

(4)　the identity of the receiver, fiscal agent or similar officer and the date of his or her appointment.

(b)　If an order confirming a plan of reorganization, arrangement or liquidation has been entered by a court or governmental authority having supervision or jurisdiction over substantially all of the assets or business of the registrant or its parent, disclose the following;

(1)　the identity of the court or governmental authority;

(2)　the date that the order confirming the plan was entered by the court or governmental authority;

(3)　a summary of the material features of the plan and, pursuant to Item 9.01 (Financial Statements and Exhibits), a copy of the plan as confirmed;

(4)　the number of shares or other units of the registrant or its parent issued and outstanding, the number reserved for future issuance in respect of claims and interests filed and allowed under the plan, and the aggregate total of such numbers; and

(5)　information as to the assets and liabilities of the registrant or its parent as of the date that the order confirming the plan was entered, or a date as close thereto as practicable.

Instructions.

1.　The information called for in paragraph (b)(5) of this Item 1.03 may be presented in the form in which it was furnished to the court or governmental authority.

2.　With respect to asset-backed securities, disclosure also is required under this Item 1.03 if the depositor (or servicer if the servicer signs the report on Form 10-K (17 CFR 249.310) of the issuing entity) becomes aware of any instances described in paragraph (a) or (b) of this Item with respect to the sponsor, depositor, servicer contemplated by Item 1108(a)(3) of Regulation AB (17 CFR 229.1108(a)(3)), trustee, significant obligor, enhancement or support provider contemplated by Items 1114(b) or 1115 of Regulation AB (17 CFR 229.1114(b) or 229.1115) or other material party contemplated by Item 1101(d)(1) of Regulation AB (17 CFR 1101(d)(1)). Terms used in this Instruction 2 have the same meaning as in Item 1101 of Regulation AB (17 CFR 229.1101).

* * *

FORM 8-K

Section 2—Financial Information

Item 2.01   Completion of Acquisition or Disposition of Assets.

If the registrant or any of its majority-owned subsidiaries has completed the acquisition or disposition of a significant amount of assets, otherwise than in the ordinary course of business, disclose the following information:

(a)   the date of completion of the transaction;

(b)   a brief description of the assets involved;

(c)   the identity of the person(s) from whom the assets were acquired or to whom they were sold and the nature of any material relationship, other than in respect of the transaction, between such person(s) and the registrant or any of its affiliates, or any director or officer of the registrant, or any associate of any such director or officer;

(d)   the nature and amount of consideration given or received for the assets and, if any material relationship is disclosed pursuant to paragraph (c) of this Item 2.01, the formula or principle followed in determining the amount of such consideration;

(e)   if the transaction being reported is an acquisition and if a material relationship exists between the registrant or any of its affiliates and the source(s) of the funds used in the acquisition, the identity of the source(s) of the funds unless all or any part of the consideration used is a loan made in the ordinary course of business by a bank as defined by Section 3(a)(6) of the Act, in which case the identity of such bank may be omitted provided the registrant:

(1)   has made a request for confidentiality pursuant to Section 13(d)(1)(B) of the Act; and

(2)   states in the report that the identity of the bank has been so omitted and filed separately with the Commission; and

(f)   if the registrant was a shell company, other than a business combination related shell company, as those terms are defined in Rule 12b–2 under the Exchange Act (17 CFR 240.12b–2), immediately before the transaction, the information that would be required if the registrant were filing a general form for registration of securities on Form 10 under the Exchange Act reflecting all classes of the registrant's securities subject to the reporting requirements of Section 13 (15 U.S.C. 78m) or Section 15(d) (15 U.S.C. 78o(d)) of such Act upon consummation of the transaction. Notwithstanding General Instruction B.3. to Form 8K, if any disclosure required by this Item 2.01(f) is previously reported, as that term is defined in Rule 12b–2 under the Exchange Act (17 CFR 240.12b–2), the registrant may identify the filing in which that disclosure is included instead of including that disclosure in this report.

Instructions.

1.   No information need be given as to:

(i)   any transaction between any person and any wholly-owned subsidiary of such person;

(ii)   any transaction between two or more wholly-owned subsidiaries of any person; or

(iii)   the redemption or other acquisition of securities from the public, or the sale or other disposition of securities to the public, by the issuer of such securities or by a wholly-owned subsidiary of that issuer.

2.   The term acquisition includes every purchase, acquisition by lease, exchange, merger, consolidation, succession or other acquisition, except that the term does not include the construction or development of property by or for the registrant or its subsidiaries or the acquisition of materials for such purpose. The term disposition includes every sale, disposition by lease, exchange, merger, consolidation, mortgage, assignment or hypothecation of assets, whether for the benefit of creditors or otherwise, abandonment, destruction, or other disposition.

FORM 8-K

3.   The information called for by this Item 2.01 is to be given as to each transaction or series of related transactions of the size indicated. The acquisition or disposition of securities is deemed the indirect acquisition or disposition of the assets represented by such securities if it results in the acquisition or disposition of control of such assets.

4.   An acquisition or disposition shall be deemed to involve a significant amount of assets:

(i)   if the registrant's and its other subsidiaries' equity in the net book value of such assets or the amount paid or received for the assets upon such acquisition or disposition exceeded 10% of the total assets of the registrant and its consolidated subsidiaries; or

(ii)   if it involved a business (see 17 CFR 210.11–01(d)) that is significant (see 17 CFR 210.11–01(b)).

Acquisitions of individually insignificant businesses are not required to be reported pursuant to this Item 2.01 unless they are related businesses (see 17 CFR 210.3–05(a)(3)) and are significant in the aggregate.

5.   Attention is directed to the requirements in Item 9.01 (Financial Statements and Exhibits) with respect to the filing of:

(i)   financial statements of businesses acquired;

(ii)   pro forma financial information; and

(iii)   copies of the plans of acquisition or disposition as exhibits to the report.

Item 2.02   Results of Operations and Financial Condition.

(a)   If a registrant, or any person acting on its behalf, makes any public announcement or release (including any update of an earlier announcement or release) disclosing material non-public information regarding the registrant's results of operations or financial condition for a completed quarterly or annual fiscal period, the registrant shall disclose the date of the announcement or release, briefly identify the announcement or release and include the text of that announcement or release as an exhibit.

(b)   A Form 8-K is not required to be furnished to the Commission under this Item 2.02 in the case of disclosure of material non-public information that is disclosed orally, telephonically, by webcast, by broadcast, or by similar means if:

(1)   the information is provided as part of a presentation that is complementary to, and initially occurs within 48 hours after, a related, written announcement or release that has been furnished on Form 8-K pursuant to this Item 2.02 prior to the presentation;

(2)   the presentation is broadly accessible to the public by dial-in conference call, by webcast, by broadcast or by similar means;

(3)   the financial and other statistical information contained in the presentation is provided on the registrant's website, together with any information that would be required under 17 CFR 244.100; and

(4)   the presentation was announced by a widely disseminated press release, that included instructions as to when and how to access the presentation and the location on the registrant's website where the information would be available.

Instructions.

1.   The requirements of this Item 2.02 are triggered by the disclosure of material non-public information regarding a completed fiscal year or quarter. Release of additional or updated material non-public information regarding a completed fiscal year or quarter would trigger an additional Item 2.02 requirement.

2.   The requirements of paragraph (e)(1)(i) of Item 10 of Regulation S–K (17 CFR 229.10(e)(1)(i)) shall apply to disclosures under this Item 2.02.

3.   Issuers that make earnings announcements or other disclosures of material non-public information regarding a completed fiscal year or quarter in an interim or annual report to shareholders are permitted to specify which portion of the report contains the information required to be furnished under this Item 2.02.

4.   This Item 2.02 does not apply in the case of a disclosure that is made in a quarterly report filed with the Commission on Form 10Q (17 CFR 249.308a) or an annual report filed with the Commission on Form 10-K (17 CFR 249.310).

Item 2.03   Creation of a Direct Financial Obligation or an Obligation under an Off-Balance Sheet Arrangement of a Registrant.

(a)   If the registrant becomes obligated on a direct financial obligation that is material to the registrant, disclose the following information:

(1)   the date on which the registrant becomes obligated on the direct financial obligation and a brief description of the transaction or agreement creating the obligation;

(2)   the amount of the obligation, including the terms of its payment and, if applicable, a brief description of the material terms under which it may be accelerated or increased and the nature of any recourse provisions that would enable the registrant to recover from third parties; and

(3)   a brief description of the other terms and conditions of the transaction or agreement that are material to the registrant.

(b)   If the registrant becomes directly or contingently liable for an obligation that is material to the registrant arising out of an off-balance sheet arrangement, disclose the following information:

(1)   the date on which the registrant becomes directly or contingently liable on the obligation and a brief description of the transaction or agreement creating the arrangement and obligation;

(2)   a brief description of the nature and amount of the obligation of the registrant under the arrangement, including the material terms whereby it may become a direct obligation, if applicable, or may be accelerated or increased and the nature of any recourse provisions that would enable the registrant to recover from third parties;

(3)   the maximum potential amount of future payments (undiscounted) that the registrant may be required to make, if different; and

(4)   a brief description of the other terms and conditions of the obligation or arrangement that are material to the registrant.

(c)   For purposes of this Item 2.03, direct financial obligation means any of the following:

(1)   a long-term debt obligation, as defined in Item 303(a)(5)(ii)(A) of Regulation S–K (17 CFR 229.303(a)(5)(ii)(A));

(2)   a capital lease obligation, as defined in Item 303(a)(5)(ii)(B) of Regulation S–K (17 CFR 229.303(a)(5)(ii)(B));

(3)   an operating lease obligation, as defined in Item 303(a)(5)(ii)(C) of Regulation S–K (17 CFR 229.303(a)(5)(ii)(C)); or

(4)   a short-term debt obligation that arises other than in the ordinary course of business.

(d)   For purposes of this Item 2.03, off-balance sheet arrangement has the meaning set forth in Item 303(a)(4)(ii) of Regulation S–K (17 CFR 229.303(a)(4)(ii)).

(e) For purposes of this Item 2.03, <u>short-term debt obligation</u> means a payment obligation under a borrowing arrangement that is scheduled to mature within one year, or, for those registrants that use the operating cycle concept of working capital, within a registrant's operating cycle that is longer than one year, as discussed in FASB ASC paragraph 210–10–45–3 (Balance Sheet Topic).

Instructions.

1. A registrant has no obligation to disclose information under this Item 2.03 until the registrant enters into an agreement enforceable against the registrant, whether or not subject to conditions, under which the direct financial obligation will arise or be created or issued. If there is no such agreement, the registrant must provide the disclosure within four business days after the occurrence of the closing or settlement of the transaction or arrangement under which the direct financial obligation arises or is created.

2. A registrant must provide the disclosure required by paragraph (b) of this Item 2.03 whether or not the registrant is also a party to the transaction or agreement creating the contingent obligation arising under the off-balance sheet arrangement. In the event that neither the registrant nor any affiliate of the registrant is also a party to the transaction or agreement creating the contingent obligation arising under the off-balance sheet arrangement in question, the four business day period for reporting the event under this Item 2.03 shall begin on the earlier of (i) the fourth business day after the contingent obligation is created or arises, and (ii) the day on which an executive officer, as defined in 17 CFR 240.3b–7, of the registrant becomes aware of the contingent obligation.

3. In the event that an agreement, transaction or arrangement requiring disclosure under this Item 2.03 comprises a facility, program or similar arrangement that creates or may give rise to direct financial obligations of the registrant in connection with multiple transactions, the registrant shall:

 (i) disclose the entering into of the facility, program or similar arrangement if the entering into of the facility is material to the registrant; and

 (ii) as direct financial obligations arise or are created under the facility or program, disclose the required information under this Item 2.03 to the extent that the obligations are material to the registrant (including when a series of previously undisclosed individually immaterial obligations become material in the aggregate).

4. For purposes of Item 2.03(b)(3), the maximum amount of future payments shall not be reduced by the effect of any amounts that may possibly be recovered by the registrant under recourse or collateralization provisions in any guarantee agreement, transaction or arrangement.

5. If the obligation required to be disclosed under this Item 2.03 is a security, or a term of a security, that has been or will be sold pursuant to an effective registration statement of the registrant, the registrant is not required to file a Form 8-K pursuant to this Item 2.03, provided that the prospectus relating to that sale contains the information required by this Item 2.03 and is filed within the required time period under Securities Act Rule 424 (§ 230.424 of this chapter).

Item 2.04 Triggering Events That Accelerate or Increase a Direct Financial Obligation or an Obligation under an Off-Balance Sheet Arrangement.

(a) If a triggering event causing the increase or acceleration of a direct financial obligation of the registrant occurs and the consequences of the event, taking into account those described in paragraph (a)(4) of this Item 2.04, are material to the registrant, disclose the following information:

 (1) the date of the triggering event and a brief description of the agreement or transaction under which the direct financial obligation was created and is increased or accelerated;

 (2) a brief description of the triggering event;

 (3) the amount of the direct financial obligation, as increased if applicable, and the terms of payment or acceleration that apply; and

(4)   any other material obligations of the registrant that may arise, increase, be accelerated or become direct financial obligations as a result of the triggering event or the increase or acceleration of the direct financial obligation.

(b)   If a triggering event occurs causing an obligation of the registrant under an off-balance sheet arrangement to increase or be accelerated, or causing a contingent obligation of the registrant under an off-balance sheet arrangement to become a direct financial obligation of the registrant, and the consequences of the event, taking into account those described in paragraph (b)(4) of this Item 2.04, are material to the registrant, disclose the following information:

(1)   the date of the triggering event and a brief description of the off-balance sheet arrangement;

(2)   a brief description of the triggering event;

(3)   the nature and amount of the obligation, as increased if applicable, and the terms of payment or acceleration that apply; and

(4)   any other material obligations of the registrant that may arise, increase, be accelerated or become direct financial obligations as a result of the triggering event or the increase or acceleration of the obligation under the off-balance sheet arrangement or its becoming a direct financial obligation of the registrant.

(c)   For purposes of this Item 2.04, the term direct financial obligation has the meaning provided in Item 2.03 of this form, but shall also include an obligation arising out of an off-balance sheet arrangement that is accrued under FASB ASC Section 450–20–25, Contingencies-Loss Contingencies-Recognition.

(d)   For purposes of this Item 2.04, the term off-balance sheet arrangement has the meaning provided in Item 2.03 of this form.

(e)   For purposes of this Item 2.04, a triggering event is an event, including an event of default, event of acceleration or similar event, as a result of which a direct financial obligation of the registrant or an obligation of the registrant arising under an off-balance sheet arrangement is increased or becomes accelerated or as a result of which a contingent obligation of the registrant arising out of an off-balance sheet arrangement becomes a direct financial obligation of the registrant.

Instructions.

1.   Disclosure is required if a triggering event occurs in respect of an obligation of the registrant under an off-balance sheet arrangement and the consequences are material to the registrant, whether or not the registrant is also a party to the transaction or agreement under which the triggering event occurs.

2.   No disclosure is required under this Item 2.04 unless and until a triggering event has occurred in accordance with the terms of the relevant agreement, transaction or arrangement, including, if required, the sending to the registrant of notice of the occurrence of a triggering event pursuant to the terms of the agreement, transaction or arrangement and the satisfaction of all conditions to such occurrence, except the passage of time.

3.   No disclosure is required solely by reason of this Item 2.04 if the registrant believes in good faith that no triggering event has occurred, unless the registrant has received a notice described in Instruction 2 to this Item 2.04.

4.   Where a registrant is subject to an obligation arising out of an off-balance sheet arrangement, whether or not disclosed pursuant to Item 2.03 of this form, if a triggering event occurs as a result of which under that obligation an accrual for a probable loss is required under FASB ASC Section 450–20–25, the obligation arising out of the off-balance sheet arrangement becomes a direct financial obligation as defined in this Item 2.04. In that situation, if the consequences as determined under Item 2.04(b) are material to the registrant, disclosure is required under this Item 2.04.

5.   With respect to asset-backed securities, as defined in 17 CFR 229.1101, disclosure also is required under this Item 2.04 if an early amortization, performance trigger or other event, including an event of default, has occurred under the transaction agreements for the asset-backed securities that would materially alter the payment priority or distribution of cash flows regarding the asset-backed securities or the amortization schedule for the asset-backed securities. In providing the disclosure required by this Item, identify the changes to the payment priorities, flow of funds or asset-backed securities as a result. Disclosure is required under this Item whether or not the registrant is a party to the transaction agreement that results in the occurrence identified.

Item 2.05   Costs Associated with Exit or Disposal Activities.

If the registrant's board of directors, a committee of the board of directors or the officer or officers of the registrant authorized to take such action if board action is not required, commits the registrant to an exit or disposal plan, or otherwise disposes of a long-lived asset or terminates employees under a plan of termination described in FASB ASC paragraph 420–10–25–4 (Exit or Disposal Cost Obligations Topic), under which material charges will be incurred under generally accepted accounting principles applicable to the registrant, disclose the following information:

(a)   the date of the commitment to the course of action and a description of the course of action, including the facts and circumstances leading to the expected action and the expected completion date;

(b)   for each major type of cost associated with the course of action (for example, one-time termination benefits, contract termination costs and other associated costs), an estimate of the total amount or range of amounts expected to be incurred in connection with the action;

(c)   an estimate of the total amount or range of amounts expected to be incurred in connection with the action; and

(d)   the registrant's estimate of the amount or range of amounts of the charge that will result in future cash expenditures, provided, however, that if the registrant determines that at the time of filing it is unable in good faith to make a determination of an estimate required by paragraphs (b), (c) or (d) of this Item 2.05, no disclosure of such estimate shall be required; provided further, however, that in any such event, the registrant shall file an amended report on Form 8-K under this Item 2.05 within four business days after it makes a determination of such an estimate or range of estimates.

Item 2.06   Material Impairments.

If the registrant's board of directors, a committee of the board of directors or the officer or officers of the registrant authorized to take such action if board action is not required, concludes that a material charge for impairment to one or more of its assets, including, without limitation, impairments of securities or goodwill, is required under generally accepted accounting principles applicable to the registrant, disclose the following information:

(a)   the date of the conclusion that a material charge is required and a description of the impaired asset or assets and the facts and circumstances leading to the conclusion that the charge for impairment is required;

(b)   the registrant's estimate of the amount or range of amounts of the impairment charge; and

(c)   the registrant's estimate of the amount or range of amounts of the impairment charge that will result in future cash expenditures, provided, however, that if the registrant determines that at the time of filing it is unable in good faith to make a determination of an estimate required by paragraphs (b) or (c) of this Item 2.06, no disclosure of such estimate shall be required; provided further, however, that in any such event, the registrant shall file an amended report on Form 8-K under this Item 2.06 within four business days after it makes a determination of such an estimate or range of estimates.

Instruction.

No filing is required under this Item 2.06 if the conclusion is made in connection with the preparation, review or audit of financial statements required to be included in the next periodic report

FORM 8-K

due to be filed under the Exchange Act, the periodic report is filed on a timely basis and such conclusion is disclosed in the report.

Section 3—Securities and Trading Markets

Item 3.01   Notice of Delisting or Failure to Satisfy a Continued Listing Rule or Standard; Transfer of Listing.

(a)   If the registrant has received notice from the national securities exchange or national securities association (or a facility thereof) that maintains the principal listing for any class of the registrant's common equity (as defined in Exchange Act Rule 12b–2 (17 CFR 240.12b–2)) that:

- the registrant or such class of the registrant's securities does not satisfy a rule or standard for continued listing on the exchange or association;

- the exchange has submitted an application under Exchange Act Rule 12d2–2 (17 CFR 240.12d2–2) to the Commission to delist such class of the registrant's securities; or

- the association has taken all necessary steps under its rules to delist the security from its automated inter-dealer quotation system,

the registrant must disclose:

(i)   the date that the registrant received the notice;

(ii)   the a rule or standard for continued listing on the national securities exchange or national securities association that the registrant fails, or has failed to, satisfy; and

(iii)   any action or response that, at the time of filing, the registrant has determined to take in response to the notice.

(b)   If the registrant has notified the national securities exchange or national securities association (or a facility thereof) that maintains the principal listing for any class of the registrant's common equity (as defined in Exchange Act Rule 12b–2 (17 CFR 240.12b–2)) that the registrant is aware of any material noncompliance with a rule or standard for continued listing on the exchange or association, the registrant must disclose:

(i)   the date that the registrant provided such notice to the exchange or association;

(ii)   the rule or standard for continued listing on the exchange or association that the registrant fails, or has failed, to satisfy; and

(iii)   any action or response that, at the time of filing, the registrant has determined to take regarding its noncompliance.

(c)   If the national securities exchange or national securities association (or a facility thereof) that maintains the principal listing for any class of the registrant's common equity (as defined in Exchange Act Rule 12b–2 (17 CFR 240.12b–2)), in lieu of suspending trading in or delisting such class of the registrant's securities, issues a public reprimand letter or similar communication indicating that the registrant has violated a rule or standard for continued listing on the exchange or association, the registrant must state the date, and summarize the contents of the letter or communication.

(d)   If the registrant's board of directors, a committee of the board of directors or the officer or officers of the registrant authorized to take such action if board action is not required, has taken definitive action to cause the listing of a class of its common equity to be withdrawn from the national securities exchange, or terminated from the automated inter-dealer quotation system of a registered national securities association, where such exchange or association maintains the principal listing for such class of securities, including by reason of a transfer of the listing or quotation to another securities exchange or quotation system, describe the action taken and state the date of the action.

FORM 8-K

Instructions.

1.   The registrant is not required to disclose any information required by paragraph (a) of this Item 3.01 where the delisting is a result of one of the following:

- the entire class of the security has been called for redemption, maturity or retirement; appropriate notice thereof has been given; if required by the terms of the securities, funds sufficient for the payment of all such securities have been deposited with an agency authorized to make such payments; and such funds have been made available to security holders;

- the entire class of the security has been redeemed or paid at maturity or retirement;

- the instruments representing the entire class of securities have come to evidence, by operation of law or otherwise, other securities in substitution therefor and represent no other right, except, if true, the right to receive an immediate cash payment (the right of dissenters to receive the appraised or fair value of their holdings shall not prevent the application of this provision); or

- all rights pertaining to the entire class of the security have been extinguished; provided, however, that where such an event occurs as the result of an order of a court or other governmental authority, the order shall be final, all applicable appeal periods shall have expired and no appeals shall be pending.

2.   A registrant must provide the disclosure required by paragraph (a) or (b) of this Item 3.01, as applicable, regarding any failure to satisfy a rule or standard for continued listing on the national securities exchange or national securities association (or a facility thereof) that maintains the principal listing for any class of the registrant's common equity (as defined in Exchange Act Rule 12b2 (17 CFR 240.12b–2)) even if the registrant has the benefit of a grace period or similar extension period during which it may cure the deficiency that triggers the disclosure requirement.

3.   Notices or other communications subsequent to an initial notice sent to, or by, a registrant under Item 3.01(a), (b) or (c) that continue to indicate that the registrant does not comply with the same rule or standard for continued listing that was the subject of the initial notice are not required to be filed, but may be filed voluntarily.

4.   Registrants whose securities are quoted exclusively (i.e., the securities are not otherwise listed on an exchange or association) on automated inter-dealer quotation systems are not subject to this Item 3.01 and such registrants are thus not required to file a Form 8-K pursuant to this Item 3.01 if the securities are no longer quoted on such quotation system. If a security is listed on an exchange or association and is also quoted on an automated inter-dealer quotation system, the registrant is subject to the disclosure obligations of Item 3.01 if any of the events specified in Item 3.01 occur.

Item 3.02   Unregistered Sales of Equity Securities.

(a)   If the registrant sells equity securities in a transaction that is not registered under the Securities Act, furnish the information set forth in paragraphs (a) and (c) through (e) of Item 701 of Regulation S–K (17 CFR 229.701(a) and (c) through (e)). For purposes of determining the required filing date for the Form 8-K under this Item 3.02(a), the registrant has no obligation to disclose information under this Item 3.02 until the registrant enters into an agreement enforceable against the registrant, whether or not subject to conditions, under which the equity securities are to be sold. If there is no such agreement, the registrant must provide the disclosure within four business days after the occurrence of the closing or settlement of the transaction or arrangement under which the equity securities are to be sold.

(b)   No report need be filed under this Item 3.02 if the equity securities sold, in the aggregate since its last report filed under this Item 3.02 or its last periodic report, whichever is more recent, constitute less than 1% of the number of shares outstanding of the class of equity securities sold. In the case of a smaller reporting company, no report need be filed if the equity securities sold, in the aggregate since its last report filed under this Item 3.02 or its last periodic report, whichever is more recent, constitute less than 5% of the number of shares outstanding of the class of equity securities sold.

Instructions.

1. For purposes of this Item 3.02, "the number of shares outstanding" refers to the actual number of shares of equity securities of the class outstanding and does not include outstanding securities convertible into or exchangeable for such equity securities.2. A smaller reporting company is defined under Item 10(f)(1) of Regulation S–K (17 CFR 229.10(f)(1)).

Item 3.03   Material Modification to Rights of Security Holders.

(a)   If the constituent instruments defining the rights of the holders of any class of registered securities of the registrant have been materially modified, disclose the date of the modification, the title of the class of securities involved and briefly describe the general effect of such modification upon the rights of holders of such securities.

(b)   If the rights evidenced by any class of registered securities have been materially limited or qualified by the issuance or modification of any other class of securities by the registrant, briefly disclose the date of the issuance or modification, the general effect of the issuance or modification of such other class of securities upon the rights of the holders of the registered securities.

Instruction.

Working capital restrictions and other limitations upon the payment of dividends must be reported pursuant to this Item 3.03.

Section 4—Matters Related to Accountants and Financial Statements

Item 4.01   Changes in Registrant's Certifying Accountant.

(a)   If an independent accountant who was previously engaged as the principal accountant to audit the registrant's financial statements, or an independent accountant upon whom the principal accountant expressed reliance in its report regarding a significant subsidiary, resigns (or indicates that it declines to stand for re-appointment after completion of the current audit) or is dismissed, disclose the information required by Item 304(a)(1) of Regulation S–K (17 CFR 229.304(a)(1) of this chapter), including compliance with Item 304(a)(3) of Regulation S–K (17 CFR 229.304(a)(3) of this chapter).

(b)   If a new independent accountant has been engaged as either the principal accountant to audit the registrant's financial statements or as an independent accountant on whom the principal accountant is expected to express reliance in its report regarding a significant subsidiary, the registrant must disclose the information required by Item 304(a)(2) of Regulation S–K (17 CFR 229.304(a)(2)).

Instruction.

The resignation or dismissal of an independent accountant, or its refusal to stand for re-appointment, is a reportable event separate from the engagement of a new independent accountant. On some occasions, two reports on Form 8-K are required for a single change in accountants, the first on the resignation (or refusal to stand for re-appointment) or dismissal of the former accountant and the second when the new accountant is engaged. Information required in the second Form 8-K in such situations need not be provided to the extent that it has been reported previously in the first Form 8-K.

Item 4.02   Non-Reliance on Previously Issued Financial Statements or a Related Audit Report or Completed Interim Review.

(a)   If the registrant's board of directors, a committee of the board of directors or the officer or officers of the registrant authorized to take such action if board action is not required, concludes that any previously issued financial statements, covering one or more years or interim periods for which the registrant is required to provide financial statements under Regulation S–X (17 CFR 210) should no longer be relied upon because of an error in such financial statements as addressed in FASB ASC Topic 250, Accounting Changes and Error Corrections, as may be modified, supplemented or succeeded, disclose the following information:

(1) the date of the conclusion regarding the non-reliance and an identification of the financial statements and years or periods covered that should no longer be relied upon;

(2) a brief description of the facts underlying the conclusion to the extent known to the registrant at the time of filing; and

(3) a statement of whether the audit committee, or the board of directors in the absence of an audit committee, or authorized officer or officers, discussed with the registrant's independent accountant the matters disclosed in the filing pursuant to this Item 4.02(a).

(b) If the registrant is advised by, or receives notice from, its independent accountant that disclosure should be made or action should be taken to prevent future reliance on a previously issued audit report or completed interim review related to previously issued financial statements, disclose the following information:

(1) the date on which the registrant was so advised or notified;

(2) identification of the financial statements that should no longer be relied upon;

(3) a brief description of the information provided by the accountant; and

(4) a statement of whether the audit committee, or the board of directors in the absence of an audit committee, or authorized officer or officers, discussed with the independent accountant the matters disclosed in the filing pursuant to this Item 4.02(b).

(c) If the registrant receives advisement or notice from its independent accountant requiring disclosure under paragraph (b) of this Item 4.02, the registrant must:

(1) provide the independent accountant with a copy of the disclosures it is making in response to this Item 4.02 that the independent accountant shall receive no later than the day that the disclosures are filed with the Commission;

(2) request the independent accountant to furnish to the registrant as promptly as possible a letter addressed to the Commission stating whether the independent accountant agrees with the statements made by the registrant in response to this Item 4.02 and, if not, stating the respects in which it does not agree; and

(3) amend the registrant's previously filed Form 8-K by filing the independent accountant's letter as an exhibit to the filed Form 8-K no later than two business days after the registrant's receipt of the letter.

Section 5—Corporate Governance and Management

Item 5.01 Changes in Control of Registrant.

(a) If, to the knowledge of the registrant's board of directors, a committee of the board of directors or authorized officer or officers of the registrant, a change in control of the registrant has occurred, furnish the following information:

(1) the identity of the person(s) who acquired such control;

(2) the date and a description of the transaction(s) which resulted in the change in control;

(3) the basis of the control, including the percentage of voting securities of the registrant now beneficially owned directly or indirectly by the person(s) who acquired control;

(4) the amount of the consideration used by such person(s);

(5)   the source(s) of funds used by the person(s), <u>unless</u> all or any part of the consideration used is a loan made in the ordinary course of business by a bank as defined by Section 3(a)(6) of the Act, in which case the identity of such bank may be omitted provided the person who acquired control:

(i)   has made a request for confidentiality pursuant to Section 13(d)(1)(B) of the Act; and

(ii)   states in the report that the identity of the bank has been so omitted and filed separately with the Commission.

(6)   the identity of the person(s) from whom control was assumed;

(7)   any arrangements or understandings among members of both the former and new control groups and their associates with respect to election of directors or other matters; and

(8)   if the registrant was a shell company, other than a business combination related shell company, as those terms are defined in Rule 12b–2 under the Exchange Act (17 CFR 240.12b–2), immediately before the change in control, the information that would be required if the registrant were filing a general form for registration of securities on Form 10 under the Exchange Act reflecting all classes of the registrant's securities subject to the reporting requirements of Section 13 (15 U.S.C. 78m) or Section 15(d) (15 U.S.C. 78o(d)) of such Act upon consummation of the change in control, with such information reflecting the registrant and its securities upon consummation of the transaction. Notwithstanding General Instruction B.3. to Form 8-K, if any disclosure required by this Item 5.01(a)(8) is previously reported, as that term is defined in Rule 12b–2 under the Exchange Act (17 CFR 240.12b–2), the registrant may identify the filing in which that disclosure is included instead of including that disclosure in this report.

(b)   Furnish the information required by Item 403(c) of Regulation S–K (17 CFR 229.403(c)).

Item 5.02   Departure of Directors or Certain Officers; Election of Directors; Appointment of Certain Officers; Compensatory Arrangements of Certain Officers.

(a)(1)   If a director has resigned or refuses to stand for re-election to the board of directors since the date of the last annual meeting of shareholders because of a disagreement with the registrant, known to an executive officer of the registrant, as defined in 17 CFR 240.3b–7, on any matter relating to the registrant's operations, policies or practices, or if a director has been removed for cause from the board of directors, disclose the following information:

(i)   the date of such resignation, refusal to stand for re-election or removal;

(ii)   any positions held by the director on any committee of the board of directors at the time of the director's resignation, refusal to stand for re-election or removal; and

(iii)   a brief description of the circumstances representing the disagreement that the registrant believes caused, in whole or in part, the director's resignation, refusal to stand for re-election or removal.

(2)   If the director has furnished the registrant with any written correspondence concerning the circumstances surrounding his or her resignation, refusal or removal, the registrant shall file a copy of the document as an exhibit to the report on Form 8-K.

(3)   The registrant also must:

(i)   provide the director with a copy of the disclosures it is making in response to this Item 5.02 no later than the day the registrant file the disclosures with the Commission;

(ii)   provide the director with the opportunity to furnish the registrant as promptly as possible with a letter addressed to the registrant stating whether he or she agrees with the statements made by the registrant in response to this Item 5.02 and, if not, stating the respects in which he or she does not agree; and

FORM 8-K

(iii) file any letter received by the registrant from the director with the Commission as an exhibit by an amendment to the previously filed Form 8-K within two business days after receipt by the registrant.

(b) If the registrant's principal executive officer, president, principal financial officer, principal accounting officer, principal operating officer, or any person performing similar functions, or any named executive officer, retires, resigns or is terminated from that position, or if a director retires, resigns, is removed, or refuses to stand for re-election (except in circumstances described in paragraph (a) of this Item 5.02), disclose the fact that the event has occurred and the date of the event.

(c) If the registrant appoints a new principal executive officer, president, principal financial officer, principal accounting officer, principal operating officer, or person performing similar functions, disclose the following information with respect to the newly appointed officer:

(1) the name and position of the newly appointed officer and the date of the appointment;

(2) the information required by Items 401(b), (d), (e) and Item 404(a) of Regulation S–K (17 CFR 229.401(b), (d), (e) and 229.404(a)); and

(3) a brief description of any material plan, contract or arrangement (whether or not written) to which a covered officer is a party or in which he or she participates that is entered into or material amendment in connection with the triggering event or any grant or award to any such covered person or modification thereto, under any such plan, contract or arrangement in connection with any such event.

Instruction to paragraph (c).

If the registrant intends to make a public announcement of the appointment other than by means of a report on Form 8-K, the registrant may delay filing the Form 8-K containing the disclosures required by this Item 5.02(c) until the day on which the registrant otherwise makes public announcement of the appointment of such officer.

(d) If the registrant elects a new director, except by a vote of security holders at an annual meeting or special meeting convened for such purpose, disclose the following information:

(1) the name of the newly elected director and the date of election;

(2) a brief description of any arrangement or understanding between the new director and any other persons, naming such persons, pursuant to which such director was selected as a director;

(3) the committees of the board of directors to which the new director has been, or at the time of this disclosure is expected to be, named; and

(4) the information required by Item 404(a) of Regulation S–K (17 CFR 229.404(a)).

(5) a brief description of any material plan, contract or arrangement (whether or not written) to which the director is a party or in which he or she participates that is entered into or material amendment in connection with the triggering event or any grant or award to any such covered person or modification thereto, under any such plan, contract or arrangement in connection with any such event.

(e) If the registrant enters into, adopts, or otherwise commences a material compensatory plan, contract or arrangement (whether or not written), as to which the registrant's principal executive officer, principal financial officer, or a named executive officer participates or is a party, or such compensatory plan, contract or arrangement is materially amended or modified, or a material grant or award under any such plan, contract or arrangement to any such person is made or materially modified, then the registrant shall provide a brief description of the terms and conditions of the plan, contract or arrangement and the amounts payable to the officer thereunder.

FORM 8-K

Instructions to paragraph (e).

1.   Disclosure under this Item 5.02(e) shall be required whether or not the specified event is in connection with events otherwise triggering disclosure pursuant to this Item 5.02.

2.   Grants or awards (or modifications thereto) made pursuant to a plan, contract or arrangement (whether involving cash or equity), that are materially consistent with the previously disclosed terms of such plan, contract or arrangement, need not be disclosed under this Item 5.02(e), provided the registrant has previously disclosed such terms and the grant, award or modification is disclosed when Item 402 of Regulation S–K (17 CFR 229.402) requires such disclosure.

(f)(1)   If the salary or bonus of a named executive officer cannot be calculated as of the most recent practicable date and is omitted from the Summary Compensation Table as specified in Instruction 1 to Item 402(c)(2)(iii) and (iv) of Regulation S–K, disclose the appropriate information under this Item 5.02(f) when there is a payment, grant, award, decision or other occurrence as a result of which such amounts become calculable in whole or part. Disclosure under this Item 5.02(f) shall include a new total compensation figure for the named executive officer, using the new salary or bonus information to recalculate the information that was previously provided with respect to the named executive officer in the registrant's Summary Compensation Table for which the salary and bonus information was omitted in reliance on Instruction 1 to Item 402(c)(2)(iii) and (iv) of Regulation S–K (17 CFR 229.402(c)(2)(iii) and (iv)).

(2)   As specified in Instruction 6 to Item 402(u) of Regulation S–K (17 CFR 229.402(u)), disclosure under this Item 5.02(f) with respect to the salary or bonus of a principal executive officer shall include pay ratio disclosure pursuant to Item 402(u) of Regulation S–K calculated using the new total compensation figure for the principal executive officer. Pay ratio disclosure is not required under this Item 5.02(f) until the omitted salary or bonus amounts for such principal executive officer become calculable in whole.

Instructions to Item 5.02.

1.   The disclosure requirements of this Item 5.02 do not apply to a registrant that is a wholly-owned subsidiary of an issuer with a class of securities registered under Section 12 of the Exchange Act (15 U.S.C. 78*l*), or that is required to file reports under Section 15(d) of the Exchange Act (15 U.S.C. 78o(d)).

2.   To the extent that any information called for in Item 5.02(c)(3) or Item 5.02(d)(3) or Item 5.02(d)(4) is not determined or is unavailable at the time of the required filing, the registrant shall include a statement this effect in the filing and then must file an amendment to its Form 8-K filing under this Item 5.02 containing such information within four business days after the information is determined or becomes available.

3.   The registrant need not provide information with respect to plans, contracts, and arrangements to the extent they do not discriminate in scope, terms or operation, in favor of executive officers or directors of the registrant and that are available generally to all salaried employees.

4.   For purposes of this Item, the term "named executive officer" shall refer to those executive officers for whom disclosure was required in the registrant's most recent filing with the Commission under the Securities Act (15 U.S.C. 77a *et seq.*) or Exchange Act (15 U.S.C. 78a *et seq.*) that required disclosure pursuant to Item 402(c) of Regulation S–K (17 CFR 229.402(c)).

Item 5.03   Amendments to Articles of Incorporation or Bylaws; Change in Fiscal Year.

(a)   If a registrant with a class of equity securities registered under Section 12 of the Exchange Act (15 U.S.C. 78*l*) amends its articles of incorporation or bylaws and a proposal for the amendment was not disclosed in a proxy statement or information statement filed by the registrant, disclose the following information:

(1)   the effective date of the amendment; and

FORM 8-K

(2)   a description of the provision adopted or changed by amendment and, if applicable, the previous provision.

(b)   If the registrant determines to change the fiscal year from that used in its most recent filing with the Commission other than by means of:

(1)   a submission to a vote of security holders through the solicitation of proxies or otherwise; or

(2)   an amendment to its articles of incorporation or bylaws,

disclose the date of such determination, the date of the new fiscal year end and the form (for example, Form 10-K or Form 10-Q) on which the report covering the transition period will be filed.

Instructions to Item 5.03.

1.   Refer to Item 601(b)(3) of Regulation S–K (17 CFR 229.601(b)(3)) regarding the filing of exhibits to this Item 5.03.

2.   With respect to asset-backed securities, as defined in 17 CFR 229.1101, disclosure is required under this Item 5.03 regarding any amendment to the governing documents of the issuing entity, regardless of whether the class of asset-backed securities is reporting under Section 13 or 15(d) of the Exchange Act.

Item 5.04   Temporary Suspension of Trading Under Registrant's Employee Benefit Plans.

(a)   No later than the fourth business day after which the registrant receives the notice required by section 101(i)(2)(E) of the Employment Retirement Income Security Act of 1974 (29 U.S.C. 1021(i)(2)(E)), or, if such notice is not received by the registrant, on the same date by which the registrant transmits a timely notice to an affected officer or director within the time period prescribed by Rule 104(b)(2)(i)(B) or 104(b)(2)(ii) of Regulation BTR (17 CFR 245.104(b)(2)(i)(B) or 17 CFR 245.104(b)(2)(ii)), provide the information specified in Rule 104(b) (17 CFR 245.104(b)) and the date the registrant received the notice required by section 101(i)(2)(E) of the Employment Retirement Income Security Act of 1974 (29 U.S.C. 1021(i)(2)(E)), if applicable.

(b)   On the same date by which the registrant transmits a timely updated notice to an affected officer or director, as required by the time period under Rule 104(b)(2)(iii) of Regulation BTR (17 CFR 245.104(b)(2)(iii)), provide the information specified in Rule 104(b)(3)(iii) (17 CFR 245.104(b)(2)(iii)).

Item 5.05   Amendments to the Registrant's Code of Ethics, or Waiver of a Provision of the Code of Ethics.

(a)   Briefly describe the date and nature of any amendment to a provision of the registrant's code of ethics that applies to the registrant's principal executive officer, principal financial officer, principal accounting officer or controller or persons performing similar functions and that relates to any element of the code of ethics definition enumerated in Item 406(b) of Regulations S–K (17 CFR 228.406(b)).

(b)   If the registrant has granted a waiver, including an implicit waiver, from a provision of the code of ethics to an officer or person described in paragraph (a) of this Item 5.05, and the waiver relates to one or more of the elements of the code of ethics definition referred to in paragraph (a) of this Item 5.05, briefly describe the nature of the waiver, the name of the person to whom the waiver was granted, and the date of the waiver.

(c)   The registrant does not need to provide any information pursuant to this Item 5.05 if it discloses the required information on its Internet website within four business days following the date of the amendment or waiver and the registrant has disclosed in its most recently filed annual report its Internet address and intention to provide disclosure in this manner. If the registrant elects to disclose the information required by this Item 5.05 through its website, such information must remain available on the website for at least a 12-month period. Following the 12-month period, the registrant must retain the information for a period of not less than five years. Upon request, the registrant must

FORM 8-K

furnish to the Commission or its staff a copy of any or all information retained pursuant to this requirement.

Instructions.

1.   The registrant does not need to disclose technical, administrative or other non-substantive amendments to its code of ethics.

2.   For purposes of this Item 5.05:

(i)   The term <u>waiver</u> means the approval by the registrant of a material departure from a provision of the code of ethics; and

(ii)   The term <u>implicit waiver</u> means the registrant's failure to take action within a reasonable period of time regarding a material departure from a provision of the code of ethics that has been made known to an executive officer, as defined in Rule 3b–7 (17 CFR 240.3b–7) of the registrant.

Item 5.06   Change in Shell Company Status.

If a registrant that was a shell company, other than a business combination related shell company, as those terms are defined in Rule 12b–2 under the Exchange Act (17 CFR 240.12b–2), has completed a transaction that has the effect of causing it to cease being a shell company, as defined in Rule 12b–2, disclose the material terms of the transaction. Notwithstanding General Instruction B.3. to Form 8-K, if any disclosure required by this Item 5.06 is previously reported, as that term is defined in Rule 12b–2 under the Exchange Act (17 CFR 240.12b–2), the registrant may identify the filing in which that disclosure is included instead of including that disclosure in this report.

Item 5.07   Submission of Matters to a Vote of Security Holders.

If any matter was submitted to a vote of security holders, through the solicitation of proxies or otherwise, provide the following information:

(a)   The date of the meeting and whether it was an annual or special meeting. This information must be provided only if a meeting of security holders was held.

(b)   If the meeting involved the election of directors, the name of each director elected at the meeting, as well as a brief description of each other matter voted upon at the meeting; and state the number of votes cast for, against or withheld, as well as the number of abstentions and broker non-votes as to each such matter, including a separate tabulation with respect to each nominee for office. For the vote on the frequency of shareholder advisory votes on executive compensation required by section 14A(a)(2) of the Securities Exchange Act of 1934 (15 U.S.C. 78n–1) and § 240.14a–21(b), state the number of votes cast for each of 1 year, 2 years, and 3 years, as well as the number of abstentions.

(c)   A description of the terms of any settlement between the registrant and any other participant (as defined in Instruction 3 to Item 4 of Schedule 14A (17 CFR 240.14a–101)) terminating any solicitation subject to Rule 14a–12(c), including the cost or anticipated cost to the registrant.

(d)   No later than one hundred fifty calendar days after the end of the annual or other meeting of shareholders at which shareholders voted on the frequency of shareholder votes on the compensation of executives as required by section 14A(a)(2) of the Securities Exchange Act of 1934 (15 U.S.C. 78n–1), but in no event later than sixty calendar days prior to the deadline for submission of shareholder proposals under § 240.14a–8, as disclosed in the registrant's most recent proxy statement for an annual or other meeting of shareholders relating to the election of directors at which shareholders voted on the frequency of shareholder votes on the compensation of executives as required by section 14A(a)(2) of the Securities Exchange Act of 1934 (15 U.S.C. 78n–1(a)(2)), by amendment to the most recent Form 8-K filed pursuant to (b) of this Item, disclose the company's decision in light of such vote as to how frequently the company will include a shareholder vote on the compensation of executives in its proxy materials until the next required vote on the frequency of shareholder votes on the compensation of executives.

FORM 8-K

Instruction 1 to Item 5.07. The four business day period for reporting the event under this Item 5.07, other than with respect to Item 5.07(d), shall begin to run on the day on which the meeting ended. The registrant shall disclose on Form 8-K under this Item 5.07 the preliminary voting results. The registrant shall file an amended report on Form 8-K under this Item 5.07 to disclose the final voting results within four business days after the final voting results are known. However, no preliminary voting results need be disclosed under this Item 5.07 if the registrant has disclosed final voting results on Form 8-K under this Item.

Instruction 2 to Item 5.07. If any matter has been submitted to a vote of security holders otherwise than at a meeting of such security holders, corresponding information with respect to such submission shall be provided. The solicitation of any authorization or consent (other than a proxy to vote at a stockholders' meeting) with respect to any matter shall be deemed a submission of such matter to a vote of security holders within the meaning of this item.

Instruction 3 to Item 5.07. If the registrant did not solicit proxies and the board of directors as previously reported to the Commission was re-elected in its entirety, a statement to that effect in answer to paragraph (b) will suffice as an answer thereto regarding the election of directors.

Instruction 4 to Item 5.07. If the registrant has furnished to its security holders proxy soliciting material containing the information called for by paragraph (c), the paragraph may be answered by reference to the information contained in such material.

Instruction 5 to Item 5.07. A registrant may omit the information called for by this Item 5.07 if, on the date of the filing of its report on Form 8-K, the registrant meets the following conditions:

1.   All of the registrant's equity securities are owned, either directly or indirectly, by a single person which is a reporting company under the Exchange Act and which has filed all the material required to be filed pursuant to Section 13, 14 or 15(d) thereof, as applicable; and

2.   During the preceding thirty-six calendar months and any subsequent period of days, there has not been any material default in the payment of principal, interest, a sinking or purchase fund installment, or any other material default not cured within thirty days, with respect to any indebtedness of the registrant or its subsidiaries, and there has not been any material default in the payment of rentals under material long-term leases.

Item 5.08   Shareholder Director Nominations

(a)   If the registrant did not hold an annual meeting the previous year, or if the date of this year's annual meeting has been changed by more than 30 calendar days from the date of the previous year's meeting, then the registrant is required to disclose the date by which a nominating shareholder or nominating shareholder group must submit the notice on Schedule 14N (§ 240.14n–101) required pursuant to § 240.14a–11(b)(10), which date shall be a reasonable time before the registrant mails its proxy materials for the meeting. Where a registrant is required to include shareholder director nominees in the registrant's proxy materials pursuant to either an applicable state or foreign law provision, or a provision in the registrant's governing documents, then the registrant is required to disclose the date by which a nominating shareholder or nominating shareholder group must submit the notice on Schedule 14N required pursuant to § 240.14a–18.

(b)   If the registrant is a series company as defined in Rule 18f–2(a) under the Investment Company Act of 1940 (§ 270.18f–2 of this chapter), then the registrant is required to disclose in connection with the election of directors at an annual meeting of shareholders (or, in lieu of such an annual meeting, a special meeting of shareholders) the total number of shares of the registrant outstanding and entitled to be voted (or if the votes are to be cast on a basis other than one vote per share, then the total number of votes entitled to be voted and the basis for allocating such votes) on the election of directors at such meeting of shareholders as of the end of the most recent calendar quarter.

FORM 8-K

Section 6—Asset-Backed Securities

The Items in this Section 6 apply only to asset-backed securities. Terms used in this Section 6 have the same meaning as in Item 1101 of Regulation AB (17 CFR 229.1101).

Item 6.01   ABS Informational and Computational Material.

Report under this Item any ABS informational and computational material filed in, or as an exhibit to, this report.

Item 6.02   Change of Servicer or Trustee.

If a servicer contemplated by Item 1108(a)(2) of Regulation AB (17 CFR 229.1108(a)(2)) or a trustee has resigned or has been removed, replaced or substituted, or if a new servicer contemplated by Item 1108(a)(2) of Regulation AB or trustee has been appointed, state the date the event occurred and the circumstances surrounding the change. In addition, provide the disclosure required by Item 1108(d) of Regulation AB (17 CFR 229.1108(c)), as applicable, regarding the servicer or trustee change. If a new servicer contemplated by Item 1108(a)(3) of this Regulation AB or a new trustee has been appointed, provide the information required by Item 1108(b) through (d) of Regulation AB regarding such servicer or Item 1109 of Regulation AB (17 CFR 229.1109) regarding such trustee, as applicable.

Instruction.

To the extent that any information called for by this Item regarding such servicer or trustee is not determined or is unavailable at the time of the required filing, the registrant shall include a statement to this effect in the filing and then must file an amendment to its Form 8-K filing under this Item 6.02 containing such information within four business days after the information is determined or becomes available.

Item 6.03   Change in Credit Enhancement or Other External Support.

(a) Loss of existing enhancement or support. If the depositor (or servicer if the servicer signs the report on Form 10-K (17 CFR 249.310) of the issuing entity) becomes aware that any material enhancement or support specified in Item 1114(a)(1) through (3) of Regulation AB (17 CFR 229.1114(a)(1) through (3)) or Item 1115 of Regulation AB (17 CFR 229.1115) that was previously applicable regarding one or more classes of the asset-backed securities has terminated other than by expiration of the contract on its stated termination date or as a result of all parties completing their obligations under such agreement, then disclose:

(1)   the date of the termination of the enhancement;

(2)   the identity of the parties to the agreement relating to the enhancement or support;

(3)   a brief description of the terms and conditions of the enhancement or support that are material to security holders;

(4)   a brief description of the material circumstances surrounding the termination; and

(5)   any material early termination penalties paid or to be paid out of the cash flows backing the asset-backed securities.

(b)   Addition of new enhancement or support. If the depositor (or servicer if the servicer signs the report on Form 10-K (17 CFR 249.310) of the issuing entity) becomes aware that any material enhancement specified in Item 1114(a)(1) through (3) of Regulation AB (17 CFR 229.1114(a)(1) through (3)) or Item 1115 of Regulation AB (17 CFR 229.1115) has been added with respect to one or more classes of the asset-backed securities, then provide the date of addition of the new enhancement or support and the disclosure required by Items 1114 or 1115 of Regulation AB, as applicable, with respect to such new enhancement or support.

(c)   Material change to enhancement or support. If the depositor (or servicer if the servicer signs the report on Form 10-K (17 CFR 249.310) of the issuing entity) becomes aware that any existing material enhancement or support specified in Item 1114(a)(1) through (3) of Regulation AB or Item

1115 of Regulation AB with respect to one or more classes of the asset-backed securities has been materially amended or modified, disclose:

    (1)   the date on which the agreement or agreements relating to the enhancement or support was amended or modified;

    (2)   the identity of the parties to the agreement or agreements relating to the amendment or modification; and

    (3)   a brief description of the material terms and conditions of the amendment or modification.

Instructions.

1.   Disclosure is required under this Item whether or not the registrant is a party to any agreement regarding the enhancement or support if the loss, addition or modification of such enhancement or support materially affects, directly or indirectly, the asset-backed securities, the pool assets or the cash flow underlying the asset-backed securities.

2.   To the extent that any information called for by this Item regarding the enhancement or support is not determined or is unavailable at the time of the required filing, the registrant shall include a statement to this effect in the filing and then must file an amendment to its Form 8-K filing under this Item 6.03 containing such information within four business days after the information is determined or becomes available.

3.   The instructions to Items 1.01 and 1.02 of this Form apply to this Item.

4.   Notwithstanding Items 1.01 and 1.02 of this Form, disclosure regarding changes to material enhancement or support is to be reported under this Item 6.03 in lieu of those Items.

Item 6.04   Failure to Make a Required Distribution.

If a required distribution to holders of the asset-backed securities is not made as of the required distribution date under the transaction documents, and such failure is material, identify the failure and state the nature of the failure to make the timely distribution.

Item 6.05   Securities Act Updating Disclosure.

Regarding an offering of asset-backed securities registered on Form SF-3 (17 CFR 239.45), if any material pool characteristic of the actual asset pool at the time of issuance of the asset-backed securities differs by 5% or more (other than as a result of the pool assets converting into cash in accordance with their terms) from the description of the asset pool in the prospectus filed for the offering pursuant to Securities Act Rule 424 (17 CFR 230.424), disclose the information required by Items 1111 and 1112 of Regulation AB (17 CFR 229.1111 and 17 CFR 229.1112) regarding the characteristics of the actual asset pool. If applicable, also provide information required by Items 1108 and 1110 of Regulation AB (17 CFR 229.1108 and 17 CFR 229.1110) regarding any new servicers or originators that would be required to be disclosed under those items regarding the pool assets.

Instruction.

No report is required under this Item if substantially the same information is provided in a post-effective amendment to the Securities Act registration statement or in a subsequent prospectus filed pursuant to Securities Act Rule 424 (17 CFR 230.424).

* * *

Section 7—Regulation FD

Item 7.01   Regulation FD Disclosure.

Unless filed under Item 8.01, disclose under this item only information that the registrant elects to disclose through Form 8-K pursuant to Regulation FD (17 CFR 243.100 through 243.103).

FORM 8-K

Section 8—Other Events

Item 8.01   Other Events.

The registrant may, at its option, disclose under this Item 8.01 any events, with respect to which information is not otherwise called for by this form, that the registrant deems of importance to security holders. The registrant may, at its option, file a report under this Item 8.01 disclosing the nonpublic information required to be disclosed by Regulation FD (17 CFR 243.100 through 243.103).

Section 9—Financial Statements and Exhibits

Item 9.01   Financial Statements and Exhibits.

List below the financial statements, pro forma financial information and exhibits, if any, filed as a part of this report.

(a)   Financial statements of businesses acquired.

(1)   For any business acquisition required to be described in answer to Item 2.01 of this form, financial statements of the business acquired shall be filed for the periods specified in Rule 3–05(b) of Regulation S–X (17 CFR 210.3–05(b)) or Rule 8–04(b) of Regulation S–X (17 CFR 210.8–04(b)) for smaller reporting companies.

(2)   The financial statements shall be prepared pursuant to Regulation S–X except that supporting schedules need not be filed. A manually signed accountant's report should be provided pursuant to Rule 2–02 of Regulation S–X (17 CFR 210.2–02).

(3)   With regard to the acquisition of one or more real estate properties, the financial statements and any additional information specified by Rule 3–14 of Regulation S–X (17 CFR 210.3–14) or Rule 8–06 of Regulation S–X (17 CFR 210.8–06) for smaller reporting companies.

(4)   Financial statements required by this item may be filed with the initial report, or by amendment not later than 71 calendar days after the date that the initial report on Form 8-K must be filed. If the financial statements are not included in the initial report, the registrant should so indicate in the Form 8-K report and state when the required financial statements will be filed. The registrant may, at its option, include unaudited financial statements in the initial report on Form 8-K.

(b)   Pro forma financial information.

(1)   For any transaction required to be described in answer to Item 2.01 of this form, furnish any pro forma financial information that would be required pursuant to Article 11 of Regulation S–X (17 CFR 210) or Rule 8–05 of Regulation S–X (17 CFR 210.8–05) for smaller reporting companies.

(2)   The provisions of paragraph (a)(4) of this Item 9.01 shall also apply to pro forma financial information relative to the acquired business.

(c)   Shell company transactions. The provisions of paragraph (a)(4) and (b)(2) of this Item shall not apply to the financial statements or pro forma financial information required to be filed under this Item with regard to any transaction required to be described in answer to Item 2.01 of this Form by a registrant that was a shell company, other than a business combination related shell company, as those terms are defined in Rule 12b–2 under the Exchange Act (17 CFR 240.12b–2), immediately before that transaction. Accordingly, with regard to any transaction required to be described in answer to Item 2.01 of this Form by a registrant that was a shell company, other than a business combination related shell company, immediately before that transaction, the financial statements and pro forma financial information required by this Item must be filed in the initial report. Notwithstanding General Instruction B.3. to Form 8-K, if any financial statement or any financial information required to be filed in the initial report by this Item 9.01(c) is previously reported, as that term is defined in Rule 12b–2 under the Exchange Act (17 CFR 240.12b–2), the registrant may identify the filing in which that disclosure is included instead of including that disclosure in the initial report.

(d) <u>Exhibits</u>. The exhibits shall be deemed to be filed or furnished, depending on the relevant item requiring such exhibit, in accordance with the provisions of Item 601 of Regulation S–K (17 CFR 229.601)and Instruction B.2 to this form.

Instruction.

During the period after a registrant has reported a business combination pursuant to Item 2.01 of this form, until the date on which the financial statements specified by this Item 9.01 must be filed, the registrant will be deemed current for purposes of its reporting obligations under Section 13(a) or 15(d) of the Exchange Act (15 U.S.C. 78m or 78*o*(d)). With respect to filings under the Securities Act, however, registration statements will not be declared effective and post-effective amendments to registrations statements will not be declared effective unless financial statements meeting the requirements of Rule 3–05 of Regulation S–X (17 CFR 210.3–05) are provided. In addition, offerings should not be made pursuant to effective registration statements, or pursuant to Rule 506 of Regulation D (17 CFR 230.506) where any purchasers are not accredited investors under Rule 501(a) of that Regulation, until the audited financial statements required by Rule 3–05 of Regulation S–X (17 CFR 210.3–05) are filed; provided, however, that the following offerings or sales of securities may proceed notwithstanding that financial statements of the acquired business have not been filed:

(a)   offerings or sales of securities upon the conversion of outstanding convertible securities or upon the exercise of outstanding warrants or rights;

(b)   dividend or interest reinvestment plans;

(c)   employee benefit plans;

(d)   transactions involving secondary offerings; or

(e)   sales of securities pursuant to Rule 144 (17 CFR 230.144).

FORM 10-K: ANNUAL REPORT PURSUANT TO SECTION 13 OR 15(d) OF THE SECURITIES EXCHANGE ACT OF 1934

GENERAL INSTRUCTIONS

A.   Rule as to Use of Form 10-K.

(1)   This Form shall be used for annual reports pursuant to Section 13 or 15(d) of the Securities Exchange Act of 1934 (15 U.S.C. 78m or 78*o*(d)) (the "Act") for which no other form is prescribed. This Form also shall be used for transition reports filed pursuant to Section 13 or 15(d) of the Act.

(2)   Annual reports on this Form shall be filed within the following period:

(a)   60 days after the end of the fiscal year covered by the report (75 days for fiscal years ending before December 15, 2006) for large accelerated filers (as defined in 17 CFR 240.12b–2):

(b)   75 days after the end of the fiscal year covered by the report for accelerated filers (as defined in 17 CFR 240.12b–2); and

(c)   90 days after the end of the fiscal year covered by the report for all other registrants.

(3)   Transition reports on this Form shall be filed in accordance with the requirements set forth in Rule 13a–10 (17 CFR 240.13a–10) or Rule 15d–10 (17 CFR 240.15d–10) applicable when the registrant changes its fiscal year end.

(4)   Notwithstanding paragraphs (2) and (3) of this General Instruction A., all schedules required by Article 12 of Regulation S–X (17 CFR 210.12–01—210.12–29) may, at the option of the registrant, be filed as an amendment to the report not later than 30 days after the applicable due date of the report.

* * *

FORM 10-K

D. Signature and Filing of Report.

(1)   Three complete copies of the report, including financial statements, financial statement schedules, exhibits, and all other papers and documents filed as a part thereof, and five additional copies which need not include exhibits, shall be filed with the Commission. At least one complete copy of the report, including financial statements, financial statement schedules, exhibits, and all other papers and documents filed as a part thereof, shall be filed with each exchange on which any class of securities of the registrant is registered. At least one complete copy of the report filed with the Commission and one such copy filed with each exchange shall be manually signed. Copies not manually signed shall bear typed or printed signatures.

(2)   (a) The report must be signed by the registrant, and on behalf of the registrant by its principal executive officer or officers, its principal financial officer or officers, its controller or principal accounting officer, and by at least the majority of the board of directors or persons performing similar functions. Where the registrant is a limited partnership, the report must be signed by the majority of the board of directors of any corporate general partner who signs the report.

* * *

G. Information to be Incorporated by Reference.

(1)   Attention is directed to Rule 12b–23 which provides for the incorporation by reference of information contained in certain documents in answer or partial answer to any item of a report.

(2)   The information called for by Parts I and II of this form (Items 1 through 9A or any portion thereof) may, at the registrant's option, be incorporated by reference from the registrant's annual report to security holders furnished to the Commission pursuant to Rule 14a–3(b) or Rule 14c–3(a) or from the registrant's annual report to security holders, even if not furnished to the Commission pursuant to Rule 14a–3(b) or Rule 14c–3(a), provided such annual report contains the information required by Rule 14a–3.

Note 1. In order to fulfill the requirements of Part I of Form 10-K, the incorporated portion of the annual report to security holders must contain the information required by Items 1–3 of Form 10-K; to the extent applicable.

Note 2. If any information required by Part I or Part II is incorporated by reference into an electronic format document from the annual report to security holders as provided in General Instruction G, any portion of the annual report to security holders incorporated by reference shall be filed as an exhibit in electronic format, as required by Item 601(b)(13) of Regulation S–K.

(3)   The information required by Part III (Items 10, 11, 12, 13 and 14) may be incorporated by reference from the registrant's definitive proxy statement (filed or required to be filed pursuant to Regulation 14A) or definitive information statement (filed or to be filed pursuant to Regulation 14C) which involves the election of directors, if such definitive proxy statement or information statement is filed with the Commission not later than 120 days after the end of the fiscal year covered by the Form 10-K. However, if such definitive proxy statement or information statement is not filed with the Commission in the 120-day period or is not required to be filed with the Commission by virtue of Rule 3a12–3(b) under the Exchange Act, the Items comprising the Part III information must be filed as part of the Form 10-K, or as an amendment to the Form 10-K, not later than the end of the 120-day period. It should be noted that the information regarding executive officers required by Item 401 of Regulation S–K (§ 229.401 of this chapter) may be included in Part I of Form 10-K under an appropriate caption. *See* the Instruction to Item 401 of Regulation S–K (§ 229.401 of this chapter).

* * *

H. Integrated Reports to Security Holders.

Annual reports to security holders may be combined with the required information of Form 10-K and will be suitable for filing with the Commission if the following conditions are satisfied:

FORM 10-K

(1) The combined report contains full and complete answers to all items required by Form 10-K. When responses to a certain item of required disclosure are separated within the combined report, an appropriate cross-reference should be made. If the information required by Part III of Form 10-K is omitted by virtue of General Instruction G, a definitive proxy or information statement shall be filed.

(2) The cover page and the required signatures are included. As appropriate, a cross-reference sheet should be filed indicating the location of information required by the items of the Form.

* * *

PART I

[*See* General Instruction G(2)]

Item 1. Business.

Furnish the information required by Item 101 of Regulation S–K (§ 229.101 of this chapter) except that the discussion of the development of the registrant's business need only include developments since the beginning of the fiscal year for which this report is filed.

Item 1A. Risk Factors.

Set forth, under the caption "Risk Factors," where appropriate, the risk factors described in Item 105 of Regulation S–K (§ 229.105 of this chapter) applicable to the registrant. Provide any discussion of risk factors in plain English in accordance with Rule 421(d) of the Securities Act of 1933 (§ 230.421(d) of this chapter). Smaller reporting companies are not required to provide the information required by this item.

Item 1B. Unresolved Staff Comments.

If the registrant is an accelerated filer or a large accelerated filer, as defined in Rule 12b–2 of the Exchange Act (§ 240.12b–2 of this chapter), or is a well-known seasoned issuer as defined in Rule 405 of the Securities Act (§ 230.405 of this chapter) and has received written comments from the Commission staff regarding its periodic or current reports under the Act not less than 180 days before the end of its fiscal year to which the annual report relates, and such comments remain unresolved, disclose the substance of any such unresolved comments that the registrant believes are material. Such disclosure may provide other information including the position of the registrant with respect to any such comment.

Item 2. Properties.

Furnish the information required by Item 102 of Regulation S–K (§ 229.102 of this chapter).

Item 3. Legal Proceedings.

(a) Furnish the information required by Item 103 of Regulation S–K (§ 229.103 of this chapter).

(b) As to any proceeding that was terminated during the fourth quarter of the fiscal year covered by this report, furnish information similar to that required by Item 103 of Regulation S–K (§ 229.103 of this chapter), including the date of termination and a description of the disposition thereof with respect to the registrant and its subsidiaries.

Item 4. Mine Safety Disclosures.

If applicable, provide a statement that the information concerning mine safety violations or other regulatory matters required by Section 1503(a) of the Dodd-Frank Wall Street Reform and Consumer Protection Act and Item 104 of Regulation S–K (17 CFR 229.104) is included in exhibit 95 to the annual report.

PART II

[*See* General Instruction G(2)]

FORM 10-K

Item 5. Market for Registrant's Common Equity, Related Stockholder Matters and Issuer Purchases of Equity Securities.

(a)   Furnish the information required by Item 201 of Regulation S–K (17 CFR 229.201) and Item 701 of Regulation S–K (17 CFR 229.701) as to all equity securities of the registrant sold by the registrant during the period covered by the report that were not registered under the Securities Act. If the Item 701 information previously has been included in a Quarterly Report on Form 10-Q or in a Current Report on Form 8-K (17 CFR 249.308), it need not be furnished.

(b)   If required pursuant to Rule 463 (17 CFR 230.463) of the Securities Act of 1933, furnish the information required by Item 701(f) of Regulation S–K (§ 229.701(f) of this chapter).

(c)   Furnish the information required by Item 703 of Regulation S–K (§ 229.703 of this chapter) for any repurchase made in a month within the fourth quarter of the fiscal year covered by the report. Provide disclosures covering repurchases made on a monthly basis. For example, if the fourth quarter began on January 16 and ended on April 15, the chart would show repurchases for the months from January 16 through February 15, February 16 through March 15, and March 16 through April 15.

Item 6. Selected Financial Data.

Furnish the information required by Item 301 of Regulation S–K (§ 229.301 of this chapter).

Item 7. Management's Discussion and Analysis of Financial Condition and Results of Operations.

Furnish the information required by Item 303 of Regulation S–K (§ 229.303 of this chapter).

Item 7A. Quantitative and Qualitative Disclosures About Market Risk.

Furnish the information required by Item 305 of Regulation S–K (§ 229.305 of this chapter).

Item 8. Financial Statements and Supplementary Data.

(a)   Furnish financial statements meeting the requirements of Regulation S–X (§ 210 of this chapter), except § 210.3–05 and Article 11 thereof, and the supplementary financial information required by Item 302 of Regulation S–K (§ 229.302 of this chapter). Financial statements of the registrant and its subsidiaries consolidated (as required by Rule 14a–3(b)) shall be filed under this item. Other financial statements and schedules required under Regulation S–X may be filed as "Financial Statement Schedules" pursuant to Item 15, Exhibits, Financial Statement Schedules, and Reports on Form 8-K, of this form.

* * *

Item 9. Changes in and Disagreements With Accountants on Accounting and Financial Disclosure.

Furnish the information required by Item 304(b) of Regulation S–K (§ 229.304(b) of this chapter).

* * *

PART III

[*See* General Instruction G(3)]

Item 10. Directors, Executive Officers and Corporate Governance.

Furnish the information required by Items 401, 405, 406 and 407(c)(3), (d)(4) and (d)(5) of Regulation S–K (§ 229.401, § 229.405, § 229.406 and § 229.407(c)(3), (d)(4) and (d)(5) of this chapter).

* * *

FORM 10-K

Item 12. Security Ownership of Certain Beneficial Owners and Management and Related Stockholder Matters.

Furnish the information required by Item 201(d) of Regulation S–K (§ 229.201(d) of this chapter) and Item 403 of Regulation S–K (§ 229.403 of this chapter).

Item 13. Certain Relationships and Related Transactions, and Director Independence.

Furnish the information required by Item 404 of Regulation S–K (§ 229.404 of this chapter) and Item 407(a) of Regulation S–K (§ 229.407(a) of this chapter).

Item 14. Principal Accounting Fees and Services.

Furnish the information required by Item 9(e) of Schedule 14A (§ 240.14a–101 of this chapter).

(1)   Disclose, under the caption <u>Audit Fees</u>, the aggregate fees billed for each of the last two fiscal years for professional services rendered by the principal accountant for the audit of the registrant's annual financial statements and review of financial statements included in the registrant's Form 10-Q (17 CFR 249.308a) or services that are normally provided by the accountant in connection with statutory and regulatory filings or engagements for those fiscal years.

(2)   Disclose, under the caption <u>Audit-Related Fees</u>, the aggregate fees billed in each of the last two fiscal years for assurance and related services by the principal accountant that are reasonably related to the performance of the audit or review of the registrant's financial statements and are not reported under Item 9(e)(1) of Schedule 14A. Registrants shall describe the nature of the services comprising the fees disclosed under this category.

(3)   Disclose, under the caption <u>Tax Fees</u>, the aggregate fees billed in each of the last two fiscal years for professional services rendered by the principal accountant for tax compliance, tax advice, and tax planning. Registrants shall describe the nature of the services comprising the fees disclosed under this category.

(4)   Disclose, under the caption <u>All Other Fees</u>, the aggregate fees billed in each of the last two fiscal years for products and services provided by the principal accountant, other than the services reported in Items 9(e)(1) through 9(e)(3) of Schedule 14A. Registrants shall describe the nature of the services comprising the fees disclosed under this category.

(5)   (i) Disclose the audit committee's pre-approval policies and procedures described in paragraph (c)(7)(i) of Rule 2–01 of Regulation S–X.

(ii)   Disclose the percentage of services described in each of Items 9(e)(2) through 9(e)(4) of Schedule 14A that were approved by the audit committee pursuant to paragraph (c)(7)(i)(C) of Rule 2–01 of Regulation S–X.

(6)   If greater than 50 percent, disclose the percentage of hours expended on the principal accountant's engagement to audit the registrant's financial statements for the most recent fiscal year that were attributed to work performed by persons other than the principal accountant's full-time, permanent employees.

PART IV

Item 15. Exhibits, Financial Statement Schedules.

(a)   List the following documents filed as a part of the report:

(1)   All financial statements;

(2)   Those financial statement schedules required to be filed by Item 8 of this form, and by paragraph (b) below.

(3)   Those exhibits required by Item 601 of Regulation S–K (§ 229.601 of this chapter) and by paragraph (b) below. Identify in the list each management contract or compensatory plan or arrangement required to be filed as an exhibit to this form pursuant to Item 15(b) of this report.

FORM 10-K

* * *

(c)   Registrants shall file, as financial statement schedules to this form, the financial statements required by Regulation S–X (17 CFR 210) which are excluded from the annual report to shareholders by Rule 14a–3(b) including[:]

    (1)   separate financial statements of subsidiaries not consolidated and fifty percent or less owned persons;

    (2)   separate financial statements of affiliates whose securities are pledged as collateral; and

    (3)   schedules.

Item 16. Form 10–K Summary.

Registrants may, at their option, include a summary of information required by this form, but only if each item in the summary is presented fairly and accurately and includes a hyperlink to the material contained in this form to which such item relates, including to materials contained in any exhibits filed with the form.

Instruction:

The summary shall refer only to Form 10-K disclosure that is included in the form at the time it is filed. A registrant need not update the summary to reflect information required by Part III of Form 10-K that the registrant incorporates by reference from a proxy or information statement filed after the Form 10-K, but must state in the summary that the summary does not include Part III information because that information will be incorporated by reference from a later filed proxy or information statement involving the election of directors.

* * *

Supplemental Information to be Furnished With Reports Filed Pursuant to Section 15(d) of the Act by Registrants Which Have Not Registered Securities Pursuant to Section 12 of the Act

(a)   Except to the extent that the materials enumerated in (1) and/or (2) below are specifically incorporated into this Form by reference, every registrant which files an annual report on this Form pursuant to Section 15(d) of the Act must furnish to the Commission for its information, at the time of filing its report on this Form, four copies of the following:

    (1)   Any annual report to security holders covering the registrant's last fiscal year; and

    (2)   Every proxy statement, form of proxy or other proxy soliciting material sent to more than ten of the registrant's security holders with respect to any annual or other meeting of security holders.

(b)   The foregoing material shall not be deemed to be "filed" with the Commission or otherwise subject to the liabilities of Section 18 of the Act, except to the extent that the registrant specifically incorporates it in its annual report on this Form by reference.

(c)   If no such annual report or proxy material has been sent to security holders, a statement to that effect shall be included under this caption. If such report or proxy material is to be furnished to security holders subsequent to the filing of the annual report of this Form, the registrant shall so state under this caption and shall furnish copies of such material to the Commission when it is sent to security holders.

FORM 10-Q: QUARTERLY REPORTS UNDER SECTION 13 OR 15(D) OF THE SECURITIES EXCHANGE ACT OF 1934

GENERAL INSTRUCTIONS

A. Rule as to Use of Form 10-Q.

1. Form 10-Q shall be used for quarterly reports under Section 13 or 15(d) of the Securities Exchange Act of 1934 (15 U.S.C. 78m or 78o(d)), filed pursuant to Rule 13a–13 (17 CFR 240.13a–13) or Rule 15d–13 (17 CFR 240.15d–13). A quarterly report on this form pursuant to Rule 13a–13 or Rule 15d–13 shall be filed within the following period after the end of each of the first three fiscal quarters of each fiscal year, but no report need be filed for the fourth quarter of any fiscal year:

    a. 40 days after the end of the fiscal quarter for large accelerated filers and accelerated filers (as defined in 17 CFR § 240.12b–2); and

    b. 45 days after the end of the fiscal quarter for all other registrants.

* * *

E. Integrated Reports to Security Holders.

Quarterly reports to security holders may be combined with the required information of Form 10-Q and will be suitable for filing with the Commission if the following conditions are satisfied:

1. The combined report contains full and complete answers to all items required by Part I of this form. When responses to a certain item of required disclosure are separated within the combined report, an appropriate cross-reference should be made.

2. If not included in the combined report, the cover page, appropriate responses to Part II, and the required signatures shall be included in the Form 10-Q. Additionally, as appropriate, a cross-reference sheet should be filed indicating the location of information required by the items of the form.

3. If an electronic filer files any portion of a quarterly report to security holders in combination with the required information of Form 10-Q, as provided in this instruction, only such portions filed in satisfaction of the Form 10-Q requirements shall be filed in electronic format.

F. Filed Status of Information Presented.

1. Pursuant to Rule 13a–13(d) and Rule 15d–13(d), the information presented in satisfaction of the requirements of Items 1, 2 and 3 of Part I of this form, whether included directly in a report on this form, incorporated therein by reference from a report, document or statement filed as an exhibit to Part I of this form pursuant to Instruction D(1) above, included in an integrated report pursuant to Instruction E above, or contained in a statement regarding computation of per share earnings or a letter regarding a change in accounting principles filed as an exhibit to Part I pursuant to Item 601 of Regulation S–K (§ 229.601 of this chapter), except as provided by Instruction F(2) below, shall not be deemed filed for the purpose of Section 18 of the Act or otherwise subject to the liabilities of that section of the Act but shall be subject to the other provisions of the Act.

2. Information presented in satisfaction of the requirements of this form other than those of Items 1, 2 and 3 of Part I shall be deemed filed for the purpose of Section 18 of the Act; except that, where information presented in response to Item 1 or 2 of Part I (or as an exhibit thereto) is also used to satisfy Part II requirements through incorporation by reference, only that portion of Part I (or exhibit thereto) consisting of the information required by Part II shall be deemed so filed.

G. Signature and Filing of Report.

If the report is filed in paper pursuant to a hardship exemption from electronic filing (*see* Item 201 et seq. of Regulation S–T (17 CFR 232.201 et seq.)), three complete copies of the report, including any financial statements, exhibits or other papers or documents filed as a part thereof, and five additional copies which need not include exhibits must be filed with the Commission. At least one complete copy of the report, including any financial statements, exhibits or other papers or documents filed as a part thereof, must be filed with each exchange on which any class of securities of the registrant is registered. At least one complete copy of the report filed with the Commission and one such copy filed with each exchange must be manually signed on the registrant's behalf by a duly authorized officer of the registrant and by the principal financial or chief accounting officer of the registrant. (See Rule 12b–11(d) (17 CFR 240.12b11(d).)) Copies not manually signed must bear typed or printed signatures. In the case where the principal executive officer, principal financial officer or chief accounting officer is also duly authorized to sign on behalf of the registrant, one signature is acceptable provided that the registrant clearly indicates the dual responsibilities of the signatory.

H.   Omission of Information by Certain Wholly-Owned Subsidiaries.

If on the date of the filing of its report on Form 10-Q, the registrant meets the conditions specified in paragraph (1) below, then such registrant may omit the information called for in the items specified in paragraph (2) below.

1.   Conditions for availability of the relief specified in paragraph (2) below:

a.   All of the registrant's equity securities are owned, either directly or indirectly, by a single person which is a reporting company under the Act and which has filed all the material required to be filed pursuant to Section 13, 14 or 15(d) thereof, as applicable;

b.   During the preceding thirty-six calendar months and any subsequent period of days, there has not been any material default in the payment of principal, interest, a sinking or purchase fund installment, or any other material default not cured within thirty days, with respect to any indebtedness of the registrant or its subsidiaries, and there has not been any material default in the payment of rentals under material long-term leases; and

c.   There is prominently set forth, on the cover page of the Form 10-Q, a statement that the registrant meets the conditions set forth in General Instruction H(1)(a) and (b) of Form 10-Q and is therefore filing this form with the reduced disclosure format.

2.   Registrants meeting the conditions specified in paragraph (1) above are entitled to the following relief:

a.   Such registrants may omit the information called for by Item 2 of Part I, Management's Discussion and Analysis of Financial Condition and Results of Operations, provided that the registrant includes in the Form 10-Q a management's narrative analysis of the results of operations explaining the reasons for material changes in the amount of revenue and expense items between the most recent fiscal year-to-date period presented and the corresponding year-to-date period in the preceding fiscal year. Explanations of material changes should include, but not be limited to, changes in the various elements which determine revenue and expense levels such as unit sales volume, prices charged and paid, production levels, production cost variances, labor costs and discretionary spending programs. In addition, the analysis should include an explanation of the effect of any changes in accounting principles and practices or method of application that have a material effect on net income as reported.

b.   Such registrants may omit the information called for in the following Part II Items: Item 2, Changes in Securities; Item 3, Defaults Upon Senior Securities.

c.   Such registrants may omit the information called for by Item 3 of Part I, Quantitative and Qualitative Disclosures About Market Risk.

PART I—FINANCIAL INFORMATION

Item 1.   Financial Statements.

Provide the information required by Rule 10–01 of Regulation S–X (17 CFR Part 210).A smaller reporting company, defined in Rule 12b–2 (§ 240.12b–2 of this chapter) may provide the information required by Article 8–03 of Regulation S–X (§ 210.8–03 of this chapter).

FORM 10-Q

Item 2. Management's Discussion and Analysis of Financial Condition and Results of Operations.

Furnish the information required by Item 303 of Regulation S–K (§ 229.303 of this chapter).

Item 3. Quantitative and Qualitative Disclosures About Market Risk.

Furnish the information required by Item 305 of Regulation S–K (§ 229.305 of this chapter).

Item 4. Controls and Procedures.

Furnish the information required by Item 307 of Regulation S–K (§ 229.307 of this chapter) and Item 308(c) of Regulation S–K (§ 229.308(c) of this chapter).

PART II—OTHER INFORMATION

* * *

Item 1. Legal Proceedings.

Furnish the information required by Item 103 of Regulation S–K (§ 229.103 of this chapter). As to such proceedings which have been terminated during the period covered by the report, provide similar information, including the date of termination and a description of the disposition thereof with respect to the registrant and its subsidiaries.

Instruction. A legal proceeding need only be reported in the 10-Q filed for the quarter in which it first became a reportable event and in subsequent quarters in which there have been material developments. Subsequent Form 10-Q filings in the same fiscal year in which a legal proceeding or a material development is reported should reference any previous reports in that year.

Item 1A. Risk Factors.

Set forth any material changes from risk factors as previously disclosed in the registrant's Form 10-K (§ 249.310) in response to Item 1A. to Part 1 of Form 10-K. Smaller reporting companies are not required to provide the information required by this item.

Item 2. Unregistered Sales of Equity Securities and Use of Proceeds.

(a) Furnish the information required by Item 701 of Regulation S–K (17 CFR 229.701) as to all equity securities of the registrant sold by the registrant during the period covered by the report that were not registered under the Securities Act. If the Item 701 information previously has been included in a Current Report on Form 8-K (17 CFR 249.308), however, it need not be furnished.

(b) If required pursuant to Rule 463 (17 CFR 230.463) of the Securities Act of 1933, furnish the information required by Item 701(f) of Regulation S–K (§ 229.701(f) of this chapter).

(c) Furnish the information required by Item 703 of Regulation S–K (§ 229.703 of this chapter) for any purchase made in the quarter covered by the report. Provide disclosures covering repurchases made on a monthly basis. For example, if the quarter began on January 16 and ended on April 15, the chart would show repurchases for the months from January 16 through February 15, February 16 through March 15, and March 16 through April 15.

Instruction. Working capital restrictions and other limitations upon the payment of dividends are to be reported hereunder.

Item 3. Defaults Upon Senior Securities.

(a) If there has been any material default in the payment of principal, interest, a sinking or purchase fund installment, or any other material default not cured within 30 days, with respect to any indebtedness of the registrant or any of its significant subsidiaries exceeding 5 percent of the total assets of the registrant and its consolidated subsidiaries, identify the indebtedness and state the nature of the default. In the case of such a default in the payment of principal, interest, or a sinking or purchase fund installment, state the amount of the default and the total arrearage on the date of filing this report.

Instruction. This paragraph refers only to events which have become defaults under the governing instruments, i.e., after the expiration of any period of grace and compliance with any notice requirements.

(b)   If any material arrearage in the payment of dividends has occurred or if there has been any other material delinquency not cured within 30 days, with respect to any class of preferred stock of the registrant which is registered or which ranks prior to any class of registered securities, or with respect to any class of preferred stock of any significant subsidiary of the registrant, give the title of the class and state the nature of the arrearage or delinquency. In the case of an arrearage in the payment of dividends, state the amount and the total arrearage on the date of filing this report.

Instructions to Item 3.

1.   Item 3 need not be answered as to any default or arrearage with respect to any class of securities all of which is held by, or for the account of, the registrant or its totally held subsidiaries.

2.   The information required by Item 3 need not be made if previously disclosed on a report on Form 8-K (17 CFR 249.308).

Item 4.   Mine Safety Disclosures.

If applicable, provide a statement that the information concerning mine safety violations or other regulatory matters required by Section 1503(a) of the Dodd-Frank Wall Street Reform and Consumer Protection Act and Item 104 of Regulation S–K (17 CFR 229.104) is included in exhibit 95 to the quarterly report.

Item 5.   Other Information.

(a)   The registrant must disclose under this item any information required to be disclosed in a report on Form 8-K during the period covered by this Form 10-Q, but not reported, whether or not otherwise required by this Form 10-Q. If disclosure of such information is made under this item, it need not be repeated in a report on Form 8-K which would otherwise be required to be filed with respect to such information or in a subsequent report on Form 10-Q; and

(b)   Furnish the information required by Item 407(c)(3) of Regulation S–K (§ 229.407 of this chapter).

Item 6.   Exhibits.

Furnish the exhibits required by Item 601 of Regulation S–K (§ 229.601 of this chapter).

SECTION 302 AND SECTION 906 CERTIFICATIONS

Section 302 [15 U.S.C. § 7241].   Corporate Responsibility for Financial Reports

(a)   Regulations required. The Commission shall, by rule, require, for each company filing periodic reports under section 13(a) or 15(d) of the Securities Exchange Act of 1934 (15 U.S.C. 78m, 78o(d)), that the principal executive officer or officers and the principal financial officer or officers, or persons performing similar functions, certify in each annual or quarterly report filed or submitted under either such section of such Act that—

(1)   the signing officer has reviewed the report;

(2)   based on the officer's knowledge, the report does not contain any untrue statement of a material fact or omit to state a material fact necessary in order to make the statements made, in light of the circumstances under which such statements were made, not misleading;

CERTIFICATIONS

(3) based on such officer's knowledge, the financial statements, and other financial information included in the report, fairly present in all material respects the financial condition and results of operations of the issuer as of, and for, the periods presented in the report;

(4) the signing officers—

(A) are responsible for establishing and maintaining internal controls;

(B) have designed such internal controls to ensure that material information relating to the issuer and its consolidated subsidiaries is made known to such officers by others within those entities, particularly during the period in which the periodic reports are being prepared;

(C) have evaluated the effectiveness of the issuer's internal controls as of a date within 90 days prior to the report; and

(D) have presented in the report their conclusions about the effectiveness of their internal controls based on their evaluation as of that date;

(5) the signing officers have disclosed to the issuer's auditors and the audit committee of the board of directors (or persons fulfilling the equivalent function)—

(A) all significant deficiencies in the design or operation of internal controls which could adversely affect the issuer's ability to record, process, summarize, and report financial data and have identified for the issuer's auditors any material weaknesses in internal controls; and

(B) any fraud, whether or not material, that involves management or other employees who have a significant role in the issuer's internal controls; and

(6) the signing officers have indicated in the report whether or not there were significant changes in internal controls or in other factors that could significantly affect internal controls subsequent to the date of their evaluation, including any corrective actions with regard to significant deficiencies and material weaknesses.

(b) Foreign reincorporations have no effect.—Nothing in this section shall be interpreted or applied in any way to allow any issuer to lessen the legal force of the statement required under this section, by an issuer having reincorporated or having engaged in any other transaction that resulted in the transfer of the corporate domicile or offices of the issuer from inside the United States to outside of the United States.

* * *

Section 906 [18 U.S.C. § 1350].   Failure of Corporate Officers to Certify Financial Reports

(a) Certification of periodic financial reports.—Each periodic report containing financial statements filed by an issuer with the Securities Exchange Commission pursuant to section 13(a) or 15(d) of the Securities Exchange Act of 1934 (15 U.S.C. 78m(a) or 78o(d)) shall be accompanied by a written statement by the chief executive officer and chief financial officer (or equivalent thereof) of the issuer.

(b) Content.—The statement required under subsection (a) shall certify that the periodic report containing the financial statements fully complies with the requirements of section 13(a) or 15(d) of the Securities Exchange Act [o]f 1934 (15 U.S.C. 78m or 78o(d)) and that information contained in the periodic report fairly presents, in all material respects, the financial condition and results of operations of the issuer.

* * *

SCHEDULE 13D: INFORMATION TO BE INCLUDED IN STATEMENTS FILED PURSUANT TO § 240.13D–1(a) AND AMENDMENTS THERETO FILED PURSUANT TO § 240.13D–2(a)

* * *

Item 1.   Security and Issuer.

State the title of the class of equity securities to which this statement relates and the name and address of the principal executive offices of the issuer of such securities.

Item 2.   Identity and Background.

If the person filing this statement or any person enumerated in Instruction C of this statement is a corporation, general partnership, limited partnership, syndicate or other group of persons, state its name, the state or other place of its organization, its principal business, the address of its principal office and the information required by (d) and (e) of this Item. If the person filing this statement or any person enumerated in Instruction C is a natural person, provide the information specified in (a) through (f) of this Item with respect to such person(s).

(a)   Name;

(b)   Residence or business address;

(c)   Present principal occupation or employment and the name, principal business and address of any corporation or other organization in which such employment is conducted;

(d)   Whether or not, during the last five years, such person has been convicted in a criminal proceeding (excluding traffic violations or similar misdemeanors) and, if so, give the dates, nature of conviction, name and location of court, any penalty imposed, or other disposition of the case;

(e)   Whether or not, during the last five years, such person was a party to a civil proceeding of a judicial or administrative body of competent jurisdiction and as a result of such proceeding was or is subject to a judgment, decree or final order enjoining future violations of, or prohibiting or mandating activities subject to, federal or state securities laws or finding any violation with respect to such laws; and, if so, identify and describe such proceedings and summarize the terms of such judgment, decree or final order; and

(f)   Citizenship.

Item 3.   Source and Amount of Funds or Other Consideration.

State the source and the amount of funds or other consideration used or to be used in making the purchases, and if any part of the purchase price is or will be represented by funds or other consideration borrowed or otherwise obtained for the purpose of acquiring, holding, trading or voting the securities, a description of the transaction and the names of the parties thereto. Where material, such information should also be provided with respect to prior acquisitions not previously reported pursuant to this regulation. If the source of all or any part of the funds is a loan made in the ordinary course of business by a bank, as defined in section 3(a)(6) of the Act, the name of the bank shall not be made available to the public if the person at the time of filing the statement so requests in writing and files such request, naming such bank, with the Secretary of the Commission. If the securities were acquired other than by purchase, describe the method of acquisition.

Item 4.   Purpose of Transaction.

State the purpose or purposes of the acquisition of securities of the issuer. Describe any plans or proposals which the reporting persons may have which relate to or would result in:

(a)   The acquisition by any person of additional securities of the issuer, or the disposition of securities of the issuer;

(b)   An extraordinary corporate transaction, such as a merger, reorganization or liquidation, involving the issuer or any of its subsidiaries;

(c)   A sale or transfer of a material amount of assets of the issuer or any of its subsidiaries;

(d)   Any change in the present board of directors or management of the issuer, including any plans or proposals to change the number or term of directors or to fill any existing vacancies on the board;

(e)   Any material change in the present capitalization or dividend policy of the issuer;

(f)   Any other material change in the issuer's business or corporate structure, including but not limited to, if the issuer is a registered closed-end investment company, any plans or proposals to make any changes in its investment policy for which a vote is required by section 13 of the Investment Company Act of 1940;

(g)   Changes in the issuer's charter, bylaws or instruments corresponding thereto or other actions which may impede the acquisition of control of the issuer by any person;

(h)   Causing a class of securities of the issuer to be delisted from a national securities exchange or to cease to be authorized to be quoted in an inter-dealer quotation system of a registered national securities association;

(i)   A class of equity securities of the issuer becoming eligible for termination of registration pursuant to section 12(g)(4) of the Act; or

(j)   Any action similar to any of those enumerated above.

Item 5.   Interest in Securities of the Issuer.

(a)   State the aggregate number and percentage of the class of securities identified pursuant to Item 1 (which may be based on the number of securities outstanding as contained in the most recently available filing with the Commission by the issuer unless the filing person has reason to believe such information is not current) beneficially owned (identifying those shares which there is a right to acquire) by each person named in Item 2. The above mentioned information should also be furnished with respect to persons who, together with any of the persons named in Item 2, comprise a group within the meaning of section 13(d)(3) of the Act;

(b)   For each person named in response to paragraph (a), indicate the number of shares as to which there is sole power to vote or to direct the vote, sole power to dispose or to direct the disposition, or shared power to dispose or to direct the disposition. Provide the applicable information required by Item 2 with respect to each person with whom the power to vote or to direct the vote or to dispose or direct the disposition is shared;

(c)   Describe any transactions in the class of securities reported on that were effected during the past sixty days or since the most recent filing of Schedule 13D (§ 240.13d–101), whichever is less, by the persons named in response to paragraph (a).

Instruction. The description of a transaction required by Item 5(c) shall include, but not necessarily be limited to: (1) The identity of the person covered by Item 5(c) who effected the transaction; (2) the date of transaction; (3) the amount of securities involved; (4) the price per share or unit; and (5) where and how the transaction was effected.

(d)   If any other person is known to have the right to receive or the power to direct the receipt of dividends from, or the proceeds from the sale of, such securities, a statement to that effect should be included in response to this item and, if such interest relates to more than five percent of the class, such person should be identified. A listing of the shareholders of an investment company registered under the Investment Company Act of 1940 or the beneficiaries of an employee benefit plan, pension fund or endowment fund is not required.

(e)   If applicable, state the date on which the reporting person ceased to be the beneficial owner of more than five percent of the class of securities.

Instruction. For computations regarding securities which represent a right to acquire an underlying security, *see* Rule 13d–3(d)(1) and the note thereto.

Item 6. Contracts, Arrangements, Understandings or Relationships With Respect to Securities of the Issuer.

Describe any contracts, arrangements, understandings or relationships (legal or otherwise) among the persons named in Item 2 and between such persons and any person with respect to any securities of the issuer, including but not limited to transfer or voting of any of the securities, finder's fees, joint ventures, loan or option arrangements, puts or calls, guarantees of profits, division of profits or loss, or the giving or withholding of proxies, naming the persons with whom such contracts, arrangements, understandings or relationships have been entered into. Include such information for any of the securities that are pledged or otherwise subject to a contingency the occurrence of which would give another person voting power or investment power over such securities except that disclosure of standard default and similar provisions contained in loan agreements need not be included.

Item 7. Material to be Filed as Exhibits.

The following shall be filed as exhibits: Copies of written agreements relating to the filing of joint acquisition statements as required by Rule 13d–1(k) and copies of all written agreements, contracts, arrangements, understanding, plans or proposals relating to: (1) The borrowing of funds to finance the acquisition as disclosed in Item 3; (2) the acquisition of issuer control, liquidation, sale of assets, merger, or change in business or corporate structure, or any other matter as disclosed in Item 4; and (3) the transfer or voting of the securities, finder's fees, joint ventures, options, puts, calls, guarantees of loans, guarantees against loss or of profit, or the giving or withholding of any proxy as disclosed in Item 6.

SCHEDULE 13E–3: TRANSACTION STATEMENT UNDER SECTION 13(e) OF THE SECURITIES EXCHANGE ACT OF 1934 AND RULE 13e–3 (§ 240.13e–3) THEREUNDER

* * *

GENERAL INSTRUCTIONS

A.   File eight copies of the statement, including all exhibits, with the Commission if paper filing is permitted.

B.   This filing must be accompanied by a fee payable to the Commission as required by § 240.0–11(b).

C.   If the statement is filed by a general or limited partnership, syndicate or other group, the information called for by Items 3, 5, 6, 10 and 11 must be given with respect to: (i) Each partner of the general partnership; (ii) each partner who is, or functions as, a general partner of the limited partnership; (iii) each member of the syndicate or group; and (iv) each person controlling the partner or member. If the statement is filed by a corporation or if a person referred to in (i), (ii), (iii) or (iv) of this Instruction is a corporation, the information called for by the items specified above must be given with respect to: (a) Each executive officer and director of the corporation; (b) each person controlling the corporation; and (c) each executive officer and director of any corporation or other person ultimately in control of the corporation.

D.   Depending on the type of Rule 13e–3 transaction (§ 240.13e–3(a)(3)), this statement must be filed with the Commission:

1.   At the same time as filing preliminary or definitive soliciting materials or an information statement under Regulations 14A or 14C of the Act;

2.   At the same time as filing a registration statement under the Securities Act of 1933;

3.   As soon as practicable on the date a tender offer is first published, sent or given to security holders; or

4.   At least 30 days before any purchase of securities of the class of securities subject to the Rule 13e–3 transaction, if the transaction does not involve a solicitation, an information statement, the registration of securities or a tender offer, as described in paragraphs 1, 2 or 3 of this Instruction; and

5.   If the Rule 13e–3 transaction involves a series of transactions, the issuer or affiliate must file this statement at the time indicated in paragraphs 1 through 4 of this Instruction for the first transaction and must amend the schedule promptly with respect to each subsequent transaction.

* * *

Item 1.   Summary Term Sheet

Furnish the information required by Item 1001 of Regulation M–A (§ 229.1001 of this chapter) unless information is disclosed to security holders in a prospectus that meets the requirements of § 230.421(d) of this chapter.

Item 2.   Subject Company Information

Furnish the information required by Item 1002 of Regulation M–A (§ 229.1002 of this chapter).

Item 3.   Identity and Background of Filing Person

Furnish the information required by Item 1003(a) through (c) of Regulation M–A (§ 229.1003 of this chapter).

Item 4.   Terms of the Transaction

Furnish the information required by Item 1004(a) and (c) through (f) of Regulation M–A (§ 229.1004 of this chapter).

Item 5.   Past Contacts, Transactions, Negotiations and Agreements

Furnish the information required by Item 1005(a) through (c) and (e) of Regulation M–A (§ 229.1005 of this chapter).

Item 6.   Purposes of the Transaction and Plans or Proposals

Furnish the information required by Item 1006(b) and (c)(1) through (8) of Regulation M–A (§ 229.1006 of this chapter).

Instruction to Item 6: In providing the information specified in Item 1006(c) for this item, discuss any activities or transactions that would occur after the Rule 13e–3 transaction.

Item 7.   Purposes, Alternatives, Reasons and Effects

Furnish the information required by Item 1013 of Regulation M–A (§ 229.1013 of this chapter).

Item 8.   Fairness of the Transaction

Furnish the information required by Item 1014 of Regulation M–A (§ 229.1014 of this chapter).

Item 9.   Reports, Opinions, Appraisals and Negotiations

Furnish the information required by Item 1015 of Regulation M–A (§ 229.1015 of this chapter).

Item 10.   Source and Amounts of Funds or Other Consideration

Furnish the information required by Item 1007 of Regulation M–A (§ 229.1007 of this chapter).

Item 11.   Interest in Securities of the Subject Company

Furnish the information required by Item 1008 of Regulation M–A (§ 229.1008 of this chapter).

SCHEDULE 14A

Item 12. The Solicitation or Recommendation

Furnish the information required by Item 1012(d) and (e) of Regulation M–A (§ 229.1012 of this chapter).

Item 13. Financial Statements

Furnish the information required by Item 1010(a) through (b) of Regulation M–A (§ 229.1010 of this chapter) for the issuer of the subject class of securities.

Instructions to Item 13:

1.   The disclosure materials disseminated to security holders may contain the summarized financial information required by Item 1010(c) of Regulation M–A (§ 229.1010 of this chapter) instead of the financial information required by Item 1010(a) and (b). In that case, the financial information required by Item 1010(a) and (b) of Regulation M–A must be disclosed directly or incorporated by reference in the statement. If summarized financial information is disseminated to security holders, include appropriate instructions on how more complete financial information can be obtained. If the summarized financial information is prepared on the basis of a comprehensive body of accounting principles other than U.S. GAAP, the summarized financial information must be accompanied by a reconciliation as described in Instruction 2.

2.   If the financial statements required by this Item are prepared on the basis of a comprehensive body of accounting principles other than U.S. GAAP, provide a reconciliation to U.S. GAAP in accordance with Item 17 of Form 20-F (§ 249.220f of this chapter).

3.   The filing person may incorporate by reference financial statements contained in any document filed with the Commission, solely for the purposes of this schedule, if: (a) The financial statements substantially meet the requirements of this Item; (b) an express statement is made that the financial statements are incorporated by reference; (c) the matter incorporated by reference is clearly identified by page, paragraph, caption or otherwise; and (d) if the matter incorporated by reference is not filed with this Schedule, an indication is made where the information may be inspected and copies obtained. Financial statements that are required to be presented in comparative form for two or more fiscal years or periods may not be incorporated by reference unless the material incorporated by reference includes the entire period for which the comparative data is required to be given. *See* General Instruction F to this Schedule.

Item 14. Persons/Assets, Retained, Employed, Compensated or Used

Furnish the information required by Item 1009 of Regulation M–A (§ 229.1009 of this chapter).

Item 15. Additional Information

Furnish the information required by Item 1011(b) and (c) of Regulation M–A (§ 229.1011(b) and (c) of this chapter).

Item 16. Exhibits

File as an exhibit to the Schedule all documents specified in Item 1016(a) through (d), (f) and (g) of Regulation M–A (§ 229.1016 of this chapter).

SCHEDULE 14A: INFORMATION REQUIRED IN PROXY STATEMENT

* * *

Notes: A. Where any item calls for information with respect to any matter to be acted upon and such matter involves other matters with respect to which information is called for by other items of this schedule, the information called for by such other items also shall be given. For example, where a solicitation of security holders is for the purpose of approving the authorization of additional securities which are to be used to acquire another specified company, and the registrants' security holders will not have a separate opportunity to vote upon the transaction, the solicitation to authorize the securities is also a solicitation with respect to the acquisition. Under those facts, information required by Items 11, 13 and 14 shall be furnished.

B. Where any item calls for information with respect to any matter to be acted upon at the meeting, such item need be answered in the registrant's soliciting material only with respect to proposals to be made by or on behalf of the registrant.

C. Except as otherwise specifically provided, where any item calls for information for a specified period with regard to directors, executive officers, officers or other persons holding specified positions or relationships, the information shall be given with regard to any person who held any of the specified positions or relationship at any time during the period. Information, other than information required by Item 404 of Regulation S–K (§ 229.404 of this chapter), need not be included for any portion of the period during which such person did not hold any such position or relationship, provided a statement to that effect is made.

D. Information may be incorporated by reference only in the manner and to the extent specifically permitted in the items of this schedule. Where incorporation by reference is used, the following shall apply:

1. Disclosure must not be incorporated by reference from a second document if that second document incorporates information pertinent to such disclosure by reference to a third document. A registrant incorporating any documents, or portions of documents, shall include a statement on the last page(s) of the proxy statement as to which documents, or portions of documents, are incorporated by reference. Information shall not be incorporated by reference in any case where such incorporation would render the statement incomplete, unclear or confusing.

2. If a document is incorporated by reference but not delivered to security holders, include an undertaking to provide, without charge, to each person to whom a proxy statement is delivered, upon written or oral request of such person and by first class mail or other equally prompt means within one business day of receipt of such request, a copy of any and all of the information that has been incorporated by reference in the proxy statement (not including exhibits to the information that is incorporated by reference unless such exhibits are specifically incorporated by reference into the information that the proxy statement incorporates), and the address (including title or department) and telephone numbers to which such a request is to be directed. This includes information contained in documents filed subsequent to the date on which definitive copies of the proxy statement are sent or given to security holders, up to the date of responding to the request.

3. If a document or portion of a document other than an annual report sent to security holders pursuant to the requirements of Rule 14a–3 (§ 240.14a–3 of this chapter) with respect to the same meeting or solicitation of consents or authorizations as that to which the proxy statement relates is incorporated by reference in the manner permitted by Item 13(b) or 14(e)(1) of this schedule, the proxy statement must be sent to security holders no later than 20 business days prior to the date on which the meeting of such security holders is held or, if no meeting is held, at least 20 business days prior to the date the votes, consents or authorizations may be used to effect the corporate action.

4. *Electronic filings.* If any of the information required by Items 13 or 14 of this Schedule is incorporated by reference from an annual or quarterly report to security holders, such report, or any portion thereof incorporated by reference, shall be filed in electronic format with the proxy statement. This provision shall not apply to registered investment companies.

* * *

Item 1. Date, Time and Place Information

(a) State the date, time and place of the meeting of security holders, and the complete mailing address, including ZIP Code, of the principal executive offices of the registrant, unless such information is otherwise disclosed in material furnished to security holders with or preceding the proxy statement. If action is to be taken by written consent, state the date by which consents are to be submitted if state law requires that such a date be specified or if the person soliciting intends to set a date.

(b) On the first page of the proxy statement, as delivered to security holders, state the approximate date on which the proxy statement and form of proxy are first sent or given to security holders.

(c) Furnish the information required to be in the proxy statement by Rule 14a–5(e) (§ 240.14a–5(e) of this chapter).

Item 2. Revocability of Proxy

State whether or not the person giving the proxy has the power to revoke it. If the right of revocation before the proxy is exercised is limited or is subject to compliance with any formal procedure, briefly describe such limitation or procedure.

Item 3. Dissenters' Right of Appraisal

Outline briefly the rights of appraisal or similar rights of dissenters with respect to any matter to be acted upon and indicate any statutory procedure required to be followed by dissenting security holders in order to perfect such rights. Where such rights may be exercised only within a limited time after the date of adoption of a proposal, the filing of a charter amendment or other similar act, state whether the persons solicited will be notified of such date.

Instructions. 1. Indicate whether a security holder's failure to vote against a proposal will constitute a waiver of his appraisal or similar rights and whether a vote against a proposal will be deemed to satisfy any notice requirements under State law with respect to appraisal rights. If the State law is unclear, state what position will be taken in regard to these matters.

2. Open-end investment companies registered under the Investment Company Act of 1940 are not required to respond to this item.

Item 4. Persons Making the Solicitation

(a) Solicitations not subject to Rule 14a–12(c) (§ 240.14a–12(c)). (1) If the solicitation is made by the registrant, so state. Give the name of any director of the registrant who has informed the registrant in writing that he intends to oppose any action intended to be taken by the registrant and indicate the action which he intends to oppose.

(2) If the solicitation is made otherwise than by the registrant, so state and give the names of the participants in the solicitation, as defined in paragraphs (a) (iii), (iv), (v) and (vi) of Instruction 3 to this Item.

(3) If the solicitation is to be made otherwise than by the use of the mails or pursuant to § 240.14a–16, describe the methods to be employed. If the solicitation is to be made by specially, engaged employees or paid solicitors, state (i) the material features of any contract or arrangement for such solicitation and identify the parties, and (ii) the cost or anticipated cost thereof.

(4) State the names of the persons by whom the cost of solicitation has been or will be borne, directly or indirectly.

(b) Solicitations subject to Rule 14a–12(c) (§ 240.14a–12(c)). (1) State by whom the solicitation is made and describe the methods employed and to be employed to solicit security holders.

(2) If regular employees of the registrant or any other participant in a solicitation have been or are to be employed to solicit security holders, describe the class or classes of employees to be so employed, and the manner and nature of their employment for such purpose.

(3) If specially engaged employees, representatives or other persons have been or are to be employed to solicit security holders, state (i) the material features of any contract or arrangement for such solicitation and the identity of the parties, (ii) the cost or anticipated cost thereof and

(iii) the approximate number of such employees of employees or any other person (naming such other person) who will solicit security holders.

(4) State the total amount estimated to be spent and the total expenditures to date for, in furtherance of, or in connection with the solicitation of security holders.

(5) State by whom the cost of the solicitation will be borne. If such cost is to be borne initially by any person other than the registrant, state whether reimbursement will be sought from the registrant, and, if so, whether the question of such reimbursement will be submitted to a vote of security holders.

(6) If any such solicitation is terminated pursuant to a settlement between the registrant and any other participant in such solicitation, describe the terms of such settlement, including the cost or anticipated cost thereof to the registrant.

Instructions. 1. With respect to solicitations subject to Rule 14a–12(c) (§ 240.14a–12(c)), costs and expenditures within the meaning of this Item 4 shall include fees for attorneys, accountants, public relations or financial advisers, solicitors, advertising, printing, transportation, litigation and other costs incidental to the solicitation, except that the registrant may exclude the amount of such costs represented by the amount normally expended for a solicitation for an election of directors in the absence of a contest, and costs represented by salaries and wages of regular employees and officers, provided a statement to that effect is included in the proxy statement.

2.   The information required pursuant to paragraph (b)(6) of this Item should be included in any amended or revised proxy statement or other soliciting materials relating to the same meeting or subject matter furnished to security holders by the registrant subsequent to the date of settlement.

3.   For purposes of this Item 4 and Item 5 of this Schedule 14A:

(a) The terms "participant" and "participant in a solicitation" include the following:

(i)   The registrant;

(ii) Any director of the registrant, and any nominee for whose election as a director proxies are solicited;

(iii) Any committee or group which solicits proxies, any member of such committee or group, and any person whether or not named as a member who, acting alone or with one or more other persons, directly or indirectly takes the initiative, or engages, in organizing, directing, or arranging for the financing of any such committee or group;

(iv) Any person who finances or joins with another to finance the solicitation of proxies, except persons who contribute not more than $500 and who are not otherwise participants;

(v)   Any person who lends money or furnishes credit or enters into any other arrangements, pursuant to any contract or understanding with a participant, for the purpose of financing or otherwise inducing the purchase, sale, holding or voting of securities of the registrant by any participant or other persons, in support of or in opposition to a participant; except that such terms do not include a bank, broker or dealer who, in the ordinary course of business, lends money or executes orders for the purchase or sale of securities and who is not otherwise a participant; and

(vi) Any person who solicits proxies.

(b) The terms "participant" and "participant in a solicitation" do not include:

(i)   Any person or organization retained or employed by a participant to solicit security holders and whose activities are limited to the duties required to be performed in the course of such employment;

(ii) Any person who merely transmits proxy soliciting material or performs other ministerial or clerical duties;

(iii) Any person employed by a participant in the capacity of attorney, accountant, or advertising, public relations or financial adviser, and whose activities are limited to the duties required to be performed in the course of such employment;

(iv) Any person regularly employed as an officer or employee of the registrant or any of its subsidiaries who is not otherwise a participant; or

(v) Any officer or director of, or any person regularly employed by, any other participant, if such officer, director or employee is not otherwise a participant.

Item 5. Interest of Certain Persons in Matters to Be Acted Upon

(a) Solicitations not subject to Rule 14a–12(c) (§ 240.14a–12(c)). Describe briefly any substantial interest, direct or indirect, by security holdings or otherwise, of each of the following persons in any matter to be acted upon, other than elections to office:

(1) If the solicitation is made on behalf of the registrant, each person who has been a director or executive officer of the registrant at any time since the beginning of the last fiscal year.

(2) If the solicitation is made otherwise than on behalf of the registrant, each participant in the solicitation, as defined in paragraphs (a) (iii), (iv), (v), and (vi) of Instruction 3 to Item 4 of this Schedule 14A.

(3) Each nominee for election as a director of the registrant.

(4) Each associate of any of the foregoing persons.

(5) If the solicitation is made on behalf of the registrant, furnish the information required by Item 402(t) of Regulation S–K (§ 229.402(t) of this chapter).

Instruction to paragraph (a). Except in the case of a solicitation subject to this regulation made in opposition to another solicitation subject to this regulation, this sub-item (a) shall not apply to any interest arising from the ownership of securities of the registrant where the security holder receives no extra or special benefit not shared on a pro rata basis by all other holders of the same class.

(b) Solicitation subject to Rule 14a–12(c) (§ 240.14a–12(c)). With respect to any solicitation subject to Rule 14a–12(c) (§ 240.14a–12(c)):

(1) Describe briefly any substantial interest, direct or indirect, by security holdings or otherwise, of each participant as defined in paragraphs (a) (ii), (iii), (iv), (v) and (vi) of Instruction 3 to Item 4 of this Schedule 14A, in any matter to be acted upon at the meeting, and include with respect to each participant the following information, or a fair and accurate summary thereof:

(i) Name and business address of the participant.

(ii) The participant's present principal occupation or employment and the name, principal business and address of any corporation or other organization in which such employment is carried on.

(iii) State whether or not, during the past ten years, the participant has been convicted in a criminal proceeding (excluding traffic violations or similar misdemeanors) and, if so, give dates, nature of conviction, name and location of court, and penalty imposed or other disposition of the case. A negative answer need not be included in the proxy statement or other soliciting material.

(iv) State the amount of each class of securities of the registrant which the participant owns beneficially, directly or indirectly.

(v) State the amount of each class of securities of the registrant which the participant owns of record but not beneficially.

(vi) State with respect to all securities of the registrant purchased or sold within the past two years, the dates on which they were purchased or sold and the amount purchased or sold on each such date.

(vii) If any part of the purchase price or market value of any of the shares specified in paragraph (b)(1)(vi) of this Item is represented by funds borrowed or otherwise obtained for the purpose of acquiring or holding such securities, so state and indicate the amount of the indebtedness as of the latest practicable date. If such funds were borrowed or obtained otherwise than pursuant to a margin account or bank loan in the regular course of business of a bank, broker or dealer, briefly describe the transaction, and state the names of the parties.

(viii) State whether or not the participant is, or was within the past year, a party to any contract, arrangements or understandings with any person with respect to any securities of the registrant, including, but not limited to joint ventures, loan or option arrangements, puts or calls, guarantees against loss or guarantees of profit, division of losses or profits, or the giving or withholding of proxies. If so, name the parties to such contracts, arrangements or understandings and give the details thereof.

(ix) State the amount of securities of the registrant owned beneficially, directly or indirectly, by each of the participant's associates and the name and address of each such associate.

(x) State the amount of each class of securities of any parent or subsidiary of the registrant which the participant owns beneficially, directly or indirectly.

(xi) Furnish for the participant and associates of the participant the information required by Item 404(a) of Regulation S–K (§ 229.404(a) of this chapter).

(xii) State whether or not the participant or any associates of the participant have any arrangement or understanding with any person—

(A) with respect to any future employment by the registrant or its affiliates; or

(B) with respect to any future transactions to which the registrant or any of its affiliates will or may be a party.

If so, describe such arrangement or understanding and state the names of the parties thereto.

(2) With respect to any person, other than a director or executive officer of the registrant acting solely in that capacity, who is a party to an arrangement or understanding pursuant to which a nominee for election as director is proposed to be elected, describe any substantial interest, direct or indirect, by security holdings or otherwise, that such person has in any matter to be acted upon at the meeting, and furnish the information called for by paragraphs (b)(1) (xi) and (xii) of this Item.

(3) If the solicitation is made on behalf of the registrant, furnish the information required by Item 402(t) of Regulation S–K (§ 229.402(t) of this chapter).

Instruction to paragraph (b): For purposes of this Item 5, beneficial ownership shall be determined in accordance with Rule 13d–3 under the Act (Section 240.13d–3 of this chapter).

Item 6. Voting Securities and Principal Holders Thereof

(a) As to each class of voting securities of the registrant entitled to be voted at the meeting (or by written consents or authorizations if no meeting is held), state the number of shares outstanding and the number of votes to which each class is entitled.

(b) State the record date, if any, with respect to this solicitation. If the right to vote or give consent is not to be determined, in whole or in part, by reference to a record date, indicate the criteria for the determination of security holders entitled to vote or give consent.

(c)   If action is to be taken with respect to the election of directors and if the persons solicited have cumulative voting rights: (1) Make a statement that they have such rights, (2) briefly describe such rights, (3) state briefly the conditions precedent to the exercise thereof, and (4) if discretionary authority to cumulate votes is solicited, so indicate.

(d)   Furnish the information required by Item 403 of Regulation S–K (§ 229.403 of this chapter) to the extent known by the persons on whose behalf the solicitation is made.

(e)   If, to the knowledge of the persons on whose behalf the solicitation is made, a change in control of the registrant has occurred since the beginning of its last fiscal year, state the name of the person(s) who acquired such control, the amount and the source of the consideration used by such person or persons; the basis of the control, the date and a description of the transaction(s) which resulted in the change of control and the percentage of voting securities of the registrant now beneficially owned directly or indirectly by the person(s) who acquired control; and the identity of the person(s) from whom control was assumed. If the source of all or any part of the consideration used is a loan made in the ordinary course of business by a bank as defined by section 3(a)(6) of the Act, the identity of such bank shall be omitted provided a request for confidentiality has been made pursuant to section 13(d)(1)(B) of the Act by the person(s) who acquired control. In lieu thereof, the material shall indicate that the identity of the bank has been so omitted and filed separately with the Commission.

Instructions. 1. State the terms of any loans or pledges obtained by the new control group for the purpose of acquiring control, and the names of the lenders or pledgees.

2.   Any arrangements or understandings among members of both the former and new control groups and their associates with respect to election of directors or other matters should be described.

Item 7.   Directors and Executive Officers

If action is to be taken with respect to the election of directors, furnish the following information in tabular form to the extent practicable. If, however, the solicitation is made on behalf of persons other than the registrant, the information required need be furnished only as to nominees of the persons making the solicitation.

(a)   The information required by instruction 4 to Item 103 of Regulation S–K (§ 229.103 of this chapter) with respect to directors and executive officers.

(b)   The information required by Items 401, 404(a) and (b), 405 and 407 of Regulation S–K (§§ 229.401, 229.404(a) and (b), 229.405 and 229.407 of this chapter), other than the information required by:

(i)   Paragraph (c)(3) of Item 407 of Regulation S–K (§ 229.407(c)(3) of this chapter); and

(ii)   Paragraphs (e)(4) and (e)(5) of Item 407 of Regulation S–K (§§ 229.407(e)(4) and 229.407(e)(5) of this chapter) (which are required by Item 8 of this Schedule 14A).

(c)   If a shareholder nominee or nominees are submitted to the registrant for inclusion in the registrant's proxy materials pursuant to § 240.14a–11 and the registrant is not permitted to exclude the nominee or nominees pursuant to the provisions of § 240.14a–11, the registrant must include in its proxy statement the disclosure required from the nominating shareholder or nominating shareholder group under Item 5 of § 240.14n–101 with regard to the nominee or nominees and the nominating shareholder or nominating shareholder group.

(d)   If a registrant is required to include a shareholder nominee or nominees submitted to the registrant for inclusion in the registrant's proxy materials pursuant to a procedure set forth under applicable state or foreign law, or the registrant's governing documents providing for the inclusion of shareholder director nominees in the registrant's proxy materials, the registrant must include in its proxy statement the disclosure required from the nominating shareholder or nominating shareholder group under Item 6 of § 240.14n–101 with regard to the nominee or nominees and the nominating shareholder or nominating shareholder group.

Instruction to Item 7. The information disclosed pursuant to paragraphs (c) and (d) of this Item 7 will not be deemed incorporated by reference into any filing under the Securities Act of 1933 (15 U.S.C. 77a et seq.), the Securities Exchange Act of 1934 (15 U.S.C. 78a et seq.), or the Investment Company Act of 1940 (15 U.S.C. 80a–1 et seq.), except to the extent that the registrant specifically incorporates that information by reference.

(e)   In lieu of the information required by this Item 7, investment companies registered under the Investment Company Act of 1940 (15 U.S.C. 80a) must furnish the information required by Item 22(b) of this Schedule 14A.

Item 8.   Compensation of Directors and Executive Officers

Furnish the information required by Item 402 of Regulation S–K (§ 229.402 of this chapter) and paragraphs (e)(4) and (e)(5) of Item 407 of Regulation S–K (§ 229.407(e)(4) and (e)(5) of this chapter) if action is to be taken with regard to:

(a)   The election of directors;

(b)   Any bonus, profit sharing or other compensation plan, contract or arrangement in which any director, nominee for election as a director, or executive officer of the registrant will participate;

(c)   Any pension or retirement plan in which any such person will participate; or

(d)   The granting or extension to any such person of any options, warrants or rights to purchase any securities, other than warrants or rights issued to security holders as such, on a pro rata basis.

However, if the solicitation is made on behalf of persons other than the registrant, the information required need be furnished only as to nominees of the persons making the solicitation and associates of such nominees. In the case of investment companies registered under the Investment Company Act of 1940 (15 U.S.C. 80a), furnish the information required by Item 22(b)(13) of this Schedule 14A.

Instruction. If an otherwise reportable compensation plan became subject to such requirements because of an acquisition or merger and, within one year of the acquisition or merger, such plan was terminated for purposes of prospective eligibility, the registrant may furnish a description of its obligation to the designated individuals pursuant to the compensation plan. Such description may be furnished in lieu of a description of the compensation plan in the proxy statement.

Item 9.   Independent Public Accountants

If the solicitation is made on behalf of the registrant and relates to: (1) The annual (or special meeting in lieu of annual) meeting of security holders at which directors are to be elected, or a solicitation of consents or authorizations in lieu of such meeting or (2) the election, approval or ratification of the registrant's accountant, furnish the following information describing the registrant's relationship with its independent public accountant:

(a)   The name of the principal accountant selected or being recommended to security holders for election, approval or ratification for the current year. If no accountant has been selected or recommended, so state and briefly describe the reasons therefor.

(b)   The name of the principal accountant for the fiscal year most recently completed if different from the accountant selected or recommended for the current year or if no accountant has yet been selected or recommended for the current year.

(c)   The proxy statement shall indicate: (1) Whether or not representatives of the principal accountant for the current year and for the most recently completed fiscal year are expected to be present at the security holders' meeting, (2) whether or not they will have the opportunity to make a statement if they desire to do so, and (3) whether or not such representatives are expected to be available to respond to appropriate questions.

(d)   If during the registrant's two most recent fiscal years or any subsequent interim period, (1) an independent accountant who was previously engaged as the principal accountant to audit the registrant's financial statements, or an independent accountant on whom the principal accountant expressed reliance in its report regarding a significant subsidiary, has resigned (or indicated it has declined to stand for re-election after the completion of the current audit) or was dismissed, or (2) a new independent accountant has been engaged as either the principal accountant to audit the registrant's financial statements or as an independent accountant on whom the principal accountant has expressed or is expected to express reliance in its report regarding a significant subsidiary, then, notwithstanding any previous disclosure, provide the information required by Item 304(a) of Regulation S–K (§ 229.304 of this chapter).

(e)(1)   Disclose, under the caption Audit Fees, the aggregate fees billed for each of the last two fiscal years for professional services rendered by the principal accountant for the audit of the registrant's annual financial statements and review of financial statements included in the registrant's Form 10-Q (17 CFR 249.308a) or services that are normally provided by the accountant in connection with statutory and regulatory filings or engagements for those fiscal years.

(2)   Disclose, under the caption Audit-Related Fees, the aggregate fees billed in each of the last two fiscal years for assurance and related services by the principal accountant that are reasonably related to the performance of the audit or review of the registrant's financial statements and are not reported under paragraph (e)(1) of this section. Registrants shall describe the nature of the services comprising the fees disclosed under this category.

(3)   Disclose, under the caption Tax Fees, the aggregate fees billed in each of the last two fiscal years for professional services rendered by the principal accountant for tax compliance, tax advice, and tax planning. Registrants shall describe the nature of the services comprising the fees disclosed under this category.

(4)   Disclose, under the caption All Other Fees, the aggregate fees billed in each of the last two fiscal years for products and services provided by the principal accountant, other than the services reported in paragraphs (e)(1) through (e)(3) of this section. Registrants shall describe the nature of the services comprising the fees disclosed under this category.

(5)(i)   Disclose the audit committee's pre-approval policies and procedures described in 17 CFR 210.2–01(c)(7)(i).

(ii)   Disclose the percentage of services described in each of paragraphs (e)(2) through (e)(4) of this section that were approved by the audit committee pursuant to 17 CFR 210.2–01(c)(7)(i)(C).

(6)   If greater than 50 percent, disclose the percentage of hours expended on the principal accountant's engagement to audit the registrant's financial statements for the most recent fiscal year that were attributed to work performed by persons other than the principal accountant's full-time, permanent employees.

(7)   If the registrant is an investment company, disclose the aggregate non-audit fees billed by the registrant's accountant for services rendered to the registrant, and to the registrant's investment adviser (not including any subadviser whose role is primarily portfolio management and is subcontracted with or overseen by another investment adviser), and any entity controlling, controlled by, or under common control with the adviser that provides ongoing services to the registrant for each of the last two fiscal years of the registrant.

(8)   If the registrant is an investment company, disclose whether the audit committee of the board of directors has considered whether the provision of non-audit services that were rendered to the registrant's investment adviser (not including any subadviser whose role is primarily portfolio management and is subcontracted with or overseen by another investment adviser), and any entity controlling, controlled by, or under common control with the investment adviser that provides ongoing services to the registrant that were not pre-approved pursuant to 17 CFR 210.2–01(c)(7)(ii) is compatible with maintaining the principal accountant's independence.

Instruction to Item 9(e).

SCHEDULE 14A

For purposes of Item 9(e)(2), (3), and (4), registrants that are investment companies must disclose fees billed for services rendered to the registrant and separately, disclose fees required to be approved by the investment company registrant's audit committee pursuant to 17 CFR 210.2–01(c)(7)(ii). Registered investment companies must also disclose the fee percentages as required by item 9(e)(5)(ii) for the registrant and separately, disclose the fee percentages as required by item 9(e)(5)(ii) for the fees required to be approved by the investment company registrant's audit committee pursuant to 17 CFR 210.2–01(c)(7)(ii).

Item 10. Compensation Plans

If action is to be taken with respect to any plan pursuant to which cash or noncash compensation may be paid or distributed, furnish the following information:

(a) Plans subject to security holder action. (1) Describe briefly the material features of the plan being acted upon, identify each class of persons who will be eligible to participate therein, indicate the approximate number of persons in each such class, and state the basis of such participation.

(2)(i) In the tabular format specified below, disclose the benefits or amounts that will be received by or allocated to each of the following under the plan being acted upon, if such benefits or amounts are determinable:

NEW PLAN BENEFITS
Plan Name

Name and Position	Dollar Value ($)	Number of Units
CEO		
A		
B		
C		
D		
Executive Group		
Non-Executive Director Group		
Non-Executive Officer Employee Group		

(ii) The table required by paragraph (a)(2)(i) of this Item shall provide information as to the following persons:

(A) Each person (stating name and position) specified in paragraph (a)(3) of Item 402 of Regulation S–K (§ 229.402(a)(3) of this chapter);

Instruction: In the case of investment companies registered under the Investment Company Act of 1940, furnish the information for Compensated Persons as defined in Item 22(b)(13) of this Schedule in lieu of the persons specified in paragraph (a)(3) of Item 402 of Regulation S–K (§ 229.402(a)(3) of this chapter).

(B) All current executive officers as a group;

(C) All current directors who are not executive officers as a group; and

(D) All employees, including all current officers who are not executive officers, as a group.

Instruction to New Plan Benefits Table

Additional columns should be added for each plan with respect to which security holder action is to be taken.

(iii) If the benefits or amounts specified in paragraph (a)(2)(i) of this item are not determinable, state the benefits or amounts which would have been received by or allocated to each of the following for the last completed fiscal year if the plan had been in effect, if such benefits or amounts may be determined, in the table specified in paragraph (a)(2)(i) of this Item:

(A) Each person (stating name and position) specified in paragraph (a)(3) of Item 402 of Regulation S–K (§ 229.402(a)(3) of this chapter);

(B) All current executive officers as a group;

(C) All current directors who are not executive officers as a group; and

(D) All employees, including all current officers who are not executive officers, as a group.

(3) If the plan to be acted upon can be amended, otherwise than by a vote of security holders, to increase the cost thereof to the registrant or to alter the allocation of the benefits as between the persons and groups specified in paragraph (a)(2) of this item, state the nature of the amendments which can be so made.

(b)(1) Additional information regarding specified plans subject to security holder action. With respect to any pension or retirement plan submitted for security holder action, state:

(i) The approximate total amount necessary to fund the plan with respect to past services, the period over which such amount is to be paid and the estimated annual payments necessary to pay the total amount over such period; and

(ii) The estimated annual payment to be made with respect to current services. In the case of a pension or retirement plan, information called for by paragraph (a)(2) of this Item may be furnished in the format specified by paragraph (h)(2) of Item 402 of Regulation S–K (§ 229.402(h)(2) of this chapter).

Instruction to paragraph (b)(1)(ii). In the case of investment companies registered under the Investment Company Act of 1940 (15 U.S.C. 80a), refer to Instruction 4 in Item 22(b)(13)(i) of this Schedule in lieu of paragraph (h)(2) of Item 402 of Regulation S–K (§ 229.402(h)(2) of this chapter).

(2)(i) With respect to any specific grant of or any plan containing options, warrants or rights submitted for security holder action, state:

(A) The title and amount of securities underlying such options, warrants or rights;

(B) The prices, expiration dates and other material conditions upon which the options, warrants or rights may be exercised;

(C) The consideration received or to be received by the registrant or subsidiary for the granting or extension of the options, warrants or rights;

(D) The market value of the securities underlying the options, warrants, or rights as of the latest practicable date; and

(E) In the case of options, the federal income tax consequences of the issuance and exercise of such options to the recipient and the registrant; and

(ii) State separately the amount of such options received or to be received by the following persons if such benefits or amounts are determinable:

(A) Each person (stating name and position) specified in paragraph (a)(3) of Item 402 of Regulation S–K (§ 229.402(a)(3) of this chapter);

(B) All current executive officers as a group;

(C) All current directors who are not executive officers as a group;

(D) Each nominee for election as a director;

(E) Each associate of any of such directors, executive officers or nominees;

(F) Each other person who received or is to receive 5 percent of such options, warrants or rights; and

(G) All employees, including all current officers who are not executive officers, as a group.

(c) Information regarding plans and other arrangements not subject to security holder action. Furnish the information required by Item 201(d) of Regulation S–K (§ 229.201(d) of this chapter).

Instructions to paragraph (c).

1. If action is to be taken as described in paragraph (a) of this Item with respect to the approval of a new compensation plan under which equity securities of the registrant are authorized for issuance, information about the plan shall be disclosed as required under paragraphs (a) and (b) of this Item and shall not be included in the disclosure required by Item 201(d) of Regulation S–K (§ 229.201(d) of this chapter). If action is to be taken as described in paragraph (a) of this Item with respect to the amendment or modification of an existing plan under which equity securities of the registrant are authorized for issuance, the registrant shall include information about securities previously authorized for issuance under the plan (including any outstanding options, warrants and rights previously granted pursuant to the plan and any securities remaining available for future issuance under the plan) in the disclosure required by Item 201(d) of Regulation S–K (§ 229.201(d) of this chapter). Any additional securities that are the subject of the amendments or modification of the existing plan shall be disclosed as required under paragraphs (a) and (b) of this Item and shall not be included in the Item 201(d) disclosure.

Instructions

1. The term plan as used in this Item means any plan as defined in paragraph (a)(6)(ii) of Item 402 of Regulation S–K (§ 229.402(a)(6)(ii) of this chapter).

2. If action is to be taken with respect to a material amendment or modification of an existing plan, the item shall be answered with respect to the plan as proposed to be amended or modified and shall indicate any material differences from the existing plan.

3. If the plan to be acted upon is set forth in a written document, three copies thereof shall be filed with the Commission at the time copies of the proxy statement and form of proxy are first filed pursuant to paragraph (a) or (b) of § 240.14a–6. Electronic filers shall file with the Commission a copy of such written plan document in electronic format as an appendix to the proxy statement. It need not be provided to security holders unless it is a part of the proxy statement.

4. Paragraph (b)(2)(ii) does not apply to warrants or rights to be issued to security holders as such on a pro rata basis.

5. The Commission shall be informed, as supplemental information, when the proxy statement is first filed, as to when the options, warrants or rights and the shares called for thereby will be registered under the Securities Act or, if such registration is not contemplated, the section of the Securities Act or rule of the Commission under which exemption from such registration is claimed and the facts relied upon to make the exemption available.

Item 11. Authorization or Issuance of Securities Otherwise Than for Exchange

If action is to be taken with respect to the authorization or issuance of any securities otherwise than for exchange for outstanding securities of the registrant, furnish the following information:

(a) State the title and amount of securities to be authorized or issued.

(b) Furnish the information required by Item 202 of Regulation S–K (§ 229.202 of this chapter). If the terms of the securities cannot be stated or estimated with respect to any or all of the securities to be authorized, because no offering thereof is contemplated in the proximate future, and if no further authorization by security holders for the issuance thereof is to be obtained, it should be stated that the terms of the securities to be authorized, including dividend or interest rates, conversion prices, voting rights, redemption prices, maturity dates, and similar matters will be determined by the board of directors. If the securities are additional shares of common stock of a class outstanding, the description may be omitted except for a statement of the preemptive rights, if any. Where the statutory provisions with respect to preemptive rights are so indefinite or complex that they cannot be stated in summarized form, it will suffice to make a statement in the form of an opinion of counsel as to the existence and extent of such rights.

(c)   Describe briefly the transaction in which the securities are to be issued including a statement as to (1) the nature and approximate amount of consideration received or to be received by the registrant and (2) the approximate amount devoted to each purpose so far as determinable for which the net proceeds have been or are to be used. If it is impracticable to describe the transaction in which the securities are to be issued, state the reason, indicate the purpose of the authorization of the securities, and state whether further authorization for the issuance of the securities by a vote of security holders will be solicited prior to such issuance.

(d)   If the securities are to be issued otherwise than in a public offering for cash, state the reasons for the proposed authorization or issuance and the general effect thereof upon the rights of existing security holders.

(e)   Furnish the information required by Item 13(a) of this schedule.

Item 12. Modification or Exchange of Securities

If action is to be taken with respect to the modification of any class of securities of the registrant, or the issuance or authorization for issuance of securities of the registrant in exchange for outstanding securities of the registrant furnish the following information:

(a)   If outstanding securities are to be modified, state the title and amount thereof. If securities are to be issued in exchange for outstanding securities, state the title and amount of securities to be so issued, the title and amount of outstanding securities to be exchanged therefor and the basis of the exchange.

(b)   Describe any material differences between the outstanding securities and the modified or new securities in respect of any of the matters concerning which information would be required in the description of the securities in Item 202 of Regulation S–K (§ 229.202 of this chapter).

(c)   State the reasons for the proposed modification or exchange and the general effect thereof upon the rights of existing security holders.

(d)   Furnish a brief statement as to arrears in dividends or as to defaults in principal or interest in respect to the outstanding securities which are to be modified or exchanged and such other information as may be appropriate in the particular case to disclose adequately the nature and effect of the proposed action.

(e)   Outline briefly any other material features of the proposed modification or exchange. If the plan of proposed action is set forth in a written document, file copies thereof with the Commission in accordance with § 240.14a–6.

(f)   Furnish the information required by Item 13(a) of this Schedule.

Instruction. If the existing security is presently listed and registered on a national securities exchange, state whether the registrant intends to apply for listing and registration of the new or reclassified security on such exchange or any other exchange. If the registrant does not intend to make such application, state the effect of the termination of such listing and registration.

SCHEDULE 14A

Item 13. Financial and Other Information. (*See* Notes D and E at the beginning of this Schedule.)

(a) *Information required.* If action is to be taken with respect to any matter specified in Item 11 or 12, furnish the following information:

(1) Financial statements meeting the requirements of Regulation S–X, including financial information required by Rule 3–05 and Article 11 of Regulation S–X with respect to transactions other than pursuant to which action is to be taken as described in this proxy statement (A smaller reporting company may provide the information in Rules 8–04 and 8–05 of Regulation S–X (§§ 210.8–04 and 210.8–05 of this chapter) in lieu of the financial information required by Rule 3–05 and Article 11 of Regulation S–X);

(2) Item 302 of Regulation S–K, supplementary financial information;

(3) Item 303 of Regulation S–K, management's discussion and analysis of financial condition and results of operations;

(4) Item 304 of Regulation S–K, changes in and disagreements with accountants on accounting and financial disclosure;

(5) Item 305 of Regulation S–K, quantitative and qualitative disclosures about market risk; and

(6) A statement as to whether or not representatives of the principal accountants for the current year and for the most recently completed fiscal year:

(i) Are expected to be present at the security holders' meeting;

(ii) Will have the opportunity to make a statement if they desire to do so; and

(iii) Are expected to be available to respond to appropriate questions.

(b) *Incorporation by reference.* The information required pursuant to paragraph (a) of this Item may be incorporated by reference into the proxy statement as follows:

(1) *S-3 registrants.* If the registrant meets the requirements of Form S-3 (*see* Note E to this Schedule), it may incorporate by reference to previously-filed documents any of the information required by paragraph (a) of this Item, provided that the requirements of paragraph (c) are met. Where the registrant meets the requirements of Form S-3 and has elected to furnish the required information by incorporation by reference, the registrant may elect to update the information so incorporated by reference to information in subsequently-filed documents.

(2) *All registrants.* The registrant may incorporate by reference any of the information required by paragraph (a) of this Item, provided that the information is contained in an annual report to security holders or a previously-filed statement or report, such report or statement is delivered to security holders with the proxy statement and the requirements of paragraph (c) are met.

(c) *Certain conditions applicable to incorporation by reference.* Registrants eligible to incorporate by reference into the proxy statement the information required by paragraph (a) of this Item in the manner specified by paragraphs (b)(1) and (b)(2) may do so only if:

(1) The information is not required to be included in the proxy statement pursuant to the requirement of another Item;

(2) The proxy statement identifies on the last page(s) the information incorporated by reference; and

(3) The material incorporated by reference substantially meets the requirements of this Item or the appropriate portions of this Item.

Instructions to Item 13.

SCHEDULE 14A

1. Notwithstanding the provisions of this Item, any or all of the information required by paragraph (a) of this Item not material for the exercise of prudent judgment in regard to the matter to be acted upon may be omitted. In the usual case the information is deemed material to the exercise of prudent judgment where the matter to be acted upon is the authorization or issuance of a material amount of senior securities, but the information is not deemed material where the matter to be acted upon is the authorization or issuance of common stock, otherwise than in an exchange, merger, consolidation, acquisition or similar transaction, the authorization of preferred stock without present intent to issue or the authorization of preferred stock for issuance for cash in an amount constituting fair value.

2. In order to facilitate compliance with Rule 2–02(a) of Regulation S–X, one copy of the definitive proxy statement filed with the Commission shall include a manually signed copy of the accountant's report. If the financial statements are incorporated by reference, a manually signed copy of the accountant's report shall be filed with the definitive proxy statement.

3. Notwithstanding the provisions of Regulation S–X, no schedules other than those prepared in accordance with Rules 12–15, 12–28 and 12–29 (or, for management investment companies, Rules 12–12 through 12–14) of that regulation need be furnished in the proxy statement.

4. Unless registered on a national securities exchange or otherwise required to furnish such information, registered investment companies need not furnish the information required by paragraph (a)(2) or (3) of this Item.

5. If the registrant submits preliminary proxy material incorporating by reference financial statements required by this Item, the registrant should furnish a draft of the financial statements if the document from which they are incorporated has not been filed with or furnished to the Commission.

6. A registered investment company need not comply with items (a)(2), (a)(3), and (a)(5) of this Item 13.

Item 14. Mergers, Consolidations, Acquisitions and Similar Matters. (*See* Notes A and D at the beginning of this Schedule)

Instructions to Item 14:

1. In transactions in which the consideration offered to security holders consists wholly or in part of securities registered under the Securities Act of 1933, furnish the information required by Form S-4 (§ 239.25 of this chapter), Form F-4 (§ 239.34 of this chapter), or Form N-14 (§ 239.23 of this chapter), as applicable, instead of this Item. Only a Form S-4, Form F-4, or Form N-14 must be filed in accordance with § 240.14a–6(j).

2. (a) In transactions in which the consideration offered to security holders consists wholly of cash, the information required by paragraph (c)(1) of this Item for the acquiring company need not be provided unless the information is material to an informed voting decision (*e.g.*, the security holders of the target company are voting and financing is not assured).

(b) Additionally, if only the security holders of the target company are voting:

i. The financial information in paragraphs (b)(8)–(11) of this Item for the acquiring company and the target need not be provided; and

ii. The information in paragraph (c)(2) of this Item for the target company need not be provided.

If, however, the transaction is a going-private transaction (as defined by § 240.13e–3), then the information required by paragraph (c)(2) of this Item must be provided and to the extent that the going-private rules require the information specified in paragraph (b)(8)–(b)(11) of this Item, that information must be provided as well.

SCHEDULE 14A

3. In transactions in which the consideration offered to security holders consists wholly of securities exempt from registration under the Securities Act of 1933 or a combination of exempt securities and cash, information about the acquiring company required by paragraph (c)(1) of this Item need not be provided if only the security holders of the acquiring company are voting, unless the information is material to an informed voting decision. If only the security holders of the target company are voting, information about the target company in paragraph (c)(2) of this Item need not be provided. However, the information required by paragraph (c)(2) of this Item must be provided if the transaction is a going-private (as defined by § 240.13e–3) or roll-up (as described by Item 901 of Regulation S–K (§ 229.901 of this chapter)) transaction.

4. The information required by paragraphs (b)(8)–(11) and (c) need not be provided if the plan being voted on involves only the acquiring company and one or more of its totally held subsidiaries and does not involve a liquidation or a spin off.

5. To facilitate compliance with Rule 2–02(a) of Regulation S–X (§ 210.2–02(a) of this chapter) (technical requirements relating to accountants' reports), one copy of the definitive proxy statement filed with the Commission must include a signed copy of the accountant's report. If the financial statements are incorporated by reference, a signed copy of the accountant's report must be filed with the definitive proxy statement. Signatures may be typed if the document is filed electronically on EDGAR. *See* Rule 302 of Regulation S–T (§ 232.302 of this chapter).

6. Notwithstanding the provisions of Regulation S–X, no schedules other than those prepared in accordance with § 210.12–15, § 210.12–28 and § 210.12–29 of this chapter (or, for management investment companies, §§ 210.12–12 through 210.12–14 of this chapter) of that regulation need be furnished in the proxy statement.

7. If the preliminary proxy material incorporates by reference financial statements required by this Item, a draft of the financial statements must be furnished to the Commission staff upon request if the document from which they are incorporated has not been filed with or furnished to the Commission.

(a) *Applicability.* If action is to be taken with respect to any of the following transactions, provide the information required by this Item:

(1) A merger or consolidation;

(2) An acquisition of securities of another person;

(3) An acquisition of any other going business or the assets of a going business;

(4) A sale or other transfer of all or any substantial part of assets; or

(5) A liquidation or dissolution.

(b) *Transaction information.* Provide the following information for each of the parties to the transaction unless otherwise specified:

(1) *Summary term sheet.* The information required by Item 1001 of Regulation M–A (§ 229.1001 of this chapter).

(2) *Contact information.* The name, complete mailing address and telephone number of the principal executive offices.

(3) *Business conducted.* A brief description of the general nature of the business conducted.

(4) *Terms of the transaction.* The information required by Item 1004(a)(2) of Regulation M–A (§ 229.1004 of this chapter).

(5) *Regulatory approvals.* A statement as to whether any federal or state regulatory requirements must be complied with or approval must be obtained in connection with the transaction and, if so, the status of the compliance or approval.

SCHEDULE 14A

(6)   Reports, opinions, appraisals. If a report, opinion or appraisal materially relating to the transaction has been received from an outside party, and is referred to in the proxy statement, furnish the information required by Item 1015(b) of Regulation M–A (§ 229.1015 of this chapter).

(7)   Past contacts, transactions or negotiations. The information required by Items 1005(b) and 1011(a)(1) of Regulation M–A (§ 229.1005 of this chapter and § 229.1011 of this chapter), for the parties to the transaction and their affiliates during the periods for which financial statements are presented or incorporated by reference under this Item.

(8)   Selected financial data. The selected financial data required by Item 301 of Regulation S–K (§ 229.301 of this chapter).

(9)   Pro forma selected financial data. If material, the information required by Item 301 of Regulation S–K (§ 229.301 of this chapter) for the acquiring company, showing the pro forma effect of the transaction.

(10)   Pro forma information. In a table designed to facilitate comparison, historical and pro forma per share data of the acquiring company and historical and equivalent pro forma per share data of the target company for the following Items:

(i)   Book value per share as of the date financial data is presented pursuant to Item 301 of Regulation S–K (§ 229.301 of this chapter);

(ii)   Cash dividends declared per share for the periods for which financial data is presented pursuant to Item 301 of Regulation S–K (§ 229.301 of this chapter); and

(iii)   Income (loss) per share from continuing operations for the periods for which financial data is presented pursuant to Item 301 of Regulation S–K (§ 229.301 of this chapter).

Instructions to paragraphs (b)(8), (b)(9) and (b)(10):

1.   For a business combination, present the financial information required by paragraphs (b)(9) and (b)(10) only for the most recent fiscal year and interim period. For a combination between entities under common control, present the financial information required by paragraphs (b)(9) and (b)(10) (except for information with regard to book value) for the most recent three fiscal years and interim period. For purposes of these paragraphs, book value information need only be provided for the most recent balance sheet date.

2.   Calculate the equivalent pro forma per share amounts for one share of the company being acquired by multiplying the exchange ratio times each of:

(i)   The pro forma income (loss) per share before non-recurring charges or credits directly attributable to the transaction;

(ii)   The pro forma book value per share; and

(iii)   The pro forma dividends per share of the acquiring company.

3.   Unless registered on a national securities exchange or otherwise required to furnish such information, registered investment companies need not furnish the information required by paragraphs (b)(8) and (b)(9) of this Item.

(11)   Financial information. If material, financial information required by Article 11 of Regulation S–X (§§ 210.10–01 through 229.11–03 of this chapter) with respect to this transaction.

Instructions to paragraph (b)(11):

1.   Present any Article 11 information required with respect to transactions other than those being voted upon (where not incorporated by reference) together with the pro forma information relating to the transaction being voted upon. In presenting this information, you must clearly distinguish between the transaction being voted upon and any other transaction.

SCHEDULE 14A

2. If current pro forma financial information with respect to all other transactions is incorporated by reference, you need only present the pro forma effect of this transaction.

(c) Information about the parties to the transaction. (1) Acquiring company. Furnish the information required by Part B (Registrant Information) of Form S-4 (§ 239.25 of this chapter) or Form F-4 (§ 239.34 of this chapter), as applicable, for the acquiring company. However, financial statements need only be presented for the latest two fiscal years and interim periods.

(2) Acquired company. Furnish the information required by Part C (Information with Respect to the Company Being Acquired) of Form S-4 (§ 239.25 of this chapter) or Form F-4 (§ 239.34 of this chapter), as applicable.

(d) Information about parties to the transaction: registered investment companies and business development companies. If the acquiring company or the acquired company is an investment company registered under the Investment Company Act of 1940 or a business development company as defined by Section 2(a)(48) of the Investment Company Act of 1940, provide the following information for that company instead of the information specified by paragraph (c) of this Item:

(1) Information required by Item 101 of Regulation S–K (§ 229.101 of this chapter), description of business;

(2) Information required by Item 102 of Regulation S–K (§ 229.102 of this chapter), description of property;

(3) Information required by Item 103 of Regulation S–K (§ 229.103 of this chapter), legal proceedings;

(4) Information required by Item 201(a), (b) and (c) of Regulation S–K (§ 229.201(a), (b) and (c) of this chapter), market price of and dividends on the registrant's common equity and related stockholder matters;

(5) Financial statements meeting the requirements of Regulation S–X, including financial information required by Rule 3–05 and Article 11 of Regulation S–X (§ 210.3–05 and § 210.11–01 through § 210.11–03 of this chapter) with respect to transactions other than that as to which action is to be taken as described in this proxy statement;

(6) Information required by Item 301 of Regulation S–K (§ 229.301 of this chapter), selected financial data;

(7) Information required by Item 302 of Regulation S–K (§ 229.302 of this chapter), supplementary financial information;

(8) Information required by Item 303 of Regulation S–K (§ 229.303 of this chapter), management's discussion and analysis of financial condition and results of operations; and

(9) Information required by Item 304 of Regulation S–K (§ 229.304 of this chapter), changes in and disagreements with accountants on accounting and financial disclosure.

Instruction to paragraph (d) of Item 14: Unless registered on a national securities exchange or otherwise required to furnish such information, registered investment companies need not furnish the information required by paragraphs (d)(6), (d)(7) and (d)(8) of this Item.

(e) Incorporation by reference. (1) The information required by paragraph (c) of this section may be incorporated by reference into the proxy statement to the same extent as would be permitted by Form S-4 (§ 239.25 of this chapter) or Form F-4 (§ 239.34 of this chapter), as applicable.

(2) Alternatively, the registrant may incorporate by reference into the proxy statement the information required by paragraph (c) of this Item if it is contained in an annual report sent to security holders in accordance with § 240.14a–3 of this chapter with respect to the same meeting or solicitation of consents or authorizations that the proxy statement relates to and the information substantially meets the disclosure requirements of Item 14 or Item 17 of Form S-4 (§ 239.25 of this chapter) or Form F-4 (§ 239.34 of this chapter), as applicable.

SCHEDULE 14A

Item 15. Acquisition or Disposition of Property

If action is to be taken with respect to the acquisition or disposition of any property, furnish the following information:

(a) Describe briefly the general character and location of the property.

(b) State the nature and amount of consideration to be paid or received by the registrant or any subsidiary. To the extent practicable, outline briefly the facts bearing upon the question of the fairness of the consideration.

(c) State the name and address of the transferer or transferee, as the case may be and the nature of any material relationship of such person to the registrant or any affiliate of the registrant.

(d) Outline briefly any other material features of the contract or transaction.

Item 16. Restatement of Accounts

If action is to be taken with respect to the restatement of any asset, capital, or surplus account of the registrant furnish the following information:

(a) State the nature of the restatement and the date as of which it is to be effective.

(b) Outline briefly the reasons for the restatement and for the selection of the particular effective date.

(c) State the name and amount of each account (including any reserve accounts) affected by the restatement and the effect of the restatement thereon. Tabular presentation of the amounts shall be made when appropriate, particularly in the case of recapitalizations.

(d) To the extent practicable, state whether and the extent, if any, to which, the restatement will, as of the date thereof, alter the amount available for distribution to the holders of equity securities.

Item 17. Action with Respect to Reports

If action is to be taken with respect to any report of the registrant or of its directors, officers or committees or any minutes of a meeting of its security holders, furnish the following information:

(a) State whether or not such action is to constitute approval or disapproval of any of the matters referred to in such reports or minutes.

(b) Identify each of such matters which it is intended will be approved or disapproved, and furnish the information required by the appropriate item or items of this schedule with respect to each such matter.

Item 18. Matters Not Required to Be Submitted

If action is to be taken with respect to any matter which is not required to be submitted to a vote of security holders, state the nature of such matter, the reasons for submitting it to a vote of security holders and what action is intended to be taken by the registrant in the event of a negative vote on the matter by the security holders.

Item 19. Amendment of Charter, Bylaws or Other Documents

If action is to be taken with respect to any amendment of the registrant's charter, bylaws or other documents as to which information is not required above, state briefly the reasons for and the general effect of such amendment.

Instructions. 1. Where the matter to be acted upon is the classification of directors, state whether vacancies which occur during the year may be filled by the board of directors to serve only until the next annual meeting or may be so filled for the remainder of the full term.

2. Attention is directed to the discussion of disclosure regarding anti-takeover and similar proposals in Release No. 34–15230 (October 13, 1978).

SCHEDULE 14A

Item 20. Other Proposed Action

If action is to be taken on any matter not specifically referred to in this Schedule 14A, describe briefly the substance of each such matter in substantially the same degree of detail as is required by Items 5 to 19, inclusive, of this Schedule, and, with respect to investment companies registered under the Investment Company Act of 1940, Item 22 of this Schedule. Registrants required to provide a separate shareholder vote pursuant to section 111(e)(1) of the Emergency Economic Stabilization Act of 2008 (12 U.S.C. 5221(e)(1)) and § 240.14a–20 shall disclose that they are providing such a vote as required pursuant to the Emergency Economic Stabilization Act of 2008, and briefly explain the general effect of the vote, such as whether the vote is non-binding.

Item 21. Voting Procedures

As to each matter which is to be submitted to a vote of security holders, furnish the following information:

(a) State the vote required for approval or election, other than for the approval of auditors.

(b) Disclose the method by which votes will be counted, including the treatment and effect of abstentions and broker non-votes under applicable state law as well as registrant charter and by-law provisions.

* * *

Item 23. Delivery of documents to security holders sharing an address.

If one annual report to security holders, proxy statement, or Notice of Internet Availability of Proxy Materials is being delivered to two or more security holders who share an address in accordance with § 240.14a–3(e)(1), furnish the following information:

(a) State that only one annual report to security holders, proxy statement, or Notice of Internet Availability of Proxy Materials, as applicable, is being delivered to multiple security holders sharing an address unless the registrant has received contrary instructions from one or more of the security holders;

(b) Undertake to deliver promptly upon written or oral request a separate copy of the annual report to security holders, proxy statement, or Notice of Internet Availability of Proxy Materials, as applicable, to a security holder at a shared address to which a single copy of the documents was delivered and provide instructions as to how a security holder can notify the registrant that the security holder wishes to receive a separate copy of an annual report to security holders, proxy statement, or Notice of Internet Availability of Proxy Materials, as applicable;

(c) Provide the phone number and mailing address to which a security holder can direct a notification to the registrant that the security holder wishes to receive a separate annual report to security holders, proxy statement, or Notice of Internet Availability of Proxy Materials, as applicable, in the future; and

(d) Provide instructions how security holders sharing an address can request delivery of a single copy of annual reports to security holders, proxy statements, or Notices of Internet Availability of Proxy Materials if they are receiving multiple copies of annual reports to security holders, proxy statements, or Notices of Internet Availability of Proxy Materials.

* * *

SCHEDULE TO

SCHEDULE TO: TENDER OFFER STATEMENT UNDER SECTION 14(d)(1) OR 13(e)(1) OF THE SECURITIES EXCHANGE ACT OF 1934

Securities and Exchange Commission,
Washington, D.C. 20549
Schedule TO

Tender Offer Statement under Section 14(d)(1) or 13(e)(1) of the Securities Exchange Act of 1934

(Amendment No. ___)

_____

(Name of Subject Company (issuer))

_____

(Names of Filing Persons (identifying status as offeror, issuer or other person))

_____

(Title of Class of Securities)

_____

(CUSIP Number of Class of Securities)

(Name, address, and telephone numbers of person authorized to receive notices and communications on behalf of filing persons)

Calculation of Filing Fee

Transaction valuation* Amount of filing fee

[ ] Check the box if any part of the fee is offset as provided by Rule 0–11(a)(2) and identify the filing with which the offsetting fee was previously paid. Identify the previous filing by registration statement number, or the Form or Schedule and the date of its filing.

Amount Previously Paid: _____

Form or Registration No.: _____

Filing Party: _____

Date Filed: _____

[ ] Check the box if the filing relates solely to preliminary communications made before the commencement of a tender offer.

Check the appropriate boxes below to designate any transactions to which the statement relates:

[ ] third-party tender offer subject to Rule 14d–1.

[ ] issuer tender offer subject to Rule 13e–4.

[ ] going-private transaction subject to Rule 13e–3.

[ ] amendment to Schedule 13D under Rule 13d–2.

Check the following box if the filing is a final amendment reporting the results of the tender offer: [ ]

_____

*   Set forth the amount on which the filing fee is calculated and state how it was determined.

SCHEDULE TO

If applicable, check the appropriate box(es) below to designate the appropriate rule provision(s) relied upon:

[ ] Rule 13e–4(i) (Cross-Border Issuer Tender Offer)

[ ] Rule 14d–1(d) (Cross-Border Third-Party Tender Offer)

General Instructions:

A.   File eight copies of the statement, including all exhibits, with the Commission if paper filing is permitted.

B.   This filing must be accompanied by a fee payable to the Commission as required by § 240.0–11.

C.   If the statement is filed by a general or limited partnership, syndicate or other group, the information called for by Items 3 and 5–8 for a third-party tender offer and Items 5–8 for an issuer tender offer must be given with respect to: (i) Each partner of the general partnership; (ii) each partner who is, or functions as, a general partner of the limited partnership; (iii) each member of the syndicate or group; and (iv) each person controlling the partner or member. If the statement is filed by a corporation or if a person referred to in (i), (ii), (iii) or (iv) of this Instruction is a corporation, the information called for by the items specified above must be given with respect to: (a) Each executive officer and director of the corporation; (b) each person controlling the corporation; and (c) each executive officer and director of any corporation or other person ultimately in control of the corporation.

D.   If the filing contains only preliminary communications made before the commencement of a tender offer, no signature or filing fee is required. The filer need not respond to the items in the schedule. Any pre-commencement communications that are filed under cover of this schedule need not be incorporated by reference into the schedule.

E.   If an item is inapplicable or the answer is in the negative, so state. The statement published, sent or given to security holders may omit negative and not applicable responses. If the schedule includes any information that is not published, sent or given to security holders, provide that information or specifically incorporate it by reference under the appropriate item number and heading in the schedule. Do not recite the text of disclosure requirements in the schedule or any document published, sent or given to security holders. Indicate clearly the coverage of the requirements without referring to the text of the items.

F.   Information contained in exhibits to the statement may be incorporated by reference in answer or partial answer to any item unless it would render the answer misleading, incomplete, unclear or confusing. A copy of any information that is incorporated by reference or a copy of the pertinent pages of a document containing the information must be submitted with this statement as an exhibit, unless it was previously filed with the Commission electronically on EDGAR. If an exhibit contains information responding to more than one item in the schedule, all information in that exhibit may be incorporated by reference once in response to the several items in the schedule for which it provides an answer. Information incorporated by reference is deemed filed with the Commission for all purposes of the Act.

G.   A filing person may amend its previously filed Schedule 13D (§ 240.13d–101) on Schedule TO (§ 240.14d–100) if the appropriate box on the cover page is checked to indicate a combined filing and the information called for by the fourteen disclosure items on the cover page of Schedule 13D (§ 240.13d–101) is provided on the cover page of the combined filing with respect to each filing person.

H.   The final amendment required by § 240.14d–3(b)(2) and § 240.13e–4(c)(4) will satisfy the reporting requirements of section 13(d) of the Act with respect to all securities acquired by the offeror in the tender offer.

I.   Amendments disclosing a material change in the information set forth in this statement may omit any information previously disclosed in this statement.

SCHEDULE TO

J.   If the tender offer disclosed on this statement involves a going-private transaction, a combined Schedule TO (§ 240.14d–100) and Schedule 13E–3 (§ 240.13e–100) may be filed with the Commission under cover of Schedule TO. The Rule 13e–3 box on the cover page of the Schedule TO must be checked to indicate a combined filing. All information called for by both schedules must be provided except that Items 1–3, 5, 8 and 9 of Schedule TO may be omitted to the extent those items call for information that duplicates the item requirements in Schedule 13E–3.

K.   For purposes of this statement, the following definitions apply:

(1)   The term offeror means any person who makes a tender offer or on whose behalf a tender offer is made;

(2)   The term issuer tender offer has the same meaning as in Rule 13e–4(a)(2); and

(3)   The term third-party tender offer means a tender offer that is not an issuer tender offer.

Special Instructions for Complying With Schedule TO

Under Sections 13(e), 14(d) and 23 of the Act and the rules and regulations of the Act, the Commission is authorized to solicit the information required to be supplied by this schedule.

Disclosure of the information specified in this schedule is mandatory. The information will be used for the primary purpose of disclosing tender offer and going-private transactions. This statement will be made a matter of public record. Therefore, any information given will be available for inspection by any member of the public.

Because of the public nature of the information, the Commission can use it for a variety of purposes, including referral to other governmental authorities or securities self-regulatory organizations for investigatory purposes or in connection with litigation involving the federal securities laws or other civil, criminal or regulatory statutes or provisions.

Failure to disclose the information required by this schedule may result in civil or criminal action against the persons involved for violation of the federal securities laws and rules.

Item 1.   Summary Term Sheet

Furnish the information required by Item 1001 of Regulation M–A (§ 229.1001 of this chapter) unless information is disclosed to security holders in a prospectus that meets the requirements of § 230.421(d) of this chapter.

Item 2.   Subject Company Information

Furnish the information required by Item 1002(a) through (c) of Regulation M–A (§ 229.1002 of this chapter).

Item 3.   Identity and Background of Filing Person

Furnish the information required by Item 1003(a) through (c) of Regulation M–A (§ 229.1003 of this chapter) for a third-party tender offer and the information required by Item 1003(a) of Regulation M–A (§ 229.1003 of this chapter) for an issuer tender offer.

Item 4.   Terms of the Transaction

Furnish the information required by Item 1004(a) of Regulation M–A (§ 229.1004 of this chapter) for a third-party tender offer and the information required by Item 1004(a) through (b) of Regulation M–A (§ 229.1004 of this chapter) for an issuer tender offer.

Item 5.   Past Contacts, Transactions, Negotiations and Agreements

Furnish the information required by Item 1005(a) and (b) of Regulation M–A (§ 229.1005 of this chapter) for a third-party tender offer and the information required by Item 1005(e) of Regulation M–A (§ 229.1005) for an issuer tender offer.

SCHEDULE TO

Item 6. Purposes of the Transaction and Plans or Proposals

Furnish the information required by Item 1006(a) and (c)(1) through (7) of Regulation M–A (§ 229.1006 of this chapter) for a third-party tender offer and the information required by Item 1006(a) through (c) of Regulation M–A (§ 229.1006 of this chapter) for an issuer tender offer.

Item 7. Source and Amount of Funds or Other Consideration

Furnish the information required by Item 1007(a), (b) and (d) of Regulation M–A (§ 229.1007 of this chapter).

Item 8. Interest in Securities of the Subject Company

Furnish the information required by Item 1008 of Regulation M–A (§ 229.1008 of this chapter).

Item 9. Persons/Assets, Retained, Employed, Compensated or Used

Furnish the information required by Item 1009(a) of Regulation M–A (§ 229.1009 of this chapter).

Item 10. Financial Statements

If material, furnish the information required by Item 1010(a) and (b) of Regulation M–A (§ 229.1010 of this chapter) for the issuer in an issuer tender offer and for the offeror in a third-party tender offer.

Instructions to Item 10:

1. Financial statements must be provided when the offeror's financial condition is material to security holder's decision whether to sell, tender or hold the securities sought. The facts and circumstances of a tender offer, particularly the terms of the tender offer, may influence a determination as to whether financial statements are material, and thus required to be disclosed.

2. Financial statements are not considered material when: (a) The consideration offered consists solely of cash; (b) the offer is not subject to any financing condition; and either: (c) the offeror is a public reporting company under Section 13(a) or 15(d) of the Act that files reports electronically on EDGAR, or (d) the offer is for all outstanding securities of the subject class. Financial information may be required, however, in a two-tier transaction. *See* Instruction 5 below.

3. The filing person may incorporate by reference financial statements contained in any document filed with the Commission, solely for the purposes of this schedule, if: (a) The financial statements substantially meet the requirements of this item; (b) an express statement is made that the financial statements are incorporated by reference; (c) the information incorporated by reference is clearly identified by page, paragraph, caption or otherwise; and (d) if the information incorporated by reference is not filed with this schedule, an indication is made where the information may be inspected and copies obtained. Financial statements that are required to be presented in comparative form for two or more fiscal years or periods may not be incorporated by reference unless the material incorporated by reference includes the entire period for which the comparative data is required to be given. *See* General Instruction F to this schedule.

4. If the offeror in a third-party tender offer is a natural person, and such person's financial information is material, disclose the net worth of the offeror. If the offeror's net worth is derived from material amounts of assets that are not readily marketable or there are material guarantees and contingencies, disclose the nature and approximate amount of the individual's net worth that consists of illiquid assets and the magnitude of any guarantees or contingencies that may negatively affect the natural person's net worth.

5. Pro forma financial information is required in a negotiated third-party cash tender offer when securities are intended to be offered in a subsequent merger or other transaction in which remaining target securities are acquired and the acquisition of the subject company is significant to the offeror under § 210.11–01(b)(1) of this chapter. The offeror must disclose the financial information specified in Item 3(f) and Item 5 of Form S-4 (§ 239.25 of this chapter) in the schedule filed with the Commission, but may furnish only the summary financial information specified in Item 3(d), (e) and

SCHEDULE TO

(f) of Form S-4 in the disclosure document sent to security holders. If pro forma financial information is required by this instruction, the historical financial statements specified in Item 1010 of Regulation M–A (§ 229.1010 of this chapter) are required for the bidder.

6. The disclosure materials disseminated to security holders may contain the summarized financial information specified by Item 1010(c) of Regulation M–A (§ 229.1010 of this chapter) instead of the financial information required by Item 1010(a) and (b). In that case, the financial information required by Item 1010(a) and (b) of Regulation M–A must be disclosed in the statement. If summarized financial information is disseminated to security holders, include appropriate instructions on how more complete financial information can be obtained. If the summarized financial information is prepared on the basis of a comprehensive body of accounting principles other than U.S. GAAP, the summarized financial information must be accompanied by a reconciliation as described in Instruction 8 of this Item.

7. If the offeror is not subject to the periodic reporting requirements of the Act, the financial statements required by this Item need not be audited if audited financial statements are not available or obtainable without unreasonable cost or expense. Make a statement to that effect and the reasons for their unavailability.

8. If the financial statements required by this Item are prepared on the basis of a comprehensive body of accounting principles other than U.S. GAAP, provide a reconciliation to U.S. GAAP in accordance with Item 17 of Form 20-F (§ 249.220f of this chapter), unless a reconciliation is unavailable or not obtainable without unreasonable cost or expense. At a minimum, however, when financial statements are prepared on a basis other than U.S. GAAP, a narrative description of all material variations in accounting principles, practices and methods used in preparing the non-U.S. GAAP financial statements from those accepted in the U.S. must be presented.

Item 11. Additional Information.

Furnish the information required by Item 1011(a) and (c) of Regulation M–A (§ 229.1011 of this chapter).

Item 12. Exhibits

File as an exhibit to the Schedule all documents specified by Item 1016 (a), (b), (d), (g) and (h) of Regulation M–A (§ 229.1016 of this chapter).

Item 13. Information Required by Schedule 13E–3

If the Schedule TO is combined with Schedule 13E–3 (§ 240.13e–100), set forth the information required by Schedule 13E–3 that is not included or covered by the items in Schedule TO.

Signature. After due inquiry and to the best of my knowledge and belief, I certify that the information set forth in this statement is true, complete and correct.

_____
(Signature)

_____
(Name and title)

_____
(Date)

Instruction to Signature: The statement must be signed by the filing person or that person's authorized representative. If the statement is signed on behalf of a person by an authorized representative (other than an executive officer of a corporation or general partner of a partnership), evidence of the representative's authority to sign on behalf of the person must be filed with the statement. The name and any title of each person who signs the statement must be typed or printed beneath the signature. See §§ 240.12b–11 and 240.14d–1(h) with respect to signature requirements.

SCHEDULE 14D–9

* * *

GENERAL INSTRUCTIONS

A.   File eight copies of the statement, including all exhibits, with the Commission if paper filing is permitted.

B.   If the filing contains only preliminary communications made before the commencement of a tender offer, no signature is required. The filer need not respond to the items in the schedule. Any pre-commencement communications that are filed under cover of this schedule need not be incorporated by reference into the schedule.

C.   If an item is inapplicable or the answer is in the negative, so state. The statement published, sent or given to security holders may omit negative and not applicable responses. If the schedule includes any information that is not published, sent or given to security holders, provide that information or specifically incorporate it by reference under the appropriate item number and heading in the schedule. Do not recite the text of disclosure requirements in the schedule or any document published, sent or given to security holders. Indicate clearly the coverage of the requirements without referring to the text of the items.

D.   Information contained in exhibits to the statement may be incorporated by reference in answer or partial answer to any item unless it would render the answer misleading, incomplete, unclear or confusing. A copy of any information that is incorporated by reference or a copy of the pertinent pages of a document containing the information must be submitted with this statement as an exhibit, unless it was previously filed with the Commission electronically on EDGAR. If an exhibit contains information responding to more than one item in the schedule, all information in that exhibit may be incorporated by reference once in response to the several items in the schedule for which it provides an answer. Information incorporated by reference is deemed filed with the Commission for all purposes of the Act.

E.   Amendments disclosing a material change in the information set forth in this statement may omit any information previously disclosed in this statement.

Item 1. Subject Company Information

Furnish the information required by Item 1002(a) and (b) of Regulation M–A (§ 229.1002 of this chapter).

Item 2. Identity and Background of Filing Person

Furnish the information required by Item 1003(a) and (d) of Regulation M–A (§ 229.1003 of this chapter).

Item 3. Past Contacts, Transactions, Negotiations and Agreements

Furnish the information required by Item 1005(d) of Regulation M–A (§ 229.1005 of this chapter).

Item 4. The Solicitation or Recommendation

Furnish the information required by Item 1012(a) through (c) of Regulation M–A (§ 229.1012 of this chapter).

Item 5. Person/Assets, Retained, Employed, Compensated or Used

Furnish the information required by Item 1009(a) of Regulation M–A (§ 229.1009 of this chapter).

Item 6. Interest in Securities of the Subject Company

Furnish the information required by Item 1008(b) of Regulation M–A (§ 229.1008 of this chapter).

SCHEDULE 14D–9

Item 7. Purposes of the Transaction and Plans or Proposals

Furnish the information required by Item 1006(d) of Regulation M–A (§ 229.1006 of this chapter).

Item 8. Additional Information

Furnish the information required by Item 1011(b) and (c) of Regulation M–A (§ 229.1011 of this chapter).

Item 9. Exhibits

File as an exhibit to the Schedule all documents specified by Item 1016(a), (e) and (g) of Regulation M–A (§ 229.1016 of this chapter).

* * *

G. REGULATION S–K

(Selected)

17 C.F.R. §§ 229.300 *et seq.*

_____

*Table of Contents**

_____

§ 229.303   (Item 303) Management's Discussion and Analysis of Financial Condition and Results of Operations.

(a) *Full fiscal years.* Discuss registrant's financial condition, changes in financial condition and results of operations. The discussion shall provide information as specified in paragraphs (a)(1) through (5) of this Item and also shall provide such other information that the registrant believes to be necessary to an understanding of its financial condition, changes in financial condition and results of operations. Discussions of liquidity and capital resources may be combined whenever the two topics are interrelated. Where in the registrant's judgment a discussion of segment information and/or of other subdivisions (e.g., geographic areas) of the registrant's business would be appropriate to an understanding of such business, the discussion shall focus on each relevant, reportable segment and/or other subdivision of the business and on the registrant as a whole.

(1) *Liquidity.* Identify any known trends or any known demands, commitments, events or uncertainties that will result in or that are reasonably likely to result in the registrant's liquidity increasing or decreasing in any material way. If a material deficiency is identified, indicate the course of action that the registrant has taken or proposes to take to remedy the deficiency. Also identify and separately describe internal and external sources of liquidity, and briefly discuss any material unused sources of liquid assets.

(2) *Capital resources.* (i) Describe the registrant's material commitments for capital expenditures as of the end of the latest fiscal period, and indicate the general purpose of such commitments and the anticipated source of funds needed to fulfill such commitments.

(ii) Describe any known material trends, favorable or unfavorable, in the registrant's capital resources. Indicate any expected material changes in the mix and relative cost of such resources. The discussion shall consider changes between equity, debt and any off-balance sheet financing arrangements.

(3) *Results of operations.* (i) Describe any unusual or infrequent events or transactions or any significant economic changes that materially affected the amount of reported income from continuing operations and, in each case, indicate the extent to which income was so affected. In addition, describe any other significant components of revenues or expenses that, in the

_____

* Although this table of contents lists item numbers, the items themselves are printed with their CFR sections (§ 229.[item number]). For example, Item 303 is § 229.303.

registrant's judgment, should be described in order to understand the registrant's results of operations.

(ii) Describe any known trends or uncertainties that have had or that the registrant reasonably expects will have a material favorable or unfavorable impact on net sales or revenues or income from continuing operations. If the registrant knows of events that will cause a material change in the relationship between costs and revenues (such as known future increases in costs of labor or materials or price increases or inventory adjustments), the change in the relationship shall be disclosed.

(iii) To the extent that the financial statements disclose material increases in net sales or revenues, provide a narrative discussion of the extent to which such increases are attributable to increases in prices or to increases in the volume or amount of goods or services being sold or to the introduction of new products or services.

(iv) For the three most recent fiscal years of the registrant or for those fiscal years in which the registrant has been engaged in business, whichever period is shortest, discuss the impact of inflation and changing prices on the registrant's net sales and revenues and on income from continuing operations.

(4) *Off-balance sheet arrangements.* (i) In a separately-captioned section, discuss the registrant's off-balance sheet arrangements that have or are reasonably likely to have a current or future effect on the registrant's financial condition, changes in financial condition, revenues or expenses, results of operations, liquidity, capital expenditures or capital resources that is material to investors. The disclosure shall include the items specified in paragraphs (a)(4)(i)(A), (B), (C) and (D) of this Item to the extent necessary to an understanding of such arrangements and effect and shall also include such other information that the registrant believes is necessary for such an understanding.

(A) The nature and business purpose to the registrant of such off-balance sheet arrangements;

(B) The importance to the registrant of such off-balance sheet arrangements in respect of its liquidity, capital resources, market risk support, credit risk support or other benefits;

(C) The amounts of revenues, expenses and cash flows of the registrant arising from such arrangements; the nature and amounts of any interests retained, securities issued and other indebtedness incurred by the registrant in connection with such arrangements; and the nature and amounts of any other obligations or liabilities (including contingent obligations or liabilities) of the registrant arising from such arrangements that are or are reasonably likely to become material and the triggering events or circumstances that could cause them to arise; and

(D) Any known event, demand, commitment, trend or uncertainty that will result in or is reasonably likely to result in the termination, or material reduction in availability to the registrant, of its off-balance sheet arrangements that provide material benefits to it, and the course of action that the registrant has taken or proposes to take in response to any such circumstances.

(ii) As used in this paragraph (a)(4), the term *off-balance sheet arrangement* means any transaction, agreement or other contractual arrangement to which an entity unconsolidated with the registrant is a party, under which the registrant has:

(A) Any obligation under a guarantee contract that has any of the characteristics identified in FASB ASC paragraph 460–10–15–4 (Guarantees Topic), as may be modified or supplemented, and that is not excluded from the initial recognition and measurement provisions of FASB ASC paragraphs 460–10–15–7, 460–10–25–1, and 460–10–30–1;

(B) A retained or contingent interest in assets transferred to an unconsolidated entity or similar arrangement that serves as credit, liquidity or market risk support to such entity for such assets;

(C) Any obligation, including a contingent obligation, under a contract that would be accounted for as a derivative instrument, except that it is both indexed to the registrant's own stock and classified in stockholders' equity in the registrant's statement of financial position, and therefore excluded from the scope of FASB ASC Topic 815, *Derivatives and Hedging,* pursuant to FASB ASC subparagraph 815–10–15–74(a), as may be modified or supplemented; or

(D) Any obligation, including a contingent obligation, arising out of a variable interest (as defined in the FASB ASC Master Glossary, as may be modified or supplemented) in an unconsolidated entity that is held by, and material to, the registrant, where such entity provides financing, liquidity, market risk or credit risk support to, or engages in leasing, hedging or research and development services with, the registrant.

(5) *Tabular disclosure of contractual obligations.* (i) In a tabular format, provide the information specified in this paragraph (a)(5) as of the latest fiscal year end balance sheet date with respect to the registrant's known contractual obligations specified in the table that follows this paragraph (a)(5)(i). The registrant shall provide amounts, aggregated by type of contractual obligation. The registrant may disaggregate the specified categories of contractual obligations using other categories suitable to its business, but the presentation must include all of the obligations of the registrant that fall within the specified categories. A presentation covering at least the periods specified shall be included. The tabular presentation may be accompanied by footnotes to describe provisions that create, increase or accelerate obligations, or other pertinent data to the extent necessary for an understanding of the timing and amount of the registrant's specified contractual obligations.

Contractual obligations	Payments due by period				
	Total	Less than 1 year	1–3 years	3–5 years	More than 5 years
[Long-Term Debt Obligations]					
[Capital Lease Obligations]					
[Operating Lease Obligations]					
[Purchase Obligations]					
[Other Long-Term Liabilities Reflected on the Registrant's Balance Sheet under GAAP]					
Total					

(ii) *Definitions:* The following definitions apply to this paragraph (a)(5):

(A) *Long-term debt obligation* means a payment obligation under long-term borrowings referenced in FASB ASC paragraph 470–10–50–1 (Debt Topic), as may be modified or supplemented.

(B) *Capital lease obligation* means a payment obligation under a lease classified as a capital lease pursuant to FASB ASC Topic 840, *Leases.*, as may be modified or supplemented.

(C) *Operating lease obligation* means a payment obligation under a lease classified as an operating lease and disclosed pursuant to FASB ASC Topic 840, as may be modified or supplemented.

(D) *Purchase obligation* means an agreement to purchase goods or services that is enforceable and legally binding on the registrant that specifies all significant terms, including: fixed or minimum quantities to be purchased; fixed, minimum or variable price provisions; and the approximate timing of the transaction.

Instructions to paragraph 303(a): 1. The registrant's discussion and analysis shall be of the financial statements and other statistical data that the registrant believes will enhance a reader's understanding of its financial condition, changes in financial condition, and results of operations. Generally, the discussion shall cover the periods covered by the financial statements included in the filing and the registrant may use any presentation that in the registrant's judgment enhances a reader's understanding. A smaller reporting company's discussion shall cover the two-year period required in Article 8 of Regulation S–X and may use any presentation that in the registrant's judgment enhances a reader's understanding. For registrants providing financial statements covering three years in a filing, discussion about the earliest of the three years may be omitted if such discussion was already included in the registrant's prior filings on EDGAR that required disclosure in compliance with Item 303 of Regulation S–K, provided that registrants electing not to include a discussion of the earliest year must include a statement that identifies the location in the prior filing where the omitted discussion may be found. An emerging growth company, as defined in Rule 405 of the Securities Act (§ 230.405 of this chapter) or Rule 12b–2 of the Exchange Act (§ 240.12b–2 of this chapter), may provide the discussion required in paragraph (a) of this Item for its two most recent fiscal years if, pursuant to Section 7(a) of the Securities Act of 1933 (15 U.S.C. 77g(a)), it provides audited financial statements for two years in a Securities Act registration statement for the initial public offering of the emerging growth company's common equity securities.

2.   The purpose of the discussion and analysis shall be to provide to investors and other users information relevant to an assessment of the financial condition and results of operations of the registrant as determined by evaluating the amounts and certainty of cash flows from operations and from outside sources.

3.   The discussion and analysis shall focus specifically on material events and uncertainties known to management that would cause reported financial information not to be necessarily indicative of future operating results or of future financial condition. This would include descriptions and amounts of (A) matters that would have an impact on future operations and have not had an impact in the past, and (B) matters that have had an impact on reported operations and are not expected to have an impact upon future operations.

4.   Where the consolidated financial statements reveal material changes from year to year in one or more line items, the causes for the changes shall be described to the extent necessary to an understanding of the registrant's businesses as a whole; *Provided, however,* That if the causes for a change in one line item also relate to other line items, no repetition is required and a line-by-line analysis of the financial statements as a whole is not required or generally appropriate. Registrants need not recite the amounts of changes from year to year which are readily computable from the financial statements. The discussion shall not merely repeat numerical data contained in the consolidated financial statements.

5.   The term "liquidity" as used in this Item refers to the ability of an enterprise to generate adequate amounts of cash to meet the enterprise's needs for cash. Except where it is otherwise clear from the discussion, the registrant shall indicate those balance sheet conditions or income or cash flow items which the registrant believes may be indicators of its liquidity condition. Liquidity generally

shall be discussed on both a long-term and short-term basis. The issue of liquidity shall be discussed in the context of the registrant's own business or businesses. For example a discussion of working capital may be appropriate for certain manufacturing, industrial or related operations but might be inappropriate for a bank or public utility.

6. Where financial statements presented or incorporated by reference in the registration statement are required by § 210.4–08(e)(3) of Regulation S–X [17 CFR part 210] to include disclosure of restrictions on the ability of both consolidated and unconsolidated subsidiaries to transfer funds to the registrant in the form of cash dividends, loans or advances, the discussion of liquidity shall include a discussion of the nature and extent of such restrictions and the impact such restrictions have had and are expected to have on the ability of the parent company to meet its cash obligations.

7. Any forward-looking information supplied is expressly covered by the safe harbor rule for projections. *See* Rule 175 under the Securities Act [17 CFR 230.175], Rule 3b–6 under the Exchange Act [17 CFR 240.3b–6] and Securities Act Release No. 6084 (June 25, 1979) (44 FR 38810).

* * *

Instructions to paragraph 303(a)(4): 1. No obligation to make disclosure under paragraph (a)(4) of this Item shall arise in respect of an off-balance sheet arrangement until a definitive agreement that is unconditionally binding or subject only to customary closing conditions exists or, if there is no such agreement, when settlement of the transaction occurs.

2. Registrants should aggregate off-balance sheet arrangements in groups or categories that provide material information in an efficient and understandable manner and should avoid repetition and disclosure of immaterial information. Effects that are common or similar with respect to a number of off-balance sheet arrangements must be analyzed in the aggregate to the extent the aggregation increases understanding. Distinctions in arrangements and their effects must be discussed to the extent the information is material, but the discussion should avoid repetition and disclosure of immaterial information.

3. For purposes of paragraph (a)(4) of this Item only, contingent liabilities arising out of litigation, arbitration or regulatory actions are not considered to be off-balance sheet arrangements.

4. Generally, the disclosure required by paragraph (a)(4) shall cover the most recent fiscal year. However, the discussion should address changes from the previous year where such discussion is necessary to an understanding of the disclosure.

5. In satisfying the requirements of paragraph (a)(4) of this Item, the discussion of off-balance sheet arrangements need not repeat information provided in the footnotes to the financial statements, provided that such discussion clearly cross-references to specific information in the relevant footnotes and integrates the substance of the footnotes into such discussion in a manner designed to inform readers of the significance of the information that is not included within the body of such discussion.

(b) *Interim periods.* If interim period financial statements are included or are required to be included by Article 3 of Regulation S–X (17 CFR 210), a management's discussion and analysis of the financial condition and results of operations shall be provided so as to enable the reader to assess material changes in financial condition and results of operations between the periods specified in paragraphs (b) (1) and (2) of this Item. The discussion and analysis shall include a discussion of material changes in those items specifically listed in paragraph (a) of this Item, except that the impact of inflation and changing prices on operations for interim periods need not be addressed.

(1) *Material changes in financial condition.* Discuss any material changes in financial condition from the end of the preceding fiscal year to the date of the most recent interim balance sheet provided. If the interim financial statements include an interim balance sheet as of the corresponding interim date of the preceding fiscal year, any material changes in financial condition from that date to the date of the most recent interim balance sheet provided also shall be discussed. If discussions of changes from both the end and the corresponding interim date of

the preceding fiscal year are required, the discussions may be combined at the discretion of the registrant.

(2) *Material changes in results of operations.* Discuss any material changes in the registrant's results of operations with respect to the most recent fiscal year-to-date period for which a statement of comprehensive income (or statement of operations if comprehensive income is presented in two separate but consecutive financial statements or if no other comprehensive income) is provided and the corresponding year-to-date period of the preceding fiscal year. If the registrant is required to or has elected to provide a statement of comprehensive income (or statement of operations if comprehensive income is presented in two separate but consecutive financial statements or if no other comprehensive income) for the most recent fiscal quarter, such discussion also shall cover material changes with respect to that fiscal quarter and the corresponding fiscal quarter in the preceding fiscal year. In addition, if the registrant has elected to provide a statement of comprehensive income (or statement of operations if comprehensive income is presented in two separate but consecutive financial statements or if no other comprehensive income) for the twelve-month period ended as of the date of the most recent interim balance sheet provided, the discussion also shall cover material changes with respect to that twelve-month period and the twelve-month period ended as of the corresponding interim balance sheet date of the preceding fiscal year. Notwithstanding the above, if for purposes of a registration statement a registrant subject to § 210.3–03(b) of Regulation S–X of this chapter provides a statement of comprehensive income (or statement of operations if comprehensive income is presented in two separate but consecutive financial statements or if no other comprehensive income) for the twelve-month period ended as of the date of the most recent interim balance sheet provided in lieu of the interim statements of comprehensive income (or statement of operations if comprehensive income is presented in two separate but consecutive financial statements or if no other comprehensive income) otherwise required, the discussion of material changes in that twelve-month period will be in respect to the preceding fiscal year rather than the corresponding preceding period.

Instruction 1 to paragraph (b). If interim financial statements are presented together with financial statements for full fiscal years, the discussion of the interim financial information shall be prepared pursuant to this paragraph (b) and the discussion of the full fiscal year's information shall be prepared pursuant to paragraph (a) of this Item. Such discussions may be combined.

Instruction 2 to paragraph (b)[.] In preparing the discussion and analysis required by this paragraph (b), the registrant may presume that users of the interim financial information have read or have access to the discussion and analysis required by paragraph (a) for the preceding fiscal year.

Instruction 3 to paragraph (b)[.] The discussion and analysis required by this paragraph (b) is required to focus only on material changes. Where the interim financial statements reveal material changes from period to period in one or more significant line items, the causes for the changes shall be described if they have not already been disclosed: *Provided, however,* That if the causes for a change in one line item also relate to other line items, no repetition is required. Registrants need not recite the amounts of changes from period to period which are readily computable from the financial statements. The discussion shall not merely repeat numerical data contained in the financial statements. The information provided shall include that which is available to the registrant without undue effort or expense and which does not clearly appear in the registrant's condensed interim financial statements.

Instruction 4 to paragraph (b)[.] The registrant's discussion of material changes in results of operations shall identify any significant elements of the registrant's income or loss from continuing operations which do not arise from or are not necessarily representative of the registrant's ongoing business.

Instruction 5 to paragraph (b). [Reserved]

Instruction 6 to paragraph (b)[.] Any forward-looking information supplied is expressly covered by the safe harbor rule for projections. See Rule 175 under the Securities Act [17 CFR 230.175], Rule 3b–6 under the Exchange Act [17 CFR 249.3b–6] and Securities Act Release No. 6084 (June 25, 1979) (44 FR 38810).

Instruction 7 to paragraph (b)[.] The registrant is not required to include the table required by paragraph (a)(5) of this Item for interim periods. Instead, the registrant should disclose material changes outside the ordinary course of the registrant's business in the specified contractual obligations during the interim period.

Instruction 8 to paragraph (b). The term statement of comprehensive income shall mean a statement of comprehensive income as defined in § 210.1–02 of Regulation S–X of this chapter.

(c)   *Safe harbor.* (1) The safe harbor provided in section 27A of the Securities Act of 1933 (15 U.S.C. 77z–2) and section 21E of the Securities Exchange Act of 1934 (15 U.S.C. 78u–5) ("statutory safe harbors") shall apply to forward-looking information provided pursuant to paragraphs (a)(4) and (5) of this Item, provided that the disclosure is made by: an issuer; a person acting on behalf of the issuer; an outside reviewer retained by the issuer making a statement on behalf of the issuer; or an underwriter, with respect to information provided by the issuer or information derived from information provided by the issuer.

(2)   For purposes of paragraph (c) of this Item only:

(i)   All information required by paragraphs (a)(4) and (5) of this Item is deemed to be a *forward looking statement* as that term is defined in the statutory safe harbors, except for historical facts.

(ii)   With respect to paragraph (a)(4) of this Item, the meaningful cautionary statements element of the statutory safe harbors will be satisfied if a registrant satisfies all requirements of that same paragraph (a)(4) of this Item.

(d)   *Smaller reporting companies.* A smaller reporting company, as defined by § 229.10(f)(1), may provide the information required in paragraph (a)(3)(iv) of this Item for the last two most recent fiscal years of the registrant if it provides financial information on net sales and revenues and on income from continuing operations for only two years. A smaller reporting company is not required to provide the information required by paragraph (a)(5) of this Item.

§ 229.307   (Item 307) Disclosure Controls and Procedures.

Disclose the conclusions of the registrant's principal executive and principal financial officers, or persons performing similar functions, regarding the effectiveness of the registrant's disclosure controls and procedures (as defined in § 240.13a–15(e) or § 240.15d–15(e) of this chapter) as of the end of the period covered by the report, based on the evaluation of these controls and procedures required by paragraph (b) of § 240.13a–15 or § 240.15d–15 of this chapter.

§ 229.402   (Item 402) Executive Compensation.

(a)   *General*—(1) *Treatment of foreign private issuers.* A foreign private issuer will be deemed to comply with this Item if it provides the information required by Items 6.B and 6.E.2 of Form 20–F (17 CFR 249.220f), with more detailed information provided if otherwise made publicly available or required to be disclosed by the issuer's home jurisdiction or a market in which its securities are listed or traded.

(2)   *All compensation covered.* This Item requires clear, concise and understandable disclosure of all plan and non-plan compensation awarded to, earned by, or paid to the named executive officers designated under paragraph (a)(3) of this Item, and directors covered by paragraph (k) of this Item, by any person for all services rendered in all capacities to the registrant and its subsidiaries, unless otherwise specifically excluded from disclosure in this Item. All such compensation shall be reported pursuant to this Item, even if also called for by

another requirement, including transactions between the registrant and a third party where a purpose of the transaction is to furnish compensation to any such named executive officer or director. No amount reported as compensation for one fiscal year need be reported in the same manner as compensation for a subsequent fiscal year; amounts reported as compensation for one fiscal year may be required to be reported in a different manner pursuant to this Item.

(3) *Persons covered.* Disclosure shall be provided pursuant to this Item for each of the following (the "named executive officers"):

(i) All individuals serving as the registrant's principal executive officer or acting in a similar capacity during the last completed fiscal year ("PEO"), regardless of compensation level;

(ii) All individuals serving as the registrant's principal financial officer or acting in a similar capacity during the last completed fiscal year ("PFO"), regardless of compensation level;

(iii) The registrant's three most highly compensated executive officers other than the PEO and PFO who were serving as executive officers at the end of the last completed fiscal year; and

(iv) Up to two additional individuals for whom disclosure would have been provided pursuant to paragraph (a)(3)(iii) of this Item but for the fact that the individual was not serving as an executive officer of the registrant at the end of the last completed fiscal year.

Instructions to Item 402(a)(3). 1. Determination of most highly compensated executive officers. The determination as to which executive officers are most highly compensated shall be made by reference to total compensation for the last completed fiscal year (as required to be disclosed pursuant to paragraph (c)(2)(x) of this Item) reduced by the amount required to be disclosed pursuant to paragraph (c)(2)(viii) of this Item, *provided, however,* that no disclosure need be provided for any executive officer, other than the PEO and PFO, whose total compensation, as so reduced, does not exceed $100,000.

2. *Inclusion of executive officer of subsidiary.* It may be appropriate for a registrant to include as named executive officers one or more executive officers or other employees of subsidiaries in the disclosure required by this Item. *See* Rule 3b-7 under the Exchange Act (17 CFR 240.3b-7).

3. *Exclusion of executive officer due to overseas compensation.* It may be appropriate in limited circumstances for a registrant not to include in the disclosure required by this Item an individual, other than its PEO or PFO, who is one of the registrant's most highly compensated executive officers due to the payment of amounts of cash compensation relating to overseas assignments attributed predominantly to such assignments.

(4) *Information for full fiscal year.* If the PEO or PFO served in that capacity during any part of a fiscal year with respect to which information is required, information should be provided as to all of his or her compensation for the full fiscal year. If a named executive officer (other than the PEO or PFO) served as an executive officer of the registrant (whether or not in the same position) during any part of the fiscal year with respect to which information is required, information shall be provided as to all compensation of that individual for the full fiscal year.

(5) *Omission of table or column.* A table or column may be omitted if there has been no compensation awarded to, earned by, or paid to any of the named executive officers or directors required to be reported in that table or column in any fiscal year covered by that table.

(6) *Definitions.* For purposes of this Item:

(i) The term *stock* means instruments such as common stock, restricted stock, restricted stock units, phantom stock, phantom stock units, common stock equivalent units or any similar instruments that do not have option-like features, and the term *option* means instruments such as stock options, stock appreciation rights and similar instruments with option-like features. The term *stock appreciation rights* ("SARs") refers to SARs payable in cash or stock, including SARs payable in cash or stock at the election of the registrant or a named executive officer. The term *equity* is used to refer generally to stock and/or options.

(ii) The term *plan* includes, but is not limited to, the following: Any plan, contract, authorization or arrangement, whether or not set forth in any formal document, pursuant to which cash, securities, similar instruments, or any other property may be received. A plan may be applicable to one person. Except with respect to the disclosure required by paragraph (t) of this Item, registrants may omit information regarding group life, health, hospitalization, or medical reimbursement plans that do not discriminate in scope, terms or operation, in favor of executive officers or directors of the registrant and that are available generally to all salaried employees.

(iii) The term *incentive plan* means any plan providing compensation intended to serve as incentive for performance to occur over a specified period, whether such performance is measured by reference to financial performance of the registrant or an affiliate, the registrant's stock price, or any other performance measure. An *equity incentive plan* is an incentive plan or portion of an incentive plan under which awards are granted that fall within the scope of FASB ASC Topic 718, *Compensation—Stock Compensation*. A *non-equity incentive plan* is an incentive plan or portion of an incentive plan that is not an equity incentive plan. The term *incentive plan award* means an award provided under an incentive plan.

(iv) The terms *date of grant* or *grant date* refer to the grant date determined for financial statement reporting purposes pursuant to FASB ASC Topic 718.

(v) *Closing market price* is defined as the price at which the registrant's security was last sold in the principal United States market for such security as of the date for which the closing market price is determined.

(b) *Compensation discussion and analysis.* (1) Discuss the compensation awarded to, earned by, or paid to the named executive officers. The discussion shall explain all material elements of the registrant's compensation of the named executive officers. The discussion shall describe the following:

(i) The objectives of the registrant's compensation programs;

(ii) What the compensation program is designed to reward;

(iii) Each element of compensation;

(iv) Why the registrant chooses to pay each element;

(v) How the registrant determines the amount (and, where applicable, the formula) for each element to pay;

(vi) How each compensation element and the registrant's decisions regarding that element fit into the registrant's overall compensation objectives and affect decisions regarding other elements; and

(vii) Whether and, if so, how the registrant has considered the results of the most recent shareholder advisory vote on executive compensation required by section 14A of the Exchange Act (15 U.S.C. 78n–1) or § 240.14a–20 of this chapter in determining compensation policies and decisions and, if so, how that consideration has affected the registrant's executive compensation decisions and policies.

(2) While the material information to be disclosed under Compensation Discussion and Analysis will vary depending upon the facts and circumstances, examples of such information may include, in a given case, among other things, the following:

(i) The policies for allocating between long-term and currently paid out compensation;

(ii)   The policies for allocating between cash and non-cash compensation, and among different forms of non-cash compensation;

(iii)   For long-term compensation, the basis for allocating compensation to each different form of award (such as relationship of the award to the achievement of the registrant's long-term goals, management's exposure to downside equity performance risk, correlation between cost to registrant and expected benefits to the registrant);

(iv)   How the determination is made as to when awards are granted, including awards of equity-based compensation such as options;

(v)   What specific items of corporate performance are taken into account in setting compensation policies and making compensation decisions;

(vi)   How specific forms of compensation are structured and implemented to reflect these items of the registrant's performance, including whether discretion can be or has been exercised (either to award compensation absent attainment of the relevant performance goal(s) or to reduce or increase the size of any award or payout), identifying any particular exercise of discretion, and stating whether it applied to one or more specified named executive officers or to all compensation subject to the relevant performance goal(s);

(vii)   How specific forms of compensation are structured and implemented to reflect the named executive officer's individual performance and/or individual contribution to these items of the registrant's performance, describing the elements of individual performance and/or contribution that are taken into account;

(viii)   Registrant policies and decisions regarding the adjustment or recovery of awards or payments if the relevant registrant performance measures upon which they are based are restated or otherwise adjusted in a manner that would reduce the size of an award or payment;

(ix)   The factors considered in decisions to increase or decrease compensation materially;

(x)   How compensation or amounts realizable from prior compensation are considered in setting other elements of compensation (*e.g.*, how gains from prior option or stock awards are considered in setting retirement benefits);

(xi)   With respect to any contract, agreement, plan or arrangement, whether written or unwritten, that provides for payment(s) at, following, or in connection with any termination or change-in-control, the basis for selecting particular events as triggering payment (*e.g.*, the rationale for providing a single trigger for payment in the event of a change-in-control);

(xii)   The impact of the accounting and tax treatments of the particular form of compensation;

(xiii)   The registrant's equity or other security ownership requirements or guidelines (specifying applicable amounts and forms of ownership), and any registrant policies regarding hedging the economic risk of such ownership;

(xiv)   Whether the registrant engaged in any benchmarking of total compensation, or any material element of compensation, identifying the benchmark and, if applicable, its components (including component companies); and

(xv)   The role of executive officers in determining executive compensation.

Instructions to Item 402(b). 1. The purpose of the Compensation Discussion and Analysis is to provide to investors material information that is necessary to an understanding of the registrant's compensation policies and decisions regarding the named executive officers.

2. The Compensation Discussion and Analysis should be of the information contained in the tables and otherwise disclosed pursuant to this Item. The Compensation Discussion and Analysis should also cover actions regarding executive compensation that were taken after the registrant's last fiscal year's end. Actions that should be addressed might include, as examples only, the adoption or implementation of new or modified programs and policies or specific decisions that were made or steps that were taken that could affect a fair understanding of the named executive officer's compensation for the last fiscal year. Moreover, in some situations it may be necessary to discuss prior years in order to give context to the disclosure provided.

3. The Compensation Discussion and Analysis should focus on the material principles underlying the registrant's executive compensation policies and decisions and the most important factors relevant to analysis of those policies and decisions. The Compensation Discussion and Analysis shall reflect the individual circumstances of the registrant and shall avoid boilerplate language and repetition of the more detailed information set forth in the tables and narrative disclosures that follow.

4. Registrants are not required to disclose target levels with respect to specific quantitative or qualitative performance-related factors considered by the compensation committee or the board of directors, or any other factors or criteria involving confidential trade secrets or confidential commercial or financial information, the disclosure of which would result in competitive harm for the registrant. The standard to use when determining whether disclosure would cause competitive harm for the registrant is the same standard that would apply when a registrant requests confidential treatment of confidential trade secrets or confidential commercial or financial information pursuant to Securities Act Rule 406 (17 CFR 230.406) and Exchange Act Rule 24b–2 (17 CFR 240.24b–2), each of which incorporates the criteria for non-disclosure when relying upon Exemption 4 of the Freedom of Information Act (5 U.S.C. 552(b)(4)). A registrant is not required to seek confidential treatment under the procedures in Securities Act Rule 406 and Exchange Act Rule 24b–2 if it determines that the disclosure would cause competitive harm in reliance on this instruction; however, in that case, the registrant must discuss how difficult it will be for the executive or how likely it will be for the registrant to achieve the undisclosed target levels or other factors.

5. Disclosure of target levels that are non-GAAP financial measures will not be subject to Regulation G (17 CFR 244.100—102) and Item 10(e) (§ 229.10(e)); however, disclosure must be provided as to how the number is calculated from the registrant's audited financial statements.

6. In proxy or information statements with respect to the election of directors, if the information disclosed pursuant to Item 407(i) would satisfy paragraph (b)(2)(xiii) of this Item, a registrant may refer to the information disclosed pursuant to Item 407(i).

(c) *Summary compensation table*—(1) *General.* Provide the information specified in paragraph (c)(2) of this Item, concerning the compensation of the named executive officers for each of the registrant's last three completed fiscal years, in a Summary Compensation Table in the tabular format specified below.

Summary Compensation Table

Name and principal position	Year	Salary ($)	Bonus ($)	Stock awards ($)	Option awards ($)	Non-equity incentive plan compensation ($)	Change in pension value and nonqualified deferred compensation earnings ($)	All other compensation ($)	Total ($)
(a)	(b)	(c)	(d)	(e)	(f)	(g)	(h)	(i)	(j)
PEO									

PFO						
A						
B						
C						

(2)   The Table shall include:

   (i)   The name and principal position of the named executive officer (column (a));

   (ii)   The fiscal year covered (column (b));

   (iii)   The dollar value of base salary (cash and non-cash) earned by the named executive officer during the fiscal year covered (column (c));

   (iv)   The dollar value of bonus (cash and non-cash) earned by the named executive officer during the fiscal year covered (column (d));

Instructions to Item 402(c)(2)(iii) and (iv). 1. If the amount of salary or bonus earned in a given fiscal year is not calculable through the latest practicable date, a footnote shall be included disclosing that the amount of salary or bonus is not calculable through the latest practicable date and providing the date that the amount of salary or bonus is expected to be determined, and such amount must then be disclosed in a filing under Item 5.02(f) of Form 8-K (17 CFR 249.308).

   2.   Registrants shall include in the salary column (column (c)) or bonus column (column (d)) any amount of salary or bonus forgone at the election of a named executive officer under which stock, equity-based or other forms of non-cash compensation instead have been received by the named executive officer. However, the receipt of any such form of non-cash compensation instead of salary or bonus must be disclosed in a footnote added to the salary or bonus column and, where applicable, referring to the Grants of Plan-Based Awards Table (required by paragraph (d) of this Item) where the stock, option or non-equity incentive plan award elected by the named executive officer is reported.

   (v)   For awards of stock, the aggregate grant date fair value computed in accordance with FASB ASC Topic 718 (column (e));

   (vi)   For awards of options, with or without tandem SARs (including awards that subsequently have been transferred), the aggregate grant date fair value computed in accordance with FASB ASC Topic 718 (column (f));

Instruction 1 to Item 402(c)(2)(v) and (vi). For awards reported in columns (e) and (f), include a footnote disclosing all assumptions made in the valuation by reference to a discussion of those assumptions in the registrant's financial statements, footnotes to the financial statements, or discussion in the Management's Discussion and Analysis. The sections so referenced are deemed part of the disclosure provided pursuant to this Item.

Instruction 2 to Item 402(c)(2)(v) and (vi). If at any time during the last completed fiscal year, the registrant has adjusted or amended the exercise price of options or SARs previously awarded to a named executive officer, whether through amendment, cancellation or replacement grants, or any other means ("repriced"), or otherwise has materially modified such awards, the registrant shall include, as awards required to be reported in column (f), the incremental fair value, computed as of the repricing or modification date in accordance with FASB ASC Topic 718, with respect to that repriced or modified award.

Instruction 3 to Item 402(c)(2)(v) and (vi). For any awards that are subject to performance conditions, report the value at the grant date based upon the probable outcome of such conditions. This amount should be consistent with the estimate of aggregate compensation cost to be recognized over the service period determined as of the grant date under FASB ASC Topic 718, excluding the effect of estimated forfeitures. In a footnote to the table, disclose the value of the award at the grant date assuming that the highest level of performance conditions will be achieved if an amount less than the maximum was included in the table.

(vii) The dollar value of all earnings for services performed during the fiscal year pursuant to awards under non-equity incentive plans as defined in paragraph (a)(6)(iii) of this Item, and all earnings on any outstanding awards (column (g));

Instructions to Item 402(c)(2)(vii). 1. If the relevant performance measure is satisfied during the fiscal year (including for a single year in a plan with a multi-year performance measure), the earnings are reportable for that fiscal year, even if not payable until a later date, and are not reportable again in the fiscal year when amounts are paid to the named executive officer.

2. All earnings on non-equity incentive plan compensation must be identified and quantified in a footnote to column (g), whether the earnings were paid during the fiscal year, payable during the period but deferred at the election of the named executive officer, or payable by their terms at a later date.

(viii) The sum of the amounts specified in paragraphs (c)(2)(viii)(A) and (B) of this Item (column (h)) as follows:

(A) The aggregate change in the actuarial present value of the named executive officer's accumulated benefit under all defined benefit and actuarial pension plans (including supplemental plans) from the pension plan measurement date used for financial statement reporting purposes with respect to the registrant's audited financial statements for the prior completed fiscal year to the pension plan measurement date used for financial statement reporting purposes with respect to the registrant's audited financial statements for the covered fiscal year; and

(B) Above-market or preferential earnings on compensation that is deferred on a basis that is not tax-qualified, including such earnings on nonqualified defined contribution plans;

Instructions to Item 402(c)(2)(viii). 1. The disclosure required pursuant to paragraph (c)(2)(viii)(A) of this Item applies to each plan that provides for the payment of retirement benefits, or benefits that will be paid primarily following retirement, including but not limited to tax-qualified defined benefit plans and supplemental executive retirement plans, but excluding tax-qualified defined contribution plans and nonqualified defined contribution plans. For purposes of this disclosure, the registrant should use the same amounts required to be disclosed pursuant to paragraph (h)(2)(iv) of this Item for the covered fiscal year and the amounts that were or would have been required to be reported for the executive officer pursuant to paragraph (h)(2)(iv) of this Item for the prior completed fiscal year.

2. Regarding paragraph (c)(2)(viii)(B) of this Item, interest on deferred compensation is above-market only if the rate of interest exceeds 120% of the applicable federal long-term rate, with compounding (as prescribed under section 1274(d) of the Internal Revenue Code, (26 U.S.C. 1274(d))) at the rate that corresponds most closely to the rate under the registrant's plan at the time the interest rate or formula is set. In the event of a discretionary reset of the interest rate, the requisite calculation must be made on the basis of the interest rate at the time of such reset, rather than when originally established. Only the above-market portion of the interest must be included. If the applicable interest rates vary depending upon conditions such as a minimum period of continued service, the reported

amount should be calculated assuming satisfaction of all conditions to receiving interest at the highest rate. Dividends (and dividend equivalents) on deferred compensation denominated in the registrant's stock ("deferred stock") are preferential only if earned at a rate higher than dividends on the registrant's common stock. Only the preferential portion of the dividends or equivalents must be included. Footnote or narrative disclosure may be provided explaining the registrant's criteria for determining any portion considered to be above-market.

3.   The registrant shall identify and quantify by footnote the separate amounts attributable to each of paragraphs (c)(2)(viii)(A) and (B) of this Item. Where such amount pursuant to paragraph (c)(2)(viii)(A) is negative, it should be disclosed by footnote but should not be reflected in the sum reported in column (h).

(ix) All other compensation for the covered fiscal year that the registrant could not properly report in any other column of the Summary Compensation Table (column (i)). Each compensation item that is not properly reportable in columns (c)–(h), regardless of the amount of the compensation item, must be included in column (i). Such compensation must include, but is not limited to:

(A) Perquisites and other personal benefits, or property, unless the aggregate amount of such compensation is less than $10,000;

(B) All "gross-ups" or other amounts reimbursed during the fiscal year for the payment of taxes;

(C) For any security of the registrant or its subsidiaries purchased from the registrant or its subsidiaries (through deferral of salary or bonus, or otherwise) at a discount from the market price of such security at the date of purchase, unless that discount is available generally, either to all security holders or to all salaried employees of the registrant, the compensation cost, if any, computed in accordance with FASB ASC Topic 718;

(D) The amount paid or accrued to any named executive officer pursuant to a plan or arrangement in connection with:

(1) Any termination, including without limitation through retirement, resignation, severance or constructive termination (including a change in responsibilities) of such executive officer's employment with the registrant and its subsidiaries; or

(2) A change in control of the registrant;

(E) Registrant contributions or other allocations to vested and unvested defined contribution plans;

(F) The dollar value of any insurance premiums paid by, or on behalf of, the registrant during the covered fiscal year with respect to life insurance for the benefit of a named executive officer; and

(G) The dollar value of any dividends or other earnings paid on stock or option awards, when those amounts were not factored into the grant date fair value required to be reported for the stock or option award in column (e) or (f); and

Instructions to Item 402(c)(2)(ix). 1. Non-equity incentive plan awards and earnings and earnings on stock and options, except as specified in paragraph (c)(2)(ix)(G) of this Item, are required to be reported elsewhere as provided in this Item and are not reportable as All Other Compensation in column (i).

2.   Benefits paid pursuant to defined benefit and actuarial plans are not reportable as All Other Compensation in column (i) unless accelerated pursuant to a change in control; information concerning these plans is reportable pursuant to paragraphs (c)(2)(viii)(A) and (h) of this Item.

3.   Any item reported for a named executive officer pursuant to paragraph (c)(2)(ix) of this Item that is not a perquisite or personal benefit and whose value exceeds $10,000 must be identified and quantified in a footnote to column (i). This requirement applies only to compensation for the last fiscal year. All items of compensation are required to be included in the Summary Compensation Table without regard to whether such items are required to be identified other than as specifically noted in this Item.

4.   Perquisites and personal benefits may be excluded as long as the total value of all perquisites and personal benefits for a named executive officer is less than $10,000. If the total value of all perquisites and personal benefits is $10,000 or more for any named executive officer, then each perquisite or personal benefit, regardless of its amount, must be identified by type. If perquisites and personal benefits are required to be reported for a named executive officer pursuant to this rule, then each perquisite or personal benefit that exceeds the greater of $25,000 or 10% of the total amount of perquisites and personal benefits for that officer must be quantified and disclosed in a footnote. The requirements for identification and quantification apply only to compensation for the last fiscal year. Perquisites and other personal benefits shall be valued on the basis of the aggregate incremental cost to the registrant. With respect to the perquisite or other personal benefit for which footnote quantification is required, the registrant shall describe in the footnote its methodology for computing the aggregate incremental cost. Reimbursements of taxes owed with respect to perquisites or other personal benefits must be included in column (i) and are subject to separate quantification and identification as tax reimbursements (paragraph (c)(2)(ix)(B) of this Item) even if the associated perquisites or other personal benefits are not required to be included because the total amount of all perquisites or personal benefits for an individual named executive officer is less than $10,000 or are required to be identified but are not required to be separately quantified.

5.   For purposes of paragraph (c)(2)(ix)(D) of this Item, an accrued amount is an amount for which payment has become due.

   (x)   The dollar value of total compensation for the covered fiscal year (column (j)). With respect to each named executive officer, disclose the sum of all amounts reported in columns (c) through (i).

Instructions to Item 402(c). 1. Information with respect to fiscal years prior to the last completed fiscal year will not be required if the registrant was not a reporting company pursuant to section 13(a) or 15(d) of the Exchange Act (15 U.S.C. 78m(a) or 78o(d)) at any time during that year, except that the registrant will be required to provide information for any such year if that information previously was required to be provided in response to a Commission filing requirement.

2.   All compensation values reported in the Summary Compensation Table must be reported in dollars and rounded to the nearest dollar. Reported compensation values must be reported numerically, providing a single numerical value for each grid in the table. Where compensation was paid to or received by a named executive officer in a different currency, a footnote must be provided to identify that currency and describe the rate and methodology used to convert the payment amounts to dollars.

3.   If a named executive officer is also a director who receives compensation for his or her services as a director, reflect that compensation in the Summary Compensation Table and provide a footnote identifying and itemizing such compensation and amounts. Use the categories in the Director Compensation Table required pursuant to paragraph (k) of this Item.

4.   Any amounts deferred, whether pursuant to a plan established under section 401(k) of the Internal Revenue Code (26 U.S.C. 401(k)), or otherwise, shall be included in the appropriate column for the fiscal year in which earned.

(d)   *Grants of plan-based awards table.* (1) Provide the information specified in paragraph (d)(2) of this Item, concerning each grant of an award made to a named executive officer in the last completed fiscal year under any plan, including awards that subsequently have been transferred, in the following tabular format:

Grants of Plan-Based Awards

Name	Grant date	Estimated future payouts under non-equity incentive plan awards			Estimated future payouts under equity incentive plan awards			All other stock awards: Number of shares of stock or units (#)	All other option awards: Number of securities underlying options (#)	Exercise or base price of option awards ($/Sh)	Grant date fair value of stock and option awards
		Threshold ($)	Target ($)	Maximum ($)	Threshold (#)	Target (#)	Maximum (#)				
(a)	(b)	(c)	(d)	(e)	(f)	(g)	(h)	(i)	(j)	(k)	(l)
PEO											
PFO											
A											
B											
C											

(2)   The Table shall include:

(i)   The name of the named executive officer (column (a));

(ii)   The grant date for equity-based awards reported in the table (column (b)). If such grant date is different than the date on which the compensation committee (or a committee of the board of directors performing a similar function or the full board of directors) takes action or is deemed to take action to grant such awards, a separate, adjoining column shall be added between columns (b) and (c) showing such date;

(iii)   The dollar value of the estimated future payout upon satisfaction of the conditions in question under non-equity incentive plan awards granted in the fiscal year, or the applicable range of estimated payouts denominated in dollars (threshold, target and maximum amount) (columns (c) through (e));

(iv)   The number of shares of stock, or the number of shares underlying options to be paid out or vested upon satisfaction of the conditions in question under equity incentive plan awards granted in the fiscal year, or the applicable range of estimated payouts denominated in the number of shares of stock, or the number of shares underlying options under the award (threshold, target and maximum amount) (columns (f) through (h));

(v)   The number of shares of stock granted in the fiscal year that are not required to be disclosed in columns (f) through (h) (column (i));

(vi)   The number of securities underlying options granted in the fiscal year that are not required to be disclosed in columns (f) through (h) (column (j));

(vii)   The per-share exercise or base price of the options granted in the fiscal year (column (k)). If such exercise or base price is less than the closing market price of the underlying security on the date of the grant, a separate, adjoining column showing the closing market price on the date of the grant shall be added after column (k) and

(viii)   The grant date fair value of each equity award computed in accordance with FASB ASC Topic 718 (column (l)). If at any time during the last completed fiscal year, the registrant has adjusted or amended the exercise or base price of options, SARs or similar option-like instruments previously awarded to a named executive officer, whether through amendment, cancellation or replacement grants, or any other means ("repriced"), or otherwise has materially modified such awards, the incremental fair value, computed as of the repricing or modification date in accordance with FASB ASC Topic 718, with respect to that repriced or modified award, shall be reported.

Instructions to Item 402(d). 1. Disclosure on a separate line shall be provided in the Table for each grant of an award made to a named executive officer during the fiscal year. If grants of awards were made to a named executive officer during the fiscal year under more than one plan, identify the particular plan under which each such grant was made.

2.   For grants of incentive plan awards, provide the information called for by columns (c), (d) and (e), or (f), (g) and (h), as applicable. For columns (c) and (f), *threshold* refers to the minimum amount payable for a certain level of performance under the plan. For columns (d) and (g), *target* refers to the amount payable if the specified performance target(s) are reached. For columns (e) and (h), *maximum* refers to the maximum payout possible under the plan. If the award provides only for a single estimated payout, that amount must be reported as the *target* in columns (d) and (g). In columns (d) and (g), registrants must provide a representative amount based on the previous fiscal year's performance if the target amount is not determinable.

3.   In determining if the exercise or base price of an option is less than the closing market price of the underlying security on the date of the grant, the registrant may use either the closing market price as specified in paragraph (a)(6)(v) of this Item, or if no market exists, any other formula prescribed for the security. Whenever the exercise or base price reported in column (k) is not the closing market price, describe the methodology for determining the exercise or base price either by a footnote or accompanying textual narrative.

4.   A tandem grant of two instruments, only one of which is granted under an incentive plan, such as an option granted in tandem with a performance share, need be reported only in column (i) or (j), as applicable. For example, an option granted in tandem with a performance share would be reported only as an option grant in column (j), with the tandem feature noted either by a footnote or accompanying textual narrative.

5.   Disclose the dollar amount of consideration, if any, paid by the executive officer for the award in a footnote to the appropriate column.

6.   If non-equity incentive plan awards are denominated in units or other rights, a separate, adjoining column between columns (b) and (c) shall be added quantifying the units or other rights awarded.

7.   Options, SARs and similar option-like instruments granted in connection with a repricing transaction or other material modification shall be reported in this Table. However, the disclosure required by this Table does not apply to any repricing that occurs through a pre-existing formula or mechanism in the plan or award that results in the periodic adjustment of the option or SAR exercise or base price, an antidilution provision in a plan or award, or a recapitalization or similar transaction equally affecting all holders of the class of securities underlying the options or SARs.

8.   For any equity awards that are subject to performance conditions, report in column (*l*) the value at the grant date based upon the probable outcome of such conditions. This amount should be consistent with the estimate of aggregate compensation cost to be recognized over the service period determined as of the grant date under FASB ASC Topic 718, excluding the effect of estimated forfeitures.

(e)   *Narrative disclosure to summary compensation table and grants of plan-based awards table.* (1) Provide a narrative description of any material factors necessary to an understanding of the information disclosed in the tables required by paragraphs (c) and (d) of this Item. Examples of such factors may include, in given cases, among other things:

(i)   The material terms of each named executive officer's employment agreement or arrangement, whether written or unwritten;

(ii)   If at any time during the last fiscal year, any outstanding option or other equity-based award was repriced or otherwise materially modified (such as by extension of exercise periods, the change of vesting or forfeiture conditions, the change or elimination of applicable performance criteria, or the change of the bases upon which returns are determined), a description of each such repricing or other material modification;

(iii)   The material terms of any award reported in response to paragraph (d) of this Item, including a general description of the formula or criteria to be applied in determining the amounts payable, and the vesting schedule. For example, state where applicable that dividends will be paid on stock, and if so, the applicable dividend rate and whether that rate is preferential. Describe any performance-based conditions, and any other material conditions, that are applicable to the award. For purposes of the Table required by paragraph (d) of this Item and the narrative disclosure required by paragraph (e) of this Item, performance-based conditions include both performance conditions and market conditions, as those terms are defined in FASB ASC Topic 718; and

(iv) An explanation of the amount of salary and bonus in proportion to total compensation.

Instructions to Item 402(e)(1). 1. The disclosure required by paragraph (e)(1)(ii) of this Item would not apply to any repricing that occurs through a pre-existing formula or mechanism in the plan or award that results in the periodic adjustment of the option or SAR exercise or base price, an antidilution provision in a plan or award, or a recapitalization or similar transaction equally affecting all holders of the class of securities underlying the options or SARs.

2.   Instructions 4 and 5 to Item 402(b) apply regarding disclosure pursuant to paragraph (e)(1) of this Item of target levels with respect to specific quantitative or qualitative performance-related factors considered by the compensation committee or the board of directors, or any other factors or criteria involving confidential trade secrets or confidential commercial or financial information, the disclosure of which would result in competitive harm for the registrant.

(2)   [Reserved]

(f)   *Outstanding equity awards at fiscal year-end table.* (1) Provide the information specified in paragraph (f)(2) of this Item, concerning unexercised options; stock that has not vested; and equity incentive plan awards for each named executive officer outstanding as of the end of the registrant's last completed fiscal year in the following tabular format:

Outstanding Equity Awards at Fiscal Year-End

	Option awards					Stock awards			
Name	Number of securities underlying unexercised options (#) exercisable	Number of securities underlying unexercised options (#) unexercisable	Equity incentive plan awards: number of securities underlying unexercised unearned options (#)	Option exercise price ($)	Option expiration date	Number of shares or units of stock that have not vested (#)	Market value of shares or units of stock that have not vested (#)	Equity incentive plan awards: number of unearned shares, units or other rights that have not vested (#)	Equity incentive plan awards: market or payout value of unearned shares, units or other rights that have not vested ($)
(a)	(b)	(c)	(d)	(e)	(f)	(g)	(h)	(i)	(j)
PEO									
PFO									
A									
B									
C									

(2)   The Table shall include:

(i)   The name of the named executive officer (column (a));

(ii)   On an award-by-award basis, the number of securities underlying unexercised options, including awards that have been transferred other than for value, that are exercisable and that are not reported in column (d) (column (b));

(iii)   On an award-by-award basis, the number of securities underlying unexercised options, including awards that have been transferred other than for value, that are unexercisable and that are not reported in column (d) (column (c));

(iv)   On an award-by-award basis, the total number of shares underlying unexercised options awarded under any equity incentive plan that have not been earned (column (d));

(v)   For each instrument reported in columns (b), (c) and (d), as applicable, the exercise or base price (column (e));

(vi)   For each instrument reported in columns (b), (c) and (d), as applicable, the expiration date (column (f));

(vii)   The total number of shares of stock that have not vested and that are not reported in column (i) (column (g));

(viii)   The aggregate market value of shares of stock that have not vested and that are not reported in column (j) (column (h));

(ix)   The total number of shares of stock, units or other rights awarded under any equity incentive plan that have not vested and that have not been earned, and, if applicable the number of shares underlying any such unit or right (column (i)); and

(x)   The aggregate market or payout value of shares of stock, units or other rights awarded under any equity incentive plan that have not vested and that have not been earned (column (j)).

Instructions to Item 402(f)(2). 1. Identify by footnote any award that has been transferred other than for value, disclosing the nature of the transfer.

2.   The vesting dates of options, shares of stock and equity incentive plan awards held at fiscal-year end must be disclosed by footnote to the applicable column where the outstanding award is reported.

3.   Compute the market value of stock reported in column (h) and equity incentive plan awards of stock reported in column (j) by multiplying the closing market price of the registrant's stock at the end of the last completed fiscal year by the number of shares or units of stock or the amount of equity incentive plan awards, respectively. The number of shares or units reported in columns (d) or (i), and the payout value reported in column (j), shall be based on achieving threshold performance goals, except that if the previous fiscal year's performance has exceeded the threshold, the disclosure shall be based on the next higher performance measure (target or maximum) that exceeds the previous fiscal year's performance. If the award provides only for a single estimated payout, that amount should be reported. If the target amount is not determinable, registrants must provide a representative amount based on the previous fiscal year's performance.

4.   Multiple awards may be aggregated where the expiration date and the exercise and/or base price of the instruments is identical. A single award consisting of a combination of options, SARs and/or similar option-like instruments shall be reported as separate awards with respect to each tranche with a different exercise and/or base price or expiration date.

5.   Options or stock awarded under an equity incentive plan are reported in columns (d) or (i) and (j), respectively, until the relevant performance condition has been satisfied. Once the relevant performance condition has been satisfied, even if the option or stock award is subject to forfeiture conditions, options are reported in column (b) or (c), as appropriate, until they are exercised or expire, or stock is reported in columns (g) and (h) until it vests.

(g)   *Option exercises and stock vested table.* (1) Provide the information specified in paragraph (g)(2) of this Item, concerning each exercise of stock options, SARs and similar instruments, and each vesting of stock, including restricted stock, restricted stock units and similar instruments, during the last completed fiscal year for each of the named executive officers on an aggregated basis in the following tabular format:

Option Exercises and Stock Vested

Name	Option awards		Stock awards	
	Number of shares acquired on exercise (#)	Value realized on exercise ($)	Number of shares acquired on vesting (#)	Value realized on vesting ($)
(a)	(b)	(c)	(d)	(e)
PEO				
PFO				
A				
B				
C				

(2)   The Table shall include:

    (i)   The name of the executive officer (column (a));

    (ii)   The number of securities for which the options were exercised (column (b));

    (iii)   The aggregate dollar value realized upon exercise of options, or upon the transfer of an award for value (column (c));

    (iv)   The number of shares of stock that have vested (column (d)); and

    (v)   The aggregate dollar value realized upon vesting of stock, or upon the transfer of an award for value (column (e)).

Instruction to Item 402(g)(2). Report in column (c) the aggregate dollar amount realized by the named executive officer upon exercise of the options or upon the transfer of such instruments for value. Compute the dollar amount realized upon exercise by determining the difference between the market price of the underlying securities at exercise and the exercise or base price of the options. Do not include the value of any related payment or other consideration provided (or to be provided) by the registrant to or on behalf of a named executive officer, whether in payment of the exercise price or related taxes. (Any such payment or other consideration provided by the registrant is required to be disclosed in accordance with paragraph (c)(2)(ix) of this Item.) Report in column (e) the aggregate dollar amount realized by the named executive officer upon the vesting of stock or the transfer of such instruments for value. Compute the aggregate dollar amount realized upon vesting by multiplying the number of shares of stock or units by the market value of the underlying shares on the vesting date. For any amount realized upon exercise or vesting for which receipt has been deferred, provide a footnote quantifying the amount and disclosing the terms of the deferral.

    (h)   *Pension benefits.* (1) Provide the information specified in paragraph (h)(2) of this Item with respect to each plan that provides for payments or other benefits at, following, or in connection with retirement, in the following tabular format:

Pension Benefits

Name	Plan name	Number of years credited service (#)	Present value of accumulated benefit ($)	Payments during last fiscal year ($)
(a)	(b)	(c)	(d)	(e)
PEO				
PFO				
A				
B				
C				

(2) The Table shall include:

(i) The name of the executive officer (column (a));

(ii) The name of the plan (column (b));

(iii) The number of years of service credited to the named executive officer under the plan, computed as of the same pension plan measurement date used for financial statement reporting purposes with respect to the registrant's audited financial statements for the last completed fiscal year (column (c));

(iv) The actuarial present value of the named executive officer's accumulated benefit under the plan, computed as of the same pension plan measurement date used for financial statement reporting purposes with respect to the registrant's audited financial statements for the last completed fiscal year (column (d)); and

(v) The dollar amount of any payments and benefits paid to the named executive officer during the registrant's last completed fiscal year (column (e)).

Instructions to Item 402(h)(2). 1. The disclosure required pursuant to this Table applies to each plan that provides for specified retirement payments and benefits, or payments and benefits that will be provided primarily following retirement, including but not limited to tax-qualified defined benefit plans and supplemental executive retirement plans, but excluding tax-qualified defined contribution plans and nonqualified defined contribution plans. Provide a separate row for each such plan in which the named executive officer participates.

2. For purposes of the amount(s) reported in column (d), the registrant must use the same assumptions used for financial reporting purposes under generally accepted accounting principles, except that retirement age shall be assumed to be the normal retirement age as defined in the plan, or if not so defined, the earliest time at which a participant may retire under the plan without any benefit reduction due to age. The registrant must disclose in the accompanying textual narrative the valuation method and all material assumptions applied in quantifying the present value of the current accrued benefit. A benefit specified in the plan document or the executive's contract itself is not an assumption. Registrants may satisfy all or part of this disclosure by reference to a discussion of those assumptions in the registrant's financial statements, footnotes to the financial statements, or

discussion in the Management's Discussion and Analysis. The sections so referenced are deemed part of the disclosure provided pursuant to this Item.

3. For purposes of allocating the current accrued benefit between tax qualified defined benefit plans and related supplemental plans, apply the limitations applicable to tax qualified defined benefit plans established by the Internal Revenue Code and the regulations thereunder that applied as of the pension plan measurement date.

4. If a named executive officer's number of years of credited service with respect to any plan is different from the named executive officer's number of actual years of service with the registrant, provide footnote disclosure quantifying the difference and any resulting benefit augmentation.

(3) Provide a succinct narrative description of any material factors necessary to an understanding of each plan covered by the tabular disclosure required by this paragraph. While material factors will vary depending upon the facts, examples of such factors may include, in given cases, among other things:

(i) The material terms and conditions of payments and benefits available under the plan, including the plan's normal retirement payment and benefit formula and eligibility standards, and the effect of the form of benefit elected on the amount of annual benefits. For this purpose, normal retirement means retirement at the normal retirement age as defined in the plan, or if not so defined, the earliest time at which a participant may retire under the plan without any benefit reduction due to age;

(ii) If any named executive officer is currently eligible for early retirement under any plan, identify that named executive officer and the plan, and describe the plan's early retirement payment and benefit formula and eligibility standards. For this purpose, early retirement means retirement at the early retirement age as defined in the plan, or otherwise available to the executive under the plan;

(iii) The specific elements of compensation (*e.g.*, salary, bonus, etc.) included in applying the payment and benefit formula, identifying each such element;

(iv) With respect to named executive officers' participation in multiple plans, the different purposes for each plan; and

(v) Registrant policies with regard to such matters as granting extra years of credited service.

(i) *Nonqualified defined contribution and other nonqualified deferred compensation plans.* (1) Provide the information specified in paragraph (i)(2) of this Item with respect to each defined contribution or other plan that provides for the deferral of compensation on a basis that is not tax-qualified in the following tabular format:

REGULATION S–K

Nonqualified Deferred Compensation

Name	Executive contributions in last FY ($)	Registrant contributions in last FY ($)	Aggregate earnings in last FY ($)	Aggregate withdrawals/distributions ($)	Aggregate balance at last FYE ($)
(a)	(b)	(c)	(d)	(e)	(f)
PEO					
PFO					
A					
B					
C					

(2) The Table shall include:

(i) The name of the executive officer (column (a));

(ii) The dollar amount of aggregate executive contributions during the registrant's last fiscal year (column (b));

(iii) The dollar amount of aggregate registrant contributions during the registrant's last fiscal year (column (c));

(iv) The dollar amount of aggregate interest or other earnings accrued during the registrant's last fiscal year (column (d));

(v) The aggregate dollar amount of all withdrawals by and distributions to the executive during the registrant's last fiscal year (column (e)); and

(vi) The dollar amount of total balance of the executive's account as of the end of the registrant's last fiscal year (column (f)).

Instruction to Item 402(i)(2). Provide a footnote quantifying the extent to which amounts reported in the contributions and earnings columns are reported as compensation in the last completed fiscal year in the registrant's Summary Compensation Table and amounts reported in the aggregate balance at last fiscal year end (column (f)) previously were reported as compensation to the named executive officer in the registrant's Summary Compensation Table for previous years.

(3) Provide a succinct narrative description of any material factors necessary to an understanding of each plan covered by tabular disclosure required by this paragraph. While material factors will vary depending upon the facts, examples of such factors may include, in given cases, among other things:

(i) The type(s) of compensation permitted to be deferred, and any limitations (by percentage of compensation or otherwise) on the extent to which deferral is permitted;

(ii) The measures for calculating interest or other plan earnings (including whether such measure(s) are selected by the executive or the registrant and the frequency and manner in which selections may be changed), quantifying interest rates and other earnings measures applicable during the registrant's last fiscal year; and

 (iii) Material terms with respect to payouts, withdrawals and other distributions.

 (j) *Potential payments upon termination or change-in-control.* Regarding each contract, agreement, plan or arrangement, whether written or unwritten, that provides for payment(s) to a named executive officer at, following, or in connection with any termination, including without limitation resignation, severance, retirement or a constructive termination of a named executive officer, or a change in control of the registrant or a change in the named executive officer's responsibilities, with respect to each named executive officer:

 (1) Describe and explain the specific circumstances that would trigger payment(s) or the provision of other benefits, including perquisites and health care benefits;

 (2) Describe and quantify the estimated payments and benefits that would be provided in each covered circumstance, whether they would or could be lump sum, or annual, disclosing the duration, and by whom they would be provided;

 (3) Describe and explain how the appropriate payment and benefit levels are determined under the various circumstances that trigger payments or provision of benefits;

 (4) Describe and explain any material conditions or obligations applicable to the receipt of payments or benefits, including but not limited to non-compete, non-solicitation, non-disparagement or confidentiality agreements, including the duration of such agreements and provisions regarding waiver of breach of such agreements; and

 (5) Describe any other material factors regarding each such contract, agreement, plan or arrangement.

Instructions to Item 402(j). 1. The registrant must provide quantitative disclosure under these requirements, applying the assumptions that the triggering event took place on the last business day of the registrant's last completed fiscal year, and the price per share of the registrant's securities is the closing market price as of that date. In the event that uncertainties exist as to the provision of payments and benefits or the amounts involved, the registrant is required to make a reasonable estimate (or a reasonable estimated range of amounts) applicable to the payment or benefit and disclose material assumptions underlying such estimates or estimated ranges in its disclosure. In such event, the disclosure would require forward-looking information as appropriate.

 2. Perquisites and other personal benefits or property may be excluded only if the aggregate amount of such compensation will be less than $10,000. Individual perquisites and personal benefits shall be identified and quantified as required by Instruction 4 to paragraph (c)(2)(ix) of this Item. For purposes of quantifying health care benefits, the registrant must use the assumptions used for financial reporting purposes under generally accepted accounting principles.

 3. To the extent that the form and amount of any payment or benefit that would be provided in connection with any triggering event is fully disclosed pursuant to paragraph (h) or (i) of this Item, reference may be made to that disclosure. However, to the extent that the form or amount of any such payment or benefit would be enhanced or its vesting or other provisions accelerated in connection with any triggering event, such enhancement or acceleration must be disclosed pursuant to this paragraph.

 4. Where a triggering event has actually occurred for a named executive officer and that individual was not serving as a named executive officer of the registrant at the end of the last completed fiscal year, the disclosure required by this paragraph for that named executive officer shall apply only to that triggering event.

 5. The registrant need not provide information with respect to contracts, agreements, plans or arrangements to the extent they do not discriminate in scope, terms or operation, in favor of executive officers of the registrant and that are available generally to all salaried employees.

(k) *Compensation of directors.* (1) Provide the information specified in paragraph (k)(2) of this Item, concerning the compensation of the directors for the registrant's last completed fiscal year, in the following tabular format:

Director Compensation

Name	Fees earned or paid in cash ($)	Stock awards ($)	Option awards ($)	Non-equity incentive plan compensation ($)	Change in pension value and nonqualified deferred compensation earnings	All other compensation ($)	Total ($)
(a)	(b)	(c)	(d)	(e)	(f)	(g)	(h)
A							
B							
C							
D							
E							

(2) The Table shall include:

(i)   The name of each director unless such director is also a named executive officer under paragraph (a) of this Item and his or her compensation for service as a director is fully reflected in the Summary Compensation Table pursuant to paragraph (c) of this Item and otherwise as required pursuant to paragraphs (d) through (j) of this Item (column (a));

(ii) The aggregate dollar amount of all fees earned or paid in cash for services as a director, including annual retainer fees, committee and/or chairmanship fees, and meeting fees (column (b));

(iii) For awards of stock, the aggregate grant date fair value computed in accordance with FASB ASC Topic 718 (column (c));

(iv) For awards of options, with or without tandem SARs (including awards that subsequently have been transferred), the aggregate grant date fair value computed in accordance with FASB ASC Topic 718 (column (d));

Instruction to Item 402(k)(2)(iii) and (iv). For each director, disclose by footnote to the appropriate column: the grant date fair value of each equity award computed in accordance with FASB ASC Topic 718; for each option, SAR or similar option like instrument for which the registrant has adjusted or amended the exercise or base price during the last completed fiscal year, whether through amendment, cancellation or replacement grants, or any other means ("repriced"), or otherwise has materially modified such awards, the incremental fair value, computed as of the repricing or modification date in accordance with FASB ASC Topic 718; and the aggregate number of stock awards and the aggregate number of option awards outstanding at fiscal year end. However, the disclosure required by this Instruction does not apply to any repricing that occurs through a pre-existing formula or mechanism in the plan or award that results in the periodic adjustment of the option or SAR exercise or base price, an antidilution provision in a plan or award, or a recapitalization or similar transaction equally affecting all holders of the class of securities underlying the options or SARs.

(v) The dollar value of all earnings for services performed during the fiscal year pursuant to non-equity incentive plans as defined in paragraph (a)(6)(iii) of this Item, and all earnings on any outstanding awards (column (e));

(vi) The sum of the amounts specified in paragraphs (k)(2)(vi)(A) and (B) of this Item (column (f)) as follows:

(A) The aggregate change in the actuarial present value of the director's accumulated benefit under all defined benefit and actuarial pension plans (including supplemental plans) from the pension plan measurement date used for financial statement reporting purposes with respect to the registrant's audited financial statements for the prior completed fiscal year to the pension plan measurement date used for financial statement reporting purposes with respect to the registrant's audited financial statements for the covered fiscal year; and

(B) Above-market or preferential earnings on compensation that is deferred on a basis that is not tax-qualified, including such earnings on nonqualified defined contribution plans;

(vii) All other compensation for the covered fiscal year that the registrant could not properly report in any other column of the Director Compensation Table (column (g)). Each compensation item that is not properly reportable in columns (b)–(f), regardless of the amount of the compensation item, must be included in column (g). Such compensation must include, but is not limited to:

(A) Perquisites and other personal benefits, or property, unless the aggregate amount of such compensation is less than $10,000;

(B) All "gross-ups" or other amounts reimbursed during the fiscal year for the payment of taxes;

(C) For any security of the registrant or its subsidiaries purchased from the registrant or its subsidiaries (through deferral of salary or bonus, or otherwise) at a discount from the market price of such security at the date of purchase, unless that discount is available generally, either to all security holders or to all salaried employees of the registrant, the compensation cost, if any, computed in accordance with FASB ASC Topic 718;

(D) The amount paid or accrued to any director pursuant to a plan or arrangement in connection with:

(1) The resignation, retirement or any other termination of such director; or

(2) A change in control of the registrant;

(E) Registrant contributions or other allocations to vested and unvested defined contribution plans;

(F) Consulting fees earned from, or paid or payable by the registrant and/or its subsidiaries (including joint ventures);

(G) The annual costs of payments and promises of payments pursuant to director legacy programs and similar charitable award programs;

(H) The dollar value of any insurance premiums paid by, or on behalf of, the registrant during the covered fiscal year with respect to life insurance for the benefit of a director; and

(I)   The dollar value of any dividends or other earnings paid on stock or option awards, when those amounts were not factored into the grant date fair value required to be reported for the stock or option award in column (c) or (d); and

Instructions to Item 402(k)(2)(vii). 1. Programs in which registrants agree to make donations to one or more charitable institutions in a director's name, payable by the registrant currently or upon a designated event, such as the retirement or death of the director, are charitable awards programs or director legacy programs for purposes of the disclosure required by paragraph (k)(2)(vii)(G) of this Item. Provide footnote disclosure of the total dollar amount payable under the program and other material terms of each such program for which tabular disclosure is provided.

2.   Any item reported for a director pursuant to paragraph (k)(2)(vii) of this Item that is not a perquisite or personal benefit and whose value exceeds $10,000 must be identified and quantified in a footnote to column (g). All items of compensation are required to be included in the Director Compensation Table without regard to whether such items are required to be identified other than as specifically noted in this Item.

3.   Perquisites and personal benefits may be excluded as long as the total value of all perquisites and personal benefits for a director is less than $10,000. If the total value of all perquisites and personal benefits is $10,000 or more for any director, then each perquisite or personal benefit, regardless of its amount, must be identified by type. If perquisites and personal benefits are required to be reported for a director pursuant to this rule, then each perquisite or personal benefit that exceeds the greater of $25,000 or 10% of the total amount of perquisites and personal benefits for that director must be quantified and disclosed in a footnote. Perquisites and other personal benefits shall be valued on the basis of the aggregate incremental cost to the registrant. With respect to the perquisite or other personal benefit for which footnote quantification is required, the registrant shall describe in the footnote its methodology for computing the aggregate incremental cost. Reimbursements of taxes owed with respect to perquisites or other personal benefits must be included in column (g) and are subject to separate quantification and identification as tax reimbursements (paragraph (k)(2)(vii)(B) of this Item) even if the associated perquisites or other personal benefits are not required to be included because the total amount of all perquisites or personal benefits for an individual director is less than $10,000 or are required to be identified but are not required to be separately quantified.

(viii) The dollar value of total compensation for the covered fiscal year (column (h)). With respect to each director, disclose the sum of all amounts reported in columns (b) through (g).

Instruction to Item 402(k)(2). Two or more directors may be grouped in a single row in the Table if all elements of their compensation are identical. The names of the directors for whom disclosure is presented on a group basis should be clear from the Table.

(3) *Narrative to director compensation table.* Provide a narrative description of any material factors necessary to an understanding of the director compensation disclosed in this Table. While material factors will vary depending upon the facts, examples of such factors may include, in given cases, among other things:

(i)   A description of standard compensation arrangements (such as fees for retainer, committee service, service as chairman of the board or a committee, and meeting attendance); and

(ii) Whether any director has a different compensation arrangement, identifying that director and describing the terms of that arrangement.

Instruction to Item 402(k). In addition to the Instruction to paragraphs (k)(2)(iii) and (iv) and the Instructions to paragraph (k)(2)(vii) of this Item, the following apply equally to paragraph (k) of this Item: Instructions 2 and 4 to paragraph (c) of this Item; Instructions to paragraphs (c)(2)(iii) and (iv) of this Item; Instructions to paragraphs (c)(2)(v) and (vi) of this Item; Instructions to paragraph (c)(2)(vii) of this Item; Instructions to paragraph (c)(2)(viii) of this Item; and Instructions 1 and 5 to paragraph (c)(2)(ix) of this Item. These Instructions apply to the columns in the Director Compensation Table that are analogous to the columns in the Summary Compensation Table to which they refer and to disclosures under paragraph (k) of this Item that correspond to analogous disclosures provided for in paragraph (c) of this Item to which they refer.

(*l*)   *Smaller reporting companies and emerging growth companies.* A registrant that qualifies as a "smaller reporting company," as defined by Item 10(f) (§ 229.10(f)(1)), or is an "emerging growth company," as defined in Rule 405 of the Securities Act (§ 230.405 of this chapter) or Rule 12b–2 of the Exchange Act (§ 240.12b–2 of this chapter), may provide the scaled disclosure in paragraphs (m) through (r) instead of paragraphs (a) through (k), (s), and (u) of this Item.

(m)   *Smaller reporting companies—General—*(1) *All compensation covered.* This Item requires clear, concise and understandable disclosure of all plan and non-plan compensation awarded to, earned by, or paid to the named executive officers designated under paragraph (m)(2) of this Item, and directors covered by paragraph (r) of this Item, by any person for all services rendered in all capacities to the smaller reporting company and its subsidiaries, unless otherwise specifically excluded from disclosure in this Item. All such compensation shall be reported pursuant to this Item, even if also called for by another requirement, including transactions between the smaller reporting company and a third party where a purpose of the transaction is to furnish compensation to any such named executive officer or director. No amount reported as compensation for one fiscal year need be reported in the same manner as compensation for a subsequent fiscal year; amounts reported as compensation for one fiscal year may be required to be reported in a different manner pursuant to this Item.

(2)   *Persons covered.* Disclosure shall be provided pursuant to this Item for each of the following (the "named executive officers"):

(i)   All individuals serving as the smaller reporting company's principal executive officer or acting in a similar capacity during the last completed fiscal year ("PEO"), regardless of compensation level;

(ii)   The smaller reporting company's two most highly compensated executive officers other than the PEO who were serving as executive officers at the end of the last completed fiscal year; and

(iii)   Up to two additional individuals for whom disclosure would have been provided pursuant to paragraph (m)(2)(ii) of this Item but for the fact that the individual was not serving as an executive officer of the smaller reporting company at the end of the last completed fiscal year.

Instructions to Item 402(m)(2). 1. *Determination of most highly compensated executive officers.* The determination as to which executive officers are most highly compensated shall be made by reference to total compensation for the last completed fiscal year (as required to be disclosed pursuant to paragraph (n)(2)(x) of this Item) reduced by the amount required to be disclosed pursuant to paragraph (n)(2)(viii) of this Item, *provided, however,* that no disclosure need be provided for any executive officer, other than the PEO, whose total compensation, as so reduced, does not exceed $100,000.

2.   *Inclusion of executive officer of a subsidiary.* It may be appropriate for a smaller reporting company to include as named executive officers one or more executive officers or other employees of subsidiaries in the disclosure required by this Item. *See* Rule 3b–7 under the Exchange Act (17 CFR 240.3b–7).

3.   *Exclusion of executive officer due to overseas compensation.* It may be appropriate in limited circumstances for a smaller reporting company not to include in the disclosure required by this Item an individual, other than its PEO, who is one of the smaller reporting company's most highly compensated executive officers due to the payment of amounts of cash compensation relating to overseas assignments attributed predominantly to such assignments.

(3) *Information for full fiscal year.* If the PEO served in that capacity during any part of a fiscal year with respect to which information is required, information should be provided as to all of his or her compensation for the full fiscal year. If a named executive officer (other than the PEO) served as an executive officer of the smaller reporting company (whether or not in the same position) during any part of the fiscal year with respect to which information is required, information shall be provided as to all compensation of that individual for the full fiscal year.

(4) *Omission of table or column.* A table or column may be omitted if there has been no compensation awarded to, earned by, or paid to any of the named executive officers or directors required to be reported in that table or column in any fiscal year covered by that table.

(5) *Definitions.* For purposes of this Item:

(i) The term *stock* means instruments such as common stock, restricted stock, restricted stock units, phantom stock, phantom stock units, common stock equivalent units or any similar instruments that do not have option-like features, and the term *option* means instruments such as stock options, stock appreciation rights and similar instruments with option-like features. The term *stock appreciation rights* ("*SARs*") refers to SARs payable in cash or stock, including SARs payable in cash or stock at the election of the smaller reporting company or a named executive officer. The term *equity* is used to refer generally to stock and/or options.

(ii) The term *plan* includes, but is not limited to, the following: Any plan, contract, authorization or arrangement, whether or not set forth in any formal document, pursuant to which cash, securities, similar instruments, or any other property may be received. A plan may be applicable to one person. Except with respect to disclosure required by paragraph (t) of this Item, smaller reporting companies may omit information regarding group life, health, hospitalization, or medical reimbursement plans that do not discriminate in scope, terms or operation, in favor of executive officers or directors of the smaller reporting company and that are available generally to all salaried employees.

(iii) The term *incentive plan* means any plan providing compensation intended to serve as incentive for performance to occur over a specified period, whether such performance is measured by reference to financial performance of the smaller reporting company or an affiliate, the smaller reporting company's stock price, or any other performance measure. An equity incentive plan is an incentive plan or portion of an incentive plan under which awards are granted that fall within the scope of FASB ASC Topic 718. A *non-equity incentive plan* is an incentive plan or portion of an incentive plan that is not an equity incentive plan. The term *incentive plan award* means an award provided under an incentive plan.

(iv) The terms *date of grant* or *grant date* refer to the grant date determined for financial statement reporting purposes pursuant to FASB ASC Topic 718.

(v) *Closing market price* is defined as the price at which the smaller reporting company's security was last sold in the principal United States market for such security as of the date for which the closing market price is determined.

(n) *Smaller reporting companies—Summary compensation table—*(1) *General.* Provide the information specified in paragraph (n)(2) of this Item, concerning the compensation of the named executive officers for each of the smaller reporting company's last two completed fiscal years, in a Summary Compensation Table in the tabular format specified below.

Summary Compensation Table

Name and principal position (a)	Year (b)	Salary ($) (c)	Bonus ($) (d)	Stock awards ($) (e)	Option awards ($) (f)	Nonequity incentive plan compensation ($) (g)	Nonqualified deferred compensation earnings ($) (h)	All other compensation ($) (i)	Total ($) (j)
PEO									
A									
B									

(2) The Table shall include:

(i) The name and principal position of the named executive officer (column (a));

(ii) The fiscal year covered (column (b));

(iii) The dollar value of base salary (cash and non-cash) earned by the named executive officer during the fiscal year covered (column (c));

(iv) The dollar value of bonus (cash and non-cash) earned by the named executive officer during the fiscal year covered (column (d));

Instructions to Item 402(n)(2)(iii) and (iv). 1. If the amount of salary or bonus earned in a given fiscal year is not calculable through the latest practicable date, a footnote shall be included disclosing that the amount of salary or bonus is not calculable through the latest practicable date and providing the date that the amount of salary or bonus is expected to be determined, and such amount must then be disclosed in a filing under Item 5.02(f) of Form 8-K (17 CFR 249.308).

2. Smaller reporting companies shall include in the salary column (column (c)) or bonus column (column (d)) any amount of salary or bonus forgone at the election of a named executive officer under which stock, equity-based or other forms of non-cash compensation instead have been received by the named executive officer. However, the receipt of any such form of non-cash compensation instead of salary or bonus must be disclosed in a footnote added to the salary or bonus column and, where applicable, referring to the narrative disclosure to the Summary Compensation Table (required by paragraph (*o*) of this Item) where the material terms of the stock, option or non-equity incentive plan award elected by the named executive officer are reported.

(v) For awards of stock, the aggregate grant date fair value computed in accordance with FASB ASC Topic 718 (column (e));

(vi) For awards of options, with or without tandem SARs (including awards that subsequently have been transferred), the aggregate grant date fair value computed in accordance with FASB ASC Topic 718 (column (f));

Instruction 1 to Item 402(n)(2)(v) and (n)(2)(vi). For awards reported in columns (e) and (f), include a footnote disclosing all assumptions made in the valuation by reference to a discussion of those assumptions in the smaller reporting company's financial statements, footnotes to the financial statements, or discussion in the Management's Discussion and Analysis. The sections so referenced are deemed part of the disclosure provided pursuant to this Item.

Instruction 2 to Item 402(n)(2)(v) and (n)(2)(vi). If at any time during the last completed fiscal year, the smaller reporting company has adjusted or amended the exercise price of options or SARs previously awarded to a named executive officer, whether through amendment, cancellation or replacement grants, or any other means ("repriced"), or otherwise has materially modified such awards, the smaller reporting company shall include, as awards required to be reported in column (f), the incremental fair value, computed as of the repricing or modification date in accordance with FASB ASC Topic 718, with respect to that repriced or modified award.

Instruction 3 to Item 402(n)(2)(v) and (vi). For any awards that are subject to performance conditions, report the value at the grant date based upon the probable outcome of such conditions. This amount should be consistent with the estimate of aggregate compensation cost to be recognized over the service period determined as of the grant date under FASB ASC Topic 718, excluding the effect of estimated forfeitures. In a footnote to the table, disclose the value of the award at the grant date assuming that the highest level of performance conditions will be achieved if an amount less than the maximum was included in the table.

> (vii) The dollar value of all earnings for services performed during the fiscal year pursuant to awards under non-equity incentive plans as defined in paragraph (m)(5)(iii) of this Item, and all earnings on any outstanding awards (column (g));

Instructions to Item 402(n)(2)(vii). 1. If the relevant performance measure is satisfied during the fiscal year (including for a single year in a plan with a multi-year performance measure), the earnings are reportable for that fiscal year, even if not payable until a later date, and are not reportable again in the fiscal year when amounts are paid to the named executive officer.

2.   All earnings on non-equity incentive plan compensation must be identified and quantified in a footnote to column (g), whether the earnings were paid during the fiscal year, payable during the period but deferred at the election of the named executive officer, or payable by their terms at a later date.

> (viii) Above-market or preferential earnings on compensation that is deferred on a basis that is not tax-qualified, including such earnings on nonqualified defined contribution plans (column (h));

Instruction to Item 402(n)(2)(viii). Interest on deferred compensation is above-market only if the rate of interest exceeds 120% of the applicable federal long-term rate, with compounding (as prescribed under section 1274(d) of the Internal Revenue Code, (26 U.S.C. 1274(d))) at the rate that corresponds most closely to the rate under the smaller reporting company's plan at the time the interest rate or formula is set. In the event of a discretionary reset of the interest rate, the requisite calculation must be made on the basis of the interest rate at the time of such reset, rather than when originally established. Only the above-market portion of the interest must be included. If the applicable interest rates vary depending upon conditions such as a minimum period of continued service, the reported amount should be calculated assuming satisfaction of all conditions to receiving interest at the highest rate. Dividends (and dividend equivalents) on deferred compensation denominated in the smaller reporting company's stock ("deferred stock") are preferential only if earned at a rate higher than dividends on the smaller reporting company's common stock. Only the preferential portion of the dividends or equivalents must be included. Footnote or narrative disclosure may be provided explaining the smaller reporting company's criteria for determining any portion considered to be above-market.

> (ix) All other compensation for the covered fiscal year that the smaller reporting company could not properly report in any other column of the Summary Compensation Table (column (i)). Each compensation item that is not properly reportable in columns (c) through (h), regardless of the amount of the compensation item, must be included in column (i). Such compensation must include, but is not limited to:
>
> > (A) Perquisites and other personal benefits, or property, unless the aggregate amount of such compensation is less than $10,000;
> >
> > (B) All "gross-ups" or other amounts reimbursed during the fiscal year for the payment of taxes;
> >
> > (C) For any security of the smaller reporting company or its subsidiaries purchased from the smaller reporting company or its subsidiaries (through deferral of salary or bonus, or otherwise) at a discount from the market price of such security at the date of purchase, unless that discount is available generally, either to all security

holders or to all salaried employees of the smaller reporting company, the compensation cost, if any, computed in accordance with FASB ASC Topic 718;

(D)   The amount paid or accrued to any named executive officer pursuant to a plan or arrangement in connection with:

(*1*)   Any termination, including without limitation through retirement, resignation, severance or constructive termination (including a change in responsibilities) of such executive officer's employment with the smaller reporting company and its subsidiaries; or

(*2*)   A change in control of the smaller reporting company;

(E)   Smaller reporting company contributions or other allocations to vested and unvested defined contribution plans;

(F)   The dollar value of any insurance premiums paid by, or on behalf of, the smaller reporting company during the covered fiscal year with respect to life insurance for the benefit of a named executive officer; and

(G)   The dollar value of any dividends or other earnings paid on stock or option awards, when those amounts were not factored into the grant date fair value required to be reported for the stock or option award in column (e) or (f); and

Instructions to Item 402(n)(2)(ix).

1.   Non-equity incentive plan awards and earnings and earnings on stock or options, except as specified in paragraph (n)(2)(ix)(G) of this Item, are required to be reported elsewhere as provided in this Item and are not reportable as All Other Compensation in column (i).

2.   Benefits paid pursuant to defined benefit and actuarial plans are not reportable as All Other Compensation in column (i) unless accelerated pursuant to a change in control; information concerning these plans is reportable pursuant to paragraph (q)(1) of this Item.

3.   Reimbursements of taxes owed with respect to perquisites or other personal benefits must be included in the columns as tax reimbursements (paragraph (n)(2)(ix)(B) of this Item) even if the associated perquisites or other personal benefits are not required to be included because the aggregate amount of such compensation is less than $10,000.

4.   Perquisites and other personal benefits shall be valued on the basis of the aggregate incremental cost to the smaller reporting company.

5.   For purposes of paragraph (n)(2)(ix)(D) of this Item, an accrued amount is an amount for which payment has become due.

(x)   The dollar value of total compensation for the covered fiscal year (column (j)). With respect to each named executive officer, disclose the sum of all amounts reported in columns (c) through (i).

Instructions to Item 402(n).

1.   Information with respect to the fiscal year prior to the last completed fiscal year will not be required if the smaller reporting company was not a reporting company pursuant to section 13(a) or 15(d) of the Exchange Act (15 U.S.C. 78m(a) or 78o(d)) at any time during that year, except that the smaller reporting company will be required to provide information for any such year if that information previously was required to be provided in response to a Commission filing requirement.

2.   All compensation values reported in the Summary Compensation Table must be reported in dollars and rounded to the nearest dollar. Reported compensation values must be reported numerically, providing a single numerical value for each grid in the table. Where compensation was paid to or received by a named executive officer in a different currency, a footnote must be provided to

identify that currency and describe the rate and methodology used to convert the payment amounts to dollars.

3. If a named executive officer is also a director who receives compensation for his or her services as a director, reflect that compensation in the Summary Compensation Table and provide a footnote identifying and itemizing such compensation and amounts. Use the categories in the Director Compensation Table required pursuant to paragraph (r) of this Item.

4. Any amounts deferred, whether pursuant to a plan established under section 401(k) of the Internal Revenue Code (26 U.S.C. 401(k)), or otherwise, shall be included in the appropriate column for the fiscal year in which earned.

(o) *Smaller reporting companies—Narrative disclosure to summary compensation table.* Provide a narrative description of any material factors necessary to an understanding of the information disclosed in the Table required by paragraph (n) of this Item. Examples of such factors may include, in given cases, among other things:

(1) The material terms of each named executive officer's employment agreement or arrangement, whether written or unwritten;

(2) If at any time during the last fiscal year, any outstanding option or other equity-based award was repriced or otherwise materially modified (such as by extension of exercise periods, the change of vesting or forfeiture conditions, the change or elimination of applicable performance criteria, or the change of the bases upon which returns are determined), a description of each such repricing or other material modification;

(3) The waiver or modification of any specified performance target, goal or condition to payout with respect to any amount included in non-stock incentive plan compensation or payouts reported in column (g) to the Summary Compensation Table required by paragraph (n) of this Item, stating whether the waiver or modification applied to one or more specified named executive officers or to all compensation subject to the target, goal or condition;

(4) The material terms of each grant, including but not limited to the date of exercisability, any conditions to exercisability, any tandem feature, any reload feature, any tax-reimbursement feature, and any provision that could cause the exercise price to be lowered;

(5) The material terms of any non-equity incentive plan award made to a named executive officer during the last completed fiscal year, including a general description of the formula or criteria to be applied in determining the amounts payable and vesting schedule;

(6) The method of calculating earnings on nonqualified deferred compensation plans including nonqualified defined contribution plans; and

(7) An identification to the extent material of any item included under All Other Compensation (column (i)) in the Summary Compensation Table. Identification of an item shall not be considered material if it does not exceed the greater of $25,000 or 10% of all items included in the specified category in question set forth in paragraph (n)(2)(ix) of this Item. All items of compensation are required to be included in the Summary Compensation Table without regard to whether such items are required to be identified.

Instruction to Item 402(o). The disclosure required by paragraph (o)(2) of this Item would not apply to any repricing that occurs through a pre-existing formula or mechanism in the plan or award that results in the periodic adjustment of the option or SAR exercise or base price, an antidilution provision in a plan or award, or a recapitalization or similar transaction equally affecting all holders of the class of securities underlying the options or SARs.

(p) *Smaller reporting companies—Outstanding equity awards at fiscal year-end table.* (1) Provide the information specified in paragraph (p)(2) of this Item, concerning unexercised options; stock that has not vested; and equity incentive plan awards for each named executive officer outstanding as of the end of the smaller reporting company's last completed fiscal year in the following tabular format:

Outstanding Equality Awards at Fiscal Year-End

	Option awards					Stock awards			
Name	Number of securities underlying unexercised options (#) exercisable	Number of securities underlying unexercised options (#) unexercisable	Equity incentive plan awards: Number of securities underlying unexercised unearned options (#)	Option exercise price ($)	Option expiration date	Number of shares or units of stock that have not vested (#)	Market value of shares of units of stock that have not vested ($)	Equity incentive plan awards: Number of unearned shares, units or other rights that have not vested (#)	Equity incentive plan awards: Market or payout value of unearned shares, units or other rights that have not vested ($)
(a)	(b)	(c)	(d)	(e)	(f)	(g)	(h)	(i)	(j)
PEO									
A									
B									

(2)   The Table shall include:

(i)   The name of the named executive officer (column (a));

(ii)   On an award-by-award basis, the number of securities underlying unexercised options, including awards that have been transferred other than for value, that are exercisable and that are not reported in column (d) (column (b));

(iii)   On an award-by-award basis, the number of securities underlying unexercised options, including awards that have been transferred other than for value, that are unexercisable and that are not reported in column (d) (column (c));

(iv)   On an award-by-award basis, the total number of shares underlying unexercised options awarded under any equity incentive plan that have not been earned (column (d));

(v)   For each instrument reported in columns (b), (c) and (d), as applicable, the exercise or base price (column (e));

(vi)   For each instrument reported in columns (b), (c) and (d), as applicable, the expiration date (column (f));

(vii)   The total number of shares of stock that have not vested and that are not reported in column (i) (column (g));

(viii) The aggregate market value of shares of stock that have not vested and that are not reported in column (j) (column (h));

(ix)   The total number of shares of stock, units or other rights awarded under any equity incentive plan that have not vested and that have not been earned, and, if applicable the number of shares underlying any such unit or right (column (i)); and

(x)   The aggregate market or payout value of shares of stock, units or other rights awarded under any equity incentive plan that have not vested and that have not been earned (column (j)).

Instructions to Item 402(p)(2).

1.   Identify by footnote any award that has been transferred other than for value, disclosing the nature of the transfer.

2.   The vesting dates of options, shares of stock and equity incentive plan awards held at fiscal-year end must be disclosed by footnote to the applicable column where the outstanding award is reported.

3.   Compute the market value of stock reported in column (h) and equity incentive plan awards of stock reported in column (j) by multiplying the closing market price of the smaller reporting company's stock at the end of the last completed fiscal year by the number of shares or units of stock or the amount of equity incentive plan awards, respectively. The number of shares or units reported in column (d) or (i), and the payout value reported in column (j), shall be based on achieving threshold performance goals, except that if the previous fiscal year's performance has exceeded the threshold, the disclosure shall be based on the next higher performance measure (target or maximum) that exceeds the previous fiscal year's performance. If the award provides only for a single estimated payout, that amount should be reported. If the target amount is not determinable, smaller reporting companies must provide a representative amount based on the previous fiscal year's performance.

4.   Multiple awards may be aggregated where the expiration date and the exercise and/or base price of the instruments is identical. A single award consisting of a combination of options, SARs and/or similar option-like instruments shall be reported as separate awards with respect to each tranche with a different exercise and/or base price or expiration date.

5.   Options or stock awarded under an equity incentive plan are reported in columns (d) or (i) and (j), respectively, until the relevant performance condition has been satisfied. Once the relevant performance condition has been satisfied, even if the option or stock award is subject to forfeiture conditions, options are reported in column (b) or (c), as appropriate, until they are exercised or expire, or stock is reported in columns (g) and (h) until it vests.

(q)   *Smaller reporting companies—Additional narrative disclosure.* Provide a narrative description of the following to the extent material:

(1)   The material terms of each plan that provides for the payment of retirement benefits, or benefits that will be paid primarily following retirement, including but not limited to tax-qualified defined benefit plans, supplemental executive retirement plans, tax-qualified defined contribution plans and nonqualified defined contribution plans.

(2)   The material terms of each contract, agreement, plan or arrangement, whether written or unwritten, that provides for payment(s) to a named executive officer at, following, or in connection with the resignation, retirement or other termination of a named executive officer, or a change in control of the smaller reporting company or a change in the named executive officer's responsibilities following a change in control, with respect to each named executive officer.

(r)   *Smaller reporting companies—Compensation of directors.* (1) Provide the information specified in paragraph (r)(2) of this Item, concerning the compensation of the directors for the smaller reporting company's last completed fiscal year, in the following tabular format:

Director Compensation

Name (a)	Fees earned or paid in cash ($) (b)	Stock awards ($) (c)	Option awards ($) (d)	Non-equity incentive plan compensation ($) (e)	Nonqualified deferred compensation earnings ($) (f)	All other compensation ($) (g)	Total ($) (h)
A							
B							
C							
D							
E							

(2)   The Table shall include:

(i)   The name of each director unless such director is also a named executive officer under paragraph (m) of this Item and his or her compensation for service as a director is fully reflected in the Summary Compensation Table pursuant to paragraph (n) of this Item and otherwise as required pursuant to paragraphs (o) through (q) of this Item (column (a));

(ii)   The aggregate dollar amount of all fees earned or paid in cash for services as a director, including annual retainer fees, committee and/or chairmanship fees, and meeting fees (column (b));

(iii)   For awards of stock, the aggregate grant date fair value computed in accordance with FASB ASC Topic 718 (column (c));

(iv)   For awards of options, with or without tandem SARs (including awards that subsequently have been transferred), the aggregate grant date fair value computed in accordance with FASB ASC Topic 718 (column (d));

Instruction to Item 402(r)(2)(iii) and (iv). For each director, disclose by footnote to the appropriate column, the aggregate number of stock awards and the aggregate number of option awards outstanding at fiscal year end.

(v)   The dollar value of all earnings for services performed during the fiscal year pursuant to non-equity incentive plans as defined in paragraph (m)(5)(iii) of this Item, and all earnings on any outstanding awards (column (e));

(vi)   Above-market or preferential earnings on compensation that is deferred on a basis that is not tax-qualified, including such earnings on nonqualified defined contribution plans (column (f));

(vii)   All other compensation for the covered fiscal year that the smaller reporting company could not properly report in any other column of the Director Compensation Table (column (g)). Each compensation item that is not properly reportable in columns (b) through (f), regardless of the amount of the compensation item, must be included in column (g) and must be identified and quantified in a footnote if it is deemed material in accordance with paragraph (o)(7) of this Item. Such compensation must include, but is not limited to:

(A)   Perquisites and other personal benefits, or property, unless the aggregate amount of such compensation is less than $10,000;

(B)   All "gross-ups" or other amounts reimbursed during the fiscal year for the payment of taxes;

(C) For any security of the smaller reporting company or its subsidiaries purchased from the smaller reporting company or its subsidiaries (through deferral of salary or bonus, or otherwise) at a discount from the market price of such security at the date of purchase, unless that discount is available generally, either to all security holders or to all salaried employees of the smaller reporting company, the compensation cost, if any, computed in accordance with FASB ASC Topic 718;

(D) The amount paid or accrued to any director pursuant to a plan or arrangement in connection with:

    (*1*)   The resignation, retirement or any other termination of such director; or

    (*2*)   A change in control of the smaller reporting company;

(E) Smaller reporting company contributions or other allocations to vested and unvested defined contribution plans;

(F) Consulting fees earned from, or paid or payable by the smaller reporting company and/or its subsidiaries (including joint ventures);

(G) The annual costs of payments and promises of payments pursuant to director legacy programs and similar charitable award programs;

(H) The dollar value of any insurance premiums paid by, or on behalf of, the smaller reporting company during the covered fiscal year with respect to life insurance for the benefit of a director; and

(I) The dollar value of any dividends or other earnings paid on stock or option awards, when those amounts were not factored into the grant date fair value required to be reported for the stock or option award in column (c) or (d); and

Instruction to Item 402(r)(2)(vii). Programs in which smaller reporting companies agree to make donations to one or more charitable institutions in a director's name, payable by the smaller reporting company currently or upon a designated event, such as the retirement or death of the director, are charitable awards programs or director legacy programs for purposes of the disclosure required by paragraph (r)(2)(vii)(G) of this Item. Provide footnote disclosure of the total dollar amount payable under the program and other material terms of each such program for which tabular disclosure is provided.

(viii) The dollar value of total compensation for the covered fiscal year (column (h)). With respect to each director, disclose the sum of all amounts reported in columns (b) through (g).

Instruction to Item 402(r)(2). Two or more directors may be grouped in a single row in the Table if all elements of their compensation are identical. The names of the directors for whom disclosure is presented on a group basis should be clear from the Table.

(3) *Narrative to director compensation table.* Provide a narrative description of any material factors necessary to an understanding of the director compensation disclosed in this Table. While material factors will vary depending upon the facts, examples of such factors may include, in given cases, among other things:

(i) A description of standard compensation arrangements (such as fees for retainer, committee service, service as chairman of the board or a committee, and meeting attendance); and

(ii) Whether any director has a different compensation arrangement, identifying that director and describing the terms of that arrangement.

Instruction to Item 402(r). In addition to the Instruction to paragraph (r)(2)(vii) of this Item, the following apply equally to paragraph (r) of this Item: Instructions 2 and 4 to paragraph (n) of this Item; the Instructions to paragraphs (n)(2)(iii) and (iv) of this Item; the Instructions to paragraphs (n)(2)(v) and (vi) of this Item; the Instructions to paragraph (n)(2)(vii) of this Item; the Instruction to paragraph (n)(2)(viii) of this Item; the Instructions to paragraph (n)(2)(ix) of this Item; and paragraph (o)(7) of this Item. These Instructions apply to the columns in the Director Compensation Table that are analogous to the columns in the Summary Compensation Table to which they refer and to disclosures under paragraph (r) of this Item that correspond to analogous disclosures provided for in paragraph (n) of this Item to which they refer.

(s) *Narrative disclosure of the registrant's compensation policies and practices as they relate to the registrant's risk management.* To the extent that risks arising from the registrant's compensation policies and practices for its employees are reasonably likely to have a material adverse effect on the registrant, discuss the registrant's policies and practices of compensating its employees, including non-executive officers, as they relate to risk management practices and risk-taking incentives. While the situations requiring disclosure will vary depending on the particular registrant and compensation policies and practices, situations that may trigger disclosure include, among others, compensation policies and practices: at a business unit of the company that carries a significant portion of the registrant's risk profile; at a business unit with compensation structured significantly differently than other units within the registrant; at a business unit that is significantly more profitable than others within the registrant; at a business unit where compensation expense is a significant percentage of the unit's revenues; and that vary significantly from the overall risk and reward structure of the registrant, such as when bonuses are awarded upon accomplishment of a task, while the income and risk to the registrant from the task extend over a significantly longer period of time. The purpose of this paragraph(s) is to provide investors material information concerning how the registrant compensates and incentivizes its employees that may create risks that are reasonably likely to have a material adverse effect on the registrant. While the information to be disclosed pursuant to this paragraph(s) will vary depending upon the nature of the registrant's business and the compensation approach, the following are examples of the issues that the registrant may need to address for the business units or employees discussed:

(1) The general design philosophy of the registrant's compensation policies and practices for employees whose behavior would be most affected by the incentives established by the policies and practices, as such policies and practices relate to or affect risk taking by employees on behalf of the registrant, and the manner of their implementation;

(2) The registrant's risk assessment or incentive considerations, if any, in structuring its compensation policies and practices or in awarding and paying compensation;

(3) How the registrant's compensation policies and practices relate to the realization of risks resulting from the actions of employees in both the short term and the long term, such as through policies requiring claw backs or imposing holding periods;

(4) The registrant's policies regarding adjustments to its compensation policies and practices to address changes in its risk profile;

(5) Material adjustments the registrant has made to its compensation policies and practices as a result of changes in its risk profile; and

(6) The extent to which the registrant monitors its compensation policies and practices to determine whether its risk management objectives are being met with respect to incentivizing its employees.

(t) *Golden parachute compensation.* (1) In connection with any proxy or consent solicitation material providing the disclosure required by section 14A(b)(1) of the Exchange Act (15 U.S.C. 78n–1(b)(1)) or any proxy or consent solicitation that includes disclosure under Item 14 of Schedule 14A (§ 240.14a–101 of this chapter) pursuant to Note A of Schedule 14A (excluding any proxy or consent solicitation of an "emerging growth company," as defined in Rule 405 of the Securities Act (§ 230.405 of this chapter) or Rule 12b–2 of the Exchange Act (§ 240.12b–2 of this chapter)), with respect to each named executive officer of the acquiring company and the target company, provide the information specified in paragraphs (t)(2) and (3) of this section regarding any agreement or understanding, whether written or unwritten, between such named executive officer and the acquiring company or target company, concerning any type of compensation, whether present, deferred or contingent, that is based on or otherwise relates to an acquisition, merger, consolidation, sale or other disposition of all or substantially all assets of the issuer, as follows:

Golden Parachute Compensation

Name	Cash ($)	Equity ($)	Pension/ NQDC ($)	Perquisites/ benefits ($)	Tax reimbursement ($)	Other ($)	Total ($)
(a)	(b)	(c)	(d)	(e)	(f)	(g)	(h)
PEO							
PFO							
A							
B							
C							

(2) The table shall include, for each named executive officer:

(i) The name of the named executive officer (column (a));

(ii) The aggregate dollar value of any cash severance payments, including but not limited to payments of base salary, bonus, and pro-rated non-equity incentive compensation plan payments (column (b));

(iii) The aggregate dollar value of:

(A) Stock awards for which vesting would be accelerated;

(B) In-the-money option awards for which vesting would be accelerated; and

(C) Payments in cancellation of stock and option awards (column (c));

(iv) The aggregate dollar value of pension and nonqualified deferred compensation benefit enhancements (column (d));

(v) The aggregate dollar value of perquisites and other personal benefits or property, and health care and welfare benefits (column (e));

(vi) The aggregate dollar value of any tax reimbursements (column (f));

(vii) The aggregate dollar value of any other compensation that is based on or otherwise relates to the transaction not properly reported in columns (b) through (f) (column (g)); and

(viii) The aggregate dollar value of the sum of all amounts reported in columns (b) through (g) (column (h)).

Instructions to Item 402(t)(2).

1. If this disclosure is included in a proxy or consent solicitation seeking approval of an acquisition, merger, consolidation, or proposed sale or other disposition of all or substantially all the assets of the registrant, or in a proxy or consent solicitation that includes disclosure under Item 14 of Schedule 14A (§ 240.14a–101) pursuant to Note A of Schedule 14A, the disclosure provided by this table shall be quantified assuming that the triggering event took place on the latest practicable date, and that the price per share of the registrant's securities shall be determined as follows: If the shareholders are to receive a fixed dollar amount, the price per share shall be that fixed dollar amount, and if such value is not a fixed dollar amount, the price per share shall be the average closing market price of the registrant's securities over the first five business days following the first public announcement of the transaction. Compute the dollar value of in-the-money option awards for which vesting would be accelerated by determining the difference between this price and the exercise or base price of the options. Include only compensation that is based on or otherwise relates to the subject transaction. Apply Instruction 1 to Item 402(t) with respect to those executive officers for whom

disclosure was required in the issuer's most recent filing with the Commission under the Securities Act (15 U.S.C. 77a *et seq.*) or Exchange Act (15 U.S.C. 78a *et seq.*) that required disclosure pursuant to Item 402(c).

2.   If this disclosure is included in a proxy solicitation for the annual meeting at which directors are elected for purposes of subjecting the disclosed agreements or understandings to a shareholder vote under section 14A(a)(1) of the Exchange Act (15 U.S.C. 78n–1(a)(1)), the disclosure provided by this table shall be quantified assuming that the triggering event took place on the last business day of the registrant's last completed fiscal year, and the price per share of the registrant's securities is the closing market price as of that date. Compute the dollar value of in-the-money option awards for which vesting would be accelerated by determining the difference between this price and the exercise or base price of the options.

3.   In the event that uncertainties exist as to the provision of payments and benefits or the amounts involved, the registrant is required to make a reasonable estimate applicable to the payment or benefit and disclose material assumptions underlying such estimates in its disclosure. In such event, the disclosure would require forward-looking information as appropriate.

4.   For each of columns (b) through (g), include a footnote quantifying each separate form of compensation included in the aggregate total reported. Include the value of all perquisites and other personal benefits or property. Individual perquisites and personal benefits shall be identified and quantified as required by Instruction 4 to Item 402(c)(2)(ix) of this section. For purposes of quantifying health care benefits, the registrant must use the assumptions used for financial reporting purposes under generally accepted accounting principles.

5.   For each of columns (b) through (h), include a footnote quantifying the amount payable attributable to a double-trigger arrangement (*i.e.*, amounts triggered by a change-in-control for which payment is conditioned upon the executive officer's termination without cause or resignation for good reason within a limited time period following the change-in-control), specifying the time-frame in which such termination or resignation must occur in order for the amount to become payable, and the amount payable attributable to a single-trigger arrangement (*i.e.*, amounts triggered by a change-in-control for which payment is not conditioned upon such a termination or resignation of the executive officer).

6.   A registrant conducting a shareholder advisory vote pursuant to § 240.14a–21(c) of this chapter to cover new arrangements and understandings, and/or revised terms of agreements and understandings that were previously subject to a shareholder advisory vote pursuant to § 240.14a–21(a) of this chapter, shall provide two separate tables. One table shall disclose all golden parachute compensation, including both the arrangements and amounts previously disclosed and subject to a shareholder advisory vote under section 14A(a)(1) of the Exchange Act (15 U.S.C. 78n–1(a)(1)) and § 240.14a–21(a) of this chapter and the new arrangements and understandings and/or revised terms of agreements and understandings that were previously subject to a shareholder advisory vote. The second table shall disclose only the new arrangements and/or revised terms subject to the separate shareholder vote under section 14A(b)(2) of the Exchange Act and § 240.14a–21(c) of this chapter.

7.   In cases where this Item 402(t)(2) requires disclosure of arrangements between an acquiring company and the named executive officers of the soliciting target company, the registrant shall clarify whether these agreements are included in the separate shareholder advisory vote pursuant to § 240.14a–21(c) of this chapter by providing a separate table of all agreements and understandings subject to the shareholder advisory vote required by section 14A(b)(2) of the Exchange Act (15 U.S.C. 78n–1(b)(2)) and § 240.14a–21(c) of this chapter, if different from the full scope of golden parachute compensation subject to Item 402(t) disclosure.

(3)   Provide a succinct narrative description of any material factors necessary to an understanding of each such contract, agreement, plan or arrangement and the payments quantified in the tabular disclosure required by this paragraph. Such factors shall include, but not be limited to a description of:

(i)   The specific circumstances that would trigger payment(s);

(ii)   Whether the payments would or could be lump sum, or annual, disclosing the duration, and by whom they would be provided; and

(iii)   Any material conditions or obligations applicable to the receipt of payment or benefits, including but not limited to non-compete, non-solicitation, non-disparagement or confidentiality agreements, including the duration of such agreements and provisions regarding waiver or breach of such agreements.

Instructions to Item 402(t).

1.   A registrant that does not qualify as a "smaller reporting company," as defined by § 229.10(f)(1) of this chapter, must provide the information required by this Item 402(t) with respect to the individuals covered by Items 402(a)(3)(i), (ii) and (iii) of this section. A registrant that qualifies as a "smaller reporting company," as defined by § 229.10(f)(1) of this chapter, must provide the information required by this Item 402(t) with respect to the individuals covered by Items 402(m)(2)(i) and (ii) of this section.

2.   The obligation to provide the information in this Item 402(t) shall not apply to agreements and understandings described in paragraph (t)(1) of this section with senior management of foreign private issuers, as defined in § 240.3b–4 of this chapter.

(u). *Pay ratio disclosure*—(1) *Disclose.* (i) The median of the annual total compensation of all employees of the registrant, except the PEO of the registrant;

(ii)   The annual total compensation of the PEO of the registrant; and

(iii)   The ratio of the amount in paragraph (u)(1)(i) of this Item to the amount in paragraph (u)(1)(ii) of this Item. For purposes of the ratio required by this paragraph (u)(1)(iii), the amount in paragraph (u)(1)(i) of this Item shall equal one, or, alternatively, the ratio may be expressed narratively as the multiple that the amount in paragraph (u)(1)(ii) of this Item bears to the amount in paragraph (u)(1)(i) of this Item.

(2)   For purposes of this paragraph (u):

(i)   *Total compensation* for the median of annual total compensation of all employees of the registrant and the PEO of the registrant shall be determined in accordance with paragraph (c)(2)(x) of this Item. In determining the total compensation, all references to "named executive officer" in this Item and the instructions thereto may be deemed to refer instead, as applicable, to "employee" and, for non-salaried employees, references to "base salary" and "salary" in this Item and the instructions thereto may be deemed to refer instead, as applicable, to "wages plus overtime";

(ii)   *Annual total compensation* means total compensation for the registrant's last completed fiscal year; and

(iii)   *Registrant* means the registrant and its consolidated subsidiaries.

(3)   For purposes of this paragraph (u), *employee* or *employee of the registrant* means an individual employed by the registrant or any of its consolidated subsidiaries, whether as a full-time, part-time, seasonal, or temporary worker, as of a date chosen by the registrant within the last three months of the registrant's last completed fiscal year. The definition of employee or employee of the registrant does not include those workers who are employed, and whose compensation is determined, by an unaffiliated third party but who provide services to the registrant or its consolidated subsidiaries as independent contractors or "leased" workers.

(4)   For purposes of this paragraph (u), an employee located in a jurisdiction outside the United States (a "non-U.S. employee") may be exempt from the definition of employee or employee of the registrant under either of the following conditions:

(i)   The employee is employed in a foreign jurisdiction in which the laws or regulations governing data privacy are such that, despite its reasonable efforts to obtain or process the information necessary for compliance with this paragraph (u), the registrant is unable to do so without violating such data privacy laws or regulations. The registrant's reasonable efforts shall include, at a minimum, using or seeking an exemption or other relief under any governing data privacy laws or regulations. If the registrant chooses to exclude any employees using this exemption, it shall list the excluded jurisdictions, identify the specific data privacy law or regulation, explain how complying with this paragraph (u) violates such data privacy law or regulation (including the efforts made by the registrant to use or seek an exemption or other relief under such law or regulation), and provide the approximate number of employees exempted from each jurisdiction based on this exemption. In addition, if a registrant excludes any non-U.S. employees in a particular jurisdiction under this exemption, it must exclude all non-U.S. employees in that jurisdiction. Further, the registrant shall obtain a legal opinion from counsel that opines on the inability of the registrant to obtain or process the information necessary for compliance with this paragraph (u) without violating the jurisdiction's laws or regulations governing data privacy, including the registrant's inability to obtain an exemption or other relief under any governing laws or regulations. The registrant shall file the legal opinion as an exhibit to the filing in which the pay ratio disclosure is included.

(ii)   The registrant's non-U.S. employees account for 5% or less of the registrant's total employees. In that circumstance, if the registrant chooses to exclude any non-U.S. employees under this exemption, it must exclude all non-U.S. employees. Additionally, if a registrant's non-U.S. employees exceed 5% of the registrant's total U.S. and non-U.S. employees, it may exclude up to 5% of its total employees who are non-U.S. employees; *provided, however,* if a registrant excludes any non-U.S. employees in a particular jurisdiction, it must exclude all non-U.S. employees in that jurisdiction. If more than 5% of a registrant's employees are located in any one non-U.S. jurisdiction, the registrant may not exclude any employees in that jurisdiction under this exemption.

(A)   In calculating the number of non-U.S. employees that may be excluded under this Item 402(u)(4)(ii) *("de minimis"* exemption), a registrant shall count against the total any non-U.S. employee exempted under the data privacy law exemption under Item 402(u)(4)(i) ("data privacy" exemption). A registrant may exclude any non-U.S. employee from a jurisdiction that meets the data privacy exemption, even if the number of excluded employees exceeds 5% of the registrant's total employees. If, however, the number of employees excluded under the data privacy exemption equals or exceeds 5% of the registrant's total employees, the registrant may not use the *de minimis* exemption. Additionally, if the number of employees excluded under the data privacy exemption is less than 5% of the registrant's total employees, the registrant may use the *de minimis* exemption to exclude no more than the number of non-U.S. employees that, combined with the data privacy exemption, does not exceed 5% of the registrant's total employees.

(B)   If a registrant excludes non-U.S. employees under the *de minimis* exemption, it must disclose the jurisdiction or jurisdictions from which those employees are being excluded, the approximate number of employees excluded from each jurisdiction under the *de minimis* exemption, the total number of its U.S. and non-U.S. employees irrespective of any exemption (data privacy or *de minimis*), and the total number of its U.S. and non-U.S. employees used for its *de minimis* calculation.

Instruction 1 to Item 402(u)—Disclosing the date chosen for identifying the median employee. A registrant shall disclose the date within the last three months of its last completed fiscal year that it selected pursuant to paragraph (u)(3) of this Item to identify its median employee. If the registrant changes the date it uses to identify the median employee from the prior year, the registrant shall disclose this change and provide a brief explanation about the reason or reasons for the change.

Instruction 2 to Item 402(u)—Identifying the median employee. A registrant is required to identify its median employee only once every three years and calculate total compensation for that employee each year; *provided that,* during a registrant's last completed fiscal year there has been no change in its employee population or employee compensation arrangements that it reasonably believes would result in a significant change to its pay ratio disclosure. If there have been no changes that the registrant reasonably believes would significantly affect its pay ratio disclosure, the registrant shall disclose that it is using the same median employee in its pay ratio calculation and describe briefly the basis for its reasonable belief. For example, the registrant could disclose that there has been no change in its employee population or employee compensation arrangements that it believes would significantly impact the pay ratio disclosure. If there has been a change in the registrant's employee population or employee compensation arrangements that the registrant reasonably believes would result in a significant change in its pay ratio disclosure, the registrant shall re-identify the median employee for that fiscal year. If it is no longer appropriate for the registrant to use the median employee identified in year one as the median employee in years two or three because of a change in the original median employee's circumstances that the registrant reasonably believes would result in a significant change in its pay ratio disclosure, the registrant may use another employee whose compensation is substantially similar to the original median employee based on the compensation measure used to select the original median employee.

Instruction 3 to Item 402(u)—Updating for the last completed fiscal year. Pay ratio information (i.e., the disclosure called for by paragraph (u)(1) of this Item) with respect to the registrant's last completed fiscal year is not required to be disclosed until the filing of its annual report on Form 10-K for that last completed fiscal year or, if later, the filing of a definitive proxy or information statement relating to its next annual meeting of shareholders (or written consents in lieu of such a meeting) following the end of such fiscal year; *provided that,* the required pay ratio information must, in any event, be filed as provided in General Instruction G(3) of Form 10-K (17 CFR 249.310) not later than 120 days after the end of such fiscal year.

Instruction 4 to Item 402(u)—Methodology and use of estimates. 1. Registrants may use reasonable estimates both in the methodology used to identify the median employee and in calculating the annual total compensation or any elements of total compensation for employees other than the PEO.

2. In determining the employees from which the median employee is identified, a registrant may use its employee population or statistical sampling and/or other reasonable methods.

3. A registrant may identify the median employee using annual total compensation or any other compensation measure that is consistently applied to all employees included in the calculation, such as information derived from the registrant's tax and/or payroll records. In using a compensation measure other than annual total compensation to identify the median employee, if that measure is recorded on a basis other than the registrant's fiscal year (such as information derived from tax and/or payroll records), the registrant may use the same annual period that is used to derive those amounts. Where a compensation measure other than annual total compensation is used to identify the median employee, the registrant must disclose the compensation measure used.

4. In identifying the median employee, whether using annual total compensation or any other compensation measure that is consistently applied to all employees included in the calculation, the registrant may make cost-of-living adjustments to the compensation of employees in jurisdictions other than the jurisdiction in which the PEO resides so that the compensation is adjusted to the cost of living in the jurisdiction in which the PEO resides. If the registrant uses a cost-of-living adjustment to identify the median employee, and the median employee identified is an employee in a jurisdiction other than the jurisdiction in which the PEO resides, the registrant must use the same cost-of-living adjustment in calculating the median employee's annual total compensation and disclose the median employee's jurisdiction. The registrant also shall briefly describe the cost-of-living adjustments it used to identify the median employee and briefly describe the cost-of-living adjustments it used to calculate the median employee's annual total compensation, including the measure used as the basis for the

cost-of-living adjustment. A registrant electing to present the pay ratio in this manner also shall disclose the median employee's annual total compensation and pay ratio without the cost-of-living adjustment. To calculate this pay ratio, the registrant will need to identify the median employee without using any cost-of-living adjustments.

5. The registrant shall briefly describe the methodology it used to identify the median employee. It shall also briefly describe any material assumptions, adjustments (including any cost-of-living adjustments), or estimates it used to identify the median employee or to determine total compensation or any elements of total compensation, which shall be consistently applied. The registrant shall clearly identify any estimates used. The required descriptions should be a brief overview; it is not necessary for the registrant to provide technical analyses or formulas. If a registrant changes its methodology or its material assumptions, adjustments, or estimates from those used in its pay ratio disclosure for the prior fiscal year, and if the effects of any such change are significant, the registrant shall briefly describe the change and the reasons for the change. Registrants must also disclose if they changed from using the cost-of-living adjustment to not using that adjustment and if they changed from not using the cost-of-living adjustment to using it.

6. Registrants may, at their discretion, include personal benefits that aggregate less than $10,000 and compensation under non-discriminatory benefit plans in calculating the annual total compensation of the median employee as long as these items are also included in calculating the PEO's annual total compensation. The registrant shall also explain any difference between the PEO's annual total compensation used in the pay ratio disclosure and the total compensation amounts reflected in the Summary Compensation Table, if material.

Instruction 5 to Item 402(u)—Permitted annualizing adjustments. A registrant may annualize the total compensation for all permanent employees (full-time or part-time) that were employed by the registrant for less than the full fiscal year (such as newly hired employees or permanent employees on an unpaid leave of absence during the period). A registrant may not annualize the total compensation for employees in temporary or seasonal positions. A registrant may not make a full-time equivalent adjustment for any employee.

Instruction 6 to Item 402(u)—PEO compensation not available. A registrant that is relying on Instruction 1 to Item 402(c)(2)(iii) and (iv) in connection with the salary or bonus of the PEO for the last completed fiscal year, shall disclose that the pay ratio required by paragraph (u) of this Item is not calculable until the PEO salary or bonus, as applicable, is determined and shall disclose the date that the PEO's actual total compensation is expected to be determined. The disclosure required by paragraph (u) of this Item shall then be disclosed in the filing under Item 5.02(f) of Form 8-K (17 CFR 249.308) that discloses the PEO's salary or bonus in accordance with Instruction 1 to Item 402(c)(2)(iii) and (iv).

Instruction 7 to Item 402(u)—Transition periods for registrants. 1. Upon becoming subject to the requirements of Section 13(a) or 15(d) of the Exchange Act (15 U.S.C. 78m or 78o(d)), a registrant shall comply with paragraph (u) of this Item with respect to compensation for the first fiscal year following the year in which it became subject to such requirements, but not for any fiscal year commencing before January 1, 2017. The registrant may omit the disclosure required by paragraph (u) of this Item from any filing until the filing of its annual report on Form 10-K (17 CFR 249.310) for such fiscal year or, if later, the filing of a proxy or information statement relating to its next annual meeting of shareholders (or written consents in lieu of such a meeting) following the end of such year; *provided that,* such disclosure shall, in any event, be filed as provided in General Instruction G(3) of Form 10-K not later than 120 days after the end of such fiscal year.

2. A registrant may omit any employees that became its employees as the result of the business combination or acquisition of a business for the fiscal year in which the transaction becomes effective, but the registrant must disclose the approximate number of employees it is omitting. Those employees shall be included in the total employee count for the triennial calculations of the median employee in the year following the transaction for purposes of evaluating whether a significant change had

occurred. The registrant shall identify the acquired business excluded for the fiscal year in which the business combination or acquisition becomes effective.

3.   A registrant shall comply with paragraph (u) of this Item with respect to compensation for the first fiscal year commencing on or after the date the registrant ceases to be a smaller reporting company, but not for any fiscal year commencing before January 1, 2017.

Instruction 8 to Item 402(u)—Emerging growth companies. A registrant is not required to comply with paragraph (u) of this Item if it is an emerging growth company as defined in Section 2(a)(19) of the Securities Act (15 U.S.C. 77(b)(a)(19)) or Section 3(a)(80) of the Exchange Act (15 U.S.C. 78c(a)(80)). A registrant shall comply with paragraph (u) of this Item with respect to compensation for the first fiscal year commencing on or after the date the registrant ceases to be an emerging growth company, but not for any fiscal year commencing before January 1, 2017.

Instruction 9 to Item 402(u)—Additional information. Registrants may present additional information, including additional ratios, to supplement the required ratio, but are not required to do so. Any additional information shall be clearly identified, not misleading, and not presented with greater prominence than the required ratio.

Instruction 10 to Item 402(u)—Multiple PEOs during the year. A registrant with more than one non-concurrent PEO serving during its fiscal year may calculate the annual total compensation for its PEO in either of the following manners:

1.   The registrant may calculate the compensation provided to each person who served as PEO during the year for the time he or she served as PEO and combine those figures; or

2.   The registrant may look to the PEO serving in that position on the date it selects to identify the median employee and annualize that PEO's compensation.

Regardless of the alternative selected, the registrant shall disclose which option it chose and how it calculated its PEO's annual total compensation.

Instruction 11 to Item 402(u)—Employees' personally identifiable information. Registrants are not required to, and should not, disclose any personally identifiable information about that employee other than his or her compensation. Registrants may choose to generally identify an employee's position to put the employee's compensation in context, but registrants are not required to provide this information and should not do so if providing the information could identify any specific individual.

INSTRUCTION TO ITEM 402. Specify the applicable fiscal year in the title to each table required under this Item which calls for disclosure as of or for a completed fiscal year.

§ 229.406   (Item 406) Code of Ethics.

(a)   Disclose whether the registrant has adopted a code of ethics that applies to the registrant's principal executive officer, principal financial officer, principal accounting officer or controller, or persons performing similar functions. If the registrant has not adopted such a code of ethics, explain why it has not done so.

(b)   For purposes of this Item 406, the term *code of ethics* means written standards that are reasonably designed to deter wrongdoing and to promote:

(1)   Honest and ethical conduct, including the ethical handling of actual or apparent conflicts of interest between personal and professional relationships;

(2)   Full, fair, accurate, timely, and understandable disclosure in reports and documents that a registrant files with, or submits to, the Commission and in other public communications made by the registrant;

(3)   Compliance with applicable governmental laws, rules and regulations;

(4)   The prompt internal reporting of violations of the code to an appropriate person or persons identified in the code; and

(5)   Accountability for adherence to the code.

(c)   The registrant must:

(1)   File with the Commission a copy of its code of ethics that applies to the registrant's principal executive officer, principal financial officer, principal accounting officer or controller, or persons performing similar functions, as an exhibit to its annual report;

(2)   Post the text of such code of ethics on its Internet website and disclose, in its annual report, its Internet address and the fact that it has posted such code of ethics on its Internet Web site; or

(3)   Undertake in its annual report filed with the Commission to provide to any person without charge, upon request, a copy of such code of ethics and explain the manner in which such request may be made.

(d)   If the registrant intends to satisfy the disclosure requirement under Item 5.05 of Form 8-K regarding an amendment to, or a waiver from, a provision of its code of ethics that applies to the registrant's principal executive officer, principal financial officer, principal accounting officer or controller, or persons performing similar functions and that relates to any element of the code of ethics definition enumerated in paragraph (b) of this Item by posting such information on its internet website, disclose the registrant's internet address and such intention.

Instructions to Item 406. 1. A registrant may have separate codes of ethics for different types of officers. Furthermore, a *code of ethics* within the meaning of paragraph (b) of this Item may be a portion of a broader document that addresses additional topics or that applies to more persons than those specified in paragraph (a). In satisfying the requirements of paragraph (c), a registrant need only file, post or provide the portions of a broader document that constitutes a *code of ethics* as defined in paragraph (b) and that apply to the persons specified in paragraph (a).

2.   If a registrant elects to satisfy paragraph (c) of this Item by posting its code of ethics on its website pursuant to paragraph (c)(2), the code of ethics must remain accessible on its Web site for as long as the registrant remains subject to the requirements of this Item and chooses to comply with this Item by posting its code on its Web site pursuant to paragraph (c)(2).

§ 229.407   (Item 407) Corporate Governance.

(a)   *Director independence.* Identify each director and, when the disclosure called for by this paragraph is being presented in a proxy or information statement relating to the election of directors, each nominee for director, that is independent under the independence standards applicable to the registrant under paragraph (a)(1) of this Item. In addition, if such independence standards contain independence requirements for committees of the board of directors, identify each director that is a member of the compensation, nominating or audit committee that is not independent under such committee independence standards. If the registrant does not have a separately designated audit, nominating or compensation committee or committee performing similar functions, the registrant must provide the disclosure of directors that are not independent with respect to all members of the board of directors applying such committee independence standards.

(1)   In determining whether or not the director or nominee for director is independent for the purposes of paragraph (a) of this Item, the registrant shall use the applicable definition of independence, as follows:

(i)   If the registrant is a listed issuer whose securities are listed on a national securities exchange or in an inter-dealer quotation system which has requirements that a majority of the board of directors be independent, the registrant's definition of independence that it uses for determining if a majority of the board of directors is independent in compliance with the listing standards applicable to the registrant. When determining whether the members of a committee of the board of directors are independent, the registrant's definition of independence that it uses for determining if the members of that specific committee are independent in compliance with the independence standards applicable for the members of the specific committee in the listing standards of the national securities exchange or inter-dealer quotation system that the registrant uses for determining if a majority of the board of directors are independent. If the registrant does not have independence standards for a committee, the independence standards for that specific committee in the listing standards of the national securities exchange or inter-dealer quotation system that the registrant uses for determining if a majority of the board of directors are independent.

(ii)　If the registrant is not a listed issuer, a definition of independence of a national securities exchange or of an inter-dealer quotation system which has requirements that a majority of the board of directors be independent, and state which definition is used. Whatever such definition the registrant chooses, it must use the same definition with respect to all directors and nominees for director. When determining whether the members of a specific committee of the board of directors are independent, if the national securities exchange or national securities association whose standards are used has independence standards for the members of a specific committee, use those committee specific standards.

(iii)　If the information called for by paragraph (a) of this Item is being presented in a registration statement on Form S-1 (§ 239.11 of this chapter) under the Securities Act or on a Form 10 (§ 249.210 of this chapter) under the Exchange Act where the registrant has applied for listing with a national securities exchange or in an inter-dealer quotation system that has requirements that a majority of the board of directors be independent, the definition of independence that the registrant uses for determining if a majority of the board of directors is independent, and the definition of independence that the registrant uses for determining if members of the specific committee of the board of directors are independent, that is in compliance with the independence listing standards of the national securities exchange or inter-dealer quotation system on which it has applied for listing, or if the registrant has not adopted such definitions, the independence standards for determining if the majority of the board of directors is independent and if members of the committee of the board of directors are independent of that national securities exchange or inter-dealer quotation system.

(2)　If the registrant uses its own definitions for determining whether its directors and nominees for director, and members of specific committees of the board of directors, are independent, disclose whether these definitions are available to security holders on the registrant's Web site. If so, provide the registrant's Web site address. If not, include a copy of these policies in an appendix to the registrant's proxy statement or information statement that is provided to security holders at least once every three fiscal years or if the policies have been materially amended since the beginning of the registrant's last fiscal year. If a current copy of the policies is not available to security holders on the registrant's Web site, and is not included as an appendix to the registrant's proxy statement or information statement, identify the most recent fiscal year in which the policies were so included in satisfaction of this requirement.

(3)　For each director and nominee for director that is identified as independent, describe, by specific category or type, any transactions, relationships or arrangements not disclosed pursuant to Item 404(a) (§ 229.404(a)), or for investment companies, Item 22(b) of Schedule 14A (§ 240.14a–101 of this chapter), that were considered by the board of directors under the applicable independence definitions in determining that the director is independent.

Instructions to Item 407(a). 1. If the registrant is a listed issuer whose securities are listed on a national securities exchange or in an inter-dealer quotation system which has requirements that a majority of the board of directors be independent, and also has exemptions to those requirements (for independence of a majority of the board of directors or committee member independence) upon which the registrant relied, disclose the exemption relied upon and explain the basis for the registrant's conclusion that such exemption is applicable. The same disclosure should be provided if the registrant is not a listed issuer and the national securities exchange or inter-dealer quotation system selected by the registrant has exemptions that are applicable to the registrant. Any national securities exchange or inter-dealer quotation system which has requirements that at least 50 percent of the members of a small business issuer's board of directors must be independent shall be considered a national securities exchange or inter-dealer quotation system which has requirements that a majority of the board of directors be independent for the purposes of the disclosure required by paragraph (a) of this Item.

2. Registrants shall provide the disclosure required by paragraph (a) of this Item for any person who served as a director during any part of the last completed fiscal year, except that no information called for by paragraph (a) of this Item need be given in a registration statement filed at a time when the registrant is not subject to the reporting requirements of section 13(a) or 15(d) of the Exchange Act (15 U.S.C. 78m(a) or 78 o (d)) respecting any director who is no longer a director at the time of effectiveness of the registration statement.

3. The description of the specific categories or types of transactions, relationships or arrangements required by paragraph (a)(3) of this Item must be provided in such detail as is necessary to fully describe the nature of the transactions, relationships or arrangements.

(b) *Board meetings and committees; annual meeting attendance.* (1) State the total number of meetings of the board of directors (including regularly scheduled and special meetings) which were held during the last full fiscal year. Name each incumbent director who during the last full fiscal year attended fewer than 75 percent of the aggregate of:

    (i) The total number of meetings of the board of directors (held during the period for which he has been a director); and

    (ii) The total number of meetings held by all committees of the board on which he served (during the periods that he served).

(2) Describe the registrant's policy, if any, with regard to board members' attendance at annual meetings of security holders and state the number of board members who attended the prior year's annual meeting.

Instruction to Item 407(b)(2). In lieu of providing the information required by paragraph (b)(2) of this Item in the proxy statement, the registrant may instead provide the registrant's Web site address where such information appears.

(3) State whether or not the registrant has standing audit, nominating and compensation committees of the board of directors, or committees performing similar functions. If the registrant has such committees, however designated, identify each committee member, state the number of committee meetings held by each such committee during the last fiscal year and describe briefly the functions performed by each such committee. Such disclosure need not be provided to the extent it is duplicative of disclosure provided in accordance with paragraph (c), (d) or (e) of this Item.

(c) *Nominating committee.* (1) If the registrant does not have a standing nominating committee or committee performing similar functions, state the basis for the view of the board of directors that it is appropriate for the registrant not to have such a committee and identify each director who participates in the consideration of director nominees.

(2) Provide the following information regarding the registrant's director nomination process:

    (i) State whether or not the nominating committee has a charter. If the nominating committee has a charter, provide the disclosure required by Instruction 2 to this Item regarding the nominating committee charter;

    (ii) If the nominating committee has a policy with regard to the consideration of any director candidates recommended by security holders, provide a description of the material elements of that policy, which shall include, but need not be limited to, a statement as to whether the committee will consider director candidates recommended by security holders;

(iii) If the nominating committee does not have a policy with regard to the consideration of any director candidates recommended by security holders, state that fact and state the basis for the view of the board of directors that it is appropriate for the registrant not to have such a policy;

(iv) If the nominating committee will consider candidates recommended by security holders, describe the procedures to be followed by security holders in submitting such recommendations;

(v) Describe any specific minimum qualifications that the nominating committee believes must be met by a nominating committee-recommended nominee for a position on the registrant's board of directors, and describe any specific qualities or skills that the nominating committee believes are necessary for one or more of the registrant's directors to possess;

(vi) Describe the nominating committee's process for identifying and evaluating nominees for director, including nominees recommended by security holders, and any differences in the manner in which the nominating committee evaluates nominees for director based on whether the nominee is recommended by a security holder, and whether, and if so how, the nominating committee (or the board) considers diversity in identifying nominees for director. If the nominating committee (or the board) has a policy with regard to the consideration of diversity in identifying director nominees, describe how this policy is implemented, as well as how the nominating committee (or the board) assesses the effectiveness of its policy;

(vii) With regard to each nominee approved by the nominating committee for inclusion on the registrant's proxy card (other than nominees who are executive officers or who are directors standing for re-election), state which one or more of the following categories of persons or entities recommended that nominee: Security holder, non-management director, chief executive officer, other executive officer, third-party search firm, or other specified source. With regard to each such nominee approved by a nominating committee of an investment company, state which one or more of the following additional categories of persons or entities recommended that nominee: Security holder, director, chief executive officer, other executive officer, or employee of the investment company's investment adviser, principal underwriter, or any affiliated person of the investment adviser or principal underwriter;

(viii) If the registrant pays a fee to any third party or parties to identify or evaluate or assist in identifying or evaluating potential nominees, disclose the function performed by each such third party; and

(ix) If the registrant's nominating committee received, by a date not later than the 120th calendar day before the date of the registrant's proxy statement released to security holders in connection with the previous year's annual meeting, a recommended nominee from a security holder that beneficially owned more than 5% of the registrant's voting common stock for at least one year as of the date the recommendation was made, or from a group of security holders that beneficially owned, in the aggregate, more than 5% of the registrant's voting common stock, with each of the securities used to calculate that ownership held for at least one year as of the date the recommendation was made, identify the candidate and the security holder or security holder group that recommended the candidate and disclose whether the nominating committee chose to nominate the candidate, *provided, however,* that no such identification or disclosure is required without the written consent of both the security holder or security holder group and the candidate to be so identified.

Instructions to Item 407(c)(2)(ix). 1. For purposes of paragraph (c)(2)(ix) of this Item, the percentage of securities held by a nominating security holder may be determined using information set forth in the registrant's most recent quarterly or annual report, and any current report subsequent thereto, filed with the Commission pursuant to the Exchange Act (or, in the case of a registrant that is an investment company registered under the Investment Company Act of 1940, the registrant's most recent report on Form N-CSR (§§ 249.331 and 274.128 of this chapter)), unless the party relying on such report knows or has reason to believe that the information contained therein is inaccurate.

2.   For purposes of the registrant's obligation to provide the disclosure specified in paragraph (c)(2)(ix) of this Item, where the date of the annual meeting has been changed by more than 30 days from the date of the previous year's meeting, the obligation under that Item will arise where the registrant receives the security holder recommendation a reasonable time before the registrant begins to print and mail its proxy materials.

3.   For purposes of paragraph (c)(2)(ix) of this Item, the percentage of securities held by a recommending security holder, as well as the holding period of those securities, may be determined by the registrant if the security holder is the registered holder of the securities. If the security holder is not the registered owner of the securities, he or she can submit one of the following to the registrant to evidence the required ownership percentage and holding period:

a.   A written statement from the "record" holder of the securities (usually a broker or bank) verifying that, at the time the security holder made the recommendation, he or she had held the required securities for at least one year; or

b.   If the security holder has filed a Schedule 13D (§ 240.13d–101 of this chapter), Schedule 13G (§ 240.13d–102 of this chapter), Form 3 (§ 249.103 of this chapter), Form 4 (§ 249.104 of this chapter), and/or Form 5 (§ 249.105 of this chapter), or amendments to those documents or updated forms, reflecting ownership of the securities as of or before the date of the recommendation, a copy of the schedule and/or form, and any subsequent amendments reporting a change in ownership level, as well as a written statement that the security holder continuously held the securities for the one-year period as of the date of the recommendation.

4.   For purposes of the registrant's obligation to provide the disclosure specified in paragraph (c)(2)(ix) of this Item, the security holder or group must have provided to the registrant, at the time of the recommendation, the written consent of all parties to be identified and, where the security holder or group members are not registered holders, proof that the security holder or group satisfied the required ownership percentage and holding period as of the date of the recommendation.

Instruction to Item 407(c)(2). For purposes of paragraph (c)(2) of this Item, the term *nominating committee* refers not only to nominating committees and committees performing similar functions, but also to groups of directors fulfilling the role of a nominating committee, including the entire board of directors.

(3)   Describe any material changes to the procedures by which security holders may recommend nominees to the registrant's board of directors, where those changes were implemented after the registrant last provided disclosure in response to the requirements of paragraph (c)(2)(iv) of this Item, or paragraph (c)(3) of this Item.

Instructions to Item 407(c)(3). 1. The disclosure required in paragraph (c)(3) of this Item need only be provided in a registrant's quarterly or annual reports.

2.   For purposes of paragraph (c)(3) of this Item, adoption of procedures by which security holders may recommend nominees to the registrant's board of directors, where the registrant's most recent disclosure in response to the requirements of paragraph (c)(2)(iv) of this Item, or paragraph (c)(3) of this Item, indicated that the registrant did not have in place such procedures, will constitute a material change.

(d) *Audit committee.* (1) State whether or not the audit committee has a charter. If the audit committee has a charter, provide the disclosure required by Instruction 2 to this Item regarding the audit committee charter.

(2) If a listed issuer's board of directors determines, in accordance with the listing standards applicable to the issuer, to appoint a director to the audit committee who is not independent (apart from the requirements in § 240.10A–3 of this chapter), including as a result of exceptional or limited or similar circumstances, disclose the nature of the relationship that makes that individual not independent and the reasons for the board of directors' determination.

(3)(i) The audit committee must state whether:

(A) The audit committee has reviewed and discussed the audited financial statements with management;

(B) The audit committee has discussed with the independent auditors the matters required to be discussed by the applicable requirements of the Public Company Accounting Oversight Board ("PCAOB") and the Commission;

(C) The audit committee has received the written disclosures and the letter from the independent accountant required by applicable requirements of the Public Company Accounting Oversight Board regarding the independent accountant's communications with the audit committee concerning independence, and has discussed with the independent accountant the independent accountant's independence; and

(D) Based on the review and discussions referred to in paragraphs (d)(3)(i)(A) through (d)(3)(i)(C) of this Item, the audit committee recommended to the board of directors that the audited financial statements be included in the company's annual report on Form 10-K (17 CFR 249.310) (or, for closed-end investment companies registered under the Investment Company Act of 1940 (15 U.S.C. 80a–1 *et seq.*), the annual report to shareholders required by section 30(e) of the Investment Company Act of 1940 (15 U.S.C. 80a–29(e)) and Rule 30d–1 (17 CFR 270.30d–1) thereunder) for the last fiscal year for filing with the Commission.

(ii) The name of each member of the company's audit committee (or, in the absence of an audit committee, the board committee performing equivalent functions or the entire board of directors) must appear below the disclosure required by paragraph (d)(3)(i) of this Item.

(4)(i) If the registrant meets the following requirements, provide the disclosure in paragraph (d)(4)(ii) of this Item:

(A) The registrant is a listed issuer, as defined in § 240.10A–3 of this chapter;

(B) The registrant is filing an annual report on Form 10-K (§ 249.310 of this chapter) or a proxy statement or information statement pursuant to the Exchange Act (15 U.S.C. 78a *et seq.*) if action is to be taken with respect to the election of directors; and

(C) The registrant is neither:

(1) A subsidiary of another listed issuer that is relying on the exemption in § 240.10A–3(c)(2) of this chapter; nor

(2) Relying on any of the exemptions in § 240.10A–3(c)(4) through (c)(7) of this chapter.

(ii)(A) State whether or not the registrant has a separately-designated standing audit committee established in accordance with section 3(a)(58)(A) of the Exchange Act (15 U.S.C. 78c(a)(58)(A)), or a committee performing similar functions. If the registrant has such a committee, however designated, identify each committee member. If the entire board of directors is acting as the registrant's audit committee as specified in section 3(a)(58)(B) of the Exchange Act (15 U.S.C. 78c(a)(58)(B)), so state.

(B) If applicable, provide the disclosure required by § 240.10A–3(d) of this chapter regarding an exemption from the listing standards for audit committees.

(5) *Audit committee financial expert.* (i)(A) Disclose that the registrant's board of directors has determined that the registrant either:

(*1*) Has at least one audit committee financial expert serving on its audit committee; or

(*2*) Does not have an audit committee financial expert serving on its audit committee.

(B) If the registrant provides the disclosure required by paragraph (d)(5)(i)(A)(*1*) of this Item, it must disclose the name of the audit committee financial expert and whether that person is independent, as *independence* for audit committee members is defined in the listing standards applicable to the listed issuer.

(C) If the registrant provides the disclosure required by paragraph (d)(5)(i)(A)(*2*) of this Item, it must explain why it does not have an audit committee financial expert.

Instruction to Item 407(d)(5)(i). If the registrant's board of directors has determined that the registrant has more than one audit committee financial expert serving on its audit committee, the registrant may, but is not required to, disclose the names of those additional persons. A registrant choosing to identify such persons must indicate whether they are independent pursuant to paragraph (d)(5)(i)(B) of this Item.

(ii) For purposes of this Item, an *audit committee financial expert* means a person who has the following attributes:

(A) An understanding of generally accepted accounting principles and financial statements;

(B) The ability to assess the general application of such principles in connection with the accounting for estimates, accruals and reserves;

(C) Experience preparing, auditing, analyzing or evaluating financial statements that present a breadth and level of complexity of accounting issues that are generally comparable to the breadth and complexity of issues that can reasonably be expected to be raised by the registrant's financial statements, or experience actively supervising one or more persons engaged in such activities;

(D) An understanding of internal control over financial reporting; and

(E) An understanding of audit committee functions.

(iii) A person shall have acquired such attributes through:

(A) Education and experience as a principal financial officer, principal accounting officer, controller, public accountant or auditor or experience in one or more positions that involve the performance of similar functions;

(B) Experience actively supervising a principal financial officer, principal accounting officer, controller, public accountant, auditor or person performing similar functions;

(C) Experience overseeing or assessing the performance of companies or public accountants with respect to the preparation, auditing or evaluation of financial statements; or

(D) Other relevant experience.

(iv) *Safe harbor.* (A) A person who is determined to be an audit committee financial expert will not be deemed an *expert* for any purpose, including without limitation for purposes of section 11 of the Securities Act (15 U.S.C. 77k), as a result of being designated or identified as an audit committee financial expert pursuant to this Item 407.

(B) The designation or identification of a person as an audit committee financial expert pursuant to this Item 407 does not impose on such person any duties, obligations or liability that are greater than the duties, obligations and liability imposed on such person as a member of the audit committee and board of directors in the absence of such designation or identification.

(C) The designation or identification of a person as an audit committee financial expert pursuant to this Item does not affect the duties, obligations or liability of any other member of the audit committee or board of directors.

Instructions to Item 407(d)(5). 1. The disclosure under paragraph (d)(5) of this Item is required only in a registrant's annual report. The registrant need not provide the disclosure required by paragraph (d)(5) of this Item in a proxy or information statement unless that registrant is electing to incorporate this information by reference from the proxy or information statement into its annual report pursuant to General Instruction G(3) to Form 10-K (17 CFR 249.310).

2. If a person qualifies as an audit committee financial expert by means of having held a position described in paragraph (d)(5)(iii)(D) of this Item, the registrant shall provide a brief listing of that person's relevant experience. Such disclosure may be made by reference to disclosures required under Item 401(e) (§ 229.401(e)).

3. In the case of a foreign private issuer with a two-tier board of directors, for purposes of paragraph (d)(5) of this Item, the term *board of directors* means the supervisory or non-management board. In the case of a foreign private issuer meeting the requirements of § 240.10A–3(c)(3) of this chapter, for purposes of paragraph (d)(5) of this Item, the term *board of directors* means the issuer's board of auditors (or similar body) or statutory auditors, as applicable. Also, in the case of a foreign private issuer, the term *generally accepted accounting principles* in paragraph (d)(5)(ii)(A) of this Item means the body of generally accepted accounting principles used by that issuer in its primary financial statements filed with the Commission.

4. A registrant that is an Asset-Backed Issuer (as defined in § 229.1101) is not required to disclose the information required by paragraph (d)(5) of this Item.

Instructions to Item 407(d). 1. The information required by paragraphs (d)(1)–(3) of this Item shall not be deemed to be "soliciting material," or to be "filed" with the Commission or subject to Regulation 14A or 14C (17 CFR 240.14a–1 through 240.14b–2 or 240.14c–1 through 240.14c–101), other than as provided in this Item, or to the liabilities of section 18 of the Exchange Act (15 U.S.C. 78r), except to the extent that the registrant specifically requests that the information be treated as soliciting material or specifically incorporates it by reference into a document filed under the Securities Act or the Exchange Act. Such information will not be deemed to be incorporated by reference into any filing under the Securities Act or the Exchange Act, except to the extent that the registrant specifically incorporates it by reference.

2. The disclosure required by paragraphs (d)(1)–(3) of this Item need only be provided one time during any fiscal year.

3. The disclosure required by paragraph (d)(3) of this Item need not be provided in any filings other than a registrant's proxy or information statement relating to an annual meeting of security holders at which directors are to be elected (or special meeting or written consents in lieu of such meeting).

(e) *Compensation committee.* (1) If the registrant does not have a standing compensation committee or committee performing similar functions, state the basis for the view of the board of directors that it is appropriate for the registrant not to have such a committee and identify each director who participates in the consideration of executive officer and director compensation.

(2)   State whether or not the compensation committee has a charter. If the compensation committee has a charter, provide the disclosure required by Instruction 2 to this Item regarding the compensation committee charter.

(3)   Provide a narrative description of the registrant's processes and procedures for the consideration and determination of executive and director compensation, including:

(i)(A)   The scope of authority of the compensation committee (or persons performing the equivalent functions); and

(B)   The extent to which the compensation committee (or persons performing the equivalent functions) may delegate any authority described in paragraph (e)(3)(i)(A) of this Item to other persons, specifying what authority may be so delegated and to whom;

(ii)   Any role of executive officers in determining or recommending the amount or form of executive and director compensation; and

(iii) Any role of compensation consultants in determining or recommending the amount or form of executive and director compensation (other than any role *limited* to consulting on any broad-based plan that does not discriminate in scope, terms, or operation, in favor of executive officers or directors of the registrant, and that is available generally to all salaried employees; or providing information that either is not customized for a particular registrant or that is customized based on parameters that are not developed by the compensation consultant, and about which the compensation consultant does not provide advice) during the registrant's last completed fiscal year, identifying such consultants, stating whether such consultants were engaged directly by the compensation committee (or persons performing the equivalent functions) or any other person, describing the nature and scope of their assignment, and the material elements of the instructions or directions given to the consultants with respect to the performance of their duties under the engagement:

(A)   If such compensation consultant was engaged by the compensation committee (or persons performing the equivalent functions) to provide advice or recommendations on the amount or form of executive and director compensation (other than any role *limited* to consulting on any broad-based plan that does not discriminate in scope, terms, or operation, in favor of executive officers or directors of the registrant, and that is available generally to all salaried employees; or providing information that either is not customized for a particular registrant or that is customized based on parameters that are not developed by the compensation consultant, and about which the compensation consultant does not provide advice) and the compensation consultant or its affiliates also provided additional services to the registrant or its affiliates in an amount in excess of $120,000 during the registrant's last completed fiscal year, then disclose the aggregate fees for determining or recommending the amount or form of executive and director compensation and the aggregate fees for such additional services. Disclose whether the decision to engage the compensation consultant or its affiliates for these other services was made, or recommended, by management, and whether the compensation committee or the board approved such other services of the compensation consultant or its affiliates.

(B) If the compensation committee (or persons performing the equivalent functions) has not engaged a compensation consultant, but management has engaged a compensation consultant to provide advice or recommendations on the amount or form of executive and director compensation (other than any role *limited* to consulting on any broad-based plan that does not discriminate in scope, terms, or operation, in favor of executive officers or directors of the registrant, and that is available generally to all salaried employees; or providing information that either is not customized for a particular registrant or that is customized based on parameters that are not developed by the compensation consultant, and about which the compensation consultant does not provide advice) and such compensation consultant or its affiliates has provided additional services to the registrant in an amount in excess of $120,000 during the registrant's last completed fiscal year, then disclose the aggregate fees for determining or recommending the amount or form of executive and director compensation and the aggregate fees for any additional services provided by the compensation consultant or its affiliates.

(iv) With regard to any compensation consultant identified in response to Item 407(e)(3)(iii) whose work has raised any conflict of interest, disclose the nature of the conflict and how the conflict is being addressed.

Instruction to Item 407(e)(3)(iv). For purposes of this paragraph (e)(3)(iv), the factors listed in § 240.10C–1(b)(4)(i) through (vi) of this chapter are among the factors that should be considered in determining whether a conflict of interest exists.

(4)　Under the caption "Compensation Committee Interlocks and Insider Participation":

(i)　Identify each person who served as a member of the compensation committee of the registrant's board of directors (or board committee performing equivalent functions) during the last completed fiscal year, indicating each committee member who:

(A)　Was, during the fiscal year, an officer or employee of the registrant;

(B)　Was formerly an officer of the registrant; or

(C)　Had any relationship requiring disclosure by the registrant under any paragraph of Item 404 (§ 229.404). In this event, the disclosure required by Item 404 (§ 229.404) shall accompany such identification.

(ii)　If the registrant has no compensation committee (or other board committee performing equivalent functions), the registrant shall identify each officer and employee of the registrant, and any former officer of the registrant, who, during the last completed fiscal year, participated in deliberations of the registrant's board of directors concerning executive officer compensation.

(iii)　Describe any of the following relationships that existed during the last completed fiscal year:

(A)　An executive officer of the registrant served as a member of the compensation committee (or other board committee performing equivalent functions or, in the absence of any such committee, the entire board of directors) of another entity, one of whose executive officers served on the compensation committee (or other board committee performing equivalent functions or, in the absence of any such committee, the entire board of directors) of the registrant;

(B)　An executive officer of the registrant served as a director of another entity, one of whose executive officers served on the compensation committee (or other board committee performing equivalent functions or, in the absence of any such committee, the entire board of directors) of the registrant; and

(C)　An executive officer of the registrant served as a member of the compensation committee (or other board committee performing equivalent functions or, in the absence of any such committee, the entire board of directors) of another entity, one of whose executive officers served as a director of the registrant.

(iv) Disclosure required under paragraph (e)(4)(iii) of this Item regarding a compensation committee member or other director of the registrant who also served as an executive officer of another entity shall be accompanied by the disclosure called for by Item 404 with respect to that person.

Instruction to Item 407(e)(4). For purposes of paragraph (e)(4) of this Item, the term *entity* shall not include an entity exempt from tax under section 501(c)(3) of the Internal Revenue Code (26 U.S.C. 501(c)(3)).

(5)   Under the caption "Compensation Committee Report:"

(i)   The compensation committee (or other board committee performing equivalent functions or, in the absence of any such committee, the entire board of directors) must state whether:

(A)   The compensation committee has reviewed and discussed the Compensation Discussion and Analysis required by Item 402(b) (§ 229.402(b)) with management; and

(B)   Based on the review and discussions referred to in paragraph (e)(5)(i)(A) of this Item, the compensation committee recommended to the board of directors that the Compensation Discussion and Analysis be included in the registrant's annual report on Form 10-K (§ 249.310 of this chapter), proxy statement on Schedule 14A (§ 240.14a–101 of this chapter) or information statement on Schedule 14C (§ 240.14c–101 of this chapter).

(ii)   The name of each member of the registrant's compensation committee (or other board committee performing equivalent functions or, in the absence of any such committee, the entire board of directors) must appear below the disclosure required by paragraph (e)(5)(i) of this Item.

Instructions to Item 407(e)(5). 1. The information required by paragraph (e)(5) of this Item shall not be deemed to be "soliciting material," or to be "filed" with the Commission or subject to Regulation 14A or 14C (17 CFR 240.14a–1 through 240.14b–2 or 240.14c–1 through 240.14c–101), other than as provided in this Item, or to the liabilities of section 18 of the Exchange Act (15 U.S.C. 78r), except to the extent that the registrant specifically requests that the information be treated as soliciting material or specifically incorporates it by reference into a document filed under the Securities Act or the Exchange Act.

2.   The disclosure required by paragraph (e)(5) of this Item need not be provided in any filings other than an annual report on Form 10-K (§ 249.310 of this chapter), a proxy statement on Schedule 14A (§ 240.14a–101 of this chapter) or an information statement on Schedule 14C (§ 240.14c–101 of this chapter). Such information will not be deemed to be incorporated by reference into any filing under the Securities Act or the Exchange Act, except to the extent that the registrant specifically incorporates it by reference. If the registrant elects to incorporate this information by reference from the proxy or information statement into its annual report on Form 10-K pursuant to General Instruction G(3) to Form 10-K, the disclosure required by paragraph (e)(5) of this Item will be deemed furnished in the annual report on Form 10-K and will not be deemed incorporated by reference into any filing under the Securities Act or the Exchange Act as a result as a result of furnishing the disclosure in this manner.

3.   The disclosure required by paragraph (e)(5) of this Item need only be provided one time during any fiscal year.

(f)   *Shareholder communications.* (1) State whether or not the registrant's board of directors provides a process for security holders to send communications to the board of directors and, if the registrant does not have such a process for security holders to send communications to the board of directors, state the basis for the view of the board of directors that it is appropriate for the registrant not to have such a process.

(2)   If the registrant has a process for security holders to send communications to the board of directors:

(i)   Describe the manner in which security holders can send communications to the board and, if applicable, to specified individual directors; and

(ii) If all security holder communications are not sent directly to board members, describe the registrant's process for determining which communications will be relayed to board members.

Instructions to Item 407(f). 1. In lieu of providing the information required by paragraph (f)(2) of this Item in the proxy statement, the registrant may instead provide the registrant's Web site address where such information appears.

2. For purposes of the disclosure required by paragraph (f)(2)(ii) of this Item, a registrant's process for collecting and organizing security holder communications, as well as similar or related activities, need not be disclosed provided that the registrant's process is approved by a majority of the independent directors or, in the case of a registrant that is an investment company, a majority of the directors who are not "interested persons" of the investment company as defined in section 2(a)(19) of the Investment Company Act of 1940 (15 U.S.C. 80a–2(a)(19)).

3. For purposes of this paragraph, communications from an officer or director of the registrant will not be viewed as "security holder communications." Communications from an employee or agent of the registrant will be viewed as "security holder communications" for purposes of this paragraph only if those communications are made solely in such employee's or agent's capacity as a security holder.

4. For purposes of this paragraph, security holder proposals submitted pursuant to § 240.14a–8 of this chapter, and communications made in connection with such proposals, will not be viewed as "security holder communications."

(g) *Smaller reporting companies and emerging growth companies.*

(1) A registrant that qualifies as a "smaller reporting company," as defined by § 229.10(f)(1), is not required to provide:

(i) The disclosure required in paragraph (d)(5) of this Item in its first annual report filed pursuant to Section 13(a) or 15(d) of the Exchange Act (15 U.S.C. 78m(a) or 78o(d)) following the effective date of its first registration statement filed under the Securities Act (15 U.S.C. 77a et seq.) or Exchange Act (15 U.S.C. 78a et seq.); and

(ii) The disclosure required by paragraphs (e)(4) and (e)(5) of this Item.

(2) A registrant that qualifies as an "emerging growth company," as defined in Rule 405 of the Securities Act (§ 230.405 of this chapter) or Rule 12b–2 of the Exchange Act (§ 240.12b–2 of this chapter), is not required to provide the disclosure required by paragraph (e)(5) of this Item.

(h) *Board leadership structure and role in risk oversight.* Briefly describe the leadership structure of the registrant's board, such as whether the same person serves as both principal executive officer and chairman of the board, or whether two individuals serve in those positions, and, in the case of a registrant that is an investment company, whether the chairman of the board is an "interested person" of the registrant as defined in section 2(a)(19) of the Investment Company Act (15 U.S.C. 80a–2(a)(19)). If one person serves as both principal executive officer and chairman of the board, or if the chairman of the board of a registrant that is an investment company is an "interested person" of the registrant, disclose whether the registrant has a lead independent director and what specific role the lead independent director plays in the leadership of the board. This disclosure should indicate why the registrant has determined that its leadership structure is appropriate given the specific characteristics or circumstances of the registrant. In addition, disclose the extent of the board's role in the risk oversight of the registrant, such as how the board administers its oversight function, and the effect that this has on the board's leadership structure.

(i) *Employee, officer and director hedging.* In proxy or information statements with respect to the election of directors:

(1) Describe any practices or policies that the registrant has adopted regarding the ability of employees (including officers) or directors of the registrant, or any of their designees, to

purchase financial instruments (including prepaid variable forward contracts, equity swaps, collars, and exchange funds), or otherwise engage in transactions, that hedge or offset, or are designed to hedge or offset, any decrease in the market value of registrant equity securities—

(i)   Granted to the employee or director by the registrant as part of the compensation of the employee or director; or

(ii)   Held, directly or indirectly, by the employee or director.

(2)   A description provided pursuant to paragraph (1) shall provide a fair and accurate summary of the practices or policies that apply, including the categories of persons covered, or disclose the practices or policies in full.

(3)   A description provided pursuant to paragraph (1) shall also describe any categories of hedging transactions that are specifically permitted and any categories of such transactions specifically disallowed.

(4)   If the registrant does not have any such practices or policies regarding hedging, the registrant shall disclose that fact or state that the transactions described in paragraph (1) above are generally permitted.

Instructions to Item 407(i).

1.   For purposes of this Item 407(i), "registrant equity securities" means those equity securities as defined in section 3(a)(11) of the Exchange Act (15 U.S.C. 78c(a)(11)) and § 240.3a11–1 of this chapter) that are issued by the registrant or by any parent or subsidiary of the registrant or any subsidiary of any parent of the registrant.

2.   The information required by this Item 407(i) will not be deemed to be incorporated by reference into any filing under the Securities Act or the Exchange Act, except to the extent that the registrant specifically incorporates it by reference.

Instructions to Item 407. 1. For purposes of this Item:

a.   *Listed issuer* means a listed issuer as defined in § 240.10A–3 of this chapter;

b.   *National securities exchange* means a national securities exchange registered pursuant to section 6(a) of the Exchange Act (15 U.S.C. 78f(a));

c.   *Inter-dealer quotation system* means an automated inter-dealer quotation system of a national securities association registered pursuant to section 15A(a) of the Exchange Act (15 U.S.C. 78o–3(a)); and

d.   *National securities association* means a national securities association registered pursuant to section 15A(a) of the Exchange Act (15 U.S.C. 78o–3(a)) that has been approved by the Commission (as that definition may be modified or supplemented).

2.   With respect to paragraphs (c)(2)(i), (d)(1) and (e)(2) of this Item, disclose whether a current copy of the applicable committee charter is available to security holders on the registrant's Web site, and if so, provide the registrant's Web site address. If a current copy of the charter is not available to security holders on the registrant's Web site, include a copy of the charter in an appendix to the registrant's proxy or information statement that is provided to security holders at least once every three fiscal years, or if the charter has been materially amended since the beginning of the registrant's last fiscal year. If a current copy of the charter is not available to security holders on the registrant's Web site, and is not included as an appendix to the registrant's proxy or information statement, identify in which of the prior fiscal years the charter was so included in satisfaction of this requirement.

§ 229.504   (Item 504) Use of Proceeds.

State the principal purposes for which the net proceeds to the registrant from the securities to be offered are intended to be used and the approximate amount intended to be used for each such purpose.

Where registrant has no current specific plan for the proceeds, or a significant portion thereof, the registrant shall so state and discuss the principal reasons for the offering.

Instructions to Item 504:

1.   Where less than all the securities to be offered may be sold and more than one use is listed for the proceeds, indicate the order of priority of such purposes and discuss the registrant's plans if substantially less than the maximum proceeds are obtained. Such discussion need not be included if underwriting arrangements with respect to such securities are such that, if any securities are sold to the public, it reasonably can be expected that the actual proceeds will not be substantially less than the aggregate proceeds to the registrant shown pursuant to Item 501 of Regulation S–K (§ 229.501).

2.   Details of proposed expenditures need not be given; for example, there need be furnished only a brief outline of any program of construction or addition of equipment. Consideration should be given as to the need to include a discussion of certain matters addressed in the discussion and analysis of registrant's financial condition and results of operations, such as liquidity and capital expenditures.

3.   If any material amounts of other funds are necessary to accomplish the specified purposes for which the proceeds are to be obtained, state the amounts of such other funds needed for each such specified purpose and the sources thereof.

4.   If any material part of the proceeds is to be used to discharge indebtedness, set forth the interest rate and maturity of such indebtedness. If the indebtedness to be discharged was incurred within one year, describe the use of the proceeds of such indebtedness other than short-term borrowings used for working capital.

5.   If any material amount of the proceeds is to be used to acquire assets, otherwise than in the ordinary course of business, describe briefly and state the cost of the assets and, where such assets are to be acquired from affiliates of the registrant or their associates, give the names of the persons from whom they are to be acquired and set forth the principle followed in determining the cost to the registrant.

6.   Where the registrant indicates that the proceeds may, or will, be used to finance acquisitions of other businesses, the identity of such businesses, if known, or, if not known, the nature of the businesses to be sought, the status of any negotiations with respect to the acquisition, and a brief description of such business shall be included. Where, however, pro forma financial statements reflecting such acquisition are not required by Regulation S–X (17 CFR 210.01 through 210.12–29), including Rule 8–05 for smaller reporting companies, to be included in the registration statement, the possible terms of any transaction, the identification of the parties thereto or the nature of the business sought need not be disclosed, to the extent that the registrant reasonably determines that public disclosure of such information would jeopardize the acquisition. Where Regulation S–X, including Rule 8–04 for smaller reporting companies, as applicable, would require financial statements of the business to be acquired to be included, the description of the business to be acquired shall be more detailed.

7.   The registrant may reserve the right to change the use of proceeds, provided that such reservation is due to certain contingencies that are discussed specifically and the alternatives to such use in that event are indicated.

H. REGULATION FD

(Selected)

17 C.F.R. §§ 243.100 *et seq.*

Table of Contents[*]

---

§ 243.100   General Rule Regarding Selective Disclosure.

(a) Whenever an issuer, or any person acting on its behalf, discloses any material nonpublic information regarding that issuer or its securities to any person described in paragraph (b)(1) of this section, the issuer shall make public disclosure of that information as provided in § 243.101(e):

(1) Simultaneously, in the case of an intentional disclosure; and

(2) Promptly, in the case of a non-intentional disclosure.

(b)(1) Except as provided in paragraph (b)(2) of this section, paragraph (a) of this section shall apply to a disclosure made to any person outside the issuer:

(i) Who is a broker or dealer, or a person associated with a broker or dealer, as those terms are defined in Section 3(a) of the Securities Exchange Act of 1934 (15 U.S.C. 78c(a));

(ii) Who is an investment adviser, as that term is defined in Section 202(a)(11) of the Investment Advisers Act of 1940 (15 U.S.C. 80b–2(a)(11)); an institutional investment manager, as that term is defined in Section 13(f)(6) of the Securities Exchange Act of 1934 (15 U.S.C. 78m(f)(6)), that filed a report on Form 13F (17 CFR 249.325) with the Commission for the most recent quarter ended prior to the date of the disclosure; or a person associated with either of the foregoing. For purposes of this paragraph, a "person associated with an investment adviser or institutional investment manager" has the meaning set forth in Section 202(a)(17) of the Investment Advisers Act of 1940 (15 U.S.C. 80b–2(a)(17)), assuming for these purposes that an institutional investment manager is an investment adviser;

(iii) Who is an investment company, as defined in Section 3 of the Investment Company Act of 1940 (15 U.S.C. 80a–3), or who would be an investment company but for Section 3(c)(1) (15 U.S.C. 80a–3(c)(1)) or Section 3(c)(7) (15 U.S.C. 80a–3(c)(7)) thereof, or an affiliated person of either of the foregoing. For purposes of this paragraph, "affiliated person" means only those persons described in Section 2(a)(3)(C), (D), (E), and (F) of the Investment Company Act of 1940 (15 U.S.C. 80a–2(a)(3)(C), (D), (E), and (F)), assuming for these purposes that a person who would be an investment company but for Section 3(c)(1) (15 U.S.C. 80a–3(c)(1)) or Section 3(c)(7) (15 U.S.C. 80a–3(c)(7)) of the Investment Company Act of 1940 is an investment company; or

---

[*] Although this table of contents lists rule numbers, the rules themselves are printed with their CFR sections (§ 243.[rule number]). For example, Rule 100 is § 243.100.

(iv) Who is a holder of the issuer's securities, under circumstances in which it is reasonably foreseeable that the person will purchase or sell the issuer's securities on the basis of the information.

(2) Paragraph (a) of this section shall not apply to a disclosure made:

(i) To a person who owes a duty of trust or confidence to the issuer (such as an attorney, investment banker, or accountant);

(ii) To a person who expressly agrees to maintain the disclosed information in confidence;

(iii) In connection with a securities offering registered under the Securities Act, other than an offering of the type described in any of Rule 415(a)(1)(i) through (vi) under the Securities Act (§ 230.415(a)(1)(i) through (vi) of this chapter) (except an offering of the type described in Rule 415(a)(1)(i) under the Securities Act (§ 230.415(a)(1)(i) of this chapter) also involving a registered offering, whether or not underwritten, for capital formation purposes for the account of the issuer (unless the issuer's offering is being registered for the purpose of evading the requirements of this section)), if the disclosure is by any of the following means:

(A) A registration statement filed under the Securities Act, including a prospectus contained therein;

(B) A free writing prospectus used after filing of the registration statement for the offering or a communication falling within the exception to the definition of prospectus contained in clause (a) of section 2(a)(10) of the Securities Act;

(C) Any other Section 10(b) prospectus;

(D) A notice permitted by Rule 135 under the Securities Act (§ 230.135 of this chapter);

(E) A communication permitted by Rule 134 under the Securities Act (§ 230.134 of this chapter); or

(F) An oral communication made in connection with the registered securities offering after filing of the registration statement for the offering under the Securities Act.

§ 243.101   Definitions.

This section defines certain terms as used in Regulation FD (§§ 243.100–243.103).

(a) *Intentional.* A selective disclosure of material nonpublic information is "intentional" when the person making the disclosure either knows, or is reckless in not knowing, that the information he or she is communicating is both material and nonpublic.

(b) *Issuer.* An "issuer" subject to this regulation is one that has a class of securities registered under Section 12 of the Securities Exchange Act of 1934 (15 U.S.C. 78l), or is required to file reports under Section 15(d) of the Securities Exchange Act of 1934 (15 U.S.C. 78o(d)), including any closed-end investment company (as defined in Section 5(a)(2) of the Investment Company Act of 1940) (15 U.S.C. 80a–5(a)(2)), but not including any other investment company or any foreign government or foreign private issuer, as those terms are defined in Rule 405 under the Securities Act (§ 230.405 of this chapter).

(c) *Person acting on behalf of an issuer.* "Person acting on behalf of an issuer" means any senior official of the issuer (or, in the case of a closed-end investment company, a senior official of the issuer's investment adviser), or any other officer, employee, or agent of an issuer who regularly communicates with any person described in § 243.100(b)(1)(i), (ii), or (iii), or with holders of the issuer's securities. An officer, director, employee, or agent of an issuer who discloses material nonpublic information in breach of a duty of trust or confidence to the issuer shall not be considered to be acting on behalf of the issuer.

(d) *Promptly.* "Promptly" means as soon as reasonably practicable (but in no event after the later of 24 hours or the commencement of the next day's trading on the New York Stock Exchange) after a senior official of the issuer (or, in the case of a closed-end investment company, a senior official of the issuer's investment adviser) learns that there has been a non-intentional disclosure by the issuer or person acting on behalf of the issuer of information that the senior official knows, or is reckless in not knowing, is both material and nonpublic.

(e) *Public disclosure.* (1) Except as provided in paragraph (e)(2) of this section, an issuer shall make the "public disclosure" of information required by § 243.100(a) by furnishing to or filing with the Commission a Form 8-K (17 CFR 249.308) disclosing that information.

(2) An issuer shall be exempt from the requirement to furnish or file a Form 8-K if it instead disseminates the information through another method (or combination of methods) of disclosure that is reasonably designed to provide broad, non-exclusionary distribution of the information to the public.

(f) *Senior official.* "Senior official" means any director, executive officer (as defined in § 240.3b–7 of this chapter), investor relations or public relations officer, or other person with similar functions.

(g) *Securities offering.* For purposes of § 243.100(b)(2)(iv):

(1) *Underwritten offerings.* A securities offering that is underwritten commences when the issuer reaches an understanding with the broker-dealer that is to act as managing underwriter and continues until the later of the end of the period during which a dealer must deliver a prospectus or the sale of the securities (unless the offering is sooner terminated);

(2) *Non-underwritten offerings.* A securities offering that is not underwritten:

(i) If covered by Rule 415(a)(1)(x) (§ 230.415(a)(1)(x) of this chapter), commences when the issuer makes its first bona fide offer in a takedown of securities and continues until the later of the end of the period during which each dealer must deliver a prospectus or the sale of the securities in that takedown (unless the takedown is sooner terminated);

(ii) If a business combination as defined in Rule 165(f)(1) (§ 230.165(f)(1) of this chapter), commences when the first public announcement of the transaction is made and continues until the completion of the vote or the expiration of the tender offer, as applicable (unless the transaction is sooner terminated);

(iii) If an offering other than those specified in paragraphs (a) and (b) of this section, commences when the issuer files a registration statement and continues until the later of the end of the period during which each dealer must deliver a prospectus or the sale of the securities (unless the offering is sooner terminated).

§ 243.102   No Effect on Antifraud Liability.

No failure to make a public disclosure required solely by § 243.100 shall be deemed to be a violation of Rule 10b–5 (17 CFR 240.10b–5) under the Securities Exchange Act.

§ 243.103   No Effect on Exchange Act Reporting Status.

A failure to make a public disclosure required solely by § 243.100 shall not affect whether:

(a) For purposes of Forms S-2 (17 CFR 239.12), S-3 (17 CFR 239.13), S-8 (17 CFR 239.16b) and SF-3 (17 CFR 239.45) under the Securities Act, an issuer is deemed to have filed all the material required to be filed pursuant to Section 13 or 15(d) of the Securities Exchange Act of 1934 (15 U.S.C. 78m or 78o(d)) or, where applicable, has made those filings in a timely manner; or

(b)   There is adequate current public information about the issuer for purposes of § 230.144(c) of this chapter (Rule 144(c)).

I. REGULATION M-A

17 C.F.R. §§ 229.1000 *et seq.*

Table of Contents*

---

§ 229.1000   (Item 1000) Definitions.

The following definitions apply to the terms used in Regulation M–A (§§ 229.1000 through 229.1016), unless specified otherwise:

(a) *Associate* has the same meaning as in § 240.12b–2 of this chapter;

(b) *Instruction C* means General Instruction C to Schedule 13E–3 (§ 240.13e–100 of this chapter) and General Instruction C to Schedule TO (§ 240.14d–100 of this chapter);

(c) *Issuer tender offer* has the same meaning as in § 240.13e–4(a)(2) of this chapter;

(d) *Offeror* means any person who makes a tender offer or on whose behalf a tender offer is made;

(e) *Rule 13e–3 transaction* has the same meaning as in § 240.13e–3(a)(3) of this chapter;

(f) *Subject company* means the company or entity whose securities are sought to be acquired in the transaction (*e.g.*, the target), or that is otherwise the subject of the transaction;

(g) *Subject securities* means the securities or class of securities that are sought to be acquired in the transaction or that are otherwise the subject of the transaction; and

(h) *Third-party tender offer* means a tender offer that is not an issuer tender offer.

---

* Although this table of contents lists item numbers, the items themselves are printed with their CFR sections (§ 229.[item number]). For example, Item 1000 is § 229.1000.

§ 229.1001　　　(Item 1001) Summary Term Sheet.

Summary term sheet. Provide security holders with a summary term sheet that is written in plain English. The summary term sheet must briefly describe in bullet point format the most material terms of the proposed transaction. The summary term sheet must provide security holders with sufficient information to understand the essential features and significance of the proposed transaction. The bullet points must cross-reference a more detailed discussion contained in the disclosure document that is disseminated to security holders.

Instructions to Item 1001: 1. The summary term sheet must not recite all information contained in the disclosure document that will be provided to security holders. The summary term sheet is intended to serve as an overview of all material matters that are presented in the accompanying documents provided to security holders.

2.　　The summary term sheet must begin on the first or second page of the disclosure document provided to security holders.

3.　　Refer to Rule 421(b) and (d) of Regulation C of the Securities Act (§ 230.421 of this chapter) for a description of plain English disclosure.

§ 229.1002　　　(Item 1002) Subject Company Information.

(a)　*Name and address.* State the name of the subject company (or the issuer in the case of an issuer tender offer), and the address and telephone number of its principal executive offices.

(b)　*Securities.* State the exact title and number of shares outstanding of the subject class of equity securities as of the most recent practicable date. This may be based upon information in the most recently available filing with the Commission by the subject company unless the filing person has more current information.

(c)　*Trading market and price.* Identify the principal market in which the subject securities are traded and state the high and low sales prices for the subject securities in the principal market (or, if there is no principal market, the range of high and low bid quotations and the source of the quotations) for each quarter during the past two years. If there is no established trading market for the securities (except for limited or sporadic quotations), so state.

(d)　*Dividends.* State the frequency and amount of any dividends paid during the past two years with respect to the subject securities. Briefly describe any restriction on the subject company's current or future ability to pay dividends. If the filing person is not the subject company, furnish this information to the extent known after making reasonable inquiry.

(e)　*Prior public offerings.* If the filing person has made an underwritten public offering of the subject securities for cash during the past three years that was registered under the Securities Act of 1933 or exempt from registration under Regulation A (§ 230.251 through § 230.263 of this chapter), state the date of the offering, the amount of securities offered, the offering price per share (adjusted for stock splits, stock dividends, etc. as appropriate) and the aggregate proceeds received by the filing person.

(f)　*Prior stock purchases.* If the filing person purchased any subject securities during the past two years, state the amount of the securities purchased, the range of prices paid and the average purchase price for each quarter during that period. Affiliates need not give information for purchases made before becoming an affiliate.

§ 229.1003　　　(Item 1003) Identity and Background of Filing Person.

(a)　*Name and address.* State the name, business address and business telephone number of each filing person. Also state the name and address of each person specified in Instruction C to the schedule (except for Schedule 14D–9 (§ 240.14d–101 of this chapter)). If the filing person is an affiliate of the subject company, state the nature of the affiliation. If the filing person is the subject company, so state.

(b) *Business and background of entities.* If any filing person (other than the subject company) or any person specified in Instruction C to the schedule is not a natural person, state the person's principal business, state or other place of organization, and the information required by paragraphs (c)(3) and (c)(4) of this section for each person.

(c) *Business and background of natural persons.* If any filing person or any person specified in Instruction C to the schedule is a natural person, provide the following information for each person:

(1) Current principal occupation or employment and the name, principal business and address of any corporation or other organization in which the employment or occupation is conducted;

(2) Material occupations, positions, offices or employment during the past five years, giving the starting and ending dates of each and the name, principal business and address of any corporation or other organization in which the occupation, position, office or employment was carried on;

(3) A statement whether or not the person was convicted in a criminal proceeding during the past five years (excluding traffic violations or similar misdemeanors). If the person was convicted, describe the criminal proceeding, including the dates, nature of conviction, name and location of court, and penalty imposed or other disposition of the case;

(4) A statement whether or not the person was a party to any judicial or administrative proceeding during the past five years (except for matters that were dismissed without sanction or settlement) that resulted in a judgment, decree or final order enjoining the person from future violations of, or prohibiting activities subject to, federal or state securities laws, or a finding of any violation of federal or state securities laws. Describe the proceeding, including a summary of the terms of the judgment, decree or final order; and

(5) Country of citizenship.

(d) *Tender offer.* Identify the tender offer and the class of securities to which the offer relates, the name of the offeror and its address (which may be based on the offeror's Schedule TO (§ 240.14d–100 of this chapter) filed with the Commission).

Instruction to Item 1003. If the filing person is making information relating to the transaction available on the Internet, state the address where the information can be found.

§ 229.1004 (Item 1004) Terms of the Transaction.

(a) *Material terms.* State the material terms of the transaction.

(1) *Tender offers.* In the case of a tender offer, the information must include:

(i) The total number and class of securities sought in the offer;

(ii) The type and amount of consideration offered to security holders;

(iii) The scheduled expiration date;

(iv) Whether a subsequent offering period will be available, if the transaction is a third-party tender offer;

(v) Whether the offer may be extended, and if so, how it could be extended;

(vi) The dates before and after which security holders may withdraw securities tendered in the offer;

(vii) The procedures for tendering and withdrawing securities;

(viii) The manner in which securities will be accepted for payment;

(ix) If the offer is for less than all securities of a class, the periods for accepting securities on a pro rata basis and the offeror's present intentions in the event that the offer is oversubscribed;

(x) An explanation of any material differences in the rights of security holders as a result of the transaction, if material;

(xi) A brief statement as to the accounting treatment of the transaction, if material; and

(xii) The federal income tax consequences of the transaction, if material.

(2) *Mergers or similar transactions.* In the case of a merger or similar transaction, the information must include:

(i) A brief description of the transaction;

(ii) The consideration offered to security holders;

(iii) The reasons for engaging in the transaction;

(iv) The vote required for approval of the transaction;

(v) An explanation of any material differences in the rights of security holders as a result of the transaction, if material;

(vi) A brief statement as to the accounting treatment of the transaction, if material; and

(vii) The federal income tax consequences of the transaction, if material.

Instruction to Item 1004(a): If the consideration offered includes securities exempt from registration under the Securities Act of 1933, provide a description of the securities that complies with Item 202 of Regulation S–K (§ 229.202). This description is not required if the issuer of the securities meets the requirements of General Instructions I.A, I.B.1 or I.B.2, as applicable, or I.C. of Form S-3 (§ 239.13 of this chapter) and elects to furnish information by incorporation by reference; only capital stock is to be issued; and securities of the same class are registered under section 12 of the Exchange Act and either are listed for trading or admitted to unlisted trading privileges on a national securities exchange; or are securities for which bid and offer quotations are reported in an automated quotations system operated by a national securities association.

(b) *Purchases.* State whether any securities are to be purchased from any officer, director or affiliate of the subject company and provide the details of each transaction.

(c) *Different terms.* Describe any term or arrangement in the Rule 13e–3 transaction that treats any subject security holders differently from other subject security holders.

(d) *Appraisal rights.* State whether or not dissenting security holders are entitled to any appraisal rights. If so, summarize the appraisal rights. If there are no appraisal rights available under state law for security holders who object to the transaction, briefly outline any other rights that may be available to security holders under the law.

(e) *Provisions for unaffiliated security holders.* Describe any provision made by the filing person in connection with the transaction to grant unaffiliated security holders access to the corporate files of the filing person or to obtain counsel or appraisal services at the expense of the filing person. If none, so state.

(f) *Eligibility for listing or trading.* If the transaction involves the offer of securities of the filing person in exchange for equity securities held by unaffiliated security holders of the subject company, describe whether or not the filing person will take steps to assure that the securities offered are or will be eligible for trading on an automated quotations system operated by a national securities association.

§ 229.1005   (Item 1005) Past Contacts, Transactions, Negotiations and Agreements.

(a)   *Transactions.* Briefly state the nature and approximate dollar amount of any transaction, other than those described in paragraphs (b) or (c) of this section, that occurred during the past two years, between the filing person (including any person specified in Instruction C of the schedule) and;

(1)   The subject company or any of its affiliates that are not natural persons if the aggregate value of the transactions is more than one percent of the subject company's consolidated revenues for:

(i)   The fiscal year when the transaction occurred; or

(ii)   The past portion of the current fiscal year, if the transaction occurred in the current year; and

Instruction to Item 1005(a)(1): The information required by this Item may be based on information in the subject company's most recent filing with the Commission, unless the filing person has reason to believe the information is not accurate.

(2)   Any executive officer, director or affiliate of the subject company that is a natural person if the aggregate value of the transaction or series of similar transactions with that person exceeds $60,000.

(b)   *Significant corporate events.* Describe any negotiations, transactions or material contacts during the past two years between the filing person (including subsidiaries of the filing person and any person specified in Instruction C of the schedule) and the subject company or its affiliates concerning any:

(1)   Merger;

(2)   Consolidation;

(3)   Acquisition;

(4)   Tender offer for or other acquisition of any class of the subject company's securities;

(5)   Election of the subject company's directors; or

(6)   Sale or other transfer of a material amount of assets of the subject company.

(c)   *Negotiations or contacts.* Describe any negotiations or material contacts concerning the matters referred to in paragraph (b) of this section during the past two years between:

(1)   Any affiliates of the subject company; or

(2)   The subject company or any of its affiliates and any person not affiliated with the subject company who would have a direct interest in such matters.

Instruction to paragraphs (b) and (c) of Item 1005: Identify the person who initiated the contacts or negotiations.

(d)   *Conflicts of interest.* If material, describe any agreement, arrangement or understanding and any actual or potential conflict of interest between the filing person or its affiliates and:

(1)   The subject company, its executive officers, directors or affiliates; or

(2)   The offeror, its executive officers, directors or affiliates.

Instruction to Item 1005(d): If the filing person is the subject company, no disclosure called for by this paragraph is required in the document disseminated to security holders, so long as substantially the same information was filed with the Commission previously and disclosed in a proxy statement, report or other communication sent to security holders by the subject company in the past year. The document disseminated to security holders, however, must refer specifically to the discussion in the proxy statement, report or other communication that was sent to security holders previously. The information also must be filed as an exhibit to the schedule.

(e) *Agreements involving the subject company's securities.* Describe any agreement, arrangement, or understanding, whether or not legally enforceable, between the filing person (including any person specified in Instruction C of the schedule) and any other person with respect to any securities of the subject company. Name all persons that are a party to the agreements, arrangements, or understandings and describe all material provisions.

Instructions to Item 1005(e) 1. The information required by this Item includes: the transfer or voting of securities, joint ventures, loan or option arrangements, puts or calls, guarantees of loans, guarantees against loss, or the giving or withholding of proxies, consents or authorizations.

2.   Include information for any securities that are pledged or otherwise subject to a contingency, the occurrence of which would give another person the power to direct the voting or disposition of the subject securities. No disclosure, however, is required about standard default and similar provisions contained in loan agreements.

§ 229.1006   (Item 1006) Purposes of the Transaction and Plans or Proposals.

(a)   *Purposes.* State the purposes of the transaction.

(b)   *Use of securities acquired.* Indicate whether the securities acquired in the transaction will be retained, retired, held in treasury, or otherwise disposed of.

(c)   *Plans.* Describe any plans, proposals or negotiations that relate to or would result in:

(1)   Any extraordinary transaction, such as a merger, reorganization or liquidation, involving the subject company or any of its subsidiaries;

(2)   Any purchase, sale or transfer of a material amount of assets of the subject company or any of its subsidiaries;

(3)   Any material change in the present dividend rate or policy, or indebtedness or capitalization of the subject company;

(4)   Any change in the present board of directors or management of the subject company, including, but not limited to, any plans or proposals to change the number or the term of directors or to fill any existing vacancies on the board or to change any material term of the employment contract of any executive officer;

(5)   Any other material change in the subject company's corporate structure or business, including, if the subject company is a registered closed-end investment company, any plans or proposals to make any changes in its investment policy for which a vote would be required by Section 13 of the Investment Company Act of 1940 (15 U.S.C. 80a–13);

(6)   Any class of equity securities of the subject company to be delisted from a national securities exchange or cease to be authorized to be quoted in an automated quotations system operated by a national securities association;

(7)   Any class of equity securities of the subject company becoming eligible for termination of registration under section 12(g)(4) of the Act (15 U.S.C. 78l);

(8)   The suspension of the subject company's obligation to file reports under Section 15(d) of the Act (15 U.S.C. 78o);

(9)   The acquisition by any person of additional securities of the subject company, or the disposition of securities of the subject company; or

(10) Any changes in the subject company's charter, bylaws or other governing instruments or other actions that could impede the acquisition of control of the subject company.

(d)   *Subject company negotiations.* If the filing person is the subject company:

(1)   State whether or not that person is undertaking or engaged in any negotiations in response to the tender offer that relate to:

(i) A tender offer or other acquisition of the subject company's securities by the filing person, any of its subsidiaries, or any other person; or

(ii) Any of the matters referred to in paragraphs (c)(1) through (c)(3) of this section; and

(2) Describe any transaction, board resolution, agreement in principle, or signed contract that is entered into in response to the tender offer that relates to one or more of the matters referred to in paragraph (d)(1) of this section.

Instruction to Item 1006(d)(1): If an agreement in principle has not been reached at the time of filing, no disclosure under paragraph (d)(1) of this section is required of the possible terms of or the parties to the transaction if in the opinion of the board of directors of the subject company disclosure would jeopardize continuation of the negotiations. In that case, disclosure indicating that negotiations are being undertaken or are underway and are in the preliminary stages is sufficient.

§ 229.1007 (Item 1007) Source and Amount of Funds or Other Consideration.

(a) *Source of funds.* State the specific sources and total amount of funds or other consideration to be used in the transaction. If the transaction involves a tender offer, disclose the amount of funds or other consideration required to purchase the maximum amount of securities sought in the offer.

(b) *Conditions.* State any material conditions to the financing discussed in response to paragraph (a) of this section. Disclose any alternative financing arrangements or alternative financing plans in the event the primary financing plans fall through. If none, so state.

(c) *Expenses.* Furnish a reasonably itemized statement of all expenses incurred or estimated to be incurred in connection with the transaction including, but not limited to, filing, legal, accounting and appraisal fees, solicitation expenses and printing costs and state whether or not the subject company has paid or will be responsible for paying any or all expenses.

(d) *Borrowed funds.* If all or any part of the funds or other consideration required is, or is expected, to be borrowed, directly or indirectly, for the purpose of the transaction:

(1) Provide a summary of each loan agreement or arrangement containing the identity of the parties, the term, the collateral, the stated and effective interest rates, and any other material terms or conditions of the loan; and

(2) Briefly describe any plans or arrangements to finance or repay the loan, or, if no plans or arrangements have been made, so state.

Instruction to Item 1007(d): If the transaction is a third-party tender offer and the source of all or any part of the funds used in the transaction is to come from a loan made in the ordinary course of business by a bank as defined by section 3(a)(6) of the Act (15 U.S.C. 78c), the name of the bank will not be made available to the public if the filing person so requests in writing and files the request, naming the bank, with the Secretary of the Commission.

§ 229.1008 (Item 1008) Interest in Securities of the Subject Company.

(a) *Securities ownership.* State the aggregate number and percentage of subject securities that are beneficially owned by each person named in response to Item 1003 of Regulation M–A (§ 229.1003) and by each associate and majority-owned subsidiary of those persons. Give the name and address of any associate or subsidiary.

Instructions to Item 1008(a). 1. For purposes of this section, beneficial ownership is determined in accordance with Rule 13d–3 (§ 240.13d–3 of this chapter) under the Exchange Act. Identify the shares that the person has a right to acquire.

2.   The information required by this section may be based on the number of outstanding securities disclosed in the subject company's most recently available filing with the Commission, unless the filing person has more current information.

3.   The information required by this section with respect to officers, directors and associates of the subject company must be given to the extent known after making reasonable inquiry.

(b)   *Securities transactions.* Describe any transaction in the subject securities during the past 60 days. The description of transactions required must include, but not necessarily be limited to:

(1)   The identity of the persons specified in the Instruction to this section who effected the transaction;

(2)   The date of the transaction;

(3)   The amount of securities involved;

(4)   The price per share; and

(5)   Where and how the transaction was effected.

Instructions to Item 1008(b). 1. Provide the required transaction information for the following persons:

(a)   The filing person (for all schedules);

(b)   Any person named in Instruction C of the schedule and any associate or majority-owned subsidiary of the issuer or filing person (for all schedules except Schedule 14D–9 (§ 240.14d–101 of this chapter));

(c)   Any executive officer, director, affiliate or subsidiary of the filing person (for Schedule 14D–9 (§ 240.14d–101 of this chapter));

(d)   The issuer and any executive officer or director of any subsidiary of the issuer or filing person (for an issuer tender offer on Schedule TO (§ 240.14d–100 of this chapter)); and

(e)   The issuer and any pension, profit-sharing or similar plan of the issuer or affiliate filing the schedule (for a going-private transaction on Schedule 13E–3 (§ 240.13e–100 of this chapter)).

2.   Provide the information required by this Item if it is available to the filing person at the time the statement is initially filed with the Commission. If the information is not initially available, it must be obtained and filed with the Commission promptly, but in no event later than three business days after the date of the initial filing, and if material, disclosed in a manner reasonably designed to inform security holders. The procedure specified by this instruction is provided to maintain the confidentiality of information in order to avoid possible misuse of inside information.

§ 229.1009   (Item 1009) Persons/Assets, Retained, Employed, Compensated or Used.

(a)   *Solicitations or recommendations.* Identify all persons and classes of persons that are directly or indirectly employed, retained, or to be compensated to make solicitations or recommendations in connection with the transaction. Provide a summary of all material terms of employment, retainer or other arrangement for compensation.

(b)   *Employees and corporate assets.* Identify any officer, class of employees or corporate assets of the subject company that has been or will be employed or used by the filing person in connection with the transaction. Describe the purpose for their employment or use.

Instruction to Item 1009(b): Provide all information required by this Item except for the information required by paragraph (a) of this section and Item 1007 of Regulation M–A (§ 229.1007).

§ 229.1010   (Item 1010) Financial Statements.

(a)   *Financial information.* Furnish the following financial information:

(1) Audited financial statements for the two fiscal years required to be filed with the company's most recent annual report under sections 13 and 15(d) of the Exchange Act (15 U.S.C. 78m; 15 U.S.C. 78o);

(2) Unaudited balance sheets, comparative year-to-date statements of comprehensive income (as defined in § 210.1–02 of Regulation S-X of this chapter) and related earnings per share data and statements of cash flows required to be included in the company's most recent quarterly report filed under the Exchange Act; and

(3) [Reserved]

(4) Book value per share as of the date of the most recent balance sheet presented.

(b) *Pro forma information.* If material, furnish pro forma information disclosing the effect of the transaction on:

(1) The company's balance sheet as of the date of the most recent balance sheet presented under paragraph (a) of this section;

(2) The company's statement of comprehensive income and earnings per share for the most recent fiscal year and the latest interim period provided under paragraph (a)(2) of this section; and

(3) The company's book value per share as of the date of the most recent balance sheet presented under paragraph (a) of this section.

(c) *Summary information.* Furnish a fair and adequate summary of the information specified in paragraphs (a) and (b) of this section for the same periods specified. A fair and adequate summary includes:

(1) The summarized financial information specified in § 210.1–02(bb)(1) of this chapter;

(2) Income per common share from continuing operations (basic and diluted, if applicable);

(3) Net income per common share (basic and diluted, if applicable);

(4) [Reserved]

(5) Book value per share as of the date of the most recent balance sheet; and

(6) If material, pro forma data for the summarized financial information specified in paragraphs (c)(1) through (c)(5) of this section disclosing the effect of the transaction.

§ 229.1011   (Item 1011) Additional Information.

(a) *Agreements, regulatory requirements and legal proceedings.* If material to a security holder's decision whether to sell, tender or hold the securities sought in the tender offer, furnish the following information:

(1) Any present or proposed material agreement, arrangement, understanding or relationship between the offeror or any of its executive officers, directors, controlling persons or subsidiaries and the subject company or any of its executive officers, directors, controlling persons or subsidiaries (other than any agreement, arrangement or understanding disclosed under any other sections of Regulation M–A (§§ 229.1000 through 229.1016));

Instruction to paragraph (a)(1): In an issuer tender offer disclose any material agreement, arrangement, understanding or relationship between the offeror and any of its executive officers, directors, controlling persons or subsidiaries.

(2) To the extent known by the offeror after reasonable investigation, the applicable regulatory requirements which must be complied with or approvals which must be obtained in connection with the tender offer;

(3) The applicability of any anti-trust laws;

(4)   The applicability of margin requirements under section 7 of the Act (15 U.S.C. 78g) and the applicable regulations; and

(5)   Any material pending legal proceedings relating to the tender offer, including the name and location of the court or agency in which the proceedings are pending, the date instituted, the principal parties, and a brief summary of the proceedings and the relief sought.

Instruction to Item 1011(a)(5): A copy of any document relating to a major development (such as pleadings, an answer, complaint, temporary restraining order, injunction, opinion, judgment or order) in a material pending legal proceeding must be furnished promptly to the Commission staff on a supplemental basis.

(b)   Furnish the information required by Item 402(t)(2) and (3) of this part (§ 229.402(t)(2) and (3)) and in the tabular format set forth in Item 402(t)(1) of this part (§ 229.402(t)(1)) with respect to each named executive officer

(1)   Of the subject company in a Rule 13e–3 transaction; or

(2)   Of the issuer whose securities are the subject of a third-party tender offer, regarding any agreement or understanding, whether written or unwritten, between such named executive officer and the subject company, issuer, bidder, or the acquiring company, as applicable, concerning any type of compensation, whether present, deferred or contingent, that is based upon or otherwise relates to the Rule 13e–3 transaction or third-party tender offer.

Instructions to Item 1011(b).

1.   The obligation to provide the information in paragraph (b) of this section shall not apply where the issuer whose securities are the subject of the Rule 13e–3 transaction or tender offer is a foreign private issuer, as defined in § 240.3b–4 of this chapter, or an emerging growth company, as defined in Rule 405 of the Securities Act (§ 230.405 of this chapter) or Rule 12b–2 of the Exchange Act (§ 240.12b–2 of this chapter).

2.   For purposes of Instruction 1 to Item 402(t)(2) of this part: If the disclosure is included in a Schedule 13E–3 (§ 240.13e–100 of this chapter) or Schedule 14D–9 (§ 240.14d–101 of this chapter), the disclosure provided by this table shall be quantified assuming that the triggering event took place on the latest practicable date and that the price per share of the securities of the subject company in a Rule 13e–3 transaction, or of the issuer whose securities are the subject of the third-party tender offer, shall be determined as follows: If the shareholders are to receive a fixed dollar amount, the price per share shall be that fixed dollar amount, and if such value is not a fixed dollar amount, the price per share shall be the average closing market price of such securities over the first five business days following the first public announcement of the transaction. Compute the dollar value of in-the-money option awards for which vesting would be accelerated by determining the difference between this price and the exercise or base price of the options. Include only compensation that is based on or otherwise relates to the subject transaction. Apply Instruction 1 to Item 402(t) with respect to those executive officers for whom disclosure was required in the most recent filing by the subject company in a Rule 13e–3 transaction or by the issuer whose securities are the subject of a third-party tender offer, with the Commission under the Securities Act (15 U.S.C. 77a *et seq.*) or Exchange Act (15 U.S.C. 78a *et seq.*) that required disclosure pursuant to Item 402(c).

(c)   *Other material information.* Furnish such additional material information, if any, as may be necessary to make the required statements, in light of the circumstances under which they are made, not materially misleading.

§ 229.1012   (Item 1012) The Solicitation or Recommendation.

(a)   *Solicitation or recommendation.* State the nature of the solicitation or the recommendation. If this statement relates to a recommendation, state whether the filing person is advising holders of the subject securities to accept or reject the tender offer or to take other action with respect to the tender offer and, if so, describe the other action recommended. If the filing person is the subject company and is not making a recommendation, state whether the subject company is expressing no opinion and is remaining neutral toward the tender offer or is unable to take a position with respect to the tender offer.

(b) *Reasons.* State the reasons for the position (including the inability to take a position) stated in paragraph (a) of this section. Conclusory statements such as "The tender offer is in the best interests of shareholders" are not considered sufficient disclosure.

(c) *Intent to tender.* To the extent known by the filing person after making reasonable inquiry, state whether the filing person or any executive officer, director, affiliate or subsidiary of the filing person currently intends to tender, sell or hold the subject securities that are held of record or beneficially owned by that person.

(d) *Intent to tender or vote in a going-private transaction.* To the extent known by the filing person after making reasonable inquiry, state whether or not any executive officer, director or affiliate of the issuer (or any person specified in Instruction C to the schedule) currently intends to tender or sell subject securities owned or held by that person and/or how each person currently intends to vote subject securities, including any securities the person has proxy authority for. State the reasons for the intended action.

Instruction to Item 1012(d): Provide the information required by this section if it is available to the filing person at the time the statement is initially filed with the Commission. If the information is not available, it must be filed with the Commission promptly, but in no event later than three business days after the date of the initial filing, and if material, disclosed in a manner reasonably designed to inform security holders.

(e) *Recommendations of others.* To the extent known by the filing person after making reasonable inquiry, state whether or not any person specified in paragraph (d) of this section has made a recommendation either in support of or opposed to the transaction and the reasons for the recommendation.

§ 229.1013   (Item 1013) Purposes, Alternatives, Reasons and Effects in a Going-Private Transaction.

(a) *Purposes.* State the purposes for the Rule 13e–3 transaction.

(b) *Alternatives.* If the subject company or affiliate considered alternative means to accomplish the stated purposes, briefly describe the alternatives and state the reasons for their rejection.

(c) *Reasons.* State the reasons for the structure of the Rule 13e–3 transaction and for undertaking the transaction at this time.

(d) *Effects.* Describe the effects of the Rule 13e–3 transaction on the subject company, its affiliates and unaffiliated security holders, including the federal tax consequences of the transaction.

Instructions to Item 1013: 1. Conclusory statements will not be considered sufficient disclosure in response to this section.

2.   The description required by paragraph (d) of this section must include a reasonably detailed discussion of both the benefits and detriments of the Rule 13e–3 transaction to the subject company, its affiliates and unaffiliated security holders. The benefits and detriments of the Rule 13e–3 transaction must be quantified to the extent practicable.

3.   If this statement is filed by an affiliate of the subject company, the description required by paragraph (d) of this section must include, but not be limited to, the effect of the Rule 13e–3 transaction on the affiliate's interest in the net book value and net earnings of the subject company in terms of both dollar amounts and percentages.

§ 229.1014   (Item 1014) Fairness of the Going-Private Transaction.

(a) *Fairness.* State whether the subject company or affiliate filing the statement reasonably believes that the Rule 13e–3 transaction is fair or unfair to unaffiliated security holders. If any director dissented to or abstained from voting on the Rule 13e–3 transaction, identify the director, and indicate, if known, after making reasonable inquiry, the reasons for the dissent or abstention.

(b) *Factors considered in determining fairness.* Discuss in reasonable detail the material factors upon which the belief stated in paragraph (a) of this section is based and, to the extent practicable, the weight assigned to each factor. The discussion must include an analysis of the extent, if any, to which the filing person's beliefs are based on the factors described in Instruction 2 of this section, paragraphs (c), (d) and (e) of this section and Item 1015 of Regulation M–A (§ 229.1015).

(c) *Approval of security holders.* State whether or not the transaction is structured so that approval of at least a majority of unaffiliated security holders is required.

(d) *Unaffiliated representative.* State whether or not a majority of directors who are not employees of the subject company has retained an unaffiliated representative to act solely on behalf of unaffiliated security holders for purposes of negotiating the terms of the Rule 13e–3 transaction and/or preparing a report concerning the fairness of the transaction.

(e) *Approval of directors.* State whether or not the Rule 13e–3 transaction was approved by a majority of the directors of the subject company who are not employees of the subject company.

(f) *Other offers.* If any offer of the type described in paragraph (viii) of Instruction 2 to this section has been received, describe the offer and state the reasons for its rejection.

Instructions to Item 1014: 1. A statement that the issuer or affiliate has no reasonable belief as to the fairness of the Rule 13e–3 transaction to unaffiliated security holders will not be considered sufficient disclosure in response to paragraph (a) of this section.

2.   The factors that are important in determining the fairness of a transaction to unaffiliated security holders and the weight, if any, that should be given to them in a particular context will vary. Normally such factors will include, among others, those referred to in paragraphs (c), (d) and (e) of this section and whether the consideration offered to unaffiliated security holders constitutes fair value in relation to:

     (i)   Current market prices;

     (ii)   Historical market prices;

     (iii)   Net book value;

     (iv)   Going concern value;

     (v)   Liquidation value;

     (vi)   Purchase prices paid in previous purchases disclosed in response to Item 1002(f) of Regulation M–A (§ 229.1002(f));

     (vii) Any report, opinion, or appraisal described in Item 1015 of Regulation M–A (§ 229.1015); and

     (viii) Firm offers of which the subject company or affiliate is aware made by any unaffiliated person, other than the filing persons, during the past two years for:

         (A)   The merger or consolidation of the subject company with or into another company, or *vice versa;*

         (B)   The sale or other transfer of all or any substantial part of the assets of the subject company; or

         (C)   A purchase of the subject company's securities that would enable the holder to exercise control of the subject company.

3. Conclusory statements, such as "The Rule 13e–3 transaction is fair to unaffiliated security holders in relation to net book value, going concern value and future prospects of the issuer" will not be considered sufficient disclosure in response to paragraph (b) of this section.

§ 229.1015 (Item 1015) Reports, Opinions, Appraisals and Negotiations.

(a) *Report, opinion or appraisal.* State whether or not the subject company or affiliate has received any report, opinion (other than an opinion of counsel) or appraisal from an outside party that is materially related to the Rule 13e–3 transaction, including, but not limited to: Any report, opinion or appraisal relating to the consideration or the fairness of the consideration to be offered to security holders or the fairness of the transaction to the issuer or affiliate or to security holders who are not affiliates.

(b) *Preparer and summary of the report, opinion or appraisal.* For each report, opinion or appraisal described in response to paragraph (a) of this section or any negotiation or report described in response to Item 1014(d) of Regulation M–A (§ 229.1014) or Item 14(b)(6) of Schedule 14A (§ 240.14a–101 of this chapter) concerning the terms of the transaction:

(1) Identify the outside party and/or unaffiliated representative;

(2) Briefly describe the qualifications of the outside party and/or unaffiliated representative;

(3) Describe the method of selection of the outside party and/or unaffiliated representative;

(4) Describe any material relationship that existed during the past two years or is mutually understood to be contemplated and any compensation received or to be received as a result of the relationship between:

(i) The outside party, its affiliates, and/or unaffiliated representative; and

(ii) The subject company or its affiliates;

(5) If the report, opinion or appraisal relates to the fairness of the consideration, state whether the subject company or affiliate determined the amount of consideration to be paid or whether the outside party recommended the amount of consideration to be paid; and

(6) Furnish a summary concerning the negotiation, report, opinion or appraisal. The summary must include, but need not be limited to, the procedures followed; the findings and recommendations; the bases for and methods of arriving at such findings and recommendations; instructions received from the subject company or affiliate; and any limitation imposed by the subject company or affiliate on the scope of the investigation.

Instruction to Item 1015(b): The information called for by paragraphs (b)(1), (2) and (3) of this section must be given with respect to the firm that provides the report, opinion or appraisal rather than the employees of the firm that prepared the report.

(c) *Availability of documents.* Furnish a statement to the effect that the report, opinion or appraisal will be made available for inspection and copying at the principal executive offices of the subject company or affiliate during its regular business hours by any interested equity security holder of the subject company or representative who has been so designated in writing. This statement also may provide that a copy of the report, opinion or appraisal will be transmitted by the subject company or affiliate to any interested equity security holder of the subject company or representative who has been so designated in writing upon written request and at the expense of the requesting security holder.

§ 229.1016 (Item 1016) Exhibits.

File as an exhibit to the schedule:

(a)   Any disclosure materials furnished to security holders by or on behalf of the filing person, including:

    (1)   Tender offer materials (including transmittal letter);

    (2)   Solicitation or recommendation (including those referred to in Item 1012 of Regulation M–A (§ 229.1012));

    (3)   Going-private disclosure document;

    (4)   Prospectus used in connection with an exchange offer where securities are registered under the Securities Act of 1933; and

    (5)   Any other disclosure materials;

(b)   Any loan agreement referred to in response to Item 1007(d) of Regulation M–A (§ 229.1007(d));

Instruction to Item 1016(b): If the filing relates to a third-party tender offer and a request is made under Item 1007(d) of Regulation M–A (§ 229.1007(d)), the identity of the bank providing financing may be omitted from the loan agreement filed as an exhibit.

(c)   Any report, opinion or appraisal referred to in response to Item 1014(d) or Item 1015 of Regulation M–A (§ 229.1014(d) or § 229.1015);

(d)   Any document setting forth the terms of any agreement, arrangement, understanding or relationship referred to in response to Item 1005(e) or Item 1011(a)(1) of Regulation M–A (§ 229.1005(e) or § 229.1011(a)(1));

(e)   Any agreement, arrangement or understanding referred to in response to § 229.1005(d), or the pertinent portions of any proxy statement, report or other communication containing the disclosure required by Item 1005(d) of Regulation M–A (§ 229.1005(d));

(f)   A detailed statement describing security holders' appraisal rights and the procedures for exercising those appraisal rights referred to in response to Item 1004(d) of Regulation M–A (§ 229.1004(d));

(g)   Any written instruction, form or other material that is furnished to persons making an oral solicitation or recommendation by or on behalf of the filing person for their use directly or indirectly in connection with the transaction; and

(h)   Any written opinion prepared by legal counsel at the filing person's request and communicated to the filing person pertaining to the tax consequences of the transaction.

* * *

J. SECURITIES LITIGATION UNIFORM STANDARDS ACT OF 1998

Table of Contents

* * *

An Act to amend the Securities Act of 1933 and the Securities Exchange Act of 1934 to limit the conduct of securities class actions under State law, and for other purposes.

§ 1.   Short Title

This Act may be cited as the "Securities Litigation Uniform Standards Act of 1998".

§ 2.   Findings

The Congress finds that—

(1)   the Private Securities Litigation Reform Act of 1995 sought to prevent abuses in private securities fraud lawsuits;

(2)   since enactment of that legislation, considerable evidence has been presented to Congress that a number of securities class action lawsuits have shifted from Federal to State courts;

(3)   this shift has prevented that Act from fully achieving its objectives;

(4)   State securities regulation is of continuing importance, together with Federal regulation of securities, to protect investors and promote strong financial markets; and

(5)   in order to prevent certain State private securities class action lawsuits alleging fraud from being used to frustrate the objectives of the Private Securities Litigation Reform Act of 1995, it is appropriate to enact national standards for securities class action lawsuits involving nationally traded securities, while preserving the appropriate enforcement powers of State securities regulators and not changing the current treatment of individual lawsuits.

TITLE I—SECURITIES LITIGATION UNIFORM STANDARDS

§ 101.   Limitation on Remedies

(a)   AMENDMENTS TO THE SECURITIES ACT OF 1933.—

(1)   AMENDMENT.—Section 16 of the Securities Act of 1933 is amended to read as follows:

"SEC. 16. ADDITIONAL REMEDIES; LIMITATION ON REMEDIES.

"(a) REMEDIES ADDITIONAL.—Except as provided in subsection (b), the rights and remedies provided by this title shall be in addition to any and all other rights and remedies that may exist at law or in equity.

"(b) CLASS ACTION LIMITATIONS.—No covered class action based upon the statutory or common law of any State or subdivision thereof may be maintained in any State or Federal court by any private party alleging—

"(1) an untrue statement or omission of a material fact in connection with the purchase or sale of a covered security; or

"(2) that the defendant used or employed any manipulative or deceptive device or contrivance in connection with the purchase or sale of a covered security.

"(c) REMOVAL OF COVERED CLASS ACTIONS.—Any covered class action brought in any State court involving a covered security, as set forth in subsection (b), shall be removable to the Federal district court for the district in which the action is pending, and shall be subject to subsection (b).

"(d) PRESERVATION OF CERTAIN ACTIONS.—

"(1) ACTIONS UNDER STATE LAW OF STATE OF INCORPORATION.—

"(A) ACTIONS PRESERVED.—Notwithstanding subsection (b) or (c), a covered class action described in subparagraph (B) of this paragraph that is based upon the statutory or common law of the State in which the issuer is incorporated (in the case of a corporation) or organized (in the case of any other entity) may be maintained in a State or Federal court by a private party.

"(B) PERMISSIBLE ACTIONS.—A covered class action is described in this subparagraph if it involves—

"(i) the purchase or sale of securities by the issuer or an affiliate of the issuer exclusively from or to holders of equity securities of the issuer; or

"(ii) any recommendation, position, or other communication with respect to the sale of securities of the issuer that—

"(I) is made by or on behalf of the issuer or an affiliate of the issuer to holders of equity securities of the issuer; and

"(II) concerns decisions of those equity holders with respect to voting their securities, acting in response to a tender or exchange offer, or exercising dissenters" or appraisal rights.

"(2) STATE ACTIONS.—

"(A) IN GENERAL.—Notwithstanding any other provision of this section, nothing in this section may be construed to preclude a State or political subdivision thereof or a State pension plan from bringing an action involving a covered security on its own behalf, or as a member of a class comprised solely of other States, political subdivisions, or State pension plans that are named plaintiffs, and that have authorized participation, in such action.

"(B) STATE PENSION PLAN DEFINED.—For purposes of this paragraph, the term 'State pension plan' means a pension plan established and maintained for its employees by the government of the State or political subdivision thereof, or by any agency or instrumentality thereof.

"(3) ACTIONS UNDER CONTRACTUAL AGREEMENTS BETWEEN ISSUERS AND INDENTURE TRUSTEES.—Notwithstanding subsection (b) or (c), a covered class action that seeks to enforce a contractual agreement between an issuer and an indenture trustee may be maintained in a State or Federal court by a party to the agreement or a successor to such party.

"(4) REMAND OF REMOVED ACTIONS.—In an action that has been removed from a State court pursuant to subsection (c), if the Federal court determines that the action may be maintained in State court pursuant to this subsection, the Federal court shall remand such action to such State court.

"(e) PRESERVATION OF STATE JURISDICTION.—The securities commission (or any agency or office performing like functions) of any State shall retain jurisdiction under the laws of such State to investigate and bring enforcement actions.

"(f) DEFINITIONS.—For purposes of this section, the following definitions shall apply:

"(1) AFFILIATE OF THE ISSUER.—The term 'affiliate of the issuer' means a person that directly or indirectly, through one or more intermediaries, controls or is controlled by or is under common control with, the issuer.

"(2) COVERED CLASS ACTION—

"(A) IN GENERAL.—The term 'covered class action' means—

"(i) any single lawsuit in which—

"(I) damages are sought on behalf of more than 50 persons or prospective class members, and questions of law or fact common to those persons or members of the prospective class, without reference to issues of individualized reliance on an alleged misstatement or omission, predominate over any questions affecting only individual persons or members; or

"(II) one or more named parties seek to recover damages on a representative basis on behalf of themselves and other unnamed parties similarly situated, and questions of law or fact common to those persons or members of the prospective class predominate over any questions affecting only individual persons or members; or

"(ii) any group of lawsuits filed in or pending in the same court and involving common questions of law or fact, in which—

"(I) damages are sought on behalf of more than 50 persons; and

"(II) the lawsuits are joined, consolidated, or otherwise proceed as a single action for any purpose.

"(B) EXCEPTION FOR DERIVATIVE ACTIONS.—Notwithstanding subparagraph (A), the term 'covered class action' does not include an exclusively derivative action brought by one or more shareholders on behalf of a corporation.

"(C) COUNTING OF CERTAIN CLASS MEMBERS.—For purposes of this paragraph, a corporation, investment company, pension plan, partnership, or other entity, shall be treated as one person or prospective class member, but only if the entity is not established for the purpose of participating in the action.

"(D) RULE OF CONSTRUCTION.—Nothing in this paragraph shall be construed to affect the discretion of a State court in determining whether actions filed in such court should be joined, consolidated, or otherwise allowed to proceed as a single action.

"(3) COVERED SECURITY.—The term 'covered security' means a security that satisfies the standards for a covered security specified in paragraph (1) or (2) of section 18(b) at the time during which it is alleged that the misrepresentation, omission, or manipulative or deceptive conduct occurred, except that such term shall not include any debt security that is exempt from registration under this title pursuant to rules issued by the Commission under section 4(2).".

(2) CIRCUMVENTION OF STAY OF DISCOVERY.—Section 27(b) of the Securities Act of 1933 is amended by inserting after paragraph (3) the following new paragraph:

"(4) CIRCUMVENTION OF STAY OF DISCOVERY.—Upon a proper showing, a court may stay discovery proceedings in any private action in a State court as necessary in aid of its jurisdiction, or to protect or effectuate its judgments, in an action subject to a stay of discovery pursuant to this subsection.".

(3) CONFORMING AMENDMENTS.—Section 22(a) of the Securities Act of 1933 is amended—

(A) by inserting "except as provided in section 16 with respect to covered class actions," after "Territorial courts,"; and

(B) by striking "No case" and inserting" Except as provided in section 16(c), no case".

(b) AMENDMENTS TO THE SECURITIES EXCHANGE ACT OF 1934—

(1) AMENDMENT.—Section 28 of the Securities Exchange Act of 1934 is amended—

(A) in subsection (a), by striking "The rights and remedies" and inserting "Except as provided in subsection (f), the rights and remedies"; and

(B) by adding at the end the following new subsection:

"(f) LIMITATIONS ON REMEDIES.—

"(1) CLASS ACTION LIMITATIONS.—No covered class action based upon the statutory or common law of any State or subdivision thereof may be maintained in any State or Federal court by any private party alleging—

"(A) a misrepresentation or omission of a material fact in connection with the purchase or sale of a covered security; or

"(B) that the defendant used or employed any manipulative or deceptive device or contrivance in connection with the purchase or sale of a covered security.

"(2) REMOVAL OF COVERED CLASS ACTIONS.—Any covered class action brought in any State court involving a covered security, as set forth in paragraph (1), shall be removable to the Federal district court for the district in which the action is pending, and shall be subject to paragraph (1).

"(3) PRESERVATION OF CERTAIN ACTIONS—

"(A) ACTIONS UNDER STATE LAW OF STATE OF INCORPORATION.—

"(i) ACTIONS PRESERVED.—Notwithstanding paragraph (1) or (2), a covered class action described in clause (ii) of this subparagraph that is based upon the statutory or common law of the State in which the issuer is incorporated (in the case of a corporation) or organized (in the case of any other entity) may be maintained in a State or Federal court by a private party.

"(ii) PERMISSIBLE ACTIONS.—A covered class action is described in this clause if it involves—

"(I) the purchase or sale of securities by the issuer or an affiliate of the issuer exclusively from or to holders of equity securities of the issuer; or

"(II) any recommendation, position, or other communication with respect to the sale of securities of an issuer that—

"(aa) is made by or on behalf of the issuer or an affiliate of the issuer to holders of equity securities of the issuer; and

"(bb) concerns decisions of such equity holders with respect to voting their securities, acting in response to a tender or exchange offer, or exercising dissenters' or appraisal rights.

"(B) STATE ACTIONS.—

"(i) IN GENERAL.—Notwithstanding any other provision of this subsection, nothing in this subsection may be construed to preclude a State or political subdivision thereof or a

State pension plan from bringing an action involving a covered security on its own behalf, or as a member of a class comprised solely of other States, political subdivisions, or State pension plans that are named plaintiffs, and that have authorized participation, in such action.

"(ii) STATE PENSION PLAN DEFINED.—For purposes of this subparagraph, the term 'State pension plan' means a pension plan established and maintained for its employees by the government of a State or political subdivision thereof, or by any agency or instrumentality thereof.

"(C) ACTIONS UNDER CONTRACTUAL AGREEMENTS BETWEEN ISSUERS AND INDENTURE TRUSTEES.—Notwithstanding paragraph (1) or (2), a covered class action that seeks to enforce a contractual agreement between an issuer and an indenture trustee may be maintained in a State or Federal court by a party to the agreement or a successor to such party.

"(D) REMAND OF REMOVED ACTIONS.—In an action that has been removed from a State court pursuant to paragraph (2), if the Federal court determines that the action may be maintained in State court pursuant to this subsection, the Federal court shall remand such action to such State court.

"(4) PRESERVATION OF STATE JURISDICTION.—The securities commission (or any agency or office performing like functions) of any State shall retain jurisdiction under the laws of such State to investigate and bring enforcement actions.

"(5) DEFINITIONS.—For purposes of this subsection, the following definitions shall apply:

"(A) AFFILIATE OF THE ISSUER.—The term 'affiliate of the issuer' means a person that directly or indirectly, through one or more intermediaries, controls or is controlled by or is under common control with, the issuer.

"(B) COVERED CLASS ACTION.—The term 'covered class action' means—

"(i)   any single lawsuit in which—

"(I)   damages are sought on behalf of more than 50 persons or prospective class members, and questions of law or fact common to those persons or members of the prospective class, without reference to issues of individualized reliance on an alleged misstatement or omission, predominate over any questions affecting only individual persons or members; or

"(II) one or more named parties seek to recover damages on a representative basis on behalf of themselves and other unnamed parties similarly situated, and questions of law or fact common to those persons or members of the prospective class predominate over any questions affecting only individual persons or members; or

"(ii) any group of lawsuits filed in or pending in the same court and involving common questions of law or fact, in which—

"(I)   damages are sought on behalf of more than 50 persons; and

"(II) the lawsuits are joined, consolidated, or otherwise proceed as a single action for any purpose.

"(C) EXCEPTION FOR DERIVATIVE ACTIONS.—Notwithstanding subparagraph (B), the term 'covered class action' does not include an exclusively derivative action brought by one or more shareholders on behalf of a corporation.

"(D) COUNTING OF CERTAIN CLASS MEMBERS.—For purposes of this paragraph, a corporation, investment company, pension plan, partnership, or other entity, shall be treated as one person or prospective class member, but only if the entity is not established for the purpose of participating in the action.

"(E) COVERED SECURITY.—The term 'covered security' means a security that satisfies the standards for a covered security specified in paragraph (1) or (2) of section 18(b) of the Securities Act of 1933, at the time during which it is alleged that the misrepresentation, omission, or manipulative or deceptive conduct occurred, except that such term shall not include any debt security that is exempt from registration under the Securities Act of 1933 pursuant to rules issued by the Commission under section 4(2) of that Act.

"(F) RULE OF CONSTRUCTION.—Nothing in this paragraph shall be construed to affect the discretion of a State court in determining whether actions filed in such court should be joined, consolidated, or otherwise allowed to proceed as a single action.".

(2) CIRCUMVENTION OF STAY OF DISCOVERY.—Section 21D(b)(3) of the Securities Exchange Act of 1934 is amended by adding at the end the following new subparagraph:

"(D) CIRCUMVENTION OF STAY OF DISCOVERY.—Upon a proper showing, a court may stay discovery proceedings in any private action in a State court, as necessary in aid of its jurisdiction, or to protect or effectuate its judgments, in an action subject to a stay of discovery pursuant to this paragraph.".

(c) APPLICABILITY.—The amendments made by this section shall not affect or apply to any action commenced before and pending on the date of enactment of this Act.

§ 102.   Promotion of Reciprocal Subpoena Enforcement

(a) Commission action.—The Securities and Exchange Commission, in consultation with State securities commissions (or any agencies or offices performing like functions), shall seek to encourage the adoption of State laws providing for reciprocal enforcement by State securities commissions of subpoenas issued by another State securities commission seeking to compel persons to attend, testify in, or produce documents or records in connection with an action or investigation by a State securities commission of an alleged violation of State securities laws.

(b) Report.—Not later than 24 months after the date of enactment of this Act, the Securities and Exchange Commission (hereafter in this section referred to as the "Commission") shall submit a report to the Congress—

(1) identifying the States that have adopted laws described in subsection (a);

(2) describing the actions undertaken by the Commission and State securities commissions to promote the adoption of such laws; and

(3) identifying any further actions that the Commission recommends for such purposes.

K. SARBANES-OXLEY ACT OF 2002

Pub. L. No. 107–204

(codified as amended in scattered sections of 15 U.S.C.)

An Act To protect investors by improving the accuracy and reliability of corporate disclosures made pursuant to the securities laws, and for other purposes.

Be it enacted by the Senate and House of Representatives of the United States of America in Congress assembled,

---

Table of Contents

SARBANES-OXLEY ACT OF 2002

TITLE IV—ENHANCED FINANCIAL DISCLOSURES

TITLE V—ANALYST CONFLICTS OF INTEREST

TITLE VI—COMMISSION RESOURCES AND AUTHORITY

TITLE VII—STUDIES AND REPORTS

TITLE VIII—CORPORATE AND CRIMINAL FRAUD ACCOUNTABILITY

TITLE IX—WHITE-COLLAR CRIME PENALTY ENHANCEMENTS

TITLE X—CORPORATE TAX RETURNS

TITLE XI—CORPORATE FRAUD ACCOUNTABILITY

§ 1. Short Title; Table of Contents

* * *

§ 2. Definitions

(a) IN GENERAL.—In this Act, the following definitions shall apply:

(1) APPROPRIATE STATE REGULATORY AUTHORITY.—The term "appropriate State regulatory authority" means the State agency or other authority responsible for the licensure or other regulation of the practice of accounting in the State or States having jurisdiction over a registered public accounting firm or associated person thereof, with respect to the matter in question.

(2) AUDIT.—The term "audit" means an examination of the financial statements of any issuer by an independent public accounting firm in accordance with the rules of the Board or the Commission (or, for the period preceding the adoption of applicable rules of the Board under section 103, in accordance with then-applicable generally accepted auditing and related standards for such purposes), for the purpose of expressing an opinion on such statements.

(3) AUDIT COMMITTEE.—The term "audit committee" means—

(A) a committee (or equivalent body) established by and amongst the board of directors of an issuer for the purpose of overseeing the accounting and financial reporting processes of the issuer and audits of the financial statements of the issuer; and

(B) if no such committee exists with respect to an issuer, the entire board of directors of the issuer.

(4) AUDIT REPORT.—The term "audit report" means a document or other record—

(A) prepared following an audit performed for purposes of compliance by an issuer with the requirements of the securities laws; and

(B) in which a public accounting firm either—

(i) sets forth the opinion of that firm regarding a financial statement, report, or other document; or

(ii) asserts that no such opinion can be expressed.

(5) BOARD.—The term "Board" means the Public Company Accounting Oversight Board established under section 101.

(6) COMMISSION.—The term "Commission" means the Securities and Exchange Commission.

(7) ISSUER.—The term "issuer" means an issuer (as defined in section 3 of the Securities Exchange Act of 1934), the securities of which are registered under section 12 of that Act, or that is required to file reports under section 15(d), or that files or has filed a registration statement that has not yet become effective under the Securities Act of 1933, and that it has not withdrawn.

(8) NON-AUDIT SERVICES.—The term "non-audit services" means any professional services provided to an issuer by a registered public accounting firm, other than those provided to an issuer in connection with an audit or a review of the financial statements of an issuer.

(9) PERSON ASSOCIATED WITH A PUBLIC ACCOUNTING FIRM.—

(A) IN GENERAL.—The terms "person associated with a public accounting firm" (or with a "registered public accounting firm") and "associated person of a public accounting firm" (or of a "registered public accounting firm") mean any individual proprietor, partner, shareholder, principal, accountant, or other professional employee of a public accounting firm, or any other independent contractor or entity that, in connection with the preparation or issuance of any audit report—

(i) shares in the profits of, or receives compensation in any other form from, that firm; or

(ii) participates as agent or otherwise on behalf of such accounting firm in any activity of that firm.

(B) EXEMPTION AUTHORITY.—The Board may, by rule, exempt persons engaged only in ministerial tasks from the definition in subparagraph (A), to the extent that the Board determines that any such exemption is consistent with the purposes of this Act, the public interest, or the protection of investors.

(10) PROFESSIONAL STANDARDS.—The term "professional standards" means—

(A) accounting principles that are—

(i) established by the standard setting body described in section 19(b) of the Securities Act of 1933, as amended by this Act, or prescribed by the Commission under section 19(a) of that Act or section 13(b) of the Securities Exchange Act of 1934; and

(ii) relevant to audit reports for particular issuers, or dealt with in the quality control system of a particular registered public accounting firm; and

(B) auditing standards, standards for attestation engagements, quality control policies and procedures, ethical and competency standards, and independence standards (including rules implementing title II) that the Board or the Commission determines—

(i) relate to the preparation or issuance of audit reports for issuers; and

(ii) are established or adopted by the Board under section 103(a), or are promulgated as rules of the Commission.

(11) PUBLIC ACCOUNTING FIRM.—The term "public accounting firm" means—

(A) a proprietorship, partnership, incorporated association, corporation, limited liability company, limited liability partnership, or other legal entity that is engaged in the practice of public accounting or preparing or issuing audit reports; and

(B) to the extent so designated by the rules of the Board, any associated person of any entity described in subparagraph (A).

(12) REGISTERED PUBLIC ACCOUNTING FIRM.—The term "registered public accounting firm" means a public accounting firm registered with the Board in accordance with this Act.

(13) RULES OF THE BOARD.—The term "rules of the Board" means the bylaws and rules of the Board (as submitted to, and approved, modified, or amended by the Commission, in accordance with section 107), and those stated policies, practices, and interpretations of the Board that the Commission, by rule, may deem to be rules of the Board, as necessary or appropriate in the public interest or for the protection of investors.

(14) SECURITY.—The term "security" has the same meaning as in section 3(a) of the Securities Exchange Act of 1934.

(15) SECURITIES LAWS.—The term "securities laws" means the provisions of law referred to in section 3(a)(47) of the Securities Exchange Act of 1934, as amended by this Act, and includes the rules, regulations, and orders issued by the Commission thereunder.

(16) STATE.—The term "State" means any State of the United States, the District of Columbia, Puerto Rico, the Virgin Islands, or any other territory or possession of the United States.

(b) CONFORMING AMENDMENT.—Section 3(a)(47) of the Securities Exchange Act of 1934 is amended by inserting "the Sarbanes-Oxley Act of 2002," before "the Public".

§ 3. Commission Rules and Enforcement

(a) REGULATORY ACTION.—The Commission shall promulgate such rules and regulations, as may be necessary or appropriate in the public interest or for the protection of investors, and in furtherance of this Act.

(b) ENFORCEMENT.—

(1) IN GENERAL.—A violation by any person of this Act, any rule or regulation of the Commission issued under this Act, or any rule of the Board shall be treated for all purposes in the same manner as a violation of the Securities Exchange Act of 1934 or the rules and regulations issued thereunder, consistent with the provisions of this Act, and any such person shall be subject to the same penalties, and to the same extent, as for a violation of that Act or such rules or regulations.

(2) INVESTIGATIONS, INJUNCTIONS, AND PROSECUTION OF OFFENSES.—Section 21 of the Securities Exchange Act of 1934 is amended—

(A) in subsection (a)(1), by inserting "the rules of the Public Company Accounting Oversight Board, of which such person is a registered public accounting firm or a person associated with such a firm," after "is a participant,";

(B) in subsection (d)(1), by inserting "the rules of the Public Company Accounting Oversight Board, of which such person is a registered public accounting firm or a person associated with such a firm," after "is a participant,";

(C) in subsection (e), by inserting "the rules of the Public Company Accounting Oversight Board, of which such person is a registered public accounting firm or a person associated with such a firm," after "is a participant,"; and

(D) in subsection (f), by inserting "or the Public Company Accounting Oversight Board" after "self-regulatory organization" each place that term appears.

(3) CEASE-AND-DESIST PROCEEDINGS.—Section 21C(c)(2) of the Securities Exchange Act of 1934 is amended by inserting "registered public accounting firm (as defined in section 2 of the Sarbanes-Oxley Act of 2002)," after "government securities dealer,".

(4) ENFORCEMENT BY FEDERAL BANKING AGENCIES.—Section 12(i) of the Securities Exchange Act of 1934 is amended by—

(A) striking "sections 12," each place it appears and inserting "sections 10A(m), 12,"; and

(B) striking "and 16," each place it appears and inserting "and 16 of this Act, and sections 302, 303, 304, 306, 401(b), 404, 406, and 407 of the Sarbanes-Oxley Act of 2002,".

(c) EFFECT ON COMMISSION AUTHORITY.—Nothing in this Act or the rules of the Board shall be construed to impair or limit—

(1) the authority of the Commission to regulate the accounting profession, accounting firms, or persons associated with such firms for purposes of enforcement of the securities laws;

(2) the authority of the Commission to set standards for accounting or auditing practices or auditor independence, derived from other provisions of the securities laws or the rules or regulations thereunder, for purposes of the preparation and issuance of any audit report, or otherwise under applicable law; or

(3) the ability of the Commission to take, on the initiative of the Commission, legal, administrative, or disciplinary action against any registered public accounting firm or any associated person thereof.

TITLE I—PUBLIC COMPANY ACCOUNTING OVERSIGHT BOARD

§ 101.   Establishment; Administrative Provisions

(a) ESTABLISHMENT OF BOARD.—There is established the Public Company Accounting Oversight Board, to oversee the audit of public companies that are subject to the securities laws, and related matters, in order to protect the interests of investors and further the public interest in the preparation of informative, accurate, and independent audit reports for companies the securities of which are sold to, and held by and for, public investors. The Board shall be a body corporate, operate as a nonprofit corporation, and have succession until dissolved by an Act of Congress.

(b) STATUS.—The Board shall not be an agency or establishment of the United States Government, and, except as otherwise provided in this Act, shall be subject to, and have all the powers conferred upon a nonprofit corporation by, the District of Columbia Nonprofit Corporation Act. No member or person employed by, or agent for, the Board shall be deemed to be an officer or employee of or agent for the Federal Government by reason of such service.

(c) DUTIES OF THE BOARD.—The Board shall, subject to action by the Commission under section 107, and once a determination is made by the Commission under subsection (d) of this section—

(1) register public accounting firms that prepare audit reports for issuers, in accordance with section 102;

(2) establish or adopt, or both, by rule, auditing, quality control, ethics, independence, and other standards relating to the preparation of audit reports for issuers, in accordance with section 103;

(3) conduct inspections of registered public accounting firms, in accordance with section 104 and the rules of the Board;

(4) conduct investigations and disciplinary proceedings concerning, and impose appropriate sanctions where justified upon, registered public accounting firms and associated persons of such firms, in accordance with section 105;

(5) perform such other duties or functions as the Board (or the Commission, by rule or order) determines are necessary or appropriate to promote high professional standards among, and improve the quality of audit services offered by, registered public accounting firms and associated persons thereof, or otherwise to carry out this Act, in order to protect investors, or to further the public interest;

(6) enforce compliance with this Act, the rules of the Board, professional standards, and the securities laws relating to the preparation and issuance of audit reports and the obligations and liabilities of accountants with respect thereto, by registered public accounting firms and associated persons thereof; and

(7) set the budget and manage the operations of the Board and the staff of the Board.

(d) COMMISSION DETERMINATION.—The members of the Board shall take such action (including hiring of staff, proposal of rules, and adoption of initial and transitional auditing and other professional standards) as may be necessary or appropriate to enable the Commission to determine, not later than 270 days after the date of enactment of this Act, that the Board is so organized and has the capacity to carry out the requirements of this title, and to enforce compliance with this title by registered public accounting firms and associated persons thereof. The Commission shall be responsible, prior to the appointment of the Board, for the planning for the establishment and administrative transition to the Board's operation.

(e) BOARD MEMBERSHIP.—

(1) COMPOSITION.—The Board shall have 5 members, appointed from among prominent individuals of integrity and reputation who have a demonstrated commitment to the interests of investors and the public, and an understanding of the responsibilities for and nature of the financial disclosures required of issuers under the securities laws and the obligations of accountants with respect to the preparation and issuance of audit reports with respect to such disclosures.

(2) LIMITATION.—Two members, and only 2 members, of the Board shall be or have been certified public accountants pursuant to the laws of 1 or more States, provided that, if 1 of those 2 members is the chairperson, he or she may not have been a practicing certified public accountant for at least 5 years prior to his or her appointment to the Board.

(3) FULL-TIME INDEPENDENT SERVICE.—Each member of the Board shall serve on a full-time basis, and may not, concurrent with service on the Board, be employed by any other person or engage in any other professional or business activity. No member of the Board may share in any of the profits of, or receive payments from, a public accounting firm (or any other person, as determined by rule of the Commission), other than fixed continuing payments, subject to such conditions as the Commission may impose, under standard arrangements for the retirement of members of public accounting firms.

(4) APPOINTMENT OF BOARD MEMBERS.—

(A) INITIAL BOARD.—Not later than 90 days after the date of enactment of this Act, the Commission, after consultation with the Chairman of the Board of Governors of the Federal Reserve System and the Secretary of the Treasury, shall appoint the chairperson and other initial members of the Board, and shall designate a term of service for each.

(B) VACANCIES.—A vacancy on the Board shall not affect the powers of the Board, but shall be filled in the same manner as provided for appointments under this section.

(5) TERM OF SERVICE.—

(A) IN GENERAL.—The term of service of each Board member shall be 5 years, and until a successor is appointed, except that—

(i) the terms of office of the initial Board members (other than the chairperson) shall expire in annual increments, 1 on each of the first 4 anniversaries of the initial date of appointment; and

(ii) any Board member appointed to fill a vacancy occurring before the expiration of the term for which the predecessor was appointed shall be appointed only for the remainder of that term.

(B) TERM LIMITATION.—No person may serve as a member of the Board, or as chairperson of the Board, for more than 2 terms, whether or not such terms of service are consecutive.

(6) REMOVAL FROM OFFICE.—A member of the Board may be removed by the Commission from office, in accordance with section 107(d)(3), for good cause shown before the expiration of the term of that member.

(f) POWERS OF THE BOARD.—In addition to any authority granted to the Board otherwise in this Act, the Board shall have the power, subject to section 107—

(1) to sue and be sued, complain and defend, in its corporate name and through its own counsel, with the approval of the Commission, in any Federal, State, or other court;

(2)   to conduct its operations and maintain offices, and to exercise all other rights and powers authorized by this Act, in any State, without regard to any qualification, licensing, or other provision of law in effect in such State (or a political subdivision thereof);

(3)   to lease, purchase, accept gifts or donations of or otherwise acquire, improve, use, sell, exchange, or convey, all of or an interest in any property, wherever situated;

(4)   to appoint such employees, accountants, attorneys, and other agents as may be necessary or appropriate, and to determine their qualifications, define their duties, and fix their salaries or other compensation (at a level that is comparable to private sector self-regulatory, accounting, technical, supervisory, or other staff or management positions);

(5)   to allocate, assess, and collect accounting support fees established pursuant to section 109, for the Board, and other fees and charges imposed under this title; and

(6)   to enter into contracts, execute instruments, incur liabilities, and do any and all other acts and things necessary, appropriate, or incidental to the conduct of its operations and the exercise of its obligations, rights, and powers imposed or granted by this title.

(g)   RULES OF THE BOARD.—The rules of the Board shall, subject to the approval of the Commission—

(1)   provide for the operation and administration of the Board, the exercise of its authority, and the performance of its responsibilities under this Act;

(2)   permit, as the Board determines necessary or appropriate, delegation by the Board of any of its functions to an individual member or employee of the Board, or to a division of the Board, including functions with respect to hearing, determining, ordering, certifying, reporting, or otherwise acting as to any matter, except that—

(A)   the Board shall retain a discretionary right to review any action pursuant to any such delegated function, upon its own motion;

(B)   a person shall be entitled to a review by the Board with respect to any matter so delegated, and the decision of the Board upon such review shall be deemed to be the action of the Board for all purposes (including appeal or review thereof); and

(C)   if the right to exercise a review described in subparagraph (A) is declined, or if no such review is sought within the time stated in the rules of the Board, then the action taken by the holder of such delegation shall for all purposes, including appeal or review thereof, be deemed to be the action of the Board;

(3)   establish ethics rules and standards of conduct for Board members and staff, including a bar on practice before the Board (and the Commission, with respect to Board-related matters) of 1 year for former members of the Board, and appropriate periods (not to exceed 1 year) for former staff of the Board; and

(4)   provide as otherwise required by this Act.

(h)   ANNUAL REPORT TO THE COMMISSION.—The Board shall submit an annual report (including its audited financial statements) to the Commission, and the Commission shall transmit a copy of that report to the Committee on Banking, Housing, and Urban Affairs of the Senate, and the Committee on Financial Services of the House of Representatives, not later than 30 days after the date of receipt of that report by the Commission.

§ 102.   Registration With the Board

(a)   MANDATORY REGISTRATION.—Beginning 180 days after the date of the determination of the Commission under section 101(d), it shall be unlawful for any person that is not a registered public accounting firm to prepare or issue, or to participate in the preparation or issuance of, any audit report with respect to any issuer.

(b) APPLICATIONS FOR REGISTRATION.—

(1) FORM OF APPLICATION.—A public accounting firm shall use such form as the Board may prescribe, by rule, to apply for registration under this section.

(2) CONTENTS OF APPLICATIONS.—Each public accounting firm shall submit, as part of its application for registration, in such detail as the Board shall specify—

(A) the names of all issuers for which the firm prepared or issued audit reports during the immediately preceding calendar year, and for which the firm expects to prepare or issue audit reports during the current calendar year;

(B) the annual fees received by the firm from each such issuer for audit services, other accounting services, and non-audit services, respectively;

(C) such other current financial information for the most recently completed fiscal year of the firm as the Board may reasonably request;

(D) a statement of the quality control policies of the firm for its accounting and auditing practices;

(E) a list of all accountants associated with the firm who participate in or contribute to the preparation of audit reports, stating the license or certification number of each such person, as well as the State license numbers of the firm itself;

(F) information relating to criminal, civil, or administrative actions or disciplinary proceedings pending against the firm or any associated person of the firm in connection with any audit report;

(G) copies of any periodic or annual disclosure filed by an issuer with the Commission during the immediately preceding calendar year which discloses accounting disagreements between such issuer and the firm in connection with an audit report furnished or prepared by the firm for such issuer; and

(H) such other information as the rules of the Board or the Commission shall specify as necessary or appropriate in the public interest or for the protection of investors.

(3) CONSENTS.—Each application for registration under this subsection shall include—

(A) a consent executed by the public accounting firm to cooperation in and compliance with any request for testimony or the production of documents made by the Board in the furtherance of its authority and responsibilities under this title (and an agreement to secure and enforce similar consents from each of the associated persons of the public accounting firm as a condition of their continued employment by or other association with such firm); and

(B) a statement that such firm understands and agrees that cooperation and compliance, as described in the consent required by subparagraph (A), and the securing and enforcement of such consents from its associated persons, in accordance with the rules of the Board, shall be a condition to the continuing effectiveness of the registration of the firm with the Board.

(c) ACTION ON APPLICATIONS.—

(1) TIMING.—The Board shall approve a completed application for registration not later than 45 days after the date of receipt of the application, in accordance with the rules of the Board, unless the Board, prior to such date, issues a written notice of disapproval to, or requests more information from, the prospective registrant.

(2) TREATMENT.—A written notice of disapproval of a completed application under paragraph (1) for registration shall be treated as a disciplinary sanction for purposes of sections 105(d) and 107(c).

(d) PERIODIC REPORTS.—Each registered public accounting firm shall submit an annual report to the Board, and may be required to report more frequently, as necessary to update the information contained in its application for registration under this section, and to provide to the Board such additional information as the Board or the Commission may specify, in accordance with subsection (b)(2).

(e) PUBLIC AVAILABILITY.—Registration applications and annual reports required by this subsection, or such portions of such applications or reports as may be designated under rules of the Board, shall be made available for public inspection, subject to rules of the Board or the Commission, and to applicable laws relating to the confidentiality of proprietary, personal, or other information contained in such applications or reports, provided that, in all events, the Board shall protect from public disclosure information reasonably identified by the subject accounting firm as proprietary information.

(f) REGISTRATION AND ANNUAL FEES.—The Board shall assess and collect a registration fee and an annual fee from each registered public accounting firm, in amounts that are sufficient to recover the costs of processing and reviewing applications and annual reports.

§ 103. Auditing, Quality Control, and Independence Standards and Rules

(a) AUDITING, QUALITY CONTROL, AND ETHICS STANDARDS.—

(1) IN GENERAL.—The Board shall, by rule, establish, including, to the extent it determines appropriate, through adoption of standards proposed by 1 or more professional groups of accountants designated pursuant to paragraph (3)(A) or advisory groups convened pursuant to paragraph (4), and amend or otherwise modify or alter, such auditing and related attestation standards, such quality control standards, and such ethics standards to be used by registered public accounting firms in the preparation and issuance of audit reports, as required by this Act or the rules of the Commission, or as may be necessary or appropriate in the public interest or for the protection of investors.

(2) RULE REQUIREMENTS.—In carrying out paragraph (1), the Board—

(A) shall include in the auditing standards that it adopts, requirements that each registered public accounting firm shall—

(i) prepare, and maintain for a period of not less than 7 years, audit work papers, and other information related to any audit report, in sufficient detail to support the conclusions reached in such report;

(ii) provide a concurring or second partner review and approval of such audit report (and other related information), and concurring approval in its issuance, by a qualified person (as prescribed by the Board) associated with the public accounting firm, other than the person in charge of the audit, or by an independent reviewer (as prescribed by the Board); and

(iii) describe in each audit report the scope of the auditor's testing of the internal control structure and procedures of the issuer, required by section 404(b), and present (in such report or in a separate report)—

(I) the findings of the auditor from such testing;

(II) an evaluation of whether such internal control structure and procedures—

(aa) include maintenance of records that in reasonable detail accurately and fairly reflect the transactions and dispositions of the assets of the issuer;

(bb) provide reasonable assurance that transactions are recorded as necessary to permit preparation of financial statements in accordance with generally accepted accounting principles, and that receipts and expenditures of the issuer are being made only in accordance with authorizations of management and directors of the issuer; and

(III) a description, at a minimum, of material weaknesses in such internal controls, and of any material noncompliance found on the basis of such testing.

(B) shall include, in the quality control standards that it adopts with respect to the issuance of audit reports, requirements for every registered public accounting firm relating to—

(i) monitoring of professional ethics and independence from issuers on behalf of which the firm issues audit reports;

(ii) consultation within such firm on accounting and auditing questions;

(iii) supervision of audit work;

(iv) hiring, professional development, and advancement of personnel;

(v) the acceptance and continuation of engagements;

(vi) internal inspection; and

(vii) such other requirements as the Board may prescribe, subject to subsection (a)(1).

(3) AUTHORITY TO ADOPT OTHER STANDARDS.—

(A) IN GENERAL.—In carrying out this subsection, the Board—

(i) may adopt as its rules, subject to the terms of section 107, any portion of any statement of auditing standards or other professional standards that the Board determines satisfy the requirements of paragraph (1), and that were proposed by 1 or more professional groups of accountants that shall be designated or recognized by the Board, by rule, for such purpose, pursuant to this paragraph or 1 or more advisory groups convened pursuant to paragraph (4); and

(ii) notwithstanding clause (i), shall retain full authority to modify, supplement, revise, or subsequently amend, modify, or repeal, in whole or in part, any portion of any statement described in clause (i).

(B) INITIAL AND TRANSITIONAL STANDARDS.—The Board shall adopt standards described in subparagraph (A)(i) as initial or transitional standards, to the extent the Board determines necessary, prior to a determination of the Commission under section 101(d), and such standards shall be separately approved by the Commission at the time of that determination, without regard to the procedures required by section 107 that otherwise would apply to the approval of rules of the Board.

(4) ADVISORY GROUPS.—The Board shall convene, or authorize its staff to convene, such expert advisory groups as may be appropriate, which may include practicing accountants and other experts, as well as representatives of other interested groups, subject to such rules as the Board may prescribe to prevent conflicts of interest, to make recommendations concerning the content (including proposed drafts) of auditing, quality control, ethics, independence, or other standards required to be established under this section.

(b) INDEPENDENCE STANDARDS AND RULES.—The Board shall establish such rules as may be necessary or appropriate in the public interest or for the protection of investors, to implement, or as authorized under, title II of this Act.

(c) COOPERATION WITH DESIGNATED PROFESSIONAL GROUPS OF ACCOUNTANTS AND ADVISORY GROUPS.—

(1) IN GENERAL.—The Board shall cooperate on an ongoing basis with professional groups of accountants designated under subsection (a)(3)(A) and advisory groups convened under subsection (a)(4) in the examination of the need for changes in any standards subject to its authority under subsection (a), recommend issues for inclusion on the agendas of such designated professional groups of accountants or advisory groups, and take such other steps as it deems appropriate to increase the effectiveness of the standard setting process.

(2) BOARD RESPONSES.—The Board shall respond in a timely fashion to requests from designated professional groups of accountants and advisory groups referred to in paragraph (1) for any changes in standards over which the Board has authority.

(d) EVALUATION OF STANDARD SETTING PROCESS.—The Board shall include in the annual report required by section 101(h) the results of its standard setting responsibilities during the period to which the report relates, including a discussion of the work of the Board with any designated professional groups of accountants and advisory groups described in paragraphs (3)(A) and (4) of subsection (a), and its pending issues agenda for future standard setting projects.

§ 104.   Inspections of Registered Public Accounting Firms

(a) IN GENERAL.—The Board shall conduct a continuing program of inspections to assess the degree of compliance of each registered public accounting firm and associated persons of that firm with this Act, the rules of the Board, the rules of the Commission, or professional standards, in connection with its performance of audits, issuance of audit reports, and related matters involving issuers.

(b) INSPECTION FREQUENCY.—

(1) IN GENERAL.—Subject to paragraph (2), inspections required by this section shall be conducted—

(A) annually with respect to each registered public accounting firm that regularly provides audit reports for more than 100 issuers; and

(B) not less frequently than once every 3 years with respect to each registered public accounting firm that regularly provides audit reports for 100 or fewer issuers.

(2) ADJUSTMENTS TO SCHEDULES.—The Board may, by rule, adjust the inspection schedules set under paragraph (1) if the Board finds that different inspection schedules are consistent with the purposes of this Act, the public interest, and the protection of investors. The Board may conduct special inspections at the request of the Commission or upon its own motion.

(c) PROCEDURES.—The Board shall, in each inspection under this section, and in accordance with its rules for such inspections—

(1) identify any act or practice or omission to act by the registered public accounting firm, or by any associated person thereof, revealed by such inspection that may be in violation of this Act, the rules of the Board, the rules of the Commission, the firm's own quality control policies, or professional standards;

(2) report any such act, practice, or omission, if appropriate, to the Commission and each appropriate State regulatory authority; and

(3) begin a formal investigation or take disciplinary action, if appropriate, with respect to any such violation, in accordance with this Act and the rules of the Board.

(d) CONDUCT OF INSPECTIONS.—In conducting an inspection of a registered public accounting firm under this section, the Board shall—

(1) inspect and review selected audit and review engagements of the firm (which may include audit engagements that are the subject of ongoing litigation or other controversy between the firm and 1 or more third parties), performed at various offices and by various associated persons of the firm, as selected by the Board;

(2) evaluate the sufficiency of the quality control system of the firm, and the manner of the documentation and communication of that system by the firm; and

(3) perform such other testing of the audit, supervisory, and quality control procedures of the firm as are necessary or appropriate in light of the purpose of the inspection and the responsibilities of the Board.

(e)   RECORD RETENTION.—The rules of the Board may require the retention by registered public accounting firms for inspection purposes of records whose retention is not otherwise required by section 103 or the rules issued thereunder.

(f)   PROCEDURES FOR REVIEW.—The rules of the Board shall provide a procedure for the review of and response to a draft inspection report by the registered public accounting firm under inspection. The Board shall take such action with respect to such response as it considers appropriate (including revising the draft report or continuing or supplementing its inspection activities before issuing a final report), but the text of any such response, appropriately redacted to protect information reasonably identified by the accounting firm as confidential, shall be attached to and made part of the inspection report.

(g)   REPORT.—A written report of the findings of the Board for each inspection under this section, subject to subsection (h), shall be—

(1)   transmitted, in appropriate detail, to the Commission and each appropriate State regulatory authority, accompanied by any letter or comments by the Board or the inspector, and any letter of response from the registered public accounting firm; and

(2)   made available in appropriate detail to the public (subject to section 105(b)(5)(A), and to the protection of such confidential and proprietary information as the Board may determine to be appropriate, or as may be required by law), except that no portions of the inspection report that deal with criticisms of or potential defects in the quality control systems of the firm under inspection shall be made public if those criticisms or defects are addressed by the firm, to the satisfaction of the Board, not later than 12 months after the date of the inspection report.

(h)   INTERIM COMMISSION REVIEW.—

(1)   REVIEWABLE MATTERS.—A registered public accounting firm may seek review by the Commission, pursuant to such rules as the Commission shall promulgate, if the firm—

(A)   has provided the Board with a response, pursuant to rules issued by the Board under subsection (f), to the substance of particular items in a draft inspection report, and disagrees with the assessments contained in any final report prepared by the Board following such response; or

(B)   disagrees with the determination of the Board that criticisms or defects identified in an inspection report have not been addressed to the satisfaction of the Board within 12 months of the date of the inspection report, for purposes of subsection (g)(2).

(2)   TREATMENT OF REVIEW.—Any decision of the Commission with respect to a review under paragraph (1) shall not be reviewable under section 25 of the Securities Exchange Act of 1934, or deemed to be "final agency action" for purposes of section 704 of title 5, United States Code.

(3)   TIMING.—Review under paragraph (1) may be sought during the 30-day period following the date of the event giving rise to the review under subparagraph (A) or (B) of paragraph (1).

§ 105.   Investigations and Disciplinary Proceedings

(a)   IN GENERAL.—The Board shall establish, by rule, subject to the requirements of this section, fair procedures for the investigation and disciplining of registered public accounting firms and associated persons of such firms.

(b)   INVESTIGATIONS.—

(1)   AUTHORITY.—In accordance with the rules of the Board, the Board may conduct an investigation of any act or practice, or omission to act, by a registered public accounting firm, any associated person of such firm, or both, that may violate any provision of this Act, the rules of the Board, the provisions of the securities laws relating to the preparation and issuance of audit reports and the obligations and liabilities of accountants with respect thereto, including the rules of the

Commission issued under this Act, or professional standards, regardless of how the act, practice, or omission is brought to the attention of the Board.

(2) TESTIMONY AND DOCUMENT PRODUCTION.—In addition to such other actions as the Board determines to be necessary or appropriate, the rules of the Board may—

(A) require the testimony of the firm or of any person associated with a registered public accounting firm, with respect to any matter that the Board considers relevant or material to an investigation;

(B) require the production of audit work papers and any other document or information in the possession of a registered public accounting firm or any associated person thereof, wherever domiciled, that the Board considers relevant or material to the investigation, and may inspect the books and records of such firm or associated person to verify the accuracy of any documents or information supplied;

(C) request the testimony of, and production of any document in the possession of, any other person, including any client of a registered public accounting firm that the Board considers relevant or material to an investigation under this section, with appropriate notice, subject to the needs of the investigation, as permitted under the rules of the Board; and

(D) provide for procedures to seek issuance by the Commission, in a manner established by the Commission, of a subpoena to require the testimony of, and production of any document in the possession of, any person, including any client of a registered public accounting firm, that the Board considers relevant or material to an investigation under this section.

(3) NONCOOPERATION WITH INVESTIGATIONS.—

(A) IN GENERAL.—If a registered public accounting firm or any associated person thereof refuses to testify, produce documents, or otherwise cooperate with the Board in connection with an investigation under this section, the Board may—

(i) suspend or bar such person from being associated with a registered public accounting firm, or require the registered public accounting firm to end such association;

(ii) suspend or revoke the registration of the public accounting firm; and

(iii) invoke such other lesser sanctions as the Board considers appropriate, and as specified by rule of the Board.

(B) PROCEDURE.—Any action taken by the Board under this paragraph shall be subject to the terms of section 107(c).

(4) COORDINATION AND REFERRAL OF INVESTIGATIONS.—

(A) COORDINATION.—The Board shall notify the Commission of any pending Board investigation involving a potential violation of the securities laws, and thereafter coordinate its work with the work of the Commission's Division of Enforcement, as necessary to protect an ongoing Commission investigation.

(B) REFERRAL.—The Board may refer an investigation under this section—

(i) to the Commission;

(ii) to any other Federal functional regulator (as defined in section 509 of the Gramm-Leach-Bliley Act), in the case of an investigation that concerns an audit report for an institution that is subject to the jurisdiction of such regulator; and

(iii) at the direction of the Commission, to—

(I) the Attorney General of the United States;

(II) the attorney general of 1 or more States; and

(III) the appropriate State regulatory authority.

(5) USE OF DOCUMENTS.—

(A) CONFIDENTIALITY.—Except as provided in subparagraph (B), all documents and information prepared or received by or specifically for the Board, and deliberations of the Board and its employees and agents, in connection with an inspection under section 104 or with an investigation under this section, shall be confidential and privileged as an evidentiary matter (and shall not be subject to civil discovery or other legal process) in any proceeding in any Federal or State court or administrative agency, and shall be exempt from disclosure, in the hands of an agency or establishment of the Federal Government, under the Freedom of Information Act (5 U.S.C. 552a), or otherwise, unless and until presented in connection with a public proceeding or released in accordance with subsection (c).

(B) AVAILABILITY TO GOVERNMENT AGENCIES.—Without the loss of its status as confidential and privileged in the hands of the Board, all information referred to in subparagraph (A) may—

(i) be made available to the Commission; and

(ii) in the discretion of the Board, when determined by the Board to be necessary to accomplish the purposes of this Act or to protect investors, be made available to—

(I) the Attorney General of the United States;

(II) the appropriate Federal functional regulator (as defined in section 509 of the Gramm-Leach-Bliley Act), other than the Commission, with respect to an audit report for an institution subject to the jurisdiction of such regulator;

(III) State attorneys general in connection with any criminal investigation; and

(IV) any appropriate State regulatory authority,

each of which shall maintain such information as confidential and privileged.

(6) IMMUNITY.—Any employee of the Board engaged in carrying out an investigation under this Act shall be immune from any civil liability arising out of such investigation in the same manner and to the same extent as an employee of the Federal Government in similar circumstances.

(c) DISCIPLINARY PROCEDURES.—

(1) NOTIFICATION; RECORDKEEPING.—The rules of the Board shall provide that in any proceeding by the Board to determine whether a registered public accounting firm, or an associated person thereof, should be disciplined, the Board shall—

(A) bring specific charges with respect to the firm or associated person;

(B) notify such firm or associated person of, and provide to the firm or associated person an opportunity to defend against, such charges; and

(C) keep a record of the proceedings.

(2) PUBLIC HEARINGS.—Hearings under this section shall not be public, unless otherwise ordered by the Board for good cause shown, with the consent of the parties to such hearing.

(3) SUPPORTING STATEMENT.—A determination by the Board to impose a sanction under this subsection shall be supported by a statement setting forth—

(A) each act or practice in which the registered public accounting firm, or associated person, has engaged (or omitted to engage), or that forms a basis for all or a part of such sanction;

(B) the specific provision of this Act, the securities laws, the rules of the Board, or professional standards which the Board determines has been violated; and

(C) the sanction imposed, including a justification for that sanction.

(4) SANCTIONS.—If the Board finds, based on all of the facts and circumstances, that a registered public accounting firm or associated person thereof has engaged in any act or practice, or omitted to act, in violation of this Act, the rules of the Board, the provisions of the securities laws relating to the preparation and issuance of audit reports and the obligations and liabilities of accountants with respect thereto, including the rules of the Commission issued under this Act, or professional standards, the Board may impose such disciplinary or remedial sanctions as it determines appropriate, subject to applicable limitations under paragraph (5), including—

    (A) temporary suspension or permanent revocation of registration under this title;

    (B) temporary or permanent suspension or bar of a person from further association with any registered public accounting firm;

    (C) temporary or permanent limitation on the activities, functions, or operations of such firm or person (other than in connection with required additional professional education or training);

    (D) a civil money penalty for each such violation, in an amount equal to—

        (i) not more than $100,000 for a natural person or $2,000,000 for any other person; and

        (ii) in any case to which paragraph (5) applies, not more than $750,000 for a natural person or $15,000,000 for any other person;

    (E) censure;

    (F) required additional professional education or training; or

    (G) any other appropriate sanction provided for in the rules of the Board.

(5) INTENTIONAL OR OTHER KNOWING CONDUCT.—The sanctions and penalties described in subparagraphs (A) through (C) and (D)(ii) of paragraph (4) shall only apply to—

    (A) intentional or knowing conduct, including reckless conduct, that results in violation of the applicable statutory, regulatory, or professional standard; or

    (B) repeated instances of negligent conduct, each resulting in a violation of the applicable statutory, regulatory, or professional standard.

(6) FAILURE TO SUPERVISE.—

    (A) IN GENERAL.—The Board may impose sanctions under this section on a registered accounting firm or upon the supervisory personnel of such firm, if the Board finds that—

        (i) the firm has failed reasonably to supervise an associated person, either as required by the rules of the Board relating to auditing or quality control standards, or otherwise, with a view to preventing violations of this Act, the rules of the Board, the provisions of the securities laws relating to the preparation and issuance of audit reports and the obligations and liabilities of accountants with respect thereto, including the rules of the Commission under this Act, or professional standards; and

        (ii) such associated person commits a violation of this Act, or any of such rules, laws, or standards.

    (B) RULE OF CONSTRUCTION.—No associated person of a registered public accounting firm shall be deemed to have failed reasonably to supervise any other person for purposes of subparagraph (A), if—

        (i) there have been established in and for that firm procedures, and a system for applying such procedures, that comply with applicable rules of the Board and that would reasonably be expected to prevent and detect any such violation by such associated person; and

(ii) such person has reasonably discharged the duties and obligations incumbent upon that person by reason of such procedures and system, and had no reasonable cause to believe that such procedures and system were not being complied with.

(7) EFFECT OF SUSPENSION.—

(A) ASSOCIATION WITH A PUBLIC ACCOUNTING FIRM.—It shall be unlawful for any person that is suspended or barred from being associated with a registered public accounting firm under this subsection willfully to become or remain associated with any registered public accounting firm, or for any registered public accounting firm that knew, or, in the exercise of reasonable care should have known, of the suspension or bar, to permit such an association, without the consent of the Board or the Commission.

(B) ASSOCIATION WITH AN ISSUER.—It shall be unlawful for any person that is suspended or barred from being associated with an issuer under this subsection willfully to become or remain associated with any issuer in an accountancy or a financial management capacity, and for any issuer that knew, or in the exercise of reasonable care should have known, of such suspension or bar, to permit such an association, without the consent of the Board or the Commission.

(d) REPORTING OF SANCTIONS.—

(1) RECIPIENTS.—If the Board imposes a disciplinary sanction, in accordance with this section, the Board shall report the sanction to—

(A) the Commission;

(B) any appropriate State regulatory authority or any foreign accountancy licensing board with which such firm or person is licensed or certified; and

(C) the public (once any stay on the imposition of such sanction has been lifted).

(2) CONTENTS.—The information reported under paragraph (1) shall include—

(A) the name of the sanctioned person;

(B) a description of the sanction and the basis for its imposition; and

(C) such other information as the Board deems appropriate.

(e) STAY OF SANCTIONS.—

(1) IN GENERAL.—Application to the Commission for review, or the institution by the Commission of review, of any disciplinary action of the Board shall operate as a stay of any such disciplinary action, unless and until the Commission orders (summarily or after notice and opportunity for hearing on the question of a stay, which hearing may consist solely of the submission of affidavits or presentation of oral arguments) that no such stay shall continue to operate.

(2) EXPEDITED PROCEDURES.—The Commission shall establish for appropriate cases an expedited procedure for consideration and determination of the question of the duration of a stay pending review of any disciplinary action of the Board under this subsection.

§ 106. Foreign Public Accounting Firms

(a) APPLICABILITY TO CERTAIN FOREIGN FIRMS.—

(1) IN GENERAL.—Any foreign public accounting firm that prepares or furnishes an audit report with respect to any issuer, shall be subject to this Act and the rules of the Board and the Commission issued under this Act, in the same manner and to the same extent as a public accounting firm that is organized and operates under the laws of the United States or any State, except that registration pursuant to section 102 shall not by itself provide a basis for subjecting such a foreign public accounting firm to the jurisdiction of the Federal or State courts, other than with respect to controversies between such firms and the Board.

(2) BOARD AUTHORITY.—The Board may, by rule, determine that a foreign public accounting firm (or a class of such firms) that does not issue audit reports nonetheless plays such a substantial role in the preparation and furnishing of such reports for particular issuers, that it is necessary or appropriate, in light of the purposes of this Act and in the public interest or for the protection of investors, that such firm (or class of firms) should be treated as a public accounting firm (or firms) for purposes of registration under, and oversight by the Board in accordance with, this title.

(b) PRODUCTION OF AUDIT WORKPAPERS.—

(1) CONSENT BY FOREIGN FIRMS.—If a foreign public accounting firm issues an opinion or otherwise performs material services upon which a registered public accounting firm relies in issuing all or part of any audit report or any opinion contained in an audit report, that foreign public accounting firm shall be deemed to have consented—

(A) to produce its audit workpapers for the Board or the Commission in connection with any investigation by either body with respect to that audit report; and

(B) to be subject to the jurisdiction of the courts of the United States for purposes of enforcement of any request for production of such workpapers.

(2) CONSENT BY DOMESTIC FIRMS.—A registered public accounting firm that relies upon the opinion of a foreign public accounting firm, as described in paragraph (1), shall be deemed—

(A) to have consented to supplying the audit workpapers of that foreign public accounting firm in response to a request for production by the Board or the Commission; and

(B) to have secured the agreement of that foreign public accounting firm to such production, as a condition of its reliance on the opinion of that foreign public accounting firm.

(c) EXEMPTION AUTHORITY.—The Commission, and the Board, subject to the approval of the Commission, may, by rule, regulation, or order, and as the Commission (or Board) determines necessary or appropriate in the public interest or for the protection of investors, either unconditionally or upon specified terms and conditions exempt any foreign public accounting firm, or any class of such firms, from any provision of this Act or the rules of the Board or the Commission issued under this Act.

(d) DEFINITION.—In this section, the term "foreign public accounting firm" means a public accounting firm that is organized and operates under the laws of a foreign government or political subdivision thereof.

§ 107.   Commission Oversight of the Board

(a) GENERAL OVERSIGHT RESPONSIBILITY.—The Commission shall have oversight and enforcement authority over the Board, as provided in this Act. The provisions of section 17(a)(1) of the Securities Exchange Act of 1934, and of section 17(b)(1) of the Securities Exchange Act of 1934 shall apply to the Board as fully as if the Board were a "registered securities association" for purposes of those sections 17(a)(1) and 17(b)(1).

(b) RULES OF THE BOARD.—

(1) DEFINITION.—In this section, the term "proposed rule" means any proposed rule of the Board, and any modification of any such rule.

(2) PRIOR APPROVAL REQUIRED.—No rule of the Board shall become effective without prior approval of the Commission in accordance with this section, other than as provided in section 103(a)(3)(B) with respect to initial or transitional standards.

(3) APPROVAL CRITERIA.—The Commission shall approve a proposed rule, if it finds that the rule is consistent with the requirements of this Act and the securities laws, or is necessary or appropriate in the public interest or for the protection of investors.

(4) PROPOSED RULE PROCEDURES.—The provisions of paragraphs (1) through (3) of section 19(b) of the Securities Exchange Act of 1934 shall govern the proposed rules of the Board, as fully as if the Board were a "registered securities association" for purposes of that section 19(b), except that, for purposes of this paragraph—

(A) the phrase "consistent with the requirements of this title and the rules and regulations thereunder applicable to such organization" in section 19(b)(2) of that Act shall be deemed to read "consistent with the requirements of title I of the Sarbanes-Oxley Act of 2002, and the rules and regulations issued thereunder applicable to such organization, or as necessary or appropriate in the public interest or for the protection of investors"; and

(B) the phrase "otherwise in furtherance of the purposes of this title" in section 19(b)(3)(C) of that Act shall be deemed to read "otherwise in furtherance of the purposes of title I of the Sarbanes-Oxley Act of 2002".

(5) COMMISSION AUTHORITY TO AMEND RULES OF THE BOARD.—The provisions of section 19(c) of the Securities Exchange Act of 1934 (15 U.S.C. 78s(c)) shall govern the abrogation, deletion, or addition to portions of the rules of the Board by the Commission as fully as if the Board were a "registered securities association" for purposes of that section 19(c), except that the phrase "to conform its rules to the requirements of this title and the rules and regulations thereunder applicable to such organization, or otherwise in furtherance of the purposes of this title" in section 19(c) of that Act shall, for purposes of this paragraph, be deemed to read "to assure the fair administration of the Public Company Accounting Oversight Board, conform the rules promulgated by that Board to the requirements of title I of the Sarbanes-Oxley Act of 2002, or otherwise further the purposes of that Act, the securities laws, and the rules and regulations thereunder applicable to that Board".

(c) COMMISSION REVIEW OF DISCIPLINARY ACTION TAKEN BY THE BOARD.—

(1) NOTICE OF SANCTION.—The Board shall promptly file notice with the Commission of any final sanction on any registered public accounting firm or on any associated person thereof, in such form and containing such information as the Commission, by rule, may prescribe.

(2) REVIEW OF SANCTIONS.—The provisions of sections 19(d)(2) and 19(e)(1) of the Securities Exchange Act of 1934 shall govern the review by the Commission of final disciplinary sanctions imposed by the Board (including sanctions imposed under section 105(b)(3) of this Act for noncooperation in an investigation of the Board), as fully as if the Board were a self-regulatory organization and the Commission were the appropriate regulatory agency for such organization for purposes of those sections 19(d)(2) and 19(e)(1), except that, for purposes of this paragraph—

(A) section 105(e) of this Act (rather than that section 19(d)(2)) shall govern the extent to which application for, or institution by the Commission on its own motion of, review of any disciplinary action of the Board operates as a stay of such action;

(B) references in that section 19(e)(1) to "members" of such an organization shall be deemed to be references to registered public accounting firms;

(C) the phrase "consistent with the purposes of this title" in that section 19(e)(1) shall be deemed to read "consistent with the purposes of this title and title I of the Sarbanes-Oxley Act of 2002";

(D) references to rules of the Municipal Securities Rulemaking Board in that section 19(e)(1) shall not apply; and

(E) the reference to section 19(e)(2) of the Securities Exchange Act of 1934 shall refer instead to section 107(c)(3) of this Act.

(3) COMMISSION MODIFICATION AUTHORITY.—The Commission may enhance, modify, cancel, reduce, or require the remission of a sanction imposed by the Board upon a registered public accounting firm or associated person thereof, if the Commission, having due regard for the public

interest and the protection of investors, finds, after a proceeding in accordance with this subsection, that the sanction—

(A) is not necessary or appropriate in furtherance of this Act or the securities laws; or

(B) is excessive, oppressive, inadequate, or otherwise not appropriate to the finding or the basis on which the sanction was imposed.

(d) CENSURE OF THE BOARD; OTHER SANCTIONS.—

(1) RESCISSION OF BOARD AUTHORITY.—The Commission, by rule, consistent with the public interest, the protection of investors, and the other purposes of this Act and the securities laws, may relieve the Board of any responsibility to enforce compliance with any provision of this Act, the securities laws, the rules of the Board, or professional standards.

(2) CENSURE OF THE BOARD; LIMITATIONS.—The Commission may, by order, as it determines necessary or appropriate in the public interest, for the protection of investors, or otherwise in furtherance of the purposes of this Act or the securities laws, censure or impose limitations upon the activities, functions, and operations of the Board, if the Commission finds, on the record, after notice and opportunity for a hearing, that the Board—

(A) has violated or is unable to comply with any provision of this Act, the rules of the Board, or the securities laws; or

(B) without reasonable justification or excuse, has failed to enforce compliance with any such provision or rule, or any professional standard by a registered public accounting firm or an associated person thereof.

(3) CENSURE OF BOARD MEMBERS; REMOVAL FROM OFFICE.—The Commission may, as necessary or appropriate in the public interest, for the protection of investors, or otherwise in furtherance of the purposes of this Act or the securities laws, remove from office or censure any member of the Board, if the Commission finds, on the record, after notice and opportunity for a hearing, that such member—

(A) has willfully violated any provision of this Act, the rules of the Board, or the securities laws;

(B) has willfully abused the authority of that member; or

(C) without reasonable justification or excuse, has failed to enforce compliance with any such provision or rule, or any professional standard by any registered public accounting firm or any associated person thereof.

§ 108. Accounting Standards

(a) AMENDMENT TO SECURITIES ACT OF 1933.—Section 19 of the Securities Act of 1933 is amended—

(1) by redesignating subsections (b) and (c) as subsections (c) and (d), respectively; and

(2) by inserting after subsection (a) the following:

"(b) RECOGNITION OF ACCOUNTING STANDARDS.—

"(1) IN GENERAL.—In carrying out its authority under subsection (a) and under section 13(b) of the Securities Exchange Act of 1934, the Commission may recognize, as 'generally accepted' for purposes of the securities laws, any accounting principles established by a standard setting body—

"(A) that—

"(i) is organized as a private entity;

"(ii) has, for administrative and operational purposes, a board of trustees (or equivalent body) serving in the public interest, the majority of whom are not, concurrent with their service on such board, and have not been during the 2-year period preceding such service, associated persons of any registered public accounting firm;

"(iii) is funded as provided in section 109 of the Sarbanes-Oxley Act of 2002;

"(iv) has adopted procedures to ensure prompt consideration, by majority vote of its members, of changes to accounting principles necessary to reflect emerging accounting issues and changing business practices; and

"(v) considers, in adopting accounting principles, the need to keep standards current in order to reflect changes in the business environment, the extent to which international convergence on high quality accounting standards is necessary or appropriate in the public interest and for the protection of investors; and

"(B) that the Commission determines has the capacity to assist the Commission in fulfilling the requirements of subsection (a) and section 13(b) of the Securities Exchange Act of 1934, because, at a minimum, the standard setting body is capable of improving the accuracy and effectiveness of financial reporting and the protection of investors under the securities laws.

"(2) ANNUAL REPORT.—A standard setting body described in paragraph (1) shall submit an annual report to the Commission and the public, containing audited financial statements of that standard setting body.".

(b) COMMISSION AUTHORITY.—The Commission shall promulgate such rules and regulations to carry out section 19(b) of the Securities Act of 1933, as added by this section, as it deems necessary or appropriate in the public interest or for the protection of investors.

(c) NO EFFECT ON COMMISSION POWERS.—Nothing in this Act, including this section and the amendment made by this section, shall be construed to impair or limit the authority of the Commission to establish accounting principles or standards for purposes of enforcement of the securities laws.

(d) STUDY AND REPORT ON ADOPTING PRINCIPLES-BASED ACCOUNTING.—

(1) STUDY.—

(A) IN GENERAL.—The Commission shall conduct a study on the adoption by the United States financial reporting system of a principles-based accounting system.

(B) STUDY TOPICS.—The study required by subparagraph (A) shall include an examination of—

(i) the extent to which principles-based accounting and financial reporting exists in the United States;

(ii) the length of time required for change from a rules-based to a principles-based financial reporting system;

(iii) the feasibility of and proposed methods by which a principles-based system may be implemented; and

(iv) a thorough economic analysis of the implementation of a principles-based system.

(2) REPORT.—Not later than 1 year after the date of enactment of this Act, the Commission shall submit a report on the results of the study required by paragraph (1) to the Committee on Banking, Housing, and Urban Affairs of the Senate and the Committee on Financial Services of the House of Representatives.

§ 109.   Funding

(a) IN GENERAL.—The Board, and the standard setting body designated pursuant to section 19(b) of the Securities Act of 1933, as amended by section 108, shall be funded as provided in this section.

(b) ANNUAL BUDGETS.—The Board and the standard setting body referred to in subsection (a) shall each establish a budget for each fiscal year, which shall be reviewed and approved according to their respective internal procedures not less than 1 month prior to the commencement of the fiscal year to which the budget pertains (or at the beginning of the Board's first fiscal year, which may be a short fiscal year). The budget of the Board shall be subject to approval by the Commission. The budget for the first fiscal year of the Board shall be prepared and approved promptly following the appointment of the initial five Board members, to permit action by the Board of the organizational tasks contemplated by section 101(d).

(c) SOURCES AND USES OF FUNDS.—

(1) RECOVERABLE BUDGET EXPENSES.—The budget of the Board (reduced by any registration or annual fees received under section 102(e) for the year preceding the year for which the budget is being computed), and all of the budget of the standard setting body referred to in subsection (a), for each fiscal year of each of those 2 entities, shall be payable from annual accounting support fees, in accordance with subsections (d) and (e). Accounting support fees and other receipts of the Board and of such standard-setting body shall not be considered public monies of the United States.

(2) FUNDS GENERATED FROM THE COLLECTION OF MONETARY PENALTIES.— Subject to the availability in advance in an appropriations Act, and notwithstanding subsection (i), all funds collected by the Board as a result of the assessment of monetary penalties shall be used to fund a merit scholarship program for undergraduate and graduate students enrolled in accredited accounting degree programs, which program is to be administered by the Board or by an entity or agent identified by the Board.

(d) ANNUAL ACCOUNTING SUPPORT FEE FOR THE BOARD.—

(1) ESTABLISHMENT OF FEE.—The Board shall establish, with the approval of the Commission, a reasonable annual accounting support fee (or a formula for the computation thereof), as may be necessary or appropriate to establish and maintain the Board. Such fee may also cover costs incurred in the Board's first fiscal year (which may be a short fiscal year), or may be levied separately with respect to such short fiscal year.

(2) ASSESSMENTS.—The rules of the Board under paragraph (1) shall provide for the equitable allocation, assessment, and collection by the Board (or an agent appointed by the Board) of the fee established under paragraph (1), among issuers, in accordance with subsection (g), allowing for differentiation among classes of issuers, as appropriate.

(e) ANNUAL ACCOUNTING SUPPORT FEE FOR STANDARD SETTING BODY.—The annual accounting support fee for the standard setting body referred to in subsection (a)—

(1) shall be allocated in accordance with subsection (g), and assessed and collected against each issuer, on behalf of the standard setting body, by 1 or more appropriate designated collection agents, as may be necessary or appropriate to pay for the budget and provide for the expenses of that standard setting body, and to provide for an independent, stable source of funding for such body, subject to review by the Commission; and

(2) may differentiate among different classes of issuers.

(f) LIMITATION ON FEE.—The amount of fees collected under this section for a fiscal year on behalf of the Board or the standards setting body, as the case may be, shall not exceed the recoverable budget expenses of the Board or body, respectively (which may include operating, capital, and accrued items), referred to in subsection (c)(1).

(g) ALLOCATION OF ACCOUNTING SUPPORT FEES AMONG ISSUERS.—Any amount due from issuers (or a particular class of issuers) under this section to fund the budget of the Board or the standard setting body referred to in subsection (a) shall be allocated among and payable by each issuer (or each issuer in a particular class, as applicable) in an amount equal to the total of such amount, multiplied by a fraction—

(1) the numerator of which is the average monthly equity market capitalization of the issuer for the 12-month period immediately preceding the beginning of the fiscal year to which such budget relates; and

(2) the denominator of which is the average monthly equity market capitalization of all such issuers for such 12-month period.

(h) CONFORMING AMENDMENTS.—Section 13(b)(2) of the Securities Exchange Act of 1934 is amended—

(1) in subparagraph (A), by striking "and" at the end; and

(2) in subparagraph (B), by striking the period at the end and inserting the following: "; and" (C) notwithstanding any other provision of law, pay the allocable share of such issuer of a reasonable annual accounting support fee or fees, determined in accordance with section 109 of the Sarbanes-Oxley Act of 2002.".

(i) RULE OF CONSTRUCTION.—Nothing in this section shall be construed to render either the Board, the standard setting body referred to in subsection (a), or both, subject to procedures in Congress to authorize or appropriate public funds, or to prevent such organization from utilizing additional sources of revenue for its activities, such as earnings from publication sales, provided that each additional source of revenue shall not jeopardize, in the judgment of the Commission, the actual and perceived independence of such organization.

(j) START-UP EXPENSES OF THE BOARD.—From the unexpended balances of the appropriations to the Commission for fiscal year 2003, the Secretary of the Treasury is authorized to advance to the Board not to exceed the amount necessary to cover the expenses of the Board during its first fiscal year (which may be a short fiscal year).

TITLE II—AUDITOR INDEPENDENCE

§ 201. Services Outside the Scope of Practice of Auditors

(a) PROHIBITED ACTIVITIES.—Section 10A of the Securities Exchange Act of 1934 is amended by adding at the end the following:

"(g) PROHIBITED ACTIVITIES.—Except as provided in subsection (h), it shall be unlawful for a registered public accounting firm (and any associated person of that firm, to the extent determined appropriate by the Commission) that performs for any issuer any audit required by this title or the rules of the Commission under this title or, beginning 180 days after the date of commencement of the operations of the Public Company Accounting Oversight Board established under section 101 of the Sarbanes-Oxley Act of 2002 (in this section referred to as the 'Board'), the rules of the Board, to provide to that issuer, contemporaneously with the audit, any non-audit service, including—

"(1) bookkeeping or other services related to the accounting records or financial statements of the audit client;

"(2) financial information systems design and implementation;

"(3) appraisal or valuation services, fairness opinions, or contribution-in-kind reports;

"(4) actuarial services;

"(5) internal audit outsourcing services;

"(6) management functions or human resources;

"(7) broker or dealer, investment adviser, or investment banking services;

"(8) legal services and expert services unrelated to the audit; and

"(9) any other service that the Board determines, by regulation, is impermissible.

"(h) PREAPPROVAL REQUIRED FOR NON-AUDIT SERVICES.—A registered public accounting firm may engage in any non-audit service, including tax services, that is not described in any of paragraphs (1) through (9) of subsection (g) for an audit client, only if the activity is approved in advance by the audit committee of the issuer, in accordance with subsection (i).".

(b) EXEMPTION AUTHORITY.—The Board may, on a case by case basis, exempt any person, issuer, public accounting firm, or transaction from the prohibition on the provision of services under section 10A(g) of the Securities Exchange Act of 1934 (as added by this section), to the extent that such exemption is necessary or appropriate in the public interest and is consistent with the protection of investors, and subject to review by the Commission in the same manner as for rules of the Board under section 107.

§ 202. Preapproval Requirements

Section 10A of the Securities Exchange Act of 1934, as amended by this Act, is amended by adding at the end the following:

"(i) PREAPPROVAL REQUIREMENTS.—

"(1) IN GENERAL.—

"(A) AUDIT COMMITTEE ACTION.—All auditing services (which may entail providing comfort letters in connection with securities underwritings or statutory audits required for insurance companies for purposes of State law) and non-audit services, other than as provided in subparagraph (B), provided to an issuer by the auditor of the issuer shall be preapproved by the audit committee of the issuer.

"(B) DE MINIMUS EXCEPTION.—The preapproval requirement under subparagraph (A) is waived with respect to the provision of non-audit services for an issuer, if—

"(i) the aggregate amount of all such non-audit services provided to the issuer constitutes not more than 5 percent of the total amount of revenues paid by the issuer to its auditor during the fiscal year in which the nonaudit services are provided;

"(ii) such services were not recognized by the issuer at the time of the engagement to be non-audit services; and

"(iii) such services are promptly brought to the attention of the audit committee of the issuer and approved prior to the completion of the audit by the audit committee or by 1 or more members of the audit committee who are members of the board of directors to whom authority to grant such approvals has been delegated by the audit committee.

"(2) DISCLOSURE TO INVESTORS.—Approval by an audit committee of an issuer under this subsection of a non-audit service to be performed by the auditor of the issuer shall be disclosed to investors in periodic reports required by section 13(a).

"(3) DELEGATION AUTHORITY.—The audit committee of an issuer may delegate to 1 or more designated members of the audit committee who are independent directors of the board of directors, the authority to grant preapprovals required by this subsection. The decisions of any member to whom authority is delegated under this paragraph to preapprove an activity under this subsection shall be presented to the full audit committee at each of its scheduled meetings.

"(4) APPROVAL OF AUDIT SERVICES FOR OTHER PURPOSES.—In carrying out its duties under subsection (m)(2), if the audit committee of an issuer approves an audit service within the scope of the engagement of the auditor, such audit service shall be deemed to have been preapproved for purposes of this subsection.".

§ 203. Audit Partner Rotation

Section 10A of the Securities Exchange Act of 1934, as amended by this Act, is amended by adding at the end the following:

"(j) AUDIT PARTNER ROTATION.—It shall be unlawful for a registered public accounting firm to provide audit services to an issuer if the lead (or coordinating) audit partner (having primary responsibility for the audit), or the audit partner responsible for reviewing the audit, has performed audit services for that issuer in each of the 5 previous fiscal years of that issuer.".

§ 204. Auditor Reports to Audit Committees

Section 10A of the Securities Exchange Act of 1934, as amended by this Act, is amended by adding at the end the following:

"(k) REPORTS TO AUDIT COMMITTEES.—Each registered public accounting firm that performs for any issuer any audit required by this title shall timely report to the audit committee of the issuer—

"(1) all critical accounting policies and practices to be used;

"(2) all alternative treatments of financial information within generally accepted accounting principles that have been discussed with management officials of the issuer, ramifications of the use of such alternative disclosures and treatments, and the treatment preferred by the registered public accounting firm; and

"(3) other material written communications between the registered public accounting firm and the management of the issuer, such as any management letter or schedule of unadjusted differences.".

§ 205. Conforming Amendments

(a) DEFINITIONS.—Section 3(a) of the Securities Exchange Act of 1934 is amended by adding at the end the following:

"(58) AUDIT COMMITTEE.—The term 'audit committee' means—

"(A) a committee (or equivalent body) established by and amongst the board of directors of an issuer for the purpose of overseeing the accounting and financial reporting processes of the issuer and audits of the financial statements of the issuer; and

"(B) if no such committee exists with respect to an issuer, the entire board of directors of the issuer.

"(59) REGISTERED PUBLIC ACCOUNTING FIRM.—The term 'registered public accounting firm' has the same meaning as in section 2 of the Sarbanes-Oxley Act of 2002.".

(b) AUDITOR REQUIREMENTS.—Section 10A of the Securities Exchange Act of 1934 is amended—

(1) by striking "an independent public accountant" each place that term appears and inserting "a registered public accounting firm";

(2) by striking "the independent public accountant" each place that term appears and inserting "the registered public accounting firm";

(3) in subsection (c), by striking "No independent public accountant" and inserting "No registered public accounting firm"; and

(4)   in subsection (b)—

(A)   by striking "the accountant" each place that term appears and inserting "the firm";

(B)   by striking "such accountant" each place that term appears and inserting "such firm"; and

(C)   in paragraph (4), by striking "the accountant's report" and inserting "the report of the firm".

(c)   OTHER REFERENCES.—The Securities Exchange Act of 1934 is amended—

(1)   in section 12(b)(1), by striking "independent public accountants" each place that term appears and inserting "a registered public accounting firm"; and

(2)   in subsections (e) and (i) of section 17, by striking "an independent public accountant" each place that term appears and inserting "a registered public accounting firm".

(d)   CONFORMING AMENDMENT.—Section 10A(f) of the Securities Exchange Act of 1934 is amended—

(1)   by striking "DEFINITION" and inserting "DEFINITIONS"; and

(2)   by adding at the end the following: "As used in this section, the term 'issuer' means an issuer (as defined in section 3), the securities of which are registered under section 12, or that is required to file reports pursuant to section 15(d), or that files or has filed a registration statement that has not yet become effective under the Securities Act of 1933, and that it has not withdrawn.".

§ 206.   Conflicts of Interest

Section 10A of the Securities Exchange Act of 1934, as amended by this Act, is amended by adding at the end the following:

"(*l*)   CONFLICTS OF INTEREST.—It shall be unlawful for a registered public accounting firm to perform for an issuer any audit service required by this title, if a chief executive officer, controller, chief financial officer, chief accounting officer, or any person serving in an equivalent position for the issuer, was employed by that registered independent public accounting firm and participated in any capacity in the audit of that issuer during the 1-year period preceding the date of the initiation of the audit.".

§ 207.   Study of Mandatory Rotation of Registered Public Accounting Firms

(a)   STUDY AND REVIEW REQUIRED.—The Comptroller General of the United States shall conduct a study and review of the potential effects of requiring the mandatory rotation of registered public accounting firms.

(b)   REPORT REQUIRED.—Not later than 1 year after the date of enactment of this Act, the Comptroller General shall submit a report to the Committee on Banking, Housing, and Urban Affairs of the Senate and the Committee on Financial Services of the House of Representatives on the results of the study and review required by this section.

(c)   DEFINITION.—For purposes of this section, the term "mandatory rotation" refers to the imposition of a limit on the period of years in which a particular registered public accounting firm may be the auditor of record for a particular issuer.

§ 208.   Commission Authority

(a)   COMMISSION REGULATIONS.—Not later than 180 days after the date of enactment of this Act, the Commission shall issue final regulations to carry out each of subsections (g) through (*l*) of section 10A of the Securities Exchange Act of 1934, as added by this title.

(b) AUDITOR INDEPENDENCE.—It shall be unlawful for any registered public accounting firm (or an associated person thereof, as applicable) to prepare or issue any audit report with respect to any issuer, if the firm or associated person engages in any activity with respect to that issuer prohibited by any of subsections (g) through (*l*) of section 10A of the Securities Exchange Act of 1934, as added by this title, or any rule or regulation of the Commission or of the Board issued thereunder.

§ 209. Considerations by Appropriate State Regulatory Authorities

In supervising nonregistered public accounting firms and their associated persons, appropriate State regulatory authorities should make an independent determination of the proper standards applicable, particularly taking into consideration the size and nature of the business of the accounting firms they supervise and the size and nature of the business of the clients of those firms. The standards applied by the Board under this Act should not be presumed to be applicable for purposes of this section for small and medium sized nonregistered public accounting firms.

TITLE III—CORPORATE RESPONSIBILITY

§ 301. Public Company Audit Committees

Section 10A of the Securities Exchange Act of 1934 is amended by adding at the end the following:

"(m) STANDARDS RELATING TO AUDIT COMMITTEES.—

"(1) COMMISSION RULES.—

"(A) IN GENERAL.—Effective not later than 270 days after the date of enactment of this subsection, the Commission shall, by rule, direct the national securities exchanges and national securities associations to prohibit the listing of any security of an issuer that is not in compliance with the requirements of any portion of paragraphs (2) through (6).

"(B) OPPORTUNITY TO CURE DEFECTS.—The rules of the Commission under subparagraph (A) shall provide for appropriate procedures for an issuer to have an opportunity to cure any defects that would be the basis for a prohibition under subparagraph (A), before the imposition of such prohibition.

"(2) RESPONSIBILITIES RELATING TO REGISTERED PUBLIC ACCOUNTING FIRMS.—The audit committee of each issuer, in its capacity as a committee of the board of directors, shall be directly responsible for the appointment, compensation, and oversight of the work of any registered public accounting firm employed by that issuer (including resolution of disagreements between management and the auditor regarding financial reporting) for the purpose of preparing or issuing an audit report or related work, and each such registered public accounting firm shall report directly to the audit committee.

"(3) INDEPENDENCE.—

"(A) IN GENERAL.—Each member of the audit committee of the issuer shall be a member of the board of directors of the issuer, and shall otherwise be independent.

"(B) CRITERIA.—In order to be considered to be independent for purposes of this paragraph, a member of an audit committee of an issuer may not, other than in his or her capacity as a member of the audit committee, the board of directors, or any other board committee—

"(i) accept any consulting, advisory, or other compensatory fee from the issuer; or

"(ii) be an affiliated person of the issuer or any subsidiary thereof.

"(C) EXEMPTION AUTHORITY.—The Commission may exempt from the requirements of subparagraph (B) a particular relationship with respect to audit committee members, as the Commission determines appropriate in light of the circumstances.

"(4) COMPLAINTS.—Each audit committee shall establish procedures for—

"(A) the receipt, retention, and treatment of complaints received by the issuer regarding accounting, internal accounting controls, or auditing matters; and

"(B) the confidential, anonymous submission by employees of the issuer of concerns regarding questionable accounting or auditing matters.

"(5) AUTHORITY TO ENGAGE ADVISERS.—Each audit committee shall have the authority to engage independent counsel and other advisers, as it determines necessary to carry out its duties.

"(6) FUNDING.—Each issuer shall provide for appropriate funding, as determined by the audit committee, in its capacity as a committee of the board of directors, for payment of compensation—

"(A) to the registered public accounting firm employed by the issuer for the purpose of rendering or issuing an audit report; and

"(B) to any advisers employed by the audit committee under paragraph (5).".

§ 302. Corporate Responsibility for Financial Reports

(a) REGULATIONS REQUIRED.—The Commission shall, by rule, require, for each company filing periodic reports under section 13(a) or 15(d) of the Securities Exchange Act of 1934, that the principal executive officer or officers and the principal financial officer or officers, or persons performing similar functions, certify in each annual or quarterly report filed or submitted under either such section of such Act that—

(1) the signing officer has reviewed the report;

(2) based on the officer's knowledge, the report does not contain any untrue statement of a material fact or omit to state a material fact necessary in order to make the statements made, in light of the circumstances under which such statements were made, not misleading;

(3) based on such officer's knowledge, the financial statements, and other financial information included in the report, fairly present in all material respects the financial condition and results of operations of the issuer as of, and for, the periods presented in the report;

(4) the signing officers—

(A) are responsible for establishing and maintaining internal controls;

(B) have designed such internal controls to ensure that material information relating to the issuer and its consolidated subsidiaries is made known to such officers by others within those entities, particularly during the period in which the periodic reports are being prepared;

(C) have evaluated the effectiveness of the issuer's internal controls as of a date within 90 days prior to the report; and

(D) have presented in the report their conclusions about the effectiveness of their internal controls based on their evaluation as of that date;

(5) the signing officers have disclosed to the issuer's auditors and the audit committee of the board of directors (or persons fulfilling the equivalent function)—

(A) all significant deficiencies in the design or operation of internal controls which could adversely affect the issuer's ability to record, process, summarize, and report financial data and have identified for the issuer's auditors any material weaknesses in internal controls; and

(B) any fraud, whether or not material, that involves management or other employees who have a significant role in the issuer's internal controls; and

(6) the signing officers have indicated in the report whether or not there were significant changes in internal controls or in other factors that could significantly affect internal controls

subsequent to the date of their evaluation, including any corrective actions with regard to significant deficiencies and material weaknesses.

(b) FOREIGN REINCORPORATIONS HAVE NO EFFECT.—Nothing in this section 302 shall be interpreted or applied in any way to allow any issuer to lessen the legal force of the statement required under this section 302, by an issuer having reincorporated or having engaged in any other transaction that resulted in the transfer of the corporate domicile or offices of the issuer from inside the United States to outside of the United States.

(c) DEADLINE.—The rules required by subsection (a) shall be effective not later than 30 days after the date of enactment of this Act.

§ 303. Improper Influence on Conduct of Audits

(a) RULES TO PROHIBIT.—It shall be unlawful, in contravention of such rules or regulations as the Commission shall prescribe as necessary and appropriate in the public interest or for the protection of investors, for any officer or director of an issuer, or any other person acting under the direction thereof, to take any action to fraudulently influence, coerce, manipulate, or mislead any independent public or certified accountant engaged in the performance of an audit of the financial statements of that issuer for the purpose of rendering such financial statements materially misleading.

(b) ENFORCEMENT.—In any civil proceeding, the Commission shall have exclusive authority to enforce this section and any rule or regulation issued under this section.

(c) NO PREEMPTION OF OTHER LAW.—The provisions of subsection (a) shall be in addition to, and shall not supersede or preempt, any other provision of law or any rule or regulation issued thereunder.

(d) DEADLINE FOR RULEMAKING.—The Commission shall—

(1) propose the rules or regulations required by this section, not later than 90 days after the date of enactment of this Act; and

(2) issue final rules or regulations required by this section, not later than 270 days after that date of enactment.

§ 304. Forfeiture of Certain Bonuses and Profits

(a) ADDITIONAL COMPENSATION PRIOR TO NONCOMPLIANCE WITH COMMISSION FINANCIAL REPORTING REQUIREMENTS.—If an issuer is required to prepare an accounting restatement due to the material noncompliance of the issuer, as a result of misconduct, with any financial reporting requirement under the securities laws, the chief executive officer and chief financial officer of the issuer shall reimburse the issuer for—

(1) any bonus or other incentive-based or equity-based compensation received by that person from the issuer during the 12-month period following the first public issuance or filing with the Commission (whichever first occurs) of the financial document embodying such financial reporting requirement; and

(2) any profits realized from the sale of securities of the issuer during that 12-month period.

(b) COMMISSION EXEMPTION AUTHORITY.—The Commission may exempt any person from the application of subsection (a), as it deems necessary and appropriate.

§ 305. Officer and Director Bars and Penalties

(a) UNFITNESS STANDARD.—

(1) SECURITIES EXCHANGE ACT OF 1934.—Section 21(d)(2) of the Securities Exchange Act of 1934 is amended by striking "substantial unfitness" and inserting "unfitness".

(2) SECURITIES ACT OF 1933.—Section 20(e) of the Securities Act of 1933 is amended by striking "substantial unfitness" and inserting "unfitness".

(b) EQUITABLE RELIEF.—Section 21(d) of the Securities Exchange Act of 1934 is amended by adding at the end the following:

"(5) EQUITABLE RELIEF.—In any action or proceeding brought or instituted by the Commission under any provision of the securities laws, the Commission may seek, and any Federal court may grant, any equitable relief that may be appropriate or necessary for the benefit of investors.".

§ 306. Insider Trades During Pension Fund Blackout Periods

(a) PROHIBITION OF INSIDER TRADING DURING PENSION FUND BLACKOUT PERIODS.—

(1) IN GENERAL.—Except to the extent otherwise provided by rule of the Commission pursuant to paragraph (3), it shall be unlawful for any director or executive officer of an issuer of any equity security (other than an exempted security), directly or indirectly, to purchase, sell, or otherwise acquire or transfer any equity security of the issuer (other than an exempted security) during any blackout period with respect to such equity security if such director or officer acquires such equity security in connection with his or her service or employment as a director or executive officer.

(2) REMEDY.—

(A) IN GENERAL.—Any profit realized by a director or executive officer referred to in paragraph (1) from any purchase, sale, or other acquisition or transfer in violation of this subsection shall inure to and be recoverable by the issuer, irrespective of any intention on the part of such director or executive officer in entering into the transaction.

(B) ACTIONS TO RECOVER PROFITS.—An action to recover profits in accordance with this subsection may be instituted at law or in equity in any court of competent jurisdiction by the issuer, or by the owner of any security of the issuer in the name and in behalf of the issuer if the issuer fails or refuses to bring such action within 60 days after the date of request, or fails diligently to prosecute the action thereafter, except that no such suit shall be brought more than 2 years after the date on which such profit was realized.

(3) RULEMAKING AUTHORIZED.—The Commission shall, in consultation with the Secretary of Labor, issue rules to clarify the application of this subsection and to prevent evasion thereof. Such rules shall provide for the application of the requirements of paragraph (1) with respect to entities treated as a single employer with respect to an issuer under section 414(b), (c), (m), or (o) of the Internal Revenue Code of 1986 to the extent necessary to clarify the application of such requirements and to prevent evasion thereof. Such rules may also provide for appropriate exceptions from the requirements of this subsection, including exceptions for purchases pursuant to an automatic dividend reinvestment program or purchases or sales made pursuant to an advance election.

(4) BLACKOUT PERIOD.—For purposes of this subsection, the term "blackout period", with respect to the equity securities of any issuer—

(A) means any period of more than 3 consecutive business days during which the ability of not fewer than 50 percent of the participants or beneficiaries under all individual account plans maintained by the issuer to purchase, sell, or otherwise acquire or transfer an interest in any equity of such issuer held in such an individual account plan is temporarily suspended by the issuer or by a fiduciary of the plan; and

(B) does not include, under regulations which shall be prescribed by the Commission—

(i) a regularly scheduled period in which the participants and beneficiaries may not purchase, sell, or otherwise acquire or transfer an interest in any equity of such issuer, if such period is—

    (I) incorporated into the individual account plan; and

    (II) timely disclosed to employees before becoming participants under the individual account plan or as a subsequent amendment to the plan; or

    (ii) any suspension described in subparagraph (A) that is imposed solely in connection with persons becoming participants or beneficiaries, or ceasing to be participants or beneficiaries, in an individual account plan by reason of a corporate merger, acquisition, divestiture, or similar transaction involving the plan or plan sponsor.

    (5) INDIVIDUAL ACCOUNT PLAN.—For purposes of this subsection, the term "individual account plan" has the meaning provided in section 3(34) of the Employee Retirement Income Security Act of 1974, except that such term shall not include a one-participant retirement plan (within the meaning of section 101(i)(8)(B) of such Act).

    (6) NOTICE TO DIRECTORS, EXECUTIVE OFFICERS, AND THE COMMISSION.—In any case in which a director or executive officer is subject to the requirements of this subsection in connection with a blackout period (as defined in paragraph (4)) with respect to any equity securities, the issuer of such equity securities shall timely notify such director or officer and the Securities and Exchange Commission of such blackout period.

    (b) NOTICE REQUIREMENTS TO PARTICIPANTS AND BENEFICIARIES UNDER ERISA.—

    (1) IN GENERAL.—Section 101 of the Employee Retirement Income Security Act of 1974 is amended by redesignating the second subsection (h) as subsection (j), and by inserting after the first subsection (h) the following new subsection:

    "(i) NOTICE OF BLACKOUT PERIODS TO PARTICIPANT OR BENEFICIARY UNDER INDIVIDUAL ACCOUNT PLAN.—

    "(1) DUTIES OF PLAN ADMINISTRATOR.—In advance of the commencement of any blackout period with respect to an individual account plan, the plan administrator shall notify the plan participants and beneficiaries who are affected by such action in accordance with this subsection.

    "(2) NOTICE REQUIREMENTS.—

    "(A) IN GENERAL.—The notices described in paragraph (1) shall be written in a manner calculated to be understood by the average plan participant and shall include—

    "(i) the reasons for the blackout period,

    "(ii) an identification of the investments and other rights affected,

    "(iii) the expected beginning date and length of the blackout period,

    "(iv) in the case of investments affected, a statement that the participant or beneficiary should evaluate the appropriateness of their current investment decisions in light of their inability to direct or diversify assets credited to their accounts during the blackout period, and

    "(v) such other matters as the Secretary may require by regulation.

    "(B) NOTICE TO PARTICIPANTS AND BENEFICIARIES.—Except as otherwise provided in this subsection, notices described in paragraph (1) shall be furnished to all participants and beneficiaries under the plan to whom the blackout period applies at least 30 days in advance of the blackout period.

    "(C) EXCEPTION TO 30-DAY NOTICE REQUIREMENT.—In any case in which—

    "(i) a deferral of the blackout period would violate the requirements of subparagraph (A) or (B) of section 404(a)(1), and a fiduciary of the plan reasonably so determines in writing, or "(ii) the inability to provide the 30-day advance notice is due to events that were unforeseeable or circumstances beyond the reasonable control of the plan administrator, and a fiduciary of the plan reasonably so determines in writing, subparagraph (B) shall not apply, and the notice shall be furnished to all participants and beneficiaries under the plan to whom the blackout period applies as soon as reasonably possible under the circumstances unless such a notice in advance of the termination of the blackout period is impracticable.

"(D) WRITTEN NOTICE.—The notice required to be provided under this subsection shall be in writing, except that such notice may be in electronic or other form to the extent that such form is reasonably accessible to the recipient.

"(E) NOTICE TO ISSUERS OF EMPLOYER SECURITIES SUBJECT TO BLACKOUT PERIOD.—In the case of any blackout period in connection with an individual account plan, the plan administrator shall provide timely notice of such blackout period to the issuer of any employer securities subject to such blackout period.

"(3) EXCEPTION FOR BLACKOUT PERIODS WITH LIMITED APPLICABILITY.—In any case in which the blackout period applies only to 1 or more participants or beneficiaries in connection with a merger, acquisition, divestiture, or similar transaction involving the plan or plan sponsor and occurs solely in connection with becoming or ceasing to be a participant or beneficiary under the plan by reason of such merger, acquisition, divestiture, or transaction, the requirement of this subsection that the notice be provided to all participants and beneficiaries shall be treated as met if the notice required under paragraph (1) is provided to such participants or beneficiaries to whom the blackout period applies as soon as reasonably practicable.

"(4) CHANGES IN LENGTH OF BLACKOUT PERIOD.—If, following the furnishing of the notice pursuant to this subsection, there is a change in the beginning date or length of the blackout period (specified in such notice pursuant to paragraph (2)(A)(iii)), the administrator shall provide affected participants and beneficiaries notice of the change as soon as reasonably practicable. In relation to the extended blackout period, such notice shall meet the requirements of paragraph (2)(D) and shall specify any material change in the matters referred to in clauses (i) through (v) of paragraph (2)(A).

"(5) REGULATORY EXCEPTIONS.—The Secretary may provide by regulation for additional exceptions to the requirements of this subsection which the Secretary determines are in the interests of participants and beneficiaries.

"(6) GUIDANCE AND MODEL NOTICES.—The Secretary shall issue guidance and model notices which meet the requirements of this subsection.

"(7) BLACKOUT PERIOD.—For purposes of this subsection—

"(A) IN GENERAL.—The term 'blackout period' means, in connection with an individual account plan, any period for which any ability of participants or beneficiaries under the plan, which is otherwise available under the terms of such plan, to direct or diversify assets credited to their accounts, to obtain loans from the plan, or to obtain distributions from the plan is temporarily suspended, limited, or restricted, if such suspension, limitation, or restriction is for any period of more than 3 consecutive business days.

"(B) EXCLUSIONS.—The term 'blackout period' does not include a suspension, limitation, or restriction—

"(i) which occurs by reason of the application of the securities laws (as defined in section 3(a)(47) of the Securities Exchange Act of 1934),

"(ii) which is a change to the plan which provides for a regularly scheduled suspension, limitation, or restriction which is disclosed to participants or beneficiaries through any summary of material modifications, any materials describing specific investment alternatives under the plan, or any changes thereto, or "(iii) which applies only to 1 or more individuals, each of whom is the participant, an alternate payee (as defined in section 206(d)(3)(K)), or any other beneficiary pursuant to a qualified domestic relations order (as defined in section 206(d)(3)(B)(i)).

"(8) INDIVIDUAL ACCOUNT PLAN.—

"(A) IN GENERAL.—For purposes of this subsection, the term 'individual account plan' shall have the meaning provided such term in section 3(34), except that such term shall not include a one-participant retirement plan.

"(B) ONE-PARTICIPANT RETIREMENT PLAN.—For purposes of subparagraph (A), the term 'one-participant retirement plan' means a retirement plan that—

"(i) on the first day of the plan year—

"(I) covered only the employer (and the employer's spouse) and the employer owned the entire business (whether or not incorporated), or

"(II) covered only one or more partners (and their spouses) in a business partnership (including partners in an S or C corporation (as defined in section 1361(a) of the Internal Revenue Code of 1986)),

"(ii) meets the minimum coverage requirements of section 410(b) of the Internal Revenue Code of 1986 (as in effect on the date of the enactment of this paragraph) without being combined with any other plan of the business that covers the employees of the business,

"(iii) does not provide benefits to anyone except the employer (and the employer's spouse) or the partners (and their spouses),

"(iv) does not cover a business that is a member of an affiliated service group, a controlled group of corporations, or a group of businesses under common control, and

"(v) does not cover a business that leases employees.".

(2) ISSUANCE OF INITIAL GUIDANCE AND MODEL NOTICE.—The Secretary of Labor shall issue initial guidance and a model notice pursuant to section 101(i)(6) of the Employee Retirement Income Security Act of 1974 (as added by this subsection) not later than January 1, 2003. Not later than 75 days after the date of the enactment of this Act, the Secretary shall promulgate interim final rules necessary to carry out the amendments made by this subsection.

(3) CIVIL PENALTIES FOR FAILURE TO PROVIDE NOTICE.—Section 502 of such Act is amended—

(A) in subsection (a)(6), by striking "(5), or (6)" and inserting "(5), (6), or (7)";

(B) by redesignating paragraph (7) of subsection (c) as paragraph (8); and

(C) by inserting after paragraph (6) of subsection (c) the following new paragraph:

"(7) The Secretary may assess a civil penalty against a plan administrator of up to $100 a day from the date of the plan administrator's failure or refusal to provide notice to participants and beneficiaries in accordance with section 101(i). For purposes of this paragraph, each violation with respect to any single participant or beneficiary shall be treated as a separate violation.".

(3) PLAN AMENDMENTS.—If any amendment made by this subsection requires an amendment to any plan, such plan amendment shall not be required to be made before the first plan year beginning on or after the effective date of this section, if—

(A) during the period after such amendment made by this subsection takes effect and before such first plan year, the plan is operated in good faith compliance with the requirements of such amendment made by this subsection, and

(B) such plan amendment applies retroactively to the period after such amendment made by this subsection takes effect and before such first plan year.

(c) EFFECTIVE DATE.—The provisions of this section (including the amendments made thereby) shall take effect 180 days after the date of the enactment of this Act. Good faith compliance with the requirements of such provisions in advance of the issuance of applicable regulations thereunder shall be treated as compliance with such provisions.

§ 307. Rules of Professional Responsibility for Attorneys

Not later than 180 days after the date of enactment of this Act, the Commission shall issue rules, in the public interest and for the protection of investors, setting forth minimum standards of professional conduct for attorneys appearing and practicing before the Commission in any way in the representation of issuers, including a rule—

(1) requiring an attorney to report evidence of a material violation of securities law or breach of fiduciary duty or similar violation by the company or any agent thereof, to the chief legal counsel or the chief executive officer of the company (or the equivalent thereof); and

(2) if the counsel or officer does not appropriately respond to the evidence (adopting, as necessary, appropriate remedial measures or sanctions with respect to the violation), requiring the attorney to report the evidence to the audit committee of the board of directors of the issuer or to another committee of the board of directors comprised solely of directors not employed directly or indirectly by the issuer, or to the board of directors.

§ 308. Fair Funds for Investors

(a) CIVIL PENALTIES ADDED TO DISGORGEMENT FUNDS FOR THE RELIEF OF VICTIMS.—If in any judicial or administrative action brought by the Commission under the securities laws (as such term is defined in section 3(a)(47) of the Securities Exchange Act of 1934 (15 U.S.C. 78c(a)(47)) the Commission obtains an order requiring disgorgement against any person for a violation of such laws or the rules or regulations thereunder, or such person agrees in settlement of any such action to such disgorgement, and the Commission also obtains pursuant to such laws a civil penalty against such person, the amount of such civil penalty shall, on the motion or at the direction of the Commission, be added to and become part of the disgorgement fund for the benefit of the victims of such violation.

(b) ACCEPTANCE OF ADDITIONAL DONATIONS.—The Commission is authorized to accept, hold, administer, and utilize gifts, bequests and devises of property, both real and personal, to the United States for a disgorgement fund described in subsection (a). Such gifts, bequests, and devises of money and proceeds from sales of other property received as gifts, bequests, or devises shall be deposited in the disgorgement fund and shall be available for allocation in accordance with subsection (a).

(c) STUDY REQUIRED.—

(1) SUBJECT OF STUDY.—The Commission shall review and analyze—

(A) enforcement actions by the Commission over the five years preceding the date of the enactment of this Act that have included proceedings to obtain civil penalties or disgorgements to identify areas where such proceedings may be utilized to efficiently, effectively, and fairly provide restitution for injured investors; and

(B) other methods to more efficiently, effectively, and fairly provide restitution to injured investors, including methods to improve the collection rates for civil penalties and disgorgements.

(2) REPORT REQUIRED.—The Commission shall report its findings to the Committee on Financial Services of the House of Representatives and the Committee on Banking, Housing, and Urban Affairs of the Senate within 180 days after of the date of the enactment of this Act, and shall

use such findings to revise its rules and regulations as necessary. The report shall include a discussion of regulatory or legislative actions that are recommended or that may be necessary to address concerns identified in the study.

(d)   CONFORMING AMENDMENTS.—Each of the following provisions is amended by inserting ", except as otherwise provided in section 308 of the Sarbanes-Oxley Act of 2002" after "Treasury of the United States":

(1)   Section 21(d)(3)(C)(i) of the Securities Exchange Act of 1934.

(2)   Section 21A(d)(1) of such Act.

(3)   Section 20(d)(3)(A) of the Securities Act of 1933.

(4)   Section 42(e)(3)(A) of the Investment Company Act of 1940.

(5)   Section 209(e)(3)(A) of the Investment Advisers Act of 1940.

(e)   DEFINITION.—As used in this section, the term "disgorgement fund" means a fund established in any administrative or judicial proceeding described in subsection (a).

TITLE IV—ENHANCED FINANCIAL DISCLOSURES

§ 401.   Disclosures in Periodic Reports

(a)   DISCLOSURES REQUIRED.—Section 13 of the Securities Exchange Act of 1934 is amended by adding at the end the following:

"(i)   ACCURACY OF FINANCIAL REPORTS.—Each financial report that contains financial statements, and that is required to be prepared in accordance with (or reconciled to) generally accepted accounting principles under this title and filed with the Commission shall reflect all material correcting adjustments that have been identified by a registered public accounting firm in accordance with generally accepted accounting principles and the rules and regulations of the Commission.

"(j)   OFF-BALANCE SHEET TRANSACTIONS.—Not later than 180 days after the date of enactment of the Sarbanes-Oxley Act of 2002, the Commission shall issue final rules providing that each annual and quarterly financial report required to be filed with the Commission shall disclose all material off-balance sheet transactions, arrangements, obligations (including contingent obligations), and other relationships of the issuer with unconsolidated entities or other persons, that may have a material current or future effect on financial condition, changes in financial condition, results of operations, liquidity, capital expenditures, capital resources, or significant components of revenues or expenses.".

(b)   COMMISSION RULES ON PRO FORMA FIGURES.—Not later than 180 days after the date of enactment of the Sarbanes-Oxley Act [of] 2002, the Commission shall issue final rules providing that pro forma financial information included in any periodic or other report filed with the Commission pursuant to the securities laws, or in any public disclosure or press or other release, shall be presented in a manner that—

(1)   does not contain an untrue statement of a material fact or omit to state a material fact necessary in order to make the pro forma financial information, in light of the circumstances under which it is presented, not misleading; and

(2)   reconciles it with the financial condition and results of operations of the issuer under generally accepted accounting principles.

(c)   STUDY AND REPORT ON SPECIAL PURPOSE ENTITIES.—

(1)   STUDY REQUIRED.—The Commission shall, not later than 1 year after the effective date of adoption of off-balance sheet disclosure rules required by section 13(j) of the Securities Exchange

Act of 1934, as added by this section, complete a study of filings by issuers and their disclosures to determine—

  (A) the extent of off-balance sheet transactions, including assets, liabilities, leases, losses, and the use of special purpose entities; and

  (B) whether generally accepted accounting rules result in financial statements of issuers reflecting the economics of such off-balance sheet transactions to investors in a transparent fashion.

  (2) REPORT AND RECOMMENDATIONS.—Not later than 6 months after the date of completion of the study required by paragraph (1), the Commission shall submit a report to the President, the Committee on Banking, Housing, and Urban Affairs of the Senate, and the Committee on Financial Services of the House of Representatives, setting forth—

  (A) the amount or an estimate of the amount of off-balance sheet transactions, including assets, liabilities, leases, and losses of, and the use of special purpose entities by, issuers filing periodic reports pursuant to section 13 or 15 of the Securities Exchange Act of 1934;

  (B) the extent to which special purpose entities are used to facilitate off-balance sheet transactions;

  (C) whether generally accepted accounting principles or the rules of the Commission result in financial statements of issuers reflecting the economics of such transactions to investors in a transparent fashion;

  (D) whether generally accepted accounting principles specifically result in the consolidation of special purpose entities sponsored by an issuer in cases in which the issuer has the majority of the risks and rewards of the special purpose entity; and

  (E) any recommendations of the Commission for improving the transparency and quality of reporting off-balance sheet transactions in the financial statements and disclosures required to be filed by an issuer with the Commission.

§ 402. Enhanced Conflict of Interest Provisions

  (a) PROHIBITION ON PERSONAL LOANS TO EXECUTIVES.—Section 13 of the Securities Exchange Act of 1934, as amended by this Act, is amended by adding at the end the following:

  "(k) PROHIBITION ON PERSONAL LOANS TO EXECUTIVES.—

  "(1) IN GENERAL.—It shall be unlawful for any issuer (as defined in section 2 of the Sarbanes-Oxley Act of 2002), directly or indirectly, including through any subsidiary, to extend or maintain credit, to arrange for the extension of credit, or to renew an extension of credit, in the form of a personal loan to or for any director or executive officer (or equivalent thereof) of that issuer. An extension of credit maintained by the issuer on the date of enactment of this subsection shall not be subject to the provisions of this subsection, provided that there is no material modification to any term of any such extension of credit or any renewal of any such extension of credit on or after that date of enactment.

  "(2) LIMITATION.—Paragraph (1) does not preclude any home improvement and manufactured home loans (as that term is defined in section 5 of the Home Owners' Loan Act), consumer credit (as defined in section 103 of the Truth in Lending Act), or any extension of credit under an open end credit plan (as defined in section 103 of the Truth in Lending Act), or a charge card (as defined in section 127(c)(4)(e) of the Truth in Lending Act), or any extension of credit by a broker or dealer registered under section 15 of this title to an employee of that broker or dealer to buy, trade, or carry securities, that is permitted under rules or regulations of the Board of Governors of the Federal Reserve System pursuant to section 7 of this title (other than an extension of credit that would be used to purchase the stock of that issuer), that is—

"(A) made or provided in the ordinary course of the consumer credit business of such issuer;

"(B) of a type that is generally made available by such issuer to the public; and

"(C) made by such issuer on market terms, or terms that are no more favorable than those offered by the issuer to the general public for such extensions of credit.

"(3) RULE OF CONSTRUCTION FOR CERTAIN LOANS.—Paragraph (1) does not apply to any loan made or maintained by an insured depository institution (as defined in section 3 of the Federal Deposit Insurance Act), if the loan is subject to the insider lending restrictions of section 22(h) of the Federal Reserve Act.".

§ 403. Disclosures of Transactions Involving Management and Principal Stockholders

(a) AMENDMENT.—Section 16 of the Securities Exchange Act of 1934 is amended by striking the heading of such section and subsection (a) and inserting the following:

"SEC. 16. DIRECTORS, OFFICERS, AND PRINCIPAL STOCKHOLDERS.

"(a) DISCLOSURES REQUIRED.—

"(1) DIRECTORS, OFFICERS, AND PRINCIPAL STOCKHOLDERS REQUIRED TO FILE.—Every person who is directly or indirectly the beneficial owner of more than 10 percent of any class of any equity security (other than an exempted security) which is registered pursuant to section 12, or who is a director or an officer of the issuer of such security, shall file the statements required by this subsection with the Commission (and, if such security is registered on a national securities exchange, also with the exchange).

"(2) TIME OF FILING.—The statements required by this subsection shall be filed—

"(A) at the time of the registration of such security on a national securities exchange or by the effective date of a registration statement filed pursuant to section 12(g);

"(B) within 10 days after he or she becomes such beneficial owner, director, or officer;

"(C) if there has been a change in such ownership, or if such person shall have purchased or sold a security-based swap agreement (as defined in section 206(b) of the Gramm-Leach-Bliley Act) involving such equity security, before the end of the second business day following the day on which the subject transaction has been executed, or at such other time as the Commission shall establish, by rule, in any case in which the Commission determines that such 2-day period is not feasible.

"(3) CONTENTS OF STATEMENTS.—A statement filed—

"(A) under subparagraph (A) or (B) of paragraph (2) shall contain a statement of the amount of all equity securities of such issuer of which the filing person is the beneficial owner; and

"(B) under subparagraph (C) of such paragraph shall indicate ownership by the filing person at the date of filing, any such changes in such ownership, and such purchases and sales of the security-based swap agreements as have occurred since the most recent such filing under such subparagraph.

"(4) ELECTRONIC FILING AND AVAILABILITY.—Beginning not later than 1 year after the date of enactment of the Sarbanes-Oxley Act of 2002—

"(A) a statement filed under subparagraph (C) of paragraph (2) shall be filed electronically;

"(B) the Commission shall provide each such statement on a publicly accessible Internet site not later than the end of the business day following that filing; and

"(C) the issuer (if the issuer maintains a corporate website) shall provide that statement on that corporate website, not later than the end of the business day following that filing.".

(b)   EFFECTIVE DATE.—The amendment made by this section shall be effective 30 days after the date of the enactment of this Act.

§ 404.   Management Assessment of Internal Controls

(a)   RULES REQUIRED.—The Commission shall prescribe rules requiring each annual report required by section 13(a) or 15(d) of the Securities Exchange Act of 1934 to contain an internal control report, which shall—

(1)   state the responsibility of management for establishing and maintaining an adequate internal control structure and procedures for financial reporting; and

(2)   contain an assessment, as of the end of the most recent fiscal year of the issuer, of the effectiveness of the internal control structure and procedures of the issuer for financial reporting.

(b)   INTERNAL CONTROL EVALUATION AND REPORTING.—With respect to the internal control assessment required by subsection (a), each registered public accounting firm that prepares or issues the audit report for the issuer shall attest to, and report on, the assessment made by the management of the issuer. An attestation made under this subsection shall be made in accordance with standards for attestation engagements issued or adopted by the Board. Any such attestation shall not be the subject of a separate engagement.

§ 405.   Exemption

Nothing in section 401, 402, or 404, the amendments made by those sections, or the rules of the Commission under those sections shall apply to any investment company registered under section 8 of the Investment Company Act of 1940.

§ 406.   Code of Ethics for Senior Financial Officers

(a)   CODE OF ETHICS DISCLOSURE.—The Commission shall issue rules to require each issuer, together with periodic reports required pursuant to section 13(a) or 15(d) of the Securities Exchange Act of 1934, to disclose whether or not, and if not, the reason therefor, such issuer has adopted a code of ethics for senior financial officers, applicable to its principal financial officer and comptroller or principal accounting officer, or persons performing similar functions.

(b)   CHANGES IN CODES OF ETHICS.—The Commission shall revise its regulations concerning matters requiring prompt disclosure on Form 8-K (or any successor thereto) to require the immediate disclosure, by means of the filing of such form, dissemination by the Internet or by other electronic means, by any issuer of any change in or waiver of the code of ethics for senior financial officers.

(c)   DEFINITION.—In this section, the term "code of ethics" means such standards as are reasonably necessary to promote—

(1)   honest and ethical conduct, including the ethical handling of actual or apparent conflicts of interest between personal and professional relationships;

(2)   full, fair, accurate, timely, and understandable disclosure in the periodic reports required to be filed by the issuer; and

(3)   compliance with applicable governmental rules and regulations.

(d)   DEADLINE FOR RULEMAKING.—The Commission shall—

(1)   propose rules to implement this section, not later than 90 days after the date of enactment of this Act; and

(2)   issue final rules to implement this section, not later than 180 days after that date of enactment.

§ 407. Disclosure of Audit Committee Financial Expert

(a) RULES DEFINING "FINANCIAL EXPERT".—The Commission shall issue rules, as necessary or appropriate in the public interest and consistent with the protection of investors, to require each issuer, together with periodic reports required pursuant to sections 13(a) and 15(d) of the Securities Exchange Act of 1934, to disclose whether or not, and if not, the reasons therefor, the audit committee of that issuer is comprised of at least 1 member who is a financial expert, as such term is defined by the Commission.

(b) CONSIDERATIONS.—In defining the term "financial expert" for purposes of subsection (a), the Commission shall consider whether a person has, through education and experience as a public accountant or auditor or a principal financial officer, comptroller, or principal accounting officer of an issuer, or from a position involving the performance of similar functions—

(1) an understanding of generally accepted accounting principles and financial statements;

(2) experience in—

(A) the preparation or auditing of financial statements of generally comparable issuers; and

(B) the application of such principles in connection with the accounting for estimates, accruals, and reserves;

(3) experience with internal accounting controls; and

(4) an understanding of audit committee functions.

(c) DEADLINE FOR RULEMAKING.—The Commission shall—

(1) propose rules to implement this section, not later than 90 days after the date of enactment of this Act; and

(2) issue final rules to implement this section, not later than 180 days after that date of enactment.

§ 408. Enhanced Review of Periodic Disclosures by Issuers

(a) REGULAR AND SYSTEMATIC REVIEW.—The Commission shall review disclosures made by issuers reporting under section 13(a) of the Securities Exchange Act of 1934 (including reports filed on Form 10-K), and which have a class of securities listed on a national securities exchange or traded on an automated quotation facility of a national securities association, on a regular and systematic basis for the protection of investors. Such review shall include a review of an issuer's financial statement.

(b) REVIEW CRITERIA.—For purposes of scheduling the reviews required by subsection (a), the Commission shall consider, among other factors—

(1) issuers that have issued material restatements of financial results;

(2) issuers that experience significant volatility in their stock price as compared to other issuers;

(3) issuers with the largest market capitalization;

(4) emerging companies with disparities in price to earning ratios;

(5) issuers whose operations significantly affect any material sector of the economy; and

(6) any other factors that the Commission may consider relevant.

(c) MINIMUM REVIEW PERIOD.—In no event shall an issuer required to file reports under section 13(a) or 15(d) of the Securities Exchange Act of 1934 be reviewed under this section less frequently than once every 3 years.

§ 409.   Real Time Issuer Disclosures

Section 13 of the Securities Exchange Act of 1934, as amended by this Act, is amended by adding at the end the following:

"(*l*) REAL TIME ISSUER DISCLOSURES.—Each issuer reporting under section 13(a) or 15(d) shall disclose to the public on a rapid and current basis such additional information concerning material changes in the financial condition or operations of the issuer, in plain English, which may include trend and qualitative information and graphic presentations, as the Commission determines, by rule, is necessary or useful for the protection of investors and in the public interest.".

TITLE V—ANALYST CONFLICTS OF INTEREST

§ 501.   Treatment of Securities Analysts by Registered Securities Associations and National Securities Exchanges

(a) RULES REGARDING SECURITIES ANALYSTS.—The Securities Exchange Act of 1934 is amended by inserting after section 15C the following new section:

"SEC. 15D. SECURITIES ANALYSTS AND RESEARCH REPORTS.

"(a) ANALYST PROTECTIONS.—The Commission, or upon the authorization and direction of the Commission, a registered securities association or national securities exchange, shall have adopted, not later than 1 year after the date of enactment of this section, rules reasonably designed to address conflicts of interest that can arise when securities analysts recommend equity securities in research reports and public appearances, in order to improve the objectivity of research and provide investors with more useful and reliable information, including rules designed—

"(1) to foster greater public confidence in securities research, and to protect the objectivity and independence of securities analysts, by—

"(A) restricting the prepublication clearance or approval of research reports by persons employed by the broker or dealer who are engaged in investment banking activities, or persons not directly responsible for investment research, other than legal or compliance staff;

"(B) limiting the supervision and compensatory evaluation of securities analysts to officials employed by the broker or dealer who are not engaged in investment banking activities; and

"(C) requiring that a broker or dealer and persons employed by a broker or dealer who are involved with investment banking activities may not, directly or indirectly, retaliate against or threaten to retaliate against any securities analyst employed by that broker or dealer or its affiliates as a result of an adverse, negative, or otherwise unfavorable research report that may adversely affect the present or prospective investment banking relationship of the broker or dealer with the issuer that is the subject of the research report, except that such rules may not limit the authority of a broker or dealer to discipline a securities analyst for causes other than such research report in accordance with the policies and procedures of the firm;

"(2) to define periods during which brokers or dealers who have participated, or are to participate, in a public offering of securities as underwriters or dealers should not publish or otherwise distribute research reports relating to such securities or to the issuer of such securities;

"(3) to establish structural and institutional safeguards within registered brokers or dealers to assure that securities analysts are separated by appropriate informational partitions within the firm from the review, pressure, or oversight of those whose involvement in investment banking activities might potentially bias their judgment or supervision; and

"(4) to address such other issues as the Commission, or such association or exchange, determines appropriate.

"(b) DISCLOSURE.—The Commission, or upon the authorization and direction of the Commission, a registered securities association or national securities exchange, shall have adopted, not later than 1 year after the date of enactment of this section, rules reasonably designed to require each securities analyst to disclose in public appearances, and each registered broker or dealer to disclose in each research report, as applicable, conflicts of interest that are known or should have been known by the securities analyst or the broker or dealer, to exist at the time of the appearance or the date of distribution of the report, including—

"(1) the extent to which the securities analyst has debt or equity investments in the issuer that is the subject of the appearance or research report;

"(2) whether any compensation has been received by the registered broker or dealer, or any affiliate thereof, including the securities analyst, from the issuer that is the subject of the appearance or research report, subject to such exemptions as the Commission may determine appropriate and necessary to prevent disclosure by virtue of this paragraph of material non-public information regarding specific potential future investment banking transactions of such issuer, as is appropriate in the public interest and consistent with the protection of investors;

"(3) whether an issuer, the securities of which are recommended in the appearance or research report, currently is, or during the 1-year period preceding the date of the appearance or date of distribution of the report has been, a client of the registered broker or dealer, and if so, stating the types of services provided to the issuer;

"(4) whether the securities analyst received compensation with respect to a research report, based upon (among any other factors) the investment banking revenues (either generally or specifically earned from the issuer being analyzed) of the registered broker or dealer; and

"(5) such other disclosures of conflicts of interest that are material to investors, research analysts, or the broker or dealer as the Commission, or such association or exchange, determines appropriate.

"(c) DEFINITIONS.—In this section—

"(1) the term 'securities analyst' means any associated person of a registered broker or dealer that is principally responsible for, and any associated person who reports directly or indirectly to a securities analyst in connection with, the preparation of the substance of a research report, whether or not any such person has the job title of 'securities analyst'; and

"(2) the term 'research report' means a written or electronic communication that includes an analysis of equity securities of individual companies or industries, and that provides information reasonably sufficient upon which to base an investment decision.".

(b) ENFORCEMENT.—Section 21B(a) of the Securities Exchange Act of 1934 is amended by inserting "15D," before "15B".

(c) COMMISSION AUTHORITY.—The Commission may promulgate and amend its regulations, or direct a registered securities association or national securities exchange to promulgate and amend its rules, to carry out section 15D of the Securities Exchange Act of 1934, as added by this section, as is necessary for the protection of investors and in the public interest.

TITLE VI—COMMISSION RESOURCES AND AUTHORITY

§ 601.   Authorization of Appropriations

Section 35 of the Securities Exchange Act of 1934 is amended to read as follows:

"SEC. 35. AUTHORIZATION OF APPROPRIATIONS.

"In addition to any other funds authorized to be appropriated to the Commission, there are authorized to be appropriated to carry out the functions, powers, and duties of the Commission, $776,000,000 for fiscal year 2003, of which—

"(1) $102,700,000 shall be available to fund additional compensation, including salaries and benefits, as authorized in the Investor and Capital Markets Fee Relief Act;

"(2) $108,400,000 shall be available for information technology, security enhancements, and recovery and mitigation activities in light of the terrorist attacks of September 11, 2001; and

"(3) $98,000,000 shall be available to add not fewer than an additional 200 qualified professionals to provide enhanced oversight of auditors and audit services required by the Federal securities laws, and to improve Commission investigative and disciplinary efforts with respect to such auditors and services, as well as for additional professional support staff necessary to strengthen the programs of the Commission involving Full Disclosure and Prevention and Suppression of Fraud, risk management, industry technology review, compliance, inspections, examinations, market regulation, and investment management.".

§ 602. Appearance and Practice Before the Commission

The Securities Exchange Act of 1934 is amended by inserting after section 4B the following:

"SEC. 4C. APPEARANCE AND PRACTICE BEFORE THE COMMISSION.

"(a) AUTHORITY TO CENSURE.—The Commission may censure any person, or deny, temporarily or permanently, to any person the privilege of appearing or practicing before the Commission in any way, if that person is found by the Commission, after notice and opportunity for hearing in the matter—

"(1) not to possess the requisite qualifications to represent others;

"(2) to be lacking in character or integrity, or to have engaged in unethical or improper professional conduct; or

"(3) to have willfully violated, or willfully aided and abetted the violation of, any provision of the securities laws or the rules and regulations issued thereunder.

"(b) DEFINITION.—With respect to any registered public accounting firm or associated person, for purposes of this section, the term 'improper professional conduct' means—

"(1) intentional or knowing conduct, including reckless conduct, that results in a violation of applicable professional standards; and

"(2) negligent conduct in the form of—

"(A) a single instance of highly unreasonable conduct that results in a violation of applicable professional standards in circumstances in which the registered public accounting firm or associated person knows, or should know, that heightened scrutiny is warranted; or

"(B) repeated instances of unreasonable conduct, each resulting in a violation of applicable professional standards, that indicate a lack of competence to practice before the Commission.".

§ 603. Federal Court Authority to Impose Penny Stock Bars

(a) Securities Exchange Act of 1934—Section 21(d) of the Securities Exchange Act of 1934, as amended by this Act, is amended by adding at the end the following:

"(6) AUTHORITY OF A COURT TO PROHIBIT PERSONS FROM PARTICIPATING IN AN OFFERING OF PENNY STOCK.—

"(A) IN GENERAL.—In any proceeding under paragraph (1) against any person participating in, or, at the time of the alleged misconduct who was participating in, an offering of penny stock, the court may prohibit that person from participating in an offering of penny stock, conditionally or unconditionally, and permanently or for such period of time as the court shall determine.

"(B) DEFINITION.—For purposes of this paragraph, the term 'person participating in an offering of penny stock' includes any person engaging in activities with a broker, dealer, or issuer for purposes of issuing, trading, or inducing or attempting to induce the purchase or sale of, any penny stock. The Commission may, by rule or regulation, define such term to include other activities, and may, by rule, regulation, or order, exempt any person or class of persons, in whole or in part, conditionally or unconditionally, from inclusion in such term.".

(b) Securities Act of 1933.—Section 20 of the Securities Act of 1933 is amended by adding at the end the following:

"(g) AUTHORITY OF A COURT TO PROHIBIT PERSONS FROM PARTICIPATING IN AN OFFERING OF PENNY STOCK.—

"(1) IN GENERAL.—In any proceeding under subsection (a) against any person participating in, or, at the time of the alleged misconduct, who was participating in, an offering of penny stock, the court may prohibit that person from participating in an offering of penny stock, conditionally or unconditionally, and permanently or for such period of time as the court shall determine.

"(2) DEFINITION.—For purposes of this subsection, the term 'person participating in an offering of penny stock' includes any person engaging in activities with a broker, dealer, or issuer for purposes of issuing, trading, or inducing or attempting to induce the purchase or sale of, any penny stock. The Commission may, by rule or regulation, define such term to include other activities, and may, by rule, regulation, or order, exempt any person or class of persons, in whole or in part, conditionally or unconditionally, from inclusion in such term.".

§ 604. Qualifications of Associated Persons of Brokers and Dealers

(a) BROKERS AND DEALERS.—Section 15(b)(4) of the Securities Exchange Act of 1934 is amended—

(1) by striking subparagraph (F) and inserting the following:

"(F) is subject to any order of the Commission barring or suspending the right of the person to be associated with a broker or dealer;"; and

(2) in subparagraph (G), by striking the period at the end and inserting the following: "; or

"(H) is subject to any final order of a State securities commission (or any agency or officer performing like functions), State authority that supervises or examines banks, savings associations, or credit unions, State insurance commission (or any agency or office performing like functions), an appropriate Federal banking agency (as defined in section 3 of the Federal Deposit Insurance Act), or the National Credit Union Administration, that—

"(i) bars such person from association with an entity regulated by such commission, authority, agency, or officer, or from engaging in the business of securities, insurance, banking, savings association activities, or credit union activities; or

"(ii) constitutes a final order based on violations of any laws or regulations that prohibit fraudulent, manipulative, or deceptive conduct.".

(b) INVESTMENT ADVISERS.—Section 203(e) of the Investment Advisers Act of 1940 is amended—

(1) by striking paragraph (7) and inserting the following:

"(7) is subject to any order of the Commission barring or suspending the right of the person to be associated with an investment adviser;";

(2) in paragraph (8), by striking the period at the end and inserting "; or"; and

(3) by adding at the end the following:

"(9) is subject to any final order of a State securities commission (or any agency or officer performing like functions), State authority that supervises or examines banks, savings associations, or credit unions, State insurance commission (or any agency or office performing like functions), an appropriate Federal banking agency (as defined in section 3 of the Federal Deposit Insurance Act), or the National Credit Union Administration, that—

"(A) bars such person from association with an entity regulated by such commission, authority, agency, or officer, or from engaging in the business of securities, insurance, banking, savings association activities, or credit union activities; or

"(B) constitutes a final order based on violations of any laws or regulations that prohibit fraudulent, manipulative, or deceptive conduct.".

(c) CONFORMING AMENDMENTS.—

(1) SECURITIES EXCHANGE ACT OF 1934.—The Securities Exchange Act of 1934 is amended—

(A) in section 3(a)(39)(F)—

(i) by striking "or (G)" and inserting "(H), or (G)"; and

(ii) by inserting ", or is subject to an order or finding," before "enumerated";

(B) in each of section 15(b)(6)(A)(i), paragraphs (2) and (4) of section 15B(c), and subparagraphs (A) and (C) of section 15C(c)(1)—

(i) by striking "or (G)" each place that term appears and inserting "(H), or (G)"; and

(ii) by striking "or omission" each place that term appears, and inserting ", or is subject to an order or finding,"; and

(C) in each of paragraphs (3)(A) and (4)(C) of section 17A(c)—

(i) by striking "or (G)" each place that term appears and inserting "(H), or (G)"; and

(ii) by inserting ", or is subject to an order or finding," before "enumerated" each place that term appears.

(2) INVESTMENT ADVISERS ACT OF 1940.—Section 203(f) of the Investment Advisers Act of 1940 is amended—

(A) by striking "or (8)" and inserting "(8), or (9)"; and

(B) by inserting "or (3)" after "paragraph (2)".

TITLE VII—STUDIES AND REPORTS

§ 701.   GAO Study and Report Regarding Consolidation of Public Accounting Firms

(a) STUDY REQUIRED.—The Comptroller General of the United States shall conduct a study—

(1) to identify—

(A) the factors that have led to the consolidation of public accounting firms since 1989 and the consequent reduction in the number of firms capable of providing audit services to large national and multi-national business organizations that are subject to the securities laws;

(B) the present and future impact of the condition described in subparagraph (A) on capital formation and securities markets, both domestic and international; and

(C) solutions to any problems identified under subparagraph (B), including ways to increase competition and the number of firms capable of providing audit services to large national and multinational business organizations that are subject to the securities laws;

(2) of the problems, if any, faced by business organizations that have resulted from limited competition among public accounting firms, including—

(A) higher costs;

(B) lower quality of services;

(C) impairment of auditor independence; or

(D) lack of choice; and

(3) whether and to what extent Federal or State regulations impede competition among public accounting firms.

(b) CONSULTATION.—In planning and conducting the study under this section, the Comptroller General shall consult with—

(1) the Commission;

(2) the regulatory agencies that perform functions similar to the Commission within the other member countries of the Group of Seven Industrialized Nations;

(3) the Department of Justice; and

(4) any other public or private sector organization that the Comptroller General considers appropriate.

(c) REPORT REQUIRED.—Not later than 1 year after the date of enactment of this Act, the Comptroller General shall submit a report on the results of the study required by this section to the Committee on Banking, Housing, and Urban Affairs of the Senate and the Committee on Financial Services of the House of Representatives.

§ 702. Commission Study and Report Regarding Credit Rating Agencies

(a) STUDY REQUIRED.—

(1) IN GENERAL.—The Commission shall conduct a study of the role and function of credit rating agencies in the operation of the securities market.

(2) AREAS OF CONSIDERATION.—The study required by this subsection shall examine—

(A) the role of credit rating agencies in the evaluation of issuers of securities;

(B) the importance of that role to investors and the functioning of the securities markets;

(C) any impediments to the accurate appraisal by credit rating agencies of the financial resources and risks of issuers of securities;

(D) any barriers to entry into the business of acting as a credit rating agency, and any measures needed to remove such barriers;

(E) any measures which may be required to improve the dissemination of information concerning such resources and risks when credit rating agencies announce credit ratings; and

(F) any conflicts of interest in the operation of credit rating agencies and measures to prevent such conflicts or ameliorate the consequences of such conflicts.

(b) REPORT REQUIRED.—The Commission shall submit a report on the study required by subsection (a) to the President, the Committee on Financial Services of the House of Representatives, and the Committee on Banking, Housing, and Urban Affairs of the Senate not later than 180 days after the date of enactment of this Act.

§ 703. Study and Report on Violators and Violations

(a) STUDY.—The Commission shall conduct a study to determine, based upon information for the period from January 1, 1998, to December 31, 2001—

(1) the number of securities professionals, defined as public accountants, public accounting firms, investment bankers, investment advisers, brokers, dealers, attorneys, and other securities professionals practicing before the Commission—

(A) who have been found to have aided and abetted a violation of the Federal securities laws, including rules or regulations promulgated thereunder (collectively referred to in this section as "Federal securities laws"), but who have not been sanctioned, disciplined, or otherwise penalized as a primary violator in any administrative action or civil proceeding, including in any settlement of such an action or proceeding (referred to in this section as "aiders and abettors"); and

(B) who have been found to have been primary violators of the Federal securities laws;

(2) a description of the Federal securities laws violations committed by aiders and abettors and by primary violators, including—

(A) the specific provision of the Federal securities laws violated;

(B) the specific sanctions and penalties imposed upon such aiders and abettors and primary violators, including the amount of any monetary penalties assessed upon and collected from such persons;

(C) the occurrence of multiple violations by the same person or persons, either as an aider or abettor or as a primary violator; and

(D) whether, as to each such violator, disciplinary sanctions have been imposed, including any censure, suspension, temporary bar, or permanent bar to practice before the Commission; and

(3) the amount of disgorgement, restitution, or any other fines or payments that the Commission has assessed upon and collected from, aiders and abettors and from primary violators.

(b) REPORT.—A report based upon the study conducted pursuant to subsection (a) shall be submitted to the Committee on Banking, Housing, and Urban Affairs of the Senate, and the Committee on Financial Services of the House of Representatives not later than 6 months after the date of enactment of this Act.

§ 704. Study of Enforcement Actions

(a) STUDY REQUIRED.—The Commission shall review and analyze all enforcement actions by the Commission involving violations of reporting requirements imposed under the securities laws, and restatements of financial statements, over the 5-year period preceding the date of enactment of this Act, to identify areas of reporting that are most susceptible to fraud, inappropriate manipulation, or inappropriate earnings management, such as revenue recognition and the accounting treatment of off-balance sheet special purpose entities.

(b) REPORT REQUIRED.—The Commission shall report its findings to the Committee on Financial Services of the House of Representatives and the Committee on Banking, Housing, and Urban Affairs of the Senate, not later than 180 days after the date of enactment of this Act, and shall use such findings to revise its rules and regulations, as necessary. The report shall include a discussion of regulatory or legislative steps that are recommended or that may be necessary to address concerns identified in the study.

§ 705.   **Study of Investment Banks**

(a)   GAO STUDY.—The Comptroller General of the United States shall conduct a study on whether investment banks and financial advisers assisted public companies in manipulating their earnings and obfuscating their true financial condition. The study should address the rule of investment banks and financial advisers—

(1)   in the collapse of the Enron Corporation, including with respect to the design and implementation of derivatives transactions, transactions involving special purpose vehicles, and other financial arrangements that may have had the effect of altering the company's reported financial statements in ways that obscured the true financial picture of the company;

(2)   in the failure of Global Crossing, including with respect to transactions involving swaps of fiberoptic cable capacity, in the designing transactions that may have had the effect of altering the company's reported financial statements in ways that obscured the true financial picture of the company; and

(3)   generally, in creating and marketing transactions which may have been designed solely to enable companies to manipulate revenue streams, obtain loans, or move liabilities off balance sheets without altering the economic and business risks faced by the companies or any other mechanism to obscure a company's financial picture.

(b)   REPORT.—The Comptroller General shall report to Congress not later than 180 days after the date of enactment of this Act on the results of the study required by this section. The report shall include a discussion of regulatory or legislative steps that are recommended or that may be necessary to address concerns identified in the study.

TITLE VIII—CORPORATE AND CRIMINAL FRAUD ACCOUNTABILITY

§ 801.   **Short Title**

This title may be cited as the "Corporate and Criminal Fraud Accountability Act of 2002".

§ 802.   **Criminal Penalties for Altering Documents**

(a)   IN GENERAL.—Chapter 73 of title 18, United States Code, is amended by adding at the end the following:

"§ 1519.   Destruction, alteration, or falsification of records in Federal investigations and bankruptcy

'Whoever knowingly alters, destroys, mutilates, conceals, covers up, falsifies, or makes a false entry in any record, document, or tangible object with the intent to impede, obstruct, or influence the investigation or proper administration of any matter within the jurisdiction of any department or agency of the United States or any case filed under title 11, or in relation to or contemplation of any such matter or case, shall be fined under this title, imprisoned not more than 20 years, or both.

"§ 1520.   Destruction of corporate audit records

"(a)(1)   Any accountant who conducts an audit of an issuer of securities to which section 10A(a) of the Securities Exchange Act of 1934 applies, shall maintain all audit or review workpapers for a period of 5 years from the end of the fiscal period in which the audit or review was concluded.

"(2) The Securities and Exchange Commission shall promulgate, within 180 days, after adequate notice and an opportunity for comment, such rules and regulations, as are reasonably necessary, relating to the retention of relevant records such as workpapers, documents that form the basis of an audit or review, memoranda, correspondence, communications, other documents, and records (including electronic records) which are created, sent, or received in connection with an audit or review and contain conclusions, opinions, analyses, or financial data relating to such an audit or review, which is conducted by any accountant who conducts an audit of an issuer of securities to which section 10A(a) of the Securities Exchange Act of 1934 applies. The Commission may, from time to time, amend or supplement the rules and regulations that it is required to promulgate under this section, after adequate notice and an opportunity for comment, in order to ensure that such rules and regulations adequately comport with the purposes of this section.

"(b) Whoever knowingly and willfully violates subsection (a)(1), or any rule or regulation promulgated by the Securities and Exchange Commission under subsection (a)(2), shall be fined under this title, imprisoned not more than 10 years, or both.

"(c) Nothing in this section shall be deemed to diminish or relieve any person of any other duty or obligation imposed by Federal or State law or regulation to maintain, or refrain from destroying, any document.".

(b) CLERICAL AMENDMENT.—The table of sections at the beginning of chapter 73 of title 18, United States Code, is amended by adding at the end the following new items:

"1519.   Destruction, alteration, or falsification of records in Federal investigations and bankruptcy.

"1520.   Destruction of corporate audit records.".

§ 803.   Debts Nondischargeable if Incurred in Violation of Securities Fraud Laws

Section 523(a) of title 11, United States Code, is amended—

(1)   in paragraph (17), by striking "or" after the semicolon;

(2)   in paragraph (18), by striking the period at the end and inserting "; or"; and

(3)   by adding at the end, the following:

"(19) that—

"(A) is for—

"(i)   the violation of any of the Federal securities laws (as that term is defined in section 3(a)(47) of the Securities Exchange Act of 1934), any of the State securities laws, or any regulation or order issued under such Federal or State securities laws; or

"(ii) common law fraud, deceit, or manipulation in connection with the purchase or sale of any security; and

"(B) results from—

"(i)   any judgment, order, consent order, or decree entered in any Federal or State judicial or administrative proceeding;

"(ii) any settlement agreement entered into by the debtor; or

"(iii) any court or administrative order for any damages, fine, penalty, citation, restitutionary payment, disgorgement payment, attorney fee, cost, or other payment owed by the debtor.".

§ 804.   Statute of Limitations for Securities Fraud

(a)   IN GENERAL.—Section 1658 of title 28, United States Code, is amended—

(1)   by inserting "(a)" before "Except"; and

(2)   by adding at the end the following:

"(b) Notwithstanding subsection (a), a private right of action that involves a claim of fraud, deceit, manipulation, or contrivance in contravention of a regulatory requirement concerning the securities laws, as defined in section 3(a)(47) of the Securities Exchange Act of 1934, may be brought not later than the earlier of—

"(1) 2 years after the discovery of the facts constituting the violation; or

"(2) 5 years after such violation.".

(b) EFFECTIVE DATE.—The limitations period provided by section 1658(b) of title 28, United States Code, as added by this section, shall apply to all proceedings addressed by this section that are commenced on or after the date of enactment of this Act.

(c) NO CREATION OF ACTIONS.—Nothing in this section shall create a new, private right of action.

§ 805. Review of Federal Sentencing Guidelines for Obstruction of Justice and Extensive Criminal Fraud

(a) ENHANCEMENT OF FRAUD AND OBSTRUCTION OF JUSTICE SENTENCES.— Pursuant to section 994 of title 28, United States Code, and in accordance with this section, the United States Sentencing Commission shall review and amend, as appropriate, the Federal Sentencing Guidelines and related policy statements to ensure that—

(1) the base offense level and existing enhancements contained in United States Sentencing Guideline 2J1.2 relating to obstruction of justice are sufficient to deter and punish that activity;

(2) the enhancements and specific offense characteristics relating to obstruction of justice are adequate in cases where—

(A) the destruction, alteration, or fabrication of evidence involves—

(i) a large amount of evidence, a large number of participants, or is otherwise extensive;

(ii) the selection of evidence that is particularly probative or essential to the investigation; or

(iii) more than minimal planning; or

(B) the offense involved abuse of a special skill or a position of trust;

(3) the guideline offense levels and enhancements for violations of section 1519 or 1520 of title 18, United States Code, as added by this title, are sufficient to deter and punish that activity;

(4) a specific offense characteristic enhancing sentencing is provided under United States Sentencing Guideline 2B1.1 (as in effect on the date of enactment of this Act) for a fraud offense that endangers the solvency or financial security of a substantial number of victims; and

(5) the guidelines that apply to organizations in United States Sentencing Guidelines, chapter 8, are sufficient to deter and punish organizational criminal misconduct.

(b) EMERGENCY AUTHORITY AND DEADLINE FOR COMMISSION ACTION.—The United States Sentencing Commission is requested to promulgate the guidelines or amendments provided for under this section as soon as practicable, and in any event not later than 180 days after the date of enactment of this Act, in accordance with the procedures set forth in section 219(a) of the Sentencing Reform Act of 1987, as though the authority under that Act had not expired.

§ 806. Protection for Employees of Publicly Traded Companies Who Provide Evidence of Fraud

(a) IN GENERAL.—Chapter 73 of title 18, United States Code, is amended by inserting after section 1514 the following:

"§ 1514A. Civil action to protect against retaliation in fraud cases

"(a) WHISTLEBLOWER PROTECTION FOR EMPLOYEES OF PUBLICLY TRADED COMPANIES.—No company with a class of securities registered under section 12 of the Securities Exchange Act of 1934, or that is required to file reports under section 15(d) of the Securities Exchange Act of 1934, or any officer, employee, contractor, subcontractor, or agent of such company, may discharge, demote, suspend, threaten, harass, or in any other manner discriminate against an employee in the terms and conditions of employment because of any lawful act done by the employee—

"(1) to provide information, cause information to be provided, or otherwise assist in an investigation regarding any conduct which the employee reasonably believes constitutes a violation of section 1341, 1343, 1344, or 1348, any rule or regulation of the Securities and Exchange Commission, or any provision of Federal law relating to fraud against shareholders, when the information or assistance is provided to or the investigation is conducted by—

"(A) a Federal regulatory or law enforcement agency;

"(B) any Member of Congress or any committee of Congress; or

"(C) a person with supervisory authority over the employee (or such other person working for the employer who has the authority to investigate, discover, or terminate misconduct); or

"(2) to file, cause to be filed, testify, participate in, or otherwise assist in a proceeding filed or about to be filed (with any knowledge of the employer) relating to an alleged violation of section 1341, 1343, 1344, or 1348, any rule or regulation of the Securities and Exchange Commission, or any provision of Federal law relating to fraud against shareholders.

"(b) ENFORCEMENT ACTION.—

"(1) IN GENERAL.—A person who alleges discharge or other discrimination by any person in violation of subsection (a) may seek relief under subsection (c), by—

"(A) filing a complaint with the Secretary of Labor; or

"(B) if the Secretary has not issued a final decision within 180 days of the filing of the complaint and there is no showing that such delay is due to the bad faith of the claimant, bringing an action at law or equity for de novo review in the appropriate district court of the United States, which shall have jurisdiction over such an action without regard to the amount in controversy.

"(2) PROCEDURE.—

"(A) IN GENERAL.—An action under paragraph (1)(A) shall be governed under the rules and procedures set forth in section 42121(b) of title 49, United States Code.

"(B) EXCEPTION.—Notification made under section 42121(b)(1) of title 49, United States Code, shall be made to the person named in the complaint and to the employer.

"(C) BURDENS OF PROOF.—An action brought under paragraph (1)(B) shall be governed by the legal burdens of proof set forth in section 42121(b) of title 49, United States Code.

"(D) STATUTE OF LIMITATIONS.—An action under paragraph (1) shall be commenced not later than 90 days after the date on which the violation occurs.

"(c) REMEDIES.—

"(1) IN GENERAL.—An employee prevailing in any action under subsection (b)(1) shall be entitled to all relief necessary to make the employee whole.

"(2) COMPENSATORY DAMAGES.—Relief for any action under paragraph (1) shall include—

"(A) reinstatement with the same seniority status that the employee would have had, but for the discrimination;

"(B) the amount of back pay, with interest; and

"(C) compensation for any special damages sustained as a result of the discrimination, including litigation costs, expert witness fees, and reasonable attorney fees.

"(d) RIGHTS RETAINED BY EMPLOYEE.—Nothing in this section shall be deemed to diminish the rights, privileges, or remedies of any employee under any Federal or State law, or under any collective bargaining agreement.".

(b) CLERICAL AMENDMENT.—The table of sections at the beginning of chapter 73 of title 18, United States Code, is amended by inserting after the item relating to section 1514 the following new item:

"1514A. Civil action to protect against retaliation in fraud cases.".

§ 807. Criminal Penalties for Defrauding Shareholders of Publicly Traded Companies

(a) IN GENERAL.—Chapter 63 of title 18, United States Code, is amended by adding at the end the following:

"§ 1348. Securities fraud

"Whoever knowingly executes, or attempts to execute, a scheme or artifice—

"(1) to defraud any person in connection with any security of an issuer with a class of securities registered under section 12 of the Securities Exchange Act of 1934 or that is required to file reports under section 15(d) of the Securities Exchange Act of 1934; or

"(2) to obtain, by means of false or fraudulent pretenses, representations, or promises, any money or property in connection with the purchase or sale of any security of an issuer with a class of securities registered under section 12 of the Securities Exchange Act of 1934 or that is required to file reports under section 15(d) of the Securities Exchange Act of 1934;

shall be fined under this title, or imprisoned not more than 25 years, or both.".

(b) CLERICAL AMENDMENT.—The table of sections at the beginning of chapter 63 of title 18, United States Code, is amended by adding at the end the following new item:

"1348. Securities fraud.".

TITLE IX—WHITE-COLLAR CRIME PENALTY ENHANCEMENTS

§ 901. Short Title

This title may be cited as the "White-Collar Crime Penalty Enhancement Act of 2002".

§ 902. Attempts and Conspiracies to Commit Criminal Fraud Offenses

(a) IN GENERAL.—Chapter 63 of title 18, United States Code, is amended by inserting after section 1348 as added by this Act the following:

"§ 1349. Attempt and conspiracy

"Any person who attempts or conspires to commit any offense under this chapter shall be subject to the same penalties as those prescribed for the offense, the commission of which was the object of the attempt or conspiracy.

(b) CLERICAL AMENDMENT.—The table of sections at the beginning of chapter 63 of title 18, United States Code, is amended by adding at the end the following new item:

"1349. Attempt and conspiracy.".

§ 903.   Criminal Penalties for Mail and Wire Fraud

(a) MAIL FRAUD.—Section 1341 of title 18, United States Code, is amended by striking "five" and inserting "20".

(b) WIRE FRAUD.—Section 1343 of title 18, United States Code, is amended by striking "five" and inserting "20".

§ 904.   Criminal Penalties for Violations of the Employee Retirement Income Security Act of 1974

Section 501 of the Employee Retirement Income Security Act of 1974 is amended—

(1)   by striking "$5,000" and inserting "$100,000";

(2)   by striking "one year" and inserting "10 years"; and

(3)   by striking "$100,000" and inserting "$500,000".

§ 905.   Amendment to Sentencing Guidelines Relating to Certain White-Collar Offenses

(a) DIRECTIVE TO THE UNITED STATES SENTENCING COMMISSION.—Pursuant to its authority under section 994(p) of title 18, United States Code, and in accordance with this section, the United States Sentencing Commission shall review and, as appropriate, amend the Federal Sentencing Guidelines and related policy statements to implement the provisions of this Act.

(b) REQUIREMENTS.—In carrying out this section, the Sentencing Commission shall—

(1)   ensure that the sentencing guidelines and policy statements reflect the serious nature of the offenses and the penalties set forth in this Act, the growing incidence of serious fraud offenses which are identified above, and the need to modify the sentencing guidelines and policy statements to deter, prevent, and punish such offenses;

(2)   consider the extent to which the guidelines and policy statements adequately address whether the guideline offense levels and enhancements for violations of the sections amended by this Act are sufficient to deter and punish such offenses, and specifically, are adequate in view of the statutory increases in penalties contained in this Act;

(3)   assure reasonable consistency with other relevant directives and sentencing guidelines;

(4)   account for any additional aggravating or mitigating circumstances that might justify exceptions to the generally applicable sentencing ranges;

(5)   make any necessary conforming changes to the sentencing guidelines; and

(6)   assure that the guidelines adequately meet the purposes of sentencing, as set forth in section 3553(a)(2) of title 18, United States Code.

(c) EMERGENCY AUTHORITY AND DEADLINE FOR COMMISSION ACTION.—The United States Sentencing Commission is requested to promulgate the guidelines or amendments provided for under this section as soon as practicable, and in any event not later than 180 days after the date of enactment of this Act, in accordance with the procedures set forth in section 219(a) of the Sentencing Reform Act of 1987, as though the authority under that Act had not expired.

§ 906.   Corporate Responsibility for Financial Reports

(a) IN GENERAL.—Chapter 63 of title 18, United States Code, is amended by inserting after section 1349, as created by this Act, the following:

"§ 1350.   Failure of corporate officers to certify financial reports

"(a) CERTIFICATION OF PERIODIC FINANCIAL REPORTS.—Each periodic report containing financial statements filed by an issuer with the Securities Exchange Commission pursuant to section 13(a) or 15(d) of the Securities Exchange Act of 1934 shall be accompanied by a written statement by the chief executive officer and chief financial officer (or equivalent thereof) of the issuer.

"(b) CONTENT.—The statement required under subsection (a) shall certify that the periodic report containing the financial statements fully complies with the requirements of section 13(a) or 15(d) of the Securities Exchange Act of 1934 and that information contained in the periodic report fairly presents, in all material respects, the financial condition and results of operations of the issuer.

"(c) CRIMINAL PENALTIES.—Whoever—

"(1) certifies any statement as set forth in subsections (a) and (b) of this section knowing that the periodic report accompanying the statement does not comport with all the requirements set forth in this section shall be fined not more than $1,000,000 or imprisoned not more than 10 years, or both; or

"(2) willfully certifies any statement as set forth in subsections (a) and (b) of this section knowing that the periodic report accompanying the statement does not comport with all the requirements set forth in this section shall be fined not more than $5,000,000, or imprisoned not more than 20 years, or both.".

(b) CLERICAL AMENDMENT.—The table of sections at the beginning of chapter 63 of title 18, United States Code, is amended by adding at the end the following:

"1350. Failure of corporate officers to certify financial reports.".

TITLE X—CORPORATE TAX RETURNS

§ 1001. Sense of the Senate Regarding the Signing of Corporate Tax Returns by Chief Executive Officers

It is the sense of the Senate that the Federal income tax return of a corporation should be signed by the chief executive officer of such corporation.

TITLE XI—CORPORATE FRAUD ACCOUNTABILITY

§ 1101. Short Title

This title may be cited as the "Corporate Fraud Accountability Act of 2002".

§ 1102. Tampering With a Record or Otherwise Impeding an Official Proceeding

Section 1512 of title 18, United States Code, is amended—

(1) by redesignating subsections (c) through (i) as subsections (d) through (j), respectively; and

(2) by inserting after subsection (b) the following new subsection:

"(c) Whoever corruptly—

"(1) alters, destroys, mutilates, or conceals a record, document, or other object, or attempts to do so, with the intent to impair the object's integrity or availability for use in an official proceeding; or

"(2) otherwise obstructs, influences, or impedes any official proceeding, or attempts to do so,

shall be fined under this title or imprisoned not more than 20 years, or both.".

§ 1103. Temporary Freeze Authority for the Securities and Exchange Commission

(a) IN GENERAL.—Section 21C(c) of the Securities Exchange Act of 1934 is amended by adding at the end the following:

"(3) TEMPORARY FREEZE.—

"(A) IN GENERAL.—

"(i) ISSUANCE OF TEMPORARY ORDER.—Whenever, during the course of a lawful investigation involving possible violations of the Federal securities laws by an issuer of publicly traded securities or any of its directors, officers, partners, controlling persons, agents, or employees, it shall appear to the Commission that it is likely that the issuer will make extraordinary payments (whether compensation or otherwise) to any of the foregoing persons, the Commission may petition a Federal district court for a temporary order requiring the issuer to escrow, subject to court supervision, those payments in an interest-bearing account for 45 days.

"(ii) STANDARD.—A temporary order shall be entered under clause (i), only after notice and opportunity for a hearing, unless the court determines that notice and hearing prior to entry of the order would be impracticable or contrary to the public interest.

"(iii) EFFECTIVE PERIOD.—A temporary order issued under clause (i) shall—

"(I)　become effective immediately;

"(II)　be served upon the parties subject to it; and

"(III) unless set aside, limited or suspended by a court of competent jurisdiction, shall remain effective and enforceable for 45 days.

"(iv) EXTENSIONS AUTHORIZED.—The effective period of an order under this subparagraph may be extended by the court upon good cause shown for not longer than 45 additional days, provided that the combined period of the order shall not exceed 90 days.

"(B) PROCESS ON DETERMINATION OF VIOLATIONS.—

"(i) VIOLATIONS CHARGED.—If the issuer or other person described in subparagraph (A) is charged with any violation of the Federal securities laws before the expiration of the effective period of a temporary order under subparagraph (A) (including any applicable extension period), the order shall remain in effect, subject to court approval, until the conclusion of any legal proceedings related thereto, and the affected issuer or other person, shall have the right to petition the court for review of the order.

"(ii) VIOLATIONS NOT CHARGED.—If the issuer or other person described in subparagraph (A) is not charged with any violation of the Federal securities laws before the expiration of the effective period of a temporary order under subparagraph (A) (including any applicable extension period), the escrow shall terminate at the expiration of the 45-day effective period (or the expiration of any extension period, as applicable), and the disputed payments (with accrued interest) shall be returned to the issuer or other affected person.".

(b) TECHNICAL AMENDMENT.—Section 21C(c)(2) of the Securities Exchange Act of 1934 is amended by striking "This" and inserting "paragraph (1)".

§ 1104. Amendment to the Federal Sentencing Guidelines

(a) REQUEST FOR IMMEDIATE CONSIDERATION BY THE UNITED STATES SENTENCING COMMISSION.—Pursuant to its authority under section 994(p) of title 28, United States Code, and in accordance with this section, the United States Sentencing Commission is requested to—

(1) promptly review the sentencing guidelines applicable to securities and accounting fraud and related offenses;

(2) expeditiously consider the promulgation of new sentencing guidelines or amendments to existing sentencing guidelines to provide an enhancement for officers or directors of publicly traded corporations who commit fraud and related offenses; and

(3) submit to Congress an explanation of actions taken by the Sentencing Commission pursuant to paragraph (2) and any additional policy recommendations the Sentencing Commission may have for combating offenses described in paragraph (1).

(b) CONSIDERATIONS IN REVIEW.—In carrying out this section, the Sentencing Commission is requested to—

(1) ensure that the sentencing guidelines and policy statements reflect the serious nature of securities, pension, and accounting fraud and the need for aggressive and appropriate law enforcement action to prevent such offenses;

(2) assure reasonable consistency with other relevant directives and with other guidelines;

(3) account for any aggravating or mitigating circumstances that might justify exceptions, including circumstances for which the sentencing guidelines currently provide sentencing enhancements;

(4) ensure that guideline offense levels and enhancements for an obstruction of justice offense are adequate in cases where documents or other physical evidence are actually destroyed or fabricated;

(5) ensure that the guideline offense levels and enhancements under United States Sentencing Guideline 2B1.1 (as in effect on the date of enactment of this Act) are sufficient for a fraud offense when the number of victims adversely involved is significantly greater than 50;

(6) make any necessary conforming changes to the sentencing guidelines; and

(7) assure that the guidelines adequately meet the purposes of sentencing as set forth in section 3553 (a)(2) of title 18, United States Code.

(c) EMERGENCY AUTHORITY AND DEADLINE FOR COMMISSION ACTION.—The United States Sentencing Commission is requested to promulgate the guidelines or amendments provided for under this section as soon as practicable, and in any event not later than the 180 days after the date of enactment of this Act, in accordance with the procedures sent forth in section 21(a) of the Sentencing Reform Act of 1987, as though the authority under that Act had not expired.

§ 1105. Authority of the Commission to Prohibit Persons From Serving as Officers or Directors

(a) SECURITIES EXCHANGE ACT OF 1934.—Section 21C of the Securities Exchange Act of 1934 is amended by adding at the end the following:

"(f) AUTHORITY OF THE COMMISSION TO PROHIBIT PERSONS FROM SERVING AS OFFICERS OR DIRECTORS.—In any cease-and-desist proceeding under subsection (a), the Commission may issue an order to prohibit, conditionally or unconditionally, and permanently or for such period of time as it shall determine, any person who has violated section 10(b) or the rules or regulations thereunder, from acting as an officer or director of any issuer that has a class of securities registered pursuant to section 12, or that is required to file reports pursuant to section 15(d), if the conduct of that person demonstrates unfitness to serve as an officer or director of any such issuer.".

(b) SECURITIES ACT OF 1933.—Section 8A of the Securities Act of 1933 is amended by adding at the end of the following:

"(f) AUTHORITY OF THE COMMISSION TO PROHIBIT PERSONS FROM SERVING AS OFFICERS OR DIRECTORS.—In any cease-and-desist proceeding under subsection (a), the Commission may issue an order to prohibit, conditionally or unconditionally, and permanently or for such period of time as it shall determine, any person who has violated section 17(a)(1) or the rules or regulations thereunder, from acting as an officer or director of any issuer that has a class of securities registered pursuant to section 12 of the Securities Exchange Act of 1934, or that is required to file reports pursuant to section 15(d) of that Act, if the conduct of that person demonstrates unfitness to serve as an officer or director of any such issuer.".

§ 1106.   Increased Criminal Penalties Under Securities Exchange Act of 1934

Section 32(a) of the Securities Exchange Act of 1934 is amended—

(1)   by striking "$1,000,000, or imprisoned not more than 10 years" and inserting "$5,000,000, or imprisoned not more than 20 years"; and

(2)   by striking "$2,500,000" and inserting "$25,000,000".

§ 1107.   Retaliation Against Informants

(a)   IN GENERAL.—Section 1513 of title 18, United States Code, is amended by adding at the end the following:

"(e) Whoever knowingly, with the intent to retaliate, takes any action harmful to any person, including interference with the lawful employment or livelihood of any person, for providing to a law enforcement officer any truthful information relating to the commission or possible commission of any Federal offense, shall be fined under this title or imprisoned not more than 10 years, or both.".

Approved July 30, 2002.

L. APPEARANCE AND PRACTICE BEFORE THE COMMISSION

17 C.F.R. § 201.102

---

§ 201.102   Appearance and Practice Before the Commission.

* * *

(e) *Suspension and disbarment*—(1) *Generally.* The Commission may censure a person or deny, temporarily or permanently, the privilege of appearing or practicing before it in any way to any person who is found by the Commission after notice and opportunity for hearing in the matter:

(i) Not to possess the requisite qualifications to represent others; or

(ii) To be lacking in character or integrity or to have engaged in unethical or improper professional conduct; or

(iii) To have willfully violated, or willfully aided and abetted the violation of any provision of the Federal securities laws or the rules and regulations thereunder.

(iv) With respect to persons licensed to practice as accountants, "improper professional conduct" under § 201.102(e)(1)(ii) means:

(A) Intentional or knowing conduct, including reckless conduct, that results in a violation of applicable professional standards; or

(B) Either of the following two types of negligent conduct:

(1) A single instance of highly unreasonable conduct that results in a violation of applicable professional standards in circumstances in which an accountant knows, or should know, that heightened scrutiny is warranted.

(2) Repeated instances of unreasonable conduct, each resulting in a violation of applicable professional standards, that indicate a lack of competence to practice before the Commission.

(2) *Certain professionals and convicted persons.* Any attorney who has been suspended or disbarred by a court of the United States or of any State; or any person whose license to practice as an accountant, engineer, or other professional or expert has been revoked or suspended in any State; or any person who has been convicted of a felony or a misdemeanor involving moral turpitude shall be forthwith suspended from appearing or practicing before the Commission. A disbarment, suspension, revocation or conviction within the meaning of this section shall be deemed to have occurred when the disbarring, suspending, revoking or convicting agency or tribunal enters its judgment or order, including a judgment or order on a plea of nolo contendere, regardless of whether an appeal of such judgment or order is pending or could be taken.

(3) *Temporary suspensions.* An order of temporary suspension shall become effective upon service on the respondent. No order of temporary suspension shall be entered by the Commission pursuant to paragraph (e)(3)(i) of this section more than 90 days after the date on which the final judgment or order entered in a judicial or administrative proceeding described in paragraph (e)(3)(i)(A) or (e)(3)(i)(B) of this section has become effective, whether upon completion of review or appeal procedures or because further review or appeal procedures are no longer available.

(i) The Commission, with due regard to the public interest and without preliminary hearing, may, by order, temporarily suspend from appearing or practicing before it any attorney, accountant, engineer, or other professional or expert who has been by name:

(A)   Permanently enjoined by any court of competent jurisdiction, by reason of his or her misconduct in an action brought by the Commission, from violating or aiding and abetting the violation of any provision of the Federal securities laws or of the rules and regulations thereunder; or

(B)   Found by any court of competent jurisdiction in an action brought by the Commission to which he or she is a party or found by the Commission in any administrative proceeding to which he or she is a party to have violated (unless the violation was found not to have been willful) or aided and abetted the violation of any provision of the Federal securities laws or of the rules and regulations thereunder.

(ii)   Any person temporarily suspended from appearing and practicing before the Commission in accordance with paragraph (e)(3)(i) of this section may, within 30 days after service upon him or her of the order of temporary suspension, petition the Commission to lift the temporary suspension. If no petition has been received by the Commission within 30 days after service of the order, the suspension shall become permanent.

(iii)   Within 30 days after the filing of a petition in accordance with paragraph (e)(3)(ii) of this section, the Commission shall either lift the temporary suspension, or set the matter down for hearing at a time and place designated by the Commission, or both, and, after opportunity for hearing, may censure the petitioner or disqualify the petitioner from appearing or practicing before the Commission for a period of time or permanently. In every case in which the temporary suspension has not been lifted, every hearing held and other action taken pursuant to this paragraph (e)(3) shall be expedited in accordance with § 201.500. If the hearing is held before a hearing officer, the time limits set forth in § 201.540 will govern review of the hearing officer's initial decision.

(iv)   In any hearing held on a petition filed in accordance with paragraph (e)(3)(ii) of this section, the staff of the Commission shall show either that the petitioner has been enjoined as described in paragraph (e)(3)(i)(A) of this section or that the petitioner has been found to have committed or aided and abetted violations as described in paragraph (e)(3)(i)(B) of this section and that showing, without more, may be the basis for censure or disqualification. Once that showing has been made, the burden shall be upon the petitioner to show cause why he or she should not be censured or temporarily or permanently disqualified from appearing and practicing before the Commission. In any such hearing, the petitioner may not contest any finding made against him or her or fact admitted by him or her in the judicial or administrative proceeding upon which the proceeding under this paragraph (e)(3) is predicated. A person who has consented to the entry of a permanent injunction as described in paragraph (e)(3)(i)(A) of this section without admitting the facts set forth in the complaint shall be presumed for all purposes under this paragraph (e)(3) to have been enjoined by reason of the misconduct alleged in the complaint.

(4)   *Filing of prior orders.* Any person appearing or practicing before the Commission who has been the subject of an order, judgment, decree, or finding as set forth in paragraph (e)(3) of this section shall promptly file with the Secretary a copy thereof (together with any related opinion or statement of the agency or tribunal involved). Failure to file any such paper, order, judgment, decree or finding shall not impair the operation of any other provision of this section.

(5)   *Reinstatement.* (i) An application for reinstatement of a person permanently suspended or disqualified under paragraph (e)(1) or (e)(3) of this section may be made at any time, and the applicant may, in the Commission's discretion, be afforded a hearing; however, the suspension or disqualification shall continue unless and until the applicant has been reinstated by the Commission for good cause shown.

(ii)   Any person suspended under paragraph (e)(2) of this section shall be reinstated by the Commission, upon appropriate application, if all the grounds for application of the provisions of that paragraph are subsequently removed by a reversal of the conviction or termination of the suspension, disbarment, or revocation. An application for reinstatement on any other grounds by any person suspended under paragraph (e)(2) of this section may be filed at any time and the applicant shall be accorded an opportunity for a hearing in the matter; however, such suspension shall continue unless and until the applicant has been reinstated by order of the Commission for good cause shown.

(6) *Other proceedings not precluded.* A proceeding brought under paragraph (e)(1), (e)(2) or (e)(3) of this section shall not preclude another proceeding brought under these same paragraphs.

(7) *Public hearings.* All hearings held under this paragraph (e) shall be public unless otherwise ordered by the Commission on its own motion or after considering the motion of a party.

(f) *Practice defined.* For the purposes of these Rules of Practice, practicing before the Commission shall include, but shall not be limited to:

(1) Transacting any business with the Commission; and

(2) The preparation of any statement, opinion or other paper by any attorney, accountant, engineer or other professional or expert, filed with the Commission in any registration statement, notification, application, report or other document with the consent of such attorney, accountant, engineer or other professional or expert.

PREPARANCE AND PRACTICE

termination of the suspension, disbarment, or revocation. An application for reinstatement to be made thereafter by any person suspended under paragraph (e)(2) of this section may be filed at any time and the applicant shall be accorded an opportunity for a hearing in the matter; however, such suspension shall continue unless and until the applicant has been reinstated by order of the Commission for good cause shown.

(f) Other proceedings not precluded. A proceeding brought under paragraph (b), (e)(2) or (e)(3) of this section shall not preclude another proceeding under these same paragraphs.

(7) Public nature of hearings. Held under this paragraph (e) shall be public unless otherwise ordered by the Commission on its own motion or after considering the motion of a party.

(h) Practice for the purposes of these Rules of Practice, practice before the Commission shall include but shall not be limited to:

(9) Transacting any business with the Commission; and

(i) The preparation of any statement, opinion or other paper by any attorney, accountant, engineer or other professional in a document in any registration statement, application, amendment, report or other document with the consent of such attorney, accountant, engineer or other professional of expert.

M. STANDARDS OF PROFESSIONAL CONDUCT FOR ATTORNEYS APPEARING AND PRACTICING BEFORE THE COMMISSION IN THE REPRESENTATION OF AN ISSUER

17 C.F.R. §§ 205.1 *et seq.*

Table of Sections

Section

205.1	Purpose and Scope.
205.2	Definitions.
205.3	Issuer as Client.
205.4	Responsibilities of Supervisory Attorneys.
205.5	Responsibilities of a Subordinate Attorney.
205.6	Sanctions and Discipline.
205.7	No Private Right of Action.

---

§ 205.1 Purpose and Scope.

This part sets forth minimum standards of professional conduct for attorneys appearing and practicing before the Commission in the representation of an issuer. These standards supplement applicable standards of any jurisdiction where an attorney is admitted or practices and are not intended to limit the ability of any jurisdiction to impose additional obligations on an attorney not inconsistent with the application of this part. Where the standards of a state or other United States jurisdiction where an attorney is admitted or practices conflict with this part, this part shall govern.

§ 205.2 Definitions.

For purposes of this part, the following definitions apply:

(a) *Appearing and practicing* before the Commission:

    (1) Means:

        (i) Transacting any business with the Commission, including communications in any form;

        (ii) Representing an issuer in a Commission administrative proceeding or in connection with any Commission investigation, inquiry, information request, or subpoena;

        (iii) Providing advice in respect of the United States securities laws or the Commission's rules or regulations thereunder regarding any document that the attorney has notice will be filed with or submitted to, or incorporated into any document that will be filed with or submitted to, the Commission, including the provision of such advice in the context of preparing, or participating in the preparation of, any such document; or

        (iv) Advising an issuer as to whether information or a statement, opinion, or other writing is required under the United States securities laws or the Commission's rules or regulations thereunder to be filed with or submitted to, or incorporated into any document that will be filed with or submitted to, the Commission; but

(2)   Does not include an attorney who:

(i)   Conducts the activities in paragraphs (a)(1)(i) through (a)(1)(iv) of this section other than in the context of providing legal services to an issuer with whom the attorney has an attorney-client relationship; or

(ii)   Is a non-appearing foreign attorney.

(b)   *Appropriate response* means a response to an attorney regarding reported evidence of a material violation as a result of which the attorney reasonably believes:

(1)   That no material violation, as defined in paragraph (i) of this section, has occurred, is ongoing, or is about to occur;

(2)   That the issuer has, as necessary, adopted appropriate remedial measures, including appropriate steps or sanctions to stop any material violations that are ongoing, to prevent any material violation that has yet to occur, and to remedy or otherwise appropriately address any material violation that has already occurred and to minimize the likelihood of its recurrence; or

(3)   That the issuer, with the consent of the issuer's board of directors, a committee thereof to whom a report could be made pursuant to § 205.3(b)(3), or a qualified legal compliance committee, has retained or directed an attorney to review the reported evidence of a material violation and either:

(i)   Has substantially implemented any remedial recommendations made by such attorney after a reasonable investigation and evaluation of the reported evidence; or

(ii)   Has been advised that such attorney may, consistent with his or her professional obligations, assert a colorable defense on behalf of the issuer (or the issuer's officer, director, employee, or agent, as the case may be) in any investigation or judicial or administrative proceeding relating to the reported evidence of a material violation.

(c)   *Attorney* means any person who is admitted, licensed, or otherwise qualified to practice law in any jurisdiction, domestic or foreign, or who holds himself or herself out as admitted, licensed, or otherwise qualified to practice law.

(d)   *Breach of fiduciary duty* refers to any breach of fiduciary or similar duty to the issuer recognized under an applicable Federal or State statute or at common law, including but not limited to misfeasance, nonfeasance, abdication of duty, abuse of trust, and approval of unlawful transactions.

(e)   *Evidence of a material violation* means credible evidence, based upon which it would be unreasonable, under the circumstances, for a prudent and competent attorney not to conclude that it is reasonably likely that a material violation has occurred, is ongoing, or is about to occur.

(f)   *Foreign government issuer* means a foreign issuer as defined in 17 CFR 230.405 eligible to register securities on Schedule B of the Securities Act of 1933 (15 U.S.C. 77a *et seq.*, Schedule B).

(g)   *In the representation of an issuer* means providing legal services as an attorney for an issuer, regardless of whether the attorney is employed or retained by the issuer.

(h)   *Issuer* means an issuer (as defined in section 3 of the Securities Exchange Act of 1934 (15 U.S.C. 78c)), the securities of which are registered under section 12 of that Act (15 U.S.C. 78*l*), or that is required to file reports under section 15(d) of that Act (15 U.S.C. 78o(d)), or that files or has filed a registration statement that has not yet become effective under the Securities Act of 1933 (15 U.S.C. 77a *et seq.*), and that it has not withdrawn, but does not include a foreign government issuer. For purposes of paragraphs (a) and (g) of this section, the term "issuer" includes any person controlled by an issuer, where an attorney provides legal services to such person on behalf of, or at the behest, or for the benefit of the issuer, regardless of whether the attorney is employed or retained by the issuer.

(i)   *Material violation* means a material violation of an applicable United States federal or state securities law, a material breach of fiduciary duty arising under United States federal or state law, or a similar material violation of any United States federal or state law.

(j)   *Non-appearing foreign attorney* means an attorney:

(1)   Who is admitted to practice law in a jurisdiction outside the United States;

(2)   Who does not hold himself or herself out as practicing, and does not give legal advice regarding, United States federal or state securities or other laws (except as provided in paragraph (j)(3)(ii) of this section); and

(3)   Who:

(i)   Conducts activities that would constitute appearing and practicing before the Commission only incidentally to, and in the ordinary course of, the practice of law in a jurisdiction outside the United States; or

(ii)   Is appearing and practicing before the Commission only in consultation with counsel, other than a non-appearing foreign attorney, admitted or licensed to practice in a state or other United States jurisdiction.

(k)   *Qualified legal compliance committee* means a committee of an issuer (which also may be an audit or other committee of the issuer) that:

(1)   Consists of at least one member of the issuer's audit committee (or, if the issuer has no audit committee, one member from an equivalent committee of independent directors) and two or more members of the issuer's board of directors who are not employed, directly or indirectly, by the issuer and who are not, in the case of a registered investment company, "interested persons" as defined in section 2(a)(19) of the Investment Company Act of 1940 (15 U.S.C. 80a–2(a)(19));

(2)   Has adopted written procedures for the confidential receipt, retention, and consideration of any report of evidence of a material violation under § 205.3;

(3)   Has been duly established by the issuer's board of directors, with the authority and responsibility:

(i)   To inform the issuer's chief legal officer and chief executive officer (or the equivalents thereof) of any report of evidence of a material violation (except in the circumstances described in § 205.3(b)(4));

(ii)   To determine whether an investigation is necessary regarding any report of evidence of a material violation by the issuer, its officers, directors, employees or agents and, if it determines an investigation is necessary or appropriate, to:

(A)   Notify the audit committee or the full board of directors;

(B)   Initiate an investigation, which may be conducted either by the chief legal officer (or the equivalent thereof) or by outside attorneys; and

(C)   Retain such additional expert personnel as the committee deems necessary; and

(iii)   At the conclusion of any such investigation, to:

(A)   Recommend, by majority vote, that the issuer implement an appropriate response to evidence of a material violation; and

(B)   Inform the chief legal officer and the chief executive officer (or the equivalents thereof) and the board of directors of the results of any such investigation under this section and the appropriate remedial measures to be adopted; and

(4)   Has the authority and responsibility, acting by majority vote, to take all other appropriate action, including the authority to notify the Commission in the event that the issuer fails in any material respect to implement an appropriate response that the qualified legal compliance committee has recommended the issuer to take.

(*l*)   *Reasonable* or *reasonably* denotes, with respect to the actions of an attorney, conduct that would not be unreasonable for a prudent and competent attorney.

(m)   *Reasonably believes* means that an attorney believes the matter in question and that the circumstances are such that the belief is not unreasonable.

(n)   *Report* means to make known to directly, either in person, by telephone, by e-mail, electronically, or in writing.

§ 205.3   Issuer as Client.

(a)   *Representing an issuer.* An attorney appearing and practicing before the Commission in the representation of an issuer owes his or her professional and ethical duties to the issuer as an organization. That the attorney may work with and advise the issuer's officers, directors, or employees in the course of representing the issuer does not make such individuals the attorney's clients.

(b)   *Duty to report evidence of a material violation.* (1) If an attorney, appearing and practicing before the Commission in the representation of an issuer, becomes aware of evidence of a material violation by the issuer or by any officer, director, employee, or agent of the issuer, the attorney shall report such evidence to the issuer's chief legal officer (or the equivalent thereof) or to both the issuer's chief legal officer and its chief executive officer (or the equivalents thereof) forthwith. By communicating such information to the issuer's officers or directors, an attorney does not reveal client confidences or secrets or privileged or otherwise protected information related to the attorney's representation of an issuer.

(2)   The chief legal officer (or the equivalent thereof) shall cause such inquiry into the evidence of a material violation as he or she reasonably believes is appropriate to determine whether the material violation described in the report has occurred, is ongoing, or is about to occur. If the chief legal officer (or the equivalent thereof) determines no material violation has occurred, is ongoing, or is about to occur, he or she shall notify the reporting attorney and advise the reporting attorney of the basis for such determination. Unless the chief legal officer (or the equivalent thereof) reasonably believes that no material violation has occurred, is ongoing, or is about to occur, he or she shall take all reasonable steps to cause the issuer to adopt an appropriate response, and shall advise the reporting attorney thereof. In lieu of causing an inquiry under this paragraph (b), a chief legal officer (or the equivalent thereof) may refer a report of evidence of a material violation to a qualified legal compliance committee under paragraph (c)(2) of this section if the issuer has duly established a qualified legal compliance committee prior to the report of evidence of a material violation.

(3)   Unless an attorney who has made a report under paragraph (b)(1) of this section reasonably believes that the chief legal officer or the chief executive officer of the issuer (or the equivalent thereof) has provided an appropriate response within a reasonable time, the attorney shall report the evidence of a material violation to:

(i)   The audit committee of the issuer's board of directors;

(ii)   Another committee of the issuer's board of directors consisting solely of directors who are not employed, directly or indirectly, by the issuer and are not, in the case of a registered investment company, "interested persons" as defined in section 2(a)(19) of the Investment Company Act of 1940 (15 U.S.C. 80a–2(a)(19)) (if the issuer's board of directors has no audit committee); or

(iii)   The issuer's board of directors (if the issuer's board of directors has no committee consisting solely of directors who are not employed, directly or indirectly, by the issuer and are not, in the case of a registered investment company, "interested persons" as defined in section 2(a)(19) of the Investment Company Act of 1940 (15 U.S.C. 80a–2(a)(19))).

(4)   If an attorney reasonably believes that it would be futile to report evidence of a material violation to the issuer's chief legal officer and chief executive officer (or the equivalents thereof)

under paragraph (b)(1) of this section, the attorney may report such evidence as provided under paragraph (b)(3) of this section.

(5) An attorney retained or directed by an issuer to investigate evidence of a material violation reported under paragraph (b)(1), (b)(3), or (b)(4) of this section shall be deemed to be appearing and practicing before the Commission. Directing or retaining an attorney to investigate reported evidence of a material violation does not relieve an officer or director of the issuer to whom such evidence has been reported under paragraph (b)(1), (b)(3), or (b)(4) of this section from a duty to respond to the reporting attorney.

(6) An attorney shall not have any obligation to report evidence of a material violation under this paragraph (b) if:

(i) The attorney was retained or directed by the issuer's chief legal officer (or the equivalent thereof) to investigate such evidence of a material violation and:

(A) The attorney reports the results of such investigation to the chief legal officer (or the equivalent thereof); and

(B) Except where the attorney and the chief legal officer (or the equivalent thereof) each reasonably believes that no material violation has occurred, is ongoing, or is about to occur, the chief legal officer (or the equivalent thereof) reports the results of the investigation to the issuer's board of directors, a committee thereof to whom a report could be made pursuant to paragraph (b)(3) of this section, or a qualified legal compliance committee; or

(ii) The attorney was retained or directed by the chief legal officer (or the equivalent thereof) to assert, consistent with his or her professional obligations, a colorable defense on behalf of the issuer (or the issuer's officer, director, employee, or agent, as the case may be) in any investigation or judicial or administrative proceeding relating to such evidence of a material violation, and the chief legal officer (or the equivalent thereof) provides reasonable and timely reports on the progress and outcome of such proceeding to the issuer's board of directors, a committee thereof to whom a report could be made pursuant to paragraph (b)(3) of this section, or a qualified legal compliance committee.

(7) An attorney shall not have any obligation to report evidence of a material violation under this paragraph (b) if such attorney was retained or directed by a qualified legal compliance committee:

(i) To investigate such evidence of a material violation; or

(ii) To assert, consistent with his or her professional obligations, a colorable defense on behalf of the issuer (or the issuer's officer, director, employee, or agent, as the case may be) in any investigation or judicial or administrative proceeding relating to such evidence of a material violation.

(8) An attorney who receives what he or she reasonably believes is an appropriate and timely response to a report he or she has made pursuant to paragraph (b)(1), (b)(3), or (b)(4) of this section need do nothing more under this section with respect to his or her report.

(9) An attorney who does not reasonably believe that the issuer has made an appropriate response within a reasonable time to the report or reports made pursuant to paragraph (b)(1), (b)(3), or (b)(4) of this section shall explain his or her reasons therefor to the chief legal officer (or the equivalent thereof), the chief executive officer (or the equivalent thereof), and directors to whom the attorney reported the evidence of a material violation pursuant to paragraph (b)(1), (b)(3), or (b)(4) of this section.

(10) An attorney formerly employed or retained by an issuer who has reported evidence of a material violation under this part and reasonably believes that he or she has been discharged for so doing may notify the issuer's board of directors or any committee thereof that he or she believes

that he or she has been discharged for reporting evidence of a material violation under this section.

(c) *Alternative reporting procedures for attorneys retained or employed by an issuer that has established a qualified legal compliance committee.* (1) If an attorney, appearing and practicing before the Commission in the representation of an issuer, becomes aware of evidence of a material violation by the issuer or by any officer, director, employee, or agent of the issuer, the attorney may, as an alternative to the reporting requirements of paragraph (b) of this section, report such evidence to a qualified legal compliance committee, if the issuer has previously formed such a committee. An attorney who reports evidence of a material violation to such a qualified legal compliance committee has satisfied his or her obligation to report such evidence and is not required to assess the issuer's response to the reported evidence of a material violation.

(2) A chief legal officer (or the equivalent thereof) may refer a report of evidence of a material violation to a previously established qualified legal compliance committee in lieu of causing an inquiry to be conducted under paragraph (b)(2) of this section. The chief legal officer (or the equivalent thereof) shall inform the reporting attorney that the report has been referred to a qualified legal compliance committee. Thereafter, pursuant to the requirements under § 205.2(k), the qualified legal compliance committee shall be responsible for responding to the evidence of a material violation reported to it under this paragraph (c).

(d) *Issuer confidences.* (1) Any report under this section (or the contemporaneous record thereof) or any response thereto (or the contemporaneous record thereof) may be used by an attorney in connection with any investigation, proceeding, or litigation in which the attorney's compliance with this part is in issue.

(2) An attorney appearing and practicing before the Commission in the representation of an issuer may reveal to the Commission, without the issuer's consent, confidential information related to the representation to the extent the attorney reasonably believes necessary:

(i) To prevent the issuer from committing a material violation that is likely to cause substantial injury to the financial interest or property of the issuer or investors;

(ii) To prevent the issuer, in a Commission investigation or administrative proceeding from committing perjury, proscribed in 18 U.S.C. 1621; suborning perjury, proscribed in 18 U.S.C. 1622; or committing any act proscribed in 18 U.S.C. 1001 that is likely to perpetrate a fraud upon the Commission; or

(iii) To rectify the consequences of a material violation by the issuer that caused, or may cause, substantial injury to the financial interest or property of the issuer or investors in the furtherance of which the attorney's services were used.

§ 205.4   Responsibilities of Supervisory Attorneys.

(a) An attorney supervising or directing another attorney who is appearing and practicing before the Commission in the representation of an issuer is a supervisory attorney. An issuer's chief legal officer (or the equivalent thereof) is a supervisory attorney under this section.

(b) A supervisory attorney shall make reasonable efforts to ensure that a subordinate attorney, as defined in § 205.5(a), that he or she supervises or directs conforms to this part. To the extent a subordinate attorney appears and practices before the Commission in the representation of an issuer, that subordinate attorney's supervisory attorneys also appear and practice before the Commission.

(c) A supervisory attorney is responsible for complying with the reporting requirements in § 205.3 when a subordinate attorney has reported to the supervisory attorney evidence of a material violation.

(d)   A supervisory attorney who has received a report of evidence of a material violation from a subordinate attorney under § 205.3 may report such evidence to the issuer's qualified legal compliance committee if the issuer has duly formed such a committee.

§ 205.5   Responsibilities of a Subordinate Attorney.

(a)   An attorney who appears and practices before the Commission in the representation of an issuer on a matter under the supervision or direction of another attorney (other than under the direct supervision or direction of the issuer's chief legal officer (or the equivalent thereof)) is a subordinate attorney.

(b)   A subordinate attorney shall comply with this part notwithstanding that the subordinate attorney acted at the direction of or under the supervision of another person.

(c)   A subordinate attorney complies with § 205.3 if the subordinate attorney reports to his or her supervising attorney under § 205.3(b) evidence of a material violation of which the subordinate attorney has become aware in appearing and practicing before the Commission.

(d)   A subordinate attorney may take the steps permitted or required by § 205.3(b) or (c) if the subordinate attorney reasonably believes that a supervisory attorney to whom he or she has reported evidence of a material violation under § 205.3(b) has failed to comply with § 205.3.

§ 205.6   Sanctions and Discipline.

(a)   A violation of this part by any attorney appearing and practicing before the Commission in the representation of an issuer shall subject such attorney to the civil penalties and remedies for a violation of the federal securities laws available to the Commission in an action brought by the Commission thereunder.

(b)   An attorney appearing and practicing before the Commission who violates any provision of this part is subject to the disciplinary authority of the Commission, regardless of whether the attorney may also be subject to discipline for the same conduct in a jurisdiction where the attorney is admitted or practices. An administrative disciplinary proceeding initiated by the Commission for violation of this part may result in an attorney being censured, or being temporarily or permanently denied the privilege of appearing or practicing before the Commission.

(c)   An attorney who complies in good faith with the provisions of this part shall not be subject to discipline or otherwise liable under inconsistent standards imposed by any state or other United States jurisdiction where the attorney is admitted or practices.

(d)   An attorney practicing outside the United States shall not be required to comply with the requirements of this part to the extent that such compliance is prohibited by applicable foreign law.

§ 205.7   No Private Right of Action.

(a)   Nothing in this part is intended to, or does, create a private right of action against any attorney, law firm, or issuer based upon compliance or noncompliance with its provisions.

(b)   Authority to enforce compliance with this part is vested exclusively in the Commission.

VI. UNIFORM FRAUDULENT TRANSFER ACT (1984)

Table of Contents

§ 1. Definitions

As used in this [Act]:

(1) "Affiliate" means:

    (i) a person who directly or indirectly owns, controls, or holds with power to vote, 20 percent or more of the outstanding voting securities of the debtor, other than a person who holds the securities,

        (A) as a fiduciary or agent without sole discretionary power to vote the securities; or

        (B) solely to secure a debt, if the person has not exercised the power to vote;

    (ii) a corporation 20 percent or more of whose outstanding voting securities are directly or indirectly owned, controlled, or held with power to vote, by the debtor or a person who directly or indirectly owns, controls, or holds, with power to vote, 20 percent or more of the outstanding voting securities of the debtor, other than a person who holds the securities,

        (A) as a fiduciary or agent without sole power to vote the securities; or

        (B) solely to secure a debt, if the person has not in fact exercised the power to vote;

    (iii) a person whose business is operated by the debtor under a lease or other agreement, or a person substantially all of whose assets are controlled by the debtor; or

    (iv) a person who operates the debtor's business under a lease or other agreement or controls substantially all of the debtor's assets.

(2) "Asset" means property of a debtor, but the term does not include:

    (i) property to the extent it is encumbered by a valid lien;

    (ii) property to the extent it is generally exempt under nonbankruptcy law; or

    (iii) an interest in property held in tenancy by the entireties to the extent it is not subject to process by a creditor holding a claim against only one tenant.

(3) "Claim" means a right to payment, whether or not the right is reduced to judgment, liquidated, unliquidated, fixed, contingent, matured, unmatured, disputed, undisputed, legal, equitable, secured, or unsecured.

(4) "Creditor" means a person who has a claim.

(5) "Debt" means liability on a claim.

(6) "Debtor" means a person who is liable on a claim.

(7) "Insider" includes:

    (i) if the debtor is an individual,

        (A) a relative of the debtor or of a general partner of the debtor;

        (B) a partnership in which the debtor is a general partner;

        (C) a general partner in a partnership described in clause (B); or

        (D) a corporation of which the debtor is a director, officer, or person in control;

    (ii) if the debtor is a corporation,

        (A) a director of the debtor;

        (B) an officer of the debtor;

        (C) a person in control of the debtor;

        (D) a partnership in which the debtor is a general partner;

        (E) a general partner in a partnership described in clause (D); or

        (F) a relative of a general partner, director, officer, or person in control of the debtor;

    (iii) if the debtor is a partnership,

        (A) a general partner in the debtor;

        (B) a relative of a general partner in, a general partner of, or a person in control of the debtor;

        (C) another partnership in which the debtor is a general partner;

        (D) a general partner in a partnership described in clause (C); or

        (E) a person in control of the debtor;

    (iv) an affiliate, or an insider of an affiliate as if the affiliate were the debtor; and

    (v) a managing agent of the debtor.

(8) "Lien" means a charge against or an interest in property to secure payment of a debt or performance of an obligation, and includes a security interest created by agreement, a judicial lien obtained by legal or equitable process or proceedings, a common-law lien, or a statutory lien.

(9) "Person" means an individual, partnership, corporation, association, organization, government or governmental subdivision or agency, business trust, estate, trust, or any other legal or commercial entity.

(10) "Property" means anything that may be the subject of ownership.

(11) "Relative" means an individual related by consanguinity within the third degree as determined by the common law, a spouse, or an individual related to a spouse within the third degree as so determined, and includes an individual in an adoptive relationship within the third degree.

(12) "Transfer" means every mode, direct or indirect, absolute or conditional, voluntary or involuntary, of disposing of or parting with an asset or an interest in an asset, and includes payment of money, release, lease, and creation of a lien or other encumbrance.

(13) "Valid lien" means a lien that is effective against the holder of a judicial lien subsequently obtained by legal or equitable process or proceedings.

§ 2. Insolvency

(a) A debtor is insolvent if the sum of the debtor's debts is greater than all of the debtor's assets at a fair valuation.

(b) A debtor who is generally not paying his [or her] debts as they become due is presumed to be insolvent.

(c) A partnership is insolvent under subsection (a) if the sum of the partnership's debts is greater than the aggregate, at a fair valuation, of all of the partnership's assets and the sum of the excess of the value of each general partner's nonpartnership assets over the partner's nonpartnership debts.

(d) Assets under this section do not include property that has been transferred, concealed, or removed with intent to hinder, delay, or defraud creditors or that has been transferred in a manner making the transfer voidable under this [Act].

(e) Debts under this section do not include an obligation to the extent it is secured by a valid lien on property of the debtor not included as an asset.

§ 3. Value

(a) Value is given for a transfer or an obligation if, in exchange for the transfer or obligation, property is transferred or an antecedent debt is secured or satisfied, but value does not include an unperformed promise made otherwise than in the ordinary course of the promisor's business to furnish support to the debtor or another person.

(b) For the purposes of Sections 4(a)(2) and 5, a person gives a reasonably equivalent value if the person acquires an interest of the debtor in an asset pursuant to a regularly conducted, noncollusive foreclosure sale or execution of a power of sale for the acquisition or disposition of the interest of the debtor upon default under a mortgage, deed of trust, or security agreement.

(c) A transfer is made for present value if the exchange between the debtor and the transferee is intended by them to be contemporaneous and is in fact substantially contemporaneous.

§ 4. Transfers Fraudulent as to Present and Future Creditors

(a) A transfer made or obligation incurred by a debtor is fraudulent as to a creditor, whether the creditor's claim arose before or after the transfer was made or the obligation was incurred, if the debtor made the transfer or incurred the obligation:

(1) with actual intent to hinder, delay, or defraud any creditor of the debtor; or

(2) without receiving a reasonably equivalent value in exchange for the transfer or obligation, and the debtor:

(i) was engaged or was about to engage in a business or a transaction for which the remaining assets of the debtor were unreasonably small in relation to the business or transaction; or

(ii) intended to incur, or believed or reasonably should have believed that he [or she] would incur, debts beyond his [or her] ability to pay as they became due.

(b) In determining actual intent under subsection (a)(1), consideration may be given, among other factors, to whether:

    (1)   the transfer or obligation was to an insider;

    (2)   the debtor retained possession or control of the property transferred after the transfer;

    (3)   the transfer or obligation was disclosed or concealed;

    (4)   before the transfer was made or obligation was incurred, the debtor had been sued or threatened with suit;

    (5)   the transfer was of substantially all the debtor's assets;

    (6)   the debtor absconded;

    (7)   the debtor removed or concealed assets;

    (8)   the value of the consideration received by the debtor was reasonably equivalent to the value of the asset transferred or the amount of the obligation incurred;

    (9)   the debtor was insolvent or became insolvent shortly after the transfer was made or the obligation was incurred;

    (10)   the transfer occurred shortly before or shortly after a substantial debt was incurred; and

    (11)   the debtor transferred the essential assets of the business to a lienor who transferred the assets to an insider of the debtor.

§ 5.   Transfers Fraudulent as to Present Creditors

(a) A transfer made or obligation incurred by a debtor is fraudulent as to a creditor whose claim arose before the transfer was made or the obligation was incurred if the debtor made the transfer or incurred the obligation without receiving a reasonably equivalent value in exchange for the transfer or obligation and the debtor was insolvent at that time or the debtor became insolvent as a result of the transfer or obligation.

(b) A transfer made by a debtor is fraudulent as to a creditor whose claim arose before the transfer was made if the transfer was made to an insider for an antecedent debt, the debtor was insolvent at that time, and the insider had reasonable cause to believe that the debtor was insolvent.

§ 6.   When Transfer Is Made or Obligation Is Incurred

For the purposes of this [Act]:

    (1)   a transfer is made:

        (i)   with respect to an asset that is real property other than a fixture, but including the interest of a seller or purchaser under a contract for the sale of the asset, when the transfer is so far perfected that a good-faith purchaser of the asset from the debtor against whom applicable law permits the transfer to be perfected cannot acquire an interest in the asset that is superior to the interest of the transferee; and

        (ii)   with respect to an asset that is not real property or that is a fixture, when the transfer is so far perfected that a creditor on a simple contract cannot acquire a judicial lien otherwise than under this [Act] that is superior to the interest of the transferee;

    (2)   if applicable law permits the transfer to be perfected as provided in paragraph (1) and the transfer is not so perfected before the commencement of an action for relief under this [Act], the transfer is deemed made immediately before the commencement of the action;

    (3)   if applicable law does not permit the transfer to be perfected as provided in paragraph (1), the transfer is made when it becomes effective between the debtor and the transferee;

(4) a transfer is not made until the debtor has acquired rights in the asset transferred;

(5) an obligation is incurred:

    (i) if oral, when it becomes effective between the parties; or

    (ii) if evidenced by a writing, when the writing executed by the obligor is delivered to or for the benefit of the obligee.

§ 7. Remedies of Creditors

(a) In an action for relief against a transfer or obligation under this [Act], a creditor, subject to the limitations in Section 8, may obtain:

    (1) avoidance of the transfer or obligation to the extent necessary to satisfy the creditor's claim;

    [(2) an attachment or other provisional remedy against the asset transferred or other property of the transferee in accordance with the procedure prescribed by [ ];]

    (3) subject to applicable principles of equity and in accordance with applicable rules of civil procedure,

        (i) an injunction against further disposition by the debtor or a transferee, or both, of the asset transferred or of other property;

        (ii) appointment of a receiver to take charge of the asset transferred or of other property of the transferee; or

        (iii) any other relief the circumstances may require.

(b) If a creditor has obtained a judgment on a claim against the debtor, the creditor, if the court so orders, may levy execution on the asset transferred or its proceeds.

§ 8. Defenses, Liability, and Protection of Transferee

(a) A transfer or obligation is not voidable under Section 4(a)(1) against a person who took in good faith and for a reasonably equivalent value or against any subsequent transferee or obligee.

(b) Except as otherwise provided in this section, to the extent a transfer is voidable in an action by a creditor under Section 7(a)(1), the creditor may recover judgment for the value of the asset transferred, as adjusted under subsection (c), or the amount necessary to satisfy the creditor's claim, whichever is less. The judgment may be entered against:

    (1) the first transferee of the asset or the person for whose benefit the transfer was made; or

    (2) any subsequent transferee other than a good faith transferee who took for value or from any subsequent transferee.

(c) If the judgment under subsection (b) is based upon the value of the asset transferred, the judgment must be for an amount equal to the value of the asset at the time of the transfer, subject to adjustment as the equities may require.

(d) Notwithstanding voidability of a transfer or an obligation under this [Act], a good-faith transferee or obligee is entitled, to the extent of the value given the debtor for the transfer or obligation, to

    (1) a lien on or a right to retain any interest in the asset transferred;

    (2) enforcement of any obligation incurred; or

    (3) a reduction in the amount of the liability on the judgment.

(e) A transfer is not voidable under Section 4(a)(2) or Section 5 if the transfer results from:

(1)　termination of a lease upon default by the debtor when the termination is pursuant to the lease and applicable law; or

(2)　enforcement of a security interest in compliance with Article 9 of the Uniform Commercial Code.

(f)　A transfer is not voidable under Section 5(b):

(1)　to the extent the insider gave new value to or for the benefit of the debtor after the transfer was made unless the new value was secured by a valid lien;

(2)　if made in the ordinary course of business or financial affairs of the debtor and the insider; or

(3)　if made pursuant to a good-faith effort to rehabilitate the debtor and the transfer secured present value given for that purpose as well as an antecedent debt of the debtor.

§ 9.　　Extinguishment of [Claim for Relief] [Cause of Action]

A [claim for relief] [cause of action] with respect to a fraudulent transfer or obligation under this [Act] is extinguished unless action is brought:

(a)　under Section 4(a)(1), within 4 years after the transfer was made or the obligation was incurred or, if later, within one year after the transfer or obligation was or could reasonably have been discovered by the claimant;

(b)　under Section 4(a)(2) or 5(a), within 4 years after the transfer was made or the obligation was incurred; or

(c)　under Section 5(b), within one year after the transfer was made or the obligation was incurred.

§ 10.　　Supplementary Provisions

Unless displaced by the provisions of this [Act], the principles of law and equity, including the law merchant and the law relating to principal and agent, estoppel, laches, fraud, misrepresentation, duress, coercion, mistake, insolvency, or other validating or invalidating cause, supplement its provisions.

§ 11.　　Uniformity of Application and Construction

This [Act] shall be applied and construed to effectuate its general purpose to make uniform the law with respect to the subject of this [Act] among states enacting it.

§ 12.　　Short Title

This [Act] may be cited as the Uniform Fraudulent Transfer Act.

§ 13.　　Repeal

The following acts and all other acts and parts of acts inconsistent herewith are hereby repealed.

VII. UNIFORM VOIDABLE TRANSACTIONS ACT

(Formerly Uniform Fraudulent Transfer Act)

(As Amended in 2014)

Table of Contents

---

* * *

PREFATORY NOTE (2014 AMENDMENTS)

In 2014 the Uniform Law Commission approved a set of amendments to the Uniform Fraudulent Transfer Act. The amendments changed the title of the Act to the Uniform Voidable Transactions Act. The amendment project was instituted to address a small number of narrowly-defined issues, and was not a comprehensive revision. The principal features of the amendments are listed below. Further explanation of provisions added or revised by the amendments may be found in the comments to those provisions.

Choice of Law. The amendments add a new § 10, which sets forth a choice of law rule applicable to claims for relief of the nature governed by the Act.

Evidentiary Matters. New §§ 4(c), 5(c), 8(g), and 8(h) add uniform rules allocating the burden of proof and defining the standard of proof with respect to claims for relief and defenses under the Act. Language in the former comments to § 2 relating to the presumption of insolvency created by § 2(b) has been moved to the text of that provision, the better to assure its uniform application.

Deletion of the Special Definition of "Insolvency" for Partnerships. Section 2(c) of the Act as originally written set forth a special definition of "insolvency" applicable to partnerships. The amendments delete original § 2(c), with the result that the general definition of "insolvency" in § 2(a) now applies to partnerships. One reason for this change is that original § 2(c) gave a partnership full credit for the net worth of each of its general partners. That makes sense only if each general partner is liable for all debts of the partnership, but such is not necessarily the case under modern partnership statutes. A more fundamental reason is that the general definition of "insolvency" in § 2(a) does not credit a non-partnership debtor with any part of the net worth of its guarantors. To the extent that a general partner is liable for the debts of the partnership, that liability is analogous to that of a guarantor. There is no good reason to define "insolvency" differently for a partnership debtor than for a non-partnership debtor whose debts are guaranteed by contract.

Defenses. The amendments refine in relatively minor respects several provisions relating to defenses available to a transferee or obligee, as follows:

(1)   As originally written, § 8(a) created a complete defense to an action under § 4(a)(1) (which renders voidable a transfer made or obligation incurred with actual intent to hinder, delay, or defraud any creditor of the debtor) if the transferee or obligee takes in good faith and for a reasonably equivalent value. The amendments add to § 8(a) the further requirement that the reasonably equivalent value must be given the debtor.

(2)   Section 8(b), derived from Bankruptcy Code §§ 550(a), (b) (1984), creates a defense for a subsequent transferee (that is, a transferee other than the first transferee) that takes in good faith and for value, and for any subsequent good-faith transferee from such a person.

The amendments clarify the meaning of § 8(b) by rewording it to follow more closely the wording of Bankruptcy Code §§ 550(a), (b) (which is substantially unchanged as of 2014). Among other things, the amendments make clear that the defense applies to recovery of or from the transferred property or its proceeds, by levy or otherwise, as well as to an action for a money judgment.

(3)   Section 8(e)(2) as originally written created a defense to an action under § 4(a)(2) or § 5 to avoid a transfer if the transfer results from enforcement of a security interest in compliance with Article 9 of the Uniform Commercial Code. The amendments exclude from that defense acceptance of collateral in full or partial satisfaction of the obligation it secures (a remedy sometimes referred to as "strict foreclosure").

Series Organizations. A new § 11 provides that each "protected series" of a "series organization" is to be treated as a person for purposes of the Act, even if it is not treated as a person for other purposes. This change responds to the emergence of the "series organization" as a significant form of business organization.

Medium Neutrality. In order to accommodate modern technology, the references in the Act to a "writing" have been replaced with "record," and related changes made.

Style. The amendments make a number of stylistic changes that are not intended to change the meaning of the Act. For example, the amended Act consistently uses the word "voidable" to denote a transfer or obligation for which the Act provides a remedy. As originally written the Act sometimes inconsistently used the word "fraudulent." No change in meaning is intended. See § 15, Comment 4. Likewise, the retitling of the Act is not intended to change its meaning. See § 15, Comment 1.

Official Comments. Comments were added explaining provisions added or revised by the amendments, and the original comments were supplemented and otherwise refreshed.

§ 1. Definitions.

As used in this [Act]:

(1)   "Affiliate" means:

(i)   a person that directly or indirectly owns, controls, or holds with power to vote, 20 percent or more of the outstanding voting securities of the debtor, other than a person that holds the securities:

(A)   as a fiduciary or agent without sole discretionary power to vote the securities; or

(B)   solely to secure a debt, if the person has not in fact exercised the power to vote;

(ii)   a corporation 20 percent or more of whose outstanding voting securities are directly or indirectly owned, controlled, or held with power to vote, by the debtor or a person that directly or indirectly owns, controls, or holds, with power to vote, 20 percent or more of the outstanding voting securities of the debtor, other than a person that holds the securities:

(A)   as a fiduciary or agent without sole discretionary power to vote the securities; or

    (B) solely to secure a debt, if the person has not in fact exercised the power to vote;

    (iii) a person whose business is operated by the debtor under a lease or other agreement, or a person substantially all of whose assets are controlled by the debtor; or

    (iv) a person that operates the debtor's business under a lease or other agreement or controls substantially all of the debtor's assets.

(2) "Asset" means property of a debtor, but the term does not include:

    (i) property to the extent it is encumbered by a valid lien;

    (ii) property to the extent it is generally exempt under nonbankruptcy law; or

    (iii) an interest in property held in tenancy by the entireties to the extent it is not subject to process by a creditor holding a claim against only one tenant.

(3) "Claim", except as used in "claim for relief", means a right to payment, whether or not the right is reduced to judgment, liquidated, unliquidated, fixed, contingent, matured, unmatured, disputed, undisputed, legal, equitable, secured, or unsecured.

(4) "Creditor" means a person that has a claim.

(5) "Debt" means liability on a claim.

(6) "Debtor" means a person that is liable on a claim.

(7) "Electronic" means relating to technology having electrical, digital, magnetic, wireless, optical, electromagnetic, or similar capabilities.

(8) "Insider" includes:

    (i) if the debtor is an individual:

        (A) a relative of the debtor or of a general partner of the debtor;

        (B) a partnership in which the debtor is a general partner;

        (C) a general partner in a partnership described in clause (B); or

        (D) a corporation of which the debtor is a director, officer, or person in control;

    (ii) if the debtor is a corporation:

        (A) a director of the debtor;

        (B) an officer of the debtor;

        (C) a person in control of the debtor;

        (D) a partnership in which the debtor is a general partner;

        (E) a general partner in a partnership described in clause (D); or

        (F) a relative of a general partner, director, officer, or person in control of the debtor;

    (iii) if the debtor is a partnership:

        (A) a general partner in the debtor;

        (B) a relative of a general partner in, a general partner of, or a person in control of the debtor;

        (C) another partnership in which the debtor is a general partner;

        (D) a general partner in a partnership described in clause (C); or

        (E) a person in control of the debtor;

    (iv) an affiliate, or an insider of an affiliate as if the affiliate were the debtor; and

    (v)   a managing agent of the debtor.

    (9) "Lien" means a charge against or an interest in property to secure payment of a debt or performance of an obligation, and includes a security interest created by agreement, a judicial lien obtained by legal or equitable process or proceedings, a common-law lien, or a statutory lien.

    (10) "Organization" means a person other than an individual.

    (11) "Person" means an individual, estate, partnership, association, trust, business or nonprofit entity, public corporation, government or governmental subdivision, agency, or instrumentality, or other legal or commercial entity.

    (12) "Property" means anything that may be the subject of ownership.

    (13) "Record" means information that is inscribed on a tangible medium or that is stored in an electronic or other medium and is retrievable in perceivable form.

    (14) "Relative" means an individual related by consanguinity within the third degree as determined by the common law, a spouse, or an individual related to a spouse within the third degree as so determined, and includes an individual in an adoptive relationship within the third degree.

    (15) "Sign" means, with present intent to authenticate or adopt a record:

        (i)   to execute or adopt a tangible symbol; or

        (ii)   to attach to or logically associate with the record an electronic symbol, sound, or process.

    (16) "Transfer" means every mode, direct or indirect, absolute or conditional, voluntary or involuntary, of disposing of or parting with an asset or an interest in an asset, and includes payment of money, release, lease, license, and creation of a lien or other encumbrance.

    (17) "Valid lien" means a lien that is effective against the holder of a judicial lien subsequently obtained by legal or equitable process or proceedings.

§ 2. Insolvency.

    (a)   A debtor is insolvent if, at a fair valuation, the sum of the debtor's debts is greater than the sum of the debtor's assets.

    (b)   A debtor that is generally not paying the debtor's debts as they become due other than as a result of a bona fide dispute is presumed to be insolvent. The presumption imposes on the party against which the presumption is directed the burden of proving that the nonexistence of insolvency is more probable than its existence.

    (c)   Assets under this section do not include property that has been transferred, concealed, or removed with intent to hinder, delay, or defraud creditors or that has been transferred in a manner making the transfer voidable under this [Act].

    (d)   Debts under this section do not include an obligation to the extent it is secured by a valid lien on property of the debtor not included as an asset.

§ 3. Value.

    (a)   Value is given for a transfer or an obligation if, in exchange for the transfer or obligation, property is transferred or an antecedent debt is secured or satisfied, but value does not include an unperformed promise made otherwise than in the ordinary course of the promisor's business to furnish support to the debtor or another person.

    (b)   For the purposes of Section 4(a)(2) and Section 5, a person gives a reasonably equivalent value if the person acquires an interest of the debtor in an asset pursuant to a regularly conducted, noncollusive foreclosure sale or execution of a power of sale for the acquisition or disposition of the interest of the debtor upon default under a mortgage, deed of trust, or security agreement.

(c)   A transfer is made for present value if the exchange between the debtor and the transferee is intended by them to be contemporaneous and is in fact substantially contemporaneous.

§ 4. Transfer or Obligation Voidable as to Present or Future Creditor.

(a)   A transfer made or obligation incurred by a debtor is voidable as to a creditor, whether the creditor's claim arose before or after the transfer was made or the obligation was incurred, if the debtor made the transfer or incurred the obligation:

(1)   with actual intent to hinder, delay, or defraud any creditor of the debtor; or

(2)   without receiving a reasonably equivalent value in exchange for the transfer or obligation, and the debtor:

(i)   was engaged or was about to engage in a business or a transaction for which the remaining assets of the debtor were unreasonably small in relation to the business or transaction; or

(ii)   intended to incur, or believed or reasonably should have believed that the debtor would incur, debts beyond the debtor's ability to pay as they became due.

(b)   In determining actual intent under subsection (a)(1), consideration may be given, among other factors, to whether:

(1)   the transfer or obligation was to an insider;

(2)   the debtor retained possession or control of the property transferred after the transfer;

(3)   the transfer or obligation was disclosed or concealed;

(4)   before the transfer was made or obligation was incurred, the debtor had been sued or threatened with suit;

(5)   the transfer was of substantially all the debtor's assets;

(6)   the debtor absconded;

(7)   the debtor removed or concealed assets;

(8)   the value of the consideration received by the debtor was reasonably equivalent to the value of the asset transferred or the amount of the obligation incurred;

(9)   the debtor was insolvent or became insolvent shortly after the transfer was made or the obligation was incurred;

(10) the transfer occurred shortly before or shortly after a substantial debt was incurred; and

(11) the debtor transferred the essential assets of the business to a lienor that transferred the assets to an insider of the debtor.

(c)   A creditor making a claim for relief under subsection (a) has the burden of proving the elements of the claim for relief by a preponderance of the evidence.

§ 5. Transfer or Obligation Voidable as to Present Creditor.

(a)   A transfer made or obligation incurred by a debtor is voidable as to a creditor whose claim arose before the transfer was made or the obligation was incurred if the debtor made the transfer or incurred the obligation without receiving a reasonably equivalent value in exchange for the transfer or obligation and the debtor was insolvent at that time or the debtor became insolvent as a result of the transfer or obligation.

(b)   A transfer made by a debtor is voidable as to a creditor whose claim arose before the transfer was made if the transfer was made to an insider for an antecedent debt, the debtor was insolvent at that time, and the insider had reasonable cause to believe that the debtor was insolvent.

(c)   Subject to Section 2(b), a creditor making a claim for relief under subsection (a) or (b) has the burden of proving the elements of the claim for relief by a preponderance of the evidence.

§ 6. When Transfer Is Made or Obligation Is Incurred.

For the purposes of this [Act]:

(1)   a transfer is made:

(i)   with respect to an asset that is real property other than a fixture, but including the interest of a seller or purchaser under a contract for the sale of the asset, when the transfer is so far perfected that a good-faith purchaser of the asset from the debtor against which applicable law permits the transfer to be perfected cannot acquire an interest in the asset that is superior to the interest of the transferee; and

(ii)   with respect to an asset that is not real property or that is a fixture, when the transfer is so far perfected that a creditor on a simple contract cannot acquire a judicial lien otherwise than under this [Act] that is superior to the interest of the transferee;

(2)   if applicable law permits the transfer to be perfected as provided in paragraph (1) and the transfer is not so perfected before the commencement of an action for relief under this [Act], the transfer is deemed made immediately before the commencement of the action;

(3)   if applicable law does not permit the transfer to be perfected as provided in paragraph (1), the transfer is made when it becomes effective between the debtor and the transferee;

(4)   a transfer is not made until the debtor has acquired rights in the asset transferred; and

(5)   an obligation is incurred:

(i)   if oral, when it becomes effective between the parties; or

(ii)   if evidenced by a record, when the record signed by the obligor is delivered to or for the benefit of the obligee.

§ 7. Remedies of Creditor.

(a)   In an action for relief against a transfer or obligation under this [Act], a creditor, subject to the limitations in Section 8, may obtain:

(1)   avoidance of the transfer or obligation to the extent necessary to satisfy the creditor's claim;

(2)   an attachment or other provisional remedy against the asset transferred or other property of the transferee if available under applicable law; and

(3)   subject to applicable principles of equity and in accordance with applicable rules of civil procedure:

(i)   an injunction against further disposition by the debtor or a transferee, or both, of the asset transferred or of other property;

(ii)   appointment of a receiver to take charge of the asset transferred or of other property of the transferee; or

(iii)   any other relief the circumstances may require.

(b)   If a creditor has obtained a judgment on a claim against the debtor, the creditor, if the court so orders, may levy execution on the asset transferred or its proceeds.

§ 8. Defenses, Liability, and Protection of Transferee or Obligee.

(a) A transfer or obligation is not voidable under Section 4(a)(1) against a person that took in good faith and for a reasonably equivalent value given the debtor or against any subsequent transferee or obligee.

(b) To the extent a transfer is avoidable in an action by a creditor under Section 7(a)(1), the following rules apply:

(1) Except as otherwise provided in this section, the creditor may recover judgment for the value of the asset transferred, as adjusted under subsection (c), or the amount necessary to satisfy the creditor's claim, whichever is less. The judgment may be entered against:

(i) the first transferee of the asset or the person for whose benefit the transfer was made; or

(ii) an immediate or mediate transferee of the first transferee, other than:

(A) a good-faith transferee that took for value; or

(B) an immediate or mediate good-faith transferee of a person described in clause (A).

(2) Recovery pursuant to Section 7(a)(1) or (b) of or from the asset transferred or its proceeds, by levy or otherwise, is available only against a person described in paragraph (1)(i) or (ii).

(c) If the judgment under subsection (b) is based upon the value of the asset transferred, the judgment must be for an amount equal to the value of the asset at the time of the transfer, subject to adjustment as the equities may require.

(d) Notwithstanding voidability of a transfer or an obligation under this [Act], a good-faith transferee or obligee is entitled, to the extent of the value given the debtor for the transfer or obligation, to:

(1) a lien on or a right to retain an interest in the asset transferred;

(2) enforcement of an obligation incurred; or

(3) a reduction in the amount of the liability on the judgment.

(e) A transfer is not voidable under Section 4(a)(2) or Section 5 if the transfer results from:

(1) termination of a lease upon default by the debtor when the termination is pursuant to the lease and applicable law; or

(2) enforcement of a security interest in compliance with Article 9 of the Uniform Commercial Code, other than acceptance of collateral in full or partial satisfaction of the obligation it secures.

(f) A transfer is not voidable under Section 5(b):

(1) to the extent the insider gave new value to or for the benefit of the debtor after the transfer was made, except to the extent the new value was secured by a valid lien;

(2) if made in the ordinary course of business or financial affairs of the debtor and the insider; or

(3) if made pursuant to a good-faith effort to rehabilitate the debtor and the transfer secured present value given for that purpose as well as an antecedent debt of the debtor.

(g) The following rules determine the burden of proving matters referred to in this section:

(1) A party that seeks to invoke subsection (a), (d), (e), or (f) has the burden of proving the applicability of that subsection.

(2)   Except as otherwise provided in paragraphs (3) and (4), the creditor has the burden of proving each applicable element of subsection (b) or (c).

(3)   The transferee has the burden of proving the applicability to the transferee of subsection (b)(1)(ii)(A) or (B).

(4)   A party that seeks adjustment under subsection (c) has the burden of proving the adjustment.

(h)   The standard of proof required to establish matters referred to in this section is preponderance of the evidence.

§ 9. Extinguishment of Claim for Relief.

A claim for relief with respect to a transfer or obligation under this [Act] is extinguished unless action is brought:

(a)   under Section 4(a)(1), not later than four years after the transfer was made or the obligation was incurred or, if later, not later than one year after the transfer or obligation was or could reasonably have been discovered by the claimant;

(b)   under Section 4(a)(2) or 5(a), not later than four years after the transfer was made or the obligation was incurred; or

(c)   under Section 5(b), not later than one year after the transfer was made.

§ 10. Governing Law.

(a)   In this section, the following rules determine a debtor's location:

(1)   A debtor who is an individual is located at the individual's principal residence.

(2)   A debtor that is an organization and has only one place of business is located at its place of business.

(3)   A debtor that is an organization and has more than one place of business is located at its chief executive office.

(b)   A claim for relief in the nature of a claim for relief under this [Act] is governed by the local law of the jurisdiction in which the debtor is located when the transfer is made or the obligation is incurred.

§ 11. Application to Series Organization.

(a)   In this section:

(1)   "Protected series" means an arrangement, however denominated, created by a series organization that, pursuant to the law under which the series organization is organized, has the characteristics set forth in paragraph (2).

(2)   "Series organization" means an organization that, pursuant to the law under which it is organized, has the following characteristics:

(i)   The organic record of the organization provides for creation by the organization of one or more protected series, however denominated, with respect to specified property of the organization, and for records to be maintained for each protected series that identify the property of or associated with the protected series.

(ii)   Debt incurred or existing with respect to the activities of, or property of or associated with, a particular protected series is enforceable against the property of or associated with the protected series only, and not against the property of or associated with the organization or other protected series of the organization.

(iii) Debt incurred or existing with respect to the activities or property of the organization is enforceable against the property of the organization only, and not against the property of or associated with a protected series of the organization.

(b) A series organization and each protected series of the organization is a separate person for purposes of this [Act], even if for other purposes a protected series is not a person separate from the organization or other protected series of the organization.

Legislative Note: This section should be enacted even if the enacting jurisdiction does not itself have legislation enabling the creation of protected series. For example, in such an enacting jurisdiction this section will apply if a protected series of a series organization organized under the law of a different jurisdiction makes a transfer to another protected series of that organization and, under applicable choice of law rules, the voidability of the transfer is governed by the law of the enacting jurisdiction.

§ 12. Supplementary Provisions.

Unless displaced by the provisions of this [Act], the principles of law and equity, including the law merchant and the law relating to principal and agent, estoppel, laches, fraud, misrepresentation, duress, coercion, mistake, insolvency, or other validating or invalidating cause, supplement its provisions.

§ 13. Uniformity of Application and Construction.

This [Act] shall be applied and construed to effectuate its general purpose to make uniform the law with respect to the subject of this [Act] among states enacting it.

§ 14. Relation to Electronic Signatures In Global and National Commerce Act.

This [Act] modifies, limits, or supersedes the Electronic Signatures in Global and National Commerce Act, 15 U.S.C. Section 7001 et seq., but does not modify, limit, or supersede Section 101(c) of that act, 15 U.S.C. Section 7001(c), or authorize electronic delivery of any of the notices described in Section 103(b) of that act, 15 U.S.C. Section 7003(b).

§ 15. Short Title.

This [Act], which was formerly cited as the Uniform Fraudulent Transfer Act, may be cited as the Uniform Voidable Transactions Act.

§ 16. Repeals; Conforming Amendments.

(a) . . . .

(b) . . . .

(c) . . . .

Legislative Note: The legislation enacting the 2014 amendments in a jurisdiction in which the act is already in force should provide as follows: (i) the amendments apply to a transfer made or obligation incurred on or after the effective date of the enacting legislation, (ii) the amendments do not apply to a transfer made or obligation incurred before the effective date of the enacting legislation, (iii) the amendments do not apply to a right of action that has accrued before the effective date of the enacting legislation, and (iv) for the foregoing purposes a transfer is made and an obligation is incurred at the time provided in Section 6 of the act. In addition, the enacting legislation should revise any reference to the act by its former title in other permanent legislation of the enacting jurisdiction.

VIII. FEDERAL RULES OF CIVIL PROCEDURE

(Selected)

Table of Contents

Rule 23. Class Actions

(a) **Prerequisites.** One or more members of a class may sue or be sued as representative parties on behalf of all members only if:

 (1) the class is so numerous that joinder of all members is impracticable;

 (2) there are questions of law or fact common to the class;

 (3) the claims or defenses of the representative parties are typical of the claims or defenses of the class; and

 (4) the representative parties will fairly and adequately protect the interests of the class.

(b) **Types of Class Actions.** A class action may be maintained if Rule 23(a) is satisfied and if:

 (1) prosecuting separate actions by or against individual class members would create a risk of:

  (A) inconsistent or varying adjudications with respect to individual class members that would establish incompatible standards of conduct for the party opposing the class; or

  (B) adjudications with respect to individual class members that, as a practical matter, would be dispositive of the interests of the other members not parties to the individual adjudications or would substantially impair or impede their ability to protect their interests;

 (2) the party opposing the class has acted or refused to act on grounds that apply generally to the class, so that final injunctive relief or corresponding declaratory relief is appropriate respecting the class as a whole; or

 (3) the court finds that the questions of law or fact common to class members predominate over any questions affecting only individual members, and that a class action is superior to other available methods for fairly and efficiently adjudicating the controversy. The matters pertinent to these findings include:

  (A) the class members' interests in individually controlling the prosecution or defense of separate actions;

  (B) the extent and nature of any litigation concerning the controversy already begun by or against class members;

  (C) the desirability or undesirability of concentrating the litigation of the claims in the particular forum; and

  (D) the likely difficulties in managing a class action.

(c) **Certification Order; Notice to Class Members; Judgment; Issues Classes; Subclasses.**

 (1) *Certification Order.*

(A) *Time to Issue.* At an early practicable time after a person sues or is sued as a class representative, the court must determine by order whether to certify the action as a class action.

(B) *Defining the Class; Appointing Class Counsel.* An order that certifies a class action must define the class and the class claims, issues, or defenses, and must appoint class counsel under Rule 23(g).

(C) *Altering or Amending the Order.* An order that grants or denies class certification may be altered or amended before final judgment.

(2) *Notice.*

(A) *For (b)(1) or (b)(2) Classes.* For any class certified under Rule 23(b)(1) or (b)(2), the court may direct appropriate notice to the class.

(B) *For (b)(3) Classes.* For any class certified under Rule 23(b)(3)—or upon ordering notice under Rule 23(e)(1) to a class proposed to be certified for purposes of settlement under Rule 23(b)(3)—the court must direct to class members the best notice that is practicable under the circumstances, including individual notice to all members who can be identified through reasonable effort. The notice may be by one or more of the following: United States mail, electronic means, or other appropriate means. The notice must clearly and concisely state in plain, easily understood language:

    (i)   the nature of the action;

    (ii)   the definition of the class certified;

    (iii)   the class claims, issues, or defenses;

    (iv)   that a class member may enter an appearance through an attorney if the member so desires;

    (v)   that the court will exclude from the class any member who requests exclusion;

    (vi)   the time and manner for requesting exclusion; and

    (vii) the binding effect of a class judgment on members under Rule 23(c)(3).

(3) *Judgment.* Whether or not favorable to the class, the judgment in a class action must:

(A)   for any class certified under Rule 23(b)(1) or (b)(2), include and describe those whom the court finds to be class members; and

(B)   for any class certified under Rule 23(b)(3), include and specify or describe those to whom the Rule 23(c)(2) notice was directed, who have not requested exclusion, and whom the court finds to be class members.

(4) *Particular Issues.* When appropriate, an action may be brought or maintained as a class action with respect to particular issues.

(5) *Subclasses.* When appropriate, a class may be divided into subclasses that are each treated as a class under this rule.

(d) **Conducting the Action.**

(1) *In General.* In conducting an action under this rule, the court may issue orders that:

(A)   determine the course of proceedings or prescribe measures to prevent undue repetition or complication in presenting evidence or argument;

(B)   require—to protect class members and fairly conduct the action—giving appropriate notice to some or all class members of:

    (i)   any step in the action;

(ii)   the proposed extent of the judgment; or

(iii)   the members' opportunity to signify whether they consider the representation fair and adequate, to intervene and present claims or defenses, or to otherwise come into the action;

(C)   impose conditions on the representative parties or on intervenors;

(D)   require that the pleadings be amended to eliminate allegations about representation of absent persons and that the action proceed accordingly; or

(E)   deal with similar procedural matters.

(2)   *Combining and Amending Orders.* An order under Rule 23(d)(1) may be altered or amended from time to time and may be combined with an order under Rule 16.

(e)   **Settlement, Voluntary Dismissal, or Compromise.** The claims, issues, or defenses of a certified class—or a class proposed to be certified for purposes of settlement—may be settled, voluntarily dismissed, or compromised only with the court's approval. The following procedures apply to a proposed settlement, voluntary dismissal, or compromise:

(1)   *Notice to the Class.*

(A)   *Information That Parties Must Provide to the Court.* The parties must provide the court with information sufficient to enable it to determine whether to give notice of the proposal to the class.

(B)   *Grounds for a Decision to Give Notice.* The court must direct notice in a reasonable manner to all class members who would be bound by the proposal if giving notice is justified by the parties' showing that the court will likely be able to:

(i)   approve the proposal under Rule 23(e)(2); and

(ii)   certify the class for purposes of judgment on the proposal.

(2)   *Approval of the Proposal.* If the proposal would bind class members, the court may approve it only after a hearing and only on finding that it is fair, reasonable, and adequate after considering whether:

(A)   the class representatives and class counsel have adequately represented the class;

(B)   the proposal was negotiated at arm's length;

(C)   the relief provided for the class is adequate, taking into account:

(i)   the costs, risks, and delay of trial and appeal;

(ii)   the effectiveness of any proposed method of distributing relief to the class, including the method of processing class-member claims;

(iii)   the terms of any proposed award of attorney's fees, including timing of payment; and

(iv)   any agreement required to be identified under Rule 23(e)(3); and

(D)   the proposal treats class members equitably relative to each other.

(3)   *Identifying Agreements.* The parties seeking approval must file a statement identifying any agreement made in connection with the proposal.

(4)   *New Opportunity to be Excluded.* If the class action was previously certified under Rule 23(b)(3), the court may refuse to approve a settlement unless it affords a new opportunity to request exclusion to individual class members who had an earlier opportunity to request exclusion but did not do so.

(5)   *Class-Member Objections.*

(A) *In General.* Any class member may object to the proposal if it requires court approval under this subdivision (e). The objection must state whether it applies only to the objector, to a specific subset of the class, or to the entire class, and also state with specificity the grounds for the objection.

(B) *Court Approval Required for Payment in Connection with an Objection.* Unless approved by the court after a hearing, no payment or other consideration may be provided in connection with:

    (i)   forgoing or withdrawing an objection, or

    (ii)   forgoing, dismissing, or abandoning an appeal from a judgment approving the proposal.

(C) *Procedure for Approval After an Appeal.* If approval under Rule 23(e)(5)(B) has not been obtained before an appeal is docketed in the court of appeals, the procedure of Rule 62.1 applies while the appeal remains pending.

(f) **Appeals.** A court of appeals may permit an appeal from an order granting or denying class-action certification under this rule, but not from an order under Rule 23(e)(1). A party must file a petition for permission to appeal with the circuit clerk within 14 days after the order is entered, or within 45 days after the order is entered if any party is the United States, a United States agency, or a United States officer or employee sued for an act or omission occurring in connection with duties performed on the United States' behalf. An appeal does not stay proceedings in the district court unless the district judge or the court of appeals so orders.

(g) **Class Counsel.**

(1) *Appointing Class Counsel.* Unless a statute provides otherwise, a court that certifies a class must appoint class counsel. In appointing class counsel, the court:

    (A)   must consider:

        (i)   the work counsel has done in identifying or investigating potential claims in the action;

        (ii)   counsel's experience in handling class actions, other complex litigation, and the types of claims asserted in the action;

        (iii)   counsel's knowledge of the applicable law; and

        (iv)   the resources that counsel will commit to representing the class;

    (B)   may consider any other matter pertinent to counsel's ability to fairly and adequately represent the interests of the class;

    (C)   may order potential class counsel to provide information on any subject pertinent to the appointment and to propose terms for attorney's fees and nontaxable costs;

    (D)   may include in the appointing order provisions about the award of attorney's fees or nontaxable costs under Rule 23(h); and

    (E)   may make further orders in connection with the appointment.

(2) *Standard for Appointing Class Counsel.* When one applicant seeks appointment as class counsel, the court may appoint that applicant only if the applicant is adequate under Rule 23(g)(1) and (4). If more than one adequate applicant seeks appointment, the court must appoint the applicant best able to represent the interests of the class.

(3) *Interim Counsel.* The court may designate interim counsel to act on behalf of a putative class before determining whether to certify the action as a class action.

(4) *Duty of Class Counsel.* Class counsel must fairly and adequately represent the interests of the class.

(h) **Attorney's Fees and Nontaxable Costs.** In a certified class action, the court may award reasonable attorney's fees and nontaxable costs that are authorized by law or by the parties' agreement. The following procedures apply:

(1) A claim for an award must be made by motion under Rule 54(d)(2), subject to the provisions of this subdivision (h), at a time the court sets. Notice of the motion must be served on all parties and, for motions by class counsel, directed to class members in a reasonable manner.

(2) A class member, or a party from whom payment is sought, may object to the motion.

(3) The court may hold a hearing and must find the facts and state its legal conclusions under Rule 52(a).

(4) The court may refer issues related to the amount of the award to a special master or a magistrate judge, as provided in Rule 54(d)(2)(D).

Rule 23.1. Derivative Actions

(a) **Prerequisites.** This rule applies when one or more shareholders or members of a corporation or an unincorporated association bring a derivative action to enforce a right that the corporation or association may properly assert but has failed to enforce. The derivative action may not be maintained if it appears that the plaintiff does not fairly and adequately represent the interests of shareholders or members who are similarly situated in enforcing the right of the corporation or association.

(b) **Pleading Requirements.** The complaint must be verified and must:

(1) allege that the plaintiff was a shareholder or member at the time of the transaction complained of, or that the plaintiff's share or membership later devolved on it by operation of law;

(2) allege that the action is not a collusive one to confer jurisdiction that the court would otherwise lack; and

(3) state with particularity:

(A) any effort by the plaintiff to obtain the desired action from the directors or comparable authority and, if necessary, from the shareholders or members; and

(B) the reasons for not obtaining the action or not making the effort.

(c) **Settlement, Dismissal, and Compromise.** A derivative action may be settled, voluntarily dismissed, or compromised only with the court's approval. Notice of a proposed settlement, voluntary dismissal, or compromise must be given to shareholders or members in the manner that the court orders.

IX. DELAWARE CHANCERY COURT RULES

(Selected)

Table of Contents

Rule 23.   Class Actions

(a) Requisites to class action. One or more members of a class may sue or be sued as representative parties on behalf of all only if (1) the class is so numerous that joinder of all members is impracticable, (2) there are questions of law or fact common to the class, (3) the claims or defenses of the representative parties are typical of the claims or defenses of the class, and (4) the representative parties will fairly and adequately protect the interests of the class.

(aa) Each person seeking to serve as a representative party on behalf of a class pursuant to this Rule shall file with the Register in Chancery an affidavit stating that the person has not received, been promised or offered and will not accept any form of compensation, directly or indirectly, for prosecuting or serving as a representative party in the class action in which the person or entity is a named party except for (i) such damages or other relief as the Court may award such person as a member of the class, (ii) such fees, costs or other payments as the Court expressly approves to be paid to or on behalf of such a person, or (iii) reimbursement, paid by such person's attorneys, of actual and reasonable out-of-pocket expenditures incurred directly in connection with the prosecution of the action. The affidavit required by this subpart shall be filed within 10 days after the earliest of the affiant filing the complaint, filing a motion to intervene in the action or filing a motion seeking appointment as a representative party in the action. An affidavit provided pursuant to this subpart shall not be construed to be a waiver of the attorney-client privilege.

(b) Class actions maintainable. An action may be maintained as a class action if the prerequisites of paragraph (a) are satisfied, and in addition:

(1) The prosecution of separate actions by or against individual members of the class would create a risk of:

(A) Inconsistent or varying adjudications with respect to individual members of the class which would establish incompatible standards of conduct for the party opposing the class, or

(B) Adjudications with respect to individual members of the class which would as a practical matter be dispositive of the interests of the other members not parties to the adjudications or substantially impair or impede their ability to protect their interests; or

(2) The party opposing the class has acted or refused to act on grounds generally applicable to the class, thereby making appropriate final injunctive relief or corresponding declaratory relief with respect to the class as a whole; or

(3) The Court finds that the questions of law or fact common to the members of the class predominate over any questions affecting only individual members, and that a class action is superior to other available methods for the fair and efficient adjudication of the controversy. The matter pertinent to the findings include:

(A) The interest of members of the class in individually controlling the prosecution or defense of separate actions;

(B) The extent and nature of any litigation concerning the controversy already commenced by or against members of the class;

(C) The desirability or undesirability of concentrating the litigation of the claims in the particular forum;

(D) The difficulties likely to be encountered in the management of a class action.

(c) Determination by order whether class action to be maintained; notice; judgment; actions conducted partially as class actions.

(1) As soon as practicable after the commencement of an action brought as a class action, the Court shall determine by order whether it is to be so maintained. An order under this paragraph may be conditional, and may be altered or amended before the decision on the merits.

(2) In any class action maintained under paragraph (b)(3), the Court shall direct to the members of the class the best notice practicable under the circumstances, including individual notice to all members who can be identified through reasonable effort. The notice shall advise each member that:

(A) The Court will exclude a member from the class if the member so requests by a specified date;

(B) The judgment, whether favorable or not, will include all members who do not request exclusion; and

(C) Any member who does not request exclusion may, if the member desires, enter an appearance through his counsel.

(3) The judgment in an action maintained as a class action under paragraph (b)(1) or (b)(2), whether or not favorable to the class, shall include and describe those whom the Court finds to be members of the class. The judgment in an action maintained as a class action under paragraph (b)(3), whether or not favorable to the class, shall include and specify or describe those to whom the notice provided in paragraph (c)(2) was directed, and who have not requested exclusion, and whom the Court finds to be members of the class.

(4) When appropriate (A) an action may be brought or maintained as a class action with respect to particular issues, or (B) a class may be divided into subclasses and each subclass treated as a class, and the provisions of this rule shall then be construed and applied accordingly.

(d) Orders in conduct of actions. In the conduct of actions to which this rule applies, the Court may make appropriate orders: (1) Determining the course of proceedings or prescribing measures to prevent undue repetition or complication in the presentation of evidence or argument; (2) requiring, for the protection of the members of the class or otherwise for the fair conduct of the action, that notice be given in such manner as the Court directs to some or all of the members of any step in the action, or of the proposed extent of the judgment, or of the opportunity of members to signify whether they consider the representation fair and adequate, to intervene and present claims or defenses, or otherwise to come into the action; (3) imposing conditions on the representative parties or on intervenors; (4) requiring that the pleadings be amended to eliminate therefrom allegations as to representation of absent persons, and that the action proceed accordingly; (5) dealing with similar procedural matters. The orders may be combined with an order under Rule 16, and may be altered or amended as may be desirable from time to time.

(e) Dismissal or compromise. Subject to the provisions of Rule 15(aaa), a class action shall not be dismissed or compromised without the approval of the Court, and notice by mail, publication or otherwise of the proposed dismissal or compromise shall be given to all members of the class in such manner as the Court directs; except that if the dismissal is to be without prejudice to the class or with prejudice to the plaintiff only, then such dismissal shall be ordered without notice thereof if there is a showing that no compensation in any form has passed directly or indirectly from any of the defendants to the plaintiff or plaintiff's attorney and that no promise to give any such compensation has been made. At the time that any party moves or otherwise applies to the Court for approval of a compromise of all or any part of a class action, each representative party in such action shall file with the Register in Chancery a further affidavit in the form required by section (aa) of this rule.

Rule 23.1.   Derivative Actions by Shareholders

(a) In a derivative action brought by one or more shareholders or members to enforce a right of a corporation or of an unincorporated association, the corporation or association having failed to enforce a right which may properly be asserted by it, the complaint shall allege that the plaintiff was a shareholder or member at the time of the transaction of which the plaintiff complains or that the plaintiff's share or membership thereafter devolved on the plaintiff by operation of law. The complaint shall also allege with particularity the efforts, if any, made by the plaintiff to obtain the action the plaintiff desires from the directors or comparable authority and the reasons for the plaintiff's failure to obtain the action or for not making the effort.

(b) Each person seeking to serve as a representative plaintiff on behalf of a corporation or unincorporated association pursuant to this Rule shall file with the Register in Chancery an affidavit stating that the person has not received, been promised or offered and will not accept any form of compensation, directly or indirectly, for prosecuting or serving as a representative party in the derivative action in which the person or entity is a named party except (i) such fees, costs or other payments as the Court expressly approves to be paid to or on behalf of such person, or (ii) reimbursement, paid by such person's attorneys, of actual and reasonable out-of-pocket expenditures incurred directly in connection with the prosecution of the action. The affidavit required by this subpart shall be filed within 10 days after the earliest of the affiant filing the complaint, filing a motion to intervene in the action or filing a motion seeking appointment as a representative party in the action. An affidavit provided pursuant to this subpart shall not be construed to be a waiver of the attorney-client privilege.

(c) The action shall not be dismissed or compromised without the approval of the Court, and notice by mail, publication or otherwise of the proposed dismissal or compromise shall be given to shareholders or members in such manner as the Court directs; except that if the dismissal is to be without prejudice or with prejudice to the plaintiff only, then such dismissal shall be ordered without notice thereof if there is a showing that no compensation in any form has passed directly or indirectly from any of the defendants to the plaintiff or plaintiff's attorney and that no promise to give any such compensation has been made. At the time that any party moves or otherwise applies to the Court for approval of a compromise of all or any part of a derivative action, each representative plaintiff in such action shall file with the Register in Chancery a further affidavit in the form required by subpart (b) of this rule.

(d) For the purposes of this Rule, an "unincorporated association" includes a statutory trust, business trust, limited liability company and a partnership (whether general or limited), and a "member" includes a person permitted by applicable law to bring a derivative action to enforce a right or such an unincorporated association.

X. INTERNAL REVENUE SERVICE "CHECK THE BOX" REGULATIONS

(Selected)

26 C.F.R. §§ 301.7701 *et seq.*

Table of Contents

---

§ 301.7701–2   Business Entities; Definitions.

(a) *Business entities.* For purposes of this section and § 301.7701–3, a *business entity* is any entity recognized for federal tax purposes (including an entity with a single owner that may be disregarded as an entity separate from its owner under § 301.7701–3) that is not properly classified as a trust under § 301.7701–4 or otherwise subject to special treatment under the Internal Revenue Code. A business entity with two or more members is classified for federal tax purposes as either a corporation or a partnership. A business entity with only one owner is classified as a corporation or is disregarded; if the entity is disregarded, its activities are treated in the same manner as a sole proprietorship, branch, or division of the owner. But see paragraphs (c)(2)(iii) through (vi) of this section for special rules that apply to an eligible entity that is otherwise disregarded as an entity separate from its owner.

(b) *Corporations.* For federal tax purposes, the term *corporation* means—

(1) A business entity organized under a Federal or State statute, or under a statute of a federally recognized Indian tribe, if the statute describes or refers to the entity as incorporated or as a corporation, body corporate, or body politic;

(2) An association (as determined under § 301.7701–3);

(3) A business entity organized under a State statute, if the statute describes or refers to the entity as a joint-stock company or joint-stock association;

(4) An insurance company;

(5) A State-chartered business entity conducting banking activities, if any of its deposits are insured under the Federal Deposit Insurance Act, as amended, 12 U.S.C. 1811 *et seq.*, or a similar federal statute;

(6) A business entity wholly owned by a State or any political subdivision thereof, or a business entity wholly owned by a foreign government or any other entity described in § 1.892–2T;

(7) A business entity that is taxable as a corporation under a provision of the Internal Revenue Code other than section 7701(a)(3); and

(8) *Certain foreign entities*—(i) *In general.* Except as provided in paragraphs (b)(8)(ii) and (d) of this section, the following business entities formed in the following jurisdictions:

American Samoa, Corporation

Argentina, Sociedad Anonima

Australia, Public Limited Company

Austria, Aktiengesellschaft

Barbados, Limited Company

Belgium, Societe Anonyme

Belize, Public Limited Company

Bolivia, Sociedad Anonima

Brazil, Sociedade Anonima

Bulgaria, Aktsionerno Druzhestvo.

Canada, Corporation and Company

Chile, Sociedad Anonima

People's Republic of China, Gufen Youxian Gongsi

Republic of China (Taiwan), Ku-fen Yu-hsien Kung-szu

Colombia, Sociedad Anonima

Costa Rica, Sociedad Anonima

Cyprus, Public Limited Company

Czech Republic, Akciova Spolecnost

Denmark, Aktieselskab

Ecuador, Sociedad Anonima or Compania Anonima

Egypt, Sharikat Al-Mossahamah

El Salvador, Sociedad Anonima

Estonia, Aktsiaselts

European Economic Area/European Union, Societas Europaea

Finland, Julkinen Osakeyhtio/Publikt Aktiebolag

France, Societe Anonyme

Germany, Aktiengesellschaft

Greece, Anonymos Etairia

Guam, Corporation

Guatemala, Sociedad Anonima

Guyana, Public Limited Company

Honduras, Sociedad Anonima

Hong Kong, Public Limited Company

Hungary, Reszvenytarsasag

Iceland, Hlutafelag

India, Public Limited Company

Indonesia, Perseroan Terbuka

Ireland, Public Limited Company

Israel, Public Limited Company

Italy, Societa per Azioni

Jamaica, Public Limited Company

Japan, Kabushiki Kaisha

Kazakstan, Ashyk Aktsionerlik Kogham

Republic of Korea, Chusik Hoesa

Latvia, Akciju Sabiedriba

Liberia, Corporation

Liechtenstein, Aktiengesellschaft

Lithuania, Akcine Bendroves

Luxembourg, Societe Anonyme

Malaysia, Berhad

Malta, Public Limited Company

Mexico, Sociedad Anonima

Morocco, Societe Anonyme

Netherlands, Naamloze Vennootschap

New Zealand, Limited Company

Nicaragua, Compania Anonima

Nigeria, Public Limited Company

Northern Mariana Islands, Corporation

Norway, Allment Aksjeselskap

Pakistan, Public Limited Company

Panama, Sociedad Anonima

Paraguay, Sociedad Anonima

Peru, Sociedad Anonima

Philippines, Stock Corporation

Poland, Spolka Akcyjna

Portugal, Sociedade Anonima

Puerto Rico, Corporation

Romania, Societate pe Actiuni

Russia, Otkrytoye Aktsionernoy Obshchestvo

Saudi Arabia, Sharikat Al-Mossahamah

Singapore, Public Limited Company

Slovak Republic, Akciova Spolocnost

Slovenia, Delniska Druzba

South Africa, Public Limited Company

Spain, Sociedad Anonima

Surinam, Naamloze Vennootschap

Sweden, Publika Aktiebolag

Switzerland, Aktiengesellschaft

Thailand, Borisat Chamkad (Mahachon)

Trinidad and Tobago, Limited Company

Tunisia, Societe Anonyme

Turkey, Anonim Sirket

Ukraine, Aktsionerne Tovaristvo Vidkritogo Tipu

United Kingdom, Public Limited Company

United States Virgin Islands, Corporation

Uruguay, Sociedad Anonima

Venezuela, Sociedad Anonima or Compania Anonima

(ii) *Clarification of list of corporations in paragraph (b)(8)(i) of this section*—(A) *Exceptions in certain cases.* The following entities will not be treated as corporations under paragraph (b)(8)(i) of this section:

(1) With regard to Canada, a Nova Scotia Unlimited Liability Company (or any other company or corporation all of whose owners have unlimited liability pursuant to federal or provincial law).

(2) With regard to India, a company deemed to be a public limited company solely by operation of section 43A(1) (relating to corporate ownership of the company), section 43A(1A) (relating to annual average turnover), or section 43A(1B) (relating to ownership interests in other companies) of the Companies Act, 1956 (or any combination of these), provided that the organizational documents of such deemed public limited company continue to meet the requirements of section 3(1)(iii) of the Companies Act, 1956.

(3) With regard to Malaysia, a Sendirian Berhad.

(B) *Inclusions in certain cases.* With regard to Mexico, the term Sociedad Anonima includes a Sociedad Anonima that chooses to apply the variable capital provision of Mexican corporate law (Sociedad Anonima de Capital Variable).

(iii) *Public companies.* For purposes of paragraph (b)(8)(i) of this section, with regard to Cyprus, Hong Kong, and Jamaica, the term Public Limited Company includes any Limited Company that is not defined as a private company under the corporate laws of those jurisdictions. In all other cases, where the term Public Limited Company is not defined, that term shall include any Limited Company defined as a public company under the corporate laws of the relevant jurisdiction.

(iv) *Limited companies.* For purposes of this paragraph (b)(8), any reference to a Limited Company includes, as the case may be, companies limited by shares and companies limited by guarantee.

(v) *Multilingual countries.* Different linguistic renderings of the name of an entity listed in paragraph (b)(8)(i) of this section shall be disregarded. For example, an entity formed under the laws of Switzerland as a Societe Anonyme will be a corporation and treated in the same manner as an Aktiengesellschaft.

(9) *Business entities with multiple charters.* (i) An entity created or organized under the laws of more than one jurisdiction if the rules of this section would treat it as a corporation with reference to any one of the jurisdictions in which it is created or organized. Such an entity may elect its classification under § 301.7701–3, subject to the limitations of those provisions, only if it is created or organized in each jurisdiction in a manner that meets the definition of an eligible entity in § 301.7701–3(a). The determination of a business entity's corporate or non-corporate classification is made independently from the determination of whether the entity is domestic or foreign. See § 301.7701–5 for the rules that determine whether a business entity is domestic or foreign.

(ii) *Examples.* The following examples illustrate the rule of this paragraph (b)(9):

Example 1. (i) *Facts.* X is an entity with a single owner organized under the laws of Country A as an entity that is listed in paragraph (b)(8)(i) of this section. Under the rules of this section, such an entity is a corporation for Federal tax purposes and under § 301.7701–3(a) is unable to elect its classification. Several years after its formation, X files a certificate of domestication in State B as a limited liability company (LLC). Under the laws of State B, X is considered to be created or organized in State B as an LLC upon the filing of the certificate of domestication and is therefore subject to the laws of State B. Under the rules of this section and § 301.7701–3, an LLC with a single owner organized only in State B is disregarded as an entity separate from its owner for Federal tax purposes (absent an election to be treated as an association). Neither Country A nor State B law requires X to terminate its charter in Country A as a result of the domestication, and in fact X does not terminate its Country A charter. Consequently, X is now organized in more than one jurisdiction.

(ii) *Result.* X remains organized under the laws of Country A as an entity that is listed in paragraph (b)(8)(i) of this section, and as such, it is an entity that is treated as a corporation under the rules of this section. Therefore, X is a corporation for Federal tax purposes because the rules of this section would treat X as a corporation with reference to one of the jurisdictions in which it is created or organized. Because X is organized in Country A in a manner that does not meet the definition of an eligible entity in § 301.7701–3(a), it is unable to elect its classification.

Example 2. (i) *Facts.* Y is an entity that is incorporated under the laws of State A and has two shareholders. Under the rules of this section, an entity incorporated under the laws of State A is a corporation for Federal tax purposes and under § 301.7701–3(a) is unable to elect its classification. Several years after its formation, Y files a certificate of continuance in Country B as an unlimited company. Under the laws of Country B, upon filing a certificate of continuance, Y is treated as organized in Country B. Under the rules of this section and § 301.7701–3, an unlimited company organized only in Country B that has more than one owner is treated as a partnership for Federal tax purposes (absent an election to be treated as an association). Neither State A nor Country B law requires Y to terminate its charter in State A as a result of the continuance, and in fact Y does not terminate its State A charter. Consequently, Y is now organized in more than one jurisdiction.

(ii) *Result.* Y remains organized in State A as a corporation, an entity that is treated as a corporation under the rules of this section. Therefore, Y is a corporation for Federal tax purposes because the rules of this section would treat Y as a corporation with reference to one of the jurisdictions in which it is created or organized. Because Y is organized in State A in a manner that does not meet the definition of an eligible entity in § 301.7701–3(a), it is unable to elect its classification.

Example 3. (i) *Facts.* Z is an entity that has more than one owner and that is recognized under the laws of Country A as an unlimited company organized in Country A. Z is organized in Country A in a manner that meets the definition of an eligible entity in § 301.7701–3(a). Under the rules of this section and § 301.7701–3, an unlimited company organized only in Country A with more than one owner is treated as a partnership for Federal tax purposes (absent an election to be treated as an association). At the time Z was formed, it was also organized as a private limited company under the laws of Country B. Z is organized in Country B in a manner that meets the definition of an eligible entity in § 301.7701–3(a). Under the rules of this section and § 301.7701–3, a private limited company organized only in Country B is treated as a corporation for Federal tax purposes (absent an election to be treated as a partnership). Thus, Z is organized in more than one jurisdiction. Z has not made any entity classification elections under § 301.7701–3.

(ii) *Result.* Z is organized in Country B as a private limited company, an entity that is treated (absent an election to the contrary) as a corporation under the rules of this section. However, because Z is organized in each jurisdiction in a manner that meets the definition of an eligible entity in § 301.7701–3(a), it may elect its classification under § 301.7701–3, subject to the limitations of those provisions.

Example 4. (i) *Facts.* P is an entity with more than one owner organized in Country A as a general partnership. Under the rules of this section and § 301.7701–3, an eligible entity with more than one owner in Country A is treated as a partnership for federal tax purposes (absent an election to be treated as an association). P files a certificate of continuance in Country B as an unlimited company. Under the rules of this section and § 301.7701–3, an unlimited company in Country B with more than one owner is treated as a partnership for federal tax purposes (absent an election to be treated as an association). P is not required under either the laws of Country A or Country B to terminate the general partnership in Country A, and in fact P does not terminate its Country A partnership. P is now organized in more than one jurisdiction. P has not made any entity classification elections under § 301.7701–3.

(ii) *Result.* P's organization in both Country A and Country B would result in P being classified as a partnership. Therefore, since the rules of this section would not treat P as a corporation with reference to any jurisdiction in which it is created or organized, it is not a corporation for federal tax purposes.

(c) *Other business entities.* For federal tax purposes—

(1) The term *partnership* means a business entity that is not a corporation under paragraph (b) of this section and that has at least two members.

(2) *Wholly owned entities*—(i) *In general.* Except as otherwise provided in this paragraph (c), a business entity that has a single owner and is not a corporation under paragraph (b) of this section is disregarded as an entity separate from its owner.

(ii) *Special rule for certain business entities.* If the single owner of a business entity is a bank (as defined in section 581, or, in the case of a foreign bank, as defined in section 585(a)(2)(B) without regard to the second sentence thereof), then the special rules applicable to banks under the Internal Revenue Code will continue to apply to the single owner as if the wholly owned entity were a separate entity. For this purpose, the special rules applicable to banks under the Internal Revenue Code do not include the rules under sections 864(c), 882(c), and 884.

(iii) *Tax liabilities of certain disregarded entities*—(A) *In general.* An entity that is disregarded as separate from its owner for any purpose under this section is treated as an entity separate from its owner for purposes of—

(*1*) Federal tax liabilities of the entity with respect to any taxable period for which the entity was not disregarded;

(*2*) Federal tax liabilities of any other entity for which the entity is liable; and

(*3*) Refunds or credits of Federal tax.

(B) *Examples*. The following examples illustrate the application of paragraph (c)(2)(iii)(A) of this section:

Example 1. In 2006, X, a domestic corporation that reports its taxes on a calendar year basis, merges into Z, a domestic LLC wholly owned by Y that is disregarded as an entity separate from Y, in a state law merger. X was not a member of a consolidated group at any time during its taxable year ending in December 2005. Under the applicable state law, Z is the successor to X and is liable for all of X's debts. In 2009, the Internal Revenue Service (IRS) seeks to extend the period of limitations on assessment for X's 2005 taxable year. Because Z is the successor to X and is liable for X's 2005 taxes that remain unpaid, Z is the proper party to sign the consent to extend the period of limitations.

Example 2. The facts are the same as in *Example 1,* except that in 2007, the IRS determines that X miscalculated and underreported its income tax liability for 2005. Because Z is the successor to X and is liable for X's 2005 taxes that remain unpaid, the deficiency may be assessed against Z and, in the event that Z fails to pay the liability after notice and demand, a general tax lien will arise against all of Z's property and rights to property.

(iv) *Special rule for employment tax purposes—*

(A) *In general.* Except as provided in paragraph (c)(2)(iv)(C) of this section, paragraph (c)(2)(i) of this section (relating to certain wholly owned entities) does not apply to taxes imposed under Subtitle C—Employment Taxes and Collection of Income Tax (Chapters 21, 22, 23, 23A, 24, and 25 of the Internal Revenue Code).

(B) *Treatment of entity.* Except as provided in paragraph (c)(2)(iv)(C) of this section, an entity that is disregarded as an entity separate from its owner for any purpose under this section is treated as a corporation with respect to taxes imposed under Subtitle C—Employment Taxes and Collection of Income Tax (Chapters 21, 22, 23, 23A, 24, and 25 of the Internal Revenue Code). For special rules regarding the application of certain employment tax exceptions, see § § 31.3121(b)(3)–1(d), 31.3127–1(b), and 31.3306(c)(5)–1(d) of this chapter.

(C) *Special rules.* (*1*) Paragraphs (c)(2)(iv)(A) and (B) of this section do not apply to withholding requirements imposed by section 3406 (backup withholding). Thus, in the case of an entity that is disregarded as an entity separate from its owner for any purpose under this section, the owner is subject to the withholding requirements imposed by section 3406 (backup withholding).

(*2*) Paragraph (c)(2)(i) of this section applies to taxes imposed under subtitle A of the Code, including Chapter 2—Tax on Self-Employment Income. Thus, an entity that is treated in the same manner as a sole proprietorship under paragraph (a) of this section is not treated as a corporation for purposes of employing its owner; instead, the entity is disregarded as an entity separate from its owner for this purpose and is not the employer of its owner. The owner will be subject to self-employment tax on self-employment income with respect to the entity's activities. Also, if a partnership is the owner of an entity that is disregarded as an entity separate from its owner for any purpose under this section, the entity is not treated as a corporation for purposes of employing a partner of the partnership that owns the entity; instead, the entity is disregarded as an entity separate from the partnership for this purpose and is not the employer of any partner of the partnership that owns the entity. A partner of a partnership that owns an entity that is disregarded as an entity separate from its owner for any purpose under this section is subject to the same self-employment tax rules as a partner of a partnership that does not own an entity that is disregarded as an entity separate from its owner for any purpose under this section.

(D) *Example.* The following example illustrates the application of paragraph (c)(2)(iv) of this section:

Example. (i) LLCA is an eligible entity owned by individual A and is generally disregarded as an entity separate from its owner for Federal tax purposes. However, LLCA is treated as an entity separate from its owner for purposes of subtitle C of the Internal Revenue Code. LLCA has employees and pays wages as defined in sections 3121(a), 3306(b), and 3401(a).

(ii) LLCA is subject to the provisions of subtitle C of the Internal Revenue Code and related provisions under 26 CFR subchapter C, Employment Taxes and Collection of Income Tax at Source, parts 31 through 39. Accordingly, LLCA is required to perform such acts as are required of an employer under those provisions of the Internal Revenue Code and regulations thereunder that apply. All provisions of law (including penalties) and the regulations prescribed in pursuance of law applicable to employers in respect of such acts are applicable to LLCA. Thus, for example, LLCA is liable for income tax withholding, Federal Insurance Contributions Act (FICA) taxes, and Federal Unemployment Tax Act (FUTA) taxes. See sections 3402 and 3403 (relating to income tax withholding); 3102(b) and 3111 (relating to FICA taxes), and 3301 (relating to FUTA taxes). In addition, LLCA must file under its name and EIN the applicable Forms in the 94X series, for example, Form 941, "Employer's Quarterly Employment Tax Return," Form 940, "Employer's Annual Federal Unemployment Tax Return;" file with the Social Security Administration and furnish to LLCA's employees statements on Forms W-2, "Wage and Tax Statement;" and make timely employment tax deposits. See § § 31.6011(a)–1, 31.6011(a)–3, 31.6051–1, 31.6051–2, and 31.6302–1 of this chapter.

(iii) A is self-employed for purposes of subtitle A, chapter 2, Tax on Self-Employment Income, of the Internal Revenue Code. Thus, A is subject to tax under section 1401 on A's net earnings from self-employment with respect to LLCA's activities. A is not an employee of LLCA for purposes of subtitle C of the Internal Revenue Code. Because LLCA is treated as a sole proprietorship of A for income tax purposes, A is entitled to deduct trade or business expenses paid or incurred with respect to activities carried on through LLCA, including the employer's share of employment taxes imposed under sections 3111 and 3301, on A's Form 1040, Schedule C, "Profit or Loss for Business (Sole Proprietorship)."

(v) *Special rule for certain excise tax purposes—(A) In general.* Paragraph (c)(2)(i) of this section (relating to certain wholly owned entities) does not apply for purposes of—

(*1*) Federal tax liabilities imposed by Chapters 31, 32 (other than section 4181), 33, 34, 35, 36 (other than section 4461), 38, and 49 of the Internal Revenue Code, or any floor stocks tax imposed on articles subject to any of these taxes;

(*2*) Collection of tax imposed by Chapters 33 and 49 of the Internal Revenue Code;

(*3*)   Registration under sections 4101, 4222, 4412;

(*4*)   Claims of a credit (other than a credit under section 34), refund, or payment related to a tax described in paragraph (c)(2)(v)(A)(*1*) of this section or under section 6426 or 6427; and

(*5*)   Assessment and collection of an assessable payment imposed by section 4980H and reporting required by section 6056.

(B)   *Treatment of entity.* An entity that is disregarded as an entity separate from its owner for any purpose under this section is treated as a corporation with respect to items described in paragraph (c)(2)(v)(A) of this section.

(C)   *Example.* The following example illustrates the provisions of this paragraph (c)(2)(v):

Example. (i) LLCB is an eligible entity that has a single owner, B. LLCB is generally disregarded as an entity separate from its owner. However, under paragraph (c)(2)(v) of this section, LLCB is treated as an entity separate from its owner for certain purposes relating to excise taxes.

(ii)   LLCB mines coal from a coal mine located in the United States. Section 4121 of chapter 32 of the Internal Revenue Code imposes a tax on the producer's sale of such coal. Section 48.4121–1(a) of this chapter defines a "producer" generally as the person in whom is vested ownership of the coal under state law immediately after the coal is severed from the ground. LLCB is the person that owns the coal under state law immediately after it is severed from the ground. Under paragraph (c)(2)(v)(A)(*1*) of this section, LLCB is the producer of the coal and is liable for tax on its sale of such coal under chapter 32 of the Internal Revenue Code. LLCB must report and pay tax on Form 720, "Quarterly Federal Excise Tax Return," under its own name and taxpayer identification number.

(iii)   LLCB uses undyed diesel fuel in an earthmover that is not registered or required to be registered for highway use. Such use is an off-highway business use of the fuel. Under section 6427(*l*), the ultimate purchaser is allowed to claim an income tax credit or payment related to the tax imposed on diesel fuel used in an off-highway business use. Under paragraph (c)(2)(v) of this section, for purposes of the credit or payment allowed under section 6427(*l*), LLCB is the person that could claim the amount on its Form 720 or on a Form 8849, "Claim for Refund of Excise Taxes." Alternatively, if LLCB did not claim a payment during the time prescribed in section 6427(i)(2) for making a claim under section 6427, § 1.34–1 of this chapter provides that B, the owner of LLCB, could claim the income tax credit allowed under section 34 for the nontaxable use of diesel fuel by LLCB.

(iv)   Assume the same facts as in paragraph (c)(2)(v)(C) *Example* (i) and (ii) of this section. If LLCB does not pay the tax on its sale of coal under chapter 32 of the Internal Revenue Code, any notice of lien the Internal Revenue Service files will be filed as if LLCB were a corporation.

(vi)   *Special rule for reporting under section 6038A*—(A) *In general.* An entity that is disregarded as an entity separate from its owner for any purpose under this section is treated as an entity separate from its owner and classified as a corporation for purposes of section 6038A if—

(*1*)   The entity is a domestic entity; and

(*2*)   One foreign person has direct or indirect sole ownership of the entity.

(B) *Definitions*—(*1*) *Indirect sole ownership.* For purposes of paragraph (c)(2)(vi)(A)(*2*) of this section, indirect sole ownership means ownership by one person entirely through one or more other entities disregarded as entities separate from their owners or through one or more grantor trusts, regardless of whether any such disregarded entity or grantor trust is domestic or foreign.

(*2*) *Entity disregarded as separate from its owner.* For purposes of paragraph (c)(2)(vi)(B)(*1*) of this section, an entity disregarded as an entity separate from its owner is an entity described in paragraph (c)(2)(i) of this section.

(*3*) *Grantor trust.* For purposes of paragraph (c)(2)(vi)(B)(*1*) of this section, a grantor trust is any portion of a trust that is treated as owned by the grantor or another person under subpart E of subchapter J of chapter 1 of the Code.

(C) *Taxable year.* The taxable year of an entity classified as a corporation for section 6038A purposes pursuant to paragraph (c)(2)(vi)(A) of this section is—

(*1*) The same as the taxable year of the foreign person described in paragraph (c)(2)(vi)(A)(*2*) of this section, if that foreign person has a U.S. income tax or information return filing obligation for its taxable year; or

(*2*) The calendar year, if paragraph (c)(2)(vi)(C)(*1*) of this section does not apply, unless otherwise provided in forms, instructions, or published guidance.

(d) *Special rule for certain foreign business entities*—(1) *In general.* Except as provided in paragraph (d)(3) of this section, a foreign business entity described in paragraph (b)(8)(i) of this section will not be treated as a corporation under paragraph (b)(8)(i) of this section if—

(i) The entity was in existence on May 8, 1996;

(ii) The entity's classification was relevant (as defined in § 301.7701-3(d)) on May 8, 1996;

(iii) No person (including the entity) for whom the entity's classification was relevant on May 8, 1996, treats the entity as a corporation for purposes of filing such person's federal income tax returns, information returns, and withholding documents for the taxable year including May 8, 1996;

(iv) Any change in the entity's claimed classification within the sixty months prior to May 8, 1996, occurred solely as a result of a change in the organizational documents of the entity, and the entity and all members of the entity recognized the federal tax consequences of any change in the entity's classification within the sixty months prior to May 8, 1996;

(v) A reasonable basis (within the meaning of section 6662) existed on May 8, 1996, for treating the entity as other than a corporation; and

(vi) Neither the entity nor any member was notified in writing on or before May 8, 1996, that the classification of the entity was under examination (in which case the entity's classification will be determined in the examination).

(2) *Binding contract rule.* If a foreign business entity described in paragraph (b)(8)(i) of this section is formed after May 8, 1996, pursuant to a written binding contract (including an accepted bid to develop a project) in effect on May 8, 1996, and all times thereafter, in which the parties agreed to engage (directly or indirectly) in an active and substantial business operation in the jurisdiction in which the entity is formed, paragraph (d)(1) of this section will be applied to that entity by substituting the date of the entity's formation for May 8, 1996.

(3) *Termination of grandfather status*—(i) *In general.* An entity that is not treated as a corporation under paragraph (b)(8)(i) of this section by reason of paragraph (d)(1) or (d)(2) of this

section will be treated permanently as a corporation under paragraph (b)(8)(i) of this section from the earliest of:

(A) The effective date of an election to be treated as an association under § 301.7701-3;

(B) A termination of the partnership under section 708(b)(1)(B) (regarding sale or exchange of 50 percent or more of the total interest in an entity's capital or profits within a twelve month period);

(C) A division of the partnership under section 708(b)(2)(B); or

(D) The date any person or persons, who were not owners of the entity as of November 29, 1999, own in the aggregate a 50 percent or greater interest in the entity.

(ii) *Special rule for certain entities.* For purposes of paragraph (d)(2) of this section, paragraph (d)(3)(i)(B) of this section shall not apply if the sale or exchange of interests in the entity is to a related person (within the meaning of sections 267(b) and 707(b)) and occurs no later than twelve months after the date of the formation of the entity.

(e) *Effective/applicability date.* (1) Except as otherwise provided in this paragraph (e), the rules of this section apply as of January 1, 1997, except that paragraph (b)(6) of this section applies on or after January 14, 2002, to a business entity wholly owned by a foreign government regardless of any prior entity classification, and paragraph (c)(2)(ii) of this section applies to taxable years beginning after January 12, 2001. The reference to the Finnish, Maltese, and Norwegian entities in paragraph (b)(8)(i) of this section is applicable on November 29, 1999. The reference to the Trinidadian entity in paragraph (b)(8)(i) of this section applies to entities formed on or after November 29, 1999. Any Maltese or Norwegian entity that becomes an eligible entity as a result of paragraph (b)(8)(i) of this section in effect on November 29, 1999, may elect by February 14, 2000, to be classified for Federal tax purposes as an entity other than a corporation retroactive to any period from and including January 1, 1997. Any Finnish entity that becomes an eligible entity as a result of paragraph (b)(8)(i) of this section in effect on November 29, 1999, may elect by February 14, 2000, to be classified for Federal tax purposes as an entity other than a corporation retroactive to any period from and including September 1, 1997. However, paragraph (d)(3)(i)(D) of this section applies on or after October 22, 2003.

(2) Paragraph (c)(2)(iii) of this section applies on and after September 14, 2009. For rules that apply before September 14, 2009, see 26 CFR part 301, revised as of April 1, 2009.

(3)(i) *General rule.* Except as provided in paragraph (e)(3)(ii) of this section, the rules of paragraph (b)(9) of this section apply as of August 12, 2004, to all business entities existing on or after that date.

(ii) *Transition rule.* For business entities created or organized under the laws of more than one jurisdiction as of August 12, 2004, the rules of paragraph (b)(9) of this section apply as of May 1, 2006. These entities, however, may rely on the rules of paragraph (b)(9) of this section as of August 12, 2004.

(4) The reference to the Estonian, Latvian, Liechtenstein, Lithuanian, and Slovenian entities in paragraph (b)(8)(i) of this section applies to such entities formed on or after October 7, 2004, and to any such entity formed before such date from the date any person or persons, who were not owners of the entity as of October 7, 2004, own in the aggregate a 50 percent or greater interest in the entity. The reference to the European Economic Area/European Union entity in paragraph (b)(8)(i) of this section applies to such entities formed on or after October 8, 2004.

(5)(i) Except as provided in this paragraph (e)(5), paragraph (c)(2)(iv) of this section applies with respect to wages paid on or after January 1, 2009.

(ii)   Paragraph (c)(2)(iv)(B) applies with respect to wages paid on or after September 14, 2009. For rules that apply before September 14, 2009, see 26 CFR part 301 revised as of April 1, 2009.

(iii)   Paragraph (c)(2)(iv)(C)(*1*) of this section applies with respect to wages paid on or after November 1, 2011. For rules that apply before November 1, 2011, see 26 CFR part 301, revised as of April 1, 2011. However, taxpayers may apply paragraph (c)(2)(iv)(C)(*1*) of this section with respect to wages paid on or after January 1, 2009.

(6)(i) Except as provided in this paragraph (e)(6), paragraph (c)(2)(v) of this section applies to liabilities imposed and actions first required or permitted in periods beginning on or after January 1, 2008.

(ii)   Paragraphs (c)(2)(v)(B) and (c)(2)(v)(C) *Example* (iv) of this section apply on and after September 14, 2009.

(iii)   Paragraph (c)(2)(v)(A)(*5*) of this section applies for periods after December 31, 2014.

(iv)   References to Chapter 49 in paragraph (c)(2)(v) of this section apply to taxes imposed on amounts paid on or after July 1, 2012.

(7)   The reference to the Bulgarian entity in paragraph (b)(8)(i) of this section applies to such entities formed on or after January 1, 2007, and to any such entity formed before such date from the date that, in the aggregate, a 50 percent or more interest in such entity is owned by any person or persons who were not owners of the entity as of January 1, 2007. For purposes of the preceding sentence, the term *interest* means—

(i)   In the case of a partnership, a capital or profits interest; and

(ii)   In the case of a corporation, an equity interest measured by vote or value.

(8)   Paragraph (c)(2)(iv)(C)(2) of this section applies on the later of—

(i)   August 1, 2016; or

(ii)   The first day of the latest-starting plan year beginning after May 4, 2016, and on or before May 4, 2017, of an affected plan (based on the plans adopted before, and the plan years in effect as of, May 4, 2016) sponsored by an entity that is disregarded as an entity separate from its owner for any purpose under this section. For rules that apply before the applicability date of paragraph (c)(2)(iv)(C)(2) of this section, see 26 CFR part 301 revised as of April 1, 2016. For the purposes of this paragraph (e)(8)—

(A)   An affected plan includes any qualified plan, health plan, or section 125 cafeteria plan if the plan benefits participants whose employment status is affected by paragraph (c)(2)(iv)(C)(2) of this section;

(B)   A qualified plan means a plan, contract, pension, or trust described in paragraph (A) or (B) of section 219(g)(5) (other than paragraph (A)(iii)); and

(C)   A health plan means an arrangement described under § 1.105–5 of this chapter.

(9)   *Reporting required under section 6038A.* Paragraph (c)(2)(vi) of this section applies to taxable years of entities beginning after December 31, 2016, and ending on or after December 13, 2017.

§ 301.7701–3   Classification of Certain Business Entities.

(a)   *In general.* A business entity that is not classified as a corporation under § 301.7701–2(b) (1), (3), (4), (5), (6), (7), or (8) (an *eligible entity*) can elect its classification for federal tax purposes as provided in this section. An eligible entity with at least two members can elect to be classified as either an association (and thus a corporation under §301.7701–2(b)(2)) or a partnership, and an eligible entity with a single owner can elect to be classified as an association or to be disregarded as an entity separate from its owner. Paragraph (b) of this section provides a default classification for an eligible entity that does not make an election. Thus, elections are necessary only when an eligible entity chooses to be classified initially as other than the default classification or when an eligible entity chooses to change its classification. An entity whose classification is determined under the default classification retains that classification (regardless of any changes in the members' liability that occurs at any time during the time that the entity's classification is relevant as defined in paragraph (d) of this section) until the entity makes an election to change that classification under paragraph (c)(1) of this section. Paragraph (c) of this section provides rules for making express elections. Paragraph (d) of this section provides special rules for foreign eligible entities. Paragraph (e) of this section provides special rules for classifying entities resulting from partnership terminations and divisions under section 708(b). Paragraph (f) of this section sets forth the effective date of this section and a special rule relating to prior periods.

(b) *Classification of eligible entities that do not file an election*—(1) *Domestic eligible entities.* Except as provided in paragraph (b)(3) of this section, unless the entity elects otherwise, a domestic eligible entity is—

(i) A partnership if it has two or more members; or

(ii) Disregarded as an entity separate from its owner if it has a single owner.

(2) *Foreign eligible entities*—(i) *In general.* Except as provided in paragraph (b)(3) of this section, unless the entity elects otherwise, a foreign eligible entity is—

(A) A partnership if it has two or more members and at least one member does not have limited liability;

(B) An association if all members have limited liability; or

(C) Disregarded as an entity separate from its owner if it has a single owner that does not have limited liability.

(ii) *Definition of limited liability.* For purposes of paragraph (b)(2)(i) of this section, a member of a foreign eligible entity has limited liability if the member has no personal liability for the debts of or claims against the entity by reason of being a member. This determination is based solely on the statute or law pursuant to which the entity is organized, except that if the underlying statute or law allows the entity to specify in its organizational documents whether the members will have limited liability, the organizational documents may also be relevant. For purposes of this section, a member has personal liability if the creditors of the entity may seek satisfaction of all or any portion of the debts or claims against the entity from the member as such. A member has personal liability for purposes of this paragraph even if the member makes an agreement under which another person (whether or not a member of the entity) assumes such liability or agrees to indemnify that member for any such liability.

(3) *Existing eligible entities*—(i) *In general.* Unless the entity elects otherwise, an eligible entity in existence prior to the effective date of this section will have the same classification that the entity claimed under §§301.7701–1 through 301.7701–3 as in effect on the date prior to the effective date of this section; except that if an eligible entity with a single owner claimed to be a partnership under those regulations, the entity will be disregarded as an entity separate from its owner under this paragraph (b)(3)(i). For special rules regarding the classification of such entities prior to the effective date of this section, see paragraph (h)(2) of this section.

    (ii)   *Special rules.* For purposes of paragraph (b)(3)(i) of this section, a foreign eligible entity is treated as being in existence prior to the effective date of this section only if the entity's classification was relevant (as defined in paragraph (d) of this section) at any time during the sixty months prior to the effective date of this section. If an entity claimed different classifications prior to the effective date of this section, the entity's classification for purposes of paragraph (b)(3)(i) of this section is the last classification claimed by the entity. If a foreign eligible entity's classification is relevant prior to the effective date of this section, but no federal tax or information return is filed or the federal tax or information return does not indicate the classification of the entity, the entity's classification for the period prior to the effective date of this section is determined under the regulations in effect on the date prior to the effective date of this section.

    (c)   *Elections*—(1) *Time and place for filing*—(i) *In general.* Except as provided in paragraphs (c)(1) (iv) and (v) of this section, an eligible entity may elect to be classified other than as provided under paragraph (b) of this section, or to change its classification, by filing Form 8832, Entity Classification Election, with the service center designated on Form 8832. An election will not be accepted unless all of the information required by the form and instructions, including the taxpayer identifying number of the entity, is provided on Form 8832. See § 301.6109–1 for rules on applying for and displaying Employer Identification Numbers.

    (ii)   *Further notification of elections.* An eligible entity required to file a Federal tax or information return for the taxable year for which an election is made under § 301.7701–3(c)(1)(i) must attach a copy of its Form 8832 to its Federal tax or information return for that year. If the entity is not required to file a return for that year, a copy of its Form 8832 ("Entity Classification Election") must be attached to the Federal income tax or information return of any direct or indirect owner of the entity for the taxable year of the owner that includes the date on which the election was effective. An indirect owner of the entity does not have to attach a copy of the Form 8832 to its return if an entity in which it has an interest is already filing a copy of the Form 8832 with its return. If an entity, or one of its direct or indirect owners, fails to attach a copy of a Form 8832 to its return as directed in this section, an otherwise valid election under § 301.7701–3(c)(1)(i) will not be invalidated, but the non-filing party may be subject to penalties, including any applicable penalties if the Federal tax or information returns are inconsistent with the entity's election under § 301.7701–3(c)(1)(i). In the case of returns for taxable years beginning after December 31, 2002, the copy of Form 8832 attached to a return pursuant to this paragraph (c)(1)(ii) is not required to be a signed copy.

    (iii)   *Effective date of election.* An election made under paragraph (c)(1)(i) of this section will be effective on the date specified by the entity on Form 8832 or on the date filed if no such date is specified on the election form. The effective date specified on Form 8832 can not be more than 75 days prior to the date on which the election is filed and can not be more than 12 months after the date on which the election is filed. If an election specifies an effective date more than 75 days prior to the date on which the election is filed, it will be effective 75 days prior to the date it was filed. If an election specifies an effective date more than 12 months from the date on which the election is filed, it will be effective 12 months after the date it was filed. If an election specifies an effective date before January 1, 1997, it will be effective as of January 1, 1997. If a purchasing corporation makes an election under section 338 regarding an acquired subsidiary, an election under paragraph (c)(1)(i) of this section for the acquired subsidiary can be effective no earlier than the day after the acquisition date (within the meaning of section 338(h)(2)).

    (iv)   *Limitation.* If an eligible entity makes an election under paragraph (c)(1)(i) of this section to change its classification (other than an election made by an existing entity to change its classification as of the effective date of this section), the entity cannot change its classification by election again during the sixty months succeeding the effective date of the election. However, the Commissioner may permit the entity to change its classification by election within the sixty months if more than fifty percent of the ownership interests in the entity as of the effective date of the subsequent election are owned by persons that did not own any interests in the entity on the filing date or on the effective date of the entity's prior election. An election by a newly formed eligible entity that is effective on the date of formation is not considered a change for purposes of this paragraph (c)(1)(iv).

(v) *Deemed elections*—(A) *Exempt organizations.* An eligible entity that has been determined to be, or claims to be, exempt from taxation under section 501(a) is treated as having made an election under this section to be classified as an association. Such election will be effective as of the first day for which exemption is claimed or determined to apply, regardless of when the claim or determination is made, and will remain in effect unless an election is made under paragraph (c)(1)(i) of this section after the date the claim for exempt status is withdrawn or rejected or the date the determination of exempt status is revoked.

(B) *Real estate investment trusts.* An eligible entity that files an election under section 856(c)(1) to be treated as a real estate investment trust is treated as having made an election under this section to be classified as an association. Such election will be effective as of the first day the entity is treated as a real estate investment trust.

(C) *S corporations.* An eligible entity that timely elects to be an S corporation under section 1362(a)(1) is treated as having made an election under this section to be classified as an association, provided that (as of the effective date of the election under section 1362(a)(1)) the entity meets all other requirements to qualify as a small business corporation under section 1361(b). Subject to § 301.7701–3(c)(1)(iv), the deemed election to be classified as an association will apply as of the effective date of the S corporation election and will remain in effect until the entity makes a valid election, under § 301.7701–3(c)(1)(i), to be classified as other than an association.

(vi) *Examples.* The following examples illustrate the rules of this paragraph (c)(1):

Example 1. On July 1, 1998, X, a domestic corporation, purchases a 10% interest in Y, an eligible entity formed under Country A law in 1990. The entity's classification was not relevant to any person for federal tax or information purposes prior to X's acquisition of an interest in Y. Thus, Y is not considered to be in existence on the effective date of this section for purposes of paragraph (b)(3) of this section. Under the applicable Country A statute, all members of Y have limited liability as defined in paragraph (b)(2)(ii) of this section. Accordingly, Y is classified as an association under paragraph (b)(2)(i)(B) of this section unless it elects under this paragraph (c) to be classified as a partnership. To be classified as a partnership as of July 1, 1998, Y must file a Form 8832 by September 14, 1998. See paragraph (c)(1)(i) of this section. Because an election cannot be effective more than 75 days prior to the date on which it is filed, if Y files its Form 8832 after September 14, 1998, it will be classified as an association from July 1, 1998, until the effective date of the election. In that case, it could not change its classification by election under this paragraph (c) during the sixty months succeeding the effective date of the election.

Example 2. (i) Z is an eligible entity formed under Country B law and is in existence on the effective date of this section within the meaning of paragraph (b)(3) of this section. Prior to the effective date of this section, Z claimed to be classified as an association. Unless Z files an election under this paragraph (c), it will continue to be classified as an association under paragraph (b)(3) of this section.

(ii) Z files a Form 8832 pursuant to this paragraph (c) to be classified as a partnership, effective as of the effective date of this section. Z can file an election to be classified as an association at any time thereafter, but then would not be permitted to change its classification by election during the sixty months succeeding the effective date of that subsequent election.

(2) *Authorized signatures*—(i) *In general.* An election made under paragraph (c)(1)(i) of this section must be signed by—

    (A) Each member of the electing entity who is an owner at the time the election is filed; or

    (B) Any officer, manager, or member of the electing entity who is authorized (under local law or the entity's organizational documents) to make the election and who represents to having such authorization under penalties of perjury.

(ii) *Retroactive elections.* For purposes of paragraph (c)(2)(i) of this section, if an election under paragraph (c)(1)(i) of this section is to be effective for any period prior to the time that it is filed, each person who was an owner between the date the election is to be effective and the date the election is filed, and who is not an owner at the time the election is filed, must also sign the election.

(iii) *Changes in classification.* For paragraph (c)(2)(i) of this section, if an election under paragraph (c)(1)(i) of this section is made to change the classification of an entity, each person who was an owner on the date that any transactions under paragraph (g) of this section are deemed to occur, and who is not an owner at the time the election is filed, must also sign the election. This paragraph (c)(2)(iii) applies to elections filed on or after November 29, 1999.

(d) *Special rules for foreign eligible entities*—(1) *Definition of relevance*—(i) *General rule.* For purposes of this section, a foreign eligible entity's classification is relevant when its classification affects the liability of any person for federal tax or information purposes. For example, a foreign entity's classification would be relevant if U.S. income was paid to the entity and the determination by the withholding agent of the amount to be withheld under chapter 3 of the Internal Revenue Code (if any) would vary depending upon whether the entity is classified as a partnership or as an association. Thus, the classification might affect the documentation that the withholding agent must receive from the entity, the type of tax or information return to file, or how the return must be prepared. The date that the classification of a foreign eligible entity is relevant is the date an event occurs that creates an obligation to file a federal tax return, information return, or statement for which the classification of the entity must be determined. Thus, the classification of a foreign entity is relevant, for example, on the date that an interest in the entity is acquired which will require a U.S. person to file an information return on Form 5471.

    (ii) *Deemed relevance*—(A) *General rule.* For purposes of this section, except as provided in paragraph (d)(1)(ii)(B) of this section, the classification for Federal tax purposes of a foreign eligible entity that files Form 8832, "Entity Classification Election", shall be deemed to be relevant only on the date the entity classification election is effective.

        (B) *Exception.* If the classification of a foreign eligible entity is relevant within the meaning of paragraph (d)(1)(i) of this section, then the rule in paragraph (d)(1)(ii)(A) of this section shall not apply.

(2) *Entities the classification of which has never been relevant.* If the classification of a foreign eligible entity has never been relevant (as defined in paragraph (d)(1) of this section), then the entity's classification will initially be determined pursuant to the provisions of paragraph (b)(2) of this section when the classification of the entity first becomes relevant (as defined in paragraph (d)(1)(i) of this section).

(3) *Special rule when classification is no longer relevant.* If the classification of a foreign eligible entity is not relevant (as defined in paragraph (d)(1) of this section) for 60 consecutive months, then the entity's classification will initially be determined pursuant to the provisions of paragraph (b)(2) of this section when the classification of the foreign eligible entity becomes relevant (as defined in paragraph (d)(1)(i) of this section). The date that the classification of a foreign entity is not relevant is the date an event occurs that causes the classification to no longer be relevant, or, if no event occurs in a taxable year that causes the classification to be relevant, then the date is the first day of that taxable year.

(4) *Effective date.* Paragraphs (d)(1)(ii), (d)(2), and (d)(3) of this section apply on or after October 22, 2003.

(e) *Coordination with section 708(b).* Except as provided in § 301.7701–2(d)(3) (regarding termination of grandfather status for certain foreign business entities), an entity resulting from a transaction described in section 708(b)(1)(B) (partnership termination due to sales or exchanges) or section 708(b)(2)(B) (partnership division) is a partnership.

(f) *Changes in number of members of an entity*—(1) *Associations.* The classification of an eligible entity as an association is not affected by any change in the number of members of the entity.

(2) *Partnerships and single member entities.* An eligible entity classified as a partnership becomes disregarded as an entity separate from its owner when the entity's membership is reduced to one member. A single member entity disregarded as an entity separate from its owner is classified as a partnership when the entity has more than one member. If an elective classification change under paragraph (c) of this section is effective at the same time as a membership change described in this paragraph (f)(2), the deemed transactions in paragraph (g) of this section resulting from the elective change preempt the transactions that would result from the change in membership.

(3) *Effect on sixty month limitation.* A change in the number of members of an entity does not result in the creation of a new entity for purposes of the sixty month limitation on elections under paragraph (c)(1)(iv) of this section.

(4) *Examples.* The following examples illustrate the application of this paragraph (f):

Example 1. A, a U.S. person, owns a domestic eligible entity that is disregarded as an entity separate from its owner. On January 1, 1998, *B*, a U.S. person, buys a 50 percent interest in the entity from *A*. Under this paragraph (f), the entity is classified as a partnership when *B* acquires an interest in the entity. However, *A* and *B* elect to have the entity classified as an association effective on January 1, 1998. Thus, *B* is treated as buying shares of stock on January 1, 1998. (Under paragraph (c)(1)(iv) of this section, this election is treated as a change in classification so that the entity generally cannot change its classification by election again during the sixty months succeeding the effective date of the election.) Under paragraph (g)(1) of this section, *A* is treated as contributing the assets and liabilities of the entity to the newly formed association immediately before the close of December 31, 1997. Because *A* does not retain control of the association as required by section 351, *A*'s contribution will be a taxable event. Therefore, under section 1012, the association will take a fair market value basis in the assets contributed by *A*, and *A* will have a fair market value basis in the stock received. *A* will have no additional gain upon the sale of stock to *B*, and *B* will have a cost basis in the stock purchased from *A*.

Example 2. (i) On April 1, 1998, *A* and *B*, U.S. persons, form *X*, a foreign eligible entity treated as an association under the default provisions of paragraph (b)(2)(i) of this section, does not make an election to be classified as a partnership. *A* subsequently purchases all of *B*'s interest in *X*.

(ii) Under paragraph (f)(1) of this section, *X* continues to be classified as an association. *X*, however, can subsequently elect to be disregarded as an entity separate from

A. The sixty month limitation of paragraph (c)(1)(iv) of this section does not prevent X from making an election because X has not made a prior election under paragraph (c)(1)(i) of this section.

Example 3. (i) On April 1, 1998, A and B, U.S. persons, form X, a foreign eligible entity. X is treated as an association under the default provisions of paragraph (b)(2)(i) of this section, and X does not make an election to be classified as a partnership. On January 1, 1999, X elects to be classified as a partnership effective on that date. Under the sixty month limitation of paragraph (c)(1)(iv) of this section, X cannot elect to be classified as an association until January 1, 2004 (*i.e.*, sixty months after the effective date of the election to be classified as a partnership).

(ii) On June 1, 2000, A purchases all of B's interest in X. After A's purchase of B's interest, X can no longer be classified as a partnership because X has only one member. Under paragraph (f)(2) of this section, X is disregarded as an entity separate from A when A becomes the only member of X. X, however, is not treated as a new entity for purposes of paragraph (c)(1)(iv) of this section. As a result, the sixty month limitation of paragraph (c)(1)(iv) of this section continues to apply to X, and X cannot elect to be classified as an association until January 1, 2004 (*i.e.*, sixty months after January 1, 1999, the effective date of the election by X to be classified as a partnership).

(5) *Effective date.* This paragraph (f) applies as of November 29, 1999.

(g) *Elective changes in classification*—(1) *Deemed treatment of elective change*—(i) *Partnership to association.* If an eligible entity classified as a partnership elects under paragraph (c)(1)(i) of this section to be classified as an association, the following is deemed to occur: The partnership contributes all of its assets and liabilities to the association in exchange for stock in the association, and immediately thereafter, the partnership liquidates by distributing the stock of the association to its partners.

(ii) *Association to partnership.* If an eligible entity classified as an association elects under paragraph (c)(1)(i) of this section to be classified as a partnership, the following is deemed to occur: The association distributes all of its assets and liabilities to its shareholders in liquidation of the association, and immediately thereafter, the shareholders contribute all of the distributed assets and liabilities to a newly formed partnership.

(iii) *Association to disregarded entity.* If an eligible entity classified as an association elects under paragraph (c)(1)(i) of this section to be disregarded as an entity separate from its owner, the following is deemed to occur: The association distributes all of its assets and liabilities to its single owner in liquidation of the association.

(iv) *Disregarded entity to an association.* If an eligible entity that is disregarded as an entity separate from its owner elects under paragraph (c)(1)(i) of this section to be classified as an association, the following is deemed to occur: The owner of the eligible entity contributes all of the assets and liabilities of the entity to the association in exchange for ~~st~~ock of the association.

Effect of elective changes—(i) *In general.* The tax treatment of a change in the ~~classificatio~~n of an entity for federal tax purposes by election under paragraph (c)(1)(i) of this ~~section is dete~~rmined under all relevant provisions of the Internal Revenue Code and general ~~principles of tax~~ law, including the step transaction doctrine.

~~Adop~~*tion of plan of liquidation.* For purposes of satisfying the requirement of ~~adoption of a plan~~ of liquidation under section 332, unless a formal plan of liquidation that ~~provides for an el~~ection to be classified as a partnership or to be disregarded as an entity ~~separate from its own~~er is adopted on an earlier date, the making, by an association, of an ~~election under paragr~~aph (c)(1)(i) of this section to be classified as a partnership or to be ~~disregarded as an e~~ntity separate from its owner is considered to be the adoption of a plan of liquidation immediately before the deemed liquidation described in paragraph (g)(1)(ii) or (iii) of this section. This paragraph (g)(2)(ii) applies to elections filed on or after December 17, 2001. Taxpayers may apply this paragraph (g)(2)(ii) retroactively to elections filed before December 17, 2001, if the corporate owner claiming treatment under section 332 and its subsidiary making the election take consistent positions with respect to the federal tax consequences of the election.

(3) *Timing of election*—(i) *In general.* An election under paragraph (c)(1)(i) of this section that changes the classification of an eligible entity for federal tax purposes is treated as occurring at the start of the day for which the election is effective. Any transactions that are deemed to occur under this paragraph (g) as a result of a change in classification are treated as occurring immediately before the close of the day before the election is effective. For example, if an election is made to change the classification of an entity from an association to a partnership effective on January 1, the deemed transactions specified in paragraph (g)(1)(ii) of this section (including the liquidation of the association) are treated as occurring immediately before the close of December 31 and must be reported by the owners of the entity on December 31. Thus, the last day of the association's taxable year will be December 31 and the first day of the partnership's taxable year will be January 1.

(ii) *Coordination with section 338 election.* A purchasing corporation that makes a qualified stock purchase of an eligible entity taxed as a corporation may make an election under section 338 regarding the acquisition if it satisfies the requirements for the election, and may also make an election to change the classification of the target corporation. If a taxpayer makes an election under section 338 regarding its acquisition of another entity taxable as a corporation and makes an election under paragraph (c) of this section for the acquired corporation (effective at the earliest possible date as provided by paragraph (c)(1)(iii) of this section), the transactions under paragraph (g) of this section are deemed to occur immediately after the deemed asset purchase by the new target corporation under section 338.

(iii) *Application to successive elections in tiered situations.* When elections under paragraph (c)(1)(i) of this section for a series of tiered entities are effective on the same date, the eligible entities may specify the order of the elections on Form 8832. If no order is specified for the elections, any transactions that are deemed to occur in this paragraph (g) as a result of the classification change will be treated as occurring first for the highest tier entity's classification change, then for the next highest tier entity's classification change, and so forth down the chain of entities until all the transactions under this paragraph (g) have occurred. For example, Parent, a corporation, wholly owns all of the interest of an eligible entity classified as an association (S1), which wholly owns another eligible entity classified as an association (S2), which wholly owns another eligible entity classified as an association (S3). Elections under paragraph (c)(1)(i) of this section are filed to classify S1, S2, and S3 each as disregarded as an entity separate from its owner effective on the same day. If no order is specified for the elections, the following transactions are deemed to occur under this paragraph (g) as a result of the elections, with each successive transaction occurring on the same day immediately after the preceding transaction S1 is treated as liquidating into Parent, then S2 is treated as liquidating into Parent, and finally S3 is treated as liquidating into Parent.

(4) *Effective date.* Except as otherwise provided in paragraph (g)(2)(ii) of this section, t[...] paragraph (g) applies to elections that are filed on or after November 29, 1999. Taxpayers [...] apply this paragraph (g) retroactively to elections filed before November 29, 1999 if all taxp[...] affected by the deemed transactions file consistently with this paragraph (g).

(h)   *Effective date*—(1) *In general.* Except as otherwise provided in this section, the rules of this section are applicable as of January 1, 1997.

(2)   *Prior treatment of existing entities.* In the case of a business entity that is not described in § 301.7701–2(b) (1), (3), (4), (5), (6), or (7), and that was in existence prior to January 1, 1997, the entity's claimed classification(s) will be respected for all periods prior to January 1, 1997, if—

(i)   The entity had a reasonable basis (within the meaning of section 6662) for its claimed classification;

(ii)   The entity and all members of the entity recognized the federal tax consequences of any change in the entity's classification within the sixty months prior to January 1, 1997; and

(iii)   Neither the entity nor any member was notified in writing on or before May 8, 1996, that the classification of the entity was under examination (in which case the entity's classification will be determined in the examination).

(3)   *Deemed elections for S corporations.* Paragraph (c)(1)(v)(C) of this section applies to timely S corporation elections under section 1362(a) filed on or after July 20, 2004. Eligible entities that filed timely S elections before July 20, 2004 may also rely on the provisions of the regulation.

PRESENT AND FUTURE VALUE TABLES

Present Value of One Dollar Per Year for _n_ Years

Years	1%	2%	3%	4%	5%	6%	7%	8%	9%	10%
1	0.9901	0.9804	0.9709	0.9615	0.9524	0.9434	0.9346	0.9259	0.9174	0.9091
2	1.9704	1.9416	1.9135	1.8861	1.8594	1.8334	1.8080	1.7833	1.7591	1.7355
3	2.9410	2.8839	2.8286	2.7751	2.7232	2.6730	2.6243	2.5771	2.5313	2.4869
4	3.9020	3.8077	3.7171	3.6299	3.5460	3.4651	3.3872	3.3121	3.2397	3.1699
5	4.8534	4.7135	4.5797	4.4518	4.3295	4.2124	4.1002	3.9927	3.8897	3.7908
6	5.7955	5.6014	5.4172	5.2421	5.0757	4.9173	4.7665	4.6229	4.4859	4.3553
7	6.7282	6.4720	6.2303	6.0021	5.7864	5.5824	5.3893	5.2064	5.0330	4.8684
8	7.6517	7.3255	7.0197	6.7327	6.4632	6.2098	5.9713	5.7466	5.5348	5.3349
9	8.5660	8.1622	7.7861	7.4353	7.1078	6.8017	6.5152	6.2469	5.9952	5.7590
10	9.4713	8.9826	8.5302	8.1109	7.7217	7.3601	7.0236	6.7101	6.4177	6.1446
11	10.3676	9.7868	9.2526	8.7605	8.3064	7.8869	7.4987	7.1390	6.8052	6.4951
12	11.2551	10.5753	9.9540	9.3851	8.8633	8.3838	7.9427	7.5361	7.1607	6.8137
13	12.1337	11.3484	10.6350	9.9856	9.3936	8.8527	8.3577	7.9038	7.4869	7.1034
14	13.0037	12.1062	11.2961	10.5631	9.8986	9.2950	8.7455	8.2442	7.7862	7.3667
15	13.8651	12.8493	11.9379	11.1184	10.3797	9.7122	9.1079	8.5595	8.0607	7.6061
20	18.0456	16.3514	14.8775	13.5903	12.4622	11.4699	10.5940	9.8181	9.1285	8.5136
25	22.0232	19.5235	17.4131	15.6221	14.0939	12.7834	11.6536	10.6748	9.8226	9.0770
50	39.1961	31.4236	25.7298	21.4822	18.2559	15.7619	13.8007	12.2335	10.9617	9.9148
100	63.0289	43.0984	31.5989	24.5050	19.8479	16.6175	14.2693	12.4943	11.1091	9.9993

Assumption: Payment made at the end of each year.